WITHDRAWN
UTSA Libraries

RENEWALS 458-4574

Handbook to Bach's
Sacred Cantata Texts

Handbook to Bach's
Sacred Cantata Texts

An Interlinear Translation with Reference
Guide to Biblical Quotations and Allusions

Melvin P. Unger

Scarecrow Press, Inc.
Lanham, Md., & London

SCARECROW PRESS, INC.

Published in the United States of America
by Scarecrow Press, Inc.
4720 Boston Way
Lanham, Maryland 20706

4 Pleydell Gardens, Folkestone
Kent CT20 2DN, England

Copyright © 1996 by Melvin P. Unger

Scripture quotations in this publication are from the Revised Standard
Version of the Bible, copyright 1946, 1952, 1971 by the Division of
Christian Education of the National Council of the Churches of Christ
in the USA, and used by permission.

All rights reserved. No part of this publication may be reproduced,
stored in a retrieval system, or transmitted in any form or by any
means, electronic, mechanical, photocopying, recording, or otherwise,
without the prior permission of the publisher.

British Cataloguing-in-Publication Information Available

Library of Congress Cataloging-in-Publication Data

Unger, Melvin P., 1950–
Handbook to Bach's sacred cantata texts : an interlinear translation with
reference guide to Biblical quotations and allusions / by Melvin P. Unger
p. cm.
English and German
Includes indexes.
1. Bach, Johann Sebastian, 1685–1750, Cantatas. 2. Cantatas, Sacred—
Librettos. 3. Bach, Johann Sebastian, 1685–1750—Religion. 4. Bible—
In Literature. I. Bach, Johann Sebastian, 1685–1750. Cantatas. Librettos.
English and German. Selections. II. Title.
ML410.B1U52   1996   782.2'40268—dc20   95-14499   CIP

ISBN 0-8108-2979-7 (cloth : alk. paper)

Printed in the United States of America

♾™ The paper used in this publication meets the minimum requirements of
American National Standard for Information Sciences—Permanence of
Paper for Printed Library Materials, ANSI Z39.48–1984.

This book is dedicated

to

Betty,

who kept assuring me our life would be less hectic once the book was finished…

Jeremy,

who thought I was carrying the concept of self-discipline a bit far…

Timothy,

who kept asking excitedly, "Is the book finished now?"…

and Andrew,

who had to rely on his older brothers for attention.

Table of Contents

Dedication   *iii*

Foreword   *ix*

Acknowledgments   *x*

Preface   *xi*

——————

SACRED CANTATAS

BWV 1	*1*	BWV 20	*66*	BWV 38	*134*
BWV 2	*5*			BWV 39	*137*
BWV 3	*8*	BWV 21	*73*	BWV 40	*142*
BWV 4	*11*	BWV 22	*78*		
BWV 5	*15*	BWV 23	*81*	BWV 41	*146*
BWV 6	*19*	BWV 24	*84*	BWV 42	*150*
BWV 7	*22*	BWV 25	*88*	BWV 43	*152*
BWV 8	*26*	BWV 26	*91*	BWV 44	*158*
BWV 9	*29*	BWV 27	*94*	BWV 45	*160*
BWV 10	*34*	BWV 28	*97*	BWV 46	*164*
		BWV 29	*100*	BWV 47	*167*
BWV 11	*38*	BWV 30	*104*	BWV 48	*170*
BWV 12	*43*			BWV 49	*173*
BWV 13	*45*	BWV 31	*110*	BWV 50	*177*
BWV 14	*48*	BWV 32	*115*		
BWV 15	*51*	BWV 33	*119*	BWV 51	*177*
BWV 16	*51*	BWV 34	*122*	BWV 52	*180*
BWV 17	*55*	BWV 35	*125*	BWV 53	*183*
BWV 18	*58*	BWV 36	*128*	BWV 54	*183*
BWV 19	*62*	BWV 37	*131*	BWV 55	*185*

BWV 56	188	BWV 96	342	BWV 136	471
BWV 57	192	BWV 97	345	BWV 137	474
BWV 58	196	BWV 98	349	BWV 138	476
BWV 59	199	BWV 99	352	BWV 139	482
BWV 60	202	BWV 100	355	BWV 140	485
BWV 61	206	BWV 101	359	BWV 141	490
BWV 62	209	BWV 102	363	BWV 142	490
BWV 63	212	BWV 103	367	BWV 143	490
BWV 64	216	BWV 104	370	BWV 144	493
BWV 65	220	BWV 105	373	BWV 145	496
BWV 66	224	BWV 106	376	BWV 146	499
BWV 67	228	BWV 107	378	BWV 147	503
BWV 68	231	BWV 108	382	BWV 148	509
BWV 69	233	BWV 109	384	BWV 149	512
BWV 70	237	BWV 110	387	BWV 150	516
BWV 71	243	BWV 111	389	BWV 151	518
BWV 72	246	BWV 112	392	BWV 152	521
BWV 73	250	BWV 113	395	BWV 153	525
BWV 74	254	BWV 114	400	BWV 154	530
BWV 75	257	BWV 115	404	BWV 155	534
BWV 76	263	BWV 116	408	BWV 156	538
BWV 77	270	BWV 117	411	BWV 157	541
BWV 78	273	BWV 118	415	BWV 158	545
BWV 79	277	BWV 119	415	BWV 159	548
BWV 80	280	BWV 120	420	BWV 160	553
BWV 81	285	BWV 121	423	BWV 161	553
BWV 82	288	BWV 122	426	BWV 162	557
BWV 83	291	BWV 123	429	BWV 163	561
BWV 84	294	BWV 124	429	BWV 164	565
BWV 85	297	BWV 125	432	BWV 165	569
BWV 86	299	BWV 126	438	BWV 166	573
BWV 87	302	BWV 127	442	BWV 167	576
BWV 88	302	BWV 128	445	BWV 168	580
BWV 89	309	BWV 129	448	BWV 169	584
BWV 90	312	BWV 130	451	BWV 170	588
BWV 91	315	BWV 131	454	BWV 171	592
BWV 92	318	BWV 132	456	BWV 172	596
BWV 93	326	BWV 133	460	BWV 173	599
BWV 94	331	BWV 134	463	BWV 174	603
BWV 95	337	BWV 135	468	BWV 175	606

BWV 176   *609*   BWV 186   *648*   BWV 196   *687*
BWV 177   *612*   BWV 187   *656*   BWV 197   *688*
BWV 178   *616*   BWV 188   *660*   BWV 198   *693*
BWV 179   *622*   BWV 189   *663*   BWV 199   *698*
BWV 180   *625*   BWV 190   *663*   BWV 200   *703*

BWV 181   *630*   BWV 191   *669*   BWV 248   *704*
BWV 182   *633*   BWV 192   *670*   BWV 249   *733*
BWV 183   *637*   BWV 193   *672*
BWV 184   *639*   BWV 194   *674*
BWV 185   *644*   BWV 195   *684*

———————

Selected Bibliography   738

Alphabetical Index of Movement Summaries   742

Alphabetical Index of Chorale Stanzas   754

Index of Chorale Stanzas Appearing More than Once   761

Index of Scriptural Quotations and Strict Paraphrases   762

Alphabetical Index of Librettists   763

Index of First Performance Dates   764

Index of Cantatas in Chronological Order   768

Index of Cantatas in Liturgical Order   772

Alphabetical Index of Cantatas with Chronological Order Numbers   773

About the Author   777

Foreword

J. S. Bach's church cantatas are the center of his lifework. From the early years in Mühlhausen and Weimar until his last years as *Thomaskantor* in Leipzig, he had to compose, rehearse, and perform them. Therefore, really to know Bach, one must study his cantatas.

The cantatas were written for church services; thus each related to the theme of a given day within the liturgical year. To understand the relation between their texts and the scriptures—which in Bach's time were common knowledge—is of utmost importance. It is therefore a joy for me to introduce to you this work by Melvin Unger. It lists with thorough completeness the connections between the cantata texts and their biblical background. This extensive work is an important source for all who want to further their understanding of Bach's church cantatas. It will also be a needed help to those who program, interpret, and perform this wonderful music.

Helmuth Rilling

Acknowledgments

I am indebted to several persons whose work contributed directly or indirectly to my own. Helmuth Rilling initially stimulated my interest in the Bach cantatas during my studies with him in the mid–1970s at the music conservatory in Frankfurt. His recordings, especially the earlier ones with copious notes by Manfred Schreier, Marianne Helms, and Artur Hirsch among others, provided useful points of comparison throughout my work. So, too, did Z. Philip Ambrose's translation of the cantata texts, which appeared with the completion of Rilling's record series. Alfred Dürr's two-volume set on Bach's cantatas was a constant source of inspiration, and I relied on his work, as well as the *Bach Compendium* by Hans-Joachim Schulze and Christoph Wolff for pertinent information regarding librettists and dates. Without English and German computer Bibles by Reteaco Inc. (Toronto), and the Deutsche Bibelgesellschaft (Stuttgart) respectively, the scope of this book would have overwhelmed me. I owe a particularly great debt of thanks to my mother, Susie Unger, who proofread the manuscript, checking all references for accuracy. A timely research grant by The American Choral Directors Association allowed me to travel to the University of Oregon for the 1991 Bach Festival, and so provided some much-needed encouragement. I also received support and advice from a number of music scholars including John Hill of the University of Illinois, Alfred Mann of the Eastman School of Music, and Don Franklin of the University of Pittsburgh. My colleague, Werner Waitkus, graciously provided assistance in translating some of the more obscure German passages. Finally, my wife assumed many of my other duties, both domestic and professional, so that I could devote more time to the completion of this manuscript. To these all, as well as to others who encouraged me by their belief in this project, I offer my sincere thanks.

The Bible text in this publication is from the Revised Standard Version, copyright 1946, 1952, New Testament Section, Second Edition 1971 by the Division of Christian Education of the National Council of the Churches of Christ in the United States of America and is used by permission.

Preface

With the exception of some avant-garde works, vocal music has always concerned itself with words and their meanings; with the literary images and concepts of poetry and narrative. This concern appears heightened at certain times or in particular genres. Such is unquestionably true of the German church cantata during the time of J. S. Bach (1685–1750).

Defined functionally rather than structurally or stylistically, the German church cantata originally went by a variety of names and embraced a diversity of forms and styles. It was placed between the Gospel reading and the Sermon of the Lutheran liturgy and culminated a long tradition of "sermon music" that sought to teach and persuade the listener.[1] Its text was written with this didactic purpose foremost in mind and, therefore, usually explored the themes of the day's sermon, which were determined by the prescribed scriptural lessons.[2] Most of the cantata librettists were clergymen "who took the substance of their poetry from their sermons..."[3] Thus the church cantata grew into a fully developed genre largely because it was regarded as a significant medium for the proclamation, amplification, and interpretation of scripture.[4] "According to Lutheran thinking everything finally depended on...whether...new musical forms...could become 'vessels and bearers of ecclesiastical proclamation' and ecclesiastical confession."[5]

Given this didactic role, the cantata typically incorporated numerous allusions to scriptural passages or themes into its libretto. Unfortunately, many of these remain enigmatic to the twentieth-century musician for they presuppose a much closer familiarity with the Bible than is common today. Frequently the allusions are sketchy, at best, and the listener must supply the substance and context from a personal store of biblical phrases, images, or stories. The purpose of this book is to reconstruct something of the receptive framework for Bach's cantata texts; to identify the significant biblical themes that, in Bach's day, would have informed and illuminated listeners' perceptions as they heard these texts on a Sunday morning.

If some of the texts strike modern readers as overly sentimental and others as too moralistic, they should be reminded that poets of cantata texts were more interested in theological persuasiveness than in beauty. A leading librettist of the time, Erdmann Neumeister, expressed this sentiment in the foreword to his publication of 1704:

> In this style I have preferred to retain biblical and theological modes of expression. For it seems to me that a magnificent ornamentation of language in human artistry and wisdom can impede the spirit and charm in sacred poetry as greatly as it may promote both in political verse.[6]

Because the text-music relationship figured so prominently in the cantata's origin and development, it is imperative that both musical *and* literary dimensions be included in one's approach to the genre. Otherwise, neither a comprehensive understanding nor an authentic interpretation will be possible. Of course, one might argue that composers were typically less concerned with these matters than clergymen. It is true some composers had only superficial regard for the cantata's liturgical role. Indeed, because Bach composed so little sacred music after his first five years in Leipzig, some scholars conclude he had little personal commitment to the vocation of church musician and probably only wrote church works to the extent his position as Cantor required it.[7] From this perspective any demonstrable text-music relationships in Bach's cantatas result not so much from devout preoccupation with theological themes as from conformity to a general method of composition.[8]

The rediscovery of Bach's Bible fundamentally challenges this view.[9] This three-volume work[10] is really a Bible and commentary in one, for it contains, in addition to the Bible text, commentaries from Luther's writings. The editor was Abraham Calov (1612–1686), a prominent Lutheran theologian. In creating his commentary, Calov essentially arranged Luther's various writings in Biblical order. When he could not find suitable commentaries from Luther's works, he supplied his own.

Throughout these volumes Bach added underlinings, corrections, and marginal notations attesting an "interest in and concern for the integrity and significance of the Biblical text."[11] While some of the markings may have anticipated a "coming battle against the unmusical members of Town Council,"[12] others bear no relation to the responsibilities of a church musician and can only signify a genuine interest in the study of Scripture and theology. Taken as a whole, the Calov Bible provides strong evidence that Bach took keen interest in theological study and, hence, would have regarded the church cantata as a significant medium for theological proclamation.

Moreover, while Bach certainly expressed dissatisfaction with his duties as church composer in Leipzig, he never allowed his church compositions to become prosaic like other disenchanted composers—such as Mozart—did. "Anyone seeking a basic orientation for the interpretation of Bach's music cannot ignore [Bach's] self-concept [as a church musician] and the priority he evidenced in his life's work."[13]

The study of text-music relations in Bach's vocal works has been discredited in the eyes of many by the sometimes fanciful approaches taken by Albert Schweizer and W. Gillies Whittaker, among others.[14] Given the confirmation of Bach's interest in scripture and theology, renewed efforts to explore this relationship are warranted. Indeed, cantata performances ignoring the text-music relationship will consistently fail to communicate Bach's deepest intent, which—being essentially dramatic in nature—gives each cantata an individuality derived from its libretto.

A weakness of previous studies is their preoccupation with the literal meanings of individual words and phrases. New studies must look for relationships between more general literary themes and their musical settings. Because cantata librettists often developed theological themes through a sequential series of scriptural allusions, the full import of a text emerges only after individual allusions interact in the reader's mind. Only then does a meaningful study of text-music relations become possible.

The following work attempts to provide the literary basis for such interpretive analyses by reproducing excerpts from biblical passages to which the cantata librettos allude. To keep the scope of this work within manageable limits we omitted almost all editorial explanations of connections or relationships. The resulting format will require some study and contemplation on the part of the reader, especially where allusions are conceptual, rather than verbal, in nature. While verbal allusions point to specific biblical passages, conceptual allusions refer to more general biblical themes and may, therefore, often be represented by any of several scriptural excerpts. Where allusion is made to a theological tenet derived from diverse biblical passages—especially if that concept is progressively developed in the scriptures—the reader must consider the given extracts (and

the references we could merely cite for lack of space) as a blended whole. In isolation, none of the given passages portray the composite literary figure or image.[15] Taken together and in succession, however, they provide a kind of biblical *Fortspinnung*, a sequential unfolding of scriptural concepts undergirding the libretto. Furthermore, when disparate themes or images are juxtaposed, the dynamic interaction between them engenders new perspectives that go beyond either of the parent ideas, especially when they are presented in their original (scriptural) contexts. To discuss all these would have extended this book unduly, hence we must entrust some exegetical work to the reader.

A final cautionary reminder regarding the titles of the cantatas may serve useful. Since a cantata's title is merely the first line of its libretto, it does not necessarily portray the cantata's literary thrust. Especially where the poet develops his or her theme gradually, the first line may actually mislead someone unfamiliar with the rest of the libretto. The reader will readily recognize those cantatas where this is so.

EXPLANATORY NOTES

The Format

To make finding individual cantatas easy, we have ordered them according to Bachwerkverzeichniss (BWV) numbers rather than their position in the liturgical church year. For each cantata we provide reference numbers indicating the work's locations in the *Neue Bach Ausgabe* and the *Bach Compendium*. Next comes the cantata's liturgical designation, along with the BWV numbers (in chronological order)[16] of other cantatas written for that occasion. The prescribed lessons are then identified with brief summaries. If a cantata was revised to suit a new liturgical occasion, we note the circumstances and identify the new scriptural lessons. Where the librettist is known, this name is provided as well.

Occasionally Bach reused music from earlier works in his church cantatas. Often this required fitting a new text to the borrowed music. Notwithstanding any musical changes that Bach might make to effect a better match between text and music, it is clear the text is no longer the dominant partner in the relationship. Because such parodies are important in discussions regarding text-music relations, we have identified them whenever they were known to us.[17]

Immediately following the heading of each cantata movement, a one-line caption appears, summarizing the literary theme of that movement. These summaries are intended to help focus the literary thrust of each movement for the reader. They are later compiled in an alphabetical index for anyone wishing to compare specific themes in Bach's cantatas.

Our summaries of chorale stanzas require special mention. Chorales represent corporate expressions of the church even when their language and sentiment is intensely personal. This corporate perspective must be inferred from the chorale's liturgical role and is not necessarily explicit in the chorale texts nor their summary captions. Furthermore, since chorales usually appear at the ends of cantatas, they tend to take on the contexts of the foregoing movements. For this reason, captions of identical chorales may differ substantially from one cantata to the next. Of course, this contrast in literary emphasis becomes evident in our choice of scriptures as well.

The cantata texts themselves appear in three different type faces according to their kind. Chorales appear in bold type, freely composed texts in regular type, and Bible texts in italics.

The Translations

In keeping with our interlinear format, we translated the cantata texts word-for-word wherever possible. Despite occasionally awkward sentence structure, such an interlinear translation provides the performer with the information for making expressive differentiations among individual words. In cases where this approach leaves the meaning unclear, an additional line within brackets rephrases the text: { }. Where the English word is not a precise equivalent, or where additional words are needed, these words appear in parentheses: ( ).[18]

Drum   laß ich ihn nur walten.
Therefore allow I him just to-rule.
{Therefore I just allow him sovereign
control.}

Es   mag die Welt
(Now) may the world

Unser Heil   ist kommen
Our Salvation (has) come

Was   frag ich nach der Welt
What (care) I   for the world

Sometimes we have not translated a German word at all, because its English equivalent is unnecessary. Thus, for exam-

ple, reflexive pronouns—so common in German—are usually omitted in translation.

wenn sie sich wenden
If   they -   turn

Double negatives are omitted according to English usage.

Aber   niemals nicht geschehn
But (let it) never   - come-to-pass

Where a German verb has a separable prefix, the English equivalent often appears in the earlier position.

Wohn uns mit deiner Güte   bei
Attend us with thy kindness -
       [beiwohnen = to attend]

The context determines whether or not to translate articles. Sometimes an article is intended to singularize the following noun.

Wo   findet meine Seele *die* Ruhe?
Where finds   my   soul - rest?

In this example, it is possible that "rest" refers to the eternal "sabbath rest" discussed in the letter to the Hebrews (i.e. heaven). If so, the article should be translated to indicate that a special rest is meant:

Where finds my soul *that* rest?[19]

Sometimes indefinite articles are better translated as possessive pronouns.

was   der Seele begehrt
what (*my*) soul   desires

instead of:

what *the* soul desires

German words with several meanings pose a particular challenge. Thus, for example, "Not" can signify need, want, necessity, distress, misery, trouble, urgency, difficulty, peril, or danger. Usually the differences among options are slight, and the context makes the best choice obvious.

Wenn alle Besserung   weicht aus dem Herzen fort?
If   all improvement retreats out of-the heart   - ?
{If all desire to change retreats out of the heart?}

Although "Besserung" can mean amelioration, the context here suggests a volitional act, hence, reformation or a desire to change.

Because German sentence structure sometimes places object before subject, a change to passive voice may be needed in English if the word order is to be retained.

Wenn ihn   der Glaube   faßt
When it (by) -   faith *is-grasped*
{When faith grasps it}

Archaic forms of address ("thee", "thy", "thine") have been avoided except where poetically desirable, specifically: addresses to God, the soul, human emotions, or elements of nature.

In poetic German the use of "wollen" is common.

[Er] will uns...erhöhn

Here the verb "will" indicates an assured future action but also intent. Rather than translating such a phrase "he *intends* us to exalt", we usually chose "he *would* us exalt" unless this made the action seem conditional. If the element of intent seemed particularly unimportant we translated it "he *shall* us exalt".

Literal quotations of scripture appear italicized. We translated such *dicta* in our usual word-for-word manner and it will not surprise the reader that these translations are less idiomatic than the Revised Standard Version appearing opposite. At times, however, there are substantive discrepancies between our translation and the RSV because the German and English versions do not agree in their renderings of the original Greek and Hebrew texts. For our purposes, the German version (hence, also, our interlinear English translation) is the more relevant for— whether or not it accurately reflects the original Hebrew or Greek meaning—it represents the understanding of the eighteenth-century German churchgoer.[20]

All chorale texts (whether Bach used the chorale tunes or not) appear in bold type. Texts that paraphrase chorales without ever quoting them directly appear in regular type and the chorale stanza that served as the movement's model is identified in each case.[21]

The Scriptural Excerpts

Scriptural allusions in Bach's cantata texts may be differentiated into four groups.

1. literal biblical quotations (*dicta*)
2. biblical paraphrases
3. allusions to specific biblical passages
4. allusions to general biblical themes or images

To recreate the eighteenth-century listener's mindset we have set forth relevant scriptures according to the following procedural guidelines.

Cantata texts that quote Scripture more or less verbatim are italicized in the first column and their English equivalents italicized in the right-hand column. Loose paraphrases of Scripture[22] appear in regular type, their RSV equivalents in the column opposite. Additional scriptures supporting the general themes of these passages then follow. Occasionally the RSV does not include material found in the German version. The reason for the discrepancy is that the German version apparently followed a different Hebrew or Greek manuscript. In such instances we have supplied the missing English text from marginal notes found in the RSV.[23]

When a text quotes or alludes to a passage appearing more than once in the Bible, the more appropriate one for the given context is reproduced. Thus, in the case of "a bruised reed he will not break", either Is. 42:3 or Mt. 12:20 is given, depending on the context, and the alternate location cited. Where two or more passages are identical and equally well-known, the reference is given thus: "Ps. 46:7/11". (Verse 11 is identical to verse 7.)

When an allusion refers to a general biblical theme or image rather than a specific passage, representative scriptures are provided, then others cited. Since passages from the Gospels often have parallel equivalents in the other Gospels; these are cited when appropriate.

When allusion is made to one of the lections of the day, the relevant lesson excerpts are reproduced with asterisks. Though such passages have, at times, only a loose connection with the themes of the cantata text, they receive priority for they constituted part of the liturgy and Bach's listeners, upon hearing the cantata, would immediately have thought of them. Where Bach reused a cantata text in a new liturgical context, we identify both sets of lessons.

Since versification in the English and German Bibles is not identical, readers wishing to check passages in the Lutheran translation will experience some inconvenience finding them. Nonsynchronization happens most frequently in the Psalms but occasionally elsewhere as well. Thus, for example, the epistle for the third Sunday after Epiphany is Romans 12:16–21 in the English Bible (beginning with "Never be conceited"), while the parallel passage in the German Bible is Romans 12:17–21.

As indicated above, our translations of *dicta* do not always correspond with the RSV renderings opposite because the German and English Bible translations themselves do not agree. Such discrepancies also tend to obscure some biblical allusions. To help clarify them we added parenthetical German phrases based on the 1545 edition of Luther's translation.[24]

The scriptural passages usually appear in chronological order, that is, the order in which the allusions appear within the libretto. Unfortunately, when disparate ideas, phrases, or images with heterogenous origins are presented consecutively in their respective contexts, they no longer connect as easily or coherently as they did in the libretto. Furthermore, when a passage is quoted at length, more than one of the cantata's images or concepts sometimes appear but in an order or context different from that found in the cantata. This tends to impede quick reading of the right-hand column. To aid the reader we have removed distracting words and phrases or, occasionally, rearranged the passages into sequences that offer better syntactical connections. The reason for allowing biblical excerpts to flow one into the other without assigning them to specific lines of the cantata text is that, in many cases, a "one-on-one" format would be too restrictive, obscuring multiple secondary or intertwining relationships between cantata libretto and given biblical passages. We hope that the most obvious connections

between our columns will immediately become apparent to the reader, and that the more complex relationships will reveal themselves upon deeper reflection.

NOTES

1. Alfred Dürr, *Die Kantaten von Johann Sebastian Bach mit ihren Texten,* 2 vols. (Kassel: Bärenreiter, 1985), 1:18. In the most literal sense, the cantata came between Gospel and creedal hymn; during the last stanza of the latter the minister ascended the pulpit.

2. The *Christmas Oratorio* represents an interesting departure from the normal pattern in that three of its six cantatas quote from lessons one day removed from their own. Cantatas II and III (intended for the second and third days of Christmas, respectively) each quote from the Gospel of the day preceding their own, while Cantata V quotes from the lesson of the day following. Since the Gospel lesson was always read immediately prior to the performance of the cantata, one can imagine a certain puzzlement on the part of listeners who first heard the day's lesson spoken, then the Gospel of the previous day sung. Why were the texts deliberately shifted in this manner?

Probably, this disengagement from the schedule of lessons was motivated by a desire for a unified and compelling story. Thus, by extending the first Gospel to the second day and shifting the second Gospel to the third day, the librettist could omit the third lesson, which is not narrative in the usual sense and would have stalled the forward thrust of the story. (See John 1:1-14.) Furthermore, by dividing the Gospel for Epiphany (the sixth and last of the series) between the fifth and sixth days, the poet could omit the account of Mary and Joseph's flight to Egypt, which, in fifth place, could not logically precede the appearance of the magi. Thus, the resulting libretto is a unified oratorio cycle.

However, nonsynchronization between lessons and libretto may be justified in another way, as well. The temporal shifts effectively portray a duality between "recalling" and "anticipating," an important theme in the libretto. Thus movements 30-32 (in one of the two cantatas that quote previous days' lessons) stress the former (e.g. "Maria behielt alle diese Worte"; "mein Herz soll es bewahren") and 51-52 (in the cantata that quotes from a subsequent lesson) the latter (e.g. "wann wird die Zeit erscheinen").

3. Paul Friedrich Brausch, "Die Kantate: Ein Beitrag zur Geschichte der deutschen Dichtungsgattung" (dissertation, University of Heidelberg, 1921) quoted in Günther Stiller,

Johann Sebastian Bach and Liturgical Life in Leipzig, trans. Herbert J. A. Bouman, Daniel F. Poellot, Hilton C. Oswald, ed. Robin A. Leaver (St. Louis: Concordia, 1984), p. 143.

   4. Stiller, p. 151.

   5. Stiller, p. 143; Melvin P. Unger, *The German Choral Church Compositions of Johann David Heinichen (1683-1729)* (New York: Peter Lang, 1990), p. 64.

   6. Quoted in Max Seiffert, Foreword to "Johann Philipp Krieger," Vol. 53/54 (1916) of *Denkmäler Deutscher Tonkunst* (Leipzig: Breitkopf & Härtel, 1892-1931), p. LXXVI, trans. M. Unger.

   7. See Robin A. Leaver, *J. S. Bach and Scripture, Glosses from the Calov Bible Commentary* (St. Louis: Concordia, 1985), p. 14.

   8. J. A. Westrup, *Bach Cantatas* (British Broadcasting Corporation, 1966; Seattle: University of Washington Press edition, 1969), pp. 7, 17-18.

   9. Gerhard Herz, "Toward a New Image of Bach," *BACH:The Journal of the Riemenschneider Bach Institute* 1 (October 1970): 9-27; 2 (January 1971): 7-27. Reprinted 16 (January 1985): 12-52. See also Howard H. Cox, *The Calov Bible of J. S. Bach* (Ann Arbor: UMI Research Press, 1985), "Bach's Conception of his Office," *BACH* 20 (Spring 1989): 22-30; "Bach's Knowledge of the Bible," in *A Bach Tribute. Essays in Honor of William H. Scheide*, Kassel & Chapel Hill, 1993, pp. 87-99.

   10. It is actually six volumes bound as three. See Leaver, p. 22.

   11. Leaver, p. 29.

   12. D. Arnold, *Bach* (Oxford, 1984), pp. 58-59, quoted in Leaver, p. 21.

   13. Helmuth Rilling, "Bach's Significance," trans. Gordon Paine, *The Choral Journal* 25 (June 1985), p. 8.

   14. Albert Schweitzer, *J. S. Bach,* trans. Ernest Newman, 2 vols. (London: Breitkopf and Härtel, reissued Boston: Bruce Humphries Publishers, 1962); W. Gillies Whittaker, *The Cantatas of Johann Sebastian Bach,* 2 vols. (London: Oxford University Press, 1959, reissued, 1964).

   15. One such composite literary image is that of Christ, the bridegroom, entering the believer's heart.

   16. We have based this order on dates provided by Hans-Joachim Schulze and Christoph Wolff in their *Bach Compendium,* 2 vols. (Frankfurt: C. F. Peters, 1988). Compare also Artur Hirsch, "Johann Sebastian Bach's Cantatas in Chronological Order," *BACH* 11 (July1980): 18-35 and Artur Hirsch's chronological list found in Z. Philip Ambrose, *The Texts to Johann Sebastian Bach's Church Cantatas* (Neuhausen-Stuttgart: Hänssler-Verlag, 1984, pp. 479-485.

   17. In these matters we found that the *Bach Compendium* and Dürr do not always agree. See, for example, BWV 11. For a concise summary of scholarly discussions regarding the Bach's parody process, see Hans-Joachim Schulze, "The Parody Process in Bach's Music: An Old Problem Reconsidered," *BACH* 20 (Spring 1989): 7-21.

   18. Minor liberties in translation have been taken without notice. Thus a German noun may be translated as an adjective: "keinen Nutzen" becomes "nothing profitable" (without parentheses) in BWV 181-1.

   19. See also the example quoted later: "Wenn ihn *der* Glaube faßt."

   20. Although the Revised Standard Version (1946-1952; second edition of the New Testament, 1971) does not approximate the German Bible as closely as other English translations do, its wider acceptance and usage made it the more desirable choice.

   21. For information about chorale stanzas we relied primarily on Dürr, *Die Kantaten* and Hans-Joachim Schulze and Christoph Wolff, *Bach Compendium.* Unfortunately, these sources do not always agree (particularly with regard to dates) nor are they always self-consistent.

   22. For an example, see BWV 135.

   23. For an example of such an omission, see Lk. 24:36.

   24. The Luther translation has undergone continual revision to the present day. The 1545 edition was the last one in Luther's own hand and we chose this as our standard. Another edition by Dieckmann was widely disseminated after 1703. What is at issue, of course, is which version would be most familiar to the librettists and churchgoers of Bach's time. See H. Strathmann, "Bibelübersetzungen. VI. Bibelrevision als kirchlich-theologisches Problem," *Die Religion in Geschichte und Gegenwart*, 3d ed., edited by Kurt Galling (Tübingen: J. C. B Mohr [Paul Siebeck], 1957-1965), vol. 1, p. 1220. Should readers attempt to check passages against the 1545 edition, they will sometimes find chapter division to be different there from that in more modern editions, and versification nonexistent.

BWV 1
Wie schön leuchtet der Morgenstern
(NBA I/28; BC A173)

The Annunciation: Mar. 25 (BWV [182], 1)
*Is. 7:10–16 (The Messiah's birth prophesied)
*Lk. 1:26–38 (The angel Gabriel announces birth of Jesus to Mary)
Librettist: Unknown

1. Chorus (Chorale Vs. 1)
●Christ the morning star, root of Jesse, bridegroom (1–1)
Wie schön leuchtet der Morgenstern
How beautiful shines the morning star
{How beautiful the morning star shines}

Voll Gnad und Wahrheit von dem Herrn,
Full-of grace and truth from the Lord,

Die süße Wurzel Jesse!
The sweet root (of) Jesse!

Du Sohn Davids aus Jakobs Stamm,
Thou son (of) David of Jacob's tribe,

Mein König und mein Bräutigam,
My king and my bridegroom,

Hast mir mein Herz besessen,
(Thou) hast - my heart posessed,
{Thou hast posessed my heart,}

Lieblich,
Lovely,

Freundlich,
Kind,

Schön und herrlich, groß und ehrlich,
Beautiful and glorious, great and honorable,

reich von Gaben,
rich in gifts,

Hoch und sehr prächtig erhaben.
High and very magnificently elevated.

Num. 24:17. ...A star shall come forth out of Jacob, and a scepter shall rise out of Israel...
Is. 11:1, 10. There shall come forth a shoot from the stump of Jesse... In that day the root of Jesse shall stand as an ensign to the peoples; him shall the nations seek... (Also Is. 53:2.)
Rom. 15:12. ...The root of Jesse shall come...in him shall the Gentiles hope.
***Lk. 1:32–33.** He will be great, and will be called the Son of the Most High; and the Lord God will give to him the throne of his father David, and he will reign over the house of Jacob for ever; and of his kingdom there will be no end.
Mt. 2:2 [Magi]: ...We have seen his star in the East...
Heb. 1:1–5, 8. In many and various ways God spoke of old to our fathers by the prophets; but in these last days he has spoken to us by a Son, whom he appointed the heir of all things, through whom also he created the world. He reflects the glory of God and bears the very stamp of his nature, upholding the universe by his word of power. When he had made purification for sins, he sat down at the right hand of the Majesty on high, having become as much superior to angels as the name he has obtained is more excellent that theirs. For to what angel did God ever say, "Thou art my Son..."? But of the Son he says, "Thy throne, O God, is for ever and ever..."
Jn. 1:14. [In Christ] the Word became flesh and dwelt among us, full of grace and truth (Luther: Gnade und Wahrheit); we have beheld his glory...
Rev. 22:16 [Christ]: ...I am the root and the offspring of David, the bright and morning star. (Also 2 Pet. 1:19.)
Jn. 7:42. Has not the scripture said that the Christ is descended from [King] David...? (Also Mt. 22:41–42, Rom. 1:3.)
Ps. 44:4. [O Lord,] thou art my King and my God, who ordainest victories for Jacob.
S. of S. 4:9 [Bridegroom]: You have ravished my heart (Luther: du hast mir das Herz genommen)...
Mt. 25:1 [Christ]: ...The kingdom of heaven shall be compared to ten maidens who...went to meet the bridegroom.
Mt. 9:15. Jesus said [concerning his disciples]... "Can the wedding guests mourn as long as the bridegroom is with them?"...
Jn. 3:26–30. ...John...answered [concerning Jesus], "He who has the bride is the bridegroom...He must increase, but I must decrease."
Rev. 17:14. ...He is Lord of lords and King of kings... (Also Rev. 19:16.)
1 Pet. 3:22. [Christ] has gone into heaven and is at the right hand of God, with angels, authorities, and powers subject to him. (Also Mk. 16:19, Acts 2:33, 5:31.)
Eph. 4:8. ...It is said, "When he ascended on high he led a host of captives, and he gave gifts to men." (Also Rom. 11:29, Jms. 1:17.)
Ps. 95:3. The Lord is a great God, and a great King above all gods. (Also Ps. 97:9, Ex. 18:11; Ps. 83:18.)
***Lk. 1:31–33.** Behold, you [Mary] will conceive in your womb and bear a son, and you shall call his name Jesus. He will be great, and will be called the Son of the Most High; and the Lord God will give to him the throne of his father David, and he will reign over the house of Jacob for ever; and of his kingdom there will be no end.
Phil. 2:9. ...God has highly exalted him...
Jn. 1:14. ...We beheld his glory, glory as of the only Son from the Father.

2. Tenor Recit. (Based on Chorale Vs. 2)
●Annunciation: Joyous, long-awaited news (1–2)
    Du wahrer Gottes und Marien Sohn,
(O) thou true   God   and Mary's son,

Du König derer Auserwählten,
Thou king of-the chosen-ones,

Wie süß ist uns dies Lebenswort,
How sweet is to-us this word-of-life,
{How sweet this word of life is to us,}

Nach   dem die ersten Väter schon
According-to which the first fathers already

So Jahr' als Tage zählten,
 - Years as days counted,
{Counted years as days,}

Das   Gabriel mit Freuden dort
Which Gabriel with joy   there
{Which Gabriel promised with joy there}

In Bethlehem verheißen!
In Bethlehem promised!
{In Bethlehem!}

O Süßigkeit, o Himmelsbrot,
O sweetness, O bread-of-heaven,

Das   weder Grab, Gefahr, noch Tod
Which neither grave, danger, nor death

Aus   unsern Herzen   reißen.
Out-of our   hearts (can) snatch.
{Can snatch out of our hearts.}

3. Soprano Aria (Based on Chorale Vs. 3)
●Divine fire: Yearning for its filling (1–3)
Erfüllet, ihr himmlischen göttlichen Flammen,
 Fill up, you heavenly   divine   flames,

Die nach euch verlangende gläuben de Brust!
The for you   longing,   believing breast!
{These believing breasts that long for you!}

Die Seelen empfinden die kräftigsten Triebe
(Our) souls experience the most-powerful urges

Der brünstigsten Liebe
Of most-passionate love

Und schmecken auf Erden die himmlische Lust.
And   taste   on earth the   heavenly pleasure.
{And taste on earth the pleasures of heaven.}

Jn. 17:3 [Christ]: [I pray]...that they know thee the only true God, and Jesus Christ whom thou hast sent.
1 Jn. 5:20. ...We are in him who is true, in his Son Jesus Christ. This is the true God and eternal life.
Eph. 1:4, 5. ...He chose us in him before the foundation of the world... He destined us in love to be his sons...
Jn. 6:68. Simon Peter answered [Jesus], "Lord, to whom shall we go? You have the words of eternal life..."
Ps. 119:103. [O Lord,] how sweet are thy words to my taste, sweeter than honey to my mouth! (Also Ps. 19:9–10.)
Mt. 13:17 [Christ]: Truly, I say to you, many prophets and righteous men longed to see what you see, and did not see it, and to hear what you hear, and did not hear it. (Also 1 Pet. 1:10–12.)
Col. 1:26. The mystery hidden for ages and generations [has] now [been] made manifest to his saints.
2 Pet. 3:8, 9. ...With the Lord one day is as a thousand years and a thousand years as one day. The Lord is not slow about his promise as some count slowness...
*Lk. 1:26, 27. In the sixth month the angel Gabriel was sent from God ...to a virgin...and the virgin's name was Mary.
*Is. 7:14. ...Behold, a young woman shall conceive and bear a son, and shall call his name Immanuel.
Mt. 2:5, 6. [The chief priests and scribes] told [Herod], "[The Christ is to be born] in Bethlehem of Judea; for so it is written by the prophet: 'And you, O Bethlehem, in the land of Judah, are by no means least among the rulers of Judah; for from you shall come a ruler who will govern my people Israel.'"
Jn. 6:48, 51 [Christ]: I am the bread of life...I am the living bread which came down from heaven; if any one eats of this bread, he will live for ever; and the bread which I shall give for the life of the world is my flesh. (Also Jn. 6:33.)
Rom. 8:38–39. ...Neither death, nor life, nor angels, nor principalities, nor things present, nor things to come, nor powers, nor height, nor depth, nor anything else in all creation, will be able to separate us from the love of God in Christ Jesus our Lord.
Jn. 10:28 [Christ]: I give them eternal life...and no one shall snatch them out of my hand.

Eph. 3:19. [May you]...be filled with all the fulness of God.
Mt. 22:37 [Christ]: You shall love the Lord your God with all your heart, and with all your soul, and with all your mind.
Ps. 73:25. [O Lord,] whom have I in heaven but thee? And there is nothing upon earth that I desire besides thee.
Lk. 3:16 [John]: ...[The one who is coming] will baptize you with the Holy Spirit and with fire.
Acts 2:1–3. When the day of Pentecost had come...there appeared to them tongues as of fire, distributed and resting on each one of them.
Lk. 24:32. [The disciples] said to each other, "Did not our hearts burn within us while he talked to us on the road...?"
S. of S. 3:4 [Bride]: ...I found him whom my soul loves. I held him, and would not let him go...
Ps. 16:11. [O Lord,] ...in thy presence there is fulness of joy, in thy right hand are pleasures for evermore.
Ps. 34:8. O taste and see that the Lord is good!...
Heb. 6:4. ...those who have...tasted the heavenly gift, and have become partakers of the Holy Spirit, and have tasted the goodness of the word of God... (Also 1 Pet. 2:3.)

4. Bass Recit. (Based on Chorale Vs. 4 & 5)
●Light from God promises blessing greater than earthly (1-4)
Ein irdscher Glanz, ein leiblich Licht
A   worldly   lustre,   a corporeal light

Rührt meine Seele nicht;
Stirs   my   soul   not;

Ein Freudenschein ist mir von Gott entstanden,
A   light-of-joy   - to-me from God   has-arisen,
{A light of joy from God has arisen to me;}

Denn ein vollkommnes Gut,
For   a   perfect   posession—

Des Heilands Leib und Blut,
The   Savior's   body and blood—

Ist zur Erquickung da.
Is for restoration there.
{Is found there for our restoration.}

So muß uns ja
So must us indeed
{So must indeed}

Der überreiche Segen,
The overflowing blessing,

Der uns von Ewigkeit bestimmt
Which for-us from eternity (was) determined
{Which was determined for us from eternity,}

Und unser Glaube zu sich nimmt,
And our   faith   to itself does-take,
{And which our faith takes to itself,}

Zum Dank   und Preis bewegen.
To thanksgiving and praise   move.
{Move us to thanksgiving and praise.}

5. Tenor Aria (Based on Chorale Vs. 6)
●Praise to God: Music as thanksgiving and sacrifice (1-5)
Unser Mund und   Ton der Saiten
Our   mouth and (the) sound of   strings

Sollen   dir
Shall (for) thee
{Shall prepare for thee}

Für   und für
For-ever and ever

Dank   und Opfer zubereiten.
Thanksgiving and sacrifice prepare.
{Thanksgiving and sacrifice.}

Col. 3:2. Set your minds on things that are above, not on things that are on earth.
1 Jn. 2:15-17. Do not love the world or the things in the world. If any one loves the world, love for the Father is not in him. For all that is in the world, the lust of the flesh and the lust of the eyes and the pride of life, is not of the Father but is of the world. And the world passes away, and the lust of it; but he who does the will of God abides for ever.
1 Pet. 2:9. You are a chosen race, a royal priesthood, a holy nation, God's own people, that you may declare the wonderful deeds of him who called you out of darkness into his marvelous light.
Is. 9:2. The people who walked in darkness have seen a great light...
Is. 60:1-3. Arise, shine; for your light has come, and the glory of the Lord has risen upon you. For behold, darkness shall cover the earth, and thick darkness the peoples; but the Lord will arise upon you, and his glory will be seen upon you. And nations shall come to your light, and kings to the brightness of your rising.
Lk. 2:32 [Nunc dimittis]. [O Lord, thou hast prepared] a light for revelation to the Gentiles, and for glory to thy people Israel.
Ps. 27:1. The Lord is my light...
Ps. 16:5. The Lord is my chosen portion (Luther: Gut)...
Ps. 73:25. [O Lord,] whom have I in heaven but thee? And there is nothing upon earth that I desire besides thee.
Jn. 6:35. Jesus said to them, "I am the bread of life; he who comes to me shall not hunger, and he who believes in me shall never thirst."
Jn. 6:54 [Christ]: "He who eats my flesh and drinks my blood has eternal life, and I will raise him up at the last day."
1 Pet. 3:9. ...To this you have been called, that you may obtain a blessing.
2 Tim. 1:9. ...the grace which he gave us...ages ago.
1 Cor. 2:7, 9-10. ...God decreed [his secret plan] before the ages for our glorification...As it is written, "What no eye has seen, nor ear heard, nor the heart of man conceived, what God has prepared for those who love him," God has revealed to us through the Spirit... (Eph. 3:9, Col. 1:26)
Eph. 1:3. Blessed be the God...who has blessed us in Christ with every spiritual blessing in the heavenly places...
Rom. 3:24-25. [All] are justified by his grace as a gift, through the redemption which is in Christ Jesus, whom God put forward...to be received by faith.
Eph. 1:6. To the praise of his glorious grace which he freely bestowed on us in the Beloved.

Ps. 34:1. I will bless the Lord at all times; his praise shall continually be in my mouth.
Ps. 71:15. [O Lord,] my mouth will tell of thy righteous acts, of thy deeds of salvation all the day, for their number is past my knowledge.
Ps. 33:1-3. Rejoice in the Lord, O you righteous! Praise befits the upright. Praise the Lord with the lyre, make melody to him with the harp of ten strings! Sing to him a new song, play skilfully on the strings (Luther: Saitenspiel), with loud shouts.
Ps. 89:1. I will sing of thy steadfast love, O Lord, for ever...
Ps. 119:108. Accept my offerings of praise, O Lord...
Ps. 50:14, 23. Offer to God a sacrifice of thanksgiving, and pay your vows to the Most High...He who brings thanksgiving as his sacrifice honors me... (Also Ps. 69:30-31.)

Herz und Sinnen sind erhoben,
Heart and senses are lifted-up,

Lebenslang
Lifelong

Mit Gesang,
With song,

Großer König, dich zu loben.
Great king, thee to praise.
{Great king, to praise thee.}

6. Chorale (Vs 7) (See also 49-6.)
●Christ, our Alpha and Omega, shall return for us (1-6)
Wie bin ich doch so herzlich froh,
How am I indeed so heartily glad,
{How I am indeed so heartily glad,}

Daß mein Schatz ist das A und O,
That my treasure is the Alpha and Omega,

Der Anfang und das Ende;
The beginning and the end;

Er wird mich doch zu seinem Preis
He will me indeed to his glory
{He will indeed, to his glory}

Aufnehmen in das Paradeis,
Take-up into - paradise,
{Take me up into paradise,}

Des klopf ich in die Hände.
For-this clap I - (my) hands.
{For this I clap my hands.}

Amen! Amen!
Amen! Amen!

Komm, du schöne Freudenkrone, bleib nicht lange,
Come, thou beautiful crown-of-joy, tarry not long,

Deiner wart ich mit Verlangen.
For-thee wait I with longing.
{For thee I wait with longing.}

Heb. 13:15-16. ...Let us continually offer up a sacrifice of praise to God, that is, the fruit of lips that acknowledge his name. Do not neglect to do good and to share what you have, for such sacrifices are pleasing to God.
1 Cor. 14:14. ..I will sing with the spirit and I will sing with the mind also.
Ps. 146:2. I will praise the Lord as long as I live; I will sing praises to my God while I have being. (Also Ps. 63:4, 104:33, 145:2.)
Ps. 95:3. For the Lord is a great God, and a great King above all gods. (Also Ps. 97:9, Ex. 18:11.)
*****Lk. 1:33.** An he will reign over the house of Jacob for ever; and of his kingdom there will be no end.

S. of S. 6:3 [Bride]: I am my beloved's and my beloved is mine...
Rev. 1:8. "I am the Alpha and the Omega," (Luther: das A und das O, der Anfang und das Ende) says the Lord God, who is and who was and who is to come, the Almighty.
Rev. 21:6, 22:13 [God]: ...I am the Alpha and the Omega...the beginning and the end.
Jn. 14:3 [Christ]: When I go and prepare a place for you, I will come again and will take you to myself, that where I am you may be also.
Eph. 5:27. [Christ desires to] present the church to himself in splendor, without spot or wrinkle or any such thing, that she might be holy and without blemish.
2 Cor. 5:1. We know that if the earthly tent we live in is destroyed, we have a building from God, a house not made with hands, eternal in the heavens.
Lk. 23:43 [Christ]: ...Today you will be with me in Paradise.
Jms. 1:12. Blessed is the man who endures trial, for when he has stood the test he will receive the crown of life which God has promised to those who love him. (See also 2 Tim. 4:8, 1 Pet. 5:4, Rev. 2:10.)
Is. 28:5. In that day the Lord of hosts will be a crown of glory, and a diadem of beauty, to the remnant of his people.
Acts 1:11. ...This Jesus, who was taken up from you into heaven, will come in the same way as you saw him go into heaven.
Rev. 22:20. He who testifies to these things says, "Surely I am coming soon." Amen. Come, Lord Jesus!
Rev. 3:11 [Christ]: I am coming soon; hold fast what you have, so that no one may seize your crown. (Also Rev. 22:7.)
Rev. 22:7, 12 [Christ]: Behold, I am coming soon...Behold, I am coming soon, bringing my recompense, to repay every one for what he has done.
Phil. 3:20-21. Our commonwealth is in heaven, and from it we await a Savior, the Lord Jesus Christ, who will change our lowly body to be like his glorious body, by the power which enables him even to subject all things to himself.

BWV 2
Ach Gott, vom Himmel sieh darein
(NBA I/16; BC A98)

2. S. after Trinity (BWV 76, 2)
*1 Jn. 3:3–18 (Whoever does not do right or love his brother is not of God)
*Lk. 14:16–24 (Parable of the great banquet)
Librettist: Unknown

1. Chorus (Chorale Vs. 1)
●Apostasy: A prayer for aid in time of apostasy (2-1)
Ach Gott, vom Himmel sieh darein
Ah, God, from heaven look into-this

Und laß dich's doch erbarmen!
And let thyself please have-mercy!
{And please have mercy on us!}

Wie wenig sind der Heilgen dein,
How few are the saints of-thine,
{How few are thy saints,}

Verlassen sind wir Armen;
Forsaken are we needy-ones;

Dein Wort man nicht läßt haben wahr,
Thy Word one not allows to-be true,
{Thy Word is not held to be true,}

Der Glaub is auch verloschen gar
- Faith is also extinguished entirely
{Faith is also entirely extinguished}

Bei allen Menschenkindern.
Among all mankind.

2. Tenor Recit. (Based on Chorale Vs. 2)
●Apostasy: False teachers are like whited sepulchres (2-2)
Sie lehren eitel falsche List,
They teach empty (and) false craftiness,

Was wider Gott und seine Wahrheit ist;
Which opposed-to God and his truth is;
{Which is opposed to God and his truth;}

Und was der eigen Witz erdenket,
And what the individual wit conceives,

—O Jammer! der die Kirche schmerzlich kränket—
—O wretchedness, which (does) the church painfully vex—
{—O wretchedness that sorely vexes the church—}

Das muß anstatt der Bibel stehn.
That must instead-of the Bible stand.
{That must stand instead of the Bible.}

Der eine wählet dies, der andre das,
The one chooses this, the other that,

Lam. 4:49–50. My eyes will flow without ceasing, without respite, until the Lord from heaven looks down and sees (Luther: vom Himmel herabschaue und sehe darein). (Also Ps. 33:13, 102:19–20.)
Ps. 12:1, 8. Help, Lord; for there is no longer any that is godly; for the faithful have vanished from among the sons of men...On every side the wicked prowl, as vileness is exalted among the sons of men.
***1 Jn. 3:10.** By this it may be seen who are the children of God, and who are the children of the devil: whoever does not do right is not of God, nor he who does not love his brother.
Mic. 7:2. The godly man has perished from the earth, and there is none upright among men... (See also Mt. 7:14, Lk. 13:23, 1 Pet. 3:20.)
1 Kings 19:10. [Elijah] said, "I have been very jealous for the Lord, the God of hosts...and I, even I only, am left; and they seek my life, to take it away."
Job 20:19. For [the godless] has crushed and abandoned the poor (Luther: unterdrückt und verlassen den Armen)...
1 Tim. 4:1–2. Now the Spirit expressly says that in later times some will depart from the faith by giving heed to deceitful spirits and doctrines of demons, through the pretensions of liars... (Also Lk. 18:8.)
1 Tim. 6:20, 21. ...Avoid the godless chatter and contradictions of what is falsely called knowledge, for by professing it some have missed the mark as regards the faith...

***1 Jn. 3:7–8.** Little children, let not one deceive you. He who does right is righteous. He who commits sin is of the devil; for the devil has sinned from the beginning. The reason the Son of God appeared was to destroy the works of the devil.
1 Jn. 4:1. Beloved, do not believe every spirit, but test the spirits to see whether they are of God; for many false prophets have gone out into the world.
2 Pet. 3:17. You therefore, beloved...beware lest you be carried away with the error of lawless men and lose your own stability.
2 Tim. 3:8, 13. ...So these men also oppose the truth, men of corrupt mind and counterfeit faith...Evil men and impostors will go on from bad to worse, deceivers and deceived.
2 Jn. 1:7. For many deceivers have gone out into the world, men who will not acknowledge the coming of Jesus Christ in the flesh; such a one is the deceiver and the antichrist.
Rom. 1:21–22, 25. ...[Men] became futile in their thinking and their senseless minds were darkened. Claiming to be wise, they became fools...they exchanged the truth about God for a lie...
2 Pet. 2:15. Forsaking the right way they have gone astray; they have followed the way of Balaam...who loved gain from wrongdoing.

5

Die törichte Vernunft ist ihr Kompaß;
- Foolish reason is their compass;

Sie gleichen denen Totengräbern,
They resemble - dead-men's-graves,

Die, ob sie zwar von außen schön,
Which, though they indeed from the-outside (look) beautiful,

Nur Stank und Moder in sich fassen
Only stench and rottenness contain

Und lauter Unflat sehen lassen.
And sheer filth exhibit.

3. Alto Aria (Based on Chorale Vs. 3)
●Apostasy: Prayer to stop false teachers (2–3)
Tilg, o Gott, die Lehren,
Eradicate, O God, the teachings,

So dein Wort verkehren!
Which thy Word pervert!

Wehre doch der Ketzerei
Restrain please (all) heresy

Und allen Rottengeistern;
And all hordes-of-spirits;

Denn sie sprechen ohne Scheu:
For they speak without timidity:

Trotz dem, der uns will meistern!
Defiance against-him, who us wants-to rule!
{Defiance against him who would be our ruler!}

4. Bass Recit. (Based on Chorale Vs. 4)
●God hears the oppressed when they cry to him (2–4)
Die Armen sind verstört,
The poor are disquieted,

Ihr seufzend Ach, ihr ängstlich Klagen
Their sighing "ah," their frightened plaints,

Bei soviel Kreuz und Not,
In (all-the) cross and deprivation

Wodurch die Feinde fromme Seelen plagen,
Through-which the enemies pious souls do-plague,
{Through which pious souls are plagued by their enemies,}

Dringt in das Gnadenohr des Allerhöchsten ein.
Penetrates into the ear-of-grace of-the Most-High - .

Darum spricht Gott: Ich muß ihr Helfer sein!
Therefore speaks God: I must their Helper be!

1 Cor. 3:19–21. The wisdom of this world is folly with God. For it is written, "He catches the wise in their craftiness," and again, "The Lord knows that the thoughts of the wise are futile." So let no one boast of men...
Col. 2:8. See to it that no one makes a prey of you by philosophy and empty deceit, according to human tradition, according to the elemental spirits of the universe, and not according to Christ. (Also Mt. 11:25, Lk. 10:21, 2 Pet. 2:1.)
Mt. 23:27, 28 [Christ]: ...You are like whitewashed tombs, which outwardly appear beautiful, but within they are full of dead men's bones and all uncleanness. So you also outwardly appear righteous to men, but within you are full of hypocrisy and iniquity.

*1 Jn. 3:8. ...The reason the Son of God appeared was to destroy the works of the devil. (Also Heb. 2:14.)
Jer. 23:28–32 [God]: Let the prophet who has a dream tell the dream, but let him who has my word speak my word faithfully...Is not my word like fire, says the Lord, and like a hammer which breaks the rock in pieces? Therefore, behold, I am against the prophets...who steal my words from one another...who use their tongues and say, "Says the Lord." Behold, I am against those who prophesy lying dreams...who...lead my people astray by their lies and their recklessness, when I did not send them or charge them...
Ps. 36:1. Transgression speaks to the wicked deep in his heart; there is no fear of God before his eyes. (Also Ps. 55:19.)
Ps. 22:16. Yea dogs are round about me; a company of evildoers (Luther: Bösen Rotte) encircle me...
2 Pet. 2:10. Bold and wilful, they are not afraid to revile the glorious ones...
Jude 1:8, 10. ...These men...reject authority, and revile the glorious ones...These men revile what they do not understand...

*1 Jn. 3:12–13. [Do] not be like Cain who was of the evil one and murdered his brother. And why did he murder him? Because his own deeds were evil and his brother's righteous. Do not wonder, brethren, that the world hates you.
Jn. 15:18–19 [Christ]: If the world hates you, know that it has hated me before it hated you. If you were of the world, the world would love its own; but because you are not of the world, but I chose you out of the world, therefore the world hates you. (Also Jn. 17:14, Mt. 5:10–12, 10:24–25.)
Is. 57:1–2. The righteous man perishes, and no one lays it to heart; devout men are taken away, while no one understands.
Mt. 16:24. If any man would come after me, let him deny himself and take up his cross and follow me.
Mt. 5:4, 10. Blessed are those who mourn, for they shall be comforted ...Blessed are those who are persecuted for righteousness' sake, for theirs is the kingdom of heaven.
*Lk. 14:21. So the servant came and reported this to his master. Then the householder in anger said to his servant, "Go out quickly to the

Ich hab ihr Flehn erhört,
I have their entreaties heard,

Der Hilfe Morgenrot,
- Help's dawning,

Der reinen Wahrheit heller Sonnenschein
- Pure truth's bright sunshine

Soll sie mit neuer Kraft,
Shall them with renewed strength,
{Shall—with renewed strength,}

Die Trost und Leben schafft,
Which comfort and life creates,
{Which creates comfort and life—}

Erquicken und erfreun.
Revive and gladden.
{Revive and gladden them.}

Ich will mich ihrer Not erbarmen,
I will - (upon) their distress have mercy,

Mein heilsam Wort
My healing Word

Soll sein die Kraft der Armen.
Shall be the strength of-the poor.

5. Tenor Aria (Based on Chorale Vs. 5)
●Affliction purifies the Christian; be patient! (2–5)
Durchs Feuer wird das Silber rein,
Through fire is - silver purified,
{Through fire silver is purified,}

Durchs Kreuz das Wort bewährt erfunden.
Through (the) cross the word authenticated is-discovered.
{Through cross-bearing we see the word authenticated.}

Drum soll ein Christ zu allen Stunden
Therefore shall a Christian at all hours
{Therefore a Christian shall at all times}

Im Kreuz und Not geduldig sein.
In cross and distress patient be.
{Be patient in cross and distress.}

6. Chorale (Vs. 6)
●Prayer: Let not evil infiltrate us (2–6)
Das wollst du, Gott, bewahren rein
That mayest thou, God, preserve pure
{May thou, O God, preserve that pure}

Für diesem arg'n Geschlechte;
From this evil generation;

streets and lanes of the city, and bring in the poor and maimed and blind and lame."
Ps. 9:9. The Lord is a stonghold for the oppressed...
Ps. 69:33. For the Lord hears the needy, and does not despise his own that are in bonds.
Ps. 12:5. "Because the poor are despoiled, because the needy groan, I will now arise," says the Lord...
Heb. 13:6. Hence we can confidently say, "The Lord is my helper, I will not be afraid; what can man do to me?"
***1 Jn. 3:8.** ...The reason the Son of God appeared was to destroy the works of the devil. (Also Heb. 2:14.)
Ex. 3:7. Then the Lord said, "I have seen the affliction of my people who are in Egypt, and have heard their cry..." (Also Ex. 6:5.)
Is. 40:28–31. Have you not known? Have you not heard? The Lord is the everlasting God, the Creator of the ends of the earth. He does not faint or grow weary, his understanding is unsearchable. He gives power to the faint, and to him who has no might he increases strength. Even youths shall faint and be weary, and young men shall fall exhausted; but they who wait for the Lord shall renew their strength, they shall mount up with wings like eagles, they shall run and not be weary, they shall walk and not faint.
1 Cor. 1:18. The word of the cross is folly to those who are perishing, but to us who are being saved it is the power of God.
Ps. 119:25. [O Lord,] my soul cleaves to the dust; revive me according to thy word!

Ps. 66:10. For thou, O God, hast tested us; thou hast tried us as silver is tried. (Also Prov. 17:3, Prov. 25:4, 27:21.)
Mal. 3:3. For he is like a refiner's fire...he will sit as a refiner and purifier of silver, and he will purify the sons of Levi and refine them like gold and silver...
1 Cor. 3:12–13. Now if any one builds on the foundation with gold, silver, precious stones...it will be revealed with fire, and the fire will test what sort of work each one has done.
Mt. 16:24 [Christ]: If any man would come after me, let him deny himself and take up his cross and follow me. (Also 10:38.)
1 Pet. 4:12–13. Beloved, do not be surprised at the fiery ordeal which comes upon you to prove you, as though something strange were happening to you. But rejoice in so far as you share Christ's sufferings, that you may also rejoice and be glad when his glory is revealed. (Also Jms. 1:2–4, 12).

***1 Jn. 3:10.** By this it may be seen who are the children of God, and who are the children of the devil: whoever does not do right is not of God, nor he who does not love his brother.
***Lk. 14:24 [Christ]:** I tell you, none of those men who were invited shall taste my banquet.
Lk. 11:29. When the crowds were increasing, [Jesus] began to say, "This generation is an evil generation..."

Und laß uns dir   befohlen sein,
And may we to-you commended be,

Daß sich's in uns   nicht flechte.
That it   in us (does) not entwine.

Der gottlos Hauf sich   umher   findt,
The godless multitude -   round-about (us) is-found

Wo solche lose Leute sind
When such wanton persons are

In   deinem Volk erhaben.
Amongst thy   people prominent.
{Prominent amongst thy people.}

Acts 2:40. And [Peter] testified with many other words...saying, "Save yourselves from this crooked generation."

2 Pet. 2:1. ...There will be false teachers among you, who will secretly bring in destructive heresies...bringing upon themselves swift destruction. (Also Gal 2:4.)

Col. 2:8. See to it that no one makes a prey of you by philosophy and empty deceit...

Jude 1:3–4. ...I found it necessary to write appealing to you to contend for the faith which was once for all delivered to the saints. For admission has been secretly gained by some who long ago were designated for this condemnation, ungodly persons who pervert the grace of our God into licentiousness and deny our only Master and Lord, Jesus Christ...

2 Thess. 2:15. So then, brethren, stand firm and hold to the traditions which you were taught by us, either by word of mouth or by letter.

BWV 3
Ach Gott, wie manches Herzeleid I
(NBA I/5; BC A33)

2. S. after Epiphany (BWV 155, 3, 13)
*Rom. 12:6–16[1] (Diversity of gifts, exemplary conduct)
*Jn. 2:1–11 (Jesus attends the wedding at Cana)
[1]End: "men of low estate."
Librettist: Unknown

1. Chorus (Chorale Vs. 1) (See also 44–4, 58–1.)
●Prayer of lament: the narrow way full of affliction (3-1)
Ach, Gott, wie manches Herzeleid
Ah,   God, how many-a   grief

Begegnet mir zu dieser Zeit!
Meets   me in this   time!
{I encounter in this time!}

Der schmale Weg ist   trübsalvoll,
The narrow   way is affliction-filled,

Den ich zum Himmel wandern soll.
Which I to heaven   travel must.
{Which I must travel to heaven.}

*Rom. 12:12, 14. Rejoice in your hope, be patient in tribulation, be constant in prayer...Bless those who persecute you; bless and do not curse them.

Job 14:1. Man that is born of woman is of few days, and full of trouble. (Also Job 5:7.)

2 Tim. 3:12. Indeed all who desire to live a godly life in Christ Jesus will be persecuted.

Jn. 16:33 [Christ]: I have said this to you, that in me you may have peace. In the world you have tribulation...

Acts 14:22. ...Through many tribulations (Luther: Trübsal) we must enter the kingdom of God.

Mt. 7:14. For the gate is narrow and the way is hard, that leads to life, and those who find it are few.

Mt. 16:24 [Christ]: If any man would come after me, let him deny himself and take up his cross and follow me.

1 Pet. 4:12–13. Beloved, do not be surprised at the fiery ordeal which comes upon you to prove you, as though something strange were happening to you. But rejoice in so far as you share Christ's sufferings, that you may also rejoice and be glad when his glory is revealed.

2. Chorale (Vs. 2) & S.A.T.B. Recits.
●Flesh recalcitrant; but God became man to help us (3-2)
      Wie   schwerlich   läßt sich Fleisch und Blut
(With) how much-difficulty (is) -   flesh and blood—

Tenor Recit:
So nur nach Irdischem und Eitlem trachtet
Which only - the-earthly and the-vain seeks

Und weder Gott noch Himmel achtet,
And neither God nor   heaven regards—

      Zwingen zu dem ewigen Gut!
      Coerced   to the eternal good!

*Rom. 12:9. ...Hate what is evil, hold fast to what is good.

Jer. 17:9. The heart is deceitful above all things, and desperately corrupt; who can understand it?

Col. 3:2. Set your minds on things that are above, not on things that are on earth.

Mk. 10:24. ...Jesus said to them again, "Children, how hard it is to enter the kingdom of God!"

Rom. 7:15–25. I do not understand my own actions. For I do not do what I want, but I do the very thing I hate. Now if I do what I do not want, I agree that the law is good. So then it is no longer I that do it, but sin which dwells within me. For I know that nothing good dwells within me, that is, in my flesh. I can will what is right, but I cannot do it. For I do not do the good I want, but the evil I do not want is what

Alto Recit:
Da du, o Jesu, nun mein alles bist,
Since thou, O Jesu, now my all art,
{Since thou, O Jesu, art now my all,}

Und doch mein Fleisch so widerspenstig ist.
And still my flesh so recalcitrant is.
{And still my flesh is so recalcitrant.}

Wo soll ich mich denn wenden hin?
Where shall I - then turn - ?

Soprano Recit:
Das Fleisch ist schwach, doch will der Geist;
The flesh is weak, yet (is-willing) the spirit;
{The flesh is weak, yet the spirit is willing;}

So hilf du mir, der du mein Herze weißt.
So help thou me, - thou (who) my heart knowest.

Zu dir, o Jesu, steht mein Sinn.
To thee, O Jesu, is-inclined my disposition.
{To thee, O Jesu, is my disposition inclined.}

Bass Recit. (Based on Chorale Vss. 3–5, BC: 3–4):
Wer deinem Rat und deiner Hilfe traut,
Whoever thy counsel and thy help trusts,

Der hat wohl nie auf falschen Grund gebaut,
He has indeed ne'er on false foundation built,

Da du der ganzen Welt zum Trost gekommen,
Since thou to-the whole world for comfort hast-come,

Und unser Fleisch an dich genommen,
And our flesh on thyself taken,
{And hast taken our flesh upon thyself,}

So rettet uns dein Sterben
Thus saves us thy dying
{Thus thy dying saves us}

Vom endlichen Verderben.
From ultimate destruction.

Drum schmecke doch ein gläubiges Gemüte
Therefore taste indeed a believing disposition
{Therefore, a believing disposition ought to taste}

Des Heilands Freundlichkeit und Güte.
The Savior's kindness and goodness.

3. Bass Aria (Based on Chorale Vs. 6; BC: 5–6 & 8)
●Suffering outwardly; rejoicing inwardly (3-3)
Empfind ich Höllenangst und Pein,
Experience I hell's-fear and torment,
{Even though I experience hell's fear and torment}

I do. Now if I do what I do not want, it is no longer I that do it, but sin which dwells within me. So I find it to be a law that when I want to do right, evil lies close at hand. For I delight in the law of God, in my inmost self, but I see in my members another law at war with the law of my mind and making me captive to the law of sin which dwells in my members. Wretched man that I am! Who will deliver me from this body of death? Thanks be to God through Jesus Christ our Lord! So then, I of myself serve the law of God with my mind, but with my flesh I serve the law of sin. (Also Gal. 5:17.)

Jn. 6:68. Lord, to whom shall we go? You have the words of eternal life.

Ps. 73:25. [O Lord,] whom have I in heaven but thee? And there is nothing upon earth that I desire besides thee.

Mk. 14:38. Watch and pray that you may not enter into temptation; the spirit indeed is willing, but the flesh is weak.

1 Sam. 16:7. ...Man looks on the outward appearance, but the Lord looks on the heart. (Also Lk. 16:15.)

Jn. 21:17. ...[Jesus] said to him the third time, "Simon, son of John, do you love me?" Peter was grieved...and he said to him, "Lord, you know everything; you know that I love you."

Prov. 3:5–6. Trust in the Lord with all your heart, and do not rely on your own insight. In all your ways acknowledge him, and he will make straight your paths.

Ps. 73:24. [O Lord,] thou dost guide me with thy counsel, and afterward thou wilt receive me to glory. (Also Ps. 33:11.)

*Jn. 2:5. Jesus' mother said to the servants, "Do whatever he tells you."

Mt. 7:26 [Christ]: Every one who hears these words of mine and does not do them will be like a foolish man who built his house upon the sand.

Rom. 8:3. God has done what the law, weakened by the flesh, could not do: sending his own Son in the likeness of sinful flesh and for sin, he condemned sin in the flesh. (Also Jn. 1:12, Heb. 2:14.)

Jn. 1:14. The Word became flesh...

2 Cor. 1:5. ...Through Christ we share abundantly in comfort...

Rom. 5:8. God shows his love for us in that while we were yet sinners Christ died for us.

1 Pet. 3:18. For Christ also died for sins once for all, the righteous for the unrighteous, that he might bring us to God, being put to death in the flesh but made alive in the spirit.

Ps. 34:8. O taste and see that the Lord is good!...

*Jn. 2:9–10. When the steward of the feast tasted the water now become wine...[he] called the bridegroom and said to him, "Every man serves the good wine first; and when men have drunk freely, then the poor wine; but you have kept the good wine until now."

Ps. 106:1. O give thanks to the Lord, for he is good; for his steadfast love endures for ever!

2 Cor. 4:16–18. So we do not lose heart. Though our outer nature is wasting away, our inner nature is being renewed every day. For this slight momentary affliction is preparing for us an eternal weight of glory beyond all comparison, because we look not to the things that are seen but to the things that are unseen; for the things that are seen

9

Doch muß beständig in dem Herzen
Yet must constantly in (my) heart

Ein rechter Freudenhimmel sein.
A veritable heaven-of-joy be.

Ich darf nur Jesu Namen nennen,
I need only Jesus' name to-name,
{I only need to pray in Jesus' name,}

Der kann auch unermeßne Schmerzen
He can even immeasurable griefs

Als einen leichten Nebel trennen.
Like a light mist (dispell).
{Dispell like a light mist.}

4. Tenor Recit. (Based on Chorale Vss. 7–14; BC: 7–10)
●Languishing yet relying on Jesus' steadfast love (3–4)
Es mag mir Leib und Geist verschmachten,
(Now) let (my) body and soul languish,

Bist du, o Jesu, mein
(If) thou, O Jesu, (art) mine

Und ich bin dein,
And I am thine,

Will ich's nicht achten.
Will I-it not regard.
{I will not regard it.}

Dein treuer Mund
Thy faithful mouth

Und dein unendlich Lieben,
And thy unending loving,

Das unverändert stets geblieben,
That unchanging has-ever remained,
{That has ever remained unchanging,}

Erhält mir noch dein ersten Bund,
Preserves for-me still thy first covenant,

Der meine Brust mit Freudigkeit erfüllet
Which my breast with gladness fills
{Which fills my breast with gladness}

Und auch des Todes Furcht, des Grabes Schrecken stillet.
And also - death's fear, the grave's terror calms.
{And also calms the fear of death, the terror of the grave.}

Fällt Not und Mangel gleich von allen Seiten ein,
Attacks distress and dearth even-though from all sides -,
{Though distress and dearth should attack from all sides,}

Mein Jesu wird mein Schatz und Reichtum sein.
My Jesu will my treasure and wealth be.
{My Jesu will be my treasure and wealth.}

are transient, but the things that are unseen are eternal. (Also Col. 3:1–3.)
1 Pet. 1:6–7. In this you rejoice, though now for a little while you may have to suffer various trials, so that the genuineness of your faith, more precious than gold which though perishable is tested by fire, may redound to praise and glory and honor at the revelation of Jesus Christ. (Also Jms. 1:2.)
Jn. 16:24 [Christ]: Hitherto you have asked nothing in my name; ask, and you will receive, that your joy may be full.
Ps. 30:5. ...Weeping may tarry for the night, but joy comes with the morning.
Is. 35:10/51:11. And the ransomed of the Lord shall return, and come to Zion with singing; everlasting joy shall be upon their heads; they shall obtain joy and gladness, and sorrow and sighing shall flee away.

Ps. 73:25–26. [O Lord,] whom have I in heaven but thee? And there is nothing upon earth that I desire besides thee. My flesh and my heart may fail (Luther: verschmachtet), but God is the strength of my heart and my portion for ever.
2 Cor. 4:16. So we do not lose heart. Though our outer nature is wasting away, our inner nature is being renewed every day.
1 Jn. 3:1. See what love the Father has given us, that we should be called children of God...
S. of S. 2:16 [Bride]: My beloved is mine and I am his... (Also S. of S. 6:3.)
Ps. 100:5. The Lord is good; his steadfast love endures for ever, and his faithfulness to all generations. (Also Ps. 106:1, 107:1, 118:1.)
Deut. 7:9. ...the faithful God who keeps covenant and steadfast love with those who love him and keep his commandments...
Is. 54:10. For the mountains may depart and the hills be removed, but my steadfast love shall not depart from you and my covenant of peace shall not be removed, says the Lord...
Jer. 31:33 [God]: This is the covenant which I will make...I will put my law within them, and I will write it upon their hearts; and I will be their God, and they shall be my people.
Lk. 1:67, 68, 27. Zechariah was filled with the Holy Spirit, and prophesied, saying, "Blessed be the Lord God of Israel, for he has visited and redeemed his people...to perform the mercy promised to our fathers, and to remember his holy covenant..."
Heb. 2:14–15. ...[Christ] himself likewise partook of the same nature, that through death he might destroy him who has the power of death, that is, the devil, and deliver all those who through fear of death were subject to lifelong bondage.
1 Cor. 15:55. O death, where is thy victory? O death, where is thy sting?
2 Cor. 8:9. You know the grace of our Lord Jesus Christ, that though he was rich, yet for your sake he became poor, so that by his poverty you might become rich.
Hab. 3:17–19. Though the fig tree do not blossom, nor fruit be on the vines, the produce of the olive fail and the fields yield no food, the flock be cut off from the fold and there be no herd in the stalls, yet I will rejoice in the Lord, I will joy in the God of my salvation. God, the Lord, is my strength...
Rom. 8:18. I consider that the sufferings of this present time are not worth comparing with the glory that is to be revealed to us. (Also 2 Cor. 4:17.)

5. Soprano & Alto Duet (Based on Chorale Vss. 15-16; BC: 15-17)
●Suffering, yet I can sing by faith (3-5)
Wenn Sorgen auf mich dringen,
Wenn cares upon me   press,

Will ich in Freudigkeit
Will I   in joyousness
{Will I joyously}

Zu meinem Jesu singen.
To my   Jesus sing.

Mein Kreuz hilft Jesus tragen,
My   cross helps Jesus carry,
{Jesus helps carry my cross,}

Drum   will ich gläubig sagen:
Therefore will I believing say:

Es dient zum besten   allezeit.
It serves for the-best at-all-times.

*Rom. 12:12, 14.** Rejoice in your hope, be patient in tribulation, be constant in prayer...Bless those who persecute you; bless and do not curse them.
Acts 16:23, 25. And when they had inflicted many blows upon [Paul and Silas], they threw them into prison...But about midnight Paul and Silas were praying and singing hymns to God...
Mt. 10:38 [Christ]: He who does not take his cross and follow me is not worthy of me.
Jn. 19:17. ...Jesus...went out bearing his own cross...
Mt. 27:32. As they went out, they came upon a man of Cyrene, Simon by name; this man they compelled to carry [Jesus'] cross.
2 Cor. 1:5. As we share abundantly in Christ's sufferings, so through Christ we share abundantly in comfort too.
Jms. 1:2-4. Count it all joy, my brethren, when you meet various trials, for you know that the testing of your faith produces steadfastness. And let steadfastness have its full effect, that you may be perfect and complete, lacking in nothing. (Also 1:12, 1 Pet. 4:12-14, 5:10.)
Rom. 8:28. We know that in everything God works for good with those who love him...

6. Chorale (Vs. 18) (See also 153-9.)
●Prayer: That I live or die in Christ (3-6)
Erhalt mein Herz im Glauben rein,
Preserve my heart in faith   pure,
{Preserve my heart pure in faith,}

So leb und sterb ich dir   allein.
So live and die I to-thee alone.
{Thus will I live and die to thee alone}

Jesu, mein Trost, hör mein Begier,
Jesu,   my comfort, hear my longing,

O mein Heiland, wär ich bei dir.
O my   Savior,   were I with thee.

Ps. 86:11. Teach me thy way, O Lord, that I may walk in thy truth; unite my heart (Luther: erhalte mein Herz) to fear thy name.
1 Thess. 5:23. May the God of peace himself sanctify you wholly; and may your spirit and soul and body be kept sound and blameless at the coming of our Lord Jesus Christ.
Jude 1:24. Now to him who is able to keep you from falling and to present you without blemish before the presence of his glory with rejoicing...
Rom. 14:7-8. None of us lives to himself, and none of us dies to himself. If we live, we live to the Lord, and if we die, we die to the Lord; so then, whether we live or whether we die, we are the Lord's.
2 Cor. 5:8-9. ...We would rather be away from the body and at home with the Lord...Whether we are at home or away, we make it our aim to please him.
Phil. 1:21. For to me to live is Christ, and to die is gain.

BWV 4
Christ lag in Todesbanden
(NBA I/9; BC A54a/b)

Easter Sunday (BWV 4, 31, 249)
*1 Cor. 5:6-8 (Christ, our paschal lamb has been sacrificed)
*Mk. 16:1-8 (The resurrection of Christ)
Librettist: Chorale (Martin Luther)

1. Sinfonia

2. Chorus (Chorale Vs. 1)
●Christ died for our sins; rose for our life! (4-2)
Christ lag in Todesbanden
Christ lay in death's-bonds

*Mk. 16:6.** And [the angel] said to them, "Do not be amazed; you seek Jesus of Nazareth, who was crucified. He has risen, he is not here; see the place where they laid him."
Ps. 18:4-5. The cords of death (Luther: Todes Bande) encompassed me, the torrents of perdition assailed me; the cords of Sheol entangled me, the snares of death confronted me. (Also 2 Sam. 22:5-6, Ps. 116:3.)
*1 Cor. 5:7.** ...Christ, our paschal lamb, has been sacrificed. Mt. 20:28. ...The Son of man came...to give his life as a ransom for many.

Für unsre Sünd gegeben,
For   our   sin   given,

Er ist wieder erstanden
He is   again   risen

Und hat uns bracht das Leben;
And has   us brought -   life;
{And has brought us new life;}

Des   wir sollen fröhlich sein,
For-that we shall   joyful   be,

Gott loben und ihm dankbar sein,
God   praise and him thankful be,
{Shall praise God and be thankful to him,}

Und singen Halleluja,   Halleluja!
And   sing   Hallelujah, Hallelujah!

3. Soprano & Alto Duet (Chorale Vs. 2)
●Sin caused us all to be enslaved by death (4-3)
Den Tod niemand zwingen kunnt
 - Death no-one master could
{There was no one who could master death}

Bei   allen Menschenkindern,
Amongst all   mankind,

Das macht' alles unser Sünd,
That does   all   our   sin,
{Our sin caused all that;}

Kein Unschuld war zu finden.
No   innocence was to be-found.

Davon   kam der Tod so bald
Because-of-that came - death so soon
{Because of that death came so soon}

Und nahm über uns Gewalt,
And gained over us   power,
{And gained power over us,}

Hielt uns in seinem Reich gefangen.
Held us in   its   kingdom captive.
{Held us captive in its kingdom.}

Halleluja!
Hallelujah!

4. Tenor Aria (Chorale Vs. 3)
●Christ conquered sin and death for us (4-4)
Jesus Christus, Gottes Sohn,
Jesus   Christ, God's   Son,

An unser Statt ist kommen
In   our   place has come

Jn. 3:16. For God so loved the world that he gave his only Son, that whoever believes in him should not perish but have eternal life.
Eph. 5:2. ...Christ loved us and gave himself up for us, a fragrant offering and sacrifice to God.
Jn. 10:10 [Christ]: ...I came that they may have life, and have it abundantly.
Jn. 20:31. These [things] are written that you may believe that Jesus is the Christ, the Son of God, and that believing you may have life in his name.
Rom. 6:23. ...The free gift of God is eternal life in Christ Jesus our Lord.
1 Jn. 5:11. This is the testimony, that God gave us eternal life, and this life is in his Son.
Rom. 5:10. For if, while we were enemies we were reconciled to God by the death of his Son, much more, now that we are reconciled, shall we be saved by his life.
*1 Cor. 5:8. Let us, therefore, celebrate the festival...
Rev. 19:6. Then I heard what seemed to be the voice of a great multitude...crying, "Hallelujah!..."

Rom. 5:12, 17, 19. ...Sin came into the world through one man and death through sin, and so death spread to all men because all men sinned...Because of one man's trespass, death reigned through that one man...By one man's disobedience many were made sinners...
Gen. 2:16–17. The Lord commanded the man, saying, "You may freely eat of every tree of the garden; but of the tree of the knowledge of good and evil you shall not eat, for in the day that you eat of it you shall die."
Rom. 6:23. The wages of sin is death...
Rom. 3:23. All have sinned and fall short of the glory of God... (Also Prov. 20:9.)
Rom. 3:10–12. As it is written: "None is righteous, no, not one; no one understands, no one seeks for God. All have turned aside, together they have gone wrong; no one does good, not even one."
Heb. 2:14–15. Since therefore the children share in flesh and blood, [Christ] himself likewise partook of the same nature, that through death he might destroy him who has the power of death, that is, the devil, and deliver all those who through fear of death were subject to lifelong bondage.
1 Cor. 15:21–22. As by a man came death, by a man has come also the resurrection of the dead. For as in Adam all die, so also in Christ shall all be made alive.
Rev. 19:1. After this I heard what seemed to be the loud voice of a great multitude in heaven, crying, "Hallelujah! Salvation and glory and power belong to our God." (Also Rev. 19:3, 4, 6.)

*1 Cor. 5:7. ...Christ, our paschal lamb, has been sacrificed.
Heb. 9:22. Indeed, under the law almost everything is purified with blood, and without the shedding of blood there is no forgiveness of sins.
1 Jn. 4:10. In this is love, not that we loved God but that he loved us and sent his Son to be the expiation for our sins.

Und hat die Sünde weggetan,
And has - sin removed,
{And has removed our sin,}

Damit dem Tod genommen
With-that (also) from death taken

All sein Recht und sein Gewalt,
All its claim and its power,

Da bleibet nichts denn Tods Gestalt,
Thus remains nothing but death's form,
{Thus nothing remains but death's outward form;}

Den Stach'l hat er verloren.
The sting has it lost.
{It has lost its sting.}

Halleluja!
Hallelujah!

5. Chorus (Chorale Vs. 4)
•Life devoured death by dying (4–5)
Es war ein wunderlicher Krieg,
It was a peculiar war,

Da Tod und Leben rungen,
When death and life struggled,

Das Leben behielt den Sieg,
- Life gained the victory,

Es hat den Tod verschlungen.
It has - death devoured.
{It has devoured death.}

Die Schrift hat verkündigt das,
The Scripture has proclaimed this:

Wie ein Tod den andern frass,
How one death the other devoured,

Ein Spott aus dem Tod ist worden.
A mockery of - death - became.
{And made a mockery of death.}

Halleluja!
Hallelujah!

6. Bass Aria (Chorale Vs. 5) (See also 158-4.)
•Christ died as our paschal lamb (4–6)
Hier ist das rechte Osterlamm,
Here is the proper Easter-lamb,

Davon Gott hat geboten,
Of-which God has commanded,

Rom. 5:7–8. Why, one will hardly die for a righteous man—though perhaps for a good man one will dare even to die. But God shows his love for us in that while we were yet sinners Christ died for us.
2 Cor. 5:21. For our sake he made him to be sin who knew no sin, so that in him we might become the righteousness of God.
Heb. 9:26. ...He has appeared once for all at the end of the age to put away sin by the sacrifice of himself.
Heb. 2:14–15. Since therefore the children share in flesh and blood, [Christ] himself likewise partook of the same nature, that through death he might destroy him who has the power of death, that is, the devil, and deliver all those who through fear of death were subject to lifelong bondage.
1 Cor. 15:25–26. He must reign until he has put all his enemies under his feet. The last enemy to be destroyed is death. (Also Is. 25:8.)
Rom. 6:9. For we know that Christ being raised from the dead will never die again; death no longer has dominion over him.
2 Tim. 1:10. ...through the appearing of our Savior Christ Jesus, who abolished death and brought life and immortality to light...
1 Cor. 15:55. ...O death, where is thy sting?

Heb. 2:14–15. ...[Christ] himself likewise partook of the same nature, that through death he might destroy him who has the power of death, that is, the devil...
1 Cor. 15:25–26. He must reign until he has put all his enemies under his feet. The last enemy to be destroyed is death.
Acts 2:24–27. God raised [Christ] up, having loosed the pangs of death, because it was not possible for him to be held by it. For David says concerning him, "I saw the Lord always before me, for he is at my right hand that I may not be shaken; therefore my heart was glad, and my tongue rejoiced; moreover my flesh will dwell in hope. For thou wilt not abandon my soul to Hades, nor let thy Holy One see corruption."
Rom. 6:9. We know that Christ being raised from the dead will never die again; death no longer has dominion over him.
1 Cor. 15:54–55. ...Then shall come to pass the saying that is written: "Death is swallowed up in victory." O death, where is thy victory? O death, where is thy sting?
Is. 25:8–9. He will swallow up death for ever (Luther: Tod verschlingen ewiglich), and the Lord God will wipe away tears from all faces, and the reproach of his people he will take away from all the earth; for the Lord has spoken. It will be said on that day, "Lo, this is our God; we have waited for him, that he might save us. This is the Lord; we have waited for him; let us be glad and rejoice in his salvation."

*1 Cor. 5:7. ...For Christ, our paschal lamb, has been sacrificed.
1 Pet. 2:24. He himself bore our sins in his body on the tree...By his wounds you have been healed.
Heb. 9:22. Indeed, under the law almost everything is purified with blood, and without the shedding of blood there is no forgiveness of sins.
Ex. 12:1, 3, 5, 7, 11–13. The Lord said to Moses and Aaron in the land of Egypt...Tell all the congregation of Israel that on the tenth day of this month they shall take every man a lamb...Your lamb shall be

Das ist hoch an des Kreuzes Stamm
It   has high on the cross's   trunk

In heisser Lieb gebraten,
In   hot   love   broiled,

Des Blut zeichnet unser Tür,
Its blood marks   our door,

Das hält der Glaub dem Tode für,
That displays - faith to Death - ,
{Our faith shows this blood to approaching Death,}

Der Würger kann uns nicht mehr schaden.
The destroyer can us   no   more   harm.
{And so the destroyer can harm us no more.}

Halleluja!
Hallelujah!

7. Soprano & Tenor Duet (Chorale Vs. 6)
●Paschal feast: we celebrate it in the light of joy (4–7)
So feiern wir das hohe Fest
So celebrate we the high feast
{So we celebrate the high feast}

Mit Herzensfreud und Wonne,
With joy-of-heart and   bliss,

Das uns der Herre scheinen lässt,
Which to-us the Lord   shine   lets,
{Which to us the Lord lets shine,}

Er is selber die Sonne,
He is himself the sun,

Der durch seiner Gnade Glanz
Which through his   grace's brightness

Erleuchtet unsre Herzen ganz,
Illuminates our   hearts entirely,

Der Sünden Nacht ist verschwunden.
 - Sin's   night has   vanished.

Halleluja!
Hallelujah!

8. Chorale (Vs. 7)
●Unleavened bread: We eat only it, which is Christ (4–8)
Wir essen und wir leben wohl
We eat   and we live indeed

In rechten Osterfladen,
(On) true   Easter-bread,

without blemish...Then they shall take some of the blood, and put it on the two door posts and the lintel of the houses...It is the Lord's passover. For I will pass through the land of Egypt that night, and I will smite all the first-born in the land of Egypt, both man and beast... The blood shall be a sign for you...and when I see the blood, I will pass over you...
Jn. 1:29. ...[John] saw Jesus coming toward him, and said, "Behold, the Lamb of God, who takes away the sin of the world!"
Is. 53:7, 10. He was oppressed, and he was afflicted, yet he opened not his mouth; like a lamb that is led to the slaughter, and like a sheep that before its shearers is dumb, so he opened not his mouth...Yet it was the will of the Lord to bruise him; he has put him to grief; when he makes himself an offering for sin...
Rev. 5:12. ...Worthy is the Lamb who was slain, to receive power and wealth and wisdom and might and honor and glory and blessing!
Rev. 20:6. Blessed and holy is he who shares in the first resurrection! Over such the second death has no power...

*1 Cor. 5:8. Let us, therefore, celebrate the festival, not with the old leaven, the leaven of malice and evil, but with the unleavened bread of sincerity and truth.
Ex. 12:14–15, 17. This day shall be for you a memorial day, and you shall keep it as a feast to the Lord...Seven days you shall eat unleavened bread; on the first day you shall put away leaven out of your houses...And you shall observe the feast of unleavened bread, for on this very day I brought your hosts out of the land of Egypt...
2 Cor. 4:6. It is the God who said, "Let light shine out of darkness," who has shone in our hearts to give the light of the knowledge of the glory of God in the face of Christ.
Rev. 1:16–18. ...His face was like the sun shining in full strength...He laid his right hand upon me, saying, "...I am the first and the last, and the living one; I died, and behold I am alive for evermore, and I have the keys of Death and Hades."
Rev. 21:23. The city has no need of sun or moon to shine upon it, for the glory of God is its light, and its lamp is the Lamb.
Rev. 22:5. And night shall be no more; they need no light of lamp or sun, for the Lord God will be their light...
Jn. 1:5. The light shines in the darkness, and the darkness has not overcome it.
1 Jn. 2:8. ...The darkness is passing away and the true light is already shining. (Also 1 Pet. 2:9.)

*1 Cor. 5:6–8. Your boasting is not good. Do you not know that a little leaven leavens the whole lump? Cleanse out the old leaven that you may be a new lump, as you really are unleavened. For Christ our paschal lamb, has been sacrificed. Let us, therefore, celebrate the festival, not with the old leaven, the leaven of malice and evil, but with the unleavened bread of sincerity and truth.
Ex. 12:14–15, 17. This day shall be for you a memorial day, and you shall keep it as a feast to the Lord...Seven days you shall eat unleavened bread; on the first day you shall put away leaven our of

Der alte Sauerteig nicht soll
The old   leaven   not shall
{The old leaven shall not}

Sein bei dem Wort der Gnaden,
Be with the word of   grace,

Christus will   die Koste sein
Christ   wants (our)   fare to-be
{Christ wants to be our fare}

Und speisen die Seel allein,
And   feed   the soul alone,

Der Glaub will   keins andern leben.
  - Faith would nought other   live (upon).
{Faith would live on nought else.}

Halleluja!
Hallelujah!

BWV 5
Wo soll ich fliehen hin
(NBA I/24; BC A145)

19. S. after Trinity (BWV 48, 5, 56)
*Eph. 4:22-28 (Exhortation to put on the new nature)
*Mt. 9:1-8 (Jesus heals the paralytic)
Librettist: Unknown

1. Chorus (Chorale Vs. 1)
●Where can I turn with my many sins? (5-1)
Wo   soll ich fliehen hin,
Where shall I   flee   - ,

Weil ich beschweret bin
For   I   encumbered am
{Since I am so encumbered}

Mit   viel und großen Sünden?
With many and   great   sins?

Wo   soll ich Rettung finden?
Where shall I   salvation find?
{Where shall I find salvation?}

Wenn   alle Welt herkäme,
Were (the) entire world to-come-here,

Mein Angst sie   nicht wegnähme.
My anxiety it (could) not take-away.
{It could still not take away my anxiety.}

your houses...And you shall observe the feast of unleavened bread, for on this very day I brought your hosts out of the land of Egypt...
Mt. 4:4. [Jesus said], "It is written, 'Man shall not live by bread alone, but by every word that proceeds from the mouth of God.'" (See Deut. 8:3, also Lk. 4:4.)
Acts 20:32. Now I commend you to God and to the word of his grace, which is able to build you up and to give you the inheritance among all those who are sanctified.
Eph. 4:22-24. Put off your old nature which belongs to your former manner of life and is corrupt through deceitful lusts, and be renewed in the spirit of your minds, and put on the new nature, created after the likeness of God in true righteousness and holiness. (Also Col. 3:9-10, 2 Pet. 1:9.)
Mt. 26:26. Now as they were eating, Jesus took bread, and blessed, and broke it, and gave it to the disciples and said, "Take, eat; this is my body."
Jn. 6:48-51 [Christ]: I am the bread of life. Your fathers ate the manna in the wilderness, and they died. This is the bread which comes down from heaven, that a man may eat of it and not die. I am the living bread which came down from heaven; if any one eats of this bread, he will live for ever; and the bread which I shall give for the life of the world is my flesh. (Also Rev. 2:17.)

*Eph. 4:22.** Put off your old nature which belongs to your former manner of life and is corrupt through deceitful lusts. (Also Col. 3:9-10.)
Is. 1:4. Ah, sinful nation, a people laden with iniquity...
Ps. 139:7-12. [O Lord,] whither shall I go from thy Spirit? Or whither shall I flee from thy presence? If I ascend to heaven, thou art there! If I make my bed in Sheol, thou art there! If I take the wings of the morning and dwell in the uttermost parts of the sea, even there thy hand shall lead me, and thy right hand shall hold me. If I say, "Let only darkness cover me, and the light about me be night," even the darkness is not dark to thee, the night is bright as the day; for darkness is as light with thee.
Rom. 7:18, 24. For I know that nothing good dwells within me, that is, in my flesh. I can will what is right, but I cannot do it...Wretched man that I am! Who will deliver me from this body of death?
Lk. 9:25. What does it profit a man if he gains the whole world and loses or forfeits himself? (Also Mt. 16:26, Mk. 8:36.)
Mk. 2:7. Who can forgive sins but God alone?
*Mt. 9:5-6** [Christ]: "Which is easier, to say, 'Your sins are forgiven,' or to say, 'Rise and walk'? But that you may know that the Son of man has authority on earth to forgive sins"—he then said to the paralytic—"Rise, take up your bed and go home." (Also Mk. 2:8-11, Lk. 5:21-24.)

2. Bass Recit. (Based on Chorale Vss. 2–3)
●Sins abhorrent to God; in Christ we find cleansing (5–2)
Der Sünden Wust   hat mich nicht nur befleckt,
-   Sin's rubbish   has me   not only   stained,
{Sin's rubbish has not only stained me,}

Er hat   vielmehr   den ganzen Geist bedeckt,
It has, much-more, (my) whole   spirit covered,
{But has covered my whole spirit,}

Gott müßte   mich als unrein von   sich treiben;
God would-have me as unclean from himself to-drive;
{God would have to drive me from himself as one unclean;}

Doch weil ein Tropfen   heilges Blut
Yet because a   droplet (of) holy blood

So   große Wunder tut,
Such great wonders does,
{Can do such great wonders,}

Kann ich noch unverstoßen bleiben.
Can I   still unrejected   remain.
{I can still remain unrejected.}

Die Wunden sind ein offnes Meer,
(His) wounds are an open sea,

Dahin   ich meine Sünden senke,
Wherein I   my   sins   submerge,

Und wenn ich mich zu diesem Strome lenke,
And when I   myself to this   stream do-guide,
{And when I turn to this stream,}

So   macht er mich von meinen Flecken leer.
Then makes he me from my   stains (clean).
{Then he cleanses me from my stains.}

3. Tenor Aria (Based on Chorale Vs. 4)
●Fountain of blood cleanses me (5–3)
Ergieße dich reichlich, du göttliche Quelle,
Overflow - profusely, thou divine   spring,

Ach, walle mit blutigen Strömen auf mich.
Ah, well-up with bloody rivers   over me.

Es   fühlet mein Herze die tröstliche Stunde,
(Now) feels my   heart the comforting hour,
{My heart feels the comforting hour,}

Nun sinken die drückenden Lasten zu Grunde,
Now sink   the pressing   burdens to the-bottom,
{Now my pressing burdens sink to the bottom,}

Es wäschet die sündlichen Flecken von sich.
It washes the sinful   stains off itself.
{Now my heart washes itself clean of the sinful stains.}

*Eph. 4:22–24. Put off your old nature which belongs to your former manner of life and is corrupt through deceitful lusts, and be renewed in the spirit of your minds, and put on the new nature, created after the likeness of God in true righteousness and holiness. (Also Col. 3:9–10.)

Lam. 4:14. [Those who had been judged for their many sins] wandered, blind, through the streets, so defiled with blood that none could touch their garments.

Is. 59:3. Your hands are defiled with blood and your fingers with iniquity... (Also 2 Cor. 7:1.)

Jer. 7:13–15. And now, because you have done all these things, says the Lord...I will cast you out of my sight...

Ps. 31:22. [O Lord]...I am driven far (Luther: verstoßen) from thy sight...

Gen. 3:24. [God] drove out the man; and at the east of the garden of Eden he placed the cherubim, and a flaming sword which turned every way, to guard the way to the tree of life.

Ps. 24:3, 4. ...Who shall stand in his holy place? He who has clean hands and a pure heart...

Eph. 2:13. But now in Christ Jesus you who once were far off have been brought near in the blood of Christ.

Is. 53:5. He was wounded for our transgressions, he was bruised for our iniquities; upon him was the chastisement that made us whole, and with his stripes we are healed. (Also 1 Pet. 2:24.)

Mic. 7:19. ...[O Lord,] thou wilt cast all our sins into the depths of the sea...

2 Kings 5:10. And Elisha sent a messenger to [Naaman the leper], saying, "Go and wash in the Jordan seven times, and your flesh shall be restored, and you shall be clean."

Ps. 46:4. There is a river whose streams make glad the city of God...

1 Jn. 1:7. ...The blood of Jesus his Son cleanses us from all sin.

*Mt. 9:2 [Christ]: ...Take heart, my son; your sins are forgiven.

Zech. 13:1. On that day there shall be a fountain opened for the house of David and the inhabitants of Jerusalem to cleanse them from sin and uncleanness.

Jer. 2:22. Though you wash yourself with lye and use much soap, the stain of your guilt is still before me, says the Lord God.

Ps. 51: 2, 7. [O Lord,] wash me thoroughly from my iniquity, and cleanse me from my sin!...Purge me with hyssop, and I shall be clean; wash me, and I shall be whiter than snow.

1 Jn. 1:7. ...The blood of Jesus his Son cleanses us from all sin. (blood: also 1 Pet. 1:18–19, Rev. 5:9)

Is. 10:27. And in that day his burden will depart from your shoulder, and his yoke will be destroyed from your neck.

Mt. 11:28 [Christ]: Come to me, all who labor and are heavy laden, and I will give you rest.

Is. 1:18. ...Though your sins are like scarlet, they shall be as white as snow; though they are red like crimson, they shall become like wool.

Acts. 22:16. ...Be baptised, and wash away your sins, calling on his name. (Also Tit. 3:5.)

4. Alto Recit. (Based on Chorale Vss. 5–7)
●Jesus forgives, frees, and comforts us (5-4)
Mein treuer Heiland tröstet mich,
My faithful Savior comforts me,

Es sei verscharrt in seinem Grabe,
(May) it be covered-over in his grave—

Was ich gesündigt habe;
Whatever I sinned have;
{Whatever I have sinned;}

Ist mein Verbrechen noch so groß,
Is my offence yet so great,
{Though my offence be ever so great,}

Er macht mich frei und los.
He makes me free and released.

Wenn Gläubige die Zuflucht bei ihm finden,
When believers - refuge with him find,

Muß Angst und Pein
Must dread and torment
{Then dread and torment must}

Nicht mehr gefährlich sein
No longer dangerous be
{Be dangerous no longer}

Und alsobald verschwinden;
And forthwith vanish;

Ihr Seelenschatz, ihr höchstes Gut
Their soul's-treasure, their highest posession

Ist Jesu unschätzbares Blut;
Is Jesus' inestimable blood;

Es ist ihr Schutz vor Teufel, Tod und Sünden,
It is their protection from devil, death, and sins,

In dem sie überwinden.
In which they overcome.

5. Bass Aria (Based on Chorale Vs. 8)
●Accuser commanded to be silent (5-5)
Verstumme, Höllenheer,
Be-silent, hell's-host,

Du machst mich nicht verzagt!
You make me not disheartened!
{You do not dishearten me!}

Ich darf dies Blut dir zeigen,
I may this blood you show,
{I may show this blood to you,}

Is. 40:1–2. Comfort, comfort my people, says your God. Speak tenderly to Jerusalem, and cry to her that her warfare is ended, that her iniquity is pardoned...
Is. 49:13. ...The Lord has comforted his people...
Mt. 5:4. Blessed are those who mourn, for they shall be comforted.
Is. 1:18. ...Though your sins are like scarlet, they shall be as white as snow...
Rom. 6:4. We were buried therefore with him by baptism into death, so that as Christ was raised from the dead by the glory of the Father, we too might walk in newness of life. (Also Col. 2:12.)
Rev. 1:5. ...To him who loves us and has freed us from our sins by his blood...
Rom. 5:20. ...Where sin increased, grace abounded all the more.
Rom. 6:23. For the wages of sin is death, but the free gift of God is eternal life in Christ Jesus our Lord.
Ps. 57:1. Be merciful to me, O God...for in thee my soul takes refuge; in the shadow of thy wings I will take refuge (Luther: Zuflucht)... (Zuflucht: also Ps. 57:1, Jer. 16:19, Heb. 6:18)
Rom. 8:1. There is therefore now no condemnation for those who are in Christ Jesus...Who shall bring any charge against God's elect? It is God who justifies; who is to condemn? Is it Christ Jesus, who died, yes, who was raised from the dead, who is at the right hand of God, who indeed intercedes for us?
Heb. 10:22. Let us draw near with a true heart in full assurance of faith, with our hearts sprinkled clean from an evil conscience and our bodies washed with pure water.
1 Pet. 1:18–19. You know that you were ransomed from the futile ways inherited from your fathers, not with perishable things such as silver or gold, but with the precious blood of Christ, like that of a lamb without blemish or spot.
Rom. 8:35–39. Who shall separate us from the love of Christ? Shall tribulation, or distress, or persecution, or famine, or nakedness, or peril, or sword? As it is written, "For thy sake we are being killed all the day long; we are regarded as sheep to be slaughtered." No, in all these things we are more than conquerors through him who loved us. For I am sure that neither death, nor life, nor angels, nor principalities, nor things present, nor things to come, nor powers, nor height, nor depth, nor anything else in all creation, will be able to separate us from the love of God in Christ Jesus our Lord.
Rev. 12:11. They have conquered...by the blood of the Lamb...

*Mt. 9:3–7. ...And behold, some of the scribes said to themselves, "This man is blaspheming." But Jesus, knowing their thoughts, said, "Why do you think evil in your hearts? For which is easier, to say, 'Your sins are forgiven,' or to say, 'Rise and walk'? But that you may know that the Son of man has authority on earth to forgive sins"—he then said to the paralytic—"Rise, take up your bed and go home." And he rose and went home.
Rev. 12:10. ...The accuser of our brethren has been thrown down, who accuses them day and night before our God.
Mk. 1:34. ... [Christ] would not permit the demons to speak...

So mußt du plötzlich schweigen,
So must you suddenly hush,
{Then you must suddenly hush,}

Es ist in Gott gewagt.
It is in God ventured.
{It is ventured in God.}

6. Soprano Recit. (Based on Chorale Vss. 9–10)
●Christ's blood is powerful enough for entire world (5–6)
Ich bin ja nur das kleinste Teil der Welt,
I am indeed only the smallest part of-the world,

Und da des Blutes edler Saft
And since the blood's noble liquid

Unendlich große Kraft
Infinitely great power

Bewährt erhält,
Proven contains,
{And since the blood's noble liquid has been proven to contain
infinitely great power,}

Daß jeder Tropfen, so auch noch so klein,
So-that each droplet, be-it ever so small,

Die ganze Welt kann rein
The entire world can clean
{Can make the entire world}

Von Sünden machen,
Of sins make,
{Clean of sin,}

So laß dein Blut
So-then let thy blood

Ja nicht an mir verderben,
Indeed not on me (be-wasted),
{Indeed not be wasted on me,}

Es komme mir zugut,
(May) it (serve) to-my advantage,

Daß ich den Himmel kann ererben.
That I - heaven can inherit.
{So that I can inherit heaven.}

7. Chorale (Vs. 11) (See also 163-6.)
●Prayer: That I avoid sin & maintain union with Christ (5–7)
Führ auch mein Herz und Sinn
(Bring) also my heart and mind

Durch deinen Geist dahin,
Through thy Spirit thither,
{Through thy Spirit to the point,}

Rom. 8:33–34. Who shall bring any charge against God's elect? It is God who justifies; who is to condemn? Is it Christ Jesus, who died, yes, who was raised from the dead, who is at the right hand of God, who indeed intercedes for us?
Ex. 12:13 [God]: The blood shall be a sign for you...when I see the blood, I will pass over you...
1 Tim. 1:1. ...Christ Jesus our hope.

Ps. 8:3–4. [O Lord,] when I look at thy heavens, the work of thy fingers, the moon and the stars which thou hast established; what is man that thou art mindful of him, and the son of man that thou dost care for him? (Also Ps. 144:3.)
1 Pet. 1:18–19. You know that you were ransomed from the futile ways inherited from your fathers, not with perishable things such as silver or gold, but with the precious blood of Christ, like that of a lamb without blemish or spot.
Heb. 12:24. ...Jesus [is] the mediator of a new covenant, and...the sprinkled blood...speaks more graciously than the blood of Abel.
Heb. 9:13, 14. If the sprinkling of defiled persons with the blood of goats and bulls...sanctifies for the purification of the flesh, how much more shall the blood of Christ, who through the eternal Spirit offered himself without blemish to God, purify your conscience from dead works to serve the living God.
Mt. 26:28 [Christ]: This is my blood of the covenant, which is poured out for many for the forgiveness of sins.
1 Jn. 1:7. ...The blood of Jesus his Son cleanses us from all sin.
Heb. 10:12. When Christ had offered for all time a single sacrifice for sins, he sat down at the right hand of God.
2 Cor. 6:1. ...We entreat you not to accept the grace of God in vain.
Heb. 26, 29. For if we sin deliberately after receiving the knowledge of the truth, there no longer remains a sacrifice for sins...How much worse punishment do you think will be deserved by the man who has spurned the Son of God, and profaned the blood of the covenant by which he was sanctified, and outraged the Spirit of grace?
Jn. 3:16–17. God so loved the world that he gave his only Son, that whoever believes in him should not perish but have eternal life. For God sent the Son into the world, not to condemn the world, but that the world might be saved through him.
Mt. 25:34. Then the King will say to those at his right hand, "Come, O blessed of my Father, inherit the kingdom prepared for you from the foundation of the world."

*Eph. 4:22–23. Put off your old nature which belongs to your former manner of life and is corrupt through deceitful lusts, and be renewed in the spirit of your minds, and put on the new nature, created after the likeness of God in true righteousness and holiness.
1 Thess. 5:21–22. Test everything; hold fast what is good, abstain from every form of evil.

Daß ich mög alles meiden,
That I may all-things shun,
{That I would shun all things}

Was mich und dich kann scheiden,
That me and thee could part,
{That could separate me and thee,}

Und ich an deinem Leibe
And I of thy body

Ein Gliedmaß ewig bleibe.
A member eternally remain.
{And that I would remain a member of thy body eternally.}

BWV 6
Bleib bei uns, denn es will Abend werden
(NBA I/10; BC A57)

Easter Monday (BWV 66, 6)
*Acts 10:34–43. (Peter preaches to Cornelius' household)
*Lk. 24:13–35. (Jesus meets the disciples on the way to Emmaus)
Librettist: Unknown; perhaps Christian Weiß the elder

1. Chorus
●Prayer: Remain with us for night approaches: Lk. 24:29 (6-1)
Bleib bei uns, denn es will Abend werden,
Abide with us, for it would evening become,

und der Tag hat sich geneiget.
and - day has - declined.

2. Alto Aria
●Prayer: O Christ, remain our light (6-2)
Hochgelobter Gottessohn,
Highly-praised Son-of-God,

Laß es dir nicht sein entgegen,
Let it to-thee not be contrary,
{Let it not be objectionable to thee,}

Daß wir itzt vor deinem Thron
That we now before thy throne

Eine Bitte niederlegen:
One request lay-down:
{Lay down one request:}

Bleib, ach bleibe unser Licht,
Remain, ah, remain our light,

Weil die Finsternis einbricht.
For the darkness breaks-in.

Is. 59:2. Your iniquities have made a separation between you and your God, and your sins have hid his face from you so that he does not hear.
Jn. 14:15 [Christ]: If you love me, you will keep my commandments.
1 Jn. 4:13, 15–16. By this we know that we abide in him and he in us, because he has given us of his own Spirit...Whoever confesses that Jesus is the Son of God, God abides in him, and he in God...He who abides in love abides in God, and God abides in him. (Also Jn. 15:4, 6.)
1 Cor. 12:12, 27. For just as the body is one and has many members, and all the members of the body, though many, are one body, so it is with Christ...Now you are the body of Christ and individually members of it.
Eph. 1:22–23. ...the church, which is his body, the fulness of him who fills all in all. (Also Eph. 4:15–16, Col. 2:19.)

*Lk. 24:13–15, 28–31. That very day two of them were going to a village named Emmaus, about seven miles from Jerusalem, and talking with each other about all these things that had happened. While they were talking and discussing together, Jesus himself drew near and went with them. But their eyes were kept from recognizing him...So they drew near to the village to which they were going. He appeared to be going further, but they constrained [Jesus], saying, *"Stay with us, for it is toward evening and the day is now far spent."* So he went in to stay with them. When he was a table with them, he took the bread and blessed, and broke it, and gave it to them. And their eyes were opened and they recognized him; and he vanished out of their sight.

1 Jn. 1:5. ...God is light and in him is no darkness at all. (Also Jn. 1:5.)
Acts 26:22–23. ...I stand here testifying...what the prophets and Moses said would come to pass: that the Christ must suffer, and that, by being the first to rise from the dead, he would proclaim light both to the people and to the Gentiles.
Heb. 4:15–16. We have not a high priest who is unable to sympathize with our weaknesses, but one who in every respect has been tempted as we are, yet without sin. Let us then with confidence draw near to the throne of grace, that we may receive mercy and find grace to help in time of need.
Ps. 27:1. The Lord is my light and my salvation; whom shall I fear?...
Is. 60:19/20. ...The Lord will be your everlasting light...
Jn. 8:12. Jesus spoke to them, saying, "I am the light of the world; he who follows me will not walk in darkness, but will have the light of life."
2 Cor. 4:6. It is the God who said, "Let light shine out of darkness," who has shone in our hearts to give the light of the knowledge of the glory of God in the face of Christ.
Jn. 3:19. And this is the judgment, that the light has come into the world, and men loved darkness rather than light, because their deeds were evil.

3. Chorale: Soprano
●Prayer: Thy Word is our light, help us keep it to end (6-3)
Ach bleib bei uns, Herr Jesu Christ,
Ah, abide with us, Lord Jesus Christ,

Weil es nun Abend worden ist,
For it now evening become has,
{For it has now become evening,}

Dein göttlich Wort, das helle Licht,
Thy divine Word, that bright light,
{Do not let thy divine Word, that bright light,}

Laß ja bei uns auslöschen nicht.
Let indeed among us be-extinguished not.
{Be extinguished among us.}

///

In dieser letzt'n betrübten Zeit
In this last sad time

Verleih uns, Herr, Beständigkeit,
Grant us, Lord, steadfastness,

Daß wir dein Wort und Sakrament
That we thy Word and Sacrament
{That we might keep thy Word and Sacrament}

Rein b'halten bis an unser End.
Pure keep until - our end.
{Pure until our end.}

4. Bass Recit.
●Darkness has triumphed in many places (6-4)
Es hat die Dunkelheit
(Now) has the darkness

An vielen Orten überhand genommen.
In many places (the) upper-hand taken.
{Taken the upper hand in many places.}

Woher ist aber dieses kommen?
Wherefrom is, however, this come?
{But how has this happened?}

Bloß daher, weil sowohl die Kleinen als die Großen
Simply by-this, because (both) - small (and) - great
{Simply by this, that both small and great}

Nicht in Gerechtigkeit
Not in righteousness

Vor dir, o Gott, gewandelt
Before thee, O God, have-walked
{Have not walked, O God, in righteousness before thee,}

*Lk. 24:29. But they constrained [Jesus], saying, *"Stay with us, for it is toward evening and the day is now far spent."*
Jn. 9:4–5 [Christ]: We must work the works of him who sent me, while it is day; night comes, when no one can work. As long as I am in the world, I am the light of the world.
Ps. 119:105. [O Lord,] thy word is a lamp to my feet and a light to my path.
Prov. 6:23. For the commandment is a lamp and the teaching a light...
Mt. 25:8. And the foolish [virgins] said to the wise, "Give us some of your oil, for our lamps are going out."
Is. 42:3. A bruised reed he will not break, and a dimly burning wick he will not quench... (Also Mt. 12:20.)

2 Pet. 3:3. ...You must understand this, that scoffers will come in the last days with scoffing, following their own passions...
1 Jn. 2:18. Children, it is the last hour; and as you have heard that antichrist is coming, so now many antichrists have come; therefore we know that it is the last hour.
1 Cor. 16:13. Be watchful, stand firm in your faith, be courageous, be strong. (Also Eph. 6:14, 2 Pet. 3:17.)
Rev. 3:10–11 [Christ]: Because you have kept my word of patient endurance, I will keep you from the hour of trial which is coming on the whole world, to try those who dwell upon the earth. I am coming soon; hold fast what you have, so that no one may seize your crown.
Mt. 24:13. He who endures to the end will be saved. (Also Mt. 24:13, Mk. 13:13, Lk. 21:19.)
Heb. 3:14. We share in Christ, if only we hold our first confidence firm to the end.

Jn. 3:19. ...Men loved darkness rather than light, because their deeds were evil.
Jn. 9:4 [Christ]: We must work the works of him who sent me, while it is day; night comes, when no one can work.
2 Tim. 3:1–5. But understand this, that in the last days there will come times of stress. For men will be lovers of self, lovers of money, proud, arrogant, abusive, disobedient to their parents, ungrateful, unholy, inhuman, implacable, slanderers, profligates, fierce, haters of good, treacherous, reckless, swollen with conceit, lovers of pleasure rather than lovers of God...
Mic. 7:2. The godly man has perished from the earth, and there is none upright among men...
Rom. 3:10–12. ...None is righteous, no, not one; no one understands, no one seeks for God. All have turned aside, together they have gone wrong; no one does good, not even one. (Also Rom. 3:23.)
Is. 53:6. All we like sheep have gone astray; we have turned every one to his own way...
Is. 59:9. Therefore justice is far from us, and righteousness does not overtake us; we look for light, and behold, darkness, and for brightness, but we walk in gloom.

Und wider ihre Christenpflicht gehandelt.
And contrary-to their Christian-duty acted.
{And have acted contrary to their Christian duty.}

Drum hast du auch den Leuchter umgestoßen.
Therefore hast thou also (their) lampstand overthrown.
{Therefore thou hast also overthrown their lampstand.}

5. Tenor Aria
●Prayer: Jesus, keep us with the light of thy Word (6-5)
Jesu, laß uns auf dich sehen,
Jesu, let us to thee look,
{Jeus, let us look to thee,}

Daß wir nicht
That we (would) not

Auf den Sündenwegen gehen.
Upon the paths-of-sin go.
{Walk upon the paths of sin.}

Laß das Licht
Let the light

Deines Worts uns heller scheinen
Of-thy Word to-us brighter shine
{Of thy Word shine more brightly to us}

Und dich jederzeit treu meinen.
And (let) thyself at-all-times faithful (be-disposed).
{And remain favorably disposed to us forever.}

6. Chorale
●Prayer for King of Kings to protect Christendom (6-6)
Beweis dein Macht, Herr Jesu Christ,
Demonstrate thy might, Lord Jesus Christ,

Der du Herr aller Herren bist;
Who (the) Lord of-all Lords art;
{Thou who art the Lord of all lords;}

Beschirm dein arme Christenheit,
Preserve thy poor Christendom,

Daß sie dich lob in Ewigkeit.
That it (might) thee praise to (all) eternity.

Eph. 5:11–13. Take no part in the unfruitful works of darkness, but instead expose them. For it is a shame even to speak of the things that they do in secret; but when anything is exposed by the light it becomes visible, for anything that becomes visible is light.
Rev. 2:5 [Christ]: Remember then from what you have fallen, repent and do the works you did at first. If not, I will come to you and remove your lampstand from its place, unless you repent. (Also Jer. 25:10.)

Heb. 12:1–2. ...Let us run with perseverance the race that is set before us, looking to Jesus the pioneer and perfecter of our faith, who for the joy that was set before him endured the cross, despising the shame, and is seated at the right hand of the throne of God.
Ps. 119:9–11. How can a young man keep his way pure? By guarding it according to thy word. With my whole heart I seek thee; let me not wander from thy commandments! I have laid up thy word in my heart, that I might not sin against thee.
Mt. 7:13–14. Enter by the narrow gate; for the gate is wide and the way is easy, that leads to destruction, and those who enter by it are many. For the gate is narrow and the way is hard, that leads to life, and those who find it are few.
Ps. 119:105. [O Lord,] thy word is a lamp to my feet and a light to my path.
Prov. 6:23. For the commandment is a lamp and the teaching a light...
2 Pet. 1:19. We have the prophetic word made more sure. You will do well to pay attention to this as to a lamp shining in a dark place, until the day dawns and the morning star rises in your hearts.
Ps. 51:11. [O Lord,] cast me not away from thy presence, and take not thy holy Spirit from me.

Ps. 17:7. Wondrously show thy steadfast love, O savior of those who seek refuge from their adversaries at thy right hand.
Rev. 17:14. ...The Lamb will conquer them, for he is Lord of lords and King of kings, and those with him are called and chosen and faithful.
Ps. 17:8. [O Lord,] keep me as the apple of the eye; hide me (Luther: beschirme mich) in the shadow of thy wings.
Prov. 2:7–8. ...[The Lord] is a shield to those who walk in integrity, guarding the paths of justice and preserving the way of his saints (Luther: beschirmt die Frommen). (Also Prov. 18:10.)
Rom. 9:5. ...God who is over all be blessed for ever. Amen. (Also Rom. 1:25.)
Rom. 11:36. From him and through him and to him are all things. To him be glory for ever. Amen.

BWV 7
Christ unser Herr zum Jordan kam
(NBA I/29; BC A177)

Feast of St. John the Baptist: June 24 (BWV 167, 7, 30)
*Is. 40:1–5. (A voice crying in the wilderness)
*Lk. 1:57–80. (Birth of John the Baptist and song of Zacharias)
Librettist: Unknown

1. Chorus (Chorale Vs. 1)
●Jesus' baptism commences his ministry: bath for sin (7-1)
Christ unser Herr zum Jordan kam
Christ   our   Lord to-the Jordan came

Nach   seines Vaters Willen,
According-to his   Father's will,

Von Sankt Johanns die Taufe nahm,
From   St.   John   - baptism took,

Sein Werk und Amt zu erfüllen;
His   work and office to fulfill;

Da   wollt er   stiften   uns ein Bad,
There wanted he to-establish for-us a   bath,
{There he wanted to establish a bath for us,}

Zu waschen uns von   Sünden,
To   wash   us from (our) sins,

Ersäufen auch den bittern Tod
To-drown also   -   bitter death

Durch sein selbst Blut und Wunden;
Through his own   blood and wounds;

Es   galt ein neues Leben.
(This) yielded a   new   life.
{And thus he brought to us new life.}

2. Bass Aria (Based on Chorale Vs. 2)
●Baptism: See what God has said it means (7-2)
Merkt und hört, ihr Menschenkinder,
Mark and hear, you children-of-mankind,

Was Gott selbst die Taufe heißt!
What God himself - baptism calls!
{What God himself calls baptism!}

Es muß   zwar   hier Wasser sein,
It must, to-be-sure, here water be,
{It must, to be sure, be water here,}

Doch schlecht Wasser nicht allein.
Though simple   water   not alone.
{Though not simple water alone.}

Mt. 3:1–3, 5–6. In those days came John the Baptist, preaching in the wilderness of Judea, "Repent, for the kingdom of heaven is at hand." For this is he who was spoken of by the prophet Isaiah when he said, "The voice of one crying in the wilderness: Prepare the way of the Lord, make his paths straight."...Then went out to him Jerusalem and all Judea and all the region about the Jordan, and they were baptized by him in the river Jordan, confessing their sins. (Also Mk. 1:1–3, Jn. 1:19–23, *Is. 40:3–5.)
Mt. 3:13–15. Then Jesus came from Galilee to the Jordan to John, to be baptized by him. John would have prevented him, saying, "I need to be baptized by you, and do you come to me?" But Jesus answered him, "Let it be so now; for thus it is fitting for us to fulfil all righteousness." Then he consented.
Acts 19:2–4. [Paul] said to [the Corinthian believers], "Did you receive the Holy Spirit when you believed?" And they said, "No, we have never even heard that there is a Holy Spirit." And he said, "Into what then were you baptized?" They said, "Into John's baptism." And Paul said, "John baptized with the baptism of repentance, telling the people to believe in the one who was to come after him, that is, Jesus." On hearing this, they were baptized in the name of the Lord Jesus.
Acts 22:16. ...Rise and be baptised, and wash away your sins, calling on his name.
Tit. 3:5. [God] saved us...by the washing (Luther: das Bad) of regeneration and renewal in the Holy Spirit. (Also Heb. 10:22.)
Rev. 1:5. ...[He] has freed us from our sins by his blood...
Heb. 2:14–15. Since therefore the children share in flesh and blood, [Christ] himself likewise partook of the same nature, that through death he might destroy him who has the power of death, that is, the devil, and deliver all those who through fear of death were subject to lifelong bondage. (Also 1 Cor. 15:54, Is. 25:8, Rom. 6:9.)
1 Pet. 2:24. ...By his wounds you have been healed. (Also Is. 53:5.)
2 Cor. 5:17. Therefore, if any one is in Christ, he is a new creation; the old has passed away, behold, the new has come.

Rom. 6:4. We were buried therefore with him by baptism into death, so that as Christ was raised from the dead by the glory of the Father, we too might walk in newness of life.
Eph. 4:5. [There is] one Lord, one faith, one baptism.
Col. 2:12. And you were buried with him in baptism, in which you were also raised with him through faith in the working of God, who raised him from the dead.
1 Pet. 3:21. Baptism, which corresponds to [Noah's experience] now saves you, not as a removal of dirt from the body but as an appeal to God for a clear conscience, through the resurrection of Jesus Christ.
Eph. 5:26. ...Christ loved the church and gave himself up for her, that he might sanctify her, having cleansed her by the washing of water with the word.

Gottes Wort und Gottes Geist
God's Word and God's Spirit

Tauft und reiniget die Sünder.
Baptizes and cleanses - sinners.

3. Tenor Recit. (Based on Chorale Vs. 3)
●Christ's baptism: God's object lesson; hear him! (7–3)
Dies hat Gott klar
This has God clearly
{This God has clearly}

Mit Worten und mit Bildern dargetan,
With words and with pictures demonstrated,

Am Jordan ließ der Vater offenbar
At-the Jordan let the Father plainly
{At the Jordan the Father let}

Die Stimme bei der Taufe Christi hören;
(His) voice at the baptism of-Christ be-heard;
{His voice be plainly heard at the baptism of Christ;}

Er *sprach: Dies ist mein lieber Sohn,*
He said: This is my beloved Son,

An diesem hab ich Wohlgefallen,
In this-one have I pleasure,

Er is vom hohen Himmelsthron
He is from-the high throne-of-heaven
{He is come from the high throne of heaven}

Der Welt zugut
The world to-advantage
{For the world's benefit}

In niedriger Gestalt gekommen
In lowly form come
{In lowly form}

Und hat das Fleisch und Blut
And has the flesh and blood

Der Menschenkinder angenommen;
Of mankind taken-on;
{And has taken on human flesh and blood;}

Den nehmet nun als euren Heiland an
Him accept now as your Savior -
{Accept him now as your Savior}

Und höret seine teuren Lehren!
And hear his precious teachings!

Jn. 15:3 [Christ]: You are already made clean by the word which I have spoken to you.
Acts 2:38. Peter said to them, "Repent, and be baptized every one of you in the name of Jesus Christ for the forgiveness of your sins; and you shall receive the gift of the Holy Spirit." (Also 1 Cor. 12:13, Gal. 3:27.)

Mt. 3:16–17. And when Jesus was baptized, he went up immediately from the water, and behold, the heavens were opened and he saw the Spirit of God descending like a dove, and alighting on him; and lo, a voice from heaven, *saying, "This is my beloved Son, with whom I am well pleased."*
Jn. 1:32. And John bore witness, "I saw the Spirit descend as a dove from heaven, and it remained on him."
Mt. 17:1–6. And...Jesus took with him Peter and James and John his brother, and led them up a high mountain apart. And he was transfigured before them, and his face shone like the sun, and his garments became white as light. And behold, there appeared to them Moses and Elijah, talking with him. And Peter said to Jesus, "Lord, it is well that we are here; if you wish, I will make three booths here, one for you and one for Moses and one for Elijah." He was still speaking, when lo, a bright cloud overshadowed them, and a voice from the cloud said, "This is my beloved Son, with whom I am well pleased; listen to him." When the disciples heard this, they fell on their faces, and were filled with awe.
Phil. 2:6–9. [Christ Jesus], who, though he was in the form of God, did not count equality with God a thing to be grasped, but emptied himself, taking the form of a servant, being born in the likeness of men. And being found in human form he humbled himself and became obedient unto death, even death on a cross. Therefore God has highly exalted him and bestowed on him the name which is above every name.
2 Cor. 8:9. You know the grace of our Lord Jesus Christ, that though he was rich, yet for your sake he became poor, so that by his poverty you might become rich. (Also Eph. 2:7, 3:16, Col. 1:27, 2:2–3.)
Heb. 2:14. Since therefore the children share in flesh and blood, [Christ] himself likewise partook of the same nature, that through death he might destroy him who has the power of death, that is, the devil.
Rom. 8:3. ...sending his own Son in the likeness of sinful flesh...
Jn. 1:14. And the Word became flesh and dwelt among us, full of grace and truth; we have beheld his glory, glory as of the only Son from the Father. (Also Jn. 1:17.)
Jn. 1:12. But to all who received him, who believed in his name, he gave power to become children of God.
Jn. 12:48–49. He who rejects me and does not receive my sayings has a judge; the word that I have spoken will be his judge on the last day. For I have not spoken on my own authority; the Father who sent me has himself given me commandment what to say and what to speak.

4. Tenor Aria (Based on Chorale Vs. 4)
●Christ's baptism shows baptism confirmed by Trinity (7-4)
Des Vaters Stimme ließ sich hören,
The Father's voice let itself be-heard,
{The Father let his voice be heard,}

Der Sohn, der uns mit Blut erkauft,
The Son, who us with blood has-bought,
{The Son, who bought us with his blood,}

Ward als ein wahrer Mensch getauft.
Was as a very man baptized.
{Was baptized as a man.}

Der Geist erschien im Bild der Tauben,
The Spirit appeared in-the likeness of doves,

Damit wir ohne Zweifel glauben,
So-that we without doubt (might) believe

Es habe die Dreifaltigkeit
(That it was) - the Trinity (who)

Uns selbst die Taufe zubereit'.
For-us - baptism did-establish.
{Established baptism for us.}

5. Bass Recit. (Based on Chorale Vs. 5)
●Baptism: Christ commanded disciples to baptize (7-5)
Als Jesus dort nach seinen Leiden
When Jesus there after his suffering

Und nach dem Auferstehn
And after the resurrection

Aus dieser Welt zum Vater wollte gehn,
Out-of this world to-the Father wished to-go,

Sprach er zu seinen Jüngern:
Said he to his disciples:
{He said to his disciples:}

Geht hin in alle Welt und lehret alle Heiden,
Go forth into all-the world and teach all heathen,

Wer gläubet und getaufet wird auf Erden,
Whoever believes and baptized is on earth,

Der soll gerecht und selig werden.
He shall righteous and blessed become.

6. Alto Aria (Based on Chorale Vs. 6)
●Baptism: We are lost unless we believe and are baptized (7-6)
Menschen, glaubt doch dieser Gnade,
(O) people, believe, please, (in) this grace,

Mt. 3:13–17. Then Jesus came from Galilee to the Jordan to John, to be baptized by him. John would have prevented him, saying, "I need to be baptized by you, and do you come to me?" But Jesus answered him, "Let it be so now; for thus it is fitting for us to fulfil all righteousness." Then he consented. And when Jesus was baptized, he went up immediately from the water, and behold, the heavens were opened and he saw the **Spirit** of God descending like a dove, and alighting on him; and lo, a voice from [the **Father** in] heaven, saying, "This is my beloved **Son**, with whom I am well pleased." [Father, Son, and Spirit = Trinity]
Jn. 1:32–33. And John bore witness, "I saw the Spirit descend as a dove from heaven, and it remained on him. I myself did not know him; but he who sent me to baptize with water said to me, 'He on whom you see the Spirit descend and remain, this is he who baptizes with the Holy Spirit.'"
Acts 19:4. ...John baptized with the baptism of repentance, telling the people to believe in the one who was to come after him, that is, Jesus.
Mk. 10:45. The Son of man...came not to be served but to serve, and to give his life as a ransom for many. (Also Mt. 20:28; 1 Pet. 1:18–19.)
Mt. 28:16–19. And Jesus...said to [his disciples], "All authority in heaven and on earth has been given to me. Go therefore and make disciples of all nations, baptizing them in the name of the Father and of the Son and of the Holy Spirit."
Mk. 16:15–16. [Jesus] said to them, "Go into all the world and preach the gospel to the whole creation. He who believes and is baptized will be saved..."

Mt. 28:16–20. Now the eleven disciples went to Galilee, to the mountain to which Jesus had directed them. And when they saw him they worshiped him; but some doubted. And Jesus came and said to them, "All authority in heaven and on earth has been given to me. *Go therefore and make disciples of all nations,* baptizing them in the name of the Father and of the Son and of the Holy Spirit, teaching them to observe all that I have commanded you; and lo, I am with you always to the close of the age."
Mk. 16:14–17. Afterward [Jesus] appeared to the eleven themselves as they sat at table...And he said to them *"Go into all the world and preach the gospel to the whole creation. He who believes and is baptized will be saved;* but he who does not believe will be condemned. And... signs will accompany those who believe..."
Acts 1:8–9. [Jesus said to his disciples,] "You shall receive power when the Holy Spirit has come upon you; and you shall be my witnesses in Jerusalem and in all Judea and Samaria and to the end of the earth." And when he had said this, as they were looking on, he was lifted up, and a cloud took him out of their sight.
Mk. 16:19. So then the Lord Jesus, after he had spoken to them, was taken up into heaven, and sat down at the right hand of God.

Jn. 8:24 [Christ]: I told you that you would die in your sins, for you will die in your sins unless you believe that I am he.
Eph. 2:4–5. But God...even when we were dead through our trespasses, made us alive together with Christ (by grace you have been saved)... (Also Eph. 2:1–2.)

Daß ihr nicht in Sünden sterbt,
That you (do) not in (your) sins die,
{That you do not die in your sins,}

Noch im Höllenpfuhl verderbt!
Nor in hell's-slough perish!
{Nor perish in hell's slough!}

Menschenwerk und -heiligkeit
Human-works and holiness

Gilt vor Gott zu keiner Zeit.
Count before God at no time.
{Count at no time before God.}

Sünden sind uns angeboren,
Sins are us inborn,
{Sin is inborn in us,}

Wir sind von Natur verloren;
We are by nature lost;
{We are lost by nature;}

Glaub und Taufe macht sie rein,
Faith and baptism makes them clean,
{Faith and baptism cleanses our works,}

Daß sie nicht verdammlich sein.
That they not damnable are.
{That they are not damnable.}

7. Chorale (Vs. 7)
●Baptism: Eye sees water, faith sees blood of Christ (7-7)
Das Aug allein das Wasser sieht,
(Our) eye only the water sees,
{Our eye sees only the water,}

Wie Menschen Wasser gießen,
How people (the) water pour,
{How people pour the water,}

Der Glaub allein die Kraft versteht
- Faith alone the power comprehends
{Faith alone comprehends the power}

Des Blutes Jesu Christi,
Of-the blood-of Jesus Christ,
{Of Jesus Christ's blood,}

Und ist für ihm ein rote Flut
And (it) is for him a red torrent
{And for him who believes it is a red torrent}

Von Christi Blut gefärbet,
By Christ's blood colored,
{Colored by Christ's blood,}

Die allen Schaden heilet gut
Which all (the) harm heals well
{Which heals all the harm}

Rom. 1:16–17. ...[The gospel] is the power of God for salvation to every one who has faith...For in it the righteousness of God is revealed through faith for faith; as it is written, "He who through faith is righteous shall live."
Rom. 3:28. For we hold that a man is justified by faith apart from works of law.
Tit. 3:5. He saved us, not because of deeds done by us in righteousness, but in virtue of his own mercy...
Heb. 9:14. How much more shall the blood of Christ, who through the eternal Spirit offered himself without blemish to God, purify your conscience from dead works... (Also Rom. 11:5–6.)
Gal. 2:16. ...Know that a man is not justified by works of the law... because by works of the law shall no one be justified.
Jn. 3:3, 5–6. Jesus answered, "Truly, truly, I say to you, unless one is born anew, he cannot see the kingdom of God...Truly, truly, I say to you, unless one is born of water and the Spirit, he cannot enter the kingdom of God. That which is born of the flesh is flesh, and that which is born of the Spirit is spirit." (Also Ps. 51:5.)
Mk. 16:16. He who believes and is baptized will be saved; but he who does not believe will be condemned.
Eph. 2:3. ...We were by nature children of wrath like the rest of mankind.
Eph. 2:8–10. For by grace you have been saved through faith; and this is not your own doing, it is the gift of God—not because of works, lest any man should boast. For we are his workmanship, created in Christ Jesus for good works, which God prepared beforehand, that we should walk in them.
Jms. 2:14, 17. What does it profit, my brethren, if a man says he has faith but has not works? Can his faith save him?...Faith by itself, if it has no works, is dead.

1 Cor. 2:12–14. Now we have received not the spirit of the world, but the Spirit which is from God, that we might understand the gifts bestowed on us by God. And we impart this in words not taught by human wisdom but taught by the Spirit, interpreting spiritual truths to those who possess the Spirit. The unspiritual man does not receive the gifts of the Spirit of God, for they are folly to him, and he is not able to understand them because they are spiritually discerned.
1 Cor. 1:18. The word of the cross is folly to those who are perishing, but to us who are being saved it is the power of God.
Rom. 1:16. I am not ashamed of the gospel: it is the power of God for salvation to every one who has faith...
Heb. 13:12, 20. ...Jesus...suffered...in order to sanctify the people through his own blood... Now may...God...by the blood of the eternal covenant, equip you with everything good...
1 Pet. 1:1–2. ...[You are]...chosen and destined by God the Father and sanctified by the Spirit for obedience to Jesus Christ and for sprinkling with his blood...
1 Jn. 1:7. ...The blood of Jesus his Son cleanses us from all sin.
Rev. 7:14. ...[The righteous] have washed their robes and made them white in the blood of the Lamb. (Also Rev. 12:11.)
Rev. 19:13. He is clad in a robe dipped in blood, and the name by which he is called is The Word of God.
Rom. 5:12, 17–19. Sin came into the world through one man and death through sin, and so death spread to all men because all men sinned... If, because of one man's trespass, death reigned through that one man, much more will those who receive the abundance of grace and the free gift of righteousness reign in life through the one man Jesus Christ. Then as one man's trespass led to condemnation for all men, so one man's act of righteousness leads to acquittal and life for

Von Adam her geerbet,
(Which) from Adam (was) inherited,
{Inherited from Adam,}

Auch von uns selbst begangen.
And by ourselves - committed.
{And committed by ourselves.}

all men. For as by one man's disobedience many were made sinners, so by one man's obedience many will be made righteous.
1 Cor. 15:22. For as in Adam all die, so also in Christ shall all be made alive.
Mt. 26:27–28. [Jesus] took a cup, and when he had given thanks he gave it to them, saying, "Drink of it, all of you; for this is my blood of the covenant, which is poured out for many for the forgiveness of sins."

BWV 8
Liebster Gott, wann werd ich sterben
(NBA I/23; BC A137a/b)

16 S. after Trinity (BWV 161, 95, 8, 27)
*Eph. 3:13–21 (Paul's prayer for the Ephesians; that they be spiritually strengthened)
*Lk. 7:11–17 (Jesus raises young man of Nain from the dead)
Librettist: Unknown

1. Chorus (Chorale Vs. 1)
●Death: Our imminent legacy from Adam (8-1)
Liebster Gott, wann werd ich sterben?
Dearest God, when shall I die?

Meine Zeit läuft immer hin,
My time runs continually on,
{My days run ever on,}

Und des alten Adams Erben,
And - old Adam's heirs,

Unter denen ich auch bin,
Among whom I, too, am,

Haben dies zum Vaterteil,
Have this for-a patrimony,

Daß sie eine kleine Weil
That they (for) a little while

Arm und elend sein auf Erden
Poor and miserable are on earth

Und dann selber Erde werden.
And then themselves earth become.
{And then become earth themselves.}

*Lk. 7:11–12. Soon afterward [Jesus] went to a city called Nain, and his disciples and a great crowd went with him. As he drew near to the gate of the city, behold, a man who had died was being carried out, the only son of his mother, and she was a widow; and a large crowd from the city was with her.
Ps. 90:12. [O Lord,] teach us to number our days that we may get a heart of wisdom.
Ps. 103:15–16. As for man, his days are like grass; he flourishes like a flower of the field; for the wind passes over it, and it is gone, and its place knows it no more. (Also Is. 40:6–7, Jms. 1:10–11, 1 Pet. 1:24.)
Jms. 4:13–15. Come now, you who say, "Today or tomorrow we will go into such and such a town and spend a year there and trade and get gain"; whereas you do not know about tomorrow. What is your life? For you are a mist that appears for a little time and then vanishes. Instead you ought to say, "If the Lord wills, we shall live and we shall do this or that."
Rom. 5:12. As sin came into the world through one man and death through sin, and so death spread to all men because all men sinned.
Ps. 39:5. [O Lord,] behold, thou hast made my days a few handbreadths, and my lifetime is as nothing in thy sight. Surely every man stands as a mere breath!
Ps. 104:29. ...When thou takest away their breath, they die and return to their dust.
Ec. 3:20. All go to one place; all are from the dust, and all turn to dust again.

2. Tenor Aria (Based on Chorale Vs. 2)
●Death: The body even now bends toward the dust (8-2)
Was willst du dich, mein Geist, entsetzen,
Why wouldst thou - , (O) my spirit, be-horrified,

Wenn meine letzte Stunde schlägt?
When my last hour strikes?

Heb. 9:27. ...It is appointed for men to die once...
Ecc. 9:12. Man does not know his time...
2 Cor. 4:7, 12. We have this treasure in earthen vessels, to show that the transcendent power belongs to God and not to us...so death is at work in us...
2 Cor. 5:1–4. We know that if the earthly tent we live in is destroyed,

Mein Leib neigt täglich sich zur Erden,
My body bends daily - toward earth,

Und da muß seine Ruhstatt werden,
And there must its resting-place (be),
{And there its resting place must be,}

Wohin man so viel tausend trägt.
Whereto they so many thousand carry.
{Whereto so many thousands are carried.}

3. Alto Recit. (Based on Chorale Vs. 3)
●Anxiety concerning death (8–3)
Zwar fühlt mein schwaches Herz
Indeed feels my weak heart
{Indeed, my weak heart feels}

Furcht, Sorge, Schmerz:
Fear, worry, (and) pain:

Wo wird mein Leib die Ruhe finden?
Where shall my body (its) rest find?
{Where shall my body find its rest?}

Wer wird die Seele doch
Who will the soul indeed

Vom aufgelegten Sündenjoch
From (its) (oppressing) yoke-of-sin

Befreien und entbinden?
Set-free and release?
{Who will indeed set the soul free and released from its oppressing yoke of sin?}

Das Meine wird zerstreut,
What's mine will-be scattered,

Und wohin werden meine Lieben
And whereto will my loved-ones

In ihrer Traurigkeit
In their sorrow

Zertrennt, vertrieben?
Be-separated, (or) scattered?

4. Bass Aria (Based on Chorale Vs. 4)
●Away anxieties! Jesus calls me to a glorious future! (8–4)
Doch weichet, ihr tollen, vergeblichen Sorgen!
Yet retreat, you frantic, futile anxieties!

Mich rufet mein Jesus: wer sollte nicht gehn?
Me calls my Jesus: who would not go?
{My Jesus calls me, who would not go?}

we have a building from God, a house not made with hands, eternal in the heavens. Here indeed we groan, and long to put on our heavenly dwelling, so that by putting it on we may not be found naked. For while we are still in this tent, we sigh with anxiety; not that we would be unclothed, but that we would be further clothed, so that what is mortal may be swallowed up by life.
Ecc. 12:1, 3, 7. Remember also your Creator in the days of your youth, before the evil days come...in the day when...strong men are bent...and the dust returns to the earth as it was, and the spirit returns to God who gave it. (Also Gen. 3:19. Ecc. 3:20.)

*Lk. 7:11–12. ...[Jesus] went to a city called Nain, and his disciples and a great crowd went with him. As he drew near to the gate of the city, behold, a man who had died was being carried out, the only son of his mother, and she was a widow; and a large crowd from the city was with her.
Jer. 45:3. ...Woe is me! for the Lord has added sorrow to my pain; I am weary with my groaning, and I find no rest (Luther: Ruhe).
Ps. 18:4–6. The cords of death (Luther: des Todes Bande) encompassed me, the torrents of perdition assailed me; the cords of Sheol entangled me, the snares of death confronted me. In my distress I called upon the Lord...
Ps. 116:3. The snares of death encompassed me; the pangs of Sheol laid hold on me; I suffered distress and anguish.
Ps. 55:4–6. My heart is in anguish within me, the terrors of death have fallen upon me. Fear and trembling come upon me, and horror overwhelms me. And I say, "O that I had wings like a dove! I would fly away and be at rest."
Rom. 7:22–24. I delight in the law of God, in my inmost self, but I see in my members another law at war with the law of my mind and making me captive to the law of sin which dwells in my members. Wretched man that I am! Who will deliver me from this body of death?
Is. 1:4. Ah, sinful nation, a people laden with iniquity...
Jn. 8:34. Jesus said... "Truly, truly, I say to you, every one who commits sin is a slave to sin."
Rom. 6:16. ...You are slaves of the one whom you obey, either of sin, which leads to death, or of obedience, which leads to righteousness. (Also 2 Pet. 2:19.)
Mt. 11:29 [Christ]: Take my yoke upon you, and learn from me; for I am gentle and lowly in heart, and you will find rest for your souls. For my yoke is easy, and my burden is light.
Heb. 4:9. So then, there remains a sabbath rest for the people of God.
1 Tim. 6:7. We brought nothing into the world, and we cannot take anything out of the world. (Also Job 21:21.)

*Eph. 3:13, 16–19. I ask you not to lose heart over what I am suffering for you, which is your glory...That according to the riches of his glory [the Father] may grant you to be strengthened with might through his Spirit in the inner man, and that Christ may dwell in your hearts through faith; that you, being rooted and grounded in love, may have power to comprehend...what is the breadth and length and height and depth, and to know the love of Christ which surpasses knowledge, that you may be filled with all the fulness of God.
2 Cor. 5:1–10. We know that if the earthly tent we live in is destroyed, we have a building from God, a house not made with hands, eternal in the heavens...So we are always of good courage; we know that while we are at home in the body we are away from the Lord...We are of

Nichts, was mir gefällt,
Nought, which me pleases,

Besitzet die Welt.
Posesses the world.
{The world posesses nought that I desire.}

Erscheine mir, seliger, fröhlicher Morgen,
Appear   to-me, blessed, happy   morning,

Verkläret und herrlich vor Jesu zu stehn.
Transfigured and glorious before Jesus to stand.
{When I shall stand before Jesus transfigured and glorious.}

5. Soprano Recit. (Based on Chorale Vs. 4)
●Rejecting the world; looking to blessings hereafter (8–5)
Behalte nur, o Welt, das Meine!
Keep   then, O world, what's mine!

Du nimmst ja selbst mein Fleisch und mein Gebeine,
You take, after-all, even my flesh and my limbs,
{You indeed take my very flesh and limbs,}

So nimm auch meine Armut hin!
So take also my poverty away!
{So take away my poverty also!}

Genug, daß mir aus Gottes Überfluß
Enough, that to-me out-of God's abundance
(It is enough that, from God's abundance,)

Das höchste Gut noch werden muß;
The highest good yet happen must;
{The highest good must yet happen to me;}

Genug, daß ich dort reich und selig bin.
Enough, that I there rich and blessed (shall) be.

Was aber ist von mir zu erben,
What, however, is (there) (for) me to inherit,
{What, however shall I inherit,}

good courage, and we would rather be away from the body and at home with the Lord. (Also Phil. 1:21, 23.)
2 Pet. 1:14. ...I know that the putting off of my body will be soon, as our Lord Jesus Christ showed me.
Mt. 25:34 [Christ]: Come, O blessed of my Father, inherit the kingdom prepared for you from the foundation of the world.
***Lk. 7:14.** And [Jesus] said [to the young man of Nain], "Young man, I say to you, arise."
Jn. 10:3. [Christ]: ...The sheep hear [the shepherd's] voice, and he calls his own sheep by name and leads them out.
Ps. 23:1, 4. The Lord is my shepherd...even though I walk through the valley of the shadow of death, I fear no evil...
Ps. 73:25. [O Lord,] whom have I in heaven but thee? And there is nothing upon earth that I desire besides thee.
1 Jn. 2:15–17. Do not love the world or the things in the world. If any one loves the world, love for the Father is not in him. (Also Jms. 4:4.)
Ps. 30:5. ...Weeping may tarry for the night, but joy comes with the morning.
1 Jn. 3:2. Beloved, we are God's children now; it does not yet appear what we shall be, but we know that when he appears we shall be like him, for we shall see him as he is.
Mt. 17:2. [Jesus] was transfigured...and his face shone like the sun, and his garments became white as light.
Phil. 3:20–21. Our commonwealth is in heaven, and from it we await a Savior, the Lord Jesus Christ, who will change our lowly body to be like his glorious body, by the power which enables him even to subject all things to himself.

1 Tim. 6:7. We brought nothing into the world, and we cannot take anything out of the world.
Gen. 3:19. In the sweat of your face you shall eat bread till you return to the ground, for out of it you were taken; you are dust, and to dust you shall return.
Jms. 2:5. ...Has not God chosen those who are poor in the world to be rich in faith and heirs of the kingdom which he has promised to those who love him?
***Eph. 3:19–20.** ...The love of Christ...surpasses knowledge...Now to him who...is able to do far more abundantly than all that we ask or think...
1 Cor. 2:9. As it is written, "What no eye has seen, nor ear heard, nor the heart of man conceived, what God has prepared for those who love him"...
2 Cor. 4:17. For this slight momentary affliction is preparing for us an eternal weight of glory beyond all comparison.
Rom. 8:18. I consider that the sufferings of this present time are not worth comparing with the glory that is to be revealed to us.
1 Jn. 3:2. Beloved, we are God's children now; it does not yet appear what we shall be, but we know that when he appears we shall be like him, for we shall see him as he is.
Col. 3:24. ...From the Lord you will receive the inheritance as your reward... (Also 1 Pet. 1:4–5.)
Ps. 16:5. The Lord is my chosen portion and my cup (Luther: Gut und Teil); thou holdest my lot (Luther: Erbteil).
Ps. 119:57. The Lord is my portion (Luther: Erbe)...

Als meines Gottes   Vatertreu?
But   my   God's paternal-faithfulness?

Die wird   ja   alle Morgen neu
It   is indeed all mornings new
{It is new every morning}

Und kann nicht sterben.
And can   not   die.

6. Chorale (Vs. 5) (partially based on setting by D. Vetter)
●Prayer: Lord of life and death, let me die well (8–6)
Herrscher über Tod und Leben,
Ruler   over death and life,

Mach einmal mein Ende gut,
Make some-day my   end   good,

Lehre mich den Geist aufgeben
Teach me the spirit to-give-up
{Teach me to give up my spirit}

Mit   recht wohlgefaßtem   Mut.
With (a) truly well-composed disposition.
{With complete composure.}

Hilf, daß ich ein ehrlich Grab
Help, that I   an honorable grave

Neben frommen Christen   hab
Next-to devout Christians will-have

Und auch endlich in der Erde
And also finally in the earth

Nimmermehr zuschanden werde!
Nevermore   to-shame   be-put!
{Nevermore be put to shame!}

BWV 9
Es ist das Heil uns kommen her
(NBA I/17; BC A107)

6. S. after Trinity (BWV 170, 9)
*Rom. 6:3–11 (Through Christ's death believers die to sin)
*Mt. 5:20–26 (From Sermon on the Mount: True righteous-
ness is characterized by love of one's neighbor)
Librettist: Unknown

1. Chorus (Chorale Vs. 1)
●Salvation has come: faith, not works, count with God (9–1)
Es   ist das Heil   uns kommen her
(Now) is - salvation to-us come hither

Lk. 16:25. But Abraham said, "Son, remember that you in your lifetime received your good things, and Lazarus in like manner evil things; but now he is comforted here, and you are in anguish."
Lam. 3:22–23. The steadfast love of the Lord never ceases, his mercies never come to an end; they are new every morning; great is thy faithfulness. (Also Ps. 90:14.)
Ps. 106:1, 107:1, 118:1. ...His steadfast love endures for ever!
Ps. 63:3. ...Thy steadfast love is better than life...

Rev. 1:17–18 [Christ]: ...Fear not, I am the first and the last, and the living one; I died, and behold I am alive for evermore, and I have the keys of Death and Hades. (Also Jn. 5:26, Rom. 6:9, 2 Tim. 1:10.)
Mt. 10:22 [Christ]: ...He who endures to the end will be saved. (Also Mt. 24:13, Mk. 13:13, Lk. 21:19.)
Ps. 31:5. [O Lord,] into thy hand I commit my spirit...
Lk. 23:46. Then Jesus, crying with a loud voice, said, "Father, into thy hands I commit my spirit!"
2 Tim. 4:6–8. For I am already on the point of being sacrificed; the time of my departure has come. I have fought the good fight, I have finished the race, I have kept the faith. Henceforth there is laid up for me the crown of righteousness, which the Lord, the righteous judge, will award to me on that Day, and not only to me but also to all who have loved his appearing.
Heb. 12:1. Therefore, since we are surrounded by so great a cloud of witnesses...let us run with perseverance the race that is set before us.
Heb. 13:7. Remember your leaders, those who spoke to you the word of God; consider the outcome (Luther: Ende) of their life, and imitate their faith.
Num. 23:10. ...Let me die the death of the righteous, and let my end be like his!
1 Cor. 15:19–20. If for this life only we have hoped in Christ, we are of all men most to be pitied. But in fact Christ has been raised from the dead, the first fruits of those who have fallen asleep.
1 Cor. 6:14. God raised the Lord and will also raise us up by his power. (Also Jn. 6:40/44/54, Rom. 8:11.)
1 Pet. 2:6. ...He who believes in him will not be put to shame. (Also Rom. 9:33, Ps. 22:4–5, Is. 45:17.)

Lk. 1:68–69. Blessed be the Lord God of Israel, for he has visited and redeemed his people, and has raised up a horn of salvation for us...
Rev. 12:10. ...Now the salvation and the power and the kingdom of our God...have come...

Von Gnad und lauter Güte.
Of   grace and sheer kindness.

Die Werk, die helfen nimmermehr,
- Works, they avail   nevermore,

Sie mögen   nicht behüten.
They (can) (us) not protect.
{They can not make us secure.}

Der Glaub sieht   Jesum Christum an,
- Faith looks (to) Jesus   Christ - ,

Der hat g'nug für uns all getan,
He has enough for us all done,
{He has done enough for us all,}

Er ist der Mittler worden.
He is the mediator become.
{He has become our mediator.}

2. Bass Recit. (Based on Chorale Vss. 2-4)
●Law given to show us we were too weak to keep it (9-2)
Gott gab uns ein Gesetz, doch waren wir zu schwach,
God gave us a law, yet were we too weak,
{God gave us a law, yet we were too weak}

Daß wir es hätten halten können.
That we it have kept could.
{To keep it.}

Wir gingen nur den Sünden nach,
We went only - sins after,
{We pursued only sin,}

Kein Mensch war fromm zu nennen;
No person (could) godly (be) called;
{There was no one who could be called godly;}

Der Geist blieb an dem Fleische kleben
The spirit remained to the flesh stuck
{The spirit remained stuck to the flesh}

Und wagte nicht zu widerstreben.
And ventured not to resist (it).

Wir sollten in   Gesetze gehn
We were in (God's) laws to-walk
{We were to walk in God's laws}

Und dort als wie in einem Spiegel sehn,
And there as if in a mirror to-see,
{And to see there, as in a mirror,}

Jn. 1:14. The Word became flesh and dwelt among us, full of grace and truth...
Eph. 2:7-9. That in the coming ages he might show the immeasurable riches of his grace in kindness toward us in Christ Jesus. For by grace you have been saved through faith; and this is not your own doing, it is the gift of God—not because of works, lest any man should boast.
Gal. 2:16. ...By works of the law shall no one be justified.
***Mt. 5:20 [Christ]:** For I tell you, unless your righteousness exceeds that of the scribes and Pharisees, you will never enter the kingdom of heaven.
Tit. 3:4-7. When the goodness and loving kindness of God our Savior appeared, he saved us, not because of deeds done by us in righteousness, but in virtue of his own mercy, by the washing of regeneration and renewal in the Holy Spirit, which he poured out upon us richly through Jesus Christ our Savior so that we might be justified by his grace and become heirs in hope of eternal life.
Heb. 12:2. [We look] to Jesus the pioneer and perfecter of our faith...
Heb. 2:9. ...[Christ came] so that...he might taste death for every one.
1 Tim. 2:5-6. For there is one God, and there is one mediator between God and men, the man Christ Jesus, who gave himself as a ransom for all... (Also Heb. 9:15, Heb. 12:24.)

Jn. 7:19. Did not Moses give you the law? Yet none of you keeps the law.
Acts 15:10. ...Why do you make a trial of God by putting a yoke upon the neck of the disciples which neither our fathers nor we have been able to bear?
Rom. 7:15-25. I do not understand my own actions. For I do not do what I want, but I do the very thing I hate. Now if I do what I do not want, I agree that the law is good. So then it is no longer I that do it, but sin which dwells within me. For I know that nothing good dwells within me, that is, in my flesh. I can will what is right, but I cannot do it. For I do not do the good I want, but the evil I do not want is what I do. Now if I do what I do not want, it is no longer I that do it, but sin which dwells within me. So I find it to be a law that when I want to do right, evil lies close at hand. For I delight in the law of God, in my inmost self, but I see in my members another law at war with the law of my mind and making me captive to the law of sin which dwells in my members. Wretched man that I am! Who will deliver me from this body of death? Thanks be to God through Jesus Christ our Lord! So then, I of myself serve the law of God with my mind, but with my flesh I serve the law of sin. (Also Gal. 5:17.)
Rom. 8:3. God has done what the law, weakened by the flesh, could not do...
Is. 53:6. All we like sheep have gone astray; we have turned every one to his own way...
Rom. 3:10-12, 23. As it is written: "None is righteous, no, not one; no one understands, no one seeks for God. All have turned aside, together they have gone wrong; no one does good, not even one."...All have sinned and fall short of the glory of God. (Also Prov. 20:9.)
Rom. 8:7-8. ...The mind that is set on the flesh is hostile to God; it does not submit to God's law, indeed it cannot; and those who are in the flesh cannot please God.

Wie unsere Natur unartig sei;
How   our   nature ill-behaved be;
{How ill-behaved our nature is;}

Und   dennoch bleiben wir dabei.
And   nevertheless persist we therewith.
{Yet we persist nevertheless in our ways.}

Aus eigner   Kraft war niemand fähig,
Of one's-own strength was no-one able,
{No one was able in their own strength}

Der Sünden   Unart   zu verlassen,
-    Sin's bad-behavior to   forsake,
{To forsake sin's evil ways,}

        Er möcht auch alle Kraft zusammenfassen.
(Though) (one) might even all strength summon-together.
{Even though one might try with all one's strength.}

3. Tenor Aria
●Sinking into the abyss with no one to help (9–3)
Wir waren schon zu   tief gesunken,
We were already too deeply sunk,

Der Abgrund   schluckt uns völlig ein,
The   abyss was-swallowing us entirely - ,

Die Tiefe   drohte   schon den Tod,
The Deep threatened already (with) death,

Und dennoch konnt in solcher Not
And   still   could in   such   distress

Uns keine Hand behilflich sein.
To-us no hand   helpful   be.
{No hand be helpful to us.}

4. Bass Recit. (Based on Chorale Vss. 5–7)
●Christ fulfilled law, providing salvation by faith (9–4)
Doch mußte das Gesetz erfüllet werden;
Yet   had   the   law   fulfilled to-be;
{Yet the law had to be fulfilled;}

Deswegen   kam das Heil   der Erden,
For-that-reason came the Salvation of-the earth,
{For that reason the Salvation of the earth came,}

Des Höchsten Sohn, der hat es selbst erfüllt
The Highest's Son, he has it himself fulfilled
{The Son of the Highest; he has fulfilled it himself}

Und seines Vaters Zorn gestillt.
And   his Father's wrath quieted.
{And quieted his Father's wrath.}

Jms. 1:23–25. If any one is a hearer of the word and not a doer, he is like a man who observes his natural face in a mirror; for he observes himself and goes away and at once forgets what he was like. But he who looks into the perfect law, the law of liberty, and perseveres...shall be blessed in his doing.
Rom. 3:20. ...Through the law comes knowledge of sin.
Rom. 7:7, 13. If it had not been for the law, I should not have known sin...that sin might be shown to be sin, and through the commandment might become sinful beyond measure. (Also Gal. 3:19, 22, 24.)
Rom. 7:15–24. I do not understand my own actions. For I do not do what I want, but I do the very thing I hate...I know that nothing good dwells within me, that is, in my flesh. I can will what is right, but I cannot do it. For I do not do the good I want, but the evil I do not want is what I do...Wretched man that I am! Who will deliver me from this body of death?
Jn. 8:34. ...Every one who commits sin is a slave to sin.
2 Pet. 2:19. ...For whatever overcomes a man, to that he is enslaved. (Also Rom. 6:16.)
*Rom. 6:6. ...that we might no longer be enslaved to sin.

Ps. 69:1–3, 13–15. Save me, O God! For the waters have come up to my neck. I sink in deep mire, where there is no foothold; I have come into deep waters, and the flood sweeps over me. I am weary with my crying; my throat is parched. My eyes grow dim with waiting for my God... With thy faithful help rescue me from sinking in the mire; let me be delivered from my enemies and from the deep waters. Let not the flood sweep over me, or the deep swallow me up, or the pit close its mouth over me. (Also Ps. 124:2–5.)
Ps. 130:1–2. Out of the depths I cry to thee, O Lord! Lord, hear my voice!
Is. 63:5. I looked, but there was no one to help...
Ps. 22:11. Be not far from me, for trouble is near and there is none to help. (Also 2 Sam. 22: 41, Ps. 18:41, 107:12.)
Ps. 108:6. That thy beloved may be delivered, give help by thy right hand, and answer me!
Ps. 119:173. [O Lord,] let thy hand be ready to help me...

Mt. 5:17 [Christ]: Think not that I have come to abolish the law and the prophets; I have come not to abolish them but to fulfil them.
Rom. 10:4. Christ is the end of the law (Luther: Gesetzes Ende), that every one who has faith may be justified.
Jn. 3:16–17. For God so loved the world that he gave his only Son, that whoever believes in him should not perish but have eternal life. For God sent the Son into the world, not to condemn the world, but that the world might be saved through him.
1 Jn. 4:14. And we have seen and testify that the Father has sent his Son as the Savior of the world.
Acts 13:38–39. ....Through [Christ] forgiveness of sins is proclaimed to you, and by him every one that believes is freed from everything from which you could not be freed by the law of Moses.
Rom. 1:18. The wrath of God is revealed...against all ungodliness and wickedness...

Durch   sein unschuldig Sterben
Through his   guiltless   dying

Ließ er uns Hilf erwerben.
Let he us   help   acquire.
{He let us acquire help.}

Wer   nun demselben traut,
Whoever now the-same   trusts,
{Whowever now trusts in him,}

Wer   auf sein Leiden baut,
Whoever on   his passion builds,
{Whoever builds on his passion,}

Der gehet nicht verloren.
He goes   not   lost.
{Will not be lost.}

Der Himmel is für   den   erkoren,
 -   Heaven is for that-one chosen,
{Heaven is chosen for the one}

Der wahren Glauben mit sich bringt
Who true   faith with him brings

Und fest um Jesu   Arme schlingt.
And fast about Jesus (his) arms entwines.
{Who comes in true faith and entwines his arms about Jesus.}

5. Soprano & Alto Duet (Based on Chorale Vs. 8)
●Faith, not works makes us righteous before God (9-5)
Herr, du siehst   statt   guter Werke
Lord, thou dost-look intead-of good works
{Lord thou dost not regard good works but rather dost look}

Auf des Herzens Glaubensstärke,
Upon the heart's   strength-of-faith,

Nur den Glauben nimmst du an.
Only -   faith   acceptest thou - .
{Only faith dost thou accept.}

Nur der Glaube macht gerecht,
Only - faith   makes righteous,
{Faith alone can make us righteous,}

Alles andre scheint zu schlecht,
All   else appears too   base,

Als daß es uns helfen kann.
Than that it us   help   can.
{Than that it could help us.}

6. Bass Recit. (Based on Chorale Vss. 9-11)
●Law discloses sin; gospel gives future beyond death (9-6)
Wenn wir die Sünd aus dem Gesetz erkennen,
When we - sin from the law   recognize,
{When we recognize sin from the law,}

Rom. 5:8. But God shows his love for us in that while we were yet sinners Christ died for us.

2 Cor. 5:21. For our sake [God] made him to be sin who knew no sin, so that in him we might become the righteousness of God.

Rom. 5:9. Since, therefore, we are now justified by [Christ's] blood, much more shall we be saved by him from the wrath of God.

*Rom. 6:6-8. We know that our old self was crucified with [Christ] so that the sinful body might be destroyed, and we might no longer be enslaved to sin. For he who has died is freed from sin. But if we have died with Christ, we believe that we shall also live with him.

1 Pet. 2:22, 24. He committed no sin; no guile was found on his lips... He himself bore our sins in his body on the tree, that we might die to sin and live to righteousness. By his wounds you have been healed.

Jn. 3:36 [Christ]: He who believes in the Son has eternal life; he who does not obey the Son shall not see life, but the wrath of God rests upon him.

Mt. 7:24 [Christ]: Every one then who hears these words of mine and does them will be like a wise man who built his house upon the rock. (Also Mt. 16:18, 1 Cor. 3:11-12.)

Jn. 3:16. ...Whoever believes in [the Son will] not perish but have eternal life.

Col. 1:5. [This is] the hope laid up for you in heaven...

Heb. 11:13, 16. [Many previously] died in faith...Therefore God is not ashamed to be called their God, for he has prepared for them a city.

S. of S. 3:4 [Bride]: ...I found him whom my soul loves. I held him, and would not let him go... (Also Gen. 32:26.)

*Rom. 6:4, 8. We were buried therefore with him by baptism into death, so that as Christ was raised from the dead by the glory of the Father, we too might walk in newness of life...But if we have died with Christ, we believe that we shall also live with him.

Rom. 3:28. For we hold that a man is justified by faith apart from works of law.

Gal. 2:16. ...A man is not justified by works of the law...because by works of the law shall no one be justified.

Rom. 10:4. For Christ is the end of the law, that every one who has faith may be justified.

Rom. 1:17. ...He who through faith is righteous shall live.

Heb. 10:38. But my righteous one shall live by faith.

Gal. 3:11. Now it is evident that no man is justified before God by the law; for "He who through faith is righteous shall live."

Eph. 2:8-9. For by grace you have been saved through faith; and this is not your own doing, it is the gift of God—not because of works, lest any man should boast.

Is. 64:6. ...All our righteous deeds are like a polluted garment.

Heb. 9:14. ...The blood of Christ...purify your conscience from dead works...

Rom. 3:20. ...Through the law comes knowledge of sin.

Rom. 7:7-8, 11-14. ...If it had not been for the law, I should not have known sin. I should not have known what it is to covet if the law had not said, "You shall not covet." But sin, finding opportunity in the commandment, wrought in me all kinds of covetousness...Sin, finding opportunity in the commandment, deceived me and by it killed me...

So   schlägt es das Gewissen nieder;
Then strikes it the conscience down;
{Then it strkes down our conscience;}

Doch ist das unser Trost zu nennen,
Yet is that our comfort to name,
{Yet we can call that our comfort,}

Daß wir im Evangelio
That we in-the gospel

Gleich wieder froh
Directly again happy

Und freudig werden:
And joyous become:

Dies   stärket unsern Glauben wieder.
This strengthens our   faith   again.

Drauf   hoffen wir der Zeit,
Thereupon await we the time,
{Thereupon we await the time,}

Die Gottes Gütigkeit
Which God's goodness

Uns zugesaget hat,
For-us appointed has,
{Has appointed for us,}

Doch aber auch aus weisem Rat
Yet, however, also out-of wise counsel
{Yet also, wisely,}

Die Stunde uns   verschwiegen.
The hour from-us (has) kept-secret.
{Kept the hour secret from us.}

Jedoch, wir lassen uns begnügen,
Still,   we let ourselves be-contented (that),

Er weiß es, wenn es nötig ist,
He knows it, when it necessary is,
{He knows when it must come,}

Und brauchet keine List
And employs   no cunning

An uns; wir dürfen auf ihn bauen
With us; we may upon him build
{With us; we may build upon him}

Und ihm allein vertrauen.
And him alone   trust.
{And trust him alone.}

The law is holy, and the commandment is holy and just and good. Did that which is good, then, bring death to me? By no means! It was sin, working death in me through what is good, in order that sin might be shown to be sin, and through the commandment might become sinful beyond measure. We know that the law is spiritual; but I am carnal, sold under sin.

Gal. 3:19–24. Why then the law? It was added because of transgressions...But the scripture consigned all things to sin...So that the law was our custodian until Christ came...

Rom. 5:20. ...Where sin increased, grace abounded all the more.

*Rom. 6:3–10. Do you not know that all of us who have been baptized into Christ Jesus were baptized into his death? We were buried therefore with him by baptism into death, so that as Christ was raised from the dead by the glory of the Father, we too might walk in newness of life. For if we have been united with him in a death like his, we shall certainly be united with him in a resurrection like his. We know that our old self was crucified with him so that the sinful body might be destroyed, and we might no longer be enslaved to sin. For he who has died is freed from sin. But if we have died with Christ, we believe that we shall also live with him. For we know that Christ being raised from the dead will never die again; death no longer has dominion over him.

Rom. 7:24–8:2. ...Who will deliver me from this body of death? Thanks be to God through Jesus Christ our Lord!...There is therefore now no condemnation for those who are in Christ Jesus. For the law of the Spirit of life in Christ Jesus has set me free from the law of sin and death.

2 Sam. 14:14. We must all die, we are like water spilt on the ground, which cannot be gathered again.

Heb. 9:27. ...It is appointed for men to die once... (Also Ecc. 3:1–2.)

Acts 1:7. [Jesus] said... "It is not for you to know times or seasons which the Father has fixed by his own authority."

Jms. 4:13–15. Come now, you who say, "Today or tomorrow we will go into such and such a town and spend a year there and trade and get gain"; whereas you do not know about tomorrow. What is your life? For you are a mist that appears for a little time and then vanishes. Instead you ought to say, "If the Lord wills, we shall live and we shall do this or that."

Ps. 31:14–15. But I trust in thee, O Lord, I say, "Thou art my God." My times are in thy hand...

Ps. 23:4. Even though I walk through the valley of the shadow of death, I fear no evil; for thou art with me...

Ps. 116:15. Precious in the sight of the Lord is the death of his saints.

1 Pet. 2:6. It stands in scripture: "Behold, I am laying in Zion a stone, a cornerstone chosen and precious, and he who believes in him will not be put to shame."

1 Pet. 2:22, 24. He committed no sin; no guile was found on his lips... He himself bore our sins in his body on the tree, that we might die to sin and live to righteousness...

Mt. 7:24 [Christ]: Every one then who hears these words of mine and does them will be like a wise man who built his house upon the rock... (Also 1 Cor. 3:12.)

Jn. 14:1–2. Let not your hearts be troubled; believe in God, believe also in me. In my Father's house are many rooms; if it were not so, would I have told you that I go to prepare a place for you?

7. Chorale (Vs. 12) (See also 155–5, 186–6.)
●Believe his Word rather than appearances (9–7)
Ob   sich's anließ, als wollt er nicht,
Though it   appear, as-if wanted he not,
{Though it appear as if he were not intending to help you,}

Laß dich es nicht erschrecken;
Let you it not   frighten;
{Let it not frighten you;}

Denn wo er ist am besten mit,
For where he is - best with (you),
{For where he is most with you,}

Da   will er's nicht entdecken.
There would he-it not   disclose.
{There he would not disclose it.}

Sein Wort laß dir   gewisser sein,
His Word let to-you more-certain be,
{Let his Word become more certain to you,}

Und ob dein Herz spräch lauter Nein,
And though your heart say   only "No,"

So laß doch   dir nicht grauen.
Yet let nevertheless yourself not be-terrified.
{Yet let yourself nevertheless not be terrified.}

Lk. 24:15, 16, 28–31. While [the disciples on the road to Emmaus] were talking and discussing together, Jesus himself drew near and went with them. But their eyes were kept from recognizing him...So they drew near to the village to which they were going. [Jesus] appeared to be going further, but they constrained him, saying, "Stay with us..."...When he was at table with them...their eyes were opened and they recognized him; and he vanished out of their sight...
Jn. 20:29. ...Blessed are those who have not seen and yet believe.
Rom. 8:24–25. ...Now hope that is seen is not hope. For who hopes for what he sees? But if we hope for what we do not see, we wait for it with patience.
Heb. 11:1. Now faith is the assurance of things hoped for, the conviction of things not seen.
2 Pet. 1:19. And we have the prophetic word made more sure. You will do well to pay attention to this as to a lamp shining in a dark place, until the day dawns and the morning star rises in your hearts.
2 Cor. 1:18–20. As surely as God is faithful, our word to you has not been Yes and No. For the Son of God, Jesus Christ...was not Yes and No; but in him it is always Yes. For all the promises of God find their Yes in him. That is why we utter the Amen through him, to the glory of God.
1 Jn. 3:19–20. By this we shall know that we are of the truth, and reassure our hearts before him whenever our hearts condemn us; for God is greater than our hearts...

BWV 10
Meine Seel erhebt den Herren
(NBA I/28; BC A175)

The Visitation: July 2 (BWV 147, 10)
*Is. 11:1–5 (Prophecy concerning the Messiah)
*Lk. 1:39–56 (Mary's visit to Elizabeth, Magnificat)
Librettist: Unknown

1. Chorus (Chorale Vss. 1–2)
●Magnificat: Mary as favored among women: Lk. 1:46–48 (10–1)
Meine Seel erhebt den Herren,
My   soul exalts the Lord,

Und mein Geist freuet sich   Gottes, meines Heilandes;
And my spirit rejoices - (in) God,   my   Savior;

///

Denn er hat seine elende Magd angesehen.
For he has his (lowly) maid regarded.

Siehe, von nun an werden mich selig preisen
Lo, from now on will   me blessed praise

        alle Kindeskind.
        all children's children.
{From now on all generations will call me blessed.}

Mt. 1:20–23. ...An angel of the Lord appeared to [Joseph] in a dream saying, "Joseph, son of David, do not fear to take Mary your wife, for that which is conceived in her is of the Holy Spirit; she will bear a son, and you shall call his name Jesus, for he will save his people from their sins." All this took place to fulfil what the Lord had spoken by the prophet: "Behold, a virgin shall conceive and bear a son, and his name shall be called Emmanuel" (which means, God with us). (See Is. 7:14.)
***Lk. 1:46–48.** And Mary said, "My soul magnifies the Lord, and my spirit rejoices in God my Savior, for he has regarded the low estate of his handmaiden. For behold, henceforth all generations will call me blessed..."*
1 Sam. 2:1–2. Hannah also prayed and said, "My heart exults in the Lord; my strength is exalted in the Lord. My mouth derides my enemies, because I rejoice in thy salvation. There is none holy like the Lord, there is none besides thee; there is no rock like our God."
Ps. 34:2–3. My soul makes its boast in the Lord; let the afflicted hear and be glad. O magnify the Lord with me, and let us exalt his name together!
Ps. 103:17. The steadfast love of the Lord is from everlasting to everlasting upon those who fear him, and his righteousness to children's children.
Ps. 145:4. One generation shall laud thy works to another, and shall declare thy mighty acts.

2. Soprano Aria (Based on Chorale Vs. 3: Lk. 1:49)
●Magnificat: The holy, mighty God has blessed richly (10-2)
Herr, der du stark und mächtig bist,
Lord, thou-who strong and mighty art,

Gott, dessen Name heilig ist,
God, whose name holy is,
{O God, whose name is holy,}

Wie wunderbar sind deine Werke!
How marvellous are thy works!

Du siehest mich Elenden an,
Thou regardest (this) wretched-one - ,

Du hast an mir so viel getan,
Thou hast (for) me so much done,
{Thou has done so much for me,}

Daß ich nicht alles zähl und merke.
That I not all (of it could) count (or) note.
{That I could not count or take note of it all.}

3. Tenor Recit. (Based on Chorale Vss. 4–5: Lk. 1:50-51)
●Magnificat: God helps lowly but scatters proud (10-3)
Des Höchsten Güt und Treu
The Highest's goodness and faithfulness

Wird alle Morgen neu
Is all mornings new
{Is new every morning}

Und währet immer für und für
And endures always (for) ever and ever

Bei denen, die allhier
For those, who here

Auf seine Hilfe schaun
To his help look
{Look to his help}

Und ihm in wahrer Furcht vertraun.
And him in true fear do-trust.
{And trust him in true faith.}

Hingegen übt er auch Gewalt
On-the-other-hand exercises he also force
{On the other hand he also exercises force}

Mit seinem Arm
With his arm

An denen, welche weder kalt
Upon those, who neither cold
{Upon those, who are neither cold}

Noch warm
Nor warm

*Lk. 1:49. For he who is mighty has done great things for me, and holy is his name.

1 Sam. 2:2. There is none holy like the Lord, there is none besides thee; there is no rock like our God. (Also Ps. 111:9, Is. 57:15.)

*Is. 11:4–5. With righteousness he shall judge the poor, and decide with equity for the meek of the earth; and he shall smite the earth with the rod of his mouth, and with the breath of his lips he shall slay the wicked. Righteousness shall be the girdle of his waist, and faithfulness the girdle of his loins.

Ps. 92:5. How great are thy works, O Lord!

Ps. 9:18. The needy shall not always be forgotten, and the hope of the poor shall not perish for ever.

Job 5:9. Who does great things and unsearchable, marvelous things without number.

Ps. 40:5. Thou hast multiplied, O Lord my God, thy wondrous deeds and thy thoughts toward us...Were I to proclaim and tell of them, they would be more than can be numbered.

Ps. 71:15. [O Lord,] my mouth will tell of thy righteous acts, of thy deeds of salvation all the day, for their number is past my knowledge. (Also Ps. 139:17–18.)

*Lk. 1:50. And his mercy is on those who fear him from generation to generation.

Lam. 3:22–23. The steadfast love of the Lord never ceases, his mercies never come to an end; they are new every morning; great is thy faithfulness. (Also Ps. 90:14.)

Ps. 103:17–18. The steadfast love of the Lord is from everlasting to everlasting upon those who fear him, and his righteousness to children's children to those who keep his covenant and remember to do his commandments.

Ps. 100:4–5. ...Give thanks to him, bless his name! For the Lord is good; his steadfast love endures for ever, and his faithfulness to all generations.

Ps. 124:8. Our help is in the name of the Lord, who made heaven and earth.

1 Sam. 2:9. He will guard the feet of his faithful ones; but the wicked shall be cut off in darkness; for not by might shall a man prevail.

Prov. 15:29. The Lord is far from the wicked, but he hears the prayer of the righteous.

*Is. 11:4–5. But with righteousness he shall judge the poor, and decide with equity for the meek of the earth; and he shall smite the earth with the rod of his mouth, and with the breath of his lips he shall slay the wicked. Righteousness shall be the girdle of his waist, and faithfulness the girdle of his loins.

*Lk. 1:51. He has shown strength with his arm, he has scattered the proud in the imagination of their hearts.

1 Sam. 2:4, 10. The bows of the mighty are broken, but the feeble gird on strength...The adversaries of the Lord shall be broken to pieces; against them he will thunder in heaven.

Rev. 3:14–17. To the angel of the church in Laodicea write:..."I know your works: you are neither cold nor hot! So, because you are lukewarm, and neither cold nor hot, I will spew you out of my mouth. For you say, I am rich, I have prospered, and I need nothing; not knowing that you are wretched, pitiable, poor, blind, and naked."

Im Glauben und im Lieben sein;
In believing (or) in loving are;
{In believing or in loving;}

Die   nacket, bloß und blind,
Those-who naked, bare, and blind,
{Those who are naked, bare, and blind,}

Die voller Stolz und Hoffart sind,
Who full-of pride and haughtiness are,
{Who are full of pride and haughtiness,}

Will seine Hand wie Spreu zerstreun.
Would his hand like chaff   scatter.
{Would his hand scatter like chaff.}

4. Bass Aria (Based on Chorale Vss. 6–7: Lk. 1:52–53)
●Magnificat: God casts down proud, exalts lowly (10–4)
Gewaltige stößt Gott vom   Stuhl
Mighty-ones casts God from (their) seat(s)
{God casts mighty ones from their seats}

Hinunter in den Schwefelpfuhl;
Down   into the pit-of-brimstone;

Die Niedern pflegt Gott zu erhöhen,
The lowly tends God to   exalt,
{God is given to exalting the lowly,}

Daß   sie wie Stern am Himmel stehen.
So-that they like stars in heaven stand.
{So that they stand like the stars in heaven.}

Die Reichen läßt Gott bloß und leer,
The rich   leaves God bare and empty,
{God leaves the rich bare and empty,}

Die Hungrigen füllt er mit Gaben,
The hungry fills he with gifts,
{He fills the hungry with gifts,}

Daß   sie auf seinem Gnadenmeer
So-that they upon his   sea-of-grace

Stets Reichtum und die Fülle haben.
Ever riches and - abundance have.
{Ever have riches and abundance.}

5. Alto & Tenor Duet (Chorale Vs. 8)
●Magnificat: God remembers his mercy: Lk. 1:54 (10–5)
Er denket   der Barmherzigkeit
He remembers (his)   mercy

Und hilft seinem Diener Israel auf.
And helps his servant Israel up.

Mt. 23:23–24. Woe to you, scribes and Pharisees, hypocrites!...You blind guides...
1 Sam. 2:3. Talk no more so very proudly, let not arrogance come from your mouth; for the Lord is a God of knowledge, and by him actions are weighed.
Ps. 138:6. For though the Lord is high, he regards the lowly; but the haughty he knows from afar.
Prov. 15:25. The Lord tears down the house of the proud, but maintains the widow's boundaries.
Is. 2:12. The Lord of hosts has a day against all that is proud and lofty, against all that is lifted up and high.
Mt. 3:12. His winnowing fork is in his hand, and he will clear his threshing floor and gather his wheat into the granary, but the chaff he will burn with unquenchable fire.
Ps. 1:4. The wicked are..like chaff which the wind drives away.

***Lk. 1:52–53.** He has put down the mighty from their thrones, and exalted those of low degree; he has filled the hungry with good things, and the rich he has sent empty away.
2 Sam. 22:28. Thou dost deliver a humble people, but thy eyes are upon the haughty to bring them down.
Ps. 138:6. For though the Lord is high, he regards the lowly; but the haughty he knows from afar.
Prov. 15:25. The Lord tears down the house of the proud, but maintains the widow's boundaries.
***Is. 11:4.** With righteousness he shall judge the poor, and decide with equity for the meek of the earth; and he shall smite the earth with the rod of his mouth, and with the breath of his lips he shall slay the wicked.
Rev. 19:20. ...[The beast and the false prophet] were thrown alive into the lake of fire that burns with sulphur.
1 Sam. 2:4–5, 7–8. The bows of the mighty are broken, but the feeble gird on strength. Those who were full have hired themselves out for bread, but those who were hungry have ceased to hunger...The Lord makes poor and makes rich; he brings low, he also exalts. He raises up the poor from the dust; he lifts the needy from the ash heap, to make them sit with princes and inherit a seat of honor...
Ps. 75:6–7. For not from the east or from the west comes lifing up; but it is God who executes judgment, putting down one and lifting up another.
Mt. 23:12. Whoever exalts himself will be humbled, and whoever humbles himself will be exalted.
Jms. 4:6. ...Therefore it says, "God opposes the proud, but gives grace to the humble." (Also Prov. 3:34, 1 Pet. 5:6.)
Mt. 19:23. And Jesus said..."Truly, I say to you, it will be hard for a rich man to enter the kingdom of heaven."
Ps. 107:9. For he satisfies him who is thirsty, and the hungry he fills with good things.

***Lk. 1:54–55.** *He has helped his servant Israel, in remembrance of his mercy,* as he spoke to our fathers, to Abraham and to his posterity for ever.
Ps. 98:3. He has remembered his steadfast love and faithfulness to the house of Israel...
***Lk. 1:54–55.** He has helped his servant Israel, in remembrance of his mercy, as he spoke to our fathers, to Abraham and to his posterity for ever.

6. Tenor Recit. (Based on Chorale Vs. 9: Lk. 1:55)
●Magnificat: Promise to Abraham fulfilled (10–6)
Was Gott den Vätern   alter Zeiten
What God to-the fathers of-ancient times

Geredet und verheißen hat,
Said   and promised   -,

Erfüllt er auch im Werk und in der Tat.
Fulfills he also   in action and in - deed.
{That he also fulfills in action and in deed.}

Was Gott dem Abraham,
What God to Abraham,

Als   er zu ihm in seine Hütten kam,
When he to him in his   tents came,

Versprochen und geschworen,
Pledged   and   swore,
{What God pledged and swore to Abraham when he came to him
in his tents,}

Ist,   da die Zeit erfüllet war, geschehen.
Has—when the time was-fulfilled—happened.

Sein Same mußte sich so sehr
His seed   had,   - as greatly
{His seed had to spread out as greatly}

Wie Sand am   Meer
As   sand by (the) sea

Und Stern am Firmament ausbreiten,
And stars in-the firmament, to-spread-out,
{And stars in the firmament;}

Der Heiland ward geboren,
The Savior   was   born,

Das ewge Wort ließ sich im Fleische sehen,
The eternal Word let itself in   flesh be-seen,
{The eternal Word appeared in the flesh,}

Das menschliche Geschlecht von Tod und allem Bösen
The   human   race   from death and all   evil
{To redeem the human race from death and all evil}

Und von des Satans Sklaverei
And from - Satan's slavery

Aus   lauter Liebe zu erlösen;
Out-of sheer love, to redeem;
{Out of sheer love;}

Drum bleibt's darbei,
So   it-remains-with-this,

Daß Gottes Wort voll   Gnad und Wahrheit sei.
That God's Word full (of) grace and   truth   is.

*Lk. 1:67–70, 72–73. Zechariah was filled with the Holy Spirit, and prophesied, saying, "Blessed be the Lord God of Israel, for he has visited and redeemed his people, and has raised up a horn of salvation for us...as he spoke by the mouth of his holy prophets from of old...to perform the mercy promised to our fathers, and to remember his holy covenant, the oath which he swore to our father Abraham."
Gen. 12:1–3. Now the Lord said to Abram, "Go from your country and your kindred...to the land that I will show you. And I will make of you a great nation, and I will bless you, and make your name great, so that you will be a blessing."
Heb. 11:8–9. By faith Abraham obeyed when he was called to go out to a place which he was to receive as an inheritance; and he went out, not knowing where he was to go. By faith he sojourned in the land of promise, as in a foreign land, living in tents with Isaac and Jacob, heirs with him of the same promise.
Gen. 13:14, 16. The Lord said to Abram, after Lot had separated from him..."I will make your descendants as the dust of the earth; so that if one can count the dust of the earth, your descendants also can be counted."
Gen. 17:15–19. And God said to Abraham, "As for Sarai your wife... Sarah shall be her name...I will bless her, and she will be a mother of nations; kings of peoples shall come from her...Sarah your wife shall bear you a son, and you shall call his name Isaac. I will establish my covenant with him as an everlasting covenant for his descendants after him."
Gen. 18:1, 10. And the Lord appeared to him...as he sat at the door of his tent...The Lord said, "I will surely return to you in the spring, and Sarah your wife shall have a son."
Gen. 22:15–17. And the angel of the Lord called to Abraham...and said, "By myself I have sworn, says the Lord, because you have...not withheld your son, your only son, I will indeed bless you, and I will multiply your descendants as the stars of heaven and as the sand which is on the seashore."
Gen. 28:13–14. And behold, the Lord...said [to Jacob], "I am the Lord, the God of Abraham your father and the God of Isaac; the land on which you lie I will give to you and to your descendants; and your descendants shall be like the dust of the earth..."
Acts 3:25. You are the sons of the prophets and of the covenant which God gave to your fathers, saying to Abraham, "And in your posterity shall all the families of the earth be blessed."
Gal. 3:16. Now the promises were made to Abraham and to his offspring. It does not say, "And to offsprings," referring to many; but, referring to one, "And to your offspring," which is Christ.
Gal. 4:4–7. But when the time had fully come, God sent forth his Son ...to redeem those who were under the law, so that we might receive adoption as sons. And because you are sons, God has sent the Spirit of his Son into our hearts, crying, "Abba! Father!" So through God you are no longer a slave but a son, and if a son then an heir.
Jn. 8:34. ...Every one who commits sin is a slave to sin. (Also Jn. 8:34, Rom. 6:16, 20, 2 Pet. 2:19, 2 Tim. 2:26, Tit. 3:3.)
1 Jn. 4:14. We have seen and testify that the Father has sent his Son as the Savior of the world.
Jn. 1:14. The [eternal] Word became flesh and dwelt among us, full of grace and truth...

7. Chorale (Vss. 10–11)
●Doxology: Praise to Father, Son, and Holy Ghost (10-7)
Lob und Preis sei   Gott dem Vater und dem Sohn
Laud and praise be (to) God the Father and the Son

Und dem Heiligen Geiste,
And the   Holy   Ghost,

Wie es war im   Angang,   jetzt und immerdar
As   it was in-the beginning, (is) now and evermore

Und von Ewigkeit zu Ewigkeit, Amen.
And from eternity to eternity,   Amen.

BWV 11 Ascension Oratorio
Lobet Gott in seinen Reichen
(NBA II/8; BC D9)

Ascension (BWV 37, 128, 43, 11)
*Acts 1:1–11 (Holy Spirit promised, Christ's ascension)
*Mk. 16:14–20 (Great commission, Christ's ascension)
Librettist: Unknown. Some movements were adapted from earlier works.

1. Chorus (Adapted from BWV Anh. 18; BC: BWV 36b)
●Praise God in his glory! (11-1)
Lobet Gott in seinen Reichen,
Praise God in his   realms,

Preiset ihn in seinen Ehren,
Praise him in his   honors,
{Praise him in his glory,}

Rühmet ihn in seiner Pracht!
Extol   him in his   pomp!

Sucht sein Lob   recht zu vergleichen,
Seek   his praise properly to compare,
(Seek his praise properly to describe,}

Wenn ihr mit gesamten Chören
When you with   united   choirs

Ihm ein Lied zu Ehren macht!
Him a song for honor do-make!
{A song of honor for him do make!}

2. Tenor Recit. (Evangelist)
●Ascension of Christ: Lk. 24:50–51 (11-2)
Der Herr Jesus hub seine Hände auf
The Lord Jesus lifted his   hands up

und segnete seine Jünger, und es geschah,
and blessed his   disciples, and it happened, (that)

da er sie segnete, schied er von ihnen.
as he them blessed, departed he from them.

1 Tim. 1:17. To the King of ages, immortal, invisible, the only God, be honor and glory for ever and ever. Amen. (Also Phil. 4:20.)
Ps. 41:13. Blessed be the Lord, the God of Israel, from everlasting to everlasting! Amen and Amen. (Doxology: also Ps. 72:19, 89:52, 106:48, 150:6, Rom. 11:36, Jude 1:25)
Mt. 28:19. ...in the name of the Father and of the Son and of the Holy Spirit.
Rev. 4:8. The four living creatures, each of them with six wings...day and night they never cease to sing, "Holy, holy, holy, is the Lord God Almighty, who was and is and is to come!"
Rev. 7:11–12. And all the angels...fell on their faces before the throne and worshiped God, saying, "Amen! Blessing and glory and wisdom and thanksgiving and honor and power and might be to our God for ever and ever! Amen."

*Mk. 16:19. So then the Lord Jesus, after he had spoken to [his disciples], was taken up into heaven, and sat down at the right hand of God.
Heb. 1:3. ...When [Christ] had made purification for sins, he sat down at the right hand of the Majesty on high.
1 Pet. 3:22. [Christ] has [now] gone into heaven and is at the right hand of God, with angels, authorities, and powers subject to him. (Also Acts 2:33, 5:31, Heb. 10:12, 12:2.)
Mk. 14:62 [Christ]: ...You will see the Son of man seated at the right hand of Power, and coming with the clouds of heaven.
1 Chron. 29:11. Thine, O Lord, is the greatness, and the power, and the glory, and the victory, and the majesty; for all that is in the heavens and in the earth is thine; thine is the Kingdom, O Lord, and thou art exalted as head above all. (Also Ps. 19:1.)
Is. 46:5 [God]: To whom will you liken me and make me equal, and compare me, that we may be alike?
Ps. 89:6. Who in the skies can be compared to the Lord? Who among the heavenly beings is like the Lord...?
Rev. 4:8–11. And the four living creatures...day and night...never cease to sing, "Holy, holy, holy, is the Lord God Almighty, who was and is and is to come!"...The twenty-four elders fall down before him who is seated on the throne and worship him who lives for ever and ever; they cast their crowns before the throne, singing, "Worthy art thou, our Lord and God, to receive glory and honor and power..."

Lk. 24:50–51. *Then he led them out as far as Bethany, and lifting up his hands he blessed them. While he blessed them, he parted from them,* and was carried up into heaven.
Jn. 3:12–13 [Christ]: If I have told you earthly things and you do not believe, how can you believe if I tell you heavenly things? No one has ascended into heaven but he who descended from heaven, the Son of man. (Also Eph. 4:8–9.)

3. Bass Recit.
●Ascension of Christ: The grief of bereavement (11–3)
Ach, Jesu, ist dein Abschied schon so nah?
Ah, Jesus, is thy   parting   already so near?

Ach, ist denn schon die Stunde da,
Ah, is then already the hour here,
{Ah, is then the hour already here,}

Da wir dich von uns lassen sollen?
When we thee from us release (must)?
{When we must let thee part from us?}

Ach, siehe, wie die heißen Tränen
Ah, see how the hot   tears

Von unsern blassen Wangen rollen,
From our pale   cheeks roll,

Wie wir uns nach dir sehnen,
How we -   for thee do-yearn,

Wie uns fast aller Trost gebricht.
How for-us nearly all consolation is-gone.
{How nearly all consolation is gone for us.}

Ach, weiche doch noch nicht!
Ah,   leave indeed not yet!
{Ah, please do not leave yet!}

4. Alto Aria (Adapted from unnumbered wedding cantata)
●Prayer: Plea for Christ not to leave (11–4)
Ach, bleibe doch,   mein liebstes Leben,
Ah, stay please, (O) my dearest life,

Ach, fliehe nicht so bald von mir!
Ah, flee   not so soon from me!
{Ah, do not flee so soon from me!}

Dein Abschied und dein frühes Scheiden
Thy departure and thy early   parting

Bringt mir das allergrößte Leiden,
Brings me the greatest-of-all suffering,

Jn. 13:31, 33, 36. ...Jesus said...“Little children, yet a little while I am with you. You will seek me; and as I said to the Jews so now I say to you, ‘Where I am going you cannot come.’”...Simon Peter said to him “Lord, where are you going?” Jesus answered, “Where I am going you cannot follow me now; but you shall follow afterward.”

Jn. 14:5, 9, 18, 27–28. Thomas said to him, “Lord, we do not know where you are going; how can we know the way?”...Jesus said to him... “I will not leave you desolate; I will come to you...Let not your hearts be troubled, neither let them be afraid. You heard me say to you, ‘I go away, and I will come to you.’ If you loved me, you would have rejoiced, because I go to the Father; for the Father is greater than I.” (Also Jn. 14:1, 16:20–22.)

*Acts 1:7. [Jesus] said to them, “It is not for you to know times or seasons which the Father has fixed by his own authority.”

Ps. 73:25. [O Lord,] whom have I in heaven but thee? And there is nothing upon earth that I desire besides thee.

S. of S. 3:4 [Bride]: ...I found him whom my soul loves. I held him, and would not let him go...

Lk. 7:37–38. Behold, a woman of the city, who was a sinner...brought an alabaster flask of ointment, and standing behind [Jesus] at his feet, weeping, she began to wet his feet with her tears, and wiped them with the hair of her head, and kissed his feet, and anointed them with the ointment.

Rev. 7:17, 21:4. ...God will wipe away every tear from their eyes.

Jn. 20:11–17. [After Jesus’ resurrection] Mary stood weeping outside the tomb, and as she wept she stooped to look into the tomb; and she saw two angels in white, sitting where the body of Jesus had lain...They said to her, “Woman, why are you weeping?” She said to them, “Because they have taken away my Lord, and I do not know where they have laid him.” Saying this, she turned round and saw Jesus standing, but she did not know that it was Jesus. Jesus said to her, “Woman, why are you weeping? Whom do you seek?” Supposing him to be the gardener, she said to him, “Sir, if you have carried him away, tell me where you have laid him, and I will take him away.” Jesus said to her, “Mary.” She turned and said to him in Hebrew, “Rabboni!” (which means Teacher). Jesus said to her, “Do not hold me, for I have not yet ascended to the Father, to my God and your God.”

Gen. 32:26. He said, “Let me go, for the day is breaking.” But Jacob said, “I will not let you go, unless you bless me.”

Lk. 24:50–51. Then [Jesus] led [the disciples] out as far as Bethany, and lifting up his hands he blessed them. While he blessed them, he parted from them...

Lk. 24:28–29. [When Jesus and the two disciples] drew near to [Emmaus]...[Jesus] appeared to be going further, but they constrained him, saying, “Stay with us, for it is toward evening...”

Ruth 1:16 [Ruth]: Entreat me not to leave you or to return from following you; for where you go I will go, and where you lodge I will lodge; your people shall be my people, and your God my God...

Jn. 16:4–7, 13 [Christ]: I have said these things to you, that when their hour comes you may remember that I told you of them. I did not say these things to you from the beginning, because I was with you. But now I am going to him who sent me; yet none of you asks me,

Ach ja, so bleibe doch noch hier;
Ah yes, so stay please yet here;
{Ah yes, so stay here yet a while;}

Sonst werd ich ganz von Schmerz umgeben.
Otherwise will I completely with grief be-surrounded.
{Otherwise I will be completely overwhelmed with grief.}

"Where are you going?" But because I have said these things to you, sorrow has filled your hearts. Nevertheless I tell you the truth: it is to your advantage that I go away, for if I do not go away, the Counselor will not come to you; but if I go, I will send him to you...When the Spirit of truth comes, he will guide you into all the truth...He will glorify me, for he will take what is mine and declare it to you.
Heb. 13:5. ...He has said, "I will never fail you nor forsake you."

5. Tenor Recit. (Evangelist)
●Ascension of Christ in a cloud: Acts 1:9, Mk. 16:19 (11–5)
Und ward aufgehoben zusehends und fuhr auf gen
And was lifted-up visibly and went up toward

Himmel, eine Wolke nahm ihn weg vor ihren Augen,
heaven, (and) a cloud took him away before their eyes,

und er sitzet zur rechten Hand Gottes.
and he sits to-the right hand of-God.

*Acts 1:9. And when he had said this, as they were looking on, *he was lifted up, and a cloud took him out of their sight.*
*Mk. 16:19. So then the Lord Jesus, after he had spoken to them, *was taken up into heaven, and sat down at the right hand of God.*
Heb. 10:12–13. When Christ had offered for all time a single sacrifice for sins, he sat down at the right hand of God, then to wait until his enemies should be made a stool for his feet. (See Ps. 110:1, Acts 7:55, Col. 3:1, 1 Pet. 3:22.)

6. Chorale
●Ascension of Christ: All things put under his feet (11–6)
Nun lieget alles unter dir,
Now lies all under thee,
{Now all lies under thee,}

Dich selbst nur ausgenommen;
Thine-own self only excepted;
{With the exception of thine own self;}

Die Engel müssen für und für
The angels must for-ever and ever

Dir aufzuwarten kommen.
Thee to-attend come.
{Come to attend thee.}

Die Fürsten stehn auch auf der Bahn
- Princes stand also on the way
{Princes also stand on the way}

Und sind dir willig untertan;
And are to-thee willingly subject;
{And are willingly subject to thee;}

Luft, Wasser, Feuer, Erden
Air, water, fire, (and) earth

Muß dir zu Dienste werden.
Must thee to service (be-put).
{Must be placed in thy service.}

1 Cor. 15:27. God has put all things in subjection under his feet. But when it says, "All things are put in subjection under him," it is plain that he is excepted who put all things under him. (Also Heb. 2:8, Phil. 3:21, 1 Pet. 3:22.)
Eph. 1:20–22. ...When he raised him from the dead and made him sit at his right hand in the heavenly places, far above all rule and authority and power and dominion, and above every name that is named, not only in this age but also in that which is to come; and he has put all things under his feet and has made him the head over all things...
Heb. 1:3–5, 8, 13–14. ...When he had made purification for sins, he sat down at the right hand of the Majesty on high, having become as much superior to angels as the name he has obtained is more excellent that theirs. For to what angel did God ever say, "Thou art my Son..."? But of the Son he says, "Thy throne, O God, is for ever and ever..." But to what angel has he ever said, "Sit at my right hand, till I make thy enemies a stool for thy feet"? Are they not all ministering spirits sent forth to serve...?
Rev. 7:14. ...These are they who have come out of the great tribulation ...therefore are they before the throne of God, and serve him day and night...
Phil. 2:9–11. Therefore God has highly exalted him and bestowed on him the name which is above every name, that at the name of Jesus every knee should bow, in heaven and on earth and under the earth, and every tongue confess that Jesus Christ is Lord, to the glory of God the Father.
Rev. 17:14. ...He is the Lord of lords and King of kings... (Also Rev. 19:16.)
Mt. 8:26–27. ...Then [Jesus] rose and rebuked the winds and the sea; and there was a great calm. And the men marveled, saying, "What sort of man is this, that even winds and sea obey him?"

7a. Tenor & Bass Recit. (Evangelist & Angels)
● Ascension: Angels proclaim his return: Acts 1:10–11 (11–7a)
Und da sie ihm nachsahen gen Himmel fahren siehe, da
And as they him watched to heaven go, lo, there

stunden bei ihnen zwei Männer in weißen Kleidern, welche
stood by them two men in white clothes, who

auch sagten: Ihr Männer von Galiläa, was stehet ihr und
also said: You men of Galilee, why stand you and

sehet gen Himmel? Dieser Jesus, welcher von euch ist
gaze toward heaven? This Jesus, who from you is

aufgenommen gen Himmel, wird kommen, wie ihr ihn
taken-up toward heaven, will come, as you him

gesehen habt gen Himmel fahren.
have-seen to heaven go.
{This Jesus...will come in the same manner as you have seen him
go to heaven.}

7b. Alto Recit.
● Christ's return: Prayer that it might be soon (11–7b)
Ach ja! so komme bald zurück:
Ah yes! So come soon back:
{Ah yes! So return soon:}

Tilg einst mein trauriges Gebärden,
Erase some-day my sad demeanor,

Sonst wird mir jeder Augenblick
Otherwise will (my) every moment
{Otherwise my every moment will}

Verhaßt und Jahren ähnlich werden.
Hated and (like) years similar become.
{Be hated and seem like years.}

7c. Tenor Recit. (Evangelist)
● Ascension: Disciples return: Lk. 24:52, Acts 1:12 (11–7c)
Sie aber beteten ihn an, wandten um
They, however, worshiped him - , turned around

gen Jerusalem von dem Berge,
toward Jerusalem from the mountain,

der da heißet der Ölberg,
which - is-called the Mount-of-Olives,

welcher ist nahe bei Jerusalem
which is near to Jerusalem

und liegt einen Sabbater-Weg davon,
and lies a Sabbath-journey away,

*Acts 1:10–11. *And while they were gazing into heaven as he went, behold, two men stood by them in white robes, and said, "Men of Galilee, why do you stand looking into heaven? This Jesus, who was taken up from you into heaven, will come in the same way as you saw him go into heaven."*
Mt. 24:30. Then will appear the sign of the Son of man in heaven, and then all the tribes of the earth will mourn, and they will see the Son of man coming on the clouds of heaven with power and great glory.
Jn. 14:3 [Christ]: When I go and prepare a place for you, I will come again and will take you to myself, that where I am you may be also.
1 Thess. 4:16–18. For the Lord himself will descend from heaven with a cry of command, with the archangel's call, and with the sound of the trumpet of God. And the dead in Christ will rise first; then we who are alive, who are left, shall be caught up together with them in clouds to meet the Lord in the air; and so we shall always be with the Lord. Therefore comfort one another with these words.

Rev. 22:20. He who testifies to these things says, "Surely I am coming soon." Amen. Come, Lord Jesus!
2 Tim. 4:8. Henceforth there is laid up for me the crown of righteousness, which the Lord, the righteous judge, will award to me on that Day, and not only to me but also to all who have loved his appearing.
Jn. 14:3 [Christ]: ...I will come again and will take you to myself, that where I am you may be also.
1 Thess. 4:18. Therefore comfort one another with these words.
2 Pet. 3:11–12. ...What sort of persons ought you to be in lives of holiness and godliness, waiting for and hastening the coming of the day of God...
2 Pet. 3:8–9. Do not ignore this one fact, beloved, that with the Lord one day is as a thousand years, and a thousand years as one day. The Lord is not slow about his promise as some count slowness...

Acts 1:4–5. ...[Jesus] charged them not to depart from Jerusalem, but to wait for the promise of the Father, which, he said, "you heard from me, for John baptized with water, but before many days you shall be baptized with the Holy Spirit."
Lk. 24:52. (Luther inserts: *But they worshiped him...*) *And they returned to Jerusalem with great joy...*
Acts 1:12–14. *Then they returned to Jerusalem from the mount called Olivet, which is near Jerusalem, a sabbath day's journey away;* and when they had entered, they went up to the upper room, where they were staying, Peter and John and James and Andrew, Philip and Thomas, Bartholomew and Matthew, James the son of Alphaeus and Simon the Zealot and Judas the son of James. All these with one accord devoted themselves to prayer...

und sie kehreten wieder gen Jerusalem
and they turned   again   toward Jerusalem

mit großer Freude.
with great   joy.

8. Soprano Aria (Adapted from unnumbered wedding cantata)
●Ascension: His love stays here as prospect of heaven (11–8)
Jesu, deine Gnadenblicke
Jesus, thy   glances-of-grace

Kann ich   doch   beständig sehn.
Can   I   nevertheless constantly see.

Deine Liebe bleibt zurücke,
Thy   love stays behind,

Daß   ich mich hier in der Zeit
So-that I myself here in (this) time

An   der künftgen Herrlichkeit
With that future   splendor

Schon voraus   im Geist   erquicke,
Already in-advance in-the spirit (can) refresh,
{So that I can nurture my spirit now already with that future glory,}

Wenn wir einst dort vor   dir stehn.
When we one-day there before thee stand.
{When one day we stand there before thee.}

9. Chorus (Chorale)
●Christ's return: Longing for it to be soon (11–9)
Wenn soll es doch geschehen,
When shall it indeed happen,

Wenn kömmt die liebe Zeit,
When comes the beloved time,

Daß ich ihn werde sehen
When I him will behold
{When I will behold him}

In seiner Herrlichkeit?
In   his   glory?

Du Tag, wenn wirst du sein,
Thou day, when wilt thou be,

Daß   wir den Heiland grüßen,
(When) we the Savior   greet,

Daß   wir den Heiland küssen?
(When) we the Savior   kiss?

Komm, stelle dich doch ein!
Come, present thyself please - !

Jn. 14:16–20 [Christ]: I will pray the Father, and he will give you another Counselor, to be with you for ever, even the Spirit of truth, whom the world cannot receive, because it neither sees him nor knows him; you know him, for he dwells with you, and will be in you. I will not leave you desolate; I will come to you. Yet a little while, and the world will see me no more, but you will see me; because I live, you will live also. In that day you will know that I am in my Father, and you in me, and I in you. (Also Jn. 16:12–15.)
Rom. 8:38–39. I am sure that neither death, nor life, nor angels, nor principalities, nor things present, nor things to come, nor powers, nor height, nor depth, nor anything else in all creation, will be able to separate us from the love of God in Christ Jesus our Lord.
Eph. 3:16–19. [I pray] that according to the riches of his glory he may grant you to be strengthened with might through his Spirit in the inner man, and that Christ may dwell in your hearts through faith; that you, being rooted and grounded in love, may have power to comprehend with all the saints what is the breadth and length and height and depth, and to know the love of Christ which surpasses knowledge, that you may be filled with all the fulness of God.
Rom. 5:2. ...We rejoice in our hope of sharing the glory of God. (Also Col. 1:27.)
Rev. 20:12. And I saw the dead, great and small, standing before the throne...
1 Thess. 4:17. ...So we shall always be with the Lord.

*Acts 1:7. [Jesus] said to them, "It is not for you to know times or seasons which the Father has fixed by his own authority."
1 Thess. 4:16–18. The Lord himself will descend from heaven with a cry of command, with the archangel's call, and with the sound of the trumpet of God. And the dead in Christ will rise first; then we who are alive, who are left, shall be caught up together with them in clouds to meet the Lord in the air; and so we shall always be with the Lord. Therefore comfort one another with these words.
Rom. 8:19, 23. The creation waits with eager longing for the revealing of the sons of God...and not only the creation, but we ourselves, who have the first fruits of the Spirit, groan inwardly as we wait for adoption as sons, the redemption of our bodies.
1 Jn. 3:2. Beloved, we are God's children now; it does not yet appear what we shall be, but we know that when he appears we shall be like him, for we shall see him as he is.
Mt. 24:36. But of that day and hour no one knows, not even the angels of heaven, nor the Son, but the Father only.
Mt. 25:13. Watch therefore, for you know neither the day nor the hour.
1 Thess. 5:2. For you yourselves know well that the day of the Lord will come like a thief in the night. (Also 2 Pet. 3:10.)
Rev. 22:20. ...Come, Lord Jesus!

BWV 12
Weinen, Klagen, Sorgen, Zagen
(NBA I/11; BC A68)

Jubilate: 3. S. after Easter (BWV 12, 103, 146)
*1 Pet. 2:11–20 (Be subject to all human orders)
*Jn. 16:16–23[1] (Jesus' farewell to his disciples)
[1]End: "nothing of me."
Librettist: perhaps Salomon Franck

1. Sinfonia

2. Chorus
●Affliction is the Christian's lot in life (12-2)
Weinen, Klagen,
Weeping, wailing,

Sorgen,   Zagen,
Worrying, fearing,

Angst   und Not
Anguish and need

Sind der Christen   Tränenbrot,
Are   the Christian's bread-of-tears,

Die   das Zeichen Jesu tragen.
Those-who the   sign of-Jesus bear.

3. Alto Recit.
●Tribulation precedes entrance to kingdom: Acts 14:22 (12-3)
Wir müssen durch viel Trübsal
We   must   through much tribulation

in   das Reich Gottes eingehen.
into the kingdom of-God   enter.

4. Alto Aria
●Cross and crown related; Christ's wounds our comfort (12-4)
Kreuz und Krone sind verbunden,
Cross and   crown are   tied-together,

Kampf und Kleinod sind vereint.
Battle   and treasure are   united.

Christen haben alle Stunden
Christians have   at-all hours

Ihre   Qual   und ihren Feind,
Their   torment and   their   foe,

Doch ihr   Trost sind Christi Wunden.
Yet their comfort is Christ's wounds.
{Yet they find comfort in Christ's wounds.}

*Jn. 16:20–22 [Christ]: Truly, truly, I say to you, you will weep and lament, but the world will rejoice; you will be sorrowful, but your sorrow will turn into joy. When a woman is in travail she has sorrow, because her hour has come; but when she is delivered of the child, she no longer remembers the anguish (Luther: Angst), for joy that a child is born into the world. So you have sorrow now, but I will see you again and your hearts will rejoice, and no one will take your joy from you.

*1 Pet. 2:20. ...If when you do right and suffer for it you take it patiently, you have God's approval.

2 Tim. 3:12. Indeed all who desire to live a godly life in Christ Jesus will be persecuted. (Also Mk. 10:38–39, Jn. 15:20.)

Jms. 1:2–4. Count it all joy, my brethren, when you meet various trials, for you know that the testing of your faith produces steadfastness. And let steadfastness have its full effect, that you may be perfect and complete, lacking in nothing. (Also Jms. 1:12.)

1 Pet. 4:12–13. Beloved, do not be surprised at the fiery ordeal which comes upon you to prove you, as though something strange were happening to you. But rejoice in so far as you share Christ's sufferings, that you may also rejoice and be glad when his glory is revealed. (Also 1 Pet. 5:10.)

2 Cor. 4:7–10. But we have this treasure in earthen vessels, to show that the transcendent power belongs to God and not to us. We are afflicted in every way, but not crushed; perplexed, but not driven to despair; persecuted, but not forsaken; struck down, but not destroyed; always carrying in the body the death of Jesus, so that the life of Jesus may also be manifested in our bodies.

Gal. 6:17 [Paul]: ...I bear on my body the marks of Jesus. (Luther: Ich trage die Malzeichen des Herrn Jesu an meinem Leibe.)

Acts 14:22. ...*Through many tribulations we must enter the kingdom of God.*

Jn. 16:33 [Christ]: I have said this to you, that in me you may have peace. In the world you have tribulation; but be of good cheer, I have overcome the world.

Mt. 7:14. The gate is narrow and the way is hard, that leads to life, and those who find it are few.

Rev. 2:10 [Christ]:..Be faithful unto death, and I will give you the crown of life.

1 Cor. 9:24. ...In a race all the runners compete, but only one receives the prize (Luther: Kleinod).

*Jn. 16:20. ...Your sorrow will turn into joy.

Mt. 16:24–25. Then Jesus told his disciples, "If any man would come after me, let him deny himself and take up his cross and follow me. For whoever would save his life will lose it, and whoever loses his life for my sake will find it." (Also Mk. 10:31.)

2 Tim. 2:11–12. The saying is sure: If we have died with him, we shall also live with him; if we endure, we shall also reign with him... (Also 1 Pet. 4:12–13, Rom. 8:17.)

1 Pet. 5:4. And when the chief Shepherd is manifested you will obtain the unfading crown of glory.

2 Tim. 4:7–8. I have fought the good fight, I have finished the race, I have kept the faith. Henceforth there is laid up for me the crown of righteousness, which the Lord, the righteous judge, will award to me on that Day...

2 Cor. 1:5. For as we share abundantly in Christ's sufferings, so through Christ we share abundantly in comfort too.

1 Pet. 2:224. ...By his wounds you have been healed.

5. Bass Aria

●Discipleship: Willing acceptance of the cross (12-5)

Ich folge Christo nach,
I   follow Christ after,
{I follow after Christ,}

Von ihm will ich nicht lassen
From him would I   not   part

Im Wohl und Ungemach,
In prosperity and   privation,

Im Leben und Erblassen.
In living and growing-pale.
{In life and death.}

Ich küsse Christi Schmach,
I   kiss   Christ's disgrace,

Ich will sein Kreuz umfassen.
I would his cross   embrace.

Ich folge Christo nach,
I   follow Christ after,
{I follow after Christ,}

Von ihm will ich nicht lassen.
From him would I   not   part.

6. Tenor Aria

●Reward comes after suffering; this is our comfort (12-6)

Sei getreu, alle   Pein
Be faithful, all (the) pain

Wird doch nur ein Kleines sein.
Will indeed only a   trifle be.

Nach dem Regen
After the   rain

Blüht   der Segen,
Blossoms the blessing,

Alles   Wetter geht vorbei.
All (bad) weather goes by.

Sei getreu, sei getreu!
Be faithful, be faithful!

7. Chorale (See also 75-14, 99-6, 100-6.)

●God's sovereignty: In affliction God comforts (12-7)

Was   Gott tut, das ist wohlgetan,
Whatever God does, that is   well-done,

Mt. 26:33, 35. Peter declared to [Jesus], "Though they all fall away...I will never fall away."

*1 Pet. 2:20–21. ...If when you do right and suffer for it you take it patiently, you have God's approval. For to this you have been called, because Christ also suffered for you, leaving you an example, that you should follow in his steps.

Mt. 13:21. ...When tribulation or persecution arises on account of the word, immediately [the one with no root in himself] falls away.

Jn. 6:66–68. After this many of his disciples drew back and no longer went about with him. Jesus said to the twelve, "Do you also wish to go away?" Simon Peter answered him, "Lord, to whom shall we go? You have the words of eternal life..."

Lk. 14:27 [Christ]: Whoever does not bear his own cross and come after me, cannot be my disciple.

Jn. 15:20 [Christ]: A servant is not greater than his master. If they persecuted me, they will persecute you...

Phil. 4:11–12. ...I have learned, in whatever state I am, to be content... in any and all circumstances I have learned the secret of facing plenty and hunger, abundance and want.

Phil. 1:20–21. ...[My goal is] that...now as always Christ will be honored in my body, whether by life or by death. For to me to live is Christ, and to die is gain.

Heb. 12:2. Looking to Jesus the pioneer and perfecter of our faith, who for the joy that was set before him endured the cross, despising the shame...

Gal. 6:14. Far be it from me to glory except in the cross of our Lord Jesus Christ, by which the world has been crucified to me, and I to the world.

1 Cor. 15:58. Therefore, my beloved brethren, be steadfast, immovable, always abounding in the work of the Lord...

Gal. 6:9. And let us not grow weary in well-doing, for in due season we shall reap, if we do not lose heart.

Rom. 8:18. ...The sufferings of this present time are not worth comparing with the glory that is to be revealed to us. (Also 2 Cor. 4:17.)

1 Pet. 5:10. And after you have suffered a little while, the God of all grace, who has called you to his eternal glory in Christ, will himself restore, establish, and strengthen you.

Heb. 3:14. For we share in Christ, if only we hold our first confidence firm to the end. (Also Heb. 10:36.)

1 Pet. 3:9. ...To this you have been called, that you may obtain a blessing.

*Jn. 16:20–22 [Christ]: Truly, truly, I say to you, you will weep and lament, but the world will rejoice; you will be sorrowful, but your sorrow will turn into joy. When a woman is in travail she has sorrow, because her hour has come; but when she is delivered of the child, she no longer remembers the anguish, for joy that a child is born into the world. So you have sorrow now, but I will see you again and your hearts will rejoice, and no one will take your joy from you.

Rev. 2:10 [Christ]: ...Be faithful unto death, and I will give you the crown of life.

Mk. 7:37. And [the people] were astonished beyond measure [at Jesus], saying, "He has done all things well..."

Rom. 8:28, 31–32, 35, 37–39. We know that in everything God works for good with those who love him, who are called according to his

Dabei will ich verbleiben,
In-that would I abide,
{In that I want to abide,}

Es mag mich auf die rauhe Bahn
(Now) may me on a harsh course

Not, Tod und Elend treiben,
Want, death, and distress drive,
{If I be driven on a harsh course by want, death, and distress,}

So wird Gott mich
Then will God me
{Then will God}

Ganz väterlich
Right fatherly

In seinem Armen halten:
In his arms hold:
{Hold me in his arms:}

Drum laß ich ihn nur walten.
Therefore allow I him just to-rule.
{Therefore I just allow him sovereign control.}

BWV 13
Meine Seufzer, meine Tränen
(NBA I/5; BC A34)

2. S. after Epiphany (BWV 155, 3, 13)
*Rom. 12:6–16[1] (Diversity of gifts, exemplary conduct)
*Jn. 2:1–11 (Wedding at Cana)
[1]End: "men of low estate"
Librettist: Georg Christian Lehms

1. Tenor Aria
●Despair: My days are filled with sighs and tears (13–1)
Meine Seufzer, meine Tränen
My sighs, my tears

Können nicht zu zählen sein.
Can not - counted be.
{Can not be counted.}

Wenn sich täglich Wehmut findet
When - daily gloom occurs
{When each day is filled with gloom}

Und der Jammer nicht verschwindet,
And - misery (does) not pass-away,

Ach! so muß uns diese Pein
Ah, then must for-us this torment
{Ah, then must this torment}

Schon den Weg zum Tode bahnen.
Already the pathway to death pave.
{Already pave the pathway to death for us.}

purpose...What then shall we say to this? If God is for us, who is against us? He who did not spare his own Son but gave him up for us all, will he not also give us all things with him?...Who shall separate us from the love of Christ? Shall tribulation, or distress, or persecution, or famine, or nakedness, or peril, or sword?...No, in all these things we are more than conquerors through him who loved us. For I am sure that neither death, nor life, nor angels, nor principalities, nor things present, nor things to come, nor powers, nor height, nor depth, nor anything else in all creation, will be able to separate us from the love of God in Christ Jesus our Lord. (Also 2 Cor. 1:5.)
Ps. 103:11, 13. As the heavens are high above the earth, so great is his steadfast love (Luther: läßt er seine Gnade walten) toward those who fear him... As a father pities his children, so the Lord pities those who fear him. (See also Mk. 10:14, 16.)
Mk. 9:36–37. And [Jesus] took a child...and [took] him in his arms... (Also Mk. 10:14–16.)
Is. 40:11. He will feed his flock like a shepherd, he will gather the lambs in his arms, he will carry them in his bosom...
Rev. 21:3–4. ...God himself will be with them; he will wipe away every tear from their eyes, and death shall be no more, neither shall there be mourning nor crying nor pain any more, for the former things have passed away. (Also Rev. 7:15–17, Is. 25:8.)
1 Pet. 4:19. Therefore let those who suffer according to God's will do right and entrust their souls to a faithful Creator.

*Rom. 12:12. ...Be patient in tribulation, be constant in prayer.
Ps. 6:6–7. I am weary with my moaning; every night I flood my bed with tears; I drench my couch with my weeping. My eye wastes away because of grief, it grows weak because of all my foes. (Also Jer. 45:3.)
Ps. 42:1–3. As a hart longs for flowing streams, so longs my soul for thee, O God. My soul thirsts for God, for the living God. When shall I come and behold the face of God? My tears have been my food day and night, while men say to me continually, "Where is your God?" (Also Ps. 80:5.)
Ps. 56:8. [O Lord,] thou hast kept count of my tossings; put thou my tears in thy bottle!
Ps. 80:5. Thou hast fed them with the bread of tears, and given them tears to drink in full measure.
Job 16:20. My friends scorn me; my eye pours out tears to God.
Job 16:16. My face is red with weeping, and on my eyelids is deep darkness.
Ps. 13:3. Consider and answer me, O Lord my God; lighten my eyes, lest I sleep the sleep of death. (Also Ps. 143:7.)
Ps. 18:4. The cords of death encompassed me, the torrents of perdition assailed me; the cords of Sheol entangled me, the snares of death confronted me. (Also 2 Sam. 22:5–6.)

2. Alto Recit.

●Despair: I cry to God but he does not answer (13-2)

Mein liebster Gott läßt mich
My dearest God lets me

Annoch vergebens rufen
Hitherto in-vain call
{Call hitherto in vain}

Und mir in meinem Weinen
And (lets) to-me in my weeping

Noch keinen Trost erscheinen.
Still no comfort appear.
{And lets no comfort appear to me in my weeping.}

Die Stunde lässet sich
The hour lets itself

Zwar wohl von ferne sehen,
Indeed from afar be-seen,
{Indeed, the hour can be seen from afar,}

Allein ich muß doch noch vergebens flehen.
But I must nevertheless still in-vain supplicate.
{But I must nevertheless still supplicate in vain.}

3. Chorale: Alto

●Despair: God's promise to help has not come true (13-3)

Der Gott, der mir hat versprochen
The God, who me has promised
{The God who has promised me}

Seinen Beistand jederzeit,
His assistance at-all-times,

Der lässt sich vergebens suchen
He lets himself in-vain be-sought
{He lets himself be sought in vain}

Itzt in meiner Traurigkeit.
Now in my sadness.

Ach! Will er denn für und für
Ah! Will he then forever and ever

Grausam zürnen über mir,
Horribly be-angry with me,
{Be horribly angry with me,}

Kann und will er sich der Armen
Can and would he - (on) the poor

Itzt nicht wie vorhin erbarmen?
Now not as formerly have-mercy?
{Could and would he not have mercy on the poor as formerly?}

Ps. 130:1–2. Out of the depths I cry to thee, O Lord! Lord, hear my voice! Let thy ears be attentive to the voice of my supplications!

Job 31:35. Oh, that I had one to hear me! (Here is my signature! let the Almighty answer me!)

Ps. 27:7–9. Hear, O Lord, when I cry aloud, be gracious to me and answer me! Thou hast said, "Seek ye my face." My heart says to thee, "Thy face, Lord, do I seek." Hide not thy face from me.

Ps. 143:1. Hear my prayer, O Lord; give ear to my supplications! In thy faithfulness answer me, in thy righteousness!

Prov. 1:28 [God]: They will call upon me, but I will not answer; they will seek me diligently but will not find me.

Is. 59:2. Your iniquities have made a separation between you and your God, and your sins have hid his face from you so that he does not hear.

S. of S. 5:6 [Bride]: I opened to my beloved, but my beloved had turned and gone. My soul failed me when he spoke. I sought him, but found him not; I called him, but he gave no answer.

Ps. 10:1. Why dost thou stand afar off, O Lord?

Ps. 13:1–2. How long, O Lord? Wilt thou forget me for ever? How long wilt thou hide thy face from me? How long must I bear pain in my soul, and have sorrow in my heart all the day? (Also Ps. 6:3–4, 42:9, 44:24, 69:17, 88:14, 89:46, 90:13–15, 102:2, 143:7, Lam. 1:21, Hab. 1:2.)

Mt. 28:20 [Christ]: ...Lo, I am with you always, to the close of the age.

Josh. 1:5–6 [God]: ...As I was with Moses, so I will be with you; I will not fail you or forsake you. Be strong and of good courage... (Also Deut. 31:6.)

Heb. 13:5–6. ...He has said, "I will never fail you nor forsake you." Hence we can confidently say, "The Lord is my helper, I will not be afraid; what can man do to me?"

Ps. 79:5. How long, O Lord? Wilt thou be angry for ever?

Ps. 80:4. O Lord God of hosts, how long wilt thou be angry with thy people's prayers? (Also Ps. 85:5.)

Ps. 77:7–9. Will the Lord spurn for ever, and never again be favorable? Has his steadfast love for ever ceased? Are his promises at an end for all time? Has God forgotten to be gracious? Has he in anger shut up his compassion?

Is. 57:16 [God]: I will not contend for ever, nor will I always be angry.

Jer. 3:12 [God]: ...I will not be angry for ever.

Ps. 103:8–10. The Lord is merciful and gracious, slow to anger and abounding in steadfast love. He will not always chide, nor will he keep his anger for ever. He does not deal with us according to our sins, nor requite us according to our iniquities.

Lam. 3:31–32. For the Lord will not cast off for ever, but, though he cause grief, he will have compassion...

Ps. 69:33. For the Lord hears the needy...

Ps. 89:49. Lord, where is thy steadfast love of old, which by thy faithfulness thou didst swear...? (Also Mal. 3:6.)

4. Soprano Recit.
●Hope: Sorrow real yet God can change it to joy (13-4)
Mein Kummer nimmet zu
My trouble increases

Und raubt mir alle Ruh,
And robs me (of) all rest,

Mein Jammerkrug ist ganz
My (cup)-of-woe is completely

Mit Tränen angefüllet,
With tears filled,
{Filled with tears,}

Und diese Not wird nicht gestillet,
And this distress is not stilled,

So mich ganz unempfindlich macht.
Which me completely senseless makes.
{Which makes me completely senseless.}

Der Sorgen Kummernacht
- Sorrow's night-of-care

Drückt mein beklemmtes Herz darnieder,
Presses my oppressed heart down,

Drum sing ich lauter Jammerlieder.
Therefore sing I only songs-of-lamentation.
{Therefore I sing only songs of lamentation.}

Doch, Seele, nein,
Yet, soul, no,

Sei nur getrost in deiner Pein:
Be just comforted in your pain:
{Be comforted in your pain:}

Gott kann den Wermutsaft
God can the wormwood's-juice
{God can transform the wormwood's juice}

Gar leicht in Freudenwein verkehren
Quite easily into wine-of-gladness transform
{Quite easily into the wine of gladness}

Und dir alsdenn viel tausend Lust gewähren.
And you thereupon many thousand pleasures grant.
{And thereupon grant you many thousand pleasures.}

5. Bass Aria
●Hope gained by looking to heaven; weeping of no use (13-5)
Ächzen und erbärmlich Weinen
Groaning and pitiable weeping

Ps. 77:2. In the day of my trouble I seek the Lord; in the night my hand is stretched out without wearying; my soul refuses to be comforted.

Ps. 22:2. O my God, I cry by day, but thou dost not answer; and by night, but find no rest.

Ps. 6:6. I am weary with my moaning; every night I flood my bed with tears... (Also Jer. 45:3.)

Ps. 56:8. Thou hast kept count of my tossings; put thou my tears in thy bottle! Are they not in thy book?

Ps. 42:6. ...My soul is cast down within me...

Ps. 38:6-8, 10, 13-14. I am utterly bowed down and prostrate; all the day I go about mourning. For my loins are filled with burning, and there is no soundness in my flesh. I am utterly spent and crushed; I groan because of the tumult of my heart...My heart throbs, my strength fails me; and the light of my eyes—it also has gone from me... I am like a deaf man, I do not hear, like a dumb man who does not open his mouth. Yea, I am like a man who does not hear...

Ps. 88:1. O Lord, my God, I call for help by day; I cry out in the night before thee!

Lam. 1:20, 22. Behold, O Lord, for I am in distress, my soul is in tumult, my heart is wrung within me...my groans are many and my heart is faint.

Ps. 13:2. How long must I bear pain in my soul, and have sorrow in my heart all the day?

Ps. 42:5/11/43:5. Why are you cast down, O my soul?...Hope in God; for I shall again praise him, my help and my God.

Lam. 3:15. He has filled me with bitterness, he has sated me with wormwood.

Ps. 90:15. [O Lord,] make us glad as many days as thou hast afflicted us, and as many years as we have seen evil.

*Jn. 2:3-4, 7-10. When the wine gave out, the mother of Jesus said to him, "They have no wine." And Jesus said to her, "O woman, what have you to do with me? My hour has not yet come"...Jesus said to [the servants], "Fill the jars with water." And they filled them up to the brim. He said to them,"Now draw some out, and take it to the steward of the feast." So they took it. When the steward of the feast tasted the water now become wine...[he] called the bridegroom and said to him, "Every man serves the good wine first...but you have kept the good wine until now." (Also Ps. 94:19.)

Ps. 27:14. Wait for the Lord; be strong, and let your heart take courage (Luther: sei getrost und unverzagt)...

Jer. 31:13-14 [God]: Then shall the maidens rejoice in the dance, and the young men and the old shall be merry. I will turn their mourning into joy, I will comfort them, and give them gladness for sorrow. I will feast the soul of the priests with abundance, and my people shall be satisfied with my goodness, says the Lord.

Ps. 30:11. [O Lord,] thou hast turned for me my mourning into dancing; thou hast loosed my sackcloth and girded me with gladness.

Ps. 16:11. [O Lord]...in thy presence there is fulness of joy, in thy right hand are pleasures for evermore.

Mt. 6:27 [Christ]: Which of you by being anxious can add one cubit to his span of life?

Hilft   der Sorgen Krankheit nicht;
Helps (our) cares' sickness   not;
{Does not help the sickness of anxious care;}

Aber wer   gen Himmel siehet
But whoever toward heaven looks
{But whoever looks toward heaven}

Und sich da um Trost bemühet,
And   -   there for comfort strives,

Dem kann leicht ein Freudenlicht
To-him can easily   a light-of-gladness

In der Trauerbrust erscheinen.
In (his) grieving-breast appear.
{To him can a light of gladness easily appear in his breast.}

6. Chorale (Added later to libretto by someone: J. S. Bach?)
        (See also 44-7, 97-9.)
●Hope: Exhortation to trust God's sovereignty (13-6)
So sei   nun, Seele, deine
So be, therefore, soul,   thine (own self true)

Und traue dem alleine,
And trust him   alone,

Der dich erschaffen hat;
Who thee created   hath;

  Es gehe, wie es   gehe,
(Let) it happen, as it (may) happen,

Dein Vater in der Höhe,
Thy father in the highest,

Der weiß zu allen Sachen Rat.
He knows for all   matters counsel.

Phil. 4:6. Have no anxiety about anything, but in everything by prayer and supplication with thanksgiving let your requests be made known to God.
Mt. 6:25–26 [Christ]: Therefore I tell you, do not be anxious about your life, what you shall eat or what you shall drink, nor about your body, what you shall put on. Is not life more than food, and the body more than clothing? Look at the birds of the air: they neither sow nor reap nor gather into barns, and yet your heavenly Father feeds them. Are you not of more value than they?
1 Pet. 5:7. Cast all your anxieties on him, for he cares about you. (Also Ps. 42:5/11/43:5.)
Ps. 30:5. His anger is but for a moment, and his favor is for a lifetime. Weeping may tarry for the night, but joy comes with the morning.
Ps. 126:5–6. May those who sow in tears reap with shouts of joy! He that goes forth weeping, bearing the seed for sowing, shall come home with shouts of joy, bringing his sheaves with him.
Jn. 16:20. ...Your sorrow will turn into joy.

*Rom. 12:12. ...Be patient in tribulation...
Lk. 21:19 [Christ]: By your endurance you will gain your lives (Luther: Fasset eure Seele mit Geduld).
Ps. 62:1–2. For God alone my soul waits in silence; from him comes my salvation. He only is my rock and my salvation, my fortress; I shall not be greatly moved. (Also Ps. 62:5–6.)
1 Pet. 4:19. Therefore let those who suffer according to God's will do right and entrust their souls to a faithful Creator.
Is. 64:8. ...O Lord, thou art our Father; we are the clay, and thou art our potter; we are all the work of thy hand.
Lk. 22:41–42. And [Jesus] withdrew from them about a stone's throw, and knelt down and prayed, "Father, if thou art willing, remove this cup from me; nevertheless not my will, but thine, be done." (Also Jn. 5:30.)
Prov. 3:5–6. Trust in the Lord with all your heart, and do not rely on your own insight. In all your ways acknowledge him, and he will make straight your paths.
Mt. 6:30–32 [Christ]: If God so clothes the grass of the field, which today is alive and tomorrow is thrown into the oven, will he not much more clothe you, O men of little faith? Therefore do not be anxious, saying, "What shall we eat?" or "What shall we drink?" or "What shall we wear?" For the Gentiles seek all these things; and your heavenly Father knows that you need them all.
Ps. 73:24. [O Lord,] thou dost guide me with thy counsel, and afterward thou wilt receive me to glory.

BWV 14
Wär Gott nicht mit uns diese Zeit
(NBA I/6; BC A40)

4. S. after Epiphany (BWV 81, 14)
*Rom. 13:8–10 (Love is the fulfilling of the law)
*Mt. 8:23–27 (Jesus calms the sea)
Librettist: Unknown

1. Chorus (Chorale Vs. 1)
●God's children lost without his aid: Ps. 124:1-3 (14-1)
Wär Gott nicht mit uns   diese Zeit,
Were God not with us (in) this time,

*Mt. 8:23–26. And when he got into the boat, his disciples followed him. And behold, there arose a great storm on the sea, so that the boat was being swamped by the waves; but he was asleep. And they went and woke him, saying, "Save, Lord; we are perishing." And he said to them, "Why are you afraid, O men of little faith?" Then he rose and rebuked the winds and the sea; and there was a great calm.
Ps. 124:1–3. *If it had not been the Lord who was on our side, let Israel now say—if it had not been the Lord who was on our side, when men rose up against us, then they would have swallowed us up alive...*

So soll Israel sagen,
So shall Israel   say,

Wär Gott nicht mit uns   diese Zeit,
Were God not with us (in) this time,

Wir hätten müssen verzagen,
We would-have-had-to despair,

Die   so ein armes Häuflein sind,
We-who such a poor little-band are,
{We who are such a poor little band,}

Veracht' von so viel   Menschenkind,
Despised by so many (of)   mankind,

Die an uns setzen alle.
Who - us attack all.
{Who all attack us.}

2. Soprano Aria
●Murderous foe too strong for our small strength (14-2)
Unsre Stärke heißt zu schwach,
Our   strength is too small,

Unserm Feind zu widerstehen.
Our   foe to   withstand.
{To withstand our foe.}

Stünd uns nicht der Höchste bei,
Stood us not the Most-high by,
{If the Almighty had not helped us,}

Würd uns ihre Tyrannei
Would - their tyranny
{Their tyranny would}

Bald bis an das   Leben   gehen.
Soon to - - (our very) life have-extended.
{Soon have taken our very lives.}

3. Tenor Recit. (Based on Chorale Vs. 2)
●Foes would have killed us if God had not intervened:
Ps. 124:3-5 (paraphrase) (14-3)
Ja, hätt es Gott nur zugegeben,
Yes, had it God but allowed,
{Yes, had God but allowed it,}

Wir wären längst nicht mehr am Leben,
We would long no more (be) living,
{We would have perished long ago,}

Sie   rissen uns aus Rachgier hin,
They would-have-torn us out-of vindictiveness forth,
{In vindictiveness they would have carried us away,}

So zornig ist auf uns ihr   Sinn.
So angry is toward us their disposition.
{So angry is their disposition toward us.}

Ps. 94:17. If the Lord had not been my help, my soul would soon have dwelt in the land of silence. (Also Ps. 129:1.)
2 Cor. 1:8–10. For we do not want you to be ignorant, brethren, of the affliction we experienced in Asia; for we were so utterly, unbearably crushed that we despaired of life itself. Why, we felt that we had received the sentence of death; but that was to make us rely not on ourselves but on God who raises the dead; he delivered us from so deadly a peril, and he will deliver us; on him we have set our hope that he will deliver us again.
Ps. 119:141. I am small and despised...
1 Cor. 1:26–28. For consider your call, brethren; not many of you were wise according to worldly standards, not many were powerful, not many were of noble birth; but God chose what is foolish in the world to shame the wise, God chose what is weak...to shame the strong, God chose what is low and despised in the world, even things that are not, to bring to nothing things that are.
2 Tim. 3:12. ...All who desire to live a godly life in Christ Jesus will be persecuted. (Also Jn. 15:20.)

Ps. 124:1–3. If it had not been the Lord who was on our side...when men rose up against us, then they would have swallowed us up alive...
Amos 7:2. O Lord God...How can Jacob stand? He is so small!
Ps. 38:19. Those who are my foes without cause are mighty, and many are those who hate me...
Ps. 18:17 / 2 Sam. 22:18. He delivered me from my strong enemy, and from those who hated me; for they were too mighty for me.
Ps. 31:13. Yea, I hear the whispering of many—terror on every side!—as they scheme together against me, as they plot to take my life.
Ps. 38:12. Those who seek my life lay their snares, those who seek my hurt speak of ruin, and meditate treachery all the day long.
2 Cor. 1:8. ...We were so utterly, unbearably crushed that we despaired of life itself.
*Mt. 8:25. And [the disciples] went and woke [Jesus], saying, "Save, Lord; we are perishing."
2 Tim. 4:17. But the Lord stood by me...So I was rescued...

Ps. 124:1–3. If it had not been the Lord who was on our side...when men rose up against us, then they would have swallowed us up alive...
Ps. 119:92. [O Lord,] if thy law had not been by delight, I should have perished in my affliction.
Ps. 7:2. ...Like a lion they rend me, dragging me away, with none to rescue.
Ps. 17:12. They are like a lion eager to tear, as a young lion lurking in ambush.
*Mt. 8:24. And behold, there arose a great storm on the sea, so that the boat was being swamped by the waves...
2 Sam. 22:5–6. The waves of death encompassed me, the torrents of perdition assailed me; the cords of Sheol entangled me, the snares of death confronted me. (Also Ps. 18:4–5.)
Ps. 18:4–6. The cords of death encompassed me, the torrents of perdition assailed me; the cords of Sheol entangled me, the snares of death confronted me. In my distress I called upon the Lord; to my God I cried for help.

Es   hätt uns ihre Wut
(Now) would us their rage (have)

Wie eine wilde Flut
Like a wild torrent

Und als beschäumte Wasser überschwemmet,
And like foamed-up waters   inundated,
{Their rage would have inundated us like a wild torrent,}

Und niemand hätte die Gewalt gehemmet.
And no one would (their) might have-arrested.
{And no one would have arrested their might.}

4. Bass Aria
●Deliverance from the furious waves of our foe (14-4)
Gott, bei deinem starken Schätzen
God, by thy   strong protecting

Sind wir vor den Feinden frei.
Are we from (our) foes (set) free.
{We are set free from our foes.}

Wenn sie sich als wilde Wellen
When they - like wild waves

Uns aus Grimm entgegenstellen,
Us in fury   oppose,
{In fury oppose us,}

Stehn uns deine Hände bei.
Stand us thy hands by.
{Thy hands assist us.}

5. Chorale (Vs. 3)
●Thanks to God that we escaped like a bird:
Ps. 124:6-8 (paraphrase) (14-5)
Gott   Lob und Dank, der nicht zugab,
(To) God (be) praise and thanks, who (did) not allow,

Daß ihr Schlund uns möcht fangen.
That their throat us might capture.

Wie ein Vogel des Stricks kömmt ab,
Like a bird whose snare comes off,

Ist unsre Seel entgangen:
Has our soul escaped:

Strick ist entzwei, und wir sind frei;
(The) snare is in-two, and we are free;

Des Herren Name steht uns bei,
The Lord's name stands us by,
{The Lord's name assists us,}

Des Gottes Himmels und Erden.
The God of-heaven and earth.

Ps. 69:1-2. Save me, O God! For the waters have come up to my neck. I sink in deep mire, where there is no foothold; I have come into deep waters, and the flood sweeps over me.
Jonah 2:3. ...The flood was round about me; all thy waves and thy billows passed over me.
Ps. 124:3-5. ...*When their anger was kindled against us; then the flood would have swept us away, the torrent would have gone over us; then over us would have gone the raging waters.*
2 Sam. 22:17-20 / Ps. 18:16-19. He reached from on high, he took me, he drew me out of many waters. He delivered me from my strong enemy, from those who hated me; for they were too mighty for me. They came upon me in the day of my calamity; but the Lord was my stay. He brought me forth into a broad place; he delivered me, because he delighted in me.

*Mt. 8:26. And [Jesus] said to [the disciples], "Why are you afraid, O men of little faith?" Then he rose and rebuked the winds and the sea; and there was a great calm.
Ps. 106:10. So he saved them from the hand of the foe, and delivered them from the power of the enemy.
Ps. 34:4. I sought the Lord, and he answered me, and delivered me from all my fears.
Ps. 59:9. O my Strength, I will sing praises to thee; for thou, O God, art my fortress. (Also 2 Sam. 22:2 / Ps. 18:2, Ps. 62:2, 6; 94:22; 144:2.)
Ps. 65:7. [O Lord, thou] dost still the roaring of the seas, the roaring of their waves, the tumult of the peoples.
Is. 17:12. Ah, the thunder of many peoples, they thunder like the thundering of the sea! Ah, the roar of nations, they roar like the roaring of mighty waters!
Ps. 89:9. [O Lord,] thou dost rule the raging of the sea; when its waves rise, thou stillest them.
Is. 59:1. Behold, the Lord's hand is not shortened, that it cannot save, or his ear dull, that it cannot hear.

Ps. 124:3, 6-8. *They would have swallowed us up alive...Blessed be the Lord, who has not given us as prey to their teeth! We have escaped as a bird from the snare of the fowlers; the snare is broken, and we have escaped! Our help is in the name of the Lord, who made heaven and earth.*
Hab. 1:13. ...The wicked swallows up the man more righteous than he.
Ps. 79:7. They have devoured Jacob...
Ps. 91:1-6. He who dwells in the shelter of the Most High, who abides in the shadow of the Almighty, will say to the Lord, "My refuge and my fortress; my God, in whom I trust." For he will deliver you from the snare of the fowler and from the deadly pestilence; he will cover you with his pinions, and under his wings you will find refuge; his faithfulness is a shield and buckler. You will not fear the terror of the night, nor the arrow that flies by day, nor the pestilence that stalks in darkness, nor the destruction that wastes at noonday.
Ps. 20:7. Some boast of chariots, and some of horses; but we boast of the name of the Lord our God. (Also Ps. 83:18.)
Jer. 17:7. Blessed is the man who trusts in the Lord, whose trust is the Lord.
Ps. 121:2. My help comes from the Lord, who made heaven and earth.
*Mt. 8:27. And the [disciples] marveled, saying, "What sort of man is this, that even winds and sea obey him?"

BWV 15
Denn du wirst meine Seele nicht in der Hölle lassen

This cantata was composed by Johann Ludwig Bach.

BWV 16
Herr Gott, dich loben wir
(NBA I/4; BC A23)

New Year/Circumcision and Name of Jesus
(BWV 143, 190, 41, 16, 171, 248-IV)
*Gal. 3:23–29 (Through faith we are heirs of the promise)
*Lk. 2:21 (Circumcision and naming of Jesus)
Librettist: Georg Christian Lehms

1. Chorus (Chorale - Te Deum) (See also 190-1 & 190-2.)
●Te Deum: Lord, we praise thee! (16-1)
Herr Gott, dich loben wir,
Lord God, thee praise we,
{Lord God, we praise thee;}

Herr Gott, wir danken dir.
Lord God, we thank thee.

Dich, Gott Vater in Ewigkeit,
Thee, God Father through (all) eternity,
{Thee, O Father God throughout all eternity,}

Ehret die Welt weit und breit.
Doth-honor the world far and wide.
{Doth the world honor far and wide.}

2. Bass Recit.
●Praise God with ardent songs for blessings to Zion (16-2)
So stimmen wir
So begin-to-sing we
{So we begin to sing}

Bei dieser frohen Zeit
At this happy time

Mit heißer Andacht an
With ardent devotion -

Und legen dir,
And lay (before) thee,

O Gott, auf dieses neue Jahr
O God, upon (the coming of) this new year

Das erste Herzensopfer dar.
(Our) first heart's-sacrifice -.
{Our heart's first offering.}

Was hast du nicht von Ewigkeit
What hast thou not from eternity (already)

Für Heil an uns getan,
For salvation for us done,
{For our salvation done,}

1 Chron. 29:13. ...We thank thee, our God, and praise thy glorious name.
Ps. 75:1. We give thanks to thee, O God; we give thanks; we call on thy name and recount thy wondrous deeds.
Ps. 66:4. All the earth worships thee; they sing praises to thee, sing praises to thy name.
Ps. 79:13. We thy people, the flock of thy pasture, will give thanks to thee for ever; from generation to generation we will recount thy praise. (Also Ps. 105:2, 6 / 1 Chron. 16:9, 13.)
Ps. 115:18. We will bless the Lord from this time forth and for evermore. Praise the Lord! (Also Dan. 2:20.)
Ps. 138:4–5. [O Lord,] all the kings of the earth shall praise thee, O Lord, for they have heard the words of thy mouth; and they shall sing of the ways of the Lord, for great is the glory of the Lord.
Ps. 98:3–4. ...All the ends of the earth have seen the victory of our God. Make a joyful noise to the Lord, all the earth; break forth into joyous song and sing praises!
Ps. 48:10. As thy name, O God, so thy praise reaches to the ends of the earth...

Ps. 9:2. I will be glad and exult in thee, I will sing praise to thy name, O Most High.
Ps. 95:1. O come, let us sing to the Lord; let us make a joyful noise to the rock of our salvation.
Ps. 34:1–3. I will bless the Lord at all times; his praise shall continually be in my mouth. My soul makes its boast in the Lord; let the afflicted hear and be glad. O magnify the Lord with me, and let us exalt his name together!
Ps. 5:11. Let all who take refuge in thee rejoice, let them ever sing for joy; and do thou defend them, that those who love thy name may exult in thee.
Mt. 22:37. ...You shall love the Lord your God with all your heart, and with all your soul, and with all your mind.
Ex. 23:19. The first of the first fruits of your ground you shall bring into the house of the Lord your God. (Also Ex. 34:26.)
Lev. 23:10 [God]: ...When you come into the land which I give you and reap its harvest, you shall bring the sheaf of the first fruits of your harvest to the priest.
Ps. 50:14, 23. Offer to God a sacrifice of thanksgiving...He who brings thanksgiving as his sacrifice honors me...
Ps. 69:30–31. I will praise the name of God with a song; I will magnify him with thanksgiving. This will please the Lord more than an ox or a bull with horns and hoofs.
Heb. 13:15. ...Let us continually offer up a sacrifice of praise to God, that is, the fruit of lips that acknowledge his name. (Also Ps. 51:15–17.)

Und   was   muß unsre Brust
And how-much must   our   breast

Noch jetzt vor   Lieb und   Treu verspüren!
Even now of (thy) love and faithfulness perceive!
{Perceive even now of thy love and faithfulness!}

Dein Zion sieht vollkommne Ruh,
Thy Zion beholds perfect   rest,
{Thy Zion experiences perfect rest,}

Es fällt ihm   Glück und Segen zu;
(Now) falls (to his lot) prosperity and blessing - ;
{Prosperity and blessing falls to his lot;}

Der Tempel schallt
The temple resounds

Von Psaltern und von Harfen,
With psaltery and with harps,

Und unsre Seele   wallt,
And our   soul effervesces,

Wenn wir nur Andachtsglut in Herz und Mund führen.
If   we but devotion's-ardor in heart and mouth do-carry.
{If we but carry devotion's ardor in our hearts and mouths.}

O, sollte darum nicht ein neues Lied erklingen
Oh, ought therefore not   a   new song ring-out
{Oh, should not a new song ring out for this?}

Und wir in heißer Liebe singen?
And we in ardent love   sing?

3. Bass Aria & Chorus
●Praise God for blessings that are new each morning (16-3)
Chorus:
Laßt uns jauchzen, laßt uns freuen:
Let us   exult,   let us rejoice:

Gottes Güt und   Treu
God's goodness and faithfulness

Bleibet alle Morgen neu.
Remains all mornings new.
{Is new every morning.}

Bass:
Krönt und segnet seine Hand,
Crowns and blesses his   hand,
{If his hand crowns and blesses,}

Ach so glaubt, daß unser Stand
Ah, then believe, that our condition

Ewig,   ewig glücklich   sei.
Eternally, eternally happy (shall) be.

Ps. 117:2. For great is his steadfast love toward us; and the faithfulness of the Lord endures for ever. Praise the Lord!

Ps. 103:17. But the steadfast love of the Lord is from everlasting to everlasting upon those who fear him...

Jms. 1:17. Every good endowment and every perfect gift is from above, coming down from the Father of lights with whom there is no variation or shadow due to change.

Eph. 1:3. Blessed be the God and Father of our Lord Jesus Christ, who has blessed us in Christ with every spiritual blessing in the heavenly places...

Ps. 147:12–14. Praise the Lord, O Jerusalem! Praise your God, O Zion! For he strengthens the bars of your gates; he blesses your sons within you. He makes peace in your borders; he fills you with the finest of the wheat.

Ps. 48:1. Great is the Lord and greatly to be praised in the city of our God! His holy mountain, beautiful in elevation, is the joy of all the earth, Mount Zion...the city of the great King.

Heb. 12:22. You have come to Mount Zion and to the city of the living God, the heavenly Jerusalem...

*Gal. 3:29. If you are Christ's, then you are Abraham's offspring, heirs according to promise.

2 Chron. 5:1, 11–12, 14. Thus all the work that Solomon did for the house of the Lord was finished...Now when the priests came out of the holy place (...with cymbals, harps, and lyres...), and when the song was raised, with trumpets and cymbals and other musical instruments, in praise to the Lord, "For he is good, for his steadfast love endures for ever," the house...of the Lord, was filled with a cloud...for the glory of the Lord filled the house of God.

Ps. 40:3. He put a new song in my mouth, a song of praise to our God...

Acts 4:20. We cannot but speak of what we have seen and heard.

Ps. 95:1–2. O come, let us sing to the Lord; let us make a joyful noise to the rock of our salvation! Let us come into his presence with thanksgiving; let us make a joyful noise to him with songs of praise!

Lam. 3:22–23. The steadfast love of the Lord never ceases, his mercies never come to an end; they are new every morning; great is thy faithfulness. (Also Ps. 90:14.)

Ps. 107:1 / 118:1 / 136:1. O give thanks to the Lord, for he is good; for his steadfast love endures for ever!

1 Kings 8:15 / 2 Chron. 6:4. ...Blessed be the Lord, the God of Israel, who with his hand has fulfilled what he promised with his mouth...

Ps. 95:7. ...We are...the sheep of his hand.

Ps. 104:28. [O Lord]...when thou openest thy hand, they are filled with good things...

Ps. 103:2, 4. Bless the Lord, O my soul, and forget not all his benefits ...who crowns you with steadfast love and mercy. (Also 1 Pet. 5:6.)

Ps. 92:12. The righteous flourish like the palm tree, and grow like a cedar in Lebanon.

Ps. 23:6. Surely goodness and mercy shall follow me all the days of my life; and I shall dwell in the house of the Lord for ever.

4. Alto Recit.

●Future blessing requested on church, school, & state (16-4)

Ach treuer Hort,
Ah, faithful refuge,

Beschütz auch fernerhin dein wertes Wort,
Protect   also henceforth thy precious Word,
{Protect thy precious Word henceforth as well,}

Beschütze Kirch und Schule,
Protect   church and school,

So wird dein Reich   vermehrt
So shall thy kingdom (be) increased

Und Satans arge List   gestört;
And Satan's evil cunning disturbed;

Erhalte nur den Frieden
Preserve - the   peace

Und die beliebte Ruh,
And (our) beloved quiet,

So ist   uns schon genug beschiede n,
So is (to) us already sufficient allotted,
{Then we have already been given sufficient,}

Und   uns fällt lauter Wohlsein zu.
And (to) us falls sheer well-being - .
{And nought but well-being falls to our lot.}

Ach! Gott, du wirst das Land
Ah! God, thou wilt the land

Noch   ferner wässern,
Yet furthermore water,
{Water henceforth as well,}

Du wirst es stets verbessern,
Thou wilt it continually improve,
{Thou wilt continually improve it,}

Du wirst es selbst mit deiner Hand
Thou wilt it even with thy   hand
{Thou wilt build it with thy very hand}

Und deinem Segen bauen.
And thy   blessing build (up).
{And thy blessing.}

Wohl   uns, wenn wir
Blessed (are) we, if   we

Dir   für und für,
In-thee forever and ever,
{Trust in thee forever and ever,}

Mein Jesus und mein Heil, vertrauen.
My   Jesus and my Salvation, trust.
{O my Jesus and my Salvation.}

2 Thess. 3:1. Finally, brethren, pray for us, that the word of the Lord may speed on and triumph, as it did among you.

1 Tim. 2:1-2. ...I urge that supplications, prayers, intercessions, and thanksgivings be made for all men, for kings and all who are in high positions, that we may lead a quiet and peaceable life, godly and respectful in every way.

Mt. 6:9-10. Pray then like this: Our Father who art in heaven, Hallowed be thy name. Thy kingdom come, Thy will be done, On earth as it is in heaven.

Mt. 13:31-32. The kingdom of heaven is like a grain of mustard seed... it is the smallest of all seeds, but when it has grown it is the greatest of shrubs and becomes a tree, so that the birds of the air come and make nests in its branches.

Eph. 6:11-12. Put on the whole armor of God, that you may be able to stand against the wiles (Luther: listigen Anläufe) of the devil. For we are not contending against flesh and blood, but against the principalities, against the powers, against the world rulers of this present darkness, against the spiritual hosts of wickedness in the heavenly places.

Ps. 29:11. May the Lord give strength to his people! May the Lord bless his people with peace!

Ps. 28:8-9. The Lord is the strength of his people, he is the saving refuge of his anointed. O save thy people, and bless thy heritage; be thou their shepherd, and carry them for ever.

Lev. 26:6 [God]: I will give peace in the land, and you shall lie down, and none shall make you afraid...and the sword shall not go through your land.

Deut. 26:15. [O Lord,] look down from thy holy habitation, from heaven, and bless thy people Israel and the ground which thou hast given us, as thou didst swear to our fathers...

Ezek. 34:26 [God]: ...I will send down the showers in their season; they shall be showers of blessing.

Ps. 65:9, 11. [O Lord,] thou visitest the earth and waterest it, thou greatly enrichest it; the river of God is full of water...Thou crownest the year with thy bounty...

Ps. 33:12. Blessed is the nation whose God is the Lord, the people whom he has chosen as his heritage!

Deut. 28:1-8, 12. And if you obey the voice of the Lord your God, being careful to do all his commandments...the Lord your God will set you high above all the nations of the earth. And all these blessings shall come upon you and overtake you...Blessed shall you be in the city, and blessed shall you be in the field. Blessed shall be the fruit of your body, and the fruit of your ground, and the fruit of your beasts, the increase of your cattle, and the young of your flock. Blessed shall be your basket and your kneading-trough. Blessed shall you be when you come in, and blessed shall you be when you go out. The Lord will cause your enemies who rise against you to be defeated before you; they shall come out against you one way, and flee before you seven ways. The Lord will command the blessing upon your barns, and in all that you undertake; and he will bless you in the land which the Lord your God gives you...The Lord will open to you his good treasury the heavens, to give the rain of your land in its season and to bless all the work of your hands...

Is. 12:2. Behold, God is my salvation; I will trust, and will not be afraid; for the Lord God is my strength and my song, and he has become my salvation.

5. Tenor Aria
●Future blessing: Jesus alone shall be our wealth (16-5)

Geliebter Jesu, du allein
Beloved   Jesu, Thou alone

Sollst meiner Seelen Reichtum sein.
Shalt   my   soul's   wealth   be.
{Shalt be the wealth of my soul.}

Wir wollen dich   vor allen Schätzen
We   would thee before all   treasures
{We would place thee before all other treasures}

In unser treues Herze setzen,
In   our   faithful heart   place,
{Within our faithful heart,}

Ja, wenn das Lebensband zerreißt,
Yea, when the   life-cord   breaks, (then)

Stimmt   unser gottvergnügter Geist
Chimes-in our   God-satisfied spirit
{Our God-satisfied spirit}

Noch mit den Lippen sehnlich ein:
Yet with (our) lips yearningly - :
{Chimes in yearningly with our lips:}

Geliebter Jesu, du allein
Beloved   Jesus, thou alone

Sollst meiner Seelen Reichtum sein.
Shalt   my   soul's   wealth   be.
{Shalt be the wealth of my soul.}

6. Chorale (Added later to libretto by someone: J. S. Bach?)
    (See also 28-6)
●Thanks for blessings in Christ; prayer for new year (16-6)
All solch dein Güt   wir preisen,
All this   thy goodness we praise,

   Vater ins Himmels Thron,
(O) Father, on heaven's throne,

Die   du uns tust beweisen
Which thou to-us dost   show

Durch Christum, deinen Sohn,
Through Christ,   thy   Son,

Und bitten ferner   dich,
And   ask furthermore of-thee,

Gib uns ein friedlich Jahre,
Give us a peaceful year;

Vor allem Leid bewahre
From all   harm protect

Und nähr uns mildiglich.
And feed us tenderly.

2 Cor. 8:9. You know the grace of our Lord Jesus Christ, that though he was rich, yet for your sake he became poor, so that by his poverty you might become rich.

2 Cor. 9:15. Thanks be to God for his inexpressible gift!

Lam. 3:24. "The Lord is my portion," says my soul, "therefore I will hope in him."

Ps. 73:25. [O Lord,] whom have I in heaven but thee? And there is nothing upon earth that I desire besides thee.

Phil. 3:8–9. Indeed I count everything as loss because of the surpassing worth of knowing Christ Jesus my Lord. For his sake I have suffered the loss of all things and count them as refuse, in order that I may gain Christ and be found in him...

Mt. 6:19–21. Do not lay up for yourselves treasures on earth, where moth and rust consume and where thieves break in and steal, but lay up for yourselves treasures in heaven...For where your treasure is, there will your heart be also.

Ecc. 12:1, 3, 6–7. Remember also your Creator in the days of your youth, before the evil days come, and the years draw nigh, when you will say, "I have no pleasure in them"...in the day when the keepers of the house tremble, and the strong men are bent...before the silver cord is snapped, or the golden bowl is broken, or the pitcher is broken at the fountain, or the wheel broken at the cistern, and the dust returns to the earth as it was, and the spirit returns to God who gave it.

Lk. 12:16–17, 19–21. And [Jesus] told them a parable, saying, "The land of a rich man brought forth plentifully; and he thought to himself ...'I will say to my soul, Soul, you have ample goods laid up for many years; take your ease, eat, drink and be merry.' But God said to him, 'Fool! This night your soul is required of you; and the things you have prepared, whose will they be?' So is he who lays up treasure for himself, and is not rich toward God."

Jms. 1:17. Every good endowment and every perfect gift is from above, coming down from the Father of lights...

Ps. 31:19, 21. [O Lord,] how abundant is thy goodness, which thou hast laid up for those who fear thee, and wrought for those who take refuge in thee...Blessed be the Lord, for he has wondrously shown his steadfast love to me...

Eph. 1:3. Blessed be the God and Father of our Lord Jesus Christ, who has blessed us in Christ with every spiritual blessing in the heavenly places...

Eph. 2:7. That in the coming ages he might show the immeasurable riches of his grace in kindness toward us in Christ Jesus.

Ps. 84:11. ...No good thing does the Lord withhold from those who walk uprightly.

Ps. 29:11. May the Lord give strength to his people! May the Lord bless his people with peace! (Also Ps. 122:6–7, 147:14.)

Ps. 12:7. Do thou, O Lord, protect us...

Ps. 121:2, 7–8. My help comes from the Lord, who made heaven and earth...The Lord will keep you from all evil; he will keep your life. The Lord will keep your going out and your coming in from this time forth and for evermore.

Ps. 37:3. Trust in the Lord, and do good; so you will dwell in the land, and enjoy security (Luther: nähre dich redlich).

Is. 40:11. He will feed his flock like a shepherd, he will gather the lambs in his arms, he will carry them in his bosom, and gently lead those that are with young. (Also Ezek. 34:11–16, Ps. 23:1–2, Rev. 7:17.)

BWV 17
Wer Dank opfert, der preiset mich
(NBA I/21; BC A131)

14. S. after Trinity (BWV 25, 78, 17)
*Gal. 5:16–24 (Work of the flesh and fruit of the Spirit)
*Lk. 17:11–19 (Jesus heals ten lepers)
Librettist: perhaps Christoph Helm

Part I

1. Chorus
●Thanksgiving as a sacrifice of praise: Ps. 50:23 (17-1)
Wer Dank opfert, der preiset mich, und das
He-who thanksgiving offers, he praises me, and that

ist der Weg, daß ich ihm zeige das Heil Gottes.
is the way, that I him will-show the salvation of-God.

2. Alto Recit.
●Nature testifies of God's majesty (17-2)
Es muß die ganze Welt ein stummer Zeuge werden
(Now) must the whole world a mute witness (be)
{The whole world must give mute testimony}

Von Gottes hoher Majestät,
To God's exalted majesty:

Luft, Wasser, Firmament und Erden,
Air, water, firmament, and earth,

Wenn ihre Ordnung als in Schnuren geht;
When their ordering as-if on rails does-go;
{When their ordering runs like clockwork;}

Ihn preiset die Natur mit ungezählten Gaben,
Him praises - nature with (the) countless gifts,
{Nature praises him with the countless gifts,}

Die er ihr in den Schoß gelegt,
Which he - in (her) lap has-laid,
{Which he has laid in her lap,}

Und was den Odem hegt,
And whatever - breath contains,
{And whatever has breath,}

Will noch mehr Anteil an ihm haben,
Shall still greater portion in him have,
{Shall have a still greater portion in him,}

Wenn es zu seinem Ruhm so Zung als Fittich regt.
When it for his glory (both) tongue (and) pinion stirs.
{When it stirs tongue as well as pinion to his glory.}

3. Soprano Aria
●God's attributes can be seen in heavens: Ps. 36:5 (17-3)
Herr, dein Güte reicht, so weit der Himmel ist,
Lord, thy kindness extends, as far-as the heavens (are),

*Lk. 17:15–16. One of them, when he saw that he was healed, turned back, praising God with a loud voice; and he fell on his face at Jesus' feet, giving him thanks...
Ps. 50:14, 23. Offer to God a sacrifice of thanksgiving, and pay your vows to the Most High...*He who brings thanksgiving as his sacrifice honors me; to him who orders his way aright I will show the salvation of God!*
Heb. 13:15. Through [Christ] then let us continually offer up a sacrifice of praise to God, that is, the fruit of lips that acknowledge his name. (Also Ps. 51:15–17.)
Ps. 69:30–31. I will praise the name of God with a song; I will magnify him with thanksgiving. This will please the Lord more than an ox or a bull with horns and hoofs. (Also Ps. 116:17.)

Ps. 8:9. O Lord, our Lord, how majestic is thy name in all the earth!
Rom. 1:20. Ever since the creation of the world his invisible nature, namely, his eternal power and deity, has been clearly perceived in the things that have been made.
Ps. 19:1–2, 4. The heavens are telling the glory of God; and the firmament proclaims his handiwork. Day to day pours forth speech, and night to night declares knowledge...their voice (Luther: Schnur) goes out through all the earth...
Ps. 8:3–4. [O Lord,] when I look at thy heavens, the work of thy fingers, the moon and the stars which thou hast extablished; what is man that thou art mindful of him...?
Ps. 89:11. The heavens are thine, the earth also is thine; the world and all that is in it, thou hast founded them.
Ps. 136:1, 4–9. O give thanks to the Lord, for he is good...to him who alone does great wonders...who by understanding made the heavens...who spread out the earth upon the waters...who made the great lights...the sun to rule over the day...the moon and stars to rule over the night...
Ps. 145:10. All thy works shall give thanks to thee, O Lord, and all thy saints shall bless thee!
Ps. 150:6. Let everything that breathes praise the Lord!
Ps. 34:1. I will bless the Lord at all times; his praise shall continually be in my mouth.
Ps. 51:15. O Lord, open thou my lips, and my mouth shall show forth thy praise.
Ps. 63:5. ...My mouth praises thee with joyful lips. (Also Ps. 71:8, 15; 109:30; 119:108; 145:21; 149:6.)
Ps. 89:1. I will sing of thy steadfast love, O Lord, for ever; with my mouth I will proclaim thy faithfulness to all generations.

Ps. 36:5. *Thy steadfast love, O Lord, extends to the heavens, thy faithfulness to the clouds.*
Ps. 57:10. For thy steadfast love is great to the heavens, thy faithfulness to the clouds. (Also Ps. 108:4.)

Und deine Wahrheit langt, so weit die Wolken gehen.
And thy   truth   reaches, as far-as the   clouds   go.

Wüßt ich gleich sonsten nicht,
Knew I   though otherwise not,
{Though I would otherwise not know,}

       wie herrlich groß du bist,
       how gloriously great thou art,

So könnt ich es gar leicht aus deinen Werken sehen.
Yet could I   it quite easily in   thy   works   see.
{Yet I could see it quite easily in thy works.}

Wie sollt man dich mit Dank dafür
How should one thee with thanks for-that

      nicht stetig preisen?
      not constantly praise?
{How should one not constantly praise thee for that with thanks?}

Da   du uns wilt den Weg des Heils
Since thou us wouldst the way of Salvation

      hingegen weisen.
      in-return   show.
{Since thou wouldst show us the way of Salvation in return.}

Part II

4. Tenor Recit.
●Samaritan leper returns to give thanks: Lk. 17:15–16 (17-4)
Einer aber   unter ihnen, da er sahe daß er gesund
One, however, among them, when he saw that he healthy

worden war, kehrete um   und preisete Gott
become was,   turned around and praised God

mit   lauter Stimme und fiel auf sein Angesicht
with (a) loud   voice and fell on his   face

zu seinen Füßen und danket ihm,
at his   feet   and thanked him,

und das war ein Samariter.
and he was a Samaritan.

5. Tenor Aria
●Songs of praise only gift of thanks I can bring (17-5)
Welch Übermaß der Güte
What   excess of goodness
{What abundance of blessing}

Schenkst du mir!
Givest   thou to-me!
{Thou dost give to me!}

Ps. 108:3–4. I will give thanks to thee, O Lord, among the peoples, I will sing praises to thee among the nations. For thy steadfast love is great above the heavens, thy faithfulness reaches to the clouds.
Rom. 1:19–20. What can be known about God is plain to [men] because God has shown it to them. Ever since the creation of the world his invisible nature, namely, his eternal power and deity, has been clearly perceived in the things that have been made. So they are without excuse...
Jn. 10:37–38 [Christ]: If I am not doing the works of my Father, then do not believe me; but if I do them, even though you do not believe me, believe the works, that you may know and understand that the Father is in me and I am in the Father. (Also Jn. 14:11.)
Ps. 103:22. Bless the Lord, all his works, in all places of his dominion. Bless the Lord, O my soul!
Ps. 50:14. Offer to God a sacrifice of thanksgiving...
Ps. 147:1. Praise the Lord! For it is good to sing praises to our God; for he is gracious, and a song of praise is seemly.
Ps. 50:23 [God]: He who brings thanksgiving as his sacrifice honors me...
*Lk. 17:11–18. On the way to Jerusalem [Jesus] was passing along between Samaria and Galilee. And as he entered a village, he was met by ten lepers, who stood at a distance and lifted up their voices and said, "Jesus, Master, have mercy on us." When he saw them he said to them, "Go and show yourselves to the priests." And as they went they were cleansed. Then one of them, when he saw that he was healed, turned back, praising God with a loud voice; and he fell on his face at Jesus' feet, giving him thanks. Now he was a Samaritan. Then said Jesus, "Were not ten cleansed? Where are the nine? Was no one found to return and give praise to God except this foreigner?"

*Lk. 17:15–16. *Then one of [the lepers], when he saw that he was healed, turned back, praising God with a loud voice; and he fell on his face at Jesus' feet, giving him thanks. Now he was a Samaritan.*
Jn. 4:9. [A] Samaritan woman said to [Jesus], "How is it that you, a Jew, ask a drink of me, a woman of Samaria?" For Jews have no dealings with Samaritans.
Lk. 7:37–39. And behold, a woman of the city, who was a sinner, when she learned that [Jesus] was at table in the Pharisee's house, brought an alabaster flask of ointment, and standing behind him at his feet, weeping, she began to wet his feet with her tears, and wiped them with the hair of her head, and kissed his feet, and anointed them with the ointment. Now when the Pharisee who had invited him saw it, he said to himself, "If this man were a prophet, he would have known who and what sort of woman this is who is touching him, for she is a sinner."

Ps. 31:19, 21. [O Lord,] how abundant is thy goodness, which thou hast laid up for those who fear thee, and wrought for those who take refuge in thee, in the sight of the sons of men!...Blessed be the Lord, for he has wondrously shown his steadfast love to me...
Ps. 116:12. What shall I render (Luther: vergelten) to the Lord for all his bounty to me?

Doch was gibt mein Gemüte
Yet   what giveth my disposition

Dir   dafür?
To-thee for-that?
{To thee in return?}

Herr, ich weiß   sonst   nichts zu bringen,
Lord, I   know otherwise (of) nothing to   bring,
{Lord, I know of nought else to bring}

Als   dir   Dank und Lob zu singen.
But to-thee thanks and praise to   sing.
{But to sing praise and thanks to thee.}

Ps. 51:15–16. O Lord, open thou my lips, and my mouth shall show forth thy praise. For thou hast no delight in sacrifice; were I to give a burnt offering, thou wouldst not be pleased.
Ps. 40:6–10. Sacrifice and offering thou dost not desire; but thou hast given me an open ear. Burnt offering and sin offering thou hast not required. Then I said, "Lo, I come...I delight to do thy will, O my God..." I have told the glad news of deliverance in the great congregation; lo, I have not restrained my lips, as thou knowest, O Lord. I have not hid thy saving help within my heart, I have spoken of thy faithfulness and thy salvation; I have not concealed thy steadfast love and thy faithfulness from the great congregation.
Ps. 145:7. They shall pour forth the fame of thy abundant goodness, and shall sing aloud of thy righteousness. (Also Is. 63:7.)

6. Bass Recit.
●Blessings of body and spirit are gifts of grace (17–6)
Sieh   meinen Willen an, ich kenne, was ich bin:
Regard my   will   - , I   know, what I am:
{Have regard for my intentions; I acknowledge what I am:}

Leib, Leben und Verstand, Gesundheit, Kraft   und Sinn,
Body, life and   reason,   health,   strength, and mind,

Der   du mich läßt   mit frohem Mund genießen,
Which thou me lettest with rejoicing mouth   enjoy,
{Which thou dost let me enjoy with rejoicing mouth,}

Sind Ströme deiner Gnad, die   du auf mich läßt fließen.
Are   streams of-thy   grace, which thou upon me lettest   flow.

Lieb, Fried, Gerechtigkeit und Freud in deinem Geist
Love, peace, righteousness, and   joy   in   thy   Spirit

Sind   Schätz, dadurch du mir schon hier
Are (the) treasures, by-which thou me already here

ein Vorbild weist,
an   example showest,
{Are the treasures by which thou showest me an example here already,}

Was Gutes du gedenkst mir dorten zuzuteilen
What good thou dost-intend me   there to-apportion
{Of the good thou dost intend to apportion to me there}

Und mich an Leib und Seel vollkommentlich zu heilen.
And   me in body and soul   perfectly   to heal.
{And by which thou dost make me perfectly whole in body and soul.}

Jms. 1:17. Every good endowment and every perfect gift is from above, coming down from the Father of lights with whom there is no variation or shadow due to change.
Ps. 36:7–8. How precious is thy steadfast love, O God! The children of men take refuge in the shadow of thy wings. They feast on the abundance of thy house, and thou givest them drink from the river of thy delights.
Mt. 7:11. If you then, who are evil, know how to give good gifts to your children, how much more will your Father who is in heaven give good things to those who ask him!
1 Cor. 4:7. ...What have you that you did not receive? If then you received it, why do you boast as if it were not a gift?
Rom. 14:17. For the kingdom of God is...righteousness and peace and joy in the Holy Spirit.
*****Gal. 5:22–23.** The fruit of the Spirit is love, joy, peace, patience, kindness, goodness, faithfulness, gentleness, self-control; against such there is no law.
Eph. 1:13–14. In [Christ] you also, who have heard the word of truth, the gospel of your salvation, and have believed in him, were sealed with the promised Holy Spirit, which is the guarantee of our inheritance until we acquire possession of it, to the praise of his glory. (See also 2 Cor. 5:5, Col. 1:12, 3:24, Heb. 9:15, 1 Pet. 1:3–5.)
1 Cor. 2:9–10. But, as it is written, "What no eye has seen, nor ear heard, nor the heart of man conceived, what God has prepared for those who love him," God has revealed to us through the Spirit...
Rom. 8:23–24. ...We ourselves, who have the first fruits of the Spirit, groan inwardly as we wait for adoption as sons, the redemption of our bodies. For in this hope we were saved...
1 Cor. 15:42–43. So is it with the resurrection of the dead. What is sown is perishable, what is raised is imperishable.

7. Chorale
●Fatherly mercy: God knows we are dust: Ps. 103:13–16 (17–7)
Wie sich ein Vatr erbarmet
As   -   a father takes-pity

Üb'r seine junge Kindlein klein:
Upon his   young children small;

Ps. 103:13–16. As a father pities his children, so the Lord pities those who fear him. For he knows our frame; he remembers that we are dust. As for man, his days are like grass; he flourishes like a flower of the field; for the wind passes over it, and it is gone, and its place knows it no more. (Also Ps. 102:3, 11.)

So   tut der Herr   uns Armen,
So (also) does the Lord (upon) us poor-ones,

So wir ihn kindlich fürchten rein.
If   we him child-like do-fear purely.
{If we but fear him with childlike simplicity.}

Er kennt das arme Gemächte,
He knows (us) poor creatures,

Gott weiß, wir sind nur Staub.
God knows, we are but dust.

Gleich wie das Gras vom Rechen,
Just   like - grass (after) raking,

Ein Blum und fallendes Laub,
A flower, and falling foliage,

Der Wind nur drüber wehet,
The wind just over-it blows,
{The wind just blows over it,}

So ist es nimmer da:
Then is it no-longer there:
{And it is no longer there:}

Also der Mensch vergehet,
So - man passes-away,

Sein End, das ist ihm nah.
His end, it is for-him near.
{His end is always near.}

Is. 40:6–8. ...All flesh is grass, and all its beauty is like the flower of the field. The grass withers, the flower fades, when the breath of the Lord blows upon it; surely the people is grass. The grass withers, the flower fades; but the word of our God will stand for ever. (Also 1 Pet. 1:24.)

Job 14:1–2. Man that is born of a woman is of few days, and full of trouble. He comes forth like a flower, and withers; he flees like a shadow, and continues not.

Jms. 1:10–11. ...Like the flower of the grass he will pass away. For the sun rises with its scorching heat and withers the grass; its flower falls, and its beauty perishes. So will the rich man fade away in the midst of his pursuits.

2 Sam. 14:14. We must all die, we are like water spilt on the ground, which cannot be gathered again.

Jms. 4:13–15. Come now, you who say, "Today or tomorrow we will go into such and such a town and spend a year there and trade and get gain"; whereas you do not know about tomorrow. What is your life? For you are a mist that appears for a little time and then vanishes. Instead you ought to say, "If the Lord wills, we shall live and we shall do this or that."

Ps. 90:5–6, 9–10, 12. [O Lord,] thou dost sweep men away; they are like a dream, like grass which is renewed in the morning: in the morning it flourishes and is renewed; in the evening it fades and withers...For all our days pass away under thy wrath, our years come to an end like a sigh. The years of our life are threescore and ten, or even by reason of strength fourscore; yet their span is but toil and trouble; they are soon gone, and we fly away...So teach us to number our days that we may get a heart of wisdom.

Ps. 39:4–6. Lord, let me know my end, and what is the measure of my days; let me know how fleeting my life is! Behold, thou hast made my days a few handbreadths, and my lifetime is as nothing in thy sight. Surely every man stands as a mere breath! Surely man goes about as a shadow!...

BWV 18
Gleichwie der Regen und Schnee vom Himmel fällt
(NBA I/7; BC A44 a/b)

Sexagesima (BWV 18, 181, 126)
*2 Cor. 11:19–12:9 (God's power is made perfect in weakness)
*Lk. 8:4–15 (Parable of the sower)
Librettist: Erdmann Neumeister

1. Sinfonia

2. Bass Recit.
●Vox Christi: My Word will produce fruit: Is. 55:10–11 (18-2)
Gleichwie der Regen und Schnee vom Himmel fällt
Just-as   the   rain and snow from heaven falls

und nicht wieder dahin kommet, sondern feuchtet
and not again thither comes, but-rather moistens

die Erde und macht sie fruchtbar und wachsend,
the earth and makes it fruitful and (fertile),

daß sie gibt Samen zu säen und Brot zu essen;
so-that it gives seed for sowing and bread for eating;

Is. 55:10–11 [God]: *For as the rain and the snow come down from heaven, and return not thither but water the earth, making it bring forth and sprout, giving seed to the sower and bread to the eater, so shall my word be that goes forth from my mouth; it shall not return to me empty, but it shall accomplish that which I purpose, and prosper in the thing for which I sent it.*

***Lk. 8:4–15.** [Jesus] said in a parable: "A sower went out to sow his seed; and as he sowed, some fell along the path, and was trodden under foot, and the birds of the air devoured it. And some fell on the rock; and as it grew up, it withered away, because it had no moisture. And some fell among thorns; and the thorns grew with it and choked

Also soll das Wort, so aus meinem Munde gehet,
So shall the Word, which out-of my mouth goes,

auch sein; es soll nicht wieder zu mir leer kommen,
also be; it shall not return to me empty - ,

sondern tun, das mir gefället, und soll ihm
but-rather do, what me pleases, and shall -

gelingen, dazu ich's sende.
succeed, for-that (for which) I-it send.
{and shall accomplish that for which I sent it}

3. Tenor/Bass Recit. & S.A.T.B. Litany (Chorale)
●Prayer: Let my heart be like fertile soil (18-3)
Tenor:
Mein Gott, hier wird mein Herze sein:
My God, here shall my heart be:
{My God, here is my heart:}

Ich öffne dir's in meines Jesu Namen;
I open it-to-thee in my Jesus' name;

So streue deinen Samen
So scatter thy seed

Als in ein gutes Land hinein.
As-if upon - good land - .

Mein Gott, hier wird mein Herze sein:
My God, here shall my heart be:
{My God, here is my heart:}

Laß solches Frucht, und hundertfältig, bringen.
Let (it) fruit, and one-hundredfold, bring.
{Let it bring forth fruit, a hundredfold.}

O Herr, Herr, hilf! o Herr, laß wohlgelingen!
O Lord, Lord, help! O Lord, let (it) succeed-well!

S.A.T.B:
Du wollest deinen Geist und Kraft zum Worte geben.
(Mayest-thou) thy Spirit and strength to-the Word give.
{Bless the Word with thy Spirit and strength.}

Erhör uns, lieber Herre Gott!
Hear us, dear Lord God!

Bass:
Nur wehre, treuer Vater, wehre,
Only forbid, faithful Father, forbid,

Daß mich und keinen Christen nicht
That me and no Christian -

Des Teufels Trug verkehre.
The devil's deceit (should) pervert.
{That the devil's deceit should lead me or any other Christian astray.}

it. And some fell into good soil and grew, and yielded a hundredfold."
...And when his disciples asked him what this parable meant, he said, "...The seed is the word of God. The ones along the path are those who have heard; then the devil comes and takes away the word from their hearts, that they may not believe and be saved. And the ones on the rock are those who, when they hear the word, receive it with joy; but these have no root, they believe for a while and in time of temptation fall away. And as for what fell among thorns, they are those who hear, but as they go on their way they are choked by the cares and riches and pleasures of life, and their fruit does not mature. And as for that in the good soil, they are those who, hearing the word, hold it fast in an honest and good heart, and bring forth fruit with patience."

*Lk. 8:15. And as for that in the good soil, they are those who, hearing the word, hold it fast in an honest and good heart, and bring forth fruit with patience.
1 Jn. 3:9. No one born of God commits sin; for God's nature (Luther: Same) abides in him...
Col. 3:16. Let the word of Christ dwell in you richly...
Jms. 1:21. Therefore put away all filthiness...and receive with meekness the implanted word, which is able to save your souls. (Also Acts 20:32, 1 Thess. 2:13.)
Acts 20:32. ...I commend you to God and to the word of his grace, which is able to build you up and to give you the inheritance among all those who are sanctified.
Eph. 3:17. [I pray]...that Christ may dwell in your hearts through faith.
Rom. 10:9-10. If you confess with your lips that Jesus is Lord and believe in your heart that God raised him from the dead, you will be saved. For man believes with his heart and so is justified, and he confesses with his lips and so is saved. (Also 1 Jn. 4:15.)
Heb. 3:7-8, 12. Therefore, as the Holy Spirit says, "Today, when you hear his voice, do not harden your hearts as in the rebellion, on the day of testing in the wilderness."...Take care, brethren, lest there be in any of you an evil, unbelieving heart, leading you to fall away from the living God.
Heb. 10:16. "This is the covenant that I will make with them after those days, says the Lord: I will put my laws on their hearts, and write them on their minds."
*Lk. 8:8. And some [seed] fell into good soil and grew and yielded a hundredfold.
Is. 55:10-11 [God]: As the rain and the snow come down from heaven, and return not thither but water the earth, making it bring forth and sprout, giving seed to the sower and bread to the eater, so shall my word be that goes forth from my mouth; it shall not return to me empty...
Ps. 118:25. *Save us, we beseech thee, O Lord! O Lord, we beseech thee, give us success!*
Is. 55:11 [God]: ...[My word] shall accomplish that which I purpose, and prosper in the thing for which I sent it.
Phil. 2:13. God is at work in you...
Phil. 1:6. I am sure that he who began a good work in you will bring it to completion at the day of Jesus Christ.
2 Thess. 3:1-2. ...Brethren, pray for us, that the word of the Lord may speed on and triumph...and that we may be delivered from wicked and evil men; for not all have faith.
Gal. 1:7. ...There are some who...want to pervert the gospel of Christ.
Eph. 6:11-12. Put on the whole armor of God, that you may be able to stand against the wiles of the devil. For we are not contending

Sein Sinn ist ganz dahin gericht',
His mind is completely thereto directed,

Uns deines Wortes zu berauben
Us of-thy Word to rob
{To rob us of thy Word}

Mit aller Seligkeit.
With all (its) blessedness.

S.A.T.B:
Den Satan unter unsre Füße treten.
- Satan beneath our feet tread.
{Tread Satan beneath our feet.}

Erhör uns, lieber Herre Gott!
Hear us, dear Lord God!

Tenor:
Ach! viel' verleugnen Wort und Glauben
Ah! Many deny Word and Faith

Und fallen ab wie faules Obst,
And fall away like rotten fruit,

Wenn sie Verfolgung sollen leiden.
When they persecution must suffer.
{When they must suffer persecution.}

So stürzen sie in ewig Herzeleid,
Thus plunge they into eternal grief,
{Thus they plunge into eternal grief,}

Da sie ein zeitlich Weh vermeiden.
Because they a temporal woe avoid.
{Because they avoid a temporal woe.}

S.A.T.B:
Und uns für des Türken und des Papsts
And (do) us from the Turk's and the Pope's
{And from the Turk's and the Pope's}

Grausamen Mord und Lästerungen,
Horrible murder and revilings,

Wüten und Toben väterlich behüten.
Raging and storming, fatherlike protect.
{Raging and storming, fatherlike protect us.}

Erhör uns, lieber Herre Gott!
Hear us, dear Lord God!

Bass:
Ein andrer sorgt nur für den Bauch;
Another cares only for (his) stomach;

Inzwischen wird der Seele ganz vergessen;
Meanwhile is (his) soul entirely forgotten;
{Meanwhile, his soul is entirely forgotten;}

against flesh and blood, but against the principalities, against the powers, against the world rulers of this present darkness, against the spiritual hosts of wickedness in the heavenly places.
1 Pet. 5:8. Your adversary the devil prowls around like a roaring lion, seeking some one to devour.
Rev. 12:9. ...The great dragon...that ancient serpent, who is called the Devil and Satan, [is] the deceiver of the whole world... (Also 1 Jn. 5:19, 2 Jn. 1:7.)
Jn. 8:44 [Christ]: ...The devil...was a murderer from the beginning, and has nothing to do with the truth, because there is no truth in him. When he lies, he speaks according to his own nature, for he is a liar and the father of lies.
*Lk. 8:12 [Christ]: The ones along the path are those who have heard; then the devil comes and takes away the word from their hearts, that they may not believe and be saved.
Jn. 15:7 [Christ]: If you abide in me, and my words abide in you, ask whatever you will, and it shall be done for you.
Gen. 3:14-15. The Lord God said to the serpent, "Because you have done this...I will put enmity between you and the woman, and between your seed and her seed; he shall bruise your head, and you shall bruise his heel."
Ps. 91:11, 13. [The Lord] will give his angels charge of you...You will tread on the lion and the adder, the young lion and the serpent you will trample under foot.
Lk. 10:18-19. And [Jesus] said to them, "I saw Satan fall like lightning from heaven. Behold, I have given you authority to tread upon serpents and scorpions, and over all the power of the enemy; and nothing shall hurt you."
*Lk. 8:13. ...[Some] believe for a while and in time of temptation fall away.
Mt. 24:11-12 [Christ]: Many false prophets will arise and lead many astray. And because wickedness is multiplied, most men's love will grow cold.
Heb. 6:4-6. It is impossible to restore again to repentance those who have once been enlightened, who have tasted the heavenly gift...if they then commit apostasy...
Heb. 10:26-27. For if we sin deliberately after receiving the knowledge of the truth, there no longer remains a sacrifice for sins, but a fearful prospect of judgment, and a fury of fire which will consume the adversaries.
Lk. 16:25. Abraham said, "Son, remember that you in your lifetime received your good things, and Lazarus in like manner evil things; but now he is comforted here, and you are in anguish."
Ps. 72:4. May [God] defend the cause of the poor of the people, give deliverance to the needy, and crush the oppressor (Luther: Lästerer)!
2 Tim. 3:1-5. But understand this, that in the last days there will come times of stress. For men will be lovers of self, lovers of money, proud, arrogant, abusive (Luther: Lästerer), disobedient to their parents, ungrateful, unholy, inhuman, implacable, slanderers, profligates, fierce, haters of good, treacherous, reckless, swollen with conceit, lovers of pleasure rather than lovers of God, holding the form of religion but denying the power of it.
*Lk. 8:14. ...They are choked by the cares and riches and pleasures of life.
Rom. 16:18. Such persons do not serve our Lord Christ, but their own appetites (Luther: Bauche)...

Der Mammon auch
- Mammon, too,

Hat vieler Herz bessessen.
Has many hearts posessed.
{Has posessed many hearts.}

So kann das Wort zu keiner Kraft gelangen.
Thus can the Word - no power attain.
{Thus the Word can not attain any influence.}

Und wieviel Seelen hält
And how-many souls holds

Die Wollust nicht gefangen?
- Pleasure not captive?
{And how many souls does pleasure not hold captive?}

So sehr verführet sie die Welt,
So greatly seduces them the world,
{So greatly does the world seduce them—}

Die Welt, die ihnen muß anstatt des Himmels stehen,
The world, which for-them must in-place-of heaven stand,
{The world which, for them must take the place of heaven—}

Darüber sie vom Himmel irregehen.
On-account-of-which they from heaven go-astray.
{On account of which they go astray from heaven.}

Alle Irrige und Verführte wiederbringen.
All straying and seduced-ones bring-back.
{Bring back all straying and seduced ones.}

Erhör uns, lieber Herre Gott!
Hear us, dear Lord God!

4. Soprano Aria
●God's Word is my true treasure, all else is trickery! (18-4)
Mein Seelenschatz ist Gottes Wort;
My soul's-treasure is God's Word;

Außer dem sind alle Schätze
Beside it are all treasures
{Beside it all treasures are}

Solche Netze,
(Mere) nets,

Welche Welt und Satan stricken,
Which world and Satan knit,

Schnöde Seelen zu berücken.
Base souls to ensnare.

Fort mit allen, fort, nur fort!
Away with all (of them), away, just away!

Mein Seelenschatz ist Gottes Wort.
My soul's-treasure is God's Word.

1 Cor. 6:13. "Food is meant for the stomach and the stomach for food"—and God will destroy both one and the other.
Phil. 3:19. Their end is destruction, their god is the belly, and they glory in their shame, with minds set on earthly things.
Mt. 6:24 [Christ]: No one can serve two masters...You cannot serve God and mammon. (Also Lk. 16:13.)
Mt. 19:23-24. And Jesus said..."I tell you, it is easier for a camel to go through the eye of a needle than for a rich man to enter the kingdom of God."
1 Tim. 6:9. Those who desire to be rich fall into temptation, into a snare, into many senseless and hurtful desires that plunge men into ruin and destruction.
2 Pet. 2:19. ...They themselves are slaves of corruption; for whatever overcomes a man, to that he is enslaved.
2 Tim. 3:4. [They will be]...lovers of pleasure rather than lovers of God...
Tit. 3:3. [We were]...slaves to various passions and pleasures...
1 Jn. 2:15-16. Do not love the world or the things in the world. If any one loves the world, love for the Father is not in him. For all that is in the world, the lust of the flesh and the lust of the eyes and the pride of life, is not of the Father but is of the world.
Jms. 4:4. Unfaithful creatures! Do you not know that friendship with the world is enmity with God? Therefore whoever wishes to be a friend of the world makes himself an enemy of God.
2 Pet. 2:15. Forsaking the right way they have gone astray; they have followed the way of Balaam, the son of Beor, who loved gain from wrongdoing...
Jms. 5:19-20. My brethren, if any one among you wanders from the truth and some one brings him back, let him know that whoever brings back a sinner from the error of his way will save his soul from death and will cover a multitude of sins.

Ps. 119:14, 47, 97, 103. [O Lord,] in the way of thy testimonies I delight as much as in all riches...for I find my delight in thy commandments, which I love...Oh, how I love thy law! It is my meditation all the day...How sweet are thy words to my taste, sweeter than honey to my mouth!
Ps. 19:9-10. ...The ordinances of the Lord are true, and righteous altogether. More to be desired are they than gold, even much fine gold; sweeter also than honey and drippings of the honeycomb.
1 Tim. 6:9. But those who desire to be rich fall...into a snare... (Also 2 Pet. 2:15, Jude 1:11.)
Jms. 4:4. ...Do you not know that friendship with the world is enmity with God? Therefore whoever wishes to be a friend of the world makes himself an enemy of God.
Lk. 4:5-7. And the devil took [Jesus] up, and showed him all the kingdoms of the world in a moment of time, and said to him, "To you I will give all this authority and their glory...if you...will worship me, it shall all be yours."
Jms. 4:7. Resist the devil and he will flee from you.
Mt. 4:10. Then Jesus said to him, "Begone, Satan!..."
Mt. 16:23. But [Jesus] turned and said to Peter, "Get behind me, Satan! You are a hindrance to me; for you are not on the side of God, but of men."

5. Chorale
●Prayer: Do not take Word away, it is our confidence (18-5)
Ich bitt, o Herr, aus   Herzens Grund,
I   ask, O Lord, from (my) heart's bottom,
{I ask, O Lord, from the bottom of my heart,}

Du   wollst nicht von mir nehmen
Thou wouldst not from me   take

Dein heilges Wort aus meinem Mund;
Thy   holy Word out-of   my   mouth;

So wird mich nicht beschämen
So will me   not   shame

Mein Sünd und Schuld, denn in dein   Huld
My   sin and guilt,   for in thy graciousness
{So will my sin and guilt not shame me, for in thy graciousness,}

Setz ich all mein Vertrauen:
Place I   all my confidence:
{I place all my confidence:}

Wer   sich nur fest darauf verläßt,
Whoever -   just firmly on-that relies,

Der wird den Tod nicht schauen.
He will   - death not   see.
{He will not see death.}

BWV 19
Es erhub sich ein Streit
(NBA I/30; BC A180)

St. Michael's Day: Sept. 29 (BWV 130, 19, 149, 50)
*Rev. 12:7-12 (The archangel Michael battles with the dragon)
*Mt. 18:1-11 (The kingdom of heaven belongs to children; their angels behold the face of God)
Librettist: Unknown; based on a poem by Picander (Christian Friedrich Henrici)

1. Chorus (Unrelated to Picander's poem)
●Angel Michael battles with Satan, the dragon (19-1)
Es   erhub sich ein   Streit.
(There) arose -   a (great) fight.

Die rasende Schlange, der höllische Drache
That raving snake,   the infernal dragon

Stürmt wider den Himmel mit wütender Rache.
Storms against -   heaven with furious vengeance.

Aber Michael bezwingt
But Michael vanquishes (the foe)

Ps. 119:43. [O Lord,] take not the word of truth utterly out of my mouth, for my hope is in thy ordinances.
Deut. 30:14. The word is very near you; it is in your mouth and in your heart, so that you can do it.
Rom. 10:8-11, 13. What does [the righteousness based on faith] say? The word is near you, on your lips (Luther: Munde) and in your heart (that is, the word of faith which we preach); because if you confess with your lips that Jesus is Lord and believe in your heart that God raised him from the dead, you will be saved. For man believes with his heart and so is justified, and he confesses with his lips and so is saved. The scripture says, "No one who believes in him will be put to shame." ...For, "every one who calls upon the name of the Lord will be saved."
1 Pet. 2:6. For it stands in scripture: "Behold, I am laying in Zion a stone, a cornerstone chosen and precious, and he who believes in him will not be put to shame."
Mt. 10:32 [Christ]: Every one who acknowledges me before men, I also will acknowledge before my Father who is in heaven.
Jn. 5:24 [Christ]: Truly, truly, I say to you, he who hears my word and believes him who sent me, has eternal life; he does not come into judgment, but has passed from death to life.
Eph. 2:8-9. For by grace you have been saved through faith; and this is not your own doing, it is the gift of God—not because of works, lest any man should boast.
Jn. 8:51 [Christ]: Truly, truly, I say to you, if any one keeps my word, he will never see death.

*Rev. 12:7-9. Now war arose in heaven, Michael and his angels fighting against the dragon; and the dragon and his angels fought, but they were defeated and there was no longer any place for them in heaven. And the great dragon was thrown down, that ancient serpent, who is called the Devil and Satan, the deceiver of the whole world—he was thrown down to the earth, and his angels were thrown down with him.
Gen. 3:1, 4-5. Now the serpent was more subtle than any other wild creature that the Lord God had made. He said to the woman, "Did God say, 'You shall not eat of any tree of the garden'?...You will not die. For God knows that when you eat of it your eyes will be opened, and you will be like God, knowing good and evil."
Gen. 3:14-15. The Lord God said to the serpent, "Because you have done this...I will put enmity between you and the woman, and between your seed and her seed; he shall bruise your head, and you shall bruise his heel." (Also Rom. 16:20.)

Und die Schar, die ihn umringt,
And the host, that him enrcircles,
{And the host, that encircles him,}

Stürzt   des Satans Grausamkeit.
Overthrows - Satan's   ferocity.

2. Bass Recit. (Unrelated to Picander's poem)
●Angel host has defeated the dragon; praise God! (19-2)
Gottlob!   der Drache liegt.
Praise-God! the dragon   lies.

Der unerschaffne Michael
The non-created Michael

Und seiner Engel Heer
And   his   angelic host

Hat ihn besiegt.
Has him defeated.
{Has defeated him.}

Dort liegt er in der Finsternis
There lies he in the darkness
{There he lies in the darkness}

Mit Ketten angebunden,
With chains   tied-up,
{Tied up with chains,}

Und seine Stätte wird nicht mehr
And his abode is   no more

Im Himmelreich gefunden.
In heaven's-kingdom found.
{To be found in heaven's kingdom.}

Wir stehen sicher und gewiß
We stand   secure and sure

Und wenn uns gleich sein Brüllen schrecket,
And though us   -   his roaring frightens,
{And though his roaring frightens us,}

So wird   doch   unser Leib und Seel
So will nevertheless our body and soul

Mit Engeln zugedecket.
By angels be-covered.
{By angels be protected.}

3. Soprano Aria (Excerpted from Picander's poem)
●Angel host encamps around God's people (19-3)
Gott schickt uns Mahanaim zu;
God   sends us Mahanaim - ;

        Wir stehen oder gehen,
(Whether) we stop   or   go,

Eph. 6:11-12. Put on the whole armor of God, that you may be able to stand against the wiles of the devil. For we are not contending against flesh and blood, but against the principalities, against the powers, against the world rulers of this present darkness, against the spiritual hosts of wickedness in the heavenly places. (Also 1 Pet. 5:8.)

*Rev. 12:7-8. Now war arose in heaven, Michael and his angels fighting against the dragon; and the dragon and his angels fought, but they were defeated... (Also Dan. 12:1, Jude 1:9.)
Rev. 20:1-3, 7-10. Then [in my vision] I saw an angel coming down from heaven, holding in his hand the key of the bottomless pit and a great chain. And he seized the dragon, that ancient serpent, who is the Devil and Satan, and bound him for a thousand years, and threw him into the pit, and shut it and sealed it over him, that he should deceive the nations no more, till the thousand years were ended...And when the thousand years are ended, Satan will be loosed from his prison and will come out to deceive the nations...And they marched up...and surrounded the camp of the saints and the beloved city; but fire came down from heaven and consumed them, and the devil who had deceived them was thrown into the lake of fire and sulphur where the beast and the false prophet were, and they will be tormented day and night for ever and ever.
2 Pet. 2:4-6, 9. If God did not spare the angels when they sinned, but cast them into hell and committed them to pits of nether gloom to be kept until the judgment; if he did not spare the ancient world, but preserved Noah, a herald of righteousness, with seven other persons, when he brought a flood upon the world of the ungodly; if by turning the cities of Sodom and Gomorrah to ashes he condemned them to extinction and made them an example to those who were to be ungodly...then the Lord knows how to rescue the godly from trial, and to keep the unrighteous under punishment until the day of judgment.
Jn. 12:30-31. Jesus answered, "...Now is the judgment of this world, now shall the ruler of this world be cast out."
Jn. 16:11. ...The ruler of this world is judged.
1 Pet. 5:8-9. Be sober, be watchful. Your adversary the devil prowls around like a roaring lion, seeking some one to devour. Resist him, firm in your faith, knowing that the same experience of suffering is required of your brotherhood throughout the world.
1 Jn. 4:4. Little children, you are of God, and have overcome them; for he who is in you is greater than he who is in the world.
*Mt. 18:10 [Christ]: See that you do not despise one of these little ones; for I tell you that in heaven their angels always behold the face of my Father who is in heaven.
Ps. 91:4, 10-11. [The Lord] will cover you with his pinions, and under his wings you will find refuge...No evil shall befall you, no scourge come near your tent. For he will give his angels charge of you to guard you in all your ways.

Gen. 32:1-2. Jacob went on his way and the angels of God met him; and when Jacob saw them he said, "This is God's army!" So he called the name of that place Mahanaim.
Ps. 27:1, 3. The Lord is my light and my salvation; whom shall I fear? The Lord is the stronghold of my life; of whom shall I be afraid?... Though a host encamp against me, my heart shall not fear; though war arise against me, yet I will be confident.

So können wir in sichrer Ruh
So can we in safe repose
{We can in safe repose}

Vor unsern Feinden stehen.
Before our enemies stand.

Es lagert sich, so nah als fern,
(Now) encamps - , (both) near (and) far,

Um uns der Engel unsers Herrn
Around us the angel of-our Lord

Mit Feuer, Roß und Wagen.
With fire, steed, and chariot.

4. Tenor Recit. (Loosely based on Picander's poem)
●Man is only a worm yet God protects him with angels (19-4)
Was ist der schnöde Mensch, das Erdenkind?
What is - base man, (this) child-of-earth?

Ein Wurm, ein armer Sünder.
A worm, a poor sinner.

Schaut, wie ihn selbst der Herr so liebgewinnt,
Look, how of-him himself the Lord so fond-has-become,
{Look how fond the Lord himself is of him,}

Daß er ihn nicht zu niedrig schätzet
That he him not too lowly regards
{That he does not consider him too lowly}

Und ihm die Himmelskinder,
And (around) him the children-of-heaven,
{To place around him the children of heaven—}

Der Seraphinen Heer,
That seraphim host—

Zu seiner Wacht und Gegenwehr,
For his guard and defence,

Zu seinem Schutze setzet.
For his protection places.
{For his protection.}

5. Tenor Aria (Loosely based on Picander's poem)
●Angels addressed: Protect me and teach me to sing! (19-5)
Bleibt, ihr Engel, bleibt bei mir!
Stay, you angels, stay by me!

Führet mich auf beiden Seiten,
Lead me from both sides,
{Walk on both sides of me,}

Daß mein Fuß nicht möge gleiten!
That my foot may-not slip!

Ps. 23:5. [O Lord,] thou preparest a table before me in the presence of my enemies...
Ps. 34:7. The angel of the Lord encamps around those who fear him, and delivers them.
2 Kings 6:15-18. When the servant of the man of God rose early in the morning and went out, behold, an army with horses and chariots was round about the city. And the servant said, "Alas, my master! What shall we do?" [Elisha] said, "Fear not, for those who are with us are more than those who are with them." Then Elisha prayed, and said, "O Lord, I pray thee, open his eyes that he may see." So the Lord opened the eyes of the young man, and he saw; and behold, the mountain was full of horses and chariots of fire around about Elisha. And when the Syrians came down...[the Lord] struck them with blindness...

Ps. 8:3-5. [O Lord,] when I look at thy heavens, the work of thy fingers, the moon and the stars which thou hast established; what is man that thou art mindful of him, and the son of man that thou dost care for him? Yet thou hast made him little less than God, and dost crown him with glory and honor. (Also Ps. 144:3, Heb. 2:5-8.)
Ps. 22:6. But I am a worm, and no man; scorned by men, and despised by the people.
Job 25:5-6. Behold, even the moon is not bright and the stars are not clean in his sight; how much less man, who is a maggot, and the son of man, who is a worm!
Is. 41:14. Fear not, you worm Jacob, you men of Israel! I will help you, says the Lord...
Heb. 1:14. Are [angels] not all ministering spirits sent forth to serve, for the sake of those who are to obtain salvation?
*Mt. 18:10. ...Their angels always behold the face of my Father who is in heaven.
Ps. 91:9-11. Because you have made the Lord your refuge...no evil shall befall you...For he will give his angels charge of you to guard you in all your ways.
Mt. 26:52-53. Then Jesus said... "...Do you think that I cannot appeal to my Father, and he will at once send me more than twelve legions of angels?"
Ps. 68:17. With mighty chariotry, twice ten thousand, thousands upon thousands, the Lord came from Sinai into the holy place.

Gen. 24:6-7. Abraham said to [his servant]..."The Lord...will send his angel before you..."
Ex. 23:20 [God]: Behold, I send an angel before you, to guard you on the way and to bring you to the place which I have prepared.
Ex. 32:34 [God]: But now go, lead the people to the place of which I have spoken to you; behold, my angel shall go before you.
Ps. 73:2. But as for me, my feet had almost stumbled, my steps had well-nigh slipped.
Ps. 66:8-9. Bless our God...who...has not let our feet slip.
Ps. 121:3. He will not let your foot be moved...

Aber lernt mich auch allhier
But teach me also here

Euer großes Heilig singen
Your great "Sanctus" to-sing

Und dem Höchsten Dank zu singen!
And to-the Most-High thanks to sing!
{And to sing thanks to the Most High!}

6. Soprano Recit. (Loosely based on Picander's poem)
•Angels are our chariot to heaven, let us love them (19-6)
Laßt uns das Angesicht
Let us the countenance

Der frommen Engel lieben
Of devout angels love
{Let us cherish the countenance of devout angels}

Und sie mit unsern Sünden nicht
And them with our sins not

Vertreiben oder auch betrüben.
Drive-away or also grieve.
{And not drive them away or grieve them with our sins.}

So sein sie, wenn der Herr gebeut,
Thus are they, if the Lord (should) command (us)
{Thus, if the Lord should command us}

Der Welt Valet zu sagen,
The world farewell to bid,
{To bid farewell to the world—}

Zu unsrer Seligkeit
To our blessedness—
{They are—to our blessedness—}

Auch unser Himmelswagen.
Also our chariot-to-heaven.

7. Chorale (Unrelated to Picander's poem)
•Prayer: Keep my soul in death until the resurrection (19-7)
Laß dein' Engel mit mir fahren
Let thine angel with me go

Auf Elias Wagen rot
On Elijah's chariot red

Und mein Seele wohl bewahren,
And my soul well protect,

Wie Lazrum nach seinem Tod.
Like Lazarus after his death.
{As they did Lazarus after his death.}

Laß sie ruhn in deinem Schoß,
Let it rest in thy (bosom),

Is. 6:1–3. ...I saw the Lord sitting upon a throne, high and lifted up; and his train filled the temple. Above him stood the seraphim; each had six wings: with two he covered his face, and with two he covered his feet, and with two he flew. And one called to another and said: "Holy, holy, holy is the Lord of hosts; the whole earth is full of his glory."
Rev. 4:8. And the four living creatures, each of them with six wings... day and night they never cease to sing, "Holy, holy, holy, is the Lord God Almighty, who was and is and is to come!"

*Mt. 18:10 [Christ]: ...I tell you that in heaven their angels always behold the face of my Father who is in heaven.
Ex. 23:20 [God]: Behold, I send an angel before you, to guard you on the way and to bring you to the place which I have prepared.
Ps. 91:11. [The Lord] will give his angels charge of you to guard you in all your ways. (Also Mt. 4:6, Lk. 4:10.)
Heb. 3:15. ...Today, when you hear his voice, do not harden your hearts as in the rebellion. (Also Heb. 3:8, 4:6–11.)
Eph. 4:30. Do not grieve the Holy Spirit of God, in whom you were sealed for the day of redemption.
Num. 22:31–32. The Lord opened the eyes of Balaam, and he saw the angel of the Lord standing in the way, with his drawnsword in his hand; and he bowed his head, and fell on his face. And the angel of the Lord said to him, "...Behold, I have come forth to withstand you, because your way is perverse before me." (Also 2 Pet. 2:15–16.)
Ex. 23:20 [God]: ...I send an angel...to bring you to the place which I have prepared.
2 Tim. 4:6–8. ...The time of my departure has come. I have fought the good fight, I have finished the race, I have kept the faith. Henceforth there is laid up for me the crown of righteousness, which the Lord, the righteous judge, will award to me on that Day, and not only to me but also to all who have loved his appearing.
2 Kings 2:11–12. And as [Elijah and Elisha] still went on and talked, behold, a chariot of fire and horses of fire separated the two of them. And Elijah went up by a whirlwind into heaven. And Elisha saw it and he cried, "My father, my father! the chariots of Israel and its horsemen!" And he saw him no more.

Lk. 16:19–25. There was a rich man, who was clothed in purple and fine linen and who feasted sumptuously every day. And at his gate lay a poor man named Lazarus, full of sores, who desired to be fed with what fell from the rich man's table; moreover the dogs came and licked his sores. The poor man died and was carried by the angels to Abraham's bosom. The rich man also died and was buried; and in Hades, being in torment, he lifted up his eyes, and saw Abraham far off and Lazarus in his bosom. And he called out, "Father Abraham, have mercy upon me, and send Lazarus to dip the end of his finger in water and cool my tongue; for I am in anguish in this flame." But Abraham said, "Son, remember that you in your lifetime received your good things, and Lazarus in like manner evil things; but now he is comforted here, and you are in anguish."
Rom. 8:23. We ourselves, who have the first fruits of the Spirit, groan inwardly as we wait for adoption as sons, the redemption of our bodies.

Erfüll sie mit Freud und Trost,
Fill it with happiness and comfort,

Bis der Leib kommt aus der Erde
Until (my) body comes out-of the earth

Und mit ihr vereinigt werde.
And with it (re)united be.

BWV 20
O Ewigkeit, du Donnerwort II
(NBA I/15; BC A95)

1. S. after Trinity (BWV 75, 20, 39)
*1 Jn. 4:16–21 (God is love; we ought also to love)
*Lk. 16:19–31 (Parable of rich man and Lazarus)
Librettist: Unknown. This work begins Bach's cycle of chorale cantatas.

Part I

1. Chorus (Chorale Vs. 1) (See also 60-1.)
●Eternity is a thunderous word that frightens me! (20-1)
O Ewigkeit, du Donnerwort,
O eternity, thou thund'rous-word,

O Schwert, das durch die Seele bohrt,
O sword, which through (one's) soul pierces,

O Anfang sonder Ende!
O beginning without end!

O Ewigkeit, Zeit ohne Zeit,
O eternity, time without time,

Ich weiß vor großer Traurigkeit
I know because-of (my) great sadness
{Because of my great sadness I do not know}

Nicht, wo ich mich hinwende.
Not, where I - (might) turn-to.
{Where to turn.}

Mein ganz erschrocken Herz erbebt,
My completely frightened heart quakes (so much),

Daß mir die Zung am Gaumen klebt.
That - (my) tongue to (my) palate sticks.
{That my tongue sticks to my palate.}

2. Tenor Recit. (Based on Chorale Vs. 2)
●Eternal damnation is like nothing on earth (20-2)
Kein Unglück ist in aller Welt zu finden,
No misfortune is in all-the world to be-found,

Das ewig dauernd sei:
That ever-lasting is:
{That is everlasting:}

1 Cor. 15:42, 44, 52–53. So it is with the resurrection of the dead. What is sown is perishable, what is raised is imperishable...It is sown a physical body, it is raised a spiritual body...For the trumpet will sound, and the dead will be raised imperishable, and we shall be changed. For this perishable nature must put on the imperishable, and this mortal nature must put on immortality.

*Lk. 16:22–24. ...The rich man also died and was buried; and in Hades, being in torment, he lifted up his eyes, and saw Abraham far off and Lazarus in his bosom. And he called out, "Father Abraham, have mercy upon me, and send Lazarus to dip the end of his finger in water and cool my tongue; for I am in anguish in this flame."
Rev. 14:10–11. ...[The damned] shall be tormented with fire and sulphur in the presence of the holy angels and in the presence of the Lamb. And the smoke of their torment goes up for ever and ever...
Ps. 90:2, 4. [O Lord,] ...from everlasting to everlasting thou art God... For a thousand years in thy sight are but as yesterday when it is past, or as a watch in the night.
2 Pet. 3:8. Do not ignore this one fact, beloved, that with the Lord one day is as a thousand years, and a thousand years as one day.
Rev. 1:8. "I am the Alpha and the Omega (Luther: das A und das O, der Anfang und das Ende)," says the Lord God, who is and who was and who is to come, the Almighty.
Rev. 22:13. I am the Alpha and the Omega, the first and the last, the beginning and the end. (Also Rev. 21:6.)
Heb. 4:12. The word of God is living and active, sharper than any two-edged sword (Luther: Schwert), piercing to the division of soul and spirit, of joints and marrow...
Ps. 22:14–15. I am poured like water, and all my bones are out of joint; my heart is like wax, it is melted within my breast; my strength is dried up like a potsherd, and my tongue cleaves to my jaws (Luther: Gaumen); thou dost lay me in the dust of death. (Also Job 29:10.)
*1 Jn. 4:17–18. In this is love perfected with us, that we may have confidence for the day of judgment... There is no fear in love, but perfect love casts out fear. For fear has to do with punishment, and he who fears is not perfected in love.

Ecc. 8:6. Every matter has its time and way, although man's trouble lies heavy upon him. (Also Ecc. 3:1.)
2 Cor. 4:18. ...The things that are seen are transient, but the things that are unseen are eternal.
Mt. 24:35. [Even] heaven and earth will pass away...
Rev. 14:11. ...[But] the smoke of their torment goes up for ever and ever...

Es   muß   doch   endlich   mit   der Zeit
(Each)   must   indeed   ultimately   in   (the course of) - time

               einmal   verschwinden.
               (eventually)   vanish.

Ach! aber ach! die Pein der Ewigkeit hat nur kein Ziel;
Ah! but ah! The pain of eternity has just no end;

Sie   treibet   fort   und   fort   ihr   Marterspiel,
It   (goes)   on   and   on   (with)   its   torturous-drama,

Ja, wie selbst Jesus spricht,
Yes, as even Jesus says,

Aus ihr   ist kein Erlösung nicht.
From it (there) is   no   redmption   - .

3. **Tenor Aria** (Based on Chorale Vs. 3)
●Eternal flames of hell are no frivolous matter (20–3)
Ewigkeit, du   machst mir bange,
Eternity, thou dost-make me anxious,

Ewig,   ewig ist zu lange!
Forever, forever is too long!

Ach, hier   gilt fürwahr (k)ein Scherz.
Ah, (this) allows truly   no   (joking).
{Ah, this truly allows for no joking.}

Flammen, die   auf ewig brennen,
Flames,   which   for-ever   burn,

Ist kein Feuer gleich zu nennen;
Are no   fire   similar to   name;
{Have no equal;}

Es   erschrickt   und   bebt mein Herz,
(Now)   becomes-alarmed and   trembles my   heart,
{My heart becomes alarmed and trembles,}

Wenn ich diese Pein bedenke
When I   this   pain consider
{When I consider this pain}

Und den Sinn zur Höllen lenke.
And (my) mind to   hell   direct.
{And turn my thoughts to the reality of hell.}

4. **Bass Recit.** (Based on Chorale Vss. 5–6 of 16 stanzas[1])
●Damnation that never ends: attempts to imagine it (20–4)
     Gesetzt,   es dau'rte der Verdammten Qual
(Even) supposing, (now) lasted   the   damned-ones' torture
{Even supposing the torture of the damned lasted}

*Lk. 16:24–26. [The rich man] called out, "Father Abraham, have mercy upon me...for I am in anguish in this flame." But Abraham said, "Son, remember that you in your lifetime received your good things, and Lazarus in like manner evil things; but now he is comforted here, and you are in anguish. And besides all this, between us and you a great chasm has been fixed, in order that those who would pass from here to you may not be able, and none may cross from there to us."
Mk. 9:47–48. If your eye causes you to sin, pluck it out; it is better for you to enter the kingdom of God with one eye than with two eyes to be thrown into hell, where their worm does not die, and the fire is not quenched. (Also Mt. 10:28.)
2 Pet. 2:4, 9. If God did not spare the angels when they sinned, but cast them into hell and committed them to pits of nether gloom to be kept until the judgment...then the Lord knows how to rescue the godly from trial, and to keep the unrighteous under punishment until the day of judgment. (Also Jude 1:6, Rev. 14:9–11, Rev. 20:1–2, 10.)
*Lk. 16:26. ...Those who would pass from here to you may not be able, and none may cross from there to us.

Mt. 10:28. Do not fear those who kill the body but cannot kill the soul; rather fear him who can destroy both soul and body in hell.
Rev. 14:9–11. If any one worships the beast and its image, and receives a mark on his forehead or on his hand, he also shall drink the wine of God's wrath, poured unmixed into the cup of his anger, and he shall be tormented with fire and sulphur in the presence of the holy angels and in the presence of the Lamb. And the smoke of their torment goes up for ever and ever; and they have no rest, day or night...
Mt. 25:41. Then [God] will say to those at his left hand, "Depart from me, you cursed, into the eternal fire prepared for the devil and his angels."
Jude 1:6–7. The angels that did not keep their own position but left their proper dwelling have been kept by him in eternal chains in the nether gloom until the judgment of the great day. Just as Sodom and Gomorrah and the surrounding cities, which likewise acted immorally and indulged in unnatural lust, serve as an example by undergoing a punishment of eternal fire.
Is. 34:9–10. The streams of Edom shall be turned into pitch, and her soil into brimstone; her land shall become burning pitch. Night and day it shall not be quenched; its smoke shall go up for ever.
Rev. 19:3. ...The smoke from her goes up for ever and ever.
Mt. 18:8–9. ...It is better for you to enter life maimed or lame than with two hands or two feet to be thrown into the eternal fire...It is better for you to enter life with one eye than with two eyes to be thrown into the hell of fire.
Mk. 9:47–48. And if your eye causes you to sin, pluck it out; it is better for you to enter the kingdom of God with one eye than with two eyes to be thrown into hell, where their worm does not die, and the fire is not quenched.

2 Pet. 3:8. Do not ignore this one fact, beloved, that with the Lord one day is as a thousand years, and a thousand years as one day.

---

[1]The chorale by Johann Rist (1642) was printed in both 12- and 16-stanza versions. See Dürr, *Die Kantaten*, p. 440.

So viele Jahr, als an der Zahl
As many years, as in the sum
{As many years as there were in the sum}

Auf Erden Gras, am Himmel Sterne wären;
On earth (blades) of-grass, (as) in heaven stars were;
{Of blades of grass on earth, or stars in heaven;}

Gesetzt, es sei die Pein so weit hinaus gestellt,
(Even) supposing, - were the pain so long spread-out,
{Even supposing the pain were stretched out as long}

Als Menschen in der Welt
As (there) people in the world
{As a line of all the people who have been in the world}

Von Anbeginn gewesen,
From (the) earliest-beginning have-been,
{From the earliest beginning,}

So wäre doch zuletzt
So were nevertheless finally

Derselben Ziel und Maß gesetzt:
Its end and measure fixed:
{So were its end and measure still fixed in the end:}

Sie müßte doch einmal aufhören.
It would indeed one-day (have-to) cease.

Nun aber, wenn du die Gefahr,
Now however, when you the peril,
{Now however, when you have endured the peril,}

Verdammter! tausend Millionen Jahr
O-Damned-one, a-thousand million years

Mit allen Teufeln ausgestanden,
With all-the devils (have) endured,
{With all the devils,}

So ist doch nie der Schluß vorhanden;
So is still ne'er the end at-hand;
{So is the end still ne'er at hand;}

Die Zeit, so niemand zählen kann,
The time-span, which no-one can-reckon,

Fängt jeden Augenblick
Begins each moment—

Zu deiner Seelen ewgem Ungelück
To your soul's eternal distress—

Sich stets von neuem an.
- Continually - anew - .

Ps. 90:2, 4. [O Lord,] before the mountains were brought forth, or ever thou hadst formed the earth and the world, from everlasting to everlasting thou art God...For a thousand years in thy sight are but as yesterday when it is past, or as a watch in the night.
Ps. 102:25–27. Of old thou didst lay the foundation of the earth, and the heavens are the work of thy hands. They will perish, but thou dost endure; they will all wear out like a garment. Thou changest them like raiment, and they pass away; but thou art the same, and thy years have no end.
Gen. 15:5. And [the Lord] brought [Abraham] outside and said, "Look toward heaven, and number the stars, if you are able to number them ...So shall your descendants be." (Also Gen. 13:16.)
Num. 23:10. Who can count the dust of Jacob, or number the fourth part of Israel?...
Ps. 139:18. If I would count them, they are more than the sand.
Jer. 33:22. As the host of heaven cannot be numbered and the sands of the sea cannot be measured...
Job 38:37. Who can number the clouds by wisdom?
Sirach (Apocrypha) 1:2. The sand of the sea, the drops of rain, and the days of eternity—who can count them?
Ecc. 3:1. For everything there is a season, and a time for every matter under heaven.
Acts 17:26. [God] made from one every nation of men to live on all the face of the earth, having determined allotted periods and the boundaries of their habitation. (See also Ps. 74:16, Deut. 32:8.)
Rev. 10:5–6. The angel whom I saw standing on sea and land lifted up his right hand to heaven and swore...that there should be no more delay (Luther: das hinfort keine Zeit [= time] mehr sein soll).
Mt. 25:41. Then [the Lord] will say to those at his left hand, "Depart from me, you cursed, into the eternal fire prepared for the devil and his angels."
2 Pet. 2:4, 9. If God did not spare the angels when they sinned, but cast them into hell and committed them to pits of nether gloom to be kept until the judgment...then the Lord knows how to rescue the godly from trial, and to keep the unrighteous under punishment until the day of judgment. (Also Rev. 14:9–11.)
Jude 1:6–7. The angels that did not keep their own position but left their proper dwelling have been kept by him in eternal chains in the nether gloom until the judgment of the great day. Just as Sodom and Gomorrah and the surrounding cities, which likewise acted immorally and indulged in unnatural lust, serve as an example by undergoing a punishment of eternal fire.
Rev. 20:1–3, 7–10. I saw an angel coming down from heaven, holding in his hand the key of the bottomless pit and a great chain. And he seized the dragon, that ancient serpent, who is the Devil and Satan, and bound him for a thousand years, and threw him into the pit, and shut it and sealed it over him...till the thousand years were ended...And when the thousand years are ended, Satan will be loosed from his prison and will come out to deceive the nations...And they marched up ...and surrounded the camp of the saints and the beloved city; but fire but fire came down from heaven and consumed them, and the devil who had deceived them was thrown into the lake of fire and sulphur where the beast and the false prophet were, and they will be tormented day and night for ever and ever.
Rev. 19:3. ...The smoke from her goes up for ever and ever.

5. Bass Aria (Based on Chorale Vs. 9 of 16-stanza version)
●God is just: eternal damnation for temporal sin (20-5)
Gott ist gerecht in seinen Werken:
God is just in his deeds:

Auf kurze Sünden dieser Welt
For brief sins of-this world

Hat er **so lange Pein bestellt;**
Has he such lengthy pain appointed;

Ach wollte doch die Welt dies merken!
Ah, would indeed the world this note!
{Ah, would the world indeed take note of this!}

Kurz ist die Zeit, der Tod geschwind,
Short is - time, - death (is) swift,

Bedenke dies, o Menschenkind!
Ponder this, O child-of-mankind!

6. Alto Aria (Based on Chorale Vs. 10 of 16-stanza version)
●Exhortation to flee sin and its judgment (20-6)
O Mensch, errette deine Seele,
O man, deliver your soul,

Entfliehe Satans Sklaverei
Flee Satan's slavery

Und mache dich von Sünden frei,
And make yourself of sins free,
{And free yourself of sin,}

Damit in jener Schwefelhöhle
So-that in yonder cavern-of-brimstone,

Der Tod, so die Verdammten plagt,
- Death, which the damned-ones plagues,
{Death—which torments those who are damned—}

Nicht deine Seele ewig nagt.
Not your soul eternally gnaws.
{Will not eternally gnaw at your soul.}

O Mensch, errette deine Seele!
O man, deliver your soul!

7. Chorale (Vs. 11 of 16-stanza version)
●Eternal torments will end when God ceases to be (20-7)
Solang ein Gott im Himmel lebt
As-long-as a God in heaven lives
{As long as there is a God in heaven}

Ps. 145:17. The Lord is just in all his ways, and kind in all his doings. (Also Rev. 15:3, 16:7.)
Job 8:3. Does God pervert justice? Or does the Almighty pervert the right? (Also Deut. 32:4.)
2 Chron. 19:7. ...There is no perversion of justice with the Lord our God...
Dan. 9:14. Therefore the Lord has kept ready the calamity and has brought it upon us; for the Lord our God is righteous in all the works which he has done...
Ps. 39:4-6. Lord, let me know my end, and what is the measure of my days; let me know how fleeting my life is! Behold, thou hast made my days a few handbreadths, and my lifetime is as nothing in thy sight. Surely every man stands as a mere breath! Surely man goes about as a shadow!...
Rom. 3:5. ...What shall we say? That God is unjust to inflict wrath on us? (I speak in a human way.) By no means! For then how could God judge the world?
Heb. 11:24-26. By faith Moses...refused to be called the son of Pharaoh's daughter, choosing rather to share ill-treatment with the people of God than to enjoy the fleeting pleasures of sin...for he looked to the reward.

Acts 2:40. [Peter]...exhorted [the people], saying, "Save yourselves from this crooked generation."
1 Cor. 6:9-10. Do you not know that the unrighteous will not inherit the kingdom of God? Do not be deceived; neither the immoral, nor idolaters, nor adulterers, nor sexual perverts, nor thieves, nor the greedy, nor drunkards, nor revilers, nor robbers will inherit the kingdom of God.
Jn. 8:34. ...Every one who commits sin is a slave to sin.
Rom. 6:16. ...You are slaves of the one whom you obey, either of sin, which leads to death, or of obedience, which leads to righteousness. (Also Rom. 6:20, 2 Pet. 2:19, 2 Tim. 2:26, Tit. 3:3.)
Col. 3:5-6. Put to death therefore what is earthly in you: fornication, impurity, passion, evil desire, and covetousness, which is idolatry. On account of these the wrath of God is coming...
Gal. 5:21. ...I warn you, as I warned you before, that those who do such things shall not inherit the kingdom of God.
*Lk. 16:27-31. And [the rich man] said, "Then I beg you, father, to send [Lazarus] to my father's house, for I have five brothers, so that he may warn them, lest they also come into this place of torment." But Abraham said, "They have Moses and the prophets; let them hear them." And he said, "No, father Abraham; but if some one goes to them from the dead, they will repent." He said to him, "If they do not hear Moses and the prophets, neither will they be convinced if some one should rise from the dead."
Mt. 3:7-8. When [John] saw many of the Pharisees and Sadducees coming for baptism, he said to them, "You brood of vipers! Who warned you to flee from the wrath to come? Bear fruit that befits repentance." (Also Lk. 3:3-8.)
Gen. 19:17. When the [angels] had brought [Lot and his family] forth, they said, "Flee for your life...lest you be consumed."

Gen. 1:1-2. In the beginning...the Spirit of God was moving (Luther: schwebte) on the face of the waters. (Also 2 Sam. 22:11, Ps. 18:10, 97:2.)
Hab. 1:12. Art thou not from everlasting, O Lord my God...?
Ps. 90:2. ...From everlasting to everlasting thou art God.

Und über alle Wolken schwebt,
And above all clouds hovers,
{Who hovers above the clouds,}

Wird solche Marter währen:
Will such torments last:

Es wird sie plagen Kält und Hitz,
(Then) will them plague cold and heat,
{Cold and heat will plague them there, as well as}

Angst, Hunger, Schrecken, Feu'r und Blitz
Fear, hunger, terror, fire, and lightening;

Und sie doch nicht verzehren.
And them still not consume.
{And still not consume them.}

Denn wird sich enden diese Pein,
For (then) will - end this pain,
{For this pain will end}

Wenn Gott nicht mehr wird ewig sein.
When God no more will eternal be.
{When God is no longer eternal.}

Ps. 102:27. [O Lord,] thou art the same, and thy years have no end.
Rev. 14:11. [So] the smoke of their torment goes up for ever and ever...
Rev. 16:8. [An] angel poured his bowl [of God's wrath] on the sun, and it was allowed to scorch men with fire; men were scorched by the fierce heat...
Rev. 7:15–16. [But the righteous] are...before the throne of God...the sun shall not strike them nor any scorching heat. (Also Ps. 121:5–6.)
Rev. 16:17. [Another] angel poured his bowl into the air, and...there were flashes of lightning, voices, peals of thunder, and a great earthquake such as had never been since men were on the earth, so great was that earthquake.
Ps. 91:7. ...But it will not come near you. You will only look with your eyes and see the recompense of the wicked.
Is. 43:2. ...When you walk through fire you shall not be burned, and the flame shall not consume you.
Dan. 3:20, 22, 24–25. [Nebuchadnezzar] ordered certain mighty men of his army to bind Shadrach, Meshach, and Abednego, and to cast them into the burning fiery furnace...Because...the furnace [was] very hot, the flame of the fire slew those men...Then King Nebuchadnezzar was astonished..."I see four men loose, walking in the midst of the fire and they are not hurt; (Luther: unversehrt) and the appearance of the fourth is like a son of the gods." (Also Ex. 3:2.)
Mk. 9:47–8 [Christ]: ...[Beware lest you be] thrown into hell, where their worm does not die, and the fire is not quenched.
Rev. 19:3. ...The smoke from her goes up for ever and ever.

Part II

8. Bass Aria (Based on Chorale Vs. 13 of 16-stanza version)
●Awake, lost sheep before trumpet of judgment sounds! (20-8)
Wacht auf, wacht auf, verlornen Schafe,
Wake up, wake up, lost sheep,

Ermuntert euch vom Sündenschlafe
Arouse yourselves from sin's-sleep

Und bessert euer Leben bald!
And better your life soon!

Wacht auf, eh die Posaune schallt,
Wake up, ere the trumpet sounds,

Die euch mit Schrecken aus der Gruft
Which you in terror out-of the tomb
{Which calls you in terror out of the tomb}

Zum Richter aller Welt vor das Gerichte ruft!
To-the judge of-all-the world before the tribunal calls!
{Before the tribunal to the judge of all the world!}

Is. 53:6. All we like sheep have gone astray; we have turned every one to his own way... (Also Ps. 119:176, Mt. 18:12.)
Eph. 5:14. Therefore it is said, "Awake, O sleeper, and arise from the dead, and Christ shall give you light." (Is. 60:1)
Mt. 24:42. Watch therefore, for you do not know on what day your Lord is coming.
1 Thess. 5:6. So then let us not sleep, as others do, but let us keep awake and be sober. (Also Rom. 13:11.)
Jer. 26:13. Now therefore amend your ways and your doings, and obey the voice of the Lord your God, and the Lord will repent of the evil which he has pronounced against you.
Mt. 24:31. [The Lord] will send out his angels with a loud trumpet call, and they will gather his elect from the four winds...
1 Thess. 4:16–17. For the Lord himself will descend from heaven with a cry of command, with the archangel's call, and with the sound of the trumpet of God. And the dead in Christ will rise first; then we who are alive, who are left, shall be caught up together with them in clouds to meet the Lord in the air... (Also Mt. 24:31, 1 Cor. 15:51–52.)
2 Tim. 4:1. ...God and Christ Jesus who is to judge the living and the dead... (Also Rom. 14:12, 2 Cor. 5:10, Rev. 20:12.)

9. Alto Recit. (Based on Chorale Vss. 13–14 of 16 stanzas)
●Death always imminent; forsake lusts of the world! (20-9)
Verlaß, o Mensch, die Wollust dieser Welt,
Forsake, O man, the pleasure of-this world,

Pracht, Hoffart, Reichtum, Ehr und Geld;
Pomp, pride, wealth, honor, and money;

1 Jn. 2:15–17. Do not love the world or the things in the world. If any one loves the world, love for the Father is not in him. For all that is in the world, the lust of the flesh and the lust of the eyes and the pride of life, is not of the Father but is of the world. And the world passes away, and the lust of it; but he who does the will of God abides for ever. (Also Jms. 4:4.)

Bedenke doch
Ponder   indeed

In dieser Zeit annoch,
In this time yet,

Da   dir der Baum des Lebens   grünet,
While (for) you the tree of life (is still) green,
{While the tree of life is still green for you,}

Was dir zu deinem Friede dienet!
What - for your peace serves!
{What serves for your peace!}

Vielleicht ist dies der letzte Tag,
Perhaps is this the last day,
{Perhaps this is the last day,}

Kein Mensch weiß, wenn er sterben mag.
No person knows, when he may-die.

Wie leicht, wie bald
How easily, how quickly

Ist mancher tot und kalt!
Is many-a-one dead and cold!

Man kann noch diese Nacht
They (could) even this night

Den Sarg vor deine Türe bringen.
The coffin before your door bring.
{Bring the coffin to your door.}

Drum sei vor allen Dingen
Therefore be, above all things,
{Therefore, above all things, be}

Auf deiner Seelen Heil bedacht!
Of your soul's welfare mindful!
{Mindful of your soul's welfare!}

10. Alto & Tenor Duet (Based on Chorale Vs. 15 of 16)
●World & sin rejected to avoid fate of rich man (20–10)
O Menschenkind,
O child-of-mankind,

Hör auf geschwind,
Cease quickly,

Die Sünd und Welt zu lieben,
 -   Sin and world to love,

Daß nicht die Pein,
That not that pain,

Wo Heulen und Zähnklappen sein,
Where wailing and gnashing-of-teeth are (found),

Jms. 5:1, 5. Come now, you rich, weep and howl for the miseries that are coming upon you...You have lived on the earth in luxury and in pleasure... (Also Ps. 49:12, 16–20.)
Ps. 90:12. [O Lord,] teach us to number our days that we may get a heart of wisdom.
Heb. 3:7–8. Therefore, as the Holy Spirit says, "Today, when you hear his voice, do not harden your hearts as in the rebellion..."
Lk. 19:41–42. And when [Jesus] drew near and saw the city he wept over it, saying, "Would that even today you knew the things that make for peace! (Luther: was zu deinem Frieden dient!)..." (Also Is. 48:18.)
Ecc. 12:1–7. Remember also your Creator in the days of your youth, before the evil days come, and the years draw nigh, when you will say, "I have no pleasure in them"...in the day when the keepers of the house tremble, and the strong men are bent...before the silver cord is snapped, or the golden bowl is broken, or the pitcher is broken at the fountain, or the wheel broken at the cistern, and the dust returns to the earth as it was, and the spirit returns to God who gave it.
Ps. 49:16–20. Be not afraid when one becomes rich, when the glory of his house increases. For when he dies he will carry nothing away; his glory will not go down after him...Though a man gets praise when he does well for himself, he will go to the generation of his fathers, who will never more see the light. Man cannot abide in his pomp, he is like the beasts that perish. (Also Ps. 52:7.)
Ps. 62:9. Men of low estate are but a breath, men of high estate are a delusion; in the balances they go up; they are together lighter than a breath.
Ps. 89:48. What man can live and never see death? Who can deliver his soul from the power of Sheol?
Jms. 4:14–15. You do not know about tomorrow. What is your life? For you are a mist that appears for a little time and then vanishes.
Ps. 102:3. For my days pass away like smoke...
Lk. 12:20–21. But God said to [the rich man], "Fool! This night your soul is required of you; and the things you have prepared, whose will they be?" So is he who lays up treasure for himself, and is not rich toward God.
Mk. 8:36–37. For what does it profit a man, to gain the whole world and forfeit his life? For what can a man give in return for his life? (Luther: damit er seine Seele löse?)

1 Jn. 2:15–17. Do not love the world or the things in the world. If any one loves the world, love for the Father is not in him. For all that is in the world, the lust of the flesh and the lust of the eyes and the pride of life, is not of the Father but is of the world. And the world passes away, and the lust of it; but he who does the will of God abides for ever.
Jms. 4:4. Unfaithful creatures! Do you not know that friendship with the world is enmity with God? Therefore whoever wishes to be a friend of the world makes himself an enemy of God.
Mt. 6:24. No one can serve two masters; for either he will hate the one and love the other, or he will be devoted to the one and despise the other. You cannot serve God and mammon. (Also Lk. 16:13.)
Ps. 52:7. See the man who would not make God his refuge, but trusted in the abundance of his riches, and sought refuge in his wealth!

Dich ewig   mag betrüben!
You eternally may   grieve!

Ach   spiegle dich   am reichen Mann,
Ah see-your-reflection in-the rich   man,

Der in der   Qual
Who in that torment

Auch nicht einmal
Even not   once
{Not even once}

Ein Tröpflein   Wasser haben kann!
A   droplet (of) water   may-have!

11. Chorale (Vs. 16 of 16-stanza version)
●Eternity is a frightening word, receive me Jesus! (20–11)
O Ewigkeit, du   Donnerwort,
O eternity, thou thund'rous-word,

O Schwert, das durch   die   Seele bohrt,
O sword, which through (one's) soul pierces,

O Anfang sonder Ende!
O beginning without end!

O Ewigkeit, Zeit ohne Zeit,
O eternity, time without time,

Ich weiß   vor   großer Traurigkeit
I know on-account-of great   sadness
{Because of my great sadness I do not know}

Nicht, wo ich mich   hinwende.
Not, where I   - (might) turn-to.
{Where to turn.}

Nimm du mich, wenn es dir gefällt,
Take thou me,   if it thee pleases,
{Take thou me, if it pleases thee,}

Herr Jesu, in dein Freudenzelt!
Lord Jesus, into thy   tent-of-joy!

Mt. 8:12. ...[They] will be thrown into the outer darkness; there men will weep and gash their teeth.
Mt. 13:41–42. The Son of man will send his angels, and they will gather out of his kingdom all causes of sin and all evildoers, and throw them into the furnace of fire; there men will weep and gnash their teeth. (Also Mt. 13:50, 22:13, 24:51, 25:30, Lk. 13:28.)
***Lk. 16:24–26.** And [the rich man] called out, "Father Abraham, have mercy upon me, and send Lazarus to dip the end of his finger in water and cool my tongue; for I am in anguish in this flame." But Abraham said, "Son, remember that you in your lifetime received your good things, and Lazarus in like manner evil things; but now he is comforted here, and you are in anguish. And besides all this, between us and you a great chasm has been fixed, in order that those who would pass from here to you may not be able, and none may cross from there to us."

Job 37:5. God thunders wondrously with his voice; he does great things which we cannot comprehend.
Ps. 90:2, 4. [O Lord,] before the mountains were brought forth, or ever thou hadst formed the earth and the world, from everlasting to everlasting thou art God...For a thousand years in thy sight are but as yesterday when it is past, or as a watch in the night.
2 Pet. 3:8. Do not ignore this one fact, beloved, that with the Lord one day is as a thousand years, and a thousand years as one day.
Rev. 1:8. "I am the Alpha and the Omega," (Luther: das A und das O, der Anfang und das Ende) says the Lord God, who is and who was and who is to come, the Almighty.
Rev. 22:13. I am the Alpha and the Omega, the first and the last, the beginning and the end. (Also Rev. 21:6.)
Is. 57:15. ...the high and lofty One who inhabits eternity, whose name is Holy...
Heb. 4:12. The word of God is living and active, sharper than any two-edged sword (Luther: Schwert), piercing to the division of soul and spirit, of joints and marrow, and discerning the thoughts and intentions of the heart.
Is. 45:22 [God]: Turn to me and be saved all the ends of the earth! For I am God, and there is no other.
Acts 7:59. And as they were stoning Stephen, he prayed, "Lord Jesus, receive my spirit."
Ps. 16:11. [O Lord,] thou dost show me the path of life; in thy presence there is fulness of joy, in thy right hand are pleasures for evermore.

BWV 21
Ich hatte viel Bekümmernis
(NBA I/16; BC A99a-c)

3. S. after Trinity or *"per ogni tempo"* (for any time) (BWV 21, 135)
*1 Pet. 5:6–11 (Cast all your cares on God)
*Lk. 15:1–10 (Parable of the lost sheep and lost coin)
Librettist: perhaps Salomon Franck. Mvts. 3–9 perhaps based on chorale by Johann Rist: **Jammer hat mich ganz umgeben** (1642). This cantata was probably revised one or more times.

Part I

1. Sinfonia

2. Chorus
●God comforted me in my grief: Ps. 94:19 (21-2)
Ich hatte viel Bekümmernis in meinem Herzen;
I had much grief in my heart;

aber deine Tröstungen erquicken meine Seele.
but thy consolations revive my soul.

3. Soprano Aria
●Lamentation: Sighings, tears, etc. fill my days (21-3)
Seufzer, Tränen, Kummer, Not,
Sighings, tears, care, need,

Ängstlichs Sehnen, Furcht und Tod
Anxious yearning, fear, and death

Nagen mein beklemmtes Herz
Gnaw (at) my oppressed heart

Ich empfinde Jammer, Schmerz.
I experience misery (and) suffering.

4. Tenor Recit.
●Prayer: God, why have you turned from me? (21-4)
Wie hast du dich, mein Gott,
(Why) hast thou - , (O) my God,

In meiner Not,
In my distress,

In meiner Furcht und Zagen
In my fear and trepidation,

Denn ganz von mir gewandt?
Then completely (away) from me turned?
{Then completely turned away from me in my distress, in my fear and trepidation?}

Ach! kennst du nicht dein Kind?
Ah! Knowest thou not thy child?
{Ah! Dost thou not recognize thy child?}

*1 Pet. 5:7. Cast all your anxieties on him, for he cares about you.
Ps. 94:19. *When the cares of my heart are many, thy consolations cheer my soul.* (Also Ps. 23:3, 119:25.)
Is. 57:15. Thus says the high and lofty One who inhabits eternity, whose name is Holy: "I dwell in the high and holy place, and also with him who is of a contrite and humble spirit, to revive the spirit of the humble, and to revive the heart of the contrite."
Is. 66:13 [God]: As one whom his mother comforts, so I will comfort you; you shall be comforted in Jerusalem.

Job 30:16–17. ...My soul is poured out within me; days of affliction have taken hold of me. The night racks my bones, and the pain that gnaws me takes no rest.
Ps. 6:6–7. I am weary with my moaning; every night I flood my bed with tears; I drench my couch with my weeping. My eye wastes away because of grief, it grows weak because of all my foes. (Also Jer. 45:3.)
Jer. 45:3. Woe is me! for the Lord has added sorrow (Luther: Jammer) to my pain (Luther: Schmerz); I am weary with my groaning (Luther: ich seufze mich müde), and I find no rest.
Ps. 31:9–10. ...I am in distress; my eye is wasted from grief, my soul and my body also. For my life is spent with sorrow, and my years with sighing; my strength fails because of my misery, and my bones waste away. (Also Ps. 13:2, 38:3.)

Judges 6:13. And Gideon said to him, "Pray, sir, if the Lord is with us, why then has all this befallen us? And where are all his wonderful deeds which our fathers recounted to us...? But now the Lord has cast us off..."
Ps. 22:1–2. My God, my God, why hast thou forsaken me? Why art thou so far from helping me, from the words of my groaning? O my God, I cry by day, but thou dost not answer; and by night, but find no rest.
Mt. 27:46. [As he hung on the cross, at] about the ninth hour Jesus cried with a loud voice, "Eli, Eli, lama sabachthani?" that is, "My God, my God, why hast thou forsaken me?"
Ps. 42:9. I say to God, my rock: "Why hast thou forgotten me?"
Ps. 10:1. Why dost thou stand afar off, O Lord? Why dost thou hide thyself in times of trouble?
Ps. 42:3. My tears have been my food day and night, while men say to me continually, "Where is your God?"
Ex. 32:11–13. Moses besought the Lord his God, and said, "O Lord, why does thy wrath burn hot against thy people, whom thou hast brought forth out of the land of Egypt with great power and with a mighty hand? Why should the Egyptians say, 'With evil intent did he

Ach! hörst du nicht das Klagen
Ah! Hearest thou not the lamentation

Von denen, die dir sind
Of those, who (to) thee are
{Of those, who are related to thee}

Mit Bund und Treu verwandt?
By covenant and fidelity related?
{By covenant and fidelity?}

Du warest meine Lust
Thou wast my delight

Und bist mir grausam worden;
And (now) art to-me cruel become;
{And art now become cruel to me;}

Ich suche dich an allen Orten,
I seek thee in all places,
{I seek thee everywhere,}

Ich ruf und schrei dir nach,
I call and cry thee after,
{I call and cry after thee,}

Allein: mein Weh und Ach!
But my "Woe and Ah"

Scheint itzt, als sei es dir ganz unbewußt.
Seems now, as were it (to) thee completely unknown.
{Now seems as if it were completely unknown to thee.}

5. Tenor Aria
●Waves of affliction overwhelm my boat (21-5)
Bäche von gesalznen Zähren,
Streams of salted tears,

Fluten rauschen stets einher.
Torrents rush continually along.

Sturm und Wellen mich versehren,
Storm and waves me disable,
{Storm and waves disable me,}

Und dies trübsalsvolle Meer
And this tribulation-filled sea

Will mir Geist und Leben schwächen,
Would (my) spirit and life weaken;

Mast und Anker wollen brechen,
Mast and anchor would break,
{Mast and anchor are near breaking,}

Hier versink ich in den Grund,
Here sink I (to) the bottom,

Dort seh in der Hölle Schlund.
There see (I) into - hell's gorge.

bring them forth, to slay them in the mountains, and to consume them from the face of the earth'? Turn from thy fierce wrath, and repent of this evil against thy people. Remember Abraham, Isaac, and Israel, thy servants, to whom thou didst swear by thine own self, and didst say to them, 'I will multiply your descendants as the stars of heaven, and all this land that I have promised I will give to your descendants, and they shall inherit it for ever.'"
Is. 64:8–9. ...O Lord, thou art our Father; we are the clay, and thou art our potter; we are all the work of thy hand. Be not exceedingly angry, O Lord, and remember not iniquity for ever. Behold, consider, we are all thy people.
Deut. 7:9. Know therefore that the Lord your God is God, the faithful God who keeps covenant and steadfast love with those who love him and keep his commandments, to a thousand generations. (Also Is. 61:8, Jer. 33:20–21.)
Lam. 5:20–22. Why dost thou forget us for ever, why dost thou so long forsake us? Restore us to thyself, O Lord, that we may be restored! Or hast thou utterly rejected us? Art thou exceedingly angry with us?
Job 30:19–21. God has cast me into the mire, and I have become like dust and ashes. I cry to thee and thou dost not answer me; I stand, and thou dost not heed me. Thou hast turned cruel (Luther: einen Grausamen) to me; with the might of thy hand thou dost persecute me.
S. of S. 3:1 [Bride]: Upon my bed by night I sought him whom my soul loves; I sought him, but found him not; I called him, but he gave no answer. (Also S. of S. 5:6.)
Ps. 39:12. Hear my prayer, O Lord, and give ear to my cry; hold not thy peace at my tears!...
Hab. 1:2. O Lord, how long shall I cry for help, and thou wilt not hear? Or cry to thee "Violence!" and thou wilt not save? (Also Ps. 6:2–4, 6–7, Ps. 13:1–3, 5, 86:3, 88:1, 89:46, 90:13–15, Is. 38:13.)

Ps. 6:6–7. I am weary with my moaning; every night I flood my bed with tears; I drench my couch with my weeping. My eye wastes away because of grief, it grows weak because of all my foes. (Also Jer. 45:3.)
Ps. 42:3. My tears have been my food day and night, while men say to me continually, "Where is your God?"
Ps. 69:1–3, 13–15. Save me, O God! For the waters have come up to my neck. I sink in deep mire, where there is no foothold; I have come into deep waters, and the flood sweeps over me. I am weary with my crying; my throat is parched. My eyes grow dim with waiting for my God... With thy faithful help rescue me from sinking in the mire; let me be delivered from my enemies and from the deep waters. Let not the flood sweep over me, or the deep swallow me up, or the pit close its mouth over me.
Jonah 2:3. For thou didst cast me into the deep, into the heart of the seas, and the flood was round about me; all thy waves and thy billows passed over me.
Ps. 124:1, 4–5. If it had not been the Lord who was on our side...then the flood would have swept us away, the torrent would have gone over us, then over us would have gone the raging waters.
Is. 5:14. Therefore Sheol has enlarged its appetite (Luther: die Seele weit aufgesperrt; later version has: Schlund weit aufgesperrt) and opened its mouth beyond measure (Luther: Rachen aufgetan ohne alle Maß)...

6. Chorus

●Exhortation to soul: Why are you cast down? Ps. 42:12 (21-6)

Was betrübst du   dich, meine Seele, und bist
Why grievest thou thyself, my   soul,   and art

so unruhig   in   mir? Harre auf Gott; denn ich
so restless within me? Wait upon God;   for I

werde ihm noch danken, daß er meines Angesichtes
will   him yet thank, that he   my   countenance's

Hülfe und mein Gott ist.
help and   my   God is.

Ps. 42:5/11/43:5. *Why are you cast down, O my soul, and why are you disquieted within me? Hope in God; for I shall again praise him, my help and my God.*
Lam. 3:24. "The Lord is my portion," says my soul, "therefore I will hope in him."
Ps. 124:8. Our help is in the name of the Lord, who made heaven and earth.
Ps. 27:13-14. I believe that I shall see the goodness of the Lord in the land of the living! Wait for the Lord; be strong, and let your heart take courage; yea, wait for the Lord!
Ps. 31:24. Be strong, and let your heart take courage, all you who wait for the Lord! (Also 37:7, 9, 34, 38:15, 39:7, 130:5-7, Is. 8:17, 33:2, Lam. 3:25-26, Mic. 7:7.)

Part II

7. Soprano & Bass Recit.

●Dialogue (Christ & Believer): Fear vs. comfort (21-7)

Ach Jesu, meine Ruh,
Ah Jesus, my repose,

Mein Licht, wo bleibest du?
My   light, where stayest thou?

O Seele sieh! Ich bin bei dir.
O Soul look! I   am with thee.

Bei mir?
With me?

Hier ist ja   lauter Nacht.
Here is indeed nought-but night.

Ich bin dein treuer Freund,
I   am thy faithful friend,

Der auch im Dunkeln wacht,
Who also in-the darkness keeps-watch,
{Who also keeps watch in the darkness,}

Wo   lauter Schalken seind.
Where nought-but rogues   are (to be found).

Brich doch mit deinem Glanz und Licht des Trostes ein.
Break please with thy radiance and light of comfort in.
{Please break in with thy radiance and light.}

Die Stunde kömmet schon,
The hour   comes already,

Da deines Kampfes Kron
When thy   battle's crown

Dir wird ein süßes Labsal sein.
(For) thee will a sweet refreshment be.
(Will be a sweet refreshment for thee.}

Mt. 11:28-29 [Christ]: Come to me, all who labor and are heavy laden, and I will give you rest. Take my yoke upon you, and learn from me; for I am gentle and lowly in heart, and you will find rest for your souls.
***1 Pet. 5:7.** Cast all your anxieties on him, for he cares about you. (Also Phil. 4:6.)
Jn. 8:12. Again Jesus spoke to them, saying, "I am the light of the world; he who follows me will not walk in darkness, but will have the light of life." (Also Jn. 1:4, 9:5, 11:9, 12:46, Ps. 27:1, 36:9.)
S. of S. 3:1 [Bride]: Upon my bed by night I sought him whom my soul loves; I sought him, but found him not; I called him, but he gave no answer. (Also S. of S. 5:6.)
Mt. 28:20 [Christ]: ...Lo, I am with you always, to the close of the age.
Job 7:3. I am allotted months of emptiness, and nights of misery are apportioned to me.
Ps. 121:3-4. ...He who keeps you will not slumber. Behold, he who keeps Israel will neither slumber nor sleep.
Ps. 139:12. [O Lord,] even the darkness is not dark to thee, the night is bright as the day; for darkness is as light with thee.
1 Thess. 5:5, 7. You are all sons of light and sons of the day; we are not of the night or of darkness...For those who sleep sleep at night, and those who get drunk are drunk at night.
Is. 60:19-20. The sun shall be no more your light by day, nor for brightness shall the moon give light to you by night; but the Lord will be your everlasting light, and your everlasting God will be your glory. Your sun shall no more go down, nor your moon withdraw itself; for the Lord will be your everlasting light, and your days of mourning shall be ended. (Also Is. 9:2, 60:1.)
Ps. 97:11. Light dawns for the righteous, and joy for the upright in heart.
***1 Pet. 5:10.** And after you have suffered a little while, the God of all grace, who has called you to his eternal glory in Christ, will himself restore, establish, and strengthen you.
2 Tim. 4:6-8. ...The time of my departure has come. I have fought the good fight, I have finished the race, I have kept the faith. Henceforth there is laid up for me the crown of righteousness... (Also Jms. 1:12.)
Rev. 2:10 [Christ]: Do not fear what you are about to suffer...Be faithful unto death, and I will give you the crown of life.

8. Soprano & Bass Duet

●Dialogue (Christ & Believer): Despair vs. comfort (21-8)

Believer:
Komm, mein Jesu, und erquicke
Come, my Jesus, and revive

    Christ:
    Ja, ich komme und erquicke
    Yes, I come and revive

Und erfreu mit deinem Blicke!
And gladden with thy glance!

    Dich mit meinem Gnadenblicke.
    Thee with my glance-of-grace.

Diese Seele,
This soul,

    Deine Seele,
    Thy soul,

Die soll sterben
It shall die

    Die soll leben
    It shall live

Und nicht leben
And not live

    Und nicht sterben
    And not die

Und in ihrer Unglückshöhle
And in its cavern-of-misfortune

    Hier aus dieser Wunden Höhle
    Here out-of this wound's-hollow

Ganz verderben.
Completely be-ruined.

    Sollst du erben
    Shalt thou inherit

Ich muß stets in Kummer schweben,
I must continually in care hover,

    Heil durch diesen Saft der Reben.
    Salvation through this juice of-the vine.

Ja, ach ja, ich bin verloren!
Yes, ah yes, I am lost!

    Nein, ach nein, du bist erkoren!
    No, ah no, thou art chosen!

Nein, ach nein, du hassest mich!
No, ah no, thou hatest me!

*1 Pet. 5:7. Cast all your anxieties on him, for he cares about you. (Also Phil. 4:6.)

Ps. 119:25, 28, 81, 107, 116. [O Lord,] my soul cleaves to the dust; revive me (Luther: erquicke mich) according to thy word!...My soul melts away for sorrow; strengthen me according to thy word!...My soul languishes for thy salvation; I hope in thy word...I am sorely afflicted; give me life, O Lord, according to thy word!...Uphold me according to thy promise, that I may live, and let me not be put to shame in my hope!

Rev. 22:20. He who testifies to these things says, "Surely I am coming soon." Amen. Come, Lord Jesus!

Rev. 3:11 [Christ]: I am coming soon; hold fast what you have, so that no one may seize your crown.

Jer. 31:25 [God]: For I will satisfy the weary soul, and every languishing soul I will replenish.

Ps. 34:5. Look to him, and be radiant; so your faces shall never be ashamed.

Ps. 116:3. The snares of death encompassed me; the pangs of Sheol laid hold on me; I suffered distress and anguish. (Also 2 Sam. 22:5-6, Ps. 18:4-5.)

Ps. 30:9-10. What profit is there in my death, if I go down to the Pit? Will the dust praise thee? Will it tell of thy faithfulness? Hear, O Lord, and be gracious to me! O Lord, be thou my helper!

Ps. 55:4-5. My heart is in anguish within me, the terrors of death have fallen upon me. Fear and trembling come upon me, and horror overwhelms me. (Also Job 17:13-15, Job 30:23.)

Is. 38:10. ...In the noontide of my days I must depart; I am consigned to the gates of Sheol...I shall look upon man no more among the inhabitants of the world.

Is. 38:1. ...Isaiah the prophet...came to [King Hezekiah], and said to him, "...Set your house in order; for you shall die, you shall not recover (Luther: sterben und nicht lebendig bleiben)."

Ps. 118:17. I shall not die, but I shall live, and recount the deeds of the Lord. (Also Hab. 1:12.)

1 Jn. 5:11. ...God gave us eternal life...in his Son.

Jn. 11:25-26. Jesus said to [Martha], "I am the resurrection and the life; he who believes in me, though he die, yet shall he live, and whoever lives and believes in me shall never die. Do you believe this?" (Also Jn. 14:19.)

Acts 14:22. [But]...through many tribulations we must enter the kingdom of God.

1 Sam. 21:10, 22:1-2. David rose and fled...from [King] Saul...and escaped to the cave (Luther: Höhle) of Adullam...and every one who was in distress, and every one who was in debt, and every one who was discontented, gathered to him...

2 Cor. 1:5. As we share abundantly in Christ's sufferings, so through Christ we share abundantly in comfort too.

Jn. 20:27. [Jesus] said to Thomas, "Put your finger here, and see my hands; and put out your hand, and place it in my [wound's hollow]; do not be faithless, but believing."

1 Pet. 2:24. He himself bore our sins in his body on the tree, that we might die to sin and live to righteousness. By his wounds you have been healed. (Also Is. 53:5.)

Mt. 26:27-29. And [Jesus] took a cup, and when he had given thanks he gave it to them, saying, "Drink of it, all of you; for this is my blood of the covenant, which is poured out for many for the forgiveness of sins. I tell you I shall not drink again of this fruit of the vine until that day when I drink it new with you in my Father's kingdom."

Eph. 1:7. In him we have redemption through his blood...

Jn. 15:16 [Christ]: You did not choose me, but I chose you...

Ja, ach ja, ich liebe dich!
Yes, ah yes, I love thee!

Ach, Jesu,   durchsüße   mir Seele und Herze!
Ah, Jesus, thoroughly-sweeten (my) soul and heart!

Entweichet, ihr Sorgen, verschwinde, du Schmerze!
Vanish,   ye cares,   disappear,   thou sorrow!

1 Thess. 1:4. For we know, brethren beloved by God, that he has chosen you. (Also Eph. 1:4, Ps. 65:4.)

2 Cor. 1:19-20. The Son of God, Jesus Christ...was not Yes and No; but in him it is always Yes. For all the promises of God find their Yes in him. That is why we utter the Amen through him, to the glory of God.

Rom. 8:35, 37. Who shall separate us from the love of Christ? Shall tribulation, or distress, or persecution, or famine, or nakedness, or peril, or sword?...No, in all these things we are more than conquerors through him who loved us.

9. Chorus & Chorale

●Comfort extended to the soul: Ps. 116:7 (21-9)
Sei nun wieder zufrieden, meine Seele,
Be now again content,   my   soul,

denn der Herr tut   dir Guts.
for   the Lord does to-thee good.

Chorale (Vss. 2 & 5) (See also 93-2 & 93-5.)
Was helfen uns die schweren Sorgen,
What profit us (our) grievous worries?
{What do our grievous worries profit us?}

Was   hilft uns unser Weh und Ach?
What profits us   our   woe and "ah"?
{What does our "Woe" and "Ah" profit us?}

Was hilft es, daß wir alle Morgen
What helps it, that we all mornings
{What does it profit, that each morning we}

Beseufzen unser Ungemach?
Sigh-about   our   hardship?

Wir machen unser Kreuz und Leid
We make   our   cross and sorrow

Nur größer durch die Traurigkeit.
Only greater through -   sadness.

///

Denk nicht in deiner Drangsalshitze,
Think not in   thy   heat-of-affliction,

Daß du von Gott verlassen seist,
That thou by God forsaken art,

Und daß Gott der im Schoße sitze,
And that God him on-his lap   sets,
{And that God him to-his bosom takes,}

Der sich mit stetem Glücke speist.
Who - (on) constant fortune feeds.

Die folgend Zeit verändert viel
The following age changes many-things

Und setzet   jeglichem sein Ziel.
And determines (for) everyone his final-end.

Ps. 116:7-8, 10. *Return, O my soul, to your rest; for the Lord has dealt bountifully with you.* For thou hast delivered my soul from death, my eyes from tears, my feet from stumbling...I kept my faith, even when I said, "I am greatly afflicted".

Ps. 73:14. All the day long I have been stricken, and chastened every morning.

*1 Pet. 5:7. Cast all your anxieties on him, for he cares about you.

Mt. 6:25, 27-32, 34 [Christ]: Therefore I tell you, do not be anxious about your life, what you shall eat or what you shall drink, nor about your body, what you shall put on. Is not life more than food, and the body more than clothing?...And which of you by being anxious can add one cubit to his span of life? And why are you anxious about clothing? Consider the lilies of the field...even Solomon in all his glory was not arrayed like one of these. But if God so clothes the grass of the field... will he not much more clothe you, O men of little faith? Therefore do not be anxious, saying, "What shall we eat?" or "What shall we drink?" or "What shall we wear?" For the Gentiles seek all these things; and your heavenly Father knows that you need them all...Therefore do not be anxious about tomorrow, for tomorrow will be anxious for itself. Let the day's own trouble be sufficient for the day.

Is. 49:14-15. But Zion said, "The Lord has forsaken me, my Lord has forgotten me. Can a woman forget her sucking child, that she should have no compassion on the son of her womb?" Even these may forget, yet I will not forget you.

Heb. 13:5-6. ...He has said, "I will never fail you nor forsake you." (Also Deut. 31:6, 8; Josh. 1:5.)

Lk. 16:19-25. There was a rich man, who was clothed in purple and fine linen and who feasted sumptuously every day. And at his gate lay a poor man named Lazarus...The poor man died and was carried by the angels to Abraham's bosom (Luther: Schoß). The rich man also died and was buried; and in Hades, being in torment, he lifted up his eyes, and saw Abraham far off and Lazarus in his bosom...Abraham said, "Son, remember that you in your lifetime received your good things, and Lazarus in like manner evil things; but now he is comforted here, and you are in anguish..."

Lk. 6:24-25. [Christ]: Woe to you that are rich, for you have received your consolation. Woe to you that are full now, for you shall hunger. Woe to you that laugh now, for you shall mourn and weep.

Mt. 19:30. Many that are first will be last, and the last first.

Mt. 25:46. And they will go away into eternal punishment, but the righteous into eternal life. (Also Dan. 12:2, Rom. 2:7-8.)

10. Tenor Aria

●Sorrow turned to joy; water of weeping into wine (21-10)

Erfreue dich, Seele, erfreue dich, Herze,
Rejoice (O), soul,   rejoice (O), heart,

Entweiche nun, Kummer, verschwinde, du Schmerze!
Vanish   now, care;   disappear, thou sorrow!

Verwandle dich,   Weinen, in lauteren Wein,
Transform thyself, (O) weeping, into pure wine,

Es   wird nun mein ächzen ein Jauchzen mir   sein.
(Now) will now my groaning an   exulting for-me (become).
{My groaning will now become exulting for me.}

Es   brennet und flammet die reineste Kerze
(Now) burns and blazes   the purest candle

Der Liebe, des Trostes in   Seele und Brust,
Of love, of comfort, in (my) soul and breast,

Weil Jesus mich tröstet mit himmlischer Lust.
For Jesus me comforts with heavenly   delight.
{For Jesus comforts me with heavenly delight.}

11. Chorus

●Lamb is worthy to receive all honor: Rev. 5:12-13 (21-11)

Das Lamm, das erwürget ist, ist würdig zu nehmen
The lamb, that   slain (was), is worthy to receive

Kraft und Reichtum und Weisheit und Stärke und
power and wealth   and wisdom and strength and

Ehre und Preis und Lob. Lob und Ehre und Preis und
honor and praise and laud. Laud and honor and praise and

Gewalt sei unserm Gott von Ewigkeit zu Ewigkeit.
might   be to-our God from eternity to eternity.

Amen, alleluja!
Amen, alleluia!

BWV 22
Jesus nahm zu sich die Zwölfe
(NBA I/8; BC A48)

Estomihi (Quinquagesima) (BWV 23, 22, 127, 159)
*1 Cor. 13:1-13 (In praise of love)
*Lk. 18:31-43 (Jesus and the twelve go to Jerusalem, healing of a blind man)
Librettist: Unknown

1. Tenor/Bass Arioso & Chorus

●Jesus foretells his death: Lk. 18:31, 34 (22-1)
Tenor (Evangelist):
Jesus nahm zu sich die Zwölfe und sprach:
Jesus took to himself the twelve and said:

Ps. 126:5-6. May those who sow in tears reap with shouts of joy! He that goes forth weeping, bearing the seed for sowing, shall come home with shouts of joy, bringing his sheaves with him. (Also Jer. 31:13, Ps. 30:11.)

Rev. 7:17. ...And God shall wipe away every tear from their eyes.

Lk. 6:20-23. Blessed are you poor, for yours is the kingdom of God. Blessed are you that hunger now, for you shall be satisfied. Blessed are you that weep now, for you shall laugh. Blessed are you when men hate you, and when they exclude you and revile you, and cast out your name as evil, on account of the Son of man! Rejoice in that day, and leap for joy, for behold, your reward is great in heaven; for so their fathers did to the prophets.

Jn. 2:1-3, 7-10. On the third day there was a marriage at Cana in Galilee, and...Jesus also was invited to the marriage...When the wine gave out...Jesus said to [the servants], "Fill the jars with water." And they filled them up to the brim. He said to them, "Now draw some out, and take it to the steward of the feast." So they took it. When the steward of the feast tasted the water now become wine, and did not know where it came from...[he]...called the bridegroom and said to him, "Every man serves the good wine first...then the poor wine; but you have kept the good wine until now."

Rev. 5:11-14. Then I looked, and I heard around the throne and the living creatures and the elders the voice of many angels, numbering myriads of myriads and thousands of thousands, saying with a loud voice, *"Worthy is the Lamb who was slain, to receive power and wealth and wisdom and might and honor and glory and blessing!"* And I heard every creature in heaven and on earth and under the earth and in the sea, and all therein, saying, *"To him who sits upon the throne and to the Lamb be blessing and honor and glory and might for ever and ever!"* And the four living creatures said, *"Amen!"* and the elders fell down and worshiped.

Rev. 1:5-6. ...To him who loves us and has freed us from our sins by his blood and made us a kingdom, priests to his God and Father, to him be glory and dominion for ever and ever. Amen. (Also 1 Tim. 6:16.)

Lk. 18:31-34. And taking the twelve, [Jesus] said to them, "Behold, we are going up to Jerusalem, and everything that is written of the Son of man by the prophets will be accomplished. For he will be delivered to the Gentiles, and will be mocked and shamefully treated and spit upon; they will scourge him and kill him, and on the third day he will rise." But they understood none of these things; this saying was hid from them, and they did not grasp what was said.

Is. 53:3-7, 10 [Messianic prophecy]. He was despised and rejected by men; a man of sorrows, and acquainted with grief; and as one from whom men hide their faces he was despised, and we esteemed him not. Surely he has borne our griefs and carried our sorrows; yet we

Bass (Christ):
Sehet, wir gehn hinauf gen Jerusalem,
Behold, we are-going up to Jerusalem,

und es wird alles vollendet werden,
and it will all accomplished be,

was geschrieben ist von des Menschen Sohn.
that written is of the Son-of-man.

Chorus:
Sie aber vernahmen der keines und wußten nicht,
They, however, understood of-it nothing and knew not,

was das gesaget war.
what that being-spoken was.
{what he meant.}

2. Alto Aria
●Accompanying Christ to his passion as his disciples did
(22-2)
Mein Jesu, ziehe mich nach dir,
My Jesus, draw me to thee;

Ich bin bereit, ich will von hier
I am prepared, I will from here (depart)

Und nach Jerusalem zu deinen Leiden gehn.
And to Jerusalem to thy passion go.
{And go to Jerusalem to thy passion.}

Wohl mir, wenn ich die Wichtigkeit
Well (for) me, if I the importance
{I am blessed if I can fully understand the importance}

Von dieser Leid- und Sterbenszeit
Of this suffering- and dying-time

Zu meinem Troste kann durchgehends wohl verstehn!
For my consolation can thoroughly well understand!
{For my consolation!}

3. Bass Recit.
●Flesh & blood understands Mt. Tabor but not Golgotha
(22-3)
Mein Jesu, ziehe mich, so werd ich laufen,
My Jesus, draw me, then will I run,

Denn Fleisch und Blut verstehet ganz und gar,
For flesh and blood understands absolutely,

Nebst deinen Jüngern nicht, was das gesaget war.
Along-with thy disciples, not what that being-spoken meant.
{For flesh and blood, like thy disciples, can not understand at all what this means.}

Es sehnt sich nach der Welt und nach dem größtem Haufen;
It yearns - for the world and for the greatest crowd;

esteemed him stricken, smitten by God, and afflicted. But he was wounded for our transgressions, he was bruised for our iniquities; upon him was the chastisement that made us whole, and with his stripes we are healed...The Lord has laid on him the iniquity of us all. He was oppressed, and he was afflicted, yet he opened not his mouth; like a lamb that is led to the slaughter, and like a sheep that before its shearers is dumb, so he opened not his mouth...Yet it was the will of the Lord to bruise him; he has put him to grief; when he makes himself an offering for sin... (Also Ps. 22, Zech. 13:7.)
Lk. 24:25-27. And [Jesus] said to [the disciples], "O foolish men, and slow of heart to believe all that the prophets have spoken! Was it not necessary that the Christ should suffer these things and enter into his glory?" And beginning with Moses and all the prophets, he interpreted to them in all the scriptures the things concerning himself. (Also 1 Cor. 15:3-5.)

*Lk. 18:31. [Jesus took] the twelve (Luther: Jesus nahm zu sich die Zwölfe)...
Jn. 12:30, 32-33. Jesus [said], "...I, when I am lifted up from the earth, will draw all men to myself (Luther: sie alle zu mir ziehen)." He said this to show by what death he was to die. (Also Jn. 6:43-44.)
Mt. 26:35. Peter said to [Jesus], "Even if I must die with you, I will not deny you." And so said all the disciples. (Also Lk. 22:33-34.)
Acts 21:13. Paul answered, "...I am ready not only to be imprisoned but even to die at Jerusalem for the name of the Lord Jesus."
Mt. 20:20-22. The mother of the sons of Zebedee came up to him, with her sons...And he said to her, "What do you want?" She said to him, "Command that these two sons of mine may sit, one at your right hand and one at your left, in your kingdom." But Jesus answered, "You do not know what you are asking. Are you able to drink the cup that I am to drink?" They said to him, "We are able."
*Lk. 18:34. But they understood none of these things; this saying was hid from them, and they did not grasp what was said.

S. of S. 1:4 [Bride]: Draw me after you, let us make haste... (Luther: Zieh mich dir nach, so laufen wir)
Jn. 12:30, 32-33. Jesus [said], "...I, when I am lifted up from the earth, will draw all men to myself." He said this to show by what death he was to die. (Also Jn. 6:43-44.)
*Lk. 18:34. But they understood none of these things; this saying was hid from them, and they did not grasp what was said.
1 Cor. 2:12-14. Now we have received not the spirit of the world, but the Spirit which is from God, that we might understand the gifts bestowed on us by God. And we impart this in words not taught by human wisdom but taught by the Spirit, interpreting spiritual truths to those who possess the Spirit. The unspiritual man does not receive the gifts of the Spirit of God, for they are folly to him, and he is not able to understand them because they are spiritually discerned.

Sie wollen beiderseits, wenn du verkläret bist,
They want, both-of-them, when thou transfigured art,
{Indeed, both thy disciples and my flesh and blood—when they see thee transfigured—want}

Zwar eine feste Burg auf Tabors Berge bauen;
Indeed a secure fortress on Tabor's mount to-build;
{To build a secure fortress on Tabor's mount;}

Hingegen Golgatha, so voller Leiden ist,
As-against Golgatha, (which) so full-of suffering is,

In deiner Niedrigkeit mit keinem Auge schauen.
In thy lowliness with no eye to-behold.
{On Golgotha, however, which is so filled with suffering, they do not wish to behold thee in thy lowliness.}

Ach! kreuzige bei mir in der verderbten Brust
Ah! crucify in me—in (my) corrupted breast—

Zuvörderst diese Welt und die verbotne Lust,
First-of-all this world and (all) forbidden pleasure,

So werd ich, was du sagst, vollkommen wohl verstehen
Then will I, what thou dost-say, perfectly well understand
{Then I will comprehend thy words completely}

Und nach Jerusalem mit tausend Freuden gehen.
And to Jerusalem with (a) thousand joys go.
{And go to Jerusalem with a thousand joys in my heart.}

4. Tenor Aria
●Prayer: Crucify fleshly desires in me (22–4)
   Mein alles in allem, mein ewiges Gut,
(O) my all in all, my eternal possession,

Verbeßre das Herze, verändre den Mut;
Improve (my) heart, change (my) disposition;

Schlag alles darnieder,
Strike everything down,

Was dieser Entsagung des Fleisches zuwider!
That to-this renunciation of-the flesh is-contrary!

Doch wenn ich nun geistlich ertötet da bin,
Yet when I - spiritually mortified there am,
{Yet when I am put to death spiritually there,}

So ziehe mich nach dir in Friede dahin!
Then draw me to thee in peace forth!
{Then draw me forth to thee in peace!}

5. Chorale (See also 96–6, 132–6, 164–6.)
●Prayer: Crucify the old nature so the new nature may live (22–5)
Ertöt uns durch dein Güte,
Mortify us through thy goodness,

Gal. 5:17. The desires of the flesh are against the Spirit, and the desires of the Spirit are against the flesh; for these are opposed to each other, to prevent you from doing what you would.
Mk. 9:2–6. ...Jesus took with him Peter and James and John, and led them up a high mountain apart by themselves; and he was transfigured before them, and his garments became glistening, intensely white, as no fuller on earth could bleach them. And there appeared to them Elijah with Moses; and they were talking to Jesus. And Peter said to Jesus, "Master, it is well that we are here; let us make three booths, one for you and one for Moses and one for Elijah." For he did not know what to say, for they were exceedingly afraid. (Also Mt. 17:1–9.)
Jn. 19:17–18. They took Jesus, and he went out bearing his own cross, to the place called the place of a skull, which is called in Hebrew Golgotha. There they crucified him...
Phil. 2:5–8. Have this mind among yourselves, which is yours in Christ Jesus, who, though he was in the form of God, did not count equality with God a thing to be grasped, but emptied himself, taking the form of a servant, being born in the likeness of men. And being found in human form he humbled himself and became obedient unto death, even death on a cross. **Gal. 2:20.** I have been crucified with Christ; it is no longer I who live, but Christ who lives in me...
Gal. 5:24. And those who belong to Christ Jesus have crucified the flesh with its passions and desires.
Gal. 6:14. Far be it from me to glory except in the cross of our Lord Jesus Christ, by which the world has been crucified to me, and I to the world.
Jn. 11:16. Thomas...said to his fellow disciples, "Let us also go, that we may die with him."

Eph. 1:22–23. ...him who fills all in all.
Col. 3:11. ...Christ is all, and in all.
Ps. 73:25. [O Lord,] whom have I in heaven but thee? And there is nothing upon earth that I desire besides thee.
1 Jn. 2:15–17. Do not love the world or the things in the world. If any one loves the world, love for the Father is not in him. For all that is in the world, the lust of the flesh and the lust of the eyes and the pride of life is not of the Father but is of the world. And the world passes away, and the lust of it; but he who does the will of God abides for ever. (Also Jms. 4:4.)
Rom. 8:12–13. So then, brethren, we are debtors, not to the flesh, to live according to the flesh—for if you live according to the flesh you will die, but if by the Spirit you put to death the deeds of the body you will live.
Gal. 6:8. For he who sows to his own flesh will from the flesh reap corruption; but he who sows to the Spirit will from the Spirit reap eternal life.
Col. 3:5. Put to death therefore what is earthly in you...
S. of S. 1:4 [Bride]: Draw me after you, let us make haste... (Luther: Zieh mich dir nach, so laufen wir)
Lk. 2:29. Lord, now lettest thou thy servant depart in peace...

Heb. 12:5–6. ...My son, do not regard lightly the discipline of the Lord, nor lose courage when you are punished by him. For the Lord disciplines him whom he loves, and chastises every son whom he receives.

Erweck uns durch dein Gnad;
Awaken us through thy grace;

Den alten Menschen kränke,
The old man mortify,

Daß der neu' leben mag
So-that the new may-live

Wohl hie auf dieser Erden,
Indeed here on this earth,

Den Sinn und all Begehren
(And so-that) (our) mind and all (our) desires

Und G'danken hab'n zu dir.
And thoughts (be-directed) towards thee.

BWV 23
Du wahrer Gott und Davids Sohn
(NBA I/8; BC A47a-c)

Estomihi (Quinquagesima) (BWV 23, 22, 127, 159)
*1 Cor. 13:1–13 (In praise of love)
*Lk. 18:31–43 (Jesus and the twelve go to Jerusalem, healing of a blind man)
Librettist: Unknown (Last movement apparently added at a later date by Bach)

1. Soprano & Alto Duet
●Prayer: Jesus, Son of David (Messiah), have mercy on me! (23-1)
Du wahrer Gott und Davids Sohn,
Thou true God and David's son,

Der du von Ewigkeit in der Erntfernung schon
Who from eternity in the distance already
{Who from distant eternity already}

Mein Herzeleid und meine Leibespein
My grief and my body's-torment

Umständlich angesehn,
In-every-detail hath-seen,

Erbarm dich mein!
Have-mercy - on-me!

Und laß durch deine Wunderhand,
And grant (that) by thy miracle-hand,

1 Pet. 4:1–2. Since therefore Christ suffered in the flesh, arm yourselves with the same thought, for whoever has suffered in the flesh has ceased from sin, so as to live for the rest of the time in the flesh no longer by human passions but by the will of God.
Rom. 6:3–8. Do you not know that all of us who have been baptized into Christ Jesus were baptized into his death? We were buried therefore with him by baptism into death, so that as Christ was raised from the dead by the glory of the Father, we too might walk in newness of life. For if we have been united with him in a death like his, we shall certainly be united with him in a resurrection like his. We know that our old self was crucified with him so that the sinful body might be destroyed, and we might no longer be enslaved to sin. For he who has died is freed from sin. But if we have died with Christ, we believe that we shall also live with him. (Also Col. 2:12–14, Gal. 2:20.)
Eph. 4:22–24. Put off your old nature which belongs to your former manner of life and is corrupt through deceitful lusts, and be renewed in the spirit of your minds, and put on the new nature, created after the likeness of God in true righteousness and holiness. (Also Col. 3:9–10.)
2 Cor. 5:15. [Christ] died for all, that those who live might live no longer for themselves but for him who for their sake died and was raised. (Also 2 Cor. 5:9, Eph. 5:10.)
Col. 3:17. Whatever you do, in word or deed, do everything in the name of the Lord Jesus...

Rom. 1:1–5. ...The gospel of God [was] promised beforehand through his prophets in the holy scriptures, the gospel concerning his Son, who was descended from David according to the flesh and designated Son of God...Jesus Christ our Lord, through whom we have received grace...
*Lk. 18:35–43. As [Jesus] drew near to Jericho, a blind man was sitting by the roadside begging; and hearing a multitude going by, he inquired what this meant. They told him, "Jesus of Nazareth is passing by." And he cried, "Jesus, Son of David, have mercy on me!" And those who were in front rebuked him, telling him to be silent; but he cried out all the more, "Son of David, have mercy on me!" And Jesus stopped, and commanded him to be brought to him; and when he came near, he asked him, "What do you want me to do for you?" He said, "Lord, let me receive my sight." And Jesus said to him, "Receive your sight; your faith has made you well." And immediately he received his sight and followed him, glorifying God; and all the people, when they saw it, gave praise to God.
Ps. 38:9–10. Lord, all my longing is known to thee, my sighing is not hidden from thee. My heart throbs, my strength fails me; and the light of my eyes—it also has gone from me.
Ps. 139:16. ...[O Lord,] in thy book were written, every one of them, the days that were formed for me, when as yet there was none of them.
Is. 35:5–6 [Messianic prophecy]. Then the eyes of the blind shall be opened, and the ears of the deaf unstopped; then the lame man shall leap like a hart, and the tongue of the dumb sing for joy...
Lk. 4:17–19, 21. [Jesus] opened the book...where it was written..."He has sent me to proclaim release to the captives and recovering of sight to the blind"...And he began to say to them, "Today this scripture has been fulfilled in your hearing."

Die   so viel Böses abgewandt,
Which so much evil   hath-averted (for others),

Mir   gleichfalls Hülf und Trost geschehen!
To-me similarly help and comfort might-come!

2. Tenor Recit.
●Prayer: Pass not by without healing & blessing me (23-2)
Ach, gehe nicht vorüber;
Ah, pass not by;

Du aller Menschen Heil,
Thou all people's salvation,
{O thou salvation of all people,}

      Bist   ja erschienen,
(For thou) didst indeed appear,

Die Kranken und nicht die Gesunden zu bedienen.
The sick and not the healthy to serve.

Drum   nehm ich ebenfalls an deiner Allmacht teil;
Therefore share I likewise in thy omnipotence - ;
{Therefore I likewise share in thy ominpotence;}

Ich sehe dich   auf diesen Wegen,
I'll look (to) thee (from) on these paths,

Worauf man
Upon-which they

Mich hat wollen legen,
Me had wanted to-lay,
{Upon which they wanted to lay me,}

Auch in der Blindheit an.
Even in (my) blindness - .

Ich fasse mich
I take-myself-in-hand

Und lasse dich
And release thee

Nicht ohne deinen Segen.
Not without thy blessing.
{And will not release thee without thy blessing.}

3. Chorus
●Eyes of all wait upon the Lord: grant me light (23-3)
Aller Augen warten,   Herr,
All eyes wait, (O) Lord,

Du allmächtger Gott, auf dich!
Thou almighty God, upon thee!

Mt. 11:2–5. When John heard in prison about the deeds of the Christ, he sent word..."Are you he who is to come, or shall we look for another?" And Jesus answered..."Go and tell John what you hear and see: the blind receive their sight..." (Also Jn. 9:30–33, Jn. 10:21.)

*Lk. 18:38–39. And [the blind man sitting by the roadside] cried, "Jesus, Son of David, have mercy on me!" And those who were in front rebuked him, telling him to be silent... (Also Mt. 9:27, 20:30.)
Lam. 1:12. Is it nothing to you, all you who pass by?
Lk. 10:30–33. Jesus replied, "A man was going down from Jerusalem to Jericho, and he fell among robbers, who stripped him and beat him, and departed, leaving him half dead. Now by chance a priest was going down that road; and when he saw him he passed by on the other side. So likewise a Levite...passed by on the other side. But a Samaritan...when he saw him, he had compassion..."
Lk. 5:31–32. Jesus [said], "Those who are well have no need of a physician, but those who are sick; I have not come to call the righteous, but sinners to repentance." (Also Mt. 9:12, Mk. 2:17; Ps. 147:3.)
1 Tim. 1:15. Christ Jesus came into the world to save sinners.
1 Jn. 4:14. We have seen and testify that the Father has sent his Son as the Savior of the world.
*Lk. 18:35–40. As [Jesus] drew near to Jericho, a blind man was sitting by the roadside begging; and hearing a multitude going by, he inquired what this meant. They told him, "Jesus of Nazareth is passing by." And he cried, "Jesus, Son of David, have mercy on me!" And those who were in front rebuked him, telling him to be silent; but he cried out all the more, "Son of David, have mercy on me!" And Jesus stopped...
Rev. 3:17 [Christ]: You say, "I am rich, I have prospered, and I need nothing; not knowing that you are wretched, pitiable, poor, blind..."
Ps. 119:81–82. [O Lord,] my soul languishes for thy salvation (Luther: Heil)...My eyes fail with watching for thy promise; I ask, "When wilt thou comfort me?"
Lk. 21:19 [Christ]: By your endurance you will gain your lives (Luther: Fasset eure Seele mit Geduld).
Ps. 63:8. [O Lord,] my soul clings to thee...
Gen. 32:24, 26–28. Jacob was left alone; and a man wrestled with him until the breaking of the day...Then [the man] said, "Let me go, for the day is breaking." But Jacob said, "I will not let you go, unless you bless me." And he said to him, "What is your name?" And he said, "Jacob." Then he said, "Your name shall no more be called Jacob, but Israel, for you have striven with God and with men, and have prevailed."

Ps. 145:15. The eyes of all look to thee, and thou givest them their food in due season. (Also Ps. 104:27, 111:5.)
Ps. 119:81–82. [O Lord,] my soul languishes for thy salvation...My eyes fail with watching for thy promise; I ask, "When wilt thou comfort me?"

Und die meinen sonderlich.
And those of-mine particularly.
{And my eyes particularly.}

Gib denselben Kraft und Licht,
Grant them strength and light,

Laß sie nicht
Leave them not

Immerdar in Finsternissen!
Evermore in darkness!

Künftig soll dein Wink allein
In-the-future shall thy beckoning alone
{In the future thy beckoning alone shall}

Der geliebte Mittelpunkt
The beloved centre (of)

Aller ihrer Werke sein.
All their works be.

Bis du sie einst durch den Tod
Until thou them one-day in - death

Wiederum gedenkst zu schliessen.
Once-again decide to close.
{Until one day in death, thou wilt decide to close them once again.}

4. Chorale
●Agnus Dei: Lamb of God, have mercy on us! (23–4)
Christe, du Lamm Gottes,
Christ, thou Lamb of-God,

Der du trägst die Sünd der Welt,
Thou-who dost-bear the sin of-the world,

Erbarm dich unser!
Have-mercy - on-us!

///

Christe, du Lamm Gottes,
Christ, thou Lamb of-God,

Der du trägst die Sünd der Welt,
Thou-who dost-bear the sin of-the world,

Erbarm dich unser!
Have-mercy - on-us!

///

Christe, du Lamm Gottes,
Christ, thou Lamb of-God,

Der du trägst die Sünd der Welt,
Thou-who dost-bear the sin of-the world,

Ps. 62:5. For God alone my soul waits in silence, for my hope is from him.

Ps. 69:3. I am weary with my crying; my throat is parched. My eyes grow dim with waiting for my God.

Ps. 123:2. Behold, as the eyes of servants look to the hand of their master, as the eyes of a maid to the hand of her mistress, so our eyes look to the Lord our God, till he have mercy upon us. (Also Ps. 25:5, 25:15, 27:14, 37:7, 130:5.)

Is. 40:31. They who wait for the Lord shall renew their strength, they shall mount up with wings like eagles, they shall run and not be weary, they shall walk and not faint.

Lam. 3:25–26. The Lord is good to those who wait for him, to the soul that seeks him. It is good that one should wait quietly for the salvation of the Lord.

Ps. 27:1. The Lord is my light and my salvation...

Ps. 36:9. For with thee [O Lord] is the fountain of life; in thy light do we see light.

Jn. 8:12. Again Jesus spoke to them, saying, "I am the light of the world; he who follows me will not walk in darkness, but will have the light of life."

Mt. 6:22–23 [Christ]: The eye is the lamp of the body. So, if your eye is sound, your whole body will be full of light; but if your eye is not sound, your whole body will be full of darkness. If then the light in you is darkness, how great is the darkness!

1 Pet. 2:9. But you are a chosen race, a royal priesthood, a holy nation, God's own people, that you may declare the wonderful deeds of him who called you out of darkness into his marvelous light.

2 Cor. 5:8–9. We are of good courage, and we would rather be away from the body and at home with the Lord. So whether we are at home or away, we make it our aim to please him. (Also Phil. 1:21–23.)

*Lk. 18:38. And [the blind man] cried, "Jesus, Son of David, have mercy on me!"

Jn. 1:29. The next day [John] saw Jesus coming toward him, and said, "Behold, the Lamb of God, who takes away the sin of the world!" (Also Jn. 1:36.)

Is. 53:3–7, 10. He was despised and rejected by men; a man of sorrows, and acquainted with grief; and as one from whom men hide their faces he was despised, and we esteemed him not. Surely he has borne our griefs and carried our sorrows; yet we esteemed him stricken, smitten by God, and afflicted. But he was wounded for our transgressions, he was bruised for our iniquities; upon him was the chastisement that made us whole, and with his stripes we are healed... The Lord has laid on him the iniquity of us all. He was oppressed, and he was afflicted, yet he opened not his mouth; like a lamb that is led to the slaughter, and like a sheep that before its shearers is dumb, so he opened not his mouth...Yet it was the will of the Lord to bruise him; he has put him to grief; when he makes himself an offering for sin... (Also Ps. 22, Zech. 13:7.)

Rev. 5:6, 9. Between the throne and the four living creatures and among the elders, I saw a Lamb standing, as though it had been slain... and they sang a new song, saying, "Worthy art thou...for thou wast slain and by thy blood didst ransom men for God from every tribe and tongue and people and nation." (Also Rev. 5:12.)

1 Pet. 1:18–19. You know that you were ransomed from the futile ways inherited from your fathers, not with perishable things such as silver or gold, but with the precious blood of Christ, like that of a lamb without blemish or spot. (Also 1 Jn. 1:7.)

83

Gib uns dein' Frieden! Amen.
Give us   thy   peace! Amen.

Ps. 29:11. ...May the Lord bless his people with peace!

BWV 24
Ein ungefärbt Gemüte
(NBA I/17; BC A102)

4. S. after Trinity (BWV 185, 24, 177)
*Rom. 8:18–23 (All creation eagerly longs for the revealing of the sons of God)
*Lk. 6:36–42 (Sermon on the mount: Be merciful, do not judge)
Librettist: Erdmann Neumeister

1. Alto Aria
●Sincerity is a mark of the Christian (24-1)
Ein ungefärbt Gemüte
An unfeigned   spirit

Von deutscher Treu und Güte
Of   German fidelity and kindness

Macht uns vor Gott und Menschen schön.
Makes us before God and   people beautiful.
{Makes us beautiful before God and people.}

Der Christen Tun und Handel,
- Christians' deeds and dealings,

Ihr ganzer Lebenswandel
Their entire   lifestyle

Soll auf dergleichen Fuße stehn.
Should on   such-a footing stand.
{Should stand on such a footing.}

2. Tenor Recit.
●Honesty is rare; we are not honest by nature (24-2)
Die Redlichkeit
- Honesty

Ist eine von den Gottesgaben.
Is one of - God's-gifts.

Daß sie bei unrer Zeit
That it in our time

So wenig Menschen haben,
So few   people possess,
{That so few people possess it in our time}

Das macht, sie bitten Gott nicht drum.
That is-because, they ask God not for-it.
{Is because they do not ask God for it.}

Denn von Natur geht unsers Herzens Dichten
For, by nature - our   heart's imaginings

*Lk. 6:42. How can you say to your brother, "Brother, let me take out the speck that is in your eye," when you yourself do not see the log that is in your own eye? You hypocrite, first take the log out of your own eye, and then you will see clearly to take out the speck that is in your brother's eye.
1 Tim. 1:5. The aim of our charge is love that issues from a pure heart and a good conscience and sincere (Luther: ungefärbtem) faith.
1 Pet. 1:22. Having purified your souls by your obedience to the truth for a sincere love of the brethren (Luther: ungefärbter Bruderliebe), love one another earnestly from the heart.
Mt. 23:27–28. Woe to you, scribes and Pharisees, hypocrites! for you are like whitewashed tombs, which outwardly appear beautiful, but within they are full of dead men's bones and all uncleanness. So you also outwardly appear righteous to men, but within you are full of hypocrisy and iniquity. (Also Lk. 11:44.)
Mt. 5:37. Let what you say be simply "Yes" or "No"; anything more than this comes from evil.
1 Sam. 16:7. ...Man looks on the outward appearance, but the Lord looks on the heart. (Also Lk. 16:15.)
Tit. 2:7–8. Show yourself in all respects a model of good deeds, and in your teaching show integrity, gravity, and sound speech that cannot be censured, so that an opponent may be put to shame, having nothing evil to say of us.
2 Cor. 8:21. We aim at what is honorable (Luther: redlich) not only in the Lord's sight but also in the sight of men.

Gal. 5:22–23. The fruit of the Spirit is love, joy, peace, patience, kindness, goodness, faithfulness, gentleness, self-control...
1 Cor. 2:12. We have received...the Spirit which is from God, that we might understand the gifts bestowed on us by God.
Jms. 4:2. ...You do not have, because you do not ask. You ask and do not receive, because you ask wrongly, to spend it on your passions.
2 Tim. 3:1–5. Understand this, that in the last days there will come times of stress. For men will be lovers of self, lovers of money, proud, arrogant, abusive, disobedient to their parents, ungrateful, unholy, inhuman, implacable, slanderers, profligates, fierce, haters of good, treacherous, reckless, swollen with conceit, lovers of pleasure rather than lovers of God, holding the form of religion but denying the power of it. Avoid such people.
Prov. 26:23–26. Like the glaze covering an earthen vessel are smooth lips with an evil heart. He who hates, dissembles with his lips and harbors deceit in his heart; when he speaks graciously, believe him not, for there are seven abominations in his heart; though his hatred be covered with guile, his wickedness will be exposed in the assembly. (Also Job 15:34–35, Ps. 28:3, 62:4.)
Jer. 17:9. The heart is deceitful above all things, and desperately corrupt...

Mit lauter Bösem um:
With nothing-but evil are-occupied:
{Are occupied with nothing but evil:}
      [umgehen = to be occupied with]

Soll's seinen Weg auf etwas Gutes richten,
Shall-it its course to something good direct,
{If our heart is to direct itself toward something good,}

So muß es Gott durch seinen Geist regieren
Then must it God through his Spirit rule
{Then God must rule it through his Spirit}

Und auf der Bahn der Tugend führen.
And upon the path of virtue lead (it).

Verlangst du Gott zum Freunde,
Desire you God as friend,
{If you desire God as your friend,}

So mache dir den Nächsten nicht zum Feinde
Then make - (your) neighbor not into-an enemy
{Then do not make an enemy of your neighbor}

Durch Falschheit, Trug und List!
Through falsity, deceit, and cunning!

Ein Christ
A Christian

Soll sich der Taubenart bestreben
Shall - (for) the dove's-manner strive
{Should strive to be like the dove}

Und ohne Falsch und Tücke leben.
And without dishonesty and malice live.
{And live without dishonesty and malice.}

Mach aus dir selbst ein solches Bild,
Make of your-self a such likeness,
{Make of yourself the kind of person}

Wie du den Nächsten haben wilt!
As you (your) neighbor have would (be)!
{You would have your neighbor be!}

Gen. 6:5. The Lord saw that the wickedness of man was great in the earth, and that every imagination of the thoughts of his heart (Luther: Dichten und Trachten) was only evil continually.

Rom. 7:18. I know that nothing good dwells within me, that is, in my flesh. I can will what is right, but I cannot do it.

Gal. 5:16–18. But I say, walk by the Spirit, and do not gratify the desires of the flesh. For the desires of the flesh are against the Spirit, and the desires of the Spirit are against the flesh; for these are opposed to each other...But if you are led (Luther: regiert) by the Spirit you are not under the law.

Phil. 2:13. For God is at work in you, both to will and to work for his good pleasure.

1 Jn. 4:19–21. We love, because he first loved us. If any one says, "I love God," and hates his brother, he is a liar; for he who does not love his brother whom he has seen, cannot love God whom he has not seen. And this commandment we have from him, that he who loves God should love his brother also.

1 Jn. 2:4–5. He who says "I know him" but disobeys his commandments is a liar, and the truth is not in him; but whoever keeps his word, in him truly love for God is perfected. (Also 1 Jn. 1:6, 3:17.)

*Lk. 6:35–36, 42. Love your enemies, and do good...and you will be sons of the Most High; for he is kind...Be merciful, even as your Father is merciful...Or how can you say to your brother, "Brother, let me take out the speck that is in your eye," when you yourself do not see the log that is in your own eye? You hypocrite, first take the log out of your own eye, and then you will see clearly to take out the speck that is in your brother's eye.

Mt. 5:9 [Christ]: Blessed are the peacemakers, for they shall be called sons of God.

Rom. 12:18. If possible, so far as it depends upon you, live peaceably with all.

Jms. 3:17–18. The wisdom from above is first pure, then peaceable, gentle, open to reason, full of mercy and good fruits, without uncertainty or insincerity. And the harvest of righteousness is sown in peace by those who make peace.

1 Pet. 2:1. So put away all malice and all guile and insincerity and envy and all slander.

Eph. 4:31–32. Let all bitterness and wrath and anger and clamor and slander be put away from you, with all malice, and be kind to one another, tenderhearted, forgiving one another, as God in Christ forgave you.

Lk. 6:31. And as you wish that men would do to you, do so to them.

Mt. 22:39 [Christ]: ...You shall love your neighbor as yourself. (Also Mk. 12:31, Lk. 10:27, Lev. 19:18.)

3. Chorus
●Golden Rule is central: Mt. 7:12 (24–3)
Alles nun, das ihr wollet, daß euch
Everything then, that you would, that to-you

die Leute tun sollen, das tut ihr ihnen.
- people do should, that do - to-them.

Mt. 7:12. *So whatever you wish that men would do to you, do so to them; for this is the law and the prophets.* (Also Lk. 6:31.)
Lev. 19:18. ...You shall love your neighbor as yourself...
Gal. 5:14. For the whole law is fulfilled in one word, "You shall love your neighbor as yourself." (Also Mt. 19:19.)

4. Bass Recit.
●Hypocrisy & dishonesty, etc. is of the devil (24-4)
Die Heuchelei
  - Hypocrisy

Ist eine Brut, die Belial gehecket.
Is a brood, that Belial hatches.

Wer   sich   in ihre Larve stecket,
Whoever himself into its larva puts,
{Whovever puts himself into hypocrisy's larvae,}

Der trägt des Teufels Liberei.
He wears the devil's livery.

Wie? lassen sich   denn Christen
What? Allow themselves then Christians
{What? Do Christians allow themselves}

Dergleichen auch gelüsten?
The-like   even to-covet?
{To covet this?}

    Gott sei's geklagt! die Redlichkeit ist teuer.
(To) God be-it lamented! - Sincerity is rare.

Manch teuflisch Ungeheuer
Many-a devilish monster

Sieht   wie ein Engel aus.
Appears like an angel - .

    Man kehrt den Wolf hinein,
(If) one (allows) the wolf   in,

Den Schafspelz kehrt man raus.
The sheep's-skin sweeps one out.
{Then is the sheep's skin swept out.}

Wie könnt es ärger sein?
How could it worse be?
{What could be worse?}

Verleumden, Schmähn und Richten,
Slandering,   reviling, and judging,

Verdammen und Vernichten
Damning   and demolishing

Ist überall gemein.
Ist everywhere common.

So geht es dort, so geht es hier.
So goes it there, so goes it here.
{We see it both there and here.}

    Der liebe Gott behüte mich dafür!
(May) the dear God protect me from-that!

*Lk. 6:42. How can you say to your brother, "Brother, let me take out the speck that is in your eye," when you yourself do not see the log that is in your own eye? You hypocrite, first take the log out of your own eye, and then you will see clearly to take out the speck that is in your brother's eye.
Jn. 8:44. You are of your father the devil...He was a murderer from the beginning, and has nothing to do with the truth, because there is no truth in him. When he lies, he speaks according to his own nature, for he is a liar and the father of lies.
1 Jn. 5:19. ...The whole world is in the power of the evil one.
2 Cor. 6:15. What accord has Christ with Belial? Or what has a believer in common with an unbeliever?
Jms. 1:15. Desire when it has conceived gives birth to sin; and sin when it is full-grown brings forth death.
Eph. 4:17-24. Now...you must no longer live as the Gentiles do, in the futility of their minds...Put off your old nature which belongs to your former manner of life and is corrupt through deceitful lusts, and be renewed in the spirit of your minds, and put on the new nature, created after the likeness of God in true righteousness and holiness.
2 Cor. 11:13-15. For such men are false apostles, deceitful workmen, disguising themselves as apostles of Christ. And no wonder, for even Satan disguises himself as an angel of light. So it is not strange if his servants also disguise themselves as servants of righteousness...
Mt. 7:15-16. Beware of false prophets, who come to you in sheep's clothing but inwardly are ravenous wolves. You will know them by their fruits...
2 Tim. 3:1-5. But understand this, that in the last days there will come times of stress. For men will be lovers of self, lovers of money, proud, arrogant, abusive, disobedient to their parents, ungrateful, unholy, inhuman, implacable, slanderers, profligates, fierce, haters of good, treacherous, reckless, swollen with conceit, lovers of pleasure rather than lovers of God, holding the form of religion but denying the power of it. Avoid such people.
2 Tim. 3:13. Evil men and impostors will go on from bad to worse, deceivers and deceived. (Also 2 Jn. 1:7.)
2 Pet. 2:1-3. ...There will be false teachers among you, who will secretly bring in destructive heresies, even denying the Master who bought them, bringing upon themselves swift destruction. And many will follow their licentiousness, and because of them the way of truth will be reviled. And in their greed they will exploit you with false words... (Also 2 Pet. 2:10-19, 2 Jn. 1:7.)
Phil. 3:18-19. Many, of whom I have often told you and now tell you even with tears, live as enemies of the cross of Christ. Their end is destruction, their god is the belly, and they glory in their shame, with minds set on earthly things.
Jms. 4:1-2. What causes wars, and what causes fightings among you? Is it not your passions that are at war in your members? You desire and do not have; so you kill. And you covet and cannot obtain; so you fight and wage war...
2 Tim. 4:18. The Lord will rescue me from every evil and save me for his heavenly kingdom. To him be the glory for ever and ever. Amen.

5. Tenor Aria

●Integrity makes us like God and angels (24-5)
　　Treu　　und Wahrheit sei der Grund
(Let) faithfulness and　Truth　　be the basis

　　Aller deiner Sinnen,
(Of) all　　your thinking,

Wie von　　außen Wort und Mund,
As　on (the) outside word and mouth,

　　Sei das Herz von　　innen.
(So) be　the heart　on (the) inside.

Gütig sein und tugendreich
Kind　being and　virtuous
{Being kind and virtuous}

Macht uns Gott und Engeln gleich.
Makes us　God and　angels　like.
{Makes us like God and the angels.}

6. Chorale

●Prayer: Source of all, grant health to body and soul (24-6)
O Gott, du　frommer Gott,
O God, thou righteous God,

Du Brunnquell aller Gaben,
Thou　fount　of-all　gifts,

Ohn　den　nichts ist, was ist,
Without whom nothing is　that is,

Von　dem wir　alles　haben,
From whom we everything have,
{From whom we have everything:}

　　Gesunden Leib gib mir,
(A)　healthy　body give me,
{Give me a healthy body,}

Und　　daß in solchem Leib
And (grant) that in　such-a　body
{And grant that I would have in such a body}

Ein unverletzte Seel
An　uncorrupted soul

Und rein Gewissen bleib.
And pure conscience remain.
{And conscience.}

Ps. 15:1-2. O Lord, who shall sojourn in thy tent? Who shall dwell on thy holy hill? He who walks blamelessly, and does what is right, and speaks truth from his heart.

Prov. 8:6-7. Hear, for I will speak noble things, and from my lips will come what is right; for my mouth will utter truth; wickedness is an abomination to my lips.

Eph. 4:25. Therefore, putting away falsehood, let every one speak the truth with his neighbor...

Mt. 23:27-28 [Christ]: Woe to you, scribes and Pharisees, hypocrites! for you are like whitewashed tombs, which outwardly appear beautiful, but within they are full of dead men's bones and all uncleanness. So you also outwardly appear righteous to men, but within you are full of hypocrisy and iniquity.

Gal. 5:22-23. But the fruit of the Spirit is love, joy, peace, patience, kindness, goodness, faithfulness, gentleness, self-control; against such there is no law.

1 Pet. 1:15-16. But as he who called you is holy, be holy yourselves in all your conduct; since it is written, "You shall be holy, for I am holy."

Deut. 32:4. ...A God of faithfulness and without iniquity, just and right (Luther: fromm) is he.

Ps. 25:8. Good and upright (Luther: fromm) is the Lord... (Also Ps. 92:15.)

Jms. 1:17. Every good endowment and every perfect gift is from above, coming down from the Father of lights with whom there is no variation or shadow due to change. (Also Mt. 7:11.)

Jn. 1:1-3. In the beginning was the Word, and the Word was with God, and the Word was God. He was in the beginning with God; all things were made through him, and without him was not anything made that was made.

Jn. 3:27. ...No one can receive anything except what is given him from heaven.

1 Thess. 5:23. May the God of peace himself sanctify you wholly; and may your spirit and soul and body be kept sound and blameless at the coming of our Lord Jesus Christ.

3 Jn. 2. Beloved, I pray that all may go well with you and that you may be in health; I know that it is well with your soul.

Acts 24:16. So I always take pains to have a clear conscience (Luther: unverletzt Gewissen) toward God and toward men.

2 Cor. 1:12. For our boast is this, the testimony of our conscience that we have behaved in the world, and still more toward you, with holiness and godly sincerity...

2 Tim. 1:3. I thank God whom I serve with a clear conscience...

BWV 25
Es ist nichts Gesundes an meinem Leibe
(NBA I/21; BC A129)

14. S. after Trinity (BWV 25, 78, 17)
*Gal. 5:16–24 (Work of the flesh and fruit of the Spirit)
*Lk. 17:11–19 (Jesus heals ten lepers)
Librettist: Johann Jacob Rambach

1. Chorus
●Sickness: Nothing sound is in my body: Ps. 38:3 (25-1)
Es   ist nichts Gesundes an meinem Leibe
(There) is nothing   sound   in   my   body

vor   deinem Dräuen und   ist kein Friede
because-of thy   menacing and (there) is no peace

in meinen Gebeinen   vor   meiner Sünde.
in   my   bones because-of my   sin.

2. Tenor Recit.
●Leprosy of sin has infected entire world (25-2)
Die ganze Welt ist nur ein Hospital,
The entire world is but a hospital,

Wo   Menschen von   unzählbar großer Zahl
Where people of (an) innumerably large number
{Where an innumerably large number of people}

Und auch die Kinder in der Wiegen
And even the children in (their) cradles

An Krankheit hart darniederliegen.
In   sickness severe   lie.
{Lie in severe sickness.}

Den einen quälet in der Brust
The one is-tortured in (his) breast (by)

Ein hitzges Fieber   böser Lust;
A   hot   fever (of) evil   lust;

Der andre lieget krank
The other lies   sick

An   eigner Ehre häßlichem Gestank;
With (his) own honor's repulsive   stench;

Den dritten   zehrt   die Geldsucht ab
The third (is) consumed (by) - avarice -

Und   stürzt ihn vor der Zeit ins Grab.
And (it) hurls him before (his) time into-the grave.
{And it hurls him into the grave before his time.}

Der erste Fall hat jedermann beflecket
The first fall has everyone   stained
{The original fall has stained everyone.}

Ps. 38:1–8. O Lord, rebuke me not in thy anger, nor chasten me in thy wrath! For thy arrows have sunk into me, and thy hand has come down on me. *There is no soundness in my flesh because of thy indignation; there is no health in my bones because of my sin.* For my iniquities have gone over my head; they weigh like a burden too heavy for me. My wounds grow foul and fester because of my foolishness, I am utterly bowed down and prostrate; all the day I go about mourning. For my loins are filled with burning, and there is no soundness in my flesh. I am utterly spent and crushed; I groan because of the tumult of my heart.

Is. 1:6. From the sole of the foot even to the head, there is no soundness in it, but bruises and sores and bleeding wounds; they are not pressed out, or bound up, or softened with oil.

Ps. 6:2. ...O Lord, heal me, for my bones are troubled.

Ps. 102:3. For my days pass away like smoke, and my bones burn like a furnace.

*Lk. 17:11–13. On the way to Jerusalem [Jesus] was passing along between Samaria and Galilee. And as he entered a village, he was met by ten lepers, who stood at a distance and lifted up their voices and said, "Jesus, Master, have mercy on us."

Rom. 8:22–23. We know that the whole creation has been groaning in travail together until now; and not only the creation, but we ourselves, who have the first fruits of the Spirit, groan inwardly as we wait for adoption as sons, the redemption of our bodies.

Ps. 14:2–3. The Lord looks down from heaven upon the children of men, to see if there are any that act wisely, that seek after God. They have all gone astray, they are all alike corrupt; there is none that does good, no, not one.

Rom. 3:10–18, 23. As it is written: "None is righteous, no, not one; no one understands, no one seeks for God. All have turned aside, together they have gone wrong; no one does good, not even one..."All have sinned and fall short of the glory of God. (Also Prov. 20:9.)

Tit. 3:3. We ourselves were once foolish, disobedient, led astray, slaves to various passions and pleasures...

*Gal. 5:19–21. Now the works of the flesh are plain: fornication, impurity, licentiousness, idolatry, sorcery, enmity, strife, jealousy, anger, selfishness, dissension, party spirit, envy, drunkenness, carousing, and the like. I warn you, as I warned you before, that those who do such things shall not inherit the kingdom of God.

1 Jn. 2:16. All that is in the world, the lust of the flesh and the lust of the eyes and the pride of life, is not of the father but is of the world. (See also Mt. 5:28.)

Lk. 20:45–47. ...[Jesus] said to his disciples, "Beware of the scribes, who like to go about in long robes, and love salutations in the market places and the best seats in the synagogues and the places of honor at feasts, who devour widows' houses and for a pretense make long prayers. They will receive the greater condemnation."

Jn. 12:43. They loved the praise of men more than the praise of God.

Und mit dem Sündenaussatz angestecket.
And with the leprosy-of-sin infected.
{And infected them with the leprosy of sin.}

Ach! dieses Gift durchwühlt auch meine Glieder.
Ah! This poison ransacks also my members.

Wo find ich Armer Arzenei?
Where find I poor-one medicine?
{Where can this poor one find medicine?}

Wer stehet mir in meinem Elend bei?
Who stands me in my wretchedness by?
{Who will help me in my wretchedness?}

Wer ist mein Arzt, wer hilft mir wieder?
Who is my physician, who helps me back?
{Who is my physician; who helps to restore me?}

3. Bass Aria

●Jesus as physician; the balm of Gilead for sin (25-3)
Ach, wo hol ich Armer Rat?
Ah, where fetch I poor-one counsel?
{Ah, where can this poor one find counsel?}

Meinen Aussatz, meine Beulen
My leprosy, my boils

Kann kein Kraut noch Pflaster heilen
Can no herb nor plaster heal

Als die Salb aus Gilead.
But the (balm) of Gilead.

Du, mein Arzt, Herr Jesu, nur
Thou, my physician, Lord Jesus, alone

Weißt die beste Seelenkur.
Knowest the best soul-cure.

4. Soprano Recit.

●Prayer for healing & cleansing; promise to praise God (25-4)
O Jesu, lieber Meister,
O Jesus, dear master,

Zu dir flieh ich;
To thee flee I;
{To thee I flee;}

Ach, stärke die geschwächten Lebensgeister!
Ah, strengthen (my) weakened vital-spirits!

Lk. 12:15. And [Jesus] said to [the people], "Take heed, and beware of all covetousness; for a man's life does not consist in the abundance of his possessions."
1 Tim. 6:9–10. Those who desire to be rich fall into temptation, into a snare, into many senseless and hurtful desires that plunge men into ruin and destruction. For the love of money is the root of all evils...
Rom. 5:12, 17–19. Sin came into the world through one man and death through sin, and so death spread to all men because all men sinned...because of one man's trespass, death reigned through that one man...one man's trespass led to condemnation for all men...by one man's disobedience many were made sinners...
1 Cor. 15:21–22. ...By a man came death...In Adam all die...
Rom. 7:24. Wretched man that I am! Who will deliver me from this body of death?
Is. 63:5. I looked, but there was no one to help... (Luther: niemand enthielt mich)
Ex. 15:26. ...I am the Lord, your healer (Luther: Arzt).

Lam. 4:17. Our eyes failed, ever watching vainly for help...
Ps. 38:3–8. [O Lord,] there is no soundness in my flesh because of thy indignation; there is no health in my bones because of my sin. For my iniquities have gone over my head; they weigh like a burden too heavy for me. My wounds grow foul and fester because of my foolishness, I am utterly bowed down and prostrate; all the day I go about mourning. For my loins are filled with burning, and there is no soundness in my flesh. I am utterly spent and crushed; I groan because of the tumult of my heart.
Deut. 28:27, 60–61. [When the Lord punishes you, he] will smite you with the boils of Egypt, and with the ulcers and the scurvy and the itch, of which you cannot be healed...And he will bring upon you again all the diseases of Egypt, which you were afraid of; and they shall cleave to you. Every sickness also, and every affliction which is not recorded in the book of this law, the Lord will bring upon you, until you are destroyed.
Wisdom (Apocrypha) 16:12. Neither herb nor poultice cured them, but it was thy word, O Lord, which heals all men.
Jer. 8:22. Is there no balm in Gilead? Is there no physician there? Why then has the health of the daughter of my people not been restored? (Also Jer. 46:11; 14:19, 30:13, 46:11.)
Lk. 5:31–32. Jesus [said]... "Those who are well have no need of a physician, but those who are sick; I have not come to call the righteous, but sinners to repentance."
Ps. 147:3. He heals the brokenhearted, and binds up their wounds. (Also Is. 57:18.)

*Lk. 17:11–13. On the way to Jerusalem [Jesus] was passing along between Samaria and Galilee. And as he entered a village, he was met by ten lepers, who stood at a distance and lifted up their voices and said, "Jesus, Master, have mercy on us."
Ps. 13:2–3. [O Lord,] how long must I bear pain in my soul, and have sorrow in my heart all the day?...Consider and answer me, O Lord my God; lighten my eyes, lest I sleep the sleep of death.
Is. 42:3 [Messianic prophecy]. A bruised reed he will not break, and a dimly burning wick he will not quench... (Also Mt. 12:20.)

Erbarme dich,
Have-mercy - ,

Du   Arzt und Helfer aller   Kranken,
Thou physician and helper of-all (the) sick,

Verstoß mich nicht
Cast-off me   not
{Cast me not away}

Von deinem Angesicht!
From   thy   countenance!

Mein Heiland, mach mich von Sündenaussatz rein,
My   Savior, make me   of   sin's-leprosy clean,
{My Savior, make me clean of sin's leprosy,}

So   will ich dir
Then will I to-thee
{Then I will dedicate to thee}

Mein ganzes Herz   dafür
My   whole heart (in return)

Zum steten Opfer   weihn
As-a continual sacrifice dedicate
{As a continual sacrifice}

Und   lebenslang für deine Hülfe danken.
And (thee) life-long for thy   help   thank.
{And thank thee all my life for thy help.}

Is. 61:1 [Messianic prophecy]. The Spirit of the Lord God is upon me, because the Lord has anointed me to bring good tidings to the afflicted; he has sent me to bind up the brokenhearted... (Also Lk. 4:18–19.)

Heb. 12:12–13. Therefore lift your drooping hands and strengthen your weak knees, and make straight paths for your feet, so that what is lame may not be put out of joint but rather be healed. (Also Is. 35:3–4, Rev. 3:2.)

Ps. 51:1–2, 10–11. Have mercy on me, O God, according to thy steadfast love...Wash me thoroughly from my iniquity, and cleanse me from my sin!...Create in me a clean heart, O God, and put a new and right spirit within me. Cast me not away from thy presence... (Also Ps. 31:22, Jer. 7:15.)

*Lk. 17:15–18. One of [the lepers], when he saw that he was healed, turned back, praising God with a loud voice; and he fell on his face at Jesus' feet, giving him thanks. Now he was a Samaritan. Then said Jesus, "Were not ten cleansed? Where are the nine? Was no one found to return and give praise to God except this foreigner?"

Rom. 12:1. I appeal to you therefore, brethren, by the mercies of God, to present your bodies as a living sacrifice, holy and acceptable to God, which is your spiritual worship. (Also Rom. 6:13.)

Ps. 51:15–17. O Lord, open thou my lips, and my mouth shall show forth thy praise. For thou hast no delight in sacrifice; were I to give a burnt offering, thou wouldst not be pleased. The sacrifice acceptable to God is a broken spirit; a broken and contrite heart, O God, thou wilt not despise. (Also Mt. 15:7–8.)

Ps. 138:1. I give thee thanks, O Lord, with my whole heart... (Also Is. 65:14, Zeph. 3:14.)

Ps. 104:33. I will sing to the Lord as long as I live; I will sing praise to my God while I have being. (Also Ps. 63:4, 146:2.)

5. Soprano Aria
●Prayer: Accept my imperfect, earthly songs (25-5)
Öffne   meinen schlechten Liedern,
Open (to) my   poor   songs,

    Jesu, dein Genadenohr!
(O) Jesus, thine ear-of-grace!

Wenn ich   dort im höhern Chor
When I (someday over) there in-the higher choir
{When someday I sing over there in the heavenly choir}

Werde mit den Engeln singen,
Will   with the angels   sing,
{With the angels,}

    Soll mein Danklied   besser klingen.
(Then) will my song-of-thanks better sound.
{Then my song of thanks will sound better.}

*Lk. 17:15–18. One of [the lepers], when he saw that he was healed, turned back, praising God with a loud voice.

Ps. 119:108. Accept my offerings of praise, O Lord...

Heb. 13:15. Through [Christ] then, let us continually offer up a sacrifice of praise to God, that is, the fruit of lips that acknowledge his name. (Also Ps. 50:14, 23.)

Ps. 19:14. [O Lord,] let the words of my mouth and the meditation of my heart be acceptable in thy sight...

Ps. 120–134 (titles). A Song of Ascents (Luther: Ein Lied im höhern Chor)

Rev. 5:11. ...[In paradise] I heard around the throne and the living creatures and the elders the voice of many angels, numbering myriads of myriads and thousands of thousands, saying with a loud voice, "Worthy is the Lamb who was slain, to receive power and wealth and wisdom and might and honor and glory and blessing!"

6. Chorale
●Eternal praise for divine deliverance (25-6)
Ich will alle meine Tage
I would all   my   days
{Throughout my days I would}

*Lk. 17:14–18. When [Jesus] saw [the ten lepers] he said to them, "Go and show yourselves to the priests." And as they went they were cleansed. Then one of them, when he saw that he was healed, turned

Rühmen deine starke Hand,
Extol   thy   strong hand,

Daß du meine Plag und Klage
That thou my vexation and lamentation

Hast so herzlich abgewandt.
Hast so cordially   removed.

Nicht nur in der Sterblichkeit
Not only in -   mortality
{Not only in this life}

Soll dein Ruhm sein ausgebreit':
Shall thy fame   be spread-abroad:

Ich will's auch hernach erweisen
I   want-it also hereafter to-render
{I want to sing it hereafter as well}

Und dort ewiglich dich preisen.
And there eternally thee to-praise.
{And praise thee there eternally.}

BWV 26
Ach wie flüchtig, ach wie nichtig
(NBA I/27; BC A162)

24. S. after Trinity (BWV 60, 26)
*Col. 1:9–14 (Paul's prayer for the Colossians)
*Mt. 9:18–26 (Jesus raises Jairus' daughter from the dead; on the way, he heals the woman who touched his garment)
Librettist: Unknown

1. Chorus (Chorale Vs. 1)
●Transience of life is like a mist that disappears (26-1)
Ach wie flüchtig, ach wie nichtig
Ah, how transient, ah, how ephemeral

Ist der Menschen Leben!
Is (a) mortal's   life!

Wie ein Nebel bald entstehet,
Just-as a mist quickly forms,

Und auch wieder bald vergehet,
And likewise again quickly vanishes,

So ist unser Leben, sehet!
So is our   life, behold!
{Lo, so is our life!}

2. Tenor Aria (Based on Chorale Vs. 2)
●Time passes like a rushing stream of water (26-2)
So schnell ein rauschend Wasser schießt,
As fast (as) - rushing water gushes,

back, praising God with a loud voice; and he fell on his face at Jesus' feet, giving him thanks. Now he was a Samaritan. Then said Jesus, "Were not ten cleansed? Where are the nine? Was no one found to return and give praise to God except this foreigner?"
Rev. 14:2–3. I heard a voice from heaven like the sound of many waters and like the sound of thunder; the voice I heard was like the sound of harpers playing on their harps, and they sing a new song before the throne and before the four living creatures and before the elders. No one could learn that song except the hundred and forty-four thousand who had been redeemed from the earth.
Rev. 5:11–12. Then I looked, and I heard around the throne and the living creatures and the elders the voice of many angels, numbering myriads of myriads and thousands of thousands, saying with a loud voice, "Worthy is the Lamb who was slain..."
Rev. 15:3. And they sing the song of Moses, the servant of God, and the song of the Lamb, saying, "Great and wonderful are thy deeds, O Lord God the Almighty!..."
Ps. 104:33. I will sing to the Lord as long as I live; I will sing praise to my God while I have being.
Ps. 146:2. I will praise the Lord as long as I live; I will sing praises to my God while I have being. (Also Ps. 145:2.)
Ps. 63:4. So I will bless thee as long as I live...

*Mt. 9:18.** While [Jesus] was thus speaking to them, behold, a ruler came and knelt before him, saying, "My daughter has just died; but come and lay your hand on her, and she will live."
Ps. 39:4–6. Lord, let me know my end, and what is the measure of my days; let me know how fleeting my life is! Behold, thou hast made my days a few handbreadths, and my lifetime is as nothing in thy sight. Surely every man stands as a mere breath! Surely man goes about as a shadow!...
Jms. 4:14. ...You do not know about tomorrow. What is your life? For you are a mist that appears for a little time and then vanishes.
Job 7:7. Remember that my life is a breath...
Job 9:25. My days are swifter than a runner; they flee away, they see no good.
Ps. 78:39. [God] remembered that they were but flesh, a wind that passes and comes not again.
Ps. 102:3. For my days pass away like smoke...My days are like an evening shadow; I wither away like grass.

Job 7:6. My days are swifter than a weaver's shuttle, and come to their end without hope.
Job 9:25–26. My days are swifter than a runner; they flee away, they see no good. They go by like skiffs of reed, like an eagle swooping on the prey.

So eilen unser Lebenstage.
So hasten our life's-days.

Die Zeit vergeht, die Stunden eilen,
The time passes, the hours hasten,

Wie sich die Tropfen plötzlich teilen,
Just-like - - droplets suddenly break-up,

Wenn alles in den Abgrund schießt.
When everything into the abyss gushes.
{When everything gushes into the abyss.}

3. Alto Recit. (Based on Chorale Vss. 3–9)
●Time brings joy, beauty, learning, etc. to an end (26-3)
Die Freude wird zur Traurigkeit,
- Joy is-turned into sadness,

Die Schönheit fällt als eine Blume,
- Beauty falls like a flower,

Die größte Stärke wird geschwächt,
The greatest strength is weakened,

Es ändert sich das Glücke mit der Zeit,
- Changed-is - - fortune with - time,
{Fortune changes with time,}

Bald ist es aus mit Ehr und Ruhme,
Soon is ended - honor and fame,
{Soon honor and fame is ended,}

Die Wissenschaft und was ein Mensche dichtet,
- Learning and what a person invents,

Wird endlich durch das Grab vernichtet.
Is finally by the grave annihilated.
{Is finally annihilated by the grave.}

4. Bass Aria (Based on Chorale Vs. 10)
●Temporal treasures a seduction: they vanish quickly (26-4)
An irdische Schätze das Herze zu hängen,
Upon earthly treasures the heart to (set),
{To set the heart upon earthly treasures,}

Ist eine Verführung der törichten Welt.
Is a seduction of-the foolish world.

Wie leichtlich entstehen verzehrende Gluten,
How easily are-formed all-consuming embers,
{How easily all-consuming embers are formed,}

Wie rauschen und reißen die wallenden Fluten,
How rush and tear the seething torrents,
{How seething torrents rush and tear,}

Ps. 90:3–6, 9–10, 12. [O Lord,] thou turnest man back to the dust, and sayest, "Turn back, O children of men!" For a thousand years in thy sight are but as yesterday when it is past, or as a watch in the night. Thou dost sweep men away; they are like a dream, like grass which is renewed in the morning: in the morning it flourishes and is renewed; in the evening it fades and withers...For all our days pass away under thy wrath, our years come to an end like a sigh. The years of our life are threescore and ten, or even by reason of strength fourscore; yet their span is but toil and trouble; they are soon gone, and we fly away ...So teach us to number our days that we may get a heart of wisdom. (Also Ps. 39:5–6, 103:14–16, Job 7:7.)
Prov. 27:20. Sheol and Abaddon [i.e. the nether world] are never satisfied...

Jms. 4:9. Be wretched and mourn and weep. Let your laughter be turned to mourning and your joy to dejection (Luther: Traurigkeit).
Job 14:1–2. Man that is born of a woman is of few days, and full of trouble. He comes forth like a flower, and withers; he flees like a shadow, and continues not.
Is. 40:6–8. ...All flesh is grass, and all its beauty is like the fower of the field. The grass withers, the flower fades, when the breath of the Lord blows upon it; surely the people is grass. The grass withers, the flower fades; but the word of our God will stand for ever. (Also 1 Pet. 1:24, Ps. 103:15–16.)
Ecc. 12:1–3. Remember also your Creator in the days of your youth, before the evil days come, and the years draw nigh, when you will say, "I have no pleasure in them"...in the days when the keepers of the house tremble, and the strong men are bent...
Ps. 49:16–20. Be not afraid when one becomes rich, when the glory of his house increases. For when he dies he will carry nothing away; his glory will not go down after him...Though a man gets praise when he does well for himself, he will go to the generation of his fathers, who will never more see the light. Man cannot abide in his pomp, he is like the beasts that perish. (Also Ps. 52:7, 62:9–11, 89:48.)
Job 1:21. And [Job] said, "Naked I came from my mother's womb, and naked shall I return..."

Mt. 6:19–21. Do not lay up for yourselves treasures on earth, where moth and rust consume and where thieves break in and steal, but lay up for yourselves treasures in heaven, where neither moth nor rust consumes and where thieves do not break in and steal. For where your treasure is, there will your heart be also.
Ecc. 9:11–12. I saw that under the sun the race is not to the swift, nor the battle to the strong, nor bread to the wise, nor riches to the intelligent, nor favor to the men of skill; but time and chance happen to them all. For man does not know his time. Like fish which are taken in an evil net, and like birds which are caught in a snare, so the sons of men are snared at an evil time, when it suddenly falls upon them.
1 Jn. 2:15–17. Do not love the world or the things in the world...For all that is in the world...is not of the Father but is of the world. And the world passes away, and the lust of it; but he who does the will of God abides for ever.

Bis   alles   zerschmettert in Trümmern   zerfällt.
Until everything shattered   into wreckage disintegrates.
{Until everything is shattered, disintegrating into wreckage.}

5. Soprano Recit. (Based on Chorale Vss. 11–12)
•Death brings down the greatest splendor (26-5)
Die höchste Herrlichkeit und Pracht
The (greatest) majesty   and pomp

Umhüllt   zuletzt   des Todes Nacht.
Is-enveloped in-the-end (by) - death's night.

Wer   gleichsam als ein Gott gesessen,
He-who as-it-were as a god   has-sat,
{He who has sat like a god,}

Entgeht dem Staub und Asche nicht,
Eludes the dust and ashes not,
{Does not elude dust and ashes,}

Und wenn die letzte Stunde schläget,
And when that last   hour strikes,

Daß   man ihn zu der Erde träget,
(When) they him to the earth carry,
{When they carry him to earth,}

Und seiner Hoheit Grund   zerbricht,
And his greatness' foundation breaks-to-pieces,
{And the foundation of his greatness breaks to pieces,}

Wird seiner ganz vergessen.
Will   he completely forgotten (be).
{Then he will be completely forgotten.}

6. Chorale (Vs. 13)
•Transience of the earthly; whoever fears God abides (26–6)
Ach wie flüchtig, ach wie nichtig
Ah, how transient, ah, how ephemeral

Sind der Menschen Sachen!
Are (all) mortals' matters!
{Are all human matters!}

Alles,   alles, was wir sehen,
Everyting, everything, that we see,

Das muß fallen und vergehen.
It   must fall and pass-away.

Wer   Gott fürcht', bleibt ewig stehen.
Whoever God fears, remains eternally standing.
{But he who fears God will stand forever.}

Mt. 16:26. For what will it profit a man, if he gains the whole world and forfeits his life? Or what shall a man give in return for his life?

Ps. 49:16–20. Be not afraid when one becomes rich, when the glory of his house increases. For when he dies he will carry nothing away; his glory will not go down after him...Though a man gets praise when he does well for himself, he will go to the generation of his fathers, who will never more see the light. Man cannot abide in his pomp, he is like the beasts that perish. (Also Ps. 89:48.)
Jms. 4:13–15, 5:1. Come now, you who say, "Today or tomorrow we will go into such and such a town and spend a year there and trade and get gain"; whereas you do not know about tomorrow. What is your life? For you are a mist that appears for a little time and then vanishes. Instead you ought to say, "If the Lord wills, we shall live and we shall do this or that."...Come now, you rich, weep and howl for the miseries that are coming upon you...
Lk. 12:20–21. God said to [the rich man], "Fool! This night your soul is required of you; and the things you have prepared, whose will they be?" So is he who lays up treasure for himself, and is not rich toward God. (Also 1 Tim. 6:6–7.)
Acts 12:21–23. On an appointed day Herod put on his royal robes, took his seat upon the throne, and made an oration to [the people of Tyre and Sidon]. And the people shouted, "The voice of a god, and not of man!" Immediatedly an angel of the Lord smote him, because he did not give God the glory; and he was eaten by worms and died.
Ps. 103:15–16. As for man, his days are like grass; he flourishes like a flower of the field; for the wind passes over it, and it is gone, and its place knows it no more.
Ecc. 3:20. All go to one place; all are from the dust, and all turn to dust again. (Also Ps. 146:4.)

Ps. 39:4–6. Lord, let me know my end, and what is the measure of my days; let me know how fleeting my life is! Behold, thou hast made my days a few handbreadths, and my lifetime is as nothing in thy sight. Surely every man stands as a mere breath! Surely man goes about as a shadow!...
Mt. 24:35 [Christ]: Heaven and earth will pass away, but my words will not pass away.
1 Jn. 2:17. The world passes away, and the lust of it; but he who does the will of God abides for ever.
Ps. 15:1–2, 5. O Lord, who shall sojourn in thy tent?...He who walks blamelessly, and does what is right...He who does these things shall never be moved.
Ps. 16:8. I keep the Lord always before me; because he is at my right hand, I shall not be moved.
Ps. 125:1. Those who trust in the Lord are like Mount Zion, which cannot be moved, but abides for ever.

BWV 27
Wer weiß, wie nahe mir mein Ende
(NBA I/23; BC A138)

16. S. after Trinity (BWV 161, 95, 8, 27)
*Eph. 3:13–21 (Paul's prayer for the Ephesians; that they be spiritually strengthened)
*Lk. 7:11–17 (Jesus raises young man of Nain from the dead)
Librettist: Unknown. Movement 6 is borrowed from Johann Rosenmüller.

1. Chorale & Soprano, Alto, & Tenor Recits. (Chorale: see also 166–6)
●Death comes at any time, only God knows how soon (27-1)
S.A.T.B:
Wer weiß, wie nahe mir mein Ende?
Who knows, how near to-me my end (is)?

Soprano Recit:
Das weiß der liebe Gott allein,
That knows the dear God alone,
{That only the dear God knows,}

Ob meine Wallfahrt auf der Erden
Whether my pilgrimage on - earth

Kurz oder länger möge sein.
Short or longer may be.

S.A.T.B:
Hin geht die Zeit, her kommt der Tod,
Hence goes - time, hither comes - death,
{Time departs, death approaches,}

Alto Recit:
Und endlich kommt es doch so weit,
And finally comes it indeed so far,
{And finally the point is reached,}

Daß sie zusammentreffen werden.
(Where) they meet - .

S.A.T.B:
Ach, wie geschwinde und behende
Ah, how swiftly and adroitly

Kann kommen meine Todesnot!
Can come my death's-trial!

Tenor Recit:
Wer weiß, ob heute nicht
Who knows, whether (even) today not
{Who knows, whether perhaps even today}

Mein Mund die letzten Worte spricht!
My mouth (its) last words will-speak!

Drum bet ich alle Zeit:
Therefore pray I at-all times:
{Therefore I pray at all times:

*Lk. 7:11–12, 14. Soon afterward [Jesus] went to a city called Nain, and his disciples and a great crowd went with him. As he drew near to the gate of the city, behold, a man who had died was being carried out, the only son of his mother, and she was a widow; and a large crowd from the city was with her...And [Jesus] came and touched the bier...and he said, "Young man, I say to you, arise."
Ecc. 9:12. Man does not know his time. Like fish which are taken in an evil net, and like birds which are caught in a snare, so the sons of men are snared at an evil time, when it suddenly falls upon them.
Ps. 39:4–6. Lord, let me know my end, and what is the measure of my days; let me know how fleeting my life is! Behold, thou hast made my days a few handbreadths, and my lifetime is as nothing in thy sight. Surely every man stands as a mere breath! Surely man goes about as a shadow!...
Job 14:1–2, 5. Man that is born of woman is of few days, and full of trouble. He comes forth like a flower, and withers; he flees like a shadow, and continues not...His days are determined, and the number of his months is with thee, and thou hast appointed his bounds that he cannot pass...
Ps. 90:3–6, 9–10, 12. [O Lord,] thou turnest man back to the dust, and sayest, "Turn back, O children of men!" For a thousand years in thy sight are but as yesterday when it is past, or as a watch in the night. Thou dost sweep men away; they are like a dream, like grass which is renewed in the morning: in the morning it flourishes and is renewed; in the evening it fades and withers...For all our days pass away under thy wrath, our years come to an end like a sigh. The years of our life are threescore and ten, or even by reason of strength fourscore; yet their span is but toil and trouble; they are soon gone, and we fly away ...So teach us to number our days that we may get a heart of wisdom. (Also Ps. 103:14–16, Job 7:7.)
Jms. 4:13–15. Come now, you who say, "Today or tomorrow we will go into such and such a town and spend a year there and trade and get gain"; whereas you do not know about tomorrow. What is your life? For you are a mist that appears for a little time and then vanishes. Instead you ought to say, "If the Lord wills, we shall live and we shall do this or that."
Lk. 12:20. But God said to [the rich man], "Fool! This night your soul is required of you; and the things you have prepared, whose will they be?"
Heb. 3:7–8, 13. Therefore, as the Holy Spirit says, "Today, when you hear his voice, do not harden your hearts as in the rebellion..."
Num. 23:10. ...Let me die the death of the righteous, and let my end be like his! (Also Heb. 13:7.)

S.A.T.B:
Mein Gott, ich bitt durch Christi Blut,
My   God, I   pray through Christ's blood,

Mach's nur mit meinem Ende gut!
Make-it but with   my   end well!
{Just make it well with my end!}

2. Tenor Recit.
●Goal of my life is to prepare for death (27-2)
Mein Leben hat kein ander Ziel,
My   life   has no   other goal,

Als daß ich möge selig sterben
Than that I   may blessedly die

Und meines Glaubens Anteil erben;
And my   faith's portion inherit;

Drum   leb ich allezeit
Therefore live I at-all-times
{Therefore I live at all times}

Zum   Grabe fertig und bereit,
For-the grave ready and prepared,
{Ready and prepared for the grave,}

Und was das Werk der Hände tut,
And what the work of-(my) hands does,
{And the work I do with my hands,}

Ist gleichsam,   ob ich sicher wüßte,
Is the-same, (as) if I assuredly knew,
{Is no different than if I knew for certain}

Daß ich noch heute sterben müßte:
That I   yet today die   had-to:
{That I had to die today:}

Denn: Ende gut macht alles   gut!
For: End good makes everything good!
{For "All is well that ends well!"}

3. Alto Aria (First two lines based on Neumeister aria)
●Death is welcome; I take afflictions to the grave (27-3)
Willkommen! will ich sagen,
"Welcome!" will I   say,

Wenn der Tod   ans   Bette tritt.
When - death up-to-(my) bed steps.
{When death steps up to my bed.}

Fröhlich will ich folgen, wenn er ruft,
Joyfully will I follow, when he calls,
{When he calls, I will follow joyfully}

In die Gruft,
Into the tomb;

Ecc. 7:1–2, 8. ...The day of death [is better] than the day of birth...for this is the end of all men, and the living will lay it to heart...Better is the end of a thing than its beginning...
Ps. 116:15. Precious in the sight of the Lord is the death of his saints.

Phil. 3:8–14. Indeed I count everything as loss because of the surpassing worth of knowing Christ Jesus my Lord. For his sake I have suffered the loss of all things, and count them as refuse, in order that I may gain Christ and be found in him, not having a righteousness of my own, based on law, but that which is through faith in Christ...that I may know him and the power of his resurrection, and may share his sufferings, becoming like him in his death, that if possible I may attain the resurrection from the dead. Not that I have already obtained this or am already perfect; but I press on to make it my own...I press on toward the goal for the prize of the upward call of God in Christ Jesus.
Ps. 39:4. Lord, let me know my end, and what is the measure of my days (Luther: daß...mein Leben ein Ziel hat)...
Acts 20:24. I do not account my life of any value nor as precious to myself, if only I may accomplish my course and the ministry which I received...
Acts 21:13. Then Paul answered, "What are you doing, weeping and breaking my heart? For I am ready not only to be imprisoned but even to die at Jerusalem for the name of the Lord Jesus."
1 Pet. 1:3–4. ...We have been born anew to a living hope...and to an inheritance which is imperishable, undefiled, and unfading, kept in heaven for you.
2 Tim. 4:6–8, 18. ...The time of my departure has come. I have fought the good fight, I have finished the race, I have kept the faith. Henceforth there is laid up for me the crown of righteousness, which the Lord, the righteous judge, will award to me on that Day, and not only to me but also to all who have loved his appearing...The Lord will rescue me from every evil and save me for his heavenly kingdom...
Rom. 14:7–8. None of us lives to himself, and none of us dies to himself. If we live, we live to the Lord, and if we die, we die to the Lord; so then, whether we live or whether we die, we are the Lord's. (Also Phil. 1:21, 2 Cor. 5:9.)

Ecc. 7:1–2, 8. ...The day of death [is better] than the day of birth. It is better to go to the house of mourning than to go to the house of feasting; for this is the end of all men, and the living will lay it to heart...Better is the end of a thing than its beginning...
Phil. 1:21–24. To me to live is Christ, and to die is gain. If it is to be life in the flesh, that means fruitful labor for me. Yet which I shall choose I cannot tell. I am hard pressed between the two. My desire is to depart and be with Christ, for that is far better. But to remain in the flesh is more necessary on your account. (Also 2 Cor. 5:6–10.)
Rev. 21:4. [God] will wipe away every tear from their eyes, and death shall be no more, neither shall there be mourning nor crying nor pain any more, for the former things have passed away.

Alle meine Plagen
All   my   afflictions

Nehm ich mit.
Take   I   with (me).
{I'll take with me.}

4. Soprano Recit.
•Yearning for heaven where the Lamb and bridegroom is
(27–4)
Ach,   wer doch schon im Himmel wär!
Ah, (would that) (I) indeed already in heaven were!
{Ah, how I wish I were already in heaven!}

Ich habe Lust zu scheiden
I   have desire to depart
{I would like to depart}

Und mit dem Lamm,
And with the lamb,
{And with the lamb,}

Das   aller Frommen   Bräutigam,
(Who-is-of) all-the righteous (the) bridegroom,
{The bridegroom of all the righteous,}

Mich in der Seligkeit zu weiden.
Myself in - blessedness to pasture.
{Find blessed pasture.}

        Flügel   her!
(Ye) wings (come) hither!

Ach,   wer doch   schon im Himmel wär!
Ah, (would that) (I) indeed already in   heaven were!
{Ah, how I wish I were already in heaven!}

5. Bass Aria
•Farewell world! I am going to heaven! (27–5)
Gute Nacht, du Weltgetümmel!
Good night, thou worldly-tumult!

Jezt mach ich mit dir Beschluß;
Now make   I with thee conclusion;
{Now I make an end with thee;}

Ich steh schon mit einem Fuß
I   stand already with one foot
{I stand with one foot already}

Bei dem lieben Gott im Himmel.
With (my) dear God in heaven.

6. Chorale (Movement borrowed from Johann Rosenmüller)
•Farewell to the world; comparing world and heaven (27–6)
Welt,   ade! ich bin dein müde,
World, farewell! I am of-thee weary,

1 Cor. 15:49–50. Just as we have borne the image of the man of dust, we shall also bear the image of the man of heaven. I tell you this, brethren: flesh and blood cannot inherit the kingdom of God, nor does the perishable inherit the imperishable. (Also 2 Cor. 5:1–4.)
Is. 25:8. [The Lord] will swallow up death for ever (Luther: Tod verschlingen ewiglich), and the Lord God will wipe away tears from all faces...

Phil. 1:23. ...My desire is to depart (Luther: Ich habe Lust abzuscheiden) and be with Christ, for that is far better.
2 Cor. 5:6–8. We are always of good courage; we know that while we are at home in the body we are away from the Lord, for we walk by faith, not by sight...We would rather be away from the body and at home with the Lord.
Heb. 11:13, 16. These [heroes] all died in faith...having acknowledged that they were strangers and exiles on the earth...As it is, they desire a better country, that is, a heavenly one. Therefore God is not ashamed to be called their God, for he has prepared for them a city.
Rev. 7:17. The Lamb in the midst of the throne will be their shepherd, and he will guide them to springs of living water; and God will wipe away every tear from their eyes.
Ps. 23:1–3. The Lord is my shepherd, I shall not want; he makes me lie down in green pastures. He leads me beside still waters; he restores my soul...
Rev. 21:9. ...One of the seven angels...spoke to me, saying, "Come, I will show you the Bride, the wife of the Lamb."
Rev. 19:6–9. Then I heard what seemed to be the voice of a great multitude crying, "Hallelujah! For the Lord our God the Almighty reigns. Let us rejoice and exult and give him the glory, for the marriage of the Lamb has come, and his Bride has made herself ready..." And the angel said to me, "Write this: Blessed are those who are invited to the marriage supper of the Lamb."... (Also Mt. 22:1–2, Mt. 25:1–13.)
Ps. 55:6. ...O that I had wings like a dove! I would fly away and be at rest.
1 Jn. 2:15. Do not love the world or the things in the world. If any one loves the world, love for the Father is not in him.
Jms. 4:4. ...Do you not know that friendship with the world is enmity with God? Therefore whoever wishes to be a friend of the world makes himself an enemy of God.
Jn. 15:19 [Christ]: If you were of the world, the world would love its own; but because you are not of the world, but I chose you out of the world, therefore the world hates you.
Jn. 16:33 [Christ]: I have said this to you, that in me you may have peace. In the world you have tribulation; but be of good cheer, I have overcome the world.
Rom. 12:2. Do not be conformed to this world but be transformed by the renewal of your mind...
Col. 3:1–3. ...Seek the things that are above, where Christ is, seated at the right hand of God. Set your minds on things that are above, not on things that are on earth. For you have died and your life is hid with Christ in God.

Heb. 4:9–11. So then, there remains a sabbath rest for the people of God; for whoever enters God's rest also ceases from his labors as God did from his. Let us therefore strive to enter that rest...

Ich will nach dem Himmel zu,
I would to - heaven (go),

Da wird sein der rechte Friede
There will be - true peace
{There I will find true peace}

Und die ewge, stolze Ruh.
And - eternal, splendid rest.

Welt, bei dir ist Krieg und Streit,
World, with thee is war and strife,

Nichts denn lauter Eitelkeit,
Nothing but sheer vanity,

In dem Himmel allezeit
In - heaven at-all-times,

Friede, Freud und Seligkeit.
Peace, joy, and blessedness.

BWV 28
Gottlob! nun geht das Jahr zu Ende
(NBA I/3; BC A20)

1. S. after Christmas (BWV 152, 122, 28)
*Gal. 4:1–7 (Through Christ we come of age and are free from the law)
*Lk. 2:33–40 (Simeon and Hanna prophesy of Christ)
Librettist: Erdmann Neumeister

1. Soprano Aria
●Old year comes to close: praise God for blessings (28–1)
Gottlob! nun geht das Jahr zu Ende,
Praise-God! Now (comes) the year to (an) end,
{Praise God! Now the year comes to an end,}

Das neue rücket schon heran.
The new (one) advances already (towards-us).

Gedenke, meine Seele, dran,
Ponder, my soul, on-this,

Wieviel dir deines Gottes Hände
How-much to-thee thy God's hands

Im alten Jahre Guts getan!
In-the old year good have-done!
{How much good thy God's hands have done thee this past year!}

Stimm ihm ein frohes Danklied an;
Strike-up for-him a happy song-of-thanks - ;

So wird er ferner dein gedenken
Thus will he furthermore thee remember
{Thus will he furthermore remember thee}

Rev. 14:13. And I heard a voice from heaven saying, "Write this: Blessed are the dead who die in the Lord henceforth." "Blessed indeed," says the Spirit, "that they may rest from their labors, for their deeds follow them!"

Jms. 4:1–2, 4. What causes wars, and what causes fightings among you? Is it not your passions that are at war in your members? You desire and do not have; so you kill. And you covet and cannot obtain; so you fight and wage war... Unfaithful creatures! Do you not know that friendship with the world is enmity with God? Therefore whoever wishes to be a friend of the world makes himself an enemy of God.

Mt. 24:6. ...You will hear of wars and rumors of wars...

Eph. 4:17–18. ...The Gentiles [live] in the futility (Luther: Eitelkeit) of their minds; they are darkened in their understanding...

Jn. 14:3 [Christ]: ...I go and prepare a place for you...

Lk. 16:22–25. The poor man died and was carried by the angels to Abraham's bosom...Abraham said [to the rich man], "Son, remember that you in your lifetime received your good things, and Lazarus in like manner evil things; but now he is comforted here, and you are in anguish..."

Mt. 25:21. [The] master said to [his faithful servant], "Well done, good and faithful servant; you have been faithful over a little, I will set you over much; enter into the joy of your master."

Ps. 65:11. [O Lord,] thou crownest the year with thy bounty...

Ps. 77:11–14. I will call to mind the deeds of the Lord; yea, I will remember thy wonders of old. I will meditate on all thy work, and muse on thy mighty deeds. Thy way, O God, is holy. What god is great like our God? Thou art the God who workest wonders, who hast manifested thy might among the peoples.

Ps. 111:7. The works of his hand are faithful and just...

Ps. 143:5. [O Lord,] I remember the days of old, I meditate on all that thou hast done; I muse on what thy hands have wrought.

Ps. 9:1–2. I will give thanks to the Lord with my whole heart; I will tell of all thy wonderful deeds. I will be glad and exult in thee, I will sing praise to thy name, O Most High. (Also Ps. 105:1–2 / 1 Chron. 16:8–9, Ps. 107:21–22, Is. 25:1.)

Ps. 145:1–2, 4. I will extol thee, my God and King, and bless thy name for ever and ever...Great is the Lord, and greatly to be praised, and his greatness is unsearchable. One generation shall laud thy works to another, and shall declare thy mighty acts.

Is. 63:7. I will recount the steadfast love of the Lord, the praises of the Lord, according to all that the Lord has granted us, and the great goodness to the house of Israel which he has granted them according to his mercy, according to the abundance of his steadfast love.

Ps. 116:7. Return, O my soul, to your rest; for the Lord has dealt bountifully with you.

Ps. 50:14, 23. Offer to God a sacrifice of thanksgiving, and pay your vows to the Most High...He who brings thanksgiving as his sacrifice honors me; to him who orders his way aright I will show the salvation of God!

Und mehr zum neuen Jahre schenken.
And more for-the new   year   give.
{And give thee more for the new year.}

2. Chorus (Chorale) (Perhaps taken from older work)
●Exhortation: Bless the Lord, O my soul: Ps. 103:1-6[1] (28-2)
       [1]paraphrase

Nun   lob, mein Seel, den Herren,
Now praise, my soul,   the Lord,
{Now praise the Lord, O my soul,}

Was   in mir ist, den Namen sein!
Whatever in me is,   the name of-his!
{All that is in me, praise his name!}

Sein Wohltat   tut er mehren,
His benefaction doth he increase,

Vergiß es nicht, o Herze mein!
Forget it not, O heart of-mine!

      Hat dir dein Sünd vergeben
(He) hath thee thy sin   forgiven
{He hath forgiven thy sin,}

Und heilt dein Schwachheit groß,
And heals thy   weakness   great,
{And heals thy great weakness,}

Errett' dein armes Leben,
Saves   thy   poor   life,

Nimmt dich in seinen Schoß.
Takes   thee (to) his   bosom.

Mit reichem Trost beschüttet,
With rich   comfort showers,
{Showers rich comfort upon thee,}

Verjüngt,   dem Adler gleich.
Rejuvenates, the eagle similar.
{Rejuvenates thee like an eagle.}

Der Kön'g schafft Recht, behütet,
The king works justice: guards

Die   leid'n in seinem Reich.
Those (who) suffer in   his kingdom.

3. Bass Recit. & Arioso
●Vox Christi: God's promise of blessing: Jer. 32:41 (28-3)
So spricht der Herr; Es soll mir eine Lust sein,
Thus says the Lord; It shall to-me a pleasure be,

daß ich ihnen Gutes tun soll, und ich will
that I to-them kindness shall-do, and I will

Ps. 28:7. ...My heart exults, and with my song I give thanks to him.
Ps. 23:6. Surely goodness and mercy shall follow me all the days of my life... (Also Ps. 112:4–7.)

Ps. 103:1–13. *Bless the Lord, O my soul; and all that is within me, bless his holy name! Bless the Lord, O my soul, and forget not all his benefits, who forgives all your iniquity, who heals all your diseases, who redeems your life from the Pit, who crowns you with steadfast love and mercy, who satisfies you with good as long as you live so that your youth is renewed like the eagle's. The Lord works vindication and justice for all who are oppressed*...The Lord is merciful and gracious, slow to anger and abounding in steadfast love...He does not deal with us according to our sins, nor requite us according to our iniquities. For as the heavens are high above the earth, so great is his steadfast love toward those who fear him; as far as the east is from the west, so far does he remove our transgressions from us. As a father pities his children, so the Lord pities those who fear him.
Ps. 107:1–2, 8–9, 15–16, 21–22, 31–32. O give thanks to the Lord, for he is good; for his steadfast love endures for ever! Let the redeemed of the Lord say so, whom he has redeemed from trouble...Let them thank the Lord for his steadfast love, for his wonderful works to the sons of men! For he satisfies him who is thirsty and the hungry he fills with good things...And let them offer sacrifices of thanksgiving, and tell of his deeds in songs of joy!...Let them extol him in the congregation of the people, and praise him in the assembly of the elders.
Ps. 5:12. For thou dost bless the righteous, O Lord; thou dost cover him with favor as with a shield.
Is. 40:29–31. He gives power to the faint, and to him who has no might he increases strength. Even youths shall faint and be weary, and young men shall fall exhausted; but they who wait for the Lord shall renew their strength, they shall mount up with wings like eagles, they shall run and not be weary, they shall walk and not faint.
Ps. 146:5, 7. Happy is he whose help is the God of Jacob, whose hope is in the Lord his God...Who executes justice (Luther: Recht schafft) for the oppressed; who gives food to the hungry... (Also Ps. 135:14.)
Ps. 146:9. The Lord watches over the sojourners, he upholds the widow and the fatherless...
Ps. 10:14. [O Lord,] thou dost see; yea thou dost note trouble and vexation, that thou mayest take it into thy hands; the hapless commits himself to thee; thou hast been the helper of the fatherless.

Jer. 32:28, 40–41. Therefore, *thus says the Lord:* ...I will make with them an everlasting covenant, that I will not turn away from doing good to them; and I will put the fear of me in their hearts, that they may not turn from me. *I will rejoice in doing them good, and I will plant them in this land in faithfulness, with all my heart and all my soul.*
1 Chron. 17:9 [God]: I will appoint a place for my people Israel, and will plant them, that they may dwell in their own place, and be disturbed no more...

sie   in diesem Lande pflanzen reulich,
them in   this   land   plant faithfully,

von   ganzem Herzen und von   ganzer Seelen.
(with) (my) whole   heart   and (with) (my) whole   soul.

4. Tenor Recit.
●God is fountain, light, treasure, to his followers (28-4)
Gott ist ein Quell,   wo   lauter   Güte fleußt;
God is a fountain, where nothing-but goodness flows;

Gott ist ein Licht, wo   lauter Gnade scheinet;
God is a light, where nothing-but grace shines;

Gott ist ein Schatz, der lauter Segen heißt;
God is a treasure, that nothing-but blessing signifies;

Gott ist ein Herr, der's treu und herzlich meinet.
God is a Lord, who-it faithfully and heartfelt intends.
{God is a Lord whose intentions are faithful and heartfelt.}

Wer   ihn im Glauben liebt, in Liebe kindlich ehrt,
Whoever him in faith   loves, in love childlike honors,
{Whoever loves him in faith, honors him in childlike love,}

Sein Wort von   Herzen hört
His Word from (the) heart heeds
{Heeds his word from the heart,}

Und sich von bösen Wegen kehrt,
And - from evil   ways does-turn,
{And turns from evil ways,}

Dem gibt er sich mit allen Gaben.
To-him gives he himself with all   gifts.
{To him he gives himself with every gift.}

Wer   Gott hat, der muß alles haben.
Whoever God has, he must everything have.
{Whoever has God, must have everything.}

5. Alto & Tenor Duet
●New Year's prayer for blessing as in the past year (28-5)
Gott hat uns im heurigen Jahre gesegnet,
God has us in the-current year blessed,
{God has blessed us in the current year,}

Daß Wohltun und Wohlsein einander begegnet.
So-that good-deed and good-health each-other have-met.

Wir loben ihn herzlich und bitten darneben,
We praise him heartily and ask in-addition,

Er woll auch ein glückliches neues Jahr geben.
(That) he would also a prosperous new year grant.
{That he would also grant us a prosperous new year.}

Deut. 30:9. ...The Lord will again take delight in prospering you, as he took delight in your fathers.
Zeph. 3:17. The Lord, your God, is in your midst...he will rejoice over you with gladness, he will renew you in his love; he will exult over you with loud singing as on a day of festival.

Col. 3:11. ...Christ is all and in all.
Ps. 36:9. [O Lord]...with thee is the **fountain** of life; in thy light do we see light. (Also Jer. 2:13.)
Jn. 4:14 [Christ]: Whoever drinks of the water that I shall give him will never thirst; the water that I shall give him will become in him a spring of water welling up to eternal life. (Also Jn. 6:35, 7:38.)
Ps. 27:1. The Lord is my **light** and my salvation... (Also 1 Pet. 2:9.)
Jn. 8:12. Jesus spoke to them, saying, "I am the light of the world." (Also 2 Cor. 4:6.)
Mt. 13:44. The kingdom of heaven is like **treasure** (Luther: Schatz) hidden in a field, which a man found and covered up; then in his joy he goes and sells all that he has and buys that field.
Ps. 73:25. [O Lord,] whom have I in heaven but thee? And there is nothing upon earth that I desire besides thee.
Jer. 31:3 [God]: ...I have loved you with an everlasting love; therefore I have continued my faithfulness to you.
Jer. 29:11. I know the plans I have for you, says the Lord, plans for welfare and not for evil, to give you a future and a hope.
Mt. 7:11. If you then, who are evil, know how to give good gifts to your children, how much more will your Father who is in heaven give good things to those who ask him!
Mt. 22:37. You shall love the Lord your God with all your heart, and with all your soul, and with all your mind.
Mk. 10:14-15. Jesus...said to them, "...Whoever does not receive the kingdom of God like a child shall not enter it."
Ps. 119:10. [O Lord,] with my whole heart I seek thee; let me not wander from thy commandments! (Also 2 Chron. 15:15, Jer. 29:13.)
2 Chron. 7:14 [God]: If my people who are called by my name humble themselves, and pray and seek my face, and turn from their wicked ways, then I will hear from heaven, and will forgive their sin and heal their land.
Rom. 8:32. He who did not spare his own Son but gave him up for us all, will he not also give us all things with him?

Ps. 67:6-7. The earth has yielded its increase; God, our God, has blessed us. God has blessed us...
1 Sam. 7:12. Then Samuel took a stone and set it up between Mizpah and Jeshanah, and called its name Ebenezer, for he said, "Hitherto the Lord has helped us."
Ps. 85:1-2, 9-12. Lord, thou wast favorable to thy land; thou didst restore the fortunes of Jacob. Thou didst forgive the iniquity of thy people; thou didst pardon all their sin...Surely his salvation is at hand for those who fear him, that glory may dwell in our land. Steadfast love (Luther: and faithfulness will meet; righteousness and peace will kiss each other. Faithfulness will spring up from the ground, and righteousness will look down from the sky. Yea, the Lord will give what is good, and and our land will yield its increase.

Wir hoffen's   von   seiner beharrlichen Güte
We hope-it because-of his   persevering kindness

Und preisen's im voraus mit dankbarm Gemüte.
And extol-it in advance with thankful   spirit.

6. Chorale (See also 16-6.)
●New Years prayer; thanks for blessings in Christ (28-6)
All solch dein   Güt   wir preisen,
All this   thy goodness we praise,

Vater ins Himmels Thron,
(O) Father, on heaven's throne,

Die   du uns tust beweisen
Which thou to-us dost   show

Durch Christum, deinen Sohn,
Through Christ,   thy Son,

Und bitten ferner   dich:
And ask furthermore of-thee:

Gib uns ein friedsam Jahre,
Give us   a peaceful year;

Für allem Leid bewahre
From all harm protect

Und nähr uns mildiglich.
And feed us   tenderly.

Ps. 32:10. ...Steadfast love surrounds him who trusts in the Lord (Luther: wer aber auf den Herrn hofft, den wird die Güte umfangen). **Heb. 11:1.** Now faith is the assurance of things hoped for, the conviction of things not seen.

Jms. 1:17. Every good endowment and every perfect gift is from above, coming down from the Father of lights... (Also Mt. 7:11.)
Ps. 31:19, 21. [O Lord,] how abundant is thy goodness, which thou hast laid up for those who fear thee, and wrought for those who take refuge in thee...Blessed be the Lord, for he has wondrously shown his steadfast love to me...
Eph. 1:3. Blessed be the God and Father of our Lord Jesus Christ, who has blessed us in Christ with every spiritual blessing in the heavenly places...
Eph. 2:7. That in the coming ages he might show the immeasurable riches of his grace in kindness toward us in Christ Jesus.
Ps. 84:11. ...No good thing does the Lord withhold from those who walk uprightly.
Ps. 29:11. May the Lord give strength to his people! May the Lord bless his people with peace! (Also Ps. 122:6-7, 147:14.)
Ps. 12:7. Do thou, O Lord, protect us...
Ps. 121:2, 7-8. My help comes from the Lord, who made heaven and earth...The Lord will keep you from all evil; he will keep your life. The Lord will keep your going out and your coming in from this time forth and for evermore.
Ps. 37:3. Trust in the Lord, and do good; so you will dwell in the land, and enjoy security (Luther: nähre dich redlich).
Is. 40:11. He will feed his flock like a shepherd, he will gather the lambs in his arms, he will carry them in his bosom, and gently lead those that are with young. (Also Ezek. 34:11-16, Ps. 23:1-2, Rev. 7:17.)

BWV 29
Wir danken dir, Gott, wir danken dir
(NBA I/32; BC B8)

Change of Town Council (BWV 71, 119, 193, 120, 29, 69)
Librettist: Unknown

1. Sinfonia (Adapted from BWV 120a-4)

2. Chorus
●Thanks to God & proclamation of his wonders: Ps. 75:1 (29-2)
Wir danken dir,   Gott, wir danken dir und verkündigen
We   thank thee, (O) God, we thank thee and   proclaim

deine Wunder.
thy   wonders.

Ps. 75:1. *We give thanks to thee, O God; we give thanks; we call on thy name and recount thy wondrous deeds.*
1 Chron. 29:13. ...We thank thee, our God, and praise thy glorious name.
Ps. 79:13. We thy people, the flock of thy pasture, will give thanks to thee for ever; from generation to generation we will recount thy praise.
Ps. 9:1-2. I will give thanks to the Lord with my whole heart; I will tell of all thy wonderful deeds. I will be glad and exult in thee, I will sing praise to thy name, O Most High. (Also Ps. 105:1-2 / 1 Chron. 16:8-9, Ps. 107:21-22, Is. 25:1.)
Ps. 77:14. [O Lord,] thou art the God who workest wonders, who hast manifested thy might among the peoples. (Also 1 Chron. 16:9, 12 / Ps. 105:2, 5.)

3. Tenor Aria
●Praise to God that Zion is still his city (29-3)
Halleluja,   Stärk und Macht
Hallelujah, strength, and might

Rev. 5:11-12. Then I...heard around the throne...the voice of many angels...saying with a loud voice, "Worthy is the Lamb who was slain, to receive power (Luther: Kraft) and wealth and wisdom and might (Luther: Stärke) and honor and glory and blessing!"

Sei   des Allerhöchsten Namen!
Be-to   the   Most-High's   name!

Zion ist noch seine Stadt,
Zion is   still   his   city,

Da   er seine Wohnung hat,
Where he his   dwelling has,

Da   er noch bei unserm Samen
Where he still with   our   seed

An der Väter Bund   gedacht.
-   The fathers' covenant remembers.
{Where he still remembers his covenant to our fathers with us, the offspring.}

4. Bass Recit.
●Praise to God for blessing our city and borders (29–4)
Gottlob!   es geht uns wohl!
Praise-God! It goes for-us well!
{Praise God! We are greatly blessed!}

Gott ist noch unsre Zuversicht,
God is   still   our confidence,

Sein Schutz, sein Trost und Licht
His protection, his comfort and light

Beschirmt die Stadt und die Paläste.
Shields   the city and the palaces.

Sein Flügel hält die Mauern feste.
His pinions hold the walls   secure.

Er läßt uns allerorten   segnen,
He allows us in-all-places to-be-blessed,
{He blesses us in all places;}

Der Treue,   die den Frieden küßt,
That faithfulness, which -   peace kisses,
{The faithfulness that kisses peace,}

Muß   für   und für
Must forever and ever

Gerechtigkeit begegnen.
(By) righteousness   be-met.

Wo   ist   ein solches Volk wie wir,
Where is (there) a such people as we,
{Where is there such a people as we,}

Dem   Gott so nah und gnädig ist!
To-whom God so near and gracious is!
{To whom God is so near and gracious?}

Ps. 76:2. His abode has been established in Salem, his dwelling place in Zion. (Also Ps. 9:11, 87:2, 135:21, Is. 8:18.)
Heb. 12:22. But you have come to Mount Zion and to the city of the living God, the heavenly Jerusalem...
Gal. 3:8–9, 29. The scripture, foreseeing that God would justify the Gentiles by faith, preached the gospel beforehand to Abraham, saying, "In you shall all the nations be blessed." So then, those who are men of faith are blessed with Abraham who had faith...that in Christ Jesus the blessing of Abraham might come upon the Gentiles...And if you are Christ's, then you are Abraham's offspring, heirs according to promise. (Also Lk. 1:67–68, 72.)
Lk. 1:54–55. [The Lord] has helped his servant Israel, in remembrance of his mercy, as he spoke to our fathers, to Abraham and to his posterity for ever. (Also Lk. 1:67–68, 72.)

Ps. 67:5–7. Let the peoples praise thee, O God; let all the peoples praise thee! The earth has yielded its increase; God, our God, has blessed us. God has blessed us; let all the ends of the earth fear him!
Ps. 33:12. Blessed is the nation whose God is the Lord, the people whom he has chosen as his heritage!
Ps. 89:15–17. Blessed are the people who know the festal shout, who walk, O Lord, in the light of thy countenance, who exult in thy name all the day, and extol thy righteousness. For thou art the glory of their strength; by thy favor our horn is exalted.
Ps. 46:1, 7. God is our refuge (Luther: Zuversicht) and strength, a very present help in trouble...The Lord of hosts is with us; the God of Jacob is our refuge. (Zuversicht: also
Ps. 61:3, 62:7, 71:5, 7, 142:5; Schutz: 2 Sam. 22:2 / Ps. 18:2, Ps. 59:9, 17, 94:22)
Ps. 48:3. Within her citadels (Luther: Palästen) God has shown himself a sure defense (Luther: Schutz).
Ps. 122:6–7. Pray for the peace of Jerusalem! "...Peace be within your walls, and security within your towers!" (Also Is. 26:1–3.)
Ps. 85:1, 9–14. Lord, thou wast favorable to thy land... Surely his salvation is at hand for those who fear him, that glory may dwell in our land. Steadfast love and faithfulness will meet; righteousness and peace will kiss each other. Faithfulness will spring up from the ground, and righteousness will look down from the sky. Yea the Lord will give what is good, and our land will yield its increase. Righteousness will go before him, and make his footsteps a way.
Ps. 36:7. How precious is thy steadfast love, O God! The children of men take refuge in the shadow of thy wings. (Also Ps. 17:8, 36:7, 57:1, 61:4, 91:1–6 Deut. 32:10–11.)
Deut. 4:7–8. *For what great nation is there that has a god so near to it as the Lord our God is to us,* whenever we call upon him? And what great nation is there, that has statutes and ordinances so righteous as all this law which I set before you this day? (Also 2 Sam. 7:23.)

5. Soprano Aria
●National blessing requested of God (29-5)

Gedenk   an uns mit deiner Liebe,
Be-mindful of us with thy   love,

Schleuß uns in dein Erbarmen ein!
Envelop us (with) thy   mercy - !

Segne die, so uns regieren,
Bless those, who us   govern,

Die uns leiten, schützen,   führen,
Who us lead,   protect, (and) guide,

Segne, die   gehorsam sein!
Bless, those (who) obedient are!
{And bless all loyal subjects!}

6. Alto Recit. & Chorus
●National response to continued blessing (29-6)

Vergiß es   ferner nicht, mit deiner Hand
Forget - furthermore not, with thy   hand
{Forget not in the future}

Uns Gutes zu erweisen;
Us good to show;
{To show good to us with thy hand;}

So soll
So shall

Dich unsre Stadt und unser Land,
Thee our   city and our   land,

Das deiner Ehre voll,
Which of-thy honor is-full,
{So shall our city and our land, which is filled with thy honor, praise thee,}

Mit Opfern und mit   Danken preisen,
With sacrifices and with thanksgiving, praise,
{With sacrifices and with thanksgiving,}

Und alles   Volk soll sagen:
And all (the) people shall say:

Amen!
Amen!

7. Alto Aria
●Hallelujah, strength and might to name of Almighty (29-7)

Halleluja, Stärk und Macht
Hallelujah, strength, and might

Sei des allerhöchsten Namen!
Be to-the Most-High's   name!

Ps. 28:8–9. The Lord is the strength of his people, he is the saving refuge of his anointed. O save thy people, and bless thy heritage; be thou their shepherd, and carry them for ever. (Also Deut. 26:15, Is. 33:2.)

2 Chron. 6:42. ...Remember thy steadfast love for David thy servant. (Also Ps. 98:3.)

Ps. 103:13. As a father pities his children, so the Lord pities those who fear him.

Mal. 1:9. ...Entreat the favor of God, that he may be gracious to us.

1 Tim. 2:1–2. ...I urge that supplications, prayers, intercessions, and thanksgivings be made for all men, for kings and all who are in high positions, that we may lead a quiet and peaceable life, godly and respectful in every way.

Rom. 13:1–2. Let every person be subject to the governing authorities. For there is no authority except from God, and those that exist have been instituted by God. Therefore he who resists the authorities resists what God has appointed, and those who resist will incur judgment.

Ps. 77:9. Has God forgotten to be gracious?...

Deut. 26:15. Look down from thy holy habitation, from heaven, and bless thy people Israel and the ground which thou hast given us, as thou didst swear to our fathers...

Ps. 28:8–9. The Lord is the strength of his people, he is the saving refuge of his anointed. O save thy people, and bless thy heritage; be thou their shepherd, and carry them for ever.

Ps. 3:8. Deliverance belongs to the Lord; thy blessing be upon thy people!

Ps. 79:13. Then we thy people, the flock of thy pasture, will give thanks to thee for ever; from generation to generation we will recount thy praise.

Is. 43:21 [God]: ...[I will bless] my chosen people, the people whom I formed for myself that they might declare my praise.

Ps. 126:1–2. When the Lord restored the fortunes of Zion, we were like those who dream. Then our mouth was filled with laughter, and our tongue with shouts of joy; then they said among the nations, "The Lord has done great things for them."

Ps. 50:23 [God]: He who brings thanksgiving as his sacrifice honors me...

Ps. 147:12–14. Praise the Lord, O Jerusalem! Praise your God, O Zion! For he strengthens the bars of your gates; he blesses your sons within you. He makes peace in your borders; he fills you with the finest of the wheat...

Deut. 27:15–26. ...And all the people shall say, "Amen."...

Neh. 8:6. And Ezra blessed the Lord, the great God; and all the people answered, "Amen, Amen." (Also Deut. 27:15–26.)

Rev. 5:11–12. Then I...heard around the throne...the voice of many angels, numbering myriads of myriads and thousands of thousands, saying with a loud voice, "Worthy is the Lamb who was slain, to receive power (Luther: Kraft) and wealth and wisdom and might (Luther: Stärke) and honor and glory and blessing!"

Ps. 9:2. I will be glad and exult in thee, I will sing praise to thy name, O Most High.

8. Chorale (See also 51–4, 167–5.)

●Prayer of praise and dedication to Trinity (29–8)

Sei Lob und Preis mit Ehren
- Laud and praise with honors (to)

Gott   Vater, Sohn,   Heiligem Geist!
God (the) Father, Son, (and) Holy Ghost!

Der woll in uns vermehren,
(May) he - in us   increase

Was   er uns aus Gnaden verheißt,
That-which he to-us out-of grace does-promise,

Daß   wir ihm fest   vertrauen,
So-that we him firmly (would) trust,
{So that we would firmly trust him,}

Gänzlich verlassn auf ihn,
Completely rely   on him,

Von   Herzen auf ihn bauen,
With (all our) heart upon him build,

Daß   unsr Herz, Mut und Sinn
So-that our heart, mettle, and mind

Ihm   tröstlich solln anhangen;
To-him cheerfully would   adhere;

Drauf   singen wir zur Stund:
Thereupon sing we at-this hour:

Amen, wir werden's erlangen,
Amen, we will-it   attain,

Glaubn wir aus Herzens Grund.
(If) believe we from heart's bottom.
{If we believe with all our heart.}

Rev. 7:11–12. All the angels stood round the throne and round the elders and the four living creatures, and they fell on their faces before the throne and worshiped God, saying, "Amen! Blessing and glory and wisdom and thanksgiving and honor and power and might be to our God for ever and ever! Amen."

1 Thess. 3:12–13. May the Lord make you increase (Luther: euch vermehre)...so that he may establish your hearts unblamable in holiness before our God and Father...

Phil. 1:6, 9. I am sure that he who began a good work in you will bring it to completion at the day of Jesus Christ...And it is my prayer that your love may abound more and more, with knowledge and all discernment... (Also Ps. 138:8.)

1 Jn. 2:24–25. Let what you heard from the beginning abide in you. If what you heard from the beginning abides in you, then you will abide in the Son and in the Father. And this is what he has promised us, eternal life.

2 Thess. 2:16–17. Now may our Lord Jesus Christ himself, and God our Father, who loved us and gave us eternal comfort and good hope through grace, comfort your hearts and establish them in every good work and word.

Mt. 7:24 [Christ]: Every one then who hears these words of mine and does them will be like a wise man who built his house upon the rock...

1 Cor. 3:11. For no other foundation can any one lay than that which is laid, which is Jesus Christ.

Mt. 22:37–38. ...You shall love the Lord your God with all your heart, and with all your soul, and with all your mind. This is the great and first commandment. (Also Deut. 6:5.)

Deut. 10:20. You shall fear the Lord your God; you shall serve him and cleave to him (Luther: ihm anhangen)... (Also Deut. 13:4.)

Ps. 63:8. [O Lord,] my soul clings to thee (Luther: hanget dir an)... (Also 2 Kings 18:6.)

1 Thess. 5:23. May the God of peace himself sanctify you wholly; and may your spirit and soul and body be kept sound and blameless at the coming of our Lord Jesus Christ.

1 Cor. 9:24. Do you not know that in a race all the runners compete, but only one receives (Luther: erlangt) the prize? So run that you may obtain it.

Phil. 3:12, 14–15. Not that I have already obtained this or am already perfect; but I press on to make it my own...I press on toward the goal for the prize of the upward call of God in Christ Jesus. Let those of us who are mature be thus minded...

Heb. 10:39. We are not of those who shrink back and are destroyed, but of those who have faith and keep their souls.

BWV 30
Freue dich, erloste Schar
(NBA I/29; BC A178)

Feast of St. John the Baptist: June 24 (BWV 167, 7, 30)
*Is. 40:1–5 (A voice crying in the wilderness)
*Lk. 1:57–80 (Birth of John the Baptist and song of Zacharias)
Librettist: perhaps Picander (Christian Friedrich Henrici)
BWV 30 is a parody of BWV 30a, which has a secular text, probably by Picander.

Part I

1. Chorus (Parody)
●Rejoice in Zion's tents, O redeemed multitude! (30-1)
Freue dich,   erlöste Schar,
Rejoice - , (O) redeemed throng,

Freue dich in   Sions Hütten.
Rejoice - within Zion's   tents.

Dein Gedeihen hat itzund
Thy flourishing hath now
{Thy future prosperity hath now}

Einen rechten festen Grund,
A   truly   secure foundation,
{A truly secure basis,}

Dich mit   Wohl zu überschütten.
Thee with well-being to   shower.
{To shower thee with blessings.}

2. Bass Recit. (Mostly new; some similarity to BWV 30a)
●Salvation, for which the fathers longed, has come (30-2)
Wir haben Rast,
We have repose,

Und des Gesetzes Last
And the   law's burden

Ist   abgetan.
(Has-been) removed.

Nichts soll uns diese Ruhe stören,
Nothing shall for-us this   rest disturb,
{Nothing shall distrub this rest for us,}

Die unsre liebe Väter oft
Which our beloved fathers oft

Gewünscht, verlanget und gehofft.
Wished-for, yearned-for, and hoped-for.

Wohlan,
Now-then!

Is. 33:20. Look upon Zion, the city of our appointed feasts! Your eyes will see Jerusalem, a quiet habitation, an immovable tent, whose stakes will never be plucked up, nor will any of its cords be broken.
Ps. 97:1, 8. The Lord reigns; let the earth rejoice; let the many coastlands be glad!...Zion hears and is glad, and the daughters of Judah rejoice, because of thy judgments, O God.
Ps. 149:1–2, 4. Praise the Lord! Sing to the Lord a new song, his praise in the assembly of the faithful! Let Israel be glad in his Maker, let the sons of Zion rejoice in their King!...For the Lord takes pleasure in his people...
***Lk. 1:67–71, 74–76.** And [John's] father Zechariah was filled with the Holy Spirit, and prophesied, saying, "Blessed be the Lord God of Israel, for he has visited and redeemed his people, and has raised up a horn of salvation for us in the house of his servant David, as he spoke by the mouth of his holy prophets from of old, that we should be saved from our enemies, and from the hand of all who hate us... that we, being delivered from the hand of our enemies, might serve him without fear, in holiness and righteousness before him all the days of our life. And you, child, will be called the prophet of the Most High; for you will go before the Lord to prepare his ways."

Rom. 8:2–3. The law of the Spirit of life in Christ Jesus has set me free from the law of sin and death. For God has done what the law, weakened by the flesh, could not do: sending his own Son...
Rom. 6:14. For sin will have no dominion over you since you are not under law but under grace.
Mt. 11:28–30 [Christ]: Come to me, all who labor and are heavy laden, and I will give you rest. Take my yoke upon you, and learn from me; for I am gentle and lowly in heart, and you will find rest for your souls. For my yoke is easy, and my burden is light.
Mt. 13:17 [Christ]: Truly, I say to you, many prophets and righteous men longed to see what you see, and did not see it, and to hear what you hear, and did not hear it.
1 Pet. 1:10–12. The prophets who prophesied of the grace that was to be yours searched and inquired about this salvation; they inquired what person or time was indicated by the Spirit of Christ within them when predicting the sufferings of Christ and the subsequent glory. It was revealed to them that they were serving not themselves but you, in the things which have now been announced to you by those who preached the good news to you through the Holy Spirit sent from heaven, things into which angels long to look. (Also Rom. 16:25–26, Eph. 3:4–6, 9, Col. 1:26.)

Es freue sich, wer immer kann,
- Rejoice -, who-so-ever can,
{Whoever can, rejoice,}

Und stimme seinem Gott zu Ehren
And strike-up to-his God for honor

Ein Loblied an,
A song-of-praise -,
{And strike up a song of praise to his God for honor,}

Und das im höhern Chor,
And all-of-that in-the higher choir,
{And all of that in the choir of ascents,}

Ja, singt einander vor!
Yes, sing to-one-another!

3. Bass Aria (Parody)
•John the Baptist: Praise God for sending his servant! (30-3)
Gelobet sei Gott, gelobet sein Name,
Praised be God, praised (be) his name,
{Praise be to God, praise be to his name,}

Der treulich gehalten Versprechen und Eid!
Who faithfully has-kept (his) promise and oath!

Sein treuer Diener ist geboren,
His faithful servant is born,

Der längstens darzu auserkoren,
Who long-ago for-this (was) elected,
{Who was elected long ago for this,}

Daß er den Weg dem Herrn bereit'.
That he the way of-the Lord (should) prepare.
{That he should prepare the way of the Lord.}

4. Alto Recit. (Newly composed)
•John the Baptist: A herald announcing the King (30-4)
Der Herold kömmt und meldt den König an,
The herald comes and announces the king -,

Er ruft; drum säumet nicht
He calls; therefore delay not
{He calls; therefore do not delay}

Und macht euch auf
And get yourselves up

Mit einem schnellen Lauf,
With a fast pace;

Eilt dieser Stimme nach!
Hasten this voice after!
{Hasten after this voice!}

Sie zeigt den Weg, sie zeigt das Licht,
It shows the way, it shows the light,

*Lk. 1:68. Blessed be the Lord God of Israel, for he has visited and redeemed his people.
Ps. 5:11. [O Lord,] let all who take refuge in thee rejoice, let them ever sing for joy...
Ps. 69:30. I will praise the name of God with a song; I will magnify (Luther: hoch ehren) him with thanksgiving.
Ps. 66:1–4. Make a joyful noise to God, all the earth; sing the glory of his name (Luther: Ehren seinem Namen)... (Also Ps. 30:4, 95:1, 149:1, Is. 42:10, etc.)
Ps. 68:3–4. Let the righteous be joyful; let them exult before God; let them be jubilant with joy! Sing to God, sing praises to his name; lift up a song to him...
Ps. 120–134 (titles). A Song of Ascents. (Luther: Ein Lied im höhern Chor)
Eph. 5:18–19. ...Be filled with the Spirit, addressing one another in psalms and hymns and spiritual songs, singing and making melody to the Lord with all your heart. (Also Col. 3:16.)

*Lk. 1:68, 72–73, 76. Blessed be the Lord God of Israel, for he has visited his people...to perform the mercy promised to our fathers, and to remember his holy covenant, the oath which he swore to our father Abraham...And you, child...will go before the Lord to prepare his ways...
Deut. 7:9. Know therefore that the Lord your God is God, the faithful God who keeps covenant and steadfast love with those who love him and keep his commandments, to a thousand generations.
Ps. 105:1–2, 8–10 / 1 Chron. 16:8–9, 15–16. O give thanks to the Lord, call on his name, make known his deeds among the peoples! Sing to him, sing praises to him, tell of all his wonderful works!...He is mindful of his covenant for ever, of the word that he commanded, for a thousand generations, the covenant which he made with Abraham, his sworn promise to Isaac, which he confirmed to Jacob as a statute, to Israel as an everlasting covenant...

*Is. 40:3. A voice cries: "In the wilderness prepare the way of the Lord, make straight in the desert a highway for our God."
Jn. 1:19–23. And this is the testimony of John, when the Jews sent priests and Levites from Jerusalem to ask him, "Who are you?" He confessed, he did not deny, but confessed, "I am not the Christ." And they asked him, "What then? Are you Elijah?" He said, "I am not." "Are you the prophet?" And he answered, "No." They said to him then, "Who are you? Let us have an answer for those who sent us. What do you say about yourself?" He said, "I am the voice of one crying in the wilderness, 'Make straight the way of the Lord,' as the prophet Isaiah said." (Also Mt. 3:3.)
Heb. 4:7. Today, when you hear his voice, do not harden your hearts. (Also Ps. 95:7–8.)
Mt. 21:24–27. Jesus answered [the chief priests and elders], "...The baptism of John, whence was it? From heaven or from men?" And they argued with one another, "If we say, 'From heaven,' he will say to us, 'Why then did you not believe him?' But if we say, 'From men,' we are afraid of the multitude; for all hold that John was a prophet." So they answered Jesus, "We do not know."

105

Wodurch wir jene selge Auen
By-which we those blessed pastures

Dereinst gewißlich können schauen.
Someday assuredly can behold.

5. Alto Aria (Parody)
●Invitation of grace is offered by the Savior! (30-5)
Kommt, ihr angefochtnen Sünder,
Come, you sorely-tried sinners,

Eilt und lauft, ihr Adamskinder,
Hasten and run, you children-of-Adam,

Euer Heiland ruft und schreit!
Your Savior calls and cries!

Kommet, ihr verirrten Schafe,
Come, you lost sheep,

Stehet auf vom Sündenschlafe,
Rise up from sin's-sleep,

Denn itzt ist die Gnadenzeit!
For now is the time-of-grace!

6. Chorale (Newly composed)
●John the Baptist: A voice crying in the wilderness (30-6)
Eine Stimme läßt sich hören
A voice lets itself be-heard
{A voice is heard}

In der Wüsten weit und breit,
In the desert far and wide,

Alle Menschen zu bekehren:
All people to convert:

Macht dem Herrn den Weg bereit,
Make (for) the Lord the way prepared,
{Prepare the way of the Lord,}

Machet Gott ein ebne Bahn,
Make (for) God a level pathway,
{Make a level pathway for God;}

Alle Welt soll heben an,
All (the) world should commence

Alle Täler zu erhöhen,
All (the) valleys to exalt,
{To exalt the valleys,}

Daß die Berge niedrig stehen.
That the mountains low (may) stand.
{That the mountains may be made low.}

Jn. 1:9, 15. The true light that enlightens every man was coming into the world...John bore witness to him, and cried, "This was he of whom I said, 'He who comes after me, ranks before me, for he was before me.'"
Jn. 14:6. Jesus said..."I am the way, and the truth, and the life..."

Mk. 6:34. As [Jesus] went ashore he saw a great throng, and he had compassion on them, because they were like sheep without a shepherd; and he began to teach them many things.
Mt. 11:28–30 [Christ]: Come to me, all who labor and are heavy laden, and I will give you rest...You will find rest for your souls.
1 Cor. 15:22. For as in Adam all die, so also in Christ shall all be made alive.
Is. 53:6. All we like sheep have gone astray; we have turned every one to his own way; and the Lord has laid on him the iniquity of us all. (Also Mt. 18:12–13.)
Mt. 25:1, 5–6. Then the kingdom of heaven shall be compared to ten maidens who took their lamps and went to meet the bridegroom...As the bridegroom was delayed, they all slumbered and slept. But at midnight there was a cry, "Behold, the bridegroom! Come out to meet him."
Eph. 5:14. Therefore it is said, "Awake, O sleeper, and arise from the dead, and Christ shall give you light."
1 Thess. 5:6. So then let us not sleep, as others do, but let us keep awake and be sober. (Also Rom. 13:11.)
Tit. 2:11. For the grace of God has appeared for the salvation of all men.

***Is. 40:3–5.** A voice cries: "In the wilderness prepare the way of the Lord, make straight in the desert a highway for our God. Every valley shall be lifted up, and every mountain and hill be made low; the uneven ground shall become level, and the rough places a plain. And the glory of the Lord shall be revealed, and all flesh shall see it together, for the mouth of the Lord has spoken."
Lk. 3:2–6. The word of God came to John the son of Zechariah in the wilderness; and he went into all the region about the Jordan, preaching a baptism of repentance for the forgiveness of sins. As it is written in the book of the words of Isaiah the prophet, "The voice of one crying in the wilderness: Prepare the way of the Lord, make his paths straight. Every valley shall be filled, and every mountain and hill shall be brought low, and the crooked shall be made straight, and the rough ways shall be made smooth; and all flesh shall see the salvation of God."
Mt. 3:1–6. In those days came John the Baptist, preaching in the wilderness of Judea, "Repent, for the kingdom of heaven is at hand." For this is he who was spoken of by the prophet Isaiah...Now John wore a garment of camel's hair, and a leather girdle around his waist; and his food was locusts and wild honey. Then went out to him Jerusalem and all Judea and all the region about the Jordan, and they were baptized by him in the river Jordan, confessing their sins. (Also Mk. 1:3, Jn. 1:23.)

Part II

7. Bass Recit. (Newly composed)
●Individual's response to God who fulfilled promise (30–7)
So bist du denn, mein Heil,   bedacht,
So art thou then, my Salvation, intentioned,
{Thus thou dost intend, O my Salvation,}

Den Bund, den du gemacht
The covenant, which thou didst-make
{To faithfully keep the covenant, which thou didst make}

Mit unsern Vätern, treu zu halten
With our   fathers, faithfully to keep
{With our fathers,}

Und in Genaden über uns zu walten;
And in   grace over us to hold-sway;

Drum   will ich mich mit allem Fleiß
Therefore will I - with all diligence

Dahin bestreben,
Thereto strive,
{To that end strive,}

Dir,   treuer Gott, auf dein Geheiß
For-thee, faithful God, at thy bidding

In Heiligkeit und Gottesfurcht zu leben.
In holiness   and   godly-fear to live.
{To live in holiness and godly fear for thee at thy bidding, O faithful God.}

8. Bass Aria (Parody)
●Forsaking what God hates; loving what he loves (30–8)
Ich will nun hassen
I will now hate

Und alles   lassen,
And everything forsake,
{And forsake everything,}

Was dir, mein Gott, zuwider ist.
That to-thee, my God, offensive is.
{That is offensive to thee, O my God.}

Ich will dich nicht betrüben,
I would thee not   grieve,
{I would not grieve thee,}

Hingegen   herzlich lieben,
But-on-the-contrary heartily love,

Weil   du mir so genädig bist.
Because thou to-me so gracious art.
{Because thou art so gracious to me.}

*Lk. 1:68, 72–73, 76. Blessed be the Lord God of Israel, for he has visited his people...to perform the mercy promised to our fathers, and to remember his holy covenant, the oath which he swore to our father Abraham...And you, child...will go before the Lord to prepare his ways...
Deut. 7:9. Know therefore that the Lord your God is God, the faithful God who keeps covenant and steadfast love with those who love him and keep his commandments, to a thousand generations.
Acts 3:25–26. You are the sons of the prophets and of the covenant which God gave to your fathers, saying to Abraham, "And in your posterity shall all the families of the earth be blessed." God, having raised up his servant, sent him to you...to bless you in turning every one of you from your wickedness.
Gal. 3:14, 16, 29. In Christ Jesus the blessing of Abraham [came] upon the Gentiles, that we might receive the promise of the Spirit through faith...Now the promises were made to Abraham and to his offspring... which is Christ...And if you are Christ's, then you are Abraham's offspring, heirs according to promise.
2 Pet. 1:5–7, 10–11. [Because God has allowed us to become partakers of the divine nature by his precious and very great promises] make every effort (Luther: Fleiß) to supplement your faith with virtue, and virtue with knowledge, and knowledge with self-control, and self-control with steadfastness, and steadfastness with godliness, and godliness with brotherly affection, and brotherly affection with love... Therefore, brethren, be the more zealous (Luther: tut desto mehr Fleiß) to confirm your call and election, for if you do this you will never fall; so there will be richly provided for you an entrance into the eternal kingdom of our Lord and Savior Jesus Christ.

Lk. 14:25–27. Now great multitudes accompanied [Jesus]; and he turned and said to them, "If any one comes to me and does not hate his own father and mother and wife and children and brothers and sisters, yes, and even his own life, he cannot be my disciple. Whoever does not bear his own cross and come after me, cannot be my disciple." (Also Mt. 10:37–38.)
Mt. 6:24 [Christ]: No one can serve two masters; for either he will hate the one and love the other, or he will be devoted to the one and despise the other. You cannot serve God and mammon. (Also Lk. 16:13.)
1 Jn. 2:15–17. Do not love the world or the things in the world. If any one loves the world, love for the Father is not in him. For all that is in the world, the lust of the flesh and the lust of the eyes and the pride of life, is not of the Father but is of the world. And the world passes away, and the lust of it; but he who does the will of God abides for ever.
Jms. 4:4. Unfaithful creatures! Do you not know that friendship with the world is enmity with God? Therefore whoever wishes to be a friend of the world makes himself an enemy of God.
Eph. 4:30. And do not grieve the Holy Spirit of God, in whom you were sealed for the day of redemption.
1 Pet. 2:1, 3. So put away all malice and all guile and insincerity and envy and all slander...for you have tasted the kindness of the Lord.

9. Soprano Recit. (Mostly new; some similarity to BWV 30a)
●Resolve to serve & praise despite fickle tendencies (30-9)
Und ob wohl sonst der Unbestand
And, although usually - inconstancy
{And, although inconstancy is usually}

Den schwachen Menschen ist verwandt,
(To) weak humans is related,
{Characteristic of weak humans,}

So sei hiermit   doch   zugesagt:
So let herewith nevertheless (this) be-said-in-addition:
{Let this nevertheless be said in addition herewith:}

So oft die Morgenröte tagt,
As oft-as the dawn becomes-day,

So lang ein Tag den andern folgen läßt,
As long-as one day the other follows - ,
{As long as one day follows the other,}

So lange will ich   steif   und fest,
So long will I, unbending and steadfast,

Mein Gott, durch deinen Geist
My God, through thy Spirit

Dir   ganz und gar zu Ehren leben.
For-thee completely for honor live.
{Completely for thine honor live.}

Dich soll sowohl mein Herz als Mund
Thee shall as-well my heart as mouth

Nach   dem mit dir gemachten Bund
According to-the with thee made covenant

Mit wohlverdientem Lob erheben.
With well-deserved praise exalt.
{Thee shall my heart as well as my mouth exalt with well-deserved praise according to the covenant made with thee.}

10. Soprano Aria (Parody)
●Longing for heavenly pastures, tents of Kedar (30-10)
Eilt,   ihr Stunden, kommt herbei,
Hasten, ye hours,   come near,

Bringt mich bald in jene Auen!
Bring me soon into yonder pastures!

Ich will mit der heilgen Schar
I will with the holy multitude
{With the holy multitude I will build}

Meinem Gott ein'   Dankaltar
My   God an altar-of-thanksgiving
{An altar of thanksgiving to my God}

Jn. 6:66. After this many of [Jesus'] disciples drew back and no longer went about with him.
Mt. 26:41. ...The spirit indeed is willing, but the flesh is weak.
1 Jn. 2:19. They went out from us, but they were not of us; for if they had been of us, they would have continued with us; but they went out, that it might be plain that they all are not of us.
2 Tim. 2:12–13. If we endure, we shall also reign with him; if we deny him, he also will deny us; if we are faithless, he remains faithful—for he cannot deny himself.
Jer. 33:19–21. The word of the Lord came to Jeremiah: "Thus says the Lord: If you can break my covenant with the day and my covenant with the night, so that day and night will not come at their appointed time, then also my covenant with David my servant may be broken..." (Also Jer. 31:36.)
Josh. 24:15. ...Choose this day whom you will serve...but as for me and my house, we will serve the Lord.
Acts 21:13. Then Paul answered, "...I am ready not only to be imprisoned but even to die at Jerusalem for the name of the Lord Jesus."
Heb. 10:36–39. You have need of endurance, so that you may do the will of God and receive what is promised. "For yet a little while, and the coming one shall come and shall not tarry; but my righteous one shall live by faith, and if he shrinks back, my soul has no pleasure in him." But we are not of those who shrink back and are destroyed, but of those who have faith and keep their souls.
Rom. 10:9–10. If you confess with your lips (Luther: Munde) that Jesus is Lord and believe in your heart that God raised him from the dead, you will be saved. For man believes with his heart and so is justified, and he confesses with his lips (Luther: Munde) and so is saved.
Ps. 103:17–18. But the steadfast love of the Lord is from everlasting to everlasting upon those who fear him, and his righteousness to children's children, to those who keep his covenant and remember to do his commandments.
Ps. 34:1. ...His praise shall continually be in my mouth. (Also Ps. 40:3, 51:15, 63:3, 71:8, 109:30.)
Heb. 13:15. ...Let us continually offer up a sacrifice of praise to God, that is, the fruit of lips that acknowledge his name. (Also Ps. 50:14, 23.)

Phil. 1:21–23. To me to live is Christ, and to die is gain...My desire is to depart and be with Christ, for that is far better.
Ps. 100:3. ...We are his people, and the sheep of his pasture.
Is. 60:7. All the flocks of Kedar shall be gathered to you...They shall come up with acceptance on my altar... [Note: Kedar was known for its flocks but also its warriors. See Ps. 120:5–6, Is. 21:16–17, 42:11, Jer. 49:28, Ezek. 27:21]
Rev. 7:17. [In heaven] the Lamb in the midst of the throne will be their shepherd, and he will guide them to springs of living water; and God will wipe away every tear from their eyes. (Also Is. 40:11.)
Rev. 14:1–3. Then I looked, and lo, on Mount Zion stood the Lamb, and with him a hundred and forty-four thousand who had his name and his Father's name written on their foreheads. And I heard a voice from heaven like the sound of many waters and like the sound of thunder; the voice I heard was like the sound of harpers playing on their harps, and they sing a new song before the throne and before the

In   den Hütten   Kedar bauen,
Within the tents (of) Kedar   build,
{Within the tents of Kedar,}

Bis ich ewig dankbar sei.
Until I eternally thankful be.
{Until I give thanks in eternity.}

11. Tenor Recit. (Newly composed)
●Patience! Soon life's imperfections gone in heaven (30–11)
Geduld, der angenehme Tag
Patience! That   pleasant   day

Kann nicht mehr weit   und lange sein,
Can   no longer distant (nor) long   be,
{Can not be distant or long any more,}

Da   du von aller   Plag
When thou from all (the) vexation

Der Unvollkommenheit der Erden,
Of-the imperfection(s)   of earth,

Die   dich,   mein Herz, gefangen hält,
Which thee, (O) my   heart,   captive   holds,

Vollkommen wirst befreiet werden.
Completely   wilt set-free   be.
{When thou wilt be set completely free from all the vexation of
the imperfections of earth, which holds thee captive, O my heart,}

Der Wunsch trifft   endlich ein,
(Thy) wish comes-true at-last   - ,

Da   du mit den erlösten Seelen
When thou with the redeemed souls

In der Vollkommenheit
In that   perfection

Von diesem Tod des Leibes bist befreit,
From this   death of-the body art set-free,

Da wird dich keine Not   mehr quälen.
Then will thee no   distress any-more torment.
{Then will no distress torment thee any longer.}

12. Chorus (Parody)
●Rejoice in Zion's pastures (heavenly Jerusalem)! (30–12)
Freue dich,   geheilgte Schar,
Rejoice - , (O) sanctified multitude,

Freue dich in Sions Auen!
Rejoice - in Zion's pastures!

four living creatures and before the elders. No one could learn that song except the hundred and forty-four thousand who had been redeemed from the earth.
Ps. 79:13. Then we thy people, the flock of thy pasture, will give thanks to thee [O Lord] for ever...
Ps. 111:1. ...I will give thanks to the Lord with my whole heart, in the company of the upright, in the congregation.

2 Tim. 4:6–7. ...The time of my departure has come. I have fought the good fight, I have finished the race, I have kept the faith.
Jms. 5:7–9. Be patient, therefore, brethren, until the coming of the Lord. Behold, the farmer waits for the precious fruit of the earth, being patient over it until it receives the early and the late rain. You also be patient. Establish your hearts, for the coming of the Lord is at hand.
*Lk. 1:78–79. ...The day shall dawn upon us from on high to give light to those who sit in darkness and in the shadow of death, to guide our feet into the way of peace.
Rom. 13:11–12. ...You know what hour it is, how it is full time now for you to wake from sleep. For salvation is nearer to us now than when we first believed; the night is far gone, the day is at hand.
1 Cor. 13:10. When the perfect comes, the imperfect will pass away.
Rom. 8:19, 21–24. For the creation waits with eager longing for the revealing of the sons of God...because the creation itself will be set free from its bondage to decay and obtain the glorious liberty of the children of God. We know that the whole creation has been groaning in travail together until now; and not only the creation, but we ourselves, who have the first fruits of the Spirit, groan inwardly as we wait for adoption as sons, the redemption of our bodies. For in this hope we were saved...
Rom. 7:24–25. Wretched man that I am! Who will deliver me from this body of death? (Luther: dem Leibe dieses Todes) Thanks be to God through Jesus Christ our Lord!
1 Cor. 15:53. For this perishable nature must put on the imperishable, and this mortal nature must put on immortality.
Rev. 7:9–10, 14–17. After this I looked, and behold, a great multitude which no man could number...crying out with a loud voice, "Salvation belongs to our God who sits upon the throne, and to the Lamb!"... These are they who have come out of the great tribulation...they shall hunger no more, neither thirst any more...and God will wipe away every tear from their eyes.

Is. 65:17–19, 25 [God]: Behold, I create new heavens and a new earth; and the former things shall not be remembered or come into mind. But be glad and rejoice for ever in that which I create; for behold, I create Jerusalem a rejoicing, and her people a joy. I will rejoice in Jerusalem, and be glad in my people; no more shall be heard in it the sound of weeping and the cry of distress...The wolf and the lamb shall feed together, the lion shall eat straw like the ox; and dust shall be the serpent's food. They shall not hurt or destroy in all my holy mountain, says the Lord.

Deiner Freude Herrlichkeit,
Thy   joy's   glory,

Deiner Selbstzufriedenheit
Thy   self-content

Wird die   Zeit kein Ende schauen.
Will (of-its) time no   end   see.
{Will see no end.}

BWV 31
Der Himmel lacht! die Erde jubilieret
(NBA I/9; BC A55a/b)

Easter Sunday (BWV 4, 31, 249)
*1 Cor. 5:6–8 (Christ, our paschal lamb, has been sacrificed)
*Mk. 16:1–8 (The resurrection of Christ)
Librettist: Salomon Franck

1. Sonata

2. Chorus
●Resurrection of Christ: Heaven and earth rejoice (31-2)
Der Himmel lacht! die Erde jubilieret
 - Heaven laughs! - Earth   exults,

Und was sie trägt in ihrem Schoß;
And (all) she carries in her bosom (rejoices too);

Der Schöpfer lebt! der Höchste triumphieret
The Creator lives! The Most-High triumphs

Und ist von   Todesbanden   los.
And is from (the) bonds-of-death set-free.

Der   sich das Grab zur   Ruh erlesen.
He-who - the grave for (his) rest selected.
{He who chose the grave for his rest—}

Der   Heiligste   kann nicht verwesen.
The Most-Holy-One can   not see-corruption.

3. Bass Recit.
●Resurrection: Alpha & Omega has keys to death & hell
(31-3)
   Erwünschter Tag! sei, Seele, wieder froh!
(O) wished-for day! Be, soul,   again happy!
{This is the day we have longed for! O soul, be happy again!}

Rev. 7:17. For the Lamb in the midst of the throne will be their shepherd, and he will guide them to springs of living water; and God will wipe away every tear from their eyes. (Also Is. 40:11.)
Rev. 21:1–4. Then I saw a new heaven and a new earth...And I saw the holy city, new Jerusalem, coming down out of heaven from God...and I heard a loud voice from the throne saying, "Behold, the dwelling of God is with men. He will dwell with them, and they shall be his people, and God himself will be with them; he will wipe away every tear from their eyes, and death shall be no more, neither shall there be mourning nor crying nor pain any more, for the former things have passed away."
Rev. 22:5. And night shall be no more...for the Lord God will be their light, and they shall reign for ever and ever.

1 Chron. 16:31. Let the heavens be glad, and let the earth rejoice, and let them say among the nations, "The Lord reigns!"
Rev. 12:12. Rejoice then, O heaven and you that dwell therein! **Is. 44:23.** Sing, O heavens, for the Lord has done it; shout, O depths of the earth; break forth into singing, O mountains, O forest, and every tree in it!
***Mk. 16:6.** [The angel] said to [the women who had come to the tomb], "Do not be amazed; you seek Jesus of Nazareth, who was crucified. He has risen, he is not here..."
Lk. 24:34. ...The Lord has risen indeed...!
Acts 2:31. [The patriarch David] foresaw and spoke of the resurrection of the Christ, that he was not abandoned to Hades, nor did his flesh see corruption. (See Ps. 16:10.)
Ps. 18:4–5. The cords of death (Luther: des Todes Bande) encompassed me, the torrents of perdition assailed me; the cords of Sheol entangled me, the snares of death confronted me. (Also 2 Sam. 22:5–6.)
Ps. 16:10. [But] thou dost not give me up to Sheol, or let thy godly one see the Pit.
Acts 2:24. God raised [Christ] up, having loosed the pangs of death, because it was not possible for him to be held by it.
Jn. 1:1–4. In the beginning was the Word, and the Word was with God, and the Word was God. He was in the beginning with God; all things were made through him, and without him was not anything made that was made. In him was life, and the life was the light of men. (Also Col. 1:15–16, Heb. 1:2.)
1 Cor. 15:54–55. ...Death is swallowed up in victory. O death, where is thy victory? O death, where is thy sting?
Ps. 16:10. [O Lord,] thou dost not give me up to Sheol, or let thy godly one see the Pit (Luther: daß dein Heiliger verwese).
Acts 2:31. [David] foresaw and spoke of the resurrection of the Christ, that he was not abandoned to Hades, nor did his flesh see corruption.
Acts 13:37. He whom God raised up saw no corruption.

Lk. 18:31–33. Taking the twelve, [Jesus had] said to them, "Behold, we are going up to Jerusalem, and everything that is written of the Son of man by the prophets will be accomplished. For he will be delivered to the Gentiles...They will scourge him and kill him, and on the third day he will rise."

Das A und O,
The Alpha and Omega,

Der erst und auch der letzte,
The first and also the last,

Den unsre schwere Schuld in Todeskerker setzte,
Who our grievous guilt in death's-dungeon did-place,

Ist nun gerissen aus der Not!
Is now snatched out-of - distress!
{Has now been snatched out of distress!}

Der Herr war tot,
The Lord was dead,

Und sieh, er lebet wieder;
And behold, he lives again;

Lebt unser Haupt, so leben auch die Glieder.
Lives our Head, then live also (his) members.
{If our Head lives, then his members shall live also.}

Der Herr hat in der Hand
The Lord has in (his) hand

Des Todes und der Hölle Schlüssel!
Of death and - hell (the) keys!
{The keys of death and hell!}

Der sein Gewand
He-who his garment
{He who splashed his garment}

Blutrot bespritzt in seinem bittern Leiden,
Blood-red splashed in his bitter passion,
{Blood-red in his bitter passion,}

Will heute sich mit Schmuck und Ehren kleiden.
Will today himself with finery and honor(s) clothe.
{Will today clothe himself with finery and honor.}

4. Bass Aria
●Christ exalted because he suffered and died (31–4)
Fürst des Lebens, starker Streiter,
Prince of life, strong combatant,
{O Prince of life, mighty warrior,}

Jn. 16:20, 22 [Christ]: Truly, truly, I say to you, you will weep and lament...you will be sorrowful, but your sorrow will turn into joy...I will see you again and your hearts will rejoice, and no one will take your joy from you.
Mt. 28:6. ...[Christ] has risen, as he said...
Rev. 5:5. ...Lo, the Lion of the tribe of Judah, the Root of David, has conquered...
Rev. 22:13. [He is]...the Alpha and the Omega, the first and the last, the beginning and the end. (Also Rev. 1:8, 21:6, Is. 44:6.)
Rom. 6:23. The wages of [our] sin is death...
Rom. 5:8. But God shows his love for us in that while we were yet sinners Christ died for us.
Is. 53:10. It was the will of the Lord to bruise him; he has put him to grief; when he makes himself an offering for sin...
2 Cor. 5:21. For our sake he made him to be sin who knew no sin, so that in him we might become the righteousness of God.
Rev. 2:8. [He is]...the first and the last, who died and came to life...
Mt. 28:6. ...[Christ] has risen, as he said.
Acts 2:24. God raised [Christ] up, having loosed the pangs of death, because it was not possible for him to be held by it.
Rom. 6:9. We know that Christ being raised from the dead will never die again; death no longer has dominion over him.
1 Cor. 15:20, 23. ...Christ has been raised from the dead, the first fruits of those who have fallen asleep...Christ the first fruits, then at his coming those who belong to Christ. (Also Jn. 6:40/44/54, Rom. 8:11.)
Rev. 1:17–18 [Christ]: ...Fear not, I am the first and the last, and the living one; I died, and behold I am alive for evermore, and I have the keys of Death and Hades. (Also Rev. 20:1.)
1 Cor. 15:25–26. He must reign until he has put all his enemies under his feet. The last enemy to be destroyed is death.
Heb. 2:9. ...He [has tasted] death for every one.
Is. 63:2–3. Why is thy apparel red, and thy garments like his that treads in the wine press? I have trodden the wine press [of God's wrath] alone, and from the peoples no one was with me...Their lifeblood is sprinkled upon my garments, and I have stained all my raiment.
Is. 53:5–6. He was wounded for our transgressions...
1 Pet. 2:24. ...By his wounds [we] have been healed.
Lk. 22:44. ...[When Jesus prayed in the garden of Gethsemane before his crucifixion,] his sweat became like great drops of blood...
Jn. 19:34. [When] one of the soldiers pierced his side with a spear...at once there came out blood and water.
Heb. 2:9. [Now] we see Jesus...crowned with glory and honor because of the suffering of death...
Phil. 2:8–11. ...He humbled himself and became obedient unto death, even death on a cross. Therefore God has highly exalted him and bestowed on him the name which is above every name, that at the name of Jesus every knee should bow, in heaven and on earth and under the earth, and every tongue confess that Jesus Christ is Lord...
Rev. 3:4–5 [Christ]: ...[The righteous] shall walk with me in white, for they are worthy. He who conquers shall be clad thus in white garments...

Acts 3:14–15. You...killed the Author of life (Luther: Fürsten des Lebens), whom God raised from the dead.
1 Cor. 15:54. Death is swallowed up in victory. (Also Heb. 2:14.)

Hochgelobter Gottessohn!
Highly-praised Son-of-God!

Hebet dich des Kreuzes Leiter
Lifts   thee the   cross's ladder
{Does the cross's ladder lift thee}

Auf den höchsten Ehrenthron?
To   the   highest throne-of-honor?

Wird,   was dich zuvor gebunden,
Becomes, what thee previously bound,
{Does what previously bound thee become}

Nun dein Schmuck und Edelstein?
Now thine adornment and   jewel?

Müssen deine Purpurwunden
Must   thy wounds-of-purple

Deiner Klarheit Strahlen sein?
Thy   brightness' rays   be?
{Become the rays of thy brilliance?}

5. Tenor Recit.
●Resurrected with Christ: we flee sin and bear fruit (31-5)
So stehe dann, du   gottergebne Seele,
So rise,   then, thou to-God-devoted soul,
{So rise, then, O soul devoted to God,}

Mit Christo geistlich auf!
With Christ, spiritually up!
{Rise up spiritually with Christ!}

Tritt   an den neuen Lebenslauf!
Set-out on the   new life's-course!

Auf! von den toten Werken!
Up from (thy) dead   works!

Laß, daß dein Heiland in dir lebt,
Let - thy Savior in thee live,
{Allow thy Savior to live in thee,}

An deinem Leben merken!
In   thy   life be-observed!
{To be observed in thy life!}

Der Weinstock, der jetzt blüht,
The grape-vine, which now blooms,

Trägt keine toten Reben!
Bears no   dead vines!

Der Lebensbaum läßt seine Zweige leben!
The tree-of-life (makes) its branches live!

Rev. 17:14. ...He is Lord of lords and King of kings...
Jn. 12:24. Unless a grain of wheat falls into the earth and dies, it remains alone; but if it dies, it bears much fruit.
Jn. 3:14–15. As Moses lifted up the serpent in the wilderness, so must the Son of man be lifted up, that whoever believes in him may have eternal life.
Jn. 12:32 [Christ]: And I, when I am lifted up from the earth, will draw all men to myself.
Phil. 2:8–11. ...He humbled himself and became obedient unto death, even death on a cross. Therefore God has highly exalted him and bestowed on him the name which is above every name, that at the name of Jesus every knee should bow, in heaven and on earth and under the earth, and every tongue confess that Jesus Christ is Lord, to the glory of God the Father.
Heb. 2:9. We see Jesus, who for a little while was made lower than the angels, crowned with glory and honor because of the suffering of death, so that by the grace of God he might taste death for every one. (Also Heb. 12:2.)
Eph. 1:20–22. ...[God] raised him from the dead and made him sit at his right hand in the heavenly places, far above all rule and authority and power and dominion, and above every name that is named, not only in this age but also in that which is to come; and he has put all things under his feet...
Mk. 15:17. And [the soldiers] clothed [Jesus] in a purple cloak...and they began to salute him, "Hail, King of the Jews!"

Rom. 6:1–5, 12. What shall we say then? Are we to continue in sin that grace may abound? By no means! How can we who died to sin still live in it? Do you not know that all of us who have been baptized into Christ Jesus were baptized into his death? We were buried therefore with him by baptism into death, so that as Christ was raised from the dead by the glory of the Father, we too might walk in newness of life. For if we have been united with him in a death like his, we shall certainly be united with him in a resurrection like his... But if we have died with Christ, we believe that we shall also live with him...Let not sin therefore reign in your mortal bodies... (Also Col. 2:12–13.)
Col. 3:1–2. If then you have been raised with Christ, seek the things that are above, where Christ is, seated at the right hand of God. Set your minds on things that are above, not on things that are on earth.
Heb. 9:14. ...The blood of Christ [shall]...purify your conscience from dead works to serve the living God.
Gal. 2:20. I have been crucified with Christ; it is no longer I who live, but Christ who lives in me; and the life I now live in the flesh I live by faith in the Son of God who loved me and gave himself for me. (Also Eph. 3:17.)
Jn. 15:1–2, 6, 8. [Jeusus said,] "I am the true vine, and my Father is the vinedresser. Every branch of mine that bears no fruit, he takes away, and every branch that does bear fruit he prunes, that it may bear more fruit...If a man does not abide in me, he is cast forth as a branch and withers; and the branches are gathered, thrown into the fire and burned...By this my Father is glorified, that you bear much fruit, and so prove to be my disciples."
Sirach (Apocrypha) 2:2. Flee from sin as from a snake...
*****Mk. 16:8.** And [the women] went out and fled from the tomb...
2 Pet. 2:20–23. If, after [having] escaped the defilements of the world through the knowledge of our Lord and Savior Jesus Christ, [men] are

Ein Christe flieht
A Christian flees

Ganz eilend von dem Grabe!
Very speedily from the   grave!

Er läßt den Stein,
He leaves the stone,

Er läßt das Tuch der Sünden
He leaves the cloth of   sins

Dahinten
Behind

Und will   mit Christo lebend sein.
And would with Christ   living   be.
{And would rather live with Christ.}

6. Tenor Aria
●Spiritual death and resurrection: old and new life (31-6)
Adam muß in uns verwesen,
Adam must in us   decay,

Soll der neue Mensch genesen,
Shall the new   man   recover,
{If the new man shall recover—}

Der nach Gott geschaffen ist.
Who after God   created   is.
{The new man who is created in God's image.}

Du mußt geistlich auferstehen
You must spiritually resurrected (be)

Und aus Sündengräbern gehen,
And out-of sins'-graves   go,
{And leave the graves of sin,}

Wenn du Christi Gliedmaß bist.
If   you Christ's   limb   are.
{If you are a member of Christ's body.}

7. Soprano Recit.
●Union with Christ in suffering and exaltation (31-7)
Weil dann das Haupt sein Glied
For   as   the head its limb

Natürlich nach sich zieht,
By-nature after itself draws,
{By nature with it carries,}

again entangled in them and overpowered, the last state has become worse for them than the first. For it would have been better for them never to have known the way of righteousness than after knowing it to turn back from the holy commandment delivered to them. It has happened to them according to the true proverb, The dog turns back to his own vomit, and the sow is washed only to wallow in the mire.
Heb. 12:1-2. ...Let us...lay aside every weight, and sin which clings so closely, and let us run with perseverance the race that is set before us, looking to Jesus the pioneer and perfecter of our faith, who for the joy that was set before him endured the cross, despising the shame, and is seated at the right hand of the throne of God.
Jn. 20:1, 3, 6-7. On the first day of the week Mary Magdalene came to the tomb early...and saw that the stone had been taken away from the tomb...Peter then came out with the other disciple...He saw the linen cloths lying, and the napkin, which had been on his head...
Is. 64:6. ...All our righteous deeds are like a polluted garment.
Rom. 6:4. ...As Christ was raised from the dead by the glory of the Father, we too [can now] walk in newness of life.
Lk. 24:5. And [the two men in dazzling apparel] said to [the women at the tomb], "Why do you seek the living among the dead?"

1 Cor. 15:22. As in Adam all die, so also in Christ shall all be made alive.
Rom. 5:12. Therefore...sin came into the world through one man and death through sin, and so death spread to all men because all men sinned.
Eph. 4:22-24. Put off your old nature which belongs to your former manner of life and is corrupt through deceitful lusts, and be renewed in the spirit of your minds, and put on the new nature, created after the likeness of God in true righteousness and holiness.
Col. 3:5, 9-10. Put to death therefore what is earthly in you...seeing that you have put off the old nature with its practices and have put on the new nature, which is being renewed in knowledge after the image of its creator.
2 Cor 4:16. Though our outer nature is wasting away, our inner nature is being renewed every day. (Also 1 Cor. 15:42.)
1 Cor. 6:15. Do you not know that your bodies are members of Christ?
1 Cor. 12:27. Now you are the body of Christ and individually members of it. (Also Eph. 5:30.)
Col. 3:1-2. If then you have been raised with Christ, seek the things that are above...

Eph. 5:23, 30. Christ is the head of the church, his body...We are members of his body.
Rom. 8:38-39. I am sure that neither death, nor life, nor angels, nor principalities, nor things present, nor things to come, nor powers, nor height, nor depth, nor anything else in all creation, will be able to separate us from the love of God in Christ Jesus our Lord.
2 Tim. 2:11-12. The saying is sure: If we have died with him, we shall also live with him; if we endure, we shall also reign with him...

So kann mich nichts von Jesu scheiden.
So can me nothing from Jesus separate.
{In the same way, nought can separate me from Jesus.}

Muß ich mit Christo leiden,
Must I with Christ suffer,
{If I must suffer with Christ,}

So werd ich auch nach dieser Zeit
Then will I also after this time

Mit Christo wieder auferstehen
With Christ again arise

Zur Ehr und Herrlichkeit
To honor and splendor

Und Gott in meinem Fleische sehen.
And God in my flesh see.
{And see God in my flesh.}

1 Pet. 4:13. Rejoice in so far as you share Christ's sufferings, that you may also rejoice and be glad when his glory is revealed.
Rom. 8:17. ...[We are] fellow heirs with Christ, provided we suffer with him in order that we may also be glorified with him.
Rom. 5:2. Through him we have obtained access to this grace in which we stand, and we rejoice in our hope of sharing the glory of God.
Phil. 3:10–11. [My goal is] that I may know him and the power of his resurrection, and may share his sufferings, becoming like him in his death, that if possible I may attain the resurrection from the dead.
Rom. 8:17. If children, then heirs, heirs of God and fellow heirs with Christ, provided we suffer with him in order that we may also be glorified with him.
1 Cor. 15:51–52. Lo! I tell you a mystery. We shall not all sleep, but we shall all be changed...at the last trumpet. For the trumpet will sound, and the dead will be raised imperishable, and we shall be changed.
Job 19:25–26. For I know that my Redeemer lives, and at last he will stand upon the earth; and after my skin has been thus destroyed, then from my flesh (Luther German: in meinem Fleisch) I shall see God.

8. Soprano Aria
●Yearning for death and light of heaven (31–8)
Letzte Stunde, brich herein,
(O) final hour, break (forth),

Mir die Augen zuzudrücken!
My - eyes to-close!
{When thou shalt close my eyes!}

Laß mich Jesu Freudenschein
Let me Jesus' ray-of-gladness
{Let me behold Jesus' ray of gladness,}

Und sein helles Licht erblicken,
And his brilliant light behold,
{And his brilliant light,}

Laß mich Engeln ähnlich sein!
Let me (to) angels similar be!
{Let me become like the angels!}

Letzte Stunde, brich herein!
(O) final hour, break (forth)!

1 Jn. 2:18. Children, it is the last hour...
1 Cor. 15:51–53. We shall all be changed...at the last trumpet. For the trumpet will sound, and the dead will be raised imperishable...
Phil. 1:21. To me to live is Christ, and to die is gain.
2 Cor. 5:6–8. So we are always of good courage; we know that while we are at home in the body we are away from the Lord, for we walk by faith, not by sight. We are of good courage, and we would rather be away from the body and at home with the Lord.
Jn. 8:12. Again Jesus spoke to them, saying, "I am the light of the world..."
Mt. 17:2. And [Jesus] was transfigured before them, and his face shone like the sun, and his garments became white as light.
Rev. 21:23, 24. The [heavenly] city has no need of sun or moon to shine upon it, for the glory of God is its light, and its lamp is the Lamb. By its light shall the nations walk...
1 Jn. 3:2. It does not yet appear what we shall be, but we know that when he appears we shall be like him...
Mt. 22:30. In the resurrection they...are like angels in heaven.
Lk. 20:36. They cannot die any more, because they are equal to angels and are sons of God, being sons of the resurrection.

9. Chorale
●Yearning for death's sleep: Christ will awaken me (31–9)
So fahr ich hin zu Jesu Christ,
Thus go I forth to Jesus Christ,

Mein' Arm tu ich ausstrecken;
My arm do I stretch-out;

So schlaf ich ein und ruhe fein,
Thus fall-asleep I - and rest well,
{Thus I fall asleep and rest well,}

Lk. 2:28–29. [Simeon] took [Jesus] up in his arms and blessed God and said, "Lord, now lettest thou thy servant depart in peace, according to thy word."
2 Tim. 4:6–8. ...The time of my departure has come. I have fought the good fight, I have finished the race, I have kept the faith. Henceforth there is laid up for me the crown of righteousness, which the Lord, the righteous judge, will award to me on that Day...
1 Thess. 4:13–14. We would not have you ignorant, brethren, concerning those who are asleep, that you may not grieve as others do who have no hope. For since we believe that Jesus died and rose

Kein Mensch kann mich aufwecken,
No one can me awaken,

Denn Jesus Christus, Gottes Sohn,
Than Jesus Christ, God's Son,

Der wird die Himmelstür auftun,
He will the door-of-heaven open;

Mich führn zum ewgen Leben.
Me lead to everlasting life.
{And lead me to everlasting life.}

BWV 32
Liebster Jesu, mein Verlangen
(NBA I/5; BC A31)

1. S. after Epiphany (BWV 154, 124, 32)
*Rom. 12:1-6[1] (Christian duty: present yourselves as living sacrifices to God)
*Lk. 2:41–52 (The twelve-year-old Jesus in the temple)
[1]End: "given to us."
Librettist: Georg Christian Lehms

1. Soprano Aria
●Voice of believing soul: Where find I thee, Jesus? (32-1)
Liebster Jesu, mein Verlangen,
Dearest Jesus, (O) my desire,

Sage mir, wo find ich dich?
Tell me, where find I thee?
{Tell me, where do I find thee?}

Soll ich dich so bald verlieren
Shall I thee so soon lose
{Shall I lose thee so soon}

Und nicht ferner bei mir spüren?
And no more with me sense?
{And no more sense thee with me?}

Ach! mein Hort, erfreue mich,
Ah! my refuge, gladden me,

Laß dich höchst vergnügt umfangen.
Allow thyself most delightedly (to be) embraced.

2. Bass Recit.
●Vox Christi: Why did you seek me? Lk. 2:49 (32-2)
Was ist's, daß du mich gesuchet? Weißt du
Why is-it, that ye me sought? Know ye

nicht, daß ich sein muß in dem,
not, that I be must in that,

das meines Vaters ist?
which my Father's is?

again, even so, through Jesus, God will bring with him those who have fallen asleep.
1 Cor. 15:20. ...Christ has been raised from the dead, the first fruits of those who have fallen asleep.
2 Pet. 1:10–11. Therefore, brethren, be the more zealous to confirm your call and election, for if you do this you will never fall; so there will be richly provided for you an entrance into the eternal kingdom of our Lord and Savior Jesus Christ.
Mt. 25:34. Then the King will say to those at his right hand, "Come, O blessed of my Father, inherit the kingdom prepared for you from the foundation of the world."
Mt. 25:21. [The] master said to [his] servant, "Well done, good and faithful servant...enter into the joy of your master."

*Lk. 2:41–46.** Now [Jesus'] parents went to Jerusalem every year at the feast of the Passover. And when he was twelve years old, they went up according to custom; and...as they were returning, the boy Jesus stayed behind in Jerusalem. His parents did not know it... supposing him to be in the company...and they sought him among their kinsfolk and acquaintances; and when they did not find him, they returned to Jerusalem, seeking him. After three days they found him in the temple...
S. of S. 3:1 [Bride]: I sought him whom my soul loves; I sought him, but found him not; I called him, but he gave no answer.
Ps. 42:1. As a hart longs for flowing streams, so longs my soul for thee, O God.
Job 23:3. Oh, that I knew where I might find him, that I might come even to his seat!
Deut. 4:29. You will seek the Lord your God, and you will find him, if you search after him with all your heart and with all your soul. (Also Jer. 29:12-14.)
Ps. 86:4. Gladden the soul (Luther: erfreue die Seele) of thy servant, for to thee, O Lord, do I lift up my soul (Luther: nach dir, Herr, verlangt mich). (Also Ps. 25:1.)

*Lk. 2:46, 48–49.** After three days they found [Jesus] in the temple, sitting among the teachers, listening to them and asking them questions...And his mother said to him, "Son, why have you treated us so? Behold, your father and I have been looking for you anxiously." And he said to them, *"How is it that you sought me? Did you not know that I must be in my Father's house?"*
Jn. 6:38 [Christ]: I have come down from heaven, not to do my own will, but the will of him who sent me. (Also Jn. 4:34, 5:30.)

3. Bass Aria
●Vox Christi: You will find me in the house of God (32-3)
Hier, in meines Vaters Stätte,
Here, in my Father's abode,

Findt mich ein betrübter Geist.
Finds me a downcast spirit.
{A downcast spirit can find me.}

Da kannst du mich sicher finden
There canst thou me surely find
{Here thou canst surely find me}

Und dein Herz mit mir verbinden,
And thy heart with me unite,
{And unite thy heart with me,}

Weil dies meine Wohnung heißt.
Because this my dwelling is-called.
{For this is called my dwelling.}

4. Soprano/Bass Recit. (Dialogue)
●Dialogue (Christ and Soul); they meet in God's house (32-4)
Soprano (Soul):
Ach! heiliger und großer Gott,
Ah, holy and great God,

So will ich mir
Thus will I -

Denn hier bei dir
Then here with thee
{Then here in thy presence}

Beständig Trost und Hilfe suchen.
Continually comfort and help seek.
{Continually seek comfort and help.}

Bass (Vox Christi):
Wirst du den Erdentand verfluchen
Wilt thou - earth's-bauble curse
{If thou wilt earth's bauble curse}

Und nur in diese Wohnung gehn,
And just into this dwelling go,
{And just enter this dwelling,}

So kannst du hier und dort bestehn.
Then canst thou here and yonder stand (the test).

Soprano: (Rhymed paraphrase of Ps. 84:1-2)
Wie lieblich ist doch deine Wohnung,
How lovely is indeed thy dwelling,

Herr, starker Zebaoth;
Lord, strong Sabaoth;

Mein Geist verlangt
My spirit longs

*Lk. 2:46, 48–49. After three days they found [Jesus] in the temple... And his mother said to him, "Son, why have you treated us so? Behold, your father and I have been looking for you anxiously." And he said to them, "How is it that you sought me? Did you not know that I must be in my Father's house?"
Ps. 34:4. I sought the Lord, and he answered me...
Jer. 29:12–14 [God]: Then you will call upon me and come and pray to me, and I will hear you. You will seek me and find me; when you seek me with all your heart, I will be found by you, says the Lord... (Also Deut. 4:29.)
Jms. 4:8. Draw near to God and he will draw near to you.
Ps. 73:2, 16–17. As for me, my feet had almost stumbled, my steps had well-nigh slipped...but when I thought how to understand this, it seemed to me a wearisome task, until I went into the sanctuary of God...
S. of S. 3:4 [Bride]: I found him whom my soul loves. I held him, and would not let him go...

Ps. 73:26. ...God is the strength of my heart and my portion for ever.
Ps. 84:4, 10, 12. [O Lord,] blessed are those who dwell in thy house, ever singing thy praise!...For a day in thy courts is better than a thousand elsewhere. I would rather be a doorkeeper in the house of my God than dwell in the tents of wickedness...blessed is the man who trusts in thee!
Ps. 27:4–5. One thing have I asked of the Lord, that will I seek after; that I may dwell in the house of the Lord all the days of my life, to behold the beauty of the Lord, and to inquire in his temple. For he will hide me in his shelter...
1 Jn. 2:15. Do not love the world or the things in the world. If any one loves the world, love for the Father is not in him.
Lk. 16:15. ...What is exalted among men is an abomination in the sight of God.
Jms. 4:4. Unfaithful creatures! Do you not know that friendship with the world is enmity with God? Therefore whoever wishes to be a friend of the world makes himself an enemy of God.
Mt. 6:24. No one can serve two masters; for either he will hate the one and love the other, or he will be devoted to the one and despise the other. You cannot serve God and mammon. (Also Lk. 16:13.)
Mt. 6:33. But seek first his kingdom and his righteousness, and all these things shall be yours as well.
Ps. 26:8–9. O Lord, I love the habitation of thy house, and the place where thy glory dwells. Sweep me not away with sinners, nor my life with bloodthirsty men...
Ps. 92:12–13. The righteous flourish like the palm tree, and grow like a cedar in Lebanon. They are planted in the house of the Lord, they flourish in the courts of our God.
Ps. 84:1–2. How lovely is thy dwelling place, O Lord of hosts! My soul longs, yea, faints for the courts of the Lord; my heart and flesh sing for joy to the living God.
Ps. 27:4. One thing have I asked of the Lord, that will I seek after; that I may dwell in the house of the Lord all the days of my life, to behold the beauty of the Lord, and to inquire in his temple.
Ps. 42:1–2. As a hart longs for flowing streams, so longs my soul for thee, O God. My soul thirsts for God, for the living God. When shall I come and behold the face of God?

Nach dem, was   nur in deinem
For   that, which only in   thy

      Hofe   prangt.
      court is-resplendently-displayed.

Mein Leib und Seele freuet sich
My body and soul rejoice -

In dem lebendgen Gott:
In the   living   God:

Ach! Jesu, meine Brust liebt dich nur ewiglich.
Ah! Jesus, my breast loves thee alone eternally.

Bass:
So kannst du glücklich sein,
Thus canst thou happy   be,

Wenn   Herz und Geist
When (thy) heart and spirit

Aus   Liebe gegen mich entzündet heißt.
Out-of love toward me   kindled (are).
{In love toward me are kindled.}

Soprano:
Ach! dieses Wort, das itzo schon
Ah!   this   word, that now already

Mein Herz aus Babels Grenzen reißt,
My   heart out-of Babel's borders snatches,
{Snatches my heart out of Babylon's borders,}

Fass'   ich mir andachtsvoll in meiner Seele ein.
(Embrace) I -   devoutly within my   soul -.
{Do I embrace devotedly within my soul.}

5. Soprano & Bass Duet
●Dialogue (Christ and believing Soul): Mystical union (32–5)
Soprano & Bass:
Nun verschwinden alle Plagen,
Now   do-vanish   all vexations,

Nun verschwindet Ach und Schmerz.
Now   does-vanish "Ah" and "woe".

Soprano:
Nun will ich nicht von dir lassen,
Now will I   not from thee depart,
{Now I will not depart from thee,}

Bass:
Und ich   dich auch stets umfassen.
And I (will) thee also continually embrace.
{And I will also continually embrace thee.}

Ps. 122:1. I was glad when they said to me, "Let us go to the house of the Lord!"

Deut. 6:4–5. Hear, O Israel: The Lord our God is one Lord; and you shall love the Lord your God with all your heart, and with all your soul, and with all your might.

Jn. 21:17. [Jesus] said to [Peter] the third time, "Simon, son of John, do you love me?" Peter was grieved because he said to him the third time, "Do you love me?" And he said to him, "Lord, you know everything; you know that I love you."

Mt. 22:37–38. And [Jesus] said to him, "You shall love the Lord your God with all your heart, and with all your soul, and with all your mind. This is the great and first commandment." (Also Deut. 6:4–5.)

Ps. 37:4. Take delight in the Lord, and he will give you the desires of your heart.

Rev. 2:4 [Christ]: I have this against you, that you have abandoned the love you had at first...

2 Tim. 4:10. Demas, in love with this present world, has deserted me...

Jms. 4:4. ...Do you not know that friendship with the world is enmity with God?...

2 Cor. 6:14–15. ...What partnership have righteousness and iniquity? Or what fellowship has light with darkness? What accord has Christ with Belial?. Or what has a believer in common with an unbeliever?

Ps. 137:1–3. By the waters of Babylon (Luther: Wassern zu Babel), there we sat down and wept...for there our captors required of us songs...saying, "Sing us one of the songs of Zion!"

Rev. 17:3–5. And I saw a woman sitting on a scarlet beast...The woman was arrayed in purple and scarlet, and bedecked with gold and jewels and pearls, holding in her hand a golden cup full of abominations and the impuities of her fornication; and on her forehead was written a name of mystery: "Babylon the great, mother of harlots and of earth's abominations." (Also Rev. 14:8.)

1 Jn. 2:15. Do not love the world or the things in the world. If any one loves the world, love for the Father is not in him.

Ps. 119:11. [O Lord,] I have laid up thy word in my heart, that I might not sin against thee.

Rev. 21:3–4. ...Behold, the dwelling of God is with men. He will dwell with them, and they shall be his people, and God himself will be with them; he will wipe away every tear from their eyes, and death shall be no more, neither shall there be mourning nor crying nor pain any more, for the former things have passed away.

Ps. 73:25. [O Lord,] whom have I in heaven but thee? And there is nothing upon earth that I desire besides thee.

Jn. 6:66–68. After this many of his disciples drew back and no longer went about with him. Jesus said to the twelve, "Do you also wish to go away?" Simon Peter answered him, "Lord, to whom shall we go? You have the words of eternal life..."

Gen. 32:26. ...Jacob said, "I will not let you go, unless you bless me."

S. of S. 3:4 [Bride]: ...I found him whom my soul loves. I held him, and would not let him go...

S. of S. 2:16 [Bride]: My beloved is mine and I am his... (Also S. of S. 6:3.)

Soprano:
Nun vergnüget sich mein Herz
Now   enjoys   itself my heart
{Now my heart enjoys itself}

Bass:
Und kann   voll Freude sagen:
And can, filled-with joy,   say:

Soprano & Bass:
Nun verschwinden alle Plagen,
Now   do-vanish   all vexations,

Nun verschwindet Ach und Schmerz!
Now does-vanish "Ah" and   "woe"!

6. Chorale (Added by someone: J. S. Bach?)
●Prayer: Open to me the portals of thy sweet blessing (32–6)
Mein Gott, öffne mir die Pforten
My   God, open to-me the portals

Solcher Gnad und Gütigkeit,
Of-this   grace and kindness,

Laß mich allzeit   allerorten
Let me at-all-times (and) in-all-places

Schmecken deine Süßigkeit!
Taste   thy sweetness!

Liebe mich und treib mich an,
Love me   and urge me   on,

Daß ich dich, so gut ich kann,
That I thee, as best I can,
{That I might, as best I can,}

Wiederum umfang und liebe
In-return   embrace and love
{In return embrace and love thee}

Und   ja nun nicht mehr betrübe.
And indeed now no more do-grieve.
{And indeed now no more grieve thee.}

S. of S. 2:6 [Bride]: O that his left hand were under my head, and that his right hand embraced me!
Ps. 37:4. Take delight in the Lord, and he will give you the desires of your heart.
Mt. 22:37. You shall love the Lord your God with all your heart, and with all your soul, and with all your mind.
Rev. 7:15–17. Therefore are [the righteous] before the throne of God, and serve him day and night within his temple; and he who sits upon the throne will shelter them with his presence. They shall hunger no more, neither thirst any more; the sun shall not strike them, nor any scorching heat. For the Lamb in the midst of the throne will be their shepherd, and he will guide them to springs of living water; and God will wipe away every tear from their eyes.

Gen. 28:12–14, 16–17. And [Jacob] dreamed that there was a ladder set up on the earth, and the top of it reached to heaven; and behold, the angels of God were ascending and descending on it! And behold, the Lord stood above it and said, "I am the Lord...the land on which you lie I will give to you and to your descendants; and your descendants shall be like the dust of the earth..." Then Jacob awoke from his sleep and said, "Surely the Lord is in this place; and I did not know it." And he was afraid, and said, "How awesome is this place! This is none other than the house of God, and this is the gate (Luther: Pforte) of heaven."
Mal. 3:10. Bring the full tithes into the storehouse, that there may be food in my house; and thereby put me to the test, says the Lord of hosts, if I will not open the windows of heaven for you and pour down for you an overflowing blessing.
Ps. 78:23–25. [God] commanded the skies above, and opened the doors of heaven (Luther: Türen des Himmels); and he rained down upon them manna to eat, and gave them the grain of heaven. Man ate the bread of the angels; he sent them food in abundance. (See Ex. 16.)
Ps. 34:8. O taste and see that the Lord is good! Happy is the man who takes refuge in him!
1 Pet. 2:3. You have tasted the kindness of the Lord.
Rom. 8:14. All who are led by the Spirit of God (Luther: welche der Geist...treibt) are sons of God.
Ps. 116:12. What shall I render to the Lord for all his bounty to me?
Mt. 22:37. You shall love the Lord your God with all your heart...
Eph. 4:30. Do not grieve the Holy Spirit of God, in whom you were sealed for the day of redemption.

BWV 33
Allein zu dir, Herr Jesu Christ
(NBA I/21; BC A127)

13. S. after Trinity (BWV 77, 33, 164)
*Gal. 3:15–22 (The purpose of the Law)
*Lk. 10:23–37 (The greatest commandment, parable of the good Samaritan)
Librettist: Unknown

1. Chorus (Chorale Vs. 1)
●Hope is placed in Christ alone; only he can help (33-1)
Allein zu dir, Herr Jesu Christ,
Alone toward thee, Lord Jesus Christ,
{O Lord Jesus Christ,}

Mein Hoffnung steht auf Erden;
My hope is-inclined on earth;
{My hope on earth lies only in thee;}

Ich weiß, daß du mein Tröster bist,
I know, that thou my comforter art,
{I know thou art my comforter,}

Kein Trost mag mir sonst werden.
No comfort (can) (there) for-me otherwise be.
{Besides thee, there is no other comfort for me.}

Von Anbeginn ist nichts erkorn,
From (the) beginning has nothing been-ordained,
{From the beginning nothing has been ordained,}

Auf Erden war kein Mensch geborn,
On earth (has) no person (ever) been-born,
{No person ever been born,}

Der mir aus Nöten helfen kann.
Who me out-of distress help can.
{Who could help me out of my distress.)

Ich ruf dich an,
I call (on) thee - ,

Zu dem ich mein Vertrauen hab.
(In) whom I my trust have.
{In whom I have placed my trust.}

2. Bass Recit. (Based on Chorale Vs. 2)
●Law shows me guilty; repentance brings forgiveness (33-2)
Mein Gott und Richter, wilt du mich
My God and judge, wouldst thou me

     aus dem Gesetze fragen,
     out-of the law question,
{My God and judge, if thou wouldst examine me by the law,}

So kann ich nicht,
Then (could) I not,
{Then I could never—}

*Lk. 10:27. ...You shall love the Lord your God with all your heart, and with all your soul, and with all your strength, and with all your mind; and your neighbor as yourself. (Mt. 22:37–40, Mk. 12:30–31, Deut. 6:5)
Ps. 39:7. Now, Lord, for what do I wait? My hope is in thee.
Ps. 62:5. For God alone my soul waits in silence, for my hope is from him.
Ps. 130:5–6. I wait for the Lord, my soul waits, and in his word I hope; my soul waits for the Lord more than watchmen for the morning, more than watchmen for the morning.
Ps. 119:114, 116. [O Lord,] thou art my hiding place and my shield; I hope in thy word...Uphold me according to thy promise, that I may live, and let me not be put to shame in my hope!
Ps. 2:12. ...Blessed are all who take refuge in him.
Ps. 7:1. O Lord my God, in thee do I take refuge...
Ps. 16:1–2. Preserve me, O God, for in thee I take refuge. I say to the Lord, "Thou art my Lord; I have no good apart from thee."
Ps. 73:28. But for me it is good to be near God; I have made the Lord God my refuge...
Ps. 91:1–2. He who dwells in the shelter of the Most High, who abides in the shadow of the Almighty, will say to the Lord, "My refuge and my fortress; my God, in whom I trust."
Acts 4:12. And there is salvation in no one else, for there is no other name under heaven given among men by which we must be saved.
1 Tim. 2:5–6. For there is one God, and there is one mediator between God and men, the man Christ Jesus, who gave himself as a ransom for all.
1 Tim. 1:1. ...Christ Jesus our hope...
1 Cor. 15:17. If Christ has not been raised, your faith is futile and you are still in your sins.
1 Pet. 1:21. Through him you have confidence in God, who raised him from the dead and gave him glory, so that your faith and hope are in God.
Lk. 18:38. [The blind man] cried, "Jesus, Son of David, have mercy on me!"

2 Tim. 4:1. Christ Jesus...is to judge the living and the dead...
Acts 10:42. ...[Christ] is the one ordained by God to be judge of the living and the dead.
Ps. 51:3. I know my transgressions, and my sin is ever before me.
Ps. 130:3. If thou, O Lord, shouldst mark iniquities, Lord, who could stand?
Ps. 143:2. Enter not into judgment with thy servant; for no man living is righteous before thee.
Gal. 2:16. ...A man is not justified by works of the law... because by works of the law shall no one be justified.

119

Weil   mein Gewissen widerspricht,
Because my conscience contradicts (me)—

Auf   tausend eines sagen.
In (a) thousand once answer.
{Once in a thousand times answer.}

An Seelenkräften arm und an der Liebe bloß,
In strength-of-soul poor and of - love bare,
{I am weak in soul and lacking in love,}

Und **meine Sünd ist schwer und übergroß;**
And my sin is grievous and enormous;

Doch weil sie mich von   Herzen reuen,
Yet, because they me from (my) heart grieve,
{Yet because these sins grieve me deeply,}

Wirst du, mein Gott und Hort,
Wilt thou, my God and refuge,
{Thou wilt, my God and refuge,}

Durch ein Vergebungswort
Through a word-of-forgivness

Mich wiederum erfreuen.
Me   anew   gladden.
{Gladden me anew.}

3. Alto Aria (Based on Chorale Vs. 2)
●Christ's forgiveness sufficient for great sin (33–3)
Wie furchtsam wankten meine Schritte,
How fearfully waver my   steps,
{How fearully my steps waver,}

Doch Jesus hört auf meine Bitte
Yet Jesus hears - my petition

Und zeigt mich seinem Vater an.
And shows me (to) his Father - .

Mich drückten Sündenlasten nieder,
Me   weighed burdens-of-sin down,
{Burdens of sin weighed me down,}

Doch hilft mir Jesu   Trostwort   wieder,
Yet helps me Jesus' word-of-comfort again,
{Yet Jesus' word of comfort reassures me,}

Daß er für mich genug   getan.
That he for me enough (has) done.
{That he has done enough for me.}

4. Tenor Recit. (Based on Chorale Vs. 3)
●Prayer of confession; faith will produce good deeds (33–4)
Mein Gott, verwirf mich nicht,
My God, cast me not—

Rom. 3:20. No human being will be justified in his sight by works of the law, since through the law comes knowledge of sin. (Also Rom. 7:7, 13, Gal. 3:11.)
***Gal. 3:19, 22, 24.** Why then the law? It was added because of transgressions...But the scripture consigned all things to sin...So that the law was our custodian until Christ came...
Job 9:2–3. ...How can a man be just before God? If one wished to contend with him, one could not answer him once in a thousand times.
Rom. 2:15. [Men] show that what the law requires is written on their hearts, while their conscience also bears witness and their conflicting thoughts accuse...them...
Rom. 3:23. All have sinned and fall short of the glory of God.
Is. 53:6. All we like sheep have gone astray; we have turned every one to his own way... (Also Rom. 3:10–12.)
1 Tim. 1:15. The saying is sure and worth of full acceptance, that Christ Jesus came into the world to save sinners. And I am the foremost of sinners...
Ps. 32:5. [O Lord,] I acknowledged my sin to thee, and I did not hide my iniquity; I said, "I will confess my transgressions to the Lord"; then thou didst forgive the guilt of my sin.
Ps. 103:12. As far as the east is from the west, so far does he remove our transgressions from us.
1 Jn. 1:8–9. If we say we have no sin, we deceive ourselves, and the truth is not in us. If we confess our sins, he is faithful and just, and will forgive our sins and cleanse us from all unrighteousness.
Ps. 51:2. [O Lord,] wash me thoroughly from my iniquity, and cleanse me from my sin!

Heb. 10:23. Let us hold fast the confession of our hope without wavering (Luther: wanken)...
Ps. 78:37–38. [The people's] heart was not steadfast toward [God]; they were not true to his covenant. Yet he, being compassionate, forgave their iniquity, and did not destroy them; he restrained his anger often, and did not stir up all his wrath.
Is. 1:4. Ah, sinful nation, a people laden with iniquity...
1 Jn. 2:1–2. ...If any one does sin, we have an advocate with the Father, Jesus Christ the righteous; and he is the expiation for our sins, and not for ours only but also for the sins of the whole world. (Also Is. 1:18.)
Heb. 7:25. ...[Christ] is able for all time to save those who draw near to God through him, since he always lives to make intercession for them. (Also Heb. 9:24.)
Rom. 8:34. Who is to comdemn? Is it Christ Jesus, who died, yes, who was raised from the dead, who is at the right hand of God, who indeed intercedes for us?
Heb. 10:10, 14. ...We have been sanctified through the offering of the body of Jesus Christ once for all...For by a single offering he has perfected for all time those who are sanctified.

Ps. 51:10–12. Create in me a clean heart, O God, and put a new and right spirit within me. Cast me not away from thy presence, and take not thy holy Spirit from me. Restore to me the joy of thy salvation, and uphold me with a willing spirit. (Also Jer. 7:15.)

Wiewohl ich dein Gebot noch täglich übertrete,
Although I thy law still daily transgress—

Von deinem Angesicht!
From thy countenance!

Das kleinste ist mir schon zu halten viel zu schwer;
The smallest is for-me already to keep much too hard;
{The smallest one is already much too hard for me to keep;}

Doch, wenn ich um nichts mehr
Yet if I for nothing more

Als Jesu Beistand bete,
Than Jesus' aid do-pray,

So wird mich kein Gewissensstreit
Then will - no battle-of-conscience

Der Zuversicht berauben;
(My) confidence rob;
{Rob me of my conficence;}

Gib mir nur aus Barmherzigkeit
Give me but out-of (thy) mercy
{Just give me by thy mercy}

Den wahren Christenglauben!
- True Christian-faith!

So stellt er sich mit guten Früchten ein
Then appears it - with good fruit -
{Then my faith will yield good fruit}

Und wird durch Liebe tätig sein.
And will through love active be.
{Expressing itself in love.}

5. Tenor & Bass Duet (Based on Chorale Vs. 3)
●Prayer to love God with complete devotion (33-5)
Gott, der du die Liebe heißt,
(O) God, thou-who - love art-called,

Ach, entzünde meinen Geist,
Ah, kindle my spirit,

Laß zu dir vor allen Dingen
Let toward thee, above all things,

Mein Liebe kräftig dringen!
My love powerfully press!
{Let my love desire thee above all else!}

Gib, daß ich aus reinem Triebe
Grant, that I out-of pure (devotion)

Ecc. 7:20. Surely there is not a righteous man on earth who does good and never sins. (Also Rom. 3:23, Jms. 3:2.)
Ps. 51:3. I know my transgressions, and my sin is ever before me.
Rom. 7:15-18. I do not understand my own actions. For I do not do what I want, but I do the very thing I hate. Now if I do what I do not want, I agree that the law is good. So then it is no longer I that do it, but sin which dwells within me. For I know that nothing good dwells within me, that is, in my flesh. I can will what is right, but I cannot do it.
Gal. 2:16. ...A man is not justified by works of the law...because by works of the law shall no one be justified.
Acts 15:10-11. Why do you make trial of God by putting a yoke upon the neck of the disciples which neither our fathers nor we have been able to bear? But we believe that we shall be saved through the grace of the Lord Jesus...
Rom. 8:1. There is therefore now no condemnation for those who are in Christ Jesus.
Rom. 3:28. For we hold that a man is justified by faith apart from works of law.
1 Jn. 3:19-20. By this we shall know that we are of the truth, and reassure our hearts before him whenever our hearts condemn us; for God is greater than our hearts.
Heb. 10:35. Therefore do not throw away your confidence, which has a great reward.
Jn. 15:16 [Christ]: You did not choose me, but I chose you and appointed you that you should go and bear fruit and that your fruit should abide...
Mt. 7:16. You will know them by their fruits...
Jms. 2:17. Faith by itself, if it has no works, is dead.
Gal. 5:22-23. The fruit of the Spirit is love, joy, peace, patience, kindness, goodness, faithfulness, gentleness, self-control; against such there is no law.
Gal. 5:6. In Christ Jesus neither circumcision nor uncircumcision is of any avail, but faith working through love.
1 Jn. 3:23. This is his commandment, that we should believe in the name of his Son Jesus Christ and love one another...
1 Cor. 13:13. So faith, hope, love abide, these three; but the greatest of these is love.

1 Jn. 4:7-8, 11-12. Beloved, let us love one another; for love is of God, and he who loves is born of God and knows God. He who does not love does not know God; for God is love...Beloved, if God so loved us, we also ought to love one another. No man has ever seen God; if we love one another, God abides in us and his love is perfected in us.
***Lk. 10:27.** ...You shall love the Lord your God with all your heart, and with all your soul, and with all your strength, and with all your mind; and your neighbor as yourself. (Also Mt. 22:37-40, Mk. 12:30-31, Deut. 6:5.)
Lk. 14:25-27. Now great multitudes accompanied [Jesus]; and he turned and said to them, "If any one comes to me and does not hate his own father and mother and wife and children and brothers and sisters, yes, and even his own life, he cannot be my disciple." (Also Mt. 10:37-38.)
Phil. 3:7-10. ...Whatever gain I had, I counted as loss for the sake of Christ. Indeed I count everything as loss because of the surpassing worth of knowing Christ Jesus my Lord. For his sake I have suffered the loss of all things, and count them as refuse, in order that I may

Als mich selbst den Nächsten   liebe;
As   my-self   (my) neighbor (would) love;
{Would love my neighbor as myself;}

Stören Feinde meine Ruh,
Disturb enemies my   rest,
{Should enemies disturb my rest,}

      Sende du mir   Hülfe zu!
(Then) send thou to-me (thy) help - !

6. Chorale (Vs. 4)
●Doxology: Glory to Father, Son, and Holy Ghost (33–6)
Ehr   sei Gott in dem höchsten Thron,
Praise be-to God on the highest   throne,

Dem Vater aller   Güte,
The father of-all goodness,

Und Jesu Christ, sein'm liebsten Sohn,
And Jesus Christ, his   dearest Son,

Der uns allzeit behüte,
Who us at-all-times protects,

Und Gott dem Heiligen Geiste,
And God   the   Holy   Ghost,

Der uns sein Hülf allzeit leiste,
Who us his help at-all-times affords,

Damit wir ihm gefällig   sein,
So-that we to-him pleasing (might) be,

Hier in dieser Zeit
Here in this time

Und folgends in der Ewigkeit.
And hereafter in - eternity.

gain Christ and be found in him, not having a righteousness of my own, based on law, but that which is through faith in Christ, the righteousness from God that depends on faith; that I may know him and the power of his resurrection...
Mt. 5:43–46, 48 [Christ]: You have heard that it was said, "You shall love your neighbor and hate your enemy." But I say to you, Love your enemies...so that you may be sons of your Father who is in heaven; for he makes his sun rise on the evil and on the good, and sends rain on the just and on the unjust. For if you love those who love you, what reward have you? Do not even the tax collectors do the same?...You, therefore, must be perfect, as your heavenly Father is perfect.

Lk. 2:14. Glory to God in the highest...
1 Tim. 1:17. To the King of ages, immortal, invisible, the only God, be honor and glory for ever and ever. Amen. (Also Phil. 4:20.)
Ps. 41:13. Blessed be the Lord, the God of Israel, from everlasting to everlasting! Amen and Amen. (Doxology: also Ps. 72:19, 89:52, 106:48, 150:6, Rom. 11:36, Jude 1:25)
Mt. 28:19. ...in the name of the Father and of the Son and of the Holy Spirit.
Mt. 3:16–17. When Jesus was baptized, he went up immediately from the water, and behold, the heavens were opened and he saw the **Spirit** of God descending like a dove, and alighting on him; and lo, [the **Father**'s] voice from heaven, saying, "This is my beloved **Son**, with whom I am well pleased."
Jms. 1:17. Every good endowment and every perfect gift is from above, coming down from the Father of lights with whom there is no variation or shadow due to change.
Jn. 10:11, 27–28. [Christ said,] "I am the good shepherd...my sheep... follow me; and I give them eternal life, and they shall never perish, and no one shall snatch them out of my hand."
Jn. 14:16–17 [Christ]: I will pray the Father, and he will give you another Counselor, to be with you for ever, even the Spirit of truth...
Rom. 8:26. Likewise the Spirit helps us in our weakness...
2 Cor. 5:6, 9. ...While we are at home in the body we are away from the Lord...Whether we are at home or away, we make it our aim to please him.
Eph. 5:10. Try to learn what is pleasing to the Lord.
Col. 3:17. Whatever you do, in word or deed, do everything in the name of the Lord Jesus...

BWV 34
O ewiges Feuer, o Ursprung der Liebe
(NBA I/13; BC A84)

Pentecost (BWV 172, 59, 74, 34)
*Acts 2:1–13 (Outpouring of the Holy Spirit)
*Jn. 14:23–31 (Jesus' farewell; he promises to send the Holy Spirit)
Librettist: Unknown. BWV 30 is a parody of wedding cantata BWV 34a.

1. Chorus (Parody)
●Prayer: Send love's fire into our hearts, thy temple (34–1)
O ewiges Feuer, o Ursprung der Liebe,
O eternal fire, O fount of love,

*Acts 2:1–4. When the day of Pentecost had come, they were all together in one place. And suddenly a sound came from heaven like the rush of a mighty wind, and it filled all the house where they were sitting. And there appeared to them tongues as of fire, distributed and resting on each one of them. And they were all filled with the Holy Spirit and began to speak in other tongues, as the Spirit gave them utterance. (Also Jn. 1:33, Lk. 3:16.)
*Jn. 14:23 [Christ]: If a man loves me, he will keep my word, and my Father will love him, and we will come to him and make our home with him.
1 Jn. 4:7–8, 11–12. Beloved, let us love one another; for love is of God, and he who loves is born of God and knows God. He who does not love does not know God; for God is love...Beloved, if God so

Entzünde die Herzen und   weihe   sie ein.
Kindle   (our) hearts and consecrate them - .

Laß himmlische Flammen durchdringen und wallen,
Let heavenly   flames   push-through and well-up,

Wir wünschen, o Höchster, dein Tempel zu sein,
We   desire,   O Most-High, thy temple to be,

Ach, laß   dir die Seelen im Glauben gefallen.
Ah, grant-that thee (our) souls in faith may-please.
{Ah, grant that our souls might please thee by faith.}

2. Tenor Recit. (Newly composed)
●Prayer: Take up residence in our heart as promised (34-2)
Herr, unsre Herzen halten   dir
Lord, our   hearts hold (out) to-thee

Dein Wort der Wahrheit für:
Thy Word of   truth   - :

Du   willst bei Menschen gerne sein,
Thou desirest with mankind gladly to-be,

Drum   sei das Herze dein;
Therefore be (my) heart thine;
{Therefore take my heart;}

Herr, ziehe gnädig   ein.
Lord, enter graciously therein.

Ein solch erwähltes Heiligtum
A   such   chosen   shrine
{Such a chosen shrine}

Hat selbst den größten Ruhm.
Has e'en the greatest renown.

3. Alto Aria (Parody)
●God indwells the elect: what greater blessing is there? (34-3)
Wohl   euch, ihr auserwählten Seelen,
Blessed (are) ye, ye elect   souls

Die Gott zur Wohnung ausersehn.
Whom God for (his) dwelling hath-chosen.

Wer kann ein größer Heil erwählen?
Who can a greater happiness choose?
{Who could find greater happiness?}

Wer kann des Segens Menge zählen?
Who can these blessings' great-number reckon?
{Who can count this great host of blessings?}

Und dieses ist vom Herrn geschehn.
And this (has) of-the Lord happened.
{And this is all the Lord's doing.}

loved us, we also ought to love one another. No man has ever seen God; if we love one another, God abides in us and his love is perfected in us.
1 Cor. 3:16–17. Do you not know that you are God's temple and that God's Spirit dwells in you?...God's temple is holy, and that temple you are.
2 Cor. 6:16. What agreement has the temple of God with idols? For we are the temple of the living God; as God said, "I will live in them and move among them, and I will be their God, and they shall be my people."
Eph. 5:10. Try to learn what is pleasing to the Lord. (Also 2 Cor 5:9.)
Heb. 11:6. Without faith it is impossible to please him...

*Jn. 14:23 [Christ]: If a man loves me, he will keep my word, and my Father will love him, and we will come to him and make our home with him. (Also Lev. 26:11–12.)
Rev. 3:20 [Christ]: Behold, I stand at the door and knock; if any one hears my voice and opens the door, I will come in to him and eat with him, and he with me.
Rev. 21:1–3. Then I saw a new heaven and a new earth...And I saw the holy city, new Jerusalem, coming down out of heaven from God...and I heard a loud voice from the throne saying, "Behold, the dwelling of God is with men. He will dwell with them, and they shall be his people, and God himself will be with them."
Eph. 3:16–17. [I pray] yhat according to the riches of his glory he may grant you to be strengthened with might through his Spirit in the inner man, and that Christ may dwell in your hearts through faith...
2 Cor. 6:16–18. What agreement has the temple of God with idols? For we are the temple of the living God; as God said, "I will live in them and move among them, and I will be their God, and they shall be my people." Therefore come out from them and be separate from them, says the Lord, and touch nothing unclean; then I will welcome you, and I will be a father to you, and you shall be my sons and daughters, says the Lord Almighty.

1 Pet. 2:9–10. You are a chosen race, a royal priesthood, a holy nation, God's own people, that you may declare the wonderful deeds of him who called you out of darkness into his marvelous light. Once you were no people but now you are God's people; once you had not received mercy but now you have received mercy.
Deut. 10:14–15. Behold, to the Lord your God belong heaven and the heaven of heavens, the earth with all that is in it; yet the Lord set his heart in love upon your fathers and chose their descendants after them, you above all peoples, as at this day.
*Jn. 14:23 [Christ]: If a man loves me, he will keep my word, and my Father will love him, and we will come to him and make our home with him. (Also Jn. 14:16–17.)
Ps. 40:5. Thou hast multiplied, O Lord my God, thy wondrous deeds and thy thoughts toward us; none can compare with thee! Were I to proclaim and tell of them, they would be more than can be numbered. (Also Ps. 71:15.)
Ps. 118:23. This is the Lord's doing (Luther: das ist vom Herrn geschehen); it is marvelous in our eyes. (Also Mt. 21:42–43.)

4. Bass Recit. (Newly composed)
●God's chosen dwelling receives his blessing (34-4)
Erwählt sich Gott die heilgen Hütten
Chooses - God the holy tabernacles
{If God chooses the holy tabernacles,}

Die er mit Heil bewohnt,
Which he with salvation will-inhabit,

So muß er auch den Segen auf sie schütten,
Then must he also (his) blessing upon them pour,
{Then he must also pour his blessing upon them,}

So wird der Sitz des Heiligtums belohnt.
Thus is the seat of-the sanctuary rewarded.

Der Herr ruft über sein geweihtes Haus
The Lord proclaims over his consecrated house

Das Wort des Segens aus:
This word of blessing - :

5. Chorus (Parody)
●Peace be upon Israel; God blesses with peace (34-5)
Friede über Israel.
Peace (be) upon Israel.

Dankt den höchsten Wunderhänden,
Give-thanks to-the highest wonder-working-hands,

Dankt, Gott hat an euch gedacht.
Give-thanks, God has of you thought.
{Give thanks, God has remembered you.}

Ja, sein Segen wirkt mit Macht,
Yea, his blessing works with might,

Friede über Israel,
Peace upon Israel,

Friede über euch zu senden.
Peace upon you to send.

*Jn. 14:23 [Christ]: If a man loves me, he will keep my word, and my Father will love him, and we will come to him and make our home with him.
Zech. 2:10-11. Sing and rejoice, and I will dwell in the midst of you, says the Lord. And many nations shall join themselves to the Lord in that day, and shall be my people; and I will dwell in the midst of you, and you shall know that the Lord of hosts has sent me to you. (Also Zech. 8:3, 8:8.)
Rev. 21:3-4. ...I heard a loud voice from the throne saying, "Behold, the dwelling of God is with men. He will dwell with them, and they shall be his people, and God himself will be with them..."
Eph. 3:17. ...that Christ may dwell in your hearts through faith.
Jn. 7:37-39. On the last day of the feast, the great day, Jesus stood up and proclaimed, "If any one thirst, let him come to me and drink. He who believes in me, as the scripture has said, 'Out of his heart shall flow rivers of living water.'" Now this he said about the Spirit, which those who believed in him were to receive...

Ps. 128:5-6. The Lord bless you from Zion! May you see the prosperity of Jerusalem all the days of your life! May you see your children's children! *Peace be upon Israel!*
*Jn. 14:26-27 [Christ]: The Counselor, the Holy Spirit, whom the Father will send in my name, he will teach you all things...Peace I leave with you; my peace I give to you; not as the world gives do I give to you. Let not your hearts be troubled, neither let them be afraid.
Rom. 14:17. The kingdom of God is...righteousness and peace and joy in the Holy Spirit.
Rom. 8:6. ...To set the mind on the Spirit is life and peace. **Ps. 85:8-9.** [God the Lord]...will speak peace to his people, to his saints, to those who turn to him in their hearts. Surely his salvation is at hand for those who fear him, that glory may dwell in our land.
Is. 52:7, 10. How beautiful upon the mountains are the feet of him who brings good tidings, who publishes peace, who brings good tidings of good, who publishes salvation...all the ends of the earth shall see the salvation of our God.
Ps. 107:1-2, 21-22. O give thanks to the Lord, for he is good; for his steadfast love endures for ever! Let the redeemed of the Lord say so... Let them thank the Lord for his steadfast love, for his wonderful works to the sons of men! And let them offer sacrifices of thanksgiving, and tell of his deeds in songs of joy! (Also 107:8, 15, 31-32.)
Ps. 29:11. May the Lord give strength to his people! May the Lord bless his people with peace!

BWV 35
Geist und Seele wird verwirret
(NBA I/20; BC A125)

12. S. after Trinity (BWV 137, 35)
*2 Cor. 3:4–11 (The new covenant shines more brightly than the old)
*Mk. 7:31–37 (Jesus heals man who was deaf and dumb)
Librettist: Georg Christian Lehms

Part I

1. Sinfonia (Adapted from earlier instrumental work)

2. Alto Aria (Adapted from earlier instrumental work)
●God's wonders make us speechless with astonishment (35-2)
Geist und Seele wird   verwirret,
Spirit and soul becomes bewildered,

Wenn sie dich, mein Gott, betracht'.
When it thee, my God, considers.

Denn die Wunder, so sie   kennet
For   the wonders, which it hath-experienced

Und   das Volk mit Jauchzen nennet,
And (which) the people with exultation   tell,

Hat sie taub und stumm gemacht.
Hath it deaf and dumb   made.
{Hath made it deaf and dumb.}

3. Alto Recit.
●God heals deaf, dumb, blind: we marvel (35-3)
Ich wundre mich;
I   marvel   - ;

Denn alles, was man sieht,
For everything, that one doth-see,
{For everything that we see,}

Muß uns Verwundrung geben.
Must us astonishment   give.
{Astonishes us.}

Betracht ich dich,
Consider I thee,
{If I consider thee,}

Du   teurer Gottessohn,
Thou precious Son-of-God,

So   flieht
Then doth-flee

Vernunft und auch Verstand davon.
Reason   and also understanding hence.
{Then reason and understanding leave me.}

*Mk. 7:32–37.** They brought to [Jesus] a man who was deaf and had an impediment in his speech; and they besought him to lay his hand upon him. And taking him aside from the multitude privately, he put his fingers into his ears, and he spat and touched his tongue; and looking up to heaven, he sighed, and said to him, "Ephphata," that is, "Be opened," And his ears were opened, his tongue was released, and he spoke plainly. And he charged them to tell no one; but the more he charged them, the more zealously they proclaimed it. And they were astonished beyond measure, saying, "He has done all things well; he even makes the deaf hear and the dumb speak."
Ps. 38:13–14. I am like a deaf man, I do not hear, like a dumb man who does not open his mouth. Yea, I am like a man who does not hear, and in whose mouth are no rebukes.
Ps. 126:1–2. When the Lord restored the fortunes of Zion, we were like those who dream. Then our mouth was filled with laughter, and our tongue with shouts of joy; then they said among the nations, "The Lord has done great things for them."

*Mk. 7:37.** [The people] were astonished beyond measure [at Jesus], saying, "He has done all things well; he even makes the deaf hear and the dumb speak."
Is. 35:5–6. The eyes of the blind shall be opened, and the ears of the deaf unstopped; then shall the lame man leap like a hart, and the tongue of the dumb sing for joy...
Mt. 15:30–31. Great crowds came to [Jesus], bringing with them the lame, the maimed, the blind, the dumb, and many others, and they put them at his feet, and he healed them, so that the throng wondered, when they saw the dumb speaking, the maimed whole, the lame walking, and the blind seeing; and they glorified the God of Israel.
Mk. 6:2. ...Many who heard [Jesus] were astonished, saying, "Where did this man get all this? What is the wisdom given to him? What mighty works are wrought by his hands!" (Also Mt. 13:54.)
Mk. 5:20. [The healed demoniac] went away and began to proclaim in the Decapolis how much Jesus had done for him; and all men marveled.
Ps. 77:11–14. I will call to mind the deeds of the Lord... I will meditate on all thy work, and muse on thy mighty deeds. Thy way, O God, is holy. What god is great like our God? Thou art the God who workest wonders, who hast manifested thy might among the peoples.

Du machst es eben,
Thou dost-make it thus,

Daß sonst ein Wunderwerk
That (what were) otherwise (considered) a miracle

vor dir was Schlechtes ist.
(next-to) thee something inferior is.
{That what would otherwise be considered a miracle is nothing next to thee.}

Du bist
Thou art

Dem Namen, Tun und Amte nach erst wunderreich,
(In) name, deed, and ministry - foremostly wonderful,

Dir ist kein Wunderding auf dieser Erde gleich.
To-thee is no marvel on this earth equal.
{No marvel on earth is equal to thee.}

Den Tauben gibst du das Gehör,
The deaf givest thou (their) hearing,

Den Stummen ihre Sprache wieder,
The dumb their speech again,

Ja, was noch mehr,
Yes, what (is) even more,

Du öffnest auf ein Wort die blinden Augenlider.
Thou openest with one word - blind eyelids.

Dies, dies sind Wunderwerke,
These, these are miracle-works,

Und ihre Stärke
And their power

Ist auch der Engel Chor nicht mächtig auszusprechen.
Is even the angel choir not mighty (enough) to-express.
{Not even the angel choir is not mighty enough to express.}

4. Alto Aria
●God has done all things well: daily blessings (35–4)
Gott hat alles wohl gemacht.
God has all-things well done.
{God has done all things well.}

Seine Liebe, seine Treu
His love, his faithfulness

Wird uns alleTage neu.
Is for-us all days new.
{Is renewed for us every day.}

Wenn uns Angst und Kummer drücket,
If us fear and anxiousness oppresses,
{If fear and anxiousness oppress us,}

Heb. 8:6. ...Christ has obtained a ministry which is as much more excellent than the old as the covenant he mediates is better, since it is enacted on better promises.
*2 Cor. 3:7–11. Now if the dispensation (Luther: Amt) of death, carved in letters on stone, came with such splendor that the Israelites could not look at Moses' face because of its brightness, fading as this was, will not the dispensation of the spirit be attended with greater splendor? For if there was splendor in the dispensation of condemnation, the dispensation of righteousness must far exceed it in splendor. Indeed, in this case, what once had splendor has come to have no splendor at all, because of the splendor that surpasses it. For if what faded away came with splendor, what is permanent must have much more splendor.
Rev. 15:3. [In paradise] they sing the song of Moses, the servant of God, and the song of the Lamb, saying, "Great and wonderful are thy deeds, O Lord God the Almighty!..."
Ps. 40:5. ...[O Lord,] none can compare with thee (Luther: dir ist nichts gleich)!
Mt. 9:27, 29–31. ...Two blind men followed [Jesus], crying aloud, "Have mercy on us, Son of David." ...He touched their eyes, saying, "According to your faith be it done to you." And their eyes were opened... But they went away and spread his fame through all that district. (Also Mt. 20:30ff.)
Lk. 7:19–23. John, calling to him two of his disciples, sent them to he Lord, saying, "Are you he who is to come, or shall we look for another?" ...In that hour he cured many of diseases and plagues and evil spirits, and on many that were blind he bestowed sight. And he answered them, "Go and tell John what you have seen and heard: the blind receive their sight, the lame walk, lepers are cleansed, and the deaf hear, the dead are raised up, the poor have good news preached to them. And blessed is he who takes no offense at me."
Lk. 4:17–21. ...[Jesus] opened the book and found the place where it was written, "The Spirit of the Lord is upon me, because he has anointed me to preach good news to the poor. He has sent me to proclaim release to the captives and recovering of sight to the blind, to set at liberty those who are oppressed, to proclaim the acceptable year of the Lord." And he closed the book...and began to say to them, "Today this scripture has been fulfilled in your hearing."
Ps. 146:7–8. ...The Lord sets the prisoners free; the Lord opens the eyes of the blind. The Lord lifts up those who are bowed down; the Lord loves the righteous.
Ps. 89:5. Let the heavens praise thy wonders, O Lord, thy faithfulness in the assembly of the holy ones!

*Mk. 7:37. And they were astonished beyond measure [at Jesus], saying, "He *has done all things well;* he even makes the deaf hear and the dumb speak."
Lam. 3:22–23. The steadfast love of the Lord never ceases, his mercies never come to an end; they are new every morning; great is thy faithfulness. (Also Ps. 90:14.)
1 Pet. 5:7. Cast all your anxieties on him, for he cares about you.
Ps. 27:1, 3. The Lord is my light and my salvation; whom shall I fear? The Lord is the stronghold of my life; of whom shall I be afraid?... Though a host encamp against me, my heart shall not fear; though war arise against me, yet I will be confident. (Also Ps. 118:6, Rom. 8:31–39.)
Ps. 119:76. [O Lord,] let thy steadfast love be ready to comfort me according to thy promise to thy servant.

Hat er reichen Trost geschicket,
Has he rich comfort sent,
{He has sent us us rich comfort,}

Weil er täglich für uns wacht:
For he daily (over) us watches:
{For he watches over us daily:}

Gott hat alles wohl gemacht.
God has all-things well done.
{God has done all things well.}

Part II

5. Sinfonia (Adapted from earlier instrumental work)

6. Alto Recit.
●Prayer of application: Touch my ears & tongue (35–6)
Ach, starker Gott, laß mich
Ah, mighty God, let me

Doch dieses stets bedenken,
Indeed this constantly consider,

So kann ich dich
So can I thee
{Then I can,}

Vergnügt in meine Seele senken.
Satisfied into my   soul (implant).
{Fully satisfied, implant thee into my soul.}

Laß mir dein süßes Hephata
Let - thy sweet Ephphatha

Das ganz verstockte Herz erweichen;
(My) completely hardened heart soften;
{Soften my completely hardened heart;}

Ach! lege nur den Gnadenfinger in die Ohren,
Ah, lay - (thy) finger-of-grace in (my) ears,

Sonst bin ich gleich verloren.
Otherwise am I (definitely) lost.
{Otherwise I am definitely lost.}

Rühr auch das Zungenband
Touch also (my) tongue's-bond

Mit deiner starken Hand,
With thy   mighty hand,

Damit ich diese Wunderzeichen
So-that I these wonder-signs
{So that I might praise these miracles}

In heilger Andacht preise
In holy worship praise
{In holy worship}

Is. 66:13 [God]: As one whom his mother comforts, so I will comfort you; you shall be comforted in Jerusalem.
2 Cor. 1:3–5. Blessed be the God and Father of our Lord Jesus Christ, the Father of mercies and God of all comfort, who comforts us in all our affliction, so that we may be able to comfort those who are in any affliction, with the comfort with which we ourselves are comforted by God. For as we share abundantly in Christ's sufferings, so through Christ we share abundantly in comfort too.
Ps. 121:3–6. ...He who keeps you will not slumber. Behold, he who keeps Israel will neither slumber nor sleep. The Lord is your keeper; the Lord is your shade on your right hand. The sun shall not smite you by day, nor the moon by night.

Ps. 77:11–14. I will call to mind the deeds of the Lord; yea, I will remember thy wonders of old. I will meditate on all thy work, and muse on thy mighty deeds. Thy way, O God, is holy. What god is great like our God? Thou art the God who workest wonders, who hast manifested thy might among the peoples.
Ps. 143:5. ...I meditate on all that thou hast done; I muse on what thy hands have wrought. (Also Ps. 105:5 / 1 Chron. 16:12.)
Col. 3:16. Let the word of Christ dwell in you richly...
Col. 1:27. ...Christ in you, the hope of glory.
Jn. 14:23. Jesus [said], "If a man loves me, he will keep my word, and my Father will love him, and we will come to him and make our home with him."
Eph. 3:17. ...that Christ may dwell in your hearts through faith.
Mt. 13:16 [Christ]: Blessed are your eyes, for they see, and your ears, for they hear.
*Mk. 7:32–35. They brought to [Jesus] a man who was deaf and had an impediment in his speech...And...he put his fingers into his ears, and he spat and touched his tongue; and looking up to heaven, he sighed, and said to him, "Ephphatha," that is, "Be opened," And his ears were opened, his tongue was released, and he spoke plainly.
Rev. 3:17 [Christ]: You say, "I am rich, I have prospered, and I need nothing; not knowing that you are wretched, pitiable, poor, blind, and naked."
Heb. 3:7–9. Therefore, as the Holy Spirit says, "Today, when you hear his voice, do not harden your hearts as in the rebellion, on the day of testing in the wilderness, where your fathers put me to the test and saw my works for forty years..."
Mt. 11:15 [Christ]: He who has ears to hear, let him hear. (Also Mt. 13:9, 43; Mk. 4:9, 23; Lk. 8:8, 14:35.)
Jn. 9:41 [Christ]: ...If you were blind, you would have no guilt, but now that you say, 'We see,' your guilt remains.
2 Cor. 3:14, 16, 18. Only through Christ is [the veil] taken away...when a man turns to the Lord the veil is removed... And we all, with unveiled face, beholding the glory of the Lord, are being changed into his likeness from one degree of glory to another...
Rom. 10:9–10. If you confess with your lips that Jesus is Lord and believe in your heart that God raised him from the dead, you will be saved. For man believes with his heart and so is justified, and he confesses with his lips and so is saved.
Mt. 10:32. Every one who acknowledges me before men, I also will acknowledge before my Father who is in heaven.
Ps. 40:9–10. ...Lo, I have not restrained my lips, as thou knowest, O Lord. I have not hid thy saving help within my heart, I have spoken of thy faithfulness and thy salvation; I have not concealed thy steadfast love and thy faithfulness from the great congregation.

Und mich als Kind und Erb erweise.
And myself as (a) child and heir demonstrate.
{And show myself to be a child and heir.}

7. Alto Aria
●Yearning for death and heaven, our true inheritance (35-7)
Ich wünsche nur bei Gott zu leben,
I desire only with God to live,

Ach! wäre doch die Zeit schon da,
Ah! Were indeed the time already at-hand,

Ein fröhliches Halleluja
A joyous hallelujah
{To commence a joyous hallelujah}

Mit allen Engeln anzuheben!
With all (the) angels to-commence!
{With all the angels!}

Mein liebster Jesu, löse doch
My dearest Jesu, loose please

Das jammerreiche Schmerzensjoch
This misery-laden yoke-of-pain

Und laß mich bald in deinen Händen
And let me soon in thy hands

Mein martervolles Leben enden.
My torment-laden life end.
{And let me end my torment-laden life soon in thy hands.}

Ps. 22:25. [O Lord,] from thee comes my praise in the great congregation; my vows I will pay before those who fear him.

2 Cor. 5:6-8. So we are always of good courage; we know that while we are at home in the body we are away from the Lord, for we walk by faith, not by sight. We are of good courage, and we would rather be away from the body and at home with the Lord.
Phil. 1:21-23. For me to live is Christ, and to die is gain...Yet which I shall choose I cannot tell. I am hard pressed between the two. My desire is to depart and be with Christ for that is far better.
Rev. 5:9-12. And [in heaven] they sang a new song, saying, "Worthy art thou...for thou wast slain and by thy blood didst ransom men for God from every tribe and tongue and people and nation, and hast made them a kingdom and priests to our God, and they shall reign on earth." Then I looked, and I heard around the throne and the living creatures and the elders the voice of many angels, numbering myriads of myriads and thousands of thousands, saying with a loud voice, "Worthy is the Lamb who was slain, to receive power and wealth and wisdom and might and honor and glory and blessing!" (Also Rev. 4:8-11.)
Mt. 11:29-30 [Christ]: Take my yoke upon you, and learn from me; for I am gentle and lowly in heart, and you will find rest for your souls. For my yoke is easy, and my burden is light.
Rom. 8:18. I consider that the sufferings of this present time are not worth comparing with the glory that is to be revealed to us.
Ps. 31:5. Into thy hand I commit my spirit... (Also Lk. 23:46.)

BWV 36
Schwingt freudig euch empor
(NBA I/1; BC A3a/b)

1 S. in Advent (BWV 61, 62, 36)
*Rom. 13:11-14 (Night is almost gone, lay aside deeds of darkness)
*Mt. 21:1-9 (Christ's triumphal entry into Jerusalem)
Librettist: probably Picander (Christian Friedrich Henrici)
(Parody: Movements 1, 3, 5, & 7 taken from BWV 36c)

1. Chorus (Parody)
●Advent: The Lord of Glory draws near to Zion! (36-1)
Schwingt freudig euch empor zu den erhabnen Sternen,
Soar joyfully - aloft to the sublime stars,

Ihr Zungen, die ihr itzt in Zion fröhlich seid!
Ye tongues, who - now in Zion joyous are!

Doch haltet ein! Der Schall darf sich nicht weit entfernen,
Yet stop! The sound (need) - not far (carry),
{Yet stop! The sound need not go far,}

Is. 62:11. Behold, the Lord has proclaimed to the end of the earth: Say to the daughter of Zion, "Behold, your salvation comes; behold, his reward is with him, and his recompense before him."
Zech. 9:9. Rejoice greatly, O daughter of Zion! Shout aloud, O daughter of Jerusalem! Lo, your king comes to you; triumphant and victorious is he, humble and riding on an ass, on a colt the foal of an ass.
Ps. 126:1-2. When the Lord restored the fortunes of Zion, we were like those who dream. Then our mouth was filled with laughter, and our tongue with shouts of joy; then they said among the nations, "The Lord has done great things for them."
*Mt. 21:4-9. [These events] took place to fulfil what was spoken by the prophet, saying, "Tell the daughter of Zion, Behold, your king is coming to you, humble, and mounted on an ass, and on a colt, the foal of an ass." The disciples went and did as Jesus had directed them; they brought the ass and the colt, and put their garments on them, and he

Es   naht sich selbst   zu euch
(Now) draweth -   -   (near) to you

der Herr der Herrlichkeit.
the Lord of   glory.
{For the Lord of glory already draweth near to you.}

2. Chorale: Soprano & Alto (Vs. 1) (See also 61-1, 62-1.)
●Advent: The Savior of the Gentiles is coming! (36-2)
Nun komm,   der Heiden Heiland,
Now come, (O thou) the Gentiles' Savior,

Der Jungfrauen Kind erkannt,
(As) the   virgin's   child made-known,

Des sich wundert   alle   Welt,
At-this -   doth-marvel the-whole world,
{At this the whole world doth marvel,}

Gott solch Geburt   ihm   bestellt.
(That) God such (a) birth (for) him hath-ordained.

3. Tenor Aria (Parody)
●Love draws the heart gently to Jesus like a bride (36-3)
Die Liebe zieht mit sanften Schritten
- Love draws with soft   footsteps

Sein Treugeliebtes allgemach.
Its   beloved   gradually.
{Love draws its beloved gradually with soft footsteps.}

Gleichwie es eine Braut entzücket,
Just-as   - a   bride is-enchanted,

Wenn sie den Bräutigam erblicket,
When she the bridegroom beholds,

So folgt ein Herz auch Jesu nach.
So follows a heart also Jesus after.
{So also does a heart follow after Jesus.}

4. Chorale (Vs. 6 of Wie schön leuchtet der Morgenstern)
●Advent: Meet king Jesus, my bridegroom, with music! (36-4)
Zwingt die Saiten in Cythara
Compel the strings in Cythera

Und laßt die süße Musica
And let - sweet music

Ganz freudenreich erschallen,
Right joyously   resound,

Daß ich möge mit   Jesulein,
That I   may with (my) little-Jesus—
{That I may with my sweet Jesus—}

sat theron. Most of the crowd spread their garments on the road, and others cut branches from the trees and spread them on the road. And the crowds that went before him and that followed him shouted, "Hosanna to the Son of David! Blessed is he who comes in the name of the Lord! Hosanna in the highest!"

Lk. 2:30–32 [Nunc dimittis]. Mine eyes have seen thy salvation which thou hast prepared in the presence of all peoples, a light for revelation to the Gentiles...
Is. 49:6 [God]: ...I will give you as a light to the nations, that my salvation may reach to the end of the earth.
Acts 26:23. ...[The prophets and Moses foretold that Christ] would proclaim light both to the people and to the Gentiles.
Mt. 1:22–23. All this took place to fulfil what the Lord had spoken by the prophet: "Behold, a virgin shall conceive and bear a son, and his name shall be called Emmanuel" (which means, God with us).
Phil. 2:6–7. [Christ Jesus], who, though he was in the form of God, did not count equality with God a thing to be grasped, but emptied himself, taking the form of a servant, being born in the likeness of men.

S. of S. 1:4 [Bride]: Draw me after you, let us make haste... (Luther: Zieh mich dir nach, so laufen wir)
Jn. 12:30, 32. Jesus answered, "...I, when I am lifted up from the earth, will draw all men to myself."
Jn. 3:27–29. John answered..."I am not the Christ...He who has the bride is the bridegroom; the friend of the bridegroom, who stands and hears him, rejoices greatly at the bridegroom's voice; therefore this joy of mine is now full."
Mt. 25:1. The kingdom of heaven shall be compared to ten maidens who took their lamps and went to meet the bridegroom. (Also Ps. 45:13–15.)
Rev. 21:2, 9. And I saw the holy city, new Jerusalem, coming down out of heaven from God, prepared as a bride adorned for her husband... Then came one of the seven angels...and spoke to me, saying, "Come I will show you the Bride, the wife of the Lamb."
Jn. 10:27 [Christ]: My sheep hear my voice, and I know them, and they follow me...
S. of S. 6:3 [Bride]: I am my beloved's and my beloved is mine...

*Mt. 21:9. ...Hosanna to the Son of David! Blessed is he who comes in the name of the Lord! Hosanna in the highest!
S. of S. 3:11. Go forth, O daughters of Zion, and behold King Solomon, with the crown with which his mother crowned him on the day of his wedding, on the day of the gladness of his heart.
Ps. 150:3–6. Praise him with trumpet sound; praise him with lute and harp! Praise him with timbrel and dance; praise him with strings and pipe! Praise him with sounding cymbals; praise him with loud clashing cymbals! Let everything that breathes praise the Lord! Praise the Lord!
S. of S. 6:3 [Bride]: I am my beloved's and my beloved is mine...
Rev. 21:2, 9. I saw the holy city, new Jerusalem, coming down out of heaven from God, prepared as a bride adorned for her husband...Then

Dem wunderschönen Bräutigam mein,
That exquisite bridegroom of-mine—

In steter Liebe wallen!
In constant love travel!
{Move in constant love!}

Singet,
Sing,

Springet,
Spring,

Jubilieret, triumphieret, dankt dem Herren!
Shout-with-joy, exult, thank the Lord!

Groß ist der König der Ehren.
Great is the King of (all) honors.

came one of the seven angels...and spoke to me, saying, "Come I will show you the Bride, the wife of the Lamb."
2 Cor. 11:2. ...I betrothed you to Christ to present you as a pure bride to her one husband.
Eph. 5:25–27. ...Christ loved the church and gave himself up for her, that he might sanctify her, having cleansed her by the washing of water with the word, that he might present the church to himself in splendor, without spot or wrinkle or any such thing, that she might be holy and without blemish.
Ps. 48:1. Great is the Lord and greatly to be praised in the city of our God!
Ps. 96:1, 4. O sing to the Lord a new song; sing to the Lord, all the earth!...For great is the Lord, and greatly to be praised; he is to be feared above all gods. (Also 1 Chron. 16:23–25, 34.)
Ps. 145:1–3. I will extol thee, my God and King, and bless thy name for ever and ever. Every day I will bless thee, and praise thy name for ever and ever. Great is the Lord, and greatly to be praised, and his greatness is unsearchable.

Part II

5. Bass Aria (Parody)
●Advent: Welcome, heavenly bridegroom, into my heart! (36–5)
Willkommen, werter Schatz!
Welcome, precious treasure!

Die Lieb und Glaube machet Platz
- Love and faith make room

Vor dich in meinem Herzen rein,
For thee in my heart pure,
{For thee in this pure heart,}

Zieh bei mir ein!
Come-dwell with me - !

Eph. 3:17. [I pray]...that Christ may dwell in your hearts through faith.
Col. 1:27. ...Christ in you, the hope of glory.
Lk. 2:7. [Mary] gave birth to her first-born son and wrapped him in swaddling cloths, and laid him in a manger, because there was no place for them in the inn.
Jn. 14:23. Jesus answered him, "If a man loves me, he will keep my word, and my Father will love him, and we will come to him and make our home with him."
2 Cor. 6:16. ...We are the temple of the living God; as God said, "I will live in them and move among them, and I will be their God, and they shall be my people."
1 Jn. 2:23–25. ...He who confesses the Son has the Father also. Let what you heard from the beginning abide in you. If what you heard from the beginning abides in you, then you will abide in the Son and in the Father. (See also Jn. 14:7.)

6. Chorale: Tenor (Vs. 6 of **Nun komm, der Heiden Heiland**)
●Prayer: Conquer flesh so it may hold thy divine power (36–6)
Der du bist dem Vater gleich,
Thou-who art (to) the Father equal,

Führ hinaus den Sieg im Fleisch,
Lead forth (thy) victory in-the flesh,

Daß dein ewig Gotts Gewalt
That thy eternal divine power

In uns das krank Fleisch enthalt.
In us the sick flesh may-contain.
{Henceforth may be held within our sick human flesh.}

Jn. 1:1, 14. In the beginning was the Word, and the Word was with God, and the Word was God...And the Word became flesh and dwelt among us, full of grace and truth... (Also Jn. 10:30, Jn. 14:11, Col. 2:9.)
Mt. 26:41. ...The spirit indeed is willing, but the flesh is weak. (Also Mk.14:38.)
Rom. 7:18. For I know that nothing good dwells within me, that is, in my flesh. I can will what is right, but I cannot do it. Rom. 8:3. God has done what the law, weakened by the flesh, could not do: sending his own Son in the likeness of sinful flesh and for sin, he condemned sin in the flesh...
Rom. 8:7–9. ...The mind that is set on the flesh is hostile to God; it does not submit to God's law, indeed it cannot; and those who are in the flesh cannot please God. But you are not in the flesh, you are in the Spirit, if in fact the Spirit of God dwells in you...

7. Soprano Aria (Parody)
●Praises that are weak but sincere heard in heaven (36–7)
Auch mit gedämpften, schwachen Stimmen
Even with subdued, weak voices

Heb. 13:15. ...Let us continually offer up a sacrifice of praise to God, that is, the fruit of lips that acknowledge his name...

Wird Gottes Majestät verehrt.
Is God's majesty honored.
{Can God's majesty be honored.}

Denn schallet nur der Geist darbei,
For resounds only the spirit thereby,
{For, as long as the spirit resounds thereby,}

So ist ihm solches ein Geschrei,
Then is to-him such (sound) a shouting,

Das er im Himmel selber hört.
That he in heaven himself hears.
{Which he himself can hear in heaven.}

8. Chorale (Vs. 8 of **Nun komm, der Heiden Heiland**)
    (See also 62-6.)
●Doxology: Praise to Father, Son, and Holy Ghost (36-8)
Lob sei Gott, dem Vater, g'ton,
Praise be-to God, the Father, given,

Lob sei Gott, sein'm eingen Sohn,
Praise be-to God, his only Son,

Lob sei Gott, dem Heilgen Geist,
Praise be-to God, the Holy Ghost,

Immer und in Ewigkeit!
Ever and in Eternity!

BWV 37
Wer da gläubet und getauft wird
(NBA I/12; BC A75)

Ascension (BWV 37, 128, 43, 11)
*Acts 1:1-11 (Holy Spirit promised, Christ's ascension)
*Mk. 16:14-20 (Great commission, Christ's ascension)
Librettist: Unknown; perhaps Christian Weiß the elder

1. Chorus
●Faith and baptism lead to salvation: Mk. 16:16 (37-1)
Wer da gläubet und getauft wird,
Whoever believes and baptized is,

der wird selig werden.
he will saved (be).

2. Tenor Aria
●Faith is the sign of Jesus' love for his own (37-2)
Der Glaube ist das Pfand der Liebe,
- Faith is the guarantee of-that love,

Die Jesus für die Seinen hegt.
Which Jesus for those (who are) his own preserves.
{Which Jesus keeps for those who are his own.}

Ps. 100:1. Make a joyful noise to he Lord... (Also Ps. 66:1; 81:1; 95:1, 2; 98:4, 6.)
Jn. 4:23. The hour is coming, and now is, when the true worshipers will worship the Father in spirit and truth, for such the Father seeks to worship him.
Mt. 21:15-17. But when the chief priests and the scribes saw the wonderful things that he did, and the children crying out in the temple, "Hosanna to the Son of David!" they were indignant; and they said to him, "Do you hear what these are saying?" And Jesus said to them, "Yes; have you never read, 'Out of the mouth of babes and sucklings thou hast brought perfect praise'?" (See Ps. 8:2; also Lk. 19:36-40.)
Lk. 19:39-40. Some of the Pharisees in the multitude said to him, "Teacher, rebuke your disciples." He answered, "I tell you, if these were silent, the very stones would cry out."

Lk. 2:14. Glory to God in the highest...
1 Tim. 1:17. To the King of ages, immortal, invisible, the only God, be honor and glory for ever and ever. Amen. (Also Phil. 4:20.)
Ps. 41:13. Blessed be the Lord, the God of Israel, from everlasting to everlasting! Amen and Amen. (Doxology: also Ps. 72:19, 89:52, 106:48, 150:6, Rom. 11:36, Jude 1:25)
Mt. 28:19. ...in the name of the Father and of the Son and of the Holy Spirit.
Rev. 7:11-12. And all the angels stood round the throne and round the elders and the four living creatures, and they fell on their faces before the throne and worshiped God, saying, "Amen! Blessing and glory and wisdom and thanksgiving and honor and power and might be to our God for ever and ever! Amen."

Mk. 16:14-19. Afterward [Jesus] appeared to the eleven themselves as they sat at table...And he said to them "Go into all the world and preach the gospel to the whole creation. *He who believes and is baptized will be saved;* but he who does not believe will be condemned. And these signs will accompany those who believe..." So then the Lord Jesus, after he had spoken to them, was taken up into heaven, and sat down at the right hand of God.

1 Pet. 1:7. ...[May] the genuineness of your faith, more precious than gold which though perishable is tested by fire,...redound to praise and glory and honor at the revelation of Jesus Christ.
Eph. 1:13-14. In [Christ] you also, who have heard the word of truth, the gospel of your salvation, and have believed in him, were sealed with the promised Holy Spirit, which is the guarantee (Luther: Pfand) of our inheritance until we acquire possession of it... (Also 2 Cor. 5:5.)

Drum   hat er bloß aus   Liebestriebe,
Therefore has he soley out-of love's-impulse,

Da   er ins Lebensbuch mich schriebe,
When he into-the book-of-life (my name) wrote,

Mir   dieses Kleinod beigelegt.
On-me this   jewel   bestowed.
{Therefore he has bestowed this jewel on me soley out of love's impulse when he wrote my name into the book of life.}

3. Chorale: Soprano & Alto
●Thanks for love given in Christ; betrothal to Christ (37-3)
Herr Gott Vater, mein starker Held!
Lord God Father, my   strong champion!

Du hast mich ewig   vor   der Welt
Thou hast me eternally before the world (was formed)
{Thou hast loved me eternally before the foundation of the world}

In deinem Sohn geliebet.
In   thy   Son   loved.
{In thy Son.}

Dein Sohn hat mich ihm selbst vertraut,
Thy   Son hath me to-him-self betrothed;
{Thy Son hath betrothed himself to me:}

Er ist mein Schatz, ich bin sein Braut,
He is   my treasure, I am   his bride,

Sehr hoch   in ihm erfreuet.
Very (greatly) in him delighted.

Eia!
Eia!

Eia!
Eia!

Himmlisch Leben wird er geben mir dort oben;
Heavenly   life   will he give   me there above;

Ewig   soll mein Herz ihn loben.
Eternally shall my   heart him praise.
{Eternally shall my heart praise him.}

4. Bass Recit.
●Faith alone, not good works, brings justification (37-4)
Ihr Sterblichen, verlanget ihr,
You mortals,   desire   you,
{You mortals, do you desire,}

Mit mir
With me

Das Antlitz   Gottes anzuschauen?
The countenance of-God   to-see?

Jn. 10:28 [Christ]: I give them eternal life...and no one shall snatch them out of my hand.
Lk. 10:20 [Christ]: ...Rejoice that your names are written in heaven.
Rev. 21:27. Nothing unclean shall enter [the heavenly city], nor any one who practices abomination or falsehood, but only those who are written in the Lamb's book of life. (Also Rev. 3:5, 13:8, 20:12, Phil. 4:3.)
Phil. 3:14. I press on toward the goal for the prize (Luther: Kleinod) of the upward call of God in Christ Jesus. (Kleinod: also Luther: 1 Cor. 9:24)

Eph. 1:3–5. ...The God and Father of our Lord Jesus Christ...chose us in him before the foundation of the world...He destined us in love to be his sons through Jesus Christ... (Also 1 Pet. 1:18–20.)
Lk. 10:20 [Christ]: ...Rejoice that your names are written in heaven.
Rev. 13:8. ...[God's enemies are those] whose name [have] not been written before the foundation of the world in the book of life of the Lamb that was slain.
Hos. 2:20 [God]: I will betroth you to me in faithfulness; and you shall know the Lord.
2 Cor. 11:2 [Paul]: ...I betrothed you to Christ to present you as a pure bride to her one husband.
Eph. 5:25–27. ...Christ loved the church and gave himself up for her, that he might sanctify her, having cleansed her by the washing of water with the word, that he might present the church to himself in splendor, without spot or wrinkle or any such thing, that she might be holy and without blemish.
S. of S. 6:3 [Bride]: I am my beloved's and my beloved is mine...
Mt. 25:34. Then the King will say to those at his right hand, "Come, O blessed of my Father, inherit the kingdom prepared for you from the foundation of the world." (Also Mt. 25:46.)
Lk. 18:29–30. And [Jesus] said to them, "Truly, I say to you, there is no man who has left house or wife or brothers or parents or children, for the sake of the kingdom of God, who will not receive manifold more in this time, and in the age to come eternal life."
1 Jn. 2:25. This is what [Christ] has promised us, eternal life.
Ps. 145:2. [O Lord,] every day I will bless thee, and praise thy name for ever and ever.
Ps. 86:12. I give thanks to thee, O Lord my God, with my whole heart, and I will glorify thy name for ever. (Also Ps. 104:33, 146:2.)

Ex. 33:20. [God] said, "You cannot see my face; for man shall not see me and live." (Also Gen. 32:30, Jn. 1:14, 18, 14:9.)
Jn. 1:18. No one has ever seen God; the only Son, who is in the bosom of the Father, he has made him known. (Also 1 Jn. 3:2.)
Mt. 5:8 [Christ]: Blessed are the pure in heart, for they shall see God.
Heb. 12:14. Strive for...the holiness without which no one will see the Lord.
Rom. 3:20, 28. No human being will be justified in his sight by works of the law, since through the law comes knowledge of sin...For we hold that a man is justified by faith apart from works of law.

So   dürft ihr nicht auf gute Werke bauen;
Then may you not on good works   build;
{Then you may not build on good works;}

Denn ob sich wohl ein Christ
For though - indeed a Christian

Muß in den guten Werken üben,
Must - - good   works practice,
{Must exercise himself in good works,}

Weil   es der ernste Wille Gottes ist,
Because it the solemn will of-God is,

So macht der Glaube doch allein,
Yet ensures -   faith indeed alone,
{Yet faith alone ensures,}

Daß wir vor Gott gerecht und selig sein.
That we before God righteous and saved are.
{That we are righteous before God and saved.}

5. Bass Aria
●Faith brings salvation, baptism is its seal (37–5)
Der Glaube schafft der Seele   Flügel,
-    Faith provides the soul (with) wings,

Daß sie sich in den Himmel schwingt,
That it - into -   heaven   soars,

Die Taufe ist das Gnadensiegel,
- Baptism is the seal-of-grace,

Das uns den Segen Gottes bringt;
Which us the blessing of-God brings;
{Which brings us the blessing of God;}

Und daher   heißt   ein selger Christ,
And therefore is-(he)-called a blessed Christian,

Wer gläubet und getaufet ist.
Who believes and baptized is.
{Who believes and is baptized.}

6. Chorale
●Prayer: Grant me faith, forgive my sins as promised (37–6)
Den Glauben mir verleihe
-    Faith to-me grant
{Grant me faith}

An dein' Sohn Jesum Christ,
In thy Son Jesus Christ,

Mein Sünd mir auch verzeihe
My sins - also forgive
{Forgive also my sins}

Allhier zu dieser Frist.
Here (in) this time.

Gal. 2:16. ...A man is not justified by works of the law...because by works of the law shall no one be justified.
Eph. 2:8–9. By grace you have been saved through faith; and this is not your own doing, it is the gift of God—not because of works, lest any man should boast.
Jms. 2:14–17, 26. [But] what does it profit, my brethren, if a man says he has faith but has not works? Can his faith save him? If a brother or sister is ill-clad and in lack of daily food, and one of you says to them, "Go in peace, be warmed and filled," without giving them the things needed for the body, what does it profit? So faith by itself, if it has no works, is dead...For as the body apart from the spirit is dead, so faith apart from works is dead.
Heb. 11:6. [But] without faith it is impossible to please him. For whoever would draw near to God must believe that he exists and that he rewards those who seek him.
Rom. 1:16–17. I am not ashamed of the gospel: it is the power of God for salvation to every one who has faith...For in it the righteousness of God is revealed through faith for faith; as it is written, "He who through faith is righteous shall live."

Heb. 11:6. Without faith it is impossible to please him. For whoever would draw near to God must believe that he exists and that he rewards those who seek him.
Is. 40:31. But they who wait for the Lord shall renew their strength, they shall mount up with wings like eagles, they shall run and not be weary, they shall walk and not faint.
***Mk. 16:16.** He who believes and is baptized will be saved; but he who does not believe will be condemned.
***Acts 1:5.** John baptized with water, but before many days you shall be baptized with the Holy Spirit. (Also Acts 11:16.)
Acts 2:39, 41. And Peter said to them, "Repent, and be baptized every one of you in the name of Jesus Christ for the forgiveness of your sins; and you shall receive the gift of the Holy Spirit."...So those who received his word were baptized, and there were added that day about three thousand souls.
Acts 18:8. ...Many of the Corinthians hearing Paul believed and were baptized.
Acts 22:16. ...Rise and be baptised, and wash away your sins, calling on his name.

***Mk. 16:14.** Afterward [Christ] appeared to the eleven themselves as they sat at table; and he upraided them for their unbelief and hardness of heart, because they had not believed those who saw him after he had risen.
Jn. 3:16–17. God so loved the world that he gave his only Son, that whoever believes in him should not perish but have eternal life. For God sent the Son into the world, not to condemn the world, but that the world might be saved through him. (Also Jn. 8:24.)
Jn. 11:25–26 [Christ]: ...I am the resurrection and the life; he who believes in me, though he die, yet shall he live, and whoever lives and believes in me shall never die...
Acts 26:18 [Christ]: ...that they may receive forgiveness of sins and a place among those who are sanctified by faith in me.
1 Cor. 1:9. God is faithful, by whom you were called into the fellowship of his Son, Jesus Christ our Lord.

Du wirst mir nicht versagen,
Thou wilt me not refuse,

Was du verheißen hast,
What thou promised hast,
{What thou hast promised,}

Daß er mein Sünd tu tragen
That he my sins (will) bear

Und lös mich von der Last.
And free me from (its) burden.

Heb. 10:23. Let us hold fast the confession of our hope without wavering, for he who promised is faithful. (Also Num. 23:19, 2 Tim. 2:13.)
1 Jn. 2:25. This is what he has promised us, eternal life.
Jn. 1:29. The next day [John] saw Jesus coming toward him, and said, "Behold, the Lamb of God, who takes away (Luther: trägt) the sin of the world!" (Also Jn. 1:36.)
Is. 1:4. Ah, sinful nation, a people laden with iniquity...
Mt. 11:28–30 [Christ]: Come to me, all who labor and are heavy laden, and I will give you rest. Take my yoke upon you, and learn from me; for I am gentle and lowly in heart, and you will find rest for your souls. For my yoke is easy, and my burden is light.

BWV 38
Aus tiefer Not schrei ich zu dir
(NBA I/25; BC A152)

21. S. after Trinity (BWV 109, 38, 98, 188)
*Eph. 6:10-17 (The armor of the Christian)
*Jn. 4:46[1]-54 (Christ heals the son of a royal official)
[1]Begin: "And at Capernaum there was an official..."
Librettist: Unknown

1. Chorus (Chorale Vs. 1)
●Out of the depths I cry to thee: Ps. 130:1-3 (38-1)
Aus tiefer Not schrei ich zu dir,
Out-of deep distress cry I to thee,

Herr Gott, erhör mein Rufen;
Lord God, hear-favorably my calling;
{Lord God, hear my supplication;}

Dein gnädig Ohr neig her zu mir
Thy gracious ear bend toward me

Und meiner Bitt sie öffne!
And to-my petition it open!
{And open it to my petition!}

Denn so du willst das sehen an,
For if thou intendest that to-regard,
{For if thou wilt regard}

Was Sünd und Unrecht ist getan,
What (of) sin and unrighteousness (hath) been-done,
{Deeds of sin and unrighteousness,}

Wer kann, Herr, vor dir bleiben?
Who can, Lord, before thee remain?
{Who can stand before thee, O Lord?}

2. Alto Recit. (Based on Chorale Vs. 2)
●Salvation brought by Jesus' grace alone (38-2)
In Jesu Gnade wird allein
In Jesus' grace (there) will alone
{Only in Jesus' grace}

*Jn. 4:46–47. ...At Capernaum there was an official whose son was ill. When he heard that Jesus had come from Judea to Galilee, he went and begged him to come down and heal his son, for he was at the point of death.
Ps. 130:1–3. Out of the depths I cry to thee, O Lord! Lord, hear my voice! Let thy ears be attentive to the voice of my supplications! If thou, O Lord, shouldst mark iniquities, Lord, who could stand!
Ps. 69:1–2, 15. Save me, O God! For the waters have come up to my neck. I sink in deep mire, where there is no foothold; I have come into deep waters, and the flood sweeps over me...Let not the flood sweep over me, or the deep swallow me up, or the pit close its mouth over me.
Ps. 28:2. Hear the voice of my supplication as I cry to thee for help, as I lift up my hands toward thy most holy sanctuary.
Ps. 76:7. But thou, terrible art thou! Who can stand before thee when once thy anger is roused?
Ps. 143:2. Enter not into judgment with thy servant; for no man living is righteous before thee.
Mal. 3:2–3. Who can endure the day of his coming, and who can stand when he appears? For he is like a refiner's fire...He will sit as a refiner and purifier of silver, and he will purify the sons of Levi and refine them like gold and silver...
Rev. 6:17. For the great day of...wrath has come, and who can stand before it?

Ps. 130:4. But there is forgiveness with thee [O Lord], that thou mayest be feared.
Eph. 2:8–9. By grace you have been saved through faith; and this is not your own doing, it is the gift of God—not because of works, lest any man should boast.

Der Trost vor uns und die Vergebung sein,
- Comfort for us and - forgiveness be,
{Can we find comfort and pardon,}

Weil durch des Satans Trug und List
Because by - Satan's deceit and craftiness

Der Menschen ganzes Leben
- Mankind's entire life

Vor Gott ein Sündengreuel ist.
Before God an abomination-of-sin is.
{Has become an abomination of sin before God.}

Was könnte nun
What could (then)

Die Geistesfreudigkeit zu unserm Beten geben,
- Joyousness-of-spirit to our praying give,
{What then could give us joyousness of spirit in our praying,}

Wo Jesu Geist und Wort nicht neue Wunder tun?
If Jesus' Spirit and Word (did) not new wonders do?
{If Jesus' Spirit and Word did not do new wonders?}

3. Tenor Aria (Based on Chorale Vs. 3)
●Jesus' word comes to comfort me in my suffering (38–3)
Ich höre mitten in den Leiden
I hear in-the-midst-of (my) sufferings

Ein Trostwort, so mein Jesus spricht.
A word-of-comfort, which my Jesus speaks.

Drum, o geängstigtes Gemüte,
Therefore, O frightened disposition,

Vertraue deines Gottes Güte,
Trust thy God's goodness,

Sein Wort besteht und fehlet nicht,
His Word stands-firm and fails not,
{His Word stands frim and will not fail,}

Sein Trost wird niemals von dir scheiden!
His comfort will ne'er from thee depart!

4. Soprano Recit.
●Jesus' word brings salvation despite weak faith (38–4)
Ach!
Ah!

Eph. 2:1–3. You he made alive, when you were dead through the trespasses and sins in which you once walked, following the course of the world, following the prince of the power of the air, the spirit that is now at work in the sons of disobedience. Among these we all once lived in the passions of our flesh, following the desires of body and mind...

Jn. 8:44 [Christ]: You are of your father the devil, and your will is to do your father's desires. He was a murderer from the beginning, and has nothing to do with the truth, because there is no truth in him. When he lies, he speaks according to his own nature, for he is a liar and the father of lies.

2 Cor. 11:14. ...Satan disguises himself as an angel of light.

Gen. 6:5. The Lord saw that the wickedness of man was great in the earth, and that every imagination of the thoughts of his heart was only evil continually.

Eph. 2:3. ...We were by nature children of wrath like the rest of mankind.

Rom. 3:10–12, 23. As it is written: "None is righteous, no, not one; no one understands, no one seeks for God. All have turned aside, together they have gone wrong; no one does good, not even one."...All have sinned and fall short of the glory of God. (Also Is. 53:6.)

Ps. 14:2–3. The Lord looks down from heaven upon the children of men, to see if there are any that act wisely, that seek after God. They have all gone astray, they are all alike corrupt (Luther: sind ein Greuel mit ihrem Wesen); there is none that does good, no, not one. (Also Is. 64:6, Jer. 17:9, Lk. 16:5, Tit. 1:16.)

Ps. 130:7–8. O Israel, hope in the Lord! For with the Lord there is steadfast love, and with him is plenteous redemption. And he will redeem Israel from all his iniquities.

***Jn. 4:48.** Jesus...said to [the official], "Unless you see signs and wonders you will not believe."

Ps. 130:5. I wait for the Lord...and in his word I hope.

***Jn. 4:49–53.** The official said to [Jesus], "Sir, come down before my child dies." Jesus said to him, "Go; your son will live." The man believed the word that Jesus spoke to him and went his way. As he was going down, his servants met him and told him that his son was living. So he asked them the hour when he began to mend, and they said to him, "Yesterday at the seventh hour the fever left him." The father knew that was the hour when Jesus had said to him, "Your son will live"; and he himself believed, and all his household.

Ps. 42:5/11/43:5. Why are you cast down, O my soul, and why are you disquieted within me? Hope in God; for I shall again praise him, my help and my God. (Also Ps. 71:5.)

Mk. 13:31 [God]: Heaven and earth will pass away, but my words will not pass away.

1 Kings 8:56. ...Not one word has failed of all his good promise...

Is. 54:10. ...My steadfast love shall not depart from you and my covenant of peace shall not be removed, says the Lord, who has compassion on you.

Rom. 8:35, 38–39. Who shall separate us from the love of Christ?...For I am sure that [nothing]...in all creation, will be able to separate us from the love of God in Christ Jesus our Lord.

Mk. 9:23–24. Jesus said to [the man with the sick child], "If you can! All things are possible to him who believes." Immediately the father of the child cried out and said, "I believe; help my unbelief!"

Daß mein Glaube   noch so schwach,
That my   faith (is) still so   weak,

Und daß ich mein Vertrauen
And that I   my confidence
{And that I have to build my confidence}

Auf feuchtem Grunde muß erbauen!
On   moist   ground must construct!
{On soft ground!}

Wie ofte müssen   neue Zeichen
How oft   must (I have) new signs

Mein Herz erweichen!
My   heart to-soften!
{To soften my heart!}

Wie? kennst du deinen Helfer nicht,
What? Knowest thou thy   helper not,

Der nur ein einzig Trostwort   spricht,
Who but a   single word-of-comfort speaks,

Und   gleich   erscheint,
And immediately (there) appears,

Eh   deine Schwachheit es vermeint,
Before thy   weakness   it imagines,
{Before thy weakness can imagine it,}

Die Rettungsstunde.
The hour-of-salvation.

Vertraue nur der Allmachtshand und seiner Wahrheit Munde!
Trust   just the Almighty's-hand and his   Mouth-of-Truth!
{So just trust the hand of the Almighty and his word of truth!}

Jms. 1:6–8. Let [us] ask in faith, with no doubting, for he who doubts is like a wave of the sea that is driven and tossed by the wind. For that person must not suppose that a double-minded man, unstable in all his ways, will receive anything from the Lord.

Lk. 24:25–27 [Christ]: ....O foolish men, and slow of heart to believe all that the prophets have spoken!

*Jn. 4:48 [Christ]: Unless you see signs and wonders you will not believe.

Jn. 10:37–38 [Christ]: If I am not doing the works of my Father, then do not believe me; but if I do them, even though you do not believe me, believe the works, that you may know and understand that the Father is in me and I am in the Father.

Jn. 2:23. ...Many believed in [Jesus'] name when they saw the signs which he did. (Also Jn. 7:31, 11:45.)

Jn. 20:30–31. Now Jesus did many other signs in the presence of the disciples, which are not written in this book; but these are written that you may believe that Jesus is the Christ, the Son of God, and that believing you may have life in his name.

*Jn. 4:50, 53. Jesus said to [the official], "Go; your son will live." The man believed the word that Jesus spoke to him and went his way...The father knew that was the hour when Jesus had said to him, "Your son will live"; and he himself believed, and all his household.

Mt. 8:8–10. [A] centurion answered [Christ], "Lord, I am not worthy to have you come under my roof; but only say the word, and my servant will be healed. For I am a man under authority, with soldiers under me; and I say to one, 'Go,' and he goes, and to another, 'Come,' and he comes, and to my slave, 'Do this,' and he does it." When Jesus heard him, he marveled, and said to those who followed him, "Truly, I say to you, not even in Israel have I found such faith."

Is. 46:12–13 [God]: ...I bring near my deliverance, it is not far off, and my salvation will not tarry...

Lk. 17:5–6. The apostles said to the Lord, "Increase our faith!" And the Lord said, "If you had faith as a grain of mustard seed, you could say to this sycamine tree, 'Be rooted up, and be planted in the sea,' and it would obey you." (Also Mt. 17:20.)

5. Soprano, Alto, & Bass Trio (Based on Chorale Vs. 4)
●Morning of comfort comes; Jesus rescues us (38-5)
Wenn meine Trübsal als   mit Ketten
When   my tribulation as (if) with chains

Ein Unglück an dem andern hält,
One misfortune to the other (binds),

So wird mich doch mein Heil erretten,
Then shall me nevertheless my Salvation rescue,
{Then shall my Salvation nevertheless rescue me,}

Daß   alles plötzlich von mir fällt.
So-that all-of-it suddenly off me falls.
{So that it all suddenly falls off me.}

Wie bald erscheint des Trostes Morgen
How soon appears   - Comfort's morning
{How quickly Comfort's morning appears}

Ps. 130:6. My soul waits for the Lord more than watchmen for the morning, more than watchmen for the morning.

Job 30:16–17. ...My soul is poured out within me; days of affliction have taken hold of me. The night racks my bones, and the pain that gnaws me takes no rest.

Mic. 7:7. But...I will look to the Lord, I will wait for the God of my salvation; my God will hear me.

Jms. 5:11. You have heard of the steadfastness of Job, and you have seen the purpose of the Lord, how the Lord is compassionate and merciful.

Is. 51:5. [God's] deliverance draws near speedily...

Acts 12:7. And behold, an angel of the Lord appeared...and he struck Peter on the side and woke him, saying, "Get up quickly." And the chains fell off his hands.

Ps. 30:5. ...Weeping may tarry for the night, but joy comes with the morning.

Rom. 13:11–12. ...For salvation is nearer to us now than when we first believed; the night is far gone, the day is at hand...

Auf diese Nacht der Not und Sorgen!
Upon this night of distress and anxiety!

6. Chorale (Vs. 5)
●Unlimited redemption available from God our shepherd
(38-6)
Ob bei uns ist der Sünden viel,
Though with us (there) (are) - sins many,
{Though there is much sin with us,}

Bei Gott ist viel mehr Gnade;
With God (there) is much more grace;

Sein Hand zu helfen hat kein Ziel,
His hand for helping has no limit,

Wie groß auch sei der Schade.
However great - may-be the injury.

Er ist allein der gute Hirt,
He is alone the good shepherd,
{He alone is the good shepherd,}

Der Israel erlösen wird
Who Israel deliver will
{Who will deliver Israel}

Aus seinen Sünden allen.
From his sins all.
{From all his sins.}

BWV 39
Brich dem Hungrigen dein Brot
(NBA I/15; BC A96)

1. S. after Trinity (BWV 75, 20, 39)
*1 Jn. 4:16–21 (God is love; we ought also to love)
*Lk. 16:19–31 (Parable of rich man and Lazarus)
Librettist: perhaps Christoph Helm

Part I

1. Chorus
●Religion acceptable to God helps the poor: Is. 58:7–8 (39-1)
Brich dem Hungrigen dein Brot und die,
Break (with) the hungry your bread, and those,

so im Elend sind, führe ins Haus!
who in distress are, (take) into (your) house!

So du einen nacket siehest, so kleide ihn
If you someone naked see, then clothe him

und entzeuch dich nicht von deinem Fleisch.
and withdraw yourself not from your (own) flesh.

Alsdenn wird dein Licht herfürbrechen
Then will your light break-forth

Rev. 21:4. [God] will wipe away every tear from their eyes, and death shall be no more, neither shall there be mourning nor crying nor pain any more, for the former things have passed away.

Mt. 19:25. When the disciples heard [Jesus' words] they were greatly astonished, saying, "Who then can be saved?" But Jesus looked at them and said to them, "With men this is impossible, but with God all things are possible." (Also Mk. 10:26–27, Lk. 18:26–27.)
Rom. 5:20. ...Where sin increased, grace abounded all the more.
Jer. 32:27 [God]: Behold, I am the Lord, the God of all flesh; is anything too hard for me? (Also Gen. 18:14.)
Is. 50:2 [God]: ...Is my hand shortened, that it cannot redeem? Or have I no power to deliver? (Also Is. 59:1.)
1 Tim. 1:15. The saying is sure and worth of full acceptance, that Christ Jesus came into the world to save sinners. And I am the foremost of sinners...
Jn. 10:11, 27–28 [Christ]: I am the good shepherd. The good shepherd lays down his life for the sheep...My sheep hear my voice, and I know them, and they follow me; and I give them eternal life, and they shall never perish, and no one shall snatch them out of my hand. (Also Mt. 18:12–13.)
Ps. 130:7–8. O Israel, hope in the Lord! For with the Lord there is steadfast love, and with him is plenteous redemption. And he will redeem Israel from all his iniquities. (Also Ps. 25:22.)
Mt. 1:21. ...You shall call his name Jesus, for he will save his people from their sins.
Acts 4:12. And there is salvation in no one else, for there is no other name under heaven given among men by which we must be saved.

Is. 58:6–9 [God]: Is not this the fast that I choose: to loose the bonds of wickedness, to undo the thongs of the yoke, to let the oppressed go free, and to break every yoke? *Is it not to share your bread with the hungry, and bring the homeless poor into your house; when you see the naked, to cover him, and not to hide yourself from your own flesh? Then shall your light break forth like the dawn, and your healing shall spring up speedily; your righteousness shall go before you, the glory of the Lord shall be your rear guard.* Then you shall call, and the Lord will answer; you shall cry, and he will say, Here I am.
*Lk. 16:19–25. There was a rich man, who was clothed in purple and fine linen and who feasted sumptuously every day. And at his gate lay a poor man named Lazarus, full of sores, who desired to be fed with what fell from the rich man's table; moreover the dogs came and licked his sores. The poor man died and was carried by the angels to Abraham's bosom. The rich man also died and was buried; and in Hades, being in torment, he lifted up his eyes, and saw Abraham far off and Lazarus in his bosom. And he called out, "Father Abraham,

wie die Morgenröte, und deine Besserung
as   the   dawn,   and   your   recovery

wird schnell wachsen, und deine Gerechtigkeit
will   quickly   increase,   and   your   righteousness

wird vor dir hergehen, und die Herrlichkeit
will   before   you   go-forth,   and   the   glory

des Herrn wird dich zu sich nehmen.
of-the Lord   will   you   to itself   take.

2. Bass Recit.
•Wealth is a blessing of God meant to be shared (39–2)
Der   reiche Gott wirft seinen Überfluß
(Our) wealthy God casts   his   abundance

Auf uns, die wir ohn ihn
Upon us,   (who) without him

          auch nicht den Odem haben.
          even   not (our) breath have.
{Upon us, who would not even have breath without him.}

Sein ist es,   was   wir sind;
His   is   it, that-which we are;

          er gibt   nur den Genuß,
          he gives   (us) just (its)   use,
{His is all that we are and have; he just gives us its use,}

Doch nicht, daß uns allein
Though not, so-that us   alone

          nur seine Schätze   laben.
          -   his   treasures (should) delight.

Sie sind der Probestein,
They are the touchstone,

          wodurch er macht bekannt,
          by-which he makes   known

Daß er der Armut auch die Notdurft ausgespendet,
That he to poverty also the necessities has-dispensed,
{That he has also provided the poor with their necessities,}

Als   er mit milder Hand,
When he with liberal hand,

Was jener nötig ist,   uns reichlich zugewendet.
What to-(them) needful is, (on) us richly   bestows.
{Richly bestows on us what is needful to them.}

Wir sollen ihm für sein gelehntes Gut
We should to-him for his   lent   blessing(s)
{We are not asked—for the blessings lent to us—}

have mercy upon me, and send Lazarus to dip the end of his finger in water and cool my tongue; for I am in anguish in this flame." But Abraham said, "Son, remember that you in your lifetime received your good things, and Lazarus in like manner evil things; but now he is comforted here, and you are in anguish."
Jms. 1:27. Religion that is pure and undefiled before God and the Father is this: to visit orphans and widows in their affliction, and to keep oneself unstained from the world. (Also Mt. 25:35–40.)
Prov. 4:18. The path of the righteous is like the light of dawn, which shines brighter and brighter until full day.

Jms. 1:17. Every good endowment and every perfect gift is from above, coming down from the Father of lights with whom there is no variation or shadow due to change.
Ps. 145:15. [O Lord,] the eyes of all look to thee, and thou givest them their food in due season. (Also Ps. 104:27, 111:5.)
Job 12:10. In his hand is the life of every living thing and the breath of all mankind.
Acts 17:28. In him we live and move and have our being...
1 Cor. 4:7. ...What have you that you did not receive? If then you received it, why do you boast as if it were not a gift?
1 Chron. 29:14. [O Lord]...all things come from thee, and of thy own have we given thee.
1 Tim. 6:17–19. As for the rich in this world, charge them not to be haughty, nor to set their hopes on uncertain riches but on God who richly furnishes us with everything to enjoy. They are to do good, to be rich in good deeds, liberal and generous, thus laying up for themselves a good foundation for the future...
Lk. 6:38. Give, and it will be given to you; good measure, pressed down, shaken together, running over, will be put into your lap. For the measure you give will be the measure you get back.
1 Jn. 3:17–18. But if any one has the world's goods and sees his brother in need, yet closes his heart against him, how does God's love abide in him? Little children, let us not love in word or speech but in deed and in truth.
Acts 20:35. In all things I have shown you that by so toiling one must help the weak, remembering the words of the Lord Jesus, how he said, "It is more blessed to give than to receive."
Mt. 10:8. Heal the sick, raise the dead, cleanse lepers, cast out demons. You received without paying, give without pay.
Mt. 26:11. You will always have the poor with you...
Acts 4:34–35. There was not a needy person among [the early believers], for as many as were possessors of lands or houses sold them, and brought the proceeds of what was sold and laid it at the apostles' feet; and distribution was made to each as any had need. (Also Acts 2:45.)
Mal. 3:10. Bring the full tithes into the storehouse, that there may be food in my house; and thereby put me to the test, says the Lord of hosts, if I will not open the windows of heaven for you and pour down for you an overflowing blessing.
Mic. 6:6–8. With what shall I come before the Lord, and bow myself before God on high? Shall I come before him with burnt offerings, with calves a year old? Will the Lord be pleased with thousands of rams, with ten thousands of rivers of oil? Shall I give my first-born for

Die Zinse nicht in seine Scheunen bringen;
The tithe not into his storehouses bring;
{To bring the tithe into his storehouses;}

Barmherzigkeit, die auf dem Nächsten ruht,
Mercy, which on (one's) neighbor rests,
{Rather, mercy shown to one's neighbor}

Kann mehr als alle Gab ihm an das Herze dringen.
Can more than all gifts - to (his) heart penetrate.
{Touches his heart more than any gift.}

3. Alto Aria
●Charity makes us like God & earns heavenly blessing (39-3)
Seinem Schöpfer noch auf Erden
(One's) creator already on earth

    Nur im Schatten ähnlich werden,
(Even) just in shadow similar to-become,
{Even dimly to resemble,}

Ist im Vorschmack selig sein.
Is in foretaste blessed (to) be.
{Is a foretaste of bliss.}

Sein Erbarmen nachzuahmen,
His mercy to-imitate,
{Imitating his mercy,}

Streuet hier des Segens Samen,
Scatters here that blessing's seed,
{Scatters here the seed of that blessing,}

Den wir dorten bringen ein.
Which we over-there (will) bring in.
{Which we will reap over there.}

Part II

4. Bass Aria
●Sharing pleases God; do not neglect it: Heb. 13:16 (39-4)
Wohlzutun und mitzuteilen vergesset nicht;
To-do-good and to-share forget not;

denn solche Opfer gefallen Gott wohl.
for such sacrifices please God well.

5. Soprano Aria
●All we have is given by God; he has need of nothing (39-5)
Höchster, was ich habe,
Most-High, what I have,

Ist nur deine Gabe.
Is but thy gift.

Wenn vor deinem Angesicht
If before thy face

---

my transgression, the fruit of my body for the sin of my soul? He has showed you, O man, what is good; and what does the Lord require of you but to do justice, and to love kindness, and to walk humbly with your God?
Ps. 40:6–8. [O Lord,] sacrifice and offering thou dost not desire; but thou hast given me an open ear. Burnt offering and sin offering thou hast not required. Then I said, "Lo, I come...I delight to do thy will, O my God; thy law is within my heart." (Also Ps. 51:16–17.)

*1 Jn. 4:7, 11, 19. Beloved, let us love one another; for love is of God, and he who loves is born of God and knows God...Beloved, if God so loved us, we also ought to love one another...We love, because he first loved us.
1 Jn. 3:2. Beloved, we are God's children now; it does not yet appear what we shall be, but we know that when he appears we shall be like him, for we shall see him as he is.
Mt. 5:7. Blessed are the merciful, for they shall obtain mercy.
Mt. 5:44–45, 48. ...Love your enemies...so that you may be sons of your Father who is in heaven...You, therefore, must be perfect, as your heavenly Father is perfect.
Mt. 19:21. Jesus said to [the rich young man], "If you would be perfect, go, sell what you possess and give to the poor, and you will have treasure in heaven; and come, follow me." (Also Mt. 25:34–36.)
Prov. 19:17. He who is kind to the poor lends to the Lord, and he will repay him for his deed...
Ps. 126:5–6. May those who sow in tears reap with shouts of joy! He that goes forth weeping, bearing the seed for sowing, shall come home with shouts of joy, bringing his sheaves with him. (Also Gal. 6:7–8, 2 Cor. 9:6–12.)

Heb. 13:16. *Do not neglect to do good and to share what you have, for such sacrifices are pleasing to God.*
Rom. 12:13. Contribute to the needs of the saints, practice hospitality.
Eph. 4:28. Let the thief no longer steal, but rather let him labor, doing honest work with his hands, so that he may be able to give to those in need.
Mic. 6:8. He has showed you, O man, what is good; and what does the Lord require of you but to do justice, and to love kindness, and to walk humbly with your God?

1 Chron. 29:12, 14. [O Lord,] both riches and honor come from thee, and thou rulest over all...All things come from thee, and of thy own have we given thee.
1 Cor. 4:7. ...What have you that you did not receive? If then you received it, why do you boast as if it were not a gift?
Jms. 1:17. Every good endowment and every perfect gift is from above, coming down from the Father of lights with whom there is no variation or shadow due to change.
Jn. 3:27. No one can receive anything except what is given him from heaven...

Ich schon mit dem meinen
I indeed with that-of mine
{I—with whatever I own—}

Dankbar wollt erscheinen,
Grateful should-want to-appear,

Wilt du doch kein Opfer nicht.
Wouldst-desire thou still no sacrifice - .
{Then wouldst thou still desire no sacrifice from me.}

6. Alto Recit.
●Gratitude: What can I do for God's blessings? (39–6)
Wie soll ich dir, o Herr, denn sattsamlich vergelten,
How shall I thee, O Lord, then sufficiently repay,
{How then, shall I sufficiently repay thee, O Lord,}

Was du an Leib und Seel mir hast
For-what thou for body and soul for-me hast

zugutgetan?
beneficially-done?
{For what thou for my body and soul hast beneficially done?}

Ja, was ich noch empfang, und solches gar nicht selten,
Yes, which I still receive, and that indeed not seldom,

Weil ich mich jede Stund noch deiner rühmen kann?
Since I - every hour still thee praise can?
{Since I can still praise thee every hour?}

Ich hab nichts als den Geist, dir eigen
I have nothing but (my) spirit, to-thee for-thine-own

zu ergeben,
to surrender,
{For thyself, I have nothing to give but my spirit,}

Dem Nächsten die Begierd, daß ich ihm
For-my neighbor, the desire, that I to-him

dienstbar werd,
available-for-service would-be,
{For my neighbor, the desire to be of service to him,}

Der Armut, was du mir gegönnt in diesem Leben,
For-the (poor), what thou me hast-granted in this life,
{For the poor, whatever thou hast granted me in this life,}

Ps. 51:15–17. O Lord, open thou my lips, and my mouth shall show forth thy praise. For thou hast no delight in sacrifice; were I to give a burnt offering, thou wouldst not be pleased. The sacrifice acceptable to God is a broken spirit; a broken and contrite heart, O God, thou wilt not despise. (Also Ps. 40:6–8, Mic. 6:6–8.)
Mt. 9:13 [Christ]: Go and learn what this means, "I desire mercy, and not sacrifice."... (Also Mt. 12:7.)
Hos. 6:6 [God]: For I desire steadfast love and not sacrifice, the knowledge of God, rather than burnt offerings.

Ps. 116:12. What shall I render (Luther: vergelten) to the Lord for all his bounty to me?
Acts 17:25.. [God is not] served by human hands, as though he needed anything, since he himself gives to all men life and breath and everything.
Ps. 13:6. I will sing to the Lord, because he as dealt bountifully with me. (Also Ps. 67:5–7.)
Ps. 116:7. Return, O my soul, to your rest; for the Lord has dealt bountifully with you.
Ps. 37:25–26. I have been young, and now am old; yet I have not seen the righteous forsaken or his children begging bread. He is ever giving liberally and lending, and his children become a blessing.
Lam. 3:22–23. The steadfast love of the Lord never ceases, his mercies never come to an end; they are new every morning; great is thy faithfulness.
Rom. 2:4. Do you presume upon the riches of his kindness...? Do you not know that God's kindness is meant to lead you to repentance?
Jms. 4:5. Do you suppose it is in vain that the scripture says, "He yearns jealously over the spirit which he has made to dwell in us"?
Ex. 20:3, 5 [God]: You shall have no other gods before me...I the Lord your God am a jealous God...
Mt. 6:24. No one can serve two masters; for either he will hate the one and love the other, or he will be devoted to the one and despise the other. You cannot serve God and mammon. (Also Lk. 16:13.)
Lk. 10:27. ...You shall love the Lord your God with all your heart, and with all your soul, and with all your strength, and with all your mind; and your neighbor as yourself. (Mt. 22:37–40, Mk. 12:30–31, Deut. 6:5, Lev. 19:18)
Ps. 41:1. Blessed is he who considers the poor!
Prov. 14:21. He who despises his neighbor is a sinner, but happy is he who is kind to the poor.
*Lk. 16:19–25. There was a rich man, who was clothed in purple and fine linen and who feasted sumptuously every day. And at his gate lay a poor man named Lazarus, full of sores, who desired to be fed with what fell from the rich man's table; moreover the dogs came and licked his sores. The poor man died and was carried by the angels to Abraham's bosom. The rich man also died and was buried; and in Hades, being in torment, he lifted up his eyes, and saw Abraham far off and Lazarus in his bosom. And he called out, "Father Abraham, have mercy upon me, and send Lazarus to dip the end of his finger in water and cool my tongue; for I am in anguish in this flame." But Abraham said, "Son, remember that you in your lifetime received your good things, and Lazarus in like manner evil things; but now he is comforted here, and you are in anguish." (Also Heb. 4:9.)

Und, wenn es dir gefällt, den schwachen Leib der Erd.
And, when it thee pleases, (my) weak body for-the earth.
{And when it pleases thee, my weak body for the earth.}

Ich bringe, was ich kann, Herr, laß er dir behagen,
I bring, what I can, Lord; let it thee suit,
{I bring what I can, Lord; let it please thee,}

Daß ich, was du versprichst,
That I, what thou dost-promise,

      auch einst davon mög tragen.
      also someday away may carry.
{That I also may someday take with me what thou dost promise.}

7. Chorale
●Blessed are the merciful; they shall receive mercy (39-7)
Selig sind, die aus Erbarmen
Blessed are those-who out-of pity

Sich annehmen fremder Not,
  - Take-upon (themselves) (others') distress,

Sind mitleidig mit den Armen,
Are sympathetic to the poor,

Bitten treulich für sie Gott.
Pray faithfully for them (to) God.

Die behülflich sind mit Rat,
Who helpful are with counsel,

Auch, womöglich, mit der Tat,
Also, where-possible, (in) - deed,

    Werden wieder Hülf empfangen
(They) shall in-turn help receive

Und Barmherzigkeit erlangen.
And mercy obtain.

Prov. 21:13. He who closes his ear to the cry of the poor will himself cry out and not be heard.
Prov. 14:31. He who oppresses a poor man insults his Maker, but he who is kind to the needy honors him.
*Lk. 16:22. The poor man died and was carried by the angels to Abraham's bosom...The rich man also died...
Ps. 103:14-16. [God] knows our frame; he remembers that we are dust. As for man, his days are like grass; he flourishes like a flower of the field; for the wind passes over it, and it is gone, and its place knows it no more.
Gen. 3:19. ...You are dust, and to dust you shall return.
1 Jn. 2:25. This is what [Christ] has promised us, eternal life.
Mt. 16:25 [Christ]: Whoever would save his life will lose it, and whoever loses his life for my sake will find it.
Heb. 10:23. Let us hold fast the confession of our hope without wavering, for he who promised is faithful.

Mt. 5:7. Blessed are the merciful, for they shall obtain mercy.
Ps. 41:1. Blessed is he who considers the poor!
Lk. 6:30-31. Give to every one who begs from you; and of him who takes away your goods do not ask them again. And as you wish that men would do to you, do so to them. (Also Mt. 7:12.)
Mt. 25:34-40. Then the King will say to those at his right hand, "Come, O blessed of my Father, inherit the kingdom prepared for you from the foundation of the world; for I was hungry and you gave me food, I was thirsty and you gave me drink, I was a stranger and you welcomed me, I was naked and you clothed me, I was sick and you visited me, I was in prison and you came to me." Then the righteous will answer him, "Lord, when did we see thee hungry and feed thee, or thirsty and give thee drink? And when did we see thee a stranger and welcome thee, or naked and clothe thee? And when did we see thee sick or in prison and vist thee?" And the King will answer them, "Truly, I say to you, as you did it to one of the least of these my brethren, you did it to me."
Rom. 12:13. Contribute to the needs of the saints, practice hospitality.
1 Jn. 3:17-18. But if any one has the world's goods and sees his brother in need, yet closes his heart against him, how does God's love abide in him? Little children, let us not love in word or speech but in deed and in truth. (Also Jms. 2:14-16.)

BWV 40
Dazu ist erschienen der Sohn Gottes
(NBA I/3; BC A12)

2. Day of Christmas (BWV 40, 121, 57, 248-II)
*Tit. 3:4–7 (The mercy of God appeared in Christ)
*Lk. 2:15–20 (The shepherds go to the manger)

This day also celebrated as the festival of St. Stephen the Martyr:
*Acts 6:8–15; 7:54–60 (Martyrdom of Stephen)
*Mt. 23:34–39 (Jesus' lament: Jerusalem kills the prophets sent to her)
Librettist: Unknown

1. Chorus
●Christ came to destroy works of devil: 1 Jn. 3:8 (40-1)
Dazu   ist erschienen der Sohn   Gottes,
For-this-purpose (has) appeared the Son (of) God,

daß er die Werke des Teufels   zerstöre.
that he the works of-the devil (might) destroy.

2. Tenor Recit.
●Incarnation: Word became flesh; the Lord became servant (40-2)
Das Wort ward Fleisch und wohnet in der Welt,
The Word became flesh and dwells in the world,

Das Licht der Welt bestrahlt den Kreis der Erden,
The Light of-the world illuminates the circle of-the earth,

Der große Gottessohn
The great Son-of-God

Verläßt   des Himmels Thron,
Relinquishes -   heaven's throne,

Und seiner Majestät   gefällt,
And His   Majesty (it) pleases,
{And it pleases His Majesty,}

Ein kleines Menschenkind zu werden.
A   little   human-child to become.
{To become a little child.}

Bedenkt doch diesen Tausch, wer nur gedenken kann;
Consider indeed this exchange, whoever think   can;
{Consider this exchange, whoever possesses thought;}

Der König wird ein Untertan,
The king becomes a   subject,

Der Herr erscheinet als ein Knecht
The Lord appears   as a servant

Und wird dem menschlichen Geschlecht—
And (is) for-the   human   race—

1 Jn. 3:8. He who commits sin is of the devil; for the devil has sinned from the beginning. *The reason the Son of God appeared was to destroy the works of the devil.*
Heb. 2:14–15. Since therefore the children share in flesh and blood, [Christ] himself likewise partook of the same nature, that through death he might destroy him who has the power of death, that is, the devil, and deliver all those who through fear of death were subject to lifelong bondage.
Jn. 16:8, 11 [Christ]: When [the Counselor] comes, he will convince the world concerning sin and righteousness and judgment...concerning judgment, because the ruler of this world is judged.

Jn. 1:14. The Word became flesh and dwelt among us, full of grace and truth; we have beheld his glory, glory as of the only Son from the Father. (Also Jn. 1:17.)
Jn. 1:9, 15. The true light that enlightens every man was coming into the world...John bore witness to him, and cried, "This was he of whom I said, 'He who comes after me, ranks before me, for he was before me.'"
Jn. 8:12. Jesus spoke to [the people], saying, "I am the light of the world; he who follows me will not walk in darkness, but will have the light of life."
Is. 60:1, 3. Arise, shine; for your light has come, and the glory of the Lord has risen upon you...and nations shall come to your light, and kings to the brightness of your rising... (Also Is. 9:2.)
1 Jn. 4:14. We have seen and testify that the Father has sent his Son as the Savior of the world.
Heb. 1:1–2. In many and various ways God spoke of old to our fathers by the prophets; but in these last days he has spoken to us by a Son, whom he appointed the heir of all things, through whom also he created the world.
1 Tim. 3:16. Great indeed, we confess, is the mystery of our religion: [Christ] was manifested in the flesh...
Phil. 2:5–8. ...Christ Jesus, who, though he was in the form of God, did not count equality with God a thing to be grasped, but emptied himself, taking the form of a servant, being born in the likeness of men. And being found in human form he humbled himself and became obedient unto death, even death on a cross.
Jn. 13:5, 12–15. [Jesus] poured water into a basin, and began to wash the disciples' feet, and to wipe them with the towel with which he was girded...He said to them, "Do you know what I have done to you? You call me Teacher and Lord; and you are right, for so I am. If I then, your Lord and Teacher, have washed your feet, you also ought to wash one another's feet. For I have given you an example, that you

O süßes Wort in aller Ohren!—
O sweet word in everyone's ears!—

Zu Trost und Heil geboren.
For comfort and salvation born.
{And is born to bring comfort and salvation to the human race—O sweet word in everyone's ears!}

3. Chorale
●Christ is with us, who can condemn us? (40-3)
Die Sünd macht Leid;
- Sin produces sorrow;

Christus bringt Freud,
Christ brings joy,

Weil er zu Trost in diese Welt ist kommen.
Because he for comfort into this world (has) come.

Mit uns ist Gott
With us is God
{God is now with us}

Nun in der Not:
Now in (our) need:
{In our need:}

Wer ist, der uns als Christen kann verdammen?
Who is-there, who us as Christians can condemn?

4. Bass Aria
●Serpent, he who will bruise your head is born! (40-4)
Höllische Schlange,
Infernal serpent,

Wird dir nicht bange?
Becomest (thou) not fearful?

Der dir den Kopf als ein Sieger zerknickt,
Who thee (thy) head as a victor crushes,
{The one who crushes thy head as victor,}

Ist nun geboren,
Is now born,

Und die verloren,
And those who-are-lost,

Werden mit ewigem Frieden beglückt.
(Are) with eternal peace blessed.
{Are now blessed with eternal peace.}

5. Alto Recit.
●Serpent brought death; woman's seed brings salvation (40-5)
Die Schlange, so im Paradies
The serpent, that in paradise

also should do as I have done to you."
2 Cor. 8:9. You know the grace of our Lord Jesus Christ, that though he was rich, yet for your sake he became poor, so that by his poverty you might become rich.
Mt. 20:28 [Christ]: The Son of Man came not to be served but to serve, and to give his life as a ransom for many.

Ps. 38:4. My iniquities have gone over my head; they weigh like a burden too heavy for me. (Also Ps. 51:3.)
Rom. 6:23. The wages of sin is death, but the free gift of God is eternal life in Christ Jesus our Lord.
Lk. 2:10–11. And the angel said to [the shepherds], "Be not afraid; for behold, I bring you good news of a great joy which will come to all the people; for to you is born this day in the city of David a Savior, who is Christ the Lord." (See Lk. 4:18–21.)
Is. 7:14. ...Behold, a young woman shall conceive and bear a son, and shall call his name Immanuel.
Mt. 1:23. ...His name shall be called Emmanuel (which means, God with us).
Ps. 91:15 [God]: When he calls to me, I will answer him; I will be with him in trouble (Luther: Not), I will rescue him...
Jn. 3:17. For God sent the Son into the world, not to condemn the world, but that the world might be saved through him. (Also Jn. 12:47, 10:10.)
Rom. 8:33–34. Who shall bring any charge against God's elect? It is God who justifies; who is to condemn? Is it Christ Jesus, who died, yes, who was raised from the dead, who is at the right hand of God, who indeed intercedes for us?

Gen. 3:14–15. The Lord God said to the serpent, "Because you have done [deceived Eve]..I will put enmity between you and the woman, and between your seed and her seed; he shall bruise your head, and you shall bruise his heel."
Rom. 16:20. ...The God of peace will soon crush Satan under your feet...
Rev. 12:9. And the great dragon was thrown down, that ancient serpent, who is called the Devil and Satan, the deceiver of the whole world...
Rev. 20:1–3. Then I saw an angel coming down from heaven, holding in his hand the key of the bottomless pit and a great chain. And he seized the dragon, that ancient serpent, who is the Devil and Satan, and bound him for a thousand years, and threw him into the pit...
Gal. 4:4. When the time had fully come, God sent forth his Son, born of woman...
Lk. 2:11. To you is born this day in the city of David a Savior, who is Christ the Lord.
Is. 9:6. To us a child is born, to us a son is given; and the government will be upon his shoulder, and his name will be called "Wonderful Counselor, Mighty God, Everlasting Father, Prince of Peace."
Lk. 2:14. Glory to God in the highest, and on earth peace among men with whom he is pleased!

Gen. 3:1, 4–6, 14–15, 22–24. Now the serpent was more subtle than any other wild creature that the Lord God had made. He said to the

Auf alle Adamskinder
Upon all (the) children-of-Adam

Das Gift der Seelen fallen ließ,
The poison of souls to-fall did-cause,
{Did cause the soul's poison to fall,}

Bringt uns nicht mehr Gefahr;
Brings us no more danger;

Des Weibes Samen stellt sich dar,
The woman's seed presents itself - ,
{The woman's seed appears,}

Der Heiland ist ins Fleisch gekommen
The Savior is in-the flesh come
{The Savior has come in the flesh,}

Und hat ihr alles Gift benommen.
And has from-it all-the venom removed.
{And has taken all its venom away.}

Drum sei getrost! betrübter Sünder.
Therefore be of-good-cheer, troubled sinner!

6. Chorale
●Serpent vanquished by Christ's passion (40-6)
Schüttle deinen Kopf und sprich:
Shake thy head and say:

Fleuch, du alte Schlange!
Flee, thou ancient serpent!

Was erneurst du deinen Stich,
Why renewest thou thy sting;
{Why dost thou try to renew thy sting;}

Machst mir angst und bange?
Makest me fearful and anxious?
{Making me fearful and anxious?}

Ist dir doch der Kopf zerknickt,
(Now) is - indeed (thy) head crushed,
{For now is thy head crushed,}

Und ich bin durchs Leiden
And I am through-the passion
{And, by the passion}

Meines Heilands dir entrückt
Of-my Savior (from) thee carried-off
{Of my Savior, I am snatched from thee and carried off}

In den Saal der Freuden.
Into the hall of delights.

woman, "Did God say, 'You shall not eat of any tree of the garden'?... You will not die. For God knows that when you eat of it your eyes will be opened, and you will be like God, knowing good and evil." So when the woman saw that the tree was good for food, and that it was a delight to the eyes, and that the tree was to be desired to make one wise, she took of its fruit and ate; and she also gave some to her husband, and he ate...The Lord God said to the serpent, "Because you have done this...I will put enmity between you and the woman, and between your seed and her seed; he shall bruise your head, and you shall bruise his heel."...Then the Lord God said, "Behold, the man has become like one of us, knowing good and evil; and now, lest he put forth his hand and take also of the tree of life, and eat, and live for ever"—therefore the Lord God sent him forth from the garden of Eden...He drove out the man; and at the east of the garden of Eden he placed the cherubim, and a flaming sword which turned every way, to guard the way to the tree of life.
1 Cor. 15:21–22. As by a man came death, by a man has come also the resurrection of the dead. For as in Adam all die, so also in Christ shall all be made alive.
Lk. 2:11. To you is born this day in the city of David a Savior, who is Christ the Lord.
Rom. 8:3. God has done what the law, weakened by the flesh, could not do: sending his own Son in the likeness of sinful flesh and for sin, he condemned sin in the flesh.
Jn. 1:14. And the Word became flesh and dwelt among us...

Mk. 15:29–30. Those who passed by [Jesus on the cross] derided him, wagging their heads (Luther: schüttelten ihre Häupter), and saying, "Aha! You who would destroy the temple and build it in three days, save yourself, and come down from the cross!"
Lk. 24:26. Was it not necessary that the Christ should suffer these things and enter into his glory?
Gen. 3:14–15. The Lord God said to the serpent, "Because you have [deceived Eve]...I will put enmity between you and the woman, and between your seed and her seed; he shall bruise your head, and you shall bruise his heel."
Jn. 3:14–15. As Moses lifted up the serpent in the wilderness, so must the Son of man be lifted up, that whoever believes in him may have eternal life.
Heb. 2:14–15. Since therefore the children share in flesh and blood, [Christ] himself likewise partook of the same nature that through death he might destroy him who has the power of death, that is, the devil, and deliver all those who through fear of death were subject to lifelong bondage.
1 Cor. 15:55–56. O death, where is thy victory? O death, where is thy sting? The sting of death is sin...
1 Pet. 3:18. Christ...died for sins once for all, the righteous for the unrighteous, that he might bring us to God...
Lk. 23:43. ...Today you will be with me in Paradise.
*Acts 7:55–56. But [Stephen], full of the Holy Spirit, gazed into heaven and saw the glory of God, and Jesus standing at the right hand of God; and he said, "Behold, I see the heavens opened, and the Son of man standing at the right hand of God." (Also Ps. 16:11.)

7. Tenor Aria
●Jesus will gather us like chicks in hell's storm (40-7)
Christenkinder, freuet euch!
Christian-children, rejoice!

Wütet schon das Höllenreich,
Rages even-though the kingdom-of-hell,
{Though the kingdom of hell rage,}

Will euch Satans Grimm erschrecken:
Should you Satan's fury frighten:
{Though Satan's fury frighten you:}

Jesus, der erretten kann,
Jesus, who rescue can,
{Jesus, who can save,}

Nimmt sich seiner Küchlein an
Takes to-himself his little-chicks -
{Takes his little chicks to himself}

Und will sie mit Flügeln decken.
And would them with (his) wings cover.
{And covers them with his wings.}

8. Chorale
●Prayer: Bless Christendom, grant a peaceful year (40-8)
Jesu, nimm dich deiner Glieder
Jesu, receive (these) thy members

Ferner in Genaden an;
(Henceforth) in grace - ;

Schenke, was man bitten kann,
Grant, (all) (that) one might-ask,

Zu erquicken deine Brüder:
To refresh thy brethren:

Gib der ganzen Christenschar
Give the entire Christian-throng

Frieden und ein selges Jahr!
Peace and a blessed year!

Freude, Freude über Freude!
Joy, joy above joy!

Christus wehret allem Leide.
Christ wards-off all sorrow.

Phil. 4:4. Rejoice in the Lord always; again I will say, Rejoice.
Ps. 27:1, 3. ...The Lord is the stronghold of my life; of whom shall I be afraid?...Though a host encamp against me, my heart shall not fear; though war arise against me, yet I will be confident.
1 Pet. 5:8. ...Your adversary the devil prowls around like a roaring lion, seeking some one to devour. (Also Jms. 4:7.)
Eph. 6:11–12. Put on the whole armor of God, that you may be able to stand against the wiles of the devil. For we are not contending against flesh and blood, but against the principalities, against the powers, against the world rulers of this present darkness, against the spiritual hosts of wickedness in the heavenly places.
*Mt. 23:37 [Christ]: ...How often would I have gathered your children together as a hen gathers her brood under her wings...
Ps. 91:1–4. He who dwells in the shelter of the Most High, who abides in the shadow of the Almighty, will say to the Lord, "My refuge and my fortress; my God, in whom I trust." For he will deliver you from the snare of the fowler and from the deadly pestilence; he will cover you with his pinions, and under his wings you will find refuge; his faithfulness is a shield and buckler.
Ps. 36:7. How precious is thy steadfast love, O God! The children of men take refuge in the shadow of thy wings. (Also Ps. 57:1, 63:7.)

*Mt. 23:37 [Christ]: ...How often would I have gathered your children together as a hen gathers her brood under her wings...
Ps. 94:14. The Lord will not forsake his people; he will not abandon his heritage. (Also Ps. 37:28.)
Ps. 100:3. ...We are his people, and the sheep of his pasture. (Also Ps. 95:6–7.)
1 Cor. 12:12, 27. Just as the body is one and has many members, and all the members of the body, though many, are one body, so it is with Christ...Now you are the body of Christ and individually members of it.
Col. 1:18. He is the head of the body, the church; he is the beginning, the first-born from the dead, that in everything he might be pre-eminent.
Col. 2:19. [Hold] fast to the Head, from whom the whole body, nourished and knit together...grows with a growth that is from God.
Rom. 12:5. We, though many, are one body in Christ, and individually members one of another.
Heb. 2:11–12. He who sanctifies and those who are sanctified have all one origin. That is why he is not ashamed to call them brethren, saying, "I will proclaim thy name to my brethren, in the midst of the congregation I will praise thee." (Also Mk. 3:34–35.)
Ps. 29:11. May the Lord give strength to his people! May the Lord bless his people with peace! (Also Ps. 122:6–7, 147:14.)
Ps. 3:8. Deliverance belongs to the Lord; thy blessing be upon thy people!
Is. 35:10/51:11. And the ransomed of the Lord shall return, and come to Zion with singing; everlasting joy shall be upon their heads; they shall obtain joy and gladness, and sorrow and sighing shall flee away.

Wonne, Wonne, über Wonne!
Bliss,   bliss, above bliss!

Er ist die Genadensonne.
He is the   sun-of-grace.

BWV 41
Jesu, nun sei gepreiset
(NBA I/4; BC A22)

New Year/Circumcision and Name of Jesus (BWV 143, 190, 41, 16, 171, 248-IV)
*Gal. 3:23–29 (Through faith we are heirs of the promise)
*Luke 2:21 (Circumcision and naming of Jesus)
Librettist: Unknown

1. Chorus (Chorale Vs. 1)
●New Year: Thanks for old year; prayer for new (41–1)
    Jesu, nun sei gepreiset
(O) Jesu, now be praised

Zu   diesem neuen Jahr
At (the beginning of) this   new   year

Für dein Güt,   uns beweiset
For thy goodness, to-us shown
{For thy goodness, shown to us}

In aller Not   und G'fahr,
In all trouble and danger;

Daß wir haben erlebet
That we   have (witnessed)

Die neu fröhliche Zeit,
The new   joyful   age,
{The joyful new age,}

Die   voller Gnaden schwebet
Which full-of grace   soars
{Which soars full of grace}

Und ewger Seligkeit;
And eternal blessedness;

Daß wir in guter   Stille
That we in goodly quietness

Das alt Jahr hab'n erfüllet.
The old year have completed.

Wir wolln uns   dir   ergeben
We want ourselves to-thee to-surrender
{We want to surrender ourselves to thee}

Itzund und immerdar,
Now   and evermore;

Ps. 36:7–8. How precious is thy steadfast love, O God! The children of men take refuge in the shadow of thy wings. They feast on the abundance of thy house, and thou givest them drink from the river of thy delights.

Ps. 119:108. Accept my offerings of praise, O Lord...
Ps. 40:5. Thou hast multiplied, O Lord my God, thy wondrous deeds and thy thoughts toward us...Were I to proclaim and tell of them, they would be more than can be numbered.
Ps. 106:1–2. O give thanks to the Lord, for he is good; for his steadfast love endures for ever! Who can utter the mighty doings of the Lord, or show forth all his praise?
Ps. 31:21. Blessed be the Lord, for he has wondrously shown his steadfast love to me (Luther: eine wunderliche Güte mir beweiset)...
Ps. 75:1. We give thanks to thee, O God; we give thanks; we call on thy name and recount thy wondrous deeds.
Ps. 36:7–8. How precious is thy steadfast love, O God! The children of men take refuge in the shadow of thy wings. They feast on the abundance of thy house, and thou givest them drink from the river of thy delights.
Ps. 56:12–13. My vows to thee I must perform, O God; I will render thank offerings to thee. For thou hast delivered my soul from death, yea, my feet from falling, that I may walk before God in the light of life. (Also Ps. 86:12–13.)
2 Cor. 1:10. He delivered us from so deadly a peril, and he will deliver us; on him we have set our hope that he will deliver us again.
Ps. 116:6. ...When I was brought low, he saved me.
Ps. 28:7. The Lord is my strength and my shield; in him my heart trusts; so I am helped, and my heart exults, and with my song I give thanks to him.
Ps. 65:11. [O Lord,] thou crownest the year with thy bounty...
Ps. 144:15. Happy the people to whom such blessings fall! Happy the people whose God is the Lord!
Ps. 33:12. Blessed is the nation whose God is the Lord, the people whom he has chosen as his heritage!
1 Tim. 2:1–2. ...I urge that supplications, prayers, intercessions, and thanksgivings be made for all men, for kings and all who are in high positions, that we may lead a quiet and peaceable life, godly and respectful in every way.
Eph. 5:10. And try to learn what is pleasing to the Lord.
2 Chron. 30:8. ...Yield yourselves to the Lord...
Rom. 12:1–2. I appeal to you...by the mercies of God, to present your bodies as a living sacrifice, holy and acceptable to God, which is your spiritual worship. Do not be conformed to this world but be transformed by the renewal of your mind, that you may prove what is the will of God, what is good and acceptable and perfect.

Behüte   Leib, Seel und Leben
Protect (our) body, soul, and   life

Hinfort   durchs   ganze Jahr!
Henceforth throughout-the entire year!

2. Soprano Aria (Includes reference to Chorale Vs. 2)
●New Year: Prayer to end year as well as it is begun (41–2)
Laß uns, o höchster Gott, **das Jahr vollbringen,**
Let us, O most-high God, the year complete,
{Let us, O God most high, complete this year,}

Damit das Ende so wie dessen Anfang sei.
So-that the end   like   its   beginning be.

Es   stehe deine Hand uns bei,
(May) stand thy   hand us by,
{May thy hand be with us,}

Daß   künftig   bei des Jahres Schluß
That in-the-future, at the year's   close,

Wir bei des Segens Überfluß
We with (thy) blessing's profusion

Wie itzt ein Halleluja   singen.
As now, a hallelujah (may) sing.

3. Alto Recit. (Includes reference to Chorale Vs. 2)
●God's sovereignty is Alpha and Omega in weal & woe (41–3)
Ach! deine Hand, dein Segen muß allein
Ah,   thy hand, thy blessing must alone
{Ah, thy hand, thy blessing alone must be}

Das A und O,   der Anfang und das Ende sein.
The Alpha and Omega, the beginning and the end be.
{The Alpha and Omega, the beginning and the end.}

Das Leben trägest du in deiner Hand,
 -   Life carriest thou in thy   hand,

Und unsre Tage sind bei dir geschrieben;
And our   days are with thee written;
{And our days are written with thee;}

Dein Auge steht auf Stadt und Land;
Thine eye (rests) on town and country;

Du   zählest unser Wohl und kennest unser Leiden,
Thou dost-reckon our weal and dost-know our affliction,

Ach! gib von beiden,
Ah, grant of   both,

Was   deine Weisheit will,
Whatever thy   wisdom will,

1 Cor. 6:19–20. ...You are not your own; you were bought with a price. (Also 1 Cor. 7:23.)
1 Thess. 5:23. May the God of peace himself sanctify you wholly; and may your spirit and soul and body be kept sound and blameless at the coming of our Lord Jesus Christ.

Ecc. 7:8. Better is the end of a thing than its beginning...
Is. 46:9–10. ...I am God...declaring the end from the beginning and from ancient times things not yet done...
Ps. 65:11. [O Lord,] thou crownest the year with thy bounty...
1 Chron. 4:10. ...Oh that thou wouldst bless me and enlarge my border, and that thy hand might be with me...
Ps. 119:173. [O Lord,] let thy hand be ready to help me...
Ps. 144:12–15. May our sons in their youth be like plants full grown, our daughters like corner pillars cut for the structure of a palace; may our garners be full, providing all manner of store; may our sheep bring forth thousands and ten thousands in our fields; may our cattle be heavy with young, suffering no mischance or failure in bearing; may there be no cry of distress in our streets! Happy the people to whom such blessings fall! Happy the people whose God is the Lord! (Also Deut. 28:3–12.)
Ezek. 34:26 [God]: ...I will send down the showers in their season; they shall be showers of blessing.
Ps. 146:10. The Lord will reign for ever, thy God, O Zion, to all generations. Praise the Lord (Luther: Hallelujah)!

Ps. 127:1. Unless the Lord builds the house, those who build it labor in vain. Unless the Lord watches over the city, the watchman stays awake in vain.
Ps. 31:14–15. But I trust in thee, O Lord, I say, "Thou art my God." My times are in thy hand...
Acts 17:25. [God]...gives to all men life and breath and everything.
Job 12:10. In his hand is the life of every living thing and the breath of all mankind. (Also Ps. 104:27, 145:15–16.)
Rev. 22:13 [Christ]: I am the Alpha and the Omega, the first and the last, the beginning and the end. (Also Rev. 1:8, 21:6, Is. 44:6.)
Ps. 139:16. [O Lord] ...in thy book were written, every one of them, the days that were formed for me, when as yet there was none of them.
Ps. 56:8. [O Lord,] thou hast kept count of my tossings; put thou my tears in thy bottle! Are they not in thy book?
Job 31:4. Does not he see my ways, and number all my steps?
Job 23:10. He knows the way that I take; when he has tried me, I shall come forth as gold.
Prov. 5:21. For a man's ways are before the eyes of the Lord, and he watches all his paths.
Deut. 28:3. Blessed shall you be in the city, and blessed shall you be in the field...
Prov. 30:8–9. [O Lord,] ...give me neither poverty nor riches; feed me with the food that is needful for me, lest I be full, and deny thee, and say, "Who is the Lord?" or lest I be poor, and steal, and profane the name of my God.
Phil. 4:11–12. ...I have learned, in whatever state I am, to be content...

worzu   dich dein Erbarmen angetrieben.
to-whatever thee thy   mercy   doth-impell.
(to whatever thy mercy doth impell thee.}

4. Tenor Aria (Includes reference to Chorale Vs. 2)
●Prayer: Add spiritual blessings to our temporal ones (41–4)
Woferne   du den edlen Frieden
In-so-far-as thou the noble peace

Für unsern Leib und Stand   beschieden,
For our body and station (hast) allotted,

So laß der Seele doch **dein selig machend Wort.**
So grant the soul indeed thy   beatific   word.

Wenn uns dies Heil begegnet,
If   us this welfare meets,
{If we are granted this welfare,}

So sind wir hier gesegnet
Then are we here blessed
{Then we are blessed here}

Und   Auserwählte dort!
And (thine) elect   there!
{And are thine elect over there!}

5. Bass Recit. & Chorus (Includes reference to Chorale Vs. 2)
●Prayer: Defeat Satan who seeks to harm thine elect (41–5)
Doch weil der Feind bei Tag und Nacht
Yet since the enemy by day and night

Zu unserm Schaden wacht
For our   harm does-watch
{Seeks to do us harm}

Und unsre Ruhe   will verstören,
And our tranquility would disturb,
{And disturb our tranquility,}

So   wollest du, o Herre Gott, erhören,
Therefore (mayest) thou, O Lord God,   hear (us),

Wenn wir in heiliger Gemeine beten:
When we in holy   community pray:

S.A.T.B:
Den Satan unter unsre Füße treten.
 - Satan under our   feet to-tread.

So bleiben wir zu deinem Ruhm
Then remain we to thy   praise

all circumstances I have learned the secret of facing plenty and
hunger, abundance and want.

Ps. 147:14. [The Lord] makes peace in your borders; he fills you with
the finest of the wheat...
Jn. 14:27 [Christ]: Peace I leave with you; my peace I give to you...
1 Cor. 7:15. ...God has called us to peace.
Ps. 119:43. [O Lord,] take not the word of truth utterly out of my
mouth, for my hope is in thy ordinances.
Acts 20:32. I commend you to God and to the word of his grace,
which is able to build you up and to give you the inheritance among
all those who are sanctified.
Jms. 1:21. ...Receive with meekness the implanted word, which is able
to save your souls. (Also Acts 20:32, 1 Thess. 2:13.)
Col. 3:16. Let the word of Christ dwell in you richly...
Jn. 5:24 [Christ]: Truly, truly, I say to you, he who hears my word and
believes...has eternal life... (Also Jn. 8:51.)
3 Jn. 1:2. Beloved, I pray that all may go well with you and that you
may be in health; I know that it is well with your soul.
1 Pet. 2:9. You are a chosen race, a royal priesthood, a holy nation,
God's own people...
2 Thess. 2:13. ...God chose you from the beginning to be saved,
through sanctification by the Spirit and belief in the truth. (Also Jn.
15:16, Ps. 33:12.)
Mt. 22:14. Many are called, but few are chosen.
Rev. 17:14. ...Those with [Christ] are called and chosen...
Mk. 10:30. [They] will...receive a hundredfold now in this time, houses
and brothers and sisters and mothers and children and lands, with
persecutions, and in the age to come eternal life.

1 Pet. 5:8. Be sober, be watchful. Your adversary the devil prowls
around like a roaring lion, seeking some one to devour. (Also Job 1:7,
2:2.)
Rev. 12:10. ...The accuser of our brethren...who accuses them day and
night before our God.
Eph. 6:11–12. Put on the whole armor of God, that you may be able
to stand against the wiles of the devil. For we are not contending
against flesh and blood, but against...the spiritual hosts of wickedness
in the heavenly places.
2 Cor. 10:3–4. For though we live in the world we are not carrying on
a worldly war, for the weapons of our warfare are not worldly but
have divine power to destroy strongholds.
Gen. 3:14–15. The Lord God said to the serpent, "Because you have
done this...I will put enmity between you and the woman, and between
your seed and her seed; he shall bruise your head, and you shall bruise
his heel."
Rom. 16:20. ...The God of peace will soon crush Satan under your
feet...
Deut. 7:6. For you are a people holy to the Lord your God; the Lord
your God has chosen you to be a people for his own possession, out
of all the peoples that are on the face of the earth. (Also Ex. 19:5.)
Ps. 33:12. Blessed is the nation whose God is the Lord, the people
whom he has chosen as his heritage!

Dein auserwähltes Eigentum
Thine elect possesion

Und können auch nach Kreuz und Leiden
And can also after cross and suffering

Zur Herrlichkeit von hinnen scheiden.
To glory from here depart.
{Depart from here to glory.}

6. Chorale (Vs. 3) (BC: Vs. 6)
●New Year: Committing year to God in praise & faith (41–6)
Dein ist allein die Ehre,
Thine is alone the honor,

Dein ist allein der Ruhm;
Thine is alone the praise;

Geduld im Kreuz uns lehre,
Patience in cross(-bearing) us teach,
{Teach us patience in cross-bearing,}

Regier all unser Tun,
Rule all our doing,

Bis wir fröhlich abscheiden
Till we joyfully depart

Ins ewig Himmelreich,
Into-the eternal kingdom-of-heaven

Zu wahrem Fried und Freude,
To true peace and joy,

Den Heilgen Gottes gleich.
The saints of-God (made) similar.

Indes mach's mit uns allen
Meanwhile do with us all

Nach deinem Wohlgefallen:
According-to thy pleasure:

Solchs singet heut ohn' Scherzen
Thus sings today without jesting
{Thus sings today most earnestly}

Die christgläubige Schar
The Christ-believing throng

Und wünscht mit Mund und Herzen
And wishes with mouth and heart
{And asks with mouth and heart for}

Ein seligs neues Jahr.
A blessed new year.

Ps. 135:4. The Lord has chosen Jacob for himself, Israel as his own possession (Luther: Eigentum). (Also Deut. 14:2.)
Jer. 13:11 [God]: ...that they might be for me a people, a name, a praise, and a glory...
Gal. 3:29. And if you are Christ's, then you are Abraham's offspring, heirs according to promise.
Rom. 8:18. I consider that the sufferings of the present time are not worth comparing with the glory that is to be revealed to us. (Also 1 Pet. 4:13, Jms. 1:12.)
Rom. 5:2. ...We rejoice in our hope of sharing the glory of God.

Ps. 115:1. Not to us, O Lord, not to us, but to thy name give glory, for the sake of thy steadfast love and thy faithfulness! (Also Is. 48:11.)
1 Tim. 1:17. To the King of ages, immortal, invisible, the only God, be honor and glory for ever and ever. Amen. (Also Rom. 16:27, Jude 1:25.)
Mt. 10:38 [Christ]: He who does not take his cross and follow me is not worthy of me. (Also Mt. 16:24, Mk.8:34, Lk.9:23.)
Jms. 1:12. Blessed is the man who endures trial, for when he has stood the test he will receive the crown of life which God has promised to those who love him.
Heb. 10:36–39. For you have need of endurance (Luther: Geduld), so that you may do the will of God and receive what is promised. "For yet a little while, and the coming one shall come and shall not tarry; but my righteous one shall live by faith, and if he shrinks back, my soul has no pleasure in him." But we are not of those who shrink back and are destroyed, but of those who have faith and keep their souls.
Jms. 4:7. Submit yourselves therefore to God...
1 Cor. 10:31. ...Whatever you do, do all to the glory of God.
2 Cor. 5:9. Whether we are at home or away, we make it our aim to please him.
2 Tim. 4:6–8. ...The time of my departure has come. I have fought the good fight, I have finished the race, I have kept the faith. Henceforth there is laid up for me the crown of righteousness, which the Lord, the righteous judge, will award to me on that Day, and not only to me but also to all who have loved his appearing.
1 Jn. 3:2. Beloved, we are God's children now; it does not yet appear what we shall be, but we know that when he appears we shall be like him, for we shall see him as he is.
Mt. 22:30. In the resurrection [we]...are like angels in heaven. (Also Lk. 20:36.)
1 Pet. 4:19. Therefore let those who suffer according to God's will do right and entrust their souls to a faithful Creator.
Mt. 26:39. ...My Father, if it be possible, let this cup pass from me; nevertheless, not as I will, but as thou wilt.
Acts 21:14. ...The will of the Lord be done. (Also Jms. 4:15.)
Ps. 28:8–9. The Lord is the strength of his people, he is the saving refuge of his anointed. O save thy people, and bless thy heritage; be thou their shepherd, and carry them for ever. (Also Deut. 26:15, Ps. 29:11.)
Ps. 115:12. ...The Lord has been mindful of us; he will bless us...

BWV 42
Am Abend aber desselbigen Sabbats
(NBA I/11; BC A63)

Quasimodogeniti: 1. S. after Easter (BWV 67, 42)
*1 Jn. 5:4–10 (Overcoming the world through faith; God's witness concerning his Son)
*Jn. 20:19–31 (Jesus appears twice to his disciples after his resurrection; unbelieving Thomas)
Librettist: Unknown; perhaps Christian Weiß the elder

1. Sinfonia (Probably from nonextant instrumental work)

2. Tenor Recit.
●Jesus appears to disciples secretly gathered: Jn. 20:19 (42-2)
Am   Abend   aber desselbigen Sabbats,
(On-the) evening, however, of-the-same Sabbath,

da   die Jünger versammlet und die Türen
when the disciples   gathered   and the doors

verschlossen waren aus Furcht vor den Juden,
locked   were (for) fear   of the Jews,

kam Jesus und   trat mitten ein.
came Jesus and entered amidst - (them).

*Jn. 20:19, 26. *On the evening of that day, the first day of the week, the doors being shut where the disciples were, for fear of the Jews, Jesus came and stood among them* and said to them, "Peace be with you." ...Eight days later, his disciples were again in the house, and Thomas was with them. The doors were shut, but Jesus came and stood among them, and said, "Peace be with you."
Lk. 24:36–37. As they were saying this, Jesus himself stood among them. But they were startled and frightened, and supposed that they saw a spirit.

3. Alto Aria
●Christ present where 2 or 3 are gathered in his name (42-3)
Wo   zwei und drei versammlet sind
Where two (or) three assembled   are

In Jesu teurem Namen,
In Jesus' precious name,

Da   stellt sich Jesus mitten ein
There appears - Jesus amidst - (them)

Und spricht darzu das Amen.
And speaks thereto the "Amen."

Denn was aus Lieb und Not geschieht,
For   what out-of love and need happens,
{For what is done out of love and need,}

Das bricht des Höchsten Ordnung nicht.
That breaks the Most-High's order   not.
{That does not break the regulation of the Most High.}

Mt. 18:19–20 [Christ]: I say to you, if two of you agree on earth about anything they ask, it will be done for them by my Father in heaven. For where two or three are gathered in my name, there am I in the midst of them.
1 Jn. 5:14. And this is the confidence which we have in [the Son of God], that if we ask anything according to his will he hears us.
Jn. 14:13–14 [Christ]: Whatever you ask in my name, I will do it, that the Father may be glorified in the Son; if you ask anything in my name, I will do it. (Also Jn. 16:23.)
Jn. 15:16 [Christ]: You did not choose me, but I chose you and appointed you that you should go and bear fruit and that your fruit should abide; so that whatever you ask the Father in my name, he may give it to you.
Jn. 15:7 [Christ]: If you abide in me, and my words abide in you, ask whatever you will, and it shall be done for you.
2 Cor. 1:20. For all the promises of God find their Yes in [Christ]. That is why we utter the Amen through him, to the glory of God.
Gal. 5:22–23. But the fruit of the Spirit is love, joy, peace, patience, kindness, goodness, faithfulness, gentleness, self-control; against such there is no law.

4. Chorale: Soprano & Tenor
●Despair not when under foe's attack, little band! (42-4)
Verzage nicht, o Häuflein klein,
Despair not, O   little-band,

Obgleich die Feinde   willens   sein,
Although (your) foes of-the-intention are,

Rom. 11:5. ...At the present time there is a remnant, chosen by grace.
Lk. 12:32. Fear not, little flock, for it is your Father's good pleasure to give you the kingdom.
*Jn. 20:19. On the evening of that day, the first day of the week, the doors being shut where the disciples were, for fear of the Jews...

150

Dich gänzlich zu verstören,
You completely to disquiet,

Und suchen deinen Untergang,
And (to) seek your downfall,

Davon dir wird recht angst und bang:
Whereof you (become) right fearful and alarmed:

Es wird nicht lange währen.
It will not long last.
{It will not last long.}

5. Bass Recit.

•Jesus appears to gathered disciples: a lesson for us (42-5)
Man kann hiervon ein schön Exempel sehen
One can in-this a beautiful example see
{One can see a beautiful example here}

An dem, was zu Jerusalem geschehen;
From that, which in Jerusalem did-happen;
{In what happened in Jerusalem;}

Denn da die Jünger sich versammlet hatten
For when the disciples themselves assembled had
{For when the disciples had gathered}

Im finstern Schatten,
In dark shadows,

Aus Furcht vor denen Juden,
(For) fear of the Jews,

So trat mein Heiland mitten ein,
Then stepped-in my Savior amidst - (them),
{Then my Savior stepped in amidst them,}

Zum Zeugnis, daß er seiner Kirche Schutz will sein.
For-a testimony, that he his church's protection will be.

Drum laßt die Feinde wüten!
Therefore let the foes rage!

6. Bass Aria

•Jesus is a shield for believers in persecution (42-6)
Jesus ist ein Schild der Seinen,
Jesus is a shield (for) his-own,

Wenn sie die Verfolgung trifft.
When them - persecution strikes.
{When persecution strikes them.}

Ihnen muß die Sonne scheinen
For-them must the sun shine
{The sun must shine for them}

Mit der goldnen Überschrift:
With (this) golden superscript:

Jn. 15:20 [Christ]: Remember the word that I said to you, "A servant is not greater than his master." If they persecuted me, they will persecute you...
Ps. 11:2. For lo, the wicked bend the bow, they have fitted their arrow to the string, to shoot in the dark at the upright in heart. (Also Ps. 13:3–4, 25:19, 27:2, 136:23–24.)
Ps. 37:1–2, 10, 12–13. Fret not yourself because of the wicked, be not envious of wrongdoers! For they will soon fade like the grass, and wither like the green herb...Yet a littlewhile, and the wicked will be no more; though you look well at his place, he will not be there...The wicked plots against the righteous, and gnashes his teeth at him; but the Lord laughs at the wicked, for he sees that his day is coming. (Also Ps. 37:14–15, 20, 32–33, 35–38.)

*Jn. 20:19. On the evening of that day, the first day of the week, the doors being shut where the disciples were, for fear of the Jews, Jesus came and stood among them and said to them, "Peace be with you."
Mt. 18:19–20 [Christ]: I say to you, if two of you agree on earth about anything they ask, it will be done for them by my Father in heaven. For where two or three are gathered in my name, there am I in the midst of them.
Ps. 28:8. The Lord is the strength of his people, he is the saving refuge of his anointed.
Mt. 16:18 [Christ]: I tell you...on this rock I will build my church, and the powers of death shall not prevail against it.
Jn. 16:33 [Christ]: I have said this to you, that in me you may have peace. In the world you have tribulation; but be of good cheer, I have overcome the world.
Jn. 1:5. The light shines in the darkness, and the darkness has not overcome it.
*1 Jn. 5:4–5. For whatever is born of God overcomes the world; and this is the victory that overcomes the world, our faith. Who is it that overcomes the world but he who believes that Jesus is the Son of God?
Mt. 28:16–20. Now the eleven disciples went to Galilee, to the mountain to which Jesus had directed them. And when they saw him they worshiped him; but some doubted. And Jesus came and said to them, "All authority in heaven and on earth has been given to me. Go therefore and make disciples of all nations, baptizing them in the name of the Father and of the Son and of the Holy Spirit, teaching them to observe all that I have commanded you; and lo, I am with you always to the close of the age."

Ps. 84:11. For the Lord God is a sun and shield...
Ps. 18:30 / 2 Sam. 22:31. ...He is a shield for all those who take refuge in him. (Also Ps. 33:20, 115:9–11, Prov. 30:5.)
Ps. 28:7. The Lord is my strength and my shield; in him my heart trusts; so I am helped, and my heart exults, and with my song I give thanks to him.
*1 Jn. 5:4–5. For whatever is born of God overcomes the world; and this is the victory that overcomes the world, our faith. Who is it that overcomes the world but he who believes that Jesus is the Son of God?
Mt. 10:28. Do not fear those who kill the body but cannot kill the soul; rather fear him who can destroy both soul and body in hell.
Acts 18:9–10. The Lord said to Paul one night in a vision, "Do not be afraid, but speak and do not be silent; for I am with you, and no man shall attack you to harm you..."

Jesus ist ein Schild der Seinen,
Jesus is a shield for his-own,

Wenn sie die Verfolgung trifft.
When them - persecution strikes.
{When persecution strikes them.}

7. Chorale (See also 126-6.)
●Prayer: Grant us peace and good government (42-7)
Verleih uns Frieden gnädichlich,
Grant us peace graciously,

Herr Gott, zu unsern Zeiten;
Lord God, for our times;

Es ist doch ja kein andrer nicht,
(There) is - indeed no other - ,

Der für uns könnte streiten,
Who for us could fight,

Denn du, unser Gott, alleine.
Than thou, our God, alone.

///

Gib unsern Fürsten und aller Obrigkeit
Give our princes and all government

Fried und gut Regiment,
Peace and good governance,

Daß wir unter ihnen
That we under them

Ein geruhig und stilles Leben führen mögen
A peaceful and quiet life may-lead

In aller Gottseligkeit und Ehrbarkeit.
In all godliness and respectability.

Amen.
Amen.

Jn. 10:27–29 [Christ]: My sheep hear my voice, and I know them, and they follow me; and I give them eternal life, and they shall never perish, and no one shall snatch them out of my hand. My Father, who has given them to me, is greater than all, and no one is able to snatch them out of the Father's hand.

Ps. 29:11. May the Lord give strength to his people! May the Lord bless his people with peace! (Also Ps. 122:6–7, 128:5–6, Is. 26:1–3.)
Is. 55:12. For you shall go out in joy, and be led forth in peace; the mountains and the hills before you shall break forth into singing, and all the trees of the field shall clap their hands. (Also Lev. 26:6.)
Ex. 14:13–14. And Moses said to the people, "Fear not, stand firm, and see the salvation of the Lord, which he will work for you today... The Lord will fight for you, and you have only to be still."
Deut. 3:22. You shall not fear them; for it is the Lord your God who fights for you. (Also Ex. 15:3, Deut. 1:30.)
Ps. 124:1–3. If it had not been the Lord who was on our side, let Israel now say—if it had not been the Lord who was on our side, when men rose up against us, then they would have swallowed us up alive, when their anger was kindled against us.

1 Tim. 2:1–2. First of all, then, I urge that supplications, prayers, intercessions, and thanksgivings be made for all men, for kings and all who are in high positions, that we may lead a quiet and peaceable life, godly and respectful in every way.
Rom. 13:1–2. Let every person be subject to the governing authorities. For there is no authority except from God, and those that exist have been instituted by God. Therefore he who resists the authorities resists what God has appointed, and those who resist will incur judgment. (Also Tit. 3:1.)
1 Pet. 2:13–14. Be subject for the Lord's sake to every human institution, whether it be to the emperor as supreme, or to governors as sent by him to punish those who do wrong and to praise those who do right.
Ps. 29:11. May the Lord give strength to his people! May the Lord bless his people with peace!
Ps. 147:12–14. Praise the Lord, O Jerusalem! Praise your God, O Zion! For he strengthens the bars of your gates; he blesses your sons within you. He makes peace in your borders...

BWV 43
Gott fähret auf mit Jauchzen
(NBA I/12; BC A77)

Ascension (BWV 37, 128, 43, 11)
*Acts 1:1–11 (Holy Spirit promised, Christ's ascension)
*Mk. 16:14–20 (Great commission, Christ's ascension)
Librettist: perhaps Christoph Helm

Part I

1. Chorus
●God has gone up with a shout: Ps. 47:5-6 (43-1)
Gott fähret auf mit Jauchzen und der Herr
God goes up with joyful-shouting and the Lord

*Acts 1:9–11. And when he had said this, as they were looking on, he was lifted up, and a cloud took him out of their sight. And while they were gazing into heaven as he went, behold, two men stood by them in white robes, and said, "Men of Galilee, why do you stand looking into heaven? This Jesus, who was taken up from you into heaven, will come in the same way as you saw him go into heaven."
Ps. 47:5–6. *God has gone up with a shout, the Lord with the sound of*

mit heller Posaunen. Lobsinget, lobsinget Gott,
with ringing trumpets. Sing-praises, sing-praises to-God,

lobsinget, lobsinget unserm Könige.
sing-praises, sing-praises to-our King.

2. Tenor Recit.
●Christ as victor: The heavenly host praises him (43-2)
Es will der Höchste sich
(Now) - would the Most-High for-himself

ein Siegsgepräng bereiten,
a pageantry-of-victory prepare,
{Now would the Most High prepare a pageantry of victory for himself,}

Da die Gefängnisse er selbst gefangen führt.
Since the prisons he himself captive leads.
{Since he himself leads captivity captive.}

Wer jauchzt ihm zu? Wer ist's,
Who cheers him - ? Who is-there,

der die Posaunen rührt?
who the trumpets (will-sound)?

Wer gehet ihm zur Seiten?
Who goes - to-(his) side?

Ist es nicht Gottes Heer,
Is it not God's host,

Das seines Namens Ehr,
Who of-his name's honor,

Heil, Preis, Reich, Kraft und Macht
Salvation, praise, kingdom, strength, and might

mit lauter Stimme singet
with loud voice does-sing

Und ihm nun ewiglich ein Halleluja bringet.
And him now eternally a "hallelujah" brings?

3. Tenor Aria
●Christ as victor over all: thousands praise him (43-3)
Ja tausend mal tausend begleiten den Wagen,
Yes, (a) thousand times (a) thousand accompany the chariot,

Dem König der Kön'ge lobsingend zu sagen,
The King of Kings in-songs-of-praise to tell,

Daß Erde und Himmel sich unter ihm schmiegt
That earth and heaven - beneath him bends

Und was er bezwungen, nun gänzlich erliegt.
And what he has-vanquished, now entirely lies-defeated.

a trumpet. Sing praises to God, sing praises! Sing praises to our King, sing praises!
Ps. 98:6. With trumpets and the sound of the horn make a joyful noise before the King, the Lord!

Ps. 68:24-27. Thy solemn processions are seen, O God, the processions of my God, my King, into the sanctuary—the singers in front, the minstrels last, between them maidens playing timbrels: "Bless God in the great congregation, the Lord, O you who are of Israel's fountain!" There is Benjamin, the least of them, in the lead, the princes of Judah in their throng, the princes of Zebulun, the princes of Naphtali.
Ps. 24:7-8, 10. Lift up your heads, O gates! and be lifted up, O ancient doors! that the King of glory may come in. Who is the King of glory? The Lord, strong and mighty, the Lord, mighty in battle!...He is the King of glory! (Also Ps. 24:9.) [Note: The church has traditionally used this psalm to celebrate Christ's ascension. See N.I.V. Study Bible, p. 808]
Ps. 68:18. [O Lord,] thou didst ascend the high mount, leading captives in thy train, and receiving gifts among men, even among the rebellious, that the Lord God may dwell there.
Eph. 4:8. Therefore it is said, "When he ascended on high he led a host of captives, and he gave gifts to men."
Ps. 68:11. The Lord gives the command; great is the host of those who bore the tidings; "The kings of the armies, they flee, they flee!"
1 Kings 22:19 / 2 Chron. 18:18. ...I saw the Lord sitting on his throne, and all the host of heaven (Luther: himmlische Heer) standing on his right hand and on his left.
Rev. 5:11-13. Then I looked, and I heard around the throne and the living creatures and the elders the voice of many angels, numbering myriads of myriads and thousands of thousands, saying with a loud voice, "Worthy is the Lamb who was slain, to receive power and wealth and wisdom and might and honor and glory and blessing!" And I heard every creature in heaven and on earth and under the earth and in the sea, and all therein, saying, "To him who sits upon the throne and to the Lamb be blessing and honor and glory and might for ever and ever!" (Also Rev. 4:8-11, 7:11-12.)
Rev. 19:6-7. Then I heard what seemed to be the voice of a great multitude...crying, "Hallelujah! For the Lord our God the Almighty reigns. Let us rejoice and exult and give him the glory..."

Ps. 68:17. With mighty chariotry, twice ten thousand, thousands upon thousands, the Lord came from Sinai into the holy place. (Also Dan. 7:10.)
Rev. 5:11-12. Then I looked, and I heard around the throne and the living creatures and the elders the voice of many angels, numbering myriads of myriads and thousands of thousands, saying with a loud voice, "Worthy is the Lamb who was slain..." (Also 1 Tim. 6:15-16, Rev. 17:14, 19:16.)
1 Pet. 3:22. [Christ] has gone into heaven and is at the right hand of God, with angels, authorities, and powers subject to him. (Also Heb. 2:7-8, 1 Cor. 15:25.)
Phil. 2:9-11. God has highly exalted him and bestowed on him the name which is above every name, that at the name of Jesus every knee should bow, in heaven and on earth and under the earth, and every tongue confess that Jesus Christ is Lord, to the glory of God the Father.

153

4. Soprano Recit.
●Ascension of Christ: Mk. 16:19 (43–4)
Und der Herr, nachdem er mit ihnen geredet hatte,
And the Lord,　after　he with them　had-spoken,

ward er aufgehoben gen Himmel und　　　sitzet
was　-　lifted-up　to　heaven　and (now) sits

zur　rechten Hand Gottes.
at-the right　hand of-God.

5. Soprano Aria (Strophic Poem Vs. 1)
●Ascension of Christ: Jesus has finished his work (43–5)
Mein Jesus hat nunmehr
My　Jesus has　now

Das Heilandwerk vollendet
(His) work-as-Savior completed

Und　nimmt die Wiederkehr
And (makes) (his)　return

Zu dem, der ihn gesendet.
To him, who him　sent.
{To him who sent him.}

Er schließt der Erde Lauf,
He finishes (his) earthly race;

Ihr Himmel, öffnet euch
Ye heavens, open　-

Und nehmt ihn　　　wieder auf!
And receive him (once) again　-!

Part II

6. Bass Recit. (Poem Vs. 2)
●Christ as victor over Satan, death, and sin (43–6)
　　Es kommt der Helden　Held,
(Now) -　comes the champion's champion

Des　　Satans Fürst und Schrecken,
(Who) (is) Satan's prince and　terror,

Der selbst den Tod gefällt,
Who even　-　death felled,
{Who felled even death itself,}

Getilgt　der Sünden Flecken,
Blotted-out　-　sin's　stains,

Zerstreut der Feinde Hauf;
Scattered　the enemy horde;

Ihr Kräfte,　eilt herbei
Ye powers, hasten here

*Mk. 16:19. *So then the Lord Jesus, after he had spoken to them, was taken up into heaven, and sat down at the right hand of God.*
*Acts 1:9. And when [Jesus] had said this, as they were looking on, he was lifted up, and a cloud took him out of their sight.
Lk. 24:50–51. Then he led them out as far as Bethany, and lifting up his hands he blessed them. While he blessed them, he parted from them, and was carried up into heaven.

Jn. 19:28–30. After this Jesus, knowing that all was now finished, said (to fulfil the scripture), "I thirst." A bowl full of vinegar stood there; so they put a sponge full of the vinegar on hyssop and held it to his mouth. When Jesus had received the vinegar, he said, "It is finished"; and he bowed his head and gave up his spirit.
Jn. 17:1, 4–5, 11, 13. [Jesus]...lifted up his eyes to heaven and said, "Father, the hour has come; glorify thy Son that the Son may glorify thee...I glorified thee on earth, having accomplished the work which thou gavest me to do; and now, Father, glorify thou me in thy own presence with the glory which I had with thee before the world was made...And now I am no more in the world, but they are in the world, and I am coming to thee... But now I am coming to thee; and these things I speak in the world, that they may have my joy fulfilled in themselves."
Heb. 10:12–13. But when Christ had offered for all time a single sacrifice for sins, he sat down at the right hand of God, then to wait until his enemies should be made a stool for his feet. (Also Ps. 110:1.)
Ps. 24:7/9. Lift up your heads, O gates! and be lifted up, O ancient doors! that the King of glory (Luther: König der Ehren) may come in. [Note: The church has traditionally used this psalm to celebrate Christ's ascension.]

Rev. 5:5. ...Lo, the Lion of the tribe of Judah, the Root of David, has conquered...
Col. 2:15. He disarmed the principalities and powers and made a public example of them, triumphing over them in him.
Heb. 2:14–15. ...[Christ] himself likewise partook of the same nature, that through death he might destroy him who has the power of death, that is, the devil, and deliver all those who through fear of death were subject to lifelong bondage.
1 Jn. 3:8. ...The reason the Son of God appeared was to destroy the works of the devil.
1 Cor. 15:54–57. ...Then shall come to pass the saying that is written: "Death is swallowed up in victory." O death, where is thy victory? O death, where is thy sting? The sting of death is sin, and the power of sin is the law. But thanks be to God, who gives us the victory through our Lord Jesus Christ.
Is. 43:25 [God]: I, I am He who blots out (Luther: tilge) your transgressions for my own sake, and I will not remember your sins. (Also Is 44:22.)
Is. 53:12 [God]: I will divide him a portion with the great, and he shall divide the spoil with the strong; because he poured out his soul to

Und holt den Sieger auf.
And hoist the   victor   up.
{And carry the victor high.}

7. Bass Aria (Poem Vs. 3)
●Christ as victor trod the winepress to save the lost (43-7)
Er ist's, der ganz allein
He it-is, who all   alone

Die   Kelter   hat getreten
The wine-press has trodden

Voll   Schmerzen, Qual   und Pein,
Full-of suffering, torment, and pain,

Verlorne zu erretten
Lost-ones to   save

Durch einen teuren Kauf.
Through a   costly purchase.

Ihr Thronen, mühet euch
Ye thro-nes,   (stir) yourselves

Und setzt ihm Kränze auf!
And set on-him garlands - !
{And set garlands upon him!}

8. Alto Recit. (Poem Vs. 4)
●Ascension: Christ receives the appointed kingdom (43-8)
Der Vater hat ihm   ja
The Father has him indeed

Ein ewig   Reich bestimmet:
An eternal kingdom allotted:

Nun ist die Stunde nah,
Now is the   hour at-hand,

Da   er die Krone nimmet
When he the crown receives

Vor   tausend Ungemach.
For (bearing a) thousand hardships.

Ich stehe hier am Weg
I   stand here by-the-way

Und schau ihm freudig nach.
And gaze him happily after.
{And gaze after him happily.}

9. Alto Aria (Poem Vs. 5)
●Christ victorious can be seen at God's right hand (43-9)
Ich sehe schon   im Geist,
I   see   already in-the spirit,

death, and was numbered with the transgressors; yet he bore the sin of many and made intercession for the transgressors.

Is. 63:2-3. Why is thy apparel red, and thy garments like his that treads in the wine press? I have trodden the wine press alone, and from the peoples no one was with me; I trod them in my anger and trampled them in my wrath; their lifeblood is sprinkled upon my garments, and I have stained all my raiment. **Rev. 14:10, 19-20.** [He who worships the beast and his image] shall drink the wine of God's wrath...So the angel swung his sickle on the earth and gathered the vintage of the earth, and threw it into the great wine press of the wrath of God; and the wine press was trodden outside the city...
Heb. 12:2. [Let us look] to Jesus the pioneer and perfecter of our faith, who for the joy that was set before him endured the cross, despising the shame, and is seated at the right hand of the throne of God.
1 Pet. 1:18-19. You know that you were ransomed from the futile ways inherited from your fathers, not with perishable things such as silver or gold, but with the precious blood of Christ, like that of a lamb without blemish or spot. (Also 1 Cor. 6:20, 7:23.)
Lk. 19:10. The Son of man came to seek and to save the lost.
Rev. 19:11-13. Then I saw heaven opened, and behold, a white horse! He who sat upon it is called Faithful and True...His eyes are like a flame of fire, and on his head are many diadems...He is clad in a robe dipped in blood, and the name by which he is called is The Word of God. (Also Rev. 6:2.)

Heb. 2:9. But we see Jesus, who for a little while was made lower than the angels, crowned with glory and honor because of the suffering of death... (Also Heb. 12:2.)
Lk. 22:29-30 [Christ]: I assign to you, as my Father assigned to me, a kingdom, that you may eat and drink at my table in my kingdom, and sit on thrones judging the twelve tribes of Israel.
Col. 1:13-14. He has delivered us from the dominion of darkness and transferred us to the kingdom of his beloved Son, in whom we have redemption, the forgiveness of sins.
2 Tim. 2:12. We shall also reign with him... (Also 1 Pet. 1:21.)
Acts 2:32-33. This Jesus God raised up...being therefore exalted at the right hand of God...
Phil. 2:9-11. God has highly exalted him and bestowed on him the name which is above every name, that at the name of Jesus every knee should bow, in heaven and on earth and under the earth, and every tongue confess that Jesus Christ is Lord, to the glory of God the Father.
*Acts 1:10-11. And while [the disciples] were gazing into heaven as he went, behold, two men stood by them in white robes, and said, "Men of Galilee, why do you stand looking into heaven? This Jesus, who was taken up from you into heaven, will come in the same way as you saw him go into heaven."

Acts 7:55-56. [Stephen], full of the Holy Spirit, gazed into heaven and saw the glory of God, and Jesus standing at the right hand of God; and he said, "Behold, I see the heavens opened, and the Son of man standing at the right hand of God."

Wie er zu Gottes Rechten
How he at God's right (hand)

Auf seine Feinde schmeißt,
Upon his enemies hurls (judgment),

Zu helfen seinen Knechten
To help his servants

Aus Jammer, Not und Schmach.
Out-of wretchedness, distress, and humiliation.

Ich stehe hier am Weg
I stand here by-the way

Und schau ihm sehnlich nach.
And gaze him yearningly after.
{And gaze yearningly after him.}

10. Soprano Recit. (Poem Vs. 6)
●Ascension: Christ goes to prepare a place for me (43-10)
Er will mir neben sich
He would for-me next-to himself
{He would, at his side,}

Die Wohnung zubereiten,
(My) dwelling prepare,

Damit ich ewiglich
So-that I eternally

Ihm stehe an der Seiten,
- Stand at (his) side,

Befreit von Weh und Ach!
Freed from woe and "Ah"!

Ich stehe hier am Weg
I stand here by-the way

Und ruf ihm dankbar nach.
And call him thankfully after.
{And call after him thankfully.}

11. Chorale
●Ascension: Christ victorious; yearning to join him (43-11)
Du Lebensfürst, Herr Jesu Christ,
Thou Prince-of-Life, Lord Jesus Christ,

Der du bist aufgenommen
(Who) art taken-up

Gen Himmel, da dein Vater ist
To heaven, where thy Father is

Ps. 110:1–2, 5–6. The Lord says to my lord: "Sit at my right hand, till I make your enemies your footstool." The Lord sends forth from Zion your mighty scepter. Rule in the midst of your foes!...The Lord is at your right hand; he will shatter kings on the day of his wrath. He will execute judgment among the nations, filling them with corpses; he will shatter chiefs over the wide earth.
1 Cor. 15:25. [Christ] must reign until he has put all his enemies under his feet.
Eph. 1:20–22. ...When [God] raised him from the dead and made him sit at his right hand in the heavenly places, far above all rule and authority and power and dominion, and above every name that is named, not only in this age but also in that which is to come; and he has put all things under his feet and has made him the head over all things...
Lk. 1:52–53. [The Lord] has put down the mighty from their thrones, and exalted those of low degree; he has filled the hungry with good things, and the rich he has sent empty away. (Also 1 Sam. 2:7–10, Ps. 113:7–8.)
*****Acts 1:9.** And when [Jesus] had said this, as they were looking on, he was lifted up, and a cloud took him out of their sight.

Jn. 14:1–3 [Christ]: Let not your hearts be troubled; believe in God, believe also in me. In my Father's house are many rooms; if it were not so, would I have told you that I go to prepare a place for you? And when I go and prepare a place for you, I will come again and will take you to myself, that where I am you may be also.
Jn. 12:26 [Christ]: ...Where I am, there shall my servant be also; if any one serves me, the Father will honor him.
2 Tim. 2:11–12. The saying is sure: If we have died with him, we shall also live with him; if we endure, we shall also reign with him... (Also Rom. 8:17, 1 Pet. 4:13.)
Rev. 20:6. Blessed and holy is he who shares in the first resurrection! Over such the second death has no power, but they shall be priests of God and of Christ, and they shall reign with him a thousand years.
Mt. 25:34. Then the King will say to those at his right hand, "Come, O blessed of my Father, inherit the kingdom prepared for you from the foundation of the world..."
Rev. 21:4. [God] will wipe away every tear from their eyes, and death shall be no more, neither shall there be mourning nor crying nor pain any more, for the former things have passed away. (Also Rev. 7:15–17.)
*****Acts 1:9.** And when [Jesus] had said this, as they were looking on, he was lifted up, and a cloud took him out of their sight.

Acts 3:15. ...the Author of life (Luther: Fürsten des Lebens), whom God raised from the dead.
Heb. 10:12. But when Christ had offered for all time a single sacrifice for sins, he sat down at the right hand of God.
Acts 5:31. God exalted him at his right hand as Leader and Savior...
1 Jn. 3:8. ...The reason the Son of God appeared was to destroy the works of the devil.

Und die Gemein der Frommen,
And the community of-the godly;

Wie soll ich deinen großen Sieg,
How shall I thy great victory,

Den du durch einen schweren Krieg
Which thou through a difficult warfare

Erworben hast, recht preisen
Obtained hast, fittingly praise

Und dir g'nug Ehr erweisen?
And thee sufficient honor render?
{How shall I fittingly praise thy great victory, which thou hast obtained through a difficult warfare, and render thee sufficient honor?}

///

Zieh uns dir nach, so laufen wir,
Draw us thee after, so run we,
{Draw us after thee, and we will run,}

Gib uns des Glaubens Flügel!
Give us - faith's wings!

Hilf, daß wir fliehen weit von hier
Help, that we (might) flee far from here

Auf Israelis Hügel!
(To) Israel's hills!

Mein Gott! wenn fahr ich doch dahin,
My God! When travel I indeed thither,
{My God, when shall I indeed travel thither,}

Woselbst ich ewig fröhlich bin?
To-the-place-where I eternally happy (will-be)?

Wenn werd ich vor dir stehen,
When shall I before thee stand,
{When shall I stand before thee,}

Dein Angesicht zu sehen?
Thy countenance to see?

Rev. 3:21 [Christ]: He who conquers, I will grant him to sit with me on my throne, as I myself conquered and sat down with my Father on his throne.
Heb. 2:14–15. ...[Christ] himself likewise partook of the same nature, that through death he might destroy him who has the power of death, that is, the devil, and deliver all those who through fear of death were subject to lifelong bondage.
Col. 2:15. He disarmed the principalities and powers and made a public example of them, triumphing over them in him.
1 Cor. 15:54–57. When the perishable puts on the imperishable, and the mortal puts on immortality, then shall come to pass the saying that is written: "Death is swallowed up in victory." O death, where is thy victory? O death, where is thy sting? The sting of death is sin, and the power of sin is the law. But thanks be to God, who gives us the victory through our Lord Jesus Christ.

Mt. 14:28. Peter anwered [Jesus], "Lord, if it is you, bid me come to you..."
S. of S. 1:4. Draw me after you, let us make haste... (Luther: Zieh mich dir nach, so laufen wir)
Jn. 12:30, 32. Jesus answered, "...I, when I am lifted up from the earth, will draw all men to myself."
Heb. 12:1–2. ...Let us run with perseverance the race that is set before us, looking to Jesus the pioneer and perfecter of our faith, who for the joy that was set before him endured the cross, despising the shame, and is seated at the right hand of the throne of God.
1 Thess. 4:16–18. The Lord himself will descend from heaven with a cry of command, with the archangel's call, and with the sound of the trumpet of God. And the dead in Christ will rise first; then we who are alive, who are left, shall be caught up together with them in clouds to meet the Lord in the air; and so we shall always be with the Lord. Therefore comfort one another with these words.
Ps. 55:5–6. ...O that I had wings like a dove! I would fly away and be at rest.
Is. 40:31. They who wait for the Lord shall renew their strength, they shall mount up with wings like eagles, they shall run and not be weary, they shall walk and not faint.
Heb. 12:22. But you have come to Mount Zion and to the city of the living God, the heavenly Jerusalem...
1 Jn. 3:2. ...We shall be like him, for we shall see him as he is. (Also Rev. 22:4.)
1 Cor. 13:12. For now we see in a mirror dimly, but then face to face. Now I know in part; then I shall understand fully, even as I have been fully understood.

BWV 44
Sie werden euch in den Bann tun I
(NBA I/12; BC A78)

Exaudi: 1. S. after Ascension (BWV 44, 183)
*1 Pet. 4:7[1]-11 (Exhortation to serve one another with the gift each has received)
*Jn. 15:26-16:4 (Farewell address of Jesus: Holy Spirit promised, persecution foretold)
[1]Begin: "Therefore keep sane and sober..."
Librettist: Unknown; perhaps Christian Weiß the elder

1. Tenor & Bass Duet
●Persecution of disciples foretold: Jn. 16:2 (44-1)
Sie werden euch in den   Bann   tun.
They will   you into - excommunication place.
{They will excommunicate you.}

2. Chorus
●Persecutors think they please God: Jn. 16:2 (44-2)
Es   kömmt aber die Zeit, daß,   wer euch tötet,
(There) comes however (a) time, (when), whoever you   kills,
{There will come a a time, however, when, whoever kills you,}

wird meinen, er tue Gott eine Dienst daran.
will   think, he does God a   service thereby.

3. Alto Aria
●Persecution awaits true disciples of Christ (44-3)
Christen müssen auf der Erden
Christians must   on - earth

Christi wahre Jünger sein.
Christ's true disciples be.

Auf sie warten alle Stunden,
For-them awaits at-all hours—

Bis sie selig überwinden,
Till they blessedly overcome—

Marter, Bann und schwere Pein.
Torture, ban, and grievous pain.

4. Chorale: Tenor (See also 58-1, 3-1.)
●Affliction fills the narrow path of pilgrimage (44-4)
Ach Gott, wie manches Herzeleid
Ah, God, how many-a   grief

Begegnet mir zu dieser Zeit.
Meets   me in this time.

Der schmale Weg ist trübsalvoll,
The narrow   way is affliction-filled,

Jn. 16:1-4 [Christ]: I have said all this to you to keep you from falling away. *They will put you out of the synagogues; indeed, the hour is coming when whoever kills you will think he is offering service to God.* And they will do this because they have not known the Father, nor me. But I have said these things to you, that when their hour comes you may remember that I told you of them...
Lk. 21:12 [Christ]: ...They will lay their hands on you and persecute you, delivering you up to the synagogues and prisons, and you will be brought before kings and governors for my name's sake.
Jn. 9:22. ...The Jews had already agreed that if any one should confess him to be Christ, he was to be put out of the synagogue (Luther: in den Bann getan würde).
Gal. 1:13-14 [Paul]: You have heard of my former life in Judaism, how I persecuted the church of God violently and tried to destroy it; and I advanced in Judaism beyond many of my own age among my people, so extremely zealous was I for the traditions of my fathers. (Also Phil. 3:4-6.)

2 Tim. 3:12. Indeed all who desire to live a godly life in Christ Jesus will be persecuted.
Jn. 15:19-20 [Christ]: If you were of the world, the world would love its own; but because you are not of the world, but I chose you out of the world, therefore the world hates you. Remember the word that I said to you, "A servant is not greater than his master." If they persecuted me, they will persecute you.
Mt. 5:10-12. Blessed are those who are persecuted for righteousness' sake, for theirs is the kingdom of heaven. Blessed are you when men revile you and persecute you and utter all kinds of evil against you falsely on my account. Rejoice and be glad, for your reward is great in heaven, for so men persecuted the prophets who were before you.
Rev. 2:7 [Christ]: ...To him who conquers I will grant to eat of the tree of life, which is in the paradise of God. (Also Rev. 2:11, 2:17, 2:26, 3:5, 3:12, 3:21, 21:7.)

Jn. 16:33 [Christ]: I have said this to you, that in me you may have peace. In the world you have tribulation; but be of good cheer, I have overcome the world.
Mt. 7:14 [Christ]: The gate is narrow and the way is hard, that leads to life, and those who find it are few.
Mt. 16:24 [Christ]: If any man would come after me, let him deny himself and take up his cross and follow me.
1 Pet. 4:12-13. Beloved, do not be surprised at the fiery ordeal which comes upon you to prove you, as though something strange were happening to you. But rejoice in so far as you share Christ's sufferings,

Den ich zum Himmel wandern soll.
Which I to heaven travel must.
{The narrow way, which I must travel to heaven, is filled with affliction.}

that you may also rejoice and be glad when his glory is revealed.
Acts 14:22. ...Through many tribulations (Luther: Trübsal) we must enter the kingdom of God.

5. Bass Recit.
●Antichrist persecutes, hates our teaching but in vain (44-5)
Es sucht der Antichrist,
(Now) seeks the Antichrist,

Das große Ungeheuer,
That great monster,
{The Antichrist, that great monster, seeks}

Mit Schwert und Feuer
With sword and fire

Die Glieder Christi zu verfolgen,
The members of-Christ to persecute,
{To persecute the members of Christ,}

Weil ihre Lehre ihm zuwider ist.
Because their teaching to-him repugnant is.
{Because their teaching is repugnant to him.}

Er bildet sich dabei wohl ein,
He flatters himself therewith no-doubt - ,

Es müsse sein Tun Gott gefällig sein.
(That) - must his actions to-God pleasing be.
{That his actions must be pleasing to God.}

Allein, es gleichen Christen denen Palmenzweigen,
But, (now) resemble Christians - palm-branches,
{But Christians resemble palm branches,}

Die durch die Last nur desto höher steigen.
Which, through (their) load, just that-much higher climb.

1 Jn. 2:18. Children, it is the last hour; and as you have heard that antichrist is coming, so now many antichrists have come; therefore we know that it is the last hour. (Also 2 Thess. 2:3-4.)
1 Pet. 5:8. Be sober, be watchful. Your adversary the devil prowls around like a roaring lion, seeking some one to devour.
Heb. 11:35-37. ...Some [heroes of faith were tortured, refusing to accept release, that they might rise again to a better life. Others suffered mockings and scourging, and even chains and imprisonment. They were stoned, they were sawn in two, they were killed with the sword; they went about in skins of sheep and goats, destitute, afflicted, ill-treated...
2 Tim. 4:3-4. The time is coming when people will not endure sound teaching, but having itching ears they will accumulate for themselves teachers to suit their own likings, and will turn away from listening to the truth and wander into myths.
***Jn. 16:2-3 [Christ]:** ...Indeed, the hour is coming when whoever kills you will think he is offering service to God. And they will do this because they have not known the Father, nor me.
Rom. 10:2. I bear them witness that they have a zeal for God, but it is not enlightened.
1 Pet. 1:6-7. In this you rejoice, though now for a little while you may have to suffer various trials, so that the genuineness of your faith, more precious than gold which though perishable is tested by fire, may redound to praise and glory and honor at the revelation of Jesus Christ.
Jms. 1:2-4. Count it all joy, my brethren, when you meet various trials, for you know that the testing of your faith produces steadfastness. And let steadfastness have its full effect, that you may be perfect and complete, lacking in nothing.

6. Soprano Aria
●Persecution's storms: God watches over church (44-6)
Es ist und bleibt der Christen Trost,
It is and remains the Christian's comfort,

Daß Gott vor seine Kirche wacht.
That God (over) his church does-watch.

Denn wenn sich gleich die Wetter türmen,
For even-though the storms pile-up,

So hat doch nach den Trübsalstürmen
Yet has nevertheless after the storms-of-tribulation
{Yet soon after the storms of tribulation,}

Die Freudensonne bald gelacht.
The sun-of-gladness soon laughed.
{The sun of gladness laughs.}

Mt. 16:18 [Christ]: ...On this rock I will build my church, and the powers of death shall not prevail against it.
Ps. 121:3-4. ...He who keeps you will not slumber. Behold, he who keeps Israel will neither slumber nor sleep.
Ps. 30:5. ...Weeping may tarry for the night, but joy comes with the morning.
2 Tim. 2:11-12. The saying is sure: If we have died with him, we shall also live with him; if we endure, we shall also reign with him...
Rom. 8:18. I consider that the sufferings of this present time are not worth comparing with the glory that is to be revealed to us. (Also 2 Cor. 4:17.)
1 Pet. 5:9-10. Resist [the devil], firm in your faith, knowing that the same experience of suffering is required of your brotherhood throughout the world. And after you have suffered a little while, the God of all grace, who has called you to his eternal glory in Christ, will himself restore, establish, and strengthen you.

7. Chorale (See also 13-6, 97-9.)
●Exhortation to trust sovereignty of God (44-7)
So sei nun, Seele, deine
So be therefore, (O) soul, thine (own self true)

Und traue dem alleine,
And trust him alone,

Der dich erschaffen hat.
Who thee created hath.

Es gehe, wie es gehe,
(Let) it happen, as it (may) happen,

Dein Vater in der Höhe,
Thy father in the highest,

Der weiß zu allen Sachen Rat.
He knows for all matters counsel.

BWV 45
Es ist dir gesagt, Mensch, was gut ist
(NBA I/18; BC A113)

8. S. after Trinity (BWV 136, 178, 45)
*Rom. 8:12-17 (All who are led by the Spirit of God are sons of God)
*Mt. 7:15-23 (Sermon on the Mount: beware of false prophets, you will know them by their fruits)
Librettist: perhaps Christoph Helm

Part I

1. Chorus
●Righteous living is what God requires: Mic. 6:8 (45-1)
Es ist dir gesagt, Mensch, was gut ist und was
It (has) you been-told, (O) Man, what good is and what

der Herr von dir fordert, nämlich: Gottes Wort halten
the Lord of you demands, namely: God's Word to-hold,

und Liebe üben und demütig sein vor deinem Gott.
and love to-practice, and humble to-be before your God.

2. Tenor Recit.
●God's will is made known, servants must obey (45-2)
Der Höchste läßt mich seinen Willen wissen
The Most-High lets me his will know
{The Most High lets me know his will}

Und was ihm wohlgefällt;
And what to-him is-well-pleasing;
{And what is well-pleasing to him;}

Er hat sein Wort zur Richtschnur dargestellt,
He has his Word as plumb-line provided,

Lk. 21:19 [Christ]: By your endurance you will gain your lives (Luther: Fasset eure Seele mit Geduld).
Ps. 62:1-2. For God alone my soul waits in silence; from him comes my salvation. He only is my rock and my salvation, my fortress; I shall not be greatly moved. (Also Ps. 62:5-6.)
1 Pet. 4:19. Therefore let those who suffer according to God's will do right and entrust their souls to a faithful Creator.
Is. 64:8. ...O Lord, thou art our Father; we are the clay, and thou art our potter; we are all the work of thy hand.
Lk. 22:41-42. And [Jesus] withdrew from them about a stone's throw, and knelt down and prayed, "Father, if thou art willing, remove this cup from me; nevertheless not my will, but thine, be done."
Jn. 5:30 [Christ]: ...I seek not my own will but the will of him who sent me.
Jms. 5:10-11. As an example of suffering and patience, brethren, take the prophets who spoke in the name of the Lord. Behold, we call those happy who were steadfast. You have heard of the steadfastness of Job, and you have seen the purpose of the Lord, how the Lord is compassionate and merciful.
Ps. 73:24. [O Lord,] thou dost guide me with thy counsel (Luther: Rat), and afterward thou wilt receive me to glory.

*Mt. 7:16-19, 21 [Christ]: You will know them by their fruits. Are grapes gathered from thorns, or figs from thistles? So, every sound tree bears good fruit, but the bad tree bears evil fruit. A sound tree cannot bear evil fruit, nor can a bad tree bear good fruit...Not every one who says to me, "Lord, Lord," shall enter the kingdom of heaven, but he who does the will of my Father who is in heaven.
Mic. 6:6-8. With what shall I come before the Lord, and bow myself before God on high? Shall I come before him with burnt offerings, with calves a year old? Will the Lord be pleased with thousands of rams, with ten thousands of rivers of oil? Shall I give my first-born for my transgression, the fruit of my body for the sin of my soul? *He has showed you, O man, what is good; and what does the Lord require of you but to do justice, and to love kindness, and to walk humbly with your God?* (Also Ps. 40:6-8.)
Jms. 1:22. Be doers of the word, and not hearers only, deceiving yourselves.

Mic. 6:8. He has showed you, O man, what is good; and what does the Lord require...
Is. 28:17 [God]: I will make justice the line (Luther: Richtschnur), and righteousness the plummet...
Lk. 11:28. [Jesus] said, "Blessed rather are those who hear the word of God and keep it!" (Also Lk. 8:21.)
1 Jn. 2:4-5. He who says "I know him" but disobeys his commandments is a liar, and the truth is not in him; but whoever keeps his word, in him truly love for God is perfected. (Also 1 Jn. 1:6, 3:17, 5:3.)
Ps. 119:1-6. Blessed are those whose way is blameless, who walk in the law of the Lord! Blessed are those who keep his testimonies, who

Wornach   mein Fuß soll sein geflissen
According-to-which my foot is to-be diligently

Allzeit   einherzugehn
At-all-times proceeding
{According to which my foot is to proceed diligently at all times,}

Mit Furcht, mit Demut und mit Liebe
With fear, with humility, and with love,

Als Proben des Gehorsams, den ich   übe,
As tests of-my obedience, which I (must) practice,

Um als ein treuer Knecht dereinsten
So-that as a faithful servant in-the-future

        zu bestehn.
        (I) be-proven.
{So that I be proven a faithful servant some day.}

3. Tenor Aria
●Servants of God will have to give strict account (45-3)
Weiß ich Gottes Rechte,
Know I God's justice,
{If I know God's justice,}

Was ist's, das mir helfen kann,
What is-there, that me can-help,
{What can help me,}

Wenn er   mir als seinem Knechte
When he (from) me as his   servant

Fordert   scharfe Rechnung an?
Demands (a) strict   account - ?

    Seele, denke dich zu retten,
(O) Soul, plan thyself to save,
{O Soul, plan to save thyself;}

Auf Gehorsam folget Lohn;
Upon obedience follows reward;

Qual   und Hohn
Torment and derision

Drohet deinem Übertreten!
Threatens thy transgressing!

Part II

4. Bass Arioso (Vox Christi)
●Judgment Day: Many rejected as evildoers: Mt. 7:22-23
(45-4)
Es werden viele zu mir sagen an jenem Tage:
(Then) will many to me say on that day:
{Then many will say to me on that day:}

seek him with their whole heart, who also do no wrong, but walk in his ways! Thou hast commanded thy precepts to be kept diligently. O that my ways may be steadfast in keeping thy statutes! Then I shall not be put to shame, having my eyes fixed on all thy commandments. **Ps. 5:8.** Lead me, O Lord, in thy righteousness...make thy way straight before me.
Heb. 12:13. Make straight paths for your feet, so that what is lame may not be put out of joint but rather be healed.
Ps. 119:105. [O Lord,] thy word is a lamp to my feet and a light to my path. (Also Ps. 119:11, 119, 130.)
Deut. 10:12-13. And now, Israel, what does the Lord your God require of you, but to fear the Lord your God, to walk in all his ways, to love him, to serve the Lord your God with all your heart and with all your soul, and to keep the commandments and statutes of the Lord...
Deut. 5:33. You shall walk in all the way which the Lord your God has commanded you, that you may live, and that it may go well with you...
1 Sam. 15:22. ...Behold, to obey is better than sacrifice, and to hearken than the fat of rams. (Also Hos. 6:6.)
Jn. 15:14 [Christ]: You are my friends if you do what I command you.

Rom. 2:6-8. [God] will render to every man according to his works: to those who by patience in well-doing seek for glory and honor and immortality, he will give eternal life; but for those who are factious and do not obey the truth, but obey wickedness, there will be wrath and fury.
2 Cor. 5:10. For we must all appear before the judgment seat of Christ, so that each one may receive good or evil, according to what he has done in the body. (Also Mt. 16:27, Acts 10:42, 1 Pet. 4:5, 2 Tim. 4:1, Rev. 20:12.)
Lk. 12:42-47. And the Lord said, "Who then is the faithful and wise steward, whom his master will set over his household, to give them their portion of food at the proper time? Blessed is that servant whom his master when he comes will find so doing. Truly, I say to you, he will set him over all his possessions. But if that servant says to himself, 'My master is delayed in coming,' and begins to beat the menservants and the maidservants, and to eat and drink and get drunk, the master of that servant will come on a day when he does not expect him and at an hour he does not know, and will punish him, and put him with the unfaithful. And that servant who knew his master's will, but did not make ready or act according to his will, shall receive a severe beating." (Also Mt. 24:45-51, 18:23-35, 25:14-30.)
Mt. 13:41-42. The Son of man will send his angels, and they will gather out of his kingdom all causes of sin and all evildoers, and throw them into the furnace of fire; there men will weep and gnash their teeth. (Also Mt. 13:50, 22:13, 24:51, 25:30, Lk. 13:28.)
***Rom. 8:13.** If you live according to the flesh you will die, but if by the Spirit you put to death the deeds of the body you will live. (Also 1 Pet. 1:17.)

***Mt. 7:21-27** [Christ]: Not every one who says to me, "Lord, Lord," shall enter the kingdom of heaven, but he who does the will of my Father who is in heaven. *On that day many will say to me, "Lord, Lord, did we not prophesy in your name, and cast out demons in your name,*

Herr, Herr, haben wir nicht in deinem Namen
Lord, Lord, have we not in thy name

geweissaget, haben wir nicht in deinem Namen
prophesied; have we not in thy name

Teufel ausgetrieben, haben wir nicht in deinem Namen
demons cast-out; have we not in thy name

viel Taten getan? Denn werde ich ihnen bekennen:
many works performed? Then will I to-them declare:

Ich habe euch noch nie erkannt, weichet alle
I have you yet never known, depart all (of you)
{I have never known you; depart from me, all of you,}

von mir, ihr Übeltäter!
from me, ye evildoers!
{ye evildoers!}

5. Alto Aria
●Acknowledging Christ sincerely before men (45-5)
Wer Gott bekennt
Whoever God acknowledges

Aus wahrem Herzensgrund,
From-the true bottom-of-his-heart,
{Whoever sincerely acknowledges God from the bottom of his heart,}

Den will er auch bekennen.
Him will he also acknowledge.

Denn der muß ewig brennen,
For he must eternally burn,

Der einzig mit dem Mund
Who only with (his) mouth

Ihn Herren nennt.
Him Lord calls.
{For whoever calls him Lord with his mouth only must eternally burn.}

6. Alto Recit.
●Judgment self-determined; God helps us do his will (45-6)
So wird denn Herz und Mund selbst
So will therefore (my own) heart and mouth themselves

von mir Richter sein,
(my) judge be,
{So my heart and mouth themselves will be my judge,}

Und Gott will mir den Lohn
And God will me the reward

and do many mighty works in your name?" And then will I declare to them, "I never knew you; depart from me, you evildoers." Every one then who hears these words of mine and does them will be like a wise man who built his house upon the rock; and the rain fell, and the floods came, and the winds blew and beat upon that house, but it did not fall, because it had been founded on the rock. And every one who hears these words of mine and does not do them will be like a foolish man who built his house upon the sand; and the rain fell, and the floods came, and the winds blew and beat against that house, and it fell; and great was the fall of it. (Also Lk. 6:43–49.)
Rom. 2:13. For it is not the hearers of the law who are righteous before God but the doers of the law who will be justified.
Jms. 1:22. Be doers of the word, and not hearers only, deceiving yourselves.
Lk. 6:46 [Christ]: Why do you call me "Lord, Lord," and not do what I tell you?

Mt. 10:32–33 [Christ]: So every one who acknowledges me before men, I also will acknowledge before my Father who is in heaven; but whoever denies me before men, I also will deny before my Father who is in heaven. (Also Lk. 12:8–9.)
2 Tim. 2:11–12. The saying is sure: If we have died with him, we shall also live with him; if we endure, we shall also reign with him; if we deny him, he also will deny us.
Rom. 10:9–10. If you confess with your lips (Luther: Munde) that Jesus is Lord and believe in your heart that God raised him from the dead, you will be saved. For man believes with his heart and so is justified, and he confesses with his lips (Luther: Munde) and so is saved.
***Mt. 7:15–16, 19, 23 [Christ]:** Beware of false prophets, who come to you in sheep's clothing but inwardly are ravenous wolves. You will know them by their fruits...Every tree that does not bear good fruit is cut down and thrown into the fire...I [will] declare to them, "I never knew you; depart from me, you evildoers."
2 Tim. 2:19. God's firm foundation stands, bearing this seal: "The Lord knows those who are his," and, "Let every one who names the name of the Lord depart from iniquity."
Mt. 13:41–42. The Son of man will send his angels, and they will gather out of his kingdom all causes of sin and all evildoers, and throw them into the furnace of fire; there men will weep and gnash their teeth. (Also Mt. 13:50, 22:13, 24:51, 25:30, Lk. 13:28.)

Lk. 19:22. [A master who was settling accounts with his servants] said to [his slothful servant], "I will condemn you out of your own mouth, you wicked servant..."
Mt. 7:16. You will know [men] by their fruits...
Lk. 6:43–45. No good tree bears bad fruit, nor again does a bad tree bear good fruit; for each tree is known by its own fruit. For figs are not gathered from thorns, nor are grapes picked from a bramble bush. The good man out of the good treasure of his heart produces good, and the evil man out of his evil treasure produces evil; for out of the abundance of the heart his mouth speaks.

nach   meinem Sinn   erteilen:
according-to my   inclination apportion:
{And God will apportion the reward to me according to my inclination:}

Trifft   nun mein Wandel nicht nach seinen Worten ein,
(Accords) now   my   walk   not   with   his   words - ,
{If my walk does not accord with his words,}

Wer will hernach   der Seelen Schaden heilen?
Who will afterwards (my) soul's   harm   heal?
{Who will heal my soul's harm afterwards?}

Was mach ich mir denn   selber Hindernis?
Why create I   -   then for-myself hindrance?
{Why do I hinder my own way?}

Des Herren Wille muß geschehen,
The Lord's will must happen,

Doch ist sein Beistand auch gewiß,
Yet is his   support also sure,

Daß er sein Werk durch mich mög wohl vollendet sehen.
So-that he his work through me may well-accomplished see.
{So that he can see his work accomplished in me.}

7. Chorale
●Prayer: Grant that I do thy will diligently (45–7)
Gib, daß ich tu mit   Fleiß
Grant that I do with diligence

Was   mir zu tun gebühret,
What for-me to do   is-fitting,
{That which is fitting for me to do,}

Worzu mich dein Befehl
To-which me   thy command

In meinem Stande führet!
In   my   situation leads!

Gib, daß ich's tue bald,
Grant that I-it do quickly,
{Grant that I do it quickly,}

Zu der Zeit, da ich soll;
At the time, that I ought;

Und wenn ich's tu, so gib,
And when I-it do, then grant,
{And when I do it, then grant}

Daß es gerate wohl!
That it turn-out well!

Mt. 12:33–37. [Christ]: Either make the tree good, and its fruit good; or make the tree bad, and its fruit bad; for the tree is known by its fruit. You brood of vipers! how can you speak good, when you are evil? For out of the abundance of the heart the mouth speaks. The good man out of his good treasure brings forth good, and the evil man out of his evil treasure brings forth evil. I tell you, on the day of judgment men will render account for every careless word they utter; for by your words you will be justified, and by your words you will be condemned.
Lk. 6:46 [Christ]: Why do you call me "Lord, Lord," and not do what I tell you? (Also Mt. 12:50, Mk. 3:35.)
Jms. 4:17. Whoever knows what is right to do and fails to do it, for him it is sin.
Lk. 12:47. And that servant who knew his master's will, but did not make ready or act according to his will, shall receive a severe beating.
Phil. 1:6. I am sure that he who began a good work in you will bring it to completion at the day of Jesus Christ.
Phil. 2:13. For God is at work in you, both to will and to work for his good pleasure. (Also 1 Thess. 4:3.)
1 Thess. 4:3. This is the will of God, your sanctification...
Ps. 138:8. The Lord will fulfil his purpose for me; thy steadfast love, O Lord, endures for ever. Do not forsake the work of thy hands.

*Mt. 7:21 [Christ]: Not every one who says to me, "Lord, Lord," shall enter the kingdom of heaven, but he who does the will of my Father who is in heaven.
Jms. 1:22–25. Be doers of the word, and not hearers only, deceiving yourselves. For if any one is a hearer of the word and not a doer, he is like a man who observes his natural face in a mirror; for he observes himself and goes away and at once forgets what he was like. But he who looks into the perfect law, the law of liberty, and perseveres, being no hearer that forgets but a doer that acts, he shall be blessed in his doing. (Also Mt. 7:21, Lk. 6:46.)
Heb. 6:11–12. We desire each one of you to show the same earnestness in realizing the full assurance of hope until the end, so that you may not be sluggish, but imitators of those who through faith and patience inherit the promises.
Rom. 12:6–8. Having gifts that differ according to the grace given to us, let us use them: if prophecy, in proportion to our faith; if service, in our serving; he who teaches, in his teaching; he who exhorts, in his exhortation; he who contributes, in liberality; he who gives aid, with zeal; he who does acts of mercy, with cheerfulness.
Phil. 2:13. God is at work in you, both to will and to work for his good pleasure.
Mt. 21:28–29 [Christ]: A man had two sons; and he went to the first and said, "Son, go and work in the vineyard today." And he answered, "I will not"; but afterward he repented and went...
Ps. 40:8. I delight to do thy will, O my God; thy law is within my heart.
Neh. 1:11. O Lord, let thy ear be attentive to the prayer of thy servant, and to the prayer of thy servants who delight to fear thy name; and give success to thy servant today.
Ps. 90:17. [O Lord,] let the favor of the Lord our God be upon us, and establish thou the work of our hands upon us, yea, the work of our hands establish thou it.

BWV 46
Schauet doch und sehet, ob irgendein Schmerz sei
(NBA I/19; BC A117)

10. S. after Trinity (BWV 46, 101, 102)
*1 Cor. 12:1-11 (There is a diversity of gifts but one Spirit)
*Lk. 19:41-48 (Jesus foretells destruction of Jerusalem and drives traders out of temple)
Librettist: Unknown

1. Chorus
●Sorrow: Is there any like mine? Lam. 1:12 (46-1)
Schauet doch und sehet, ob irgendein Schmerz
Behold, indeed, and see, if any grief (there)

sei wie mein Schmerz, der mich troffen hat.
be like my grief, which me has-struck.

Denn der Herr hat mich voll Jammers gemacht
For the Lord has me full of-wretchedness made

am Tage seines grimmigen Zorns.
on-the day of-his furious wrath.

Lam. 1:12. Is it nothing to you, all you who pass by? *Look and see if there is any sorrow like my sorrow which was brought upon me, which the Lord inflicted on the day of his fierce anger.*
*Lk. 19:41-44. When [Jesus] drew near and saw the city he wept over it, saying, "Would that even today you knew the things that make for peace! But now they are hid from your eyes. For the days shall come upon you, when your enemies will cast up a bank about you and surround you, and hem you in on every side, and dash you to the ground, you and your children within you, and they will not leave one stone upon another in you; because you did not know the time of your visitation."

2. Tenor Recit.
●Jerusalem brings flood of judgment on itself (46-2)
So klage du, zerstörte Gottesstadt,
So lament thou, (O) destroyed city-of-God,

Du armer Stein- und Aschenhaufen!
Thou poor stone- and ash-heap!

Laß ganze Bäche Tränen laufen,
Let whole streams of-tears run,

Weil dich betroffen hat
For thee befallen hath
{For thee hath befallen}

Ein unersetzlicher Verlust
An irreparable loss

Der allerhöchsten Huld,
Of-the most-precious favor,

So du entbehren mußt
Which thou do-without must
{Which thou must now do without}

Durch deine Schuld.
Through thine-own fault.

Du wurdest wie Gomorra zugerichtet,
Thou wast like Gomorrah treated,
{Thou wast treated like Gomorrah,}

Wiewohl nicht gar vernichtet.
Although not entirely annihilated.

Lk. 21:20-24 [Christ]: When you see Jerusalem surrounded by armies, then know that its desolation has come near. Then let those who are in Judea flee to the mountains, and let those who are inside the city depart, and let not those who are out in the country enter it; for these are days of vengeance, to fulfil all that is written. Alas for those who are with child and for those who give suck in those days! For great distress shall be upon the earth and wrath upon this people; they will fall by the edge of the sword, and be led captive among all nations; and Jerusalem will be trodden down by the Gentiles, until the times of the Gentiles are fulfilled.
Lk. 23:28-30. Jesus turning to them said, "Daughters of Jerusalem, do not weep for me, but weep for yourselves and for your children. For behold, the days are coming when they will say, 'Blessed are the barren, and the wombs that never bore, and the breasts that never gave suck!' Then they will begin to say to the mountains, 'Fall on us'; and to the hills, 'Cover us.'"
Jer. 9:1. O that my head were waters, and my eyes a fountain of tears, that I might weep day and night for the slain of the daughter of my people!
Lam. 2:11. My eyes are spent with weeping; my soul is in tumult; my heart is poured out in grief because of the destruction of the daughter of my people, because infants and babes faint in the streets of the city.
Lam. 1:16. For these things I weep; my eyes flow with tears; for a comforter is far from me, one to revive my courage; my children are desolate, for the enemy has prevailed.
Gen. 19:24-25. Then the Lord rained on Sodom and Gomorrah brimstone and fire from the Lord out of heaven; and he overthrew those cities, and all the valley, and all the inhabitants of the cities, and what grew on the ground.
Is. 1:9. If the Lord of hosts had not left us a few survivors, we should have been like Sodom, and become like Gomorrah.

O besser! wärest du in Grund zerstört,
O better, wert thou (to-thy) foundation destroyed,
{It were better if thou hadst been destroyed to thy foundations,}

Als daß man Christi Feind jetzt in dir lästern hört.
Than that one Christ's foe now in thee blaspheming hear.
{Than that one now hear Christ's foe blaspheming within thee.}

Du achtest Jesu Tränen nicht,
Thou heedest Jesus' tears not,
{Thou didst not heed Jesus' tears,}

So achte nun des Eifers Wasserwogen,
So heed now (his) zeal's watery-billows,
{So heed now the zeal of his watery billows,}

Die du selbst über dich gezogen,
Which thou - upon thyself hast-drawn,

Da Gott, nach viel Geduld,
When God, after much patience,

Den Stab zum Urteil bricht.
The rod for judgment (wields).

3. Bass Aria

•God's judgment breaks like a storm on Jerusalem (46-3)
Dein Wetter zog sich auf von weiten,
Thy storm drew - (on) from afar,

Doch dessen Strahl bricht endlich ein
Yet its flash breaks finally (forth)
{Yet its flash will finally break forth}

Und muß dir unerträglich sein,
And must for-thee unbearable be,
{And will be unbearable for thee,}

Da überhäufte Sünden
When overly-piled-up sins
{When thy high mound of sins}

Der Rache Blitz entzünden
- Vengeance's lightning kindle
{Kindle the lightning of his veangeance}

Und dir den Untergang bereiten.
And for-thee thy downfall prepare.
{And prepare thy downfall.}

4. Alto Recit.

•Judgment not reserved for Jerusalem alone (46-4)
Doch bildet euch, o Sünder, ja nicht ein,
Yet imagine - , O sinners, indeed not - ,
{Yet do not imagine, O sinners}

Mt. 24:15-18 [Christ]: When you see the desolating sacrilege spoken of by the prophet Daniel standing in the holy place (let the reader understand), then let those who are in Judea flee to the mountains; let him who is on the housetop not go down to take what is in his house; and let him who is in the field not turn back to take his mantle...
2 Thess. 2:3-4. ...That day will not come, unless the rebellion comes first, and the man of lawlessness is revealed, the son of perdition, who opposes and exalts himself against every so-called god or object of worship, so that he takes his seat in the temple of God, proclaiming himself to be God.
*Lk. 19:41. When [Jesus] drew near and saw the city he wept over it...
Mt. 23:37-38 [Christ]: O Jerusalem, Jerusalem, killing the prophets and stoning those who are sent to you! How often would I have gathered your children together as a hen gathers her brood under her wings, and you would not! Behold, your house is forsaken and desolate.
Gen. 6:17 [God]: Behold, I will bring a flood of waters upon the earth, to destroy all flesh in which is the breath of life from under heaven; everything that is on the earth shall die.
Deut. 32:16. [The people] stirred [God] to jealousy (Luther: Eifer) with strange gods; with abominable practices they provoked him to anger. (Also Ex. 20:5, 34:14, Deut 4:24, etc.)
Is. 11:4. ...He shall smite the earth with the rod of his mouth, and with the breath of his lips he shall slay the wicked.

Gen. 7:11-12. In the six hundredth year of Noah's life...all the fountains of the great deep burst forth, and the windows of the heavens were opened. And rain fell upon the earth forty days and forty nights.
Is. 30:27-28, 30. Behold, the name of the Lord comes from far, burning with his anger, and in thick rising smoke; his lips are full of indignation, and his tongue is like a devouring fire; his breath is like an overflowing stream that reaches up to the neck; to sift the nations with the sieve of destruction, and to place on the jaws of the peoples a bridle that leads astray...The Lord will cause his majestic voice to be heard and the descending blow of his arm to be seen, in furious anger and a flame of devouring fire, with a cloudburst and tempest and hailstones.
Rev. 18:5. [Babylon's] sins are heaped high as heaven, and God has remembered her iniquities. (Also Ezra 9:6, Jer. 51:9.)
Is. 29:5-6. ...In an instant, suddenly, you will be visited by the Lord of hosts with thunder and with earthquake and great noise, with whirlwind and tempest, and the flame of a devouring fire. (Also Is. 40:10.)
2 Thess. 1:7-8. ...The Lord Jesus [will be] revealed from heaven with his mighty angels in flaming fire (Luther: Feuerflammen), inflicting vengeance (Luther: Rache) upon those who do not know God and upon those who do not obey the gospel of our Lord Jesus.

Lk. 13:3/5 [Christ]: I tell you...unless you repent you will all likewise perish.
Rom. 2:1-9. Therefore you have no excuse, O man, whoever you are, when you judge another; for in passing judgment upon him you

165

Es sei Jerusalem allein
It   be   Jerusalem   alone   (that)
{That it was Jerusalem alone}

Vor   andern   Sünden voll gewesen!
More-than others (with) sins   filled was!
{That was so sinful!}

Man kann bereits   von   euch dies Urteil lesen:
One   can already concerning you   this judgment read:
{One can already read this judgment concerning you:}

Weil   ihr   euch   nicht bessert
Because you yourselves (do) not reform
{Because you do not change your ways}

Und täglich die Sünden vergrößert,
And daily (your) sins   increase,
{And daily increase your sins,}

So   müsset ihr alle so schrecklich umkommen.
Therefore must you all so   terribly   perish.
{Therefore all of you must terribly perish.}

5. Alto Aria
●Jesus would shelter righteous like sheep or chicks (46-5)
Doch Jesus will auch bei der Strafe
Yet   Jesus desires even in - punishment

Der Frommen Schild und Beistand sein,
The righteous' shield and support to-be,

Er sammelt sie als seine Schafe,
He gathers them as   his   sheep,

Als seine Küchlein liebreich ein;
As his   chicks,   lovingly in;
{He gathers them lovingly, as his sheep, as his chicks;}

Wenn Wetter der Rache die Sünder belohnen,
When storms of vengeance - sinners   reward,
{When storms of vengeance reward sinners for their deeds,}

Hilft er, daß   Fromme sicher wohnen.
Helps he, that (the) righteous securely dwell.
{He ensures that the righteous dwell securely.}

6. Chorale
●Prayer: Spare us in judgment for Jesus' sake (46-6)
O großer Gott von   Treu,
O   great God of faithfulness,

Weil vor   dir niemand gilt
Since before thee no-one is-worthy

Als dein Sohn Jesus Christ,
But thy Son Jesus Christ,

condemn yourself, because you, the judge, are doing the very same things. We know that the judgment of God rightly falls upon those who do such things. Do you suppose, O man, that when you judge those who do such things and yet do them yourself, you will escape the judgment of God? Or do you presume upon the riches of his kindness and forbearance and patience? Do you not know that God's kindness is meant to lead you to repentance? But by your hard and impenitent heart you are storing up wrath for yourself on the day of wrath when God's righteous judgment will be revealed. For he will render to every man according to his works: to those who by patience in well-doing seek for glory and honor and immortality, he will give eternal life; but for those who are factious and do not obey the truth, but obey wickedness, there will be wrath and fury. There will be tribulation and distress for every human being who does evil, the Jew first and also the Greek...

Heb. 12:25. See that you do not refuse him who is speaking. For if they did not escape when they refused him who warned them on earth, much less shall we escape if we reject him who warns from heaven. (Also Heb. 2:3.)

Jer. 26:13. Now therefore amend your ways and your doings, and obey the voice of the Lord your God, and the Lord will repent of the evil which he has pronounced against you.

Ps. 27:5. [The Lord] will hide me in his shelter in the day of trouble; he will conceal me under the cover of his tent, he will set me high upon a rock.

Job 14:13. O that thou wouldest hide me in Sheol, that thou wouldest conceal me until thy wrath be past, that thou wouldest appoint me a set time, and remember me! (Also Zeph. 2:3.)

Is. 40:11. He will feed his flock like a shepherd, he will gather the lambs in his arms, he will carry them in his bosom, and gently lead those that are with young.

Jn. 10:11, 14, 27–28 [Christ]: I am the good shepherd. The good shepherd lays down his life for the sheep...I am the good shepherd; I know my own and my own know me, as the Father knows me and I know the Father...My sheep hear my voice, and I know them, and they follow me; and I give them eternal life, and they shall never perish, and no one shall snatch them out of my hand.

Mt. 23:37 [Christ]: ...How often would I have gathered your children together as a hen gathers her brood under her wings, and you would not!

Ps. 57:1. Be merciful to me, O God, be merciful to me, for in thee my soul takes refuge; in the shadow of thy wings I will take refuge, till the storms of destruction pass by. (Also Ps. 17:8, 36:7, 63:7, 91:4, Deut. 32:10–11.)

1 Pet. 2:22, 24. [Christ] committed no sin; no guile was found on his lips...He himself bore our sins in his body on the tree, that we might die to sin and live to righteousness. By his wounds you have been healed.

Acts 4:12. And there is salvation in no one else, for there is no other name under heaven given among men by which we must be saved. (Also Jn. 14:6.)

Mt. 19:17. [Jesus] said to [the man], "Why do you ask me about what is good? (Luther: Was heißest du mich gut?) One there is who is good..."

Der deinen Zorn gestillt,
Who thy wrath hath-stilled,

So sieh doch an die Wunden sein,
Then look please on the wounds of-his,
{Then please look on his wounds,}

Sein Marter, Angst und schwere Pein;
His torment, fear, and grievous pain;

Um seinetwillen schone,
For his-sake spare (us),

Uns nicht nach Sünden lohne.
And not according-to (our) sins reward (us).
{And reward us not according to our sins.}

Rom. 3:10–12, 23. As it is written: "None is righteous, no, not one; no one understands, no one seeks for God. All have turned aside, together they have gone wrong; no one does good, not even one."...All have sinned and fall short of the glory of God.
Rom. 5:9. Since, therefore, we are now justified by his blood, much more shall we be saved by him from the wrath of God.
Eph. 4:32. ...God in Christ forgave you.
1 Jn. 2:12. ...Your sins are forgiven for his sake.
1 Cor. 5:7. ...For Christ, our paschal lamb, has been sacrificed (Luther: für uns geopfert).
Ps. 103:8, 10–13. The Lord is merciful and gracious, slow to anger and abounding in steadfast love...He does not deal with us according to our sins, nor requite us according to our iniquities. For as the heavens are high above the earth, so great is his steadfast love toward those who fear him; as far as the east is from the west, so far does he remove our transgressions from us. As a father pities his children, so the Lord pities those who fear him.

BWV 47
Wer sich selbst erhöhet, der soll erniedrigetwerden
(NBA I/23; BC A141)

17. S. after Trinity (BWV 148, 114, 47)
*Eph. 4:1–6 (Exhortation to unity in the Spirit)
*Lk. 14:1–11 (Jesus heals man on the Sabbath, exhortation to humility)
Librettist: Johann Friedrich Helbig

1. Chorus
●Whoever exalts himself shall be humbled: Lk. 14:11 (47-1)
Wer sich selbst erhöhet, der soll erniedriget werden,
Whoever him-self exalts, he shall humbled be,

und wer sich selbst erniedriget, der soll erhöhet werden.
and whoever him-self humbles, he shall exalted be.

2. Soprano Aria
●Humility is mark of true Christian; God hates pride (47-2)
Wer ein wahrer Christ will heißen,
Whoever a true Christian would be-called,
{Whoever would be called a true Christian,}

Muß der Demut sich befleißen;
Must (to) meekness himself devote;

Demut stammt aus Jesu Reich.
Meekness originates (with) Jesus' kingdom.

Hoffart ist dem Teufel gleich;
Arrogance is the devil like;
{Arrogance is of the devil;}

Gott pflegt alle die zu hassen,
God nurtures all those to hate,
{God nurtures hatred for those,}

***Lk. 14:7–11.** Now [Jesus] told a parable to those who were invited, when he marked how they chose the places of honor, saying to them, "When you are invited by any one to a marriage feast, do not sit down in a place of honor, lest a more eminent man than you be invited by him; and he who invited you both will come and say to you, 'Give place to this man,' and then you will begin with shame to take the lowest place. But when you are invited, go and sit in the lowest place, so that when your host comes he may say to you, 'Friend, go up higher'; then you will be honored in the presence of all who sit at table with you. *For every one who exalts himself will be humbled, and he who humbles himself will be exalted.*" (Also Mt. 23:10–12, Lk. 18:14, Jms. 4:10, Prov. 29:23, Job 22:29, Ezek. 21:26.)

***Eph. 4:1–2.** I therefore, a prisoner for the Lord, beg you to lead a life worthy of the calling to which you have been called, with all lowliness and meekness... (Also Phil. 2:3, Col. 3:12.)
Is. 57:15. For thus says the high and lofty One who inhabits eternity, whose name is Holy: "I dwell in the high and holy place, and also with him who is of a contrite and humble spirit, to revive the spirit of the humble, and to revive the heart of the contrite."
Mt. 5:5. Blessed are the meek, for they shall inherit the earth.
Is. 14:12–15. How you are fallen from heaven, O Day Star [= Lucifer], son of Dawn! How you are cut down to the ground, you who laid the nations low! You said in your heart, "I will ascend to heaven; above the stars of God I will set my throne on high; I will sit on the mount of assembly in the far north; I will ascend above the heights of the clouds, I will make myself like the Most High." But you are brought down to Sheol, to the depths of the Pit. (Also Jude 1:6, 2 Pet. 2:4.)

So   den   Stolz   nicht fahren lassen.
Who (their) pride (do) not   let   go.
{Who do not let go of their pride.}

3. Bass Recit.
●Humility: Man is but dust, should he exalt himself? (47-3)
Der Mensch ist Kot, Stank, Asch und Erde;
 - Mankind is mud, stench, ashes, and earth;

Ist's möglich, daß vom Übermut,
Is-it possible, that by arrogance,

Als einer Teufelsbrut,
Like a   devil's-brood,

Er noch   bezaubert werde?
He still (should) enchanted be?
{Is it possible for him still to be enchanted by arrogance, that devil's brood?}

Ach Jesus, Gottes Sohn,
Ah, Jesus, God's Son,

Der Schöpfer aller Dinge,
The Creator of-all things,

Ward unsertwegen niedrig und geringe,
Became for-our-sake lowly and unimportant,
{Became lowly and insignificant for our sake,}

Er duld'te Schmach und Hohn;
He endured humiliation and scorn;

Und du, du armer Wurm,   suchst dich zu brüsten?
And you, you wretched worm, (do you) seek - to boast?

Gehört sich das vor einen Christen?
Is-proper   that for a   Christian?
{Is that proper for a Christian?}

Geh, schäme dich, du stolze Kreatur,
Go, shame yourself, you proud created-one,

Tu Buß und folge Christi Spur;
Repent and follow Christ's footprints;
{Repent and follow Christ's footsteps;}

Wirf dich   vor Gott im Geiste gläubig nieder!
Cast yourself before God in spirit, believing, down!
{Cast yourself down spiritually before God, in faith!}

Zu seiner Zeit erhöht er dich auch wieder.
In his time will-exalt he you also again.
{In his time he will exalt you again.}

4. Bass Aria
●Prayer: Grant humility that I not forfeit salvation (47-4)
Jesu, beuge doch mein Herze
Jesus, bow indeed my spirit
{Jesus, please make my spirit bow}

Prov. 6:16–17. There are six things wich the Lord hates, seven which are an abomination to him: haughty eyes... (Also Prov. 16:5, 21:4, Is. 2:12, 13:11, Lk. 1:51, Jms. 4:6, 1 Pet. 5:5.)

Gen. 3:19. In the sweat of your face you shall eat bread till you return to the ground, for out of it you were taken; you are dust, and to dust you shall return.
Gen. 18:27. Abraham answered, "Behold, I have taken upon myself to speak to the Lord, I who am but dust and ashes." (Also Job 4:19, 2 Cor. 5:1.)
Job 25:5–6. Behold, even the moon is not bright and the stars are not clean in his sight; how much less man, who is a maggot, and the son of man, who is a worm!
Phil. 2:5–9. Have this mind among yourselves, which is yours in Christ Jesus, who, though he was in the form of God, did not count equality with God a thing to be grasped, but emptied himself, taking the form of a servant, being born in the likeness of men. And being found in human form he humbled himself and became obedient unto death, even death on a cross. Therefore God has highly exalted him and bestowed on him the name which is above every name.
Ps. 22:6–8. I am a worm, and no man; scorned by men, and despised by the people. All who see me mock at me, they make mouths at me, they wag their heads; "He committed his cause to the Lord; let him deliver him, let him rescue him, for he delights in him!"
Ps. 22:6–8. I am...scorned by men, and despised by the people. All who see me mock at me, they make mouths at me, they wag their heads; "He committed his cause to the Lord; let him deliver him, let him rescue him, for he delights in him!"
Is. 50:6. I gave my back to the smiters, and my cheeks to those who pulled out the beard; I hid not my face from shame and spitting.
Jn. 13:13–15 [Christ]: You call me Teacher and Lord; and you are right, for so I am. If I then, your Lord and Teacher, have washed your feet, you also ought to wash one another's feet. For I have given you an example, that you also should do as I have done to you.
Jn. 15:20 [Christ]: Remember the word that I said to you, "A servant is not greater than his master." If they persecuted me, they will persecute you.
1 Cor. 4:7. ...What have you that you did not receive? If then you received it, why do you boast as if it were not a gift? (Also 1 Chron. 29:14.)
Rom. 1:25. ...[Men] served the creature rather than the Creator...
Mt. 23:11–12 [Christ]: He who is greatest among you shall be your servant; whoever exalts himself will be humbled, and whoever humbles himself will be exalted. (Also Lk. 18:14.)
1 Pet. 5:5–6. ...Clothe yourselves, all of you, with humility toward one another, for "God opposes the proud, but gives grace to the humble." Humble yourselves therefore under the mighty hand of God, that in due time he may exalt you.

2 Chron. 7:14 [God]: If my people who are called by my name humble themselves, and pray and seek my face, and turn from their wicked ways, then I will hear from heaven, and will forgive their sin and heal their land.

Unter deine starke Hand,
Beneath thy strong hand,

Daß ich nicht mein Heil verscherze
That I not my salvation frivolously-forfeit
{That I not frivolously forfeit my salvation}

Wie der erste Höllenbrand.
Like that first firebrand-of-hell.

Laß mich deine Demut suchen
Let me thy meekness seek

Und den Hochmut ganz verfluchen;
And - arrogance entirely curse;

Gib mir einen niedern Sinn,
Grant me a lowly disposition,

Daß ich dir gefällig bin!
That I to-thee pleasing might-be!

5. Chorale
●Temporal honor given up for eternal reward (47–5)
Der zeitlichen Ehrn will ich gern entbehrn,
- Temporal honors will I gladly dispense-with,

Du wollst mir nur das Ewge gewährn,
(If) thou wouldst me just that (which is) eternal grant,
{If thou wouldst just grant me that which is eternal,}

Das du erworben hast
Which thou hast-gained

Durch deinen herben, bittern Tod.
Through thy harsh, bitter death.

Das bitt ich dich, mein Herr und Gott.
This ask I of-thee, my Lord and God.

Jude 1:6. The angels that did not keep their own position but left their proper dwelling have been kept by him in eternal chains in the nether gloom until the judgment of the great day.
Lk. 10:18. [Jesus] said to them, "I saw Satan fall like lightning from heaven."
2 Pet. 2:4, 9. If God did not spare the angels when they sinned, but cast them into hell and committed them to pits of nether gloom to be kept until the judgment...then the Lord knows how...to keep the unrighteous under punishment until the day of judgment.
Mt. 11:29 [Christ]: Take my yoke upon you, and learn from me; for I am gentle and lowly in heart...
Jms. 4:10. Humble yourselves before the Lord and he will exalt you.
2 Chron. 34:27. Because your heart was penitent and you humbled yourself before God when you heard his words against this place and its inhabitants, and you have humbled yourself before me, and have rent your clothes and wept before me, I also have heard you, says the Lord.
Job 22:29. For God abases the proud, but he saves the lowly.

Ps. 49:12–13. Man cannot abide in his pomp, he is like the beasts that perish. This is the fate of those who have foolish confidence, the end of those who are pleased with their portion. (Also Ps. 49:16–20.)
Mt. 16:25 [Christ]: Whoever would save his life will lose it, and whoever loses his life for my sake will find it. (Also Mk. 8:35, Lk. 9:24.)
Jms. 4:4. ...Whoever wishes to be a friend of the world makes himself an enemy of God. (Also 1 Jn. 2:15–17, Lk. 16:15.)
Jn. 5:44. ...Seek the glory that comes from the only God...
Phil. 3:4, 7 [Paul]: ...If any other man thinks he has reason for confidence in the flesh, I have more...But whatever gain I had, I counted as loss the the sake of Christ. (Also 1 Thess. 2:6.)
2 Cor. 4:17–18. For this slight momentary affliction is preparing for us an eternal weight of glory beyond all comparison, because we look not to the things that are seen but to the things that are unseen; for the things that are seen are transient, but the things that are unseen are eternal.
Col. 3:1–3. If then you have been raised with Christ, seek the things that are above, where Christ is, seated at the right hand of God. Set your minds on things that are above, not on things that are on earth. For you have died and your life is hid with Christ in God.
Jn. 3:16. For God so loved the world that he gave his only Son, that whoever believes in him should not perish but have eternal life.
Heb. 2:9. We see Jesus, who for a little while was made lower than the angels, crowned with glory and honor because of the suffering of death, so that by the grace of God he might taste death for every one.
Rom. 5:2. Through him we have obtained access to this grace in which we stand, and we rejoice in our hope of sharing the glory of God.

BWV 48
Ich elender Mensch, wer wird mich erlösen
(NBA I/24; BC A144)

19. S. after Trinity (BWV 48, 5, 56)
*Eph. 4:22–28 (Exhortation to put on the new nature)
*Mt. 9:1–8 (Jesus heals the paralytic)
Librettist: Unknown

1. Chorus
●Wretched man that I am, who will deliver me? Rom. 7:24 (48-1)
Ich elender Mensch, wer wird mich erlösen
I, wretched man, who will me deliver

vom Leibe dieses Todes?
from-the body of-this death?

2. Alto Recit.
●Sin is a poison that infects body; even more the soul (48-2)
O Schmerz, o Elend, so mich trifft,
O pain, O misery, which me strikes,

Indem der Sünden Gift
In-that - sin's poison

Bei mir in Brust und Adern wütet:
With me in breast and veins rages:
{In my breast and veins does rage:}

Die Welt wird mir ein
The world becomes (for) me a

Siech- und Sterbehaus,
house-of-sickness and house-of-death,

Der Leib muß seine Plagen
The body must its plagues

Bis zu dem Grabe mit sich tragen.
- To the grave with it carry.
{The body must carry its plagues with it to the grave.}

Allein die Seele fühlet den stärksten Gift,
But the soul feels the strongest poison,
{But it is the soul that feels the strongest poison,}

Damit sie angestecket;
With-which it is-infected;

Drum, wenn der Schmerz den Leib des Todes trifft,
Thus, when - pain (this) body of death strikes,
{Thus, when suffering strikes this body of death,}

Wenn ihr der Kreuzkelch bitter schmecket,
When to-it the cross's-cup bitter tastes,
{When the cross's cup tastes bitter to it,}

Rom. 7:15, 18–19, 22–25. I do not understand my own actions. For I do not do what I want, but I do the very thing I hate...For I know that nothing good dwells within me, that is, in my flesh. I can will what is right, but I cannot do it. For I do not do the good I want, but the evil I do not want is what I do...I delight in the law of God, in my inmost self, but I see in my members another law at war with the law of my mind and making me captive to the law of sin which dwells in my members. *Wretched man that I am! Who will deliver me from this body of death?* Thanks be to God through Jesus Christ our Lord! So then, I of myself serve the law of God with my mind, but with my flesh I serve the law of sin.

Rom. 5:12, 17, 19. Therefore...sin came into the world through one man and death through sin, and so death spread to all men because all men sinned...Because of one man's trespass, death reigned through that one man...By one man's disobedience many were made sinners...
1 Cor. 15:21–22. ...By a man came death...In Adam all die...
Rom. 6:23. The wages of sin is death...
Rom. 8:19–24, 26. ...Creation waits with eager longing for the revealing of the sons of God; for the creation was subjected to futility, not of its own will but by the will of him who subjected it in hope; because the creation itself will be set free from its bondage to decay and obtain the glorious liberty of the children of God. We know that the whole creation has been groaning in travail together until now; and not only the creation, but we ourselves, who have the first fruits of the Spirit, groan inwardly as we wait for adoption as sons, the redemption of our bodies. For in this hope we were saved...Likewise the Spirit helps us in our weakness; for we do not know how to pray as we ought, but the Spirit himself intercedes for us with sighs too deep for words.
***Eph. 4:22–24.** Put off your old nature which belongs to your former manner of life and is corrupt through deceitful lusts, and be renewed in the spirit of your minds, and put on the new nature, created after the likeness of God in true righteousness and holiness.
Col. 3:5–6, 9. Put to death therefore what is earthly in you: fornication, impurity, passion, evil desire, and covetousness, which is idolatry. On account of these the wrath of God is coming...[Put off] the old nature with its practices.
Rom. 7:24. ...Who will deliver me from this body of death?
Mt. 16:24 [Christ]: If any man would come after me, let him deny himself and take up his cross and follow me. (Also Mt. 10:38.)
Gal. 5:24. Those who belong to Christ Jesus have crucified the flesh with its passions and desires.
Mk. 10:38–39. But Jesus said to them..."Are you able to drink the cup that I drink, or to be baptized with the baptism with which I am baptized?" And they said to him, "We are able." And Jesus said to them, "The cup that I drink you will drink; and with the baptism with which I am baptized, you will be baptized..." (Also Mt. 20:20–22.)

So treibt er ihr ein brünstig Seufzen aus.
Then forces (that cup) from-it a passionate sigh - .
{Then that cup forces a passionate sigh from it.}

3. Chorale
●Sin's wage is suffering: I would rather suffer now (48-3)
Soll's ja so sein,
Shall-it then thus be,
{If it then be so,}

Daß Straf und Pein
That punishment and pain

Auf Sünde folgen müssen,
 - Sin follow must,
{Must follow sin,}

So fahr hier fort
Then proceed here - (to afflict me)

Und schone dort
And spare (over) there

Und laß mich hier wohl büßen.
And let me here indeed do-penance.

4. Alto Aria
●Prayer: Destroy my sinful flesh but spare my soul (48-4)
Ach, lege das Sodom der sündlichen Glieder,
Ah, lay the Sodom of-(my) sinful members,
{Destroy the Sodom of my sinful members,}

Wofern es dein Wille, zerstöret darnieder!
To-the-extent it (be) thy will, destroyed down!
{To the extent that it be necessary!}

Nur schone der Seele und mache sie rein,
Only spare (my) soul and make it pure,

Um vor dich ein heiliges Zion zu sein.
In-order before thee a holy Zion to be.
{So that it may be a holy Zion before thee.}

5. Tenor Recit.
●Christ does wonders among the weak and dead (48-5)
Hier aber tut des Heilands Hand
Here, however, does the Savior's hand
{Here, however, the Savior's hand does wonders}

Auch unter denen Toten Wunder.
Even among (the) dead wonders.
{Even among the dead.}

Scheint deine Seele gleich erstorben,
Seems your soul even-as-if (it had) died,
{Though it seem as though your soul had died,}

Rom. 8:23, 26. ...We..groan inwardly as we wait for adoption as sons, the redemption of our bodies...the Spirit himself intercedes for us with sighs too deep for words.

Gen. 2:16–17. The Lord commanded the man [Adam], saying, "You may freely eat of every tree of the garden; but of the tree of the knowledge of good and evil you shall not eat, for in the day that you eat of it you shall die."
Rom. 6:23. The wages of sin is death, but the free gift of God is eternal life in Christ Jesus our Lord. (Also Rom. 1:18.)
Rom. 1:18. The wrath of God is revealed from heaven against all ungodliness and wickedness of men who by their wickedness suppress the truth.
Rom. 8:12–13. So then, brethren, we are debtors, not to the flesh, to live according to the flesh—for if you live according to the flesh you will die, but if by the Spirit you put to death the deeds of the body you will live. (Also Gal. 6:8.)
Rev. 3:19 [Christ]: Those whom I love, I reprove and chasten; so be zealous and repent.
1 Cor. 11:32. When we are judged by the Lord, we are chastened so that we may not be condemned along with the world. (Also Heb. 12:7–11.)
1 Pet. 4:1–2. ...Whoever has suffered in the flesh has ceased from sin, so as to live for the rest of the time in the flesh no longer by human passions but by the will of God.

*Eph. 4:22. Put off your old nature which belongs to your former manner of life and is corrupt through deceitful lusts.
Gal. 5:24. Those who belong to Christ Jesus have crucified the flesh with its passions and desires.
Col. 3:5–6. Put to death therefore what is earthly in you: fornication, impurity, passion, evil desire, and covetousness, which is idolatry. On account of these the wrath of God is coming.
1 Cor. 5:5. ...Deliver this man to Satan for the destruction of the flesh, that his spirit may be saved in the day of the Lord Jesus.
Rom. 6:6–7. We know that our old self was crucified with him so that the sinful body might be destroyed, and we might no longer be enslaved to sin. For he who has died is freed from sin.
1 Cor. 3:16–17. Do you not know that you are God's temple and that God's Spirit dwells in you?...God's temple is holy, and that temple you are.

*Mt. 9:2–7. Behold, they brought to [Jesus] a paralytic, lying on his bed; and when Jesus saw their faith he said to the paralytic, "Take heart, my son; your sins are forgiven." And behold, some of the scribes said to themselves, "This man is blaspheming." But Jesus, knowing their thoughts, said, "Why do you think evil in your hearts? For which is easier, to say, 'Your sins are forgiven,' or to say, 'Rise and walk'? But that you may know that the Son of man has authority on earth to forgive sins"—he then said to the paralytic—"Rise, take up your bed and go home." And he rose and went home.
Ps. 88:10. [O Lord,] dost thou wonders for the dead?...
Mt. 19:25. When the disciples heard [Jesus' words] they were greatly astonished, saying, "Who then can be saved?" But Jesus looked at

Der   Leib geschwächt und ganz verdorben,
(Your) body weakened and completely ruined,

Doch   wird   uns Jesu Kraft bekannt.
Nevertheless (is-made) to-us Jesus' power known.
{Nevertheless Jesus' power is made known to us.}

Er weiß   im   geistlich Schwachen
He knows (how) in-(those) spiritually   weak

Den Leib gesund, die Seele stark zu machen.
The body healthy, the soul strong to   make.
{He knows how to make the body healthy, the soul strong in those who are spiritually weak.}

6. Tenor Aria
●Jesus heals our body and soul by faith (48-6)
Vergibt mir Jesus meine Sünden,
Forgives me Jesus   my   sins,
{If Jesus forgives my sins,}

So   wird   mir Leib und Seel gesund.
Then become (my) body and soul   well.
{Then my body and soul become well.}

Er kann die Toten lebend machen
He can the dead   alive   make
{He can make the dead alive}

Und zeigt sich kräftig in den Schwachen,
And shows himself mighty in the   weak,

Er hält den längst geschloßnen Bund,
He keeps the long-ago contracted covenant,
{He keeps the age-old covenant,}

Daß wir im Glauben Hilfe   finden.
That we by   faith   help (will) find.
{That we can find help through faith.}

7. Chorale
●Prayer: I turn to Jesus for relief in my heartache (48-7)
Herr Jesu Christ,   einiger Trost,
Lord Jesus Christ, (my) only comfort,

Zu dir will ich mich wenden;
To thee will I -   turn;

them and said to them, "With men this is impossible, but with God all things are possible." (Also Mk. 10:26–27, Lk. 18:26–27.)
Mk. 2:16–17. The scribes of the Pharisees...said..."Why does he eat with tax collectors and sinners?" And when Jesus heard it, he said to them, "Those who are well have no need of a physician, but those who are sick; I came not to call the righteous, but sinners."
Eph. 2:1–2. And you [Christ] made alive, when you were dead through the trespasses and sins in which you once walked...
2 Cor. 12:9. [Christ] said to me, "My grace is sufficient for you, for my power is made perfect in weakness."...
Is. 59:1. Behold, the Lord's hand is not shortened, that it cannot save, or his ear dull, that it cannot hear. (Also Is. 50:2, Num. 11:23.)

*Mt. 9:4–6.** Jesus...said, "...Which is easier, to say, 'Your sins are forgiven,' or to say, 'Rise and walk'? But that you may know that the Son of man has authority on earth to forgive sins"—[Jesus] then said to the paralytic—"Rise, take up your bed and go home." And he rose and went home.
1 Thess. 5:23. May the God of peace himself sanctify you wholly; and may your spirit and soul and body be kept sound...
Jn. 10:10 [Christ]: ...I came that they may have life, and have it abundantly.
Eph. 2:4–5. ...Even when we were dead through our trespasses, [God] made us alive together with Christ...
Lk. 4:18–19 [Christ]: ...[The Lord] has anointed me to preach good news to the poor. He has sent me to proclaim release to the captives and recovering of sight to the blind, to set at liberty those who are oppressed, to proclaim the acceptable year of the Lord.
2 Cor. 12:9 [Christ]: ...My grace is sufficient for you, for my power is made perfect in weakness...
Jms. 5:15–16. [Your] prayer of faith will save [a] sick man, and the Lord will raise him up; and if he has commited sins, he will be forgiven. Therefore confess your sins to one another, and pray for one another, that you may be healed...
Gal. 3:8–9, 14, 26, 29. The scripture, foreseeing that God would justify the Gentiles by faith, preached the gospel beforehand to Abraham, saying, "In you shall all the nations be blessed." So then, those who are men of faith are blessed with Abraham who had faith...that in Christ Jesus the blessing of Abraham might come upon the Gentiles, that we might receive the promise of the Spirit through faith...for in Christ Jesus you are all sons of God, through faith...And if you are Christ's, then you are Abraham's offspring, heirs according to promise.
Deut. 7:9. Know therefore that the Lord your God is God, the faithful God who keeps covenant and steadfast love with those who love him...

Ps. 73:25–26. [O Lord,] whom have I in heaven but thee? And there is nothing upon earth that I desire besides thee. My flesh and my heart may fail, but God is the strength of my heart and my portion for ever.
2 Cor. 1:3–5. Blessed be the God and Father of our Lord Jesus Christ, the Father of mercies and God of all comfort, who comforts us in all our affliction, so that we may be able to comfort those who are in any affliction, with the comfort with which we ourselves are comforted by

Mein Herzleid ist dir wohl bewußt,
My heartache is to-thee well known,

Du kannst und wirst es enden.
Thou canst and wilt it end.

In deinen Willen sei's gestellt,
In thy will (may) it-be placed,

Mach's, lieber Gott, wie dir's gefällt:
Do, dear God, as it-thee pleases:

Dein bin und will ich bleiben.
Thine am (I) and will I remain.
{Thine I am and thine I will remain.}

BWV 49
Ich geh und suche mit Verlangen
(NBA I/25; BC A150)

20. S. after Trinity (BWV 162, 180, 49)
*Eph. 5:15-21 (Exhortation to walk carefully, be filled with
the Spirit)
*Mt. 22:1-14 (Parable of the royal wedding feast)
Librettist: Unknown

1. Sinfonia (Taken from nonextant instrumental work)

2. Bass Aria (Vox Christi)
●Bridegroom seeks bride, his perfect dove (49-2)
Ich geh und suche mit Verlangen
I go and search with longing (for)
{I go and search longingly for}

Dich, meine Taube, schönste Braut.
Thee, my dove, fairest bride.

Sag an, wo bist du hingegangen,
Tell (me), where art thou gone,

Daß dich mein Auge nicht mehr schaut?
That thee mine eye no longer doth-see?
{That mine eye no longer seeth thee?}

3. Soprano & Bass Recit. (Dialogue between Christ & Soul)
●Dialogue: Wedding banquet is ready for the bride (49-3)
Bass:
Mein Mahl ist zubereit'
My feast is prepared

Und meine Hochzeittafel fertig,
And my marriage-banquet (is) ready,

Nur meine Braut ist noch nicht gegenwörtig.
Only my bride is yet not present.

God. For as we share abundantly in Christ's sufferings, so through Christ we share abundantly in comfort too.
1 Pet. 4:19. Therefore let those who suffer according to God's will do right and entrust their souls to a faithful Creator.
Job 23:10. [God] he knows the way that I take; when he has tried me, I shall come forth as gold.
Mt. 26:39. Going a little farther [in the garden of Gethsemane, Jesus] fell on his face and prayed, "My Father, if it be possible, let this cup pass from me; nevertheless, not as I will, but as thou wilt."
1 Pet. 5:10. And after you have suffered a little while, the God of all grace, who has called you to his eternal glory in Christ, will himself restore, establish, and strengthen you.
1 Cor. 15:58. Therefore, my beloved brethren, be steadfast, immovable, always abounding in the work of the Lord...

S. of S. 6:9 [Bridegroom]: My dove, my perfect one, is only one, the darling of her mother, flawless to her that bore her... (Also S. of S. 2:14, 5:2.)
S. of S. 3:1-3 [Bride]: Upon my bed by night I sought him whom my soul loves; I sought him, but found him not; I called him, but he gave no answer. "I will rise now and go about the city, in the streets and in the squares; I will seek him whom my soul loves." I sought him, but found him not. The watchmen found me, as they went about in the city. "Have you seen him whom my soul loves?"
S. of S. 5:6 [Bride]: I opened to my beloved, but my beloved had turned and gone. My soul failed me when he spoke. I sought him, but found him not; I called him, but he gave no answer.

***Mt. 22:1-14.** Again Jesus spoke to [the people] in parables, saying, "The kingdom of heaven may be compared to a king who gave a marriage feast for his son, and sent his servants to call those who were invited to the marriage feast; but they would not come. Again he sent other servants, saying 'Tell those who are invited, Behold, I have made ready my dinner, my oxen and my fat calves are killed, and everything is ready; come to the marriage feast.' But they made light of it and went off, one to his farm, another to his business, while the rest seized his servants, treated them shamefully and killed them. The king was angry, and he sent his troops and destroyed those murderers and burned their city. Then he said to his servants, 'The wedding is ready, but those invited were not worthy. Go therefore to the thoroughfares,

Soprano:
Mein Jesus redt von mir;
My   Jesus speaks of me;

O Stimme, welche mich erfreut!
O voice, which me gladdens!

Bass:
Ich geh und suche mit Verlangen
I   go and search with longing (for)
{I go and search longingly for}

Dich, meine Taube, schönste Braut.
Thee, my dove, fairest bride.

Soprano:
Mein Bräutigam, ich falle   dir zu Füßen.
My bridegroom, I   fall (before) thee at (thy) feet.

Bass & Soprano:
Komm, [Schönste/Schönster], komm und laß dich
küssen,
Come, [fairest/fairest],   come and let thyself (be)
kissed,

[Du sollst mein/Laß mich dein] fettes Mahl genießen
[Thou shalt my/Let me   thy] (sumptuous) meal enjoy

[Komm, liebe Braut und/Mein Bräutigam! ich] eile nun,
[Come, dear bride and/My bridegroom! I] hasten now,

Die Hochzeitkleider anzutun.
(My) wedding-raiment to-put-on.

4. Soprano Aria (Believing Soul)
●Bride lovely in salvation's garment of righteousness (49-4)
Ich bin herrlich, ich bin schön,
I am glorious, I am lovely,

Meinen Heiland zu entzünden.
My   Savior to impassion.

Seines Heils Gerechtigkeit
His   salvation's righteousness

Ist mein Schmuck und Ehrenkleid;
Is my adornment and ceremonial-dress;

Und damit will ich bestehn,
And therewith will I   stand (the test),

Wenn ich werd in'n Himmel gehn.
When I (do) into heaven go.
{When I to heaven go.}

and invite to the marriage feast as many as you find.' And those servants went out into the streets and gathered all whom they found, both bad and good; so the wedding hall was filled with guests. But when the king came in to look at the guests, he saw there a man who had no wedding garment; and he said to him, 'Friend, how did you get in here without a wedding garment?' And he was speechless. Then the king said to the attendants, 'Bind him hand and foot, and cast him into the outer darkness; there men will weep and gnash their teeth.' For many are called, but few are chosen." (Also Mt. 8:11, 25:1-13, 26:29, 14:15-24.)

Rev. 21:2, 9. I saw the holy city, new Jerusalem, coming down out of heaven from God, prepared as a bride adorned for her husband...Then came one of the seven angels...and spoke to me, saying, "Come I will show you the Bride, the wife of the Lamb." (Also Ps. 45:15.)

Lk. 7:37-38. ...A woman of the city, who was a sinner...[stood at Jesus'] feet, weeping, [and] began to wet his feet with her tears, and wiped them with the hair of her head, and kissed his feet.. (Also Jn. 11:2, Jn. 12:1-8, Mk. 14:1-9.)

Rev. 19:7-9. ...The marriage of the Lamb has come, and his Bride has made herself ready; it was granted her to be clothed with fine linen, bright and pure...Blessed are those who are invited to the marriage supper of the Lamb... (Also Lk. 14:15.)

Lk. 13:29. Men will come from east and west, and from north and south, and sit at table in the kingdom of God.

Is. 25:6. On this mountain the Lord of hosts will make for all peoples a feast of fat things (Luther: ein fettes Mahl), a feast of wine on the lees... (Also Rev. 19:7-9.)

*Mt. 22:12. ..."Friend, how did you get in here without a wedding garment?"...

Rev. 3:5 [Christ]: He who conquers shall be clad thus in white garments, and I will not blot his name out of the book of life...

S. of S. 1:5 [Bride]: I am very dark, but comely, O daughters of Jerusalem...

S. of S. 7:6 [Bridegroom]: How fair and pleasant you are, O loved one, delectable maiden! (Also S. of S. 4:1, 7.)

S. of S. 7:10 [Bride]: I am my beloved's, and his desire is for me.

Is. 61:10. I will greatly rejoice in the Lord, my soul shall exult in my God; for he has clothed me with the garments of salvation, he has covered me with the robe of righteousness, as a bridegroom decks himself with a garland, and as a bride adorns herself with her jewels. (Also Ezek. 16:9-13.)

Eph. 5:25-27. ...Christ loved the church and gave himself up for her, that he might sanctify her, having cleansed her by the washing of water with the word, that he might present the church to himself in splendor, without spot or wrinkle or any such thing, that she might be holy and without blemish.

*Mt. 22:11-12. But when the king came in to look at the guests, he saw there a man who had no wedding garment; and he said to him, 'Friend, how did you get in here without a wedding garment?' And he was speechless.

Rev. 7:14. ...[The righteous] have washed their robes and made them white in the blood of the Lamb. (Also Rev. 3:5, 3:18, 4:4, 7:9, 19:14.)

5. Soprano & Bass Recit. (Dialogue between Christ & Soul)
●Dialogue: Bridegroom & Bride (Christ & Believer) (49-5)
Soprano:
Mein Glaube hat mich selbst so angezogen.
My faith has (my) self thus clothed.
{See how my faith has clothed me.}

Bass:
So bleibt mein Herze dir gewogen,
Thus remains my heart toward-thee well-disposed,
{Thus my heart remains well-disposed toward thee.}

So will ich mich mit dir
Thus will I myself (to) thee

In Ewigkeit vertrauen und verloben.
In eternity entrust and betroth.
{Thus will I entrust and betroth myself to thee in eternity.}

Soprano:
Wie wohl ist mir!
How well is (it for) me!
{How fortunate I am!}

Der Himmel ist mir aufgehoben:
- Heaven (has) for-me been-provided:
{Heaven has been provided for me:}

Die Majestät ruft selbst und sendet ihre Knechte,
(His) Majesty calls himself and sends (his) servants,
{His Majesty himself calls, and sends his servants,}

Daß das gefallene Geschlechte
So-that the fallen race

Im Himmelssaal
In heaven's-hall

Bei dem Erlösungsmahl
At - salvation's-meal

Zu Gaste möge sein,
(A) guest may be,

Hier komm ich, Jesu, laß mich ein!
Here come I, Jesus, let me in!
{Here I come, O Jesus, let me in!}

Bass:
Sei bis in Tod getreu,
Be unto death faithful,
{Be faithful unto death,}

So leg ich dir die Lebenskrone bei.
So confer I (on) thee the crown-of-life -.
{And I will confer on thee the crown of life.}

*Mt. 22:11-12. When the king came in to look at the guests, he saw there a man who had no wedding garment; and he said to him, 'Friend, how did you get in here without a wedding garment?' And he was speechless.
Is. 64:6. ...All our righteous deeds are like a polluted garment.
Rev. 3:5 [Christ]: He who conquers shall be clad thus in white garments, and I will not blot his name out of the book of life; I will confess his name before my Father and before his angels.
Phil. 3:9. ...Not having a righteousness of my own, based on law, but that which is through faith in Christ, the righteousness from God that depends on faith...
Tit. 3:4-7. When the goodness and loving kindness of God our Savior appeared, he saved us, not because of deeds done by us in righteousness, but in virtue of his own mercy, by the washing of regeneration and renewal in the Holy Spirit, which he poured out upon us richly through Jesus Christ our Savior so that we might be justified by his grace and become heirs in hope of eternal life.
Hos. 2:19-20 [God]: I will betroth you to me for ever; I will betroth you to me in righteousness and in justice, in steadfast love, and in mercy. I will betroth you to me in faithfulness; and you shall know the Lord.
*Mt. 22:8-10. [The king] said to his servants, 'The wedding is ready, but those invited were not worthy. Go therefore to the thoroughfares, and invite to the marriage feast as many as you find.' And those servants went out into the streets and gathered all whom they found, both bad and good; so the wedding hall was filled with guests.
Mt. 26:27-29. And [Jesus] took a cup, and when he had given thanks he gave it to [his disciples], saying, "Drink of it, all of you; for this is my blood of the covenant, which is poured out for many for the forgiveness of sins. I tell you I shall not drink again of this fruit of the vine until that day when I drink it new with you in my Father's kingdom." (Also Lk. 22:17-18.)
Rev. 19:6-9. Then I heard what seemed to be the voice of a great multitude...crying, "Hallelujah! For the Lord our God the Almighty reigns. Let us rejoice and exult and give him the glory, for the marriage of the Lamb has come, and his Bride has made herself ready; it was granted her to be clothed with fine linen, bright and pure"—for the fine linen is the righteous deeds of the saints. And the angel said to me, "Write this: Blessed are those who are invited to the marriage supper of the Lamb."...
Mt. 25:1, 6, 10-13 [Christ]: The kingdom of heaven shall be compared to ten maidens who took their lamps and went to meet the bridegroom...At midnight there was a cry, "Behold, the bridegroom! Come out to meet him."...And those who were ready went in with him to the marriage feast; and the door was shut. Afterward the other maidens came also, saying, "Lord, lord, open to us." But he replied, "Truly, I say to you, I do not know you." Watch therefore, for you know neither the day nor the hour.
Rev. 2:10 [Christ]: *Be faithful unto death, and I will give you the crown of life.* (Also Rev. 3:11.)
2 Tim. 4:6-8. ...The time of my departure has come. I have fought the good fight, I have finished the race, I have kept the faith. Henceforth there is laid up for me the crown of righteousness, which the Lord, the righteous judge, will award to me on that Day, and not only to me but also to all who have loved his appearing. (Also Jms. 1:12.)

6. Bass Aria & Soprano Chorale (Christ & Believer)
    (See also 1-6.)
●Dialogue (Christ & Believer): United in paradise (49-6)
Dich hab ich je und je geliebet,
Thee have I ever and ever loved,
{I have loved thee for ever and ever,}

    Wie bin ich doch so herzlich froh,
    How am I indeed so heartily glad,
    {How I am indeed so heartily glad,}

    Daß mein Schatz ist das A und O,
    That my treasure is the Alpha and Omega,

    Der Anfang und das Ende.
    The beginning and the end.

Und darum zieh ich dich zu mir.
And therefore draw I thee to me.

    Er wird mich doch zu seinem Preis
    He will me indeed to his glory
    {He will indeed, to his glory}

    Aufnehmen in das Paradeis;
    Take-up into - paradise;
    {Take me up into paradise,}

    Des klopf ich in die Hände.
    For-this clap I - (my) hands.
    {For this I clap my hands.}

Ich komme bald,
I come soon,

    Amen! Amen!
    Amen! Amen!

Ich stehe vor der Tür,
I stand before the door,

    Komm, du schöne Freudenkrone, bleib nicht lange!
    Come, thou beautiful crown-of-joy, tarry not long!

Mach auf, mein Aufenthalt!
Make open, (O) mine abode!
{Open up to me, O mine abode!}

    Deiner wart ich mit Verlangen.
    Thee await I with longing.
    {For thee I wait with longing.}

Dich hab ich je und je geliebet,
Thee have I ever and ever loved,
{I have loved thee for ever and ever,}

Jer. 31:3 [God]: *...I have loved you with an everlasting love;* therefore I have continued my faithfulness to you. (Luther: Ich hab dich je und je geliebet; darum habe ich dich zu mir gezogen aus lauter Güte.)
S. of S. 6:3 [Bride]: I am my beloved's and my beloved is mine...
Rev. 1:8. "I am the Alpha and the Omega," (Luther: das A und das O, der Anfang und das Ende) says the Lord God, who is and who was and who is to come, the Almighty.
Rev. 21:6. ...I am the Alpha and the Omega, the beginning and the end... (Also Rev. 22:18.)
Mal. 3:6. For I the Lord do not change...
Ps. 25:6. Be mindful of thy mercy, O Lord, and of thy steadfast love, for they have been from of old.
Jn. 6:43-44. Jesus answered them, "...No one can come to me unless the Father who sent me draws him; and I will raise him up at the last day." (Also Jn. 12:32.)
S. of S. 1:4. Draw me after you, let us make haste... (Luther: Zieh mich dir nach, so laufen wir)
Jn. 14:3 [Christ]: When I go and prepare a place for you, I will come again and will take you to myself, that where I am you may be also.
Eph. 5:27. [Christ desires to] present the church to himself in splendor, without spot or wrinkle or any such thing, that she might be holy and without blemish.
2 Cor. 5:1. We know that if the earthly tent we live in is destroyed, we have a building from God, a house not made with hands, eternal in the heavens.
Lk. 23:43 [Christ]: ...Today you will be with me in Paradise.
Jms. 1:12. Blessed is the man who endures trial, for when he has stood the test he will receive the crown of life which God has promised to those who love him.
2 Tim. 4:8. Henceforth there is laid up for me the crown of righteousness, which the Lord, the righteous judge, will award to me on that day, and not only to me but also to all who have loved his appearing.
1 Pet. 5:4. When the chief Shepherd is manifested you will obtain the unfading crown of glory.
Is. 28:5. In that day the Lord of hosts will be a crown of glory, and a diadem of beauty, to the remnant of his people. Acts 1:11. ...This Jesus, who was taken up from you into heaven, will come in the same way as you saw him go into heaven. (Also Jms. 1:12, Rev. 2:10.)
1 Thess. 1:10. ...Wait for his Son from heaven...
Rev. 22:20. He who testifies to these things says, "Surely I am coming soon." Amen. Come, Lord Jesus!
Rev. 3:20 [Christ]: Behold, I stand at the door and knock; if any one hears my voice and opens the door, I will come in to him and eat with him, and he with me.
Jms. 5:8-9. ...Establish your hearts, for the coming of the Lord is at hand...behold, the Judge is standing at the doors.
Rev. 22:7. Behold, I am coming soon...
Rev. 3:11. I am coming soon; hold fast what you have, so that no one may seize your crown. (Also Rev. 22:12, 20.)
Phil. 3:20-21. Our commonwealth is in heaven, and from it we await a Savior, the Lord Jesus Christ, who will change our lowly body to be like his glorious body, by the power which enables him even to subject all things to himself.

Und darum zieh ich dich zu mir.
And therefore draw I thee to me.

Jer. 31:3 [God]: ...I have loved you with an everlasting love; therefore I have continued my faithfulness to you. (Luther: Ich hab dich je und je geliebt; darum habe ich dich zu mir gezogen aus lauter Güte.)

BWV 50
Nun ist das Heil und die Kraft
(Single movement; perhaps fragment of longer work)
(NBA I/30; BC A194)

Perhaps St. Michael's Day: Sept. 29 (BWV 130, 19, 149, 50)
*Rev. 12:7-12 (The archangel Michael battles with the dragon)
*Mt. 18:1-11 (The kingdom of heaven belongs to children; their angels behold the face of God)
Librettist: Unknown. Perhaps an adaptation of an earlier work.

1. Chorus
●Victory of Christ's kingdom over Satan: Rev. 12:10[1] (50-1)
   [1]The biblical passage has been modified somewhat.
Nun ist das Heil und die Kraft und das Reich
Now (has) the salvation and the power and the kingdom

und die Macht unsers Gottes seines Christus worden,
and the might of-our God   his Christ (come),

weil   der verworfen ist, der sie verklagete
because he cast-down is, who them accused

Tag und Nacht vor Gott.
day and night before God.

*Rev. 12:7-12. Now war arose in heaven, Michael and his angels fighting against the dragon; and the dragon and his angels fought, but they were defeated and there was no longer any place for them in heaven. And the great dragon was thrown down, that ancient serpent, who is called the Devil and Satan, the deceiver of the whole world—he was thrown down to the earth, and his angels were thrown down with him. And I heard a loud voice in heaven, saying, *"Now the salvation and the power and the kingdom of our God and the authority of his Christ have come, for the accuser of our brethren has been thrown down, who accuses them day and night before our God."* (Also Zech. 3:1-2, Job 1:9-11.)
1 Jn. 3:8. ...The reason the Son of God appeared was to destroy the works of the devil. (Also Heb. 2:14.)
Rev. 20:1-3, 7-10. Then I saw an angel coming down from heaven, holding in his hand the key of the bottomless pit and a great chain. And he seized the dragon, that ancient serpent, who is the Devil and Satan, and bound him for a thousand years, and threw him into the pit, and shut it and sealed it over him, that he should deceive the nations no more, till the thousand years were ended...And when the thousand years are ended, Satan will be loosed from his prison and will come out to deceive the nations...And they marched up...and surrounded the camp of the saints and the beloved city; but fire came down from heaven and consumed them, and the devil who had deceived them was thrown into the lake of fire and sulphur where the beast and the false prophet were, and they will be tormented day and night for ever and ever.

BWV 51
Jauchzet Gott in allen Landen
(NBA I/22; BC A134)

15. S. after Trinity; *"et In ogni Tempo"* (and at any time) (BWV 138, 99, 51)
*Gal. 5:25-6:10 (Exhortation to walk in the Spirit)
*Mt. 6:24-34 (Sermon on the Mount: Exhortation not to be anxious but to seek the kingdom of God)
Librettist: Unknown

1. Soprano Aria
●Praise God all ye lands, for his help in trouble! (51-1)
Jauchzet   Gott in allen Landen!
Shout-with-joy (to) God in all   lands!
{Shout with joy to God in every land!}

Was der Himmel und die Welt
What the heavens and the world
{Whatever the heavens and the earth}

Ps. 66:1-2, 4. Make a joyful noise to God, all the earth; sing the glory of his name; give to him glorious praise!...All the earth worships thee...
Ps. 100:1-2. Make a joyful noise to the Lord, all the lands! Serve the Lord with gladness! Come into his presence with singing! (Also Ps. 81:1, 95:1, 2, 98:4, 6.)
Ps. 148:1-5, 7-12. Praise the Lord! Praise the Lord from the heavens, praise him in the heights! Praise him, all his angels, praise him, all his host! Praise him, sun and moon, praise him, all you shining stars! Praise him, you highest heavens, and you waters above the heavens! Let them praise the name of the Lord!...Praise the Lord from the earth, you sea monsters and all deeps, fire and hail, snow and frost, stormy wind fulfilling his command! Mountains and all hills, fruit trees and all cedars! Beasts and all cattle, creeping things and flying birds! Kings of the earth and all peoples, princes and all rulers of the earth! Young men and maidens together, old men and children!
Ps. 107:1-2. O give thanks to the Lord, for he is good; for his steadfast love endures for ever! Let the redeemed of the Lord say so, whom he has redeemed from trouble (Luther: Not).

An Geschöpfen in   sich   hält,
Of created-things in themselves contain,
{Contain of created things,}

Müssen dessen Ruhm erhöhen,
Must   (his)   fame   exalt,

Und wir wollen unserm Gott
And we   would   to-our God

Gleichfalls itzt ein Opfer bringen,
Likewise   now a sacrifice bring,

Daß er uns in   Kreuz und Not
(For) he us amidst cross   and trouble

Allezeit   hat beigestanden.
At-all-times has   stood-by.
{For he has stood by us at all times in cross and trouble.}

2. Soprano Recit.
●Praising God in his temple for his daily blessings (51-2)
Wir beten   zu   dem Tempel an,
We worship toward the   temple -,
{We worship at the temple,}

Da   Gottes Ehre wohnet,
Where God's glory dwells,

Da dessen Treu,
Since (his) faithfulness,

So   täglich neu,
Which (is) daily new,
{Which is new every day,}

Mit lauter Segen   lohnet.
With sheer blessing (us) recompenses.
{Brings us sheer blessing.}

Wir preisen, was er an uns hat getan.
We praise, what he (for) us has done.

Muß gleich der schwache Mund
Must though (our) weak   mouth

     von seinen Wundern lallen,
     of   his   wonders stammer,
{Though our weak mouth can only stammer of his wonders,}

So kann ein schlechtes Lob
So can   a poorly-rendered praise

     ihm dennoch wohlgefallen.
     him nevertheless please-well.
{So will a poorly-rendered praise please him nevertheless.}

Ps. 150:6. Let everything that breathes praise the Lord!...
Ps. 66:13-14, 20. [O Lord,] I will come into thy house with burnt offerings (Luther: Brandopfer); I will pay thee my vows, that which my lips uttered and my mouth promised when I was in trouble...Blessed be God, because he has not rejected my prayer or removed his steadfast love from me!
Heb. 13:15. ...Let us continually offer up a sacrifice of praise to God, that is, the fruit of lips that acknowledge his name. (Also Ps. 51:15–17.)
Ps. 56:12–13. My vows to thee I must perform, O God; I will render thank offerings to thee. For thou hast delivered my soul from death, yea, my feet from falling... (Also Ps. 86:12–13, 116:8.)
Ps. 34:19. Many are the afflictions of the righteous; but the Lord delivers him out of them all.
2 Tim. 4:17. The Lord stood by me...
*****Mt. 6:30.** If God so clothes the grass of the field, which today is alive and tomorrow is thrown into the oven, will he not much more clothe you, O men of little faith?

Ps. 5:7. I through the abundance of thy steadfast love will enter thy house [O Lord], I will worship toward thy holy temple in the fear of thee. (Also Dan. 6:10, Jonah 2:7.)
Ps. 26:8. O Lord, I love the habitation of thy house, and the place where thy glory dwells (Luther: da deine Ehre wohnet).
Ps. 138:2. I bowed down toward thy holy temple and give thanks to thy name for thy steadfast love and thy faithfulness (Luther: Güte und Treue); for thou hast exalted above everything thy name and thy word.
2 Chron. 7:1–3. When Solomon had ended his prayer, fire came down from heaven and consumed the burnt offering and the sacrifices, and the glory of the Lord (Luther: Herrlichkeit des Herrn) filled the temple. And the priests could not enter the house of the Lord, because the glory of the Lord filled the Lord's house. When all the children of Israel saw the fire come down and the glory of the Lord upon the temple, they bowed down with their faces to the earth on the pavement, and worshiped... (Also 1 Kings 8:10–11.)
Lam. 3:22–23. The steadfast love of the Lord never ceases, his mercies never come to an end; they are new every morning... (Also Ps. 90:14.)
Ps. 126:3. The Lord has done great things for us; we are glad. (Also 1 Sam. 12:24, Lk. 1:49.)
Ps. 50:23 [God]: He who brings thanksgiving as his sacrifice honors me...
Lk. 19:37, 39–40. As [Jesus] was now drawing near, at the descent of the Mount of Olives, the whole multitude of the disciples began to rejoice and praise God with a loud voice for all the mighty works that they had seen... And some of the Pharisees in the multitude said to him, "Teacher, rebuke your disciples." He answered, "I tell you, if these were silent, the very stones would cry out."
Heb. 13:15. ...Let us continually offer up a sacrifice of praise to God, that is, the fruit of lips that acknowledge his name.

3. Soprano Aria
●Prayer: Bless us anew each morning & we will live godly (51-3)

Höchster, mache deine Güte
(O) Most-High, make   thy goodness
{O Most High make thy goodness}

Ferner   alle Morgen neu.
Henceforth all mornings new.
{New every morning henceforth.}

So   soll vor die   Vatertreu
Then shall for the Father's-faithfulness

Auch ein dankbares Gemüte
Also (our) grateful   spirit
{Our grateful spirit also}

Durch ein frommes Leben weisen,
Through a   godly   life   show,
{Show by a godly life,}

Daß wir deine Kinder heißen.
That we   thy children are-called.
{That we are called thy children.}

4. Chorale: Soprano (See also 29-8, 167-5.)
●Prayer of praise and dedication to Trinity (51-4)
Sei Lob und Preis mit Ehren
   - Laud and praise with honors (to)

Gott   Vater, Sohn,   Heiligem Geist!
God (the) Father, Son, (and) Holy   Ghost!

Der woll in uns vermehren,
(May) he - in us   increase

Was   er uns aus Gnaden verheißt,
That-which he to-us out-of grace does-promise,

Daß wir ihm fest   vertrauen,
So-that we him firmly (would) trust,
{So that we would firmly trust him,}

Gänzlich uns   lass'n auf ihn,
Completely ourselves entrust (to) him,
{Completely rely on him,}

Ps. 90:14. [O Lord,] satisfy us in the morning with thy steadfast love, that we may rejoice and be glad all our days.
Mt. 6:11. Give us this day our daily bread. (Also Lk. 11:3.)
Lam. 3:22-23. ...[The Lord's] mercies...are new every morning...
*Mt. 6:25-26, 28-30, 34 [Christ]: I tell you, do not be anxious about your life...Is not life more than food, and the body more than clothing? Look at the birds of the air; they neither sow nor reap nor gather into barns, and yet your heavenly Father feeds them. Are you not of more value than they?...And why are you anxious about clothing? Consider the lilies of the field, how they grow; they neither toil nor spin; yet I tell you, even Solomon in all his glory was not arrayed like one of these. But if God so clothes the grass of the field, which today is alive and tomorrow is thrown into the oven, will he not much more clothe you, O men of little faith? Therefore do not be anxious about tomorrow, for tomorrow will be anxious for itself...
Rom. 12:1. I appeal to you therefore, brethren, by the mercies of God, to present your bodies as a living sacrifice, holy and acceptable to God, which is your spiritual worship.
Ps. 50:14, 23. Offer to God a sacrifice of thanksgiving, and pay your vows to the Most High...He who brings thanksgiving as his sacrifice honors me; to him who orders his way aright I will show the salvation of God!
1 Sam. 15:22. ...Has the Lord as great delight in burnt offerings and sacrifices, as in obeying the voice of the Lord? Behold, to obey is better than sacrifice... (Also Jms. 2:26.)
2 Tim. 2:19. ...Let every one who names the name of the Lord depart from iniquity.
Mt. 5:48 [Christ]: You, therefore, must be perfect, as your heavenly Father is perfect. (Also Lk. 6:32-36, 1 Pet. 1:15-16.)
Mt. 5:9. Blessed are the peacemakers, for they shall be called sons of God (Luther: Gottes Kinder heißen). (Also 1 Jn. 3:1.)

Rev. 7:11-12. All the angels stood round the throne and round the elders and the four living creatures, and they fell on their faces before the throne and worshiped God, saying, "Amen! Blessing and glory and wisdom and thanksgiving and honor and power and might be to our God for ever and ever! Amen."
1 Thess. 3:12-13. May the Lord make you increase (Luther: euch vermehre)...so that he may establish your hearts unblamable in holiness before our God and Father...
Phil. 1:6, 9. I am sure that he who began a good work in you will bring it to completion at the day of Jesus Christ...And it is my prayer that your love may abound more and more, with knowledge and all discernment... (Also Ps. 138:8.)
1 Jn. 2:24-25. Let what you heard from the beginning abide in you. If what you heard from the beginning abides in you, then you will abide in the Son and in the Father. And this is what he has promised us, eternal life.
2 Thess. 2:16-17. Now may our Lord Jesus Christ himself, and God our Father, who loved us and gave us eternal comfort and good hope through grace, comfort your hearts and establish them in every good work and word.
Mt. 7:24 [Christ]: Every one then who hears these words of mine and does them will be like a wise man who built his house upon the rock...
1 Cor. 3:11. For no other foundation can any one lay than that which is laid, which is Jesus Christ.

Von   Herzen auf ihn bauen,
With (all our) heart upon him build,

Daß uns'r Herz, Mut und Sinn
So-that our heart, mettle, and mind

Ihm festiglich anhangen;
To-him firmly would-adhere;

Drauf   singen wir zur Stund:
Thereupon sing we at-this hour:

Amen! wir werdn's erlangen,
Amen! We will-it attain,

    Glaub'n wir von Herzensgrund.
(If) believe we from heart's-bottom.
{If we believe with all our heart.}

5. Soprano Aria
●Alleluia (51–5)
Alleluja!
Alleluia!

Mt. 22:37–38. [Jesus] said to him, "You shall love the Lord your God with all your heart (Luther: Herzen), and with all your soul (Luther: Seele), and with all your mind (Luther: Gemüte). This is the great and first commandment." (Also Deut. 6:5.)
Deut. 10:20. You shall fear the Lord your God; you shall serve him and cleave to him (Luther: ihm anhangen)... (Also Deut. 13:4.)
Ps. 63:8. [O Lord,] my soul clings to thee (Luther: hanget dir an)... (Also 2 Kings 18:6.)
1 Thess. 5:23. May the God of peace himself sanctify you wholly; and may your spirit and soul and body be kept sound and blameless at the coming of our Lord Jesus Christ.
Phil. 3:12, 14–15. Not that I have already obtained this or am already perfect; but I press on to make it my own...I press on toward the goal for the prize of the upward call of God in Christ Jesus. Let those of us who are mature be thus minded...
Heb. 10:39. We are not of those who shrink back and are destroyed, but of those who have faith and keep their souls.

Rev. 19:1. After this I heard what seemed to be the loud voice of a great multitude in heaven, crying, "Hallelujah! Salvation and glory and power belong to our God." (Also Rev. 19:3, 4, 6.)

BWV 52
Falsche Welt, dir trau ich nicht
(NBA I/26; BC A160)

23. S. after Trinity (BWV 163, 139, 52)
*Phil. 3:17–21 (Our citizenship is in heaven.)
*Mt. 22:15–22 (The Pharisees try to trap Jesus with the question: "Is it lawful to pay taxes to Ceasar?")
Librettist: Unknown

1. Sinfonia (Taken from an earlier work)

2. Soprano Recit.
●Hypocrisy and deceit is rampant in the world (52–2)
Falsche Welt, dir trau ich nicht!
Deceitful world, thee trust I not!
{Deceitful world, I trust thee not!}

Hier muß ich unter Skorpionen
Here must I amidst scorpions

Und unter falschen Schlangen wohnen.
And amidst deceitful serpents dwell.

Dein Angesicht,
Thy countenance,

Das noch so freundlich ist,
Which ever so friendly is,
{Which is ever so friendly,}

Sinnt auf ein heimliches Verderben:
Devises a secret destruction:

***Mt. 22:15–18.** Then the Pharisees went and took counsel how to entangle [Jesus] in his talk. And they sent their disciples to him, along with the Herodians, saying, "Teacher, we know that you are true, and teach the way of God truthfully, and care for no man; for you do not regard the position of men. Tell us, then, what you think. Is it lawful to pay taxes to Caesar, or not?" But Jesus, aware of their malice, said, "Why put me to the test, you hypocrites?"
Ezek. 2:6. And you, son of man, be not afraid of them, nor be afraid of their words, though...you sit upon scorpions (Luther: du wohnst unter den Skorpionen); be not afraid of their words, nor be dismayed at their looks, for they are a rebellious house.
Gen. 3:1, 4, 13. Now the serpent was more subtle than any other wild creature that the Lord God had made. He said to the woman, "Did God say, 'You shall not eat of any tree of the garden'?...You will not die..." Then the Lord God said to the woman, "What is this that you have done?" The woman said, "The serpent beguiled me, and I ate."
Mt. 12:34 [Christ]: You brood of vipers! how can you speak good, when you are evil? For out of the abundance of the heart the mouth speaks. (Also Mt. 23:33.)

Wenn Joab küßt,
When Joab kisses,

So muß ein frommer Abner sterben.
Then must a righteous Abner die.

Die Redlichkeit ist aus der Welt verbannt,
- Sincerity is (from) the world banished,
{Sincerity has been banished from the world,}

Die Falschheit hat sie fortgetrieben,
- Deceit has it driven-away,
{Deceit has driven it away,}

Nun ist die Heuchelei
Now has - hypocrisy
{And hyporcrisy now}

An ihrer Stelle blieben.
In its stead remained.
{Remains in its stead.}

Der beste Freund ist ungetreu,
The best friend is untrue,

O jämmerlicher Stand!
O wretched condition!

3. Soprano Aria
●Hypocritical world hates me but God is my friend! (52-3)
Immerhin, immerhin,
For-all-that, for-all-that,

Wenn ich gleich verstoßen bin!
Though I - dispossessed be!
{Even if I be dispossessed!}

Ist die falsche Welt mein Feind,
Is the false world my foe,
{Though the false world be my foe,}

O so bleibt doch Gott mein Freund,
Oh, then remains nevertheless God my friend,
{Oh, then God remains as my friend nevertheless;}

Der es redlich mit mir meint.
Who it sincerely with me intends.
{He holds sincere intentions toward me.}

4. Soprano Recit.
●Faithfulness of God preserves me when worlds attacks (52-4)
Gott ist getreu!
God is faithful!

Er wird, er kann mich nicht verlassen;
He will, he can me not forsake;

Prov. 26:23–24. Like the glaze covering an earthen vessel are smooth lips with an evil heart. He who hates, dissembles with his lips and harbors deceit in his heart. (Also Ps. 28:3, 62:4.)
Mt. 23:27–28 [Christ]: Woe to you, scribes and Pharisees, hypocrites! for you are like whitewashed tombs, which outwardly appear beautiful, but within they are full of dead men's bones and all uncleanness. So you also outwardly appear righteous to men, but within you are full of hypocrisy and iniquity.
2 Sam. 3:27–29. When Abner returned to Hebron, Joab took him aside into the midst of the gate to speak with him privately, and there he smote him in the belly, so that he died...Afterward, when David heard of it, he said, "I and my kingdom are for ever guiltless before the Lord for the blood of Abner the son of Ner. May it fall upon the head of Joab, and upon all his father's house..."
Mic. 7:2. The godly man has perished from the earth, and there is none upright among men...
Rom. 3:12–13. All have turned aside, together they have gone wrong; no one does good, not even one. Their throat is an open grave, they use their tongues to deceive. The venom of asps is under their lips. (Also Jer. 17:9, Is. 1:6.)
Lk. 22:47–48. While [Jesus] was still speaking, there came a crowd, and the man called Judas, one of the twelve, was leading them. He drew near to Jesus to kiss him; but Jesus said to him, "Judas, would you betray the Son of man with a kiss?"
2 Tim. 3:8, 13. ...So these men also oppose the truth, men of corrupt mind and counterfeit faith...Evil men and impostors will go on from bad to worse, deceivers and deceived. (Also 2 Jn. 1:7.)

Jms. 4:4. Unfaithful creatures! Do you not know that friendship with the world is enmity with God? Therefore whoever wishes to be a friend of the world makes himself an enemy of God.
1 Jn. 2:15–17. Do not love the world or the things in the world. If any one loves the world, love for the Father is not in him. For all that is in the world, the lust of the flesh and the lust of the eyes and the pride of life, is not of the Father but is of the world. And the world passes away, and the lust of it; but he who does the will of God abides for ever.
Jn. 15:18–19 [Christ]: If the world hates you, know that it has hated me before it hated you. If you were of the world, the world would love its own; but because you are not of the world, but I chose you out of the world, therefore the world hates you.
Jn. 15:15 [Christ]: No longer do I call you servants, for the servant does not know what his master is doing; but I have called you friends...
Jer. 29:11. For I know the plans I have for you, says the Lord, plans for welfare and not for evil, to give you a future and a hope. (Also Prov. 23:18.)
Rom. 8:32. He who did not spare his own Son but gave him up for us all, will he not also give us all things with him? (Also Mt. 7:11.)

1 Cor. 10:13. ...[But] *God is faithful* (Luther: Aber Gott ist getreu)...
Rom. 3:4. ...Let God be true though every man be false...
2 Tim. 2:13. ...If we are faithless, he remains faithful—for he cannot deny himself.
Heb. 13:5–6. ...[God] has said, "I will never fail you nor forsake you." Hence we can confidently say, "The Lord is my helper, I will not be

Will mich die Welt in ihrer Raserei
Would me the world in its raging

In ihre Schlingen fassen,
In its snares seize,
{Would the world, raging, catch me in its snare,}

So steht mir seine Hülfe bei.
Then stands me his help by.
{Then his help stands by me.}

Auf seine Freundschaft will ich bauen
Upon his friendship will I build,

Und meine Seele, Geist und Sinn
And (will) my soul, spirit, and mind

Und alles, was ich bin,
And all that I am,

Ihm anvertrauen.
To-him entrust.
{Entrust to him.}

5. Soprano Aria
●Faithfulness to God avowed; world scorned (52-5)
Ich halt es mit dem lieben Gott,
I side - with the dear God,

Die Welt mag nur alleine bleiben.
The world (can) just alone-by-itself remain.
{The world can just remain alone by itself.}

Gott mit mir, und ich mit Gott,
God with me, and I with God,

Also kann ich selber Spott
Thus can I, myself, ridicule
{Thus I can direct ridicule, myself,}

Mit den falschen Zungen treiben.
(Toward) those deceitful tongues (direct).
{At those deceitful tongues.}

6. Chorale
●Prayer: I trust in thee; let me not be confounded! (52-6)
In dich hab ich gehoffet, Herr,
In thee have I hoped, (O) Lord,

Hilf, daß ich nicht zuschanden werd,
Help, that I not confounded be,
{Help that I be not confounded,}

afraid; what can man do to me?" (See Deut. 31:6, 8; Josh. 1:5.)
Mt. 10:16–20 [Christ]: Behold, I send you out as sheep in the midst of wolves; so be wise as serpents and innocent as doves. Beware of men; for they will deliver you up to councils, and flog you in their synagogues, and you will be dragged before governors and kings for my sake, to bear testimony before them and the Gentiles. When they deliver you up, do not be anxious how you are to speak or what you are to say; for what you are to say will be given to you in that hour; for it is not you who speak, but the Spirit of your Father speaking through you. (Also Jn. 15:20.)
Jn. 16:33 [Christ]: I have said this to you, that in me you may have peace. In the world you have tribulation; but be of good cheer, I have overcome the world.
1 Jn. 4:4. Little children, you are of God, and have overcome them; for he who is in you is greater than he who is in the world.
Mt. 7:24–25 [Christ]: Every one then who hears these words of mine and does them will be like a wise man who built his house upon the rock; and the rain fell, and the floods came, and the winds blew and beat upon that house, but it did not fall, because it had been founded on the rock.
1 Pet. 4:19. Therefore let those who suffer according to God's will do right and entrust their souls to a faithful Creator.
1 Thess. 5:23. May the God of peace himself sanctify you wholly; and may your spirit and soul and body be kept sound and blameless at the coming of our Lord Jesus Christ. (Also 2 Tim. 1:12.)

Ps. 73:28. But for me it is good to be near God (Luther: daß ich mich zu Gott halte); I have made the Lord God my refuge...
Jms. 4:4. Unfaithful creatures! Do you not know that friendship with the world is enmity with God? Therefore whoever wishes to be a friend of the world makes himself an enemy of God.
Josh. 24:15. ...Choose this day whom you will serve...but as for me and my house, we will serve the Lord.
Jms. 1:27. Religion that is pure and undefiled before God and the Father is this...to keep oneself unstained from the world.
S. of S. 6:3 [Bride]: I am my beloved's and my beloved is mine...
Ps. 118:6–7. With the Lord on my side I do not fear. What can man do to me? The Lord is on my side to help me; I shall look in triumph on those who hate me. (Also Ps. 56:4, Rom. 8:31.)
Ps. 37:12–13. The wicked plots against the righteous, and gnashes his teeth at him; but the Lord laughs at the wicked, for he sees that his day is coming.
Ps. 52:6. The righteous shall see, and fear, and shall laugh at him... (Also Job 22:19, Ps. 2:4, 59:8.)

Ps. 25:2–3. O my God, in thee I trust, let me not be put to shame; let not my enemies exult over me. Yea, let none that wait for thee be put to shame; let them be ashamed who are wantonly treacherous.
Ps. 71:1. In thee, O Lord, do I take refuge; let me never be put to shame!
Ps. 25:20. Oh guard my life, and deliver me; let me not be put to shame, for I take refuge in thee. (Also Ps. 31:1, 31:17.)

Noch ewiglich   zu Spotte!
Nor   eternally (be put) to ridicule!

Das bitt ich   dich,
That ask I (of) thee,
{That I ask of thee,}

Erhalte mich
Uphold me

In deiner   Treu,   Herr Gotte!
In   thy faithfulness, Lord God!

BWV 53
Schlage doch gewünschte Stunde

This cantata was probably composed by Georg Melchior Hoffmann. See Dürr, *Die Kantaten*, p. 1003.

BWV 54
Widerstehe doch der Sünde
(NBA I/18; BC A51)

Oculi: 3. S. in Lent (BWV 54 only)
*Eph. 5:1-9 (Exhortation to pure living)
*Lk. 11:14-28 (Accusation that Christ drove out demons by Beelzebul)
Alfred Dürr suggests this cantata also suits the 7. S. after Trinity (See Dürr, *Die Kantaten*, pp. 292-293.)
+Rom. 6:19-23 (The wages of sin is death but the gift of God is eternal life)
+Mk. 8:1-9 (Jesus feeds the four thousand)
Librettist: Georg Christian Lehms

1. Alto Aria
●Sin: Resist it or its poison will eventually kill you (54-1)
Widerstehe doch der Sünde,
Resist   indeed -   sin,
{Be sure to resist sin,}

Sonst   ergreifet dich ihr Gift.
Otherwise seizes   you its poison.
{Or its poison will seize you.}

Laß dich nicht den   Satan   blenden;
Let yourself not   - (by) Satan (be) blinded;

Denn   die   Gottes Ehre schänden,
For   those-who God's glory profane,

Trifft ein Fluch, der tödlich ist.
Strikes a curse, that deadly is.
{A deadly curse will strike.}

Is. 50:7. For the Lord God helps me; therefore I have not been confounded; therefore I have set my face like a flint, and I know that I shall not be put to shame.
Is. 54:4. Fear not, for you will not be ashamed; be not confounded, for you will not be put to shame; for you will forget the shame of your youth, and the reproach of your widowhood you will remember no more. (Also Jer. 17:18.)
1 Pet. 2:6 [God]: Behold, I am laying in Zion a stone, a cornerstone chosen and precious, and he who believes in him will not be put to shame. (Also Ps. 22:4-5, Is.45:17.)
Ps. 40:11. Do not thou, O Lord, withhold thy mercy from me, let thy steadfast love and thy faithfulness ever preserve me!

+**Rom. 6:19-22.** I am speaking in human terms, because of your natural limitations. For just as you once yielded your members to impurity and to greater and greater iniquity, so now yield your members to righteousness for sanctification. When you were slaves of sin, you were free in regard to righteousness. But then what return did you get from the things of which you are now ashamed? The end of those things is death. But now that you have been set free from sin and have become slaves of God, the return you get is sanctification and its end, eternal life. (Also Rom. 6:12.)
1 Jn. 2:1. My little children, I am writing this to you so that you may not sin...
Rom. 8:6. To set the mind on the flesh is death, but to set the mind on the Spirit is life and peace.
Gal. 6:7-8. Do not be deceived; God is not mocked, for whatever a man sows, that he will also reap. For he who sows to his own flesh will from the flesh reap corruption; but he who sows to the Sprit will from the Spirit reap eternal life.
2 Cor. 4:4. ...The god of this world has blinded the minds of the unbelievers, to keep them from seeing the light of the gospel of the glory of Christ... (Also 1 Jn. 2:11.)
***Eph. 5:6-8.** Let no one deceive you with empty words, for it is because of these things that the wrath of God comes upon the sons of disobedience...Once you were darkness, but now you are light in the Lord; walk as children of light. (Also Heb. 10:29-30.)

2. Alto Recit.

●Sin outwardly appealing but like a whitewashed tomb (54–2)

Die   Art verruchter Sünden
The manner of-vile   sin
{The appearance of vile sin}

Ist zwar von   außen wunderschön;
Is indeed from (the) outside very-beautiful;
{Is indeed very beautiful outwardly;}

Allein man muß
But   one must

Hernach   mit Kummer und Verdruß
Afterwards with trouble and vexation

Viel Ungemach empfinden.
Much hardship experience.
{Experience much hardship.}

Von   außen ist sie Gold;
From (the) outside is it gold;
{From the outside it is gold;}

Doch, will man weiter gehn,
Yet, would one further go,
{Yet if one goes further,}

So zeigt sich nur ein leerer Schatten
Then emerges only an empty shadow

Und   übertünchtes Grab.
And (a) whitewashed tomb.

Sie ist den Sodomsäpfeln gleich,
It is (to) Sodom's-apples similar,
{It is similiar to Sodom's apples,}

Und   die   sich   mit derselben gatten,
And those-who themselves with the-same unite,
{And those who unite themselves with the same,}

Gelangen nicht in Gottes Reich.
Attain   not - God's kingdom.
{Do not attain God's kingdom.}

Sie ist als wie ein scharfes Schwert,
It is   like   a   sharp   sword,

Das uns durch Leib und Seele   fährt.
Which us through body and soul does-pierce.
{Which pierces through our body and soul.}

Tit. 2:11–12. The grace of God...[trains] us to renounce irreligion and worldly passions, and to live sober, upright, and godly lives in this world.

Mt. 23:27–28 [Christ]: Woe to you, scribes and Pharisees, hypocrites! for you are like whitewashed tombs, which outwardly appear beautiful, but within they are full of dead men's bones and all uncleanness. So you also outwardly appear righteous to men, but within you are full of hypocrisy and iniquity. (Also Lk. 11:44.)

2 Cor. 11:14. ...Satan disguises himself as an angel of light.

Mt. 18:7 [Christ]: Woe to the world for temptations to sin!... (Also Lk. 17:1.)

Heb. 12:15–17. See to it...that no one be immoral or irreligious like Esau, who sold his birthright for a single meal. For you know that afterward, when he desired to inherit the blessing, he was rejected, for he found no chance to repent, though he sought it with tears.

Rom. 8:5–6. Those who live according to the flesh set their minds on the things of the flesh...To set the mind on the flesh is death...

Jms. 1:15. Desire when it has conceived gives birth to sin; and sin when it is full-grown brings forth death.

Tit. 3:3. We ourselves were once foolish, disobedient, led astray, slaves to various passions and pleasures...

Rom. 7:11. Sin, finding opportunity in the commandment, deceived me and by it killed me. (Also Heb. 3:13.)

Prov. 23:31–32. Do not look at wine when it is red, when it sparkles in the cup and goes down smoothly. At the last it bites like a serpent, and stings like an adder.

Prov. 5:3–5. The lips of a loose woman drip honey, and her speech is smoother than oil; but in the end she is bitter as wormwood, sharp as a two-edged sword. Her feet go down to death; her steps follow the path to Sheol. (Also Prov. 6:25–29, 6:32, 7:24–27, 9:17–18.)

Josephus IV:483–485. ...It is said that, owing to the impiety of its inhabitants, [Sodom] was consumed by thunderbolts; and in fact vestiges of the divine fire and faint traces of five cities are still visible. Still, too, may one see ashes reproduced in the fruits, which from their outward appearance would be thought edible, but on being plucked with the hand dissolve into smoke and ashes. [Translated by H. St. J. Thackeray. See also BWV 95–2, 179–3.]

Deut. 32:32–33 [Moses]: [This people's] vine comes from the vine of Sodom, and from the fields of Gomorrah; their grapes are grapes of poison, their clusters are bitter; their wine is the poison of serpents, and the cruel venom of asps.

Jude 1:7. ...Sodom and Gomorrah and the surrounding cities, which likewise acted immorally and indulged in unnatural lust, serve as an example by undergoing a punishment of eternal fire.

1 Cor. 6:9. Do you not know that the unrighteous will not inherit the kingdom of God?...

1 Tim. 6:10. ...It is through this craving that some have wandered away from the faith and pierced their hearts with many pangs.

3. Alto Aria

●Siners are of the devil; resist him and he flees (54–3)

Wer   Sünde tut,   der ist vom Teufel,
Whoever sin commits, he is of-the devil,

1 Jn. 3:8. *He who commits sin is of the devil;* for the devil has sinned from the beginning. The reason the Son of God appeared was to destroy the works of the devil.

Jn. 8:44 [Christ]: You are of your father the devil, and your will is to

Denn dieser hat sie aufgebracht;
For (he) has it reared;
{For the devil is the father of sin;}

Doch wenn man ihren schnöden Banden
Yet (once) one its base bonds
{Yet if one resists sin's base bonds}

Mit rechter Andacht widerstanden,
With true devotion has-resisted, (then)
{With true devotion, then}

Hat sie sich gleich davongemacht.
Has it - immediately taken-flight.
{Sin immediately takes flight.}

BWV 55
Ich armer Mensch, ich Sündenknecht
(NBA I/26; BC A157)

22. S. after Trinity (BWV 89, 115, 55)
*Phil. 1:3–11 (Paul's prayer for the church at Philippi)
*Mt. 18:23–35 (The parable of the unforgiving servant)
Librettist: Unknown

1. Tenor Aria
●Fear of judgment: I recognize my sin (55-1)
Ich armer Mensch, ich Sündenknecht,
I, wretched man, I servant-of-sin,
I, who am such a wretched man; I, who am such a servant-of-sin,}

Ich geh vor Gottes Angesichte
I go before God's face

Mit Furcht und Zittern zum Gerichte.
With fear and trembling unto judgment.

Er ist gerecht, ich ungerecht.
He is righteous, I, unrighteous.

Ich armer Mensch, ich Sündenknecht!
I, wretched man, I, servant-of-sin!
I, who am such a wretched man; I, who am such a servant-of-sin!}

2. Tenor Recit.
●Fear of judgment: My sin is great, where can I flee? (55-2)
Ich habe wider Gott gehandelt
I have against God acted
{I have acted against God}

Und bin demselben Pfad,
And have that path,

Den er mir vorgeschrieben hat,
Which he for-me prescribed - ,

do your father's desires. He was a murderer from the beginning, and has nothing to do with the truth, because there is no truth in him. When he lies, he speaks according to his own nature, for he is a liar and the father of lies.
+Rom. 6:20. When you were slaves of sin, you were free in regard to righteousness.
2 Pet. 2:19. ...[Though such men promise freedom] they themselves are slaves of corruption; for whatever overcomes a man, to that he is enslaved. (Also Jn. 8:34, Rom. 6:16.)
Jms. 4:7. Submit yourselves therefore to God. Resist the devil and he will flee from you.
1 Pet. 5:8–9. Be sober, be watchful. Your adversary the devil prowls around like a roaring lion, seeking some one to devour. Resist him, firm in your faith...
*Lk. 11:14. Now [Jesus] was casting out a demon...

*Mt. 18:23–34. The kingdom of heaven may be compared to a king who wished to settle accounts with his servants. When he began the reckoning, one was brought to him who owed him ten thousand talents; and as he could not pay, his lord ordered him to be sold, with his wife and children and all that he had, and payment to be made. So the servant fell on his knees, imploring him, "Lord, have patience with me, and I will pay you everything." And out of pity for him the lord of that servant released him and forgave him the debt (Luther: Schuld). But that same servant as he went out came upon one of his fellow servants who owed him a hundred denarii, and seizing him by the throat he said, "Pay what you owe." So his fellow servant fell down and besought him, "Have patience with me, and I will pay you." He refused and went and put him in prison till he should pay the debt. When his fellow servants saw what had taken place, they were greatly distressed, and they went and reported to their lord all that had taken place. Then his lord summoned him and said to him, "You wicked servant! I forgave you all that debt because you besought me; and should not you have had mercy on your fellow servant, as I had mercy on you?" And in anger his lord delivered him to the jailers, till he should pay all his debt.
Rom. 14:10, 12. ...We shall all stand before the judgment seat of God... Each of us shall give account of himself to God. (Also 2 Cor. 5:10.)

Deut. 5:33. You shall walk in all the way which the Lord your God has commanded you, that you may live...
Ezek. 11:12 [God]: ...You have not walked in my statutes, nor executed my ordinances...
Jer. 3:25. Let us lie down in our shame, and let our dishonor cover us; for we have sinned against the Lord our God...we have not obeyed the voice of the Lord our God.
Lk. 15:21. The [prodigal] son said to [his father], "Father, I have sinned against heaven and before you; I am no longer worthy to be called your son."

Nicht nachgewandelt.
Not   followed.

Wohin?   soll   ich der Morgenröte Flügel
Where-to? Should I   -   dawn's wings
{Where to? If I should elect}

Zu meiner Flucht erkiesen,
For my   flight elect,
{The wings of dawn for my flight,}

Die   mich zum   letzten Meere wiesen,
Which me to-the (farthest) sea would-direct,
{To take me to the farthest sea,}

So   wird mich doch die Hand des Allerhöchsten finden
Then would me   still the hand of-the Most-High   find
{Then the hand of the Most High would still find me}

Und   mir die Sündenrute binden.
And for-me - sin's-rod   bind.
{And with the rod of sin chastise me.}

Ach ja!
Ah yes!

Wenn gleich die Höll ein Bette
If   even   - hell a bed
{Even if hell had a bed}

Vor mich und meine Sünden hätte,
For me and my   sins   had,
{For me and my sins,}

So wäre   doch   der Grimm des Höchsten   da.
So would nevertheless the fury of-the Most-High be-there.
{The fury of the Most High would still be there.}

Die Erde schützt mich nicht,
The earth protects me   not,

Sie droht mich   Scheusal zu verschlingen,
It threatens me—(a) monster—to devour,
{It threatens to devour the monster that I am,}

Und will ich mich zum Himmel schwingen,
And would I -   to heaven   ascend,
{And if I would ascend to heaven,}

Da wohnet Gott, der mir das Urteil spricht.
There dwells God, who (my) - judgment utters.
{Then God dwells there, who utters my judgment.}

3. Tenor Aria
●Prayer: Have mercy on me, a sinner, for Jesus' sake (55–3)
Erbarme dich!
Have-mercy - !

Ps. 76:7. But thou, [O Lord,] terrible art thou! Who can stand before thee when once thy anger is roused?
Nah. 1:6. Who can stand before his indignation? Who can endure the heat of his anger? His wrath is poured out like fire, and the rocks are broken asunder by him.
Ps. 139:7–12. [O Lord,] whither shall I go from thy Spirit? Or whither shall I flee from thy presence? If I ascend to heaven, thou art there! If I make my bed in Sheol (Luther: Hölle), thou art there! If I take the wings of the morning and dwell in the uttermost parts of the sea, even there thy hand shall lead me, and thy right hand shall hold me. If I say, "Let only darkness cover me, and the light about me be night," even the darkness is not dark to thee, the night is bright as the day; for darkness is as light with thee.
Jer. 23:23–24. Am I a God at hand, says the Lord, and not a God afar off? Can a man hide himself in secret places so that I cannot see him? says the Lord. Do I not fill heaven and earth? says the Lord. (Also Jonah 1:3.)
Deut. 28:15, 37. If you will not obey the voice of the Lord your God or be careful to do all his commandments and his statutes which I command you this day, then all these curses shall come upon you and overtake you...And you shall become a horror (Luther: Scheusal), a proverb, and a byword, among all the peoples where the Lord will lead you away.
Rev. 6:15–17. ...Every one, slave and free, hid in the caves and among the rocks of the mountains, calling to the mountains and rocks, "Fall on us and hide us from the face of him who is seated on the throne, and from the wrath of the Lamb; for the great day of their wrath has come, and who can stand before it?" (Also Is. 2:19, Hos. 10:8, Lk. 23:30.)
Num. 16:31–35. As [Moses] finished speaking all these words, the ground under them split asunder; and the earth opened its mouth and swallowed them up, with their households and all the men that belonged to Korah and all their goods. So they and all that belonged to them went down alive into Sheol (Luther: Hölle); and the earth closed over them, and they perished from the midst of the assembly. And all Israel that were round about them fled at their cry; for they said, "Lest the earth swallow us up!" And fire came forth from the Lord, and consumed the two hundred and fifty men offering the incense. (Also Ps. 21:9.)
Rev. 14:7. And [an angel] said with a loud voice, "Fear God and give him glory, for the hour of his judgment has come..."
Rev. 20:11–12. I saw a great white throne and him who sat upon it; from his presence earth and sky fled away, and no place was found for them. And I saw the dead, great and small, standing before the throne, and books were opened. Also another book was opened, which is the book of life. And the dead were judged by what was written in the books, by what they had done.
Ps. 33:13–15. The Lord looks down from heaven, he sees all the sons of men; from where he sits enthroned he looks forth on all the inhabitants of the earth, he who fashions the hearts of all, and observes all their deeds.

*Mt. 18:26–27. The servant fell on his knees, imploring [his master], "Lord, have patience with me, and I will pay you everything." And out of pity for him the lord of that servant released him and forgave him the debt.

Laß die Tränen dich erweichen,
Let (my) tears thee soften,
{Let my tears soften thee,}

Laß sie dir zu Herzen reichen;
Let them - to (thy) heart reach;
{Let them reach to thy heart;}

Laß um Jesu Christi willen
Let, for Jesus Christ's sake,

Deinen Zorn des Eifers stillen!
(The) wrath of-(thy) zeal be-quieted!
{Thy zealous wrath be quieted!}

Erbarme dich!
Have-mercy - !

4. Tenor Recit.
●Atonement: In judgment I plead Christ's saving work (55-4)
Erbarme dich!
Have-mercy - !

Jedoch nun
Yet now

Tröst ich mich,
Comfort I myself (that)
{I comfort myself that}

Ich will nicht für Gerichte stehen
I will not before (his) judgment stand

Und lieber vor dem Gnadenthron
(But) rather before the throne-of-grace

Zu meinem frommen Vater gehen.
To my righteous father go.

Ich halt ihm seinen Sohn,
I hold (before) him his Son,
{I hold his Son before him,}

Sein Leiden, sein Erlösen für,
His passion, his redemption - :

Wie er für meine Schuld
How he for my debt (of sin)

Bezahlet und genug getan,
Has-paid, and enough (has) done,

Und bitt ihn um Geduld,
And ask him for forbearance;

Hinfüro will ich's nicht mehr tun.
Henceforth would I-it no more do.
{Henceforth would I sin no more.}

Lk. 18:13. [A] tax collector, standing far off, would not even lift up his eyes to heaven, but beat his breast, saying, "God be merciful to me a sinner!"

Lk. 7:37–38, 44, 47–48. And behold, a woman of the city, who was a sinner, when she learned that [Jesus] was at table in the Pharisee's house, brought an alabaster flask of ointment, and standing behind him at his feet, weeping, she began to wet his feet with her tears, and wiped them with the hair of her head, and kissed his feet, and anointed them with the ointment...Then turning toward the woman he said to Simon, "Do you see this woman?...I tell you, her sins, which are many, are forgiven, for she loved much; but he who is forgiven little, loves little." And he said to her, "Your sins are forgiven." (Also Jn. 11:2, Jn. 12:1–8, Mk. 14:1–9.)

Ps. 51:17. The sacrifice acceptable to God is a broken spirit; a broken and contrite heart, O God, thou wilt not despise.

Jn. 5:22–24 [Christ]: The Father judges no one, but has given all judgment to the Son, that all may honor the Son, even as they honor the Father. He who does not honor the Son does not honor the Father who sent him. Truly, truly, I say to you, he who hears my word and believes him who sent me, has eternal life; he does not come into judgment, but has passed from death to life.

1 Jn. 4:16–18. So we know and believe the love God has for us...In this is love perfected with us, that we may have confidence for the day of judgment...There is no fear in love, but perfect love casts out fear. For fear has to do with punishment, and he who fears is not perfected in love.

Rom. 8:1. There is therefore now no condemnation for those who are in Christ Jesus.

Rom. 8:33–34. Who shall bring any charge against God's elect? It is God who justifies; who is to condemn? Is it Christ Jesus, who died, yes, who was raised from the dead, who is at the right hand of God, who indeed intercedes for us?

Heb. 4:14–16. Since then we have a great high priest who has passed through the heavens, Jesus, the Son of God, let us hold fast our confession. For we have not a high priest who is unable to sympathize with our weaknesses, but one who in every respect has been tempted as we are, yet without sin. Let us then with confidence draw near to the throne of grace, that we may receive mercy and find grace to help in time of need.

Rom. 5:8–10. God shows his love for us in that while we were yet sinners Christ died for us. Since, therefore, we are now justified by his blood, much more shall we be saved by him from the wrath of God. For if while we were enemies we were reconciled to God by the death of his Son, much more, now that we are reconciled, shall we be saved by his life.

Gal. 3:13. Christ redeemed us from the curse of the law, having become a curse for us—for it is written, "Cursed be every one who hangs on a tree." (Also 1 Pet. 3:18.)

1 Pet. 1:18–19. You know that you were ransomed from the futile ways inherited from your fathers, not with perishable things such as silver or gold, but with the precious blood of Christ, like that of a lamb without blemish or spot. (Also Rev. 5:9.)

*Mt. 18:26–27. The servant fell on his knees, imploring [his master], "Lord, have patience (Luther: Geduld) with me..."

Jn. 8:10–11. Jesus looked up and said to [the woman caught in adultery], "Woman, where are they? Has no one condemned you?"

So nimmt mich Gott zu Gnaden wieder an.
Thus receives me God into grace again - .
{Thus God receives me into his grace again.}

5. Chorale
●Prayer of repentance, returning to God (55-5)
Bin ich gleich von dir gewichen,
(Have) I although from thee withdrawn,
{Though I have turned from thee,}

Stell ich mich doch wieder ein;
Present I myself indeed again - ;
{I return again to thee;}

Hat uns doch dein Sohn verglichen
(For) us indeed thy Son hath-reconciled
{For thy Son hath indeed reconciled us}

Durch sein Angst und Todespein.
Through his anguish and pangs-of-death.

Ich verleugne nicht die Schuld,
I deny not (my) guilt,

Aber deine Gnad und Huld
But thy grace and favor

Ist viel größer als die Sünde,
Is much greater than the sin,

Die ich stets in mir befinde.
Which I ever within me find.
{Which I ever find within me.}

BWV 56
Ich will den Kreuzstab gerne tragen
(NBA I/24; BC A146)

19. S. after Trinity (BWV 48, 5, 56)
*Eph. 4:22-28 (Exhortation to put on the new nature)
*Mt. 9:1-8 (Jesus heals the paralytic)
Librettist: Unknown

1. Bass Aria
●Carrying the cross: it leads me to paradise (56-1)
Ich will den Kreuzstab gerne tragen,
I will the crosier gladly carry,

She said, "No one, Lord." And Jesus said, "Neither do I condemn you; go, and do not sin again." (Also Jn. 5:14.)
Rom. 6:1-2. What shall we say then? Are we to continue in sin that grace may abound? By no means! How can we who died to sin still live in it?...

Mal. 3:7. From the days of your fathers you have turned aside from my statutes and have not kept them. Return to me, and I will return to you, says the Lord of hosts...
1 Pet. 2:25. For you were straying like sheep, but have now returned to the Shepherd and Guardian of your souls.
Lk. 15:20-21. And [the prodigal son] arose and came to his father. But while he was yet at a distance, his father saw him and had compassion, and ran and embraced him and kissed him. And the son said to him, "Father, I have sinned against heaven and before you; I am no longer worthy to be called your son."
Is. 53:6. All we like sheep have gone astray; we have turned every one to his own way; and the Lord has laid on him the iniquity of us all.
Col. 1:19-22. For in [Christ] all the fulness of God was pleased to dwell, and through him to reconcile to himself all things, whether on earth or in heaven, making peace by the blood of his cross. And you, who once were estranged and hostile in mind, doing evil deeds, he has now reconciled in his body of flesh by his death, in order to present you holy and blameless and irreproachable before him.
Rom. 5:2, 20. Through [Christ] we have obtained access to this grace in which we stand, and we rejoice in our hope of sharing the glory of God... Where sin increased, grace abounded all the more. (Also 1 Pet. 3:18.)
Rom. 7:18, 24-25. For I know that nothing good dwells within me, that is, in my flesh...Wretched man that I am! Who will deliver me from this body of death? Thanks be to God through Jesus Christ our Lord!...
1 Tim. 1:15-16. The saying is sure and worth of full acceptance, that Christ Jesus came into the world to save sinners. And I am the foremost of sinners; but I received mercy...that...Jesus Christ might display his perfect patience for an example to those who were to believe in him for eternal life.

Mt. 16:24-25. Then Jesus told his disciples, "If any man would come after me, let him deny himself and take up his cross and follow me. For whoever would save his life will lose it, and whoever loses his life for my sake will find it." (Also Mt. 10:38.)
1 Pet. 1:6-7. ...Now for a little while you may have to suffer various trials, so that the genuineness of your faith, more precious than gold which though perishable is tested by fire, may redound to praise and glory and honor at the revelation of Jesus Christ.

Er kömmt von Gottes lieber Hand.
It comes from God's dear hand.

Der führet mich nach meinen Plagen
He leads me, after my troubles (are over),

Zu Gott, in das gelobte Land.
To God, into the Promised Land.

Da leg ich den Kummer auf einmal ins Grab,
There lay I (my) cares all-at-once into-the grave,
{There I lay my cares into the grave all at once,}

Da wischt mir die Tränen mein Heiland selbst ab.
There wipes - (my) tears my Savior himself away.
{There my Savior himself wipes away my tears.}

2. Bass Recit.
●Life is like a journey by ship through stormy seas (56-2)
Mein Wandel auf der Welt
My (sojourn) in the world

Ist einer Schiffahrt gleich:
Is (to) a journey-by-ship similar:

Betrübnis, Kreuz und Not
Sadness, cross, and trouble

Sind Wellen, welche mich bedecken
Are billows, which me cover

Und auf den Tod
And (nigh) unto - death

Mich täglich schrecken;
Me daily frighten;
{Daily fighten me;}

Mein Anker aber, der mich hält,
My anchor, however, which me holds,
{The anchor that holds me, however,}

Ist die Barmherzigkeit,
Is the compassion,

Womit mein Gott mich oft erfreut.
With-which my God me often gladdens.
{With which my God often gladdens me.}

Der rufet so zu mir:
He calls thus to me:

Ich bin bei dir,
I am with you,

Ich will dich nicht verlassen noch versäumen!
I will you not leave nor forsake!
{I will not leave you nor forsake you!}

Rom. 8:18. I consider that the sufferings of this present time are not worth comparing with the glory that is to be revealed to us. (Also 2 Cor. 4:17.)
***Mt. 9:2.** And behold, they brought to [Jesus] a paralytic, lying on his bed; and when Jesus saw their faith he said to the paralytic, "Take heart, my son; your sins are forgiven."
Heb. 4:8-9. If Joshua had given [the Israelites] rest [in Canaan], God would not speak later of another day. So then, there remains a sabbath rest for the people of God.
Rev. 14:13. ...Blessed are the dead who die in the Lord henceforth. "Blessed indeed," says the Spirit, "that they may rest from their labors, for their deeds follow them!"
Rev. 21:3-4. ...[Then] God himself will be with them; he will wipe away every tear from their eyes, and death shall be no more, neither shall there be mourning nor crying nor pain any more, for the former things have passed away. (Also Rev. 7:15-17 [see below: 56-4], Is. 25:8.)

***Mt. 9:1.** Getting into a boat [Jesus] crossed over and came to his own city.
2 Sam. 22:5-6. The waves of death encompassed me, the torrents of perdition assailed me; the cords of Sheol entangled me, the snares of death confronted me.
Ps. 18:4-6. The cords of death encompassed me, the torrents of perdition assailed me; the cords of Sheol entangled me, the snares of death confronted me.
Ps. 124:2-5. ...When their anger was kindled against us; then the flood would have swept us away, the torrent would have gone over us; then over us would have gone the raging waters.
Ps. 69:1-3, 13-15. Save me, O God! For the waters have come up to my neck. I sink in deep mire, where there is no foothold; I have come into deep waters, and the flood sweeps over me. I am weary with my crying; my throat is parched. My eyes grow dim with waiting for my God... With thy faithful help rescue me from sinking in the mire; let me be delivered from my enemies and from the deep waters. Let not the flood sweep over me, or the deep swallow me up, or the pit close its mouth over me.
Heb. 6:19-20. We have this as a sure and steadfast anchor of the soul, a hope that enters into the inner shrine behind the [temple] curtain, where Jesus has gone as a forerunner on our behalf, having become a high priest for ever after the order of Melchizedek.
Mt. 28:20 [Christ]: ...Lo, I am with you always, to the close of the age.
Heb. 13:5-6. [God] has said, "I will never fail you nor forsake you (Luther: dich nicht verlassen noch versäumen)." Hence we can confidently say, "The Lord is my helper, I will not be afraid; what can man do to me?"
Josh. 1:1, 5. The Lord said to Joshua..."...No man shall be able to stand before you all the days of your life; as I was with Moses, so I will be with you; I will not fail you or forsake you." (Also Deut. 31:6-8.)
Heb. 11:13, 16. These [heroes] all died in faith...having acknowledged that they were strangers and exiles on the earth...As it is, they desire a better country, that is, a heavenly one. Therefore God is not ashamed to be called their God, for he has prepared for them a city.
Heb. 13:14. For here we have no lasting city, but we seek the city which is to come.

Und wenn das wütenvolle Schäumen
And when the furious foaming

Sein Ende hat,
Its end has,
{Comes to an end,}

So tret ich aus dem Schiff in meine Stadt,
Then step I out-of the ship into my city,
{Then I step out of the ship into my city,}

Die ist das Himmelreich,
Which is the kingdom-of-heaven,

Wohin ich mit den Frommen
Whereto I with the righteous

Aus vieler Trübsal werde kommen.
Out-of much tribulation will come.

Rev. 7:14. ...These are they who have come out of the great tribulation...
Acts 14:22. ...Through many tribulations we must enter the kingdom of God.
Rev. 21:2, 9, 23–24, 27. And I saw the holy city, new Jerusalem, coming down out of heaven from God, prepared as a bride adorned for her husband...Then came one of the seven angels...and spoke to me, saying, "Come I will show you the Bride, the wife of the Lamb."... And the city has no need of sun or moon to shine upon it, for the glory of God is its light, and its lamp is the Lamb. By its light shall the nations walk...But nothing unclean shall enter [the heavenly city], nor any one who practices abomination or falsehood, but only those who are written in the Lamb's book of life.
Acts 14:22. ...Through many tribulations we must enter the kingdom of God.
Rev. 7:14–15. ...These are they who have come out of the great tribulation...therefore are they before the throne of God, and serve him day and night...

3. Bass Aria

●Heaven anticipated; freed like an eagle (56-3)
Endlich, endlich wird mein Joch
Finally, finally must my yoke

Wieder von mir weichen müssen.
Again from me (be-lifted) - .

Da krieg ich in dem Herren Kraft,
Then gain I in the Lord strength,
{Then will I gain strength in the Lord,}

Da hab ich Adlers Eigenschaft,
Then have I (the) eagle's characteristic,
{Then will I become like the eagle,}

Da fahr ich auf von dieser Erden
Then mount I up from this earth
{Then will I mount up from this earth}

Und laufe sonder matt zu werden.
And run without weary to become.
{And run without becoming weary.}

O gescheh es heute noch!
O (that it would) happen - today yet!

Mt. 11:28–30 [Christ]: Come to me, all who labor and are heavy laden, and I will give you rest. Take my yoke upon you, and learn from me; for I am gentle and lowly in heart, and you will find rest for your souls. For my yoke is easy, and my burden is light.
Is. 10:27. And in that day his burden will depart (Luther: weichen müssen) from your shoulder, and his yoke will be destroyed from your neck. (Also Lev. 26:13, Is. 9:4, 14:25.)
Is. 40:28–31. Have you not known? Have you not heard? The Lord is the everlasting God, the Creator of the ends of the earth. He does not faint or grow weary, his understanding is unsearchable. He gives power to the faint, and to him who has no might he increases strength. Even youths shall faint and be weary, and young men shall fall exhausted; but they who wait for the Lord shall renew their strength, they shall mount up with wings like eagles, they shall run and not be weary, they shall walk and not faint.
2 Cor. 5:8. We are of good courage, and we would rather be away from the body and at home with the Lord.
Phil. 1:21–23. For to me to live is Christ, and to die is gain. If it is to be life in the flesh, that means fruitful labor for me. Yet which I shall choose I cannot tell. I am hard pressed between the two. My desire is to depart and be with Christ, for that is far better.

4. Bass Recit. & Arioso

●Yearning for heaven; my inheritance: rest & comfort (56-4)
Ich stehe fertig und bereit,
I stand ready and prepared,

Das Erbe meiner Seligkeit
The inheritance of-my salvation
{To receive the inheritance of my salvation}

Mit Sehnen und Verlangen
With yearning and longing

1 Pet. 1:3–5. Blessed be the God and Father of our Lord Jesus Christ! By his great mercy we have been born anew to a living hope through the resurrection of Jesus Christ from the dead, and to an inheritance which is imperishable, undefiled, and unfading, kept in heaven for you, who by God's power are guarded through faith for a salvation ready to be revealed in the last time. (Also Mt. 25:34.)
Col. 1:12. ...[The Father] has qualified us to share in the inheritance of the saints in light.

Von Jesu Händen zu empfangen.
From Jesus' hands to receive.
{From Jesus' hands.}

Wie wohl wird mir geschehn,
How well will (it) for-me (be),
{How well it will be for me,}

Wenn ich den Port der Ruhe werde sehn:
When I the harbour of rest will see:

///

Da leg ich den Kummer auf einmal ins Grab,
There lay I (my) cares all-at-once into-the grave,
{There I lay my cares into the grave all at once,}

Da wischt mir die Tränen mein Heiland selbst ab.
There wipes - (my) tears my Savior himself away.
{There my Savior himself wipes away my tears.}

5. Chorale
●Yearning for death: it brings me to port of rest (56-5)
Komm, o Tod, du Schlafes Bruder,
Come, O death, thou sleep's brother,
{Come, O death, thou brother to sleep,}

Komm und führe mich nur fort;
Come and lead me just away;
{Come and just lead me away;}

Löse meines Schiffleins Ruder,
Loosen my little-ship's rudder,

Bringe mich an sichern Port.
Bring me to (the) secure port.

Es mag, wer da will, dich scheuen,
(Let), whoever (may) wish, thee shun,
{Let whoever may wish shun thee,}

Du kannst mich vielmehr erfreuen;
Thou canst me on-the-contrary delight;
{On the contrary, thou canst delight me;}

Denn durch dich komm ich herein
For through thee come I inside

Zu dem schönsten Jesulein.
To the fairest Jesus-child.

Col. 3:24. ...From the Lord you will receive the inheritance as your reward...
Heb. 9:15. ...[Christ] is the mediator of a new covenant, so that those who are called may receive the promised eternal inheritance...
Rom. 8:23-24. ...We ourselves, who have the first fruits of the Spirit, groan inwardly as we wait for adoption as sons, the redemption of our bodies. For in this hope we were saved... (Also Eph. 1:13-14.)
Heb. 4:9. So then, there remains a sabbath rest for the people of God.
Rev. 14:13. ...Blessed are the dead who die in the Lord henceforth... that they may rest from their labors, for their deeds follow them!

Rev. 7:15-17. Therefore [the righteous who have come through the tribulation] are...before the throne of God, and serve him day and night within his temple; and he who sits upon the throne will shelter them with his presence. They shall hunger no more, neither thirst any more; the sun shall not strike them, nor any scorching heat. For the Lamb in the midst of the throne will be their shepherd, and he will guide them to springs of living water; and God will wipe away every tear from their eyes. (Also Rev. 21:4 [see above: 56-1], Is. 25:8.)

Jn. 11:11-15. ...[Jesus] said to them, "Our friend Lazarus has fallen asleep, but I go to awake him out of sleep." The disciples said to him, "Lord, if he has fallen asleep, he will recover." Now Jesus had spoken of his death, but they thought that he meant taking rest in sleep. Then Jesus told them plainly, "Lazarus is dead; and for your sake I am glad that I was not there, so that you may believe. But let us go to him." (Also Mt. 9:24, Mk. 5:39, Lk. 8:52.)
*Mt. 9:1. Getting into a boat [Jesus] crossed over and came to his own city.
Heb. 13:14. Here we have no lasting city, but we seek the city which is to come. (Also Heb. 11:10, 16.)
2 Cor. 5:8. We are of good courage, and we would rather be away from the body and at home with the Lord.
1 Cor. 15:54-55. When the perishable puts on the imperishable, and the mortal puts on immortality, then shall come to pass the saying that is written: "Death is swallowed up in victory." O death, where is thy victory? O death, where is thy sting?
Heb. 2:14-15. Since therefore the children share in flesh and blood, [Christ] himself likewise partook of the same nature, that through death he might destroy him who has the power of death, that is, the devil, and deliver all those who through fear of death were subject to lifelong bondage.
Rom. 5:2. Through [Christ] we have obtained access to this grace in which we stand, and we rejoice in our hope of sharing the glory of God.
Phil. 1:21, 23. For to me to live is Christ, and to die is gain...My desire is to depart and be with Christ, for that is far better.

BWV 57
Selig ist der Mann
(NBA I/3; BC A14)

2. Day of Christmas (BWV 40, 121, 57, 248-II)
*Tit. 3:4–7 (The mercy of God appeared in Christ)
*Lk. 2:15–20 (The shepherds go to the manger)

This day also celebrated as the festival of St. Stephen the Martyr:
*Acts 6:8–7:2 & 7:51–59 (The stoning of Stephen)
*Mt. 23:34–39 (Jesus' lament: Jerusalem kills the prophets sent to her)
Librettist: Georg Christian Lehms

1. Bass Aria (Voice of Christ)[1]
●Trials: Whoever endures receives the crown: Jms. 1:12 (57-1)
Selig ist der Mann, der die Anfechtung erduldet;
Blessed is the man, who - trial endures;

denn, nachdem er bewähret ist, wird er die Krone
for, after he proven is, will he the crown

des Lebens empfangen.
of life receive.

2. Soprano Recit. (Voice of the believing soul)[1]
●Hope of heaven comforts me in present suffering (57-2)
Ach! dieser süße Trost
Ah! this sweet comfort

Erquickt auch mir mein Herz,
Revives even - my heart,

Das sonst in Ach und Schmerz
Which otherwise in "Ah" and grief

Sein ewig Leiden findet
(Nought but) endless suffering (experiences)

Und sich als wie ein Wurm in seinem Blute windet.
And - like - a worm in its (own) blood writhes.

Ich muß als wie ein Schaf
I must like - a sheep

Bei tausend rauhen Wölfen leben;
Amidst (a) thousand savage wolves live;

Ich bin ein recht verlaßnes Lamm,
I am a truly forsaken lamb,

Und muß mich ihrer Wut
And must myself (to) their rage

*Acts 7:55–58. [Stephen], full of the Holy Spirit, gazed into heaven and saw the glory of God, and Jesus standing at the right hand of God; and he said, "Behold, I see the heavens opened, and the Son of man standing at the right hand of God." But they cried out with a loud voice and stopped their ears and rushed together upon him. Then they cast him out of the city and stoned him...
*Mt. 23:34–35 [Christ]: I send you prophets and wise men and scribes, some of whom you will kill and crucify, and some you will scourge in your synagogues and persecute from town to town, that upon you may come all the righteous blood shed on earth, from the blood of innocent Abel to the blood of Zechariah...whom you murdered...
Jms. 1:12. *Blessed is the man who endures trial, for when he has stood the test he will receive the crown (Greek: stephanos) of life* which God has promised to those who love him. (Also Jms. 1:2–4.)
1 Pet. 4:12–13. Beloved, do not be surprised at the fiery ordeal which comes upon you to prove you, as though something strange were happening to you. But rejoice in so far as you share Christ's sufferings, that you may also rejoice and be glad when his glory is revealed.

1 Pet. 1:3–7. Blessed be the God and Father of our Lord Jesus Christ! By his great mercy we have been born anew to a living hope through the resurrection of Jesus Christ from the dead, and to an inheritance which is imperishable, undefiled, and unfading, kept in heaven for you, who by God's power are guarded through faith for a salvation ready to be revealed in the last time. In this you rejoice, though now for a little while you may have to suffer various trials, so that the genuineness of your faith, more precious than gold which though perishable is tested by fire, may redound to praise and glory and honor at the revelation of Jesus Christ.
Jn. 16:33 [Christ]: I have said this to you, that in me you may have peace. In the world you have tribulation; but be of good cheer, I have overcome the world.
Mt. 10:16–18 [Christ]: Behold, I send you out as sheep in the midst of wolves; so be wise as serpents and innocent as doves. Beware of men; for they will deliver you up to councils, and flog you in their synagogues, and you will be dragged before governors and kings for my sake, to bear testimony before them and the Gentiles.
*Acts 6:8–10, 12–13, 15, 7:54–60. And Stephen, full of grace and power, did great wonders and signs among the people. Then some... arose and disputed with Stephen. But they could not withsand the wisdom and the Spirit with which he spoke...And they stirred up the people and the elders and the scribes, and they came upon him and seized him and brought him before the council, and set up false witnesses...And gazing at him, all who sat in the council saw that his face was like the face of an angel...Now when they heard these things

---

[1]The manuscript designates the persons of this dialogue as "Jesus" and "Anima".

Und Grausamkeit ergeben.
And   ferocity   surrender.
{And must surrender myself to their rage and ferocity.}

Was Abeln dort betraf,
What Abel there befell,

Erpresset mir auch diese Tränenflut.
Exacts   from-me also this flood-of-tears.

Ach! Jesu, wüßt ich hier
Ah! Jesu, knew I here

Nicht Trost von dir,
(No) comfort from thee,
{Ah, Jesu, if I knew no comfort from thee here,}

So müßte   Mut und   Herze brechen,
Then would (my) courage and (my) heart   break,
{Then my courage and my heart would break,}

Und voller Trauer sprechen:
And full-of mourning say:

3. Soprano Aria (Voice of the believing soul)
●Christ's love: I could not bear to live without it (57–3)
Ich wünschte   mir den Tod, den Tod,
I   would-wish (for) myself - death, - death,
{I would wish death for myself—death,}

Wenn du, mein Jesu, mich   nicht liebtest.
If   thou, my Jesus, me (didst) not   love.
{If thou, O my Jesus, didst not love me.}

Ja wenn du mich annoch betrübtest,
Yea, if thou me   still didst-grieve,
{Yea, if thou wouldst leave me grieving,}

So hätt ich mehr als   Höllennot.
Then had I more than (the) pain-of-hell.
{Then I would suffer more greatly than from the pain of hell.}

4. Soprano/Bass Recit. (Dialogue of Christ & believer)
●Dialogue (Christ and Believer): Christ extends hand (57–4)
Bass:
Ich reiche dir   die Hand
I   hold-out to-thee (my) hand
{I hold out my hand to thee}

Und auch damit das Herze.
And also therewith (my) heart.

---

they ground their teeth against him. But he, full of the Holy Spirit, gazed into heaven and saw the glory of God, and Jesus standing at the right hand of God; and he said, "Behold, I see the heavens opened, and the Son of man standing at the right hand of God." But they cried out with a loud voice and stopped their ears and rushed together upon him. Then they cast him out of the city and stoned him...And as they were stoning Stephen, he prayed, "Lord Jesus, receive my spirit." And he knelt down and cried with a loud voice, "Lord, do not hold this sin against them." And when he had said this he fell asleep.
Gen. 4:8. Cain said to Abel his brother, "Let us go out to the field." And when they were in the field, Cain rose up against his brother Abel, and killed him. (Also *Mt. 23:35.)
Lam. 1:16. For these things I weep; my eyes flow with tears; for a comforter is far from me, one to revive my courage; my children are desolate, for the enemy has prevailed.
Ps. 42:3. My tears have been my food day and night...
Ps. 6:6. I am weary with my moaning; every night I flood my bed with tears... (Also Ps. 42:3, 69:3, Jer. 45:3.)
2 Cor. 1:3–5. Blessed be the God and Father of our Lord Jesus Christ, the Father of mercies and God of all comfort, who comforts us in all our affliction...For as we share abundantly in Christ's sufferings, so through Christ we share abundantly in comfort too.

Rom. 8:35–39. Who shall separate us from the love of Christ? Shall tribulation, or distress, or persecution, or famine, or nakedness, or peril, or sword? As it is written, "For thy sake we are being killed all the day long; we are regarded as sheep to be slaughtered." No, in all these things we are more than conquerors through him who loved us. For I am sure that neither death, nor life, nor angels, nor principalities, nor things present, nor things to come, nor powers, nor height, nor depth, nor anything else in all creation, will be able to separate us from the love of God in Christ Jesus our Lord.
Ps. 63:3. [O Lord,] thy steadfast love is better than life...
Ps. 73:25–26. Whom have I in heaven but thee? And there is nothing upon earth that I desire besides thee. My flesh and my heart may fail, but God is the strength of my heart and my portion for ever.
Phil. 3:8–10. Indeed I count everything as loss because of the surpassing worth of knowing Christ Jesus my Lord. For his sake I have suffered the loss of all things, and count them as refuse, in order that I may gain Christ and be found in him, not having a righteousness of my own, based on law, but that which is through faith in Christ...that I may know him and the power of his resurrection, and may share his sufferings, becoming like him in his death...

Jer. 32:17, 21. Ah Lord God! It is thou who hast made the heavens and the earth by thy great power and by thy outstretched arm! Nothing is too hard for thee...Thou didst bring thy people Israel out of the land of Egypt with signs and wonders, with a strong hand and outstretched arm... (Also Deut. 4:34, 5:15, 7:19, 11:2.)
Ps. 108:6. [O Lord,] that thy beloved may be delivered, give help by thy right hand, and answer me! (Also Ps. 60:5.)
Ps. 73:18–19. Truly thou dost set [thine enemies] in slippery places;

Soprano:
Ach! süßes Liebespfand,
Ah! sweet pledge-of-love,

Du kannst die Feinde stürzen
Thou canst (my) enemies overthrow

Und ihren Grimm verkürzen.
And their fury curtail.

5. Bass Aria (Vox Christi)
●Divine aid against enemies assured; sun will shine (57-5)
Ja, ja, ich kann die Feinde schlagen,
Yea, Yea, I can (thine) enemies defeat,
{Yea, yea, I can defeat thine enemies,}

Die dich nur stets bei mir verklagen,
Who thee just constantly before me accuse,
{Who just constantly accuse thee before me,}

Drum fasse dich, bedrängter Geist.
Therefore compose thyself, oppressed spirit.

Bedrängter Geist, hör auf zu weinen,
Oppressed spirit, cease to weep,
{Oppressed spirit, cease thy weeping,}

Die Sonne wird noch helle scheinen,
The sun will yet brightly shine,

Die dir itzt Kummerwolken weist.
Which thee now clouds-of-care doth-show.
{Which now shows thee nought but clouds of care.}

6. Soprano & Bass Recit. (Dialogue of Christ & believer)
●Dialogue (Christ and Believer): Yearning for death (57-6)
Bass:
In meinem Schoß liegt Ruh und Leben,
In my bosom doth-lie rest and life,

Dies will ich dir einst ewig geben.
This will I thee some-day eternally give.
{This will I someday eternally give to thee.}

Soprano:
Ach! Jesu, wär ich schon bei dir,
Ah! Jesus, were I already with thee,

Ach striche mir
Ah, grazed -

Der Wind schon über Gruft und Grab,
The wind already over (my) tomb and grave,
{Ah, if only the wind already grazed over my tomb and grave,}

thou dost make them fall to ruin (Luther: stürzest sie zu Boden). How they are destroyed in a moment, swept away utterly by terrors!
Lk. 1:51–53. He has shown strength with his arm, he has scattered the proud in the imagination of their hearts. He has put down the mighty from their thrones, and exalted those of low degree; he has filled the hungry with good things, and the rich he has sent empty away.
Col. 2:15. [Christ] disarmed the principalities and powers and made a public example of them, triumphing over them in him.

Ps. 37:12–13. The wicked plots against the righteous, and gnashes his teeth at him; but the Lord laughs at the wicked, for he sees that his day is coming.
Prov. 21:30. No wisdom, no understanding, no counsel, can avail against the Lord.
Is. 50:2 [God]: ...Is my hand shortened, that it cannot redeem? Or have I no power to deliver? (Also Is. 59:1.)
Jn. 16:33 [Christ]: I have said this to you, that in me you may have peace. In the world you have tribulation; but be of good cheer, I have overcome the world.
1 Jn. 4:4. Little children, you are of God, and have overcome them; for he who is in you is greater than he who is in the world.
Rev. 12:10. ...The accuser of our brethren has been thrown down, who accuses them day and night before our God.
***Acts 6:11–13.** They secretly instigated men [against Jesus]...who said, "We have heard him speak blasphemous words against Moses and God." And they stirred up the people and the elders and the scribes, and they came upon him and seized him and brought him before the council, and set up false witnesses who said, "This man never ceases to speak words against this holy place and the law..."
Rom. 8:31. What then shall we say to this? If God is for us, who is against us? (Also Ps. 27:1, 118:6.)
Lk. 21:19 [Christ]: By your endurance you will gain your lives (Luther: Fasset eure Seele mit Geduld).
Ps. 30:5. ...Weeping may tarry for the night, but joy comes with the morning.

Lk. 16:19–25. There was a rich man, who was clothed in purple and fine linen and who feasted sumptuously every day. And at his gate lay a poor man named Lazarus, full of sores, who desired to be fed with what fell from the rich man's table; moreover the dogs came and licked his sores. The poor man died and was carried by the angels to Abraham's bosom (Luther: Schoß). The rich man also died and was buried; and in Hades, being in torment, he lifted up his eyes, and saw Abraham far off and Lazarus in his bosom. And he called out, "Father Abraham, have mercy upon me, and send Lazarus to dip the end of his finger in water and cool my tongue; for I am in anguish in this flame." But Abraham said, "Son, remember that you in your lifetime received your good things, and Lazarus in like manner evil things; but now he is comforted here, and you are in anguish."
Rev. 14:13. "...Blessed are the dead who die in the Lord henceforth." "Blessed indeed," says the Spirit, "that they may rest from their labors, for their deeds follow them!"

So könnt ich alle Not besiegen.
Then could I all trouble conquer.

Wohl denen, die im Sarge liegen
Blessed (are) they, who in-a coffin lie

Und auf den Schall der Engel hoffen!
And for the sound of-the angels wait-expectantly!
{And wait expectantly for the angels' trumpet call!}

Ach! Jesu, mache mir doch nur,
Ah! Jesus, make for-me indeed - ,

Wie Stephano, den Himmel offen!
As (thou didst for) Stephen, the heaven(s) open!
{Ah, Jesus, open the heavens for me, as thou didst for Stephen!}

Mein Herz ist schon bereit,
My heart is already prepared,

Zu dir hinaufzusteigen.
To thee to-ascend.
{To ascend to thee.}

Komm, komm, vergnügte Zeit!
Come, come, delightful time!

Du magst mir Gruft und Grab
Thou mayest me tomb and grave

Und meinen Jesum zeigen.
And my Jesus show.
{Thou mayest show me tomb and grave, as well as my Jesus.}

7. Soprano Aria (Voice of the believing soul)
●Yearning for death: Prayer offering soul to God (57-7)
Ich ende behende mein irdisches Leben,
I end quickly my earthly life;
{I end my earthly life quickly;}

Mit Freuden zu scheiden verlang ich jetzt eben.
With (these) enjoyments to part desire I now - .
{To part now with these enjoyments is my desire.}

Mein Heiland, ich sterbe mit höchster Begier,
My Savior, I die with (the) greatest eagerness,

Hier hast du die Seele, was schenkest du mir?
Here hast thou (my) soul; what givest thou me?

1 Thess. 4:16. The Lord himself will descend from heaven with a cry of command, with the archangel's call, and with the sound of the trumpet of God. And the dead in Christ will rise first.
1 Cor. 15:42, 51–53. So it is with the resurrection of the dead. What is sown is perishable, what is raised is imperishable...Lo! I tell you a mystery. We shall not all sleep, but we shall all be changed, in a moment, in the twinkling of an eye, at the last trumpet. For the trumpet will sound, and the dead will be raised imperishable, and we shall be changed. For this perishable nature must put on the imperishable, and this mortal nature must put on immortality.
2 Cor. 5:6–8. So we are always of good courage; we know that while we are at home in the body we are away from the Lord, for we walk by faith, not by sight. We are of good courage, and we would rather be away from the body and at home with the Lord.
***Acts 7:56, 59.** And [Stephen] said, "Behold, I see the heavens opened, and the Son of man standing at the right hand of God"...And as they were stoning Stephen, he prayed, "Lord Jesus, receive my spirit."
Ps. 57:7. My heart is steadfast (Luther: Mein Herz ist bereit), O God, my heart is steadfast! I will sing and make melody!
2 Tim. 4:6, 8. ...The time of my departure has come...Henceforth there is laid up for me the crown of righteousness, which the Lord, the righteous judge, will award to me on that Day, and not only to me but also to all who have loved his appearing.
Lk. 23:46. Then Jesus, crying with a loud voice, said, "Father, into thy hands I commit my spirit!" And having said this he breathed his last. (Also Ps. 31:5.)
Ps. 16:11. [O Lord,] thou dost show me the path of life; in thy presence there is fulness of joy, in thy right hand are pleasures for evermore.
1 Thess. 4:17–18. ...So we shall always be with the Lord. Therefore comfort one another with these words.

2 Tim. 4:6–8. I am already on the point of being sacrificed; the time of my departure has come. I have fought the good fight, I have finished the race, I have kept the faith. Henceforth there is laid up for me the crown of righteousness, which the Lord, the righteous judge, will award to me on that Day, and not only to me but also to all who have loved his appearing.
1 Jn. 2:15–17. Do not love the world or the things in the world. If any one loves the world, love for the Father is not in him. For all that is in the world, the lust of the flesh and the lust of the eyes and the pride of life, is not of the Father but is of the world. And the world passes away, and the lust of it; but he who does the will of God abides for ever.
Ecc. 12:7. The dust returns to the earth as it was, and the spirit returns to God who gave it.
Ps. 31:5. [O Lord,] into thy hand I commit my spirit... (Also Lk. 23:46.)
1 Jn. 2:25. This is what [Christ] has promised us, eternal life.

8. Chorale (Voice of Christ)
- Vox Christi: Eternal bliss assured (57-8)

Richte dich, Liebste,
Govern thyself, dearest,

    nach   meinem Gefallen und gläube,
    according-to my   pleasure, and believe,

Daß ich dein Seelenfreund immer und ewig verbleibe,
That I   thy soul's-friend always and eternally will-remain,

Der dich ergötzt
Who thee delight
{I, who delight thee}

Und in den Himmel ersetzt
And into - heaven remove (thee)

Aus   dem gemarterten Leibe.
Out-of (this-thy) tortured   body.

Jer. 31:3 [God]: ...I have loved you with an everlasting love...
Is. 62:5. ...As the bridegroom rejoices over the bride, so shall your God rejoice over you.
Jn. 15:14 [Christ]: You are my friends if you do what I command you.
Col. 1:10. [May you]...lead a life worthy of the Lord, fully pleasing to him, bearing fruit in every good work...
Mt. 28:20 [Christ]: ...Lo, I am with you always...
Jn. 14:1-3 [Christ]: Let not your hearts be troubled; believe in God, believe also in me. In my Father's house are many rooms; if it were not so, would I have told you that I go to prepare a place for you? And when I go and prepare a place for you, I will come again and will take you to myself, that where I am you may be also.
Ps. 94:19. [O Lord,] when the cares of my heart are many, thy consolations cheer (Luther: ergötzten) my soul.
2 Cor. 5:1-4. For we know that if the earthly tent we live in is destroyed, we have a building from God, a house not made with hands, eternal in the heavens. Here indeed we groan, and long to put on our heavenly dwelling, so that by putting it on we may not be found naked. For while we are still in this tent, we sigh with anxiety; not that we would be unclothed, but that we would be further clothed, so that what is mortal may be swallowed up by life.

BWV 58
Ach Gott, wie manches Herzeleid II
(NBA I/4; BC A26a/b)

1. S. after New Year (BWV 153, 58, 248-V)
*1 Pet. 4:12-19 (Sharing the sufferings of Christ)
*Mt. 2:13-23 (Mary & Joseph's flight to Eygpt)
Librettist: Unknown

1. Soprano Chorale/Bass Aria (Believer vs. Vox Christi)
    (Chorale: see also 3-1, 44-4)
- Dialogue (Believer & Christ): Way to heaven is hard (58-1)

Ach Gott, wie manches Herzeleid
Ah God, how many-a   grief

Begegnet mir zu dieser Zeit!
Meets   me in this time!
{I encounter in this time!}

    Nur   Geduld, Geduld, mein Herze,
    Only (have) patience, patience, my heart,

    Es ist eine böse Zeit.
    It is an evil time.

Der schmale Weg ist Trübsals voll,
The narrow way is affliction-filled,

Den ich zum Himmel wandern soll.
Which I to heaven travel must.
{The narrow way, which I must travel to heaven, is filled with affliction.}

Mt. 7:14. The gate is narrow and the way is hard, that leads to life, and those who find it are few.
Mt. 16:24 [Christ]: If any man would come after me, let him deny himself and take up his cross and follow me.
***1 Pet. 4:12-13.** Beloved, do not be surprised at the fiery ordeal which comes upon you to prove you, as though something strange were happening to you. But rejoice in so far as you share Christ's sufferings, that you may also rejoice and be glad when his glory is revealed.
Eph. 5:15-16. Look carefully then how you walk, not as unwise men but as wise, making the most of the time, because the days are evil.
Jms. 5:7-8, 10-11. Be patient, therefore, brethren, until the coming of the Lord. Behold, the farmer waits for the precious fruit of the earth, being patient over it until it receives the early and the late rain. You also be patient. Establish your hearts, for the coming of the Lord is at hand...As an example of suffering and patience, brethren, take the prophets who spoke in the name of the Lord. Behold, we call those happy who were steadfast. You have heard of the steadfastness of Job, and you have seen the purpose of the Lord, how the Lord is compassionate and merciful.
1 Pet. 1:6-7. In this you rejoice, though now for a little while you may have to suffer various trials, so that the genuineness of your faith,

Doch der Gang zur Seligkeit
Yet   the   path to blessedness

Führt zur Freude nach dem Schmerze.
Leads to   joy   after - sorrow.

2. Bass Recit.

●Persecution: God rescues us like Joseph from Herod (58–2)
Verfolgt dich gleich die arge Welt,
Persecutes thee - the wicked world,
{Though the wicked world persecute thee,}

So hast du dennoch Gott zum Freunde,
Yet hast thou nevertheless God for-a friend,
{Yet hast thou God for a friend,}

Der wider deine Feinde
Who against thy   foes

Dir stets den Rücken hält.
- Continually thy   rear doth-guard.
{Who continually doth guard thy rear against thy foes.}

Und wenn der wütende Herodes
And although (that) raging Herod

Das Urteil eines schmähen Todes
The sentence of-a reviling death
{Passes a sentence of ignominious death}

Gleich über unsern Heiland fällt,
- Upon our   Savior passes,
{Upon our Savior,}

So kommt ein Engel in der Nacht,
Yet comes an angel in the night;
{Yet an angel comes in the night;}

Der lässet Joseph träumen,
He lets Joseph dream,

Daß er   dem Würger soll entfliehen
That he (from) the destroyer should flee

Und nach Ägypten ziehen.
And to   Egypt move.

Gott hat ein Wort, das dich vertrauend macht.
God hath a word, which thee trustful doth-make.
{God hath a word, that doth make thee trust him.}

Er spricht: wenn   Berg und Hügel niedersinken,
He saith: (Though) mountain and hill sink-down,

Wenn dich die Flut des Wassers will ertrinken,
(Though) thee the flood of waters would drown,
{Though the flood of waters would come nigh to drowning you,}

more precious than gold which though perishable is tested by fire, may redound to praise and glory and honor at the revelation of Jesus Christ.

1 Pet. 5:10. And after you have suffered a little while, the God of all grace, who has called you to his eternal glory in Christ, will himself restore, establish, and strengthen you.

Jn. 15:20 [Christ]: Remember the word that I said to you, "A servant is not greater than his master." If they persecuted me, they will persecute you.

Jn. 16:33 [Christ]: I have said this to you, that in me you may have peace. In the world you have tribulation; but be of good cheer, I have overcome the world.

Ps. 27:10. My father and my mother have forsaken me, but the Lord will take me up.

Ps. 145:18. The Lord is near to all who call upon him...

Jn. 15:15 [Christ]: No longer do I call you servants...but I have called you friends...

Ps. 118:6–7. With the Lord on my side I do not fear. What can man do to me? The Lord is on my side to help me; I shall look in triumph on those who hate me. (Also Ps. 27:1, Ps. 56:4.)

Ex. 14:13–14. And Moses said to the people, "Fear not, stand firm, and see the salvation of the Lord, which he will work for you today; for the Egyptians whom you see [overtaking you] today, you shall never see again. The Lord will fight for you, and you have only to be still." (Also Deut. 1:30, 20:4.)

Ps. 121:2–8. My help comes from the Lord, who made heaven and earth. He will not let your foot be moved, he who keeps you will not slumber. Behold, he who keeps Israel will neither slumber nor sleep. The Lord is your keeper; the Lord is your shade on your right hand. The sun shall not smite you by day, nor the moon by night. The Lord will keep you from all evil; he will keep your life. The Lord will keep your going out and your coming in from this time forth and for evermore.

*Mt. 2:13–16. Now when they had departed, behold, an angel of the Lord appeared to Joseph in a dream and said, "Rise, take the child and his mother, and flee to Egypt, and remain there till I tell you; for Herod is about to search for the child, to destroy him." And he rose and took the child and his mother by night, and departed to Egypt, and remained there until the death of Herod. This was to fulfil what the Lord had spoken by the prophet, "Out of Egypt have I called my son." Then Herod, when he saw that he had been tricked by the wise men, was in a furious rage, and he sent and killed all the male children in Bethlehem and in all that region who were two years old or under, according to the time which he had ascertained from the wise men.

Is. 54:10. For the mountains may depart and the hills be removed, but my steadfast love shall not depart from you and my covenant of peace shall not be removed, says the Lord, who has compassion on you.

Mt. 24:35 [Christ]: Heaven and earth will pass away, but my words will not pass away. (Also Mk. 13:31.)

Is. 43:1–2 [God]: ...Fear not, for I have redeemed you; I have called you by name, you are mine. When you pass through the waters I will be with you; and through the rivers, they shall not overwhelm you; when you walk through fire you shall not be burned, and the flame shall not consume you.

Mt. 28:20 [Christ]: ...Lo, I am with you always, to the close of the age.

So   will ich dich   doch   nicht
(Yet) will I   thee nevertheless not

      verlassen noch versäumen.
      leave   nor   forsake.
{Yet will I never leave thee nor forsake thee.}

3. Soprano Aria
●Affliction: God is my confidence so I am content (58-3)
Ich bin vergnügt in meinem Leiden,
I   am   content in   my   suffering,

Denn Gott ist meine Zuversicht.
For   God   is   my   confidence.

Ich habe   sichern Brief und Siegel,
I   have (a) sure   charter and   seal,

Und dieses ist der feste Riegel,
And   this   is the solid   bolt (on my door),

Den   bricht auch selbst die Hölle nicht.
(Which) breaks indeed even -   hell not.
{Which even hell cannot break.}

4. Soprano Recit.
●Persecution: God shows me a new land (58-4)
Kann es die Welt nicht lassen,
Can   - the world not refrain,
{Though the world cannot refrain,}

Mich zu verfolgen und zu hassen,
Me   to persecute and to   hate,
{From persecuting me or hating me,}

So weist mir Gottes Hand
So shows me God's hand
{God's hand shows me}

Ein andres Land.
A   different land.

Ach! könnt es heute noch geschehen,
Ah! Could it today yet   happen,
{Ah, if it could only happen even today yet,}

Daß ich mein Eden möchte sehen!
That I   my   Eden   might behold!
{That I might behold my Eden!}

5. Soprano Chorale/Bass Aria
●Dialogue (Christ & Believer): Way to heaven worth it (58-5)
Ich hab vor mir ein schwere Reis'
I have before me a   difficult journey (that leads)

Zu dir ins Himmels Paradeis,
To thee, into heaven's paradise,

Ps. 48:14. This is God, our God for ever and ever. He will be our guide for ever.
Heb. 13:5–6. ...He has said, "I will never fail you nor forsake (Luther: nicht verlassen noch versäumen)." Hence we can confidently say, "The Lord is my helper, I will not be afraid; what can man do to me?" (Deut. 31:6, 8; Josh. 1:5)

*1 Pet. 4:13. Rejoice in so far as you share Christ's sufferings...
Ps. 71:5. For thou, O Lord, art my hope, my trust (Luther: Zuversicht), O Lord... (Also Ps. 61:3, 71:7, 142:5.)
Ezek. 37:26. [God]: "I will make a covenant..it shall be an everlasting covenant with them..." (Also Is. 54:10.)
2 Tim. 2:19. But God's firm foundation stands, bearing this seal: "The Lord knows those who are his"...
Rev. 9:4. ...The seal of God [was] upon their foreheads.
Eph. 1:13–14. In [Christ] you also, who have heard the word of truth, the gospel of your salvation, and have believed in him, were sealed with the promised Holy Spirit, which is the guarantee of our inheritance until we acquire possession of it, to the praise of his glory. (Also 2 Cor. 5:5, Heb. 9:15.)
Mt. 16:18 [Christ]: ...On this rock I will build my church, and the powers of death (Luther: Pforten der Hölle) shall not prevail against it.

*Mt. 2:13. ...An angel of the Lord appeared to Joseph in a dream and said, "Rise, take the child and his mother, and flee to Egypt..."
Jn. 15:18, 20 [Christ]: If the world hates you, know that it has hated me before it hated you...If they persecuted me, they will persecute you. (Also Jn. 17:14, Mt. 5:10–12, 10:24–25, 1 Jn. 3:13.)
Heb. 11:13, 16. [Many] died in faith...having acknowledged that they were strangers and exiles on the earth...As it is, they desire a better country, that is, a heavenly one. Therefore God is not ashamed to be called their God, for he has prepared for them a city. (Also Heb. 13:14.)
Rev. 2:7. ...To him who conquers I will grant to eat of the tree of life, which is in the paradise of God.
Gen. 2:8–9. ...In Eden, in the east...[God] put the man whom he had formed... The Lord God made to grow every tree that is pleasant to the sight and good for food, the tree of life also in the midst of the garden...
Rev. 22:1–3. [In paradise, the angel] showed me the river of the water of life, bright as crystal, flowing from the throne of God and of the Lamb through the middle of the street of the city; also, on either side of the river, the tree of life with its twelve kinds of fruit, yielding its fruit each month; and the leaves of the tree were for the healing of the nations.

Acts 14:22. ...Through many tribulations (Luther: Trübsal) we must enter the kingdom of God.
Mt. 7:14. For the gate is narrow and the way is hard, that leads to life, and those who find it are few.
Mt. 16:24 [Christ]: If any man would come after me, let him deny himself and take up his cross and follow me.
*Mt. 2:13. ...An angel of the Lord appeared to Joseph in a dream and said, "Rise, take the child and his mother, and flee to Egypt..."

Nur getrost, getrost, ihr Herzen,
Just be-of-good-cheer, be-of-good-cheer, ye hearts,

Hier ist Angst, dort Herrlichkeit!
Here (there) is fear, there glory!

Da ist mein rechtes Vaterland,
There is my true fatherland,
{There my true fatherland is,}

Daran du dein Blut hast gewandt.
Whereto thou thy blood hast devoted.
{For which thou thy blood didst shed.}

Und die Freude jener Zeit
And the joy of-that time

Überwieget alle Schmerzen.
Outweighs all sorrows.

BWV 59
Wer mich liebet, der wird mein Wort halten I
(NBA I/13; BC A82)

Pentecost (BWV 172, 59, 74, 34)
*Acts 2:1–13 (Outpouring of the Holy Spirit)
*Jn. 14:23–31 (Jesus' farewell; he promises to send the Holy Spirit)
Librettist: Erdmann Neumeister

1. Soprano & Bass Duet
●Promise of God's indwelling: Jn. 14:23 (59-1)
Wer mich liebet, der wird mein Wort halten,
Whoever me loves, he will my word keep,

und mein Vater wird ihn lieben, und wir
and my father will him love, and we

werden zu ihm kommen und Wohnung bei ihm machen.
will to him come and (our) dwelling with him make.

2. Soprano Recit.
●Pentecost: God honors mortals by indwelling them (59-2)
O, was sind das für Ehren,
Oh, what are (then) those (kind of) honors,
{Oh, what places of honor are those,}

Worzu uns Jesus setzt?
To-which us Jesus (leads)?
{To which Jesus leads us?}

Der uns so würdig schätzt,
He-who us so worthy reckons,
{He reckons us so worthy,}

Heb. 11:13–16. These [heroes] all died in faith...having acknowledged that they were strangers and exiles on the earth. For people who speak thus make it clear that they are seeking a homeland (Luther: Vaterland). If they had been thinking of that land from which they had gone out, they would have had opportunity to return. But as it is, they desire a better country, that is, a heavenly one. Therefore God is not ashamed to be called their God, for he has prepared for them a city.
Mt. 5:10–12. Blessed are those who are persecuted for righteousness' sake, for theirs is the kingdom of heaven. Blessed are you when men revile you and persecute you and utter all kinds of evil against you falsely on my account. Rejoice and be glad (Luther: seid fröhlich und getrost), for your reward is great in heaven, for so men persecuted the prophets who were before you.
Rom. 8:18. I consider that the sufferings of this present time are not worth comparing with the glory that is to be revealed to us. (Also 2 Cor. 4:17.)

*Jn. 14:16–20, 23, 26.** I will pray the Father, and he will give you another Counselor, to be with you for ever, even the Spirit of truth, whom the world cannot receive, because it neither sees him nor knows him; you know him, for he dwells with you, and will be in you. I will not leave you desolate; I will come to you. Yet a little while, and the world will see me no more, but you will see me; because I live, you will live also. In that day you will know that I am in my Father, and you in me, and I in you... *If a man loves me, he will keep my word, and my Father will love him, and we will come to him and make our home with him...*The Counselor, the Holy Spirit, whom the Father will send in my name, he will teach you all things, and bring to your remembrance all that I have said to you.

Ps. 8:3–5. [O Lord,] when I look at thy heavens, the work of thy fingers, the moon and the stars which thou hast established; what is man that thou art mindful of him, and the son of man that thou dost care for him? Yet thou hast made him little less than God, and dost crown him with glory and honor. 1 Jn. 3:1. See what love the Father has given us, that we should be called children of God; and so we are...
Jn. 1:12. To all who received [Christ], who believed in his name, he gave power to become children of God.
Rev. 3:20 [Christ]: Behold, I stand at the door and knock; if any one hears my voice and opens the door, I will come in to him and eat with him, and he with me.
*Jn. 14:23 [Christ]:** ...We will come to him and make our home with him.
*Acts 2:1–4.** When the day of Pentecost had come, they were all together in one place. And suddenly a sound came from heaven like

Daß er verheißt,
That he promises,

Samt   Vater und dem Heilgen Geist
With (the) Father and the   Holy   Ghost

In   unsre Herzen einzukehren.
Into our   hearts   to-enter.

O, was   sind das   für Ehren?
Oh, what (then) are those (kind of) honors?
{Oh, what honors are those?}

Der Mensch ist Staub,
 -    Man   is   dust,

Der Eitelkeit ihr Raub,
Of   vanity (the) prey,
{Vanity's prey,}

Der Müh und Arbeit   Trauerspiel
Of   care and   toil   (the) tragic-drama
{Toil and trouble's tragic drama,}

Und alles Elends   Zweck und Ziel.
And of-all misery (the) object and goal.
{And all misery's object and goal.}

Wie nun? Der Allerhöchste spricht,
How then? The   Most-High   says,

Er   will   in unsern Seelen
He desires in   our   souls

Die Wohnung   sich   erwählen.
(A)   dwelling for-himself to-elect.
{He desires to elect our souls as his dwelling.}

Ach, was tut Gottes Liebe nicht?
Ah, what does God's   love   not (all do)?

Ach, daß doch, wie er wollte,
Ah,   that indeed, as he wished,

Ihn auch ein jeder lieben sollte.
Him - everyone love would.
{Ah, if only—as he wished—everyone would love him.}

3. Chorale
●Pentecost: Prayer & praise for Holy Ghost (59-3)
Komm, Heiliger Geist, Herre Gott,
Come,   Holy Ghost, Lord God,

Erfüll mit deiner Gnaden Gut
Fill   with   thy   grace's blessing

Deiner Gläubigen   Herz, Mut und Sinn.
Thy   believers (in) heart, will, and mind.

the rush of a mighty wind, and it filled all the house where they were sitting. And there appeared to them tongues as of fire, distributed and resting on each one of them. And they were all filled with the Holy Spirit and began to speak in other tongues, as the Spirit gave them utterance.

Ps. 144:3–4. O Lord, what is man that thou dost regard him, or the son of man that thou dost think of him: Man is like a breath, his days are like a passing shadow.

Ps. 103:14–16. [God] knows our frame; he remembers that we are dust. As for man, his days are like grass; he flourishes like a flower of the field; for the wind passes over it, and it is gone, and its place knows it no more.

Ps. 90:3, 5–6, 9–10, 12. [O Lord,] thou turnest man back to the dust, and sayest, "Turn back, O children of men!"...Thou dost sweep men away; they are like a dream, like grass which is renewed in the morning: in the morning it flourishes and is renewed; in the evening it fades and withers...For all our days pass away under thy wrath, our years come to an end like a sigh. The years of our life are threescore and ten, or even by reason of strength fourscore; yet their span is but toil and trouble (Luther: Mühe und Arbeit); they are soon gone, and we fly away...So teach us to number our days that we may get a heart of wisdom.

Rom. 8:20–21. For the creation was subjected to futility (Luther: Eitelkeit)...[It] will be set free from its bondage to decay and obtain the glorious liberty of the children of God.

Ecc. 3:20. All go to one place; all are from the dust, and all turn to dust again.

Job 14:1–2. Man that is born of woman is of few days, and full of trouble. He comes forth like a flower, and withers; he flees like a shadow, and continues not. (Also Job 5:7.)

Is. 57:15. Thus says the high and lofty One who inhabits eternity, whose name is Holy: "I dwell in the high and holy place, and also with him who is of a contrite and humble spirit, to revive the spirit of the humble, and to revive the heart of the contrite."

Ezek. 37:26–27 [God]: I will make a covenant of peace with them...My dwelling place shall be with them; and I will be their God, and they shall be my people. (Also Is. 54:10, Jer. 24:7, 31:31–33, Ezek. 11:19–20, 37:26–27, Heb. 8:7–11.)

2 Cor. 6:16, 18. ...We are the temple of the living God; as God said, "I will live in them and move among them, and I will be their God, and they shall be my people...I will be a father to you, and you shall be my sons and daughters..."

Jn. 14:23 [Christ]: ...If a man loves me...my Father will love him, and we will come to him and make our home with him.

Mt. 22:37–38. ...You shall love the Lord your God with all your heart... This is the great and first commandment.

Eph. 5:18–19. ...Be filled with the Spirit, addressing one another in psalms and hymns and spiritual songs, singing and making melody to the Lord with all your heart.

*Acts 2:2–8. Suddenly a sound came from heaven...and there appeared to them tongues as of fire, distributed and resting on each one of them. And they were all filled with the Holy Spirit and began to speak in other tongues, as the Spirit gave them utterance. Now there were dwelling in Jerusalem Jews, devout men from every nation under heaven. And at this sound the multitude came together, and they

Dein brünstig Lieb entzünd in ihn'n.
Thine ardent love   kindle in them.
{Kindle thy ardent love within them.}

O Herr, durch deines Lichtes Glanz
O Lord,   by   thy   light's lustre (thou)

Zu dem Glauben versammlet hast
To -   faith   gathered hast
{Hast gathered to faith}

Das Volk aus aller Welt Zungen;
  - People from all-the world's tongues;
{People of every tongue in the world;}

Das sei dir, Herr, zu Lob gesungen.
That be to-thee, Lord, for praise sung.
{May that be sung to thy praise, Lord.}

Alleluja, alleluja.
Alleluia, alleluia.

4. Bass Aria
●Pentecost: God dwells in us; we shall live with him (59-4)
Die Welt mit allen Königreichen,
The world with all (its) kingdoms,

Die Welt mit aller Herrlichkeit
The world with all (its) glory

Kann dieser Herrlichkeit nicht gleichen,
Can this   glory   not   equal,
{Can not equal this glory,}

Womit uns unser Gott erfreut:
Wherewith us   our   God gladdens:
{Wherewith our God gladdens us:}

Daß er in unsern Herzen thronet
That he in   our   hearts enthrones (himself)
{That he enthrones himself in our hearts}

Und wie in einem Himmel wohnet.
And (there) as in   a   heaven dwells.
{And makes this his heavenly dwelling.}

Ach Gott, wie selig sind wir doch,
Ah God, how blessed are we indeed,

Wie selig werden wir erst noch,
How blessed will we some-day yet (be),

Wenn wir nach dieser Zeit der Erden
When we after this time (on) earth

were bewildered, because each one heard them speaking in his own language. And they were amazed and wondered, saying, "Are not all these who are speaking Galileans? And how is it that we hear, each of us in his own native language?"

2 Cor. 4:6. It is the God who said, "Let light shine out of darkness," who has shone in our hearts to give the light of the knowledge of the glory of God in the face of Christ.

Heb. 1:3. [Christ] reflects the glory of God (Luther: der Glanz seiner Herrlichkeit)...

Is. 60:1, 3–4. Arise, shine; for your light has come, and the glory of the Lord has risen upon you...and nations shall come to your light, and kings to the brightness of your rising. Lift up your eyes round about, and see; they all gather together, they come to you.

1 Pet. 2:9–10. You are a chosen race, a royal priesthood, a holy nation, God's own people, that you may declare the wonderful deeds of him who called you out of darkness into his marvelous light. Once you were no people but now you are God's people...

Rev. 5:6, 9. And between the throne and the four living creatures and among the elders, I saw a Lamb standing, as though it had been slain... and they sang a new song, saying, "Worthy art thou...for thou wast slain and by thy blood didst ransom men for God from every tribe and tongue and people and nation."

Phil. 3:8–11. Indeed I count everything as loss because of the surpassing worth of knowing Christ Jesus my Lord. For his sake I have suffered the loss of all things, and count them as refuse, in order that I may gain Christ and be found in him, not having a righteousness of my own, based on law, but that which is through faith in Christ...that I may know him and the power of his resurrection, and may share his sufferings, becoming like him in his death, that if possible I may attain the resurrection from the dead.

1 Cor. 3:16–17. Do you not know that you are God's temple and that God's Spirit dwells in you?...God's temple is holy, and that temple you are. (Also 2 Cor. 6:16–17.)

*Jn. 14:17 [Christ]: ...[The Counselor] dwells with you, and will be in you.

Jn. 17:21, 23 [Christ]: [I ask, O Father]...even as thou, Father, art in me, and I in thee, that they also may be in us, so that the world may believe that thou hast sent me...I in them and thou in me...

1 Jn. 4:15–16. Whoever confesses that Jesus is the Son of God, God abides in him, and he in God. So we know and believe the love God has for us. God is love, and he who abides in love abides in God, and God abides in him.

1 Jn. 4:13. By this we know that we abide in him and he in us, because he has given us of his own Spirit. (Also 1 Jn. 3:24.)

Jn. 14:1–3. [Jesus]: "Let not your hearts be troubled; believe in God, believe also in me. In my Father's house are many rooms; if it were not so, would I have told you that I go to prepare a place for you? And when I go and prepare a place for you, I will come again and will take you to myself, that where I am you may be also."

1 Thess. 4:17–18. ...So we shall always be with the Lord. Therefore comfort one another with these words.

Bei   dir im Himmel wohnen werden.
With thee in heaven   shall-dwell.

Rom. 8:18. I consider that the sufferings of this present time are not worth comparing with the glory that is to be revealed to us.
2 Cor. 4:17. For this slight momentary (Luther: zeitlich) affliction is preparing for us an eternal weight of glory beyond all comparison.

BWV 60
O Ewigkeit, du Donnerwort I[1]
(NBA I/27; BC A161)

24. S. after Trinity (BWV 60, 26)
*Col. 1:9–14 (Paul's prayer for the Colossians)
*Mt. 9:18–26 (Jesus raises Jairus' daughter from the dead; on the way, he heals the woman who touched his garment)
[1]The manuscript title identifies this cantata as a dialogue between Fear and Hope.
Librettist: Unknown

1. Alto & Tenor Duet (Dialogue: Fear vs. Hope)
        (Chorale: see also 20-1)
•Dialogue: Fear of eternity; Hope's response (60-1)
Alto (Fear's lament):
O Ewigkeit, du   Donnerwort,
O eternity, thou thund'rous-word,

O Schwert, das durch   die Seele bohrt,
O sword, which through (one's) soul pierces,

O Anfang sonder Ende!
O beginning without end!

O Ewigkeit, Zeit ohne Zeit,
O eternity, time without time,

Ich weiß   vor   großer Traurigkeit
I know because-of (my) great   sadness
{Because of my great sadness I do not know}

Nicht, wo ich mich   hinwende;
Not, where I   - (might) turn-to;
{Where to turn.}

Mein ganz erschrockenes Herze bebt,
My completely frightened   heart quakes (so much),

Daß mir die Zung am   Gaumen klebt.
That - (my) tongue to (my) palate sticks.
{That my tongue sticks to my palate.}

   Tenor (Hope's response - Gen. 49:18/Ps. 119:166):
   Herr, ich warte auf dein Heil.
   Lord, I   wait for thy salvation.

2. Alto & Tenor Recit. (Dialogue: Fear vs. Hope)
•Dialogue: Fear vs. Hope as I consider death (60-2)
Alto (Fear):
O schwerer Gang   zum letzten Kampf und Streite!
O difficult passage to-(my) final   fight   and battle!

Job 37:5. God thunders wondrously with his voice; he does great things which we cannot comprehend.
Ps. 90:2, 4. [O Lord,] before the mountains were brought forth, or ever thou hadst formed the earth and the world, from everlasting to everlasting thou art God...For a thousand years in thy sight are but as yesterday when it is past, or as a watch in the night.
Heb. 4:12. The word of God is living and active, sharper than any two-edged sword, piercing to the division of soul and spirit, of joints and marrow, and discerning the thoughts and intentions of the heart.
Is. 57:15 [God]: [I am] the high and lofty One who inhabits eternity, whose name is Holy...
Rev. 1:8. "I am the Alpha and the Omega," (Luther: das A und das O, der Anfang und das Ende) says the Lord God, who is and who was and who is to come, the Almighty.
Rev. 22:13 [God]: I am the Alpha and the Omega, the first and the last, the beginning and the end. (Also Rev. 21:6.)
Is. 45:22 [God]: Turn to me and be saved all the ends of the earth! For I am God, and there is no other.
Ps. 22:14–15. I am poured like water, and all my bones are out of joint; my heart is like wax, it is melted within my breast; my strength is dried up like a potsherd, and my tongue cleaves to my jaws (Luther: Gaumen); thou dost lay me in the dust of death.
1 Jn. 4:18. There is no fear in love, but perfect love casts out fear. For fear has to do with punishment, and he who fears is not perfected in love.
Gen. 49:18. *I wait for thy salvation, O Lord.* (Also Ps. 119:166.)

Heb. 9:27. ...It is appointed for men to die once, and after that comes judgment.

Tenor (Hope):
Mein Beistand ist schon da,
My   helper is already there,

Mein Heiland steht mir ja
My   Savior stands - indeed

Mit   Trost   zur Seite.
With comfort at-(my) side.

Alto:
Die Todesangst, der letzte Schmerz
The fear-of-death, the final   pain

Ereilt   und überfällt mein Herz
Overtakes and   seizes   my   heart

Und martert diese Glieder.
And torments these members (of mine).

Tenor:
Ich lege diesen Leib vor Gott zum Opfer nieder.
I   lay   this body before God as-a sacrifice down.
{I lay down this body before God as a sacrifice.}

Ist gleich der Trübsal Feuer   heiß,
- Although - affliction's fire (be) hot,

Genug,   es reinigt mich zu Gottes Preis.
(It is) enough (that) it purifies me to God's praise.

Alto:
Doch nun wird sich der Sünden große Schuld
Yet now will - (my) sins' great guilt

vor mein Gesichte stellen.
before my   face   appear.

Tenor:
Gott wird deswegen   doch
God will on-that-account nevertheless

kein Todesurteil fällen.
no sentence-of-death pass.
{pass no sentence of death.}

Er gibt ein Ende den Versuchungsplagen,
He (sets) a limit to-the plagues-of-temptation,

Daß man sie kann ertragen.
That one them can   bear.
{That one can bear them.}

3. Alto & Tenor Aria (Dialogue: Fear vs. Hope)
●Dialogue: Fear vs. Hope as I consider death (60-3)
Alto (Fear):
Mein letztes Lager will mich schrecken,
My   final   bed would me   terrify,
{My deathbed terrifies me,}

Ps. 18:4–5. The cords of death encompassed me, the torrents of perdition assailed me; the cords of Sheol entangled me, the snares of death confronted me. (Also 2 Sam. 22:5–6.)
Heb. 2:14–15. ...[Christ]...partook of [human] nature, that through death he might...deliver all those who through fear of death were subject to lifelong bondage.
Ps. 22:11. [O Lord,] be not far from me, for trouble is near and there is none to help.
Mt. 28:20 [Christ]: ...Lo, I am with you always to the close of the age.
Ps. 28:7. The Lord is my strength and my shield; in him my heart trusts; so I am helped, and my heart exults, and with my song I give thanks to him.
2 Cor. 1:5. As we share abundantly in Christ's sufferings, so through Christ we share abundantly in comfort too.
Ps. 116:3. The snares of death encompassed me; the pangs of Sheol (Luther: Angst der Hölle) laid hold on me; I suffered distress and anguish.
Ps. 69:1–3. Save me, O God! For the waters have come up to my neck. I sink in deep mire, where there is no foothold; I have come into deep waters, and the flood sweeps over me. I am weary with my crying; my throat is parched. My eyes grow dim with waiting for my God...
1 Pet. 4:19. Let those who suffer according to God's will do right and entrust their souls to a faithful Creator.
Rom. 12:1. I appeal to you...to present your bodies as a living sacrifice, holy and acceptable to God, which is your spiritual worship.
1 Pet. 4:12. Beloved, do not be surprised at the fiery ordeal which comes upon you to prove you, as though something strange were happening to you. (Also Jms. 1:2–4, 12, 1 Pet. 5:10.)
Dan. 3:21. [Daniel's three friends] were bound...and they were cast into the burning fiery furnace.
1 Pet. 1:6–7. In this you rejoice, though now for a little while you may have to suffer various trials, so that the genuineness of your faith, more precious than gold which though perishable is tested by fire, may redound to praise and glory and honor at the revelation of Jesus Christ. (Also Prov. 17:3, 25:4, Mal. 3:3.)
1 Jn. 3:19–20. By this we shall know that we are of the truth, and reassure our hearts before him whenever our hearts condemn us; for God is greater than our hearts...
Rom. 2:15–16. ...What the law requires is written on [men's] hearts, while their conscience also bears witness and their conflicting thoughts accuse or perhaps excuse them on that day when...God judges the secrets of men by Christ Jesus.
1 Tim. 1:15. ...Christ Jesus came into the world to save sinners. And I am the foremost of sinners...
Rom. 6:23. The wages of sin is death, but the free gift of God is eternal life in Christ Jesus our Lord.
1 Jn. 3:14. We know that we have passed out of death into life...
1 Cor. 10:13. ...God...will not let you be tempted beyond your strength, but with the temptation will also provide the way of escape, that you may be able to endure it.

Ps. 6:6. I am weary with my moaning; every night I flood my bed with tears; I drench my couch (Luther: Lager) with my weeping. (Also Jer. 45:3.)
Heb. 2:15–16. ...[Christ]...partook of [human] nature that through death he might destroy him who has the power of death, that is, the devil,

Tenor (Hope):
Mich wird des Heilands Hand bedecken,
Me will the Savior's hand cover,
{The Savior's hand will cover me,}

Alto:
Des Glaubens Schwachheit sinket fast,
(My) faith's weakness sinks nearly,
{My faith nearly fails,}

Tenor:
Mein Jesus trägt mit mir die Last.
My Jesus bears with me the burden.
{My Jesus helps me bear this burden.}

Alto:
Das offne Grab sieht greulich aus,
The open grave looks horrible -,

Tenor:
Es wird mir doch ein Friedenshaus.
It becomes for-me, however, a house-of-peace.

and deliver all those who through fear of death were subject to lifelong bondage.

Ex. 33:21–23. The Lord said [to Moses], "Behold, there is a place by me where you shall stand upon the rock; and while my glory passes by I will put you in a cleft of the rock, andI will cover you with my hand until I have passed by..."

Is. 49:2. ...In the shadow of his hand he hid me (Luther: hat er mich bedeckt)... (Also Is. 51:16.)

Mt. 14:28–31. Peter answered [Jesus], "Lord, if it is you, bid me come to you on the water." [Jesus] said, "Come." So Peter got out of the boat and walked on the water and came to Jesus; but when he saw the wind, he was afraid, and beginning to sink he cried out, "Lord, save me." Jesus immediately reached out his hand and caught him, saying to him, "O man of little faith, why did you doubt?"

Mt. 11:28–30 [Christ]: Come to me, all who labor and are heavy laden, and I will give you rest. Take my yoke upon you, and learn from me; for I am gentle and lowly in heart, and you will find rest for your souls. For my yoke is easy, and my burden is light.

Mt. 10:28 [Christ]: And do not fear those who kill the body but cannot kill the soul...

Rev. 14:13. ...Blessed are the dead who die in the Lord henceforth... that they may rest from their labors, for their deeds follow them!

4. Alto & Bass Recit. (Dialogue: Fear vs. Christ)
●Dialogue: Fear vs. Christ's word as I consider death (60–4)
Alto (Fear):
Der Tod bleibt doch der menschlichen Natur verhaßt
- Death remains nevertheless to human nature hateful

Und reißet fast
And (casts) nearly

Die Hoffnung ganz zu Boden.
(All) (our) hope completely to (the) ground.

Bass (Christ):
Selig sind die Toten;
Blessed are the dead;

Alto:
Ach! Aber ach, wieviel Gefahr
Ah! But ah, how-much peril

Stellt sich der Seele dar,
Presents itself to-my soul -,
{My soul will encounter,}

Den Sterbeweg zu gehen!
The path-of-death to walk!
{In walking the path to death!}

Vielleicht wird ihr der Höllenrachen
Perhaps will to-it the jaws-of-hell
{Perhaps the jaws of hell...}

Den Tod erschrecklich machen,
- Death frightful make,
{Will make death frightful to my soul,}

*Mt. 9:18, 23–25. While [Jesus] was thus speaking to them, behold, a ruler came in and knelt before him, saying, "My daughter has just died; but come and lay your hand on her, and she will live."...And when Jesus came to the ruler's house, and saw the flute players, and the crowd making a tumult, he said, "Depart; for the girl is not dead but sleeping." And they laughed at him. But when the crowd had been put outside, he went in and took her by the hand, and the girl arose.

Job 17:13–15. If I look for Sheol as my house, if I spread my couch in darkness, if I say to the pit, "You are my father," and to the worm, "My mother," or "My sister," where then is my hope? Who will see my hope?

1 Cor. 15:26. The last enemy to be destroyed is death.

Rom. 8:19–24. For the creation waits with eager longing for the revealing of the sons of God; for the creation was subjected to futility, not of its own will but by the will of him who subjected it in hope; because the creation itself will be set free from its bondage to decay and obtain the glorious liberty of the children of God. We know that the whole

creation has been groaning in travail together until now; and not only the creation, but we ourselves, who have the first fruits of the Spirit, groan inwardly as we wait for adoption as sons, the redemption of our bodies. For in this hope we were saved...

Rev. 14:13. And I heard a voice from heaven saying, "Write this: *Blessed are the dead* who die in the Lord henceforth. "Blessed indeed," says the Spirit, "that they may rest from their labors, for their deeds follow them!"

Is. 5:14. Sheol (Luther: Hölle) has enlarged its appetite and opened its mouth beyond measure (Luther: Rachen aufgetan ohne alle Maß)...

1 Pet. 5:8–10. Be sober, be watchful. Your adversary the devil prowls

Wenn er sie zu verschlingen sucht;
When (they) it - to-devour do-seek;
{When those jaws seek to devour it;}

Vielleicht ist sie bereits verflucht
Perhaps is it already damned
{Perhaps it is already damned}

Zum ewigen Verderben.
To eternal destruction.

Bass:
Selig sind die Toten, die in dem Herren sterben;
Blessed are the dead, who in the Lord die;

Alto:
Wenn ich im Herren sterbe,
If I in-the Lord die,
{If I die in the Lord,}

Ist denn die Seligkeit mein Teil und Erbe?
Is then (eternal) salvation my portion and inheritance?

Der Leib wird ja der Würmer Speise!
(My) body becomes indeed - worms' fare!
{Indeed, my body becomes the fare of worms!}

Ja, werden meine Glieder
Yes, (turn) my members
{Yes, if my members turn}

Zu Staub und Erde wieder,
To dust and earth again,

Da ich ein Kind des Todes heiße,
Since I a child of death am-called,
{Since I am by nature mortal}

So schein ich ja im Grabe zu verderben.
Then appear I indeed within-the grave to perish.
{Then it would seem that I will perish in the grave.}

Bass:
Selig sind die Toten, die in dem Herren sterben,
Blessed are the dead, who in the Lord die,

von nun an.
from now on.

Alto:
Wohlan!
Well-then!

Soll ich von nun an selig sein:
Shall I from now on blessed be,
{If I am to be blessed from now on,}

So stelle dich, o Hoffnung, wieder ein!
Then present thyself, O hope, again - !
{Then return again, O hope!}

around like a roaring lion, seeking some one to devour (Luther: verschlinge). (Also Ps. 22:12–13, 21.)

Num. 16:31–33. And as [Moses] finished speaking all these words, the ground under them split asunder; and the earth opened its mouth and swallowed them up, with their households and all the men that belonged to Korah and all their goods. So they and all that belonged to them went down alive into Sheol (Luther: Hölle); and the earth closed over them, and they perished from the midst of the assembly.

Heb. 10:26–27. If we sin deliberately after receiving the knowledge of the truth, there no longer remains a sacrifice for sins, but a fearful prospect of judgment, and a fury of fire which will consume the adversaries.

Jn. 3:18. He who believes in him is not condemned; he who does not believe is condemned already, because he has not believed in the name of the only Son of God.

Rev. 14:13. And I heard a voice from heaven saying, "Write this: *Blessed are the dead who die in the Lord* henceforth." "Blessed indeed," says the Spirit, "that they may rest from their labors, for their deeds follow them!"

Job 21:23, 25–26. One dies in full prosperity...Another dies in bitterness of soul...They lie down alike in the dust, and the worms cover them.

Job 19:25–26. I know that my Redeemer lives...and after my skin has been thus destroyed, then from my flesh (Luther German: in meinem Fleisch) I shall see God.

1 Cor. 15:49–50. Just as we have borne the image of the man of dust, we shall also bear the image of the man of heaven. I tell you this, brethren: flesh and blood cannot inherit the kingdom of God, nor does the perishable inherit the imperishable.

Col. 3:24. ...From the Lord you will receive the inheritance as your reward...

*Col. 1:11–12. May you be strengthened with all power, according to his glorious might, for all endurance and patience with joy, giving thanks to the Father, who has qualified us to share in the inheritance of the saints in light. (Also Eph. 1:13–14, Heb. 9:15.)

1 Pet. 1:3–5. Blessed be the God and Father of our Lord Jesus Christ! By his great mercy we have been born anew to a living hope through the resurrection of Jesus Christ from the dead, and to an inheritance which is imperishable, undefiled, and unfading, kept in heaven for you, who by God's power are guarded through faith for a salvation ready to be revealed in the last time.

Rev. 14:13. And I heard a voice from heaven saying, "Write this: *Blessed are the dead who die in the Lord henceforth.*" "Blessed indeed," says the Spirit, "that they may rest from their labors, for their deeds follow them!"

1 Cor. 15:17–20. If Christ has not been raised, your faith is futile and you are still in your sins. Then those also who have fallen asleep in Christ have perished. If for this life only we have hoped in Christ, we are of all men most to be pitied. But in fact Christ has been raised from the dead, the first fruits of those who have fallen asleep. (Also Jn. 6:40/44/54, 8:11.)

2 Cor. 5:6–8. So we are always of good courage; we know that while we are at home in the body we are away from the Lord, for we walk by faith, not by sight. We are of good courage, and we would rather be away from the body and at home with the Lord.

Phil. 1:21–23. To me to live is Christ, and to die is gain...Which I shall choose I cannot tell. I am hard pressed between the two. My desire is to depart and be with Christ, for that is far better.

Mein Leib mag ohne Furcht im Schlafe ruhn,
My body may without fear in sleep rest,
{My body may rest in its sleep without fear,}

Der Geist kann einen Blick in jene Freude tun.
(My) spirit can a glance into yonder happiness (cast).
{My spirit can already see into yonder bliss.}

5. Chorale
●Hope's response to Christ's word: Death not feared (60-5)
Es ist genug;
It is enough;

Herr, wenn es dir gefällt,
Lord, if it thee pleases,
{Lord if it pleases thee,}

So spanne mich doch aus!
Then put-to-rest me indeed - !
{Then indeed put me to rest!}

Mein Jesus kömmt;
My Jesus comes;

Nun gute Nacht, o Welt!
Now good night, O world!

Ich fahr ins Himmelshaus,
I travel into heaven's-dwelling,

Ich fahre sicher hin mit Frieden,
I depart securely - in peace,

Mein großer Jammer bleibt danieden.
My great misery remains below.

Es ist genug.
It is enough.

*Mt. 9:23-25. When Jesus came to the ruler's house, and saw the flute players, and the crowd making a tumult, he said, "Depart; for the girl is not dead but sleeping." And they laughed at him. But when the crowd had been put outside, he went in and took her by the hand, and the girl arose. (Also Acts 7:54-60.)

Mk. 14:41-42. And [Jesus] came the third time [to his disciples], and said to them, "Are you still sleeping and taking your rest? *It is enough;* the hour has come; the Son of man is betrayed into the hands of sinners. Rise, let us be going..."
Mk. 14:35-36. And going a little farther, [Jesus] fell on the ground and prayed that, if it were possible, the hour might pass from him. And he said, "Abba, Father, all things are possible to thee; remove this cup from me; yet not what I will, but what thou wilt."
*Mt. 9:24. [Jesus] said [to the crowd], "Depart; for the girl is not dead but sleeping." And they laughed at him.
Jn. 11:11-15. ...[Jesus] said to them, "Our friend Lazarus has fallen asleep, but I go to awake him out of sleep." The disciples said to him, "Lord, if he has fallen asleep, he will recover." Now Jesus had spoken of his death, but they thought that he meant taking rest in sleep. Then Jesus told them plainly, "Lazarus is dead; and for your sake I am glad that I was not there, so that you may believe. But let us go to him."
Lk. 2:28-29. [Simeon] took [Jesus] up in his arms and blessed God and said, "Lord, now lettest thou thy servant depart in peace, according to thy word."
2 Cor. 5:1-4. We know that if the earthly tent we live in is destroyed, we have a building from God, a house not made with hands, eternal in the heavens. Here indeed we groan, and long to put on our heavenly dwelling, so that by putting it on we may not be found naked. For while we are still in this tent, we sigh with anxiety; not that we would be unclothed, but that we would be further clothed, so that what is mortal may be swallowed up by life.
Rev. 21:4. ...Death shall be no more, neither shall there be mourning nor crying nor pain any more, for the former things have passed away. (Also Rev. 7:15-17.)

BWV 61
Nun komm, der Heiden Heiland I
(NBA I/1; BC A1)

1. S. in Advent (BWV 61, 62, 36)
*Rom. 13:11-14 (Night is almost gone, lay aside deeds of darkness)
*Mt. 21:1-9 (Christ's triumphal entry into Jerusalem)
Librettist: Erdmann Neumeister

1. Chorus (Chorale Overture) (See also 36-2, 62-1.)
●Advent prayer: Come, Savior of the Gentiles! (61-1)
Nun komm, der Heiden Heiland,
Now come, (O thou) the Gentiles' Savior,

*Mt. 21:6-10. The disciples went and did as Jesus had directed them; they brought the ass and the colt, and put their garments on them, and he sat thereon. Most of the crowd spread their garments on the road, and others cut branches from the trees and spread them on the road. And the crowds that went before him and that followed him shouted, "Hosanna to the Son of David! Blessed is he who comes in the name of the Lord! Hosanna in the highest!" And when he entered Jerusalem, all the city was stirred, saying, "Who is this?"
Lk. 2:30-32. Mine eyes have seen thy salvation which thou hast prepared in the presence of all peoples, a light for revelation to the Gentiles, and for glory to thy people Israel. (Also Is. 49:6.)

Der Jungfrauen Kind   erkannt,
(As) the   virgin's child (made) known,

Des sich wundert alle Welt:
At-this - doth-marvel the-whole world,
{At this the whole world doth marvel,}

Gott solch Geburt   ihm   bestellt.
(That) God such (a) birth (for) him hath-ordained.

2. Tenor Recit.
●Advent: Christ's coming brings ever new blessings (61-2)
Der Heiland ist gekommen,
The Savior has   come,

Hat unser armes Fleisch und Blut
Has our   poor   flesh and blood

An sich genommen
On himself taken

Und nimmet uns zu Blutsverwandten an.
And receives us as   blood-relatives   - .

O allerhöchstes Gut,
O most-precious possession,

Was hast du nicht   an uns getan?
What hast thou not (all) for us   done?

Was tust du nicht
What dost thou not

Noch täglich an den   Deinen?
Yet   daily for those (who are) thine?

Du kommst und läßt dein Licht
Thou comest and lettest thy light

Mit vollem Segen scheinen.
With full   blessing shine.

3. Tenor Aria
●New Year's prayer: Come & bless thy church! (61-3)
Komm, Jesu, komm zu deiner Kirche
Come, Jesus, come to   thy   church

Und gib ein selig neues Jahr.
And grant a blessed new year.

Befördre deines Namens Ehre,
Advance thy   name's honor,

Is. 7:14. The Lord himself will give you a sign. Behold, a young woman shall conceive and bear a son, and shall call his name Immanuel. (Also Mt. 1:22–23.)
Phil. 2:6–7. [Christ Jesus], who, though he was in the form of God, did not count equality with God a thing to be grasped, but emptied himself, taking the form of a servant, being born in the likeness of men.

Lk. 2:10–11. The angel said to [the shepherds], "...To you is born this day in the city of David a Savior, who is Christ the Lord."
Jn. 1:14. The Word became flesh and dwelt among us...
Rom. 8:3. ...[God sent] his own Son in the likeness of sinful flesh...
1 Tim. 3:16. Great indeed, we confess, is the mystery of our religion: He was manifested in the flesh... (Also Phil. 2:6–7.)
Heb. 2:14. Since...the children share in flesh and blood, [Christ] himself likewise partook of the same nature...
Heb. 2:11. He who sanctifies and those who are sanctified have all one origin. That is why he is not ashamed to call them brethren.
Jn. 1:12. To all who received [Christ], who believed in his name, he gave power to become children of God.
2 Tim. 2:19. God's firm foundation stands, bearing this seal: "The Lord knows those who are his"...
Ps. 16:5. The Lord is my chosen portion and my cup (Luther: Gut und Teil)... (Also Ps. 73:25.)
Lam. 3:22–23. The steadfast love of the Lord never ceases, his mercies never come to an end; they are new every morning; great is thy faithfulness. (Also Ps. 90:14.)
Ps. 68:19. Blessed be the Lord, who daily bears us up; God is our salvation.
Is. 9:2. The people who walked in darkness have seen a great light; those who dwelt in a land of deep darkness, on them has light shined. (Also Is. 49:6.)
Jn. 1:4–5, 9. In [Christ] was life, and the life was the light of men. The light shines in the darkness, and the darkness has not overcome it... The true light that enlightens every man was coming into the world.
1 Jn. 2:8. ...The darkness is passing away and the true light is already shining. (Also 2 Cor. 4:6.)
*Rom. 13:12. ...The night is far gone, the day is at hand...

*Mt. 21:8–10. Most of the crowd spread their garments on the road, and others cut branches from the trees and spread them on the road. And the crowds that went before him and that followed him shouted, "Hosanna to the Son of David! Blessed is he who comes in the name of the Lord! Hosanna in the highest!" And when he entered Jerusalem, all the city was stirred...
Ps. 72:19. Blessed be his glorious name (Luther: sein herrlicher Name) for ever; may his glory (Luther: Ehre) fill the whole earth! Amen and Amen!
Deut. 26:15. [O Lord,] look down from thy holy habitation, from heaven, and bless thy people...
Is. 48:11 [God]: For my own sake, for my own sake, I do it, for how should my name be profaned? My glory I will not give to another.
Ps. 31:3. [O Lord,] thou art my rock and my fortress; for thy name's sake lead me and guide me. (Also Ps. 23:3.)

Erhalte die gesunde Lehre
Preserve the sound teaching

2 Thess. 3:1. ...[May] the word of the Lord...speed on and triumph...
2 Tim. 4:3–4. The time is coming when people will not endure sound teaching (Luther: heilsame Lehre), but having itching ears they will accumulate for themselves teachers to suit their own likings, and will turn away from listening to the truth and wander into myths. (Also Tit. 1:9.)

Und segne Kanzel und Altar.
And bless pulpit and altar.

Ps. 28:8–9. The Lord is the strength of his people...O [Lord,] save thy people, and bless thy heritage; be thou their shepherd, and carry them for ever. (Also Ps. 29:11.)

4. Bass Recit.
●Vox Christi: I stand at the door & knock: Rev. 3:20 (61–4)
Siehe, ich stehe vor der Tür und klopfe an. So jemand
Behold, I stand before the door and knock - . If anyone

meine Stimme hören wird und die Tür auftun, zu dem werde
my voice hears and the door opens, to him will

ich eingehen und das Abendmahl mit ihm halten
I enter and the evening-meal with him celebrate

und er mit mir.
and he with me.

Rev. 3:20 [Christ]: *Behold, I stand at the door and knock; if any one hears my voice and opens the door, I will come in to him and eat with him, and he with me.*
Rev. 19:6–9. Then I heard what seemed to be the voice of a great multitude, like the sound of many waters and like the sound of mighty thunderpeals, crying, "Hallelujah! For the Lord our God the Almighty reigns. Let us rejoice and exult and give him the glory, for the marriage of the Lamb has come, and his Bride has made herself ready; it was granted her to be clothed with fine linen, bright and pure"—for the fine linen is the righteous deeds of the saints. And the angel said to me, "Write this: Blessed are those who are invited to the marriage supper of the Lamb."...

5. Soprano Aria
●Advent: Preparing my heart to be his dwelling (61–5)
Öffne dich, mein ganzes Herze,
Open thyself, my whole heart,
{Open wide to him, O heart of mine,}

Jesus kommt und ziehet ein.
Jesus comes and moves in.

Bin ich gleich nur Staub und Erde,
Am I though but dust and earth,
{Though I am but dust and earth,}

Will er mich doch nicht verschmähn,
Would he me yet not scorn,
{Yet he would not disdain}

Seine Lust an mir zu sehn,
His pleasure in me to (find),
{To find his pleasure in me,}

Daß ich seine Wohnung werde,
So-that I his dwelling become,
{So that I become his dwelling,}

O wie selig werd' ich sein!
Oh, how blessed shall I be!
{Oh, how blessed I shall be!}

Zech. 9:9. Rejoice greatly, O daughter of Zion! Shout aloud, O daughter of Jerusalem! Lo, your king comes to you; triumphant and victorious is he, humble and riding on an ass, on a colt the foal of an ass.
Ezek. 37:26–27 [God]: I will make a covenant of peace with [my people]; it shall be an everlasting covenant with them; and I will bless them and multiply them, and will set my sanctuary in the midst of them for evermore. My dwelling place shall be with them; and I will be their God, and they shall be my people.
Jn. 14:23. Jesus [said], "If a man loves me...my Father will love him, and we will come to him and make our home with him."
Ps. 51:17. ...A broken and contrite heart, O God, thou wilt not despise.
I Sam. 12:22. For the Lord will not cast away his people, for his great name's sake, because it has pleased the LORD to make you a people for himself.
Rev. 21:3–4. ...Behold, the dwelling of God is with men. He will dwell with them, and they shall be his people, and God himself will be with them.
Ps. 8:4. [O Lord,] what is man that thou art mindful of him, and the son of man that thou dost care for him?
Gen. 2:7. The Lord God formed man of dust from the ground...
Gen. 3:19. ... You are dust, and to dust you shall return.
2 Cor. 4:7. We have this treasure in earthen vessels...
1 Cor. 3:16–17. Do you not know that you are God's temple and that God's Spirit dwells in you?... God's temple is holy, and that temple you are. (Also 1 Cor. 6:19–20.)

6. Chorale
●Advent prayer: Come, my crown of joy, do not tarry! (61–6)
Amen, Amen:
Amen, amen:

Rev. 1:7. Behold, he is coming with the clouds, and every eye will see him...Even so. Amen.
Rev. 22:20. He who testifies to these things says, "Surely I am coming soon." Amen. Come, Lord Jesus!

Komm,   du schöne Freudenkrone, bleib nicht lange!
Come, (O) thou beautiful crown-of-joy,   tarry not long!

Deiner wart' ich mit Verlangen.
Thee   await I with longing.
{I wait for thee with yearning.}

BWV 62
Nun komm, der Heiden Heiland II
(NBA I/1; BC A2)

1. S. in Advent (BWV 61, 62, 36)
*Rom. 13:11-14 (Night is almost gone, lay aside deeds of darkness)
*Mt. 21:1-9 (Christ's triumphal entry into Jerusalem)
Librettest: Unknown

1. Chorus (Chorale Vs. 1) (See also 36-2, 61-1.)
●Advent prayer: Come, Savior of the Gentiles! (62-1)
Nun komm,   der Heiden Heiland,
Now come, (O thou) the Gentiles' Savior,

     Der Jungfrauen Kind   erkannt,
(As) the   virgin's   child (made) known,

Des sich wundert   alle Welt:
At-this - doth-marvel the-whole world,
{At this the whole world doth marvel,}

     Gott solch Geburt   ihm   bestellt.
(That) God such (a) birth (for) him hath-ordained.

2. Tenor Aria (Loosely based on Chorale Vss. 2 & 3)
●Advent mystery: Ruler of heaven comes to earth (62-2)
Bewundert, o Menschen,   dies große Geheimnis:
Marvel,   O   people, (at) this great   mystery:

Der höchste Beherrscher erscheinet der Welt.
The highest   ruler   appears to-the world.

Hier werden die Schätze des Himmels entdecket,
Here (are) the treasures of heaven discovered,

Hier wird uns ein göttliches Manna bestellt,
Here is for-us a   divine   manna appointed,

O Wunder! die Keuschheit wird gar nicht beflecket.
O wonder! - Virginity   is not-at-all blemished.

Heb. 10:37. For yet a little while, and the coming one shall come and shall not tarry.
Is. 28:5. In that day the Lord of hosts will be a crown of glory, and a diadem of beauty, to the remnant of his people.
Rev. 3:11 [Christ]: I am coming soon; hold fast what you have, so that no one may seize your crown. (crown: also 2 Tim. 4:8, 1 Pet. 5:4, Jms. 1:12, Rev. 2:10)

*Mt. 21:6-10. The disciples went and did as Jesus had directed them; they brought the ass and the colt, and put their garments on them, and he sat thereon. Most of the crowd spread their garments on the road, and others cut branches from the trees and spread them on the road. And the crowds that went before him and that followed him shouted, "Hosanna to the Son of David! Blessed is he who comes in the name of the Lord! Hosanna in the highest!" And when he entered Jerusalem, all the city was stirred, saying, "Who is this?"
Lk. 2:30-32. Mine eyes have seen thy salvation which thou hast prepared in the presence of all peoples, a light for revelation to the Gentiles, and for glory to thy people Israel. (Also Is. 49:6.)
Mt. 1:22-23. All this took place to fulfil what the Lord had spoken by the prophet: "Behold, a virgin shall conceive and bear a son, and his name shall be called Emmanuel" (which means, God with us). (See Is. 7:14.)
Phil. 2:6-7. [Christ Jesus], who, though he was in the form of God, did not count equality with God a thing to be grasped, but emptied himself, taking the form of a servant, being born in the likeness of men.
1 Tim. 3:16. Great indeed, we confess, is the mystery of our religion: [Christ] was manifested in the flesh, vindicated in the Spirit, seen by angels, preached among the nations, believed on in the world, taken up in glory. (Also Col. 1:27.)
Heb. 1:3. [Christ] reflects the glory of God and bears the very stamp of his nature, upholding the universe by his word of power...
Deut. 10:17. For the Lord your God is God of gods and Lord of lords...
2 Cor. 8:9. You know the grace of our Lord Jesus Christ, that though he was rich, yet for your sake he became poor, so that by his poverty you might become rich.
Eph. 1:18. ...That you may know...what are the riches of his glorious inheritance...
Rev. 2:17 [Christ]: ...To him who conquers I will give some of the hidden manna... (Also Ex. 16:31.)
Jn. 6:51 [Christ]: I am the living bread which came down from heaven; if any one eats of this bread, he will live for ever; and the bread which I shall give for the life of the world is my flesh.
Mt. 1:18. Now the birth of Jesus Christ took place in this way. When his mother Mary had been betrothed to Joseph, before they came together she was found to be with child of the Holy Spirit.

3. Bass Recit. (Based on Chorale Vss. 4 & 5)
●Advent: God's Son, the champion of Judah, comes (62-3)
So geht aus Gottes Herrlichkeit und Thron
Thus goes from God's glory and throne

Sein eingeborner Sohn.
His only-begotten Son.

Der Held aus Juda bricht herein,
The champion of Judah breaks (forth),

Den Weg mit Freudigkeit zu laufen
(His) course with joy to run
{To run his course with joy}

Und uns Gefallne zu erkaufen.
And us fallen-ones to redeem.

O heller Glanz, o wunderbarer Segensschein!
O bright gleam, O wonderful light-of-blessing!

4. Bass Aria (Based on Chorale Vs. 6)
●Advent prayer: Show thyself mighty in human flesh! (62-4)
Streite, siege, starker Held!
Fight, conquer, (O) strong champion!

Sei vor uns im Fleische kräftig!
Be for us in-the flesh mighty!
{Show thyself mighty for us in the flesh!}

Sei geschäftig,
Be active,

Das Vermögen in uns Schwachen
The power (that is) in us weak-ones

Stark zu machen!
Strong to make!
{To make our weak human power strong!}

1 Jn. 4:14. We have seen and testify that the Father has sent his Son as the Savior of the world.
Jn. 3:16. God so loved the world that he gave his only Son...
Phil. 2:6–7. Though he was in the form of God, [Christ] did not count equality with God a thing to be grasped, but emptied himself, taking the form of a servant, being born in the likeness of men. (Also Heb. 1:3.)
Mt. 2:1–6. Now when Jesus was born in Bethlehem of Judea in the days of Herod the king, behold, wise men from the East came to Jerusalem, saying, "Where is he who has been born king of the Jews? For we have seen his star in the East, and have come to worship him." When Herod the king heard this, he was troubled, and all Jerusalem with him; and assembling all the chief priests and scribes of the people, he inquired of them where the Christ was to be born. They told him, "In Bethlehem of Judea; for so it is written by the prophet: 'And you, O Bethlehem, in the land of Judah, are by no means least among the rulers of Judah; for from you shall come a ruler who will govern my people Israel.'" (See Mic. 5:2, also Jn. 7:42.)
Gen. 49:10. The scepter shall not depart from Judah, nor the ruler's staff from between his feet, until he comes to whom it belongs (bis der Held komme)...
Ps. 19:5. ...A strong man (Luther: Held) runs...[the] course with joy.
Heb. 12:1–2. ...Let us run with perseverance the race that is set before us, looking to Jesus the pioneer and perfecter of our faith, who for the joy that was set before him endured the cross, despising the shame, and is seated at the right hand of the throne of God.
Tit. 2:11. The grace of God has appeared for the salvation of all men.
Rev. 5:9. ...[O Lord,] thou wast slain and by thy blood didst ransom (Luther: hast erkauft) men for God from every tribe and tongue and people and nation. (Also 1 Cor. 6:19–20, 1 Cor. 7:23.)
2 Cor. 4:6. It is the God who said, "Let light shine out of darkness," who has shone in our hearts to give the light of the knowledge of the glory of God in the face of Christ. (Also Mal. 4:2, Is. 60:1, 3, 19.)

Is. 9:6. To us a child is born, to us a son is given; and the government will be upon his shoulder, and his name will be called "Wonderful Counselor, Mighty God (Luther: Kraft, Held), Everlasting Father, Prince of Peace."
Rom. 8:3–4. God has done what the law, weakened by the flesh, could not do: sending his own Son in the likeness of sinful flesh and for sin, he condemned sin in the flesh, in order that the just requirement of the law might be fulfilled in us, who walk not according to the flesh but according to the Spirit.
Mt. 26:41. ...The spirit indeed is willing, but the flesh is weak.
Lam. 3:18. Gone is my glory (Luther: mein Vermögen ist dahin)...
Jer. 20:11. The Lord is with me as a dread warrior...
2 Cor. 12:9. But [the Lord] said to me, "My grace is sufficient for you, for my power is made perfect in weakness."...
Phil. 2:13. For God is at work in you, both to will and to work for his good pleasure. (Also Heb. 13:20–21.)
Heb. 2:14. Since therefore the children share in flesh and blood, [Christ] himself likewise partook of the same nature, that through death he might destroy him who has the power of death, that is, the devil...
1 Jn. 3:8. ...The reason the Son of God appeared was to destroy the works of the devil.

5. Soprano & Alto Recit. (Based on Chorale Vs. 7)
●Advent: Praise to God for glorious gift in manger! (62-5)
Wir ehren diese Herrlichkeit
We honor this glory

Und nahen nun zu deiner Krippen
And draw-near now to thy crib

Und preisen mit erfreuten Lippen,
And praise with gladdened lips,

Was du uns zubereit';
What thou for-us hast-prepared;

Die Dunkelheit verstört' uns nicht
The darkness troubled us not

Und sahen dein unendlich Licht.
(When we) saw thy everlasting light.

6. Chorale (Vs. 8) (See also 36-8.)
●Doxology: Praise to Father, Son, and Holy Ghost (62-6)
Lob sei Gott, dem Vater, ton,
Praise be-to God, the Father, given,

Lob sei Gott, sein'm ein'gen Sohn,
Praise be-to God, his only Son,

Lob sei Gott, dem Heilgen Geist,
Praise be-to God, the Holy Ghost,

Immer und in Ewigkeit!
Ever and in Eternity!

Lk. 2:15-16. When the angels went away from them into heaven, the shepherds said to one another, "Let us go over to Bethlehem and see this thing that has happened, which the Lord has made known to us." And they went with haste, and found Mary and Joseph, and the babe lying in a manger.
Lk. 2:28-32. [Simeon] took [Jesus] up in his arms and blessed God and said, "Lord, now lettest thou thy servant depart in peace, according to thy word; for mine eyes have seen thy salvation which thou hast prepared in the presence of all peoples, a light for revelation to the Gentiles, and for glory to thy people Israel." (Also Is. 9:2, 42:6, 49:6, 52:10, 60:1-3.)
Jn. 1:4-5, 14. In [Christ] was life, and the life was the light of men. The light shines in the darkness, and the darkness has not overcome it...And the Word became flesh and dwelt among us, full of grace and truth; we have beheld his glory (Luther: Herrlichkeit), glory as of the only Son from the Father.
*Rom. 13:11-12. ...You know what hour it is, how it is full time now for you to wake from sleep...the night is far gone, the day is at hand...

*Mt. 21:9. ...Hosanna to the Son of David! Blessed is he who comes in the name of the Lord! Hosanna in the highest!
Lk. 2:14. Glory to God in the highest...
2 Cor. 9:15. Thanks be to God for his inexpressible gift!
1 Tim. 1:17. To the King of ages, immortal, invisible, the only God, be honor and glory for ever and ever. Amen. (Also Phil. 4:20.)
Ps. 41:13. Blessed be the Lord, the God of Israel, from everlasting to everlasting! Amen and Amen. (Doxology: also Ps. 72:19, 89:52, 106:48, 150:6, Rom. 11:36, Jude 1:25)
Mt. 28:19. ...in the name of the Father and of the Son and of the Holy Spirit.
Rev. 7:11-12. And all the angels stood round the throne and round the elders and the four living creatures, and they fell on their faces before the throne and worshiped God, saying, "Amen! Blessing and glory and wisdom and thanksgiving and honor and power and might be to our God for ever and ever! Amen."

BWV 63
Christen, ätzet diesen Tag
(NBA I/2; BC A8)

Christmas Day (BWV 63, 91, 110, 248-I, 191)
*Tit. 2:11–14 (The grace of God has appeared) or:
*Is. 9:2–7 (The people who walked in darkness have seen a great light; unto us a child is born)
*Lk. 2:1–14 (The birth of Christ, announcement to the shepherds, the praise of the angels)
Librettist: perhaps Johann Michael Heineccius

1. Chorus
●Christmas: Commemorate this day and render thanks (63-1)
Christen, ätzet diesen Tag
Christians, etch this day

In Metall und Marmorsteine.
In metal and marble-stones.

Kommt und eilt mit mir zur Krippen
Come and hasten with me to-the manger

Und erweist mit frohen Lippen
And show with joyful lips

Euren Dank und eure Pflicht;
Your thanks and your obligation;

Denn der Strahl, so da einbricht,
For the ray (of light), which there breaks-in,
{For the ray of light which breaks in there,}

Zeigt sich euch zum Gnadenscheine.
Proves-to-be for-you (a) sign-of-grace.
{Will prove to be a sign of grace for you.}

2. Alto Recit.
●Christmas: Blessed day when God came to deliver us (63-2)
O selger Tag! o ungemeines Heute,
O blessed day! O extraordinary "today",

An dem das Heil der Welt,
On which the Salvation of-the world—

Der Schilo, den Gott schon im Paradies
That Shiloh, which God already in Paradise

Dem menschlichen Geschlecht verhieß,
To-the human race did-promise—

*Lk. 2:10–11, 15–16. The angel said to [the shepherds], "Be not afraid; for behold, I bring you good news of a great joy which will come to all the people; for to you is born this day in the city of David a Savior, who is Christ the Lord." When the angels went away from them into heaven, the shepherds said to one another, "Let us go over to Bethlehem and see this thing that has happened, which the Lord has made known to us." And they went with haste, and found Mary and Joseph, and the babe lying in a manger.
Deut. 4:9. Only take heed...lest you forget the things which your eyes have seen...
Ex. 13:3. And Moses said to the people, "Remember this day, in which you came out of Egypt...for by strength of hand the Lord brought you out from this place..."
1 Sam. 7:12. Samuel took a stone and set it up...and called its name Ebenezer, for he said, "Hitherto the Lord has helped us."
*Tit. 2:11. For the grace of God has appeared for the salvation of all men.
Ps. 50:14, 23 [God]: Offer to God a sacrifice of thanksgiving, and pay your vows to the Most High...He who brings thanksgiving as his sacrifice honors me... (Also Ps. 22:25.)
2 Cor. 9:15. Thanks be to God for his inexpressible gift!
*Is. 9:2. The people who walked in darkness have seen a great light; those who dwelt in a land of deep darkness, on them has light shined. (Also Mt. 4:16, 2 Cor. 4:6.)

Ps. 118:24. This is the day which the Lord has made; let us rejoice and be glad in it.
1 Jn. 4:14. We have seen and testify that the Father has sent his Son as the Savior of the world.
Acts 13:32–33. And we bring you the good news that what God promised to the fathers, this he has fulfilled to us their children...as also it is written in the second psalm, 'Thou art my Son, **today** I have begotten thee.'
Heb. 1:5–6. To what angel did God ever say, "Thou art my Son, **today** I have begotten thee"? Or again, "I will be to him a father, and he shall be to me a son"? And again, when he brings the first-born into the world, he says, "Let all God's angels worship him."
Gen. 3:14–15. The Lord God [had] said to the serpent [in Eden], "Because you have [deceived Eve]...I will put enmity between you and the woman, and between your seed and her seed; he shall bruise your head, and you shall bruise his heel."
1 Jn. 3:8. ...The devil has sinned from the beginning. The reason the Son of God appeared was to destroy the works of the devil. (Also Heb. 2:14.)

Nunmehro   sich vollkommen dargestellt
Now   (has) itself in-perfection presented
{Now comes in its perfection}

Und suchet Israel von der Gefangenschaft
And seeks Israel from the   captivity

       und Sklavenketten
       and   slave-chains

Des Satans zu erretten.
Of Satan to deliver.
{Seeking to deliver Israel from the captivity and slave-chains of
Satan.}

    Du liebster Gott, was sind wir arme   doch?
(O) thou dear God, what are we poor-ones indeed?

Ein abgefallnes Volk,   so dich verlassen;
An   apostate   people, that thee forsake;
{An apostate people that forsake thee;}

Und dennoch willst du uns nicht hassen;
And still (dost) thou us   not   hate;
{And still thou dost not hate us;}

Denn eh wir sollen noch nach   dem Verdienst
For ere we must yet according to-(our) deserving

    zu   Boden liegen,
    on-the ground lie,
{For ere we must lie in ruin as we deserve,}

Eh   muß die Gottheit sich bequemen,
Ere-that must the Godhead   condescend,

Die menschliche Natur an sich zu nehmen
-     Human   nature upon itself to take

Und auf der Erden
And on the earth

Im   Hirtenstall zu einem Kinde werden.
In-a shepherd's-stall - a   child become.

Lk. 4:17–21. ...[Jesus] opened the book and found the place where it was written, "The Spirit of the Lord is upon me, because he has anointed me to preach good news to the poor. He has sent me to proclaim release to the captives and recovering of sight to the blind, to set at liberty those who are oppressed, to proclaim the acceptable year of the Lord." And he closed the book...and began to say to them, "Today (Luther: heute) this scripture has been fulfilled in your hearing." (See Is. 61:1–2.)

Ex. 6:6 [God]: ...I am the Lord, and I will bring you [Israel] out from under the burdens of the Egyptians, and I will deliver you from their bondage, and I will redeem you...

1 Jn. 5:19. ...The whole world is in the power of the evil one. (Also 2 Tim.2:26.)

Deut. 9:1. Hear, O Israel; you are to pass over the Jordan [into the Promised Land] this day...

Josh. 18:10. And Joshua cast lots for [the tribes of Israel] in **Shiloh** before the Lord; and there Joshua apportioned the [Promised] land to the people of Israel, to each his portion.

Ps. 78:54–56. [The Lord] brought [Israel] to his holy land, to the mountain which his right hand had won. He drove out nations before them; he apportioned them for a possession and settled the tribes of Israel in their tents. Yet they tested and rebelled against the Most High God, and did not observe his testimonies...

2 Kings 17:16. [But] they forsook all the commandments of the Lord their God...

Ps. 78:60. [Then the Lord] forsook his dwelling at **Shiloh**, the tent where he dwelt among men.

2 Chron. 15:3–4. For a long time Israel was without the true God...but when in their distress they turned to the Lord, the God of Israel, and sought him, he was found by them.

2 Chron. 7:14 [God]: If my people who are called by my name humble themselves, and pray and seek my face, and turn from their wicked ways, then I will hear from heaven, and will forgive their sin and heal their land.

Ps. 130:7–8. O Israel, hope in the Lord! For with...him is plenteous redemption. And he will redeem Israel from all his iniquities. (Also Ps. 25:22, Lk. 24:21.)

Rom. 3:10–12, 23. ...None is righteous, no, not one; no one understands, no one seeks for God. All have turned aside, together they have gone wrong; no one does good, not even one...All have sinned and fall short of the glory of God.

Rom. 5:8. But God shows his love for us in that while we were yet sinners Christ died for us.

1 Jn. 3:8. He who commits sin is of the devil; for the devil has sinned from the beginning. The reason the Son of God appeared was to destroy the works of the devil.

Acts 13:38–39. Let it be known to you...that through [Christ] forgiveness of sins is proclaimed to you, and by him every one that believes is freed from everything from which you could not be freed by the law of Moses. (Also Rev. 1:5.)

Ps. 103:8, 10. The Lord is merciful and gracious, slow to anger and abounding in steadfast love...He does not deal with us according to our sins, nor requite us according to our iniquities. (Also 2 Cor. 5:19.)

Heb. 2:14–15. Since therefore the children share in flesh and blood, [Christ] himself likewise partook of the same nature, that through death he might destroy him who has the power of death, that is, the devil, and deliver all those who through fear of death were subject to lifelong bondage.

Phil. 2:6–7. Though [Christ] was in the form of God, [he] did not count equality with God a thing to be grasped, but emptied himself, taking the form of a servant, being born in the likeness of men.

O unbegreifliches, doch seliges   Verfügen!
O incomprehensible, yet blessed disposition-of-events!

3. Soprano & Bass Duet
●Christmas, God's gift of salvation: we build on it (63-3)
    Gott, du hast es wohl gefüget,
(O) God, thou hast it well-disposed,
{O God, thou hast disposed that well,}

Was uns itzo widerfährt.
What us now befallen-hath.
{Which now hath befallen us.}

Drum   laßt uns auf ihn   stets   trauen
Therefore let us (in) him constantly trust
{Therefore let us trust him constantly}

Und auf seine Gnade bauen,
And upon his grace build,
{And build upon his grace}

Denn er hat uns dies beschert,
For he has on-us this bestowed,
{For he has bestowed this on us,}

Was uns ewig nun vergnüget.
Which us eternally now delights.
{This which now eternally delights us.}

4. Tenor Recit.
●Christmas: The lion of Judah has appeared to free us (63-4)
So   kehret sich nun heut
Thus is-transformed now today

Das bange Leid,
The anxious sorrow,

Mit welchem Israel   geängstet und beladen,
With which Israel (has been) frightened and burdened,

In lauter Heil und Gnaden.
Into sheer well-being and favor.

Der Löw' aus Davids Stamme ist erschienen,
The lion of David's tribe (has) appeared,

Sein Bogen ist gespannt, das Schwert is schon gewetzt,
His bow is bent, the sword is already whetted,

Womit   er uns in   vor'ge Freiheit setzt.
With-which he us to (our) former freedom sets.
{With which he puts us back into our former freedom.}

5. Alto & Tenor Duet
●Christmas: Celebrate and give thanks for salvation (63-5)
Ruft und fleht den Himmel an,
Call and entreat - heaven - ;

Lk. 2:16. And [the shepherds] went with haste, and found Mary and Joseph, and the babe lying in a manger.

Mk. 7:37. ...He has done all things well...
Ps. 126:2. Then our mouth was filled with laughter, and our tongue with shouts of joy; then they said among the nations, "The Lord has done great things for them."
***Tit. 2:11.** For the grace of God has appeared for the salvation of all men.
1 Cor. 3:11-14. No other foundation can any one lay than that which is laid, which is Jesus Christ. Now if any one builds on the foundation with gold, silver, precious stones, wood, hay, straw—each man's work will become manifest; for the Day will disclose it, because it will be revealed with fire, and the fire will test what sort of work each one has done. If the work which any man has built on the foundation survives, he will receive a reward. (Also Mt. 7:24.)
Jn. 3:16. God so loved the world that he gave his only Son, that whoever believes in him should not perish but have eternal life. For God sent the Son into the world, not to condemn the world, but that the world might be saved through him.
1 Jn. 4:14. We have seen and testify that the Father has sent his Son as the Savior of the world.
2 Cor. 9:15. Thanks be to God for his inexpressible gift!
Ps. 16:11. [O Lord,] thou dost show me the path of life; in thy presence there is fulness of joy, in thy right hand are pleasures for evermore.

***Is. 9:2-4.** The people who walked in darkness have seen a great light; those who dwelt in a land of deep darkness, on them has light shined. Thou hast multiplied the nation, thou hast increased its joy; they rejoice before thee as with joy at the harvest, as men rejoice when they divide the spoil. For the yoke of his burden, and the staff for his shoulder, the rod of his oppressor, thou hast broken as on the day of Midian. (Also Is. 10:27, 14:25.)
Jer. 31:13 [God]: ...I will turn their mourning into joy, I will comfort them, and give them gladness for sorrow.
Jn. 16:20 [Christ]: ...Your sorrow will turn into joy.
Mt. 11:28 [Christ]: Come to me, all who labor and are heavy laden, and I will give you rest. (Also Is. 1:4.)
Rev. 5:5. ...Weep not; lo, the Lion of the tribe of Judah, the Root of David, has conquered...
Gen. 49:9-10. Judah is a lion's whelp...The scepter shall not depart from Judah...until he comes to whom it belongs; and to him shall be the obedience of the peoples.
Ps. 7:12-13. ...God will whet his sword; he has bent and strung his bow; he has prepared his deadly weapons, making his arrows fiery shafts.
Gal. 5:1. For freedom Christ has set us free...
Rom. 8:2. The law of the Spirit of life in Christ Jesus has set me free from the law of sin and death.

Lk. 2:14. Glory to God in the highest, and on earth peace among men with whom he is pleased!
Ps. 32:11. Be glad in the Lord, and rejoice, O righteous, and shout for joy, all you upright in heart!

Kommt, ihr Christen, kommt zum Reihen,
Come, ye Christians, come to-the roundelay,

Ihr sollt euch ob dem erfreuen,
Ye shall - over that rejoice,

Was Gott hat anheut getan!
What God has today done!
{What God has done today!}

Da uns seine Huld verpfleget
For us his favor feeds
{For his favor feeds us}

Und mit so viel Heil beleget,
And with so much prosperity covers (us),

Daß man nicht g'nug danken kann.
That one (him) not enough can-thank.
{That one can not thank him enough.}

6. Bass Recit.
●Christmas: Let your ardor ascend to God like flames! (63-6)
Verdoppelt euch demnach,
Redouble yourselves accordingly,

ihr heißen Andachtsflammen,
ye hot flames-of-devotion,

Und schlagt in Demut brünstiglich zusammen!
And strike in humility ardently together!
{And strike together in ardent humility!}

Steigt fröhlich himmelan,
Mount joyfully heavenward,

Und danket Gott für dies, was er getan!
And thank God for this, what he hath-done!
{And thank God for that which he hath done!}

7. Chorus
●Christmas prayer: Look with favor on us worshipers (63-7)
Höchster, schau in Gnaden an
Most-High, look with favor upon

Diese Glut gebückter Seelen!
These (with) ardor bowed souls!
{These souls bowed in ardent love!}

Laß den Dank, den wir dir bringen,
Let the thanks, which we to-thee do-bring,

Angenehme vor Dir klingen,
Pleasant before thee sound,
{Sound pleasant before thee,}

Laß uns stets in Segen gehn,
Let us ever in blessing walk,

Ps. 98:1. O sing to the Lord a new song, for he has done marvelous things!...

Ps. 118:24. This is the day which the Lord has made; let us rejoice and be glad in it.

Ps. 126:3. The Lord has done great things for us; we are glad. (Also 1 Sam. 12:24, Lk. 1:49.)

Ps. 150:3–4. Praise him with trumpet sound; praise him with lute and harp! Praise him with timbrel and dance...

Jer. 31:13 [God]: ...The maidens [shall] rejoice in the dance, and the young men and the old shall be merry. I will turn their mourning into joy, I will comfort them, and give them gladness for sorrow. (Also Ps. 30:11.)

Ezek. 34:23–24 [God]: I will set up over them one shepherd, my servant David, and he shall feed them: he shall feed them and be their shepherd. And I, the Lord, will be their God, and my servant David shall be prince among them; I, the Lord, have spoken.

Ps. 116:12. What shall I render to the Lord for all his bounty to me?

Ps. 50:14, 23 [God]: Offer to God a sacrifice of thanksgiving...He who brings thanksgiving as his sacrifice honors me...

2 Cor. 9:15. Thanks be to God for his inexpressible gift!

Ps. 116:12. What shall I render (Luther: vergelten) to the Lord for all his bounty to me?

Mt. 22:38. [Jesus] said to [the man who questioned him about the greatest commandment in the law], "You shall love the Lord your God with all your heart, and with all your soul, and with all your mind. This is the great and first commandment." (See Deut. 6:5.)

Phil. 1: 9. It is my prayer that your love may abound more and more, with knowledge and all discernment...

Ps. 84:2. My soul longs, yea, faints for the courts of the Lord; my heart and flesh sing for joy to the living God.

Ps. 42:1–2. As a hart longs for flowing streams, so longs my soul for thee, O God. My soul thirsts for God, for the living God. When shall I come and behold the face of God?

Lk. 1:46–49. And Mary said, "My soul magnifies the Lord, and my spirit rejoices in God my Savior, for he has regarded the low estate of his handmaiden. For behold, henceforth all generations will call me blessed; for he who is mighty has done great things for me, and holy is his name."

Ps. 95:1–2, 6. O come, let us sing to the Lord; let us make a joyful noise to the rock of our salvation! Let us come into his presence with thanksgiving; let us make a joyful noise to him with songs of praise!... O come, let us worship and bow down, let us kneel before the Lord, our Maker!

Mt. 2:11. Going into the house [the wise men] saw the child with Mary his mother, and they fell down and worshiped him. Then, opening their treasures, they offered him gifts, gold and frankincense and myrrh.

Ps. 119:108. Accept my offerings of praise, O Lord...

Ps. 19:14. Let the words of my mouth and the meditation of my heart be acceptable in thy sight...

Ps. 67:1. May God be gracious to us and bless us and make his face to shine upon us.

Ps. 28:8–9. The Lord is the strength of his people...O save thy people, and bless thy heritage; be thou their shepherd, and carry them for ever. (Also Deut. 26:15, 29:11.)

Eph. 6:12. For we are not contending against flesh and blood, but against the principalities, against the powers, against the world rulers of this present darkness, against the spiritual hosts of wickedness in the heavenly places.

Aber   niemals nicht geschehn,
But (let it) never   -   come-to-pass,

Daß uns Satan möge quälen.
That us   Satan should torment.
{That Satan should torment us.}

1 Pet. 5:8. ...[Our] adversary the devil prowls around like a roaring lion, seeking some one to devour.
Ps. 3:8. Deliverance belongs to the Lord; thy blessing be upon thy people!
1 Jn. 3:8. ...The reason the Son of God appeared was to destroy the works of the devil.

BWV 64
Sehet, welch eine Liebe hat uns der Vater erzeiget
(NBA I/3; BC A15)

3. Day of Christmas (BWV 64, 133, 151, 248-III)
*Heb. 1:1–14 (God spoke through his Son, who is superior to the angels)
*Jn. 1:1–14 (Prologue: In the beginning was the Word...and the Word became flesh)
Librettist: Johann Knauer (Libretto has been shortened, then expanded with two chorales.)

1. Chorus
●God's love shown: we are God's children: 1 Jn. 3:1 (64-1)
Sehet, welch eine Liebe hat uns der Vater erzeiget,
Behold, what   a   love has to-us the Father shown,

daß wir Gottes Kinder heißen.
that we God's children are-called.

1 Jn. 3:1. *See what love the Father has given us, that we should be called children of God;* and so we are...
***Jn. 1:12.** To all who received [Christ], who believed in his name, [Christ] gave power to become children of God.
Rom. 8:15–17. ...You have received the spirit of sonship. When we cry, "Abba! Father!" it is the Spirit himself bearing witness with our spirit that we are children of God, and if children, then heirs, heirs of God and fellow heirs with Christ...
Gal. 4:4–7. When the time had fully come, God sent forth his Son, born of woman, born under the law, to redeem those who were under the law, so that we might receive adoption as sons. And because you are sons, God has sent the Spirit of his Son into our hearts, crying, "Abba! Father!" So through God you are no longer a slave but a son, and if a son then an heir.

2. Chorale (Added to original libretto) (See also 91-6, 248-28.)
●God's love shown in Christ's birth: give thanks! (64-2)
Das hat er alles uns getan,
That has he all for-us done,
{All that he has done for us,}

Sein groß Lieb zu zeigen an.
His great love to   show.
{To show his great love.}

     Des freu sich alle Christenheit
(Let) over-this rejoice all Christendom
{Let all Christendom rejoice over this}

Und dank ihm des   in   Ewigkeit.
And thank him for-this (through) (all) eternity.

Kyrieleis!
Kyrieleis!

Ps. 126:3. The Lord has done great things for us; we are glad.
Jn. 3:16. God so loved the world that he gave his only Son, that whoever believes in him should not perish but have eternal life.
1 Jn. 4:9–10. In this the love of God was made manifest among us, that God sent his only Son into the world, so that we might live through him. In this is love, not that we loved God but that he loved us and sent his Son to be the expiation for our sins.
Phil. 2:6–8. Though he was in the form of God, [Christ Jesus] did not count equality with God a thing to be grasped, but emptied himself, taking the form of a servant, being born in the likeness of men. And being found in human form he humbled himself and became obedient unto death, even death on a cross. **Rom. 5:8.** God shows his love for us in that while we were yet sinners Christ died for us.
2 Cor. 9:15. Thanks be to God for his inexpressible gift!
2 John 1:3. Grace, mercy, and peace will be with us, from God the Father and from Jesus Christ the Father's Son...
Rev. 7:12. Amen! Blessing and glory and wisdom and thanksgiving and honor and power and might be to our God for ever and ever! Amen.

3. Alto Recit.
●World rejected in view of possessing heaven's riches (64-3)
Geh, Welt! behalte nur das   Deine,
Go, world! Keep   -   what (is) thine,

Ich will und mag nichts von dir haben,
I (seek) and desire nought from thee - ,

1 Jn. 2:15–17. Do not love the world or the things in the world. If any one loves the world, love for the Father is not in him. For all that is in the world, the lust of the flesh and the lust of the eyes and the pride of life, is not of the Father but is of the world. And the world passes away, and the lust of it; but he who does the will of God abides for ever.

Der Himmel ist nun meine,
- Heaven is now mine,

An diesem soll sich meine Seele laben.
With this shall itself my soul refresh.
{My soul shall refresh itself with this.}

Dein Gold ist ein vergänglich Gut,
Thy gold is a transient possession,

Dein Reichtum ist geborget,
Thy wealth is borrowed,

Wer dies besitzt, der ist gar schlecht versorget.
Whoever this posseses, he is indeed poorly provided-for.
{Whoever posesses only this is indeed poorly provided for.}

Drum sag ich mit getrostem Mut:
Therefore say I with confident courage:
{Therefore I say with confident courage:}

4. Chorale (Added to original libretto) (See also 94-1.)
•World rejected for pleasure of having Jesus (64-4)
Was frag ich nach der Welt
What (care) I for the world
{What do I care for the world}

Und allen ihren Schätzen,
And all its treasures,

Wenn ich mich nur an dir,
If I myself only in thee,

Mein Jesu, kann ergötzen!
My Jesus, can delight!
{If I can only delight myself in thee, O my Jesus!}

Dich hab ich einzig mir
Thee have I alone before-me

Zur Wollust vorgestellt:
For (my) pleasure placed:
{I have chosen thee alone for my pleasure:}

Du, du bist meine Lust;
Thou, thou art my delight;

Was frag ich nach der Welt!
What (care) I for the world!
{What do I care for the world!}

5. Soprano Aria
•World's riches pass away; Jesus' gifts are eternal (64-5)
Was die Welt
What the world

In sich hält,
In itself contains,

Jms. 4:4. ...Do you not know that friendship with the world is enmity with God? Therefore whoever wishes to be a friend of the world makes himself an enemy of God.
2 Cor. 5:1. We know that if the earthly tent we live in is destroyed, we have a building from God, a house not made with hands, eternal in the heavens.
Jn. 14:1–3 [Christ]: Let not your hearts be troubled...In my Father's house are many rooms; if it were not so, would I have told you that I go to prepare a place for you? And when I go and prepare a place for you, I will come again and will take you to myself, that where I am you may be also. (Also 1 Cor. 2:9.)
Rom. 5:2. ...We rejoice in our hope of sharing the glory of God
Mt. 6:19–20. Do not lay up for yourselves treasures on earth, where moth and rust consume and where thieves break in and steal, but lay up for yourselves treasures in heaven, where neither moth nor rust consumes and where thieves do not break in and steal.
Mt. 16:26. For what will it profit a man, if he gains the whole world and forfeits his life? Or what shall a man give in return for his life? (Also Mk. 8:36–37, Lk. 9:25.)

2 Cor. 4:16–18. So we do not lose heart. Though our outer nature is wasting away, our inner nature is being renewed every day. For this slight momentary affliction is preparing for us an eternal weight of glory beyond all comparison, because we look not to the things that are seen but to the things that are unseen; for the things that are seen are transient, but the things that are unseen are eternal.
Col. 3:1–3. If then you have been raised with Christ, seek the things that are above, where Christ is, seated at the right hand of God. Set your minds on things that are above, not on things that are on earth. For you have died and your life is hid with Christ in God.
Ps. 73:25–26. [O Lord,] whom have I in heaven but thee? (Luther: Wenn ich nur dich habe...) And there is nothing upon earth that I desire besides thee. My flesh and my heart may fail, but God is the strength of my heart and my portion for ever.
Ps. 94:19. [O Lord,] when the cares of my heart are many, thy consolations cheer (Luther: ergötzen) my soul.
Ps. 16:11. ...In thy presence there is fulness of joy, in thy right hand are pleasures for evermore.
Ps. 37:4. Take delight (Luther: Lust) in the Lord...
S. of S. 6:3 [Bride]: I am my beloved's and my beloved is mine...
1 Jn. 2:15. Do not love the world or the things in the world. If any one loves the world, love for the Father is not in him.
Jms. 4:4. Unfaithful creatures! Do you not know that friendship with the world is enmity with God? Therefore whoever wishes to be a friend of the world makes himself an enemy of God.

1 Jn. 2:16–17. All that is in the world, the lust of the flesh and the lust of the eyes and the pride of life, is not of the Father but is of the world. And the world passes away, and the lust of it; but he who does the will of God abides for ever.
Jms. 4:13–14, 5:1. Come now, you who say, "Today or tomorrow we will go into such and such a town and spend a year there and trade and get gain"; whereas you do not know about tomorrow. What is

Muß als wie ein Rauch vergehen.
Must like - smoke pass-away.
{Must pass away like smoke.}

Aber was mir Jesus gibt
But what me Jesus gives
{But what Jesus gives me}

Und was meine Seele liebt,
And what my soul loves,

Bleibet fest und ewig stehen.
Remains firm and eternally standing.
{Stands firm for ever.}

6. Bass Recit.
●Christ's birth makes heaven certain; yearning for it (64–6)
Der Himmel bleibet mir gewiß,
  - Heaven remains for-me certain,
{Heaven remains certain for me,}

Und den besitz ich schon im Glauben.
And it possess I already in faith.
{And I possess it already in faith.}

Der Tod, die Welt und Sünde,
  - Death, the world, and sin,

Ja selbst das ganze Höllenheer
Yes, even the entire host-of-hell

Kann mir, als einem Gotteskinde,
Can (not) from-me, as a child-of-God,

Denselben nun und nimmermehr
(It) now (nor) (ever)

Aus meiner Seele rauben.
Out-of my soul rob.
{Can never—since I am a child of God—steal it from out of my soul.}

Nur dies, nur einzig dies macht mir noch Kümmernis,
Only this, only soley this causes me still concern,
{Only this, only this one thing still causes me concern,}

Daß ich noch länger soll auf dieser Welt verweilen;
That I yet longer (must) in this world tarry;
{That I must yet longer in this world tarry;}

Denn Jesus will den Himmel mit mir teilen,
For Jesus would - heaven with me share,

Und dazu hat er mich erkoren,
And for-that has he me chosen,
{And for that he has chosen me;}

Deswegen ist er Mensch geboren.
For-that-reason (was) he (as a) human born.
{For that reason he was born as a human being.}

your life? For you are a mist that appears for a little time and then vanishes...Come now, you rich, weep and howl for the miseries that are coming upon you...
Ps. 102:3, 11. My days pass away like smoke, and my bones burn like a furnace...My days are like an evening shadow; I wither away like grass.
Jms. 1:10–11. ...Like the flower of the grass [the rich man] will pass away. For the sun rises with its scorching heat and withers the grass; its flower falls, and its beauty perishes. So will the rich man fade away in the midst of his pursuits.
Mk. 13:31 [Christ]: Heaven and earth will pass away, but my words will not pass away. (Also Mt. 24:35, Lk. 21:33, Is. 40:8, Ps. 102:25–26.)
Heb. 13:8. Jesus Christ is the same yesterday and today and for ever.

2 Pet. 1:11. There will be richly provided for you an entrance into the eternal kingdom of our Lord...
1 Pet. 1:3–4. ...By [God's] great mercy we have been born anew to a living hope through the resurrection of Jesus Christ from the dead, and to an inheritance which is imperishable, undefiled, and unfading, kept in heaven for you.
Rom. 5:2. Through [Christ] we have obtained access to this grace in which we stand, and we rejoice in our hope of sharing the glory of God.
Heb. 13:14. Here we have no lasting city, but we seek the city which is to come. (Also Heb. 11:16.)
Heb. 11:1. Now faith is the assurance of things hoped for, the conviction of things not seen.
Jn. 10:28 [Christ]: I give them eternal life, and they shall never perish, and no one shall snatch them out of my hand.
Rom. 8:38–39. I am sure that neither death, nor life, nor angels, nor principalities, nor things present, nor things to come, nor powers, nor height, nor depth, nor anything else in all creation, will be able to separate us from the love of God in Christ Jesus our Lord.
Jn. 16:33 [Christ]: I have said this to you, that in me you may have peace. In the world you have tribulation; but be of good cheer, I have overcome the world. (Also 1 Jn. 4:4, 5:4–5.)
2 Cor. 5:1–8. We know that if the earthly tent we live in is destroyed, we have a building from God, a house not made with hands, eternal in the heavens. Here indeed we groan, and long to put on our heavenly dwelling, so that by putting it on we may not be found naked. For while we are still in this tent, we sigh with anxiety; not that we would be unclothed, but that we would be further clothed, so that what is mortal may be swallowed up by life. He who has prepared us for this very thing is God, who has given us the Spirit as a guarantee. So we are always of good courage; we know that while we are at home in the body we are away from the Lord, for we walk by faith, not by sight. We are of good courage, and we would rather be away from the body and at home with the Lord.
Phil. 1:21, 23. To me to live is Christ, and to die is gain...My desire is to depart and be with Christ, for that is far better.
2 Thess. 2:14. To this [God] called you through our gospel, so that you may obtain the glory of our Lord Jesus Christ.
Jn. 14:3 [Christ]: When I go and prepare a place for you, I will come again and will take you to myself, that where I am you may be also.

7. Alto Aria
●World surrendered for heaven and eternal life (64-7)
Von der Welt verlang ich nichts,
From the world desire I nothing,

Wenn ich nur den Himmel erbe.
If   I but - heaven inherit.

Alles, alles geb   ich hin,
All,   all surrender I -,
{I surrender all else,}

Weil ich   genug versichert bin,
For I sufficiently assured am,
{For I am sufficiently assured,}

Daß ich ewig nicht verderbe.
That I eternally not shall-perish.
{That I shall not perish eternally.}

8. Chorale
●World and this life given farewell (64-8)
Gute Nacht, o Wesen
Good night, O existence

Das die Welt   erlesen!
That the world hath-chosen!

Mir gefällst du nicht.
Me pleasest thou not.
{Thou dost not please me.}

Gute Nacht, ihr Sünden,
Good night, ye sins,

Bleibet weit dahinten,
Remain far behind,

Kommt nicht mehr ans Licht!
Come no more to light!

Gute Nacht, du Stolz und Pracht!
Good night, thou pride and pomp!

1 Jn. 2:15. Do not love the world or the things in the world....
Mt. 19:29 [Christ]: Everyone who has left houses or brothers or sisters or father or mother or children or lands, for my name's sake, will receive a hundredfold, and inherit eternal life.
Mt. 25:34. Then the King will say to those at his right hand, "Come, O blessed of my Father, inherit the kingdom prepared for you from the foundation of the world."
Phil. 3:7-8. Whatever gain I had, I counted as loss for the sake of Christ. Indeed I count everything as loss because of the surpassing worth of knowing Christ Jesus my Lord...
Lk. 16:19-25. There was a rich man, who was clothed in purple and fine linen and who feasted sumptuously every day. And at his gate lay a poor man named Lazarus, full of sores, who desired to be fed with what fell from the rich man's table; moreover the dogs came and licked his sores. The poor man died and was carried by the angels to Abraham's bosom. The rich man also died and was buried; and in Hades, being in torment, he lifted up his eyes, and saw Abraham far off and Lazarus in his bosom. And he called out, "Father Abraham, have mercy upon me..." But Abraham said, "Son, remember that you in your lifetime received your good things, and Lazarus in like manner evil things; but now he is comforted here, and you are in anguish."

Phil. 1:23. ...My desire is to depart and be with Christ...
2 Tim. 4:6. ...The time of my departure has come.
Heb. 11:14-16. People who speak thus make it clear that they are seeking a homeland. If they had been thinking of that land from which they had gone out, they would have had opportunity to return. But as it is, they desire a better country, that is, a heavenly one... (Also Heb. 13:14.)
Jms. 4:4. Unfaithful creatures! Do you not know that friendship with the world is enmity with God? Therefore whoever wishes to be a friend of the world makes himself an enemy of God.
1 Jn. 2:15-17. Do not love the world or the things in the world. If any one loves the world, love for the Father is not in him. For all that is in the world, the lust of the flesh and the lust of the eyes and the pride of life, is not of the Father but is of the world. And the world passes away, and the lust of it; but he who does the will of God abides for ever.
Rom. 6:1-9, 12. What shall we say then? Are we to continue in sin that grace may abound? By no means! How can we who died to sin still live in it? Do you not know that all of us who have been baptized into Christ Jesus were baptized into his death? We were buried therefore with him by baptism into death, so that as Christ was raised from the dead by the glory of the Father, we too might walk in newness of life. For if we have been united with him in a death like his, we shall certainly be united with him in a resurrection like his. We know that our old self was crucified with him so that the sinful body might be destroyed, and we might no longer be enslaved to sin. For he who has died is freed from sin. But if we have died with Christ, we believe that we shall also live with him. For we know that Christ being raised from the dead will never die again; death no longer has dominion over him...Let not sin therefore reign in your mortal bodies, to make you obey their passions.

Dir sei ganz, du Lasterleben,
Thee be completely, thou life-of-wickedness,

Gute Nacht gegeben!
"Good night" given!

BWV 65
Sie werden aus Saba alle kommen
(NBA I/5; BC A27)

Epiphany (BWV 65, 123, 248-VI, [200])
*Is. 60:1–6 (Prophecy: the Lord will shine upon you and nations will come to your light)
*Mt. 2:1–12 (The Magi come from the East)
Librettist: Unknown

1. Chorus
●Epiphany: Visitors from Sheba prophesied: Is. 60:6 (65-1)
Sie werden aus Saba alle kommen, Gold und Weihrauch
They will out-of Sheba all come, gold and frankincense

bringen, und des Herren Lob verkündigen.
bring, and the Lord's praise proclaim.

2. Chorale
●Epiphany: Prophecy fulfilled; Kings brought gifts (65-2)
Die Kön'ge aus Saba kamen dar,
The kings out-of Sheba came thence;

Gold, Weihrauch, Myrrhen brachten sie dar,
Gold, frankincense, myrrh brought they forth,

Alleluja!
Alleluia!

3. Bass Recit.
●Epiphany: What gift can I bring to Christ? (65-3)
Was dort Jesaias vorhergesehn,
What there Isaiah saw-beforehand,

Das ist zu Bethlehem geschehn.
That has in Bethlehem (now) happened.

Hier stellen sich die Weisen
Here present themselves the wise men
{Here the wise men present themselves}

Bei Jesu Krippen ein
At Jesus' manger -

Und wollen ihn als ihren König preisen.
And would him as their king praise.

Gold, Weihrauch, Myrrhen sind
Gold, frankincense, myrrh are

Col. 3:1–3. If then you have been raised with Christ, seek the things that are above, where Christ is, seated at the right hand of God. Set your minds on things that are above, not on things that are on earth. For you have died and your life is hid with Christ in God. (Also 2 Cor. 4:16–18.)

*Is. 60:6. A multitude of camels shall cover you, the young camels of Midian and Ephah; *all those from Sheba shall come. They shall bring gold and frankincense, and shall proclaim the praise of the Lord.*

*Mt. 2:1–2, 9–11. Now when Jesus was born in Bethlehem of Judea in the days of Herod the king, behold, wise men from the East came to Jerusalem, saying, "Where is he who has been born king of the Jews? For we have seen his star in the East, and have come to worship him." ...When they had heard the king they went their way; and lo, the star which they had seen in the East went before them, till it came to rest over the place where the child was. When they saw the star, they rejoiced exceedingly with great joy; and going into the house they saw the child with Mary his mother, and they fell down and worshiped him. Then, opening their treasures, they offered him gifts, gold and frankincense and myrrh.

*Is. 60:1, 3–6. Arise, shine; for your light has come, and the glory of the Lord has risen upon you...and nations shall come to your light, and kings to the brightness of your rising. Lift up your eyes round about, and see; they all gather together, they come to you...Then you shall see and be radiant, your heart shall thrill and rejoice...A multitude of camels shall cover you, the young camels of Midian and Ephah; all those from Sheba shall come. They shall bring gold and frankincense, and shall proclaim the praise of the Lord.
Is. 42:6–7 [God]: I am the Lord...I have given you as a covenant to the people, a light to the nations, to open the eyes that are blind, to bring out the prisoners from the dungeon, from the prison those who sit in darkness.
Is. 49:6. ...I will give you as a light to the nations, that my salvation may reach to the end of the earth.
1 Pet. 1:10–12. The prophets who prophesied of the grace that was to be yours searched and inquired about this salvation; they inquired what person or time was indicated by the Spirit of Christ within them

Die köstlichen Geschenke,
The precious gifts,

Womit sie dieses Jesuskind
With-which they this Jesus-child

Zu Bethlehem im Stall beehren.
At Bethlehem in-the stable do-honor.

Mein Jesu, wenn ich itzt an meine Pflicht gedenke,
My Jesus, if I now - my duty bear-in-mind,

Muß ich mich auch zu deiner Krippe kehren
(Then) must I - also to thy manger turn

Und gleichfalls dankbar sein:
And likewise thankful be:

Denn dieser Tag ist mir ein Tag der Freuden,
For this day is for-me a day of gladness,
{For this day is a day of gladness for me,}

Da du, o Lebensfürst,
When thou, O Prince-of-life,

Das Licht der Heiden
The Light of-the Gentiles
{Dost become the Light of the Gentiles}

Und ihr Erlöser wirst.
And their Redeemer becomest.
{And their Redeemer.}

Was aber bring ich wohl, du Himmelskönig?
What, however, bring I indeed, thou Heaven's-king?
{But what, indeed, might I bring, O thou King of Heaven?}

Ist dir mein Herze nicht zuwenig,
(If) for-thee my heart (be) not too-little,

So nimm es gnädig an,
Then accept it graciously - ,

Weil ich nichts Edlers bringen kann.
For I nothing more-noble can-bring.

4. Bass Aria
●Epiphany: Gold compared with heart as a fitting gift (65–4)
Gold aus Ophir ist zu schlecht,
Gold out-of Ophir is too inferior,

Weg, nur weg mit eitlen Gaben,
Away, - away with (the) empty gifts,

Die ihr aus der Erde brecht!
Which you out-of the earth do-tear!

Jesus will das Herze haben.
Jesus wants the heart to-have.
{Jesus wants to have the heart.}

when predicting the sufferings of Christ and the subsequent glory. It was revealed to them that they were serving not themselves but you, in the things which have now been announced to you by those whopreached the good news to you through the Holy Spirit sent from heaven, things into which angels long to look.
Acts 26:22–23. ...[This is] what the prophets and Moses said would come to pass: that the Christ...would proclaim light both to the people and to the Gentiles.
*Mt. 2:10–11. When [the wise men] saw the star, they rejoiced exceedingly with great joy; and going into the house they saw the child with Mary his mother, and they fell down and worshiped him. Then, opening their treasures, they offered him gifts, gold and frankincense and myrrh.
Ps. 118:24. This is the day which the Lord has made; let us rejoice and be glad in it. (Also Ps. 126:2–3.)
Ps. 107:21–22. Let [God's people] thank the Lord for his steadfast love, for his wonderful works to the sons of men! And let them offer sacrifices of thanksgiving, and tell of his deeds in songs of joy! (Also Ps. 107:15.)
Ps. 50:14, 23 [God]: Offer to God a sacrifice of thanksgiving, and pay your vows to the Most High...He who brings thanksgiving as his sacrifice honors me... (als Heb. 13:15)
Lk. 17:15–18. One of [the ten lepers], when he saw that he was healed, turned back, praising God with a loud voice; and he fell on his face at Jesus' feet, giving him thanks. Now he was a Samaritan. Then said Jesus, "Were not ten cleansed? Where are the nine? Was no one found to return and give praise to God except this foreigner?"
Lk. 2:30–32 [Nunc dimittis]. Mine eyes have seen thy salvation which thou hast prepared in the presence of all peoples, a light for revelation to the Gentiles, and for glory to thy people Israel.
Is. 9:2. The people who walked in darkness have seen a great light; those who dwelt in a land of deep darkness, on them has light shined. (Also Mt. 4:16, 2 Cor. 4:6, Rev. 21:23–24.)
*Is. 60:3. Nations shall come to your light, and kings to the brightness of your rising. (Also Is. 42:6–7, 49:6.)
*Mt. 2:1–2. ...Wise men from the East came to Jerusalem, saying, "Where is he who has been born king of the Jews? For we have seen his star in the East, and have come to worship him."
Ps. 116:12. What shall I render to the Lord for all his bounty to me?
Rom. 12:1. I appeal to you therefore, brethren, by the mercies of God, to present your bodies as a living sacrifice, holy and acceptable to God, which is your spiritual worship.
Hos. 6:6 [God]: For I desire steadfast love and not sacrifice, the knowledge of God, rather than burnt offerings.

1 Kings 9:27–28. Hiram sent with the fleet his servants, seamen who were familiar with the sea, together with the servants of Solomon; and they went to Ophir, and brought from there gold, to the amount of four hundred and twenty talents; and they brought it to King Solomon. (Gold of Ophir: see also 1 Kings 22:48, 1 Chron. 29:4, 2 Chron 8:18, Job 22:23–26, 28:16, Ps. 45:9)
Ps. 116:12. What shall I render to the Lord for all his bounty to me?
Mk. 7:6–7. And [Jesus] said to [the scribes and Pharisees], "Well did Isaiah prophesy of you hypocrites, as it is written, 'This people honors me with their lips, but their heart is far from me; in vain do they worship me...'" (Also Is. 29:13, Mt. 15:8–9.)

Schenke dies, o Christenschar,
Give   this, O Christian-throng,

Jesu   zu dem neuen Jahr!
To-Jesus for the   new   year!

5. Tenor Recit.
●Epiphany: My votive gifts of faith, prayer, patience (65–5)
Verschmähe nicht,
Disdain   not,

    Du,   meiner Seelen Licht,
(O) thou, (who art) my   soul's light,

Mein Herz, das ich in Demut zu dir bringe;
My heart, which I in humility to thee bring;

Es schließt ja solche Dinge
It includes indeed such things
{Indeed, it includes those things}

In sich   zugleich   mit ein,
Within itself at-the-same-time - -,

Die deines Geistes Früchte sein.
Which thy Spirit's fruits are.
{Which are the fruits of thy Spirit:}

Des Glaubens Gold, der Weihrauch des Gebets,
-   Faith's   gold, the frankincense of prayer,

Die Myrrhen der Geduld sind meine Gaben,
The myrrh of patience are   my   gifts;

Die sollst du, Jesu, für   und für
Them shalt thou, Jesus, for-ever and ever
{Them shalt thou have forever and ever, O Jesus,}

Zum   Eigentum und zum Geschenke haben.
As (thy) possession and as-a   gift   have.
{As thine own posession and as thy gift.}

Gib   aber dich auch selber mir,
Give, however, - also thyself to-me,
{However, give thyself also to me,}

So machst du mich zum Reichsten auf der Erden;
Then makest thou me (the) richest-person on - earth;

Denn, hab ich dich, so muß
For,   have I thee, then must
{For if I have thee, then must}

Des größten Reichtums Überfluß
The greatest wealth's abundance

Mir dermaleinst im Himmel werden.
(Mine) hereafter in heaven become.
{Become mine hereafter in heaven.}

1 Sam. 15:22. ...Behold, to obey is better than sacrifice, and to hearken than the fat of rams.
Ps. 51:17. The sacrifice acceptable to God is a broken spirit; a broken and contrite heart, O God, thou wilt not despise. (Also Ps. 40:6–10.)

*Mt. 2:11. ...They offered him gifts, gold and frankincense and myrrh.
Ps. 116:12. What shall I render to the Lord...?
Ps. 51:17. ...A broken and contrite heart, O God, thou wilt not despise.
Is. 57:15. Thus says the high and lofty One who inhabits eternity, whose name is Holy: "I dwell in the high and holy place, and also with him who is of a contrite and humble spirit..."
Jn. 6:35, 37. Jesus said to them, "...Him who comes to me I will not cast out."
Mk. 12:41–44. [Jesus] sat down opposite the treasury, and watched the multitude putting money into the treasury. Many rich people put in large sums. And a poor widow came, and put in two copper coins, which make a penny. And he called his disciples to him, and said to them, "Truly, I say to you, this poor widow has put in more than all those who are contributing to the treasury. For they all contributed out of their abundance; but she out of her poverty has put in everything she had, her whole living."
Mt. 22:37 [Christ]: ...You shall love the Lord your God with all your heart...
Jn. 4:23–24 [Christ]: ...True worshipers will worship the Father in spirit and truth, for such the Father seeks to worship him. God is spirit, and those who worship him must worship in spirit and truth.
Gal. 5:22–23. The fruit of the Spirit is love, joy, peace, patience, kindness, goodness, faithfulness, gentleness, self-control...
1 Pet. 1:6. ...Your **faith** [is] more precious than gold...
Ps. 141:2. [O Lord,] let my **prayer** be counted as incense before thee, and the lifting up of my hands as an evening sacrifice! (Also Rev. 5:8, 8:3–4.)
Lk. 8:15. ...Hearing the word, [those whose hearts have been prepared] hold it fast in an honest and good heart, and bring forth fruit with **patience** (Luther: Geduld).
Heb. 10:36. You have need of endurance (Luther: Geduld), so that you may do the will of God and receive what is promised.
Ps. 73:25. [O Lord,] whom have I in heaven but thee? And there is nothing upon earth that I desire besides thee. (Luther: Wenn ich nur dich habe, so frage ich nichts nach Himmel und Erde.)
S. of S. 6:3 [Bride]: I am my beloved's and my beloved is mine...
Jer. 32:38 [God]: They shall be my people, and I will be their God. (Also Jer. 24:7, 31:33.)
2 Cor. 8:9. You know the grace of our Lord Jesus Christ, that though he was rich, yet for your sake he became poor, so that by his poverty you might become rich. (Also Eph. 2:7, 3:16, Col. 1:27, 2:2–3.)
2 Cor. 9:15. Thanks be to God for his inexpressible gift!
1 Cor. 2:9. As it is written, "What no eye has seen, nor ear heard, nor the heart of man conceived, what God has prepared for those who love him"... (Also Rom. 8:18.)

6. Tenor Aria
●Epiphany: My votive gift is my heart and all I am (65–6)
Nimm mich   dir   zu eigen hin,
Take   me to-thyself to   own   -,

Nimm mein Herze zum Geschenke.
Take   my   heart as-a   gift.

Alles, alles, was ich bin,
All,   all,   that I   am,

    Was ich rede, tu und denke,
(All) that I   speak, do, and   think,

Soll, mein Heiland, nur allein
Shall, my   Savior,   solely

Dir   zum Dienst gewidmet sein.
To-thee for   service dedicated   be.
{To thee for thy service be dedicated.}

7. Chorale[1] (See also 92–7.)
●Epiphany: Prayer of personal surrender (65–7)
Ei nun, mein Gott, so fall ich dir
Ah now,   my God, thus fall I   -
{Ah now, my God, thus do I fall}

Getrost   in deine Hände.
Confidently into thy   hands.

Nimm mich und mach es so mit mir
Take   me   and make it thus with me
{Take me and accomplish thy will with me}

Bis an mein letztes Ende,
Until -   my   final   end,

Wie du wohl weißt,   daß meinem Geist
As   thou well knowest (how); that for-my   spirit

Dadurch sein Nutz   entstehe,
Thereby   its benefit (may) be-fostered,

Und deine Ehr je mehr und mehr
And   thy   honor ever more and more

Sich in mir selbst   erhöhe.
(May) in me   -   (be) heightened.
{And that thy honor be exalted in me more and more.}

Mt. 22:37–38. [Jesus] said to [the man], "You shall love the Lord your God with all your heart, and with all your soul, and with all your mind. This is the great and first commandment."
Jer. 24:7 [God]: I will give them a heart to know that I am the Lord; and they shall be my people and I will be their God, for they shall return to me with their whole heart.
Rom. 12:1. ...Present your bodies as a living sacrifice, holy and acceptable to God, which is your spiritual worship.
Col. 3:17. And whatever you do, in word or deed, do everything in the name of the Lord Jesus, giving thanks to God the Father through him.
1 Cor. 10:31. So, whether you eat or drink, or whatever you do, do all to the glory of God.
1 Cor. 6:19–20. Do you not know that your body is a temple of the Holy Spirit within you, which you have from God? You are not your own; you were bought with a price. So glorify God in your body. (Also 1 Cor. 3:16; 7:23.)
Phil. 1:21–22. To me to live is Christ, and to die is gain. If it is to be life in the flesh, that means fruitful labor for me...

2 Sam. 24:14. David said to Gad, "I am in great distress; let us fall into the hand of the Lord, for his mercy is great..." (Also 1 Chron. 21:13.)
Ps. 31:5. Into thy hand I commit my spirit; thou hast redeemed me, O Lord, faithful God. (Also Lk. 23:46.)
Rom. 8:28. We know that in everything God works for good with those who love him, who are called according to his purpose.
Heb. 12:5–6, 10–11. ...My son, do not regard lightly the discipline of the Lord, nor lose courage when you are punished by him. For the Lord disciplines him whom he loves, and chastises every son whom he receives...He disciplines us for our good, that we may share his holiness. For the moment all discipline seems painful rather than pleasant; later it yields the peaceful fruit of righteousness to those who have been trained by it. (Also Prov. 3:11–12.)
1 Pet. 1:6–7. In this you rejoice, though now for a little while you may have to suffer various trials, so that the genuineness of your faith, more precious than gold which though perishable is tested by fire, may redound to praise and glory and honor at the revelation of Jesus Christ. (Also Jms. 1:2–4, 1 Pet. 4:19.)
1 Cor. 1:8. [God] will sustain you to the end, guiltless in the day of our Lord Jesus Christ.
Phil. 1:20–21. [My hope is that]...Christ will be honored in my body, whether by life or by death. For to me to live is Christ, and to die is gain.

---

[1]Original without text; this text added by Carl Friedrich Zelter after 1800.

BWV 66
Erfreut euch, ihr Herzen
(NBA I/10; BC A56)

Easter Monday (BWV 66, 6)
*Acts 10:34–43 (Peter preaches to Cornelius' household)
*Lk. 24:13–35 (Jesus meets the disciples on the way to Emmaus)
Librettist: Unknown. This cantata was adapted from BWV 66a.

1. Chorus
●Easter: Rejoice & put away sorrow; Christ is risen (66–1)
Erfreut euch, ihr Herzen,
Rejoice,   ye   hearts,

Entweichet, ihr Schmerzen,
Disappear,   ye   sorrows,

Es   lebet der Heiland und herrschet in euch.
(Now) lives the Savior and   reigns in you.
{The Savior lives and reigns in you.}

Ihr könnet verjagen
Ye can put-to-flight

Das Trauern, das Fürchten, das ängstliche Zagen,
 - Grieving, - fearing,   -   anxious trepidation,

Der Heiland erquicket sein geistliches Reich.
The Savior comforts   his   spiritual kingdom.

2. Bass Recit.
●Easter: Resurrection made everything turn out well (66–2)
Es   bricht das Grab und damit unsre Not,
(Now) breaks the grave and therewith our distress,
{The grave breaks and therewith our distress;}

Der Mund verkündigt Gottes Taten;
(My) mouth proclaims God's deeds;

Der Heiland lebt, so ist in Not und Tod
The Savior lives; thus has in distress and death

Den Gläubigen   vollkommen wohl geraten.
For believers (everything) perfectly well turned-out.
{The Savior lives; thus everything in this distress and death has turned out perfectly well for believers.}

3. Bass Aria
●Easter: Jesus appears; thank God for his goodness! (66–3)
Lasset dem Höchsten ein Danklied erschallen
Let   to-the Most-High a song-of-thanks resound
{Let a song of thanks resound to the Most High}

Mt. 28:5–8. The angel said to the women, "Do not be afraid; for I know that you seek Jesus who was crucified. He is not here; for he has risen, as he said. Come, see the place where he lay. Then go quickly and tell his disciples that he has risen from the dead, and behold, he is going before you to Galilee; there you will see him. Lo, I have told you." So they departed quickly from the tomb with fear and great joy, and ran to tell his disciples.
*Lk. 24:13–15. That very day two of [the disciples] were going to a village named Emmaus, about seven miles from Jerusalem, and talking with each other about all these things that had happened. While they were talking and discussing together, Jesus himself drew near [after his resurrection] and went with them.
Jn. 14:18 [Christ]: I will not leave you desolate; I will come to you. Yet a little while, and the world will see me no more, but you will see me...
Jn. 16:20–22 [Christ]: Truly, truly, I say to you, you will weep and lament, but the world will rejoice; you will be sorrowful, but your sorrow will turn into joy. When a woman is in travail she has sorrow, because her hour has come; but when she is delivered of the child, she no longer remembers the anguish, for joy that a child is born into the world. So you have sorrow now, but I will see you again and your hearts will rejoice, and no one will take your joy from you.

Acts 2:24–27. But God raised [Christ] up, having loosed the pangs of death, because it was not possible for him to be held by it. For David says concerning him, "I saw the Lord always before me, for he is at my right hand that I may not be shaken; therefore my heart was glad, and my tongue rejoiced; moreover my flesh will dwell in hope. For thou wilt not abandon my soul to Hades, nor let thy Holy One see corruption."
*Lk. 24:25–26, 33, 35. And [Christ] said to [the disciples], "O foolish men, and slow of heart to believe all that the prophets have spoken! Was it not necessary that the Christ should suffer these things and enter into his glory?"...And they rose that same hour and returned to Jerusalem; and they found the eleven gathered together and those who were with them...Then they told what had happened on the road... (Also Ps. 71:15.)
Jn. 16:20–21 [Christ]: ...You will be sorrowful, but your sorrow will turn into joy. When a woman is in travail she has sorrow, because her hour has come; but when she is delivered of the child, she no longer remembers the anguish, for joy that a child is born into the world.

*Lk. 24:15. While [two of the disciples] were talking and discussing together, Jesus himself drew near [after his resurrection) and went with them.
Ps. 89:1–2. I will sing of thy steadfast love, O Lord, for ever; with my mouth I will proclaim thy faithfulness to all generations. For thy

Vor sein Erbarmen und ewige Treu.
For his mercy and everlasting faithfulness.

Jesus erscheinet, uns Friede zu geben,
Jesus appears, us peace to give,
{Jesus appears, to give us peace;}

Jesus berufet uns, mit ihm zu leben.
Jesus calls us, with him to live.

Täglich wird seine Barmherzigkeit neu.
Daily is his compassion new.
{His compassion is new each day.}

4. Alto/Tenor Recit. & Arioso (Dialogue)
●Dialogue: Fear vs. Hope regarding resurrection (66–4)
Tenor (Hope):
Bei Jesu Leben freudig sein
In Jesus' life joyful to-be
{Being joyful in Jesus' life}

Ist unsrer Brust ein heller Sonnenschein.
Is to-our breast - bright sunshine.
{Is like bright sunshine in our breast.}

Mit Trost erfüllt auf seinen Heiland schauen
With comfort filled upon one's Savior to-look
{To look upon one's Savior filled with comfort}

Und in sich selbst ein Himmelreich erbauen,
And within one's self a kingdom-of-heaven to-build,
{And to build a kingdom of heaven within oneself,}

Ist wahrer Christen Eigentum.
Is true Christians' (heritage).
{Is the heritage of true Christians.}

Doch weil ich hier ein himmlisch Labsal habe,
But since I here a heavenly refreshment have,
{But since I have a heavenly refreshment here,}

So sucht mein Geist hier seine Lust und Ruh,
Thus seeks my spirit here its delight and rest,
{My spirit shall seek here its delight and rest,}

Mein Heiland ruft mir kräftig zu:
My Savior calls to-me (loudly) - :

»Mein Grab und Sterben bringt euch Leben,
"My grave and dying brings you life,

Mein Auferstehn ist euer Trost.«
My rising is your comfort."

Mein Mund will zwar ein Opfer geben,
My mouth would indeed an offering give (to you),
{My mouth would indeed give an offering to you,}

Mein Heiland, doch wie klein,
(O) my Savior; yet how small,

steadfast love was established for ever, thy faithfulness is firm as the heavens.
Jn. 20:19. On the evening of that day, the first day of the week, the doors being shut where the disciples were, for fear of the Jews, Jesus came and stood among them and said to them, "Peace be with you." (Also Jn. 20:26.)
2 Tim. 1:9–10. [God]...saved us and called us...through...our Savior Christ Jesus, who abolished death and brought life and immortality to light through the gospel. (Also Rom. 6:8–9, Gal. 2:20.)
Lam. 3:22–23. The steadfast love of the Lord never ceases, his mercies never come to an end; they are new every morning; great is thy faithfulness. (Also Ps. 90:14.)

*Lk. 24:15–16, 30–33, 35. While [the disciples on the road to Emmaus] were talking and discussing together, Jesus himself drew near and went with them. But their eyes were kept from recognizing him...When he was at table with them...their eyes were opened and they recognized him; and he vanished out of their sight. They said to each other, "Did not our hearts burn within us while he talked to us on the road, while he opened to us the scriptures?" And they rose that same hour and returned to Jerusalem; and they found the eleven gathered together...Then they told what had happened on the road, and how he was known to them in the breaking of the bread.
2 Cor. 4:3–4, 6. ...If our gospel is veiled, it is veiled only to those who are perishing. In their case the god of this world has blinded the minds of the unbelievers, to keep them from seeing the light of the gospel of the glory of Christ...For it is the God who said, "Let light shine out of darkness," who has shone in our hearts...
Mt. 3:2 [John]: ...The kingdom of heaven (Luther: das Himmelreich) is at hand. (Also Mt. 4:17.)
Lk. 17:20–21 [Christ]: ...The kingdom of God is not coming with signs to be observed; nor will they say, "Lo, here it is!" or "There!" for behold, the kingdom of God is in the midst of you (Luther: inwendig in euch).
Rom. 14:17. For the kingdom of God is...righteousness and peace and joy in the Holy Spirit.
Jude 1:20. ...Beloved, build yourselves up on your most holy faith; pray in the Holy Spirit. (Also Mt. 7:24, 1 Cor. 3:10–11.)
Eph. 3:16–19. [I pray that God]...may grant you to be strengthened with might through his Spirit in the inner man, and that Christ may dwell in your hearts through faith...
Ps. 37:4. Take delight (Luther: Lust) in the Lord...
Mt. 11:28 [Christ]: Come to me...and I will give you rest.
Jn. 10:10 [Christ]: ...I came that they may have life, and have it abundantly.
Jn. 14:19 [Christ]: ...Because I live, you will live also.
1 Thess. 5:10. [He] died for us so that whether we wake or sleep we might live with him. (Also Mt. 20:28, Mk. 10:45.)
Col. 2:13, 15. You, who were dead...God made alive together with [Christ], having forgiven us all our trespasses...He disarmed the principalities and powers and made a public example of them, triumphing over them in him.
Heb. 13:15. Through [Christ] then, let us continually offer up a sacrifice of praise to God, that is, the fruit of lips that acknowledge his name. (Also Ps. 50:14, 23, Ps. 51:15–17.)

Wie wenig, wie so gar geringe
How little, how even trifling
{How little, even trifling}

Wird es vor dir, o großer Sieger, sein,
Will it before thee, O great victor, be,
{Will it seem before thee, O great victor,}

Wenn ich vor dich ein Sieg- und Danklied bringe.
If I before thee a triumph- and thanks-song bring.
{If I bring a song of triumph and thanksgiving to thee.}

Tenor & Alto (Hope vs. Fear):
Mein/Kein Auge sieht den Heiland auferweckt,
  My/No eye sees the Savior restored-to-life,

Es hält ihn nicht/noch der Tod in Banden
(Now) holds him not/still - death in (its) bonds

Tenor (Hope):
Wie, darf noch Furcht in einer Brust entstehn?
What, may still fear in (any) breast arise?
{What, may fear still arise in any breast?}

  Alto (Fear):
  Läßt wohl das Grab die Toten aus?
  Gives-up indeed the grave (its) dead - ?
  {Will the grave indeed give up its dead?}

Tenor:
Wenn Gott in einem Grabe lieget,
If God in a grave lies,
{If God lies in a grave,}

So halten Grab und Tod ihn nicht.
Then hold grave and death him not.
{Then grave and death will not hold him.}

  Alto:
  Ach Gott! der du den Tod besieget,
  Ah God! Thou who - death hast-conquered,

  Dir weicht des Grabes Stein, das Siegel bricht,
  To-thee yields the grave's stone; the seal breaks;

  Ich glaube, aber hilf mir Schwachen,
  I believe, but help my weakness,

  Du kannst mich stärker machen;
  Thou canst me stronger make;
  {Thou canst make me stronger;}

  Besiege mich und meinen Zeifelmut,
  Conquer me and my doubting-disposition,

  Der Gott, der Wunder tut,
  The God, who wonders does,
  {The God who does wonders,}

  Hat meinen Geist durch Trostes Kraft gestärket,
  Has my spirit through comfort's power strengthened,
  {Has strengthened my spirit through comfort's power,}

Ps. 50:14, 23. [God]: Offer to God a sacrifice of thanksgiving...He who brings thanksgiving as his sacrifice honors me...

Ps. 71:8. My mouth is filled with thy praise, and with thy glory all the day. (Also Ps. 109:30.)

Ps. 116:12. What shall I render to the Lord for all his bounty to me?

Ps. 8:4. [O Lord,] what is man that thou art mindful of him, and the son of man that thou dost care for him? (Also Ps. 144:3.)

Hope vs. Fear:

Mk. 5:36. ...Jesus said... "Do not fear, only believe."

Heb. 11:1. Now faith is the assurance of things hoped for...

1 Cor. 15:17, 20. If Christ has not been raised, your faith is futile...In fact Christ has been raised from the dead...

1 Pet. 1:21. Through him you have confidence in God, who raised him from the dead and gave him glory, so that your faith and hope are in God.

*Lk. 24:18–25. One of [the disciples], named Cleopas, answered [Jesus], "Are you the only visitor to Jerusalem who does not know the things that have happened there in these days?" And he said to them, "What things?" And they said to him, "Concerning Jesus of Nazareth, who was a prophet mighty in deed and word before God and all the people, and how our chief priests and rulers delivered him up to be condemned to death, and crucified him. But we had hoped (Luther: *hofften*) that he was the one to redeem Israel. Yes, and besides all this, it is now the third day since this happened. Moreover, some women of our company amazed us (Luther: haben uns *erschreckt*). They were at the tomb early in the morning and did not find his body; and they came back saying that they had even seen a vision of angels, who said that he was alive. Some of those who were with us went to the tomb, and found it just as the women had said; but him they did not see." And he said to them, "O foolish men, and slow of heart to believe...!"

Job 14:14. If a man die, shall he live again?...

Acts 2:24. God raised [Christ] up, having loosed the pangs of death, because it was not possible for him to be held by it.

Acts 13:34–35. As for the fact that [God] raised him from the dead...he says also in another psalm, "Thou wilt not let thy Holy One see corruption." (Also Ps. 16:10, Acts 13:37.)

Mt. 27:62–66. ...The chief priests and the Pharisees gathered before Pilate and said, "Sir, we remember how that impostor said, while he was still alive, 'After three days I will rise again.' Therefore order the sepulchre to be made secure until the third day, lest his disciples go and steal him away, and tell the people, 'He has risen from the dead,' and the last fraud will be worse than the first." Pilate said to them, "...Go, and make it as secure as you can." So they went and made the sepulchre secure by sealing the stone and setting a guard.

1 Cor. 15:54–55. ...Death is swallowed up in victory. O death, where is thy victory? O death, where is thy sting?

Jn. 20:25–27. ...But [Thomas] said, "Unless I see in his hands the print of the nails, and placed my finger in the mark of the nails, and place my hand in his side, I will not believe." Eight days later, his disciples were again in the house, and Thomas was with them. The doors were shut, but Jesus came and stood among them, and said, "Peace be with you." Then he said to Thomas, "Put your finger here, and see my hands; and put out your hand, and place it in my side; do not be faithless, but believing."

Mk. 9:24. ...The father of the [sick] child cried out and said, "I believe; help my unbelief!"

*Lk. 24:29–31. ...So [Jesus] went in to stay with [the disciples]. When he was at table with them, he took bread and blessed, and broke it,

Daß er den auferstandnen Jesum merket.
So-that it the risen Jesus perceives.
{So that it perceives the risen Jesus.}

5. Alto & Tenor Duet
●Dialogue: Fear Vs. Hope that Christ is taken away (66-5)
Ich furchte zwar/nicht des Grabes Finsternissen
I feared indeed/not the grave's darkness

Und klagete/hoffete,
And lamented/hoped,

mein Heil sei nun/nicht entrissen.
(that) my Salvation be now/not snatched-away.

Nun ist mein Herze voller Trost,
Now is my heart full-of comfort,

Und wenn sich auch ein Feind erbost,
And even-if - - a foe gets-angry,
{And though my foe gets angry,}

Will ich in Gott zu siegen wissen.
Would I in God (how) to conquer know.
{I will know how to conquer in God.}

6. Chorale
●Alleluia! Christ is our comfort (66-6)
Alleluja! Alleluja! Alleluja!
Alleluia! Alleluia! Alleluia!

Des solln wir alle froh sein,
For-this shall we all joyful be,

Christus will unser Trost sein,
Christ would our comfort be,

Kyrie eleis!
Kyrie eleis!

and gave it to them. And their eyes were opened and they recognized him; and he vanished out of their sight.

Jn. 20:11–18. But Mary stood weeping outside the tomb, and as she wept she stooped to look into the tomb; and she saw two angels in white, sitting where the body of Jesus had lain, one at the head and one at the feet. They said to her, "Woman, why are you weeping?" She said to them, "Because they have taken away my Lord, and I do not know where they have laid him." Saying this, she turned round and saw Jesus standing, but she did not know that it was Jesus. Jesus said to her, "Woman, why are you weeping? Whom do you seek?" Supposing him to be the gardener, she said to him, "Sir, if you have carried him away, tell me where you have laid him, and I will take him away." Jesus said to her "Mary." She turned and said to him in Hebrew, "Rabboni!" (which means Teacher). Jesus said to her, "Do not hold me, for I have not yet ascended to the Father; but go to my brethren and say to them, I am ascending to my Father and your Father, to my God and your God." Mary Magdalene went and said to the disciples, "I have seen the Lord"; and she told them that he had said these things to her.
Ps. 27:1. The Lord is my light and my salvation; whom shall I fear?...
1 Cor. 15:57. Thanks be to God, who gives us the victory through our Lord Jesus Christ. (Also Heb. 2:14.)
Rom. 8:37. In all these things we are more than conquerors through him who loved us.

Rev. 19:6–7. Then I heard what seemed to be the voice of a great multitude, like the sound of many waters and like the sound of mighty thunderpeals, crying, "Hallelujah! For the Lord our God the Almighty reigns. Let us rejoice and exult and give him the glory..." (Also 19:1, 3–4.)
Rev. 21:3–4. ...Behold, the dwelling of God is with men. He will dwell with them, and they shall be his people, and God himself will be with them; he will wipe away every tear from their eyes, and death shall be no more, neither shall there be mourning nor crying nor pain any more, for the former things have passed away. (Also Rev. 7:15–17, Is. 25:8.)
2 Cor. 1:3–5. Blessed be the God and Father of our Lord Jesus Christ, the Father of mercies and God of all comfort, who comforts us in all our affliction, so that we may be able to comfort those who are in any affliction, with the comfort with which we ourselves are comforted by God. For as we share abundantly in Christ's sufferings, so through Christ we share abundantly in comfort too.
2 Jn. 1:3. Grace, mercy, and peace will be with us, from God the Father and from Jesus Christ the Father's Son, in truth and love.

BWV 67
Halt im Gedächtnis Jesum Christ
(NBA I/11; BC A62)

Quasimodogeniti: 1. S. after Easter (BWV 67, 42)
*1 Jn. 5:4–10 (Overcoming the world through faith; God's witness concerning his Son)
*Jn. 20:19–31 (Jesus appears twice to his disciples after his resurrection; unbelieving Thomas)
Librettist: perhaps Salomon Franck

1. Chorus
●Remember Christ, risen from the dead: 2 Tim. 2:8 (67-1)
Halt im Gedächtnis Jesum Christ,
Hold in remembrance Jesus Christ,

der auferstanden ist von den Toten.
who   risen   is from the dead.
{who is risen from the dead.}

2. Tenor Aria
●Christ risen but I still experience inner strife (67-2)
Mein Jesus ist erstanden,
My   Jesus is   arisen,

Allein, was schreckt mich noch?
But   why   fear   (I)   still?
{But why am I still afraid?}

Mein Glaube kennt des Heilands Sieg,
My   faith   knows the Savior's conquest,

Doch fühlt mein Herze Streit und Krieg,
Yet experiences my heart strife and warfare,
{Yet my heart experiences strife and warfare,}

Mein Heil, erscheine doch!
My Salvation, appear please!
{O my Salvation, please appear!}

3. Alto Recit.
●Jesus conquered death, yet I still experience fear (67-3)
Mein Jesu, heißest du des Todes Gift
My   Jesus, art-called thou - death's poison
{My Jesus, if thou art called death's poison}

Und eine Pestilenz der Hölle:
And a   plague   to hell:

Ach, daß mich noch Gefahr und Schrecken trifft?
Ah, (why-do) me still peril and   terror strike?
{Ah, why does terror and a sense of peril still strike me?}

2 Tim. 2:8. *Remember Jesus Christ, risen from the dead,* descended from David, as preached in my gospel.
Ps. 77:11. I will call to mind the deeds of the Lord...
Lam. 3:21. This I call to mind, and therefore I have hope.
1 Thess. 4:14. Since we believe that Jesus died and rose again, even so, through Jesus, God will bring with him those who have fallen asleep.
*1 Jn. 5:4–5, 10. ...This is the victory that overcomes the world, our faith. Who is it that overcomes the world but he who believes that Jesus is the Son of God?...He who believes in the Son of God has the testimony in himself. He who does not believe God has made him a liar, because he has not believed in the testimony God has borne to his Son.
Ps. 16:8. I keep the Lord always before me...
Heb. 12:1–2. ...Let us run with perseverance the race that is set before us, looking to Jesus the pioneer and perfecter of our faith, who for the joy that was set before him endured the cross, despising the shame, and is seated at the right hand of the throne of God.

*Jn. 20:25–29. ...But [Thomas] said to them, "Unless I see in [Jesus'] hands the print of the nails, and place my finger in the mark of the nails, and place my hand in his side, I will not believe." Eight days later, his disciples were again in the house, and Thomas was with them. The doors were shut, but Jesus came and stood among them, and said, "Peace be with you." Then [Jesus] said to Thomas, "Put your finger here, and see my hands; and put out your hand, and place it in my side; do not be faithless, but believing." Thomas answered him, "My Lord and my God!" Jesus said to him, "Have you believed because you have seen me? Blessed are those who have not seen and yet believe."
Ps. 42:5/11/43:5. Why are you cast down, O my soul, and why are you disquieted with me?...
1 Cor. 15:16–20. If the dead are not raised, then Christ has not been raised. If Christ has not been raised, your faith is futile and you are still in your sins. Then those also who have fallen asleep in Christ have perished. If for this life only we have hoped in Christ, we are of all men most to be pitied. But in fact Christ has been raised from the dead, the first fruits of those who have fallen asleep. (Also Jn. 6:40/44/54, Rom. 8:11.)
Heb. 11:1. Now faith is the assurance of things hoped for, the conviction of things not seen.

Hos. 13:14. ...O Death, where are your plagues? O Sheol, where is your destruction?... (Luther: Tod, ich will dir ein Gift sein; Hölle, ich will dir eine Pestilenz sein.)
Is. 25:8. He will swallow up death for ever...
1 Cor. 15:25–26. [Christ] must reign until he has put all his enemies under his feet. The last enemy to be destroyed is death.
2 Tim. 1:10. ...Our Savior Christ Jesus...abolished death and brought life and immortality to light...
Heb. 2:14–15. Since therefore the children share in flesh and blood, [Christ] himself likewise partook of the same nature, that through death he might destroy him who has the power of death, that is, the devil, and deliver all those who through fear of death were subject to lifelong bondage.

Du   legtest selbst auf unsre Zungen
Thou didst-lay even on   our   tongues
{Thou didst lay on our very tongues}

Ein   Loblied,   welches wir gesungen:
A song-of-praise, which we did-sing:

1 Jn. 3:8. ...The devil has sinned from the beginning. The reason the Son of God appeared was to destroy the works of the devil.
Ps. 40:3. He put a new song in my mouth, a song of praise to our God. (Also Ps. 71:8.)

4. Chorale
●Song of praise for Christ's victory in resurrection (67-4)
Erschienen ist der herrlich Tag,
Appeared   is   the glorious day,
{The glorious day has appeared,}

Dran   sich niemand gnug freuen mag:
Over-which -   no-one enough can-rejoice:
{Over which we can not rejoice enough:}

Christ, unser Herr, heut triumphiert,
Christ,   our Lord, today triumphs,
{Christ, our Lord, triumphs today,}

All sein Feind er gefangen führt.
All his foes he captive leads.

Alleluja!
Alleluia!

Ps. 118:24. This is the day which the Lord has made; let us rejoice and be glad in it.
Is. 25:8–9. He will swallow up death for ever, and the Lord God will wipe away tears from all faces, and the reproach of his people he will take away from all the earth; for the Lord has spoken. It will be said on that day, "Lo, this is our God; we have waited for him, that he might save us. This is the Lord; we have waited for him; let us be glad and rejoice in his salvation."
Eph. 4:8–10. Therefore it is said, "When [Christ] ascended on high he led a host of captives, and he gave gifts to men." (In saying, "He ascended," what does it mean but that he had also descended into the lower parts of the earth? He who descended is he who also ascended far above all the heavens, that he might fill all things.)
Rev. 19:1. After this I heard what seemed to be the loud voice of a great multitude in heaven, crying, "Hallelujah! Salvation and glory and power belong to our God." (Hallelujah: also Rev. 19:3, 4, 6)

5. Alto Recit.
●Fear of foe still with me but God will work in me (67-5)
Doch scheinet fast,
Yet (it) seems almost,
{Yet it almost seems}

Daß mich der Feinde Rest,
(As-if) me the   foe's remnant,
{As if the foe's remnant,}

Den ich zu groß und allzu schrecklich finde,
Whom I too great and all-too dreadful find,
{Whom I find too great and all too dreadful,}

Nicht ruhig bleiben läßt.
Not peaceful to-remain allows.
{Will not leave me in peace.}

Doch, wenn du mir den Sieg erworben hast,
Yet, (after) thou for-me the victory hast-won,

So   streite selbst mit mir, mit deinem Kinde:
Then contend even with me, with thy child:

Ja, ja, wir spüren schon im Glauben,
Yes, yes, we perceive already in faith,

Daß du, o   Friedefürst,
That thou, O Prince-of-Peace,

Dein Wort und Werk an uns erfüllen wirst.
Thy word and work in us   wilt-fulfill.

*Jn. 20:19. On the evening of that day, the first day of the week, the doors being shut where the disciples were, for fear of the Jews...
*1 Jn. 5:4–5. Whatever is born of God overcomes the world; and this is the victory that overcomes the world, our faith. Who is it that overcomes the world but he who believes that Jesus is the Son of God? (See also 1 Jn. 4:4.)
Jn. 16:33 [Christ]: I have said this to you, that in me you may have peace. In the world you have tribulation; but be of good cheer, I have overcome the world.
Mk. 9:23–24. Jesus said to [the man], "If you can! All things are possible to him who believes." Immediately the father of the child cried out and said, "I believe; help my unbelief!" Phil. 2:13. God is at work in you, both to will and to work for his good pleasure.
Gen. 32:24, 26. Jacob was left alone; and [the Lord] wrestled with him until the breaking of the day...[and] Jacob said, "I will not let you go, unless you bless me."
Heb. 12:5–6, 10. ...My son, do not regard lightly the discipline of the Lord, nor lose courage when you are punished by him. For the Lord disciplines him whom he loves, and chastises every son whom he receives...He disciplines us for our good, that we may share his holiness.
Phil. 1:6. I am sure that he who began a good work in you will bring it to completion at the day of Jesus Christ. (Also Ps. 138:8.)
*Jn. 20:19. Jesus came and...said to them, *"Peace be with you."*
Is. 9:6. ...His name will be called "...Prince of Peace."
2 Thess. 1:11–12. To this end we always pray for you, that our God may make you worthy of his call, and may fulfil every good resolve and work of faith by his power, so that the name of our Lord Jesus may be glorified in you, and you in him, according to the grace of our God and the Lord Jesus Christ.

6. Bass Aria & S.A.T. Trio
● Vox Christi: Peace be with you: Jn. 20:19, 21 (67–6)
Bass (Christ):
Friede sei mit euch!
Peace be with you!

Soprano, Alto, Tenor:
Wohl uns!   Jesus hilft uns kämpfen
(How-blessed-are-we!) Jesus helps us do-battle

Und die Wut der Feinde dämpfen,
And the rage of-the enemies to-dampen,

Hölle, Satan, weich!
Hell, Satan, retreat!

Bass:
Friede sei mit euch!
Peace be with you!

Soprano, Alto, Tenor:
Jesus holet uns zum Frieden
Jesus fetches us to peace

Und erquicket in uns Müden
And revives in us weary-ones

Geist und Leib zugleich.
Spirit and body alike.

Bass:
Friede sei mit euch!
Peace be with you!

Soprano, Alto, Tenor:
O Herr, hilf   und laß   gelingen,
O Lord, help (us) and let (us) succeed,

Durch den Tod hindurchzudringen
Through - death to-press-through
{To press through death}

In dein Ehrenreich!
Into thy kingdom-of-glory!

Bass:
Friede sei mit euch!
Peace be with you!

7. Chorale (See also 116–1, 143–2.)
● Jesus as Lord & Prince of Peace confessed by church (67–7)
Du   Friedefürst, Herr Jesu Christ,
Thou Prince-of-peace, Lord Jesus Christ,

Wahr' Mensch und wahrer Gott,
True   man   and   true God,

Ein starker Nothelfer   du bist
A   strong Helper-in-need thou art

*Jn. 20:19–21. On the evening of that day, the first day of the week, the doors being shut where the disciples were, for fear of the Jews, Jesus came and stood among them and said to them, *"Peace be with you."* When he had said this, he showed them his hands and his side. Then the disciples were glad when they saw the Lord. Jesus said to them again, *"Peace be with you. As the Father has sent me, even so I send you."*
*1 Jn. 5:4–5. Whatever is born of God overcomes the world; and this is the victory that overcomes the world, our faith. Who is it that overcomes the world but he who believes that Jesus is the Son of God?
Jms. 4:7. ...Resist the devil and he will flee from you.
Rom. 16:20. ...The God of peace will soon crush Satan under your feet...
Eph. 6:11–12. Put on the whole armor of God, that you may be able to stand against the wiles of the devil. For we are not contending against flesh and blood, but against the principalities, against the powers, against the world rulers of this present darkness, against the spiritual hosts of wickedness in the heavenly places.
*Jn. 20:21. Jesus said to them again, *"Peace be with you..."*
Jn. 14:27. Peace I leave with you; my peace I give to you; not as the world gives do I give to you. Let not your hearts be troubled, neither let them be afraid.
1 Cor. 7:15. ...God has called us to peace.
Mt. 11:28–30 [Christ]: Come to me, all who labor and are heavy laden, and I will give you rest. Take my yoke upon you, and learn from me; for I am gentle and lowly in heart, and you will find rest for your souls. For my yoke is easy, and my burden is light.
Ps. 23:1–3. The Lord is my shepherd...He leads me beside still waters; he restores my soul...
1 Thess. 5:23. May the God of peace himself sanctify you wholly; and may your spirit and soul and body be kept sound and blameless at the coming of our Lord Jesus Christ.
Mt. 10:28. Do not fear those who kill the body but cannot kill the soul... (Also Heb. 12:4.)
Rev. 2:10–11. Do not fear what you are about to suffer...Be faithful unto death, and I will give you the crown of life...He who conquers shall not be hurt by the second death.
Rev. 14:13. ...Blessed are the dead who die in the Lord henceforth... that they may rest from their labors, for their deeds follow them!
Num. 23:10. ...Let me die the death of the righteous, and let my end be like his!
Ps. 73:24. ...Afterward thou wilt receive me to glory.

*Jn. 20:19. ...Jesus came and stood among them and said to them, "Peace be with you."
Is. 9:6. To us a child is born, to us a son is given; and the government will be upon his shoulder, and his name will be called "Wonderful Counselor, Mighty God, Everlasting Father, Prince of Peace."
Ps. 124:8. Our help is in the name of the Lord...
1 Jn. 5:20. ...We are in him who is true, in his Son Jesus Christ. This is the true God and eternal life. (Also Jn. 17:3.)

Im Leben und im Tod:
In   life   and   in   death:

Drum   wir allein
Therefore we   alone

Im   Namen dein
In (the) name of-thine

Zu deinem Vater schreien.
To   thy   Father   do-cry.
{Therefore we cry to thy Father in thy name alone.}

BWV 68
Also hat Gott die Welt geliebt
(NBA I/14; BC A86)

2. Day of Pentecost (BWV 173, 68, 174)
*Acts 10:42–48 (The Holy Spirit descends on the Gentiles at Cornelius' house while Peter preaches)
*Jn. 3:16–21 (God sent his Son so that the world might be saved through him.)
Librettist: Christiane Mariane von Ziegler (Libretto modified)

1. Chorale

●God sent his Son so all might have eternal life: Jn. 3:16 (paraphrase) (68-1)
Also hat Gott die Welt geliebt,
Thus has God the world loved,
{For God so loved the world,}

Daß er uns seinen Sohn gegeben.
That he to-us his   Son did-give.
{That he gave us his Son.}

Wer   sich im Glauben ihm ergibt,
Whoever himself in   faith   to-him gives,
{Whoever gives himself to him in faith,}

Der soll   dort   ewig   bei ihm leben.
He shall (over) there eternally with him live.
{Will live eternally over there with him.}

Wer   glaubt, daß Jesus ihm geboren,
Whoever believes, that Jesus for-him was-born,
{Whoever believes that Jesus was born for him,}

Der bleibet ewig unverloren,
He remains eternally unforlorn,
{He will never perish,}

Und   ist kein Leid, das den betrübt,
And (there) is no sorrow that him can-grieve,
{And no sorrow can grieve the one}

Den Gott und auch sein Jesus liebt.
Whom God and also   his   Jesus loves.

Ps. 34:17. When the righteous cry for help, the Lord hears, and delivers them out of all their troubles (Luther: Not).
Dan. 6:27. He delivers and rescues (Luther: Er ist ein Erlöser und Nothelfer)...
Ps. 140:7. O Lord, my Lord, my strong deliverer...
Ps. 33:21. Yea, our heart is glad in him, because we trust in his holy name.
Jn. 14:13–14 [Christ]: Whatever you ask in my name, I will do it, that the Father may be glorified in the Son; if you ask anything in my name, I will do it. (Also Jn. 15:16, 16:23–24.)
Lk. 18:7–8 [Christ]: Will not God vindicate his elect, who cry to him day and night? Will he delay long over them? I tell you, he will vindicate them speedily...

*Jn. 3:14–17. As Moses lifted up the serpent in the wilderness, so must the Son of man be lifted up, that whoever believes in him may have eternal life. *For God so loved the world that he gave his only Son, that whoever believes in him should not perish (Luther: verloren werden) but have eternal life.* For God sent the Son into the world, not to condemn the world, but that the world might be saved through him.
1 Jn. 4:9–10. In this the love of God was made manifest among us, that God sent his only Son into the world, so that we might live through him. In this is love, not that we loved God but that he loved us and sent his Son to be the expiation for our sins.
Rom. 5:8. God shows his love for us in that while we were yet sinners Christ died for us.
Eph. 2:4–6. God, who is rich in mercy, out of the great love with which he loved us, even when we were dead through our trespasses, made us alive together with Christ (by grace you have been saved), and raised us up with him, and made us sit with him in the heavenly places in Christ Jesus...
Jn. 11:25–26. Jesus said to [Martha], "I am the resurrection and the life; he who believes in me, though he die, yet shall he live, and whoever lives and believes in me shall never die. Do you believe this?"
1 Jn. 5:11–12. This is the testimony, that God gave us eternal life, and this life is in his Son. He who has the Son has life; he who has not the Son of God has not life.
1 Jn. 1:3. ...Our fellowship is with the Father and with his Son Jesus Christ.
1 Jn. 2:23–25. No one who denies the Son has the Father. He who confesses the Son has the Father also. Let what you heard from the beginning abide in you. If what you heard from the beginning abides in you, then you will abide in the Son and in the Father. And this is what he has promised us, eternal life.
Rom. 8:32. He who did not spare his own Son but gave him up for us all, will he not also give us all things with him?

2. Soprano Aria (Adapted from BWV 208–13)
●Rejoice, O my heart, because thy Jesus has come! (68-2)
Mein gläubiges Herze,
(O) my believing heart,

Frohlocke, sing, scherze,
Rejoice, sing, jest,

Dein Jesus is da!
Thy Jesus is here!

Weg Jammer, weg Klagen,
Away misery! Away lamentation!

Ich will euch nur sagen:
I would to-you simply say:

Mein Jesus ist nah.
My Jesus is near!

3. Bass Recit.
●Christ came not to judge but save; no one excluded (68-3)
Ich bin mit Petro nicht vermessen,
I am with Peter not mistaken,

Was mich getrost und freudig macht,
Which me consoled and joyful makes,
{This consoles me and makes me joyful,}

Daß mich mein Jesus nicht vergessen.
That me my Jesus not forgotten (has).
{That my Jesus has not forgotten me.}

Er kam nicht nur, die Welt zu richten,
He came not only, the world to judge,

Nein, nein, er wollte Sünd und Schuld
No, no, he wanted sin and guilt

Als Mittler zwischen Gott und Mensch
As mediator between God and mankind

vor diesmal schlichten.
- now to-arbitrate.
{No, no, as mediator between God and mankind, he came this time to arbitrate sin and guilt.}

4. Bass Aria (Taken from BWV 208-7)
●Confession of faith: sufficiency of Christ's salvation (68-4)
Du bist geboren mir zugute,
Thou art born me for-benefit,
{Thou art born for my benefit,}

Jn. 3:17. God sent the Son into the world...
Jn. 3:16. ...that whoever believes in him should not perish but have eternal life.
1 Jn. 4:10, 14. In this is love, not that we loved God but that he loved us and sent his Son...And we have seen and testify that the Father has sent his Son as the Savior of the world.
1 Sam. 2:1–2. ...My heart exults in the Lord...I rejoice in thy salvation [O Lord]. (Also Ps. 13:5.)
Zeph. 3:14. Sing aloud, O daughter of Zion; shout, O Israel! Rejoice and exult with all your heart...!
Gal. 4:6. ...God has sent the Spirit of his Son into our hearts, crying, "Abba! Father!"
1 Jn. 4:13. By this we know that we abide in him and he in us, because he has given us of his own Spirit. (Also 1 Jn. 3:24.)
*Acts 10:45. The believers from among the circumcised who came with Peter were amazed, because the gift of the Holy Spirit had been poured out even on the Gentiles.
Rom. 5:5. ...God's love has been poured into our hearts through the Holy Spirit which has been given to us.
S. of S. 3:4 [Bride]: ...I found him whom my soul loves. I held him, and would not let him go...
Mt. 28:20 [Christ]: ...Lo, I am with you always to the close of the age.
Phil. 4:4–5. Rejoice in the Lord always; again I will say, Rejoice...The Lord is at hand (Luther: Der Herr ist nahe).

*Acts 10:34–36, 43–45. Peter opened his mouth and said [to the Gentiles at Caesarea]: "Truly I perceive that God shows no partiality, but in every nation any one who fears him and does what is right is acceptable to him. You know the word which he sent to Israel, preaching good news of peace by Jesus Christ...To him all the prophets bear witness that every one who believes in him receives forgiveness of sins through his name." While Peter was still saying this, the Holy Spirit fell on all who heard the word. And the believers from among the circumcised who came with Peter were amazed, because the gift of the Holy Spirit had been poured out even on the Gentiles. (Also Acts 10:47.)
Acts 15:7–9. [In Jerusalem,] after there had been much debate, Peter rose and said to them, "...God who knows the heart bore witness to [the Gentiles], giving them the Holy Spirit just as he did to us; and he made no distinction between us and them, but cleansed their hearts by faith."
*Jn. 3:17–18. God sent the Son into the world, not to condemn the world, but that the world might be saved through him. He who believes in him is not condemned; he who does not believe is condemned already, because he has not believed in the name of the only Son of God. (Also Jn. 5:22–24.)
1 Tim. 2:5–6. For there is one God, and there is one mediator between God and men, the man Christ Jesus, who gave himself as a ransom for all. (Also Heb. 9:15, 12:24.)

*Jn. 3:16–17. ...[God] gave his only Son, that whoever believes in him should not perish but have eternal life...Whoever believes in him [will] not perish but have eternal life. For God sent the Son into the world, not to condemn the world, but that the world might be saved through him.
Jn. 10:10 [Christ]: ...I came that they may have life, and have it abundantly.

Das glaub ich, mir ist wohl zumute,
This believe I; I am in-good-spirits,
{This I believe and am in good spirits,}

Weil du vor mich genung getan.
Because thou for me enough (hast) done.

Das Rund der Erden mag gleich brechen,
The circle of-the earth may well break,
{Should the circle of the earth break,}

Will mir der Satan widersprechen,
Would me - Satan oppose,
{Should Satan should oppose me,}

So bet ich dich, mein Heiland, an.
Then pray I to-thee, my Savior - .
{Then I will pray to thee my Savior.}

5. Chorus
●Judgment escaped by faith in the Son: Jn. 3:18 (68–5)
Wer an ihn gläubet, der wird nicht gerichtet;
Whoever in him believes, he will not be-judged;

wer aber nicht gläubet, der ist schon gerichtet;
Whoever, however, not believes, he is already judged;

denn er gläubet nicht an den Namen
for he believes not on the name

des eingebornen Sohnes Gottes.
of-the only-begotten Son of-God.

BWV 69
Lobe den Herrn, meine Seele II
(NBA I/32; BC B10)

Change of Town Council (BWV 71, 119, 193, 120, 29, 69)
This cantata is a revision of BWV 69a, which had been written
for 12 S. after Trinity. Libretto of 69a was a modified version
of a text by Johann Knauer.
+2 Cor. 3:4–11 (The new covenant shines more brightly than
the old)
+Mk. 7:31–37 (Jesus heals man who was deaf and dumb)
Librettist: Unknown

1. Chorus (From BWV 69a)
●Praise the Lord, O my soul, for blessings: Ps. 103:2 (69–1)
Lobe den Herrn, meine Seele, und vergiß nicht,
Praise the Lord, my soul, and forget not,

was er dir Gutes getan hat!
what he for-thee good done hath!
{all the good he hath done for thee!}

Rom. 8:31, 33–34. What then shall we say to this? If God is for us, who is against us?...Who shall bring any charge against God's elect? It is God who justifies; who is to condemn? Is it Christ Jesus, who died, yes, who was raised from the dead, who is at the right hand of God, who indeed intercedes for us? (Also 1 Jn. 2:1, Heb. 7:25.)
Ps. 27:1. The Lord is my light and my salvation; whom shall I fear?...
Jn. 16:33 [Christ]: ...Be of good cheer, I have overcome the world. (Also 1 Jn. 2:13, 14; 4:4.)
Mt. 24:35 [Christ]: Heaven and earth will pass away, but my words will not pass away. (Also Mk. 13:31, Lk. 21:33.)
Eph. 6:11–12. Put on the whole armor of God, that you may be able to stand against the wiles of the devil. For we are not contending against flesh and blood, but against the principalities, against the powers, against the world rulers of this present darkness, against the spiritual hosts of wickedness in the heavenly places. (Also 1 Pet. 5:8.)
1 Jn. 3:8. ...The reason the Son of God appeared was to destroy the works of the devil. (Also Heb. 2:14.)

Jn. 3:18. He who believes in him is not condemned; he who does not believe is condemned already, because he has not believed in the name of the only Son of God.
Jn. 5:22–24 [Christ]: The Father judges no one, but has given all judgment to the Son, that all may honor the Son, even as they honor the Father. He who does not honor the Son does not honor the Father who sent him. Truly, truly, I say to you, he who hears my word and believes him who sent me, has eternal life; he does not come into judgment, but has passed from death to life. (Also 1 Jn. 5:13.)
1 Jn. 2:22–23. Who is the liar but he who denies that Jesus is the Christ? This is the antichrist, he who denies the Father and the Son. No one who denies the Son has the Father. He who confesses the Son has the Father also.

Ps. 103:1–2. Bless the Lord, O my soul; and all that is within me, bless his holy name! *Bless the Lord, O my soul, and forget not all his benefits.*
Ps. 104:1. Bless the Lord, O my soul! O Lord my God, thou art very great! Thou art clothed with honor and majesty.

2. Soprano Recit. (New to this version)
●Praise to God for his sustenance of all creatures (69–2)
Wie groß ist Gottes Güte doch!
How great is God's kindness indeed!

Er bracht uns an das Licht,
He brought us to the light,

Und er erhält uns noch.
And he sustains us still.

Wo findet man nur eine Kreatur,
Where finds one even one creature,
{Where can one find even one creature,}

Der es an Unterhalt gebricht?
For-whom - - sustenance is-wanting?

Betrachte doch, mein Geist,
Observe indeed, (O) my spirit,

Der Allmacht unverdeckte Spur,
The Almighty's unconcealed trace,

Die auch im kleinen
Which even in small (things)

sich recht groß erweist.
itself downright great proves-to-be.
{Which, even in small things, proves to be great.}

Ach! möcht es mir, o Höchster, doch gelingen,
Ah! might it for-me, O Most-High, indeed succeed,
{Ah!, that I might indeed succeed, O Most High,}

Ein würdig Danklied dir zu bringen!
A worthy song-of-thanks to-thee to bring!
{To bring before thee a worthy song of thanks!}

Doch, sollt es mir hierbei an Kräften fehlen,
Yet, should it for-me in-this of powers fail,
{Yet, should in this my powers fail,}

So will ich doch, Herr, deinen Ruhm erzählen.
So would I nevertheless, Lord, thy praise tell.
{I nevertheless want to tell thy praise, O Lord.}

3. Alto Aria (From BWV 69a)
●Rise, O my soul, & sing a song of thanks to God! (69–3)
Meine Seele,
My soul,

Auf! erzähle,
Rise! tell,

Was dir Gott erwiesen hat!
What to-thee God hath-shown!
{What favor God hath shown to thee!}

Ps. 31:19. O how abundant is thy goodness (Luther: Wie groß ist deine Güte)...! (Also Ps. 103:11.)
Ps. 139:12–16. [O Lord,] the darkness is not dark to thee, the night is bright as the day; for darkness is as light with thee. For thou didst form my inward parts, thou didst knit me together in my mother's womb. I praise thee, for thou art fearful and wonderful. Wonderful are thy works! Thou knowest me right well; my frame was not hidden from thee, when I was being made in secret, intricately wrought in the depths of the earth. Thy eyes beheld my unformed substance; in thy book were written, every one of them, the days that were formed for me, when as yet there was none of them.
Ps. 145:15–16. The eyes of all look to thee, and thou givest them their food in due season. Thou openest thy hand, thou satisfiest the desire of every living thing. (Also Ps. 104:27, 111:5, Job 12:10.)
Mt. 10:29–31 [Christ]: Are not two sparrows sold for a penny? And not one of them will fall to the ground without your Father's will. But even the hairs of your head are all numbered. Fear not, therefore; you are of more value than many sparrows. (Also Lk. 12:6–7.)
Mt. 6:25–26, 28–30 [Christ]: ...Do not be anxious about your life, what you shall eat or what you shall drink, nor about your body, what you shall put on...Look at the birds of the air: they neither sow nor reap nor gather into barns, and yet your heavenly Father feeds them. Are you not of more value than they?...And why are you anxious about clothing? Consider the lilies of the field, how they grow; they neither toil nor spin; yet I tell you, even Solomon in all his glory was not arrayed like one of these. But if God so clothes the grass of the field, which today is alive and tomorrow is thrown into the oven, will he not much more clothe you, O men of little faith?
Heb. 13:15. Through [Christ] then, let us continually offer up a sacrifice of praise to God, that is, the fruit of lips that acknowledge his name.
Ps. 50:14, 23 [God]: Offer to God a sacrifice of thanksgiving, and pay your vows to the Most High...He who brings thanksgiving as his sacrifice honors me... (Also Ps. 51:15–17.)
Ps. 147:7. Sing to the Lord with thanksgiving...
Is. 42:10. Sing to the Lord a new song, his praise (Luther: Ruhm) from the end of the earth...
Is. 43:21. ...that [my people] might declare my praise (Luther: meinen Ruhm erzählen).
Ps. 89:1. I will sing of thy steadfast love, O Lord, for ever; with my mouth I will proclaim thy faithfulness to all generations.

Ps. 103:1. Bless the Lord, O my soul; and all that is within me, bless his holy name!
Ps. 105:1–2 / 1 Chron. 16:8–9. O give thanks to the Lord, call on his name, make known his deeds among the peoples! Sing to him, sing praises to him, tell of all his wonderful works!
Ps. 75:1. We give thanks to thee, O God; we give thanks; we call on thy name and recount thy wondrous deeds. (Also Ps. 9:1, 107:22, Is. 25:1.)
+Mk. 7:33–36. ...[Jesus] put his fingers into [the man's] ears, and he spat and touched his tongue; and...said to him, "Ephphata," that is, "Be

Rühme seine Wundertat,
Extol his wondrous-work,

Laß, dem Höchsten zu gefallen,
Let, the Most-High to please,
{To please the Most High, let}

Ihm ein frohes Danklied schallen!
To-him a joyous song-of-thanks resound!
{A joyous song of thanks resound to him!}

4. Tenor Recit. (New to this version)
●Praise God for the blessing of good government (69-4)
Der Herr hat große Ding an uns getan.
The Lord has great things for us done.
{The Lord has done great things for us.}

Denn er versorget und erhält,
For he provides and sustains,

Beschützet und regiert die Welt.
Protects and rules the world.

Er tut mehr, als man sagen kann.
He does more, than one can-tell.

Jedoch, nur eines zu gedenken:
Nevertheless, only one-thing (more) to consider:
{Nevertheless, consider one other thing:}

Was könnt uns Gott wohl Beßres schenken,
What could to-us God indeed better-thing give,
{What better thing could God give us,}

Als daß er unsrer Obrigkeit
Than that he to-our government

Den Geist der Weisheit gibet,
The spirit of wisdom would-give,

Die denn zu jeder Zeit
Which indeed at all times

Das Böse straft, das Gute liebet?
- Evil punishes, - good cherishes?

Ja, die bei Tag und Nacht
Yes, which - day and night

Für unsre Wohlfahrt wacht?
For our well-being keeps-watch?

Laßt uns dafür den Höchsten preisen;
Let us for-that the Most-High praise;
{Let us praise the Most High for that;}

Auf! ruft ihn an,
Rise! Call-to him -,

opened," And his ears were opened, his tongue was released, and he spoke plainly. And he charged them to tell no one; but the more he charged them, the more zealously they proclaimed it.
Mk. 5:19. [Jesus]...said to [the healed demoniac], "Go home to your friends, and tell them how much the Lord has done for you, and how he has had mercy on you."
Ps. 13:6. I will sing to the Lord, because he as dealt bountifully with me.
Lk. 1:49. For he who is mighty has done great things for me, and holy is his name.

Ps. 126:3. The Lord has done great things for us; we are glad. (Also 1 Sam. 12:24.)
Is. 25:1. Lord, thou art my God; I will exalt thee, I will praise thy name, for thou hast done wonderful things...
Ps. 98:1. O sing to the Lord a new song, for he has done marvelous things!...
Joel 2:21. ...Rejoice, for the Lord has done great things!
Ps. 111:5. He provides food for those who fear him; he is ever mindful of his covenant.
Job 12:10. In his hand is the life of every living thing and the breath of all mankind.
Ps. 145:15. [O Lord,] the eyes of all look to thee, and thou givest them their food in due season.
Ps. 103:19. The Lord has established his throne in the heavens, and his kingdom rules over all.
Ps. 22:28. Dominion belongs to the Lord, and he rules over the nations.
Ps. 97:1. The Lord reigns; let the earth rejoice; let the many coastlands be glad!
Ps. 40:5. Thou hast multiplied, O Lord my God, thy wondrous deeds and thy thoughts toward us...Were I to proclaim and tell of them, they would be more than can be numbered.
1 Kings 3:5-6, 9-14. At Gibeon the Lord appeared to Solomon in a dream by night; and God said, "Ask what I shall give you." And Solomon said, "...Give thy servant...an understanding mind to govern thy people, that I may discern between good and evil; for who is able to govern this thy great people?" It pleased the Lord that Solomon had asked this. And God said to him, "Because you have asked this, and have not asked for yourself long life or riches or the life of your enemies, but have asked for yourself understanding to discern what is right, behold, I now do according to your word. Behold, I give you a wise and discerning mind, so that none like you has been before you and none like you shall arise after you. I give you also what you have not asked, both riches and honor, so that no other king shall compare with you, all your days. And if you will walk in my ways, keeping my statutes and my commandments, as your father David walked, then I will lengthen your days."
1 Pet. 2:13-14. Be subject for the Lord's sake to every human institution, whether it be to the emperor as supreme, or to governors as sent by him to punish those who do wrong and to praise those who do right.
Rom. 13:1-5. Let every person be subject to the governing authorities. For there is no authority except from God, and those that exist have been instituted by God. Therefore he who resists the authorities resists what God has appointed, and those who resist will incur judgment. For rulers are not a terror to good conduct, but to bad. Would you have no fear of him who is in authority? Then do what is good, and

Daß er sich auch noch fernerhin
That he himself also yet henceforth

so gnädig woll erweisen.
so gracious might prove-to-be.
{That he might prove to be so gracious to us in the future as
well.}

Was unserm Lande schaden kann,
Whatever our land could-harm,
{Whatever could harm our land,}

Wirst du, o Höchster, von uns wenden
Wilt thou, O Most-High, away-from us turn
{Wilt thou, O Most High avert from us}

Und uns erwünschte Hilfe senden.
And us (the) desired help send.
{And send us the help we desire.}

Ja, ja, du wirst in Kreuz und Nöten
Yes, yes, thou wilt in cross(-bearing) and difficulties

Uns züchtigen, jedoch nicht töten.
Us chastise, yet not slay.
{Chasten us, yet not slay us.}

you will receive his approval, for he is God's servant for your good. But if you do wrong, be afraid, for he does not bear the sword in vain; he is the servant of God to execute his wrath on the wrongdoer. Therefore one must be subject, not only to avoid God's wrath but also for the sake of conscience.
Tit. 3:1. Remind [your listeners] to be submissive to rulers and authorities, to be obedient...
1 Tim. 2:1–2. ...I urge that supplications, prayers, intercessions, and thanksgivings be made for all men, for kings and all who are in high positions, that we may lead a quiet and peaceable life, godly and respectful in every way. (Also Lk. 1:74–75.)
Ps. 28:8–9. The Lord is the strength of his people, he is the saving refuge of his anointed. O save thy people, and bless thy heritage; be thou their shepherd, and carry them for ever. Deut. 26:15. [O Lord,] look down from thy holy habitation, from heaven, and bless thy people Israel and the ground which thou hast given us, as thou didst swear to our fathers... (Also Ps. 29:11.)
Ps. 3:8. Deliverance belongs to the Lord; [O Lord,] thy blessing be upon thy people!
Ps. 103:8–9. The Lord is merciful and gracious, slow to anger and abounding in steadfast love. He will not always chide, nor will he keep his anger for ever.
Heb. 12:5–6, 10. ...My son, do not regard lightly the discipline of the Lord, nor lose courage when you are punished by him. For the Lord disciplines him whom he loves...He disciplines us for our good, that we may share his holiness. (Also Prov. 3:11–12, Jms. 1:2–4, 1 Pet. 1:6–7.)
Ps. 118:18. The Lord has chastened me sorely, but he has not given me over to death.
2 Cor. 6:9. [We are]...as punished, and yet not killed. (Also Jer. 4:27, 5:10, 5:18, 30:11, 46:28, Ezek. 20:17.)

5. Bass Aria (Taken unchanged from BWV 69a)
●Prayer: Preserve & keep me; then will I praise God (69-5)
Mein Erlöser und Erhalter,
My Redeemer and Sustainer,

Nimm mich stets in Hut und Wacht!
Take me continually into (thy) keeping and watch!

Steh mir bei in Kreuz und Leiden,
Stand me by in cross and suffering,
{Stand by me in cross-bearing and suffering,}

Alsdann singt mein Mund mit Freuden:
Thereupon sings my mouth with joy:

Gott hat alles wohlgemacht.
God has all-things done-well.
{God has done all things well.}

Ps. 138:7–8. [O Lord,] though I walk in the midst of trouble, thou dost preserve my life...and thy right hand delivers me. The Lord will fulfil his purpose for me; thy steadfast love, O Lord, endures for ever. Do not forsake the work of thy hands.
Ps. 25:20. Oh guard my life, and deliver me; let me not be put to shame, for I take refuge in thee.
Ps. 54:4. Behold, God is my helper (Luther: Gott steht mir bei); the Lord is the upholder of my life (Luther: erhält meine Seele).
Ps. 61:4. ...Oh to be safe under the shelter of thy wings! (Also Ps. 27:5.)
1 Pet. 4:19. Let those who suffer according to God's will do right and entrust their souls to a faithful Creator.
2 Tim. 4:17. The Lord stood by me...So I was rescued...
Ps. 89:1–2. I will sing of thy steadfast love, O Lord, for ever; with my mouth I will proclaim thy faithfulness...
+**Mk. 7:37.** [The people] were astonished beyond measure [at Jesus' miracles], saying, "He has done all things well..."

6. Chorale (New to this version) (See also 76-14.)
●Praise to God by people for national blessings (69-6)
Es danke, Gott, und lobe dich
(Let) thank (thee), God, and praise thee

Ps. 67:5–7. Let the peoples praise thee, O God; let all the peoples praise thee! The earth has yielded its increase; God, our God, has blessed us. God has blessed us; let all the ends of the earth fear him!

Das Volk   in guten Taten.
The people with good deeds.
{May thy people thank and praise thee, God, with good deeds.}

Das Land bringt Frucht und bessert sich,
The land   bears fruit and improves - ,

Dein Wort ist   wohl geraten.
Thy Word (has) well-succeeded.

    Uns segne Vater und der Sohn,
(May) us bless Father and the Son,
{May the Father and the Son bless us,}

    Uns segne Gott der Heilge Geist,
(May) us   bless God the Holy Ghost,
{May God the Holy Ghost bless us, too,}

Dem   alle Welt die Ehre   tut,
To-whom all-the world - honor (ascribes),
{To whom all the world ascribes honor,}

Vor ihm sich fürchte allermeist,
 - Him -   fear   most-of-all,
{May we fear him above all,}

Und sprecht von Herzen: Amen!
And   say from-the-heart: Amen!

BWV 70
Wachet! betet! betet! wachet!
(NBA I/27; BC A165)

26. S. after Trinity (no other cantatas)
*2 Pet. 3:3–13 (Heaven and earth will be destroyed on the Day of the Lord.)
*Mt. 25:31–46 (The judgment of the world)
This cantata is an expansion of BWV 70a, for the 2. S. of Advent:
+Rom. 15:4–13 (Christ called the Gentiles as was promised)
+Lk. 21:25–36 (Return of Christ: Watch and pray so you will be ready)
Librettist: Revisions perhaps by J. S. Bach; librettist of 70a was Salomon Franck

1. Chorus (Unchanged from BWV 70a)
●Watch and pray; be prepared for Day of Judgment! (70-1)
Wachet! betet! betet! wachet!
Watch!   Pray! Pray! Watch!

Seid bereit
Be prepared

Allezeit,
At-all-times,

Bis   der Herr der Herrlichkeit
Until (the time when) the Lord of   Glory

Tit. 3:8, 14. ...Insist...that those who have believed in God may be careful to apply themselves to good deeds... Let our people learn to apply themselves to good deeds... (Also Tit. 1:16, 2:14.)
Lk. 1:74–75. ...That we...might serve [the Lord]...in holiness and righteousness before him all the days of our life.
Lev. 25:18–19 [God]: Therefore you shall do my statutes, and keep my ordinances and perform them; so you will dwell in the land securely. The land will yield its fruit, and you will eat your fill, and dwell in it securely. (Also Lev. 26:3–4, Deut. 28:11.)
Is. 55:10–11 [God]: As the rain and the snow come down from heaven, and return not thither but water the earth, making it bring forth and sprout, giving seed to the sower and bread to the eater, so shall my word be that goes forth from my mouth; it shall not return to me empty, but it shall accomplish that which I purpose, and prosper in the thing for which I sent it. (Also Mt. 13:23, Mk. 4:20.)
Deut. 26:15. [O Lord,] look down from thy holy habitation, from heaven, and bless thy people... (Also Ps. 28:9.)
Mt. 28:19. ...in the name of the Father and of the Son and of the Holy Spirit.
Ps. 66:4. [O Lord,] all the earth worships thee; they sing praises to thee, sing praises to thy name.
Deut. 6:13. You shall fear the Lord your God; you shall serve him... (Also Deut. 10:20, 13:4, Is. 8:13, Mt. 10:28.)
Ps. 9:1. I will give thanks to the Lord with my whole heart...
Ps. 106:48. Blessed be the Lord, the God of Israel, from everlasting to everlasting! And let all the people say, "Amen!" Praise the Lord!

+**Lk. 21:36 [Christ]:** Watch at all times, praying that you may have strength to escape all these things that will take place, and to stand before the Son of man. (Also Mk. 14:38, Mt. 26:41.)
+**Lk. 21:25–28, 34–35 [Christ]:** There will be signs in sun and moon and stars, and upon the earth distress of nations in perplexity at the roaring of the sea and the waves, men fainting with fear and with foreboding of what is coming on the world; for the powers of the heavens will be shaken. And then they will see the Son of man coming on the world; for the powers of the heavens will be shaken. And then they will see the Son of man coming in a cloud with power and great glory. Now when these things begin to take place, look up and raise your heads, because your redemption is drawing near...But take heed to yourselves lest your hearts be weighed down with dissipation and drunkenness and cares of this life, and that day come upon you suddenly like a snare; for it will come upon all who dwell upon the face of the whole earth.
***Mt. 25:31–34, 41 [Christ]:** When the Son of man comes in his glory, and all the angels with him, then he will sit on his glorious throne. Before him will be gathered all the nations, and he will separate them one from another as a shepherd separates the sheep from the goats, and he will place the sheep at his right hand, but the goats at the left. Then the King will say to those at his right hand, "Come, O blessed of my Father, inherit the kingdom prepared for you from the foundation of the world." ...Then he will say to those at his left hand,

Dieser   Welt ein Ende machet.
With-this world an   end   makes.
{Makes an end with this world.}

2. Bass Recit. (New addition)
●Last Day: Frightening for sinners, joyful for chosen (70-2)
Erschrecket, ihr verstockten Sünder!
Be alarmed, you   stubborn   sinners!

Ein Tag bricht an,
A   day breaks - ,

Vor   dem   sich   niemand bergen kann:
From which themselves none   hide   can;
{From which none can hide;}

Er   eilt mit dir zum strengen Rechte,
(It) speeds - you to   strict   justice,

O! sündliches Geschlechte,
O   sinful   generation,

Zum ewgen Herzeleide.
To   eternal sorrow-of-heart.

Doch euch, erwählte Gotteskinder,
But   to-you, chosen children-of-God,

Ist er ein Anfang wahrer Freude.
Is (it) (the) beginning of-true   joy.
{It is the beginning of true joy.}

Der Heiland holet euch, wenn alles   fällt und bricht,
The Savior fetches you—when everything falls and breaks—

Vor   sein erhöhtes Angesicht;
Before his   exalted countenance;

Drum   zaget nicht!
Therefore be-dismayed not!
{Therefore, be not dismayed!}

3. Alto Aria (Unchanged from BWV 70a)
●Last Day: Yearning for exodus out of this world (70-3)
Wann kömmt der Tag, an dem wir ziehen
When comes the day, on which we move
{When will the day come, on which we move}

Aus   dem Ägypten dieser Welt?
Out-of the   Egypt of-this world?

Ach! laßt uns bald aus Sodom fliehen,
Ah,   let us soon out-of Sodom flee,

Eh uns das Feuer überfällt!
Ere us   the   fire   falls-upon!
{Ere the fire falls upon us!}

"Depart from me, you cursed, into the eternal fire prepared for the devil and his angels."

*2 Pet. 3:3–4, 10. First of all you must understand this, that scoffers will come in the last days with scoffing, following their own passions and saying, "Where is the promise of his coming?"...But the day of the Lord will come like a thief, and then the heavens will pass away with a loud noise, and the elements will be dissolved with fire, and the earth and the works that are upon it will be burned up.
Jer. 19:15. Thus says the Lord of hosts, the God of Israel, Behold, I am bringing upon this city and upon all its towns all the evil that I have pronounced against it, because they have stiffened their neck, refusing to hear my words.
Mal. 3:2. Who can endure the day of his coming, and who can stand when he appears?
Nah. 1:6. Who can stand before his indignation? Who can endure the heat of his anger? His wrath is poured out like fire, and the rocks are broken asunder by him.
Rev. 6:15–17. Then the kings of the earth and the great men and the generals and the rich and the strong, and every one, slave and free, hid in the caves and among the rocks of the mountains, calling to the mountains and rocks, "Fall on us and hide us from the face of him who is seated on the throne, and from the wrath of the Lamb; for the great day of their wrath has come, and who can stand before it?" (Also Is. 2:19, Hos. 10:8, Lk. 23:30.)
1 Thess. 4:16–18, 5:4. The Lord himself will descend from heaven with a cry of command, with the archangel's call, and with the sound of the trumpet of God. And the dead in Christ will rise first; then we who are alive, who are left, shall be caught up together with them in clouds to meet the Lord in the air; and so we shall always be with the Lord. Therefore comfort one another with these words...You are not in darkness, brethren for that day to surprise you like a thief.
*Mt. 25:34 [Christ]: Then the King will say to those at his right hand, "Come, O blessed of my Father, inherit the kingdom prepared for you from the foundation of the world."
Josh. 8:1. ...Do not fear or be dismayed... (Luther: Fürchte dich nicht und zage nicht)

Ex. 13:18. God led the people round by the way of the wilderness toward the Red Sea. And the people of Israel went up out of the land of Egypt... (Also Acts 13:17.)
Gen. 19:17, 24. And when the [angels] had brought [Lot and his family] forth, they said, "Flee for your life; do not look back or stop anywhere in the valley; flee to the hills, lest you be consumed." Then the Lord rained on Sodom and Gomorrah brimstone and fire from the Lord out of heaven.
*2 Pet. 3:10. But the day of the Lord will come like a thief, and then the heavens will pass away with a loud noise, and the elements will be dissolved with fire, and the earth and the works that are upon it will be burned up.
1 Thess. 5:3. When people say, "There is peace and security," then sudden destruction will come upon them...
*2 Pet. 3:3–4. First of all you must understand this, that scoffers will come in the last days with scoffing, following their own passions and

Wacht, Seelen, auf von Sicherheit
Awake (O) Souls, - from complacency

Und glaubt, es ist die letzte Zeit!
And believe, it is the last age!
{And believe it is the last hour!}

4. Tenor Recit. (New addition)
●Yearning for heaven; spirit is willing, flesh weak (70-4)
Auch bei dem himmlischen Verlangen
Even in (our) heavenly longing

Hält unser Leib den Geist gefangen;
Holds our body the spirit captive;
{Our body holds the spirit captive;}

Es legt die Welt durch ihre Tücke
(Now) lays the world through its knavery
{For the world lays, through its knavery,}

Den Frommen Netz und Stricke.
For-the godly (a) net and snares.
{A net and snares for the godly.}

Der Geist ist willig, doch das Fleisch ist schwach;
The spirit is willing, but the flesh is weak;

Dies preßt uns aus ein jammervolles Ach!
This forces from-us - a pitiable "Alas!"

5. Soprano Aria (Unchanged from BWV 70a)
●Last Day will come despite scoffers (70-5)
Laß der Spötter Zungen schmähen,
Let the scoffers' tongues revile,

Es wird doch und muß geschehen,
It will nevertheless and must happen,
{Nevertheless, it will and has to happen,}

Daß wir Jesum werden sehen
That we Jesus will see

Auf den Wolken, in den Höhen.
On the clouds, in the heights.

Welt und Himmel mag vergehen,
World and heaven may pass-away,

Christi Wort muß fest bestehen.
Christ's word must firm endure.

Laßt der Spötter Zungen schmähen;
Let the scoffer's tongues revile;

Es wird doch und muß geschehen!
It will nevertheless and must happen!
{Nevertheless, it will and has to happen!}

saying, "Where is the promise of his coming? For ever since the fathers fell asleep, all things have continued as they were from the beginning of creation."...
1 Jn. 2:18. Children, it is the last hour; and as you have heard that antichrist is coming, so now many antichrists have come; therefore we know that it is the last hour.

Rom. 7:15, 18–25. I do not understand my own actions. For I do not do what I want, but I do the very thing I hate...I can will what is right, but I cannot do it. For I do not do the good I want, but the evil I do not want is what I do. Now if I do what I do not want, it is no longer I that do it, but sin which dwells within me. So I find it to be a law that when I want to do right, evil lies close at hand. For I delight in the law of God, in my inmost self, but I see in my members another law at war with the law of my mind and making me captive to the law of sin which dwells in my members. Wretched man that I am! Who will deliver me from this body of death? Thanks be to God through Jesus Christ our Lord! So then, I of myself serve the law of God with my mind, but with my flesh I serve the law of sin.
Mk. 14:38 [Christ]: Watch and pray that you may not enter into temptation; the spirit indeed is willing, but the flesh is weak. (Also Mt. 26:41.)
Rom. 8:23. ...We ourselves, who have the first fruits of the Spirit, groan inwardly as we wait for adoption as sons, the redemption of our bodies.

*2 Pet. 3:3–9. ...You must understand this, that scoffers will come in the last days with scoffing, following their own passions and saying, "Where is the promise of his coming? For ever since the fathers fell asleep, all things have continued as they were from the beginning of creation." They deliberately ignore this fact, that by the word of God heavens existed long ago, and an earth formed out of water and by means of water, through which the world that then existed was deluged with water and perished. But by the same word the heavens and earth that now exist have been stored up for fire, being kept until the day of judgment and destruction of ungodly men. But do not ignore this one fact, beloved, that with the Lord one day is as a thousand years, and a thousand years as one day. The Lord is not slow about his promise as some count slowness, but is forbearing toward you, not wishing that any should perish, but that all should reach repentance.
Mt. 24:30–31 [Christ]: Then will appear the sign of the Son of man in heaven, and then all the tribes of the earth will mourn, and they will see the Son of man coming on the clouds of heaven with power and great glory; and he will send out his angels with a loud trumpet call, and they will gather his elect from the four winds, from one end of heaven to the other. (Also Acts 1:11, 1 Thess. 4:16–18, Rev. 1:7.)
+Lk. 21:33 [Christ]: Heaven and earth will pass away, but my words will not pass away. (Also Mt. 24:35, Mk. 13:31.)
Is. 43:13. I am God, and also henceforth I am He; there is none who can deliver from my hand; I work and who can hinder it? (Also Is. 14:27, Job 9:12, 11:10, 42:2–3.)

6. Tenor Recit. (New Addition)
●Last Day: God remembers his servants (70-6)
Jedoch bei dem unartigen Geschlechte
Yet amidst this wicked generation

Denkt Gott an seine Knechte,
Remembers God - his servants,
{God remembers his servants,}

Daß diese böse Art
So-that this evil sort

Sie ferner nicht verletzet,
Them henceforth not injure,
{Will not injure them henceforth,}

Indem er sie in seiner Hand bewahrt
(For) he them in his hand preserves
{For he preserves them in his hand}

Und in ein himmlisch Eden setzet.
And into a heavenly Eden sets.
{And brings them to a heavenly Eden.}

7. Chorale (New addition)
●Last Day anticipated: Joy as soul thinks of heaven (70-7)
Freu dich sehr, o meine Seele,
Rejoice - greatly, O my soul,

Und vergiß all Not und Qual,
And forget all distress and torment,

Weil dich nun Christus, dein Herre,
For thee now Christ, thy Lord,
{For Christ, thy Lord,}

Ruft aus diesem Jammertal!
Calls out-of this vale-of-misery!
{Now calls thee out of this vale of misery!}

Seine Freud und Herrlichkeit
His joy and glory

Sollt du sehn in Ewigkeit,
Shalt thou see in eternity,

Mit den Engeln jubilieren,
With the angels shout-with-joy,

In Ewigkeit triumphiere n.
In eternity exult.

Acts 2:40. ...Save yourselves from this crooked generation (Luther: unartigen Leuten).
2 Pet. 2:7, 9. If he rescued righteous Lot...then the Lord knows how to rescue the godly from trial, and to keep the unrighteous under punishment until the day of judgment.
Ps. 97:10. The Lord loves those who hate evil; he preserves the lives of his saints; he delivers them from the hand of the wicked. (Also Ps. 31:3, 145:20.)
Jn. 10:27-29 [Christ]: My sheep...shall never perish, and no one shall snatch them out of my hand. My Father, who has given them to me, is greater than all, and no one is able to snatch them out of the Father's hand.
Deut. 32:9-10. The Lord's portion is his people...he encircled him, he cared for him, he kept him as the apple of his eye.
Gen. 2:8-9. The Lord God planted a garden in Eden, in the east; and there he put the man whom he had formed. And out of the ground the Lord God made to grow every tree that is pleasant to the sight and good for food, the tree of life also in the midst of the garden... (Also Rev. 2:7.)
Rev. 22:1-3. Then [the angel] showed me the river of the water of life, bright as crystal, flowing from the throne of God and of the Lamb through the middle of the street of the [heavenly] city; also, on either side of the river, the tree of life with its twelve kinds of fruit, yielding its fruit each month; and the leaves of the tree were for the healing of the nations.
Rom. 5:2. ...We rejoice in our hope of sharing the glory of God.

Mt. 5:10-12 [Christ]: Blessed are those who are persecuted for righteousness' sake, for theirs is the kingdom of heaven. Blessed are you when men revile you and persecute you...Rejoice and be glad, for your reward is great in heaven...
Jn. 14:1-3 [Christ]: Let not your hearts be troubled; believe in God, believe also in me. In my Father's house are many rooms; if it were not so, would I have told you that I go to prepare a place for you? And when I go and prepare a place for you, I will come again and will take you to myself, that where I am you may be also.
Rom. 5:2. ...We rejoice in our hope of sharing the glory of God.
1 Jn. 3:2. ...It does not yet appear what we shall be, but we know that when he appears we shall be like him, for we shall see him as he is.
Rom. 8:18. I consider that the sufferings of this present time are not worth comparing with the glory that is to be revealed to us. (Also 2 Cor. 4:17.)
Lk. 16:25. Abraham said, "Son, remember that you in your lifetime received your good things, and Lazarus in like manner evil things; but now he is comforted here [in heaven], and you are in anguish."
Rev. 5:11-12. Then I looked, and I heard around the throne and the living creatures and the elders the voice of many angels, numbering myriads of myriads and thousands of thousands, saying with a loud voice, "Worthy is the Lamb who was slain, to receive power and wealth and wisdom and might and honor and glory and blessing!"

Part II

8. Tenor Aria (Unchanged from BWV 70a)
●Last Day: Lift up your heads, O ye righteous! (70-8)
Hebt euer Haupt empor
Lift your heads aloft

Und seid getrost, ihr Frommen,
And be of-good-cheer, you godly-ones,

Zu eurer Seelen Flor!
To your souls' blooming!
{To the flourishing of your souls!}

Ihr sollt in Eden grünen,
You shall in Eden flourish,

Gott ewiglich zu dienen.
God eternally to serve.
{To serve God eternally.}

9. Bass Recit. (New addition)
●Last day: Frightening, yet Jesus comforts me (70-9)
Ach, soll nicht dieser große Tag,
Ah, should not this great day,

Der Welt Verfall
The world's collapse

Und der Posaunen Schall,
And the trumpet's peal,

Der unerhörte letzte Schlag,
The unprecedented final blow,

Des Richters ausgesprochne Worte,
Of-the judge's uttered words,

Des Höllenrachens offne Pforte
- Hell's-jaws open portal
{The open portal of hell's jaws,}

In meinem Sinn
In my mind
{Awaken in my mind}

Viel Zweifel, Furcht und Schrecken,
Much doubt, fear, and terror,

Der ich ein Kind der Sünden bin,
(Since) I a child of sin am,
{Since I am a child of sin?}

Is. 51:6. Lift up your eyes to the heavens, and look at the earth beneath; for the heavens will vanish like smoke, the earth will wear out like a garment, and they who dwell in it will die like gnats; but my salvation will be for ever, and my deliverance will never be ended.
Lk. 21:28 [Christ]: Now when these things begin to take place, look up and raise your heads, because your redemption is drawing near.
Hos. 14:7 [God]: ...[My people] shall flourish as a garden; they shall blossom as the vine, their fragrance shall be like the wine of Lebanon. (Also Ps. 92:12–13, Prov. 11:28, Is. 66:14.)
Rev. 7:15-17. Therefore are [the righteous] before the throne of God, and serve him day and night within his temple; and he who sits upon the throne will shelter them with his presence. They shall hunger no more, neither thirst any more; the sun shall not strike them, nor any scorching heat. For the Lamb in the midst of the throne will be their shepherd, and he will guide them to springs of living water; and God will wipe away every tear from their eyes. (Also Rev. 21:4, Is. 25:8.)

*2 Pet. 3:7, 10. ...The heavens and earth that now exist have been stored up for fire, being kept until the day of judgment and destruction of ungodly men...The day of the Lord will come like a thief, and then the heavens will pass away with a loud noise, and the elements will be dissolved with fire, and the earth and the works that are upon it will be burned up.
*Mt. 25:31–34, 41 [Christ]: When the Son of man comes in his glory, and all the angels with him, then he will sit on his glorious throne. Before him will be gathered all the nations, and he will separate them one from another as a shepherd separates the sheep from the goats, and he will place the sheep at his right hand, but the goats at the left. Then the King will say to those at his right hand, "Come, O blessed of my Father, inherit the kingdom prepared for you from the foundation of the world." ...Then he will say to those at his left hand, "Depart from me, you cursed, into the eternal fire prepared for the devil and his angels."
Ps. 96:13. ...He comes to judge the earth... (Also Ps. 98:9.)
1 Thess. 4:16. For the Lord himself will descend from heaven with a cry of command, with the archangel's call, and with the sound of the trumpet of God...
Mt. 13:41–42. The Son of man will send his angels, and they will gather out of his kingdom all causes of sin and all evildoers, and throw them into the furnace of fire...
Is. 5:14. Sheol (Luther: Hölle) has enlarged its appetite and opened its mouth beyond measure (Luther: Rachen aufgetan ohne alle Maß)...
Zeph. 1:14-16, 2:3. The great day of the Lord is near, near and hastening fast; the sound of the day of the Lord is bitter, the mighty man cries aloud there. A day of wrath is that day, a day of distress and anguish, a day of ruin and devastation, a day of darkness and gloom, a day of clouds and thick darkness, a day of trumpet blast and battle cry...Seek the Lord, all you humble of the land, who do his commands; seek righteousness, seek humility; perhaps you may be hidden on the day of the wrath of the Lord.
Joel 2:11. ...The day of the Lord is great and very terrible; who can endure it? (Also Joel 2:30–31, Amos 5:18, Acts 17:31, Thess. 5:2.)

Erwecken?
Awaken?
{ - }

Jedoch, es gehet meiner Seelen
Yet,   (now) rises in-my soul

Ein Freudenschein, ein Licht des Trostes auf.
A   ray-of-joy,   a light of comfort - .

Der Heiland kann sein Herze nicht verhehlen,
The Savior can his heart not conceal,

So   vor Erbarmen bricht,
Which in   pity   breaks,

Sein Gnadenarm verläßt mich nicht.
His arm-of-mercy forsakes me not.

Wohlan, so ende ich mit Freuden meinen Lauf.
Well-then, so end I with joy   my course.
{Well then, I will finish my course with joy.}

10. Bass Aria (Unchanged from BWV 70a)
●Last Day anticipated despite cataclysmic events (70–10)
Seligster   Erquickungstag,
Most-blessed day-of-refreshment,

Führe mich zu deinen Zimmern!
Lead me to thy chambers!

Schalle, knalle, letzter Schlag,
Resound, explode, final   blow;

Welt und Himmel, geht zu Trümmern!
World and heaven, go to   pieces!

Jesus führet mich zur Stille,
Jesus leads me to quietness,

An den Ort,   da Lust und Fülle.
To the place, where delight and abundance (are).

11. Chorale (Unchanged from BWV 70a)
●Rejection of world in favor of Jesus (70–11)
Nicht nach   Welt, nach Himmel nicht
Not   for (the) world, for heaven not

1 Jn. 4:17–18. In this is love perfected with us, that we may have confidence for the day of judgment, because as he is so are we in this world. There is no fear in love, but perfect love casts out fear. For fear has to do with punishment, and he who fears is not perfected in love.
Jn. 5:24 [Christ]: ...He who hears my word and believes him who sent me, has eternal life; he does not come into judgment, but has passed from death to life. (Also Rom. 6:23, 8:1.)
Ps. 103:8–12. The Lord is merciful and gracious, slow to anger and abounding in steadfast love. He will not always chide, nor will he keep his anger for ever. He does not deal with us according to our sins, nor requite us according to our iniquities. For as the heavens are high above the earth, so great is his steadfast love (Luther: läßt er seine Gnade walten) toward those who fear him; as far as the east is from the west, so far does he remove our transgressions from us.
Jer. 31:20 [God]: Is Ephraim my dear son? Is he my darling child? For as often as I speak against him, I do remember him still. Therefore my heart yearns for him (Luther: bricht mir mein Herz); I will surely have mercy on him, says the Lord.
Rom. 8:31, 33–34. What then shall we say to this? If God is for us, who is against us?...Who shall bring any charge against God's elect? It is God who justifies; who is to condemn?
2 Tim. 4:7–8. I have fought the good fight, I have finished the race, I have kept the faith. Henceforth there is laid up for me the crown of righteousness, which the Lord, the righteous judge, will award to me on that Day, and not only to me but also to all who have loved his appearing.

Rev. 21:1–4. Then I saw a new heaven and a new earth; for the first heaven and the first earth had passed away, and the sea was no more. And I saw the holy city, new Jerusalem, coming down out of heaven from God, prepared as a bride adorned for her husband; and I heard a loud voice from the throne saying, "Behold, the dwelling of God is with men. He will dwell with them, and they shall be his people, and God himself will be with them; he will wipe away every tear from their eyes, and death shall be no more, neither shall there be mourning nor crying nor pain any more, for the former things have passed away."
Jn. 14:1–3 [Christ]: Let not your hearts be troubled; believe in God, believe also in me. In my Father's house are many rooms; if it were not so, would I have told you that I go to prepare a place for you? And when I go and prepare a place for you, I will come again and will take you to myself, that where I am you may be also.
Heb. 12:28. Therefore let us be grateful for receiving a kingdom that cannot be shaken...
Ps. 16:11. [O Lord,] thou dost show me the path of life; in thy presence there is fulness of joy, in thy right hand are pleasures for evermore.

1 Jn. 2:15–17. Do not love the world or the things in the world. If any one loves the world, love for the Father is not in him. For all that is in the world, the lust of the flesh and the lust of the eyes and the pride of life, is not of the Father but is of the world. And the world passes away, and the lust of it; but he who does the will of God abides for ever. (Also Jms. 4:4.)

Meine Seele wünscht und sehnet.
(Does) my soul wish and yearn.

Jesum wünsch ich und sein Licht,
Jesus desire I and his light,
{I desire Jesus and his light,}

Der mich hat mit Gott versöhnet,
Who me has with God reconciled,
{Who me with God did reconcile,}

Der mich freiet vom Gericht,
Who me frees from judgment,
{Who frees me from judgment;}

Meinen Jesum laß ich nicht.
My Jesus leave I not.
{I will not let my Jesus go.}

BWV 71
Gott ist mein König
(NBA I/32; BC B1)

Change of Town Council in Mühlhausen (BWV 71, 119, 193, 120, 29, 69)
No specific lessons
Librettist: Unknown; perhaps Georg Christian Eilmar

1. Chorus
●Old age reminisces about God's help: Ps. 74:12[1] (71-1)
Gott ist mein König von altersher,
God is my king from of-old,

der alle Hilfe tut, so auf Erden geschieht.
who all (the) help does, which on earth occurs.
{from whom all help on earth comes.}

2. Tenor Aria & Soprano Chorale
●Old age too feeble for new tasks: 2 Sam. 19:35, 37 (71-2)
Tenor:
Ich bin nun achtzig Jahr, warum soll dein Knecht
I am now eighty years, why should thy servant

sich mehr beschweren? Ich will umkehren,
 - further complain? I will turn-back,

daß ich sterbe in meiner Stadt, bei meines Vaters
that I die in my city, beside my father's

Ps. 73:25. [O Lord,] whom have I in heaven but thee? And there is nothing upon earth that I desire besides thee.
Phil. 1:21. To me to live is Christ, and to die is gain.
Jn. 8:12. Jesus spoke to them, saying, "I am the light of the world; he who follows me will not walk in darkness, but will have the light of life."
Ps. 36:9. [O Lord,] with thee is the fountain of life; in thy light do we see light.
Rom. 5:1-2, 10. Therefore, since we are justified by faith, we have peace with God through our Lord Jesus Christ. Through him we have obtained access to this grace in which we stand, and we rejoice in our hope of sharing the glory of God...For if, while we were enemies we were reconciled to God by the death of his Son, much more, now that we are reconciled, shall we be saved by his life. (Also 2 Cor. 5:18.)
Jn. 5:24 [Christ]: ...He who hears my word and believes him who sent me, has eternal life; he does not come into judgment, but has passed from death to life.
Acts 4:12. And there is salvation in no one else, for there is no other name under heaven given among men by which we must be saved. (Also Jn. 14:6.)
S. of S. 3:4 [Bride]: ...I found him whom my soul loves. I held him, and would not let him go... (Also Gen. 32:26.)
Rev. 3:11 [Christ]: I am coming soon; hold fast what you have, so that no one may seize your crown.

Ps. 74:12. *God my King is from of old, working salvation in the midst of the earth.*[1]
Ps. 44:1, 4. We have heard with our ears, O God, our fathers have told us, what deeds thou didst perform in their days in the days of old ...Thou art my King and my God, who ordainest victories for Jacob.
Ps. 135:13-14. Thy name, O Lord, endures for ever, thy renown, O Lord, throughout all ages. For the Lord will vindicate his people, and have compassion on his servants.
Job 8:8-9. Inquire, I pray you, of bygone ages, and consider what the fathers have found; for we are but of yesterday, and know nothing, for our days on earth are a shadow.

2 Sam. 19:33-35, 37. King [David] said to Barzillai, "Come over with me, and I will provide for you with me in Jerusalem." But Barzillai said to the king "How many years have I still to live, that I should go up with the king to Jerusalem? *I am this day eighty ears old; can I discern what is pleasant and what is not? Can your servant taste what he eats or what he drinks? Can I still listen to the voice of singing men and singing women? Why then should your servant be an added burden to my lord the king?*...Pray let your servant return, that I may die in my own city, near the grave of my father and my mother. But here

[1]This verse is the central line in the original Hebrew psalm text. The literary device of placing a key thematic line at the very center of a psalm was common. See N.I.V. Study Bible, note to Ps. 6:6.

und meiner Mutter Grab.
and   my   mother's grave.

Soprano:
Soll ich auf dieser Welt
Should I (in) this world
{If I should in this world}

Mein Leben höher bringen,
My   life higher bring,
{My life extend,}

Durch manchen sauren Tritt
By   many-a bitter step (should)

Hindurch ins Alter dringen,
Through into old-age press,

Soprano:
So gib   Geduld, vor Sünd
Then grant (me) patience; from sin

Und Schanden mich bewahr,
And disgrace   me   protect,
{And disgrace protect me,}

Auf daß ich tragen mag
So that I might-wear

Soprano:
Mit Ehren graues Haar.
With honor gray   hair.
{Gray hair with honor.}

3. S.A.T.B. Quartet
●Old age: Blessing to old age: Deut. 33:25; Gen. 21:22 (71-3)
    Dein Alter sei wie deine Jugend,
(May) your old-age be like your   youth,

und Gott ist mit dir in allem, das du tust.
and God is with you in all   that you do.

4. Bass Arioso
●God ordains course of whole universe: Ps. 74:16–17 (71-4)
Tag und Nacht ist dein. Du machest, daß beide,
Day and night is thine. Thou ordainest, that both,

Sonn und Gestirn, ihren gewissen Lauf haben.
Sun and stars, their fixed   course have.

Du setzest einem jeglichen Lande seine Grenze.
Thou settest (for)   every   land   its   borders.

is your servant Chimham; let him go over with my lord the king; and do for him whatever seems good to you."
Ps. 90:10. The years of our life are threescore and ten, or even by reason of strength fourscore; yet their span is but toil and trouble; they are soon gone, and we fly away.
Ps. 71:9, 17–20. [O Lord,] do not cast me off in the time of old age; forsake me not when my strength is spent...O God, from my youth thou hast taught me, and I still proclaim thy wondrous deeds. So even to old age and gray hairs, O God, do not forsake me, till I proclaim thy might to all the generations to come. Thy power and thy righteousness, O God, reach the high heavens. Thou who hast done great things, O God who is like thee? Thou who hast made me see many sore troubles wilt revive me again; from the depths of the earth thou wilt bring me up again.
Is. 46:4 [God]: Even to your old age I am He, and to gray hairs I will carry you.
Prov. 16:31. A hoary head is a crown of glory; it is gained in a righteous life.
Tit. 2:2. Bid the older men be temperate, serious, sensible, sound in faith, in love and in steadfastness.
Mt. 10:22. ...He who endures to the end will be saved. (Also Mt. 24:13, Mk. 13:13, Lk. 21:19.)
Gal. 6:9. And let us not grow weary in well-doing, for in due season we shall reap, if we do not lose heart.
Rev. 2:10 [Christ]: Do not fear what you are about to suffer...Be faithful unto death, and I will give you the crown of life.
Jude 1:24–25. Now to him who is able to keep you from falling and to present you without blemish before the presence of his glory with rejoicing, to the only God, our Savior through Jesus Christ our Lord, be glory, majesty, dominion, and authority...Amen.

Deut. 33:25. Your bars shall be iron and bronze; and *as your days, so shall your strength be.*
Gen. 21:22. At that time Abimelech and Phicol the commander of his army said to Abraham, *"God is with you in all that you do."*
Deut. 4:40. Therefore you shall keep [God's] statutes and his commandments, which I command you this day, that it may go well with you, and with your children after you, and that you may prolong your days in the land which the Lord your God gives you for ever. (Also Deut. 5:33.)

Ps. 74:16–17, 19. *Thine is the day, thine also the night; thou hast established the luminaries and the sun. Thou hast fixed all the bounds of the earth; thou hast made summer and winter. Jer. 31:35–36.* Thus says the Lord, who gives the sun for light by day and the fixed order of the moon and the stars for light by night, who stirs up the sea so that its waves roar—the Lord of hosts is his name; "If this fixed order departs from before me, says the Lord, then shall the descendants of Israel cease from being a nation before me for ever." (Also Amos 5:8, Ps. 19:5–6, 74:16.)
Acts 17:26. [God] made from one [man] every nation of men to live on all the face of the earth, having determined allotted periods and the boundaries of their habitation. (Also Deut. 32:8.)

5. Alto Aria
●Praise to God for mighty power which keeps our land (71-5)
Durch mächtige Kraft
With   mighty   power

Erhältst   du unsre Grenzen,
Preservest thou   our   borders,

Hier muß der Friede glänzen,
Here must - peace shine,
{Here peace must shine,}

Wenn Mord und   Kriegessturm
Though murder and (the) storm-of-war

Sich allerorts   erhebt.
- Everywhere (else) arise.
{Arise everywhere else.}

Wenn Kron und Zepter bebt,
If   crown and scepter shake,

    Hast du das Heil geschafft
(Then) hast thou - salvation provided

Durch mächtige Kraft!
Through mighty power!

6. Chorus
●Prayer for protection from enemies: Ps. 74:19 (71-6)
Du wollest dem Feinde nicht geben
(Mayest) thou   -   to-the foe   not   give

die Seele deiner Turteltauben.
the soul of-thy   turtledoves.

7. Chorus
●Prayer for continued blessing on new government (71-7)
Das neue Regiment
(This) new government

Auf jeglichen Wegen
(In)   every endeavor

Bekröne mit Segen!
Crown with blessing!
{Please crown this new government with blessing in every endeavor!}

Friede,   Ruh und Wohlergehen
Harmony, peace, and prosperity

Müsse stets   zur Seite stehen
Must constantly   attend

Dem neuen Regiment.
(This) new government.

///

Ps. 125:1-5. Those who trust in the Lord are like Mount Zion, which cannot be moved, but abides for ever. As the mountains are round about Jerusalem, so the Lord is round about his people, from this time forth and for evermore. For the scepter of wickedness shall not rest upon the land allotted to the righteous, lest the righteous put forth their hands to do wrong. Do good, O Lord, to those who are good, and to those who are upright in their hearts! But those who turn aside upon their crooked ways the Lord will lead away with evildoers! Peace be in Israel!
Mt. 24:6. You will hear of wars and rumors of wars; see that you are not alarmed...
Ps. 147:12-14. Praise the Lord, O Jerusalem! Praise your God, O Zion! For he strengthens the bars of your gates; he blesses your sons within you. He makes peace in your borders; he fills you with the finest of the wheat.
Ps. 28:8-9. The Lord is the strength of his people, he is the saving refuge of his anointed. O save thy people, and bless thy heritage; be thou their shepherd, and carry them for ever.
Ps. 68:32, 34-35. Sing to God, O kingdoms of the earth; sing praises to the Lord...Ascribe power to God whose majesty is over Israel, and his power is in the skies. Terrible is God in his sanctuary, the God of Israel, he gives power and strength to his people. Blessed be God! (Also Ps. 29:1, 10-11.)

Ps. 74:19. *Do not deliver the soul of thy dove to the wild beasts;* do not forget the life of thy poor for ever.
Is. 59:11. ...We moan and moan like doves; we look for justice, but there is none, for salvation, but it is far from us. (Also Is. 38:14, S. of S. 6:9.)
Ps. 17:7-9. Wondrously show thy steadfast love, O savior of those who seek refuge from their adversaries at thy right hand. Keep me as the apple of the eye; hide me in the shadow of thy wings, from the wicked who despoil me, my deadly enemies who surround me.

Ps. 28:8-9. The Lord is the strength of his people, he is the saving refuge of his anointed. O save thy people, and bless thy heritage; be thou their shepherd, and carry them for ever.
Ps. 29:11. May the Lord give strength to his people! May the Lord bless his people with peace! (Also Ps. 3:8.)
Ps. 115:12-15. The Lord has been mindful of us; he will bless us; he will bless the house of Israel; he will bless the house of Aaron; he will bless those who fear the Lord, both small and great. May the Lord give you increase, you and your children! May you be blessed by the Lord, who made heaven and earth!
Ps. 128:5-6. The Lord bless you from Zion! May you see the prosperity of Jerusalem all the days of your life! May you see your children's children! Peace be upon Israel!
Ps. 144:12-15. May our sons in their youth be like plants full grown, our daughters like corner pillars cut for the structure of a palace; may our garners be full, providing all manner of store; may our sheep bring forth thousands and ten thousands in our fields; may our cattle be heavy with young, suffering no mischance or failure in bearing; may there be no cry of distress in our streets! Happy the people to whom such blessings fall! Happy the people whose God is the Lord! (Also Ps. 33:12.)

Glück,   Heil   und großer Sieg
Fortune, prosperity, and great victory

Muß täglich von neuen
Must daily   anew

Dich, Joseph, erfreuen,
Thee, Joseph, delight,
{Must delight thee, Joseph, anew each day,}

Daß an allen Ort und Landen
That in every region and territory

Ganz   beständig sei vorhanden
Altogether steadfast might-be present

Glück,   Heil   und großer Sieg!
Fortune, prosperity, and great victory!

Lam. 3:22–23. The steadfast love of the Lord never ceases, his mercies never come to an end; they are new every morning; great is thy faithfulness. (Also Ps. 90:14.)

Deut. 33:1, 13–16. This is the blessing with which Moses the man of God blessed the children of Israel before his death...And of Joseph he said, "Blessed by the Lord be his land, with the choicest gifts of heaven above, and of the deep that couches beneath, with the choicest fruits of the sun, and the rich yield of the months, with the finest produce of the ancient mountains, and the abundance of the everlasting hills, with the best gifts of the earth and its fulness, and the favor of him that dwelt in the bush. Let these come upon the head of Joseph, and upon the crown of the head of him that is prince among his brothers."

Ps. 147:13–14. [The Lord] strengthens the bars of your gates; he blesses your sons within you. He makes peace in your borders; he fills you with the finest of the wheat.

Ps. 3:9. Deliverance belongs to the Lord; thy blessing be upon thy people!

BWV 72
Alles nur nach Gottes Willen
(NBA I/6; BC A37)

3. S. after Epiphany (BWV 73, 111, 72, 156)
*Rom. 12:16[1]–21 (Overcoming evil with good)
*Mt. 8:1–13 (Jesus heals a leper; the centurion from Capernaum comes to Jesus)
[1]Begin: "Never be conceited."
Librettist: Salomon Franck

1. Chorus
●God's sovereign will trusted in good & bad times (72-1)
Alles   nur   nach Gottes Willen,
All-things only according-to God's will,

So   bei Lust als   Traurigkeit,
Thus (may it be) in delight as (in) sadness,

So   bei gut als   böser Zeit.
Thus (may it be) in good as (in) evil times.

Gottes Wille soll mich stillen
God's will shall me quieten
{God's will shall quieten me}

Bei Gewölk und   Sonnenschein.
Amidst cloud and (amidst) sunshine.

Alles   nur   nach   Gottes Willen!
Everything only according-to God's   will!

Dies soll meine Losung sein.
This shall my watchword be.

*Mt. 8:1–3. When [Jesus] came down from the mountain, great crowds followed him; and behold, a leper came to him and knelt before him, saying, "Lord, if you will, you can make me clean." And he stretched out his hand and touched him, saying, "I will; be clean." And immediately his leprosy was cleansed.

Mt. 26:39, 42. Going a little farther [in the garden of Gethsemane, Jesus] fell on his face and prayed, "My Father, if it be possible, let this cup pass from me; nevertheless, not as I will, but as thou wilt." ... Again, for the second time, he went away and prayed, "My Father, if this cannot pass unless I drink it, thy will be done."

Mt. 6:9–10 [Christ]: Pray then like this: Our Father who art in heaven, Hallowed be thy name. Thy kingdom come, Thy will be done, On earth as it is in heaven.

Ps. 62:1. For God alone my soul waits in silence... (Luther: Meine Seele ist stille zu Gott)

Ps. 131:2. I have calmed and quieted my soul, like a child quieted at its mother's breast; like a child that is quieted is my soul. (Also Lam. 3:26).

Job 1:21. [Job] said, "Naked I came from my mother's womb, and naked shall I return; the Lord gave, and the Lord has taken away; blessed be the name of the Lord."

Job 2:10. But [Job] said to [his wife], "You speak as one of the foolish women would speak. Shall we receive good at the hand of God, and shall we not receive evil?" In all this Job did not sin with his lips.

1 Pet. 4:19. Therefore let those who suffer according to God's will do right and entrust their souls to a faithful Creator.

2a. Alto Recit.
●God's sovereign will: Submission brings blessings (72-2a)
O selger   Christ,
O blessed (is the) Christian,
{How blessed is the Christian,}

        der allzeit seinen   Willen
        who always   his (own) will

In Gottes Willen senkt, es gehe wie es   gehe,
In God's   will submerges, it go   as it (may) go,
{To God's will submits, no matter what happens}

Bei Wohl und Wehe.
In weal and woe.

Herr, so du willt,
Lord, if thou wilt,

        so muß sich alles   fügen!
        then must - all-things accomodate-themselves!

Herr, so du willt, so kannst du mich vergnügen!
Lord, if thou wilt, then canst thou me   satisfy!

Herr, so du willt,   verschwindet meine Pein!
Lord, if thou wilt, (then) vanishes   my   pain!

Herr, so du willt,   werd ich gesund und rein!
Lord, if thou wilt, (then) become I healthy and clean!

Herr, so du willt,   wird Traurigkeit zur Freude!
Lord, if thou wilt, (then) (turns) sadness   to   joy!

Herr, so du willt,   find ich auf Dornen   Weide!
Lord, if thou wilt, (then) find I amidst thorns (a) pasture!

Herr, so du willt,   werd ich einst selig sein!
Lord, if thou wilt, (then) will I one-day blessed be!

Herr, so du willt,
Lord, if thou wilt,

—laß mich dies Wort   im Glauben fassen
—let me this expression by   faith   grasp

Und meine Seele stillen!—
And my   soul   quieten!—

Herr, so du willt, so sterb ich nicht,
Lord, if thou wilt, then die I   not,
{Lord, if thou wilt, then I shall not die,}

Ob   Leib und Leben mich verlassen,
Even-though body and life   me   forsake,

Wenn mir dein Geist dies Wort ins   Herze spricht!
If   -   thy Spirit this word into (my) heart speaks!
{If thy Spirit speaks this word into my heart!}

Mt. 26:39, 42. Going a little farther [Jesus] fell on his face and prayed, "My Father, if it be possible, let this cup pass from me; nevertheless, not as I will, but as thou wilt." ...Again, for the second time, he went away and prayed, "My Father, if this cannot pass unless I drink it, thy will be done."
Mt. 6:9–10 [Christ]: Pray then like this: Our Father who art in heaven, Hallowed be thy name. Thy kingdom come, Thy will be done...
Job 1:21. ...The Lord gave, and the Lord has taken away; blessed be the name of the Lord.
Job 2:10. ...Shall we receive good at the hand of God, and shall we not receive evil?...
Dan. 3:16–18. Shadrach, Meshach, and Abednego answered the king, "O Nebuchadnezzar, we have no need to answer you in this matter. If it be so, our God whom we serve is able to deliver us from the burning fiery furnace; and he will deliver us out of your hand, O king. But if not, be it known to you, O king, that we will not serve your gods or worship the golden image which you have set up."
Mk. 10:27. ...[Christ]: With men it is impossible, but not with God; for all things are possible with God. (Also Mt. 19:26, Lk. 18:27.)
***Mt. 8:3.** [Jesus] stretched out his hand and touched [the leper], saying, "I will; be clean." And immediately his leprosy was cleansed.
Ps. 30:11. [O Lord,] thou hast turned for me my mourning into dancing; thou hast loosed my sackcloth and girded me with gladness. (Also Ps. 30:5, 126:6.)
Jer. 31:13 [God]: Then shall the maidens rejoice in the dance, and the young men and the old shall be merry. I will turn their mourning into joy, I will comfort them, and give them gladness for sorrow. (Also Ps. 30:11.)
Ezek. 28:24. For the house of Israel there shall be no more a brier to prick or a thorn to hurt them...
Is. 35:6. Waters shall break forth in the wilderness, and streams in the desert. (Also Is. 43:19–20.)
Is. 55:13. Instead of the thorn shall come up the cypress; instead of the brier shall come up the myrtle...
***Mt. 8:5–10.** As [Jesus] entered Capernaum, a centurion came forward to him, beseeching him and saying, "Lord, my servant is lying paralyzed at home, in terrible distress." And he said to him, "I will come and heal him." But the centurion answered him, "Lord, I am not worthy to have you come under my roof; but only say the word, and my servant will be healed. For I am a man under authority, with soldiers under me; and I say to one, 'Go,' and he goes, and to another, 'Come,' and he comes, and to my slave, 'Do this,' and he does it." When Jesus heard him, he marveled, and said to those who followed him, "Truly, I say to you, not even in Israel have I found such faith."
Ps. 62:1. For God alone my soul waits in silence (Luther: meine Seele ist stille zu Gott); from him comes my salvation.
Jn. 11:25–26. Jesus said to [Martha], "I am the resurrection and the life; he who believes in me, though he die, yet shall he live, and whoever lives and believes in me shall never die. Do you believe this?"

2b. Alto Aria

●God's sovereign will: I shall trust it always (72-2b)
Mit allem, was ich hab und bin,
With all,   that I have and am,

Will ich mich   Jesu lassen,
Will I myself (to) Jesus relinquish,
{Will I relinquish myself to Jesus,}

Kann gleich mein schwacher Geist und Sinn
Can though my   weak   spirit and mind
{Though my weak spirit and mind can}

Des Höchsten   Rat nicht fassen;
The Most-High's counsel not comprehend;

        Er führe mich nur immer hin
(Yet may) he lead   me -   ever forth
{Yet I allow him to lead me ever forth}

Auf   Dorn- und Rosenstraßen!
Upon (paths of) thorn (or) (paths)-of-roses!

3. Bass Recit.

●God's sovereign will is that he should bless you! (72–3)
So glaube nun!
So believe now!

Dein Heiland saget: Ich will's tun!
Thy Savior says: I will-it do!
{Thy Savior says: I will do it!}

Er pflegt die Gnadenhand
He is-given (his) hand-of-grace

Noch willigst auszustrecken,
Yet willingly to-extend,
{He is given to stretching out his hand willingly,}

Wenn Kreuz und Leiden dich erschrecken,
When cross and suffering thee frighten,
{When cross and suffering frighten thee,}

Er kennet deine Not und   löst dein Kreuzesband.
He knows thy   need and loosens thy   cross's-fetter.

Er   stärkt,   was   schwach,
He strengthens, what (is) weak,

Und will das niedre Dach
And will the lowly roof

Der armen Herzen nicht verschmähen,
Of poor   hearts   not   despise,

Darunter   gnädig einzugehen.
Thereunder graciously to-enter.
{And will not despise to enter graciously under the lowly roof of poor hearts.}

Ps. 31:14–15. But I trust in thee, O Lord, I say, "Thou art my God." My times are in thy hand...

Rom. 14:8. If we live, we live to the Lord, and if we die, we die to the Lord; so then, whether we live or whether we die, we are the Lord's. (Phil. 1:21, 2 Cor. 5:9)

1 Pet. 4:19. Therefore let those who suffer according to God's will do right and entrust their souls to a faithful Creator.

1 Pet. 5:7. Cast all your anxieties on him, for he cares about you.

Job 11:7–9. Can you find out the deep things of God? Can you find out the limit of the Almighty? It is higher than heaven—what can you do? Deeper than Sheol—what can you know? Its measure is longer than the earth, and broader than the sea.

Is. 55:9. For as the heavens are higher than the earth, so are my ways higher than your ways and my thoughts than your thoughts [says the Lord]. (Also Prov. 20:24.)

Job 12:13. With God are wisdom and might; he has counsel and understanding. (Also Ps. 33:11.)

Ps. 131:1–2. O Lord, my heart is not lifted up, my eyes are not raised too high; I do not occupy myself with things too great and too marvelous for me. But I have calmed and quieted my soul, like a child quieted at its mother's breast; like a child that is quieted is my soul.

*Mt. 8:1–3. When [Jesus] came down from the mountain, great crowds followed him; and behold, a leper came to him and knelt before him, saying, "Lord, if you will, you can make me clean." And he stretched out his hand and touched him, saying, "I will; be clean." And immediately his leprosy was cleansed.

Ezek. 34:16 [God]: I will seek the lost, and I will bring back the strayed, and I will bind up the crippled, and I will strengthen the weak, and the fat and the strong I will watch over; I will feed them in justice.

Jer. 29:11. I know the plans I have for you, says the Lord, plans for welfare and not for evil, to give you a future and a hope. (Also Prov. 23:18.)

Ps. 102:17. [The Lord] will regard the prayer of the destitute, and will not despise their supplication.

Acts 14:22. ...Through many tribulations we must enter the kingdom of God.

Mt. 10:38 [Christ]: He who does not take his cross and follow me is not worthy of me.

Mt. 16:24 [Christ]: If any man would come after me, let him deny himself and take up his cross and follow me. (Also Mk. 8:34, Lk. 9:23.)

Ps. 34:19. Many are the afflictions of the righteous; but the Lord delivers him out of them all.

*Mt. 8:5–8. As [Jesus] entered Capernaum, a centurion came forward to him, beseeching him and saying, "Lord, my servant is lying paralyzed at home, in terrible distress." And he said to him, "I will come and heal him." But the centurion answered him, "Lord, I am not worthy to have you come under my roof; but only say the word, and my servant will be healed."

Job 36:5. Behold, God is mighty, and does not despise any...

Is. 57:15. For thus says the high and lofty One who inhabits eternity, whose name is Holy: "I dwell in the high and holy place, and also with him who is of a contrite and humble spirit, to revive the spirit of the humble, and to revive the heart of the contrite."

4. Soprano Aria
●God's sovereign will is to sweeten thy cross! (72–4)
Mein Jesus will es tun, er will dein Kreuz versüßen.
My Jesus would it do; he would thy cross sweeten.
{My Jesus wants to do it; he will sweeten thy cross.}

Obgleich dein Herze liegt in viel Bekümmernissen,
Though thy heart lie in many   afflictions,

Soll es   doch   sanft und still
Shall it nevertheless gently and quietly

　　　in seinen Armen ruhn,
　　　in   his   arms   rest,
{It shall nevertheless rest gently and quietly in his arms,}

Wenn ihn   der Glaube faßt;
If   it (by) -   faith is-grasped;

　　　mein Jesus will es tun!
　　　my   Jesus will it do!
　　　(my Jesus will do it!}

5. Chorale (See also 111–1, 144–6.)
●God's sovereign will desired at all times (72–5)
Was   mein Gott will, das g'scheh allzeit,
Whatever my God wills, that be-done always,

Sein Will, der ist der beste,
His will, it is the best,

Zu helfen den'n er ist bereit,
To help all-them he is prepared,

Die an ihn glauben feste.
Who on him believe steadfastly.

Der hilft aus Not,   der fromme Gott,
He helps out-of trouble, (this) righteous God,

Und züchtiget mit Maßen.
And chastises with measure.

Wer   Gott vertraut, fest auf ihn baut,
Whoever (in) God trusts, firmly on him builds,

Den will er nicht verlassen.
Him will he not   forsake.

Mt. 8:3. And [Jesus] stretched out his hand and touched him, saying, "I will; be clean."...
Mk. 8:34 [Christ]: ...If any man would come after me, let him...take up his cross and follow me. (Also Mt. 10:38, 16:24, Lk. 9:23.)
Ps. 94:19. [O Lord,] when the cares of my heart are many, thy consolations cheer my soul.
Jn. 10:10, 14–15, 27–28 [Christ]: ...I came that they may have life, and have it abundantly...I am the good shepherd; I know my own and my own know me, as the Father knows me and I know the Father; and I lay down my life for the sheep...My sheep hear my voice, and I know them, and they follow me; and I give them eternal life, and they shall never perish, and no one shall snatch them out of my hand.
Ps. 131:2. I have calmed and quieted my soul, like a child quieted at its mother's breast...
Lam. 3:26. It is good that one should wait quietly for the salvation of the Lord.
***Mt. 8:10, 13.** When Jesus heard him, he marveled, and said to those who followed him, "Truly, I say to you, not even in Israel have I found such faith..." And to the centurion Jesus said, "Go; be it done for you as you have believed." And the servant was healed at that very moment.

Mt. 26:39. ...[O Lord,] not as I will, but as thou wilt.
Mt. 6:10. Thy kingdom come, Thy will be done...
Rom. 8:28. We know that in everything God works for good with those who love him, who are called according to his purpose.
Ps. 33:18–19. Behold, the eye of the Lord is on those who fear him, on those who hope in his steadfast love, that he may deliver their soul from death, and keep them alive in famine.
Jer. 30:11. For I am with you to save you, says the Lord; I will make a full end of all the nations among whom I scattered you, but of you I will not make a full end. I will chasten you in just measure (Luther: züchtigen...mit Maßen), and I will by no means leave you unpunished. (Also Jer. 4:27, 5:10, 5:18, 46:28, Ezek. 20:17.)
Heb. 12:6. The Lord disciplines him whom he loves, and chastises every son whom he receives.
Mt. 7:24 [Christ]: Every one then who hears these words of mine and does them will be like a wise man who built his house upon the rock.
1 Cor. 3:11. No other foundation can any one lay than that which is laid, which is Jesus Christ.
Mt. 28:20 [Jesus]: ...Lo, I am with you always to the close of the age.
Heb. 13:5. ...He has said, "I will never fail you nor forsake you."

BWV 73
Herr, wie du willt, so schick's mit mir
(NBA I/6; BC A35)

3. S. after Epiphany (BWV 73, 111, 72, 156)
*Rom. 12:16[1]-21 (Overcoming evil with good)
*Mt. 8:1-13 (Jesus heals a leper; the centurion from Capernaum comes to Jesus)
[1]Begin: "Never be conceited."
Librettist: Unknown

1. Chorale & S. T. B. Recits. (Chorale: see also 156-6)
●God's sovereign will to be trusted even in suffering (73-1)
Chorale:
Herr, wie du willt, so schick's mit mir
Lord, as thou wilt, so ordain-it for me

Im Leben und im Sterben!
In living and in dying!

Tenor:
Ach! aber ach! wieviel
Alas! But alas! How-much

Läßt mich dein Wille leiden!
Lets me thy will suffer!
{How much thy will lets me suffer!}

Mein Leben ist des Unglücks Ziel,
My life is - misfortune's target,

Da Jammer und Verdruß
For misery and vexation

Mich lebend foltern muß,
Me (while I am) living torment must,
{Must torment me in life,}

Und kaum will meine Not im Sterben von mir scheiden.
And hardly would my suffering in dying from me depart.
{And my suffering hardly leaves me in death.}

Chorale:
Allein zu dir steht mein Begier,
Only toward thee (is) my desire,
{Toward thee only is my desire,}

Herr, laß mich nicht verderben!
Lord, let me not perish!

Bass:
Du bist mein Helfer, Trost und Hort,
Thou art my helper, consolation, and refuge,

So der Betrübten Tränen zählet
Who the dejected-ones' tears dost-count

Und ihre Zuversicht,
And their confidence,
{And dost not break their confidence,}

*Mt. 8:1-3. When [Jesus] came down from the mountain, great crowds followed him; and behold, a leper came to him and knelt before him, saying, "Lord, if you will, you can make me clean." And he stretched out his hand and touched him, saying, "I will; be clean." And immediately his leprosy was cleansed.
*Mt. 8:5-7. As [Jesus] entered Capernaum, a centurion came forward to him, beseeching him and saying, "Lord, my servant is lying paralyzed at home, in terrible distress." And he said to him, "I will come and heal him."
Mk. 14:35-36. Going a little farther [in the garden of Gethsemane, Jesus] fell on the ground and prayed that, if it were possible, the hour might pass from him. And he said, "Abba, Father, all things are possible to thee; remove this cup from me; yet not what I will, but what thou wilt."
Job 7:2-3, 5-7, 13-16. Like a slave who longs for the shadow, and like a hireling who looks for his wages, so I am allotted months of emptiness, and nights of misery are apportioned to me...My flesh is clothed with worms and dirt; my skin hardens, then breaks out afresh. My days are swifter than a weaver's shuttle, and come to their end without hope. Remember that my life is a breath; my eye will never again see good...When I say, "My bed will comfort me, my couch will ease my complaint," then thou dost scare me with dreams and terrify me with visions, so that I would choose strangling and death rather than my bones. I loathe my life; I would not live for ever. Let me alone, for my days are a breath.
Ps. 38:9-10. Lord, all my longing (Luther: Begierde) is known to thee, my sighing is not hidden from thee. My heart throbs, my strength fails me; and the light of my eyes—it also has gone from me.
Ps. 42:1-2. As a hart longs for flowing streams, so longs my soul for thee, O God. My soul thirsts for God, for the living God. When shall I come and behold the face of God?
Ps. 73:25-26. Whom have I in heaven but thee? And there is nothing upon earth that I desire besides thee. My flesh and my heart may fail, but God is the strength of my heart and my portion for ever.
Ps. 54:4. Behold, God is my helper; the Lord is the upholder of my life.
Ps. 18:2. The Lord is my rock, and my fortress, and my deliverer, my God, my rock (Luther: Hort), in whom I take refuge, my shield, and the horn of my salvation, my stronghold. (Helfer: also Ps. 40:17)
Ps. 56:8. [O Lord,] thou hast kept count of my tossings; put thou my tears in thy bottle! Are they not in thy book?
Ps. 71:5. For thou, O Lord, art my hope, my trust (Luther: Zuversicht), O Lord, from my youth. (Also Ps. 61:3, 71:7; 142:5.)
Ps. 103:13-14. As a father pities his children, so the Lord pities those who fear him. For he knows our frame; he remembers that we are dust.

Das schwache Rohr, nicht gar zerbricht;
That fragile reed, not completely breaks:
{That fragile reed:}

Und weil du mich erwählet,
And because thou me (hast) chosen,

So sprich ein Trost- und Freudenwort!
Therefore speak a (word of) comfort; - (a) word-of-joy!

Chorale:
Erhalt mich nur in deiner Huld,
Preserve me only in thy favor,
{Only preserve me in thy favor,}

Sonst wie du willt, gib mir Geduld,
Otherwise (do) as thou wilt; give me patience,

Denn dein Will ist der beste.
For thy will is - best.

Soprano:
Dein Wille zwar ist ein versiegelt Buch,
Thy will indeed is a sealed book,

Da Menschenweisheit nichts vernimmt;
(In-which) human-wisdom nothing understands;
{In which human wisdom nought can understand;}

Der Segen scheint uns oft ein Fluch,
The blessing seems to-us often a curse,

Die Züchtigung ergrimmte Strafe,
(Our) discipline angry punishment,

Die Ruhe, so du in dem Todesschlafe
That rest, which thou in the sleep-of-death
{That rest which thou hast appointed}

Uns einst bestimmt,
For-us (hast) one-day appointed,
{For us one day in the sleep of death,}

Ein Eingang zu der Hölle.
(Seems) an entrance into - hell.

Doch macht dein Geist uns dieses Irrtums frei
Yet makes thy Spirit us from-this error free
{Yet thy Spirit frees us from this error}

Und zeigt, daß uns dein Wille heilsam sei.
And shows (us) that for-us thy will wholesome is.
{And shows us that thy will is wholesome for us.}

Herr, wie du willt!
Lord, as thou wilt!

Is. 42:3. A bruised reed he will not break, and a dimly burning wick he will not quench. (Also Mt. 12:20.)
1 Pet. 2:9. You are a chosen race, a royal priesthood, a holy nation, God's own people... (Also Ps. 95:6–7, 100:3.)
Jn. 15:16 [Christ]: You did not choose me, but I chose you and appointed you that you should go and bear fruit and that your fruit should abide; so that whatever you ask the Father in my name, he may give it to you. (Also 1 Thess. 1:4.)
Heb. 10:36–39. [But] you have need of endurance (Luther: Geduld), so that you may do the will of God and receive what is promised.
Jms. 5:10–11. As an example of suffering and patience, brethren, take the prophets who spoke in the name of the Lord. Behold, we call those happy who were steadfast. You have heard of the steadfastness of Job, and you have seen the purpose of the Lord, how the Lord is compassionate and merciful.
Rom. 5:3–5. ...We rejoice in our sufferings, knowing that suffering produces endurance, and endurance produces character, and character produces hope, and hope does not disappoint us...
Is. 45:11. Thus says the Lord, the Holy One of Israel, and his Maker: "Will you question me about my children, or command me concerning the work of my hands?"
Prov. 3:5–6. Trust in the Lord with all your heart, and do not rely on your own insight.
Is. 29:11–12. The vision of all this has become to you like the words of a book that is sealed. When men give it to one who can read, saying, "Read this," he says, "I cannot, for it is sealed." And when they give the book to one who cannot read, saying, "Read this," he says, "I cannot read."
1 Cor. 2:16. Who has known the mind of the Lord so as to instruct him?... (Also Is. 40:13–14, Rom. 11:34.)
Is. 55:9 [God]: As the heavens are higher than the earth, so are my ways higher than your ways and my thoughts than your thoughts. (Also Prov. 20:24.)
1 Cor. 1:25. The foolishness of God is wiser than men, and the weakness of God is stronger than men.
Deut. 30:19 [God]: ...I have set before you life and death, blessing and curse (Luther: Segen und Fluch)... (Also Josh. 8:34.)
Heb. 12:5–7. ...My son, do not regard lightly the discipline of the Lord, nor lose courage when you are punished by him. For the Lord disciplines him whom he loves, and chastises every son whom he receives. It is for discipline that you have to endure. God is treating you as sons; for what son is there whom his father does not discipline?
Jer. 30:11 [God]: ...Of you I will not make a full end. I will chasten you in just measure (Luther: züchtigen...mit Maßen)... (Also Jer. 4:27, 5:10, 5:18, 46:28, Ezek. 20:17.)
Heb. 4:9–11. So then, there remains a sabbath rest for the people of God; for whoever enters God's rest also ceases from his labors as God did from his. Let us therefore strive to enter that rest...
Rev. 14:13. ...Blessed are the dead who die in the Lord henceforth... that they may rest from their labors, for their deeds follow them!
Rom. 8:28. We know that in everything God works for good with those who love him, who are called according to his purpose.
1 Pet. 4:19. Therefore let those who suffer according to God's will do right and entrust their souls to a faithful Creator.

2. Tenor Aria

●Prayer: Pour Spirit of joy into my despairing heart (73-2)
Ach senke doch den Geist der   Freuden
Ah,   (pour) please the   Spirit of (all) joy

Dem Herzen ein!
(My) heart into!
{Into my heart!}

Es   will oft bei mir   geistlich Kranken
(Now) would often (in) me—(who am a) spiritual invalid—

Die Freudigkeit und Hoffnung wanken
-   Joy   and hope   falter
{Joy and hope often falter in me, who am such a spiritual invalid,}

Und   zaghaft sein.
And (I) fainthearted be.
{And I become fainthearted.}

3. Bass Recit.

●Human will perverse: it vacillates & rejects dying (73-3)
Ach, unser Wille bleibt verkehrt,
Ah,   our   will remains perverse,

Bald trotzig, bald verzagt,
Now defiant, now despondent,

Des Sterbens will er nie   gedenken;
-   Dying wants it never to-bear-in-mind;
{It never wants to consider death;}

Allein ein Christ,   in Gottes Geist gelehrt,
Only a Christian, through God's Spirit taught,

Lernt sich in Gottes Willen senken
Learns himself in God's   will to-submerge
{Learns to submerge himself in God's will}

Und sagt:
And says:

Rom. 12:12. Rejoice in your hope, be patient in tribulation...
Ps. 51:12. [O Lord,] restore to me the joy of thy salvation, and uphold me with a willing spirit.
Lk. 11:13 [Christ]: ...[How gladly] will the heavenly Father give the Holy Spirit to those who ask him!
1 Cor. 2:12, 14. We have received not the spirit of the world, but the Spirit which is from God, that we might understand the gifts bestowed on us by God...The unspiritual man does not receive the gifts of the Spirit of God, for they are folly to him, and he is not able to understand them because they are spiritually discerned.
Gal. 5:22. The fruit of the Spirit is love, joy, peace...
Heb. 10:23. Let us hold fast the confession of our hope without wavering (Luther: wanken), for he who promised is faithful.
Heb. 12:12–13. Therefore lift your drooping hands and strengthen your weak knees, and make straight paths for your feet, so that what is lame may not be put out of joint but rather be healed.
Jms. 1:6–8. But let [a man] ask in faith, with no doubting, for he who doubts is like a wave of the sea that is driven and tossed by the wind. For that person must not suppose that a double-minded man, unstable in all his ways, will receive anything from the Lord.
Ps. 119:123. [O Lord,] my eyes fail with watching for thy salvation, and for the fulfilment of thy righteous promise.
Josh. 8:1. The Lord said to Joshua, "Do not fear or be dismayed..." (Luther: Fürchte dich nicht und zage nicht) (Also 1 Chron. 22:13.)

Rom. 8:7. The mind that is set on the flesh is hostile to God; it does not submit to God's law, indeed it cannot.
Jer. 17:9. The heart is deceitful above all things, and desperately corrupt; who can understand it?
Rom. 2:15. ...[In sinners' hearts] their conflicting thoughts accuse or perhaps excuse them...
Heb. 9:27. ...It is appointed for men to die once, and after that comes judgment.
Jms. 4:13–16. Come now, you who say, "Today or tomorrow we will go into such and such a town and spend a year there and trade and get gain"; whereas you do not know about tomorrow. What is your life? For you are a mist that appears for a little time and then vanishes. Instead you ought to say, "If the Lord wills, we shall live and we shall do this or that." As it is, you boast in your arrogance. All such boasting is evil.
Ps. 90:12. [O Lord,] teach us to number our days that we may get a heart of wisdom.
1 Cor. 2:16. Who has known the mind of the Lord so as to instruct him? But we have the mind of Christ.
Rom. 12:2. Do not be conformed to this world but be transformed by the renewal of your mind, that you may prove what is the will of God, what is good and acceptable and perfect.
Mt. 26:39. ...[O Lord,] not as I will, but as thou wilt. (Also Mk. 14:36.)

4. Bass Aria

●God's sovereign will accepted; acceptance of death (73–4)
Herr, so du willt,
Lord, if thou wilt,

So preßt, ihr Todesschmerzen,
Then press, ye pangs-of-death,

Die Seufzer aus dem Herzen,
(These) groans out-of (my) heart,

Wenn mein Gebet nur vor dir gilt.
If my prayer only before thee be-acceptable.
{If only my prayer be acceptable to thee.}

///

Herr, so du willt,
Lord, if thou wilt,

So lege meine Glieder
Then lay my members
{Then lay down my members}

In Staub und Asche nieder,
In dust and ashes down—
{In dust and ashes—}

Dies höchst verderbte Sündenbild,
This most corrupted image-of-sin,

///

Herr, so du willt,
Lord, if thou wilt,

So schlagt, ihr Leichenglocken,
Then strike, ye bells-of-death,

Ich folge unerschrocken,
I follow unfrightened;

Mein Jammer ist nunmehr gestillt.
My misery is henceforth stilled.

Ps. 116:3. The snares of death encompassed me; the pangs of Sheol laid hold on me; I suffered distress and anguish. (Also Ps. 18:4–5, 2 Sam. 22:5–6).)
Rom. 8:23. ...We ourselves, who have the first fruits of the Spirit, groan inwardly as we wait for adoption as sons, the redemption of our bodies...
2 Cor. 5:2–4. Here indeed we groan, and long to put on our heavenly dwelling, so that by putting it on we may not be found naked. For while we are still in this tent, we sigh with anxiety...
Mt. 26:38. [Jesus] said to [his disciples], "My soul is very sorrowful, even to death..."
Heb. 2:15. [Christ]...[delivered] all those who through fear of death were subject to lifelong bondage.
1 Jn. 4:16–18. So we know and believe the love God has for us...In this is love perfected with us, that we may` have confidence for the day of judgment...There is no fear in love, but perfect love casts out fear. For fear has to do with punishment, and he who fears is not perfected in love.
Prov. 15:29. The Lord...hears the prayer of the righteous.
1 Pet. 3:12. For the eyes of the Lord are upon the righteous, and his ears are open to their prayer.

Ecc. 12:7. The dust returns to the earth as it was, and the spirit returns to God who gave it. (Also Gen. 3:19. Ps. 104:29, Ecc. 3:20.)
2 Cor. 4:7, 12. We have this treasure in earthen vessels...So death is at work in us...
2 Cor. 5:1–4. We know that if the earthly tent we live in is destroyed, we have a building from God, a house not made with hands, eternal in the heavens. Here indeed we groan, and long to put on our heavenly dwelling, so that by putting it on we may not be found naked. For while we are still in this tent, we sigh with anxiety; not that we would be unclothed, but that we would be further clothed, so that what is mortal may be swallowed up by life.
Ps. 51:5. Behold, I was brought forth in iniquity (Luther: aus sündlichem Samen gezeugt), and in sin did my mother conceive me.
Rom. 7:18, 24–25. I know that nothing good dwells within me, that is, in my flesh. I can will what is right, but I cannot do it...Wretched man that I am! Who will deliver me from this body of death? Thanks be to God through Jesus Christ our Lord!

2 Cor. 5:6–8. So we are always of good courage; we know that while we are at home in the body we are away from the Lord, for we walk by faith, not by sight. We are of good courage, and we would rather be away from the body and at home with the Lord.
Ps. 23:4. Even though I walk through the valley of the shadow of death, I fear no evil; for thou art with me...
Phil. 1:21, 23. To me...to die is gain...My desire is to depart and be with Christ, for that is far better.
Rev. 21:4. [God] will wipe away every tear from their eyes, and death shall be no more, neither shall there be mourning nor crying nor pain any more, for the former things have passed away.

5. Chorale
● God's will is to extend grace to us in Christ (73-5)
Das ist des Vaters Wille;
This is   the   Father's will;

Der uns erschaffen hat;
Who us   created   has;
{He who has created us;}

Sein Sohn hat   Guts   die Fülle
His   Son   has (of) good-things the fill

Erworben und Genad;
Gained   and   grace;
{His Son has gained the fill of all good things with grace;}

Auch Gott der Heilge Geist
Also, God the Holy   Ghost

Im Glauben uns regieret,
By   faith   us   governs,
{Governs us by faith,}

Zum   Reich des Himmels führet.
To-the kingdom of   heaven   leads.
{And leads us to the kingdom of heaven.}

Ihm   sei Lob, Ehr und Preis!
To-him be laud, honor, and praise!

BWV 74
Wer mich liebet der wird mein Wort halten II
(NBA I/13; BC A83)

Pentecost (BWV 172, 59, 74, 34)
*Acts 2:1–13 (Outpouring of the Holy Spirit)
*Jn. 14:23–31 (Jesus' farewell: He promises to send the Holy Spirit)
Librettist: Christiane Mariane von Ziegler. Text modified by someone: J. S. Bach? At least some movements are based on earlier musical material.

1. Chorus (Adapted from BWV 59-1)
● Vox Christi: Holy Spirit promised: Jn. 14:23 (74-1)
Wer   mich liebet, der wird mein Wort halten,
Whoever me loves,   he will my   word keep,

und mein Vater wird ihn lieben, und wir werden
and my Father will ihn love,   and we   will

zu ihm kommen und   Wohnung bei ihm machen.
to him   come and (our) abode with him make.

Jn. 6:40 [Christ]: This is the will of my Father, that every one who sees the Son and believes in him should have eternal life; and I will raise him up at the last day.
Jn. 1:16–17. From [Christ's] fulness have we all received, grace upon grace. For the law was given through Moses; grace and truth came through Jesus Christ.
Rom. 3:24. [We] are justified by his grace as a gift, through the redemption which is in Christ Jesus.
Rom. 5:18. Then as one man's trespass led to condemnation for all men, so one man's act of righteousness leads to acquittal and life for all men.
Rom. 8:7–11, 14. The mind that is set on the flesh is hostile to God; it does not submit to God's law, indeed it cannot; and those who are in the flesh cannot please God. But you are not in the flesh, you are in the Spirit, if in fact the Spirit of God dwells in you. Any one who does not have the Spirit of Christ does not belong to him. But if Christ is in you, although your bodies are dead because of sin, your spirits are alive because of righteousness. If the Spirit of him who raised Jesus from the dead dwells in you, he who raised Christ Jesus from the dead will give life to your mortal bodies also through his Spirit which dwells in you...For all who are led by the Spirit of God are sons of God.
Jude 1:25. To the only God, our Savior through Jesus Christ our Lord, be glory, majesty, dominion, and authority, before all time and now and for ever. Amen.
Rom. 16:27. To the only wise God be glory for evermore through Jesus Christ! Amen.

***Jn. 14:23.** Jesus answered him, "If a man loves me, he will keep my word, and my Father will love him, and we will come to him and make our home with him."*
Jn. 14:21 [Christ]: He who has my commandments and keeps them, he it is who loves me; and he who loves me will be loved by my Father, and I will love him and manifest myself to him.
Jn. 14:16–20 [Christ]: I will pray the Father, and he will give you another Counselor, to be with you for ever, even the Spirit of truth, whom the world cannot receive, because it neither sees him nor knows him; you know him, for he dwells with you, and will be in you. I will not leave you desolate; I will come to you. Yet a little while, and the world will see me no more, but you will see me; because I live, you will live also. In that day you will know that I am in my Father, and you in me, and I in you.

2. Soprano Aria (Adapted from BWV 59-4)
●Prayer claiming God's promise to indwell our hearts (74-2)
Komm, komm, mein Herze steht dir offen,
Come, come, my heart (is) to-thee open,
{Come, come, my heart is open to thee,}

Ach, laß es deine Wohnung sein!
Ah, let it thy dwelling be!

Ich liebe dich, so muß ich hoffen:
I love thee, so must I expect
{I love thee, so I can expect}

Dein Wort trifft itzo bei mir ein;
(That) thy Word will-be-fulfilled now in me - ;
{That thy Word will now be fulfilled in me;}

Denn wer dich sucht, fürcht', liebt und ehret,
For whoever thee seeks, fears, loves, and honors,
{For whoever seeks, fears, loves, and honors thee,}

Dem ist der Vater zugetan.
To-him is the Father devoted.

Ich zweifle nicht, ich bin erhöret,
I doubt not, I have-been (favorably) heard,

Daß ich mich dein getrösten kann.
So-that I myself in-thee comfort can.
{So now I can comfort myself in thee.}

3. Alto Recit.
●Prayer: My heart is prepared as thy dwelling (74-3)
Die Wohnung ist bereit.
(Thy) dwelling is prepared.

Du findst ein Herz,
Thou dost-find (here) a heart,

das dir allein ergeben,
that to-thee alone is-surrendered,

Drum laß mich nicht erleben,
Therefore let me never experience,

Daß du gedenkst, von mir zu gehn.
That thou shouldst-plan, from me to go.

Das laß ich nimmermehr, ach, nimmermehr geschehen!
That allow I nevermore, ah, nevermore to-happen!
{That I will never, ah, never allow!}

4. Bass Aria
●Vox Christi: I will come again: Jn. 14:28 (74-4)
Ich gehe hin und komme wieder zu euch. Hättet ihr
I go thither and come again to you. Had you (held)

Jn. 1:12. To all who received [Christ], who believed in his name, he gave power to become children of God.
Mt. 10:40 [Christ]: ...He who receives me receives him who sent me. (Also Mt. 10:40, 18:5, Mk. 9:37, Lk. 9:48, Jn. 13:20.)
Rev. 3:20 [Christ]: Behold, I stand at the door and knock; if any one hears my voice and opens the door, I will come in to him and eat with him, and he with me.
S. of S. 5:2 [Bride]: I slept, but my heart was awake. Hark! my beloved is knocking, "Open to me, my sister, my love, my dove, my perfect one..."
*Jn. 14:23. Jesus [said]... "If a man loves me, he will keep my word, and my Father will love him, and we will come to him and make our home with him." (Also Jn. 14:21.)
Mt. 22:37-38. [Jesus] said... "You shall love the Lord your God with all your heart, and with all your soul, and with all your mind. This is the great and first commandment." (See Deut. 6:5.)
1 Jn. 4:13, 15-16. By this we know that we abide in him and he in us, because he has given us of his own Spirit..Whoever confesses that Jesus is the Son of God, God abides in him, and he in God...He who abides in love abides in God, and God abides in him. (Also Jn. 15:4, 6; 17:21-23, 1 Jn. 3:24.)
Eph. 3:17, 19. ...that Christ may dwell in your hearts through faith... that you may be filled with all the fulness of God.
1 Cor. 3:16. Do you not know that you are God's temple and that God's Spirit dwells in you?
1 Jn. 5:14-15. This is the confidence which we have in him, that if we ask anything according to his will he hears us. And if we know that he hears us in whatever we ask, we know that we have obtained the requests made of him.

*Jn. 14:23 [Christ]: ...We will come to him and make our home with him.
2 Cor. 6:16-17. ...God said, "I will live in them and move among them, and I will be their God, and they shall be my people. Therefore come out from them and be separate from them..."
Mt. 6:24 [Christ]: No one can serve two masters; for either he will hate the one and love the other, or he will be devoted to the one and despise the other. You cannot serve God and mammon. (Also Lk. 16:13.)
Ex. 20:3, 5 [God]: You shall have no other gods before me..I the Lord your God am a jealous God... (Also Deut. 5:7.)
Jn. 14:18, 20 [Christ]: I will not leave you desolate; I will come to you ...In that day you will know that I am in my Father, and you in me, and I in you.
Ps. 38:21. Do not forsake me, O Lord! O my God, be not far from me! (Also Ps. 71:9, 18; 119:121; 138:8.)
S. of S. 3:4 [Bride]: ...I found him whom my soul loves. I held him, and would not let him go... (Also Gen. 32:26.)
Mt. 28:20 [Christ]: ...Lo, I am with you always to the close of the age.
Josh. 1:5, 9 [God]: ...I will not fail you or forsake you...The Lord your God is with you wherever you go. (Also Deut. 31:6-8, Heb. 13:5.)

*Jn. 14:28 [Christ]: You heard me say to you, *"I go away, and I will come to you." If you loved me, you would have rejoiced,* because I go to the Father; for the Father is greater than I.
Jn. 14:1, 3, 18. Let not your hearts be troubled; believe in God,

mich lieb, so würdet ihr   euch freuen.
me   dear, then would you (have) rejoiced.

5. Tenor Aria
●Rejoice for Christ will return, though Satan attacks! (74-5)
Kommt, eilet, stimmet Sait und Lieder
Come, hasten, tune   strings and songs

In muntern und erfreuten Ton.
In   lively and gladdened sound.

Geht er gleich weg, so kömmt er wieder,
Goes he though away, so comes he again,
{Though he go away, he will come again,}

Der hochgelobte Gottessohn.
The highly-exalted Son-of-God.

Der Satan wird indes versuchen,
- Satan will meanwhile attempt,

Den Deinigen   gar   sehr zu fluchen.
- Thine-own (people) indeed greatly to curse.

Er ist mir hinderlich,
He is to-me obstructive,

So glaub ich, Herr, an dich.
So believe I, Lord, in thee.
{But I believe, O Lord, in thee.}

6. Bass Recit.
●Condemnation removed for those in Christ: Rom. 8:1 (74-6)
Es   ist nichts   Verdammliches   an denen,
(There) is nothing worthy-of-condemnation in those,

die in Christo Jesu sind.
who in Christ Jesus are.

7. Alto Aria
●Christ's blood alone saves from hell & makes us heirs (74-7)
Nichts kann mich erretten
Nothing can me   save
{Nothing can save me}

Von höllischen Ketten
From hell's   chains

believe also in me...When I go and prepare a place for you, I will come again and will take you to myself, that where I am you may be also...I will not leave you desolate; I will come to you.

Zech. 9:9. Rejoice greatly, O daughter of Zion! Shout aloud, O daughter of Jerusalem! Lo, your king comes to you; triumphant and victorious is he...
Ps. 33:1–3. Rejoice in the Lord, O you righteous! Praise befits the upright. Praise the Lord with the lyre, make melody to him with the harp of ten strings! Sing to him a new song, play skilfully on the strings, with loud shouts. (Also Ps. 57:8–9, 81:2–3, 149:2–3.)
Acts 1:10–11. While [the disciples] were gazing into heaven as [Jesus ascended], behold, two men stood by them in white robes, and said, "Men of Galilee, why do you stand looking into heaven? This Jesus, who was taken up from you into heaven, will come in the same way as you saw him go into heaven."
Jn. 14:3, 18 [Christ]: ...I will come again and will take you to myself, that where I am you may be also...I will not leave you desolate; I will come to you.
Heb. 10:12–13. When Christ had offered for all time a single sacrifice for sins, he sat down at the right hand of God, then to wait until his enemies should be made a stool for his feet. (Also Ps. 110:1, Acts 7:55, Col. 3:1, 1 Pet. 3:22.)
Rev. 12:12. Rejoice...O heaven and you that dwell therein! But woe to you, O earth and sea, for the devil has come down to you in great wrath, because he knows that his time is short!
1 Pet. 5:8–9. Be sober, be watchful. Your adversary the devil prowls around like a roaring lion, seeking some one to devour. Resist him, firm in your faith, knowing that the same experience of suffering is required of your brotherhood throughout the world. (Also Eph. 6:11–12.)
Jn. 16:33 [Christ]: I have said this to you, that in me you may have peace. In the world you have tribulation; but be of good cheer, I have overcome the world.
Mt. 16:27 [Christ]: The Son of man [will] come with his angels in the glory of his Father, and then he will repay every man for what he has done.

Rom. 8:1–4. *There is therefore now no condemnation for those who are in Christ Jesus.* For the law of the Spirit of life in Christ Jesus has set me free from the law of sin and death. For God has done what the law, weakened by the flesh, could not do: sending his own Son in the likeness of sinful flesh and for sin, he condemned sin in the flesh, in order that the just requirement of the law might be fulfilled in us, who walk not according to the flesh but according to the Spirit.

Acts 4:12. There is salvation in no one else [than in Christ], for there is no other name under heaven given among men by which we must be saved.
Eph. 2:1–2. And you [God] made alive, when you were dead through the trespasses and sins in which you once walked, following the course of the world, following the prince of the power of the air, the spirit that is now at work in the sons of disobedience.
Jude 1:6. And the angels that did not keep their own position but left their proper dwelling have been kept by [God] in eternal chains in the nether gloom until the judgment of the great day. (Also 2 Pet. 2:4.)

Als, Jesu, dein Blut.
But, Jesus, thy blood.

Dein Leiden, dein Sterben
Thy passion, thy dying

Macht mich ja zum Erben:
Makes me indeed (an) heir:
{Indeed makes me an heir:}

Ich lache der Wut.
I laugh (at) (hell's) fury.

1 Pet. 1:18–19. You know that you were ransomed from the futile ways inherited from your fathers, not with perishable things such as silver or gold, but with the precious blood of Christ, like that of a lamb without blemish or spot. (Also Rev. 5:9.)
1 Jn. 1:7. ...The blood of Jesus his Son cleanses us from all sin.
Gal. 4:4–7. When the time had fully come, God sent forth his Son...to redeem those who were under the law, so that we might receive adoption as sons. And because you are sons, God has sent the Spirit of his Son into our hearts, crying, "Abba! Father!" So through God you are no longer a slave but a son, and if a son then an heir. (Also Col. 3:24.)
1 Jn. 4:4. Little children, you are of God, and have overcome them; for he who is in you is greater than he who is in the world. (Also Jn. 16:33.)
Ps. 52:6. The righteous shall see [God's judgment on the enemy], and fear, and shall laugh at him... (Also Ps. 2:4, 59:8, Prov. 1:26.)

8. Chorale
●Salvation is a gift of which no one is worthy (74-8)
Kein Menschenkind hier auf der Erd
No child-of-man here on the earth

Ist dieser edlen Gabe wert,
Is of-this noble gift worthy,
{Is worthy of this noble gift,}

Bei uns ist kein Verdienen;
In us (there) is no merit;

Hier gilt gar nichts als Lieb und Gnad,
Here is-effective indeed nothing but love and grace,
{Indeed, nothing is effective but love and grace here,}

Die Christus uns verdienet hat
Which Christ for-us earned has
{Which Christ has earned for us}

Mit Büßen und Versühnen.
With (his) atonement and reconciliation.

Eph. 1:7–8, 2:8–9. In [Christ] we have redemption through his blood, the forgiveness of our trespasses, according to the riches of his grace which he lavished upon us...For by grace you have been saved through faith...it is the gift of God—not because of works, lest any man should boast.
Rom. 3:10–12, 23–25. As it is written: "None is righteous, no, not one; no one understands, no one seeks for God. All have turned aside, together they have gone wrong; no one does good, not even one." ...All have sinned and fall short of the glory of God, they are justified by his grace as a gift, through the redemption which is in Christ Jesus, whom God put forward as an expiation by his blood, to be received by faith...
Rom. 5:11, 17. ...We rejoice in God through our Lord Jesus Christ, through whom we have now received our reconciliation...If, because of one man's trespass, death reigned through that one man, much more will those who receive the abundance of grace and the free gift of righteousness reign in life through the one man Jesus Christ. (Also Rom. 5:21.)
Phil. 3:8–9 ...[My desire is] that I may gain Christ and be found in him, not having a righteousness of my own, based on law, but that which is through faith in Christ, the righteousness from God that depends on faith.

BWV 75
Die Elenden sollen essen
(NBA I/15; BC A94)

1. Sunday after Trinity (BWV 75, 20, 39)
*1 Jn. 4:16-21 (God is love; we ought also to love)
*Lk. 16:19-31 (Parable of rich man and Lazarus)
Librettist: Unknown

1. Chorus
●Poverty vs. wealth: The hungry shall eat: Ps. 22:26 (75-1)
Die Elenden sollen essen, daß sie satt werden,
The afflicted shall eat, so-that they satiated become,

Ps. 22:26. *The afflicted shall eat and be satisfied; those who seek him shall praise the Lord! May your hearts live for ever!*
Joel 2:26. You shall eat in plenty and be satisfied, and praise the name of the Lord your God, who has dealt wondrously with you. And my people shall never again be put to shame.

und   die   nach dem Herrn fragen, werden ihn preisen.
and they-who after the Lord inquire,   will   him praise.

Euer Herz soll ewiglich leben.
Your heart shall eternally live.

2. Bass Recit.
•Poverty vs. wealth: Earthly wealth can lead to hell (75-2)
Was   hilft des Purpurs Majestät, da sie vergeht?
What profits - purple's majesty, since it passes-away?
{Of what use is the majesty of royal purple, since it passes away?}

Was   hilft der größte Überfluß,
What profits the greatest abundance,
{Of what use is the greatest abundance,}

Weil alles, so wir sehen, verschwinden muß?
Since all, that we see,   must-pass-away?

     Was hilft der Kitzel   eitler Sinnen,
(Of) what use the tickling (of) frivolous senses,

Denn unser Leib muß selbst   von hinnen?
For   our body must itself (depart) from hence?

Ach wie geschwind ist es geschehen,
Ah how   quickly   does it   happen,

Daß Reichtum,   Wollust,   Pracht
That riches, sensual-pleasure, (and) pomp

Den Geist zur Hölle macht!
(Our) spirit to hell (do-send)!

3. Tenor Aria
•Poverty vs. wealth: Jesus shall be everything to me (75-3)
Mein Jesus soll mein alles sein.
My   Jesus shall my   all be.
{My Jesus shall be my all.}

Mein Purpur is sein teures Blut,
My   purple is his costly blood,

Er selbst mein allerhöchstes Gut
He himself my   most-precious posession,

Und seines Geistes Liebesglut
And his   Spirit's embers-of-love
{And the ardor his Spirit puts within in me}

Mein allersüß'ster Freudenwein.
My   sweetest-of-all wine-of-joy.
{The sweetest wine of joy.}

Lk. 1:53 [Magnificat]. [The Lord] has filled the hungry with good things, and the rich he has sent empty away.

Jn. 6:48, 51 [Christ]: I am the bread of life...I am the living bread which came down from heaven; if any one eats of this bread, he will live for ever; and the bread which I shall give for the life of the world is my flesh.

*Lk. 16:19–21. There was a rich man, who was clothed in purple...and who feasted sumptuously every day. And at his gate lay a poor man named Lazarus, full of sores, who desired to be fed with what fell from the rich man's table...

Ps. 49:16–20. Be not afraid when one becomes rich, when the glory of his house increases. For when he dies he will carry nothing away; his glory will not go down after him...Though a man gets praise when he does well for himself, he will go to the generation of his fathers, who will never more see the light. Man cannot abide in his pomp, he is like the beasts that perish. (Also Ps. 52:7, 62:9–11, 89:48.)

Mt. 16:26 [Christ]: What will it profit a man, if he gains the whole world and forfeits his life?

1 Jn. 2:17. The world passes away, and the lust of it; but he who does the will of God abides for ever.

Mt. 10:28 [Christ]: Do not fear those who kill the body but cannot kill the soul; rather fear him who can destroy both soul and body in hell. (Also 1 Cor. 6:13.)

Mt. 19:23–24. Jesus said to his disciples, "Truly, I say to you, it will be hard for a rich man to enter the kingdom of heaven. Again I tell you, it is easier for a camel to go through the eye of a needle than for a rich man to enter the kingdom of God." (Also Mk. 10:23, Lk. 18:24.)

1 Tim. 6:9. Those who desire to be rich fall into temptation, into a snare, into many senseless and hurtful desires that plunge men into ruin and destruction.

*Lk. 16:23. The rich man also died...and in Hades, being in torment, he lifted up his eyes, and saw Abraham far off and Lazarus in his bosom.

Col. 3:11. ...Christ is all and in all.

Mk. 15:17. [The soldiers] clothed [Jesus] in a purple cloak, and plaiting a crown of thorns they put it on him.

1 Pet. 1:18–19. You know that you were ransomed...with the precious blood of Christ...

1 Jn. 1:7. ...The blood of Jesus...cleanses us from all sin.

Rev. 5:9. And [in paradise] they sang a new song, saying, "Worthy art thou...for thou wast slain and by thy blood didst ransom men for God from every tribe and tongue and people and nation."

Ps. 16:5. The Lord is my chosen portion and my cup (Luther: Gut und Teil)...

Ps. 73:25–26. [O Lord,] whom have I in heaven but thee? And there is nothing upon earth that I desire besides thee. My flesh and my heart may fail, but God is the strength of my heart and my portion for ever.

Lk. 3:16. [The one who is coming]...will baptize you with the Holy Spirit and with fire. (Also Mt. 3:11.)

Eph. 5:18. Do not get drunk with wine, for that is debauchery; but be filled with the Spirit...

Rom. 5:5. ...God's love has been poured into our hearts through the Holy Spirit which has been given to us.

1 Cor. 12:13. ...[We] all were made to drink of one Spirit.

258

4. Tenor Recit.
●Poverty vs. wealth: positions reversed in eternity (75-4)
Gott stürzet und erhöhet
God overthrows and raises-up

In Zeit und Ewigkeit!
In time and eternity!

Wer   in der Welt den Himmel sucht,
Whoever in the world - heaven seeks,
{Whoever seeks heaven in the world,}

Wird dort verflucht.
Will there be-cursed.

Wer   aber   hier die Hölle überstehet,
Who, however, here - hell overcomes,
{But whoever overcomes hell here,}

Wird dort   erfreut.
Will there be-gladdened.

5. Soprano Aria
●Afflictions accepted with joy in view of heaven (75-5)
Ich nehme mein Leiden mit Freuden auf mich.
I   take   my   affliction with   joy   upon myself.
{I accept my affliction with joy.}

Wer   Lazarus' Plagen
Whoever Lazarus' misery

Geduldig ertragen,
Patiently has-borne,

Den nehmen die Engel zu   sich.
Him   take   the angels to themselves.
{Will be received by the angels.}

6. Soprano Recit.
●Contentment experienced while journeying to heaven (75-6)
Indes   schenkt Gott ein gut Gewissen,
Meanwhile grants God   a   good conscience,
{Meanwhile God grants a good conscience,}

Dabei   ein Christe kann
Whereby a Christian can

Ein kleines Gut
A   small posession

Mit großer Lust genießen.
With great pleasure enjoy.
{Enjoy modest posessions with great pleasure.}

Ja,   führt er auch durch   lange   Not
Yes, leads he even through prolonged distress
{Yes, even if he leads us through prolonged distress}

1 Sam. 2:7–8. The Lord makes poor and makes rich; he brings low, he also exalts. He raises up the poor from the dust; he lifts the needy from the ash heap, to make them sit with princes and inherit a seat of honor... (Also Ps. 75:6–7, 113:7–8.)
Lk. 1:52. He has put down the mighty from their thrones, and exalted those of low degree. (Also Ezek. 21:26.)
Lk. 14:11. For every one who exalts himself will be humbled, and he who humbles himself will be exalted. (Also Lk. 18:14.)
*Lk. 16:25. But Abraham said [to the rich man], "Son, remember that you in your lifetime received your good things, and Lazarus in like manner evil things; but now he is comforted here, and you are in anguish."
Mt. 19:30. Many that are first will be last, and the last first.
Rom. 8:18. I consider that the sufferings of this present time are not worth comparing with the glory that is to be revealed to us. (Also 2 Cor. 4:17.)
*Lk. 16:22. The poor man died and was carried by the angels to Abraham's bosom.
Rev. 2:7 [Christ]: ...To him who conquers I will grant to eat of the tree of life, which is in the paradise of God. (Also Rev. 2:11, 2:17, 2:26, 3:5, 3:12, 3:21, 21:7.)

2 Cor. 4:17. This slight momentary affliction is preparing for us an eternal weight of glory beyond all comparison. (Also Rom. 8:18.)
1 Pet. 1:6. In this you rejoice, though now for a little while you may have to suffer various trials.
Jms. 1:12. Blessed is the man who endures trial, for when he has stood the test he will receive the crown of life which God has promised to those who love him. (Also Jms. 1:2–4.)
Rev. 2:3 [Christ]: I know you are enduring patiently and bearing up for my name's sake, and you have not grown weary. (Also Gal. 6:9.)
*Lk. 16:22. The poor man died and was carried by the angels to Abraham's bosom.

1 Tim. 1:19. [Hold] faith and a good conscience...
Ps. 37:16. Better is a little that the righteous has than the abundance of many wicked.
Prov. 15:16. Better is a little with the fear of the Lord than great treasure and trouble with it.
1 Tim. 6:6. There is great gain in godliness with contentment.
Mk. 10:29-30. Jesus said, "Truly, I say to you, there is no one who has left house or brothers or sisters of mother or father or children or lands, for my sake and for the gospel, who will not receive a hundredfold now in this time, houses and brothers and sisters and mothers and children and lands, with persecutions, and in the age to come eternal life." (Also Mt. 19:29, Lk. 18:29–30.)
*Lk. 16:25. Abraham said [to the rich man], "Son, remember that you in your lifetime received your good things, and Lazarus in like manner evil things; but now he is comforted here, and you are in anguish."
Rom. 8:18. I consider that the sufferings of this present time are not worth comparing with the glory that is to be revealed to us.

Zum Tod,
To death,

So ist es doch am Ende wohlgetan.
So is it still in-the end well-done.
{It is still well done in the end.}

7. Chorale (See also 100-5.)
●Future glory much greater than present sufferings (75-7)
Was Gott tut, das ist wohlgetan.
Whatever God does, that is well-done.

Muß ich den Kelch gleich schmecken,
Must I the cup though taste,
{Though I must drink the cup,}

Der bitter ist nach meinem Wahn,
That bitter is according-to my delusion,
{That, in my delusion, seems bitter to me,}

Laß ich mich doch nicht schrecken,
Allow I myself nevertheless not to-be-frightened,
{I nevertheless allow myself not to be frightened,}

Weil doch zuletzt
For nevertheless in-the-end

Ich werd ergötzt
I will-be delighted

Mit süßem Trost im Herzen;
With sweet comfort in (my) heart;

Da weichen alle Schmerzen.
Then retreat all sufferings.
{Then will all sufferings retreat.}

Part II

8. Sinfonia

9. Alto Recit.
●Poverty vs. wealth: Believer also spiritually poor (75-9)
Nur eines kränkt
Only one-thing grieves

Ein christliches Gemüte
A Christian disposition

Wenn es an seines Geistes Armut denkt.
When it of its soul's poverty thinks.
{When it thinks of its soul's poverty.}

Es gläubt zwar Gottes Güte,
It believes indeed (in) God's goodness,

2 Cor. 4:17. For this slight momentary affliction is preparing for us an eternal weight of glory beyond all comparison.
2 Cor. 5:1. We know that if the earthly tent we live in is destroyed, we have a building from God, a house not made with hands, eternal in the heavens.
Mt. 10:22 [Christ]: ...He who endures to the end will be saved. (Also Mt. 24:13, Mk. 13:13, Lk. 21:19.)

Mk. 7:37. And [the people] were astonished beyond measure [at Jesus], saying, "He has done all things well..."
Job 2:10. ...Shall we receive good at the hand of God, and shall we not receive evil?
Mt. 20:20-23. The mother of the sons of Zebedee came up to [Jesus], with her sons...And he said to her, "What do you want?" She said to him, "Command that these two sons of mine may sit, one at your right hand and one at your left, in your kingdom." But Jesus answered, "You do not know what you are asking. Are you able to drink the cup that I am to drink?" They said to him, "We are able." He said to them, "You will drink my cup, but to sit at my right hand and at my left is not mine to grant, but it is for those for whom it has been prepared by my Father." (Also Mk. 10:38-39, Mt. 26:27-28.)
Lk. 22:41-42. And [Jesus]...knelt down and prayed, "Father, if thou art willing, remove this cup from me; nevertheless not my will, but thine, be done."
Jn. 18:11. Jesus said to Peter, "...Shall I not drink the cup which the Father has given me?"
2 Cor. 1:5. As we share abundantly in Christ's sufferings, so through Christ we share abundantly in comfort too.
2 Tim. 2:12. If we endure [with Christ], we shall also reign with him... (Also Rom. 8:17, 1 Pet. 4:13.)
*Lk. 16:25. "...Now [Lazarus] is comforted here [in heaven]..."
Ps. 94:19. ...[O Lord,] thy consolations cheer (Luther: ergötzen) my soul.
Ps. 16:11. ...In thy presence there is fulness of joy, in thy right hand are pleasures for evermore.
Rev. 21:3-4. ...God himself will be with [men]; he will wipe away every tear from their eyes, and death shall be no more, neither shall there be mourning nor crying nor pain any more, for the former things have passed away. (Also Is. 25:8.)

Mt. 5:3 [Christ]: Blessed are the poor in spirit, for theirs is the kingdom of heaven.
Rom. 7:15, 18-20, 22-25. I do not understand my own actions. For I do not do what I want, but I do the very thing I hate... For I know that nothing good dwells within me, that is, in my flesh. I can will what is right, but I cannot do it. For I do not do the good I want, but the evil I do not want is what I do. Now if I do what I do not want, it is no longer I that do it, but sin which dwells within me...For I delight in the law of God, in my inmost self, but I see in my members another law at war with the law of my mind and making me captive to the law of sin which dwells in my members. Wretched man that I am! Who will deliver me from this body of death? Thanks be to God through Jesus Christ our Lord! So then, I of myself serve the law of God with my mind, but with my flesh I serve the law of sin.

Die   alles   neu erschafft;
Which all-things new creates;
{Which makes all things new;}

Doch mangelt ihm die Kraft,
Still   lacks   it the strength,
{Yet it lacks the strength,}

Dem überirdschen Leben
To-the spiritual   life

Das Wachstum und die Frucht zu geben.
  -    Growth   and -   fruit to give.
{To make the spiritual life produce growth and fruit.}

10. Alto Aria
●Spiritual wealth given by Christ through Spirit (75–10)
Jesus macht mich geistlich reich.
Jesus makes me spiritually rich.

Kann ich seinen Geist empfangen,
Can I   his   Spirit   receive,
{If I but his Spirit can receive,}

Will ich weiter nichts verlangen;
Would I further nothing desire;
{I desire nothing further;}

Denn mein Leben wächst zugleich.
For   my   life   grows (thereby).

Jesus macht mich geistlich reich.
Jesus makes me spiritually rich.

11. Bass Recit.
●Eternal wealth ours if we abide in Christ, deny self (75–11)
Wer   nur in Jesu bleibt,
Whoever just in Jesus abides,

Die Selbstverleugnung treibt,
  -    Self-denial   practices,

Daß   er in Gottes Liebe
So-that he in God's love

Sich gläubig übe,
Himself in-faith exercises,
{So that he practices the love of God in faith,}

Hat, wenn das Irdische verschwunden,
Has, when the temporal has-passed-away,

Sich selbst und Gott gefunden.
Him-self   and God   found.
{Found himself and God.}

2 Cor. 5:17. If any one is in Christ, he is a new creation; the old has passed away, behold, the new has come.
Col. 3:1–2. If then you have been raised with Christ, seek the things that are above...Set your minds on things that are above, not on things that are on earth.
Eph. 4:22–24. Put off your old nature which belongs to your former manner of life and is corrupt through deceitful lusts, and be renewed in the spirit of your minds, and put on the new nature, created after the likeness of God in true righteousness and holiness. (Also Col. 3:9–10.)
Jn. 15:4, 8 [Christ]: ...As the branch cannot bear fruit by itself, unless it abides in the vine, neither can you, unless you abide in me...By this my Father is glorified, that you bear much fruit, and so prove to be my disciples.

1 Cor. 1:5. In every way you were enriched in [Christ]...
2 Cor. 8:9. For you know the grace of our Lord Jesus Christ, that though he was rich, yet for your sake he became poor, so that by his poverty you might become rich.
Eph. 2:7. ...the immeasurable riches of his grace in kindness toward us in Christ Jesus. (Also Eph. 3:8.)
Rev. 2:9 [Christ]: I know your tribulation and your poverty (but you are rich)...
Col. 1:27. ...God chose to make known how great among the Gentiles are the riches of the glory of this mystery, which is Christ in you, the hope of glory. (Also Col. 2:2–3.)
Eph. 3:16. According to the riches of his glory [may he] grant you to be strengthened with might through his Spirit in the inner man...
1 Jn. 4:13. By this we know that we abide in him and he in us, because he has given us of his own Spirit.
Gal. 5:22–23. The fruit of the Spirit is love, joy, peace, patience, kindness, goodness, faithfulness, gentleness, self-control; against such there is no law.

Jn. 15:4, 6, 9–10 [Christ]: Abide in me, and I in you. As the branch cannot bear fruit by itself, unless it abides in the vine, neither can you, unless you abide in me...If a man does not abide in me, he is cast forth as a branch and withers; and the branches are gathered, thrown into the fire and burned...As the Father has loved me, so have I loved you; abide in my love. If you keep my commandments, you will abide in my love, just as I have kept my Father's commandments and abide in his love. (Also Jn. 6:56, *1 Jn. 4:16.)
1 Jn. 3:24. All who keep [Christ's] commandments abide in him, and he in them...
Mt. 16:24 [Christ]: If any man would come after me, let him deny himself and take up his cross and follow me...
Lk. 6:27, 32, 35 [Christ]: ...Love your enemies, do good to those who hate you...If you love those who love you, what credit is that to you? For even sinners love those who love them...But love your enemies... and you will be sons of the Most High; for he is kind to the ungrateful and the selfish.
Gal. 5:6. In Christ Jesus [nothing] is of any avail, but faith working through love.
Mt. 16:25 [Christ]: ...Whoever loses his life for my sake will find it. (Also Mk. 8:35–37.)
1 Jn. 2:17. ...The world passes away, and the lust of it; but he who does the will of God abides for ever.

12. Bass Aria
●Love for Jesus and faith in him confessed (75-12)
Mein Herze glaubt und liebt.
My   heart believes and loves.

Denn Jesu süße Flammen,
For   Jesus' sweet flames,

Aus den' die meinen stammen,
From which those of-mine originate,
{From which mine originate,}

Gehn über mich zusammen,
Go   over   me   altogether,

Weil   er sich mir ergibt.
Because he himself to-me devotes.
{Because he devotes himself to me.}

13. Tenor Recit.
●Wealth vs. poverty: Rejecting world for Christ (75-13)
O Armut, der kein Reichtum gleicht!
O poverty, that no   wealth equals!
{O poverty that no wealth can equal!}

Wenn aus dem Herzen
If   out-of the heart

Die ganze Welt entweicht,
The whole world (retreats),

Und Jesus nur allein   regiert.
And Jesus only alone (there) reigns.
{And Jesus alone therein reigns.}

So wird ein Christ zu Gott geführt!
So (is) a Christian to God   led!
{Thus a Christian is led to God!}

Gib, Gott, daß wir es nicht verscherzen.
Grant, God, that we it not frivolously-forfeit.
{Grant, O God, that we might not frivolously forfeit it.}

14. Chorale (See also 12-7, 99-6, 100-6.)
●God's sovereign will accepted, even affliction (75-14)
Was   Gott tut, das ist wohlgetan,
Whatever God does, that is well-done,

Gal. 5:6. In Christ Jesus [nothing] is of any avail, but faith working through love.
*1 Jn. 4:16–21. So we know and believe the love God has for us. God is love, and he who abides in love abides in God, and God abides in him. In this is love perfected with us, that we may have confidence for the day of judgment, because as he is so are we in this world. There is no fear in love, but perfect love casts out fear. For fear has to do with punishment, and he who fears is not perfected in love. We love, because he first loved us. If any one says, "I love God," and hates his brother, he is a liar; for he who does not love his brother whom he has seen, cannot love God whom he has not seen. And this commandment we have from him, that he who loves God should love his brother also.
Mt. 3:11. [Christ] will baptize you with the Holy Spirit and with fire. (Also Lk. 3:16.)
Acts 2:1–4. When the day of Pentecost had come...a sound came from heaven like the rush of a mighty wind, and it filled all the house where [the disciples] were sitting. And there appeared to them tongues as of fire, distributed and resting on each one of them. And they were all filled with the Holy Spirit...
Rom. 5:5. ...God's love has been poured into our hearts through the Holy Spirit which has been given to us.
*Lk. 16:24. [But the rich man] called out, "Father Abraham, have mercy upon me, and send Lazarus to dip the end of his finger in water and cool my tongue; for I am in anguish in this flame (Luther: Flamme)."

*Lk. 16:20–21. At [the rich man's] gate lay a poor man named Lazarus, full of sores, who desired to be fed with what fell from the rich man's table...
Rev. 2:9 [Christ]: I know your tribulation and your poverty (but you are rich)...
Jms. 2:5. ...Has not God chosen those who are poor in the world to be rich in faith and heirs of the kingdom which he has promised to those who love him?
2 Cor. 8:9. You know the grace of our Lord Jesus Christ, that though he was rich, yet for your sake he became poor, so that by his poverty you might become rich. (Also Eph. 2:7, 3:16, Col. 1:27, 2:2, Rev. 2:9.)
Ps. 73:25. [O Lord,] whom have I in heaven but thee? And there is nothing upon earth that I desire besides thee.
1 Jn. 2:15. Do not love the world or the things in the world. If any one loves the world, love for the Father is not in him.
Mt. 6:24. No one can serve two masters...You cannot serve God and mammon.
Phil. 3:7–8. Whatever gain I had, I counted as loss the the sake of Christ. Indeed I count everything as loss because of the surpassing worth of knowing Christ Jesus my Lord...
*Lk. 16:22. The poor man died and was carried by the angels to Abraham's bosom...

Mk. 7:37. [The people] were astonished beyond measure [at Jesus], saying, "He has done all things well..."
Rom. 8:28. We know that in everything God works for good with those who love him, who are called according to his purpose.

Dabei will ich verbleiben.
In-that want I   to-abide.
{In that I want to abide.}

Es   mag mich auf die rauhe Bahn
(Now) may me   on   a harsh course

Not, Tod und Elend treiben,
Want, death, and distress drive,
{If I be driven on a harsh course by want, death, and distress,}

So wird Gott mich
Then will God me
{Then will God}

Ganz väterlich
Right fatherly

In seinen Armen halten:
In his   arms   hold:
{Hold me in his arms:}

Drum   laß ich ihn nur walten.
Therefore allow I him just to-rule.
{Therefore I just allow him sovereign control.}

BWV 76
Die Himmel erzählen die Ehre Gottes
(NBA I/16; BC A97, A185)

2. S. after Trinity (BWV 76, 2)
*1 Jn. 3:13–18 (Whoever does not do right or love his brother
is not of God)
*Lk. 14:16–24 (Parable of the great banquet)
Librettist: Unknown

Part I

1. Chorus
●Heavens tell the glory of God: Ps. 19:1, 3 (76–1)
Die Himmel erzählen die Ehre Gottes,
The heavens   tell   the glory of-God,

und die Feste verkünkiget seiner Hände Werk.
and the firmament proclaims   his   handiwork.

Es ist keine Sprache noch Rede,
There is no language nor speech,

da   man nicht ihre Stimme höre.
(in-which) one not their voice hears.
{In which one does not hear their voice.}

Rom. 8:18. I consider that the sufferings of this present time are not worth comparing with the glory that is to be revealed to us.
2 Cor. 4:17. For this slight momentary affliction is preparing for us an eternal weight of glory beyond all comparison.
2 Cor. 1:5. For as we share abundantly in Christ's sufferings, so through Christ we share abundantly in comfort too. (Also 1 Pet. 4:13.)
***Lk. 16:22.** The poor man died and was carried by the angels to Abraham's bosom...
Ps. 103:11, 13. As the heavens are high above the earth, so great is [God's] steadfast love (Luther: läßt er seine Gnade walten) toward those who fear him...As a father pities his children, so the Lord pities those who fear him.
Mk. 10:14–16. Jesus...said... "Let the children come to me, do not hinder them; for to such belongs the kingdom of God. Truly, I say to you, whoever does not receive the kingdom of God like a child shall not enter it." And he took them in his arms and blessed them, laying his hands upon them. (Also Mk. 9:36–37, Is. 40:11.)
Rev. 21:3–4. ...God himself will be with them; he will wipe away every tear from their eyes, and death shall be no more, neither shall there be mourning nor crying nor pain any more, for the former things have passed away. (Also Is. 25:8.)
1 Pet. 4:19. Therefore let those who suffer according to God's will do right and entrust their souls to a faithful Creator.

Ps. 19:1–4. *The heavens are telling the glory of God; and the firmament proclaims his handiwork.* Day to day pours forth speech, and night to night declares knowledge. *There is no speech, nor are there words; their voice is not heard* (Luther: da man nicht ihre Stimme höre); Yet their voice goes out through all the earth, and their words to the end of the world...
1 Chron. 29:11. Thine, O Lord, is the greatness, and the power, and the glory, and the victory, and the majesty; for all that is in the heavens and in the earth is thine; thine is the Kingdom, O Lord, and thou art exalted as head above all.
Ps. 97:6. The heavens proclaim his righteousness; and all the peoples behold his glory.
Hab. 3:3. ...[God's] glory covered the heavens and the earth was full of his praise.

2. Tenor Rect.

●Nature & grace tell of God's gracious invitation (76-2)

So   läßt   sich   Gott nicht unbezeuget!
Thus leaves himself God not untestified!
{Thus God does not leave himself without testimony!}

Natur und Gnade redt alle Menschen an:
Nature and grace address all   people   - (thus):

Dies alles hat   ja   Gott getan,
This all has indeed God done,
{All this has been done by God,}

Daß   sich   die Himmel regen
To-the-extent-that themselves the heavens animate
{To the extent that the heavens are animated}

Und Geist und Körper sich   bewegen.
And soul and body themselves bestir.
{And body and soul are stirred.}

Gott selbst hat sich zu euch geneiget
God himself has -   to you inclined
{God himself has inclined himself to you}

 Und ruft durch   Boten   ohne Zahl:
And calls through messengers without number:

Auf, kommt zu meinem Liebesmahl!
Rise, come to   my   love-feast!

3. Soprano Aria

●Exhortation: Heed God's invitation of grace in Christ (76-3)

Hört, ihr Völker, Gottes Stimme,
Hear, ye peoples, God's voice,

Eilt   zu seinem Gnadenthron!
Hasten to   his   throne-of-grace!

Aller Dinge   Grund   und   Ende
Of-all things (the) foundation and termination

Ist sein eingeborner Sohn:
Is his   only-begotten Son:

Daß   sich   alles zu ihm wende.
So-that - all-things to him turn.
{Let all creation turn to him.}

Rom. 1:19–20. What can be known about God is plain to [all] because God has shown it to them. Ever since the creation of the world his invisible nature, namely, his eternal power and deity, has been clearly perceived in the things that have been made. So they are without excuse.

Jn. 1:1–3. In the beginning was the Word, and the Word was with God, and the Word was God. He was in the beginning with God; all things were made through him, and without him was not anything made that was made.

Col. 1:15–17. [Christ] is the image of the invisible God, the first-born of all creation; for in him all things were created, in heaven and on earth, visible and invisible, whether thrones or dominions or principalities or authorities—all things were created through him and for him. He is before all things, and in him all things hold together.

Ps. 147:4. [The Lord] determines the number of the stars, he gives to all of them their names. (Also Gen. 15:5.)

Ps. 19:1–4. The heavens are telling the glory of God; and the firmament proclaims his handiwork. Day to day pours forth speech, and night to night declares knowledge. There is no speech, nor are there words; their voice is not heard; Yet their voice goes out through all the earth, and their words to the end of the world...

*Lk. 14:16–18. ...A man once gave a great banquet, and invited many; and at the time for the banquet he sent his servant to say to those who had been invited, "Come; for all is now ready." But they all alike began to make excuses...

Rev. 19:9. ...Blessed are those who are invited to the marriage supper of the Lamb...

*Lk. 14:16–18 [Christ]: ...A man...sent his servant to say to those who had been invited, "Come; for all is now ready." But they all alike began to make excuses...

Mt. 21:37–38 [Christ]: ...[An owner of a vineyard sent servants to the tenants of his vineyard and, when they mistreated his messengers, he] sent his son to them, saying "They will respect my son." ...When the tenants saw the son, they said to themselves, "This is the heir..." (Also Mk. 12:6–7, Lk. 20:13–14.)

Mt. 17:5. [At Christ's transfiguration]...a voice from the cloud said, "This is my beloved Son, with whom I am well pleased; listen to him."

Ps. 86:9. [O Lord,] all the nations thou hast made shall come and bow down before thee, O Lord, and shall glorify thy name. (Also Zeph. 2:11, Rev. 15:4.)

Jn. 3:17. God sent [his] Son into the world...that the world might be saved through him.

Col. 1:15–17. [Christ] is the image of the invisible God, the first-born of all creation; for in him all things were created...all things were created through him and for him. He is before all things, and in him all things hold together.

Jn. 1:1–3, 14. In the beginning was the Word, and the Word was with God, and the Word was God. He was in the beginning with God; all things were made through him, and without him was not anything made that was made...And the Word became flesh and dwelt among us, full of grace and truth; we have beheld his glory, glory as of the only Son from the Father.

1 Jn. 4:9. In this the love of God was made manifest among us, that God sent his only Son into the world, so that we might live through him. (Also Jn. 3:16, 18.)

4. Bass Recit.

●God's invitation of grace spurned by many (76-4)

Wer aber hört,
Who, though, heeds (this invitation),
{Who heeds this invitation, though,}

Da sich der größte Haufen
Since - the greatest horde
{Since the majority}

Zu andern Göttern kehrt?
To other gods does-turn?
{Turns to other gods?}

Der älteste Götze eigner Lust
The oldest god (of) individual inclination
[Götze = idol, false deity]

Beherrscht der Menschen Brust.
Controls the human breast.

Die Weisen brüten Torheit aus,
The wise hatch folly -,

Und Belial sitzt wohl in Gottes Haus,
And Belial sits apparently in God's house,
{And Belial apparently sits in God's house,}

Weil auch die Christen selbst von Christo laufen.
Since even - Christians, (too), from Christ do-run.

5. Bass Aria

●God's invitation rejected by perverse; I will accept (76-5)

Fahr hin, abgöttische Zunft!
Go away, idolatrous band!

Sollt sich die Welt gleich verkehren,
Should - the world though turn-perverse,
{Even though the world should turn perverse,}

Will ich doch Christum verehren,
Will I still Christ honor,
{I will still honor Christ,}

Er ist das Licht der Vernunft.
He is the light of reason.

6. Alto Recit.

●God's invitation came to us Gentiles & enlightened us (76-6)

Du hast uns, Herr, von allen Straßen
Thou hast us, Lord, from all thoroughfares
{Thou hast called us, O Lord, from every thoroughfare}

Zur dir geruft,
To thyself called,
{To thyself,}

Jn. 12:37-38. Though [Jesus] had done so many signs before [the people], yet they did not believe in him; it was that the word spoken by the prophet Isaiah might be fulfilled: "Lord, who has believed our report...?" (See Is. 53:1.)

*Lk. 14:18. ...They all alike began to make excuses...

Rom. 1:18, 21-23, 25. The wrath of God is revealed from heaven against all ungodliness and wickedness of men who by their wickedness suppress the truth...Although they knew God they did not honor him as God or give thanks to him, but they became futile in their thinking and their senseless minds were darkened. Claiming to be wise, they became fools, and exchanged the glory of the immortal God for images resembling mortal man or birds or animals or reptiles ...They exchanged the truth about God for a lie and worshiped and served the creature rather than the Creator... (Also Gen. 3:6, Mt. 7:13-14, 1 Cor. 1:19-20, 25.)

Is. 53:6. All we like sheep have gone astray; we have turned every one to his own way...

Mt. 21:12-13. Jesus entered the temple of God and drove out all who sold and bought in the temple...He said to them, "It is written, 'My house shall be called a house of prayer'; but you make it a den of robbers." (Also Jn. 2:15.)

2 Cor. 6:15-18. What accord has Christ with Belial? Or what has a believer in common with an unbeliever? What agreement has the temple of God with idols? For we are the temple of the living God; as God said, "I will live in them and move among them, and I will be their God, and they shall be my people. Therefore come out from them and be separate from them, says the Lord, and touch nothing unclean; then I will welcome you, and I will be a father to you, and you shall be my sons and daughters, says the Lord Almighty."

1 Cor. 10:7. Do not be idolaters (Luther: Abgöttische) as some of [the Israelites] were; as it is written, "The people sat down to eat and drink and rose up to dance."

Rom. 1:28. Since [men] did not see fit to acknowledge God, God gave them up to a base mind (Luther: verkehrten Sinn) and to improper conduct.

Mt. 26:33. Peter declared to [Jesus], "Though they all fall away because of you, I will never fall away."

2 Cor. 4:3-4. ...If our gospel is veiled, it is veiled only to those who are perishing. In their case the god of this world has blinded the minds of the unbelievers, to keep them from seeing the light of the gospel of the glory of Christ, who is the likeness of God. (Also 1 Jn. 2:11.)

Jn. 1:9. [In Christ] the true light that enlightens every man was coming into the world. (Also Mt. 11:25, Lk. 10:21.)

*Lk. 14:16-18, 21-24 [Christ]: ...A man once gave a great banquet, and invited many; and at the time for the banquet he sent his servant to say to those who had been invited, "Come; for all is now ready." But they all alike began to make excuses...So the servant came and reported this to his master. Then the householder in anger said to his servant, "Go out quickly to the streets and lanes of the city, and bring in the poor and maimed and blind and lame." And the servant said, "Sir, what you commanded has been done, and still there is room." And the master said to the servant, "Go out to the highways and

Als   wir   in Finsternis der   Heiden saßen,
When we (still) in-the darkness of-the Gentiles sat,
{While we still sat in the darkness of the Gentiles,}

Und,   wie das Licht die Luft
And, (just) as   -   light the air

Belebet und erquickt,
Quickens and revives, (so hast thou)

Uns auch erleuchtet und belebet,
Us also enlightened and quickened,

Ja   mit dir selbst gespeiset und getränket
Yea, (hast us) with thy-self   fed   and given-to-drink

Und deinen Geist geschenket,
And thy   Spirit   given,
{And given us thy Spirit,}

Der   stets   in unserm Geiste schwebet.
Who constantly within our   soul   moves.
{Who constantly moves within our soul.}

Drum   sei dir dies Gebet   demütigst zugeschickt:
Therefore be to-thee this prayer (now) humbly   sent:

hedges, and compel people to come in, that my house may be filled.
For I tell you, none of those men who were invited shall taste my banquet."
Acts 28:28. Let it be known to you then that this salvation of God has been sent to the Gentiles; they will listen.
Mt. 8:11–12 [Christ]: I tell you, many will come from east and west and sit at table with Abraham, Isaac, and Jacob in the kingdom of heaven, while the sons of the kingdom will be thrown into the outer darkness... (Also Lk. 13:29, Rom. 11:11.)
Mt. 4:16. The people who sat in darkness have seen a great light, and for those who sat in the region and shadow of death light has dawned. (Also Is. 9:2, Ps. 107:10–11, Lk. 1:79.)
Col. 2:13. You, who were dead in trespasses and the uncircumcision of your flesh, God made alive...
Eph. 2:1–2. You [God] made alive, when you were dead through the trespasses and sins in which you once walked, following the course of this world... (Also Col. 2:13.)
Jn. 6:54 [Christ]: He who eats my flesh and drinks my blood has eternal life, and I will raise him up at the last day. (Also Mt. 26:26–28.)
Jn. 4:14 [Christ]: Whoever drinks of the water that I shall give him will never thirst; the water that I shall give him will become in him a spring of water welling up to eternal life.
Jn. 6:48, 51 [Christ]: I am the bread of life...if any one eats of this bread, he will live for ever...
1 Jn. 3:24. ...By this we know that he abides in us, by the Spirit which he has given us. (Also 1 Jn. 4:13.)
2 Cor. 1:22. He has put his seal upon us and given us his Spirit in our hearts as a guarantee. (Also Acts 5:32, Rom. 5:5, 1 Cor 12:13, 2 Cor. 5:5.)

7. Chorale
●Prayer that God bless us & bring salvation to others (76-7)
Es woll   uns Gott genädig sein
(Now-may) to-us God gracious be
{May God be gracious to us}

Und seinen Segen geben;
And   his   blessing give;
{And give his blessing;}

    Sein   Antlitz uns mit hellem Schein
(May) his countenance us with bright lustre
{May his countenance illuminate us mightily}

Erleucht zum ewgen Leben,
Illuminate to eternal life,
{To eternal life,}

Daß wir erkennen seine Werk,
So-that we acknowledge his   work,

Und was ihm   lieb auf Erden,
And what to-him is-dear on earth,
{And what is dear to him on earth,}

Und   Jesus Christus Heil und Stärk
And (that) Jesus Christ's salvation and power

Ps. 67:1–2. May God be gracious to us and bless us and make his face to shine upon us, that thy way may be known upon earth, thy saving power among all nations.
Num. 6:24–26. The Lord bless you and keep you: The Lord make his face to shine upon you, and be gracious to you: The Lord lift up his countenance upon you, and give you peace.
Jn. 1:4–5. In [Christ] was life, and the life was the light of men. The light shines in the darkness, and the darkness has not overcome it.
Jn. 8:12. Again Jesus spoke to them, saying, "I am the light of the world; he who follows me will not walk in darkness, but will have the light of life." (Also Ps. 36:9.)
Rom. 1:20–21. Ever since the creation of the world his invisible nature, namely, his eternal power and deity, has been clearly perceived in the things that have been made. So they are without excuse; for although they knew God they did not honor him as God or give thanks to him, but they became futile in their thinking and their senseless minds were darkened.
Col. 1:9–10. ...We have not ceased to pray for you, asking that you may be filled with the knowledge of his will in all spiritual wisdom and understanding, to lead a life worthy of the Lord, fully pleasing to him, bearing fruit in every good work and increasing in the knowledge of God. (Also Heb. 13:21.)
2 Cor. 5:9. ...We make it our aim to please him. (Also Eph. 5:10, Rom. 14:8.)

Bekannt den Heiden werden
Known to-the Gentiles become
{Might become known to the Gentiles}

Und sie zu Gott bekehren.
And they to God convert.
{And they be converted to God.}

Part II

8. Sinfonia

9. Bass Recit.
●God's people to reflect his glory despite persecution (76-9)
Gott segne noch die treue Schar,
God bless (then) the faithful throng,

Damit sie seine Ehre
That they his glory

Durch Glauben, Liebe, Heiligkeit
Through faith, love, (and) holiness

Erweise und vemehre.
Might-demonstrate and increase.

Sie ist der Himmel auf der Erden
They are - heaven on the earth
{They represent heaven on this earth}

Und muß durch steten Streit
And must through constant strife,

Mit Haß und mit Gefahr
By hate and by danger
{Hate, and danger}

In dieser Welt gereinigt werden.
In this world purified be.
{In this world be purified.}

10. Tenor Aria
●Favor of this world rejected in favor of Christ (76-10)
Hasse nur, hasse mich recht,
Hate, then, hate me thoroughly,

Feindlichs Geschlecht!
Hostile generation!

Christum gläubig zu umfassen
Christ in-faith to embrace
{In order to embrace Christ in faith}

2 Pet. 3:9. [God does not wish]...that any should perish, but that all should reach repentance.
Mt. 28:19 [Christ]: Go...and make disciples of all nations, baptizing them in the name of the Father and of the Son and of the Holy Spirit.
*Lk. 14:23. Go out to the highways and hedges, and compel people to come in, that my house may be filled.
Acts 26:19–20 [Paul]: I...declared...to the Gentiles, that they should repent and turn to God and perform deeds worthy of their repentance. (Also Acts 13:47, 17:30, 28:28.)

Ps. 67:1–2. May God...bless us and make his face to shine upon us, that [his] way may be known upon earth, [his] saving power among all nations.
1 Tim. 6:11. As for you, man of God, ...aim at righteousness, godliness, faith, love, steadfastness, gentleness. (Also 1 Tim. 2:15, 2 Tim. 2:22b.)
1 Pet. 1:15–16. As he who called you is holy, be holy yourselves in all your conduct; since it is written, "You shall be holy, for I am holy." (See Lev. 20:26.)
1 Pet. 2:12. Maintain good conduct among the Gentiles, so that...they may see your good deeds and glorify God on the day of visitation.
Acts 13:47. ...The Lord has commanded us, saying, "I have set you to be a light for the Gentiles, that you may bring salvation to the uttermost parts of the earth."
Acts 1:8 [Christ]: ...You shall be my witnesses... (Also Is. 43:10.)
Heb. 12:1. ...a cloud of witnesses...
Rom. 1:19–20. What can be known about God is plain to [men] because God has shown it to them. Ever since the creation of the world his...eternal power and deity, has been clearly perceived in the things that have been made.
Ps. 19:1. The heavens are telling the glory of God; and the firmament proclaims his handiwork.
Mt. 5:14, 16. You are the light of the world...Let your light so shine before men, that they may see your good works and give glory to your Father who is in heaven.
*1 Jn. 3:13. Do not wonder, brethren, that the world hates you. (Also Jn. 15:18–21, Jn. 17:14, Mt. 5:10–12, 10:24–25.)
1 Pet. 1:6–7. In this you rejoice, though now for a little while you may have to suffer various trials, so that the genuineness of your faith, more precious than gold which though perishable is tested by fire, may redound to praise and glory and honor at the revelation of Jesus Christ.
Jms. 1:2–3. Count it all joy, my brethren, when you meet various trials, for you know that the testing of your faith produces steadfastness. (Also Jms. 1:12, 1 Pet. 4:12–14.)

Jn. 15:18–19 [Christ]: If the world hates you, know that it has hated me before it hated you. If you were of the world, the world would love its own; but because you are not of the world, but I chose you out of the world, therefore the world hates you. (Also Jn. 17:14, Mt. 5:10–12, 10:24–25.)
1 Jn. 3:13. Do not wonder, brethren, that the world hates you.
2 Tim. 3:12. Indeed all who desire to live a godly life in Christ Jesus will be persecuted.
Phil. 3:8–11. ...For [Christ's] sake I have suffered the loss of all things, and count them as refuse, in order that I may gain Christ and be found in him, not having a righteousness of my own, based on law, but that which is through faith in Christ, the righteousness from God that

Will ich alle Freude lassen.
Would I all happiness relinquish.
{I am willing to relinquish all happiness.}

11. Alto Recit.
●Heavenly feast of love's sweet manna already begun (76–11)
Ich fühle schon im Geist,
I perceive already in (my) spirit,

Wie Christus mir
How Christ to-me

Der Liebe Süßigkeit erweist
- Love's sweetness shows

Und mich mit Manna speist,
And me with manna feeds,

Damit sich unter uns allhier
So-that - amongst us here

Die brüderliche Treue
- Brotherly fidelity

Stets stärke und verneue.
Constantly (may) strengthen and renew (itself).
{Constantly may be strengthened and renewed.}

12. Alto Aria
●Brotherly love shown us in Christ to be our example (76–12)
Liebt, ihr Christen, in der Tat!
Love, ye Christians, in - deed!
{O Christians, show your love in your deeds!}

Jesus stirbet für die Brüder,
Jesus dies for the brethren,

Und sie sterben für sich wieder,
And they die for (each-other) in-turn,

Weil er sich verbunden hat.
Because he himself (to them) bound has.
{Because he has made a bond with them.}

13. Tenor Recit.
●Firmament of godly souls shall declare love of God (76–13)
So soll die Christenheit
Thus shall - Christendom

Die Liebe Gottes preisen
The love of-God praise
{Praise the love of God}

depends on faith; that I may know him and the power of his resurrection, and may share his sufferings, becoming like him in his death, that if possible I may attain the resurrection from the dead.

Rom. 5:5. Hope does not disappoint us, because God's love has been poured into our hearts through the Holy Spirit which has been given to us.
Ps. 78:23–25. ...[God] rained down upon [the Israelites] manna to eat, and gave them the grain of heaven. Man ate the bread of the angels; he sent them food in abundance. (Also Ex. 16:31, 35, Jn. 6:32–35, Rev. 2:17.)
Jn. 6:30–35. They said to [Jesus], "Then what sign do you do, that we may see, and believe you? What work do you perform? Our fathers ate the manna in the wilderness..." Jesus then said to them, "Truly, truly, I say to you, it was not Moses who gave you the bread from heaven; my Father gives you the true bread from heaven. For the bread of God is that which comes down from heaven, and gives life to the world." They said to him, "Lord, give us this bread always." Jesus said to them, "I am the bread of life; he who comes to me shall not hunger, and he who believes in me shall never thirst." (Also Jn. 6:50–51, 58.)
Rev. 2:17 [Christ]: ...To him who conquers I will give some of the hidden manna...
Is. 40:11. He will feed his flock like a shepherd...
***Lk. 14:16.** ...A man once gave a great banquet, and invited many.
***1 Jn. 3:14.** We know that we have passed out of death into life, because we love the brethren. He who does not love abides in death.
2 Thess. 1:3. ...Your faith is growing abundantly, and the love of every one of you for one another is increasing.

***1 Jn. 3:11, 16, 18, 23.** This is the message which you have heard from the beginning, that we whould love one another...By this we know love, that he laid down his life for us; and we ought to lay down our lives for the brethren...Little children, let us not love in word or speech but in deed and in truth...This is his commandment, that we should believe in the name of his Son Jesus Christ and love one another... (Also Jms. 2:14–16, Jn. 15:12, 17.)
Jn. 15:13 [Christ]: Greater love has no man than this, that a man lay down his life for his friends. (Also Rom. 5:7–8.)
1 Jn. 4:19–21. We love, because he first loved us. If any one says, "I love God," and hates his brother, he is a liar; for he who does not love his brother whom he has seen, cannot love God whom he has not seen. And this commandment we have from him, that he who loves God should love his brother also. (See Jn. 13:34–35.)

Ps. 106:1. Praise the Lord! O give thanks to the Lord, for he is good; for his steadfast love endures for ever.
Ps. 63:3. [O Lord,] because thy steadfast love is better than life, my lips will praise thee.
Ps. 79:13. We thy people, the flock of thy pasture, will give thanks to thee for ever; from generation to generation we will recount thy praise. (Also 1 Chron. 16:9, 12, Ps. 105:2, 6.)
1 Jn. 3:1. See what love the Father has given us, that we should be called children of God; and so we are...
1 Jn. 4:7–12. Beloved, let us love one another; for love is of God, and he who loves is born of God and knows God. He who does not love

268

Und sie an sich erweisen:
And it in itself demonstrate:
{And give evidence of this love in its actions:}

Bis in die Ewigkeit
Until - - eternity

Die Himmel frommer Seelen
The firmament of-godly souls (shall)

Gott und sein Lob erzählen.
God and his praise declare.
{Proclaim God and his praise.}

14. Chorale (See also 69-6.)
●God's praise expressed by his people in good deeds (76-14)
Es danke, Gott, und lobe dich
(Let) thank (thee), God, and praise thee

Das Volk in guten Taten;
The people with good deeds;
{May thy people thank and praise thee, God, with good deeds;}

Das Land bringt Frucht und bessert sich,
The land bears fruit and improves - ,

Dein Wort ist wohl geraten.
Thy Word (has) well-succeeded.

Uns segne Vater und der Sohn,
(May) us bless Father and the Son,
{May the Father and the Son bless us,}

Uns segne Gott, der Heilge Geist,
(May) us bless God, the Holy Ghost,
{May God the Holy Ghost bless us, too,}

Dem alle Welt die Ehre tu,
To-whom all-the world - honor (ascribes),
{To whom all the world ascribes honor,}

does not know God; for God is love. In this the love of God was made manifest among us, that God sent his only Son into the world, so that we might live through him. In this is love, not that we loved God but that he loved us and sent his Son to be the expiation for our sins. Beloved, if God so loved us, we also ought to love one another. No man has ever seen God; if we love one another, God abides in us and his love is perfected in us.
Jn. 13:35 [Christ]: By this all men will know that you are my disciples, if you have love for one another. (Also Jn. 15:12, 17, 1 Thess. 4:9, *1 Jn. 3:11.)
Ps. 96:2–3. Sing to the Lord, bless his name...Declare his glory among the nations, his marvelous works among all the peoples! (Also Ps. 102:21–22, Is. 66:19.)
Dan. 2:20. ...Blessed be the name of God for ever and ever... (Also Ps. 86:12, 113:2, 115:18, 145:1–2, Dan. 2:20.)
Ps. 148:1–4. Praise the Lord! Praise the Lord from the heavens, praise him in the heights! Praise him, all his angels, praise him, all his host! Praise him, sun and moon, praise him, all you shining stars! Praise him, you highest heavens...
Dan. 12:3. Those who are wise shall shine like the brightness of the firmament; and those who turn many to righteousness, like the stars for ever and ever.
Eph. 2:6. [God] raised us up with [Christ], and made us sit with him in the heavenly places...
Rev. 19:1. ...[In my vision] I heard what seemed to be the loud voice of a great multitude in heaven, crying, "Hallelujah! Salvation and glory and power belong to our God."
Ps. 19:1. The heavens are telling the glory of God; and the firmament proclaims his handiwork.

Ps. 67:5–7. Let the peoples praise thee, O God; let all the peoples praise thee! The earth has yielded its increase; God, our God, has blessed us. God has blessed us; let all the ends of the earth fear him!
Tit. 3:8. ...Those who have believed in God [should] be careful to apply themselves to good deeds... (Also Tit. 1:16, 2:14, 3:14.)
1 Pet. 2:12. Maintain good conduct among the Gentiles, so that...they may see your good deeds and glorify God... (Also Mt. 5:16.)
Lev. 25:18–19 [God]: You shall do my statutes, and keep my ordinances and perform them; so you will dwell in the land securely. The land will yield its fruit, and you will eat your fill, and dwell in it securely. (Also Lev. 26:3–4, Deut. 28:11.)
Is. 55:10–11 [God]: As the rain and the snow come down from heaven, and return not thither but water the earth, making it bring forth and sprout, giving seed to the sower and bread to the eater, so shall my word be that goes forth from my mouth; it shall not return to me empty, but it shall accomplish that which I purpose, and prosper in the thing for which I sent it. (Also Mt. 13:18, Mk. 4:14, 20.)
Ps. 115:12–15. The Lord has been mindful of us; he will bless us...he will bless those who fear the Lord, both small and great. May the Lord give you increase, you and your children! May you be blessed by the Lord, who made heaven and earth!
Ps. 66:4. [O Lord,] all the earth worships thee; they sing praises to thee, sing praises to thy name.
Mt. 28:19. ...in the name of the Father and of the Son and of the Holy Spirit.
1 Pet. 1:17. If you invoke as Father him who judges each one impartially according to his deeds, conduct yourselves with fear throughout the time of your exile [on earth].

Für ihm sich fürchte allermeist
\- Him - fear most-of-all,
{May we fear him above all,}

Und sprech von Herzen: Amen!
And say from-the-heart: Amen!

BWV 77
Du sollt Gott, deinen Herren, lieben
(NBA I/21; BC A126)

13. S. after Trinity (BWV 77, 33, 164)
*Gal. 3:15–22 (The purpose of the Law)
*Lk. 10:23–37 (The greatest commandment; parable of the good Samaritan)
Librettist: Johann Knauer, modified.

1. Chorus
●Love God with all your heart, soul, mind: Lk. 10:27 (77-1)
Du sollt Gott, deinen Herren, lieben
You shall God, your Lord, love

von ganzem Herzen, von ganzer Seele,
with (your) whole heart, with (your) whole soul,

von allen Kräften und von ganzem Gemüte
with all (your) powers and with all (your) mind,

und deinen Nächsten als dich selbst.
and your neighbor as your self.

2. Bass Recit.
●God's favor sure for those who love God completely (77-2)
So muß es sein!
So must it be!

Gott will das Herz für sich alleine haben.
God desires the heart for himself alone to-have.
{God desires to have our hearts for himself alone.}

Man muß den Herrn von ganzer Seele
One must the Lord with (one's) whole soul
{One must choose the Lord with all of one's soul}

Zu seiner Lust erwählen
As one's delight choose
{As one's delight}

Und sich nicht mehr erfreun,
And - (never) more pleasure-find,
{And never find greater pleasure,}

Als wenn er das Gemüte
Than when he (our) disposition
{Than when he kindles our disposition}

Deut. 10:12. ...What does the Lord your God require of you, but to fear the Lord your God, to walk in all his ways, to love him, to serve the Lord your God with all your heart...?
Ps. 9:1. I will give thanks to the Lord with my whole heart; I will tell of all thy wonderful deeds.
Ps. 106:48. Blessed be the Lord, the God of Israel, from everlasting to everlasting! And let all the people say, "Amen!" Praise the Lord!

*Lk. 10:25–27.** And behold, a lawyer stood up to put [Jesus] to the test, saying, "Teacher, what shall I do to inherit eternal life?" And he said to him, "What is written in the law...?" And he answered, *"You shall love the Lord your God with all your heart, and with all your soul, and with all your strength, and with all your mind; and your neighbor as yourself."* (Also Mt. 22:37–40, Mk. 12:30–31.)
Deut. 6:4–5. Hear, O Israel: The Lord our God is one Lord; and you shall love the Lord your God with all your heart, and with all your soul, and with all your might.
Lev. 19:17–18 [God]: You shall not hate your brother in your heart... but you shall love your neighbor as yourself: I am the Lord.
Lk. 6:32, 35–36 [Christ]: If you love those who love you, what credit is that to you? For even sinners love those who love them...But love your enemies, and do good...and you will be sons of the Most High; for he is kind...Be merciful, even as your Father is merciful.
1 Jn. 3:17–18. If any one has the world's goods and sees his brother in need, yet closes his heart against him, how does God's love abide in him? Little children, let us not love in word or speech but in deed and in truth. (Also Jms. 2:14–16.)

*Lk. 10:25, 27.** ...What shall I do to inherit eternal life?...You shall love the Lord your God with all your heart, and with all your soul, and with all your strength, and with all your mind...
Mk. 12:33. To love [God] with all the heart, and with all the understanding, and with all the strength, and to love one's neighbor as oneself, is much more than all whole burnt offerings and sacrifices.
Gal. 5:6. For in Christ Jesus [nothing] is of any avail, but faith working through love.
Ex. 20:3, 5 [God]: You shall have no other gods before me...I the Lord your God am a jealous God... (Also Deut. 5:7.)
Rev. 2:4 [Christ]: I have this against you, that you have abandoned the love you had at first.
Ps. 73:25. [O Lord,] whom have I in heaven but thee? And there is nothing upon earth that I desire besides thee.
Phil. 3:8–9. ...I count everything as loss because of the surpassing worth of knowing Christ Jesus my Lord. For his sake I have suffered the loss of all things, and count them as refuse, in order that I may gain Christ and be found in him...
Ps. 37:4. Take delight (Luther: Lust) in the Lord, and he will give you the desires of your heart.
Rom. 5:5. ...God's love has been poured into our hearts through the Holy Spirit which has been given to us.

Durch seinen Geist entzündt,
Through his   Spirit kindles,
{By his Spirit,}

Weil wir nur seiner Huld und Güte
For we - (of) his grace and kindness

Alsdenn erst recht versichert sind.
Then   only truly assured are.
{For only then are we truly assured of his grace and kindness.}

3. Soprano Aria
●Love for God declared; prayer that it be constant (77-3)
Mein Gott, ich liebe dich von   Herzen,
My God, I love thee with (all my) heart,

Mein ganzes Leben hangt dir an.
My   entire   life clings-to thee - .

Laß mich doch dein   Gebot   erkennen
Let me indeed thy commandment discern

Und in Liebe so entbrennen,
And with love so be-kindled,

Daß ich dich ewig lieben kann.
That I   thee eternally can-love.
{That I can eternally love thee.}

4. Tenor Recit.
●Prayer for a compassionate heart toward neighbor (77-4)
Gib mir dabei, mein Gott! ein Samariterherz,
Grant me as-well, my God, a Samaritan's-heart,

Daß ich   zugleich   den Nächsten liebe
That I at-the-same-time (my) neighbor would-love
{That I would also love my neighbor}

Und mich bei seinem Schmerz
And - in his   pain
{And when he is in pain}

Auch über ihn betrübe,
Also about him be-distressed,
{Be distressed about him, in turn;}

Damit ich   nicht bei ihm vorübergeh
So-that I (would) not - him pass-by
{So that I would not pass him by}

2 Chron. 16:9. The eyes of the Lord run to and fro throughout the whole earth, to show his might in behalf of those whose heart is blameless toward him...

Deut. 11:13-15. If you will obey [the] commandments which I command you this day, to love the Lord your God, and to serve him with all your heart and with all your soul, he will give the rain for your land in its season, the early rain and the later rain, that you may gather in your grain and your wine and your oil. And he will give grass in your fields for your cattle, and you shall eat and be full...

Mt. 6:33. But seek first his kingdom and his righteousness, and all these things shall be yours as well. (Also 1 Cor. 2:9.)

Mt. 22:37-40 [Parallel Gospel account]. [Jesus] said to him, "You shall love the Lord your God with all your heart, and with all your soul, and with all your mind. This is the great and first commandment. And a second is like it, You shall love your neighbor as yourself. On these two commandments depend (Luther: hanget) all the law and the prophets."

Deut. 13:4. You shall walk after the Lord your God and fear him, and keep his commandments and obey his voice, and you shall serve him and cleave to him (Luther: ihm anhangen). (Also Deut. 10:20, Ps. 63:8, 2 Kings 18:6.)

Jn. 21:15-17. When [the disciples and Jesus] had finished breakfast, Jesus said to Simon Peter, "Simon, son of John, do you love me more than these?" He said to him, "Yes, Lord; you know that I love you." He said to him, "Feed my lambs." A second time he said to him, "Simon, son of John, do you love me?" He said to him, "Yes, Lord; you know that I love you." He said to him, "Tend my sheep." He said to him the third time, "Simon, son of John, do you love me?" Peter was grieved because he said to him the third time, "Do you love me?" and he said to him, "Lord, you know everything; you know that I love you."

Lk. 10:25-37. ...A lawyer stood up to put [Jesus] to the test, saying, "Teacher, what shall I do to inherit eternal life?" He said to him, "What is written in the law? How do you read?" And he answered, "You shall love the Lord your God with all your heart, and with all your soul, and with all your strength, and with all your mind; and your neighbor as yourself." And he said to him, "You have answered right; do this, and you will live." But he, desiring to justify himself, said to Jesus, "And who is my neighbor?" Jesus replied, "A man was going down from Jerusalem to Jericho, and he fell among robbers, who stripped him and beat him, and departed, leaving him half dead. Now by chance a priest was going down that road; and when he saw him he passed by on the other side. So likewise a Levite, when he came to the place and saw him, passed by on the other side. But a Samaritan, as he journeyed, came to where he was; and when he saw him, he had compassion, and went to him and bound up his wounds, pouring on oil and wine; then he set him on his own beast and brought him to an inn, and took care of him...Which of these three, do you think, proved neighbor to the man who fell among the robbers?" He said, "The one who showed mercy on him." And Jesus said to him, "Go and do likewise."

Und   ihn in seiner   Not   nicht lasse.
And (would) him in his   distress not leave.
{And leave him in his distress.}

Gib,   daß ich Eigenliebe   hasse,
Grant, that I   self-love (would) hate,

So wirst du   mir dereinst das Freudenleben
Then wilt thou to-me some-day that life-of-gladness
{Then thou wilt someday give to me that life of gladness—}

Nach   meinem Wunsch, jedoch aus Gnaden geben.
According-to my   wish, nevertheless by   grace, give.
{According to my desire—yet nevertheless by grace.}

5. Alto Aria
●Love imperfect: I want to love yet lack the power (77-5)
Ach, es bleibt in meiner Liebe
Ah, there (is) in my   love

Lauter   Unvollkommenheit!
Nought-but imperfection!

Hab ich oftmals gleich den Willen,
Have I often though the inclination,
{Though I often have the inclination,}

Was Gott saget, zu erfüllen,
What God says, to perform,
{To do what God says,}

Fehlt   mir's   doch   an Möglichkeit.
Is-wanting in-me nevertheless (the) potentiality.
{Nevertheless, I find the power lacking in me.}

6. Chorale[1]
●Prayer: Dwell in me by a faith expressed through love (77-6)
Herr, durch den Glauben wohn in mir,
Lord, through -   faith   live in me,

Laß ihn sich immer   stärken,
Let it   - always grow-stronger,

Daß er sei fruchtbar für   und für
That it be fruitful forever and ever

Und reich in guten Werken;
And rich in good   works;

2 Tim. 3:1-2. ...In the last days...men will be lovers of self...
Phil. 2:4-7, 9. Let each of you look not only to his own interests, but also to the interests of others. Have this mind among yourselves, which is yours in Christ Jesus, who, though he was in the form of God, did not count equality with God a thing to be grasped, but emptied himself, taking the form of a servant...Therefore God has highly exalted him and bestowed on him the name which is above every name.
Mt. 25:34-40. [In the judgment] the King will say to those at his right hand, "Come, O blessed of my Father, inherit the kingdom prepared for you from the foundation of the world; for I was hungry and you gave me food, I was thirsty and you gave me drink, I was a stranger and you welcomed me, I was naked and you clothed me, I was sick and you visited me, I was in prison and you came to me." Then the righteous will answer him, "Lord, when did we see thee hungry and feed thee, or thirsty and give thee drink? And when did we see thee a stranger and welcome thee, or naked and clothe thee? And when did we see thee sick or in prison and vist thee?" And the King will answer them, "Truly, I say to you, as you did it to one of the least of these my brethren, you did it to me."

1 Jn. 4:12. ...If we love one another, God abides in us and his love is perfected in us. (Also Col. 3:14.)
Phil. 3:12-14. Not that I have already obtained this or am already perfect; but I press on to make it my own...One thing I do, forgetting what lies behind and straining forward to what lies ahead, I press on toward the goal for the prize of the upward call of God in Christ Jesus...
Rom. 7:15, 18, 22-24. I do not understand my own actions. For I do not do what I want, but I do the very thing I hate...For I know that nothing good dwells within me, that is, in my flesh. I can will what is right, but I cannot do it...For I delight in the law of God, in my inmost self, but I see in my members another law at war with the law of my mind and making me captive to the law of sin which dwells in my members. Wretched man that I am! Who will deliver me from this body of death?
Mk. 14:38. ...The spirit indeed is willing, but the flesh is weak. (Also Mt. 26:41.)

Eph. 3:16-17. [May God]...grant you to be strengthened with might through his Spirit in the inner man...that Christ may dwell in your hearts through faith...
2 Thess. 1:3. ...Your faith is growing abundantly, and the love of every one of you for one another is increasing.
Jn. 15:8 [Christ]: By this my Father is glorified, that you bear much fruit, and so prove to be my disciples.
Gal. 5:22-23. The fruit of the Spirit is love, joy, peace, patience, kindness, goodness, faithfulness, gentleness, self- control; against such there is no law.
Jms. 2:14-16. What does it profit, my brethren, if a man says he has faith but has not works? Can his faith save him? If a brother or sister is ill-clad and in lack of daily food, and one of you says to them, "Go in peace, be warmed and filled," without giving them the things needed for the body, what does it profit?

---

[1]Chorale untexted in autograph score. This text has been suggested by Werner Neumann. In his original (separately published) libretto Knauer used Vss. 11 & 12 of **Dies sind die heiligen zehn Gebot** [Luther, 1524]. For another suggestion see BC A126.

Daß er sei tätig durch die Lieb,
That it be active in - love,

Mit Freuden und Geduld sich üb,
In joy and patience itself exercise,
{Exercise itself in joy and patience,}

Dem Nächsten fort zu dienen.
(My) neighbor (ever) to serve.

BWV 78
Jesu, der du meine Seele
(NBA I/21; BC A130)

14. S. after Trinity (BWV 25, 78, 17)
*Gal. 5:16–24 (Work of the flesh and fruit of the Spirit)
*Lk. 17:11–19 (Jesus heals ten lepers)
Librettist: Unknown

1. Chorus (Chorale Vs. 1)
●Jesus' passion tore my soul from darkness (78-1)
Jesu, der du meine Seele
Jesus, who thou my soul
{Jesus, thou who my soul}

Hast durch deinen bittern Tod
Hast through thy bitter death

Aus des Teufels finstern Höhle
Out-of the devil's dark cavern

Und der schweren Seelennot
And - oppressive affliction-of-soul

Kräftiglich herausgerissen
Forcefully torn-out (to freedom)

Und mich solches lassen wissen
And me (this) let know
{And hast assured me of this}

Durch dein angenehmes Wort,
Through thy pleasant Word,

Sei doch itzt, o Gott, mein Hort!
Be indeed now, O God, my refuge!

2. Soprano & Alto Duet (Based on Chorale Vs. 2)
●Hastening to Jesus for healing with feeble steps (78-2)
Wir eilen mit schwachen, doch emsigen Schritten,
We hasten with weak, yet eager steps,

1 Jn. 3:17–18. If any one has the world's goods and sees his brother in need, yet closes his heart against him, how does God's love abide in him? Little children, let us not love in word or speech but in deed and in truth.
1 Tim. 6:18. ...Be rich in good deeds, liberal and generous.
Gal. 5:6. In Christ Jesus neither circumcision nor uncircumcision is of any avail, but faith working through love (Luther: Glaube der durch die Liebe tätig ist).
Col. 1:11. May you be strengthened...for all endurance and patience with joy.
***Lk. 10:27.** ...You shall love...your neighbor as yourself. (Also Lev. 19:18.)

Ps. 116:8. [O Lord,] thou hast delivered my soul from death... (Also Ps. 56:13.)
Heb. 2:14–15. Since...the children share in flesh and blood, [Christ] himself likewise partook of the same nature, that through death he might destroy him who has the power of death, that is, the devil, and deliver all those who through fear of death were subject to lifelong bondage.
Rom. 6:23. The wages of sin is death, but the free gift of God is eternal life in Christ Jesus our Lord.
Eph. 2:4–6. God, who is rich in mercy, out of the great love with which he loved us, even when we were dead through our trespasses, made us alive together with Christ...and raised us up with him, and made us sit with him in the heavenly places in Christ Jesus. (Also Rom. 6:4, Col 2:12–13.)
1 Jn. 3:8. ...The reason the Son of God appeared was to destroy the works of the devil.
Eph. 4:8–10. Therefore it is said, "When he ascended on high he led a host of captives, and he gave gifts to men." (In saying, "He ascended," what does it mean but that he had also descended into the lower parts of the earth? He who descended is he who also ascended far above all the heavens, that he might fill all things.)
1 Cor. 15:25–26. [Christ] must reign until he has put all his enemies under his feet. The last enemy to be destroyed is death.
2 Tim. 1:10. ...Our Savior Christ Jesus...abolished death and brought life and immortality to light... (Also Jn. 11:25–26.)
1 Pet. 3:18. Christ...died for sins once for all, the righteous for the unrighteous, that he might bring us to God, being put to death in the flesh but made alive in the spirit.
Rom. 5:6, 8. While we were still weak, at the right time Christ died for the ungodly...God shows his love for us in that while we were yet sinners Christ died for us.
Ps. 18:2. The Lord is my rock, and my fortress, and my deliverer, my God, my rock (Luther: Hort), in whom I take refuge, my shield, and the horn of my salvation, my stronghold.

Heb. 4:16. Let us then with confidence draw near...that we may receive mercy and find grace to help in time of need.
***Lk. 17:11–13.** On the way to Jerusalem [Jesus] was passing along between Samaria and Galilee. And as he entered a village, he was met by ten lepers, who stood at a distance and lifted up their voices and said, "Jesus, Master, have mercy on us."

O Jesu, o Meister, zu helfen zu dir.
O Jesus, O master, for   help   to thee.

Du suchest die Kranken und Irrenden treulich.
Thou seekest the sick   and erring faithfully.

Ach höre, wie wir
Ah hear, how we

Die Stimmen erheben, um Hülfe zu bitten!
(Our) voices   raise, for help do entreat (thee)!

Es   sei uns dein gnädiges   Antlitz   erfreulich!
(Now) be to-us thy gracious countenance gratifying!
{May thy gracious countenance smile upon us!}

Lk. 5:31–32. Jesus [said], "Those who are well have no need of a physician, but those who are sick; I have not come to call the righteous, but sinners to repentance." (Also Mt. 9:12–13, Mk. 2:17.)
Lk. 15:4–7 [Christ]: What man of you, having a hundred sheep, if he has lost one of them does not leave the ninety-nine in the wilderness, and go after the one which is lost, until he finds it? And when he has found it, he lays it on his shoulders, rejoicing. And when he comes home, he calls together his friends and his neighbors, saying to them, "Rejoice with me, for I have found my sheep which was lost." Just so, I tell you, there will be more joy in heaven over one sinner who repents than over ninety-nine righteous persons who need no repentance. (Also Mt. 18:12–14.)
Ps. 67:1. May God be gracious to us and bless us and make his face to shine upon us... (Also Ps. 4:6, 31:16, 80:3/7/19, Num. 6:24–26.)

3. Tenor Recit. (Based on Chorale Vss. 3–5)
●Confession of sinful nature: it makes me transgress (78–3)
Ach! ich bin ein Kind der Sünden
Ah! I am a child of sin,

Ach! ich irre weit und breit.
Ah! I stray far and wide.

Der Sünden Aussatz, so an mir zu finden,
- Sin's leprosy, which in me can-be found,

Verläßt mich nicht   in dieser Sterblichkeit.
Leaves me not (in peace) in this   mortal-life.
{Never leaves me in peace in this mortal life.}

Mein Wille trachtet nur nach Bösen.
My   will strives only after evil.

Der Geist zwar spricht: ach! wer wird mich erlösen?
(My) spirit indeed says: Alas! who will me deliver?

Aber Fleisch und Blut zu zwingen
But   flesh and blood to overcome

Und das Gute zu vollbringen,
And the good to accomplish,

Ist über   alle meine Kraft.
Is greater-than all my strength.

Will ich den Schaden nicht verhehlen,
Would I the wrong   not conceal,
{If I would not conceal my sin,}

So kann ich nicht, wie oft ich fehle, zählen.
So can I not, how often I fail, count.
{Then I must admit, I cannot count the times I fail.}

Drum nehm ich nun der Sünden Schmerz und Pein
Therefore take I now - sin's suffering and pain

Ps. 51:5. Behold, I was brought forth in iniquity, and in sin did my mother conceive me.
*Gal. 5:17. The desires of the flesh are against the Spirit, and the desires of the Spirit are against the flesh; for these are opposed to each other, to prevent you from doing what you would.
Is. 53:6. All we like sheep have gone astray; we have turned every one to his own way... (Also Gen. 6:5.)
Jer. 30:12–13. Thus says the Lord: Your hurt is incurable, and your wound is grievous. There is none to uphold your cause, no medicine for your wound, no healing for you.
*Lk. 17:12–13. ...[Jesus] was met by ten lepers, who stood at a distance and lifted up their voices and said, "Jesus, Master, have mercy on us."
Lev. 13:9–10, 45–46. When a man is afflicted with leprosy, he shall be brought to the priest; and the priest shall make an examination...The leper who has the disease shall wear torn clothes and let the hair of his head hang loose, and he shall cover his upper lip and cry. "Unclean, unclean." He shall remain unclean as long as he has the disease; he is unclean; he shall dwell alone in a habitation outside the camp.
Gen. 6:5. The Lord saw that the wickedness of man was great in the earth, and that every imagination of the thoughts of his heart (Luther: Dichten und Trachten) was only evil continually.
Ps. 34:14. Depart from evil, and do good; seek peace, and pursue it. (Also Is. 1:16–17, Amos 5:14–15.)
Col. 3:2. Set your minds (Luther: trachtet) on things that are above, not on things that are on earth.
Rom. 7:15, 18–20, 24–25. I do not understand my own actions. For I do not do what I want, but I do the very thing I hate...For I know that nothing good dwells within me, that is, in my flesh. I can will what is right, but I cannot do it. For I do not do the good I want, but the evil I do not want is what I do. Now if I do what I do not want, it is no longer I that do it, but sin which dwells within me...Wretched man that I am! Who will deliver me from this body of death? Thanks be to God through Jesus Christ our Lord!...
Mt. 26:41. ...The spirit indeed is willing, but the flesh is weak. (Also Mk. 14:38.)

Und meiner Sorgen Bürde,
And   my   sorrows' burden—

So   mir   sonst unerträglich würde,
Which for-me otherwise unbearable would-be—
{Which would otherwise be unbearable for me—and}

Ich liefre sie   dir,   Jesu, seufzend ein.
I deliver them (up) to-thee, Jesus, with-groaning - .

Rechne   nicht die Missetat,
Reckon (against me) not   the   misdeed(s),
{Do not reckon the misdeeds against me,}

Die   dich, Herr, erzürnet hat!
Which thee, Lord, have-angered!
{Which have angered thee, O Lord!}

4. Tenor Aria (Based on Chorale Vss. 6–7)
●Christ's blood cancels guilt and makes us victorious (78-4)
Das Blut, so   meine Schuld durchstreicht,
The blood, which (does) my   guilt   strike-out,
{The blood which strikes out my guilt,}

Macht mir das Herze wieder leicht
Makes - (my) heart   again   light
{Makes my heart light again}

Und spricht mich frei.
And pronounces me free.

Ruft mich der Höllen Heer zum Streite,
Calls me - hell's host   to   battle,
{Should hell's host call me to battle}

So stehet Jesus mir zur Seite,
Then stands Jesus (at my) side,
{Then Jesus stands at my side,}

Daß ich beherzt und sieghaft sei.
So-that I encouraged and victorious am.
{So that I am encouraged and victorious.}

5. Bass Recit. (Based on Chorale Vss. 8–10)
●Christ's passion led to blessing; I offer my heart (78-5)
Die Wunden, Nägel, Kron und Grab,
The wounds, nails, crown, and grave,

Die Schläge, so man dort dem Heiland gab,
The blows, which (they) there the Savior gave,

Sind ihm nunmehr o Siegeszeichen
Are for-him   now   symbols-of-victory

Und können mir verneute Kräfte reichen.
And can to-me renewed powers   give.
{And can give me renewed powers.}

Ps. 32:5. [O Lord,] I acknowledged my sin to thee, and I did not hide my iniquity (Luther: verhehle meine Missetat nicht); I said, "I will confess my transgressions to the Lord"; then thou didst forgive the guilt of my sin.
Ps. 38:4. For my iniquities have gone over my head; they weigh like a burden too heavy for me.
Mt. 11:28–30 [Christ]: Come to me, all who...are heavy laden, and I will give you rest. Take my yoke upon you, and learn from me; for I am gentle and lowly in heart, and you will find rest for your souls. For my yoke is easy, and my burden is light.
Ps. 32:1–2. Blessed is he whose transgression is forgiven, whose sin is covered. Blessed is the man to whom the Lord imputes no iniquity (Luther: Missetat nicht zurechnet)... (Also Rom. 4:7–8.)
Mic. 7:18–19. Who is a God like thee, pardoning iniquity and passing over transgression for the remnant of his inheritance? He does not retain his anger for ever because he delights in steadfast love. He will again have compassion upon us, he will tread our iniquities under foot. Thou wilt cast all our sins into the depths of the sea. (Also Ps. 103:12, Rom. 4:7–8.)

Col. 1:19–22. In [Christ] all the fulness of God was pleased to dwell, and through him to reconcile to himself all things, whether on earth or in heaven, making peace by the blood of his cross. And you, who once were estranged and hostile in mind, doing evil deeds, he has now reconciled in his body of flesh by his death, in order to present you holy and blameless and irreproachable before him.
Col. 2:13–15. You, who were dead in trespasses and the uncircumcision of your flesh, God made alive together with him, having forgiven us all our trespasses, having canceled the bond which stood against us with its legal demands; this he set aside, nailing it to the cross. He disarmed the principalities and powers and made a public example of them, triumphing over them in him. (Also Eph. 6:12, 1 Pet. 5:8.)
Rom. 8:33. Who shall bring any charge against God's elect? It is God who justifies.
1 Cor. 10:13. ...God is faithful, and he will not let you be tempted beyond your strength, but with the temptation will also provide the way of escape...
Rom. 8:31. What then shall we say to this? If God is for us, who is against us? (Also 2 Cor. 2:14.)
Ps. 118:6–7. With the Lord on my side I do not fear...The Lord is on my side to help me; I shall look in triumph on those who hate me.

Mt. 27:26, 28–31. Then [Pilate] released for [the people] Barabbas, and having scourged Jesus, delivered him to be crucified...And they stripped him and put a scarlet robe upon him, and plaiting a crown of thorns they put it on [Jesus'] head, and put a reed in his right hand. And kneeling before him they mocked him, saying, "Hail, King of the Jews!" And they spat upon him, and took the reed and struck him on the head. And when they had mocked him, they stripped him of the robe, and put his own clothes on him, and led him away to crucify him. (Also Mk. 15:15–20, Lk. 23:24–25, Jn. 19:1–16, 20:25, 27–28.)
Heb. 2:14–15. ...[Christ] partook of [human] nature, that through death he might destroy him who has the power of death, that is, the devil,

Wenn ein erschreckliches Gericht
When a dreadful court-of-justice

Den Fluch für die Verdammten spricht,
The curse upon the damned pronounces,

So kehrst du ihn in Segen.
Then turnest thou it into blessing.

Mich kann kein Schmerz und keine Pein bewegen,
Me can no suffering and no pain stir,
{No suffering and no pain can stir me,}

Weil sie mein Heiland kennt;
For of-them my Savior knows;
{For my Savior knows of them;}

Und da dein Herz für mich in Liebe brennt,
And since thy heart for me with love burns,
{And since thy heart burns for me with love,}

So lege ich hinwieder
So lay I in-return

Das meine vor dich nieder.
(Whatever-is) mine before thee down.
{I will, in return, lay down before thee whatever is mine.}

Dies mein Herz, mit Leid vermenget,
This my heart, with sorrow mixed,

So dein teures Blut besprenget,
Which thy precious blood does-sprinkle,
{Sprinkled with thy precious blood,}

So am Kreuz vergossen ist,
Which on-the cross shed (was),
{Which was shed on the cross,}

Geb ich dir, Herr Jesu Christ.
Give I to-thee, Lord Jesus Christ.
{I give to thee, Lord Jesus Christ.}

6. Bass Aria (Based on Chorale Vs. 11)
●Christ calms our accusing conscience and gives hope (78-6)
Nun du wirst mein Gewissen stillen,
Now thou wilt my conscience quieten,

So wider mich um Rache schreit,
Which against me for vengeance cries,

Ja, deine Treue wird's erfüllen,
Yes, thy faithfulness will-it accomplish,

Weil mir dein Wort die Hoffnung beut.
For to-me thy Word - hope does-offer.
{For thy Word offers me hope.}

and deliver all those who through fear of death were subject to lifelong bondage. (Also Phil. 2:5–8.)

1 Pet. 2:24. [Christ] himself bore our sins in his body on the tree, that we might die to sin and live to righteousness. By his wounds you have been healed. (Also Is. 53:5, 11–12, Gal. 3:13, Acts 5:30.)

Rom. 6:23. For the wages of sin is death, but the free gift of God is eternal life in Christ Jesus our Lord.

Col. 2:13–15. ...God made [you] alive together with [Christ]...having canceled the bond which stood against us with its legal demands; this he set aside, nailing it to the cross. He disarmed the principalities and powers and made a public example of them, triumphing over them in him.

1 Jn. 4:16–18. So we know and believe the love God has for us. God is love, and he who abides in love abides in God, and God abides in him. In this is love perfected with us, that we may have confidence for the day of judgment...There is no fear in love, but perfect love casts out fear. For fear has to do with punishment, and he who fears is not perfected in love. (Also Jn. 3:16–17, 13:1.)

Rom. 8:32. He who did not spare his own Son but gave him up for us all, will he not also give us all things with him?

1 Pet. 4:19. Therefore let those who suffer according to God's will do right and entrust (Luther: befehlen) their souls to a faithful Creator.

Job 23:10. [God] knows the way that I take; when he has tried me, I shall come forth as gold.

Ps. 139:3. ...[He is] acquainted with all my ways.

Rom. 12:1. I appeal to you therefore, brethren, by the mercies of God, to present your bodies as a living sacrifice, holy and acceptable to God, which is your spiritual worship.

Phil. 3:8–9. ...I count everything as loss because of the surpassing worth of knowing Christ Jesus my Lord. For his sake I have suffered the loss of all things, and count them as refuse, in order that I may gain Christ and be found in him, not having a righteousness of my own, based on law, but that which is through faith in Christ...

1 Pet. 1:18–19. You know that you were ransomed from the futile ways inherited from your fathers, not with perishable things such as silver or gold, but with the precious blood of Christ... (Also Eph. 2:13, 1 Jn. 1:7, Heb. 13:12, Rev. 5:9.)

Ps. 116:12. What shall I render to the Lord for all his bounty to me?

Ps. 51:17. The sacrifice acceptable to God is a broken spirit; a broken and contrite heart, O God, thou wilt not despise.

1 Jn. 3:19–21. By this we shall know that we are of the truth, and reassure our hearts before him whenever our hearts condemn us; for God is greater than our hearts, and he knows everything. Beloved, if our hearts do not condemn us, we have confidence before God.

1 Jn. 1:9. If we confess our sins, he is faithful and just, and will forgive our sins and cleanse us from all unrighteousness.

1 Thess. 5:24. He who calls you is faithful, and he will do it. (Also 2 Thess. 3:3.)

Rom. 8:1. There is therefore now no condemnation for those who are in Christ Jesus.

Rom. 8:33–34, 38–39. Who shall bring any charge against God's elect? It is God who justifies; who is to condemn? Is it Christ Jesus, who died, yes, who was raised from the dead, who is at the right hand of

Wenn Christen an dich glauben,
If   Christians on thee believe,
{If Christians believe on thee,}

Wird sie kein Feind in   Ewigkeit
Will them no   foe   in (all) eternity
{No foe will them in all eternity}

Aus deinen Händen rauben.
Out of-thy   hands   steal.

7. Chorale (Vs. 12)
●Prayer of faith in face of sin & death (78-7)
Herr, ich glaube, hilf mir Schwachen,
Lord, I   believe; help (this) weak-one,

Laß mich ja verzagen nicht;
Let me indeed despair   not;
{Let me indeed not despair;}

Du,   du kannst mich stärker machen,
Thou, thou canst   me stronger make,

Wenn mich Sünd und Tod anficht.
When me   sin and death assail.

Deiner Güte will ich trauen,
Thy kindness will I   trust,

Bis ich fröhlich werde schauen
Till I   joyfully shall   behold

Dich, Herr Jesu, nach dem Streit
Thee, Lord Jesus, after   the battle

In der süßen Ewigkeit.
In - sweet   eternity.

BWV 79
Gott der Herr ist Sonn und Schild
(NBA I/31; BC A184)

Reformation Day (BWV 80, 79)
*2 Thess. 2:3-8 (Prophecy concerning man of lawlessness)
*Rev. 14:6-8 (An angel announces eternal gospel and judgment)
Librettist: Unknown; perhaps Christian Weiß the elder, perhaps Erdmann Neumeister

1. Chorus
●God is sun & shield for righteous: Ps. 84:11 (79-1)
Gott der Herr ist Sonn und Schild. Der Herr
God the Lord is sun   and shield. The Lord

gibt Gnade und Ehre, er wird   kein Gutes
gives grace and honor, he will (let) no good-thing

God, who indeed intercedes for us?...For I am sure that neither death, nor life, nor angels, nor principalities, nor things present, nor things to come, nor powers, nor height, nor depth, nor anything else in all creation, will be able to separate us from the love of God in Christ Jesus our Lord.
Jn. 10:27-29 [Christ]: My sheep hear my voice, and I know them, and they follow me; and I give them eternal life, and they shall never perish, and no one shall snatch them out of my hand. My Father, who has given them to me, is greater than all, and no one is able to snatch them out of the Father's hand.

Mk. 9:24. The father of the child cried out [to Jesus] and said, "I believe; help my unbelief!"
Ps. 6:2. Be gracious to me, O Lord, for I am languishing (Luther: ich bin schwach); O Lord, heal me, for my bones are troubled.
Ps. 119:28. [O Lord,] my soul melts away for sorrow; strengthen me according to thy word!
Rom. 5:6. While we were still weak, at the right time Christ died for the ungodly.
Rom. 8:26. Likewise the Spirit helps us in our weakness; for we do not know how to pray as we ought, but the Spirit himself intercedes for us with sighs too deep for words.
Rom. 16:25. [God]...is able to strengthen you...
Ps. 23:4. Even though I walk through the valley of the shadow of death, I fear no evil; for thou art with me...
2 Tim. 4:6-8. I am already on the point of being sacrificed; the time of my departure has come. I have fought the good fight, I have finished the race, I have kept the faith. Henceforth there is laid up for me the crown of righteousness, which the Lord, the righteous judge, will award to me on that Day, and not only to me but also to all who have loved his appearing.
Job 19:25-26. I know that my Redeemer lives, and at last he will stand upon the earth; and after my skin has been thus destroyed, then from my flesh I shall see God.
1 Thess. 4:17. Then we who are alive, who are left, shall be caught up together with them in clouds to meet the Lord in the air; and so we shall always be with the Lord.
1 Jn. 3:2. ...We know that when he appears we shall be like him, for we shall see him as he is.

Ps. 84:11. *The Lord God is a sun and shield; he bestows favor and honor. No good thing does the Lord withhold from those who walk uprightly.*
Ps. 5:12. Thou dost bless the righteous, O Lord; thou dost cover him with favor as with a shield.
Ps. 18:30 / 2 Sam. 22:31. This God—his way is perfect; the promise of the Lord proves true; he is a shield for all those who take refuge in him. (Also Ps. 18:2, 35.)

mangeln lassen den Frommen.
be-lacking   for-the righteous.
{He will not let the righteous lack any good thing.}

2. Alto Aria
●God as sun & shield: Gratefulness for his protection (79-2)
Gott ist unsre Sonn und Schild!
God is   our   sun   and shield!

Darum   rühmet dessen Güte
Therefore extols   his   goodness

Unser dankbares Gemüte,
Our   thankful   spirit,
{Therefore our thankful spirit extols the goodness}

Die   er für sein Häuflein   hegt.
Which he for his little-band preserves.
{That he preserves for his little band.}

Denn er will uns ferner   schützen,
For   he will us furthermore protect,
{For he will protect us furthermore,}

Ob   die Feinde   Pfeile schnitzen
Though (our) foes (their) arrows sharpen
{Though our foes sharpen their arrows}

Und ein   Lästerhund   gleich billt.
And a   blasphemous-hound should howl.

3. Chorale (See also 192-1.)
●Thanks for blessings since infancy: Sir. 50:22 (79-3)
Nun danket   alle   Gott
Now thank (ye) all (our) God

Mit Herzen, Mund und Händen,
With heart,   mouth, and   hands,

Der große Dinge tut
Who great things does
{Who does great things}

An uns und allen Enden,
For us (in)   all   quarters,

Der uns von   Mutterleib
Who to-us from (the) womb

Und   Kindesbeinen an
And (from) infancy   on

Unzählig viel zugut
Countless much good

Und   noch itzund getan.
And (still) even now has-done.
{Who has done countless much good to us from the womb and from infancy on, and even now.}

Ps. 33:20. Our soul waits for the Lord; he is our help and shield.
Rom. 8:32. He who did not spare his own Son but gave him up for us all, will he not also give us all things with him?

Ps. 28:7. The Lord is my strength and my shield; in him my heart trusts; so I am helped, and my heart exults, and with my song I give thanks to him. (Also Ps. 115:9–11.)
Ps. 106:1. O give thanks to the Lord, for he is good; for his steadfast love (Luther: Güte) endures for ever! (Also Ps. 135:3, 147:1.)
Ps. 5:11. [O Lord,] let all who take refuge in thee rejoice, let them ever sing for joy (Luther: ewig rühmen); and do thou defend them, that those who love thy name may exult in thee.
Ps. 145:6–7. Men shall proclaim the might of thy terrible acts, and I will declare thy greatness. They shall pour forth the fame of thy abundant goodness...
Lk. 12:32. Fear not, little flock, for it is your Father's good pleasure to give you the kingdom.
Eph. 6:16. ...[Arm yourselves with] the shield of faith, with which you can quench all the flaming darts (Luther: Pfeile) of the evil one. (Also Ps. 57:4.)
*2 Thess. 2:3–4, 8. Let no one deceive you in any way; for [the day of Christ's return] will not come, unless the rebellion comes first, and the man of lawlessness is revealed, the son of perdition, who opposes and exalts himself against every so-called god or object of worship, so that he takes his seat in the temple of God, proclaiming himself to be God ...And then the lawless one will be revealed, and the Lord Jesus will slay him with the breath of his mouth and destroy him by his appearing and his coming.

Sirach (Apocrypha) 50:22–23 [= Sirach 50:24–26 of German Bible]. *And now bless the God of all, who in every way does great things; who exalts our days from birth, and deals with us according to his mercy.* (Luther: Nun danket alle Gott, der große Dinge tut an allen Enden, der uns von Mutterleib an lebendig erhält und tut uns alles Gute.)
Ps. 111:1. Praise the Lord. I will give thanks to the Lord with my whole heart... (Also Ps. 86:12, 109:30.)
Ps. 109:30. With my mouth I will give great thanks to the Lord... (Also Ps. 145:21.)
Ps. 47:1. Clap your hands, all peoples! Shout to God with loud songs of joy! (Also Is. 12:6, 44:23.)
Ps. 75:1. We give thanks to thee, O God; we give thanks; we call on thy name and recount thy wondrous deeds.
Ps. 145:10. All thy works shall give thanks to thee, O Lord, and all thy saints shall bless thee!
Lk. 1:49. For he who is mighty has done great things for me, and holy is his name.
1 Sam. 12:24. ...Consider what great things he has done for you.
Ps. 126:3. The Lord has done great things for us; we are glad.
Ps. 71:5–6. For thou, O Lord, art my hope, my trust, O Lord, from my youth. Upon thee I have leaned from my birth; thou art he who took me from my mother's womb (Luther: Mutterleibe). My praise is continually of thee. (Also Ps. 22:10, Jer. 1:5.)
Job 9:10. [God] does great things beyond understanding, and marvelous things without number. (Also Job 5:9, Ps. 40:5, 71:15, 139:17–18.)

4. Bass Recit.

●Praise for knowledge of salvation; prayer for others (79-4)

Gottlob,   wir wissen
Thank-God, we   know

Den rechten Weg zur Seligkeit;
The   right   way to salvation;

Denn, Jesu, du hast ihn uns durch dein Wort gewiesen,
For, Jesus, thou hast it to-us through thy Word shown,
{For Jesus, thou hast shown it to us through thy Word,}

Drum   bleibt dein Name jederzeit gepriesen.
Therefore continues thy name at-all-times to-be-praised.
{Therefore thy name continues to be praised at all times.}

Weil   aber   viele noch
Since, however, many still

Zu dieser Zeit
At this   time

An fremdem Joch
A   foreign yoke

Aus   Blindheit ziehen müssen,
Because-of (their) blindness   must-pull,
{However, since many still must bear an alien yoke because of
their blindness,}

Ach! so   erbarme dich
Ah! therefore have-mercy
{Ah, therefore graciously have mercy}

Auch ihrer gnädiglich,
Also on-them graciously,
{Also upon them,}

Daß sie den rechten Weg erkennen
That they the true   way might-discern

Und dich bloß ihren Mittler nennen.
And thee just as-their mediator name.
{And that they might just name thee as their mediator.}

5. Soprano & Bass Duet

●Prayer for protection and the light of God's Word (79-5)

Gott, ach Gott, verlaß die Deinen
God, ah God, forsake - thine-own

Nimmermehr!
Nevermore!

Laß dein Wort uns helle scheinen;
Let thy Word over-us brightly shine;

Obgleich   sehr
Even-though greatly

1 Jn. 3:14. We know that we have passed out of death into life... (Also
1 Jn. 4:6.)
Eph. 1:9. [God] has made known to us...the mystery of his will,
according to his purpose which he set forth in Christ. (Also Col.
1:25-27.)
Rom. 16:25-26. ...[The] gospel...is now disclosed and through the
prophetic writings is made known to all nations, according to the
command of the eternal God, to bring about the obedience of faith.
*Rev. 14:6. I saw another angel flying in midheaven, with an eternal
gospel to proclaim to those who dwell on earth, to every nation and
tribe and tongue and people.
Jn. 14:4-6. [Jesus said to the disciples,] "You know the way where I
am going." Thomas said to him, "Lord, we do not know where you are
going; how can we know the way?" Jesus said to him, "I am the way,
and the truth, and the life; no one comes to the Father, but by me."
Mt. 7:13-14 [Christ]: ...The way is easy, that leads to destruction, and
those who enter by it are many...The way is hard, that leads to life,
and those who find it are few.
Phil. 3:18-19. Many, of whom I have often told you and now tell you
even with tears, live as enemies of the cross of Christ. Their end is
destruction...
Eph. 4:17-18. ...The Gentiles [live] in the futility of their minds; they
are darkened in their understanding, alienated from the life of God...
Jn. 10:16 [Christ]: I have other sheep, that are not of this fold; I must
bring them also, and they will heed my voice. So there shall be one
flock, one shepherd.
Mt. 11:28-30 [Christ]: Come to me, all who labor and are heavy
laden, and I will give you rest. Take my yoke upon you, and learn
from me; for I am gentle and lowly in heart, and you will find rest for
your souls. For my yoke is easy, and my burden is light.
2 Cor. 6:14-15. Do not be mismated (Luther: ziehet nicht am fremden
Joch) with unbelievers. For what partnership have righteousness and
iniquity? Or what fellowship has light with darkness? What accord has
Christ with Belial? Or what has a believer in common with an
unbeliever?
1 Tim. 2:5-6. There is one God, and there is one mediator between
God and men, the man Christ Jesus, who gave himself as a ransom for
all. (Also Heb. 9:15, 12:24, Acts 4:12.)

Ps. 94:14. The Lord will not forsake his people; he will not abandon
his heritage.
Ps. 27:9. Hide not thy face from me...forsake me not, O God of my
salvation!
Ps. 119:41-43. Let thy steadfast love come to me, O Lord, thy
salvation according to thy promise; then shall I have an answer for
those who taunt me, for I trust in thy word. And take not the word of
truth utterly out of my mouth, for my hope is in thy ordinances.
Ps. 119:105. [O Lord,] thy word is a lamp to my feet and a light to my
path. (Also 2 Pet. 1:19.)
Acts 4:25-26. ...Why did the Gentiles rage, and the peoples imagine
vain things? The kings of the earth set themselves in array, and the
rulers were gathered together, against the Lord and against his
Anointed. (Also Ps. 2:1.)

Wider uns die Feinde toben,
Against us (our) foes do-rage,
{Even though our foes rage greatly against us,}

So soll unser Mund dich loben.
Yet shall our mouth thee praise.
{Yet shall our mouth praise thee.}

6. Chorale
●Prayer for protection & preservation in the truth (79–6)
Erhalt uns in der Wahrheit,
Preserve us in the truth,

Gib ewigliche Freiheit,
Grant (us) everlasting freedom,

Zu preisen deinen Namen
To praise thy name

Durch Jesum Christum. Amen.
Through Jesus Christ. Amen.

*Rev. 14:7. Fear God and give him glory, for the hour of his judgment has come; and worship him who made heaven and earth, the sea and the fountains of water.
Ps. 27:3. Though a host encamp against me, my heart shall not fear; though war arise against me, yet I will be confident.
Ps. 34:1. I will bless the Lord at all times; his praise shall continually be in my mouth. (Also Ps. 40:3. 51:15, 63:3, 71:8, 109:30, Heb. 13:15.)

Ps. 86:11. Teach me thy way, O Lord, that I may walk in thy truth...
Jn. 8:31, 36 [Christ]: ...If you continue in my word, you are truly my disciples, and you will know the the truth, and the truth will make you free...If the Son makes you free, you will be free indeed.
Gal. 2:4. ...False brethren secretly...slipped in to spy out our freedom... (Also Jude 1:4.)
2 Cor. 3:17. Now the Lord is the Spirit, and where the Spirit of the Lord is, there is freedom.
Gal. 5:1. For freedom Christ has set us free; stand fast therefore, and do not submit again to a yoke of slavery. (Also Gal. 5:13.)
Heb. 13:15. Through [Christ] then, let us continually offer up a sacrifice of praise to God, that is, the fruit of lips that acknowledge his name.
Jude 1:25. To the only God, our Savior through Jesus Christ our Lord, be glory, majesty, dominion, and authority, before all time and now and for ever. Amen. (Also Rom. 16:27.)

BWV 80
Ein feste Burg ist unser Gott
(NBA I/31; BC A183a/b)

Reformation Day (BWV 80, 79)
*2 Thess. 2:3–8 (Prophecy concerning man of lawlessness)
*Rev. 14:6–8 (An angel announces eternal gospel and judgment)

BWV 80 was constructed from BWV 80a, an earlier version intended for Oculi (3. S. in Lent):
+Eph. 5:1–9 (Be imitators of God: walk in love; walk as children of light)
+Lk. 11:14–28 (Jesus accused of casting out demons by Beelzebul)
Librettist: Salomon Franck (80a); revisions perhaps by J. S. Bach.

1. Chorus (Chorale Vs. 1) (New to this version)
●Mighty fortress is our God against ancient foe (80–1)
Ein feste Burg ist unser Gott,
A mighty fortress is our God,

Ein gute Wehr und Waffen;
A good defence and weapon;

Er hilft uns frei aus aller Not,
He helps us free from all distress

Ps. 18:2. The Lord is my rock, and my fortress (Luther: Burg), and my deliverer, my God, my rock, in whom I take refuge, my shield, and the horn of my salvation, my stronghold. (Also Ps. 31:2, 62:2, 6; 91:1–2, 94:22; 144:2.)
Ps. 35:1–2. Contend, O Lord, with those who contend with me; fight against those who fight against me! Take hold of shield and buckler (Luther: Schild und Waffen), and rise for my help!
1 Pet. 5:8. Be sober, be watchful. Your adversary the devil prowls around like a roaring lion, seeking some one to devour.
Eph. 6:11–12. Put on the whole armor of God, that you may be able to stand against the wiles (Luther: listigen Anläufe) of the devil. For we are not contending against flesh and blood, but against the

Die uns itzt hat betroffen.
Which us now has befallen.

Der alte böse Feind,
The ancient evil foe,

Mit Ernst er's itzt meint,
With seriousness he-it now intends,
{He comes with serious intent,}

Groß Macht und viel List
Great power and much cunning

Sein grausam Rüstung ist,
His fearsome armor is,

Auf Erd ist nicht seinsgleichen.
On earth is not his-equal.

2. Bass Aria and Soprano Chorale (Vs. 2)
●Battle led by Christ; victory assured for God's child (80-2)
Alles, was von Gott geboren,
All, that of God is-born,

Ist zum Siegen auserkoren.
Is for victory chosen.
{Has been chosen for victory.}

Mit unserer Macht ist nichts getan,
With our might is nothing done,
{With our might can nothing be done,}

Wir sind gar bald verloren.
We are very soon lost.

Es streit' vor uns der rechte Mann,
(Now) fights for us the right man,
{The right man does fight for us,}

Den Gott selbst hat erkoren.
Whom God himself has chosen.

Wer bei Christi Blutpanier
Whoever (to) Christ's banner-of-blood

In der Taufe Treu geschworen,
In - baptism loyalty has-sworn,
{Whoever has sworn loyalty to Christ's banner of blood in baptism,}

Siegt in Christ für und für.
Conquers in Christ forever and ever.

Fragst du, wer er ist?
Ask you, who he is?
{Do you ask who this is?}

Er heißt Jesus Christ,
He (is) called Jesus Christ,

principalities, against the powers, against the world rulers of this present darkness, against the spiritual hosts of wickedness in the heavenly places.
*2 Thess. 2:3–4, 8. Let no one deceive you in any way; for [the day of the Lord] will not come, unless the rebellion comes first, and the man of lawlessness is revealed, the son of perdition, who opposes and exalts himself against every so-called god or object of worship, so that he takes his seat in the temple of God, proclaiming himself to be God ...And then the lawless one will be revealed, and the Lord Jesus will slay him with the breath of his mouth and destroy him by his appearing and his coming.
Rev. 12:9. And the great dragon was thrown down, that ancient serpent, who is called the Devil and Satan, the deceiver of the whole world—he was thrown down to the earth, and his angels were thrown down with him.
1 Jn. 3:8. ...The devil has sinned from the beginning. The reason the Son of God appeared was to destroy the works of the devil.

1 Jn. 5:4–5. Whatever is born of God overcomes the world; and this is the victory that overcomes the world, our faith. Who is it that overcomes the world but he who believes that Jesus is the Son of God? (Also 1 Jn. 2:13–14, 4:4, Jn. 16:33.)
1 Cor. 15:57. Thanks be to God, who gives us the victory through our Lord Jesus Christ.
Ps. 124:2–3. If it had not been the Lord who was on our side...they would have swallowed us up alive...
Jn. 15:5 [Christ]: ...Apart from me you can do nothing.
Ps. 20:5–6. May we shout for joy over your victory, and in the name of our God set up our banners (Luther: Panier)!...Now I know the Lord will help his anointed...
Rev. 12:11. [The righteous] have conquered [Satan] by the blood of the Lamb...
Heb. 2:14. Since therefore the children share in flesh and blood, [Christ] himself likewise partook of the same nature, that through death he might destroy him who has the power of death, that is, the devil.
1 Jn. 3:8. ...The reason the Son of God appeared was to destroy the works of the devil.
Heb. 5:4–5. And one does not take the honor upon himself, but he is called by God, just as Aaron was. So also Christ did not exalt himself... but was appointed by him who said to him, "Thou art my Son, today I have begotten thee".
Gal. 3:27. As many of you as were baptized into Christ have put on Christ. (Also Rom. 13:14.)
Rom. 6:3–4. Do you not know that all of us who have been baptized into Christ Jesus were baptized into his death? We were buried therefore with him by baptism into death, so that as Christ was raised from the dead by the glory of the Father, we too might walk in newness of life.
Rom. 8:37–39. ...We are more than conquerors through him who loved us. For I am sure that neither death, nor life, nor angels, nor principalities, nor things present, nor things to come, nor powers, nor height, nor depth, nor anything else in all creation, will be able to separate us from the love of God in Christ Jesus our Lord.
Rev. 17:14. ...The Lamb will conquer...for he is Lord of lords and King of kings, and those with him are called and chosen and faithful (Luther: Auserwählten und Gläubigen).

Der Herre Zebaoth,
The Lord Sabaoth,

Und   ist kein andrer Gott,
And (there) is no   other god;

Das   Feld muß er behalten.
The (battle)-field must he retain.

Alles, was von Gott geboren,
All,   that of God is-born,

Ist zum Siegen auserkoren.
Is for victory   chosen.
{Has been chosen for victory.}

3. Bass Recit.
●Ponder Christ's love which enlists us to the fight (80–3)
Erwäge doch, Kind Gottes, die so große Liebe,
Ponder indeed, child of-God, the so great love,
{Ponder indeed, O child of God, this love so great,}

Da   Jesus sich
Inasmuch-as Jesus himself
{Inasmuch as Jesus}

Mit seinem Blute   dir verschriebe,
With his   blood to-thee did-pledge,
{Pledged himself to thee with his blood,}

Womit er dich
By-which he thee

Zum Kriege wider Satans Heer und wider Welt und Sünde
To   war against Satan's host and against world and sin

Geworben hat!
Enlisted hath!

Gib nicht in deiner Seele
Allow not within thy   soul

Dem Satan und den Lastern statt!
 - Satan and - wickedness place!
{Give no place within thy soul to Satan and wickedness!}

Laß nicht dein Herz,
Let not thy heart,

Den Himmel Gottes auf der Erden,
The heaven of-God on - earth,
{God's heaven on earth,}

Zur Wüste werden!
To-a wilderness become!
{Become a wilderness!}

Bereue deine Schuld mit Schmerz,
Repent of-thy guilt with sorrow,

Rev. 19:11–13. I saw heaven opened, and behold, a white horse! He who sat upon it is called Faithful and True, and in righteousness he judges and makes war. His eyes are like a flame of fire, and on his head are many diadems; and he has a name inscribed which no one knows but himself. He is clad in a robe dipped in blood, and the name by which he is called is The Word of God. (Also Rev. 6:2.)
Is. 6:1–3. ...I saw the Lord sitting upon a throne, high and lifted up... Above him stood the seraphim...and one called to another and said: "Holy, holy, holy is the Lord of hosts (Luther: Zebaoth); the whole earth is full of his glory." ("Zebaoth": also Ps. 80:5, 8, 20)
Deut. 4:35. ...The Lord is God; there is no other besides him... (Also Deut. 4:39, 1 Kings 8:60, Is. 45:5, 14, 18, 21, 22; 46:9.)
1 Jn. 5:4. Whatever is born of God overcomes the world...

1 Jn. 3:1. See what love the Father has given us, that we should be called children of God; and so we are...
1 Pet. 1:18–19. You know that you were ransomed from the futile ways inherited from your fathers, not with perishable things such as silver or gold, but with the precious blood of Christ, like that of a lamb without blemish or spot.
1 Cor. 6:19–20. ...You are not your own; you were bought with a price... (Also 1 Cor. 7:23.)
Ex. 32:26. Moses stood in the gate of the camp, and said, "Who is on the Lord's side? Come to me."...
Jms. 4:4, 7. ...Do you not know that friendship with the world is enmity with God? Therefore whoever wishes to be a friend of the world makes himself an enemy of God...Submit yourselves therefore to God. Resist the devil and he will flee from you. (Also 1 Jn. 2:15–17, Mt. 6:24.)
Eph. 6:11. Put on the whole armor of God...
1 Tim. 6:12. Fight the good fight of the faith...
+Lk. 11:14–15. Now [Jesus] was casting out a demon... But some of them said, "He casts out demons by Beelzebul, the prince of demons."
Mk. 3:23, 28–30. And [Jesus]...said to them in parables, "How can Satan cast out Satan?...Truly, I say to you, all sins will be forgiven the sons of men, and whatever blasphemies (Luther: Gotteslästerungen) they utter; but whoever blasphemes against the Holy Spirit never has forgiveness, but is guilty of an eternal sin"—for they had said, "He has an unclean spirit." (Also Mt. 12:31.)
+Lk. 11:19–20, 23–26. [Jesus said,] "If I cast out demons by Beelzebul, by whom do your sons cast them out? Therefore they shall be your judges. But if it is by the finger of God that I cast out demons, then the kingdom of God has come upon you...He who is not with me is against me, and he who does not gather with me scatters. When the unclean spirit has gone out of a man, he passes through waterless places (Luther: dürre Stätten) seeking rest; and finding none he says, 'I will return to my house from which I came.' And when he comes he finds it swept and put in order. Then he goes and brings seven other spirits more evil than himself; and they enter and dwell there; and the last state of that man becomes worse than the first."
1 Cor. 3:16. Do you not know that you are God's temple and that God's Spirit dwells in you?
1 Jn. 3:24. All who keep his commandments abide in [Christ], and he in them. And by this we know that he abides in us, by the Spirit which

Daß Christi Geist mit dir sich fest   verbinde!
That Christ's spirit with thee - firmly (might) unite!

4. Soprano Aria
●World & Satan rejected; Christ invited into heart (80-4)
Komm in mein Herzenshaus,
Come into my heart's-house,

Herr Jesu, mein Verlangen!
(O) Lord, Jesus, my desire!

Treib Welt und Satan aus
Drive world and Satan out

Und laß dein Bild in mir erneuert prangen!
And let thine image in me renewed be-resplendent!
{And let thine image be resplendent anew in me!}

Weg, schnöder Sündengraus!
Away, vile horror-of-sin!

5. Chorale (Vs. 3) (New to this version)
●Devil not to be feared because he has been judged (80-5)
Und wenn die Welt voll Teufel wär
And if the world full-of devils were

Und wollten uns verschlingen,
And wanted us to-devour,
{Who wanted to devour us,}

So fürchten wir uns nicht so sehr,
Then fear we - not so greatly,
{We would not greatly fear,}

Es soll uns doch gelingen.
It shall for-us nevertheless succeed.
{We shall succeed nevertheless.}

Der Fürst dieser Welt,
The prince of-this world,

Wie saur er sich stellt,
However surly he himself presents,
{However ferocious he may appear,}

Tut er uns doch nicht,
Does he (harm) to-us nevertheless not,
{Does us no harm,}

Das macht, er ist gericht',
That is, he is judged,

Ein Wörtlein kann ihn fällen.
A little-word can him fell.
{A little word can fell him.}

he has given us. (Also 1 Jn. 3:24, 4:13, Acts 5:32, Rom. 5:5, 2 Cor. 1:22, 5:5.)

+**Lk. 11:14.** Now [Jesus] was casting out a demon...
Jn. 14:23. Jesus answered him, "If a man loves me, he will keep my word, and my Father will love him, and we will come to him and make our home with him." (See also Jn. 14:21.)
Eph. 3:17. ...that Christ may dwell in your hearts through faith...
1 Jn. 2:15. Do not love the world or the things in the world. If any one loves the world, love for the Father is not in him. (Also Jms. 4:4.)
Mt. 6:24 [Christ]: No one can serve two masters; for either he will hate the one and love the other, or he will be devoted to the one and despise the other. You cannot serve God and mammon. (Also Lk. 16:13.)
+**Eph. 5:1.** Therefore be imitators of God, as beloved children.
Gal. 3:27. For as many of you as were baptized into Christ have put on Christ.
Gal. 4:19. My little children, with whom I am again in travail until Christ be formed in you! (Also Rom. 13:14.)

+**Lk. 11:14.** Now [Jesus] was casting out a demon...
1 Jn. 5:19. ...The whole world is in the power of the evil one.
1 Pet. 5:8-9. Be sober, be watchful. Your adversary the devil prowls around like a roaring lion, seeking some one to devour (Luther: verschlinge). Resist him, firm in your faith...
Eph. 6:11-12. Put on the whole armor of God, that you may be able to stand against the wiles (Luther: listigen Anläufe) of the devil. For we are not contending against flesh and blood, but against the principalities, against the powers, against the world rulers of this present darkness, against the spiritual hosts of wickedness in the heavenly places.
2 Cor. 10:3-4. For though we live in the world we are not carrying on a worldly war, for the weapons of our warfare are not worldly but have divine power to destroy strongholds.
Jn. 12:30-31 [Christ]: ...Now is the judgment of this world, now shall the ruler of this world be cast out.
Jn. 16:11 [Christ]: ...The ruler of this world is judged.
Eph. 2:1-2. And you [God] made alive, when you were dead through the trespasses and sins in which you once walked, following the course of the world, following the prince of the power of the air, the spirit that is now at work in the sons of disobedience.
1 Jn. 3:8. ...The reason the Son of God appeared was to destroy the works of the devil.
Heb. 2:14. ...[Christ] himself likewise partook of the same nature, that through death he might destroy him who has the power of death, that is, the devil.
*****2 Thess. 2:8.** And then the lawless one will be revealed, and the Lord Jesus will slay him with the breath of his mouth and destroy him by his appearing and his coming.
Rev. 12:10-11. And I heard a loud voice in heaven, saying, "Now the salvation and the power and the kingdom of our God and the authority of his Christ have come, for the accuser of our brethren has been thrown down, who accuses them day and night before our God. And they have conquered him by the blood of the Lamb and by the word of their testimony, for they loved not their lives unto death."

6. Tenor Recit.
●Stand firm with Christ in battle; victory assured (80–6)
So stehe dann bei Christi blutgefärbten Fahne,
So stand then by Christ's blood-stained banner,

O Seele, fest
O Soul, firm
{So stand firm, then, by Christ's blood-stained banner, O Soul,}

Und glaube, daß dein Haupt   dich nicht verläßt,
And believe, that thy head (doth) thee not forsake,

Ja, daß sein Sieg
Yea, that thy victory

Auch dir den Weg zu deiner Krone bahne!
Also for-thee the way to thy crown doth-pave!

Tritt freudig an den Krieg!
Step joyfully into - battle!

Wirst du nur Gottes Wort
Wilt thou but God's Word

So hören als bewahren,
(Both) hear as-well-as keep,

So wird der Feind gezwungen auszufahren,
Then will the foe be-forced to-leave,

Dein Heiland bleibt dein Hort!
Thy Savior remains thy refuge!

7. Alto & Tenor Duet (Some word changes in this version)
●Victory sure for those holding God in hearts by faith (80–7)
Wie selig sind doch die,
How blessed are indeed those,

    die Gott im Munde tragen,
    who God in-their mouths do-hold,

Doch selger ist das Herz,
Yet more-blessed is the heart,

    das ihn im Glauben trägt!
    that him in faith does-hold!

Es bleibet unbesiegt und kann die Feinde schlagen
It remains unconquered and can the foes defeat

Acts 11:23. [Barnabas] exhorted them all to remain faithful to the Lord with steadfast purpose.
1 Pet. 5:8–9. Be sober, be watchful. Your adversary the devil prowls around like a roaring lion, seeking some one to devour. Resist him, firm in your faith...
Rev. 17:14. ...The Lamb will conquer...for he is Lord of lords and King of kings, and those with him are called and chosen and faithful. (Also Rev. 19:16, Ps. 98:9.)
Rev. 12:11. And [the righteous] have conquered...by the blood of the Lamb and by the word of their testimony...
Rom. 8:37–39. ...We are more than conquerors through him who loved us. For I am sure that neither death, nor life, nor angels, nor principalities, nor things present, nor things to come, nor powers, nor height, nor depth, nor anything else in all creation, will be able to separate us from the love of God in Christ Jesus our Lord.
Eph. 5:23. Christ is the head of the church, his body. (Also Eph. 4:15.)
2 Tim. 2:11–12. The saying is sure: If we have died with him, we shall also live with him; if we endure, we shall also reign with him... (Also Rom. 8:17, 1 Pet. 4:13.)
2 Tim. 4:8. Henceforth there is laid up for me the crown of righteousness, which the Lord, the righteous judge, will award to me on that Day, and not only to me but also to all who have loved his appearing.
Rev. 2:10–11 [Christ]: Do not fear what you are about to suffer. Behold, the devil is about to throw some of you into prison, that you may be tested, and for ten days you will have tribulation. Be faithful unto death, and I will give you the crown of life. (Also Jms. 1:12.)
Deut. 31:7–8. ...Be strong and of good courage... It is the Lord who goes before you; he will be with you, he will not fail you or forsake you; do not fear or be dismayed. (Also Josh. 1:7, 9.)
Eph. 6:17. And take the helmet of salvation, and the sword of the Spirit, which is the word of God.
Jms. 1:22. But be doers of the word, and not hearers only, deceiving yourselves.
Jms. 4:7. Submit yourselves therefore to God. Resist the devil and he will flee from you.
+Lk. 11:14. Now [Jesus] was casting out a demon...
2 Sam. 22:2–3. [David] said, "The Lord is my rock (Luther: Fels), and my fortress...my rock (Luther: Hort), in whom I take refuge..." (Also 1 Sam. 2:2, Ps. 18:2, 46.)

Rom. 10:9–10. If you confess with your lips (Luther: Munde) that Jesus is Lord and believe in your heart that God raised him from the dead, you will be saved. For man believes with his heart and so is justified, and he confesses with his lips (Luther: Munde) and so is saved.
1 Jn. 4:15. Whoever confesses that Jesus is the Son of God, God abides in him, and he in God.
Eph. 3:16–19. [I pray] that according to the riches of his glory [God] may grant you to be strengthened with might through his Spirit in the inner man, and that Christ may dwell in your hearts through faith; that you, being rooted and grounded in love, may have power to comprehend with all the saints what is the breadth and length and height and depth, and to know the love of Christ which surpasses knowledge, that you may be filled with all the fulness of God.
1 Jn. 5:4. Whatever is born of God overcomes the world; and this is the victory that overcomes the world, our faith.

Und wird zuletzt gekrönt, wenn es den Tod erlegt.
And will at-last be-crowned, when it - death has-slain.
{And will at last be crowned when it has overcome death.}

8. Chorale (Vs. 4) (BWV 80a has Vs. 2 instead)
●Victory ultimately assured despite temporal losses (80–8)
Das Wort sie sollen lassen stahn
That word they must let stand

Und kein Dank dazu haben.
And no thanks thereto have.
{No thanks to their own efforts.}

Er ist bei uns wohl auf dem Plan
He is with us indeed according to-the plan

Mit seinem Geist und Gaben.
With his Spirit and gifts.

Nehmen sie uns den Leib,
Take they from-us (our) body,
{Though they take from us our body,}

Gut, Ehr, Kind und Weib,
Possesion, honor, child, and wife,

Laß fahren dahin,
Let (all these) go hence,
{Let them have all these things,}

Sie habens kein Gewinn;
They have no gain;
{They gain nothing thereby;}

Das Reich muß uns doch bleiben.
The kingdom must for-us nevertheless remain.
{There still remains for us the kingdom.}

BWV 81
Jesus schläft, was soll ich hoffen
(NBA I/6; BC A39)

4. S. after Epiphany (BWV 81, 14)
*Rom. 13:8–10 (Love is the fulfilling of the law)
*Mt. 8:23–27 (Jesus calms the sea)
Librettist: Unknown

1. Alto Aria
●Jesus sleeps in boat during storm; I am without hope (81–1)
Jesus schläft, was soll ich hoffen?
Jesus sleeps, (how can) I hope?

Rev. 2:10–11 [Christ]: Do not fear what you are about to suffer. Behold, the devil is about to throw some of you into prison, that you may be tested, and for ten days you will have tribulation. Be faithful unto death, and I will give you the crown of life. He who has an ear, let him hear what the Spirit says to the churches. He who conquers shall not be hurt by the second death.

Is. 40:8. The grass withers, the flower fades; but the word of our God will stand for ever. (Also 1 Pet. 1:24–25.)
Mk. 13:31. Heaven and earth will pass away, but my words will not pass away. (Also Mt. 24:35.)
***2 Thess. 2:8.** And then the lawless one will be revealed, and the Lord Jesus will slay him with the breath of his mouth and destroy him by his appearing and his coming.
1 Cor. 2:9–10, 12. As it is written, "What no eye has seen, nor ear heard, nor the heart of man conceived, what God has prepared for those who love him," God has revealed to us through the Spirit. For the Spirit searches everything, even the depths of God…Now we have received not the spirit of the world, but the Spirit which is from God, that we might understand the gifts bestowed on us by God.
Rom. 11:29. For the gifts and call of God are irrevocable.
Mt. 10:28 [Christ]: Do not fear those who kill the body but cannot kill the soul; rather fear him who can destroy both soul and body in hell.
Phil. 3:7–11. Whatever gain I had, I counted as loss for the sake of Christ. Indeed I count everything as loss because of the surpassing worth of knowing Christ Jesus my Lord. For his sake I have suffered the loss of all things, and count them as refuse, in order that I may gain Christ and be found in him, not having a righteousness of my own, based on law, but that which is through faith in Christ, the righteousness from God that depends on faith; that I may know him and the power of his resurrection, and may share his sufferings, becoming like him in his death, that if possible I may attain the resurrection from the dead.
Rom. 8:18. I consider that the sufferings of this present time are not worth comparing with the glory that is to be revealed to us.
2 Cor. 4:17. For this slight momentary affliction is preparing for us an eternal weight of glory beyond all comparison. (Also Rom. 8:18.)

***Mt. 8:23-26.** And when [Jesus] got into the boat, his disciples followed him. And behold, there arose a great storm on the sea, so that the boat was being swamped by the waves; but he was asleep. And they went and woke him, saying, "Save, Lord; we are perishing." And he said to them, "Why are you afraid, O men of little faith?" Then he rose and rebuked the winds and the sea; and there was a great calm.

Seh ich nicht
See I not
{Do I not already see}

Mit erblaßtem Angesicht
With ashen face

Schon des Todes Abgrund offen?
Already - death's abyss (gaping) open?
{Death's abyss gaping open?}

2. Tenor Recit.

●Prayer: Why dost thou stand far off in my peril? (81–2)
Herr! warum trittest du so ferne?
Lord! Why (standest) thou so far-off?

Warum verbirgst du dich zur Zeit der Not,
Why hidest thou thyself in-a time of need,

Da alles mir ein kläglich End droht?
When everything me (with) a deplorable end threatens?
{When everything threatens me with a deplorable end?}

Ach, wird dein Auge nicht durch meine Not beweget,
Ah, (is) thine eye not by my need moved,
{Ah, does my need not move thine eye,}

So sonsten nie zu schlummern pfleget?
Which otherwise never to slumber is-wont?
{Which otherwise is never wont to slumber?}

Du wiesest ja mit einem Sterne
Thou didst-show indeed with a star
{Indeed, with a star thou didst show}

Vordem den neubekehrten Weisen,
In-former-times the newly-converted wise-men,
{In former times, the newly converted wise men,}

Den rechten Weg zu reisen.
The right way to journey.

Ach leite mich durch deiner Augen Licht,
Ah, lead me by thine eyes' light,

Weil dieser Weg nichts als Gefahr verspricht.
Because this course nothing but danger promises.
{Because this course promises nothing but danger.}

3. Tenor Aria

●Storm waves of Belial assail the Christian (81–3)
Die schäumenden Wellen von Belials Bächen
The foaming waves of Belial's waters

Verdoppeln die Wut.
Redouble their rage.

Ps. 107:23–30. Some went down to the sea in ships, doing business on the great waters; they saw the deeds of the Lord, his wondrous works in the deep. For he commanded, and raised the stormy wind, which lifted up the waves of the sea. They mounted up to heaven, they went down to the depths (Luther: Abgrund); their courage melted away in their evil plight; they reeled and staggered like drunken men, and were at their wits' end. Then they cried to the Lord in their trouble, and he delivered them from their distress; he made the storm be still, and the waves of the sea were hushed. Then they were glad because they had quiet, and he brought them to their desired haven.

*Mt. 8:25. And [The disciples] went and woke [Jesus], saying, "Save, Lord; we are perishing."
Ps. 22:1–2, 11. My God, my God, why hast thou forsaken me? Why art thou so far from helping me, from the words of my groaning? O my God, I cry by day, but thou dost not answer; and by night, but find no rest...Be not far from me, for trouble is near and there is none to help.
Ps. 13:1. How long, O Lord? Wilt thou forget me for ever? How long wilt thou hide thy face from me?
Ps. 102:2. Do not hide thy face from me in the day of my distress! Incline thy ear to me; answer me speedily in the day when I call!
Ps. 143:7. Make haste to answer me, O Lord! My spirit fails! Hide not thy face from me, lest I be like those who go down to the Pit. (Also Ps. 13:1, 44:24, 69:17, 88:14.)
Ps. 33:18–19. Behold, the eye of the Lord is on those who fear him, on those who hope in his steadfast love, that he may deliver their soul from death...
Ps. 77:9. Has God forgotten to be gracious?...
Ps. 121:3–4. He will not let your foot be moved, he who keeps you will not slumber. Behold, he who keeps Israel will neither slumber nor sleep.
Ps. 33:18–19. Behold, the eye of the Lord is on those who fear him, on those who hope in his steadfast love, that he may deliver their soul from death, and keep them alive in famine. (Also Ps. 34:15.)
Mt. 2:1–2, 9–10. Now when Jesus was born in Bethlehem of Judea in the days of Herod the king, behold, wise men from the East came to Jerusalem, saying, "Where is he who has been born king of the Jews? For we have seen his star in the East, and have come to worship him." ...When they had heard the king they went their way; and lo, the star which they had seen in the East went before them, till it came to rest over the place where the child was. When they saw the star, they rejoiced exceedingly with great joy.
Ps. 32:8 [God]: I will instruct you and teach you the way you should go; I will counsel you with my eye upon you (Luther: mit meinen Augen leiten).

*Mt. 8:24. Behold, there arose a great storm on the sea, so that the boat was being swamped by the waves...
Ps. 69:1–2, 15. Save me, O God! For the waters have come up to my neck. I sink in deep mire, where there is no foothold; I have come into deep waters, and the flood sweeps over me...Let not the flood sweep over me, or the deep swallow me up, or the pit close its mouth over me.
1 Pet. 5:8–9. Be sober, be watchful. Your adversary the devil prowls around like a roaring lion, seeking some one to devour. Resist him, firm in your faith...
2 Cor. 6:15. What accord has Christ with Belial? Or what has a believer in common with an unbeliever?

Ein Christ soll zwar wie Felsen stehn,
A Christian shall indeed like boulders stand,
{A Christian shall indeed stand like a boulder,}

Wenn Trübsalswinde   um   ihn gehn,
When winds-of-affliction around him go,

Doch suchet die stürmende Flut
Yet   seeks   the storming torrent
{Yet this storming torrent seeks}

Die Kräfte des   Glaubens zu schwächen.
The strength of (his) faith   to   weaken.

4. Bass Arioso
●Vox Christi: O ye of little faith, why fear? Mt. 8:26 (81–4)
Ihr Kleingläubigen, warum seid ihr so furchtsam?
Ye of-little-faith,   why   are ye so   fearful?

5. Bass Aria
●Christ's rebuke to raging sea: Be still! (81–5)
Schweig, aufgetürmtes Meer!
Be-still,   towering   sea!

Verstumme, Sturm und Wind!
Grow-dumb,   storm and wind!

Dir   sei dein Ziel gesetzet,
For-thee be thy boundary set,
{May thy boundary be set for thee,}

Damit mein auserwähltes Kind
So-that my   chosen   child

Kein Unfall   je verletzet.
No   mishap (shall) ever injure.
{So that no mishap shall ever injure my chosen child.}

6. Alto Recit.
●Relief that Christ speaks a word and calms the storm (81–6)
Wohl mir, mein Jesus spricht ein Wort,
Blest (am-I); my Jesus speaks   a word,

Mein Helfer ist erwacht,
My   helper is awakened,

So   muß der Wellen Sturm, des Unglücks Nacht
Thus must the waves' storm, - misfortune's night,

Und aller Kummer   fort.
And all sorrow (be) gone.

Ex. 14:13–14. Moses said to the people, "Fear not, stand firm, and see the salvation of the Lord, which he will work for you today; for the Egyptians whom you see today, you shall never see again. The Lord will fight for you, and you have only to be still."
1 Cor. 16:13. Be watchful, stand firm in your faith, be courageous, be strong. (Also Phil. 4:1, 2 Thess. 2:15.)
Mt. 16:18 [Christ]: ...On this rock I will build my church, and the powers of death shall not prevail against it.
Mt. 7:24–25 [Christ]: Every one then who hears these words of mine and does them will be like a wise man who built his house upon the rock; and the rain fell, and the floods came, and the winds blew and beat upon that house, but it did not fall, because it had been founded on the rock.

*Mt. 8:26. And [Jesus] said to them, *"Why are you afraid, O men of little faith?"*
Mt. 17:20. ...I say to you, if you have faith as a grain of mustard seed, you will say to this mountain, "Move from here to there," and it will move; and nothing will be impossible to you. (Also Mt. 6:30, 14:31, 16:8, Lk. 12:28.)

*Mt. 8:26. ...Then [Jesus] rose and rebuked the winds and the sea; and there was a great calm.
Ps. 65:7. [God doth] still the roaring of the seas, the roaring of their waves, the tumult of the peoples.
Ps. 89:9. [O Lord,] thou dost rule the raging of the sea; when its waves rise, thou stillest them.
Ps. 107:29–30. He made the storm be still, and the waves of the sea were hushed. Then they were glad because they had quiet, and he brought them to their desired haven.
Jer. 5:22 [God]: I placed the sand as the bound for the sea, a perpetual barrier which it cannot pass; though the waves toss, they cannot prevail, though they roar, they cannot pass over it. (Also Ps. 104:9, Job 38:11.)
Ps. 91:11–12. [The Lord] will give his angels charge of you to guard you in all your ways. On their hands they will bear you up, lest you dash your foot against a stone. (Also Mt. 4:6, Lk. 4:10.)

*Mt. 8:27. And the men marveled, saying, "What sort of man is this, that even winds and sea obey him?"
Heb. 1:3. [Christ] reflects the glory of God and bears the very stamp of his nature, upholding the universe by his word of power. (power of God's word: also Heb. 11:3, 2 Pet. 3:5)
Lk. 7:6–7. Jesus went with [the elders sent by the centurion]. When he was not far from the house, the centurion sent friends to him, saying to him, "Lord, do not trouble yourself, for I am not worthy to have you come under my roof; therefore I did not presume to come to you. But say the word, and let my servant be healed."
Ps. 35:23. Bestir thyself, and awake for my right, for my cause, my God and my Lord!
Ps. 44:23. Rouse thyself! Why sleepest thou, O Lord? Awake! Do not cast us off for ever! (Also Ps. 59:4.)

7. Chorale
●Christ shelters me in storm; keeps me safe from foe (81-7)
Unter deinen Schirmen
Beneath thy   shelter

Bin ich vor den Stürmen
Am I from the   storms
{I am free from the storms}

Aller Feinde frei.
Of-all foes free.
{Of all foes.}

Laß den Satan wittern,
Let - Satan bluster,

Laß den Feind erbittern,
Let the foe become-incensed,

Mir steht Jesus bei.
Me stands Jesus by.
{Jesus stands by me.}

Ob   es jetzt gleich
Though - now -   (thunder)

kracht und   blitzt,
cracks and (lightning) flashes,

Ob   gleich Sünd und Hölle schrecken,
Though - sin and hell   frighten,

Jesus will mich decken.
Jesus will me   cover.
{Jesus will cover me.}

Ps. 91:1-6. He who dwells in the shelter (Luther: Schirm) of the Most High, who abides in the shadow of the Almighty, will say to the Lord, "My refuge and my fortress; my God, in whom I trust." For he will deliver you from the snare of the fowler and from the deadly pestilence; he will cover (Luther: decken) you with his pinions, and under his wings you will find refuge; his faithfulness is a shield (Luther: Schirm) and buckler. You will not fear the terror of the night, nor the arrow that flies by day, nor the pestilence that stalks in darkness, nor the destruction that wastes at noonday.

Rev. 12:7-11. Now war arose in heaven, Michael and his angels fighting against the dragon; and the dragon and his angels fought, but they were defeated and there was no longer any place for them in heaven. And the great dragon was thrown down, that ancient serpent, who is called the Devil and Satan, the deceiver of the whole world—he was thrown down to the earth, and his angels were thrown down with him. And I heard a loud voice in heaven, saying, "Now the salvation and the power and the kingdom of our God and the authority of his Christ have come, for the accuser of our brethren has been thrown down, who accuses them day and night before our God. And they have conquered him by the blood of the Lamb and by the word of their testimony..."

Ps. 124:1-5. If it had not been the Lord who was on our side...when men rose up against us, then they would have swallowed us up alive, when their anger was kindled against us; then the flood would have swept us away, the torrent would have gone over us; then over us would have gone the raging waters.

Rev. 16:18. ...There were flashes of lightning, voices, peals of thunder, and a great earthquake such as had never been since men were on the earth, so great was that earthquake. (Also Rev. 8:5, 11:19.)

2 Tim. 4:17. But the Lord stood by me...So I was rescued...

Ps. 91:4. He will cover you with his pinions...

BWV 82
Ich habe genug
(NBA I/28; BC A169/a-d)

Mary's Purification (Candlemas) (BWV 83, 125, 82, 157, 158, [161], [200])
*Mal. 3:1-4 (The Lord will suddenly come to his temple and purify his people)
*Lk. 2:22-32 (Mary presents Jesus at the temple; Nunc dimittis)
Librettist: Unknown

1. Bass Aria
●Voice of Simeon (Nunc dimittis): Lk. 2:29-32 (82-1)
Ich habe   genug,
I   have (now) enough,

Ich habe den Heiland, das Hoffen der Frommen,
I   have the Savior, the hope of-the godly,
{I have taken the Savior, the hope of the godly,}

*Mal. 3:1 [God]: Behold, I send my messenger to prepare the way before me, and the Lord whom you seek will suddenly come to his temple; the messenger of the covenant in whom you delight, behold, he is coming, says the Lord of hosts.

*Lk. 2:22, 24-32. And when the time came for their purification according to the law of Moses, [Mary and Joseph] brought [Jesus] up to Jerusalem to present him to the Lord...and to offer a sacrifice

Auf meine begierigen Arme genommen;
(In) my eager arms taken;
{In my eager arms;}

Ich habe genug!
I have (now) enough!

Ich hab ihn erblickt,
I have him seen,
{I have seen him,}

Mein Glaube hat Jesum ans Herze gedrückt;
My faith has Jesus to-my heart pressed;
{My faith has pressed Jesus to my heart;}

Nun wünsch ich, noch heute mit Freuden
Now wish I, yet today with joy

Von hinnen zu scheiden.
From here to depart.
{Now I wish I could depart from here today yet with joy.}

2. Bass Recit.
●Yearning to depart with Simeon & be with Christ (82-2)
Ich habe genug.
I have (now) enough.

Mein Trost ist nur allein,
My consolation is (this) alone,

Daß Jesus mein und ich sein eigen möchte sein.
That Jesus mine (own) and I his own might be.

Im Glauben halt ich ihn,
In faith hold I him,

Da seh ich auch mit Simeon
Thus see I also with Simeon
{Thus I also see with Simeon}

Die Freude jenes Lebens schon.
The joy of-yonder life already.

Laßt uns mit diesem Manne ziehn!
Let us with this man go!

Ach! möchte mich von meines Leibes Ketten
Ah, would-that me from my body's chains

Der Herr erretten;
The Lord (might) deliver;
{Ah, if only the Lord would deliver me from my body's chains;}

Ach! wäre doch mein Abshied hier,
Ah, were indeed my departure at-hand,

Mit Freuden sagt ich, Welt, zu dir:
With joy said I (then), (O) world, to thee:

according to what is said in the law of the Lord...Now there was a man in Jerusalem, whose name was Simeon, and this man was righteous and devout, looking for the consolation of Israel, and the Holy Spirit was upon him. And it had been revealed to him by the Holy Spirit that he should not see death before he had seen the Lord's Christ. And inspired by the Spirit he came into the temple; and when the parents brought in the child Jesus, to do for him according to the custom of the law, he took him up in his arms and blessed God and said, "Lord, now lettest thou thy servant depart in peace, according to thy word; for mine eyes have seen thy salvation which thou hast prepared in the presence of all peoples, a light for revelation to the Gentiles, and for glory to thy people Israel." (See Is. 42:6, 49:6, 52:10.)
Phil. 1:20–23. ...[My hope is] that...Christ will be honored in my body, whether by life or by death. For to me to live is Christ, and to die is gain. If it is to be life in the flesh, that means fruitful labor for me. Yet which I shall choose I cannot tell. I am hard pressed between the two. My desire is to depart and be with Christ, for that is far better.
2 Cor. 5:6–8. So we are always of good courage; we know that while we are at home in the body we are away from the Lord, for we walk by faith, not by sight. We are of good courage, and we would rather be away from the body and at home with the Lord.

Phil. 3:7–11. Whatever gain I had, I counted as loss for the sake of Christ. Indeed I count everything as loss because of the surpassing worth of knowing Christ Jesus my Lord. For his sake I have suffered the loss of all things, and count them as refuse, in order that I may gain Christ and be found in him, not having a righteousness of my own, based on law, but that which is through faith in Christ, the righteousness from God that depends on faith; that I may know him and the power of his resurrection, and may share his sufferings, becoming like him in his death, that if possible I may attain the resurrection from the dead.
2 Tim. 2:19. ...The Lord knows those who are his...
S. of S. 6:3 [Bride]: I am my beloved's and my beloved is mine...
S. of S. 3:4 [Bride]: ...I found him whom my soul loves. I held him, and would not let him go... (Also Gen. 32:26.)
*****Lk. 2:28–29.** [Simeon] took [Jesus] up in his arms and blessed God and said, "Lord, now lettest thou thy servant depart in peace..."
2 Tim. 4:6–8. ...The time of my departure has come. I have fought the good fight, I have finished the race, I have kept the faith. Henceforth there is laid up for me the crown of righteousness, which the Lord, the righteous judge, will award to me on that Day, and not only to me but also to all who have loved his appearing. (Also Jms. 1:12, Rev. 2:10.)
Heb. 11:10. [We look] forward to the city which has foundations, whose builder and maker is God.
Rom. 7:24–25. ...Who will deliver me from this body of death? Thanks be to God through Jesus Christ our Lord!...
2 Cor. 5:1–4. We know that if the earthly tent we live in is destroyed, we have a building from God, a house not made with hands, eternal in the heavens. Here indeed we groan, and long to put on our heavenly dwelling, so that by putting it on we may not be found naked. For while we are still in this tent, we sigh with anxiety; not that we would be unclothed, but that we would be further clothed, so that what is mortal may be swallowed up by life. (Also 2 Pet. 1:14.)
2 Cor. 5:8. ...We would rather be away from the body and at home with the Lord. (Also Phil. 1:23.)

Ich habe   genug.
I   have (had)   enough.

Jms. 4:4. ...Do you not know that friendship with the world is enmity with God? Therefore whoever wishes to be a friend of the world makes himself an enemy of God.

1 Jn. 2:17. The world passes away, and the lust of it; but he who does the will of God abides for ever.

3. Bass Aria
●Yearning for death: Here is only misery, there peace (82–3)
Schlummert ein, ihr matten Augen,
    Fall-asleep,   ye weary   eyes,

Fallet sanft und selig zu!
Fall   softly and blessedly shut!

    Welt, ich bleibe nicht mehr hier,
(O) world, I remain no longer here,

Hab ich doch kein Teil an dir,
Have I indeed no part in thee,
{For I have indeed no part in thee,}

Das   der Seele könnte taugen.
That (to-my) soul   might bring-benefit.

Hier muß ich   das Elend bauen,
Here must I (with) - misery reckon,

Aber dort, dort werd ich schauen
But there, there shall I   see

Süßen Frieden, stille Ruh.
Sweet   peace, quiet rest.

*Lk. 2:29.** Lord, now lettest thou thy servant depart in peace...
Rev. 14:13. And I heard a voice from heaven saying, "Write this: Blessed are the dead who die in the Lord henceforth." "Blessed indeed," says the Spirit, "that they may rest from their labors, for their deeds follow them!"
1 Jn. 2:15–17. Do not love the world or the things in the world. If any one loves the world, love for the Father is not in him. For all that is in the world, the lust of the flesh and the lust of the eyes and the pride of life, is not of the Father but is of the world. And the world passes away, and the lust of it; but he who does the will of God abides for ever.
Lk. 16:19–25. There was a rich man, who was clothed in purple and fine linen and who feasted sumptuously every day. And at his gate lay a poor man named Lazarus, full of sores, who desired to be fed with what fell from the rich man's table; moreover the dogs came and licked his sores. The poor man died and was carried by the angels to Abraham's bosom. The rich man also died and was buried; and in Hades, being in torment, he lifted up his eyes, and saw Abraham far off and Lazarus in his bosom. And he called out, "Father Abraham, have mercy upon me, and send Lazarus to dip the end of his finger in water and cool my tongue; for I am in anguish in this flame." But Abraham said, "Son, remember that you in your lifetime received your good things, and Lazarus in like manner evil things; but now he is comforted here, and you are in anguish." (Also Heb. 4:9.)

4. Bass Recit.
●Yearning to die and begin rest; farewell to world (82–4)
Mein Gott! wenn kömmt das schöne: Nun!
My   God! When comes that beautiful (word), "Now!"

Da ich im Friede fahren werde
When I in peace   will-depart
{When I will depart in peace}

Und   in dem Sande   kühler Erde
And (both here) in the sand (of-the) cool earth

Und dort bei dir im Schoße ruhn?
And there with thee in-thy bosom rest?

Der Abschied   ist   gemacht,
(My) farewell hath-been made,

    Welt, gute Nacht!
(O) world, good night!

5. Bass Aria
●Yearning for death as escape from woe (82–5)
Ich freue mich auf meinen Tod,
I   look-forward to   my   death,

*Lk. 2:29.** Lord, now lettest thou thy servant depart in peace...
Rev. 14:13. ...Blessed are the dead who die in the Lord henceforth... that they may rest from their labors, for their deeds follow them!
Phil. 1:23. ...My desire is to depart and be with Christ, for that is far better.
2 Cor. 5:8. We are of good courage, and we would rather be away from the body and at home with the Lord.
Lk. 16:22. The poor man died and was carried by the angels to Abraham's bosom.
Gen. 3:19. ...till you return to the ground, for out of it you were taken; you are dust, and to dust you shall return.
Ecc. 12:7. The dust returns to the earth as it was, and the spirit returns to God who gave it. (Also Ecc. 3:20.)
2 Tim. 4:6–7. I am already on the point of being sacrificed; the time of my departure has come. I have fought the good fight, I have finished the race, I have kept the faith.
Jms. 4:4. ...Whoever wishes to be a friend of the world makes himself an enemy of God. (Also 1 Jn. 2:15–17.)

Rom. 8:19–24. ...Creation waits with eager longing for the revealing of the sons of God; for the creation was subjected to futility, not of its own will but by the will of him who subjected it in hope; because the creation itself will be set free from its bondage to decay and obtain the glorious liberty of the children of God. We know that the whole

Ach, hätt' er sich schon eingefunden.
Ah, had it - already appeared.
{Ah, if only it had already come.}

Da entkomm ich aller Not,
Then escape I all woe,
{Then I will escape all woe}

Die mich noch auf der Welt gebunden.
That me now-yet on the earth does-bind.
{That still binds me now on earth.}

BWV 83
Erfreute Zeit im neuen Bunde
(NBA I/28; BC A167)

Mary's Purification (Candlemas) (BWV 83, 125, 82, 157, 158, [161], [200])
*Mal. 3:1–4 (The Lord will suddenly come to his temple and purify his people)
*Lk. 2:22–32 (Mary presents Jesus at the temple; Nunc dimittis)
Librettist: Unknown

1. Alto Aria
●Death welcomed by believers of new covenant (83-1)
Erfreute Zeit im neuen Bunde,
(O) joyous age of-the new covenant,

Da unser Glaube Jesum hält.
When our faith Jesus holds.
{When our faith holds Jesus.}

Wie freudig wird zur letzten Stunde
How gladly (is) in-(our) last hour

Die Ruhestatt, das Grab bestellt!
That resting-place, the grave, ordered!
{How gladly do we order, in our last hour, that resting place, our grave!}

2. Bass Aria (Chorale) and Recit.
●Voice of Simeon (Nunc dimittis): Lk. 2:29–31 (83-2)
Herr, nun lässest du deinen Diener
Lord, now lettest thou thy servant

in Friede fahren, wie du gesaget hast.
in peace depart, as thou hast-said.

Was uns als Menschen schrecklich scheint,
What to-us as humans frightful seems,
{What seems frightful to us as humans,}

Ist uns ein Eingang zu dem Leben.
Is for-us an entrance to - life.

creation has been groaning in travail together until now; and not only the creation, but we ourselves, who have the first fruits of the Spirit, groan inwardly as we wait for adoption as sons, the redemption of our bodies. For in this hope we were saved...
Rom. 5:2. ...We rejoice in our hope of sharing the glory of God.
Rev. 21:3–4. ...Behold, the dwelling of God [will be] with men. He will dwell with them, and they shall be his people, and God himself will be with them; he will wipe away every tear from their eyes, and death shall be no more, neither shall there be mourning nor crying nor pain any more, for the former things have passed away. (Also Rev. 7:15–17, Is. 25:8.)

Jer. 31:33 [God]: This is the covenant which I will make...I will put my law within them, and I will write it upon their hearts; and I will be their God, and they shall be my people.
Heb. 12:24. ...Jesus [is] the mediator of a new covenant...
Lk. 22:20. ...[Jesus took] the cup after supper, saying, "This cup which is poured out for you is the new covenant in my blood."
Heb. 9:15. Therefore he is the mediator of a new covenant, so that those who are called may receive the promised eternal inheritance, since a death has occurred which redeems them from the transgressions under the first covenant. (Also Heb. 12:24.)
Heb. 2:14–15. Since...the children share in flesh and blood, [Christ] himself likewise partook of the same nature, that through death he might destroy him who has the power of death, that is, the devil, and deliver all those who through fear of death were subject to lifelong bondage.
2 Tim. 1:10. ...Our Savior Christ Jesus...abolished death and brought life and immortality to light... (Also 1 Cor. 15:25–26.)

*Lk. 2:25–29. Now there was a man in Jerusalem, whose name was Simeon, and this man was righteous and devout, looking for the consolation of Israel, and the Holy Spirit was upon him. And it had been revealed to him by the Holy Spirit that he should not see death before he had seen the Lord's Christ. And inspired by the Spirit he came into the temple; and when the parents brought in the child Jesus, to do for him according to the custom of the law, he took him up in his arms and blessed God and said, *"Lord, now lettest thou thy servant depart in peace, according to thy word."*
Phil. 1:21, 23. To me to live is Christ, and to die is gain...My desire is to depart and be with Christ, for that is far better.
Lk. 23:43. [Jesus] said to [the thief on the cross] "Truly, I say to you, today you will be with me in Paradise."

Es   ist der Tod
(Now) is - death
{Death is}

Ein Ende dieser Zeit und   Not,
(The) end to-this time and (this) woe,

Ein Pfand,   so   uns der Herr gegeben
A guarantee, which to-us the Lord has-given
{A guarantee, which the Lord has given to us}

Zum Zeichen, daß er's herzlich meint
As-a   sign,   that he-it (well) means
{As a sign that he means well with us}

Und uns will nach vollbrachtem Ringen
And us will after   completed struggling
{And will bring us, after completed struggling}

Zum Friede bringen.
To   peace   bring.
{To peace.}

Und weil der Heiland nun
And since the Savior now
{And since the Savior now is}

Der Augen Trost,   des Herzens Labsal ist,
To-our eyes consolation, to-our heart refreshment is,
{Consolation to our eyes, refreshment to our heart,}

Was Wunder, daß ein Herz des Todes Furcht vergißt!
What wonder, that a heart - death's fear forgets!
{Small wonder that our heart forgets the fear of death!}

Es kann erfreut den Ausspruch tun:
It can with-joy the   saying   (utter):

Denn meine Augen haben deinen Heiland gesehen,
For   mine   eyes   have   thy   Savior   seen,

welchen du bereitet hast für allen Völkern.
whom   thou prepared hast for all peoples.
{whom thou hast prepared for all peoples.}

3. Tenor Aria
●Encouragement to pray fervently in care-filled times (83-3)
Eile, Herze, voll Freudigkeit
Hasten, heart, full-of joyousness

Vor   den Gnadenstuhl zu treten!
Before the throne-of-grace to step!
{To step before the throne of grace!}

Du sollst deinen Trost empfangen
Thou shalt thy consolation receive

Und Barmherzigkeit erlangen,
And   mercy   obtain,

2 Cor. 5:6-8. So we are always of good courage; we know that while we are at home in the body we are away from the Lord, for we walk by faith, not by sight. We are of good courage, and we would rather be away from the body and at home with the Lord.
Rev. 21:3-4. ...Behold, the dwelling of God is with men. He will dwell with them, and they shall be his people, and God himself will be with them; he will wipe away every tear from their eyes, and death shall be no more, neither shall there be mourning nor crying nor pain any more, for the former things have passed away. (Also Rev. 7:15-17, Is. 25:8.)
2 Tim. 4:6-8. ...The time of my departure has come. I have fought the good fight, I have finished the race, I have kept the faith. Henceforth there is laid up for me the crown of righteousness, which the Lord, the righteous judge, will award to me on that Day, and not only to me but also to all who have loved his appearing. (Also 1 Pet. 5:10.)
Heb. 4:9-10. So then, there remains a sabbath rest for the people of God; for whoever enters God's rest also ceases from his labors as God did from his.
Lk. 16:19-22. There was a rich man, who was clothed in purple and fine linen and who feasted sumptuously every day. And at his gate lay a poor man named Lazarus, full of sores, who desired to be fed with what fell from the rich man's table; moreover the dogs came and licked his sores. The poor man died and was carried by the angels to Abraham's bosom...
Rev. 21:4. [God] will wipe away every tear from their eyes, and death shall be no more, neither shall there be mourning nor crying nor pain any more, for the former things have passed away. (Also Is. 25:8. Rev. 7:15-17.)
Jn. 16:21-22 [Christ]: When a woman is in travail she has sorrow, because her hour has come; but when she is delivered of the child, she no longer remembers the anguish, for joy that a child is born into the world. So you have sorrow now, but I will see you again and your hearts will rejoice, and no one will take your joy from you.
*Lk. 2:29-32. Lord, now lettest thou thy servant depart in peace, according to thy word; _for mine eyes have seen thy salvation which thou hast prepared in the presence of all peoples,_ a light for revelation to the Gentiles, and for glory to thy people Israel.
Ps. 27:1. The Lord is my light and my salvation...
Ps. 23:4. Even though I walk through the valley of the shadow of death, I fear no evil; for thou art with me; thy rod and thy staff, they comfort me. (Also Is. 43:2.)

Heb. 4:14-16. Since then we have a great high priest who has passed through the heavens, Jesus, the Son of God, let us hold fast our confession. For we have not a high priest who is unable to sympathize with our weaknesses, but one who in every respect has been tempted as we are, yet without sin. Let us then with confidence draw near to the throne of grace, that we may receive mercy and find grace to help in time of need.
1 Jn. 5:14-15. And this is the confidence which we have in [Christ], that if we ask anything according to his will he hears us. And if we know that he hears us in whatever we ask, we know that we have obtained the requests made of him.
Lk. 18:1. And [Jesus] told them a parable, to the effect that they ought always to pray and not lose heart.
1 Thess. 5:17. Pray constantly. (Also Rom. 12:12.)

Ja,   bei kummervoller Zeit,
Yea, (do-hasten) in-a care-filled time,

Stark am Geiste, kräftig beten.
Strong in spirit, vigorously, to-pray.
{To pray vigorously, strong in spirit.}

4. Alto Recit.
●Darkness of death & doubt turned to light by Christ (83-4)
Ja,   merkt dein Glaube noch viel Finsternis,
Yea, perceives thy faith yet much darkness,
{Yea, though thy faith perceive much darkness yet,}

Dein Heiland kann der Zweifel Schatten trennen;
Thy Savior can - doubts' shadows dissolve;

Ja, wenn des Grabes Nacht
Yea, when the grave's night

Die letzte Stunde schrecklich macht,
(Thy) final hour frightful makes,
{Makes thy final hour frightful,}

So wirst du doch gewiß
Then shalt thou nevertheless assuredly

Sein helles Licht im Tode selbst erkennen.
His bright light in death itself recognize.
{Recognize his bright light in death itself.}

5. Chorale (See also 125-6.)
●Christ is light for the Gentiles & glory of Israel (83-5)
Er ist das Heil und selig Licht
He is the salvation and blessed light

Für die Heiden,
For the Gentiles,

Zu erleuchten, die dich kennen nicht,
To enlighten, those-who thee know not,
{To enlighten those who know thee not,}

Und zu weiden.
And to pasture (them).

Er ist deins Volks Israel
He is (for) thy people Israel

Der Preis, Ehr, Freud und Wonne.
The glory, honor, joy, and bliss.

Eph. 6:18. Pray at all times in the Spirit, with all prayer and supplication... (Also Jude 1:20.)
Jms. 5:16. ...The prayer of a righteous man has great power in its effects. Elijah was a man of like nature with ourselves and he prayed fervently that it might not rain, and for three years and six months it did not rain on the earth. Then he prayed again and the heaven gave rain, and the earth brought forth its fruit.

Ps. 23:4. Even though I walk through the valley of the shadow of death, I fear no evil; for thou art with me; thy rod and thy staff, they comfort me. (Also Mt. 4:16, Lk. 1:79.)
Heb. 2:14-15. Since therefore the children share in flesh and blood, [Christ] himself likewise partook of the same nature, that through death he might destroy him who has the power of death, that is, the devil, and deliver all those who through fear of death were subject to lifelong bondage.
Is. 43:1-2. Now thus says the Lord, he who created you, O Jacob, he who formed you, O Israel: "Fear not, for I have redeemed you; I have called you by name, you are mine. When you pass through the waters I will be with you; and through the rivers, they shall not overwhelm you; when you walk through fire you shall not be burned, and the flame shall not consume you."
Mk. 5:36. ...Jesus said... "Do not fear, only believe." (Also Lk. 8:50.)
Ps. 27:1. The Lord is my light and my salvation; whom shall I fear?...
Ps. 36:9. [O Lord,] with thee is the fountain of life; in thy light do we see light.
Ps. 116:15. Precious in the sight of the Lord is the death of his saints.

*****Lk. 2:30-32.** Mine eyes have seen thy salvation which thou hast prepared in the presence of all peoples, a light for revelation to the Gentiles, and for glory to thy people Israel.
Is. 42:6-7 [God]: I am the Lord, I have called you in righteousness, I have taken you by the hand and kept you; I have given you as a covenant to the people, a light to the nations, to open the eyes that are blind, to bring out the prisoners from the dungeon, from the prison those who sit in darkness.
Is. 49:6 [God]: ...I will give you as a light to the nations, that my salvation may reach to the end of the earth. (Also Acts 26:23, 13:47.)
Acts 4:12. And there is salvation in no one else [than in Christ], for there is no other name under heaven given among men by which we must be saved.
Is. 40:11. He will feed his flock like a shepherd, he will gather the lambs in his arms, he will carry them in his bosom, and gently lead those that are with young.
Rev. 7:17. The Lamb in the midst of the throne will be their shepherd, and he will guide them to springs of living water; and God will wipe away every tear from their eyes. (Also Ezek. 34:11-16, Ps. 23:1-2.)
Is. 28:5. In that day the Lord of hosts will be a crown of glory, and a diadem of beauty, to the remnant of his people.
Deut. 10:21. He is your praise (Luther: Ruhm); he is your God...

BWV 84
Ich bin vergnügt mit meinem Glücke
(NBA I/7; BC A43)

Septuagesima (BWV 144, 92, 84)
*1 Cor. 9:24–10:5 (Run the race so as to obtain the prize)
*Mt. 20:1–16 (The parable of the vineyard laborers)
Librettist: Picander (Christian Friedrich Henrici)

1. Soprano Aria
●Contentment with what I have, though it be little (84-1)
Ich bin vergnügt mit meinem Glücke,
I   am content with my   fortune,
{I am content with my lot,}

Das   mir der liebe Gott beschert.
Which on-me the dear God has-bestowed.
{Which the dear God has bestowed on me.}

Soll ich nicht reiche Fülle haben,
Shall I   not   rich   abundance have,
{If I am not to have rich abundance,}

So   dank ich ihm für kleine Gaben
Then thank I   him for small gifts
{Then I thank him for small gifts}

Und bin auch nicht derselben wert.
And am even   not of-those worthy.
{And am not worthy even of those.}

2. Soprano Recit.
●God owes me nothing; I have but done my duty (84-2)
Gott ist mir ja   nichts schuldig,
God   - me indeed nothing owes,
{God indeed owes me nothing,}

Und wenn er mir   was   gibt,
And when he to-me something gives,
{And when he gives something to me,}

So   zeigt   er mir, daß er mich liebt;
So demonstrates he to-me that he me loves;
{He demonstrates to me that he loves me;}

Ich kann mir nichts bei ihm verdienen,
I   can   - nothing from him   earn,
{I can never put him in my debt,}

Denn was ich tu, ist   meine Pflicht.
For whatever I do, is (but) my   duty.

Ja! wenn mein Tun gleich noch so gut geschienen,
Yes, when my dealings even yet so good have-appeared,
{Yes, though my dealings appear yet so noble,}

So hab ich   doch   nichts Rechtes ausgericht'.
So have I nevertheless nothing of-worth accomplished.
{So have I nevertheless accomplished nothing of worth.}

*Mt. 20:1–16. The kingdom of heaven is like a householder who went out early in the morning to hire laborers for his vineyard. After agreeing with the laborers for a denarius (Luther: Groschen) a day, he sent them into his vineyard. And going out about the third hour he saw others standing idle in the market place; and to them he said, "You go into the vineyard too, and whatever is right I will give you." So they went. Going out again about the sixth hour and the ninth hour, he did the same. And about the eleventh hour he went out and found others standing; and he said to them, "Why do you stand here idle all day?" They said to him, "Because no one has hired us." He said to them, "You go into the vineyard too." And when evening came, the owner of the vineyard said to his steward, "Call the laborers and pay them their wages, beginning with the last, up to the first." And when those hired about the eleventh hour came, each of them received a denarius. Now when the first came, they thought they would receive more; but each of them also received a denarius. And on receiving it they grumbled at the householder, saying, "These last worked only one hour, and you have made them equal to us who have borne the burden of the day and the scorching heat." But he replied to one of them, "Friend, I am doing you no wrong; did you not agree with me for a denarius? Take what belongs to you, and go; I choose to give to this last as I give to you. Am I not allowed to do what I choose with what belongs to me? Or do you begrudge my generosity?" So the last will be first, and the first last.

Phil. 4:11–12. [I do not] complain of want; for I have learned, in whatever state I am, to be content. I know how to be abased, and I know how to abound; in any and all circumstances I have learned the secret of facing plenty and hunger, abundance and want.
Job 41:11 [God]: Who has given to me, that I should repay him? Whatever is under the whole heaven is mine.
Gen. 32:10. I am not worthy of the least of all the steadfast love and all the faithfulness which thou hast shown to thy servant...
Lk. 17:7–10. Will any one of you, who has a servant plowing or keeping sheep, say to him when he has come in from the field, "Come at once and sit down at table"? Will he not rather say to him, "Prepare and serve me, till I eat and drink; and afterward you shall eat and drink"? Does he thank the servant because he did what was commanded? So you also, when you have done all that is commanded you, say, "We are unworthy servants; we have only done what was our duty."
Heb. 13:5–6. Keep your life free from love of money, and be content with what you have; for he has said, "I will never fail you nor forsake you." Hence we can confidently say, "The Lord is my helper, I will not be afraid; what can man do to me?" (Deut. 31:6, 8; Josh. 1:5)

Doch ist der Mensch so ungeduldig,
Yet is - man so impatient,
{Yet human nature is so impatient,}

Daß er sich oft betrübt,
That he himself often grieves,
{That one often becomes downcast,}

Wenn ihm der liebe Gott nicht überflüssig gibt.
If him the dear God not superabundantly (blesses).
{If the dear God does not superabundantly bless him.}

Hat er uns nicht so lange Zeit
Has he us not (for) so long (a) time
{Has he not all this long time}

Umsonst ernähret und gekleidet
Freely nourished and clothed
{Freely nourished and clothed us}

Und will uns einsten seliglich
And intends us one-day blessedly
{And intends one day to blessedly exalt us}

In seine Herrlichkeit erhöhn?
Into his glory to-exalt?
{Into his glory?}

Es ist genug für mich,
It is enough for me,

Daß ich nicht hungrig darf zu Bette gehn.
That I not hungry (must) to bed go.
{That I do not have to go to bed hungry.}

3. Soprano Aria
●Contentment with my lot though others have more (84–3)
Ich esse mit Freuden mein weniges Brot
I eat with gladness my bit-of bread

Und gönne dem Nächsten von Herzen das Seine.
And grant (my) neighbor from-my heart what's his.
{And sincerely do not begrudge my neighbor what is his.}

Ein ruhig Gewissen, ein fröhlicher Geist,
A peaceful conscience, a happy spirit,

Ein dankbares Herze, das lobet und preist,
A thankful heart, that lauds and praises,

Vermehret den Segen, verzuckert die Not.
Multiplies (one's) blessing, sweetens (one's) necessity.

4. Soprano Recit.
●Contentment now; looking to eternal compensation (84–4)
Im Schweiße meines Angesichts
In-the sweat of-my face

Lk. 12:15–21. [Jesus] said... "Take heed, and beware of all covetousness; for a man's life does not consist in the abundance of his possessions."
*Mt. 20:10–11. When the first [laborers] came, they thought they would receive more; but each of them also received a denarius. And on receiving it they grumbled at the householder...
Prov. 28:25. A greedy man stirs up strife, but he who trusts in the Lord will be enriched. (Also Prov. 27:20, Ecc. 4:8.)
Ps. 73:2–3, 13. ...My feet had almost stumbled, my steps had well-nigh slipped. For I was envious of the arrogant, when I saw the prosperity of the wicked... All in vain have I kept my heart clean and washed my hands in innocence.
Prov. 23:17–18. Let not your heart envy sinners, but continue in the fear of the Lord all the day. Surely there is a future, and your hope will not be cut off. (Also Prov. 3:31.)
Ps. 37:25. I have been young, and now am old; yet I have not seen the righteous forsaken or his children begging bread.
Neh. 9:21. Forty years didst thou sustain [the Israelites] in the wilderness, and they lacked nothing; their clothes did not wear out and their feet did not swell. (Also Deut. 29:5.)
Mt. 6:25–26 [Christ]: I tell you, do not be anxious about your life, what you shall eat or what you shall drink, nor about your body, what you shall put on. Is not life more than food, and the body more than clothing? Look at the birds of the air; they neither sow nor reap nor gather into barns, and yet your heavenly Father feeds them... (Also Mt. 6:27–34.)
1 Pet. 5:4, 6. And when the chief Shepherd is manifested you will obtain the unfading crown of glory...Humble yourselves therefore under the mighty hand of God, that in due time he may exalt you. (Also Jms. 4:6.)
1 Tim. 6:8–9. If we have food and clothing, with these we shall be content. But those who desire to be rich fall into temptation, into a snare, into many senseless and hurtful desires that plunge men into ruin and destruction.

Ecc. 5:18–19. Behold, what I have seen to be good and to be fitting is to eat and drink and find enjoyment in all the toil with which one toils under the sun the few days of his life which God has given him, for this is his lot. Every man also to whom God has given wealth and possessions and power to enjoy them, and to accept his lot and find enjoyment in his toil—this is the will of God. (Also Ecc. 2:24–25, 3:12–13, 9:7.)
*Mt. 20:13–15. ...Friend, I am doing you no wrong; did you not agree with me for a denarius? Take what belongs to you, and go; I choose to give to this last as I give to you. Am I not allowed to do what I choose with what belongs to me? Or do you begrudge my generosity?
1 Tim. 6:6–7. There is great gain in godliness with contentment; for we brought nothing into the world, and we cannot take anything out of the world.

Gen. 3:19. In the sweat of your face you shall eat bread till you return to the ground, for out of it you were taken; you are dust, and to dust you shall return.

Will ich indes mein Brot genießen,
Will I meanwhile my bread enjoy,
{Will I meanwhile enjoy my bread,}

Und wenn mein Lebenslauf,
And when my life's-course,

Mein Lebensabend wird beschließen,
My life's-evening, will come-to-a-close,

So teilt mir Gott den Groschen aus,
Then apportions to-me God (my) pence -,
{Then God will apportion to me my pence,}

Da steht der Himmel drauf.
For-that vouches - heaven -.
{Heaven has vouched for that.}

O! wenn ich diese Gabe
Oh! if I this gift

Zu meinem Gnadenlohne habe,
For my compensation-of-grace possess,

So brauch ich weiter nichts.
Then need I furthermore nothing.
{Then I have need of nothing else.}

5. Chorale
●Contentment now since eternal well-being is assured (84-5)
Ich leb indes in dir vergnüget
I live, meanwhile, in thee content

Und sterb ohn alle Kümmernis,
And die without (any) cares,

Mir gnüget, wie es mein Gott füget,
Me satisfies, how - my God directs,
{I am satisfied with the way my God directs matters,}

Ich glaub und bin es ganz gewiß:
I believe and am of-it completely sure:
{I believe and am completely sure of this:}

Durch deine Gnad und Christi Blut
Through thy grace and Christ's blood

Machst du's mit meinem Ende gut.
Makest thou-it with my end well.
{Thou dost make it well with mine end.}

Ecc. 2:24–25. There is nothing better for a man than that he should eat and drink, and find enjoyment in his toil. This also, I saw, is from the hand of God; for apart from him who can eat or who can have enjoyment? (Also Ecc. 3:12–13, 5:18–19, 9:7.)
*Mt. 20:8–10. When evening came, the owner of the vineyard said to his steward, "Call the laborers and pay them their wages, beginning with the last, up to the first." And when those hired about the eleventh hour came, each of them received a denarius. Now when the first came, they thought they would receive more; but each of them also received a denarius (Luther: Groschen).
2 Tim. 4:6–8. ...The time of my departure has come. I have fought the good fight, I have finished the race (Luther: Lauf vollendet), I have kept the faith. Henceforth there is laid up for me the crown of righteousness, which the Lord, the righteous judge, will award to me on that Day, and not only to me but also to all who have loved his appearing. (Also Jms. 1:12, Rev. 2:10.)
Lk. 18:29–30 [Christ]: ...There is no man who has left house or wife or brothers or parents or children, for the sake of the kingdom of God, who will not receive manifold more in this time, and in the age to come eternal life.
2 Cor. 4:17. This slight momentary affliction is preparing for us an eternal weight of glory beyond all comparison. (Also Rom. 8:18.)
Eph. 2:8–9. By grace you have been saved through faith; and this is not your own doing, it is the gift of God—not because of works, lest any man should boast.
Rom. 11:6. But if it is by grace, it is no longer on the basis of works; otherwise grace would no longer be grace.

1 Tim. 6:6–8. There is great gain in godliness with contentment; for we brought nothing into the world, and we cannot take anything out of the world; but if we have food and clothing, with these we shall be content.
Phil. 4:6–7. Have no anxiety about anything, but in everything by prayer and supplication with thanksgiving let your requests be made known to God. And the peace of God, which passes all understanding, will keep your hearts and your minds in Christ Jesus.
Rom. 8:28. We know that in everything God works for good with those who love him, who are called according to his purpose.
Jms. 2:5. ...Has not God chosen those who are poor in the world to be rich in faith and heirs of the kingdom which he has promised to those who love him? (Also Lk. 6:21.)
Heb. 6:19–20. We have this as a sure and steadfast anchor of the soul, a hope that enters into the inner shrine behind the [temple] curtain, where Jesus has gone as a forerunner on our behalf, having become a high priest for ever...
Rom. 5:2. Through [Christ] we have obtained access to this grace in which we stand, and we rejoice in our hope of sharing the glory of God...
Eph. 2:13. ...In Christ Jesus you who once were far off have been brought near in the blood of Christ. (Also Heb. 9:14, 1 Pet. 1:18–19, Rev. 1:5.)
1 Jn. 4:16–17. So we know and believe the love God has for us. God is love, and he who abides in love abides in God, and God abides in him. In this is love perfected with us, that we may have confidence for the day of judgment...
Num. 23:10. ...Let me die the death of the righteous, and let my end be like his!
1 Cor. 1:7–8. ...Our Lord Jesus Christ...will sustain you to the end, guiltless in the day of our Lord Jesus Christ.

BWV 85
Ich bin ein guter Hirt
(NBA I/11; BC A66)

Misericordias Domini: 2. S. after Easter (BWV 104, 85, 112)
*1 Pet. 2:21–25 (Christ as example; you have returned to the shepherd of your souls)
*Jn. 10:11–16 (Jesus declares himself to be the good Shepherd)
Librettist: Unknown; perhaps Christian Weiß the elder

1. Bass Aria
●Vox Christi: I am the good shepherd: Jn. 10:12 (85-1)
Ich bin ein guter Hirt, ein guter Hirt läßt
I am a good shepherd, a good shepherd gives-up

sein Leben für die Schafe.
his life for the sheep.

2. Alto Aria
●Jesus as good shepherd: he gave his life for sheep (85-2)
Jesus ist ein guter Hirt;
Jesus is a good shepherd;

Denn er hat bereits sein Leben
For he has already his life

Für die Schafe hingegeben,
For the sheep given-up,
{For he has given up his life for the sheep,}

Die ihm niemand rauben wird.
Which from-him no-one shall-steal.
{And no one shall steal them from him.}

Jesus ist ein guter Hirt.
Jesus is a good shepherd.

3. Chorale: Soprano (See also 104-6.)
●Shepherd Psalm: Paraphrase of Ps. 23:1–2 (85-3)
Der Herr ist mein getreuer Hirt,
The Lord is my faithful shepherd,

Dem ich mich ganz vertraue,
To-whom I myself completely entrust,
{To whom I completely entrust myself,}

Zur Weid er mich, sein Schäflein, führt
To-a pasture he me, his little-sheep, leads
{To a pasture he leads me, his little sheep}

Auf schöner grünen Aue,
Upon-a beautiful green meadow,

Jn. 10:10–15. [Jesus said,] "The thief comes only to steal and kill and destroy; I came that they may have life, and have it abundantly. I am the good shepherd. The good shepherd lays down his life for the sheep. He who is a hireling and not a shepherd, whose own the sheep are not, sees the wolf coming and leaves the sheep and flees; and the wolf snatches them and scatters them. He flees because he is a hireling and cares nothing for the sheep. I am the good shepherd; I know my own and my own know me, as the Father knows me and I know the Father; and I lay down my life for the sheep."

Jn. 10:17–18, 27–30 [Christ]: For this reason the Father loves me, because I lay down my life, that I may take it again. No one takes it from me, but I lay it down of my own accord. I have power to lay it down, and I have power to take it again; this charge I have received from my Father...My sheep hear my voice, and I know them, and they follow me; and I give them eternal life, and they shall never perish, and no one shall snatch them out of my hand. My Father, who has given them to me, is greater than all, and no one is able to snatch them out of the Father's hand. I and the Father are one.
Rom. 5:7–8. Why, one will hardly die for a righteous man—though perhaps for a good man one will dare even to die. But God shows his love for us in that while we were yet sinners Christ died for us. (Also Jn. 15:13.)
1 Tim. 2:5–6. There is one God, and there is one mediator between God and men, the man Christ Jesus, who gave himself as a ransom for all... (Also Eph. 5:2, Tit. 2:14.)
Jn. 6:39 [Christ]: This is the will of him who sent me, that I should lose nothing of all that he has given me, but raise it up at the last day.

Ps. 23:1–3. The Lord is my shepherd, I shall not want; he makes me lie down in green pastures. He leads me beside still waters; he restores my soul. He leads me in paths of righteousness for his name's sake.
Ezek. 34:14–16 [God]: I will feed them with good pasture, and upon the mountain heights of Israel shall be their pasture; there they shall lie down in good grazing land, and on fat pasture they shall feed on the mountains of Israel. I myself will be the shepherd of my sheep, and I will make them lie down, says the Lord God. I will seek the lost, and I will bring back the strayed, and I will bind up the crippled, and I will strengthen the weak...
*Jn. 10:14, 27 [Christ]: I am the good shepherd; I know my own and my own know me...My sheep hear my voice, and I know them, and they follow me. (Also Rev. 7:15–17.)
*1 Pet. 2:25. You were straying like sheep, but have now returned to the Shepherd and Guardian of your souls.

Zum frischen Wasser leit er mich,
To   fresh   waters leads he me,
{He leads me to fresh waters,}

Mein Seel zu laben kräftiglich
My   soul to restore mightily
{To restore my soul mightily}

Durchs   selig Wort der Gnaden.
Through-the blessed word of   grace.

4. Tenor Recit.
●Shepherd watches sheep when hirelings sleep (85-4)
Wenn die Mietlinge schlafen,
When the hirelings   sleep,

Da   wachet dieser Hirt bei seinen Schafen,
Then keeps-watch this shepherd by his   sheep,
{Then this shepherd keeps watch over his sheep,}

So daß ein jedes in gewünschter Ruh
So that (each one) in   welcome   rest

Die   Trift und Weide kann genießen,
The meadow and pasture can   enjoy,
{Can enjoy the meadow and pasture,}

In welcher Lebensströme fließen.
In   which   streams-of-life do-flow.

Denn suchet der Höllenwolf gleich einzudringen,
For   seeks the wolf-of-hell (indeed) to-invade,
{For if the wolf of hell should indeed seek to invade,}

Die Schafe zu verschlingen,
The sheep to   devour,

So hält ihm dieser Hirt   doch seinen Rachen zu.
Then holds - this shepherd indeed his   jaws shut.
{Then this shepherd holds his jaws shut.}

5. Tenor Aria
●Jesus as shepherd shows his love by dying for sheep (85-5)
Seht, was die Liebe tut.
See, what - love does.

Mein Jesus hält in guter Hut
My   Jesus holds in good keeping

Die Seinen   feste eingeschlossen
- His-own—securely   enclosed

Und hat am Kreuzesstamm vergossen
And has on-the cross's-beam   poured-out
{And has, on the cross, poured out}

1 Pet. 2:2. Like newborn babes, long for the pure spiritual milk, that by it you may grow up to salvation; for you have tasted the kindness of the Lord.
Mt. 4:4 [Christ]: It is written, "Man shall not live by bread alone, but by every word that proceeds from the mouth of God." (See Deut. 8:3, also Lk. 4:4.)
Ps. 119:25, 28, 81. [O Lord,] my soul cleaves to the dust; revive me according to thy word!...My soul melts away for sorrow; strengthen me according to thy word!...My soul languishes for thy salvation; I hope in thy word. (Also Ps. 119:107, 116.)

*****Jn. 10:10-15 [Christ]:** The thief comes only to steal and kill and destroy; I came that they may have life, and have it abundantly. I am the good shepherd. The good shepherd lays down his life for the sheep. He who is a hireling (Luther: Mietling) and not a shepherd, whose own the sheep are not, sees the wolf coming and leaves the sheep and flees; and the wolf snatches them and scatters them. He flees because he is a hireling and cares nothing for the sheep. I am the good shepherd; I know my own and my own know me, as the Father knows me and I know the Father; and I lay down my life for the sheep.
Jn. 10:9 [Christ]: I am the door; if any one enters by me, he will be saved, and will go in and out and find pasture.
Ps. 23:1-3. The Lord is my shepherd, I shall not want; he makes me lie down in green pastures. He leads me beside still waters; he restores my soul.
Rev. 7:17. The Lamb in the midst of the throne will be their shepherd, and he will guide them to springs of living water... (Also Rev. 21:6, 22:1, 22:17.)
Jn. 4:14 [Christ]: Whoever drinks of the water that I shall give him will never thirst; the water that I shall give him will become in him a spring of water welling up to eternal life.
Jn. 10:28-29 [Christ]: I give them eternal life, and they shall never perish, and no one shall snatch them out of my hand.
1 Pet. 5:8. Be sober, be watchful. Your adversary the devil prowls around like a roaring lion, seeking some one to devour. (Also Ps. 22:21.)
2 Tim. 4:17. The Lord stood by me and gave me strength...So I was rescued from the lion's mouth. (Also 1 Sam. 17:34-35, Dan. 6:22, Heb. 11:33.)

*****Jn. 10:11 [Christ]:** I am the good shepherd. The good shepherd lays down his life for the sheep.
Jn. 15:13 [Christ]: Greater love has no man than this, that a man lay down his life for his friends.
*****Jn. 10:14-15, 27-29 [Christ]:** I am the good shepherd; I know my own and my own know me, as the Father knows me and I know the Father...My sheep hear my voice, and I know them, and they follow me; and I give them eternal life, and they shall never perish, and no one shall snatch them out of my hand. My Father, who has given them to me, is greater than all, and no one is able to snatch them out of the Father's hand.
*****1 Pet. 2:24.** [Christ] himself bore our sins in his body on the tree, that we might die to sin and live to righteousness. (Also Gal. 3:13.)

Für sie sein teures Blut.
For them his precious blood.
{His precious blood for them.}

6. Chorale
●God as shepherd: I need not fear anything (85–6)
Ist   Gott   mein Schutz und treuer Hirt,
(With) God (as) my   shelter and true shepherd,

Kein Unglück mich berühren wird.
No misfortune me   shall-touch.
{No misfortune shall touch me.}

Weicht, alle   meine Feinde,
Retreat, all (you) my   foes,

Die ihr   mir stiftet Angst und Pein,
You-who for-me cause fear and pain,
{You who cause me fear and pain,}

Es wird zu eurem Schaden sein,
It will to your   harm be,
{It will be to your harm,}

Ich habe Gott zum Freunde.
I have God for-a friend.

BWV 86
Wahrlich, wahrlich, ich sage euch
(NBA I/12; BC A73)

Rogate: 5. S. after Easter (BWV 86, 87)
*Jms. 1:22–27 (Be doers of the word and not hearers only)
*Jn. 16:23[1]–30 (Christ's farewell: Ask anything of the Father in my name)
[1]Begin: "Truly, truly, I say"
Librettist: Unknown; perhaps Christian Weiß the elder

1. Bass Aria
●Vox Christi: I will grant your requests: Jn. 16:23 (86–1)
Wahrlich, wahrlich, ich sage euch, so ihr den Vater
Truly,   truly,   I   say to-you, if you of-the Father

etwas   bitten werdet in meinem Namen, so wird er's
something shall-request in   my   name, then will he-it

euch geben.
to-you give.

1 Pet. 1:18–19. You know that you were ransomed...with the precious blood of Christ...like that of a lamb without blemish or spot. (Also Rev. 5:9.)

Ps. 23:1, 4. The Lord is my shepherd...Even though I walk through the valley of the shadow of death, I fear no evil (Luther: Unglück); for thou art with me; thy rod and thy staff, they comfort me.
*****Jn. 10:14, 27–28 [Christ]:** I am the good shepherd...My sheep hear my voice, and I know them, and they follow me; and I give them eternal life, and they shall never perish, and no one shall snatch them out of my hand.
Ps. 118:6–7. With the Lord on my side I do not fear. What can man do to me? The Lord is on my side to help me; I shall look in triumph on those who hate me. (Also Ps. 27:1, Ps. 56:4, 2 Cor. 2:14.)
Rom. 8:31, 37. What then shall we say to this? If God is for us, who is against us?...In all these things we are more than conquerors through him who loved us.
Deut. 1:30. The Lord your God who goes before you will himself fight for you...
Ps. 7:12–16. ...God will whet his sword; he has bent and strung his bow; he has prepared his deadly weapons, making his arrows fiery shafts. Behold the wicked man conceives evil...He makes a pit, digging it out, and falls into the hole which he has made. His mischief returns upon his own head, and on his own pate his violence descends. (Also Ps. 35:8, 141:10.)
Zech. 2:8. ...He who touches you touches the apple of [God's] eye.
Jn. 15:15 [Christ]: No longer do I call you servants...but I have called you friends...

*****Jn. 16:23–24 [Christ]:** *...Truly, truly, I say to you, if you ask anything of the Father, he will give it to you in my name.* Hitherto you have asked nothing in my name; ask, and you will receive, that your joy may be full.
Jn. 14:13–14 [Christ]: Whatever you ask in my name, I will do it, that the Father may be glorified in the Son; if you ask anything in my name, I will do it.
Jn. 15:15–16 [Christ]: No longer do I call you servants, for the servant does not know what his master is doing; but I have called you friends, for all that I have heard from my Father I have made known to you. You did not choose me, but I chose you and appointed you that you should go and bear fruit and that your fruit should abide; so that whatever you ask the Father in my name, he may give it to you.

2. Alto Aria

●Confidence in face of trouble, that prayers are heard (86-2)

Ich will   doch   wohl Rosen brechen,
I   will, however, indeed roses   (gather),

Wenn   mich gleich die Dornen stechen.
Even-though me -   the thorns   prick.
{Even though the thorns prick me.}

Denn ich bin der Zuversicht,
For   I   am of-the conviction,
{For I have confidence}

Daß mein Bitten   und mein Flehen
That my petitioning and my   entreating

Gott gewiß zu Herzen gehen,
God assuredly to   heart   go,
{Assuredly reach God's heart,}

Weil es mir sein Wort verspricht.
For (this) me his Word promises.
{For his Word assures me of this.}

3. Chorale: Soprano

●Promises of God's Word are sure & bring us to heaven
(86-3)

Und was der ewig   gütig Gott
And what the eternally gracious God

In seinem Wort versprochen hat,
In his   Word   has-promised,

Geschworn bei seinem Namen,
Sworn   by   his   name,

Das hält und gibt er g'wiß   fürwahr.
That keeps and grants he assuredly - .
{That will he assuredly fulfil and grant.}

      Der helf uns zu   der Engel Schar
(May) he help us to (reach) the angel   host

Durch Jesum Christum, Amen!
Through Jesus Christ. Amen!

4. Tenor Recit.

●Promises of God fulfilled, unlike those of world (86-4)

Gott macht es nicht gleich wie die Welt,
God   acts   not   as   the world (does),
{God does not act like the world,}

S. of S. 6:2 [Bride]: My beloved has gone down to his garden...to gather lilies (Luther: Rosen breche).

Hab. 3:17–19. Though the fig tree do not blossom, nor fruit be on the vines...yet I will rejoice in the Lord, I will joy in the God of my salvation. God, the Lord, is my strength...

Ps. 130:6. I wait for the Lord, my soul waits, and in his word I hope.

Ps. 42:42:5/11/43:5. Why are you cast down, O my soul, and why are you disquieted within me? Hope in God; for I shall again praise him, my help and my God.

Rom. 8:24–25, 28. ...Now hope that is seen is not hope. For who hopes for what he sees? But if we hope for what we do not see, we wait for it with patience...We know that in everything God works for good with those who love him, who are called according to his purpose.

Heb. 11:1. Faith is the assurance of things hoped for, the conviction of things not seen.

Rom. 5:5. And hope does not disappoint us, because God's love has been poured into our hearts through the Holy Spirit which has been given to us.

Ps. 27:13–14. I believe that I shall see the goodness of the Lord in the land of the living! Wait for the Lord; be strong, and let your heart take courage; yea, wait for the Lord! (Also Ps. 31:24, 38:15, 39:7, 62:1–2, 130:5–6, 131:2.)

Eph. 6:18. Pray at all times in the Spirit, with all prayer and supplication (Luther: Bitten und Flehen)... (Also Phil. 4:6.)

Ps. 6:9. The Lord has heard my supplication (Luther: Flehen); the Lord accepts my prayer. (Also Ps. 116:1.)

Mt. 7:11 [Christ]: If you then, who are evil, know how to give good gifts to your children, how much more will your Father who is in heaven give good things to those who ask him!

Mt. 24:35 [Christ]: Heaven and earth will pass away, but my words will not pass away. (Also Mk. 13:31, Lk. 21:33, Is. 40:8, Ps. 102:25–27.)

Heb. 6:13–15. When God made a promise to Abraham, since he had no one greater by whom to swear, he swore by himself, saying, "Surely, I will bless you and mulitiply you." And thus Abraham, having patiently endured, obtained the promise.

2 Tim. 2:13. If we are faithless, [God] remains faithful—for he cannot deny himself. (Also Rom. 3:4.)

2 Pet. 1:3–4. His divine power has granted to us all things that pertain to life and godliness, through the knowledge of him who called us to his own glory and excellence, by which he has granted to us his precious and very great promises...

1 Jn. 2:25. And this is what he has promised us, eternal life.

2 Cor. 1:20. All the promises of God find their Yes in [Christ]. That is why we utter the Amen through him, to the glory of God.

Rom. 5:2. Through [Christ] we have obtained access to this grace in which we stand, and we rejoice in our hope of sharing the glory of God.

Jn. 14:27 [Christ]: ...Not as the world gives do I give to you. Let not your hearts be troubled, neither let them be afraid.

Rom. 3:4. ...Let God be true though every man be false... (Also 2 Tim. 2:13, Ps. 116:11.)

2 Cor. 1:18–20. As surely as God is faithful, our word to you has not been Yes and No. For the Son of God, Jesus Christ...was not Yes and No; but in him it is always Yes. For all the promises of God find their

Die   viel verspricht und wenig hält;
Which much promises and   little keeps;
{Which promises much and keeps little;}

Denn was   er zusagt, muß geschehen,
For whatever he assents-to, must   happen,

Daß man daran kann seine Lust und Freude sehen.
So-that one thereby can   his pleasure and   joy   see.
{So that one can see God's pleasure and joy thereby.}

5. Tenor Aria
●Prayers answered eventually, though help be deferred (86-5)
Gott hilft gewiß;
God helps assuredly;

Wird gleich die Hülfe   aufgeschoben,
 - Although - help (be) deferred,
{Just because help may be deferred,}

Wird sie doch   drum   nicht aufgehoben.
Is   it   yet for-that-reason not withdrawn.
{Does not mean it is withdrawn.}

Denn Gottes Wort bezeiget dies:
For   God's Word declares this:

Gott hilft gewiß!
God helps assuredly!

6. Chorale (See also 186–11.)
●Hope rewarded in God's own time; he may be trusted (86-6)
Die Hoffnung wart' der rechten Zeit,
(Our) hope awaits the   right time,

Was   Gottes Wort zusaget;
For-what God's Word does-promise;
{When we shall receive what God's Word has promised.}

Wenn das geschehen soll zur Freud,
When that   shall-happen to-our joy,
{Just when this is to happen to our joy—}

     Setzt Gott kein g'wisse Tage.
(Then) sets God no specific day.
{Just what particular day—has not been indicated by God.}

Er weiß wohl, wenn's am besten ist,
He knows well, when-it - best is,
{He knows well when it is best,}

Yes in him. That is why we utter the Amen through him, to the glory of God.
Lk. 12:32 [Christ]: Fear not, little flock, for it is your Father's good pleasure to give you the kingdom.
Mt. 7:7, 11 [Christ]: Ask, and it will be given you...If you...who are evil, know how to give good gifts to your children, how much more will your Father who is in heaven give good things to those who ask him! (Also Lk. 11:9–13, Rom. 8:32.)
Prov. 15:8. The sacrifice of the wicked is an abomination to the Lord, but the prayer of the upright is his delight. (Also Prov. 15:29.)

Lk. 18:7–8 [Christ]: Will not God vindicate his elect, who cry to him day and night? Will he delay long over them? I tell you, he will vindicate them speedily. Nevertheless, when the Son of God comes, will he find faith on the earth?
Ps. 40:17. As for me, I am poor and needy; but the Lord takes thought for me. Thou art my help and my deliverer; do not tarry, O my God! (Also Ps. 70:5.)
2 Pet. 3:3–4, 8–9. ...You must understand this, that scoffers will come in the last days with scoffing...saying, "Where is the promise of his coming? For ever since the fathers fell asleep, all things have continued as they were from the beginning of creation."...But do not ignore this one fact, beloved, that with the Lord one day is as a thousand years, and a thousand years as one day. The Lord is not slow about his promise as some count slowness...
Heb. 10:36–38. You have need of endurance (Luther: Geduld), so that you may do the will of God and receive what is promised. "For yet a little while, and the coming one shall come and shall not tarry; but my righteous one shall live by faith, and if he shrinks back, my soul has no pleasure in him."

Gal. 6:9. Let us not grow weary in well-doing, for in due season (Luther: zu seiner Zeit) we shall reap, if we do not lose heart. (Also Rev. 2:3.)
Heb. 10:36. You have need of endurance, so that you may do the will of God and receive what is promised.
Rom. 8:24–26, 28. In...hope we were saved. Now hope that is seen is not hope. For who hopes for what he sees? But if we hope for what we do not see, we wait for it with patience. Likewise the Spirit helps us in our weakness; for we do not know how to pray as we ought, but the Spirit himself intercedes for us with sighs too deep for words...We know that in everything God works for good with those who love him, who are called according to his purpose.
Acts 1:7. [Jesus] said to [his disciples], "It is not for you to know times or seasons which the Father has fixed by his own authority."
Ps. 37:5. Commit your way to the Lord; trust in him, and he will act.
Lam. 3:25–27, 31–32. The Lord is good to those who wait for him...It is good that one should wait quietly for the salvation of the Lord...For the Lord will not cast off for ever, but, though he cause grief, he will have compassion according to the abundance of his steadfast love.
Gal. 4:4. When the time had fully come, God sent forth his Son...
Rom. 5:6. ...At the right time Christ died for the ungodly.
2 Pet. 3:8–9. Do not ignore this one fact, beloved, that with the Lord one day is as a thousand years, and a thousand years as one day. The Lord is not slow about his promise as some count slowness...

Und braucht an uns kein arge List;
And employs on us no malicious cunning;
{And employs no malicious cunning on us;}

Des solln wir ihm vertrauen.
For-this are we him to-trust.
{For this we are to trust him.}

BWV 87
Bisher habt ihr nichts gebeten in meinem Namen
(NBA I/12; BC A74)

Rogate: 5. S. after Easter (BWV 86, 87)
*Jms. 1:22–27 (Be doers of the word and not hearers only)
*Jn. 16:23[1]–30 (Christ's farewell: Ask anything of the Father in my name)
[1]Begin: "Truly, truly, I say"
Librettist: Christiane Mariane von Ziegler (Libretto greatly modified)

1. Bass Aria
●Vox Christi: You have not asked in my name: Jn. 16:24 (87-1)
Bisher habt ihr nichts gebeten in meinem Namen.
Hitherto have you nothing asked in my name.

2. Alto Recit.
●Failure to pray despite deliberate transgressions (87-2)
O Wort, das Geist und Seel erschreckt!
O word, that spirit and soul alarms!

Ihr Menschen, merkt den Zuruf, was dahinter steckt!
You people, perceive (his) call, what behind-it lies!
{You people, take note of his call, and the reason for it!}

Ihr habt Gesetz und Evangelium vorsätzlich übertreten,
You have Law and Gospel deliberately transgressed,

Und diesfalls möcht' ihr ungesäumt
And therefore (should) you immediately

In Buß und Andacht beten.
In penitence and devotion pray.

3. Alto Aria
●Prayer of confession; request for advocacy (87-3)
Vergib, o Vater, unsre Schuld
Forgive, O Father, our guilt

Ps. 130:5. I wait for the Lord, my soul waits, and in his word I hope.
Tit. 1:2–3. [We have been given] hope of eternal life which God, who never lies, promised ages ago and at the proper time manifested in his word...
Rev. 3:14. ...the words of the Amen, the faithful and true witness, the beginning of God's creation.
Ps. 31:14–15. I trust in thee, O Lord, I say, "Thou art my God." My times are in thy hand...

*Jn. 16:23–24 [Christ]:** ...Truly, truly, I say to you, if you ask anything of the Father, he will give it to you in my name. *Hitherto you have asked nothing in my name;* ask, and you will receive, that your joy may be full.
Jn. 14:13–14 [Christ]: Whatever you ask in my name, I will do it, that the Father may be glorified in the Son; if you ask anything in my name, I will do it. (Also Jn. 15:16.)

Jms. 4:2–3. ...You do not have, because you do not ask. You ask and do not receive, because you ask wrongly, to spend it on your passions.
Is. 43:22, 24 [God]: ...You did not call upon me, O Jacob; but you have been weary of me, O Israel!...You have burdened me with your sins, you have wearied me with your iniquities.
Ps. 14:2–4. The Lord looks down from heaven upon the children of men, to see if there are any that act wisely, that seek after God. They have all gone astray, they are all alike corrupt; there is none that does good, no, not one. Have they no knowledge, all the evildoers who eat up my people as they eat bread, and do not call upon the Lord? (Also Ps. 53:4.)
Rev. 2:5 [Christ]: Remember then from what you have fallen, repent and do the works you did at first. If not, I will come to you and remove your lampstand from its place, unless you repent. (Also Mt. 11:21, Lk. 10:13.)

2 Chron. 7:14 [God]: If my people who are called by my name humble themselves, and pray and seek my face, and turn from their wicked ways, then I will hear from heaven, and will forgive their sin and heal their land. (Also 1 Jn. 1:9.)
Heb. 4:15–16. We have not a high priest who is unable to sympathize with our weaknesses, but one who in every respect has been tempted

Und habe noch mit uns Geduld,
And have yet with us patience,
{And have patience with us yet,}

Wenn wir in Andacht beten
When we in devotion pray

Und sagen,   Herr, auf dein Geheiß:
And say, (O) Lord, upon thy bidding:

Ach, rede nicht mehr sprüchwortsweis,
Ah, speak no more epigramatically,

Hilf uns vielmehr vertreten!
Help us rather advocate!
{Help us rather, and be our advocate!}

as we are, yet without sin. Let us then with confidence draw near to the throne of grace, that we may receive mercy and find grace to help in time of need.

Mt. 18:26–27. The servant fell on his knees, imploring [his master], "Lord, have patience (Luther: Geduld) with me, and I will pay you everything." And out of pity for him the lord of that servant released him and forgave him the debt (Luther: Schuld).

***Jn. 16:23, 25–27, 29 [Christ]:** "...Truly, truly, I say to you, if you ask anything of the Father, he will give it to you in my name... I have said this to you in figures (Luther: Sprichwort); the hour is coming when I shall no longer speak to you in figures but tell you plainly of the Father. In that day you will ask in my name; and I do not say to you that I shall pray the Father for you; for the Father himself loves you, because you have loved me and have believed that I came from the Father..." His disciples said, "Ah, now you are speaking plainly, not in any figure!..."

1 Jn. 2:1–2. ...My little children, I am writing this to you so that you may not sin; but if any one does sin, we have an advocate with the Father, Jesus Christ the righteous; and he is the expiation for our sins...

1 Jn. 1:9. If we confess our sins, he is faithful and just, and will forgive our sins and cleanse us from all unrighteousness.

Rom. 8:34. Is it Christ Jesus who is at the right hand of God, who indeed intercedes for us (Luther: vertritt uns)? (Also Heb. 7:25.)

4. Tenor Recit. (Not in Ziegler's original poem)
●Pardon for sin sought since God sees contrite heart (87-4)
Wenn unsre Schuld bis an den Himmel steigt,
When our guilt up to - heaven climbs,
{When our guilt piles up to heaven,}

Du siehst und kennest ja mein Herz,
Thou seest and knowest indeed my heart,
{Thou dost indeed see and know my heart,}

das nichts vor dir verschweigt;
which nothing before thee conceals;
{which does not attempt to conceal anything from thee;}

Drum suche mich zu trösten!
Therefore seek me to comfort!
{Therefore come and comfort me!}

Ezra 9:6. O my God, I am ashamed and blush to lift my face to thee, my God, for our iniquities have risen higher than our heads, and our guilt (Luther: Schuld) has mounted up to the heavens. (Also Rev. 18:5.)

Is. 1:18. Come now, let us reason together, says the Lord: though your sins are like scarlet, they shall be as white as snow; though they are red like crimson, they shall become like wool.

Ps. 32:3, 5. When I declared not my sin, my body wasted away through my groaning all day long... I acknowledged my sin to thee, and I did not hide my iniquity; I said, "I will confess my transgressions to the Lord"; then thou didst forgive the guilt of my sin. (Also Job 31:33, 37.)

1 Sam. 16:7. ...Man looks on the outward appearance, but the Lord looks on the heart. (Also Lk. 16:15, Jn. 2:25.)

Jn. 21:17. [Jesus] said to [Peter] the third time, "Simon, son of John, do you love me?" Peter was grieved because he said to him the third time, "Do you love me?" and he said to him, "Lord, you know everything; you know that I love you."

5. Bass Aria
●Vox Christi: World of fear overcome: Jn. 16:33 (87-5)
In der Welt habt ihr Angst; aber seid getrost,
In the world have you fear; but be of-good-cheer,

ich habe die Welt überwunden.
I have the world overcome.

***Jn. 16:33 [Christ]:** I have said this to you, that in me you may have peace. *In the world you have tribulation; but be of good cheer, I have overcome the world.*

1 Jn. 5:4–5. Whatever is born of God overcomes the world; and this is the victory that overcomes the world, our faith. Who is it that overcomes the world but he who believes that Jesus is the Son of God? (See also 1 Jn. 4:4, Jn. 16:33.)

6. Tenor Aria
●Suffering accepted; Christ will help & comfort (87-6)
Ich will leiden, ich will schweigen,
I would suffer, I would keep-silent,

***Jn. 16:33 [Christ]:** ...Be of good cheer, I have overcome the world.

1 Pet. 4:19. Therefore let those who suffer according to God's will do right and entrust their souls to a faithful Creator.

Jesus wird mir   Hülf erzeigen,
Jesus will to-me (his) help   show,
{Jesus will reveal his help to me,}

Denn er   tröst' mich nach dem Schmerz.
For   he comforts me after (my) suffering.

Weicht, ihr Sorgen, Trauer,   Klagen,
(Depart), ye sorrows, mourning, lamentations,

Denn warum sollt ich verzagen?
For   why should I   despair?

Fasse   dich, betrübtes Herz!
Compose thyself, troubled heart!

7. Chorale
● Suffering turned into joy if Jesus loves me (87-7)
Muß ich sein betrübet?
Must I   be troubled?

So mich Jesus liebet,
If   me Jesus loves,
{If Jesus loves me,}

     Ist mir aller Schmerz
(Then) is to-me all   pain
{Then all pain is}

Über   Honig süße,
More-than honey sweet,
{Sweeter than honey to me,}

   Tausend Zuckerküsse
(A) thousand (sweet-kisses)

Drücket er ans   Herz.
Presses he upon-(my) heart.

Wenn   die Pein sich stellet ein,
Whenever - pain -   sets in,

Seine Liebe macht zur Freuden
His   love turns into   joy

Auch das bittre Leiden.
Even - bitter suffering.
{His love turns even bitter suffering into joy.}

Ps. 131:2. I have calmed and quieted my soul, like a child quieted at its mother's breast...
Rev. 2:10 [Christ]: Do not fear what you are about to suffer...For ten days you will have tribulation. Be faithful unto death, and I will give you the crown of life.
2 Tim. 2:11–12. The saying is sure: If we have died with him, we shall also live with him; if we endure, we shall also reign with him... (Also Rom. 8:17, 1 Pet. 4:13.)
Rev. 7:16–17. [Then] they shall hunger no more, neither thirst any more; the sun shall not strike them, nor any scorching heat. For the Lamb in the midst of the throne will be their shepherd, and he will guide them to springs of living water; and God will wipe away every tear from their eyes. (Also Rev. 21:4, Is. 25:8.)
Ps. 42:5–6. Why are you cast down (Luther: betrübst du dich), O my soul, and why are you disquieted within me?...My soul is cast down within me...Hope in God; for I shall again praise him, my help and my God...
Lk. 21:19 [Christ]: By your endurance you will gain your lives (Luther: Fasset eure Seele mit Geduld).

Hab. 3:17–18. Though the fig tree do not blossom, nor fruit be on the vines, the produce of the olive fail and the fields yield no food, the flock be cut off from the fold and there be no herd in the stalls, yet I will rejoice in the Lord, I will joy in the God of my salvation.
Ps. 73:25, 26. [O Lord,] whom have I in heaven but thee? And there is nothing upon earth that I desire besides thee. My flesh and my heart may fail, but God is the strength of my heart and my portion for ever.
Ps. 36:7. How precious is thy steadfast love, O God! The children of men take refuge in the shadow of thy wings.
Ps. 119:103. How sweet are thy words to my taste, sweeter than honey to my mouth! (Also Ps. 19:9–10.)
2 Cor. 1:3–5. Blessed be the God and Father of our Lord Jesus Christ, the Father of mercies and God of all comfort, who comforts us in all our affliction...For as we share abundantly in Christ's sufferings, so through Christ we share abundantly in comfort too.
1 Pet. 4:13. Rejoice in so far as you share Christ's sufferings, that you may also rejoice and be glad when his glory is revealed.
Rom. 8:18. I consider that the sufferings of this present time are not worth comparing with the glory that is to be revealed to us. (Also 2 Cor. 4:17.)
Rom. 8:35–39. Who shall separate us from the love of Christ? Shall tribulation, or distress, or persecution, or famine, or nakedness, or peril, or sword? As it is written, "For thy sake we are being killed all the day long; we are regarded as sheep to be slaughtered." No, in all these things we are more than conquerors through him who loved us. For I am sure that neither death, nor life, nor angels, nor principalities, nor things present, nor things to come, nor powers, nor height, nor depth, nor anything else in all creation, will be able to separate us from the love of God in Christ Jesus our Lord.

BWV 88
Siehe, ich will viel Fischer aussenden
(NBA I/17; BC A105)

5. S. after Trinity (BWV 93, 88)
*1 Pet. 3:8-15[1] (Turn from evil and choose right; sanctify Christ in your hearts)
*Lk. 5:1-11 (Peter's great catch of fish)
[1]End: "Christ the Lord"
Librettist: Unknown; perhaps Christoph Helm. Johann Ludwig Bach also set this libretto to music.

Part I

1. Bass Aria
●God seeks people by sending fishermen: Jer. 16:16 (88-1)
Siehe, ich will viel Fischer aussenden,
Behold, I will many fishermen send-out,

spricht der Herr, die sollen sie fischen.
says the Lord, (and) they shall them (catch).

Und darnach will ich viel Jäger aussenden,
And thereafter will I many hunters send-out, (and)

die sollen sie fahen auf allen Bergen und
they shall them hunt upon all (the) mountains and

auf allen Hügeln und in allen Steinritzen.
upon all (the) hills and in all rock-clefts.

2. Tenor Recit.
●God seeks sinners even though we reject him (88-2)
Wie leichtlich könnte doch der Höchste uns entbehren
How easily could indeed the Most-High us dispense-with
{How easily could the Most High dispense with us}

Und seine Gnade von uns kehren,
And his grace from us turn,
{And turn his grace from us,}

Wenn der verkehrte Sinn
When (our) perverted disposition

sich böslich von ihm trennt
- wickedly from him parts
{wickedly turns from him}

Und mit verstocktem Mut
And with stubborn spirit

In sein Verderben rennt.
To its ruin runs.
{Runs to its ruin.}

Was aber tut
What, however, does

Jer. 16:14-16. Therefore, behold, the days are coming, says the Lord, when it shall no longer be said, "As the Lord lives who brought up the people of Israel out of the land of Egypt," but "As the Lord lives who brought up the people of Israel out of the north country and out of all the countries where he had driven them." For I will bring them back to their own land which I gave to their fathers. *Behold, I am sending for many fishers, says the Lord, and they shall catch them; and afterwards I will send for many hunters, and they shall hunt them from every mountain and every hill, and out of the clefts of the rocks.*
Hab. 1:14-15. For thou makest men like the fish of the sea, like crawling things that have no ruler. He brings all of them up with a hook, he drags them out with his net, he gathers them in his seine; so he rejoices and exults. (Also Am. 4:2, Is. 2:21.)
***Lk. 5:10.** ...Jesus said to Simon, "Do not be afraid; henceforth you will be catching men."

Rom. 10:21 [God]: ...All day long I have held out my hands to a disobedient and contrary people. (See Is. 65:1-2.)
Mt. 13:15 [Christ]: For this people's heart has grown dull (Luther: verstockt), and their ears are heavy of hearing, and their eyes they have closed, lest they should perceive with their eyes, and hear with their ears, and understand with their heart, and turn for me to heal them. (See Is. 6:9-10, also Acts 28:27.)
Mt. 23:37 [Christ]: O Jerusalem, Jerusalem, killing the prophets and stoning those who are sent to you! How often would I have gathered your children together as a hen gathers her brood under her wings, and you would not!
Rom. 3:10-12, 15-18. As it is written: "None is righteous, no, not one; no one understands, no one seeks for God. All have turned aside, together they have gone wrong; no one does good, not even one... Their feet are swift to shed blood, in their paths are ruin and misery, and the way of peace they do not know. There is no fear of God before their eyes." (Also Is. 43:22-25.)
Rom. 1:28. Since they did not see fit to acknowledge God, God gave them up to a base mind (Luther: verkehrten Sinn) and to improper conduct...
Ps. 103:10-13. He does not deal with us according to our sins, nor requite us according to our iniquities. For as the heavens are high above the earth, so great is his steadfast love toward those who fear him; as far as the east is from the west, so far does he remove our

Sein vatertreu Gemüte?
His paternally-faithful spirit (do)?

Tritt er mit seiner Güte
Withdraws he with his goodness
{Does he withdraw with his goodness}

Von uns, gleich so wie wir von ihm, zurück,
From us, just as we (do) from him - ?

Und überläßt er uns der Feinde List und Tück?
And relinquishes he us to-the foe's cunning and spite?
{And does he relinquish us to the foe's cunning and spite?}

3. Tenor Aria
●God seeks us when we stray from proper path (88-3)
Nein, Gott ist allezeit geflissen,
No, God is at-all-times intent,

Uns auf gutem Wege zu wissen
Us on (the) good path to (keep)
{To keep us on the good path}

Unter seiner Gnade Schein.
Beneath his grace's radiance.
{Beneath the radiance of his grace.}

Ja, wenn wir verirret sein
Yes, when we astray (have-gone)

Und die rechte Bahn verlassen,
And the right way (have) abandoned,

Will er uns gar suchen lassen.
Would he (have) us indeed sought-for.
{He indeed seeks for us.}

Part II

4. Tenor/Bass Arioso (Evangelist & Christ)
●Simon Peter sent by Christ to fish for men: Lk. 5:10 (88-4)
Tenor:
Jesus sprach zu Simon:
Jesus said to Simon:

Bass:
Fürchte dich nicht; denn von nun an wirst
Fear thou not; for from now on wilt

du Menschen fahen.
thou men catch.

5. Soprano & Alto Duet
●God's blessing assured if we are faithful stewards (88-5)
Beruft Gott selbst, so muß der Segen
Calls God himself, so must (his) blessing
{If God himself calls us, then must his blessing}

transgressions from us. As a father pities his children, so the Lord pities those who fear him.
2 Tim. 2:13. If we are faithless, he remains faithful—for he cannot deny himself. (Also Rom. 3:3–4.)
1 Jn. 4:10. In this is love, not that we loved God but that he loved us and sent his Son to be the expiation for our sins.
Rom. 5:8. God shows his love for us in that while we were yet sinners Christ died for us.
Heb. 3:12–13. Take care, brethren, lest there be in any of you an evil, unbelieving heart...that none of you may be hardened (Luther: verstockt) by the deceitfulness of sin (Luther: Betrug der Sünde).
2 Cor. 11:14. ...Even Satan disguises himself as an angel of light. (Also Rev. 12:9.)

Mt. 7:13–14 [Christ]: Enter by the narrow gate; for the gate is wide and the way is easy, that leads to destruction, and those who enter by it are many. For the gate is narrow and the way is hard, that leads to life, and those who find it are few.
Is. 53:6. All we like sheep have gone astray; we have turned every one to his own way... (Also Ps. 14:3, 119:176.)
Ezek. 34:11, 16. Thus says the Lord God: Behold, I, I myself will search for my sheep...I will seek the lost, and I will bring back the strayed, and I will bind up the crippled, and I will strengthen the weak... (Also Lk. 19:10.)
Is. 30:21. And your ears shall hear a word behind you, saying, "This is the way, walk in it," when you turn to the right or when you turn to the left. (Also Jer. 42:3.)
Jer. 10:23. I know, O Lord, that the way of man is not in himself, that it is not in man who walks to direct his steps.
Mt. 18:12–13 [Christ]: If a man has a hundred sheep, and one of them has gone astray, does he not leave the ninety-nine on the mountains and go in search of the one that went astray? And if he finds it, truly, I say to you, he rejoices over it more than over the ninety-nine that never went astray...

*Lk. 5:5–11. Simon answered, "Master, we toiled all night and took nothing! But at your word I will let down the nets." And when they had done this, they enclosed a great shoal of fish; and as their nets were breaking, they beckoned to their partners in the other boat to come and help them. And they came and filled both the boats, so that they began to sink. But when Simon Peter saw it, he fell down at Jesus' knees, saying, "Depart from me, for I am a sinful man, O Lord." For he was astonished, and all that were with him, at the catch of fish which they had taken; and so also were James and John, sons of Zebedee, who were partners with Simon. And *Jesus said to Simon, "Do not be afraid; henceforth you will be catching men."* And when they had brought their boats to land, they left everything and followed him.

*Lk. 5:4–7. When [Jesus] had ceased speaking, he said to Simon, "Put out into the deep and let down your nets for a catch." And Simon answered, "Master, we toiled all night and took nothing! But at your word I will let down the nets." And when they had done this, they enclosed a great shoal of fish; and as their nets were breaking, they beckoned to their partners in the other boat to come and help them...

Auf allem unsern Tun
Upon all our doing

Im Übermaße ruhn,
In abundance rest,

Stünd uns gleich Furcht und Sorg entgegen.
Stood us even-though fear and care opposed.
{Though fear and care should stand opposed to us.}

Das Pfund, so er uns ausgetan,
The talent, which he to-us has-distributed,

Will er mit Wucher wiederhaben;
Would he with interest have-back;
{Would he have back with interest;}

Wenn wir es nur nicht selbst vergraben,
If we it only not ourselves bury,
{If only we do not bury it ourselves,}

So hilft er gern, damit es fruchten kann.
Then helps he gladly, so-that it bear-fruit may.
{Then he gladly helps so that it may bear fruit.}

6. Soprano Recit.
●God's commissioning assures success despite obstacles (88–6)
Was kann dich denn in deinem Wandel schrecken,
What can thee then in thy way frighten,
{What is there to frighten thee in thy way,}

Wenn dir, mein Herz, Gott selbst die Hände reicht?
If to-thee, (O) my heart, God himself (his) hands extends?
{If God himself extends his hands to thee, O my heart?}

Vor dessen bloßem Wink schon
Before whose mere beckoning already

alles Unglück weicht,
all misfortune retreats,

Und der dich mächtiglich kann schützen und bedecken.
And who thee mightily can protect and cover.
{And who can mightily protect and cover thee.}

Kommt Mühe, Überlast, Neid,
Comes trouble, overburden, envy,

Plag und Falschheit her
vexation and falsehood (near)
{If trouble, overburden, envy, vexation, and falsehood come near}

Und trachtet, was du tust, zu stören und zu hindern,
And seek, whatever thou doest, to disrupt and to hinder,

Laß Trug und Ungemach
(Then) let deceit and hardship

2 Tim. 1:9–10. [God]...called us with a holy calling...
Rom. 11:29. The gifts and call of God are irrevocable.
1 Cor. 4:1–2. This is how one should regard us, as servants of Christ... Moreover it is required of stewards that they be found trustworthy.
Mt. 25:14–19, 24–27 [Christ]: It will be as when a man going on a journey called his servants and entrusted to them his property; to one he gave five talents, to another two, to another one, to each according to his ability. Then he went away. He who had received the five talents went at once and traded with them; and he made five talents more. So also, he who had the two talents made two talents more. But he who had received the one talent went and dug in the ground and hid his master's money. Now after a long time the master of those servants came and settled accounts with them...He also who had received the one talent came forward, saying, "Master, I knew you to be a hard man, reaping where you did not sow, and gathering where you did not winnow; so I was afraid, and I went and hid your talent in the ground. Here you have what is yours." But his master answered him, "You wicked and slothful servant! You knew that I reap where I have not sowed and gather where I have not winnowed? Then you ought to have invested my money with the bankers, and at my coming I should have received what was my own with interest."
Jn. 15:8, 16 [Christ]: By this my Father is glorified, that you bear much fruit, and so prove to be my disciples...I chose you and appointed you that you should go and bear fruit and that your fruit should abide...

Mt. 14:28–31. Peter answered [Jesus], "Lord, if it is you, bid me come to you on the water." He said, "Come." So Peter got out of the boat and walked on the water and came to Jesus; but when he saw the wind, he was afraid, and beginning to sink he cried out, "Lord, save me." Jesus immediately reached out his hand and caught him, saying to him, "O man of little faith, why did you doubt?"
Mt. 8:23–27. When [Jesus] got into the boat, his disciples followed him. And behold, there arose a great storm on the sea, so that the boat was being swamped by the waves; but he was asleep. And they went and woke him, saying, "Save, Lord; we are perishing." And he said to them, "Why are you afraid, O men of little faith?" Then he rose and rebuked the winds and the sea; and there was a great calm. And the men marveled, saying, "What sort of man is this, that even winds and sea obey him?"
Is. 14:27. The Lord of hosts has purposed, and who will annul it? His hand is stretched out, and who will turn it back? (Also Job 9:12, 11:10, 42:2.)
Rom. 8:33–39. Who shall bring any charge against God's elect? It is God who justifies; who is to condemn? Is it Christ Jesus, who died, yes, who was raised from the dead, who is at the right hand of God, who indeed intercedes for us? Who shall separate us from the love of Christ? Shall tribulation, or distress, or persecution, or famine, or nakedness, or peril, or sword? As it is written, "For thy sake we are being killed all the day long; we are regarded as sheep to be slaughtered." No, in all these things we are more than conquerors through him who loved us. For I am sure that neither death, nor life, nor angels, nor principalities, nor things present, nor things to come, nor powers, nor height, nor depth, nor anything else in all creation, will be able to separate us from the love of God in Christ Jesus our Lord. (Also Is. 58:7–9.)

den   Vorsatz nicht vermindern;
(thy) resolution   not   diminish;

Das Werk, so   er bestimmt,
The work, which he   allots,

        wird   keinem   je   zu schwer.
        will (for) no-one ever (be) too hard.

Geh allzeit   freudig fort,
Go at-all-times joyfully forth,

        du wirst am Ende sehen,
        thou wilt in-the end   see,

Daß,   was   dich eh gequält,
That, whatever thee ever tortured,
{That all that ever tortured thee,}

        dir sei zu Nutz geschehen!
        thee - for profit occured!
        {did for thy profit occur!}

7. Chorale (See also 93–7.)
●Perform allotted tasks, trusting God's sovereignty (88–7)
Sing, bet und geh auf Gottes Wegen,
Sing, pray, and walk in God's   ways,

Verricht   das   Deine nur getreu
Perform (what is) thine only faithfully
{Just perform thine own tasks faithfully}

Und trau des Himmels reichem Segen,
And trust -   heaven's   rich   blessing,

So   wird er bei dir werden neu;
Then will it by thee become new;
{Then his blessing will be renewed with thee;}

Denn welcher seine Zuversicht
For   whoever his confidence
{For whoever places his confidence}

Auf Gott setzt, den verläßt er nicht.
(In) God places, him forsakes he not.
{In God, is never forsaken by him.}

2 Cor. 4:7–10. But we have this treasure in earthen vessels, to show that the transcendent power belongs to God and not to us. We are afflicted in every way, but not crushed; perplexed, but not driven to despair; persecuted, but not forsaken; struck down, but not destroyed; always carrying in the body the death of Jesus, so that the life of Jesus may also be manifested in our bodies.
Mt. 11:28–30 [Christ]: Come to me, all who labor and are heavy laden, and I will give you rest. Take my yoke upon you, and learn from me; for I am gentle and lowly in heart, and you will find rest for your souls. For my yoke is easy, and my burden is light.
Rom. 8:28. We know that in everything God works for good with those who love him, who are called according to his purpose.
Jms. 1:2–4. Count it all joy, my brethren, when you meet various trials, for you know that the testing of your faith produces steadfastness. And let steadfastness have its full effect, that you may be perfect and complete, lacking in nothing. (Also 1 Pet. 1:6–7.)
Heb. 12:11. For the moment all discipline seems painful rather than pleasant; later it yields the peaceful fruit of righteousness to those who have been trained by it.

2 Tim. 4:5. As for you, always be steady, endure suffering...fulfil your ministry. (Also 2 Cor. 4:1.)
Col. 3:16–17. Let the word of Christ dwell in you richly...and sing psalms and hymns and spiritual songs with thankfulness in your hearts to God. And whatever you do, in word or deed, do everything in the name of the Lord Jesus, giving thanks to God the Father through him. (Eph. 5:19–20)
1 Cor. 4:1–2. This is how one should regard us, as servants of Christ and stewards of the mysteries of God. Moreover it is required of stewards that they be found trustworthy.
Prov. 3:5–6. Trust in the Lord with all your heart, and do not rely on your own insight. In all your ways acknowledge him, and he will make straight your paths.
Ps. 37:5. Commit your way to the Lord; trust in him, and he will act.
Deut. 28:12. The Lord will open to you his good treasury the heavens, to give the rain of your land in its season and to bless all the work of your hands...
Lam. 3:22–23. The steadfast love of the Lord never ceases, his mercies never come to an end; they are new every morning; great is thy faithfulness. (Also Ps. 90:14, 92:2.)
Ps. 9:10. And those who know thy name put their trust in thee, for thou, O Lord, hast not forsaken those who seek thee. (Also Ps. 25:2, 146:3–5.)
Deut. 31:8. It is the Lord who goes before you; he will be with you, he will not fail you or forsake you; do not fear or be dismayed. (Also Josh. 1:7, 9, Heb. 13:5.)

BWV 89
Was soll ich aus dir machen, Ephraim
(NBA I/26; BC A155)

22. S. after Trinity (BWV 89, 115, 55)
*Phil. 1:3–11 (Paul's prayer for the church at Philippi)
*Mt. 18:23–35 (The parable of the unforgiving servant)
Librettist: Unknown

1. Bass Aria
●Voice of God: Israel deserves no mercy: Hos. 11:8 (89-1)
Was soll ich aus dir machen, Ephraim?
What shall I of thee make, Ephraim?
{O Ephraim, what shall I make of thee?}

Soll ich dich schützen, Israel? Soll ich nicht billig
Shall I thee protect, Israel? Shall I not simply

ein Adama aus dir machen und dich wie Zeboim zurichten?
an Adamah of thee make, and thee like Zeboiim treat?

Aber mein Herz ist anders Sinnes,
But my heart is of-different mind,

meine Barmherzigkeit ist zu brünstig.
(for) my compassion is too ardent.

2. Alto Recit.
●Judgment well-deserved; man himself shows no mercy (89-2)
Ja, freilich sollte Gott
Yes, to-be-sure, should God
{Yes, to be sure, God should}

Ein Wort zum Urteil sprechen
A Word (of) judgment speak

Und seines Namens Spott
And his name's derision
{And the derision of his name}

An seinen Feinden rächen.
Upon his foes avenge.

Unzählbar ist die Rechnung deiner Sünden,
Countless is the sum of-your sins,

Und hätte Gott auch gleich Geduld,
And had God even though patience (with you),
{And even if God should have patience with you,}

Verwirft doch dein feindseliges Gemüte
Rejects nevertheless your hostile spirit
{Your hostile spirit nevertheless rejects}

Die angebotne Güte
(His) proffered kindness

Hos. 11:8–9 [God]: *How can I give you up, O Ephraim! How can I hand you over, O Israel! How can I make you like Admah! How can I treat you like Zeboiim! My heart recoils within me, my compassion grows warm and tender. I will not execute my fierce anger, I will not again destroy Ephraim; for I am God and not man, the Holy One in your midst, and I will not come to destroy. (Also Hos. 6:4.)*
Deut. 29:23. The whole land [will be] brimstone and salt, and a burnt-out waste, unsown, and growing nothing, where no grass can sprout, an overthrow like that of Sodom and Gomorrah, Admah and Zeboiim, which the Lord overthrew in his anger and wrath.
Gen. 19:24–25. The Lord rained on Sodom and Gomorrah brimstone and fire from the Lord out of heaven; and he overthrew those cities, and all the valley, and all the inhabitants of the cities, and what grew on the ground.
Ps. 103:8–13. The Lord is merciful and gracious, slow to anger and abounding in steadfast love. He will not always chide, nor will he keep his anger for ever. He does not deal with us according to our sins, nor requite us according to our iniquities. For as the heavens are high above the earth, so great is his steadfast love toward those who fear him; as far as the east is from the west, so far does he remove our transgressions from us. As a father pities his children, so the Lord pities those who fear him.

Ezek. 20:21–22 [God]: [My people] rebelled against me; they did not walk in my statutes...I thought I would pour out my wrath upon them and spend my anger against them in the wilderness. But I withheld my hand...
Ezra 9:6. ...Our iniquities have risen higher than our heads, and our guilt has mounted up to the heavens. (Also Rev. 18:5.)
Jer. 5:1, 3. Run to and fro through the streets of Jerusalem, look and take note! Search her squares to see if you can find a man, one who does justice and seeks truth... [God has] smitten them, but they felt no anguish... They refused to take correction. They have made their faces harder than rock; they have refused to repent.
Ps. 74:10. How long, O God, is the foe to scoff? Is the enemy to revile thy name for ever?
*Mt. 18:23–35 [Christ]: The kingdom of heaven may be compared to a king who wished to settle accounts with his servants. When he began the reckoning, one was brought to him who owed him ten thousand talents; and as he could not pay, his lord ordered him to be sold, with his wife and children and all that he had, and payment to be made. So the servant fell on his knees, imploring him, "Lord, have patience with me, and I will pay you everything." And out of pity for him the lord of that servant released him and forgave him the debt. But that same servant as he went out came upon one of his fellow servants who owed him a hundred denarii, and seizing him by the throat he said, "Pay what you owe." So his fellow servant fell down and besought him, "Have patience with me, and I will pay you." He refused and went and put him in prison till he should pay the debt. When his fellow servants saw what had taken place, they were greatly distressed, and they went and reported to their lord all that had taken place. Then his lord summoned him and said to him, "You wicked servant! I forgave you

Und drückt den Nächsten um die Schuld;
And presses (your) neighbor for (payment of) the debt;

So muß die Rache sich entzünden.
So must (his) vengeance - be-kindled.
{Therefore his vengeance must be kindled.}

3. Alto Aria
●Judgment like that of Sodom falls on unmerciful (89–3)
Ein unbarmherziges Gerichte
A merciless judgment

Wird über dich gewiß ergehn.
Will upon you surely fall.
{Will surely fall upon you.}

Die Rache fängt bei denen an,
- Vengeance begins with those -,

Die nicht Barmherzigkeit getan,
Who not compassion have-shown,
{Who have not shown compassion,}

Und machet sie wie Sodom ganz zunichte.
And makes them like Sodom completely to-nothing.
{And annihilates them completely like Sodom.}

4. Soprano Recit.
●Sins' debt forgiven in Jesus who is end of the law (89–4)
Wohlan! mein Herze legt Zorn,
Well-then! My heart lays wrath,

Zank und Zwietracht hin;
quarrelling, and dissension away;

Es ist bereit, dem Nächsten zu vergeben.
It is prepared, (its) neighbor to forgive.

Allein, wie schrecket mich mein sündenvolles Leben,
Yet, how alarms me my sinful life,
{Yet how my sinful life alarms me—}

Daß ich vor Gott in Schulden bin!
That I before God in debt am!
{That I am so indebted before God!}

Doch Jesu Blut
Yet Jesus' blood

Macht diese Rechnung gut,
Makes this account good,
{Pays this account,}

all that debt because you besought me; and should not you have had mercy on your fellow servant, as I had mercy on you?" And in anger his lord delivered him to the jailers, till he should pay all his debt. So also my heavenly Father will do to every one of you, if you do not forgive your brother from your heart.

Jms. 2:13. Judgment is without mercy to one who has shown no mercy; yet mercy triumphs over judgment.
***Mt. 18:32–35 [Christ]:** Then [the servant's] lord summoned him and said to him, "You wicked servant! I forgave you all that debt because you besought me; and should not you have had mercy on your fellow servant, as I had mercy on you?" And in anger his lord delivered him to the jailers, till he should pay all his debt. So also my heavenly Father will do to every one of you, if you do not forgive your brother from your heart.
Mt. 5:7 [Christ]: Blessed are the merciful, for they shall obtain mercy.
Mt. 6:14–15 [Christ]: For if you forgive men their trespasses, your heavenly Father also will forgive you; but if you do not forgive men their trespasses, neither will your Father forgive your trespasses. (Also Mk. 11:25.)
Gen. 19:24–25. Then the Lord rained on Sodom and Gomorrah brimstone and fire from the Lord out of heaven; and he overthrew those cities, and all the valley, and all the inhabitants of the cities, and what grew on the ground.

Gal. 5:19–21. Now the works of the flesh are plain: fornication, impurity, licentiousness, idolatry, sorcery, enmity, strife, jealousy, anger (Luther: Zorn), selfishness, (Luther: Zank) dissension (Luther: Zwietracht), party spirit, envy, drunkenness, carousing, and the like. I warn you, as I warned you before, that those who do such things shall not inherit the kingdom of God.
Eph. 4:31–32. Let all bitterness and wrath (Luther: Grimm) and anger (Luther: Zorn) and clamor and slander be put away from you, with all malice, and be kind to one another, tenderhearted, forgiving one another, as God in Christ forgave you. (Also Col. 3:8, 1 Cor. 1:10.)
***Phil. 1:9.** ...It is my prayer that your love may abound more and more, with knowledge and all discernment.
Acts 13:38–39. Let it be known...that through [Christ] forgiveness of sins is proclaimed to you, and by him every one that believes is freed from everything from which you could not be freed by the law of Moses. (Also Rev. 1:5.)
Rom. 10:4. Christ is the end of the law (Luther: Gesetzes Ende), that every one who has faith may be justified.
Gal. 3:23–26. Now before faith came, we were confined under the law, kept under restraint until faith should be revealed. So that the law was our custodian until Christ came, that we might be justified by faith. But now that faith has come, we are no longer under a custodian; for in Christ Jesus you are all sons of God, through faith.
Mt. 5:17 [Christ]: Think not that I have come to abolish the law and the prophets; I have come not to abolish them but to fulfil them.
Mk. 10:45 [Christ]: The Son of man came...to give his life as a ransom (Luther: Bezahlung) for many. (Also Mt. 20:28.)

Wenn ich zu ihm, als des Gesetzes Ende,
If I to him, as the law's (appointed) end,

Mich gläubig wende.
Myself in-faith do-turn.
{If, in faith, I turn to him—the law's appointed end.}

5. Soprano Aria
•Sin's account paid by Jesus' drops of blood (89–5)
Gerechter Gott, ach, rechnest du?
Righteous God, ah, countest thou?
{O righteous God, ah, art thou keeping an account?}

So werde ich zum Heil der Seelen
Then will I for-the salvation of-(my) soul

Die Tropfen Blut von Jesu zählen.
The drops-of blood of Jesus count.
{Count the drops of blood that Jesus shed.}

Ach! rechne mir die Summe zu!
Ah, put-to-my-account that sum -!
{Ah, put that sum to my account!}

Ja, weil sie niemand kann ergründen,
Yes, since them no-one can fathom,
{Yes, since no one can determine their number,}

Bedeckt sie meine Schuld und Sünden.
Cover they my debt and sins.
{They are sufficient to cover my debt and sin.}

6. Chorale
•Shortcomings acknowledged; adequacy in Christ's blood (89–6)
Mir mangelt zwar sehr viel,
(I) lack indeed very much,
{I indeed lack very much,}

Doch, was ich haben will,
Yet, what I would-have,
{Yet what I desire,}

Ist alles mir zugute
Is all to-me for-benefit
{Is all attained to my benefit}

Erlangt mit deinem Blute,
Attained by thy blood,
{By thy blood,}

Damit ich überwinde
So-that I do-conquer

1 Jn. 1:7. ...The blood of Jesus...cleanses us from all sin...If we confess our sins, he is faithful and just, and will forgive our sins and cleanse us from all unrighteousness.
Col. 2:13–14. And you...God made alive together with him, having forgiven us all our trespasses, having canceled the bond which stood against us with its legal demands; this he set aside, nailing it to the cross...

Ps. 130:1–3. Out of the depths I cry to thee, O Lord! Lord, hear my voice! Let thy ears be attentive to the voice of my supplications! If thou, O Lord, shouldst mark iniquities, Lord, who could stand!
Ps. 76:7. [O Lord,] terrible art thou! Who can stand before thee when once thy anger is roused?
Nah. 1:6. Who can stand before his indignation? Who can endure the heat of his anger? His wrath is poured out like fire, and the rocks are broken asunder by him.
Mal. 3:1–2. Who can endure the day of his coming, and who can stand when he appears?
1 Jn. 1:7. ...The blood of Jesus his Son cleanses us from all sin.
1 Pet. 1:18–19. You know that you were ransomed from the futile ways inherited from your fathers, not with perishable things such as silver or gold, but with the precious blood of Christ, like that of a lamb without blemish or spot. (Also Rev. 5:9.)
Eph. 3:17–19. [I pray]...that you, being rooted and grounded in love, may have power to comprehend with all the saints what is the breadth and length and height and depth, and to know the love of Christ which surpasses knowledge...
Mt. 26:28 [Christ]: This is my blood of the covenant, which is poured out for many for the forgiveness of sins.

Rom. 7:18. Nothing good dwells within me...I can will what is right, but I cannot do it.
Rom. 3:28. ...A man is justified by faith apart from works of law.
Rom. 5:9–11. Since...we are now justified by his blood, much more shall we be saved by him from the wrath of God.
Eph. 2:8–9. By grace you have been saved through faith...it is the gift of God—not because of works...
Tit. 3:5–7. ...He saved us, not because of deeds done by us in righteousness, but in virtue of his own mercy, by the washing of regeneration and renewal in the Holy Spirit, which he poured out upon us richly through Jesus Christ our Savior so that we might be justified by his grace and become heirs in hope of eternal life.
Col. 2:13–15. You, who were dead in trespasses and the uncircumcision of your flesh, God made alive together with him, having forgiven us all our trespasses, having canceled the bond which stood against us with its legal demands; this he set aside, nailing it to the cross. He disarmed the principalities and powers and made a public example of them, triumphing over them in him.
Rom. 8:33–34, 37. Who shall bring any charge against God's elect? It is God who justifies; who is to condemn? Is it Christ Jesus, who died, yes, who was raised from the dead, who is at the right hand of God, who indeed intercedes for us?...We are more than conquerors through him who loved us.
Rev. 12:10–11. ...Now the salvation and the power and the kingdom of our God and the authority of his Christ have come, for the accuser of

Tod, Teufel, Höll und Sünde.
Death, devil, hell, and sin.

our brethren has been thrown down, who accuses them day and night before our God. And they have conquered him by the blood of the Lamb...

BWV 90
Es reißet euch ein schrecklich Ende
(NBA I/27; BC A163)

25. S. after Trinity (BWV 90, 116)
*1 Thess. 4:13–18 (Christ will return with the archangel's call and the sound of the trumpet)
*Mt. 24:15–28 (There will be great tribulation at the end of the world)
Librettist: Unknown

1. Tenor Aria
●Judgment is imminent yet sinners disregard judge (90-1)
Es reißet euch ein schrecklich Ende,
(Now) (comes-upon) you a frightful end,
{A frightful end is coming upon you,}

Ihr sündlichen Verächter, hin.
You sinful scorners - .

Der Sünden Maß ist voll gemessen,
(Your) sin's measure is measured-full,

Doch euer ganz verstockter Sinn
Yet your completely impenitent spirit

Hat seines Richters ganz vergessen.
Has its judge completely forgotten.
{Has completely forgotten its judge.}

Mal. 4:1. Behold, the day comes, burning like an oven, when all the arrogant and all evildoers (Luther: Verächter) will be stubble; the day that comes shall burn them up, says the Lord of hosts, so that it will leave them neither root nor branch. (Also Ps. 25:3.)
*Mt. 24:21 [Christ]: Then there will be great tribulation, such as has not been from the beginning of the world until now, no, and never will be.
Heb. 10:26–27. If we sin deliberately after receiving the knowledge of the truth, there no longer remains a sacrifice for sins, but a fearful prospect of judgment, and a fury of fire which will consume the adversaries. (Also Heb. 9:27, Joel 2:11, 30–31, Amos 5:18–20, 2 Pet. 3:7, 10.)
Mt. 23:32–33 [Christ]: Fill up, then, the measure (Luther: Maß) of your fathers. You serpents, you brood of vipers, how are you to escape being sentenced to hell? (Also 1 Thess. 2:16.)
Rom. 2:5–10. By your hard and impenitent heart you are storing up wrath for yourself on the day of wrath when God's righteous judgment will be revealed. For he will render to every man according to his works: to those who by patience in well-doing seek for glory and honor and immortality, he will give eternal life; but for those who are factious and do not obey the truth, but obey wickedness, there will be wrath and fury. There will be tribulation and distress for every human being who does evil, the Jew first and also the Greek...

2. Alto Recit.
●God's kindness is in vain: no repentance produced (90-2)
Des Höchsten Güte wird von Tag zu Tage neu,
The Most-High's kindness is from day to day new,
{The kindness of the Most High is new from day to day.}

Der Undank aber sündigt stets auf Gnade.
- Ingratitude, however, sins constantly upon grace.

O, ein verzweifelt böser Schade,
Oh, (this is) a desperately bad injury,

So dich in dein Verderben führt.
Which you to your ruin leads.
{Which leads you to your ruin.}

Ach! wird dein Herze nicht gerührt?
Ah, is your heart not stirred?

Daß Gottes Güte dich
So-that God's kindness you

Lam. 3:22–23. The steadfast love of the Lord never ceases, his mercies never come to an end; they are new every morning; great is thy faithfulness. (Also Ps. 90:14, 92:2.)
2 Tim. 3:1–5. But understand this, that in the last days there will come times of stress. For men will be lovers of self, lovers of money, proud, arrogant, abusive, disobedient to their parents, ungrateful, unholy, inhuman, implacable, slanderers, profligates, fierce, haters of good, treacherous, reckless, swollen with conceit, lovers of pleasure rather than lovers of God, holding the form of religion but denying the power of it. Avoid such people.
Rom. 5:20. ...Where sin increased, grace abounded all the more.
Rom. 6:1. What shall we say then? Are we to continue in sin that grace may abound?
Jer. 30:12–13. Thus says the Lord: Your hurt is incurable (Luther: verzweifelt böse), and your wound is grievous. There is none to uphold your cause, no medicine for your wound, no healing for you.
Ps. 103:10. [The Lord] does not deal with us according to our sins, nor requite us according to our iniquities.
Lk. 6:35. ...The Most High...is kind to the ungrateful and the selfish...

Zur wahren Buße leitet?
To true repentance leads?
{So that you are led to repentance by God's kindness?}

Sein treues Herze lässet sich
His faithful heart lets itself

Zu ungezählter Wohltat schauen:
In countless benefits be-seen:

Bald läßt er Tempel auferbauen,
Now lets he temples be-erected,
{Now he lets temples be erected,}

Bald wird die Aue zubereitet,
Now is the meadow prepared,

Auf die des Wortes Manna fällt,
Upon which the Word's manna falls

So dich erhält.
Which you sustains.

Jedoch, o! Bosheit dieses Lebens,
Yet, —Oh, (the) spitefulness of (human) life—

Die Wohltat ist an dir vergebens.
- Good-deeds are (spent) on you in-vain.

3. Bass Aria
•Judgment: Light of Word taken from desecrated temple
(90-3)
So löschet im Eifer der rächende Richter
Thus will-extinguish in (his) zeal the avenging judge
{Thus will the avenging judge, in his zeal, extinguish}

Den Leuchter des Wortes zur Strafe doch aus.
The lampstand of-(his) Word for punishment indeed - .
{The lampstand of his Word as punishment.}

Ihr müsset, o Sünder, durch euer Verschulden
You must, O sinners, through your (own) fault

Den Greuel an heiliger Stätte erdulden,
The abomination in (the) holy place endure,
{Endure the abomination in the holy place,}

Ihr machet aus Tempeln ein mörderisch Haus.
You make of temples a murderous house.

Mt. 5:45. ...He makes his sun rise on the evil and on the good, and sends rain on the just and on the unjust.
Rom. 2:4. Do you not know that God's kindness is meant to lead you to repentance?
Ps. 40:5. Thou hast multiplied, O Lord my God, thy wondrous deeds and thy thoughts toward us...Were I to proclaim and tell of them, they would be more than can be numbered. (Also Ps. 71:15, 139:17–18.)
Is. 11:1, 10. There shall come forth a shoot from the stump of Jesse, and a branch shall grow out of his roots...In that day the root of Jesse shall stand as an ensign to the peoples; him shall the nations seek...
Zech. 6:12–13. ...Behold, the man whose name is the Branch: for he shall grow up in his place, and he shall build the temple of the Lord. It is he who shall build the temple of the Lord... (Also Mk. 14:58, Jn. 2:18–21.)
Mal. 3:1. Behold...the Lord whom you seek will suddenly come to his temple; the messenger of the covenant in whom you delight, behold, he is coming, says the Lord of hosts.
Ezek. 34:11, 14–15. Thus says the Lord God: Behold, I, I myself will search for my sheep...I will feed them with good pasture...I myself will be the shepherd of my sheep...
Jn. 10:7, 9. Jesus...said to them, "...I am the door of the sheep...If any one enters by me, he will be saved, and will go in and out and find pasture."
Jn. 6:48–51. [Jesus said,] "I am the bread of life. Your fathers ate the manna in the wilderness, and they died. This is the bread which comes down from heaven, that a man may eat of it and not die. I am the living bread which came down from heaven; if any one eats of this bread, he will live for ever; and the bread which I shall give for the life of the world is my flesh." (Also Rev. 2:17.)
Rom. 2:4–5. Do you presume upon the riches of his kindness and forbearance and patience? Do you not know that God's kindness is meant to lead you to repentance? But by your hard and impenitent heart you are storing up wrath for yourself on the day of wrath when God's righteous judgment will be revealed.

Rev. 2:4–5 [Christ]: I have this against you, that you have abandoned the love you had at first. Remember then from what you have fallen, repent and do the works you did at first. If not, I will come to you and remove your lampstand from its place (Luther: Leuchter wegstoßen von seiner Stätte), unless you repent.
*Mt. 24:15–17 [Christ]: When you see the desolating sacrilege (Luther: Greuel der Verwüstung) spoken of by the prophet Daniel standing in the holy place (let the reader understand), then let those who are in Judea flee to the mountains; let him who is on the housetop not go down to take what is in his house. (Also Dan. 9:27, 11:31, 12:11, 2 Thess. 2:3–4, 8.)
Mt. 21:12–13. Jesus entered the temple of God and drove out all who sold and bought in the temple, and he overturned the tables of the moneychangers and the seats of those who sold pigeons. He said to them, "It is written, 'My house shall be called a house of prayer'; but you make it a den of robbers." (Also Mk. 11:17, Lk. 19:46, Jn. 2:15, Is. 56:7, Jer. 7:11.)

4. Tenor Recit.
●Elect protected by God & Word in time of judgment (90-4)
Doch Gottes Auge sieht auf uns als Auserwählte:
Yet God's eye looks on us as chosen-ones:

Und wenn kein Mensch der Feinde Menge   zählte,
And though no man the foe's number could-count,

So schützt uns doch der Held in Israel,
Yet protects us nevertheless the champion in Israel,
{Yet the champion in Israel nevertheless protects us,}

Es hemmt sein Arm der Feinde Lauf
(Now) checks his arm the foe's course
{His arm checks the foe's course}

Und hilft uns auf:
And helps us up:

Des Wortes Kraft wird in Gefahr
The Word's power will, in peril,

Um so viel mehr erkannt und offenbar.
(Just) that much more recognized and manifested (be).
{Be just that much more recognized and manifested.}

5. Chorale (See also 101-7.)
●Prayer for blessing & spiritual protection on nation (90-5)
Leit uns mit deiner rechten Hand
Lead us with thy right hand

Und segne unser Stadt und Land;
And bless our city and land;

Gib uns allzeit dein heilges Wort,
Give us always thy holy Word,

Behüt   fürs Teufels List und Mord;
Protect (us) from-the devil's cunning and murder;

Verleih ein selges Stündelein,
Grant a blessed little-hour,

Auf daß wir ewig bei dir sein!
So that we eternally with thee might-be!

Ps. 33:18–19. Behold, the eye of the Lord is on those who fear him, on those who hope in his steadfast love, that he may deliver their soul from death...
*Mt. 24:21–22, 24, 31 [Christ]: There will be great tribulation, such as has not been from the beginning of the world until now, no, and never will be. And if those days had not been shortened, no human being would be saved; but for the sake of the elect (Luther: Auserwählten) those days will be shortened...For false Christs and false prophets will arise and show great signs and wonders, so as to lead astray, if possible, even the elect (Luther: Auserwählten)...and he will send out his angels with a loud trumpet call, and they will gather his elect (Luther: Auserwählten) from the four winds, from one end of heaven to the other.
Jer. 20:11. The Lord is with me as a dread warrior (Luther: starker Held); therefore my persecutors will stumble, they will not overcome me. (Also Is. 9:6.)
Is. 52:10. The Lord has bared his holy arm before the eyes of all the nations; and all the ends of the earth shall see the salvation of our God. (Also Lk. 1:51.)
Joel 2:11. The Lord utters his voice before his army...he that executes his word is powerful...
Heb. 4:12. The word of God is living and active, sharper than any two-edged sword... (Also 1 Cor. 1:18.)
Rev. 19:11, 13–14. I saw heaven opened, and behold, a white horse! He who sat upon it...is clad in a robe dipped in blood, and the name by which he is called is The Word of God. And the armies of heaven... followed him...

Ps. 60:5. [O Lord,] that thy beloved may be delivered, give victory by thy right hand and answer us! (Also Ps. 89:13.)
Ps. 139:9–10. If I...dwell in the uttermost parts of the sea, even there thy hand shall lead me, and thy right hand shall hold me. (Also Ps. 16:11, 63:8, 108:6.)
Deut. 26:15. Look down from thy holy habitation, from heaven, and bless thy people Israel and the ground which thou hast given us, as thou didst swear to our fathers...
Ps. 28:9. O save thy people, and bless thy heritage...
Ps. 119:43. And take not the word of truth utterly out of my mouth, for my hope is in thy ordinances. (Also Ps. 138:2.)
Ps. 3:8. Deliverance belongs to the Lord; thy blessing be upon thy people!
1 Pet. 5:8. Be sober, be watchful. Your adversary the devil prowls around like a roaring lion, seeking some one to devour.
Eph. 6:11, 16–17. Put on the whole armor of God, that you may be able to stand against the wiles (Luther: listigen Anläufe) of the devil... [Take] the shield of faith, with which you can quench all the flaming darts of the evil one. And take the helmet of salvation, and the sword of the Spirit, which is the word of God.
Phil. 1:6. I am sure that he who began a good work in you will bring it to completion at the day of Jesus Christ.
Rev. 2:7 [Christ]: ...To him who conquers I will grant to eat of the tree of life, which is in the paradise of God.
1 Thess. 4:17. ...So we shall always be with the Lord.

BWV 91
Gelobet seist du, Jesu Christ
(NBA I/2; BC A9a/b)

Christmas Day (BWV 63, 91, 110, 248-I, 191)
*Tit. 2:11–14 (The grace of God has appeared)
or: *Is. 9:2–7 (The people who walked in darkness have seen a great light; unto us a child is born)
*Lk. 2:1–14 (The birth of Christ, announcement to the shepherds, the praise of the angels)
Librettist: Unknown

1. Chorus (Chorale Vs. 1)
●Incarnation: Praise to Christ for his human birth (91-1)
Gelobet seist du, Jesu Christ,
Blessed   be thou, Jesus Christ,

Daß du   Mensch geboren bist
That thou (as a) (man)   wast-born

Von einer Jungfrau, das ist wahr,
Of   a   virgin,   this is   true,

Des   freuet sich der Engel Schar.
Over-this rejoices   the angel host.

Kyrie eleis!
Kyrie eleis!

2. Soprano Recit. and Chorale (Vs. 2)
●Incarnation: Eternal good clothed in flesh & blood (91-2)
Der Glanz   der höchsten Herrlichkeit,
The radiance of-the highest   glory,

Das Ebenbild von Gottes Wesen,
The   image   of God's essence,

Hat in   bestimmter Zeit
Has, at (the) appointed time,

Sich   einen   Wohnplatz auserlesen.
For-himself a place-of-residence chosen.
{Chosen a place of residence for himself.}

Des ewgen Vaters einigs Kind,
The eternal Father's only child,

Das ewge Licht von Licht geboren,
The eternal light of light born,
{The eternal light born of light,}

Izt man in der Krippe findt.
Now one in the manger finds.
{Is now found in the manger.}

O Menschen, schauet an,
O   people,   behold,

Mt. 1:20–23. [The angel said to Joseph,] "...That which is conceived in [Mary] is of the Holy Spirit; she will bear a son, and you shall call his name Jesus, for he will save his people from their sins." All this took place to fulfil what the Lord had spoken by the prophet: "Behold, a virgin shall conceive and bear a son, and his name shall be called Emmanuel" (which means, God with us).
Is. 7:14. The Lord himself will give you a sign. Behold, a young woman shall conceive and bear a son, and shall call his name Immanuel.
***Lk. 2:10–14.** The angel said to [the shepherds], "Be not afraid; for behold, I bring you good news of a great joy which will come to all the people; for to you is born this day in the city of David a Savior, who is Christ the Lord. And this will be a sign for you: you will find a babe wrapped in swaddling cloths and lying in a manger." And suddenly there was with the angel a multitude of the heavenly host praising God and saying, "Glory to God in the highest, and on earth peace among men with whom he is pleased!"
2 Jn. 1:3. Grace, mercy, and peace will be with us, from God the Father and from Jesus Christ the Father's Son, in truth and love.

Heb. 1:3. [Christ] reflects the glory of God (Luther: der Glanz seiner Herrlichkeit) and bears the very stamp of his nature (Luther: das Ebenbild seines Wesens), upholding the universe by his word of power... (Also 2 Cor. 4:4, Col. 1:15.)
Phil. 2:5–7. Have this mind among yourselves, which is yours in Christ Jesus, who, though he was in the form of God, did not count equality with God a thing to be grasped, but emptied himself, taking the form of a servant, being born in the likeness of men.
Jn. 1:1, 14, 18. In the beginning was the Word, and the Word was with God, and the Word was God...And the Word became flesh and dwelt among us, full of grace and truth; we have beheld his glory, glory as of the only Son of the Father...No one has ever seen God; the only Son, who is in the bosom of the Father, he has made him known.
Gal. 4:4–5. But when the time had fully come, God sent forth his Son, born of woman, born under the law, to redeem those who were under the law, so that we might receive adoption as sons.
***Is. 9:2.** The people who walked in darkness have seen a great light; those who dwelt in a land of deep darkness, on them has light shined. (Also Mt. 4:16, 2 Cor. 4:6.)
1 Jn. 1:5. This is the message we have heard...and proclaim to you, that God is light and in him is no darkness at all. (Also Ps. 36:9–10.)
1 Tim. 6:15–16. ...the King of kings and Lord of lords, who alone has immortality and dwells in unapproachable light...
Jn. 1:9. [In Christ] the true light that enlightens every man was coming into the world. (Also Jn. 1:4.)
Jn. 3:16. God so loved the world that he gave his only Son, that

Was hier der Liebe Kraft getan!
What here - love's power has-done!

In unser armes Fleisch und Blut,
In our poor flesh and blood—

(Und war denn dieses nicht verflucht, verdammt, verloren?)
And was then this not cursed, condemned, lost?—
{Which was cursed, condemned, and lost—}

Verkleidet sich das ewge Gut.
Clothes itself the eternal good.
{The eternal good is clothed.}

So wird es ja zum Segen auserkoren.
Thus is it indeed for blessing chosen.
{Thus it has indeed been chosen for blessing.}

3. Tenor Aria (Based on Chorale Vss. 3–4)
●Incarnation: The eternal light becomes a tiny child (91-3)
Gott, dem der Erden Kreis zu klein,
God, for-whom the earth's circle (is) too small,

Den weder Welt noch Himmel fassen,
Whom neither world nor heaven (can) contain,

Will in der engen Krippe sein.
Would in the cramped manger be.
{Chooses to be in the cramped manger.}

Erscheinet uns dies ewge Licht,
Appears to-us this eternal light,
{If this eternal light appears to us,}

So wird hinfüro Gott uns nicht
Then will henceforth God us not

Als dieses Lichtes Kinder hassen.
As this light's children hate.
{Then God will henceforth not hate us, for we are now the children of this light.}

4. Bass Recit. (Based on Chorale Vs. 5)
●Christmas: Prepare to receive Creator as thy guest! (91-4)
O Christenheit!
O Christendom!

Wohlan, so mache dich bereit,
(Come), then get thyself prepared,

whoever believes in him should not perish but have eternal life.
1 Jn. 4:9–10. In this the love of God was made manifest among us, that God sent his only Son into the world, so that we might live through him. In this is love, not that we loved God but that he loved us and sent his Son to be the expiation for our sins.
Rom. 8:3. For God has done what the law, weakened by the flesh, could not do: sending his own Son in the likeness of sinful flesh and for sin, he condemned sin in the flesh.
Heb. 2:14–15. Since...the children share in flesh and blood, [Christ] himself likewise partook of the same nature, that through death he might destroy him who has the power of death, that is, the devil, and deliver all those who through fear of death were subject to lifelong bondage. (Also Phil. 2:7–8.)
Eph. 1:5–6. [God] destined us in love to be his sons through Jesus Christ, according to the purpose of his will, to the praise of his glorious grace which he freely bestowed on us in the Beloved.

Is. 40:22. It is [God] who sits above the circle of the earth, and its inhabitants are like grasshoppers; who stretches out the heavens like a curtain, and spreads them like a tent to dwell in.
2 Chron. 2:6. Who is able to build [our God] a house, since heaven, even highest heaven, cannot contain him?... (Also 2 Chron. 6:18, 1 Kings 8:27.)
Is. 66:1. Thus says the Lord: "Heaven is my throne and the earth is my footstool; what is the house which you would build for me, and what is the place of my rest?" (Also Acts 7:48–49, 17:24.)
Phil. 2:6–7. ...Though he was in the form of God, [Christ Jesus] did not count equality with God a thing to be grasped, but emptied himself, taking the form of a servant, being born in the likeness of men.
2 Cor. 8:9. You know the grace of our Lord Jesus Christ, that though he was rich, yet for your sake he became poor...
***Is. 9:2.** The people who walked in darkness have seen a great light; those who dwelt in a land of deep darkness, on them has light shined.
Jn. 1:9. The true light that enlightens every man was coming into the world.
1 Tim. 6:15–16. ...the blessed and only Sovereign, the King of kings and Lord of lords, who alone has immortality and dwells in unapproachable light, whom no man has ever seen or can see...
Eph. 5:8. Once you were darkness, but now you are light in the Lord; walk as children of light.
Jn. 12:36 [Christ]: While you have the light, believe in the light, that you may become sons of light. (Also 1 Thess. 5:5.)
Jn. 16:27 [Christ]: The Father himself loves you, because you have loved me and have believed that I came from the Father.

Jn. 1:1–3, 9–12. In the beginning was the Word, and the Word was with God, and the Word was God. He was in the beginning with God; all things were made through him, and without him was not anything made that was made...The true light that enlightens every man was coming into the world. He was in the world, and the world was made through him, yet the world knew him not. He came to his own home, and his own people received him not. But to all who received him, who believed in his name, he gave power to become children of God.

Bei dir den Schöpfer zu empfangen.
- - The Creator to receive.

Der große Gottessohn
The great Son-of-God

Kömmt als ein Gast zu dir gegangen.
Comes as a guest to thee (descending).

Ach, laß dein Herz durch diese Liebe rühren;
Ah, let thy heart by this love be-stirred;

Er kömmt zu dir, um dich vor seinen Thron
He comes to thee, - thee before his throne

Durch dieses Jammertal zu führen.
Through this vale-of-tears to lead.
{He comes to thee, to lead thee through this vale of tears before his throne.}

5. Soprano & Alto Duet (Based on Chorale Vs. 6)
●Incarnation: Christ became poor so we might be rich (91-5)
Die Armut, so Gott auf sich nimmt,
(This) poverty, which God on himself takes,

Hat uns ein ewig Heil bestimmt,
Has for-us an eternal salvation appointed,
{Has appointed for us an eternal salvation,}

Den Überfluß an Himmelsschätzen.
The overflowing-abundance of heaven's-treasures.

Sein menschlich Wesen machet euch
His mortal nature makes you

Den Engelsherrlichkeiten gleich,
The splendor-of-angels equal,
{Equal with the splendor of angels,}

Euch zu der Engel Chor zu setzen.
You to the angels' choir to (appoint).
{To place you in the angels' choir.}

6. Chorale (Vs. 7) (See also 64-2, 248-28.)
●Christmas: Let all praise God for this gift of love! (91-6)
Das hat er alles uns getan,
That has he all for-us done,
{All that has he done for us,}

Mt. 10:40 [Christ]: He who receives you receives me, and he who receives me receives him who sent me. (Also Jn. 13:20.)
1 Jn. 3:1. See what love the Father has given us, that we should be called children of God; and so we are...
1 Jn. 4:9–10. In this the love of God was made manifest among us, that God sent his only Son into the world, so that we might live through him. In this is love, not that we loved God but that he loved us and sent his Son to be the expiation for our sins. (Also Jn. 3:16, 18.)
Heb. 2:10–11, 14–15. It was fitting that he, for whom and by whom all things exist, in bringing many sons to glory, should make the pioneer of their salvation perfect through suffering. For he who sanctifies and those who are sanctified have all one origin. That is why he is not ashamed to call them brethren...Since therefore the children share in flesh and blood, he himself likewise partook of the same nature, that through death he might destroy him who has the power of death, that is, the devil, and deliver all those who through fear of death were subject to lifelong bondage.
Ezek. 34:11, 15–16. Thus says the Lord God: Behold...I myself will be the shepherd of my sheep...I will seek the lost, and I will bring back the strayed... (Also Ps. 23:1–2, Is. 40:11, Rev. 7:17.)
Jn. 10:11, 27 [Christ]: I am the good shepherd. The good shepherd lays down his life for the sheep...My sheep hear my voice, and I know them, and they follow me.
Jn. 14:3 [Christ]: ...I...will take you to myself, that where I am you may be also. (Also Heb. 12:1–2.)
Acts 14:22. ...Through many tribulations we must enter the kingdom of God.
Rev. 7:14–15. ...These [clothed in white robes] are they who have come out of the great tribulation...therefore are they before the throne of God...

2 Cor. 8:9. You know the grace of our Lord Jesus Christ, that though he was rich, yet for your sake he became poor, so that by his poverty you might become rich. (Also Eph. 2:7, 3:16, Col. 1:27, 2:2.)
Heb. 2:9–11, 14–15. We see Jesus, who for a little while was made lower than the angels, crowned with glory and honor because of the suffering of death, so that by the grace of God he might taste death for every one. For it was fitting that he, for whom and by whom all things exist, in bringing many sons to glory, should make the pioneer of their salvation perfect through suffering. For he who sanctifies and those who are sanctified have all one origin. That is why he is not ashamed to call them brethren...Since therefore the children share in flesh and blood, [Christ] himself likewise partook of the same nature, that through death he might destroy him who has the power of death, that is, the devil, and deliver all those who through fear of death were subject to lifelong bondage.
1 Pet. 1:3–4. ...By his great mercy we have been born anew...to an inheritance which is imperishable, undefiled, and unfading, kept in heaven for you.
Mt. 22:30. In the resurrection [we]...are like angels in heaven. (Also Lk. 20:36.)

Ps. 126:3. The Lord has done great things for us; we are glad.
Jn. 3:16. God so loved the world that he gave his only Son, that whoever believes in him should not perish but have eternal life.

Sein groß Lieb zu zeigen an;
His great love to show;
{To show his great love;}

Des freu sich alle Christenheit
(Let) over-this rejoice all Christendom
{Let all Christendom rejoice over this}

Und dank ihm des in Ewigkeit.
And thank him for-this (through) (all) eternity.

Kyrie eleis!
Kyrie eleis!

1 Jn. 4:9–10. In this the love of God was made manifest among us, that God sent his only Son into the world, so that we might live through him. In this is love, not that we loved God but that he loved us and sent his Son to be the expiation for our sins.

Phil. 2:6–8. Though he was in the form of God, [Christ Jesus] did not count equality with God a thing to be grasped, but emptied himself, taking the form of a servant, being born in the likeness of men. And being found in human form he humbled himself and became obedient unto death, even death on a cross.

1 Jn. 4:10. In this is love, not that we loved God but that he loved us and sent his Son to be the expiation for our sins.

Rom. 5:8. God shows his love for us in that while we were yet sinners Christ died for us.

2 Cor. 9:15. Thanks be to God for his inexpressible gift!

2 Jn. 1:3. Grace, mercy, and peace will be with us, from God the Father and from Jesus Christ the Father's Son, in truth and love.

Rev. 7:12. Amen! Blessing and glory and wisdom and thanksgiving and honor and power and might be to our God for ever and ever! Amen. (Also 1 Tim. 1:17, Rev. 5:13, Rev. 1:5–6.)

BWV 92
Ich hab in Gottes Herz und Sinn
(NBA I/7; BC A42)

Septuagesima[1] (BWV 144, 92, 84)
*1 Cor. 9:24–10:5 (Run the race so as to obtain the prize)
*Mt. 20:1–16 (The parable of the vineyard laborers)
Librettist: Unknown

1. Chorus (Chorale Vs. 1)
●God's ways are best; what seems bad is my gain (92–1)
Ich hab in Gottes Herz und Sinn
I have to God's heart and mind

Mein Herz und Sinn ergeben,
My (own) heart and mind surrendered,

Was böse scheint, ist mein Gewinn,
What bad seems, is my gain,
{What seems bad, is my gain,}

Der Tod selbst ist mein Leben.
- Death itself is (for-me) life.
{Death itself is life for me.}

Ich bin ein Sohn des, der den Thron
I am a son of-him, who the throne

Des Himmels aufgezogen;
Of heaven has-mounted;

Ps. 131:1–2. O Lord, my heart is not lifted up, my eyes are not raised too high; I do not occupy myself with things too great and too marvelous for me. But I have calmed and quieted my soul, like a child quieted at its mother's breast; like a child that is quieted is my soul.

Lk. 22:41–42. [Jesus]...knelt down and prayed, "Father, if thou art willing, remove this cup from me; nevertheless not my will, but thine, be done."

Is. 55:8–9. For my thoughts are not your thoughts, neither are your ways my ways, says the Lord. For as the heavens are higher than the earth, so are my ways higher than your ways and my thoughts than your thoughts. (Also Job 11:7–9, 12:13.)

Phil. 1:21. To me to live is Christ, and to die is gain.

Rom. 8:28. We know that in everything God works for good with those who love him, who are called according to his purpose...

Gen. 50:19–20. Joseph said to [his brothers], "...You meant evil against me; but God meant it for good."

Rom. 8:32. He who did not spare his own Son but gave him up for us all, will he not also give us all things with him?

Mt. 7:11. If you...who are evil, know how to give good gifts to your children, how much more will your Father who is in heaven give good things to those who ask him! (Also Lk. 11:13.)

Heb. 12:5–7, 9–11. ...My son, do not regard lightly the discipline of the Lord, nor lose courage when you are punished by him. For the Lord

---

[1]Artur Hirsch suggests that this cantata may originally have been intended for the 4. S. after Epiphany, which has, as its Gospel, the story of Christ calming the storm (*Mt. 8:23–27). He conjectures that both poet and composer may not have realized until later that, because Easter was coming early in that year (1725), the 4. S. after Epiphany would be omitted, and Septuagesima would follow instead. See notes to Hänssler recording #98717.

Ob   er gleich schlägt   und   Kreuz auflegt,
Though he   -   strike (me) and (a) cross impose,

Bleibt   doch sein Herz gewogen.
Remains yet   his heart well-disposed.
{Yet his heart remains well-disposed.}

2. Bass: Chorale (Vs. 2) and Recit.
●Love of God constant despite billows & storms (92-2)
Es kann mir fehlen nimmermehr!
It can me   fail   nevermore!
{It can never fail me!}

Es   müssen eh'r,
(Now) must sooner
{Sooner must—}

Wie selbst der treue Zeuge spricht,
As   even the faithful witness says—

Mit Prasseln und mit grausem Knallen
With rattling and with horrible exploding

Die Berge und die Hügel fallen:
The mountains and the hills collapse:
{The mountains and the hills collapse with rattling and with
horrible exploding:}

Mein Heiland aber trüget   nicht,
My   Savior, though, deceives (me) not,

Mein Vater muß mich lieben.
My   father must me   love.
{My father must love me.}

Durch Jesu rotes Blut
Through Jesus' crimson blood

        bin ich in seine Hand geschrieben;
        am I upon his hand   written;
        {am I written upon his hand;}

Er schützt mich doch!
He protects me indeed!

Wenn er mich auch gleich   wirft ins Meer,
If   he me indeed - (should) cast into-the sea,
{Even if he should cast me into the sea,}

So   lebt der Herr auf großen Wassern noch,
Then lives the Lord upon great waters (too),
{Then I will find he lives upon mighty waters too,}

Der hat mir selbst mein Leben zugeteilt,
He has me even   my   life   allotted,
{He has my very life allotted,}

Drum   werden sie mich nicht ersäufen.
Therefore will they me   not   drown.
{Therefore the waters will not drown me.}

disciplines him whom he loves, and discipline us and we respected
them. Shall we not much more be subject to the Father of spirits and
live?...For the moment all discipline seems painful rather than
pleasant; later it yields the peaceful fruit of righteousness...

Is. 54:10. The mountains may depart and the hills be removed
(Luther: Berge weichen und Hügel hinfallen), but my steadfast love
shall not depart from you and my covenant of peace shall not be
removed, says the Lord, who has compassion on you. (Also Ezek.
37:26.)
Mt. 24:29, 35 [Christ]: ...After the tribulation of those days the sun
will be darkened, and the moon will not give its light, and the stars
will fall from heaven, and the powers of the heavens will be shaken...
Heaven and earth will pass away, but my words will not pass away.
(Also Mk. 13:31, Lk. 21:33, Is. 40:8, Ps. 102:25-27.)
2 Pet. 3:10. The day of the Lord will come like a thief, and then the
heavens will pass away with a loud noise, and the elements will be
dissolved with fire, and the earth and the works that are upon it will
be burned up.
Lk. 23:30. Then [men] will begin to say to the mountains, 'Fall on us';
and to the hills, 'Cover us.' (Also Rev. 6:16.)
Ps. 102:25-28. [O Lord, the earth and the heavens] will perish, but
thou dost endure; they will all wear out like a garment. Thou changest
them like raiment, and they pass away; but thou art the same, and thy
years have no end.
Ps. 119:89-90. For ever, O Lord, thy word is firmly fixed in the
heavens. Thy faithfulness endures to all generations...
2 Tim. 2:13. If we are faithless, he remains faithful—for he cannot
deny himself. (Also Rom. 3:4.)
Jn. 14:21 [Christ]: ...He who loves me will be loved by my Father, and
I will love him and manifest myself to him. (Also Jn. 14:23, 16:26-27.)
Is. 49:16 [God]: Behold, I have graven you on the palms of my
hands...
Eph. 2:13. Now in Christ Jesus you who once were far off have been
brought near in the blood of Christ. (Also Heb. 9:14, Rev. 1:5.)
Heb. 10:19. ...We have confidence to enter the sanctuary by the blood
of Jesus... (Also Heb. 13:20, 1 Pet. 1:18-19, 1 Jn. 1:7, Rev. 5:9.)
Ps. 34:15, 17, 19. The eyes of the Lord are toward the righteous, and
his ears toward their cry...When the righteous cry for help, the Lord
hears, and delivers them out of all their troubles...Many are the
afflictions of the righteous; but the Lord delivers him out of them all.
Jonah 2:3. Thou didst cast me into the deep, into the heart of the
seas, and the flood was round about me; all thy waves and thy billows
passed over me.
Mt. 8:23-26. When [Jesus] got into the boat, his disciples followed
him. And behold, there arose a great storm on the sea, so that the
boat was being swamped by the waves; but he was asleep. And they
went and woke him, saying, "Save, Lord; we are perishing." And he
said to them, "Why are you afraid, O men of little faith?" Then he
rose and rebuked the winds and the sea; and there was a great calm.
(Also Mk. 4:35-39.)
Ps. 69:1, 15. Save me, O God! For the waters have come up to my
neck...Let not the flood sweep over me, or the deep swallow me up...
(Also Ps. 18:16, 77:19, 124:4-5, 144:7.)

319

Wenn mich die Wellen schon ergreifen
Even-if me the waves - seize
{Even if the waves should seize me}

Und ihre Wut mit mir zum Abgrund eilt,
And their fury with me to-the abyss hasten,
{And their fury hasten with me to the abyss,}

So will er mich nur üben,
So would he me just test,
{He is just testing me,}

Ob ich an Jonam werde denken,
Whether I of Jonah will think,
{Whether I will think of Jonah,}

Ob ich den Sinn mit Petro auf ihn werde lenken.
Whether I (my) mind with Peter to him will direct.
{Whether I will direct my mind to him as Peter did.}

Er will mich stark im Glauben machen,
He would me strong in faith make,
{He would make me strong in faith,}

Er will für meine Seele wachen
He would over my soul watch

Und mein Gemüt,
And my disposition—

Das immer wankt und weicht,
Which always vacillates and yields—

In seiner Güt,
In his goodness—

Der an Beständigkeit nichts gleicht,
Which in steadfastness nothing equals—
{Which is unmatched in steadfastness—}

Gewöhnen festzustehen.
Accustom to-stand-firmly.
{Help to stand firmly.}

Mein Fuß soll fest
My foot shall firmly

Bis an der Tage letzten Rest
Until the days' last remainder
{Until my last remaining days}

Sich hier auf diesen Felsen gründen.
Itself here upon this rock ground.
{Ground itself upon this rock.}

Halt ich denn Stand,
Hold I (my) position,
{If I hold my position,}

Und lasse mich in felsenfestem Glauben finden,
And let myself in rock-firm faith be-found,

Ps. 29:3. The voice of the Lord is upon the waters; the God of glory thunders, the Lord, upon many waters. (Also Is. 51:10.)

Is. 43:1–2. ...Thus says the Lord, he who created you, O Jacob, he who formed you, O Israel: "Fear not, for I have redeemed you; I have called you by name, you are mine. When you pass through the waters I will be with you; and through the rivers, they shall not overwhelm you..." (Also Ps. 32:6, 46:1–3, 7.)

Heb. 12:11. ...All discipline seems painful rather than pleasant; later it yields the peaceful fruit of righteousness to those who have been trained (Luther: geübt) by it.

Prov. 3:11. My son, do not despise the Lord's discipline or be weary of his reproof, for the Lord reproves him whom he loves, as a father the son in whom he delights. (Also Heb. 12:5–7.)

*1 Cor. 9:25–27. Every athlete exercises self-control in all things. They do it to receive a perishable wreath, but we an imperishable. Well, I do not run aimlessly, I do not box as one beating the air; but I pommel my body and subdue it...

Jms. 1:2–4. Count it all joy, my brethren, when you meet various trials, for you know that the testing of your faith produces steadfastness. And let steadfastness have its full effect, that you may be perfect and complete, lacking in nothing. (Also 1 Pet. 1:6–7.)

Jonah 1:11–12, 17. Then [the sailors] said to [Jonah], "What shall we do to you, that the sea may quiet down for us?" For the sea grew more and more tempestuous. He said to them, "Take me up and throw me into the sea; then the sea will quiet down for you; for I know it is because of me that this great tempest has come upon you." ...And the Lord appointed a great fish to swallow up Jonah; and Jonah was in the belly of the fish three days and three nights.

Mt. 14:28–31. Peter answered [Jesus], "Lord, if it is you, bid me come to you on the water." He said, "Come." So Peter got out of the boat and walked on the water and came to Jesus; but when he saw the wind, he was afraid, and beginning to sink he cried out, "Lord, save me." Jesus immediately reached out his hand and caught him, saying to him, "O man of little faith, why did you doubt?"

Heb. 10:23, 36–38. Let us hold fast the confession of our hope without wavering (Luther: wanken), for he who promised is faithful...For you have need of endurance, so that you may do the will of God and receive what is promised. "For yet a little while, and the coming one shall come and shall not tarry; but my righteous one shall live by faith, and if he shrinks back, my soul has no pleasure in him."

Jms. 1:6–8. ...He who doubts is like a wave of the sea that is driven and tossed by the wind. For that person must not suppose that a double-minded man, unstable in all his ways, will receive anything from the Lord.

1 Cor. 15:58. Therefore, my beloved brethren, be steadfast, immovable... (Also 1 Cor. 16:13, Eph. 6:14, Phil. 4:1, 2 Thess. 2:15, 2 Pet. 3:17.)

Heb. 6:19. We have [our hope] as a sure and steadfast anchor of the soul...

1 Pet. 2:6. It stands in scripture: "Behold, I am laying in Zion a stone, a cornerstone chosen and precious, and he who believes in him will not be put to shame."

Mt. 16:16–18. Simon Peter replied, "You are the Christ, the Son of the living God." And Jesus answered him, "Blessed are you, Simon Bar-Jona! For flesh and blood has not revealed this to you, but my Father who is in heaven." And I tell you, you are Peter, and on this rock I will build my church, and the powers of death shall not prevail against it.

Weiß seine Hand,
(Then) knows his hand,

Die er mir schon vom Himmel beut,
Which he to-me already from heaven extends,

Zu rechter Zeit
At-the proper time

Mich wieder zu erhöhen.
(How) me again to raise-up.
{Then his hand, which he already extends to me from heaven, knows how to raise me up again at the proper time.}

3. Tenor Aria (Based on Chorale Vs. 4)
●Storms of life break whatever God does not hold (92-3)
Seht, seht! wie reißt, wie bricht, wie fällt,
See, see! How (everything) tears, - breaks, - falls,

Was Gottes starker Arm nicht hält.
That God's strong arm (does) not hold.

Seht aber fest und unbeweglich prangen,
Behold, however, firm and immutably resplendent,

Was unser Held mit seiner Macht umfangen.
That-which our champion with his might has-surrounded.

Laßt Satan wüten, rasen, krachen,
Let Satan rage, rave, roar,

Der starke Gott wird uns unüberwindlich machen.
The mighty God will us unconquerable make.
{The mighty God will make us unconquerable.}

4. Chorale: Alto (Vs. 5)
●God's wisdom perfect; he knows when to allow grief (92-4)
Zudem ist Weisheit und Verstand
In-addition is wisdom and understanding

Bei ihm ohn alle Maßen,
With him beyond all measure,
{In addition, he has wisdom and understanding beyond all measure,}

Zeit, Ort und Stund ist ihm bekannt,
Time, place, and hour is to-him known,
{Time, place, and hour is known to him,}

*1 Cor. 10:4. All [our fathers] drank the same supernatural drink. For they drank from the supernatural Rock which followed them, and the Rock was Christ.
Eph. 2:19-21. So then you are no longer strangers and sojourners, but you are fellow citizens with the saints and members of the household of God, built upon the foundation of the apostles and prophets, Christ Jesus himself being the cornerstone, in whom the whole structure is joined together and grows into a holy temple in the Lord. (Also 1 Cor. 3:11.)
Ps. 37:34. Wait for the Lord, and keep to his way, and he will exalt you...
1 Pet. 5:6. Humble yourselves therefore under the mighty hand of God, that in due time (Luther: zu seiner Zeit) he may exalt you. (Also Ps. 75:6-7, Ezek. 21:26.)
Mt. 23:12 [Christ]: Whoever exalts himself will be humbled, and whoever humbles himself will be exalted. (Also Lk. 18:14.)

Col. 1:15-17. [Christ] is the image of the invisible God, the first-born of all creation; for in him all things were created, in heaven and on earth, visible and invisible, whether thrones or dominions or principalities or authorities—all things were created through him and for him. He is before all things, and in him all things hold together.
Job 12:10. In his hand is the life of every living thing and the breath of all mankind.
Ps. 104:27-29. [O Lord,] these all look to thee, to give them their food in due season. When thou givest to them, they gather it up; when thou openest thy hand, they are filled with good things. When thou hidest thy face, they are dismayed; when thou takest away their breath, they die and return to their dust.
Ps. 127:1. Unless the Lord builds the house, those who build it labor in vain...
Mt. 16:18 [Christ]: ...On this rock I will build my church, and the powers of death shall not prevail against it.
Ps. 46:1-3. God is our refuge (Luther: Zuversicht) and strength, a very present help in trouble. Therefore we will not fear though the earth should change, though the mountains shake in the heart of the sea; though its waters roar and foam, though the mountains tremble with its tumult.
Rom. 8:35-37. Who shall separate us from the love of Christ? Shall tribulation, or distress, or persecution, or famine, or nakedness, or peril, or sword? As it is written, "For thy sake we are being killed all the day long; we are regarded as sheep to be slaughtered." No, in all these things we are more than conquerors through him who loved us.

Job 12:13-14. With God are wisdom and might; he has counsel and understanding. If he tears down, none can rebuild...
Is. 55:8-9. My thoughts are not your thoughts, neither are your ways my ways, says the Lord. For as the heavens are higher than the earth, so are my ways higher than your ways and my thoughts than your thoughts.
Job 11:7-9. Can you find out the deep things of God? Can you find out the limit of the Almighty? It is higher than heaven—what can you do? Deeper than Sheol—what can you know? Its measure is longer than the earth, and broader than the sea.
Job 9:10. [God] does great things beyond understanding, and marvelous things without number. (Also Job 5:9, 12:16.)
1 Kings 4:29-30. God gave Solomon wisdom and understanding (Luther: Weisheit und Verstand) beyond measure, and largeness of

Zu tun und auch zu lassen.
To do and also to leave (undone).

Er weiß, wenn Freud, er weiß, wenn Leid
He knows, when joy, he knows, when grief

Uns, seinen Kindern, diene,
Us, his children, (best) does-serve,
{Serves us, his children, best,}

Und was er tut, ist alles gut,
And whatever he does, is all good,
{And all that he does is good,}

Ob's noch so traurig schiene.
Even-though-it yet so sad may-seem.
{Even if it seem ever so sad.}

5. Tenor Recit. (Loosely based on Chorale Vss. 6, 8)
●Sufferings faced with faith & patience as Christ did (92-5)
Wir wollen nun nicht länger zagen
We would now no longer falter-faintheartedly

Und uns mit Fleisch und Blut,
And - with flesh and blood—

Weil wir in Gottes Hut,
Because we (are) in God's keeping—

So furchtsam wie bisher befragen.
So fearfully, as hitherto, consult.
{And consult with flesh and blood so fearfully as hitherto, because we are in God's keeping.}

Ich denke dran,
I think of-this,

Wie Jesus nicht gefürcht das tausendfache Leiden;
How Jesus (did) not fear (his) thousandfold suffering;

Er sah es an
He regarded it -

Als eine Quelle ewger Freuden.
As a source (of) everlasting joy.

Und dir, mein Christ,
And for-you, my (dear) Christian,

Wird deine Angst und Qual, dein bitter Kreuz und Pein
Will your fear and torment, your bitter cross and pain
{Your fear and torment, your bitter cross and pain will}

Um Jesu willen Heil und Zucker sein.
For Jesus' sake, prosperity and (sweetness) be.
{Be prosperity and sweetness for Jesus' sake.}
[Zucker = sugar]

mind like the sand on the seashore, so that Solomon's wisdom surpassed the wisdom of all the people of the east, and all the wisdom of Egypt.

Ps. 31:14-15. I trust in thee, O Lord, I say, "Thou art my God." My times are in thy hand...

Job 23:10. He knows the way that I take; when he has tried me, I shall come forth as gold.

Rom. 8:28. We know that in everything God works for good with those who love him, who are called according to his purpose.

Heb. 12:5-7, 11. ...My son, do not regard lightly the discipline of the Lord, nor lose courage when you are punished by him. For the Lord disciplines him whom he loves, and chastises every son whom he receives. It is for discipline that you have to endure. God is treating you as sons; for what son is there whom his father does not discipline? ...For the moment all discipline seems painful rather than pleasant; later it yields the peaceful fruit of righteousness to those who have been trained by it. (Also Prov. 3:11.)

Gal. 1:15-16 [Paul]: When he who had set me apart before I was born, and had called me through his grace...I did not confer with flesh and blood.

Jer. 17:5, 7. Thus says the Lord: "Cursed is the man who trusts in man ...whose heart turns away from the Lord...Blessed is the man who trusts in the Lord, whose trust is the Lord." (Also Is. 30:1-3.)

Prov. 3:5-6. Trust in the Lord with all your heart, and do not rely on your own insight. In all your ways acknowledge him, and he will make straight your paths.

1 Pet. 5:7. Cast all your anxieties on him, for he cares about you.

Ps. 121:2-8. My help comes from the Lord, who made heaven and earth. He will not let your foot be moved, he who keeps you will not slumber. Behold, he who keeps Israel will neither slumber nor sleep. The Lord is your keeper; the Lord is your shade on your right hand. The sun shall not smite you by day, nor the moon by night. The Lord will keep you from all evil; he will keep your life. The Lord will keep your going out and your coming in from this time forth and for evermore.

Heb. 12:1-2. Let us run with perseverance the race that is set before us, looking to Jesus the pioneer and perfecter of our faith, who for the joy that was set before him endured the cross, despising the shame, and is seated at the right hand of the throne of God. (Also Mt. 26:38-39.)

Mt. 26:38-39. [In Gethsemane, Jesus] said to [his disciples], "My soul is very sorrowful, even to death; remain here, and watch with me." And going a little farther he fell on his face and prayed, "My Father, if it be possible, let this cup pass from me; nevertheless, not as I will, but as thou wilt."

1 Pet. 4:1-2. Since therefore Christ suffered in the flesh, arm yourselves with the same thought, for whoever has suffered in the flesh has ceased from sin, so as to live for the rest of the time in the flesh no longer by human passions but by the will of God.

Mt. 10:38 [Christ]: He who does not take his cross and follow me is not worthy of me. (Also Mt. 16:24.)

Mt. 5:10-12 [Christ]: Blessed are those who are persecuted for righteousness' sake, for theirs is the kingdom of heaven. Blessed are

Vertraue Gottes   Huld
Trust   God's graciousness

Und merke noch, was   nötig   ist:
And mark   yet, what needful is:
{And mark yet, what is needful for you:}

Geduld! Geduld!
Patience! patience!

6. Bass Aria (Based on Chorale Vs. 9)
●Storms produce fruit; trusting God's discipline (92–6)
Das Brausen von den rauhen Winden
The blustering of -   raw   winds

Macht, daß wir volle Ähren   finden.
Ensures, that we full heads (of grain) do-find.

Des Kreuzes Ungestüm schafft bei den Christen Frucht,
The cross's   tempest produces in (a) Christian fruit,
{The cross's tempest produces fruit in a Christian,}

Drum   laßt uns alle unser Leben
Therefore let us all   our   life
{Therefore let all of us surrender our lives completely}

Dem weisen Herrscher ganz ergeben.
To-(our) wise   ruler   completely surrender.
{To our wise ruler.}

Küßt seines Sohnes Hand, verehrt die treue   Zucht.
Kiss his   Son's   hand; revere (his) faithful discipline.

7. Chorale (Vs. 10) **& S.A.T.B. Recits.** (Chorale: see also 65–7)
●Surrendering to God; accepting hardship as beneficial (92–7)
Ei nun, mein Gott, so fall ich dir
Ah, now my God, thus fall I -
{Ah now, my God, thus do I fall}

Getrost   in deine Hände.
Confidently into thy   hands.

Bass:
So spricht der   gottgelaßne Geist,
Thus speaks the to-God-entrusted spirit,
{Thus speaks the spirit to God entrusted,}

Wenn er des Heilands Brudersinn
When it the Savior's brotherly-disposition
{When it praises in faith the Savior's brotherly disposition}

Und Gottes Treue   gläubig preist.
And God's faithfulness in-faith does-praise.
{And God's faithfulness.}

Nimm mich, und mache es mit mir
Take   me, and   do - with me

you when men revile you and persecute you and utter all kinds of evil against you falsely on my account. Rejoice and be glad, for your reward is great in heaven, for so men persecuted the prophets who were before you.
1 Pet. 4:19. Therefore let those who suffer according to God's will do right and entrust their souls to a faithful Creator.
Heb. 10:36. For you have need of endurance (Luther: Geduld), so that you may do the will of God and receive what is promised. (Also Lk. 21:19.)

Jms. 1:2–4. Count it all joy, my brethren, when you meet various trials, for you know that the testing of your faith produces steadfastness. And let steadfastness have its full effect, that you may be perfect and complete, lacking in nothing. (Also Jms. 1:12, 1 Pet. 4:12–14, 5:10.)
Jn. 15:1–2, 8, 16 [Christ]: I am the true vine, and my Father is the vinedresser. Every branch of mine that bears no fruit, he takes away, and every branch that does bear fruit he prunes, that it may bear more fruit...By this my Father is glorified, that you bear much fruit, and so prove to be my disciples...You did not choose me, but I chose you and appointed you that you should go and bear fruit and that your fruit should abide... (Also Gal. 5:22–23.)
1 Pet. 4:19. Therefore let those who suffer according to God's will do right and entrust their souls to a faithful Creator.
Job 5:17. Behold, happy is the man whom God reproves; therefore despise not the chastening (Luther: Züchtigung) of the Almighty.
Prov. 3:11. My son, do not despise the Lord's discipline or be weary of his reproof, for the Lord reproves him whom he loves, as a father the son in whom he delights. (Also Heb. 12:5–7, 11.)

2 Sam. 24:14. David said to Gad, "I am in great distress; let us fall into the hand of the Lord, for his mercy is great; but let me not fall into the hand of man." (Also 1 Chron. 21:13.)
Mt. 26:38–39. [Jesus] said to [his disciples], "My soul is very sorrowful, even to death; remain here, and watch with me." And going a little farther he fell on his face and prayed, "My Father, if it be possible, let this cup pass from me; nevertheless, not as I will, but as thou wilt."
Ps. 31:5. Into thy hand I commit my spirit; thou hast redeemed me, O Lord, faithful God.
Lk. 23:46. Then Jesus, crying with a loud voice, said, "Father, into thy hands I commit my spirit!" And having said this he breathed his last.
Heb. 2:10–12. It was fitting that he, for whom and by whom all things exist, in bringing many sons to glory, should make the pioneer of their salvation perfect through suffering. For he who sanctifies and those who are sanctified have all one origin. That is why he is not ashamed to call them brethren, saying, "I will proclaim thy name to my brethren, in the midst of the congregation I will praise thee."
Phil. 1:6. I am sure that he who began a good work in you will bring it to completion at the day of Jesus Christ.
Jms. 1:2–4. Count it all joy, my brethren, when you meet various trials, for you know that the testing of your faith produces steadfastness. And let steadfastness have its full effect, that you may

Bis an mein letztes Ende,
Until - my final end,

Tenor:
Ich weiß gewiß,
I know assuredly,

Daß ich ohnfehlbar selig bin,
That I without-fail blest am,
{That I am blest without fail,}

Wenn meine Not und mein Bekümmernis
If my distress and my affliction

Von dir so wird geendigt werden:
By thee thus will concluded be:
{By thee will thus concluded be:}

Wie du wohl weißt, daß meinem Geist
As thou well knowest (how); that for-my spirit

Dadurch sein Nutz entstehe,
Thereby its benefit (may) be-fostered,

Alto:
Daß schon auf dieser Erden,
So-that already on this earth,

Dem Satan zum Verdruß,
- Satan for vexation,
{To Satan's vexation,}

Dein Himmelreich sich in mir zeigen muß
Thy kindom-of-heaven - in me must-appear

Und deine Ehr je mehr und mehr
And thy honor ever more and more

Sich in ihr selbst erhöhe.
(May) in it - (be) heightened.
{And that thy honor be exalted in me more and more.}

Soprano:
So kann mein Herz nach deinem Willen
Thus can my heart according to-thy will

Sich, o mein Jesu, selig stillen,
Itself, O my Jesus, blessedly quieten,
{O my Jesus, blessedly quieten itself,}

Und ich kann bei gedämpften Saiten
And I can with muted strings

Dem Friedensfürst ein neues Lied bereiten.
The Prince-of-Peace a new song prepare.
{Prepare a new song for the Prince of Peace.}

be perfect and complete, lacking in nothing. (Also Jms. 1:12.)
1 Pet. 4:12–13, 19. Beloved, do not be surprised at the fiery ordeal which comes upon you to prove you, as though something strange were happening to you. But rejoice in so far as you share Christ's sufferings, that you may also rejoice and be glad when his glory is revealed...Therefore let those who suffer according to God's will do right and entrust their souls to a faithful Creator.
1 Pet. 5:10. And after you have suffered a little while, the God of all grace, who has called you to his eternal glory in Christ, will himself restore, establish, and strengthen you.
Jms. 5:10–11. As an example of suffering and patience, brethren, take the prophets who spoke in the name of the Lord. Behold, we call those happy who were steadfast. You have heard of the steadfastness of Job, and you have seen the purpose of the Lord, how the Lord is compassionate and merciful.
Ps. 94:19. When the cares (Luther: Bekümmernis) of my heart are many, [the Lord's] consolations cheer my soul.
Rom. 8:28. We know that in everything God works for good with those who love him, who are called according to his purpose.
Prov. 3:11. My son, do not despise the Lord's discipline or be weary of his reproof, for the Lord reproves him whom he loves, as a father the son in whom he delights.
Heb. 12:11. For the moment all discipline seems painful rather than pleasant; later it yields the peaceful fruit of righteousness to those who have been trained by it.
1 Pet. 4:1–2. ...Whoever has suffered in the flesh has ceased from sin, so as to live for the rest of the time in the flesh no longer by human passions but by the will of God.
1 Jn. 3:8. He who commits sin is of the devil; for the devil has sinned from the beginning. The reason the Son of God appeared was to destroy the works of the devil.
Lk. 17:21 [Christ]: ...Behold, the kingdom of God is in the midst of you (Luther: inwendig in euch).
2 Cor. 3:18. We all, with unveiled face, beholding the glory of the Lord, are being changed into his likeness from one degree of glory to another; for this comes from the Lord who is the Spirit. (Also Gal. 4:19, Eph. 4:24, Col. 3:10.)
Mt. 26:39. ...Not as I will, but as thou wilt.
Ps. 131:1–2. O Lord, my heart is not lifted up, my eyes are not raised too high; I do not occupy myself with things too great and too marvelous for me. But I have calmed and quieted my soul, like a child quieted at its mother's breast; like a child that is quieted is my soul. (Also Is. 55:8–9, 62:1, 6.)
Phil. 4:6–7. Have no anxiety about anything, but in everything by prayer and supplication with thanksgiving let your requests be made known to God. And the peace of God, which passes all understanding, will keep your hearts and your minds in Christ Jesus.
1 Pet. 4:19. Therefore let those who suffer according to God's will do right and entrust their souls to a faithful Creator.
Hab. 3:17–18. Though the fig tree do not blossom, nor fruit be on the vines, the produce of the olive fail and the fields yield no food, the flock be cut off from the fold and there be no herd in the stalls, yet I will rejoice in the Lord...
Ps. 33:2–3. Praise the Lord with the lyre...Sing to him a new song, play skilfully on the strings (Luther: Saitenspiel)... (Also Ps. 57:8–9, 81:2–3, 149:2–3.)

8. Soprano Aria (Loosely based on Chorale Vs. 11)
●Trusting the shepherd of my soul despite affliction (92–8)
Meinem Hirten bleib ich treu.
To-my shepherd remain I faithful.
{To my shepherd will I remain faithful.}

Will er mir den Kreuzkelch füllen,
Would he for-me the cross's-chalice fill,

Ruh ich ganz in seinem Willen,
(Then) rest I completely in his will,
{Then I shall rest completely in his will,}

Er steht mir im Leiden bei.
He stands (by) me in suffering - .

Es wird dennoch, nach dem Weinen,
(Then) will nevertheless, after (my) weeping,
{For, after my weeping}

Jesu Sonne wieder scheinen.
Jesus' sun again shine.
{Jesus' sun shall shine again.}

Meinem Hirten bleib ich treu.
To-my shepherd remain I faithful.
{To my shepherd will I remain faithful.}

Jesu leb ich, der wird walten,
(For) Jesus live I, he shall rule,
{For Jesus I live, he shall rule;}

Freu dich, Herz, du sollst erkalten,
Rejoice, (O) heart, thou shalt grow-cold,
{Rejoice, O heart, thou canst now grow cold,}

Jesus hat genug getan.
Jesus hath enough achieved.
{Jesus hath achieved enough.}

Amen: Vater, nimm mich an!
Amen: Father, receive me - !

9. Chorale (Vs. 12)
●Affliction-filled ways accepted in faith (92–9)
Soll ich denn auch des Todes Weg
Should I then also (upon) the way-of-death

Und finstre Straße reisen,
And (upon) dark roads travel,

Wohlan! ich tret auf Bahn und Steg,
Well-then! I step (out) upon (the) course and path,

Den mir dein' Augen weisen.
Which to-me thine eyes do-show.
{To which thine eyes direct me.}

Du bist mein Hirt, der alles wird
Thou art my shepherd, who all-things will

Ps. 23:1. The Lord is my shepherd, I shall not want; he makes me lie down in green pastures...
Jn. 10:14–15, 27–28 [Christ]: I am the good shepherd; I know my own and my own know me, as the Father knows me and I know the Father; and I lay down my life for the sheep...My sheep hear my voice, and I know them, and they follow me; and I give them eternal life, and they shall never perish, and no one shall snatch them out of my hand.
1 Pet. 2:25. You were straying like sheep, but have now returned to the Shepherd and Guardian of your souls.
Mk. 10:38–39. Jesus said to [his disciples]..."Are you able to drink the cup that I drink, or to be baptized with the baptism with which I am baptized?" And they said to him, "We are able." And Jesus said to them, "The cup that I drink you will drink; and with the baptism with which I am baptized, you will be baptized..." (Also Mt. 20:20–22.)
Mt. 11:29–30 [Christ]: Take my yoke upon you, and learn from me; for I am gentle and lowly in heart, and you will find rest for your souls. For my yoke is easy, and my burden is light.
2 Cor. 1:3–4. Blessed be the God and Father of our Lord Jesus Christ ...who comforts us in all our affliction... (Also Ps. 86:17, Rom. 8:38–39.)
1 Pet. 5:10. And after you have suffered a little while, the God of all grace, who has called you to his eternal glory in Christ, will himself restore, establish, and strengthen you.
Ps. 126:6. ...He that goes forth weeping, bearing the seed for sowing, shall come home with shouts of joy, bringing his sheaves with him.
Rev. 21:4. [God] will wipe away every tear from their eyes, and death shall be no more, neither shall there be mourning nor crying nor pain any more, for the former things have passed away. (Also Rev. 7:15–17, Is. 25:8.)
2 Cor. 5:1. For we know that if the earthly tent we live in is destroyed, we have a building from God, a house not made with hands, eternal in the heavens.
Phil. 1:21, 23. To me to live is Christ, and to die is gain...My desire is to depart and be with Christ, for that is far better.
2 Cor. 5:6, 8. So we are always of good courage...and we would rather be away from the body and at home with the Lord.
Acts 7:59. And as they were stoning Stephen, he prayed, "Lord Jesus, receive my spirit."

Ps. 23:4. Even though I walk through the valley of the shadow of death, I fear no evil; for thou art with me; thy rod and thy staff, they comfort me. (Also Is. 43:2.)
Job 19:8. [The Lord] has walled up my way, so that I cannot pass, and he has set darkness upon my paths.
Job 23:10. But he knows the way that I take; when he has tried me, I shall come forth as gold.
Ps. 32:8 [God]: I will instruct you and teach you the way you should go; I will counsel you with my eye upon you (Luther: mit meinen Augen leiten).
Ps. 33:18–19. Behold, the eye of the Lord is on those who fear him, on those who hope in his steadfast love, that he may deliver their soul from death, and keep them alive in famine. (Also Ps. 34:15.)
Ps. 73:24. [O Lord,] thou dost guide me with thy counsel, and afterward thou wilt receive me to glory.
Ps. 23:1. The Lord is my shepherd, I shall not want...

Zu solchem Ende kehren,
To such-a conclusion (bring),

Daß ich einmal in deinem Saal
That I one-day within thy hall

Dich ewig möge ehren.
Thee eternally may honor.
{Eternally may honor thee.}

Jn. 10:14, 27–28 [Christ]: I am the good shepherd; I know my own and my own know me...My sheep hear my voice, and I know them, and they follow me; and I give them eternal life, and they shall never perish, and no one shall snatch them out of my hand.
Jn. 14:1–3 [Christ]: Let not your hearts be troubled; believe in God, believe also in me. In my Father's house are many rooms; if it were not so, would I have told you that I go to prepare a place for you? And when I go and prepare a place for you, I will come again and will take you to myself, that where I am you may be also.

BWV 93
Wer nur den lieben Gott läßt walten
(NBA I/17; BC A104)

5. S. after Trinity (BWV 93, 88)
*1 Pet. 3:8–15[1] (Turn from evil and choose right; sanctify Christ in your hearts)
*Lk. 5:1–11 (Peter's great catch of fish)
[1]End: "Christ the Lord."
Librettist: Unknown

1. Chorus (Chorale Vs. 1)
●Trusting God's ways is like building on solid ground (93-1)
Wer nur den lieben Gott läßt walten
Whoever just the dear God allows to-rule
{Whoever just allows the dear God to rule}

Und hoffet auf ihn allezeit,
And hopes in him always,

Den wird er wunderlich erhalten
Him will he wondrously uphold

In allem Kreuz und Traurigkeit.
In (every) cross and (in all) sadness.

Wer Gott, dem Allerhöchsten, traut,
Whoever God, the Most-High, trusts,

Der hat auf keinen Sand gebaut.
He has on no sand built.
{He has not built on sand.}

Ps. 146:5. Happy is he whose help is the God of Jacob, whose hope (Luther: Hoffnung) is in the Lord his God.
Jer. 17:7. Blessed is the man who trusts in the Lord, whose trust is the Lord. (Also Ps. 32:10, 84:12.)
*Lk. 5:4–5. [Jesus] said to Simon, "Put out into the deep and let down your nets for a catch." And Simon answered, "Master, we toiled all night and took nothing! But at your word I will let down the nets."
Prov. 3:5–6. Trust in the Lord with all your heart, and do not rely on your own insight. In all your ways acknowledge him, and he will make straight your paths.
Ps. 34:19. Many are the afflictions of the righteous; but the Lord delivers him out of them all.
*1 Pet. 3:14–15. Even if you...suffer for righteousness' sake, you will be blessed. Have no fear...nor be troubled, but in your hearts reverence Christ as Lord.
Mk. 8:34 [Christ]: ...If any man would come after me, let him deny himself and take up his cross and follow me.
Mt. 7:24–27 [Christ]: Every one then who hears these words of mine and does them will be like a wise man who built his house upon the rock; and the rain fell, and the floods came, and the winds blew and beat upon that house, but it did not fall, because it had been founded on the rock. And every one who hears these words of mine and does not do them will be like a foolish man who built his house upon the sand; and the rain fell, and the floods came, and the winds blew and beat against that house, and it fell; and great was the fall of it. (Also Lk. 6:46–49.)

2. Bass: Recit. & Chorale (Vs. 2) (Chorale: see also 21-9)
●Sorrows are best born with composure (93-2)
Was helfen uns die schweren Sorgen?
What profit us (our) grievous worries?
{What do our grievous worries profit us?}

Sie drücken nur das Herz
They weigh-down just the heart
{They just weigh down our hearts}

Mit Zentnerpein,
With (the) pain-of-a-hundredweight,

Ps. 38:6–10, 13–14. I am utterly bowed down and prostrate; all the day I go about mourning. For my loins are filled with burning, and there is no soundness in my flesh. I am utterly spent and crushed; I groan because of the tumult of my heart. Lord, all my longing is known to thee, my sighing is not hidden from thee. My heart throbs, my strength fails me; and the light of my eyes—it also has gone from me... I am like a deaf man, I do not hear, like a dumb man who does not open his mouth. Yea, I am like a man who does not hear...
Ps. 42:3. My tears have been my food day and night, while men say to me continually, "Where is your God?" (Ps. 79:10, 80:5, Job 30:16–17)

mit   tausend Angst und Schmerz.
with (a) thousand fears and sufferings.

Was hilft uns unser Weh und Ach?
What profits us   our   woe and "ah"?
{What does our "Woe" and "Ah" profit us?}

Es bringt   nur bittres Ungemach.
It brings (us) only bitter   distress.

Was hilft es, daß wir alle   Morgen
What profits it, that we all (our) mornings
{What does it profit, that we each morning}

Mit Seufzen von dem Schlaf aufstehn
With sighing from (our) sleep   arise

Und mit beträntem Angesicht des Nachts zu Bette gehn?
And with tear-stained face   at night to bed do-go?

Wir machen unser Kreuz und Leid
We   make   our cross and sorrow

Durch bange Traurigkeit nur größer.
Through anxious sadness only greater.
{We only make our cross and sorrow greater through anxious sadness.}

Drum   tut ein Christ viel besser
Therefore does a Christian much better (if)
{Therefore a Christian does much better if}

Er trägt sein Kreuz mit christlicher Gelassenheit.
He bears his cross with Christlike   composure.

3. Tenor Aria (Based on Chorale Vs. 3)
●Patience in affliction is rewarded by Father's help (93-3)
Man   halte nur ein wenig stille,
One (should) (be) but a   little quiet,
{One should just be quiet a little,}

Wenn sich die Kreuzesstunde naht,
When - the cross's-hour draws-near,

Denn unsres Gottes Gnadenwille
For   our God's   goodwill

Verläßt uns nie mit Rat und Tat.
Forsakes us never in (word) and deed.

Gott, der die Auserwählten kennt,
God, who the   elect   knows,
{God, who knows his elect,}

Gott, der sich uns ein Vater nennt,
God, who himself - (our) father calls,
{God, who calls himself our father,}

Wird endlich allen Kummer wenden
Will in-the-end all   trouble turn-away

Ps. 31:9–11. ...My eye is wasted from grief, my soul and my body also. For my life is spent with sorrow, and my years with sighing; my strength fails because of my misery, and my bones waste away. I am the scorn of all my adversaries, a horror to my neighbors, an object of dread to my acquaintances; those who see me in the street flee from me.

2 Cor. 1:8–10. We do not want you to be ignorant, brethren, of the affliction we experienced in Asia; for we were so utterly, unbearably crushed that we despaired of life itself. Why, we felt that we had received the sentence of death; but that was to make us rely not on ourselves but on God who raises the dead; he delivered us from so deadly a peril, and he will deliver us; on him we have set our hope that he will deliver us again.

Ps. 6:6–7. I am weary with my moaning; every night I flood my bed with tears; I drench my couch with my weeping. My eye wastes away because of grief, it grows weak because of all my foes.

Jer. 45:3. ...I am weary with my groaning (Luther: ich seufze mich müde), and I find no rest.

Mt. 10:38 [Christ]: He who does not take his cross and follow me is not worthy of me. (Also Mt. 16:24, Mk. 8:34, Lk. 9:23.)

Mt. 16:24–25. Jesus told his disciples, "If any man would come after me, let him deny himself and take up his cross and follow me. For whoever would save his life will lose it, and whoever loses his life for my sake will find it."

Ps. 131:2. I have calmed and quieted my soul, like a child quieted at its mother's breast; like a child that is quieted is my soul.

Jms. 5:10–11. As an example of suffering and patience, brethren, take the prophets who spoke in the name of the Lord. Behold, we call those happy who were steadfast. You have heard of the steadfastness of Job, and you have seen the purpose of the Lord, how the Lord is compassionate and merciful.

Lam. 3:24–26. "The Lord is my portion," says my soul, "therefore I will hope in him."...It is good that one should wait quietly for the salvation of the Lord. (Also Ps. 62:1-2, 5-8.)

Ps. 131:1–2. O Lord, my heart is not lifted up, my eyes are not raised too high; I do not occupy myself with things too great and too marvelous for me. But I have calmed and quieted my soul, like a child quieted at its mother's breast; like a child that is quieted is my soul.

Mk. 14:41–42. [Jesus] came...and said to [his disciples], "...The hour has come (Luther: die Stunde ist gekommen); the Son of man is betrayed into the hands of sinners. Rise, let us be going..."

Ps. 23:4. Even though I walk through the valley of the shadow of death, I fear no evil; for thou art with me; thy rod and thy staff, they comfort me.

Heb. 13:5. ...[God] has said, "I will never fail you nor forsake you (Luther: dich nicht verlassen noch versäumen)."

Ps. 73:24. [O Lord,] thou dost guide me with thy counsel (Luther: Rat), and afterward thou wilt receive me to glory.

Prov. 8:14. I [the wisdom of God] have counsel and sound wisdom (Luther: Rat und Tat), I have insight, I have strength.

Lk. 18:7–8 [Christ]: Will not God vindicate his elect (Luther: Auserwählten), who cry to him day and night?...I tell you, he will vindicate them speedily...

1 Pet. 5:10. After you have suffered a little while, the God of all grace, who has called you to his eternal glory in Christ, will himself restore, establish, and strengthen you.

Und seinen Kindern Hilfe senden.
And to-his children help send.
{And send help to his children.}

Ps. 103:13. As a father pities his children, so the Lord pities those who fear him.

1 Jn. 3:1. See what love the Father has given us, that we should be called children of God; and so we are...

4. Soprano & Alto Duet (Chorale Vs. 4)
●Appointed time of joy determined by God for us (93-4)
Er kennt die rechten Freudenstunden,
He knows the proper hours-for-joy,
{He knows the proper hour for joy,}

Er weiß wohl, wenn es nützlich sei;
He knows well, when it profitable be;

Wenn er uns nur hat treu erfunden
If he us only has faithful found
{If only he has found us faithful}

Und merket keine Heuchelei,
And notes no hypocrisy,

So kömmt Gott, eh wir uns versehn,
Then comes God, before we (know-it),
{Then God comes, before we know it,}

Und lässet uns viel Guts geschehn.
And lets to-us much good happen.
{And lets much good happen to us.}

Lam. 3:25-26. The Lord is good to those who wait for him, to the soul that seeks him. It is good that one should wait quietly for the salvation of the Lord.

*1 Pet. 3:10-12. He that would love life and see good days, let him keep his tongue from evil and his lips from speaking guile; let him turn away from evil and do right; let him seek peace and pursue it. For the eyes of the Lord are upon the righteous, and his ears are open to their prayer...

Ps. 84:11. ...No good thing does the Lord withhold from those who walk uprightly.

Gal. 6:9. Let us not grow weary in well-doing, for in due season we shall reap, if we do not lose heart. (Rev. 2:3)

Ps. 40:17. As for me, I am poor and needy; but the Lord takes thought for me. Thou art my help and my deliverer; do not tarry, O my God!

Rom. 8:28. We know that in everything God works for good with those who love him, who are called according to his purpose. (Heb. 12:11)

Ps. 27:13-14. I believe that I shall see the goodness of the Lord in the land of the living! Wait for the Lord; be strong, and let your heart take courage; yea, wait for the Lord! (Also Ps. 37:7, 9, 34; 130:5-7.)

5. Tenor: Recit. & Chorale (Vs. 5) (Chorale: see also 21-9)
●Affliction: Think not that God has forsaken you! (93-5)
Denk nicht in deiner Drangsalshitze,
Think not in thy heat-of-affliction,

Wenn Blitz und Donner kracht
When lightning and thunder crack

Und dir ein schwüles Wetter bange macht,
And thee a sultry storm (doth) anxious make,
{And a sultry storm doth make thee anxious,}

Daß du von Gott verlassen seist.
That thou by God forsaken art.

Gott bleibt auch in der größten Not,
God remains even in the greatest distress,

Ja gar bis in den Tod
Yes, even unto - - death

Mit seiner Gnade bei den Seinen.
With his mercy near his own.

Du darfst nicht meinen,
Thou must not think,

Daß dieser Gott im Schoße sitze,
That this-one God on-his lap sets,
{That God takes him to his bosom,}

Ps. 46:1-3. God is our refuge (Luther: Zuversicht) and strength, a very present help in trouble. Therefore we will not fear though the earth should change, though the mountains shake in the heart of the sea; though its waters roar and foam, though the mountains tremble with its tumult. (Also 1 Pet. 4:12-13, Jms. 1:2-4, 12, 5:10-11.)

Rom. 8:35, 38-39. Who shall separate us from the love of Christ? Shall tribulation, or distress, or persecution, or famine, or nakedness, or peril, or sword?...I am sure that neither death, nor life, nor angels, nor principalities, nor things present, nor things to come, nor powers, nor height, nor depth, nor anything else in all creation, will be able to separate us from the love of God in Christ Jesus...

Mt. 28:20 [Christ]: ...Lo, I am with you always, to the close of the age.

Heb. 13:5-6. ...He has said, "I will never fail you nor forsake you." Hence we can confidently say, "The Lord is my helper, I will not be afraid..." (Also Deut. 31:6, 8; Josh. 1:5.)

Ps. 23:4. Even though I walk through the valley of the shadow of death, I fear no evil; for thou art with me...

2 Tim. 2:19. God's firm foundation stands, bearing this seal: "The Lord knows those who are his (Luther: der Herr kennt die Seinen)"...

Lk. 16:19-25. There was a rich man, who was clothed in purple and fine linen and who feasted sumptuously every day. And at his gate lay a poor man named Lazarus, full of sores, who desired to be fed with what fell from the rich man's table; moreover the dogs came and licked his sores. The poor man died and was carried by the angels to Abraham's bosom. The rich man also died and was buried; and in Hades, being in torment, he lifted up his eyes, and saw Abraham far off and Lazarus in his bosom. And he called out, "Father Abraham,

Der täglich, wie der reiche Mann,
Who daily, like the rich man,

In Lust und Freuden leben kann.
In pleasure and joy can-live.

Der sich mit stetem Glücke speist,
He-who himself with constant fortune feeds,
{He who on constant fortune feeds,}

Bei lauter guten Tagen,
Amidst nothing-but good days,

Muß oft zuletzt,
Must often in-the-end,

Nachdem er sich an eitler Lust ergötzt,
After he himself with vain pleasure has-amused,
{After he has amused himself with vain pleasure,}

»Der Tod in Töpfen!« sagen.
" - Death (is) in (the) pots!" utter.
{Utter, "Poison is in the pot!"}

Die Folgezeit verändert viel!
The following-age changes many-things!

Hat Petrus gleich die ganze Nacht
Has Peter though the entire night

Mit leerer Arbeit zugebracht
In empty toil spent
{Though Peter has spent the entire night in empty toil}

Und nichts gefangen:
And nothing caught:

Auf Jesu Wort kann er noch einen Zug erlangen.
At Jesus' word can he yet a catch procure.

Drum traue nur in Armut, Kreuz und Pein
Therefore trust (then) amidst poverty, cross, and pain
{Therefore, just keep trusting despite poverty, cross, and pain}

Auf deines Jesu Güte
In thy Jesus' kindness

Mit gläubigem Gemüte.
With believing disposition.

Nach Regen gibt er Sonnenschein
After rain gives he sunshine
{After rain he gives sunshine}

Und setzet jeglichem sein Ziel.
And appoints for-everyone his final-end.

have mercy upon me..." But Abraham said, "Son, remember that you in your lifetime received your good things, and Lazarus in like manner evil things; but now he is comforted here, and you are in anguish." (Also Heb. 4:9.)

Jms. 5:1, 3–5, 7–8. Come now, you rich, weep and howl for the miseries that are coming upon you...You have laid up treasure for the last days. Behold, the wages of the laborers who mowed your fields, which you kept back by fraud, cry out; and the cries of the harvesters have reached the ears of the Lord of hosts. You have lived on the earth in luxury and in pleasure; you have fattened your hearts in a day of slaughter... Be patient, therefore, brethren, until the coming of the Lord. Behold, the farmer waits for the precious fruit of the earth, being patient over it until it receives the early and the late rain. You also be patient. Establish your hearts, for the coming of the Lord is at hand.

Mk. 10:31 [Christ]: But many that are first will be last, and the last first.

Prov. 14:12. There is a way which seems right to a man, but its end is the way to death. (Also Prov. 16:25.)

2 Kings 4:38–40. Elisha came...to Gilgal when there was a famine in the land. And as the sons of the prophets were sitting before him, he said to his servant, "Set on the great pot, and boil pottage for the sons of the prophets." One of them went out into the field to gather herbs, and found a wild vine and gathered from it his lap full of wild gourds, and came and cut them up into the pot of pottage, not knowing what they were. And they poured out for the men to eat. But while they were eating of the pottage, they cried out, "O man of God, there is death in the pot!" And they could not eat it.

Prov. 12:28. In the path of righteousness is life, but the way of error leads to death.

Jms. 5:7. Be patient, therefore, brethren, until the coming of the Lord...

*Lk. 5:4–9. ...[Jesus] said to Simon, "Put out into the deep and let down your nets for a catch." And Simon answered, "Master, we toiled all night and took nothing! But at your word I will let down the nets." And when they had done this, they enclosed a great shoal of fish; and as their nets were breaking, they beckoned to their partners in the other boat to come and help them. And they came and filled both the boats, so that they began to sink. But when Simon Peter saw it, he fell down at Jesus' knees, saying, "Depart from me, for I am a sinful man, O Lord." For he was astonished, and all that were with him, at the catch of fish which they had taken.

Prov. 3:5. Trust in the Lord with all your heart, and do not rely on your own insight.

Ps. 30:5. ...Weeping may tarry for the night, but joy comes with the morning. (Also Ps. 126:5–6.)

Jer. 31:13 [God]: ...I will turn their mourning into joy, I will comfort them, and give them gladness for sorrow.

Job 14:5. [Man's] days are determined, and the number of his months is with thee, and thou hast appointed his bounds (Luther: du hast ein Ziel gesetzt) that he cannot pass...

Ps. 31:14–15. But I trust in thee, O Lord, I say, "Thou art my God." My times are in thy hand...

Ps. 73:24. [O Lord,] thou dost guide me with thy counsel, and afterward thou wilt receive me to glory.

6. Soprano Aria (Based on Chorale Vs. 6)
●Trusting God who exalts the poor & humbles the rich (93–6)
Ich will auf den Herren schaun
I will to the Lord look
{I will look to the Lord}

Und stets meinem Gott vertraun.
And constantly my God trust.
{And constantly trust my God.}

Er ist der rechte Wundermann.
He is the true man-of-miracles.

Der die Reichen arm und bloß
He-is-the-one-who the rich-ones poor and bare

Und die Armen reich und groß
And the poor-ones rich and great

Nach seinem Willen machen kann.
According-to his will can-make.
{He is the one who—as he wills—can make the rich poor and bare;
the poor rich and great.}

7. Chorale (Vs. 7) (See also 88–7.)
●Blessing for those who faithfully walk in God's ways (93–7)
Sing, bet und geh auf Gottes Wegen,
Sing, pray, and walk in God's ways,

Verricht das Deine nur getreu
Perform (what is) thine only faithfully
{Just perform thine own tasks faithfully}

Und trau des Himmels reichem Segen,
And trust - heaven's rich blessing,

So wird er bei dir werden neu;
Then will it by thee become new;
{Then his blessing will be renewed with thee;}

Denn welcher seine Zuversicht
For whoever his confidence
{For whoever places his confidence}

Auf Gott setzt, den verläßt er nicht.
(In) God places, him forsakes he not.
{In God, is never forsaken by him.}

Mic. 7:7. But as for me, I will look to the Lord, I will wait for the God of my salvation; my God will hear me.

Ps. 17:6–7. I call upon thee, for thou wilt answer me, O God; incline thy ear to me, hear my words. Wondrously show thy steadfast love, O savior of those who seek refuge from their adversaries at thy right hand.

Ps. 118:8–9. It is better to take refuge in the Lord than to put confidence in man. It is better to take refuge in the Lord than to put confidence in princes.

Lk. 1:51–53. He has shown strength with his arm, he has scattered the proud in the imagination of their hearts. He has put down the mighty from their thrones, and exalted those of low degree; he has filled the hungry with good things, and the rich he has sent empty away.

Ps. 107:9. He satisfies him who is thirsty, and the hungry he fills with good things.

1 Sam. 2:7–8. The Lord makes poor and makes rich; he brings low, he also exalts. He raises up the poor from the dust; he lifts the needy from the ash heap, to make them sit with princes and inherit a seat of honor... (Also Ps. 113:7–8.)

Mk. 10:31 [Christ]: Many that are first will be last, and the last first. (Also Mt. 19:30.)

Gal. 6:9. Let us not grow weary in well-doing, for in due season we shall reap, if we do not lose heart. (Rev. 2:3)

1 Pet. 4:19. Let those who suffer according to God's will do right and entrust their souls to a faithful Creator.

2 Tim. 4:5. ...Always be steady, endure suffering...fulfil your ministry.

1 Cor. 4:1–2. This is how one should regard us, as servants of Christ and stewards of the mysteries of God. Moreover it is required of stewards that they be found trustworthy.

Rev. 2:10 [Christ]: ...Be faithful unto death (Luther: sei getreu bis an den Tod)...

Deut. 28:12. The Lord will open to you his good treasury the heavens, to give the rain of your land in its season and to bless all the work of your hands...

Ps. 84:11. For the Lord God...bestows favor and honor. No good thing does the Lord withhold from those who walk uprightly. (Also Jms. 1:17.)

Lam. 3:22–23. The steadfast love of the Lord never ceases, his mercies never come to an end; they are new every morning; great is thy faithfulness. (Also Ps. 90:14, 92:2.)

Ps. 9:10. And those who know thy name put their trust in thee, for thou, O Lord, hast not forsaken those who seek thee. (Also Ps. 25:2, 146:3–5.)

Deut. 31:8. It is the Lord who goes before you; he will be with you, he will not fail you or forsake you; do not fear or be dismayed. (Also Deut. 31:6, Josh. 1:7, 9, Heb. 13:5.)

BWV 94
Was frag ich nach der Welt
(NBA I/19; BC A115)

9. S. after Trinity (BWV 105, 94, 168)
*1 Cor. 10:6–13 (Consider and avoid the sins of the Israelites in the wilderness)
*Lk. 16:1–9 (Parable of the dishonest steward)
Librettist: Unknown

1. Chorus (Chorale Vs. 1) (See also 64–4.)
●World and its treasures rejected in favor of Christ (94–1)
Was frag ich nach der Welt
What (care) I   for   the world
{What do I care for the world}

Und allen ihren Schätzen,
And   all   its   treasures,

Wenn ich mich nur an dir,
If   I   myself only in thee,

Mein Jesu, kann ergötzen!
My   Jesus, can   delight!
{If I can only delight myself in thee, O my Jesus!}

Dich hab ich einzig   mir
Thee have I   alone before-me

Zur   Wollust vorgestellt,
For (my) pleasure   placed,
{I have chosen thee alone for my pleasure,}

Du,   du bist meine Ruh:
Thou, thou art   my   rest;

Was frag ich nach der Welt!
What (care) I   for   the world!
{What do I care for the world!}

2. Bass Aria (Based on Chorale Vs. 2)
●World passes away but Christ remains my confidence (94–2)
Die Welt ist wie ein Rauch und Schatten,
The world is like - smoke and shadow,

Der   bald verschwindet und vergeht,
Which soon   vanishes   and passes-away,

Weil sie nur   kurze Zeit besteht.
Because it only (a) short time endures.
{Because it only lasts a short time.}

Wenn aber   alles   fällt und bricht,
When, however, everything collapses and breaks,

Bleibt Jesus meine Zuversicht,
Remains Jesus my   confidence,
{Then Jesus remains my confidence,}

1 Jn. 2:15–17. Do not love the world or the things in the world. If any one loves the world, love for the Father is not in him. For all that is in the world, the lust of the flesh and the lust of the eyes and the pride of life, is not of the Father but is of the world. And the world passes away, and the lust of it; but he who does the will of God abides for ever. (Also Jms. 4:4.)
Col. 3:1–3. If then you have been raised with Christ, seek the things that are above, where Christ is, seated at the right hand of God. Set your minds on things that are above, not on things that are on earth. For you have died and your life is hid with Christ in God.
2 Cor. 4:18. We look not to the things that are seen but to the things that are unseen; for the things that are seen are transient, but the things that are unseen are eternal.
***1 Cor. 10:7.** Do not be idolaters as some of [the Israelites] were; as it is written, "The people sat down to eat and drink and rose up to dance."
Mt. 4:10. Then Jesus said to [Satan], "Begone, Satan! for it is written, 'You shall worship the Lord your God and him only shall you serve.'" (Also Lk. 4:8, Deut. 6:13–14.)
Ps. 73:25–26. [O Lord,] whom have I in heaven but thee? (Luther: Wenn ich nur dich habe...) And there is nothing upon earth that I desire besides thee. My flesh and my heart may fail, but God is the strength of my heart and my portion for ever.
Ps. 94:19. When the cares of my heart are many, thy consolations cheer (Luther: ergötzen) my soul.
Mt. 11:28–30 [Christ]: Come to me, all who labor and are heavy laden, and I will give you rest. Take my yoke upon you, and learn from me; for I am gentle and lowly in heart, and you will find rest for your souls. For my yoke is easy, and my burden is light.

Is. 51:6. Lift up your eyes to the heavens, and look at the earth beneath; for the heavens will vanish like smoke, the earth will wear out like a garment, and they who dwell in it will die like gnats; but my salvation will be for ever, and my deliverance will never be ended. (Also Ps. 102:3, 11.)
1 Jn. 2:17. The world passes away, and the lust of it; but he who does the will of God abides for ever.
Jms. 4:14, 5:1. ...What is your life? For you are a mist that appears for a little time and then vanishes...Come now, you rich, weep and howl for the miseries that are coming upon you... (Also Jms. 1:10–11.)
Mt. 24:35 [Christ]: Heaven and earth will pass away, but my words will not pass away. (Also Mk. 13:31, Lk. 21:33.)
Ps. 46:1–3. God is our refuge (Luther: Zuversicht) and strength, a very present help in trouble. Therefore we will not fear though the earth should change, though the mountains shake in the heart of the sea; though its waters roar and foam, though the mountains tremble with its tumult.

An dem sich meine Seele hält.
To whom - my soul clings.
{To him my soul clings.}

Darum: was frag ich nach der Welt!
Therefore: What (care) I for the world!
{Therefore: What do I care for the world!}

3. Tenor: Recit. & Chorale (Vs. 3)
●Worldly success is temporal; I choose Jesus (94–3)
Die Welt sucht Ehr und Ruhm
The world seeks honor and fame

Bei hocherhabnen Leuten.
From highly-prominent people.

Ein Stolzer baut die prächtigsten Paläste,
(The) proud-man builds the most-magnificent palaces,

Er sucht das höchste Ehrenamt,
He seeks the highest office-of-honor,

Er kleidet sich aufs beste
He clothes himself in-the best-way-possible

In Purpur, Gold, in Silber, Seid und Samt.
In purple, gold, in silver, silk, and velvet.

Sein Name soll vor allen
His name must before all

In jedem Teil der Welt erschallen.
In every part of-the world resound.

Sein Hochmuts-Turm
His tower-of-pride

Soll durch die Luft bis an die Wolken dringen,
Must through the air to - the clouds press,
{Must press through the air to the clouds,}

Er trachtet nur nach hohen Dingen
He seeks only after lofty things

Und denkt nicht einmal dran,
And thinks not once on-this,

Wie bald doch diese gleiten.
How quickly indeed these slip-away.

Oft bläset eine schale Luft
Oft blows a vapid breeze
{Oft a vapid breeze blows}

Den stolzen Leib auf einmal in die Gruft,
The proud body suddenly into the tomb,

Und da verschwindet alle Pracht,
And then vanishes all (the) pomp,

Ps. 63:8. [O Lord], my soul clings to thee (Luther: hanget dir an)... (Also Deut. 10:20, 13:4, 2 Kings 18:6.)
***Lk. 16:9, 13 [Christ]:** I tell you, make friends for yourselves by means of unrighteous mammon, so that when it fails they may receive you into the eternal habitations...No servant can serve two masters; for either he will hate the one and love the other, or he will be devoted to the one and despise the other. You cannot serve God and mammon.

Lk. 7:24–25. ...[Jesus] began to speak to the crowds concerning John [the Baptist], "...What then did you go out to see? A man clothed in soft clothing? Behold, those who are gorgeously appareled and live in luxury are in kings' courts."
Prov. 14:20. The poor is disliked even by his neighbor, but the rich has many friends. (Also Prov. 19:6–7.)
Lk. 16:19–25. There was a rich man, who was clothed in purple and fine linen and who feasted sumptuously every day. And at his gate lay a poor man named Lazarus, full of sores, who desired to be fed with what fell from the rich man's table; moreover the dogs came and licked his sores. The poor man died and was carried by the angels to Abraham's bosom. The rich man also died and was buried; and in Hades, being in torment, he lifted up his eyes, and saw Abraham far off and Lazarus in his bosom. And he called out, "Father Abraham, have mercy upon me, and send Lazarus to dip the end of his finger in water and cool my tongue; for I am in anguish in this flame." But Abraham said, "Son, remember that you in your lifetime received your good things, and Lazarus in like manner evil things; but now he is comforted here, and you are in anguish." (Also Heb. 4:9.)
Prov. 30:13. There are those—how lofty are their eyes, how high their eyelids lift!
Gen. 11:4–9. Then [the men of the earth] said, "Come, let us build ourselves a city, and a tower with its top in the heavens, and let us make a name for ourselves, lest we be scattered abroad upon the face of the whole earth." And the Lord came down to see the city and the tower, which the sons of men had built. And the Lord said, "Behold, they are one people, and they have all one language; and this is only the beginning of what they will do; and nothing that they propose to do will now be impossible for them. Come, let us go down, and there confuse their language, that they may not understand one another's speech." So the Lord scattered them abroad from there over the face of all the earth, and they left off building the city. Therefore its name was called Babel, because there the Lord scattered them abroad over the face of all the earth.
Lk. 12:15–21. [Jesus] said to [his disciples], "Take heed, and beware of all covetousness; for a man's life does not consist in the abundance of his possessions." And he told them a parable, saying, "The land of a rich man brought forth plentifully; and he thought to himself, 'What shall I do, for I have nowhere to store my crops?' And he said, 'I will do this: I will pull down my barns, and build larger ones; and there I will store all my grain and my goods, And I will say to my soul, Soul, you have ample goods laid up for many years; take your ease, eat, drink and be merry,' But God said to him, 'Fool! This night your soul is required of you; and the things you have prepared, whose will they be?' So is he who lays up treasure for himself, and is not rich toward God."

Wormit   der arme Erdenwurm
Of-which that poor earthly-worm

Hier in der Welt so großen Staat gemacht.
Here in the world such great display did-make.

Ach! solcher   eitler   Tand
Ah!   such (a) frivolous bauble

Wird weit   von mir aus meiner Brust verbannt.
Is   far (away) from me out-of my breast banned.
{Is banned far from my breast.}

Dies aber, was mein Herz
This, however, which my   heart

Vor anderm   rühmlich   hält,
Above all-else as-praiseworthy holds,

Was   Christen wahren Ruhm und wahre Ehre gibet,
Which to-Christians true   glory and true honor accords,

Und was mein Geist,
And which my spirit—

Der   sich der Eitelkeit entreißt,
Which itself from vanity rescues—
{Rescuing itself from vanity—}

Anstatt der Pracht und Hoffart liebet,
Instead of pomp and pride does-love,

Ist Jesus nur allein,
Is Jesus only alone,

Und dieser soll's auch ewig sein.
And this-one shall-it also ever be.
{And he shall also remain it throughout eternity.}

Gesetzt, daß mich die Welt
Granted, that me the world

Darum für töricht hält:
For-this as foolish considers:
{Granted that the world considers me foolish for this:}

Was frag ich nach der Welt!
What (care) I   for   the world!
{What do I care for the world!}

4. Alto Aria (Based on Chorale Vs. 4)
●World deluded by Mammon; Jesus is true wealth (94-4)
Betörte Welt, betörte Welt!
Deluded world, deluded world!

Auch dein Reichtum, Gut und Geld
Even your riches, wealth, and money

Ist Betrug und falscher Schein.
Is deception and false   pretence.

Mk. 8:36–37 [Christ]: What does it profit a man, to gain the whole world and forfeit his life? For what can a man give in return for his life? (Also Mt. 16:26, Lk. 9:25.)
Job 25:6. ...The son of man...is a worm! (Also Ps. 22:6.)
Ps. 49:16–20. Be not afraid when one becomes rich, when the glory of his house increases. For when he dies he will carry nothing away; his glory will not go down after him...Though a man gets praise when he does well for himself, he will go to the generation of his fathers, who will never more see the light. Man cannot abide in his pomp, he is like the beasts that perish. (Also Ps. 52:7, 62:9–11, 89:48, 146:4.)
Job 17:13–16. If I look for Sheol as my house, if I spread my couch in darkness, if I say to the pit, "You are my father," and to the worm, "My mother," or "My sister," where then is my hope? Who will see my hope? Will it go down to the bars of Sheol? Shall we descend together into the dust?
1 Pet. 5:5–6. ...God opposes the proud, but gives grace to the humble. Humble yourselves therefore under the mighty hand of God, that in due time he may exalt you. (Also Mt. 23:12, Prov. 29:23, Job 22:29, Ezek. 21:26, Lk. 18:14, Jms. 4:6, 10.)
Rom. 2:6–7. [God] will render to every man according to his works: to those who by patience in well-doing seek for glory and honor and immortality, he will give eternal life.
Phil. 3:7–9. Whatever gain I had, I counted as loss for the sake of Christ. Indeed I count everything as loss because of the surpassing worth of knowing Christ Jesus my Lord. For his sake I have suffered the loss of all things, and count them as refuse, in order that I may gain Christ and be found in him...
Ps. 73:25. [O Lord,] whom have I in heaven but thee? And there is nothing upon earth that I desire besides thee.
1 Cor. 1:26–28. Consider your call, brethren; not many of you were wise according to worldly standards, not many were powerful, not many were of noble birth; but God chose what is foolish in the world to shame the wise, God chose what is weak...to shame the strong, God chose what is low and despised in the world, even things that are not, to bring to nothing things that are.
1 Cor. 4:10. We are fools for Christ's sake, but you are wise in Christ. We are weak, but you are strong. You are held in honor, but we in disrepute. (Also 1 Cor. 1:18, Acts 17:18.)
1 Cor. 3:18–19, 21. Let no one deceive himself. If any one among you thinks that he is wise in this age, let him become a fool that he may become wise. For the wisdom of this world is folly with God...So let no one boast of men...
Jms. 4:4. ...Whoever wishes to be a friend of the world makes himself an enemy of God.
1 Jn. 2:17. The world passes away, and the lust of it; but he who does the will of God abides for ever.

1 Tim. 6:10. The love of money is the root of all evils; it is through this craving that some have wandered away from the faith and pierced their hearts with many pangs.
Lk. 12:15–21. And [Jesus] said to them, "Take heed, and beware of all covetousness; for a man's life does not consist in the abundance of his possessions." And he told them a parable, saying, "The land of a rich man brought forth plentifully; and he thought to himself, 'What shall I do, for I have nowhere to store my crops?' And he said, 'I will do this: I will pull down my barns, and build larger ones; and there I will store all my grain and my goods, And I will say to my soul, Soul, you

Du magst den eitlen Mammon zählen,
You may - vain mammon count,

Ich will dafür mir Jesum wählen;
I will instead for-myself Jesus choose;
{I will instead choose Jesus for myself;}

Jesus, Jesus soll allein
Jesus, Jesus shall alone

Meiner Seelen Reichtum sein.
My soul's wealth be.

Betörte Welt, betörte Welt!
Deluded world, deluded world!

5. Bass: Recit. & Chorale (Vs. 5)
●World's ridicule accepted for sake of heaven's honor (94-5)
Die Welt bekümmert sich.
The world is-troubled.

Was muß doch wohl der Kummer sein?
What (can) indeed (its) care be?

O Torheit! dieses macht ihr Pein:
O folly! This gives it torment:
{O folly! This is what torments it:}

Im Fall sie wird verachtet.
In case it be scorned.

Welt schäme dich!
World be-ashamed!

Gott hat dich ja so sehr geliebet,
God hath thee indeed so greatly loved,
{God hath indeed so greatly loved thee,}

Daß er sein eingebor nes Kind
That he his only-begotten child

Für deine Sünd
For thy sin

Zur größten Schmach um deine Ehre gibet,
To (the) greatest disgrace for thy honor doth-give,
{That he delivered up his only Son to the greatest disgrace for thy honor,}

Und du willst nicht um Jesu willen leiden?
And thou wouldst not for Jesus' sake suffer?

Die Traurigkeit der Welt is niemals größer,
The sadness of-the world is never [seen to be] greater,

Als wenn man ihr mit List
Than when one - with artifice

have ample goods laid up for many years; take your ease, eat, drink and be merry,' But God said to him, 'Fool! This night your soul is required of you; and the things you have prepared, whose will they be?' So is he who lays up treasure for himself, and is not rich toward God."
*Lk. 16:9, 13 [Christ]: I tell you, make friends for yourselves by means of unrighteous mammon, so that when it fails they may receive you into the eternal habitations...No servant can serve two masters; for either he will hate the one and love the other, or he will be devoted to the one and despise the other. You cannot serve God and mammon.
Mt. 19:29-30 [Christ]: And everyone who has left houses or brothers or sisters or father or mother or children or lands, for my name's sake, will receive a hundredfold, and inherit eternal life. But many that are first will be last, and the last first. (Also Mk. 10:29-31, Lk. 18:29-30.)

Jn. 5:44 [Christ]: How can you believe, who receive glory from one another and do not seek the glory that comes from the only God?
1 Cor. 3:21. ...Let no one boast of men...
*Lk. 16:3-4. The steward said to himself, "What shall I do, since my master is taking the stewardship away from me? I am not strong enough to dig, and I am ashamed to beg (Luther: so schäme ich mich zu betteln). I have decided what to do, so that people may receive me into their houses (Luther: mich in ihre Häuser nehmen) when I am put out of the stewardship."
Jn. 12:42-43. ...Many even of the authorities believed in [Jesus], but for fear of the Pharisees they did not confess it, lest they should be put out of the synagogue: for they loved the praise of men more than the praise of God.
Jms. 4:4. Unfaithful creatures! Do you not know that friendship with the world is enmity with God? Therefore whoever wishes to be a friend of the world makes himself an enemy of God. (Also 1 Jn. 2:15-17.)
Jn. 3:16. God so loved the world that he gave his only Son, that whoever believes in him should not perish but have eternal life.
1 Jn. 4:9-10. In this the love of God was made manifest among us, that God sent his only Son into the world, so that we might live through him. In this is love, not that we loved God but that he loved us and sent his Son to be the expiation for our sins.
2 Cor. 8:9. You know the grace of our Lord Jesus Christ, that though he was rich, yet for your sake he became poor, so that by his poverty you might become rich. (Also Eph. 2:7, 3:16, Col. 1:27, 2:2-3.)
Is. 53:3-7, 10. He was despised and rejected by men; a man of sorrows, and acquainted with grief; and as one from whom men hide their faces he was despised, and we esteemed him not. Surely he has borne our griefs and carried our sorrows; yet we esteemed him stricken, smitten by God, and afflicted. But he was wounded for our transgressions, he was bruised for our iniquities; upon him was the chastisement that made us whole, and with his stripes we are healed... The Lord has laid on him the iniquity of us all. He was oppressed, and he was afflicted, yet he opened not his mouth; like a lamb that is led to the slaughter, and like a sheep that before its shearers is dumb, so he opened not his mouth...Yet it was the will of the Lord to bruise him; he has put him to grief; when he makes himself an offering for sin... (Also 1 Pet. 2:24.)

Nach ihren   Ehren trachtet.
After   its (worldly) honors strives.
{Than when one strives with artifice for its worldly honors.}

Es ist   ja   besser,
It   is indeed better (that)

Ich trage Christi Schmach,
I   carry Christ's disgrace,

Solang   es ihm gefällt.
For-as-long-as it him pleases.
{For as long as it may please him.}

Es ist   ja   nur ein Leiden dieser Zeit,
It   is, after-all, only a suffering of-this age,

Ich weiß gewiß,   daß mich die Ewigkeit
I   know assuredly, that me - eternity
{I know assuredly that eternity will}

Dafür   mit Preis und Ehren krönet;
For-this with praise and honor will-crown;
{Crown me for this with praise and honor;}

Ob   mich die Welt
Though me the world

Verspottet und verhönet,
Ridicule   and deride,
{Though the world ridicule and deride me}

Ob   sie mich gleich verächtlich   hält,
Though it me   - contemptuously (treat),
{Though it treat me contemptuously,}

Wenn mich mein Jesus ehrt:
If   me   my Jesus honors:
{If my Jesus honors me:}

Was frag ich nach der Welt!
What (care) I for the world!
{What do I care for the world!}

6. Tenor Aria (Based on Chorale Vs. 6)
●Worldly pleasures are empty illusions (94–6)
Die Welt kann ihre Lust und Freud,
The world can its pleasure and joy—

Das Blendwerk schnöder Eitelkeit,
That optical-illusion of-base conceit—

Nicht hoch genug erhöhen.
Not highly enough (praise).

Sie wühlt, nur gelben Kot zu finden,
It   digs, only yellow mud to find,

1 Pet. 2:21. To this you have been called, because Christ also suffered for you, leaving you an example, that you should follow in his steps.
1 Pet. 4:1–2. Since therefore Christ suffered in the flesh, arm yourselves with the same thought, for whoever has suffered in the flesh has ceased from sin, so as to live for the rest of the time in the flesh no longer by human passions but by the will of God.
1 Pet. 4:13–14, 16. Rejoice in so far as you share Christ's sufferings, that you may also rejoice and be glad when his glory is revealed. If you are reproached for the name of Christ, you are blessed, because the spirit of glory and of God rests upon you...If one suffers as a Christian, let him not be ashamed, but under that name let him glorify God.
Rom. 8:18. I consider that the sufferings of this present time are not worth comparing with the glory that is to be revealed to us. (Also 2 Cor. 4:17.)
1 Pet. 4:19, 5:4. Therefore let those who suffer according to God's will do right and entrust their souls to a faithful
Creator...And when the chief Shepherd is manifested you will obtain the unfading crown of glory. (Also Jms. 1:12.)
Lk. 6:20–26 [Christ]: Blessed are you poor, for yours is the kingdom of God. Blessed are you that hunger now, for you shall be satisfied. Blessed are you that weep now, for you shall laugh. Blessed are you when men hate you, and when they exclude you and revile you, and cast out your name as evil, on account of the Son of man! Rejoice in that day, and leap for joy, for behold, your reward is great in heaven; for so their fathers did to the prophets. But woe to you that are rich, for you have received your consolation. Woe to you that are full now, for you shall hunger. Woe to you that laugh now, for you shall mourn and weep. Woe to you, when all men speak well of you, for so their fathers did to the false prophets. (Also Mt. 5:11–12.)
2 Tim. 2:11–12. The saying is sure: If we have died with him, we shall also live with him; if we endure, we shall also reign with him; if we deny him, he also will deny us.
Rev. 3:4–5 [Christ]: ...They shall walk with me in white, for they are worthy. He who conquers shall be clad thus in white garments...[and] I will confess his name before my Father and before his angels. (Also Jn. 12:26.)
1 Jn. 2:17. The world passes away, and the lust of it; but he who does the will of God abides for ever.

Ecc. 1:14. I have seen everything that is done under the sun; and behold, all is vanity and a striving after wind. (Also Ecc. 1:2, 2:17.)
Eph. 4:17–18. ...You must no longer live as the Gentiles do, in the futility (Luther: Eitelkeit) of their minds; they are darkened in their understanding, alienated from the life of God because of the ignorance that is in them, due to their hardness of heart.
Phil. 3:19. Their end is destruction, their god is the belly, and they glory in their shame, with minds set on earthly things.
Rom. 8:5–6. Those who live according to the flesh set their minds on the things of the flesh, but those who live according to the Spirit set their minds on the things of the Spirit. To set the mind on the flesh

Gleich einem Maulwurf in den Gründen
Like   a   mole   in the bottoms

Und läßt dafür den Himmel stehen.
And leaves for-that - heaven stand (unheeded).
{And for that leaves heaven stand unheeded.}

7. Soprano Aria (Based on Chorale Vs. 6)
●World rejected as loathsome; true riches in Jesus (94-7)
Es   halt es mit der blinden Welt,
(Now) (let him) hold - to the blind world,

Wer nichts auf seine Seele hält,
Who nothing for his soul (does-care),

Mir ekelt vor der Erden.
(I) find-loathsome the earth.
{The earth is loathsome to me.}

Ich will nur meinen Jesum lieben
I   will only   my   Jesus love
{I will love my Jesus alone}

Und mich in Buß und Glauben üben,
And myself in repentance and faith exercise,
{And exercise myself in repentance and faith,}

So kann ich reich und selig werden.
Thus can I wealthy and blessed become.
{Thus can I become truly wealthy and blessed.}

8. Chorale (Vss. 7 & 8)
●World rejected for pleasure of having Jesus (94-8)
Was frag ich nach der Welt!
What (care) I for the world!

Im Hui muß sie verschwinden,
In-a trice must it vanish,

Ihr Ansehn kann durchaus
Its eminence can certainly

Den blassen Tod nicht binden.
-   Pale death not bind.
{Pale death will certainly not be bound by its eminence.}

Die Güter müssen fort,
(All) possessions must be-put-away,

Und alle Lust verfällt;
And all pleasure decline;

Bleibt Jesus nur bei mir:
Remains Jesus only with me:
{If only Jesus remains with me:}

is death, but to set the mind on the Spirit is life and peace.
Col. 3:1–3. If then you have been raised with Christ, seek the things that are above, where Christ is, seated at the right hand of God. Set your minds on things that are above, not on things that are on earth. For you have died and your life is hid with Christ in God.

Jms. 4:4. Unfaithful creatures! Do you not know that friendship with the world is enmity with God? Therefore whoever wishes to be a friend of the world makes himself an enemy of God.
1 Jn. 2:15–17. Do not love the world or the things in the world. If any one loves the world, love for the Father is not in him. For all that is in the world, the lust of the flesh and the lust of the eyes and the pride of life, is not of the Father but is of the world. And the world passes away, and the lust of it; but he who does the will of God abides for ever.
Ps. 73:25. [O Lord,] whom have I in heaven but thee? And there is nothing upon earth that I desire besides thee.
Col. 1:27. ...God chose to make known how great...are the riches of the glory of this mystery, which is Christ in you, the hope of glory. (Also Eph. 2:7.)
2 Cor. 8:9. You know the grace of our Lord Jesus Christ, that though he was rich, yet for your sake he became poor, so that by his poverty you might become rich.
1 Cor. 1:5. In every way you were enriched in [Christ]...
Mt. 16:24–25. Jesus told his disciples, "If any man would come after me, let him deny himself and take up his cross and follow me. For whoever would save his life will lose it, and whoever loses his life for my sake will find it." (Also Mk. 8:34–35, Lk. 9:23–24; Mt. 10:38, 19:29–30.)

1 Jn. 2:15–17. Do not love the world or the things in the world. If any one loves the world, love for the Father is not in him. For all that is in the world, the lust of the flesh and the lust of the eyes and the pride of life, is not of the Father but is of the world. And the world passes away, and the lust of it...
Ps. 49:16–20. Be not afraid when one becomes rich, when the glory of his house increases. For when he dies he will carry nothing away; his glory will not go down after him...Though a man gets praise when he does well for himself, he will go to the generation of his fathers, who will never more see the light. Man cannot abide in his pomp, he is like the beasts that perish. (Also Ps. 52:7, 62:9–11.)
Ps. 89:48. What man can live and never see death?...
Ps. 146:3–4. Put not your trust in princes, in a son of man, in whom there is no help. When his breath departs he returns to his earth; on that very day his plans perish.
Ecc. 5:15. As he came from his mother's womb he shall go again, naked as he came, and shall take nothing for his toil, which he may carry away in his hand. (Also Job 1:21.)
1 Tim. 6:7. We brought nothing into the world, and we cannot take anything out of the world.
Ps. 73:25–26. [O Lord,] whom have I in heaven but thee? And there is nothing upon earth that I desire besides thee. My flesh and my heart may fail, but God is the strength of my heart and my portion for ever.
Mt. 24:35. Heaven and earth will pass away, but my words will not pass away. (Also Mk. 13:31, Lk. 21:33, Is. 40:8.)

Was frag ich nach der Welt!
What (care) I   for the world!
{What do I care for the world!}

///

Was frag ich nach der Welt!
What (care) I   for   the world!
{What do I care for the world!}

Mein Jesus ist mein Leben,
My   Jesus is my   life,

Mein Schatz, mein Eigentum,
My   treasure, my   possession,

Dem   ich mich   ganz   ergeben,
To-whom I myself completely have-surrendered,
{To whom I have completely surrendered myself;}

Mein ganzes   Himmelreich,
(He is) my   entire kingdom-of-heaven,

Und   was   mir sonst gefällt.
And whatever me otherwise pleases.
{And whatever else pleases me.}

Drum   sag ich noch einmal:
Therefore say I   yet once-more:

Was frag ich nach der Welt!
What (care) I   for   the world!
{What do I care for the world!}

BWV 95
Christus, der ist mein Leben
(NBA I/23; BC A136)

16. S. after Trinity (BWV 161, 95, 8, 27)
*Eph. 3:13-21 (Paul's prayer for the Ephesians; that they be spiritually strengthened)
*Lk. 7:11-17 (Resurrection of boy at Nain)
Librettist: Unknown

1. Chorus (Chorales) & Tenor Recit. (Chorales: see also 106-3b, 125-1)
●Yearning for death: Christ is my life, death is gain (95-1)
Chorale:
Christus, der ist mein Leben,
Christ,   he   is   my   life,

Sterben ist mein Gewinn;
Dying   is   my   gain;

Dem   tu ich mich ergeben,
To-him do I myself surrender,
{To him do I surrender myself,}

Mt. 28:20 [Christ]: ...Lo, I am with you always, to the close of the age. (Also Ps. 48:14.)

Jms. 4:4. Unfaithful creatures! Do you not know that friendship with the world is enmity with God? Therefore whoever wishes to be a friend of the world makes himself an enemy of God.
Lk. 16:13. No servant can serve two masters; for either he will hate the one and love the other, or he will be devoted to the one and despise the other. You cannot serve God and mammon. (Also Mt. 6:24.)
Mt. 22:37-38. And [Jesus] said to [the man], "You shall love the Lord your God with all your heart, and with all your soul, and with all your mind. This is the great and first commandment."
Phil. 1:21. To me to live is Christ (Luther: Denn Christus ist mein Leben), and to die is gain.
Mt. 13:44-46. The kingdom of heaven (Luther: Himmelreich) is like treasure (Luther: Schatz) hidden in a field, which a man found and covered up; then in his joy he goes and sells all that he has and buys that field. Again, the kingdom of heaven is like a merchant in search of fine pearls, who, on finding one pearl of great value, went and sold all that he had and bought it.
Ps. 73:25-26. [O Lord,] whom have I in heaven but thee? And there is nothing upon earth that I desire besides thee...God is the strength of my heart and my portion for ever.
1 Jn. 2:15. Do not love the world or the things in the world. If any one loves the world, love for the Father is not in him.
Jms. 1:27. Religion that is pure and undefiled before God and the Father is this: ...to keep oneself unstained from the world.

*Lk. 7:11-12, 14. Soon afterward [Jesus] went to a city called Nain, and his disciples and a great crowd went with him. As he drew near to the gate of the city, behold, a man who had died was being carried out, the only son of his mother, and she was a widow; and a large crowd from the city was with her...And [Jesus] came and touched the bier...and he said, "Young man, I say to you, arise."
Phil. 1:21. *To me to live is Christ* (Luther: Denn Christus ist mein Leben), and *to die is gain* (Luther: und sterben ist mein Gewinn).
Jn. 17:3. This is eternal life, that they know thee the only true God, and Jesus Christ whom thou hast sent.

Mit Freud fahr ich dahin.
With   joy   depart   I   thither.

Tenor Recit:
Mit Freuden,
Mith   joy,

Ja   mit   Herzenslust
Yes, with delight-of-heart

Will ich von hinnen scheiden.
Will   I   from hence   depart.

Und   hieß es   heute noch: Du mußt!
And if-it-were-commanded today   yet: You must!

So   bin ich willig und   bereit,
Then am I   willing and prepared,
{Then I am willing and prepared to bring}

Den armen Leib, die abgezehrten Glieder,
(My) poor body, (my)   wasted   members,

Das Kleid der Sterblichkeit
This garb of   mortality

Der   Erde wieder
To-the earth back
{Back to the earth}

In   ihren Schoß zu bringen.
Into its   bosom to   bring.
{Into its bosom.}

Mein Sterbelied ist schon gemacht;
My   funeral-song is already   made;

Ach, dürft ich's heute   singen!
Ah, might I-it today (yet) sing!
{Ah, might I sing it yet today!}

Chorale:
Mit   Fried und Freud ich fahr dahin,
With peace and   joy   I   depart thither,

Nach   Gottes Willen,
According-to God's   will,

Getrost   ist mir mein Herz und   Sinn,
Consoled is   -   my heart and disposition,

Sanft und stille.
Placid and still.

Wie Gott mir verheißen hat:
As   God me   promised has:
{As God promised me:}

Der Tod ist mein Schlaf worden.
- Death has   my   sleep become.
{Death has become sleep for me.}

Col. 3:4. When Christ who is our life appears, then you also will appear with him in glory.

Phil. 2:23. My desire is to depart and be with Christ, for that is far better.

2 Cor. 5:6–9. So we are always of good courage; we know that while we are at home in the body we are away from the Lord, for we walk by faith, not by sight. We are of good courage, and we would rather be away from the body and at home with the Lord. So whether we are at home or away, we make it our aim to please him.

Heb. 9:27. ...It is appointed for men to die...

Sirach (Apocrypha) 14:17. All living beings become old like a garment, for the decree from of old is, "You must surely die!" (Luther: Du mußt sterben!)

2 Cor. 5:1–4. We know that if the earthly tent we live in is destroyed, we have a building from God, a house not made with hands, eternal in the heavens. Here indeed we groan, and long to put on our heavenly dwelling, so that by putting it on we may not be found naked. For while we are still in this tent, we sigh with anxiety; not that we would be unclothed, but that we would be further clothed, so that what is mortal may be swallowed up by life. (Also 2 Pet. 1:14.)

Rom. 7:24–25. Wretched man that I am! Who will deliver me from this body of death? Thanks be to God through Jesus Christ our Lord!...

1 Cor. 15:40, 42–44, 49–58. There are celestial bodies and there are terrestrial bodies; but the glory of the celestial is one, and the glory of the terrestrial is another...So it is with the resurrection of the dead. What is sown is perishable, what is raised is imperishable. It is sown in dishonor, it is raised in glory. It is sown in weakness, it is raised in power. It is sown a physical body, it is raised a spiritual body...Just as we have borne the image of the man of dust, we shall also bear the image of the man of heaven. I tell you this, brethren: flesh and blood cannot inherit the kingdom of God, nor does the perishable inherit the imperishable. Lo! I tell you a mystery. We shall not all sleep, but we shall all be changed, in a moment, in the twinkling of an eye, at the last trumpet. For the trumpet will sound, and the dead will be raised imperishable, and we shall be changed. For this perishable nature must put on the imperishable, and this mortal nature must put on immortality. When the perishable puts on the imperishable, and the mortal puts on immortality, then shall come to pass the saying that is written: "Death is swallowed up in victory." O death, where is thy victory? O death, where is thy sting? The sting of death is sin, and the power of sin is the law. But thanks be to God, who gives us the victory through our Lord Jesus Christ. Therefore, my beloved brethren, be steadfast, immovable, always abounding in the work of the Lord, knowing that in the Lord your labor is not in vain. (Also Heb. 2:14.)

Phil. 1:23. ...My desire is to depart and be with Christ, for that is far better.

Lk. 2:29. Lord, now lettest thou thy servant depart in peace, according to thy word.

Ps. 131:2. I have calmed and quieted my soul, like a child quieted at its mother's breast; like a child that is quieted is my soul.

Lk. 8:52–53. ...[Jesus] said, "Do not weep; for she is not dead but sleeping." And they laughed at him, knowing that she was dead.

2. Soprano Recit.
●Worldly pleasures deceitful; rejected for heaven (95-2)
Nun, falsche Welt!
Now, deceitful world!

Nun hab ich weiter nichts mit dir zu tun;
Now have I further nothing with thee to do;
{Now I have nothing further to do with thee;}

Mein Haus ist schon bestellt,
My house is already prepared,

Ich kann weit sanfter ruhn,
I can far-more softly rest (there),

Als da ich sonst bei dir,
Than (ever) I otherwise (did) with thee, (where)

An deines Babels Flüssen,
Beside thy Babel's streams,

Das Wollustsalz verschlucken müssen,
 - Debauchery's-salt to-swallow (I) was-forced,
{Debauchery's salt I had to swallow,}

Wenn ich an deinem Lustrevier
When I in thy pleasure-quarters

Nur Sodomsäpfel konnte brechen.
Only Sodom's-apples could (gather).

Nein, nein! nun kann ich mit gelaßnerm Mute sprechen:
No, no! Now can I with more-composed spirit say:

3. Chorale: Soprano
●World rejected & given farewell; heaven anticipated (95-3)
Valet will ich dir geben,
Farewell would I give-thee,

Du arge, falsche Welt,
Thou wicked, deceitful world,

Dein sündlich böses Leben
Thy sinful, evil life

Durchaus mir nicht gefällt.
Absolutely me not doth-please.
{Pleases me absolutely not.}

Im Himmel ist gut wohnen,
In heaven is fair dwelling,

Jms. 4:4. Unfaithful creatures! Do you not know that friendship with the world is enmity with God? Therefore whoever wishes to be a friend of the world makes himself an enemy of God. (Also 1 Jn. 2:15-17.)

Jn. 14:1-3 [Christ]: Let not your hearts be troubled; believe in God, believe also in me. In my Father's house are many rooms; if it were not so, would I have told you that I go to prepare a place for you? And when I go and prepare a place for you, I will come again and will take you to myself, that where I am you may be also.

Heb. 13:14. Here we have no lasting city, but we seek the city which is to come.

Ps. 137:1-3. By the waters of Babylon (Luther: Wassern zu Babel), there we sat down and wept, when we remembered Zion. On the willows there we hung up our lyres. For there our captors required of us songs...saying, "Sing us one of the songs of Zion!"

Acts 2:40. ...Save yourselves from this crooked generation.

2 Pet. 2:6, 9. If by turning the cities of Sodom and Gomorrah to ashes [God]...made them an example to those who were to be ungodly...then the Lord knows how to...keep the unrighteous under punishment until the day of judgment. (Also Jude 1:7.)

Gen. 19:24-26. The Lord rained on Sodom and Gomorrah brimstone and fire from the Lord out of heaven; and he overthrew those cities, and all the valley, and all the inhabitants of the cities, and what grew on the ground. But Lot's wife behind him looked back, and she became a pillar of salt.

Josephus IV:483-485. ...It is said that, owing to the impiety of its inhabitants, [Sodom] was consumed by thunderbolts; and in fact vestiges of the divine fire and faint traces of five cities are still visible. Still, too, may one see ashes reproduced in the fruits, which from their outward appearance would be thought edible, but on being plucked with the hand dissolve into smoke and ashes. [Translated by H. St. J. Thackeray. See also BWV 54-2, 179-3.]

Is. 57:20-21. The wicked are like the tossing sea; for it cannot rest, and its waters toss up mire and dirt. There is no peace...for the wicked. (Also Is. 48:22.)

Jn. 16:33 [Christ]: I have said this to you, that in me you may have peace. In the world you have tribulation; but be of good cheer, I have overcome the world. (Also 1 Jn. 2:13, 14; 4:4.)

1 Jn. 2:15-17. Do not love the world or the things in the world. If any one loves the world, love for the Father is not in him. For all that is in the world, the lust of the flesh and the lust of the eyes and the pride of life, is not of the Father but is of the world. And the world passes away, and the lust of it; but he who does the will of God abides for ever. (Also Jms. 4:4.)

Rev. 21:3-4. I heard a loud voice from the throne saying, "Behold, the dwelling of God is with men. He will dwell with them, and they shall be his people, and God himself will be with them; he will wipe away every tear from their eyes, and death shall be no more, neither shall there be mourning nor crying nor pain any more, for the former things have passed away." (Also Is. 25:8.)

Jn. 12:26 [Christ]: If any one serves me, he must follow me; and where I am, there shall my servant be also; if any one serves me, the Father will honor him.

1 Cor. 3:13-14. Each man's work will become manifest; for the Day will disclose it, because it will be revealed with fire, and the fire will

Hinauf   steht mein Begier.
Upwards (I-direct) my longing.

Da wird Gott ewig   lohnen
There will God eternally reward

Dem,   der ihm dient allhier.
The-one, who him serves here.

4. Tenor Recit.
●Yearning for death: it will mark the end of all woe (95-4)
Ach könnte mir doch bald so wohl geschehn,
Ah, could me indeed soon such good   befall,
{Ah, might I indeed be so blessed,}

Daß ich den Tod,
That I - death,

Das Ende aller Not,
The end of-all woe,

In meinen Gliedern könnte sehn;
In   my   members could   see;

Ich wollte ihn zu meinem Leibgedinge wählen
I would it as   my   jointure   choose

Und alle Stunden nach ihm zählen.
And all   hours   by it number.
{And each hour by it number.}

5. Tenor Aria
●Yearning for death: may the hour soon strike! (95-5)
Ach, schlage doch bald, selge Stunde,
Ah,   strike please soon, blessed hour,
{Ah, O blessed hour, please soon strike,}

Den allerletzten Glockenschlag!
(Thy) very-last   (clock's-)chime!

Komm, komm, ich reiche   dir die Hände,
Come,   come, I stretch-out to-thee (my) hands,
{Come, come, I stretch out my hands to thee,}

Komm, mache meiner Not ein Ende,
Come, make of-my woe an end,

Du längst erseufzter Sterbenstag!
Thou long sighed-for day-of-death!
{Thou long yearned-for day of death!}

6. Bass Recit.
●Death is gateway to God; Christ wakes me from sleep (95-6)
Denn ich weiß dies
For   I   know this

Und glaub es ganz gewiß,
And believe it most certainly,

test what sort of work each one has done. If the work which any man has built on the foundation survives, he will receive a reward. (Also 2 Cor. 5:10.)
2 Tim. 4:6–8. ...The time of my departure has come. I have fought the good fight, I have finished the race, I have kept the faith. Henceforth there is laid up for me the crown of righteousness, which the Lord, the righteous judge, will award to me on that Day, and not only to me but also to all who have loved his appearing.

Rev. 14:13. And I heard a voice from heaven saying, "Write this: Blessed are the dead who die in the Lord henceforth." "Blessed indeed," says the Spirit, "that they may rest from their labors, for their deeds follow them!"
2 Cor. 4:7, 12. We have this treasure in earthen vessels, to show that the transcendent power belongs to God and not to us...So death is at work in us...
Phil. 1:20–21, 23. [My hope is]...that...Christ will be honored in my body, whether by life or by death. For to me to live is Christ, and to die is gain...My desire is to depart and be with Christ, for that is far better. (Also 2 Cor. 5:8.)
2 Cor. 5:1–4. For we know that if the earthly tent we live in is destroyed, we have a building from God, a house not made with hands, eternal in the heavens. Here indeed we groan, and long to put on our heavenly dwelling, so that by putting it on we may not be found naked. For while we are still in this tent, we sigh with anxiety; not that we would be unclothed, but that we would be further clothed, so that what is mortal may be swallowed up by life.
2 Cor. 5:8. ...We would rather be away from the body and at home with the Lord.

Job 14:5. [Man's] days are determined, and the number of his months is with thee, and thou hast appointed his bounds that he cannot pass...
Heb. 9:27. ...It is appointed for men to die once...
2 Cor. 5:2–4. Here indeed we groan, and long to put on our heavenly dwelling, so that by putting it on we may not be found naked. For while we are still in this tent, we sigh with anxiety; not that we would be unclothed, but that we would be further clothed, so that what is mortal may be swallowed up by life.
Rom. 8:22–24, 26. We know that the whole creation has been groaning in travail together until now; and not only the creation, but we ourselves, who have the first fruits of the Spirit, groan inwardly as we wait for adoption as sons, the redemption of our bodies. For in this hope we were saved...Likewise the Spirit helps us in our weakness; for we do not know how to pray as we ought, but the Spirit himself intercedes for us with sighs too deep for words (Luther: unaussprechlichem Seufzen).

Job 19:25–26. I know that my Redeemer lives...and after my skin has been thus destroyed, then from my flesh I shall see God.
Jn. 14:1–3 [Christ]: Let not your hearts be troubled; believe in God, believe also in me. In my Father's house are many rooms...And when I go and prepare a place for you, I will come again and will take you to myself, that where I am you may be also.

Daß ich aus meinem Grabe
That I from my grave

Ganz einen sichern Zugang zu dem Vater habe.
Altogether a sure admittance to the Father have.

Mein Tod ist nur ein Schlaff,
My death is but a sleep,

Dadurch der Leib,
Through-which (my) body,

        der hier von Sorgen abgenommen,
        which here by sorrows was-diminished,

Zur Ruhe kommen.
To rest comes.
{Comes to rest.}

Sucht nun ein Hirte sein verlornes Schaf,
Seeks then a shepherd his lost sheep,
{If, then, a shepherd seeks his lost sheep,}

Wie sollte Jesus mich nicht wieder finden,
How should Jesus me not once-again find,
{How should Jesus not once again find me,}

Da er mein Haupt und ich sein Gliedmaß bin!
Since he my head and I his member am!

So kann ich nun mit frohen Sinnen
Thus can I now with joyful disposition

Mein selig Auferstehn auf meinen Heiland gründen.
My blessed resurrection upon my Savior ground.

7. Chorale
●Resurrection of Christ assures my ascension (95–7)
Weil du vom Tod erstanden bist,
Because thou from death arisen art,

Werd ich im Grab nicht bleiben;
Shall I in-the grave not remain;
{In the grave I shall not remain;}

Dein letztes Wort mein Auffahrt ist,
Thy final word my ascension is,

Todsfurcht kannst du vertreiben.
Fear-of-death canst thou drive-away.

Denn wo du bist, da komm ich hin,
For where thou art, there (will) I-come - ,

Daß ich stets bei dir leb und bin;
That I always with thee (may) live and be;

Jn. 12:26 [Christ]: If any one serves me, he must follow me; and where I am, there shall my servant be also; if any one serves me, the Father will honor him.
Eph. 2:18. Through [Christ] we...have access (Luther: Zugang) in one Spirit to the Father.
Lk. 8:52–53. ...[Jesus] said, "Do not weep; for she is not dead but sleeping." And they laughed at him, knowing that she was dead.
1 Thess. 4:13–14. But we would not have you ignorant, brethren, concerning those who are asleep, that you may not grieve as others do who have no hope. For since we believe that Jesus died and rose again, even so, through Jesus, God will bring with him those who have fallen asleep.
Heb. 4:9. So then, there remains a sabbath rest for the people of God. (Also Heb. 4:1.)
Rev. 14:13. And I heard a voice from heaven saying, "Write this: Blessed are the dead who die in the Lord henceforth." "Blessed indeed," says the Spirit, "that they may rest from their labors, for their deeds follow them!"
Mt. 18:12–13 [Christ]: If a man has a hundred sheep, and one of them has gone astray, does he not leave the ninety-nine on the mountains and go in search of the one that went astray? And if he finds it, truly, I say to you, he rejoices over it more than over the ninety-nine that never went astray...
Ps. 16:10. [O Lord,] thou dost not give me up to Sheol, or let thy godly one see the Pit (Luther: daß dein Heiliger verwese). (Also Acts 2:27, 13:35.)
Eph. 5:23, 29–30. ...Christ is the head of the church, his body...No man ever hates his own flesh, but nourishes and cherishes it, as Christ does the church, because we are members of his body. (Also Eph. 3:6, 4:15–16, Rom. 12:4–5, 1 Cor. 12:12, 27.)
1 Cor. 15:20, 23. ...Christ has been raised from the dead, the first fruits of those who have fallen asleep...Christ the first fruits, then at his coming those who belong to Christ. Rom. 8:11. If the Spirit of him who raised Jesus from the dead dwells in you, he who raised Christ Jesus from the dead will give life to your mortal bodies also through his Spirit which dwells in you. (Also Jn. 6:40/44/54.)

1 Cor. 15:21–23. As by a man came death, by a man has come also the resurrection of the dead. For as in Adam all die, so also in Christ shall all be made alive. But each in his own order: Christ the first fruits, then at his coming those who belong to Christ. (Also Rom. 6:8–10.)
Jn. 14:19 [Christ]:...Because I live, you will live also.
1 Thess. 4:16. The Lord himself will descend from heaven with a cry of command, with the archangel's call, and with the sound of the trumpet of God. And the dead in Christ will rise first.
***Lk. 7:14.** And [Jesus] said, "Young man, I say to you, arise."
1 Cor. 15:54–55. When the perishable puts on the imperishable, and the mortal puts on immortality, then shall come to pass the saying that is written: "Death is swallowed up in victory." O death, where is thy victory? O death, where is thy sting?
Heb. 2:14–15. Since...the children share in flesh and blood, [Christ] himself likewise partook of the same nature, that through death he might destroy him who has the power of death, that is, the devil, and deliver all those who through fear of death were subject to lifelong bondage.
Jn. 12:26 [Christ]: If any one serves me, he must follow me; and where I am, there shall my servant be also; if any one serves me, the Father will honor him. (Also Jn. 14:3.)

Drum   fahr ich hin mit Freuden.
Therefore depart I - with joy.
{Therefore I depart with joy.}

Lk. 2:29. Lord, now lettest thou thy servant depart in peace, according to thy word.

BWV 96
Herr Christ, der einge Gottessohn
(NBA I/24; BC A142)

18. S. after Trinity (BWV 96, 169)
*1 Cor. 1:4–9 (Paul's prayer of thanks for the blessings of the Gospel in Corinth)
*Mt. 22:34–46 (Jesus identifies the greatest commandments and asks the Pharisees whose Son Christ is)
Librettist: Unknown

1. Chorus (Chorale Vs. 1)
●Christ is only begotten Son of God & morning star (96-1)
Herr Christ, der einge Gottessohn,
Lord Christ, the only Son-of-God,

Vaters   in Ewigkeit,
(Who was) the-Father's in eternity,

Aus seinem Herzen entsprossen,
Out-of his   heart was-sprouted,
{Who originated out of his heart,}

Gleichwie   geschrieben steht,
Just-as (it) written   stands,
{Just as it stands written;}

Er ist der Morgensterne,
He is the morning-star,

Sein' Glanz streckt er so ferne
His radiance extends he so far
{His radiance does he extend so far that it is}

Vor   andern Sternen   klar.
Beyond (all) other   stars (more) bright.

2. Alto Recit. (Based on Chorale Vs. 2)
●Incarnation: Love shown when God became son of David (96-2)
O Wunderkraft der Liebe,
O wondrous-power of love,

Wenn Gott an sein Geschöpfe denket,
When God of his creation   thinks,
{When God remembers his creation,}

Wenn sich die Herrlichkeit
When (now) (his) glory

Im   letzten Teil der Zeit
In (this) last portion of time
{In these latter days}

*Mt. 22:41–46. ...Jesus asked [the Pharisees] a question, saying, "What do you think of the Christ? Whose son is he?" They said to him, "The son of David." He said to them, "How is it then that David, inspired by the Spirit, calls him Lord, saying, 'The Lord said to my Lord, Sit at my right hand, till I put thy enemies under thy feet'? If David thus calls him Lord, how is he his son?" And no one was able to answer him a word, nor from that day did any one dare to ask him any more questions.
Jn. 1:1, 14, 18. In the beginning was the Word, and the Word was with God, and the Word was God...And the Word became flesh and dwelt among us, full of grace and truth; we have beheld his glory, glory as of the only Son from the Father...No one has ever seen God; the only Son, who is in the bosom of the Father, he has made him known. (Also Jn. 3:18, 1 Jn. 4:9.)
Heb. 1:3, 5–6. He reflects the glory of God (Luther: der Glanz seiner Herrlichkeit) and bears the very stamp of his nature...For to what angel did God ever say, "Thou art my Son, today I have begotten thee"? Or again, "I will be to him a father, and he shall be to me a son"? And again, when he brings the first-born into the world, he says, "Let all God's angels worship him."
Jn. 14:9, 11. Jesus said to [Philip], "...He who has seen me has seen the Father; how can you say, 'Show us the Father'?...Believe me that I am in the Father and the Father in me..." (Also Jn. 10:30.)
Rev. 22:16 [Christ]: ...I am the root and the offspring of David, the bright and morning star. (Also 2 Pet. 1:19, Rev. 2:28.)
Jn. 8:12. Again Jesus spoke to them, saying, "I am the light of the world; he who follows me will not walk in darkness, but will have the light of life." (Also Jn. 1:4, 9:5, 11:9, 12:46, Ps. 36:9.)

1 Jn. 4:9. In this the love of God was made manifest among us, that God sent his only Son into the world, so that we might live through him.
Jn. 3:16. For God so loved the world that he gave his only Son, that whoever believes in him should not perish but have eternal life.
Jn. 1:14. And the Word became flesh and dwelt among us, full of grace and truth; we have beheld his glory, glory as of the only Son from the Father. (See also Is. 40:5.)
Heb. 1:1–3. In many and various ways God spoke of old to our fathers by the prophets; but in these last days he has spoken to us by a Son, whom he appointed the heir of all things, through whom also he created the world. He reflects the glory of God (Luther: der Glanz seiner Herrlichkeit)...
Gal. 4:4–5. When the time had fully come, God sent forth his Son, born of woman...so that we might receive adoption as sons. (Also Rom. 16:25–26.)

Zur Erde senket.
To earth descends.

O unbegreifliche, geheime Macht!
O incomprehensible, mysterious might!

Es trägt ein auserwählter Leib
(Here) bears a chosen body

Den großen Gottessohn,
The great Son-of-God,

Den David schon
Whom David already

Im Geist als seinen Herrn verehrte,
In-the spirit as his Lord did-honor,

Da dies gebenedeite Weib
In-that this favored woman

In unverletzter Keuschheit bliebe.
In unviolated chastity remains.

O reiche Segenskraft!
O rich power-of-blessing!

so sich auf uns ergossen,
which - upon us (is) poured-out,

Da er den Himmel auf, die Hölle zugeschlossen.
In-that he - heaven has-opened, (and) hell locked-shut.

3. Tenor Aria (Based on Chorale Vs. 3)
●Prayer that Christ illuminate & kindle the soul (96–3)
Ach, ziehe die Seele mit Seilen der Liebe,
Ah, draw this soul (of mine) with cords of love,

O Jesu, ach zeige dich kräftig in ihr.
O Jesus, ah, manifest thyself powerfully in it.

Erleuchte sie, daß sie dich gläubig erkenne,
Illuminate it, that it thee in-faith might-recognize,
{Illuminate it, that it might recognize thee in faith,}

Phil. 2:6–7. ...Though he was in the form of God, [Christ Jesus] did not count equality with God a thing to be grasped, but emptied himself, taking the form of a servant, being born in the likeness of men.
*Mt. 22:41–45. ...Jesus asked them... "What do you think of the Christ? Whose son is he?" They said to him, "The son of David." He said to them, "How is it then that David, inspired by the Spirit, calls him Lord, saying, 'The Lord said to my Lord, Sit at my right hand...'? If David thus calls him Lord, how is he his son?" (Also Rom. 1:3–4.)
Heb. 10:5. ...When Christ came into the world, he said, "...A body hast thou prepared for me." (See Ps. 40:6–8.)
Lk. 1:26, 27–28, 30–31, 35. In the sixth month the angel Gabriel was sent from God...to a virgin...and the virgin's name was Mary. And he came to her and said, "Hail, O favored one, the Lord is with you!...Do not be afraid, Mary, for you have found favor with God. And behold, you will conceive in your womb and bear a son, and you shall call his name Jesus...The Holy Spirit will come upon you, and the power of the Most High will overshadow you; therefore the child to be born will be called holy, the Son of God."
Lk. 1:41–42. ...Elizabeth...exclaimed [to Mary] with a loud cry, "Blessed are you among women (Luther: gebenedeit bist du unter den Weibern)...!"
Is. 44:3 [God]: ...I will pour my Spirit upon your descendants, and my blessing on your offspring.
Eph. 1:3. Blessed be the God and Father of our Lord Jesus Christ, who has blessed us in Christ with every spiritual blessing...
Rom. 5:5, 9. ...God's love has been poured into our hearts through the Holy Spirit which has been given to us...Since, therefore, we are now justified by his blood, much more shall we be saved by him from the wrath of God.
Heb. 9:24. For Christ has entered...into heaven itself, now to appear in the presence of God on our behalf. (Also Eph. 2:18.)

Hos. 11:4 [God]: I led them with cords of compassion, with bands of love (Luther: Seilen der Liebe)... (Also Jer. 31:3.)
Jn. 12:30, 32. [Jesus said,] "...I, when I am lifted up from the earth, will draw all men to myself." (Also Jn. 6:44, 65; S. of S. 1:4.)
Phil. 2:13. God is at work in you, both to will and to work for his good pleasure.
*1 Cor. 1:6. ... The testimony to Christ was confirmed among you (Luther: in euch kräftig geworden ist).
Jn. 8:12. Jesus spoke to them, saying, "I am the light of the world; he who follows me will not walk in darkness, but will have the light of life." (Also Jn. 1:4, 9:5, 11:9, 12:46.)
Jn. 1:9. [In Christ] the true light that enlightens every man was coming into the world. (Also Eph. 1:17–18, 4:18.)
Jn. 17:3. This is eternal life, that they know...Jesus Christ (Luther: Jesum Christi erkennen)...
1 Cor. 12:3. ...No one can say "Jesus is Lord" except by the Holy Spirit.
Rom. 5:5. ...God's love has been poured into our hearts through the Holy Spirit which has been given to us.
Acts 2:1–4. When the day of Pentecost had come, [the disciples] were all together in one place. And suddenly a sound came from heaven like the rush of a mighty wind, and it filled all the house where they were sitting. And there appeared to them tongues as of fire,

Gib, daß sie mit heiligen Flammen entbrenne,
Grant, that it with holy flames be-kindled,

Ach würke ein gläubiges Dürsten nach dir.
Ah, bring-about a believing thirsting for thee.
{Ah create a believing thirst for thee.}

4. Soprano Recit. (Based on Chorale Vs. 4)
●Prayer that God enlighten soul & lead to right path (96-4)
Ach, führe mich, o Gott, zum rechten Wege,
Ah, lead me, O God, to-the right way,

Mich, der ich unerleuchtet bin,
I, who - unenlightened am,

Der ich nach meines Fleisches Sinn
Who - according-to my flesh's disposition

So oft zu irren pflege;
So oft to err am-wont;

Jedoch gehst du nur mir zur Seiten,
Yet walkest thou only at-my side,
{Yet, if only thou dost walk with me,}

Willst du mich nur mit deinen Augen leiten,
Wilt thou me but with thine eyes guide,
{If only thou wilt guide me with thine eyes,}

So gehet meine Bahn
Then leads my course
{Then my course}

Gewiß zum Himmel an.
Surely to heaven - .
{Surely leads to heaven.}

5. Bass Aria (Based on Chorale Vs. 4)
●Prayer that God guide my wayward steps (96-5)
Bald zur Rechten, bald zur Linken
Now to-the right, now to-the left

Lenkt sich mein verirrter Schritt.
Turns - my wayward step.

Gehe doch, mein Heiland, mit,
Walk please, my Savior, along (with me),
{Please walk, my Savior, along with me,}

Laß mich in Gefahr nicht sinken,
Let me into danger not fall,
{Let me not fall into danger,}

Laß mich ja dein weises Führen
Let me indeed thy wise leading

distributed and resting on each one of them. And they were all filled with the Holy Spirit... (Also Mt. 3:11, Lk. 3:16.)
Jn. 7:37-39. On the last day of the feast, the great day, Jesus stood up and proclaimed, "If any one thirst, let him come to me and drink. He who believes in me, as the scripture has said, 'Out of his heart shall flow rivers of living water.'" Now this he said about the Spirit, which those who believed in him were to receive... (Also Is. 12:3, 44:3, Joel 2:28, Acts 2:18.)
Ps. 42:1-2. As a hart longs for flowing streams, so longs my soul for thee, O God. My soul thirsts for God, for the living God...

Ps. 27:11. Teach me thy way, O Lord; and lead me on a level path because of my enemies. (Also Ps. 143:8, 10.)
Prov. 14:12. There is a way which seems right to a man, but its end is the way to death. (Also Prov. 16:25.)
Eph. 4:17-18. ...You must no longer live as the Gentiles do, in the futility of their minds; they are darkened in their understanding, alienated from the life of God because of the ignorance that is in them, due to their hardness of heart. Rom. 8:5-6. For those who live according to the flesh set their minds on the things of the flesh, but those who live according to the Spirit set their minds on the things of the Spirit. To set the mind on the flesh is death, but to set the mind on the Spirit is life and peace. (Also Rom. 1:21, Gal. 5:16, Phil. 3:19, Col. 3:1-3.)
Is. 53:6. All we like sheep have gone astray; we have turned every one to his own way...
Ps. 119:176. I have gone astray like a lost sheep...
Ps. 16:11. [O Lord,] thou dost show me the path of life... (Also Ps. 25:9, Mt. 18:12.)
Ps. 32:8 [God]: I will instruct you and teach you the way you should go; I will counsel you with my eye upon you. (Also Ps. 33:18, 34:15.)
Is. 30:21. Your ears shall hear a word behind you, saying, "This is the way, walk in it," when you turn to the right or when you turn to the left. (Also Jer. 42:3.)
Ps. 73:24. Thou dost guide me with thy counsel, and afterward thou wilt receive me to glory.
***1 Cor. 1:7-8.** ...As you wait for the revealing of our Lord Jesus Christ; who will sustain you to the end, guiltless in the day of our Lord Jesus Christ.

Deut. 5:32. You shall be careful to do therefore as the Lord your God has commanded you; you shall not turn aside to the right hand or to the left. (Also Deut. 17:11, 20, 28:14, Josh. 1:7, Prov. 4:27, Is. 30:21.)
1 Pet. 2:25. You were straying like sheep, but have now returned to the Shepherd and Guardian of your souls.
Is. 53:6. All we like sheep have gone astray... (Also Ps. 14:3, 119:176, Rom. 3:10-12, Mt. 18:12.)
Ps. 69:1-2, 15. Save me, O God! For the waters have come up to my neck. I sink in deep mire, where there is no foothold; I have come into deep waters, and the flood sweeps over me...Let not the flood sweep over me, or the deep swallow me up, or the pit close its mouth over me. (Also 2 Sam. 22:5-6, Ps. 18:16, 124:4-5, 144:7.)
Gen. 28:16-17. Then Jacob awoke from his sleep and said, "Surely the Lord is in this place; and I did not know it." And he was afraid, and said, "How awesome is this place! This is none other than the house of God, and this is the gate of heaven (Luther: Pforte des Himmels)."

Bis zur Himmelspforte spüren.
Up to heaven's-portal experience.

6. Chorale (Vs. 5) (See also 22–5, 132–6, 164–6.)
●Prayer that old nature would die & new nature live (96–6)
Ertöt uns durch dein Güte,
Mortify us through thy goodness,

Erweck uns durch dein Gnad;
Awaken us through thy grace;

Den alten Menschen kränke,
The old man mortify,

Daß er neu Leben hab
So-that it new life may-have

Wohl hier auf dieser Erden,
Indeed here on this earth,

          Den Sinn und all Begierden
(And so-that) (our) mind and all (our) desires

Und G'danken hab'n zu dir.
And thoughts (be-directed) towards thee.

BWV 97
In allen meinen Taten
(NBA I/34; BC A189)

Occasion Unknown (BWV 131, 150, 117, 192, 100, 97)
Perhaps for 5. S. after Trinity or for a wedding.
Librettist: Chorale (Paul Fleming)

1. Chorus (Chorale Vs. 1)
●God's counsel needed for successful endeavors (97–1)
In allen meinen Taten
In all my doings

Laß ich den Höchsten raten,
Allow I the Most-High to-counsel (me),
{I allow the Most High to counsel me,}

Der alles kann und hat,
Who all-things can and has;

Er muß zu allen Dingen,
He must in all things,

Soll's anders wohl gelingen,
Shall-it otherwise well succeed,
{If it is otherwise to succeed,}

Ps. 73:24. [O Lord,] thou dost guide me with thy counsel (Luther: Rat), and afterward thou wilt receive me to glory.

Heb. 12:5–6. ...My son, do not regard lightly the discipline of the Lord, nor lose courage when you are punished by him. For the Lord disciplines him whom he loves, and chastises every son whom he receives.
Rom. 8:13. ...If by the Spirit you put to death the deeds of the body you will live. (Also 1 Pet. 4:1.)
Rom. 6:3–8. Do you not know that all of us who have been baptized into Christ Jesus were baptized into his death? We were buried therefore with him by baptism into death, so that as Christ was raised from the dead by the glory of the Father, we too might walk in newness of life. For if we have been united with him in a death like his, we shall certainly be united with him in a resurrection like his. We know that our old self was crucified with him so that the sinful body might be destroyed, and we might no longer be enslaved to sin. For he who has died is freed from sin. But if we have died with Christ, we believe that we shall also live with him. (Also Col. 2:12–14, Gal. 2:20.)
Eph. 4:22–24. Put off your old nature which belongs to your former manner of life and is corrupt through deceitful lusts, and be renewed in the spirit of your minds, and put on the new nature, created after the likeness of God in true righteousness and holiness. (Also Col. 3:2.)
Col. 3:9–10. ...Seeing that you have put off the old nature with its practices and have put on the new nature, which is being renewed in knowledge after the image of its creator.
2 Cor. 5:15. [Christ] died for all, that those who live might live no longer for themselves but for him who for their sake died and was raised. (Also 2 Cor. 5:9, Eph. 5:10.)
Col. 3:17. Whatever you do, in word or deed, do everything in the name of the Lord Jesus...

Prov. 3:5–6. Trust in the Lord with all your heart, and do not rely on your own insight. In all your ways acknowledge him, and he will make straight your paths.
Prov. 2:6–7. For the Lord gives wisdom; from his mouth come knowledge and understanding, he stores up sound wisdom for the upright...
Ps. 147:5. Great is our Lord, and abundant in power; his understanding is beyond measure. (Also Ps. 33:11, Is. 28:29.)
Ps. 24:1. The earth is the Lord's and the fulness thereof... Ps. 50:10–12 [God]: Every beast of the forest is mine, the cattle on a thousand hills. I know all the birds of the air, and all that moves in the field is mine. If I were hungry, I would not tell you; for the world and all that is in it is mine. (Also Ex. 19:5.)
Jer. 32:27 [God]: Behold, I am the Lord, the God of all flesh; is anything too hard for me? (Also Gen. 18:14, Is. 59:1.)
Mt. 28:18. Jesus...said..."All authority in heaven and on earth has been given to me."
Prov. 8:14. I [wisdom] have counsel and sound wisdom (Luther: Rat und Tat), I have insight, I have strength.
Prov. 24:3–5. By wisdom a house is built, and by understanding it is established.
Ps. 16:7. I bless the Lord who gives me counsel...
Ps. 73:24. Thou dost guide me with thy counsel (Luther: Rat), and afterward thou wilt receive me to glory.

Selbst geben   Rat und Tat.
Himself grant (help by) word and deed.

Jer. 32:18–19. ...O great and mighty God whose name is the Lord of hosts, great in counsel and mighty in deed (Luther: groß von Rat und mächtig von Tat)...

2. Bass Aria (Chorale Vs. 2)
●Success not guaranteed by human effort but God's will (97–2)

Nichts ist es spat und frühe
Nought is it late (or) early
{Nothing comes of it late or early}

Ps. 127:1–2. Unless the Lord builds the house, those who build it labor in vain. Unless the Lord watches over the city, the watchman stays awake in vain. It is in vain that you rise up early and go late to rest, eating the bread of anxious toil; for he gives to his beloved sleep.

Um   alle meine Mühe,
Despite all my efforts,

Prov. 10:22. The blessing of the Lord makes rich, and he adds no sorrow (Luther: Mühe) with it.

Mein Sorgen ist umsonst.
My trouble is for-nought.

Prov. 3:5–6. Trust in the Lord with all your heart, and do not rely on your own insight. In all your ways acknowledge him, and he will make straight your paths.

Er mag's mit meinen Sachen
He may with my affairs

Ps. 37:5. Commit your way to the Lord; trust in him, and he will act.
Ps. 90:17. Let the favor of the Lord our God be upon us, and establish thou the work of our hands upon us, yea, the work of our hands establish thou it.

Nach   seinem Willen machen,
According-to his will do,
{He may do with my affairs according to His will,}

Is. 26:12. O Lord...thou hast wrought for us all our works.
Jer. 10:23. I know, O Lord, that the way of man is not in himself, that it is not in man who walks to direct his steps. (Also Is. 30:21.)
Acts 21:14. ...The will of the Lord be done.

Ich stell's in seine Gunst.
I place-it into his goodwill.
{I entrust it to his goodwill.}

Mt. 6:9–10. Pray then like this: Our Father who art in heaven, Hallowed be thy name. Thy kingdom come, Thy will be done, On earth as it is in heaven. (Also Mk. 14:35–36, Mt. 26:39, 42.)

3. Tenor Recit. (Chorale Vs. 3)
●God's will is best for me; I gladly accept it (97–3)

Es kann mir nichts geschehen,
(Now) can to-me nothing happen,
{Nothing can happen to me,}

Rom. 8:28. We know that in everything God works for good with those who love him, who are called according to his purpose.
Ps. 31:14–15. But I trust in thee, O Lord, I say, "Thou art my God." My times are in thy hand...
Heb. 12:5–7, 9–10. ...My son, do not regard lightly the discipline of the Lord, nor lose courage when you are punished by him. For the Lord disciplines him whom he loves, and chastises every son whom he receives. It is for discipline that you have to endure. God is treating you as sons; for what son is there whom his father does not discipline? ...He disciplines us for our good, that we may share his holiness. For the moment all discipline seems painful rather than pleasant; later it yields the peaceful fruit of righteousness to those who have been trained by it. (Also Jms. 1:2–4, 1 Pet. 1:6–7, Jer. 30:11.)
Prov. 3:11. My son, do not despise the Lord's discipline or be weary of his reproof, for the Lord reproves him whom he loves, as a father the son in whom he delights.
Job 2:10. ...Shall we receive good at the hand of God, and shall we not receive evil? (Also Job 1:21.)
Job 23:10. But he knows the way that I take; when he has tried me, I shall come forth as gold.

Als was er hat versehen,
But whatever he has (ordered),

Und was mir selig ist:
And whatever for-me blessed is:
{And whatever is blessed for me:}

Ich nehm es, wie er's gibet:
I take it, as he-it gives:
{I take it as he gives it:}

Was ihm von mir beliebet,
What him regarding me pleases,
{Whatever he would desire for me,}

Das hab ich auch erkiest.
That have I also chosen.

4. Tenor Aria (Chorale Vs. 4)
●God's grace keeps from harm if commandments obeyed (97–4)

Ich traue seiner Gnaden,
I trust in-his grace,

2 Thess. 3:3. The Lord is faithful; he will strengthen you and guard you from evil.

Die mich vor allem Schaden,
Which me from all harm,
{Which protects me from all harm,}

Ps. 121:2–8. My help comes from the Lord, who made heaven and earth. He will not let your foot be moved, he who keeps you will not slumber. Behold, he who keeps Israel will neither slumber nor sleep. The Lord is your keeper; the Lord is your shade on your right hand. The sun shall not smite you by day, nor the moon by night. The Lord

Vor allem Übel schützt.
From all evil protects.
{From all evil.}

Leb ich nach seinen Gesetzen,
Live I according-to his commandments,
{If I live according-to his commandments,}

So wird mich nichts verletzen,
Then will me nothing hurt,
{Then will nothing hurt me,}

Nichts fehlen, was mir nützt.
Nothing (will I) lack, of-that-which for-me is-profitable.
{Nothing will I lack of that which is profitable for me.}

5. Alto Recit. (Chorale Vs. 5)
●God's grace sought in forgiveness of sins (97-5)
 Er wolle meiner Sünden
(May) he - from-my sins

In Gnaden mich entbinden,
In mercy me release,
{In mercy may he free me from my sins,}

Durchstreichen meine Schuld!
Strike-out my guilt!

Er wird auf mein Verbrechen
He will upon my offences

Nicht stracks das Urteil sprechen
Not straightway the verdict speak
{He will not pass sentence straightway on my offences}

Und haben noch Geduld.
And (will) have yet forbearance.
{But will yet show forbearance.}

6. Alto Aria (Chorale Vs. 6)
●God's Word comforts in all circumstances of life (97-6)
Leg ich mich späte nieder,
Lay I me late down,
{Though I retire late,}

Erwache frühe wieder,
Awaken early again,

Lieg oder ziehe fort,
Lie or proceed,
{Rest or proceed,}

In Schwachheit und in Banden,
In weakness and in bonds,

Und was mir stößt zuhanden,
And (in) whatever me strikes close-at-hand,
{And in whatever strikes me close at hand,}

will keep you from all evil; he will keep your life. The Lord will keep your going out and your coming in from this time forth and for evermore.
Deut. 4:40. Therefore you shall keep his statutes and his commandments...that it may go well with you... (Also Ex. 20:6, Deut. 5:10, 5:29, 5:33, 7:9, 30:9–10, 1 Jn. 3:22, 24.)
Deut. 28:2. All these blessings shall come upon you and overtake you, if you obey the voice of the Lord your God.
Jn. 15:10 [Christ]: If you keep my commandments, you will abide in my love...
1 Jn. 5:3. For this is the love of God, that we keep his commandments. And his commandments are not burdensome.
Ps. 91:10. No evil shall befall you, no scourge come near your tent.
Ps. 84:11. For the Lord God is a sun and shield; he bestows favor and honor. No good thing does the Lord withhold from those who walk uprightly. (Lam. 3:25–26)
Ps. 34:10. The young lions suffer want and hunger; but those who seek the Lord lack no good thing.

Rev. 1:5–6. ...[He] has freed us from our sins by his blood and made us a kingdom, priests to his God and Father... (Also Acts 13:38–39.)
Col. 2:13–14. You, who were dead in trespasses and the uncircumcision of your flesh, God made alive together with him, having forgiven us all our trespasses, having canceled the bond which stood against us with its legal demands; this he set aside, nailing it to the cross.
Ps. 103:8–12. The Lord is merciful and gracious, slow to anger and abounding in steadfast love. He will not always chide, nor will he keep his anger for ever. He does not deal with us according to our sins, nor requite us according to our iniquities. For as the heavens are high above the earth, so great is his steadfast love toward those who fear him; as far as the east is from the west, so far does he remove our transgressions from us.
2 Pet. 3:9. The Lord is...forbearing toward you, not wishing that any should perish, but that all should reach repentance.
Mt. 18:26–27. The [indebted] servant fell on his knees, imploring [his master], "Lord, have patience (Luther: Geduld) with me, and I will pay you everything." And out of pity for him the lord of that servant released him and forgave him the debt.

Ps. 127:2. It is in vain that you rise up early and go late to rest, eating the bread of anxious toil; for he gives to his beloved sleep.
Josh. 1:5, 9 [God]: I will be with you; I will not fail you or forsake you ...Be strong and of good courage; be not frightened, neither be dismayed; for the Lord your God is with you wherever you go. (Also Deut. 31:6–8, Heb. 13:5.)
Is. 43:1–2 [God]: ...Fear not, for I have redeemed you; I have called you by name, you are mine. When you pass through the waters I will be with you; and through the rivers, they shall not overwhelm you; when you walk through fire you shall not be burned, and the flame shall not consume you.
2 Cor. 6:4–5. As servants of God we commend ourselves in every way: through great endurance, in afflictions, hardships, calamities, beatings, imprisonments, tumults, labors, watching, hunger. (Also Heb. 11:35–38, 2 Cor. 11:23–27.)
Ps. 119:25, 28. My soul cleaves to the dust; revive me according to thy word!...My soul melts away for sorrow; strengthen me according to thy word! (Also Ps. 119:81, 107, 116.)

So tröstet mich sein Wort.
Still comforts me   his Word.
{Still his Word comforts me.}

Ps. 119:103. [O Lord,] how sweet are thy words to my taste, sweeter than honey to my mouth! (Also Ps. 19:9–10.)

7. Soprano & Bass Duet (Chorale Vs. 7)
●Misfortune accepted if God has chosen it for me (97-7)
Hat er es denn beschlossen,
Has he it then   decided,
{If he has decided it,}

So will ich unverdrossen
Then would I   unflagging

An mein Verhängnis gehn!
To my   fate   go!

Kein Unfall unter allen
No misfortune amongst all-of-them
{Amongst all the misfortunes that befall me}

Wird mir zu harte fallen,
Will me too harsh befall,
{None will be too harsh;}

Ich will ihn überstehn.
I will it surmount.
{I will surmount it.}

Lk. 22:41–42. [Jesus] withdrew from them about a stone's throw, and knelt down and prayed, "Father, if thou art willing, remove this cup from me; nevertheless not my will, but thine, be done."
Acts 21:13. ...I am ready not only to be imprisoned but even to die at Jerusalem for the name of the Lord Jesus.
Rom. 8:18. I consider that the sufferings of this present time are not worth comparing with the glory that is to be revealed to us.
2 Cor. 12:7–10. To keep me from being too elated by the abundance of revelations, a thorn was given me in the flesh, a messenger of Satan, to harass me, to keep me from being too elated. Three times I besought the Lord about this, that it should leave me; but he said to me, "My grace is sufficient for you, for my power is made perfect in weakness." I will all the more gladly boast of my weaknesses, that the power of Christ may rest upon me. For the sake of Christ, then, I am content with weaknesses, insults, hardships, persecutions, and calamities; for when I am weak, then I am strong.
1 Cor. 10:13. No temptation has overtaken you that is not common to man. God is faithful, and he will not let you be tempted beyond your strength, but with the temptation will also provide the way of escape, that you may be able to endure it.

8. Soprano Aria (Chorale Vs. 8)
●God's will accepted regarding life or death (97-8)
Ihm hab ich mich ergeben
To-him have I myself surrendered
{To him have I surrendered myself}

Zu sterben und zu leben,
To die   (or) to live,

Sobald er mir gebeut.
Whenever he me   bids.
{Whenever he bids me.}

Es sei heut oder morgen,
(Whether) it be today or tomorrow,

Dafür laß ich ihn sorgen;
About-that let I him care;
{I let him care about that;}

Er weiß die rechte Zeit.
He knows the proper time.

Phil. 1:20–23. [I desire]...that...Christ will be honored in my body, whether by life or by death. For to me to live is Christ, and to die is gain. If it is to be life in the flesh, that means fruitful labor for me. Yet which I shall choose I cannot tell. I am hard pressed between the two. My desire is to depart and be with Christ, for that is far better.
Jn. 12:24–25, 27–28 [Christ]: Unless a grain of wheat falls into the earth and dies, it remains alone; but if it dies, it bears much fruit. He who loves his life loses it, and he who hates his life in this world will keep it for eternal life...Now is my soul troubled. And what shall I say? "Father, save me from this hour"? No, for this purpose I have come to this hour. Father glorify thy name... (Also Mt. 10:38, 16:24–25, Mk. 8:34–35, Lk. 9:23–24.)
2 Cor. 5:6–9. So we are always of good courage; we know that while we are at home in the body we are away from the Lord, for we walk by faith, not by sight. We are of good courage, and we would rather be away from the body and at home with the Lord. So whether we are at home or away, we make it our aim to please him.
Ps. 31:14–15. But I trust in thee, O Lord, I say, "Thou art my God." My times are in thy hand... (Also Job 14:5.)

9. Chorale (Vs. 9) (See also 13-6, 44-7.)
●God's wisdom trusted; his providence accepted (97-9)
So sei nun, Seele, deine
So be, therefore, (O) soul,   thine (own self true)

Lk. 21:19 [Christ]: By your endurance you will gain your lives (Luther: Fasset eure Seele mit Geduld).
Ps. 62:1–2. For God alone my soul waits in silence; from him comes my salvation. He only is my rock and my salvation, my fortress; I shall not be greatly moved. (Also Ps. 62:5–6.)

Und traue dem alleine,
And trust him alone,

Der dich erschaffen hat;
Who thee created hath;

Es gehe, wie es gehe,
(Let) it happen, as it (may) happen,

Dein Vater in der Höhe,
Thy father in the highest,

Weiß allen Sachen Rat.
Knows (for) all matters counsel.

BWV 98
Was Gott tut, das ist wohlgetan II
(NBA I/25; BC A153)

21. S. after Trinity (BWV 109, 38, 98, 188)
*Eph. 6:10-17 (The armor of the Christian)
*Jn. 4:46[1]-54 (Christ heals the son of a royal official)
[1]Begin: "And at Capernaum there was an official..."
Librettist: Unknown

1. Chorus (Chorale) (See also 99-1, 100-1, 144-3.)
●God's sovereign will trusted & accepted (98-1)
Was Gott tut, das ist wohlgetan,
Whatever God does, that is well-done,

Es bleibt gerecht sein Wille;
(Now) remains just his will;
{His will remains just;}

Wie er fängt meine Sachen an,
In-whatever-way he deals-with my affairs - ,

Will ich ihm halten stille.
Will I to-him submit quietly.
{Will I submit to him quietly.}

Er ist mein Gott,
He is my God,

Der in der Not
Who in - distress

Mich wohl weiß zu erhalten;
Me well knows (how) to sustain;
{Knows well how to sustain me;}

Drum laß ich ihn nur walten.
Therefore allow I him just to-rule.
{Therefore I will just allow him to rule.}

1 Pet. 4:19. Therefore let those who suffer according to God's will do right and entrust their souls to a faithful Creator.
Is. 64:8. O Lord, thou art our Father; we are the clay, and thou art our potter; we are all the work of thy hand.
Lk. 22:42 [Christ]: Father, if thou art willing, remove this cup from me; nevertheless not my will, but thine, be done.
Jn. 5:30 [Christ]: ...I seek not my own will but the will of him who sent me.
Jms. 5:10-11. As an example of suffering and patience, brethren, take the prophets who spoke in the name of the Lord. Behold, we call those happy who were steadfast. You have heard of the steadfastness of Job, and you have seen the purpose of the Lord, how the Lord is compassionate and merciful.
Mt. 6:30-32 [Christ]: If God so clothes the grass of the field, which today is alive and tomorrow is thrown into the oven, will he not much more clothe you, O men of little faith? Therefore do not be anxious, saying, "What shall we eat?" or "What shall we drink?" or "What shall we wear?" For the Gentiles seek all these things; and your heavenly Father knows that you need them all.
Ps. 73:24. [O Lord,] thou dost guide me with thy counsel, and afterward thou wilt receive me to glory.

Mk. 7:37. ...He has done all things well...
Deut. 32:4. ...A God of faithfulness and without iniquity, just and right is he.
Rom. 8:28, 31-32. We know that in everything God works for good with those who love him, who are called according to his purpose... What then shall we say to this? If God is for us, who is against us? He who did not spare his own Son but gave him up for us all, will he not also give us all things with him?
Ps. 145:17. The Lord is just (Luther: gerecht) in all his ways, and kind in all his doings. (Also Rev. 15:3, 16:7.)
1 Pet. 4:19. Therefore let those who suffer according to God's will do right and entrust their souls to a faithful Creator.
Is. 45:9. Woe to him who strives with his Maker, an earthen vessel with the potter! Does the clay say to him who fashions it, "What are you making"?... (Also Rom. 9:21.)
Prov. 3:5-6. Trust in the Lord with all your heart, and do not rely on your own insight. In all your ways acknowledge him, and he will make straight your paths.
Ps. 34:15, 17-19. The eyes of the Lord are toward the righteous, and his ears toward their cry...When the righteous cry for help, the Lord hears, and delivers them out of all their troubles (Luther: Not). The Lord is near to the brokenhearted, and saves the crushed in spirit. Many are the afflictions of the righteous; but the Lord delivers him out of them all.
Ps. 131:1-2. O Lord, my heart is not lifted up, my eyes are not raised too high; I do not occupy myself with things too great and too marvelous for me. But I have calmed and quieted my soul, like a child quieted at its mother's breast; like a child that is quieted is my soul.
Lam. 3:26. It is good that one should wait quietly for the salvation of the Lord. (Also Ps. 62:1, 5.)
Ps. 145:14. The Lord upholds (Luther: erhält) all who are falling, and raises up all who are bowed down. (Also Ps. 17:5, 63:8, 119:116, 146:9, Is. 42:1.)

2. Tenor Recit.

●Prayer for help; declaration of confidence in God (98–2)

Ach Gott! wenn wirst du mich einmal
Ah God! When wilt thou me at-last
{Ah God, When wilt thou finally deliver me}

Von meiner Leidensqual,
From my suffering's-torment, (and)

Von meiner Angst befreien?
From my fear deliver?
{From my fear?}

Wie lange soll ich Tag und Nacht
How long must I day and night

Um Hilfe schreien?
For help cry?
{Cry for help?}

Und ist kein Retter da!
And (there) is no Savior at-hand!

Der Herr ist denen allen nah,
The Lord is to-those all nigh,
{The Lord is nigh to all those,}

Die seiner Macht
Who (in) his might

Und seiner Huld vertrauen.
And his favor trust.

Drum will ich meine Zuversicht
Therefore would I my confidence

Auf Gott alleine bauen,
Upon God alone build,

Denn er verläßt die Seinen nicht.
For he forsakes his own not.
{For he forsakes not his own.}

3. Soprano Aria

●Weeping ceases despite heavy yoke; God abandons none (98–3)

Hört, ihr Augen, auf zu weinen!
Cease, ye eyes, - to weep!

Trag ich doch
Bear I indeed
{Indeed I shall bear}

Mit Geduld mein schweres Joch.
With patience my heavy yoke.

Gott, der Vater, lebet noch,
God, the Father, liveth still,

Von den Seinen
Of his own,

*Jn. 4:46–47. ...At Capernaum there was an official whose son was ill. When he heard that Jesus had come from Judea to Galilee, he went and begged him to come down and heal his son, for he was at the point of death.

Hab. 1:2. O Lord, how long shall I cry for help, and thou wilt not hear?...

Ps. 6:2–3, 6–7. Be gracious to me, O Lord, for I am languishing; O Lord, heal me, for my bones are troubled. My soul also is sorely troubled. But thou, O Lord—how long?...I am weary with my moaning; every night I flood my bed with tears; I drench my couch with my weeping. My eye wastes away because of grief, it grows weak because of all my foes. (Also Jer. 45:3.)

Ps. 22:1–2, 11. My God, my God, why hast thou forsaken me? Why art thou so far from helping me, from the words of my groaning? O my God, I cry by day, but thou dost not answer; and by night, but find no rest...Be not far from me, for trouble (Luther: Angst) is near and there is none to help. (Also Ps. 13:1–3, 5, 89:46, 90:13–15, 86:3, 88:1, Is. 38:13.)

Lk. 18:7–8 [Christ]: Will not God vindicate his elect, who cry to him day and night? Will he delay long over them? I tell you, he will vindicate them speedily...

Ps. 145:18. The Lord is near to all who call upon him, to all who call upon him in truth. (Also Ps. 34:18.)

Ps. 142:5. I cry to thee, O Lord; I say, Thou art my refuge (Luther: Zuversicht), my portion in the land of the living. (Also Ps. 61:3, 71:5, 7.)

Ps. 62:5–8. For God alone my soul waits in silence, for my hope is from him. He only is my rock and my salvation, my fortress; I shall not be shaken. On God rests my deliverance and my honor; my mighty rock, my refuge (Luther: Zuversicht) is God. Trust in him at all times, O people; pour out your heart before him; God is a refuge for us.

Mt. 7:24–25 [Christ]: Every one then who hears these words of mine and does them will be like a wise man who built his house upon the rock; and the rain fell, and the floods came, and the winds blew and beat upon that house, but it did not fall, because it had been founded on the rock.

Ps. 94:14. For the Lord will not forsake his people; he will not abandon his heritage. (Also 2 Tim. 2:19.)

Ps. 37:28. For the Lord loves justice; he will not forsake his saints....

Lam. 3:22–33. The steadfast love of the Lord never ceases, his mercies never come to an end; they are new every morning; great is thy faithfulness. "The Lord is my portion," says my soul, "therefore I will hope in him." The Lord is good to those who wait for him, to the soul that seeks him. It is good that one should wait quietly for the salvation of the Lord. It is good for a man that he bear the yoke in his youth. Let him sit alone in silence when he has laid it on him; let him put his mouth in the dust—there may yet be hope; let him give his cheek to the smiter, and be filled with insults. For the Lord will not cast off for ever, but, though he cause grief, he will have compassion according to the abundance of his steadfast love; for he does not willingly afflict or grieve the sons of men.

Ps. 103:13. As a father pities his children, so the Lord pities those who fear him.

Rev. 21:4. He will wipe away every tear from their eyes, and death

Läßt er keinen.
Abandons he none.

Hört, ihr Augen, auf zu weinen!
Cease, ye eyes, - to weep!

4. Alto Recit.
●God compassionate; his promise to hear our prayers (98–4)
Gott hat ein Herz, das des Erbarmens Überfluß;
God has a heart, which (with) compassion overflows;
{God has a heart that overflows with compassion;}

Und wenn der Mund vor seinen Ohren klagt
And when (my) mouth before his ears cries
{And when my mouth cries in his hearing}

Und ihm des Kreuzes Schmerz
And him (of) (my) cross's pain
{And tells him of my cross's pain}

Im Glauben und Vertrauen sagt,
In faith and confidence tells,
{In faith and confidence,}

So bricht in ihm das Herz,
Then breaks in him the heart,
{Then his heart breaks,}

Daß er sich über uns erbarmen muß.
So-that he - upon us take-pity must.
{So that he must take pity upon us.}

Er hält sein Wort;
He keeps his word;

Er saget: Klopfet an,
He says: Knock - ,

So wird euch aufgetan!
Then will for-you (it) be-opened!
{And it will be opened for you!}

Drum laßt uns alsofort,
Therefore let us from-now-on,

Wenn wir in höchsten Nöten schweben,
When we in (the) greatest (of) distresses hover,

Das Herz zu Gott allein erheben!
(Our) heart to God alone lift-up!

5. Bass Aria
●Persevering in prayer until God hears & blesses (98–5)
Meinen Jesum laß ich nicht,
My Jesus leave I not,
{I will not my Jesus go,}

shall be no more, neither shall there be mourning nor crying nor pain any more, for the former things have passed away. (Also Ps. 37:28, Is. 25:8.)
Ps. 30:5. For his anger is but for a moment, and his favor is for a lifetime. Weeping may tarry for the night, but joy comes with the morning.

*Jn. 4:46–47, 49–51. ...At Capernaum there was an official whose son was ill. When he heard that Jesus had come from Judea to Galilee, he went and begged him to come down and heal his son, for he was at the point of death...The official said to him, "Sir, come down before my child dies." Jesus said to him, "Go; your son will live." The man believed the word that Jesus spoke to him and went his way. As he was going down, his servants met him and told him that his son was living.
Ps. 103:8, 11, 13–14. The Lord is merciful and gracious, slow to anger and abounding in steadfast love...For as the heavens are high above the earth, so great is his steadfast love toward those who fear him...As a father pities his children, so the Lord pities those who fear him. For he knows our frame; he remembers that we are dust.
Jer. 31:20 [God]: Is Ephraim my dear son? Is he my darling child?... Therefore my heart yearns for him (Luther: bricht mir mein Herz); I will surely have mercy on him (Luther: sein erbarmen), says the Lord.
Mt. 7:7–11 [Christ]: Ask, and it will be given you; seek, and you will find; knock, and it will be opened to you. For every one who asks receives, and he who seeks finds, and to him who knocks it will be opened. For what man of you, if his son asks him for bread, will give him a stone? Or if he asks for a fish, will give him a serpent? If you then, who are evil, know how to give good gifts to your children, how much more will your Father who is in heaven give good things to those who ask him! (Also Lk. 11:9–13, Rom. 8:32.)
Lam. 2:19. Arise, cry out in the night, at the beginning of the watches! Pour out your heart like water before the presence of the Lord!...
Lam. 3:41. Let us lift up our hearts and hands to God in heaven.
Heb. 4:15–16. For we have not a high priest who is unable to sympathize with our weaknesses, but one who in every respect has been tempted as we are, yet without sin. Let us then with confidence draw near to the throne of grace, that we may receive mercy and find grace to help in time of need.
1 Pet. 5:7. Cast all your anxieties on him, for he cares about you.
Phil. 4:6–7. Have no anxiety about anything, but in everything by prayer and supplication with thanksgiving let your requests be made known to God. And the peace of God, which passes all understanding, will keep your hearts and your minds in Christ Jesus.
Ps. 55:22. Cast your burden on the Lord, and he will sustain you; he will never permit the righteous to be moved.

Gen. 32:24, 26. Jacob was left alone; and a man wrestled with him until the breaking of the day...Then [the man] said, "Let me go, for the day is breaking." But Jacob said, "I will not let you go, unless you bless me."

Bis mich erst sein Angesicht
Until me first his countenance
{Until his countenance}

Wird   erhören   oder segnen.
Will grant-favorable-hearing (to me) or   bless (me).

Er allein
He alone

Soll mein Schutz in   allem   sein,
Shall my   shield in all-those-things be,

Was mir   Übels kann begegnen.
Which me (with) misfortune may   confront.
{In which I could encounter misfortune.}

BWV 99
Was Gott tu, das ist wohlgetan I
(NBA I/22; BC A133)

15. S. after Trinity (BWV 138, 99, 51)
*Gal. 5:25–6:10 (Exhortation to walk in the Spirit)
*Mt. 6:24–34 (Sermon on the Mount: Exhortation not to be
anxious but to seek the kingdom of God)
Librettist: Unknown

1. Chorus (Chorale Vs. 1) (See also 98-1, 100-1, 144-3.)
●God's sovereign will trusted & accepted (99-1)
Was   Gott tut, das ist wohlgetan,
Whatever God does, that is well-done,

Es   bleibt gerecht sein Wille;
(Now) remains just   his   will;
{His will remains just;}

Wie   er fängt meine Sachen an,
In-whatever-way he deals-with my   affairs - ,

Will ich ihm halten stille.
Will I to-him submit quietly.
{Will I submit to him quietly.}

Er ist mein Gott,
He is my   God,

Der in der Not
Who in - distress

Mich wohl weiß   zu erhalten;
Me   well knows (how) to sustain;
{Knows well how to sustain me;}

Drum   laß ich ihn nur walten.
Therefore allow I him just to-rule.
{Therefore I will just allow him to rule.}

Lk. 18:1–8. And [Jesus] told them a parable, to the effect that they ought always to pray and not lose heart. He said, "In a certain city there was a judge who neither feared God nor regarded man; and there was a widow in that city who kept coming to him and saying, 'Vindicate me against my adversary.' For a while he refused; but afterward he said to himself, 'Though I neither fear God nor regard man, yet because this widow bothers me, I will vindicate her, or she will wear me out by her continual coming.'" And the Lord said, "Hear what the unrighteous judge says. And will not God vindicate his elect, who cry to him day and night? Will he delay long over them? I tell you, he will vindicate them speedily. Nevertheless, when the Son of man comes, will he find faith on earth?"
Ps. 91:1–2. He who dwells in the shelter of the Most High, who abides in the shadow of the Almighty, will say to the Lord, "My refuge and my fortress; my God, in whom I trust."
Ps. 121:7–8. The Lord will keep you from all evil; he will keep your life. The Lord will keep your going out and your coming in from this time forth and for evermore.

Mk. 7:37. ...He has done all things well...
Deut. 32:4. ...A God of faithfulness and without iniquity, just and right is he.
Rom. 8:28–39. We know that in everything God works for good with those who love him, who are called according to his purpose...What then shall we say to this? If God is for us, who is against us? He who did not spare his own Son but gave him up for us all, will he not also give us all things with him?...Who shall separate us from the love of Christ? Shall tribulation, or distress, or persecution, or famine, or nakedness, or peril, or sword?...No, in all these things we are more than conquerors through him who loved us. For I am sure that neither death, nor life, nor angels, nor principalities, nor things present, nor things to come, nor powers, nor height, nor depth, nor anything else in all creation, will be able to separate us from the love of God in Christ Jesus our Lord.
Ps. 145:17. The Lord is just (Luther: gerecht) in all his ways, and kind in all his doings. (Also Rev. 15:3, 16:7.)
***Mt. 6:30–32.** If God so clothes the grass of the field, which today is alive and tomorrow is thrown into the oven, will he not much more clothe you, O men of little faith? Therefore do not be anxious, saying, "What shall we eat?" or "What shall we drink?" or "What shall we wear?" For the Gentiles seek all these things; and your heavenly Father knows that you need them all.
1 Pet. 4:19. Therefore let those who suffer according to God's will do right and entrust their souls to a faithful Creator.
Is. 45:9. Woe to him who strives with his Maker, an earthen vessel with the potter! Does the clay say to him who fashions it, "What are you making"?... (Also Rom. 9:21.)
Lam. 3:26. It is good that one should wait quietly for the salvation of the Lord. (Also Ps. 62:1, 5; 131:1–2.)
Ps. 145:14. The Lord upholds (Luther: erhält) all who are falling, and raises up all who are bowed down. (Also Ps. 17:5, 63:8, 119:116, 146:9, Is. 42:1.)

2. Bass Recit. (Based on Chorale Vs. 2)
●Word of God assures me of his help in misfortune (99–2)
Sein Wort der Wahrheit stehet fest
His Word of truth stands fast

Und wird mich nicht betrügen,
And will me not deceive,

Weil es die Gläubigen nicht fallen noch verderben läßt.
For it - believers not fall nor perish lets.
{For it will not let believers fall nor perish.}

Ja, weil es mich den Weg zum Leben führet,
Yes, for it me (in) the way to life leads,
{Yes, for it leads me in the way to life,}

So faßt mein Herze sich und lässet sich begnügen
Thus composes my heart itself and lets itself be-content
{Thus my heart composes itself and is content}

An Gottes Vatertreu und Huld
With God's paternal-faithfulness and graciousness

Und hat Geduld,
And has patience,

Wenn mich ein Unfall rühret.
When me a mishap touches.
{When I experience mishap.}

Gott kann mit seinen Allmachtshänden
God can with his almighty-hands

Mein Unglück wenden.
My misfortune turn-around.
{Avert my misfortune.}

3. Tenor Aria (Based on Chorale Vs. 3)
●Cup given us may be bitter but is our medicine (99–3)
Erschüttre dich nur nicht, verzagte Seele,
Shudder - not, disheartened soul,

Wenn dir der Kreuzeskelch so bitter schmeckt!
When to-thee the cross's-cup so bitter tastes!

Gott ist dein weiser Arzt und Wundermann,
God is thy wise physician and man-of-wonders,

So dir kein tödlich Gift einschenken kann,
Who for-thee no fatal poison can-pour,
{Who can pour no fatal poison for thee,}

Mt. 24:35 [Christ]: Heaven and earth will pass away, but my words will not pass away. (Also Mk. 13:31, Lk. 21:33, Is. 40:8.)
Prov. 30:5. Every word of God proves true; he is a shield to those who take refuge in him. (Also Rom. 3:4.)
Ps. 119:105. [O Lord,] thy word is a lamp to my feet and a light to my path.
Ps. 16:11. Thou dost show me the path of life (Luther: Weg zum Leben)...
Mt. 10:29–31 [Christ]: Are not two sparrows sold for a penny? And not one of them will fall to the ground without your Father's will. But even the hairs of your head are all numbered. Fear not, therefore; you are of more value than many sparrows. (Also Lk. 12:6–7.)
Ps. 145:14. The Lord upholds (Luther: erhält) all who are falling, and raises up all who are bowed down. (Also Ps. 17:5, 63:8, 119:116, 146:9, Is. 42:1, 1 Cor. 1:8.)
Ps. 103:11, 13. For as the heavens are high above the earth, so great is his steadfast love toward those who fear him...As a father pities his children, so the Lord pities those who fear him.
Rom. 12:12. Rejoice in your hope, be patient in tribulation, be constant in prayer. (Also Jms. 5:7–9.)
Jms. 1:3. You know that the testing of your faith produces steadfastness (Luther: Geduld). (Also Jms. 1:12, 1 Pet. 4:12–14, Heb. 10:36.)
Is. 59:1. Behold, the Lord's hand is not shortened, that it cannot save, or his ear dull, that it cannot hear. (Also Is. 50:2.)
1 Pet. 5:10. And after you have suffered a little while, the God of all grace...will himself restore, establish, and strengthen you.
Jer. 31:13 [God]: ...I will turn their mourning into joy, I will comfort them, and give them gladness for sorrow.
Ps. 90:15. [O Lord,] make us glad as many days as thou hast afflicted us, and as many years as we have seen evil.

Mk. 14:35–36. Going a little farther, [Jesus] fell on the ground and prayed that, if it were possible, the hour might pass from him. And he said, "Abba, Father, all things are possible to thee; remove this cup from me; yet not what I will, but what thou wilt." (Also Mk. 10:38–39, Mt. 20:22–23, 26:27, 39, Jn. 18:11.)
Job 5:18. [The Lord] wounds, but he binds up; he smites, but his hands heal.
Mk. 2:17. ...[Jesus] said to them, "Those who are well have no need of a physician, but those who are sick; I came not to call the righteous, but sinners." (Also Lk. 5:30–32.)
Rom. 8:28. We know that in everything God works for good with those who love him, who are called according to his purpose. Heb. 12:11. For the moment all discipline seems painful rather than pleasant; later it yields the peaceful fruit of righteousness to those who have been trained by it. (Also Rom. 5:3–5, Jms. 1:2–4, 1 Pet. 1:6–7.)
Prov. 3:11. My son, do not despise the Lord's discipline or be weary of his reproof, for the Lord reproves him whom he loves, as a father the son in whom he delights. (Also Heb. 12:5–7, 11.)
Mt. 7:9–11 [Christ]: For what man of you, if his son asks him for bread, will give him a stone? Or if he asks for a fish, will give him a serpent? If you then, who are evil, know how to give good gifts to your children, how much more will your Father who is in heaven

Obgleich die Süßigkeit verborgen steckt.
Although (its) sweetness hidden lies.

4. Alto Recit. (Based on Chorale Vs. 4)
●Faith in affliction; it is based on eternal covenant (99-4)
Nun, der von Ewigkeit geschloß'ne Bund
Now, that from eternity contracted covenant
{Now that covenant sealed from eternity}

Bleibt meines Glaubens Grund.
Remains my faith's foundation.

Er spricht mit Zuversicht
It says with confidence

Im Tod und Leben:
In death and life:

Gott ist mein Licht,
God is my light,

Ihm will ich mich ergeben.
To-him will I - surrender.

Und haben alle Tage
And have all days

Gleich ihre eigne Plage,
Though, their own vexation,
{And though each day has its own vexation,}

Doch auf das überstandne Leid,
Yet upon - endured suffering,

Wenn man genug geweinet,
When one enough (has) wept,

Kommt endlich die Errettungszeit,
Comes finally the time-of-deliverance,
{The time of deliverance finally comes,}

Da Gottes treuer Sinn erscheinet.
When God's faithful inclination becomes-apparent.

5. Soprano & Alto Aria (Duet) (Based on Chorale Vs. 5)
●Cross bitter to flesh; endure it for future reward (99-5)
Wenn des Kreuzes Bitterkeiten
When the cross's bitter-sorrows

Mit des Fleisches Schwachheit streiten,
With the flesh's weakness struggle,
{Struggle against the weakness of the flesh,}

Ist dennoch wohlgetan.
Is (it) nevertheless well-done.
{It is nevertheless well done.}

give good things to those who ask him! (Also Lk. 11:9-13, Rom. 8:32.)
Jn. 13:7. Jesus answered [Peter], "What I am doing you do not know now, but afterward you will understand."

Ps. 105:8 / 1 Chron. 16:15. [The Lord] is mindful of his covenant for ever... (Also Ps. 111:5, 9.)
Ps. 89:28 [God]: My steadfast love I will keep for him for ever, and my covenant will stand firm for him.
Heb. 13:20. ...by the blood of the eternal covenant...
2 Tim. 2:19. God's firm foundation (Luther: Grund) stands, bearing this seal: "The Lord knows those who are his," and, "Let every one who names the name of the Lord depart from iniquity."
Phil. 1:20-21. It is my eager expectation and hope...that...Christ will be honored in my body, whether by life or by death. For to me to live is Christ, and to die is gain. (Also 2 Cor. 5:8.)
Ps. 27:1. The Lord is my light and my salvation; whom shall I fear?... (Also Ps. 56:4, 118:6, Rom. 8:31-39.)
Jn. 8:12. Again Jesus spoke to them, saying, "I am the light of the world; he who follows me will not walk in darkness, but will have the light of life." (Also Jn. 1:4, 9:5, 11:9, 12:46, Ps. 36:9.)
***Mt. 6:34 [Christ]:** Therefore do not be anxious about tomorrow, for tomorrow will be anxious for itself. Let the day's own trouble be sufficient for the day.
1 Pet. 5:10. And after you have suffered a little while, the God of all grace, who has called you to his eternal glory in Christ, will himself restore, establish, and strengthen you. Jms. 5:10-11. As an example of suffering and patience, brethren, take the prophets who spoke in the name of the Lord. Behold, we call those happy who were steadfast. You have heard of the steadfastness of Job, and you have seen the purpose of the Lord, how the Lord is compassionate and merciful.
Rev. 2:10 [Christ]: Do not fear what you are about to suffer...Be faithful unto death, and I will give you the crown of life.
Ps. 30:5. ...Weeping may tarry for the night, but joy comes with the morning.
Ps. 126:6. He that goes forth weeping, bearing the seed for sowing, shall come home with shouts of joy, bringing his sheaves with him.
Rev. 21:4. [God] will wipe away every tear from their eyes, and death shall be no more, neither shall there be mourning nor crying nor pain any more, for the former things have passed away. (Also Is. 25:8.)

Mk. 14:38 [Christ]: ...The spirit indeed is willing, but the flesh is weak. (Also Mt. 26:41.)
Gal. 5:17. For the desires of the flesh are against the Spirit, and the desires of the Spirit are against the flesh; for these are opposed to each other, to prevent you from doing what you would.
***Gal. 6:8.** He who sows to his own flesh will from the flesh reap corruption; but he who sows to the Sprit will from the Spirit reap eternal life. (Also Rom. 8:13, Gal. 5:24.)
Mt. 16:24-25. Then Jesus told his disciples, "If any man would come after me, let him deny himself and take up his cross and follow me. For whoever would save his life will lose it, and whoever loses his life for my sake will find it." (Also Mt. 10:38, Mk. 8:34-35, Lk. 9:23-24.)

Wer   das Kreuz durch falschen Wahn
Whoever the cross through erroneous delusion

Sich vor unerträglich schätzet,
  - As unbearable reckons,
{Whoever reckons the cross unbearable through erroneous delusion,}

Wird auch künftig nicht ergötzet.
Will   also hereafter not be-delighted.
{Will not receive eternal delight hereafter.}

6. Chorale (Vs. 6) (See also 12-7, 75-14, 100-6.)
●God's sovereign will accepted, even affliction (99-6)
Was   Gott tut, das ist wohlgetan,
Whatever God does, that is well-done,

Dabei will ich verbleiben.
In-that want I   to-abide.
{In that I want to abide.}

Es   mag mich auf die rauhe Bahn
(Now) may me on   a harsh course

Not, Tod und Elend treiben,
Want, death, and distress drive,
{If I be driven on a harsh course by want, death, and distress,}

So wird Gott mich
Then will God   me
{Then will God}

Ganz väterlich
Right fatherly

In seinen Armen halten,
In   his   arms   hold,
{Hold me in his arms;}

Drum   laß ich ihn nur walten.
Therefore allow I him just to-rule.
{Therefore I just allow him sovereign control.}

BWV 100
Was Gott tut, das ist wohlgetan III
(NBA I/34; BC A191)

Occasion Unknown (BWV 131, 150, 117, 192, 100, 97)
Perhaps 12. S. after Trinity or for a wedding.
Librettist: Chorale (Samuel Rodigast)

1. Chorus (Chorale Vs. 1) (Revised from BWV 99-1) (See
     also 98-1, 99-1, 144-3.)
●God's sovereign ways trusted and accepted as just (100-1)
Was   Gott tut, das ist wohlgetan,
Whatever God does, that is   well-done,

*Gal. 6:5, 9. Each man will have to bear his own load...And let us not grow weary in well-doing, for in due season we shall reap, if we do not lose heart. (Also Rev. 2:3.)
1 Cor. 10:13. No temptation has overtaken you that is not common to man. God is faithful, and he will not let you be tempted beyond your strength, but with the temptation will also provide the way of escape, that you may be able to endure it.
2 Tim. 2:11-12. The saying is sure: If we have died with him, we shall also live with him; if we endure, we shall also reign with him; if we deny him, he also will deny us. (Also Rom. 8:17, 1 Pet. 4:13.)

Mk. 7:37. [The people] were astonished beyond measure [at Jesus], saying, "He has done all things well..."
Rom. 8:28. We know that in everything God works for good with those who love him, who are called according to his purpose.
Rom. 8:18. I consider that the sufferings of this present time are not worth comparing with the glory that is to be revealed to us.
2 Cor. 4:17. For this slight momentary affliction is preparing for us an eternal weight of glory beyond all comparison.
2 Cor. 1:5. For as we share abundantly in Christ's sufferings, so through Christ we share abundantly in comfort too. (Also 1 Pet. 4:13.)
Lk. 16:22. The poor man died and was carried by the angels to Abraham's bosom...
Ps. 103:11, 13. As the heavens are high above the earth, so great is his steadfast love (Luther: läßt er seine Gnade walten) toward those who fear him...As a father pities his children, so the Lord pities those who fear him.
Mk. 10:14-16. Jesus...said to them, "Let the children come to me, do not hinder them; for to such belongs the kingdom of God. Truly, I say to you, whoever does not receive the kingdom of God like a child shall not enter it." And he took them in his arms and blessed them, laying his hands upon them. (Also Mk. 9:36-37, Is. 40:11.)
Rev. 21:3-4. ...God himself will be with them; he will wipe away every tear from their eyes, and death shall be no more, neither shall there be mourning nor crying nor pain any more, for the former things have passed away. (Also Is. 25:8.)
1 Pet. 4:19. Therefore let those who suffer according to God's will do right and entrust their souls to a faithful Creator.

Mk. 7:37. [The people] were astonished beyond measure [at Jesus], saying, "He has done all things well..."

Es   bleibt gerecht sein Wille;
(Now) remains just   his   will;
{His will remains just;}

Wie   er   fängt   meine   Sachen   an,
In-whatever-way he deals-with my   affairs - ,

Will ich ihm halten stille.
Will I to-him submit quietly.
{Will I submit to him quietly.}

Er ist mein Gott,
He is my God,

Der in der Not
Who in - distress

Mich wohl weiß   zu erhalten;
Me   well knows (how) to sustain;
{Knows well how to sustain me;}

Drum   laß ich ihn nur walten.
Therefore allow I him just to-rule.
{Therefore I will just allow him to rule.}

2. Alto & Tenor Duet (Chorale Vs. 2)
●God's ways trusted; he will change my misfortune (100-2)
Was   Gott tut, das ist wohlgetan,
Whatever God does, that is well-done,

Er wird mich nicht betrügen;
He will me   not deceive;
{He will not deceive me;}

Er führet mich auf rechter Bahn,
He leads   me   on the-right course,

So   laß ich mich begnügen
Therefore let I myself be-content
{Therefore I content myself}

An seiner Huld
With his graciousness

Und hab Geduld,
And have patience;

Er wird mein Unglück wenden,
He will my misfortune change,
{He will change my misfortune;}

Es steht in seinen Händen.
It (lies) in his   hands.

Ps. 145:17. The Lord is just in all his ways, and kind in all his doings. (Also Deut. 32:4.)

Rom. 8:28, 32. We know that in everything God works for good with those who love him, who are called according to his purpose...He who did not spare his own Son but gave him up for us all, will he not also give us all things with him?

Mt. 26:39, 42. Going a little farther [Jesus] fell on his face and prayed, "My Father, if it be possible, let this cup pass from me; nevertheless, not as I will, but as thou wilt."...Again, for the second time, he went away and prayed, "My Father, if this cannot pass unless I drink it, thy will be done."

1 Pet. 4:19. Let those who suffer according to God's will do right and entrust their souls to a faithful Creator.

Lam. 3:26. It is good that one should wait quietly for the salvation of the Lord.

Ps. 62:1. For God alone my soul waits in silence (Luther: meine Seele ist stille zu Gott); from him comes my salvation. (Also Ps. 62:5.)

Ps. 131:1–2. O Lord, my heart is not lifted up, my eyes are not raised too high; I do not occupy myself with things too great and too marvelous for me. But I have calmed and quieted my soul, like a child quieted at its mother's breast; like a child that is quieted is my soul.

Ps. 145:14. The Lord upholds (Luther: erhält) all who are falling, and raises up all who are bowed down. (erhalten: also Ps. 63:8, 119:116, 146:9, Is. 42:1)

Jms. 4:7. Submit yourselves therefore to God...

Mt. 6:9–10. Pray then like this:...Thy kingdom come, Thy will be done, On earth as it is in heaven.

Rom. 8:28. We know that in everything God works for good with those who love him...

Prov. 30:5. Every word of God proves true; he is a shield to those who take refuge in him. (Also Rom. 3:4.)

Ps. 25:9. He leads the humble in what is right, and teaches the humble his way. (Also Ps. 16:11, Is. 30:11.)

Ps. 27:11. Teach me thy way, O Lord; and lead me on a level path (Luther: richtiger Bahn)... (Also Ps. 143:8, 10.)

Prov. 14:2. He who walks in uprightness fears the Lord... (Luther: Wer den Herrn fürchtet der gehet auf rechter Bahn)

Ps. 145:8–9. The Lord is gracious and merciful, slow to anger and abounding in steadfast love. The Lord is good to all, and his compassion is over all that he has made. (Also Ps. 103:8, 11–13.)

Ps. 63:8. [O Lord,] my soul clings to thee; thy right hand upholds me. (Also Ps. 119:116, 145:14, 146:9.)

Rom. 12:12. Rejoice in your hope, be patient in tribulation, be constant in prayer. (Also Jms. 5:7–9.)

Jms. 1:3. You know that the testing of your faith produces steadfastness (Luther: Geduld). (Also Jms. 1:12, 5:10–11, 1 Pet. 4:12–14.)

1 Pet. 5:10. And after you have suffered a little while, the God of all grace...will himself restore, establish, and strengthen you.

Jer. 31:13 [God]: ...I will turn their mourning into joy, I will comfort them, and give them gladness for sorrow.

Ps. 10:14. [O Lord,] thou dost see; yea thou dost note trouble and vexation, that thou mayest take it into thy hands (Luther: es steht in deinen Händen)... (Also Ps. 31:15.)

3. Soprano Aria (Chorale Vs. 3)

●God's ways trusted though they be like medicine (100–3)

Was   Gott tut, das ist wohlgetan,
Whatever God does, that is   well-done,

Er wird mich wohl bedenken;
He will me indeed consider;
{He will indeed think of me;}

Er, als mein Arzt und Wundermann,
He, as   my physician and man-of-wonders,

Wird mir nicht Gift einschenken
Will for-me not poison   pour
{Will not give me posion}

Vor Arzenei.
For medicine.

Gott ist getreu,
God is faithful,

Drum   will ich auf ihn bauen
Therefore will I upon him build
{Therefore I will build upon him}

Und seiner Gnade trauen.
And   his   grace   trust.
{And trust his grace.}

Jer. 29:11. I know the plans I have for you, says the Lord, plans for welfare and not for evil, to give you a future and a hope. (Also Ps. 139:16–17.)

Job 5:18. [God] wounds, but he binds up; he smites, but his hands heal.

Mk. 2:17. [Jesus]...said to them, "Those who are well have no need of a physician, but those who are sick; I came not to call the righteous, but sinners." (Also Lk. 5:31–32.)

Mt. 7:9–11 [Christ]: What man of you, if his son asks him for bread, will give him a stone? Or if he asks for a fish, will give him a serpent? If you then, who are evil, know how to give good gifts to your children, how much more will your Father who is in heaven give good things to those who ask him! (Also Lk. 11:9–13, Rom. 8:32.)

Mk. 14:35–36. Going a little farther, [Jesus] fell on the ground and prayed that, if it were possible, the hour might pass from him. And he said, "Abba, Father, all things are possible to thee; remove this cup from me; yet not what I will, but what thou wilt." (Also Mk. 10:38–39, Mt. 20:22–23, 26:27, 39, Jn. 18:11.)

1 Cor. 10:13. No temptation has overtaken you that is not common to man. God is faithful (Luther: Aber Gott ist getreu), and he will not let you be tempted beyond your strength, but with the temptation will also provide the way of escape, that you may be able to endure it.

Mt. 7:24–26 [Christ]: Every one then who hears these words of mine and does them will be like a wise man who built his house upon the rock; and the rain fell, and the floods came, and the winds blew and beat upon that house, but it did not fall, because it had been founded on the rock. (Also Col. 2:6–7, 1 Thess. 5:11, Jude 1:20.)

Jn. 13:7. Jesus answered [Peter], "What I am doing you do not know now, but afterward you will understand."

4. Bass Aria (Chorale Vs. 4)

●God & his ways trusted; his purpose revealed someday (100–4)

Was   Gott tut, das ist wohlgetan,
Whatever God does, that is   well-done,

Er ist mein Licht, mein Leben,
He is my light,   my   life,

Der mir nichts Böses gönnen kann,
Who me   nothing evil   can-wish,
{Who can wish me no evil,}

Ich will   mich ihm ergeben
I would   myself to-him surrender
{I would surrender myself to him}

In Freud und Leid!
In joy and sorrow!

Es   kommt die Zeit,
There comes the time,
{The time will come,}

Da öffentlich erscheinet,
When openly is-manifested,
{When it becomes manifest,}

Ps. 27:1. The Lord is my light and my salvation; whom shall I fear?... (Also Ps. 56:4, 118:6, Rom. 8:31–39.)

Phil. 1:21. To me to live is Christ (Luther: Denn Christus ist mein Leben)...

Jn. 8:12. Jesus [said]... "I am the light of the world; he who follows me will not walk in darkness, but will have the light of life." (Also Jn. 1:4, 9:5, 11:9, 12:46, Ps. 36:9.)

Ps. 139:16–18. ...In thy book were written, every one of them, the days that were formed for me, when as yet there was none of them. How precious to me are thy thoughts, O God! How vast is the sum of them! If I would count them, they are more than the sand. When I awake, I am still with thee.

Job 1:21. [Job] said, "Naked I came from my mother's womb, and naked shall I return; the Lord gave, and the Lord has taken away; blessed be the name of the Lord."

1 Pet. 5:10. After you have suffered a little while, the God of all grace, who has called you to his eternal glory in Christ, will himself restore, establish, and strengthen you. **Jms. 5:11.** ...You have heard of the steadfastness of Job, and you have seen the purpose of the Lord, how the Lord is compassionate and merciful.

Heb. 12:5–6, 11. ...My son, do not regard lightly the discipline of the Lord, nor lose courage when you are punished by him. For the Lord disciplines him whom he loves, and chastises every son whom he receives...For the moment all discipline seems painful rather than pleasant; later it yields the peaceful fruit of righteousness to those who have been trained by it.

Wie treulich er es meinet.
How faithful he it intended.
{How faithful his intentions are.}

Ps. 30:5. ...Weeping may tarry for the night, but joy comes with the morning.

5. Alto Aria (Chorale Vs. 5) (See also 75-7.)
●Future comfort greater than present cup of suffering (100-5)
Was   Gott tut, das ist wohlgetan,
Whatever God does, that is   well-done,

Muß ich den Kelch gleich schmecken,
Must I   the cup   though   taste,
{Though I must drink the cup,}

Der bitter ist   nach   meinem Wahn,
That bitter is according-to   my   delusion,
{That, in my delusion, seems bitter to me,}

Laß ich mich   doch   nicht schrecken,
Allow I myself nevertheless not to-be-frightened,
{I nevertheless allow myself not to be frightened,}

Weil   doch   zuletzt
For nevertheless in-the-end

Ich werd ergötzt
I   will-be delighted

Mit süßem Trost im   Herzen;
With sweet comfort in (my) heart;

Da weichen alle Schmerzen.
Then retreat   all   sufferings.
{Then will all sufferings retreat.}

Rev. 2:10 [Christ]: Do not fear what you are about to suffer...Be faithful unto death, and I will give you the crown of life.
Mt. 20:20–23. The mother of the sons of Zebedee came up to [Jesus], with her sons...And he said to her, "What do you want?" She said to him, "Command that these two sons of mine may sit, one at your right hand and one at your left, in your kingdom." But Jesus answered, "You do not know what you are asking. Are you able to drink the cup that I am to drink?" They said to him, "We are able." He said to them, "You will drink my cup, but to sit at my right hand and at my left is not mine to grant, but it is for those for whom it has been prepared by my Father." (Also Mk. 10:38–39, Mt. 26:27–28, Jn. 18:11.)
Lk. 22:41–42. [Jesus]...knelt down and prayed, "Father, if thou art willing, remove this cup from me; nevertheless not my will, but thine, be done." (Also Jn 18:11.)
2 Cor. 4:17. This slight momentary affliction is preparing for us an eternal weight of glory beyond all comparison. (Also Rom. 8:18.)
Lk. 16:22, 25. The poor man [Lazarus] died and was carried by the angels to Abraham's bosom. The rich man also died and was buried... But Abraham said, "Son, remember that you in your lifetime received your good things, and Lazarus in like manner evil things; but now he is comforted here, and you are in anguish." (Also Heb. 4:9.)
Ps. 94:19. [O Lord]...thy consolations cheer (Luther: ergötzen) my soul.
Rev. 21:3–4. ...God himself will be with them; he will wipe away every tear from their eyes, and death shall be no more, neither shall there be mourning nor crying nor pain any more, for the former things have passed away. (Also Is. 25:8.)

6. Chorale (Vs. 6) (Taken from BWV 75-14) (See also 12-7, 75-14, 99-6.)
●God's sovereign ways accepted, even affliction (100-6)
Was   Gott tut, das ist wohlgetan,
Whatever God does, that is   well-done,

Darbei will ich verbleiben.
In-that want I   to-abide.
{In that I want to abide.}

Es   mag mich auf die rauhe Bahn
(Now) may me   on   a   harsh course

Not, Tod und Elend treiben,
Want, death, and distress drive,
{If I be driven on a harsh course by want, death, and distress,}

So   wird Gott mich
Then will God me
{Then will God}

Mk. 7:37. ...He has done all things well...
Rom. 8:28. We know that in everything God works for good with those who love him, who are called according to his purpose.
Rom. 8:18. I consider that the sufferings of this present time are not worth comparing with the glory that is to be revealed to us.
2 Cor. 4:17. For this slight momentary affliction is preparing for us an eternal weight of glory beyond all comparison.
2 Cor. 1:5. For as we share abundantly in Christ's sufferings, so through Christ we share abundantly in comfort too.
1 Pet. 4:13. But rejoice in so far as you share Christ's sufferings, that you may also rejoice and be glad when his glory is revealed.
1 Pet. 4:19. Therefore let those who suffer according to God's will do right and entrust their souls to a faithful Creator.
Ps. 103:11, 13. As the heavens are high above the earth, so great is his steadfast love (Luther: läßt er seine Gnade walten) toward those who fear him...As a father pities his children, so the Lord pities those who fear him.
Mk. 10:14, 16. Jesus...said to them, "Let the children come to me, do not hinder them; for to such belongs the kingdom of God..." And he took them in his arms... (Also Mk. 9:36–37, Is. 40:11.)

Ganz väterlich
Right fatherly

In seinen Armen halten;
In his arms hold;
{Hold me in his arms;}

Drum laß ich ihn nur walten.
Therefore allow I him just to-rule.
{Therefore I just allow him sovereign control.}

BWV 101
Nimm von uns, Herr, du treuer Gott
(NBA I/19; BC A118)

10. S. after Trinity (BWV 46, 101, 102)
*1 Cor. 12:1-11 (There is a diversity of gifts but one Spirit)
*Lk. 19:41-48 (Jesus foretells destruction of Jerusalem and drives traders out of temple)
Librettist: Unknown

1. Chorus (Chorale Vs. 1)
●Prayer: Spare us from judgment of national disasters (101-1)
Nimm von uns, Herr, du treuer Gott,
Take from us, (O) Lord, thou faithful God,

Die schwere Straf und große Not,
The severe punishment and great distress,

Die wir mit Sünden ohne Zahl
Which we for sins without number

Verdienet haben allzumal.
Earned have altogether.
{Which we all have earned for sins without number.}

Behüt für Krieg und teurer Zeit,
Protect from war and dearth times,
{Protect us from times of war and dearth,}

Für Seuchen, Feur und großem Leid.
From pestilences, fire, and great suffering.

2. Tenor Aria (Based on Chorale Vs. 2)
●Prayer: Spare us from war, our deserved judgment (101-2)
Handle nicht nach deinen Rechten
Deal not according to-thy right

Mit uns bösen Sündenknechten,
With us evil servants-of-sin,
{Deal not with us servants of sin according to thy right,}

Laß das Schwert der Feinde ruhn!
Let the sword of (our) foes rest!

Lk. 16:22. The poor man died and was carried by the angels to Abraham's bosom...
Rev. 21:3-4. ...God himself will be with them; he will wipe away every tear from their eyes, and death shall be no more, neither shall there be mourning nor crying nor pain any more, for the former things have passed away. (Also Rev. 7:17, Is. 25:8.)
Is. 40:11. He will feed his flock like a shepherd, he will gather the lambs in his arms, he will carry them in his bosom, and gently lead those that are with young.

*Lk. 19:41-44. When [Jesus] drew near and saw the city he wept over it, saying, "Would that even today you knew the things that make for peace! But now they are hid from your eyes. For the days shall come upon you, when your enemies will cast up a bank about you and surround you, and hem you in on every side, and dash you to the ground, you and your children within you, and they will not leave one stone upon another in you; because you did not know the time of your visitation."
Rev. 18:5. [Babylon's] sins are heaped high as heaven, and God has remembered her iniquities. (Also Ezra 9:6, Jer. 51:9.)
Deut. 28:15, 21-22. If you will not obey the voice of the Lord your God or be careful to do all his commandments and his statutes...then all these curses shall come upon you and overtake you...The Lord will make the pestilence cleave to you until he has consumed you off the land which you are entering to take possession of it. The Lord will smite you with consumption, and with fever, inflammation, and fiery heat, and with drought, and with blasting, and with mildew; they shall pursue you until you perish.
2 Chron. 20:9. [O Lord,] if evil comes upon us, the sword, judgment, or pestilence, or famine, we will stand before this house, and before thee, for thy name is in this house, and cry to thee in our affliction, and thou wilt hear and save.
Jer. 14:7. Though our iniquities testify against us, act, O Lord, for thy name's sake; for our backslidings are many, we have sinned against thee. (Also Jer. 14:20.)
Ps. 29:11. ...May the Lord bless his people with peace! (Also Ps. 122:6-7, 128:6, 147:14.)

Ps. 130:3-4. If thou, O Lord, shouldst mark iniquities, Lord, who could stand! But there is forgiveness with thee...
Ps. 103:10-12. He does not deal with us according to our sins, nor requite us according to our iniquities. For as the heavens are high above the earth, so great is his steadfast love toward those who fear him; as far as the east is from the west, so far does he remove our transgressions from us.
Is. 1:4. Ah, sinful nation, a people laden with iniquity...
Jn. 8:34. ...Every one who commits sin is a slave to sin (Luther: der Sünden Knecht). (Also Rom. 6:16, 20, Tit. 3:3, 2 Pet. 2:19.)

Höchster, höre unser Flehen,
Most-High, hear our entreaty,

Daß wir nicht durch sündlich Tun
That we not through sinful conduct
{That we do not perish because of sinful conduct}

Wie Jerusalem vergehen!
Like Jerusalem perish!
{Like Jerusalem!}

3. Soprano Recit. and Chorale (Vs. 3)
●Prayer: Peace comes from thee; keep us faithful (101-3)
Ach! Herr Gott, durch die Treue dein
Ah, Lord God, through the faithfulness of-thine
{Ah, Lord God, by thy faithfulness}

Wird unser Land in Fried und Ruhe sein.
Will our land in peace and quiet be.
{Our land will rest in peace and quiet.}

Wenn uns ein Unglückswetter droht,
When us - misfortune's-storm threatens,
{When misfortune's storm threatens us,}

So rufen wir,
Then call we,
{Then we call,}

Barmherzger Gott, zu dir
Compassionate God, to thee

In solcher Not:
In (that) distress:

Mit Trost und Rettung uns erschein!
With comfort and salvation to-us appear!
{Appear to us with comfort and salvation!}

Du kannst dem feindlichen Zerstören
Thou canst the foe's-hostile destruction
{Thou canst ward off the foe's hostile destruction}

Durch deine Macht und Hülfe wehren.
Through thy might and help ward-off.
{Through thy might and help.}

Beweis an uns deine große Gnad
Manifest in us thy great grace
{Manifest thy great grace in us}

Und straf uns nicht auf frischer Tat,
And punish us not for recent deed,
{And punish us not in the very act,}

Wenn unsre Füße wanken wollten
If our feet to-waver should-be-inclined
{If our feet should be inclined to waver}

Lev. 26:21, 25 [God]: If you walk contrary to me...I will bring a sword upon you, that shall execute vengeance for the covenant; and if you gather within your cities I will send pestilence among you, and you shall be delivered into the hand of the enemy.
Jer. 47:6-7. Ah, sword of the Lord! How long till you are quiet? Put yourself into your scabbard, rest and be still! How can it be quiet, when the Lord has given it a charge?... (Also Jer. 15:5-9.)
*Lk. 19:43 [Christ]: The days shall come upon you, when your enemies will cast up a bank about you and surround you, and hem you in on every side.

*Lk. 19:41-42. When [Jesus] drew near and saw the city he wept over it, saying, "Would that even today you knew the things that make for peace..."
Lk. 13:32, 34-35. And Jesus said to them, "...O Jerusalem, Jerusalem, killing the prophets and stoning those who are sent to you! How often would I have gathered your children together as a hen gathers her brood under her wings, and you would not! Behold, your house is forsaken..." (Also Mt. 23:37-38.)
Lev. 26:3-4, 6 [God]: If you walk in my statutes and observe my commandments and do them, then I will give you your rains in their season, and the land shall yield its increase, and the trees of the field shall yield their fruit...And I will give peace in the land, and you shall lie down, and none shall make you afraid; and I will remove evil beasts from the land, and the sword shall not go through your land. (See also Deut. 28.)
Ps. 28:8-9. The Lord is the strength of his people, he is the saving refuge of his anointed. O save thy people, and bless thy heritage; be thou their shepherd, and carry them for ever.
Ps. 80:1-3. Give ear, O Shepherd of Israel, thou who leadest Joseph like a flock! Thou who art enthroned upon the cherubim, shine forth (Luther: erscheine, der du sitzest über den Cherubim!)...Stir up thy might, and come to save us! Restore us, O God; let thy face shine, that we may be saved!
Ps. 17:6-7. I call upon thee, for thou wilt answer me, O God; incline thy ear to me, hear my words. Wondrously show (Luther: beweise) thy steadfast love, O savior of those who seek refuge from their adversaries at thy right hand.
Ps. 130:3-4. If thou, O Lord, shouldst mark iniquities, Lord, who could stand! But there is forgiveness with thee...
Ps. 103:10-11. [The Lord] does not deal with us according to our sins, nor requite us according to our iniquities. For as the heavens are high above the earth, so great is his steadfast love toward those who fear him.
Jn. 8:3-5, 7, 9-11. The scribes and the Pharisees brought a woman who had been caught in adultery, and placing her in the midst they said to him, "Teacher, this woman has been caught in the act (Luther: auf frischer Tat) of adultery. Now in the law Moses commanded us to stone such. What do you say about her?"...He stood up and said to them, "Let him who is without sin among you be the first to throw a stone at her."...But when they heard it, they went away, one by one... Jesus looked up and said to her, "Woman, where are they? Has no one condemned you?" She said, "No one, Lord." And Jesus said, "Neither do I condemn you; go, and do not sin again."
Rom. 3:10-12. As it is written: "None is righteous, no, not one...no one seeks for God. All have turned aside, together they have gone wrong; no one does good, not even one."

Und wir aus Schwachheit strauchen sollten.
And we out-of weakness should-stumble.
{And we should stumble out of weakness.}

Wohn uns mit deiner Güte bei
Attend us with thy kindness -

Und gib, daß wir
And grant, that we

Nur nach dem Guten streben,
Only after the good (would) strive,
{Would strive only after the good,}

Damit allhier
So-that here

Und auch in jenem Leben
And also in yonder life

Dein Zorn und Grimm fern von uns sei.
Thy wrath and fury far from us (might) be.

4. Bass Aria (Based on Chorale Vs. 4)
•Prayer: Spare us from thy zealous wrath! (101-4)
Warum willst du so zornig sein?
Why wouldst thou so wrathful be?

Es schlagen deines Eifers Flammen
(Now) strike thy zeal's flames

Schon über unserm Haupt zusammen.
Already above our head together.
{Thy zeal's flames already strike together above our heads.}

Ach, stelle doch die Strafen ein
Ah, suspend indeed the sentence -
{Ah, please suspend the sentence}

Und trag aus väterlicher Huld
And (have) out-of paternal grace
{And out of paternal grace, have}

Mit unserm schwachen Fleisch Geduld!
With our weak flesh patience!
{Patience with our weak flesh!}

5. Tenor Recit. & Chorale (Vs. 5)
•Sinful nature, devil & world makes us prone to sin (101-5)
Die Sünd hat uns verderbet sehr.
- Sin has us corrupted greatly.
{Sin has corrupted us greatly.}

So müssen auch die Frömmsten sagen
Thus must also the godliest say
{Thus even the godliest must say}

Und mit betränten Augen klagen:
And with tear-filled eyes bewail (that):

Is. 59:7. Their feet run to evil...
Prov. 4:26. Take heed to the path of your feet, then all your ways will be sure. (Also Jer. 14:10.)
Ps. 73:2. But as for me, my feet had almost stumbled (Luther: gestrauchelt), my steps had well-nigh slipped. (strauchen: also Ps. 119:165, Is. 35:3, Heb. 12:13)
Amos 5:14-15. Seek good, and not evil, that you may live; and so the Lord, the God of hosts, will be with you, as you have said. Hate evil, and love good, and establish justice in the gate; it may be that the Lord, the God of hosts, will be gracious to the remnant of Joseph. (Also Is. 1:16-17, also Ps. 34:14, Mt. 6:33.)
Rom. 1:18. For the wrath of God is revealed from heaven against all ungodliness and wickedness of men...
Dan. 9:16, 18. O Lord, according to all thy righteous acts, let thy anger and thy wrath (Luther: Zorn und Grimm) turn away from thy city Jerusalem, thy holy hill; because for our sins, and for the iniquities of our fathers, Jerusalem and thy people have become a byword among all who are round about us...for we do not present our supplications before thee on the ground of our righteousness, but on the ground of thy great mercy.

*Lk. 19:45-46. And [Jesus] entered the temple and began to drive out those who sold, saying to them, "It is written, 'My house shall be a house of prayer'; but you have made it a den of robbers." (Also Mt. 21:12-13, Mk. 11:15-17.)
Jn. 2:14-17. In the temple [Jesus] found those who were selling...And making a whip of cords, he drove them all, with the sheep and oxen out of the temple...And he told those who sold pigeons, "Take these things away; you shall not make my Father's house a house of trade." His disciples remembered that it was written, "Zeal for thy house will consume me." (See Ps. 69:9.)
Num. 12:11. Aaron said to Moses, "Oh, my lord, do not punish us because we have done foolishly and have sinned."
Ps. 103:8-10, 13-14. The Lord is merciful and gracious, slow to anger and abounding in steadfast love. He will not always chide, nor will he keep his anger for ever. He does not deal with us according to our sins, nor requite us according to our iniquities...As a father pities his children, so the Lord pities those who fear him. For he knows our frame; he remembers that we are dust. (Also Ex. 34:6, Ps. 145:8-9.)
Mk. 14:38. ...The spirit indeed is willing, but the flesh is weak. (Also Mt. 26:41, Rom. 7:18.)

Rom. 5:12. ...Sin came into the world through one man and death through sin, and so death spread to all men because all men sinned.
Jn. 8:34. Jesus [said]... "Truly, truly, I say to you, every one who commits sin is a slave to sin." (Also Rom. 6:16, 20.)
2 Pet. 2:19. ...For whatever overcomes a man, to that he is enslaved. (Also Tit. 3:3.)
Rom. 7:15-24. I do not understand my own actions. For I do not do what I want, but I do the very thing I hate. Now if I do what I do not want, I agree that the law is good. So then it is no longer I that do it, but sin which dwells within me. For I know that nothing good dwells within me, that is, in my flesh. I can will what is right, but I cannot do

Der Teufel plagt uns noch viel mehr.
The devil plagues us yet much more.
{The devil still plagues us greatly.}

Ja, dieser böse Geist,
Yes, this evil spirit,

Der schon von Anbeginn ein Mörder heißt,
Who already from (the) beginning a murderer is-called,
{Who is called a murderer already from the beginning,}

Sucht uns um unser Heil zu bringen
Seeks us (without) our salvation to bring-about
{Seeks to deprive us of our salvation}

Und als ein Löwe zu verschlingen.
And like a lion (us) to devour.
{And to devour us like a lion.}

Die Welt, auch unser Fleisch und Blut
The world, even our (own) flesh and blood

Uns allezeit verführen tut.
Us always leads-astray - .
{Always leads us astray.}

Wir treffen hier auf dieser schmalen Bahn
We encounter here on this narrow way

Sehr viele Hindernis im Guten an.
(A) great many obstacles to the-good - .
[antreffen = to encounter]

Solch Elend kennst du, Herr, allein:
Such misery knowest thou, Lord, alone:

Hilf, Helfer, hilf uns Schwachen,
Help, (O) Helper, help us weak-ones,

Du kannst uns stärker machen!
Thou canst us stronger make!
{Thou canst make us stronger!}

Ach, laß uns dir befohlen sein.
Ah, let us to-thee commended be.
{Ah, let us be commended to thee.}

6. Soprano & Alto Duet (Based on Chorale Vs. 6)
●Prayer: Remember Jesus' death & have mercy on me!
(101-6)
Gedenk an Jesu bittern Tod!
Remember - Jesus' bitter death!

Nimm, Vater, deines Sohnes Schmerzen
Take, (O) Father, thy Son's sufferings

Und seiner Wunden Pein zu Herzen,
And his wounds' pain to heart,

Die sind ja für die ganze Welt
They are, after-all, for the entire world

it. For I do not do the good I want, but the evil I do not want is what I do. Now if I do what I do not want, it is no longer I that do it, but sin which dwells within me. So I find it to be a law that when I want to do right, evil lies close at hand. For I delight in the law of God, in my inmost self, but I see in my members another law at war with the law of my mind and making me captive to the law of sin which dwells in my members. Wretched man that I am! Who will deliver me from this body of death? (Also Gal. 5:17.)
Jn. 8:44 [Christ]: You are of your father the devil, and your will is to do your father's desires. He was a murderer from the beginning, and has nothing to do with the truth, because there is no truth in him. When he lies, he speaks according to his own nature, for he is a liar and the father of lies.
1 Jn. 3:8. He who commits sin is of the devil; for the devil has sinned from the beginning. The reason the Son of God appeared was to destroy the works of the devil. (Also Heb. 2:14.)
1 Pet. 5:8. Be sober, be watchful. Your adversary the devil prowls around like a roaring lion, seeking some one to devour.
Jms. 1:13–14. Let no one say when he is tempted, "I am tempted by God"; for God cannot be tempted with evil and he himself tempts no one; but each person is tempted when he is lured and enticed by his own desire.
Mt. 18:7 [Christ]: Woe to the world for temptations to sin! For it is necesssary that temptations come, but woe to the man by whom the temptation comes! (Also Lk. 17:1.)
Jms. 4:4. Unfaithful creatures! Do you not know that friendship with the world is enmity with God? Therefore whoever wishes to be a friend of the world makes himself an enemy of God. (Also 1 Jn. 2:15–17.)
Mt. 7:13–14 [Christ]: Enter by the narrow gate; for the gate is wide and the way is easy, that leads to destruction, and those who enter by it are many. For the gate is narrow and the way is hard, that leads to life, and those who find it are few.
Ps. 30:10. Hear, O Lord, and be gracious to me! O Lord, be thou my helper! (Also Ps. 54:4.)
2 Thess. 3:3. The Lord is faithful; he will strengthen you and guard you from evil. (Also Rom. 16:25.)
Heb. 4:15–16. For we have not a high priest who is unable to sympathize with our weaknesses, but one who in every respect has been tempted as we are, yet without sin. Let us then with confidence draw near to the throne of grace, that we may receive mercy and find grace to help in time of need.

Is. 53: 5–6. He was wounded for our transgressions, he was bruised for our iniquities; upon him was the chastisement that made us whole, and with his stripes we are healed...All we like sheep have gone astray; we have turned every one to his own way; and the Lord has laid on him the iniquity of us all.
2 Cor. 5:21. For our sake [God] made him to be sin who knew no sin, so that in him we might become the righteousness of God.
Rom. 5:8. God shows his love for us in that while we were yet sinners Christ died for us.
Rom. 8:3. For God has done what the law, weakened by the flesh, could not do: sending his own Son in the likeness of sinful flesh and for sin, he condemned sin in the flesh.
Rom. 8:33–34. Who shall bring any charge against God's elect? It is God who justifies; who is to condemn? Is it Christ Jesus, who died,

Die Zahlung und das Lösegeld;
The payment and the ransom;

Erzeig auch mir zu aller Zeit,
Show also to-me at all times,

Barmherzger Gott, Barmherzigkeit!
Merciful God, (thy) mercy!

Ich seufze stets in meiner Not:
I sigh continually in my distress:

Gedenk an Jesu bittern Tod!
Remember - Jesus' bitter death!

7. Chorale (Vs. 7) (See also 90–5.)
●Prayer for blessing on nation & spiritual protection (101-7)
Leit uns mit deiner rechten Hand
Lead us with thy right hand

Und segne unser Stadt und Land;
And bless our city and land;

Gib uns allzeit dein heilges Wort,
Give us alway thy holy Word,

Behüt für's Teufels List und Mord;
Protect (us) from-the devil's cunning and murder;

Verleih ein selges Stündelein,
Grant a blessed little-hour,

Auf daß wir ewig bei dir sein!
So that we eternally with thee might-be!

BWV 102
Herr, deine Augen sehen nach dem Glauben
(NBA I/19; BC A119)

10. S. after Trinity (BWV 46, 101, 102)
*1 Cor. 12:1–11 (There is a diversity of gifts but one Spirit)
*Lk. 19:41–48 (Jesus foretells destruction of Jerusalem and drives traders out of temple)
Librettist: perhaps Christoph Helm

Part I

1. Chorus
●Impenitence: God's discipline in vain: Jer. 5:3 (102-1)
Herr, deine Augen sehen nach dem Glauben!
Lord, thine eyes look for - faith!

yes, who was raised from the dead, who is at the right hand of God, who indeed intercedes for us? (Also 1 Jn. 2:1, Heb. 7:25.)
Mt. 20:28 [Christ]: ...The Son of Man came not to be served but to serve, and to give his life as a ransom (Luther: Bezahlung) for many. (Also Mk. 10:45, 1 Tim. 2:5–6, Rev. 5:9–10.)
Rom. 8:26. Likewise the Spirit helps us in our weakness; for we do not know how to pray as we ought, but the Spirit himself intercedes for us with sighs too deep for words.
Ps. 51:1–2, 10–11. Have mercy on me, O God, according to thy steadfast love; according to thy abundant mercy blot out my transgressions. Wash me thoroughly from my iniquity, and cleanse me from my sin!...Create in me a clean heart, O God, and put a new and right spirit within me. Cast me not away from thy presence, and take not thy holy Spirit from me.

Ps. 60:5. [O Lord,] that thy beloved may be delivered, give victory by thy right hand and answer us! (Also Ps. 89:13.)
Ps. 139:9–10. If I...dwell in the uttermost parts of the sea, even there thy hand shall lead me, and thy right hand shall hold me. (Also Ps. 16:11, 63:8, 108:6.)
Deut. 26:15. [O Lord,] look down from thy holy habitation, from heaven, and bless thy people Israel and the ground which thou hast given us, as thou didst swear to our fathers...
Ps. 28:9. O save thy people, and bless thy heritage...
Ps. 119:43. And take not the word of truth utterly out of my mouth, for my hope is in thy ordinances. (Also Ps. 138:2.)
Ps. 3:8. Deliverance belongs to the Lord; thy blessing be upon thy people!
1 Pet. 5:8. Be sober, be watchful. Your adversary the devil prowls around like a roaring lion, seeking some one to devour.
Eph. 6:11, 16–17. Put on the whole armor of God, that you may be able to stand against the wiles (Luther: listigen Anläufe) of the devil... [Take] the shield of faith, with which you can quench all the flaming darts of the evil one. And take the helmet of salvation, and the sword of the Spirit, which is the word of God.
Phil. 1:6. I am sure that he who began a good work in you will bring it to completion at the day of Jesus Christ.
Rev. 2:7 [Christ]: ...To him who conquers I will grant to eat of the tree of life, which is in the paradise of God.
1 Thess. 4:17. ...So we shall always be with the Lord.

*Lk. 19:41–44.** When [Jesus] drew near and saw the city he wept over it, saying, "Would that even today you knew the things that make for peace! But now they are hid from your eyes. For the days shall come upon you, when your enemies will cast up a bank about you and surround you, and hem you in on every side, and dash you to the ground, you and your children within you, and they will not leave one stone upon another in you; because you did not know the time of your visitation."

Du schlägest sie, aber sie fühlen's nicht;
Thou dost-strike them, but they feel-it not;

du   plagest   sie, aber sie bessern   sich   nicht.
thou dost-plague them, but they reform themselves not.

Sie haben ein härter Angesicht denn ein Fels
They have a harder   face   than a rock
{They have a face harder than rock}

und wollen sich   nicht bekehren!
and   will themselves not   convert!
{and will not be converted!}

2. Bass Recit.
●Impenitence nullifies God's attempts to work in us (102-2)
Wo   ist das Ebenbild, das Gott uns   eingepräget,
Where is the image,   that God in-us (has) imprinted,

Wenn der verkehrte Will sich ihm zuwiderleget?
If   the perverted will itself against-it-sets?
{If our perverted will sets itself against it?}

Wo   ist die Kraft von seinem Wort,
Where is the power of   his   Word,

Wenn alle Besserung weicht aus dem Herzen fort?
If   all improvement retreats out-of-the heart   - ?
{If all desire to change retreats from our heart?}

Der Höchste suchet uns durch Sanftmut zwar zu zähmen,
The Most-High seeks us   with gentleness indeed to tame,
{The Most High indeed seeks to tame us with gentleness,}

Ob   der verirrte Geist sich   wollte noch bequemen;
So-that the wayward spirit - might-want yet to-comply;
{So that the wayward spirit might yet want to comply;}

Doch, fährt er fort in dem verstockten Sinn,
Yet, continues it - with - (a) stubborn disposition,
{Yet, if it persists in its stubborness,}

So   gibt er ihn in's Herzens Dünkel hin.
Then surrenders he it to-the heart's darkness - .
{Then he surrenders it to the darkness of its heart.}

3. Alto Aria
●Impenitence: Woe to the soul that persists in it! (102-3)
Weh der Seele, die den Schaden
Woe to-that soul, who the harm (to itself)

Jer. 5:1, 3. Run to and fro through the streets of Jerusalem, look and take note! Search her squares to see if you can find a man, one who does justice and seeks truth; that I may pardon her...*O Lord, do not thy eyes look for truth? Thou hast smitten them, but they felt no anguish; thou hast consumed them, but they refused to take correction. They have made their faces harder than rock; they have refused to repent.* (Also Jer. 26:13.)
Is. 1:5 [God]: Why will you still be smitten that you continue to rebel?... (Also Is. 9:13, Jer. 2:30, Zeph. 3:2.)
Jer. 19:15. Thus says the Lord of hosts, the God of Israel, Behold, I am bringing upon this city and upon all its towns all the evil that I have pronounced against it, because they have stiffened their neck, refusing to hear my words. (Also Jer. 7:26.)

Gen. 1:26–27. God said, "Let us make man in our image, after our likeness..." So God created man in his own image, in the image of God he created him; male and female he created them.
1 Pet. 1:15–16. As he who called you is holy, be holy yourselves in all your conduct; since it is written, "You shall be holy, for I am holy." (See Lev. 11:44.)
Ps. 138:2. ...[O Lord,] thou hast exalted above everything thy name and thy word.
Heb. 4:12. The word of God is living and active, sharper than any two-edged sword, piercing to the division of soul and spirit, of joints and marrow, and discerning the thoughts and intentions of the heart. (Also 1 Thess. 1:5.)
Is. 55:10–11 [God]: ...[My word] shall not return to me empty, but it shall accomplish that which I purpose...
Jer. 7:25–26 [God]: ...I have persistently sent all my servants the prophets to [my people], day after day; yet they did not listen to me, or incline their ear, but stiffened their neck... (Also Jer. 19:15.)
Rom. 2:4. ...Do you not know that God's kindness is meant to lead you to repentance?
Mt. 11:29–30 [Christ]: Take my yoke upon you, and learn from me; for I am gentle and lowly in heart, and you will find rest for your souls. For my yoke is easy, and my burden is light.
Ps. 81:11, 13 [God]: But my people did not listen to my voice...O that my people would listen to me, that Israel would walk in my ways!
Rom. 1:21–23, 28–29. Although [men] knew God they did not honor him as God or give thanks to him, but they became futile in their thinking and their senseless minds were darkened. Claiming to be wise, they became fools, and exchanged the glory of the immortal God for images resembling mortal man or birds or animals or reptiles...And since they did not see fit to acknowledge God, God gave them up to a base mind (Luther: verkehrten Sinn) and to improper conduct. They were filled with all manner of wickedness... (Also Rom. 11:8–10, Eph. 4:17–18.)
Jn. 12:40. [God] has blinded their eyes and hardened their heart, lest they should see with their eyes and perceive with their heart, and turn for me to heal them. (Also Is. 6:9–10, Ex. 9:12, 10:1, Deut. 2:30.)

Rom. 2:5–8. By your hard and impenitent heart you are storing up wrath for yourself on the day of wrath when God's righteous judgment will be revealed. For he will render to every man according to his works: to those who by patience in well-doing seek for glory and

Nicht mehr kennt
No   longer discerns

Und, die Straf auf sich zu laden,
And, the punishment on itself to load,
{And, loading up punishment for itself,}

Störrig   rennt,
Headstrong runs,
{Runs headlong;}

Ja von ihres Gottes Gnaden
Yes, from its   God's   grace

Selbst sich trennt.
  - Itself separates.
{Yes, separates itself from the very grace of its God.}

4. Bass Arioso
●Impenitence: God's forbearance will end! Rom. 2:4–5
(102–4)
Verachtest du den Reichtum seiner Gnade,
Despisest thou the   riches   of-his grace,

Geduld und Langmütigkeit? Weißest du nicht,
patience and forbearance?   Knowest thou not,

daß dich Gottes Güte zur Buße   locket?
that thee God's goodness to repentance coaxeth?

Du   aber   nach   deinem verstockten und
Thou, however, because-of   thy   obstinate and

unbußfertigen Herzen häufest dir selbst
impenitent   heart, heapest-up for-thy-self

den Zorn auf den Tag des   Zorns
  - wrath on the day of (the) wrath

und der Offenbarung des gerechten Gerichts Gottes.
and the   revelation of-the righteous judgment of-God.

Part II

5. Tenor Aria
●Exhortation to repent: Think of your judgment! (102–5)
Erschecke   doch
Be-frightened indeed

Du allzu sichre Seele!
Thou all-too sure soul!

Denk, was   dich würdig zähle
Think of-what (punishment) thee deserving reckons

Der Sünden Joch.
  - Sin's yoke.
{Think what punishment thy sin's yoke will have earned thee.}

honor and immortality, he will give eternal life; but for those who are factious and do not obey the truth, but obey wickedness, there will be wrath and fury.
1 Thess. 2:16. ...[These men who resist God] always...fill up the measure of their sins. But God's wrath has come upon them at last! (Also Mt. 23:32.)
Heb. 10:26–30. If we sin deliberately after receiving the knowledge of the truth, there no longer remains a sacrifice for sins, but a fearful prospect of judgment, and a fury of fire which will consume the adversaries. A man who has violated the law of Moses dies without mercy at the testimony of two or three witnesses. How much worse punishment do you think will be deserved by the man who has spurned the Son of God, and profaned the blood of the covenant by which he was sanctified, and outraged the Spirit of grace? For we know him who said, "Vengeance is mine, I will repay." And again, "The Lord will judge his people." (Also Is. 59:1–2.)

Rom. 2:1–9. Therefore you have no excuse, O man, whoever you are, when you judge another; for in passing judgment upon him you condemn yourself, because you, the judge, are doing the very same things. We know that the judgment of God rightly falls upon those who do such things. Do you suppose, O man, that when you judge those who do such things and yet do them yourself, you will escape the judgment of God? *Or do you presume upon the riches of his kindness and forbearance and patience? Do you not know that God's kindness is meant to lead you to repentance? But by your hard and impenitent heart you are storing up wrath for yourself on the day of wrath when God's righteous judgment will be revealed.* For he will render to every man according to his works: to those who by patience in well-doing seek for glory and honor and immortality, he will give eternal life; but for those who are factious and do not obey the truth, but obey wickedness, there will be wrath and fury. There will be tribulation and distress for every human being who does evil, the Jew first and also the Greek...
*Lk. 19:43–44 [Christ]: The days shall come upon you, when your enemies will cast up a bank about you and surround you, and hem you in on every side, and dash you to the ground, you and your children within you, and they will not leave one stone upon another in you...

1 Thess. 5:2–3. You yourselves know well that the day of the Lord will come like a thief in the night. When people say, "There is peace and security," then sudden destruction will come upon them as travail comes upon a woman with child, and there will be no escape.
Is. 13:6–9. Wail, for the day of the Lord is near; as destruction from the Almighty it will come! Therefore all hands will be feeble, and every man's heart will melt, and they will be dismayed. Pangs and agony will seize them; they will be in anguish like a woman in travail. They will look aghast at one another; their faces will be aflame. Behold the day of the Lord comes, cruel, with wrath and fierce anger, to make the earth a desolation and to destroy its sinners from it.
Rom. 6:23. The wages of sin is death...
Rom. 6:16. Do you not know that if you yield yourselves to any one as obedient slaves, you are slaves of the one whom you obey, either

Die   Gottteslangmut   geht   auf einem Fuß von Blei,
The   forbearance-of-God   treads with   a   foot   of   lead,
{The forbearance of God treads with leaden foot,}

Damit   der Zorn   hernach   dir
So-that (his)   wrath   hereafter   for-thee

desto   schwerer   sei.
so-much   graver   (will) be.
{So that his wrath hereafter will be so much graver for thee.}

6. Alto Recit.
●Exhortation to repent: Waiting is very dangerous! (102–6)
Bei Warten   ist Gefahr;
In   waiting   (there) is   danger;

Willt   du die   Zeit   verlieren?
Wouldst thou the (opportunity)   lose?

Der Gott,   der ehmals   gnädig war,
The God,   who formerly   merciful was,
{The God who was formerly merciful,}

Kann leichtlich dich vor seinen Richtstuhl führen.
Can   easily   thee before his   judgment-seat   lead.
{Can easily lead thee before his judgment seat.}

Wo   bleibt sodann die   Buß?
Where remains   then   - repentance?
{Where is repentance then?}

Es ist ein   Augenblick,
It   is (the)   twinkling-of-an-eye,

Der Zeit und Ewigkeit, der Leib und Seele scheidet;
That time and eternity,   the body and   soul   separates;
{That separates time and eternity, body and soul;}

Verblendter Sinn, ach kehre doch zurück,
Blinded   mind,   ah, turn   indeed back,
{Blinded mind, ah, do turn back,}

Daß   dich dieselbe Stund nicht finde unbereitet!
So-that thee that-same hour   not   find   unprepared!
{So that the hour not find thee unprepared!}

7. Chorale
●Exhortation to repent: Life can quickly end! (102–7)
Heut lebst du,   heut bekehre dich!
Today livest thou; today be-converted   - !

Eh   morgen kömmt, kann's   ändern sich;
Before morning comes,   can (times) change   - ;

Wer   heut ist frisch, gesund und rot,
He-who today is   fresh,   healthy,   and ruddy,

---

of sin, which leads to death, or of obedience, which leads to righteousness? (Also Jn. 8:34, 2 Pet. 2:19.)

Heb. 12:25. See that you do not refuse him who is speaking. For if they did not escape when they refused him who warned them on earth, much less shall we escape if we reject him who warns from heaven.

Heb. 10:29. How much worse punishment do you think will be deserved by the man who has spurned the Son of God, and profaned the blood of the covenant by which he was sanctified, and outraged the Spirit of grace?

Heb. 3:7–11. Therefore, as the Holy Spirit says, "Today, when you hear his voice, do not harden your hearts as in the rebellion, on the day of testing in the wilderness, where your fathers put me to the test and saw my works for forty years. Therefore I was provoked with that generation, and said, 'They always go astray in their hearts; they have not known my ways.' As I swore in my wrath, 'They shall never enter my rest.'"

Heb. 12:15–17. See to it that no one fail to obtain the grace of God... that no one be immoral or irreligious like Esau, who sold his birthright for a single meal. For you know that afterward, when he desired to inherit the blessing, he was rejected, for he found no chance to repent, though he sought it with tears. (Also Heb. 2:3, 12:25.)

Jms. 4:14. You do not know about tomorrow. What is your life? For you are a mist that appears for a little time and then vanishes.

Prov. 27:1. Do not boast about tomorrow, for you do not know what a day may bring forth.

Ps. 39:5. Surely every man stands as a mere breath! Surely every man goes about as a shadow! (Also Ps. 90:12, Job 14:5.)

***Lk. 19:44 [Christ]:** ...You did not know the time of your visitation.

Ps. 81:11, 13 [God]: My people did not listen to my voice...O that my people would listen to me...

2 Cor. 4:3–4. ...If our gospel is veiled, it is veiled only to those who are perishing. In their case the god of this world has blinded the minds (Luther: Sinn verblendet hat) of the unbelievers, to keep them from seeing the light of the gospel... (Also Is. 44:18, Jn. 12:40, Rom. 11:10, 1 Jn. 2:11.)

Rom. 14:10–12. ...We shall all stand before the judgment seat of God; for it is written, "As I live, says the Lord, every knee shall bow to me, and every tongue shall give praise to God." So each of us shall give account of himself to God. (Also 2 Cor. 5:10, Heb. 9:27.)

Prov. 27:1. Do not boast about tomorrow, for you do not know what a day may bring forth.

Jms. 4:13–15. Come now, you who say, "Today or tomorrow we will go into such and such a town and spend a year there and trade and get gain"; whereas you do not know about tomorrow. What is your life? For you are a mist that appears for a little time and then vanishes. Instead you ought to say, "If the Lord wills, we shall live and we shall do this or that."

Ist morgen krank, ja   wohl   gar tot.
Is tomorrow sick, yes, (sometimes) indeed even dead.

So du nun stirbest ohne   Buß,
If thou now diest without repentance,

Dein Leib und Seel dort brennen muß.
Thy body and soul yonder must-burn.

///

Hilf, o Herr Jesu, hilf du mir,
Help, O Lord Jesus, help thou me,

Daß ich noch heute komm zu dir
That I yet today come to thee

Und Buße tu   den Augenblick,
And repent (in) that moment

Eh mich der schnelle Tod   hinrück,
Ere me - sudden death snatches-away,
{Ere sudden death snatches me away,}

Auf daß ich heut und jederzeit
So that I today and evermore

Zu meiner Heimfahrt sei bereit.
For my home-going be prepared.
{Be prepared for my homegoing.}

BWV 103
Ihr werdet weinen und heulen
(NBA I/11; BC A69)

Jubilate: 3. S. after Easter (BWV 12, 103, 146)
*1 Pet. 2:11–20 (Be subject to all human orders)
*Jn. 16:16–23[1] (Jesus' farewell to his disciples)
[1]End: "nothing of me."
Librettist: Christiane Mariane von Ziegler (Text shortened and modified by someone: J. S. Bach?)

1. Chorus and Bass solo
●Weeping foretold; it will turn to joy: Jn. 16:20 (103-1)
Chorus:
Ihr werdet weinen und heulen,
You will weep and wail,

aber die Welt wird sich freuen.
but the world will rejoice.

Bass:
Ihr aber werdet traurig sein.
You, however, will sorrowful be.

Doch eure Traurigkeit soll
Yet your sorrow shall

Ps. 90:12. So teach us to number our days that we may get a heart of wisdom.
Ps. 39:4–6. Lord, let me know my end, and what is the measure of my days; let me know how fleeting my life is! Behold, thou hast made my days a few handbreadths, and my lifetime is as nothing in thy sight. Surely every man stands as a mere breath! Surely man goes about as a shadow!... (Also Ps. 103:14–16, Job 7:7, Jms. 1:10–11.)
Mt. 10:28 [Christ]: Do not fear those who kill the body but cannot kill the soul; rather fear him who can destroy both soul and body in hell. (Also Lk. 12:5.)
***Lk. 19:42, 44 [Christ]:** Would that even today you knew the things that make for peace!...You did not know the time of your visitation.
Ecc. 12:1. Remember also your Creator in the days of your youth...
Jn. 14:6. Jesus said..."I am the way, and the truth, and the life; no one comes to the Father, but by me." (Also Acts 4:12.)
Jn. 6:43–44. Jesus answered them, "...No one can come to me unless the Father who sent me draws him; and I will raise him up at the last day."
Heb. 3:13. Exhort one another every day, as long as it is called "today," that none of you may be hardened by the deceitfulness of sin. For we share in Christ, if only we hold our first confidence firm to the end, while it is said, "Today, when you hear his voice, do not harden your hearts as in the rebellion." (Also Heb. 4:6–11.)
Ps. 39:5. [O Lord,] behold, thou hast made my days a few handbreadths...
Lk. 12:17–20. ...A rich man...thought to himself...I will pull down my barns, and build larger ones...and I will say to my soul..."Eat, drink, and be merry." But God said to him, "Fool! This night your soul is required of you; and the things you have prepared, whose will they be?"

***Jn. 16:20–23 [Christ]:** Truly, truly, I say to you, *you will weep and lament, but the world will rejoice; you will be sorrowful, but your sorrow will turn into joy.* When a woman is in travail she has sorrow, because her hour has come; but when she is delivered of the child, she no longer remembers the anguish, for joy that a child is born into the world. So you have sorrow now, but I will see you again and your hearts will rejoice, and no one will take your joy from you. In that day you will ask nothing of me...
Jn. 15:18–19 [Christ]: If the world hates you, know that it has hated me before it hated you. If you were of the world, the world would love its own; but because you are not of the world, but I chose you out of the world, therefore the world hates you. (Also Jn. 17:14, Mt. 5:10–12, 10:24–25, 1 Jn. 3:13.)
Jer. 31:13 [God]: ...I will turn their mourning into joy, I will comfort them, and give them gladness for sorrow. (Also Ps. 30:11, 90:15.)

in Freude verkehret werden.
into joy transformed be.
{shall be transformed into joy.}

Ps. 30:5. ...Weeping may tarry for the night, but joy comes with the morning. (Also Ps. 30:11, 126:5.)

2. Tenor Recit.
●Weeping because Jesus, our refuge, taken from us (103–2)
Wer sollte nicht in Klagen untergehn,
Who would not amidst lamentation go-under,
{Who would not sink in lamentation,}

Wenn uns der Liebste wird entrissen?
If from-us (our) beloved (were) torn-away?
{If our beloved is torn from us?}

Der Seele Heil, die Zuflucht kranker Herzen
(Our) soul's salvation, the refuge (of) sick hearts

Acht' nicht auf unsre Schmerzen.
Pays-heed not to our sorrows.
{Pays no heed to our sorrows.}

Jn. 13:31, 33, 36. ...Jesus said..."Little children, yet a little while I am with you. You will seek me; and as I said to the Jews so now I say to you, 'Where I am going you cannot come.'"...Simon Peter said to him, "Lord, where are you going?" Jesus answered, "Where I am going you cannot follow me now; but you shall follow afterward."
Mt. 9:14–15. The disciples of John came to [Jesus], saying, "Why do we and the Pharisees fast, but your disciples do not fast?" And Jesus said to them, "Can the wedding guests mourn as long as the bridegroom is with them? The days will come, when the bridegroom is taken away from them, and then they will fast." (Also Mk. 2:19–20, Lk. 5:34–35.)
Ps. 73:25. [O Lord,] whom have I in heaven but thee? And there is nothing upon earth that I desire besides thee.
Ps. 27:1. The Lord is my light and my salvation (Luther: Heil)...
Joel 3:16. ...The Lord is a refuge (Luther: Zuflucht) to his people.
Ps. 22:1–2. My God, my God, why hast thou forsaken me? Why art thou so far from helping me, from the words of my groaning? O my God, I cry by day, but thou dost not answer; and by night, but find no rest. (Also Ps. 6:2–4, 6–7, 13:1–3, 5, 86:3, 88:1, Is. 38:13.)

3. Alto Aria
●Christ as physician & balm; our only hope (103–3)
Kein Arzt ist außer dir zu finden,
No physician is other-than thou to (be) found,
{No physician is to be found other than thou,}

Ich suche durch ganz Gilead;
(Though) I search through all Gilead;

Wer heilt die Wunden meiner Sünden,
Who will-heal the wounds of-my sins,

Weil man hier keinen Balsam hat?
Since one here no balm has?
{Since there is no balm here?}

Verbirgst du dich, so muß ich sterben.
Hidest thou thyself, then must I die.
{If thou hidest thyself, then I must die.}

Erbarme dich, ach, höre doch!
Have-mercy, ah, hear (me) please!

Du suchest ja nicht mein Verderben,
Thou seekest indeed not my ruin,
{Surely thou dost not seek my ruin,}

Wohlan, so hofft mein Herze noch.
Well! Then hopes my heart still.
{Well! Then my heart still has hope.}

Jer. 8:21–22. For the wound of the daughter of my people is my heart wounded, I mourn, and dismay has taken hold on me. Is there no balm in Gilead? Is there no physician there? Why then has the health of the daughter of my people not been restored? (Also Gen. 37:25, Jer. 46:11.)
Mk. 2:17. ...Jesus...said to them, "Those who are well have no need of a physician, but those who are sick; I came not to call the righteous, but sinners." (Also Lk. 5:30–31.)
Jer. 30:17. I will restore health to you, and your wounds I will heal, says the Lord... (Also Is. 57:18, Jer. 3:22, 33:6, Hos. 6:1, 14:4.)
2 Chron. 7:14 [God]: If my people...seek my face...I will hear from heaven, and will forgive their sin and heal their land. (Also Ex. 15:26.)
Ps. 73:25. [O Lord,] whom have I in heaven but thee? And there is nothing upon earth that I desire besides thee.
Ps. 143:7. Make haste to answer me, O Lord! My spirit fails! Hide not thy face from me, lest I be like those who go down to the Pit. (Also Ps. 13:1, 44:24, 69:17, 88:14, 102:2.)
Ps. 104:29. When thou hidest thy face, they are dismayed; when thou takest away their breath, they die and return to their dust.
Ps. 30:8–10. To thee, O Lord, I cried; and to the Lord I made supplication: "What profit is there in my death, if I go down to the Pit? Will the dust praise thee? Will it tell of thy faithfulness? Hear, O Lord, and be gracious to me! O Lord, be thou my helper!"
Prov. 23:18. Surely there is a future, and your hope will not be cut off.
Jn. 3:17. For God sent the Son into the world, not to condemn the world, but that the world might be saved through him.

4. Alto Recit.

●Sorrow will turn to joy when Christ returns (103-4)

Du wirst mich nach der Angst
Thou wilt me after (my) anguish
{After my anguish, thou wilt}

      auch wiederum erquicken;
      also again revive;
      (also revive me again;}

So will ich mich zu deiner Ankunft schicken,
Therefore will I myself for thine arrival prepare,
{Therefore I will prepare myself for thine arrival,}

Ich traue dem Verheißungswort,
I trust the word-of-promise,

Daß meine Traurigkeit
That my sorrow

In Freude soll verkehret werden.
Into joy shall transformed be.
{Shall be transformed into joy.}

5. Tenor Aria

●Sorrow will turn to joy; I will see Jesus again (103-5)

Erholet euch, betrübte Sinnen,
Recover yourselves (now), (O) distressed senses,

Ihr tut euch selber allzu weh.
Ye cause your-selves too-much woe.

Laßt von dem traurigen Beginnen,
Leave-off - your sorrowful undertakings,

Eh ich in Tränen untergeh,
Ere I in tears go-under,

Mein Jesus läßt sich wieder sehen,
My Jesus lets himself again be-seen,
{My Jesus will again appear.}

O Freude, der nichts gleichen kann!
O joy, which nothing can-equal!

Wie wohl ist mir dadurch geschehen,
What-good is to-me thereby come,
{How greatly I am benefitted by this,}

Nimm, nimm mein Herz zum Opfer an.
Receive, receive, my heart as-(my) offering - .

6. Chorale

●Sorrow brief & will turn to joy; Jesus comforts us (103-6)

Ich hab dich einen Augenblick,
I have thee for-a moment,
{For a moment, I have thee,}

*Jn. 16:20–22 [Christ]: ...You will be sorrowful, but your sorrow will turn into joy. When a woman is in travail she has sorrow, because her hour has come; but when she is delivered of the child, she no longer remembers the anguish (Luther: Angst), for joy that a child is born into the world. So you have sorrow (Luther: Traurigkeit) now, but I will see you again and your hearts will rejoice, and no one will take your joy from you.
Ps. 30:7. [O Lord]...thou didst hide thy face, I was dismayed.
Is. 54:7–8 [God]: For a brief moment I forsook you, but with great compassion I will gather you...for a moment I hid my face from you, but with everlasting love I will have compassion on you, says the Lord, your Redeemer.
Jn. 14:1, 3 [Christ]: Let not your hearts be troubled; believe in God, believe also in me...I will come again and will take you to myself, that where I am you may be also.
Jn. 14:16–18 [Christ]: I will pray the Father, and he will give you another Counselor, to be with you for ever, even the Spirit of truth...I will not leave you desolate; I will come to you.

Ps. 42:3, 5/11. My tears have been my food day and night, while men say to me continually, "Where is your God?"...Why are you cast down, O my soul, and why are you disquieted within me? Hope in God; for I shall again praise him, my help and my God.
Ps. 6:6–7. I am weary with my moaning; every night I flood my bed with tears; I drench my couch with my weeping. My eye wastes away because of grief, it grows weak because of all my foes. (Also Jer. 45:3.)
Ps. 90:15. [O Lord,] make us glad as many days as thou hast afflicted us, and as many years as we have seen evil.
Jn. 14:18 [Christ]: I will not leave you desolate; I will come to you.
*Jn. 16:22 [Christ]: You have sorrow now, but I will see you again and your hearts will rejoice, and no one will take your joy from you.
Acts 1:10–11. And while they were gazing into heaven as [Jesus ascended], behold, two men stood by them in white robes, and said, "Men of Galilee, why do you stand looking into heaven? This Jesus, who was taken up from you into heaven, will come in the same way as you saw him go into heaven."
Rom. 12:1. I appeal to you therefore, brethren, by the mercies of God, to present your bodies as a living sacrifice, holy and acceptable to God, which is your spiritual worship.
Eph. 3:17. That Christ may dwell in your hearts through faith...

Is. 54:7–8 [God]: For a brief moment I forsook you, but with great compassion I will gather you. In overflowing wrath for a moment I hid my face from you, but with everlasting love I will have compassion on you, says the Lord, your Redeemer.
Ps. 30:5–12. His anger is but for a moment, and his favor is for a lifetime. Weeping may tarry for the night, but joy comes with the

O liebes Kind, verlassen:
O   dear   child,   forsaken:

Sieh   aber,   sieh,   mit großem Glück
Behold however, behold, with   great   fortune
{But lo, with great fortune}

Und Trost   ohn alle Maßen
And comfort beyond all measure

Will ich   dir   schon die Freudenkron
Will I   upon-thee already the crown-of-joy

Aufsetzen und   verehren;
Place   and (thee) honor;
{Will I already place the crown of joy upon thee and honor thee;}

Dein kurzes Leid   soll sich in Freud
Thy   brief suffering shall - into joy
{Thy brief suffering shall be transformed into joy}

Und ewig   Wohl   verkehren.
And eternal well-being be-transformed.
{And eternal well-being.}

morning. As for me, I said in my prosperity, "I shall never be moved." By thy favor, O Lord, thou hadst established me as a strong mountain; thou didst hide thy face, I was dismayed. To thee, O Lord, I cried; and to the Lord I made supplication: "What profit is there in my death, if I go down to the Pit? Will the dust praise thee? Will it tell of thy faithfulness? Hear, O Lord, and be gracious to me! O Lord, be thou my helper!" Thou hast turned for me my mourning into dancing; thou hast loosed my sackcloth and girded me with gladness, that my soul may praise thee and not be silent. O Lord my God, I will give thanks to thee for ever.
2 Cor. 1:3–4. Blessed be the God and Father of our Lord Jesus Christ, the Father of mercies and God of all comfort, who comforts us in all our affliction...
Rev. 21:3–4. ...God himself will be with them; he will wipe away every tear from their eyes...
2 Tim. 4:8. Henceforth there is laid up for me the crown of righteousness, which the Lord, the righteous judge, will award to me on that Day, and not only to me but also to all who have loved his appearing. (Also Jms. 1:12, Rev. 2:10.)
Rom. 8:18. I consider that the sufferings of this present time are not worth comparing with the glory that is to be revealed to us.
2 Cor. 4:17. For this slight momentary affliction is preparing for us an eternal weight of glory beyond all comparison.
*Jn. 16:20 [Christ]: ...Your sorrow will turn into joy.

BWV 104
Du hirte Israel, höre
(NBA I/11; BC A65)

Misericordias Domini: 2. S. after Easter (BWV 104, 85, 112)
*1 Pet. 2:21–25 (Christ as example; you have returned to the shepherd of your souls)
*Jn. 10:11–16 (Jesus declares himself to be the good Shepherd)
Librettist: Unknown; perhaps Christian Weiß the elder

1. Chorus
●Shepherd of Israel sought in prayer: Ps. 80:1 (104–1)
Du   Hirte   Israel,   höre,   der du Joseph
Thou shepherd of-Israel, hear (us), thou-who Joseph

hütest   wie der Schafe, erscheine, der du sitzest
dost-shelter like - sheep, appear, thou-who dost-sit

über Cherubim.
above cherubim.

2. Tenor Recit.
●Shepherd on high cares for me, why should I worry? (104–2)
Der höchste   Hirte   sorgt vor mich,
The highest shepherd cares for me,
{The greatest shepherd cares for me}

Ps. 80:1–3. *Give ear, O Shepherd of Israel, thou who leadest Joseph like a flock! Thou who art enthroned upon the cherubim, shine forth...Stir up thy might, and come to save us! Restore us, O God; let thy face shine, that we may be saved!*
Ps. 100:3. Know that the Lord is God! It is he that made us, and we are his; we are his people, and the sheep of his pasture. (Also Ps. 95:6–7.)
*Jn. 10:14 [Christ]: I am the good shepherd...
Ex. 25:22 [God]: ...From above the mercy seat, from between the two cherubim that are upon the ark of the testimony, I will speak with you of all that I will give you in commandment for the people of Israel.
*1 Pet. 2:25. You were straying like sheep, but have now returned to the Shepherd and Guardian of your souls.
2 Kings 19:15–16. Hezekiah prayed before the Lord, and said: "O Lord the God of Israel, who art enthroned above the cherubim, thou art the God, thou alone, of all the kingdoms of the earth; thou hast made heaven and earth. Incline thy ear, O Lord, and hear; open thy eyes, O Lord, and see..." (Also Is. 37:15; Ps. 99:1, 1 Sam. 4:4, 2 Sam. 6:2.)

*Jn. 10:14 [Christ]: I am the good shepherd...
Jn. 10:27–28 [Christ]: My sheep hear my voice, and I know them, and they follow me; and I give them eternal life, and they shall never perish, and no one shall snatch them out of my hand.
Ps. 23:1–4. The Lord is my shepherd, I shall not want; he makes me lie down in green pastures. He leads me beside still waters; he restores

Was nützen   meine Sorgen?
What profit (me) my   worries?
{What do my worries profit me?}

Es   wird ja   alle Morgen
(Now) (is) indeed every morning

Des Hirtens   Güte neu.
The Shepherd's kindness new.
{Indeed the Shepherd's kindness is new every morning.}

Mein Herz, so   fasse dich,
My   heart, then compose thyself,

Gott ist getreu.
God is faithful.

3. Tenor Aria
●Shepherd hidden; Fearful, I cry "abba" in faith (104-3)
Verbirgt mein Hirte   sich zu lange,
Hides   my shepherd himself too long,
{If my shepherd hides himself too long,}

Macht mir die Wüste allzu bange,
Makes me the desert all-too anxious,
{If the desert makes me all too anxious,}

Mein schwacher Schritt eilt   dennoch   fort.
My   feeble   step hastens nevertheless onward.

Mein Mund schreit nach dir,
My   mouth cries   to thee,

Und du,   mein Hirte,   wirkst in mir
And thou, (O) my shepherd, dost-produce in me

Ein gläubig Abba durch dein Wort.
A   believing "abba" through thy Word.

4. Bass Recit.
●Pasture is Word of God, sheepfold is heaven (104-4)
Ja, dieses   Wort ist meiner Seelen Speise,
Yes, this (same) Word is my   soul's   food,

Ein Labsal meiner Brust,
A   tonic to-my breast,

my soul...Even though I walk through the valley of the shadow of death, I fear no evil; for thou art with me; thy rod and thy staff, they comfort me.
Mt. 6:25, 30–31 [Christ]: I tell you, do not be anxious about your life, what you shall eat or what you shall drink, nor about your body, what you shall put on...If God so clothes the grass of the field, which today is alive and tomorrow is thrown into the oven, will he not much more clothe you, O men of little faith? Therefore do not be anxious...
Lam. 3:22–23. The steadfast love of the Lord never ceases, his mercies never come to an end; they are new every morning; great is thy faithfulness. (Also Ps. 90:14, 92:2.)
1 Pet. 5:7. Cast all your anxieties on him, for he cares about you. (Also Phil. 4:6, 1 Cor. 10:13.)
Lk. 21:19 [Christ]: By your endurance you will gain your lives (Luther: Fasset eure Seele mit Geduld).
1 Cor. 10:13. ...*God is faithful* (Luther: Gott ist getreu)...

Mt. 9:36. When [Jesus] saw the crowds, he had compassion for them, because they were harassed and helpless, like sheep without a shepherd. (Also Mk 6:34; 1 Kings 22:17 / 2 Chron. 18:16, Ps. 119:176; Ezek. 34:12.)
Is. 54:7–8 [God]: For a brief moment I forsook you, but with great compassion I will gather you...for a moment I hid my face from you, but with everlasting love I will have compassion on you, says the Lord, your Redeemer.
Ps. 22:1–2. My God, my God, why hast thou forsaken me? Why art thou so far from helping me, from the words of my groaning? O my God, I cry by day, but thou dost not answer; and by night, but find no rest.
Ps. 107:4–6. Some [of God's people] wandered in desert wastes, finding no way to a city to dwell in; hungry and thirsty, their soul fainted within them. Then they cried to the Lord in their trouble, and he delivered them from their distress.
Lk. 15:4 [Christ]: What man of you, having a hundred sheep, if he has lost one of them does not leave the ninety-nine in the wilderness, and go after the one which is lost, until he finds it? (Also Mt. 18:12–13.)
Is. 35:4. Say to those who are of a fearful heart, "Be strong, fear not! Behold, your God...will come and save you."
Jn. 20:29. Jesus said to [Thomas], "Have you believed because you have seen me? Blessed are those who have not seen and yet believe."
Rom. 8:15–17. For you did not receive the spirit of slavery to fall back into fear, but you have received the spirit of sonship. When we cry, "Abba! Father!" it is the Spirit himself bearing witness with our spirit that we are children of God, and if children, then heirs... (abba: also Mk. 14:36, Gal. 4:6)

Mt. 4:4 [Christ]: ...Man shall not live by bread alone, but by every word that proceeds from the mouth of God. (Also Deut. 8:3, Lk. 4:4.)
Josh. 1:8. This book of the law shall not depart out of your mouth, but you shall meditate on it day and night...
Ps. 119:47–48, 92, 103. [O Lord,] I find my delight in thy commandments, which I love. I revere thy commandments, which I love, and I will meditate on thy statutes...If thy law had not been my

Die Weide, die ich meine Lust,
The pasture, which I, my pleasure,
{The pasture, which I call my pleasure,}

Des Himmels Vorschmack, ja mein alles heiße.
- Heaven's foretaste, yes, my all do-call.
{The foretaste of heaven, yes, my all.}

Ach! sammle nur, o guter Hirte,
Ah, gather (then), O good shepherd,

Uns Arme und Verirrte;
Us poor and straying-ones;

Ach laß den Weg nur bald geendet sein
Ah, let (this) (difficult) path but soon ended be
{Ah, just let this difficult path soon be ended}

Und führe uns in deinen Schafstall ein!
And lead us into thy sheepfold - !

5. Bass Aria
●Flock of Jesus receive kindness now & reward later (104-5)
Beglückte Herde, Jesu Schafe,
Fortunate flock, Jesus' sheep,

Die Welt ist euch ein Himmelreich.
The world is (now) for-you a kingdom-of-heaven.

Hier schmeckt ihr Jesu Güte schon
Here taste you Jesus' kindness (now) already
{Here you already taste Jesus' kindness}

Und hoffet noch des Glaubens Lohn
And hope yet (for) faith's compensation

Nach einem sanften Todesschlafe.
After a gentle sleep-of-death.

6. Chorale (See also 85-3.)
●Shepherd's Psalm: Ps. 23:1-2 (104-6)
Der Herr ist mein getreuer Hirt,
The Lord is my faithful shepherd,

Dem ich mich ganz vertraue,
To-whom I myself completely entrust,
{To whom I completely entrust myself,}

delight, I should have perished in my affliction...How sweet are thy words to my taste, sweeter than honey to my mouth!
Ps. 23:1. The Lord is my shepherd, I shall not want; he makes me lie down in green pastures...
Ezek. 34:14-15 [God]: I will feed them with good pasture...I myself will be the shepherd of my sheep...
*Jn. 10:14 [Christ]: I am the good shepherd...
Is. 40:11. He will feed his flock like a shepherd, he will gather the lambs in his arms, he will carry them in his bosom, and gently lead those that are with young.
Is. 53:6. All we like sheep have gone astray; we have turned every one to his own way... (Also Ps. 14:3, 119:176, Mt. 18:12.)
Ezek. 34:11-12 [God]: ...Behold, I, I myself will search for my sheep, and will seek them out. As a shepherd seeks out his flock when some of his sheep have been scattered abroad, so will I seek out my sheep, and I will rescue them from all places where they have been scattered... (Also Rev. 7:17.)
Jn. 10:1-3, 27-28 [Christ]: Truly, truly, I say to you, he who does not enter the sheepfold (Luther: Schafstall) by the door but climbs in by another way, that man is a thief and a robber; but he who enters by the door is the shepherd of the sheep...My sheep hear my voice, and I know them, and they follow me; and I give them eternal life, and they shall never perish, and no one shall snatch them out of my hand.

Ps. 95:7. ...We are the people of his pasture, and the sheep of his hand. (Also Ps. 100:3.)
*1 Pet. 2:25. You were straying like sheep, but have now returned to the Shepherd and Guardian of your souls.
Rom. 8:32. He who did not spare his own Son but gave him up for us all, will he not also give us all things with him?
Lk. 17:20-21. Being asked by the Pharisees when the kingdom of God was coming, [Jesus] answered them, "...The kingdom of God is in the midst of you (Luther: inwendig in euch)."
Ps. 34:8. O taste and see that the Lord is good!...
1 Pet. 2:3. You have tasted the kindness of the Lord.
Mk. 10:29-30. Jesus said, "Truly, I say to you, there is no one who has left house or brothers or sisters of mother or father or children or lands, for my sake and for the gospel, who will not receive a hundredfold now in this time...and in the age to come eternal life." (Also Mt. 19:29, Lk. 18:29-30.)
Jn. 11:25-26. Jesus said to [Martha], "I am the resurrection and the life; he who believes in me, though he die, yet shall he live, and whoever lives and believes in me shall never die..."
1 Jn. 2:25. This is what he has promised us, eternal life.
Lk. 6:23. ...Your reward (Luther: Lohn) is great in heaven...

Ps. 23:1-3. *The Lord is my shepherd, I shall not want; he makes me lie down in green pastures. He leads me beside still waters; he restores my soul. He leads me in paths of righteousness for his name's sake.*
Ezek. 34:14-16 [God]: I will feed them with good pasture, and upon the mountain heights of Israel shall be their pasture; there they shall lie down in good grazing land, and on fat pasture they shall feed on the mountains of Israel. I myself will be the shepherd of my sheep, and I will make them lie down, says the Lord God. I will seek the lost,

Zur Weid er mich, sein Schäflein, führt,
To-a pasture he me, his little-sheep, leads,
{To a pasture he leads me, his little sheep,}

Auf schöner grüner Aue,
Upon-a beautiful green meadow,

Zum frischen Wasser leit' er mich,
To fresh waters leads he me,
{He leads me to fresh waters,}

Mein Seel zu laben kräftiglich
My soul to restore powerfully
{To restore my soul mightily}

Durchs selig Wort der Gnaden.
Through-the blessed word of grace.

and I will bring back the strayed, and I will bind up the crippled, and I will strengthen the weak...
*Jn. 10:14, 27 [Christ]: I am the good shepherd; I know my own and my own know me...My sheep hear my voice, and I know them, and they follow me.
*1 Pet. 2:25. You were straying like sheep, but have now returned to the Shepherd and Guardian of your souls.
1 Pet. 2:2. Like newborn babes, long for the pure spiritual milk, that by it you may grow up to salvation; for you have tasted the kindness of the Lord.
Mt. 4:4 [Christ]: It is written, "Man shall not live by bread alone, but by every word that proceeds from the mouth of God." (See Deut. 8:3, also Lk. 4:4.)
Ps. 119:25, 28, 81, 107, 116. [O Lord,] my soul cleaves to the dust; revive me according to thy word!...My soul melts away for sorrow; strengthen me according to thy word!...My soul languishes for thy salvation; I hope in thy word...I am sorely afflicted; give me life, O Lord, according to thy word!...Uphold me according to thy promise, that I may live, and let me not be put to shame in my hope!

BWV 105
Herr, gehe nicht ins Gericht mit deinem Knecht
(NBA I/19; BC A114)

9. S. after Trinity (BWV 105, 94, 168)
*1 Cor. 10:6–13 (Consider and avoid the sins of the Israelites in the wilderness)
*Lk. 16:1–9 (Parable of the dishonest steward)
Librettist: Unknown

1. Chorus
●Guilt: No one justified before God: Ps. 143:2 (105–1)
Herr, gehe nicht ins Gericht mit deinem Knecht.
Lord, (enter) not into judgment with thy servant.

Denn vor dir wird kein Lebendiger gerecht.
since before thee will no living-one be-justified.

Ps. 143:2. *Enter not into judgment with thy servant; for no man living is righteous before thee.*
Ps. 130:3. If thou, O Lord, shouldst mark iniquities, Lord, who could stand!
Ps. 76:7. But thou, terrible art thou! Who can stand before thee when once thy anger is roused?
Nah. 1:6. Who can stand before [God's] indignation? Who can endure the heat of his anger? His wrath is poured out like fire, and the rocks are broken asunder by him. (Also: Mal. 3:2, Rev. 6:17.)
Gal. 3:11. Now it is evident that no man is justified before God by the law; for "He who through faith is righteous shall live." (Also Rom. 3:20.)

2. Alto Recit.
●Confession of sin; plea not to be cast away (105–2)
Mein Gott, verwirf mich nicht,
My God, cast-away me not,
{My God, cast me not away,}

Indem ich mich in Demut vor dir beuge,
For I - in humility before thee bow,

Von deinem Angesicht.
From thy face.
{My God, do not cast me away from before thy face for I bow in humility before thee.}

Ich weiß, wie groß dein Zorn und mein Verbrechen ist,
I know, however great thy wrath and my offence is,

Jer. 7:15. [God]: I will cast you out of my sight...
Ps. 27:9. [O Lord,] hide not thy face from me. Turn not thy servant away in anger, thou who hast been my help. Cast me not off, forsake me not, O God of my salvation!
2 Chron. 7:14 [God]: If my people who are called by my name humble themselves, and pray and seek my face, and turn from their wicked ways, then I will hear from heaven, and will forgive their sin and heal their land. (Also 1 Jn. 1:9.)
Ps. 51:1–3, 11, 15–17. Have mercy on me, O God, according to thy steadfast love; according to thy abundant mercy blot out my transgressions. Wash me thoroughly from my iniquity, and cleanse me from my sin! For I know my transgressions, and my sin is ever before me...Cast me not away from thy presence, and take not thy holy Spirit from me...O Lord, open thou my lips, and my mouth shall show forth

Daß du zugleich ein schneller Zeuge
That thou (both) a ready witness

Und ein gerechter Richter bist.
And a righteous judge art.

Ich lege dir ein frei Bekenntnis dar
I lay before-thee a free confession down
{I freely make confession}

Und stürze mich nicht in Gefahr,
And cast myself not into (the) danger,

Die Fehler meiner Seelen
The errors of-my soul

Zu leugnen, zu verhehlen.
To deny, to conceal.
{Of denying or concealing the errors of my soul.}

thy praise. For thou hast no delight in sacrifice; were I to give a burnt offering, thou wouldst not be pleased. The sacrifice acceptable to God is a broken spirit; a broken and contrite heart, O God, thou wilt not despise.
Mal. 3:5 [God]: I will draw near to you for judgment; I will be a swift witness (Luther: schneller Zeuge) against the sorcerers, against the adulterers, against those who swear falsely, against those who oppress the hireling in his wages, the widow and the orphan, against those who thrust aside the sojourner, and do not fear me, says the Lord...
Rom. 1:18. For the wrath of God is revealed from heaven against all ungodliness and wickedness of men who by their wickedness suppress the truth.
Ps. 7:11. God is a righteous judge...
Ps. 32:3, 5. When I declared not my sin, my body wasted away through my groaning all day long...I acknowledged my sin to thee, and I did not hide (Luther: verhehlte nicht) my iniquity; I said, "I will confess my transgressions to the Lord"; then thou didst forgive the guilt of my sin. (Also Job 31:33, 37.)

3. Soprano Aria
●Conscience tortures sinner; accuses & excuses him (105-3)
Wie zittern und wanken
How (do) tremble and vacillate

Der Sünder Gedanken,
The sinner's thoughts,
{How sinners' thoughts tremble and vacillate,}

Indem sie sich untereinander verklagen
In-that they - one-another accuse
{In that they accuse one another}

Und wiederum sich zu entschuldigen wagen.
And then-again themselves to excuse do-venture.
{And then again venture to excuse themselves.}

So wird ein geängstigt Gewissen
Thus is a frightened conscience

Durch eigene Folter zerrissen.
By (its) own torture torn.

Rom. 2:13–16. It is not the hearers of the law who are righteous before God but the doers of the law who will be justified. When Gentiles who have not the law do by nature what the law requires, they are a law to themselves, even though they do not have the law. They show that what the law requires is written on their hearts, while their conscience also bears witness and their conflicting thoughts accuse or perhaps excuse them on that day when, according to my gospel, God judges the secrets of men by Christ Jesus. (Also 2 Cor. 5:10.)
Heb. 10:26–31. If we sin deliberately after receiving the knowledge of the truth, there no longer remains a sacrifice for sins, but a fearful prospect of judgment, and a fury of fire which will consume the adversaries. A man who has violated the law of Moses dies without mercy at the testimony of two or three three witnesses. How much worse punishment do you think will be deserved by the man who has spurned the Son of God, and profaned the blood of the covenant by which he was sanctified, and outraged the Spirit of grace? For we know him who said, "Vengeance is mine, I will repay." And again, "The Lord will judge his people." It is a fearful thing to fall into the hands of the living God.

4. Bass Recit.
●Debt of sin paid by Christ on the cross (105-4)
Wohl aber dem, der seinen Bürgen weiß,
Happy however (is) he, who his guarantor knows,

Der alle Schuld ersetzet,
Who (for) all debt makes-substitution,
{The one who makes substitution for all sin,}

So wird die Handschrift ausgetan,
Thus is the bond cancelled,

Jer. 9:24 [God]: Let him who glories glory in this, that he understands and knows me, that I am the Lord...
1 Tim. 2:5–6. There is one God, and there is one mediator between God and men, the man Christ Jesus, who gave himself as a ransom for all...
2 Tim. 1:12. I am not ashamed, for I know whom I have believed...
1 Pet. 1:18–19. ...You were ransomed...not with perishable things such as silver or gold, but with the precious blood of Christ, like that of a lamb without blemish or spot.
Ps. 103:10. [The Lord] does not deal with us according to our sins, nor requite us according to our iniquities.
*Lk. 16:5–6. Summoning his master's debtors one by one, [the steward] said to the first, 'How much do you owe my master?' He said, 'A hundred measures of oil.' And he said to him, 'Take your bill and sit down quickly and write fifty.'

Wenn Jesus sie mit Blute netzet.
If   Jesus it with blood sprinkles.
{If Jesus sprinkles it with blood.}

Er heftet sie ans Kreuze selber an,
He fastens it to-the cross himself - ,

Er wird von deinen Gütern,   Leib und Leben,
He will of   your possessions, body, and life—

Wenn deine Sterbestunde schlägt,
When your dying-hour   strikes—

Dem Vater selbst die Rechnung übergeben.
To-the Father himself the account   hand-over.
{He himself will hand over the account of your possessions, body,
and life to the Father when your hour of death strikes.}

So   mag man deinen Leib, den man zum Grabe trägt,
Thus may one your   body, which one to-the grave carries,
{Thus one may cover your body, which is carried to the grave,}

Mit Sand und Staub beschütten,
With sand and dust   cover,
{With sand and dust;}

Dein Heiland öffnet dir die ewgen Hütten.
Your Savior opens to-you the eternal shelter.

5. Tenor Aria
●Mammon & world rejected in favor of Christ (105–5)
Kann ich nur Jesum mir zum Freunde machen,
Can I but Jesus - (my) friend   make,
{If I can but make Jesus my friend,}

So   gilt der Mammon nichts bei mir.
Then (means) - Mammon nothing to me.
{Then Mammon means nothing to me.}

Ich finde kein Vergnügen hier
I find no   pleasure here

Bei dieser eitlen Welt und   irdschen Sachen.
In   this   vain world and (in) earthly things.

Col. 2:13–14. You, who were dead in trespasses and the uncircumcision of your flesh, God made alive together with him, having forgiven us all our trespasses, having canceled the bond which stood against us with its legal demands; this he set aside, nailing it to the cross. (Also 2 Cor. 5:21.)
Heb. 9:13–14. If the sprinkling of defiled persons with the blood of goats and bulls...sanctifies for the purification of the flesh, how much more shall the blood of Christ... (Also 1 Jn. 1:7.)
1 Cor. 4:1–2. This is how one should regard us, as servants of Christ and stewards...Moreover it is required of stewards that they be found trustworthy. (Also 1 Pet. 4:10.)
*Lk. 16:1–2. [Jesus] also said to the disciples, "There was a rich man who had a steward, and charges were brought to him that this man was wasting his goods. And he called him and said to him, 'What is this that I hear about you? Turn in the account (Luther: Rechnung) of your stewardship...'"
Heb. 9:27. ...It is appointed for men to die once, and after that comes judgment.
1 Jn. 2:1–2. ...If any one does sin, we have an advocate with the Father, Jesus Christ the righteous; and he is the expiation for our sins, and not for ours only but also for the sins of the whole world.
1 Cor. 15:55. O death, where is thy victory? O death, where is thy sting?
Ecc. 3:20. ...All are from the dust, and all turn to dust again. (Also Gen. 3:19, Ps. 146:4, Ecc. 12:7.)
2 Cor. 5:1. We know that if the earthly tent we live in is destroyed, we have a building from God, a house not made with hands, eternal in the heavens.
Mt. 6:19–21. Do not lay up for yourselves treasures on earth, where moth and rust consume and where thieves break in and steal, but lay up for yourselves treasures in heaven, where neither moth nor rust consumes and where thieves do not break in and steal. For where your treasure is, there will your heart be also.
*Lk. 16:9 [Christ]: Make friends for yourselves by means of unrighteous mammon, so that when it fails they may receive you into the eternal habitations (Luther: ewigen Hütten).
Jn. 14:3 [Christ]: When I go and prepare a place for you, I will come again and will take you to myself, that where I am you may be also.

*Lk. 16:9 [Christ]: Make friends for yourselves by means of unrighteous mammon, so that when it fails they may receive you into the eternal habitations (Luther: ewigen Hütten).
Lk. 16:13 [Christ]: No servant can serve two masters; for either he will hate the one and love the other, or he will be devoted to the one and despise the other. You cannot serve God and mammon. (Also Mt. 6:24.)
Jms. 4:4. Unfaithful creatures! Do you not know that friendship with the world is enmity with God? Therefore whoever wishes to be a friend of the world makes himself an enemy of God.
1 Jn. 2:15–17. Do not love the world or the things in the world. If any one loves the world, love for the Father is not in him. For all that is in the world, the lust of the flesh and the lust of the eyes and the pride of life, is not of the Father but is of the world. And the world passes away, and the lust of it; but he who does the will of God abides for ever.

6. Chorale

●Conscience stilled by God; promise of eternal life (105–6)

Nun, ich weiß, du wirst mir stillen
Now, I know, thou wilt - still

Mein Gewissen, das mich plagt.
My conscience, which me plagues.
{My conscience, which plagues me.}

Es wird deine Treu erfüllen,
(Now) will thy faithfulness fulfil,

Was du selber hast gesagt:
What thou thyself hast said:

Daß auf dieser weiten Erden
That on this wide earth

Keiner soll verloren werden,
No-one shall lost be,
{No one shall perish,}

Sondern ewig leben soll,
But eternally shall-live,

Wenn er nur ist Glaubens voll.
If he but is of-faith full.
{If only he is filled with faith.}

1 Jn. 3:19–21. By this we shall know that we are of the truth, and reassure our hearts before him whenever our hearts condemn us; for God is greater than our hearts, and he knows everything. Beloved, if our hearts do not condemn us, we have confidence before God.

1 Jn. 4:16–18. So we know and believe the love God has for us. God is love, and he who abides in love abides in God, and God abides in him. In this is love perfected with us, that we may have confidence for the day of judgment, because as he is so are we in this world. There is no fear in love, but perfect love casts out fear. For fear has to do with punishment, and he who fears is not perfected in love.

Rom. 5:20. ...Where sin increased, grace abounded all the more.

Heb. 10:22–23. Let us draw near with a true heart in full assurance of faith, with our hearts sprinkled clean from an evil conscience and our bodies washed with pure water. Let us hold fast the confession of our hope without wavering, for he who promised is faithful. (Also 2 Tim. 2:13.)

Heb. 9:14. How much more shall the blood of Christ, who through the eternal Spirit offered himself without blemish to God, purify your conscience from dead works to serve the living God.

Jn. 3:16–17. For God so loved the world that he gave his only Son, that whoever believes in him should not perish (Luther: verloren werden) but have eternal life. For God sent the Son into the world, not to condemn the world, but that the world might be saved through him.

Rom. 1:16–17. ...[The gospel] is the power of God for salvation to every one who has faith...For in it the righteousness of God is revealed through faith for faith; as it is written, "He who through faith is righteous shall live." (See Hab. 2:4.)

BWV 106
Gottes Zeit ist die allerbeste Zeit
(NBA I/34; BC B18)

Actus tragicus - Cantata for a funeral service (BWV 106, 157, 198)
Librettist: Unknown; 2c–3b based on scriptural compilation by Johann Olearius (1611–1684)

1. Sonatina

2a. Chorus

●God's time is best; for living or dying: Acts 17:28 (106–2a)

Gottes Zeit ist die allerbeste Zeit.
God's time is the very-best time.

In ihm leben, weben und sind wir, solange er will.
In him live, move, and are we, as-long-as he wills.
{In him we live, move, and have our being, as long as he wills it.}

In ihm sterben wir zur rechten Zeit, wenn er will.
In him die we at-the right time, when he wills.
{In him we die at the right time, whenever he wills it.}

Ps. 31:14–15. I trust in thee, O Lord, I say, "Thou art my God." My times are in thy hand...

Acts 17:27–28. [God] is not far from each one of us, for *"In him we live and move and have our being";* as even some of your poets have said, "For we are indeed his offspring."

Col. 1:17. He is before all things, and in him all things hold together.

Jms. 4:13–15. Come now, you who say, "Today or tomorrow we will go into such and such a town and spend a year there and trade and get gain"; whereas you do not know about tomorrow. What is your life? For you are a mist that appears for a little time and then vanishes. Instead you ought to say, "If the Lord wills, we shall live and we shall do this or that."

2b. Tenor Arioso
●Death inevitable; prayer to be reminded: Ps. 90:12 (106-2b)
Ach, Herr, *lehre uns bedenken, daß wir sterben*
Ah, Lord, teach us to-bear-in-mind, that we die

müssen, auf daß wir klug werden.
must, so that we wise become.

2c. Bass Aria
●Death is coming; set your house in order: Is. 38:1 (106-2c)
Bestelle dein Haus; denn du wirst sterben
Set-in-order your house; for you will die
{Set your house in order for you will die}

und nicht lebendig bleiben!
and not living continue!
{and not continue living!}

2d. Chorus (Alto, Tenor, Bass) and Soprano Arioso
●Death decreed for all: Sir. 14:17, Rev. 22:20 (106-2d)
Es ist der alte Bund: Mensch, *du mußt sterben!*
It is the ancient covenant: man, thou must die!

Soprano:
Ja, komm, Herr Jesu!
Yes, come, Lord Jesus!

3a. Alto Aria
●Death: Committing spirit into God's hand: Ps. 31:5 (106-3a)
In deine Hände befehl ich meinen Geist;
Into thy hand commit I my spirit;

du hast mich erlöset, Herr, du getreuer Gott.
thou hast me redeemed, Lord, thou faithful God.

3b. Bass Arioso and Alto Chorale (Chorale: see also 95-1, 125-1)
●Death accepted with joy as entrance to paradise (106-3b)
Heute wirst du mit mir im Paradies sein.
Today will you with me in paradise be.
{Today you will be with me in paradise.}

Chorale:
Mit Fried und Freud ich fahr dahin
With peace and joy I depart thither

In Gottes Willen,
According-to God's will,

Getrost ist mir mein Herz und Sinn,
Consoled is - my heart and disposition,

Ps. 90:10, 12. The years of our life are threescore and ten, or even by reason of strength fourscore; yet their span is but toil and trouble; they are soon gone, and we fly away...*So teach us to number our days that we may get a heart of wisdom.*
Ps. 103:14–16. [God] knows our frame; he remembers that we are dust. As for man, his days are like grass; he flourishes like a flower of the field; for the wind passes over it, and it is gone, and its place knows it no more. (Also Ps. 39:5–6, 90:3–12, Job 7:7.)

Is. 38:1. ...Isaiah the prophet...came to [King Hezekiah], and said to him, "Thus says the Lord: *Set your house in order; for you shall die, you shall not recover."*
Lk. 12:17–20. ...A rich man...thought to himself...I will pull down my barns, and build larger ones...and I will say to my soul..."eat, drink, and be merry." But God said to him, "Fool! This night your soul is required of you; and the things you have prepared, whose will they be?"

Sirach (Apocrypha) 14:17–19. All living beings become old like a garment, for *the decree from of old is, "You must surely die!"* Like flourishing leaves on a spreading tree which sheds some and puts forth others, so are the generations of flesh and blood: one dies and another is born. Every product decays and ceases to exist, and the man who made it will pass away with it.
Rom. 5:12, 17, 19. ...Sin came into the world through one man and death through sin, and so death spread to all men because all men sinned...Because of one man's trespass, death reigned through that one man...By one man's disobedience many were were made sinners... (See Gen. 3:3, 19; also Rom. 6:23.)
Heb. 9:27. ...It is appointed for men to die once...
Rev. 22:20. He who testifies to these things says, "Surely I am coming soon." *Amen. Come, Lord Jesus!*

Ps. 31:5. *Into thy hand I commit my spirit; thou hast redeemed me, O Lord, faithful God.*
Lk. 23:46. Then Jesus, crying with a loud voice, said, "Father, into thy hands I commit my spirit!" And having said this he breathed his last.
1 Pet. 4:19. Let those who suffer according to God's will do right and entrust their souls to a faithful Creator.

Lk. 23:43. [Jesus] said to [the thief on the cross] "Truly, I say to you, *today you will be with me in Paradise."*
Lk. 2:29. Lord, now lettest thou thy servant depart in peace, according to thy word.
2 Cor. 5:6–9. So we are always of good courage (Luther: getrost); we know that while we are at home in the body we are away from the Lord, for we walk by faith, not by sight. We are of good courage, and we would rather be away from the body and at home with the Lord. So whether we are at home or away, we make it our aim to please him.
Phil. 1:23. ...My desire is to depart and be with Christ, for that is far better.
Ps. 131:2. I have calmed and quieted my soul, like a child quieted at its mother's breast; like a child that is quieted is my soul. (Also Ps. 62:1, 5.)

Sanft und stille.
Placid and still.

Wie Gott mir verheißen hat:
As God me promised has:
{As God promised me:}

Der Tod ist mein Schlaf worden.
- Death has my sleep become.
{Death has become sleep for me.}

4. Chorale
●Doxology; prayer for victory through Jesus (106-4)
Glorie, Lob, Ehr und Herrlichkeit
Glory, praise, honor, and majesty

Sei dir, Gott Vater und Sohn bereit',
Be to-thee, God (the) Father and Son given,

Dem Heilgen Geist mit Namen!
(And) the Holy Ghost by name!

Die göttlich Kraft
(May) the divine power

Mach uns sieghaft
Make us triumphant

Durch Jesum Christum, Amen.
Through Jesus Christ, Amen.

BWV 107
Was willst du dich betrüben
(NBA I/18; BC A109)

7. S. after Trinity (BWV 186, 107, 187)
*Rom. 6:19-23 (The wages of sin is death but the gift of God is eternal life)
*Mk. 8:1-9 (Jesus feeds the four thousand)
Librettist: Chorale (Johann Heermann)

1. Chorale (Vs. 1)
●Doubt not, but trust him who is called Immanuel (107-1)
Was willst du dich betrüben,
Why wouldst thou - grieve,

O meine liebe Seel?
O my dear soul?

Ergib dich, den zu lieben,
Devote thyself, him to love,
{Devote thyself to loving him,}

Der heißt Immanuel!
Who is-called Emmanuel!

1 Cor. 15:55. O death, where is thy victory? O death, where is thy sting?
Lk. 8:52-53. ...[Jesus] said, "Do not weep; for she is not dead but sleeping." And they laughed at him, knowing that she was dead.
1 Cor. 15:42, 51-52. So it is with the resurrection of the dead. What is sown is perishable, what is raised is imperishable...Lo! I tell you a mystery. We shall not all sleep, but we shall all be changed, in a moment, in the twinkling of an eye, at the last trumpet...

Mt. 28:18-19. Jesus came and said to [his disciples], "All authority in heaven and on earth has been given to me. Go therefore and make disciples of all nations, baptizing them in the name of the Father and of the Son and of the Holy Spirit."
2 Cor. 2:14. Thanks be to God, who in Christ always leads us in triumph...
Heb. 2:14-15. Since...the children share in flesh and blood, [Christ] himself likewise partook of the same nature, that through death he might destroy him who has the power of death, that is, the devil, and deliver all those who through fear of death were subject to lifelong bondage. (Also 1 Jn. 3:8, 2 Tim. 1:10, Is. 25:8.)
Rom. 6:23. For the wages of sin is death, but the free gift of God is eternal life in Christ Jesus our Lord.
Rom. 8:37-39. ...In all these things we are more than conquerors through him who loved us. For I am sure that neither death, nor life, nor angels, nor principalities, nor things present, nor things to come, nor powers, nor height, nor depth, nor anything else in all creation, will be able to separate us from the love of God in Christ Jesus our Lord.

Mk. 8:1-2, 4, 6, 8-9. In those days, when again a great crowd had gathered, and they had nothing to eat, [Jesus] called his disciples to him, and said to them, "I have compassion on the crowd, because they have been with me now three days, and have nothing to eat"...His disciples answered him, "How can one feed these men with bread here in the desert?"...He...took the seven loaves, and having given thanks he broke them and gave them to his disciples to set before the people; and they set them before the crowd...And they ate, and were satisfied... And there were about four thousand people.
Mk. 8:17-20. Jesus said to [his disciples], "Why do you discuss the fact that you have no bread? Do you not yet perceive or understand? Are your hearts hardened?...When I broke the five loaves for the five thousand, how many baskets full of broken pieces did you take up?... And the seven for the four thousand, how many baskets full of broken pieces did you take up?...Do you not yet understand?"
Ps. 42:5, 11; 43:5. Why are you cast down (Luther: betrübst du dich), O my soul, and why are you disquieted within me? Hope in God; for I shall again praise him, my help and my God.

Vertraue ihm allein,
Trust   him alone,

Er wird gut   alles machen
He will good all-things make
{He will make all things good}

Und fördern deine Sachen,
And further thy   affairs,

Wie dir's wird selig sein!
As to-thee will blessed be!
{In ways that will be blessed for thee!}

2. Bass Recit. (Chorale Vs. 2)
●Faithfulness of God to those who trust him (107-2)
Denn Gott verlässet keinen,
For   God forsakes no-one,

Der sich auf ihn verläßt,
Who - upon him relies,

Er bleibt getreu den Seinen,
He remains faithful to   his-own,

Die ihm vertrauen fest.
Who him   trust   firmly.
{Whoever trusts firmly in him.}

Läßt   sich's an wunderlich,
Appears it -   strange,
{Though matters appear strange,}

So laß dir   doch   nicht grauen!
(Yet) let thyself nevertheless not be-terrified!

Mit Freuden wirst du schauen,
With joy   wilt thou behold,

Wie Gott wird retten dich.
How God will rescue thee.

3. Bass Aria (Chorale Vs. 3)
●God's sovereignty complete & may be relied upon (107-3)
Auf ihn magst du es wagen
Upon him mayest thou it venture
{Thou mayest venture it upon him}

Mit unerschrocknem Mut,
With   undaunted   spirit,

Du wirst mit ihm erjagen,
Thou wilt with him apprehend,
{Thou wilt apprehend with him,}

Was   dir ist nütz und gut.
What for-thee is profitable and good.

Mt. 6:33. Seek first [God's] kingdom and his righteousness, and all these things shall be yours as well.
Mt. 22:37 [Christ]: ...You shall love the Lord your God with all your heart, and with all your soul, and with all your mind. (Also Deut. 6:5.)
Mt. 1:23. ...His name shall be called Emmanuel which means, God with us. (See Is. 7:14.)
Ps. 118:8. It is better to take refuge (Luther: vertrauen) in the Lord than to put confidence in man. (Also Ps. 18:30.)
Rom. 8:28. We know that in everything God works for good with those who love him... (Also Heb. 12:11.)
Ps. 37:23. The steps of a man are from the Lord (Luther: von dem Herrn...gefördert), and he establishes him in whose way he delights. (Also Ps. 90:17.)

Josh. 1:5, 9 [God]: ...As I was with Moses, so I will be with you; I will not fail you or forsake you...Be strong and of good courage; be not frightened, neither be dismayed; for the Lord your God is with you wherever you go.
Heb. 13:5-6. ...[God] has said, "I will never fail you nor forsake you." Hence we can confidently say, "The Lord is my helper, I will not be afraid; what can man do to me?"
Ps. 37:28. The Lord loves justice; he will not forsake his saints. The righteous shall be preserved for ever, but the children of the wicked shall be cut off.
Ps. 94:14. For the Lord will not forsake his people; he will not abandon his heritage. (Also 1 Kings 6:13, Is. 42:16.)
Deut. 31:6. Be strong and of good courage, do not fear or be in dread of them (Luther: vor ihnen grauen); for it is the Lord your God who goes with you; he will not fail you or forsake you. (Also Deut. 31:8.)
Ex. 14:13-14. And Moses said to the people, "Fear not, stand firm, and see the salvation of the Lord, which he will work for you today; for the Egyptians whom you see today, you shall never see again. The Lord will fight for you, and you have only to be still."
Lk. 18:7-8. Will not God vindicate (Luther: retten) his elect, who cry to him day and night? Will he delay long over them? I tell you, he will vindicate them speedily. Nevertheless, when the Son of God comes, will he find faith on the earth?

Mt. 7:24-25 [Christ]: Every one then who hears these words of mine and does them will be like a wise man who built his house upon the rock; and the rain fell, and the floods came, and the winds blew and beat upon that house, but it did not fall, because it had been founded on the rock.
Jer. 17:7-8. Blessed is the man who trusts in the Lord, whose trust is the Lord. He is like a tree planted by water, that sends out its roots by the stream, and does not fear when heat comes, for its leaves remain green, and is not anxious in the year of drought, for it does not cease to bear fruit. (Also Ps. 40:4, 146:3-5.)
Ps. 9:9-10. The Lord is a stronghold...in times of trouble. And those who know thy name put their trust in thee...
Rom. 8:28. We know that in everything God works for good with those who love him, who are called according to his purpose. (Also Heb. 12:11, Ps. 18:30.)
Ps. 84:11. The Lord God is a sun and shield; he bestows favor and

Was Gott beschlossen hat,
What God decided hath,
{What God hath decided,}

Das kann niemand hindern
That can no-one hinder

Aus allen Menschenkindern,
Of all humankind,
{That no one of all mankind can hinder,}

Es geht nach seinem Rat.
It goes according-to his counsel.

4. Tenor Aria (Chorale Vs. 4)
•Satan cannot prevail against thee; God is with thee! (107-4)
Wenn auch gleich aus der Höllen
Though even - out-of - hell

Der Satan wollte sich
- Satan would himself

Dir selbst entgegenstellen
Thee - oppose
{Oppose thee}

Und toben wider dich,
And rage against thee,

So muß er doch mit Spott
So must he yet amidst ridicule

Von seinen Ränken lassen,
From his intrigues desist,

Damit er dich will fassen;
With-which he thee would seize;

Denn dein Werk fördert Gott.
For thy work is-furthered-by God.

5. Soprano Aria (Chorale Vs. 5)
•God's sovereignty complete: to accomplish or hinder (107-5)
Er richt's zu seinen Ehren
He directs-it for his honor
{He directs matters for his honor}

Und deiner Seligkeit;
And thy blessedness;

Soll's sein, kein Mensch kann's wehren,
If-it's to-be, (then) no man can-it prevent,

Und wär's ihm noch so leid.
- Be-it for-him yet ever-so disagreeable.
{No matter how much he may dislike it.}

honor. No good thing does the Lord withhold from those who walk uprightly. (Also Ps. 34:10.)
Is. 43:13 [God]: I am God, and also henceforth I am He; there is none who can deliver from my hand; I work and who can hinder it?
Prov. 21:30. No wisdom, no understanding, no counsel, can avail against the Lord.
Is. 14:27. For the Lord of hosts has purposed, and who will annul it? His hand is stretched out, and who will turn it back? (Also Job 9:12, 11:10, 42:2–3.)
Rev. 3:8 [Christ]: ...I have set before you an open door, which no one is able to shut...
Is. 28:29. This also comes form the Lord of hosts; he is wonderful in counsel, and excellent in wisdom.

1 Pet. 5:8–10. Be sober, be watchful. Your adversary the devil prowls around like a roaring lion, seeking some one to devour. Resist him, firm in your faith, knowing that the same experience of suffering is required of your brotherhood throughout the world. And after you have suffered a little while, the God of all grace, who has called you to his eternal glory in Christ, will himself restore, establish, and strengthen you.
Eph. 6:11–12. Put on the whole armor of God, that you may be able to stand against the wiles of the devil. For we are not contending against flesh and blood, but against the principalities, against the powers, against the world rulers of this present darkness, against the spiritual hosts of wickedness in the heavenly places.
2 Cor. 11:14–15. ...Even Satan disguises himself as an angel of light. So it is not strange if his servants also disguise themselves as servants of righteousness... (Also 2 Cor. 2:11, Rev. 12:9.)
Mt. 16:18 [Christ]: ...I will build my church, and the powers of death (Luther: Pforten der Hölle) shall not prevail against it.
Ps. 138:8. The Lord will fulfil his purpose for me...
Job 22:19. The righteous see [the fall of their wicked adversaries] and are glad; the innocent laugh them to scorn. (Also Ps. 59:8.)
Ps. 90:17. Let the favor of the Lord our God be upon us, and establish (Luther: fördere) thou the work of our hands upon us, yea, the work of our hands establish thou it.

Rom. 8:28. We know that in everything God works for good with those who love him, who are called according to his purpose.
***Rom. 6:22.** ...The return you get is sanctification and its end, eternal life.
***Mk. 8:6, 8–9.** And [Jesus] commanded the crowd to sit down on the ground; and he took the seven loaves, and having given thanks he broke them and gave them to his disciples to set before the people... And they ate, and were satisfied...And there were about four thousand people.
Ps. 85:9. Surely his salvation is at hand for those who fear him, that glory may dwell in our land. (Also Is. 46:13.)
Jn. 14:13 [Christ]: Whatever you ask in my name, I will do it, that the Father may be glorified in the Son.
Is. 46:9–11 [God]: ...I am God, and there is no other; I am God, and there is none like me, declaring the end from the beginning and from

Will's denn Gott haben nicht,
Will-it then God have not,
{But if God would not have it happen,}

So kann's niemand forttreiben,
Then can-it no-one make-to-continue,
{Then no one can accomplish it,}

Es muß zurücke bleiben,
It must be-left,
{It must remain undone;}

Was Gott will, das geschicht.
What God wills, that (is-what) happens.

6. Tenor Aria (Chorale Vs. 6)
●Trusting God's sovereignty & yielding to his will (107-6)
Drum ich mich ihm ergebe,
Therefore I myself to-him yield,
{Therefore I yield myself to him,}

Ihm sei es heimgestellt;
To-him be it entrusted;

Nach nichts ich sonst mehr strebe,
For nothing (will) I else further strive,
{For I will strive for nothing else,}

Denn nur, was ihm gefällt.
Than only, what him pleases.
{Than only what pleases him.)

Drauf wart ich und bin still,
Thereupon wait I and am still,
{I wait upon that, and am still,}

Sein Will, der ist der beste,
His will, it is the best,

Das glaub ich steif und feste,
That believe I unbendingly and firmly,
{I believe that unbendingly and firmly,}

Gott mach es, wie er will!
(May) God do it, as he would!

7. Chorale (Vs. 7)
●Praise & honor to God for his protection & blessing (107-7)
Herr, gib, daß ich dein Ehre
Lord, grant, that I thine honor—

Ja all mein Leben lang
Yes, all my life long—

Von Herzengrund vermehre,
From (the) bottom-of-my-heart might-increase,

ancient times things not yet done, saying, "My counsel shall stand, and I will accomplish all my purpose,"...I have spoken, and I will bring it to pass; I have purposed, and I will do it. (Also Is. 55:10–11.)
2 Chron. 20:6. O Lord, God of our fathers, art thou not God in heaven? Dost thou not rule over all the kingdoms of the nations? In thy hand are power and might, so that none is able to withstand thee.
Job 23:13–14. He is unchangeable and who can turn him? What he desires, that he does. For he will complete what he appoints for me; and many such things are in his mind. (Also Prov. 21:30.)
Dan. 4:35. ...[The Lord] does according to his will in the host of heaven and among the inhabitants of the earth; and none can stay his hand or say to him, "What doest thou?"

Rom. 6:13. ...Yield yourselves to God...and your members to God as instruments of righteousness.
Mt. 6:10. Thy kingdom come, Thy will be done, On earth as it is in heaven. (Also Acts 21:14.)
2 Cor. 5:9. ...We make it our aim to please him. (Also Eph. 5:10.)
Jn. 6:38 [Christ]: I have come down from heaven, not to do my own will, but the will of him who sent me. (Also Jn. 4:34, 5:30.)
Lk. 22:41–42. [Jesus] withdrew from them about a stone's throw, and knelt down and prayed, "Father, if thou art willing, remove this cup from me; nevertheless not my will, but thine, be done." (Also Mt. 6:10, 26:39–42, Mk. 14:35–36.)
Is. 55:8–9. My thoughts are not your thoughts, neither are your ways my ways, says the Lord. For as the heavens are higher than the earth, so are my ways higher than your ways and my thoughts than your thoughts. (Also Job 12:13.)
Is. 45:9. Woe to him who strives with his Maker, an earthen vessel with the potter! Does the clay say to him who fashions it, "What are you making"?... (Also Rom. 9:21.)
Job 5:8. As for me, I would seek God, and to God would I commit my cause.
Ps. 131:1–2. O Lord, my heart is not lifted up, my eyes are not raised too high; I do not occupy myself with things too great and too marvelous for me. But I have calmed and quieted my soul, like a child quieted at its mother's breast; like a child that is quieted is my soul.
Lam. 3:25–26. The Lord is good to those who wait for him, to the soul that seeks him. It is good that one should wait quietly for the salvation of the Lord.

Ps. 115:1. Not to us, O Lord, not to us, but to thy name give glory (Luther: Ehre), for the sake of thy steadfast love and thy faithfulness!
Ps. 116:17. I will offer to thee the sacrifice of thanksgiving and call on the name of the Lord.
Ps. 86:12. I give thanks to thee, O Lord my God, with my whole heart, and I will glorify thy name for ever.
Ps. 104:33. I will sing to the Lord as long as I live (Luther: mein Leben lang); I will sing praise to my God while I have being. (Also Ps. 9:1, 63:4, 138:1, 146:2.)
Mt. 28:19. ...in the name of the Father and of the Son and of the Holy Spirit.

Dir   sage Lob und Dank!
To-thee express praise and thanks!

O Vater, Sohn und Geist,
O Father, Son, and Spirit,

Der du aus lauter Gnaden
Who - out-of sheer mercy

Abwendest Not und Schaden,
Dost-avert distress and   harm,

Sei immerdar gepreist!
Be   evermore praised!

Ps. 111:1–2, 4–6, 9. Praise the Lord. I will give thanks to the Lord with my whole heart, in the company of the upright, in the congregation. Great are the works of the Lord...The Lord is gracious and merciful. He provides food for those who fear him...He has shown his people the power of his works...He sent redemption to his people; he has commanded his covenant for ever...

Ps. 103:2–5, 8. Bless the Lord, O my soul, and forget not all his benefits, who forgives all your iniquity, who heals all your diseases, who redeems your life from the Pit, who crowns you with steadfast love and mercy, who satisfies you with good as long as you live...The Lord is merciful and gracious, slow to anger and abounding in steadfast love.

Ps. 121:7–8. The Lord will keep you from all evil; he will keep your life. The Lord will keep your going out and your coming in from this time forth and for evermore.

Ps. 145:2. [O Lord,] every day I will bless thee, and praise thy name for ever and ever.

BWV 108
Es ist euch gut, daß ich hingehe
(NBA I/12; BC A72)

Cantate: 4. S. after Easter (BWV 166, 108)
*Jms. 1:17–21 (All good gifts come from above; be doers of the Word)
*Jn. 16:5–15 (Jesus' farewell: promise to send the Holy Spirit)
Librettist: Christiane Mariane von Ziegler (Text shortened by someone: J. S. Bach?)

1. Bass Aria
●Vox Christi: I will send the Comforter: Jn. 16:7 (108-1)
Es ist euch   gut, daß ich hingehe;
It is for-you good, that I   depart;

denn so ich   nicht hingehe,   kömmt der Tröster
for   if I (do) not depart, (then) comes the Comforter

nicht zu euch. So ich aber gehe,   will ich
not   to you. If I however go, (then) will I

ihn zu euch senden.
him to you   send.

*Jn. 16:4–11 [Christ]: ...I did not say these things to you from the beginning, because I was with you. But now I am going to him who sent me; yet none of you asks me, "Where are you going?" But because I have said these things to you, sorrow has filled your hearts. Nevertheless I tell you the truth: *it is to your advantage that I go away, for if I do not go away, the Counselor will not come to you; but if I go, I will send him to you.* And when he comes, he will convince the world concerning sin and righteousness and judgment: concerning sin, because they do not believe in me; concerning righteousness, because I go to the Father, and you will see me no more; concerning judgment, because the ruler of this world is judged.

2. Tenor Aria
●Certainty of salvation based on Jesus' parting words (108-2)
Mich kann kein Zweifel stören,
Me   can   no   doubt   deter,
{No doubt can deter me,}

Auf dein Wort, Herr, zu hören.
Upon thy word, Lord, to hearken.
{From hearkening to thy word.}

Jn. 14:1–3, 11 [Christ]: Let not your hearts be troubled; believe in God, believe also in me. In my Father's house are many rooms; if it were not so, would I have told you that I go to prepare a place for you? And when I go and prepare a place for you, I will come again and will take you to myself, that where I am you may be also...Believe me that I am in the Father and the Father in me; or believe me for the sake of the works themselves.

Ich glaube, gehst du fort,
I   believe, goest thou away,
{I believe that if thou dost go away,}

So kann ich mich getrösten,
Then can I myself comfort,
{Then I can comfort myself,}

Daß ich zu   den Erlösten
That I amongst the redeemed
{That, with the redeemed, I}

Komm   an   gewünschten Port.
Shall-arrive at (the) desired   port.

3. Tenor Recit.
●Certainty of salvation based on coming of Spirit (108-3)
Dein Geist wird mich also regieren,
Thy Spirit will me so   rule,
{Thy Spirit will rule me in such a way}

Daß ich auf   rechter Bahne geh;
That I on (the) right course shall-go;
{That I go on the right course;}

Durch deinen Hingang kommt er   ja   zu mir,
Through thy   departure comes he indeed to me,
{Through thy departure he indeed comes to me,}

Ich frage sorgensvoll: Ach, ist er nicht schon hier?
I   ask anxiously: "Ah, is he not   yet here?"

4. Chorus
●Spirit will come & lead into all truth: Jn. 16:13 (108-4)
Wenn aber   jener, der Geist der Wahrheit,
When, however, that-one—the Spirit of   truth—

kommen wird, der wird euch in alle Wahrheit leiten.
will-come,   he will you into all   truth   lead.

Denn er wird nicht von ihm selber reden, sondern
For he will not   of him-self speak, but-rather

was er hören wird, das wird er reden;
what he will-hear, that will he speak;

und was   zukünftig ist, wird er verkündigen.
and what in-the-future is, will he   proclaim.

5. Alto Aria
●Prayer for blessing; to be led in God's ways forever (108-5)
Was mein Herz von dir begehrt,
What my heart of thee desires,
{What my heart desires from thee,}

Jn. 12:26 [Christ]: If any one serves me, he must follow me; and where I am, there shall my servant be also...

Jn. 16:27–31. [Jesus said,] "...You have loved me and have believed that I came from the Father. I came from the Father and have come into the world; again, I am leaving the world and going to the Father." His disciples said, "Ah, now you are speaking plainly, not in any figure! Now we know that you know all things, and need none to question you; by this we believe that you came from God." Jesus answered them, "Do you now believe?"

Lk. 23:43. [Jesus] said to [the thief on the cross] "Truly, I say to you, today you will be with me in Paradise."

Heb. 4:9–11. So then, there remains a sabbath rest for the people of God; for whoever enters God's rest also ceases from his labors as God did from his. Let us therefore strive to enter that rest...

*Jn. 16:13 [Christ]: When the Spirit of truth comes, he will guide you into all the truth...

1 Jn. 2:27. The anointing which you received from [God] abides in you, and you have no need that any one should teach you; as his anointing teaches you about everything...

Rom. 8:14. All who are led by the Spirit of God are sons of God.

Prov. 2:20. So you will walk in the way of good men and keep to the paths of the righteous. (Also Is. 2:3, Mic. 4:2.)

Ps. 143:8, 10. [O Lord]...teach me the way I should go, for to thee I lift up my soul...Teach me to do thy will, for thou art my God! Let thy good spirit lead me on a level path! (Also Ps. 27:11, Prov. 14:2.)

Gal. 5:16–18. ...Walk by the Spirit, and do not gratify the desires of the flesh. For the desires of the flesh are against the Spirit, and the desires of the Spirit are against the flesh; for these are opposed to each other, to prevent you from doing what you would. But if you are led by the Spirit you are not under the law. (Also Rom. 8:9–11.)

*Jn. 16:12–15 [Christ]: I have yet many things to say to you, but you cannot bear them now. *When the Spirit of truth comes, he will guide you into all the truth; for he will not speak on his own authority, but whatever he hears he will speak, and he will declare to you the things that are to come.* He will glorify me, for he will take what is mine and declare it to you. All that the Father has is mine; therefore I said that he will take what is mine and declare it to you.

Jn. 14:16–17, 26 [Christ]: I will pray the Father, and he will give you another Counselor, to be with you for ever, even the Spirit of truth, whom the world cannot receive, because it neither sees him nor knows him; you know him, for he dwells with you, and will be in you...The Counselor, the Holy Spirit, whom the Father will send in my name, he will teach you all things, and bring to your remembrance all that I have said to you.

Jn. 16:23–24 [Christ]: In that day you will ask nothing of me. Truly, truly, I say to you, if you ask anything of the Father, he will give it to you in my name. Hitherto you have asked nothing in my name; ask, and you will receive, that your joy may be full. (Also Jn. 14:13, 15:16.)

Ach, das wird mir wohl   gewährt.
Ah,   that will to-me indeed be-imparted.
{Ah, that will indeed be imparted to me.}

Überschütte mich mit Segen,
Cover   me with blessing,

Führe mich auf deinen Wegen,
Lead   me upon thy   ways,

Daß   ich in der Ewigkeit
So-that I in - eternity

Schaue   deine Herrlichkeit!
Will-behold thy   glory!

6. Chorale
•Spirit leads all who love God in paths of blessing (108–6)
Dein Geist, den Gott vom Himmel gibt,
Thy Spirit, whom God from heaven gives,

Der leitet alles, was ihn liebt,
He leads   all, who him love,
{He leads all who love him,}

Auf wohl gebähntem Wege.
On   well-paved   ways.

Er setzt und richtet unsren Fuß,
He places and directs   our   foot,

Daß er nicht anders treten muß,
That it not elsewhere tread   - ,
{That it does not tread elsewhere}

Als wo man findt den Segen.
But where one finds - blessing.
{Than where blessing is to be found.}

BWV 109
Ich glaube, lieber Herr
(NBA I/25; BC A151)

21. S. after Trinity (BWV 109, 38, 98, 188)
*Eph. 6:10–17 (The armor of the Christian)
*Jn. 4:46[1]–54 (Christ heals the son of a royal official)
[1]Begin: "And at Capernaum there was an official..."
Librettist: Unknown

1. Chorus
•Faith confessed despite circumstance: Mk. 9:24 (109–1)
Ich glaube, lieber Herr, hilf meinem Unglauben!
I believe; dear Lord, help   my   unbelief!

Ps. 145:19. [The Lord] fulfils the desire of all who fear him (Luther: was die Gottesfürchtigen begehren), he also hears their cry, and saves them. (Also Ps. 84:11.)
Is. 44:3 [God]: I will pour water on the thirsty land, and streams on the dry ground; I will pour my Spirit upon your descendants, and my blessing on your offspring.
Mal. 3:10. ...Put me to the test, says the Lord of hosts, if I will not open the windows of heaven for you and pour down for you an overflowing blessing.
Ps. 139:24. [O Lord]...lead me in the way everlasting! (Also Ps. 119:35, 143:10.)
Ps. 73:24. [O Lord,] thou dost guide me with thy counsel, and afterward thou wilt receive me to glory.
Jn. 17:24 [Christ]: Father, I desire that they also, whom thou hast given me, may be with me where I am, to behold my glory which thou hast given me in thy love for me before the foundation of the world.

*Jn. 16:13 [Christ]:** When the Spirit of truth comes, he will guide you into all the truth...he will declare to you the things that are to come.
1 Jn. 2:27. The anointing which you received from [God] abides in you, and you have no need that any one should teach you; as his anointing teaches you about everything...
Jn. 14:26 [Christ]: The Counselor, the Holy Spirit, whom the Father will send in my name, he will teach you all things, and bring to your remembrance all that I have said to you.
Jn. 14:21 [Christ]: He who has my commandments and keeps them, he it is who loves me; and he who loves me will be loved by my Father, and I will love him and manifest myself to him. (See also Jn. 14:23.)
Is. 26:7. [O Lord,] the way of the righteous is level; thou dost make smooth the path of the righteous. (Also Ps. 27:11, 119:35, 139:24, 143:10, Prov. 15:19.)
Ps. 25:10. All the paths of the Lord are steadfast love and faithfulness... (Also Prov. 3:17.)
Ps. 84:11. ...No good thing does the Lord withhold from those who walk uprightly. (Also Ps. 34:10.)
Ps. 121:2–3. My help comes from the Lord, who made heaven and earth. He will not let your foot be moved, he who keeps you will not slumber.
Prov. 3:23, 26. Then you will walk on your way securely and your foot will not stumble...For the Lord will be your confidence and will keep your foot from being caught.

*Jn. 4:46–48.** ...At Capernaum there was an official whose son was ill. When he heard that Jesus had come from Judea to Galilee, he went and begged him to come down and heal his son, for he was at the point of death. Jesus therefore said to him, "Unless you see signs and wonders you will not believe."
Mk. 9:17–18, 22–24. One of the crowd [said to Jesus], "Teacher, I brought my son to you, for he has a dumb spirit; and wherever it seizes him, it dashes him down; and he foams and grinds his teeth and becomes rigid; and I asked your disciples to cast it out, and they were not able...but if you can do anything, have pity on us and help us." And Jesus said to him, "If you can! All things are possible to him who believes." Immediately the father of the child cried out and said, "I believe; help my unbelief!"

2. Tenor Recit.

●Hope vs. Fear: vacillation between the two (109-2)

Des Herren Hand ist ja noch nicht verkürzt,
The Lord's hand is indeed yet   not shortened,
{Indeed, the Lord's hand has not been shortened,}

Mir kann geholfen werden.
I   can helped   be.
{I can be helped.}

Ach nein, ich sinke schon zur Erden
Ah no,   I   sink already to-the ground
{Ah no, I sink to the ground already}

Vor Sorge, daß sie mich zu Boden stürzt.
With worry, - it me to-the ground casts.
{With worry; it casts me to the ground.}

Der Höchste   will,   sein Vaterherze bricht.
The Most-High is-willing; his father's-heart breaks.

Ach nein! er hört die Sünder nicht.
Ah no! He hears (us) sinners not.

Er wird, er muß dir   bald zu helfen eilen,
He will, he must to-thee soon to help hasten,
{He will, he must soon hasten to help thee,}

Um deine Not zu heilen.
- Thy distress to heal.

Ach nein, es bleibet mir um Trost   sehr bange;
Ah no, (still) remain (I) for consolation very anxious;
{Ah no, I still remain very anxious for consolation;}

Ach Herr, wie lange?
Ah Lord, how long?

Num. 11:23. The Lord said to Moses, "Is the Lord's hand shortened? Now you shall see whether my word will come true for you or not."
Is. 59:1. Behold, the Lord's hand is not shortened, that it cannot save, or his ear dull, that it cannot hear. (Also Is. 50:2.)
Ps. 42:3, 5, 11; 43:5. My tears have been my food day and night, while men say to me continually, "Where is your God?"...Why are you cast down, O my soul, and why are you disquieted within me? Hope in God; for I shall again praise him, my help and my God.
Jer. 31:20. Is Ephraim my dear son? Is he my darling child? For as often as I speak against him, I do remember him still. Therefore my heart yearns for him (Luther: bricht mir mein Herz); I will surely have mercy on him, says the Lord.
Ps. 103:13. As a father pities his children, so the Lord pities those who fear him.
Mk. 1:40-41. A leper came to [Jesus] beseeching him, and kneeling said to him, "If you will, you can make me clean." Moved with pity, he stretched out his hand and touched him, and said to him, "I will; be clean." (Also Mt. 8:2-3, Lk. 5:12-13.)
Is. 59:1-2. Behold, the Lord's hand is not shortened, that it cannot save, or his ear dull, that it cannot hear. But your iniquities have made a separation between you and your God, and your sins have hid his face from you so that he does not hear. (Also Jn. 9:31.)
Is. 38:17. Lo, it was for my welfare that I had great bitterness (Luther: um Trost war mir sehr bange); but thou hast held back my life from the pit of destruction, for thou hast cast all my sins behind thy back.
Ps. 13:1. How long, O Lord? Wilt thou forget me for ever? How long wilt thou hide thy face from me? (Also Ps. 6:3-4, 89:46, 90:13-15, Ps. 22:1-2, 86:3, 88:1, Is. 38:13.)
Ps. 90:13, 15. Return, O Lord! How long? Have pity on thy servants!... Make us glad as many days as thou hast afflicted us, and as many years as we have seen evil.

3. Tenor Aria

●Hope vs. Fear: Doubt lets faith's wick almost go out (109-3)

Wie zweifelhaftig ist mein Hoffen,
How   irresolute is   my hoping,

Wie wanket mein geängstigt Herz!
How wavers my   anxious heart!
{How my anxious heart wavers!}

Des Glaubens Docht glimmt kaum hervor,
- Faith's   wick glimmers hardly forth,
{Faith's wick hardly glimmers,}

Es   bricht dies fast zerstoßne Rohr,
(Now) breaks this almost bruised reed,
{This bruised reed almost breaks,}

Mk. 9:17, 22. One of the crowd answered [Jesus], "Teacher...If you can do anything, have pity on us and help us."
Rom. 8:24-25. ...Hope that is seen is not hope. For who hopes for what he sees? But if we hope for what we do not see, we wait for it with patience.
Jms. 1:5-8. ...Let [us] ask God, who gives to all men generously and without reproaching, and it will be given him. But let [us] ask in faith, with no doubting, for he who doubts is like a wave of the sea that is driven and tossed by the wind. For that person must not suppose that a double-minded man, unstable in all his ways, will receive anything from the Lord.
Heb. 10:23. Let us hold fast the confession of our hope without wavering (Luther: wanken), for he who promised is faithful.
Mk. 9:24. ...[O Lord,] I believe; help my unbelief!
Mt. 12:18-21 [God]: Behold, my servant whom I have chosen, my beloved with whom my soul is well pleased...He will not wrangle or cry aloud, nor will any one hear his voice in the streets; he will not break a bruised reed or quench a smoldering wick, till he brings justice to victory; and in his name will the Gentiles hope. (See Is. 42:1-3.)

Die Furcht macht   stetig   neuen Schmerz.
(My) fear   gives (me) constantly   new   grief.

Is. 40:11. He will feed his flock like a shepherd, he will gather the lambs in his arms, he will carry them in his bosom, and gently lead those that are with young.

4. Alto Recit.
●Faith in the promise that Jesus will act (109-4)
O fasse dich, du zweifelhafter Mut,
O compose thyself, thou irresolute disposition,

Weil Jesus jetzt noch Wunder tut!
For Jesus now still wonders doth!
{For Jesus now still doth wonders!}

Die Glaubensaugen werden schauen
The eyes-of-faith shall behold

Das Heil des Herrn;
The salvation of-the Lord;

Scheint die Erfüllung allzufern,
Seems the fulfilment all-too-distant,
{If its fulfilment seems all too distant,}

So kannst du doch auf die Verheißung bauen.
Yet canst thou nevertheless on the promise build.
{Thou canst nevertheless build on the promise.}

Ps. 42:3, 5, 11; 43:5. ...Why are you cast down, O my soul, and why are you disquieted within me? Hope in God; for I shall again praise him, my help and my God.
Lk. 21:19 [Christ]: By your endurance you will gain your lives (Luther: Fasset eure Seele mit Geduld).
*Jn. 4:48, 50. Jesus therefore said to [the man] "Unless you see signs and wonders you will not believe...Go; your son will live."...
Ps. 119:123. [O Lord,] my eyes fail with watching for thy salvation, and for the fulfilment of thy righteous promise.
Jn. 11:40. Jesus said... "Did I not tell you that if you would believe you would see the glory of God?"
Jn. 20:29. Jesus said to [Thomas], "Have you believed because you have seen me? Blessed are those who have not seen and yet believe."
Rom. 8:24-25. In this hope we were saved. Now hope that is seen is not hope. For who hopes for what he sees? But if we hope for what we do not see, we wait for it with patience.
Heb. 11:1. Now faith is the assurance of things hoped for, the conviction of things not seen.
Mt. 7:24 [Christ]: Every one then who hears these words of mine and does them will be like a wise man who built his house upon the rock.
Ps. 130:5-6. I wait for the Lord, my soul waits, and in his word I hope; my soul waits for the Lord more than watchmen for the morning, more than watchmen for the morning.

5. Alto Aria
●Christ helps his own in battle between doubt & faith (109-5)
Der Heiland kennet ja die Seinen,
The Savior knows indeed his own,
{The Savior indeed knows his own,}

Wenn ihre Hoffnung hilflos liegt.
When their hope helpless lies.
{When their hope lies helpless.}

Wenn Fleisch und Geist in ihnen streiten,
When flesh and spirit within them fight,

So steht er ihnen selbst zur Seiten,
Then stands he (by) them, himself by (their) side,
{Then he himself will stand by their side,}

Damit zuletzt der Glaube siegt.
So-that at-last - faith triumphs.

2 Tim. 2:19. God's firm foundation (Luther: Grund) stands, bearing this seal: "The Lord knows those who are his" (Luther: der Herr kennt die Seinen)...
Jn. 10:14, 28 [Christ]: I am the good shepherd; I know my own and my own know me...I give them eternal life, and they shall never perish, and no one shall snatch them out of my hand.
Ps. 103:14. [God] knows our frame; he remembers that we are dust.
Mk. 14:38 [Christ]: Watch and pray that you may not enter into temptation; the spirit indeed is willing, but the flesh is weak. (Also Mt. 26:41.)
Gal. 5:17. For the desires of the flesh are against the Spirit, and the desires of the Spirit are against the flesh; for these are opposed to each other, to prevent you from doing what you would. (Also Rom. 7:15-23.)
Mk. 9:24. Immediately the father of the child cried out and said, "I believe; help my unbelief!"
1 Jn. 5:4. Whatever is born of God overcomes the world; and this is the victory that overcomes the world, our faith.

6. Chorale
●Whoever trusts in God shall never be put to shame (109-6)
Wer   hofft in Gott und   dem vertraut,
Whoever hopes in God and (in) him trusts,

Der wird nimmer   zuschanden;
He will never (be-put) to-shame;

Ps. 25:1-3, 20. To thee, O Lord, I lift up soul, O my God, in thee I trust, let me not be put to shame; let not my enemies exult over me. Yea, let none that wait for thee be put to shame...Oh guard my life, and deliver me; let me not be put to shame, for I take refuge in thee.
Ps. 119:116. [O Lord,] uphold me according to thy promise, that I may live, and let me not be put to shame in my hope! (Also Ps. 31:17, 74:21, 119:6, 31, Is. 45:17, 49:23, 50:7, 54:4.)

Denn wer   auf diesen Felsen baut,
For whoever on this   rock builds—

Ob   ihm gleich geht zuhanden
Even-though him   -   befalls

Viel   Unfalls hie, hab ich   doch   nie
Much misfortune here— I-have nevertheless never

Den Menschen sehen fallen,
That   man   seen   fall,
{Seen that man fall,}

Der sich verläßt auf Gottes Trost;
Who   relies   on God's comfort;

Er hilft sein' Gläubgen allen.
He helps his believing-ones all.
{He helps all of his believing ones.}

BWV 110
Unser Mund sei voll Lachens
(NBA I/2; BC A10)

Christmas Day (BWV 63, 91, 110, 248-I, 191)
*Tit. 2:11–14 (The grace of God has appeared)
or: *Is. 9:2–7 (The people who walked in darkness have seen a great light; unto us a child is born)
*Lk. 2:1–14 (The birth of Christ, announcement to the shepherds, the praise of the angels)
Librettist: Georg Christian Lehms. This cantata is adapted from some pre-existing movements.

1. Chorus (Music from BWV 1069)
●Laughter for great things God has done: Ps. 126:2–3 (110-1)
  Unser Mund sei voll Lachens und unsre Zunge
(May) our mouth be full-of laughter and our tongue

voll Rühmens. Denn der Herr hat Großes
full-of praises.   For the Lord hath great-things

an uns getan.
for us done.

2. Tenor Aria
●Incarnation: Praise God for coming down from heaven (110–2)
Ihr Gedanken und ihr Sinnen,
Ye thoughts and ye senses,

Schwinget euch anitzt von hinnen,
Soar-aloft   -   now from hence,

Steiget schleunig himmelan
Climb   swiftly heavenward

Und bedenkt, was Gott getan!
And consider, what God hath-done!

Mt. 7:24 [Christ]: Every one...who hears these words of mine and does them will be like a wise man who built his house upon the rock.
1 Pet. 2:6. It stands in scripture: "Behold, I am laying in Zion a stone, a cornerstone chosen and precious, and he who believes in him will not be put to shame." (See Is. 28:16, also Rom. 9:33, Eph. 2:20.)
1 Cor. 3:11. For no other foundation can any one lay than that which is laid, which is Jesus Christ.
Ps. 37:23–25, 28. The steps of a man are from the Lord, and he establishes him in whose way he delights; though he fall, he shall not be cast headlong, for the Lord is the stay of his hand. I have been young, and now am old; yet I have not seen the righteous forsaken or his children begging bread...For the Lord loves justice; he will not forsake his saints...
Ps. 94:14. For the Lord will not forsake his people; he will not abandon his heritage.
Ps. 37:28. The Lord loves justice; he will not forsake his saints. (Also 1 Kings 6:13, Is. 42:16.)

*Lk. 2:10–11. And the angel said to [the shepherds], "Be not afraid; for behold, I bring you good news of a great joy which will come to all the people; for to you is born this day in the city of David a Savior, who is Christ the Lord."
Ps. 126:1–3. When the Lord restored the fortunes of Zion, we were like those who dream. *Then our mouth was filled with laughter, and our tongue with shouts of joy;* then they said among the nations, "The Lord has done great things for them." *The Lord has done great things for us;* we are glad. (Also 1 Sam. 12:24, Lk. 1:49.)
Ps. 118:24. This is the day which the Lord has made; let us rejoice and be glad in it.
Job 8:21. He will yet fill your mouth with laughter, and your lips with shouting.
Joel 2:21. Fear not, O land; be glad and rejoice, for the Lord has done great things! (Also Is. 44:23.)

Ps. 113:4–6. The Lord is high above all nations, and his glory above the heavens! Who is like the Lord our God, who is seated on high, who looks far down upon the heavens and the earth? (Also Ps. 97:9, 99:2.)
Phil. 2:5–7. ...Though [Christ Jesus] was in the form of God, [he] did not count equality with God a thing to be grasped, but emptied himself, taking the form of a servant, being born in the likeness of men. (Also Jn. 17:5.)
*Lk. 2:13–14. And suddenly there was with the angel a multitude of the heavenly host praising God and saying, "Glory to God in the highest..."
Ps. 103:2. Bless the Lord, O my soul; and all that is within me, bless his holy name! Bless the Lord, O my soul, and forget not all his benefits (Luther: was er mir Gutes getan hat).

Er wird Mensch, und (um) dies   allein,
He becomes human, and   for   this (reason) alone,

Daß wir Himmels Kinder   sein.
That we heaven's children (should) be.
{That we should become children of heaven.}

3. Bass Recit.
●God's greatness is beyond all else: Jer. 10:6 (110-3)
Dir,   Herr, ist niemand gleich. Du bist groß, und dein
To-thee, Lord, is no-one   equal. Thou art great, and thy

Name ist groß und   kannst's mit der Tat beweisen.
name is great, and (thou) canst-it with - deeds prove.

4. Alto Aria
●Incarnation: Man lowly yet exalted in incarnation (110-4)
Ach Herr, was ist ein Menschenkind,
Ah Lord, what is a child-of-mankind,

Daß du sein Heil so schmerzlich suchest?
That thou his salvation so   painfully dost-seek?

Ein Wurm, den du verfluchest,
A   worm, whom thou dost-curse,

Wenn Höll und Satan um ihn sind;
When hell and Satan about him are;

Doch auch dein Sohn, den Seel und Geist
Yet   also thy son, whom soul and spirit

Aus Liebe seinen Erben   heißt.
Out-of love (their) inheritance do-call.
{Out of love call their inheritance.}

5. Soprano & Tenor Duet (Music from BWV 243a)
●Glory to God in the highest: Lk. 2:14 (110-5)
Ehre sei Gott in der Höhe und Friede auf Erden und
Glory be-to God in the highest and peace on earth and

den Menschen ein Wohlgefallen!
to mankind   -   goodwill!

6. Bass Aria
●Praise to God: Humans exhorted to musical praise (110-6)
Wacht auf, ihr Adern und ihr Glieder,
Wake up, ye (sinews) and ye members,

Heb. 2:14. Since therefore the children share in flesh and blood, [Christ] himself likewise partook of the same nature...
1 Jn. 3:1. See what love the Father has given us, that we should be called children of God; and so we are...
Rom. 9:8. ...It is not the children of the flesh who are the children of God, but the children of the promise are reckoned as descendants. (Also Jn. 1:12.)

Jer. 10:6. *There is none like thee, O Lord; thou art great, and thy name is great in might.* (Also Ps. 40:5.)
Ex. 15:11. Who is like thee, O Lord, among the gods? Who is like thee, majestic in holiness, terrible in glorious deeds, doing wonders?
Is. 6:1. ...I saw the Lord sitting upon a throne, high and lifted up; and his train filled the temple...

Ps. 144:3. O Lord, what is man that thou dost regard him, or the son of man that thou dost think of him? (Also Ps. 8:3–5, Heb. 2:5–8.)
Job 25:5–6. Behold, even the moon is not bright and the stars are not clean in his sight; how much less man, who is a maggot, and the son of man, who is a worm! (Also Ps. 22:6, Is. 41:14.)
Ps. 138:6. Though the Lord is high, he regards the lowly...
***Lk. 2:11.** To you is born this day...a Savior...
Rom. 8:3. God has done what the law, weakened by the flesh, could not do: sending his own Son in the likeness of sinful flesh and for sin, he condemned sin in the flesh. (Also Jn. 1:12, Heb. 2:14.)
Heb. 1:2. In these last days he has spoken to us by a Son, whom he appointed the heir (Luther: Erben) of all things...
Gal. 4:4–7. When the time had fully come, God sent forth his Son, born of woman, born under the law, to redeem those who were under the law, so that we might receive adoption as sons. And because you are sons, God has sent the Spirit of his Son into our hearts, crying, "Abba! Father!" So through God you are no longer a slave but a son, and if a son then an heir (Luther: Erben Gottes). (Also Col 3:24.)
1 Cor. 15:49–50. Just as we have borne the image of the man of dust, we shall also bear the image of the man of heaven. I tell you this, brethren: flesh and blood cannot inherit (Luther: ererben) the kingdom of God, nor does the perishable inherit the imperishable. (Also 2 Cor. 5:1–4.)

***Lk. 2:10–14.** And the angel said to [the shepherds], "Be not afraid; for behold, I bring you good news of a great joy which will come to all the people; for to you is born this day in the city of David a Savior, who is Christ the Lord. And this will be a sign for you: you will find a babe wrapped in swaddling cloths and lying in a manger." And suddenly there was with the angel a multitude of the heavenly host praising God and saying, *"Glory to God in the highest, and on earth peace among men with whom he is pleased!"*

Ps. 57:8. Awake, my soul! Awake, O harp and lyre! I will awake the dawn!
Ps. 103:2. Bless the Lord, O my soul; and all that is within me, bless his holy name!...

Und singt dergleichen Freudenlieder,
And sing such songs-of-joy,
{And sing the kind of joyful songs,}

Die unserm Gott gefällig sein.
Which to-our God pleasing are.
{Which are pleasing to our God.}

Und ihr, ihr andachtsvollen Saiten,
And ye, ye worshipful strings,

Sollt ihm ein solches Lob bereiten,
(Ye) shall him - such praise prepare,
{Ye shall prepare him the kind of praise}

Dabei sich Herz und Geist erfreun.
In-which - heart and spirit rejoice.

7. Chorale
●Alleluia: Corporate praise to God for this day (110-7)
Alleluja! Alleluja! Gelobt sei Gott,
Alleluia! Alleluia! Praised be God;
{Alleluia! Alleluia! Praise be to God;}

Singen wir all aus unsers Herzens Grunde.
Sing we all from our hearts' bottom.
{Let us all sing from the bottom of our hearts.}

Denn Gott hat heut gemacht solch Freud,
For God hath today wrought such joy,

Die wir vergessen solln zu keiner Stunde.
Which we forget shall at no hour.
{Which we shall not forget at any time.}

BWV 111
Was mein Gott will, das g'scheh allzeit
(NBA I/6; BC A36)

3. S. after Epiphany (BWV 73, 111, 72, 156)
*Rom. 12:16[1]-21 (Overcoming evil with good)
*Mt. 8:1-13 (Jesus heals a leper; the centurion from Capernaum comes to Jesus)
[1]Begin: "Never be conceited."
Librettist: Unknown

1. Chorus (Chorale Vs. 1) (See also 72-5, 144-6.)
●God's will trusted & accepted, building on him (111-1)
Was mein Gott will, das g'scheh allzeit,
Whatever my God wills, that be-done always,

Sein Will, der ist der beste;
His will, it is the best;

Zu helfen den'n er ist bereit,
To help all-them he is prepared,

Ps. 22:3. [O Lord,] thou art...enthroned on the praises of Israel.
Ps. 71:23. [O Lord,] my lips will shout for joy, when I sing praises to thee; my soul also, which thou hast rescued.
Ps. 47:1. Clap your hands, all peoples! Shout to God with loud songs of joy! (Also Ps. 107:22, Is. 12:6, 44:23.)
Ps. 50:23 [God]: He who brings thanksgiving as his sacrifice honors me... (Also Ps. 50:14, Heb. 13:15.)
Ps. 33:1-3. Rejoice in the Lord, O you righteous! Praise befits the upright. Praise the Lord with the lyre, make melody to him with the harp of ten strings! Sing to him a new song, play skilfully on the strings (Luther: Saitenspiel), with loud shouts. (Also Ps. 81:2-3.)
Ps. 16:9. ...My heart is glad, and my soul rejoices...
Ps. 149:1, 4. Praise the Lord! Sing to the Lord a new song, his praise in the assembly of the faithful!...For the Lord takes pleasure in his people...

*Lk. 2:10-11, 14. ...I bring you good news of a great joy...To you is born this day in the city of David a Savior...Glory to God in the highest, and on earth peace among men with whom he is pleased!
Rev. 19:1. ...Hallelujah! Salvation and glory and power belong to our God... (Also Rev. 19:3, 4, 6.)
Ps. 138:1. I give thee thanks, O Lord, with my whole heart...
Zeph. 3:14. Sing aloud, O daughter of Zion; shout, O Israel! Rejoice and exult with all your heart...
Ps. 118:24. This is the day which the Lord has made; let us rejoice and be glad in it.
Ps. 126:3. The Lord has done great things for us; we are glad. (Also 1 Sam. 12:24, Lk. 1:49.)
Ps. 103:2. Bless the Lord, O my soul; and all that is within me, bless his holy name! Bless the Lord, O my soul, and forget not all his benefits.

*Mt. 8:1-3. When [Jesus] came down from the mountain, great crowds followed him; and behold, a leper came to him and knelt before him, saying, "Lord, if you will, you can make me clean." And he stretched out his hand and touched him, saying, "I will; be clean." And immediately his leprosy was cleansed.
Mt. 26:39. ...Not as I will, but as thou wilt.
Mt. 6:10. Thy kingdom come, Thy will be done...
Rom. 8:28. We know that in everything God works for good with those who love him, who are called according to his purpose.
Ps. 33:18-19. Behold, the eye of the Lord is on those who fear him, on those who hope in his steadfast love, that he may deliver their soul from death, and keep them alive in famine.

Die an ihn gläuben feste.
Who on him believe steadfastly.

Er hilft aus Not, der fromme Gott,
He helps out-of trouble, (this) righteous God,

Und züchtiget mit Maßen:
And chastises with measure:

Wer Gott vertraut, fest auf ihn baut,
Whoever (in) God trusts, firmly on him builds,

Den will er nicht verlassen.
Him will he not forsake.

2. Bass Aria (Based on Chorale Vs. 2)
●Fear not but trust God; no one can stop his plans! (111–2)
Entsetze dich, mein Herze, nicht,
Be-frightened - , my heart, not,
{My heart, do not be frightened,}

Gott ist dein Trost und Zuversicht
God is thy consolation and confidence

Und deiner Seele Leben.
And thy soul's life.

Ja, was sein weiser Rat bedacht,
Yes, whatever his wise counsel hath-decided,

Dem kann die Welt und Menschenmacht
That can the world and human-might

Unmöglich widerstreben.
Impossibly resist.

3. Alto Recit. (Based on Chorale Vs. 2)
●God as refuge; fleeing him like Jonah did is foolish (111–3)
O Törichter! der sich von Gott entzieht
O foolish-one, who himself from God withdraws
{O foolish one, who withdraws from God}

Und wie ein Jonas dort
And like a Jonah there

Vor Gottes Angesichte flieht;
From God's face does-flee;

Auch unser Denken ist ihm offenbar,
Even our thinking is to-him manifest,
{He knows even our thoughts,}

Und unsers Hauptes Haar
And our head's hair(s)
{And all the hairs on our head}

Hat er gezählet.
Has he counted.

Jer. 30:11. For I am with you to save you, says the Lord; I will make a full end of all the nations among whom I scattered you, but of you I will not make a full end. I will chasten you in just measure (Luther: züchtigen...mit Maßen), and I will by no means leave you unpunished. (Also Jer. 4:27, 5:10, 5:18, 46:28, Ezek. 20:17.)
Heb. 12:6. For the Lord disciplines him whom he loves, and chastises every son whom he receives. (Also Prov. 3:11, Heb. 12:5–7, 11.)
Mt. 7:24 [Christ]: Every one then who hears these words of mine and does them will be like a wise man who built his house upon the rock.
1 Cor. 3:11. For no other foundation can any one lay than that which is laid, which is Jesus Christ.
Mt. 28:20 [Christ]: ...Lo, I am with you always to the close of the age.
Heb. 13:5. ...He has said, "I will never fail you nor forsake you..."

Josh. 1:9. ...Be strong and of good courage; be not frightened, neither be dismayed (Luther: entsetze dich nicht); for the Lord your God is with you wherever you go. (entsetzen: also Mk. 16:6, Lk. 21:9)
Ps. 46:1. God is our refuge (Luther: Zuversicht) and strength, a very present help in trouble.
Ps. 61:3. [O Lord,] thou art my refuge (Luther: Zuversicht), a strong tower against the enemy.
Ps. 27:1. The Lord is my light and my salvation; whom shall I fear? The Lord is the stronghold of my life; of whom shall I be afraid? (Also Ps. 56:4, 118:6, Rom. 8:31–39.)
Ps. 33:11. The counsel (Luther: Rat) of the Lord stands for ever, the thoughts of his heart to all generations. (Also Is. 28:29, 40:13–14, Jer. 32:19.)
Prov. 21:30. No wisdom, no understanding, no counsel, can avail against the Lord. (Also Is. 43:13, Job 9:12. 11:10.)
***Mt. 8:8–9.** The centurion answered [Jesus], "Lord, I am not worthy to have you come under my roof; but only say the word, and my servant will be healed. For I am a man under authority, with soldiers under me; and I say to one, 'Go,' and he goes, and to another, 'Come,' and he comes, and to my slave, 'Do this,' and he does it."

Jonah 1:1–3. Now the word of the Lord came to Jonah the son of Amittai, saying, "Arise, go to Nineveh, that great city, and cry against it; for their wickedness has come up before me." But Jonah rose to flee to Tarshish from the presence of the Lord. He went down to Joppa and found a ship going to Tarshish; so he paid the fare, and went on board, to go with them to Tarshish, away from the presence of the Lord.
Ps. 139:7. [O Lord,] whither shall I go from thy Spirit? Or whither shall I flee from thy presence? (Also Jer. 23:24.)
Ps. 139:1–3. O Lord, thou hast searched me and known me! Thou knowest when I sit down and when I rise up; thou discernest my thoughts from afar. Thou searchest out my path and my lying down, and art acquainted with all my ways.
Mt. 10:29–31 [Christ]: Are not two sparrows sold for a penny? And not one of them will fall to the ground without your Father's will. But even the hairs of your head are all numbered. Fear not, therefore; you are of more value than many sparrows. (Also Lk. 12:6–7, Mt. 6:25–30.)
Ps. 2:12. ...Blessed are all who take refuge in him (Luther: auf ihn trauen). (Also: Ps. 34:8, 146:5.)

Wohl   dem, der diesen Schutz erwählet
Happy (is) he, who this refuge chooses
{Happy is he who chooses this refuge}

Im gläubigen Vertrauen,
In believing reliance,

Auf dessen Schluß und Wort
Upon his conclusion and word

Mit Hoffnung und Geduld zu schauen.
With hope and patience to look.
{To look with hope and patience to his conclusion and word.}

4. Alto & Tenor Duet (Based on Chorale Vs. 3)
●God's will accepted & followed, even to death (111–4)
So geh ich mit beherzten Schritten,
So walk I with emboldened steps,
{Thus I walk with emboldened steps,}

Auch wenn mich Gott zum Grabe führt.
Even if me God to-the grave does-lead.
{Even if God leads me to the grave.}

Gott hat die Tage aufgeschrieben,
God has (my) days recorded,

So wird, wenn seine Hand mich rührt,
So shall, if his hand me touches,
{So shall, if he touches me with his hand,}

Des Todes Bitterkeit vertrieben.
- Death's bitterness be-driven-away.

5. Soprano Aria (Based on Chorale Vs. 3)
●Death: Prayer that faith may conquer in death's hour (111–5)
Drum   wenn der Tod zuletzt den Geist
Therefore when - death at-last (my) spirit
{Therefore when death in the end tears my spirit}

Noch mit Gewalt aus seinem Körper reißt,
Yet with force out-of its body tears,
{Yet forcefully out of this body,}

So nimm ihn, Gott in   treue Vaterhände!
Then take it, God, to (thy) faithful father's-hands!

Wenn Teufel, Tod und Sünde   mich bekriegt
When devil, death, and sin, (against) me make-war
{When devil, death, and sin make war against me}

Und meine Sterbekissen
And my deathbed's-pillow

Ein Kampfplatz werden müssen,
A battlefield become must,
{A battlefield must become,}

Ps. 146:5. Happy is he (Luther: wohl dem) whose help is the God of Jacob, whose hope (Luther: Hoffnung) is in the Lord his God. (Also Ps. 40:4, 84:12.)
Ps. 46:7, 11. The Lord of hosts is with us; the God of Jacob is our refuge (Luther: Schutz).
2 Cor. 1:9. ...[Our affliction served] to make us rely not on ourselves (Luther: daß wir unser Vertrauen nicht auf uns selbst stellen) but on God...
Ps. 130:5–6. I wait for the Lord, my soul waits, and in his word I hope; my soul waits for the Lord more than watchmen for the morning, more than watchmen for the morning.
Rom. 8:24–25. In this hope we were saved. Now hope that is seen is not hope. For who hopes for what he sees? But if we hope for what we do not see, we wait for it with patience. (Also Rom. 15:4, Gal. 5:5.)

Acts 21:13–14. Paul answered, "What are you doing, weeping and breaking my heart? For I am ready not only to be imprisoned but even to die at Jerusalem for the name of the Lord Jesus." And when he would not be persuaded, we ceased and said, "The will of the Lord be done."
Ps. 23:4. Even though I walk through the valley of the shadow of death, I fear no evil; for thou art with me; thy rod and thy staff, they comfort me.
Ps. 139:16. [O Lord]...in thy book were written, every one of them, the days that were formed for me, when as yet there was none of them.
Ps. 31:14–15. I trust in thee, O Lord... My times are in thy hand...
*Mt. 8:3. And [Jesus] stretched out his hand and touched [the man], saying, "I will; be clean." And immediately his leprosy was cleansed.
Heb. 2:14–15. ...[Christ] himself likewise partook of the same nature, that through death he might...deliver all those who through fear of death were subject to lifelong bondage.
1 Sam. 15:32. ...Surely the bitterness of death is past (Luther: also muß man des Todes Bitterkeit vertreiben).

2 Cor. 5:1–8. We know that if the earthly tent we live in is destroyed, we have a building from God, a house not made with hands, eternal in the heavens. Here indeed we groan, and long to put on our heavenly dwelling, so that by putting it on we may not be found naked. For while we are still in this tent, we sigh with anxiety; not that we would be unclothed, but that we would be further clothed, so that what is mortal may be swallowed up by life. He who has prepared us for this very thing is God, who has given us the Spirit as a guarantee. So we are always of good courage; we know that while we are at home in the body we are away from the Lord, for we walk by faith, not by sight. We are of good courage, and we would rather be away from the body and at home with the Lord.
Ps. 31:5. Into thy hand I commit my spirit; thou hast redeemed me, O Lord, faithful God. (Also Lk. 23:46.)
Num. 23:10. ...Let me die the death of the righteous, and let my end be like his!
1 Cor. 15:26. The last enemy to be destroyed is death.
Heb. 12:4. In your struggle against sin you have not yet resisted to the point of shedding your blood.
Eph. 6:11–12. Put on the whole armor of God...For we are...contending against the principalities, against the powers, against the world rulers of this present darkness... (Also 1 Pet. 5:8.)

So   hilf,   damit in dir mein Glaube   siegt!
Then help, so-that in thee my   faith may-conquer!

O seliges, gewünschtes Ende!
O blessed,   desired   end!

6. Chorale (Vs. 4)
●Prayer for victory when temptation assails (111-6)
Noch eins, Herr, will   ich bitten dich,
Yet one-thing, Lord, would I   ask of-thee,

Du wirst mir's nicht versagen:
Thou wilt me-it not   refuse:
{Thou wilt not refuse it to me:}

Wann mich der böse Geist anficht,
When me the evil spirit assails,
{When the evil spirit assails me,}

Laß mich doch nicht verzagen.
Let me indeed not   despair.

Hilf, steur und wehr, ach Gott, mein Herr,
Help, direct, and defend, ah God, my Lord,

Zu   Ehren deinem Namen.
To (the) honor of-thy name.

Wer   das begehrt, dem wird's gewährt;
Whoever that desires, to-him will-it be-granted;

Drauf sprech ich fröhlich: Amen.
To-that say I joyously: "Amen."

2 Tim. 4:7-8. I have fought the good fight, I have finished the race, I have kept the faith. Henceforth there is laid up for me the crown of righteousness...
Rev. 2:10 [Christ]: ...Be faithful unto death (Luther: sei getreu bis an den Tod), and I will give you the crown of life.

Jn. 17:15 [Christ]: I do not pray that thou shouldst take them out of the world, but that thou shouldst keep them from the evil one. (Also Lk. 22:32.)
1 Pet. 5:8-10. Be sober, be watchful. Your adversary the devil prowls around like a roaring lion, seeking some one to devour. Resist him, firm in your faith, knowing that the same experience of suffering is required of your brotherhood throughout the world. And after you have suffered a little while, the God of all grace, who has called you to his eternal glory in Christ, will himself restore, establish, and strengthen you. (Also Eph. 6:11-12.)
Mt. 26:41 [Christ]: Watch and pray that you may not enter into temptation (Luther: Anfechtung); the spirit indeed is willing, but the flesh is weak. (Also Mk. 14:38.)
***Rom. 12:21.** Do not be overcome by evil, but overcome evil with good.
Ps. 31:3. Yea, [O Lord,] thou art my rock and my fortress; for thy name's sake lead me and guide me.
Phil. 1:6. ...He who began a good work in you will bring it to completion at the day of Jesus Christ.
Rom. 8:37. In all these things we are more than conquerors through him who loved us.
Ps. 23:3. ...He leads me in paths of righteousness for his name's sake.
Mt. 5:6 [Christ]: Blessed are those who hunger and thirst for righteousness, for they shall be satisfied.
1 Jn. 5:14. And this is the confidence which we have in him, that if we ask anything according to his will he hears us.
Ps. 145:19. He fulfils the desire of all who fear him (Luther: was die Gottesfürchtigen begehren), he also hears their cry, and saves them.

BWV 112
Der Herr ist mein getreuer Hirt
(NBA I/11; BC A67)

Misericordias Domini: 2. S. after Easter (BWV 104, 85, 112)
*1 Pet. 2:21-25 (Christ as example; you have returned to the shepherd of your souls)
*Jn. 10:11-16 (Jesus declares himself to be the good Shepherd)
Librettist: Chorale (Wolfgang Meuslin)

1. Chorus (Chorale Vs.1) (Perhaps from an earlier work)
●Shepherd's Psalm: paraphrase of Ps. 23:1-2 (112-1)
Der Herr ist mein getreuer Hirt,
The Lord is my faithful shepherd,

Hält mich in seiner Hute,
Holds me in his   care,

Darin mir gar   nichts mangeln wird
Wherein (I) absolutely nothing   lack shall
{Wherein I shall lack absolutely nothing}

Ps. 23:1-2. *The Lord is my shepherd, I shall not want; he makes me lie down in green pastures...*
Ezek. 34:14-16 [God]: I will feed [my sheep] with good pasture, and upon the mountain heights of Israel shall be their pasture; there they shall lie down in good grazing land, and on fat pasture they shall feed on the mountains of Israel. I myself will be the shepherd of my sheep, and I will make them lie down, says the Lord God. I will seek the lost, and I will bring back the strayed, and I will bind up the crippled, and I will strengthen the weak...
***Jn. 10:14-15, 27-29 [Christ]:** I am the good shepherd; I know my own and my own know me, as the Father knows me and I know the Father; and I lay down my life for the sheep...My sheep hear my voice, and I know them, and they follow me; and I give them eternal life, and they shall never perish, and no one shall snatch them out of my hand. My Father, who has given them to me, is greater than all, and no one is able to snatch them out of the Father's hand.
***1 Pet. 2:25.** You were straying like sheep, but have now returned to the Shepherd and Guardian of your souls.

Irgend an einem Gute,
Of-any   a   good-thing,
{Of any good thing,}

Er weidet mich ohn Unterlaß,
He pastures me without ceasing,

Darauf wächst das wohlschmeckend Gras
(There) grows the   tasty   grass

Seines heilsamen Wortes.
Of-his   healing   Word.

2. Alto Aria (Chorale Vs. 2)
•Shepherd's Psalm: paraphrase of Ps. 23:2–3 (112-2)
Zum reinen Wasser er mich weist,
To   pure   water he me directs,
{To pure water he directs me,}

Das mich erquicken tue.
Which me refreshes   - .
{Which refreshes me.}

Das ist sein fronheiliger Geist,
That is his sacred-Holy Ghost;

Der macht mich wohlgemute.
He makest me of-good-cheer.

Er führet mich auf   rechter Straß
He leads me on (the) right road

Seiner   Geboten   ohn   Ablaß
Of-his commandments without ceasing

Von wegen   seines Namens willen.
On-account-of   his   name's sake.

3. Bass Arioso & Recit. (Chorale Vs. 3)
•Shepherd's Psalm: paraphrase of Ps. 23:4 (112-3)
Und   ob   ich wandert im finstern Tal,
And though I wander in-the dark   vale,

Fürcht ich kein Ungelücke
Fear   I   no misfortune
{I fear no misfortune}

In Verfolgung, Leiden, Trübsal
In persecution, suffering, tribulation,

Und dieser Welte Tücke;
And this world's trickery;

Denn du bist bei mir stetiglich,
For thou art with me constantly,

Dein Stab und Stecken trösten mich,
Thy staff and rod   comfort me,

Ps. 84:11. The Lord God is a sun and shield; he bestows favor and honor. No good thing does the Lord withhold from those who walk uprightly. (Also Ps. 34:10, Jms. 1:17.)
Mt. 4:4. ...Man shall not live by bread alone, but by every word that proceeds from the mouth of God. (Also Deut. 8:3.)
Josh. 1:8. This book of the law shall not depart out of your mouth, but you shall meditate on it day and night...
Ps. 119:103. [O Lord,] how sweet are thy words to my taste, sweeter than honey to my mouth! (Also Ps. 19:9–10.)
Wisdom (Apocrypha) 16:12. Neither herb nor poultice cured them, but it was thy word, O Lord, which heals all men. (Also Jer. 8:22, 14:19, 30:13.)

Ps. 23:2–3. *...He leads me beside still waters; he restores my soul. He leads me in paths of righteousness for his name's sake.*
Jn. 4:14 [Christ]: Whoever drinks of the water that I shall give him will never thirst; the water that I shall give him will become in him a spring of water welling up to eternal life. (Also Rev. 7:17, 21:6, 22:1, 22:17.)
Is. 44:3 [God]: I will pour water on the thirsty land, and streams on the dry ground; I will pour my Spirit upon your descendants, and my blessing on your offspring. (Also Is. 32:15.)
1 Cor. 12:13. ...[We] all were made to drink of one Spirit.
Mt. 3:11 [John the Baptist]: I baptize you with water... [Christ] will baptize you with the Holy Spirit and with fire. (Also Mk. 1:8, Lk. 3:16, Jn. 3:5, Acts 1:5.)
Jn. 16:13 [Christ]: When the Spirit of truth comes, he will guide you into all the truth... (Also Jn. 14:26, 1 Jn. 2:29.)
Ps. 119:35. [O Lord,] lead me in the path of thy commandments, for I delight in it. (Also Ps. 119:105–106, 143:10, 139:24.)
*1 Pet. 2:25. You were straying like sheep, but have now returned to the Shepherd and Guardian of your souls.
Ps. 31:3. [O Lord,] thou art my rock and my fortress; for thy name's sake lead me and guide me. (Also Ps. 25:9–10, Ps. 16:11.)

Ps. 23:4. *Even though I walk through the valley of the shadow of death, I fear no evil; for thou art with me; thy rod and thy staff, they comfort me.*
Ezek. 34:12 [God]: ...So will I seek out my sheep, and I will rescue them from all places where they have been scattered on a day of clouds and thick darkness...
Jn. 10:29 [Christ]: My Father, who has given [the sheep] to me, is greater than all, and no one is able to snatch them out of the Father's hand.
Jn. 16:33 [Christ]: I have said this to you, that in me you may have peace. In the world you have tribulation; but be of good cheer, I have overcome the world. (Also 1 Jn. 2:13, 14; 4:4.)
Ps. 27:1. The Lord is my light and my salvation; whom shall I fear?... (Also Ps. 56:4, 118:6.)
Rom. 8:35, 38–39. Who shall separate us from the love of Christ? Shall tribulation, or distress, or persecution, or famine, or nakedness, or peril, or sword?...I am sure that neither death, nor life, nor angels, nor principalities, nor things present, nor things to come, nor powers, nor height, nor depth, nor anything else in all creation, will be able to separate us from the love of God in Christ Jesus our Lord. (Also 2 Cor. 4:7–10, 12, 2 Cor. 12:9–10.)

Auf dein Wort ich mich   lasse.
(To) thy Word I myself relinquish.
{I trust in thy Word.}

4. Soprano & Tenor Duet (Chorale Vs. 4)
●Shepherd's Psalm: paraphrase of Ps. 23:5 (112-4)
Du   bereitest für mir einen Tisch
Thou preparest for me a   table

Vor   mein' Feinden allenthalben,
Before my   enemies everywhere,

Machst mein Herze   unverzagt   und frisch,
Makest my   heart undisheartened and fresh,
{Dost cheer and revive my heart,}

Mein Haupt tust du   mir salben
My   head dost thou for-me anoint

Mit deinem Geist, der Freuden Öl,
With thy   Spirit, -   joy's oil,

Und schenkest voll ein meiner Seel
And   pourest full -   my soul
{And dost fill my soul}
            [einschenken = to pour in, to fill]

Deiner geistlichen Freuden.
With-thy spiritual   joys.

5. Chorale (Vs. 5)
●Shepherd's Psalm: paraphrase of Ps. 23:6 (112-5)
Gutes   und die Barmherzigkeit
Goodness and -   mercy

Folgen mir nach im Leben,
Follow me   -   in life,

Und ich werd bleiben allezeit
And I   will remain evermore

Im   Haus des Herren eben,
In-the house of-the Lord   - :

Auf Erd in christlicher Gemein
On earth in   Christian communion

Und nach dem Tod da werd ich sein
And after - death then will I be

Bei Christo, meinem Herren.
With Christ,   my   Lord.

Ps. 119:114. [O Lord,] thou art my hiding place and my shield; I hope in thy word. (Also Ps. 119:42, 43, 49, 81.)

Ps. 23:5. *Thou preparest a table before me in the presence of my enemies; thou anointest my head with oil, my cup overflows.*
Ps. 78:19-20, 25. [In the desert, the Israelites] spoke against God, saying, "Can God spread a table in the wilderness?" He smote the rock so that water gushed out and streams overflowed...Man ate of the bread of the angels; he sent them food in abundance.
Ezek. 34:14-15 [God]: I will feed [my sheep] with good pasture, and upon the mountain heights of Israel shall be their pasture; there they shall lie down in good grazing land, and on fat pasture they shall feed on the mountains of Israel. I myself will be the shepherd of my sheep, and I will make them lie down, says the Lord God.
Ps. 31:19, 24. [O Lord,] how abundant is thy goodness, which thou hast laid up for those who fear thee, and wrought for those who take refuge in thee, in the sight of the sons of men!...Be strong, and let your heart take courage (Luther: seid getrost und unverzagt), all you who wait for the Lord! (Also Ps. 27:14, 112:7.)
Ps. 92:10. [O Lord,] thou hast exalted my horn like that of the wild ox, thou hast poured over me fresh oil.
Is. 44:3 [God]: ...I will pour my Spirit upon your descendants, and my blessing on your offspring.
Jn. 7:37-39. On the last day of the feast, the great day, Jesus stood up and proclaimed, "If any one thirst, let him come to me and drink. He who believes in me, as the scripture has said, 'Out of his heart shall flow rivers of living water.'" Now this he said about the Spirit, which those who believed in him were to receive... (Also Joel 2:28, Acts 2:18.)
1 Cor. 12:13. ...[We] all were made to drink of one Spirit.

Ps. 23:6. *Surely goodness and mercy shall follow me all the days of my life; and I shall dwell in the house of the Lord for ever.*
Ps. 27:4. One thing have I asked of the Lord, that will I seek after; that I may dwell in the house of the Lord all the days of my life, to behold the beauty of the Lord, and to inquire in his temple.
2 Cor. 6:16. ...We are the temple of the living God; as God said, "I will live in them and move among them, and I will be their God, and they shall be my people."
1 Tim. 3:15. ...The household of God...is the church of the living God, the pillar and bulwark of the truth.
1 Jn. 1:3, 7. That which we have seen and heard we proclaim also to you, so that you may have fellowship (Luther: Gemeinschaft) with us, and our fellowship is with the Father and with his Son Jesus Christ...If we walk in the light, as he is in the light, we have fellowship (Luther: Gemeinschaft) with one another...
Phil. 1:21-24. ...To me to live is Christ, and to die is gain...Yet which I shall choose I cannot tell. I am hard pressed between the two. My desire is to depart and be with Christ, for that is far better. But to remain in the flesh is more necessary on your account.
2 Cor. 5:6-8. So we are always of good courage; we know that while we are at home in the body we are away from the Lord, for we walk by faith, not by sight. We are of good courage, and we would rather be away from the body and at home with the Lord.
1 Thess. 4:17. ...So we shall always be with the Lord. (Also Jn. 14:3.)

BWV 113
Herr Jesu Christ, du höchstes Gut
(NBA I/20; BC A122)

11. S. after Trinity (BWV 199, 179, 113)
*1 Cor. 15:1–10 (Paul writes of his apostleship and lists post-resurrection appearances of Jesus)
*Lk. 18:9–14 (Parable of the Pharisee and the tax collector in the temple to pray)
Librettist: Unknown

1. Chorus (Chorale Vs. 1)
●Prayer: Lord of all grace, see how burdened I am with sin! (113-1)
Herr Jesu Christ, du höchstes Gut,
Lord Jesus Christ, thou highest good,

Du Brunnquell aller Gnaden,
Thou wellspring of-all grace,

Sieh doch, wie ich in meinem Mut
See, please, how I within my dispositon
{See how in my heart}

Mit Schmerzen bin beladen
With sorrows am laden
{I am laden with sorrows}

Und in mir hab der Pfeile viel,
And in me have - arrows many,
{And have many arrows within me,}

Die im Gewissen ohne Ziel
Which in (my) conscience without end

Mich armen Sünder drücken.
(Me) poor sinner oppress.
{Oppress this poor sinner.}

2. Chorale: Alto (Vs. 2) (See also 131-2.)
●Prayer: Have mercy on me, burdened with sin! (113-2)
Erbarm dich mein in solcher Last,
Have-mercy on-me (who-has) such (a) burden,
{Have mercy on me with my great burden,}

Nimm sie aus meinem Herzen,
Take it out-of my heart,

Dieweil du sie gebüßet hast
Since thou for-it atoned hast
{Since thou hast atoned for it}

Am Holz mit Todesschmerzen,
On-the (tree) with death's-pangs,

Ps. 16:5. The Lord is my chosen portion (Luther: Gut)...
Ps. 73:25. [O Lord,] whom have I in heaven but thee? And there is nothing upon earth that I desire besides thee.
Jms. 1:17. Every good endowment and every perfect gift is from above, coming down from the Father of lights with whom there is no variation or shadow due to change.
Ps. 69:16. Answer me, O Lord, for thy steadfast love is good; according to thy abundant mercy, turn to me. (Also Ps. 103:8, 10–12.)
Is. 1:4. Ah, sinful nation, a people laden with iniquity...
Rom. 2:15. ...What the law requires is written on [men's] hearts, while their conscience also bears witness and their conflicting thoughts accuse or perhaps excuse them...
1 Tim. 6:10. ...Some have wandered away from the faith and pierced their hearts with many pangs.
Ps. 38:1–8. O Lord, rebuke me not in thy anger, nor chasten me in thy wrath! For thy arrows have sunk into me, and thy hand has come down on me. There is no soundness in my flesh because of thy indignation; there is no health in my bones because of my sin. For my iniquities have gone over my head; they weigh like a burden too heavy for me. My wounds grow foul and fester because of my foolishness, I am utterly bowed down and prostrate; all the day I go about mourning. For my loins are filled with burning, and there is no soundness in my flesh. I am utterly spent and crushed; I groan because of the tumult of my heart.
Ps. 86:5–6. Thou, O Lord, art good and forgiving (Luther: gut und gnädig), abounding in steadfast love (Luther: Güte) to all who call on thee.
*Lk. 18:13. ...God be merciful to me a sinner!

Ps. 51:1–3. Have mercy on me, O God, according to thy steadfast love; according to thy abundant mercy blot out my transgressions. Wash me thoroughly from my iniquity, and cleanse me from my sin! For I know my transgressions, and my sin is ever before me.
Ps. 38:3–4. There is no soundness in my flesh because of thy indignation; there is no health in my bones because of my sin. For my iniquities have gone over my head; they weigh like a burden too heavy for me.
*Lk. 18:9–14. [Jesus]...told this parable to some who trusted in themselves that they were righteous and despised others: "Two men went up into the temple to pray, one a Pharisee and the other a tax collector. The Pharisee stood and prayed thus with himself, 'God, I thank thee that I am not like other men, extortioners, unjust, adulterers, or even like this tax collector. I fast twice a week, I give tithes of all that I get.' But the tax collector, standing far off, would

Auf daß ich nicht für großem Weh
So that I not in great woe
{So that I do not go to ruin in great woe}

In   meinen Sünden untergeh,
Amidst   my   sins   go-under,
{Amidst my sins,}

Noch ewiglich verzage.
Nor   evermore despair.

3. Bass Aria (Based on Chorale Vs. 3)
●Trembling seizes me when I think of my sin (113-3)
Fürwahr, wenn mir das kömmet ein,
Truly,   when to-me it   occurs,
{Truly, when it occurs to me,}

Daß ich nicht recht vor Gott gewandelt
That I   not rightly before God have-walked
{That I have not walked rightly before God}

Und täglich wider ihn   mißhandelt,
And daily against him have-done-wrong,
{And have daily done wrong against him,}

So   quält mich Zittern, Furcht und Pein.
Then torments me trembling, fear, and pain.
{Then trembling, fear, and pain torments me.}

Ich weiß, daß mir das Herze bräche,
I   know, that - (my) heart would-break,

Wenn mir dein Wort nicht Trost verspräche.
If   me thy Word not comfort did-promise.
{If thy Word did not promise me comfort.}

4. Bass Recit. & Chorale (Vs. 4)
●Conscience pangs turn to joy of reconciliation (113-4)
Jedoch dein heilsam Wort, das macht
But   thy   healing Word, it (assures)

Mit seinem süßen Singen,
With its   sweet singing,

Daß meine Brust,
That my   breast,

Der   vormals lauter Angst bewußt,
Which formerly nought-but fear knew,

Sich wieder kräftig kann erquicken.
Itself again mightily can   revive.
{Can mightily revive itself again.}

not even lift up his eyes to heaven, but beat his breast, saying, 'God be merciful to me a sinner!' I tell you, this man went down to his house justified rather than the other; for every one who exalts himself will be humbled, but he who humbles himself will be exalted."
1 Pet. 2:24. [Christ] himself bore our sins in his body on the tree, that we might die to sin and live to righteousness. By his wounds you have been healed. (Also Is. 53:5, 11–12, Gal. 3:13, Heb. 10:10, 14.)
Rom. 6:23. For the wages of sin is death, but the free gift of God is eternal life in Christ Jesus our Lord.

Heb. 10:26–27. If we sin deliberately after receiving the knowledge of the truth, there no longer remains a sacrifice for sins, but a fearful prospect of judgment, and a fury of fire which will consume the adversaries. (Also Heb. 9:27.)
Rom. 1:18. For the wrath of God is revealed from heaven against all ungodliness and wickedness of men who by their wickedness suppress the truth.
Mic. 6:8. [God] has showed you, O man, what is good; and what does the Lord require of you but to do justice, and to love kindness, and to walk humbly with your God?
Ps. 130:1–3. Out of the depths I cry to thee, O Lord! Lord, hear my voice! Let thy ears be attentive to the voice of my supplications! If thou, O Lord, shouldst mark iniquities, Lord, who could stand! (Also Ps. 76:7, 143:2, Nah. 1:6, Mal. 3:2, Rev. 6:17.)
Ps. 119:120. [O Lord,] my flesh trembles for fear of thee, and I am afraid of thy judgments.
Ps. 32:3–4. When I declared not my sin, my body wasted away through my groaning all day long. For day and night thy hand was heavy upon me; my strength was dried up as by the heat of summer.
1 Jn. 1:8–9. If we say we have no sin, we deceive ourselves, and the truth is not in us. If we confess our sins, he is faithful and just, and will forgive our sins and cleanse us from all unrighteousness.

Ps. 32:1–2, 5, 11. Blessed is he whose transgression is forgiven, whose sin is covered. Blessed is the man to whom the Lord imputes no iniquity, and in whose spirit there is no deceit...I acknowledged my sin to thee, and I did not hide my iniquity; I said, "I will confess my transgressions to the Lord"; then thou didst forgive the guilt of my sin ...Be glad in the Lord, and rejoice, O righteous, and shout for joy, all you upright in heart! (Also Rom. 4:7–8, Job 31:33.)
*Lk. 18:13–14. The tax collector, standing far off, would not even lift up his eyes to heaven, but beat his breast, saying, "God be merciful to me a sinner!" ...This man went down to his house justified rather than the other; for every one who exalts himself will be humbled, but he who humbles himself will be exalted.
Ps. 32:3. When I declared not my sin, my body wasted away through my groaning all day long.

Das jammervolle Herz
This woeful heart

Empfindet nun nach tränenreichem Schmerz
Perceives now after tear-filled pain

Den hellen Schein von Jesu Gnadenblicken;
The bright radiance of Jesus' glances-of-mercy;

Sein Wort hat mir so vielen Trost gebracht,
His Word has me so much comfort brought,
{His Word has brought me so much comfort,}

Daß mir das Herze wieder lacht,
That - (my) heart again laughs,
{That my heart laughs again,}

Als wenn's beginnt zu springen.
As though-it were-beginning to spring.

Wie wohl ist meiner Seelen!
How blest is my soul!

Das nagende Gewissen kann mich nicht länger quälen,
(My) nagging conscience can me no longer torment,
{My nagging conscience can no longer torment me,}

Dieweil Gott alle Gnad verheißt,
Since God all grace does-promise, (and)
{Since God promises all his grace and}

Hiernächst die Gläubigen und Frommen
After-this (all) believers and righteous-ones
{After this feeds all believers and righteous ones}

Mit Himmelsmanna speist,
With heaven's-manna does-feed,
{With heaven's manna,}

Wenn wir nur mit zerknirschtem Geist
If we but with remorseful spirit

Zu unserm Jesu kommen.
To our Jesus do-come.
{Come to our Jesus.}

5. Tenor Aria (Based on Chorale Vs. 5)
●Word of comfort & life: Jesus accepts sinners (113-5)
Jesus nimmt die Sünder an:
Jesus accepts - sinners - :

Süßes Wort voll Trost und Leben!
Sweet word (of) comfort and life!

Er schenkt die wahre Seelenruh
He gives - true rest-of-soul

Und rufet jedem tröstlich zu:
And calls-to each-one comfortingly - :

Ps. 40:12. ...My iniquities have overtaken me, till I cannot see; they are more than the hairs of my head; my heart fails me. (Also Ps. 38:4, Ezra 9:6.)

Ps. 38:8. ...I groan because of the tumult of my heart.

Ps. 51:1–3, 7–12. Have mercy on me, O God, according to thy steadfast love; according to thy abundant mercy blot out my transgressions. Wash me thoroughly from my iniquity, and cleanse me from my sin! For I know my transgressions, and my sin is ever before me...Purge me with hyssop, and I shall be clean; wash me, and I shall be whiter than snow. Fill me with joy and gladness; let the bones which thou hast broken rejoice. Hide thy face from my sins, and blot out all my iniquities. Create in me a clean heart, O God, and put a new and right spirit within me. Cast me not away from thy presence, and take not thy holy Spirit from me. Restore to me the joy of thy salvation, and uphold me with a willing spirit.

2 Chron. 7:14 [God]: If my people who are called by my name humble themselves, and pray and seek my face, and turn from their wicked ways, then I will hear from heaven, and will forgive their sin and heal their land. (Also 1 Kings 8:33–34, 2 Chron. 6:24–25, Is. 1:18.)

Jer. 31:13 [God]: Then the maidens rejoice in the dance, and the young men and the old shall be merry. I will turn their mourning into joy, I will comfort them, and give them gladness for sorrow. (Also Ps. 30:11.)

Rom. 5:20. ...Where sin increased, grace abounded all the more.

Is. 40:11. He will feed his flock like a shepherd...

Rev. 2:17 [Christ]: ...To him who conquers I will give some of the hidden manna... (Also Jn. 6:48–51.)

Jn. 6:35–37. Jesus said to them, "I am the bread of life; he who comes to me shall not hunger, and he who believes in me shall never thirst... All that the Father gives me will come to me; and him who comes to me I will not cast out."

Is. 57:15. For thus says the high and lofty One who inhabits eternity, whose name is Holy: "I dwell in the high and holy place, and also with him who is of a contrite and humble spirit, to revive the spirit of the humble, and to revive the heart of the contrite."

Ps. 51:16–17. [O Lord,] thou hast no delight in sacrifice; were I to give a burnt offering, thou wouldst not be pleased. The sacrifice acceptable to God is a broken spirit; a broken and contrite heart, O God, thou wilt not despise.

1 Jn. 1:8–9. If we say we have no sin, we deceive ourselves, and the truth is not in us. If we confess our sins, he is faithful and just, and will forgive our sins and cleanse us from all unrighteousness.

Ps. 30:5. His anger is but for a moment, and his favor is for a lifetime. Weeping may tarry for the night, but joy comes with the morning.

Lk. 15:2. The Pharisees and the scribes murmured [against Jesus], saying, "This man receives sinners and eats with them." (Also Mk. 2:17, Lk. 5:30–31, 1 Tim. 1:15.)

Mt. 11:28 [Christ]: Come to me, all who labor and are heavy laden, and I will give you rest.

Lk. 7:37–38, 44, 47–48. ...A woman of the city, who was a sinner, when she learned that [Jesus] was at table in the Pharisee's house, brought an alabaster flask of ointment, and standing behind him at his feet, weeping, she began to wet his feet with her tears, and wiped them with the hair of her head, and kissed his feet, and anointed them with the ointment...Then turning toward the woman [Jesus] said to Simon, "Do you see this woman?...I tell you, her sins, which are many, are forgiven, for she loved much; but he who is forgiven little, loves little." And he said to her, "Your sins are forgiven."

Dein Sünd ist dir vergeben!
Thy   sin is thee forgiven!
{Thy sin is forgiven thee!}

6. Tenor Recit. (Based on Chorale Vs. 6)
●Christ invites sinners to come and be cleansed (113–6)
Der Heiland nimmt die Sünder an:
The Savior   accepts - sinners - :

Wie lieblich klingt das Wort in meinen Ohren!
How lovely rings this word in   my   ears!

Es ruft: »Kommt her zu mir,
It calls: "Come hither to me,

Die ihr mühselig und   beladen,
All-who (labor)   and (are) burdened,

Kommt her zum Brunnquell aller Gnaden,
Come hither to-the wellspring of-all grace,

Ich hab euch mir zu   Freunden auserkoren!«
I   have you - as (my) friends   chosen!"
{I have chosen you as my friends!}

Auf dieses Wort will ich zu dir
At   this word would I to thee
{At this word would I come to thee}

Wie der bußfertige Zöllner treten
Like the penitent publican (come)
{Like the penitent publican}

Und mit demütigem Geist »Gott, sei mir gnädig!« beten.
And with   humble   spirit, "God, be to-me merciful!" pray.
{And with humble spirit pray, "God be merciful to me!"}

Ach, tröste meinen blöden Mut
Ah, comfort my   (dull) spirit

Und mache mich durch dein vergoßnes Blut
And make me, through thy   spilled   blood

Von allen Sünden rein,
From all   sins   clean,
{And make me clean of all my sins through thy spilled blood,}

So werd ich auch wie David und Manasse,
So will I also like David and Manasseh—

Wenn ich dabei
If   I therewith

Dich stets   in Lieb und Treu
Thee constantly in love and faithfulness

Mit meinem Glaubensarm umfasse,
With my   arms-of-faith do-embrace—

Mt. 9:2. And behold, they brought to [Jesus] a paralytic, lying on his bed; and when Jesus saw their faith he said to the paralytic, "Take heart, my son; your sins are forgiven."

1 Tim. 1:15. The saying is sure and worth of full acceptance, that Christ Jesus came into the world to save sinners. And I am the foremost of sinners...
Mt. 9:10–13. As [Jesus] sat at table in the house, behold, many tax collectors and sinners came and sat down with Jesus and his disciples. And when the Pharisees saw this, they said to his disciples, "Why does your teacher eat with tax collectors and sinners?" But when he heard it, he said, "Those who are well have no need of a physician, but those who are sick. Go and learn what this means, 'I desire mercy, and not sacrifice.' For I came not to call the righteous, but sinners." (Also Mk. 2:17, Lk. 5:32.)
Mt. 11:28–30 [Christ]: Come to me, all who labor and are heavy laden, and I will give you rest. Take my yoke upon you, and learn from me; for I am gentle and lowly in heart, and you will find rest for your souls. For my yoke is easy, and my burden is light. (Also Jer. 6:16, Is. 1:18.)
Heb. 10:22. Let us draw near with a true heart in full assurance of faith, with our hearts sprinkled clean from an evil conscience...
Tit. 2:14. For the grace of God has appeared for the salvation of all men.
Jn. 15:15–16 [Christ]: No longer do I call you servants, for the servant does not know what his master is doing; but I have called you friends... You did not choose me, but I chose you and appointed you that you should go and bear fruit...
*Lk. 18:13–14 [Christ]: The tax collector, standing far off, would not even lift up his eyes to heaven, but beat his breast, saying, "God be merciful to me a sinner!" ...This man went down to his house justified rather than the other; for every one who exalts himself will be humbled, but he who humbles himself will be exalted.
1 Pet. 1:18–19. You know that you were ransomed from the futile ways inherited from your fathers, not with perishable things such as silver or gold, but with the precious blood of Christ, like that of a lamb without blemish or spot.
Mt. 26:27–28. And [Jesus] took a cup, and when he had given thanks he gave it to them, saying, "Drink of it, all of you; for this is my blood of the covenant, which is poured out for many for the forgiveness of sins." (Also Mk. 14:24.)
1 Jn. 1:7–9. ...The blood of Jesus his Son cleanses us from all sin. If we say we have no sin, we deceive ourselves, and the truth is not in us. If we confess our sins, he is faithful and just, and will forgive our sins and cleanse us from all unrighteousness. (blood of Christ: also Eph. 2:13, Heb. 13:12, Rev. 5:9)
2 Sam. 12:13. David said to Nathan, "I have sinned against the Lord," And Nathan said to David, "The Lord also has put away your sin."
2 Chron. 33:12–13. And when [Manasseh] was in distress he entreated the favor of the Lord his God and humbled himself greatly before the God of his fathers. He prayed to him and God received his entreaty and heard his supplication and brought him again to Jerusalem into his kingdom. Then Manasseh knew that the Lord was God.
1 Jn. 3:1–3. See what love the Father has given us, that we should be called children of God; and so we are...

Hinfort ein Kind des Himmels sein.
Henceforth a child of heaven be.

7. Soprano & Alto Duet (Based on Chorale Vs. 7)
●Prayer: Forgive me & break sin's yoke (113–7)
Ach Herr, mein Gott, vergib mir's doch,
Ah Lord, my God, forgive me-for-that please,

Wormit ich deinen Zorn erreget,
Wherewith I thine anger have-aroused,

Zerbrich das schwere Sündenjoch,
Break the heavy yoke-of-sin,

Das mir der Satan auferleget,
Which (on) me - Satan hath-laid,

Daß sich mein Herz zufrieden gebe
That - my heart (may) rest-contented

Und dir zum Preis und Ruhm hinfort
And - for (thy) praise and glory henceforth

Nach deinem Wort
According-to thy Word

In kindlichem Gehorsam lebe.
In childlike obedience live.

8. Chorale (Vs. 8) (See also 168–6.)
●Prayer: Strengthen, heal, wash me; take me home (113–8)
Stärk mich mit deinem Freudengeist,
Strengthen me with thy spirit-of-joy,

Heil mich mit deinen Wunden,
Heal me with thy wounds,

Wasch mich mit deinem Todesschweiß
Wash me with thy sweat-of-death

In meiner letzten Stunden;
In my last hours;

Mt. 18:2–4. Calling to him a child, [Jesus] put him in the midst of them, and said, "Truly, I say to you, unless you turn and become like children, you will never enter the kingdom of heaven. Whoever humbles himself like this child, he is the greatest in the kingdom of heaven."

*Lk. 18:13. The tax collector, standing far off, would not even lift up his eyes to heaven, but beat his breast, saying, "God be merciful to me a sinner!"
Ps. 38:1. O Lord, rebuke me not in thy anger (Luther: Zorn)...
Rom. 1:18. The wrath of God is revealed from heaven against all ungodliness and wickedness of men...
1 Jn. 1:9. If we confess our sins, he is faithful and just, and will forgive our sins and cleanse us from all unrighteousness.
Is. 10:27. In that day his burden will depart from your shoulder, and his yoke will be destroyed from your neck. (Also Is. 9:4, 14:25, Ps. 81:6.)
Rom. 6:16. Do you not know that if you yield yourselves to any one as obedient slaves, you are slaves of the one whom you obey, either of sin, which leads to death, or of obedience, which leads to righteousness? (Also Jn. 8:34, 2 Pet. 2:19.)
Mt. 11:29–30 [Christ]: Take my yoke upon you...for I am gentle and lowly in heart, and you will find rest for your souls. For my yoke is easy, and my burden is light. (Also Jer. 6:16.)
Ps. 51:2, 13, 15. [O Lord,] wash me thoroughly from my iniquity, and cleanse me from my sin!...Then will I teach transgressors thy ways, and sinners will return to thee...O Lord, open thou my lips, and my mouth shall show forth thy praise.
Ps. 131:1–2. O Lord...I have calmed and quieted my soul, like a child quieted at its mother's breast; like a child that is quieted is my soul.
Lk. 18:17 [Christ]: Truly, I say to you, whoever does not receive the kingdom of God like a child shall not enter it. (Also Mk. 9:36–37, 10:14–16, Mt. 18:1–4.)
Eph. 5:8–10. ...Walk as children of light (for the fruit of light is found in all that is good and right and true), and try to learn what is pleasing to the Lord.
1 Jn. 5:3. This is the love of God, that we keep his commandments. And his commandments are not burdensome. (See also Jn. 14:15, 1 Jn. 2:5, 2 Jn. 1:6.)

Ps. 41:4. ...O Lord, be gracious to me; heal me, for I have sinned against thee!
Ps. 51:12. Restore to me the joy of thy salvation...
Jer. 17:14. Heal me, O Lord, and I shall be healed; save me, and I shall be saved; for thou art my praise.
Is. 53:5. He was wounded for our transgressions, he was bruised for our iniquities; upon him was the chastisement that made us whole, and with his stripes we are healed.
1 Pet. 2:24. [Christ] himself bore our sins in his body on the tree, that we might die to sin and live to righteousness. By his wounds you have been healed.
Lk. 22:44. Being in an agony [before his death, Jesus] prayed more earnestly; and his sweat became like great drops of blood falling down upon the ground.
Ps. 51:2, 7. [O Lord,] wash me thoroughly from my iniquity, and cleanse me from my sin!...Wash me and I shall be whiter than snow. (Also Tit. 3:5, Rev. 7:14.)

Und nimm mich einst,   wenn   dir's gefällt,
And take me one-day, whenever it-thee pleases,
{And take me one day, whenever it pleases thee,}

In wahrem Glauben von der Welt
In true faith from the world

Zu deinen Auserwählten!
To thy chosen-ones!

BWV 114
Ach, lieben Christen, seid getrost
(NBA I/23; BC A139)

17. S. after Trinity (BWV 148, 114, 47)
*Eph. 4:1–6 (Exhortation to unity in the Spirit)
*Lk. 14:1–11 (Jesus heals man on the sabbath, exhortation to humility)
Librettist: Unknown

1. Chorus (Chorale Vs. 1)
●Chastisement of the Lord is well deserved by all (114-1)
Ach, lieben Christen, seid getrost,
Ah, dear Christians, be comforted;

Wie tut ihr so verzagen!
Why do you so despair?

Weil uns der Herr heimsuchen tut,
Since us the Lord does-afflict,
{Since the Lord afflicts us,}

Laßt uns von   Herzen sagen:
Let us from (our) hearts say:
{Let us then say from our hearts:}

Die   Straf   wir wohl verdienet han,
The punishment we indeed deserved have,
{We have indeed deserved our punishment,}

Solchs muß bekennen jedermann,
(This) must confess everyone,
{This everyone must confess,}

Niemand darf sich ausschließen.
No-one can himself exclude.
{No one can exclude himself.}

2. Tenor Aria (Based on Chorale Vs. 2)
●Refuge only in Christ; where else could I turn? (114-2)
Wo wird in diesem Jammertale
Where will, in this vale-of-tears,

Num. 23:10. ...Let me die the death of the righteous, and let my end be like his! (Also Heb. 13:7.)
2 Tim. 4:6–8. The time of my departure has come. I have fought the good fight, I have finished the race, I have kept the faith. Henceforth there is laid up for me the crown of righteousness, which the Lord, the righteous judge, will award to me on that Day, and not only to me but also to all who have loved his appearing.
Ps. 31:5. Into thy hand I commit my spirit; thou hast redeemed me, O Lord, faithful God. (Also Lk. 23:46.)
Rom. 5:2. ...We rejoice in our hope of sharing the glory of God.
1 Thess. 4:17. ...So we shall always be with the Lord.
Rev. 17:14. ...He is Lord of lords and King of kings, and those with him are called and chosen and faithful. (Also 1 Pet. 2:9.)

Hos. 9:7. The days of punishment (Luther: Heimsuchung) have come...
Prov. 3:11. My son, do not despise the Lord's discipline or be weary of his reproof, for the Lord reproves him whom he loves, as a father the son in whom he delights.
Heb. 12:5–7, 9–11. ...My son, do not regard lightly the discipline of the Lord, nor lose courage (Luther: verzage nicht) when you are punished by him. For the Lord disciplines him whom he loves, and chastises every son whom he receives. It is for discipline that you have to endure. God is treating you as sons; for what son is there whom his father does not discipline?...Besides this, we have had earthly fathers to discipline us and we respected them. Shall we not much more be subject to the Father of spirits and live? For they disciplined us for a short time at their pleasure, but he disciplines us for our good, that we may share his holiness. For the moment all discipline seems painful rather than pleasant; later it yields the peaceful fruit of righteousness to those who have been trained by it. (Also Jms. 1:2–4, 1 Pet. 1:6–7.)
1 Cor. 11:32. When we are judged by the Lord, we are chastened so that we may not be condemned along with the world.
Rev. 3:19 [Christ]: Those whom I love, I reprove and chasten; so be zealous and repent. (Also Jer. 30:11.)
Rom. 3:10–12, 23. It is written: "None is righteous, no, not one; no one understands, no one seeks for God. All have turned aside, together they have gone wrong; no one does good, not even one...All have sinned and fall short of the glory of God." (Also Ps. 14:1–3, Prov. 20:9, Jer. 17:9, Is. 1:6.)

2 Chron. 14:11. ...O Lord, there is none like thee to help...Help us, O Lord our God, for we rely on thee...
Ps. 22:11. Be not far from me, for trouble is near and there is none to help. (Also Ps. 107:12.)

Für meinen Geist die Zuflucht sein?
For my spirit - refuge be (found)?
{Refuge be found for my spirit?}

Allein zu Jesu Vaterhänden
Only to Jesus' fatherly-hands

Will ich mich in der Schwachheit wenden;
Would I - in (my) weakness turn;
{Would I turn in my weakness;}

Sonst weiß ich weder aus noch ein.
Otherwise know I neither out nor in.
{Otherwise, I am at my wit's end.}

3. Bass Recit. (Loosely based on Chorale Vs. 2)
●Affliction caused by sin-seeking nature & pride (114-3)
O Sünder, trage mit Geduld,
O sinner, bear with patience,

Was du durch deine Schuld
What you through your (own) fault (upon)

Dir selber zugezogen!
Your-self have-drawn!

Das Unrecht säufst du ja
- Injustice drink you indeed

Wie Wasser in dich ein,
Like water - - in,
{For you drink in injustice like water,}

Und diese Sünden Wassersucht
And this sin's-dropsy
{And this sick thirsting after sin}

Ist zum Verderben da
Is for destruction (destined)

Und wird dir tödlich sein.
And will for-you fatal be.
{And will prove fatal for you.}

Der Hochmut aß vordem von der verbotnen Frucht,
- Pride ate in-former-times of the forbidden fruit,
{In former times pride ate of the forbidden fruit,}

Gott gleich zu werden;
God equal to become;
{To become equal with God;}

Wie oft erhebst du dich mit schwülstigen Gebärden,
How oft raise you yourself with pompous bearing,
{How oft you raise yourself with pompous bearing,}

Daß du erniedrigt werden mußt.
So-that you humbled must-be.
{So now you must be humbled.}

Jn. 6:68. Simon Peter answered [Jesus], "Lord, to whom shall we go? You have the words of eternal life..."
Heb. 10:22. Let us draw near with a true heart in full assurance of faith...
Heb. 6:18. So that...we who have fled for refuge (Luther: Zuflucht) might have strong encouragement to seize the hope set before us. (Zuflucht: Ps. 57:1, Jer. 16:19)
Deut. 33:27. The eternal God is your dwelling place, and underneath are the everlasting arms...
Ps. 103:13-14. As a father pities his children, so the Lord pities those who fear him. He knows our frame; he remembers that we are dust.
2 Cor. 12:9. [The Lord] said to me, "My grace is sufficient for you, for my power is made perfect in weakness." I will all the more gladly boast of my weaknesses, that the power of Christ may rest upon me.

Mic. 7:9. I will bear the indignation of the Lord because I have sinned against him, until he pleads my cause...
Gal. 6:7-8. Do not be deceived; God is not mocked, for whatever a man sows, that he will also reap. For he who sows to his own flesh will from the flesh reap corruption; but he who sows to the Sprit will from the Spirit reap eternal life. (Also Jer. 17:9-10, 32:19, Rom. 2:6.)
Gal. 5:17, 19-21. For the desires of the flesh are against the Spirit, and the desires of the Spirit are against the flesh...Now the works of the flesh are plain: fornication, impurity, licentiousness, idolatry, sorcery, enmity, strife, jealousy, anger, selfishness, dissension, party spirit, envy, drunkenness, carousing, and the like. I warn you...those who do such things shall not inherit the kingdom of God.
Job 15:15-16. Behold, God puts no trust in his holy ones, and the heavens are not clean in his sight; how much less one who is abominable and corrupt, a man who drinks iniquity like water (Luther: Unrecht säuft wie Wasser)!
Rom. 1:29, 32. [Men] were filled with all manner of wickedness... Though they know God's decree that those who do such things deserve to die, they not only do them but approve those who practice them.
Rom. 6:23. The wages of sin is death... (Also Rom. 6:21.)
Gen. 3:1, 4-6. The serpent...said to the woman, "Did God say, 'You shall not eat of any tree of the garden'?...You will not die. For God knows that when you eat of it your eyes will be opened, and you will be like God, knowing good and evil." So when the woman saw that the tree was good for food, and that it was a delight to the eyes, and that the tree was to be desired to make one wise, she took of its fruit and ate; and she also gave some to her husband, and he ate.
Prov. 16:18. Pride goes before destruction, and a haughty spirit before a fall.
***Lk. 14:1-2, 4, 7-11.** One sabbath when [Jesus] went to dine at the house of a ruler who belonged to the Pharisees...there was a man before him who had dropsy (Luther: wassersüchtig)...Then he took him and healed him, and let him go...Now [Jesus] told a parable to those who were invited, when he marked how they chose the places of honor, saying to them, "When you are invited by any one to a marriage feast, do not sit down in a place of honor, lest a more eminent man than you be invited by him; and he who invited you both will come and say to you, 'Give place to this man,' and then you will begin with shame to take the lowest place. But when you are invited,

Wohlan, bereite deine Brust,
Well-then, prepare your breast,

Daß sie den Tod und Grab nicht scheut,
That it (away from) death and grave (does) not shy,
{So-that it does not shy away from death and the grave,}

So kömmst du durch ein selig Sterben
So come you through a blessed dying
{Thus you will come through a blessed death}

Aus diesem sündlichen Verderben
Out-of this sinful corruption

Zur Unschuld und zur Herrlichkeit.
To innocence and to glory.

4. Chorale: Soprano (Vs. 3)
●Grain of wheat dies to produce fruit; so our body (114-4)
Kein Frucht das Weizenkörnlein bringt,
No fruit the grain-of-wheat produces, (unless)
{No grain of wheat produces fruit unless}

Es fall denn in die Erden;
It fall - into the earth;

So muß auch unser irdscher Leib
Thus must also our earthly body

Zu Staub und Aschen werden,
To dust and ashes (turn),

Eh er kömmt zu der Herrlichkeit,
Before it come to the glory,

Die du, Herr Christ, uns hast bereit'
Which thou, Lord Christ, for-us hast prepared

Durch deinen Gang zum Vater.
Through thy going to-the Father.
{Through thy ascension to the Father.}

5. Alto Aria (Based on Chorale Vs. 4)
●Death, my way to freedom, no longer frightens me (114-5)
Du machst, o Tod, mir nun nicht ferner bange,
Thou makest, O death, me now no longer afraid,
{No longer dost thou make me afraid, O death,}

Wenn ich durch dich die Freihei nur erlange,
If I through thee - freedom only (can) attain,
{If I can only attain freedom through thee,}

go and sit in the lowest place, so that when your host comes he may say to you, 'Friend, go up higher'; then you will be honored in the presence of all who sit at table with you. For every one who exalts himself will be humbled, and he who humbles himself will be exalted." (Also Job 22:29, Prov. 29:23, Mt. 23:10–12, Lk. 18:14, *Eph. 4:1–2.)
2 Cor. 5:2–4. Here indeed we groan, and long to put on our heavenly dwelling... For while we are still in this tent, we sigh with anxiety...that what is mortal may be swallowed up by life.
Rev. 14:13. ...Blessed are the dead who die in the Lord henceforth... that they may rest from their labors, for their deeds follow them!
1 Cor. 15:50. Flesh and blood cannot inherit the kingdom of God, nor does the perishable inherit the imperishable.
2 Cor. 5:1. We know that if the earthly tent we live in is destroyed, we have a building from God, a house not made with hands, eternal in the heavens.

Jn. 12:24–26 [Christ]: Unless a grain of wheat falls into the earth and dies, it remains alone; but if it dies, it bears much fruit. He who loves his life loses it, and he who hates his life in this world will keep it for eternal life. If any one serves me, he must follow me; and where I am, there shall my servant be also; if any one serves me, the Father will honor him.
2 Cor. 4:7, 9–10, 16–17, 5:1–2, 4. But we have this treasure in earthen vessels, to show that the transcendent power belongs to God and not to us. We are afflicted in every way...always carrying in the body the death of Jesus, so that the life of Jesus may also be manifested in our bodies...We do not lose heart. Though our outer nature is wasting away, our inner nature is being renewed every day. For this slight momentary affliction is preparing for us an eternal weight of glory beyond all comparison...For we know that if the earthly tent we live in is destroyed, we have a building from God, a house not made with hands, eternal in the heavens. Here indeed we groan, and long to put on our heavenly dwelling...While we are still in this tent, we sigh with anxiety...that what is mortal may be swallowed up by life. (Also 2 Pet. 1:14, Rom. 7:24–25.)
Jn. 14:1–3 [Christ]: Let not your hearts be troubled; believe in God, believe also in me. In my Father's house are many rooms; if it were not so, would I have told you that I go to prepare a place for you? And when I go and prepare a place for you, I will come again and will take you to myself, that where I am you may be also. (Also Jn. 12:26.)

Jn. 12:24–25 [Christ]: ...If [a grain of wheat] dies, it bears much fruit... He who hates his life in this world will keep it for eternal life.
Rom. 6:7. For he who has died is freed from sin.
1 Cor. 15:42–44, 49–52. So it is with the resurrection of the dead. What is sown is perishable, what is raised is imperishable. It is sown in dishonor, it is raised in glory. It is sown in weakness, it is raised in power. It is sown a physical body, it is raised a spiritual body...Just as we have borne the image of the man of dust, we shall also bear the image of the man of heaven...Flesh and blood cannot inherit the kingdom of God...Lo! I tell you a mystery. We shall not all sleep, but we shall all be changed, in a moment, in the twinkling of an eye, at the last trumpet... (Also 1 Thess. 4:16–18.)

Es muß ja so einmal gestorben sein.
(One) must indeed thus one-day die - .
{Then I must indeed one day die.}

Mit Simeon will ich in Friede fahren,
With Simeon would I in peace depart,
{With Simeon would I depart in peace,}

Mein Heiland will mich in der Gruft bewahren
My Savior will me within the tomb protect
{My Savior will protect me within the tomb}

Und ruft mich einst zu sich verklärt und rein.
And call me one-day to himself transfigured and pure.

2 Tim. 4:6–8. ...The time of my departure has come. I have fought the good fight, I have finished the race, I have kept the faith. Henceforth there is laid up for me the crown of righteousness, which the Lord, the righteous judge, will award to me on that Day, and not only to me but also to all who have loved his appearing.
Phil. 1:21–23. To me to live is Christ, and to die is gain...Which I shall choose I cannot tell. I am hard pressed between the two. My desire is to depart and be with Christ, for that is far better. (Also 2 Cor. 5:8.)
Lk. 2:27–30. ...[Simeon] came into the temple; and when the parents brought in the child Jesus...he took him up in his arms and blessed God and said, "Lord, now lettest thou thy servant depart in peace, according to thy word; for mine eyes have seen thy salvation."
Phil. 3:20–21. Our commonwealth is in heaven, and from it we await a Savior, the Lord Jesus Christ, who will change our lowly body to be like his glorious body... (Also Mk. 9:2, Eph. 5:27, Rev. 19:8.)
1 Jn. 3:2. ...It does not yet appear what we shall be, but we know that when he appears we shall be like him, for we shall see him as he is.

6. Tenor Recit. (Based on Chorale Vs. 5)
●Commit body & soul to God for your eternal welfare
(114-6)
Indes bedenke deine Seele
Meanwhile think-of your soul

Und stelle sie dem Heiland dar;
And present it to-the Savior - ;

Gib deinen Leib und deine Glieder
Return your body and your members

Gott, der sie dir gegeben, wieder.
To-God, who them to-you gave - .
{To God who gave them to you.}
        [wiedergeben = to return]

Er sorgt und wacht,
He cares and watches,

Und so wird seiner Liebe Macht
And so (is) his love's might

Im Tod und Leben offenbar.
In death and life made-manifest.

1 Thess. 5:23. May the God of peace himself sanctify you wholly; and may your spirit and soul and body be kept sound and blameless at the coming of our Lord Jesus Christ.
Rom. 12:1. ...Present your bodies as a living sacrifice, holy and acceptable to God, which is your spiritual worship.
1 Cor. 6:19–20. Do you not know that your body is a temple of the Holy Spirit within you, which you have from God? You are not your own; you were bought with a price. So glorify God in your body. (Also 1 Cor. 3:16; 7:23.)
Rom. 6:19–22. ...Just as you once yielded your members to impurity and to greater and greater iniquity, so now yield your members to righteousness for sanctification. When you were slaves of sin, you were free in regard to righteousness. But then what return did you get from the things of which you are now ashamed? The end of those things is death. But now that you have been set free from sin and have become slaves of God, the return you get is sanctification and its end, eternal life.
2 Cor. 4:16, 5:6–9. So we do not lose heart. Though our outer nature is wasting away, our inner nature is being renewed every day. For this slight momentary affliction is preparing for us an eternal weight of glory beyond all comparison, because we look not to the things that are seen but to the things that are unseen; for the things that are seen are transient, but the things that are unseen are eternal. So we are always of good courage; we know that while we are at home in the body we are away from the Lord, for we walk by faith, not by sight. We are of good courage, and we would rather be away from the body and at home with the Lord. So whether we are at home or away, we make it our aim to please him. (Also Phil. 1:20–24.)

7. Chorale (Vs. 6)
●In life or death, Christ saves us from Adam's curse (114-7)
   Wir wachen oder schlafen ein,
(Whether) we   wake   or   go-to-sleep,

So sind wir   doch   des Herren;
So   are we nevertheless the Lord's;

Auf Christum wir getaufet sein,
In   Christ we baptized are,
{We are baptized into Christ;}

Der kann dem Satan wehren.
He can - Satan ward-off.
{He can ward off Satan.}

Durch Adam auf uns kömmt der Tod,
Through Adam upon us comes - death,
{Through Adam death comes upon us,}

Christus   hilft uns aus aller Not.
Christ (however) helps us out-of all distress.

Drum   loben wir den Herren.
Therefore praise we the Lord.
{Therefore we praise the Lord.}

Rom. 14:7-8. None of us lives to himself, and none of us dies to himself. If we live, we live to the Lord, and if we die, we die to the Lord; so then, whether we live or whether we die, we are the Lord's. **Phil. 1:20-21.** It is my eager expectation and hope...that...Christ will be honored in my body, whether by life or by death. For to me to live is Christ, and to die is gain.
Rom. 6:3-5. Do you not know that all of us who have been baptized into Christ Jesus were baptized into his death? We were buried therefore with him by baptism into death, so that as Christ was raised from the dead by the glory of the Father, we too might walk in newness of life. For if we have been united with him in a death like his, we shall certainly be united with him in a resurrection like his.
Heb. 2:14. ...[Christ] himself likewise partook of the same nature, that through death he might destroy him who has the power of death, that is, the devil. (Also 1 Jn. 3:8, Is. 25:8.)
1 Cor. 15:22, 47, 49, 57. For as in Adam all die, so also in Christ shall all be made alive...The first man was from the earth, a man of dust; the second man is from heaven...Just as we have borne the image of the man of dust, we shall also bear the image of the man of heaven... Thanks be to God, who gives us the victory through our Lord Jesus Christ. (Also Rom. 6:8-10.)

BWV 115
Mache dich, mein Geist, bereit
(NBA I/26; BC A156)

22. S. after Trinity (BWV 89, 115, 55)
*Phil. 1:3-11 (Paul's prayer for the church at Philippi)
*Mt. 18:23-35 (The parable of the unforgiving servant)
Librettist: Unknown

1. Chorus (Chorale Vs. 1)
●Prepare for judgment day: watch and pray! (115-1)
Mache dich, mein Geist, bereit,
Get   thyself, my   soul, prepared,

Wache, fleh und bete,
Watch, implore, and pray,

Daß dich nicht die böse Zeit
That thee not the evil time
{That the evil time doth not}

Unverhofft   betrete;
Unexpectedly befalleth;
{Unexpectedly befall thee;}

Denn es ist
For (now) has

Satans List
Satan's craftiness

Lk. 21:34-36 [Christ]: Take heed to yourselves lest your hearts be weighed down with dissipation and drunkenness and cares of this life, and that day come upon you suddenly like a snare; for it will come upon all who dwell upon the face of the whole earth. But watch at all times, praying that you may have strength to escape all these things that will take place, and to stand before the Son of man.
2 Cor. 5:10. For we must all appear before the judgment seat of Christ, so that each one may receive good or evil, according to what he has done in the body. (Also 1 Cor. 3:12, Rom. 14:10-12, Heb. 9:27.)
Mt. 12:36-37 [Christ]: I tell you, on the day of judgment men will render account for every careless word they utter; for by your words you will be justified, and by your words you will be condemned.
***Mt. 18:32-34.** Then [the lord of the unforgiving servant] summoned [his servant] and said to him, "You wicked servant! I forgave you all that debt because you besought me; and should not you have had mercy on your fellow servant, as I had mercy on you?" And in anger his lord delivered him to the jailers, till he should pay all his debt.
1 Thess. 5:1-4. As to the times and the seasons, brethren, you have no need to have anything written to you. For you yourselves know well that the day of the Lord will come like a thief in the night. When people say, "There is peace and security," then sudden destruction will come upon them as travail comes upon a woman with child, and there will be no escape. But you are not in darkness, brethren for that day to surprise you like a thief. (Also 2 Pet. 3:10.)

Über viele Frommen
Upon many righteous
{Come upon many righteous}

Zur Versuchung kommen.
(In) temptation come.
{In temptation.}

2. Alto Aria (Based on Chorale Vs. 2)
●Sleeping still? Judgment will awaken you! (115–2)
Ach schläfrige Seele, wie? ruhest du noch?
Ah sleepy soul, what? Rest you still?
{Ah sleepy soul, what? Do you still rest?}

Ermuntre dich doch!
Rouse yourself - !

Es möchte die Strafe dich plötzlich erwecken
(Soon) may - judgment you suddenly awaken
{Judgment may suddenly awaken you,}

Und, wo du nicht wachest,
And, if you (do) not watch,

Im Schlafe des ewigen Todes bedecken.
In-the sleep of eternal death cover.
{It may cover you with the sleep of eternal death.}

3. Bass Recit. (Based on Chorale Vss. 3–6)
●God keeps watch, hates dark, desires enlightenment (115–3)
Gott, so vor deine Seele wacht,
God, who over your soul does-watch,

Hat Abscheu an der Sünden Nacht;
Has abhorrence to - sin's night;

Er sendet dir sein Gnadenlicht
He sends you his light-of-grace

Und will vor diese Gaben,
And wants (of you)—for these gifts,

Die er so reichlich dir verspricht,
Which he so richly to-you promises—
{Which he so richly promises you—}

Nur offne Geistesaugen haben.
Only (of you) open eyes-of-the-spirit to-have.
{Only that your spiritual eyes be opened.}

Des Satans List ist ohne Grund,
- Satan's stratagem is without reason
{Without reason, Satan's stratagem is}

Mk. 13:32–33. Of that day or that hour no one knows, not even the angels in heaven, nor the Son, but only the Father. Take heed, watch; for you do not know when the time will come.
Mt. 26:41. Watch and pray that you may not enter into temptation; the spirit indeed is willing, but the flesh is weak. (Also Mk. 14:38, Mt. 24:42, 25:13.)

Mk. 14:41–42. And [Jesus] came the third time, and said to [the disciples], "Are you still sleeping and taking your rest? It is enough; the hour has come; the Son of man is betrayed into the hands of sinners. Rise, let us be going..." (Also Mt. 26:45, Lk. 22:46.)
Rom. 13:11–12. ...You know what hour it is, how it is full time now for you to wake from sleep. For salvation is nearer to us now than when we first believed; the night is far gone, the day is at hand. Let us then cast off the works of darkness...
Eph. 5:14. Therefore it is said, "Awake, O sleeper, and arise from the dead, and Christ shall give you light." (See Is. 60:1.)
1 Thess. 5:2–3, 6. For you yourselves know well that the day of the Lord will come like a thief in the night. When people say, "There is peace and security," then sudden destruction will come upon them as travail comes upon a woman with child, and there will be no escape... So then let us not sleep, as others do, but let us keep awake and be sober.

Ps. 121:3–4, 7. [The Lord] will not let your foot be moved, he who keeps you will not slumber. Behold, he who keeps Israel will neither slumber nor sleep...The Lord will keep you from all evil; he will keep your life.
1 Pet. 3:12. The eyes of the Lord are upon the righteous, and his ears are open to their prayer. But the face of the Lord is against those that do evil.
1 Thess. 5:6–7. Let us not sleep, as others do, but let us keep awake and be sober. For those who sleep sleep at night, and those who get drunk are drunk at night.
Prov. 15:9. The way of the wicked is an abomination to the Lord, but he loves him who pursues righteousness. (Also Prov. 6:16–19, Hab. 1:13, Lk. 16:15.)
Eph. 5:12–13. It is a shame even to speak of the things that they do in secret.
2 Cor. 4:6. It is the God who said, "Let light shine out of darkness," who has shone in our hearts... (Also 1 Pet. 2:9.)
2 Cor. 11:14. ...Satan disguises himself as an angel of light.
1 Pet. 5:8. Be sober, be watchful. Your adversary the devil prowls around like a roaring lion, seeking some one to devour.
Ps. 35:7. Without cause [my enemies] hid their net for me; without cause they dug a pit for my life.
Eph. 5:6–10. Let no one deceive you with empty words, for it is because of these things that the wrath of God comes upon the sons of disobedience. Therefore do not associate with them, for once you were darkness, but now you are light in the Lord; walk as children of light (for the fruit of light is found in all that is good and right and true), and try to learn what is pleasing to the Lord.

Die Sünder zu bestricken;
- Sinners to ensnare;
{To ensnare sinners;}

Brichst du nun selbst den Gnadenbund,
Break you now yourself the covenant-of-grace,
{If you yourself break the convenant of grace,}

Wirst du die Hülfe nie erblicken.
Will you (his) help never see.
{You will never see help.}

Die ganze Welt und ihre Glieder
The whole world and its members

Sind nichts als falsche Brüder;
Are nothing but false brethren;

Doch macht dein Fleisch und Blut hiebei
Yet (seeks) your flesh and blood (from-them)
{Yet your flesh and blood seeks from them}

Sich lauter Schmeichelei.
- Nothing-but flattery.

Eph. 1:17-18. May [God]...give you a spirit of wisdom and of revelation in the knowledge of him, having the eyes of your hearts enlightened, that you may know what is the hope to which he has called you, what are the riches of his glorious inheritance in the saints.
1 Cor. 2:12. Now we have received not the spirit of the world, but the Spirit which is from God, that we might understand the gifts bestowed on us by God. (Also 2 Cor. 2:14.)
Heb. 10:28-29. A man who has violated the law of Moses dies without mercy at the testimony of two or three witnesses. How much worse punishment do you think will be deserved by the man who has spurned the Son of God, and profaned the blood of the covenant by which he was sanctified, and outraged the Spirit of grace? (Also Heb. 6:4-6.)
2 Pet. 2:20-21. If, after they have escaped the defilements of the world through the knowledge of our Lord and Savior Jesus Christ, they are again entangled in them and overpowered, the last state has become worse for them than the first. For it would have been better for them never to have known the way of righteousness than after knowing it to turn back from the holy commandment delivered to them.
Jms. 4:4. Unfaithful creatures! Do you not know that friendship with the world is enmity with God? Therefore whoever wishes to be a friend of the world makes himself an enemy of God. (Also 1 Jn. 2:15-17.)
Gal. 2:4. ...False brethren...slipped in... (Also 2 Cor. 11:26, 1 Jn. 2:19, Jude 1:4.)
Jn. 12:43. They loved the praise of men more than the praise of God. (Also Jn. 5:44.)
Prov. 29:5. A man who flatters his neighbor spreads a net for his feet.

4. Soprano Aria (Based on Chorale Vs. 7)
●Pray as you watch: beg for mercy on your debt (115-4)
Bete aber auch dabei
Pray, however, also therewith

Mitten in dem Wachen!
Amidst (your) watching!

Bitte bei der großen Schuld
Ask, in (your) great debt,

Deinen Richter um Geduld,
Of-your judge to-have forbearance,
{That your judge have forbearance,}

Soll er dich von Sünden frei
(If) he you from sin free

Und gereinigt machen!
And cleansed (is to) make!
{If he is to make you pure and free from sin!}

Mt. 26:41 [Christ]: Watch and pray that you may not enter into temptation; the spirit indeed is willing, but the flesh is weak.
Lk. 21:36 [Christ]: Watch at all times, praying that you may have strength to escape all these things that will take place, and to stand before the Son of man.
*Mt. 18:23-27 [Christ]: Therefore the kingdom of heaven may be compared to a king who wished to settle accounts with his servants. When he began the reckoning, one was brought to him who owed him ten thousand talents; and as he could not pay, his lord ordered him to be sold, with his wife and children and all that he had, and payment to be made. So the servant fell on his knees, imploring him, "Lord, have patience (Luther: Geduld) with me, and I will pay you everything." And out of pity for him the lord of that servant released him and forgave him the debt...
1 Jn. 1:8-9. If we say we have no sin, we deceive ourselves, and the truth is not in us. If we confess our sins, he is faithful and just, and will forgive our sins and cleanse us from all unrighteousness.

5. Tenor Recit. (Based on Chorale Vss. 8-9)
●Lord hears our cry in Christ's name; wants to help (115-5)
Er sehnet sich nach unserm Schreien,
He yearns - after our crying,
{He is drawn by our crying,}

Ps. 34:17. When the righteous cry for help, the Lord hears... (Also Ps. 116:2, 145:18-19.)
Lk. 18:7-8 [Christ]: Will not God vindicate his elect, who cry to him day and night? Will he delay long over them? I tell you, he will vindicate them speedily...

Er neigt sein gnädig Ohr hierauf;
He bows his gracious ear hereupon;
{He bows his gracious ear to it;}

Wenn Feinde sich auf unsern Schaden freuen,
When foes - over our harm rejoice,

So siegen wir in seiner Kraft:
Then triumph we in his power:
{Then we triumph in his power:}

Indem sein Sohn, in dem wir beten,
Since his Son, in whom we pray,

Uns Mut und Kräfte schafft
Us (with) courage and strength furnishes
{Furnishes us with courage and strength}

Und will als Helfer zu uns treten.
And would as helper to us (come).
{And comes to us as helper.}

6. Chorale (Vs. 10)
●Judgment Day is near so let us watch & pray (115-6)
Drum so laßt uns immerdar
Therefore, then let us evermore

Wachen, flehen, beten,
Watch, implore, pray,

Weil die Angst, Not und Gefahr
For - fear, distress, and danger

Immer näher treten;
Ever closer tread;

Denn die Zeit
For the time

Ist nicht weit,
Is not far,

Da uns Gott wird richten
When us God will judge
{When God will judge us}

Und die Welt vernichten.
And the world destroy.

Ps. 10:17. O Lord, thou wilt hear the desire of the meek; thou wilt strengthen their heart, thou wilt incline thy ear.
Is. 30:18–19. Therefore the Lord waits to be gracious to you...He will surely be gracious to you at the sound of your cry; when he hears it, he will answer you.
Ps. 30:1–2. I will extol thee, O Lord, for thou hast drawn me up, and hast not let my foes rejoice over me. O Lord my God, I cried to thee for help, and thou hast healed me.
Mic. 7:7–8. As for me, I will look to the Lord, I will wait for the God of my salvation; my God will hear me. Rejoice not over me, O my enemy; when I fall, I shall rise; when I sit in darkness, the Lord will be a light to me. (Also Ps. 13:3–4.)
Ps. 79:9. Help us, O God of our salvation, for the glory of thy name; deliver us...
Jn. 14:13–14 [Christ]: Whatever you ask in my name, I will do it, that the Father may be glorified in the Son; if you ask anything in my name, I will do it. (Also Jn. 15:16, 16:23–24.)
Col. 1:11. May you be strengthened with all power, according to his glorious might... (Also Phil. 4:13.)
Rom. 8:37. In all these things we are more than conquerors through him who loved us.

Lk. 21:34–36 [Christ]: Take heed to yourselves lest your hearts be weighed down with dissipation and drunkenness and cares of this life, and that day come upon you suddenly like a snare; for it will come upon all who dwell upon the face of the whole earth. But watch at all times, praying that you may have strength to escape all these things that will take place, and to stand before the Son of man.
Joel 2:1–2. Blow the trumpet in Zion; sound the alarm on my holy mountain! Let all the inhabitants of the land tremble, for the day of the Lord is coming, it is near, a day of darkness and gloom, a day of clouds and thick darkness!... (Also Joel 1:15, Zeph.1:7.)
Rom. 13:11–12. ...You know what hour it is, how it is full time now for you to wake from sleep. For salvation is nearer to us now than when we first believed; the night is far gone, the day is at hand. Let us then cast off the works of darkness...
1 Pet. 4:5. [Those who live in profligacy] will give account to him who is ready to judge the living and the dead.
2 Pet. 3:10–12. But the day of the Lord will come like a thief, and then the heavens will pass away with a loud noise, and the elements will be dissolved with fire, and the earth and the works that are upon it will be burned up. Since all these things are thus to be dissolved, what sort of persons ought you to be in lives of holiness and godliness, waiting for and hastening the coming of the day of God, because of which the heavens will be kindled and dissolved, and the elements will melt with fire!

BWV 116
Du Friedefürst, Herr Jesu Christ
(NBA I/27; BC A164)

25. S. after Trinity (BWV 90, 116)
*1 Thess. 4:13–18 (Christ will return with the archangel's call and the sound of the trumpet)
*Mt. 24:15–28 (There will be great tribulation at the end of the world)
Librettist: Unknown

1. Chorus (Chorale Vs. 1) (See also 67-7, 143-2.)
●Christ is our helper; we cry to God in his name (116-1)
Du   Friedefürst, Herr Jesu Christ,
Thou Prince-of-peace, Lord Jesus Christ,

Wahr' Mensch und wahrer Gott,
True   man   and   true God,

Ein starker   Nothelfer   du bist
A   strong Helper-in-need thou art

Im Leben und im Tod.
In   life and in death.

Drum   wir allein
Therefore we alone

Im   Namen dein
In (the) name of-thine

Zu deinem Vater schreien.
To   thy   Father do-cry.
{Therefore we cry to thy Father in thy name alone.}

2. Alto Aria (Based on Chorale Vs. 2)
●Menacing judgment & peril; we cry out in his name (116-2)
Ach, unaussprechlich ist die Not
Ah,   unspeakable   is (our) peril

Und des erzürnten Richters Dräuen!
And the wrathful   judge's menacing!

Kaum, daß wir noch in dieser Angst,
Scarce, (can) we yet in   this terror—
{Scarce can we in our terror}

Wie du, o Jesu, selbst verlangst,
As thou, O Jesus, thyself dost-ask (of us)—
{Do what thou, O Jesus, dost ask of us:}

Zu Gott in deinem Namen schreien.
To God in   thy   name   cry.
{Cry to God in thy name.}

Is. 9:6. To us a child is born, to us a son is given; and the government will be upon his shoulder, and his name will be called "Wonderful Counselor, Mighty God, Everlasting Father, Prince of Peace (Luther: Friedfürst)."
Col. 2:9. In [Christ] the whole fulness of deity dwells bodily...
1 Jn. 5:20. ...We are in him who is true, in his Son Jesus Christ. This is the true God and eternal life. (Also Jn. 17:3.)
Ps. 124:8. Our help is in the name of the Lord...
Ps. 54:4. Behold, God is my helper; the Lord is the upholder of my life.
Dan. 6:27. He delivers and rescues (Luther: Er ist ein Erlöser und Nothelfer), he works signs and wonders...
Ps. 61:2–3. [O God]...lead thou me to the rock that is higher than I; for thou art my refuge, a strong tower against the enemy.
Ps. 142:5. I cry to thee, O Lord; I say, Thou art my refuge, my portion in the land of the living. (Also Ps. 130:1.)
Ps. 79:9. Help us, O God of our salvation, for the glory of thy name; deliver us...for thy name's sake!
Jn. 14:13–14 [Christ]: Whatever you ask in my name, I will do it, that the Father may be glorified in the Son; if you ask anything in my name, I will do it.
Jn. 16:23–24 [Christ]: ...Truly, truly, I say to you, if you ask anything of the Father, he will give it to you in my name. Hitherto you have asked nothing in my name; ask, and you will receive, that your joy may be full. (Also Jn. 15:16.)
Lk. 18:7–8 [Christ]: Will not God vindicate his elect, who cry to him day and night? Will he delay long over them? I tell you, he will vindicate them speedily...

***Mt. 24:21–22 [Christ]:** Then there will be great tribulation, such as has not been from the beginning of the world until now, no, and never will be. And if those days had not been shortened, no human being would be saved; but for the sake of the elect those days will be shortened.
Lk. 21:20, 22 [Christ]: But when you see Jerusalem surrounded by armies, then know that its desolation has come near...These are days of vengeance, to fulfil all that is written.
Nah. 1:6. Who can stand before [the Lord's] indignation? Who can endure the heat of his anger? His wrath is poured out like fire, and the rocks are broken asunder by him. (Also Jer. 7:20, Rom. 1:18, Rom. 2:5, Rev. 6:17, 19:15.)
Ps. 79:9. Help us, O God of our salvation, for the glory of thy name; deliver us, and forgive our sins, for thy name's sake! (Also Ps. 25:11, 143:11, Jer. 14:7, 21.)
Jn. 16:24 [Christ]: Hitherto you have asked nothing in my name; ask, and you will receive, that your joy may be full. Jn. 14:13–14 [Christ]: Whatever you ask in my name, I will do it, that the Father may be glorified in the Son; if you ask anything in my name, I will do it. (Also Jn. 15:16, 16:23.)

3. Tenor Recit. (Based on Chorale Vs. 3)
●Reminding Jesus that he is a God of love and peace (116–3)
Gedenke doch,
Remember, please,

O Jesu, daß du noch
O Jesus, that thou still

Ein Fürst des Friedens heißest!
A Prince of Peace art-called!

Aus Liebe wolltest du dein Wort uns senden.
In love didst-desire thou thy Word to-us to-send.
{In love didst thou send thy Word to us.}

Will sich dein Herz auf einmal von uns wenden,
Would - (then) thy heart suddenly from us turn,
{Wouldst thou then suddenly turn thy heart from us,}

Der du so große Hülfe sonst beweisest?
Thou-who such great help otherwise dost-show?

4. Soprano, Tenor & Bass Trio (Based on Chorale Vs. 4)
●We confess our sin & beg for mercy shown in Christ (116–4)
Ach, wir bekennen unsre Schuld
Ah, we confess our guilt

Und bitten nichts als um Geduld
And beg (for) nothing but - forbearance

Und um dein unermeßlich Lieben.
And for thy immeasurable love.

Es brach ja dein erbarmend Herz,
(For) broke indeed thy compassionate heart,
{For thy commpassionate heart indeed did break,}

Als der Gefallnen Schmerz
When the fallen-ones' pain

Dich zu uns in die Welt getrieben.
Thee to us into the world drove.
{Drove thee into the world to us.}

5. Alto Recit. (Based on Chorale Vss. 5–6)
●Prayer: Rescue us from the chastisement of war (116–5)
Ach, laß uns durch die scharfen Ruten
Ah, let us through the sharp (blows of the rod)

Nicht allzu heftig bluten!
Not all-too severely bleed!
{Ah, do not let us bleed too severely from the sharp blows of thy rod!}

Is. 9:6. For to us a child is born, to us a son is given; and the government will be upon his shoulder, and his name will be called "Wonderful Counselor, Mighty God, Everlasting Father, Prince of Peace (Luther: Friedefürst)."
Phil. 4:9. ...The God of peace will be with you.
Jn. 1:1, 14, 18. In the beginning was the Word, and the Word was with God, and the Word was God...And the Word became flesh and dwelt among us, full of grace and truth; we have beheld his glory, glory as of the only Son of the Father...No one has ever seen God; the only Son, who is in the bosom of the Father, he has made him known.
Jn. 3:16. For God so loved the world that he gave his only Son, that whoever believes in him should not perish but have eternal life.
Rom. 5:8. God shows his love for us in that while we were yet sinners Christ died for us.
1 Jn. 4:10. In this is love, not that we loved God but that he loved us and sent his Son to be the expiation for our sins.
Ps. 89:49. Lord, where is thy steadfast love of old, which by thy faithfulness thou didst swear to David?
Mal. 3:6. I the Lord do not change; therefore you, O sons of Jacob, are not consumed.

Mt. 18:23–27 [Christ]: The kingdom of heaven may be compared to a king who wished to settle accounts with his servants. When he began the reckoning, one was brought to him who owed him ten thousand talents; and as he could not pay, his lord ordered him to be sold, with his wife and children and all that he had, and payment to be made. So the servant fell on his knees, imploring him, "Lord, have patience (Luther: Geduld) with me, and I will pay you everything." And out of pity for him the lord of that servant released him and forgave him the debt (Luther: Schuld).
Jer. 14:20. We acknowledge our wickedness, O Lord, and the iniquity of our fathers, for we have sinned against thee.
1 Jn. 1:9. If we confess our sins, he is faithful and just, and will forgive our sins and cleanse us from all unrighteousness. (Also 2 Chron. 7:14, 1 Kings 8:33–34.)
Jer. 31:20 [God]: Is Ephraim my dear son? Is he my darling child? For as often as I speak against him, I do remember him still. Therefore my heart yearns for him (Luther: bricht mir mein Herz); I will surely have mercy on him (Luther: sein erbarmen), says the Lord.
Jn. 3:16–17. God so loved the world that he gave his only Son...God sent the Son into the world, not to condemn the world, but that the world might be saved through him.
1 Jn. 4:10. In this is love, not that we loved God but that he loved us and sent his Son to be the expiation for our sins. (Also Gal. 4:4.)

Ps. 89:30–33. If [David's] children forsake my law and do not walk according to my ordinances, if they violate my statutes (Luther: Ordnungen) and do not keep my commandments, then I will punish their transgression with the rod (Luther: Rute) and their iniquity with scourges; but I will not remove from him my steadfast love, or be false to my faithfulness.
Jer. 9:13–16. The Lord says: "Because [my people] have forsaken my law which I set before them, and have not obeyed my voice, or walked in accord with it, but have stubbornly followed their own hearts... behold, I will feed this people with wormwood, and give them poisonous water to drink. I will scatter them among the nations whom

O Gott, der du ein Gott der Ordnung bist,
O God, thou-who a God of order art,
{O God, thou who art a God of good order,}

Du weißt, was bei der Feinde Grimm
Thou knowest, what in the foe's fury

Für Grausamkeit und Unrecht ist.
Of cruelty and injustice (there) is.
{Thou knowest what cruelty and injustice there is in the foe's fury.}

Wohlan, so strecke deine Hand
Now-then, - stretch (out) thy hand

Auf ein erschreckt geplagtes Land,
Over (this) terrified, plagued land,

Die kann der Feinde Macht bezwingen
It can the foe's might conquer
{It can the conquer the foe's might}

Und uns beständig Friede bringen!
And us lasting peace bring!
{And bring us lasting peace!}

6. Chorale (Vs. 7)
●Prayer: Enlighten mind & heart as only Christ can (116-6)
Erleucht auch unser Sinn und Herz
Illumine also our mind and heart

Durch den Geist deiner Gnad,
Through the Spirit of-thy grace,

Daß wir nicht treiben draus ein Scherz,
That we not make of-it a jest,
{That we not make a jest of it—}

Der unsrer Seelen schad.
Which our souls would-harm.
{A jest that would harm our souls.}

O Jesu Christ,
O Jesus Christ,

Allein du bist,
Alone thou art,
{Thou art the only one,}

neither they nor their fathers have known; and I will send the sword after them, until I have consumed them."
Is. 10:5–6 [God]: Ah, Assyria, the rod (Luther: Rute) of my anger, the staff of my fury! Against a godless nation I send him, and against the people of my wrath I command him... (Also 2 Sam. 7:14–15, Ps. 89:31–32.)
Jer. 30:11. I am with you to save you, says the Lord; I will make a full end of all the nations among whom I scattered you, but of you I will not make a full end. I will chasten you in just measure and I will by no means leave you unpunished. (Also Jer. 4:27, 5:10, 5:18, 46:28, Ezek. 20:17.)
Hab. 1:12–13. ...Thou, O Rock, hast established [our foe] for chastisement. Thou who art of purer eyes than to behold evil and canst not look on wrong, why dost thou look on faithless men, and art silent when the wicked swallows up the man more righteous than he? (Also Ps. 94:20.)
Ps. 125:4–5. Do good, O Lord, to those who are good, and to those who are upright in their hearts! But those who turn aside upon their crooked ways the Lord will lead away with evildoers! Peace be in Israel!
Ps. 138:7. [O Lord,] though I walk in the midst of trouble, thou dost preserve my life; thou dost stretch out thy hand against the wrath of my enemies, and thy right hand delivers me. (Also Deut. 7:17–19, Ex. 6:6.)
Ps. 29:11. May the Lord give strength to his people! May the Lord bless his people with peace! (Also Ps. 122:6–7, 128:5–6, 147:14, Is. 26:1–3.)

2 Cor. 4:6. It is the God who said, "Let light shine out of darkness," who has shone in our hearts to give the light of the knowledge of the glory of God in the face of Christ. (Also Eph. 1:18, Jn. 1:9.)
1 Cor. 2:12, 14, 16. We have received not the spirit of the world, but the Spirit which is from God, that we might understand the gifts bestowed on us by God...The unspiritual man does not receive the gifts of the Spirit of God, for they are folly to him, and he is not able to understand them because they are spiritually discerned...Who has known the mind of the Lord so as to instruct him? But we have the mind of Christ.
Heb. 10:15–17. The Holy Spirit also bears witness to us; for after saying, "This is the covenant that I will make with them after those days, says the Lord: I will put my laws on their hearts, and write them on their minds (Luther: Sinn)," then he adds, "I will remember their sins and their misdeeds no more." (Also Heb. 8:10, Jer. 31:33.)
Heb. 12:5–7, 10–11. ...My son, do not regard lightly the discipline of the Lord...The Lord disciplines him whom he loves, and chastises every son whom he receives. It is for discipline that you have to endure...He disciplines us for our good, that we may share his holiness. For the moment all discipline seems painful rather than pleasant; later it yields the peaceful fruit of righteousness to those who have been trained by it. (Also Prov. 3:11–12, 1 Cor. 11:32, Rev. 3:19.)
1 Pet. 2:25. You were straying like sheep, but have now returned to the Shepherd and Guardian of your souls.
Acts 4:12. And there is salvation in no one else, for there is no other name under heaven given among men by which we must be saved. (Also Jn. 14:6.)

Der solch's wohl kann ausrichten.
Who (this) indeed can accomplish.
{Who can accomplish this.}

BWV 117
Sei Lob und Ehr dem höchsten Gut
(NBA I/34; BC A187)

Occasion Unknown (BWV 131, 150, 117, 192, 100, 97)
Librettist: Chorale (Johann Jakob Schütz) A number of
movements are possibly adapted from pre-existing works.

1. Chorus (Chorale Vs. 1)
●Praise & honor to God who does wonders and comforts
(117-1)

      Sei Lob und Ehr dem höchsten Gut,
(Let there) be praise and honor to-the highest good,

Dem Vater aller Güte,
To-the Father of-all goodness,

Dem Gott, der alle Wunder tut,
To-the God, who all wonders does,
{To the God who does all wonders,}

Dem Gott, der mein Gemüte
To-the God, who my spirit
{To the God who fills my spirit}

Mit seinem reichen Trost erfüllt,
With his rich consolation fills,
{With his abundant consolation,}

Dem Gott, der allen Jammer stillt.
To-the God, who all sorrow stills.
{To the God, who stills all sorrow.}

Gebt unserm Gott die Ehre!
Give our God the glory!

2. Bass Recit. (Chorale Vs. 2)
●Praise to God from heaven's host & all creatures (117-2)
Es danken dir die Himmelsheer,
(Now) thanks thee the host-of-heaven,
{The host of heaven gives thanks to thee,}

O Herrscher aller Thronen,
O ruler of-all thrones,

Und die auf Erden, Luft und Meer
And all-those upon (the) earth, air, and sea (who)

In deinem Schatten wohnen,
In thy shade do-dwell—

Die preisen deine Schöpfermacht,
They praise thy creative-power,

Phil. 1:6, 9. I am sure that he who began a good work in you will bring it to completion at the day of Jesus Christ...And it is my prayer that your love may abound more and more, with knowledge and all discernment...

Ps. 72:18–19. Blessed be the Lord, the God of Israel, who alone does wondrous things. Blessed be his glorious name for ever; may his glory fill the whole earth! Amen and Amen! (Also Ps. 41:13, 106:48.)
Ps. 77:14. [O Lord,] thou art the God who workest wonders, who hast manifested thy might among the peoples.
1 Chron. 16:8–10 / Ps. 105:1–3. O give thanks to the Lord, call on his name, make known his deeds among the peoples! Sing to him, sing praises to him, tell of all his wonderful works! Glory in his holy name; let the hearts of those who seek the Lord rejoice!
Jms. 1:17. Every good endowment and every perfect gift is from above, coming down from the Father of lights with whom there is no variation or shadow due to change.
2 Cor. 1:3–5. Blessed be the God and Father of our Lord Jesus Christ, the Father of mercies and God of all comfort, who comforts us in all our affliction, so that we may be able to comfort those who are in any affliction, with the comfort with which we ourselves are comforted by God. For as we share abundantly in Christ's sufferings, so through Christ we share abundantly in comfort too.
Ps. 10:14. [O Lord,] thou dost see; yea thou dost note trouble and vexation (Luther: Jammer), that thou mayest take it into thy hands; the hapless commits himself to thee; thou hast been the helper of the fatherless. (Jammer: also Ps. 25:18, 116:3)
Deut. 32:3. I will proclaim the name of the Lord. Ascribe greatness to our God! (Luther: Gebt unserm Gott allein die Ehre!)

Rev. 5:11–13. ...I heard around the throne...the voice of many angels, numbering myriads of myriads and thousands of thousands, saying with a loud voice, "Worthy is the Lamb who was slain, to receive power and wealth and wisdom and might and honor and glory and blessing!" And I heard every creature in heaven and on earth and under the earth and in the sea, and all therein, saying, "To him who sits upon the throne and to the Lamb be blessing and honor and glory and might for ever and ever!" (Also Rev. 4:8–11.)
Rev. 17:14. ...He is Lord of lords and King of kings... (Also Rev. 19:16, Phil. 2:9–10.)
Ps. 104:24, 27–28. O Lord, how manifold are thy works! In wisdom hast thou made them all; the earth is full of thy creatures...These all look to thee, to give them their food in due season. When thou givest to them, they gather it up; when thou openest thy hand, they are filled with good things. (Also Ps. 121:5–6, 145:15–16, Is. 25:4.)
Ps. 148:2–3, 5, 7–11. Praise him, all his angels, praise him, all his host! Praise him, sun and moon, praise him, all you shining stars!... For he

Die alles also wohl bedacht.
Which everything (has) (so) well thought-out.
{Which has thought out everything so well.}

Gebt unserm Gott die Ehre!
Give our God the glory!

3. Tenor Aria (Chorale Vs. 3)
●Praise to God for sustaining his creation (117-3)
Was unser Gott geschaffen hat,
Whatever our God created has,
{Whatever our God has created,}

Das will er auch erhalten;
That will he also sustain;

Darüber will er früh und spat
Over-that will he early and late

Mit seiner Gnade walten.
With his grace hold-sway.

In seinem ganzen Königreich
In his entire kingdom

Ist alles recht und alles gleich.
Is all just and all equal.
{All things are just and equal.}

Gebt unserm Gott die Ehre!
Give our God the glory!

4. Chorale (Vs. 4)
●Praise to God for help when I cried to him in need (117-4)
Ich rief dem Herrn in meiner Not:
I called to-the Lord in my distress:

Ach Gott, vernimm mein Schreien!
Ah Lord, hearken-to my crying!

Da half mein Helfer mir vom Tod
Then helped my Helper me from death
{Then my Helper helped me from death}

Und ließ mir Trost gedeihen.
And let (my) comfort flourish.

Drum dank, ach Gott, drum dank ich dir;
Therefore thank, ah God, therefore thank I thee;
{Therefore I thank thee, ah God, I thank thee:}

Ach danket, danket Gott mit mir!
Ah thank, thank God with me!

Gebt unserm Gott die Ehre!
Give our God the glory!

commanded and they were created...Praise the Lord from the earth, you sea monsters and all deeps, fire and hail, snow and frost, stormy wind fulfilling his command! Mountains and all hills, fruit trees and all cedars! Beasts and all cattle, creeping things and flying birds! Kings of the earth and all peoples...

Ps. 104:10-18, 24, 27-28. [O Lord,] thou makest springs gush forth in the valleys; they flow between the hills, they give drink to every beast of the field; the wild asses quench their thirst. By them the birds of the air have their habitation; they sing among the branches. From thy lofty abode thou waterest the mountains; the earth is satisfied with the fruit of thy work. Thou dost cause the grass to grow for the cattle, and plants for man to cultivate, that he may bring forth food from the earth, and wine to gladden the heart of man, oil to make his face shine, and bread to strengthen man's heart. The trees of the Lord are watered abundantly, the cedars of Lebanon which he planted. In them the birds build their nests; the stork has her home in the fir trees. The high mountains are for the wild goats; the rocks are a refuge for the badgers...O Lord, how manifold are thy works! In wisdom hast thou made them all; the earth is full of thy creatures...These all look to thee, to give them their food in due season. When thou givest to them, they gather it up; when thou openest thy hand, they are filled with good things. (Also Ps. 145:15-16, 147:7-9, 14-18, Col. 1:16-17.)
Ps. 145:17. The Lord is just in all his ways, and kind in all his doings. (just: also Deut 32:4, Rev. 15:3, 16:7)
Ps. 103:6, 11. The Lord works vindication and justice for all who are oppressed...As the heavens are high above the earth, so great is his steadfast love (Luther: läßt er seine Gnade walten) toward those who fear him.

Ps. 116:1, 3-6. I love the Lord, because he has heard my voice and my supplications...The snares of death encompassed me; the pangs of Sheol laid hold on me; I suffered distress and anguish. Then I called on the name of the Lord: "O Lord, I beseech thee, save my life!" Gracious is the Lord, and righteous; our God is merciful. The Lord preserves the simple; when I was brought low, he saved me.
Ps. 18:4-6. The cords of death encompassed me, the torrents of perdition assailed me; the cords of Sheol entangled me, the snares of death confronted me. In my distress I called upon the Lord; to my God I cried for help. From his temple he heard my voice, and my cry to him reached his ears.
Ps. 34:4, 6. I sought the Lord, and he answered me, and delivered me from all my fears...This poor man cried, and the Lord heard him, and saved him out of all his troubles.
Ps. 40:1-3. I waited patiently for the Lord; he inclined to me and heard my cry. He drew me up from the desolate pit, out of the miry bog, and set my feet upon a rock, making my steps secure. He put a new song in my mouth, a song of praise to our God. Many will see and fear, and put their trust in the Lord.
Ps. 34:1-3. I will bless the Lord at all times; his praise shall continually be in my mouth. My soul makes its boast in the Lord; let the afflicted hear and be glad. O magnify the Lord with me, and let us exalt his name together!

5. Alto Recit. (Chorale Vs. 5)
●Praise to God for never deserting his people (117-5)
Der Herr ist   noch und nimmer nicht
The Lord is (not) (now) and   never (was)

Von seinem Volk geschieden,
From his   people   parted,

Er bleibet ihre Zuversicht,
He remains their confidence,

Ihr   Segen,   Heil und Frieden;
Their blessing, salvation, and peace;

Mit   Mutterhänden leitet er
With maternal-hands leads he

Die Seinen stetig   hin und her.
His own continually to and fro.

Gebt unserm Gott die Ehre!
Give   our   God the glory!

6. Bass Aria (Chorale Vs. 6)
●Praise to God: Creator himself supplies our needs (117-6)
Wenn Trost und Hülf ermangeln muß,
When solace and help is-found-wanting,

Die   alle Welt erzeiget,
Which all-the world renders,
{When any solace and help rendered by the world fails,}

So kömmt, so hilft der   Überfluß,
Then comes, then helps - (He-who-is) Abundance (itself),

Der Schöpfer selbst, und neiget
The Creator himself, and inclines

Die Vateraugen denen zu,
(His) fatherly-eyes to-them,

Die sonsten nirgend finden Ruh.
Who otherwise nowhere find repose.

Gebt unserm Gott die Ehre!
Give   our   God the glory!

7. Alto Aria (Chorale Vs. 7)
●Praising God all life long; reaching all the earth (117-7)
Ich will dich all mein Leben lang,
I   will thee all my   life   long,

O Gott, von nun an ehren;
O God, from now on honor;
{From now on, I will honor thee, O God, all my life long;}

Man soll, o Gott, den Lobgesang
They shall, O God, (my) song-of-praise

Ps. 94:14. The Lord will not forsake his people; he will not abandon his heritage. (Also Ps. 37:28, Is. 42:16, 1 Kings 6:13, Heb. 13:5.)
Ps. 46:1–2. God is our refuge (Luther: Zuversicht) and strength, a very present help in trouble. Therefore we will not fear... (Zuversicht: also Ps. 61:3, 62:7, 71:5, 7, 91:2, 142:5)
Eph. 1:3. Blessed be the God and Father of our Lord Jesus Christ, who has blessed us in Christ with every spiritual blessing (Luther: Segen)...
Gal. 3:14. In Christ Jesus the blessing of Abraham [came] upon the Gentiles...
Ps. 27:1. The Lord is my light and my salvation (Luther: Heil); whom shall I fear?...
Eph. 2:14. ...[Christ] is our peace (Luther: Friede)...
Is. 66:13 [God]: As one whom his mother comforts, so I will comfort you...
Jn. 10:14, 27 [Christ]: I am the good shepherd; I know my own and my own know me...My sheep hear my voice, and I know them, and they follow me... (Also Ps. 100:3, Ps. 95:6–7.)
Ps. 121:8. The Lord will keep your going out and your coming in from this time forth and for evermore.

Ps. 146:3–7. Put not your trust in princes, in a son of man, in whom there is no help. When his breath departs he returns to his earth; on that very day his plans perish. Happy is he whose help is the God of Jacob, whose hope is in the Lord his God, who made heaven and earth, the sea, and all that is in them; who keeps faith for ever; who executes justice for the oppressed; who gives food to the hungry... (Also Ps. 118:8, Jer. 17:7.)
Mal. 3:10. ...Put me to the test, says the Lord of hosts, if I will not open the windows of heaven for you and pour down for you an overflowing blessing. (Also Ps. 50:10–11.)
Ps. 27:10. My father and my mother have forsaken me, but the Lord will take me up.
Ps. 34:15, 17–19. The eyes of the Lord are toward the righteous, and his ears toward their cry...When the righteous cry for help, the Lord hears, and delivers them out of all their troubles. The Lord is near to the brokenhearted, and saves the crushed in spirit. Many are the afflictions of the righteous; but the Lord delivers him out of them all. (Also Ps. 10:17, 116:2, 145:19.)
Ps. 103:13. As a father pities his children, so the Lord pities those who fear him.
Mt. 11:28 [Christ]: Come to me, all who labor and are heavy laden, and I will give you rest. (Also Jer. 6:16.)
Ps. 115:1. Not to us, O Lord...but to thy name give glory, for the sake of thy steadfast love and thy faithfulness!...

Ps. 104:33. I will sing to the Lord as long as I live (Luther: mein Leben lang); I will sing praise to my God while I have being.
Ps. 63:4. So I will bless thee as long as I live; I will lift up my hands and call on thy name.
Ps. 145:1–2. I will extol thee, my God and King, and bless thy name for ever and ever. Every day I will bless thee, and praise thy name for ever and ever. (Also Ps. 146:2.)
Ps. 40:3. [The Lord] put a new song in my mouth, a song of praise to our God. Many will see and fear, and put their trust in the Lord.

An allen Orten hören.
In all places hear.
{O God, my song of praise shall be heard by people everywhere.}

       Mein ganzes Herz ermuntre sich,
(Let) my whole heart arouse itself,

       Mein Geist und Leib erfreue sich.
(Let) my soul and body rejoice - .

Gebt unserm Gott die Ehre!
Give our God the glory!

Is. 24:16. From the ends of the earth we hear songs of praise, of glory to the Righteous One...

Ps. 48:10. As thy name, O God, so thy praise reaches to the ends of the earth...

Ps. 67:5, 7. Let the peoples praise thee, O God; let all the peoples praise thee!...God has blessed us; let all the ends of the earth fear him! (Also Ps. 98:3–4.)

Ps. 117:1–2. Praise the Lord, all nations! Extol him, all peoples! For great is his steadfast love toward us...

Ps. 103:22. Bless the Lord, all his works, in all places of his dominion. Bless the Lord, O my soul!

Ps. 84:2. ...My heart and flesh (Luther: Leib und Seele) sing for joy to the living God.

Lk. 1:46–47. And Mary said, "My soul magnifies the Lord, and my spirit rejoices in God my Savior."

8. Tenor Recit. (Chorale Vs. 8)
●Praise to God: Praise him all who confess his name! (117-8)
Ihr, die ihr Christi Namen nennt,
You, who - Christ's name (use),

Gebt unserm Gott die Ehre!
Give our God the glory!

Ihr, die ihr Gottes Macht bekennt,
You, who - God's might confess,

Gebt unserm Gott die Ehre!
Give our God the glory!

Die falschen Götzen macht zu Spott,
- False gods put to ridicule,

Der Herr ist Gott, der Herr ist Gott:
The Lord is God, the Lord is God:

Gebt unserm Gott die Ehre!
Give our God the glory!

Ps. 107:1-2. O give thanks to the Lord, for he is good; for his steadfast love endures for ever! Let the redeemed of the Lord say so, whom he has redeemed from trouble.

1 Cor. 1:2. ...All those who in every place call on the name of our Lord Jesus Christ...

Ps. 77:13-14. ...What god is great like our God? Thou art the God who workest wonders, who hast manifested thy might among the peoples. (Also Deut. 4:7, Ps. 113:5.)

1 Chron. 16:36. Blessed be the Lord, the God of Israel, from everlasting to everlasting!...

1 Kings 18:27, 36–38, 39. At noon Elijah mocked [the prophets of Baal], saying, "Cry aloud, for he is a god; either he is musing, or he has gone aside, or he is on a journey, or perhaps he is asleep and must be awakened." ...And at the time of the offering of the oblation, Elijah the prophet came near and said, "O Lord, God of Abraham, Isaac, and Israel, let it be known this day that thou art God in Israel, and that I am thy servant, and that I have done all these things at thy word. Answer me, O Lord, answer me, that this people may know that thou, O Lord, art God, and that thou hast turned their hearts back." Then the fire of the Lord fell, and consumed the burnt offering...And when all the people saw it, they fell on their faces; and they said, *"The Lord, he is God; the Lord, he is God."* (Also Ps. 115:4–8, 135:15–18, Jer. 10:8.)

9. Chorus (Chorale Vs. 9)
●Praise to God: Rejoice before Lord & pay your vows! (117-9)
So kommet vor sein Angesicht
So come before his face

Mit jauchzenvollem Springen;
With jubilant leaping;

Bezahlet die gelobte Pflicht
Discharge (your) pledged vow(s)

Und laßt uns fröhlich singen:
And let us joyfully sing:

Gott hat es alles wohl bedacht
God has it all well planned
{God has planned it all well}

Ps. 95:1-3. O come, let us sing to the Lord; let us make a joyful noise to the rock of our salvation! Let us come into his presence with thanksgiving; let us make a joyful noise to him with songs of praise! For the Lord is a great God, and a great King above all gods.

Ps. 100:1-2. Make a joyful noise to he Lord, all the lands! Serve the Lord with gladness! Come into his presence with singing! (Also Ps. 66:1, 81:1-2, 98:4-6.)

Ps. 149:1-3. Praise the Lord! Sing to the Lord a new song, his praise in the assembly of the faithful! Let Israel be glad in his Maker, let the sons of Zion rejoice in their King! Let them praise his name with dancing, making melody to him with timbrel and lyre!

Ps. 50:14. Offer to God a sacrifice of thanksgiving, and pay your vows to the Most High.

Ps. 22:25. [O Lord,] from thee comes my praise in the great congregation; my vows I will pay before those who fear him. (Also Ps. 61:8, 66:13, 116:14, 18.)

Und alles, alles recht gemacht.
And all-things, all-things rightly done.

Gebt unserm Gott die Ehre!
Give our God the glory!

Mk. 7:37. ...He has done all things well...

2 Sam. 22:31 / Ps. 18:30. This God—his way is perfect; the promise of the Lord proves true; he is a shield for all those who take refuge in him. (Also Rom. 8:28.)

Ps. 68:3–4. Let the righteous be joyful; let them exult before God; let them be jubilant with joy! Sing to God, sing praises to his name; lift up a song to him...

BWV 118
O Jesu Christ, meins Lebens Licht (Motet)
NBA III/1; BC B23a/b

This work by J. S. Bach is not classified as a cantata.

BWV 119
Preise, Jerusalem, den Herrn
(NBA I/32; BC B3)

Change of Town Council (BWV 71, 119, 193, 120, 29, 69)
Librettist: Unknown

1. Chorus (Probably adapted from a pre-existing instrumental work)
●Praise God for blessing Jerusalem: Ps. 147:12–14 (119–1)
Preise, Jerusalem, den Herrn, lobe, Zion,
Praise, (O) Jerusalem, the Lord; extol, (O) Zion,

deinen Gott! Denn er machet fest die Riegel
thy God! For he makes fast the bars

deiner Tore und segnet deine Kinder drinnen,
of-thy gates and blesses thy children therein,

er schaffet deinen Grenzen Frieden.
he procures for-thy borders peace.

Ps. 147:12–14. *Praise the Lord, O Jerusalem! Praise your God, O Zion! For he strengthens the bars of your gates; he blesses your sons within you. He makes peace in your borders; he fills you with the finest of the wheat.*

Ps. 122:2–4. Our feet have been standing within your gates, O Jerusalem! Jerusalem, built as a city which is bound firmly together, to which the tribes go up, the tribes of the Lord, as was decreed for Israel, to give thanks to the name of the Lord. (Also Ps. 102:21.)

Ps. 65:1–2. Praise is due to thee, O God, in Zion; and to thee shall vows be performed, O thou who hearest prayer!...

Ps. 29:11. May the Lord give strength to his people! May the Lord bless his people with peace!

Ps. 122:6–7. Pray for the peace of Jerusalem! "May they prosper who love you! Peace be within your walls, and security within your towers!" (Also Ps. 48:1–3, Is. 26:1–3.)

2. Tenor Recit.
●Blessed is the land & city in which God dwells (119–2)
Gesegnet Land, glückselge Stadt,
Blessed land, (O) happy city,

Woselbst der Herr sein Herd und Feuer hat!
The-very-place-where the Lord his hearth and fire has!
{The very place where the Lord has his hearth and fire!}

Wie kann Gott besser lohnen,
How can God better reward,
{How can God reward any nation better,}

Als wo er Ehre läßt in einem Lande wohnen?
Than where he glory lets in a land reside?
{Than by letting his glory reside in the land?}

Wie kann er eine Stadt
How can he a city
{How can he bless a city}

Ps. 33:12. Blessed is the nation whose God is the Lord, the people whom he has chosen as his heritage!

Ex. 29:45 [God]: I will dwell among the people of Israel, and will be their God. (Also Zech. 2:10–11, Zech. 8:8.)

Ezek. 37:26–27 [God]: I will make a covenant of peace with them; it shall be an everlasting covenant with them; and I will bless them and multiply them, and will set my sanctuary in the midst of them for evermore. My dwelling place shall be with them; and I will be their God, and they shall be my people. (Also Is. 54:10.)

Ex. 19:5–6 [God]: Now therefore, if you will obey my voice and keep my covenant, you shall be my own possession among all peoples; for all the earth is mine, and you shall be to me a kingdom of priests and a holy nation...

Deut. 7:6. You are a people holy to the Lord your God; the Lord your God has chosen you to be a people for his own possession, out of all the peoples that are on the face of the earth. (Also 1 Pet. 2:5, 9.)

Ps. 85:1, 9–14. Lord, thou wast favorable to thy land...Surely his salvation is at hand for those who fear him, that glory (Luther: Ehre) may dwell in our land. Steadfast love and faithfulness (Luther: Güte

Mit reicherm Nachdruck segnen,
With richer emphasis bless,
{With richer emphasis,}

Als wo er Güt und Treu
Than where he kindness and faithfulness

einander läßt begegnen,
   -     allows to-meet,
{Than where he allows kindness and faithfulness to meet,}

Wo er Gerechtigkeit und Friede
Where he righteousness and peace

Zu küssen niemals müde,
To kiss never (would be) tired,

Nicht müde, niemals satt
Not tired, never satiated

Zu werden, teur verheißen, auch in der Tat erfüllet hat?
To become, dearly promised, also in - fact fulfilled has?
{Than where he promised that righteousness and peace would never tire of kissing each other, and has also fulfilled it?}

Da ist der Schluß gemacht:
Therefore is the conclusion made:

Gesegnet Land, glückselge Stadt!
Blessed land, (O) happy city!

3. Tenor Aria

●Consider God's blessing on city of Linden-trees (119-3)
Wohl dir, du Volk der Linden,
(It is) well for-thee, thou people of-the Linden-trees,

Wohl dir, du hast es gut!
(It is) well for-thee; thou art-well-off!

Wieviel an Gottes Segen
How-much (of this) upon God's blessing
{How much of this depended upon God's blessing}

Und seiner Huld gelegen,
And his favor depended—
{And his favor—}

Die überschwenglich tut,
Which extravagantly manifests-itself—

Kannst du an dir befinden.
Canst thou in thee discover.
{Thou canst discover in thyself.}

4. Bass Recit.

●Thank God for his blessings through good government (119-4)
So herrlich stehst du, liebe Stadt!
(How) glorious standest thou, dear city!
{How glorious is thy position, dear city!}

und Treue) will meet; righteousness and peace (Luther: Gerechtigkeit und Friede) will kiss each other. Faithfulness (Luther: Treue) will spring up from the ground, and righteousness will look down from the sky. Yea the Lord will give what is good, and our land will yield its increase. Righteousness will go before him, and make his footsteps a way.

Ps. 72:1–3, 7. Give the king thy justice, O God, and thy righteousness to the royal son! May he judge thy people with righteousness, and thy poor with justice! Let the mountains bear prosperity for thy people, and the hills, in righteousness!...In his days may righteousness flourish, and peace abound, till the moon be no more!

Is. 32:16–18. Then justice will dwell in the wilderness, and righteousness abide in the fruitful field. And the effect of righteousness will be peace, and the result of righteousness, quietness and trust for ever. My people will abide in a peaceful habitation, in secure dwellings, and in quiet resting places.

Zech. 8:8 [God]: I will bring them to dwell in the midst of Jerusalem; and they shall be my people and I will be their God, in faithfulness and in righteousness.

Deut. 28:2–3. All these blessings shall come upon you and overtake you, if you obey the voice of the Lord your God. Blessed shall you be in the city, and blessed shall you be in the field...

1 Kings 8:15/2 Chron. 6:4. And [Solomon] said, "Blessed be the Lord, the God of Israel, who with his hand has fulfilled what he promised with his mouth to David my father..."

Ps. 144:15. Happy the people to whom such blessings fall! Happy the people whose God is the Lord!

Deut. 33:29. Happy are you (Luther: wohl dir) Israel! Who is like you, a people saved by the Lord, the shield of your help...

Ps. 144:15. Happy the people to whom such blessings fall! Happy the people whose God is the Lord!

Ps. 127:1. Unless the Lord builds the house, those who build it labor in vain. Unless the Lord watches over the city, the watchman stays awake in vain.

Ps. 77:11–14. I will call to mind the deeds of the Lord; yea, I will remember thy wonders of old. I will meditate on all thy work, and muse on thy mighty deeds...What god is great like our God? Thou art the God who workest wonders, who hast manifested thy might among the peoples. (Also Ps. 113:5.)

Ps. 89:15–17. Blessed are the people who know the festal shout, who walk, O Lord, in the light of thy countenance, who exult in thy name all the day, and extol thy righteousness. For thou art the glory of their strength; by thy favor our horn is exalted.

Eph. 3:20. Now to him who by the power at work within us is able to do far more abundantly (Luther: überschwenglich tun kann) than all that we ask or think, to him be glory...

Ps. 48:1–2. Great is the Lord and greatly to be praised in the city of our God!...Beautiful in elevation, is the joy of all the earth, Mount Zion...the city of the great King.

416

Du Volk, das Gott
Thou people, which God

      zum   Erbteil sich erwählet hat!
      for-his inheritance -   chosen has!
      {for his inheritance has chosen!}

Doch wohl! und aber wohl!
(How) good! (But how very) good!

      wo   man's   zu Herzen fassen
      where one-it (would) to   heart take

Und recht erkennen will,
And rightly recognize - ,
{How good—where one would take it to heart and rightly
recognize,}

Durch wen der Herr den Segen wachsen lassen.
Through whom the Lord (this) blessing grow   does-let.
{Through whom the Lord lets this blessing grow.}

Ja!
Yes!

Was bedarf es   viel?
What needs - (yet-to-be-said?)

Das Zeugnis ist schon da,
The testimony is already at-hand,

Herz und Gewissen wird uns überzeugen,
Heart and conscience will us   convince,
{Heart and conscience will convince us,}

Daß,   was   wir Gutes bei uns sehn,
That, whatever we of-good amidst us see,
{That, whatever good we experience,}

Nächst Gott durch   kluge   Obrigkeit
Next-to God, through intelligent ruling-authorities

Und durch ihr weises Regiment geschehn.
And through their wise governing (does-come).
{Next to God—comes through intelligent authorities and through
their wise governing.}

Drum   sei, geliebtes Volk,
Therefore be, beloved people,

      zu treuem   Dank   bereit,
      for sincere thanksgiving prepared,
{Therefore, be prepared, beloved people, for sincere
thanksgiving,}

Sonst   würden auch davon nicht deine Mauern schweigen!
Otherwise would even thereof not thy   walls keep-silent!
{Or else the very city walls would break their silence!}

Ps. 33:12. Blessed is the nation whose God is the Lord, the people whom he has chosen as his heritage!

Deut. 7:6. You are a people holy to the Lord your God; the Lord your God has chosen you to be a people for his own possession, out of all the peoples that are on the face of the earth. (Also Deut. 26:18)

Ex. 19:5 [God]: ...If you will obey my voice and keep my covenant, you shall be my own possession among all peoples...

Zech. 8:8. I will bring them to dwell in the midst of Jerusalem; and they shall be my people and I will be their God, in faithfulness and in righteousness.

1 Pet. 2:9. You are a chosen race, a royal priesthood, a holy nation, God's own people...

1 Sam. 13:14. ...The Lord has sought out a man after his own heart; and the Lord has appointed him to be prince over his people...

Rom. 13:1–6. Let every person be subject to the governing authorities. For there is no authority except from God, and those that exist have been instituted by God. Therefore he who resists the authorities resists what God has appointed, and those who resist will incur judgment. For rulers are not a terror to good conduct, but to bad. Would you have no fear of him who is in authority? Then do what is good, and you will receive his approval, for he is God's servant for your good... Therefore one must be subject, not only to avoid God's wrath but also for the sake of conscience. For the same reason you also pay taxes, for the authorities are ministers of God, attending to this very thing.

1 Pet. 2:13–14. Be subject for the Lord's sake to every human institution, whether it be to the emperor as supreme, or to governors as sent by him to punish those who do wrong and to praise those who do right. (See also Tit. 3:1, Jn. 19:11, Dan. 2:21.)

2 Sam. 23:3–4. ...When one rules justly over men, ruling in the fear of God, he dawns on them like the morning light, like the sun shining forth upon a cloudless morning, like rain that makes grass to sprout from the earth.

Prov. 29:4. By justice a king gives stability to the land...

Prov. 8:12, 15–16, 18, 20–21. I, wisdom, dwell in prudence, and I find knowledge and discretion...By me kings reign, and rulers decree what is just; by me princes rule, and nobles govern the earth...Riches and honor are with me, enduring wealth and prosperity...I walk in the way of righteousness, in the paths of justice, endowing with wealth those who love me, and filling their treasuries.

1 Tim. 2:1–2. First of all, then, I urge that supplications, prayers, intercessions, and thanksgivings be made for all men, for kings and all who are in high positions, that we may lead a quiet and peaceable life, godly and respectful in every way.

Ps. 67:3/5. Let the peoples praise thee, O God; let all the peoples praise thee!

Lk. 19:36–40. As [Jesus] rode along, they spread their garments on the road. As he was now drawing near, at the descent of the Mount of Olives, the whole multitude of the disciples began to rejoice and praise God with a loud voice for all the mighty works that they had seen, saying, "Blessed is the King who comes in the name of the Lord! Peace in heaven and glory in the highest!" And some of the Pharisees in the multitude said to him, "Teacher, rebuke your disciples." He answered, "I tell you, if these were silent, the very stones would cry out."

5. Alto Aria
●Government is gift and image of God (119-5)
Die Obrigkeit ist Gottes Gabe,
 - Government is God's gift,

Ja selber Gottes Ebenbild.
Yes, even God's image.

Wer ihre Macht nicht will ermessen,
Whoever its might not would (duly) measure,
{Whoever would not duly measure its might,}

Der muß auch Gottes gar vergessen:
 - Must also of-God indeed be-oblivious:
{Must also indeed be oblivious of God:}

Wie würde sonst sein Wort erfüllt?
How would otherwise his Word be-fulfilled?
{How would his Word be fulfilled otherwise?}

Rom. 13:1-4. Let every person be subject to the governing authorities (Luther: Obrigkeit). For there is no authority except from God, and those that exist have been instituted by God. Therefore he who resists the authorities resists what God has appointed, and those who resist will incur judgment. For rulers are not a terror to good conduct, but to bad. Would you have no fear of him who is in authority? Then do what is good, and you will receive his approval, for he is God's servant for your good. But if you do wrong, be afraid, for he does not bear the sword in vain; he is the servant of God to execute his wrath on the wrongdoer.
Dan. 2:21. [God]...removes kings and sets up kings... (Also Jn. 19:11.)
1 Pet. 2:13-14. Be subject for the Lord's sake to every human institution, whether it be to the emperor as supreme, or to governors as sent by him to punish those who do wrong and to praise those who do right.
Tit. 3:1. ...Be submissive to rulers and authorities...be obedient...

6. Soprano Recit.
●Offering of thanks to God at end of election day (119-6)
Nun! wir erkennen es und bringen dir,
Now-then! We recognize it and bring to-thee,

O höchster Gott, ein Opfer unsers Danks dafür.
O most-high God, an offering of-our thanks for-this.

Zumal, nachdem der heutge Tag,
Especially, after this present day,

Der Tag, den uns der Herr gemacht,
The day, which for-us the Lord did-make, (which)

Euch, teure Väter, teils von eurer Last entbunden,
You, dear elders, in-part of your burden released,
{In part, freed you, dear elders, of your burden,}

Teils auch auf euch
In-part also upon yourselves

Schlaflose Sorgenstunden
Sleepless hours-of-worry

Bei einer neuen Wahl gebracht,
With a new election did-bring,
{In part also brought upon yourselves sleepless hours of worry with a new election;}

So seufzt ein treues Volk mit Herz und Mund zugleich:
Thus sighs a faithful people with heart and mouth alike:

1 Tim. 2:1-2. First of all, then, I urge that supplications, prayers, intercessions, and thanksgivings be made for all men, for kings and all who are in high positions...
Ps. 50:14, 23 [God]: Offer to God a sacrifice of thanksgiving, and pay your vows to the Most High...He who brings thanksgiving as his sacrifice honors me... (Also Heb. 13:15, Ps. 69:30-31, 116:17-18.)
Ps. 118:24. This is the day which the Lord has made; let us rejoice and be glad in it. (Also Ps. 126:2-3.)
Dan. 2:21. [God]...sets up kings...
1 Sam. 10:21, 24. ...Finally...Saul the son of Kish was taken by lot...And Samuel said to all the people, "Do you see him whom the Lord has chosen? There is none like him among all the people." And all the people shouted, "Long live the king!"
1 Kings 1:39-40. Zadok the priest took the horn of oil from the tent, and anointed Solomon. Then they blew the trumpet; and all the people said, "Long live King Solomon!" And all the people went up after him, playing on pipes, and rejoicing with great joy, so that the earth was split by their noise.
Ps. 67:3/5. Let the peoples praise thee, O God; let all the peoples praise thee!
Ps. 79:13. [O Lord,] we thy people, the flock of thy pasture, will give thanks to thee for ever; from generation to generation we will recount thy praise.
Ps. 147:12-14. Praise the Lord, O Jerusalem! Praise your God, O Zion! For he strengthens the bars of your gates; he blesses your sons within you. He makes peace in your borders; he fills you with the finest of the wheat.
Ps. 71:23. [O Lord,] my lips will shout for joy, when I sing praises to thee; my soul also...

7. Chorus
●God's continuing blessing on governors sought (119-7)
Der Herr hat Guts an uns getan,
The Lord has good to us done,
{The Lord has done good to us,}

Ps. 126:2-3. ...They said among the nations, "The Lord has done great things for them." The Lord has done great things for us; we are glad. (Also 1 Sam. 12:24, Lk. 1:49.)

Des   sind wir alle fröhlich.
Thereof are we all   joyful.
{For this we are all joyful.}

Er   seh   die teuren Väter an
(May) he regard (our) dear elders -.

Und halte auf   unzählig
And   dwell (through) unmeasured

Und   späte lange Jahre naus
And advanced long years   -

In   ihrem Regimente Haus,
Within their government's house,
{Within their house of government,}

So wollen wir ihn preisen.
Then will we him praise.
{Then will we praise him.}

8. Alto Recit.
●Prayer: Since we are thy people, hear one final request
(119-8)
Zuletzt!
Finally!

Da   du uns,   Herr, zu deinem Volk gesetzt,
Since thou us, (O) Lord to   thy people didst-make,

So laß von deinen Frommen
Then let from   thy righteous-ones

Nur noch ein arm Gebet   vor deine Ohren kommen
Just yet one poor prayer before thine ears   come
{Just one more prayer come to thine ears}

Und höre! ja   erhöre!
And hear! Yes, grant-favorable-hearing!

Der Mund, das Herz und Seele seufzet sehre.
(Our) mouth, (our) heart, and soul sighs deeply.

9. Chorale
●Te Deum: Bless this people, thine inheritance (119-9)
Hilf deinem Volk, Herr Jesu Christ,
Help thy people, Lord Jesus Christ,

Und segne, was dein   Erbteil ist.
And bless,   what thine inheritance is.
{And bless what is thine inheritance.}

Wart und pfleg ihr' zu aller Zeit
Tend and nourish them at   all times

Und heb sie hoch in Ewigkeit!
And raise them high in eternity!

Amen.
Amen.

Ps. 67:5-7. Let the peoples praise thee, O God; let all the peoples praise thee! ...God, our God, has blessed us. God has blessed us; let all the ends of the earth fear him!
Is. 63:7. I will recount the steadfast love of the Lord, the praises of the Lord, according to all that the Lord has granted us, and the great goodness to the house of Israel which he has granted them according to his mercy, according to the abundance of his steadfast love.
Ps. 61:6-7. Prolong the life of the king; may his years endure to all generations! May he be enthroned for ever before God; bid steadfast love and faithfulness watch over him!
Prov. 20:28. Loyalty and faithfulness preserve the king, and his throne is upheld by righteousness. (Also Prov. 29:14, Ps. 61:6-8.)
Josh. 1:16-17. [The people] answered Joshua, "All that you have commanded us we will do, and wherever you send us we will go. Just as we obeyed Moses in all things, so we will obey you; only may the Lord your God be with you, as he was with Moses!"
Ps. 79:13. Then [O Lord,] we thy people, the flock of thy pasture, will give thanks to thee for ever; from generation to generation we will recount thy praise.

1 Pet. 2:9. You are a chosen race, a royal priesthood, a holy nation, God's own people...
Deut. 7:6. For you are a people holy to the Lord your God; the Lord your God has chosen you to be a people for his own possession, out of all the peoples that are on the face of the earth. (Also Ex. 19:5, Deut 26:18.)
Jn. 15:16 [Christ]: You did not choose me, but I chose you and appointed you that you should go and bear fruit and that your fruit should abide; so that whatever you ask the Father in my name, he may give it to you. (Also Jn. 14:13, 16:23.)
1 Kings 8:52-53. Let thy eyes be open to the supplication of thy servant, and to the supplication of thy people Israel, giving ear to them whenever they call to thee. For thou didst separate them from among all the peoples of the earth, to be thy heritage, as thou didst declare through Moses, thy servant, when thou didst bring our fathers out of Egypt, O Lord God. (Also 2 Chron. 6:40.)
1 Pet. 3:12. For the eyes of the Lord are upon the righteous, and his ears are open to their prayer...
Rom. 8:26. Likewise the Spirit helps us in our weakness; for we do not know how to pray as we ought, but the Spirit himself intercedes for us with sighs too deep for words.

Deut. 26:15. [O Lord,] look down from thy holy habitation, from heaven, and bless thy people Israel and the ground which thou hast given us, as thou didst swear to our fathers...
Ps. 29:11. May the Lord give strength to his people! May the Lord bless his people with peace!
Ps. 74:2. [O Lord,] remember thy congregation...which thou hast redeemed to be the tribe of thy heritage (Luther: Erbteil)! Remember Mount Zion, where thou hast dwelt.
Ps. 95:7. He is our God and we are the people of his pasture, and the sheep of his hand.
Ps. 100:3. Know that the Lord is God! It is he that made us, and we are his; we are his people, and the sheep of his pasture.
Ps. 28:9. O [Lord,] save thy people, and bless thy heritage (Luther: Erbe); be thou their shepherd, and carry them for ever (Luther: erhöhe sie ewiglich). (Also Ps. 33:12.)

BWV 120
Gott, man lobet dich in der Stille
(NBA I/32; BC B6)

Change of Town Council (BWV 71, 119, 193, 120, 29, 69)
Librettist: Unknown. Some movements apparently parodies,
details unclear.

1. Alto Aria
●Praise offered & vows paid to God in Zion: Ps. 65:1 (120-1)
Gott, man lobet dich in der Stille zu Zion,
God, one praises thee in the stillness of Zion,
{Or: God, there will be silence and praise to thee in Zion,}

und dir bezahlet man Gelübde.
and to-thee pays one vows.
{and to thee shall vows be paid.}

2. Chorus
●Voices raised in praise to God for his goodness (120-2)
Jauchzet, ihr erfreuten Stimmen,
Shout-with-joy, ye joyous voices,

Steiget bis zum Himmel nauf!
Mount up to heaven - !

Lobet Gott im Heiligtum
Praise God in (his) sanctuary

Und erhebet seinen Ruhm;
And lift-up his praise;

Seine Güte,
His kindness,

Sein erbarmendes Gemüte
His compassionate disposition

Hört zu keinen Zeiten auf!
Shall-cease at no time - !

3. Bass Recit.
●Pay vows for civic blessings, seek further blessing (120-3)
Auf, du geliebte Lindenstadt,
Up, thou beloved Linden-city,
{Rise, thou beloved city of linden trees,}

Komm, falle vor dem Höchsten nieder,
Come, fall before the Most-High down,
{Come, fall down before the Most High,}

Erkenne, wie er dich
Recognize, how he thee
{Recognize, how}

In deinem Schmuck und Pracht
In thine adornment and splendor

Ps. 65:1. *Praise is due to thee, O God, in Zion; and to thee shall vows be performed.*

Ps. 135:21. Blessed be the Lord from Zion, he who dwells in Jerusalem! Praise the Lord!

Ps. 147:12. Praise the Lord, O Jerusalem! Praise your God, O Zion!

Ps. 22:25. [O Lord,] from thee comes my praise in the great congregation; my vows I will pay before those who fear him.

Ps. 116:17-19. I will offer to thee the sacrifice of thanksgiving and call on the name of the Lord. I will pay my vows to the Lord in the presence of all his people, in the courts of the house of the Lord, in your midst, O Jerusalem. Praise the Lord! (Also Ps. 50:14, 61:8, 66:13.)

Ps. 98:4. Make a joyful noise to the Lord, all the earth; break forth into joyous song and sing praises!

Ps. 100:1-2. Make a joyful noise to he Lord, all the lands!...Come into his presence with singing! (Also Ps. 66:1, 95:1-2, 81:1-2, 98:6.)

Is. 24:14. [The people] lift up their voices, they sing for joy...

Ps. 150:1. Praise the Lord! Praise God in his sanctuary (Luther: Heiligtum); praise him in his mighty firmament!

1 Chron. 16:34. O give thanks to the Lord, for he is good; for his steadfast love endures for ever!

Ps. 145:8-9. The Lord is gracious and merciful, slow to anger and abounding in steadfast love (Luther: Güte). The Lord is good to all, and his compassion is over all that he has made. (Also Ex. 34:6, Ps. 103:8.)

Ps. 99:5, 9. Extol (Luther: erhebet) the Lord our God; worship at his footstool! Holy is he!...Extol (Luther: erhöhet) the Lord our God, and worship at his holy mountain; for the Lord our God is holy!

Ps. 100:4-5. ...Give thanks to him, bless his name! For the Lord is good; his steadfast love endures for ever, and his faithfulness to all generations. (Also Ps. 106:1, 107:1, 118:1, 136:1, 2, etc., Lam. 3:22.)

Ps. 95:6-7. O come, let us worship and bow down, let us kneel before the Lord, our Maker! For he is our God and we are the people of his pasture, and the sheep of his hand.

Ps. 72:11. May all kings fall down before [the king], all nations serve him!

Ps. 126:3. The Lord has done great things for us; we are glad.

Jer. 33:9 [God]: This city shall be to me a name of joy, a praise and a glory before all the nations of the earth who shall hear of all the good that I do for them; they shall fear and tremble because of all the good and all the prosperity I provide for it.

Ps. 102:21-22. [Let] men...declare in Zion the name of the Lord, and in Jerusalem his praise, when peoples gather together and kingdoms, to worship the Lord.

Ps. 50:14. Offer to God a sacrifice of thanksgiving, and pay your vows to the Most High.

1 Chron. 29:12-14. [O Lord,] both riches and honor come from thee,

So väterlich
So fatherlike

Erhält,   beschützt, bewacht
Preserves, protects,   guards
{He preserves, protects, and guards thee,}

Und seine Liebeshand
And   his   hand-of-love

Noch über dir beständig   hat.
Still   over thee steadfastly (doth-hold).

Wohlan,
Well-then,

Bezahle die Gelübde, die   du   dem Höchsten hast getan,
Pay   the   vows,   which thou to-the Most-High hast made,

Und singe   Dank- und Demutslieder!
And sing (songs of) thanks and songs-of-humility!

Komm, bitte, daß er Stadt und Land
Come, pray, that he town and country

Unendlich wolle mehr erquicken
Unendingly would further refresh

Und diese werte Obrigkeit,
And this worthy government,

So   heute Sitz und Wahl verneut,
Which today seat and   poll renews,

Mit vielem Segen wolle schmücken!
With many blessings would   adorn!

4. Soprano Aria
●Blessing on government brings justice & faithfulness (120-4)
Heil   und Segen
Well-being and blessing

Soll und muß zu aller Zeit
Shall and must at all times

Sich auf unsre Obrigkeit
- Upon our government

In erwünschter Fülle legen,
In desired measure (come),

Daß sich Recht und Treue müssen
So-that - justice and faithfulness   -

Miteinander freundlich küssen.
Each-other   as-friends do-kiss.

and thou rulest over all. In thy hand are power and might; and in thy hand it is to make great and to give strength to all. And now we thank thee, our God, and praise thy glorious name...For all things come from thee...

Ps. 103:13. As a father pities his children, so the Lord pities those who fear him.

Ps. 145:17, 20. The Lord is just in all his ways, and kind in all his doings...The Lord preserves all who love him...

Ps. 66:13-15, 20. [O Lord,] I will come into thy house with burnt offerings; I will pay thee my vows, that which my lips uttered and my mouth promised when I was in trouble. I will offer to thee burnt offerings of fatlings, with the smoke of the sacrifice of rams; I will make an offering of bulls and goats...Blessed be God, because he has not rejected my prayer or removed his steadfast love from me! (vows: also Ps. 22:5, 61:8, 65:1, 116:14, 17-19)

Ps. 95:1-2. O come, let us sing to the Lord; let us make a joyful noise to the rock of our salvation! Let us come into his presence with thanksgiving; let us make a joyful noise to him with songs of praise! (Also Ps. 66:1-2, 107:22, 135:3, 147:7.)

Ps. 85:6-7. [O Lord,] wilt thou not revive us again (Luther: wieder erquicken), that thy people may rejoice in thee? Show us thy steadfast love, O Lord, and grant us thy salvation.

Ps. 61:5-8. For thou, O God, hast heard my vows, thou hast given me the heritage of those who fear thy name. Prolong the life of the king; may his years endure to all generations! May he be enthroned for ever before God; bid steadfast love and faithfulness watch over him! So will I ever sing praises to thy name, as I pay my vows day after day.

1 Tim. 2:1-2. ...I urge that supplications, prayers, intercessions, and thanksgivings be made for all men, for kings and all who are in high positions (Luther: Obrigkeit), that we may lead a quiet and peaceable life, godly and respectful in every way.

Ps. 128:5-6. The Lord bless you from Zion! May you see the prosperity of Jerusalem all the days of your life! May you see your children's children! Peace be upon Israel! (Also Ps. 144:12-15.)

Rom. 13:1-2. Let every person be subject to the governing authorities (Luther: Obrigkeit). For there is no authority (Luther: Obrigkeit) except from God, and those that exist have been instituted by God. Therefore he who resists the authorities resists what God has appointed... (Also Tit. 3:1.)

1 Tim. 2:1-2. ...I urge that supplications, prayers, intercessions, and thanksgivings be made for all men, for kings and all who are in high positions (Luther: Obrigkeit), that we may lead a quiet and peaceable life, godly and respectful in every way.

Ps. 85:1, 9-12. Lord, thou wast favorable to thy land...Surely his salvation is at hand for those who fear him, that glory may dwell in our land. Steadfast love and faithfulness will meet; righteousness and peace will kiss each other. Faithfulness will spring up from the ground, and righteousness will look down from the sky. Yea, the Lord will give what is good, and our land will yield its increase. (Also: Ps. 72:1-3, 7, Is. 32:16-18, Zech. 8:8.)

5. Tenor Recit.
●Prayer for new government: righteousness & blessing (120-5)
Nun, Herr, so   weihe   selbst das Regiment
Now, Lord, - inaugurate thyself this government
{Now Lord, wouldst thou inaugurate this government thyself}

mit deinem Segen ein,
with   thy   blessing - ,

Daß alle Bosheit von uns fliehe
That all iniquity from us might-flee

Und die Gerechtigkeit in unsern Hütten   blühe,
And - righteousness in   our dwellings would-flourish,

Daß deines Vaters reiner Same
That thy   Father's pure seed

Und dein gebenede iter Name
And thy   blessed   name

Bei   uns verherrlicht möge sein!
Amongst us   glorified   might be!

6. Chorale
●Te Deum: Bless this people, thine inheritance (120-6)
Nun hilf uns, Herr, den Dienern dein,
Now help us, Lord—(these) servants of-thine,

Die mit deinm Blut erlöset sein!
Who with thy blood redeemed are!
{Who have been redeemed with thy blood!}

Laß uns im Himmel haben   teil
Let us in heaven   have (a) part

Mit den Heilgen im ewgen   Heil!
With the   saints in-that eternal Salvation!

Hilf deinem Volk, Herr Jesu Christ,
Help thy people, Lord Jesus Christ,

Und segne, was dein   Erbteil ist;
And bless, what thine inheritance is;

Wart und pfleg ihr' zu aller Zeit
Tend and nourish it at all   times

Ps. 72:1–3, 7. Give the king thy justice, O God, and thy righteousness to the royal son! May he judge thy people with righteousness, and thy poor with justice! Let the mountains bear prosperity for thy people, and the hills, in righteousness!...In his days may righteousness flourish, and peace abound, till the moon be no more!
Prov. 14:34. Righteousness exalts a nation, but sin is a reproach to any people. (Also Prov. 11:11.)
Is. 32:16–18. Then justice will dwell in the wilderness, and righteousness abide in the fruitful field. And the effect of righteousness will be peace, and the result of righteousness, quietness and trust for ever. My people will abide in a peaceful habitation, in secure dwellings, and in quiet resting places. (Also Hos. 10:12.)
Jms. 1:21. Therefore put away all...rank growth of wickedness (Luther: Bosheit) and receive with meekness the implanted word, which is able to save your souls. (Also 1 Thess. 2:13.)
Lk. 8:11. ...The seed is the word of God. (Also Is. 55:11, Mt. 13:3–30, Lk. 8:5–15.)
1 Jn. 3:9. No one born of God commits sin; for God's nature (Luther: Same) abides in him...
Col. 3:16. Let the word of Christ dwell in you richly...
Ps. 138:2. ...[O Lord,] thou hast exalted above everything thy name and thy word (Luther: du hast deinen Namen über alles herrlich gemacht durch dein Wort).
2 Thess. 1:11–12. To this end we always pray for you, that our God may make you worthy of his call, and may fulfil every good resolve and work of faith by his power, so that the name of our Lord Jesus may be glorified in you...

Ps. 28:9. O save thy people, and bless thy heritage; be thou their shepherd, and carry them for ever.
Ps. 79:9. Help us, O God of our salvation, for the glory of thy name...
Rev. 5:9. ...[O Lord,] worthy art thou...for thou wast slain and by thy blood didst ransom men for God from every tribe and tongue and people and nation, and hast made them a kingdom and priests to our God, and they shall reign on earth.
1 Pet. 1:18–19. You know that you were ransomed from the futile ways inherited from your fathers, not with perishable things such as silver or gold, but with the precious blood of Christ, like that of a lamb without blemish or spot. (Also Eph. 2:13, 1 Jn. 1:7, Heb. 13:12.)
Col. 1:11–12. May you be strengthened with all power, according to his glorious might, for all endurance and patience with joy, giving thanks to the Father, who has qualified us to share in the inheritance of the saints in light.
Deut. 26:15. [O Lord,] look down from thy holy habitation, from heaven, and bless thy people Israel and the ground which thou hast given us, as thou didst swear to our fathers...
Ps. 33:12. Blessed is the nation whose God is the Lord, the people whom he has chosen as his heritage (Luther: Erbe)!
Ps. 74:2. [O Lord,] remember thy congregation...which thou hast redeemed to be the tribe of thy heritage (Luther: Erbteil)! Remember Mount Zion, where thou hast dwelt.
Ps. 100:3. ...We are his people, and the sheep of his pasture. (Also Ps. 95:7.)
Ps. 29:11. May the Lord give strength to his people! May the Lord bless his people with peace!

Und heb sie hoch in Ewigkeit!
And raise it high in eternity!

Ps. 28:9. O save thy people, and bless thy heritage (Luther: Erbe); be thou their shepherd, and carry them for ever (Luther: erhöhe sie ewiglich).

BWV 121
Christum wir sollen loben schon
(NBA I/3; BC A13)

2. Day of Christmas (BWV 40, 121, 57, 248-II)
*Tit. 3:4–7 (The mercy of God appeared in Christ)
*Lk. 2:15–20 (The shepherds go to the manger)

This day also celebrated as the festival of St. Stephen the Martyr:
Acts 6:8–7:2 & 7:51–59 (The stoning of Stephen)
Mt. 23:34–39 (Jesus' lament: Jerusalem kills the prophets sent to her)
Librettist: Unknown

1. Chorus (Chorale Vs. 1)
●Christ's birth: Praise Son of Mary to ends of earth! (121-1)
Christum wir sollen loben schon, [schon = schön]
Christ we (shall) praise (sweetly),
{We shall praise Christ sweetly,}

Der reinen Magd Marien Sohn,
The pure maiden Maria's Son,
{Son of the pure maiden Mary,}

So weit die liebe Sonne leucht
As far-as the dear sun radiates,

Und an aller Welt Ende reicht.
And to all-the world's ends does-reach.
{Reaching to the ends of the world.}

***Lk. 2:15–20.** When the angels went away from them into heaven, the shepherds said to one another, "Let us go over to Bethlehem and see this thing that has happened, which the Lord has made known to us." And they went with haste, and found Mary and Joseph, and the babe lying in a manger. And when they saw it they made known the saying which had been told them concerning this child; and all who heard it wondered at what the shepherds told them. But Mary kept all these things, pondering them in her heart. And the shepherds returned, glorifying and praising God for all they had heard and seen, as it had been told them.
Ps. 48:10. As thy name, O God, so thy praise reaches to the ends of the earth...
Ps. 98:3–4. ...All the ends of the earth have seen the victory of our God. Make a joyful noise to the Lord, all the earth; break forth into joyous song and sing praises! (Also Ps. 22:27, 67:7.)

2. Tenor Aria (Based on Chorale Vs. 2)
●Incarnation: Creator exalts us by becoming flesh (121-2)
O du von Gott erhöhte Kreatur,
O thou by God exalted creature,
{O thou creature, exalted by God,}

Begreife nicht, nein, nein, bewundre nur:
Comprehend not, no, no, marvel only:
{Do not try to comprehend, no, just marvel at this:}

Gott will durch Fleisch des Fleisches Heil erwerben.
God would by flesh the flesh's salvation gain.

Wie groß ist doch der Schöpfer aller Dinge,
How great is indeed the Creator of-all things—

Und wie bist du verachtet und geringe,
And how art thou despised and lowly—
{And how despised and lowly thou—}

Ps. 8:3–5. [O Lord,] when I look at thy heavens, the work of thy fingers, the moon and the stars which thou hast established; what is man that thou art mindful of him, and the son of man that thou dost care for him? Yet thou hast made him little less than God, and dost crown him with glory and honor. (Also Ps. 144:3, Heb. 2:5–8.)
***Lk. 2:18–19.** All who heard [the news of Christ's birth] wondered at what the shepherds told them. But Mary kept all these things, pondering them in her heart.
Rom. 8:3–4. God has done what the law, weakened by the flesh, could not do: sending his own Son in the likeness of sinful flesh and for sin, he condemned sin in the flesh, in order that the just requirement of the law might be fulfilled in us, who walk not according to the flesh but according to the Spirit.
Phil. 2:6–8. ...Though he was in the form of God, [Christ Jesus] did not count equality with God a thing to be grasped, but emptied himself, taking the form of a servant, being born in the likeness of men. And being found in human form he humbled himself and became obedient unto death, even death on a cross.

Um dich   dadurch zu retten vom Verderben.
- Thee by-this-means to save from perdition.
{How amazing that thou art to be saved from perdition by this means, since God is the Creator of all things and thou so lowly and despised.}

3. Alto Recit. (Based on Chorale Vss. 3 & 4)
●Incarnation: Incomprehensible mystery of grace (121-3)
Der Gnade unermeßlich's Wesen
- Grace's unmeasurable essence
{The unmeasurable essence of grace}

Hat sich den Himmel nicht
Has - - heaven not
{Has not chosen heaven}

Zur   Wohnstatt auserlesen,
For-its dwelling-place chosen,
{For its dwelling place,}

Weil keine Grenze   sie umschließt.
Because no boundary (can) it circumscribe.
{Because no boundary can circumscribe it.}

Was   Wunder, daß allhie Verstand und Witz gebricht,
What (a) wonder! - In-all-this reason and wit   fails,

Ein solch Geheimnis zu ergründen,
- Such (a) mystery to   fathom,

Wenn sie sich in ein keusches Herze gießt.
When (grace) itself into a   chaste heart does-pour.
{When grace pours itself into a chaste heart.}

Gott wählet   sich   den reinen Leib zu einem Tempel
God chooses for-himself this pure body for a   temple

        seiner Ehren,
        of-his praise,
{God chooses this pure body as his temple of praise,}

Um   zu den Menschen sich mit wundervoller Art
In-order to - mankind - in   marvelous manner

        zu kehren.
        to turn.
{That he might turn to mankind in marvelous manner.}

4. Bass Aria (Based on Chorale Vs. 5)
●Response at manger: Recognizing Messiah as John did (121-4)
Johannis freudenvolles Springen
John's   joyful   leaping

Erkannte dich, mein Jesu, schon.
Recognized thee, my Jesus, already.

Heb. 2:11. He who sanctifies and those who are sanctified have all one origin. That is why he is not ashamed to call them brethren. (Also Heb. 2:14.)

*Tit. 3:4, 7. ...The goodness and loving kindness of God our Savior appeared...so that we might be justified by his grace and become heirs in hope of eternal life.
Heb. 1:1-2, 5. In these last days [God] has spoken to us by a Son...He reflects the glory of God and bears the very stamp of his nature (Luther: das Ebenbilde seines Wesens)...To what angel did God ever say, "Thou art my Son, today I have begotten thee"?...
1 Kings 8:27. Will God indeed dwell on the earth? Behold, heaven and the highest heaven cannot contain thee... (Also 2 Chron. 2:6, Is. 66:1, Acts 7:48-49, 17:24.)
2 Cor. 8:9. You know the grace of our Lord Jesus Christ, that though he was rich, yet for your sake he became poor, so that by his poverty you might become rich.
Phil. 2:5-7. ...Christ Jesus, who, though he was in the form of God, did not count equality with God a thing to be grasped, but emptied himself, taking the form of a servant, being born in the likeness of men. (Also Heb. 2:14-15.)
1 Tim. 3:16. Great indeed, we confess, is the mystery of our religion: He was manifested in the flesh...
Lk. 1:26, 27-28, 30-33, 35. In the sixth month the angel Gabriel was sent from God...to a virgin...and the virgin's name was Mary. And he came to her and said, "Hail, O favored one, the Lord is with you!...Do not be afraid, Mary, for you have found favor with God. And behold, you will conceive in your womb and bear a son, and you shall call his name Jesus. He will be great, and will be called the Son of the Most High; and the Lord God will give to him the throne of his father David, and he will reign over the house of Jacob for ever; and of his kingdom there will be no end...The Holy Spirit will come upon you, and the power of the Most High will overshadow you; therefore the child to be born will be called holy, the Son of God." (Also 1 Cor. 3:16, 6:19, 7:23.)
Heb. 10:5. When Christ came into the world, he said, "Sacrifices and offerings thou hast not desired, but a body hast thou prepared for me." (See Ps. 40:6.)
1 Cor. 3:16. Do you not know that you are God's temple and that God's Spirit dwells in you? (Also 1 Cor. 6:19.)
Jn. 1:14. The Word became flesh and dwelt among us, full of grace and truth; we have beheld his glory, glory as of the only Son of the Father.

Lk. 1:39-44. In those days Mary arose and went with haste...and she entered the house of Zechariah and greeted Elizabeth [her kinswoman, who had conceived a son who would be John the Baptist]. And when Elizabeth heard the greeting of Mary, the babe leaped in her womb; and Elizabeth was filled with the Holy Spirit and she exclaimed with a loud cry, "Blessed are you among women, and blessed is the fruit of your womb: And why is this granted me, that the mother of my Lord should come to me? For behold, when the voice of your greeting came to my ears, the babe in my womb leaped for joy."

Nun da ein Glaubensarm dich hält,
Now since an arm-of-faith thee holds,
{Now, since an arm of faith can hold thee,}

So will mein Herze von der Welt
So would my heart from the world

Zu deiner Krippe brünstig dringen.
To thy crib ardently press.

5. Soprano Aria (Based on Chorale Vss. 6 & 7)
●Response at manger: Wonder that Christ is so lowly (121–5)
Doch wie erblickt es dich in deiner Krippe?
Yet how sees it thee in thy crib?
{Yet what does it find in thy crib?}

Es seufzt mein Herz:
(Now) sighs my heart:

mit bebender und fast geschloßner Lippe
with tremulous and almost closed lips

Bringt es sein dankend Opfer dar.
Brings it its grateful offering - .
{It brings its grateful offering.}

Gott, der so unermeßlich war,
God, who so boundless was,

Nimmt Knechtsgestalt und Armut an.
Takes-upon-himself (a) servant's-form and poverty - .

Und weil er dieses uns zugutgetan,
And because he this for-our benefit-has-done,
{And because he has done this for our benefit,}

So lasset mit der Engel Chören
So let with the angel choirs

Ein jauchzend Lob- und Danklied hören!
A jubilant praise and thanksgiving-song be-heard!

6. Chorale (Vs. 8)
●Response at manger: Worshipful doxology (121–6)
Lob, Ehr und Dank sei dir gesagt,
Praise, honor, and thanks be to-thee (given),

Christ, geborn von der reinen Magd,
Christ, born of the pure maiden,

Samt Vater und dem Heilgen Geist
With Father and the Holy Ghost

Von nun an bis in Ewigkeit.
From now on until eternity.

Lk. 2:27–31. When the parents brought in the child Jesus...[Simeon] took him up in his arms and blessed God and said, "Lord, now lettest thou thy servant depart in peace, according to thy word; for mine eyes have seen thy salvation which thou hast prepared in the presence of all peoples."
Rom. 3:24–25. ...Christ Jesus, whom God put forward...to be received by faith.
*Lk. 2:16. [The shepherds] went with haste, and found Mary and Joseph, and the babe lying in a manger.
Mt. 22:37. ...You shall love the Lord...with all your heart...
1 Jn. 2:15. Do not love the world or the things in the world. If any one loves the world, love for the Father is not in him.
Jms. 4:4. ...Do you not know that friendship with the world is enmity with God? Therefore whoever wishes to be a friend of the world makes himself an enemy of God.

Lk. 2:7. [Mary] gave birth to her first-born son and wrapped him in swaddling cloths, and laid him in a manger, because there was no place for them in the inn.
Lk. 2:9–14, *15–16. An angel of the Lord appeared to [the shepherds], and the glory of the Lord shone around them, and they were filled with fear. And the angel said to them, "Be not afraid; for behold, I bring you good news of a great joy which will come to all the people; for to you is born this day in the city of David a Savior, who is Christ the Lord. And this will be a sign for you: you will find a babe wrapped in swaddling cloths and lying in a manger." And suddenly there was with the angel a multitude of the heavenly host praising God and saying, "Glory to God in the highest, and on earth peace among men with whom he is pleased!" [*Lk. 2:15–16]. When the angels went away from them into heaven, the shepherds said to one another, "Let us go over to Bethlehem and see this thing that has happened, which the Lord has made known to us." And they went with haste, and found Mary and Joseph, and the babe lying in a manger.
Phil. 2:7. [Christ] emptied himself, taking the form of a servant, being born in the likeness of men.
2 Cor. 8:9. You know the grace of our Lord Jesus Christ, that though he was rich, yet for your sake he became poor, so that by his poverty you might become rich.
Mt. 2:1, 11. Now when Jesus was born in Bethlehem of Judea in the days of Herod the king, behold, wise men from the East...and going into the house they saw the child with Mary his mother, and they fell down and worshiped him. Then, opening their treasures, they offered him gifts, gold and frankincense and myrrh.

Mt. 2:11. Going into the house [the wise men] saw the child with Mary his mother, and they fell down and worshiped him.
Lk. 2:14. Glory to God in the highest...!
Ps. 41:13. Blessed be the Lord, the God of Israel, from everlasting to everlasting! Amen and Amen. (Doxology: also Ps. 72:19, 89:52, 106:48, 150:6, Rom. 11:36)
Ps. 113:2. Blessed be the name of the Lord from this time forth and for evermore.
2 Cor. 9:15. Thanks be to God for his inexpressible gift!
Ps. 115:18. We will bless the Lord from this time forth and for evermore. Praise the Lord! (Also Dan. 2:20.)

BWV 122
Das neugeborne Kindelein
(NBA I/3; BC A19)

1. S. after Christmas (BWV 152, 122, 28)
*Gal. 4:1–7 (Through Christ we come of age and are free from the law)
*Lk. 2:33–40 (Simeon and Hanna prophesy of Christ)
Librettist: Unknown

1. Chorus (Chorale Vs. 1)
●Christ's birth brings a new year to Christendom (122-1)
Das neugeborne Kindelein,
The   new-born   little-child,

Das herzeliebe Jesulein
The   darling   little-Jesus

Bringt abermal ein neues Jahr
Brings once-again a   new   year
{Once again brings a new year}

Der auserwählten Christenschar.
To-the   chosen   Christian-throng.

2. Bass Aria (Based on Chorale Vs. 2)
●Christ's birth: Reconciling sinful mankind to God (122-2)
O Menschen, die ihr täglich sündigt,
O   people, you-who daily do-sin,

Ihr sollt der Engel Freude sein.
You shall the angels' joy   be.
{You shall be the angels' joy.}

Ihr jubilierendes Geschrei,
Their jubilant   shouting,

Daß Gott mit euch versöhnet sei,
That God with you reconciled be,
{That God has been reconciled with you,}

Hat euch den süßen   Trost   verkündigt.
Has to-you this sweet consolation made-known.
{Has made this sweet consolation known to you.}

3. Soprano Recit. (Based on Chorale Vs. 2)
●Christ's birth restores our relations with heaven (122-3)
Die Engel, welche sich   zuvor
The angels, who themselves previously
{The angels, who previously}

Vor euch als vor Verfluchten scheuen,
From you as from cursed-ones shied,
{Shied away from you as from cursed ones,}

Heb. 9:15. [Christ] is the mediator of a new covenant...
2 Cor. 5:17. ...The old has passed away, behold, the new has come.
Gal. 3:23–26. Now before faith came, we were confined under the law, kept under restraint until faith should be revealed. So that the law was our custodian until Christ came, that we might be justified by faith. But now that faith has come, we are no longer under a custodian; for in Christ Jesus you are all sons of God, through faith.
***Gal. 4:4–7.** When the time had fully come, God sent forth his Son, born of woman, born under the law, to redeem those who were under the law, so that we might receive adoption as sons. And because you are sons, God has sent the Spirit of his Son into our hearts, crying, "Abba! Father!" So through God you are no longer a slave but a son, and if a son then an heir.
1 Pet. 2:9–10. You are a chosen race, a royal priesthood, a holy nation, God's own people, that you may declare the wonderful deeds of him who called you out of darkness into his marvelous light. Once you were no people but now you are God's people; once you had not received mercy but now you have received mercy. (Also Tit. 2:14.)

Rom. 3:10–12, 23. As it is written: "None is righteous, no, not one; no one understands, no one seeks for God. All have turned aside, together they have gone wrong; no one does good, not even one." ... All have sinned and fall short of the glory of God. (Also Ps. 14:1–3, Jer. 17:9.)
Rom. 5:20. ...But where sin increased, grace abounded all the more.
Lk. 15:7, 10. ...There will be more joy in heaven over one sinner who repents than over ninety-nine righteous persons who need no repentance...There is joy before the angels of God over one sinner who repents. (Also Mt. 18:12–14.)
2 Cor. 5:18–19. All this is from God, who through Christ reconciled us to himself...that is in Christ God was reconciling the world to himself, not counting their trespasses against them, and entrusting to us the message of reconciliation... (Also Rom. 5:10, Col. 1:21–22.)
Lk. 2:13–14. Suddenly there was with the angel a multitude of the heavenly host praising God and saying, "Glory to God in the highest, and on earth peace among men with whom he is pleased!"

Heb. 1:14. Are [angels] not all ministering spirits sent forth to serve, for the sake of those who are to obtain salvation?
Lk. 2:13–14. Suddenly there was with the angel a multitude of the heavenly host praising God and saying, "Glory to God in the highest, and on earth peace among men with whom he is pleased!"
///
Gen. 3:22–24. [After Adam and Eve had sinned,] the Lord God said, "Behold, the man has become like one of us, knowing good and evil; and now, lest he put forth his hand and take also of the tree of life,

Erfüllen nun die Luft im   höhern   Chor,
Fill   now the air in-the (heavenly) choir,
{Now fill the air in the heavenly choir,}

Um über euer Heil sich zu erfreuen.
 - Over your Salvation - to rejoice.
{To rejoice over your salvation.}

Gott, so   euch aus dem Paradies
God, who (did) you out-of - paradise,
{God, who cast you out of paradise,}

Aus englischer Gemeinschaft stieß,
Out-of angelic   communion   cast,
{And communion with angels,}

Läßt euch nun wiederum auf Erden
Lets you now again   on earth

Durch seine Gegenwart vollkommen selig werden:
Through his   presence   perfectly blessed become:
{Now, by his presence, lets you become perfectly blessed again on earth:}

So danket   nun mit vollem Munde
So thank (him) now with full (voice)

Für die gewünschte Zeit im neuen Bunde.
For (this) longed-for age in-the new covenant.

---

and eat, and live for ever"—therefore the Lord God sent him forth from the garden of Eden...He drove out the man; and at the east of the garden of Eden he placed the cherubim, and a flaming sword which turned every way, to guard the way to the tree of life.
Is. 59:2. Your iniquities have made a separation between you and your God, and your sins have hid his face from you...
///
1 Pet. 1:10–12. The prophets who prophesied of the grace that was to be yours searched and inquired about this salvation; they inquired what person or time was indicated by the Spirit of Christ within them when predicting the sufferings of Christ and the subsequent glory. It was revealed to them that they were serving not themselves but you, in the things which have now been announced to you by those who preached the good news to you through the Holy Spirit sent from heaven, things into which angels long to look. (Also Rom. 16:25–26, Eph. 3:4–6, 9, Col. 1:26.)
Lk. 1:68–69. Blessed be the Lord God of Israel, for he has visited and redeemed his people, and has raised up a horn of salvation for us...
Zech. 2:10–11. Sing and rejoice, and I will dwell in the midst of you, says the Lord. (Also Zech. 2:11, Ezek. 43:9.)
Jn. 1:14. [In Christ] the Word became flesh and dwelt among us, full of grace and truth; we have beheld his glory, glory as of the only Son from the Father. (Also Mt. 1:23.)
Ps. 71:8. [O Lord,] my mouth is filled with thy praise, and with thy glory all the day. (Also Ps. 34:1, 40:3, 51:15, 63:3, 109:30, 145:21, Heb. 13:15.)
Lk. 1:68–70, 72–73. Blessed be the Lord God of Israel, for he has visited and redeemed his people, and has raised up a horn of salvation for us...as he spoke by the mouth of his holy prophets from of old...to perform the mercy promised to our fathers, and to remember his holy covenant, the oath which he swore to our father Abraham.
Heb. 12:24. ...Jesus [is the] mediator of a new covenant... (Also Jer. 31:31, 1 Cor. 11:25, Heb. 8:8–9, 13.)
Lk. 22:20. ...[Jesus took] the cup after supper, saying, "This cup which is poured out for you is the new covenant in my blood."
Heb. 9:15. Therefore [Christ] is the mediator of a new covenant, so that those who are called may receive the promised eternal inheritance, since a death has occurred which redeems them from the transgressions under the first covenant.
2 Cor. 5:17. Therefore, if any one is in Christ, he is a new creation; the old has passed away, behold, the new has come.

---

4. Soprano, Alto & Tenor Trio with Alto Chorale (Vs. 3)
●Reconciled with God: now Satan can not harm us (122-4)
Ist Gott   versöhnt   und unser Freund,
(If) God (is) reconciled (with us) and (is) our   friend,

O   wohl   uns, die wir an ihn glauben,
O (how) well (it is) for-us, who - in him believe;

Was kann uns tun der arge Feind?
What can to-us do the evil   foe?
{What can the evil foe do to us?}

Sein Grimm kann   unsern Trost   nicht rauben;
His fury   can (us of) our consolation not   rob;

Rom. 8:31. What then shall we say to this? If God is for us, who is against us? (Also Ps. 27:1, 118:6.)
Ps. 2:1. Why do the nations conspire, and the peoples plot in vain? (Also Ps. 2:2–4, Acts 4:25–28.)
Col. 1:21–22. You, who once were estranged and hostile in mind, doing evil deeds, [Christ] has now reconciled in his body of flesh by his death... (Also 1 Pet. 3:18.)
Jn. 15:15 [Christ]: No longer do I call you servants, for the servant does not know what his master is doing; but I have called you friends... (Also Heb. 2:11.)
Jn. 3:16. God so loved the world that he gave his only Son, that whoever believes in him should not perish but have eternal life.
1 Jn. 3:8. ...The reason the Son of God appeared was to destroy the works of the devil. (Also Heb. 2:14.)

Trotz Teufel und der Höllen Pfort,
(We mouth) defiance (to) devil and - hell's gates,

Ihr Wüten wird sie wenig nützen,
Their raging will them little profit,
{Their raging will profit them little,}

Das Jesulein ist unser Hort.
The Jesus-child is our refuge.

Gott ist mit uns und will uns schützen.
God is with us and will us protect.
{God is with us and will protect us.}

5. Bass Recit. (Related to Chorale Vs. 4)
●Christ's birth: the long-awaited day has come! (122-5)
Dies ist ein Tag, den selbst der Herr gemacht,
This is a day, which himself the Lord has-made,

Der seinen Sohn in diese Welt gebracht.
Who his Son into this world has-brought.
{Who brought his Son into this world.}

O selge Zeit, die nun erfüllt!
O blessed time, which now is-fulfilled!

O gläubigs Warten, das nunmehr gestillt!
O faith-filled waiting, which henceforth (is-satisfied!)

O Glaube, der sein Ende sieht!
O Faith, which its goal sees!
{O Faith, which sees its goal!}

O Liebe, die Gott zu sich zieht!
O Love, which God to itself draws!

O Freudigkeit, so durch die Trübsal dringt
O joyousness, which through - tribulation presses

Und Gott der Lippen Opfer bringt!
And to-God (its) lips' offering brings!

6. Chorale (Vs. 4)
●Christ's birth begins true year of Jubilee, rejoice! (122-6)
Es bringt das rechte Jubeljahr,
(This) brings the true Jubilee-year,

Was trauern wir denn immerdar?
Why grieve we then evermore?

Frisch auf! itzt ist es Singenszeit,
Quickly rise! Now is it time-for-singing,

1 Pet. 5:8. ...Your adversary the devil prowls around like a roaring lion, seeking some one to devour.
Mt. 16:18 [Christ]: ...I will build my church, and the powers of death (Luther: Pforten der Hölle) shall not prevail against it.
2 Sam. 22:2-3. ...The Lord is my rock (Luther: Fels), and my fortress, and my deliverer, my God, my rock (Luther: Hort), in whom I take refuge... (Hort: also 1 Sam. 2:2, 2 Sam. 22:32, 23:3, Ps. 18:2, 31, 46, 19:14)
Mt. 1:22-23. All this took place to fulfil what the Lord had spoken by the prophet: "Behold, a virgin shall conceive and bear a son, and his name shall be called Emmanuel" (which means, God with us). (See Is. 7:14.)

Ps. 118:24. This is the day which the Lord has made; let us rejoice and be glad in it. (Also Ps. 126:2-3.)
*Gal. 4:4-5. When the time had fully come, God sent forth his Son, born of woman, born under the law, to redeem those who were under the law, so that we might receive adoption as sons. (Also Jn. 3:16-17, 1 Jn. 4:9-10.)
Is. 25:9. It will be said on that day, "Lo, this is our God; we have waited for him, that he might save us..."
Lk. 2:25-26. 28-31. Now there was a man in Jerusalem, whose name was Simeon, and this man was righteous and devout, looking for the consolation of Israel, and the Holy Spirit was upon him. And it had been revealed to him by the Holy Spirit that he should not see death before he had seen the Lord's Christ...He took [the child Jesus] up in his arms and blessed God and said, "Lord, now lettest thou thy servant depart in peace, according to thy word; for mine eyes have seen thy salvation which thou hast prepared in the presence of all peoples." (Also Mt. 13:17, 1 Pet. 1:10-12.)
*Lk. 2:38. And coming up at that very hour [Anna] gave thanks to God, and spoke of him to all who were looking for the redemption of Jerusalem.
Ps. 30:5. ...Weeping may tarry for the night, but joy comes with the morning.
Heb. 13:15. Through him [Christ], let us continually offer up a sacrifice of praise to God, that is, the fruit of lips that acknowledge his name. (Also Ps. 50:14, 23, Ps. 51:15-17.)

Lev. 25:10-12. You shall hallow the fiftieth year, and proclaim liberty throughout the land to all its inhabitants; it shall be a jubilee for you, when each of you shall return to his property and each of you shall return to his family. A jubilee shall that fiftieth year be to you; in it you shall neither sow, nor reap what grows of itself, nor gather the grapes from the undressed vines. For it is a jubilee; it shall be holy to you...
Ps. 102:13. ...It is the time to favor [Zion]; the appointed time has come.
Ps. 57:8-10. Awake, my soul! Awake, O harp and lyre! I will awake the dawn! I will give thanks to thee, I will sing praises to thee among the nations. For thy steadfast love is great to the heavens, thy faithfulness to the clouds. (Also Ps. 108:1-4.)
Rom. 8:38-39. I am sure that neither death, nor life, nor angels, nor principalities, nor things present, nor things to come, nor powers, nor

Das Jesulein wendt alles Leid.
The Jesus-child turns all sorrow (into joy).

BWV 123
Liebster Immanuel, Herzog der Frommen
(NBA I/5; BC A28)

Epiphany (BWV 65, 123, 248-VI, [200])
*Is. 60:1–6 (Prophecy: the Lord will shine upon you and nations will come to your light)
*Mt. 2:1–12 (The Magi come from the East)
Librettist: Unknown

1. Chorus (Chorale Vs. 1)
●Emmanuel: Heavenly prince has captured my heart (123-1)
Liebster Immanuel, Herzog der Frommen,
Dearest Emmanuel, (prince) of-the righteous,

Du, meiner Seelen Heil, komm, komm nur bald!
Thou, my soul's salvation, come, come - soon!

Du hast mir, höchster Schatz, mein Herz genommen,
Thou hast - , (O) highest treasure, my heart captured,
{O highest treasure, thou hast captured my heart,}

So ganz vor Liebe brennt und nach dir wallt.
Which entirely with love burns and for thee wells-up.
{Which burns with love and wells up with longing for thee.}

Nichts kann auf Erden
Nothing can on earth

Mir liebers werden,
To-me dearer become,
{Become dearer to me,}

Als wenn ich meinen Jesum stets behalt.
Than that I my Jesus ever may-keep.

2. Alto Recit. (Based on Chorale Vs. 2)
●Heaven's manna delights me now on earth already (123-2)
Die Himmelssüßigkeit, der Auserwählten Lust
(He-who-is) heaven's-sweetness, the chosen-ones' delight,

Erfüllt auf Erden schon mein Herz und Brust,
Fills (now) on earth already my heart and breast,
{Fills my heart and breast now on earth already,}

Wenn ich den Jesusnamen nenne
If I the name-of-Jesus speak

Und sein verborgnes Manna kenne:
And his hidden manna know:

height, nor depth, nor anything else in all creation, will be able to separate us from the love of God in Christ Jesus our Lord.
Jer. 31:13–14 [God]: ...I will turn their mourning into joy (Luther: Trauern in Freude verkehren)... (Also Jn. 16:20.)

Mt. 1:23. Behold, a virgin shall conceive and bear a son, and his name shall be called Emmanuel (which means, God with us). (See Is. 7:14.)
*Mt. 2:1–2, 7–11. Now when Jesus was born in Bethlehem of Judea in the days of Herod the king, behold, wise men from the East came to Jerusalem, saying, "Where is he who has been born king of the Jews? For we have seen his star in the East, and have come to worship him." ...Then Herod summoned the wise men secretly and ascertained from them what time the star appeared; and he sent them to Bethlehem, saying, "Go and search diligently for the child, and when you have found him bring me word, that I too may come and worship him." When they had heard the king they went their way; and lo, the star which they had seen in the East went before them, till it came to rest over the place where the child was. When they saw the star, they rejoiced exceedingly with great joy; and going into the house they saw the child with Mary his mother, and they fell down and worshiped him. Then, opening their treasures, they offered him gifts, gold and frankincense and myrrh.
*Is. 60:1, 3–4, 6. Arise, shine; for your light has come, and the glory of the Lord has risen upon you...Nations shall come to your light, and kings to the brightness of your rising. Lift up your eyes round about, and see; they all gather together, they come to you...They shall bring gold and frankincense, and shall proclaim the praise of the Lord.
Mt. 22:37. ...You shall love the Lord your God with all your heart...
S. of S. 4:9 [Bridegroom]: You have ravished my heart (Luther: du hast mir das Herz genommen), my sister, my bride, you have ravished my heart with a glance of your eyes...
Ps. 73:25. [O Lord,] whom have I in heaven but thee? And there is nothing upon earth that I desire besides thee.

Ex. 16:13–15, 31, 35. ...In the morning dew lay round about the camp [of the Israelites]. And when the dew had gone up, there was on the face of the wilderness a fine, flake-like thing, fine as hoarfrost on the ground. When the people of Israel saw it, they said to one another, "What is it?"...And Moses said to them, "It is the bread which the Lord has given you to eat."...Now the house of Israel called its name manna; it was like coriander seed, white, and the taste of it was like wafers made with honey...And the people of Israel ate the manna forty years, till they came to a habitable land; they ate the manna, till they came to the border of the land of Canaan. (Also Ps. 78:23–25, Hos. 14:5.)
Rev. 2:17 [Christ]: ...To him who conquers I will give some of the hidden manna...
Jn. 6:30–32, 35. They said to [Jesus], "...What sign do you do, that we may see, and believe you? What work do you perform? Our fathers

Gleichwie der Tau ein dürres Land erquickt,
Just-as   the dew   a parched land   revives,
{Just as the dew revives a parched land,}

So ist mein Herz
So is my heart

Auch bei Gefahr und Schmerz
Even in peril   and   pain

In Freudigkeit durch Jesu Kraft entzückt.
To joyfulness through Jesus' power transported.
{Transported to bliss through Jesus' power.}

3. Tenor Aria (Based on Chorale Vs. 3)
●Storms of life do not frighten me, Jesus sends aid (123-3)
Auch die harte Kreuzesreise
Even the hard journey-of-the-cross

Und der Tränen bittre Speise
And -   tears' bitter fare
{And the bitter fare of tears}

Schreckt mich nicht.
Frighten me   not.
{Do not frighten me.}

Wenn die Ungewitter toben,
When the tempests   rage, (then)

Sendet Jesus mir von oben
Sends Jesus to-me from above
{Jesus sends to me from above}

Heil   und Licht.
Salvation and light.

4. Bass Recit. (Based on Chorale Vs. 4)
●Victory over hell and death is assured in Jesus (123-4)
Kein Höllenfeind kann mich verschlingen,
No   foe-from-hell can me   devour,
{No foe from hell can devour me,}

Das schreiende Gewissen   schweigt.
(My) crying   consience has-become-still.

Was sollte mich der Feinde Zahl umringen?
How should me the foe's number surround?
{How should the foe's host surround me?}

Der Tod hat selbsten keine Macht,
 - Death has itself   no   power,
{Death itself has no power,}

ate the manna in the wilderness..." Jesus then said to them, "Truly, truly, I say to you, it was not Moses who gave you the bread from heaven; my Father gives you the true bread from heaven..I am the bread of life; he who comes to me shall not hunger, and he who believes in me shall never thirst."
Hos. 14:5 [God]: I will be as the dew to Israel; he shall blossom as the lily, he shall strike root as the poplar.
Ps. 34:8. O taste and see that the Lord is good! Happy is the man who takes refuge in him!
Rom. 8:35, 38–39. Who shall separate us from the love of Christ? Shall tribulation, or distress, or persecution, or famine, or nakedness, or peril, or sword?...I am sure that neither death, nor life, nor angels, nor principalities, nor things present, nor things to come, nor powers, nor height, nor depth, nor anything else in all creation, will be able to separate us from the love of God in Christ Jesus our Lord.

Mt. 10:38 [Christ]: He who does not take his cross and follow me is not worthy of me. (Also Mt. 16:24, Mk. 8:34, Lk. 9:23.)
Mt. 5:4 [Christ]: Blessed are those who mourn, for they shall be comforted.
Ps. 42:3. My tears have been my food day and night, while men say to me continually, "Where is your God?"
Is. 43:1–2. ...Thus says the Lord..."Fear not, for I have redeemed you; I have called you by name, you are mine. When you pass through the waters I will be with you; and through the rivers, they shall not overwhelm you..."
1 Pet. 4:12. Beloved, do not be surprised at the fiery ordeal which comes upon you to prove you, as though something strange were happening to you. (Also Jms. 1:2–4, 12, 1 Pet. 5:10, 2 Tim. 3:12.)
2 Cor. 12:10. For the sake of Christ, then, I am content with weaknesses, insults, hardships, persecutions, and calamities; for when I am weak, then I am strong. (Also Rom. 8:35–39, 2 Cor. 4:7–10, 12.)
Ps. 27:1. The Lord is my light (Luther: Licht) and my salvation (Luther: Heil); whom shall I fear? The Lord is the stronghold of my life; of whom shall I be afraid? (Also Is. 49:6, Acts 13:47.)
*****Is. 60:1–22.** ...Your light has come...

1 Pet. 5:8. ...Your adversary the devil prowls around like a roaring lion, seeking some one to devour (Luther: verschlinge).
Eph. 6:12. We are not contending against flesh and blood, but against the principalities, against the powers, against the world rulers of this present darkness, against the spiritual hosts of wickedness in the heavenly places.
Rom. 8:33. Who shall bring any charge against God's elect? It is God who justifies.
1 Jn. 4:17. In this is love perfected with us, that we may have confidence for the day of judgment...
Ps. 27:3. Though a host encamp against me, my heart shall not fear; though war arise against me, yet I will be confident. (Also Ps. 118:6.)
Is. 25:8. He will swallow up death for ever... (Also 2 Tim. 1:10, Heb. 2:14.)
1 Cor. 15:54–57. When the perishable puts on the imperishable, and

Mir   aber ist der Sieg schon zugedacht,
For-me, however, is the victory already (assured),
{For me, the victory is already assured,}

Weil sich mein Helfer mir, mein Jesus, zeigt.
For himself my Helper to-me, my Jesus, shows.
{Since Jesus, my Helper, shows himself to me.}

5. Bass Aria (Based on Chorale Vs. 5)
●World rejects me, I reject it in favor of Christ (123-5)
Laß, o Welt, mich aus Verachtung
Leave, O world, me (out of) disdain
{O world, in thy disdain, leave me}

In betrübter Einsamkeit!
In sorrowful loneliness!

Jesus, der ins Fleisch gekommen
Jesus, who in-the flesh   has-come
{Jesus, who has come in the flesh}

Und mein Opfer angenommen,
And my offering   accepted,
{And accepted my offering,}

Bleibet bei mir allezeit.
Stays   with me for-all-time.

6. Chorale (Vs. 6)
●Rejecting world and yielding life to Christ (123-6)
Drum   fahrt nur immer hin, ihr Eitelkeiten,
Therefore depart - evermore - , ye vain-conceits,

Du, Jesus, du bist mein, und ich bin dein;
Thou, Jesus, thou art mine, and I   am thine;

Ich will mich von der Welt zu dir bereiten;
I would -   from the world to thee (turn);

Du sollst in meinem Herz und Munde sein.
Thou shalt in   my   heart and mouth be.

Mein ganzes Leben
My   entire life

Sei dir ergeben,
Be to-thee surrendered,

the mortal puts on immortality, then shall come to pass the saying that is written: "Death is swallowed up in victory." O death, where is thy victory? O death, where is thy sting? The sting of death is sin, and the power of sin is the law. But thanks be to God, who gives us the victory through our Lord Jesus Christ.
Rom. 8:37. In all these things we are more than conquerors through him who loved us.

Jms. 4:4. Unfaithful creatures! Do you not know that friendship with the world is enmity with God? Therefore whoever wishes to be a friend of the world makes himself an enemy of God. (Also 1 Jn. 2:15–17.)
Jn. 15:18–19 [Christ]: If the world hates you, know that it has hated me before it hated you. If you were of the world, the world would love its own; but because you are not of the world, but I chose you out of the world, therefore the world hates you. (Also Jn. 17:14, Mt. 5:10–12, 10:24–25, 1 Jn. 3:13.)
Heb. 4:15–16. [In Christ] we have not a high priest who is unable to sympathize with our weaknesses, but one who in every respect has been tempted as we are, yet without sin. Let us then with confidence draw near to the throne of grace, that we may receive mercy and find grace to help in time of need.
Jn. 1:14. The Word became flesh and dwelt among us... (Also Rom. 8:3, Heb. 2:14, 1 Tim. 3:16.)
Rom. 12:1. I appeal to you therefore, brethren, by the mercies of God, to present your bodies as a living sacrifice, holy and acceptable to God, which is your spiritual worship.
*Mt. 2:11. ...Opening their treasures, [the wise men] offered him gifts, gold and frankincense and myrrh. (Also *Is. 60:5–6.)
Ps. 51:17. The sacrifice acceptable to God is a broken spirit; a broken and contrite heart, O God, thou wilt not despise.

1 Jn. 2:15–17. Do not love the world or the things in the world. If any one loves the world, love for the Father is not in him. For all that is in the world, the lust of the flesh and the lust of the eyes and the pride of life, is not of the Father but is of the world. And the world passes away, and the lust of it; but he who does the will of God abides for ever. (Also Jms. 4:4.)
Mt. 22:37. ...You shall love the Lord your God with all your heart...
S. of S. 6:3 [Bride]: I am my beloved's and my beloved is mine...
Mt. 4:4. ...Man shall not live by bread alone, but by every word that proceeds from the mouth of God. (See Deut. 8:3, also Lk. 4:4.)
Deut. 30:14. The word is very near you; it is in your mouth and in your heart, so that you can do it.
Rom. 10:9. If you confess with your lips (Luther: Munde) that Jesus is Lord and believe in your heart that God raised him from the dead, you will be saved. (Also Rom. 10:10.)
Ps. 19:14. [O Lord,] let the words of my mouth and the meditation of my heart be acceptable in thy sight...
Ps. 71:8. My mouth is filled with thy praise... (Also Ps. 34:1, 40:3, 51:15, 63:3, 109:30, 145:21, Heb. 13:15.)
Rom. 12:1. I appeal to you therefore, brethren, by the mercies of God, to present your bodies as a living sacrifice, holy and acceptable to God, which is your spiritual worship. (Also 1 Cor. 6:19–20, 1 Cor. 3:16; 7:23.)

Bis man mich einsten legt ins Grab hinein.
Until one me some-day lays in-the grave -.
{Until someday they lay me in the grave.}

BWV 124
Meinen Jesum laß ich nicht
(NBA I/5; BC A30)

1. S. after Epiphany (BWV 154, 124, 32)
*Rom. 12:1–6[1] (Christian duty: present yourselves as living sacrifices to God)
*Lk. 2:41–52 (The twelve-year-old Jesus in the temple)
[1]End: "given to us."
Librettist: Unknown

1. Chorus (Chorale Vs. 1)
●Clinging to Jesus so not to lose him (124–1)
Meinen Jesum laß ich nicht,
My Jesus relinquish I not,
{I will not let my Jesus go,}

Weil er sich für mich gegeben,
Since he himself for me did-give,
{Since he gave himself for me,}

So erfordert meine Pflicht,
Thus demands my duty,
{Thus I am obliged}

Klettenweis an ihm zu kleben.
Vine-like to him to (cling).
{Vine-like to cling to him.}

Er ist meines Lebens Licht,
He is my life's light,

Meinen Jesum laß ich nicht.
My Jesus relinquish I not.
{I will not let my Jesus go.}

2. Tenor Recit. (Based on Chorale Vs. 2)
●Clinging to Jesus in life: Giving him all I am (124–2)
Solange sich ein Tropfen Blut
As-long-as - (yet) a drop of-blood

In Herz und Adern reget,
In (my) heart and veins does-stir,

Soll Jesus nur allein
Shall Jesus - alone

Mein Leben und mein alles sein.
My life and my all be.
{Be my life and my all.}

2 Cor. 5:9. Whether we are at home or away, we make it our aim to please him. (Also Eph. 5:10, Rom. 14:8.)
Phil. 1:20–21. ...That...Christ will be honored in my body, whether by life or by death. For to me to live is Christ, and to die is gain. (Also 2 Cor. 5:8.)

Gen. 32:26. ...I will not let you go, unless you bless me.
Jn. 6:68. Simon Peter answered [Jesus], "Lord, to whom shall we go? You have the words of eternal life..."
Gal. 2:20. ...It is no longer I who live, but Christ who lives in me; and the life I now live in the flesh I live by faith in the Son of God who loved me and gave himself for me. (gave himself: also Gal. 1:3–4, Eph. 5:2, 25, 1 Tim. 2:6, Tit. 2:14)
Ps. 63:8. [O Lord,] my soul clings to thee (Luther: hanget dir an)...
*Lk. 2:41–46. Now [Jesus'] parents went to Jerusalem every year at the feast of the Passover. And when he was twelve years old, they went up according to custom; and when the feast was ended, as they were returning, the boy Jesus stayed behind in Jerusalem. His parents did not know it, but supposing him to be in the company they went a day's journey, and they sought him among their kinsfolk and acquaintances; and when they did not find him, they returned to Jerusalem, seeking him. After three days they found him in the temple...
S. of S. 3:4. ...I found him whom my soul loves. I held him, and would not let him go...
Ps. 27:1. The Lord is my light and my salvation...The Lord is the stronghold of my life...
Jn. 8:12. Jesus spoke to them, saying, "I am the light of the world; he who follows me will not walk in darkness, but will have the light of life (Luther: Licht des Lebens)." (Also Jn. 1:4, 9:5, 11:9, 12:46, Ps. 36:9.)
Mt. 26:33. Peter declared to [Jesus], "Though they all fall away because of you, I will never fall away." (Also Mk. 14:29, Lk. 22:33–34.)

Mt. 22:37. ...You shall love the Lord your God with all your heart, and with all your soul, and with all your mind. (Also Mk. 12:30–31, Lk. 10:27, Deut. 6:5.)
Mt. 4:10. ...You shall worship the Lord your God and him only shall you serve. (Also Lk. 4:8, Deut. 6:13–14.)
2 Cor. 5:9. ...We make it our aim to please him. (Also Rom. 14:8.)
Phil. 1:21. To me to live is Christ (Luther: Denn Christus ist mein Leben), and to die is gain.
Josh. 24:15. ...As for me and my house, we will serve the Lord.
Phil. 1:20–21. ...Christ [shall] be honored in my body, whether by life or by death.
Ps. 146:2. I will praise the Lord as long as I live; I will sing praises to my God while I have being. (Also Ps. 146:2.)
Ps. 73:25. [O Lord,] whom have I in heaven but thee? And there is nothing upon earth that I desire besides thee.
Ps. 63:4. So I will bless thee as long as I live...

Mein Jesus, der an mir so große Dinge tut:
My   Jesus, who for me such great things does:
{My Jesus, who does such great things for me:}

Ich kann ja nichts   als meinen Leib und Leben
I   can indeed nothing (less) than my body and life
{I can indeed to nothing less than give my body and life}

Ihm   zum Geschenke geben.
To-him as   present   give.
{To him as present.}

3. Tenor Aria (Based on Chorale Vs. 3)
●Clinging to Jesus in the pangs of death (124–3)
Und wenn der harte Todesschlag
And when the cruel stroke-of-death

Die Sinnen schwächt, die Glieder rühret,
(My) senses weakens, (my) members touches,

Wenn der dem Fleisch verhaßte Tag
When that by-the flesh   hated   day
{When that day hated by the flesh}

Nur Furcht und Schrecken mit sich führet,
Only fear and terror   with it brings,

      Doch   tröstet sich die Zuversicht:
Then-nevertheless comforts (me) this certainty:
{Then this certainty comforts me nevertheless:}

Ich lasse meinen Jesum nicht.
I relinquish my   Jesus not.
{I will not let my Jesus go.}

4. Bass Recit. (Based on Chorale Vs. 4)
●Losing Jesus: Reunion with him after death (124–4)
Doch ach!
Yet   alas!

Welch schweres Ungemach
What   severe   hardship

Empfindet noch allhier die Seele?
Experiences yet here (my) soul?
{Must my soul yet experience here?}

Wird nicht die hart gekränkte Brust
Will not (my) sorely vexed breast

Zu   einer Wüstenei und Marterhöhle
(Become) a   wilderness and den-of-torment

Bei Jesu schmerzlichstem Verlust?
With Jesus' most-grievous   loss?
{With the most grievous loss of Jesus?}

Ps. 116:12. What shall I render to the Lord for all his bounty to me?
Ps. 126:3. The Lord has done great things for us; we are glad. (Also 1 Sam. 12:24, Lk. 1:49.)
*Rom. 12:1. I appeal to you therefore, brethren, by the mercies of God, to present your bodies as a living sacrifice, holy and acceptable to God, which is your spiritual worship.
1 Cor. 6:19–20. Do you not know that your body is a temple of the Holy Spirit within you, which you have from God? You are not your own; you were bought with a price. So glorify God in your body. (Also 1 Cor. 3:16; 7:23.)
Mt. 2:11. ...Going into the house [the wise men] saw the child [Jesus] with Mary his mother, and they fell down and worshiped him. Then, opening their treasures, they offered him gifts, gold and frankincense and myrrh. (Also Is. 60:5–6.)

Ps. 23:4. Even though I walk through the valley of the shadow of death, I fear no evil; for thou art with me...
Heb. 2:14–15. Since therefore the children share in flesh and blood, [Christ] himself likewise partook of the same nature, that through death he might destroy him who has the power of death, that is, the devil, and deliver all those who through fear of death were subject to lifelong bondage.
Is. 43:1–2. ...Thus says the Lord, he who created you, O Jacob, he who formed you, O Israel: "Fear not...When you pass through the waters I will be with you; and through the rivers, they shall not overwhelm you..."
Is. 25:8. He will swallow up death for ever, and the Lord God will wipe away tears from all faces...
2 Cor. 4:14, 16. ...He who raised the Lord Jesus will raise us also with Jesus and bring us...into his presence...So we do not lose heart. Though our outer nature is wasting away, our inner nature is being renewed every day.
Ps. 73:26. My flesh and my heart may fail, but God is the strength of my heart and my portion for ever.
Mt. 28:20 [Christ]: ...Lo, I am with you always to the close of the age. (Also Ps. 48:14.)

Jn. 16:16, 20–22 [Christ]: A little while, and you will see me no more; again a little while, and you will see me...Truly, truly, I say to you, you will weep and lament, but the world will rejoice; you will be sorrowful, but your sorrow will turn into joy. When a woman is in travail she has sorrow, because her hour has come; but when she is delivered of the child, she no longer remembers the anguish, for joy that a child is born into the world. So you have sorrow now, but I will see you again and your hearts will rejoice, and no one will take your joy from you. (Also Jn. 14:28.)
Jn. 14:3 [Christ]: ...I will come again and will take you to myself, that where I am you may be also. (Also Jn. 12:26.)
Rom. 8:18. I consider that the sufferings of this present time are not worth comparing with the glory that is to be revealed to us.
2 Cor. 4:17–18. This slight momentary affliction is preparing for us an eternal weight of glory beyond all comparison, because we look not to the things that are seen but to the things that are unseen; for the things that are seen are transient, but the things that are unseen are eternal. (Also Rom. 8:18.)

Allein mein Geist sieht gläubig auf
But-yet my spirit looks in-faith up
{But yet my spirit looks up in faith}

Und an den Ort, wo Glaub und Hoffnung prangen,
- To the place, where faith and hope shine-resplendent,

Allwo ich nach vollbrachtem Lauf
Where I, after completed course,

Dich, Jesu, ewig soll umfangen.
Thee, Jesus, evermore shall embrace.
{Where I shall evermore embrace thee, Jesus, after completing my course.}

5. Soprano & Alto Duet (Based on Chorale Vs. 5)
●Forsaking the world: Future in heaven with Jesus (124-5)
Entziehe dich eilends, mein Herze, der Welt,
Withdraw - in-haste, my heart, from-the world,
{Withdraw quickly, from the world, O my heart,}

Du findest im Himmel dein wahres Vergnügen.
Thou findest in heaven thy true pleasure.

Wenn künftig dein Auge den Heiland erblickt,
When one-day thine eye (shall) the Savior behold,

So wird erst dein sehnendes Herze erquickt,
Then will at-last thy yearning heart be-refreshed,

So wird es in Jesu zufriedengestellt.
Then will it in Jesus be-made-content.

6. Chorale (Vs. 6) (See also 154-8, 157-5.)
●Clinging to Jesus: Walking with him brings blessing (124-6)
Jesum laß ich nicht von mir,
Jesus let I not from me,
{I'll not let Jesus leave me,}

Geh ihm ewig an der Seiten;
(I'll) go with-him ever at (his) side;

Christus läßt mich für und für
Christ lets me forever and ever

Zu den Lebensbächlein leiten.
To the stream-of-life be-guided.

Selig, der mit mir so spricht:
Blessed (is he) who with me thus says:

Meinen Jesum laß ich nicht.
My Jesus relinquish I not.
{I will not let my Jesus go.}

1 Cor. 13:10, 12. When the perfect comes, the imperfect will pass away ...For now we see in a mirror dimly, but then face to face. **1 Cor. 10:13.** So faith, hope, love abide, these three; but the greatest of these is love. **Ps. 73:25.** [O Lord,] whom have I in heaven but thee?... **2 Tim. 4:6–8.** ...The time of my departure has come. I have fought the good fight, I have finished the race (Luther: Lauf vollendet), I have kept the faith. Henceforth there is laid up for me the crown of righteousness, which the Lord, the righteous judge, will award to me on that Day, and not only to me but also to all who have loved his appearing. **S. of S. 3:4 [Bride]:** ...I found him whom my soul loves. I held him, and would not let him go...

1 Jn. 2:15, 17. Do not love the world or the things in the world. If any one loves the world, love for the Father is not in him...The world passes away, and the lust of it; but he who does the will of God abides for ever. (Also Jms. 4:4.) **Ps. 16:11.** [O Lord]...in thy presence there is fulness of joy, in thy right hand are pleasures for evermore. **Jn. 16:16 [Christ]:** A little while, and you will see me no more; again a little while, and you will see me... **1 Jn. 3:2.** Beloved, we are God's children now; it does not yet appear what we shall be, but we know that when he appears we shall be like him, for we shall see him as he is. (Also 1 Cor. 13:12, Rev. 22:4.) **Rev. 21:3–4.** ... [God] will dwell with them, and they shall be his people, and God himself will be with them; he will wipe away every tear from their eyes, and death shall be no more, neither shall there be mourning nor crying nor pain any more, for the former things have passed away. (Also Rev. 7:15–17, Is. 25:8.)

Gen. 32:26. ...Jacob said, "I will not let you go, unless you bless me." (Also S. of S. 3:4.) **Lk. 9:57.** As they were going along the road, a man said to [Jesus], "I will follow you wherever you go." (Also Mt. 8:19.) **Mic. 6:8.** ...What does the Lord require of you but to...walk humbly with your God? **Ps. 23:1–3.** The Lord is my shepherd... He leads me beside still waters; he restores my soul. He leads me in paths of righteousness for his name's sake. (Also Ezek. 34:15.) **Rev. 7:17.** The Lamb in the midst of the throne will be their shepherd, and he will guide them to springs of living water; and God will wipe away every tear from their eyes. **Jn. 4:13–14.** Jesus said, "...Whoever drinks of the water that I shall give him will never thirst; the water that I shall give him will become in him a spring of water welling up to eternal life." (Also Jn. 4:10–11, 7:37–39, Is. 12:3, Rev. 21:6, 22:1, 22:17.) **Ezek. 34:31.** You are my sheep, the sheep of my pasture, and I am your God, says the Lord God. (Also Ezek. 34:11, 15, Ps. 95:6–7, 100:3, Heb. 13:20.) **Jer. 17:7.** Blessed is the man who trusts in the Lord, whose trust is the Lord. **Josh. 24:16.** The people answered, "Far be it from us that we should forsake the Lord, to serve other gods." **Phil. 1:21.** To me to live is Christ, and to die is gain.

BWV 125
Mit Fried und Freud ich fahr dahin
(NBA I/28; BC A168)

Mary's Purification (Candlemas) (BWV 83, 125, 82, 157, 158, [161], [200])
*Mal. 3:1–4 (The Lord will suddenly come to his temple and purify his people)
*Lk. 2:22–32 (Mary presents Jesus at the temple; Nunc dimittis)
Librettist: Unknown

1. Chorus (Chorale Vs. 1) (See also 95-1, 106-3b.)
●Death is welcomed with peace & joy: Simeon (125-1)
Mit Fried und Freud ich fahr dahin,
With peace and   joy   I depart thither,

In   Gottes Willen,
According-to God's   will,

Getrost ist mir mein Herz und   Sinn,
Consoled is   -   my heart and disposition,

Sanft und stille.
Placid and still.

Wie Gott mir verheißen hat,
As   God me promised has,
{As God promised me,}

Der Tod ist mein Schlaf worden.
  - Death has my   sleep become.
{Death has become sleep for me.}

2. Alto Aria (Related to Chorale Vs. 2)
●Death approaching: I look to Jesus, he looks on me (125-2)
Ich will auch mit gebrochnen Augen
I would also with (failing)   eyes
{Even with failing eyes I would look}

Nach dir, mein treuer Heiland, sehn.
To   thee, my   true   Savior, look.
{To thee, my true Savior.}

Wenngleich des Leibes Bau zerbricht,
Although   (my) body's structure breaks,

Doch fällt mein Herz und Hoffen nicht.
Yet falls my heart and hope not.
{Yet my heart and my hope do not fail.}

Mein Jesus sieht auf mich im   Sterben
My   Jesus looks upon me in (my) dying

Und lässet mir kein Leid geschehn.
And lets me no harm befall.
{And lets no harm befall me.}

*Lk. 2:29. Lord, now lettest thou thy servant depart in peace, according to thy word.
2 Cor. 5:6–9. So we are always of good courage (Luther: getrost); we know that while we are at home in the body we are away from the Lord, for we walk by faith, not by sight. We are of good courage, and we would rather be away from the body and at home with the Lord. So whether we are at home or away, we make it our aim to please him.
Phil. 1:23. ...My desire is to depart and be with Christ, for that is far better.
Ps. 131:2. I have calmed and quieted my soul, like a child quieted at its mother's breast; like a child that is quieted is my soul. (Also Ps. 62:1, 5.)
1 Cor. 15:55. O death, where is thy victory? O death, where is thy sting?
Lk. 8:52–53. ...[Jesus] said, "Do not weep; for she is not dead but sleeping." And they laughed at him, knowing that she was dead.
1 Cor. 15:42, 51–52. So it is with the resurrection of the dead. What is sown is perishable, what is raised is imperishable...Lo! I tell you a mystery. We shall not all sleep, but we shall all be changed, in a moment, in the twinkling of an eye, at the last trumpet...

*Lk. 2:25–32. Now there was a man in Jerusalem, whose name was Simeon, and this man was righteous and devout, looking for the consolation of Israel, and the Holy Spirit was upon him. And it had been revealed to him by the Holy Spirit that he should not see death before he had seen the Lord's Christ. And inspired by the Spirit he came into the temple; and when the parents brought in the child Jesus, to do for him according to the custom of the law, he took him up in his arms and blessed God and said, "Lord, now lettest thou thy servant depart in peace, according to thy word; for mine eyes have seen thy salvation which thou hast prepared in the presence of all peoples, a light for revelation to the Gentiles, and for glory to thy people Israel."
2 Cor. 4:16–17, 5:1. So we do not lose heart. Though our outer nature is wasting away, our inner nature is being renewed every day. For this slight momentary affliction is preparing for us an eternal weight of glory beyond all comparison...For we know that if the earthly tent we live in is destroyed, we have a building (Luther: Bau) from God, a house not made with hands, eternal in the heavens.
Ps. 23:4. Even though I walk through the valley of the shadow of death, I fear no evil; for thou art with me; thy rod and thy staff, they comfort me.

3. Bass Recit. and Chorale (Vs. 2)
●Death not feared: Christ our light & salvation come (125–3)
O Wunder, daß ein Herz
O wonder, that a heart

Vor   der dem Fleisch verhaßten Gruft
Before the   -   flesh-abhorrent   tomb

und gar des Todes Schmerz
and even - death's pangs

Sich nicht entsetzet!
(Is) not alarmed!
{What a wonder that a heart can be unalarmed before the flesh-
abhorrent tomb and even death's pangs!}

Das macht Christus, wahr' Gottes Sohn,
This has-done Christ, true   Son-of-God,
{That Christ has done, the true Son of God,}

Der treue Heiland,
The true Savior,

Der   auf dem Sterbebette schon
He-who on (my)   deathbed   already

Mit Himmelssüßigkeit den Geist ergötzet,
With heaven's-sweetness (my) spirit delights,
{Delights my spirit with heaven's sweetness,}

Den   du mich, Herr, hast sehen lan,
He-whom thou me, Lord, hast   let-see,
{He whom thou, Lord, hast let me see,}

Da in   erfüllter Zeit ein Glaubensarm
When, in (the) fullness-of time, (my) arm-of-faith

das Heil   des Herrn umfinge;
the Salvation of-the Lord did-embrace;
{embraced the Salvation of the Lord;}

Und machst bekannt
And dost-make known
{And thou dost make known to us}

Von   dem erhabnen Gott, dem Schöpfer aller Dinge,
Concerning the   exalted God, the creator of-all things,

Daß er sei das Leben und Heil,
That he is - Life and Salvation,

Der Menschen Trost und Teil,
  - Mankind's consolation and portion,

Ihr   Retter vom Verderben
Their Savior from destruction

*Lk. 2:29–30. Lord, now lettest thou thy servant depart in peace, according to thy word; for mine eyes have seen thy salvation which thou hast prepared.

Heb. 2:14–15. Since therefore the children share in flesh and blood, [Christ] himself likewise partook of the same nature, that through death he might destroy him who has the power of death, that is, the devil, and deliver all those who through fear of death were subject to lifelong bondage.

2 Tim. 1:10. ...Our Savior Christ Jesus...abolished death and brought life and immortality to light...

1 Cor. 15:20, 25–26, 53–55. ...Christ has been raised from the dead, the first fruits of those who have fallen asleep...He must reign until he has put all his enemies under his feet. The last enemy to be destroyed is death...For this perishable nature must put on the imperishable, and this mortal nature must put on immortality. When the perishable puts on the imperishable, and the mortal puts on immortality, then shall come to pass the saying that is written: "Death is swallowed up in victory." O death, where is thy victory? O death, where is thy sting?

Is. 25:8–9. He will swallow up death for ever, and the Lord God will wipe away tears from all faces, and the reproach of his people he will take away from all the earth; for the Lord has spoken. It will be said on that day, "Lo, this is our God; we have waited for him, that he might save us. This is the Lord; we have waited for him; let us be glad and rejoice in his salvation (Luther: Heil)."

Jn. 11:25–26. Jesus said to [Martha], "I am the resurrection and the life; he who believes in me, though he die, yet shall he live, and whoever lives and believes in me shall never die. Do you believe this?"

1 Jn. 5:20. ...We are in him who is true, in his Son Jesus Christ. This is the true God and eternal life. (Also Jn. 17:3.)

Ps. 16:11. [O Lord,] thou dost show me the path of life; in thy presence there is fulness of joy, in thy right hand are pleasures for evermore.

Ps. 94:19. When the cares of my heart are many, thy consolations cheer (Luther: ergötzen) my soul.

Phil. 1:21–23. To me to live is Christ, and to die is gain...

Heb. 4:3, 9. We who have believed enter [God's] rest...So then, there remains a sabbath rest for the people of God.

*Lk. 2:27–31. ...When the parents brought in the child Jesus, to do for him according to the custom of the law, [Simeon] took him up in his arms and blessed God and said, "Lord, now...mine eyes have seen thy salvation which thou hast prepared in the presence of all peoples."

Jn. 14:6. Jesus said... "I am the way, and the truth, and the life; no one comes to the Father, but by me."

Jn. 1:2–4. [Christ] was in the beginning with God; all things were made through him, and without him was not anything made that was made. In him was life, and the life was the light of men. (Also Jn. 8:12, 9:5, 11:9, 12:46, Ps. 36:9.)

Jn. 17:3 [Christ]: This is eternal life, that they know thee the only true God,   and Jesus Christ whom thou hast sent.

Ps. 73:25–26. [O Lord,] whom have I in heaven but thee? And there is nothing upon earth that I desire besides thee. My flesh and my heart may fail, but God is the strength of my heart and my portion (Luther: Trost und Teil) for ever.

Ps. 103:2–3. Bless the Lord, O my soul...who forgives all your iniquity, who heals all your diseases, who redeems your life from the Pit (Luther: dein Leben vom Verderben erlöst)...

Im Tod und auch im Sterben.
In death, and also   in   dying.

Jn. 8:51 [Christ]: Truly, truly, I say to you, if any one keeps my word, he will never see death.

4. Tenor & Bass Duet (Based on Chorale Vs. 3)
●Light fills world; promise of salvation by faith (125-4)
Ein unbegreiflich Licht erfüllt
An incomprehensible light fills

*Lk. 2:30–32. Mine eyes have seen thy salvation which thou hast prepared in the presence of all peoples, a light for revelation to the Gentiles, and for glory to thy people Israel.
Is. 60:1, 3, 19. Arise, shine; for your light has come, and the glory of the Lord has risen upon you...Nations shall come to your light, and kings to the brightness of your rising...The sun shall be no more your light by day...but the Lord will be your everlasting light...
2 Cor. 4:6. It is the God who said, "Let light shine out of darkness," who has shone in our hearts to give the light of the knowledge of the glory of God in the face of Christ. (Also Mal. 4:2.)
Acts 13:32–33. And we bring you the good news that what God promised to the fathers, this he has fulfilled to us their children... (Also Lk. 2:10–11.)
Jn. 3:16. For God so loved the world that he gave his only Son, that whoever believes in him should not perish but have eternal life.
Mk. 16:16. He who believes and is baptized will be saved...

den ganzen Kreis der Erden.
the   entire circle of-the earth.

Es   schallet kräftig fort und fort
(Now) resounds mightily on and on
{Loudly and continuously rings}

Ein höchst erwünscht Verheißungswort:
A most-highly desired   word-of-promise:
{This most highly desired word of promise:

Wer   glaubt, soll selig werden.
Whoever believes, shall saved   be.
{Whoever believes shall be saved.}

5. Alto Recit. (Based on Chorale Vs. 3)
●Mercy seat established, grace extended in Christ (125-5)
O unerschöpfter Schatz der Güte,
O unfathomed treasure of kindness,

Jn. 1:16. From [Christ's] fulness have we all received, grace upon grace.
Eph. 2:7. In the coming ages [God will] show the immeasurable riches of his grace in kindness (Luther: überschwenglichen Reichtum seiner Gnade durch seine Güte) toward us in Christ Jesus.
Rom. 5:6–8. While we were still weak, at the right time Christ died for the ungodly. Why, one will hardly die for a righteous man—though perhaps for a good man one will dare even to die. But God shows his love for us in that while we were yet sinners Christ died for us.
Is. 1:4. Ah, sinful nation, a people laden with iniquity...
Rom. 6:23. The wages of sin is death, but the free gift of God is eternal life in Christ Jesus our Lord.
Rom. 3:23–25. Since all have sinned and fall short of the glory of God, they are justified by his grace (Luther: Gnade) as a gift, through the redemption which is in Christ Jesus, whom God put forward as an expiation (Luther: einem Gnadenstuhl) by his blood, to be received by faith...
Lev. 16:15–16. [To make atonement for sin, the priest] shall kill the goat of the sin offering which is for the people, and bring its blood within the veil...sprinkling it upon the mercy seat (Luther: Gnadenstuhl) and before the mercy seat; thus he shall make atonement for the holy place, because of the uncleanesses of the people of Israel, and because of their transgressions, all their sins...
Heb. 9:11–12. When Christ appeared as a high priest of the good things that have come...he entered once for all into the Holy Place, taking not the blood of goats and calves but his own blood, thus securing an eternal redemption.
1 Jn. 4:10. In this is love, not that we loved God but that he loved us and sent his Son to be the expiation for our sins.
Lk. 2:34. ...[Christ] is set for the fall and rising of many in Israel, and for a sign (Luther: Zeichen)...
Is. 11:10. ...The root of Jesse shall stand as an ensign to the peoples; him shall the nations seek... (Also Is. 11:12.)

So sichs uns Menschen aufgetan:
Which - to-us humans is-disclosed:
{Which is disclosed to us humans:}

es   wird der Welt,
(now) is for-the world—

So   Zorn und Fluch auf sich geladen,
Which wrath and curse upon itself has-loaded—

Ein Stuhl der Gnaden
A   seat of mercy

Und Siegeszeichen aufgestellt,
And symbol-of-victory being-erected,
{Now a seat of mercy and a symbol of victory is being erected for the world, which has earned nothing but wrath and curse.}

Und jedes gläubige Gemüte
And every believing heart

Wird in sein Gnadenreich geladen.
Is into his kingdom-of-grace invited.
{Is invited into his kingdom of grace.}

6. Chorale (Vs. 4) (See also 83–5.)
●Christ is light and salvation for Gentiles (125–6)
Er ist das Heil und selig Licht
He is the salvation and blessed light

Für die Heiden,
For the Gentiles,

Zu erleuchten, die dich kennen nicht,
To enlighten, those-who thee know not,
{To enlighten those who know thee not,}

Und zu weiden.
And to pasture (them).

Er ist deins Volks Israel
He is (for) thy people Israel

Der Preis, Ehr, Freud und Wonne.
The glory, honor, joy, and bliss.

Jn. 3:16. For God so loved the world that he gave his only Son, that whoever believes in him should not perish but have eternal life.
Eph. 2:8–9. By grace you have been saved through faith...
Mt. 11:28 [Christ]: Come to me, all who labor and are heavy laden...
Jn. 6:37 [Christ]: ...All that the Father gives me will come to me; and him who comes to me I will not cast out.
Mt. 22:2–3 [Christ]: The kingdom of heaven may be compared to a king who gave a marriage feast for his son, and sent his servants to call those who were invited to the marriage feast... (Also Lk. 14:16–17.)

*Lk. 2:30–32. Mine eyes have seen thy salvation which thou hast prepared in the presence of all peoples, a light for revelation to the Gentiles, and for glory to thy people Israel.
Is. 42:6–7 [God]: I am the Lord, I have called you in righteousness, I have taken you by the hand and kept you; I have given you as a covenant to the people, a light to the nations, to open the eyes that are blind, to bring out the prisoners from the dungeon, from the prison those who sit in darkness.
Is. 49:6 [God]: ...I will give you as a light to the nations, that my salvation may reach to the end of the earth. (Also Acts 26:23, 13:47.)
2 Cor. 4:6. It is the God who said, "Let light shine out of darkness," who has shone in our hearts to give the light of the knowledge of the glory of God in the face of Christ. (Also Mal. 4:2, Is. 60:1, 3, 19.)
Is. 40:11. He will feed his flock like a shepherd, he will gather the lambs in his arms, he will carry them in his bosom, and gently lead those that are with young. (Also Ezek. 34:11–16, Ps. 23:1–2, Rev. 7:17.)
Deut. 10:21. He is your praise (Luther: Ruhm); he is your God...

BWV 126
Erhalt uns, Herr, bei deinem Wort
(NBA I/7; BC A46)

Sexagesima (BWV 18, 181, 126)
*2 Cor. 11:19–12:9 (God's power is made perfect in weakness)
*Lk. 8:4–15 (Parable of the sower)
Librettist: Unknown

1. Chorus (Chorale Vs. 1)
●Prayer: Preserve us from thy enemies by thy Word (126-1)
Erhalt uns, Herr, bei deinem Wort,
Preserve us, Lord, by thy Word,

Und steur' des Papsts und Türken Mord,
And fend-off the pope's and (the) Turk's (murderous-intentions),

Die Jesum Christum, deinen Sohn,
Who Jesus Christ, thy Son,
{Who would overthrow Jesus Christ, thy Son,}

Ps. 119:114–119. [O Lord,] thou art my hiding place and my shield; I hope in thy word. Depart from me, you evildoers, that I may keep the commandments of my God. Uphold me (Luther: erhalt mich) according to thy promise, that I may live, and let me not be put to shame in my hope! Hold me up, that I may be safe and have regard for thy statutes continually! Thou dost spurn all who go astray from thy statutes; yea, their cunning is in vain. All the wicked of the earth thou dost count as dross; therefore I love thy testimonies.
Heb. 4:12. The word of God is living and active, sharper than any two-edged sword...
*Lk. 8:4–5, 9–12. [Jesus] said in a parable: "A sower went out to sow his seed; and as he sowed, some fell along the path, and was trodden under foot, and the birds of the air devoured it."...And when his disciples asked him what this parable meant, he said, "...The parable is this: The seed is the word of God. The ones along the path are those who have heard; then the devil comes and takes away the word from their hearts, that they may not believe and be saved."

Stürzen   wollen von seinem Thron.
Overthrow would from   his   throne.
{From his throne.}

Phil. 3:18. Many...live as enemies of the cross of Christ.
*2 Cor. 11:25–26. ...I have been...[in] danger from my own people, danger from Gentiles...danger from false brethren.

2. Tenor Aria (Based on Chorale Vs. 2)
●Prayer: Dispel the derision of church's enemies (126-2)
Sende   deine Macht von oben,
Send (down) thy   power from above,

Herr der Herren, starker Gott!
Lord of Lords, mighty God!

Deine Kirche zu erfreuen
Thy   church to gladden
{To gladden thy church}

Und der Feinde bittern Spott
And the foe's bitter derision
{And to dispel the foe's bitter derision}

Augenblicklich zu zerstreuen.
In-an-instant   to   dispel.
{In an instant.}

Ps. 68:1–3. Let God arise, let his enemies be scattered; let those who hate him flee before him! As smoke is driven away, so drive them away; as wax melts before fire, let the wicked perish before God! But let the righteous be joyful; let them exult before God; let them be jubilant with joy! (Also Ps. 92:7–9.)
Ps. 74:22. Arise, O God, plead thy cause (Luther: Sache); remember how the impious scoff at thee all the day!
Ps. 80:6. ...Our enemies laugh among themselves (Luther: spotten unser).
Rom. 8:31. What then shall we say to this? If God is for us, who is against us? (Also Ps. 27:1, 118:6.)
Mt. 16:18 [Christ]: ...I will build my church, and the powers of death (Luther: Pforten der Hölle) shall not prevail against it.
Rev. 17:14. ...The Lamb will conquer them, for he is Lord of lords and King of kings, and those with him are called and chosen and faithful. (Also Rev. 19:16, Ps. 98:9.)
Ps. 145:20. The Lord preserves all who love him; but all the wicked he will destroy.
Ps. 6:10. All my enemies shall be ashamed and sorely troubled; they shall turn back, and be put to shame in a moment. (Also Ps. 73:19.)

3. Alto/Tenor Recit. & Chorale (Vs. 3)
●Prayer: Fight our foes: false brethren & lastly death (126-3)
Alto:
Der Menschen Gunst und Macht wird wenig nützen,
-   Human   favor and might will little profit,
{Human favor and might will profit little,}

Wenn du nicht willt das arme Häuflein schützen,
If   thou not wilt this poor little-band protect,
{If thou dost not protect this little band,}

Both:
Gott Heilger Geist, du   Tröster wert,
God, Holy Ghost, thou Comforter dear,

Tenor:
Du   weißt, daß die verfolgte Gottesstadt
Thou knowest, that the persecuted city-of-God

Den ärgsten Feind nur in sich selber hat
(Its) worst   foe but within it-self hath
{Finds its worst foe within itself}

Durch die Gefährlichkeit der falschen Brüder.
Through the   danger   of   false brethren.

Both:
Gib dein'm Volk   einerlei   Sinn auf Erd,
Give thy people one-and-the-same mind on earth,

Ps. 60:11/108:12. O grant us help against the foe, for vain is the help of man!
Ps. 127:1. ...Unless the Lord watches over the city, the watchman stays awake in vain.
Ps. 124:1–5. If it had not been the Lord who was on our side, let Israel now say—if it had not been the Lord who was on our side, when men rose up against us, then they would have swallowed us up alive, when their anger was kindled against us; then the flood would have swept us away, the torrent would have gone over us; then over us would have gone the raging waters.
2 Tim. 2:19. God's firm foundation stands, bearing this seal: "The Lord knows those who are his"...
Rom. 8:26. The Spirit helps us in our weakness; for we do not know how to pray as we ought, but the Spirit himself intercedes for us with sighs too deep for words.
Jn. 14:16–17 [Christ]: ...The Father...will give you another Counselor (Luther: Tröster), to be with you for ever, even the Spirit of truth, whom the world cannot receive, because it neither sees him nor knows him; you know him, for he dwells with you, and will be in you. (Also Jn. 14:26–27, 16:7.)
Dan. 9:19. ...O Lord, give heed and act; delay not, for thy own sake, O my God, because thy city and thy people are called by thy name.
*2 Cor. 11:25–26. ...I have been...[in] danger from my own people... danger from false brethren. (Also Gal. 2:4, 1 Jn. 2:19, Jude 1:4.)
Mt. 10:21. Brother will deliver up brother to death...
2 Pet. 2:1–3. ...There will be false teachers among you, who will secretly bring in destructive heresies...and because of them the way of

Alto:
Daß wir, an Christi Leibe   Glieder,
That we, of Christ's body (the) members,
{That we, the members of Christ's body,}

Im Glauben eins, im Leben einig   sei'n.
In   faith   one, in   life   unified might-be.
{Might be one in faith and unified in life.}

Both:
Steh bei uns in der letzten Not!
Stand by us in (our) final extremity!

Tenor:
Es   bricht alsdann   der letzte Feind herein
(Then) breaks thereupon (our) last   foe   in
{For in our final hour our last foe comes to challenge us}

Und will   den   Trost   von unsern Herzen trennen;
And would (our) consolation from our   hearts sever;
{And seeks to remove all consolation from our hearts;}

Doch laß dich da als unsern Helfer kennen.
Yet let thyself then as   our   helper be-known.
{Yet let thyself be known then as our helper.}

Both:
G'leit uns ins Leben aus dem Tod!
Lead   us into life out-of - death!

4. Bass Aria (Based on Chorale Vs. 4)
●Prayer: Cast down the pride of the enemy (126-4)
Stürze   zu   Boden, schwülstige Stolze!
Cast (down) to (the) ground,   pompous arrogance!
{Cast this pompous arrogance down to the ground!}

Mache zunichte, was sie erdacht!
Frustrate,   what it hath-devised!

Laß sie den Abgrund plötzlich verschlingen,
Let it the   abyss   suddenly devour,
{Let the abyss suddenly devour it,}

Wehre dem Toben   feindlicher Macht,
Fend-off the raging (of) hostile   might,

Laß ihr Verlangen nimmer gelingen!
Let its desire   never   succeed!

5. Tenor Recit. (Based on Chorale Vs. 5)
●God's Word manifested: God protects church in peace (126-5)
So wird dein Wort und Wahrheit offenbar
Thus is thy Word and   Truth made-manifest

truth will be reviled. And in their greed they will exploit you with false words...
Jn. 17:21, 23 [Christ]: [I pray] that [my disciples] may all be one; even as thou, Father, art in me, and I in thee, that they also may be in us, so that the world may believe that thou hast sent me...I in them and thou in me... (Also Eph. 4:1-6.)
Phil. 2:2. Complete my joy by being of the same mind (Luther: eines Sinnes), having the same love, being in full accord and of one mind. (Also Phil. 1:27, Jn. 17:23, Rom. 12:16, 1 Pet. 3:8.)
1 Cor. 12:12-13, 27. For just as the body is one and has many members, and all the members of the body, though many, are one body, so it is with Christ. For by one Spirit we were all baptized into one body—Jews, or Greeks, slaves or free—and all were made to drink of one Spirit...Now you are the body of Christ and individually members of it. (Also Rom. 12:4-5, 1 Cor. 6:15, Eph. 5:30.)
Heb. 2:14. Since therefore the children share in flesh and blood, [Christ] himself likewise partook of the same nature, that through death he might destroy him who has the power of death, that is, the devil, and deliver all those who through fear of death were subject to lifelong bondage.
1 Cor. 15:26. The last enemy to be destroyed is death.
2 Tim. 1:10. ...Our Savior Christ Jesus...abolished death and brought life and immortality to light...
Ps. 23:4. Even though I walk through the valley of the shadow of death, I fear no evil; for thou art with me...
1 Jn. 3:14. We know that we have passed out of death into life... (Also Jn. 5:24.)

Ob. 1:3-4. The pride of your heart has deceived you, you who live in the clefts of the rock, whose dwelling is high, who say in your heart, "Who will bring me down to the ground?" Though you soar aloft like the eagle, though your nest is set among the stars, thence I will bring you down, says the Lord.
Ps. 33:10. The Lord brings the counsel of the nations to nought; he frustrates the plans of the peoples.
Lk. 1:51. He has shown strength with his arm, he has scattered the proud in the imagination of their hearts.
Num. 26:10. [When God judged Korah and his rebellious companions] the earth opened its mouth and swallowed (Luther: verschlang) them up together... (See Num. 16:32.)
Rev. 20:1-3. I saw an angel coming down from heaven, holding in his hand the key of the bottomless pit (Luther: Abgrund) and a great chain. And he seized the dragon, that ancient serpent, who is the Devil and Satan, and bound him for a thousand years, and threw him into the pit...
Ps. 2:1. Why do the nations conspire (Luther: toben), and the peoples plot in vain? (Also Ps. 83:2, Acts 4:25-28.)
Ps. 112:10. ...The desire of the wicked man comes to nought. (Also Prov. 10:28, 11:7, Is. 8:10, 29:20, 40:23, Ezek. 32:12.)

Jn. 17:17. ...Thy word is truth.
Col. 1:5-6. ...The word of the truth...in the whole world...is bearing fruit and growing... (Also Acts 13:49.)
Ps. 138:2. [O Lord]...thou hast exalted above everything thy name and thy word.
Prov. 30:5. Every word of God proves true; he is a shield to those who take refuge in him.

Und stellet sich im höchsten Glanze
And presents itself in-the greatest splendor - ,

Daß du für deine Kirche wachst,
In-that thou over thy church dost-watch,

Daß du des heilgen Wortes Lehren
In-that thou the holy Word's teachings

Zum Segen fruchtbar machst;
(With) blessing fruitful dost-make;

Und willst du dich als Helfer zu uns kehren,
And wouldst thou - as helper to us turn,
{And if thou wouldst turn to us as helper,}

So wird uns denn in Frieden
So will to-us then in peace

Des Segens Überfluß beschieden.
 - Blessing's profusion be-apportioned.
{Then the profusion of these blessings will be apportioned to us in peace.}

6. Chorale (Vss. 6 & 7) (See also 42-7.)
●Prayer: Grant peace and good government (126-6)
Verleih uns Frieden gnädichlich,
Grant us peace graciously,

Herr Gott, zu unsern Zeiten;
Lord God, for our times;

Es ist doch ja kein andrer nicht,
(There) is - indeed no other - ,

Der für uns könnte streiten,
Who for us could fight,

Denn du, unser Gott, alleine.
Than thou, our God, alone.

///

Gib unserm Fürst'n und aller Obrigkeit
Give our princes and all government

Fried und gut Regiment,
Peace and good governance,

Daß wir unter ihnen
That we under them

Ein geruh'g und stilles Leben führen mögen
A peaceful and quiet life lead may
{May lead a peaceful and quiet life}

Ps. 119:41–42. Let thy steadfast love come to me, O Lord, thy salvation according to thy promise; then shall I have an answer for those who taunt me, for I trust in thy word.
Ps. 28:8. The Lord is the strength of his people, he is the saving refuge of his anointed.
Mt. 16:18 [Christ]: ...On this rock I will build my church, and the powers of death shall not prevail against it.
Is. 55:10–11 [God]: For as the rain and the snow come down from heaven, and return not thither but water the earth, making it bring forth and sprout, giving seed to the sower and bread to the eater, so shall my word be that goes forth from my mouth; it shall not return to me empty, but it shall accomplish that which I purpose, and prosper in the thing for which I sent it.
***Lk. 8:15.** As for...the good soil, they are those who, hearing the word, hold it fast in an honest and good heart, and bring forth fruit with patience. (Also Mt. 13:23, Mk. 4:20.)
Rom. 8:31. What then shall we say to this? If God is for us, who is against us? (Also Ps. 27:1, 118:6.)
Heb. 13:6. We can confidently say, "The Lord is my helper, I will not be afraid; what can man do to me?" (Also Ps. 30:10, 40:17, 70:5, 79:9, 118:6.)
Ezek. 37:26–27 [God]: I will make a covenant of peace with them; it shall be an everlasting covenant with them; and I will bless them and multiply them, and will set my sanctuary in the midst of them for evermore. My dwelling place shall be with them; and I will be their God, and they shall be my people.

Ps. 29:11. May the Lord give strength to his people! May the Lord bless his people with peace! (Also Ps. 122:6–7, 128:5–6, Is. 26:1–3.)
Is. 55:12. You shall go out in joy, and be led forth in peace; the mountains and the hills before you shall break forth into singing, and all the trees of the field shall clap their hands. (Also Lev. 26:6.)
Ex. 14:13–14. Moses said to the people, "Fear not, stand firm, and see the salvation of the Lord, which he will work for you today...The Lord will fight for you, and you have only to be still."
Deut. 3:22. You shall not fear them; for it is the Lord your God who fights for you. (Also Ex. 15:3, Deut. 1:30.)
Ps. 124:1–3. If it had not been the Lord who was on our side, let Israel now say—if it had not been the Lord who was on our side, when men rose up against us, then they would have swallowed us up alive, when their anger was kindled against us.

1 Tim. 2:1–2. First of all, then, I urge that supplications, prayers, intercessions, and thanksgivings be made for all men, for kings and all who are in high positions, that we may lead a quiet and peaceable life, godly and respectful in every way.
Rom. 13:1–2. Let every person be subject to the governing authorities. For there is no authority except from God, and those that exist have been instituted by God. Therefore he who resists the authorities resists what God has appointed, and those who resist will incur judgment. (Also Tit. 3:1.)
1 Pet. 2:13–14. Be subject for the Lord's sake to every human institution, whether it be to the emperor as supreme, or to governors as sent by him to punish those who do wrong and to praise those who do right.

In aller Gottseligkeit und Ehrbarkeit.
In all godliness and respectability.

Amen.
Amen.

BWV 127
Herr Jesu Christ, wahr' Mensch und Gott
(NBA I/8; BC A49)

Estomihi (Quinquagesima) (BWV 23, 22, 127, 159)
*1 Cor. 13:1–13 (In praise of love)
*Lk 18:31–43 (Jesus and the twelve go to Jerusalem, healing of a blind man)
Librettist: Unknown

1. Chorus (Chorale Vs. 1)
●Prayer: Christ who suffered for me, have mercy! (127-1)
Herr Jesu Christ, wahr' Mensch und Gott,
Lord Jesus Christ, true man and God,

Der du littst Marter, Angst und Spott,
Thou who-didst-suffer torture, fear, and scorn;

Für mich am Kreuz auch endlich starbst
For me on-the-cross also at-last didst-die
{Also at last didst die for me on the cross}

Und mir deins Vaters Huld erwarbst,
And for-me thy Father's favor didst-win,
{And didst win thy Father's favor for me,}

Ich bitt durchs bittre Leiden dein:
I beg through-the bitter suffering of-thine:
{I beg by thy bitter suffering:}

Du wollst mir Sünder gnädig sein.
Thou wouldst to-me (a) sinner merciful be.
{Be merciful to me, a sinner.}

2. Tenor Recit. (Based on Chorale Vss. 2 & 3)
●Jesus who suffered leads me through death to life (127-2)
Wenn alles sich zur letzten Zeit entsetzet,
When everything - at-that last (hour) is-terrified,
{When all creatures become terrified in that final hour,}

Und wenn ein kalter Todesschweiß
And when a cold sweat-of-death

Die schon erstarrten Glieder netzet,
(My) already stiffened members moistens,

Wenn meine Zunge nichts, als nur durch Seufzer spricht
When my tongue nought but - through groans speaks
{When my tongue can only groan}

Ps. 29:11. May the Lord give strength to his people! May the Lord bless his people with peace!
Ps. 147:12–14. Praise the Lord, O Jerusalem! Praise your God, O Zion! For he strengthens the bars of your gates; he blesses your sons within you. He makes peace in your borders...

*Lk. 18:31–33, 35, 38. Taking the twelve, [Jesus] said to them, "Behold, we are going up to Jerusalem, and everything that is written of the Son of man by the prophets will be accomplished. For he will be delivered to the Gentiles, and will be mocked and shamefully treated and spit upon; they will scourge him and kill him, and on the third day he will rise."...As he drew near to Jericho, a blind man was sitting by the roadside begging...And he cried, "Jesus, Son of David, have mercy on me!"
1 Pet. 2:21. ...Christ...suffered for you...
Rom. 1:3–4. ...[He] was descended from David according to the flesh and designated Son of God... (Also 1 Jn. 5:20, Jn. 17:3.)
Phil. 2:6–8. ...Though he was in the form of God, [Christ Jesus] did not count equality with God a thing to be grasped, but emptied himself...being born in the likeness of men...He humbled himself and became obedient unto death, even death on a cross.
Rom. 5:10. ...We were reconciled to God by the death of his Son... (Also Col. 1:22, Heb. 13:12.)
1 Tim. 2:5–6. For there is one God, and there is one mediator between God and men, the man Christ Jesus, who gave himself as a ransom for all...
1 Cor. 6:19–20. ...You were bought with a price... (Also 1 Pet. 1:18–19.)
2 Jn. 1:3. Grace, mercy, and peace will be with us, from God the Father and from Jesus Christ the Father's Son...
Lk. 18:13. The tax collector, standing far off, would not even lift up his eyes to heaven, but beat his breast, saying, "God be merciful to me a sinner!"

Ps. 116:3. The snares of death encompassed me; the pangs of Sheol laid hold on me; I suffered distress and anguish.
Heb. 9:27. ...It is appointed for men to die once...
Ps. 55:4–5. My heart is in anguish within me, the terrors of death have fallen upon me. Fear and trembling come upon me, and horror overwhelms me.
Ps. 22:14–15. ...My heart is like wax, it is melted within my breast; my strength is dried up like a potsherd, and my tongue cleaves to my jaws; thou dost lay me in the dust of death.
Ps. 18:4–6. The cords of death encompassed me, the torrents of perdition assailed me; the cords of Sheol entangled me, the snares of death confronted me. In my distress I called upon the Lord; to my God I cried for help...

Und dieses Herze   bricht:
And   this   heart (of mine) breaks:

Genung, daß da der Glaube weiß,
Enough, that then (my) faith knows,
{It is enough that by faith then knows,}

Daß Jesus bei mir steht,
That Jesus by me stands,
{That standing with me is Jesus,}

Der mit Geduld zu seinem Leiden geht
Who with patience to   his   passion goes
{Who goes to his own passion with patience,}

Und diesen schweren Weg auch mich geleitet
And this arduous way also me leads
{And leads me the same arduous way,}

Und mir die Ruhe zubereitet.
And for-me (my) rest prepares.
{And prepares my rest for me.}

3. Soprano Aria (Based on Chorale Vs. 4)
•Death is welcome for my soul is in his hands (127-3)
Die Seele ruht in Jesu Händen,
(My) soul rests in Jesus' hands,
{My soul will rest in Jesus' hands,}

Wenn Erde diesen Leib bedeckt.
When earth this body covers.
{When earth shall cover this body.}

Ach ruft mich bald, ihr Sterbeglocken,
Ah, call me soon, ye bells-of-death,

Ich bin zum Sterben unerschrocken,
I am of dying unterrified,
{I am not terrified of dying,}

Weil mich mein Jesus wieder weckt.
Because me my Jesus again shall-awaken.
{Because my Jesus shall awaken me again.}

4. Bass Recit. & Aria (Based on Chorale Vss. 5; 6-7)
•Prayer: Be my advocate when trumpet sounds judgment (127-4)
Wenn einstens die Posaunen schallen,
When one-day the trumpets sound,

Und wenn der Bau der Welt
And when the structure of-the world

Nebst denen Himmelsfesten
Along-with those-of-the heavenly-firmaments

Zerschmettert wird zerfallen,
Shattered, will fall-to-pieces,
{Shatters into pieces,}

Heb. 2:14–15. ...[Christ] himself likewise partook of the same nature, that through death he might destroy him who has the power of death, that is, the devil, and deliver all those who through fear of death were subject to lifelong bondage.
Is. 53:7. He was oppressed, and he was afflicted, yet he opened not his mouth; like a lamb that is led to the slaughter, and like a sheep that before its shearers is dumb, so he opened not his mouth.
Ps. 23:4. Even though I walk through the valley of the shadow of death, I fear no evil; for thou art with me; thy rod and thy staff, they comfort me.
Is. 43:2 [God]: When you pass through the waters I will be with you; and through the rivers, they shall not overwhelm you...
Jn. 14:1–3 [Christ]: Let not your hearts be troubled; believe in God, believe also in me. In my Father's house are many rooms; if it were not so, would I have told you that I go to prepare a place for you? And when I go and prepare a place for you, I will come again and will take you to myself, that where I am you may be also.
Rev. 14:13. ...Blessed are the dead who die in the Lord henceforth... that they may rest from their labors...
Heb. 4:9–10. So then, there remains a sabbath rest for the people of God; for whoever enters God's rest also ceases from his labors as God did from his. (Also Rev. 14:13.)

Lk. 23:46. Then Jesus, crying with a loud voice, said, "Father, into thy hands I commit my spirit!" And having said this he breathed his last. (Also Ps. 31:5.)
Ecc. 12:7. The dust returns to the earth as it was, and the spirit returns to God who gave it. (Also Gen. 3:19. Ps. 146:4, Ecc. 3:20.)
Phil. 1:21–23. To me to live is Christ, and to die is gain...Which I shall choose I cannot tell. I am hard pressed between the two. My desire is to depart and be with Christ, for that is far better.
2 Cor. 5:8. We are of good courage, and we would rather be away from the body and at home with the Lord.
Jn. 6:54 [Christ]: He who eats my flesh and drinks my blood has eternal life, and I will raise him up at the last day. (Also Jn. 6:40, 44.)
Rom. 6:8–9. ...We believe that we shall...live with [Christ]. For we know that Christ being raised from the dead will never die again; death no longer has dominion over him.
1 Cor. 15:20, 23. ...Christ has been raised from the dead, the first fruits of those who have fallen asleep...Christ the first fruits, then at his coming those who belong to Christ. (Also Jn. 6:40/44/54, Rom. 8:11.)

1 Thess. 4:16–17. The Lord himself will descend from heaven with a cry of command, with the archangel's call, and with the sound of the trumpet of God. And the dead in Christ will rise first. (Also Mt. 24:31, 1 Cor. 15:51–52.)
2 Pet. 3:10–12. The day of the Lord will come like a thief, and then the heavens will pass away with a loud noise, and the elements will be dissolved with fire, and the earth and the works that are upon it will be burned up. Since all these things are thus to be dissolved, what sort of persons ought you to be in lives of holiness and godliness, waiting for and hastening the coming of the day of God, because of which the heavens will be kindled and dissolved, and the elements will melt with fire!
2 Cor. 5:1, 10. We know that if the earthly tent we live in is destroyed,

So denke mein, mein Gott, im besten;
Then think on-me, my God, with favor;

Wenn sich dein Knecht einst vors Gerichte stellt,
When - thy servant one-day before-the judgment appears,

Da die Gedanken sich verklagen,
Where (my) thoughts each-other accuse,
{Where my thoughts accuse each other,}

So wollest du allein,
Then mayest thou alone,

O Jesu, mein Fürsprecher sein
O Jesus, my advocate be.

Und meiner Seele tröstlich sagen:
And to-my soul comfortingly say:

///

Fürwahr, fürwahr, euch sage ich:
Truly, truly, to-you say I:
{Truly, truly, I say to you:}

Wenn Himmel und Erde im Feuer vergehen,
Though heaven and earth in fire pass-away,
{Though heaven and earth pass away in flames,}

So soll doch ein Gläubiger ewig bestehen.
So shall nevertheless a believer eternally stand.

Er wird nicht kommen ins Gericht
He will not come into judgment

Und den Tod ewig schmecken nicht.
And (will) death eternally taste not.
{And will never taste death through all eternity.}

Nur halte dich,
Just cleave - ,

Mein Kind, an mich:
My child, to me:

Ich breche mit starker und helfender Hand
I-will break with strong and helping hand

Des Todes gewaltig geschlossenes Band.
- Death's mighty locked bond(s).

5. Chorale (Vs. 8)
●Prayer: Forgive, keep us steadfast till death (127-5)
Ach, Herr, vergib all unsre Schuld,
Ah, Lord, forgive all our guilt,

Hilf, daß wir warten mit Geduld,
Help, that we (may) wait with patience,

we have a building (Luther: Bau) from God, a house not made with hands, eternal in the heavens...We must all appear before the judgment seat of Christ, so that each one may receive good or evil, according to what he has done in the body. (Also Rom. 14:12, Heb. 9:27, 1 Cor. 3:12, Eph. 6:8.)
Rom. 2:15–16. ...[Men's] conscience also bears witness and their conflicting thoughts accuse or perhaps excuse them on that day when, according to my gospel, God judges the secrets of men by Christ Jesus.
1 Jn. 2:1–2. ...We have an advocate with the Father, Jesus Christ the righteous; and he is the expiation for our sins, and not for ours only but also for the sins of the whole world. (Also Rom. 8:34, Heb. 4:15.)
Heb. 7:25. ...[Christ] is able for all time to save those who draw near to God through him, since he always lives to make intercession for them.
Heb. 9:24. For Christ has entered, not into a sanctuary made with hands, a copy of the true one, but into heaven itself, now to appear in the presence of God on our behalf.

2 Pet. 3:10. The day of the Lord will come like a thief, and then the heavens will pass away with a loud noise, and the elements will be dissolved with fire, and the earth and the works that are upon it will be burned up.
Mk. 13:31 [Christ]: Heaven and earth will pass away, but my words will not pass away. (Also Mt. 24:35, Lk. 21:33, Ps. 102:25–28.)
Jn. 5:24 [Christ]: Truly, truly, I say to you, he who hears my word and believes him who sent me, has eternal life; he does not come into judgment, but has passed from death to life.
Jn. 8:51 [Christ]: Truly, truly, I say to you, if any one keeps my word, he will never see death. (Also Jn. 11:25–26.)
Heb. 2:9. We see Jesus, who for a little while was made lower than the angels, crowned with glory and honor because of the suffering of death, so that by the grace of God he might taste death for every one. (Also Mt. 16:28, Mk. 9:1, Lk. 9:27.)
Heb. 2:14–15. ...[Christ] himself likewise partook of the same nature, that through death he might destroy him who has the power of death, that is, the devil, and deliver all those who through fear of death were subject to lifelong bondage.
Acts 2:24. God raised [Christ] up, having loosed the pangs of death, because it was not possible for him to be held by it.
2 Tim. 1:10. ...Christ...abolished death and brought life and immortality to light... (Also 1 Cor. 15:25–26.)
Rev. 1:17–18 [Christ]: ...Fear not, I am the first and the last, and the living one; I died, and behold I am alive for evermore, and I have the keys of Death and Hades.

*Lk. 18:38. ...Jesus, Son of David, have mercy on me!
Lk. 18:13. ...God be merciful to me a sinner!
Ps. 32:1. Blessed is he whose transgression is forgiven, whose sin is covered.
Rev. 2:10 [Christ]: Do not fear what you are about to suffer...Be faithful unto death, and I will give you the crown of life.
Jms. 5:10–11. As an example of suffering and patience, brethren, take the prophets who spoke in the name of the Lord. Behold, we call those happy who were steadfast. You have heard of the steadfastness

Bis unser Stündlein kömmt herbei,
Until our little-hour comes near,

Auch   unser Glaub stets wacker sei,
Also (that) our faith ever valiant be,
{Also that our faith be ever valiant,}

Dein'm Wort zu trauen festiglich,
Thy   Word to trust   firmly,
{To trust thy Word firmly,}

Bis wir einschlafen seliglich.
Until we fall-asleep blessedly.
{Until we blessedly fall asleep.}

BWV 128
Auf Christi Himmelfahrt allein
(NBA I/12; BC A76)

Ascension (BWV 37, 128, 43, 11)
*Acts 1:1–11 (Holy Spirit promised, Christ's ascension)
*Mk. 16:14–20 (Great commission, Christ's ascension)
Librettist: Christiane Mariane von Ziegler (Text modified by someone: J. S. Bach?)

1. Chorus (Chorale)
●Ascension of Christ: The basis for my own ascension (128-1)
Auf   Christi Himmelfahrt allein
Upon Christ's ascension alone

Ich meine Nachfahrt gründe
I my-own (ascension) base
{Do I base my own}
       [Nachfahrt = a journey following in the path of another]

Und allen Zweifel, Angst und Pein
And all doubt, fear, and pain

Hiermit stets überwinde;
Herewith ever conquer;

Denn weil das Haupt im Himmel   ist,
For, because the head in heaven (now) is,
{For, because the head is now in heaven,}

Wird seine Glieder Jesus Christ
Will its members Jesus Christ
{Will Jesus Christ fetch the members}

Zu rechter Zeit nachholen.
In good time bring-after.
{In good time.}

of Job, and you have seen the purpose of the Lord, how the Lord is compassionate and merciful.
Heb. 10:36–39. You have need of endurance (Luther: Geduld), so that you may do the will of God and receive what is promised. "For yet a little while, and the coming one shall come and shall not tarry; but my righteous one shall live by faith, and if he shrinks back, my soul has no pleasure in him." But we are not of those who shrink back and are destroyed, but of those who have faith and keep their souls. (Also Col. 1:23, Tit. 1:9.)
Rev. 3:10–11 [Christ]: Because you have kept my word of patient endurance, I will keep you from the hour of trial...I am coming soon; hold fast what you have, so that no one may seize your crown.
1 Cor. 15:20, 23. ...Christ has been raised from the dead, the first fruits of those who have fallen asleep...Christ the first fruits, then at his coming those who belong to Christ. (Also Jn. 11:11, 13, Rom. 6:8–10.)
Rev. 14:13. ...Blessed are the dead who die in the Lord henceforth... that they may rest from their labors...

*Mk. 16:19. ...The Lord Jesus, after he had spoken to [his disciples], was taken up into heaven, and sat down at the right hand of God.
*Acts 1:9–11. ...As they were looking on, [Jesus] was lifted up, and a cloud took him out of their sight. And while they were gazing into heaven as he went, behold, two men stood by them in white robes, and said, "Men of Galilee, why do you stand looking into heaven? This Jesus, who was taken up from you into heaven, will come in the same way as you saw him go into heaven."
Jn. 14:1–3 [Christ]: Let not your hearts be troubled; believe in God, believe also in me In my Father's house are many rooms; if it were not so, would I have told you that I go to prepare a place for you? And when I go and prepare a place for you, I will come again and will take you to myself, that where I am you may be also.
Jn. 12:26 [Christ]: If any one serves me, he must follow me; and where I am, there shall my servant be also...
Eph. 5:23, 29–30. ...Christ is the head of the church, his body...For no man ever hates his own flesh, but nourishes and cherishes it, as Christ does the church, because we are members of his body. (Also Eph. 4:15–16.)
1 Cor. 12:27. You are the body of Christ and individually members of it. (Also Rom. 12:4–5, 1 Cor. 6:15.)
1 Thess. 4:16–17. The Lord himself will descend from heaven with a cry of command, with the archangel's call, and with the sound of the trumpet of God. And the dead in Christ will rise first; then we who are alive, who are left, shall be caught up together with them in clouds to meet the Lord in the air; and so we shall always be with the Lord.
1 Cor. 15:23. ...Christ the first fruits, then at his coming those who belong to Christ. (Also Rom. 6:8–10.)

2. Tenor Recit.
●Prayer: Come, bring me to thee in heavenly Salem (128-2)
Ich bin bereit, komm, hole mich!
I am ready; come, get me!

Hier in der Welt
Here in the world

Ist Jammer, Angst und Pein;
Is misery, fear and pain;

Hingegen dort, in Salems Zelt,
By-contrast, there, in Salem's tent,

Werd ich verkläret sein.
Will I transfigured be.
{Will I be transfigured.}

Da seh ich Gott von Angesicht zu Angesicht,
There see I God - face to face,
{There I'll see God face to face,}

Wie mir sein heilig Wort verspricht.
As me his holy Word does-promise.
{As his holy Word promises me.}

3. Bass Aria & Recit.
●Jesus at God's right hand; I will join him there (128-3)
Auf, auf, mit hellem Schall
Rise-up, rise-up, with bright sound

Verkündigt überall:
Proclaim (it) everywhere:

Mein Jesus sitzt zur Rechten!
My Jesus sits at (God's) right-hand!

Wer sucht mich anzufechten?
Who seeks me to-attack?
{Who can attack me?}

Ist er von mir genommen,
Is he from me taken,
{Though he is taken from me,}

Ich werd einst dahin kommen,
I will one-day to-that-place come,
{I will one day come to that place,}

Wo mein Erlöser lebt.
Where my Redeemer lives.

Meine Augen werden ihn in größter Klarheit schauen.
My eyes will him in (the) greatest clarity see.
{My eyes will see him in the greatest clarity.}

O könnt ich im voraus mir eine Hütte bauen!
O could I ahead-of-time for-myself a shelter build!
{O, if I could only build a shelfter for myself ahead of time!}

Jn. 14:3 [Christ]: ...I will come again and will take you to myself, that where I am you may be also. (Also Jn. 12:26.)
Rev. 22:20. He who testifies to these things says, "Surely I am coming soon." Amen. Come, Lord Jesus!
Phil. 1:21–23. To me to live is Christ, and to die is gain...Which I shall choose I cannot tell. I am hard pressed between the two. My desire is to depart and be with Christ, for that is far better. (Also 2 Cor. 5:8.)
Col. 3:1. If then you have been raised with Christ, seek the things that are above, where Christ is, seated at the right hand of God. (Also 2 Cor. 4:16–5:1.)
Ps. 76:1–2. ...[God's] name is great in Israel. His abode has been established in Salem, his dwelling place in Zion. (Salem: also Heb. 7:1–2)
Heb. 12:22. You have come to Mount Zion and to the city of the living God, the heavenly Jerusalem...
Rev. 21:2–3. I saw the holy city, new Jerusalem, coming down out of heaven from God...and I heard a loud voice from the throne saying, "Behold, the dwelling of God is with men..."
1 Jn. 3:2. ...When [Christ] appears we shall be like him, for we shall see him as he is.
Phil. 3:20–21. Our commonwealth is in heaven, and from it we await a Savior, the Lord Jesus Christ, who will change our lowly body to be like his glorious body... (Also Mt. 17:2, Mk. 9:2.)
1 Cor. 13:12. Now we see in a mirror dimly, but then face to face... (Also Rev. 22:4.)

*Mk. 16:19. So then the Lord Jesus, after he had spoken to them, was taken up into heaven, and sat down at the right hand of God. (Also Lk. 22:69, Acts 2:33, 5:31, 7:55–56, Col. 3:1, Heb. 1:3, 12:2, 1 Pet. 3:22.)
Heb. 10:12. When Christ had offered for all time a single sacrifice for sins, he sat down at the right hand of God.
Rom. 8:33–34. Who shall bring any charge against God's elect? It is God who justifies; who is to condemn? Is it Christ Jesus, who died, yes, who was raised from the dead, who is at the right hand of God, who indeed intercedes for us? (Also 1 Jn. 2:1, Heb. 7:25.)
Jn. 13:31, 33, 36. ...Jesus said..."Little children, yet a little while I am with you. You will seek me; and as I said to the Jews so now I say to you, 'Where I am going you cannot come.'"...Simon Peter said to him "Lord, where are you going?" Jesus answered, "Where I am going you cannot follow me now; but you shall follow afterward."
Jn. 14:1–3 [Christ]: Let not your hearts be troubled; believe in God, believe also in me. In my Father's house are many rooms; if it were not so, would I have told you that I go to prepare a place for you? And when I go and prepare a place for you, I will come again and will take you to myself, that where I am you may be also. (Also Jn. 12:26.)
1 Jn. 3:2. Beloved, we are God's children now; it does not yet appear what we shall be, but we know that when he appears we shall be like him, for we shall see him as he is.
1 Cor. 13:12. Now we see in a mirror dimly, but then face to face. Now I know in part; then I shall understand fully even as I have been fully understood.
Mt. 17:1–6. ...Jesus took with him Peter and James and John his brother, and led them up a high mountain apart. And he was transfigured before them, and his face shone like the sun, and his garments became white as light. And behold, there appeared to them Moses and Elijah, talking with him. And Peter said to Jesus, "Lord, it

Wohin? Vergebner Wunsch!
Whither? Useless wish!

Er wohnet nicht auf Berg und Tal,
He dwells not on hill and vale,

Sein Allmacht zeigt sich überall;
His omnipotence reveals itself everywhere;

So schweig, verwegner Mund,
So hush, presumptuous mouth,

Und suche nicht dieselbe zu ergründen!
And seek not the-same to fathom!
{And do not seek to fathom it!}

4. Alto & Tenor Duet
●Christ's exaltation to God's right hand unfathomable (128–4)
Sein Allmacht zu ergründen,
His omnipotence to fathom,
{To fathom his omnipotence,}

Wird sich kein Mensche finden,
Will - no human (be-able),

Mein Mund verstummt und schweigt.
My mouth falls-dumb and becomes-silent.

Ich sehe durch die Sterne,
I see through the stars,

Daß er sich schon von ferne
That he - already from afar
{That he already appears from afar}

Zur Rechten Gottes zeigt.
At-the right-hand of-God appears.
{At the right hand of God.}

5. Chorale
●Christ will place me at his right hand (128–5)
Alsdenn so wirst du mich
Thereupon then wilt thou me

Zu deiner Rechten stellen
At thy right-hand station
{Thereupon wilt thou station me at thy right hand}

Und mir als deinem Kind
And (upon) me as thy child

Ein gnädig Urteil fällen,
A gracious judgment pass, (and)
{And pass a gracious judgment upon me, as thy child,}

Mich bringen zu der Lust,
Me bring into that pleasure,
{And will bring me into that pleasure,}

is well that we are here; if you wish, I will make three booths here, one for you and one for Moses and one for Elijah." He was still speaking, when lo, a bright cloud overshadowed them, and a voice from the cloud said, "This is my beloved Son, with whom I am well pleased; listen to him." When the disciples heard this, they fell on their faces, and were filled with awe. (Also Mk. 9:2–6.)

Acts 7:48–50. The Most High does not dwell in houses made with hands; as the prophet says, "Heaven is my throne, and earth my footstool. What house will you build for me, says the Lord, or what is the place of my rest? Did not my hand make all these things?" (Also Is. 66:1.)

Rom. 11:34. Who has known the mind of the Lord, or who has been his counselor? (Also Is. 40:13.)

Job 42:3. I have uttered what I did not understand, things too wonderful for me, which I did not know.

1 Pet. 3:22. [Christ] has gone into heaven and is at the right hand of God, with angels, authorities, and powers subject to him.

Heb. 1:3–4. He reflects the glory of God and bears the very stamp of his nature, upholding the universe by his word of power. When he had made purification for sins, he sat down at the right hand of the Majesty on high, having become as much superior to angels as the name he has obtained is more excellent that theirs.

Phil. 2:9–10. God has highly exalted him and bestowed on him the name which is above every name, that at the name of Jesus every knee should bow, in heaven and on earth and under the earth, and every tongue confess that Jesus Christ is Lord, to the glory of God the Father.

Hab. 2:20. The Lord is in his holy temple; let all the earth keep silence before him.

Mt. 17:6. ...[The disciples]...fell on their faces, and were filled with awe.

Acts 7:55–56. [Stephen], full of the Holy Spirit, gazed into heaven and saw the glory of God, and Jesus standing at the right hand of God; and he said, "Behold, I see the heavens opened, and the Son of man standing at the right hand of God."

Mt. 20:20–23. The mother of the sons of Zebedee came up to him, with her sons...And he said to her, "What do you want?" She said to him, "Command that these two sons of mine may sit, one at your right hand and one at your left, in your kingdom." But Jesus answered, "You do not know what you are asking...To sit at my right hand and at my left is not mine to grant, but it is for those for whom it has been prepared by my Father." (Also Mk. 10:37–40.)

Mt. 25:31–34. When the Son of man comes in his glory, and all the angels with him, then he will sit on his glorious throne. Before him will be gathered all the nations, and he will separate them one from another as a shepherd separates the sheep from the goats, and he will place the sheep at his right hand, but the goats at the left. Then the King will say to those at his right hand, "Come, O blessed of my Father, inherit the kingdom prepared for you from the foundation of the world."

Jn. 5:24 [Christ]: Truly, truly, I say to you, he who hears my word and believes him who sent me, has eternal life; he does not come into judgment, but has passed from death to life.

447

Wo   deine Herrlichkeit
Where thy   glory

Ich werde schauen an
I   will   behold
{Where I will behold thy glory}

In   alle Ewigkeit.
Through all   eternity.

BWV 129
Gelobet sei der Herr, mein Gott
(NBA I/15; BC A93)

Trinity Sunday (BWV 165, [194], 176, 129)
*Rom. 11:33–36 (O the depth of the riches and wisdom and knowledge of God!)
*Jn. 3:1–15 (Discussion between Jesus and Nicodemus: You must be born anew)
Librettist: Chorale (Johann Olearius)

1. Chorus (Chorale Vs. 1)
●Praise to God the Creator: my light & life (129-1)
Gelobet sei der Herr,
Blessed be the Lord,

Mein Gott, mein Licht, mein Leben,
My   God, my   light, my   life,

Mein Schöpfer, der mir hat
My   Creator, who me hath
{My creator, who hath given me}

Mein Leib und Seel gegeben,
My   body and soul   given,
{My body and soul,}

Mein Vater, der mich schützt
My   Father, who me protects
{My Father, who protects me}

Von   Mutterleibe an,
From (my) mother's-womb on,
{Since my mother's womb,}

Der alle Augenblick
Who (each) moment (of my life)

Viel Guts an mir getan.
Much good to me hath-done.
{Hath done much good to me.}

2. Bass Aria (Chorale Vs. 2)
●Praise to God the Son: my Salvation, my life (129-2)
Gelobet sei der Herr,
Blessed be the Lord,

Ps. 16:11. [O Lord,] thou dost show me the path of life; in thy presence there is fulness of joy...pleasures for evermore.
1 Jn. 3:2. Beloved, we are God's children now; it does not yet appear what we shall be, but we know that when he appears we shall be like him, for we shall see him as he is.
1 Cor. 13:12. For now we see in a mirror dimly, but then face to face. Now I know in part; then I shall understand fully, even as I have been fully understood.

1 Kings 8:56. Blessed be the Lord (Luther: Gelobet sei der Herr)...
Ps. 113:2. Blessed be the name of the Lord (Luther: Gelobet sei des Herrn Name) from this time forth and for evermore! (Also Ps. 41:13, 72:18–19, 89:15, 115:18, 119:12, 106:48, etc...)
*Rom. 11:33, 36. O the depths of the riches and wisdom and knowledge of God! How unsearchable are his judgments and how inscrutable his ways!...For from him and through him and to him are all things. To him be glory for ever. Amen.
Ps. 27:1. The Lord is my light and my salvation...The Lord is the stronghold of my life...
Ps. 100:3. Know that the Lord is God! It is he that made us, and we are his...
Ps. 139:13–16. [O Lord,] thou didst form my inward parts, thou didst knit me together in my mother's womb. I praise thee, for thou art fearful and wonderful. Wonderful are thy works! Thou knowest me right well; my frame was not hidden from thee, when I was being made in secret, intricately wrought in the depths of the earth. Thy eyes beheld my unformed substance; in thy book were written, every one of them, the days that were formed for me, when as yet there was none of them.
Ps. 103:13. As a father pities his children, so the Lord pities those who fear him.
Ps. 22:9–10. [O Lord,] thou art he who took me from the womb; thou didst keep me safe upon my mother's breasts. Upon thee was I cast from my birth, and since my mother bore me thou hast been my God.
Ps. 71:5–6. Thou, O Lord, art my hope, my trust, O Lord, from my youth. Upon thee I have leaned from my birth; thou art he who took me from my mother's womb. My praise is continually of thee.
Ps. 116:7. ...The Lord has dealt bountifully with you (Luther: der Herr tut dir gutes)...
Lam. 3:22–23. The steadfast love of the Lord never ceases, his mercies never come to an end; they are new every morning; great is thy faithfulness.

Ex. 15:2. The Lord is my strength and my song, and he has become my salvation (Luther: Heil)...I will praise him...I will exalt him. (Also Ps. 27:1, 118:14, Is. 12:2.)

Mein Gott, mein Heil, mein Leben,
My God, my salvation, my life,

Des Vaters liebster Sohn,
The Father's dearest Son,

Der sich für mich gegeben,
Who himself for me did-give,
{Who gave himself for me,}

Der mich erlöset hat
Who me redeemed hath
{Who redeemed me}

Mit seinem teuren Blut,
With his precious blood,

Der mir im Glauben schenkt
Who to-me through faith doth-give

Sich selbst, das höchste Gut.
Him-self, the highest good.
{Who gives himself, the highest good, to me by faith.}

3. Soprano Aria (Chorale Vs. 3)
●Praise to God the Holy Ghost: my comfort & strength
(129-3)
Gelobet sei der Herr,
Blessed be the Lord,

Mein Gott, mein Trost, mein Leben,
My God, my comfort, my life,

Des Vaters werter Geist,
The Father's precious Spirit,

Den mir der Sohn gegeben,
Whom me the Son did-give,
{Who was given to me by the Son,}

Der mir mein Herz erquickt,
Who - my heart doth-revive,
{Who revives my heart,}

Der mir gibt neue Kraft,
Who to-me doth-give new strength,
{Who gives me new strength,}

Der mir in aller Not
Who me in all distress
{Who provides me in all distress}

Lk. 1:68-69. Blessed be the Lord God...for he has visited and redeemed his people, and has raised up a horn of salvation for us...
*Jn. 3:16. For God so loved the world that he gave his only Son, that whoever believes in him should not perish but have eternal life.
Gal. 1:3-4. ...Our Lord Jesus Christ...gave himself for our sins to deliver us from the present evil age...
Tit. 2:13-14. ...Our great God and Savior Jesus Christ...gave himself for us to redeem us from all iniquity... (Also Rom. 8:32, Gal. 2:20, Eph. 5:2, 5:25.)
1 Jn. 4:10. In this is love, not that we loved God but that he loved us and sent his Son to be the expiation for our sins.
1 Tim. 2:5-6. For there is one God, and there is one mediator between God and men, the man Christ Jesus, who gave himself as a ransom for all...
1 Pet. 1:18-19. You...were ransomed...not with perishable things such as silver or gold, but with the precious blood of Christ, like that of a lamb without blemish or spot. (Also Eph. 2:13, 1 Jn. 1:7, Heb. 13:12, Rev. 5:9.)
Eph. 3:17. ...that Christ may dwell in your hearts through faith...
1 Jn. 1:3. ...Our fellowship is with the Father and with his Son Jesus Christ.
Ps. 16:5. The Lord is my chosen portion and my cup (Luther: Gut und Teil)...

Ps. 73:26. [O Lord,] my flesh and my heart may fail, but God is the strength of my heart (Luther: Trost) and my portion for ever.
Jn. 14:16-17 [Christ]: I will pray the Father, and he will give you another Counselor (Luther: Tröster), to be with you for ever, even the Spirit of truth...He dwells with you, and will be in you.
1 Cor. 12:13. ...[We] all were made to drink of one Spirit.
Rom. 5:5. ...God's love has been poured into our hearts through the Holy Spirit which has been given to us.
Gal. 4:6. Because you are sons, God has sent the Spirit of his Son into our hearts, crying, "Abba! Father!" (Also Acts 5:32, 2 Cor. 1:22, 5:5, 1 Jn. 3:24, 4:13.)
Jn. 16:13-14. [Christ]: When the Spirit of truth comes, he will guide you into all the truth; for he will not speak on his own authority, but whatever he hears he will speak...He will take what is mine and declare it to you. (Also Jn. 14:26, 1 Jn. 2:27.)
*Rom. 11:33-34. O the depths of the riches and wisdom and knowledge of God! How unsearchable are his judgments and how inscrutable his ways! "For who has known the mind of the Lord, or who has been his counselor?"
Jn. 14:26 [Christ]: But the Counselor (Luther: Tröster), the Holy Spirit, whom the Father will send in my name, he will teach you all things...
Acts 1:8 [Christ]: You shall receive power (Luther: Kraft) when the Holy Spirit has come upon you...
Is. 40:29-31. [The Lord] gives power (Luther: Kraft) to the faint, and to him who has no might he increases strength. Even youths shall faint and be weary, and young men shall fall exhausted; but they who wait for the Lord shall renew their strength, they shall mount up with wings like eagles, they shall run and not be weary, they shall walk and not faint.

Rat,   Trost   und Hülfe schafft.
Counsel, comfort, and help provideth.
{With counsel, comfort, and help.}

Ps. 34:17, 19. When the righteous cry for help, the Lord hears, and delivers them out of all their troubles (Luther: Not)...Many are the afflictions of the righteous; but the Lord delivers him out of them all.

4. Alto Aria (Chorale Vs. 4)
●Praise to the Trinity, who is praised by all (129-4)
Gelobet sei der Herr,
Blessed   be the Lord,

Ps. 89:52. Blessed be the Lord for ever! Amen and Amen.
Ps. 106:48. Blessed be the Lord...from everlasting to everlasting! And let all the people say, "Amen!" Praise the Lord! (Doxology: also Ps. 41:13, 72:19)

Mein Gott, der ewig   lebet,
My   God, who eternally liveth,
{My God, who lives eternally,}

*****Rom. 11:36.** From him and through him and to him are all things. To him be glory for ever. Amen.
Ps. 150:6. Let everything that breathes praise the Lord!...

Den   alles   lobet, was
Whom all-things praise, that

Rev. 4:10. The twenty-four elders fall down before him who is seated on the throne and worship him who lives for ever and ever (Luther: von Ewigkeit zu Ewigkeit)... (Also Rev. 10:6, 15:7.)

In allen Lüften schwebet;
In all-the (skies) do-hover;
{Whom all things that hover in all the skies do praise;}

Ps. 148:1–4. Praise the Lord! Praise the Lord from the heavens, praise him in the heights! Praise him, all his angels, praise him, all his host! Praise him, sun and moon, praise him, all you shining stars! Praise him, you highest heavens, and you waters above the heavens!

Gelobet sei der Herr,
Blessed   be the Lord,

Is. 6:1–3. ...I saw the Lord sitting upon a throne, high and lifted up; and his train filled the temple. Above him stood the seraphim; each had six wings: with two he covered his face, and with two he covered his feet, and with two he flew. And one called to another and said: "Holy, holy, holy is the Lord of hosts; the whole earth is full of his glory."

Des   Name heilig heißt,
Whose name Holy is-called,
{Whose name is called Holy,}

1 Sam. 2:2. There is none holy like the Lord...

Gott   Vater, Gott der Sohn
God (the) Father, God the Son,

Is. 57:15. [He is] the high and lofty One who inhabits eternity, whose name is Holy...

Und Gott der Heilge Geist.
And God the Holy Ghost.

Mt. 28:19. ...the name of the Father and of the Son and of the Holy Spirit.

5. Chorale (Vs. 5)
●Praise to the Trinity; singing "Holy" with angels (129-5)
        Dem wir das Heilig itzt
(The-one) to-whom we that "Holy" now

*****Rom. 11:36.** From him and through him and to him are all things. To him be glory for ever. Amen.

Mit Freuden lassen klingen
With joy   let   resound
{The one to whom we now let that *Sanctus* joyfully resound}

Rev. 4:8–11. And the four living creatures, each of them with six wings, are full of eyes all round and within, and day and night they never cease to sing, "Holy, holy, holy, is the Lord God Almighty, who was and is and is to come!" And whenever the living creatures give glory and honor and thanks to him who is seated on the throne, who lives for ever and ever, the twenty-four elders fall down before him who is seated on the throne and worship him who lives for ever and ever; they cast their crowns before the throne, singing, "Worthy art thou, our Lord and God, to receive glory and honor and power, for thou didst create all things, and by thy will they existed and were created."

Und mit der Engel Schar
And with the angel host

Das Heilig, Heilig singen,
That "Holy, Holy" sing,

Den herzlich lobt   und preist
Whom heartily doth-laud and praise

Rev. 5:11–14. Then I looked, and I heard around the throne and the living creatures and the elders the voice of many angels, numbering myriads of myriads and thousands of thousands, saying with a loud voice, "Worthy is the Lamb who was slain, to receive power and wealth and wisdom and might and honor and glory and blessing!" And I heard every creature in heaven and on earth and under the earth and in the sea, and all therein, saying, "To him who sits upon the throne and to the Lamb be blessing and honor and glory and might for ever and ever!" And the four living creatures said, "Amen!" and the elders fell down and worshiped.

Die ganze Christenheit:
The entire Christendom:
{Whom the entire Christendom doth heartily laud and praise:}

Gelobet sei mein Gott
Praised be   my   God

In alle Ewigkeit!
For all   eternity!

Ps. 106:48. Blessed be the Lord, the God of Israel, from everlasting to everlasting! And let all the people say, "Amen!" Praise the Lord!

BWV 130
Herr Gott, dich loben alle wir
(NBA I/30; BC A179a/b)

St. Michael's Day: Sept. 29 (BWV 130, 19, 149, 50)
*Rev. 12:7–12 (The archangel Michael battles with the dragon)
*Mt. 18:1–11 (The kingdom of heaven belongs to children; their angels behold the face of God)
Librettist: Unknown

1. Chorus (Chorale Vs. 1)
●Angels: Praise to God for angels around God's throne (130-1)
Herr Gott, dich loben alle wir
Lord God, thee praise we-all
{Lord God, we all do praise thee}

Und sollen billig danken dir
And would willingly thank thee

Für dein Geschöpf der Engel schon,
For thy   creation, the angels, indeed,
{For thy creation, the angels,}

Die   um   dich schwebn um deinen Thron.
Who around thee hover about thy throne.
{Who hover around thee, about thy throne.}

2. Alto Recit. (Based on Chorale Vss. 2–3)
●Angels' mission: to encircle Christ and his children (130-2)
Ihr   heller Glanz und hohe Weisheit zeigt,
Their bright radiance and lofty wisdom shows,

Wie Gott   sich zu uns Menschen neigt,
How God himself to us mortals inclines,
{How God inclines himself to us mortals,}

Der solche Helden, solche Waffen
He-who such champions, such (armed-defense)

Vor uns geschaffen.
For us has-created.

Sie ruhen ihm zu Ehren nicht;
They rest him to praise not;
{They do not rest from praising him;}

Ihr ganzer Fleiß ist nur dahin gericht',
Their whole diligence is only thereto directed,
{Their efforts are focused on this:}

Daß sie, Herr Christe, um dich sein
That they, Lord Christ, around thee be
{That they encircle thee, Lord Christ}

Und um dein armes Häufelein:
And around thy poor little-band:
{And thy poor little band;}

*Mt. 18:10 [Christ]: See that you do not despise one of these little ones; for I tell you that in heaven their angels always behold the face of my Father who is in heaven.
Rev. 5:11–12. I looked, and I heard around the throne and the living creatures and the elders the voice of many angels, numbering myriads of myriads and thousands of thousands, saying with a loud voice, "Worthy is the Lamb who was slain, to receive power and wealth and wisdom and might and honor and glory and blessing!" (Also Dan. 7:10, Ps. 68:17.)
Rev. 7:11–12. All the angels stood round the throne and round the elders and the four living creatures, and they fell on their faces before the throne and worshiped God, saying, "Amen! Blessing and glory and wisdom and thanksgiving and honor and power and might be to our God for ever and ever! Amen."
Is. 6:1–3. ...I saw the Lord sitting upon a throne, high and lifted up; and his train filled the temple. Above him stood the seraphim; each had six wings: with two he covered his face, and with two he covered his feet, and with two he flew. And one called to another and said: "Holy, holy, holy is the Lord of hosts; the whole earth is full of his glory."

Rev. 7:11. All the angels stood round the throne and round the elders and the four living creatures, and they fell on their faces before the throne and worshiped God.
Rev. 4:8. And the four living creatures, each of them with six wings... day and night...never cease to sing, "Holy, holy, holy, is the Lord God Almighty, who was and is and is to come!"
Heb. 1:14. Are [angels] not all ministering spirits sent forth to serve, for the sake of those who are to obtain salvation?
Ps. 103:19–21. The Lord has established his throne in the heavens, and his kingdom rules over all...His angels, [his] mighty ones...do his word, hearkening to the voice of his word!...All his hosts, his ministers ...do his will!
Ex. 23:20 [God]: Behold, I send an angel before you, to guard you on the way and to bring you to the place which I have prepared.
Ps. 91:10–11. No evil shall befall you, no scourge come near your tent. For [the Lord] will give his angels charge of you to guard you in all your ways. (Also Lk. 4:10.)
2 Cor. 10:3–4. For though we live in the world we are not carrying on a worldly war, for the weapons of our warfare are not worldly but have divine power to destroy strongholds.
Eph. 6:11–12. Put on the whole armor of God, that you may be able to stand against the wiles of the devil. For we are not contending against flesh and blood, but against the principalities, against the powers, against the world rulers of this present darkness, against the spiritual hosts of wickedness in the heavenly places. (Also 1 Pet. 5:8.)
*Rev. 12:7–9. Now war arose in heaven, Michael and his angels fighting against the dragon; and the dragon and his angels fought, but

Wie nötig ist doch diese Wacht
How needful is indeed (their) watch

Bei Satans Grimm und Macht?
Amidst Satan's fury and might?

3. Bass Aria (Based on Chorale Vss. 4-6)
●Dragon tirelessly seeks to devour God's children (130-3)
Der alte Drache brennt vor Neid
The ancient dragon burns with envy

Und dichtet stets auf neues Leid,
And devises ever (to bring) new harm,

Daß er das kleine Häuflein trennet.
That he (our) little band divide.

Er tilgte gern, was Gottes ist,
He would-eradicate gladly, what God's is,
{He would gladly eradicate whatever belongs to God,}

Bald braucht er List,
Soon uses he craftiness,
{He is quick to use craftiness,}

Weil er nicht Rast noch Ruhe kennet.
For he neither rest nor repose knows.
{For he knows neither rest nor repose.}

4. Soprano & Tenor Recit. (Based on Chorale Vss. 7-9)
●Angels guard us like they did Daniel & his friends (130-4)
Wohl aber uns, daß Tag und Nacht
Well though for-us, that day and night
{Fortunately, though, for us that day and night}

Die Schar der Engel wacht,
The host of angels keeps-watch,

Des Satans Anschlag zu zerstören!
- Satan's assault to destroy!

Ein Daniel, so unter Löwen sitzt,
A Daniel, who among lions sits,
{A Daniel, sitting among lions,}

Erfährt, wie ihn die Hand des Engels schützt.
Discovers, how him the hand of angels does-protect.
{Discovers how the hand of angels protects him.}

Wenn dort die Glut
If there the embers

In Babels Ofen keinen Schaden tut,
In Babylon's furnace no injury (can) do,

So lassen Gläubige ein Danklied hören,
Then let believers a song-of-thanks be-heard,
{Then believers can let a song of thanks be heard;}

they were defeated and there was no longer any place for them in heaven. And the great dragon was thrown down, that ancient serpent, who is called the Devil and Satan, the deceiver of the whole world—he was thrown down to the earth, and his angels were thrown down with him.

1 Pet. 5:8. Be sober, be watchful. Your adversary the devil prowls around like a roaring lion, seeking some one to devour. (Also Lk. 22:31-32.)
*Rev. 12:7-12. War arose in heaven, Michael and his angels fighting against the dragon; and the dragon and his angels fought, but they were defeated...And the great dragon was thrown down, that ancient serpent, who is called the Devil and Satan, the deceiver of the whole world—he was thrown down to the earth, and his angels were thrown down with him. And I heard a loud voice in heaven, saying, "Now the salvation and the power and the kingdom of our God and the authority of his Christ have come, for the accuser of our brethren has been thrown down, who accuses them day and night before our God. And they have conquered him by the blood of the Lamb and by the word of their testimony, for they loved not their lives even unto death. Rejoice then, O heaven and you that dwell therein! But woe to you, O earth and sea, for the devil has come down to you in great wrath, because he knows that his time is short!" (Also Rev. 20:1-3.)
2 Cor. 11:14. ...Satan disguises himself as an angel of light. Eph. 6:11. Put on the whole armor of God, that you may be able to stand against the wiles (Luther: listigen Anläufe) of the devil.

*Mt. 18:10 [Christ]: See that you do not despise one of these little ones; for I tell you that in heaven their angels always behold the face of my Father who is in heaven.
Heb. 1:14. Are [angels] not all ministering spirits sent forth to serve, for the sake of those who are to obtain salvation? (Also Ps. 103:20-21.)
Dan. 6:16, 19, 21-22. ...King [Darius] commanded, and Daniel was brought and cast into the den of lions. The king said to Daniel, "May your God, whom you serve continually, deliver you!"...Then, at break of day, the king arose and went in haste to the den of lions...Then Daniel said to the king, "O king live for ever! My God sent his angel and shut the lions' mouths, and they have not hurt me, because I was found blameless before him; and also before you, O king, I have done no wrong."
2 Tim. 4:17. The Lord stood by me...so I was rescued from the lion's mouth. (Also Heb. 11:33.)
Dan. 3:20-21, 24-25. [King Nebuchadnezzar] ordered certain mighty men of his army to bind Shadrach, Meshach, and Abednego, and to cast them into the burning fiery furnace. Then these men were bound in their mantles, their tunics, their hats, and their other garments, and they were cast into the burning fiery furnace...Then King Nebuchadnezzar was astonished and rose up in haste. He said to his counselors, "Did we not cast three men bound into the fire?" They answered the king, "True, O king." He answered, "But I see four men loose, walking in the midst of the fire and they are not hurt; and the appearance of the fourth is like a son of the gods."
Ps. 91:9-13. Because you have made the Lord your refuge, the Most

So   stellt   sich in Gefahr
Then presents itself in danger

Noch jetzt der Engel Hülfe dar.
Even now the angels' help   - .
{Then the angels' help appears in danger, even today.}

5. Tenor Aria (Based on Chorale Vs. 10)
●Prayer: May angels protect us; take us up like Elijah (130–5)
Laß, o Fürst der Cherubinen,
Grant, O Prince of-the Cherubim (that),

Dieser Helden hohe Schar
This   heroic lofty   host

Immerdar
Evermore

Deine Gläubigen bedienen;
Thy   believers might-serve;

Daß sie auf Elias Wagen
That they in Elijah's chariot

Sie zu dir gen Himmel tragen.
Them to thee (in) heaven   carry.
{That they would carry them up to thee in heaven in Elijah's chariot.}

6. Chorale (Vss. 11–12)
●Praising God with angels; prayer that they protect us (130–6)
Darum   wir billig loben dich
Therefore we willingly praise thee

Und danken dir, Gott, ewiglich,
And   thank thee, God, eternally,

Wie auch der lieben Engel Schar
As   also the dear angel host

Dich preisen heut und immerdar.
Thee praises today and evermore.
{Praises thee today and evermore.}

///

Und bitten dich,   wollst allezeit
And ask   thee, (that thou) wouldst alway

Dieselben heißen sein   bereit,
Them   bid   to-be prepared,
{Bid them to be prepared,}

Zu schützen deine kleine Herd,
To protect thy   little flock,

So   hält dein göttlichs Wort in Wert.
Which holds thy   divine Word in esteem.

High your habitation, no evil shall befall you, no scourge come near your tent. For he will give his angels charge of you to guard you in all your ways. On their hands they will bear you up, lest you dash your foot against a stone. You will tread on the lion and the adder, the young lion and the serpent you will trample under foot. (Also Mk. 16:18, Lk. 10:19.)

Ps. 99:1. The Lord reigns...he sits enthroned upon the cherubim... (Also Ps. 80:1, 103:19–21, Is. 37:16, Ezek. 11:22.)
***Mt. 18:10 [Christ]:** See that you do not despise one of these little ones; for I tell you that in heaven their angels always behold the face of my Father who is in heaven.
Mt. 26:52–53. Then Jesus said..."Do you think that I cannot appeal to my Father, and he will at once send me more than twelve legions of angels?"
Ps. 91:11. [The Lord] will give his angels charge of you to guard you in all your ways.
Ps. 103:20–21. Bless the Lord, O you his angels, you mighty ones who do his word, hearkening to the voice of his word! Bless the Lord, all his hosts, his ministers that do his will! (Also Heb. 1:14.)
2 Kings 2:11–12. As [Elijah and Elisha] still went on and talked, behold, a chariot of fire and horses of fire separated the two of them. And Elijah went up by a whirlwind into heaven. And Elisha saw it and he cried, "My father, my father! the chariots of Israel and its horsemen!" And he saw him no more.

Ps. 145:1–2. I will extol thee, my God and King, and bless thy name for ever and ever. Every day I will bless thee, and praise thy name for ever and ever.
Rev. 5:11–14. I looked, and I heard around the throne and the living creatures and the elders the voice of many angels, numbering myriads of myriads and thousands of thousands, saying with a loud voice, "Worthy is the Lamb who was slain, to receive power and wealth and wisdom and might and honor and glory and blessing!" And I heard every creature in heaven and on earth and under the earth and in the sea, and all therein, saying, "To him who sits upon the throne and to the Lamb be blessing and honor and glory and might for ever and ever!" And the four living creatures said, "Amen!" and the elders fell down and worshiped. (Also Ps. 103:19–21, Dan. 7:10.)

Heb. 1:14. Are [angels] not all ministering spirits sent forth to serve, for the sake of those who are to obtain salvation?
Ps. 34:6–8. This poor man cried, and the Lord heard him, and saved him out of all his troubles. The angel of the Lord encamps around those who fear him, and delivers them. O taste and see that the Lord is good!...
Ps. 28:8–9. The Lord is the strength of his people, he is the saving refuge of his anointed. O save thy people, and bless thy heritage; be thou their shepherd, and carry them for ever.
Ps. 91:9–11. Because you have made the Lord your refuge, the Most High your habitation, no evil shall befall you, no scourge come near your tent. For he will give his angels charge of you to guard you in all your ways.

BWV 131
Aus der Tiefen rufe ich, Herr, zu dir
(NBA I/34; BC B25)

Occasion Unknown (BWV 131, 150, 117, 192, 100, 97)
Perhaps this cantata was intended for a day of penitence.
Librettist: perhaps Georg Christian Eilmar

1. Chorus
●Crying from the depths to the Lord: Ps. 130:1-2 (131-1)
Aus der Tiefen rufe ich, Herr, zu dir. Herr,
Out of-the depths cry I, Lord, to thee. Lord,

höre meine Stimme, laß deine Ohren merken
hear my voice, let thine ears give-heed

auf die Stimme meines Flehens!
to the voice of-my supplication!

2. Bass Arioso & Soprano Chorale (Vs. 2) (Chorale: see also
113-2)
●Sin's burden removed in Christ: Ps. 130:3-4 (131-2)
So du willt, Herr, Sünde zurechnen,
If thou wouldst, Lord, sin reckon,
{Lord, if thou shouldst keep an account of sins committed,}

Herr, wer wird bestehen?
Lord, who would stand?

Erbarm dich mein in solcher Last,
Have-mercy on-me (who-has) such (a) burden,
{Have mercy on me with my great burden,}

Nimm sie aus meinem Herzen,
Take it out of-my heart,

Dieweil du sie gebüßet hast
Since thou for-it atoned hast
{Since thou hast atoned for it}

Am Holz mit Todesschmerzen,
On-the (tree) with death's-pangs,

Denn bei dir ist die Vergebung,
For with thee (there) is - forgiveness,

    daß man dich fürchte.
    that one thee (may) fear.
    {that one may fear thee.}

Auf daß ich nicht mit großem Weh
So that I not amidst great woe
{So that I do not go to ruin in great woe}

In meinen Sünden untergeh,
Amidst my sins go-under,
{Amidst my sins,}

Noch ewiglich verzage.
Nor evermore despair.

Ps. 130:1-2. *Out of the depths I cry to thee, O Lord! Lord, hear my voice! Let thy ears be attentive to the voice of my supplications!*
Ps. 69:1-3, 13-15. Save me, O God! For the waters have come up to my neck. I sink in deep mire, where there is no foothold; I have come into deep waters, and the flood sweeps over me. I am weary with my crying; my throat is parched. My eyes grow dim with waiting for my God... With thy faithful help rescue me from sinking in the mire; let me be delivered from my enemies and from the deep waters. Let not the flood sweep over me, or the deep swallow me up, or the pit close its mouth over me. (Also Ps. 18:16, 124:4-5, 144:7.)
Ps. 42:7. ...All thy waves and thy billows have gone over me.

Ps. 130:3. *If thou, O Lord, shouldst mark iniquities, Lord, who could stand!*
Ps. 143:2. Enter not into judgment with thy servant; for no man living is righteous before thee.
Ps. 76:7. But thou, terrible art thou! Who can stand before thee when once thy anger is roused? (Also Nah. 1:6, Mal. 3:2, Rev. 6:17.)
Gal. 3:11. Now it is evident that no man is justified before God by the law; for "He who through faith is righteous shall live." (Also Rom. 3:20.)
Is. 1:4. Ah, sinful nation, a people laden with iniquity...
Mt. 11:28-30 [Christ]: Come to me, all who labor and are heavy laden, and I will give you rest. Take my yoke upon you, and learn from me; for I am gentle and lowly in heart, and you will find rest for your souls. For my yoke is easy, and my burden is light. (Also Jer. 6:16.)
1 Esdras (Apocrypha) 8:86. ...Thou, O Lord, didst lift the burden of our sins.
1 Pet. 3:18. Christ...died for sins once for all, the righteous for the unrighteous, that he might bring us to God... (Also 1 Cor. 15:3.)
1 Pet. 2:24. He himself bore our sins in his body on the tree, that we might die to sin and live to righteousness. By his wounds you have been healed. (Also Is. 53:5, 12, Acts 5:30.)
Gal. 3:13. Christ redeemed us from the curse of the law, having become a curse for us—for it is written, "Cursed be every one who hangs on a tree." (Also 1 Pet. 3:18.)
Ps. 130:4. *But there is forgiveness with thee, that thou mayest be feared.*
Ps. 103:12. As far as the east is from the west, so far does he remove our transgressions from us. (Also Is. 1:18.)
Col. 2:13-14. You, who were dead in trespasses and the uncircumcision of your flesh, God made alive together with [Christ], having forgiven us all our trespasses, having canceled the bond which stood against us with its legal demands; this he set aside, nailing it to the cross.
Jn. 3:16. God so loved the world that he gave his only Son, that whoever believes in him should not perish but have eternal life.
Jn. 8:24 [Christ]: I told you that you would die in your sins, for you will die in your sins unless you believe that I am he.

3. Chorus
●Waiting for the Lord; hoping in his Word: Ps. 130:5 (131–3)
Ich harre des Herrn, meine Seele harret,
I   wait-for the Lord,   my   soul   waits,

und ich hoffe auf sein Wort.
and   I   hope   in   his   Word.

4. Tenor Aria & Alto Chorale (Vs. 5)
●Cleansing from sin sought like David & Manasseh did
(131–4)
Meine Seele wartet auf den Herrn von einer Morgenwache
My   Soul   waits for the Lord from one morning-watch

bis zu der andern.
- to the other.

Und weil ich denn in meinem Sinn,
And because I - in   my   heart—

Wie ich zuvor geklaget,
As   I   before have-lamented—

Auch ein betrübter Sünder bin,
Also a troubled sinner am,

Den sein Gewissen naget,
Whom his conscience rankles,
{Whose conscience rankles him,}

Und wollte gern im Blute dein
And would gladly in (the) blood of-thine

Von Sünden abgewaschen sein
From (my) sins   washed   be
{And would gladly be washed from my sins in thy blood}

Wie David und Manasse.
Like David and Manasseh.

5. Chorus
●Hope in the Lord for he will pardon: Ps. 130:7–8 (131–5)
Israel hoffe auf den Herrn; denn bei dem Herrn
Israel, hope in the Lord; for with the Lord

ist die Gnade und   viel Erlösung bei ihm.
is - mercy and (there is) much redemption with him.

Und er wird Israel erlösen aus allen seinen Sünden.
And he will Israel redeem from all   of-his   sins.

Ps. 130:5. *I wait for the Lord, my soul waits, and in his word I hope.*
Ps. 33:20. Our soul waits for the Lord; he is our help and shield.
Ps. 119:81–82. [O Lord,] my soul languishes for thy salvation; I hope in thy word. My eyes fail with watching for thy promise; I ask, "When wilt thou comfort me?"
Ps. 69:3. I am weary with my crying; my throat is parched. My eyes grow dim with waiting for my God.

Ps. 130:6. *My soul waits for the Lord more than watchmen for the morning, more than watchmen for the morning.*
Ps. 32:3–5. When I declared not my sin, my body wasted away through my groaning all day long. For day and night thy hand was heavy upon me; my strength was dried up as by the heat of summer. I acknowledged my sin to thee, and I did not hide my iniquity; I said, "I will confess my transgressions to the Lord"; then thou didst forgive the guilt of my sin. (Also 1 Jn. 1:7–9.)
1 Pet. 1:18–19. You know that you were ransomed from the futile ways inherited from your fathers, not with perishable things such as silver or gold, but with the precious blood of Christ, like that of a lamb without blemish or spot. (Also Eph. 2:13, Heb. 13:12, Rev. 5:9.)
2 Sam. 12:7, 9, 13. [After King David had sinned,] Nathan said to [him], "You are the man...You have smitten Uriah the Hittite with the sword, and have taken his wife [Bathsheba] to be your wife"...David said to Nathan, "I have sinned against the Lord," And Nathan said to David, "The Lord also has put away your sin."
Ps. 51:1–2. A Psalm of David, when Nathan the prophet came to him, after he had gone in to Bathsheba. Have mercy on me, O God, according to thy steadfast love; according to thy abundant mercy blot out my transgressions. Wash me thoroughly from my iniquity, and cleanse me from my sin! (Also Ps. 38:17–18.)
2 Chron. 33:2, 11–13. [King Manasseh] did what was evil in the sight of the Lord...Therefore the Lord brought upon them the commanders of the army of the king of Assyria...And when [Manasseh] was in distress he entreated the favor of the Lord his God and humbled himself greatly before the God of his fathers. He prayed to him and God received his entreaty and heard his supplication and brought him again to Jerusalem into his kingdom...

Ps. 130:7–8. *O Israel, hope in the Lord! For with the Lord there is steadfast love, and with him is plenteous redemption. And he will redeem Israel from all his iniquities.* (Also Ps. 25:22.)
Ps. 103:2–3, 8–12. Bless the Lord, O my soul, and forget not all his benefits, who forgives all your iniquity...The Lord is merciful and gracious, slow to anger and abounding in steadfast love. He will not always chide, nor will he keep his anger for ever. He does not deal with us according to our sins, nor requite us according to our iniquities. For as the heavens are high above the earth, so great is his steadfast love toward those who fear him; as far as the east is from the west, so far does he remove our transgressions from us. (Also Is. 1:18.)

BWV 132
Bereitet die Wege, bereitet die Bahn!
(NBA I/1; BC A6)

4. S. in Advent (BWV 132)
*Phil. 4:4–7 (Exhortation to rejoice in the Lord always)
*Jn. 1:19–28 (Testimony of John the Baptist concerning himself)
Librettist: Salomon Franck

1. Soprano Aria
●Advent: Prepare the way for the coming Messiah! (132-1)
Bereitet die Wege, bereitet die Bahn!
Prepare the roads, prepare the pathway!

Bereitet die Wege
Prepare the roads

Und machet die Stege
And make the footpaths

Im Glauben und Leben
In faith and life

Dem Höchsten ganz eben,
For-the Most-High completely level,
{Completely level for the Most High,}

Messias kömmt an!
Messiah is-coming!

2. Tenor Recit.
●Advent preparation requires clearing away sin (132-2)
Willst du dich Gottes Kind und Christi Bruder nennen,
Wouldst thou thyself God's child and Christ's brother call,
{If thou wouldst call thyself God's child and Christ's brother,}

So müssen Herz und Mund den Heiland frei bekennen.
Then must heart and mouth the Savior freely confess.
{Then heart and mouth must freely confess the Savior.}

Ja, Mensch, dein ganzes Leben
Yes, (O) man, thy entire life

Muß von dem Glauben Zeugnis geben!
Must of (thy) faith testimony give!
{Must give testimony of thy faith!}

Soll Christi Wort und Lehre
(Even-if) Christ's word and teaching (should)

Auch durch dein Blut versiegelt sein,
- Through thy blood sealed be,
{Be sealed with thy blood,}

So gib dich willig drein!
- Give thyself willingly thereto!

*Jn. 1:19–23. This is the testimony of John, when the Jews sent priests and Levites from Jerusalem to ask him, "Who are you?" He confessed, he did not deny, but confessed, "I am not the Christ." And they asked him, "What then? Are you Elijah?" He said, "I am not." "Are you the prophet?" And he answered, "No." They said to him then, "Who are you? Let us have an answer for those who sent us. What do you say about yourself?" He said, "I am the voice of one crying in the wilderness, 'Make straight the way of the Lord,' as the prophet Isaiah said." (Also Mt. 3:3.)

Mt. 3:1–3, 5–6. In those days came John the Baptist, preaching in the wilderness of Judea, "Repent, for the kingdom of heaven is at hand." For this is he who was spoken of by the prophet Isaiah when he said, "The voice of one crying in the wilderness: Prepare the way of the Lord, make his paths straight."...Then went out to him Jerusalem and all Judea and all the region about the Jordan, and they were baptized by him in the river Jordan, confessing their sins. (Also Mk. 1:1–3.)

Is. 40:3–5. A voice cries: "In the wilderness prepare the way of the Lord, make straight in the desert a highway for our God. Every valley shall be lifted up, and every mountain and hill be made low; the uneven ground shall become level, and the rough places a plain. And the glory of the Lord shall be revealed, and all flesh shall see it together, for the mouth of the Lord has spoken."

Mt. 12:48, 50. [Jesus] replied to the man..."Who is my mother, and who are my brothers?...Whoever does the will of my Father in heaven is my brother, and sister, and mother." (Also Mk. 3:33–35, Lk. 8:21.)

Heb. 2:11. He who sanctifies and those who are sanctified have all one origin. That is why he is not ashamed to call them brethren.

Mt. 7:21 [Christ]: Not every one who says to me, "Lord, Lord," shall enter the kingdom of heaven, but he who does the will of my Father who is in heaven.

Rom. 10:9–10. If you confess with your lips (Luther: Munde) that Jesus is Lord and believe in your heart that God raised him from the dead, you will be saved. For man believes with his heart and so is justified, and he confesses with his lips (Luther: Munde) and so is saved. (Also Mt. 10:32–33, Lk. 12:8–9.)

Jms. 2:14, 17. What does it profit, my brethren, if a man says he has faith but has not works? Can his faith save him?...So faith by itself, if it has no works, is dead.

Mt. 7:16 [Christ]: You will know them by their fruits...

Heb. 12:4. In your struggle against sin you have not yet resisted to the point of shedding your blood.

Rev. 2:10 [Christ]: Do not fear what you are about to suffer. Behold, the devil is about to throw some of you into prison, that you may be tested, and for ten days you will have tribulation. Be faithful unto death, and I will give you the crown of life.

Acts 21:13. ...I am ready not only to be imprisoned but even to die...for the name of the Lord Jesus.

Denn dieses ist der Christen Kron und Ehre.
For   this is the Christian's crown and glory.

Indes,   mein Herz, bereite
Meanwhile, my heart, prepare

Noch heute
Yet   today

Dem Herrn die Glaubensbahn
For-the Lord the pathway-of-faith

Und räume weg die Hügel und die Höhen,
And clear away the hills and the high-places,

Die   ihm entgegen stehen!
Which to-him contrary   stand!
{Which are opposed to him!}

Wälz ab die schweren Sündensteine,
Roll away the   heavy   stones-of-sin,

Nimm deinen Heiland an,
Receive thy   Savior   - ,

Daß er mit dir im Glauben sich vereine!
That he with thee in   faith himself unite!
{That he might unite himself with thee through faith!}

3. Bass Aria
●Self-examination: The law shows us to be sinners (132–3)
Wer bist du? Frage dein Gewissen,
Who art thou? Question thy conscience,

Da wirst du sonder Heuchelei,
Then wilt thou without hypocrisy,

Ob   du, o Mensch,   falsch oder treu,
Whether thou, O man, (art) false or true,

Dein rechtes Urteil hören müssen.
Thy proper judgment have-to-hear.
{Then wilt thou hear thy proper judgment without hypocrisy: whether thou, O man, art false or true.}

Wer bist du?   Frage das Gesetze,
Who art thou? Question the law,

Das wird dir sagen, wer du bist,
It   will thee tell, who thou art,
{It will tell thee, who thou art,}

Ein Kind des Zorns in Satans Netze,
A child of wrath in Satan's net,

Ein falsch und heuchlerischer Christ.
A   false and   hypocritical Christian.

Mt. 3:3. ...Prepare the way of the Lord... (Also *Jn. 1:23.)
Is. 1:16–17. Wash yourselves; make yourselves clean; remove the evil of your doings from before my eyes; cease to do evil, learn to do good...
Mt. 5:29–30 [Christ]: If your right eye causes you to sin, pluck it out and throw it away; it is better that you lose one of your members than that your whole body be thrown into hell. And if your right hand causes you to sin, cut it off and throw it away; it is better that you lose one of your members than that your whole body go into hell. (Also Mt. 18:8–9, Mk. 9:43–47.)
Is. 1:4. Ah, sinful nation, a people laden with iniquity...
1 Esdras (Apocrypha) 8:86. ...Thou, O Lord, didst lift the burden of our sins.
Mk. 16:2–3. Very early on the first day of the week [the women] went to [Jesus'] tomb when the sun had risen. And they were saying to one another, "Who will roll away (Luther: wälzt) the stone for us from the door of the tomb?"
Heb. 12:1–2. ...Let us also lay aside every weight, and sin which clings so closely, and let us run with perseverance the race that is set before us, looking to Jesus the pioneer and perfecter of our faith...
Eph. 3:17. That Christ may dwell in your hearts through faith... (Also Col. 1:27, 2 Cor. 13:5.)
1 Cor. 6:17. He who is united to the Lord becomes one spirit with him.
Rom. 6:5–6. If we have been united with him in a death like his, we shall certainly be united with him in a resurrection like his. We know that our old self was crucified with him so that the sinful body might be destroyed, and we might no longer be enslaved to sin.

***Jn. 1:19.** ...The Jews sent priests and Levites from Jerusalem to ask [John], "Who are you?"
1 Cor. 11:28. Let a man examine himself...
Rom. 2:15–16. ...What the law requires is written on [men's] hearts, while their conscience also bears witness and their conflicting thoughts accuse or perhaps excuse them on that day when, according to my gospel, God judges the secrets of men by Christ Jesus.
Rom. 3:10–12, 23. ...None is righteous, no, not one; no one understands, no one seeks for God. All have turned aside, together they have gone wrong; no one does good, not even one...All have sinned and fall short of the glory of God. (Also Ps. 14:1–3, Is. 1:6.)
Jer. 17:9. The heart is deceitful above all things, and desperately corrupt; who can understand it?
Rom. 3:20. ...Through the law comes knowledge of sin.
Rom. 7:7, 13. If it had not been for the law, I should not have known sin...that sin might be shown to be sin, and through the commandment might become sinful beyond measure. Eph. 2:3. ...We all once lived in the passions of our flesh, following the desires of body and mind, and so we were by nature children of wrath like the rest of mankind.
Rom. 7:22–23. For I delight in the law of God, in my inmost self, but I see in my members another law at war with the law of my mind and making me captive to the law of sin which dwells in my members.
Jn. 8:34. ...Every one who commits sin is a slave to sin. (Also Rom. 6:16, 20, 2 Pet. 2:19.)

4. Alto Recit.

●Confession of unfaithfulness to God (132-4)

Ich will, mein Gott, dir frei heraus bekennen,
I would, my God, to-thee freely admit (that)

Ich habe dich bisher nicht recht bekannt.
I have thee before-now not truly confessed.
{I have not truly confessed thee before now.}

Ob Mund und Lippen gleich dich Herrn und Vater nennen,
Though mouth and lips - thee Lord and Father do-call,
{Though my mouth and lips call thee Lord and Father,}

Hat sich mein Herz doch von dir abgewandt.
Hath - my heart nevertheless from thee turned-away.
{My heart hath nevertheless turned away from thee.}

Ich habe dich verleugnet mit dem Leben!
I have thee denied with (my) life!
{I have denied thee with my life!}

Wie kannst du mir ein gutes Zeugnis geben?
How canst thou of-me a good testimony give?
{How canst thou give a good testimony of me?}

Als, Jesu, mich dein Geist und Wasserbad
When, Jesus, me thy Spirit- and water-bath
{When, O Jesus, thy bath by Spirit and water}

Gereiniget von meiner Missetat,
Cleansed of my misdeeds,
{Cleansed me of my misdeeds,}

Hab ich dir zwar stets feste Treu versprochen;
Did I to-thee indeed ever constant faithfulness promise;
{I promised thee ever constant faithfulness;}

Ach! aber ach! der Taufbund is gebrochen.
Ah! But alas! - Baptism's-covenant is broken.

Die Untreu reuet mich!
(My) faithlessness grieves me!

Ach Gott, erbarme dich,
Ah God, have-mercy,

Ach hilf, daß ich mit unverwandter Treue
Ah help, that I with unwavering faithfulness

Den Gnadenbund im Glauben stets erneue!
The covenant-of-grace in faith ever would-renew!

5. Alto Aria

●Baptism of blood & water provides clean raiment (132-5)
Christi Glieder, ach bedenket,
(O) Christ's members: Ah, consider,

Was der Heiland euch geschenket
What the Savior to-you hath-given

Ps. 32:3-5. [O Lord,] when I declared not my sin, my body wasted away through my groaning all day long. For day and night thy hand was heavy upon me; my strength was dried up as by the heat of summer. I acknowledged my sin to thee, and I did not hide my iniquity; I said, "I will confess my transgressions to the Lord"; then thou didst forgive the guilt of my sin.

Mt. 15:7-8 [Christ]: You hypocrites! Well did Isaiah prophesy of you, when he said: "This people honors me with their lips, but their heart is far from me." (See Is. 29:13.)

Deut. 23:23. You shall be careful to perform what has passed your lips, for you have voluntarily vowed to the Lord your God what you have promised with your mouth.

Jms. 1:22. Be doers of the word, and not hearers only, deceiving yourselves.

Rom. 2:13-14. For it is not the hearers of the law who are righteous before God but the doers of the law who will be justified. (Also Mt. 7:21.)

Rev. 2:4-5 [Christ]: I have this against you, that you have abandoned the love you had at first. Remember then from what you have fallen, repent and do the works you did at first. If not, I will come to you and remove your lampstand from its place, unless you repent.

Mt. 3:5-6. Then went out to [John the Baptist] Jerusalem and all Judea and all the region about the Jordan, and they were baptized by him in the river Jordan, confessing their sins. (Also Mk. 1:1-3.)

Rom. 6:3-7. Do you not know that all of us who have been baptized into Christ Jesus were baptized into his death? We were buried therefore with him by baptism into death, so that as Christ was raised from the dead by the glory of the Father, we too might walk in newness of life. For if we have been united with him in a death like his, we shall certainly be united with him in a resurrection like his. We know that our old self was crucified with him so that the sinful body might be destroyed, and we might no longer be enslaved to sin. For he who has died is freed from sin.

1 Pet. 3:21. Baptism, which corresponds to [Noah's experience] now saves you, not as a removal of dirt from the body but as an appeal to God for a clear conscience, through the resurrection of Jesus Christ.

Jer. 3:22 [God]: Return, O faithless sons, I will heal your faithlessness...

Heb. 10:28-29. A man who has violated the law of Moses dies without mercy at the testimony of two or three witnesses. How much worse punishment do you think will be deserved by the man who has spurned the Son of God, and profaned the blood of the covenant by which he was sanctified, and outraged the Spirit of grace?

Ezek. 16:9-13 [God]: I bathed you with water and washed off your blood from you, and anointed you with oil. I clothed you also with embroidered cloth and shod you with leather, I swathed you in fine linen and covered you with silk. And I decked you with ornaments, and put bracelets on your arms, and a chain on your neck. And I put a ring on your nose, and earrings in your ears, and a beautiful crown upon your head. Thus you were decked with gold and silver; and your

Durch der Taufe reines Bad!
Through - baptism's cleansing bath!

Bei der Blut- und Wasserquelle
By (means of) this blood- and water-spring

Werden eure Kleider helle,
Become your clothes bright,
{Your clothes,}

Die befleckt von Missetat.
Which spotted (were) with misdeeds.
{Which were spotted with misdeeds, become bright.}

Christus gab zum neuen Kleide
Christ gave (to you) as (your) new raiment

Roten Purpur, weiße Seide,
Crimson purple, white silk,

Diese sind der Christen Staat.
These are - Christians' finery.

6. Chorale (Missing in original source)[1] (See also 22-5, 96-6, 164-6.)
●Prayer: Crucify old nature so the new nature may live (132-6)
Ertöt uns durch dein Güte,
Mortify us through thy goodness,

Erweck uns durch dein Gnad;
Awaken us through thy grace;

Den alten Menschen kränke,
The old man mortify,

Daß der neu' leben mag
That the new may-live

Wohl hie auf dieser Erden,
Indeed here on this earth,

Den Sinn und all Begehren
(And that) (our) mind and all (our) desires

Und G'danken habn zu dir.
And thoughts (be directed) towards thee.

raiment was of fine linen, and silk, and embroidered cloth; you ate fine flour and honey and oil. You grew exceedingly beautiful, and came to regal estate.
Is. 61:10. ...My soul shall exult in my God; for he has clothed me with the garments of salvation, he has covered me with the robe of righteousness, as a bridegroom decks himself with a garland, and as a bride adorns herself with her jewels.
Tit. 3:5. He saved us...by the washing (Luther: Bad) of regeneration... (Also Heb. 10:22.)
Eph. 5:25–27. ...Christ loved the church and gave himself up for her, that he might sanctify her, having cleansed her by the washing of water with the word, that he might present the church to himself in splendor, without spot or wrinkle or any such thing, that she might be holy and without blemish. (Also Mt. 22:11–12.)
Rev. 7:9–10, 14. ...I looked, and behold, a great multitude which no man could number, from every nation, from all tribes and peoples and tongues, standing before the throne and before the Lamb, clothed in white robes, with palm branches in their hands, and crying out with a loud voice, "Salvation belongs to our God who sits upon the throne, and to the Lamb!"...These are they who have come out of the great tribulation; they have washed their robes and made them white in the blood of the Lamb.

Rom. 6:2–4, 6–7. ...How can we who died to sin still live in it? Do you not know that all of us who have been baptized into Christ Jesus were baptized into his death? We were buried therefore with him by baptism into death, so that as Christ was raised from the dead by the glory of the Father, we too might walk in newness of life...We know that our old self was crucified with him so that the sinful body might be destroyed, and we might no longer be enslaved to sin. For he who has died is freed from sin. (Also Gal. 2:20, Col. 2:12–14.)
Gal. 5:24. Those who belong to Christ Jesus have crucified the flesh with its passions and desires. (Also 1 Pet. 2:24.)
1 Pet. 4:1–2. Since therefore Christ suffered in the flesh, arm yourselves with the same thought, for whoever has suffered in the flesh has ceased from sin, so as to live for the rest of the time in the flesh no longer by human passions but by the will of God.
Heb. 12:5–6, 11. ...My son, do not regard lightly the discipline of the Lord, nor lose courage when you are punished by him. For the Lord disciplines him whom he loves, and chastises every son whom he receives...For the moment all discipline seems painful rather than pleasant; later it yields the peaceful fruit of righteousness...
Eph. 4:22–24. Put off your old nature which belongs to your former manner of life and is corrupt through deceitful lusts, and be renewed in the spirit of your minds, and put on the new nature, created after the likeness of God in true righteousness and holiness.
Col. 3:9–10. ...Seeing that you have put off the old nature with its practices and have put on the new nature, which is being renewed in knowledge after the image of its creator.
2 Cor. 5:15. [Christ] died for all, that those who live might live no longer for themselves but for him who for their sake died and was raised.
Col. 3:17. Whatever you do, in word or deed, do everything in the name of the Lord Jesus...
2 Cor. 5:9. ...We make it our aim to please him. (Also Eph. 5:10.)

---

[1]A separate publication of Franck's libretto includes this chorale.

BWV 133
Ich freue mich in dir
(NBA I/3; BC A16)

3. Day of Christmas (BWV 64, 133, 151, 248-III)
*Heb. 1:1–14 (God spoke through his Son, who is superior to the angels)
*Jn. 1:1–14 (Prologue: In the beginning was the Word...and the Word became flesh)
Librettist: Unknown

1. Chorus (Chorale Vs. 1)
●Christ's birth: A glad welcome to Jesus, my brother (133-1)
Ich freue mich in dir
I   rejoice -   in thee

Und heiße dich willkommen,
Und   bid   thee   welcome,

Mein liebes Jesulein!
My   dear   little-Jesus!

Du   hast dir vorgenommen,
Thou hast -   undertaken,

Mein Brüderlein zu sein.
My little-brother to be.
{To become my little brother.}

Ach, wie ein süßer Ton!
Ah, what a sweet sound!

Wie freundlich sieht er aus,
How friendly   -   he appears,
{How friendly he seems,}

Der große Gottessohn!
The great Son-of-God!

2. Alto Aria (Based on Chorale Vs. 2)
●Incarnation: We see God face to face! (133-2)
Getrost!   es faßt ein heilger Leib
Be-of-good-cheer! (Now) holds a   holy   body
{Be of good cheer! Now a holy body holds}

Des Höchsten unbegreiflichs Wesen.
The Most-High's incomprehensible substance.

Ich habe Gott—wie wohl ist mir geschehen!—
I   have God— how well (for) me has-happened!—
{How blessed I am—I have seen God}

Von Angesicht zu Angesicht gesehen.
 -    Face   to   face   seen.
{Face face to face!}

Ach! meine Seele muß   genesen.
Ah!   My   soul must (now) recover.

*Jn. 1:1, 14. In the beginning was the Word, and the Word was with God, and the Word was God...And the Word became flesh and dwelt among us, full of grace and truth; we have beheld his glory, glory as of the only Son of the Father.
*Heb. 1:1–2, 5–6. In many and various ways God spoke of old to our fathers by the prophets; but in these last days he has spoken to us by a Son, whom he appointed the heir of all things, through whom also he created the world...For to what angel did God ever say, "Thou art my Son, today I have begotten thee"? Or again, "I will be to him a father, and he shall be to me a son"? And again, when he brings the first-born into the world, he says, "Let all God's angels worship him."
Gal. 4:4–7. When the time had fully come, God sent forth his Son, born of woman, born under the law, to redeem those who were under the law, so that we might receive adoption as sons. And because you are sons, God has sent the Spirit of his Son into our hearts, crying, "Abba! Father!" So through God you are no longer a slave but a son, and if a son then an heir.
Heb. 2:14. Since therefore the children share in flesh and blood, [Christ] himself likewise partook of the same nature...
Heb. 2:11–12. He who sanctifies and those who are sanctified have all one origin. That is why he is not ashamed to call them brethren, saying, "I will proclaim thy name to my brethren, in the midst of the congregation I will praise thee."

*Jn. 1:14, 18. The Word became flesh and dwelt among us, full of grace and truth; we have beheld his glory, glory as of the only Son of the Father...No one has ever seen God; the only Son, who is in the bosom of the Father, he has made him known.
*Heb. 1:3. He reflects the glory of God and bears the very stamp of his nature (Luther: das Ebenbild seines Wesens)...
Phil. 2:5–7. ...Christ Jesus, who, though he was in the form of God, did not count equality with God a thing to be grasped, but emptied himself, taking the form of a servant, being born in the likeness of men.
Mt. 1:20. ...That which is conceived in [Mary] is of the Holy Spirit.
Jn. 14:9. Jesus said... "He who has seen me has seen the Father..."
Ex. 33:20. [God] said, "You cannot see my face; for man shall not see me and live."
Gen. 32:30. Jacob called the name of the place Peniel, saying, "...I have seen God face to face, and yet my life is preserved." (Luther: Ich habe Gott von Angesicht gesehen, und meine Seele ist genesen.) (Also Ps. 80:3, 19.)

3. Tenor Recit. (Based on Chorale Vs. 2)
●Christmas: God has come; we will not hide like Adam
(133–3)
Ein Adam mag sich   voller Schrecken
An Adam may, - filled-with terror
{Let Adam, filled with terror,}

Vor   Gottes Angesicht
Before God's   face
{Hide himself from God's face}

Im Paradies verstecken!
In paradise   hide   (himself)!
{In paradise!}

Der allerhöchste Gott kehrt selber bei uns ein:
The Most-High God lodges himself with us   - :
{The Host-High God himself lodges with us:}

Und so entsetzet sich mein Herze nicht;
And thus is-alarmed - my   heart not;
{And thus my heart is not alarmed;}

Es kennet sein erbarmendes Gemüte.
It knows his compassionate disposition.

Aus unermeßner Güte
Out-of unmeasured kindness

Wird   er ein kleines Kind
Becomes he a   little child
{He becomes a little child}

Und heißt mein Jesulein.
And is-called my little-Jesus.

4. Soprano Aria (Based on Chorale Vs. 3)
●Christ's birth: How sweet the news is! (133–4)
Wie lieblich klingt es in den Ohren,
How lovely rings - in (my) ears,

Dies Wort: mein Jesus ist geboren,
This word: my Jesus is born,

Wie   dringt es in das Herz hinein!
How penetrates it into (my) heart - !
{How it penetrates into my heart!}

Wer   Jesu Namen   nicht versteht
Whoever Jesus' name (does) not understand

Und wem es   nicht durchs Herze geht,
And whomever it (does) not to-the heart go,
{And whoever is not struck to the heart by this word,}

1 Jn. 2:28. And now, little children, abide in [Christ], so that when he appears we may have confidence and not shrink from him in shame at his coming.
Gen. 3:6, 8. [In the garden of Eden,] when the woman [Eve] saw that the tree was good for food, and that it was a delight to the eyes, and that the tree was to be desired to make one wise, she took of its fruit and ate; and she also gave some to her husband [Adam], and he ate... And they heard the sound of the Lord God walking in the garden in the cool of the day, and the man and his wife hid themselves from the presence of the Lord God...
Zech. 2:10–11. Sing and rejoice, O daughter of Zion; for lo, I come and I will dwell in the midst of you, says the Lord. And many nations shall join themselves to the Lord in that day, and shall be my people; and I will dwell in the midst of you, and you shall know that the Lord of hosts has sent me to you.
***Jn. 1:14.** The Word became flesh and dwelt among us...
Heb. 4:14–16. Since then we have a great high priest who has passed through the heavens, Jesus, the Son of God, let us hold fast our confession. For we have not a high priest who is unable to sympathize with our weaknesses, but one who in every respect has been tempted as we are, yet without sin. Let us then with confidence draw near to the throne of grace, that we may receive mercy and find grace to help in time of need.
Tit. 3:4–5. When the goodness and loving kindness of God our Savior appeared, he saved us, not because of deeds done by us in righteousness, but in virtue of his own mercy...
Eph. 2:7. That in the coming ages [God] might show the immeasurable riches of his grace in kindness (Luther: überschwenglichen Reichtum seiner Gnade durch seine Güte) toward us in Christ Jesus.
Jn. 3:16. For God so loved the world that he gave his only Son, that whoever believes in him should not perish but have eternal life.
Mt. 1:22–23. All this took place to fulfil what the Lord had spoken by the prophet: "Behold, a virgin shall conceive and bear a son, and his name shall be called Emmanuel" (which means, God with us). (See Is. 7:14.)

Is. 52:7. How beautiful upon the mountains are the feet of him who brings good tidings, who publishes peace, who brings good tidings of good, who publishes salvation...
Acts 13:32–33. We bring you the good news that what God promised to the fathers, this he has fulfilled to us...as also it is written in the second psalm, "Thou art my Son, today I have begotten thee."
Lk. 2:9–14, 16–20. An angel of the Lord appeared to [the shepherds], and the glory of the Lord shone around them...And the angel said to them, "...Behold, I bring you good news of a great joy which will come to all the people; for to you is born this day in the city of David a Savior, who is Christ the Lord. And this will be a sign for you: you will find a babe wrapped in swaddling cloths and lying in a manger." And suddenly there was with the angel a multitude of the heavenly host praising God and saying, "Glory to God in the highest, and on earth peace among men with whom he is pleased!"...And [the shepherds] went with haste, and found Mary and Joseph, and the babe lying in a manger. And when they saw it they made known the saying which had

Der muß   ein harter Felsen sein.
He must (indeed) a   hard   rock   be.
{Must be as hard as rock.}

5. Bass Recit. (Based on Chorale Vs. 3)
●Christ's coming to earth takes away fear of death (133-5)
Wohlan, des Todes Furcht und Schmerz
Well-then, - death's   fear   and   pain

Erwägt   nicht mein getröstet Herz.
Considers not   my comforted heart.
{Well then, my comforted heart gives no thought to death's fear and pain.}

Will   er vom Himmel sich
Would he from heaven   -

Bis zu der Erde lenken,
 - To the earth journey,

So   wird er auch an mich
Then will he also of me
{Then he will also be mindful of me}

In meiner Gruft gedenken.
In   my   tomb mindful-be.
{In my tomb.}

Wer   Jesum recht erkennt,
Whoever Jesus   truly   knows,

Der stirbt nicht, wenn er stirbt,
He dies not,   when he dies,
{He does not die when he dies,}

Sobald   er Jesum nennt.
As-soon-as he Jesus names.
{As soon as he names the name of Jesus.}

6. Chorale (Vs. 4)
●Holding fast to Jesus in life & death (133-6)
Wohlan,   so will ich mich
Well-then! Then would I   -

An dich, o Jesu, halten,
To thee, O Jesus, cleave,

Und sollte gleich die Welt
And should though the world
{Even if the world should}

been told them concerning this child; and all who heard it wondered at what the shepherds told them. But Mary kept all these things, pondering them in her heart. And the shepherds returned, glorifying and praising God for all they had heard and seen, as it had been told them.

Heb. 2:14-15. Since therefore the children share in flesh and blood, [Christ] himself likewise partook of the same nature, that through death he might destroy him who has the power of death, that is, the devil, and deliver all those who through fear of death were subject to lifelong bondage.
1 Cor. 15:25-26. [Christ] must reign until he has put all his enemies under his feet. The last enemy to be destroyed is death.
2 Tim. 1:10. ...through the appearing of our Savior Christ Jesus who abolished death and brought life and immortality to light... (Also Is. 25:8.)
1 Cor. 15:20-23. 47-49. ...Christ has been raised from the dead, the first fruits of those who have fallen asleep. For as by a man came death, by a man has come also the resurrection of the dead. For as in Adam all die, so also in Christ shall all be made alive. But each in his own order: Christ the first fruits, then at his coming those who belong to Christ...The first man was from the earth, a man of dust; the second man is from heaven. As was the man of dust, so are those who are of the dust; and as is the man of heaven, so are those who are of heaven. Just as we have borne the image of the man of dust, we shall also bear the image of the man of heaven. (Also Rom. 6:8-10.)
Jn. 11:25-26. Jesus said to [Martha], "I am the resurrection and the life; he who believes in me, though he die, yet shall he live, and whoever lives and believes in me shall never die. Do you believe this?" (Also Jn. 8:51.)
Jn. 20:31. These [things] are written that you may believe that Jesus is the Christ, the Son of God, and that believing you may have life in his name.
Mt. 1:21. ...You shall call his name Jesus, for he will save his people from their sins.
Acts 2:21. Whoever calls on the name of the Lord shall be saved.
Jn. 3:16. For God so loved the world that he gave his only Son, that whoever believes in him should not perish but have eternal life.
Rev. 2:10-11 [Christ]: ...Be faithful unto death, and I will give you the crown of life...He who conquers shall not be hurt by the second death.

Ps. 63:8. [O Lord,] my soul clings to thee...
S. of S. 3:4 [Bride]: ...I found him whom my soul loves. I held him, and would not let him go... (Also Gen. 32:26.)
Ps. 73:25, 28. [O Lord,] whom have I in heaven but thee? And there is nothing upon earth that I desire besides thee...For me it is good to be near God (Luther: daß ich mich zu Gott halte); I have made the Lord God my refuge...
Heb. 10:39. We are not of those who shrink back and are destroyed, but of those who have faith and keep their souls.
Heb. 10:23, 25. Let us hold fast the confession of our hope without wavering...and all the more as you see the Day drawing near.

In tausend Stücken spalten.
Into (a) thousand pieces split.
{Break into a thousand pieces.}

O Jesu, dir, nur dir,
O Jesus, for-thee, only for-thee,

Dir leb ich ganz allein;
For-thee live I - only;
{Will I live;}

Auf dich, allein auf dich,
In thee, only in thee,

Mein Jesu, schlaf ich ein.
My Jesus, fall-I-asleep.
{My Jesus, will I fall asleep.}
[einschlafen = to fall asleep]

BWV 134
Ein Herz, das seinen Jesum lebend weiß
(NBA I/10; BC A59a/b)

3. Easter Day (BWV 134, 145, 158)
*Acts 13:26–33 (Paul preaches of Christ's death and resurrection in synagogue at Antioch)
*Lk. 24:36–47 (Jesus appears to disciples in Jerusalem after his resurrection)
Librettist: Unknown (Much of it is a parody of BWV 134a: new text written for pre-existing music.)

1. Tenor & Alto Recit. (Music newly composed)
●Resurrected Jesus encountered and praised (134-1)
Tenor:
Ein Herz, das seinen Jesum lebend weiß,
A heart, that its Jesus (as) alive knows,
{A heart that knows Jesus to be alive,}

Empfindet Jesu neue Güte
Experiences Jesus' new kindness
{Experiences Jesus' kindness anew}

Und dichtet nur auf seines Heilands Preis.
And devises (nought) but for its Savior's praise.

Alto:
Wie freuet sich ein gläubiges Gemüte.
How rejoices - a believing disposition.
{How a believing disposition rejoices!}

2. Tenor Aria (Parody)
●Resurrection light has come: Offer praise to God! (134-2)
Auf, Gläubige, singet die lieblichen Lieder,
Arise, believers, sing the lovely songs,

Euch scheinet ein herrlich verneuetes Licht.
Upon-you shines a glorious, renewed light.

2 Pet. 3:10. But the day of the Lord will come like a thief, and then the heavens will pass away with a loud noise, and the elements will be dissolved with fire, and the earth and the works that are upon it will be burned up.
Mt. 24:35 [Christ]: Heaven and earth will pass away, but my words will not pass away. (Also Mk. 13:31, Lk. 21:33, Is. 40:8.)
Phil. 1:21. To me to live is Christ, and to die is gain. (Also 2 Cor. 5:8.)
Jn. 11:11, 13–15. ...[Jesus] said to them, "Our friend Lazarus has fallen asleep, but I go to awake him out of sleep."...Now Jesus had spoken of his death, but they thought that he meant taking rest in sleep. Then Jesus told them plainly, "Lazarus is dead; and for your sake I am glad that I was not there, so that you may believe..." (Also Lk. 8:52–53.)
1 Cor. 15:20, 23. ...Christ has been raised from the dead, the first fruits of those who have fallen asleep...Christ the first fruits, then at his coming those who belong to Christ. (Also Rom. 6:8–10.)

*Lk. 24:36–47. As [the disciples] were saying this, Jesus himself stood among them. But they were startled and frightened, and supposed that they saw a spirit. And he said to them, "Why are you troubled, and why do questionings rise in your hearts? See my hands and my feet, that it is I myself; handle me, and see; for a spirit has not flesh and bones as you see that I have." And while they still disbelieved for joy, and wondered, he said to them, "Have you anything here to eat?" They gave him a piece of broiled fish, and he took it and ate before them. Then he said to them, "These are my words which I spoke to you, while I was still with you, that everything written about me in the law of Moses and the prophets and the psalms must be fulfilled." Then he opened their minds to understand the scriptures, and said to them, "Thus it is written, that the Christ should suffer and on the third day rise from the dead, and that repentance and forgiveness of sins should be preached in his name to all nations, beginning from Jerusalem."
*Acts 13:32–33. We bring you the good news that what God promised to the fathers, this he has fulfilled to us their children by raising Jesus...

Is. 60:1–3. Arise, shine; for your light has come, and the glory of the Lord has risen upon you. For behold, darkness shall cover the earth, and thick darkness the peoples; but the Lord will arise upon you, and his glory will be seen upon you. And nations shall come to your light, and kings to the brightness of your rising.
Acts 26:22–23. ...What the prophets and Moses said would come to pass: that the Christ must suffer, and that, by being the first to rise

Der lebende Heiland gibt selige Zeiten,
The living Savior (brings) blessed times,

Auf, Seelen, ihr müsset ein Opfer bereiten,
Arise, (O) souls, ye must a sacrifice prepare,

Bezahlet dem Höchsten mit Danken die Pflicht.
Pay the Most-High with thanksgiving (your) obligation.
{Pay your obligation to the Most-High with thanksgiving.}

3. Tenor & Alto Recit. (Music newly composed)
●Christ conquered death and hell for us (134-3)
Tenor:
Wohl dir, Gott hat an dich gedacht,
Well for-thee, God has - thee remembered,
{How blessed thou art for God has remembered thee,}

O Gott geweihtes Eigentum;
O (thou) to-God consecrated possession;

Der Heiland lebt und siegt mit Macht.
The Savior lives, and conquers with might.

Zu deinem Heil, zu seinem Ruhm
To thy salvation, to his praise

Muß hier der Satan furchtsam zittern
Must here - Satan fearfully tremble
{Satan must fearfully tremble here}

Und sich die Hölle selbst erschüttern.
And - - hell itself quake.

Es stirbt der Heiland dir zu gut
(Thus) dies the Savior for-thy benefit
{The Savior dies for thy benefit}

Und fähret für dich zu der Höllen,
And travels for thee to - hell,

Sogar vergießet er sein kostbar Blut,
Even sheds he his precious blood,
{He even sheds his precious blood,}

Daß du in seinem Blute siegst,
That thou in his blood (canst) conquer,

Denn dieses kann die Feinde fällen,
For this can the foes bring-down,
{For this blood can bring down the foe,}

Und wenn der Streit dir an die Seele dringt,
And (even) if the strife - to (thy) soul does-press,

from the dead, he would proclaim light both to the people and to the Gentiles. (Also Eph. 5:14.)

Ps. 50:14, 23 [God]: Offer to God a sacrifice of thanksgiving, and pay your vows to the Most High...He who brings thanksgiving as his sacrifice honors me; to him who orders his way aright I will show the salvation of God! (Also Ps. 22:25, 61:8, 66:13-14, 116:14, 17-18, Jon. 2:9.)

Heb. 13:15. Through [Christ] then, let us continually offer up a sacrifice of praise to God, that is, the fruit of lips that acknowledge his name. (Also Ps. 51:15-17.)

Ps. 98:1-3. O sing to the Lord a new song, for he has done marvelous things! His right hand and his holy arm have gotten him victory. The Lord has made known his victory, he has revealed his vindication in the sight of the nations. He has remembered his steadfast love and faithfulness to the house of Israel...

Deut. 14:2. For you are a people holy to the Lord your God, and the Lord has chosen you to be a people for his own possession (Luther: Eigentum), out of all the peoples that are on the face of the earth. (Also 1 Pet. 2:9-10.)

Ex. 14:14. The Lord will fight for you, and you have only to be still.

Deut. 1:30. The Lord your God...will himself fight for you...

Rom. 6:4, 9. Christ was raised from the dead by the glory of the Father...We know that Christ being raised from the dead will never die again; death no longer has dominion over him.

Rom. 8:11. If the Spirit of him who raised Jesus from the dead dwells in you, he who raised Christ Jesus from the dead will give life to your mortal bodies also through his Spirit which dwells in you.

1 Cor. 15:55. O death, where is thy victory?...

Ps. 98:3. ...All the ends of the earth have seen the victory of our God.

Rev. 1:17-18 [Christ]: ...Fear not, I am the first and the last, and the living one; I died, and behold I am alive for evermore, and I have the keys of Death and Hades.

1 Pet. 1:21. Through [Christ] you have confidence in God, who raised him from the dead and gave him glory, so that your faith and hope are in God.

Rev. 12:10-11. ...Now the salvation and the power and the kingdom of our God and the authority of his Christ have come, for the accuser of our brethren has been thrown down, who accuses them day and night before our God. And they have conquered him by the blood of the Lamb...

Jms. 2:19. ...The demons believe—and shudder.

Eph. 4:9-10. In saying, "He ascended," what does it mean but that [Christ] had also descended into the lower parts of the earth? He who descended is he who also ascended far above all the heavens, that he might fill all things.

1 Jn. 3:8. ...The reason the Son of God appeared was to destroy the works of the devil.

1 Pet. 1:18-19. You know that you were ransomed from the futile ways inherited from your fathers...with the precious blood of Christ, like that of a lamb without blemish or spot. (Also Eph. 2:13, 1 Jn. 1:7, Heb. 13:12, Rev. 5:9.)

Rev. 12:11. [Our brethren] have conquered...by the blood of the Lamb ...for they loved not their lives even unto death.

Heb. 12:4. In your struggle against sin you have not yet resisted to the point of shedding your blood.

Daß du alsdann nicht überwunden   liegst.
That thou then   not   vanquished shouldst-lie.

Alto:
Der Liebe Kraft ist vor mich ein Panier
 - Love's power is before me   a standard
{Love's power is a standard before me}

Zum Heldenmut, zur Stärke in den Streiten:
For   valor,   for strength in the fighting:

Mir Siegeskronen zu bereiten,
Me crowns-of-victory to prepare,
{In order to prepare crowns of victory for me,}

Nahmst   du die Dornenkrone dir,
Didst-accept thou the crown-of-thorns - ,
{Thou didst accept the crown of thorns—}

Mein Herr, mein Gott, mein auferstandnes   Heil,
My   Lord, my God, my   risen   Salvation—

So   hat kein Feind an mir zum Schaden   teil.
Thus hath no foe on me for   harm (a) portion.
{And now no foe can harm me.}

Tenor:
Die Feinde zwar sind nicht zu   zählen.
The foes indeed (can) not (be) numberted.
{The foes indeed are more than can be numbered.}

Alto:
Gott schützt die ihm getreuen Seelen.
God protects the to-him faithful souls.
{God protects all souls who are faithful to him.}

Tenor:
Der letzte Feind ist   Grab und Tod.
The last   foe is (the) grave and death.

Alto:
Gott macht auch den zum Ende unsrer Not.
God makes even it to-be-the end of-our woe.
{And God even makes it to be the escape from earthly woes.}

4. Alto & Tenor Duet (Parody)
●Praise to God for reappearance of victorious Christ (134–4)
Wir danken und preisen dein brünstiges Lieben
We thank and praise thy   ardent   loving

Rom. 8:35–37. Who shall separate us from the love of Christ? Shall tribulation, or distress, or persecution, or famine, or nakedness, or peril, or sword? As it is written, "For thy sake we are being killed all the day long; we are regarded as sheep to be slaughtered." No, in all these things we are more than conquerors through him who loved us.
Rom. 8:17. ...[We are] fellow heirs with Christ, provided we suffer with him in order that we may also be glorified with him.
1 Pet. 4:1. Since therefore Christ suffered in the flesh, arm yourselves with the same thought, for whoever has suffered in the flesh has ceased from sin.
Is. 11:10. ....The root of Jesse shall stand as an ensign (Luther: Panier) to the peoples; him shall the nations seek...He will raise an ensign for the nations...
2 Tim. 4:6–8. ...The time of my departure has come. I have fought the good fight, I have finished the race, I have kept the faith. Henceforth there is laid up for me the crown of righteousness, which the Lord... will award to me on that Day, and not only to me but also to all who have loved his appearing. (Also Is. 28:5, 1 Pet. 5:4, Jms. 1:12, Rev. 2:10.)
Phil. 2:8–9. ...[Christ] humbled himself and became obedient unto death, even death on a cross. Therefore God has highly exalted him... (Also Heb. 12:2.)
Mt. 27:26, 28–29. ...Having scourged Jesus, [Pilate] delivered him to be crucified...And they stripped him and put a scarlet robe upon him, and plaiting a crown of thorns they put it on [Jesus'] head... (Also Mk. 15:17, Jn. 19:2, 5.)
*Acts 13:28, 30. Though [the rulers in Jerusalem] could charge [Jesus] with nothing deserving death, yet they asked Pilate to have him killed ...But God raised him from the dead. (Also Acts 2:24.)
Jn. 20:27–28. [After his resurrection, Jesus] said to Thomas, "Put your finger here, and see my hands; and put out your hand, and place it in my side; do not be faithless, but believing." Thomas answered him, "My Lord and my God!"
Eph. 1:19–22. ...The immeasurable greatness of his power [is at work] in us who believe, according to the working of his great might which he accomplished in Christ when he raised him from the dead and made him sit at his right hand in the heavenly places, far above all rule and authority and power and dominion...and he has put all things under his feet...
Ps. 25:19. Consider how many are my foes... (Also Ps. 3:1.)
Ps. 27:1, 3. The Lord is my light and my salvation; whom shall I fear? The Lord is the stronghold of my life; of whom shall I be afraid?... Though a host encamp against me, my heart shall not fear... (Also Ps. 118:6.)
1 Cor. 15:25–26. [Christ] must reign until he has put all his enemies under his feet. The last enemy to be destroyed is death. (Also Is. 25:8, 2 Tim. 1:10, 1 Cor. 15:55–56.)
1 Thess. 5:9–10. For God has not destined us for wrath, but to obtain salvation through our Lord Jesus Christ, who died for us so that whether we wake or sleep we might live with him.
Phil. 1:23. ...My desire is to depart and be with Christ, for that is far better. (Also 2 Cor. 5:8.)

Rom. 5:8. God shows his love for us in that while we were yet sinners Christ died for us.
*Acts 13:30. But God raised [Christ] from the dead.

Und bringen ein Opfer der Lippen vor dich.
And bring an offering of (our) lips before thee.

Der Sieger erwecket die freudigen Lieder,
The victor awakens (our) joyful songs,

Der Heiland erscheinet und tröstet uns wieder
The Savior appears and comforts us again

Und stärket die streitende Kirche durch sich.
And strengthens the contending church through himself.
{And strengthens the church-at-arms through himself.}

5. Tenor & Alto Recit. (Music newly composed)
●Christ's victory: May we appreciate & appropriate it (134–5)
Tenor:
Doch würke selbst
Yet bring-about, thyself,

den Dank in unserm Munde,
the giving-of-thanks in our mouth,

In dem er allzu irdisch ist;
In that it much-too earthly is;
{For it is much too earthly;}

Ja schaffe, daß zu keiner Stunde
Yes, see-to-it that at no hour

Dich und dein Werk kein menschlich Herz vergißt;
Thee and thy work (any) human heart forget;
{Any human heart forget thee and thy work;}

Ja, laß in dir das Labsal unsrer Brust
Yes, let in thee the refreshment of-our breasts
{Yes, let the refreshment of our breasts}

Und aller Herzen Trost und Lust,
And all hearts' comfort and delight,
{And the comfort and delight of all the hearts}

Die unter deiner Gnade trauen,
That beneath (the shelter of) thy mercy trust,
{Who trust in thy mercy}

Vollkommen und unendlich sein.
Perfect and neverending be.
{Be perfect and unending in thee.}

Es schließe deine Hand uns ein,
(Now) encircle thy hand us -,
{Now let thy hand encircle us,}

Heb. 13:15. Through him then, let us continually offer up a sacrifice of praise to God, that is, the fruit of lips that acknowledge his name. (Also Ps. 51:15–17, 119:108.)
*Lk. 24:36–39. As [the disciples] were saying this, Jesus himself stood among them. But they were startled and frightened, and supposed that they saw a spirit. And he said to them, "Why are you troubled, and why do questionings rise in your hearts? See my hands and my feet, that it is I myself; handle me, and see; for a spirit has not flesh and bones as you see that I have."
Deut. 1:30. The Lord your God who goes before you will himself fight for you...
Eph. 6:10–12. Finally, be strong in the Lord and in the strength of his might. Put on the whole armor of God, that you may be able to stand against the wiles (Luther: listigen Anläufe) of the devil. For we are not contending against flesh and blood, but against the principalities, against the powers, against the world rulers of this present darkness, against the spiritual hosts of wickedness in the heavenly places. (Also 1 Pet. 5:8, 2 Cor. 10:3–4, Phil. 1:28–30.)

Ps. 40:3. [The Lord] put a new song in my mouth, a song of praise to our God. Many will see and fear, and put their trust in the Lord. (Also Is. 51:16, 59:21.)
Ps. 34:1. I will bless the Lord at all times; his praise shall continually be in my mouth. (Also Ps. 63:3, 71:8, 109:30, 145:21, Heb. 13:15.)
Ps. 104:33–34. I will sing to the Lord as long as I live; I will sing praise to my God while I have being. May my meditation be pleasing to him, for I rejoice in the Lord.
Ps. 19:14. [O Lord,] let the words of my mouth and the meditation of my heart be acceptable in thy sight...
Ps. 51:15. O Lord, open thou my lips, and my mouth shall show forth thy praise.
Ps. 105:4–5. Seek the Lord and his strength, seek his presence continually! Remember the wonderful works that he has done... (Also 1 Chron. 16:11–12.)
Ps. 106:7. [O Lord,] our fathers, when they were in Egypt, did not consider thy wonderful works; they did not remember the abundance of thy steadfast love...
Ps. 106:13, 21. They soon forgot [God's] works; they did not wait for his counsel...They forgot God, their Savior, who had done great things in Egypt. (Also Ps. 78:10–11.)
Ps. 103:2. Bless the Lord, O my soul, and forget not all his benefits.
2 Cor. 6:1. ...We entreat you not to accept the grace of God in vain.
Phil. 2:13. God is at work in you, both to will and to work for his good pleasure.
Jms. 1:4. Let steadfastness have its full effect, that you may be perfect and complete, lacking in nothing.
1 Jn. 1:4. We are writing this that [your] joy may be complete.
Ps. 4:7. [God has] put more joy in my heart than...when...grain and wine abound.
Eph. 1:16–23. I...[pray]...that the God of our Lord Jesus Christ, the Father of glory, may give you a spirit of wisdom and of revelation in the knowledge of him, having the eyes of your hearts enlightened, that you may know what is the hope to which he has called you, what are the riches of his glorious inheritance in the saints, and what is the

Daß wir die Wirkung   kräftig   schauen,
That we   the efficacy powerfully might-see—

Was uns dein Tod und Sieg erwirbt,
What for-us thy death and victory doth-win,
{What thy death and victory doth win for us—}

Und daß man nun nach deinem   Auferstehen
And that (we) now after thine (own) resurrection

        Nicht stirbt, wenn man gleich zeitlich stirbt,
(Do) not   die—although (we) indeed temporally die—

Und wir dadurch zu deiner Herrlichkeit eingehen.
And we thereby into thy   glory   might-enter.

Alto:
Was   in uns ist, erhebt dich, großer Gott,
All-that within us is, exalts thee, great God,
{All that is within us exalts thee, O great God,}

Und preiset deine Huld und   Treu;
And praises   thy grace and faithfulness;

Dein Auferstehen macht sie wieder neu,
Thy resurrection makes these again new,
{Thy resurrection renews these for us;}

Dein großer Sieg macht uns von Feinden los
Thy great victory makes us from foes   free
{Thy great victory frees us from foes}

Und bringet uns zum Leben;
And brings   us   to   life;

Drum   sei dir Preis und Dank gegeben.
Therefore be to-thee praise and thanks given.
{Therefore let praise and thanks be given to thee.}

6. Chorus (Parody)
●Praise to Christ who rose victorious & comforts us (134–6)
Erschallet, ihr Himmel, erfreue dich,   Erde,
Resound,   ye heavens, rejoice   - , (O) earth,

Lobsinge   dem Höchsten, du glaubende Schar.
Sing-praise to-the Most-High, thou believing throng.

Es schauet und schmecket ein jedes Gemüte
Now seeth and tasteth   - every   heart

Des lebenden Heilands unendliche Güte,
The living   Savior's unending kindness,

Er tröstet und stellet als Sieger sich dar.
He comforts and presents as victor himself - .
{With comfort he presents himself to us as victor.}

immeasurable greatness of his power in us who believe, according to the working of his great might which he accomplished in Christ when he raised him from the dead and made him sit at his right hand in the heavenly places, far above all rule and authority and power and dominion, and above every name that is named, not only in this age but also in that which is to come; and he has put all things under his feet and has made him the head over all things for the church, which is his body, the fulness of him who fills all in all.

Rom. 6:4. ...As Christ was raised from the dead by the glory of the Father, [so] we too [may] walk in newness of life.

Jn. 11:25–26. Jesus said to [Martha], "I am the resurrection and the life; he who believes in me, though he die, yet shall he live, and whoever lives and believes in me shall never die. Do you believe this?" (Also Jn. 8:51.)

Rev. 20:6. Blessed and holy is he who shares in the first resurrection! Over such the second death has no power...

Ps. 103:1–2. Bless the Lord, O my soul; and all that is within me, bless his holy name! Bless the Lord, O my soul, and forget not all his benefits.

Acts 5:30–31. The God of our fathers raised Jesus...[and]...exalted him at his right hand as Leader and Savior, to give repentance to Israel and forgiveness of sins.

Rom. 8:33–34, 37. Who shall bring any charge against God's elect? It is God who justifies; who is to condemn? Is it Christ Jesus, who died, yes, who was raised from the dead, who is at the right hand of God?... In all these things we are more than conquerors through him who loved us.

1 Cor. 15:57. Thanks be to God, who gives us the victory through our Lord Jesus Christ.

2 Tim. 1:10. ...Our Savior Christ Jesus...abolished death and brought life and immortality to light... (Also 1 Cor. 15:25–26.)

1 Cor. 6:14. God raised the Lord and will also raise us up by his power.

Rom. 8:11. ...He who raised Christ Jesus from the dead will give life to your mortal bodies also through his Spirit which dwells in you.

*****Acts 13:32–33.** We bring you the good news that what God promised to the fathers, this he has fulfilled to us their children by raising Jesus...

Ps. 89:5. Let the heavens praise thy wonders, O Lord...

Ps. 148:1, 7, 11–12. Praise the Lord! Praise the Lord from the heavens, praise him in the heights!...Praise the Lord from the earth... Kings of the earth and all peoples, princes and all rulers of the earth! Young men and maidens together, old men and children!

Ps. 34:8. O taste and see that the Lord is good!...

1 Pet. 2:3. You have tasted the kindness of the Lord.

*****Lk. 24:36–40.** As [the disciples] were saying this, Jesus himself stood among them. But they were startled and frightened, and supposed that they saw a spirit. And he said to them, "Why are you troubled, and why do questionings rise in your hearts? See my hands and my feet, that it is I myself; handle me, and see; for a spirit has not flesh and bones as you see that I have."

BWV 135
Ach Herr, mich armen Sünder
(NBA I/16; BC A100)

3. S. after Trinity (BWV 21, 135)
*1 Pet. 5:6-11 (Cast all your cares on God)
*Lk. 15:1-10 (Parable of the lost sheep and lost coin)
Librettist: Unknown

1. Chorus (Chorale[1] Vs. 1)
●Prayer for mercy on this poor sinner (135-1)
Ach Herr, mich armen Sünder
Ah Lord, (this) poor   sinner
{Ah Lord, do not punish this poor sinner}

Straf nicht in deinem Zorn,
Punish not in   thy   wrath,
{In thy wrath,}

Dein' ernsten Grimm doch linder,
Thy   severe   anger indeed soften,

Sonst ist's mit mir verlorn.
Else   is-it with me   lost.
{Or else I am lost.}

Ach Herr, wollst   mir vergeben
Ah Lord, mayest (thou) -   forgive

Mein Sünd und gnädig sein,
My   sin and merciful be,
{My sin, and be merciful,}

Daß ich mag ewig leben,
That I   may eternally live, (and)

Entfliehn der Höllenpein.
Escape   the pangs-of-hell.

2. Tenor Recit. (Based on Chorale Vs. 2)
●Healing sought from physician of souls (135-2)
Ach heile mich, du   Arzt der Seelen,
Ah heal me, thou physician of   souls,

Ich bin sehr krank und schwach;
I   am very sick and   weak;

Man möchte die Gebeine zählen,
One could (my) bones   count,
{One can count all my bones,}

So jämmerlich hat mich mein Ungemach,
So wretchedly has -   my   hardship,

Mein Kreuz und Leiden zugericht;
My   cross and suffering dealt-with-me;

+**Ps. 6:1.** O Lord, rebuke me not in thy anger, nor chasten me in thy wrath.
Ps. 130:1-4. Out of the depths I cry to thee, O Lord! Lord, hear my voice! Let thy ears be attentive to the voice of my supplications! If thou, O Lord, shouldst mark iniquities, Lord, who could stand! But there is forgiveness with thee, that thou mayest be feared.
Ps. 143:2. [O Lord,] enter not into judgment with thy servant; for no man living is righteous before thee.
Nah. 1:6. Who can stand before his indignation? Who can endure the heat of his anger? His wrath is poured out like fire, and the rocks are broken asunder by him. (Also Ps. 76:7, Mal. 3:2, Rev. 6:17.)
Lk. 18:9-14. [Jesus]...told this parable to some who trusted in themselves that they were righteous and despised others: "Two men went up into the temple to pray, one a Pharisee and the other a tax collector. The Pharisee stood and prayed thus with himself, 'God, I thank thee that I am not like other men, extortioners, unjust, adulterers, or even like this tax collector. I fast twice a week, I give tithes of all that I get.' But the tax collector, standing far off, would not even lift up his eyes to heaven, but beat his breast, saying, 'God be merciful to me a sinner!' I tell you, this man went down to his house justified rather than the other; for every one who exalts himself will be humbled, but he who humbles himself will be exalted."
Gal. 3:11. Now it is evident that no man is justified before God by the law; for "He who through faith is righteous shall live." (Also Rom. 3:20.)
Jn. 3:16. For God so loved the world that he gave his only Son, that whoever believes in him should not perish (Luther: verloren werden) but have eternal life.

+**Ps. 6:2-4.** Be gracious to me, O Lord, for I am languishing (Luther: schwach); O Lord, heal me, for my bones are troubled. My soul also is sorely troubled. But thou, O Lord—how long? Turn, O Lord, save my life; deliver me for the sake of thy steadfast love.
Lk. 5:31-32. Jesus [said]..."Those who are well have no need of a physician, but those who are sick; I have not come to call the righteous, but sinners to repentance." (Also Mt. 9:12-13, Mk. 2:17.)
Ps. 147:3. [The Lord] heals the brokenhearted, and binds up their wounds. (Also Is. 57:18, 61:1.)
Ps. 32:3-4. When I declared not my sin, my body wasted away through my groaning all day long. For day and night thy hand was heavy upon me; my strength was dried up as by the heat of summer.
Ps. 22:17. I can count all my bones...
Ps. 38:1-8. O Lord, rebuke me not in thy anger, nor chasten me in thy

---

[1]This chorale loosely paraphrases Psalm 6. Passages from this psalm are marked [+].

Das Angesicht
(My) countenance

Ist ganz von Tränen aufgeschwollen,
Is completely with tears swollen,
{Is completely swollen with tears,}

Die, schnellen Fluten gleich,
Which, rapid torrents like,

    von Wangen abwärts rollen.
    from (my) cheeks downwards roll.

Der Seele ist von Schrecken angst und bange;
(My) soul is with terror fearful and anxious;
{My soul is fearful and anxious with terror;}

Ach, du Herr, wie so lange?
Ah, thou Lord, why so long?

3. Tenor Aria (Based on Chorale Vs. 3)
●Comfort sought; how can God be praised in death? (135-3)
Tröste mir, Jesu, mein Gemüte,
Comfort, - (O) Jesus, my spirit,

Sonst versink ich in den Tod,
Else sink I into - death,
{Or I will sink into death,}

Hilf mir, hilf mir durch deine Güte
Help me, help me by thy kindness

Aus der großen Seelennot!
Out of (this) great distress-of-soul!

Denn im Tod ist alles stille,
For in death is all still,
{For in death all is still,}

Da gedenkt man deiner nicht.
There remembers one thee not.
{There no one remembers thee.}

Liebster Jesu, ist's dein Wille,
Dearest Jesus, is-it thy will,
{Dearest Jesus, if it is thy will,}

So erfreu mein Angesicht!
Then gladden my countenance!

4. Alto Recit. (Based on Chorale Vs. 4)
●Grief & suffering has sapped all my strength (135-4)
Ich bin von Seufzen müde,
I am from sighing weary,
{I am weary with sighing,}

Mein Geist hat weder Kraft noch Macht,
My Spirit has neither strength nor might,

wrath! For thy arrows have sunk into me, and thy hand has come down on me. There is no soundness in my flesh because of thy indignation; there is no health in my bones because of my sin. For my iniquities have gone over my head; they weigh like a burden too heavy for me. My wounds grow foul and fester because of my foolishness, I am utterly bowed down and prostrate; all the day I go about mourning. For my loins are filled with burning, and there is no soundness in my flesh. I am utterly spent and crushed; I groan because of the tumult of my heart.
+Ps. 6:6-7. I am weary with my moaning; every night I flood my bed with tears; I drench my couch with my weeping. My eye wastes away because of grief, it grows weak because of all my foes. (Also Ps. 42:3, 69:3, Jer. 45:3.)
+Ps. 6:3. My soul also is sorely troubled. But thou, O Lord—how long?
Ps. 13:1-2. How long, O Lord? Wilt thou forget me for ever? How long wilt thou hide thy face from me? How long must I bear pain in my soul, and have sorrow in my heart all the day? (Also Ps. 89:46, 90:13-15.)

Ps. 119:76, 81-82. [O Lord,] let thy steadfast love be ready to comfort me according to thy promise to thy servant...My soul languishes for thy salvation; I hope in thy word. My eyes fail with watching for thy promise; I ask, "When wilt thou comfort me?"
+Ps. 6:4-5. Turn, O Lord, save my life; deliver me for the sake of thy steadfast love. For in death there is no remembrance of thee; in Sheol who can give thee praise?
*1 Pet. 5:7. Cast all your anxieties on [God], for he cares about you.
Ps. 31:16. [O Lord,] let thy face shine on thy servant; save me in thy steadfast love (Luther: hilf mir durch deine Güte)!
Ps. 13:3. Consider and answer me, O Lord my God; lighten my eyes, lest I sleep the sleep of death.
Ps. 30:8-10. To thee, O Lord, I cried; and to the Lord I made supplication: "What profit is there in my death, if I go down to the Pit? Will the dust praise thee? Will it tell of thy faithfulness? Hear, O Lord, and be gracious to me! O Lord, be thou my helper!" (Also Is. 38:18.)
Ps. 90:13-15. Return, O Lord! How long? Have pity on thy servants! Satisfy us in the morning with thy steadfast love, that we may rejoice and be glad all our days. Make us glad as many days as thou hast afflicted us, and as many years as we have seen evil.
1 Pet. 4:19. Let those who suffer according to God's will do right and entrust their souls to a faithful Creator.
Mt. 26:39. ...[Jesus] fell on his face and prayed, "My Father, if it be possible, let this cup pass from me; nevertheless, not as I will, but as thou wilt."

+Ps. 6:6-7. I am weary with my moaning; every night I flood my bed with tears; I drench my couch with my weeping. My eye wastes away because of grief, it grows weak because of all my foes. (Also Jer. 45:3.)
Jer. 45:3. ...Woe is me! for the Lord has added sorrow to my pain; I am weary with my groaning, and I find no rest.
Ps. 31:9-11. Be gracious to me, O Lord, for I am in distress; my eye

Weil ich die ganze Nacht
Because I the entire night
{Because I lie the entire night}

Oft ohne Seelenruh und Friede
Oft without peace-of-mind and tranquillity

In großem Schweiß und Tränen liege.
In great sweat and tears lie.
{In great sweat and tears.}

Ich gräme mich fast tot und bin vor Trauern alt;
I grieve - nigh to-death and am with mourning old;

Denn meine Angst ist mannigfalt.
For my fear is manifold.

5. Bass Aria (Based on Chorale Vs. 5)
●Suffering passes; Jesus comforts; foe is dispersed (135-5)
Weicht, all ihr Übeltäter,
Retreat, all you evildoers,
{Away, all you evildoers,}

Mein Jesus tröstet mich!
My Jesus comforts me!

Er läßt nach Tränen und nach Weinen
He lets—after tears and after weeping—

Die Freudensonne wieder scheinen;
The sun-of-joy again shine;
{The sun of joy shine again;}

Das Trübsalwetter ändert sich,
The storm-of-affliction transforms itself,
{The storm of affliction is transformed,}

Die Feinde müssen plötzlich fallen
- Foes must suddenly fall

Und ihre Pfeile rückwärts prallen.
And their arrows backwards (against themselves) recoil.

6. Chorale (Vs. 6)
●Doxology: Praise to Father, Son, and Holy Ghost (135-6)
Ehr sei ins Himmels Throne
Glory be in heaven's throne

Mit hohem Ruhm und Preis
With great honor and praise

Dem Vater und dem Sohne
To-the Father and the Son

is wasted from grief, my soul and my body also. For my life is spent with sorrow, and my years with sighing; my strength fails because of my misery, and my bones waste away. I am the scorn of all my adversaries, a horror to my neighbors, an object of dread to my acquaintances; those who see me in the street flee from me.
Ps. 38:1–8. O Lord, rebuke me not in thy anger, nor chasten me in thy wrath! For thy arrows have sunk into me, and thy hand has come down on me. There is no soundness in my flesh because of thy indignation; there is no health in my bones because of my sin. For my iniquities have gone over my head; they weigh like a burden too heavy for me. My wounds grow foul and fester because of my foolishness, I am utterly bowed down and prostrate; all the day I go about mourning. For my loins are filled with burning, and there is no soundness in my flesh. I am utterly spent and crushed; I groan because of the tumult of my heart.

+Ps. 6:8–10. Depart from me, all you workers of evil; for the Lord has heard the sound of my weeping. The Lord has heard my supplication; the Lord accepts my prayer. All my enemies shall be ashamed and sorely troubled; they shall turn back, and be put to shame in a moment.
Ps. 30:5. [The Lord's] anger is but for a moment, and his favor is for a lifetime. Weeping may tarry for the night, but joy comes with the morning.
Ps. 126:5–6. May those who sow in tears reap with shouts of joy! He that goes forth weeping, bearing the seed for sowing, shall come home with shouts of joy, bringing his sheaves with him.
Ps. 37:12–15. The wicked plots against the righteous, and gnashes his teeth at him; but the Lord laughs at the wicked, for he sees that his day is coming. The wicked draw the sword and bend their bows, to bring down the poor and needy, to slay those who walk uprightly; their sword shall enter their own heart, and their bows shall be broken.
Ps. 11:2. Lo, the wicked bend the bow, they have fitted their arrow to the string, to shoot in the dark at the upright in heart. (Also Ps. 91:5.)
*1 Pet. 5:8–9. Be sober, be watchful. Your adversary the devil prowls around like a roaring lion, seeking some one to devour. Resist him, firm in your faith, knowing that the same experience of suffering is required of your brotherhood throughout the world.
Ps. 7:14–16. Behold the wicked man conceives evil...He makes a pit, digging it out, and falls into the hole which he has made. His mischief returns upon his own head, and on his own pate his violence descends. (Also Prov. 26:27, Neh. 4:4.)

Ps. 41:13. Blessed be the Lord, the God of Israel, from everlasting to everlasting! Amen and Amen. (Doxology: also Ps. 72:19, 89:52, 106:48, 150:6, Rom. 11:36, Jude 1:25)
Ps. 7:17. I will give to the Lord the thanks due to his righteousness, and I will sing praise to the name of the Lord, the Most High.
Ps. 116:1–8. I love the Lord, because he has heard my voice and my supplications. Because he inclined his ear to me, therefore I will call on him as long as I live. The snares of death encompassed me; the pangs of Sheol laid hold on me; I suffered distress and anguish. Then I called on the name of the Lord: "O Lord, I beseech thee, save my

Und auch zu gleicher Weis
And also in   like manner

Dem Heilgen Geist mit Ehren
To-the Holy Ghost with glory

In alle Ewigkeit,
For all eternity,

Der woll uns all'n bescheren
May-he us   all   grant

Die ewge Seligkeit.
- Eternal blessedness.

BWV 136
Erforsche mich, Gott, und erfahre mein Herz
(NBA I/18; BC A111)

8. S. after Trinity (BWV 136, 178, 45)
*Rom. 8:12–17 (All who are led by the Spirit of God are sons
of God)
*Mt. 7:15–23 (Sermon on the Mount: beware of false
prophets, you will know them by their fruits)
Librettist: Unknown

1. Chorus
●Prayer: Search me O God & try my heart: Ps. 139:23 (136-1)
Erforsche mich, Gott, und erfahre mein Herz;
Search   me, God, and know   my heart;

prüfe mich und erfahre wie ich's meine!
try   me and discover how I-it mean!
{try me and discover my intentions!}

2. Tenor Recit.
●Heart is fallen: it bears thorns & will be judged (136-2)
Ach, daß der Fluch, so dort die Erde schlägt,
Alas, that the curse, which there the earth did-strike,

Auch derer Menschen Herz getroffen!
Also the   human   heart has-struck!

Wer kann auf gute Früchte hoffen,
Who can for good   fruit   hope,
{Who can hope for good fruit,}

Da dieser Fluch bis in die Seele dringet,
Since this curse to   the soul penetrates,
{Since this curse penetrates to the soul,}

So daß sie Sündendornen bringet
So that it thorns-of-sin   yields
{So that it bears thorns of sin}

life!" Gracious is the Lord, and righteous; our God is merciful...When
I was brought low, he saved me. Return, O my soul, to your rest; for
the Lord has dealt bountifully with you. For thou hast delivered my
soul from death, my eyes from tears, my feet from stumbling. (Also
+Ps. 6:9, 56:13.)
*1 Pet. 5:10–11. After you have suffered a little while, the God of all
grace, who has called you to his eternal glory in Christ, will himself
restore, establish, and strengthen you. To him be the dominion for
ever and ever. Amen. (Also 1 Pet. 4:11, 1 Tim. 1:17.)
Rev. 7:11–12. And all the angels stood round the throne...and they fell
on their faces before the throne and worshiped God, saying, "Amen!
Blessing and glory and wisdom and thanksgiving and honor and power
and might be to our God for ever and ever! Amen."

Ps. 139:1–3, 23–24. O Lord, thou hast searched me and known me!
Thou knowest when I sit down and when I rise up; thou discernest my
thoughts from afar. Thou searchest out my path and my lying down,
and art acquainted with all my ways...*Search me, O God, and know my
heart! Try me and know my thoughts!* And see if there be any wicked
way in me, and lead me in the way everlasting!
Ps. 19:14. Let the words of my mouth and the meditation of my heart
be acceptable in thy sight... (Also Ps. 104:34.)
Jer. 17:9–10 [God]: The heart is deceitful above all things, and
desperately corrupt; who can understand it? I the Lord search the
mind and try the heart, to give to every man according to his ways,
according to the fruit of his doings.

Gen. 3:17–18. To Adam [God] said, "Because you have...eaten of the
tree of which I commanded you, 'You shall not eat of it,' cursed is the
ground because of you; in toil you shall eat of it all the days of your
life; thorns and thistles it shall bring forth to you..."
Rom. 8:20, 23–24. ...Creation was subjected to futility, not of its own
will but by the will of him who subjected it...We know that the whole
creation has been groaning in travail together until now; and not only
the creation, but we ourselves...
Rom. 5:12. ...Sin came into the world through one man [Adam] and
death through sin, and so death spread to all men because all men
sinned...
Gen. 8:21. ...The Lord said in his heart, "I will never again curse the
ground because of man, for the imagination of man's heart is evil
from his youth..."
Jer. 17:9. The heart is deceitful above all things, and desperately
corrupt; who can understand it?

Und   Lasterdisteln   trägt.
And thistles-of-wickedness bears.
{And yields thistles of wickedness.}

Doch wollen   sich oftmals die Kinder der Höllen
Yet   would themselves often the children of   hell
{Yet would the children of hell often}

In Engel des Lichtes verstellen;
As angels of   light   disguise;
{Disguise themselves as angels of light;}

Man   soll   bei dem verderbten Wesen
One is-expected from this corrupted   essence,

Von diesen Dornen Trauben lesen.
From these thorns,   grapes to-gather.

Ein Wolf will   sich mit reiner Wolle decken,
A   wolf would himself with pure wool   cover,
{A wolf covers himself with pure wool,}

Doch bricht ein Tag herein,
Yet breaks a   day   - ,
{Yet a day is breaking,}

Der wird, ihr Heuchler, euch ein Schrecken,
Which will, you hypocrites, for-you a   terror,
{Which will be a terror for you hypocrites,}

Ja unerträglich sein.
Yes, unbearable be.
{Yes, it will be unbearable.}

3. Alto Aria
●Day of Judgment will destroy hypocrites (136-3)
Es   kömmt ein Tag
(There) comes a   day

So   das Verborgne richtet,
Which (will) the   hidden   judge,
{When all that is now hidden will be judged,}

Vor dem die Heuchelei erzittern mag.
At which - hypocrisy   quake   may.
{A day at which hypocrisy may well quake.}

Denn seines Eifers Grimm vernichtet,
For   his   zeal's wrath annihilates,

Was   Heuchelei und List erdichtet.
Whatever hypocrisy and cunning devises.

Mk. 7:20–23. [Jesus] said, "What comes out of a man is what defiles a man. For from within, out of the heart of man, come evil thoughts, fornication, theft, murder, adultery, coveting, wickedness, deceit, licentiousness, envy, slander, pride, foolishness. All these evil things come from within and they defile a man." (Also Mt. 15:18–19.)
*Mt. 7:15–20 [Christ]: Beware of false prophets, who come to you in sheep's clothing but inwardly are ravenous wolves. You will know them by their fruits. Are grapes gathered from thorns, or figs from thistles? So, every sound tree bears good fruit, but the bad tree bears evil fruit. A sound tree cannot bear evil fruit, nor can a bad tree bear good fruit. Every tree that does not bear good fruit is cut down and thrown into the fire. Thus you will know them by their fruits. (Also Mt. 12:33–35, Lk. 6:43–45, Jms. 3:11–12.)
2 Cor. 11:13–15. Such men are false apostles, deceitful workmen, disguising themselves as apostles of Christ. And no wonder, for even Satan disguises himself as an angel of light. So it is not strange if his servants also disguise themselves as servants of righteousness...
Mt. 3:10. Even now the axe is laid to the root of the trees; every tree therefore that does not bear good fruit is cut down and thrown into the fire. (Also Lk. 3:9, Jn. 15: 2, 6.)
Jer. 8:12–13 [God]: Were [my people] ashamed when they committed abomination? No, they were not at all ashamed...Therefore they shall fall among the fallen; when I punish them, they shall be overthrown, says the Lord. When I would gather them, says the Lord, there are no grapes on the vine, nor figs on the fig tree; even the leaves are withered...
*Mt. 7:22–23 [Christ]: On that day many will say to me, "Lord, Lord, did we not prophesy in your name, and cast out demons in your name, and do many mighty works in your name?" And then will I declare to them, "I never knew you; depart from me, you evildoers."

Rom. 2:6, 16. [God] will render to every man according to his works... on that day when, according to my gospel, God judges the secrets of men by Christ Jesus.
Lk. 12:1–5. ...[Jesus] began to say to his disciples first, "Beware of the leaven of the Pharisees, which is hypocrisy. Nothing is covered up that will not be revealed, or hidden that will not be known. Therefore whatever you have said in the dark shall be heard in the light, and what you have whispered in private rooms shall be proclaimed upon the housetops. I tell you, my friends, do not fear those who kill the body, and after that have no more that they can do. But I will warn you whom to fear: fear him who, after he has killed, has power to cast into hell; yes, I tell you, fear him!" (Also Mt. 10:26–28.)
Zeph. 1:14–15, 3:8 [God]: The great day of the Lord is near, near and hastening fast...A day of wrath is that day, a day of distress and anguish, a day of ruin and devastation, a day of darkness and gloom, a day of clouds and thick darkness...the day when I arise as a witness... to pour out upon them my indignation, all the heat of my anger (Luther: Zorn meines Grimmes); for in the fire of my jealous wrath (Luther: durch meines Eifers Feuer) all the earth shall be consumed. (Also Amos 5:18, Joel 2:11, 30–31, 2 Pet. 3:7, 10.)

4. Bass Recit.

●Righteousness & purity found only in Christ's blood (136-4)
Die Himmel   selber   sind nicht rein,
The heavens themselves are not pure,

Wie soll es nun ein Mensch vor diesem Richter sein?
How shall it then for-a mortal before this   judge   be?
{How will it be then for a mortal before this judge?}

Doch wer   durch Jesu   Blut   gereinigt,
Yet he-who through Jesus' blood (has-been) cleansed,

Im Glauben sich   mit ihm vereinigt,
By   faith himself with him has-united,
{Who has been united with him by faith,}

Weiß, daß er   ihm   kein hartes Urteil   spricht.
Knows, that he upon-him no harsh sentence (will-pass).
{Knows that God will pass no harsh sentence upon him.}

Kränkt ihn die Sünde noch,
Vexes him - sin   still,
{If he is still vexed by sin—}

Der Mangel   seiner Werke,
The deficiency of-his deeds—

Er hat in Christo   doch
He has in Christ nevertheless
{He finds nevertheless in Christ}

Gerechtigkeit und Stärke.
Righteousness and strength.

5. Tenor & Bass Duet

●Sin came through Adam; cleansing through Christ (136-5)
Uns treffen zwar der Sünden Flecken,
Us touch indeed - sin's   stains,
{We are indeed touched by the stains of sin,}

So   Adams Fall auf uns gebracht.
Which Adam's fall on us has-brought.
{Which Adam's fall brought upon us.}

Allein, wer   sich zu Jesu Wunden,
Yet   he-who (his-way) to Jesus' wounds,
{Yet he who has found his way to Jesus' wounds—}

Dem großen Strom   voll   Blut gefunden,
That great   stream filled-with blood, has-found,
{That great stream filled with blood—}

Job 15:15–16. Behold, God puts no trust in his holy ones, and the heavens are not clean in his sight; how much less one who is abominable and corrupt, a man who drinks iniquity like water!

Nah. 1:6. Who can stand before his indignation? Who can endure the heat of his anger? His wrath is poured out like fire, and the rocks are broken asunder by him. (Also Ps. 143:2, Mal. 3:2.)

Ps. 130:3. If thou, O Lord, shouldst mark iniquities, Lord, who could stand!

1 Jn. 1:8–9. If we say we have no sin, we deceive ourselves, and the truth is not in us. If we confess our sins, he is faithful and just, and will forgive our sins and cleanse us from all unrighteousness.

1 Jn. 1:7. ...The blood of Jesus...cleanses us from all sin. (Also 1 Pet. 1:18–19, Rev. 5:9; Eph. 2:13, Heb. 13:12.)

Gal. 2:20. I have been crucified with Christ; it is no longer I who live, but Christ who lives in me; and the life I now live in the flesh I live by faith in the Son of God who loved me and gave himself for me.

1 Cor. 6:17. He who is united to the Lord becomes one spirit with him. (Also Eph. 3:17.)

Rom. 8:33. Who shall bring any charge against God's elect? It is God who justifies.

Rom. 3:26. ...[God] justifies him who has faith in Jesus.

Rom. 5:1. Since we are justified by faith, we have peace with God through our Lord Jesus Christ.

Eph. 2:8–9. By grace you have been saved through faith; and this is not your own doing, it is the gift of God—not because of works, lest any man should boast.

Phil. 3:7–9. But whatever gain I had, I counted as loss for the sake of Christ...in order that I may gain Christ and be found in him, not having a righteousness of my own, based on law, but that which is through faith in Christ, the righteousness from God that depends on faith.

Rom. 5:8–9. God shows his love for us in that while we were yet sinners Christ died for us. Since, therefore, we are now justified by his blood, much more shall we be saved by him from the wrath of God.

1 Cor. 15:21–22. As by a man came death, by a man has come also the resurrection of the dead. For as in Adam all die, so also in Christ shall all be made alive. (Also 1 Cor. 15:45.)

Rom. 5:12, 15–17. ...Sin came into the world through one man and death through sin, and so death spread to all men because all men sinned...But the free gift is not like the trespass. For if many died through one man's trespass, much more have the grace of God and the free gift in the grace of that one man Jesus Christ abounded for many...The judgment following one trespass brought condemnation, but the free gift following many trespasses brings justification. If, because of one man's trespass, death reigned through that one man, much more will those who receive the abundance of grace and the free gift of righteousness reign in life through the one man Jesus Christ.

1 Pet. 1:18–19. You know that you were ransomed from the futile ways inherited from your fathers, not with perishable things such as silver or gold, but with the precious blood of Christ, like that of a lamb without blemish or spot.

Wird dadurch wieder rein gemacht.
Is   by-it   again   made-clean.
{Is by it made clean again.}

6. Chorale
●Blood of Christ cleanses & frees entire world (136–6)
Dein Blut, der edle Saft,
Thy blood, that noble liquid,

Hat solche Stärk und Kraft,
Hath such   power and strength,

Daß auch ein Tröpflein kleine
That even a   droplet small

Die ganze Welt kann   reine,
The entire world can (make) pure,
{Can purify the entire world,}

Ja, gar aus   Teufels Rachen
Yes, even out-of (the) devil's jaws,
{Yes, can even free us from the devil's jaws:}

Frei, los   und   ledig   machen.
Free, released, and unencumbered make.
{Released and unencumbered.}

1 Pet. 2:24. [Christ] himself bore our sins in his body on the tree, that we might die to sin and live to righteousness. By his wounds you have been healed. (Also Is. 53:5.)

Heb. 9:13–14. If the sprinkling of defiled persons with the blood of goats and bulls...sanctifies for the purification of the flesh, how much more shall the blood of Christ, who through the eternal Spirit offered himself without blemish to God, purify your conscience from dead works to serve the living God.
Rev. 5:9. [In paradise] they sang a new song, saying, "Worthy art thou ...for thou wast slain and by thy blood didst ransom men for God from every tribe and tongue and people and nation."
1 Jn. 2:2. [Christ] is the expiation for our sins, and not for ours only but also for the sins of the whole world. (Also Heb. 9:26.)
Jn. 1:29. ...[John] saw Jesus coming toward him, and said, "Behold, the Lamb of God, who takes away the sin of the world!" (Also Jn. 1:36.)
1 Jn. 5:19. ...The whole world is in the power of the evil one.
1 Jn. 3:8. ...The reason the Son of God appeared was to destroy the works of the devil. (Also Heb. 2:14.)
1 Pet. 5:8. ...Your adversary the devil prowls around like a roaring lion, seeking some one to devour.
Gal. 5:1. For freedom Christ has set us free... (Also Rom. 6:17–18, 22.)
Jn. 8:36. If the Son makes you free, you will be free indeed.

BWV 137
Lobe den Herren, den mächtigen König der Ehren
(NBA I/20; BC A124)

12. S. after Trinity (BWV 137, 35) Perhaps intended also for Feast of St. John the Baptist (June 24).
*2 Cor. 3:4–11 (The new covenant shines more brightly than the old)
*Mk. 7:31–37 (Jesus heals man who was deaf and dumb)
Librettist: Chorale (Joachim Neander)

1. Chorus (Chorale Vs. 1)
●Praise the Lord, the mighty king, with psaltry & lyre (137–1)
Lobe den Herren, den mächtigen König der Ehren,
Praise the Lord, the   mighty   king of glory,

Meine geliebte Seele, das ist mein Begehren.
(O) my beloved soul; that is   my   desire.

Kommet   zu   Hauf,
Come (together-as-a) throng,
{Come, throng together;}

Psalter und Harfen, wacht auf!
Psaltry and lyres,   awake!

Lasset die Musicam hören.
Let   the   music be-heard.

Ps. 24:7–8, 10. Lift up your heads, O gates! and be lifted up, O ancient doors! that the King of glory (Luther: König der Ehren) may come in. Who is the King of glory? The Lord, strong and mighty (Luther: stark und mächtig), the Lord, mighty in battle!...He is the King of glory!
1 Tim. 1:17. To the King of ages, immortal, invisible, the only God, be honor and glory for ever and ever. Amen.
Ps. 103:1. Bless the Lord, O my soul; and all that is within me, bless his holy name!
*Mk. 7:37. ...He has done all things well; he even makes the deaf hear and the dumb speak.
Ps. 145:1–3. I will extol thee, my God and King, and bless thy name for ever and ever. Every day I will bless thee, and praise thy name for ever and ever. Great is the Lord, and greatly to be praised, and his greatness is unsearchable.
Ps. 117:1–2. Praise the Lord, all nations! Extol him, all peoples! For great is his steadfast love toward us; and the faithfulness of the Lord endures for ever. Praise the Lord! (Also Ps. 96:1–4.)
Ps. 35:18. [O Lord,] I will thank thee in the great congregation; in the mighty throng I will praise thee. (Also Ps. 22:25.)
Ps. 108:1–3. My heart is steadfast, O God, my heart is steadfast! I will sing and make melody! Awake, my soul! Awake, O harp and lyre! I will awake the dawn! I will give thanks to thee, O Lord, among the peoples, I will sing praises to thee among the nations. (Also Ps. 57:8–10, 81:1–2.)

2. Alto Aria (Chorale Vs. 2)
●Praise the Lord who bears you on eagles' wings (137–2)
Lobe den Herren, der alles so herrlich regieret,
Praise the Lord, who all-things so gloriously doth-rule,

Der dich auf Adelers Fittichen sicher geführet,
Who thee on eagle's pinions safely hath-led,

Der dich erhält,
Who thee doth-preserve,

Wie es dir selber gefällt;
As it (doth) thee thyself please;
{Who keeps thee as thou thyself would have it;}

Hast du nicht dieses verspüret?
Hast thou this not perceived?
{Hast thou not pereived this?}

3. Soprano & Bass Duet (Chorale Vs. 3)
●Praise the Lord who fashions you, covers with wings (137–3)
Lobe den Herren, der künstlich und fein dich bereitet,
Praise the Lord, who artfully and fine thee doth-fashion,

Der dir Gesundheit verliehen, dich freundlich geleitet;
Who thee health hath-given, thee kindly hath-led;

In wieviel Not
In how-much distress

Hat nicht der gnädige Gott
Hath not the gracious God

Über dir Flügel gebreitet!
Over thee (his) wings spread!
{Spread his wings over thee!}

4. Tenor Aria (Chorale Vs. 4)
●Praise the Lord who has poured blessings on us (137–4)
Lobe den Herren, der deinen Stand sichtbar gesegnet,
Praise the Lord, who thy state visibly hath-blessed,

Der aus dem Himmel
Who (thee) from - heaven

mit Strömen der Liebe geregnet;
with streams of love hath-showered;

Denke dran,
Think on-this,

Ps. 103:19. The Lord has established his throne in the heavens, and his kingdom rules over all.
Ps. 22:27–28. All the ends of the earth shall remember and turn to the Lord; and all the families of the nations shall worship before him. For dominion belongs to the Lord, and he rules over the nations.
Ps. 103:1, 5. Bless the Lord, O my soul; and all that is within me, bless his holy name!...who satisfies you with good as long as you live so that your youth is renewed like the eagle's.
Is. 40:28–31. Have you not known? Have you not heard? The Lord is the everlasting God, the Creator of the ends of the earth. He does not faint or grow weary, his understanding is unsearchable. He gives power to the faint, and to him who has no might he increases strength. Even youths shall faint and be weary, and young men shall fall exhausted; but they who wait for the Lord shall renew their strength, they shall mount up with wings like eagles (Luther: Adler), they shall run and not be weary, they shall walk and not faint.
*Mk. 7:37. ...He has done all things well...

Ps. 119:73. [O Lord,] thy hands have made and fashioned me (Luther: mich gemacht und bereitet)... (Also Job 10:8, Is. 44:24, Jer. 1:5.)
Ps. 139:13–15. [O Lord,] thou didst form my inward parts, thou didst knit me together in my mother's womb. I praise thee, for thou art fearful and wonderful. Wonderful are thy works! Thou knowest me right well; my frame was not hidden from thee, when I was being made in secret, intricately wrought in the depths of the earth.
Ps. 103:2–3. Bless the Lord, O my soul...who heals all your diseases...
*Mk. 7:37. [The people] were astonished beyond measure [at Jesus], saying, "He has done all things well; he even makes the deaf hear and the dumb speak."
Ps. 23:1–3. The Lord is my shepherd, I shall not want; he makes me lie down in green pastures. He leads me beside still waters; he restores my soul. He leads me in paths of righteousness for his name's sake.
Ps. 34:19. Many are the afflictions of the righteous; but the Lord delivers him out of them all.
Ps. 36:7. How precious is thy steadfast love, O God! The children of men take refuge in the shadow of thy wings.
Ps. 91:4. He will cover you with his pinions, and under his wings you will find refuge... (Also Ps. 17:8, 57:1, 61:4, Deut. 32:10–11, Mt. 23:37.)

Ps. 103:2, 4, 11. Bless the Lord, O my soul; and forget not all his benefits...who crowns you with steadfast love and mercy...As the heavens are high above the earth, so great is his steadfast love toward those who fear him.
Ps. 116:7. ...O my soul...the Lord has dealt bountifully with you.
Rom. 5:5. ...God's love has been poured into our hearts through the Holy Spirit which has been given to us.
Is. 44:3 [God]: I will pour water on the thirsty land, and streams on the dry ground; I will pour my Spirit upon your descendants, and my blessing on your offspring. (Also Is. 32:15.)
Ps. 36:8. [O Lord, the children of men] feast on the abundance of thy house, and thou givest them drink from the river of thy delights.

Was der Allmächtige kann,	**Ps. 31:19, 21.** O how abundant is thy goodness, which thou hast laid up for those who fear thee...Blessed be the Lord, for he has wondrously shown his steadfast love to me... (Also Ps. 40:5, 67:5–7.)
What the Almighty can-do,	
	Eph. 3:19–21. ...The love of Christ...surpasses knowledge... To him who by the power at work within us is able to do far more abundantly than all that we ask or think, to him be glory...for ever and ever. Amen.
Der dir mit Liebe begegnet.	
Who thee with love hath-met.	

5. Chorale (Vs. 5)
●Praise the Lord: all that is in me; that hath breath (137–5)
Lobe den Herren, was in mir ist, lobe den Namen!
Praise the Lord, all-that in me is, praise (his) name!

Alles, was Odem hat,
Everything, that breath has,

    lobe mit Abrahams Samen!
    praise (him) with Abraham's seed!

Er ist dein Licht,
He is thy light,

Seele, vergiß es ja nicht;
Soul, forget it indeed not;

    Lobende, schließe mit Amen!
    (O) praising-one, close with "Amen"!

Ps. 103:1–2. Bless the Lord, O my soul; and all that is within me, bless his holy name! Bless the Lord, O my soul; and forget not all his benefits.
Ps. 150:6. Let everything that breathes praise the Lord! Praise the Lord!
Ps. 148:7, 10–12. Praise the Lord from the earth...Beasts and all cattle, creeping things and flying birds! Kings of the earth and all peoples, princes and all rulers of the earth! Young men and maidens together, old men and children!
Ps. 22:23. You who fear the Lord, praise him! All you sons of Jacob, glorify him, and stand in awe of him, all you sons of Israel!
Gal. 3:16, 29. Now the promises were made to Abraham and to his offspring...which is Christ...And if you are Christ's, then you are Abraham's offspring, heirs according to promise.
Ps. 27:1. The Lord is my light and my salvation; whom shall I fear?...
Ps. 106:48. Blessed be the Lord, the God of Israel, from everlasting to everlasting! And let all the people say, "Amen!" Praise the Lord! (Amen: also Deut. 27:15–26, Neh. 8:6)

BWV 138
Warum betrübst du dich, mein Herz
(NBA I/22; BC A132)

15. S. after Trinity (BWV 138, 99, 51)
*Gal. 5:25–6:10 (Exhortation to walk in the Spirit)
*Mt. 6:24–34 (Sermon on the Mount: Exhortation not to be anxious but to seek the kingdom of God)
Librettist: Unknown

1. Chorus (Chorale Vs. 1) & Alto & Tenor Recits.
●Dialogue: Anxious care & sorrow vs. trust in God (138–1)
Warum betrübst du dich, mein Herz?
Why troublest thou thyself, my heart?
{Why art thou troubled, my heart?}

Bekümmerst dich und trägest Schmerz
Art-anxious - and bearest sorrow

Nur um das zeitliche Gut?
Merely about - temporal possession?
{About merely temporal things?}

Ach, ich bin arm,
Ah, I am poor,

*Mt. 6:25–34 [Christ]: I tell you, do not be anxious about your life, what you shall eat or what you shall drink, nor about your body, what you shall put on. Is not life more than food, and the body more than clothing? Look at the birds of the air: they neither sow nor reap nor gather into barns, and yet your heavenly Father feeds them. Are you not of more value than they? And which of you by being anxious can add one cubit to his span of life? And why are you anxious about clothing? Consider the lilies of the field, how they grow; they neither toil nor spin; yet I tell you, even Solomon in all his glory was not arrayed like one of these. But if God so clothes the grass of the field, which today is alive and tomorrow is thrown into the oven, will he not much more clothe you, O men of little faith? Therefore do not be anxious, saying, "What shall we eat?" or "What shall we drink?" or "What shall we wear?" For the Gentiles seek all these things; and your

Mich drücken schwere Sorgen.
Me oppress heavy cares.
{Heavy cares oppress me.}

Vom Abend bis zum Morgen
From evening till - morning

Währt meine liebe Not.
Endures my dear distress.
{Endures this distress of mine.}

Daß Gott erbarm!
(May) God have-mercy!

Wer wird mich noch erlösen
Who will me yet deliver
{Who will yet deliver me}

Vom Leibe dieser bösen
From-the body of-this evil

Und argen Welt?
And wicked world?

Wie elend ist's um mich bestellt!
How wretchedly is-it for me appointed!
{How wretched is my lot!}

Ach! wär ich doch nur tot!
Ah! Were I - only dead!
{Ah, if only I were dead!}

Vertrau du deinem Herren Gott,
Trust thou (in) thy Lord God,

Der alle Ding erschaffen hat.
Who all things created hath.
{Who hath created all things.}

2. Bass Recit.[1]
●Adversity: I've been given a bitter cup of tears (138-2)
Ich bin veracht',
I am despised,

Der Herr hat mich zum Leiden
The Lord has me to suffering
{The Lord has made me to suffer}

Am Tage seines Zorns gemacht;
On-the day of-his wrath made;
{On the day of his wrath;}

Der Vorrat, hauszuhalten,
The provision, (for-my) housekeeping,
{My provision for housekeeping}

heavenly Father knows that you need them all. But seek first his kingdom and his righteousness, and all these things shall be yours as well. Therefore do not be anxious about tomorrow, for tomorrow will be anxious for itself. Let the day's own trouble be sufficient for the day.
Ps. 42:3, 42:5/11/43:5. My tears have been my food day and night, while men say to me continually, "Where is your God?"...Why are you cast down (Luther: was betrübst du dich), O my soul, and why are you disquieted within me? Hope in God; for I shall again praise him, my help and my God.
Ps. 6:6. I am weary with my moaning; every night I flood my bed with tears... (Also Ps. 69:3, Jer. 45:3.)
Ps. 55:16-17. I call upon God...Evening and morning and at noon I utter my complaint and moan...
Ps. 73:14. For all the day long I have been stricken, and chastened every morning.
Ps. 40:17. As for me, I am poor and needy...Thou art my help and my deliverer; do not tarry, O my God!
Ps. 70:5. I am poor and needy; hasten to me, O God! Thou art my help and my deliverer; O Lord, do not tarry!
Ps. 86:1. Incline thy ear, O Lord, and answer me, for I am poor and needy. (Also Ps. 109:21-24.)
Rom. 7:24. Wretched man that I am! Who will deliver me from this body of death?
Job 7:15-16. I would choose strangling and death rather than my bones. I loathe my life; I would not live for ever. Let me alone, for my days are a breath.
Job 10:1. I loathe my life; I will give free utterance to my complaint; I will speak in the bitterness of my soul. (Also Job 7:11.)
Ps. 42:5/11/43:5. ...Why are you cast down, O my soul, and why are you disquieted within me? Hope in God; for I shall again praise him, my help and my God.
Ps. 124:8. Our help is in the name of the Lord, who made heaven and earth. (Also Ps. 146:5-6.)
Is. 40:28-29. Have you not known? Have you not heard? The Lord is the everlasting God, the Creator of the ends of the earth. He does not faint or grow weary, his understanding is unsearchable. He gives power to the faint, and to him who has no might he increases strength.

Ps. 22:6-8. I am a worm, and no man; scorned by men, and despised by the people. All who see me mock at me, they make mouths at me, they wag their heads; "He committed his cause to the Lord; let him deliver him, let him rescue him, for he delights in him!"
Ps. 119:141. I am small and despised...
Lam. 1:12. Is it nothing to you, all you who pass by? Look and see if there is any sorrow like my sorrow which was brought upon me, which the Lord inflicted on the day of his fierce anger (Luther: am Tage seines grimmigen Zorns). (Also Is. 13:13, Lam. 2:1, Zeph. 2:3.)
Ruth 1:20-21. ...The Almighty has dealt very bitterly with me. I went away full, and the Lord has brought me back empty...
1 Kings 17:11-12. As [the widow of Zarephath] was going to bring [drink to the prophet Elijah], he called to her and said, "Bring me a morsel of bread in your hand." And she said, "As the Lord your God lives, I have nothing baked, only a handful of meal in a jar, and a little oil in a cruse; and now, I am gathering a couple of sticks, that I may go in and prepare it for myself and my son, that we may eat it, and die."

---

[1]In the *Neue Bach Ausgabe* the second and third movements are joined.

Ist ziemlich klein;
Is rather small;

Man schenkt mir vor den Wein der Freuden
They pour for-me as - wine of gladness
{I am given the bitter cup of tears}

Den bittern Kelch der Tränen ein.
The bitter cup of tears -.
{As my wine of gladness.}

Wie kann ich nun mein Amt mit Ruh verwalten,
How can I now my (duties) with calmness carry-out,
{How can I now calmly carry out my duties,}

Wenn Seufzer meine Speise und Tränen das Getränke sein?
When sighing my food, and tears (my) drink is?
{When siging my food is, and tears my drink?}

3. Chorale S.A.T.B. (Vs. 2) with Soprano & Alto Recits.[1]
●Dialogue: Doubting anxiety vs. trust in God (138-3)

Er kann und will dich lassen nicht,
He can and would thee leave not,
{He could and would not ever leave thee,}

Er weiß gar wohl, was dir gebricht,
He knows full well, what for-thee is-lacking,

Himmel und Erd ist sein!
Heaven and earth are his!

Soprano:
Ach, wie?
Ah, what?

Gott sorget freilich vor das Vieh,
God cares to-be-sure for the cattle,
{To be sure, God cares for the cattle,}

Er gibt den Vögeln seine Speise,
He gives the birds their food,

Er sättiget die jungen Raben,
He satisfies the young ravens,

Nur ich, ich weiß nicht, auf was Weise
Only I, I know not in what manner

Ich armes Kind
I— poor child—

Mein bißchen Brot soll haben;
My little-bit-of bread shall have;

---

*Mt. 6:25 [Christ]: ...I tell you, do not be anxious about your life, what you shall eat or what you shall drink...
Mt. 6:11. [O Lord,] give us this day our daily bread. (Also Lk. 11:3.)
Jms. 2:15–16. If a brother or sister is ill-clad and in lack of daily food, and one of you says to them, "Go in peace, be warmed and filled," without giving them the things needed for the body, what does it profit?
Jer. 48:33. Gladness and joy have been taken away from the fruitful land of Moab...the wine [ceases] from the wine presses; no one treads them with shouts of joy...
Ps. 42:3. My tears have been my food day and night...
Prov. 30:8–9. [O Lord]...give me neither poverty nor riches; feed me with the food that is needful for me, lest I be full, and deny thee, and say, "Who is the Lord?" or lest I be poor, and steal, and profane the name of my God.
Mk. 14:35–36. ...[Jesus] fell on the ground and prayed... "Abba, Father, all things are possible to thee; remove this cup from me; yet not what I will, but what thou wilt." (Also Mt 20:22–23, Mk. 10:38–39.)

Heb. 13:5–6. Keep your life free from love of money, and be content with what you have; for he has said, "I will never fail you nor forsake you." Hence we can confidently say, "The Lord is my helper, I will not be afraid; what can man do to me?"
Josh. 1:5, 9 [God]: ...As I was with Moses, so I will be with you; I will not fail you or forsake you...Be strong and of good courage; be not frightened, neither be dismayed; for the Lord your God is with you wherever you go. (Also Deut. 31:6–8.)
Job 23:10. [God] knows the way that I take; when he has tried me, I shall come forth as gold.
Ps. 31:14–15. I trust in thee, O Lord, I say, "Thou art my God." My times are in thy hand...
*Mt. 6:26 [Christ]: Look at the birds of the air: they neither sow nor reap nor gather into barns, and yet your heavenly Father feeds them. Are you not of more value than they?
Ps. 121:2. My help comes from the Lord, who made heaven and earth.
Ps. 124:8. Our help is in the name of the Lord, who made heaven and earth.
Ps. 24:1. The earth is the Lord's and the fulness thereof, the world and those who dwell therein.
Ps. 147:9. He gives to the beasts their food, and to the young ravens which cry. (Also Job 38:41.)
Ps. 145:15–16. [O Lord,] the eyes of all look to thee, and thou givest them their food in due season. Thou openest thy hand, thou satisfiest the desire of every living thing.
Ps. 50:10–12 [God]: Every beast of the forest is mine, the cattle on a thousand hills. I know all the birds of the air, and all that moves in the field is mine. If I were hungry, I would not tell you; for the world and all that is in it is mine.
*Mt. 6:31–32 [Christ]: Therefore do not be anxious, saying, "What shall we eat?" or "What shall we drink?" or "What shall we wear?" For

---

[1]In the *Neue Bach Ausgabe* the second and third movements are joined.

Wo ist jemand, der sich zu meiner Rettung findt?
Where is (there) anyone, who - to my rescue (comes)?
{Who is there to come to my rescue?}

> **Dein Vater und dein Herre Gott,**
> Thy Father and thy Lord God,

> **Der dir beisteht in aller Not.**
> Who thee stands-by in all distress.
> {Who stands by thee in all distress.}

Alto:
Ich bin verlassen,
I am forsaken,

Es scheint,
It seems,

Als wollte mich auch Gott bei meiner Armut hassen,
As would me even God in my poverty hate,
{As if even God would hate me in my poverty,}

Da er's doch immer gut mit mir gemeint.
Though he-has indeed always well toward me been-intentioned.
{Though he has indeed always been well-intentioned toward me.}

Ach Sorgen,
Ah sorrows,

Werdet ihr denn alle Morgen
Will ye then every morning

Und alle Tage wieder neu?
And every day again (be) new?

So klag ich immerfort;
Thus lament I continually;

Ach! Armut! hartes Wort,
Ah, poverty! Harsh word,

Wer steht mir denn in meinem Kummer bei?
Who stands-by me then in my grief - ?
{Who then will stand by me in my grief?}

> **Dein Vater und dein Herre Gott,**
> Thy Father and thy Lord God,

> **Der steht dir bei in aller Not.**
> He stands-by thee - in every need.

4. Tenor Recit.
●Trust in God exercised: patience in adversity (138-4)
Ach süßer Trost! Wenn Gott mich nicht verlassen
Ah sweet comfort! If God me not forsake
{Ah, sweet comfort! If God would not forsake}

the Gentiles seek all these things; and your heavenly Father knows that you need them all.
1 Kings 17:2-12. [When famine came to the land of Israel] the word of the Lord came to [Elijah], "Depart from here and turn eastward, and hide yourself by the brook Cherith...You shall drink from the brook, and I have commanded the ravens (Luther: Raben) to feed you there." So...he went...And the ravens brought him bread and meat in the evening; and he drank from the brook. And after a while the brook dried, because there was no rain in the land. Then the word of the Lord came to him, "Arise, go to Zarephath...Behold, I have commanded a widow there to feed you." So he arose and went...and when he came to the gate of the city, behold, a widow was there gathering sticks; and he called to her and said, "Bring me a little water in a vessel that I may drink." And as she was going to bring it, he called to her and said, "Bring me a morsel of bread (Luther: Bissen Brot) in your hand." And she said, "As the Lord your God lives, I have nothing baked, only a handful of meal in a jar, and a little oil in a cruse; and now, I am gathering a couple of sticks, that I may go in and prepare it for myself and my son, that we may eat it, and die."
Prov. 19:7. All a poor man's brothers hate him; how much more do his friends go far from him!
Ps. 22:1-2. My God, my God, why hast thou forsaken me? Why art thou so far from helping me, from the words of my groaning? O my God, I cry by day, but thou dost not answer; and by night, but find no rest. (Also Mt. 27:46, Mk. 15:34.)
Ps. 71:10-12. My enemies speak concerning me, those who watch for my life consult together, and say, "God has forsaken him; pursue and seize him, for there is none to deliver him." O God, be not far from me; O my God, make haste to help me!
Ps. 55:17. Evening and morning and at noon I utter my complaint and moan...
Ps. 73:14. For all the day long I have been stricken, and chastened every morning.
Ps. 90:5-6, 13-14. [O Lord,] thou dost sweep men away; they are like a dream, like grass which is renewed in the morning: in the morning it flourishes and is renewed; in the evening it fades and withers... Return, O Lord! How long? Have pity on thy servants! Satisfy us in the morning with thy steadfast love, that we may rejoice and be glad all our days.
Ps. 37:25-26. I have been young, and now am old; yet I have not seen the righteous forsaken or his children begging bread. He is ever giving liberally and lending, and his children become a blessing.
*Mt. 6:32 [Christ]: The Gentiles seek all these things; and your heavenly Father knows that you need them all.

Ps. 130:5-6. I wait for the Lord, my soul waits, and in his word I hope; my soul waits for the Lord more than watchmen for the morning, more than watchmen for the morning.
Ps. 71:10-12. My enemies speak concerning me..."God has forsaken him; pursue and seize him, for there is none to deliver him."
Heb. 13:5-6. ...[God] has said, "I will never fail you nor forsake you (Luther: dich nicht verlassen noch versäumen)." Hence we can

Und nicht versäumen will,
And not   abandon would,
{Nor abandon me,}

So kann ich in der Still
Then can I in - quietness

Und in Geduld mich fassen.
And in patience myself compose.
{Then I can compose myself in quietness and patience.}

Die Welt mag immerhin mich hassen,
The world may   still   me   hate,
{Let the world still hate me;}

So werf ich meine Sorgen
Then cast I my cares
{Then I can cast my cares}

Mit Freuden auf den Herrn,
With gladness upon the Lord,
{With gladness upon the Lord,}

Und hilft er heute nicht,
And helps he today not,
{And if he should not help today}

so   hilft er mir   doch   morgen.
then helps he me nevertheless tomorrow.
{then he will help me tomorrow.}

Nun leg ich herzlich gern
Now lay I (most) gladly
{Now will I most gladly lay}

Die Sorgen unters Kissen
(My) cares beneath-(my) pillow

Und mag nichts mehr als dies zu meinem Troste wissen:
And want nothing more than this for   my   comfort to-know:
{And want to know nothing more than this for my comfort:}

5. Bass Aria
●Trust in God exercised: calmness in suffering (138-5)
Auf Gott steht meine Zuversicht,
(In) God stands my confidence,
{My confidence rests in God,}

Mein Glaube läßt ihn walten.
My faith lets him rule.

Nun kann mich keine Sorge nagen,
Now can me no care rankle,
{Now no care can rankle me,}

Nun kann mich auch kein Armut plagen.
Now can me also no poverty plague.
{Nor can any poverty plague me now.}

confidently say, "The Lord is my helper, I will not be afraid; what can man do to me?"
Ps. 46:10–11 [God]: "Be still, and know that I am God. I am exalted among the nations, I am exalted in the earth!" The Lord of hosts is with us; the God of Jacob is our refuge.
Is. 30:15. Thus [says] the Lord God, the Holy One of Israel, "...In quietness and in trust shall be your strength."
Lk. 21:19 [Christ]: By your endurance you will gain your lives (Luther: Fasset eure Seele mit Geduld).
Ps. 131:1–2. O Lord, my heart is not lifted up, my eyes are not raised too high; I do not occupy myself with things too great and too marvelous for me. But I have calmed and quieted my soul, like a child quieted at its mother's breast; like a child that is quieted is my soul.
Lam. 3:25–26. The Lord is good to those who wait for him, to the soul that seeks him. It is good that one should wait quietly for the salvation of the Lord.
Ps. 27:3. Though a host encamp against me, my heart shall not fear; though war arise against me, yet I will be confident.
Jn. 15:18–19 [Christ]: If the world hates you, know that it has hated me before it hated you. If you were of the world, the world would love its own; but because you are not of the world, but I chose you out of the world, therefore the world hates you. (Also Jn. 17:14, Mt. 5:10–12, 10:24–25, 1 Jn. 3:13.)
1 Pet. 5:7. Cast all your anxieties on him, for he cares about you. (Also Phil. 4:6.)
Nah. 1:12. Thus says the Lord, "...Though I have afflicted you, I will afflict you no more."
Ps. 30:5. His anger is but for a moment, and his favor is for a lifetime. Weeping may tarry for the night, but joy comes with the morning.
Lam. 3:22–23. The steadfast love of the Lord never ceases, his mercies never come to an end; they are new every morning; great is thy faithfulness.
Ps. 127:1–2. Unless the Lord builds the house, those who build it labor in vain. Unless the Lord watches over the city, the watchman stays awake in vain. It is in vain that you rise up early and go late to rest, eating the bread of anxious toil; for he gives to his beloved sleep.
Ps. 4:8. In peace I will both lie down and sleep; for thou alone, O Lord, makest me dwell in safety.
Is. 12:2. Behold, God is my salvation; I will trust, and will not be afraid; for the Lord God is my strength and my song, and he has become my salvation. (Also Ps. 56:3–4.)

Ps. 62:5–8. For God alone my soul waits in silence, for my hope is from him. He only is my rock and my salvation, my fortress; I shall not be shaken. On God rests my deliverance and my honor; my mighty rock, my refuge is God. Trust in him at all times, O people; pour out your heart before him; God is a refuge (Luther: Zuversicht) for us. (Zuversicht: also Ps. 46:1, 61:3, 62:7, 71:5, 7, 91:2, 142:5).
***Mt. 6:31–32 [Christ]:** Therefore do not be anxious, saying, "What shall we eat?" or "What shall we drink?" or "What shall we wear?" For the Gentiles seek all these things; and your heavenly Father knows that you need them all.
Ps. 131:2. I have calmed and quieted my soul, like a child quieted at its mother's breast; like a child that is quieted is my soul. (Also Lam. 3:26.)
Ps. 103:13. As a father pities his children, so the Lord pities those who fear him.

Auch mitten in dem größten Leide
Even amidst the greatest suffering

Bleibt er mein Vater, meine Freude,
Remains he my Father, my joy,
{He remains my Father, my joy,}

Er will mich wunderlich erhalten.
He will me wondrously uphold.
{He will wondrously uphold me.}

6. Alto Recit.
●Trust in God exercised: all cares rejected (138-6)
Ei nun!
Well then!

So will ich auch recht sanfte ruhn.
Then would I also right softly rest.
{Then I can rest right softly.}

Euch, Sorgen, sei der Scheidebrief gegeben!
To-you sorrows, be the divorce-bill given!

Nun kann ich wie im Himmel leben.
Now can I as-though in heaven live.
{Now I can live as though I were in heaven.}

7. Chorale (Vs. 3)
●Trust in God exercised: earth affords no comfort (138-7)
Weil du mein Gott und Vater bist,
Since thou my God and Father art,
{Since thou art my God and Father,}

Dein Kind wirst du verlassen nicht,
Thy child wilt thou forsake not,
{Thou wilt not forsake thy child,}

Du väterliches Herz!
Thou fatherly heart!
{O fatherly heart!}

Ich bin ein armer Erdenkloß,
I am (but) a poor clod-of-earth,

Auf Erden weiß ich keinen Trost.
On earth know I no comfort.
{On earth I experience no comfort.}

Neh. 8:10. ...The joy of the Lord is your strength.
Phil. 4:4, 6-7, 11-13, 19. Rejoice in the Lord always; again I will say, Rejoice...Have no anxiety about anything, but in everything by prayer and supplication with thanksgiving let your requests be made known to God. And the peace of God, which passes all understanding, will keep your hearts and your minds in Christ Jesus...I have learned, in whatever state I am, to be content. I know how to be abased, and I know how to abound; in any and all circumstances I have learned the secret of facing plenty and hunger, abundance and want. I can do all things in him who strengthens me...And my God will supply every need of yours according to his riches in glory in Christ Jesus.
Ps. 145:14. The Lord upholds (Luther: erhält) all who are falling, and raises up all who are bowed down.

*Mt. 6:34 [Christ]: Therefore do not be anxious about tomorrow, for tomorrow will be anxious for itself. Let the day's own trouble be sufficient for the day.
1 Pet. 5:7. Cast all your anxieties on [God], for he cares about you.
Ps. 4:8. In peace I will both lie down and sleep; for thou alone, O Lord, makest me dwell in safety. (Also Ps. 127:2.)
Phil. 4:7. The peace of God, which passes all understanding, will keep your hearts and your minds in Christ Jesus.
*Mt. 6:28-30 [Christ]: ...Consider the lilies of the field, how they grow; they neither toil nor spin; yet I tell you, even Solomon in all his glory was not arrayed like one of these. But if God so clothes the grass of the field, which today is alive and tomorrow is thrown into the oven, will he not much more clothe you, O men of little faith?

*Mt. 6:26, 32 [Christ]: Look at the birds of the air...your heavenly Father feeds them. Are you not of more value than they?...The Gentiles seek all these things; and your heavenly Father knows that you need them all.
Ps. 103:13-16. As a father pities his children, so the Lord pities those who fear him. For he knows our frame; he remembers that we are dust. As for man, his days are like grass; he flourishes like a flower of the field; for the wind passes over it, and it is gone, and its place knows it no more. (Also Gen. 3:19, Ecc. 3:20, 12:7.)
2 Cor. 4:7-9. We have this treasure in earthen vessels, to show that the transcendent power belongs to God and not to us. We are afflicted in every way, but not crushed; perplexed, but not driven to despair; persecuted, but not forsaken; struck down, but not destroyed.
2 Cor. 15:47. The first man [Adam] was from the earth, a man of dust...
Ecc. 3:19-20. The fate of the sons of men and the fate of beasts is the same; as one dies, so dies the other. They all have the same breath... All go to one place; all are from the dust, and all turn to dust again. (Also Gen. 3:19. Ecc. 12:7, Ps. 146:4.)
2 Cor. 5:1. We know that if the earthly tent we live in is destroyed, we have a building from God, a house not made with hands, eternal in the heaven.

BWV 139
Wohl dem, der sich auf seinen Gott
(NBA I/26; BC A159)

23. S. after Trinity (BWV 163, 139, 52)
*Phil. 3:17–21 (Our citizenship is in heaven.)
*Mt. 22:15–22 (The Pharisees try to trap Jesus with the question: "Is it lawful to pay taxes to Ceasar?")
Librettist: Unknown

1. Chorus (Chorale Vs. 1)
●God as friend: Relying on him in times of opposition (139–1)
Wohl dem, der sich auf seinen Gott
Happy he, who himself (to)   his   God
{Happy is he who can entrust himself to his God}

Recht kindlich kann verlassen!
Right childlike can   entrust!
{In right childlike manner!}

Den mag gleich Sünde, Welt und Tod
Him may (indeed) sin,   world, and death
{Sin, world, and death}

Und alle Teufel hassen,
And all   devils   hate,
{And all devils may hate him,}

So bleibt er dennoch wohlvergnügt,
Yet remains he nevertheless   cheerful,
{Yet he nevertheless remains cheerful,}

Wenn er nur Gott zum Freunde kriegt.
If   he but God as   friend   gains.
{If he but gains God as his friend.}

2. Tenor Aria (Based on Chorale Vs. 2)
●God as friend means the foe presents no danger (139–2)
Gott ist mein Freund; was hilft das Toben,
God is   my   friend; what profits that raging,
{God is my friend; what does that raging profit,}

So   wider mich ein Feind erhoben!
Which against me (the)   foe   has-raised?
{Which the foe has raised against me?}

Ich bin getrost bei Neid und Haß.
I   am confident amidst envy and hatred.

Ja, redet nur die Wahrheit spärlich,
Yes, speak but the   truth   rarely,
{Yes, though you speak the truth but rarely,}

Seid immer falsch, was tut   mir das?
Be   ever   false,   what does to-me that?
{Be ever false, what does that hurt me?}

Prov. 16:20. ...Happy is he who trusts in the Lord (Luther: wohl dem der sich auf den Herrn verläßt). (Also Ps. 84:12, 146:5, Prov. 3:5–6.)
Ps. 131:1–2. O Lord, my heart is not lifted up, my eyes are not raised too high; I do not occupy myself with things too great and too marvelous for me. But I have calmed and quieted my soul, like a child quieted at its mother's breast; like a child that is quieted is my soul.
Mt. 18:2–4. Calling to him a child, [Jesus] put him in the midst of them, and said, "Truly, I say to you, unless you turn and become like children, you will never enter the kingdom of heaven. Whoever humbles himself like this child, he is the greatest in the kingdom of heaven."
Ps. 118:6–7. With the Lord on my side I do not fear. What can man do to me? The Lord is on my side to help me; I shall look in triumph on those who hate me. (Also Ps. 27:1, Ps. 56:4, Rom. 8:31, 2 Cor. 2:14.)
Eph. 6:12. We are not contending against flesh and blood, but against the principalities, against the powers, against the world rulers of this present darkness, against the spiritual hosts of wickedness in the heavenly places. (Also 1 Pet. 5:8, 2 Cor. 10:3–4, Phil. 1:28–30, 1 Jn. 5:19.)
Jn. 15:18–19 [Christ]: If the world hates you, know that it has hated me before it hated you. If you were of the world, the world would love its own; but because you are not of the world, but I chose you out of the world, therefore the world hates you. (Also Jn. 17:14, Mt. 5:10–12, 10:24–25, 1 Jn. 3:13.)
Jn. 15:15–16 [Christ]: No longer do I call you servants, for the servant does not know what his master is doing; but I have called you friends... You did not choose me, but I chose you and appointed you that you should go and bear fruit and that your fruit should abide; so that whatever you ask the Father in my name, he may give it to you.

Jn. 15:15 [Christ]: No longer do I call you servants...but I have called you friends...
Ps. 27:1, 3. The Lord is my light and my salvation; whom shall I fear? The Lord is the stronghold of my life; of whom shall I be afraid?... Though a host encamp against me, my heart shall not fear; though war arise against me, yet I will be confident.
Ps. 56:3–4. [O Lord,] when I am afraid, I put my trust in thee. In God, whose word I praise, in God I trust without a fear. What can flesh do to me? (Also Ps. 118:6–7.)
***Mt. 22:15–17.** The Pharisees went and took counsel how to entangle [Jesus] in his talk. And they sent their disciples to him, along with the Herodians, saying, "Teacher, we know that you are true, and teach the way of God truthfully, and care for no man; for you do not regard the position of men. Tell us, then, what you think..."
Jn. 2:24–25. But Jesus did not trust himself to [the people], because he knew all men and needed no one to bear witness of man; for he himself knew what was in man.
1 Jn. 4:4. Little children, you are of God, and have overcome [false spirits]; for he who is in you is greater than he who is in the world. (Also Jn. 16:33.)

Ihr Spötter seid mir ungefährlich.
You scoffers are to-me not-dangerous.
{You scoffers present no danger to me.}

3. Alto Recit.
•Christ's children sent among wolves as he too was (139-3)
Der Heiland sendet ja die Seinen
The Savior sends, indeed his own
{Indeed, the Savior sends those who are his own}

Recht mitten in der Wölfe Wut.
Directly admist - the wolves' rage.

Um ihn hat sich der Bösen Rotte
Around him has - the malicious rabble—
{Around him, the malicious rabble has—}

Zum Schaden und zum Spotte
For harm and for mocking—

Mit List gestellt;
With cunning set (itself):

Doch da sein Mund so weisen Ausspruch tut,
Yet since his mouth such wise utterance makes,
{Yet because his mouth speaks so wisely,}

So schützt er mich auch vor der Welt.
Thus protects he me also from the world.
{He can protect me from the world.}

4. Bass Aria (Based on Chorale Vs. 3)
•God as friend in times of adversity (139-4)
Das Unglück schlägt auf allen Seiten
- Misfortune wraps on all sides
{On all sides misfortune wraps}

Um mich ein zentnerschweres Band.
Around me a hundredweight (of) (chain).

Doch plötzlich erscheinet die helfende Hand.
Yet suddenly appears the helping hand.

Mir scheint des Trostes Licht von weiten;
To-me shines - comfort's light from afar;
{Comfort's light appears from afar}

Da lern ich erst, daß Gott allein
Then learn I (finally), that God alone
{Then I finally learn that God alone}

Der Menschen bester Freund muß sein.
- Man's best friend must be.

Ps. 37:12–13. The wicked plots against the righteous, and gnashes his teeth at him; but the Lord laughs at the wicked, for he sees that his day is coming.

Mt. 10:16–20 [Christ]: Behold, I send you out as sheep in the midst of wolves; so be wise as serpents and innocent as doves. Beware of men; for they will deliver you up to councils, and flog you in their synagogues, and you will be dragged before governors and kings for my sake, to bear testimony before them and the Gentiles. When they deliver you up, do not be anxious how you are to speak or what you are to say; for what you are to say will be given to you in that hour; for it is not you who speak, but the Spirit of your Father speaking through you. (Also Mt. 7:15.)
Ps. 22:16. Yea, dogs are round about me; a company of evildoers (Luther: Bösen Rotte) encircle me...
***Mt. 22:15–22.** Then the Pharisees went and took counsel how to entangle [Jesus] in his talk. And they sent their disciples to him, along with the Herodians, saying, "Teacher, we know that you are true, and teach the way of God truthfully, and care for no man; for you do not regard the position of men. Tell us, then, what you think. Is it lawful to pay taxes to Caesar, or not?" But Jesus, aware of their malice, said, "Why put me to the test, you hypocrites? Show me the money for the tax." And they brought him a coin. And Jesus said to them, "Whose likeness and inscription is this?" They said, "Caesar's." Then he said to them, "Render therefore to Caesar the things that are Caesar's, and to God the things that are God's." When they heard it, they marveled; and they left him and went away.

2 Cor. 4:6–9. ...[God]...has shone in our hearts to give the light of the knowledge of the glory of God in the face of Christ. But we have this treasure in earthen vessels, to show that the transcendent power belongs to God and not to us. We are afflicted in every way, but not crushed; perplexed, but not driven to despair; persecuted, but not forsaken; struck down, but not destroyed...
Is. 59:1. Behold, the Lord's hand is not shortened, that it cannot save, or his ear dull, that it cannot hear. (Also Is. 50:2, Num. 11:23.)
Ps. 30:5. ...Weeping may tarry for the night, but joy comes with the morning.
Ps. 37:7–10. Be still before the Lord, and wait patiently for him; fret not yourself over him who prospers in his way, over the man who carries out evil devices! Refrain from anger, and forsake wrath! Fret not yourself; it tends only to evil. For the wicked shall be cut off; but those who wait for the Lord shall possess the land. Yet a little while, and the wicked will be no more; though you look well at his place, he will not be there. (wait for the Lord: also Ps. 27:14)
Ps. 60:11/108:12. [O Lord]...grant us help against the foe, for vain is the help of man!
Ps. 146:3, 5. Put not your trust in princes, in a son of man, in whom there is no help...Happy is he whose help is the God of Jacob, whose hope is in the Lord his God...

5. Soprano Recit. (Based on Chorale Vs. 4)
●Sin's burden is greatest foe; removed by the Savior (139-5)
Ja, trag ich gleich den größten Feind in mir,
Yes, bear I though the greatest foe within me,
{Yes, though I bear the greatest foe of all within me,}

Die schwere Last der Sünden,
The heavy burden of sin,

Mein Heiland läßt mich Ruhe finden.
My Savior lets me rest find.
{My Savior grants me rest.}

Ich gebe Gott, was Gottes ist,
I give-to God, what God's is,
{I give to God what belongs to God,}

Das Innerste der Seelen.
The innermost-part of-(my) soul.

Will er sie nun erwählen,
Would he it now elect,
{If he chooses it for his own,}

So weicht der Sünden Schuld,
Then retreats - sin's guilt,

    so fällt des Satans List.
    then falls - Satan's craftiness.

6. Chorale (Vs. 5)
●God as friend allows me to to defy all foes (139-6)
Dahero   Trotz der Höllen Heer!
Therefore (we mouth) defiance to hell's host!

Trotz auch des Todes Rachen!
Defiance also to death's jaws!

Trotz aller Welt! mich kann nicht mehr
Defiance to-all-the world! Me can no more
{Defiance to all the world! Its battering}

Ihr Pochen traurig machen!
Its battering[1] sad make!
{Can no longer sadden me!}

Gott ist mein Schutz, mein Hilf und Rat;
God is my protection, my help and counsel;

[1]or "boasting"

Jms. 4:1. What causes wars, and what causes fightings among you? Is it not your passions that are at war in your members?
Jer. 17:9. The heart is deceitful above all things, and desperately corrupt...
Mt. 15:11, 18–20 [Christ]: Not what goes into the mouth defiles a man, but what comes out of the mouth, this defiles a man...What comes out of the mouth proceeds from the heart, and this defiles a man. For out of the heart come evil thoughts, murder, adultery, fornication, theft, false witness, slander. These are what defile a man... (Also Mk. 7:20–23.)
Rom. 7:15, 18–20, 24–25. I do not understand my own actions. For I do not do what I want, but I do the very thing I hate...I know that nothing good dwells within me, that is, in my flesh. I can will what is right, but I cannot do it. For I do not do the good I want, but the evil I do not want is what I do. Now if I do what I do not want, it is no longer I that do it, but sin which dwells within me...Wretched man that I am! Who will deliver me from this body of death? Thanks be to God through Jesus Christ our Lord!...
Is. 1:4. Ah, sinful nation, a people laden with iniquity...
Mt. 11:28–30 [Christ]: Come to me, all who labor and are heavy laden, and I will give you rest. Take my yoke upon you, and learn from me; for I am gentle and lowly in heart, and you will find rest for your souls. For my yoke is easy, and my burden is light. (Also Jer. 6:16.)
*****Mt. 22:21 [Christ]:** ...Render...to God the things that are God's. (Also Jms. 4:5.)
Mt. 22:37–38 [Christ]: ...You shall love the Lord your God with all your heart, and with all your soul, and with all your mind. This is the great and first commandment. (Also Rom. 12:1.)
Jn. 15:16 [Christ]: You did not choose me, but I chose you and appointed you... (Also Heb. 2:11.)
*****Mt. 22:22.** When [Jesus' questioners] heard [his answer], they marveled; and they left him and went away.

Rom. 8:31. What then shall we say to this? If God is for us, who is against us?
Eph. 6:11–12. Put on the whole armor of God, that you may be able to stand against the wiles (Luther: listigen Anläufe) of the devil. For we are not contending against flesh and blood, but against the principalities, against the powers, against the world rulers of this present darkness, against the spiritual hosts of wickedness in the heavenly places. (Also 1 Pet. 5:8, 2 Cor. 10:3–4, Phil. 1:28–30.)
Is. 5:14. ...Sheol (Luther: Hölle) has enlarged its appetite and opened its mouth (Luther: Rachen) beyond measure...
Rom. 8:37. ...We are more than conquerors through him who loved us.
Col. 2:15. [Christ] disarmed the principalities and powers and made a public example of them, triumphing over them in him.
1 Cor. 15:55. O death, where is thy victory? O death, where is thy sting?
Ps. 27:1, 3. The Lord is my light and my salvation; whom shall I fear? The Lord is the stronghold of my life; of whom shall I be afraid?... Though a host encamp against me, my heart shall not fear; though war arise against me, yet I will be confident. (Also Ps. 118:6.)

Wohl dem, der Gott zum Freunde hat!
Blessed he, who God as friend has!
{Blessed is he who has God as his friend!}

Gott ist mein Schutz, mein Hilf und Rat;
God is my protection, my help, and counsel;

Wohl dem, der Gott zum Freunde hat!
Blessed he, who God as friend has!
{Blessed is he who has God as his friend!}

BWV 140
Wachet auf, ruft uns die Stimme
(NBA I/27; BC A166)

27. S. after Trinity (BWV 140 only) During Bach's tenure in Leipzig (1723–1750), a 27th Sunday after Trinity occurred only in 1731 and 1742.
*1 Thess. 5:1-11 (Last day will come like a thief in the night; exhortation to be ready)
*Mt. 25:1-13 (Parable of the ten virgins waiting for the bridegroom)
Librettist: Unknown

1. Chorus (Chorale Vs. 1)
●Watchmen of Jerusalem announce bridegroom's arrival (140-1)
Wachet auf, ruft uns die Stimme
"Wake up!" calls to-us the voice
{"Wake up!" call the voices}

Der Wächter sehr hoch auf der Zinne,
Of-the watchmen very high upon the battlement,

Wach auf, du Stadt Jerusalem!
"Wake up, thou city (of) Jerusalem!"

Mitternacht heißt diese Stunde;
Midnight is-called this hour;
{It is at midnight that}

Sie rufen uns mit hellem Munde:
They call to-us with bright (voices):

Wo seid ihr klugen Jungfrauen?
"Where are you (O) wise virgins?

Wohl auf, der Bräutgam kömmt;
Arise-then, the bridegroom is-coming;

Steht auf, die Lampen nehmt!
Rise up, (your) lamps take!
{Rise up; take your lamps!}

Alleluja!
Alleluia!

Jn. 16:33 [Christ]: I have said this to you, that in me you may have peace. In the world you have tribulation; but be of good cheer, I have overcome the world. (Also Jms. 4:4, 1 Jn. 2:15–17.)
Jer. 17:7. Blessed is the man who trusts in the Lord, whose trust is the Lord. (Also Ps. 2:12, 40:4, 84:12, 146:5.)
Ps. 46:7/11. The Lord of hosts is with us; the God of Jacob is our refuge (Luther: Schutz). (Also Ps. 18:2, 30, 35, 48:3, 59:9, 17, 94:22.)
Ps. 73:24. [O Lord,] thou dost guide me with thy counsel (Luther: Rat), and afterward thou wilt receive me to glory.
Ps. 33:20. Our soul waits for the Lord; he is our help and shield. (Also Ps. 28:7, 115:9–11.)
Ps. 33:12. Blessed is the nation whose God is the Lord, the people whom he has chosen as his heritage!

*Mt. 25:1-13. The kingdom of heaven shall be compared to ten maidens who took their lamps and went to meet the bridegroom. Five of them were foolish, and five were wise. For when the foolish took their lamps, they took no oil with them; but the wise took flasks of oil with their lamps. As the bridegroom was delayed, they all slumbered and slept. But at midnight there was a cry, "Behold, the bridegroom! Come out to meet him." Then all those maidens rose and trimmed their lamps. And the foolish said to the wise, "Give us some of your oil, for our lamps are going out." But the wise replied, "Perhaps there will not be enough for us and for you; go rather to the dealers and buy for youselves." And while they went to buy, the bridegroom came, and those who were ready went in with him to the marriage feast; and the door was shut. Afterward the other maidens came also, saying, "Lord, lord, open to us." But he replied, "Truly, I say to you, I do not know you." Watch therefore, for you know neither the day nor the hour.
Is. 62:6 [God]: Upon your walls, O Jerusalem, I have set watchmen; all the day and all the night they shall never be silent...
Mal. 3:1. ...The Lord whom you seek will suddenly come to his temple; the messenger of the covenant in whom you delight, behold, he is coming, says the Lord of hosts.
Ps. 130:6. My soul waits for the Lord more than watchmen for the morning, more than watchmen for the morning.
*1 Thess. 5:1-7. But as to the times and the seasons, brethren, you have no need to have anything written to you. For you yourselves know well that the day of the Lord will come like a thief in the night. When people say, "There is peace and security," then sudden destruction will come upon them as travail comes upon a woman with child, and there will be no escape. But you are not in darkness, brethren for that day to surprise you like a thief. For you are all sons of light and sons of the day; we are not of the night or of darkness. So then let us not sleep, as others do, but let us keep awake and be sober. For those who sleep sleep at night, and those who get drunk are drunk at night.
Eph. 5:14. Therefore it is said, "Awake, O sleeper, and arise from the dead, and Christ shall give you light."

Macht euch bereit
Make yourselves ready
{Get ready}

Zu der Hochzeit,
For the wedding,

Ihr müsset ihm entgegengehn!
You must him go-forth-to-meet!"
{You must go forth to meet him!"}

2. Tenor Recit.
●Bridegroom's arrival from heaven announced to bride (140–2)
Er kommt, er kommt,
He comes, he comes,

Der Bräutgam kommt!
The bridegroom comes!

Ihr Töchter Zions, kommt heraus,
You daughters of-Zion, come forth,

Sein Ausgang eilet aus der Höhe
His (journey) hastens from the heights
{He hastens from the heights}

In euer Mutter Haus.
Into your mother's house.

Der Bräutgam kommt, der einem Rehe
The bridegroom comes, who a roe
{The bridegroom comes, who leaps like a roe}

Und jungen Hirsche gleich
And young buck like
{And young buck}

Auf denen Hügeln springt
On the hills leaps
{Upon the hills}

Und euch das Mahl der Hochzeit bringt.
And to-you the banquet of-the wedding brings.
{And brings you the wedding banquet.}

Wacht auf, ermuntert euch!
Wake up, rouse yourselves!

Den Bräutgam zu empfangen!
The bridegroom to receive!
{So you can receive the bridegroom!}

Dort, sehet, kommt er hergegangen.
There, lo, he-comes approaching.

Mt. 24:44. Therefore you...must be ready; for the Son of man is coming at an hour you do not expect.
S. of S. 3:11. Go forth, O daughters of Zion, and behold King Solomon, with the crown with which his mother crowned him on the day of his wedding, on the day of the gladness of his heart. (Also Ps. 45:13–15.)
Rev. 19:7, 9. ...The marriage of the Lamb has come, and his Bride has made herself ready...Blessed are those who are invited to the marriage supper of the Lamb...
Rev. 21:2. I saw the holy city, new Jerusalem, coming down out of heaven from God, prepared as a bride adorned for her husband.

*Mt. 25:6. At midnight there was a cry, "Behold, the bridegroom! Come out to meet him."
S. of S. 3:11. Go forth, O daughters of Zion, and behold King Solomon, with the crown with which his mother crowned him on the day of his wedding, on the day of the gladness of his heart.
Ps. 45:13–15. ...The princess is decked in her chamber with gold-woven robes; in many-colored robes she is led to the king, with her virgin companions, her escort, in her train. With joy and gladness they are led along as they enter the palace of the king.
Lk. 1:78–79. ...The day shall dawn upon us from on high (Luther: Aufgang aus der Höhe) to give light to those who sit in darkness and in the shadow of death, to guide our feet into the way of peace.
S. of S. 3:1–4 [Bride]: ...I sought him whom my soul loves; I sought him, but found him not; I called him, but he gave no answer. "I will rise now and go about the city, in the streets and in the squares; I will seek him whom my soul loves." I sought him, but found him not. The watchmen found me, as they went about in the city. "Have you seen him whom my soul loves?" Scarcely had I passed them, when I found him whom my soul loves. I held him, and would not let him go until I had brought him into my mother's house (Luther: Mutter Haus), and into the chamber of her that conceived me. (Also S. of S. 8:2.)
S. of S. 2:8–9. The voice of my beloved! Behold, he comes, leaping upon the mountains, bounding over the hills. My beloved is like a gazelle (Luther: Reh), or a young stag (Luther: Hirsch). Behold, there he stands behind our wall, gazing in at the windows, looking through the lattice. (Also S. of S. 2:17, 8:14.)
Rev. 19:6–9. Then I heard what seemed to be the voice of a great multitude, like the sound of many waters and like the sound of mighty thunderpeals, crying, "Hallelujah! For the Lord our God the Almighty reigns. Let us rejoice and exult and give him the glory, for the marriage of the Lamb has come, and his Bride has made herself ready; it was granted her to be clothed with fine linen, bright and pure"—for the fine linen is the righteous deeds of the saints. And the angel said to me, "Write this: Blessed are those who are invited to the marriage supper of the Lamb."...
Mt. 24:44. Therefore you also must be ready; for the Son of man is coming at an hour you do not expect.

3. Soprano & Bass Aria
●Dialogue: Bride (Soul) and Bridegroom (Christ) (140-3)
Soprano:
Wann kommst du, mein Heil?
When comest thou, my Salvation?

Bass:
Ich komme, dein Teil.
I'm coming, thy portion.

Soprano:
Ich warte mit brennendem Öle.
I wait with burning oil.

Soprano/Bass:
Eröffne / Ich-öffne den Saal
Open / I-open the hall

Zum himmlischen Mahl
For-the heavenly banquet

Soprano:
Komm, Jesu!
Come, Jesus!

Bass:
Ich komme; komm, lieblich Seele!
I'm coming; come, lovely soul!

4. Chorale: Tenor (Vs. 2)
●Bride (Zion) rejoices over bridegroom's arrival (140-4)
Zion hört die Wächter singen,
Zion hears the watchmen sing,

Das Herz tut ihr vor Freuden springen,
(Her) heart does - for joy leap,
{Her heart leaps for joy,}

Sie wachet und steht eilend auf.
She keeps-watch and rises quickly - .
{She has been keeping watch and rises quickly.}

Ihr Freund kommt vom Himmel prächtig,
Her friend comes from heaven glorious,

Von Gnaden stark, von Wahrheit mächtig,
In grace strong, in truth mighty,
{Strong in grace, mighty in truth,}

Ihr Licht wird hell, ihr Stern geht auf.
Her light becomes bright; her star rises.

Nun komm, du werte Kron,
Now come, thou precious crown,

Herr Jesu, Gottes Sohn!
Lord Jesus, God's Son!

Is. 62:5, 11. ...As the bridegroom rejoices over the bride, so shall your God rejoice over you...Behold, the Lord has proclaimed to the end of the earth: Say to the daughter of Zion, "Behold, your salvation comes; behold, his reward is with him, and his recompense before him."
Gen. 49:18. I wait for thy salvation (Luther: Heil), O Lord.
Lam. 3:24. "The Lord is my portion (Luther: Teil)," says my soul, "therefore I will hope in him." (Also Ps. 73:26.)
Ps. 16:5. The Lord is my chosen portion and my cup (Luther: Gut und Teil); thou holdest my lot. (Also Ps. 142:5.)
Mt. 24:44. ...Be ready; for the Son of man is coming at an hour you do not expect.
*Mt. 25:4, 10. The wise took flasks of oil with their lamps. And while [the foolish] went to buy, the bridegroom came, and those who were ready went in with him to the marriage feast; and the door was shut.
Mt. 22:1-3. Jesus spoke...in parables, saying, "The kingdom of heaven may be compared to a king who gave a marriage feast for his son, and sent his servants to call those who were invited to the marriage feast..."
Rev. 21:9. ....One of the seven angels...spoke to me, saying, "Come, I will show you the Bride, the wife of the Lamb."
Rev. 19:7-9. Let us rejoice and exult and give him the glory, for the marriage of the Lamb has come, and his Bride has made herself ready; it was granted her to be clothed with fine linen, bright and pure —for the fine linen is the righteous deeds of the saints. And the angel said to me, "Write this: Blessed are those who are invited to the marriage supper of the Lamb."... (Also Rev. 3:20.)
Rev. 22:20. He who testifies to these things says, "Surely I am coming soon." Amen. Come, Lord Jesus!

*Mt. 25:6-7. At midnight there was a cry, "Behold, the bridegroom! Come out to meet him." Then all those maidens rose and trimmed their lamps...
*Mt. 25:13. Watch therefore, for you know neither the day nor the hour.
Ps. 130:6. My soul waits for the Lord more than watchmen for the morning, more than watchmen for the morning.
S. of S. 3:6-7, 9-11. What is that coming up from the wilderness, like a column of smoke, perfumed with myrrh and frankincense, with all the fragrant powders of the merchant? Behold, it is the litter of Solomon! About it are sixty mighty men of the mighty men of Israel... King Solomon made himself a palanquin from the wood of Lebanon. He made its posts of silver, its back of gold, its seat of purple; it was lovingly wrought within by the daughters of Jerusalem. Go forth, O daughters of Zion, and behold King Solomon, with the crown with which his mother crowned him on the day of his wedding, on the day of the gladness of his heart.
Ps. 104:1. ...O Lord my God, thou art very great! Thou art clothed with honor and majesty. (Also Ps. 93:1.)
Jn. 1:14. The Word became flesh and dwelt among us, full of grace and truth (Luther: Gnade und Wahrheit); we have beheld his glory, glory as of the only Son from the Father.
Is. 60:1, 3. Arise, shine; for your light has come, and the glory of the Lord has risen upon you...And nations shall come to your light, and kings to the brightness of your rising.
Is. 28:5. In that day the Lord of hosts will be a crown of glory, and a diadem of beauty, to the remnant of his people.
2 Tim. 4:8. Henceforth there is laid up for me the crown of righteousness, which the Lord...will award to me on that Day, and not only to

Hosianna!
Hosanna!

Wir folgen all
We follow all

Zum Freudensaal
To   joy's-hall

Und halten mit das Abendmahl.
And hold-together the evening-meal.

5. Bass Recit.
●Vox Christi: Bride (Soul) welcomed by Christ (140-5)
So geh herein zu mir,
So (come) in   to me,

Du mir erwählte Braut!
Thou my chosen bride!

Ich habe mich mit dir
I   have myself to thee

Von Ewigkeit vertraut.
From eternity betrothed.
{I have betrothed myself to thee from eternity.}

Dich will ich auf mein Herz,
Thee would I on my heart,
{I would set thee upon my heart,}

Auf meinen Arm gleich wie ein Siegel setzen
Upon my   arm like as a   seal   set
{Upon my arm, as a seal}

Und dein betrübtes Aug ergötzen.
And thy troubled eye delight.
{And delight thy troubled eye.}

Vergiß, o Seele, nun
Forget, O soul, now

Die Angst, den Schmerz,
The fear, the pain,

Den du erdulden müssen;
Which thou to-suffer hast-had;
{Which thou hast had to suffer;}

Auf meiner Linken sollst du ruhn,
Upon my left-hand shalt thou rest,

Und meine Rechte soll dich küssen.
And my right-hand shall thee kiss.
{And my right hand shall embrace thee.}

me but also to all who have loved his appearing.
Mt. 24:44. ...Be ready; for the Son of man is coming at an hour you do not expect.
*Mt. 25:10. ...The bridegroom came, and those who were ready went in with him to the marriage feast; and the door was shut. (Ps. 45:15)
Lk. 22:17–18. And [Jesus] took a cup, and when he had given thanks he said, "Take this, and divide it among yourselves; for I tell you that from now on I shall not drink of the fruit of the vine until the kingdom of God comes."
Rev. 19:9. ...Blessed are those who are invited to the marriage supper (Luther: Abendmahl) of the Lamb...

*Mt. 25:10. And...the bridegroom came, and those who were ready went in with him to the marriage feast; and the door was shut. (Also Ps. 45:13–15.)
Eph. 5:25, 27. ...Christ loved the church and gave himself up for her... that he might present the church to himself in splendor, without spot or wrinkle or any such thing, that she might be holy and without blemish.
Hos. 2:19–20 [God]: I will betroth you to me for ever; I will betroth you to me in righteousness and in justice, in steadfast love, and in mercy. I will betroth you to me in faithfulness; and you shall know the Lord. (Also 2 Cor. 11:2.)
S. of S. 8:6 [Bridegroom]: Set me as a seal upon your heart, as a seal upon your arm; for love is strong as death, jealousy is cruel as the grave. Its flashes are flashes of fire, a most vehement flame.
Rev. 21:1–4. Then I saw a new heaven and a new earth; for the first heaven and the first earth had passed away, and the sea was no more. And I saw the holy city, new Jerusalem, coming down out of heaven from God, prepared as a bride adorned for her husband; and I heard a loud voice from the throne saying, "Behold, the dwelling of God is with men. He will dwell with them, and they shall be his people, and God himself will be with them; he will wipe away every tear from their eyes, and death shall be no more, neither shall there be mourning nor crying nor pain any more, for the former things have passed away." (Also Rev. 7:15–17.)
Is. 25:8–9. He will swallow up death for ever, and the Lord God will wipe away tears from all faces, and the reproach of his people he will take away from all the earth; for the Lord has spoken. It will be said on that day, "Lo, this is our God; we have waited for him, that he might save us. This is the Lord; we have waited for him; let us be glad and rejoice in his salvation."
Is. 54:4. ...The reproach of your widowhood you will remember no more.
S. of S. 2:6 [Bride]: O that his left hand were under my head, and that his right hand embraced me!
Mt. 20:20–23. The mother of the sons of Zebedee came up to [Jesus], with her sons...And he said to her, "What do you want?" She said to him, "Command that these two sons of mine may sit, one at your right hand and one at your left, in your kingdom." But Jesus answered, "You do not know what you are asking. Are you able to drink the cup that I am to drink?" They said to him, "We are able." He said to them, "You will drink my cup, but to sit at my right hand and at my left is not mine to grant, but it is for those for whom it has been prepared by my Father." (Also Mk. 10:37–40.)

6. Soprano & Bass Duet

●Dialogue: Love duet between Soul & Christ (140-6)

Soprano:

Mein Freund is mein,

My friend is mine,

Bass:

Und ich bin sein,

And I am his,

Both:

Die Liebe soll nichts scheiden.

(This) love shall nothing sever.

{Nothing shall sever this love.}

Soprano/Bass:

Ich-will/Du-sollst

I-will/Thou-shalt

       mit dir/mir in Himmels Rosen weiden,

       with me/thee in heaven's roses pasture,

Da Freude die Fülle, da Wonne wird sein.

Where joy (in) fullness, (and) where bliss will be.

7. Chorale (Vs. 3)

●Glory be to God for anticipated splendor of heaven (140-7)

Gloria sei dir gesungen

Gloria be to-thee sung

Mit Menschen- und englischen Zungen,

With human and angelic tongues,

Mit Harfen und mit Zimbeln schon.

With harps and with cymbals (sweet).

       [schon = schön]

Von zwölf Perlen sind die Pforten,

Of twelve pearls are the portals,

An deiner Stadt sind wir Konsorten

In thy city are we consorts

{In thy city we shall be the consorts}

Der Engel hoch um deinen Thron.

Of angels high around thy throne.

Kein Aug hat je gespürt,

No eye hath yet perceived,

Kein Ohr hat je gehört

No ear hath ever heard

Solche Freude.

Such joy.

Des sind wir froh.

Over-this are we glad.

{We rejoice over this.}

S. of S. 2:16 [Bride]: My beloved (Luther: Freund) is mine and I am his... (Also S. of S. 6:3.)

Rom. 8:35–39. Who shall separate us from the love of Christ? Shall tribulation, or distress, or persecution, or famine, or nakedness, or peril, or sword? As it is written, "For thy sake we are being killed all the day long; we are regarded as sheep to be slaughtered." No, in all these things we are more than conquerors through him who loved us. For I am sure that neither death, nor life, nor angels, nor principalities, nor things present, nor things to come, nor powers, nor height, nor depth, nor anything else in all creation, will be able to separate us from the love of God in Christ Jesus our Lord.

S. of S. 6:2–3 [Bride]: My beloved has gone down to his garden, to the bed of spices, to pasture his flock in the gardens, and to gather lilies (Luther: Rosen). I am my beloved's and my beloved is mine; he pastures his flock among the lilies (Luther: Rosen).

Rev. 7:17. The Lamb in the midst of the throne will be their shepherd, and he will guide them to springs of living water; and God will wipe away every tear from their eyes.

Ps. 16:11. [O Lord,] thou dost show me the path of life; in thy presence there is fulness of joy, in thy right hand are pleasures for evermore.

Lk. 2:13–14 [Christmas narrative]: Suddenly there was with the angel a multitude of the heavenly host praising God and saying, "Glory to God in the highest, and on earth peace among men with whom he is pleased!"

Phil. 4:20. To our God and Father be glory for ever and ever.

1 Tim. 1:17. To the King of ages, immortal, invisible, the only God, be honor and glory for ever and ever. Amen. (Also Rom. 16:27, Jude 1:25, 1 Pet. 4:11.)

Ps. 148:1–2. Praise the Lord! Praise the Lord from the heavens, praise him in the heights! Praise him, all his angels, praise him, all his host!

Ps. 150:3–6. Praise him with trumpet sound; praise him with lute and harp! Praise him with timbrel and dance; praise him with strings and pipe! Praise him with sounding cymbals; praise him with loud clashing cymbals! Let everything that breathes praise the Lord! Praise the Lord!

Rev. 7:11–12. All the angels stood round the throne and round the elders and the four living creatures, and they fell on their faces before the throne and worshiped God, saying, "Amen! Blessing and glory and wisdom and thanksgiving and honor and power and might be to our God for ever and ever! Amen." (Also Rev. 5:11–14.)

Rev. 21:10–11, 21. And in the Spirit [the angel] carried me away to a great, high mountain, and showed me the holy city Jerusalem coming down out of heaven from God, having the glory of God, its radiance like a most rare jewel, like a jasper, clear as crystal...And the twelve gates were twelve pearls, each of the gates made of a single pearl, and the street of the city was pure gold, transparent as glass.

Heb. 12:22–23. You have come to Mount Zion and to the city of the living God, the heavenly Jerusalem, and to innumerable angels in festal gathering, and to the assembly of the first-born who are enrolled in heaven...

1 Cor. 2:9–10. As it is written, "What no eye has seen, nor ear heard, nor the heart of man conceived, what God has prepared for those who love him," God has revealed to us through the Spirit...

Io, Io!
Io, io!

Ewig in dulci jubilo.
Ever in dulci jubilo.

Rom. 5:2. ...We rejoice in our hope of sharing the glory of God.
Ps. 16:11. ...[O Lord,] in thy presence there is fulness of joy, in thy right hand are pleasures for evermore.
Mt. 5:12 [Christ]: Rejoice and be glad, for your reward is great in heaven...

BWV 141
Das ist je gewißlich wahr

This cantata was composed by Georg Philipp Telemann.

BWV 142
Uns ist ein Kind geboren

This cantata was not composed by J. S. Bach. It was perhaps composed by Johann Kuhnau.

BWV 143
Lobe den Herrn, meine Seele I
(NBA I/4; BC V99: probably a spurious work)

New Year/Circumcision and Name of Jesus
(BWV 143, 190, 41, 16, 171, 248-IV)
*Gal. 3:23–29 (Through faith we are heirs of the promise)
*Luke 2:21 (Circumcision and naming of Jesus)
Librettist: Unknown

1. Chorus
●Praise the Lord, O my soul!: Ps. 146:1 (143-1)
Lobe den Herrn,   meine Seele.
Praise the Lord, (O) my   soul.

Ps. 146:1. Praise the Lord! *Praise the Lord, O my soul!*
Ps. 103:1–2. Bless the Lord, O my soul; and all that is within me, bless his holy name! Bless the Lord, O my soul, and forget not all his benefits.

2. Chorale: Soprano (Vs. 1) (See also 67-7, 116-1.)
●Christ is our helper; we cry to God in Jesus' name (143-2)
Du   Friedefürst, Herr Jesu Christ,
Thou Prince-of-peace, Lord Jesus Christ,

Wahr' Mensch und wahrer Gott,
True   man   and   true   God,

Ein starker Nothelfer   du bist
A   strong Helper-in-need thou art

Im Leben und im Tod.
In   life and in death.

Drum   wir allein
Therefore we alone

Is. 9:6. To us a child is born, to us a son is given; and the government will be upon his shoulder, and his name will be called "Wonderful Counselor, Mighty God, Everlasting Father, Prince of Peace (Luther: Friedefürst)."
Lk. 1:30–33. The angel said to [Mary], "...Behold, you will conceive in your womb and bear a son, and you shall call his name Jesus. He will be great, and will be called the Son of the Most High; and the Lord God will give to him the throne of his father David. And he will reign over the house of Jacob for ever; and of his kingdom there will be no end."
Mt. 1:21. ...You shall call his name Jesus, for he will save his people from their sins.
***Lk. 2:21.** And at the end of eight days, when he was circumcised, he was called Jesus, the name given by the angel before he was conceived in the womb.
Mt. 1:23. ...His name shall be called Emmanuel (which means, God with us). (See Is. 7:14.)
Ps. 33:20. ...The Lord...is our help and shield.
Dan. 6:26–27. ...He is the living God, enduring for ever; his kingdom shall never be destroyed, and his dominion shall be to the end. He delivers and rescues (Luther: Er ist ein Erlöser und Nothelfer)... (Nothelfer: also Jer. 14:8)

Im   Namen dein
In (the) name of-thine

Zu deinem Vater schreien.
To   thy   Father do-cry.
{Therefore we cry to thy Father in thy name alone.}

3. Tenor Recit.
●Happy is he whose help is God of Jacob: Ps. 146:5 (143–3)
Wohl dem, des Hilfe der Gott Jakobs ist,
Happy he, whose help the God of-Jacob is,
{Happy is he whose help is the God of Jacob,}

des Hoffnung auf den Herrn, seinem Gotte, stehet.
whose hope   on the Lord,   his   God   (rests).
{whose hope rests on the Lord his God.}

4. Tenor Aria
●National misfortune strikes other lands but not ours (143–4)
  Tausendfaches Unglück, Schrecken,
(A) thousandfold   misfortune, terror,

Trübsal,   Angst und schneller Tod,
Tribulation, fear, and sudden   death,

        Völker, die das Land bedecken,
(Invading) nations, who the land   cover,
{Invading nations that cover the land,}

Sorgen und sonst mehr noch   Not
Sorrows and yet   more - privation:

Sehen andre Länder zwar,
See   other lands   indeed,
{Other lands indeed see all these,}

Aber wir ein Segensjahr.
But   we a year-of-blessing.

5. Bass Aria
●God of Zion is king forever: Ps. 146:10 (143–5)
Der Herr ist König ewiglich, dein Gott,
The Lord is king   eternally, thy God, (O)

Zion, für und für.
Zion, forever and ever.

Ps. 142:5. I cry (Luther: schrei) to thee, O Lord; I say, Thou art my refuge, my portion in the land of the living. (Also Ps. 130:1.)
Jn. 14:13–14 [Christ]: Whatever you ask in my name, I will do it, that the Father may be glorified in the Son; if you ask anything in my name, I will do it. (Also Jn. 16:23–24.)
Lk. 18:7–8. Will not God vindicate his elect, who cry to him day and night? Will he delay long over them? I tell you, he will vindicate them speedily...

Ps. 146:3, 5–6. Put not your trust in princes, in a son of man, in whom there is no help...*Happy is he whose help is the God of Jacob, whose hope is in the Lord his God,* who made heaven and earth, the sea, and all that is in them; who keeps faith for ever.
Ps. 144:15. Happy the people to whom such blessings fall! Happy the people whose God is the Lord!
Ps. 71:5–6. Thou, O Lord, art my hope, my trust, O Lord, from my youth. Upon thee I have leaned from my birth; thou art he who took me from my mother's womb. My praise is continually of thee.

Ps. 91:1–11. He who dwells in the shelter of the Most High, who abides in the shadow of the Almighty, will say to the Lord, "My refuge and my fortress; my God, in whom I trust." For he will deliver you from the snare of the fowler and from the deadly pestilence; he will cover you with his pinions, and under his wings you will find refuge; his faithfulness is a shield and buckler. You will not fear the terror of the night, nor the arrow that flies by day, nor the pestilence that stalks in darkness, nor the destruction that wastes at noonday. A thousand may fall at your side, ten thousand at your right hand; but it will not come near you. You will only look with your eyes and see the recompense of the wicked. Because you have made the Lord your refuge, the Most High your habitation, no evil shall befall you, no scourge come near your tent. For he will give his angels charge of you to guard you in all your ways. (Also Is. 54:14.)
Ps. 125:1–2. Those who trust in the Lord are like Mount Zion, which cannot be moved, but abides for ever. As the mountains are round about Jerusalem, so the Lord is round about his people, from this time forth and for evermore.

Ps. 146:10. *The Lord will reign for ever, thy God, O Zion, to all generations.* Praise the Lord! (Also Ex. 15:18, Ps. 10:16, Rev. 11:15.)
Ps. 77:13. ...What god is great like our God?
Lk. 1:30–33. The angel said to [Mary], "...Behold, you will conceive in your womb and bear a son, and you shall call his name Jesus. He will be great, and will be called the Son of the Most High; and the Lord God will give to him the throne of his father David. And he will reign over the house of Jacob for ever; and of his kingdom there will be no end."
Mt. 1:23. ...His name shall be called Emmanuel (which means, God with us). (See Is. 7:14.)
*Lk. 2:21. ...When he was circumcised, he was called Jesus, the name given by the angel before he was conceived...

6. Tenor Aria
●New Year's prayer for protection and blessing (143–6)
Jesu, Retter deiner Herde,
Jesus, deliverer of-thy flock,

Bleibe ferner unser Hort,
Remain furthermore our refuge,

Daß dies Jahr uns glücklich werde,
That this year for-us auspicious be,

Halte Wacht an jedem Ort.
Keep watch in every place.

Führ, o Jesu, deine Schar
Lead, O Jesus, (this) thy throng

Bis zu jenem neuen Jahr.
Until yonder new year.
{Until the next new year.}

7. Chorus (Chorale Vs. 3)
●Prayer that Christ act as Prince of Peace for us (143–7)
Halleluja.
Hallelujah!

Gedenk, Herr, jetzund an dein Amt,
Remember, (O) Lord, now - thy office,

Daß du ein Friedfürst bist,
That thou a prince-of-peace art,
{That thou art a prince of peace,}

Und hilf uns gnädig allesamt
And help us graciously all-together

Jetzt und zu jeder Frist;
Now and in every term;
{Now and at all times;}

Laß uns hinfort
Let to-us henceforth

Dein göttlich Wort
Thy divine Word

Im Fried noch länger schallen.
In peace yet longer resound.
{Continue to resound in peace.}

Dan. 9:19. O Lord, hear; O Lord, forgive; O Lord, give heed and act; delay not, for thy own sake, O my God, because thy city and thy people are called by thy name.
Ps. 100:3. Know that the Lord is God! It is he that made us, and we are his; we are his people, and the sheep of his pasture.
Ps. 95:7. He is our God and we are the people of his pasture, and the sheep of his hand.
Jn. 10:14, 27–28 [Christ]: I am the good shepherd...My sheep hear my voice, and I know them, and they follow me; and I give them eternal life, and they shall never perish, and no one shall snatch them out of my hand.
1 Sam. 2:2. There is none holy like the Lord...there is no rock (Luther: Hort) like our God.
Ps. 29:11. May the Lord give strength to his people! May the Lord bless his people with peace! (Also Ps. 128:5–6, Is. 26:1–3.)
Ps. 127:1. ...Unless the Lord watches over the city, the watchman stays awake in vain.
Ps. 28:8–9. The Lord is the strength of his people, he is the saving refuge of his anointed. O save thy people, and bless thy heritage; be thou their shepherd, and carry them for ever. (prayer for national blessing: also Deut. 26:15, Ps. 29:11)

Ps. 146:1, 10. Praise the Lord (Luther: *Halleluja*)! Praise the Lord, O my soul!...The Lord will reign for ever, thy God, O Zion, to all generations. Praise the Lord (Luther: *Halleluja*)!
Is. 9:6. For to us a child is born, to us a son is given; and the government will be upon his shoulder, and his name will be called "...Prince of Peace."
Ps. 29:11. May the Lord give strength to his people! May the Lord bless his people with peace! (Also Is. 26:1–3.)
Ps. 128:5–6. The Lord bless you from Zion! May you see the prosperity of Jerusalem all the days of your life! May you see your children's children! Peace be upon Israel!
1 Tim. 2:1–2. ...I urge that supplications, prayers, intercessions, and thanksgivings be made for all men, for kings and all who are in high positions, that we may lead a quiet and peaceable life, godly and respectful in every way.
Ps. 122:6–7. Pray for the peace of Jerusalem! "May they prosper who love you! Peace be within your walls, and security within your towers!"
Is. 2:3. Many peoples shall come, and say: "Come, let us go up to the mountain of the Lord, to the house of the God of Jacob; that he may teach us his ways and that we may walk in his paths." For out of Zion shall go forth the law, and the word of the Lord from Jerusalem. (Also Mic. 4:2.)
Heb. 12:22–23. But you have come to Mount Zion and to the city of the living God, the heavenly Jerusalem, and to innumerable angels in festal gathering, and to the assembly of the first-born who are enrolled in heaven, and to a judge who is God of all, and to the spirits of just men made perfect.
***Gal. 3:29.** If you are Christ's, then you are Abraham's offspring, heirs according to promise.
Sirach (Apocrypha) 50:23 (= Sirach 50:25 of German Bible). May he give us gladness of heart, and grant that peace may be in our days in Israel, as in the days of old.

BWV 144
Nimm, was dein ist, und gehe hin
(NBA I/7; BC A41)

Septuagesima (BWV 144, 92, 84)
*1 Cor. 9:24–10:5 (Run the race so as to obtain the prize)
*Mt. 20:1–16 (The parable of the vineyard laborers)
Librettist: Unknown; perhaps Christian Weiß the elder

1. Chorus
●Parable of vineyard laborers (excerpt): Mt. 20:14 (144-1)
Nimm, was dein ist, und gehe hin.
Take   what yours is,   and   go   - .
{Take what is yours, and go.}

2. Alto Aria
●Contentment with one's lot exhorted (144-2)
Murre nicht,
Murmur not,

Lieber Christ,
Dear Christian,

Wenn was nicht   nach   Wunsch geschicht;
When a-matter not according-to (your) wish   (goes);
{When a matter does not go according to your wishes;}

Sondern sei mit dem zufrieden,
Rather   be with that content,
{Rather be content with that}

Was   dir dein Gott hat beschieden,
Which to-you your God has   allotted,
{Which your God has allotted to you,}

Er weiß, was   dir   nützlich ist.
He knows, what for-you profitable is.
{He knows what is profitable for you.}

3. Chorale (See also 98-1, 99-1, 100-1.)
●God's sovereign will trusted & accepted (144-3)
Was   Gott tut, das ist wohlgetan,
Whatever God does, that is well-done,

Es   bleibt gerecht sein Wille;
(Now) remains just   his will;
{His will remains just;}

Wie   er fängt meine Sachen an,
In-whatever-way he deals-with my   affairs - ,

Will ich ihm halten stille.
Will I to-him submit quietly.
{Will I submit to him quietly.}

Er ist mein Gott,
He is   my   God,

*Mt. 20:1–16. The kingdom of heaven is like a householder who went out early in the morning to hire laborers for his vineyard. After agreeing with the laborers for a denarius a day, he sent them into his vineyard. And going out about the third hour he saw others standing idle in the market place; and to them he said, "You go into the vineyard too, and whatever is right I will give you." So they went. Going out again about the sixth hour and the ninth hour, he did the same. And about the eleventh hour he went out and found others standing; and he said to them, "Why do you stand here idle all day?" They said to him, "Because no one has hired us." He said to them, "You go into the vineyard too." And when evening came, the owner of the vineyard said to his steward, "Call the laborers and pay them their wages, beginning with the last, up to the first." And when those hired about the eleventh hour came, each of them received a denarius. Now when the first came, they thought they would receive more; but each of them also received a denarius. And on receiving it they grumbled at the householder, saying, "These last worked only one hour, and you have made them equal to us who have borne the burden of the day and the scorching heat." But he replied to one of them, "Friend, I am doing you no wrong; did you not agree with me for a denarius? *Take what belongs to you, and go;* I choose to give to this last as I give to you. Am I not allowed to do what I choose with what belongs to me? Or do you begrudge my generosity?" So the last will be first, and the first last.
Heb. 13:5. Keep your life free from love of money, and be content with what you have; for [the Lord] has said, "I will never fail you nor forsake you." (Also Rom. 8:28.)

Mk. 7:37. [The people] were astonished beyond measure [at Jesus], saying, "He has done all things well..."
Ps. 145:17. The Lord is just in all his ways...
Deut. 32:4. ...A God of faithfulness...just and right is he.
Rom. 8:28, 31–32, 35, 37. We know that in everything God works for good with those who love him, who are called according to his purpose...What then shall we say to this? If God is for us, who is against us? He who did not spare his own Son but gave him up for us all, will he not also give us all things with him?...Who shall separate us from the love of Christ? Shall tribulation, or distress, or persecution, or famine, or nakedness, or peril, or sword?...No, in all these things we are more than conquerors through him who loved us.
1 Pet. 4:19. Therefore let those who suffer according to God's will do right and entrust their souls to a faithful Creator.
Ps. 62:1–2. For God alone my soul waits in silence (Luther: meine Seele ist stille zu Gott)... (Also Ps. 62:5.)
Ps. 131:1–2. O Lord, my heart is not lifted up, my eyes are not raised too high; I do not occupy myself with things too great and too marvelous for me. But I have calmed and quieted my soul, like a child

Der in der Not
Who in - distress

Mich wohl weiß   zu erhalten;
Me   well   knows (how) to   sustain;
{Knows well how to sustain me;}

Drum   lass' ich ihn nur walten.
Therefore allow I   him just to-rule.
{Therefore I will just allow him to rule.}

4. Tenor Recit.
●Discontent: Where it rules there is much grief (144-4)
Wo   die Genügsamkeit regiert
Where - contentment   rules

Und überall das Ruder führt,
And everywhere the helm controls,
{And everywhere controls the helm,}

Da   ist der Mensch vergnügt
There is - (man)   satisfied

Mit dem, wie es Gott fügt.
With that, (which) God ordains.

Dagegen,   wo die Ungenügsamkeit das Urteil spricht,
As-opposed-to where - discontent   (its) opinion speaks,

Da   stellt sich Gram und Kummer ein,
There sets-in - grief and trouble -,
{There grief and trouble sets in,}

Das Herz will nicht
The heart will not
{The heart refuses}

Zufrieden sein,
Satisfied   be,
{To be satisfied,}

Und man gedenkt nicht daran:
And one thinks not of-this:
{And one does not bear in mind that}

Was   Gott tut, das ist wohlgetan.
Whatever God does, that is well-done.

5. Soprano Aria
●Contentment is a great treasure in this life (144-5)
Genügsamkeit
Contentment

Ist ein Schatz in diesem Leben,
Is a treasure in   this   life,

Welcher kann Vergnügung geben
Which   can pleasure (bring)
{Which can bring pleasure even}

quieted at its mother's breast; like a child that is quieted is my soul.
Lam. 3:26. It is good that one should wait quietly for the salvation of the Lord.
2 Pet. 2:9. The Lord knows how to rescue the godly from trial...
Ps. 145:14. The Lord upholds (Luther: erhält) all who are falling, and raises up all who are bowed down. (Also Ps. 17:5, 63:8, 119:116, 146:9, Is. 42:1.)
Jms. 4:7. Submit yourselves therefore to God...

1 Tim. 6:6–10. There is great gain in godliness with contentment; for we brought nothing into the world, and we cannot take anything out of the world; but if we have food and clothing, with these we shall be content. But those who desire to be rich fall into temptation, into a snare, into many senseless and hurtful desires that plunge men into ruin and destruction. For the love of money is the root of all evils; it is through this craving that some have wandered away from the faith and pierced their hearts with many pangs.
Jms. 4:1–4. What causes wars, and what causes fightings among you? Is it not your passions that are at war in your members? You desire and do not have; so you kill. And you covet and cannot obtain; so you fight and wage war. You do not have, because you do not ask. You ask and do not receive, because you ask wrongly, to spend it on your passions. Unfaithful creatures! Do you not know that friendship with the world is enmity with God? Therefore whoever wishes to be a friend of the world makes himself an enemy of God.
Prov. 27:20. Sheol and Abaddon are never satisfied, and never satisfied are the eyes of man.
Ecc. 5:10. He who loves money will not be satisfied with money; nor he who loves wealth, with gain: this also is vanity.
Ecc. 6:7. All the toil of man is for his mouth, yet his appetite is not satisfied.
Ecc. 4:8. A person who has no one, either son or brother, yet there is no end to all his toil, and his eyes are never satisfied with riches, so that he never askes, "For whom am I toiling and depriving myself of pleasure?" This also is vanity and an unhappy business.
Heb. 13:5–6. Keep your life free from love of money, and be content with what you have; for he has said, "I will never fail you nor forsake you." Hence we can confidently say, "The Lord is my helper, I will not be afraid; what can man do to me?"

1 Tim. 6:6–8. There is great gain in godliness with contentment; for we brought nothing into the world, and we cannot take anything out of the world; but if we have food and clothing, with these we shall be content.
Phil. 4:11–13. [I do not] complain of want; for I have learned, in whatever state I am, to be content. I know how to be abased, and I know how to abound; in any and all circumstances I have learned the secret of facing plenty and hunger, abundance and want. I can do all things in him who strengthens me.
2 Cor. 12:7–10. To keep me from being too elated by the abundance of revelations, a thorn was given me in the flesh, a messenger of

In der größten Traurigkeit,
In the greatest sadness—

Genügsakmkeit.
Contentment.

Denn es lässet sich in allen
For it (allows) itself in all
{For it allows itself to be satisfied}

Gottes Fügung wohl gefallen
God's providence (to-be) well pleased—
{With all of God's providence—}

Genügsamkeit.
Contentment.

6. Chorale (See also 72-5, 111-1.)
•Trusting & accepting God's will, building on him (144-6)
Was mein Gott will, das g'scheh allzeit,
Whatever my God wills, that be-done always,

Sein Will, der ist der beste;
His will, it is the best;

Zu helfen den'n er ist bereit,
To help all-them he is prepared,

Die an ihn glauben feste.
Who on him believe steadfastly.

Er hilft aus Not, der fromme Gott,
He helps out-of trouble, (this) righteous God,

Und züchtiget mit Maßen.
And chastises with measure.

Wer Gott vertraut, fest auf ihn baut,
Whoever (in) God trusts, firmly on him builds,

Den will er nicht verlassen.
Him will he not forsake.

Satan, to harass me, to keep me from being too elated. Three times I besought the Lord about this, that it should leave me; but he said to me, "My grace is sufficient for you, for my power is made perfect in weakness." I will all the more gladly boast of my weaknesses, that the power of Christ may rest upon me. For the sake of Christ, then, I am content with weaknesses, insults, hardships, persecutions, and calamities; for when I am weak, then I am strong.
Rom. 8:28. We know that in everything God works for good with those who love him, who are called according to his purpose. **Ps. 18:30.** This God—his way is perfect; the promise of the Lord proves true; he is a shield for all those who take refuge in him.
Ecc. 5:18. Behold, what I have seen to be good and to be fitting is to eat and drink and find enjoyment in all the toil with which one toils under the sun the few days of his life which God has given him, for this is his lot. (Also Ecc. 2:25–26, 3:12–13, 9:7.)

Mt. 26:39. ...Not as I will, but as thou wilt.
Mt. 6:10. Thy kingdom come, Thy will be done...
Rom. 8:28. We know that in everything God works for good with those who love him...
Mt. 8:1–3. When [Jesus] came down from the mountain, great crowds followed him; and behold, a leper came to him and knelt before him, saying, "Lord, if you will, you can make me clean." And he stretched out his hand and touched him, saying, "I will; be clean."...
Mk. 9:23–24. Jesus said to [the father of the boy who was sick], "...All things are possible to him who believes." Immediately [he] cried out and said, "I believe; help my unbelief!"
Ps. 33:18–19. Behold, the eye of the Lord is on those who fear him, on those who hope in his steadfast love, that he may deliver their soul from death, and keep them alive in famine.
Jer. 30:11. For I am with you to save you, says the Lord; I will make a full end of all the nations among whom I scattered you, but of you I will not make a full end. I will chasten you in just measure (Luther: züchtigen...mit Maßen), and I will by no means leave you unpunished. (Also Jer. 4:27, 5:10, 5:18, 46:28, Ezek. 20:17.)
Heb. 12:6. The Lord disciplines him whom he loves, and chastises every son whom he receives.
Mt. 7:24 [Christ]: Every one then who hears these words of mine and does them will be like a wise man who built his house upon the rock.
1 Cor. 3:11. For no other foundation can any one lay than that which is laid, which is Jesus Christ.
Mt. 28:20 [Christ]: ...Lo, I am with you always to the close of the age.
Heb. 13:5. ...He has said, "I will never fail you nor forsake you."

BWV 145
Ich lebe, mein Herze, zu deinem Ergötzen
(NBA I/10; BC A60)

3. Easter Day (BWV 134, 145, 158)
*Acts 13:26–33 (Paul preaches of Christ's death and resurrection in synagogue at Antioch)
*Lk. 24:36–47 (Jesus appears to disciples in Jerusalem after his resurrection)
Librettist: Picander (Christian Friedrich Henrici)

1. Tenor & Soprano Duet[1] (Perhaps a parody of earlier work)
●Dialogue: Jesus & Soul list benefits of resurrection (145-1)
Tenor/Soprano
Ich lebe, mein Herze, / Du lebest, mein Jesu,
I live, (O) my (dear) heart, / Thou livest, (O) my Jesus,

zu deinem/meinem Ergötzen,
to thy/my delight,

Mein/Dein Leben erhebet dein/mein Leben empor.
My/Thy life exalts thy/my life on-high.

Die klagende Handschrift is völlig zerissen,
The indicting bond is completely torn-asunder,

Der Friede verschaffet ein ruhig Gewissen
(This) peace procures a quiet conscience
{This peace procures a clear conscience}

Und öffnet den Sündern das himmlische Tor.
And opens to sinners the heavenly gate.
{And opens the heavenly gate to sinners.}

2. Tenor Recit.
●Resurrection guarantees freedom from indictment (145-2)
Nun fordre, Moses, wie du willt,
Now demand (of us), (O) Moses, as (much as) you wish,

Das dräuende Gesetz zu üben,
The threatening law to practice,
{That we practice the threatening law,}

Ich habe meine Quittung hier
I have my receipt here

Mit Jesu Blut und Wunden unterschrieben.
With Jesus' blood and wounds signed.
{Signed with Jesus' blood and wounds.}

Dieselbe gilt,
This-same (receipt) means (that),

Ich bin erlöst, ich bin befreit
I am redeemed, I am freed

Ps. 94:19. [O Lord]...thy consolations cheer (Luther: ergötzen) my soul.
*Lk. 24:36–40, 45–47. As [the disciples] were saying this, Jesus himself stood among them. But they were startled and frightened, and supposed that they saw a spirit. And he said to them, "Why are you troubled, and why do questionings rise in your hearts? See my hands and my feet, that it is I myself; handle me, and see; for a spirit has not flesh and bones as you see that I have."...Then he opened their minds to understand the scriptures, and said to them, "Thus it is written, that the Christ should suffer and on the third day rise from the dead, and that repentance and forgiveness of sins should be preached in his name to all nations..."
*Acts 13:30–31. God raised [Christ] from the dead; and for many days he appeared to those who came up with him from Galilee to Jerusalem, who are now his witnesses to the people.
Col. 2:13–14. And you, who were dead in trespasses and the uncircumcision of your flesh, God made alive together with him, having forgiven us all our trespasses, having canceled the bond which stood against us with its legal demands; this he set aside, nailing it to the cross.
1 Pet. 3:21. Baptism...now saves you, not as a removal of dirt from the body but as an appeal to God for a clear conscience, through the resurrection of Jesus Christ. (Also Heb. 10:22.)
Rom. 5:1–2, 10. Therefore, since we are justified by faith, we have peace with God through our Lord Jesus Christ. Through him we have obtained access to this grace in which we stand, and we rejoice in our hope of sharing the glory of God...For if, while we were enemies we were reconciled to God by the death of his Son, much more, now that we are reconciled, shall we be saved by his life.

Jn. 1:17. The law was given through Moses; grace and truth came through Jesus Christ.
Jms. 2:10. Whoever keeps the whole law but fails in one point has become guilty of all of it.
Rom. 3:20–22. No human being will be justified in [God's] sight by works of the law, since through the law comes knowledge of sin. But now the righteousness of God has been manifested apart from law, although the law and the prophets bear witness to it, the righteousness of God through faith in Jesus Christ for all who believe... (Also Gal. 2:16, 3:10–14, Acts 15:10–11.)
*Lk. 24:44. Then [Jesus] said to [his disciples], "These are my words which I spoke to you, while I was still with you, that everything written about me in the law of Moses and the prophets and the psalms must be fulfilled." Then he opened their minds to understand the scriptures, and said to them, "Thus it is written, that the Christ should suffer and on the third day rise from the dead, and that repentance and forgiveness of sins should be preached in his name to all nations..."
Acts 13:38–39. ...Through this man forgiveness of sins is proclaimed to you, and by him every one that believes is freed from everything from

---

[1]Two movements precede this one in the extant source, which is a copy from the nineteenth century. Neither of these two movements' texts originate in Picander's poem. Furthermore, the second of these movements is taken from a cantata by Telemann. Hence, they should probably be excluded. See Dürr, *Die Kantaten*, pp. 327–328.

Und lebe nun mit Gott in Fried und Einigkeit,
And live now with God in peace and unity,
{And now live with God in peace and unity,}

Der Kläger wird an mir zuschanden,
The accuser is in me confounded,
{The accuser is confounded with regard to me,}

Denn Gott ist auferstanden.
For God is risen.

Mein Herz, das merke dir!
My heart, that bear-in-mind - !
{O my heart, bear that in mind!}

3. Bass Aria (Perhaps a parody of earlier work)
●Resurection is foundation for our faith (145-3)
Merke, mein Herze, beständig nur dies,
Mark, (O) my heart, steadfastly just this—

Wenn du alles sonst vergißt,
If thou all else dost-forget,
{Even if thou shouldst forget all else—}

Daß dein Heiland lebend ist;
That thy Savior alive is;
{That thy Savior is alive;}

Lasse dieses deinem Gläuben
Let this for-thy faith

Einen Grund und Feste bleiben,
A foundation and stronghold remain,
{Let this remain a foundation and stronghold for thy faith,}

Auf solche besteht er gewiß,
Upon this stands it assuredly (secure),
{Upon this it will assuredly stand secure,}

Merke, meine Herze, nur dies.
Mark, (O) my heart, just this.

4. Soprano Recit.
●Resurrection of Jesus gives me hope in death (145-4)
Mein Jesus lebt,
My Jesus lives,

Das soll mir niemand nehmen,
That shall from-me no-one take,
{That no one can take from me,}

Drum sterb ich sonder Grämen.
Therefore die I without grieving.
{Therefore I can die without grieving.}

Ich bin gewiß
I am sure

which you could not be freed by the law of Moses. (Also Rom. 5:1–2, 10.)

Col. 2:13–14. You, who were dead in trespasses and the uncircumcision of your flesh, God made alive together with him, having forgiven us all our trespasses, having canceled the bond which stood against us with its legal demands; this he set aside, nailing it to the cross.

Rom. 8:33–34. Who shall bring any charge against God's elect? It is God who justifies; who is to condemn? Is it Christ Jesus, who died, yes, who was raised from the dead, who is at the right hand of God, who indeed intercedes for us?

Rev. 12:10. ...The accuser of our brethren has been thrown down, who accuses them day and night before our God.

*Acts 13:28–33. Though [those living in Jerusalem and their rulers] could charge [Jesus] with nothing deserving death, yet they asked Pilate to have him killed. And when they had fulfilled all that was written of him, they took him down from the tree, and laid him in a tomb. But God raised him from the dead; and for many days he appeared to those who came up with him from Galilee to Jerusalem, who are now his witnesses to the people. And we bring you the good news that what God promised to the fathers, this he has fulfilled to us their children by raising Jesus...

1 Cor. 15:16–20. If the dead are not raised, then Christ has not been raised. If Christ has not been raised, your faith is futile and you are still in your sins. Then those also who have fallen asleep in Christ have perished. If for this life only we have hoped in Christ, we are of all men most to be pitied. But in fact Christ has been raised from the dead, the first fruits of those who have fallen asleep.

1 Pet. 1:18–21. You know that you were ransomed from the futile ways inherited from your fathers, not with perishable things such as silver or gold, but with the precious blood of Christ, like that of a lamb without blemish or spot. He was destined before the foundation of the world but was made manifest at the end of the times for your sake. Through him you have confidence in God, who raised him from the dead and gave him glory, so that your faith and hope are in God.

1 Cor. 15:17, 20, 54–57. If Christ has not been raised, your faith is futile...But in fact Christ has been raised from the dead, the first fruits of those who have fallen asleep...When the perishable puts on the imperishable, and the mortal puts on immortality, then shall come to pass the saying that is written: "Death is swallowed up in victory." O death, where is thy victory? O death, where is thy sting? The sting of death is sin, and the power of sin is the law. But thanks be to God, who gives us the victory through our Lord Jesus Christ.

Heb. 2:14–15. Since therefore the children share in flesh and blood, [Christ] himself likewise partook of the same nature, that through death he might destroy him who has the power of death, that is, the

Und habe das Vertrauen,
And have - confidence,

Daß mich des Grabes Finsternis
That me the grave's darkness
{That the grave's darkness raises me}

Zur Himmelsherrlichkeit erhebt;
To heaven's-glory raises;
{To heaven's glory;}

Mein Jesus lebt,
My Jesus lives,

Ich habe nun genug,
I have now enough,

Mein Herz und Sinn
My heart and mind

Will heute noch zum Himmel hin,
Would today yet to heaven (go),
{Would go to heaven even today yet,}

Selbst den Erlöser anzuschauen.
Even (my) Redeemer to-gaze-at.
{To gaze at my Redeemer himself.}

5. Chorale
●Resurrection: Praise to Christ for his resurrection (145-5)
Drum wir auch billig fröhlich sein,
Therefore we (will) also rightly joyful be,

Singen das Halleluja fein
Sing (our) "Hallelujah" fair

Und loben dich, Herr Jesu Christ;
And praise thee, Lord Jesus Christ;

Zu Trost du uns erstanden bist.
For comfort thou for-us arisen art.
{For our comfort art thou risen.}

Halleluja!
Hallelujah!

devil, and deliver all those who through fear of death were subject to lifelong bondage. (Also 2 Tim. 1:10.)
2 Cor. 5:1–8. We know that if the earthly tent we live in is destroyed, we have a building from God, a house not made with hands, eternal in the heavens. Here indeed we groan, and long to put on our heavenly dwelling, so that by putting it on we may not be found naked. For while we are still in this tent, we sigh with anxiety; not that we would be unclothed, but that we would be further clothed, so that what is mortal may be swallowed up by life. He who has prepared us for this very thing is God, who has given us the Spirit as a guarantee. So we are always of good courage; we know that while we are at home in the body we are away from the Lord, for we walk by faith, not by sight. We are of good courage, and we would rather be away from the body and at home with the Lord.
2 Thess. 2:14. To this [God] called you through our gospel, so that you may obtain the glory of our Lord Jesus Christ.
Lk. 2:29. Lord, now lettest thou thy servant depart in peace...
Phil. 1:23. ...My desire is to depart and be with Christ, for that is far better.
2 Cor. 5:8. ...We would rather be away from the body and at home with the Lord.
1 Jn. 3:1–2. See what love the Father has given us, that we should be called children of God; and so we are...Beloved, we are God's children now; it does not yet appear what we shall be, but we know that when he appears we shall be like him, for we shall see him as he is. (Also 1 Cor. 13:12.)

*Acts 13:32–33. We bring you the good news that what God promised to the fathers, this he has fulfilled to us their children by raising Jesus...
Rev. 1:17–18. ...[Christ said], "Fear not, I am the first and the last, and the living one; I died, and behold I am alive for evermore, and I have the keys of Death and Hades."
Is. 25:8–9. He will swallow up death for ever, and the Lord God will wipe away tears from all faces, and the reproach of his people he will take away from all the earth; for the Lord has spoken. It will be said on that day, "Lo, this is our God; we have waited for him, that he might save us. This is the Lord; we have waited for him; let us be glad and rejoice in his salvation."
Rev. 5:11–12. ...I heard...thousands of thousands, saying with a loud voice, "Worthy is the Lamb who was slain, to receive power and wealth and wisdom and might and honor and glory and blessing!"
Rev. 19:1. After this I heard what seemed to be the loud voice of a great multitude in heaven, crying, "Hallelujah! Salvation and glory and power belong to our God." (Also Rev. 19:6–7.)
Lk. 24:52–53. And [after Christ ascended, the disciples] returned to Jerusalem with great joy, and were continually in the temple blessing God.

BWV 146
Wir müssen durch viel Trübsal in das Reich Gottes eingehen
(NBA I/11; BC A70)

Jubilate: 3. S. after Easter (BWV 12, 103, 146)
*1 Pet. 2:11–20 (Be subject to all human orders)
*Jn. 16:16–23[1] (Jesus' farewell to his disciples)
[1]End: "nothing of me."
Librettist: Unknown

1. Sinfonia (Adapted from nonextant concerto for violin)

2. Chorus (Adapted from nonextant concerto for violin)
●Tribulation precedes entrance to kingdom: Acts 14:22 (146–2)
Wir müssen durch viel Trübsal
We must through much tribulation

in das Reich Gottes eingehen.
into the kindom of-God enter.
{enter into the kingdom of God.}

3. Alto Aria
●Sodom rejected for prospect of heaven (146–3)
Ich will nach dem Himmel zu,
I would to - heaven (go);

Schnödes Sodom, ich und du
Base Sodom, I and thou

Sind nunmehr geschieden.
Are henceforth parted.

Meines Bleibens ist nicht hier,
My abiding is not here,

Denn ich lebe doch bei dir
For I live, indeed, with thee

Nimmermehr in Frieden.
Nevermore in peace.
{For I can indeed nevermore live in peace with thee.}

4. Soprano Recit.
●Yearning for heaven because of oppression by world (146–4)
Ach! wer doch schon im Himmel wär,
Ah! If only (I) already in heaven were,
{Ah, If only I were already in heaven,}

Wie dränget mich nicht die böse Welt!
How oppresses me not the evil world!
{How this evil world oppresses me!}

Acts 14:22. *...Through many tribulations we must enter the kingdom of God.*
*Jn. 16:16, 20–22 [Christ]: A little while, and you will see me no more; again a little while, and you will see me...Truly, truly, I say to you, you will weep and lament, but the world will rejoice; you will be sorrowful, but your sorrow will turn into joy. When a woman is in travail she has sorrow, because her hour has come; but when she is delivered of the child, she no longer remembers the anguish, for joy that a child is born into the world. So you have sorrow now, but I will see you again and your hearts will rejoice, and no one will take your joy from you.
Mt. 5:10 [Christ]: Blessed are those who are persecuted for righteousness' sake, for theirs is the kingdom of heaven.
*1 Pet. 2:20. ...If when you do right and suffer for it you take it patiently, you have God's approval.

2 Tim. 3:12–13. Indeed all who desire to live a godly life in Christ Jesus will be persecuted, while evil men and impostors will go on from bad to worse... (Also 1 Pet. 4:12–13.)
Gen. 13:13. The men of Sodom were wicked, great sinners against the Lord.
Gen. 19:24–25. Then the Lord rained on Sodom and Gomorrah brimstone and fire from the Lord out of heaven; and he overthrew those cities...
Jude 1:7. ...Sodom and Gomorrah and the surrounding cities, which likewise acted immorally...serve as an example by undergoing a punishment of eternal fire.
Jms. 4:4. Unfaithful creatures! Do you not know that friendship with the world is enmity with God? Therefore whoever wishes to be a friend of the world makes himself an enemy of God.
1 Jn. 2:15. Do not love the world or the things in the world. If any one loves the world, love for the Father is not in him.
1 Jn. 5:19. ...The whole world is in the power of the evil one.
Jn. 16:33 [Christ]: I have said this to you, that in me you may have peace. In the world you have tribulation; but be of good cheer, I have overcome the world.
Col. 3:1–3. If then you have been raised with Christ, seek the things that are above, where Christ is, seated at the right hand of God. Set your minds on things that are above, not on things that are on earth. For you have died and your life is hid with Christ in God. (Also 2 Cor. 4:16–18.)

Phil. 1:21–23. To me to live is Christ, and to die is gain...Which I shall choose I cannot tell. I am hard pressed between the two. My desire is to depart and be with Christ, for that is far better.
2 Cor. 4:8–10. We are afflicted in every way, but not crushed; perplexed, but not driven to despair; persecuted, but not forsaken; struck down, but not destroyed; always carrying in the body the death of Jesus, so that the life of Jesus may also be manifested in our bodies.

Mit Weinen steh ich auf,
With weeping rise I up,
{With weeping I rise up,}

Mit Weinen leg ich mich zu Bette,
With weeping lay I me to bed,
{With weeping I lay me to bed,}

Wie   trüglich   wird mir nachgestellt!
How treacherously am I   waylaid!

Herr! merke, schaue drauf,
Lord! Mark,   look upon-it;

Sie hassen mich, und ohne Schuld,
They hate   me, and without cause,

Als wenn die Welt die Macht,
As if   the world the might,
{As if the world had the might}

Mich gar zu töten hätte;
Me even to slay did-have;
{Even to slay me;}

Und leb ich denn mit Seufzen und Geduld
And live I though with sighing and forbearance
{And even when I live with sighing and forbearance}

Verlassen und veracht',
Forsaken and despised,

So hat sie noch an meinem Leide
Then has it yet in   my suffering

Die größte Freude.
The greatest pleasure.
{Then the world takes the greatest pleasure in my suffering.}

Mein Gott, das fällt mir schwer.
My   God, that (find-I) hard.
{My God, I find that hard.}

Ach! wenn ich doch,
Ah!   If   I only,
{Ah, If only I were—}

Mein Jesu, heute noch
My   Jesus—today yet

Bei dir im Himmel wär!
With thee in heaven were!
{With thee in heaven!}

5. Soprano Aria
●Sowing in tears, reaping with joy (146-5)
Ich säe meine Zähren
I sow my   tears

Ps. 6:6–7. I am weary with my moaning; every night I flood my bed with tears; I drench my couch with my weeping. My eye wastes away because of grief, it grows weak because of all my foes. (Also Jer. 45:3.)

Ps. 42:3. My tears have been my food day and night, while men say to me continually, "Where is your God?"

Ps. 59:3–4. Lo, they lie in wait for my life; fierce men band themselves against me. For no transgression or sin of mine, O Lord, for no fault of mine, they run and make ready... (Also Ps. 35:19, 38:19, 140:2–5.)

Ps. 69:3–4. I am weary with my crying; my throat is parched. My eyes grow dim with waiting for my God. More in number than the hairs of my head are those who hate me without cause...

Ps. 35:15. At my stumbling they gathered in glee, they gathered together against me...

Ps. 56:5–6, 8. All day long they seek to injure my cause; all their thoughts are against me for evil. They band themselves together, they lurk, they watch my steps...[O Lord,] thou hast kept count of my tossings; put thou my tears in thy bottle! Are they not in thy book?

Ps. 109:2–3. For wicked and deceitful mouths are opened against me, speaking against me with lying tongues. They beset me with words of hate, and attack me without cause.

Jn. 15:18–19 [Christ]: If the world hates you, know that it has hated me before it hated you. If you were of the world, the world would love its own; but because you are not of the world, but I chose you out of the world, therefore the world hates you. (Also Jn. 17:14, Mt. 10:24–25.)

Mt. 10:22–25 [Christ]: You will be hated by all for my name's sake. But he who endures to the end will be saved. When they persecute you in one town, flee to the next; for truly, I say to you, you will not have gone through all the towns of Israel, before the Son of man comes. A disciple is not above his teacher, nor a servant above his master; it is enough for the disciple to be like his teacher, and the servant like his master. If they have called the master of the house Beelzebul, how much more will they malign those of his household.

1 Jn. 3:13. Do not wonder, brethren, that the world hates you.

Mt. 5:10–12 [Christ]: Blessed are those who are persecuted for righteousness' sake, for theirs is the kingdom of heaven. Blessed are you when men revile you and persecute you and utter all kinds of evil against you falsely on my account. Rejoice and be glad, for your reward is great in heaven, for so men persecuted the prophets who were before you.

*1 Pet. 2:19–20. For one is approved if, mindful of God, he endures pain while suffering unjustly. For what credit is it, if when you do wrong and are beaten for it you take it patiently? But if when you do right and suffer for it you take it patiently, you have God's approval.

*Jn. 16:20 [Christ]: Truly, truly, I say to you, you will weep and lament, but the world will rejoice; you will be sorrowful, but your sorrow will turn into joy.

2 Cor. 5:8. ...We would rather be away from the body and at home with the Lord.

1 Thess. 4:17. ...And so we shall always be with the Lord.

Ps. 126:5–6. May those who sow in tears reap with shouts of joy! He that goes forth weeping, bearing the seed for sowing, shall come home with shouts of joy, bringing his sheaves with him.

Mit bangem Herzen aus.
With anxious   heart   - .

Jedoch   mein Herzeleid
Nevertheless my heart's-grief

Wird mir die Herrlichkeit
Will for-me -   glory

Am   Tage der seligen Ernte gebären.
On-the day of blessed harvest bear.
{Will bear glory for me on the day of blessed harvest.}

6. Tenor Recit.
●Heaven entered only by bearing one's cross (146–6)
Ich bin bereit,
I   am prepared,

Mein Kreuz geduldig zu ertragen;
My   cross patiently to   bear;

Ich weiß, daß alle meine Plagen
I   know, that all   my   torments

        Nicht wert   der Herrlichkeit,
(Are) not worthy (to be compared with) the   glory,

Die   Gott an den erwählten Scharen
Which God to the chosen multitudes
{Which God will reveal to the chosen multitudes}

Und auch an mir wird offenbaren.
And also to mir will   reveal.
{And also to me.}

Jetzt wein ich, da   das Weltgetümmel
Now weep I, while the world's-tumult
{Now I weep, while the world's rabble}

Bei meinem Jammer fröhlich scheint.
At   my   misery happy appears.
{Appears happy at my misery.}

Bald kommt die Zeit,
Soon comes the time,
{The time is coming soon}

Da   sich mein Herz erfreut,
When -   my heart will-rejoice,

Und da die Welt einst ohne Tröster   weint.
And when the world - without comforters will-weep.

Wer   mit dem Feinde ringt und schlägt,
He-who with the foe wrestles and fights,

Dem   wird die Krone beigelegt;
On-him is the crown conferred;

*Jn. 16:20 [Christ]: ...You will be sorrowful, but your sorrow will turn into joy.
Lk. 6:20–23 [Christ]: Blessed are you poor, for yours is the kingdom of God. Blessed are you that hunger now, for you shall be satisfied. Blessed are you that weep now, for you shall laugh. Blessed are you when men hate you, and when they exclude you and revile you, and cast out your name as evil, on account of the Son of man! Rejoice in that day, and leap for joy, for behold, your reward is great in heaven; for so their fathers did to the prophets. (Also Mt. 5:11–12.)
Jer. 31:13 [God]: Then shall the maidens rejoice in the dance, and the young men and the old shall be merry. I will turn their mourning into joy, I will comfort them, and give them gladness for sorrow. (Also Ps. 30:11.)

Mt. 16:24–25. Jesus told his disciples, "If any man would come after me, let him deny himself and take up his cross and follow me. For whoever would save his life will lose it, and whoever loses his life for my sake will find it." (Also Mk. 8:34, Lk. 9:23–24.)
Mt. 10:38 [Christ]: He who does not take his cross and follow me is not worthy of me.
Rom. 8:18. I consider that the sufferings of this present time are not worth comparing with the glory that is to be revealed to us.
2 Thess. 2:14. To this [God] called you through our gospel, so that you may obtain the glory of our Lord Jesus Christ.
2 Cor. 4:16–18. So we do not lose heart...for this slight momentary affliction is preparing for us an eternal weight of glory beyond all comparison, because we look not to the things that are seen but to the things that are unseen; for the things that are seen are transient, but the things that are unseen are eternal.
*Jn. 16:20–22 [Christ]: Truly, truly, I say to you, you will weep and lament, but the world will rejoice; you will be sorrowful, but your sorrow will turn into joy. When a woman is in travail she has sorrow, because her hour has come; but when she is delivered of the child, she no longer remembers the anguish, for joy that a child is born into the world. So you have sorrow now, but I will see you again and your hearts will rejoice, and no one will take your joy from you.
Ps. 35:15. But at my stumbling they gathered in glee...
Lk. 6:24–26 [Christ]: Woe to you that are rich, for you have received your consolation. Woe to you that are full now, for you shall hunger. Woe to you that laugh now, for you shall mourn and weep. Woe to you, when all men speak well of you, for so their fathers did to the false prophets.
Mt. 8:12 [Christ]: [They]...will be thrown into the outer darkness; there men will weep and gash their teeth.
Rev. 3:21 [Christ]: He who conquers, I will grant him to sit with me on my throne, as I myself conquered and sat down with my Father on his throne.
Jms. 1:12. Blessed is the man who endures trial, for when he has stood the test he will receive the crown of life which God has promised to those who love him. (Also 2 Tim. 2:3, 5, 12, 4:6–8, 1 Pet. 5:4, Rev. 2:10.)
Mt. 7:13–14 [Christ]: Enter by the narrow gate; for the gate is wide and the way is easy, that leads to destruction, and those who enter by it are many. For the gate is narrow and the way is hard, that leads to life, and those who find it are few.

Denn Gott trägt keinen nicht mit Händen in den Himmel.	
For God bears no-one - with (his) hands to - heaven.	
{For God brings no one to heaven without effort.}	**Acts 14:22.** ...Through many tribulations we must enter the kingdom of God.

7. Tenor & Bass Duet
●Anticipation of heaven's bliss after earth's pain (146-7)

Wie will ich mich freuen,
How I-will   -   rejoice,

      wie will ich mich   laben,
      how I-will   -   indulge-in-comfort,

1 Cor. 2:9–10. But, as it is written, "What no eye has seen, nor ear heard, nor the heart of man conceived, what God has prepared for those who love him," God has revealed to us through the Spirit...

Wenn alle vergängliche Trübsal vorbei!
When all   transient   affliction is-past!

Dan. 12:3. And those who are wise shall shine like the brightness of the firmament; and those who turn many to righteousness, like the stars for ever and ever.

Da   glänz ich wie Sterne und leuchte wie   Sonne,
Then glitter I like   stars   and   shine   like (the) sun,
{Then I will glitter like the stars and shine like the sun,}

Is. 25:8–9. [The Lord] will swallow up death for ever, and the Lord God will wipe away tears from all faces, and the reproach of his people he will take away from all the earth; for the Lord has spoken. It will be said on that day, "Lo, this is our God; we have waited for him, that he might save us. This is the Lord; we have waited for him; let us be glad and rejoice in his salvation."

Da   störet   die   himmlische selige Wonne
Then disturbs (that) heavenly   blessed rapture

Kein Trauren, Heulen und   Geschrei.
No   grieving, wailing, and (no) crying.
{Then no grieving, wailing, or crying will disturb that heavenly blessed rapture.}

Rev. 21:3–4. ...Behold, the dwelling of God is with men. He will dwell with them, and they shall be his people, and God himself will be with them; he will wipe away every tear from their eyes, and death shall be no more, neither shall there be mourning nor crying nor pain any more, for the former things have passed away. (Also Rev. 7:15–17.)

8. Chorale (Untexted in source)[1]
●Anticipation of heaven where all is perfect (146-8)

Denn wer   selig dahin fähret,
For   he-who blessed thither goes,

Lk. 2:29. Lord, now lettest thou thy servant depart in peace...
Rev. 14:13. ...Blessed are the dead who die in the Lord henceforth... that they may rest from their labors, for their deeds follow them! (Also Lk. 16:19–25.)

Da   kein Tod mehr klopfet an,
Where no death more will-knock,
{Where death will never knock again,}

Heb. 4:9. ...There remains a sabbath rest for the people of God.
Rev. 21:4. ...Death shall be no more... (Also Is. 25:8.)
Prov. 10:24. ...The desire of the righteous will be granted.

Dem ist alles wohl gewähret,
To-him is   all   indeed imparted,

Heb. 11:16. ...[God] has prepared for them a city.
Heb. 12:22. You have come to Mount Zion and to the city of the living God, the heavenly Jerusalem... (Also Jn. 14:2–3.)

Was er ihm nur wünschen kann.
That he - ever desire could.
{That he could ever desire.}

Rev. 21:1–4, 10–11, 21. Then I saw a new heaven and a new earth; for the first heaven and the first earth had passed away, and the sea was no more. And I saw the holy city, new Jerusalem, coming down out of heaven from God, prepared as a bride adorned for her husband; and I heard a loud voice from the throne saying, "Behold, the dwelling of God is with men. He will dwell with them, and they shall be his people, and God himself will be with them; he will wipe away every tear from their eyes, and death shall be no more, neither shall there be mourning nor crying nor pain any more, for the former things have passed away."...And in the Spirit he carried me away to a great, high mountain, and showed me the holy city Jerusalem coming down out of heaven from God, having the glory of God, its radiance like a most rare jewel, like a jasper, clear as crystal...And the twelve gates were twelve pearls, each of the gates made of a single pearl, and the street of the city was pure gold, transparent as glass.

Er ist in der festen Stadt,
He is in that secure city,

Da   Gott seine Wohnung hat;
Where God his   dwelling has;

Er ist in das Schloß geführet,
He is into that palace   led,

Das kein Unglück nie berühret.
Which no misfortune ever touches.

---

[1]The source has music but no text. This chorale has been suggested by Rudolf Wustmann. (See Dürr, *Die Kantaten*, p. 357). In the *Neue Bach Ausgabe*, Reinmar Emans, on the suggestion of Martin Petzoldt, has chosen the first stanza of **Freu dich sehr, o meine Seele** (below). See *Bach Compendium* for a further suggestion.

▸Alternate Chorale

Freu dich sehr, o meine Seele,
Rejoice - greatly, O my soul,

Und vergiß all Not und Qual,
And forget all distress and torment,

Weil dich nun Christus, dein Herre,
For thee now Christ, thy Lord,
{For Christ, thy Lord,}

Ruft aus diesem Jammertal!
Calls out-of this vale-of-misery!
{Now calls thee out of this vale of misery!}

Aus Trübsal und großem Leid
Out-of tribulation and great sorrow

Sollst du fahren in die Freud,
Shalt thou journey into - joy,

Die kein Ohre hat gehöret
Which no ear has (ever) heard

Und in Ewigkeit auch währt.
And (which) throughout eternity also shall-endure.

BWV 147
Herz und Mund und Tat und Leben
(NBA I/28; BC A174)

The Visitation: July 2 (BWV 147, 10)
*Is. 11:1-5 (Prophecy concerning the Messiah)
*Lk. 1:39-56 (Mary's visit to Elizabeth, Magnificat)
Librettist: Unknown (Bach began this cantata in Weimar. Its original libretto was by Salomon Franck and was intended for the 4. S. of Advent. An unknown librettist expanded and modified the text for its new liturgical position and Bach then completed the musical setting. See Dürr, *Die Kantaten*, p. 744.)

4. S. of Advent
+Phil. 4:4-7 (Exhortation to rejoice in the Lord always)
+Jn. 1:19-28 (Testimony of John the Baptist concerning himself)

Part I

1. Chorus
●Confessing Christ with heart, mouth, deeds, & life (147-1)
Herz und Mund und Tat und Leben
Heart and mouth and deeds and life

Muß von Christo Zeugnis geben
Must of Christ witness give
{Must give witness of Christ}

Lk. 16:19-25. There was a rich man, who was clothed in purple and fine linen and who feasted sumptuously every day. And at his gate lay a poor man named Lazarus, full of sores, who desired to be fed with what fell from the rich man's table; moreover the dogs came and licked his sores. The poor man died and was carried by the angels to Abraham's bosom. The rich man also died and was buried; and in Hades, being in torment, he lifted up his eyes, and saw Abraham far off and Lazarus in his bosom. And he called out, "Father Abraham, have mercy upon me, and send Lazarus to dip the end of his finger in water and cool my tongue; for I am in anguish in this flame." But Abraham said, "Son, remember that you in your lifetime received your good things, and Lazarus in like manner evil things; but now he is comforted here, and you are in anguish."

Mt. 5:10-12 [Christ]: Blessed are those who are persecuted for righteousness' sake, for theirs is the kingdom of heaven. Blessed are you when men revile you and persecute you...Rejoice and be glad, for your reward is great in heaven...

1 Cor. 2:9-10. As it is written, "What no eye has seen, nor ear heard, nor the heart of man conceived, what God has prepared for those who love him," God has revealed to us through the Spirit...

Rom. 8:18. I consider that the sufferings of this present time are not worth comparing with the glory that is to be revealed to us. (Also 2 Cor. 4:17.)

Dan. 7:18. The saints of the Most High shall receive the kingdom, and possess the kingdom for ever, for ever and ever.

+Jn. 1:19-23, 25-27. This is the testimony (Luther: Zeugnis) of John, when the Jews sent priests and Levites from Jerusalem to ask him, "Who are you?" He confessed, he did not deny, but confessed, "I am not the Christ."...They asked him, "Then why are you baptizing, if you are neither the Christ, nor Elijah, nor the prophet?" John answered them, "I baptize with water; but among you stands one whom you do not know, even he who comes after me, the thong of whose sandal I am not worthy to untie."

Jn. 1:29. The next day [John] saw Jesus coming toward him, and said, "Behold, the Lamb of God, who takes away the sin of the world!" (Also Jn. 1:36.)

Mt. 16:15-16. [Jesus] said to [his disciples], "But who do you say that I am?" Simon Peter replied, "You are the Christ, the Son of the living God." (Also Mk. 8:29, Lk. 9:20.)

*Lk. 1:46-47. Mary said, "My soul magnifies the Lord, and my spirit rejoices in God my Savior."

Deut. 30:14. The word is very near you; it is in your mouth and in your heart, so that you can do it.

Rom. 10:9-10. If you confess with your lips (Luther: Munde) that Jesus is Lord and believe in your heart that God raised him from the dead, you will be saved. For man believes with his heart and so is justified, and he confesses with his lips (Luther: Munde) and so is saved.

Jms. 2:18, 26. But some one will say, "You have faith and I have works." Show me your faith apart from your works, and I by my works will show you my faith...For as the body apart from the spirit is dead, so faith apart from works is dead.

Ohne Furcht und Heuchelei,
Without fear and hypocrisy,

Daß er Gott und Heiland sei.
That he God and Savior is.
{That he is God and Savior.}

2. Tenor Recit. (New to this version)
●Magnificat: Mary's confession & our stubborn silence (147–2)
Gebenedeiter Mund!
Blessed mouth!

Maria macht ihr Innerstes der Seelen
Mary makes her inmost (feelings) of soul

Durch Dank und Rühmen kund;
Through thanks and praise known;
{Known through thanks and praise;}

Sie fänget bei sich an,
She begins with herself - ,
{Beginning with her own experience,}

Des Heilands Wunder zu erzählen,
The Savior's wonders to tell,
{She tells of the Savior's wonders,}

Was er an ihr als seiner Magd getan.
What He for her—as his maiden—has-done.

O menschliches Geschlecht,
O human race,

Des Satans und der Sünden Knecht,
Of Satan and of sin (the) servant,

Du bist befreit
You are freed

Durch Christi tröstendes Erscheinen
Through Christ's comforting appearance

Von dieser Last und Dienstbarkeit!
From this load and servitude!

Jedoch dein Mund und dein verstockt Gemüte
Yet your mouth and your stubborn heart

Verschweigt, verleugnet solche Güte;
Remains-silent, denies such kindness;

Doch wisse, daß dich nach der Schrift
Yet know, that you, according-to the Scriptures
{Yet know that, according to the Scriptures,}

Tit. 3:8. ...Those who have believed in God [should] be careful to apply themselves to good deeds... (Also Tit. 1:16, 2:14, 3:14.)
Ps. 19:14. Let the words of my mouth and the meditation of my heart be acceptable in thy sight... (Also Ps. 104:34.)
1 Cor. 10:31. So, whether you eat or drink, or whatever you do, do all to the glory of God.

Lk. 1:42. [Elizabeth] exclaimed with a loud cry [to Mary], "Blessed (Luther: gebenedeit) are you among women...!"
*Lk. 1:46–55. And Mary said, "My soul magnifies the Lord, and my spirit rejoices in God my Savior, for he has regarded the low estate of his handmaiden. For behold, henceforth all generations will call me blessed; for he who is mighty has done great things for me, and holy is his name. And his mercy is on those who fear him from generation to generation. He has shown strength with his arm, he has scattered the proud in the imagination of their hearts, he has put down the mighty from their thrones, and exalted those of low degree; he has filled the hungry with good things, and the rich he has sent empty away. He has helped his servant Israel, in remembrance of his mercy, as he spoke to our fathers, to Abraham and to his posterity for ever."
1 Sam. 2:1–2. Hannah also prayed and said, "My heart exults in the Lord; my strength is exalted in the Lord..."
Ps. 107:2, 22. Let the redeemed of the Lord say so, whom he has redeemed from trouble...
Ps. 9:1. [O Lord,] I will give thanks to the Lord with my whole heart; I will tell of all thy wonderful deeds. (Also Is. 25:1.)
Ps. 75:1. We give thanks to thee, O God; we give thanks; we call on thy name and recount thy wondrous deeds.
Is. 40:1–2. Comfort, comfort my people, says your God. Speak tenderly to Jerusalem, and cry to her that her warfare (Luther: Ritterschaft; in later edition: Dienstbarkeit) is ended, that her iniquity is pardoned...
Jn. 8:34, 36. Jesus [said], "Truly, truly, I say to you, every one who commits sin is a slave to sin."...If the Son makes you free, you will be free indeed. (Also Rom. 6:16, 20, 2 Pet. 2:19.)
Rom. 6:22. Now...you have been set free from sin...
Ps. 40:10. I have not hid thy saving help within my heart, I have spoken of thy faithfulness and thy salvation; I have not concealed thy steadfast love and thy faithfulness from the great congregation.
Mt. 26:34–35, 69–74. Jesus said to [Peter], "Truly, I say to you, this very night, before the cock crows, you will deny me three times." Peter said to him, "Even if I must die with you, I will not deny you." And so said all the disciples... Now [at the trial before Caiaphas] Peter was sitting outside in the courtyard. And a maid came up to him, and said, "You also were with Jesus the Galilean." But he denied it before them all, saying, "I do not know what you mean." And when he went out to the porch, another maid saw him, and she said to the bystanders, "This man was with Jesus of Nazareth." And again he denied it with an oath, "I do not know the man." After a little while the bystanders came up and said to Peter, "Certainly you are also one of them, for your accent betrays you." Then he began to invoke a curse on himself and to swear, "I do not know the man."...
Rom. 1:20–21. ...[Men] are without excuse; for although they knew God they did not honor him as God or give thanks to him...

Ein allzuscharfes Urteil   trifft!
An all-too-severe judgment will-strike!
{An all-too-severe judgment will strike you!}

3. Alto Aria
●Denial of Christ now means denial by him later (147-3)
Schäme dich, o Seele, nicht,
Be-ashamed, O soul, not,
{Do not be ashamed, O my soul}

Deinen Heiland zu bekennen,
Thy Savior to confess,

Soll er dich die seine nennen
Should he thee his-own call
{If he is to call thee his own}

Vor des Vaters Angesicht!
Before the Father's countenance!

Doch wer ihn auf dieser Erden
Yet he-who Him on this earth

Zu verleugnen sich nicht scheut,
To deny (does) - not hesitate,
{Yet he who does not hesitate to deny Christ on this earth,}

Soll von ihm verleugnet werden,
Shall by Him denied be,
{Shall be denied by him}

Wenn er kommt zur Herrlichkeit.
When he comes (in) glory.

4. Bass Recit. (New to this version)
●Stubbornness warned against: receive Christ today! (147-4)
Verstockung kann Gewaltige verblenden,
Stubborness can the-mighty blind,
{Stubborness can blind the mighty,}

Bis sie des Höchsten Arm vom Stuhle stößt;
Until them the Highest's arm from (their) seat casts;
{Until the arm of the Highest casts them from their seats;}

Doch dieser Arm erhebt,
Yet this arm lifts-up,

Obschon vor ihm der Erde Kreis erbebt,
Even-though before it the earth's sphere quakes,

Hingegen die Elenden,
On-the-other-hand, the afflicted,
{On the other hand, this arm—though the earth's sphere quakes before it—lifts up the afflicted}

Mt. 10:32-33 [Christ]: Every one who acknowledges me before men, I also will acknowledge before my Father who is in heaven; but whoever denies me before men, I also will deny before my Father who is in heaven. (Also Lk. 12:8-9.)

Lk. 9:23-26. And [Jesus] said to all, "If any man would come after me, let him deny himself and take up his cross daily and follow me. For whoever would save his life will lose it; and whoever loses his life for my sake, he will save it. For what does it profit a man if he gains the whole world and loses or forfeits himself? For whoever is ashamed of me and of my words, of him will the Son of man be ashamed when he comes in his glory (Luther: Herrlichkeit) and the glory of the Father and of the holy angels." (Also Mt. 10:32-33, 16:24-27, Mk. 8:34-38, Lk. 12:9.)
2 Tim. 2:11-12. The saying is sure: If we have died with him, we shall also live with him; if we endure, we shall also reign with him; if we deny him, he also will deny us.
1 Jn. 2:28. And now, little children, abide in him, so that when he appears we may have confidence and not shrink from him in shame at his coming.
Mt. 25:31-34, 41. When the Son of man comes in his glory, and all the angels with him, then he will sit on his glorious throne. Before him will be gathered all the nations, and he will separate them one from another as a shepherd separates the sheep from the goats, and he will place the sheep at his right hand, but the goats at the left. Then the King will say to those at his right hand, "Come, O blessed of my Father, inherit the kingdom prepared for you from the foundation of the world."...Then he will say to those at his left hand, "Depart from me, you cursed, into the eternal fire prepared for the devil and his angels."

*Lk. 1:46, 50-53. Mary said, "My soul magnifies the Lord...His mercy is on those who fear him from generation to generation. He has shown strength with his arm, he has scattered the proud in the imagination of their hearts, he has put down the mighty from their thrones, and exalted those of low degree; he has filled the hungry with good things, and the rich he has sent empty away."
1 Sam. 2:1-8. Hannah also prayed and said, "My heart exults in the Lord; my strength is exalted in the Lord. My mouth derides my enemies, because I rejoice in thy salvation. There is none holy like the Lord, there is none besides thee; there is no rock like our God. Talk no more so very proudly, let not arrogance come from your mouth; for the Lord is a God of knowledge, and by him actions are weighed. The bows of the mighty are broken, but the feeble gird on strength. Those who were full have hired themselves out for bread, but those who were hungry have ceased to hunger. The barren has borne seven, but she who has many children is forlorn. The Lord kills and brings to life; he brings down to Sheol and raises up. The Lord makes poor and makes rich; he brings low, he also exalts. He raises up the poor

So   er erlöst.
Whom he saves.

O hochbeglückte Christen,
O highly-favored Christians,

Auf, machet euch   bereit,
Rise, make yourselves ready,

Itzt ist die angenehme Zeit,
Now is the acceptable time,

Itzt ist der Tag des   Heils: der Heiland heißt
Now is the day of Salvation: the Savior bids

Euch   Leib und Geist
You (your) body and soul

Mit Glaubensgaben rüsten,
With faith's-gifts   to-arm,

Auf, ruft zu ihm in brünstigem Verlangen,
Rise, call to him with ardent   desire,

Um   ihn im Glauben zu empfangen!
In-order him in faith to   receive!
{In order to receive him by faith!}

5. Soprano Aria
●Prayer of Soul offering itself to Christ (147-5)
Bereite   dir,   Jesu, noch itzo die Bahn,
Prepare for-thyself, Jesus, already now the way,
{Prepare the way for thyself even now already, O Jesus;}

Mein Heiland, erwähle
My   Savior,   elect

Die gläubende Seele
This believing soul

Und siehe mit Augen der Gnade mich an!
And look with eyes of   grace upon-me!

6. Chorale (Vs. 6) (New to this version)
●Posessing Jesus is the greatest blessing & comfort (147-6)
Wohl   mir, daß ich Jesum habe,
Blest (am) I, that I   Jesus have,

O wie feste halt ich ihn,
O how firmly hold I him,
{O how firmly I hold him,}

Daß   er mir mein Herze labe,
So-that he - my heart refreshes,

Wenn ich krank und traurig bin.
When I sick and sorrowful am.

from the dust; he lifts the needy from the ash heap, to make them sit with princes and inherit a seat of honor..." (Also Ps. 113:7–9.)
2 Cor. 6:2. ...Behold, now is the acceptable time; behold, now is the day of salvation (Luther: Tage des Heils).
Heb. 3:13, 15. Exhort one another every day, as long as it is called "today," that none of you may be hardened by the deceitfulness of sin ...Today, when you hear his voice, do not harden your hearts as in the rebellion. (Also Heb. 3:7–11, 4:6–11, Ps. 95:7–8.)
1 Thess. 5:23. May the God of peace himself sanctify you wholly; and may your spirit and soul and body be kept sound and blameless at the coming of our Lord Jesus Christ.
Mt. 3:8. Bear fruit that befits repentance. (Also Mt. 7:16, 7:20, Lk. 3:8.)
Gal. 5:22–23. The fruit of the Spirit is love, joy, peace, patience, kindness, goodness, faithfulness, gentleness, self-control; against such there is no law.
Eph. 5:14. Therefore it is said, "Awake, O sleeper, and arise from the dead, and Christ shall give you light."
Mt. 25:1, 6. The kingdom of heaven shall be compared to ten maidens who took their lamps and went to meet the bridegroom...At midnight there was a cry, "Behold, the bridegroom! Come out to meet him."
Jn. 1:12. To all who received [Christ], who believed in his name, he gave power to become children of God.
Heb. 11:6. And without faith it is impossible to please him...
*Lk. 1:45. Blessed is she who believed that there would be a fulfilment of what was spoken to her from the Lord [regarding Christ's coming].

+Jn. 1:19, 23. This is the testimony of John, when the Jews sent priests and Levites from Jerusalem to ask him, "Who are you?"...He said, "I am the voice of one crying in the wilderness, 'Make straight the way of the Lord,' as the prophet Isaiah said." (Also Is. 40:3, Mt. 3:3.)
Mt. 21:5, 9. Tell the daughter of Zion, "Behold, your king is coming to you...Blessed is he who comes in the name of the Lord! Hosanna in the highest!" (See Zech. 9:9.)
Jn. 1:12. To all who received [Christ], who believed in his name, he gave power to become children of God.
Jn. 15:16 [Christ]: You did not choose me, but I chose you and appointed you that you should go and bear fruit...
2 Thess. 2:13. ...God chose you from the beginning to be saved, through sanctification by the Spirit and belief in the truth. (Also Ps. 33:12, 1 Pet. 2:9.)

S. of S. 7:10 [Bride]: I am my beloved's, and his desire is for me.
S. of S. 2:16 [Bride]: My beloved is mine and I am his... (Also S. of S. 6:3.)
S. of S. 3:1–4 [Bride]: Upon my bed by night I sought him whom my soul loves; I sought him, but found him not; I called him, but he gave no answer. "I will rise now and go about the city, in the streets and in the squares; I will seek him whom my soul loves." I sought him, but found him not. The watchmen found me, as they went about in the city. "Have you seen him whom my soul loves?" Scarcely had I passed them, when I found him whom my soul loves. I held him, and would not let him go...
Ps. 63:8. [O Lord,] my soul clings to thee (Luther: hanget dir an)...
Ps. 94:19. When the cares of my heart are many, thy consolations cheer my soul.

Jesum hab ich, der mich liebet
Jesus have I, who me does-love
{I have Jesus, who loves me}

Und sich   mir zu eigen gibet;
And himself to-me to own does-give;
{And who gives himself to me to own;}

Ach drum   laß   ich Jesum nicht,
Ah, therefore relinquish I   Jesus not,
{Ah, therefore I'll not relinquish Jesus}

Wenn mir gleich mein Herze   bricht.
Even   -   if   my   heart should-break.

Part II

7. Tenor Aria
●Confessing Christ: Jesus' help sought (147–7)
Hilf, Jesu, hilf, daß ich auch dich   bekenne
Help, Jesus, help, that I   also   thee (might) confess

In wohl und Weh, in Freud und Leid,
In weal and woe, in joy   and sorrow,

Daß ich dich   meinen Heiland nenne
That I thee (as) my   Savior might-name

Im Glauben und Gelassenheit,
In   faith and   composure,

Daß stets mein Herz von deiner Liebe brenne.
That ever   my   heart with thy   love would-burn.

8. Alto Recit. (New to this version)
●God's hand works in unseen places to move the flesh (147–8)
Der höchsten   Allmacht   Wunderhand
The   highest Omnipotent-One's miracle-hand

Wirkt im   Verborgenen   der Erden.
Works in (the) hidden-places of-the earth.

Johannes muß mit   Geist erfüllet werden,
John   must with (the) Spirit filled   be,
{John must become filled with the Spirit;}

Ps. 16:11. ...In thy presence there is fulness of joy, in thy right hand are pleasures for evermore.
Ps. 23:1–3. The Lord is my shepherd, I shall not want; he makes me lie down in green pastures. He leads me beside still waters; he restores my soul...
2 Cor. 1:5. As we share abundantly in Christ's sufferings, so through Christ we share abundantly in comfort too.
Eph. 3:16–17, 19. [May the Father] grant you to be strengthened with might through his Spirit in the inner man, and that Christ may dwell in your hearts through faith; that you, being rooted and grounded in love...may be filled with all the fulness of God.
1 Jn. 5:12. He who has the Son has life...
Ps. 73:25–26. [O Lord,] whom have I in heaven but thee? And there is nothing upon earth that I desire besides thee. My flesh and my heart may fail, but God is the strength of my heart and my portion for ever. (Also Ps. 38:8–10, 15.)
Gen. 32:26. ...Jacob said, "I will not let you go, unless you bless me."

1 Jn. 4:15. Whoever confesses (Luther: bekennt) that Jesus is the Son of God, God abides in him, and he in God. (Also 1 Jn. 4:2–3.)
Rev. 2:10 [Christ]: Do not fear what you are about to suffer...Be faithful unto death, and I will give you the crown of life.
Jms. 1:12. Blessed is the man who endures trial, for when he has stood the test he will receive the crown of life which God has promised to those who love him.
Job 2:10. [Job] said..."Shall we receive good at the hand of God, and shall we not receive evil?" In all this Job did not sin with his lips. (Also Job 6:10.)
Rev. 3:8 [Christ]: ...You have kept my word and have not denied my name. (Also Rev. 2:13.)
Mt. 26:35. Peter said to [Jesus], "Even if I must die with you, I will not deny you."... (Also Mk. 14:29, Lk. 22:33.)
Mt. 26:74–75. Then [Peter] began to invoke a curse on himself and to swear, "I do not know the man." And immediately the cock crowed. And Peter remembered the saying of Jesus, "Before the cock crows, you will deny me three times." And he went out and wept bitterly.
Rev. 2:4 [Christ]: I have this against you, that you have abandoned the love you had at first.
Jn. 21:1, 17. [After his resurrection] Jesus revealed himself again to the disciples...[and] he said to [Peter] the third time, "Simon, son of John, do you love me?" Peter was grieved because he said to him the third time, "Do you love me?" And he said to him, "Lord, you know everything; you know that I love you."

Ps. 139:13–16. [O Lord,] thou didst form my inward parts, thou didst knit me together in my mother's womb. I praise thee, for thou art fearful and wonderful. Wonderful are thy works! Thou knowest me right well; my frame was not hidden from thee, when I was being made in secret, intricately wrought in the depths of the earth. Thy eyes beheld my unformed substance; in thy book were written, every one of them, the days that were formed for me, when as yet there was none of them.
Lk. 1:13, 15. [An] angel said to [Zechariah the priest], "Do not be

Ihn zieht der Liebe Band
Him tugs - Love's bond
{Love's bond tugs him}

Bereits in seiner Mutter Leibe,
Already in his mother's womb,

Daß er den Heiland kennt,
So-that he the Savior recognizes,
{So that he recognizes the Savior,}

Ob er ihn gleich noch nicht
Though he him immediately yet not
{Though he does not yet}

Mit seinem Munde nennt,
With his mouth names,
{Call him by name,}

Er wird bewegt, er hüpft und springet,
He is stirred, he hops and jumps,

Indem Elisabeth das Wunderwerk ausspricht,
While Elizabeth the miracle expresses,
{While Elizabeth tells of the miracle,}

Indem Mariae Mund der Lippen Opfer bringet.
While Mary's mouth (her) lips' sacrifice brings.
{While Mary's mouth brings the sacrifice of her lips.}

Wenn ihr, o Gläubige, des Fleisches Schwachheit merkt,
If you, O believers, the flesh's weakness do-note,

Wenn euer Herz in Liebe brennet,
If your heart with love does-burn,

Und doch der Mund den Heiland nicht bekennet,
And yet (your) mouth the Savior (does) not confess,

Gott ist es, der euch kräftig stärkt,
God is it, who you mightily does-strengthen,
{God it is, who mightily strengthens you,}

Er will in euch des Geistes Kraft erregen,
He would in you the Spirit's power excite,

Ja Dank und Preis auf eure Zunge legen.
Yes, thanks and praise upon your tongues place.
{Yes, place thanks and praise upon your tongue.}

9. Bass Aria

●Confessing Christ: He constrains weak flesh & mouth (147-9)

Ich will von Jesu Wundern singen
I will of Jesus' wonders sing

Und ihm der Lippen Opfer bringen.
And him (my) lips' sacrifice bring.

afraid, Zechariah, for your prayer is heard, and your wife Elizabeth will bear you a son, and you shall call his name John...He will be great before the Lord, and he...will be filled with the Holy Spirit, even from his mother's womb."

*Lk. 1:39–45. In those days Mary arose and went with haste into the hill country, to a city of Judah, and she entered the house of Zechariah and greeted Elizabeth. And when Elizabeth heard the greeting of Mary, the babe leaped in her womb; and Elizabeth was filled with the Holy Spirit and she exclaimed with a loud cry, "Blessed are you among women, and blessed is the fruit of your womb: And why is this granted me, that the mother of my Lord should come to me? For behold, when the voice of your greeting came to my ears, the babe in my womb leaped for joy. And blessed is she who believed that there would be a fulfilment of what was spoken to her from the Lord."

*Lk. 1:46–47. And Mary said, "My soul magnifies the Lord, and my spirit rejoices in God my Savior."

Heb. 13:15. ...Let us continually offer up a sacrifice of praise to God, that is, the fruit of lips that acknowledge his name.

Ps. 50:14, 23 [God]: Offer to God a sacrifice of thanksgiving, and pay your vows to the Most High...He who brings thanksgiving as his sacrifice honors me; to him who orders his way aright I will show the salvation of God!

Mt. 26:41. ...The spirit indeed is willing, but the flesh is weak. (Also Mk. 14:38.)

Rom. 7:15, 18–19, 24–25. I do not understand my own actions. For I do not do what I want, but I do the very thing I hate...For I know that nothing good dwells within me, that is, in my flesh. I can will what is right, but I cannot do it. For I do not do the good I want, but the evil I do not want is what I do...Wretched man that I am! Who will deliver me from this body of death? Thanks be to God through Jesus Christ our Lord! (Also Gal. 5:17.)

1 Cor. 12:3. ...No one can say "Jesus is Lord" except by the Holy Spirit.

Phil. 1:6. I am sure that he who began a good work in you will bring it to completion at the day of Jesus Christ.

Phil. 2:13. For God is at work in you, both to will and to work for his good pleasure.

Eph. 3:16. That according to the riches of his glory he may grant you to be strengthened with might through his Spirit in the inner man. (Also Col. 1:29.)

Ps. 51:15. O Lord, open thou my lips, and my mouth shall show forth thy praise.

Ps. 40:3. [The Lord] put a new song in my mouth, a song of praise to our God. Many will see and fear, and put their trust in the Lord. (Also Ps. 34:1 63:3, 71:8, 109:30, Heb. 13:15.)

*Lk. 1:46–47, 49. And Mary said, "My soul magnifies the Lord, and my spirit rejoices in God my Savior...for he who is mighty has done great things for me..."

Heb. 13:15. ...Let us continually offer up a sacrifice of praise to God, that is, the fruit of lips that acknowledge his name. (Also Ps. 9:1, 50:14, 23, 51:15-17, 63:3, Is. 25:1.)

Jer. 31:33 [God]: This is the covenant which I will make...I will put my law within them, and I will write it upon their hearts; and I will be

Er wird   nach   seiner Liebe Bund
He will—according-to his   love's covenant—

Das schwache Fleisch, den irdschen Mund
The   weak   flesh,   the earthly mouth
{Powerfully overcome the weak flesh, the earthly mouth}

Durch heilges Feuer kräftig   zwingen.
Through holy   fire powerfully overcome.
{With holy fire.}

10. Chorale (Vs. 16) (New to this version)
●Jesus remains my delight, comfort, & sustenance (147-10)
Jesus bleibet meine Freude,
Jesus remains   my   joy,

Meines Herzens Trost und   Saft,
My   heart's comfort and (sustenance),

Jesus wehret allem Leide,
Jesus wards-off all suffering,

Er ist meines Lebens Kraft,
He is   my   life's strength,

Meiner Augen Lust und Sonne,
My   eyes' delight and sun,

Meiner Seele Schatz und Wonne;
My   soul's treasure and bliss;

Darum   laß ich Jesum nicht
Therefore allow I   Jesus not
{Therefore I do not allow Jesus}

Aus dem Herzen und Gesicht.
From (my) heart and sight.

their God, and they shall be my people. (Also Jer. 32:40, Is. 54:10, 55:3, Ezek. 37:26, Heb. 8:10, 10:15-17.)
Rom. 5:5. ...God's love has been poured into our hearts through the Holy Spirit which has been given to us.
Lk. 3:16. John answered them all, "I baptize you with water; but he who is mightier than I is coming...he will baptize you with the Holy Spirit and with fire." (Also Mt. 3:11.)
Rom. 8:3-4. God has done what the law, weakened by the flesh, could not do: sending his own Son in the likeness of sinful flesh and for sin, he condemned sin in the flesh, in order that the just requirement of the law might be fulfilled in us, who walk not according to the flesh but according to the Spirit.

*Lk. 1:47. My spirit rejoices in God my Savior.
Ps. 84:2. ...My heart and flesh sing for joy to the living God.
Mt. 22:37-38. And [Jesus] said... "You shall love the Lord your God with all your heart, and with all your soul, and with all your mind. This is the great and first commandment." (Also Mk. 12:30-31, Lk. 10:27, Deut. 6:5.)
Ps. 73:25-26. [O Lord,] whom have I in heaven but thee? And there is nothing upon earth that I desire besides thee. My flesh and my heart may fail, but God is the strength of my heart and my portion (Luther: Trost und Teil) for ever.
Ps. 27:1. The Lord is my light and my salvation; whom shall I fear? The Lord is the stronghold of my life (Luther: Lebens Kraft); of whom shall I be afraid?
1 Jn. 2:16-17. All that is in the world, the lust of the flesh and the lust of the eyes (Augen Lust) and the pride of life, is not of the Father but is of the world. And the world passes away, and the lust of it; but he who does the will of God abides for ever.
Ps. 37:4. Take delight (Luther: Lust) in the Lord, and he will give you the desires of your heart.
Gen. 32:26. ...Jacob said, "I will not let you go, unless you bless me."
S. of S. 3:4 [Bride]: ...I found him whom my soul loves. I held him, and would not let him go...

BWV 148
Bringet dem Herrn Ehre seines Namens
(NBA I/23; BC A140)

17. S. after Trinity (BWV 148, 114, 47)
*Eph. 4:1-6 (Exhortation to unity in the Spirit)
*Lk. 14:1-11 (Jesus heals man on the sabbath, exhortation to humility)
Librettist: Unknown; text derived from a poem by Picander (Christian Friedrich Henrici)

1. Chorus
●Worship: Give the Lord glory due his name: Ps. 29:2/96:8-9 (148-1)
Bringet dem Herrn   Ehre seines Namens,
Bring to-the Lord (the) glory of-his   name,
{Give to the Lord the glory due his name;}

Ps. 29:1-2. *Ascribe to the Lord, O heavenly beings, ascribe to the Lord glory and strength. Ascribe to the Lord the glory of his name; worship the Lord in holy array.*
Ps. 96:7-9/1 Chron. 16:28-30. Ascribe to the Lord, O families of the peoples, ascribe to the Lord glory and strength! Ascribe to the Lord the glory due his name; bring an offering, and come into his courts! Worship the Lord in holy array; tremble before him, all the earth! (Also Ps. 68:34-35, 2 Chron. 20:21.)
Is. 66:23. ...From sabbath to sabbath, all flesh shall come to worship before me, says the Lord.
*Lk. 14:1-4. One sabbath when [Jesus] went to dine at the house of a ruler who belonged to the Pharisees, they were watching him. And behold, there was a man before him who had dropsy (Luther: war wassersüchtig). And Jesus spoke to the lawyers and Pharisees, saying,

betet an den Herrn im heiligen Schmuck.
worship the Lord in holy array.

2. Tenor Aria
●Sabbath: Hastening with joy to God's house (148-2)
Ich eile, die Lehren
I hasten, the precepts

Des Lebens zu hören
Of life to hear

Und suche mit Freuden das heilige Haus.
And seek with joy that holy house.
{And seek that holy house with joy.}

Wie rufen so schöne
How summons so beautifully

Das frohe Getöne
That joyful noise

Zum Lobe des Höchsten die Seligen aus!
For praise of-the Most-High the (faithful) - !
{How that joyful noise so beautifully summons the faithful to the praise of the Most High!}

3. Alto Recit.
●Longing for God; He is my indwelling rest (148-3)
So wie der Hirsch nach frischem Wasser schreit,
Like as the hart for cool waters cries,

So schrei ich, Gott, zu dir.
So cry I, God, to thee.
{So I cry, O God, to thee.}

Denn alle meine Ruh
For all my rest

Ist niemand außer du.
Is none-other but thou.

Wie heilig und wie teuer
How holy and how dear

Ist, Höchster, deine Sabbatsfeier!
Is, Most-High, thy Sabbath-celebration!

Da preis ich deine Macht
There praise I thy might
{There do I praise thy might}

In der Gemeine der Gerechten.
In the assembly of-the righteous.

"Is it lawful to heal on the sabbath, or not?" But they were silent. Then he took him and healed him, and let him go.

Ex. 20:8. Remember the sabbath day... (Also Ex. 31:15, 35:2, Lev. 23:3, Deut. 5:12, Is. 58:13–14.)
Is. 2:3. Many peoples shall come, and say: "Come, let us go up to the mountain of the Lord, to the house of the God of Jacob; that he may teach us his ways and that we may walk in his paths." For out of Zion shall go forth the law, and the word of the Lord from Jerusalem. (Also Mic. 4:2.)
Ps. 122:1. I was glad when they said to me, "Let us go to the house of the Lord!" (Also Zech. 8:21.)
Ps. 119:47, 105. [O Lord,] I find my delight in thy commandments, which I love...Thy word is a lamp to my feet and a light to my path.
Jn. 6:68. Simon Peter answered him, "Lord, to whom shall we go? You have the words of eternal life..."
Prov. 19:16. He who keeps the commandment keeps his life; he who despises the word will die. (Also Ps. 119:93.)
Ps. 26:8. [O Lord,] I love the habitation of thy house, and the place where thy glory dwells. (Also Ps. 27:4, 84:1–2, 4, 10.)
Ezra 3:10–11, 13. When the builders laid the foundation of the [second] temple...[the priests and Levites] sang responsively, praising and giving thanks to the Lord...And all the people shouted with a great shout, when they praised the Lord...The people shouted with a great shout, and the sound was heard afar.
Ps. 100:1–2. Make a joyful noise to he Lord, all the lands! Serve the Lord with gladness! Come into his presence with singing! (Also Ps. 66:1, 81:1, 95:1,2, 98:4, 6.)

Ps. 42:1–2. As a hart longs for flowing streams, so longs my soul for thee, O God. My soul thirsts for God, for the living God. When shall I come and behold the face of God?
Ps. 73:25. Whom have I in heaven but thee? And there is nothing upon earth that I desire besides thee.
Ps. 84:1–2, 4, 10. How lovely is thy dwelling place, O Lord of hosts! My soul longs, yea, faints for the courts of the Lord; my heart and flesh sing for joy to the living God...Blessed are those who dwell in thy house, ever singing thy praise!...For a day in thy courts is better than a thousand elsewhere. I would rather be a doorkeeper in the house of my God than dwell in the tents of wickedness.
Is. 58:13–14. If you...call the sabbath a delight and the holy day of the Lord honorable...then you shall take delight in the Lord...
Ex. 31:15. ...The seventh day is a sabbath of solemn rest...
Mt. 11:28 [Christ]: Come to me, all who labor and are heavy laden, and I will give you rest.
Ps. 116:12. What shall I render to the Lord for all his bounty to me?
Ps. 22:22, 25. [O Lord,] I will tell of thy name to my brethren; in the midst of the congregation I will praise thee...From thee comes my praise in the great congregation; my vows I will pay before those who fear him. (Also Ps. 35:18, 116:18–19.)
Ps. 149:1–2. Praise the Lord! Sing to the Lord a new song, his praise in the assembly of the faithful! Let Israel be glad in his Maker, let the sons of Zion rejoice in their King!

O! wenn   die Kinder dieser Nacht
Oh! If (only) the children of-this night
{Oh, if only the children of this dark world}

Die Lieblichke it bedächten,
This loveliness would-consider,
{Would consider this loveliness,}

Denn Gott wohnt selbst in mir.
For   God dwells himself in me.
{For God himself dwells in me.}

4. Alto Aria
●Receiving God with heart & mouth; resting in him (148-4)
Mund und Herze steht   dir offen,
Mouth and heart stand to-thee open,
{My mouth and heart are open to thee,}

Höchster, senke dich hinein!
Most-High, settle thyself therein!

Ich in dich, und du in mich;
I   in thee, and thou in me;

Glaube, Liebe,   Dulden,   Hoffen
Faith,   love, patient-endurance, hope

Soll mein Ruhebette sein.
Shall my   bed-of-rest be.

5. Tenor Recit.
●Heavenly sabbath sought; ensured by God's indwelling
(148-5)
Bleib auch,   mein Gott, in mir
Remain also, (O) my God, in me

Und gib mir deinen Geist,
And give me   thy   Spirit,

Der mich nach   deinem Wort regiere,
Who me according-to thy   Word shall-rule,
{Who shall rule me according to thy Word,}

Daß ich so einen Wandel   führe,
That I such a   manner-of-life might-lead,

Der dir   gefällig heißt,
As to-thee pleasing (is),
{As is pleasing to thee,}

Damit ich nach der Zeit
That   I   after (this) time

In deiner Herrlichkeit,
In thy   glory,

Is. 60:1. Arise, shine; for your light has come...
Eph. 5:8. Once you were darkness, but now you are light in the Lord...
Eph. 3:17, 19. [I pray] that Christ may dwell in your hearts through faith...that you may be filled with all the fulness of God.
Col. 1:27. ...Christ in you, the hope of glory.
Jn. 14:17, 20, 23, 27 [Christ]: ...You know [the Spirit], for he dwells with you, and will be in you...In that day you will know that I am in my Father, and you in me, and I in you...If a man loves me, he will keep my word, and my Father will love him, and we will come to him and make our home with him...My peace I give to you...
1 Jn. 3:24. ...By this we know that [God] abides in us, by the Spirit which he has given us. (Also 1 Jn. 4:13.)

2 Cor. 6:11. Our mouth is open to you...our heart is wide.
Rom. 10:9-11. If you confess with your lips (Luther: Munde) that Jesus is Lord and believe in your heart that God raised him from the dead, you will be saved. For man believes with his heart and so is justified, and he confesses with his lips (Luther: Munde) and so is saved. (Also Deut. 30:14.)
Jn. 1:12. To all who received [Christ], who believed in his name, he gave power to become children of God.
Jn. 14:20 [Christ]: ...I am in my Father, and you in me, and I in you.
Mt. 11:28 [Christ]: Come to me...and I will give you rest.
Heb. 4:9. ...There remains a sabbath rest for the people of God. Ps. 46:10 [God]: Be still, and know that I am God...
Lam. 3:26. It is good that one should wait quietly for the salvation of the Lord.
Ps. 131:2. I have calmed and quieted my soul, like a child quieted at its mother's breast...
Is. 30:15. ...In quietness and in trust shall be your strength.
Ps. 37:7. Be still before the Lord, and wait patiently for him...
1 Cor. 13:7. Love bears all things, believes (Luther: glaubet) all things, hopes (Luther: hoffet) all things, endures (Luther: duldet) all things.

1 Jn. 3:24. ...By this we know that [God] abides in us, by the Spirit which he has given us.
Ps. 51:11. [O Lord]...take not thy holy Spirit from me.
Jn. 16:13 [Christ]: When the Spirit of truth comes, he will guide you into all the truth... (Also Jn. 14:26, 1 Jn. 2:27.)
Col. 3:16. Let the word of Christ dwell in you richly...
Eph. 5:8-10. ...You are light in the Lord; walk as children of light (for the fruit of light is found in all that is good and right and true)...Try to learn what is pleasing to the Lord.
Heb. 13:20-21. May the God of peace...equip you with everything good that you may do his will, working in you that which is pleasing in his sight, through Jesus Christ; to whom be glory for ever and ever. Amen.
Rev. 2:10 [Christ]: ...Be faithful unto death, and I will give you the crown of life.
Heb. 4:9-10. ...There remains a sabbath rest for the people of God; for whoever enters God's rest also ceases from his labors as God did from his.
Heb. 4:1-2, 11. While the promise of entering his rest remains, let us fear lest any of you be judged to have failed to reach it. For good news came to us just as to [the Israelites]; but the message which they heard did not benefit them, because it did not meet with faith in the

Mein lieber Gott, mit dir
My dear God, with thee

Den großen Sabbat möge halten.
That great Sabbath might celebrate.

6. Chorale[1]
●Praising Christ's name at all times (148–6)
Amen zu aller Stund
Amen at every hour

Sprech ich aus Herzensgrund;
Say I from-the bottom-of-my-heart;

Du wollest uns tun leiten,
(We pray) thou wouldst us - lead,

Herr Christ, zu allen Zeiten,
Lord Christ, at all times,

Auf daß wir deinen Namen
So that we thy name

Ewiglich preisen. Amen.
Eternally (might) praise. Amen.

hearers...Let us therefore strive to enter that rest, that no one fall by the same sort of disobedience.
Rev. 14:13. And I heard a voice from heaven saying, "Write this: Blessed are the dead who die in the Lord henceforth." "Blessed indeed," says the Spirit, "that they may rest from their labors, for their deeds follow them!"

Ps. 106:48. Blessed be the Lord, the God of Israel, from everlasting to everlasting! And let all the people say, "Amen!" Praise the Lord!
Neh. 8:6. Ezra blessed the Lord, the great God; and all the people answered, "Amen, Amen."
Jer. 42:3. [Pray] that the Lord your God may show us the way we should go, and the thing that we should do.
Is. 30:21. Your ears shall hear a word behind you, saying, "This is the way, walk in it," when you turn to the right or when you turn to the left.
Ps. 43:3–4. [O Lord,] send out thy light and thy truth; let them lead me, let them bring me to thy holy hill and to thy dwelling! Then I will go to the altar of God, to God my exceeding joy; and I will praise thee with the lyre, O God, my God.
1 Chron. 16:29, 36. Ascribe to the Lord the glory due his name; bring an offering, and come before him! Worship the Lord in holy array... Blessed be the Lord, the God of Israel, from everlasting to everlasting! Then all the people said "Amen!" and praised the Lord.
Ps. 145:20–21. The Lord preserves all who love him...Let all flesh bless his holy name for ever and ever.
Ps. 145:2. [O Lord,] every day I will bless thee, and praise thy name for ever and ever.

BWV 149
Man singet mit Freuden vom Sieg
(NBA I/30; BC A181)

St. Michael's Day: Sept. 29 (BWV 130, 19, 149, 50)
*Rev. 12:7–12 (The archangel Michael battles with the dragon)
*Mt. 18:1–11 (The kingdom of heaven belongs to children; their angels behold the face of God)
Librettist: Picander (Christian Friedrich Henrici)

1. Chorus (Parody of BWV 208-15)
●Victory song of Lord's triumph: Ps. 118:15-16 (149–1)
Man singet mit Freuden vom Sieg in den Hütten
They sing with joy of victory in the tents

der Gerechten: Die Rechte des Herrn behält
of-the righteous: The right-hand of-the Lord gains

den Sieg, die Rechte des Herrn ist erhöhet,
the victory, the right-hand of-the Lord is exalted,

die Rechte des Herrn behält den Sieg!
the right-hand of-the Lord gains the victory!

Ps. 98:1. O sing to the Lord a new song, for he has done marvelous things! His right hand and his holy arm have gotten him victory.
Ps. 118:15-16. *Hark, glad songs of victory in the tents of the righteous: "The right hand of the Lord does valiantly, the right hand of the Lord is exalted, the right hand of the Lord does valiantly!"*
Ps. 89:13. [O Lord,] thou hast a mighty arm; strong is thy hand, high thy right hand. (Also Ps. 68:3, Ex. 15:16.)
***Rev. 12:7-9.** Now war arose in heaven, Michael and his angels fighting against the dragon; and the dragon and his angels fought, but they were defeated and there was no longer any place for them in heaven. And the great dragon was thrown down, that ancient serpent, who is called the Devil and Satan, the deceiver of the whole world—he was thrown down to the earth, and his angels were thrown down with him.

---

[1]The source has music but no text. This chorale text has been suggested by a number of scholars. See Dürr, *Die Kantaten*, p. 620. For another suggestion see the *Bach Compendium*.

2. Bass Aria

●Praise to the Lamb who conquered Satan by his blood
(149–2)

Kraft und Stärke sei gesungen
(Let) power and might be sung (to)

Gott, dem Lamme, das bezwungen
God, the Lamb, who has-conquered

Und den Satanas verjagt,
And - Satan put-to-flight,
{And put Satan to flight,}

Der uns Tag und Nacht verklagt.
Who us day and night accused.
{Who accused us day and night.}

Ehr und Sieg ist auf die Frommen
Honor and victory has upon the godly
{Honor and victory has come to the godly}

Durch des Lammes Blut gekommen.
Through the lamb's blood come.
{Through the blood of the lamb.}

3. Alto Recit.

●Peace in face of foes, God's angel hosts protect me (149–3)
Ich fürchte mich
I have-fear

Vor tausend Feinden nicht,
Before a-thousand foes not,
{I have no fear before a thousand foes,}

Denn Gottes Engel lagern sich
For God's angels encamp -

Um meine Seiten her;
Around my every-side - ;

Wenn alles fällt, wenn alles bricht,
Though all (things) should-fall, though all should-break,

So bin ich doch in Ruhe.
So am I nevertheless at rest.
{I am nevertheless at rest.}

Wie wär es möglich zu verzagen?
How were it possible to despair?

Gott schickt mir ferner Roß und Wagen
God sends to-me, moreover, horse and chariot

Und ganze Herden Engel zu.
And whole hosts of-angels - .

*Rev. 12:10–12. And I heard a loud voice in heaven, saying, "Now the salvation and the power and the kingdom of our God and the authority of his Christ have come, for the accuser of our brethren has been thrown down, who accuses them day and night before our God. And they have conquered him by the blood of the Lamb and by the word of their testimony, for they loved not their lives even unto death. Rejoice then, O heaven and you that dwell therein! But woe to you, O earth and sea, for the devil has come down to you in great wrath, because he knows that his time is short!"

Rev. 20:1–3. Then I saw an angel coming down from heaven, holding in his hand the key of the bottomless pit and a great chain. And he seized the dragon, that ancient serpent, who is the Devil and Satan, and bound him for a thousand years, and threw him into the pit, and shut it and sealed it over him, that he should deceive the nations no more, till the thousand years were ended...

Rev. 17:14. ...The Lamb will conquer...for he is Lord of lords and King of kings, and those with him are called and chosen and faithful. (Also Rev. 19:16.)

1 Jn. 3:8. ...The reason the Son of God appeared was to destroy the works of the devil. (Also Heb. 2:14.)

Ps. 27:1, 3. The Lord is my light and my salvation; whom shall I fear? The Lord is the stronghold of my life; of whom shall I be afraid?... Though a host encamp against me, my heart shall not fear; though war arise against me, yet I will be confident. (Also Ps. 118:6, Rom. 8:31–39.)

Ps. 34:7. The angel of the Lord encamps around those who fear him, and delivers them.

Ps. 91:7. A thousand may fall at your side, ten thousand at your right hand; but it will not come near you. (Also Is. 54:14.)

Ps. 4:8. In peace I will both lie down and sleep; for thou alone, O Lord, makest me dwell in safety. (Also Ps. 46:1–3.)

Ps. 3:5–6. I lie down and sleep; I wake again, for the Lord sustains me. I am not afraid of ten thousands of people who have set themselves against me round about.

2 Kings 6:15–18. When the servant of [Elisha the prophet] rose early in the morning and went out, behold, an army with horses and chariots was round about the city. And the servant said, "Alas, my master! What shall we do?" [Elisha] said, "Fear not, for those who are with us are more than those who are with them." Then Elisha prayed, and said, "O Lord, I pray thee, open his eyes that he may see." So the Lord opened the eyes of the young man, and he saw; and behold, the mountain was full of horses and chariots of fire around about Elisha. And when the Syrians came down...[the Lord] struck them with blindness...

Mt. 26:52–53. Jesus said to [the disciple who had struck the slave of the high priest in the garden of Gethsemane], "...Do you think that I cannot appeal to my Father, and he will at once send me more than twelve legions of angels?"

4. Soprano Aria

●Angels of God keep watch over me wherever I go (149-4)

Gottes Engel weichen nie,
God's angels withdraw never,

Sie sind bei mir allerenden.
They are with me everywhere.

Wenn ich schlafe, wachen sie,
When I sleep, watch they,
{When I sleep they keep watch,}

Wenn ich gehe,
When I go,

Wenn ich stehe,
When I stop,

Tragen sie mich auf den Händen.
Bear they me upon (their) hands.
{They bear me upon their hands.}

5. Tenor Recit.

●Repentance sought so an angel will take me to heaven (149-5)

Ich danke dir,
I thank thee,

Mein lieber Gott, dafür;
My dear God, for-that;

Dabei verleih mir,
Therewith grant -

Daß ich mein sündlich Tun bereue,
That I my sinful conduct rue,
{That I rue my sinful conduct,}

Daß sich mein Engel drüber freue,
So - my angel over-this might-rejoice,
{So my guardian angel might rejoice over this,}

Damit er mich an meinem Sterbetage
So-that he me on my day-of-death
{So that, on the day of my death,}

In deinen Schoß zum Himmel trage.
Into thy bosom to heaven might-carry.
{He might carry me to heaven into thy bosom.}

6. Alto & Tenor Duet

●Yearning for heaven; the night watch is almost over (149-6)

Seid wachsam, ihr heiligen Wächter,
Be watchful, ye holy watchmen,

Die Nacht ist schier dahin.
The night is almost gone.

*Mt. 18:10 [Christ]: See that you do not despise one of these little ones; for I tell you that in heaven their angels always behold the face of my Father who is in heaven.

Heb. 1:14. Are [angels] not all ministering spirits sent forth to serve, for the sake of those who are to obtain salvation? (Also Ps. 103:20–21.)

Ps. 91:1–12. He who dwells in the shelter of the Most High, who abides in the shadow of the Almighty, will say to the Lord, "My refuge and my fortress; my God, in whom I trust." For he will deliver you from the snare of the fowler and from the deadly pestilence; he will cover you with his pinions, and under his wings you will find refuge; his faithfulness is a shield and buckler. You will not fear the terror of the night, nor the arrow that flies by day, nor the pestilence that stalks in darkness, nor the destruction that wastes at noonday. A thousand may fall at your side, ten thousand at your right hand; but it will not come near you. You will only look with your eyes and see the recompense of the wicked. Because you have made the Lord your refuge, the Most High your habitation, no evil shall befall you, no scourge come near your tent. For he will give his angels charge of you to guard you in all your ways. On their hands they will bear you up, lest you dash your foot against a stone. (Also Ps. 121:5–8, Mt. 4:6, Lk. 4:10–11.)

Lk. 15:4, 7–10 [Christ]: What man of you, having a hundred sheep, if he has lost one of them does not leave the ninety-nine in the wilderness, and go after the one which is lost, until he finds it?...I tell you, there will be more joy in heaven over one sinner who repents than over ninety-nine righteous persons who need no repentance. Or what woman, having ten silver coins, if she loses one coin, does not light a lamp and sweep the house and seek diligently until she finds it? And when she has found it, she calls together her friends and neighbors, saying, "Rejoice with me, for I have found the coin which I had lost." Just so, I tell you, there is joy before the angels of God over one sinner who repents. (Also Mt. 18:12–14.)

Lk. 16:19–25. There was a rich man, who was clothed in purple and fine linen and who feasted sumptuously every day. And at his gate lay a poor man named Lazarus, full of sores, who desired to be fed with what fell from the rich man's table; moreover the dogs came and licked his sores. The poor man died and was carried by the angels to Abraham's bosom (Luther: Schoß). The rich man also died and was buried; and in Hades, being in torment, he lifted up his eyes, and saw Abraham far off and Lazarus in his bosom. And he called out, "Father Abraham, have mercy upon me..." But Abraham said, "Son, remember that you in your lifetime received your good things, and Lazarus in like manner evil things; but now he is comforted here, and you are in anguish." (Also Heb. 4:9.)

Is. 62:6 [God]: Upon your walls, O Jerusalem, I have set watchmen; all the day and all the night they shall never be silent...

Is. 21:11–12. ...One is calling to me from Seir, "Watchman, what of the night? (Luther: Ist die Nacht schier hin?)..." The watchman says: "Morning comes, and also the night. If you will inquire, inquire; come back again."

Ich sehne mich und ruhe nicht,
I   yearn -   and rest not,

Bis ich vor dem Angesicht
Till I before the countenance

Meines lieben Vaters bin.
Of-my   dear Father am.

7. Chorale
●Prayer: Bring my soul to thee & raise my body on last day
(149-7)
Ach Herr, laß dein lieb Engelein
Ah Lord, let thy dear little-angel

Am   letzten End die Seele mein
At (my) final end this soul of-mine
{Carry this soul of mine at my final end}

In Abrahams Schoß tragen,
Into Abraham's bosom carry,
{Into Abraham's bosom,}

Den Leib in seim Schlafkämmerlein
(Let) (my) body in   its   sleeping-closet
{Let my body rest in its sleeping-closet}

Gar sanft ohn einge Qual und Pein
Very softly without any torment and pain
{Very softly without any torment or pain}

Ruhn bis am jüngsten Tage!
Rest till - Judgment Day!
{Till Judgment Day!}

Alsdenn vom Tod erwecke mich,
Then   from death awaken me,

Daß meine Augen   sehen dich
That my   eyes (may) see   thee

In aller Freud, o Gottes Sohn,
In total   joy, O God's Son,

Mein Heiland und Genadenthron!
My   Savior and   mercy-seat!

Herr Jesu Christ, erhöre mich, erhöre mich,
Lord Jesus Christ, hear me, hear me (favorably),
{Lord Jesus Christ, grant this to me,}

Rom. 13:11-12. ...You know what hour it is, how it is full time now for you to wake from sleep. For salvation is nearer to us now than when we first believed; the night is far gone, the day is at hand...
1 Jn. 3:2. Beloved, we are God's children now; it does not yet appear what we shall be, but we know that when he appears we shall be like him, for we shall see him as he is.
1 Cor. 13:12. For now we see in a mirror dimly, but then face to face... (Also Rev. 22:4.)
*****Mt. 18:10.** ...In heaven [the] angels always behold the face of my Father who is in heaven.

Lk. 16:22. [Lazarus] died and was carried by the angels to Abraham's bosom (Luther: Schoß)...
Jn. 6:40 [Christ]: This is the will of my Father, that every one who sees the Son and believes in him should have eternal life; and I will raise him up at the last day (Luther: jüngsten Tage). (Also Jn. 6:39, 54, 11:24-25.)
1 Cor. 15:40, 42, 50-52, 54-55. There are celestial bodies and there are terrestrial bodies...So it is with the resurrection of the dead. What is sown is perishable, what is raised is imperishable...Flesh and blood cannot inherit the kingdom of God, nor does the perishable inherit the imperishable. Lo! I tell you a mystery. We shall not all sleep, but we shall all be changed, in a moment, in the twinkling of an eye, at the last trumpet. For the trumpet will sound, and the dead will be raised imperishable, and we shall be changed...When the perishable puts on the imperishable, and the mortal puts on immortality, then shall come to pass the saying that is written: "Death is swallowed up in victory." O death, where is thy victory? O death, where is thy sting?
1 Thess. 4:13-14, 16-18. We would not have you ignorant, brethren, concerning those who are asleep, that you may not grieve as others do who have no hope. For since we believe that Jesus died and rose again, even so, through Jesus, God will bring with him those who have fallen asleep...The dead in Christ will rise first; then we who are alive, who are left, shall be caught up together with them in clouds to meet the Lord in the air; and so we shall always be with the Lord. Therefore comfort one another with these words.
Rom. 5:2. Through [Christ] we have obtained access to this grace in which we stand, and we rejoice in our hope of sharing the glory of God.
Heb. 9:11-12. When Christ appeared as a high priest of the good things that have come, then through the greater and more perfect tent (not made with hands, that is, not of this creation) he entered once for all into the Holy Place, taking not the blood of goats and calves but his own blood, thus securing an eternal redemption.
Ex. 25:1, 17, 21-22. The Lord said to Moses, "...You shall make a mercy seat (Luther: Gnadenthron) of pure gold...and you shall put the mercy seat on the top of the ark...There I will meet with you..."
Lev. 16:15-16. "Then [Aaron] shall...bring [the] blood within the veil... sprinkling it upon the mercy seat (Luther: Gnadenstuhl)...Thus he shall make atonement...because of [the people's] transgressions..."
Rom. 3:24-25. [Now we] are justified by [God's] grace as a gift, through the redemption which is in Christ Jesus, whom God put forward as an expiation (Luther: einem Gnadenstuhl) by his blood, to be received by faith...
2 Cor. 4:14. ...He who raised the Lord Jesus will raise us also with Jesus and bring us with you into his presence. (Also 1 Cor. 6:14.)

Ich will dich preisen ewiglich!
I would thee praise eternally!
{I would praise thee eternally!}

1 Jn. 3:2. Beloved, we are God's children now; it does not yet appear what we shall be, but we know that when he appears we shall be like him, for we shall see him as he is.

BWV 150
Nach dir, Herr, verlanget mich
(NBA I/41; BC B24)

Occasion Unknown (BWV 131, 150, 117, 192, 100, 97)
Perhaps this cantata was intended for a day of penitence.
Librettist: Unknown

1. Sinfonia

2. Chorus
●Prayer of hope and trust in God: Ps. 25:1–2 (150-2)
Nach dir, Herr, verlanget mich. Mein Gott, ich hoffe
For thee, Lord,   long   I.   My God, I hope
{I long, O Lord, for thee. My God, I hope}

auf dich. Laß mich nicht zuschanden werden,
in thee. Let me not   confounded   be,

daß sich meine Feinde nicht freuen über mich.
that -   my   foes   not rejoice over me.

Ps. 25:1–3. *To thee, O Lord, I lift up soul, O my God, in thee I trust, let me not be put to shame; let not my enemies exult over me.* Yea, let none that wait for thee be put to shame; let them be ashamed who are wantonly treacherous.
Ps. 86:4. Gladden the soul of thy servant, for to thee, O Lord, do I lift up my soul (Luther: nach dir, Herr, verlangt mich).
Ps. 119:114, 116. Thou art my hiding place and my shield; I hope in thy word...Uphold me according to thy promise, that I may live, and let me not be put to shame in my hope!
Ps. 35:19. [O Lord,] let not those rejoice over me who are wrongfully my foes, and let not those wink the eye who hate me without cause.

3. Soprano Aria
●Cheerfulness despite cross, storm, death, and hell (150-3)
Doch bin und bleibe ich vergnügt,
Yet am and remain I cheerful,
{Yet I am cheerful and remain so,}

Obgleich hier zeitlich   toben
Though here temporally (there) rage
{Though here in this time there rage}

Kreuz, Sturm und andre Proben,
Cross, storm, and other trials,

Tod, Höll und was   sich fügt.
Death, hell, and whatever (else) may-happen.

Ob   Unfall schlägt den treuen Knecht,
Though mishap strike the faithful servant,

Recht ist und bleibet ewig Recht.
Right is and remains ever right.

Phil. 4:11–12. ...I have learned, in whatever state I am, to be content. I know how to be abased, and I know how to abound; in any and all circumstances I have learned the secret of facing plenty and hunger, abundance and want.
2 Cor. 4:8–10, 17. We are afflicted in every way, but not crushed; perplexed, but not driven to despair; persecuted, but not forsaken; struck down, but not destroyed; always carrying in the body the death of Jesus, so that the life of Jesus may also be manifested in our bodies ...For this slight momentary (Luther: zeitlich) affliction is preparing for us an eternal weight of glory beyond all comparison. (Also Rom. 8:18.)
1 Pet. 4:12–13. Beloved, do not be surprised at the fiery ordeal which comes upon you to prove you, as though something strange were happening to you. But rejoice in so far as you share Christ's sufferings, that you may also rejoice and be glad when his glory is revealed. (Also Jms. 1:2–4, 12, 1 Pet. 5:10.)
Ps. 94:15. For justice will return to the righteous, and all the upright in heart will follow it. (Luther: Denn Recht muß doch Recht bleiben, und dem werden all frommen Herzen zufallen.)

4. Chorus
●Prayer: Lead me in thy truth; I wait on thee: Ps. 25:5 (150-4)
Leite mich in deiner Wahrheit und lehre mich;
Lead me in thy   truth   and teach me;

denn du bist der Gott, der mir hilft,
for thou art the God, who me helps,
{For thou art the God who helps me,}

Ps. 25:5. *Lead me in thy truth, and teach me, for thou art the God of my salvation; for thee I wait all the day long.*
Ps. 43:3. Oh send out thy light and thy truth; let them lead me, let them bring me to thy holy hill and to thy dwelling!
Ps. 38:15. But for thee, O Lord, do I wait (Luther: harre); it is thou, O Lord my God, who wilt answer.
Ps. 130:5–6. I wait (Luther: harre) for the Lord, my soul waits (Luther: harret), and in his word I hope; my soul waits for the Lord

täglich harre ich dein.
daily wait I upon-thee.

5. Alto, Tenor & Bass Trio
●Winds may twist cedars but not him who trusts in God (150–5)
Zedern müssen von den Winden
Cedars must from the winds

Oft viel Ungemach empfinden.
Oft much discomfort experience.
{Cedars must often experience much discomfort from the winds.}

Oftmals werden sie verkehrt.
Often become they twisted-about.
{Often they become twisted about.}

Rat und Tat auf Gott gestellet,
Word and deed (that is) upon God placed,
{Word and deed that is placed upon God,}

Achtet nicht, was widerbellet,
Heeds not, what howls-against (it),

Denn sein Wort ganz anders lehrt.
For his Word (us) entirely otherwise teaches.
{For his Word teaches us quite otherwise.}

6. Chorus
●Faith God will rescue my foot out of net: Ps. 25:15 (150–6)
Meine Augen sehen stets zu dem Herrn;
Mine eyes look ever to the Lord;

denn er wird meinen Fuß aus dem Netze ziehen.
for he will my foot out of-the net pull.
{for he will pull my foot out of the net.}

7. Chorus
●Suffering endured with God's help; future joy seen (150–7)
Meine Tage in den Leiden
My days in - suffering

Endet Gott dennoch zur Freuden;
Ends God nevertheless (in) joy;
{God nevertheless ends in joy;}

Christen auf den Dornenwegen
Christians on - thorny-paths

more than watchmen for the morning, more than watchmen for the morning.

Acts 14:22. ...Through many tribulations we must enter the kingdom of God.
Acts 8:1. ...A great persecution arose against the church in Jerusalem...
Mt. 7:24–27 [Christ]: Every one then who hears these words of mine and does them will be like a wise man who built his house upon the rock; and the rain fell, and the floods came, and the winds blew and beat upon that house, but it did not fall, because it had been founded on the rock. And every one who hears these words of mine and does not do them will be like a foolish man who built his house upon the sand; and the rain fell, and the floods came, and the winds blew and beat against that house, and it fell; and great was the fall of it. (Also Lk. 6:46–49.)
Mk. 4:16–17 [Christ]: [Some people...], when they hear the word, immediately receive it with joy; [but] they have no root in themselves, [so] endure for a while; then when tribulation or persecution arises on account of the word, immediately they fall away. (Also Lk. 8:13.)
Heb. 3:12. Take care, brethren, lest there be in any of you an evil, unbelieving heart, leading you to fall away from the living God.
Heb. 10:39. We are not of those who shrink back and are destroyed, but of those who have faith and keep their souls.
Heb. 11:24–26. By faith Moses...[chose] rather to share ill-treatment (Luther: Ungemach) with the people of God than to enjoy the fleeting pleasures of sin. He considered abuse suffered for the Christ greater wealth than the treasures of Egypt, for he looked to the reward. (Also Heb. 11:37.)
Ps. 27:1, 3. ...The Lord is the stronghold of my life; of whom shall I be afraid?...Though a host encamp against me, my heart shall not fear; though war arise against me, yet I will be confident. (Also Ps. 118:6, Is. 26:3, Rom. 8:31–39.)

Ps. 25:15. *My eyes are ever toward the Lord, for he will pluck my feet out of the net.*
Ps. 141:8–10. My eyes are toward thee, O Lord God; in thee I seek refuge; leave me not defenseless! Keep me from the trap which they have laid for me, and from the snares of evildoers! Let the wicked together fall into their own nets, while I escape. (Also Ps. 31: 4–5, 35:7–8, 123:2.)

Ps. 90:15. [O Lord,] make us glad as many days as thou hast afflicted us, and as many years as we have seen evil.
Rom. 8:18. I consider that the sufferings of this present time (Luther: dieser Zeit Leiden) are not worth comparing with the glory that is to be revealed to us.
Jms. 1:12. Blessed is the man who endures trial, for when he has stood the test he will receive the crown of life which God has promised to those who love him. (Also 1 Pet. 4:13, 5:10.)
Lk. 6:21. ...Blessed are you that weep now, for you shall laugh.
Ps. 30:5. ...Weeping may tarry for the night, but joy comes with the morning.
Ps. 126:5–6. May those who sow in tears reap with shouts of joy! He that goes forth weeping, bearing the seed for sowing, shall come home with shouts of joy, bringing his sheaves with him.

Führen Himmels Kraft und Segen.
Bear   heaven's power and blessing.

Bleibet Gott mein treuer Schatz,
Remains God my faithful treasure,
{If God remains my faithful treasure,}

    Achte ich nicht Menschenkreuz;
(Then) heed I   not   man's-cross;
{Then I heed not man's cross;}

Christus, der uns steht zur Seiten,
Christ, who - stands by-our side,

Hilft mir täglich sieghaft streiten.
Helps me daily victoriously to-fight.
{Helps me daily to fight victoriously.}

BWV 151
Süßer Trost, mein Jesus kömmt
(NBA I/3; BC A17)

3. Day of Christmas (BWV 64, 133, 151, 248-III)
*Heb. 1:1–14 (God spoke through his Son, who is superior to the angels)
*Jn. 1:1–14 (Prologue: In the beginning was the Word...and the Word became flesh)
Librettist: Georg Christian Lehms

1. Soprano Aria
●Christ's birth signifies my election for heaven (151-1)
  Süßer Trost, mein Jesus kömmt,
(O) sweet comfort, my Jesus comes,

Jesus wird anitzt geboren!
Jesus (is) now born!

Herz und Seele freuet sich,
Heart and soul rejoice,
{My heart and soul rejoice,}

Denn mein liebster Gott hat mich
For   my dearest God has me
{For my dearest God has now elected me}

Nun zum Himmel auserkoren.
Now for heaven   elected.
{For heaven.}

2. Bass Recit.
●Christmas: God sent his Son to earth to deliver us (151-2)
Erfreue dich,   mein Herz,
Rejoice - , (O) my heart,

Denn itzo weicht der Schmerz,
For   now subsides the pain,

2 Cor. 4:17. For this slight momentary affliction is preparing for us an eternal weight of glory beyond all comparison.
Phil. 1:21. To me to live is Christ, and to die is gain.
2 Cor. 1:5. For as we share abundantly in Christ's sufferings, so through Christ we share abundantly in comfort too.
2 Tim. 2:11–12. ...If we have died with him, we shall also live with him; if we endure, we shall also reign with him...
Rom. 8:17. ...[We are] fellow heirs with Christ, provided we suffer with him in order that we may also be glorified with him. (Also 1 Pet. 4:13.)
Mt. 10:38 [Christ]: He who does not take his cross and follow me is not worthy of me. (Also Mt. 16:24, Mk. 8:34, Lk. 9:23.)
Rom. 8:35–37. Who shall separate us from the love of Christ? Shall tribulation, or distress, or persecution, or famine, or nakedness, or peril, or sword? As it is written, "For thy sake we are being killed all the day long; we are regarded as sheep to be slaughtered." No, in all these things we are more than conquerors through him who loved us.

Lk. 2:10. To you is born this day in the city of David a Savior, who is Christ the Lord.
*Jn. 1:14. The Word became flesh and dwelt among us, full of grace and truth...
Is. 25:9. ...Lo, this is our God; we have waited for him, that he might save us....
Mt. 1:21. ...You shall call his name Jesus, for he will save his people from their sins.
Ps. 95:6–7. O come, let us worship and bow down, let us kneel before the Lord, our Maker! For he is our God and we are the people of his pasture, and the sheep of his hand. (Also Ps. 100:3.)
2 Thess. 2:13–14, 16–17. ...God chose you from the beginning to be saved, through sanctification by the Spirit and belief in the truth. To this he called you through our gospel, so that you may obtain the glory of our Lord Jesus Christ...Now may our Lord Jesus Christ himself, and God our Father, who loved us and gave us eternal comfort (Luther: ewigen Trost) and good hope through grace, comfort your hearts and establish them in every good work and word.
1 Pet. 2:9. You are a chosen race, a royal priesthood, a holy nation, God's own people... (Also Jn. 15:16, 1 Thess. 1:4, 2 Thess. 2:13; Ps. 65:4.)
2 Pet. 1:10–11. ...Confirm your call and election (Luther: Erwählung), for if you do this...there will be richly provided for you an entrance into the eternal kingdom of our Lord and Savior Jesus Christ.

Ps. 16:9. Therefore my heart is glad... (Luther: Darum freuet sich mein Herz...)
Is. 25:9. It will be said on that day, "Lo, this is our God; we have waited for him, that he might save us. This is the Lord; we have waited for him; let us be glad and rejoice in his salvation."
Is. 10:27. In that day his burden will depart from your shoulder (Luther: Zu der Zeit wird seine Last von deiner Schulter weichen müssen)...

Der dich so lange Zeit gedrücket.
Which thee so long (a) time hath-oppressed.
{Which hath oppressed thee for so long.}

Gott hat den liebsten Sohn,
God hath (his) dearest Son,
{God hat sent his dearest Son,}

Den er so hoch und teuer hält,
Whom he so high and dear doth-hold,
{Whom he doth regard so highly and dearly,}

Auf diese Welt geschicket.
Into this world sent.
{Into this world.}

Er läßt den Himmelsthron
He leaves - heaven's-throne

Und will die ganze Welt
And would the entire world

Aus ihren Sklavenketten
From its chains-of-slavery

Und ihrer Dienstbarkeit erretten.
And its servitude deliver.
{And would deliver the entire world from its chains of slavery and its servitude.}

O wundervolle Tat!
O wonderful deed!

Gott wird ein Mensch und will auf Erden
God becomes a man and desires on earth
{God becomes a man and is willing—upon this earth—}

Noch niedriger als wir und noch viel ärmer werden.
Even lowlier than we and yet much poorer to-become.
{To become even lowlier and much poorer than we.}

3. Alto Aria
●Christ's poverty has made us rich (151-3)
In Jesu Demut kann ich Trost,
In Jesus' lowliness can I comfort,
{In Jesus' lowliness can I find comfort,}

In seiner Armut Reichtum finden.
In his poverty, riches find.
{In his poverty, riches.}

Mir macht desselben schlechter Stand
For-me (means) his poor station
{For me, his poor station brings}

Gal. 4:4–5. When the time had fully come, God sent forth his Son, born of woman, born under the law, to redeem those who were under the law...

1 Jn. 4:9–10. In this the love of God was made manifest among us, that God sent his only Son into the world, so that we might live through him. In this is love, not that we loved God but that he loved us and sent his Son to be the expiation for our sins.

*Heb. 1:1–2, 5–6, 8. In many and various ways God spoke of old to our fathers by the prophets; but in these last days he has spoken to us by a Son, whom he appointed the heir of all things, through whom also he created the world...For to what angel did God ever say, "Thou art my Son, today I have begotten thee"? Or again, "I will be to him a father, and he shall be to me a son"? And again, when he brings the first-born into the world, he says, "Let all God's angels worship him."... Of the Son he says, "Thy throne, O God, is for ever and ever..."

Jn. 3:16. God so loved the world that he gave his only Son, that whoever believes in him should not perish but have eternal life.

Acts 13:38–39. ...Through this man forgiveness of sins is proclaimed to you, and by him every one that believes is freed from everything from which you could not be freed by the law of Moses. (Also Rev. 1:5.)

Gal. 5:1. For freedom Christ has set us free...

Jn. 8:36. If the Son makes you free, you will be free indeed.

Is. 40:1–2. Comfort, comfort my people, says your God. Speak tenderly to Jerusalem, and cry to her that her warfare (Luther: Ritterschaft; in later version: Dienstbarkeit) is ended, that her iniquity is pardoned...

Phil. 2:5–7. ...Christ Jesus...though he was in the form of God, did not count equality with God a thing to be grasped, but emptied himself, taking the form of a servant, being born in the likeness of men. (Also 2 Cor. 8:9.)

Is. 53:3. He was despised and rejected by men; a man of sorrows, and acquainted with grief...

Mt. 8:20. Jesus said... "Foxes have holes, and birds of the air have nests; but the Son of man has nowhere to lay his head." (Also Lk. 9:58.)

Ps. 22:6–8. I am a worm, and no man; scorned by men, and despised by the people. All who see me mock at me, they make mouths at me, they wag their heads; "He committed his cause to the Lord; let him deliver him, let him rescue him, for he delights in him!" [For Messianic application of this passage see Mt. 27:39–43, Mk. 15:29–32.]

Lk. 2:7. [Mary] gave birth to her first-born son and wrapped him in swaddling cloths, and laid him in a manger, because there was no place for them in the inn.

2 Cor. 8:9. You know the grace of our Lord Jesus Christ, that though he was rich, yet for your sake he became poor, so that by his poverty you might become rich.

*Jn. 1:14. The Word became flesh and dwelt among us...

Heb. 2:14–15. Since...the children share in flesh and blood, [Christ] himself likewise partook of the same nature, that through death he might destroy him who has the power of death, that is, the devil, and deliver all those who through fear of death were subject to lifelong bondage.

Nur lauter   Heil   und   Wohl   bekannt,
Nought-but prosperity and well-being   -,

Ja, seine wundervolle Hand
Yes, his   wondrous   hand

Will mir   nur   Segenskränze winden.
Will for-me nought-but wreathes-of-blessing twine.
{Will twine nought but wreathes of blessing for me.}

4. Tenor Recit.
●Christ's condescension opened heaven for us (151–4)
Du   teurer Gottessohn,
Thou precious Son-of-God,

Nun hast du mir den Himmel aufgemacht
Now hast thou for-me - heaven   opened
{Now hast thou opened heaven for me}

Und durch dein Niedrigsein
And through thy   low-estate

Das Licht der Seligkeit zuwege bracht.
The light of blessedness brought-about.
{Brought about the light of blessedness.}

Weil du nun ganz allein
Since thou now all   alone

Des Vaters Burg und Thron
The Father's citadel and throne

Aus   Liebe gegen uns verlassen,
Out-of love toward us didst-leave,

So wollen wir dich auch
So would we thee also
{So would we also hold thee}

Dafür   in unser Herze fassen.
For-this within our hearts hold.
{Within our hearts for this.}

5. Chorale
●Paradise reopened to us today (151–5)
Heut schleußt er wieder auf die Tür
Today unlocks he again   - the door
{Today he again unlocks the door}

Zum   schönen Paradeis,
To-that beautiful paradise,

Phil. 2:7–8. [Christ] emptied himself, taking the form of a servant, being born in the likeness of men. And being found in human form he humbled himself and became obedient unto death, even death on a cross.
Rom. 8:32. He who did not spare his own Son but gave him up for us all, will he not also give us all things with him?
Ps. 23:6. Surely goodness and mercy shall follow me all the days of my life...

Eph. 2:18. Through [Christ] we...have access in one Spirit to the Father. (Also Rom. 5:1–2.)
Heb. 9:15. He is the mediator of a new covenant, so that those who are called may receive the promised eternal inheritance, since a death has occurred which redeems them from the transgressions under the first covenant.
Heb. 9:1, 3, 11–12. ...The first covenant had regulations for worship and an earthly sanctuary...Behind the second curtain stood...the Holy of Holies...When Christ appeared as a high priest of the good things that have come, then through the greater and more perfect tent (not made with hands, that is, not of this creation) he entered once for all into the Holy Place, taking not the blood of goats and calves but his own blood, thus securing an eternal redemption.
Heb. 10:19–20, 22. ...Since we have confidence to enter the sanctuary by the blood of Jesus, by the new and living way which he opened for us through the curtain, that is, through his flesh...let us draw near with a true heart in full assurance of faith...
2 Cor. 4:6. For it is the God who said, "Let light shine out of darkness," who has shone in our hearts to give the light of the knowledge of the glory of God in the face of Christ.
*Jn. 1:4–5. In him was life, and the life was the light of men. The light shines in the darkness...
*Jn. 1:1, 14. In the beginning was the Word, and the Word was with God, and the Word was God...And the Word became flesh and dwelt among us...
Phil. 2:6–7. ...Though he was in the form of God, [Christ Jesus] did not count equality with God a thing to be grasped...emptied himself, taking the form of a servant, being born in the likeness of men. (Also Jn. 17:5.)
1 Jn. 4:19. We love, because he first loved us.
S. of S. 3:4 [Bride]: ...I found him whom my soul loves. I held him, and would not let him go... (Also Gen. 32:26.)
Eph. 3:17. That Christ may dwell in your hearts through faith...

Rom. 5:2. Through [Christ] we have obtained access to this grace in which we stand, and we rejoice in our hope of sharing the glory of God.
Gen. 3:17–19, 22–24. To Adam [God] said, "Because you have listened to the voice of your wife, and have eaten of the tree of which I commanded you, 'You shall not eat of it,' cursed is the ground because of you; in toil you shall eat of it all the days of your life; thorns and thistles it shall bring forth to you; and you shall eat the plants of the field." In the sweat of your face you shall eat bread till you return to the ground, for out of it you were taken; you are dust,

Der Cherub steht nicht mehr dafür,
The cherub stands   no   more before-it,
{The cherubim no longer stands before it;}

Gott   sei Lob,   Ehr   und Preis.
To-God be laud, honor, and praise.

BWV 152
Tritt auf die Glaubensbahn
(NBA I/3; BC A18)

1. S. after Christmas (BWV 152, 122, 28)
*Gal. 4:1–7 (Through Christ we come of age and are free from the law)
*Lk. 2:33–40 (Simeon and Hanna prophesy of Christ)
Librettist: Salomon Franck

1. Sinfonia

2. Bass Aria
●Cornerstone laid by God: don't stumble but believe! (152–2)
Tritt auf die Glaubensbahn,
Walk on the   path-of-faith:

Gott hat den Stein geleget,
God hath the   stone   laid,
{God hath laid the stone,}

Der   Zion hält und träget,
Which Zion holds and bears-up,
{Which holds and bears up Zion,}

   Mensch, stoße dich   nicht   dran!
(O) man,   hit   thyself not against-it!

Tritt auf die Glaubensbahn!
Walk on the   path-of-faith!

3. Bass Recit.
●Cornerstone laid in Israel for fall & rising of many (152–3)
Der Heiland   ist   gesetzt
The   Savior has-been established

In Israel zum Fall   und Auferstehen.
In Israel for   falling and   rising.

Der   edle Stein ist sonder Schuld,
(This) noble stone is   without   fault,

and to dust you shall return...Then the Lord God said, "Behold, the man has become like one of us, knowing good and evil; and now, lest he put forth his hand and take also of the tree of life, and eat, and live for ever"—therefore the Lord God sent him forth from the garden of Eden...He drove out the man; and at the east of the garden of Eden he placed the cherubim, and a flaming sword which turned every way, to guard the way to the tree of life.
Rev. 2:7 [Christ]: ...To him who conquers I will grant to eat of the tree of life, which is in the paradise of God. (Also Rev. 22:1–3.)

Is. 28:16. Thus says the Lord God, "Behold, I am laying in Zion for a foundation a stone, a tested stone, a precious cornerstone, of a sure foundation: 'He who believes will not be in haste.'"
Ps. 118:22–23. The stone which the builders rejected has become the head of the corner. This is the Lord's doing; it is marvelous in our eyes.
Is. 8:14–15. He will become a sanctuary, and a stone of offense, and a rock of stumbling to both houses of Israel, a trap and a snare to the inhabitants of Jerusalem. And many shall stumble thereon; they shall fall and be broken; they shall be snared and taken.
Mt. 21:44 [Christ]: He who falls on this stone will be broken to pieces; but when it falls on any one, it will crush him.
1 Pet. 2:6–8. It stands in scripture: "Behold, I am laying in Zion a stone, a cornerstone chosen and precious, and he who believes in him will not be put to shame." To you therefore who believe, he is precious, but for those who do not believe, "The very stone which the builders rejected has become the head of the corner," and "A stone that will make men stumble, a rock that will make them fall"; for they stumble because they disobey the word, as they were destined to do.
1 Cor. 3:11. No other foundation can any one lay than that which is laid, which is Jesus Christ.
Eph. 2:19–21. ...You are no longer strangers and sojourners, but you are fellow citizens with the saints and members of the household of God, built upon the foundation of the apostles and prophets, Christ Jesus himself being the cornerstone, in whom the whole structure is joined together and grows into a holy temple in the Lord.

*Lk. 2:33–35. [Jesus'] father and mother marveled at what was said about him; and Simeon blessed them and said to Mary his mother, "Behold, this child is set for the fall and rising of many in Israel, and for a sign that is spoken against (and a sword will pierce through your own soul also), that thoughts out of many hearts may be revealed."
Mt. 21:42–44. Jesus said... "Have you never read in the scriptures: 'The very stone which the builders rejected has become the head of the corner; this was the Lord's doing, and it is marvelous in our eyes'?

Wenn sich die böse Welt
Even-if - the wicked world

So hart an ihm verletzt,
So severely against it injures (itself),
{Injures itself so severely against it,}

Ja, über ihn zur Höllen fällt,
Yes, over it into hell does-fall,
{Yes, falls over it into hell,}

Weil sie boshaftig an ihn rennet
Because it spitefully against it runs
{Because it runs spitefully against it}

Und Gottes Huld
And God's favor

Und Gnade nicht erkennet!
And grace (does) not acknowledge!
{And does not acknowledge God's favor and grace!}

Doch selig ist
But blessed is

Ein auserwählter Christ,
An elect Christian,

Der seinen Glaubensgrund auf diesen Eckstein leget,
Who his faith's-foundation upon this cornerstone lays,
{Who lays his faith's foundation upon this cornerstone,}

Weil er dadurch Heil und Erlösung findet.
For he thereby salvation and redemption finds.
{For he finds salvation and redemption thereby.}

4. Soprano Aria
●Prayer: Cornerstone, help me to find salvation in thee
(152-4)
    Stein, der über alle Schätze,
(O) stone, which surpasses all (other) treasures,

Hilf, daß ich zu aller Zeit
Help, that I at all times

Durch den Glauben auf dich setze
Through - faith upon thee would-set

Meinen Grund der Seligkeit
My foundation for salvation,
{Help, that through faith I would set my foundation for salvation upon thee at all times,}

Und mich nicht an dir verletze,
And myself not against thee would-injure,
{And would not injure myself against thee,}

    Stein, der über alle Schätze!
(O) stone, which surpasses all (other) treasures!

Therefore I tell you, the kingdom of God will be taken away from you and given to a nation producing the fruits of it. And he who falls on this stone will be broken to pieces; but when it falls on any one, it will crush him."
1 Cor. 1:22–24. For Jews demand signs and Greeks seek wisdom, but we preach Christ crucified, a stumbling block to Jews and folly to Gentiles, but to those who are called, both Jews and Greeks, Christ the power of God and the wisdom of God.
1 Pet. 2:7–8. To you therefore who believe, [Christ] is precious, but for those who do not believe, "The very stone which the builders rejected has become the head of the corner," and "A stone that will make men stumble, a rock that will make them fall"; for they stumble because they disobey the word, as they were destined to do.
Jn. 3:17–18. God sent the Son into the world, not to condemn the world, but that the world might be saved through him. He who believes in him is not condemned; he who does not believe is condemned already, because he has not believed in the name of the only Son of God.
Mt. 7:24–27 [Christ]: Every one then who hears these words of mine and does them will be like a wise man who built his house upon the rock; and the rain fell, and the floods came, and the winds blew and beat upon that house, but it did not fall, because it had been founded on the rock. And every one who hears these words of mine and does not do them will be like a foolish man who built his house upon the sand; and the rain fell, and the floods came, and the winds blew and beat against that house, and it fell; and great was the fall of it. (Also Lk. 6:46–49.)
Rom. 1:16–17. I am not ashamed of the gospel: it is the power of God for salvation to every one who has faith, to the Jew first and also to the Greek.
Eph. 2:19–21. So then you are no longer strangers and sojourners, but you are fellow citizens with the saints and members of the household of God, built upon the foundation of the apostles and prophets, Christ Jesus himself being the cornerstone, in whom the whole structure is joined together and grows into a holy temple in the Lord.

1 Pet. 2:7. To you therefore who believe, he is precious...
Mt. 21:42–44 [Christ]: ...The very stone which the builders rejected has become the head of the corner; this was the Lord's doing, and it is marvelous in our eyes...The kingdom of God will be taken away from you and given to a nation producing the fruits of it. And he who falls on this stone will be broken to pieces; but when it falls on any one, it will crush him.
Mt. 16:15–18. [Jesus] said to them, "But who do you say that I am?" Simon Peter replied, "You are the Christ, the Son of the living God." And Jesus answered him, "Blessed are you, Simon Bar-Jona! For flesh and blood has not revealed this to you, but my Father who is in heaven." And I tell you, you are Peter, and on this rock I will build my church, and the powers of death shall not prevail against it.
Mt. 11:6 [Christ]: Blessed is he who takes no offense at me. (Also Lk. 7:23.)
Jn. 3:16. God so loved the world that he gave his only Son, that whoever believes in him should not perish but have eternal life.
Heb. 10:38–39 [God]: My righteous one shall live by faith, and if he shrinks back, my soul has no pleasure in him. But we are not of those who shrink back and are destroyed, but of those who have faith and keep their souls.

5. Bass Recit.
●Foolishness of God is greater than wisdom of world (152-5)
Es   ärgre sich die kluge Welt,
(Let) offence-take the clever world,
{Let the clever world take offence}

Daß Gottes Sohn
That God's Son

Verläßt   den hohen Ehrenthron,
Does-leave (his) lofty throne-of-honor,
{Leaves his lofty throne of honor,}

Daß er in Fleisch und Blut   sich   kleidet
That he in flesh   and blood himself does-clothe

Und   in der   Menschenheit leidet.
And (as a member of) humanity does-suffer.

Die größte Weisheit dieser Erden
The greatest wisdom of-this earth

Muß   vor   des Höchsten   Rat
Must before the Most-High's counsel
{Must—before the counsel of the Most High—}

Zur größten Torheit   werden.
The greatest foolishness become.
{Become the greatest foolishness.}

Was Gott beschlossen hat,
What God (ordained) has,
{What God has ordained,}

Kann die Vernunft doch nicht ergründen;
Can - reason indeed not   fathom;

Die blinde Leiterin verführt die geistlich Blinden.
That blind guide misleads the spiritually blind.
{That blind guide misleads those who are spiritually blind.}

6. Soprano & Bass Duet
●Dialogue (Soul & Jesus): How must Jesus be received?
(152-6)
Soul (Soprano):
Wie soll ich dich, Liebster der Seelen, umfassen?
How shall I   thee, dearest of   souls,   embrace?
{How shall I embrace thee, O dearest of souls?}

Bass (Jesus):
Du mußt dich verleugnen und alles   verlassen!
Thou must thyself renounce and   all (else) forsake!

1 Tim. 3:16. Great indeed, we confess, is the mystery of our religion: [Christ] was manifested in the flesh, vindicated in the Spirit, seen by angels, preached among the nations, believed on in the world, taken up in glory.
1 Cor. 1:22-24. Jews demand signs and Greeks seek wisdom, but we preach Christ crucified, a stumbling block to Jews and folly to Gentiles, but to those who are called, both Jews and Greeks, Christ the power of God and the wisdom of God.
Heb. 2:14-15. Since...the children share in flesh and blood, [Christ] himself likewise partook of the same nature that through death he might destroy him who has the power of death, that is, the devil, and deliver all those who through fear of death were subject to lifelong bondage.
1 Jn. 4:2-3. By this you know the Spirit of God: every spirit which confesses that Jesus Christ has come in the flesh is of God, and every spirit which does not confess Jesus is not of God. This is the spirit of antichrist, of which you heard that it was coming, and now it is in the world already. (Also 2 Jn. 1:7.)
1 Cor. 1:25-29. The foolishness of God is wiser than men, and the weakness of God is stronger than men. For consider your call, brethren; not many of you were wise according to worldly standards, not many were powerful, not many were of noble birth; but God chose what is foolish in the world to shame the wise, God chose what is weak in the world to shame the strong, God chose what is low and despised in the world, even things that are not, to bring to nothing things that are, so that no human being might boast in the presence of God.
Mt. 11:25-26. At that time Jesus declared, "I thank thee, Father, Lord of heaven and earth, that thou hast hidden these things from the wise and understanding and revealed them to babes; yea, Father, for such was thy gracious will."
Ps. 33:11. The counsel of the Lord stands for ever, the thoughts of his heart to all generations.
Prov. 3:5. Trust in the Lord with all your heart, and do not rely on your own insight.
1 Cor. 3:18-19. Let no one deceive himself. If any one among you thinks that he is wise in this age, let him become a fool that he may become wise. For the wisdom of this world is folly with God...
Prov. 14:12. There is a way which seems right to a man, but its end is the way to death. (Also Prov. 16:25.)
Lk. 6:39. Can a blind man lead a blind man? Will they not both fall into a pit? (Also Mt. 15:14.)

Hos. 2:20 [God]: I will betroth you to me in faithfulness; and you shall know the Lord. (Also 2 Cor. 11:2.)
S. of S. 3:4 [Bride]: ...I found him whom my soul loves. I held him, and would not let him go... (Also Gen. 32:26.)
Rev. 3:11. ...Hold fast what you have, so that no one may seize your crown.
Phil. 3:7-8. But whatever gain I had, I counted as loss for the sake of Christ. Indeed I count everything as loss because of the surpassing worth of knowing Christ Jesus my Lord. For his sake I have suffered the loss of all things, and count them as refuse, in order that I may gain Christ.
Mk. 10:17, 21. ....A man ran up and knelt before [Jesus], and asked him, "Good Teacher, what must I do to inherit eternal life?"...Jesus looking upon him loved him, and said to him, "You lack one thing; go sell what you have, and give to the poor...and come, follow me." (Also Mt. 19:16-21, Lk. 18:18-22.)

Wie soll ich erkennen das ewige Licht?
How shall I recognize the eternal light?

Erkenne mich gläubig und ärgre dich nicht!
Recognize me in-faith and take-offence not!
{Recognize me in faith and do not take offence!}

Komm, lehre mich, Heiland die Erde verschmähen!
Come,   teach   me,   Savior, the earth   to-despise!

Komm, Seele, durch Leiden, zur Freude zu gehen!
Come,   Soul, through suffering into   joy   to go!
{Come, O Soul, through suffering thou wilt enter joy!}

Ach, ziehe mich, Liebster, so folg ich dir nach!
Ah,   draw   me,   beloved, so follow I thee - !
{Ah, draw me, beloved, and I will follow thee!}

Dir   schenk ich die Krone
To-thee grant   I the crown
{To thee will I grant the crown}

nach Trübsal und Schmach.
after tribulation and humiliation.

Mt. 10:38 [Christ]: He who does not take his cross and follow me is not worthy of me.

Lk. 9:23-26. And [Jesus] said to all, "If any man would come after me, let him deny himself and take up his cross daily and follow me. For whoever would save his life will lose it; and whoever loses his life for my sake, he will save it. For what does it profit a man if he gains the whole world and loses or forfeits himself? For whoever is ashamed of me and of my words, of him will the Son of man be ashamed when he comes in his glory and the glory of the Father and of the holy angels." (Also Mk. 8:34-38, Mt. 16:24-27.)

Rom. 1:16-17. I am not ashamed of the gospel: it is the power of God for salvation to every one who has faith, to the Jew first and also to the Greek.

1 Cor. 1:22-24. Jews demand signs and Greeks seek wisdom, but we preach Christ crucified, a stumbling block to Jews and folly to Gentiles, but to those who are called, both Jews and Greeks, Christ the power of God and the wisdom of God.

Jn. 1:9-12. The true light that enlightens every man was coming into the world. He was in the world...yet the world knew him not. He came to his own home, and his own people received him not. But to all who received him, who believed in his name, he gave power to become children of God. (Also Jn. 3:19, 8:12, 9:5, 11:9, 12:35-36, 46, Ps. 36:9.)

Mt. 11:2-6. When John heard in prison about the deeds of the Christ, he sent word..."Are you he who is to come, or shall we look for another?" And Jesus answered..."Go and tell John what you hear and see: the blind receive their sight...and blessed is he who takes no offense at me (Luther: der sich nicht an mir ärgert)." (Also Lk. 7:20-23.)

Jms. 4:4. ...Do you not know that friendship with the world is enmity with God? Therefore whoever wishes to be a friend of the world makes himself an enemy of God.

1 Jn. 2:15. Do not love the world or the things in the world. If any one loves the world, love for the Father is not in him.

Rom. 8:18. I consider that the sufferings (Luther: Leiden) of this present time are not worth comparing with the glory that is to be revealed to us. (Also 2 Cor. 4:17.)

Mt. 8:19. A scribe came up and said to [Jesus], "Teacher, I will follow you wherever you go."

S. of S. 1:4. Draw me after you, let us make haste... (Luther: Zieh mich dir nach, so laufen wir) (Also Jer. 31:3.)

Jn. 6:43-44. Jesus answered them, "...No one can come to me unless the Father who sent me draws (Luther: ziehe) him; and I will raise him up at the last day." (Also Jn. 12:30, 32.)

Acts 14:22. ...Through many tribulations we must enter the kingdom of God.

Jms. 1:12. Blessed is the man who endures trial, for when he has stood the test he will receive the crown of life which God has promised to those who love him. (Also 2 Tim. 4:8, 1 Pet. 5:4, Rev. 2:10.)

BWV 153
Schau, lieber Gott, wie meine Feind
(NBA I/4; BC A25)

1. S. after New Year (BWV 153, 58, 248-V)
*1 Pet. 4:12-19 (Sharing the sufferings of Christ)
*Mt. 2:13-23 (Mary & Joseph's flight to Eygpt)
Librettist: Unknown

1. Chorale
●Prayer: Behold my foes; without thy help I am ruined! (153-1)

Schau, lieber Gott, wie meine Feind,
Behold, dear God, how my foes,

Damit ich stets muß kämpfen,
With-whom I ever must battle,

So listig und so mächtig seind,
So cunning and so mighty are,

Daß sie mich leichtlich dämpfen!
That they me easily subdue!
{That they easily subdue me!}

Herr, wo mich deine Gnad nicht hält,
Lord, if me thy grace (doth) not hold,
{Lord, if thy grace doth not sustain me,}

So kann der Teufel, Fleisch und Welt
Then can the devil, flesh, and world
{Then the devil, flesh, and world can}

Mich leicht in Unglück stürzen.
Me easily into disaster hurl.
{Easily hurl me into disaster.}

2. Alto Recit.
●Prayer for help in face of lions & dragons (153-2)

Mein liebster Gott, ach laß dich's doch erbarmen,
My dearest God, ah, let thyself please show-mercy,
{My dearest God, ah, please show mercy to me,}

Ach hilf doch, hilf mir Armen!
Ah, do-help, help (this) poor-wretch!

Ich wohne hier bei lauter Löwen und bei Drachen,
I dwell here amidst (many) lions and amidst dragons,

Und diese wollen mir durch Wut und Grimmigkeit
And these seek - by (their) rage and ferocity

Ps. 3:1. O Lord, how many are my foes!...
Ps. 25:19. Consider how many are my foes, and with what violent hatred they hate me. (Also Ps. 38:19, 43:1-2, 55:1-4, 56:12, 59:1-3.)
*1 Pet. 4:12-14, 16. Beloved, do not be surprised at the fiery ordeal which comes upon you to prove you, as though something strange were happening to you. But rejoice in so far as you share Christ's sufferings, that you may also rejoice and be glad when his glory is revealed. If you are reproached for the name of Christ, you are blessed, because the spirit of glory and of God rests upon you...If one suffers as a Christian, let him not be ashamed, but under that name let him glorify God.
Ps. 31:13. Yea, I hear the whispering of many—terror on every side!—as they scheme together against me, as they plot to take my life. (Also Ps. 38:12, 19.)
Ps. 62:4. They only plan to thrust (a man) down (Luther: wie sie ihn dämpfen)...
Ps. 124:2-3. If it had not been the Lord who was on our side, when men rose up against us, then they would have swallowed us up alive...
1 Jn. 5:19. ...The whole world is in the power of the evil one.
Eph. 6:11-12. Put on the whole armor of God, that you may be able to stand against the wiles of the devil. For we are not contending against flesh and blood, but against the principalities, against the powers, against the world rulers of this present darkness, against the spiritual hosts of wickedness in the heavenly places. (Also 1 Pet. 5:8, 2 Cor. 10:3-4, Phil. 1:28-30.)
Jms. 4:1. What causes wars, and what causes fightings among you? Is it not your passions that are at war in your members?
1 Pet. 2:11. ...The passions of the flesh...wage war against your soul. (Also Gal. 5:17.)
Jn. 15:18-19 [Christ]: If the world hates you, know that it has hated me before it hated you. If you were of the world, the world would love its own; but because you are not of the world, but I chose you out of the world, therefore the world hates you. (Also Jn. 17:14, Mt. 5:10-12, 10:24-25, 1 Jn. 3:13.)

Ps. 70:5. I am poor and needy; hasten to me, O God! Thou art my help and my deliverer; O Lord, do not tarry! (Also Ps. 40:17, 86:1.)
Ps. 59:1-3. Deliver me from my enemies, O my God, protect me from those who rise up against me, deliver me from those who work evil, and save me from bloodthirsty men. For, lo, they lie in wait for my life; fierce men band themselves against me...
Ps. 7:2. ...Like a lion they rend me, dragging me away, with none to rescue.
Ps. 17:12. They are like a lion eager to tear, as a young lion lurking in ambush. (Also Sirach 25:15-16.)
Ps. 22:13, 19-21. They open wide their mouths at me, like a ravening and roaring lion...But thou, O Lord, be not far off! O thou my help, hasten to my aid! Deliver my soul from the sword, my life from the

In kurzer Zeit
In short (order)

Den Garaus völlig machen.
(My) final-ruin fully to-complete.

3. Bass Arioso
●Fear not, I am with thee: Is. 41:10 (153–3)
Fürchte dich nicht, ich bin mit dir. Weiche nicht,
Fear - not, I am with you. (Waver) not,

ich bin dein Gott; ich stärke dich, ich
I am your God; I (will) strengthen you, I (will)

helfe dir auch durch die rechte Hand meiner Gerechtigkeit.
help you also by the right hand of-my righteousness.

4. Tenor Recit.
●Prayer for help in face of growing threat from foes (153–4)
Du sprichst zwar, lieber Gott, zu meiner Seelen Ruh
Thou dost-speak indeed, dear God, unto my soul's rest,

Mir einen Trost in meinen Leiden zu.
To-me a (word of) comfort in my suffering - .
{Dear God, in my suffering thou dost speak a word of comfort
unto my soul's rest.}

Ach, aber meine Plage
Ah, but my trouble

Vergrößert sich von Tag zu Tage,
Increases - from day to day,

Denn meiner Feinde sind so viel,
For my foes are so many;

Mein Leben ist ihr Ziel,
My life is their aim,

Ihr Bogen wird auf mich gespannt,
Their bows are against me drawn,
{Their bows are drawn against me,}

Sie richten ihre Pfeile zum Verderben,
They prepare their arrows for destruction,

Ich soll von ihren Händen sterben;
I am by their hands to-die;
{I am to die by their hands;}

Gott! meine Not ist dir bekannt,
God! My distress is to-thee known,
{O God! My distress is known to thee,}

Die ganze Welt wird mir zur Marterhöhle;
The whole world becomes for-me a den-of-torture;
{The whole world becomes a den of torture for me;}

power of the dog! Save me from the mouth of the lion, my afflicted soul from the horns of the wild oxen! (Also 1 Pet. 5:8.)
Ps. 38:12. Those who seek my life lay their snares, those who seek my hurt speak of ruin, and meditate treachery all the day long.

Is. 41:8–11. But you, Israel, my servant, Jacob, whom I have chosen, the offspring of Abraham, my friend; you whom I took from the ends of the earth, and called from its farthest corners, saying to you, "You are my servant, I have chosen you and not cast you off"; *fear not, for I am with you, be not dismayed, for I am your God; I will strengthen you, I will help you, I will uphold you with my victorious right hand.* Behold, all who are incensed against you shall be put to shame and confounded; those who strive against you shall be as nothing and shall perish.

Is. 41:10 [God]: Fear not, for I am with you, be not dismayed, for I am your God...
Is. 30:15. Thus said the Lord God, the Holy One of Israel, "In returning and rest you shall be saved; in quietness and in trust shall be your strength." (Also Ps. 46:10–11.)
Mt. 11:28–29 [Christ]: Come to me, all who labor and are heavy laden, and I will give you rest. Take my yoke upon you, and learn from me; for I am gentle and lowly in heart, and you will find rest for your souls. (Also Jer. 6:16.)
2 Cor. 1:3–5. Blessed be the God and Father of our Lord Jesus Christ, the Father of mercies and God of all comfort, who comforts us in all our affliction...For as we share abundantly in Christ's sufferings, so through Christ we share abundantly in comfort too.
Ps. 69:3–4. ...My eyes grow dim with waiting for my God. More in number than the hairs of my head are those who hate me without cause...
Ps. 54:1–3. Save me, O God, by thy name, and vindicate me by thy might. Hear my prayer, O God; give ear to the words of my mouth. For insolent men have risen against me, ruthless men seek my life; they do not set God before them.
Ps. 86:14. O God, insolent men have risen up against me; a band of ruthless men seek my life, and they do not set thee before them.
Ps. 38:12. Those who seek my life lay their snares, those who seek my hurt speak of ruin, and meditate treachery all the day long. (Also 1 Kings 19:10, 14, Ps. 35:4, 40:14, 70:2.)
Ps. 11:2. Lo, the wicked bend the bow, they have fitted their arrow to the string, to shoot in the dark at the upright in heart. (Also Ps. 37:14.)
Ps. 57:4. I lie in the midst of lions that greedily devour the sons of men; their teeth are spears and arrows, their tongues sharp swords. (Also Is. 5:28–29.)
Ps. 140:4. Guard me, O Lord, from the hands of the wicked... (Also Ps. 82:4.)
Lam. 3:59–60. Thou hast seen the wrong done to me, O Lord; judge thou my cause. Thou hast seen all their vengeance, all their devices against me.
***1 Pet. 4:19.** ...Let those who suffer according to God's will do right and entrust their souls to a faithful Creator.
Ps. 30:10. Hear, O Lord, and be gracious to me! O Lord, be thou my helper!

Hilf, Helfer, hilf! errette meine Seele!
Help, Helper, help! Deliver   my   soul!

5. Chorale
●God's purposes prevail despite opposition of devils (153-5)
Und ob gleich alle Teufel
And even-though all devils

Dir wollten widerstehn,
You would   oppose,
{Would oppose you,}

So wird   doch   ohne Zweifel
So will   nevertheless without doubt
{So will God nonetheless}

Gott nicht zurücke gehn;
God not   retreat;
{Never retreat;}

Was   er ihm fürgenommen
Whatever he - has-undertaken

Und was   er haben will,
And whatever he would-have,

Das muß doch endlich kommen
That must indeed finally   come (around)

Zu seinem Zweck und Ziel.
To   his   purpose and goal.

6. Tenor Aria
●Storms defied; God has promised to be with me (153-6)
Stürmt nur, stürmt, ihr   Trübsalswetter,
Storm then, storm, ye tempests-of-tribulation,

Wallt, ihr Fluten, auf mich los!
Seethe, ye torrents, upon me forth!
{Proceed, then, ye torrents, to seethe down upon me!}

Schlagt, ihr Unglücksflammen,
Beat,   ye flames-of-misfortune,

Über mich zusammen,
Above me   together,
{Beat down upon me, ye flames of misfortune,}

Stört,   ihr Feinde, meine Ruh,
Disturb, ye foes,   my rest,
{If ye disturb my rest, O my foes,}

Spricht mir doch Gott tröstlich zu:
Says   to-me indeed God comfortingly - :
{Then God says comfortingly to me:}

Ps. 54:4. Behold, God is my helper; the Lord is the upholder of my life.

1 Pet. 5:8-9. ...Your adversary the devil prowls around like a roaring lion, seeking some one to devour. Resist him, firm in your faith, knowing that the same experience of suffering is required of your brotherhood throughout the world.
Eph. 6:12. We are not contending against flesh and blood, but against the principalities, against the powers, against the world rulers of this present darkness, against the spiritual hosts of wickedness in the heavenly places.
Ps. 37:12-13. The wicked plots against the righteous, and gnashes his teeth at him; but the Lord laughs at the wicked, for he sees that his day is coming.
1 Jn. 3:8. He who commits sin is of the devil; for the devil has sinned from the beginning. The reason the Son of God appeared was to destroy the works of the devil.
Ps. 27:1, 3. The Lord is my light and my salvation (Luther: Heil); whom shall I fear? The Lord is the stronghold of my life; of whom shall I be afraid?...Though a host encamp against me, my heart shall not fear; though war arise against me, yet I will be confident. (Also Ps. 118:6.)
Rom. 8:31, 35-37. ...If God is for us, who is against us?...Who shall separate us from the love of Christ? Shall tribulation, or distress, or persecution, or famine, or nakedness, or peril, or sword? As it is written, "For thy sake we are being killed all the day long; we are regarded as sheep to be slaughtered." No, in all these things we are more than conquerors through him who loved us.
Is. 14:27. The Lord of hosts has purposed, and who will annul it? His hand is stretched out, and who will turn it back?
Is. 43:13. I am God...There is none who can deliver from my hand; I work and who can hinder it? (Also Job 9:12, 11:10, 42:2-3.)

*****1 Pet. 4:12-13.** Beloved, do not be surprised at the fiery ordeal which comes upon you to prove you, as though something strange were happening to you. But rejoice in so far as you share Christ's sufferings, that you may also rejoice and be glad when his glory is revealed. (Also Jms. 1:2-4, 12.)
Ps. 57:1. ...O God...in the shadow of thy wings I will take refuge, till the storms of destruction pass by.
Ps. 124:1, 4-5. If it had not been the Lord who was on our side...then the flood would have swept us away, the torrent would have gone over us; then over us would have gone the raging waters.
Rev. 2:10 [Christ]: Do not fear what you are about to suffer. Behold, the devil is about to throw some of you into prison, that you may be tested, and for ten days you will have tribulation....
Ps. 118:6-7. With the Lord on my side I do not fear. What can man do to me? The Lord is on my side to help me; I shall look in triumph on those who hate me.
Rom. 8:35, 37. Who shall separate us from the love of Christ? Shall tribulation, or distress, or persecution, or famine, or nakedness, or peril, or sword?...No, in all these things we are more than conquerors through him who loved us.

Ich bin dein Hort und Erretter.
I am your refuge and deliverer.

7. Bass Recit.
●Sufferings of Christchild gives us courage (153-7)
Getrost! mein Herz,
Courage! My heart,

Erdulde deinen Schmerz,
Endure thy pain,

Laß dich dein Kreuz nicht unterdrücken!
Let thee thy cross not crush!
{Let not thy cross crush thee!}

Gott wird dich schon
God will thee indeed

Zu rechter Zeit erquicken;
At-the proper time refresh;
{God will indeed refresh thee at the proper time;}

Muß doch sein lieber Sohn,
Must indeed his dear Son,
{Remember that his dear Son—}

Dein Jesus, in noch zarten Jahren
Thy Jesus, in yet tender years
{Thy Jesus—while still at a tender age,}

Viel größre Not erfahren,
Much greater affliction experience,
{Had to experience much greater affliction,}

Da ihm der Wüterich Herodes
When him the tyrant Herod
{When the tyrant Herod}

Die äußerste Gefahr des Todes
The gravest peril of death
{Threatened him with the gravest peril of death}

Mit mörderischen Fäusten droht!
With murderous fists threatens!
{With murderous fists!}

Kaum kömmt er auf die Erden,
Scarce comes he to - earth,
{Scarce had he come to earth,}

So muß er schon ein Flüchtling werden!
Then must he already a fugitive become!
{When he already had to become a fugitive!}

Wohlan, mit Jesu tröste dich
Come-then, with Jesus comfort thyself

Und glaube festiglich:
And believe steadfastly:

Ps. 18:2. The Lord is my rock, and my fortress, and my deliverer (Luther: Erretter), my God, my rock (Luther: Hort), in whom I take refuge, my shield, and the horn of my salvation, my stronghold.

Jms. 1:2-4, 12. Count it all joy, my brethren, when you meet various trials, for you know that the testing of your faith produces steadfastness. And let steadfastness have its full effect, that you may be perfect and complete, lacking in nothing...Blessed is the man who endures trial, for when he has stood the test he will receive the crown of life which God has promised to those who love him.
Rom. 12:12. Rejoice in your hope, be patient in tribulation, be constant in prayer.
Mk. 8:34 [Christ]: ...If any man would come after me, let him deny himself and take up his cross and follow me. (Also Mt. 16:24.)
Mt. 10:38 [Christ]: He who does not take his cross and follow me is not worthy of me. (Also Lk. 9:23.)
1 Pet. 5:10. After you have suffered a little while, the God of all grace, who has called you to his eternal glory in Christ, will himself restore, establish, and strengthen you.
Ps. 30:5. ...Weeping may tarry for the night, but joy comes with the morning.
Lam. 3:31-33. For the Lord will not cast off for ever, but, though he cause grief, he will have compassion according to the abundance of his steadfast love; for he does not willingly afflict or grieve the sons of men.
Heb. 12:3. Consider him who endured from sinners such hostility against himself, so that you may not grow weary or fainthearted.
1 Pet. 4:1. Since therefore Christ suffered in the flesh, arm yourselves with the same thought...
1 Pet. 2:21. For to this you have been called, because Christ also suffered for you, leaving you an example, that you should follow in his steps.
*Mt. 2:13-16. When [the wise men] had departed [from Bethlehem after worshipping the Christchild], behold, an angel of the Lord appeared to Joseph in a dream and said, "Rise, take the child and his mother, and flee to Egypt, and remain there till I tell you; for Herod is about to search for the child, to destroy him." And he rose and took the child and his mother by night, and departed to Egypt, and remained there until the death of Herod. This was to fulfil what the Lord had spoken by the prophet, "Out of Egypt have I called my son." Then Herod, when he saw that he had been tricked by the wise men, was in a furious rage, and he sent and killed all the male children in Bethlehem and in all that region who were two years old or under, according to the time which he had ascertained from the wise men.
*1 Pet. 4:12-13. Beloved, do not be surprised at the fiery ordeal which comes upon you to prove you, as though something strange were happening to you. But rejoice in so far as you share Christ's sufferings, that you may also rejoice and be glad when his glory is revealed.
2 Cor. 1:5. For as we share abundantly in Christ's sufferings, so through Christ we share abundantly in comfort too.
2 Tim. 2:11-12. The saying is sure: If we have died with him, we shall also live with him; if we endure, we shall also reign with him... (Also Rom. 8:17, 1 Pet. 4:13.)

Denjenigen, die hier mit Christo leiden,
To-those   who here with Christ suffer,

Will er das Himmelreich bescheiden.
Would he the kingdom-of-heaven apportion.

8. Alto Aria
●Suffering ends in heaven where it changes to rapture (153–8)
Soll ich meinen Lebenslauf
If   I   my   life's-course

Unter Kreuz und Trübsal   führen,
Amidst cross and tribulation (am-to-run),

Hört es   doch   im Himmel auf.
Ceases it nevertheless in heaven   - .
{It nevertheless ceases in heaven.}

Da   ist lauter Jubilieren,
In-that-place is sheer jubilation,

Daselbsten verwechselt mein Jesus das Leiden
There   transforms   my Jesus the suffering
{There my Jesus transforms suffering}

Mit seliger Wonne, mit ewigen Freuden.
Into blessed rapture, into eternal   joys.

9. Chorale
●Prayer: Help me to live faithfully until I reach heaven
(153–9)
Drum   will ich, weil ich lebe noch,
Therefore would I, while I live yet,
{Therefore would I, while I yet live,}

Das Kreuz dir fröhlich tragen nach;
The cross thee joyfully carry after;
{Joyfully follow after thee, bearing my cross;}

Mein Gott, mach mich darzu   bereit,
My   God, make me for-that prepared,
{My God, make me prepared for that,}

Es dient zum Besten allezeit!
It serves for-the best at-all-times!

///

Hilf mir mein Sach recht greifen an,
Help me my   affairs rightly to-undertake,

Daß ich mein' Lauf vollenden kann,
So-that I   my course can-complete,

Hilf mir auch zwingen Fleisch und Blut,
Help me also to-master flesh and blood,

Rev. 2:3 [Christ]: I know you are enduring patiently and bearing up for my name's sake, and you have not grown weary.
Mt. 5:10. Blessed are those who are persecuted for righteousness' sake, for theirs is the kingdom of heaven.

Lk. 6:20–23 [Christ]: Blessed are you poor, for yours is the kingdom of God. Blessed are you that hunger now, for you shall be satisfied. Blessed are you that weep now, for you shall laugh. Blessed are you when men hate you, and when they exclude you and revile you, and cast out your name as evil, on account of the Son of man! Rejoice in that day, and leap for joy, for behold, your reward is great in heaven... (Also Lk. 16:19–25.)
Rev. 21:1–4. [In my vision] I saw a new heaven and a new earth; for the first heaven and the first earth had passed away, and the sea was no more. And I saw the holy city, new Jerusalem, coming down out of heaven from God, prepared as a bride adorned for her husband; and I heard a loud voice from the throne saying, "Behold, the dwelling of God is with men. He will dwell with them, and they shall be his people, and God himself will be with them; he will wipe away every tear from their eyes, and death shall be no more, neither shall there be mourning nor crying nor pain any more, for the former things have passed away." (Also Is. 25:8. Rev. 7:15–17.)
Jer. 31:13 [God]: Then shall the maidens rejoice in the dance, and the young men and the old shall be merry. I will turn their mourning into joy, I will comfort them, and give them gladness for sorrow. (Also Ps. 30:11, 126:5–6, Jn. 16:20.)

Mk. 8:34 [Christ]: ...If any man would come after me, let him deny himself and take up his cross and follow me. (Also Mt. 10:38, 16:24, Lk. 9:23.)
2 Tim. 2:3, 11–12. Share in suffering as a good soldier of Christ Jesus ...The saying is sure: If we have died with him, we shall also live with him; if we endure, we shall also reign with him; if we deny him, he also will deny us.
Heb. 12:11. For the moment all discipline seems painful rather than pleasant; later it yields the peaceful fruit of righteousness to those who have been trained by it. (Also Rom. 5:3–5, Jms. 1:2–4.)
Rom. 8:28. We know that in everything God works for good (Luther: alle Dinge zum Besten dienen) with those who love him, who are called according to his purpose. (Also Ps. 18:30.)

2 Tim. 4:6–8. I am already on the point of being sacrificed; the time of my departure has come. I have fought the good fight, I have finished the race (Luther: Lauf vollendet), I have kept the faith. Henceforth there is laid up for me the crown of righteousness, which the Lord, the righteous judge, will award to me on that Day, and not only to me but also to all who have loved his appearing. (Also 1 Pet. 5:4, Jms. 1:12, Rev. 2:10.)
Mk. 14:38 [Christ]: Watch and pray that you may not enter into temptation; the spirit indeed is willing, but the flesh is weak. (Also Mt. 26:41.)
Gal. 5:16–17. ...Walk by the Spirit, and do not gratify the desires of

Für Sünd und Schanden mich behüt!
From sin and disgrace me protect!
{From sin and disgrace protect me!}

///

(For this chorale stanza see also 3–6.)
Erhalt mein Herz im Glauben rein,
Preserve my heart in faith pure,
{Preserve my heart pure in faith,}

So leb und sterb ich dir allein;
So live and die I to-thee alone;
{Thus will I live and die to thee alone;}

Jesu, mein Trost, hör mein Begier,
Jesu, my comfort, hear my longing,

O mein Heiland, wär ich bei dir!
O my Savior, were I with thee!

the flesh. For the desires of the flesh are against the Spirit, and the desires of the Spirit are against the flesh; for these are opposed to each other, to prevent you from doing what you would. (Also Rom. 8:9–11.)

Ps. 86:11. Teach me thy way, O Lord, that I may walk in thy truth; unite my heart (Luther: erhalte mein Herz) to fear thy name.
1 Thess. 5:23. May the God of peace himself sanctify you wholly; and may your spirit and soul and body be kept sound and blameless at the coming of our Lord Jesus Christ.
Jude 1:24. Now to him who is able to keep you from falling and to present you without blemish before the presence of his glory with rejoicing...
Rom. 14:7–8. None of us lives to himself, and none of us dies to himself. If we live, we live to the Lord, and if we die, we die to the Lord; so then, whether we live or whether we die, we are the Lord's.
2 Cor. 5:8–9. ...We would rather be away from the body and at home with the Lord...Whether we are at home or away, we make it our aim to please him.
Phil. 1:21. For to me to live is Christ, and to die is gain.

BWV 154
Mein liebster Jesus ist verloren
(NBA I/5; BC A29)

1. S. after Epiphany (BWV 154, 124, 32)
*Rom. 12:1–6[1] (Christian duty: present yourselves as living sacrifices to God)
*Lk. 2:41–52 (The twelve-year-old Jesus in the temple)
[1]End: "given to us."
Librettist: Unknown

1. Tenor Aria
●Jesus is gone; this brings despair to my soul! (154-1)
Mein liebster Jesus ist verloren:
My dearest Jesus is (vanished):
{My dearest Jesus has vanished:}

O Wort, das mir Verzweiflung bringt,
O word that to-me despair does-bring,
{O word that brings me despair,}

O Schwert, das durch die Seele dringt,
O sword that through the soul pierces,
{O sword that pierces through my soul,}

O Donnerwort in meinen Ohren.
O thunderous-word in my ears.

2. Tenor Recit.
●Jesus is gone; where might I find him whom I love? (154-2)
Wo treff ich meinen Jesum an,
Where meet I my Jesus - ?
{Where can I find Jesus?}

*Lk. 2:41–46. Now [Jesus'] parents went to Jerusalem every year at the feast of the Passover. And when he was twelve years old, they went up according to custom; and when the feast was ended, as they were returning, the boy Jesus stayed behind in Jerusalem. His parents did not know it, but supposing him to be in the company they went a day's journey, and they sought him among their kinsfolk and acquaintances; and when they did not find him, they returned to Jerusalem, seeking him. After three days they found him in the temple...
Lk. 2:34–35. [When his parents had brought Jesus to the temple to present him to the Lord as an infant] Simeon...said to Mary his mother, "Behold, this child is set for the fall and rising of many in Israel, and for a sign that is spoken against (and a sword will pierce through your own soul also), that thoughts out of many hearts may be revealed."
Job 23:3. Oh, that I knew where I might find him...
Ps. 22:2. O my God, I cry by day, but thou dost not answer; and by night, but find no rest.

*Lk. 2:43–45. ...The boy Jesus stayed behind in Jerusalem. His parents did not know it, but supposing him to be in the company they went a day's journey, and they sought him among their kinsfolk and acquaintances; and when they did not find him, they returned to Jerusalem, seeking him.
Job 23:3. Oh, that I knew where I might find him...

Wer zeiget mir die Bahn,
Who will-show me the way,

Wo meiner Seele brünstiges Verlangen,
Upon-which my soul's (most) burning desire—

Mein Heiland, hingegangen?
My Savior— has-gone?

Kein Unglück kann mich so empfindlich rühren,
No misfortune could me so deeply touch,
{No misfortune could touch me so deeply,}

Als wenn ich Jesum soll verlieren.
Than if I Jesus should lose.
{Than if I should lose Jesus.}

3. Chorale
●Prayer longing for Jesus, my all, to come (154-3)
Jesu, mein Hort und Erretter,
Jesus, my refuge and deliverer,

Jesu, meine Zuversicht,
Jesus, my confidence,

Jesu, starker Schlangentreter,
Jesus, strong serpent-crusher,

Jesu, meines Lebens Licht!
Jesus, my life's light!

Wie verlanget meinem Herzen,
How yearns my heart,

Jesulein, nach dir mit Schmerzen!
Little-Jesus, for thee with aching!
{How my heart yearns achingly, O little Jesus, for thee!}

Komm, ach komm, ich warte dein,
Come, ah come, I wait for-thee,

Komm, o liebstes Jesulein!
Come, O dearest little-Jesus!

4. Alto Aria
●Prayer: Do not hide thyself in the cloud of my sins! (154-4)
Jesu, laß dich finden,
Jesus, (please) let thyself be-found,

S. of S. 3:1–4 [Bride]: Upon my bed by night I sought him whom my soul loves; I sought him, but found him not; I called him, but he gave no answer. "I will rise now and go about the city, in the streets and in the squares; I will seek him whom my soul loves." I sought him, but found him not. The watchmen found me, as they went about in the city. "Have you seen him whom my soul loves?" Scarcely had I passed them, when I found him whom my soul loves. I held him, and would not let him go until I had brought him into my mother's house, and into the chamber of her that conceived me. (Also S. of S. 5:6.)
Ps. 42:1–2. As a hart longs for flowing streams, so longs my soul for thee, O God. My soul thirsts for God, for the living God. When shall I come and behold the face of God?
Ps. 73:25. Whom have I in heaven but thee? (Luther: Wenn ich nur dich habe...) And there is nothing upon earth that I desire besides thee.

Ps. 18:2. The Lord is my rock, and my fortress, and my deliverer (Luther: Erretter), my God, my rock (Luther: Hort), in whom I take refuge, my shield, and the horn of my salvation, my stronghold.
Ps. 142:5. I cry to thee, O Lord; I say, Thou art my refuge (Luther: Zuversicht), my portion in the land of the living. (Zuversicht: also Ps. 46:1, 61:3, 62:7, 71:5–7)
Col. 3:11. ...Christ is all and in all.
Heb. 2:9. We see Jesus, who for a little while was made lower than the angels, crowned with glory and honor because of the suffering of death, so that by the grace of God he might taste death for every one.
Col. 2:15. [Christ] disarmed the principalities and powers and made a public example of them, triumphing over them in him.
Gen. 3:14–15. The Lord God said to the serpent [in the garden of Eden], "Because you have done this...I will put enmity between you and the woman, and between your seed and her seed; he shall bruise your head, and you shall bruise his heel."
Rev. 12:9. And the great dragon was thrown down, that ancient serpent, who is called the Devil and Satan, the deceiver of the whole world...
Rom. 16:20. ...The God of peace will soon crush Satan under your feet... (Also Heb. 2:14, 1 Jn. 3:8.)
Jn. 1:4–5. In [Christ] was life, and the life was the light of men. The light shines in the darkness, and the darkness has not overcome it.
Jn. 8:12. Jesus [said]... "I am the light of the world; he who follows me will not walk in darkness, but will have the light of life." (Also Jn. 9:5, 11:9, 12:46, Ps. 36:9.)
Ps. 27:1. The Lord is my light and my salvation...
Ps. 130:5–6. I wait for the Lord, my soul waits...my soul waits for the Lord more than watchmen for the morning...
Rev. 22:20. He who testifies to these things says, "Surely I am coming soon." Amen. Come, Lord Jesus!

Jer. 29:13–14 [God]: You will seek me and find me; when you seek me with all your heart. I will be found by you, says the Lord... (Also 2 Chron. 15:15.)
S. of S. 3:1 [Bride]: Upon my bed by night I sought him whom my soul loves; I sought him, but found him not; I called him, but he gave no answer.

Laß doch meine Sünden
Let please   my   sins
{Please let my sins}

Keine dicke Wolken sein,
No   thick   clouds   be,
{Be no thick clouds,}

Wo   du dich zum   Schrecken
Wherein thou -   to (my) terror

Willst für mich verstecken,
Wouldst from me   hide,

Stelle dich bald wieder ein!
Appear - soon again - !

5. Bass Arioso
●Vox Christi: Jesus as a boy in the temple: Lk. 2:49 (154-5)
Wisset ihr nicht, daß ich sein muß in dem,
Know ye not, that I must be in that,

das meines Vaters ist?
which my   Father's is?

6. Tenor Recit.
●Jesus heard in his Word and found in Father's house (154-6)
Dies ist die Stimme meines Freundes,
This is the voice of-my   friend,

Gott   Lob und Dank!
To-God (be) praise and thanks!

Mein Jesu, mein getreuer Hort,
My Jesus, my   faithful refuge,

Läßt durch sein Wort
Lets through his Word

Sich wieder tröstlich hören;
Himself again comfortingly be-heard;
{Lets himself be heard again through his Word;}

Ich war vor Schmerzen krank,
I   was with   sorrow   sick,
{I was sick with sorrow,}

Der Jammer wollte mir das Mark
 - Misery sought - the marrow

In   Beinen fast verzehren;
Of (my) bones nigh to-consume;
{Misery was nigh consuming the marrow of my bones;}

Ps. 102:2. [O Lord,] do not hide thy face from me in the day of my distress! Incline thy ear to me; answer me speedily in the day when I call! (Also Ps. 22:1–2, 27:7, 69:17.)
Is. 59:1–2. Behold, the Lord's hand is not shortened, that it cannot save, or his ear dull, that it cannot hear. But your iniquities have made a separation between you and your God, and your sins have hid his face from you so that he does not hear. (Also Jn. 9:31.)
Ezek. 39:24 [God]: I dealt with them according to their uncleanness and their transgressions, and hid my face from them. (Also Is. 54:8, 57:17.)
Lam. 3:44. [O Lord,] thou hast wrapped thyself with a cloud so that no prayer can pass through.
Ex. 19:16. On the morning of the third day [when God was about to give his commandments to Moses and the Israelites at Mount Sinai] there were thunders and lightnings, and a thick cloud upon the mountain...

*Lk. 2:46–50. After three days they found [Jesus] in the temple, sitting among the teachers, listening to them and asking them questions; and all who heard him were amazed at his understanding and his answers. And when they saw him they were astonished; and his mother said to him, "Son, why have you treated us so? Behold, your father and I have been looking for you anxiously." And he said to them, "How is it that you sought me? *Did you not know that I must be in my Father's house?*" And they did not understand the saying which he spoke to them.

S. of S. 2:8 [Bride]: The voice of my beloved (Luther: Freundes)!...
Jn. 10:3–4. ...The sheep hear his voice, and he calls his own sheep by name and leads them out...The sheep follow him, for they know his voice.
Jn. 10:27 [Christ]: My sheep hear my voice...
Jn. 5:39 [Christ]: You search the scriptures...it is they that bear witness to me.
Jn. 14:21, 23–24, 26. [Christ]: He who has my commandments and keeps them, he it is who loves me...and I will love him and manifest myself to him...If a man loves me, he will keep my word, and my Father will love him, and we will come to him and make our home with him. He who does not love me does not keep my words; and the word which you hear is not mine but the Father's who sent me...The Counselor, the Holy Spirit, whom the Father will send in my name, he will teach you all things, and bring to your remembrance all that I have said to you.
Jn. 16:16, 20–22 [Christ]: A little while, and you will see me no more; again a little while, and you will see me...You will be sorrowful, but your sorrow will turn into joy. When a woman is in travail she has sorrow, because her hour has come; butt when she is delivered of the child, she no longer remembers the anguish, for joy that a child is born into the world. So you have sorrow (Luther: Traurigkeit) now, but I will see you again and your hearts will rejoice, and no one will take your joy from you.
S. of S. 5:6, 8 [Bride]: I opened to my beloved, but my beloved had turned and gone...I sought him, but found him not; I called him, but he gave no answer...I adjure you, O daughters of Jerusalem, if you find my beloved, that you tell him I am sick (Luther: krank) with love.

Nun aber wird mein Glaube wieder stark,
Now, however, becomes my faith again strong,
{Now, however, my faith becomes strong again,}

Nun bin ich höchst erfreut;
Now am I most gladdened;

Denn ich erblicke meiner Seele Wonne,
For I behold my soul's bliss,

Den Heiland, meine Sonne,
The Savior, my sun,

Der nach betrübter Trauernacht
Who after (a) sorrowful night-of-mourning

Durch seinen Glanz mein Herze fröhlich macht.
By his radiance my heart joyful makes.
{Makes my heart joyful with his radiance.}

Auf, Seele, mache dich bereit!
Rise, soul, make thyself ready!

Du mußt zu ihm
Thou must to him

In seines Vaters Haus, hin in den Tempel ziehn;
Into his Father's house, forth into the temple go;

Da läßt er sich in seinem Wort erblicken,
There lets he himself within his Word be-seen,
{There he lets himself be seen in his Word,}

Da will er dich im Sakrament erquicken;
There will he thee in-the Sacrament refresh;
{There he will refresh thee in the Sacrament;}

Doch, willst du würdiglich sein Fleisch und Blut genießen,
Yet, wouldst thou worthily his flesh and blood eat,
{Yet, wouldst thou eat his flesh and blood worthily,}

So mußt du Jesum auch in Buß und Glauben küssen.
Then must thou Jesus also in repentance and faith kiss.
{Then must thou also kiss Jesus in repentance and faith.}

7. Alto & Tenor Duet
●Jesus found; I will rejoice and not let him go (154-7)
Wohl mir, Jesus ist gefunden,
Well for-me! Jesus is found,

Nun bin ich nicht mehr betrübt.
Now am I no longer saddened.
{Now I am no longer saddened.}

Der, den meine Seele liebt,
He, whom my soul loves,

Ps. 22:1. My God, my God, why hast thou forsaken me? Why art thou so far from helping me, from the words of my groaning? (Also Ps. 6:2–4, 6–7, 13:1–3, 5, 86:3, 88:1–2, Is. 38:13.)
Ps. 31:10. ...My strength fails because of my misery, and my bones waste away. (Also Ps. 22:17, 38:3.)
S. of S. 3:1–4 [Bride]: Upon my bed by night I sought him whom my soul loves; I sought him, but found him not; I called him, but he gave no answer. "I will rise now and go about the city, in the streets and in the squares; I will seek him whom my soul loves." I sought him, but found him not. The watchmen found me, as they went about in the city. "Have you seen him whom my soul loves?" Scarcely had I passed them, when I found him whom my soul loves. I held him, and would not let him go...
Ps. 27:1. The Lord is my light... (Also Ps. 36:9, 2 Cor. 4:6.)
Mt. 2:10. When [the wise men] saw the star [again], they rejoiced exceedingly with great joy (Luther: wurden sie hoch erfreut).
Ps. 30:5. ...Weeping may tarry for the night, but joy comes with the morning.
Ps. 43:3–4. Oh send out thy light and thy truth; let them lead me, let them bring me to thy holy hill and to thy dwelling! Then I will go to the altar of God, to God my exceeding joy (Luther: Freude und Wonne)...
*Lk. 2:49. [Jesus] said to [his parents], "How is it that you sought me? Did you not know that I must be in my Father's house?"
Ps. 26:8. O Lord, I love the habitation of thy house, and the place where thy glory dwells.
Ps. 122:1. I was glad when they said to me, "Let us go to the house of the Lord!" (Also Is. 2:3, Mic. 4:2.)
Jn. 5:39 [Christ]: ...The scriptures...bear witness to me.
Jn. 6:54–56 [Christ]: He who eats my flesh and drinks my blood has eternal life...My flesh is food indeed, and my blood is drink indeed. He who eats my flesh and drinks my blood abides in me, and I in him.
1 Cor. 11:27–29. Whoever, therefore, eats the bread or drinks the cup of the Lord in an unworthy manner will be guilty of profaning the body and blood of the Lord. Let a man examine himself, and so eat of the bread and drink of the cup. For any one who eats and drinks without discerning the body eats and drinks judgment upon himself.
Ps. 2:11–12. Serve the Lord with fear, with trembling kiss his feet (Luther: küsset den Sohn), lest he be angry, and you perish in the way; for his wrath is quickly kindled. Blessed are all who take refuge in him.

*Lk. 2:43–46. ...His parents...sought him among their kinsfolk and acquaintances; and when they did not find him, they returned to Jerusalem, seeking him. After three days they found him in the temple, sitting among the teachers, listening to them and asking them questions.
Jn. 16:16, 20 [Christ]: ...A little while, and you will see me...You will be sorrowful, but your sorrow will turn into joy.
Jer. 29:13–14. You will seek me and find me; when you seek me with all your heart. I will be found by you, says the Lord...
S. of S. 3:4 [Bride]: ...I found him whom my soul loves. I held him,

Zeigt sich mir zur frohen Stunden.
Appears to-me in joyous hours.
{Appears to me in a joyous time.}

Ich will dich, mein Jesu, nun nimmermehr lassen,
I will thee, my Jesus, now nevermore leave,
{I will now nevermore leave thee, my Jesus,}

Ich will dich im Glauben beständig umfassen.
I will thee in faith continually embrace.
{I will continually embrace thee in faith.}

8. Chorale (See also 124-6, 157-5.)
●Clinging to Jesus; he leads me to streams of life (154-8)
Meinen Jesum laß ich nicht,
My Jesus relinquish I not,
{I'll not let Jesus go,}

Geh ihm ewig an der Seiten;
(I'll) go (with) him ever at (his) side;

Christus läßt mich für und für
Christ lets me forever and ever

Zu den Lebensbächlein leiten.
To the streams-of-life be-guided.

Selig, wer mit mir so spricht:
Blessed, (is he) who with me thus says:

Meinen Jesum laß ich nicht.
My Jesus relinquish I not.
{I will not let my Jesus go.}

BWV 155
Mein Gott, wie lang, ach lange
(NBA I/5; BC A32)

2. S. after Epiphany (BWV 155, 3, 13)
*Rom. 12:6-16[1] (Diversity of gifts, exemplary conduct)
*Jn. 2:1-11 (Jesus attends wedding at Cana)
[1]End: "men of low estate."
Librettist: Salomon Franck

1. Soprano Recit.
●Lament: My cup is filled with woe, joy's wine fails (155-1)
Mein Gott, wie lang, ach lange?
My God, how long, ah, (how) long?

Des Jammers ist zuviel!
Of misery (there) is too-much!

Ich sehe gar kein Ziel
I see absolutely no end

and would not let him go until I had brought him into my mother's house, and into the chamber of her that conceived me.
Ps. 63:8. [O Lord,] my soul clings to thee (Luther: hanget dir an)...
Ps. 73:25. [O Lord,] whom have I in heaven but thee? And there is nothing upon earth that I desire besides thee.
Gen. 32:26. ...I will not let you go, unless you bless me.
Rev. 3:11. ...Hold fast what you have, so that no one may seize your crown.
Heb. 10:39. We are not of those who shrink back and are destroyed, but of those who have faith and keep their souls.

Gen. 32:26. ...Jacob said, "I will not let you go, unless you bless me."
S. of S. 3:4 [Bride]: ...I found him whom my soul loves. I held him, and would not let him go...
Lk. 9:57. As they were going along the road, a man said to [Jesus], "I will follow you wherever you go." (Also Mt. 8:19.)
Jn. 6:66-68. After this many of his disciples drew back and no longer went about with him. Jesus said to the twelve, "Do you also wish to go away?" Simon Peter answered him, "Lord, to whom shall we go? You have the words of eternal life..."
Ps. 23:1-3. The Lord is my shepherd, I shall not want; he makes me lie down in green pastures. He leads me beside still waters; he restores my soul...
Rev. 7:17. The Lamb in the midst of the throne will be their shepherd, and he will guide them to springs of living water; and God will wipe away every tear from their eyes.
Jn. 4:13-14. Jesus said, "...Whoever drinks of the water that I shall give him will never thirst; the water that I shall give him will become in him a spring of water welling up to eternal life." (Also Jn. 4:10-11, 7:37-38, Is. 12:3, Rev. 21:6, 22:1, 22:17.)
Josh. 24:15. ...Choose this day whom you will serve...but as for me and my house, we will serve the Lord.

Ps. 13:1-3. How long, O Lord? Wilt thou forget me for ever? How long wilt thou hide thy face from me? How long must I bear pain in my soul, and have sorrow in my heart all the day?...Consider and answer me, O Lord my God; lighten my eyes, lest I sleep the sleep of death.
Ps. 6:2-4, 6-7. Be gracious to me, O Lord, for I am languishing; O Lord, heal me, for my bones are troubled. My soul also is sorely troubled. But thou, O Lord—how long? Turn, O Lord, save my life; deliver me for the sake of thy steadfast love...I am weary with my

Der Schmerzen und der Sorgen.
Of   sufferings and of sorrows.
{To my suffering and sorrow.}

Dein süßer Gnadenblick
Thy sweet look-of-grace

Hat   unter Nacht und Wolken sich verborgen,
Hath beneath night and clouds itself   hidden,
{Hath hidden itself beneath night and clouds,}

Die   Liebeshand   zieht sich, ach! ganz   zurück,
(Thy) hand-of-love withdraws itself, ah, completely - ;

Um Trost ist mir sehr bange.
For comfort am (I) very anxious.
{I long anxiously for comfort.}

Ich finde, was   mich Armen täglich kränket,
I   find, which (does) (this) poor-wretch daily   vex,
{I find—to this poor wretch's daily vexation—}

Das Tränen-maß wird stets   voll eingeschenket,
(My) tears' measure is ever (to the) full   poured,
{My cup of tears ever poured to the full,}

Der Freuden-wein gebricht;
The   wine-of-joy   fails;

Mir   sinkt fast alle Zuversicht.
For-me sinks nigh all confidence.
{For me nigh all confidence sinks.}

2. Alto & Tenor Duet
●Faith in adversity: Hope in God and wait for him! (155-2)
Du mußt glauben, du mußt hoffen,
You must believe, you must hope,

Du mußt   Gott gelassen sein!
You must (in) God   patient   be!

Jesus weiß die rechten Stunden,
Jesus knows the right   hour,

Dich mit   Hülfe zu erfreun.
You with (his) help to gladden.
{To gladden you with his help.}

Wenn die trübe Zeit verschwunden,
When the troubled time has-passed-away, (then)

Steht sein ganzes Herz   dir   offen.
Stands his whole heart to-you open.
{His whole heart stands open to you.}

3. Bass Recit.
●Affliction sent as test; wormwood will turn to wine (155-3)
So sei, o Seele, sei zufrieden!
So be, O soul, be   content!

moaning; every night I flood my bed with tears; I drench my couch with my weeping. My eye wastes away because of grief, it grows weak because of all my foes. (Also Ps. 89:46, 90:13-15; Ps. 22:1-2.)
Ps. 116:3-6. The snares of death encompassed me; the pangs of Sheol laid hold on me; I suffered distress and anguish (Luther: Jammer und Not).
Ps. 25:18. [O Lord,] consider my affliction (Luther: Jammer) and my trouble...
Ps. 44:24. Why dost thou hide thy face? Why dost thou forget our affliction and oppression?
Ps. 88:14. O Lord, why dost thou cast me off? Why dost thou hide thy face from me? (Also Ps. 69:17, 102:2. 143:7.)
Ps. 69:3. I am weary with my crying; my throat is parched. My eyes grow dim with waiting for my God.
Ps. 42:3. My tears have been my food day and night, while men say to me continually, "Where is your God?"
Lam. 3:44. Thou hast wrapped thyself with a cloud so that no prayer can pass through.
Ps. 18:11. He made darkness his covering around him, his canopy thick clouds dark with water.
Lam. 2:3. ...He has withdrawn...his right hand...
Is. 38:17. Lo, it was for my welfare that I had great bitterness (Luther: um Trost war mir sehr bange)...
Lam. 1:16. For these things I weep; my eyes flow with tears; for a comforter is far from me, one to revive my courage...
Jer. 48:33. Gladness and joy have been taken away from the fruitful land of Moab...the wine [ceases] from the wine presses; no one treads them with shouts of joy; the shouting is not the shout of joy.
*Jn. 2:1-3. On the third day there was a marriage at Cana in Galilee, and...Jesus also was invited to the marriage...When the wine gave out, the mother of Jesus said to him, "They have no wine."

*Rom. 12:12. Rejoice in your hope, be patient in tribulation (Luther: Trübsal), be constant in prayer.
Heb. 10:35-38. Therefore do not throw away your confidence, which has a great reward. For you have need of endurance, so that you may do the will of God and receive what is promised. "For yet a little while, and the coming one shall come and shall not tarry; but my righteous one shall live by faith..."
Heb. 11:1. Now faith is the assurance of things hoped for...
Ps. 130:7. O Israel, hope in the Lord! For with the Lord there is steadfast love, and with him is plenteous redemption.
1 Pet. 4:19. Let those who suffer according to God's will do right and entrust their souls to a faithful Creator.
Ps. 31:14-15. I trust in thee, O Lord, I say, "Thou art my God." My times are in thy hand...
*Jn. 2:3-5. When the wine gave out, the mother of Jesus said to him, "They have no wine." And Jesus said to her, "O woman, what have you to do with me? My hour has not yet come."
1 Pet. 5:10. After you have suffered a little while, the God of all grace, who has called you to his eternal glory in Christ, will himself restore, establish, and strengthen you.

*Rom. 12:12. Rejoice in your hope, be patient in tribulation (Luther: Trübsal), be constant in prayer.
Rom. 8:24-25. ...Now hope that is seen is not hope. For who hopes for what he sees? But if we hope for what we do not see, we wait for it with patience.

Wenn es vor deinen Augen scheint,
If it to thine eyes appear,
{If it appear to thine eyes}

Als ob dein liebster Freund
As if thy dearest friend

Sich ganz von dir geschieden;
Himself completely from thee hath-removed;
{Hath removed himself completely from thee;}

Wenn er dich kurze Zeit verläßt,
When he thee (for a) short time doth-leave,
{When he doth leave thee for a short time,}

Herz! glaube fest,
Heart, believe steadfastly,

Es wird ein Kleines sein,
It will a short-time be,
{It will only be a short time}

Da er für bittre Zähren
Till he for bitter tears

Den Trost- und Freudenwein
The (wine-of) comfort and wine-of-joy

Und Honigseim für Wermut will gewähren!
And virgin-honey for wormwood shall grant (thee)!
{Till he shall grant thee the wine of comfort and joy for bitter
tears; virgin honey for wormwood!}

Ach! denke nicht,
Ah, think not,

Daß er von Herzen dich betrübe,
That he from (his) heart thee saddens,
{That he delights to sadden thee,}

Er prüfet nur durch Leiden deine Liebe,
He tests only through suffering thy love,
{He only tests thy love through suffering,}

Er machet, daß dein Herz bei trüben Stunden weine,
He makes - thy heart in dreary hours to-weep,

Damit sein Gnadenlicht
So-that his light-of-grace

Dir desto lieblicher erscheine;
To-thee so-much lovelier appear;

Er hat, was dich ergötzt,
He hath, that-which thee delights,

Zuletzt
In-the-end

Jn. 20:29. Jesus said to [Thomas], "Have you believed because you
have seen me? Blessed are those who have not seen and yet believe."
Is. 64:7. [O Lord]...thou hast hid thy face from us...
Job 23:3. Oh, that I knew where I might find him...
S. of S. 5:6 [Bride]: I opened to my beloved (Luther: Freund), but my
beloved had turned and gone. My soul failed me when he spoke. I
sought him, but found him not; I called him, but he gave no answer.
(Also S. of S. 3:1.)
Is. 54:7–8 [God]: For a brief moment I forsook you, but with great
compassion I will gather you. In overflowing wrath for a moment I hid
my face from you, but with everlasting love I will have compassion on
you, says the Lord, your Redeemer.
Ps. 30:5. His anger is but for a moment, and his favor is for a lifetime.
Weeping may tarry for the night, but joy comes with the morning.
1 Pet. 5:10. After you have suffered a little while...[God] will himself
restore, establish, and strengthen you.
Jer. 31:13–14 [God]: I will turn their mourning into joy, I will comfort
them, and give them gladness for sorrow.
Ps. 30:11. [O Lord,] thou hast turned for me my mourning into
dancing; thou hast loosed my sackcloth and girded me with gladness.
*Jn. 2:9. The steward of the feast tasted the water now become wine,
and did not know where it came from.
///
S. of S. 4:11 [Bridegroom]: Your lips distil nectar (Luther:
Honigseim), my bride; honey and milk are under your tongue...
Prov. 5:3–5. The lips of a loose woman drip honey (Luther: (Luther:
Honigseim), and her speech is smoother than oil; but in the end she
is bitter as wormwood (Luther: Wermut)...
///
Jms. 5:10–11. As an example of suffering and patience, brethren, take
the prophets who spoke in the name of the Lord. Behold, we call
those happy who were steadfast. You have heard of the steadfastness
of Job, and you have seen the purpose of the Lord, how the Lord is
compassionate and merciful.
Lam. 3:31–33. The Lord will not cast off for ever, but, though he
cause grief, he will have compassion according to the abundance of his
steadfast love; for he does not willingly afflict or grieve the sons of
men.
Job 1:8–12. The Lord said to Satan, "Have you considered my servant
Job, that there is none like him on the earth, a blameless and upright
man, who fears God and turns away from evil?" Then Satan answered
the Lord, "Does Job fear God for nought? Hast thou not put a hedge
about him and his house and all that he has, on every side? Thou hast
blessed the work of his hands, and his possessions have increased in
the land. But put forth thy hand now, and touch all that he has, and
he will curse thee to thy face." And the Lord said to Satan, "Behold,
all that he has is in your power; only upon himself do not put forth
your hand."...
Heb. 12:5–6, 10. ...My son, do not regard lightly the discipline of the
Lord, nor lose courage when you are punished by him. For the Lord
disciplines him whom he loves, and chastises every son whom he
receives...He disciplines us for our good, that we may share his
holiness.
*Jn. 2:1, 3, 7–10. On the third day there was a marriage at Cana in
Galilee...When the wine gave out, the mother of Jesus said to him,

Zu deinem Trost   dir   vorbehalten;
For   thy comfort for-thee reserved;
{He hath reserved for thee that which delights thee, for thy comfort;}

Drum laß ihn nur, o Herz, in   allem walten!
So   let him just, O heart, in all-things rule!
{So just let him rule in all things, O heart!}

4. Soprano Aria
●Cast all your cares, your sorrows' yoke, on God (155-4)
Wirf,   mein Herze, wirf dich noch
Cast, (O) my   heart,   cast thyself yet

In   des Höchsten Liebesarme,
Into the Most-High's arms-of-love,
{Into the loving arms of the Most High,}

Daß er   deiner sich erbarme.
That he on-thee   have-mercy.
{That he have mercy on thee.}

Lege deiner Sorgen Joch,
Lay   thy   sorrows' yoke,

Und was dich bisher   beladen,
And what thee till-now hath-burdened,

Auf die Achseln seiner Gnaden.
Upon the shoulders of-his   grace.

5. Chorale (See also 9-7, 186-6.)
●Believe his Word rather than appearances (155-5)
Ob   sich's anließ, als wollt er nicht,
Though it   appear, as-if wanted he not,
{Though it appear as if he were not intending to help you,}

Laß dich es nicht erschrecken,
Let you it not   frighten,
{Let it not frighten you,}

Denn wo er ist am besten mit,
For where he is -   best with (you),
{For where he is most with you,}

Da   will er's nicht entdecken.
There would he-it not   disclose.
{There would he not disclose it.}

Sein Wort laß dir   gewisser sein,
His   Word let to-you more-certain be,
{Let his Word become more certain to you,}

Und ob dein Herz spräch lauter Nein,
And though your heart say   only "No,"

"They have no wine."...Jesus said to [the servants], "Fill the jars with water." And they filled them up to the brim. He said to them, "Now draw some out, and take it to the steward of the feast." So they took it. When the steward of the feast tasted the water now become wine, and did not know where it came from...[he]...called the bridegroom and said to him, "Every man serves the good wine first...then the poor wine; but you have kept the good wine until now."

1 Chron. 21:13. David said to Gad, "I am in great distress; let me fall into the hand of the Lord, for his mercy is very great..." (Also 2 Sam. 24:14.)
1 Pet. 5:7. Cast all your anxieties on [God], for he cares about you.
Phil. 4:6-7. Have no anxiety about anything, but in everything by prayer and supplication with thanksgiving let your requests be made known to God. And the peace of God, which passes all understanding, will keep your hearts and your minds in Christ Jesus.
Mt. 11:28-30 [Christ]: Come to me, all who labor and are heavy laden, and I will give you rest. Take my yoke upon you, and learn from me; for I am gentle and lowly in heart, and you will find rest for your souls. For my yoke is easy, and my burden is light.
Is. 10:27. In that day his burden will depart from your shoulder, and his yoke will be destroyed from your neck. (Also Is. 9:4, 14:25, Ps. 81:6.)
Is. 40:11. He will feed his flock like a shepherd, he will gather the lambs in his arms, he will carry them in his bosom, and gently lead those that are with young.

*Jn. 2:3-5. When the wine gave out, the mother of Jesus said to him, "They have no wine." And Jesus said to her, "O woman, what have you to do with me? My hour has not yet come."
Lk. 24:15, 16, 28-31. While [the disciples on the road to Emmaus] were talking and discussing together, Jesus himself drew near and went with them. But their eyes were kept from recognizing him...So they drew near to the village to which they were going. [Jesus] appeared to be going further, but they constrained him, saying, "Stay with us..."...When he was at table with them...their eyes were opened and they recognized him; and he vanished out of their sight...
Jn. 20:29. ...Blessed are those who have not seen and yet believe.
Rom. 8:24-25. ...Now hope that is seen is not hope. For who hopes for what he sees? But if we hope for what we do not see, we wait for it with patience.
Ps. 27:14. Wait for the Lord; be strong, and let your heart take courage; yea, wait for the Lord!
Heb. 11:1. Now faith is the assurance of things hoped for, the conviction of things not seen.
2 Pet. 1:19. And we have the prophetic word made more sure. You will do well to pay attention to this as to a lamp shining in a dark place, until the day dawns and the morning star rises in your hearts.
2 Cor. 1:18-20. As surely as God is faithful, our word to you has not been Yes and No. For the Son of God, Jesus Christ...was not Yes and No; but in him it is always Yes. For all the promises of God find their

So laß   doch   dir   nicht grauen.
Yet let nevertheless yourself not be-terrified.
{Yet let yourself nevertheless not be terrified.}

BWV 156
Ich steh mit einem Fuß im Grabe
(NBA I/6; BC A38)

3. S. after Epiphany (BWV 73, 111, 72, 156)
*Rom. 12:16[1]-21 (Overcoming evil with good)
*Mt. 8:1-13 (Jesus heals a leper; the centurion from
Capernaum comes to Jesus)
[1]Begin: "Never be conceited."
Librettist: Picander (Christian Friedrich Henrici)

1. Sinfonia (Perhaps from an earlier work)

2. Tenor Aria & Soprano Chorale
•Prayer: My end is near, take my soul into thy hands (156-2)
Ich steh mit einem Fuß im Grabe,
I stand with one   foot in-the grave,

>   **Mach's mit mir, Gott, nach deiner Güt**
>   Deal   with me, God, according to-thy kindness

Bald fällt der kranke Leib hinein,
Soon falls (my) ailing body thereinto,

>   **Hilf mir in meinen Leiden,**
>   Help me in   my   suffering,

Komm, lieber Gott, wenn   dir's gefällt,
Come, dear God, whenever thee-it pleases,
{Come, dear God, whenever it pleases thee,}

>   **Was ich dich bitt, versag mir nicht.**
>   What I of-thee ask,   deny me not.
>   {Do not deny me what I ask of thee.}

Ich habe schon mein Haus   bestellt,
I   have already my   house set-in-order,
{I have already set my house in order,}

>   **Wenn sich mein Seel soll scheiden,**
>   If   -   my   soul is to-depart,

>   **So nimm sie, Herr, in deine Händ.**
>   Then take it, Lord, into thy hands.

Nur laß mein Ende selig sein!
Only let my   end blessed be!

>   **Ist alles gut, wenn gut das End.**
>   All-is   good, if good the end.

Yes in him. That is why we utter the Amen through him, to the glory
of God.
1 Jn. 3:19-20. ...We shall know that we are of the truth, and reassure
our hearts before him whenever our hearts condemn us; for God is
greater than our hearts...

*Mt. 8:5-6. As [Jesus] entered Capernaum, a centurion came forward
to him, beseeching him and saying, "Lord, my servant is lying
paralyzed at home, in terrible distress."
Job 17:1. My spirit is broken (Luther: Mein Odem ist schwach), my
days are extinct (Luther: abgekürzt), the grave is ready for me.
Ps. 69:1-2, 15. ...The waters have come up to my neck. I sink in deep
mire, where there is no foothold; I have come into deep waters, and
the flood sweeps over me...Let not the flood sweep over me, or the
deep swallow me up, or the pit close its mouth over me.
Ps. 143:7. Make haste to answer me, O Lord! My spirit fails! Hide not
thy face from me, lest I be like those who go down to the Pit.
Job 33:19-22. Man is also chastened with pain upon his bed, and with
continual strife in his bones; so that his life loathes bread, and his
appetite dainty food. His flesh is so wasted away that it cannot be
seen; and his bones which were not seen stick out. His soul draws near
the Pit, and his life to those who bring death.
Ps. 102:3, 11. My days pass away like smoke, and my bones burn like
a furnace...My days are like an evening shadow; I wither away like
grass.
Ps. 13:2-3. How long must I bear pain in my soul, and have sorrow in
my heart all the day?...Consider and answer me, O Lord my God;
lighten my eyes, lest I sleep the sleep of death.
Is. 38:1. ...Isaiah the prophet...came to [King Hezekiah], and said to
him, "Thus says the Lord: Set your house in order (Luther: bestelle
dein Haus); for you shall die, you shall not recover." (Also 2 Kings
20:1, 2 Sam. 17:23.)
Ps. 31:5. [O Lord,] into thy hand I commit my spirit...
Lk. 23:46. Then Jesus, crying with a loud voice, said, "Father, into thy
hands I commit my spirit!" And having said this he breathed his last.
(Also Ps. 31:5.)
Mt. 10:22. ...He who endures to the end will be saved. (Also Mt. 24:13,
Mk. 13:13, Lk. 21:19.)
Num. 23:10. ...Let me die the death of the righteous, and let my end
be like his!
Rev. 2:10-11. Do not fear what you are about to suffer...Be faithful
unto death, and I will give you the crown of life. He who has an ear,
let him hear what the Spirit says to the churches. He who conquers
shall not be hurt by the second death.

3. Bass Recit.
●Willingness to suffer & die; yielding to God's will (156-3)
Mein Angst und   Not,
My   fear and distress,

Mein Leben und mein Tod
My   life and my death

Steht,   liebster Gott, in deinen Händen;
Stand, (O) dearest God, in thy   hands;
{Rest, O dearest God, in thy hands;}

So wirst du auch auf mich
Thus wilt thou also upon me

Dein gnädig Auge wenden.
Thy gracious eye   turn.
{Turn thy gracious eye.}

Willst   du mich meiner Sünden wegen
Wouldst thou me for-my sins   sake

Ins   Krankenbette legen,
Upon-a sickbed   lay,
{If thou wouldst lay me upon a sickbed for my sins' sake,}

Mein Gott, so bitt ich dich,
My   God, then ask I of-thee,
{My God, then I ask of thee,}

Laß deine Güte größer sein als die Gerechtigkeit;
Let thy kindness greater be than (thy) justice;
{Let thy kindness be greater than thy justice;}

Doch hast du mich darzu versehn,
Yet hast thou me for-this (ordained),
{Yet if thou hast planned for me,}

Daß mich mein Leiden   soll verzehren,
That me   my suffering should consume,
{That my suffering should consume me,}

Ich bin bereit,
I am ready,

Dein Wille soll an mir geschehn,
Thy will shall to me be-done,
{Let thy will be done to me,}

Verschone nicht und fahre fort,
Spare   not and proceed,

Laß meine Not nicht lange währen;
Let my distress not long continue;

Je länger hier, je später dort.
The longer here, the later there.

Ps. 119:143. Trouble and anguish have come upon me (Luther: Angst und Not haben mich getroffen), but thy commandments are my delight.
Ps. 31:5, 14–15. Into thy hand I commit my spirit; thou hast redeemed me, O Lord, faithful God...But I trust in thee, O Lord, I say, "Thou art my God." My times are in thy hand...
Ps. 119:153. [O Lord,] look on my affliction and deliver me...
Ps. 34:15, 17–19. The eyes of the Lord are toward the righteous, and his ears toward their cry...When the righteous cry for help, the Lord hears, and delivers them out of all their troubles. The Lord is near to the brokenhearted, and saves the crushed in spirit. Many are the afflictions of the righteous; but the Lord delivers him out of them all. (Also Ps. 33:18–19.)
Ex. 23:25 [God]: You shall serve the Lord your God...and I will take sickness away from the midst of you.
Deut. 28:58–59. If you are not careful to do all the words of this law which are written in this book, that you may fear this glorius and awful name, the Lord your God, then the Lord will bring on you and your offspring extraordinary afflictions, afflictions severe and lasting...
Ps. 107:17–20. Some [of God's people] were sick through their sinful ways, and because of their iniquities suffered affliction; they loathed any kind of food, and they drew near to the gates of death. Then they cried to the Lord in their trouble, and he delivered them from their distress; he sent forth his word, and healed them, and delivered them from destruction.
Ps. 38:1–4. O Lord, rebuke me not in thy anger, nor chasten me in thy wrath! For thy arrows have sunk into me, and thy hand has come down on me. There is no soundness in my flesh because of thy indignation; there is no health in my bones because of my sin. For my iniquities have gone over my head; they weigh like a burden too heavy for me.
Ps. 130:3. If thou, O Lord, shouldst mark iniquities, Lord, who could stand!
Ps. 143:2. Enter not into judgment with thy servant; for no man living is righteous before thee.
Ps. 103:10. [The Lord] does not deal with us according to our sins, nor requite us according to our iniquities.
Rom. 5:20. ...Where sin increased, grace abounded all the more.
Mk. 14:35–36. Going a little farther, [in the garden of Gethsemane, Jesus] fell on the ground and prayed that, if it were possible, the hour might pass from him. And he said, "Abba, Father, all things are possible to thee; remove this cup from me; yet not what I will, but what thou wilt." (Also Mt. 26:39, 42.)
Rom. 14:8. ...Whether we live or whether we die, we are the Lord's.
Phil. 1:21–23. To me to live is Christ, and to die is gain...Which I shall choose I cannot tell. I am hard pressed between the two. My desire is to depart and be with Christ, for that is far better.
2 Cor. 5:6–8. So we are always of good courage; we know that while we are at home in the body we are away from the Lord, for we walk by faith, not by sight. We are of good courage, and we would rather be away from the body and at home with the Lord.

4. Alto Aria

●Prayer of submission to God's will in all things (156-4)
Herr,   was   du willt, soll mir gefallen,
Lord, whatever thou wilt, shall me please,
{Lord whatever thou wilt is acceptable to me,}

Weil doch dein Rat   am besten gilt.
For indeed thy counsel for-the best counts.
{For thy counsel is best.}

In der Freude,
In -   joy,

In dem Leide,
In -   suffering,

Im Sterben, in Bitten   und   Flehn
In   dying,   in petition, and supplication

Laß mir allemal geschehn,
Let to-me always   happen,
{Let it always happen to me,}

Herr, wie du willt.
Lord, as thou wilt.

5. Bass Recit.

●Spiritual health desired more than physical health (156-5)
Und willst du, daß ich nicht soll kranken,
And desirest thou, that I not should suffer,

So werd ich dir von   Herzen danken;
Then will I thee from (my) heart   thank;
{Then will I thank thee from my heart;}

Doch aber   gib mir auch dabei,
Yet, however, grant to-me as-well therewith,

Daß auch in meinem frischen Leibe
That also in my   vigorous body

Die Seele sonder Krankheit   sei
(My) soul without sickness (might) be

Und allezeit gesund verbleibe.
And evermore healthy remain.

Nimm sie durch   Geist und Wort in   acht,
Take it   by (thy) Spirit and Word into (thy) care,
{Care for my soul through thy Spirit and thy Word,}

Denn dieses ist mein   Heil,
For   this is my salvation,

Und wenn mir Leib und Seel verschmacht,
And if (my) body and soul   should-fail,

*Mt. 8:1-3. When [Jesus] came down from the mountain, great crowds followed him; and behold, a leper came to him and knelt before him, saying, "Lord, if you will, you can make me clean." And he stretched out his hand and touched him, saying, "I will; be clean." And immediately his leprosy was cleansed.
Mt. 6:9-10 [Christ]: Pray...like this: Our Father who art in heaven, Hallowed be thy name. Thy kingdom come, Thy will be done, On earth as it is in heaven.
Mt. 26:39, 42. Going a little farther [in the garden of Gethsemane, Jesus] fell on his face and prayed, "My Father, if it be possible, let this cup pass from me; nevertheless, not as I will, but as thou wilt."...Again, for the second time, he went away and prayed, "My Father, if this cannot pass unless I drink it, thy will be done." (Also Mk. 14:35-36.)
1 Pet. 4:19. Therefore let those who suffer according to God's will do right and entrust their souls to a faithful Creator.
Job 12:13-15, 23. With God are wisdom and might; he has counsel and understanding (Luther: Rat und Verstand). (Also Ps. 33:11, 73:24, Is. 28:29.)
Acts 21:13-14. Then Paul answered, "What are you doing, weeping and breaking my heart? For I am ready not only to be imprisoned but even to die at Jerusalem for the name of the Lord Jesus." And when he would not be persuaded, we ceased and said, "The will of the Lord be done."

*Mt. 8:2. ...Lord, if you will, you can make me clean.
Lk. 17:14-18. When [Jesus] saw [the ten lepers standing at a distance] he said to them, "Go and show yourselves to the priests." And as they went they were cleansed. Then one of them, when he saw that he was healed, turned back, praising God with a loud voice; and he fell on his face at Jesus' feet, giving him thanks. Now he was a Samaritan. Then said Jesus, "Were not ten cleansed? Where are the nine? Was no one found to return and give praise to God except this foreigner?"
Jn. 13:8-9. ...Jesus [said to Peter], "If I do not wash you, you have no part in me." Simon Peter said to him, "Lord, not my feet only but also my hands and my head!"
1 Thess. 5:23. May...God...sanctify you wholly; and may your spirit and soul and body be kept sound and blameless at the coming of our Lord Jesus Christ.
3 Jn. 1:2. Beloved, I pray that all may go well with you and that you may be in health; I know that it is well with your soul.
1 Tim. 4:8. While bodily training is of some value, godliness is of value in every way, as it holds promise for the present life and also for the life to come.
Jms. 1:21. ...Receive with meekness the implanted word, which is able to save your souls. (Also Ps. 119:9-11, Acts 20:32, 1 Thess. 2:13.)
Ezek. 36:27. I will put my spirit within you, and cause you to walk in my statutes...
1 Jn. 3:24. All who keep his commandments abide in him, and he in them. And by this we know that he abides in us, by the Spirit which he has given us.
2 Cor. 4:16-18. So we do not lose heart. Though our outer nature is wasting away, our inner nature is being renewed every day. For this slight momentary affliction is preparing for us an eternal weight of glory beyond all comparison, because we look not to the things that are seen but to the things that are unseen; for the things that are seen are transient, but the things that are unseen are eternal.

So bist du, Gott, mein Trost und meines Herzens Teil!
Then art thou, God, my comfort and   my   heart's portion!

6. Chorale (See also 73-1.)
●Prayer: Thy will be done in living and dying (156-6)
Herr, wie du willt, so schick's mit mir
Lord, as thou wilt, so ordain-it   for me

Im Leben und im Sterben;
In living and in   dying;

Allein zu   dir steht mein Begier,
Only toward thee (is) my desire,
{Toward thee only is my desire,}

Herr, laß mich nicht verderben!
Lord, let me   not   perish!

Erhalt mich nur in deiner Huld,
Preserve me only in thy favor,
{Only preserve me in thy favor,}

Sonst   wie du willt, gib mir Geduld,
Otherwise (do) as thou wilt; give me patience,

Dein Will, der ist der beste.
Thy will, it is - best.

Ps. 73:26. My flesh and my heart may fail (Luther: verschmachtet), but God is the strength of my heart and my portion (Luther: Trost und Teil) for ever.

*Mt. 8:2–3. ...A leper came to him and knelt before [Jesus], saying, "Lord, if you will, you can make me clean." And he stretched out his hand and touched him, saying, "I will; be clean." And immediately his leprosy was cleansed.
*Mt. 8:5–7. As he entered Capernaum, a centurion came forward to him, beseeching him and saying, "Lord, my servant is lying paralyzed at home, in terrible distress." And he said to him, "I will come and heal him."
Mk. 14:35–36. Going a little farther, [in the garden of Gethsemane, Jesus] fell on the ground and prayed that, if it were possible, the hour might pass from him. And he said, "Abba, Father, all things are possible to thee; remove this cup from me; yet not what I will, but what thou wilt."
Ps. 38:9–10. Lord, all my longing is known to thee (Luther: vor dir ist alle meine Begierde), my sighing is not hidden from thee. My heart throbs, my strength fails me; and the light of my eyes—it also has gone from me. (Also Ps. 42:1–2.)
Ps. 73:25–26. Whom have I in heaven but thee? And there is nothing upon earth that I desire besides thee. My flesh and my heart may fail, but God is the strength of my heart and my portion for ever.
Jms. 1:2–4. Count it all joy, my brethren, when you meet various trials, for you know that the testing of your faith produces steadfastness (Luther: Geduld). And let steadfastness have its full effect, that you may be perfect and complete, lacking in nothing. (Also Lk. 21:19, Heb. 10:36–39.)

BWV 157
Ich lasse dich nicht, du segnest mich denn
(NBA I/34; BC A170, B20)

Funeral Service (106, 157, 198) Apparently it was later adapted for Mary's Purification (Candlemas).

Candlemas (BWV 83, 125, 82, 157, 158, [161], [200]):
*Mal. 3:1–4 (The Lord will suddenly come to his temple and purify his people)
*Lk. 2:22–32 (Mary presents Jesus at the temple; Nunc dimittis)
Librettist: Picander (Christian Friedrich Henrici)

1. Tenor & Bass Duet
●Clinging to Jesus till he blesses: Gen. 32:26 (157-1)
Ich lasse dich nicht,   du segnest mich denn!
I relinquish thee not (unless) thou bless   me   - !

2. Tenor Aria
●Clinging to Jesus for comfort; fixing faith on him (157-2)
Ich halte meinen Jesum feste,
I   hold   my   Jesus tight,

Ich laß ihn nun und ewig nicht.
I'll leave him now and eternally never.
{I'll not leave him now nor ever.}

Gen. 32:22–26. The same night [after sending gifts ahead of him to appease his brother Esau, whom he feared, Jacob] arose and took his two wives, his two maids, and his eleven children, and crossed the ford of the Jabbok. He took them and sent them across the stream, and likewise everything that he had. And Jacob was left alone; and a man wrestled with him until the breaking of the day. When the man saw that he did not prevail against Jacob, he touched the hollow of his thigh; and Jacob's thigh was put out of joint as he wrestled with him. Then he said, "Let me go, for the day is breaking." But Jacob said, *"I will not let you go, unless you bless me."*
S. of S. 3:4 [Bride:] ...I found him whom my soul loves. I held him, and would not let him go...

*Lk. 2:22, 24–28. When the time came for their purification according to the law of Moses, [Mary and Joseph] brought [Jesus] up to Jerusalem to present him to the Lord...and to offer a sacrifice according to what is said in the law of the Lord...Now there was a man in Jerusalem, whose name was Simeon, and this man was righteous and devout, looking for the consolation of Israel, and the Holy Spirit was upon him. And it had been revealed to him by the Holy Spirit that he should not see death before he had seen the Lord's Christ.

Er ist allein mein Aufenthalt,
He is alone my abode,
{He alone is my abode,}

Drum faßt mein Glaube mit Gewalt
Hence grasps my faith with might
{Hence my faith fixes itself mightily on}

Sein segenreiches Angesicht;
His blessed countenance;

Denn dieser Trost ist doch der beste:
For this comfort is indeed the best:

Ich halte meinen Jesum feste!
I hold my Jesus tight!

And inspired by the Spirit he came into the temple; and when the parents brought in the child Jesus, to do for him according to the custom of the law, he took him up in his arms and blessed God...

S. of S. 3:4 [Bride:] ...I found him whom my soul loves. I held him, and would not let him go...

Ps. 63:8. [O Lord,] my soul clings to thee...

Ps. 27:8. [O God,] thou hast said, "Seek ye my face." My heart says to thee, "Thy face, Lord, do I seek."

Ps. 73:25–26. Whom have I in heaven but thee? And there is nothing upon earth that I desire besides thee. My flesh and my heart may fail, but God is the strength of my heart and my portion (Luther: Trost und Teil) for ever.

Jn. 6:66–68. ...Many of [Jesus'] disciples drew back and no longer went about with him. Jesus said to the twelve, "Do you also wish to go away?" Simon Peter answered him, "Lord, to whom shall we go? You have the words of eternal life..."

3. Tenor Recit.

●Clinging to Jesus in trouble, who else is there? (157–3)

Mein lieber Jesu du,
My dear Jesus, thou,

Wenn ich Verdruß und Kummer leide,
When I vexation and trouble suffer,

So bist du meine Freude,
Then art thou my joy,

In Unruh meine Ruh
In unrest my rest

Und in der Angst mein sanftes Bette;
And in - (times of) fear my soft bed;

Die falsche Welt ist nicht getreu,
The false world is not true,

Der Himmel muß veralten,
The heavens must grow-old,

Die Lust der Welt vergeht wie Spreu;
The lust of-the world passes-away like chaff;

Wenn ich dich nicht, mein Jesus, hätte,
If I thee not, my Jesus, had,
{If I had not thee, my Jesus,}

An wen sollt ich mich sonsten halten?
To whom should I - (then) cling?

Drum laß ich nimmermehr von dir,
Therefore part I nevermore from thee (unless)
{Therefore I will never let thee go unless}

Dein Segen bleibe denn bei mir.
Thy blessing remain - with me.

Ps. 73:26. My flesh and my heart may fail, but God is the strength of my heart and my portion for ever.

Hab. 3:17–19. Though the fig tree do not blossom, nor fruit be on the vines, the produce of the olive fail and the fields yield no food, the flock be cut off from the fold and there be no herd in the stalls, yet I will rejoice in the Lord, I will joy in the God of my salvation. God, the Lord, is my strength...

Ps. 43:4. I will go to the altar of God, to God my exceeding joy (Luther: Freude und Wonne)...

Ps. 4:8. In peace I will both lie down and sleep; for thou alone, O Lord, makest me dwell in safety. (Also Ps. 3:5–6.)

Mt. 11:28–29 [Christ]: Come to me, all who labor and are heavy laden, and I will give you rest...You will find rest for your souls. (Also Jer. 6:16.)

Jn. 15:18–19 [Christ]: If the world hates you, know that it has hated me before it hated you. If you were of the world, the world would love its own; but because you are not of the world, but I chose you out of the world, therefore the world hates you. (Also Jn. 17:14, Mt. 5:10–12, 10:24–25, 1 Jn. 3:13.)

1 Jn. 2:15, 17. Do not love the world or the things in the world. If any one loves the world, love for the Father is not in him...And the world passes away, and the lust of it; but he who does the will of God abides for ever. (Also Jms. 4:4.)

Heb. 1:11–12. [The heavens] will perish, but thou remainest; they will all grow old like a garment, like a mantle thou wilt roll them up...

2 Pet. 3:10–12. ...The heavens will pass away with a loud noise, and the elements will be dissolved with fire, and the earth and the works that are upon it will be burned up. Since all these things are thus to be dissolved, what sort of persons ought you to be in lives of holiness and godliness, waiting for and hastening the coming of the day of God...

Mt. 3:12. [God's] winnowing fork is in his hand, and he will clear his threshing floor and gather his wheat into the granary, but the chaff (Luther: Spreu) he will burn with unquenchable fire. (Spreu: also Lk. 3:17, Job 21:18, Ps. 1:4, 35:5, Hos. 13:3)

Ps. 73:28. But for me it is good to be near God (Luther: mich zu Gott halte); I have made the Lord God my refuge...

Ps. 73:25. [O Lord,] whom have I in heaven but thee?...

Gen. 32:26. ...Jacob said, *"I will not let you go, unless you bless me."*

4. Bass Aria, Recit., & Arioso
●Clinging to Jesus affords entrance to heaven (157-4)
Ja, ja, ich halte Jesum feste,
Yes, yes, I hold Jesus fast,

So geh ich auch zum Himmel ein,
Thus enter I also - heaven - ,
{Thus I also enter heaven,}

Wo Gott und seines Lammes Gäste
Where God and his Lamb's guests

In Kronen zu der Hochzeit sein.
(Wearing) crowns at the wedding are.
{Appear at the wedding, wearing crowns.}

Da laß ich nicht, mein Heil, von dir,
There part I not, my Salvation, from thee,
{There I'll not part, O my Salvation, from thee;}

Da bleibt dein Segen auch bei mir.
There remains thy blessing also with me.
{There thy blessing also remains with me.}

///

Ei, wie vergnügt
Ah, how pleasing

Ist mir mein Sterbekasten,
Is to-me my casket,

Weil Jesus mir in Armen liegt!
For Jesus in-my arms does-lie!

So kann mein Geist recht freudig rasten!
So can my spirit right joyfully rest!

Ja, ja, ich halte Jesum feste,
Yes, yes, I hold Jesus tight,

So geh ich auch zum Himmel ein!
Thus enter I also into heaven - !
{Thus I also enter heaven!}

O schöner Ort!
O beautiful place!

Komm, sanfter Tod, und führ mich fort,
Come, gentle death, and lead me forth,

Wo Gott und seines Lammes Gäste
Where God and his Lamb's guests

In Kronen zu der Hochzeit sein.
(Wearing) crowns at the wedding are.
{Appear at the wedding, wearing crowns.}

Rev. 3:11. ...Hold fast what you have, so that no one may seize your crown.
1 Jn. 5:11-12. ...God gave us eternal life, and this life is in his Son. He who has the Son has life; he who has not the Son of God has not life.
Rev. 19:6-9. [In my vision] I heard what seemed to be the voice of a great multitude, like the sound of many waters and like the sound of mighty thunderpeals, crying, "Hallelujah! For the Lord our God the Almighty reigns. Let us rejoice and exult and give him the glory, for the marriage of the Lamb has come, and his Bride has made herself ready; it was granted her to be clothed with fine linen, bright and pure"—for the fine linen is the righteous deeds of the saints. And the angel said to me, "Write this: Blessed are those who are invited to the marriage supper of the Lamb."...
Rev. 2:10-11 [Christ]: ...Be faithful unto death, and I will give you the crown of life. (Also Is. 28:5, 2 Tim. 4:8, 1 Pet. 5:4, Jms. 1:12.)
Gen. 32:26. ...Jacob said, "I will not let you go, unless you bless me."

Phil. 1:21-23. For to me to live is Christ, and to die is gain. If it is to be life in the flesh, that means fruitful labor for me. Yet which I shall choose I cannot tell. I am hard pressed between the two. My desire is to depart and be with Christ, for that is far better. (Also 2 Cor. 5:8.)
*Lk. 2:28-32. [Simeon] took [the child Jesus] up in his arms and blessed God and said, "Lord, now lettest thou thy servant depart in peace, according to thy word; for mine eyes have seen thy salvation which thou hast prepared in the presence of all peoples, a light for revelation to the Gentiles, and for glory to thy people Israel."
Rev. 14:13. I heard a voice from heaven saying, "Write this: Blessed are the dead who die in the Lord henceforth." "Blessed indeed," says the Spirit, "that they may rest from their labors, for their deeds follow them!" (Also Heb. 4:9-11.)
*Lk. 2:28. [Simeon] took [Jesus] up in his arms...
S. of S. 3:4 [Bride:] ...I found him whom my soul loves. I held him, and would not let him go until I had brought him into my mother's house, and into the chamber of her that conceived me.
1 Jn. 5:12. He who has the Son has life; he who has not the Son of God has not life.
Jn. 13:31, 33, 36. ...Jesus said..."Little children, yet a little while I am with you. You will seek me; and as I said to the Jews so now I say to you, 'Where I am going you cannot come.'"...Simon Peter said to him "Lord, where are you going?" Jesus answered, "Where I am going you cannot follow me now; but you shall follow afterward."
Rom. 5:2. ...We rejoice in our hope of sharing the glory of God.
Mt. 22:1-2. Again Jesus spoke to them in parables, saying, "The kingdom of heaven may be compared to a king who gave a marriage feast for his son."
Rev. 19:9. ...Blessed are those who are invited to the marriage supper of the Lamb...
Rev. 21:3-4. ...[Then] the dwelling of God [will be] with men. He will dwell with them, and they shall be his people, and God himself will be

Ich bin erfreut,
I   am happy,

Das Elend dieser Zeit
The misery of-this time

Noch von mir heute abzulegen;
Yet   from me today to-lay-aside;
{I am happy to lay aside the misery of this age even today;}

Denn Jesus wartet mein im Himmel mit dem Segen.
For   Jesus   waits for-me in heaven with (his) blessing.

Da   laß ich nicht, mein Heil,   von dir,
There part I   not,   my Salvation, from thee,
{There I'll not part, O my Salvation, from thee,}

Da   bleibt dein Segen auch bei mir.
There remains thy blessing also with me.
{There thy blessing also remains with me.}

5. Chorale (See also 124–6, 154–8.)
●Clinging to Jesus, he leads me to streams of life (157-5)
Meinen Jesum   laß   ich nicht,
My   Jesus relinquish I   not,
{I will not relinquish my Jesus;}

Geh ihm   ewig an der Seiten;
(I'll) go with-him ever at (his) side;

Christus läßt mich für und für
Christ   lets me forever and ever

Zu dem Lebensbächlein leiten.
To   the   stream-of-life   be-guided.

Selig,   der mit mir so spricht:
Blessed, (is he) who with me thus says:

Meinen Jesum   laß   ich nicht.
My   Jesus relinquish I   not.
{I will not relinquish my Jesus.}

with them; he will wipe away every tear from their eyes, and death shall be no more, neither shall there be mourning nor crying nor pain any more, for the former things have passed away. (Also Rev. 7:15–17, Is. 25:8.)
2 Cor. 5:1–4. We know that if the earthly tent we live in is destroyed, we have a building from God, a house not made with hands, eternal in the heavens. Here indeed we groan, and long to put on our heavenly dwelling, so that by putting it on we may not be found naked. For while we are still in this tent, we sigh with anxiety; not that we would be unclothed, but that we would be further clothed, so that what is mortal may be swallowed up by life. (Also 2 Pet. 1:14, Rom. 7:24–25.)
1 Thess. 4:17. ...[Then] we shall always be with the Lord.
Lk. 14:16–17 [Christ]: ...A man once gave a great banquet, and invited many; and at the time for the banquet he sent his servant to say to those who had been invited, "Come; for all is now ready."
Jn. 14:2–3 [Christ]: In my Father's house are many rooms; if it were not so, would I have told you that I go to prepare a place for you? And when I go and prepare a place for you, I will come again and will take you to myself, that where I am you may be also.
Gen. 32:26. ...Jacob said, "I will not let you go, unless you bless me."

S. of S. 3:4 [Bride:] ...I found him whom my soul loves. I held him, and would not let him go...
Lk. 9:57. As they were going along the road, a man said to [Jesus], "I will follow you wherever you go." (Also Mt. 8:19.)
Ps. 23:1–3. The Lord is my shepherd, I shall not want; he makes me lie down in green pastures. He leads me beside still waters; he restores my soul. He leads me in paths of righteousness for his name's sake.
Rev. 7:17. The Lamb in the midst of the throne will be their shepherd, and he will guide them to springs of living water; and God will wipe away every tear from their eyes.
Jn. 4:13–14. Jesus said, "...Whoever drinks of the water that I shall give him will never thirst; the water that I shall give him will become in him a spring of water welling up to eternal life." (Also Jn. 4:10–11, 7:37–38, Is. 12:3, Rev. 21:6, 22:1, 22:17.)
Jn. 6:66–68. ...Many of [Jesus'] disciples drew back and no longer went about with him. Jesus said to the twelve, "Do you also wish to go away?" Simon Peter answered him, "Lord, to whom shall we go? You have the words of eternal life..."
Josh. 24:2, 15–16. Joshua said to all the people, "...Choose this day whom you will serve...but as for me and my house, we will serve the Lord." Then the people answered, "Far be it from us that we should forsake the Lord, to serve other gods."
Ps. 40:4. Blessed is the man who makes the Lord his trust... (Also Ps. 84:12, 146:3–6, Jer. 17:7.)
Phil. 1:21. To me to live is Christ, and to die is gain.

BWV 158
Der Friede sei mit dir
(NBA I/10; BC A61, A171)

3. **Easter Day** and (possibly in an earlier version) Mary's Purification (Candlemas)
3. Easter Day (BWV 134, 145, 158)
*Acts 13:26–33 (Paul preaches of Christ's death and resurrection in synagogue at Antioch)
*Lk. 24:36–47 (Jesus appears to disciples in Jerusalem after his resurrection)

Mary's Purification (Candlemas) (BWV 83, 125, 82, 157, 158, [161], [200])
+Mal. 3:1–4 (The Lord will suddenly come to his temple and purify his people)
+Lk. 2:22–32 (Mary presents Jesus at the temple; Nunc dimittis)

Librettist: Unknown

1. Bass Recit.
●Peace offered by Christ to troubled conscience (158–1)
Der Friede sei mit dir,
- Peace be with thee,

Du ängstliches Gewissen!
(O) thou anxious conscience!

Dein Mittler stehet hier,
Thy mediator stands here,

Der hat dein Schuldenbuch
He hath thy book-of-debts

Und des Gesetzes Fluch
And the Law's curse

Verglichen und zerissen.
Settled and torn-up.

Der Friede sei mit dir,
- Peace be with thee:

Der Fürste dieser Welt,
The prince of-this world,

Der deiner Seele nachgestellt,
Who for-thy soul did-lie-in-wait,
{Who did lie in wait for thy soul,}

Ist durch des Lammes Blut bezwungen und gefällt.
Is through the Lamb's blood overpowered and brought-down.
{Is overpowered and brought down through the blood of the Lamb.}

Mein Herz, was bist du so betrübt,
My heart, why art thou so troubled,

*Lk. 24:36–40. As [the disciples] were [discussing the reports of Christ's resurrection], Jesus himself stood among them and said to them, "Peace to you!" (Luther: Friede sei mit euch). But they were startled and frightened, and supposed that they saw a spirit. And he said to them, "Why are you troubled, and why do questionings rise in your hearts? See my hands and my feet, that it is I myself; handle me, and see; for a spirit has not flesh and bones as you see that I have." (Also Jn. 20:19–21.)

Jn. 14:27 [Christ]: Peace I leave with you; my peace I give to you; not as the world gives do I give to you. Let not your hearts be troubled, neither let them be afraid.

Col. 3:15. Let the peace of Christ rule in your hearts...

Is. 57:20–21. But the wicked are like the tossing sea; for it cannot rest ...There is no peace, says my God, for the wicked. (Also Is. 48:22.)

Rom. 2:15–16. [Men] show that what the law requires is written on their hearts, while their conscience (Luther: Gewissen) also bears witness and their conflicting thoughts accuse or perhaps excuse them on that day when, according to my gospel, God judges the secrets of men by Christ Jesus.

1 Jn. 3:19–21. By this we shall know that we are of the truth, and reassure our hearts before him whenever our hearts condemn us; for God is greater than our hearts, and he knows everything. Beloved, if our hearts do not condemn us, we have confidence before God.

Heb. 9:15. [Christ] is the mediator (Luther: Mittler) of a new covenant, so that those who are called may receive the promised eternal inheritance, since a death has occurred which redeems them from the transgressions under the first covenant. (Also 1 Tim. 2:5–6, Heb. 12:24.)

Gal. 3:10. For all who rely on works of the law are under a curse; for it is written, "Cursed be every one who does not abide by all things written in the book of the law, and do them." (Also Gal. 3:13.)

Col. 2:13–15. You, who were dead in trespasses and the uncircumcision of your flesh, God made alive together with him, having forgiven us all our trespasses, having canceled the bond which stood against us with its legal demands; this he set aside, nailing it to the cross. He disarmed the principalities and powers and made a public example of them, triumphing over them in him.

Jn. 12:30–31. Jesus [said], "...Now is the judgment of this world, now shall the ruler (Luther: Fürst) of this world be cast out." (Also Jn. 16:11, Eph. 2:2, 1 Jn. 5:19.)

Rev. 12:10–12. And I heard a loud voice in heaven, saying, "Now the salvation and the power and the kingdom of our God and the authority of his Christ have come, for the accuser of our brethren has been thrown down, who accuses them day and night before our God. And they have conquered him by the blood of the Lamb and by the word of their testimony, for they loved not their lives unto death. Rejoice then, O heaven and you that dwell therein!..."

Ps. 42:5/11/43:5. Why are you cast down (Luther: betrübst du dich), O my soul, and why are you disquieted within me? Hope in God; for I shall again praise him, my help and my God.

Da dich doch Gott durch Christum liebt?
Since thee indeed God through Christ loves?
{Since God indeed loves thee through Christ?}

Er selber spricht zu mir:
He himself says to me:

Der Friede sei mit dir!
- Peace be with thee!

Rom. 8:31, 33–34. ...If God is for us, who is against us?...Who shall bring any charge against God's elect? It is God who justifies; who is to condemn? Is it Christ Jesus, who died, yes, who was raised from the dead, who is at the right hand of God, who indeed intercedes for us?
1 Jn. 4:10. In this is love, not that we loved God but that he loved us and sent his Son to be the expiation for our sins.
Rom. 5:8. God shows his love for us in that while we were yet sinners Christ died for us.
2 Thess. 2:16–17. Now may our Lord Jesus Christ himself, and God our Father, who loved us and gave us eternal comfort and good hope through grace, comfort your hearts...

2. Bass Aria and Soprano Chorale (Perhaps from an earlier work)
●Farewell given to world, heaven's splendor preferred (158–2)
Welt, ade, ich bin dein müde,
World, farewell, I am of-thee weary,

Salems Hütten steh'n mir an,
Salem's (dwellings) suit me - ,

Welt, ade, ich bin dein müde,
World, farewell, I am of-thee weary,

Ich will nach dem Himmel zu,
I would to - heaven (go),

Wo ich Gott in Ruh und Friede
Where I God in rest and peace

Ewig selig schauen kann.
Eternally blessed behold can.
{Where I, in rest and peace can ever blessedly behold God.}

Da wird sein der rechte Friede
There will be - true peace
{There I will find true peace}

Und die ewig stolze Ruh.
And - eternally splendid rest.

Da bleib ich, da hab ich Vergnügen zu wohnen,
There stay I, there have I pleasure to dwell,
{There I'll remain, there I'll be delighted to dwell,}

Welt, bei dir ist Krieg und Streit,
World, with thee is war and strife,

1 Jn. 2:15. Do not love the world or the things in the world. If any one loves the world, love for the Father is not in him. (Also Jms. 4:4.)
+Lk. 2:29. Lord, now lettest thou thy servant depart in peace...
Ps. 84:10. [O Lord,] a day in thy courts is better than a thousand elsewhere. I would rather be a doorkeeper in the house of my God than dwell in the tents of wickedness.
Ps. 65:4. Blessed is he whom thou dost choose and bring near, to dwell in thy courts!...
Ps. 76:1–2. [God's] abode has been established in Salem, his dwelling place in Zion. (Salem: also Heb. 7:1–2)
Heb. 12:22. But you have come to Mount Zion and to the city of the living God, the heavenly Jerusalem...
Rev. 21:10–11, 21. In the Spirit [the angel] carried me away to a great, high mountain, and showed me the holy city Jerusalem coming down out of heaven from God, having the glory of God, its radiance like a most rare jewel, like a jasper, clear as crystal...And the twelve gates were twelve pearls, each of the gates made of a single pearl, and the street of the city was pure gold, transparent as glass.
Heb. 4:9–11. So then, there remains a sabbath rest for the people of God; for whoever enters God's rest also ceases from his labors as God did from his. Let us therefore strive to enter that rest...
Rev. 14:13. ...Blessed are the dead who die in the Lord henceforth... that they may rest from their labors, for their deeds follow them!
Rom. 8:18. ...The sufferings of this present time are not worth comparing with the glory that is to be revealed to us. (Also 2 Cor. 4:17.)
1 Cor. 13:12. Now we see in a mirror dimly, but then face to face...
Phil. 3:8–9. I count everything as loss because of the surpassing worth of knowing Christ Jesus my Lord. For his sake I have suffered the loss of all things and count them as refuse, in order that I may gain Christ and be found in him...
Jms. 4:1–2, 4. What causes wars, and what causes fightings among you? Is it not your passions that are at war in your members? You desire and do not have; so you kill. And you covet and cannot obtain; so you fight and wage war... Unfaithful creatures! Do you not know that friendship with the world is enmity with God? Therefore whoever wishes to be a friend of the world makes himself an enemy of God.
Mt. 24:6. ...You...hear of wars and rumors of wars...

Nichts denn lauter Eitelkeit;
Nothing but sheer vanity;

Da prang ich gezieret mit himmlischen Kronen.
There parade I adorned with heavenly crowns.
{There I'll proudly wear my heavenly crown.}

In dem Himmel allezeit
In - heaven (there is) at-all-times,

Friede, Freud und Seligkeit.
Peace, joy, and blessedness.

3. Bass Recit. and Arioso (Perhaps from an earlier work)
●Prayer: May I be a child of peace until I enter heaven (158-3)
Nun, Herr, regiere meinen Sinn,
Now, Lord, rule my disposition,

Damit ich auf der Welt,
So-that I on the earth—

So lang es dir, mich hier zu lassen, noch gefällt,
As long as (it) thee, me here to leave, yet pleases—
{As long as it pleases thee to leave me here—}

Ein Kind des Friedens bin,
A child of peace may-be,

Und laß mich zu dir aus meinen Leiden
And let me to thee from my afflictions

Wie Simeon in Frieden scheiden!
Like Simeon in peace depart!
{And let me—like Simeon—depart in peace from my afflictions to thee!}

Da bleib ich, da hab ich Vergnügen zu wohnen,
There stay I, there have I pleasure to dwell,
{There I'll remain, there I'll be delighted to dwell,}

Da prang ich gezieret mit himmlischen Kronen.
There parade I adorned with heavenly crowns.
{There I'll proudly wear my heavenly crown.}

4. Chorale (See also 4–6.)
●Christ died as our paschal lamb (158-4)
Hier ist das rechte Osterlamm,
Here is the proper Easter-lamb,

Eph. 4:17. ...The Gentiles [live] in the futility (Luther: Eitelkeit) of their minds...
Jn. 16:33 [Christ]: I have said this to you, that in me you may have peace. In the world you have tribulation; but be of good cheer, I have overcome the world.
1 Pet. 5:4. When the chief Shepherd is manifested you will obtain the unfading crown of glory. (crown: also Is. 28:5, 2 Tim. 4:8, Jms. 1:12, Rev. 2:10)
Ps. 16:11. [O Lord]...in thy presence there is fulness of joy, in thy right hand are pleasures for evermore.
Rev. 21:4. [In paradise, God] will wipe away every tear from their eyes, and death shall be no more, neither shall there be mourning nor crying nor pain any more, for the former things have passed away. (Also Rev. 7:15–17, Is. 25:8.)

Col. 3:15. Let the peace of Christ rule in your hearts, to which indeed you were called in the one body...
Phil. 4:7. The peace of God, which passes all understanding, will keep your hearts and your minds (Luther: Sinne)...
***Lk. 24:36.** ...Jesus himself [suddenly] stood among [his disciples] and said to them, "Peace to you (Luther: Friede sei mit euch)!" (Also Jn. 20:19–21.)
Jn. 14:27 [Christ]: Peace I leave with you; my peace I give to you; not as the world gives do I give to you. Let not your hearts be troubled, neither let them be afraid.
Heb. 12:14. Strive for peace with all men, and for the holiness without which no one will see the Lord.
Rom. 12:18. If possible, so far as it depends upon you, live peaceably with all.
Mt. 5:9 [Christ]: Blessed are the peacemakers, for they shall be called sons of God.
+Lk. 2:25-32. Now there was a man in Jerusalem, whose name was Simeon, and this man was righteous and devout, looking for the consolation of Israel, and the Holy Spirit was upon him. And it had been revealed to him by the Holy Spirit that he should not see death before he had seen the Lord's Christ. And inspired by the Spirit he came into the temple; and when the parents brought in the child Jesus, to do for him according to the custom of the law, he took him up in his arms and blessed God and said, "Lord, now lettest thou thy servant depart in peace, according to thy word; for mine eyes have seen thy salvation which thou hast prepared in the presence of all peoples, a light for revelation to the Gentiles, and for glory to thy people Israel."
2 Tim. 4:6, 8. ...The time of my departure has come...Henceforth there is laid up for me the crown of righteousness...
Jms. 1:12. Blessed is the man who endures trial, for when he has stood the test he will receive the crown of life which God has promised to those who love him. (crown: also 1 Pet. 5:4, Rev. 2:10)

1 Cor. 5:7. ...Christ, our paschal lamb, has been sacrificed.
1 Pet. 2:24. [Christ] himself bore our sins in his body on the tree...By his wounds you have been healed.

Davon   Gott hat geboten;
Of-which God has commanded;

Das ist hoch an des Kreuzes Stamm
It   has high on   the   cross's   trunk

In heisser Lieb gebraten.
In   hot   love   broiled.

Des Blut zeichnet unsre Tür,
Its blood marks   our door,

Das   hält   der Glaub dem Tode für;
That displays - faith   to   Death - ;
{Our faith shows this blood to approaching Death;}

Der Würger kann uns nicht rühren.
The destroyer can us   not   touch.
{And so the destroyer can not touch us.}

Alleluja!
Alleluia!

Heb. 9:22. Indeed, under the law almost everything is purified with blood, and without the shedding of blood there is no forgiveness of sins.

Ex. 12:1, 3, 5, 7, 11–13. The Lord said to Moses and Aaron in the land of Egypt...Tell all the congregation of Israel that on the tenth day of this month they shall take every man a lamb...Your lamb shall be without blemish...Then they shall take some of the blood, and put it on the two doorposts and the lintel of the houses...It is the Lord's passover. For I will pass through the land of Egypt that night, and I will smite all the first-born in the land of Egypt, both man and beast...The blood shall be a sign for you...and when I see the blood, I will pass over you...

*Lk. 24:46–47. ...Thus it is written, that the Christ should suffer and on the third day rise from the dead, and that repentance and forgiveness of sins should be preached in his name to all nations, beginning from Jerusalem.

Jn. 1:29. ...[John] saw Jesus coming toward him, and said, "Behold, the Lamb of God, who takes away the sin of the world!"

Is. 53:7, 10. He was oppressed, and he was afflicted, yet he opened not his mouth; like a lamb that is led to the slaughter, and like a sheep that before its shearers is dumb, so he opened not his mouth...Yet it was the will of the Lord to bruise him; he has put him to grief; when he makes himself an offering for sin...

Rev. 5:12. ...Worthy is the Lamb who was slain, to receive power and wealth and wisdom and might and honor and glory and blessing!

Heb. 2:14–15. Since therefore the children share in flesh and blood, [Christ] himself likewise partook of the same nature, that through death he might destroy him who has the power of death, that is, the devil, and deliver all those who through fear of death were subject to lifelong bondage.

Rev. 20:6. Blessed and holy is he who shares in the first resurrection! Over such the second death has no power...

BWV 159
Sehet! Wir gehn hinauf gen Jerusalem
(NBA I/8; BC A50)

Estomihi (Quinquagesima) (BWV 23, 22, 127, 159)
*1 Cor. 13:1–13 (In praise of love)
*Lk. 18:31–43 (Jesus and the twelve go to Jerusalem, healing of a blind man)
Librettist: Picander (Christian Friedrich Henrici)

1. Bass Arioso & Alto Recit.
●Dialogue regarding Jesus' plan to go to Jerusalem (159-1)
   Sehet!
   Behold!

Komm, schaue doch,   mein Sinn,
Come,   see   - , (O) my   mind,
{Come, ponder now, O my mind,}

*Lk. 18:31–34. Taking the twelve, [Jesus] said to them, *"Behold, we are going up to Jerusalem,* and everything that is written of the Son of man by the prophets will be accomplished. For he will be delivered to the Gentiles, and will be mocked and shamefully treated and spit upon; they will scourge him and kill him, and on the third day he will rise." But they understood none of these things; this saying was hid from them, and they did not grasp what was said.

Jn. 11:7–8, 16, 47–53. ...[Jesus] said to the disciples, "Let us go into Judea again." The disciples said to him, "Rabbi, the Jews were but now seeking to stone you, and are you going there again?"...Thomas... said to his fellow disciples, "Let us also go, that we may die with him." ...[And after Jesus had raised Lazarus from the dead] the chief priests

Wo   geht dein Jesus hin?
Where goes thy Jesus - ?
{Where is thy Jesus going?}

    Wir   gehn hinauf
    We are-going up

O harter Gang! hinauf?
O hard passage! Up?

O ungeheur er Berg,   den meine Sünden zeigen!
O monstrous mountain, (to) which my   sins   do-point!

Wie sauer wirst du müssen steigen!
How bitterly wilt thou have to-climb!
{How bitter will be thy climb!}

    Gen   Jerusalem.
    Toward Jerusalem.

Ach, gehe nicht!
Ah,   go   not!
{Ah, do not go!}

Dein Kreuz ist dir   schon zugericht',
Thy   cross is for-thee already prepared,
{Thy cross is already prepared for thee,}

Wo   du dich sollst zu Tode bluten;
Where thou - must to death bleed;
{Where thou must bleed to death;}

Hier sucht man Geißeln vor, dort bindt man Ruten;
Here seek they scourges - , there bind they switches,
{Here they seek scourges, there they bind switches,}

Die Bande warten dein;
  - Bonds   await thee;

Ach, gehe selber nicht hinein!
Ah,   go thyself not   in!
{Do not go into Jerusalem thyself!}

Doch bliebest   du zurücke stehen,
Yet wouldst-stay thou back   - ,
{Yet if thou wouldst stay back,}

So   müßt   ich selbst nicht nach Jerusalem,
Then were-forced I myself not   to   Jerusalem (but)
{Then I myself would be forced to go—not to Jerusalem but,}

Ach, leider   in die Hölle gehen.
Ah,   alas, (down) to - hell   to-go.
{Alas, down to hell.}

and the Pharisees gathered the council, and said, "What are we to do? For this man performs many signs. If we let him go on thus, every one will believe in him, and the Romans will come and destroy both our holy place and our nation." But one of them, Caiaphas, who was high priest that year, said to them, "You know nothing at all; you do not understand that it is expedient for you that one man should die for the people, and that the whole nation should not perish." He did not say this of his own accord, but being high priest that year he prophesied that Jesus should die for the nation, and not for the nation only, but to gather into one the children of God who are scattered abroad. So from that day on they took counsel how to put him to death.
2 Sam. 15:23, 30. [When King David had learned that his son Absalom had proclaimed himself king, he fled,] and all the country wept aloud as all the people passed by, and the king crossed the brook Kidron, and all the people passed on toward the wilderness...But David went up the ascent of the Mount of Olives, weeping as he went, barefoot and with his head covered; and all the people who were with him covered their heads, and they went up, weeping as they went.
Jn. 18:1. [After Jesus had celebrated the Passover with his disciples and had told them that one of their number would betray him,] he went forth with his disciples across the Kidron valley, where there was a garden [named Gethsemane], which he and his disciples entered.
Lk. 22:39–42, 44, 47–48, 54. And [Jesus] came out, and went, as was his custom, to the Mount of Olives [to the garden of Gethsemane]; and the disciples followed him. And when he came to the place he said to them, "Pray that you may not enter into temptation."...And he withdrew from them about a stone's throw, and knelt down and prayed, "Father, if thou art willing, remove this cup from me; nevertheless not my will, but thine, be done."...And being in an agony [Jesus] prayed more earnestly; and his sweat became like great drops of blood falling down upon the ground...While [Jesus] was still speaking, there came a crowd, and the man called Judas, one of the twelve, was leading them. He drew near to Jesus to kiss him; but Jesus said to him, "Judas, would you betray the Son of man with a kiss?"... Then they seized him and led him away...
Mt. 27:1–2, 26–31. When morning came, all the chief priests and the elders of the people took counsel against Jesus to put him to death; and they bound him (Luther: bunden ihn) and led him away and delivered him to Pilate the governor...Then [Pilate]...having scourged Jesus (Luther: Jesum ließ er geißeln), delivered him to be crucified. Then the soldiers of the governor took Jesus into the praetorium, and they gathered the whole battalion before him. And they stripped him and put a scarlet robe upon him, and plaiting a crown of thorns they put it on his head, and put a reed in his right hand. And kneeling before him they mocked him, saying, "Hail, King of the Jews!" And they spat upon him, and took the reed and struck him on the head. And when they had mocked him, they stripped him of the robe, and put his own clothes on him, and led him away to crucify him. (Also Mk. 15:1–20, Lk. 22:63–23:25, Jn. 18:28–19:17.)
Heb. 2:9. ...So that...he might taste death for every one.
1 Pet. 2:24. He himself bore our sins in his body on the tree, that we might die to sin and live to righteousness. By his wounds you have been healed.

2. Alto Aria & Soprano Chorale
•Accompanying Christ through humiliation & death (159-2)
Ich folge dir nach
I   follow thee after
{I follow after thee}

Ich will hier bei dir stehen,
I   will here by thee stand,
{I will stand here beside thee,}

Durch Speichel und Schmach;
Through spittle   and humiliation;

Verachte mich doch nicht!
Disdain   me please not!
{Please do not disdain me!}

Am   Kreuz will ich dich noch umfangen,
On-the cross would I   thee yet   embrace,

Von dir will ich nicht gehen,
From thee would I   not   go,

Bis dir dein Herze bricht.
Till thee thy heart breaks.
{Till the time comes when thy heart shall break.}

Dich laß ich nicht aus meiner Brust,
Thee let I   not from my   breast,
{I will not let thee from my breast,}

Wenn dein Haupt wird erblassen
When thy head   - grows-pale

Im   letzten Todesstoß,
In-the final stroke-of-death,

Und wenn du endlich scheiden mußt,
And when thou finally   depart   must,
{And when thou finally must depart,}

Alsdenn will ich dich fassen,
Even-then would I   thee embrace,
{Even then I would embrace thee,}

Sollst du dein Grab in mir erlangen.
Shalt thou thy grave in me   attain.
{Thou shalt find thy grave in me.}

In meinen Arm und Schoß.
In   my   arm and bosom.

3. Tenor Recit.
•Mourning for Jesus; deferring pleasure till heaven (159-3)
Nun will ich mich,
Now would I - ,

Mein Jesu, über dich
My   Jesu, for thee

Jn. 11:16. Thomas...said to his fellow disciples, "Let us also go [to Jerusalem with Jesus], that we may die with him."
Mt. 16:24–25. Jesus told his disciples, "If any man would come after me, let him deny himself and take up his cross and follow me. For whoever would save his life will lose it, and whoever loses his life for my sake will find it." (Also Mt. 10:38, Mk. 8:34–35, Lk. 9:23–24.)
Lk. 9:57. ...A man said to [Jesus], "I will follow you wherever you go." (Also Mt. 8:19.)

[From the Passion & Easter Accounts]
Mt. 26:33–35. Peter declared to [Jesus], "Though they all fall away because of you, I will never fall away." Jesus said to him, "Truly, I say to you, this very night, before the cock crows, you will deny me three times." Peter said to him, "Even if I must die with you, I will not deny you." And so said all the disciples. (Also Mk. 14:29, Lk. 22:33–34.)
Jn. 18:3, 12. Judas, procuring a band of soldiers and some officers from the chief priests and the Pharisees, went [to the garden where Jesus was] with lanterns and torches and weapons...So the band of soldiers and their captain and the officers of the Jews seized Jesus and bound him.
Mt. 26:56. ...Then all the disciples forsook him and fled. (Also Mk. 14:50.)
Jn. 19:17–18, 25. So they took Jesus, and he went out bearing his own cross, to the place called the place of a skull, which is called in Hebrew Golgotha. There they crucified him...But standing by the cross of Jesus were his mother, and his mother's sister, Mary the wife of Clopas, and Mary Magdalene.
Mt. 27:46. And about the ninth hour Jesus cried with a loud voice, "Eli, Eli, lama sabachthani?" that is, "My God, my God, why hast thou forsaken me?" (Also Mk. 15:34.)
Mt. 27:50, 55–56. And Jesus cried again with a loud voice and yielded up his spirit...There were also many women there, looking on from afar, who had followed Jesus from Galilee, ministering to him; among whom were Mary Magdalene, and Mary the mother of James and Joseph, and the mother of the sons of Zebedee.
Jn. 19:38–42. After this Joseph of Arimathea, who was a disciple of Jesus, but secretly, for fear of the Jews, asked Pilate that he might take away the body of Jesus, and Pilate gave him leave. So he came and took away his body. Nicodemus also, who had at first come to him by night, came bringing a mixture of myrrh and aloes, about a hundred pounds' weight. They took the body of Jesus, and bound it in linen cloths with the spices, as is the burial custom of the Jews. Now in the place where he was crucified there was a garden, and in the garden a new tomb where no one had ever been laid. So because of the Jewish day of Preparation, as the tomb was close at hand, they laid Jesus there.
Jn. 20:11–17. But Mary stood weeping outside the tomb, and as she wept she stooped to look into the tomb; and she saw two angels in white, sitting where the body of Jesus had lain, one at the head and one at the feet. They said to her, "Woman, why are you weeping?" She said to them, "Because they have taken away my Lord, and I do not know where they have laid him." Saying this, she turned round and saw Jesus standing, but she did not know that it was Jesus. Jesus said to her, "Woman, why are you weeping? Whom do you seek?" Supposing him to be the gardener, she said to him, "Sir, if you have carried him away, tell me where you have laid him, and I

In meinem   Winkel grämen;
In my (own) little-corner grieve;
{Now would I grieve for thee, O my Jesu, in my little corner;}

Die Welt mag immerhin
The world may evermore
{Let the world evermore}

Den Gift der Wollust zu sich nehmen,
The poison of pleasure to itself take,
{Feed on the poison of sensual pleasure,}

Ich labe mich an meinen Tränen
I'll feast - on my   tears

Und will mich eher nicht
And would - ere-that not

Nach einer Freude sehnen,
For   any enjoyment yearn,

Bis dich mein Angesicht
Till thee my countenance
{Till my countenance}

Wird in der Herrlichkeit erblicken.
Will in -   glory   see.
{Will see thee in glory.}

Bis ich durch dich erlöset   bin;
Till I through thee redeemed have-been;
{Till I have been redeemed through thee;}

Da will ich mich mit dir erquicken.
Then will I myself with thee refresh.
{Then I will find refreshment in thee.}

4. Bass Aria
●Christ's passion now over and salvation accomplished (159-4)
Es ist vollbracht,
It is finished,

Das Leid ist alle,
The pain is over,

will take him away." Jesus said to her "Mary." She turned and said to him in Hebrew, "Rabboni!" (which means Teacher). Jesus said to her, "Do not hold me, for I have not yet ascended to the Father; but go to my brethren and say to them, I am ascending to my Father and your Father, to my God and your God."
[End of Passion & Easter accounts]

Lk. 6:21 [Christ]: ...Blessed are you that weep now, for you shall laugh.
Heb. 11:24-26. By faith Moses...[chose] rather to share ill-treatment with the people of God than to enjoy the fleeting pleasures of sin. He considered abuse suffered for the Christ greater wealth than the treasures of Egypt, for he looked to the reward.
1 Jn. 2:15-17. Do not love the world or the things in the world. If any one loves the world, love for the Father is not in him. For all that is in the world, the lust of the flesh and the lust of the eyes and the pride of life, is not of the Father but is of the world. And the world passes away, and the lust of it; but he who does the will of God abides for ever. (Also Jms. 4:4.)
1 Pet. 4:13. Rejoice in so far as you share Christ's sufferings, that you may also rejoice and be glad when his glory is revealed.
2 Tim. 2:11-12. The saying is sure: If we have died with him, we shall also live with him; if we endure, we shall also reign with him... (Also Rom. 8:17.)
1 Jn. 3:2. ...[Then] we shall see him as he is.
1 Cor. 13:12. Now we see in a mirror dimly, but then face to face... (Also Rev. 22:4.)
Jn. 16:19-22. ...[Jesus] said to [his disciples], "Is this what you are asking yourselves, what I meant by saying, 'A little while, and you will not see me, and again a little while, and you will see me'? Truly, truly, I say to you, you will weep and lament, but the world will rejoice; you will be sorrowful, but your sorrow will turn into joy. When a woman is in travail she has sorrow, because her hour has come; but when she is delivered of the child, she no longer remembers the anguish, for joy that a child is born into the world. So you have sorrow now, but I will see you again and your hearts will rejoice, and no one will take your joy from you.
Rev. 7:17. [In paradise] the Lamb in the midst of the throne will be their shepherd, and he will guide them to springs of living water; and God will wipe away every tear from their eyes.

*Lk. 18:31-33. Taking the twelve, [Jesus] said to them, "...Everything that is written of the Son of man by the prophets will be accomplished. For he will be delivered to the Gentiles, and will be mocked and shamefully treated and spit upon; they will scourge him and kill him, and on the third day he will rise."
Jn. 19:28-30. After [Jesus had been nailed to the cross], knowing that all was now finished, [he] said (to fulfil the scripture), "I thirst." A bowl full of vinegar stood there; so they put a sponge full of the vinegar on hyssop and held it to his mouth. When Jesus had received the vinegar, he said, *"It is finished"* (Luther: Es ist vollbracht); and he bowed his head and gave up his spirit.

Wir sind von unserm Sündenfalle
We are from our fall-into-sin

In Gott gerecht gemacht.
In God righteous made.
{In God made righteous.}

Nun will ich eilen
Now would I hasten

Und meinem Jesu Dank erteilen,
And to-my Jesus thanks impart,

Welt, gute Nacht!
World, good night!

Es ist vollbracht!
It is finished!

Heb. 10:14. By a single offering [Christ] has perfected for all time those who are sanctified. (Also Heb. 10:10, 12.)
Rom. 3:24–25. [All who believe] are justified by [God's] grace as a gift, through the redemption which is in Christ Jesus, whom God put forward as an expiation by his blood, to be **received by faith**...
Rom. 5:17–18. If, because of one man's trespass, death reigned through that one man, much more will those who receive the abundance of grace and the free gift of righteousness reign in life through the one man Jesus Christ. Then as one man's trespass led to condemnation for all men, so one man's act of righteousness leads to acquittal and life for all men. (Also 1 Cor. 15:21–22.)
2 Cor. 9:15. Thanks be to God for his inexpressible gift!
1 Pet. 1:18–19. You know that you were ransomed from the futile ways inherited from your fathers, not with perishable things such as silver or gold, but with the precious blood of Christ, like that of a lamb without blemish or spot.
1 Cor. 6:19–20. You are not your own; you were bought with a price...
Rom. 12:2. I appeal to you...by the mercies God, ...do not be conformed to this world but be transformed by the renewal of your mind, that you may prove what is the will of God, what is good and acceptable and perfect.
1 Jn. 2:15. Do not love the world or the things in the world. If any one loves the world, love for the Father is not in him.

5. Chorale (See also 182-7.)
●Christ's passion is my joy for it offers me heaven (159-5)
Jesu, deine Passion
Jesus, thy passion

Ist mir lauter Freude,
Is for-me pure joy,
{Is pure joy for me,}

Deine Wunden, Kron und Hohn
Thy wounds, crown, and scorn

Meines Herzens Weide;
My heart's pasture;

Meine Seel auf Rosen geht,
My soul upon roses walks,
{My soul walks upon roses,}

Wenn ich dran gedenke,
When I this remember,
{When I remember that}

In dem Himmel eine Stätt
In - heaven an abode

Lk. 24:26. Was it not necessary that the Christ should suffer these things and enter into his glory?
Is. 53:3–5, 10, 12. He was despised and rejected by men; a man of sorrows, and acquainted with grief; and as one from whom men hide their faces he was despised, and we esteemed him not. Surely he has borne our griefs and carried our sorrows; yet we esteemed him stricken, smitten by God, and afflicted. But he was wounded for our transgressions, he was bruised for our iniquities; upon him was the chastisement that made us whole, and with his stripes we are healed... It was the will of the Lord to bruise him...He poured out his soul to death, and was numbered with the transgressors; yet he bore the sin of many and made intercession for the transgressors.
1 Pet. 2:24. He himself bore our sins in his body on the tree, that we might die to sin and live to righteousness. By his wounds you have been healed. (Also Gal. 3:13.)
Jn. 1:29. ...Behold, the Lamb of God, who takes away the sin of the world! (Also Jn. 1:36.)
Rev. 7:17. The Lamb...will be [the] shepherd [of his people], and he will guide them to springs of living water...
Ps. 100:3. ...We are his people, and the sheep of his pasture. (Also Ps. 95:6–7.)
S. of S. 2:16 [Bride]: My beloved is mine and I am his, he pastures his flock among the lilies (Luther: Rosen). (Also S. of S. 6:3.)
Rom. 5:2. Through [Christ] we have obtained access to this grace in which we stand, and we rejoice in our hope of sharing the glory of God.
2 Pet. 1:11. There will be richly provided for you an entrance into the eternal kingdom of our Lord and Savior Jesus Christ.

Mir deswegen schenke.
To-me by-this is-given.
{When I remember that, because of these sufferings, an abode in heaven is given to us.}

BWV 160
Ich weiß, daß mein Erlöser lebt

This cantata was composed by Georg Philipp Telemann.

BWV 161
Komm, du süße Todesstunde
(NBA I/23; BC A135a/b)

16. S. after Trinity. Later, Bach also designated it for Mary's Purification (Candlemas)
16 S. after Trinity (BWV 161, 95, 8, 27)
*Eph. 3:13–21 (Paul's prayer for the Ephesians; that they be spiritually strengthened)
*Lk. 7:11–17 (Resurrection of boy at Nain)

Mary's Purification (Candlemas) (BWV 83, 125, 82, 157, 158, [161], [200])
+Mal. 3:1–4 (The Lord will suddenly come to his temple and purify his people)
+Lk. 2:22–32 (Mary presents Jesus at the temple; Nunc dimittis)

Librettist: Salomon Franck

1. Alto Aria
●Yearning for death: Sweetness comes out of death (161-1)
Komm, du süße Todesstunde,
Come, thou sweet hour-of-death,

Da mein Geist
When my spirit

Honig speist
(On) honey shall-feed

Aus des Löwen Munde;
Out-of the lion's mouth;

Mache meinen Abschied süße,
Make my departure sweet,

Säume nicht,
Tarry not

Jn. 14:1–3 [Christ]: Let not your hearts be troubled; believe in God, believe also in me. In my Father's house are many rooms; if it were not so, would I have told you that I go to prepare a place for you? And when I go and prepare a place for you, I will come again and will take you to myself, that where I am you may be also. (Also Jn. 12:26.)

*Lk. 7:11–12, 14. ...[Jesus] went to a city called Nain, and his disciples and a great crowd went with him. As he drew near to the gate of the city, behold, a man who had died was being carried out, the only son of his mother, and she was a widow; and a large crowd from the city was with her...And [Jesus] came and touched the bier...and he said, "Young man, I say to you, arise."
Phil. 1:21. To me to live is Christ, and to die is gain.
+Lk. 2:25–30. There was a man in Jerusalem, whose name was Simeon, and this man was righteous and devout, looking for the consolation of Israel, and the Holy Spirit was upon him. And it had been revealed to him by the Holy Spirit that he should not see death before he had seen the Lord's Christ. And inspired by the Spirit he came into the temple; and when the parents brought in the child Jesus, to do for him according to the custom of the law, he took him up in his arms and blessed God and said, "Lord, now lettest thou thy servant depart in peace, according to thy word; for mine eyes have seen thy salvation."
Ps. 116:15. Precious in the sight of the Lord is the death of his saints.
Ps. 116:3. The snares of death encompassed me...
Ps. 22:21. Save me from the mouth of the lion...!
Judges 14:1–2, 5–9, 12, 14. Samson went down to Timnah, and at Timnah he saw one of the daughters of the Philistines. Then he came up, and told his father and mother, "I saw one of the daughters of the Philistines at Timnah; now get her for me as my wife."...Then Samson went down with his father and mother to Timnah, and he came to the vineyards of Timnah. And behold, a young lion roared against him; and the Spirit of the Lord came mightily upon him, and he tore the lion asunder as one tears a kid; and he had nothing in his hand. But he did not tell his father or his mother what he had done. Then he went down and talked with the woman; and she pleased Samson well. And after a while he returned to take her; and he turned aside to see the carcass of the lion, and behold, there was a swarm of bees in the body of the lion, and honey. He scraped it out into his hands, and went on, eating as he went; and he came to his father and mother, and gave some to them, and they ate. But he did not tell them that he had taken the honey from the carcass of the lion...And Samson said to [his Philistine companions], "Let me now put a riddle to you...Out of the eater came something to eat. Out of the strong came something sweet." [But] they could not...tell what the riddle was.

Letztes Licht,
Final light,

Daß ich meinen Heiland küsse.
So-that I my Savior might-kiss.

2. Tenor Recit.
●Worldly pleasures detested; death yearned for (161--2)
Welt! deine Lust ist Last!
World, thy pleasures (are) burdens!

Dein Zucker ist mir als ein Gift verhaßt!
Thy sugar is to-me like a poison detested!
{Thy sugar is to me like a detested poison!}

Dein Freudenlicht
Thy light-of-joy

Ist mein Komete,
Is my comet,
{Is my omen of harm,}

Und wo man deine Rosen bricht,
And if one (would) thy roses pick,

        Sind Dornen ohne Zahl
(Then there) are thorns without number

Zu meiner Seelen Qual!
To my soul's torment!
{Bringing torment to my soul!}

Der blasse Tod ist meine Morgenröte,
- Pale death is my rosy-dawn,

Mit solcher geht mir auf die Sonne
With (it) rises for-me - the sun

Der Herrlichkeit und Himmelswonne.
Of glory and heavenly-bliss.
{With it the sun of glory and heavenly bliss rises for me.}

Drum seufz ich recht von Herzensgrunde
Thus sigh I quite from (the) bottom-of-my-heart
{Thus do I yearn from the bottom of my heart}

Nur nach der letzten Todesstunde!
Only for (my) last hour-of-death!

Ich habe Lust, bei Christo bald zu weiden,
I have (the) desire, with Christ soon to pasture,
{I have the desire soon to pasture with Christ,}

Ich habe Lust, von dieser Welt zu scheiden.
I have (the) desire, from this world to part.
{I have the desire to part from this world.}

Jn. 12:24–25. Unless a grain of wheat falls into the earth and dies, it remains alone; but if it dies, it bears much fruit. He who loves his life loses it, and he who hates his life in this world will keep it for eternal life.
Rev. 14:13. ...Blessed are the dead who die in the Lord henceforth...
2 Cor. 5:8. ....We would rather be away from the body and at home with the Lord.

1 Jn. 2:15–17. Do not love the world or the things in the world. If any one loves the world, love for the Father is not in him. For all that is in the world, the lust of the flesh and the lust of the eyes and the pride of life, is not of the Father but is of the world. And the world passes away, and the lust of it; but he who does the will of God abides for ever.
Jms. 4:4. Unfaithful creatures! Do you not know that friendship with the world is enmity with God? Therefore whoever wishes to be a friend of the world makes himself an enemy of God.
Eph. 4:22. Put off your old nature which belongs to your former manner of life and is corrupt through deceitful lusts.
Prov. 5:3–4. The lips of a loose woman drip honey...but in the end she is bitter as wormwood, sharp as a two-edged sword. (Also Prov. 6:25–29, 32, 7:6–27.)
Prov. 23:31–32. ...[Wine] sparkles in the cup and goes down smoothly [but] at the last it bites like a serpent, and stings like an adder.
Heb. 11:24–26. By faith Moses...refused to be called the son of Pharaoh's daughter, choosing rather to share ill-treatment with the people of God than to enjoy the fleeting pleasures of sin. He considered abuse suffered for the Christ greater wealth than the treasures of Egypt, for he looked to the reward.
Rom. 8:18. ...The sufferings of this present time are not worth comparing with the glory that is to be revealed to us.
Rom. 5:2. ...We rejoice in our hope of sharing the glory of God.
Rev. 14:13. ...Blessed are the dead who die in the Lord henceforth... that they may rest from their labors, for their deeds follow them!
Prov. 4:18. The path of the righteous is like the light of dawn, which shines brighter and brighter until full day.
2 Cor. 4:16–18. ...Though our outer nature is wasting away, our inner nature is being renewed every day. For this slight momentary affliction is preparing for us an eternal weight of glory beyond all comparison, because we look not to the things that are seen but to the things that are unseen; for the things that are seen are transient, but the things that are unseen are eternal.
2 Cor. 5:1–2. For we know that if the earthly tent we live in is destroyed, we have a building from God, a house not made with hands, eternal in the heavens. Here indeed we groan (Luther: sehnen wir uns), and long to put on our heavenly dwelling.
+Lk. 2:29. Lord, now lettest thou thy servant depart in peace, according to thy word.
Phil. 1:23. ...My desire (Luther: Ich habe Lust) is to depart and be with Christ, for that is far better. (Also 2 Cor. 5:8.)
Rev. 7:17. The Lamb in the midst of the throne will be [the] shepherd [of the righteous], and he will guide them to springs of living water; and God will wipe away every tear from their eyes. (Also Rev. 21:3–4.)

3. Tenor Aria

●Yearning to depart & be with Christ in heaven (161-3)

Mein Verlangen
My wish

Ist, den Heiland zu umfangen
Is, the Savior to embrace

Und bei Christo bald zu sein.
And with Christ soon to be.

Ob ich sterblich' Asch und Erde
Though I, (being) mortal ash and earth,

Durch den Tod zermalmet werde,
By - death pulverized will-be,
{Will be ground to dust by death,}

Wird der Seele reiner Schein
Will (my) soul's pure lustre
{My soul's pure lustre will}

Dennoch gleich den Engeln prangen.
Nevertheless like the angels shine.
{Nevertheless like angels shine.}

4. Alto Recit.

●Death's sleep welcomed for Jesus will awaken me (161-4)

Der Schluß ist schon gemacht,
The conclusion is already (reached),
{I have made my decision,}

Welt, gute Nacht!
World, good night!

Und kann ich nur den Trost erwerben,
And can I but this comfort attain,
{If only I can attain this comfort,}

In Jesu Armen bald zu sterben:
In Jesus' arms soon to die:

Er ist mein sanfter Schlaf.
He is my gentle sleep.

Das kühle Grab wird mich mit Rosen decken,
The cool grave will me with roses cover,

Bis Jesus mich wird auferwecken,
Till Jesus me shall resurrect,

Bis er sein Schaf
Till he his sheep

Führt auf die süße Lebensweide,
Leads to the sweet pasture-of-life,

*Eph. 3:17, 19. [May]...Christ...dwell in your hearts through faith...that you may be filled with all the fulness of God.
Phil. 1:20–23. ...[My hope is] that...Christ will be honored in my body, whether by life or by death. For to me to live is Christ, and to die is gain. If it is to be life in the flesh, that means fruitful labor for me. Yet which I shall choose I cannot tell. I am hard pressed between the two. My desire is to depart and be with Christ, for that is far better.
2 Cor. 5:6–8. ...We know that while we are at home in the body we are away from the Lord, for we walk by faith, not by sight. We are of good courage, and we would rather be away from the body and at home with the Lord.
Ecc. 12:7. The dust returns to the earth as it was, and the spirit returns to God who gave it. (Also Ecc. 3:20, Gen. 3:19.)
1 Cor. 15:49–50, 53–54. Just as we have borne the image of the man of dust, we shall also bear the image of the man of heaven. I tell you this, brethren: flesh and blood cannot inherit the kingdom of God, nor does the perishable inherit the imperishable...For this perishable nature must put on the imperishable, and this mortal nature must put on immortality. When the perishable puts on the imperishable, and the mortal puts on immortality, then shall come to pass the saying that is written: "Death is swallowed up in victory."
Mt. 22:30. In the resurrection [we]...are like angels in heaven.

Phil. 1:21, 23. To me to live is Christ, and to die is gain...My desire is to depart and be with Christ, for that is far better.
Rev. 14:13. ...Blessed are the dead who die in the Lord...
1 Thess. 4:13–14, 16. But we would not have you ignorant, brethren, concerning those who are asleep, that you may not grieve as others do who have no hope. For since we believe that Jesus died and rose again, even so, through Jesus, God will bring with him those who have fallen asleep...The dead in Christ will rise first.
*Lk. 7:14. [Jesus] came and touched the bier...and he said, "Young man, I say to you, arise."
1 Cor. 15:51–52. ...We shall all be changed, in a moment, in the twinkling of an eye, at the last trumpet. For the trumpet will sound, and the dead will be raised imperishable, and we shall be changed.
1 Cor. 15:20, 23. ...Christ has been raised from the dead, the first fruits of those who have fallen asleep...Christ the first fruits, then at his coming those who belong to Christ. (Also Jn. 6:40/44/54, Rom. 8:11.)
Ps. 116:15. Precious in the sight of the Lord is the death of his saints.
Ps. 23:1–4. The Lord is my shepherd, I shall not want; he makes me lie down in green pastures. He leads me beside still waters; he restores my soul. He leads me in paths of righteousness for his name's sake. Even though I walk through the valley of the shadow of death, I fear no evil; for thou art with me...
Jn. 10:14–15, 27–28 [Christ]: I am the good shepherd; I know my own and my own know me, as the Father knows me and I know the Father; and I lay down my life for the sheep...My sheep hear my voice,

Daß mich der Tod von ihm nicht scheide.
So-that me - death from him (will) not separate.
{So that death will not separate me from him.}

So brich herein, du froher Todestag,
So break forth, thou happy day-of-death,

So schlage doch, du letzter Stundenschlag!
So strike then, thou final hourly-stroke!

5. Chorus
●Yearning for death: Body to earth, soul to heaven (161-5)
Wenn es meines Gottes Wille,
If it (be) my God's will,

Wünsch ich, daß des Leibes Last
Wish I, that (my) body's burden
{I would wish that by body}

Heute noch die Erde fülle,
Today yet the ground (would) fill,

Und der Geist, des Leibes Gast,
And (my) spirit, the body's guest,

Mit Unsterblichkeit sich kleide
With immortality itself clothe
{Clothe itself with immortality}

In der süßen Himmelsfreude.
In the sweet joy-of-heaven.

Jesu, komm und nimm mich fort!
Jesus, come and take me hence!

Dieses sei mein letztes Wort.
(May) this be my final word.

6. Chorale
●Body consumed in the earth but later transfigured (161-6)
Der Leib zwar in der Erden
The body indeed in the earth

Von Würmen wird verzehrt,
By worms is consumed,

Doch auferweckt soll werden,
Yet resurrected shall be,
{Yet it shall be resurrected,}

Durch Christum schön verklärt,
Through Christ (shall be) beautifully transfigured,

Wird leuchten als die Sonne
Will shine like the sun

and I know them, and they follow me; and I give them eternal life, and they shall never perish, and no one shall snatch them out of my hand.
Rev. 7:17. The Lamb in the midst of the throne will be their shepherd, and he will guide them to springs of living water; and God will wipe away every tear from their eyes.
2 Cor. 5:8. ...We would rather be away from the body and at home with the Lord.
1 Thess. 4:17. ...So we shall always be with the Lord...

2 Pet. 1:14. I know that the putting off of my body will be soon, as our Lord Jesus Christ showed me.
2 Cor. 5:1-4. We know that if the earthly tent we live in is destroyed, we have a building from God, a house not made with hands, eternal in the heavens. Here indeed we groan, and long to put on our heavenly dwelling, so that by putting it on we may not be found naked. For while we are still in this tent, we sigh with anxiety; not that we would be unclothed, but that we would be further clothed, so that what is mortal may be swallowed up by life.
1 Cor. 15:40, 42-44, 49-50, 54-55. There are celestial bodies and there are terrestrial bodies; but the glory of the celestial is one, and the glory of the terrestrial is another...So it is with the resurrection of the dead. What is sown is perishable, what is raised is imperishable. It is sown in dishonor, it is raised in glory. It is sown in weakness, it is raised in power. It is sown a physical body, it is raised a spiritual body ...Just as we have borne the image of the man of dust, we shall also bear the image of the man of heaven. I tell you this, brethren: flesh and blood cannot inherit the kingdom of God, nor does the perishable inherit the imperishable...When the perishable puts on the imperishable, and the mortal puts on immortality, then shall come to pass the saying that is written: "Death is swallowed up in victory." O death, where is thy victory? O death, where is thy sting?
+Lk. 2:29. Lord, now lettest thou thy servant depart in peace, according to thy word.

Job 21:23-26. One [person] dies in full prosperity, being wholly at ease and secure, his body full of fat and the marrow of his bones moist. Another dies in bitterness of soul, never having tasted of good. They lie down alike in the dust, and the worms cover them.
Phil. 3:20-21. But our commonwealth is in heaven, and from it we await a Savior, the Lord Jesus Christ, who will change our lowly body to be like his glorious body, by the power which enables him even to subject all things to himself.
Mt. 17:1-6. ...Jesus took with him Peter and James and John his brother, and led them up a high mountain apart. And he was transfigured (Luther: verklärt) before them, and his face shone like the sun, and his garments became white as light. And behold, there appeared to them Moses and Elijah, talking with him. And Peter said to Jesus, "Lord, it is well that we are here; if you wish, I will make three booths here, one for you and one for Moses and one for Elijah." He was still speaking, when lo, a bright cloud overshadowed them, and a voice from the cloud said, "This is my beloved Son, with whom I am well pleased; listen to him." When the disciples heard this, they fell on their faces, and were filled with awe. (Also Mk. 9:2-6.)

Und leben ohne   Not
And   live without distress

In himml'scher Freud und Wonne.
In   heavenly   joy   and   bliss.

Was schadt mir denn der Tod?
What does-harm me then   - death?
{How can death then harm me?}

BWV 162
Ach, ich sehe, itzt, da ich zur Hochzeit gehe
(NBA I/25; BC A148)

20. S. after Trinity (BWV 162, 180, 49)
*Eph. 5:15-21 (Exhortation to walk carefully, be filled with the Spirit)
*Mt. 22:1-14 (Parable of the royal wedding feast)
Librettist: Salomon Franck

1. Bass Aria
●Life & death confront me on way to heavenly wedding (162-1)
Ach! ich sehe,
Ah! I see,

Itzt, da ich zur   Hochzeit gehe,
Now, that I to-the (heavenly) wedding go,
{Now as I go to the heavenly wedding,}

Wohl und Wehe.
Weal and woe.

Seelengift   und Lebensbrot,
Poison-of-soul and bread-of-life,

Himmel, Hölle, Leben, Tod,
Heaven, hell,   life, death,

Himmelsglanz   und Höllenflammen
Heaven's-radiance and hell's-flames

Sind beisammen.
Are   together.

Jesu, hilf, daß ich   bestehe!
Jesus, help, that I (may) stand-the-test!

2. Tenor Recit.
●Wedding of heaven is great honor for earthly bride (162-2)
O großes Hochzeitsfest,
O great wedding-feast,

Darzu   der Himmelskönig
To-which the king-of-heaven

1 Cor. 15:49. We shall...bear the image of the man of heaven.
Mt. 13:43. Then the righteous will shine like the sun in the kingdom of their Father...
Rev. 21:3-4. ...God himself will be with them; he will wipe away every tear from their eyes, and death shall be no more, neither shall there be mourning nor crying nor pain any more, for the former things have passed away. (Also Is. 25:8. Rev. 7:15-17.)
Mt. 10:28 [Christ]: Do not fear those who kill the body but cannot kill the soul... (Also Lk. 12:5.)
1 Cor. 15:54-55. ...Death is swallowed up in victory. O death, where is thy victory? O death, where is thy sting?

*Mt. 22:2-3, 6-11, 13-14. ...A king...gave a marriage feast for his son, and sent his servants to call those who were invited...but they would not come...[Some of them] seized his servants...and killed them. The king was angry, and he sent his troops and destroyed those murderers and burned their city. Then he said to his servants, 'The wedding is ready, but those invited were not worthy. Go therefore to the thoroughfares, and invite to the marriage feast as many as you find.' And those servants went out into the streets and gathered all whom they found, both bad and good...When the king came in to look at the guests, he saw there a man who had no wedding garment...Then the king said to the attendants, 'Bind him hand and foot, and cast him into the outer darkness; there men will weep and gnash their teeth.' For many are called, but few are chosen.
Rev. 19:9. ...Blessed are those who are invited to the marriage supper of the Lamb...
Deut. 11:26-28. Behold, [there is] before you this day a blessing and a curse: the blessing, if you obey the commandments of the Lord your God...and the curse, if you do not obey...
Mt. 7:13-14 [Christ]: Enter by the narrow gate; for the gate is wide and the way is easy, that leads to destruction, and those who enter by it are many. For the gate is narrow and the way is hard, that leads to life, and those who find it are few.
Jn. 6:48, 51 [Christ]: I am the bread of life (Luther: Brot des Lebens) ...I am the living bread which came down from heaven; if any one eats of this bread, he will live for ever... (Also Jn. 6:35, 37.)
Deut. 30:15, 19. See, I have set before you this day life and good, death and evil...life and death, blessing and curse; therefore choose life...
Mt. 18:9 [Christ]: ...It is better for you to enter life with one eye than with two eyes to be thrown into the hell of fire. (Also Mt. 5:29-30, Mk. 9:43-47.)

*Mt. 22:1-14. ...Jesus spoke to them in parables, saying, "The kingdom of heaven may be compared to a king who gave a marriage feast for his son, and sent his servants to call those who were invited to the marriage feast; but they would not come. Again he sent other servants,

Die Menschen   rufen   läßt!
-    People be-summoned lets!
{Lets people be summoned!}

Ist denn die arme Braut,
Is then the poor bride—

Die menschliche Natur, nicht viel zu schlecht und wenig,
(Our) human   nature— not much too inferior and little,

Daß sich mit ihr der Sohn des Höchsten traut?
That - (to) her the Son of-the Most-High be-wed?

O großes Hochzeitsfest,
O great wedding-feast,

Wie ist das Fleisch zu solcher   Ehre kommen,
How is the flesh to such (an) honor come,
{How has the flesh come to such honor,}

Daß Gottes Sohn
That God's Son

Es hat auf ewig angenommen?
It has forever   accepted?
{Has forever accepted it?}

Der Himmel ist sein Thron,
- Heaven is his throne,

Die Erde dient zum Schemel seinen Füßen,
- Earth serves as-a footstool for-his feet,

Noch will er diese Welt
Yet desires he this world

Als Braut und Liebste küssen!
As bride and beloved to-kiss!
{Yet he desires to kiss this world as his bride and beloved!}

Das Hochzeitmahl ist angestellt,
The wedding-feast is prepared,

Das Mastvieh   ist   geschlachtet;
The fattened-cattle have-been slaughtered;

Wie herrlich ist doch   alles   zubereitet!
How gloriously is indeed everything made-ready!

Wie selig ist,   den   hier der Glaube leitet,
How blessed is he-whom here - faith leads,
{How blessed is he whom faith leads here,}

Und wie verflucht ist doch,   der dieses Mahl verachtet!
And how cursed is, indeed, he-who this feast   scorns!

saying 'Tell those who are invited, Behold, I have made ready my dinner, my oxen and my fat calves (Luther: Mastvieh) are killed, and everything is ready; come to the marriage feast.' But they made light of it Luther: verachteten das) and went off, one to his farm, another to his business, while the rest seized his servants, treated them shamefully and killed them. The king was angry, and he sent his troops and destroyed those murderers and burned their city. Then he said to his servants, 'The wedding is ready, but those invited were not worthy. Go therefore to the thoroughfares, and invite to the marriage feast as many as you find.' And those servants went out into the streets and gathered all whom they found, both bad and good; so the wedding hall was filled with guests. But when the king came in to look at the guests, he saw there a man who had no wedding garment; and he said to him, 'Friend, how did you get in here without a wedding garment?' And he was speechless. Then the king said to the attendants, 'Bind him hand and foot, and cast him into the outer darkness; there men will weep and gnash their teeth.' For many are called, but few are chosen." (Also Mt. 25:1–13.)

Hos. 2:19–20 [God]: I will betroth you to me for ever; I will betroth you to me in righteousness and in justice, in steadfast love, and in mercy. I will betroth you to me in faithfulness; and you shall know the Lord.

Is. 62:4–5. ...You shall be called My delight is in her, and your land Married; for the Lord delights in you and your land shall be married. For as a young man marries a virgin, so shall your sons marry you, and as the bridegroom rejoices over the bride, so shall your God rejoice over you.

Jn. 3:29. [John the Baptist said concerning Jesus], "He who has the bride is the bridegroom; the friend of the bridegroom, who stands and hears him, rejoices greatly at the bridegroom's voice..."

2 Cor. 11:2 [Paul]: ...I betrothed you to Christ to present you as a pure bride to her one husband. (Also Eph. 5:25–27, Ezek. 16:9–13, Is. 61:10.)

1 Jn. 3:1. See what love the Father has given us...

Jn. 3:16. God so loved the world that he gave his only Son...

1 Jn. 4:10. In this is love, not that we loved God but that he loved us and sent his Son...

Ps. 8:3–5. [O Lord,] when I look at thy heavens, the work of thy fingers, the moon and the stars which thou hast established; what is man that thou art mindful of him, and the son of man that thou dost care for him? Yet thou hast made him little less than God, and dost crown him with glory and honor. (Also Ps. 144:3, Heb. 2:5–8.)

Is. 66:1. Thus says the Lord: "Heaven is my throne and the earth is my footstool; what is the house which you would build for me...?" (Also Acts 7:48–49, 17:24.)

Rev. 19:6–9. Then I heard what seemed to be the voice of a great multitude, like the sound of many waters and like the sound of mighty thunderpeals, crying, "Hallelujah! For the Lord our God the Almighty reigns. Let us rejoice and exult and give him the glory, for the marriage of the Lamb has come, and his Bride has made herself ready; it was granted her to be clothed with fine linen, bright and pure"—for the fine linen is the righteous deeds of the saints. And the angel said to me, "Write this: Blessed are those who are invited to the marriage supper of the Lamb."...

3. Soprano Aria
●Prayer: Bread of Life, revive my soul, I hunger for thee
(162-3)
Jesu, Brunnquell aller Gnaden,
Jesus, fount of-all mercies,

Labe mich elenden Gast,
Refresh (this) wretched guest,

Weil du mich berufen hast!
For thou me called hast!
{For thou hast called me!}

Ich bin matt, schwach und beladen,
I am faint, weak, and burdened,

Ach! erquicke meine Seele,
Ah, revive my soul;

Ach! wie hungert mich nach dir!
Ah! How do-hunger (I) for thee!
{Ah, how I hunger for thee!}

Lebensbrot, das ich erwähle,
Bread-of-life, which I choose,

Komm, vereine dich mit mir!
Come, unite thyself (to) me!

4. Alto Recit.
●Prayer: Wedding garment of salvation sought (162-4)
Mein Jesu, laß mich nicht
My Jesus, let me not

Zur Hochzeit unbekleidet kommen,
To-the wedding ungarbed come,
{Come to the wedding ungarbed,}

Daß mich nicht treffe dein Gericht;
That me not strike thy judgment;
{That thy judgment not strike me;}

Mit Schrecken hab ich ja vernommen,
With terror did I indeed perceive,

Wie du den kühnen Hochzeitgast,
How thou that audacious wedding-guest,

Der ohne Kleid erschienen,
Who without (a wedding) garment did-appear,
{Who appeared without a wedding garment,}

Verworfen und verdammet hast!
Didst-reject and damn - !

Ich weiß auch mein Unwürdigkeit:
I know also my (own) unworthiness:

Lk. 13:29 [Christ]: Men will come from east and west, and from north and south, and sit at table in the kingdom of God.
Mt. 5:6 [Christ]: Blessed are those who hunger and thirst for righteousness, for they shall be satisfied.
Jn. 1:16. From [Christ's] fulness have we all received, grace upon grace.
Mt. 26:26-28. Now as they were eating, Jesus took bread, and blessed, and broke it, and gave it to the disciples and said, "Take, eat; this is my body." And he took a cup, and when he had given thanks he gave it to them, saying, "Drink of it, all of you; for this is my blood of the covenant, which is poured out for many for the forgiveness of sins. (Also Mk. 14:22-25, Lk. 22:17-20, 1 Cor. 11:23-26.)
Mt. 11:28-30 [Christ]: Come to me, all who labor and are heavy laden (Luther: beladen), and I will give you rest (Luther: euch erquicken). Take my yoke upon you, and learn from me; for I am gentle and lowly in heart, and you will find rest for your souls. For my yoke is easy, and my burden is light. (Also Jer. 6:16, 31:25.)
Ps. 42:1-2. As a hart longs for flowing streams, so longs my soul for thee, O God. My soul thirsts for God, for the living God. When shall I come and behold the face of God?
Jn. 6:48-51 [Christ]: I am the bread of life. Your fathers ate the manna in the wilderness, and they died. This is the bread which comes down from heaven, that a man may eat of it and not die. I am the living bread which came down from heaven; if any one eats of this bread, he will live for ever; and the bread which I shall give for the life of the world is my flesh. (Also Rev. 2:17.)

*Mt. 22:10-13. [The] servants went out into the streets and gathered all whom they found, both bad and good; so the wedding hall was filled with guests. But when the king came in to look at the guests, he saw there a man who had no wedding garment; and he said to him, 'Friend, how did you get in here without a wedding garment?' And he was speechless. Then the king said to the attendants, 'Bind him hand and foot, and cast him into the outer darkness; there men will weep and gnash their teeth.' For many are called, but few are chosen."
Is. 64:6. ...All our righteous deeds are like a polluted garment.
Rom. 3:21-25. But now the righteousness of God has been manifested apart from law...the righteousness of God through faith in Jesus Christ for all who believe. For there is no distinction; since all have sinned and fall short of the glory of God, they are justified by his grace as a gift, through the redemption which is in Christ Jesus, whom God put forward as an expiation by his blood, to be received by faith...
Rom. 1:17. ...He who through faith is righteous shall live. (See Hab. 2:4, also Rom. 3:26, 28, Gal. 3:11.)
Phil. 3:8-9. ...[My goal is] that I may gain Christ and be found in him, not having a righteousness of my own, based on law, but that which is through faith in Christ, the righteousness from God that depends on faith. (Also 1 Cor. 1:30-31.)
Is. 61:10. ...My soul shall exult in my God; for he has clothed me with the garments of salvation, he has covered me with the robe of righteousness, as a bridegroom decks himself with a garland, and as a bride adorns herself with her jewels.
Ezek. 16:10-13 [God]: I clothed you also with embroidered loth and

Ach! schenke mir des Glaubens Hochzeitkleid;
Ah! Grant me - faith's wedding-garment;

Laß dein Verdienst zu meinem Schmucke dienen!
Let thy merit as my adornment serve!
{Let thy merit serve as my adornment!}

Gib mir zum Hochzeitkleide
Grant me as-my wedding-garment

Den Rock des Heils, der Unschuld weiße Seide!
The cloak of Salvation, - innocence's white silk!
{The cloak of Salvation, the white silk of innocence!}

Ach! laß dein Blut, den hohen Purpur, decken
Ah, let thy blood, that noble purple, cover

Den alten Adamsrock und seine Lasterflecken,
The old cloak-of-Adam and its stains-of-iniquity,

So werd ich schön und rein
So will I fair and pure

Und dir willkommen sein,
And to-thee acceptable be,
{Thus will I be fair and pure and acceptable to thee,}

So werd ich würdiglich das Mahl des Lammes schmecken.
So will I worthily the meal of-the lamb taste.
{Thus will I partake worthily of the Lamb's meal.}

shod you with leather, I swathed you in fine linen and covered you with silk. And I decked you with ornaments, and put bracelets on your arms, and a chain on your neck. And I put a ring on your nose, and earrings in your ears, and a beautiful crown upon your head. Thus you were decked with gold and silver; and your raiment was of fine linen, and silk, and embroidered cloth... (Also Ps. 45:12–15.)

Rev. 19:7–8. ...The marriage of the Lamb has come, and his Bride has made herself ready; it was granted her to be clothed with fine linen, bright and pure...

Rev. 7:14. ...[The righteous] have washed their robes and made them white in the blood of the Lamb. (Also Eph. 5:25–27.)

Eph. 4:22–24. Put off your old nature which belongs to your former manner of life and is corrupt through deceitful lusts, and be renewed in the spirit of your minds, and put on the new nature, created after the likeness of God in true righteousness and holiness. (Also Col. 3:9–10.)

1 Cor. 15:22. As in Adam all die, so also in Christ shall all be made alive.

Rom. 5:17–18. If, because of one man's trespass, death reigned through that one man, much more will those who receive the abundance of grace and the free gift of righteousness reign in life through the one man Jesus Christ. Then as one man's trespass led to condemnation for all men, so one man's act of righteousness leads to acquittal and life for all men.

Eph. 2:13. ...You who once were far off have been brought near in the blood of Christ.

1 Cor. 10:16. The cup of blessing which we bless, is it not a participation in the blood of Christ? The bread which we break, is it not a participation in the body of Christ?

1 Cor. 11:27–29. Whoever, therefore, eats the bread or drinks the cup of the Lord in an unworthy manner will be guilty of profaning the body and blood of the Lord. Let a man examine himself, and so eat of the bread and drink of the cup. For any one who eats and drinks without discerning the body eats and drinks judgment upon himself.

5. Alto & Tenor Duet

●Garment of righteousness now; robe of glory later (162–5)
In meinem Gott bin ich erfreut!
In my God am I made-glad!

Die Liebesmacht hat ihn bewogen,
The power-of-love has him stirred,
{The strength of his love has stirred him,}

Daß er mir in der Gnadenzeit
So-that he me in (this) time-of-grace
{So that he has clothed me in this age of grace,}

Aus lauter Huld hat angezogen
Out-of sheer favor has clothed (with)
{Out of sheer favor,}

Die Kleider der Gerechtigkeit.
The garments of righteousness.
{With the garments of righteousness.}

Ich weiß, er wird nach diesem Leben
I know, he will after this life

Tit. 3:4–7. When the goodness and loving kindness of God our Savior appeared, he saved us, not because of deeds done by us in righteousness, but in virtue of his own mercy, by the washing of regeneration and renewal in the Holy Spirit, which he poured out upon us richly through Jesus Christ our Savior so that we might be justified by his grace and become heirs in hope of eternal life.

Is. 61:10. I will greatly rejoice in the Lord, my soul shall exult in my God; for he has clothed me with the garments of salvation, he has covered me with the robe of righteousness, as a bridegroom decks himself with a garland, and as a bride adorns herself with her jewels.

Eph. 5:25–27. ...Christ loved the church and gave himself up for her, that he might sanctify her, having cleansed her by the washing of water with the word, that he might present the church to himself in splendor, without spot or wrinkle or any such thing, that she might be holy and without blemish.

Rev. 3:5 [Christ]: He who conquers shall be clad thus in white garments, and I will not blot his name out of the book of life; I will confess his name before my Father and before his angels.

Rev. 19:7–8. Let us rejoice and exult and give him the glory, for the marriage of the Lamb has come, and his Bride has made herself ready; it was granted her to be clothed with fine linen, bright

Der Ehre weißes Kleid
- Glory's white dress

Mir auch im Himmel geben.
To-me also in heaven give.
{I know that, after this life, he will also give to me in heaven the white dress of glory.}

6. Chorale
●Heaven glimpsed with its robe and crown (162–6)
Ach, ich habe schon erblicket
Ah, I have already glimpsed

Diese große Herrlichkeit.
This great glory.

Itzund werd ich schön geschmücket
Soon-now will I (be) beautifully adorned

Mit dem weißen Himmelskleid;
With the white dress-of-heaven;

Mit der güldnen Ehrenkrone
With the golden crown-of-honor

Steh ich da für Gottes Throne,
Stand I there before God's throne,
{Shall I stand there before God's throne,}

Schaue solche Freude an,
Contemplating such joy -

Die kein Ende nehmen kann.
That no end can-ever-have.
{That can never be brought to an end.}

pure—for the fine linen is the righteous deeds of the saints.
Rev. 19:11–14. I saw heaven opened, and behold, a white horse! He who sat upon it is called Faithful and True...His eyes are like a flame of fire, and on his head are many diadems; and he has a name inscribed which no one knows but himself. He is clad in a robe dipped in blood, and the name by which he is called is The Word of God. And the armies of heaven, arrayed in fine linen, white and pure, followed him on white horses.

Rev. 7:9–10, 14–17. [In my vision] I looked, and behold, a great multitude which no man could number, from every nation, from all tribes and peoples and tongues, standing before the throne and before the Lamb, clothed in white robes, with palm branches in their hands, and crying out with a loud voice, "Salvation belongs to our God who sits upon the throne, and to the Lamb!"...These are they who have come out of the great tribulation; they have washed their robes and made them white in the blood of the Lamb. Therefore are they before the throne of God, and serve him day and night within his temple; and he who sits upon the throne will shelter them with his presence. They shall hunger no more, neither thirst any more; the sun shall not strike them, nor any scorching heat. For the Lamb in the midst of the throne will be their shepherd, and he will guide them to springs of living water; and God will wipe away every tear from their eyes.
Rev. 3:4–5 [Christ]: ...They shall walk with me in white, for they are worthy. He who conquers shall be clad thus in white garments, and I will not blot his name out of the book of life; I will confess his name before my Father and before his angels.
1 Pet. 5:4. When the chief Shepherd is manifested you will obtain the unfading crown of glory (Luther: Krone der Ehren).
Jms. 1:12. Blessed is the man who endures trial, for when he has stood the test he will receive the crown of life which God has promised to those who love him. (Also Is. 28:5, 2 Tim. 4:8, Rev. 2:10.)

BWV 163
Nur jedem das Seine
(NBA I/26; BC A158)

23. S. after Trinity (BWV 163, 139, 52)
*Phil. 3:17–21 (Our citizenship is in heaven.)
*Mt. 22:15–22 (The Pharisees try to trap Jesus with the question: "Is it lawful to pay taxes to Ceasar?")
Librettist: Salomon Franck

1. Tenor Aria
●Pay to every man what is due him (163–1)
Nur jedem das Seine!
Only to-each (his) own!

Muß Obrigkeit haben
Must governing-authorities have
{If governing authorities must have}

*Mt. 22:15–22. Then the Pharisees went and took counsel how to entangle [Jesus] in his talk. And they sent their disciples to him, along with the Herodians, saying, "Teacher, we know that you are true, and teach the way of God truthfully, and care for no man; for you do not regard the position of men. Tell us, then, what you think. Is it lawful to pay taxes to Caesar, or not?" But Jesus, aware of their malice, said, "Why put me to the test, you hypocrites? Show me the money for the tax." And they brought him a coin. And Jesus said to them, "Whose likeness and inscription is this?" They said, "Caesar's." Then he said to them, "Render therefore to Caesar the things that are Caesar's, and to God the things that are God's." When they heard it, they marveled; and they left him and went away. (Also Mt. 17:24–27.)
Rom. 13:1, 5–7. Let every person be subject to the governing authorities (Luther: Obrigkeit). For there is no authority (Luther: Obrigkeit) except from God, and those that exist have been instituted

Zoll, Steuern und Gaben,
Tariff, taxes, and donations,

Man weigere sich nicht
(Let) one refuse - not
{Then let no one refuse}

Der schuldigen Pflicht!
(Their) obliged duty!

Doch bleibet das Herze dem Höchsten alleine.
Yet remains the heart for-the Most-High alone.
{Yet the heart is reserved for the Most High alone.}

2. Bass Recit.
●Paying God, giver of all, his due: our poor hearts (163-2)
Du bist, mein Gott, der Geber aller Gaben;
Thou art, (O) my God, the giver of-all gifts;

Wir haben, was wir haben,
We have, what we have,

Allein von deiner Hand.
Alone from thy hand.
{From thy hand alone.}

Du, du hast uns gegeben
Thou, thou hast us given
{Thou, thou hast given us}

Geist, Seele, Leib und Leben
Spirit, soul, body, and life

Und Hab und Gut und Ehr und Stand!
And goods, and possesions, and honor, and station!

Was sollen wir
What should we

Denn dir
Then to-thee

Zur Dankbarkeit dafür erlegen,
In gratitude for-that pay,
{What then should we pay to thee to show our gratitude,}

Da unser ganz Vermögen
Since our entire posessions
{Sinde all our posessions}

Nur dein und gar nicht unser ist?
Only thine and absolutely not ours are?
{Are thine alone, and not ours at all?}

Doch ist noch eins, das dir, Gott, wohlgefällt:
Yet there-is still one-thing, which thee, God, doth-please:

by God...Therefore one must be subject, not only to avoid God's wrath but also for the sake of conscience. For the same reason you also pay taxes, for the authorities are ministers of God, attending to this very thing. Pay all of them their dues, taxes to whom taxes are due, revenue to whom revenue is due, respect to whom respect is due, honor to whom honor is due. (Also 1 Pet. 2:13–14, Tit. 3:1.)
Deut. 5:7 [God]: You shall have no other gods before me. (Also Ex. 20:3.)
Mt. 22:37 [Christ]: ...You shall love the Lord your God with all your heart... (Also Mk. 12:30, Lk. 10:27, Deut. 6:5.)
Jms. 4:5. Or do you suppose it is in vain that the scripture says, "He yearns jealously over the spirit which he has made to dwell in us"?
Acts 5:29. Peter and the apostles answered [the council], "We must obey God rather than men."

Jms. 1:17. Every good endowment and every perfect gift is from above, coming down from the Father...
1 Cor. 4:7. ...What have you that you did not receive? If then you received it, why do you boast as if it were not a gift?
Jn. 3:27. ...No one can receive anything except what is given him from heaven.
1 Chron. 29:1–2, 5–6, 9–12, 14, 16. David the king said to all the assembly, "...I have provided for the house of my God, so far as I was able...Who then will offer willingly, consecrating himself today to the Lord?" Then the heads of fathers' houses made their freewill offerings, as did also the leaders of the tribes, the commanders of thousands and of hundreds, and the officers over the king's work... Then the people rejoiced because these had given willingly, for with a whole heart they had offered freely to the Lord; David the king also rejoiced greatly. Therefore David blessed the Lord in the presence of all the assembly; and David said: "Blessed art thou, O Lord, the God of Israel our father, for ever and ever. Thine, O Lord, is the greatness, and the power, and the glory, and the victory, and the majesty; for all that is in the heavens and in the earth is thine; thine is the Kingdom, O Lord, and thou art exalted as head above all. Both riches and honor come from thee, and thou rulest over all. In thy hand are power and might; and in thy hand it is to make great and to give strength to all... All things come from thee, and of thy own have we given thee...O Lord our God, all this abundance that we have provided for building thee a house for thy holy name comes from thy hand and is all thy own."
Jn. 17:7. ...Everything that thou hast given me is from thee.
Ps. 116:12. What shall I render to the Lord for all his bounty to me?
Mt. 22:37–38. [Jesus] said... "You shall love the Lord your God with all your heart, and with all your soul, and with all your mind. This is the great and first commandment." (Also Mk. 12:30, Lk. 10:27, Deut. 6:5.)
Jms. 4:4–5. Unfaithful creatures! Do you not know that friendship with the world is enmity with God? Therefore whoever wishes to be a friend of the world makes himself an enemy of God. Or do you suppose it is in vain that the scripture says, "He yearns jealously over the spirit which he has made to dwell in us"?

Das Herze soll allein,
The heart shall alone,

Herr, deine Zinsmünze sein.
Lord, thy tribute-coinage be.

Ach! aber ach! ist das nicht schlechtes Geld?
Ah! But alas! Is that not inferior coin?

Der Satan hat dein Bild daran verletzet,
- Satan hath thine image there-on damaged;

Die falsche Münz ist abgesetzet.
(This) base coin is discarded.

3. Bass Aria
●Heart as coin of tribute, God's image on it restored (163-3)
Laß mein Herz die Münze sein,
Let my heart the coinage be,

Die ich dir, mein Jesu, steure!
Which I to-thee, my Jesus, pay!

Ist sie gleich nicht allzu rein,
Be it though not all-too clean,
{Though it be not all too clean,}

Ach, so komm doch und erneure,
Ah, then come please and renew,

Herr, den schönen Glanz bei ihr!
(O) Lord, the beautiful lustre in it!

Komm, arbeite, schmelz und präge,
Come, work, melt, and stamp (it),

Daß dein Ebenbild bei mir
That thine image in me

Ganz erneuert glänzen möge!
Completely restored shine may!
{May shine completely restored!}

4. Soprano & Alto Arioso
●Heart held captive by world, freed by God's grace (163-4)
Ich wollte dir,
I would to-thee,

O Gott, das Herze gerne geben;
O God, (my) heart gladly give;
{O God, I would gladly give my heart to thee;}

*Mt. 22:18-21. Jesus, aware of [the] malice [of those questioning him], said, "Why put me to the test, you hypocrites? Show me the money for the tax." And they brought him a coin. And Jesus said to them, "Whose likeness and inscription is this?"...
Gen. 1:27. God created man in his own image, in the image of God he created him; male and female he created them.
Rom. 5:12. [But]...sin came into the world through one man and death through sin, and so death spread to all men because all men sinned.
Rom. 1:21. ...[Men] became futile in their thinking and their senseless minds were darkened.
Wisdom (Apocrypha) 2:23-24. God created man for incorruption, and made him in the image of his own eternity, but through the devil's envy death entered the world, and those who belong to his party experience it.
Jer. 17:9-10. The heart is deceitful above all things, and desperately corrupt...

*Mt. 22:21. ...[Jesus] said to them, "Render therefore to Caesar the things that are Caesar's, and to God the things that are God's."
Rom. 12:1. I appeal to you therefore, brethren, by the mercies of God, to present your bodies as a living sacrifice, holy and acceptable to God, which is your spiritual worship.
2 Cor. 8:3, 5. [The believers in the churches of Macedonia] gave according to their means...and beyond their means, of their own free will...but first they gave themselves to the Lord...
Rom. 8:29. Those whom [God] foreknew he also predestined to be conformed to the image of his Son, in order that he might be the firstborn among many brethren.
Ps. 51:10. Create in me a clean heart, O God, and put a new and right spirit within me.
Mal. 3:3. [The Lord] is like a refiner's fire...he will sit as a refiner and purifier of silver, and he will purify the sons of Levi and refine them like gold and silver... (Also Prov. 17:3, 25:4, 27:21.)
Is. 1:25 [God]: I will...smelt away your dross as with lye and remove all your alloy. (Also Ezek. 22:19-22.)
2 Cor. 3:18. We all, with unveiled face, beholding the glory of the Lord, are being changed into his likeness from one degree of glory to another; for this comes from the Lord who is the Spirit. (Also Rom. 8:29.)
Eph. 4:17, 22-24. Now...you must no longer live as the Gentiles do, in the futility of their minds...Put off your old nature which belongs to your former manner of life and is corrupt through deceitful lusts, and be renewed in the spirit of your minds, and put on the new nature, created after the likeness of God in true righteousness and holiness. (Also Col. 3:10.)

Mt. 22:37 [Christ]: ...You shall love the Lord your God with all your heart...
Mt. 26:41 [Christ]: Watch and pray that you may not enter into temptation; the spirit indeed is willing, but the flesh is weak. (Also Mk. 14:34-38.)
Rom. 7:15, 18, 22-23, 25. I do not understand my own actions. For I do not do what I want, but I do the very thing I hate...For I know that

Der Will ist zwar bei mir,
The will is indeed in me,
{Indeed, I have the will to do so,}

Doch   Fleisch und Blut will immer widerstreben.
Yet (my) flesh and blood would ever strive-against (it).

Dieweil die Welt
And-since the world

Das Herz gefangen hält,
(My) heart captive holds,
{Holds my heart captive,}

So will sie sich den Raub nicht nehmen lassen;
 - Would it - the booty not be-taken let;
{It will hardly let the booty be taken from it;}

Jedoch ich muß sie hassen,
Yet   I must it hate,
{Yet I must hate the world}

Wenn ich dich lieben soll.
If   I thee shall-love.
{If I am to love thee.}

So mache doch mein Herz mit deiner Gnade voll;
So make please my heart with thy   grace full;
{So please fill my heart with thy grace;}

Leer es ganz   aus von Welt und allen Lüsten
Empty it completely - of world and all   lusts

Und mache mich zu einem rechten Christen.
And make   me into a   true   Christian.

5. Soprano & Alto Duet
●Prayer: Help me surrender myself to thee (163-5)
Nimm mich   mir   und gib mich dir!
Take   me from-myself and give me to-thee!

Nimm mich   mir   und   meinem Willen,
Take   me from-myself and (from) my   will,

Deinen Willen zu erfüllen;
Thy   will   to fulfill;

Gib dich   mir   mit deiner Güte,
Give thyself to-me (along) with thy goodness,

Daß mein Herz und mein Gemüte
That my   heart and my disposition

In dir bleibe   für und für,
In thee remain forever and ever,
{Might remain in thee forever and ever,}

nothing good dwells within me, that is, in my flesh. I can will what is right, but I cannot do it...I delight in the law of God, in my inmost self, but I see in my members another law at war with the law of my mind and making me captive to the law of sin which dwells in my members...So then, I of myself serve the law of God with my mind, but with my flesh I serve the law of sin.

Gal. 5:17. The desires of the flesh are against the Spirit, and the desires of the Spirit are against the flesh; for these are opposed to each other, to prevent you from doing what you would.

Lk. 16:13 [Christ]: No servant can serve two masters; for either he will hate the one and love the other, or he will be devoted to the one and despise the other. You cannot serve God and mammon. (Also Mt. 6:24.)

Lk. 14:25-27. Now great multitudes accompanied [Jesus]; and he turned and said to them, "If any one comes to me and does not hate his own father and mother and wife and children and brothers and sisters, yes, and even his own life, he cannot be my disciple. Whoever does not bear his own cross and come after me, cannot be my disciple." (Also Mt. 10:37-38.)

1 Jn. 2:15-17. Do not love the world or the things in the world. If any one loves the world, love for the Father is not in him. For all that is in the world, the lust of the flesh and the lust of the eyes and the pride of life, is not of the Father but is of the world. And the world passes away, and the lust of it; but he who does the will of God abides for ever.

Jms. 4:4. Unfaithful creatures! Do you not know that friendship with the world is enmity with God? Therefore whoever wishes to be a friend of the world makes himself an enemy of God.

Eph. 3:17, 19. [I pray] that Christ may dwell in your hearts through faith...that you may be filled with all the fulness of God.

Col. 1:9-10. ...We have not ceased to pray for you, asking that you may be filled with the knowledge of his will in all spiritual wisdom and understanding, to lead a life worthy of the Lord, fully pleasing to him, bearing fruit in every good work and increasing in the knowledge of God. (Also Phil. 1:9-11, 2 Thess. 1:11-12; Heb. 13:21.)

Rom. 12:1. ...Present your bodies as a living sacrifice, holy and acceptable to God, which is your spiritual worship.

Rom. 7:18-20, 24-25. I can will what is right, but I cannot do it. For I do not do the good I want, but the evil I do not want is what I do. Now if I do what I do not want, it is no longer I that do it, but sin which dwells within me...Wretched man that I am! Who will deliver me from this body of death? Thanks be to God through Jesus Christ our Lord!...

Mk. 14:36. ...Not what I will, but what thou wilt. (Also Mt. 26:39, 42.)

Phil. 2:13. God is at work in you, both to will and to work for his good pleasure.

Gal. 5:24. Those who belong to Christ Jesus have crucified the flesh with its passions and desires.

S. of S. 2:16 [Bride]: My beloved is mine and I am his... (Also S. of S. 6:3.)

Mt. 22:37-40 [Christ]: ...You shall love the Lord your God with all your heart, and with all your soul, and with all your mind (Luther: Gemüte). This is the great and first commandment. (Also Mk. 12:30, Lk. 10:27, Deut. 6:5.)

564

Nimm mich mir und gib mich dir!
Take me from-myself and give me to-thee!

6. Chorale (See also 5–7.)
●Prayer to avoid sin by Spirit's power (163–6)
Führ auch mein Herz und Sinn
(Bring) also my heart and mind

Durch deinen Geist dahin,
Through thy Spirit thither,
{Through thy Spirit to the point,}

Daß ich mög alles meiden,
That I may all-things shun,
{That I would shun all things}

Was mich und dich kann scheiden,
That me and thee could part,
{That could separate me and thee,}

Und ich an deinem Leibe
And I of thy body

Ein Gliedmaß ewig bleibe.
A member eternally remain.
{And that I would remain a member of thy body eternally.}

BWV 164
Ihr, die ihr euch von Christo nennet
(NBA I/21; BC A128)

13. S. after Trinity (BWV 77, 33, 164)
*Gal. 3:15–22 (The purpose of the Law)
*Lk. 10:23–37 (The greatest commandment; parable of the good Samaritan)
Librettist: Salomon Franck

1. Tenor Aria
●Where is your love, the mark of a Christian? (164–1)
Ihr, die ihr euch von Christo nennet,
You, who yourselves after Christ do-name,
{You, who name yourselves after Christ,}

Wo bleibet die Barmherzigkeit,
Where (is) the compassion,

Jn. 15:4–5 [Christ]: Abide in me, and I in you...apart from me you can do nothing.

Ezek. 36:26–27 [God]: A new heart I will give you, and a new spirit I will put within you; and I will take out of your flesh the heart of stone and give you a heart of flesh. And I will put my spirit within you, and cause you to walk in my statutes and be careful to observe my ordinances.
Jer. 31:33 [God]: This is the covenant which I will make...I will put my law within them, and I will write it upon their hearts (Luther: in ihr Herz geben und in ihren Sinn schreiben)... (Also Heb. 8:10, 10:16.)
2 Cor. 3:3. ...You are a letter from Christ...written not with ink but with the Spirit of the living God, not on tablets of stone but on tablets of human hearts.
2 Cor. 1:22. [God] has put his seal upon us and given us his Spirit in our hearts...
Gal. 5:16. ...Walk by the Spirit, and do not gratify the desires of the flesh.
1 Thess. 5:19. Do not quench the Spirit.
1 Thess. 5:21–22. ...Abstain from every form of evil.
Is. 59:2. Your iniquities have made a separation between you and your God...
1 Tim. 6:11. As for you, man of God, shun all this...
1 Jn. 5:3. This is the love of God, that we keep his commandments. And his commandments are not burdensome. (Also Jn. 14:15, 1 Jn. 2:5, 2 Jn. 1:6.)
1 Jn. 3:24. All who keep his commandments abide in him, and he in them. And by this we know that he abides in us, by the Spirit which he has given us. (Also Jn. 15:4, 6; 1 Jn. 4:13, 15–16.)
1 Cor. 6:17. He who is united to the Lord becomes one spirit with him.
1 Cor. 12:12, 27. Just as the body is one and has many members, and all the members of the body, though many, are one body, so it is with Christ...Now you are the body of Christ and individually members of it.

***Lk. 10:27 [Christ]:** ...You shall love the Lord your God with all your heart, and with all your soul, and with all your strength, and with all your mind; and your neighbor as yourself. (Also Mt. 22:37–40, Mk. 12:30–31, Deut. 6:5, Lev. 19:18.)
Jn. 13:34–35 [Christ]: A new commandment I give to you, that you love one another; even as I have loved you, that you also love one another. By this all men will know that you are my disciples, if you have love for one another.
Jn. 15:12, 17 [Christ]: This is my commandment, that you love one another as I have loved you...This I command you, to love one another.
1 Thess. 4:9. ...You yourselves have been taught by God to love one another.
1 Jn. 3:17–18. If any one has the world's goods and sees his brother in need, yet closes his heart against him, how does God's love abide in him? Little children, let us not love in word or speech but in deed and in truth.

Daran man Christi Glieder kennet?
By-which one Christ's members recognizes?
{By which one recognizes Christ's members?}

Sie ist von euch, ach, allzu weit.
It is from you, ah, all-too far.
{Ah, it is removed all too far from you.}

Die Herzen sollten liebreich sein,
(Your) hearts should loving be,
{Your hearts should be loving,}

So sind sie härter als ein Stein.
(Now) are they harder than a stone.
{But they are harder than stone.}

2. Bass Recit.

●Mercy taught by Christ yet we ignore the needy (164-2)
Wir hören zwar, was selbst die Liebe spricht:
We hear, indeed, what itself - love says:
{Indeed, we hear what He—who is love itself—says:}

Die mit Barmherzigkeit den Nächsten hier umfangen,
Those-who with mercy their neighbor here embrace,

Die sollen vor Gericht
They shall in-the judgment

Barmherzigkeit erlangen.
Mercy obtain.
{They shall obtain mercy in the judgment.}

Jedoch, wir achten solches nicht!
Yet, we heed this not!
{Yet we do not heed this!}

Wir hören noch des Nächsten Seufzer an!
We listen yet to-(our) neighbor's sighing - !
{Indeed, we hear our neighbor's sighing:}

Er kopft an unser Herz; doch wird's nicht aufgetan!
He knocks on our heart; yet is-it not (to-him) opened!
{He knocks upon our heart; yet we do not open to him!}

Wir sehen zwar sein Händeringen,
We see indeed his handwringing,
{We indeed see his handwringing,}

Sein Auge, das von Tränen fleußt;
His eye, which with tears flows;

Doch läßt das Herz sich nicht zur Liebe zwingen.
Yet lets (our) heart itself not to love be-compelled.
{Yet our heart is unmoved and refuses to love.}

Jms. 2:14–17. What does it profit, my brethren, if a man says he has faith but has not works? Can his faith save him? If a brother or sister is ill-clad and in lack of daily food, and one of you says to them, "Go in peace, be warmed and filled," without giving them the things needed for the body, what does it profit? So faith by itself, if it has no works, is dead.

1 Jn. 4:8, 11. He who does not love does not know God...Beloved, if God so loved us, we also ought to love one another.

1 Cor. 12:27. Now you are the body of Christ and individually members of it. (Also Rom. 12:4–5, 1 Cor. 6:15, Eph. 4:15–16, 5:23, 29–30.)

1 Jn. 3:10. By this it may be seen who are the children of God, and who are the children of the devil: whoever does not do right is not of God, nor he who does not love his brother.

Mt. 23:23 [Christ]: Woe to you, scribes and Pharisees, hypocrites! for you tithe mint and dill and cummin, and have neglected the weightier matters of the law, justice and mercy...

1 Jn. 3:11. This is the message which you have heard from the beginning, that we would love one another.

1 Jn. 4:7–8. Beloved, let us love one another; for love is of God, and he who loves is born of God and knows God. He who does not love does not know God; for God is love.

Mt. 5:7; 7:2, 7 [Christ]: Blessed are the merciful, for they shall obtain mercy...With the judgment you pronounce you will be judged, and the measure you give will be the measure you get...Ask, and it will be given you; seek, and you will find; knock, and it will be opened to you (Luther: euch aufgetan).

Prov. 3:27–28. Do not withhold good from those to whom it is due, when it is in your power to do it. Do not say to your neighbor, "Go, and come again, tomorrow I will give it"—when you have it with you.

Gal. 6:10. So then, as we have opportunity, let us do good to all men, and especially to those who are of the household of faith.

Lk. 16:19–25 [Christ]: There was a rich man, who was clothed in purple and fine linen and who feasted sumptuously every day. And at his gate lay a poor man named Lazarus, full of sores, who desired to be fed with what fell from the rich man's table; moreover the dogs came and licked his sores. The poor man died and was carried by the angels to Abraham's bosom. The rich man also died and was buried; and in Hades, being in torment, he lifted up his eyes, and saw Abraham far off and Lazarus in his bosom. And he called out, "Father Abraham, have mercy upon me, and send Lazarus to dip the end of his finger in water and cool my tongue; for I am in anguish in this flame." But Abraham said, "Son, remember that you in your lifetime received your good things, and Lazarus in like manner evil things; but now he is comforted here, and you are in anguish."

*Lk. 10:25–37. And behold, a lawyer stood up to put [Jesus] to the test, saying, "Teacher, what shall I do to inherit eternal life?" He said to him, "What is written in the law? How do you read?" And he answered, "You shall love the Lord your God with all your heart, and with all your soul, and with all your strength, and with all your mind;

Der Priester und Levit,
The priest and Levite,

Der hier zur Seite tritt,
Who here to-the side step, (they)
{Who step to the side—they}

Sind ja ein Bild liebloser Christen;
Are indeed a picture of-loveless Christians;

Sie tun, als wenn sie nichts von fremdem Elend wüßten,
They act, as if they nothing of strangers' misery know,
{They act as if they know nothing of a stranger's misery;}

Sie gießen weder Öl noch Wein
They pour neither oil nor wine

Ins Nächsten Wunden ein.
Into (their) neighbors' wounds -.

3. Alto Aria
•Sharing the pain of others makes us like God (164–3)
Nur durch Lieb und durch Erbarmen
Only through love and through (the) showing-of-mercy

Werden wir Gott selber gleich.
Become we God himself like.
{Do we become like God himself.}

Samaritergleiche Herzen
Samaritan-like hearts

Lassen fremden Schmerz sich schmerzen
Allow (a) stranger's pain themselves to-pain
{Share a stranger's pain}

Und sind an Erbarmung reich.
And are in compassion rich.
{And are rich in compassion.}

4. Tenor Recit.
•Prayer: Melt my heart so I will show love to others (164–4)
Ach, schmelze doch durch deinen Liebesstrahl
Ah, melt indeed, through thy radiance-of-love

Des kalten Herzens Stahl,
This cold heart's steel,

Daß ich die wahre Christenliebe,
That I - true Christian-love,

Mein Heiland, täglich übe,
(O) my Savior, daily (might) practise,

Daß meines Nächsten Wehe,
That my neighbor's woe—

and your neighbor as yourself." And he said to him, "You have answered right; do this, and you will live." But he, desiring to justify himself, said to Jesus, "And who is my neighbor?" Jesus replied, "A man was going down from Jerusalem to Jericho, and he fell among robbers, who stripped him and beat him, and departed, leaving him half dead. Now by chance a priest was going down that road; and when he saw him he passed by on the other side. So likewise a Levite, when he came to the place and saw him, passed by on the other side. But a Samaritan, as he journeyed, came to where he was; and when he saw him, he had compassion, and went to him and bound up his wounds, pouring on oil and wine; then he set him on his own beast and brought him to an inn, and took care of him. And the next day he took out two denarii and gave them to the innkeeper, saying, 'Take care of him; and whatever more you spend, I will repay you when I come back.' Which of these three, do you think, proved neighbor to the man who fell among the robbers?" He said, "The one who showed mercy on him." And Jesus said to him, "Go and do likewise."

Lk. 6:36 [Christ]: Be merciful, even as your Father is merciful.
1 Jn. 4:11–12, 16–17, 19–21. If God so loved us, we also ought to love one another. No man has ever seen God; if we love one another, God abides in us and his love is perfected in us...God is love, and he who abides in love abides in God, and God abides in him. In this is love perfected with us, that we may have confidence for the day of judgment...We love, because he first loved us. If any one says, "I love God," and hates his brother, he is a liar; for he who does not love his brother whom he has seen, cannot love God whom he has not seen. And this commandment we have from him, that he who loves God should love his brother also.
Lk. 6:32, 35 [Christ]: If you love those who love you, what credit is that to you? For even sinners love those who love them...But love your enemies, and do good, and lend, expecting nothing in return; and your reward will be great, and you will be sons of the Most High; for he is kind to the ungrateful and the selfish. (Also Mt. 5:43–48.)

1 Jn. 3:17. If any one has the world's goods and sees his brother in need, yet closes his heart against him, how does God's love abide in him?
Mt. 24:12 [Christ]: Because wickedness is multiplied...men's love will grow cold.
1 Jn. 4:11, 16, 19. If God so loved us, we also ought to love one another...God is love...We love, because he first loved us.
Gal. 6:10. ...As we have opportunity, let us do good to all men...
1 Cor. 12:24–27. ...God has so composed the body [of Christ]...that the members may have the same care for one another. If one member suffers, all suffer together; if one member is honored, all rejoice together. Now you are the body of Christ and individually members of it.
*Lk. 10:29–30, 33, 36–37. [The lawyer who had questioned Jesus,] desiring to justify himself, said to Jesus, "And who is my neighbor?" Jesus replied, "A man was going down from Jerusalem to Jericho, and he fell among robbers, who stripped him and beat him, and departed,

Er sei auch,   wer   er   ist,
He be, indeed, whoever he (may) be,
{No matter who he may be:}

Freund oder Feind, Heid oder Christ,
Friend   or   foe, heathen or Christian—

Mir   als mein eignes Leid zu Herzen allzeit gehe!
To-me as   my   own sorrow to heart ever go!
{Ever may touch my heart as if it were my own sorrow!}

        Mein Herz sei liebreich, sanft und mild,
(May) my heart be   loving,   tender, and mild,

So wird in mir   verklärt   dein Ebenbild.
So will in me be-transfigured thine image.
{So will thine image be transfigured in me.}

5. Soprano & Bass Duet
●Mercy and favor shown by God to those who show mercy
(164-5)
Händen, die sich nicht verschließen,
To-hands that - do-not   close (themselves against others),

Wird der Himmel aufgetan.
Will -   heaven be-opened.

Augen, die mitleidend fließen,
Eyes, which in-sympathy flow,

Sieht   der Heiland gnädig   an.
Regards the Savior with-mercy - .
{Are regarded with mercy by the Savior.}

Herzen,   die nach Liebe streben,
To-hearts, who for love   strive,

Will Gott selbst sein Herze geben.
Will God himself his heart give.
{Will God himself give his heart.}

6. Chorale (See also 22-5, 96-6, 132-6.)
●Prayer: Crucify old nature so the new nature may live
(164-6)
Ertöt uns durch dein Güte,
Mortify us through thy goodness,

Erweck uns durch dein Gnad!
Awaken us through thy grace!

Den alten Menschen kränke,
The   old   man   mortify,

leaving him half dead...But a Samaritan, as he journeyed, came to where he was; and when he saw him, he had compassion...Which of these three, do you think, proved neighbor to the man who fell among the robbers?" He said, "The one who showed mercy on him." And Jesus said to him, "Go and do likewise."
Jn. 4:9. [A] Samaritan woman said to [Jesus], "How is it that you, a Jew, ask a drink of me, a woman of Samaria?" For Jews have no dealings with Samaritans.
Mt. 5:43–45, 48 [Christ]: You have heard that it was said, "You shall love your neighbor and hate your enemy." But I say to you, Love your enemies...so that you may be sons of your Father who is in heaven; for he makes his sun rise on the evil and on the good, and sends rain on the just and on the unjust...You, therefore, must be perfect, as your heavenly Father is perfect.
2 Cor. 3:18. And we...are being changed into his likeness from one degree of glory to another; for this comes from the Lord who is the Spirit. (Also Eph. 4:22–24, Col. 3:9–10.)

Lk. 6:38 [Christ]: Give, and it will be given to you; good measure, pressed down, shaken together, running over, will be put into your lap. For the measure you give will be the measure you get back.
Deut. 28:12. The Lord will open to you his good treasury the heavens... to bless all the work of your hands...
Prov. 11:24–25; 19:17; 28:27. One man gives freely, yet grows all the richer; another withholds what he should give, and only suffers want. A liberal man will be enriched, and one who waters will himself be watered...He who is kind to the poor lends to the Lord, and he will repay him for his deed...He who gives to the poor will not want, but he who hides his eyes will get many a curse.
Job 29:12–13, 15–16; 30:25; 31:32. I delivered the poor who cried, and the fatherless who had none to help him...I caused the widow's heart to sing for joy...I was eyes to the blind, and feet to the lame. I was a father to the poor, and I searched out the cause of him whom I did not know...Did not I weep for him whose day was hard? Was not my soul grieved for the poor?...I have opened my doors to the wayfarer.
Mt. 5:7 [Christ]: Blessed are the merciful, for they shall obtain mercy.

Rom. 6:2–4, 6–7. ...How can we who died to sin still live in it? Do you not know that all of us who have been baptized into Christ Jesus were baptized into his death? We were buried therefore with him by baptism into death, so that as Christ was raised from the dead by the glory of the Father, we too might walk in newness of life...We know that our old self was crucified with him so that the sinful body might be destroyed, and we might no longer be enslaved to sin. For he who has died is freed from sin. (Also Gal. 2:20, Col. 2:12–14.)
Gal. 3:27. As many of you as were baptized into Christ have put on Christ. (Also Gal. 4:19, Rom. 13:14.)
Gal. 5:24. Those who belong to Christ Jesus have crucified the flesh with its passions and desires. (Also 1 Pet. 2:24.)
Eph. 4:22–24. Put off your old nature which belongs to your former manner of life and is corrupt through deceitful lusts, and be renewed

Daß der neu' leben mag
That the new   may-live

Wohl   hier auf dieser Erden,
Indeed here on   this   earth,

        Den Sinn und all   Begehren
(And that) (our) mind and all (our) desires

Und G'danken   habn   zu   dir.
And thoughts (be directed) towards thee.

in the spirit of your minds, and put on the new nature, created after the likeness of God in true righteousness and holiness. (Also Col. 3:9–10.)
Heb. 12:5–6, 11. ...My son, do not regard lightly the discipline of the Lord, nor lose courage when you are punished by him. For the Lord disciplines him whom he loves, and chastises every son whom he receives...For the moment all discipline seems painful rather than pleasant; later it yields the peaceful fruit of righteousness...
1 Pet. 4:1–2. Since therefore Christ suffered in the flesh, arm yourselves with the same thought, for whoever has suffered in the flesh has ceased from sin, so as to live for the rest of the time in the flesh no longer by human passions but by the will of God.
2 Cor. 5:15. [Christ] died for all, that those who live might live no longer for themselves but for him who for their sake died and was raised. (Also 2 Cor. 5:9, Eph. 5:10.)
Col. 3:17. Whatever you do, in word or deed, do everything in the name of the Lord Jesus...

BWV 165
O heilges Geist- und Wasserbad
(NBA I/15; BC A90)

Trinity Sunday (BWV 165, [194], 176, 129)
*Rom. 11:33–36 (O the depth of the riches and wisdom and knowledge of God!)
*Jn. 3:1–15 (Discussion between Jesus and Nicodemus: You must be born anew)
Librettist: Salomon Franck

1. Soprano Aria
●Baptism by Spirit & water brings us into kingdom (165-1)
O heilges Geist- und Wasserbad,
O sacred Spirit- and   water-bath,

Das Gottes Reich   uns   einverleibet
Which God's kingdom for-us incorporates
{Which puts God's kingdom within us}

Und uns ins Buch des Lebens schreibet!
And us into-the book of   life   writes!
{And writes our names into the book of life!}

O Flut,   die alle Missetat
O flood, which all   iniquity

Durch ihre Wunderkraft ertränket
Through its miraculous-power drowns
{O flood which drowns all iniquity through its miraculous power}

Und uns das neue Leben schenket!
And on-us the new life   bestows!
{And bestows the new life upon us!}

O heilges Geist- und Wasserbad!
O sacred Spirit- and water-bath!

*Jn. 3:3, 5–6. Jesus answered [Nicodemus], "Truly, truly, I say to you, unless one is born anew, he cannot see the kingdom of God...Truly, truly, I say to you, unless one is born of water and the Spirit, he cannot enter the kingdom of God. That which is born of the flesh is flesh, and that which is born of the Spirit is spirit."
Lk. 3:16. John answered them all, "I baptize you with water; but he who is mightier than I is coming, the thong of whose sandals I am not worthy to untie; he will baptize you with the Holy Spirit and with fire." (Also Mt. 3:11, Mk. 1:7–8, Jn. 1:26–27, 33.)
1 Pet. 3:21. Baptism, which corresponds to [Noah's experience] now saves you, not as a removal of dirt from the body but as an appeal to God for a clear conscience, through the resurrection of Jesus Christ.
Gen. 7:11–12, 21–22, 23. In the six hundredth year of Noah's life, in the second month, on the seventeenth day of the month, on that day all the fountains of the great deep burst forth, and the windows of the heavens were opened. And rain fell upon the earth forty days and forty nights...And all flesh died that moved upon the earth, birds, cattle, beasts, all swarming creatures that swarm upon the earth, and every man; everything on the dry land in whose nostrils was the breath of life died...Only Noah was left, and those that were with him in the ark.
Rom. 6:4. We were buried therefore with [Christ] by baptism into death, so that as Christ was raised from the dead by the glory of the Father, we too might walk in newness of life.
2 Cor. 5:17. Therefore, if any one is in Christ, he is a new creation; the old has passed away, behold, the new has come.
Col. 3:9–10. ...You have put off the old nature with its practices and have put on the new nature, which is being renewed in knowledge after the image of its creator.
Rev. 21:27. Nothing unclean shall enter [the heavenly city]...only those who are written in the Lamb's book of life. (Also Rev. 3:5, 13:8, 17:8, 20:12, 15.)
Lk. 10:20 [Christ]: Rejoice that your names are written in heaven.

2. Bass Recit.

●Baptism by water & Spirit heals us of sin's disease (165-2)
Die   sündige   Geburt verdammter Adamserben
The sin-begotten birth   of-the-cursed heirs-of-Adam
{The sinful nature inherited at birth by the cursed heirs of Adam}

Gebieret   Gottes Zorn, den Tod und das Verderben.
Gives-birth-to God's wrath, - death, and - perdition.
{Brings God's wrath, death, and perdition upon us.}

Denn was   vom Fleisch geboren ist,
For whatever of-the flesh   born   is,
{For whatever is born of the flesh,}

Ist nichts als Fleisch, von Sünden angestecket,
Is nought but flesh,   by   sin   contaminated,
{Is but fleshly, contaminated by sin,}

Vergiftet und beflecket.
Poisoned, and stained.

Wie selig ist ein Christ!
How blessed is a Christian!

Er   wird   im   Geist- und Wasserbade
He becomes in-that Spirit- and water-bath
{In that Spirit- and water-bath}

Ein Kind der Seligkeit   und Gnade.
A child of heavenly-bliss and grace.
{He becomes a child of heavenly bliss and grace.}

Er ziehet Christum an
He puts   Christ on
{He clothes himself with Christ}

Und   seiner Unschuld weiße Seide,
And (with) his   innocence's white silk,
{And with the white silk of Christ's innocence;}

Er wird mit Christi Blut, der Ehren   Purpurkleide,
He is with Christ's blood, of glory (the) purple-robe,

Im Taufbad angetan.
In baptism's-bath attired.
{In baptism's bath he is attired with Christ's blood, the purple robe of glory.}

3. Alto Aria

●Prayer: May my baptism's healing purpose ever be realized (165-3)
    Jesu, der aus großer Liebe
(O) Jesus, who, out-of great love,

In   der   Taufe mir verschriebe
In (the-rite-of) baptism to-me has-pledged
{In the rite of baptism pledged to me}

*Jn. 3:5-6 [Christ]:** Truly, truly, I say to you, unless one is born of water and the Spirit, he cannot enter the kingdom of God. That which is born of the flesh is flesh, and that which is born of the Spirit is spirit.

Ps. 51:5. Behold, I was brought forth in iniquity, and in sin did my mother conceive me.

Rom. 7:18. I know that nothing good dwells within me, that is, in my flesh...

Rom. 5:12, 17-19. ...Sin came into the world through one man and death through sin, and so death spread to all men because all men sinned...Because of one man's trespass, death reigned through that one man...One man's trespass led to condemnation for all men...By one man's disobedience many were made sinners...

Eph. 2:1-6. And you [God] made alive, when you were dead through the trespasses and sins in which you once walked, following the course of the world, following the prince of the power of the air, the spirit that is now at work in the sons of disobedience. Among these we all once lived in the passions of our flesh, following the desires of body and mind, and so we were by nature children of wrath like the rest of mankind. But God, who is rich in mercy, out of the great love with which he loved us, even when we were dead through our trespasses, made us alive together with Christ (by grace you have been saved), and raised us up with him, and made us sit with him in the heavenly places in Christ Jesus.

1 Pet. 3:21. Baptism...now saves you, not as a removal of dirt from the body but as an appeal to God for a clear conscience, through the resurrection of Jesus Christ.

Rom. 6:3-4. Do you not know that all of us who have been baptized into Christ Jesus were baptized into his death? We were buried therefore with him by baptism into death, so that as Christ was raised from the dead by the glory of the Father, we too might walk in newness of life.

Rom. 6:23. The wages of sin is death, but the free gift of God is eternal life in Christ Jesus our Lord.

1 Cor. 15:21-22, 47-49. As by a man came death, by a man has come also the resurrection of the dead. For as in Adam all die, so also in Christ shall all be made alive...The first man was from the earth, a man of dust; the second man is from heaven. As was the man of dust, so are those who are of the dust; and as is the man of heaven, so are those who are of heaven. Just as we have borne the image of the man of dust, we shall also bear the image of the man of heaven.

Ezek. 16:9-10 [God]: I bathed you with water...I swathed you in fine linen and covered you with silk.

Gal. 3:27. As many of you as were baptized into Christ have put on Christ. (Also Rom. 13:14, Eph. 4:24, Col. 3:10.)

Rev. 7:14. ...[The righteous] have washed their robes and made them white in the blood of the Lamb.

Eph. 2:4-6. God, who is rich in mercy, out of the great love with which he loved us, even when we were dead through our trespasses, made us alive together with Christ (by grace you have been saved), and raised us up with him, and made us sit with him in the heavenly places in Christ Jesus.

Mk. 16:16 [Christ]: He who believes and is baptized will be saved...

Col. 2:12-14. And you were buried with him in baptism, in which you

Leben, Heil und Seligkeit,
Life,   salvation, and blessedness,

Hilf, daß ich mich dessen   freue
Help, that I   - over-this might-rejoice
{Help that I might rejoice over this}

Und den Gnadenbund erneue
And this covenant-of-grace renew
{And renew this covenant of grace}

In   der ganzen   Lebenszeit.
(Throughout) the whole (of my) life's-span.

4. Bass Recit.
●Baptismal vows often broken, sanctification needed (165-4)
Ich habe ja,   mein Seelenbräutigam,
I   have, indeed, (O) my   soul's-bridegroom—

Da du   mich neu geboren,
When thou (didst-make) me newly born—

Dir ewig treu zu sein geschworen,
To-thee ever faithful to be   sworn,
{I have indeed sworn ever to be faithful to thee, O my soul's
bridegroom, when thou didst give me new birth,}

Hochheilges Gotteslamm;
Most-holy   Lamb-of-God;

Doch hab ich, ach! den   Taufbund   oft gebrochen
Yet have I, alas, the covenant-of-baptism often broken
{Yet, alas, I have often broken the covenant of baptism}

Und nicht erfüllt, was ich versprochen,
And not fulfilled, what I did-promise;

Erbarme,   Jesu, dich
Have-mercy, (O) Jesus - ,

Aus Gnaden über mich!
Out-of grace upon me!
{O Jesus, out of thy grace, have mercy upon me!}

Vergib mir die begangne Sünde,
Forgive me the committed sins,

Du   weißt,   mein Gott, wie schmerzlich ich empfinde
Thou knowest, (O) my God, how painfully   I   experience

---

were also raised with him through faith in the working of God, who
raised him from the dead. And you, who were dead in trespasses and
the uncircumcision of your flesh, God made alive together with him,
having forgiven us all our trespasses, having canceled the bond which
stood against us with its legal demands; this he set aside, nailing it to
the cross.

Rom. 6:4, 11–12. We were buried therefore with him by baptism into
death, so that as Christ was raised from the dead by the glory of the
Father, we too might walk in newness of life...So you also must
consider yourselves dead to sin and alive to God in Christ Jesus. Let
not sin therefore reign in your mortal bodies, to make you obey their
passions.

Col. 3:1. If then you have been raised with Christ, seek the things that
are above, where Christ is...

1 Pet. 1:3. ...By [God's] great mercy we have been born anew to a
living hope through the resurrection of Jesus Christ...

Rom. 6:4. We were buried...with him by baptism into death, so that as
Christ was raised from the dead by the glory of the Father, we too
might walk in newness of life.

*Jn. 3:3 [Christ]: ...Unless one is born anew, he cannot see the
kingdom of God..

1 Jn. 4:10. In this is love, not that we loved God but that he loved us
and sent his Son to be the expiation for our sins.

Jn. 1:29. ...[John] saw Jesus coming toward him, and said, "Behold, the
Lamb of God, who takes away the sin of the world!" (Also Jn. 1:36.)

Jer. 31:3 [God]: ...I have loved you with an everlasting love; therefore
I have continued my faithfulness to you.

Hos. 2:19 [God]: I will betroth you to me for ever...

Jer. 3:20. Surely, as a faithless wife leaves her husband, so have you
been faithless to me, O house of Israel, says the Lord.

Heb. 10:28–29. A man who has violated the law of Moses dies without
mercy at the testimony of two or three witnesses. How much worse
punishment do you think will be deserved by the man who has
spurned the Son of God, and profaned the blood of the covenant by
which he was sanctified, and outraged the Spirit of grace?

Rom. 6:2–3. ...How can we who died to sin still live in it? Do you not
know that all of us who have been baptized into Christ Jesus were
baptized into his death?

2 Cor. 11:2–3. I feel a divine jealousy for you, for I betrothed you to
Christ to present you as a pure bride to her one husband. But I am
afraid that as the serpent deceived Eve by his cunning, your thoughts
will be led astray from a sincere and pure devotion to Christ.

Gen. 3:9, 11–13. [After Adam and Eve had eaten of the forbidden
fruit in the garden of Eden], the Lord God called to the man, and said
to him, "...Have you eaten of the tree of which I commanded you not
to eat?" The man said, "The woman whom thou gavest to be with me,
she gave me fruit of the tree and I ate." Then the Lord God said to
the woman, "What is this that you have done?" The woman said, "The
serpent beguiled me, and I ate."

Rom. 5:12, 19. Sin came into the world through one man and death
through sin, and so death spread to all men...by one man's
disobedience many were made sinners...

Gen. 6:5. The Lord saw that the wickedness of man was great in the
earth, and that every imagination of the thoughts of his heart was only
evil continually.

Der alten Schlangen Stich;
The ancient serpent's sting;

Das Sündengift verderbt mir Leib und Seele,
The venom-of-sin corrupts (my) body and soul,

Hilf, daß ich gläubig dich erwähle,
Help, that I, believing, thee might-choose,
{Help that, in faith, I would choose thee,}

Blutrotes Schlangenbild,
(O) blood-red serpent-image,

Das an dem Kreuz erhöhet,
Which on the cross hath-been-raised,

Das alle Schmerzen stillt
Which all suffering doth-still

Und mich erquickt, wenn alle Kraft vergehet.
And me doth-revive, when all strength (hath-vanished).

5. Tenor Aria
●Prayer: Sanctify me till death; You conquered death & sin (165–5)
Jesu, meines Todes Tod,
(O) Jesus, (who art) my death's death,
{O Jesus, thou who art the death of my death,}

Laß in meinem Leben
Let in my life

Und in meiner letzten Not
And (also) in my last (hour's) need

Mir vor Augen schweben,
Before-mine eyes (this thought) hover,

Daß du mein Heilschlänglein seist
That thou my serpent-of-Salvation art

Für das Gift der Sünde.
For the poison of sin.

Heile, Jesu, Seel und Geist,
Heal, (O) Jesus, (my) soul and spirit,

Daß ich Leben finde!
That I life might-find!

Ps. 14:2–3. The Lord looks down from heaven upon the children of men, to see if there are any that act wisely, that seek after God. They have all gone astray, they are all alike corrupt; there is none that does good, no, not one.
Rom. 7:15, 19–20. I do not understand my own actions...For I do not do the good I want, but the evil I do not want is what I do. Now if I do what I do not want, it is no longer I that do it, but sin which dwells within me...
Lk. 18:13. ...God be merciful to me a sinner!
Num. 21:5–9. The people [of Israel] spoke against God and against Moses, "Why have you brought us up out of Egypt to die in the wilderness? For there is no food and no water, and we loathe this worthless food." Then the Lord sent fiery serpents among the people, and they bit the people, so that many people of Israel died. And the people came to Moses, and said, "We have sinned, for we have spoken against the Lord and against you; pray to the Lord, that he take away the serpents from us." So Moses prayed for the people. And the Lord said to Moses, "Make a fiery serpent, and set it on a pole; and every one who is bitten, when he sees it, shall live." So Moses made a bronze serpent, and set it on a pole; and if a serpent bit any man, he would look at the bronze serpent and live.
***Jn. 3:14–15.** As Moses lifted up the serpent in the wilderness, so must the Son of man be lifted up, that whoever believes in him may have eternal life. (Also Jn. 12:32–33.)
Heb. 12:1–2. ...Let us also lay aside every weight, and sin which clings so closely, and let us run with perseverance the race that is set before us, looking to Jesus the pioneer and perfecter of our faith, who for the joy that was set before him endured the cross...

Is. 25:8. He will swallow up death for ever, and the Lord God will wipe away tears from all faces...
2 Tim. 1:10. ...through the appearing of our Savior Christ Jesus, who abolished death and brought life and immortality to light... (Also 1 Cor. 15:25–26.)
Heb. 2:14–15. Since therefore the children share in flesh and blood, [Christ] himself likewise partook of the same nature, that through death he might destroy him who has the power of death, that is, the devil, and deliver all those who through fear of death were subject to lifelong bondage.
1 Jn. 3:8. ...The reason the Son of God appeared was to destroy the works of the devil.
Heb. 9:26. [Christ] appeared...to put away sin by the sacrifice of himself.
1 Jn. 3:5. You know that he appeared to take away sins, and in him there is no sin.
Num. 21:9. Moses made a bronze serpent, and set it on a pole; and if a serpent bit any man, he would look at the bronze serpent and live.
***Jn. 3:14–15.** As Moses lifted up the serpent in the wilderness, so must the Son of man be lifted up, that whoever believes in him may have eternal life.
Heb. 13:12. Jesus also suffered outside the gate in order to sanctify the people through his own blood.
1 Thess. 5:23. May...God...sanctify you wholly; and may your spirit and soul and body be kept sound and blameless at the coming of our Lord Jesus Christ.

6. Chorale
●Baptism, Word, and Eucharist guard us from evil (165-6)
Sein Wort, sein Tauf, sein Nachtmahl
His Word, his baptism, his supper

Dient wider allen Unfall,
Serves to-counter all calamity;

Der Heilge Geist im Glauben
The Holy Ghost in faith
{Through our faith the Holy Ghost}

Lehrt uns darauf vertrauen.
Teaches us in-this to-trust.
{Teaches us to believe this.}

BWV 166
Wo gehest du hin
(NBA I/12; BC A71)

Cantate: 4. S. after Easter (BWV 166, 108)
*Jms. 1:17-21 (All good gifts come from above; be doers of the Word)
*Jn. 16:5-15 (Jesus' farewell: promise to send the Holy Spirit)
Librettist: Unknown; perhaps Christian Weiß the elder

1. Bass Aria
●Vox Christi: Where goest thou? Jn. 16:5 (166-1)
Wo gehest du hin?
Where goest thou - ?

2. Tenor Aria
●Eternal destiny kept in mind at all times (166-2)
Ich will an den Himmel denken
I will of - heaven think
{I will think of heaven}

Und der Welt mein Herz nicht schenken.
And the world my heart not give.
{And not give the world my heart.}

Denn ich gehe oder stehe,
For (whether) I move or (rest),
{For whether I am busy or at rest,}

Jms. 1:21. ...The implanted **word**...is able to save your souls.
Mt. 7:24-25 [Christ]: Every one then who hears these words of mine and does them will be like a wise man who built his house upon the rock; and the rain fell, and the floods came, and the winds blew and beat upon that house, but it did not fall, because it had been founded on the rock.
1 Pet. 3:21. Baptism...now saves you, not as a removal of dirt from the body but as an appeal to God for a clear conscience, through the resurrection of Jesus Christ.
1 Cor. 10:16. The **cup** of blessing which we bless, is it not a participation in the blood of Christ? The **bread** which we break, is it not a participation in the body of Christ?
Jn. 6:54, 56 [Christ]: He who eats my flesh and drinks my blood has eternal life... He who eats my flesh and drinks my blood abides in me, and I in him.
Jn. 14:26-27 [Christ]: The Counselor, the **Holy Spirit**, whom the Father will send in my name, he will teach you all things...
1 Cor. 2:12-14. Now we have received not the spirit of the world, but the Spirit which is from God, that we might understand the gifts bestowed on us by God. And we impart this in words not taught by human wisdom but taught by the Spirit, interpreting spiritual truths to those who possess the Spirit. The unspiritual man does not receive the gifts of the Spirit of God, for they are folly to him, and he is not able to understand them because they are spiritually discerned.

Jn. 14:3-6. [Jesus said], "...I go and prepare a place for you, I will come again and will take you to myself, that where I am you may be also. And you know the way where I am going." Thomas said to him, "Lord, we do not know where you are going; how can we know the way?" Jesus said to him, "I am the way, and the truth, and the life; no one comes to the Father, but by me."
*Jn. 16:4-7 [Christ]: ...I did not say these things to you from the beginning, because I was with you. But now I am going to him who sent me; yet none of you asks me, "Where are you going?" But because I have said these things to you, sorrow has filled your hearts. Nevertheless I tell you the truth: it is to your advantage that I go away, for if I do not go away, the Counselor will not come to you; but if I go, I will send him to you.
Col. 3:1-3. If then you have been raised with Christ, seek the things that are above, where Christ is, seated at the right hand of God. Set your minds on things that are above, not on things that are on earth. For you have died and your life is hid with Christ in God. (Also 2 Cor. 4:18.)
Mt. 6:19-21 [Christ]: Do not lay up for yourselves treasures on earth, where moth and rust consume and where thieves break in and steal, but lay up for yourselves treasures in heaven, where neither moth nor rust consumes and where thieves do not break in and steal. For where your treasure is, there will your heart be also.
1 Jn. 2:15-17. Do not love the world or the things in the world. If any one loves the world, love for the Father is not in him. For all that is in the world, the lust of the flesh and the lust of the eyes and the pride of life, is not of the Father but is of the world. And the world passes away, and the lust of it; but he who does the will of God abides for ever. (Also Jms. 4:4.)

So liegt mir die Frag im Sinn:
(There) lies - this question in (my) mind:
{This one question preoccupies my mind:}

Mensch, ach Mensch, wo gehst du hin?
Man, ah man, where goest thou - ?

3. Chorale: Soprano
●Prayer to keep resolve firm until I reach heaven (166-3)
Ich bitte dich, Herr Jesu Christ,
I ask (of) thee, Lord Jesus Christ,

Halt mich bei den Gedanken
Hold me to these thoughts

Und laß mich ja zu keiner Frist
And let me indeed at no time

Von dieser Meinung wanken,
From this intention waver,

Sondern dabei verharren fest,
Rather in-it persist firmly,

Bis daß die Seel aus ihrem Nest
Until (my) soul out-of its nest
{Until my soul leaves its nest}

Wird in den Himmel kommen.
Will into - heaven come.
{And goes to heaven.}

4. Bass Recit.
●Worldly pleasures & life itself can vanish quickly (166-4)
Gleichwie die Regenwasser bald verfließen
Just-as the rain-waters soon subside

Und manche Farben leicht verschießen,
And many colors easily fade,
{And many colors fade quickly,}

So geht es auch der Freude in der Welt,
So is it too (with) the pleasures (of) the world,

Auf welche mancher Mensch so viele Stücken hält;
Of which many-a person so (high-an-opinion) holds;
{Which so many people regard so highly;}

Denn ob man gleich zuweilen sieht,
For though one - occasionally sees,

Daß sein gewünschtes Glücke blüht,
That his wished-for fortune blooms,
{The fortune one wished for coming true,}

So kann doch wohl in besten Tagen
Yet can nevertheless indeed in (the) best-of days

Ps. 90:10, 12. The years of our life are threescore and ten, or even by reason of strength fourscore; yet their span is but toil and trouble; they are soon gone, and we fly away...So teach us to number our days that we may get a heart of wisdom.

Heb. 10:23. Let us hold fast the confession of our hope without wavering (Luther: wanken), for he who promised is faithful.
Heb. 3:14. We share in Christ, if only we hold our first confidence firm to the end.
Rev. 2:10 [Christ]: ...Be faithful unto death, and I will give you the crown of life.
Rev. 3:11 [Christ]: I am coming soon; hold fast what you have, so that no one may seize your crown.
1 Cor. 15:58. Therefore, my beloved brethren, be steadfast, immovable, always abounding in the work of the Lord, knowing that in the Lord your labor is not in vain.
Ecc. 12:1, 6–7. Remember...your Creator in the days of your youth, before the...silver cord is snapped...and the dust returns to the earth as it was, and the spirit returns to God who gave it.
2 Cor. 5:1–4. We know that if the earthly tent we live in is destroyed, we have a building from God, a house not made with hands, eternal in the heavens. Here indeed we groan, and long to put on our heavenly dwelling, so that by putting it on we may not be found naked. For while we are still in this tent, we sigh with anxiety; not that we would be unclothed, but that we would be further clothed, so that what is mortal may be swallowed up by life.

1 Jn. 2:17. The world passes away, and the lust of it; but he who does the will of God abides for ever.
Ps. 49:12–13, 16–20. Man cannot abide in his pomp, he is like the beasts that perish. This is the fate of those who have foolish confidence, the end of those who are pleased with their portion...Be not afraid when one becomes rich, when the glory of his house increases. For when he dies he will carry nothing away; his glory will not go down after him...Though a man gets praise when he does well for himself, he will go to the generation of his fathers, who will never more see the light. Man cannot abide in his pomp, he is like the beasts that perish.
Jms. 1:10–11. ...Like the flower of the grass he will pass away. For the sun rises with its scorching heat and withers the grass; its flower falls, and its beauty perishes. So will the rich man fade away in the midst of his pursuits.
Ps. 39:4–6. Lord, let me know my end, and what is the measure of my days; let me know how fleeting my life is! Behold, thou hast made my days a few handbreadths, and my lifetime is as nothing in thy sight. Surely every man stands as a mere breath! Surely man goes about as a shadow! Surely for nought are they in turmoil; man heaps up, and knows not who will gather. (Also Lk. 12:16–21.)
Is. 40:6–7. ...All flesh is grass, and all its beauty is like the flower of the field. The grass withers, the flower fades when the breath of the

Ganz unvermut' die letzte Stunde schlagen.
Quite unexpectedly the final hour strike.
{Yet the final hour can indeed strike quite unexpectedly in the best of days.}

5. Alto Aria
●Worldly good fortune can change before nightfall (166-5)
Man nehme sich in acht,
(Let) everyone take - - heed,

Wenn das Gelücke lacht.
When (his) (good) fortune laughs.
{When good fortune smiles upon him.}

Denn es kann leicht auf Erden
For (things) can easily on earth
{For things on earth can easily}

Vor abends anders werden,
Before evening (quite) different become,
{Change dramatically before evening}

Als man am Morgen nicht gedacht.
Than one in-the morning - had-thought.
{From what one had thought in the morning.}

6. Chorale (See also 27-1.)
●Death comes at any time, only God knows how soon (166-6)
Wer weiß, wie nahe mir mein Ende?
Who knows, how near to-me my end (is)?

Hin geht die Zeit, her kommt der Tod;
Hence goes - time, hither comes - death;
{Time departs, death approaches;}

Ach, wie geschwinde und behende
Ah, how swiftly and adroitly

Kann kommen meine Todesnot.
Can come my death's-trial.

Mein Gott, ich bitt durch Christi Blut:
My God, I pray through Christ's blood:

Mach's nur mit meinem Ende gut!
Make-it but with my end well!
{Just make it well with my end!}

Lord blows upon it; surely the people is grass. (Also Ps. 102:3, 11, 103:15–16, 1 Pet. 1:24–25.)

Sirach (Apocrypha) 18:25–26. In the time of plenty think of the time of hunger; in the days of wealth think of poverty and need. From morning to evening conditions change, and all things move swiftly before the Lord.
Ps. 62:10. ...If riches increase, set not your heart on them.
Jms. 4:13–15. Come now, you who say, "Today or tomorrow we will go into such and such a town and spend a year there and trade and get gain"; whereas you do not know about tomorrow. What is your life? For you are a mist that appears for a little time and then vanishes. Instead you ought to say, "If the Lord wills, we shall live and we shall do this or that."
Ps. 90:5–6. ...[Men] are like a dream, like grass which is renewed in the morning: in the morning it flourishes and is renewed; in the evening it fades and withers.
Lk. 12:20–21. God said to [the rich man], "Fool! This night your soul is required of you; and the things you have prepared, whose will they be?" So is he who lays up treasure for himself, and is not rich toward God. (Also 1 Tim. 6:6–7.)
Ps. 90:12. [O Lord,] teach us to number our days that we may get a heart of wisdom.

Ecc. 9:12. Man does not know his time...
Job 14:1–2, 5. Man that is born of woman is of few days, and full of trouble. He comes forth like a flower, and withers; he flees like a shadow, and continues not...His days are determined, and the number of his months is with thee, and thou hast appointed his bounds that he cannot pass...
Ps. 90:3–6. [O Lord,] thou turnest man back to the dust, and sayest, "Turn back, O children of men!" For a thousand years in thy sight are but as yesterday when it is past, or as a watch in the night. Thou dost sweep men away; they are like a dream, like grass which is renewed in the morning: in the morning it flourishes and is renewed; in the evening it fades and withers.
Ps. 103:15–16. As for man, his days are like grass; he flourishes like a flower of the field; for the wind passes over it, and it is gone, and its place knows it no more.
Lk. 9:25 [Christ]: What does it profit a man if he gains the whole world and loses or forfeits himself? (Also Mt. 16:26, Mk. 8:36–37.)
Num. 23:10. ...Let me die the death of the righteous, and let my end be like his! (Also Heb. 13:7.)
Ecc. 7:1–2, 8. ...The day of death [is better] than the day of birth. It is better to go to the house of mourning than to go to the house of feasting; for this is the end of all men, and the living will lay it to heart...Better is the end of a thing than its beginning...

BWV 167
Ihr Menschen, rühmet Gottes Liebe
(NBA I/29; BC A176)

Feast of St. John the Baptist: June 24 (BWV 167, 7, 30)
*Is. 40:1–5 (A voice crying in the wilderness)
*Lk. 1:57–80 (Birth of John the Baptist and song of Zacharias)
Librettist: Unknown

1. Tenor Aria
●Praise to God for sending His Son, our Salvation (167-1)
Ihr Menschen, rühmet Gottes Liebe
Ye   people,   extol   God's   love

Und preiset seine Gütigkeit!
And praise   his   goodness!

Lobt ihn aus reinem Herzenstriebe,
Praise him out-of pure   heart's-impulse,

Daß er uns zu bestimmter Zeit
That he us at-the appointed time

Das *Horn des Heils*, den Weg zum Leben
The horn of salvation, the way to   life

An Jesu, seinem Sohn, gegeben.
In Jesus,   his   Son, has-given.
{That, at the appointed time, he has given us in Jesus the horn of salvation, the way to life.}

2. Alto Recit.
●Praise God that he sent his Son, preceded by John (167-2)
Gelobet sei der Herr Gott   Israel,
Blessed be the Lord God (of) Israel,

Der sich in Gnaden zu uns wendet
Who -   in mercy   to us   turns
{Who turns to us in mercy}

Und seinen Sohn
And his   Son
{And sends his Son}

Vom   hohen Himmelsthron
From (the) lofty throne-of-heaven

Zum   Welterlöser   sendet.
As Savior-of-the-world sends.
{As Savior of the world.}

Erst stellte sich Johannes ein
First appeared -   John   -
{First did John appear}

Ps. 106:1–2. O give thanks to the Lord, for he is good; for his steadfast love (Luther: Güte) endures for ever! Who can utter the mighty doings of the Lord, or show forth all his praise? (Also Ps. 135:3, 147:1.)
2 Cor. 9:15. Thanks be to God for his inexpressible gift!
*Lk. 1:67–70. ...Zechariah [the priest] was filled with the Holy Spirit, and prophesied, saying, "Blessed be the Lord God of Israel, for he has visited and redeemed his people, and has raised up a *horn of salvation* for us in the house of his servant David, as he spoke by the mouth of his holy prophets from of old."
Lk. 2:30–32 [Simeon]: Mine eyes have seen thy salvation which thou hast prepared in the presence of all peoples, a light for revelation to the Gentiles, and for glory to thy people Israel.
Gal. 4:4–5. When the time had fully come, God sent forth his Son, born of woman, born under the law, to redeem those who were under the law, so that we might receive adoption as sons.
Acts 4:12. And there is salvation in no one else, for there is no other name under heaven given among men by which we must be saved.
Jn. 14:6. Jesus said... "I am the way, and the truth, and the life; no one comes to the Father, but by me."
Rom. 15:8–11. ...Christ became a servant...in order to confirm the promises given to the patriarchs, and in order that the Gentiles might glorify God for his mercy. As it is written, "Therefore I will praise thee among the Gentiles, and sing to thy name"; and again it is said, "Rejoice, O Gentiles, with his people"; and again, "Praise the Lord, all Gentiles, and let all the peoples praise him".

*Lk. 1:59, 67–70, 76–79. ...And on the eighth day [when] they came to circumcise the child [who would later be known as John the Baptist]... Zechariah [his father] was filled with the Holy Spirit, and prophesied, saying, *"Blessed be the Lord God of Israel,* for he has visited and redeemed his people, and has raised up a horn of salvation for us in the house of his servant David, as he spoke by the mouth of his holy prophets from of old...And you, child, will be called the prophet of the Most High; for you will go before the Lord to prepare his ways, to give knowledge of salvation to his people in the forgiveness of their sins, through the tender mercy of our God, when the day shall dawn upon us from on high to give light to those who sit in darkness and in the shadow of death, to guide our feet into the way of peace."
Heb. 1:1–2. In many and various ways God spoke of old to our fathers by the prophets; but in these last days he has spoken to us by a Son...
1 Jn. 4:9–10. In this the love of God was made manifest among us, that God sent his only Son into the world, so that we might live through him. In this is love, not that we loved God but that he loved us and sent his Son to be the expiation for our sins.
Jn. 3:16. For God so loved the world that he gave his only Son, that whoever believes in him should not perish (Luther: verloren werden) but have eternal life. (Also Jn. 3:17–18.)

Und mußte   Weg und Bahn
And must (the) way and path
{To prepare the way and path}

Dem Heiland zubereiten;
For-the Savior   prepare;
{For the Savior;}

Hierauf   kam Jesus selber an,
Thereupon arrived Jesus himself - ,
{Then Jesus himself arrived,}

Die armen Menschenkinder
The poor   children-of-men
{To gladden the poor children of men}

Und die verlornen Sünder
And (all)   lost   sinners
{And all lost sinners}

Mit Gnad und Liebe zu erfreun
With grace and love to gladden
{With grace and love,}

Und sie zum   Himmelreich
And them to-the kingdom-of-heaven
{And to lead them to the kingdom of heaven}

in wahrer   Buß zu leiten.
in true   repentance to lead.
{In true repentance.}

3. Soprano & Alto Duet
●God's promises of a Savior have now been fulfilled (167-3)
Gottes Wort, das trüget nicht,
God's Word, - deceives not,

Es   geschieht, was er verspricht.
It (all) happens,   that he promises.
{Whatever he promises, happens}

Was er in dem Paradies
What he in that paradise
{What he already promised in that paradise}

Und vor so viel hundert Jahren
And before so many hundred years
{So many hundred years ago}

Denen   Vätern schon verhieß,
To-those fathers already promised,
{To our forefathers,}

Haben wir   gottlob   erfahren.
Have   we, praise-God, experienced.
{This, praise God, we have now experienced.}

Mt. 17:12-13. [As Jesus and his three disciples came down from the mountain where Jesus had been transfigured,] the disciples asked him, "...Why do the scribes say that first Elijah must come?" He replied, "Elijah does come, and he is to restore all things; but I tell you that Elijah has already come..." Then the disciples understood that he was speaking to them of John the Baptist. (Also Mk. 9:11-13.)
Mt. 3:1-3, 5-6. In those days came John the Baptist, preaching in the wilderness of Judea, "Repent, for the kingdom of heaven is at hand." For this is he who was spoken of by the prophet Isaiah when he said, "The voice of one crying in the wilderness: Prepare the way of the Lord, make his paths straight."...Then went out to him Jerusalem and all Judea and all the region about the Jordan, and they were baptized by him in the river Jordan, confessing their sins. (Also *Is. 40:1-5, Mk. 1:1-3, Jn. 1:19-23.)
Lk. 4:16-19, 21. And [Jesus] came to Nazareth, where he had been brought up; and he went to the synagogue...and he stood up to read... He opened the book...where it was written, "The Spirit of the Lord is upon me, because he has anointed me to preach good news to the poor, He has sent me to proclaim release to the captives and recovering of sight to the blind, to set at liberty those who are oppressed, to proclaim the acceptable year of the Lord."...And he began to say to them, "Today this scripture has been fulfilled in your hearing." (Also Is. 61:1-2, Ezek. 34:16.)
Lk. 5:32 [Christ]: I have not come to call the righteous, but sinners to repentance. (Also Mt. 9:12-13, Mk. 2:17.)
Lk. 19:10 [Christ]: The Son of man came to seek and to save the lost.

Rom. 15:8. ...Christ [came as] a servant to the circumcised to show God's truthfulness, in order to confirm the promises given to the patriarchs...
Gen. 3:14-15. The Lord God said to the serpent [in the garden of Eden], "Because you have [deceived Adam and Eve]...I will put enmity between you and the woman, and between your seed and her seed; he shall bruise your head, and you shall bruise his heel." (See also Rom. 16:20. Rev. 12:9, 1 Jn. 3:8, Heb. 2:14.)
***Lk. 1:67-70, 72-73.** Zechariah was filled with the Holy Spirit, and prophesied, saying, "Blessed be the Lord God of Israel, for he has visited and redeemed his people, and has raised up a horn of salvation for us...as he spoke by the mouth of his holy prophets from of old...to perform the mercy promised to our fathers, and to remember his holy covenant..."
Lk. 24:25-27, 32. And [Jesus] said to [the disciples on the road to Emmaus], "O foolish men, and slow of heart to believe all that the prophets have spoken! Was it not necessary that the Christ should suffer these things and enter into his glory?" And beginning with Moses and all the prophets, he interpreted to them in all the scriptures the things concerning himself. (Also Mt. 13:17, 1 Pet. 1:10-12.)
Mt. 13:17 [Christ]: Truly, I say to you, many prophets and righteous men longed to see what you see, and did not see it, and to hear what you hear, and did not hear it. (Also 1 Pet. 1:10-12.)

4. Bass Recit.
●Canticle of Zechariah: God's promises now fulfilled (167-4)
Des Weibes Samen kam,
The woman's seed came,

Nachdem die Zeit   erfüllet;
After   the time had-been-fulfilled;
{In the fullness of time;}

Der Segen, den Gott   Abraham,
The blessing, which God (to) Abraham,

Dem Glaubensheld, versprochen,
That   hero-of-faith, had-promised,

Ist wie der Glanz   der Sonne angebrochen,
Has like the radiance of-the sun   dawned,
{Has dawned like the radiance of the sun,}

Und unser Kummer ist   gestillet.
And   our   sorrow   is (now) stilled.

Ein stummer Zacharias preist
A   mute   Zacharias praises

Mit lauter Stimme Gott vor seine Wundertat,
With loud   voice God for his   miracle,
{God with a loud voice for the miracle,}

Die   er dem Volk   erzeiget hat.
Which he to-the people manifested has.
{Which he has manifested to the people.}

Bedenkt, ihr Christen, auch, was Gott an euch getan,
Consider, ye Christians, too,   what God for you has-done,
{Consider, ye Christians, too, what God has done for you,}

Und stimmet ihm ein   Loblied   an!
And strike-up to-him a   song-of-praise - !
{And strike up a song of praise to him!}

5. Chorale (See also 29-8, 51-4.)
●Prayer of praise and dedication to Trinity (167-5)
Sei Lob und Preis mit Ehren
- Laud and praise with honors (to)

Gott   Vater, Sohn,   Heiliger Geist!
God (the) Father, Son, (and) Holy   Ghost!

Gen. 3:14-15. ...God said to the serpent [in the garden of Eden], "Because you have [deceived Adam and Eve]...I will put enmity between you and the woman, and between your seed and her seed; he shall bruise your head, and you shall bruise his heel."
Gal. 4:4. When the time had fully come, God sent forth his Son, born of woman...
Gen. 12:1-2. Now the Lord [had] said to Abram, "Go from your country and your kindred...to the land that I will show you. And I will make of you a great nation, and I will bless you, and make your name great, so that you will be a blessing." (Also Gen. 18:18.)
Gal. 3:8-9, 14, 26, 29. The scripture, foreseeing that God would justify the Gentiles by faith, preached the gospel beforehand to Abraham, saying, "In you shall all the nations be blessed." So then, those who are men of faith are blessed with Abraham who had faith...that in Christ Jesus the blessing of Abraham might come upon the Gentiles... for in Christ Jesus you are all sons of God, through faith...And if you are Christ's, then you are Abraham's offspring, heirs according to promise.
*Lk. 1:68, 78-79 [Zechariah]: ...The Lord God of Israel...has visited and redeemed his people...when the day [dawns] upon us from on high to give light to those who sit in darkness...
Lk. 1:13, 15, 18-20, 22. The angel said to [Zechariah], "Do not be afraid, Zechariah...your wife Elizabeth will bear you a son, and you shall call his name John...He will be great before the Lord, and he shall drink no wine nor strong drink, and he will be filled with the Holy Spirit, even from his mother's womb." And Zechariah said to the angel, "How shall I know this? For I am an old man, and my wife is advanced in years." And the angel answered him, "I am Gabriel, who stand in the presence of God; and I was sent to speak to you, and to bring you this good news. And behold, you will be silent and unable to speak until the day that these things come to pass, because you did not believe my words, which will be bulfilled in their time."...And when he came out, he could not speak...
*Lk. 1:57-58, 62-64, 67-68, 72-73. Now the time came for Elizabeth to be delivered, and she gave birth to a son. And her neighbors and kinsfolk...rejoiced with her...And they made signs to his father, inquiring what he would have him called. And he asked for a writing tablet, and wrote, "His name is John."...And immediately his mouth was opened and his tongue loosed, and he spoke, blessing God...And... Zechariah was filled with the Holy Spirit, and prophesied, saying, "Blessed be the Lord God of Israel, for he has visited and redeemed his people...to perform the mercy promised to our fathers, and to remember his holy covenant, the oath wich he swore to our father Abraham."

Rev. 7:11-12. All the angels stood round the throne and round the elders and the four living creatures, and they fell on their faces before the throne and worshiped God, saying, "Amen! Blessing and glory and wisdom and thanksgiving and honor and power and might be to our God for ever and ever! Amen."
Jer. 31:7. ...Give praise, and say, "The Lord has saved his people..."

Der woll in uns vermehren,
(May) he - in us increase

Was er uns aus Genaden verheißt,
That-which he to-us out-of grace does-promise,

Daß wir ihm fest vertrauen,
So-that we him firmly (would) trust,
{So that we would firmly trust him,}

Gänzlich verlassn auf ihn,
Completely rely on him,

Von Herzen auf ihn bauen,
With (all our) heart upon him build,

Daß unsr Herz, Mut und Sinn
So-that our heart, mettle, and mind

Ihm festiglich anhangen;
To-him firmly would-adhere;

Darauf singn wir zur Stund:
Thereupon sing we at-this hour:

Amen, wir werdn's erlangen,
Amen, we will-it attain,

Gläubn wir aus Herzens Grund.
(If) believe we from heart's bottom.
{If we believe with all our heart.}

2 Thess. 1:11–12. To this end we always pray for you, that our God may make you worthy of his call, and may fulfil every good resolve and work of faith by his power, so that the name of our Lord Jesus may be glorified in you, and you in him, according to the grace of our God and the Lord Jesus Christ.

1 Thess. 3:12–13. ...May the Lord make you increase (Luther: vermehre)...so that he may establish your hearts unblamable in holiness before our God and Father...

Phil. 1:6, 9. I am sure that he who began a good work in you will bring it to completion at the day of Jesus Christ...And it is my prayer that your love may abound more and more, with knowledge and all discernment... (Also Ps. 138:8.)

1 Jn. 2:24–25. Let what you heard from the beginning abide in you. If what you heard from the beginning abides in you, then you will abide in the Son and in the Father. And this is what he has promised us, eternal life.

2 Thess. 2:16–17. Now may our Lord Jesus Christ himself, and God our Father, who loved us and gave us eternal comfort and good hope through grace, comfort your hearts and establish them in every good work and word.

Mt. 7:24 [Christ]: Every one then who hears these words of mine and does them will be like a wise man who built his house upon the rock...

1 Cor. 3:11. No other foundation can any one lay than that which is laid, which is Jesus Christ.

Mt. 22:37–38. [Jesus] said... "You shall love the Lord your God with all your heart (Luther: Herzen), and with all your soul (Luther: Seele), and with all your mind (Luther: Gemüte). This is the great and first commandment." (Also Deut. 6:5.)

Deut. 13:4. You shall walk after the Lord your God and fear him, and keep his commandments and obey his voice, and you shall serve him and cleave to him (Luther: ihm anhangen). (Also Deut. 10:20, 2 Kings 18:6.)

Ps. 63:8. [O Lord,] my soul clings to thee (Luther: hanget dir an)...

1 Thess. 5:23. May the God of peace himself sanctify you wholly; and may your spirit and soul and body be kept sound and blameless at the coming of our Lord Jesus Christ.

1 Cor. 9:24–27. Do you not know that in a race all the runners compete, but only one receives (Luther: erlangt) the prize? So run that you may obtain it.

Phil. 3:12, 14–15. Not that I have already obtained this or am already perfect; but I press on to make it my own...I press on toward the goal for the prize of the upward call of God in Christ Jesus. Let those of us who are mature be thus minded...

Heb. 10:39. We are not of those who shrink back and are destroyed, but of those who have faith and keep their souls.

BWV 168
Tue Rechnung! Donnerwort
(NBA I/19; BC A116)

9. S. after Trinity (BWV 105, 94, 168)
*1 Cor. 10:6–13 (Consider and avoid the sins of the Israelites in the wilderness)
*Lk. 16:1–9 (Parable of the dishonest steward)
Librettist: Salomon Franck

1. Bass Aria
●Stewardship: Frightening command to give account (168-1)
Tue Rechnung! Donnerwort,
"Give account!" (What a) thunderous-word,

Das die Felsen selbst zerspaltet,
Which the rocks themselves splits,
{Which splits the very rocks,}

Wort, wovon mein Blut erkaltet!
Word, at-which my blood chills!
{A word that chills my blood!}

Tue Rechnung! Seele, fort!
"Give account!" (O) soul, forth!

Ach, du mußt Gott wiedergeben
Ah, thou must to-God return

Seine Güter, Leib und Leben.
His goods, body, and life.
{Ah, thou must now return goods, body, and life to God.}

Tue Rechnung! Donnerwort!
"Give acount!" (What a) thunderous-word!

2. Tenor Recit.
●Stewardship: Unfaithfulness brings fear of judgment (168-2)
Es ist nur fremdes Gut,
It is but (an) other's goods,
{It is but borrowed wealth,}

Was ich in diesem Leben habe;
What I in this life have;
{Whatever I have in this life;}

Geist, Leben, Mut und Blut
Spirit, life, will, and blood,

Und Amt und Stand ist meines Gottes Gabe,
And office and station is my God's gift,

Es ist mir zum Verwalten
It is (given) to-me for administration
{It is given to me to administer}

Und treulich damit hauszuhalten
And faithfully - to-manage

*Lk. 16:1–9. [Jesus]...said to the disciples, "There was a rich man who had a steward, and charges were brought to him that this man was wasting his goods. And he called him and said to him, 'What is this that I hear about you? *Turn in the account* (Luther: tu Rechnung) of your stewardship, for you can no longer be steward.' And the steward said to himself, 'What shall I do, since my master is taking the stewardship away from me? I am not strong enough to dig, and I am ashamed to beg. I have decided what to do, so that people may receive me into their houses when I am put out of the stewardship.' So, summoning his master's debtors one by one, he said to the first, 'How much do you owe my master?' He said, 'A hundred measures of oil.' And he said to him, 'Take your bill and sit down quickly and write fifty.' Then he said to another, 'And how much do you owe?' He said, 'A hundred measures of wheat.' He said to him, 'Take your bill and write eighty.' The master commended the dishonest steward for his shrewdness; for the sons of this world are more shrewd in dealing with their own generation than the sons of light. And I tell you, make friends for yourselves by means of unrighteous mammon, so that when it fails they may receive you into the eternal habitations."

Rom. 14:10–12. ...We shall all stand before the judgment seat of God; for it is written, "As I live, says the Lord, every knee shall bow to me, and every tongue shall give praise to God." So each of us shall give account of himself to God.

2 Cor. 5:10. For we must all appear before the judgment seat of Christ, so that each one may receive good or evil, according to what he has done in the body. (Also 1 Cor. 3:12–13, Heb. 9:27.)

1 Cor. 4:7. ...What have you that you did not receive? If then you received it, why do you boast as if it were not a gift?

Jms. 1:17. Every good endowment and every perfect gift is from above, coming down from the Father of lights with whom there is no variation or shadow due to change.

1 Cor. 4:1–2. This is how one should regard us, as servants of Christ and stewards of the mysteries of God. Moreover it is required of stewards that they be found trustworthy.

1 Chron. 29:12, 14, 16. [King David prayed,] "Both riches and honor come from thee, [O Lord,] and thou rulest over all. In thy hand are power and might; and in thy hand it is to make great and to give strength to all...But who am I, and what is my people, that we should be able thus to offer willingly? For all things come from thee, and of thy own have we given thee...O Lord our God, all this abundance that we have provided for building thee a house for thy holy name comes from thy hand and is all thy own."

Jn. 3:27. ...No one can receive anything except what is given him from heaven.

***Lk. 16:1–2 [Christ]:** ...There was a rich man who had a steward, and charges were brought to him that this man was wasting his goods. And he called him and said to him, "What is this that I hear about you? Turn in the account (Luther: tu Rechnung) of your stewardship (Luther: Haushalten)..."

Von hohen Händen anvertraut.
By   lofty   hands   entrusted.

Ach! aber ach! mir graut,
Ah,   but alas! I shudder,

Wenn ich in mein Gewissen gehe
When I into my conscience go
{When I delve into my conscience}

Und meine Rechnungen so voll   Defekte sehe!
And my   accounts   so full-of deficiencies see!
{And see so many deficiencies in my accounts!}

Ich habe Tag und Nacht
I   have day and night
{Day and night I have}

Die Güter,   die   mir Gott verliehen,
The possessions, which to-me God has-lent,

Kaltsinning durchgebracht!
Indifferently   squandered!
{Indifferently squandered the posessions that God has lent me!}

Wie kann ich dir, gerechter Gott, entfliehen?
How can I thee, righteous God, escape?
{How can I escape thee, O righteous God?}

Ich rufe flehentlich:
I   call imploringly:

Ihr Berge fallt! ihr Hügel decket mich
Ye mountains fall! Ye hills cover   me

Vor Gottes Zorngerichte
From God's wrathful-judgment

Und vor dem Blitz von seinem Angesichte!
And from the lightning of   his   countenance!

3. Tenor Aria
●Stewardship: All my debts are engraved in God's book
(168-3)
Kapital und Interessen,
Principal and interest,

Meine Schulden groß und klein
My   debts   great and small,

Müssen einst verrechnet sein.
Must one-day reckoned be.
{Must one day be accounted for.}

Alles, was ich schuldig blieben,
All   that I indebted remain,
{All that I owe}

Mt. 25:14–15, 19–27 [Christ]: For [the time of reckoning] will be as when a man going on a journey called his servants and entrusted to them his property; to one he gave five talents, to another two, to another one, to each according to his ability. Then he went away...Now after a long time the master of those servants came and settled accounts with them. And he who had received the five talents came forward, bringing five talents more, saying, "Master, you delivered to me five talents; here I have made five talents more." His master said to him, "Well done, good and faithful servant; you have been faithful over a little, I will set you over much; enter into the joy of your master." And he also who had the two talents came forward, saying, "Master, you delivered to me two talents; here I have made two talents more." His master said to him, "Well done, good and faithful servant; you have been faithful over a little, I will set you over much; enter into the joy of your master." He also who had received the one talent came forward, saying, "Master, I knew you to be a hard man, reaping where you did not sow, and gathering where you did not winnow; so I was afraid, and I went and hid your talent in the ground. Here you have what is yours." But his master answered him, "You wicked and slothful servant! You knew that I reap where I have not sowed and gather where I have not winnowed? Then you ought to have invested my money with the bankers, and at my coming I should have received what was my own with interest."

Mal. 3:2. Who can endure the day of [the Lord's] coming, and who can stand when he appears?

Mt. 23:33 [Christ]: You serpents, you brood of vipers, how are you to escape being sentenced to hell?

Nah. 1:6. Who can stand before his indignation? Who can endure the heat of his anger? His wrath is poured out like fire, and the rocks are broken asunder by him.

Dan. 10:6. [In Daniel's vision a man appeared to him with a] face like the appearance of lightning...

Ps. 76:7. But thou, [O Lord], terrible art thou! Who can stand before thee when once thy anger is roused?

Ps. 139:7. [O Lord,] whither shall I go from thy Spirit? Or whither shall I flee from thy presence? (Also Jer. 23:24.)

Lk. 23:28–30 [Christ]: ...Weep for yourselves and for your children. For behold, the days are coming when they will say, "Blessed are the barren, and the wombs that never bore, and the breasts that never gave suck!" Then they will begin to say to the mountains, "Fall on us"; and to the hills, "Cover us." (Also Rev. 6:15–17.)

Mt. 18:23–25 [Christ]: The kingdom of heaven may be compared to a king who wished to settle accounts with his servants. When he began the reckoning, one was brought to him who owed him ten thousand talents; and as he could not pay, his lord ordered him to be sold, with his wife and children and all that he had, and payment to be made.

Rev. 20:11–13, 15. Then [in my vision] I saw a great white throne and him who sat upon it; from his presence earth and sky fled away, and no place was found for them. And I saw the dead, great and small, standing before the throne, and books were opened. Also another book was opened, which is the book of life. And the dead were judged by what was written in the books, by what they had done. And the sea gave up the dead in it, Death and Hades gave up the dead in them, and all were judged by what they had done...and if any one's name was

Ist in Gottes Buch geschrieben
Is in God's book   written
{Is written in God's book}

Als mit Stahl und Demantstein.
As with steel and   diamond.

4. Bass Recit.
●Judgment not feared if Christ is guarantor of debts (168–4)
Jedoch,   erschrocknes Herz, leb und verzage nicht!
But-yet, (O) frightened   heart, live, and despair not!

Tritt freudig vor   Gericht!
Step joyfully before (the) court-of-judgment!

Und überführt dich dein Gewissen,
And convicts thee thy conscience,
{And if thy conscience convicts thee that}

Du werdest hier verstummen müssen,
Thou wilt here have-to-become-silent,
{Thou wilt have to become silent there,}

So schau den Bürgen an,
Then behold thy guarantor - ,

Der alle Schulden   abgetan!
Who all debts   hath-laid-aside!
{Who hath laid all thy debts aside!}

Es ist bezahlt und völlig abgeführt,
It is paid-up and fully discharged,

Was du, o Mensch, in   Rechnung schuldig blieben;
What thou, O man, in (the) account indebted remained;
{What thou, O man, still didst owe;}

Des Lammes Blut, o   großes Lieben!
The Lamb's blood—O (what) great love!—

Hat deine Schuld durchstrichen
Hath thy debt   cancelled

Und dich mit Gott verglichen!
And thee with God reconciled!

Es ist bezahlt, du bist quittiert!
It is paid, thou art acquitted!

Indessen,
Meanwhile,

Weil   du weißt,
Because thou knowest,

Daß du   Haushalter seist,
That thou (a) steward art,

not found written in the book of life, he was thrown into the lake of fire. (Also Dan. 7:9–10.)
2 Cor. 5:10. We must all appear before the judgment seat of Christ, so that each one may receive good or evil, according to what he has done in the body.
Rom. 2:6. For [God] will render to every man according to his works. (Also Jer. 17:10.)

Mt. 18:23–27 [Christ]: Therefore the kingdom of heaven may be compared to a king who wished to settle accounts with his servants. When he began the reckoning, one was brought to him who owed him ten thousand talents; and as he could not pay, his lord ordered him to be sold, with his wife and children and all that he had, and payment to be made. So the servant fell on his knees, imploring him, "Lord, have patience with me, and I will pay you everything." And out of pity for him the lord of that servant released him and forgave him the debt (Luther: Schuld).
Col. 2:13–15. You, who were dead in trespasses and the uncircumcision of your flesh, God made alive together with him, having forgiven us all our trespasses, having canceled the bond which stood against us with its legal demands; this he set aside, nailing it to the cross. He disarmed the principalities and powers and made a public example of them, triumphing over them in him.
Heb. 10:19–22. Therefore, brethren, since we have confidence to enter the sanctuary by the blood of Jesus, by the new and living way which he opened for us through the curtain, that is, through his flesh, and since we have a great priest over the house of God, let us draw near with a true heart in full assurance of faith, with our hearts sprinkled clean from an evil conscience and our bodies washed with pure water.
1 Pet. 1:18–19. You know that you were ransomed from the futile ways inherited from your fathers, not with perishable things such as silver or gold, but with the precious blood of Christ, like that of a lamb without blemish or spot.
Rev. 5:6, 9. [In my vision]...I saw a Lamb standing, as though it had been slain...and they sang a new song, saying, "Worthy art thou...for thou wast slain and by thy blood didst ransom men for God from every tribe and tongue and people and nation."
2 Cor. 5:21. For our sake [God] made him to be sin who knew no sin, so that in him we might become the righteousness of God.
Rom. 5:8–10. God shows his love for us in that while we were yet sinners Christ died for us. Since, therefore, we are now justified by his blood, much more shall we be saved by him from the wrath of God. For if while we were enemies we were reconciled to God by the death of his Son, much more, now that we are reconciled, shall we be saved by his life.
1 Cor. 6:19–20. ...You are not your own; you were bought with a price...
1 Cor. 4:1–2. This is how one should regard us, as servants of Christ and stewards...Moreover it is required of stewards that they be found trustworthy. (Also 1 Pet. 4:10.)
***Lk. 16:3–9 [Christ]:** [A] steward said to himself, 'What shall I do, since my master is taking the stewardship away from me? I am not strong enough to dig, and I am ashamed to beg. I have decided what to do, so that people may receive me into their houses when I am put out of the stewardship.' So, summoning his master's debtors one by one, he said to the first, 'How much do you owe my master?' He said,

So   sei bemüht und unvergessen,
Therefore be concerned and never-negligent,

Den Mammon klüglich anzuwenden,
This mammon prudently to-employ,

Den Armen wohlzutun,
The poor   to-do-good,
{By helping the poor with it,}

So wirst du, wenn sich Zeit und Leben enden,
Thus wilt thou, when - time and life do-end,

In Himmelshütten sicher ruhn.
In heaven's-tents securely rest.

5. Soprano & Alto Duet
●Stewardship: Wealth used to ensure heavenly treasure
(168–5)
    Herz, zerreiß des Mammons Kette,
(O) heart, tear   - Mammon's chain,

    Hände, streuet Gutes aus!
(O) hands, scatter good (abroad)!

Machet sanft mein Sterbebette,
Make   soft   my   death-bed,
{And in doing so, make my deathbed soft,}

Bauet mir ein festes Haus,
Build me a   solid house,

Das im Himmel ewig bleibet,
Which in heaven eternally remains,

Wenn der Erden Gut zerstäubet.
When   - earthly wealth turns-to-dust.

6. Chorale (See also 113–8.)
●Prayer: Strengthen, heal, wash me; take me home (168–6)
Stärk   mich mit deinem Freudengeist,
Strengthen me with thy   spirit-of-joy,

Heil mich mit deinen Wunden,
Heal me with thy   wounds,

Wasch mich mit deinem Todesschweiß
Wash me with thy   sweat-of-death

In meiner letzten Stunden;
In my   last   hours;

'A hundred measures of oil.' And he said to him, 'Take your bill and sit down quickly and write fifty.' Then he said to another, 'And how much do you owe?' He said, 'A hundred measures of wheat.' He said to him, 'Take your bill and write eighty.' The master commended the dishonest steward for his shrewdness; for the sons of this world are more shrewd in dealing with their own generation than the sons of light. And I tell you, make friends for yourselves by means of unrighteous mammon, so that when it fails they may receive you into the eternal habitations (Luther: ewigen Hütten).
Prov. 19:17. He who is kind to the poor lends to the Lord, and he will repay him for his deed.
Mt. 19:21. Jesus said to [a rich young man], "If you would be perfect, go, sell what you possess and give to the poor, and you will have treasure in heaven; and come, follow me." (Also Mk. 10:21, Lk. 18:22.)

*Lk. 16:9 [Christ]: I tell you, make friends for yourselves by means of unrighteous mammon, so that when it fails they may receive you into the eternal habitations.
Mt. 6:24 [Christ]: No one can serve two masters; for either he will hate the one and love the other, or he will be devoted to the one and despise the other. You cannot serve God and mammon. (Also Lk. 16:13.)
Mt. 19:21–23. Jesus said to [the rich young man], "If you would be perfect, go, sell what you possess and give to the poor, and you will have treasure in heaven; and come, follow me." When the young man heard this he went away sorrowful; for he had great possessons. And Jesus said to his disciples, "Truly, I say to you, it will be hard for a rich man to enter the kingdom of heaven." (Also Mk. 10:23, Lk. 18:24, 1 Tim. 6:9–10.)
Ps. 112:5, 9. It is well with the man who deals generously and lends... He has distributed freely (Luther: er streut aus), he has given to the poor...
Mt. 6:19–20 [Christ]: Do not lay up for yourselves treasures on earth, where moth and rust consume and where thieves break in and steal, but lay up for yourselves treasures in heaven, where neither moth nor rust consumes and where thieves do not break in and steal.

Rom. 15:13. May the God of hope fill you with all joy and peace in believing, so that by the power of the Holy Spirit you may abound in hope.
Col. 1:11. May you be strengthened with all power, according to [God's] glorious might, for all endurance and patience with joy.
1 Pet. 2:24. [Christ] himself bore our sins in his body on the tree, that we might die to sin and live to righteousness. By his wounds you have been healed.
Is. 53:5. He was wounded for our transgressions, he was bruised for our iniquities; upon him was the chastisement that made us whole, and with his stripes we are healed.
Lk. 22:44. Being in an agony [in the garden of Gethsemane before his arrest, Jesus] prayed more earnestly; and his sweat became like great drops of blood falling down upon the ground.
Ps. 51:2, 7. [O Lord,] wash me thoroughly from my iniquity, and cleanse me from my sin!...Wash me and I shall be whiter than snow. (Also Tit. 3:5, Rev. 7:14.)
Num. 23:10. ...Let me die the death of the righteous, and let my end be like his! (Also Heb. 13:7.)

Und nimm mich einst,   wenn   dir's gefällt,
And   take   me   one-day, whenever it-thee pleases,
{And take me one day, whenever it pleases thee,}

In wahrem Glauben von der Welt
In   true   faith   from the world

Zu deinen Auserwählten!
To   thy   chosen-ones!

BWV 169
Gott soll allein mein Herze haben
(NBA I/24; BC A143)

18. S. after Trinity (BWV 96, 169)
*1 Cor. 1:4–9 (Paul's prayer of thanks for the blessings of the Gospel in Corinth)
*Mt. 22:34–46 (Jesus identifies the greatest commandments and asks the Pharisees whose Son Christ is)
Librettist: Unknown

1. Sinfonia (Adapted from nonextant instrumental work)

2. Alto Arioso & Recit.
●Loving God alone despite the world's wooing (169-2)
Gott soll allein mein Herze haben.
God shall alone   my   heart   have.
{God alone shall have my heart.}

Zwar   merk ich an der Welt,
Indeed observe I of the world,
{I indeed observe of the world—}

Die ihren Kot   unschätzbar hält,
Which its dirt (as) priceless   holds,

Weil sie so freundlich mit   mir tut,
Because it so   friendly (towards) me acts—
{Which, in acting so friendly towards me, shows that it considers its dirt to be priceless—}

     Sie wollte gern   allein
(That) it would dearly (all) alone

Das Liebste meiner Seele sein;
The beloved of-my soul be;
{That it would dearly have my soul's undivided loyalty;}

Doch nein: Gott soll allein mein Herze haben,
Yet no: God shall alone my   heart have,
{Yet no: God alone shall have my heart,}

Ich find in ihm das höchste Gut.
I   find in him the highest worth.

---

2 Tim. 4:6–8. The time of my departure has come. I have fought the good fight, I have finished the race, I have kept the faith. Henceforth there is laid up for me the crown of righteousness, which the Lord, the righteous judge, will award to me on that Day, and not only to me but also to all who have loved his appearing.
Ps. 31:5. Into thy hand I commit my spirit; thou hast redeemed me, O Lord, faithful God. (Also Lk. 23:46.)
Rom. 5:2. ...We rejoice in our hope of sharing the glory of God.
1 Thess. 4:17. ...So we shall always be with the Lord.
Rev. 17:14. ...He is Lord of lords and King of kings, and those with him are called and chosen and faithful. (Also 1 Pet. 2:9.)

*Mt. 22:35–40. ...A lawyer, asked [Jesus] a question, to test him. "Teacher, which is the great commandment in the law?" And he said to him, "You shall love the Lord your God with all your heart, and with all your soul, and with all your mind. This is the great and first commandment. And a second is like it, You shall love your neighbor as yourself. On these two commandments depend all the law and the prophets." (Also Mk. 12:30–31, Lk. 10:27, Deut. 6:5, Lev. 19:18.)
Mt. 4:10. Jesus said to [Satan], "Begone, Satan! for it is written, 'You shall worship the Lord your God and him only shall you serve.'" (Also Lk. 4:8, Deut. 6:13–14.)
1 Jn. 2:15–17. Do not love the world or the things in the world. If any one loves the world, love for the Father is not in him. For all that is in the world, the lust of the flesh and the lust of the eyes and the pride of life, is not of the Father but is of the world. And the world passes away, and the lust of it; but he who does the will of God abides for ever.
Jms. 4:1–4. What causes wars, and what causes fightings among you? Is it not your passions that are at war in your members? You desire and do not have; so you kill. And you covet and cannot obtain; so you fight and wage war. You do not have, because you do not ask. You ask and do not receive, because you ask wrongly, to spend it on your passions. Unfaithful creatures! Do you not know that friendship with the world is enmity with God? Therefore whoever wishes to be a friend of the world makes himself an enemy of God.
Jms. 1:27. Religion that is pure and undefiled before God and the Father is this: ...to keep oneself unstained from the world.
Jn. 15:18–19 [Christ]: If the world hates you, know that it has hated me before it hated you. If you were of the world, the world would love its own; but because you are not of the world, but I chose you out of the world, therefore the world hates you. (Also Mt. 5:10–12, 10:24–25, 1 Jn. 3:13.)
Prov. 26:23–25. Like the glaze covering an earthen vessel are smooth lips with an evil heart. He who hates, dissembles with his lips and harbors deceit in his heart; when he speaks graciously, believe him not, for there are seven abominations in his heart. (Also Ps. 28:3, 62:4.)
Jer. 17:9. The heart is deceitful above all things, and desperately corrupt...
Mt. 10:16 [Christ]: Behold, I send you out as sheep in the midst of wolves; so be wise as serpents and innocent as doves.
Heb. 11:24–26. By faith Moses...[chose] rather to share ill-treatment with the people of God than to enjoy the fleeting pleasures of sin. He

Wir sehen zwar
We see, indeed,

Auf Erden hier und dar
On earth here and there

Ein Bächlein der Zufriedenheit,
A rivulet of contentment,

Das von des Höchsten Güte quillet:
Which from the Most-High's goodness wells-up:
{Which wells up from the Most High's goodness:}

Gott aber ist der Quell, mit Strömen angefüllet,
God, however, is the fount, with streams replete,

Da schöpf ich, was mich allezeit
There draw I, what me for-all-time

Kann sattsam und wahrhaftig laben.
Can sufficiently and truly refresh.
{There I can draw that which will sufficiently and truly refresh me
for all time.}

Gott soll allein mein Herze haben.
God shall alone my heart have.
{God alone shall have my heart.}

3. Alto Aria
●Loving God alone; he is the highest worth (169-3)
Gott soll allein mein Herze haben,
God shall alone my heart have,
{God alone shall have my heart,}

Ich find in ihm das höchste Gut.
I find in him the highest (worth).

Er liebt mich in der bösen Zeit
He loves me in - hard times

Und will mich in der Seligkeit
And shall me in - (paradise)

Mit Gütern seines Hauses laben.
With (the) goods of-his house delight.
{And shall delight me in paradise with the provisions of his
house.}

considered abuse suffered for the Christ greater wealth than the
treasures of Egypt...

Mk. 10:29-30. Jesus said, "Truly, I say to you, there is no one who has
left house or brothers or sisters of mother or father or children or
lands, for my sake and for the gospel, who will not receive a
hundredfold now in this time, houses and brothers and sisters and
mothers and children and lands, with persecutions, and in the age to
come eternal life." (Also Mt. 19:29, Lk. 18:29-30.)

Jms. 1:17. Every good endowment and every perfect gift is from
above, coming down from the Father of lights with whom there is no
variation or shadow due to change. (Also Mt. 7:11.)

Ps. 36:7-9. How precious is thy steadfast love, O God! The children
of men take refuge in the shadow of thy wings. They feast on the
abundance of thy house, and thou givest them drink from the river of
thy delights. For with thee is the fountain of life (Luther: lebendige
Quelle); in thy light do we see light.

Jn. 1:4. In [Christ] was life, and the life was the light of men.

Jn. 7:37-39. On the last day of the feast [of Tabernacles], the great
day, Jesus stood up and proclaimed, "If any one thirst, let him come
to me and drink. He who believes in me, as the scripture has said,
'Out of his heart shall flow rivers of living water.'" Now this he said
about the Spirit, which those who believed in him were to receive...
(Also Is. 44:3, Joel 2:28, Acts 2:18.)

Rev. 21:6 [God]: ...To the thirsty I will give from the fountain of the
water of life without payment.

Is. 12:3. With joy you will draw water from the wells of salvation.

*Mt. 22:37 [Christ]: ...You shall love the Lord your God with all your
heart, and with all your soul, and with all your mind.

Ps. 16:5. The Lord is my chosen portion and my cup (Luther: Gut und
Teil)... (Also Ps. 119:57, 142:5, Lam. 3:24.)

Ps. 73:25. [O Lord,] whom have I in heaven but thee? And there is
nothing upon earth that I desire besides thee.

Rom. 8:35-37. Who shall separate us from the love of Christ? Shall
tribulation, or distress, or persecution, or famine, or nakedness, or
peril, or sword?...As it is written, "For thy sake we are being killed all
the day long; we are regarded as sheep to be slaughtered." No, in all
these things we are more than conquerors through him who loved us.

2 Cor. 4:17. This slight momentary affliction is preparing for us an
eternal weight of glory beyond all comparison. (Also Rom. 8:18.)

Mt. 5:12 [Christ]: ...Your reward is great in heaven...

Jn. 14:1-3 [Christ]: Let not your hearts be troubled; believe in God,
believe also in me. In my Father's house are many rooms; if it were
not so, would I have told you that I go to prepare a place for you?
And when I go and prepare a place for you, I will come again and will
take you to myself, that where I am you may be also.

Ps. 16:11. [O Lord,] thou dost show me the path of life; in thy
presence there is fulness of joy, in thy right hand are pleasures for
evermore.

4. Alto Recit.
●Love of God fully satisfies & opens heaven to us (169-4)
Was ist die Liebe Gottes?
What is the love of-God?

Des Geistes Ruh,
The spirit's rest,

Der Sinnen Lustgenieß,
The senses' satisfaction,

Der Seele Paradies.
The soul's paradise.

Sie schließt die Hölle zu,
It shuts the (gates of) hell -,

Den Himmel aber auf;
- Heaven, however, (it) opens;
   [zuschließen = to close; aufschließen = to open]

Sie ist Elias Wagen,
It is Elijah's chariot,

Da werden wir im Himmel nauf
There are we into heaven up
{In which we are carried up to heaven}

In Abrahms Schoß getragen.
Into Abraham's bosom carried.
{Into Abraham's bosom.}

Ps. 34:8. O taste and see that the Lord is good!...
Ps. 145:19. [The Lord] fulfils the desire of all who fear him...
Eph. 3:19. ...The love of Christ...surpasses knowledge...
Ps. 73:25. [O Lord]...there is nothing upon earth that I desire besides thee. (Also Ps. 37:4.)
Mt. 11:28–29 [Christ]: Come to me...and I will give you rest...You will find rest for your souls. (Also Jer. 6:16.)
Rom. 5:2. Through [Christ] we have obtained access to this grace in which we stand, and we rejoice in our hope of sharing the glory of God.
Rev. 1:17–18 [Christ]: ...Fear not, I am the first and the last, and the living one; I died, and behold I am alive for evermore, and I have the keys of Death and Hades (Luther: Hölle).
Rom. 5:8–9. God shows his love for us in that while we were yet sinners Christ died for us. Since, therefore, we are now justified by his blood, much more shall we be saved by him from the wrath of God. (Also Tit. 3:4–7.)
Jn. 14:1, 3 [Christ]: Let not your hearts be troubled; believe in God, believe also in me...When I go and prepare a place for you, I will come again and will take you to myself, that where I am you may be also. (Also Jn. 12:26.)
2 Kings 2:11. As [Elijah and Elisha] still went on and talked, behold, a chariot of fire and horses of fire separated the two of them. And Elijah went up by a whirlwind into heaven.
1 Thess. 4:17. ...So we shall always be with the Lord.
Lk. 16:19–23, 25. There was a rich man, who was clothed in purple and fine linen and who feasted sumptuously every day. And at his gate lay a poor man named Lazarus, full of sores, who desired to be fed with what fell from the rich man's table; moreover the dogs came and licked his sores. The poor man died and was carried by the angels to Abraham's bosom (Luther: Schoß). The rich man also died and was buried; and in Hades, being in torment, he lifted up his eyes and saw Abraham far off and Lazarus in his bosom...But Abraham said, "Son, remember that you in your lifetime received your good things, and Lazarus in like manner evil things; but now he is comforted here, and you are in anguish." (Also Heb. 4:9.)

5. Alto Aria (Adapted from nonextant instrumental work)
●Love of God practised; love of world put to death (169-5)
Stirb in mir,
Die within me,

   Welt und alle deine Liebe,
(O) world and all thy love,
{O world—and all my love of thee,}

Daß die Brust
That (my) breast

Sich auf Erden für und für
- On earth forever and ever

In der Liebe Gottes übe;
- The love of-God (might) practise;

Jms. 4:4. Unfaithful creatures! Do you not know that friendship with the world is enmity with God? Therefore whoever wishes to be a friend of the world makes himself an enemy of God.
Gal. 6:14. Far be it from me to glory except in the cross of our Lord Jesus Christ, by which the world has been crucified to me, and I to the world.
Gal. 5:16–17. ...Walk by the Spirit, and do not gratify the desires of the flesh. For the desires of the flesh are against the Spirit, and the desires of the Spirit are against the flesh; for these are opposed to each other, to prevent you from doing what you would.
Rom. 8:12–13. So then, brethren, we are debtors, not to the flesh, to live according to the flesh—for if you live according to the flesh you will die, but if by the Spirit you put to death the deeds of the body you will live.
Mic. 6:8. [The Lord] has showed you, O man, what is good; and what does the Lord require of you but to do justice, and to love kindness (Luther: Liebe üben), and to walk humbly with your God?

Stirb in mir,
Die within me,

Hoffart, Reichtum, Augenlust,
(O) pride, wealth, lust-of-the-eyes,

Ihr verworfnen Fleischestriebe.
Ye reprobate impulses-of-the-flesh.

6. Alto Recit.
•Loving one's neighbor required of those who love God
(169-6)
Doch meint es auch dabei
Yet means this also therewith
{But this means also}

Mit eurem Nächsten treu;
(To) your neighbor (be) true;

Denn so steht in der Schrift geschrieben:
For thus (it) stands in - Scripture written:
{For thus it is written in Scripture:}

Du sollst Gott und den Nächsten lieben.
Thou shalt God and thy neighbor love.
{Thou shalt love God and thy neighbor.}

7. Chorale (See also 197-5.)
•Loving one's neighbor: Prayer for divine help (169-7)
Du süße Liebe, schenk uns deine Gunst,
(O) thou sweet Love, grant us thy favor,

Laß uns empfinden der Liebe Brunst,
Let us experience - love's ardor,

Daß wir uns von Herzen einander lieben
That we - from (our) hearts one-another might-love
{That we might love one another from the bottom of our hearts}

Und in Friede auf einem Sinn bleiben.
And in peace, of one mind continue.
{And continue of one mind in peace.}

Kyrie eleison.
Kyrie eleison.

1 Jn. 2:15-17. Do not love the world or the things in the world. If any one loves the world, love for the Father is not in him. For all that is in the world, the lust of the flesh and the lust of the eyes (Luther: Augen Lust) and the pride of life (Luther: hoffärtiges Leben), is not of the Father but is of the world. And the world passes away, and the lust of it; but he who does the will of God abides for ever.

1 Jn. 4:7-8, 11-12, 19-21. Beloved, let us love one another; for love is of God, and he who loves is born of God and knows God. He who does not love does not know God; for God is love...Beloved, if God so loved us, we also ought to love one another. No man has ever seen God; if we love one another, God abides in us and his love is perfected in us...We love, because he first loved us. If any one says, "I love God," and hates his brother, he is a liar; for he who does not love his brother whom he has seen, cannot love God whom he has not seen. And this commandment we have from him, that he who loves God should love his brother also.
*Mt. 22:37-39 [Christ]: ...You shall love the Lord your God with all your heart, and with all your soul, and with all your mind. This is the great and first commandment. And a second is like it, You shall love your neighbor as yourself. (Also Deut. 6:5, Lev. 19:18.)

Rom. 5:5. ...God's love has been poured into our hearts through the Holy Spirit which has been given to us.
1 Jn. 4:16. So we know and believe the love God has for us. God is love, and he who abides in love abides in God, and God abides in him.
1 Pet. 1:22. Having purified your souls by your obedience to the truth for a sincere love of the brethren, love one another earnestly from the heart. (Also 1 Pet. 3:8.)
Phil. 2:1-2. So if there is any encouragement in Christ, any incentive of love, any participation in the Spirit, any affection and sympathy, complete my joy by being of the same mind (Luther: eines Sinnes), having the same love, being in full accord and of one mind. (Also Phil. 1:27, Jn. 17:21, 23, Rom. 12:16.)
Eph. 4:1-3. I...beg you to lead a life worthy of the calling to which you have been called, with all lowliness and meekness, with patience, forbearing one another in love, eager to maintain the unity of the Spirit in the bond of peace.
2 Jn. 1:3. Grace, mercy, and peace will be with us, from God the Father and from Jesus Christ the Father's Son, in truth and love.

BWV 170
Vergnügte Ruh, beliebte Seelenlust
(NBA I/17; BC A106)

6. S. after Trinity (BWV 170, 9)
*Rom. 6:3–11 (Through Christ's death believers die to sin)
*Mt. 5:20–26 (From Sermon on the Mount: True righteousness is characterized by love of one's neighbor)
Librettist: Georg Christian Lehms

1. Alto Aria
●Contentment of soul found only in concord & virtue (170-1)
  Vergnügte Ruh, beliebte Seelenlust,
(O) happy   rest, beloved joy-of-soul,
{O happy rest, sought after joy of soul,}

Dich kann man nicht bei Höllensünden,
Thee can one   not amidst hell's-sins,
{One can not find thee amidst hell's sins}

Wohl aber   Himmelseintracht finden;
But-rather (in) heaven's-concord   find;
{But rather in heaven's concord;}

Du   stärkst   allein die schwache Brust.
Thou dost-strengthen alone the   weak   breast.
{Thou alone dost strengthen the weak breast.}

Drum   sollen lauter   Tugendgaben
Therefore shall nought-but virtue's-endowments

In meinem Herzen   Wohnung haben.
In   my   heart (its) dwelling (find).

2. Alto Recit.
●Hatred manifested by a world alienated from God (170-2)
Die Welt, das Sündenhaus,
The world—that house-of-sin—

Bricht nur in   Höllenlieder aus
Breaks only with songs-of-hell forth
{Breaks forth only with songs of hell}

Und sucht durch   Haß und Neid
And seeks through hatred and envy

Des Satans Bild an sich zu tragen.
 - Satan's image - - to bear.

Ihr Mund ist voller   Ottergift,
Its mouth is filled-with (the) poison-of-vipers,

Der   oft die Unschuld tödlich trifft,
Which often - innocence fatally strikes,
{Which often fatally strikes the innocent,}

*Mt. 5:21–24 [Christ]: You have heard that it was said to the men of old, "You shall not kill; and whoever kills shall be liable to judgment." But I say to you that every one who is angry with his brother shall be liable to judgment; whoever insults his brother shall be liable to the council, and whoever says, "You fool!" shall be liable to the hell of fire. So if you are offering your gift at the altar, and there remember that your brother has something against you, leave your gift there before the altar and go; first be reconciled to your brother, and then come and offer your gift.
Ps. 133:1. Behold, how good and pleasant it is when brothers dwell in unity!
Prov. 14:30. A tranquil mind gives life to the flesh, but passion (Luther: Neid) makes the bones rot.
Mt. 11:29 [Christ]: Take my yoke upon you, and learn from me; for I am gentle and lowly in heart, and you will find rest for your souls.
Gal. 5:19–23. Now the works of the flesh are plain:...enmity, strife, jealousy, anger, selfishness, dissension, party spirit, envy...I warn you, as I warned you before, that those who do such things shall not inherit the kingdom of God. But the fruit of the Spirit is love, joy, peace, patience, kindness, goodness, faithfulness, gentleness, self-control; against such there is no law.
Eph. 4:31–32. Let all bitterness and wrath and anger and clamor and slander be put away from you, with all malice, and be kind to one another, tenderhearted, forgiving one another, as God in Christ forgave you. (Also Col. 3:8, 1 Cor. 1:10, 1 Pet. 2:1.)

Jms. 4:1–4. What causes wars, and what causes fightings among you? Is it not your passions that are at war in your members? You desire and do not have; so you kill. And you covet and cannot obtain; so you fight and wage war. You do not have, because you do not ask. You ask and do not receive, because you ask wrongly, to spend it on your passions. Unfaithful creatures! Do you not know that friendship with the world is enmity with God? Therefore whoever wishes to be a friend of the world makes himself an enemy of God. (Also 1 Jn. 2:15–17.)
Jn. 8:44 [Christ]: You are of your father the devil, and your will is to do your father's desires. He was a murderer from the beginning...
Rom. 3:10–18. As it is written: "None is righteous, no, not one; no one understands, no one seeks for God. All have turned aside, together they have gone wrong; no one does good, not even one. Their throat is an open grave, they use their tongues to deceive. The venom of asps (Luther: Otterngift) is under their lips. Their mouth is full of curses and bitterness. Their feet are swift to shed blood, in their paths are ruin and misery, and the way of peace they do not know. There is no fear of God before their eyes." (Also Ps. 5:9, 10:7, 14:1–3, 140:3, Jer. 17:9, Jms. 3:8–10.)
*Mt. 5:22 [Christ]: I say to you that every one who is angry with his brother shall be liable to judgment; whoever insults his brother

Und will allein von Racha! sagen.
And would only of "Raca!" speak.

Gerechter Gott, wie weit
Righteous God, how far
{Righteous God, how greatly}

Ist doch der Mensch von dir entfernet;
Is indeed - man from thee distanced;
{Man is alienated from thee;}

Du liebst, jedoch sein Mund
Thou lovest, yet his mouth

Macht Fluch und Feindschaft kund
Proclaims curse(s) and enmity (abroad)

Und will den Nächsten nur mit Füßen treten.
And would (his) neighbor just (under his) feet trample.
{And would just trample his neighbor underfoot.}

Ach! diese Schuld ist schwerlich zu verbeten.
Ah! This offence (can) scarcely (be) prayed-away.
{Ah, this sin is forgiven with difficulty!}

3. Alto Aria
●Pity the hearts who scoff at law against hatred! (170-3)
Wie jammern mich doch die verkehrten Herzen,
How pity (I) indeed the perverted hearts,
{How I indeed pity the perverted hearts,}

Die dir, mein Gott, so sehr zuwider sein;
Who to-thee, my God, so greatly offensive are;
{Who are so greatly offensive to thee, O my God;}

Ich zittre recht und fühle tausend Schmerzen,
I tremble quite and feel (a) thousand torments,
{I quite tremble and feel a thousand torments,}

Wenn sie sich nur an Rach und Haß erfreun.
When they - only in vengeance and hatred rejoice.
{When they find joy in nought but vengeance and hatred.}

Gerechter Gott, was magst du doch gedenken,
Righteous God, what must thou then think,

(Luther: zu seinem Bruder sagt: Racha!) shall be liable to the council, and whoever says, "You fool!" shall be liable to the hell of fire.

1 Jn. 4:8, 20–21. He who does not love does not know God; for God is love...If any one says, "I love God," and hates his brother, he is a liar; for he who does not love his brother whom he has seen, cannot love God whom he has not seen. And this commandment we have from him, that he who loves God should love his brother also.

Eph. 4:32. Be kind to one another, tenderhearted, forgiving one another, as God in Christ forgave you.

Mt. 18:23–35 [Christ]: The kingdom of heaven may be compared to a king who wished to settle accounts with his servants. When he began the reckoning, one was brought to him who owed him ten thousand talents; and as he could not pay, his lord ordered him to be sold, with his wife and children and all that he had, and payment to be made. So the servant fell on his knees, imploring him, "Lord, have patience with me, and I will pay you everything." And out of pity for him the lord of that servant released him and forgave him the debt. But that same servant, as he went out, came upon one of his fellow servants who owed him a hundred denarii, and seizing him by the throat he said, "Pay what you owe." So his fellow servant fell down and besought him, "Have patience with me, and I will pay you." He refused and went and put him in prison till he should pay the debt. When his fellow servants saw what had taken place, they were greatly distressed, and they went and reported to their lord all that had taken place. Then his lord summoned him and said to him, "You wicked servant! I forgave you all that debt because you besought me; and should not you have had mercy on your fellow servant, as I had mercy on you?" And in anger his lord delivered him to the jailers, till he should pay all his debt. So also my heavenly Father will do to every one of you, if you do not forgive your brother from your heart.

Prov. 11:20–21. Men of perverse mind (Luther: verkehrten Herzen) are an abomination to the Lord, but those of blameless ways are his delight. Be assured, an evil man will not go unpunished, but those who are righteous will be delivered.

Deut. 32:5. They have dealt corruptly with [God], they are no longer his children because of their blemish; they are a perverse and crooked generation. (verkehrt: also Acts 2:40,

Rom. 1:28, Phil. 2:15)

Gal. 5:16–21. ...Walk by the Spirit, and do not gratify the desires of the flesh. For the desires of the flesh are against the Spirit, and the desires of the Spirit are against the flesh; for these are opposed to each other, to prevent you from doing what you would. But if you are led by the Spirit you are not under the law. Now the works of the flesh are plain: fornication, impurity, licentiousness, idolatry, sorcery, enmity, strife, jealousy, anger (Luther: Zorn), selfishness, (Luther: Zank) dissension (Luther: Zwietracht), party spirit, envy, drunkenness, carousing, and the like. I warn you, as I warned you before, that those who do such things shall not inherit the kingdom of God.

Joel 2:1–2. Blow the trumpet in Zion; sound the alarm on my holy mountain! Let all the inhabitants of the land tremble, for the day of the Lord is coming, it is near, a day of darkness and gloom, a day of clouds and thick darkness!... (Also Joel 1:15, Zeph. 1:7, 2 Pet. 3:10–12.)

Wenn sie allein mit rechten Satansränken
When they but with real satanic-intrigues
{When they, by their satanic intrigues,}

Dein scharfes Strafgebot so frech verlacht.
Thy stern precept-of-judgment so insolently deride.
{Only deride thy stern warning of judgment so insolently.}

Ach! ohne Zweifel hast du so gedacht:
Ah! Without doubt hast thou thus thought:
{Ah, without doubt thou hast thought thus:}

Wie jammern mich doch die verkehrten Herzen!
How pity (I) indeed these perverted hearts!
{"How I indeed pity these perverted hearts!"}

4. Alto Recit.
●Yearning to leave hate-filled world for heaven (170-4)
Wer sollte sich demnach
Who would - accordingly
{Accordingly, who would}

Wohl hier zu leben wünschen,
Indeed here to live wish,
{Wish to live here}

Wenn man nur Haß und Ungemach
When one only hatred and hardship
{When one receives only hatred and hardship}

Vor seine Liebe sieht?
For his love sees?
{In return for one's love?}

Doch, weil ich auch den Feind
Yet, because I also (my) enemy

Wie meinen besten Freund
As my best friend,

Nach Gottes Vorschrift lieben soll,
According-to God's instruction, shall-love,
{Yet, because God instructs me also to love my enemy as my best friend,}

So flieht
Thus flees

*Mt. 5:22 [Christ]: ...Every one who is angry with his brother shall be liable to judgment; whoever insults his brother shall be liable to the council, and whoever says, "You fool!" shall be liable to the hell of fire.

Heb. 12:25. See that you do not refuse him who is speaking. For if they did not escape when they refused him who warned them on earth [at Mt. Sinai], much less shall we escape if we reject him who warns from heaven.

Heb. 3:7-9. Therefore, as the Holy Spirit says, "Today, when you hear his voice, do not harden your hearts as in the rebellion, on the day of testing in the wilderness, where your fathers put me to the test and saw my works for forty years.

2 Chron. 36:16. [God's people] kept mocking the messengers of God, despising his words, and scoffing at his prophets, till the wrath of the Lord rose against his people, till there was no remedy.

Mt. 23:37-38 [Christ]: O Jerusalem, Jerusalem, killing the prophets and stoning those who are sent to you! How often would I have gathered your children together as a hen gathers her brood under her wings, and you would not! Behold, your house is forsaken and desolate.

Ezek. 18:23. Have I any pleasure in the death of the wicked, says the Lord God, and not rather that he would turn from his way and live? (Also Ezek. 18:32.)

Acts 2:40. [Peter] testified with many other words and exhorted [the people], saying, "Save yourselves from this crooked generation." (Luther: unartigen Leuten; later version has: verkehrten Geschlecht).

Phil. 1:21-23. To me to live is Christ, and to die is gain...Which I shall choose I cannot tell. I am hard pressed between the two. My desire is to depart and be with Christ, for that is far better. (Also 2 Cor. 5:8.)

2 Cor. 5:8. ...We would rather be away from the body and at home with the Lord.

Acts 14:22. ...Through many tribulations (Luther: Trübsal) we must enter the kingdom of God.

2 Tim. 3:12. All who desire to live a godly life in Christ Jesus will be persecuted. (See also 1 Pet. 4:12-13, Jn. 15:20.)

Mt. 5:43-48 [Christ]: You have heard that it was said, "You shall love your neighbor and hate your enemy." But I say to you, Love your enemies...so that you may be sons of your Father who is in heaven; for he makes his sun rise on the evil and on the good, and sends rain on the just and on the unjust. For if you love those who love you, what reward have you? Do not even the tax collectors do the same? And if you salute only your brethren, what more are you doing than others? Do not even the Gentiles do the same? You, therefore, must be perfect, as your heavenly Father is perfect. (Also Lk. 6:32-36.)

Mt. 22:37, 39 [Christ]: You shall love the Lord your God with all your heart, and...you shall love your neighbor as yourself. (Also Mk. 12:30-31, Lk. 10:27, Deut. 6:5, Lev. 19:18.)

1 Jn. 4:7-8, 12, 16, 19-21. Beloved, let us love one another; for love is of God, and he who loves is born of God and knows God. He who does not love does not know God; for God is love...If we love one another, God abides in us and his love is perfected in us...God is love, and he who abides in love abides in God, and God abides in him...We love, because he first loved us. If any one says, "I love God," and hates

Mein Herze   Zorn und Groll
My   heart (from all) wrath and animosity

Und wünscht allein bei Gott zu leben,
And desires only with God to live,
{And desires only to live with God,}

Der selbst die Liebe heißt.
Who himself - love is-called.
{Who is called love itself.}

Ach, eintrachtvoller Geist,
Ah,   peaceable   spirit,

Wenn wird er dir   doch nur sein Himmelszion geben?
When will he to-thee indeed just his heavenly-Zion grant?
{When will he indeed finally grant his heavenly Zion to thee?}

his brother, he is a liar; for he who does not love his brother whom he has seen, cannot love God whom he has not seen. And this commandment we have from him, that he who loves God should love his brother also.
Heb. 12:14. Strive for peace with all men, and for the holiness without which no one will see the Lord.
*Mt. 5:22 [Christ]: ...Every one who is angry with his brother shall be liable to judgment; whoever insults his brother shall be liable to the council, and whoever says, "You fool!" shall be liable to the hell of fire.
Gal. 5:21. I warn you, as I warned you before, that those who do such things shall not inherit the kingdom of God.
Rev. 21:1, 3–4. [In my vision] I saw a new heaven and a new earth; for the first heaven and the first earth had passed away...and I heard a loud voice from the throne saying, "Behold, the dwelling of God is with men. He will dwell with them, and they shall be his people, and God himself will be with them; he will wipe away every tear from their eyes, and death shall be no more, neither shall there be mourning nor crying nor pain any more, for the former things have passed away." (Also Is. 25:8. Rev. 7:15–17.)

5. Alto Aria
●Loathing to live here; yearning for tranquil heaven (170-5)
Mir ekelt mehr zu leben,
(I) loath longer to live,
{I loath the thought of living longer,}

Drum   nimm mich, Jesu, hin!
Therefore take me, Jesus, hence!

Mir   graut   vor allen Sünden,
(I) have-aversion to all   sins,

Laß mich dies Wohnhaus finden,
Let me this dwelling-house find,
{Let me find this dwelling place}

Woselbst ich ruhig   bin.
Where   I at-rest (may be).
{Where I may be at rest.}

1 Jn. 2:15. Do not love the world or the things in the world. If any one loves the world, love for the Father is not in him. (Also Jms. 4:4.)
*Rom. 6:11. So you...must consider yourselves dead to sin and alive to God in Christ Jesus.
Col. 3:1–3. If then you have been raised with Christ, seek the things that are above, where Christ is, seated at the right hand of God. Set your minds on things that are above, not on things that are on earth. For you have died and your life is hid with Christ in God.
Phil. 1:23. ...My desire is to depart and be with Christ, for that is far better.
Ps. 139:19–24. O that...men of blood would depart from me, men who maliciously defy thee, who lift themselves up against thee for evil! Do I not hate them that hate thee, O Lord? And do I not loathe them that rise up against thee? I hate them with perfect hatred; I count them my enemies. Search me, O God, and know my heart! Try me and know my thoughts! And see if there be any wicked way in me, and lead me in the way everlasting!
Lk. 2:29. Lord, now lettest thou thy servant depart in peace, according to thy word.
Heb. 4:9. So then, there remains a sabbath rest for the people of God.

BWV 171
Gott, wie dein Name, so ist auch dein Ruhm
(NBA I/4; BC A24)

New Year/Circumcision and Name of Jesus
(BWV 143, 190, 41, 16, 171, 248-IV)
*Gal. 3:23–29 (Through faith we are heirs of the promise)
*Luke 2:21 (Circumcision and naming of Jesus)
Librettist: Picander (Christian Friedrich Henrici)

1. Chorus (Taken from earlier, nonextant work)
●God's name & praise reach ends of earth: Ps. 48:10 (171-1)
   Gott, wie dein Name,
(O) God, as   thy   name,

so ist auch dein Ruhm bis an der Welt Ende.
so is   also thy renown   to   the earth's ends.
{So thy renown reaches to the ends of the earth.}

2. Tenor Aria
●God's name is exalted by all creation (171-2)
Herr, so weit die Wolken gehen,
Lord, as far-as the clouds   go,

Gehet deines Namens Ruhm.
Goes   thy   name's renown.
{Lord, thy name's renown reaches to the clouds.}

Alles, was die Lippen rührt,
All   that (its) lips   stirs,
{All that stirs the lip,}

Alles, was noch Odem führt,
All   that still breath draws,
{All that draws breath,}

Wird dich in der Macht erhöhen.
Shall thee in (thy) might   exalt.
{Shall exalt thee in thy might.}

3. Alto Recit.
●Jesus' name means everything to me in the new year (171-3)
Du süßer Jesus-Name du,
Thou sweet name-of-Jesus, thou,

In dir ist meine Ruh,
In thee is   my   repose,

Du bist mein Trost auf Erden,
Thou art my comfort on earth;

Wie kann denn mir
How can then (I)
{How can I then}

Mic. 5:2, 4. ... From you [Bethlehem Ephrathah] shall come forth...one who is to be ruler in Israel, whose origin is from of old, from ancient days...He shall be great to the ends of the earth.
Ps. 48:10. *As thy name, O God, so thy praise reaches to the ends of the earth...* (Also Ps. 22:27, 67:7, 98:3.)
Ps. 148:13. Let [all peoples] praise the name of the Lord, for his name alone is exalted; his glory is above earth and heaven.
Ps. 8:1. O Lord, our Lord, how majestic is thy name in all the earth!
Ps. 30:4. Sing praises to the Lord, O you his saints, and give thanks to his holy name.
Mt. 1:21. [The angels said to Joseph,] "...You shall call [the child's] name Jesus, for he will save his people from their sins."
*Lk. 2:21. And at the end of eight days, when he was circumcised, he was called Jesus, the name given by the angel before he was conceived in the womb.

Ps. 108:3–5. [O Lord]...I will sing praises to thee among the nations. For thy steadfast love is great above the heavens, thy faithfulness reaches to the clouds. Be exalted, O God, above the heavens! Let thy glory be over all the earth! (Also Ps. 36:5, 57:10–11.)
Ps. 145:10, 21. All thy works shall give thanks to thee, O Lord, and all thy saints shall bless thee!...My mouth will speak the praise of the Lord, and let all flesh bless his holy name for ever and ever.
Ps. 148:1, 7, 10–11. Praise the Lord! Praise the Lord from the heavens, praise him in the heights!...Praise the Lord from the earth... Beasts and all cattle, creeping things and flying birds! Kings of the earth and all peoples...
Ps. 150:6. Let everything that breathes praise the Lord! Praise the Lord!
Ps. 34:1. I will bless the Lord at all times; his praise shall continually be in my mouth. (Also Ps. 40:3, 51:15, 63:3, 71:8, 109:30.)
Heb. 13:15. ...Let us continually offer up a sacrifice of praise to God, that is, the fruit of lips that acknowledge his name. (Also Ps. 50:14, 23.)

Mt. 1:21. [The angels said to Joseph,] "...You shall call [the child's] name Jesus, for he will save his people from their sins."
*Lk. 2:21. ...When [the child] was circumcised, he was called Jesus, the name given by the angel before he was conceived...
Jn. 1:12. To all who received [Christ], who believed in his name, he gave power to become children of God.
Eph. 1:3. ...The God and Father of our Lord Jesus Christ...has blessed us in Christ with every spiritual blessing...
Mt. 11:28–29 [Christ]: Come to me...and you will find rest for your souls.
2 Cor. 1:5. ...Through Christ we share abundantly in comfort... (Also 2 Thess. 2:16–17.)
Rom. 8:35–39. Who shall separate us from the love of Christ? Shall tribulation, or distress, or persecution, or famine, or nakedness, or peril, or sword?...No, in all these things we are more than conquerors through him who loved us. For I am sure that neither death, nor life,

Im   Kreuze bange werden?
Amidst-the cross anxious become?
{Become anxious when faced with my cross?}

Du bist mein festes Schloß und mein Panier,
Thou art my   secure castle and my banner,

Da   lauf ich hin,
There run I   - ,
{To which I run}

Wenn ich verfolget bin.
When I persecuted am.
{When I am persecuted.}

Du bist mein Leben und mein Licht,
Thou art my   life   and my light,

Mein Ehre, meine Zuversicht,
My   honor, my confidence,

Mein Beistand in Gefahr
My   helper in danger

Und mein Geschenk zum neuen Jahr.
And my   gift   for-the new year.

4. Soprano Aria (Parody of BWV 205-9)
●Jesus' name is my first and last word (171-4)
Jesus soll mein erstes Wort
Jesus shall my   first word
{"Jesus" shall be the first word on my lips}

In dem neuen Jahre heißen.
In the new year   (be).
{In the new year.}

Fort und fort
On and on

Lacht sein Nam in meinem Munde,
Laughs his name in my   mouth,
{His name laughs in my mouth,}

Und in meiner letzten Stunde
And in my   last   hour

Ist Jesus auch mein letztes Wort.
Is Jesus also   my   last   word.
{My last word shall also be "Jesus."}

5. Bass Recit.
●Prayer in Jesus' name: Bless us all this year! (171-5)
Und da du, Herr, gesagt:
And since thou, Lord, hast-said:

nor angels, nor principalities, nor things present, nor things to come, nor powers, nor height, nor depth, nor anything else in all creation, will be able to separate us from the love of God in Christ Jesus our Lord.

Ps. 18:2. The Lord is my rock, and my fortress, and my deliverer, my God, my rock, in whom I take refuge, my shield, and the horn of my salvation, my stronghold.

Ps. 7:1. O Lord my God, in thee do I take refuge; save me from all my pursuers, and deliver me.

Ps. 27:1, 3. The Lord is my light and my salvation; whom shall I fear? The Lord is the stronghold of my life (Luther: Lebens Kraft); of whom shall I be afraid?...Though a host encamp against me, my heart shall not fear; though war arise against me, yet I will be confident. (Also Ps. 118:6.)

Ps. 20:5-7. ...In the name of our God [we will] set up our banners (Luther: Panier)!...I know that the Lord will help his anointed; he will answer him from his holy heaven with mighty victories by his right hand. Some boast of chariots, and some of horses; but we boast of the name of the Lord our God. (Also Is. 11:10, 12.)

Ps. 62:7. On God rests my deliverance and my honor... (Luther: Bei Gott ist mein Heil, meine Ehre...)

Ps. 46:1. God is our refuge (Luther: Zuversicht) and strength... (Also Ps. 61:3, 62:7, 71:5, 7, 91:2, 142:5.)

Ps. 54:4. Behold, God is my helper (Luther: Gott steht mir bei); the Lord is the upholder of my life.

Ps. 73:25-26. [O Lord,] whom have I in heaven but thee? And there is nothing upon earth that I desire besides thee. God is...my portion (Luther: Teil) for ever. (Also Ps. 16:5, 142:5.)

1 Chron. 29:13. ...We thank thee, our God, and praise thy glorious name.

*Lk. 2:21. ...He was called Jesus...

Ps. 145:1-2. I will extol thee, my God and King, and bless thy name for ever and ever. Every day I will bless thee, and praise thy name for ever and ever. (Also Ps. 7:17, 9:2, 66:2, 69:30, 99:3, 100:4, 113:1, 135:1, 148:13, Is. 25:1.)

Rom. 10:8-11, 13. What does [the righteousness based on faith] say? The word is near you, on your lips (Luther: Munde) and in your heart (that is, the word of faith which we preach); because if you confess with your lips that Jesus is Lord and believe in your heart that God raised him from the dead, you will be saved. For man believes with his heart and so is justified, and he confesses with his lips and so is saved ...For, "every one who calls upon the name of the Lord will be saved." (Also Deut. 30:14.)

Heb. 13:15. Through [Jesus] then, let us continually offer up a sacrifice of praise to God, that is, the fruit of lips that acknowledge his name.

Rev. 22:13. [Christ is] the Alpha and the Omega, the first and the last, the beginning and the end. (Also Rev. 1:8, 21:6.)

Jn. 14:13-14 [Christ]: Whatever you ask in my name, I will do it, that the Father may be glorified in the Son; if you ask anything in my name, I will do it.

Bittet nur in meinem Namen,
Ask just in my name,
{"Just ask in my name,"}

So ist alles Ja! und Amen!
So is everything "Yes" and "Amen!"
{Thus everything will be "Yes" and "Amen!"}

So flehen wir,
So implore we,
{So we implore thee,}

Du Heiland aller Welt, zu dir:
Thou Savior of-all-the world, (of) thee:
{O Savior of all the world:}

Verstoß uns ferner nicht,
Reject us furthermore not,
{Continue not to reject us in the future,}

Behüt uns dieses Jahr
Protect us this year

Für Feuer, Pest und Kriegsgefahr!
From fire, plague, and risk-of-war!

Laß uns dein Wort, das helle Licht,
Let for-us thy Word, that bright light,
{Let thy Word, that bright light,}

Noch rein und lauter brennen;
Still pure and clear burn;
{Continue to burn pure and clear;}

Gib unsrer Obrigkeit
Show our authorities

Und dem gesamten Lande
And the entire land

Dein Heil des Segens zu erkennen;
Thy prosperity of blessing - - ;
[zu erkennen geben = to show]

Gib allezeit
Grant evermore

Glück und Heil zu allem Stande.
Happiness and prosperity to every station.

Wir bitten, Herr, in deinem Namen,
We ask, Lord, in thy name,

Sprich: ja! darzu, sprich: Amen, amen!
Say "Yes!" to-this, say: "Amen, amen!"

Jn. 15:15–16 [Christ]: No longer do I call you servants, for the servant does not know what his master is doing; but I have called you friends, for all that I have heard from my Father I have made known to you. You did not choose me, but I chose you and appointed you that you should go and bear fruit and that your fruit should abide; so that whatever you ask the Father in my name, he may give it to you.

2 Cor. 1:18–20. As surely as God is faithful, our word to you has not been Yes and No. For the Son of God, Jesus Christ...was not Yes and No; but in him it is always Yes. For all the promises of God find their Yes in him. That is why we utter the Amen through him, to the glory of God.

Rom. 8:32. He who did not spare his own Son but gave him up for us all, will he not also give us all things with him?

1 Jn. 4:14. We...testify that the Father has sent his Son as the Savior of the world.

Ps. 94:14. The Lord will not forsake his people (Luther: sein Volk nicht verstoßen)... (Also Ps. 27:9, 31:22.)

Ps. 119:169–170. Let my cry come before thee, O Lord...Let my supplication (Luther: Flehen) come before thee...

2 Chron. 20:9. [O Lord,] if evil comes upon us, the sword, judgment, or pestilence, or famine, we will...cry to thee in our affliction, and thou wilt hear and save.

2 Pet. 1:19. We have the prophetic word made more sure...as a lamp shining in a dark place...

Ps. 119:105. [O Lord,] thy word is a lamp to my feet and a light to my path.

2 Cor. 4:3–4. ...If our gospel is veiled, it is veiled only to those who are perishing. In their case the god of this world has blinded the minds of the unbelievers, to keep them from seeing the light of the gospel of the glory of Christ...

1 Tim. 2:1–2. ...I urge that supplications, prayers, intercessions, and thanksgivings be made for all men, for kings and all who are in high positions (Luther: Oberkeit), that we may lead a quiet and peaceable life...

Deut. 26:15. [O God,] look down from thy holy habitation, from heaven, and bless thy people Israel and the ground which thou hast given us, as thou didst swear to our fathers...

Ps. 28:8–9. The Lord is the strength of his people...O save thy people, and bless thy heritage; be thou their shepherd, and carry them for ever.

Ps. 144:12–15. May our sons in their youth be like plants full grown, our daughters like corner pillars cut for the structure of a palace; may our garners be full, providing all manner of store; may our sheep bring forth thousands and ten thousands in our fields; may our cattle be heavy with young, suffering no mischance or failure in bearing; may there be no cry of distress in our streets! Happy the people to whom such blessings fall! Happy the people whose God is the Lord!

Ps. 29:11. May the Lord give strength to his people! May the Lord bless his people with peace! (Also Ps. 122:6–7, 128:5–6, 147:14, Is. 26:1–3.)

Ps. 3:8. Deliverance belongs to the Lord; thy blessing be upon thy people!

Jn. 16:23–24 [Christ]: ...Truly, truly, I say to you, if you ask anything of the Father, he will give it to you in my name. Hitherto you have asked nothing in my name; ask, and you will receive, that your joy may be full.

6. Chorale (Music taken from BWV 41-6) (See also 190-7.)
●Prayer: Bless us this new year for thy name's sake (171-6)
Laß uns das Jahr vollbringen
Let us this year complete
{Let us complete this year}

Zu Lob dem Namen dein,
To (the) praise of-the name of-thine,
{To the praise of thy name,}

Daß wir demselben singen
That we (to) the-same (may) sing
{That we to thy name may sing}

In der Christen Gemein.
Within the Christian communion.

Wollst uns das Leben fristen
Mayest-thou for-us (our) life prolong

Durch dein allmächtig Hand,
By thine almighty hand,

Erhalt dein liebe Christen
Preserve (these) thy dear Christians

Und unser Vaterland!
And our fatherland!

Dein Segen zu uns wende,
Thy blessing upon us turn,

Gib Fried an allem Ende,
Grant peace in all quarters,

Gib unverfälscht im Lande
Grant unadulterated in-this land

Dein seligmachend Wort,
Thy beatific Word,

Ps. 31:3. [O Lord]...for thy name's sake lead me and guide me.
Ps. 79:9. Help us, O God of our salvation, for the glory of thy name... (Also 1 Sam. 12:22.)
Ps. 115:1. Not to us, O Lord, not to us, but to thy name give glory, for the sake of thy steadfast love and thy faithfulness!
Ps. 28:9. ...[O Lord,] bless thy heritage; be thou their shepherd, and carry them for ever.
Ps. 35:18. Then I will thank thee in the great congregation; in the mighty throng I will praise thee.
Ps. 22:22, 25. [O God,] I will tell of thy name to my brethren; in the midst of the congregation I will praise thee...From thee comes my praise in the great congregation; my vows I will pay before those who fear him. (Also Ps. 40:9-10, Ps. 107:32, 149:1, Heb. 2:12.)
Ps. 91:15-16 [God]: When [my child] calls to me, I will answer him; I will be with him in trouble, I will rescue him and honor him. With long life I will satisfy him... (Also 1 Pet. 3:10-12.)
Ps. 31:14-15. I trust in thee, O Lord...My times are in thy hand...
Jms. 4:13-15. Come now, you who say, "Today or tomorrow we will go into such and such a town and spend a year there and trade and get gain"; whereas you do not know about tomorrow. What is your life? For you are a mist that appears for a little time and then vanishes. Instead you ought to say, "If the Lord wills, we shall live and we shall do this or that."
Deut. 26:15. [O Lord,] look down from thy holy habitation, from heaven, and bless thy people Israel...
Ps. 89:13. Thou hast a mighty arm; strong is thy hand, high thy right hand.
Ps. 29:11. May the Lord give strength to his people! May the Lord bless his people with peace!
Ps. 122:6-7. Pray for the peace of Jerusalem! "May they prosper who love you! Peace be within your walls, and security within your towers!"
Ps. 147:12-14. Praise the Lord, O Jerusalem! Praise your God, O Zion! For he strengthens the bars of your gates; he blesses your sons within you. He makes peace in your borders...
Is. 2:3. Many peoples shall come, and say: "Come, let us go up to the mountain of the Lord, to the house of the God of Jacob; that he may teach us his ways and that we may walk in his paths." For out of Zion shall go forth the law, and the word of the Lord from Jerusalem. (Also Mic. 4:2.)
Jer. 23:28 [God]: ...Let him who has my word speak my word faithfully. (Also Tit. 1:9.)
Acts 20:32. I commend you...to the word of [God's] grace, which is able to build you up and to give you the inheritance among all those who are sanctified.
1 Tim. 4:1-2. Now the Spirit expressly says that in later times some will depart from the faith by giving heed to deceitful spirits and doctrines of demons, through the pretensions of liars... (Also 2 Pet. 2:1-3.)
Eph. 6:11-12. Put on the whole armor of God, that you may be able to stand against the wiles of the devil. For we are not contending against flesh and blood, but against the principalities, against the powers, against the world rulers of this present darkness, against the spiritual hosts of wickedness in the heavenly places. (Also 2 Cor. 10:3-4, Phil. 1:28-30.)

Die Teufel mach zuschanden
The devils confound
{Confound all devils}

Hier und an allem Ort!
Here and in every place!

BWV 172
Erschallet, ihr Lieder, erklinget, ihr Saiten
(NBA I/13; BC A81a-c)

Pentecost (BWV 172, 59, 74, 34)
*Acts 2:1–13 (Outpouring of the Holy Spirit)
*Jn. 14:23–31 (Jesus' farewell: He promises to send the Holy Spirit)
Librettist: probably Salomon Franck

1. Chorus
●Resound ye songs! God prepares souls as his temples (172-1)
Erschallet, ihr Lieder, erklinget, ihr Saiten!
Resound, ye songs; ring-out, ye strings!

O seligste Zeiten!
O most-blest (of) times!

Gott will sich die Seelen zu Tempeln bereiten.
God would for-himself (our) souls as temples prepare.
{God has chosen our souls as temples for himself.}

2. Bass Recit.
●Vox Christi: Promise of divine indwelling: Jn. 14:23 (172-2)
Wer mich liebet, der wird mein Wort halten,
Whoever me loves, he will my Word keep,
{He who loves me will keep my Word,}

und mein Vater wird ihn lieben, und wir
and my Father will him love, and we

werden zu ihm kommen und Wohnung
will to him come and (our) dwelling

bei ihm machen.
with him make.

3. Bass Aria
●Prayer for divine indwelling (172-3)
Heiligste Dreieinigkeit,
Most-holy Trinity,

1 Pet. 5:8. Be sober, be watchful. Your adversary the devil prowls around like a roaring lion, seeking some one to devour.
1 Jn. 3:8. ...The reason the Son of God appeared was to destroy the works of the devil. (Also Heb. 2:14.)
Ps. 31:17. Let me not be put to shame (Luther: zu Schanden werden) O Lord, for I call on thee; let the wicked be put to shame, let them go dumbfounded to Sheol (Luther: zu Schanden und geschweigt werden in der Hölle).

Ps. 66:8. Bless our God, O peoples, let the sound of his praise be heard (Luther: seinen Ruhm weit erschallen).
Ps. 47:1. Clap your hands, all peoples! Shout to God with loud songs of joy! (Also Ps. 107:22, Is. 12:6.)
Ps. 33:1–3. Rejoice in the Lord, O you righteous! Praise befits the upright. Praise the Lord with the lyre, make melody to him with the harp of ten strings! Sing to him a new song, play skilfully on the strings (Luther: Saitenspiel), with loud shouts. (Also Ps. 57:8–9, 81:2–3, 149:2–3.)
Zech. 2:10–11. Sing and rejoice, O daughter of Zion; for lo, I come and I will dwell in the midst of you, says the Lord. And many nations shall join themselves to the Lord in that day, and shall be my people; and I will dwell in the midst of you, and you shall know that the Lord of hosts has sent me to you. (Also Zech 8:3, 8:8, Ezek. 43:9.)
Rev. 21:3. ...Behold, the dwelling of God is with men. He will dwell with them, and they shall be his people, and God himself will be with them.
Jn. 14:16–17 [Christ]: I will pray the Father, and he will give you [a] Counselor (Luther: Tröster), to be with you for ever, even the Spirit of truth, whom the world cannot receive, because it neither sees him nor knows him; you know him, for he dwells with you, and will be in you.
1 Cor. 6:19. Do you not know that your body is a temple of the Holy Spirit within you, which you have from God?...

Jn. 14:23, 26. Jesus [said]..."If a man loves me, he will keep my word, and my Father will love him, and we will come to him and make our home with him...The Counselor (Luther: Tröster), the Holy Spirit, whom the Father will send in my name, he will teach you all things, and bring to your remembrance all that I have said to you." (Also Jn. 14:21, 16:7.)
*Acts 2:1–4. When the day of Pentecost had come, [the disciples] were all together in one place. And suddenly a sound came from heaven like the rush of a mighty wind, and it filled all the house where they were sitting. And there appeared to them tongues as of fire, distributed and resting on each one of them. And they were all filled with the Holy Spirit and began to speak in other tongues, as the Spirit gave them utterance.

Eph. 5:18. ...Be filled with the Spirit...
Jn. 14:23. Jesus [said]... "If a man loves me...we will come to him and make our home with him." (See also Jn. 14:21.)

Großer Gott der Ehren,
Great God of glory,

Komm doch, in der Gnadenzeit
Come, please, in this time-of-grace
{Please come, in this time of grace,}

Bei uns einzukehren,
With us   to-lodge,
{And lodge with us,}

Komm doch in   die Herzenshütten,
Come, please into (our) hearts'-tents,
{Please come into the tents of our hearts;}

Sind sie gleich gering und klein,
Are they indeed modest and small,
{Though they be modest and insignificant,}

Komm und laß dich   doch   erbitten,
Come   and let thyself indeed be-entreated,
{Come and let thyself be moved by our entreaty;}

Komm und kehre bei uns ein!
Come   and lodge with us   - !

4. Tenor Aria
●Soul, prepare thyself for the Spirit's entrance (172-4)
O Seelenparadies,
O soul's-paradise,

Das   Gottes Geist durchwehet,
Through-which God's Spirit   wafteth—

Der   bei der Schöpfung blies,
Who (also) at   -   creation was-blowing—

Der Geist, der nie vergehet;
The Spirit, who never passes-away;

        Auf,   auf,   bereite dich,
(O soul,) rise-up, rise-up (and) prepare thyself;

Der Tröster   nahet sich.
The Comforter draweth-near.

5. Soprano & Alto Duet
●Dialogue: Love duet between Soul & Holy Spirit (172-5)
Soprano:
Komm, laß mich nicht länger warten,
Come, let me not   longer wait,
{Come, let me wait no longer,}

Komm, du sanfter Himmelswind,
Come, thou gentle   heavenly-wind,

Wehe durch den Herzensgarten!
Waft through this heart's-garden!

Ezek. 11:17, 19. ...Thus says the Lord God: ...I will...put a new spirit within them... (Also Jer. 24:7, 31:31-33, Heb. 8:7-11.)
Ezek. 43:9 [God]: ...I will dwell in their midst for ever.
Ezek. 37:27 [God]: My dwelling place shall be with them; and I will be their God, and they shall be my people.
Ps. 24:7. Lift up your heads, O gates! and be lifted up, O ancient doors! that the King of glory (Luther: König der Ehren) may come in.
Eph. 3:17, 19. ...Christ [will] dwell in your hearts through faith...that you may be filled with all the fulness of God.
2 Cor. 6:16. ...As God said, "I will live in them and move among them, and I will be their God, and they shall be my people."
Is. 57:15. For thus says the high and lofty One who inhabits eternity, whose name is Holy: "I dwell in the high and holy place, and also with him who is of a contrite and humble spirit, to revive the spirit of the humble, and to revive the heart of the contrite."
Mt. 8:8. The centurion [who came to Jesus] answered him, "Lord, I am not worthy to have you come under my roof..." (Also Lk. 7:6.)
Lk. 19:5-7. When Jesus came to the place [where Zacchaeus was], he looked up and said to him, "Zacchaeus, make haste and come down; for I must stay at your house today." So he made haste and came down and received him joyfully. And when they saw it they all murmured, "He has gone in to be the guest of a man who is a sinner."

Gen. 2:8-9. The Lord God planted a garden in Eden, in the east; and there he put the man whom he had formed. And out of the ground the Lord God made to grow every tree that is pleasant to the sight and good for food, the tree of life also in the midst of the garden, and the tree of the knowledge of good and evil.
S. of S. 4:12, 16 [Bridegroom]: A garden locked is my sister, my bride ...Awake, O north wind, and come, O south wind! Blow upon my garden, let its fragrance be wafted abroad.
Gen. 1:1-2. In the beginning...the Spirit of God was moving on the face of the waters.
Jn. 3:8 [Christ]: The wind blows where it wills, and you hear the sound of it, but you do not know whence it comes or whither it goes; so it is with every one who is born of the Spirit.
Jn. 14:16-17 [Christ]: I will pray the Father, and he will give you another Counselor (Luther: Tröster), to be with you for ever, even the Spirit of truth, whom the world cannot receive, because it neither sees him nor knows him; you know him, for he dwells with you, and will be in you.
*Jn. 14:31 [Therefore]...rise, let us go...

S. of S. 4:12-5:1 [Bridegroom]: A garden locked is my sister, my bride, a garden locked, a fountain sealed. Your shoots are an orchard of pomegranates with all choicest fruits, henna with nard, nard and saffron, calamus and cinnamon, with all trees of frankincense, myrrh and aloes, with all chief spices—a garden fountain, a well of living water, and flowing streams from Lebanon. [Bride]: Awake, O north wind, and come, O south wind! Blow upon my garden, let its fragrance be wafted abroad. Let my beloved come to his garden, and eat its choicest fruits. [Bridegroom]: I come to my garden, my sister, my bride, I gather my myrrh with my spice, I eat my honeycomb with my

Alto:
Ich   erquicke dich, mein Kind.
I-will   revive   thee,   my   child.

Soprano:
Liebste Liebe, die   so süße,
Dearest love,   which (is) so sweet,

Aller Wollust   Überfluß,
Of-all delight (the) overflowing-abundance,
{The overflowing abundance of all delight;}

Ich vergeh, wenn ich dich misse.
I   perish,   if   I   thee am-without.
{I shall perish, if I do not have thee.}

Alto:
Nimm von mir den Gnadenkuß.
Accept from me the kiss-of-grace.

Soprano:
Sei im Glauben mir willkommen,
Be through faith in-me made-welcome,
{By faith I bid thee welcome,}

Höchste Liebe, komm herein!
Highest   love,   come   in!

Du   hast mir das Herz genommen.
Thou hast (my) - heart captured.
{Thou hast captured my heart.}

Alto:
Ich bin dein, und du bist mein!
I   am thine, and thou art mine!

6. Chorale
●Mystic union with Christ (172-6)
Von Gott kömmt mir ein Freudenschein,
From God comes to-me a   light-of-joy,
{A light of joy comes to me from God,}

Wenn du   mit deinen Äugelein
When thou with   thy   sweet-eyes

Mich freundlich tust anblicken.
Me with-kindness dost regard.
{When thou dost regard me kindly with thy sweet eyes.}

O Herr Jesu, mein trautes   Gut,
O Lord Jesus,   my   darling possession,

honey, I drink my wine with my milk. Eat, O friends, and drink: drink deeply, O lovers!
*Jn. 14:23 [Christ]: ...If a man loves me...my Father will love him, and we will come to him...
Jn. 14:17 [Christ]: The Spirit...dwells with you, and will be in you.
Jn. 20:22 [Christ]: ...Receive the Holy Spirit.
Mt. 11:28 [Christ]: ...Come to me...and I will give you rest (Luther: euch erquicken).
Jer. 31:3 [God]: ...I have loved you with an everlasting love...
Ps. 94:19. [O Lord,] when the cares of my heart are many, thy consolations cheer my soul.
Ps. 16:11. Thou dost show me the path of life; in thy presence there is fulness of joy, in thy right hand are pleasures for evermore.
Ps. 73:25. [O Lord,] whom have I in heaven but thee? And there is nothing upon earth that I desire besides thee.
S. of S. 4:10-11 [Bridegroom]: How sweet is your love, my sister, my bride! How much better is your love than wine, and the fragrance of your oils than any spice! Your lips distil nectar, my bride; honey and milk are under your tongue; the scent of your garments is like the scent of Lebanon.
S. of S. 1:2, 8:1 [Bride]: O that you would kiss me with the kisses of your mouth! For your love is better than wine...O that you were like a brother to me...I would kiss you, and none would despise me.
S. of S. 4:9 [Bridegroom]: You have ravished my heart (Luther: du hast mir das Herz genommen), my sister, my bride, you have ravished my heart with a glance of your eyes, with one jewel of your necklace.
S. of S. 6:2-3 [Bride]: My beloved has gone down to his garden, to the bed of spices, to pasture his flock in the gardens, and to gather lilies. I am my beloved's and my beloved is mine; he pastures his flock among the lilies. (Also S. of S. 2:16.)

*Jn. 14:23. Jesus [said]... "If a man loves me...my Father will love him, and we will come to him..."
Is. 60:1. Arise...for your light has come...
2 Cor. 4:6. It is...God...who has shone in our hearts... (Also Is. 60:1.)
Ps. 4:6. ...Lift up the light of thy countenance upon us, O Lord! (Also Ps. 89:15.)
Ps. 33:18. Behold, the eye of the Lord is on those who...hope in his steadfast love.
Lk. 1:48. He has regarded the low estate of his handmaiden.
Jer. 31:3 [God]: ...I have loved you with an everlasting love...
Hos. 2:19-20 [God]: I will betroth you to me for ever; I will betroth you to me in righteousness and in justice, in steadfast love, and in mercy. I will betroth you to me in faithfulness; and you shall know the Lord.
2 Cor. 11:2. ...I betrothed you to Christ to present you as a pure bride to her one husband. (Also Eph. 5:25-27, Ezek. 16:9-13, Is. 62:5, Jn. 3:29, Rev. 19:7-9.)
Is. 61:10. ...My soul shall exult in my God; for he has clothed me with the garments of salvation, he has covered me with the robe of righteousness, as a bridegroom decks himself with a garland, and as a bride adorns herself with her jewels.
Ps. 16:5. The Lord is my chosen portion and my cup (Luther: Gut und Teil)...

Dein Wort, dein Geist, dein Leib und Blut
Thy Word, thy Spirit, thy body and blood

Mich innerlich erquicken.
(Do) me inwardly revive.
{Inwardly revives me.}

Nimm mich
Take me

Freundlich
Kindly

In dein Arme, daß ich warme werd von Gnaden:
In thine arms, that I warm become from (thy) favor:
{In thine arms that I become warm with thy favor:}

Auf dein Wort komm ich geladen.
Upon thy Word come I invited.
{Upon thy word I come invited.}

Ps. 73:25–26. [O Lord,] whom have I in heaven but thee? And there is nothing upon earth that I desire besides thee. My flesh and my heart may fail, but God is the strength of my heart and my portion for ever.

Mt. 11:28–29 [Christ]: Come to me, all who labor and are heavy laden, and I will give you rest (Luther: euch erquicken). Take my yoke upon you, and learn from me; for I am gentle and lowly in heart, and you will find rest for your souls. (Also Jer. 31:25.)

Jn. 6:35, 37, 54–56 [Christ]: I am the bread of life; he who comes to me shall not hunger, and he who believes in me shall never thirst...All that the Father gives me will come to me; and him who comes to me I will not cast out...He who eats my flesh and drinks my blood has eternal life, and I will raise him up at the last day. For my flesh is food indeed, and my blood is drink indeed. He who eats my flesh and drinks my blood abides in me, and I in him.

1 Cor. 10:16. The cup of blessing which we bless, is it not a participation in the blood of Christ? The bread which we break, is it not a participation in the body of Christ?

Eph. 1:13. In [Christ] you...who have heard the word of truth, the gospel of your salvation, and have believed in him, were sealed with the promised Holy Spirit.

Eph. 1:3. Blessed be the God and Father of our Lord Jesus Christ, who has blessed us in Christ with every spiritual blessing in the heavenly places...

Ps. 145:8. The Lord is gracious and merciful...and abounding in steadfast love. (Also Ps. 103:8.)

Is. 40:11. He will feed his flock like a shepherd, he will gather the lambs in his arms, he will carry them in his bosom...

Rev. 22:17. The Spirit and the Bride say, "Come." ...And let him who is thirsty come, let him who desires take the water of life without price.

BWV 173
Erhöhtes Fleisch und Blut
(NBA I/14; BC A85)

2. Day of Pentecost (BWV 173, 68, 174)
*Acts 10:42–48 (The Holy Spirit descends on the Gentiles at Cornelius' house while Peter preaches)
*Jn. 3:16–21 (God sent his Son so that the world might be saved through him.)
Librettist: Unknown (This cantata is a parody of BWV 173a: new text fitted to preexisting music in all movements.)

1. Tenor Recit.
●Flesh & blood exalted by God's acceptance of it (173-1)
Erhöhtes Fleisch und Blut,
(O) exalted flesh and blood,

Das Gott selbst an sich nimmt,
Which God himself upon himself takes,
{Which God himself takes on,}

Dem er schon hier auf Erden
For-which he already here on earth
{For which, already here on earth,}

Heb. 2:14–15. Since...the children share in flesh and blood, [Christ] himself likewise partook of the same nature, that through death he might destroy him who has the power of death, that is, the devil, and deliver all those who through fear of death were subject to lifelong bondage.

Rom. 8:3–4. For God has done what the law, weakened by the flesh, could not do: sending his own Son in the likeness of sinful flesh and for sin, he condemned sin in the flesh, in order that the just requirement of the law might be fulfilled in us, who walk not according to the flesh but according to the Spirit.

Jn. 1:1, 14. In the beginning was the Word, and the Word was with God, and the Word was God...And the Word became flesh and dwelt among us... (Also 1 Tim. 3:16.)

Ein himmlisch Heil bestimmt,
A   heavenly welfare appoints,
{He appoints a heavenly blessedness,}

Des Höchsten Kind zu werden,
The Most-High's child to become,
{Which is to become a child of the Most High,}

     Erhöhtes Fleisch und Blut!
(O) exalted   flesh   and blood!

2. Tenor Aria
●Praise to God for his goodness to sanctified spirits (173-2)
Ein geheiligtes Gemüte
A   sanctified   spirit

Sieht und schmecket Gottes Güte.
Sees and   tastes   God's goodness.

Rühmet, singet, stimmt die Saiten,
Extol,   sing,   tune   the strings,

Gottes Treue auszubreiten!
God's faithfulness to-spread-abroad!
{To spread abroad God's faithfulness!}

3. Alto Aria
●Silence impossible after great things God has done (173-3)
Gott will,   o ihr Menschenkinder,
God desires, O ye children-of-men,

An euch große Dinge tun.
For you great things to-do.
{To do great things for you.}

Mund und Herze, Ohr und Blicke
Mouth and heart, ear and glances
{Mouth and heart, ear and eye}

Können nicht bei diesem Glücke
Can   not amidst this fortune
{Can not keep still amidst this fortune}

Und so heilger Freude ruhn.
And such holy   joy keep-still.
{And such holy joy.}

1 Jn. 5:1. Every one who believes that Jesus is the Christ is a child of God...
Rom. 8:14. All who are led by the Spirit of God are sons of God...It is the Spirit himself bearing witness with our spirit that we are children of God.
1 Jn. 3:1-2. See what love the Father has given us, that we should be called children of God; and so we are...Beloved, we are God's children now; it does not yet appear what we shall be, but we know that when he appears we shall be like him, for we shall see him as he is.

Rom. 8:9-10. You are not in the flesh, you are in the Spirit, if in fact the Spirit of God dwells in you. Any one who does not have the Spirit of Christ does not belong to him. But if Christ is in you, although your bodies are dead because of sin, your spirits are alive because of righteousness.
Ps. 34:8. O taste and see that the Lord is good! Happy is the man who takes refuge in him!
1 Pet. 2:3. You have tasted the kindness of the Lord.
Ps. 33:1-3. Rejoice in the Lord, O you righteous! Praise befits the upright. Praise the Lord with the lyre, make melody to him with the harp of ten strings! Sing to him a new song, play skilfully on the strings (Luther: Saitenspiel), with loud shouts. (Also Ps. 57:8-9, 81:2-3, 98:5-6, 149:2-3, Ps. 150:1-6.)
Ps. 98:4. Make a joyful noise to the Lord, all the earth; break forth into joyous song and sing praises! (Luther: singet, rühmet und lobet!) (Also Jer. 20:13.)
Ps. 71:22. I will...praise thee with the harp for thy faithfulness (Luther: Treue), O my God; I will sing praises to thee with the lyre, O Holy One of Israel. (Also Ps. 108:1-3.)

*Acts 10:44-46. While Peter was still [speaking], the Holy Spirit fell on all who heard the word. And the believers from among the circumcised who came with Peter were amazed, because the gift of the Holy Spirit had been poured out even on the Gentiles. For they heard them speaking in tongues and extolling God...
Ps. 126:1-3. When the Lord restored the fortunes of Zion, we were like those who dream. Then our mouth was filled with laughter, and our tongue with shouts of joy; then they said among the nations, "The Lord has done great things for them." The Lord has done great things for us; we are glad. (Also 1 Sam. 12:24, Lk. 1:49.)
Ps. 103:1. Bless the Lord, O my soul; and all that is within me, bless his holy name!
Lk. 19:37-40. As [Jesus] was...drawing near...the whole multitude of the disciples began to rejoice and praise God with a loud voice for all the mighty works that they had seen, saying, "Blessed is the King who comes in the name of the Lord! Peace in heaven and glory in the highest!" And some of the Pharisees in the multitude said to him, "Teacher, rebuke your disciples." He answered, "I tell you, if these were silent, the very stones would cry out."
Acts 13:52. The disciples were filled with joy and with the Holy Spirit.

4. Soprano & Bass Duet
●Praise to God for gifts of grace through his Spirit (173–4)
Bass:
So   hat Gott die Welt geliebt,
Thus has God the world loved (that)
{God has so loved the world that}

Sein Erbarmen
His   mercy

Hilft uns Armen,
Helps us poor-ones,

Daß   er seinen Sohn uns   gibt,
In-that he his   Son to-us does-give,

Gnadengaben zu genießen,
Gifts-of-grace to   enjoy,

Die   wie reiche Ströme fließen.
Which like abundant streams do-flow.

Soprano:
Sein verneuter Gnadenbund
His   renewed covenant-of-grace

Ist geschäftig
Is   active

Und wird   kräftig
And becomes mighty

In der Menschen Herz und Mund,
In the human   heart and mouth,

Daß sein Geist zu seiner Ehre
So-that his Spirit to his   honor
{So that, to his honor, his Spirit}

Gläubig zu ihm rufen   lehre.
In-faith to him to-call does-teach.
{Teaches them to call on him in faith.}

Both:
Nun wir lassen unsre Pflicht
Now we let   our obligation (its)

Jn. 3:16. God so loved the world that he gave his only Son, that whoever believes in him should not perish but have eternal life. (Also Rom. 8:3, 32.)
1 Jn. 4:9–10. In this the love of God was made manifest among us, that God sent his only Son into the world, so that we might live through him. In this is love, not that we loved God but that he loved us and sent his Son to be the expiation for our sins.
Tit. 3:4–7. When the goodness and loving kindness of God our Savior appeared, he saved us, not because of deeds done by us in righteousness, but in virtue of his own mercy, by the washing of regeneration and renewal in the Holy Spirit, which he poured out upon us richly through Jesus Christ our Savior so that we might be justified by his grace and become heirs in hope of eternal life.
Eph. 4:7–8. Grace was given to each of us according to the measure of Christ's gift. Therefore it is said, "When he ascended on high he led a host of captives, and he gave gifts to men." (Also Rom. 12:6, 1 Pet. 4:10.)
Rom. 5:5. ...God's love has been poured into our hearts through the Holy Spirit which has been given to us.
Is. 44:3. [God said,] I will pour water on the thirsty land, and streams on the dry ground; I will pour my Spirit upon your descendants... (Also Is. 32:15, Joel 2:28.)
Jer. 31:31, 33–34. Behold, the days are coming, says the Lord, when I will make a new covenant with the house of Israel and the house of Judah...This is the covenant which I will make...I will put my law within them, and I will write it upon their hearts...No longer shall each man teach his neighbor and each his brother, saying, "Know the Lord," for they shall all know me, from the least of them to the greatest, says the Lord...
2 Cor. 3:6. ...[This] new covenant, [is] not in a written code but in the Spirit; for the written code kills, but the Spirit gives life.
Heb. 9:15. [Christ] is the mediator of a new covenant...
Jn. 7:37–39. On the last day of the feast, the great day, Jesus stood up and proclaimed, "If any one thirst, let him come to me and drink. He who believes in me, as the scripture has said, 'Out of his heart shall flow rivers of living water.'" Now this he said about the Spirit, which those who believed in him were to receive... (Also Acts 2:18.)
Jn. 16:13–14 [Christ]: When the Spirit of truth comes, he will guide you into all the truth...He will glorify me, for he will take what is mine and declare it to you.
Rom. 10:8–9. What does [the new covenant of righteousness based on faith] say? The word is near you, on your lips (Luther: Munde) and in your heart (that is, the word of faith which we preach); because if you confess with your lips (Luther: Munde) that Jesus is Lord and believe in your heart that God raised him from the dead, you will be saved. (Also Deut. 30:14.)
1 Cor. 12:3. ...No one can say "Jesus is Lord" except by the Holy Spirit.
Eph. 3:20. ...By the [Spirit's] power at work within us [God] is able to do far more abundantly than all that we ask or think... (Also Phil. 1:6, 2:13.)
Rom. 8:15–16. ...[We] have received the spirit of sonship. When we cry, "Abba! Father!" it is the Spirit himself bearing witness with our spirit that we are children of God.
*****Acts 10:44–45.** While Peter was still [speaking to his Gentile

Opfer bringen,
Offering bring,

Dankend singen,
Gratefully sing,

Da sein offenbartes Licht
Because his manifested light
{For his manifested light}

Sich zu seinen Kindern neiget
- To his children does-bend
{Inclines itself to his children}

Und sich ihnen kräftig zeiget.
And itself to-them mightily does-show.
{And mightily shows itself to them.}

5. Soprano & Tenor Recit.
●Heart's ardor offered in devotion to infinite Father (173-5)
Unendlichster, den man doch Vater nennt,
(O) Infinite-One, whom (we) nevertheless "Father" call,

Wir wollen dann das Herz zum Opfer bringen,
We would then (our) heart as-an offering bring;

Aus unsrer Brust, die ganz vor Andacht brennt,
From our breast, which altogether with devotion burns,
{From our breast, which burns completely with devotion,}

Soll sich der Seufzer Glut zum Himmel schwingen.
Shall - (our) sighing's ardor to heaven soar.
{Soars the ardor of our sighing to heaven.}

6. Chorus
●Prayer: Stir our spirits with thy Spirit (173-6)
Rühre, Höchster, unsern Geist,
Stir, Most-High, our spirit,

Daß des höchsten Geistes Gaben
That the highest Spirit's gifts
{That the Holy Spirit's gifts}

Ihre Würkung in uns haben!
Their effect in us might-have!

Da dein Sohn uns beten heißt,
Since thy Son us pray does-bid,
{Since thy Son does bid us pray,}

listeners], the Holy Spirit fell on all who heard the word. And the believers from among the circumcised who came with Peter were amazed, because the gift of the Holy Spirit had been poured out even on the Gentiles. (Also Acts 11:4-17.)
Ps. 50:14. Offer to God a sacrifice of thanksgiving, and pay your vows to the Most High. (Also Ps. 22:25, 50:23, 51:15-17, 61:8, 66:13, 69:30-31, Heb. 13:15.)
Ps. 116:17. I will offer to [God] the sacrifice of thanksgiving and call on the name of the Lord.
Eph. 1:18-20. [May you have] the eyes of your hearts enlightened, that you may know...what is the immeasurable greatness of his power (Luther: überschwengliche Größe seiner Kraft) in us who believe, according to the working of his great might (Luther: nach der Wirkung seiner mächtigen Stärke) which he accomplished in Christ...
Eph. 3:4-6. ...The mystery of Christ...has now been revealed (Luther: offenbart)...by the Spirit; that is, how the Gentiles are fellow heirs, members of the same body, and partakers of the promise in Christ Jesus through the gospel.
2 Cor. 4:6. It is the God who said, "Let light shine out of darkness," who has shone in our hearts to give the light of the knowledge of the glory of God in the face of Christ.
Is. 9:2. The people who walked in darkness have seen a great light... (Also Mt. 4:16.)

Gal. 4:4-7. ...God sent forth his Son...so that we might receive adoption as sons. And because you are sons, God has sent the Spirit of his Son into our hearts, crying, "Abba! Father!" So through God you are no longer a slave but a son, and if a son then an heir.
Rom. 8:15-17. For you did not receive the spirit of slavery to fall back into fear, but you have received the spirit of sonship. When we cry, "Abba! Father!" it is the Spirit himself bearing witness with our spirit that we are children of God, and if children, then heirs, heirs of God and fellow heirs with Christ...
Rom. 8:26. Likewise the Spirit helps us in our weakness; for we do not know how to pray as we ought, but the Spirit himself intercedes for us with sighs too deep for words.

Phil. 1:6, 9. I am sure that he who began a good work in you will bring it to completion at the day of Jesus Christ...And it is my prayer that your love may abound more and more, with knowledge and all discernment...
Phil. 2:13. For God is at work in you, both to will and to work for his good pleasure.
Eph. 1:19. ...[I pray that you might know] the immeasurable greatness of his power in us who believe, according to the working (Luther: Wirkung) of his great might.
Rom. 8:16. ...When we cry, "Abba! Father!" it is the Spirit himself bearing witness with our spirit that we are children of God.
2 Cor. 1:21-22. It is God who establishes us with you in Christ...; he has put his seal upon us and given us his Spirit in our hearts as a guarantee. (given the Spirit: also Acts 5:32, Rom. 5:5, 2 Cor. 5:5, 1 Jn. 3:24, 4:13)
Jn. 16:23-24 [Christ]: ...Truly, truly, I say to you, if you ask anything of the Father, he will give it to you in my name. Hitherto you have asked nothing in my name; ask, and you will receive, that your joy may be full. (Also Jn. 14:13, 15:16.)

Wird es durch die Wolken dringen
Will it through the clouds penetrate
{Our praying will penetrate the clouds}

Und Erhörung auf uns bringen.
And (a) favorable-answer to us bring.
{And bring us a favorable answer.}

Sirach (Apocrypha) 35:17 (= Sirach 35:21 of the German Bible). The prayer of the humble pierces the clouds, and he will not be consoled until it reaches the Lord; he will not desist until the Most High visits him, and does justice for the righteous, and executes judgment. (Also Lam. 3:44.)

1 Jn. 5:14–15. This is the confidence which we have in [Christ], that if we ask anything according to his will he hears us. And if we know that he hears us in whatever we ask, we know that we have obtained the requests made of him.

BWV 174
Ich liebe den Höchsten von ganzem Gemüte
(NBA I/14; BC A87)

2. Day of Pentecost (BWV 173, 68, 174)
*Acts 10:42–48 (The Holy Spirit descends on the Gentiles at Cornelius' house while Peter preaches)
*Jn. 3:16–21 (God sent his Son so that the world might be saved through him.)
Librettist: Picander (Christian Friedrich Henrici)

1. Sinfonia (Taken from Brandenburg concerto 3–1)

2. Alto Aria
●Loving God with all one's heart because he loved us (174-2)
Ich liebe den Höchsten von ganzem Gemüte,
I love the Most-High with all-my disposition,
{I love the Most High with all my heart,}

Er hat mich auch am höchsten lieb.
He (holds) me, too, - exceeding dear.
{He also loves me exceedingly.}

Gott allein
God alone

Soll der Schatz der Seelen sein,
Shall the treasure of (all) souls be,
{Is to be the treasure of all souls;}

Da hab ich die ewige Quelle der Güte.
There have I the eternal wellspring of kindness.
{In him I possess the eternal wellspring of kindness.}

3. Tenor Recit.
●Love of God that gave Son as ransom is like no other (174-3)
O Liebe, welcher keine gleich!
O love, which (is) no-other like!
{O love which is like no other!}

O unschätzbares Lösegeld!
O priceless ransom!

Der Vater hat des Kindes Leben
The Father has (his) child's life

Mt. 22:35–38. ...A lawyer, asked [Jesus] a question, to test him. "Teacher, which is the great commandment in the law?" And he said to him, "You shall love the Lord your God with all your heart, and with all your soul, and with all your mind (Luther: Gemüte). This is the great and first commandment." (Also Mk. 12:30–31, Lk. 10:27, Deut. 6:5.)

Phil. 1:21. To me to live is Christ...

Gal. 2:20. ...I live by faith in the Son of God who loved me and gave himself for me.

***Jn. 3:16.** For God so loved the world that he gave his only Son, that whoever believes in him should not perish but have eternal life.

Deut. 5:7. [God said,] "You shall have no other gods before me." (Also Ex. 20:3.)

Mt. 4:10 [Christ]: "...It is written, 'You shall worship the Lord your God and him only shall you serve.'" (Also Lk. 4:8, Deut. 6:13–14.)

Phil. 3:8. ...I count everything as loss because of the surpassing worth of knowing Christ Jesus my Lord...

Mt. 13:44–46 [Christ]: The kingdom of heaven is like treasure hidden in a field, which a man found and covered up; then in his joy he goes and sells all that he has and buys that field. Again, the kingdom of heaven is like a merchant, on search of fine pearls, who, on finding one pearl of great value, went and sold all that he had and bought it.

Jms. 1:17. Every good endowment and every perfect gift is from above, coming down from the Father of lights with whom there is no variation or shadow due to change.

Ps. 36:9–10. [O Lord,] with thee is the fountain of life (Luther: lebendige Quelle); in thy light do we see light.

Ps. 73:25. [O Lord,] whom have I in heaven but thee? And there is nothing upon earth that I desire besides thee.

***Jn. 3:16.** God so loved the world that he gave his only Son...

1 Jn. 4:9–10. In this the love of God was made manifest among us, that God sent his only Son into the world, so that we might live through him. In this is love, not that we loved God but that he loved us and sent his Son to be the expiation for our sins.

1 Jn. 3:16. By this we know love, that he laid down his life for us...

Jn. 15:13 [Christ]: Greater love has no man than this, that a man lay down his life for his friends.

Rom. 5:6–8. While we were still weak, at the right time Christ died for the ungodly. Why, one will hardly die for a righteous man—though

Vor Sünder in den Tod gegeben
For sinners (up) to death delivered
{The Father has delivered up his child's life to death for sinners}

Und alle, die das Himmelreich
And (has) all, who the kingdom-of-heaven

Verscherzet und verloren,
Did-frivolously-forfeit and lose,

Zur Seligkeit erkoren.
To blessedness elected.
{And has elected to blessedness all who frivolously forfeited and lost the kingdom of heaven.}

Also hat Gott die Welt geliebt!
Thus has God the world loved!
{"God so loved the world!"}

Mein Herz, das merke dir
My heart, this note -
{O my heart, note this}

Und stärke dich mit diesen Worten;
And fortify thyself with these words;

Vor diesem mächtigen Panier
Before this mighty banner

Erzittern selbst die Höllenpforten.
Tremble even the gates-of-hell.
{The very gates of hell tremble.}

4. Bass Aria
●Salvation offered in love, gained by faith: believe! (174-4)
Greifet zu,
Take-hold,

Faßt das Heil, ihr Glaubenshände!
Grasp that salvation, ye hands-of-faith!

Jesus gibt sein Himmelreich
Jesus gives (to you) his kingdom-of-heaven

Und verlangt nur das von euch:
And requires only this of you: (that you)

Gläubt getreu bis an das Ende!
Believe faithfully to the end!

5. Chorale
●Prayer: I love thee above all else, even in sorrow! (174-5)
Herzlich lieb hab ich dich, o Herr.
Heartily love I thee, O Lord.
{I love thee with all my heart, O Lord.}

perhaps for a good man one will dare even to die. But God shows his love for us in that while we were yet sinners Christ died for us.
Mk. 10:45 [Christ]: The Son of man also came not to be served but to serve, and to give his life as a ransom (Luther: Bezahlung) for many.
*Jn. 3:16-17. God so loved the world that he gave his only Son, that whoever believes in him should not perish (Luther: verloren werden) but have eternal life. For God sent the Son into the world, not to condemn the world, but that the world might be saved through him. (Also 1 Thess. 5:9-10.)
Mt. 1:21. You shall call his name Jesus, for he will save his people from their sins.
Is. 11:1, 10. There shall come forth a shoot from the stump of Jesse... In that day the root of Jesse shall stand as an ensign (Luther: Panier) to the peoples; him shall the nations seek... (Also Is. 11:12.)
Mt. 16:15-18. [Jesus] said to [his disciples], "Who do you say that I am?" Simon Peter replied, "You are the Christ, the Son of the living God." And Jesus answered him, "Blessed are you, Simon Bar-Jona! For flesh and blood has not revealed this to you, but my Father who is in heaven. And I tell you, you are Peter, and on this rock I will build my church, and the powers of death (Luther: Pforten der Hölle) shall not prevail against it.
1 Jn. 3:8. ...The reason the Son of God appeared was to destroy the works of the devil.
Heb. 2:14-15. Since therefore the children share in flesh and blood, [Christ] himself likewise partook of the same nature, that through death he might destroy him who has the power of death, that is, the devil, and deliver all those who through fear of death were subject to lifelong bondage.
Col. 2:15. [Christ] disarmed the principalities and powers and made a public example of them, triumphing over them in him.
Jms. 2:19. ...Even the demons believe—and shudder.

*Jn. 3:18 [Christ]: He who believes in [the Son] is not condemned; he who does not believe is condemned already, because he has not believed in the name of the only Son of God.
Mk. 16:16 [Christ]: He who believes and is baptized will be saved; but he who does not believe will be condemned.
Rom. 10:9. If you confess with your lips that Jesus is Lord and believe in your heart that God raised him from the dead, you will be saved.
Eph. 2:8-9. For by grace you have been saved through faith; and this is not your own doing, it is the gift of God—not because of works, lest any man should boast.
Lk. 12:32 [Christ]: Fear not, little flock, for it is your Father's good pleasure to give you the kingdom.
Heb. 3:14. We share in Christ, if only we hold our first confidence firm to the end.
Rev. 2:25 [Christ]: Only hold fast what you have, until I come. (Also Rev. 3:11.)

Mt. 22:37-38 [Christ]: You shall love the Lord your God with all your heart, and with all your soul, and with all your mind. This is the great and first commandment.
Ps. 18:1. I love thee, O Lord, my strength... (Luther: Herzlich lieb habe ich dich, Herr meine Stärke...)

Ich bitt,   wollst sein von mir nicht fern
I   ask, (that thou) wouldst be from me not   far
{I ask that thou wouldst not be far from me}

Mit deiner Hülf und Gnaden.
With thy help and   grace.

Die ganze Welt erfreut mich nicht,
The entire world delights me   not,
{The entire world holds no attraction for me,}

Nach Himml und Erden frag ich nicht,
For   heaven and earth ask I   not,
{I ask not for heaven or earth,}

Wenn ich dich nur kann haben.
If   I   thee just can   have.
{If I can but have thee.}

Und wenn mir gleich mein Herz zerbricht,
And even - though my heart should-break,

So   bist du doch mein Zuversicht,
Then art thou still   my   confidence,

Mein Heil   und meines Herzens Trost,
My salvation and   my   heart's comfort,

Der mich durch sein Blut hat   erlöst.
Who me   by   his blood hath redeemed.
{Who hath redeemed me by his blood.}

Herr Jesu Christ,
Lord Jesus Christ,

Mein Gott und Herr, mein Gott und Herr,
My   God and Lord, my God and Lord,

In Schanden laß mich nimmermehr!
In   shame   leave me   nevermore!
{Let me never be put to shame!}

Ps. 22:11. [O Lord,] be not far from me, for trouble is near and there is none to help. (Also Ps. 35:22–23, 38:21–22, 71:12.)

1 Jn. 2:15–17. Do not love the world or the things in the world. If any one loves the world, love for the Father is not in him. For all that is in the world, the lust of the flesh and the lust of the eyes and the pride of life, is not of the Father but is of the world. And the world passes away, and the lust of it; but he who does the will of God abides for ever.

Jms. 4:4. Unfaithful creatures! Do you not know that friendship with the world is enmity with God? Therefore whoever wishes to be a friend of the world makes himself an enemy of God.

Ps. 73:25–26. [O Lord,] whom have I in heaven but thee? And there is nothing upon earth that I desire besides thee. (Luther: Wenn ich nur dich habe, so frage ich nichts nach Himmel und Erde.) My flesh and my heart may fail, but God is the strength of my heart and my portion (Luther: Trost und Teil) for ever.

Hab. 3:17–19. Though the fig tree do not blossom, nor fruit be on the vines, the produce of the olive fail and the fields yield no food, the flock be cut off from the fold and there be no herd in the stalls, yet I will rejoice in the Lord, I will joy in the God of my salvation. God, the Lord, is my strength...

Ps. 142:5. I cry to thee, O Lord; I say, Thou art my refuge (Luther: Zuversicht), my portion in the land of the living. (Zuversicht: also Ps. 46:1, 61:3, 62:7, 71:5, 7).

Rom. 8:35, 38–39. Who shall separate us from the love of Christ? Shall tribulation, or distress, or persecution, or famine, or nakedness, or peril, or sword?...I am sure that neither death, nor life, nor angels, nor principalities, nor things present, nor things to come, nor powers, nor height, nor depth, nor anything else in all creation, will be able to separate us from the love of God in Christ Jesus our Lord.

1 Pet. 1:18–19. You know that you were ransomed from the futile ways inherited from your fathers, not with perishable things such as silver or gold, but with the precious blood of Christ, like that of a lamb without blemish or spot. (Also Eph. 2:13, 1 Jn. 1:7, Heb. 13:12, Rev. 5:9.)

Jn. 20:27–28. [Jesus, appearing to his disciples after his resurrection] said to Thomas, "Put your finger here, and see my hands; and put out your hand, and place it in my side; do not be faithless, but believing." Thomas answered him, "My Lord and my God!"

1 Cor. 12:3. ...No one can say "Jesus is Lord" except by the Holy Spirit.

Ps. 63:8. [O Lord,] my soul clings to thee; thy right hand upholds me.

Ps. 31:1. In thee, O Lord, do I seek refuge; let me never be put to shame (Luther: laß mich nimmermehr zu Schanden werden): in thy righteousness deliver me!

Ps. 71:1. In thee, O Lord, do I take refuge; let me never be put to shame! (Also Ps. 25:2–3, 25:20, 31:17.)

BWV 175
Er rufet seinen Schafen mit Namen
(NBA I/14; BC A89)

3. Day of Pentecost (BWV 184, 175)
*Acts 8:14–17 (Baptism of Holy Ghost comes to believers in Samaria)
*Jn. 10:1–11 (Jesus identifies himself as the true shepherd)
Librettist: Christiane Mariane von Ziegler (Text greatly modified by someone: J. S. Bach?)

1. Tenor Recit.
●Shepherd calls sheep by name & leads them: Jn. 10:3 (175-1)
Er rufet seinen Schafen mit Namen
He calls his sheep by name

und führet sie hinaus.
and leads them out.

2. Alto Aria
●Yearning for shepherd and green pasture (175-2)
Komm, leite mich,
Come, lead me;

Es sehnet sich
(Now) yearns -

Mein Geist auf grüner Weide!
My spirit for green pastures!
{My spirit yearns for green pastures!}

Mein Herze schmacht',
My heart languishes,

Ächzt Tag und Nacht,
Groans day and night,

    Mein Hirte, meine Freude.
(O) my shepherd, my joy.

3. Tenor Recit.
●Yearning for God: Where do I find thee? (175-3)
Wo find' ich dich?
Where find I thee?
{O where do I find thee?}

Ach, wo bist du verborgen?
Ah, where art thou hidden?

O! Zeige dich mir bald!
Oh! Appear to-me soon!

Ich sehne mich.
I long - (for thee).

Jn. 10:3–5, 14, 27 [Christ]: ...The sheep hear [the shepherd's] voice, and *he calls his own sheep by name and leads them out.* When he has brought out all his own, he goes before them, and the sheep follow him, for they know his voice. A stranger they will not follow, but they will flee from him, for they do not know the voice of strangers...I am the good shepherd; I know my own and my own know me...My sheep hear my voice, and I know them, and they follow me.
Is. 40:11. He will feed his flock like a shepherd, he will gather the lambs in his arms, he will carry them in his bosom, and gently lead those that are with young. (Also Ezek. 34:11–16, Ps. 23:1–2, Rev. 7:17.)

Ps. 23:1–3. The Lord is my shepherd, I shall not want; he makes me lie down in green pastures. He leads me beside still waters; he restores my soul...
Ps. 42:1–2. As a hart longs for flowing streams, so longs my soul for thee, O God. My soul thirsts for God, for the living God. When shall I come and behold the face of God?
Ps. 119:28. My soul melts away for sorrow (Luther: Ich gräme mich, daß mir das Herz verschmachtet); strengthen me according to thy word!
Ps. 22:1–2. My God, my God, why hast thou forsaken me? Why art thou so far from helping me, from the words of my groaning? O my God, I cry by day, but thou dost not answer; and by night, but find no rest. (Also Ps. 6:2–4, 6–7, 13:1–3, 5, 86:3, 88:1, Is. 38:13.)
Rom. 8:22–23, 26. We know that the whole creation has been groaning in travail together until now; and not only the creation, but we ourselves, who have the first fruits of the Spirit, groan inwardly (Luther: sehnen uns auch) as we wait for adoption as sons, the redemption of our bodies...Likewise the Spirit helps us in our weakness; for we do not know how to pray as we ought, but the Spirit himself intercedes for us with sighs too deep for words (Luther: unaussprechlichem Seufzen).

Job 23:3. Oh, that I knew where I might find [God]...!
Ps. 42:3. My tears have been my food day and night, while men say to me continually, "Where is your God?" (Also Ps. 79:10.)
Ps. 13:1–2. How long, O Lord? Wilt thou forget me for ever? How long wilt thou hide thy face from me? How long must I bear pain in my soul, and have sorrow in my heart all the day?...
Ps. 143:7. Make haste to answer me, O Lord! My spirit fails! Hide not thy face from me, lest I be like those who go down to the Pit. (Also Ps. 44:24, 69:17, 88:14, 102:2, 143:7.)
Ps. 130:5–6. I wait for the Lord, my soul waits, and in his word I hope; my soul waits for the Lord more than watchmen for the morning, more than watchmen for the morning.

Brich an, erwünschter Morgen!
Break forth, desired   morning!

4. Tenor Aria (Parody of BWV 173a-7)
•Jesus recognized as true shepherd (175-4)
Es dünket mich, ich seh dich kommen,
It   seems to-me, I see thee coming,

Du   gehst   zur rechten Türe ein.
Thou dost-enter by-the right   door - .

Du wirst im Glauben aufgenommen
Thou art by faith   received

Und mußt der wahre Hirte sein.
And must the true shepherd be.

Ich kenne deine holde Stimme,
I recognize thy gracious voice,

Die   voller Lieb und Sanftmut ist,
Which (so) full-of love and gentleness is,
{Which is so loving and gentle,}

Daß ich im Geist darob   ergrimme,
That I in-my spirit at-(anyone) am-angered,
{That I am angered in my spirit at anyone}

Wer zweifelt, daß du   Heiland seist.
Who doubts, that thou (the) Savior   art.
{Who doubts that thou art the Savior.}

5. Alto/Bass Recits.
•Jesus' words not understood by reason: Jn. 10:6 (175-5)
Alto:
Sie vernahmen aber nicht, was es war,
They understood, however, not, what it was,

   das er zu ihnen gesaget hatte.
   that he to them   had-said.
   {that he had said to them.}

Ps. 30:5. ...Weeping may tarry for the night, but joy comes with the morning.

***Jn. 10:1-5 [Christ]:** Truly, truly, I say to you, he who does not enter the sheepfold by the door but climbs in by another way, that man is a thief and a robber; but he who enters by the door is the shepherd of the sheep. To him the gatekeeper opens; the sheep hear his voice, and he calls his own sheep by name and leads them out. When he has brought out all his own, he goes before them, and the sheep follow him, for they know his voice. A stranger they will not follow, but they will flee from him, for they do not know the voice of strangers.
Jn. 1:12. To all who received [Christ], who believed in his name, he gave power to become children of God.
Is. 40:11. He will feed his flock like a shepherd, he will gather the lambs in his arms, he will carry them in his bosom, and gently lead those that are with young.
Mt. 11:28-29 [Christ]: Come to me...for I am gentle (Luther: sanftmütig)...
Ps. 103:8. The Lord is merciful and gracious, slow to anger and abounding in steadfast love.
1 Kings 19:11-12. ...The Lord passed by [Elijah], and a great and strong wind rent the mountains...but the Lord was not in the wind; and after the wind an earthquake; but the Lord was not in the earthquake; and after the earthquake a fire, but the Lord was not in the fire; and after the fire a still small voice.
Jn. 10: 4-5 [Christ]: The sheep follow [the true shepherd], for they know his voice. A stranger they will not follow, but they will flee from him, for they do not know the voice of strangers.
Jn. 14:17 [Christ]: ...The world cannot receive [the Spirit of truth] because it neither sees him nor knows him; you know him, for he dwells with you, and will be in you.
1 Jn. 4:2-3. By this you know the Spirit of God: every spirit which confesses that Jesus Christ has come in the flesh is of God, and every spirit which does not confess Jesus is not of God. This is the spirit of antichrist... (Also 2 Jn. 1:7.)
Jn. 10:24-27. The Jews gathered round [Jesus] and said to him, "How long will you keep us in suspense? If you are the Christ, tell us plainly." Jesus answered them, "I told you, and you do not believe. The works that I do in my Father's name, they bear witness to me; but you do not believe, because you do not belong to my sheep. My sheep hear my voice, and I know them, and they follow me."
Jn. 12:37-38. Though [Jesus] had done so many signs before them, yet they did not believe in him.
Ps. 139:21-22. Do I not hate them that hate thee, O Lord? And do I not loathe them that rise up against thee? I hate them with perfect hatred; I count them my enemies.

***Jn. 10:6-8.** This figure Jesus used with [the people], *but they did not understand what he was saying to them.* So Jesus again said to them, "Truly, truly, I say to you, I am the door of the sheep. All who came before me are thieves and robbers..."
Is. 44:18. [Those who do not worship the true God] know not, nor do they discern; for he has shut their eyes (Luther: sie sind verblendet), so that they cannot see, and their minds, so that they cannot understand. (Also Jn. 12:40, Rom. 11:10, 2 Cor. 4:4, 1 Jn. 2:11.)

Bass:
Ach ja! Wir Menschen sind oftmals
Ah, yes! We humans are often

    den Tauben zu vergleichen:
    to deaf-persons to-be likened:
    {like the deaf:}

Wenn die verblendete Vernunft nicht weiß,
When (our) deluded reason (does) not understand,

    was er gesaget hatte.
    what he did-say.

O! Törin, merke doch, wenn Jesus mit dir spricht,
Oh! fool, note indeed, when Jesus with thee speaks,
    [Törin = female fool]

Daß es zu deinem Heil geschicht.
That it for thy salvation is-done.
{That it concerns thy salvation.}

6. Bass Aria (Perhaps from an earlier work)
●Jesus' words promise abundant life to all who follow (175-6)
Öffnet euch, ihr beiden Ohren,
Open (up), ye both ears,
{Open up, ye ears, both!}

Jesus hat euch zugeschworen,
Jesus hath to-you sworn,
{Jesus hath sworn to you}

Daß er Teufel, Tod erlegt.
That he devil (and) death does-slay.
{That he slays both devil and death.}

Gnade, Gnüge, volles Leben
Grace, plenty, abundant life

Will er allen Christen geben,
Would he to-all Christians give,
{Would he give to all Christians}

Wer ihm folgt, sein Kreuz nachträgt.
Who him follow; his cross carry.
{Who take up their cross and follow him.}

7. Chorale (Music taken from BWV 59-3)
●Spirit's help sought to accept word of new life (175-7)
Nun, werter Geist, ich folge dir;
Now, dear Spirit, I follow thee;

Hilf, daß ich suche für und für
Help, that I would-seek forever and ever

Mt. 13:10-16. Then the disciples came and said to [Jesus], "Why do you speak to [the people] in parables?" And he answered them, "To you it has been given to know the secrets of the kingdom of heaven, but to them it has not been given. For to him who has will more be given, and he will have abundance; but from him who has not, even what he has will be taken away. This is why I speak to them in parables, because seeing they do not see, and hearing they do not hear, nor do they understand. With them indeed is fulfilled the prophecy of Isaiah which says: 'You shall indeed hear but never understand, and you shall indeed see but never perceive. For this people's heart has grown dull, and their ears are heavy of hearing, and their eyes they have closed, lest they should perceive with their eyes, and hear with their ears, and understand with their heart, and turn for me to heal them.' But blessed are your eyes, for they see, and your ears, for they hear." (Also Mk. 4:11-12.)
1 Cor. 1:18-19, 25. The word of the cross is folly (Luther: Torheit) to those who are perishing, but to us who are being saved it is the power of God. For it is written, "I will destroy the wisdom of the wise, and the cleverness of the clever I will thwart."...For the foolishness of God (Luther: göttliche Torheit) is wiser than men, and the weakness of God is stronger than men. (Also Mt. 11:25, Lk. 10:21.)
*Jn. 10:10 [Christ]: ...I came that they may have life, and have it abundantly.

Mt. 13:9 [Christ]: He who has ears to hear, let him hear. (Also Mt. 11:15, 13:43; Mk. 4:9, 23; Lk. 8:8, 14:35.)
1 Jn. 3:8. ...The reason the Son of God appeared was to destroy the works of the devil.
Heb. 2:14-15. Since therefore the children share in flesh and blood, [Christ] himself likewise partook of the same nature, that through death he might destroy him who has the power of death, that is, the devil, and deliver all those who through fear of death were subject to lifelong bondage. (Also 1 Cor. 15:25-26, 2 Tim. 1:10.)
Is. 25:8. He will swallow up death for ever...
*Jn. 10:10 [Christ]: ...I came that they may have life, and have it abundantly (Luther: und volle Genüge haben sollen).
Mt. 19:21 [Christ]: ...Come, follow me. (Also Mk. 10:21, Lk. 18:21, Jn. 21:22.)
Mt. 11:28 [Christ]: Come to me...and I will give you rest.
Mk. 8:34 [Christ]: ...If any man would come after me, let him deny himself and take up his cross and follow me. (Also Mt. 10:38, 16:24, Lk. 9:23.)
Mk. 10:29-30 [Christ]: ...Truly, I say to you, there is no one who has left house or brothers or sisters of mother or father or children or lands, for my sake and for the gospel, who will not receive a hundredfold now in this time, houses and brothers and sisters and mothers and children and lands, with persecutions, and in the age to come eternal life. (Also Mt. 19:29, Lk. 18:29-30.)

Eph. 1:13. In [Christ] you also, who have heard the word of truth, the gospel of your salvation, and have believed in him, were sealed with the promised Holy Spirit.
Mt. 16:24-25. Jesus told his disciples, "If any man would come after me, let him deny himself and take up his cross and follow me. For

Nach deinem Wort ein ander Leben,
At   thy   word, a different life,
{Help that, at thy word, I would ever seek a different life,}

Das du   mir   willt   aus Gnaden geben.
Which thou to-me wouldst out-of grace   give.
{Which, out of grace, thou dost desire to give me.}

Dein Wort ist ja   der Morgenstern,
Thy Word is indeed the morning-star,

Der   herrlich leuchtet nah und fern.
Which gloriously radiates near and far.

Drum   will ich, die mich anders   lehren,
Therefore will I,   those-who me otherwise (would) teach,

In Ewigkeit, mein Gott, nicht hören.
Eternally,   my God,   not   hear.
{Therefore I will eternally refuse to hear those who would teach me otherwise.}

Alleluja, alleluja!
Alleluia, alleluia!

BWV 176
Es ist ein trotzig und verzagt Ding
(NBA I/15; BC A92)

Trinity Sunday (BWV 165, [194], 176, 129)
*Rom. 11:33–36 (O the depth of the riches and wisdom and knowledge of God!)
*Jn. 3:1–15 (Discussion between Jesus and Nicodemus: You must be born anew)
Librettist: Christiane Mariane von Ziegler (modified)

1. Chorus
●Heart is obstinate and hopeless: Jer. 17:9 (modified) (176-1)
Es ist ein trotzig und   verzagt Ding
It is an obstinate and disheartening thing

um   aller Menschen Herze.
about all   human   hearts.
{about the human heart.}

2. Alto Recit.
●Timid Nicodemus, unlike Joshua, prefers night (176-2)
Ich meine,   recht   verzagt,
I   think (it was) truly faint-hearted (of him),
          [verzagt = disheartened but also faint-hearted]

Daß Nikodemus sich bei Tage nicht,
That Nicodemus -   by   day not (but)

---

whoever would save his life will lose it, and whoever loses his life for my sake will find it." (Also Mt. 10:38–39, Mk. 8:34–35, Lk. 9:23–24. Jn. 12:24–26.)
***Jn. 10:10 [Christ]:** ...I came that they may have life, and have it abundantly.
Col. 3:1–3. If then you have been raised with Christ, seek the things that are above, where Christ is, seated at the right hand of God. Set your minds on things that are above, not on things that are on earth. For you have died and your life is hid with Christ in God. (Also 2 Cor. 4:16–18, Heb. 11:14–16.)
2 Pet. 1:19. We have the prophetic word made more sure. You will do well to pay attention to this as to a lamp shining in a dark place, until the day dawns and the morning star rises in your hearts. (Also Ps. 119:105.)
Rev. 2:26, 28 [Christ]: He who conquers and who keeps my works until the end...I will give him the morning star.
Rev. 22:16 [Christ]: ...I am the root and the offspring of David, the bright and morning star.
Jn. 1:14. [In Christ] the [eternal] Word became flesh...
Jn. 1:9. [In Christ] the true light that enlightens every man was coming into the world.
1 Jn. 4:1, 3. Beloved, do not believe every spirit, but test the spirits to see whether they are of God; for many false prophets have gone out into the world...Every spirit which does not confess Jesus is not of God. This is the spirit of antichrist, of which you heard that it was coming, and now it is in the world already. (Also 1 Jn. 2:18–20, 2 Jn. 1:7.)

Jer. 17:9–10. *The heart is deceitful above all things, and desperately corrupt* (Luther: ein trotzig und verzagt Ding); who can understand it? "I the Lord search the mind and try the heart, to give to every man according to his ways, according to the fruit of his doings."
Prov. 20:9. Who can say, "I have made my heart clean; I am pure from my sin"?
Jn. 2:25. [Jesus] knew all men and needed no one to bear witness of man; for he himself knew what was in man.

***Jn. 3:1–3.** Now there was a man of the Pharisees, named Nicodemus, a ruler of the Jews. This man came to Jesus by night and said to him, "Rabbi, we know that you are a teacher come from God; for no one can do these signs that you do, unless God is with him."
Jn. 19:38–39. ...[After Jesus' crucifixion] Joseph of Arimathea, who was a disciple of Jesus, but secretly, for fear of the Jews, asked Pilate that he might take away the body of Jesus, and Pilate gave him leave. So he came and took away his body. Nicodemus also, who had at first

Bei Nacht zu Jesus wagt.
By night to Jesus did-venture.
{That Nicodemus would not venture to visit Jesus by day but only by night.}

Die Sonne mußte dort bei Josua so lange stille stehn,
The sun was-forced - with Joshua so long still to-stand,
{In Joshua's day the sun was forced to stand still so long,}

So lange bis der Sieg vollkommen war geschehn;
So long till the victory fully had-been accomplished;
{Until the victory had been fully accomplished;}

Hier aber wünschet Nikodem:
Here however wishes Nicodemus:

O säh ich sie zu Rüste gehn!
O saw I it to rest go!
{But here Nicodemus wishes: O that the sun would go to rest!}

3. Soprano Aria
●Fear keeps me from seeking omnipotent God by day (176-3)
Dein sonst hell beliebter Schein
Thy normally bright beloved radiance
{Thy beloved radiance, normally so bright,}

Soll für mich umnebelt sein,
Must for me beclouded be,
[Nebel = fog]

Weil ich nach dem Meister frage,
While I for the master ask,
{While I seek the master,}

Denn ich scheue mich bei Tage.
For I am-fearful by day.

Niemand kann die Wunder tun,
No-one can these wonders do,
{No human could do such wonders,}

Denn sein Allmacht und sein Wesen,
For his omnipotence, and his nature,
{For his almighty power, and his nature,}

Scheint, ist göttlich auserlesen,
It-would-seem, are divinely chosen,

Gottes Geist muß auf ihm ruhn.
God's Spirit must upon him be-resting.
{God's Spirit must be resting upon him.}

4. Bass Recit.
●Fear keeps me from seeking God openly; yet I believe (176-4)
So wundre dich, o Meister, nicht,
So wonder - , O master, not
{So do not wonder, O master,}

come to him by night, came bringing a mixture of myrrh and aloes, about a hundred pounds' weight.
Jn. 7:13. For fear of the Jews no one spoke openly of [Jesus].
Jn. 12:42. Many even of the authorities believed in [Jesus], but for fear of the Pharisees they did not confess it...
2 Tim. 1:8. Do not be ashamed...of testifying to our Lord...
1 Thess. 5:4-5, 8. You are not in darkness, brethren...For you are all sons of light and sons of the day; we are not of the night or of darkness...we belong to the day...
Josh. 10:12-14. ...Joshua [spoke] to the Lord in the day when the Lord gave the Amorites over to the men of Israel; and he said in the sight of Israel, "Sun, stand thou still at Gibeon, and thou Moon in the valley of Aijalon." And the sun stood still, and the moon stayed, until the nation took vengeance on their enemies...The sun stayed in the midst of heaven, and did not hasten to go down for about a whole day. There has been no day like it before or since, when the Lord hearkened to the voice of a man; for the Lord fought for Israel. (Also Sirach 46:4.)

2 Cor. 4:3-4, 6. Even if our gospel is veiled, it is veiled only to those who are perishing. In their case the god of this world has blinded the minds of the unbelievers, to keep them from seeing the light of the gospel of the glory of Christ, who is the likeness of God...For it is the God who said, "Let light shine out of darkness," who has shone in our hearts to give the light of the knowledge of the glory of God in the face of Christ. (Also Mal. 4:2, Is. 9:2, 60:1, 3, 19.)
1 Thess. 5:5-8. For you are all sons of light and sons of the day; we are not of the night or of darkness. So then let us not sleep, as others do, but let us keep awake and be sober. For those who sleep sleep at night, and those who get drunk are drunk at night. But, since we belong to the day, let us be sober, and put on the breastplate of faith and love, and for a helmet the hope of salvation.
Mt. 10:32-33 [Christ]: Every one who acknowledges me before men, I also will acknowledge before my Father who is in heaven; but whoever denies me before men, I also will deny before my Father who is in heaven. (Also Lk. 12:8-9.)
2 Tim. 2:12. If we endure, we shall also reign with him; if we deny him, he also will deny us.
*Jn. 3:1-3. Now there was a man of the Pharisees, named Nicodemus, a ruler of the Jews. This man came to Jesus by night and said to him, "Rabbi, we know that you are a teacher come from God; for no one can do these signs that you do, unless God is with him."
Jn. 2:23. ...Many believed in [Jesus'] name when they saw the signs which he did. (Also Jn. 7:31, 11:45.)
Jn. 20:30-31. Now Jesus did many other signs in the presence of the disciples, which are not written in this book; but these are written that you may believe that Jesus is the Christ, the Son of God, and that believing you may have life in his name.

*Jn. 3:1-2. ...Nicodemus, a ruler of the Jews...came to Jesus by night...
Jn. 20:19. On the evening of [the first day after Christ's resurrection]...the doors being shut where the disciples were, for fear of the Jews...

Warum ich dich bei Nacht ausfrage!
Why   I   thee by night do-seek!
{Why I seek thee by night!}

Ich fürchte, daß bei Tage
I   fear,   that by day

Mein Ohnmacht   nicht bestehen   kann.
My powerlessness (will) not to-stand-the-test be-able.
{My powerlessness will not be able to stand the test.}

Doch tröst ich mich,
Yet comfort I myself,
{Yet I comfort myself that}

du   nimmst   mein Herz und Geist
thou dost-admit-and-accept my heart and spirit

Zum Leben auf und an,
Unto life   - - -,
[aufnehmen = to admit, annehmen = to accept]

Weil alle, die nur an dich glauben, nicht verloren werden.
For all, who just in thee believe, not   lost   shall-be.
{For all who will just believe in thee, shall not perish.}

5. Alto Aria
●Courage! God promises eternal life by faith (176-5)
Ermuntert euch,   furchtsam und schüchterne Sinne,
Rouse   yourselves, (O) fearful and   timid   faculties,

Erholet euch, höret, was Jesus verspricht:
Be-renewed; hear, what Jesus promises:

Daß ich durch den Glauben den Himmel gewinne.
That I through - faith - heaven obtain.
{That I shall obtain heaven by faith.}

Wenn die Verheißung erfüllend geschicht,
When the promise (fulfillment) (achieves),
{When the promise is finally fulfilled,}

Werd ich dort oben
Shall I   up-there

Mit   Danken   und Loben
With giving-of-thanks and extolling

Vater, Sohn und Heilgen Geist
Father, Son, and   Holy Ghost

Mt. 26:41 [Christ]: ...The spirit indeed is willing, but the flesh is weak. (Also Mk. 14:38.)
Rom. 7:15, 18–20, 24–25. I do not understand my own actions. For I do not do what I want, but I do the very thing I hate...For I know that nothing good dwells within me, that is, in my flesh. I can will what is right, but I cannot do it. For I do not do the good I want, but the evil I do not want is what I do. Now if I do what I do not want, it is no longer I that do it, but sin which dwells within me...Wretched man that I am! Who will deliver me from this body of death? Thanks be to God through Jesus Christ our Lord!...
Mk. 10:24, 26–27. ...Jesus said to [his disciples], "Children, how hard it is to enter the kingdom of God!" ...And they were exceedingly astonished, and said to him, "Then who can be saved?" Jesus looked at them and said, "With men it is impossible, but not with God; for all things are possible with God." (Also Mt. 19:23–26, Lk. 18:24–27.)
Jn. 6:35, 37. Jesus said to them, "...All that the Father gives me will come to me; and him who comes to me I will not cast out."
Mk. 5:36. ...Jesus said..."Do not fear, only believe." (Also Lk. 8:50.)
Jn. 3:16. For God so loved the world that he gave his only Son, that whoever believes in him should not perish (Luther: verloren werden) but have eternal life.

Jn. 12:42. Many even of the authorities believed in [Jesus], but for fear of the Pharisees they did not confess it...
Rev. 3:2 [Christ]: Awake, and strengthen what remains and is on the point of death, for I have not found your works perfect...
Is. 35:3–4. Strengthen the weak hands, and make firm the feeble knees. Say to those who are of a fearful heart, "Be strong, fear not!..." (Also Heb. 12:12–13.)
Lk. 8:50 [Christ]: ...Do not fear; only believe...
Lk. 22:32 [Christ]: I have prayed for you that your faith may not fail...
*Jn. 3:14–15 [Christ]: As Moses lifted up the serpent in the wilderness, so must the Son of man be lifted up, that whoever believes in him may have eternal life.
Jn. 3:16 [Christ]: For God so loved the world that he gave his only Son, that whoever believes in him should not perish but have eternal life.
Rom. 5:1–2. Therefore, since we are justified by faith, we have peace with God through our Lord Jesus Christ. Through him we have obtained access to this grace in which we stand, and we rejoice in our hope of sharing the glory of God.
Jude 1:24–25. To him who is able to keep you from falling and to present you without blemish before the presence of his glory with rejoicing, to the only God, our Savior through Jesus Christ our Lord, be glory, majesty, dominion, and authority, before all time and now and for ever. Amen.
Rev. 5:11–13. Then [in my vision] I looked, and I heard around the throne and the living creatures and the elders the voice of many angels, numbering myriads of myriads and thousands of thousands, saying with a loud voice, "Worthy is the Lamb who was slain, to receive power and wealth and wisdom and might and honor and glory and blessing!" And I heard every creature in heaven and on earth and

Preisen, der dreieinig heißt.
Praise, who triune is-called.
{Up there in heaven I shall praise Father, Son, and Holy Ghost—
who is called the triune God—with giving of thanks and extolling.}

6. Chorale
●Kingdom of heaven sought: there triune God praised (176–6)
Auf daß wir also allzugleich
So that we thus altogether
{Our goal is that we thus altogether}

Zur Himmelspforten dringen
To-the gates-of-heaven may-press

Und dermaleinst in deinem Reich
And hereafter in thy kingdom

Ohn alles Ende singen,
Without - end (may) sing,

Daß du alleine König seist,
That thou alone king art,
{That thou alone art king,}

Hoch über alle Götter,
High above all gods,

Gott Vater, Sohn und Heilger Geist,
God (the) Father, Son and Holy Ghost,

Der Frommen Schutz und Retter,
Of godly-men (the) refuge and Savior,

Ein Wesen, drei Personen.
One being (in) three persons.

under the earth and in the sea, and all therein, saying, "To him who sits upon the throne and to the Lamb be blessing and honor and glory and might for ever and ever!"
Mt. 28:19. ...in the name of the Father and of the Son and of the Holy Spirit...

*Jn. 3:3, 5. Jesus answered, "Truly, truly, I say to you, unless one is born anew, he cannot see the kingdom of God...Truly, truly, I say to you, unless one is born of water and the Spirit, he cannot enter the kingdom of God."
Rev. 11:15. ...The kingdom of the world has become the kingdom of our Lord and of his Christ, and he shall reign for ever and ever.
Rev. 4:8. And the four living creatures, each of them with six wings... day and night they never cease to sing, "Holy, holy, holy, is the Lord God Almighty, who was and is and is to come!"
1 Tim. 6:15–16. ...[He is] the blessed and only Sovereign, the King of kings and Lord of lords, who alone has immortality and dwells in unapproachable light...To him be honor and eternal dominion. Amen.
Rev. 17:14. ...He is Lord of lords and King of kings, and those with him are called and chosen and faithful. (Also Rev. 19:16.)
Ps. 95:3. The Lord is a great God, and a great King above all gods. (Also Ex. 18:11, Ps. 83:18, 97:9.)
Ps. 144:1–2. Blessed be the Lord...my stronghold (Luther: Schutz) and my deliverer (Luther: Erretter)... (Also Ps. 18:2.)
Ex. 15:13. [O Lord,] thou hast led in thy steadfast love the people whom thou hast redeemed, thou hast guided them by thy strength to thy holy abode. (Also Lk. 1:68.)
*Jn. 3:5, 13, 16. ...Unless one is born of water and the **Spirit**, he cannot enter the kingdom of God...No one has ascended into heaven but he who descended from heaven, the Son of man...**God** so loved the world that he gave his only **Son**... [Trinity = God, Son, and Spirit]
Mt. 28:19. ...in the name of the Father and of the Son and of the Holy Spirit...

BWV 177
Ich ruf zu dir, Herr Jesu Christ
(NBA I/17; BC A103)

4. S. after Trinity (BWV 185, 24, 177)
*Rom. 8:18–23 (All creation eagerly longs for the revealing of the sons of God)
*Lk. 6:36–42 (Sermon on the mount: Be merciful, do not judge)
Librettist: Chorale (Johann Agricola)

1. Chorus (Chorale Vs. 1) (See also 185–6.)
●Prayer for grace to keep true faith of God's Word (177–1)
Ich ruf zu dir, Herr Jesu Christ,
I cry to thee, Lord Jesus Christ,

Ich bitt, erhör mein Klagen,
I ask, (please) hear my crying,

Ps. 27:7–9. Hear, O Lord, when I cry aloud, be gracious to me and answer me! Thou hast said, "Seek ye my face." My heart says to thee, "Thy face, Lord, do I seek." Hide not thy face from me. Turn not thy servant away in anger, thou who hast been my help. Cast me not off, forsake me not, O God of my salvation! (Also Ps. 4:1, 17:6, 28:2, 102:1–2.)
Heb. 4:16. Let us...with confidence draw near to the throne of grace, that we may receive mercy and find grace to help in time of need.
Rev. 14:12. Here is a call for the endurance of the saints, those who keep the commandments of God and the faith of Jesus.
Heb. 10:23, 38–39. Let us hold fast the confession of our hope without wavering, for he who promised is faithful...But my righteous one shall live by faith, and if he shrinks back, my soul has no pleasure in him. But we are not of those who shrink back and are destroyed, but of those who have faith and keep their souls.

Verleih mir Gnad zu dieser   Frist,
Grant me grace for this period-of-time,

Laß mich doch nicht verzagen;
Let me indeed not   despair;

Den rechten Glauben, Herr, ich mein,
The   true   faith,   Lord, I mean,

Den wollest du mir geben,
That wouldst thou to-me give,
{Wouldst thou give that to me,}

Dir   zu leben,
For-thee to live,
{To live for thee,}

Mein'm Nächsten nütz zu sein,
To-my neighbor of-service to be,
{To be of service to my neighbor,}

Dein Wort zu halten eben.
Thy Word to keep (thus).
{And thus to keep thy Word.}

2. Alto Aria (Chorale Vs. 2)
● Prayer for hope in death; not relying on good works (177-2)
Ich bitt noch mehr, o Herre Gott,
I ask yet more, O Lord God,

Du kannst es mir wohl geben:
Thou canst it to-me indeed give:
{Thou canst indeed give it to me:}

Daß ich werd nimmermehr zu Spott,
That I be-brought nevermore to scorn,
{That I nevermore be brought to scorn;}

Die Hoffnung gib   daneben,
(And) hope give (to me) therewith,
{And give me hope also,}

Voraus, wenn ich muß   hier davon,
In-advance, when I must (from) here (depart),
{In advance, when I must depart from here,}

Daß ich dir mög vertrauen
That I thee might trust
{That I might trust thee}

Und nicht bauen
And not build

Auf alles mein Tun,
On all   my doing,
{Upon any of my works,}

Jms. 2:14–17. What does it profit, my brethren, if a man says he has faith but has not works? Can his faith save him? If a brother or sister is ill-clad and in lack of daily food, and one of you says to them, "Go in peace, be warmed and filled," without giving them the things needed for the body, what does it profit? So faith by itself, if it has no works, is dead.
Jms. 1:27. Religion that is pure and undefiled before God and the Father is this: to visit orphans and widows in their affliction, and to keep oneself unstained from the world.
Rom. 14:7–8. None of us lives to himself... If we live, we live to the Lord...
Mt. 22:35–40. ...A lawyer, asked [Jesus] a question, to test him. "Teacher, which is the great commandment in the law?" And he said to him, "You shall love the Lord your God with all your heart, and with all your soul, and with all your mind. This is the great and first commandment. And a second is like it, You shall love your neighbor as yourself. On these two commandments depend all the law and the prophets." (Also Mk. 12:30–31, Lk. 10:27, Deut. 6:5, Lev. 19:18.)
Jn. 14:23–24. Jesus [said], "If a man loves me, he will keep my word, and my Father will love him, and we will come to him and make our home with him. He who does not love me does not keep my words; and the word which you hear is not mine but the Father's who sent me." (Also Rev. 3:10.)
Lk. 11:28. [Jesus] said, "Blessed...are those who hear the word of God and keep it!"

Ps. 119:116. [O Lord,] uphold me according to thy promise, that I may live, and let me not be put to shame in my hope!
Is. 45:17. ...You shall not be put to shame or confounded (Luther: noch zu Spott werden) to all eternity.
Ps. 25:1–2. To thee, O Lord, I lift up soul, O my God, in thee I trust, let me not be put to shame... (Also Ps. 25:20, 31:1, 17, 71:1, 119:6, 31, Is. 49:23, 50:7, 54:4.)
Rom. 5:2. Through [Christ] we have obtained access to this grace in which we stand, and we rejoice in our hope of sharing the glory of God.
Gal. 5:5. ...By faith, we wait for the hope of righteousness.
Phil. 3:8–9. For [Christ's] sake I have suffered the loss of all things, and count them as refuse, in order that I may gain Christ and be found in him, not having a righteousness of my own, based on law, but that which is through faith in Christ, the righteousness from God that depends on faith. (Also Tit. 3:5.)
Jude 1:20. ...Beloved, build yourselves up on your most holy faith... (Also Col. 2:6–7, 1 Thess. 5:11.)
Mt. 7:26 [Christ]: Every one who hears these words of mine and does not do them will be like a foolish man who built his house upon the sand.
1 Jn. 3:23. This is [God's] commandment, that we should believe in the name of his Son Jesus Christ and love one another, just as he commanded us.
Gal. 2:16. ...Know that a man is not justified by works of the law, because by works of the law shall no one be justified. Eph. 2:8–9. For by grace you have been saved through faith ...it is the gift of God—not because of works, lest any man should boast. (Also Gal. 3:11.)
Rom. 3:20, 27–28. No human being will be justified in [God's] sight by works of the law...Then what becomes of our boasting? It is excluded.

Sonst wird mich's ewig reuen.
Or-else will (I-it) ever regret.
else I will ever regret it.}

3. Soprano Aria (Chorale Vs. 3)
●Prayer for forgiving spirit & Word's nourishment (177-3)
Verleih, daß ich aus   Herzensgrund
Grant,   that   I from (the) bottom-of-my-heart

Mein' Feinden mög vergeben,
My   foes   might   forgive,
{Grant that I might forgive my foes from the bottom of my heart,}

Verzeih mir auch zu dieser Stund,
Forgive me   also   at   this   hour,

Gib mir ein neues Leben;
Give me   a   new   life;

Dein Wort mein Speis laß allweg sein,
Thy Word my   food let always be,
{Let thy Word be my food alway,}

Damit   mein Seel zu nähren,
Therewith my   soul to nourish,
{To nourish my soul therewith,}

Mich zu wehren,
Me   to defend,
{To defend me}

Wenn Unglück   geht daher,
When misfortune (comes) along,

Das mich bald möcht   abkehren.
Which me easily might (cause to) turn-away.
{Which might easily cause me me to turn away from thee.}

4. Tenor Aria (Chorale Vs. 4)
●Prayer for constancy; ensured by grace, not works (177-4)
Laß mich kein Lust noch Furcht von dir
Let me   no pleasure nor   fear   from thee

In dieser Welt abwenden.
In this world divert.
{Let no pleasure or fear divert me from thee in this world.}

On what principle? On the principle of works? No, but on the principle of faith. For...a man is justified by faith apart from works of law.
Rom. 11:6. If it is by grace, it is no longer on the basis of works; otherwise grace would no longer be grace.

*****Lk. 6:36–37 [Christ]:** Be merciful, even as your Father is merciful. Judge not, and you will not be judged; condemn not, and you will not be condemned; forgive and you will be forgiven.
Mt. 6:15 [Christ]: If you do not forgive men their trespasses, neither will your Father forgive your trespasses. (Also Mt. 5:7, Mt. 18:34–35, Mk. 11:26, Jms. 2:13.)
Eph. 4:32. Be kind to one another, tenderhearted, forgiving one another, as God in Christ forgave you.
1 Jn. 1:8–9. If we say we have no sin, we deceive ourselves, and the truth is not in us. If we confess our sins, [God] is faithful and just, and will forgive our sins and cleanse us from all unrighteousness.
Mt. 6:12. [O Lord,] forgive us our debts, as we also have forgiven our debtors. (Also Lk. 11:4.)
Eph. 1:7–8. In [Christ] we have redemption through his blood, the forgiveness of our trespasses, according to the riches of his grace which he lavished upon us. (Also Acts 10:43.)
2 Cor. 5:17. Therefore, if any one is in Christ, he is a new creation; the old has passed away, behold, the new has come.
Jn. 5:21 [Christ]: As the Father raises the dead and gives them life, so also the Son gives life to whom he will.
Jn. 5:24 [Christ]: Truly, truly, I say to you, he who hears my word and believes him who sent me, has eternal life; he does not come into judgment, but has passed from death to life.
Mt. 4:4 [Christ]: ...It is written, "Man shall not live by bread alone, but by every word that proceeds from the mouth of God." (See Deut. 8:3, also Lk. 4:4.)
Jer. 15:16. [O Lord,] thy words were found, and I ate them (Luther: Indes enthalt uns dein Wort wenn wirs kriegen; later version has: Dein Wort ward meine Speise da ich's empfing)...
Acts 20:32. ...I commend you to God and to the word of his grace, which is able to build you up... (Also Heb. 5:12–14.)
Mk. 4:16–17 [Christ]: When [those who have no root in themselves] hear the word [they] immediately receive it with joy... They...endure for a while; then when tribulation or persecution arises on account of the word, immediately they fall away. (Also Lk. 18:13.)
Ps. 119:11. [O Lord,] I have laid up thy word in my heart, that I might not sin against thee.

Josh. 22:29. Far be it from us that we should rebel against the Lord, and turn away this day from following the Lord...
1 Jn. 2:15–17. Do not love the world or the things in the world. If any one loves the world, love for the Father is not in him. For all that is in the world, the lust of the flesh (Luther: Fleisches Lust) and the lust of the eyes (Luther: Augen Lust) and the pride of life, is not of the Father but is of the world. And the world passes away, and the lust of it; but he who does the will of God abides for ever. (Also Jms. 4:4.)
2 Tim. 4:10. Demas, in love with this present world, has deserted me...

Beständigsein ans End gib mir,
Constancy   until-the end give me,
{Give me constancy until the end,}

Du   hast's allein in   Händen;
Thou dost-hold-it alone in (thy) hands;
{Thou alone dost have the power;}

Und   wem   du's gibst,
And to-whomever thou-it dost-give,
{And to whomever thou dost give it,}

der hat's   umsonst:
he receives-it free-of-charge:

Es   kann niemand ererben
(Now) can   no-one   inherit
{For no one can inherit}

Noch erwerben
Nor   acquire

Durch Werke deine Gnad,
Through works   thy   grace,
{Thy grace—}

Die uns errett' vom Sterben.
Which us does-deliver from dying.
{Which delivers us from death—by good works.}

5. Chorale (Vs. 5)
●Prayer for help & protection in spiritual battle (177–5)
Ich lieg im Streit und   widerstreb,
I   lie amidst combat and (try-to) resist,
{I find myself in the midst of combat and try to resist,}

Hilf, o Herr Christ, dem Schwachen!
Help, O Lord Christ, (this) weak-one!

An deiner Gnad allein ich kleb,
To thy   grace alone I adhere,
{To thy grace alone I cling,}

Du   kannst mich stärker machen.
Thou canst   me stronger make.
{Thou canst make me stronger.}

Kömmt nun Anfechtung, Herr, so wehr,
Comes now   trial,   Lord, then restrain (it),
{And if trial should come, then Lord restrain it,}

Mk. 4:17 [Christ]: [Those who] have no root in themselves...endure for a while; then when tribulation or persecution arises on account of the word, immediately they fall away. (Also Lk. 18:13.)

Jude 1:24–25. Now to him who is able to keep you from falling and to present you without blemish before the presence of his glory with rejoicing, to the only God, our Savior through Jesus Christ our Lord, be glory...

Jn. 10:27–28 [Christ]: My sheep hear my voice, and I know them, and they follow me; and I give them eternal life, and they shall never perish, and no one shall snatch them out of my hand.

Col. 1:23. ...Continue in the faith, stable and steadfast, not shifting from the hope of the gospel which you heard...

Heb. 10:23. Let us hold fast the confession of our hope without wavering, for he who promised is faithful.

Mt. 10:22 [Christ]: ...He who endures to the end will be saved. (Also Mt. 24:13, Mk. 13:13, Lk. 21:19.)

Rev. 21:6 [God]: ...To the thirsty I will give from the fountain of the water of life without payment (Luther: umsonst). (Also Is. 55:1.)

Rom. 6:23. The wages of sin is death, but the free gift of God is eternal life in Christ Jesus our Lord.

Eph. 2:8–9. By grace you have been saved through faith; and this is not your own doing, it is the gift of God—not because of works, lest any man should boast.

Gal. 2:16. ...Know that a man is not justified by works of the law... because by works of the law shall no one be justified. (Also Rom. 3:20, 27–28, Rom. 5:15–17, 11:6.)

Gal. 3:10–11. All who rely on works of the law are under a curse; for it is written, "Cursed be every one who does not abide by all things written in the book of the law, and do them." Now it is evident that no man is justified before God by the law; for "He who through faith is righteous shall live."

Ps. 35:10. ...O Lord, who is like thee, thou who deliverest the weak from him who is too strong for him... (Also Ps. 18:17.)

Eph. 6:11–12. Put on the whole armor of God, that you may be able to stand against the wiles of the devil. For we are not contending against flesh and blood, but against the principalities, against the powers, against the world rulers of this present darkness, against the spiritual hosts of wickedness in the heavenly places. (Also 1 Pet. 5:8, 2 Cor. 10:3–4.)

Mt. 26:41 [Christ]: Watch and pray that you may not enter into temptation (Luther: Anfechtung); the spirit indeed is willing, but the flesh is weak. (Also Mk. 14:38, Lk. 8:13, 22:40, 46.)

Lk. 8:13 [Christ]: ...When [some] hear the word, [they] receive it with joy; but these have no root, they believe for a while and in time of temptation (Luther: Anfechtung) fall away.

Jms. 1:2–4, 12. Count it all joy, my brethren, when you meet various trials (Luther: Anfechtung), for you know that the testing of your faith produces steadfastness. And let steadfastness have its full effect, that you may be perfect and complete, lacking in nothing...Blessed is the man who endures trial (Luther: Anfechtung erduldet), for when he has stood the test he will receive the crown of life which God has promised to those who love him.

Daß sie mich nicht umstoßen.
That it me not overthrow.
{That it might not bring me down.}

Du kannst maßen,
Thou canst measure (it),

Daß mir's nicht bring Gefahr;
That it-to-me not bring peril;
{That it not bring peril to me;}

Ich weiß, du wirst's nicht lassen.
I know, thou wilt-it not allow.
{I know thou wilt not allow that.}

2 Thess. 3:3. The Lord is faithful; he will strengthen you and guard you from evil. (Also Rom. 16:25, 1 Pet. 5:10.)
Heb. 12:5–7. ...My son, do not regard lightly the discipline of the Lord ...For the Lord disciplines him whom he loves, and chastises every son whom he receives.
Jer. 30:11. I am with you to save you, says the Lord...I will chasten you in just measure (Luther: züchtigen...mit Maßen)...
*Lk. 6:38 [Christ]: ...The measure (Luther: Maß) you give will be the measure you get back. (Also Mt. 7:2.)
1 Cor. 10:13. No temptation has overtaken you that is not common to man. God is faithful, and he will not let you be tempted beyond your strength, but with the temptation will also provide the way of escape, that you may be able to endure it.

BWV 178
Wo Gott der Herr nicht bei uns hält
(NBA I/18; BC A112)

8. S. after Trinity (BWV 136, 178, 45)
*Rom. 8:12–17 (All who are led by the Spirit of God are sons of God)
*Mt. 7:15–23 (Sermon on the Mount: beware of false prophets, you will know them by their fruits)
Librettist: Unknown

1. Chorus (Chorale Vs. 1)
●God's help is only sure defense against the foe (178-1)
Wo Gott der Herr nicht bei uns hält,
Where God the Lord not with us (stands),
{Where God the Lord does not stand with us,}

Wenn unsre Feinde toben,
When our foes rage,

Und er unsrer Sach nicht zufällt
And (where) he our cause (does) not (support)

Im Himmel hoch dort oben,
In heaven high - above;

Wo er Israels Schutz nicht ist
Where he Israel's refuge not is
{Where he is not Israel's refuge}

Und selber bricht der Feinde List,
And himself breaks the foe's artifice,

So ist's mit uns verloren.
There is-it with (our-cause) lost.
{There our cause is lost.}

2. Alto: Chorale (Vs. 2) **and Recit.**
●Foe's plots will fail; God will protect us (178-2)
Was Menschenkraft und -witz anfäht,
What human-power and wit contrives,

Ps. 124:1–8. If it had not been the Lord who was on our side, let Israel now say—if it had not been the Lord who was on our side, when men rose up against us, then they would have swallowed us up alive, when their anger was kindled against us; then the flood would have swept us away, the torrent would have gone over us; then over us would have gone the raging waters. Blessed be the Lord, who has not given us as prey to their teeth! We have escaped as a bird from the snare of the fowlers; the snare is broken, and we have escaped! Our help is in the name of the Lord, who made heaven and earth.
Ps. 74:22–23. Arise, O God, plead thy cause (Luther: Sache); remember how the impious scoff at thee all day! Do not forget the clamor of thy foes, the uproar of thy adversaries which goes up continually!
Lam. 3:58. Thou hast taken up my cause (Luther: führe du die Sache meiner Seele), O Lord, thou hast redeemed my life.
Ps. 56:1–4. Be gracious to me, O God, for men trample upon me; all day long foemen oppress me; my enemies trample upon me all day long, for many fight against me proudly. When I am afraid, I put my trust in thee. In God, whose word I praise, in God I trust without a fear. What can flesh do to me? (Also Is. 12:2.)
Ps. 94:17. If the Lord had not been my help, my soul would soon have dwelt in the land of silence.
Ps. 46:7/11. The Lord of hosts is with us; the God of Jacob is our refuge (Luther: Schutz). (Also Ps. 18:2, 11, 48:3, 59:9, 17, 94:22.)

Ps. 31:13. Yea, I hear the whispering of many—terror on every side!— as they scheme together against me, as they plot to take my life.
Ps. 118:6–7. With the Lord on my side I do not fear. What can man

Soll uns billig nicht schrecken;
Shall us in-no-wise frighten;

Denn Gott der Höchste steht uns bei
For God the Most-High stands us by
{For God the Most High stands with us}

Und machet uns von ihren Stricken frei.
And sets us from their snares free.
{And frees us from their snares.}

Er sitzet an der höchsten Stätt,
He sits in the highest place,

Er wird ihrn Rat aufdecken.
And will their counsel expose.
{And will expose their counsel.}

Die Gott im Glauben fest umfassen,
Those-who God in faith firmly do-embrace,
{Those who firmly embrace God in faith,}

Will er niemals versäumen noch verlassen;
Will he never fail nor forsake;

Er stürzet der Verkehrten Rat
He overthrows the perverted-ones' counsel
{He overthrows the cousel of the wicked}

Und hindert ihre böse Tat.
And thwarts their evil action.

Wenn sie's aufs Klügste greifen an,
When they most-cunningly attack,

Auf Schlangenlist und falsche Ränke sinnen,
With serpent's-craftiness and deceitful intrigues do-plot,

Der Bosheit Endzweck zu gewinnen;
(Their) wickedness' goal to achieve;
{To achieve the goal of their wickedness;}

So geht doch Gott ein ander Bahn:
Then pursues indeed God an-other course:
{Then God indeed pursues another course:}

Er führt die Seinigen mit starker Hand,
He leads - his-own with powerful hand,

do to me? The Lord is on my side to help me... (Also Ps. 56:11, Rom. 8:31, 2 Cor. 2:14.)

Ps. 27:1, 3. The Lord is my light and my salvation; whom shall I fear? The Lord is the stronghold of my life; of whom shall I be afraid?... Though a host encamp against me, my heart shall not fear; though war arise against me, yet I will be confident.

Ps. 54:4. Behold, God is my helper (Luther: Gott steht mir bei); the Lord is the upholder of my life.

Ps. 140:5. Arrogant men have hidden a trap (Luther: Stricke) for me, and with cords they have spread a net, by the wayside they have set snares for me. (Also Ps. 56:5–6, 59:3–4, 124:7.)

Ps. 124:7–8. We have escaped as a bird from the snare of the fowlers; the snare is broken, and we have escaped!

Ps. 11:4–5. The Lord is in his holy temple, the Lord's throne is in heaven; his eyes behold, his eyelids test, the children of men. The Lord tests the righteous and the wicked, and his soul hates him that loves violence.

Heb. 13:5–6. ...He has said, "I will never fail you nor forsake (Luther: nicht verlassen noch versäumen)." Hence we can confidently say, "The Lord is my helper, I will not be afraid; what can man do to me?" (Also Deut. 31:6, 8; Josh. 1:5.)

Job 5:12–13. He frustrates the devices (Luther: Anschläge) of the crafty (Luther: Listigen), so that their hands achieve no success. He takes the wise in their own craftiness (Luther: Listigkeit); and the schemes of the wily are brought to a quick end (Luther: und stürzt der Verkehrten Rat).

Ps. 64:1–6. Hear my voice, O God, in my complaint; preserve my life from dread of the enemy, hide me from the secret plots of the wicked, from the scheming of evildoers, who whet their tongues like swords, who aim bitter words like arrows, shooting from ambush at the blameless, shooting at him suddenly and without fear. They hold fast to their evil purpose (Luther: bösen Anschlägen); they talk of laying snares (Luther: Stricke) secretly, thinking, "Who can see us? Who can search out our crimes (Luther: Schalkheit)? We have thought out a cunningly conceived plot (Luther: Ränke)."...

Ps. 27:2. When evildoers assail me, uttering slanders against me, my adversaries and foes, they shall stumble and fall.

2 Pet. 2:9. The Lord knows how to rescue the godly from trial...

Jn. 10:3–4 [Christ]: ...[The good shepherd] calls his own sheep by name and leads them out. When he has brought out all his own, he goes before them, and the sheep follow him, for they know his voice.

Mt. 2:7–9, 12–15. [When King Herod had ascertained where the King of the Jews was to be born, he] summoned the wise men secretly and ascertained from them what time the star appeared; and he sent them to Bethlehem, saying, "Go and search diligently for the child, and when you have found him bring me word, that I too may come and worship him." When they had heard the king they went their way [to Bethelehem]...And [God] warned [them] in a dream not to return to Herod, [so] they departed to their own country by another way. Now when they had departed, behold, an angel of the Lord appeared to Joseph in a dream and said, "Rise, take the child and his mother, and flee to Egypt, and remain there till I tell you; for Herod is about to search for the child, to destroy him." And he rose and took the child and his mother by night, and departed to Egypt, and remained there until the death of Herod...

Ex. 14:10, 13–16, 22. [After the Israelites had fled from Pharaoh in Egypt, he pursued them.] When Pharaoh drew near, the people of Israel lifted up their eyes, and behold, the Egyptians were marching

Durchs   Kreuzesmeer,   in das gelobte Land,
Through (the) sea-of-the-cross, into the Promised Land,

Da   wird er alles Unglück   wenden.
There will he all misfortune turn-around.
{There he will transform all misfortune.}

Es steht in seinen Händen.
It stands in his   hands' (power).

3. Bass Aria (Based on Chorale Vs. 3)
●Foes batter Christ's kingdom like waves do a ship (178-3)
Gleichwie die wilden Meereswellen
Just-as   the   wild   sea-billows

Mit Ungestüm ein Schiff zerschellen,
With turbulence a   ship do-dash-in-pieces,
{Dash a ship to pieces with their turbulence,}

So raset auch der Feinde Wut
So rages also the foe's fury
{So the fury of our foes also rages}

Und raubt das beste   Seelengut.
And plunders the best possessions-of-soul.
{And plunders the most precious spiritual treasure.}

Sie wollen Satans Reich erweitern,
They desire Satan's kingdom to-expand,
{They seek to expand Satan's kingdom,}

Und Christi Schifflein soll zerscheitern.
And Christ's little-ship must founder.
{And to make Christ's little ship founder.}

4. Chorale: Tenor (Vs. 4)
●Foes seek our blood but call themselves Christians (178-4)
Sie   stellen   uns wie Ketzern nach,
They lie-in-wait (for) us like heretics   - ,

Nach unserm Blut sie trachten;
For   our blood they strive;
{They strive for our blood;}

Noch rühmen sie   sich   Christen auch,
Yet   pride they themselves (on being) Christians, too,
{Yet they pride themselves on also being Christians,}

after them; and they were in great fear...And Moses said to the people, "Fear not, stand firm, and see the salvation of the Lord...The Lord will fight for you, and you have only to be still." The Lord said to Moses, "...Lift up your rod, and stretch out your hand over the sea and divide it, that the people of Israel may go on dry ground through the sea."...And the people of Israel went into the midst of the sea on dry ground, the waters being a wall to them on their right hand and on their left. (Also Ps. 136:10–24.)
Ps. 10:14. [O Lord,] thou dost see; yea thou dost note trouble and vexation, that thou mayest take it into thy hands (Luther: es steht in deinen Händen)...

Ps. 124:2–5. If it had not been the Lord who was on our side, when men rose up against us, then then they would have swallowed us up alive, when their anger was kindled against us; then the flood would have swept us away, the torrent would have gone over us; then over us would have gone the raging waters.
Mt. 8:23–25. When [Jesus] got into the boat, his disciples followed him. And behold, there arose a great storm on the sea, so that the boat was being swamped by the waves; but he was asleep. And they went and woke him, saying, "Save, Lord; we are perishing." (Also Mk. 4:35–38.)
Ps. 69:1–2, 15. Save me, O God! For the waters have come up to my neck. I sink in deep mire, where there is no foothold; I have come into deep waters, and the flood sweeps over me...Let not the flood sweep over me, or the deep swallow me up, or the pit close its mouth over me. (Also Ps. 18:16.)
Ps. 144:7. [O Lord,] stretch forth thy hand from on high, rescue me and deliver me from the many waters, from the hand of aliens.
*Mt. 7:15 [Christ]: Beware of false prophets, who come to you in sheep's clothing but inwardly are ravenous wolves.
Phil. 3:18. Many, of whom I have often told you and now tell you even with tears, live as enemies of the cross of Christ. Jude 1:12–13. ... These are..wild waves of the sea, casting up the foam of their own shame...
Jn. 8:44. [Christ said to those who opposed him,] "You are of your father the devil, and your will is to do your father's desires..."

Ps. 59:2–3. [O Lord,] save me from bloodthirsty men. For, lo, they lie in wait for my life...
2 Pet. 2:1–3. ...There will be false teachers among you, who will secretly bring in destructive heresies, even denying the Master who bought them, bringing upon themselves swift destruction. And many will follow their licentiousness, and because of them the way of truth will be reviled. And in their greed they will exploit you with false words; from of old their condemnation has not been idle, and their destruction has not been asleep.
Tit. 1:16. They profess to know God, but they deny him by their deeds...
*Mt. 7:15–23 [Christ]: Beware of false prophets, who come to you in sheep's clothing but inwardly are ravenous wolves. You will know them by their fruits. Are grapes gathered from thorns, or figs from

Die Gott allein   groß achten.
Who God alone (as) great regard.
{Who regard God alone as great.}

Ach Gott, der teure Name dein
Ah   God, the precious name of-thine
{Ah God, thy precious name}

Muß ihrer Schalkheit Deckel sein.
Must their villainy's cover be.
{Is made the cover for their villainy.}

Du wirst einmal aufwachen.
(But) thou shalt one-day awaken.

5. Chorale (Vs. 5) and A.T.B. Recits.
●Foes like a lion; champion of Judah destroys them (178-5)
Auf sperren sie den Rachen weit,
   Open   they (their) jaws   wide,
   {They open their jaws wide,}

Bass:
Nach Löwenart mit brüllendem Getöne;
In   lion-manner with roaring   noise;
{Like lions with roaring noise;}

Sie fletschen ihre Mörderzähne
They bare   their murderous-teeth

Und wollen uns verschlingen
And would   us   devour

Tenor:
Jedoch,
Nevertheless,

Lob   und Dank   sei Gott allezeit;
Praise and thanks be-to God alway;

Tenor:
Der   Held aus Juda schützt uns noch,
The   champion of Judah protects us still,

Es   wird ihn' nicht gelingen.
(Now) will (they) not succeed.
{They will not succeed.}

Alto:
Sie werden wie die Spreu vergehn,
They will   like - chaff vanish,
{They will vanish like chaff,}

thistles? So, every sound tree bears good fruit, but the bad tree bears evil fruit. A sound tree cannot bear evil fruit, nor can a bad tree bear good fruit. Every tree that does not bear good fruit is cut down and thrown into the fire. Thus you will know them by their fruits. Not every one who says to me, "Lord, Lord," shall enter the kingdom of heaven, but he who does the will of my Father who is in heaven. On that day many will say to me, "Lord, Lord, did we not prophesy in your name, and cast out demons in your name, and do many mighty works in your name?" And then will I declare to them, "I never knew you; depart from me, you evildoers."
2 Chron. 36:16. [Those who were unfaithful to God] kept mocking the messengers of God, despising his words, and scoffing at his prophets, till the wrath of the Lord rose...[and] there was no remedy.
Ps. 59:4-5. ...Rouse thyself, come to my help, and see! Thou, Lord God of hosts, art God of Israel. Awake to punish all the nations; spare none of those who treacherously plot evil.
Mt. 8:25. [The disciples] went and woke [Jesus who was asleep in the boat], saying, "Save, Lord; we are perishing."
Ps. 7:6. Arise, O Lord, in thy anger, lift thyself up against the fury of my enemies; awake, O my God; thou hast appointed a judgment. (Also Ps. 35:23, 44:23, 59:4-5, Zeph. 7:18.)

Is. 5:14. Sheol has enlarged its appetite (Luther: die Seele weit aufgesperrt; later version has: Schlund weit aufgesperrt) and opened its mouth beyond measure (Luther: Rachen aufgetan ohne alle Maß)...
Ps. 22:13, 19-21. [My enemies] open wide their mouths (Luther: Rachen) at me, like a ravening and roaring lion...But thou, O Lord, be not far off! O thou my help, hasten to my aid! Deliver my soul from the sword, my life from the power of the dog! Save me from the mouth (Luther: Rachen) of the lion, my afflicted soul from the horns of the wild oxen!
Ps. 7:1-2. O Lord my God, in thee do I take refuge; save me from all my pursuers, and deliver me, lest like a lion they rend me, dragging me away, with none to rescue. (Also Ps. 17:11-12.)
1 Pet. 5:8. Be sober, be watchful. Your adversary the devil prowls around like a roaring lion, seeking some one to devour (Luther: verschlinge).
Ps. 124:6-8. Blessed be the Lord, who has not given us as prey to their teeth! We have escaped as a bird from the snare of the fowlers; the snare is broken, and we have escaped! Our help is in the name of the Lord...
Ps. 37:12-13. The wicked plots against the righteous, and gnashes his teeth at him; but the Lord laughs at the wicked, for he sees that his day is coming.
Ezek. 34:10. Thus says the Lord God...I will rescue my sheep from their mouths, that they may not be food for them.
Rev. 5:5. Then one of the elders said to me, "Weep not; lo, the Lion of the tribe of Judah, the Root of David, has conquered..." (Also Gen. 49:9.)
2 Tim. 4:17. The Lord stood by me and gave me strength...So I was rescued from the lion's mouth. (Also Dan. 6:22, Heb. 11:33.)
Ps. 35:1, 5. Contend, O Lord, with those who contend with me; fight against those who fight against me!...Let them be like chaff before the wind, with the angel of the Lord driving them on!

Wenn seine   Gläubigen wie grüne Bäume   stehn.
When his (true) believers like green   trees (shall) stand.
{When God's true believers stand like strong green trees.}

Er wird ihrn Strick zerreißen   gar
He will their cords tear-to-pieces completely
{He will tear their cords completely to pieces}

Und   stürzen ihre falsche Lahr.
And overthrow their false teaching.

Bass:
Gott wird die törichten Propheten
God will the foolish   prophets

Mit   Feuer seines Zornes töten,
With (the) fire of-his wrath   slay,
{God will slay the foolish prophets with the fire of his wrath,}

Und ihre Ketzerei verstören.
And their heresy bring-to-ruin.
{And bring their heresy to ruin.}

Sie werden's Gott nicht wehren.
They will   God not   restrain.
{They will not restrain God from doing it.}

6. Tenor Aria (Based on Chorale Vs. 6)
●Reason silenced; hope & comfort extended in Christ (178-6)
Schweig, schweig nur, taumelnde Vernunft!
Hush,   hush (then), reeling   intellect!

Sprich nicht: Die Frommen sind verlorn,
Say   not: The righteous   are   lost,
{Do not say, "The righteous are lost";}

Das Kreuz hat sie nur neu geborn.
The cross has them but born-anew.
{The cross has but born them anew.}

Denn denen, die auf Jesum hoffen,
For to-those, who on Jesus   hope,
{For to all those who hope in Jesus,}

Steht stets die Tür der Gnaden offen;
Stands ever the door of grace   open;
{The door of grace stands open;}

Und wenn sie Kreuz und Trübsal   drückt,
And when them cross and tribulation oppresses,
{And when cross and tribulation oppresses them,}

So werden sie mit Trost erquickt.
Then are they with comfort refreshed.
{Then they are refreshed with comfort.}

Hos. 13:3. They shall be like the morning mist or like the dew that goes early away, like the chaff that swirls from the threshing floor or like smoke from a window. (chaff: also Ps. 83:13, Is. 17:13, Jer. 13:24)
Ps. 1:1, 3–4. Blessed is the man who walks not in the counsel of the wicked, nor stands in the way of sinners, nor sits in the seat of scoffers ...He is like a tree planted by streams of water, that yields its fruit in its season, and its leaf does not wither. In all that he does, he prospers. The wicked are not so, but are like chaff which the wind drives away.
1 Tim. 4:1–2. Now the Spirit expressly says that in later times some will depart from the faith by giving heed to deceitful spirits and doctrines of demons, through the pretensions of liars...
*Mt. 7:15 [Christ]: Beware of false prophets, who come to you in sheep's clothing but inwardly are ravenous wolves.
Ezek. 13:3, 6. Thus says the Lord God, Woe to the foolish prophets who follow their own spirit, and have seen nothing!...They have spoken falsehood and divined a lie...
Is. 66:15. For behold, the Lord will come in fire, and his chariots like the stormwind, to render his anger in fury, and his rebuke with flames of fire. For by fire will the Lord execute judgment, and by his sword, upon all flesh; and those slain by the Lord shall be many. (Also Ps. 21:9, Is. 30:27, 30, Ezek. 21:31, Nah. 1:6, Rev. 14:10.)

Mk. 4:38–39. But [while the storm raged, Jesus] was in the stern, asleep on the cushion; and they woke him and said to him, "Teacher, do you not care if we perish?" And he awoke and rebuked the wind, and said to the sea, "Peace! Be still!"... (Luther: Schweig und verstumme!)
Ps. 46:10 [God]: Be still, and know that I am God...
Phil. 4:6–7. Have no anxiety about anything, but in everything by prayer and supplication with thanksgiving let your requests be made known to God. And the peace of God, which passes all understanding (Luther: Vernunft), will keep your hearts and your minds in Christ Jesus.
Jms. 1:2–4. Count it all joy, my brethren, when you meet various trials, for you know that the testing of your faith produces steadfastness. And let steadfastness have its full effect, that you may be perfect and complete, lacking in nothing.
Jn. 12:24–25 [Christ]: Unless a grain of wheat falls into the earth and dies, it remains alone; but if it dies, it bears much fruit. He who loves his life loses it, and he who hates his life in this world will keep it for eternal life.
Mk. 8:34 [Christ]: ...If any man would come after me, let him deny himself and take up his cross and follow me. (Also Mt. 10:38, 16:24, Lk. 9:23.)
1 Pet. 1:3, 6. Blessed be the God and Father of our Lord Jesus Christ! By his great mercy we have been born anew to a living hope through the resurrection of Jesus Christ...In this you rejoice, though now for a little while you may have to suffer various trials...

7. Chorale (Vss. 7 & 8)
●Faith unwavering sought despite opposition (178–7)
Die Feind sind all in deiner Hand,
(Our) foes are all in thy hand,

Darzu all ihr Gedanken;
Therewith all of-their designs;

Ihr Anschläg sind dir, Herr, bekannt,
Their onslaughts are to-thee, (O) Lord, known,

Hilf nur, daß wir nicht wanken.
Help just, that we (might) not waver.
{Just help us not to waver.}

Vernunft wider den Glauben ficht,
Reason against - faith does-fight,
{Reason fights against belief,}

Aufs Künftge will sie trauen nicht,
For-the future would it trust not,
{It has no faith regarding the future,}

Da du wirst selber trösten.
When thou wilt thyself comfort (me).
{When thou thyself wilt comfort me.}

///

Den Himmel und auch die Erden
- Heaven and also - earth

Hast du, Herr Gott, gegründet;
Hast thou, (O) Lord God, established;

Dein Licht laß uns helle werden,
Thy light let for-us bright become,
{Let thy light become bright for us,}

Das Herz uns werd entzündet
(May) (our) heart - be kindled

In rechter Lieb des Glaubens dein,
With real love for-the faith of-thine,
{With real love for thy faith,}

Bis an das End beständig sein.
Until the end steadfast be.
{And be steadfast until the end.}

Die Welt laß immer murren.
The world let ever murmur.
{Not caring how much the world may murmur.}

Ps. 138:7. [O Lord,] ...thou dost stretch out thy hand against the wrath of my enemies, and thy right hand delivers me. (Also Ex. 15:6.)
Ps. 124:6–7. Blessed be the Lord, who has not given us as prey to their teeth! We have escaped as a bird from the snare of the fowlers; the snare is broken, and we have escaped!
Lam. 3:58, 60. Thou hast taken up my cause, O Lord, thou hast redeemed my life...Thou hast seen all their vengeance, all their devices (Luther: Gedanken) against me.
Ps. 64:5. They hold fast to their evil purpose (Luther: bösen Anschlägen); they talk of laying snares (Luther: Stricke) secretly, thinking, "Who can see us?"
Ps. 83:3. They lay crafty plans (Luther: listige Anschläge) against thy people...
Mk. 5:36 [Christ]: ...Do not fear, only believe. (Also Lk. 8:50.)
Heb. 10:23. Let us hold fast the confession of our hope without wavering (Luther: wanken), for he who promised is faithful. (Also Heb. 10:39.)
Mk. 9:24. Immediately the father of the [sick] child cried out and said, "I believe; help my unbelief!"
Jn. 20:29. Jesus said to [Thomas], "Have you believed because you have seen me? Blessed are those who have not seen and yet believe."
Rom. 8:24–25. In this hope we were saved. Now hope that is seen is not hope. For who hopes for what he sees? But if we hope for what we do not see, we wait for it with patience. (Also Heb. 11:1.)

Ps. 124:8. Our help is in the name of the Lord, who made heaven and earth.
Ps. 102:25. [O Lord,] of old thou didst lay the foundation of the earth (die Erde gegründet), and the heavens are the work of thy hands. (Also Ps. 89:11, Is. 45:18, 48:13, 51:13, Heb. 1:10.)
Is. 9:2. The people who walked in darkness have seen a great light; those who dwelt in a land of deep darkness, on them has light shined. (Also Mt. 4:16, Mal. 4:2, Is. 60:1, 3, 19.)
2 Cor. 4:6. For it is the God who said, "Let light shine out of darkness," who has shone in our hearts to give the light of the knowledge of the glory of God in the face of Christ.
Rom. 15:13. May the God of hope fill you with all joy and peace in believing...
2 Thess. 3:5. May the Lord direct your hearts to the love of God and to the steadfastness of Christ. (Also Col. 1:11.)
1 Cor. 15:58. Therefore, my beloved brethren, be steadfast, immovable, always abounding in the work of the Lord...
Mt. 10:22 [Christ]: ...He who endures to the end will be saved. (Also Mt. 24:13, Mk. 13:13, Lk. 21:19.)
Jn. 16:33 [Christ]:...In the world you have tribulation; but be of good cheer, I have overcome the world.
Jn. 15:18–19 [Christ]: If the world hates you, know that it has hated me before it hated you. If you were of the world, the world would love its own; but because you are not of the world, but I chose you out of the world, therefore the world hates you. (Also Jn. 17:14, Mt. 5:10–12, 10:24–25, 1 Jn. 3:13.)

BWV 179
Siehe zu, daß deine Gottesfurcht nicht Heuchelei sei
(NBA I/20; BC A121)

11. S. after Trinity (BWV 199, 179, 113)
*1 Cor. 15:1–10 (Paul writes of his apostleship and lists post-resurrection appearances of Jesus)
*Lk. 18:9–14 (Parable of the Pharisee and the tax collector in the temple to pray)
Librettist: Unknown

1. Chorus
●Hypocrisy warned against: Sirach (Apocrypha) 1:28 (179-1)
Siehe zu, daß deine Gottesfurcht nicht Heuchelei sei,
Take-heed, that thy piety not hypocrisy be,
{Take heed that thy piety not be hypocritical,}

und diene Gott nicht mit falschem Herzen!
and serve God not with (a) false heart!
{And do not serve God with a false heart!}

2. Tenor Recit.
●Hypocrisy plagues all Christendom (179-2)
Das heutge Christentum
- Today's Christendom

Ist leider schlecht bestellt:
Is, alas, in-a-bad-state:

Die meisten Christen in der Welt
Most-of-the Christians in the world

Sind laulichte Laodizäer,
Are lukewarm Laodiceans,

Und aufgeblasne Pharisäer,
And puffed-up Pharisees,

Die sich von außen fromm bezeigen
Who themselves outwardly pious present
{Who outwardly present themselves as pious}

Und wie ein Schilf den Kopf zur Erde beugen,
And like a reed (their) head(s) to-the earth bow,
{And bow their heads humbly to the earth like a reed;}

Im Herzen aber
In (their) hearts, however,

steckt ein stolzer Eigenruhm;
lurks a proud glorification-of-self;

Sie gehen zwar in Gottes Haus
They go, indeed, into God's house
{Indeed, they go into God's house}

Sirach (Apocrypha) 1:28–30. (= Sirach 1:34–38 of German Bible). *Do not disobey the fear of the Lord; do not approach him with a divided mind.* Be not a hypocrite in men's sight, and keep watch over your lips. Do not exalt yourself lest you fall, and thus bring dishonor upon yourself. The Lord will reveal your secrets and cast you down in the midst of the congregation, because you did not come in the fear of the Lord, and your heart was full of deceit.
Mt. 15:7–8 [Christ]: You hypocrites! Well did Isaiah prophesy of you, when he said: "This people honors me with their lips, but their heart is far from me." (See Is. 29:13.)

Ps. 12:1, 8. Help, Lord; for there is no longer any that is godly; for the faithful have vanished from among the sons of men...On every side the wicked prowl, as vileness is exalted among the sons of men.
Mt. 23:23–25 [Christ]: Woe to you, scribes and Pharisees, hypocrites! for you tithe mint and dill and cummin, and have neglected the weightier matters of the law, justice and mercy and faith; these you ought to have done, without neglecting the others. You blind guides, straining out a gnat and swallowing a camel! Woe to you, scribes and Pharisees, hypocrites! for you cleanse the outside of the cup and of the plate, but inside they are full of extortion and rapacity.
Rev. 3:14–17 [Christ]: To the angel of the church in Laodicea write: "...I know your works: you are neither cold nor hot! So, because you are lukewarm, and neither cold nor hot, I will spew you out of my mouth. For you say, I am rich, I have prospered, and I need nothing; not knowing that you are wretched, pitiable, poor, blind, and naked."
***Lk. 18:9–12.** [Jesus] also told this parable to some who trusted in themselves that they were righteous and despised others: "Two men went up into the temple to pray, one a Pharisee and the other a tax collector. The Pharisee stood and prayed thus with himself, 'God, I thank thee that I am not like other men, extortioners, unjust, adulterers, or even like this tax collector. I fast twice a week, I give tithes of all that I get...'"
Is. 58:5–6 [God]: Is such the fast that I choose, a day for a man to humble himself? Is it to bow down his head like a rush (Luther: Schilf), and to spread sackcloth and ashes under him? Will you call this a fast, and a day acceptable to the Lord? Is not this the fast that I choose: to loose the bonds of wickedness...?
Mt. 7:15–16 [Christ]: Beware of false prophets, who come to you in sheep's clothing but inwardly are ravenous wolves. You will know them by their fruits... (Also Mt. 12:33–35, Lk. 6:43–45.)

Und tun daselbst die äußerlichen Pflichten,
And perform there (their) outward duties,

Macht aber dies wohl einen Christen aus?
Makes, however, this indeed a Christian - ?
{However, does this, indeed, make a Christian?}

Nein! Heuchler können's auch verrichten!
No! Hypocrites can-this also perform!
{No! Hypocrites can also do these things!}

3. Tenor Aria
●Hypocrites outwardly beautiful but inwardly filthy (179-3)
Falscher Heuchler Ebenbild
False hypocrites' image
{The image of false hypocrites}

Können Sodomsäpfel heißen,
Could Sodom's-apples be-called,
{Is like that of Sodom's apples,}

Die mit Unflat angefüllt
Which with filth are-crammed

Und von außen herrlich gleißen.
And (yet) on-the outside splendidly glisten.

Heuchler, die von außen schön,
Hypocrites, (though) outwardly beautiful,

Können nicht vor Gott bestehn.
Can not before God stand.
{Can not stand before God.}

4. Bass Recit.
●True Christian admits his sin like the publican (179-4)
Wer so von innen wie von außen ist,
Whoever from within as from without is,
{Whoever is the same inwardly as outwardly,}

Der heißt ein wahrer Christ.
He is-called a true Christian.

So war der Zöllner in dem Tempel:
Thus was the publican in the temple:
{That is the way it was with the publican in the temple:}

Der schlug in Demut an die Brust,
He beat in humility - (his) breast,
{In humility he beat his breast,}

Mt. 6:2, 5, 16 [Christ]: Thus, when you give alms, sound no trumpet before you, as the hypocrites do in the synagogues and in the streets, that they may be praised by men...And when you pray, you must not be like the hypocrites; for they love to stand and pray in the synagogues and at the street corners, that they may be seen by men... And when you fast, do not look dismal, like the hypocrites, for they disfigure their faces that their fasting may be seen by men. Truly, I say to you, they have received their reward.

Mt. 23:25, 27-28 [Christ]: Woe to you, scribes and Pharisees, hypocrites! for you cleanse the outside of the cup and of the plate, but inside they are full of extortion and rapacity...Woe to you, scribes and Pharisees, hypocrites! for you are like whitewashed tombs, which outwardly appear beautiful, but within they are full of dead men's bones and all uncleanness (Luther: Unflats). So you also outwardly appear righteous to men, but within you are full of hypocrisy and iniquity. (Also Lk. 11:39, 44.)
Josephus IV:483-485. ...It is said that, owing to the impiety of its inhabitants, [Sodom] was consumed by thunderbolts; and in fact vestiges of the divine fire and faint traces of five cities are still visible. Still, too, may one see ashes reproduced in the fruits, which from their outward appearance would be thought edible, but on being plucked with the hand dissolve into smoke and ashes. [Translated by H. St. J. Thackeray. See also BWV 54-2, 95-2.]
Mt. 12:33-34 [Christ]: Either make the tree good, and its fruit good; or make the tree bad, and its fruit bad; for the tree is known by its fruit. You brood of vipers! how can you speak good, when you are evil?...
Mt. 7:21-23 [Christ]: Not every one who says to me, "Lord, Lord," shall enter the kingdom of heaven, but he who does the will of my Father who is in heaven. On that day many will say to me, "Lord, Lord, did we not prophesy in your name, and cast out demons in your name, and do many mighty works in your name?" And then will I declare to them, "I never knew you; depart from me, you evildoers."
*Lk. 18:14 [Christ]: I tell you, [the repentant tax collector] went down to his house justified rather than the [the self-righteous Pharisee]...

Is. 29:13 [God]: ...This people draw near with their mouth and honor me with their lips, while their hearts are far from me, and their fear of me is a commandment of men learned by rote. (Also Mt. 15:7-8.)
Mt. 23:27-28 [Christ]: ...You are like whitewashed tombs, which outwardly appear beautiful, but within they are full of dead men's bones and all uncleanness. So you also outwardly appear righteous to men, but within you are full of hypocrisy and iniquity.
*Lk. 18:9-14. [Jesus]...told this parable to some who trusted in themselves that they were righteous and despised others: "Two men went up into the temple to pray, one a Pharisee and the other a tax collector. The Pharisee stood and prayed thus with himself, 'God, I thank thee that I am not like other men, extortioners (Luther: Räuber), unjust, adulterers (Luther: Ehebrecher), or even like this tax collector. I fast twice a week, I give tithes of all that I get.' But the tax

Er legte sich nicht selbst ein heilig Wesen bei;
He ascribed - not to-himself a holy character - ;
{He did not claim to be holy;}

Und diesen stelle dir,
And this-one set-before you,

O Mensch, zum rühmlichen Exempel
O man, as (your) praiseworthy example

In deiner Buße für!
In your penitence - !
{In your penitence, set this man before you as your praiseworthy example!}

Bist du kein Räuber, Ehebrecher,
Are you no robber, adulterer,
{Even though you are no robber or adulterer,}

Kein ungerechter Ehrenschwächer,
No unjust slanderer,

Ach bilde dir doch ja nicht ein,
Ah, flatter yourself indeed not - (that)

Du seist deswegen engelrein!
You are for-that-reason angel-pure!

Bekenne Gott in Demut deine Sünden,
Confess-to God in humility your sins,
{In humility confess your sins to God,}

So kannst du Gnad und Hilfe finden!
Then can you grace and help find!
{And you will be able to find grace and help!}

5. Soprano Aria
●Prayer for mercy: I sink in the deep mire of sin! (179-5)
Liebster Gott, erbarme dich,
Dearest God, have-mercy,

Laß mir Trost und Gnad erscheinen!
Let to-me comfort and grace appear!
{Bring comfort and grace to me!}

Meine Sünden kränken mich
My sins vex me

Als ein Eiter in Gebeinen,
Like an abcess in (my) body,

Hilf mir, Jesu, Gottes Lamm,
Help me, Jesus, God's lamb,

collector, standing far off, would not even lift up his eyes to heaven, but beat his breast, saying, 'God be merciful to me a sinner!' I tell you, this man went down to his house justified rather than the other; for every one who exalts himself will be humbled, but he who humbles himself will be exalted."
Gal. 3:10. All who rely on works of the law are under a curse; for it is written, "Cursed be every one who does not abide by all things written in the book of the law, and do them."
Jms. 2:10. For whoever keeps the whole law but fails in one point has become guilty of all of it.
Rom. 3:10–12, 23. As it is written: "None is righteous, no, not one; no one understands, no one seeks for God. All have turned aside, together they have gone wrong; no one does good, not even one." ... All have sinned and fall short of the glory of God. (Also Ps. 14:1–3.)
Prov. 20:9. Who can say, "I have made my heart clean; I am pure from my sin"?
Mt. 7:3–5 [Christ]: Why do you see the speck that is in your brother's eye, but do not notice the log that is in your own eye? Or how can you say to your brother, "Let me take the speck out of your eye," when there is the log in your own eye? You hypocrite, first take the log out of your own eye, and then you will see clearly to take the speck out of your brother's eye. (Also Lk. 6:41–42.)
1 Jn. 1:8–9. If we say we have no sin, we deceive ourselves, and the truth is not in us. If we confess our sins, he is faithful and just, and will forgive our sins and cleanse us from all unrighteousness.
Heb. 4:14–16. Since then we have a great high priest who has passed through the heavens, Jesus, the Son of God, let us hold fast our confession. For we have not a high priest who is unable to sympathize with our weaknesses, but one who in every respect has been tempted as we are, yet without sin. Let us then with confidence draw near to the throne of grace, that we may receive mercy and find grace to help in time of need.

*Lk. 18:13. ...God be merciful to me a sinner!
Ps. 32:3–4. [O Lord,] when I declared not my sin, my body wasted away through my groaning all day long. For day and night thy hand was heavy upon me; my strength was dried up as by the heat of summer.
Hab. 3:16. ...My body trembles, my lips quiver at the sound; rotteness (Luther: Eiter) enters my bones...
Ps. 38:3–7. There is no soundness in my flesh because of thy indignation; there is no health in my bones because of my sin. For my iniquities have gone over my head; they weigh like a burden too heavy for me. My wounds grow foul and fester because of my foolishness, I am utterly bowed down and prostrate; all the day I go about mourning. For my loins are filled with burning, and there is no soundness in my flesh.
1 Pet. 1:18–19. You know that you were ransomed from the futile ways inherited from your fathers, not with perishable things such as silver or gold, but with the precious blood of Christ, like that of a lamb without blemish or spot.
Jn. 1:29. ...[John] saw Jesus coming toward him, and said, "Behold, the Lamb of God, who takes away the sin of the world!" (Also Jn. 1:36.)

Ich versink in tiefen Schlamm!
I sink-under in deep mire!

6. Chorale
●Prayer for mercy and lenient judgment (179-6)
Ich armer Mensch, ich armer Sünder
I poor mortal, I poor sinner,

Steh hier vor Gottes Angesicht.
Stand here before God's countenance.

Ach Gott, ach Gott, verfahr gelinder
Ah God, ah God, proceed more-leniently

Und geh nicht mit mir ins Gericht!
And go not with me into judgment!
{And do not enter into judgment with me!}

Erbarme dich, erbarme dich,
Have-mercy, have-mercy—

Gott, mein Erbarmer, über mich!
(O) God, my God-of-mercy—upon me!

Ps. 69:1-2, 15. Save me, O God! For the waters have come up to my neck. I sink in deep mire, where there is no foothold; I have come into deep waters, and the flood sweeps over me...Let not the flood sweep over me, or the deep swallow me up, or the pit close its mouth over me. (Also Ps. 18:16, 124:4-5, 144:7.)

2 Cor. 5:10. We must all appear before the judgment seat of Christ...
*Lk. 18:13. The tax collector, standing far off, would not even lift up his eyes to heaven, but beat his breast, saying, 'God be merciful to me a sinner!'
Ps. 51:1. Have mercy on me, O God, according to thy steadfast love; according to thy abundant mercy blot out my transgressions.
Ps. 38:1. O Lord, rebuke me not in thy anger, nor chasten me in thy wrath!
Ps. 143:2. Enter not into judgment with thy servant; for no man living is righteous before thee.
Ps. 130:3. If thou, O Lord, shouldst mark iniquities, Lord, who could stand!
Gal. 3:10-11. For all who rely on works of the law are under a curse; for it is written, "Cursed be every one who does not abide by all things written in the book of the law, and do them." Now it is evident that no man is justified before God by the law; for "He who through faith is righteous shall live."
Eph. 2:8-9. For by grace you have been saved through faith; and this is not your own doing, it is the gift of God—not because of works, lest any man should boast. (Also Rom. 3:20, 27-28, 11:6.)

BWV 180
Schmücke dich, o liebe Seele
(NBA I/25; BC A149)

20. S. after Trinity (BWV 162, 180, 49)
*Eph. 5:15-21 (Exhortation to walk carefully, be filled with the Spirit)
*Mt. 22:1-14 (Parable of the royal wedding feast)
Librettist: Unknown

1. Chorus (Chorale Vs. 1)
●Wedding feast: Prepare to receive Lord's invitation! (180-1)
Schmücke dich, o liebe Seele,
Adorn thyself, O dear soul,
{Put on thy finery, O dear soul,}

Laß die dunkle Sündenhöhle,
Leave the dark hollow-of-sin,

Komm ans helle Licht gegangen,
(And) come into-the bright light - ,

Fange herrlich an zu prangen;
Commence splendidly - to parade (about);
{Parade thy splendor;}

Is. 52:1. Awake, awake, put on your strength, O Zion, put on your beautiful garments (Luther: schmücke dich herrlich), O Jerusalem, the holy city...
Rev. 19:7-8. ...The marriage of the Lamb has come, and his Bride has made herself ready; it was granted her to be clothed with fine linen, bright and pure...
Is. 2:5. O house of Jacob, come, let us walk in the light of the Lord. (Also 2 Cor. 4:3-4, 6.)
*Mt. 22:1-14. Jesus spoke to [the people] in parables, saying, "The kingdom of heaven may be compared to a king who gave a marriage feast for his son, and sent his servants to call those who were invited to the marriage feast; but they would not come. Again he sent other servants, saying 'Tell those who are invited, Behold, I have made ready my dinner, my oxen and my fat calves are killed, and everything is ready; come to the marriage feast.' But they made light of it and went off, one to his farm, another to his business, while the rest seized his servants, treated them shamefully and killed them. The king was angry, and he sent his troops and destroyed those murderers and burned their city. Then he said to his servants, 'The wedding is ready, but those invited were not worthy. Go therefore to the thoroughfares,

Denn der Herr   voll   Heil   und Gnaden
For   the Lord, so-filled-with salvation and   grace

Läßt dich itzt zu Gaste laden.
Lets thee now as guest be-invited.
{Lets thee now be invited as his guest.}

Der   den Himmel kann verwalten,
He-who (all) heaven   can superintend,

Will   selbst Herberg in dir halten.
Would himself lodging with thee find.
{Would himself find lodging with thee.}

2. Tenor Aria (Based on Chorale Vs. 2)
●Savior knocks at thy heart's door; open to him! (180-2)
Ermuntre dich: dein Heiland klopft,
Rouse   thyself: thy Savior knocks;

Ach, öffne bald die Herzenspforte!
Ah,   open quickly (thy) heart's-door!
{Ah, open thy heart's door quickly!}

Ob   du gleich in entzückter Lust
Even-though thou   -   in overjoyed pleasure

Nur halb gebrochne Freudenworte
Only half   broken   words-of-joy

Zu deinem Jesu sagen mußt.
To   thy Jesus must-utter.
{Even though, in overjoyed pleasure, thou canst only utter half-broken words of joy to thy Jesus.}

3. Soprano Recit. (Based on Chorale Vs. 3) **& Chorale** (Vs. 4)
●Lord's table: Yearning for its blessings (180-3)
Wie teuer sind des heilgen Mahles Gaben!
How costly are the   holy banquet's gifts!

Sie   finden ihresgleichen nicht.
(One) finds   their-like   not.
{Their like is not to be found.}

Was   sonst die Welt
Whatever else the world

Für kostbar   hält,
As precious may-hold,

Sind   Tand und Eitelkeiten;
Are (but) trifles and vain-nothings;

Ein Gotteskind wünscht diesen Schatz zu haben
A   child-of-God wishes   this treasure to have
{A child of God desires this treasure}

and invite to the marriage feast as many as you find.' And those servants went out into the streets and gathered all whom they found, both bad and good; so the wedding hall was filled with guests. But when the king came in to look at the guests, he saw there a man who had no wedding garment; and he said to him, 'Friend, how did you get in here without a wedding garment?' And he was speechless. Then the king said to the attendants, 'Bind him hand and foot, and cast him into the outer darkness; there men will weep and gnash their teeth.' For many are called, but few are chosen." (Also Mt. 25:1–13.)
Jn. 14:23. Jesus [said], "If a man loves me, he will keep my word, and my Father will love him, and we will come to him and make our home with him." (Also Jn. 14:16–17, 21.)

Rev. 3:20 [Christ]: Behold, I stand at the door and knock; if any one hears my voice and opens the door, I will come in to him and eat with him, and he with me.
S. of S. 5:2–5 [Bride]: I slept, but my heart was awake. Hark! my beloved is knocking, "Open to me, my sister, my love, my dove, my perfect one; for my head is wet with dew, my locks with the drops of the night." I had put off my garment, how could I put it on? I had bathed my feet, how could I soil them? My beloved put his hand to the latch, and my heart was thrilled within me. I arose to open to my beloved, and my hands dripped with myrrh, my fingers with liquid myrrh, upon the handles of the bolt.
Acts 12:13–16. When [Peter] knocked at the door of the gateway [after being freed from prison by the angel], a maid named Rhoda came to answer. Recognizing Peter's voice, in her joy she did not open the gate but ran in and told that Peter was standing at the gate. They said to her, "You are mad." But she insisted that it was so. They said, "It is his angel!" But Peter continued knocking...

Mt. 26:26–28. Now as they were eating, Jesus took bread, and blessed, and broke it, and gave it to the disciples and said, "Take, eat; this is my body." And he took a cup, and when he had given thanks he gave it to them, saying, "Drink of it, all of you; for this is my blood of the covenant, which is poured out for many for the forgiveness of sins." (Also Mk. 14:22–25, Lk. 22:17–20, 1 Cor. 11:23–26.)
1 Cor. 10:16. The cup of blessing which we bless, is it not a participation in the blood of Christ? The bread which we break, is it not a participation in the body of Christ?
Phil. 3:7–11. Whatever gain I had, I counted as loss for the sake of Christ. Indeed I count everything as loss because of the surpassing worth of knowing Christ Jesus my Lord. For his sake I have suffered the loss of all things, and count them as refuse, in order that I may gain Christ and be found in him, not having a righteousness of my own, based on law, but that which is through faith in Christ, the righteousness from God that depends on faith; that I may know him and the power of his resurrection, and may share his sufferings, becoming like him in his death, that if possible I may attain the resurrection from the dead.
1 Jn. 2:15–17. Do not love the world or the things in the world. If any one loves the world, love for the Father is not in him. For all that is

Und spricht:
And says:

Chorale:
Ach, wie hungert mein Gemüte,
Ah, how hungers my disposition,
{Ah, how my disposition hungers—}

Menschenfreund, nach deiner Güte!
(O) friend-of-man— for thy kindness!

Ach, wie pfleg ich oft mit Tränen
Ah, how tend I often with tears

Mich nach dieser Kost zu sehnen!
-   For   this   fare to yearn!
{Ah, how often I tend to yearn for this fare with tears!}

Ach, wie pfleget mich zu dürsten
Ah, how tend (I) to thirst
{Ah, how I tend to thirst}

Nach dem Trank des Lebensfürsten!
For   the drink of-the Prince-of-Life!
{For the drink offered by the Prince of Life!}

Wünsche stets, daß mein Gebeine
Wishing   ever, that my   body

Sich durch Gott mit Gott vereine.
Itself through God with God might-unite.
{Through God might unite itself with God.}

4. Alto Recit. (Based on Chorale Vss. 5–6)
●Lord's table: A mystery beyond human understanding
(180–4)
Mein Herz fühlt in sich Furcht und Freude;
My heart feels within itself fear and joy;
{My heart feels fear and joy;}

Es wird die Furcht erregt,
(Now) is - fear aroused,
{Fear is aroused,}

Wenn es die Hoheit überlegt,
When it the grandeur ponders,
{When it ponders the grandeur,}

Wenn es sich nicht in das Geheimnis findet,
When it (its-way) not into that mystery finds,
{When it can not comprehend the mystery,}

Noch durch Vernunft dies hohe Werk ergründet.
Nor through reason this lofty work fathoms.
{Nor fathom this lofty work through reason.}

Nur Gottes Geist kann durch sein Wort uns lehren,
Only God's Spirit can through his Word us teach,
{Only God's Spirit can teach us through his Word,}

in the world, the lust of the flesh and the lust of the eyes and the of life, is not of the Father but is of the world. And the world passes away, and the lust of it; but he who does the will of God abides for ever. (Also Jms. 4:4.)
Mt. 6:19–21 [Christ]: Do not lay up for yourselves treasures on earth, where moth and rust consume and where thieves break in and steal, but lay up for yourselves treasures in heaven, where neither moth nor rust consumes and where thieves do not break in and steal. For where your treasure is, there will your heart be also.
Ps. 73:25. [O Lord,] whom have I in heaven but thee? And there is nothing upon earth that I desire besides thee.
Ps. 42:1–2. As a hart longs for flowing streams, so longs my soul for thee, O God. My soul thirsts for God, for the living God. When shall I come and behold the face of God?
Ps. 69:3. I am weary with my crying; my throat is parched. My eyes grow dim with waiting for my God.
Jn. 7:37–39. On the last day of the feast, the great day, Jesus stood up and proclaimed, "If any one thirst, let him come to me and drink. He who believes in me, as the scripture has said, 'Out of his heart shall flow rivers of living water.'"
Jn. 4:14 [Christ]: Whoever drinks of the water that I shall give him will never thirst; the water that I shall give him will become in him a spring of water welling up to eternal life. (Also Is. 12:3, 44:3, Rev. 7:17, 21:6, 22:17.)
1 Cor. 10:16. The cup of blessing which we bless, is it not a participation in the blood of Christ? The bread which we break, is it not a participation in the body of Christ?
1 Cor. 6:17. He who is united to the Lord becomes one spirit with him.
Eph. 5:23, 30. ...Christ is the head of the church, his body...We are members of his body. (Also 1 Cor. 6:15, 12:27.)

1 Tim. 3:16. Great indeed, we confess, is the mystery of our religion...
1 Cor. 1:23–24. ...We preach Christ crucified, a stumbling block to Jews and folly to Gentiles, but to those who are called, both Jews and Greeks, Christ the power of God and the wisdom of God.
1 Cor. 2:7. We impart a secret and hidden wisdom of God... (Also Col. 1:26–27, Eph. 2:7, 3:4–6, 9, Col. 2:2–3, 1 Pet. 1:10–12.)
Jn. 6:32–35, 41, 43–45, 47–56. Jesus...said... "Truly, truly, I say to you... my Father gives you the true bread from heaven. For the bread of God is that which comes down from heaven, and gives life to the world." They said to him, "Lord, give us this bread always." Jesus said to them, "I am the bread of life; he who comes to me shall not hunger, and he who believes in me shall never thirst."...The Jews then murmured at him, because he said, "I am the bread which came down from heaven."...Jesus answered them, "...No one can come to me unless the Father who sent me draws him; and I will raise him up at the last day." It is written in the prophets, 'And they shall all be taught by God.' Every one who has heard and learned from the Father comes to me. "Truly, truly, I say to you, he who believes has eternal life. I am the bread of life. Your fathers ate the manna in the wilderness, and they died. This is the bread which comes down from heaven, that a man may eat of it and not die. I am the living bread which came down

Wie   sich   allhier die Seelen nähren,
How themselves here those souls   feed,
{How those souls}

Die   sich   im Glauben zugeschickt.
Who themselves in   faith have-prepared.
{Who have prepared themselves in faith, feed themselves here.}

Die Freude aber wird gestärket,
 -    Joy, however, is strengthened,

Wenn sie des Heilands Herz erblickt
When it the Savior's heart beholds
{When it beholds the Savior's heart}

Und seiner Liebe Größe   merket.
And his   love's magnitude doth-note.
{And notes the magnitude of his love.}

5. Soprano Aria (Based on Chorale Vs. 7)
●Prayer offering weak faith to him who can illumine me (180–5)

   Lebens Sonne, Licht der Sinnen,
(O) life's sun,   light of-the senses,

   Herr, der du   mein alles bist!
(O) Lord, thou-who my   all   art!
{O Lord, who art my all!}

Du wirst meine Treue   sehen
Thou wilt   my faithfulness see
{Thou wilt see my faithfulness}

Und den Glauben nicht verschmähen,
And (my)   faith   not   disdain,
{And not disdain my faith,}

Der noch schwach und furchtsam ist.
Which still   weak   and   fearful   is.
{Which is still weak and fearful.}

from heaven; if any one eats of this bread, he will live for ever; and the bread which I shall give for the life of the world is my flesh." The Jews then disputed among themselves, saying, "How can this man give us his flesh to eat?" So Jesus said to them, "Truly, truly, I say to you, unless you eat the flesh of the Son of man and drink his blood, you have no life in you; he who eats my flesh and drinks my blood has eternal life, and I will raise him up at the last day. For my flesh is food indeed, and my blood is drink indeed. He who eats my flesh and drinks my blood abides in me, and I in him."
1 Cor. 11:23–26. ...The Lord Jesus on the night when he was betrayed took bread, and when he had given thanks, he broke it, and said, "This is my body which is for you. Do this in remembrance of me." In the same way also the cup, after supper, saying, "This is the new covenant in my blood. Do this, as often as you drink it, in remembrance of me." For as often as you eat this bread and drink the cup, you prolaim the Lord's death until he comes.
Rom. 5:7–8. Why, one will hardly die for a righteous man—though perhaps for a good man one will dare even to die. But God shows his love for us in that while we were yet sinners Christ died for us.

Jn. 1:9. [In Christ] the true light that enlightens every man was coming into the world.
Jn. 8:12. Jesus [said], "I am the light of the world; he who follows me will not walk in darkness, but will have the light of life." (Also Jn. 1:4, 9:5, 11:9, 12:46, Ps. 27:1, 36:9, 2 Cor. 4:6.)
1 Cor. 2:12. Now we have received not the spirit of the world, but the Spirit which is from God, that we might understand the gifts bestowed on us by God.
Lk. 22:19 [Christ]: ...This is my body which is given for you...
Jn. 6:51–54. [Jesus said,] "I am the living bread...; the bread which I shall give for the life of the world is my flesh." The Jews then disputed among themselves, saying, "How can this man give us his flesh to eat?" So Jesus said to them, "Truly, truly, I say to you, unless you eat the flesh of the Son of man and drink his blood, you have no life in you; he who eats my flesh and drinks my blood has eternal life, and I will raise him up at the last day."
1 Cor. 10:16. The cup of blessing which we bless, is it not a participation in the blood of Christ? The bread which we break, is it not a participation in the body of Christ?
Jn. 20:29 [Christ]: ...Blessed are those who have not seen and yet believe.
Mk. 9:23–24. ...All things are possible to him who believes. ...[O Lord] I believe; help my unbelief!
Jn. 6:35, 37. Jesus said... "...He who comes to me shall not hunger, and he who believes in me shall never thirst...All that the Father gives me will come to me; and him who comes to me I will not cast out."
Ps. 73:25–26. [O Lord,] whom have I in heaven but thee? And there is nothing upon earth that I desire besides thee. My flesh and my heart may fail, but God is the strength of my heart and my portion for ever.
Phil. 1:21–23. To me to live is Christ, and to die is gain.
Ps. 102:17. [The Lord] will regard the prayer of the destitute, and will not despise their supplication (Luther: verschmäht ihr Gebet nicht).

6. Bass Recit. (Based on Chorale Vs. 8)
●Prayer that God's love to me not be in vain (180-6)
Herr, laß an mir dein treues Lieben,
Lord, let in me thy faithful loving,
{Lord, let thy faithful loving,}

So dich vom Himmel abgetrieben,
Which thee from heaven drove,
{Which drove thee from heaven,}

Ja nicht vergeblich sein!
Indeed not in-vain be!
{Indeed not be spent on me in vain!}

Entzünde du in Liebe meinen Geist,
Kindle thou with love my spirit,

Daß er sich nur nach dem, was himmlisch heißt,
That it (its-way) only to that, which heavenly is-called,
{That it might wend its way to that which is heavenly,}

Im Glauben lenke
In faith wends
{In faith,}

Und deiner Liebe stets gedenke.
And thy love ever remembers.
{And ever remember thy love.}

7. Chorale (Vs. 9)
●Prayer: May invitation to thy table not be in vain (180-7)
Jesu, wahres Brot des Lebens,
(O) Jesus, true bread of life,

Hilf, daß ich doch nicht vergebens
Help, that I indeed not in-vain

Oder mir vielleicht zum Schaden
Or - perhaps to-my harm

Sei zu deinem Tisch geladen.
Be to thy table invited.

Laß mich durch dies Seelenessen
Let me through this spiritual-meal

Deine Liebe recht ermessen,
Thy love truly measure,

1 Jn. 4:9-10. In this the love of God was made manifest among us, that God sent his only Son into the world, so that we might live through him. In this is love, not that we loved God but that he loved us and sent his Son to be the expiation for our sins.

Jn. 3:16-18 [Christ]: God so loved the world that he gave his only Son, that whoever believes in him should not perish but have eternal life. For God sent the Son into the world, not to condemn the world, but that the world might be saved through him. He who believes in him is not condemned; he who does not believe is condemned already, because he has not believed in the name of the only Son of God.

Deut. 10:12-13. ...What does the Lord your God require of you, but to fear the Lord your God, to walk in all his ways, to love him, to serve the Lord your God with all your heart and with all your soul, and to keep the commandments and statutes of the Lord... (Also Deut. 6:5, Mt. 22:37, Mk. 12:30, Lk. 10:27.)

Col. 3:1-2. If then you have been raised with Christ, seek the things that are above, where Christ is, seated at the right hand of God. Set your minds on things that are above, not on things that are on earth.

2 Thess. 3:5. May the Lord direct your hearts to the love of God...

2 Tim. 2:8. Remember (Luther: halt im Gedächtnis) Jesus Christ...

Lk. 22:19-20. [Jesus] took bread, and when he had given thanks he broke it and gave it to [the disciples], saying, "This is my body which is given for you. Do this in remembrance of me (Luther: zu meinem Gedächtnis)." And likewise [Jesus took] the cup after supper, saying, "This cup which is poured out for you is the new covenant in my blood."

Jn. 6:30-35. [The people] said to [Jesus], "...What work do you perform? Our fathers ate the manna in the wilderness..." Jesus then said to them, "Truly, truly, I say to you, it was not Moses who gave you the bread from heaven; my Father gives you the true bread from heaven. For the bread of God is that which comes down from heaven, and gives life to the world." They said to him, "Lord, give us this bread always." Jesus said to them, "I am the bread of life; he who comes to me shall not hunger, and he who believes in me shall never thirst."

Ps. 78:23-25. [When God led the children of Israel through the wilderness] he commanded the skies above, and opened the doors of heaven; and he rained down upon them manna to eat, and gave them the grain of heaven. Man ate the bread of the angels; he sent them food in abundance.

1 Cor. 10:1-3, 5. I want you to know, brethren, that our fathers were all under the cloud, and all passed through the sea, and all were baptized into Moses in the cloud and in the sea, and all ate the same supernatural food...Nevertheless with most of them God was not pleased; for they were overthrown in the wilderness.

1 Cor. 11:27-29. Whoever...eats the bread or drinks the cup of the Lord in an unworthy manner will be guilty of profaning the body and blood of the Lord. Let a man examine himself, and so eat of the bread and drink of the cup. For any one who eats and drinks without discerning the body eats and drinks judgment upon himself.

Daß ich auch,   wie jetzt auf Erden,
That I, too, (someday) as now   on earth,

Mög ein Gast im Himmel werden.
Might a guest in heaven become.
{That I might someday become a guest at thy table in heaven as
now I am on earth.}

BWV 181
Leichtgesinnte Flattergeister
(NBA I/7; BC A45)

Sexagesima (BWV 18, 181, 126)
*2 Cor. 11:19–12:9 (God's power is made perfect in weakness)
*Lk. 8:4–15 (Parable of the sower)
Librettist: Unknown. Movement 5, perhaps other movements,
too, based on an earlier work.

1. Bass Aria
●Word rendered ineffective by fickle spirit & Belial (181-1)
Leichtgesinnte   Flattergeister
Superficially-minded fickle-spirits

Rauben   sich   des Wortes Kraft.
(Deprive) themselves of-the Word's power.

Belial mit seinen Kindern
Belial with his   children

Suchet ohnedem zu hindern,
Seeks,   moreover, to hinder (it),

Daß   es keinen Nutzen   schafft.
So-that it nothing-profitable accomplishes.
{So that it accomplishes nothing.}

2. Alto Recit.
●Word that falls on hard hearts is ineffective (181-2)
O unglückselger Stand verkehrter Seelen,
O   unhappy   state of-wayward souls,

So gleichsam an dem Wege sind;
Who as-it-were on the   path are;
{Who are—as it were—the seed along the path;}

Und wer will   doch des Satans List erzählen,
And who could indeed - Satan's cunning tell,
{And who is there that can describe Satan's cunning,}

Wenn er das Wort   dem   Herzen raubt,
When he the Word out-of-the heart steals,
{When he steals the Word out of that heart,}

Das, am Verstande blind,
Which, in discernment blind,

Lk. 22:17–19. [As Jesus ate the passover with his disciples,] he took a
cup, and when he had given thanks he said, "Take this, and divide it
among yourselves; for I tell you that from now on I shall not drink of
the fruit of the vine until the kingdom of God comes." And he took
bread, and when he had given thanks he broke it and gave it to them,
saying, "This is my body which is given for you. Do this in
remembrance of me."
Rev. 19:9. ...Blessed are those who are invited to the marriage supper
of the Lamb...

Prov. 23:9. Do not speak in the hearing of a fool, for he will despise
the wisdom of your words.
Prov. 1:20, 22. Wisdom cries aloud in the street..."How long, O simple
ones, will you love being simple? How long will scoffers delight in
their scoffing and fools hate knowledge?"
2 Tim. 3:15–17. ...The sacred writings...are able to instruct you for
salvation through faith in Christ Jesus. All scripture is inspired by God
and profitable for teaching, for reproof, for correction, and for
training in righteousness...
Heb. 4:12. The word of God is living and active, sharper than any two-
edged sword...
***Lk. 8:4–8.** [Jesus] said in a parable: "A sower went out to sow his
seed; and as he sowed, some fell along the path, and was trodden
under foot, and the birds of the air devoured it. And some fell on the
rock; and as it grew up, it withered away, because it had no moisture.
And some fell among thorns; and the thorns grew with it and choked
it. And some fell into good soil and grew, and yielded a hundredfold."
As he said this, he called out, "He who has ears to hear, let him hear."
And when his disciples asked him what this parable meant, he said,
"To you it has been given to know the secrets of the kingdom of God;
but for others they are in parables, so that seeing they may not see,
and hearing they may not understand."

***Lk. 8:5, 12 [Christ]:** ...A sower went out to sow his seed; and as he
sowed, some fell along the path, and was trodden under foot, and the
birds of the air devoured it...The ones along the path are those who
have heard; then the devil comes and takes away the word from their
hearts, that they may not believe and be saved.
2 Cor. 2:11. ...We are not ignorant of [Satan's] designs. (Also Gen.
3:4–10.)
2 Cor. 11:14. ...Satan disguises himself as an angel of light.
2 Cor. 4:3–4. ...If (the) gospel is veiled, it is veiled only to those who
are perishing. In their case the god of this world has blinded the
minds of the unbelievers, to keep them from seeing the light of the
gospel of the glory of Christ... (Also Is. 44:18, Rom. 11:8–10, 1 Jn.
2:11.)
Jn. 12:40 [God]: ...Their eyes [have been blinded] and [their heart]
hardened...lest they should see with their eyes and perceive with their
heart, and turn for me to heal them. (Also Is. 6:9–10, Ex. 9:12, 10:1,
Deut. 2:30.)
Jms. 1:19, 21–24. ...Let every man be quick to hear [God's word]...
Therefore put away all filthiness and rank growth of wickedness

Den Schaden nicht versteht noch glaubt.
The   harm   not discerns nor believes?
{Neither discerns nor believes the harm done?}

Es werden Felsenherzen,
(Now) will   hearts-of-stone,
{Hearts of stone}

So   boshaft widerstehn,
Which wickedly   resist (God's call),

Ihr eigen Heil   verscherzen
Their own salvation frivolously-forfeit
{Will frivolously forfeit their own salvation}

Und einst zugrundegehn.
And one-day   be-ruined.

Es   wirkt   ja Christi letztes Wort,
(Now) works indeed Christ's final   word,
{Indeed, Christ's final word}

Daß Felsen selbst   zerspringen;
That rocks   themselves split-in-pieces;
{Splits the very rocks asunder;}

Des Engels Hand bewegt des Grabes Stein,
The angel's hand   moves   the grave's stone,

Ja, Mosis Stab kann dort
Yes, Moses' rod   can there
{Yes, and Moses' rod}

Aus   einem Berge Wasser bringen.
Out-of   a mountain water   bring.
{Draws water there out of a mountain.}

Willst   du, o Herz, noch härter sein?
Wouldst thou, O heart, still   harder be (than these)?

3. Tenor Aria

●Word sown among worldly thorns, which will burn (181–3)
Der schädlichen Dornen unendliche Zahl,
The   harmful   thorns'   infinite number,
{The infinite number of harmful thorns:}

Die Sorgen der Wollust, die   Schätze zu mehren,
The cares of pleasure, (one's)   treasures to multiply,
{The cares of pleasure, concern to multiply one's treasures,}

Die werden das Feuer der höllischen Qual
These will   the fire of   hell's torment
{These will feed the fires of hell's torment}

In   Ewigkeit nähren.
Through eternity   feed.
{For all eternity.}

(Luther: Bosheit) and receive with meekness the implanted word, which is able to save your souls. But be doers of the word, and not hearers only, deceiving yourselves. For if any one is a hearer of the word and not a doer, he is like a man who observes his natural face in a mirror; for he observes himself and goes away and at once forgets what he was like.
Mt. 7:26–27 [Christ]: Every one who hears these words of mine and does not do them will be like a foolish man who built his house upon the sand; and the rain fell, and the floods came, and the winds blew and beat against that house, and it fell; and great was the fall of it. (Also Lk. 6:46–49.)
Jn. 12:48 [Christ]: He who rejects me and does not receive my sayings has a judge; the word that I have spoken will be his judge on the last day.
Heb. 12:25–26. See that you do not refuse him who is speaking. For if they did not escape when they refused him who warned them on earth [from Mount Sinai], much less shall we escape if we reject him who warns from heaven. His voice then shook the earth; but now he has promised, "Yet once more I will shake not only the earth but also the heaven." (See Ex. 19:18.)
Mt. 27:50–51. [As Jesus hung on the cross, he] cried [his last words] with a loud voice and yielded up his spirit. And behold, the curtain of the temple was torn in two, from top to bottom; and the earth shook, and the rocks were split.
Mt. 28:1–2. Now after the sabbath, toward the dawn of the first day of the week [after Jesus' body had been laid in the tomb], Mary Magdalene and the other Mary went to see the sepulchre. And behold, there was a great earthquake; for an angel of the Lord descended from heaven and came and rolled back the stone, and sat upon it.
Ex. 17:5–6. [In the wilderness] the Lord said to Moses, "...Behold I will stand before you there on the rock at Horeb; and you shall strike the rock, and water shall come out of it, that the people may drink." And Moses did so, in the sight of the elders of Israel. (Also Num. 20:10–11.)
Heb. 3:15. ...Today, when you hear [God's] voice, do not harden your hearts as in the rebellion. (Also Heb. 3:8, 4:6–11.)
Ezek. 36:26 [God]: A new heart I will give you...I will take out of your flesh the heart of stone and give you a heart of flesh.

*Lk. 8:7, 14 [Christ]:** And some [seed] fell among thorns; and the thorns grew with it and choked it...[This seed signifies] those who hear, but as they go on their way they are choked by the cares and riches and pleasures of life, and their fruit does not mature.
Mt. 6:19–21 [Christ]: Do not lay up for yourselves treasures on earth, where moth and rust consume and where thieves break in and steal, but lay up for yourselves treasures in heaven, where neither moth nor rust consumes and where thieves do not break in and steal. For where your treasure is, there will your heart be also.
Heb. 6:4, 7–8. It is impossible to restore again to repentance those who have once been enlightened...For land which has drunk the rain that often falls upon it, and brings forth vegetation useful to those for whose sake it is cultivated, receives a blessing from God. But if it bears thorns and thistles, it is worthless and near to being cursed; its end is to be burned.

4. Soprano Recit.
●Seed lies dormant unless soil is prepared (181-4)
Von diesen wird die Kraft erstickt,
By these is (its) strength choked,
{By these things the Word's strength is choked,}

Der edle Samme liegt vergebens,
The noble seed lies fruitless

Wer sich nicht recht im Geiste schickt,
Whoever himself not truly in-the Spirit (devotes),
{In him who does not set about}

Sein Herz beizeiten
His heart in-good-time
{To prepare his heart spiritually in good time}

Zum guten Lande zu bereiten,
Into good soil to prepare,
{To be good soil,}

Daß unser Herz der Süßigkeit en schmecket,
So-that our heart the sweetness tastes,
{So that our heart may taste the sweetness,}

So uns dies Wort entdecket,
Which to-us this Word reveals,
{Which this Word reveals to us:}

Die Kräfte dieses und des künftgen Lebens.
The power of-this and of the-future life.
{The power of this life and the life to come.}

5. Chorus (Apparently based on an earlier work)
●Prayer: Make soil of our heart receptive to thy Word (181-5)
Laß, Höchster, uns zu allen Zeiten
Grant, (O) Most-High, to-us at all times
{Grant to us, O Most High, at all times}

Des Herzens Trost, dein heilig Wort.
(Our) heart's comfort, thy holy Word.

Du kannst nach deiner Allmachtshand
Thou canst through thine almighty-hand

Allein ein fruchtbar gutes Land
Alone, a fertile good soil

In unsern Herzen zubereiten.
Within our hearts prepare.
{Thou alone, by thine almighty hand canst make our hearts to be a good, fertile soil.}

*Lk. 8:7-8, 14-15 [Christ]: Some [seed] fell among thorns; and the thorns grew with it and choked it. And some fell into good soil and grew, and yielded a hundredfold...As for what fell among thorns, they are those who hear, but as they go on their way they are choked by the cares and riches and pleasures of life, and their fruit does not mature. And as for that in the good soil, they are those who, hearing the word, hold it fast in an honest and good heart, and bring forth fruit with patience.
Ps. 19:9-10. ...The ordinances of the Lord are true, and righteous altogether. More to be desired are they than gold, even much fine gold; sweeter also than honey and drippings of the honeycomb.
Ps. 119:103. [O Lord,] how sweet are thy words to my taste, sweeter than honey to my mouth!
Jms. 1:21. ...Receive with meekness the implanted word, which is able to save your souls. (Also Acts 20:32, 1 Thess. 2:13.)
Col. 3:16. Let the word of Christ dwell in you richly...
Rom. 1:16. ...[The gospel] is the power of God for salvation to every one who has faith...
1 Cor. 1:18. The word of the cross is folly to those who are perishing, but to us who are being saved it is the power of God.
Col. 1:26-27. The mystery hidden for ages and generations [has] now [been] made manifest to his saints. To them God chose to make known how great among the Gentiles are the riches of the glory of this mystery, which is Christ in you, the hope of glory.
Eph. 1:13-14. ...You...who have heard the word of truth, the gospel of your salvation, and have believed in [Christ], were sealed with the promised Holy Spirit, which is the guarantee of our inheritance...
1 Tim. 4:8. ...Godliness is of value in every way, as it holds promise for the present life and also for the life to come (Luther: dieses und des zukünftigen Lebens).

*Lk. 8:8, 15 [Christ]: Some [seed] fell into good soil and grew, and yielded a hundredfold...As for that in the good soil, they are those who, hearing the word, hold it fast in an honest and good heart, and bring forth fruit with patience.
Rom. 15:4. Whatever was written in former days was written for our instruction, that by steadfastness (Luther: Geduld) and by the encouragement (Luther: Trost) of the scriptures we might have hope. (Also 1 Thess. 2:13.)
Jms. 1:21. ...Receive with meekness the implanted word, which is able to save your souls. (Also Acts 20:32, 1 Thess. 2:13.)
Mt. 3:8. Bear fruit that befits repentance. (Also Lk. 3:8, Rom. 7:4.)
Jn. 15:1-2, 5, 8, 16 [Christ]: I am the true vine, and my Father is the vinedresser. Every branch of mine that bears no fruit, he takes away, and every branch that does bear fruit he prunes, that it may bear more fruit...I am the vine, you are the branches. He who abides in me, and I in him, he it is that bears much fruit...By this my Father is glorified, that you bear much fruit, and so prove to be my disciples...I chose you and appointed you that you should go and bear fruit and that your fruit should abide... (Also Jer. 17:8, Ezek. 17:8, 23.)
Gal. 5:22-23. The fruit of the Spirit is love, joy, peace, patience, kindness, goodness, faithfulness, gentleness, self-control...
Lk. 13:6-9. And [Jesus] told this parable: "A man had a fig tree planted in his vineyard; and he came seeking fruit on it and found none, And he said to the vinedresser, 'Lo, these three years I have come seeking fruit on this fig tree, and I find none, Cut it down; why should it use up the ground?' And he answered him, 'Let it alone, sir, this year also, till I dig about it and put on manure. And if it bears fruit next year, well and good; but if not, you can cut it down.'"

BWV 182
Himmelskönig sei willkommen
(NBA I/8; BC A53, A172)

Palm Sunday (BWV 182 only)
*Phil. 2:5–11 (Exhortation to have the mind of Christ who took the form of a servant) or *1 Cor. 11:23–32 (Paul tells how Christ instituted Holy Communion)
*Mt. 21:1–9 (Triumphal entry of Jesus into Jerusalem)

In Leipzig, Bach reused this cantata for:
The Annunciation: Mar. 25 (BWV [182], 1)
+Is. 7:10–16 (The Messiah's birth prophesied)
+Lk. 1:26–38 (The angel Gabriel announces birth of Jesus to Mary)

Librettist: perhaps Salomon Franck

1. Sonata

2. Chorus
●King of Heaven welcomed into the Zion of our hearts (182–2)

    Himmelskönig, sei willkommen,
(O) King-of-heaven,   welcome!

Laß auch uns dein Zion sein!
Let also us thy Zion be!
{Let us, too, be thy Zion!}

Komm herein,
Come   in,

Du   hast uns das Herz genommen.
Thou hast   (our)   heart   captured.
{Thou hast captured our heart.}

3. Bass Recit.
●Vox Christi: I come to do God's will: Ps. 40:7–8 (182–3)
Siehe, ich komme, im   Buch ist von mir geschrieben;
Behold, I   come, in-the Book it-is of   me   written;

deinen Willen, mein Gott, tu ich gerne.
thy   will,   my   God, do I   gladly.

*Mt. 21:1–9 [Christ's triumphal entry into Jerusalem before his Passion]. When they drew near to Jerusalem...Jesus sent two disciples, saying to them, "Go into the village opposite you, and immediately you will find an ass tied, and a colt with her; untie them and bring them to me. If any one says anything to you, you shall say, 'The Lord has need of them,' and he will send them immediately." This took place to fulfil what was spoken by the prophet, saying, "Tell the daughter of Zion, Behold, your king is coming to you, humble, and mounted on an ass, and on a colt, the foal of an ass." The disciples went and did as Jesus had directed them; they brought the ass and the colt, and put their garments on them, and he sat theron. Most of the crowd spread their garments on the road, and others cut branches from the trees and spread them on the road. And the crowds that went before him and that followed him shouted, "Hosanna to the Son of David! Blessed is he who comes in the name of the Lord! Hosanna in the highest!" (See Zech. 9:9.)

S. of S. 3:6–7, 11. What is that coming up from the wilderness, like a column of smoke, perfumed with myrrh and frankincense, with all the fragrant powders of the merchant? Behold, it is the litter of Solomon! ...Go forth, O daughters of Zion, and behold King Solomon, with the crown with which his mother crowned him on the day of his wedding, on the day of the gladness of his heart.

S. of S. 4:9–10 [Bridegroom]: You have ravished my heart (Luther: du hast mir das Herz genommen), my sister, my bride, you have ravished my heart with a glance of your eyes, with one jewel of your necklace. How sweet is your love, my sister, my bride! How much better is your love than wine, and the fragrance of your oils than any spice!

Mt. 16:21. ...Jesus began to show his disciples that he must go to Jerusalem and suffer many things from the elders and chief priests and scribes, and be killed...

Ps. 40:7–8. I said, "*Lo, I come; in the roll of the book it is written of me; I delight to do thy will,* O my God..."

Heb. 10:5, 7–10. ...When Christ came into the world, he said, "Sacrifices and offerings thou hast not desired, but a body hast thou prepared for me...'Lo, I have come to do thy will, O God,' as it is written of me in the roll of the book." When he said above, "Thou hast neither desired nor taken pleasure in sacrifices and offerings and burnt offerings and sin offerings" (these are offered according to the law), then he added, "Lo, I have come to do thy will." He abolishes the first in order to establish the second. And by that will we have been sanctified through the offering of the body of Jesus Christ once for all. (See Ps. 40:6–8.)

Mk. 14:36. [In the garden of Gethsemane, Jesus prayed,] "Abba, Father, all things are possible to thee; remove this cup from me; yet not what I will, but what thou wilt." (Also Mt. 26:39, 42.)

4. Bass Aria

●Love made Christ leave glory & sacrifice himself (182-4)
Starkes Lieben,
(What) strong loving,

Das dich, großer Gottessohn,
Which thee, great Son-of-God,
{Which drove thee, great Son of God,}

Von dem Thron
From the throne
{From the throne}

Deiner Herrlichkeit getrieben,
Of-thy glory drove,
{Of thy glory,}

Daß du dich zum Heil der Welt
That thou thyself for-the salvation of-the world

Als ein Opfer fürgestellt,
As a sacrifice didst-offer,
{That thou didst offer thyself as a sacrifice for the salvation of the world;}

Daß du dich mit Blut verschrieben.
That thou thyself with blood didst-pledge.
{That thou didst pledge thyself with blood!}

5. Alto Aria

●Lay down your very being before the entering king (182-5)
Leget euch dem Heiland unter,
Lay yourselves (before) the Savior (down),
{Prostrate yourselves before the Savior,}

Herzen, die ihr christlich seid!
Hearts, that Christian are!
{All ye hearts that are Christian!}

Tragt ein unbeflecktes Kleid
Bring (the) unspotted garment

Eures Glaubens ihm entgegen,
Of-your faith to-meet-him,

Leib und Leben und Vermögen
(Let) body and life and possessions

Sei dem König itzt geweiht.
Be to-the king now consecrated.
{Be now consecrated to the King.}

*Phil. 2:5-9. Have this mind among yourselves, which is yours in Christ Jesus, who, though he was in the form of God, did not count equality with God a thing to be grasped, but emptied himself, taking the form of a servant, being born in the likeness of men. And being found in human form he humbled himself and became obedient unto death, even death on a cross. Therefore God has highly exalted him and bestowed on him the name which is above every name.

Jn. 1:1-3, 14, 18. In the beginning was the Word, and the Word was with God, and the Word was God. He was in the beginning with God; all things were made through him, and without him was not anything made that was made...And the Word became flesh and dwelt among us, full of grace and truth; we have beheld his glory, glory as of the only Son of the Father...No one has ever seen God; the only Son, who is in the bosom of the Father, he has made him known.

2 Cor. 8:9. You know the grace of our Lord Jesus Christ, that though he was rich, yet for your sake he became poor, so that by his poverty you might become rich.

Heb. 10:10, 14. We have been sanctified through the offering of the body of Jesus Christ once for all...For by a single offering he has perfected for all time those who are sanctified.

Eph. 5:2. ...Christ loved us and gave himself up for us, a fragrant offering and sacrifice to God. (Also Gal. 1:3-4, 2:20, Eph. 5:25, 1 Tim. 2:6, Tit. 2:14.)

Mt. 20:28 [Christ]: ...The Son of Man came not to be served but to serve, and to give his life as a ransom for many. (Also Mk. 10:45.)

1 Pet. 1:18-19. You know that you were ransomed...not with perishable things such as silver or gold, but with the precious blood of Christ, like that of a lamb without blemish or spot.

*Mt. 21:8-9. [As Jesus entered Jerusalem] most of the crowd spread their garments on the road, and others cut branches from the trees and spread them on the road. And the crowds that went before him and that followed him shouted, "Hosanna to the Son of David! Blessed is he who comes in the name of the Lord! Hosanna in the highest!"

Joel 2:13. Rend your hearts and not your garments...

Mt. 22:37 [Christ]: ...You shall love the Lord your God with all your heart, and with all your soul, and with all your mind.

Is. 61:10. ...My soul shall exult in my God; for he has clothed me with the garments of salvation, he has covered me with the robe of righteousness, as a bridegroom decks himself with a garland, and as a bride adorns herself with her jewels. (Also Ps. 45: 12-15, Eph. 5:25-27, Rev. 3:5, 19:7-8.)

Rev. 7:14. ...[The righteous] have washed their robes and made them white in the blood of the Lamb.

Heb. 10:22. Let us draw near [to God] with a true heart in full assurance of faith...

Rom. 12:1. I appeal to you...by the mercies of God, to present your bodies as a living sacrifice, holy and acceptable to God, which is your spiritual worship.

1 Cor. 10:31. So, whether you eat or drink, or whatever you do, do all to the glory of God.

Phil. 1:21-23. To me to live is Christ, and to die is gain.

6. Tenor Aria
●Staying with Jesus through persecution and woe (182–6)
Jesu, laß durch Wohl und Weh
Jesus, let through weal and woe
{Jesus, through weal and woe, let me}

Mich auch mit dir ziehen!
Me   also with thee go!
{Also go with thee!}

Schreit die Welt   nur   »Kreuzige!«,
Cries   the world nought-but "Crucify!"
{Though the world cry nought but "Crucify!"}

So laß mich nicht fliehen,
Then let me   not   flee,
{Yet let me not flee,}

Herr, vor deinem Kreuzpanier;
(O) Lord, from   thy   cross-banner;

Kron und Palmen find ich hier.
Crown and   palm   find I   here.
{Both crown and palm shall I find there.}

7. Chorus (Chorale) (See also 159–5.)
●Christ's passion is my joy for it offers me heaven (182–7)
Jesu, deine Passion
Jesus, thy passion

Ist mir lauter Freude,
Is for-me pure   joy,
{Is pure joy for me,}

Deine Wunden, Kron und Hohn
Thy   wounds, crown, and scorn

Mt. 8:19. A scribe came up and said to [Jesus], "Teacher, I will follow you wherever you go."
Jn. 11:16. Thomas...said to his fellow disciples, "Let us also go [with Jesus into Jerusalem], that we may die with him."
Mt. 26:33–35. Peter declared to [Jesus], "Though they all fall away because of you, I will never fall away." Jesus said to him, "Truly, I say to you, this very night, before the cock crows, you will deny me three times." Peter said to him, "Even if I must die with you, I will not deny you." And so said all the disciples. (Also Mk. 14:29, Lk. 22:33–34.)
Mt. 26:56. ...Then [when Jesus was arrested] all the disciples forsook him and fled. (Also Mk. 14:50.)
Jn. 19:14–15. [Pilate] said to the Jews, "Behold your King!" They cried out, "Away with him, away with him, crucify him!" Pilate said to them, "Shall I crucify your King?" The chief priests answered, "We have no king but Caesar." (Also Mt. 27:22–24, Mk. 15:13–14, Lk. 23:21.)
Jn. 3:14–15 [Christ]: As Moses lifted up the serpent in the wilderness, so must the Son of man be lifted up, that whoever believes in him may have eternal life.
Is. 11:10. In that day the root of Jesse shall stand as an ensign (Luther: Panier) to the peoples... (Also Is. 11:12.)
Heb. 2:9. We [now] see Jesus, who for a little while was made lower than the angels, crowned with glory and honor because of the suffering of death, so that by the grace of God he might taste death for every one.
2 Tim. 2:11–12. The saying is sure: If we have died with him, we shall also live with him; if we endure, we shall also reign with him... (Also Rom. 8:17, 1 Pet. 4:13.)
Jms. 1:12. Blessed is the man who endures trial, for when he has stood the test he will receive the crown of life which God has promised to those who love him. (Also 2 Tim. 4:8, 1 Pet. 5:4, Heb. 10:32–39, Rev. 2:10.)
*Mt. 21:8–9. ...[As Jesus entered Jerusalem] most of the crowd spread their garments on the road, and others cut branches from the trees and spread them on the road. And the crowds that went before him and that followed him shouted, "Hosanna to the Son of David! Blessed is he who comes in the name of the Lord! Hosanna in the highest!" (See Zech. 9:9.)
Rev. 7:9–10. ...Behold, a great multitude...standing before the throne and before the Lamb, clothed in white robes, with palm branches in their hands, and crying out with a loud voice, "Salvation belongs to our God who sits upon the throne, and to the Lamb!"

Mk. 9:31–32. [Jesus] was teaching his disciples, saying to them, "The Son of man will be delivered into the hands of men, and they will kill him; and when he is killed, after three days he will rise." (Also Mt. 16:21, 20:17–19, Mk. 8:31, 10:32–34, Lk. 9:22, 18:31–34, 24:11.)
Lk. 18:31–34. Taking the twelve, [Jesus] said to them, "Behold, we are going up to Jerusalem, and everything that is written of the Son of man by the prophets will be accomplished. For he will be delivered to the Gentiles, and will be mocked and shamefully treated and spit upon; they will scourge him and kill him, and on the third day he will rise." But they understood none of these things; this saying was hid from them, and they did not grasp what was said.
Lk. 24:26. Was it not necessary that the Christ should suffer these things and enter into his glory?

Meines Herzens Weide;
My   heart's pasture;

Meine Seel auf Rosen geht,
My   soul upon roses walks,
{My soul walks upon roses,}

Wenn ich dran gedenke,
When I   this remember,
{When I remember that}

In dem Himmel eine Stätt
In -   heaven an abode

Uns deswegen schenke.
To-us by-these is-given.
{When I remember that, because of these sufferings, an abode in heaven is given to us.}

8. Chorus
●Following Jesus into Zion; he opens way of salvation (182-8)
So lasset uns gehen in   Salem der Freuden,
So let   us   go into (that) Salem of   joy,
{So let us enter that Salem of joy;}

Begleitet den König in Lieben und Leiden.
Accompany the king in love and sorrow.

Er gehet voran
He goes before (us)

Und öffnet die Bahn.
And opens the way.

Is. 53:5. He was wounded for our transgressions, he was bruised for our iniquities; upon him was the chastisement that made us whole, and with his stripes we are healed.
1 Pet. 2:24. He himself bore our sins in his body on the tree, that we might die to sin and live to righteousness. By his wounds you have been healed. (Also Gal. 3:13.)
Jn. 1:29. ...Behold, the Lamb of God, who takes away the sin of the world! (Also Jn. 1:36.)
Rev. 7:17. The Lamb...will be [the] shepherd [of his people], and he will guide them to springs of living water...
S. of S. 2:16 [Bride]: My beloved is mine and I am his, he pastures his flock among the lilies (Luther: Rosen). (Also S. of S. 6:3.)
Jn. 14:1-3 [Christ]: Let not your hearts be troubled; believe in God, believe also in me. In my Father's house are many rooms; if it were not so, would I have told you that I go to prepare a place for you? And when I go and prepare a place for you, I will come again and will take you to myself, that where I am you may be also. (Also Jn. 12:26.)

Mk. 10:32-34. [Jesus and his disciples] were on the road, going up to Jerusalem, and Jesus was walking ahead of them; and they were amazed, and those who followed were afraid. And taking the twelve again, he began to tell them what was to happen to him, saying, "Behold, we are going up to Jerusalem; and the Son of man will be delivered to the chief priests and the scribes, and they will condemn him to death, and deliver him to the Gentiles; and they will mock him, and spit upon him, and scourge him, and kill him; and after three days he will rise." (Also Mt. 20:17-19, Lk. 18:31-33.)
Jn. 11:16. Thomas...said to his fellow disciples, "Let us also go, that we may die with him."
*Mt. 21:9. ...[As Jesus entered Jerusalem,] the crowds that went before him and that followed him shouted, "Hosanna to the Son of David! Blessed is he who comes in the name of the Lord! Hosanna in the highest!"
Heb. 12:22. You have come to Mount Zion and to the city of the living God, the heavenly Jerusalem...
Heb. 12:1-2. [Let us follow] Jesus the pioneer and perfecter of our faith, who for the joy that was set before him endured the cross, despising the shame, and is seated at the right hand of the throne of God.
Eph. 2:18. Through him we...have access in one Spirit to the Father. (Also Rom. 5:1-2.)
Heb. 10:19-22. Therefore, brethren, since we have confidence to enter the sanctuary by the blood of Jesus, by the new and living way which he opened for us through the curtain, that is, through his flesh, and since we have a great priest over the house of God, let us draw near with a true heart in full assurance of faith...

BWV 183
Sie werden euch in den Bann tun II
(NBA I/12; BC A79)

Exaudi: 1. S. after Ascension (BWV 44, 183)
*1 Pet. 4:7[1]-11 (Exhortation to serve one another with the gift each has received)
*Jn. 15:26–16:4 (Farewell address of Jesus: Holy Spirit promised, persecution foretold)
[1]Begin: "Therefore keep sane and sober..."
Librettist: Christiane Mariane von Ziegler (Text modified somewhat by someone: J. S. Bach?)

1. Bass Recit.
●Vox Christi: Persecution is coming: Jn. 16:2 (183-1)
Sie werden euch in den Bann tun,
They will you into - excommunication place;
{They will excommunicate you;}

es kömmt aber die Zeit,
(there is) coming, indeed, (a) time
{indeed, a time is coming}

daß, wer euch tötet, wird meinen,
when, whoever you kills, will think
{when, whoever kills you, will think}

er tue Gott einen Dienst daran.
he is-doing God a service thereby.

2. Tenor Aria
●Persecution & death accepted without fear (183-2)
Ich fürchte nicht des Todes Schrecken,
I fear not - death's terror,
{I do not fear the terror of death,}

Ich scheue ganz kein Ungemach.
I dread absolutely no hardship.

Denn Jesus' Schutzarm wird mich decken,
For Jesus' guarding-arm will me cover,
{For Jesus' guarding arm will cover me,}

Ich folge gern und willig nach;
I follow gladly and willingly after (him);
{I gladly and willingly follow after him;}

Wollt ihr nicht meines Lebens schonen
Would you not my life spare
{If you do not intend to spare my life}

Und glaubt, Gott einen Dienst zu tun,
And believe, God (thus) a service to do,
{And believe you are doing God a service thereby,}

*Jn. 16:1–4 [Christ]: I have said all this to you to keep you from falling away. *They will put you out of the synagogues; indeed, the hour is coming when whoever kills you will think he is offering service to God.* And they will do this because they have not known the Father, nor me. But I have said these things to you, that when their hour comes you may remember that I told you of them...
Jn. 9:22. ...The Jews had...agreed that if any one should confess [Jesus] to be Christ, he was to be put out of the synagogue (Luther: in den Bann getan würde).
Jn. 15:18–19 [Christ]: If the world hates you, know that it has hated me before it hated you. If you were of the world, the world would love its own; but because you are not of the world, but I chose you out of the world, therefore the world hates you.
1 Jn. 3:13 [Christ]: Do not wonder, brethren, that the world hates you. (Also Jn. 17:14, Mt. 5:10–12, 10:24–25.)
Acts 26:1, 9–10. ...[Recounting his former life as a persecutor of the believers] Paul stretched out his hand and [said]: "...I myself was convinced that I ought to do many things in opposing the name of Jesus of Nazareth. And I did so in Jerusalem; I not only shut up many of the saints in prison, by authority from the chief priests, but when they were put to death I cast my vote against them." (Also Acts 22:4–5, 1 Cor. 15:9, Gal. 1:13–14, 1 Tim. 1:13.)

Ps. 23:4. Even though I walk through the valley of the shadow of death, I fear no evil; for thou art with me; thy rod and thy staff, they comfort me. (Also Ps. 27:1, Is. 43:2.)
Ps. 18:4–5. The cords of death encompassed me...the snares of death confronted me. (Also Ps. 116:3.)
Lk. 12:4 [Christ]: ...Do not fear those who kill the body, and after that have no more that they can do. (Also Mt. 10:28.)
Rev. 2:10 [Christ]: Do not fear what you are about to suffer...Be faithful unto death, and I will give you the crown of life.
Ps. 116:15. Precious in the sight of the Lord is the death of his saints. (Also 1 Thess. 4:17–18, Rev. 14:13.)
Wisdom (Apocrypha) 5:16. ...With his right hand [God] will cover [the righteous], and with his arm he will shield them.
Mt. 16:24–25 [Christ]: ...If any man would come after me, let him deny himself and take up his cross and follow me. For whoever would save his life will lose it, and whoever loses his life for my sake will find it. (Also Mt. 10:38–39, Mk. 8:34–35, Lk. 9:23–24.)
Heb. 11:35–38. ...Some [believers] were tortured, refusing to accept release, that they might rise again to a better life. Others suffered mockings and scourging, and even chains and imprisonment. They were stoned, they were sawn in two, they were killed with the sword; they went about in skins of sheep and goats, destitute, afflicted, ill-treated (Luther: mit Ungemach)—of whom the world was not worthy...
*Jn. 16:2 [Christ]: ...Whoever kills you will think he is offering service to God.

Er soll euch selben noch belohnen,
He shall you - yet reward,
{He shall yet reward you;}

Wohlan, es mag dabei beruhn.
Well-then, it may therewith rest.
{Well then, let it rest at that.}

3. Alto Recit.
●Giving up life for Christ (183–3)
Ich bin bereit, mein Blut und armes Leben
I am prepared, my blood and poor life
{I am prepared to give up my blood and my poor life}

Vor dich, mein Heiland, hinzugeben,
For thee, my Savior, to-give-up,
{For thee, my Savior,}

Mein ganzer Mensch soll dir gewidmet sein;
My entire person shall to-thee dedicated be;
{My entire person shall be dedicated to thee;}

Ich tröste mich, dein Geist wird bei mir stehen,
I comfort myself, thy Spirit will by me stand,
{I comfort myself that thy Spirit will stand by me,}

Gesetzt, es sollte mir vielleicht zuviel geschehen.
Supposing it should for-me perhaps too-much (be).
{If it should ever become too much for me.}

4. Soprano Aria
●Prayer for Spirit's intercession (183–4)
Höchster Tröster, Heilger Geist,
Highest comforter, (O) Holy Spirit,

Der du mir die Wege weist,
Thou-who to-me the paths dost-show,
{Thou who dost show me the paths}

Darauf ich wandeln soll,
On-which I am-to-walk,

Hilf meine Schwachheit mit vertreten,
Help my weakness with (thy) intercession,

Denn von mir selber kann ich nicht beten,
For by my-self can I not pray;
{For by myself I can not pray,}

Ich weiß, du sorgest vor mein Wohl!
I know, thou carest for my good!

5. Chorale
●Spirit teaches us how to pray effectively (183–5)
Du bist ein Geist, der lehret,
Thou art a Spirit, who teaches,

Zech. 2:8. ...He who touches you touches the apple of [God's] eye.
Rom. 12:19. Beloved, never avenge yourselves, but leave it to the wrath of God; for it is written, "Vengeance is mine, I will repay, says the Lord."
2 Cor. 12:10. For the sake of Christ, then, I am content with weaknesses, insults, hardships, persecutions, and calamities...

Acts 21:13. Paul [said], "What are you doing, weeping and breaking my heart? For I am ready not only to be imprisoned but even to die at Jerusalem for the name of the Lord Jesus."
Lk. 22:33. [Peter] said to [Jesus], "Lord, I am ready to go with you to prison and to death." (Also Mt. 26:35, Mk. 14:29.)
Jn. 15:20–21 [Christ]: Remember the word that I said to you, "A servant is not greater than his master." If they persecuted me, they will persecute you...But all this they will do to you on my account, because they do not know him who sent me...
Mt. 10:17–20 [Christ]: ...They will deliver you up to councils, and flog you in their synagogues, and you will be dragged before governors and kings for my sake, to bear testimony before them and the Gentiles. When they deliver you up, do not be anxious how you are to speak or what you are to say; for what you are to say will be given to you in that hour; for it is not you who speak, but the Spirit of your Father speaking through you.
*Jn. 15:26 [Christ]: When the Counselor (Luther: Tröster) comes, whom I shall send to you from the Father, even the Spirit of truth, who proceeds from the Father, he will bear witness to me.

Jn. 14:16–17 [Christ]: I will pray the Father, and he will give you another Counselor (Luther: Tröster), to be with you for ever, even the Spirit of truth...you know him, for he dwells with you, and will be in you.
Jn. 14:26 [Christ]: The Counselor (Luther: Tröster), the Holy Spirit, whom the Father will send in my name, he will teach you all things, and bring to your remembrance all that I have said to you. (Also Jn. 16:7, 13, 1 Jn. 2:27.)
Is. 30:21. Your ears shall hear a word behind you, saying, "This is the way, walk in it," when you turn to the right or when you turn to the left. (Also Jer. 42:3.)
Rom. 8:26–27. The Spirit helps us in our weakness; for we do not know how to pray as we ought, but the Spirit himself intercedes for us with sighs too deep for words. And he who searches the hearts of men knows what is the mind of the Spirit, because the Spirit intercedes for the saints according to the will of God.
Jer. 29:11. For I know the plans I have for you, says the Lord, plans for welfare and not for evil, to give you a future and a hope. (Also Prov. 23:18.)

Jn. 14:26 [Christ]: The Counselor, the Holy Spirit, whom the Father will send in my name, he will teach you all things...

Wie man recht beten soll;
How one truly pray should;
{How one should truly pray;}

Dein Beten wird erhöret,
Thy praying is heard,

Dein Singen klinget wohl.
Thy singing resounds well.

Es steigt zum Himmel an,
It rises to heaven -,

Es steigt und läßt nicht abe,
It rises and lets not off,
{It rises and does not cease,}

Bis der geholfen habe,
Till he has-helped,

Der allein helfen kann.
Who alone can-help.
{Till he who alone can help has helped.}

BWV 184
Erwünschtes Freudenlicht
(NBA I/14; BC A88)

3. Day of Pentecost (BWV 184, 175)
*Acts 8:14-17 (Baptism of Holy Ghost comes to believers in Samaria)
*Jn. 10:1-11 (Jesus identifies himself as the true shepherd)
Librettist: Unknown. Movements 1-4, 6 adapted from BWV 184a.

1. Tenor Recit.
•Shepherd that was long awaited has now come (184-1)
  Erwünschtes Freudenlicht,
(O) hoped-for light-of-joy,

Das mit dem neuen Bund anbricht
Which with the new covenant dawns
{Which dawns with the new covenant}

Durch Jesum, unsern Hirten!
Through Jesus, our shepherd!

Wir, die wir sonst in Todes Tälern irrten,
We, who formerly in death's vales strayed,
{We, who formerly strayed in the vales of death,}

Empfinden reichlich nun,
Perceive richly now,
{Now experience abundantly}

Wie Gott zu uns den längst erwünschten Hirten sendet,
How God to us the long- awaited shepherd sends,
{How God sends to us the long-awaited shepherd,}

*Jn. 15:26 [Christ]: When the Counselor (Luther: Tröster) comes, whom I shall send to you from the Father, even the Spirit of truth, who proceeds from the Father, he will bear witness to me.
1 Cor. 2:11. For what person knows a man's thoughts except the spirit of the man which is in him? So also no one comprehends the thoughts of God except the Sprit of God.
Rom. 8:26. ...The Spirit helps us in our weakness; for we do not know how to pray as we ought...
*1 Pet. 4:7. ...Keep sane and sober for your prayers.
Lk. 11:1, 5-8, 11-13. [Jesus] was praying in a certain place, and when he ceased, one of his disciples said to him, "Lord, teach us to pray..." And he said to them, "Which of you who has a friend will go to him at midnight and say to him, 'Friend, lend me three loaves; for a friend of mine has arrived on a journey, and I have nothing to set before him'; and he will answer from within, 'Do not bother me; the door is now shut, and my children are with me in bed; I cannot get up and give you anything'? I tell you, though he will not get up and give him anything because he is his friend, yet because of his importunity he will rise and give him whatever he needs...What father among you, if his son asks for a fish, will instead of a fish give him a serpent; or if he asks for an egg, will give him a scorpion? If you then, who are evil, know how to give good gifts to your children, how much more will the heavenly Father give the Holy Spirit to those who ask him!"

Is. 60:1-3, 19. Arise, shine; for your light has come, and the glory of the Lord has risen upon you. For behold, darkness shall cover the earth, and thick darkness the peoples; but the Lord will arise upon you, and his glory will be seen upon you. And nations shall come to your light, and kings to the brightness of your rising...The sun shall be no more your light by day...but the Lord will be your everlasting light... (Also Is. 9:2.)
2 Cor. 4:6. It is the God who said, "Let light shine out of darkness," who has shone in our hearts to give the light of the knowledge of the glory of God in the face of Christ.
Jn. 1:9. [In Christ] the true light that enlightens every man was coming into the world.
Jn. 8:12. [Christ] ...I am the light of the world; he who follows me will not walk in darkness, but will have the light of life. (Also Jn. 1:4, 9:5, 11:9, 12:46, Ps. 36:9.)
Jn. 10:14-15, 27-28 [Christ]: I am the good shepherd; I know my own and my own know me, as the Father knows me and I know the Father; and I lay down my life for the sheep...My sheep hear my voice, and I know them, and they follow me; and I give them eternal life...
Ezek. 34:11-12, 14-16, 23-24. Thus says the Lord God: Behold, I, I myself will search for my sheep, and will seek them out. As a

Der unsre Seele speist
Who our soul feeds
{Who feeds our soul}

Und unsern Gang durch Wort und Geist
And our course through Word and Spirit
{And turns our course through Word and Spirit}

Zum rechten Wege wendet.
To-the right way turns.
{To the right way.}

Wir, sein erwähltes Volk, empfinden seine Kraft;
We, his chosen people, perceive his power;

In seiner Hand allein ist, was uns
In his hand alone is, that-which us (with)

   Labsal schafft,
   refreshment provides,
{In his hand alone is that which gives us refreshment,}

Was unser Herze kräftig stärket.
That-which our hearts mightily strengthens.
{That which strengthens our hearts mightily.}

Er liebt uns, seine Herde,
He loves us— his flock—

Die seinen Trost und Beistand merket.
Who his comfort and assistance (experience).
{Who experience his comfort and assistance.}

Er ziehet sie vom Eitlen, von der Erde,
He draws them (away) from-the vain, from the earthly,
{He draws them away from vain and earthly things,}

Auf ihn zu schauen
Upon him to gaze

Und jederzeit auf seine Huld zu trauen.
And at-all-times (in) his favor to trust.

O Hirte, so sich vor die Herde gibt,
O shepherd, who himself for the flock does-give,
{O shepherd, who gives himself for his flock,}

Der bis ins Grab und bis in Tod sie liebt!
Who till (the) grave and till - death them loves!
{Who loves them till death and the grave!}

shepherd seeks out his flock when some of his sheep have been scattered abroad, so will I seek out my sheep, and I will rescue them from all places where they have been scattered on a day of clouds and thick darkness...I will feed them with good pasture, and upon the mountain heights of Israel shall be their pasture; there they shall lie down in good grazing land, and on fat pasture they shall feed on the mountains of Israel. I myself will be the shepherd of my sheep, and I will make them lie down, says the Lord God. I will seek the lost, and I will bring back the strayed, and I will bind up the crippled, and I will strengthen the weak...And I will set up over them one shepherd, my servant David, and he shall feed them: he shall feed them and be their shepherd. And I, the Lord, will be their God, and my servant David shall be prince among them; I, the Lord, have spoken.
Ezek. 37:26–27 [God]: I will make a covenant of peace with them; it shall be an everlasting covenant with them; and I will bless them and multiply them, and will set my sanctuary in the midst of them for evermore. My dwelling place shall be with them; and I will be their God, and they shall be my people. (Also Jer. 31:31–33, Ezek. 37:26–27, Heb. 8:7–11.)
*Jn. 10:1–11. [Jesus said,] "Truly, truly, I say to you, he who does not enter the sheepfold by the door but climbs in by another way, that man is a thief and a robber; but he who enters by the door is the shepherd of the sheep. To him the gatekeeper opens; the sheep hear his voice, and he calls his own sheep by name and leads them out. When he has brought out all his own, he goes before them, and the sheep follow him, for they know his voice. A stranger they will not follow, but they will flee from him, for they do not know the voice of strangers." This figure Jesus used with them, but they did not understand what he was saying to them. So Jesus again said to them, "Truly, truly, I say to you, I am the door of the sheep. All who came before me are thieves and robbers; but the sheep did not heed them. I am the door; if any one enters by me, he will be saved, and will go in and out and find pasture. The thief comes only to steal and kill and destroy; I came that they may have life, and have it abundantly. I am the good shepherd. The good shepherd lays down his life for the sheep."
Is. 53:6. All we like sheep have gone astray; we have turned every one to his own way; and the Lord has laid on him the iniquity of us all. (Also Ps. 14:3, 119:176, Mt. 18:12.)
*Jn. 10:3. ...[The good shepherd] calls his own sheep by name and leads them out.
Jn. 10:27 [Christ]: My sheep hear my voice...and they follow me.
Jn. 6:43–44 [Christ]: ...No one can come to me unless the Father who sent me draws (Luther: ziehe) him...
Jn. 12:32 [Christ]: I, when I am lifted up from the earth, will draw all men to myself. (Also S. of S. 1:4.)
Col. 3:1–2. If...you have been raised with Christ, seek the things that are above, where Christ is, seated at the right hand of God. Set your minds on things that are above, not on things that are on earth. (Also 2 Cor. 4:16–18.)
Heb. 12:2. Looking to Jesus the pioneer and perfecter of our faith, who for the joy that was set before him endured the cross, despising the shame, and is seated at the right hand of the throne of God..
Eph. 5:2. ...Christ loved us and gave himself up for us... (Also Gal. 1:3–4, 2:20, Eph. 1 Tim. 2:6, Tit. 2:14.)
Rom. 5:7–8. Why, one will hardly die for a righteous man—though perhaps for a good man one will dare even to die. But God shows his love for us in that while we were yet sinners Christ died for us. (Also Jn. 15:13.)
Jn. 13:1. ...Jesus...having loved his own who were in the world, he loved them to the end.

Sein Arm kann denen Feinden wehren,
His   arm   can   their   foes   check,
{His arm can check their foes,}

Sein Sorgen kann uns Schafe geistlich nähren,
His   caring   can   us   sheep spiritually nourish,
{His watchful care can spiritually nourish us, who are his sheep,}

Ja, kömmt die Zeit,   durchs   finstre Tal zu gehen,
Yes, comes the time, through-the dark vale to   go,
{Yes, and when the time comes to pass through the dark vale,}

So   hilft und tröstet uns sein sanfter Stab.
Then helps and comforts us his gentle staff.
{Then his gentle staff helps and comforts us.}

Drum   folgen wir   mit Freuden bis ins Grab.
Therefore follow we (him) with joy   to (the) grave.
{Therefore we will follow him joyfully to the grave.}

Auf!   Eilt zu ihm, verklärt   vor ihm zu stehen.
Rise! Hasten to him, transfigured before him to stand.

2. Soprano & Alto Duet
●Sheep come to Jesus and scorn the enticing world (184–2)
  Gesegnete Christen, glückselige Herde,
(O) blessed Christians,   happy   flock,

Kommt, stellt   euch   bei Jesu mit Dankbarkeit ein!
Come, present yourselves before Jesus with gratitude - !

Verachtet das Locken der schmeichlenden Erde,
Scorn   the enticings of-the flattering   earth,

Daß   euer Vergnügen vollkommen kann sein!
So-that your pleasure   perfect   may be!
{So that your pleasure may be perfect!}

3. Tenor Recit.
●Rejoice, for Christ loves & defends his flock! (184–3)
So freuet euch, ihr auserwählten Seelen!
So rejoice, ye   chosen   souls!

Die Freude gründet sich in Jesu Herz.
(Your) joy is-based - in Jesus' heart.
{Your joy finds its foundation in Jesus' heart.}

---

*Jn. 10:11 [Christ]: I am the good shepherd. The good shepherd lays down his life for the sheep.

1 Jn. 4:9. In this the love of God was made manifest among us, that God sent his only Son into the world, so that we might live through him.

Jn. 10:28 [Christ]: I give [my sheep] eternal life, and they shall never perish, and no one shall snatch them out of my hand.

Ps. 89:10. [O Lord]...thou dost scatter thy enemies with thy mighty arm.

Ps. 23:1–4. The Lord is my shepherd, I shall not want; he makes me lie down in green pastures. He leads me beside still waters; he restores my soul. He leads me in paths of righteousness for his name's sake. Even though I walk through the valley of the shadow of death (Luther: finstern Tal), I fear no evil; for thou art with me; thy rod and thy staff, they comfort me.

Phil. 1:21, 23. To me to live is Christ, and to die is gain...My desire is to depart and be with Christ, for that is far better. (Also 2 Cor. 5:8.)

2 Cor. 5:1–4. For we know that if the earthly tent we live in is destroyed, we have a building from God, a house not made with hands, eternal in the heavens. Here indeed we groan, and long to put on our heavenly dwelling, so that by putting it on we may not be found naked. For while we are still in this tent, we sigh with anxiety; not that we would be unclothed, but that we would be further clothed, so that what is mortal may be swallowed up by life. (Also Phil. 3:20–21.)

Ps. 100:3. Know that the Lord is God! It is he that made us, and we are his; we are his people, and the sheep of his pasture. (Also Ps. 95:6–7.)

*Jn. 10:3–5. ...The sheep hear [the shepherd's] voice, and he calls his own sheep by name and leads them out...The sheep follow him, for they know his voice. A stranger they will not follow, but they will flee from him, for they do not know the voice of strangers.

Prov. 1:10. My son, if sinners entice you, do not consent.

Mt. 18:7. Woe to the world for temptations to sin!...

1 Jn. 2:15–17. Do not love the world or the things in the world. If any one loves the world, love for the Father is not in him. For all that is in the world, the lust of the flesh and the lust of the eyes and the pride of life, is not of the Father but is of the world. And the world passes away, and the lust of it; but he who does the will of God abides for ever. (Also Jms. 4:4, Jn. 5:44.)

Ps. 16:11. [O Lord,] thou dost show me the path of life; in thy presence there is fulness of joy, in thy right hand are pleasures for evermore.

1 Pet. 2:9–10. You are a chosen race, a royal priesthood, a holy nation, God's own people, that you may declare the wonderful deeds of him who called you out of darkness into his marvelous light. Once you were no people but now you are God's people; once you had not received mercy but now you have received mercy.

Tit. 2:13–14. ...Our great God and Savior Jesus Christ...gave himself

Dies Labsal kann kein Mensch erzählen.
This comfort can no man relate.
{This comfort is beyond telling.}

Die Freude steigt auch unterwärts
This joy reaches also downwards
{This joy also reaches down}

Zu denen, die in Sündenbanden lagen,
To those, who in sin's-bonds lay,
{To those who formerly lay in bonds of sin:}

Die hat der Held aus Juda schon zerschlagen.
Them hath the champion of Judah already broken.
{These the champion of Judah has already broken.}

Ein David steht uns bei.
A David stands us by.
{A David stands here to help us.}

Ein Heldenarm macht uns von Feinden frei.
A champion's-arm makes us of foes free.
{A champion's arm frees us of our foes.}

Wenn Gott mit Kraft die Herde schützt,
If God with strength (his) flock protects,

Wenn er im Zorn auf ihre Feinde blitzt,
If he in wrath upon her foes throws-lightning,

Wenn er den bittern Kreuzestod
If he the bitter cross's-death

Für sie nicht scheuet,
For her not shuns,
{If he does not shun the cross's death for her,}

So trifft sie ferner keine Not,
Then strikes her furthermore no distress,
{Then no distress can further strike her,}

So lebet sie in ihrem Gott erfreuet.
Then lives she in her God gladdened.
{Then she lives rejoicing in her God.}

Hier schmecket sie die edle Weide
Here tastes she the noble pasture
{Here she tastes the noble pasture}

Und hoffet dort vollkommne Himmelsfreude.
And hopes-for there perfect heavenly-joy.
{And expects over there perfect heavenly joy.}

4. Tenor Aria
●Blessings await those who know Jesus' voice (184–4)
Glück und Segen sind bereit,
Happiness and blessing are made-ready,

for us to redeem us from all iniquity and to purify for himself a people of his own who are zealous for good deeds.
1 Jn. 4:10. In this is love, not that we loved God but that he loved us and sent his Son to be the expiation for our sins.
Ps. 106:2. Who can utter the mighty doings of the Lord, or show forth all his praise?
1 Cor. 2:9–10. As it is written, "What no eye has seen, nor ear heard, nor the heart of man conceived, what God has prepared for those who love him," God has revealed to us...
Rom. 5:8. God shows his love for us in that while we were yet sinners Christ died for us.
Col. 2:13–15. You, who were dead in trespasses and the uncircumcision of your flesh, God made alive together with him, having forgiven us all our trespasses, having canceled the bond which stood against us with its legal demands; this he set aside, nailing it to the cross. He disarmed the principalities and powers and made a public example of them, triumphing over them in him.
Rev. 5:5. ...The Lion of the tribe of Judah, the Root of David, has conquered...
Ezek. 34:23 [God]: I will set up over [my people] one shepherd, my servant David...
Gen. 49:10. The scepter shall not depart from Judah...until he comes to whom it belongs (Luther: bis das der Held komme)...
Lk. 1:51. [God] has shown strength with his arm, he has scattered the proud in the imagination of their hearts.
2 Sam. 22:14–15. The Lord thundered from heaven, and the Most High uttered his voice. And he sent out arrows, and scattered them; lightning, and routed them.
*Jn. 10:11. ...The good shepherd lays down his life for the sheep. (Also Jn. 10:17–18.)
Rom. 5:7–8. Why, one will hardly die for a righteous man—though perhaps for a good man one will dare even to die. But God shows his love for us in that while we were yet sinners Christ died for us. (Also Jn. 15:13.)
Phil. 2:8. ...[Christ] humbled himself and became obedient unto death, even death on a cross. (Also Heb. 12:2.)
Rom. 8:32. He who did not spare his own Son but gave him up for us all, will he not also give us all things with him?
Ps. 23:6. Surely goodness and mercy shall follow me all the days of my life; and I shall dwell in the house of the Lord for ever.
Ps. 23:1–2. The Lord is my shepherd, I shall not want; he makes me lie down in green pastures...
Rev. 7:15–17. ...He who sits upon the throne will shelter [his people] with his presence. They shall hunger no more, neither thirst any more; the sun shall not strike them, nor any scorching heat. For the Lamb in the midst of the throne will be their shepherd, and he will guide them to springs of living water; and God will wipe away every tear from their eyes. (Also Rev. 21:4, Is. 25:8.)

*Jn. 10:4–5. ...The sheep follow [their shepherd], for they know his voice. A stranger they will not follow, but they will flee from him, for they do not know the voice of strangers.
Jn. 10:14 [Christ]: I am the good shepherd; I know my own and my own know me.

Die geweihte Schar zu krönen,
The sacred throng to crown,
{To crown the sacred throng;}

Jesus bringt die güldne Zeit,
Jesus brings the golden age,
{Jesus ushers in the golden age,}

Welche sich zu ihm gewöhnen.
To-those-who - to him have-grown-accustomed.
{To those who have learned to recognize his voice.}

5. Chorale (New to this version)
●Prayer that God will keep his own until eternity (184–5)
Herr, ich hoff je, du werdest die
Lord, I hope ever, (that) thou wilt those

In keiner Not verlassen,
In no distress abandon,

Die dein Wort recht als treue Knecht
Who thy Word truly as faithful servants
{Who grasp thy Word as faithful servants}

Im Herzn und Glauben fassen;
In heart and faith do-grasp; (that thou)
{In heart and faith; that thou}

Gibst ihn' bereit die Seligkeit
Wilt-grant to-them already (eternal) Salvation

Und läßt sie nicht verderben.
And wilt-let them not perish.
{And wilt not let them perish.}

O Herr, durch dich bitt ich, laß mich
O Lord, through thee pray I, let me
{O Lord, through thee I pray, let me}

Fröhlich und willig sterben.
Joyfully and willingly die.

6. Chorus
●Prayer: Good Shepherd, lead us to life (184–6)
Guter Hirte, Trost der Deinen,
(O) good shepherd, Comfort of those-who-are-thine-own,

Laß uns nur dein heilig Wort!
Leave us only thy holy Word!
{Just leave us thy holy Word!}

Laß dein gnädig Antlitz scheinen,
Let thy gracious countenance shine (upon us),

Bleibe unser Gott und Hort,
Remain our God and refuge,

*Jn. 10:10 [Christ]: ...I came that they may have life, and have it abundantly. (Also Jn. 10:27–28.)
1 Pet. 5:4. And when the chief Shepherd is manifested you will obtain the unfading crown of glory. (Also 2 Tim. 4:8, Jms. 1:12, Rev. 2:10.)
Rev. 21:1, 3–4. Then [in my vision] I saw a new heaven and a new earth...and I heard a loud voice from the throne saying, "Behold, the dwelling of God is with men. He will dwell with them, and they shall be his people, and God himself will be with them; he will wipe away every tear from their eyes, and death shall be no more, neither shall there be mourning nor crying nor pain any more, for the former things have passed away."

Jn. 10:27–29 [Christ]: My sheep hear my voice, and I know them, and they follow me; and I give them eternal life, and they shall never perish, and no one shall snatch them out of my hand. My Father, who has given them to me, is greater than all, and no one is able to snatch them out of the Father's hand.
Ps. 119:41–42. Let thy steadfast love come to me, O Lord, thy salvation according to thy promise...for I trust in thy word.
Ps. 40:4. Blessed is the man who makes the Lord his trust... (Also Ps. 40:4, 84:12, 146:5, Jer. 17:7.)
Heb. 13:5–6. ...He has said, "I will never fail you nor forsake you." Hence we can confidently say, "The Lord is my helper, I will not be afraid..." (Also Deut. 31:6, 8; Josh. 1:5.)
Jn. 3:16. For God so loved the world that he gave his only Son, that whoever believes in him should not perish but have eternal life.
Rom. 10:8–11, 13. What does [the righteousness based on faith] say? The word is near you, on your lips and in your heart (that is, the word of faith which we preach); because if you confess with your lips that Jesus is Lord and believe in your heart that God raised him from the dead, you will be saved. For man believes with his heart and so is justified, and he confesses with his lips and so is saved. The scripture says, "No one who believes in him will be put to shame."... For, "every one who calls upon the name of the Lord will be saved."
Num. 23:10. ...Let me die the death of the righteous, and let my end be like his! (Also Heb. 13:7.)

*Jn. 10:11 [Christ]: I am the good shepherd...
Ps. 23:1–4. The Lord is my shepherd, I shall not want; he makes me lie down in green pastures. He leads me beside still waters; he restores my soul. He leads me in paths of righteousness for his name's sake. Even though I walk through the valley of the shadow of death, I fear no evil; for thou art with me; thy rod and thy staff, they comfort me.
Ps. 119:43. [O Lord,] take not the word of truth utterly out of my mouth, for my hope is in thy ordinances.
Ps. 31:16. Let thy face shine on thy servant; save me in thy steadfast love! (Also Num. 6:24–26, Ps. 4:6, 80:3/7/19.)
Ps. 67:1–2. May God be gracious to us and bless us and make his face (Luther: Antlitz) to shine upon us, that thy way may be known upon earth, thy saving power among all nations.

Der durch allmachtsvolle Hände
Who with almighty hands

Unsern Gang zum Leben wende!
Our course to life doth-turn!
{Doth turn our steps to life everlasting!}

BWV 185
Barmherziges Herze der ewigen Liebe
(NBA I/17; BC A101)

4. S. after Trinity (BWV 185, 24, 177)
*Rom. 8:18–23 (All creation eagerly longs for the revealing of
the sons of God)
*Lk. 6:36–42 (Sermon on the mount: Be merciful, do not
judge)
Librettist: Salomon Franck

1. Soprano & Tenor Duet
●Prayer: O God of love, kindle a heart of love in me! (185-1)
Barmherziges Herze der ewigen Liebe,
(O) compassionate heart of eternal love,

Errege, bewege mein Herze durch dich;
Stir-up, move my heart through thyself;
{Stir up and move my heart with thine own;}

Damit ich Erbarmen und Gütigkeit übe,
So-that I mercy and kindness might-practice,
{So that I might practice mercy and kindness,}

O Flamme der Liebe, zerschmelze du mich!
O flame of love, melt thou me!

2. Alto Recit.
●Warning: Show mercy so that you receive mercy (185-2)
Ihr Herzen, die ihr euch
Ye hearts, who yourselves
{Ye hearts who have}

In Stein und Fels verkehrt,
Into stone and rock have-turned,
{Turned yourselves to rock and stone,}

Zerfließt und werdet weich,
Melt and become soft,

Erwägt, was euch der Heiland lehret,
Ponder, what you the Savior teaches,
{Ponder what the Savior teaches you;}

Übt, übt Barmherzigkeit
Practise, practise compassion

Und sucht noch auf der Erden
And seek (while) yet on the earth

Ps. 16:11. [O Lord,] thou dost show me the path of life; in thy
presence there is fulness of joy...
*Jn. 10:9–10 [Christ]: I am the door; if any one enters by me, he will
be saved, and will go in and out and find pasture. The thief comes
only to steal and kill and destroy; I came that they may have life, and
have it abundantly.

Neh. 9:17. ...Thou art a God ready to forgive, gracious and merciful,
slow to anger and abounding in steadfast love...
*Lk. 6:36. Be merciful, even as your Father is merciful.
1 Jn. 4:10, 16, 19–21. In this is love, not that we loved God but that
he loved us...We know and believe the love God has for us. God is
love, and he who abides in love abides in God, and God abides in him
...We love, because he first loved us. If any one says, "I love God," and
hates his brother, he is a liar; for he who does not love his brother
whom he has seen, cannot love God whom he has not seen. And this
commandment we have from him, that he who loves God should love
his brother also.
1 Jn. 3:17–18. But if any one has the world's goods and sees his
brother in need, yet closes his heart against him, how does God's love
abide in him? Little children, let us not love in word or speech but in
deed and in truth. (Also Jms. 2:14–16.)
Mic. 6:8. ...What does the Lord require of you but to do justice, and
to love kindness (Luther: Liebe üben), and to walk humbly with your
God?
Rom. 5:5. ...God's love has been poured into our hearts through the
Holy Spirit which has been given to us.
S. of S. 8:6. ...Love is strong as death...Its flashes are flashes of fire, a
most vehement flame. (Also Mt. 3:11, Lk. 3:16.)

Deut. 15:7. ...You shall not harden your heart or shut your hand
against your poor brother.
Mt. 18:28–35. [The servant whose debt had been forgiven by his
master]...came upon one of his fellow servants who owed him a
hundred denarii, and seizing him by the throat he said, "Pay what you
owe." So his fellow servant fell down and besought him, "Have
patience with me, and I will pay you." He refused and went and put
him in prison till he should pay the debt. When his fellow servants saw
what had taken place, they were greatly distressed, and they went and
reported to their lord all that had taken place. Then his lord
summoned him and said to him, "You wicked servant! I forgave you
all that debt because you besought me; and should not you have had
mercy on your fellow servant, as I had mercy on you?" And in anger
his lord delivered him to the jailers, till he should pay all his debt. So
also my heavenly Father will do to every one of you, if you do not
forgive your brother from your heart.
Sirach (Apocrypha) 35:2. (= Sirach 35:3–4 of German Bible)...He who
gives alms (Luther: Barmherzigkeit übt) sacrifices a thank offering.

Dem Vater gleich zu werden!
The Father like to become!
{To become like the Father!}

Ach! greifet nicht durch das verbotne Richten
Ah! (draw) not through that forbidden judging
{Ah, do not—through forbidden judging—}

Dem Allerhöchsten ins Gericht,
The Most-High into judgment,
{Bring divine judgment upon yourselves,}

Sonst wird sein Eifer euch zernichten.
Else will his zeal you destroy.
{Or his zealous wrath will destroy you.}

Vergebt, so wird euch auch vergeben;
Forgive, then will you also be-forgiven;

Gebt, gebt in diesem Leben;
Give, give in this life;

Macht euch ein Kapital,
Store-up for-yourselves a principal,

Das dort einmal
Which there one-day
{Which God will one day}

Gott wiederzahlt mit reichen Interessen;
God will-repay with abundant interest;
{Repay there with abundant interest;}

Denn wie ihr meßt, wird man euch wieder messen.
For as you measure, will they to-you in-return measure.
{For the measure you give, will you get in return.}

3. Alto Aria
●Sow plentifully in this age to gather a rich harvest (185–3)
Sei bemüht in dieser Zeit,
Be concerned in this age,

  Seele, reichlich auszustreuen,
(O) Soul, plentifully (seed) to-scatter,
{O soul, take care to scatter seed plentifully in this age,}

Soll die Ernte dich erfreuen
Shall the harvest thee gladden
{If the harvest is to gladden thee}

In der reichen Ewigkeit,
In that abundant eternity,

Wo, wer Gutes ausgesäet,
Where, whoever good has-sown,
{Where, whoever has sown,}

Fröhlich nach den Garben gehet.
Joyfully after the sheaves goes.
{Gathers the sheaves joyfully.}

Mt. 5:44–45, 48 [Christ]: ...Love your enemies and pray for those who persecute you, so that you may be sons of your Father who is in heaven; for he makes his sun rise on the evil and on the good, and sends rain on the just and on the unjust...You, therefore, must be perfect, as your heavenly Father is perfect.

*Lk. 6:35–38 [Christ]: Love your enemies, and do good, and lend, expecting nothing in return; and your reward will be great, and you will be sons of the Most High; for he is kind to the ungrateful and the selfish. Be merciful, even as your Father is merciful. Judge not, and you will not be judged; condemn not, and you will not be condemned; forgive and you will be forgiven; give, and it will be given to you; good measure, pressed down, shaken together, running over, will be put into your lap. For the measure you give will be the measure you get back. (Also Mt. 7:1–2.)

Mt. 6:19–20 [Christ]: Do not lay up for yourselves treasures on earth, where moth and rust consume and where thieves break in and steal, but lay up for yourselves treasures in heaven, where neither moth nor rust consumes and where thieves do not break in and steal.

Lk. 16:9 [Christ]: I tell you, make friends for yourselves by means of unrighteous mammon, so that when it fails they may receive you into the eternal habitations.

Prov. 11:24–25. One man gives freely, yet grows all the richer; another withholds what he should give, and only suffers want. A liberal man will be enriched, and one who waters will himself be watered.

Ps. 37:21. ...The righteous is generous and gives. (Also 1 Tim. 6:18.)

Prov. 19:17. He who is kind to the poor lends to the Lord, and he will repay him for his deed.

Prov. 21:13. He who closes his ear to the cry of the poor will himself cry out and not be heard.

*Lk. 6:38 [Christ]: The measure you give will be the measure you get back.

2 Cor. 9:6, 8–9. The point is this: he who sows sparingly will also reap sparingly, and he who sows bountifully will also reap bountifully...God is able to provide you with every blessing in abundance, so that you may always have enough of everything and may provide in abundance for every good work. As it is written, "He scatters abroad, he gives to the poor; his righteousness endures for ever."

Ecc. 11:6. In the morning sow your seed, and at evening withhold not your hand; for you do not know which will prosper, this or that, or whether both alike will be good.

Gal. 6:7–9. Do not be deceived; God is not mocked, for whatever a man sows, that he will also reap. For he who sows to his own flesh will from the flesh reap corruption; but he who sows to the Sprit will from the Spirit reap eternal life. And let us not grow weary in well-doing, for in due season we shall reap, if we do not lose heart.

Hos. 10:12. Sow for yourselves righteousness, reap the fruit of steadfast love; break up your fallow ground, for it is the time to seek the Lord, that he may come and rain salvation upon you.

Ps. 126:5–6. May those who sow in tears reap with shouts of joy! He that goes forth weeping, bearing the seed for sowing, shall come home with shouts of joy, bringing his sheaves with him.

4. Bass Recit.

●Blindness to own faults; splinter in neighbor's eye (185-4)

Die Eigenliebe schmeichelt sich!
-    Self-love   flatters   itself!

Bestrebe dich,
Exert   yourself,

Erst deinen   Balken auszuziehen,
First your (own) beam   to-pull-out,
{To pull out your own beam first,}

Denn magst du dich   um Splitter auch bemühen,
Then may you yourself about splinters also concern,
{Then you may concern yourself about splinters,}

Die in des Nächsten Augen   sein.
Which in (your) neighbor's eyes (may) be-found.
{Which may be found in your neighbor's eyes.}

Ist gleich dein Nächster nicht vollkommen rein,
Is indeed your neighbor not perfectly pure,
{Though your neighbor be not perfectly pure,}

So wisse, daß auch du   kein Engel,
Then know, that also you (are) no angel,
{Then remember that you, too, are no angel,}

Verbeßre deine Mängel!
Correct   your shortcomings!

Wie kann ein Blinder mit dem andern
How can one blind-man with the other
{How can one blind man}

Doch   recht und richtig wandern?
Indeed properly and correctly walk?
{Properly lead another?}

Wie, fallen sie zu ihrem Leide
What, fall they to their sorrow
{What, will they not, to their sorrow}

Nicht in die Gruben alle beide?
Not into the ditch both-of-them?
{Both fall into the ditch?}

5. Bass Aria

●Mark of Christian is non-judging generosity (185-5)

Das ist der Christen Kunst:
This is the Christian's art:

Nur Gott und sich erkennen,
Only God and oneself to-discern,

Von wahrer Liebe brennen,
With true   love to-burn,

*Lk. 6:42 [Christ]: How can you say to your brother, "Brother, let me take out the speck that is in your eye," when you yourself do not see the log that is in your own eye? You hypocrite, first take the log out of your own eye, and then you will see clearly to take out the speck that is in your brother's eye. (Also Mt. 7:3–5.)

Jn. 9:39–41. Jesus said, "For judgment I came into this world, that those who do not see may see, and that those who see may become blind." Some of the Pharisees near him heard this, and they said to him, "Are we also blind?" Jesus said to them, "If you were blind, you would have no guilt; but now that you say, 'We see,' your guilt remains."

Jn. 8:3–5, 7–11. The scribes and the Pharisees brought a woman who had been caught in adultery, and placing her in the midst they said to [Jesus], "Teacher, this woman has been caught in the act of adultery. Now in the law Moses commanded us to stone such. What do you say about her?"...He stood up and said to them, "Let him who is without sin among you be the first to throw a stone at her." And once more he bent down and wrote with his finger on the ground. But when they heard it, they went away, one by one, beginning with the eldest, and Jesus was left alone with the woman standing before him. Jesus looked up and said to her, "Woman, where are they? Has no one condemned you?" She said, "No one, Lord." And Jesus said, "Neither do I condemn you; go, and do not sin again."

Jms. 2:8–13. If you really fulfil the royal law, according to the scripture, "You shall love your neighbor as yourself," you do well. But if you show partiality, you commit sin, and are convicted by the law as transgressors. For whoever keeps the whole law but fails in one point has become guilty of all of it. For he who said, "Do not commit adultery," said also, "Do not kill." If you do not commit adultery but do kill, you have become a transgressor of the law. So speak and so act as those who are to be judged under the law of liberty. For judgment is without mercy to one who has shown no mercy; yet mercy triumphs over judgment.

Jms. 4:11–12. Do not speak evil against one another, brethren. He that speaks evil against a brother or judges his brother, speaks evil against the law and judges the law. But if you judge the law, you are not a doer of the law but a judge. There is one lawgiver and judge, he who is able to save and to destroy. But who are you that you judge your neighbor?

*Lk. 6:39. [Jesus] also told them a parable: "Can a blind man lead a blind man? Will they not both fall into a pit?" (Also Mt. 15:14.)

Rom. 14:22. The faith that you have, keep between yourself and God...

Gal. 6:3–4. If any one thinks he is something, when he is nothing, he deceives himself. But let each one test his own work... (Also 2 Cor. 10:12.)

1 Cor. 4:4. I am not aware of anything against myself, but I am not thereby acquitted. It is the Lord who judges me.

1 Chron. 28:9. ...The Lord searches all hearts, and understands every plan and thought... (Also Ps. 139:23–24, Jer. 17:10.)

1 Jn. 3:10. By this it may be seen who are the children of God, and who are the children of the devil: whoever does not do right is not of God, nor he who does not love his brother.

Jn. 13:34–35 [Christ]: A new commandment I give to you, that you love one another; even as I have loved you, that you also love one

Nicht   unzulässig richten,
Not, (as is) forbidden, to-judge,

Noch fremdes Tun vernichten,
Nor   other's deeds to-destroy,

Des   Nächsten nicht vergessen,
(One's) neighbor   not   to-forget,

Mit   reichem Maße messen:
With generous measure to-measure:

Das macht bei Gott und Menschen Gunst,
This creates with God and   men   favor,
{This creates favor with God and men,}

Das ist der Christen Kunst.
This is the Christian's art.

6. Chorale (See also 177-1.)
●Prayer for grace to keep true faith of God's Word (185-6)
Ich ruf zu dir, Herr Jesu Christ,
I   cry to thee, Lord Jesus Christ,

Ich bitt,   erhör mein Klagen,
I   ask, (please) hear my   crying,

Verleih mir Gnad zu dieser   Frist,
Grant me grace for this period-of-time,

Laß mich doch nicht verzagen;
Let me indeed not   despair;

Den rechten Weg, Herr, ich mein,
The true   way, Lord, I mean,

Den wollest du mir geben,
That wouldst thou to-me give,
{Wouldst thou give that to me,}

Dir   zu leben,
For-thee to live,
{To live for thee,}

Mein'm Nächsten nütz zu sein,
To-my   neighbor of-service to be,
{To be of service to my neighbor,}

another. By this all men will know that you are my disciples, if you have love for one another. (Also Jn. 15:12, 17, 1 Thess. 4:9, 1 Jn. 3:11.)
1 Jn. 3:23. This is his commandment, that we should believe in the name of his Son Jesus Christ and love one another, just as he commanded us.
Mt. 22:37–40 [Christ]: ...You shall love the Lord your God with all your heart, and with all your soul, and with all your mind. This is the great and first commandment. And a second is like it, You shall love your neighbor as yourself. On these two commandments depend all the law and the prophets. (Also Mk. 12:30–31, Lk. 10:27, Deut. 6:5, Lev. 19:18.)
Jms. 4:11–12. Do not speak evil against one another, brethren...Who are you that you judge your neighbor?
***Lk. 6:36–38 [Christ]:** Be merciful, even as your Father is merciful. Judge not, and you will not be judged; condemn not, and you will not be condemned; forgive and you will be forgiven; give, and it will be given to you; good measure (Luther: Maß), pressed down, shaken together, running over, will be put into your lap. For the measure (Luther: Maß) you give will be the measure you get back. (Also Mt. 7:2.)
Prov. 3:3–4. Let not loyalty and faithfulness forsake you...So you will find favor (Luther: Gunst) and good repute (Luther: Klugheit) in the sight of God and man.

Ps. 27:7–9. Hear, O Lord, when I cry aloud, be gracious to me and answer me! Thou hast said, "Seek ye my face." My heart says to thee, "Thy face, Lord, do I seek." Hide not thy face from me. Turn not thy servant away in anger, thou who hast been my help. Cast me not off, forsake me not, O God of my salvation! (Also Ps. 4:1, 17:6, 28:2, 102:1–2.)
Heb. 4:16. Let us...with confidence draw near to the throne of grace, that we may receive mercy and find grace to help in time of need.
Rev. 14:12. Here is a call for the endurance of the saints, those who keep the commandments of God and the faith of Jesus.
Heb. 10:23. Let us hold fast the confession of our hope without wavering, for he who promised is faithful.
Jms. 1:27. Religion that is pure and undefiled before God and the Father is this: to visit orphans and widows in their affliction, and to keep oneself unstained from the world.
Mt. 22:35–40. ...A lawyer, asked [Jesus] a question, to test him. "Teacher, which is the great commandment in the law?" And he said to him, "You shall love the Lord your God with all your heart, and with all your soul, and with all your mind. This is the great and first commandment. And a second is like it, You shall love your neighbor as yourself. On these two commandments depend all the law and the prophets." (Also Mk. 12:30–31, Lk. 10:27, Deut. 6:5, Lev. 19:18.)
Rom. 14:7–8. None of us lives to himself, and none of us dies to himself. If we live, we live to the Lord, and if we die, we die to the Lord; so then, whether we live or whether we die, we are the Lord's. (Also Phil. 1:21.)
2 Cor. 5:9. Whether we are at home or away, we make it our aim to please him.
Jms. 2:14–17. What does it profit, my brethren, if a man says he has faith but has not works? Can his faith save him? If a brother or sister is ill-clad and in lack of daily food, and one of you says to them, "Go in peace, be warmed and filled," without giving them the things needed for the body, what does it profit? So faith by itself, if it has no works, is dead.

Dein Wort zu halten eben.
Thy Word to   keep   (thus).
{And thus to keep thy Word.}

BWV 186
Ärgre dich, o Seele, nicht
(NBA I/18; BC A108)

7. S. after Trinity (BWV 186, 107, 187)
*Rom. 6:19–23 (The wages of sin is death but the gift of God
is eternal life)
*Mk. 8:1–9 (Jesus feeds the four thousand)
Librettist: Unknown. This libretto is a revised and expanded
version of a libretto by Salomon Franck (186a) for
3. S. of Advent (BWV 186a only)
+1 Cor. 4:1–5 (Paul as a steward of the gospel)
+Mt. 11:2–10 (John the Baptist in prison; he sends
messengers to question Jesus)

Part I

1. Chorus
●Incarnation: God became servant; do not take offence!
(186–1)
Ärgre dich,   o Seele, nicht,
Take-offence, O soul,   not,
{O soul, do not take offence,}

Daß das allerhöchste Licht,
That the all-surpassing light,

Gottes Glanz und Ebenbild,
God's radiance and   image,

Sich in Knechtsgestalt verhüllt,
Itself in servant's-form does-veil,
{Veils itself in servant's form,}

Ärgre dich,   o Seele, nicht!
Take-offence, O soul,   not!
{O soul, do not take offence!}

2. Bass Recit. (Added in this version)
●Poverty strikes Christ as well as his members (186–2)
Die Knechtsgestalt, die Not, der Mangel
  -   Servant-form,   - trouble, - deprivation

Trifft Christi Glieder nicht allein,
Strikes Christ's members not alone,
{Does not strike Christ's members alone,}

Es   will ihr Haupt selbst arm und elend sein.
(Now) seeks their head himself poor and wretched to-be.
{For their head seeks to be poor and wretched himself.}

Und ist nicht Reichtum, ist nicht Überfluß
And is not   wealth, is not   plenty

Jn. 14:23–24. Jesus [said,] "If a man loves me, he will keep my word,
and my Father will love him, and we will come to him and make our
home with him. He who does not love me does not keep my words;
and the word which you hear is not mine but the Father's who sent
me." (Also Rev. 3:10.)
Lk. 11:28. [Jesus] said, "Blessed...are those who hear the word of God
and keep it!"

+Mt. 11:2–6. When John heard in prison about the deeds of the
Christ, he sent word..."Are you he who is to come, or shall we look for
another?" And Jesus answered..."Go and tell John what you hear and
see: the blind receive their sight and the lame walk, lepers are
cleansed and the deaf hear, and the dead are raised up, and the poor
have good news preached to them. And blessed is he who takes no
offense (Luther: ärgert) at me." (Also Lk. 7:20–23.)
Heb. 1:1–3. In many and various ways God spoke of old to our fathers
by the prophets; but in these last days he has spoken to us by a Son,
whom he appointed the heir of all things, through whom also he
created the world. He reflects the glory of God (Luther: der Glanz
seiner Herrlichkeit) and bears the very stamp of his nature (Luther:
das Ebenbilde seines Wesens), upholding the universe by his word of
power...
Phil. 2:5–9. Have this mind among yourselves, which is yours in Christ
Jesus, who, though he was in the form of God, did not count equality
with God a thing to be grasped, but emptied himself, taking the form
of a servant (Luther: Knechtsgestalt), being born in the likeness of
men. And being found in human form he humbled himself and
became obedient unto death, even death on a cross. Therefore God
has highly exalted him and bestowed on him the name which is above
every name.
2 Cor. 8:9. You know the grace of our Lord Jesus Christ, that though
he was rich, yet for your sake he became poor, so that by his poverty
you might become rich.

Phil. 2:7. [Christ] emptied himself, taking the form of a servant
(Luther: Knechtsgestalt)...
Jn. 13:12–16. When [Jesus] had washed [the disciples'] feet...and
resumed his place, he said to them, "Do you know what I have done
to you? You call me Teacher and Lord; and you are right, for so I am.
If I then, your Lord and Teacher, have washed your feet, you also
ought to wash one another's feet. For I have given you an example,
that you also should do as I have done to you. Truly, truly, I say to
you, a servant is not greater than his master; nor is he who is sent
greater than he who sent him." (Also Jn. 15:20.)
Eph. 5:23. ...Christ is the head of the church, his body...
1 Cor. 12:12, 27. For just as the body is one and has many members,
and all the members of the body, though many, are one body, so it is
with Christ...Now you are the body of Christ and individually members
of it. (Also Rom. 12:4–5, Eph. 4:15–16, 5:29–30.)

Des Satans   Angel,
- Satan's baited-hook,

So man mit Sorgfalt meiden muß?
Which one with care   must-avoid?

Wird   dir   im Gegenteil
Becomes for-you, in   contrast,
{When, in contrast,}

Die Last zu viel zu tragen,
The burden too much to carry,
{Your burden becomes too much for you,}

Wenn Armut dich beschwert,
When poverty you encumbers,
{When poverty encumbers you,}

Wenn Hunger dich verzehrt,
When hunger you consumes,
{When hunger consumes you,}

Und   willst sogleich verzagen,
And (you) would forthwith despair,

So denkst du nicht an Jesum, an dein Heil.
Then think you not of Jesus, of your salvation.
{Then you are not thinking of Jesus, of your salvation.}

Hast du wie jenes Volk
Have you like that-other nation
{If you, like that other nation,}

        nicht bald   zu essen,
        not shortly something-to-eat,
        {do not shortly have something to eat;}

So seufzest du: Ach Herr,
Then sigh   you: Ah, Lord,
{Then you sigh: Ah, Lord,}

        wie lange willst   du mein vergessen?
        how long wouldst thou me   forget?
        {how long wouldst thou forget me?}

3. Bass Aria
●Doubt: Is this the one who is to help me? (186–3)
Bist du,   der   mir helfen soll,
Art thou, the-one-who me to-help is,
{Art thou the one who is to help me?}

Eilst   du nicht, mir beizustehen?
Hastenest thou not, me to-stand-by?
{Wilt thou not hasten to stand by me?}

2 Cor. 8:9. You know the grace of our Lord Jesus Christ, that though he was rich, yet for your sake he became poor...
1 Tim. 6:9–10. Those who desire to be rich fall into temptation, into a snare, into many senseless and hurtful desires that plunge men into ruin and destruction. For the love of money is the root of all evils; it is through this craving that some have wandered away from the faith and pierced their hearts with many pangs. (Also Mt. 19:23–24, Mk. 10:25, Lk. 18:24–25.)
Mt. 6:30–32. If God so clothes the grass of the field, which today is alive and tomorrow is thrown into the oven, will he not much more clothe you, O men of little faith? Therefore do not be anxious, saying, "What shall we eat?" or "What shall we drink?" or "What shall we wear?" For the Gentiles seek all these things; and your heavenly Father knows that you need them all.
*Mk. 8:1–3. In those days, when again a great crowd had gathered, and they had nothing to eat, [Jesus] called his disciples to him, and said to them, "I have compassion on the crowd, because they have been with me now three days, and have nothing to eat; and if I send them away hungry to their homes, they will faint on the way; and some of them have come a long way."
Mt. 7:14 [Christ]: ...The way is hard, that leads to life...
Acts 14:22. ...Through many tribulations we must enter the kingdom of God.
2 Cor. 1:8–10. We do not want you to be ignorant, brethren, of the affliction we experienced in Asia; for we were so utterly, unbearably crushed (Luther: beschweret) that we despaired of life itself. Why, we felt that we had received the sentence of death; but that was to make us rely not on ourselves but on God who raises the dead; he delivered us from so deadly a peril, and he will deliver us; on him we have set our hope that he will deliver us again.
Ps. 94:14. The Lord will not forsake his people; he will not abandon his heritage.
Heb. 12:1–2. ...Let us run with perseverance the race that is set before us, looking to Jesus the pioneer and perfecter of our faith, who for the joy that was set before him endured the cross, despising the shame, and is seated at the right hand of the throne of God.
Ps. 77:7–9. Will the Lord...never again be favorable? Has his steadfast love for ever ceased? Has God forgotten to be gracious? Has he in anger shut up his compassion? (Also Ps. 13:1, Is. 49:14.)
Ps. 13:1–2. How long, O Lord? Wilt thou forget me for ever? How long wilt thou hide thy face from me? How long must I bear pain in my soul, and have sorrow in my heart all the day?... (Also Ps. 6:2–4, 6–7, 13:1–2, 22:1–2, 44:24, 69:17, 88:1, 14, 89:46, 90:13–15, Is. 38:13.)

+Mt. 11:2–3. ...John...sent word [to Jesus]..."Are you he who is to come, or shall we look for another?"
Ps. 22:19. ...O Lord, be not far off! O thou my help, hasten to my aid! (Also Ps. 70:5.)
Mk. 9:22. [O Lord,] ...if you can do anything, have pity on us and help us.
*Mk. 8:1–4. ...[Jesus] called his disciples to him, and said to them, "I have compassion on the crowd, because they have been with me now three days, and have nothing to eat; and if I send them away hungry

Mein Gemüt ist zweifelsvoll,
My   mind   is full-of-doubt,

Du   verwirfst vielleicht mein Flehen;
Thou dost-reject perhaps my supplication;
{Thou dost perhaps reject my supplication;}

Doch, o Seele, zweifle nicht,
Yet, O soul, doubt   not,

Laß Vernunft dich nicht bestricken.
Let   reason thee not   ensnare.
{Let not reason ensnare thee.}

Deinen Helfer, Jakobs Licht,
Thy   helper, Jacob's light,

Kannst du in der Schrift erblicken.
Canst thou in the Scripture see.

to their homes, they will faint on the way; and some of them have come a long way." And his disciples answered him, "How can one feed these men with bread here in the desert?"

Jms. 1:6–8. ...He who doubts is like a wave of the sea that is driven and tossed by the wind. For that person must not suppose that a double-minded man, unstable in all his ways, will receive anything from the Lord.

Mk. 8:14, 16–17, 19–21. Now [the disciples] had forgotten to bring bread...And they discussed it with one another...And being aware of it, Jesus said to them, "Why do you discuss the fact that you have no bread?...When I broke the five loaves for the five thousand, how many baskets full of broken pieces did you take up?...And the seven for the four thousand, how many baskets full of broken pieces did you take up?...Do you not yet understand?"

Prov. 3:5. Trust in the Lord with all your heart, and do not rely on your own insight. (Also 1 Cor. 1:25–27.)

Ps. 102:17. He will regard the prayer of the destitute, and will not despise their supplication.

Ps. 54:4. Behold, God is my helper...

Ps. 27:1, 4–5. The Lord is my light and my salvation...

Num. 24:17. ...A star shall come forth out of Jacob, and a scepter shall rise out of Israel...

2 Cor. 1:20. All the promises of God find their Yes in [Christ]...

Jn. 5:39 [Christ]: You search the scriptures...it is they that bear witness to me.

4. Tenor Recit. (Added in this version)
●Body is temporal but Word's manna feeds our souls (186-4)
Ach, daß ein Christ so sehr
Ah,   that a Christian so much

Für seinen Körper sorgt!
About his   body should-care!

Was ist er mehr?
What is it more?
{What is it but}

Ein Bau von Erden,
A building of earth,
{An earthen building,}

Der wieder muß zur Erde werden,
Which again must into earth be-changed,
{Which must change back into earth again,}

Ein Kleid, so   nur geborgt.
A cloak, which (is) only borrowed.

Er könnte ja   das beste Teil erwählen,
He could, indeed, the best portion choose (instead),
{Instead, a Christian could indeed choose the best portion,}

So seine Hoffnung nie betrügt:
Which his hope ne'er would-betray:
{Which would ne'er betray his hope:}

2 Cor. 5:1–4. We know that if the earthly tent we live in is destroyed, we have a building (Luther: Bau) from God, a house not made with hands, eternal in the heavens. Here indeed we groan, and long to put on our heavenly dwelling, so that by putting it on we may not be found naked. For while we are still in this tent, we sigh with anxiety; not that we would be unclothed, but that we would be further clothed, so that what is mortal may be swallowed up by life.

Ecc. 12:7. The dust returns to the earth as it was, and the spirit returns to God who gave it. (Also Gen. 3:19. Ecc. 3:20.)

Mt. 6:25 [Christ]: ...Do not be anxious about your life, what you shall eat or what you shall drink, nor about your body, what you shall put on. Is not life more than food, and the body more than clothing?

Lk. 10:39–42. [Martha] had a sister called Mary, who sat at the Lord's feet and listened to his teaching. But Martha was distracted with much serving; and she went to him and said, "Lord, do you not care that my sister has left me to serve alone? Tell her then to help me." But the Lord answered her, "Martha, Martha, you are anxious and troubled about many things; one thing is needful. Mary has chosen the good portion (Luther: das gute Teil erwählt), which shall not be taken away from her."

Rom. 5:5. [Our] hope does not disappoint us...

2 Cor. 4:16–18. So we do not lose heart. Though our outer nature is wasting away, our inner nature is being renewed every day. For this slight momentary affliction is preparing for us an eternal weight of glory beyond all comparison, because we look not to the things that

Das Heil der Seelen,
The welfare of   souls,
{The welfare of his soul,}

So   in Jesu liegt.
Which in Jesus does-lie.
{Which may be found in Jesus.}

O selig! wer ihn in der Schrift erblickt,
O blessed he-who him in the Scripture does-see,
{How blessed is the one who sees Jesus in the Scripture,}

Wie er durch seine Lehren
How he through his teachings
{How, through his teachings, he sends}

Auf alle, die ihn hören,
Upon all, who him hear,
{Upon all, who hear him,}

Ein geistlich Manna schickt!
A   spiritual manna does-send!
{A spiritual manna!}

Drum,   wenn der Kummer gleich
Therefore, even-if -   sorrow   -

        das Herze   nagt und frißt,
        (your) heart should-gnaw and eat,
        {should gnaw and eat at your heart,}

So schmeckt und sehet doch, wie freundlich Jesus ist.
Then   taste   and see, indeed, how   kind   Jesus is.

5. Tenor Aria
●Savior powerfully manifested, nurturing body & soul (186–5)
Mein Heiland läßt sich merken
My   Savior lets himself be-seen

In seinen Gnadenwerken.
In   his   works-of-grace.

Da er sich   kräftig   weist,
Since he himself powerfully manifests,
{Since he powerfully manifests himself here,}

Den schwachen Geist zu lehren,
The   weak   soul to instruct,

Den matten Leib zu nähren,
The tired body to nourish:

Dies sättigt Leib und Geist.
This satiates body and soul.

are seen but to the things that are unseen; for the things that are seen are transient, but the things that are unseen are eternal. (Also Col. 3:1–3.)
Ps. 63:3. ...[O Lord,] thy steadfast love is better than life...
Ps. 119:103. How sweet are thy words to my taste, sweeter than honey to my mouth! (Also Ps. 19:9–10.)
Mt. 4:4 [Christ]: ...Man shall not live by bread alone, but by every word that proceeds from the mouth of God. (Also Deut. 8:3, Lk. 4:4.)
Ps. 78:23–25. [When God led the children of Israel through the wilderness] he commanded the skies above, and opened the doors of heaven; and he rained down upon them manna to eat, and gave them the grain of heaven. Man ate the bread of the angels; he sent them food in abundance.
*Mk. 8:6–9. ...[Jesus] took the seven loaves, and having given thanks he broke them and gave them to his disciples to set before the people; and they set them before the crowd. And they had a few small fish; and having blessed them, he commanded that these also should be set before them. And they ate, and were satisfied; and they took up the broken pieces left over, seven baskets full. And there were about four thousand people.
Jn. 6:30–35. [The people] said to [Jesus], "...What sign do you do, that we may see, and believe you? What work do you perform? Our fathers ate the manna in the wilderness..." Jesus then said to them, "Truly, truly, I say to you, it was not Moses who gave you the bread from heaven; my Father gives you the true bread from heaven. For the bread of God is that which comes down from heaven, and gives life to the world." They said to him, "Lord, give us this bread always." Jesus said to them, "I am the bread of life; he who comes to me shall not hunger, and he who believes in me shall never thirst." (Also Jn. 6:47–53, Ex. 16:13–35.)
Rev. 2:17 [Christ]: ...To him who conquers I will give some of the hidden manna...
Ps. 34:8. O taste and see that the Lord is good!...

+Mt. 11:2–6. When John heard in prison about the deeds of the Christ, he sent word [to Jesus]..."Are you he who is to come, or shall we look for another?" And Jesus answered..."Go and tell John what you hear and see: the blind receive their sight and the lame walk, lepers are cleansed and the deaf hear, and the dead are raised up, and the poor have good news preached to them. And blessed is he who takes no offense at me." (Also Lk. 7:20–23.)
Jn. 6:30–31. [The people] said to [Jesus], "...What sign do you do, that we may see, and believe you? What work do you perform? Our fathers ate the manna in the wilderness..."
*Mk. 8:6, 9. And [Jesus] took the seven loaves, and having given thanks he broke them and gave them to his disciples to set before the people...And there were about four thousand people.
Is. 55:1. Ho, every one who thirsts, come to the waters; and he who has no money, come, buy and eat! Come, buy wine and milk without money and without price.
Mt. 11:28–29 [Christ]: Come to me, all who labor and are heavy laden, and I will give you rest...You will find rest for your souls.
1 Thess. 5:23. May the God of peace himself sanctify you wholly; and may your spirit and soul and body be kept sound and blameless at the coming of our Lord Jesus Christ.

6. Chorale (Added in this version) (See also 9–7, 155–5.)
●Believe his Word rather than appearances (186–6)
Ob   sich's anließ,   als   wollt er nicht,
Though it   appear, as-if wanted he not,
{Though it appear as if he were not intending to help you,}

Laß dich es nicht erschrecken;
Let you it not   frighten;
{Let it not frighten you;}

Denn wo er ist am besten mit,
For   where he is -   best with (you),
{For where he is most with you,}

Da   will er's nicht entdecken.
There would he-it not   disclose.
{There he would not disclose it.}

Sein Wort laß dir   gewisser sein,
His   Word let to-you more-certain be,
{Let his Word become more certain to you,}

Und ob dein Herz spräch lauter Nein,
And though your heart say   only "No,"

So laß dir   doch   nicht grauen!
Yet let yourself nevertheless not be-terrified!

Part II

7. Bass Recit. (Added in this version)
●Physical dearth but spiritual nourishment (186–7)
Es ist die Welt die große Wüstenei;
(Now) is the world a great wilderness;
{The world is that great wilderness;}

Der Himmel wird zu Erz, die Erde wird zu Eisen,
The heavens turn to brass, the earth turns to iron,

Wenn Christen durch den Glauben weisen,
When Christians by (their) faith   do-show,
{And Christians show by their faith,}

Das Christi Wort ihr größter Reichtum sei;
That Christ's word their greatest wealth is;
{That their greatest wealth is Christ's word;}

Jms. 1:3. ...The testing of your faith produces steadfastness.
Mk. 6:35–37. When it grew late, [Jesus'] disciples came to him and said, "This is a lonely place, and the hour is now late; send [the people] away, to go into the country and villages round about and buy themselves something to eat." But he answered them, "You give them something to eat." And they said to him, "Shall we go and buy two hundred denarii worth of bread, and give it to them to eat?"
*Mk. 8:1–4. In those days, when again a great crowd had gathered, and they had nothing to eat, he called his disciples to him, and said to them, "I have compassion on the crowd, because they have been with me now three days, and have nothing to eat; and if I send them away hungry to their homes, they will faint on the way; and some of them have come a long way." And his disciples answered him, "How can one feed these men with bread here in the desert (Luther: Wüste)?"
Lk. 24:15, 16, 28–31. While [the disciples on the road to Emmaus] they were talking and discussing together, Jesus himself drew near and went with them. But their eyes were kept from recognizing him...So they drew near to the village to which they were going. [Jesus] appeared to be going further, but they constrained him, saying, "Stay with us..."...When he was at table with them...their eyes were opened and they recognized him; and he vanished out of their sight...
Jn. 20:29 [Christ]: ...Blessed are those who have not seen and yet believe.
Rom. 8:24–25. ...Now hope that is seen is not hope. For who hopes for what he sees? But if we hope for what we do not see, we wait for it with patience. (Also Heb. 11:1.)
Ps. 27:14. Wait for the Lord; be strong, and let your heart take courage; yea, wait for the Lord!
Heb. 11:1. Now faith is the assurance of things hoped for, the conviction of things not seen.
2 Pet. 1:19. We have the prophetic word made more sure. You will do well to pay attention to this as to a lamp shining in a dark place, until the day dawns and the morning star rises in your hearts.
2 Cor. 1:20. All the promises of God find their Yes in him. That is why we utter the Amen through him, to the glory of God.
1 Jn. 3:19–20. ...We shall know that we are of the truth, and reassure our hearts before him whenever our hearts condemn us; for God is greater than our hearts...

*Mk. 8:1–4. In those days, when again a great crowd had gathered, and they had nothing to eat, he called his disciples to him, and said to them, "I have compassion on the crowd, because they have been with me now three days, and have nothing to eat; and if I send them away hungry to their homes, they will faint on the way; and some of them have come a long way." And his disciples answered him, "How can one feed these men with bread here in the desert (Luther: Wüste)?"
Deut. 28:1, 12, 15, 22–24. If you obey the voice of the Lord your God, being careful to do all his commandments...The Lord will open to you his good treasury the heavens, to give the rain of your land in its season...But if you will not obey...the Lord will smite you with...fiery heat, and with drought, and with blasting, and with mildew; they shall pursue you until you perish. And the heavens over your head shall be brass, and the earth under you shall be iron. The Lord will make the

Der Nahrungssegen scheint
The blessing-of-sustenance seems
{Even the blessing of sustenance seems}

Von ihnen fast zu fliehen,
From them almost to flee,
{To be denied them,}

Ein steter Mangel wird beweint,
A constant dearth is bemoaned,

Damit sie nur der Welt sich desto mehr entziehen;
So-that they just the world - that-much more forsake;
{So much so that it causes them to withdraw from the world just that much more;}

Da findet erst des Heilands Wort,
Then finds finally the Savior's Word,
{Until finally the Savior's Word,}

Der höchste Schatz,
That greatest treasure,

In ihren Herzen Platz;
In their hearts (its) place;
{Finds its place in their hearts;}

Ja, jammert ihn des Volkes dort,
Yes, pitied (he) the people there,
{Yes, if he was moved to pity by the people in the biblical account,}

So muß auch hier sein Herze brechen
Then must also here his heart break
{Then his heart must also break here}

Und über sie den Segen sprechen.
And over them the blessing pronounce.
{And pronounce a blessing upon them.}

8. Soprano Aria
●Lord shows mercy to needy, giving them Word of life (186-8)
Die Armen will der Herr umarmen
The needy desires the Lord to-embrace
{The Lord desires to embrace the needy}

Mit Gnaden hier und dort;
With mercy here and there;

rain of your land powder and dust; from heaven it shall come down upon you until you are destroyed. (Also Lev. 26:18–20.)
Ecc. 8:14. There is a vanity which takes place on earth, that there are righteous men to whom it happens according to the deeds of the wicked, and there are wicked men to whom it happens according to the deeds of the righteous. I said that this is also vanity. (Also Ecc. 7:15.)
Ps. 73:3–4, 7, 12–14, 16–17, 25–26. I was envious of the arrogant, when I saw the prosperity of the wicked. For they have no pangs; their bodies are sound and sleek...Their eyes swell out with fatness, their hearts overflow with follies...Behold, these are the wicked; always at ease, they increase in riches. All in vain have I kept my heart clean and washed my hands in innocence. For all the day long I have been stricken, and chastened every morning...But when I thought how to understand this, it seemed to me a wearisome task...Then I perceived their end...[O Lord,] whom have I in heaven but thee? And there is nothing upon earth that I desire besides thee. (Luther: Wenn ich nur dich habe, so frage ich nichts nach Himmel und Erde.) My flesh and my heart may fail, but God is the strength of my heart and my portion for ever.
Mt. 5:6 [Christ]: Blessed are those who hunger and thirst for righteousness, for they shall be satisfied.
Mt. 4:1–4. [When] Jesus was led up by the Spirit into the wilderness to be tempted by the devil...he fasted forty days and forty nights, and afterward he was hungry. And the tempter came and said to him, "If you are the Son of God, command these stones to become loaves of bread." But he answered, "It is written, 'Man shall not live by bread alone, but by every word that proceeds from the mouth of God.'" (Also Mt. 13:3, 7 22; Mk. 4:7, 18–19.)
Hab. 3:17–18. Though the fig tree do not blossom, nor fruit be on the vines, the produce of the olive fail and the fields yield no food...yet I will rejoice in the Lord, I will joy in the God of my salvation.
Ps. 63:3. [O Lord,] because thy steadfast love is better than life, my lips will praise thee.
Ps. 135:14. The Lord will...have compassion on his servants.
Ps. 103:13–14. As a father pities his children, so the Lord pities those who fear him. For he knows our frame; he remembers that we are dust.
*****Mk. 8:1–2, 6.** ...When...a great crowd had gathered, and they had nothing to eat, [Jesus] called his disciples to him, and said to them, "I have compassion on the crowd (Luther: mich jammert des Volks)..." ...And he took the seven loaves, and having given thanks he broke them and gave them to his disciples to set before the people...

+Mt. 11:5. [With Christ] the blind receive their sight and the lame walk, lepers are cleansed and the deaf hear, and the dead are raised up, and the poor have good news preached to them.
Is. 41:17–18 [God]: When the poor and needy seek water, and there is none, and their tongue is parched with thirst, I the Lord will answer them...I will make the wilderness a pool of water, and the dry land springs of water.
Amos 8:11. ...[This is] not a famine of bread, nor a thirst for water, but of hearing the words of the Lord.
Jn. 7:37–39. ...Jesus stood up and proclaimed, "If any one thirst, let him come to me and drink. He who believes in me, as the scripture has said, 'Out of his heart shall flow rivers of living water.'" Now this

Er schenket ihnen aus Erbarmen
He   gives   them out-of compassion
{Out of compassion he gives them}

Den höchsten Schatz,   das Lebenswort.
The   greatest   treasure (of all): the Word-of-Life.

9. Alto Recit. (Added in this version)
●Word leads & sustains us on hard course to paradise (186–9)
Nun mag die Welt   mit ihrer Lust   vergehen;
Now (let) the world (and) its pleasures pass-away;

Bricht gleich der Mangel ein,
Sets-in although - dearth   -,
{Although dearth sets in,}

Doch kann die Seele freudig sein.
Yet   can the soul joyful   be.
{Yet the soul can remain joyful.}

Wird   durch dies Jammertal der Gang
Becomes through this vale-of-tears the path
{If the path through this vale of tears becomes}

Zu schwer, zu lang,
Too hard, too long,

In Jesu Wort liegt Heil   und Segen.
In Jesus' Word lies salvation and blessing.
{In Jesus' Word salvation and blessing can be found.}

Es ist ihres Fußes Leuchte und ein Licht auf ihren Wegen.
It is its   foot's lamp   and a light upon its   ways.

Wer   gläubig durch die Wüste   reist,
Whoever in-faith through the wilderness travels,
{Whoever travels in faith through the wilderness,}

Wird durch dies Wort getränkt,   gespeist;
Is   through this Word given-drink (and) given-food;
{Is given food and drink through this Word;}

Der Heiland öffnet selbst,   nach   diesem Worte,
The Savior opens, himself, according-to this Word,

Ihm   einst des Paradieses Pforte,
To-him one-day -   Paradise's gate,
{The Savior himself will one day open the gate of Paradise
according to this Word,}

Und nach vollbrachtem Lauf
And after completed   course
{And when their course is run}

Setzt er   den Gläubigen die Krone auf.
Places he (upon) - believers the crown -.
{He will place the crown upon believers' heads.}

he said about the Spirit, which those who believed in him were to
receive...
Jn. 14:26–27 [Christ]: The Counselor, the Holy Spirit, whom the
Father will send in my name, he will teach you all things, and bring to
your remembrance all that I have said to you. (Also Jn. 16:12–15.)
Jn. 5:24 [Christ]: ...He who hears my word and believes him who sent
me, has eternal life; he does not come into judgment, but has passed
from death to life.

1 Jn. 2:15–17. Do not love the world or the things in the world. If any
one loves the world, love for the Father is not in him. For all that is
in the world, the lust of the flesh and the lust of the eyes and the
pride of life, is not of the Father but is of the world. And the world
passes away, and the lust of it; but he who does the will of God abides
for ever.
Hab. 3:17–19. Though the fig tree do not blossom, nor fruit be on the
vines, the produce of the olive fail and the fields yield no food, the
flock be cut off from the fold and there be no herd in the stalls, yet
I will rejoice in the Lord, I will joy in the God of my salvation. God,
the Lord, is my strength...
Phil. 4:11–12. I [do not] complain of want; for I have learned, in
whatever state I am, to be content. I know how to be abased, and I
know how to abound; in any and all circumstances I have learned the
secret of facing plenty and hunger, abundance and want.
***Mk. 8:1–3.** ...When again a great crowd had gathered, and they had
nothing to eat, [Jesus] called his disciples to him, and said to them, "I
have compassion on the crowd, because they have been with me now
three days, and have nothing to eat; and if I send them away hungry
to their homes, they will faint on the way; and some of them have
come a **long way.**"
Num. 21:5. The people [of Israel] spoke against God and against
Moses, "Why have you brought us up out of Egypt to die in the
wilderness? For there is no food and no water..."
Ps. 63:1. O God, thou art my God, I seek thee, my soul thirsts for
thee; my flesh faints for thee, as in a dry and weary land where no
water is. (Also Ps. 78:15, 105:41, 107:35.)
Mt. 7:14 [Christ]: ...The way is hard, that leads to life, and those who
find it are few.
Acts 14:22. ...Through many tribulations we must enter the kingdom
of God.
Ps. 119:81–82. [O Lord,] my soul languishes for thy salvation; I hope
in thy word. (Also Ps. 119:123.)
Ps. 119:105. Thy word is a lamp to my feet and a light to my path.
Mt. 25:34 [Christ]: [In the judgment] the King will say to those at his
right hand, "Come, O blessed of my Father, inherit the kingdom
prepared for you from the foundation of the world."
Lk. 23:43 [Christ]: ...Today you will be with me in Paradise.
2 Tim. 4:6–8. I am already on the point of being sacrificed; the time
of my departure has come. I have fought the good fight, I have
finished the race (Luther: Lauf vollendet), I have kept the faith.
Henceforth there is laid up for me the crown of righteousness, which
the Lord, the righteous judge, will award to me on that Day, and not
only to me but also to all who have loved his appearing. (crown: also
1 Pet. 5:4, Jms. 1:12, Rev. 2:10)

10. Soprano & Alto Duet
●Remain faithful in suffering; a crown awaits you (186–10)
Laß,   Seele, kein Leiden
Let, (O) Soul,   no suffering
{O Soul, let no suffering}

Von Jesu dich scheiden,
From Jesus thee separate,
{Separate thee from Jesus,}

Sei,   Seele, getreu!
Be, (O) Soul, faithful!
{O Soul, be faithful!}

Dir   bleibet die Krone
For-thee remains the crown
{A crown awaits thee}

Aus Gnaden zu Lohne,
Out-of grace for reward,
{As a reward of grace,}

Wenn du von   Banden des Leibes nun frei.
When thou from (the) bonds of-the body (art) free.
{When thou wilt be free from the bonds of the body.}

Heb. 11:35–36. ...Some [believers] were tortured, refusing to accept release, that they might rise again to a better life. Others suffered mockings and scourgings, and even chains and imprisonment.
+Mt. 11:2–3. When John heard in prison about the deeds of the Christ, he sent word..."Are you he who is to come, or shall we look for another?"
Rom. 8:35, 37–39. Who shall separate us from the love of Christ? Shall tribulation, or distress, or persecution, or famine, or nakedness, or peril, or sword?...No, in all these things we are more than conquerors through him who loved us. For I am sure that neither death, nor life, nor angels, nor principalities, nor things present, nor things to come, nor powers, nor height, nor depth, nor anything else in all creation, will be able to separate us from the love of God in Christ Jesus our Lord.
Rev. 2:10 [Christ]: Do not fear what you are about to suffer...For ten days you will have tribulation. Be faithful unto death, and I will give you the crown of life.
Jms. 1:12. Blessed is the man who endures trial, for when he has stood the test he will receive the crown of life which God has promised to those who love him. (Also 2 Tim. 4:8, 1 Pet. 5:4.)
2 Pet. 1:14. I know that the putting off of my body will be soon, as our Lord Jesus Christ showed me. (Also 2 Cor. 5:1.)

11. Chorale (Replaces closing chorale of previous version)
(See also 86–6.)
●Hope rewarded in God's own time; he may be trusted (186–11)
Die Hoffnung wart' der rechten Zeit,
(Our) hope   awaits the   right time,

Was   Gottes Wort   zusaget.
For-what God's Word does-promise.
{When we shall receive what God's Word has promised.}

Wenn das geschehen soll zur Freud,
When that   shall-happen to-our joy,
{Just when this is to happen to our joy—}

Setzt Gott kein g'wisse Tage.
Sets God no specific day.
{Just what particular day—has not been indicated by God.}

Er weiß wohl, wenn's am besten ist,
He knows well, when-it - best   is,
{He knows well when it is best,}

Und braucht an uns kein arge   List,
And employs on us no malicious cunning,
{And employs no malicious cunning upon us,}

Des   solln wir ihm vertrauen.
For-this are we him to-trust.
{For this we are to trust him.}

Gal. 6:9. Let us not grow weary in well-doing, for in due season (Luther: zu seiner Zeit) we shall reap, if we do not lose heart. (Also Rev. 2:3.)
Heb. 10:36. You have need of endurance, so that you may do the will of God and receive what is promised.
2 Cor. 4:17. This slight momentary affliction is preparing for us an eternal weight of glory beyond all comparison. (Also Rom. 8:18.)
Rom. 8:23–25, 28. ...We ourselves, who have the first fruits of the Spirit, groan inwardly as we wait for adoption as sons, the redemption of our bodies. For in this hope we were saved. Now hope that is seen is not hope. For who hopes for what he sees? But if we hope for what we do not see, we wait for it with patience...We know that in everything God works for good with those who love him, who are called according to his purpose.
Acts 1:7 [Christ]: It is not for you to know times or seasons which the Father has fixed by his own authority.
2 Pet. 3:8–9. Do not ignore this one fact, beloved, that with the Lord one day is as a thousand years, and a thousand years as one day. The Lord is not slow about his promise as some count slowness...
Prov. 3:5–6. Trust in the Lord with all your heart, and do not rely on your own insight. In all your ways acknowledge him, and he will make straight your paths.
Tit. 1:2–3. [We have been given] hope of eternal life which God, who never lies, promised ages ago and at the proper time manifested in his word...
Rev. 22:6. ...These words are trustworthy and true... (Also Rev. 3:14, Prov. 30:5.)

BWV 187
Es wartet alles auf dich
(NBA I/18; BC A110)

7. S. after Trinity (BWV 186, 107, 187)
*Rom. 6:19–23 (The wages of sin is death but the gift of God
is eternal life)
*Mk. 8:1–9 (Jesus feeds the four thousand)
Librettist: perhaps Christoph Helm

Part I

1. Chorus
●Creation looks to God for sustenance: Ps. 104:27–28 (187-1)
Es   wartet alles   auf dich, daß du ihnen
(Now) wait   all (creatures) upon thee, that thou to-them
{All creatures wait upon thee to give them their}

Speise gebest zu seiner Zeit. Wenn du   ihnen gibest,
food   givest in due time. When thou to-them dost-give,
{food in due time. When thou givest to them,}

so sammlen sie,   wenn du deine Hand auftust,
then gather they (it), when thou thy hand dost-open,
{they gather it up; when thou dost open thy hand,}

so werden sie mit   Güte   gesättiget.
then are   they with good-things satisfied.
{they are satisfied with good things.}

2. Bass Recit.
●Creatures fill whole world: who could feed them all? (187-2)
Was Kreaturen   hält
What creatures are-contained-within
{Look how many creatures are contained within}

Das große Rund der Welt!
The great circle of-the world!

Schau doch die Berge an,
Behold, indeed, the mountains - ,
{Behold the mountains,}

da   sie bei tausend gehen;
where they in-the thousands do-range;

Was   zeuget nicht die Flut?
What bears-witness not the torrent?
{And what evidence does not the torrent provide?}

Es   wimmeln Ström und Seen.
(Now) do-teem streams and seas.
{Both streams and seas are teeming.}

Der Vögel großes Heer
The birds' great host

*Mk. 8:1–3. In those days, when again a great crowd had gathered,
and they had nothing to eat, [Jesus] called his disciples to him, and
said to them, "I have compassion on the crowd, because they have
been with me now three days, and have nothing to eat; and if I send
them away hungry to their homes, they will faint on the way; and
some of them have come a long way."
Ps. 145:15–16. [O Lord,] the eyes of all look to thee, and thou givest
them their food in due season. Thou openest thy hand, thou satisfiest
the desire of every living thing. (Also Ps. 111:5.)
Ps. 104:24, 27–30. O Lord, how manifold are thy works! In wisdom
hast thou made them all; the earth is full of thy creatures. *These all
look to thee, to give them their food in due season. When thou givest to
them, they gather it up; when thou openest thy hand, they are filled with
good things.* When thou hidest thy face, they are dismayed; when thou
takest away their breath, they die and return to their dust. When thou
sendest forth thy Spirit, they are created; and thou renewest the face
of the ground.
Ps. 147:9. He gives to the beasts their food, and to the young ravens
which cry. (Also Job 12:10.)

Gen. 1:20–22. [In the beginning] God said, "Let the waters bring forth
swarms of living creatures, and let birds fly above the earth across the
firmament of the heavens." So God created the great sea monsters
and every living creature that moves, with which the waters swarm...
And God blessed them, saying, "Be fruitful and multiply and fill the
waters in the seas, and let birds mulitply on the earth."
Ps. 50:10–12 [God]: Every beast of the forest is mine, the cattle on a
thousand hills. I know all the birds of the air, and all that moves in the
field is mine. If I were hungry, I would not tell you; for the world and
all that is in it is mine.
Ps. 104:24–27. O Lord, how manifold are thy works! In wisdom hast
thou made them all; the earth is full of thy creatures. Yonder is the
sea, great and wide, which teems with things innumberable (Luther:
da wimmelt's ohne Zahl), living things both small and great. There go
the ships, and Leviathan which thou didst form to sport in it. These
all look to thee, to give them their food in due season. (Also Ps.
111:5.)
Ps. 104:10–13, 16–18. Thou makest springs gush forth in the valleys;
they flow between the hills, they give drink to every beast of the field;
the wild asses quench their thirst. By them the birds of the air have
their habitation; they sing among the branches. From thy lofty abode
thou waterest the mountains; the earth is satisfied with the fruit of thy
work...The trees of the Lord are watered abundantly, the cedars of
Lebanon which he planted. In them the birds build their nests; the
stork has her home in the fir trees. The high mountains are for the
wild goats; the rocks are a refuge for the badgers...

Zieht durch die Luft zu Feld.
Moves through the air to (the) plain.

Wer nähret solche Zahl,
Who feeds such-a (large) number?

Und wer
And who

Vermag ihr wohl die Notdurft abzugeben?
Can them indeed (with) their necessities supply?
{Can indeed supply them with their necessities?}

Kann irgendein Monarch nach solcher Ehre streben?
Can any monarch to such-an honor aspire?
{Can any monarch aspire to such an honor?}

Zahlt aller Erden Gold
(Buys) all (the) earth's gold
{Could all of the earth's gold}

Ihr wohl ein einig Mal?
Them indeed a single meal?
{Indeed buy a single meal for them?}

3. Alto Aria
●Lord crowns the year with his blessing (187-3)
Du Herr, *du krönst* allein *das Jahr mit deinem Gut.*
Thou, Lord, thou crownest alone the year with thy goodness.
{Thou, Lord, thou alone crownest the year with thy bounty.}

Es träufet Fett und Segen
(Now) drips fatness and blessing
{Fatness and blessing drips}

Auf deines Fußes Wegen,
Upon thy foot's pathways,

Und deine Gnade ist's, die alles Gutes tut.
And thy grace is-it, which all good-things doeth.
{And it is thy grace which doeth all good things.

Part II

4. Bass Aria
●Vox Christi: Do not worry: Mt. 6:31–32 (187-4)
Darum sollt ihr nicht sorgen noch sagen:
Therefore shall you not worry nor say:
{Therefore you shall not worry nor say:}

Was werden wir essen, was werden wir trinken,
What will we eat, what will we drink,

Mt. 6:26 [Christ]: Look at the birds of the air: they neither sow nor reap nor gather into barns, and yet your heavenly Father feeds (Luther: nährt) them...
Ps. 145:15–16. [O Lord,] the eyes of all look to thee, and thou givest them their food in due season. Thou openest thy hand, thou satisfiest the desire of every living thing.
Is. 40:28. ...The Lord is...the Creator of the ends of the earth...His understanding is unsearchable. (Also Is. 45:18.)
Ps. 113:4–6. The Lord is high above all nations, and his glory above the heavens! Who is like the Lord our God, who is seated on high, who looks far down upon the heavens and the earth? (Also Ps. 89:6, 97:9, 99:2.)
Ps. 95:3. The Lord is a great God, and a great King above all gods. (Also Ps. 83:18, 97:9, Ex. 18:11.)
***Mk. 8:1–3, 6–9.** In those days, when...a great crowd had gathered, and they had nothing to eat, [Jesus] called his disciples to him, and said to them, "I have compassion on the crowd, because they have been with me now three days, and have nothing to eat; and if I send them away hungry to their homes, they will faint on the way; and some of them have come a long way."...And he commanded the crowd to sit down on the ground; and he took the seven loaves, and having given thanks he broke them and gave them to his disciples to set before the people; and they set them before the crowd. And they had a few small fish; and having blessed them, he commanded that these also should be set before them. And they ate, and were satisfied...And there were about four thousand people.

Ps. 65:9–13. [O Lord,] thou visitest the earth and waterest it, thou greatly enrichest it; the river of God is full of water; thou providest their grain, for so thou hast prepared it. Thou waterest its furrows abundantly, settling its ridges, softening it with showers, and blessing its growth. *Thou crownest the year with thy bounty;* the tracks of thy chariot drip with fatness (Luther: deine Fußtapfen triefen von Fett). The pastures of the wilderness drip (Luther: sind fett, daß sie triefen), the hills gird themselves with joy, the meadows clothe themselves with flocks, the valleys deck themselves with grain, they shout and sing together for joy.
Jms. 1:17. Every good endowment and every perfect gift is from above, coming down from the Father of lights with whom there is no variation or shadow due to change.

Mt. 6:25–32 [Christ]: Therefore I tell you, do not be anxious about your life, what you shall eat or what you shall drink, nor about your body, what you shall put on. Is not life more than food, and the body more than clothing? Look at the birds of the air: they neither sow nor reap nor gather into barns, and yet your heavenly Father feeds (Luther: nährt) them. Are you not of more value than they? And which of you by being anxious can add one cubit to his span of life? And why are you anxious about clothing? Consider the lilies of the field, how they grow; they neither toil nor spin; yet I tell you, even Solomon in all his glory was not arrayed like one of these. But if God so clothes the grass of the field, which today is alive and tomorrow is thrown into the oven, will he not much more clothe you, O men of little faith? *Therefore do not be anxious, saying, "What shall we eat?" or*

womit werden wir uns kleiden? Nach
wherewith will we ourselves clothe? After

solchem allen trachten die Heiden. Denn euer
all-such (things) seek the Gentiles. For your

himmlischer Vater weiß, daß ihr dies alles bedürfet.
heavenly Father knows, that you this all need.

"What shall we drink?" or "What shall we wear?" For the Gentiles seek all these things; and your heavenly Father knows that you need them all.
*Mk. 8:6, 8. ...And [Jesus] took the seven loaves, and having given thanks he broke them and gave them to his disciples to set before the people...And they ate and were satisfied...

5. Soprano Aria
●God sustains all creatures; he will also help me (187-5)
Gott versorget alles Leben,
God takes-care-of all life,

Was hienieden Odem hegt.
That here-below breath contains.
{That contains breath here below.}

Sollt er mir allein nicht geben,
Should he to-me alone not give,
{Should he not give to me alone,}

Was er allen zugesagt?
What he to-all has-promised?

Weicht, ihr Sorgen, seine Treue
Retreat, ye cares; his faithfulness

Ist auch meiner eingedenk
Is also of-me mindful
{Is mindful also of me}

Und wird ob mir täglich neue
And becomes for me daily new
{And daily becomes new for me}

Durch manch Vaterliebs Geschenk.
Through many-a paternal-love's gift.
{Through many a gift of paternal love.}

Ps. 136:25. He...gives food to all flesh...
Ps. 147:9. He gives to the beasts their food, and to the young ravens which cry.
Job 12:10. In his hand is the life of every living thing and the breath of all mankind.
Ps. 145:15-16. [O Lord,] the eyes of all look to thee, and thou givest them their food in due season. Thou openest thy hand, thou satisfiest the desire of every living thing. (Also Ps. 111:5.)
Ps. 104:27-30. These all look to thee, to give them their food in due season. When thou givest to them, they gather it up; when thou openest thy hand, they are filled with good things. When thou hidest thy face, they are dismayed; when thou takest away their breath, they die and return to their dust. When thou sendest forth thy Spirit, they are created; and thou renewest the face of the ground.
Mt. 6:26, 30-31 [Christ]: Look at the birds of the air: they neither sow nor reap nor gather into barns, and yet your heavenly Father feeds them. Are you not of more value than they?...If God so clothes the grass of the field, which today is alive and tomorrow is thrown into the oven, will he not much more clothe you, O men of little faith? Therefore do not be anxious...
Ps. 115:12-13. The Lord has been mindful of us; he will bless us...he will bless those who fear the Lord, both small and great.
Lam. 3:22-23. The steadfast love of the Lord never ceases, his mercies never come to an end; they are new every morning; great is thy faithfulness (Luther: Treue).
Ps. 103:13-14. As a father pities his children, so the Lord pities those who fear him. He knows our frame; he remembers that we are dust.
Jms. 1:17. Every good endowment and every perfect gift is from above, coming down from the Father...

6. Soprano Recit.
●Trusting God like a child; he will give me my share (187-6)
Halt ich nur fest an ihm mit kindlichem Vertrauen
Hold I just firmly to him with childlike trust
{As long as I cling tightly to him with childlike trust}

Und nehm mit Dankbarkeit, was er mir zugedacht,
And accept with gratitude, what he for-me has-destined,

So werd ich mich nie ohne Hülfe schauen,
Then will I myself ne'er without help see,
{Then I'll never experience a lack of help,}

1 Tim. 6:6, 8. There is great gain in godliness with contentment...If we have food and clothing, with these we shall be content.
Phil. 4:11-12. ...I [do not] complain of want; for I have learned, in whatever state I am, to be content. I know how to be abased, and I know how to abound; in any and all circumstances I have learned the secret of facing plenty and hunger, abundance and want.
Heb. 13:5. ...Be content with what you have; for he has said, "I will never fail you nor forsake you."
Ps. 37:25. I have been young, and now am old; yet I have not seen the righteous forsaken or his children begging bread.
Mt. 6:26-32 [Christ]: Look at the birds of the air: they neither sow

Und wie er auch vor mich die Rechnung hab gemacht.
And how he also for me the amount has calculated.
{And I will see that he has also included me in his accounting.}

Das Grämen nützet nicht, die Mühe ist verloren,
- Fretting profits not, that effort is wasted,
{Fretting is of no use; that effort is wasted,}

Die das verzagte Herz um seine Notdurft nimmt;
Which the despairing heart upon its necessity expends;
{Which the despairing heart expends, worrying about its necessity;}

Der ewig reiche Gott
The eternally rich God

hat sich die Sorge auserkoren,
has for-himself these cares chosen,
{has taken these cares upon himself,}

So weiß ich, daß er mir auch
Thus know I, that he for-me as-well,

meinen Teil bestimmt.
my portion has-appointed.
{Thus I know that he has appointed my portion for me as well.}

7. Chorale
●God as great provider; may we praise him rightly (187–7)
Gott hat die Erde zugericht',
God has the earth (created),
{God has created the earth,}

Läßt's an Nahrung mangeln nicht;
Lets-it for sustenance lack not;
{He does not let it lack for sustenance;}

Berg und Tal, die macht er naß,
Hill and vale, them makes he wet,
{He waters hill and vale,}

Daß dem Vieh auch wächst sein Gras;
So-that for-the cattle, too, may-grow the grass;
{So that, for the cattle, the grass may grow;}

Aus der Erden Wein und Brot
From-out the earth (both) wine and bread
{From the earth God produces both wine and bread}

Schaffet Gott und gibt's uns satt,
Produces God and gives-of-it to-us our-fill,
{And gives to us our fill of it,}

Daß der Mensch sein Leben hat.
That - man his life may-have.
{So that man may have his life.}

nor reap nor gather into barns, and yet your heavenly Father feeds them. Are you not of more value than they? And which of you by being anxious can add one cubit to his span of life? And why are you anxious about clothing? Consider the lilies of the field, how they grow; they neither toil nor spin; yet I tell you, even Solomon in all his glory was not arrayed like one of these. But if God so clothes the grass of the field, which today is alive and tomorrow is thrown into the oven, will he not much more clothe you, O men of little faith? Therefore do not be anxious, saying, "What shall we eat?" or "What shall we drink?" or "What shall we wear?" For the Gentiles seek all these things; and your heavenly Father knows that you need them all.
Ps. 127:2. It is in vain that you rise up early and go late to rest, eating the bread of anxious toil; for he gives to his beloved sleep. (Also Ps. 127:1.)
Mt. 6:27 [Christ]: Which of you by being anxious can add one cubit to his span of life?
1 Pet. 5:7. Cast all your anxieties on him, for he cares about you. (Also Phil. 4:6.)
Phil. 4:19. ...God will supply every need of yours according to his riches in glory in Christ Jesus.
Prov. 30:7–9. Two things I ask of thee; deny them not to me before I die: Remove far from me falsehood and lying; give me neither poverty nor riches; feed me with the food that is needful for me (Luther: mein beschieden Teil Speise), lest I be full, and deny thee, and say, "Who is the Lord?" or lest I be poor, and steal, and profane the name of my God.

Ps. 104:5–18, 23–24, 27. [O Lord,] thou didst set the earth on its foundations, so that it should never be shaken. Thou didst cover it with the deep as with a garment; the waters stood above the mountains. At thy rebuke they fled; at the sound of thy thunder they took to flight. The mountains rose, the valleys sank down to the place which thou didst appoint for them. Thou didst set a bound which they should not pass, so that they might not again cover the earth. Thou makest springs gush forth in the valleys; they flow between the hills, they give drink to every beast of the field; the wild asses quench their thirst. By them the birds of the air have their habitation; they sing among the branches. From thy lofty abode thou waterest the mountains; the earth is satisfied with the fruit of thy work. Thou dost cause the grass to grow for the cattle, and plants for man to cultivate, that he may bring forth food from the earth, and wine to gladden the heart of man, oil to make his face shine, and bread to strengthen man's heart. The trees of the Lord are watered abundantly, the cedars of Lebanon which he planted. In them the birds build their nests; the stork has her home in the fir trees. The high mountains are for the wild goats; the rocks are a refuge for the badgers...Man goes forth to his work and to his labor until the evening. O Lord, how manifold are thy works! In wisdom hast thou made them all; the earth is full of thy creatures...These all look to thee, to give them their food in due season.

///

Wir danken   sehr und bitten ihn,
We   thank (him) greatly and   ask of-him,

Daß er uns geb des Geistes Sinn,
That he to-us grant the Spirit's mind,
{That he would grant us the Spirit's mind,}

Daß wir solches recht   verstehn,
That we   this   properly might-understand,
{That we might properly understand this,}

Stets in sein' Geboten   gehn,
Ever in his   commandments might-walk,

Seinen Namen machen groß
His   name   would-magnify

In Christo ohn Unterlaß:
In Christ without ceasing:

So sing'n wir recht das Gratias.
Thus sing we truly the "Gratias!"
{Thus we can truly sing the "Gratias!"}

BWV 188
Ich habe meine Zuversicht
(NBA I/25; BC A154)

21. S. after Trinity (BWV 109, 38, 98, 188)
*Eph. 6:10–17 (The armor of the Christian)
*Jn. 4:46[1]–54 (Christ heals the son of a royal official)
[1]Begin: "And at Capernaum there was an official..."
Librettist: Picander (Christian Friedrich Henrici)

1. Sinfonia (Based on earlier, nonextant work)

2. Tenor Aria
●God is my confidence when all around me fails (188–2)
Ich habe meine Zuversicht
I   have   my   confidence
{I have placed my confidence}

Auf den getreuen Gott gericht',
To the faithful God directed,
{In the faithful God,}

Da   ruhet meine Hoffnung feste.
There rests   my   hope   firmly.
{There my hope rests securely.}

Wenn alles bricht, wenn alles   fällt,
When everything breaks, when everything collapses,

Wenn niemand Treu   und Glauben hält,
When no-one faithfulness and   faith keeps,
{When no one keeps their word,}

1 Chron. 29:13. And now we thank thee, our God, and praise thy glorious name.
Ps. 19:14. [O Lord,] let the words of my mouth and the meditation of my heart be acceptable in thy sight...
Rom. 8:26–27. ...We do not know how to pray as we ought...He who searches the hearts of men knows what is the mind of the Spirit (Luther: Geistes Sinn), because the Spirit intercedes for the saints according to the will of God.
1 Cor. 2:16. Who has known the mind of the Lord so as to instruct him? But we have the mind of Christ. (See Is. 40:13.)
Jn. 14:26 [Christ]: The Counselor, the Holy Spirit, whom the Father will send in my name, he will teach you all things...
Jn. 16:13–14 [Christ]: When the Spirit of truth comes, he will guide you into all the truth...He will glorify me...
Gal. 5:16. But I say, walk by the Spirit...
1 Jn. 3:24. All who keep [Christ's] commandments abide in him, and he in them. And by this we know that he abides in us, by the Spirit which he has given us. (Also 4:13, Acts 5:32, Rom. 5:5, 2 Cor. 1:22, 5:5.)
1 Kings 8:57–58. [May] the Lord our God be with us...that he may incline our hearts to him, to walk in all his ways, and to keep his commandments, his statutes, and his ordinances...
1 Pet. 4:11. ...In order that in everything God may be glorified through Jesus Christ. To him belong glory and dominion for ever and ever. Amen.
Jude 1:25. To the only God, our Savior through Jesus Christ our Lord, be glory, majesty, dominion, and authority, before all time and now and for ever. Amen. (Also Rom. 16:27.)

*Jn. 4:46–53.** ...At Capernaum there was an official whose son was ill. When he heard that Jesus had come from Judea to Galilee, he went and begged him to come down and heal his son, for he was at the point of death. Jesus therefore said to him, "Unless you see signs and wonders you will not believe." The official said to him, "Sir, come down before my child dies." Jesus said to him, "Go; your son will live." The man believed the word that Jesus spoke to him and went his way. As he was going down, his servants met him and told him that his son was living. So he asked them the hour when he began to mend, and they said to him, "Yesterday at the seventh hour the fever left him." The father knew that was the hour when Jesus had said to him, "Your son will live"; and he himself believed, and all his household.
Ps. 46:1–3, 7. God is our refuge (Luther: Zuversicht) and strength, a very present help in trouble. Therefore we will not fear though the earth should change, though the mountains shake in the heart of the sea; though its waters roar and foam, though the mountains tremble with its tumult...The Lord of hosts is with us; the God of Jacob is our refuge. (Zuversicht: also Ps. 61:3, 62:7, 71:5, 7, 91:2, 142:5)
Rom. 3:4. ...Let God be true though every man be false...
Is. 33:8. The highways lie waste, the wayfaring man ceases. Covenants are broken, witnesses are despised (Luther: es hält weder Treu noch Glauben)...
Ps. 73:28. But for me it is good to be near God (Luther: mich zu Gott halte); I have made the Lord God my refuge (Luther: Zuversicht)...

So ist doch Gott der allerbeste.
Then is indeed God (our) very-best (hope).
{Then is God indeed our very best hope.}

3. Bass Recit.
●God's intentions are kind despite his angry look (188-3)
Gott meint es gut mit jedermann,
God means - well with everyone,

Auch in den allergrößten Nöten.
Even in the very-worst-of troubles.

Verbirget er gleich seine Liebe,
Hides he though his love,
{Though he hide his love}

So denkt sein Herz doch heimlich dran,
Yet thinks his heart nevertheless secretly about-it,
(Yet in his heart he is thinking of it,}

Das kann er niemals nicht entziehn;
That can he never (ever) withdraw;
{He could never withdraw it;}

Und wollte mich der Herr auch töten,
And would me the Lord even slay,
{And even if the Lord should want to slay me,}

So hoff ich doch auf ihn.
Then hope I neverthless in him.
{I shall nevertheless hope in him.}

Denn sein erzürntes Angesicht
For his angered countenance

Ist anders nicht
Is nothing-other

Als eine Wolke trübe,
Than a cloud dark,
{Than a dark cloud,}

Sie hindert nur den Sonnenschein,
It hinders only the sunshine,
{It only prevents the sunshine,}

Damit durch einen sanften Regen
So-that through a gentle rain

Der Himmelssegen
The blessings-of-heaven

Um so viel reicher möge sein.
 - That much richer may be.
{Might be that much more abundant.}

Der Herr verwandelt sich in einen grausamen,
The Lord transforms himself into a ferocious (being),

---

2 Tim. 2:13. ...He remains faithful—for he cannot deny himself.
Ps. 146:5. Happy is he whose help is the God of Jacob, whose hope (Luther: Hoffnung) is in the Lord his God.

*Jn. 4:48–49. Jesus therefore said to [the man whose child was at the point of death], "Unless you see signs and wonders you will not believe." The official said to him, "Sir, come down before my child dies."
Is. 54:7–8 [God]: For a brief moment I forsook you, but with great compassion I will gather you. In overflowing wrath for a moment I hid my face from you, but with everlasting love I will have compassion on you, says the Lord, your Redeemer.
Heb. 12:5–7, 9–11. ...My son, do not regard lightly the discipline of the Lord, nor lose courage when you are punished by him. For the Lord disciplines him whom he loves, and chastises every son whom he receives. It is for discipline that you have to endure. God is treating you as sons; for what son is there whom his father does not discipline? ...Besides this, we have had earthly fathers to discipline us and we respected them. Shall we not much more be subject to the Father of spirits and live? For they disciplined us for a short time at their pleasure, but he disciplines us for our good, that we may share his holiness. For the moment all discipline seems painful rather than pleasant; later it yields the peaceful fruit of righteousness to those who have been trained by it.
Prov. 3:11–12. My son, do not despise the Lord's discipline or be weary of his reproof, for the Lord reproves him whom he loves, as a father the son in whom he delights. (Also 1 Cor. 11:32, Rev. 3:19.)
Job 13:15. Behold, [God] will slay me; I have no hope...
Lam. 3:43–44. [O Lord,] thou hast wrapped thyself with anger and pursued us, slaying without pity; thou hast wrapped thyself with a cloud so that no prayer can pass through.
Job 23:3. Oh, that I knew where I might find him, that I might come even to his seat!
Ps. 90:15. [O Lord,] make us glad as many days as thou hast afflicted us, and as many years as we have seen evil.
Ps. 103:9. [The Lord] will not always chide, nor will he keep his anger for ever.
Is. 12:1–2. You will say in that day: "I will give thanks to thee, O Lord, for though thou wast angry with me, thy anger turned away, and thou didst comfort me. Behold, God is my salvation; I will trust, and will not be afraid; for the Lord God is my strength and my song, and he has become my salvation."
Jer. 31:13 [God]: Then shall the maidens rejoice in the dance, and the young men and the old shall be merry. I will turn their mourning into joy, I will comfort them, and give them gladness for sorrow. (Also Ps. 30:11.)
Rom. 5:3–5. ...We rejoice in our sufferings, knowing that suffering produces endurance, and endurance produces character, and character produces hope, and hope does not disappoint us, because God's love has been poured into our hearts through the Holy Spirit which has been given to us.
Jms. 1:2–4. Count it all joy, my brethren, when you meet various trials, for you know that the testing of your faith produces steadfastness. And let steadfastness have its full effect, that you may be perfect and complete, lacking in nothing.

Um desto tröstlicher zu scheinen;
- So-much more-comforting to appear;
{In order to appear so much more comforting later on;}

Er will, er kann's nicht böse meinen.
He would, he could not evil intend.
{He would not, he could not mean to harm us.}

Drum   laß ich ihn nicht,   er segne mich denn.
Therefore release I him not, (until) he bless me   - .
{Therefore I will not release him until he bless me.}

4. Alto Aria
●God's ways are unfathomable but ever for our best (188-4)
Unerforschlich ist die Weise,
Unfathomable is the manner,

Wie   der Herr die Seinen führt.
In-which - God (his) own leads.
{In which God leads his own.}

Selber unser Kreuz und Pein
Even   our cross and pain

Muß zu unserm Besten sein
Must for our   best be
{Must serve for our best}

Und zu seines Namens Preise.
And for his   name's praise.

5. Soprano Recit.
●Worldly power temporal but God is an eternal refuge
(188-5)
Die Macht der Welt verlieret sich.
The might of-this world   disappears.

Wer kann auf Stand und Hoheit bauen?
Who can upon rank and noble-station build?
{Who can build upon rank and noble station?}

Gott aber bleibet ewiglich;
God, however, remains evermore;

Wohl   allen, die auf ihn vertrauen!
Blessed (are) all-they, who in him trust!
{Blessed are all they who trust in him!}

1 Pet. 1:6–7. In this you rejoice, though now for a little while you may have to suffer various trials, so that the genuineness of your faith, more precious than gold which though perishable is tested by fire, may redound to praise and glory and honor at the revelation of Jesus Christ.

Jms. 5:10-11. As an example of suffering and patience, brethren, take the prophets who spoke in the name of the Lord. Behold, we call those happy who were steadfast. You have heard of the steadfastness of Job, and you have seen the purpose of the Lord, how the Lord is compassionate and merciful.

Gen. 32:26. ...Jacob said, "I will not let you go, unless you bless me."

Prov. 20:24. A man's steps are ordered by the Lord; how then can man understand his way?

Is. 55:8–9. My thoughts are not your thoughts, neither are your ways my ways, says the Lord. For as the heavens are higher than the earth, so are my ways higher than your ways and my thoughts than your thoughts. (Also Job 11:7–9, 12:13.)

Prov. 3:5. Trust in the Lord with all your heart, and do not rely on your own insight.

Ps. 23:1, 3. The Lord is my shepherd...He leads me in paths of righteousness for his name's sake.

Jn. 10:14, 27 [Christ]: I am the good shepherd; I know my own and my own know me...My sheep hear my voice, and I know them, and they follow me.

Mk. 8:34 [Christ]: ...If any man would come after me, let him deny himself and take up his cross and follow me. (Also Mt. 10:38, 16:24, Lk. 9:23.)

Rom. 8:28. ...In everything God works for good with those who love him, who are called according to his purpose.

Phil. 1:29. It has been granted to you that for the sake of Christ you should not only believe in him but also suffer for his sake.

1 Pet. 4:13–14. Rejoice in so far as you share Christ's sufferings, that you may also rejoice and be glad when his glory is revealed. If you are reproached for the name of Christ, you are blessed, because the spirit of glory and of God rests upon you.

Ps. 49:12–13, 18–20. Man cannot abide in his pomp, he is like the beasts that perish. This is the fate of those who have foolish confidence, the end of those who are pleased with their portion... Though a man gets praise when he does well for himself, he will go to the generation of his fathers, who will never more see the light. Man cannot abide in his pomp, he is like the beasts that perish. (Also Ps. 52:7, 62:9–11.)

Ps. 146:3–5. Put not your trust in princes, in a son of man, in whom there is no help. When his breath departs he returns to his earth; on that very day his plans perish. Happy (Luther: wohl dem) is he whose help is the God of Jacob, whose hope is in the Lord his God. (Also Ps. 118:8–9.)

Is. 26:4. Trust in the Lord for ever, for the Lord God is an everlasting rock.

Ps. 40:4. Blessed is the man who makes the Lord his trust, who does not turn to the proud, to those who go astray after false gods! (Also Ps. 84:12, 146:3–6, Jer. 17:7.)

6. Chorale
●Trusting God in fear & distress; he can deliver (188–6)
Auf meinen lieben Gott
In   my   beloved God
{I shall trust my beloved God}

Trau ich in Angst und Not;
Trust I in fear and distress;
{In fear and distress;}

Er kann mich allzeit retten
He can me   ever deliver
{He can ever deliver me}

Aus Trübsal, Angst und Nöten;
From tribulation, fear, and distress;

Mein Unglück kann er wenden,
My misfortune can he alter,
{He can alter my misfortune,}

Steht   alls in seinen Händen.
It-stands all in   his   hands.
{It all rests in his hands.}

Ps. 28:7. The Lord is my strength and my shield; in him my heart trusts... (Also Ps. 18:2, 33:20, 115:9–11.)

Ps. 91:1–2. He who dwells in the shelter of the Most High, who abides in the shadow of the Almighty, will say to the Lord, "My refuge and my fortress; my God, in whom I trust."

Ps. 119:143. Trouble and anguish have come upon me (Luther: Angst und Not haben mich getroffen), but thy commandments are my delight.

Ps. 62:5–8. For God alone my soul waits in silence, for my hope is from him. He only is my rock and my salvation, my fortress; I shall not be shaken. On God rests my deliverance and my honor; my mighty rock, my refuge is God. Trust in him at all times, O people; pour out your heart before him; God is a refuge for us.

Ps. 138:7. [O Lord,] though I walk in the midst of trouble, thou dost preserve my life...and thy right hand delivers me.

Ps. 34:17. When the righteous cry for help, the Lord hears, and delivers them out of all their troubles. (Also Ps. 72:12–14, 145:19, Is. 30:18–19.)

Ps. 10:14. [O Lord,] thou dost see; yea thou dost note trouble and vexation, that thou mayest take it into thy hands (Luther: es steht in deinen Händen)... (Also Ps. 31:15.)

BWV 189
Meine Seele rühmt und preist

This cantata was probably composed by Georg Melchior Hoffmann. See Dürr, *Die Kantaten*, p. 1003.

BWV 190
Singet dem Herrn ein neues Lied
(NBA I/4; BC A21)

New Year/Circumcision and Name of Jesus
(BWV 143, 190, 41, 16, 171, 248-IV)
*Gal. 3:23–29 (Through faith we are heirs of the promise)
*Luke 2:21 (Circumcision and naming of Jesus)
Librettist: Unknown

1. Chorus (Chorale lines: see also 16–1, 190–2)
●Praise the Lord with music: Ps. 149:1, 150:4, 6 (190–1)
Singet dem Herrn ein neues Lied!
Sing   to-the Lord   a new song!

Die Gemeine der Heiligen soll ihn loben!
The assembly of   saints shall him praise!
{Let the assembly of saints praise him!}

Lobet ihn mit Pauken und Reigen,
Praise him with drums and roundelay,

lobet ihn mit Saiten und Pfeifen!
praise him with strings and pipes!

Ps. 149:1–4. *Praise the Lord! Sing to the Lord a new song, his praise in the assembly of the faithful! Let Israel be glad in his Maker, let the sons of Zion rejoice in their King! Let them praise his name with dancing, making melody to him with timbrel and lyre! For the Lord takes pleasure in his people...*

Ps. 150:1–6. Praise the Lord! Praise God in his sanctuary; praise him in his mighty firmament! Praise him for his mighty deeds; praise him according to his exceeding greatness! Praise him with trumpet sound; praise him with lute and harp! *Praise him with timbrel and dance; praise him with strings and pipe!* Praise him with sounding cymbals; praise him with loud clashing cymbals! *Let everything that breathes praise the Lord! Praise the Lord! (Luther: Halleluja!)*

Ps. 33:1–3. Rejoice in the Lord, O you righteous! Praise befits the upright. Praise the Lord with the lyre, make melody to him with the harp of ten strings! Sing to him a new song, play skilfully on the strings, with loud shouts.

Herr Gott, dich loben wir!
Lord God, thee praise we!
{Lord God, we praise thee!}

Alles, was Odem hat, lobe den Herrn!
All,   that breath has, praise the Lord!
{All that has breath, praise the Lord!}

Herr Gott, wir danken dir!
Lord God, we   thank thee!

Alleluja!
Alleluia!

2. Chorale (Te Deum) & Alto, Tenor, & Bass Recits.
    (Chorale: see also 16-1, 190-1)
●Praise to God for renewed national blessings (190-2)
    Herr Gott, dich loben wir,
    Lord God, thee praise we,
    {Lord God, we praise thee, }

Bass:
Daß du   mit diesem neuen Jahr
That thou with this   new year
{That, with this new year, thou dost grant to us}

Uns neues Glück und neuen Segen schenkest
To-us new prosperity and new   blessing dost-grant
{New prosperity and new blessing,}

Und noch in Gnaden an uns denkest.
And still with favor on us dost-think.

    Herr Gott, wir danken dir,
    Lord God, we   thank thee,

Tenor:
Daß deine Gütigkeit
That thy kindness
{That thy kindness hath}

In der vergangnen Zeit
In the   past   time
{In time past}

Das ganze Land und unsre werte Stadt
The entire land and our   fair city
{Protected the entire land and our fair city}

Vor Teurung, Pestilenz und Krieg behütet hat.
From famine, pestilence and war protected hath.
{From famine, pestilence, and war.}

    Herr Gott, dich loben wir,
    Lord God, thee praise we,
    {Lord God, we praise thee,}

Ps. 96:1–4. O sing to the Lord a new song; sing to the Lord, all the earth! Sing to the Lord, bless his name; tell of his salvation from day to day. Declare his glory among the nations, his marvelous works among all the peoples! For great is the Lord, and greatly to be praised; he is to be feared above all gods.
Ps. 81:1–3. Sing aloud to God our strength; shout for joy to the God of Jacob! Raise a song, sound the timbrel, the sweet lyre with the harp. Blow the trumpet at the new moon, at the full moon, on our feast day.
Ps. 98:5–6. Sing praises to the Lord with the lyre, with the lyre and the sound of melody! With trumpets and the sound of the horn make a joyful noise before the King, the Lord!

1 Chron. 29:13. ...We thank thee, our God, and praise thy glorious name.
Ps. 144:15. Happy the people to whom such blessings fall! Happy the people whose God is the Lord!
Deut. 26:15. [O God,] look down from thy holy habitation, from heaven, and bless thy people Israel and the ground which thou hast given us, as thou didst swear to our fathers...
Ps. 79:13. Then we thy people, the flock of thy pasture, will give thanks to thee for ever; from generation to generation we will recount thy praise.
Ps. 105:1–2, 6, 8–10. O give thanks to the Lord, call on his name, make known his deeds among the peoples! Sing to him, sing praises to him, tell of all his wonderful works!...O offspring of Abraham his servant, sons of Jacob, his chosen ones!...He is mindful of his covenant for ever, of the word that he commanded, for a thousand generations, the covenant which he made with Abraham, his sworn promise to Isaac, which he confirmed to Jacob as a statute, to Israel as an everlasting covenant... (= 1 Chron. 16:8–9, 13, 15–17).
***Gal. 3:16, 29.** Now the promises were made to Abraham and to his offspring...which is Christ...And if you are Christ's, then you are Abraham's offspring, heirs according to promise.
Ps. 9:1–2. I will give thanks to the Lord with my whole heart; I will tell of all thy wonderful deeds. I will be glad and exult in thee, I will sing praise to thy name, O Most High. (Also Ps. 105:1–2, 107:21–22, Is. 25:1.)
Ps. 75:1. We give thanks to thee, O God; we give thanks; we call on thy name and recount thy wondrous deeds.
1 Chron. 16:12–13 / Ps. 105:5–6. Remember the wonderful works that [the Lord] has done, the wonders he wrought, the judgments he uttered, O offspring of Abraham his servant, sons of Jacob, his chosen ones!
Ps. 85:1. Lord, thou wast favorable to thy land; thou didst restore the fortunes of Jacob...
Ps. 65:11. Thou crownest the year with thy bounty...
Ezek. 36:28–30 [God]: You shall dwell in the land which I gave to your fathers...And I will summon the grain and make it abundant and lay no famine upon you. I will make the fruit of the tree and the increase of the field abundant, that you may never again suffer the disgrace of famine...
Deut. 7:12–15. The Lord your God will keep with you the covenant and the steadfast love which he swore to your fathers to keep; he will love you, bless you, and multiply you...You shall be blessed above all

Alto:

Denn deine   Vatertreu
For   thy paternal-faithfulness

Hat noch kein Ende,
Hath yet   no end,

Sie wird bei uns noch alle Morgen neu.
It becomes for us still each morning new.
{It is still new each morning for us.}

Drum   falten wir,
Therefore fold we,
{Therefore we fold,}

Barmherzger Gott, dafür
Merciful   God, for-this,

In Demut unsre Hände
In humility our hands

Und sagen lebenslang
And say   lifelong
{And say throughout our lives}

Mit Mund und Herzen   Lob und Dank.
With mouth and heart (our) praise and thanks.

Herr Gott, wir danken dir!
Lord God, we   thank thee!

3. Alto Aria
●Praise God who leads us to pasture like a shepherd (190-3)
Lobe,   Zion, deinen Gott,
Praise, (O) Zion,   thy   God,
{Praise thy God, O Zion,}

Lobe deinen Gott mit Freuden,
Praise thy   God with joy,

Auf! erzähle dessen Ruhm,
Rise! Tell   (the) glory (of him),

Der in seinem Heiligtum
Who—within his   sanctuary

Fernerhin dich als dein Hirt
Henceforth thee as thy shepherd—
{Henceforth, as thy shepherd—}

Will auf grüner Auen weiden.
Shall to green pastures lead.
{Shall lead thee to green pastures.}

peoples...And the Lord will take away from you all sickness; and none of the evil diseases of Egypt, which you knew, will he inflict upon you...

Ps. 147:12-14. Praise the Lord, O Jerusalem! Praise your God, O Zion! For he strengthens the bars of your gates; he blesses your sons within you. He makes peace in your borders; he fills you with the finest of the wheat.

2 Chron. 14:6. ...[The king] had no war in those years, for the Lord gave him peace.

Jms. 1:17. Every good endowment and every perfect gift is from above, coming down from the Father...

Ps. 103:13. As a father pities his children, so the Lord pities those who fear him.

Lam. 3:22-23. The steadfast love of the Lord never ceases, his mercies never come to an end; they are new every morning; great is thy faithfulness (Luther: Treue).

Ps. 89:1-2. I will sing of thy steadfast love, O Lord, for ever; with my mouth I will proclaim thy faithfulness to all generations. For thy steadfast love was established for ever, thy faithfulness is firm as the heavens.

Ps. 117:1-2. Praise the Lord, all nations! Extol him, all peoples! For great is his steadfast love toward us; and the faithfulness of the Lord endures for ever... (Also Ps. 100:4-5, 106:1, 107:1, 118:1, 136:1, 2, etc...)

Ps. 63:3-4. [O Lord,] because thy steadfast love is better than life, my lips will praise thee. So I will bless thee as long as I live; I will lift up my hands and call on thy name. (Also Ps. 104:33, 146:2, 145:2.)

Ps. 71:8. My mouth is filled with thy praise, and with thy glory all the day. (Also Ps. 34:1, 40:3, 51:15-17, 109:30, 145:21, Heb. 13:15.)

Ps. 19:14. Let the words of my mouth and the meditation of my heart be acceptable in thy sight...

Ps. 147:12. Praise the Lord, O Jerusalem! *Praise your God, O Zion!*

Ps. 9:11. Sing praises to the Lord, who dwells in Zion! (Also Ps. 65:1, 135:21.)

Ps. 66:8-9. Bless our God, O peoples, let the sound of his praise be heard (Luther: seinen Ruhm weit erschallen)...

Ps. 150:1. Praise the Lord! Praise God in his sanctuary (Luther: Heiligtum)...

Ps. 63:1. O God, thou art my God, I seek thee, my soul thirsts for thee; my flesh faints for thee, as in a dry and weary land where no water is. So I have looked upon thee in the sanctuary (Luther: Heiligtum), beholding thy power and glory.

Ps. 23:1-3, 6. The Lord is my shepherd, I shall not want; he makes me lie down in green pastures (Luther: weidet mich auf einer grünen Aue). He leads me beside still waters; he restores my soul. He leads me in paths of righteousness for his name's sake...Surely goodness and mercy shall follow me all the days of my life; and I shall dwell in the house of the Lord for ever.

Is. 40:11. He will feed his flock like a shepherd... (Also Ezek. 34:11-16, Rev. 7:17.)

4. Bass Recit.

● New Year's wish: Only to have Jesus as shepherd (190-4)
Es wünsche sich die Welt,
(Let) desire - the world,
{Let the world desire}

Was Fleisch und Blute wohlgefällt;
What flesh and blood pleases;
{What pleases flesh and blood;}

Nur eins, *eins bitt ich von dem Herrn,*
Only one-thing, one-thing ask I of the Lord,
{Only one thing do I ask of the Lord,}

Dies eine hätt ich gern,
This one-thing would-I-like,

Daß Jesus, meine Freude,
That Jesus, my joy,

Mein treuer Hirt, mein Trost und Heil
My faithful shepherd, my consolation and salvation

Und meiner Seelen bestes Teil,
And my soul's best portion,

Mich als ein Schäflein seiner Weide
Me as a little-sheep of-his pasture
{Would embrace me as a little sheep of his pasture}

Auch dieses Jahr mit seinem Schutz umfasse
Also this year with his protection would-embrace
{This year also with his protection}

Und nimmermehr aus seinen Armen lasse.
And nevermore from his arms release.

Sein guter Geist,
(May) his good Spirit,

Der mir den Weg zum Leben weist,
Who me the path to life does-show,
{Who shows me the path to life,}

Regier und führe mich auf ebner Bahn,
Rule and lead me on (a) level path,

So fang ich dieses Jahr in Jesu Namen an.
Thus begin I this year in Jesus name - .
{Thus can I begin this year in Jesus name.}

5. Tenor & Bass Duet

● Jesus shall be everything to me; my beginning & end (190-5)
Jesus soll mein alles sein,
Jesus shall my all be,
{Jesus shall be my all,}

1 Jn. 2:15. Do not love the world or the things in the world. If any one loves the world, love for the Father is not in him. (Also Jms. 4:4.)
1 Cor. 15:50. ...Flesh and blood cannot inherit the kingdom of God, nor does the perishable inherit the imperishable.
Rom. 7:18. I know that nothing good dwells within me, that is, in my flesh...
Ps. 27:4. *One thing have I asked of the Lord, that will I seek after* (Luther: eins bitt ich vom Herrn, das hätte ich gerne); that I may dwell in the house of the Lord all the days of my life, to behold the beauty of the Lord, and to inquire in his temple.
Mt. 22:37-38 [Christ]: You shall love the Lord your God with all your heart, and with all your soul, and with all your mind. This is the great and first commandment.
Ps. 73:25-26. [O Lord,] whom have I in heaven but thee? And there is nothing upon earth that I desire besides thee. My flesh and my heart may fail, but God is the strength of my heart and my portion (Luther: Trost und Teil) for ever.
Lk. 10:39-42. [Martha] had a sister called Mary, who sat at [Jesus'] feet and listened to his teaching. But Martha was distracted with much serving; and she went to him and said, "Lord, do you not care that my sister has left me to serve alone? Tell her then to help me." But the Lord answered her, "Martha, Martha, you are anxious and troubled about many things; one thing is needful. Mary has chosen the good portion (Luther: gute Teil erwählt)..." (Also Ps. 16:5, 142:5.)
Jn. 6:68-69. ...Lord, to whom shall we go? You have the words of eternal life; and we have believed, and have come to know, that you are the Holy One of God.
Ps. 100:3. ...We are [God's] people, and the sheep of his pasture. (Also Ps. 95:6-7.)
Is. 40:11. ...He will gather the lambs in his arms, he will carry them in his bosom... (Also Ezek. 34:11-16, Rev. 7:17.)
Jn. 10:14, 27-28 [Christ]: I am the good shepherd; I know my own and my own know me...My sheep hear my voice, and I know them, and they follow me; and I give them eternal life...and no one shall snatch them out of my hand.
Jn. 14:6 [Christ]: I am the way, and the truth, and the life; no one comes to the Father, but by me.
Acts 4:12. And there is salvation in no one else, for there is no other name under heaven given among men by which we must be saved.
Ps. 16:11. [O Lord,] thou dost show me the path of life... (Also Ps. 25:9.)
Ps. 143:10. ...[O Lord,] let thy good spirit lead me on a level path!
Ps. 23:1, 3. The Lord is my shepherd...He leads me in paths of righteousness for his name's sake.
Col. 3:17. Whatever you do, in word or deed, do everything in the name of the Lord Jesus...
***Lk. 2:21.** At the end of eight days, when he was circumcised, he was called Jesus, the name given by the angel before he was conceived in the womb.

2 Thess. 1:12. [May] the name of our Lord Jesus...be glorified in you...
Mt. 1:21. ...You shall call his name Jesus, for he will save his people from their sins.
***Lk. 2:21.** ...When he was circumcised, he was called Jesus...
Phil. 2:9-11. ...God has highly exalted [Christ] and bestowed on him the name which is above every name, that at the name of Jesus every

Jesus soll mein Anfang bleiben,
Jesus shall my beginning remain,
{Jesus shall remain my beginning,}

Jesus ist mein Freudenschein,
Jesus is my light-of-joy,

Jesu will ich mich verschreiben.
To-Jesus would I myself entrust.
{To Jesus would I entrust myself.}

Jesus hilft mir durch sein Blut,
Jesus helps me through his blood,

Jesus macht mein Ende gut.
Jesus makes my end good.

6. Tenor Recit.
●Blessing sought on anointed one and entire land (190–6)
Nun, Jesus gebe,
Now, (may) Jesus grant,

Daß mit dem neuen Jahr auch sein Gesalbter lebe;
That with the new year also his annointed-one may-live;
{That his annointed one, too, may live in the coming year;}

Er segne beides, Stamm und Zweige,
(May) he bless both, trunk and branches,

Auf daß ihr Glück bis an die Wolken steige.
So that their posperity up-to the clouds may-climb.
{So that their prosperity may climb to the clouds.}

Es segne Jesus Kirch und Schul,
(Now) bless Jesus church and school,
{May Jesus bless church and school,}

Er segne alle treue Lehrer,
(May) he bless all faithful teachers,

Er segne seines Wortes Hörer;
(May) he bless his Word's hearers;

Er segne Rat und Richterstuhl;
(May) he bless council and court;

Er gieß auch über jedes Haus
(May) he pour-out also upon every house

In unsrer Stadt die Segensquellen aus;
In our city, the springs-of-blessing - ;

knee should bow, in heaven and on earth and under the earth, and every tongue confess that Jesus Christ is Lord, to the glory of God the Father.
Col. 3:11. ...Christ is all and in all.
Phil. 3:8. ...I count everything as loss because of the surpassing worth of knowing Christ Jesus my Lord.
Phil. 1:21. To me to live is Christ... (Also Ps. 73:25.)
Ps. 27:1. The Lord is my light and my salvation...
Jn. 8:12. Jesus spoke to [the people], saying, "I am the light of the world; he who follows me will not walk in darkness, but will have the light of life." (Also Jn. 1:4, 9:5, 11:9, 12:46.)
Eph. 2:13. In Christ Jesus you who once were far off have been brought near in the blood of Christ. (Also Heb. 9:14, 1 Pet. 1:18–19, Rev. 1:5.)
Rev. 1:8. "I am the Alpha and the Omega," (Luther: das A und das O, der Anfang und das Ende) says the Lord God... (Also Rev. 21:6, 22:13.)
Phil. 1:6. ...He who began a good work in you will bring it to completion at the day of Jesus Christ.
Num. 23:10. ...Let me die the death of the righteous, and let my end be like his! (Also Heb. 13:7.)

Ps. 28:8–9. The Lord is the strength of his people, he is the saving refuge of his anointed (Luther: Gesalbten). O save thy people, and bless thy heritage; be thou their shepherd, and carry them for ever.
Ps. 18:50/2 Sam. 22:51. Great triumphs he gives to his king, and shows steadfast love to his anointed (Luther: Gesalbten)... (Also Ps. 61:6–7.)
Ezek. 31:3–7 [God]: Behold, I will liken you to a cedar in Lebanon,with fair branches and forest shade, and of great height, its top among the clouds. The waters nourished it, the deep made it grow tall, making its rivers flow round the place of its planting, sending forth its streams to all the trees of the forest. So it towered high above all the trees of the forest; its boughs grew large and its branches long, from abundant water in its shoots. All the birds of the air made their nests in its boughs; under its branches all the beasts of the field brought forth their young; and under its shadow dwelt all great nations. It was beautiful in its greatness, in the length of its branches; for its roots went down to abundant waters... (Also Ps. 1:1–3, Jer. 17:7–8.)
Ps. 36:5. Thy steadfast love, O Lord, extends to the heavens, thy faithfulness to the clouds. (Also Ps. 57:10, 108:4.)
Deut. 28:2–3, 8. All these blessings shall come upon you and overtake you, if you obey the voice of the Lord your God. Blessed shall you be in the city, and blessed shall you be in the field...He will bless you in the land which the Lord your God gives you.
Ezek. 34:26 [God]: ...I will send down the showers in their season; they shall be showers of blessing.
Mal. 3:10. ...Put me to the test, says the Lord of hosts, if I will not open the windows of heaven for you and pour down for you an overflowing blessing.
Deut. 26:15. [O Lord,] look down from thy holy habitation, from

Er gebe, daß aufs neu
(May) he grant, that anew

Sich Fried und Treu
- Peace and faithfulness

In unsern Grenzen küssen mögen.
Within our borders might-kiss.
{Might kiss within our borders.}

So leben wir dies ganze Jahr im Segen.
Thus live we this entire year in blessing.
{Thus shall we live the entire year in blessing.}

7. Chorale (See also 171-6.)
●Prayer: Bless us this new year for thy name's sake (190-7)
Laß uns das Jahr vollbringen
Let us this year complete

Zu Lob dem Namen dein,
To (the) praise of-the name of-thine,
{To the praise of thy name,}

Daß wir demselben singen
That we (to) the-same (may) sing
{That we to thy name may sing}

In der Christen Gemein;
Within the Christian communion;

Wollst uns das Leben fristen
Mayest-thou for-us (our) life prolong

Durch dein allmächtig Hand,
By thine almighty hand,

Erhalt deine liebe Christen
Preserve (these) thy dear Christians

Und unser Vaterland.
And our fatherland.

Dein Segen zu uns wende,
Thy blessing upon us turn,

Gib Fried an allem Ende;
Grant peace in all quarters;

heaven, and bless thy people Israel...as thou didst swear to our fathers... (Also Ps. 29:11.)
*Gal. 3:16, 29. Now the promises were made to Abraham and to his offspring...which is Christ...And if you are Christ's, then you are Abraham's offspring, heirs according to promise.
Ps. 85:9-12. Surely his salvation is at hand for those who fear him, that glory may dwell in our land. Steadfast love and faithfulness will meet; righteousness and peace will kiss each other. Faithfulness will spring up from the ground, and righteousness will look down from the sky. Yea, the Lord will give what is good, and our land will yield its increase.
Ps. 147:14. He makes peace in your borders; he fills you with the finest of the wheat.

Ps. 31:3. [O Lord]...for thy name's sake lead me and guide me.
Ps. 79:9. Help us, O God of our salvation, for the glory of thy name... (Also 1 Sam. 12:22.)
Ps. 115:1. Not to us, O Lord, not to us, but to thy name give glory, for the sake of thy steadfast love and thy faithfulness!
Ps. 28:9. ...[O Lord,] bless thy heritage; be thou their shepherd, and carry them for ever.
Ps. 35:18. Then I will thank thee in the great congregation; in the mighty throng I will praise thee.
Ps. 22:22, 25. [O God,] I will tell of thy name to my brethren; in the midst of the congregation I will praise thee...From thee comes my praise in the great congregation; my vows I will pay before those who fear him. (Also Ps. 40:9-10, Ps. 107:32, 149:1, Heb. 2:12.)
Ps. 91:15-16 [God]: When [my child] calls to me, I will answer him; I will be with him in trouble, I will rescue him and honor him. With long life I will satisfy him...
Ps. 31:14-15. I trust in thee, O Lord...My times are in thy hand...
Jms. 4:13-15. Come now, you who say, "Today or tomorrow we will go into such and such a town and spend a year there and trade and get gain"; whereas you do not know about tomorrow. What is your life? For you are a mist that appears for a little time and then vanishes. Instead you ought to say, "If the Lord wills, we shall live and we shall do this or that."
Deut. 26:15. [O Lord,] look down from thy holy habitation, from heaven, and bless thy people Israel...
Ps. 89:13. Thou hast a mighty arm; strong is thy hand, high thy right hand.
Ps. 29:11. May the Lord give strength to his people! May the Lord bless his people with peace!
Ps. 122:6-7. Pray for the peace of Jerusalem! "May they prosper who love you! Peace be within your walls, and security within your towers!"
Ps. 147:12-14. Praise the Lord, O Jerusalem! Praise your God, O Zion! For he strengthens the bars of your gates; he blesses your sons within you. He makes peace in your borders...
Is. 2:3. Many peoples shall come, and say: "Come, let us go up to the mountain of the Lord, to the house of the God of Jacob; that he may teach us his ways and that we may walk in his paths." For out of Zion shall go forth the law, and the word of the Lord from Jerusalem. (Also Mic. 4:2.)

Gib unverfälscht im Lande
Grant unadulterated in-this land

Dein seligmachend Wort.
Thy beatific Word.

Die Heuchler mach zuschanden
The hypocrites confound
{Confound all hypocrites}

Hier und an allem Ort!
Here and in every place!

Jer. 23:28 [God]: ...Let him who has my word speak my word faithfully. (Also Tit. 1:9.)

Acts 20:32. I commend you...to the word of [God's] grace, which is able to build you up and to give you the inheritance among all those who are sanctified.

Jms. 1:22. But be doers of the word, and not hearers only, deceiving yourselves. (Also Lk. 8:21, 11:28, Jn. 15:14.)

Mt. 7:21 [Christ]: Not every one who says to me, "Lord, Lord," shall enter the kingdom of heaven, but he who does the will of my Father who is in heaven.

1 Tim. 4:1–2. Now the Spirit expressly says that in later times some will depart from the faith by giving heed to deceitful spirits and doctrines of demons, through the pretensions of liars... (Also 2 Pet. 2:1–3.)

1 Jn. 3:8. ...The reason the Son of God appeared was to destroy the works of the devil. (Also Heb. 2:14.)

Is. 33:14–15. The sinners in Zion are afraid; trembling has seized the godless (Luther: Heuchler); "Who among us can dwell with the devouring fire? Who among us can dwell with everlasting burnings?" He who walks righteously and speaks uprightly...

Ps. 31:17. Let me not be put to shame (Luther: zu Schanden werden) O Lord, for I call on thee; let the wicked be put to shame, let them go dumbfounded to Sheol (Luther: zu Schanden und geschweigt werden in der Hölle).

BWV 191
Gloria in excelsis Deo
(NBA I/2; BC E16)

Christmas Day (BWV 63, 91, 110, 248-I, 191)
*Tit. 2:11–14 (The grace of God has appeared)
or: *Is. 9:2–7 (The people who walked in darkness have seen a great light; unto us a child is born)
*Lk. 2:1–14 (The birth of Christ, announcement to the shepherds, the praise of the angels)
Librettist: Traditional doxologies

Part I

1. Chorus (From Bm Mass: Gloria)
●Doxology (Greater) Excerpt: Lk. 2:14 (191-1)
Gloria in excelsis Deo. Et in terra
Glory in (the) highest to-God. And on earth
{Glory to God in the highest. And on earth}

pax hominibus bonae voluntatis.
peace to-men of-good will.

Part II

2. Soprano & Tenor Duet (From Bm Mass: Domine Deus)
●Doxology (Lesser): Part A (191-2)
Gloria Patri et Filio et Spiritui sancto.
Glory (be to the) Father and Son and Spirit Holy.
{Glory be to the Father, and to the Son, and to the Holy Ghost.}

***Lk. 2:9–14.** An angel of the Lord appeared to [the shepherds], and the glory of the Lord shone around them, and they were filled with fear. And the angel said to them, "Be not afraid; for behold, I bring you good news of a great joy which will come to all the people; for to you is born this day in the city of David a Savior, who is Christ the Lord. And this will be a sign for you: you will find a babe wrapped in swaddling cloths and lying in a manger." And suddenly there was with the angel a multitude of the heavenly host praising God and saying, *"Glory to God in the highest, and on earth peace among men with whom he is pleased!"*

Ps. 41:13. Blessed be the Lord, the God of Israel, from everlasting to everlasting! Amen and Amen. (Doxology: also Ps. 72:19, 89:52, 106:48, and 150:6).

Rom. 11:36. From him and through him and to him are all things. To him be glory for ever. Amen.

Mt. 28:19. ...In the name of the Father and of the Son and of the Holy Spirit.

3. Chorus (From Bm Mass: Cum Sancto Spiritu)
●Doxology (Lesser): Part B (191–3)
Sicut erat in   principio   et nunc et semper
As   it-was in (the) beginning, and now and always
{As it was in the beginning, is now, and ever shall be,}

et in   saecula saeculorum, amen.
and for generations of-generations. Amen.
{World without end. Amen.)

Rev. 4:8. The four living creatures, each of them with six wings...day and night they never cease to sing, "Holy, holy, holy, is the Lord God Almighty, who was and is and is to come!"
Ps. 106:48. Blessed be the Lord, the God of Israel, from everlasting to everlasting! And let all the people say, "Amen!" Praise the Lord!
Jude 1:25. To the only God, our Savior through Jesus Christ our Lord, be glory, majesty, dominion, and authority, before all time and now and for ever. Amen. (Also Rom. 16:27.)
Heb. 13:8. Jesus Christ is the same yesterday and today and for ever.

BWV 192
Nun danket allet Gott
(NBA I/34; BC A188)

Occasion Unknown (BWV 131, 150, 117, 192, 100, 97)
Perhaps this cantata was intended for a wedding or Reformation Day.
Librettist: Chorale (Martin Rinckart)

1. Chorus (Chorale Vs. 1) (See also 79-3.)
●Thanks for blessings since infancy: Sir. 50:22 (192-1)
Nun danket   alle   Gott
Now thank (ye) all (our) God

Mit Herzen, Mund und Händen,
With heart,   mouth, and   hands,

Der große Dinge tut
Who great things does
{Who does great things}

An uns und allen Enden,
For us (in) all   quarters,

Der uns von   Mutterleib
Who to-us from (the) womb

Und   Kindesbeinen an
And (from) infancy   on

Unzählig viel zugut
Countless much good

Und   noch jetzund getan.
And (still) even now has-done.
{Who has done countless much good to us from the womb and from infancy on, and even now.}

Sirach (Apocrypha) 50:22 (= Sirach 50:24 of German Bible). And now bless the God of all, who in every way does great things; who exalts our days from birth, and deals with us according to his mercy. (Luther: Nun danket alle Gott, der große Dinge tut an allen Enden, der uns von Mutterleib an lebendig erhält und tut uns alles Gute.)
Ps. 111:1. Praise the Lord. I will give thanks to the Lord with my whole heart... (Also Ps. 86:12, 109:30.)
Ps. 109:30. With my mouth I will give great thanks to the Lord; I will praise him in the midst of the throng. (Also Ps. 145:21.)
Ps. 47:1. Clap your hands, all peoples! Shout to God with loud songs of joy! (Also Is. 12:6, 44:23.)
Ps. 75:1. We give thanks to thee, O God; we give thanks; we call on thy name and recount thy wondrous deeds.
Ps. 145:10. All thy works shall give thanks to thee, O Lord, and all thy saints shall bless thee!
Lk. 1:49. For he who is mighty has done great things for me, and holy is his name.
1 Sam. 12:24. ...Consider what great things [the Lord] has done for you.
Ps. 126:3. The Lord has done great things for us; we are glad.
Ps. 71:5–6. For thou, O Lord, art my hope, my trust, O Lord, from my youth. Upon thee I have leaned from my birth; thou art he who took me from my mother's womb (Luther: Mutterleibe). My praise is continually of thee. (Also Ps. 22:10, Jer. 1:5.)
Job 9:10. [He] does great things beyond understanding, and marvelous things without number. (Also Job 5:9.)

2. Soprano & Bass Duet (Chorale Vs. 2)
●Prayer for blessing all our days: Sir. 50:23–24 (192-2)
    Der ewig reiche Gott
(May) the eternally rich God

Woll uns bei unserm Leben
  - To-us in   our   life
{Grant to us in our life}

Sirach (Apocrypha) 50:23–24 (= Sirach 50:25–26 of German Bible). May he give us gladness of heart, and grant that peace may be in our days in Israel, as in the days of old. May he entrust to us his mercy! And let him deliver us in our days! (Luther: Er gebe uns ein fröhlich

Ein immer fröhlich Herz
An   ever   joyful   heart

Und edlen Frieden geben
And noble   peace   grant
{And noble peace,}

Und uns in seiner Gnad
And us   in   his   grace
{And preserve us in his grace}

Erhalten fort und fort
Preserve   continually
{Continually,}

Und uns aus aller   Not
And us   from all difficulty
{And deliver us from all difficulty}

Erlösen hier und   dort.
Deliver   here and (over) there.
{Everywhere.}

3. Chorus (Chorale Vs. 3)
●Doxology: Praise to Father, Son, and Holy Ghost (192–3)
Lob,   Ehr   und Preis sei Gott,
Laud, honor, and praise be-to God,

Dem Vater und dem Sohne
The Father and   the   Son

Und dem, der beiden gleich
And to-him, who to-both is-equal
{And to him who is equal to both}

Im   hohen Himmelsthrone,
On (the) high throne-of-heaven,

Dem dreieinigen Gott,
The   triune   God,

Als der ursprünglich war
As   he in-the-beginning was
{As he was in the beginning,}

Und ist und bleiben wird
And is, and remain shall
{Is now, and ever shall be,}

Jetzund und immerdar.
Now   and   evermore.

Herz und verleihe immerdar Frieden zu unsrer Zeit in Israel, und daß seine Gnade stets bei uns bleibe; und erlöse uns, solange wir leben.)
Jms. 1:17. Every good endowment and every perfect gift is from above, coming down from the Father...
Mt. 7:11 [Christ]: If you...know how to give good gifts to your children, how much more will your Father who is in heaven give good things to those who ask him!
Is. 55:12. You shall go out in joy, and be led forth in peace...
Ps. 29:11. May the Lord give strength to his people! May the Lord bless his people with peace! (Also Ps. 122:6–7, 147:14.)
Ps. 128:5–6. The Lord bless you from Zion! May you see the prosperity of Jerusalem all the days of your life! May you see your children's children! Peace be upon Israel!
Ps. 28:8–9. The Lord is the strength of his people, he is the saving refuge of his anointed. O save thy people, and bless thy heritage; be thou their shepherd, and carry them for ever. (Also Ps. 125:1–5.)
Ps. 3:8. Deliverance belongs to the Lord; thy blessing be upon thy people!
Ps. 107:1–2. O give thanks to the Lord, for he is good; for his steadfast love endures for ever! Let the redeemed of the Lord say so, whom he has redeemed (Luther: erlöst) from trouble (Luther: Not).

Lk. 2:14. Glory to God in the highest...
1 Tim. 1:17. To the King of ages, immortal, invisible, the only God, be honor and glory for ever and ever. Amen.
Phil. 4:20. To our God and Father be glory for ever and ever.
Ps. 41:13. Blessed be the Lord, the God of Israel, from everlasting to everlasting! Amen and Amen. (Doxology: also Ps. 72:19, 89:52, 106:48, 150:6)
Rom. 11:36. For from him and through him and to him are all things. To him be glory for ever. Amen.
Jude 1:25. To the only God, our Savior through Jesus Christ our Lord, be glory, majesty, dominion, and authority, before all time and now and for ever. Amen.
Rom. 16:27. To the only wise God be glory for evermore through Jesus Christ! Amen.
Mt. 28:19. ...in the name of the Father and of the Son and of the Holy Spirit.
Rev. 4:8. The four living creatures, each of them with six wings...day and night they never cease to sing, "Holy, holy, holy, is the Lord God Almighty, who was and is and is to come!"
Rev. 7:11–12. And all the angels stood round the throne and round the elders and the four living creatures, and they fell on their faces before the throne and worshiped God, saying, "Amen! Blessing and glory and wisdom and thanksgiving and honor and power and might be to our God for ever and ever! Amen."
Heb. 13:8. Jesus Christ is the same yesterday and today and for ever.
Ps. 106:48. Blessed be the Lord, the God of Israel, from everlasting to everlasting! And let all the people say, "Amen!" Praise the Lord!

BWV 193
Ihr Tore zu Zion
(NBA I/32; BC B5)

Change of Town Council (BWV 71, 119, 193, 120, 29, 69)
Librettist: Unknown. Parody of BWV 193a in movements 1, 3, 5.

1. Chorus (Parody)
●Rejoice Zion, you are God's people! (193-1)
Ihr Tore zu Zion, ihr Wohnungen Jakobs, freuet euch!
Ye gates of Zion, ye dwellings of-Jacob, rejoice!

Gott is unsers Herzens Freude,
God is our heart's joy,
{God is the joy of our heart,}

Wir sind Völker seiner Weide,
We are (the) people of-his pasture,

Ewig ist sein Königreich.
Everlasting is his kingdom.

Ps. 87:1–3. On the holy mount stands the city he founded; the Lord loves the gates of Zion more than all the dwelling places of Jacob. Glorious things are spoken of you, O city of God.
Is. 12:6. Shout, and sing for joy, O inhabitant of Zion, for great in your midst is the Holy One of Israel. (Also Ps. 48:11, 149:2, Zeph. 3:14, Zech. 2:10.)
Ps. 43:4. I will go to the altar of God, to God my exceeding joy (Luther: Freude und Wonne)... (Also Ps. 84:2.)
Ps. 95:6–7. O come, let us worship and bow down, let us kneel before the Lord, our Maker! For he is our God and we are the people of his pasture, and the sheep of his hand. (Also Ps. 100:3.)
Ps. 10:16. The Lord is king for ever and ever...
Ps. 145:13. [O Lord,] thy kingdom is an everlasting kingdom, and thy dominion endures throughout all generations...
Rev. 11:15. ...The kingdom of the world has become the kingdom of our Lord and of his Christ, and he shall reign for ever and ever. (Also Ex. 15:18, Ps. 146:10, Lk. 1:33.)

2. Soprano Recit.
●Guardian of Israel does not sleep (193-2)
Der Hüter Israels entschläft noch schlummert nicht;
The guardian of-Israel falls-asleep nor slumbers not;
{The guardian of Israel neither slumbers nor sleeps,}

Es ist annoch sein Angesicht
- - Hitherto his countenance (has been)

Der Schatten unsrer rechten Hand;
The shade (on) our right hand;

Und das gesamte Land
And the entire land

Hat sein Gewächs im Überfluß gegeben.
Has its growth in abundance yielded.
{Has yielded abundant growth.}

Wer kann dich, Herr, genug davor erheben?
Who can thee, Lord, enough for-this exalt?
{O Lord, who can exalt thee enough for this?}

Ps. 121:2–8. My help comes from the Lord, who made heaven and earth. He will not let your foot be moved, he who keeps you will not slumber. Behold, *he who keeps Israel will neither slumber nor sleep. The Lord is your keeper; the Lord is your shade on your right hand.* The sun shall not smite you by day, nor the moon by night. The Lord will keep you from all evil; he will keep your life. The Lord will keep your going out and your coming in from this time forth and for evermore.
Ps. 44:3. Not by their own sword did they win the land, nor did their own arm give them victory; but thy right hand [O Lord], and thy arm and the light of thy countenance (Luther: Angesicht); for thou didst delight in them.
Ps. 65:11–13. [O Lord,] thou crownest the year with thy bounty...The pastures of the wilderness drip, the hills gird themselves with joy, the meadow clothe themselves with flocks, the valleys deck themselves with grain, they shout and sing together for joy.
Ps. 67:6–7. The earth has yielded its increase (Luther: das Land gibt sein Gewächs); God, our God, has blessed us. God has blessed us; let all the ends of the earth fear him! (Also Joel 2:23.)
Ps. 116:12. What shall I render to the Lord for all his bounty to me?

3. Soprano Aria (Parody)
●Thanks to God for his fatherly devotion (193-3)
Gott, wir danken deiner Güte,
(O) God, we thank (thee for) thy kindness,

Denn dein väterlich Gemüte
For thy fatherly disposition (towards us)

Währet ewig für und für.
Endures forever and ever.

Ps. 106:1. Praise the Lord! O give thanks to the Lord, for he is good; for his steadfast love endures for ever (Luther: seine Güte währet ewiglich)! (Also Ps. 107:1, 118:1, 136: 1, 2, 3, etc...)
Ps. 103:2, 8, 10–13. Bless the Lord, O my soul, and forget not all his benefits....The Lord is merciful and gracious, slow to anger and abounding in steadfast love...He does not deal with us according to our sins, nor requite us according to our iniquities. For as the heavens are high above the earth, so great is his steadfast love toward those who fear him; as far as the east is from the west, so far does he

Du vergibst das Übertreten,
Thou forgivest (our) trespasses,

Du erhörest, wenn wir beten,
Thou dost-hear, when we pray,

Drum kömmt alles Fleisch zu dir.
Thus shall-come all flesh to thee.
{Thus shall all flesh come to thee.}

4. Alto Recit.
●Leipzig blessed like Jerusalem with peace & justice (193-4)
O Leipziger Jerusalem,
O Leipzig, (our) Jerusalem,

vergnüge dich an deinem Feste!
delight thyself in (this) thy festival!

Der Fried ist noch in deinen Mauern,
- Peace is still within thy walls,
{Peace still reigns within your walls,}

Es stehn annoch die Stühle zum Gericht,
(Now) stand as-yet the seats of judgment,
{The seats of justice still stand secure,}

Und die Gerechtigkeit bewohnet die Paläste.
And - righteousness resides (within) the palaces.

Ach bitte, daß dein Ruhm und Licht
Ah, pray, that thy fame and light

Also beständig möge dauern!
Thus steadfastly may endure!

5a. Alto Aria (Parody)
●Prayer for blessing on just administrators (193-5)
Sende, Herr, den Segen ein,
Send, [O] Lord, (thy) blessing (down),

Laß die wachsen und erhalten,
Let all-them increase and (be) preserved,

Die vor dich das Recht verwalten
Who before thee - justice administer
{Who administer justice before thee}

Und ein Schutz der Armen sein!
And a refuge for-the poor are!
{And act as a refuge for the poor!}

Sende, Herr, den Segen ein!
Send, [O] Lord, (thy) blessing (down)!

remove our transgressions (Luther: Übertretungen) from us. As a father pities his children, so the Lord pities those who fear him.
2 Chron. 7:14 [God]: If my people who are called by my name humble themselves, and pray and seek my face, and turn from their wicked ways, then I will hear from heaven, and will forgive their sin and heal their land. (Also 1 Kings 8:33-34, 2 Chron. 6:24-25.)
Ps. 65:1-2. Praise is due to thee, O God, in Zion; and to thee shall vows be performed, O thou who hearest prayer! To thee shall all flesh come.

Ps. 118:24. This is the day which the Lord has made; let us rejoice and be glad in it.
Zeph. 3:14. Sing aloud, O daughter of Zion...Rejoice and exult with all your heart, O daughter of Jerusalem!
Ps. 122:3-7. Jerusalem, built as a city which is bound firmly together, to which the tribes go up, the tribes of the Lord, as was decreed for Israel, to give thanks to the name of the Lord. There thrones (Luther: Stühle zum Gericht) were set, the thrones of the house of David. Pray for the peace of Jerusalem! (Luther: Wünschet Jerusalem Glück!) "May they prosper who love you! Peace (Luther: Friede) be within your walls (Luther: Mauern), and security (Luther: Glück) within your towers (Luther: Palästen)!" (Also Ps. 48:1-3.)
Prov. 29:4. By justice a king gives stability to the land...
Jer. 33:9 [God]: This city shall be to me a name of joy, a praise and a glory before all the nations of the earth who shall hear of all the good that I do for them...
Is. 49:6 [God]: ...I will give you as a light to the nations, that my salvation may reach to the end of the earth.
Mt. 5:14, 16 [Christ]: You are the light of the world. A city set on a hill cannot be hid...Let your light so shine before men, that they may see your good works and give glory to your Father who is in heaven.
Prov. 13:9. The light of the righteous rejoices, but the lamp of the wicked will be put out.

Ezek. 34:26 [God]: ...I will send down the showers in their season; they shall be showers of blessing.
Deut. 26:15. [O Lord,] look down from thy holy habitation, from heaven, and bless thy people... (Also Ps. 28:8-9.)
Ps. 72:1-8, 12-14, 17. Give the king thy justice, O God, and thy righteousness to the royal son! May he judge thy people with righteousness, and thy poor with justice! Let the mountains bear prosperity for thy people, and the hills, in righteousness! May he defend the cause of the poor of the people, giver deliverance to the needy, and crush the oppressor! May he live while the sun endures, and as long as the moon, throughout all generations! May he be like rain that falls on the mown grass, like showers that water the earth. In his days may righteousness flourish, and peace abound, till the moon be no more! May he have dominion from sea to sea...For he delivers the needy when he calls, the poor and him who has no helper. He has pity on the weak and the needy, and saves the lives of the needy. From oppression and violence he redeems their life; and precious is their blood in his sight...May his name endure for ever, his fame continue as long as the sun! My men bless themselves by him, all nations call him blessed!

5b. Recit.
(A recitative formerly fit here; it is no longer extant.)

6. Chorus
●Rejoice Zion, you are God's people! (193-6)
Ihr Tore zu Zion, ihr Wohnungen Jakobs, freuet euch!
Ye gates of Zion, ye   dwellings of-Jacob,   rejoice!

Gott is unsers Herzens Freude,
God is our   heart's   joy,

Wir sind   Völker seiner Weide,
We are (the) people of-his pasture;

Ewig   ist sein Königreich.
Everlasting is   his   kingdom.

Ps. 87:1–3. On the holy mount stands the city he founded; the Lord loves the gates of Zion more than all the dwelling places of Jacob. Glorious things are spoken of you, O city of God.
Is. 12:6. Shout, and sing for joy, O inhabitant of Zion, for great in your midst is the Holy One of Israel. (Also Ps. 48:11, 149:2, Zeph. 3:14, Zech. 2:10.)
Ps. 84:2. ...My heart and flesh sing for joy to the living God. (Also Ps. 43:4.)
Ps. 100:3. Know that the Lord is God! It is he that made us, and we are his; we are his people, and the sheep of his pasture. (Also Ps. 95:6–7.)
Ps. 146:10. The Lord will reign for ever, thy God, O Zion, to all generations. Praise the Lord (Luther: Halleluja)!
Rev. 11:15. ...The kingdom of the world has become the kingdom of our Lord and of his Christ, and he shall reign for ever and ever. (Also Ex. 15:18, Ps. 10:16, 145:13, Lk. 1:33.)

BWV 194
Höchsterwünschtes Freudenfest
(NBA I/31; BC A91a/b, B31)

Church & Organ Dedication in Störmthal (BWV 194)
*Rev. 21:2–8 (The new Jerusalem comes down from heaven)
*Lk. 19:1–10 (The conversion of Zacchaeus)
Librettist: Unknown. This cantata was adapted from secular cantata BWV 194a, which is only partially extant.

This cantata was later reused several times for:
Trinity Sunday (BWV 165, [194], 176, 129)
+Rom. 11:33–36 (O the depth of the riches and wisdom and knowledge of God!)
+Jn. 3:1–15 (Discussion between Jesus and Nicodemus: You must be born anew)

Part I

1. Chorus
●Church Dedication: A celebration of praise (194–1)
    Höchsterwünschtes Freudenfest,
(O) most-highly-desired festival-of-joy,

Das   der Herr zu seinem Ruhme
Which the Lord to   his   renown

Im   erbauten Heiligtume
In (this newly) constructed sanctuary

Uns vergnügt begehen läßt.
Us   gladly   celebrates lets.
(Lets us gladly celebrate.}

    Höchsterwünschtes Freudenfest!
(O) most-highly-desired festival-of-joy!

1 Kings 7:51–8:2, 65. All the work that King Solomon did on the house of the Lord was finished. And Solomon brought in the things which David his father had dedicated, the silver, the gold, and the vessels, and stored them in the treasuries of the house of the Lord. Then Solomon assembled the elders of Israel and all the heads of the tribes, the leaders of the fathers' houses of the people of Israel, before King Solomon in Jerusalem, to bring up the ark of the covenant of the Lord out of the city of David, which is Zion. And all the men of Israel assembled to King Solomon at the feast...So Solomon held the feast at that time, and all Israel with him, a great assembly...
Ps. 118:24. This is the day which the Lord has made; let us rejoice and be glad in it.
Ps. 126:3. The Lord has done great things for us; we are glad. (Also 1 Sam. 12:24, Lk. 1:49.)

2. Bass Recit.

●Prayer dedicating new sanctuary & our hearts to God
(194-2)

Unendlich großer Gott, ach wende dich
(O) infinite great God, ah, turn -

Zu uns, zu dem erwähleten Geschlechte,
To us, to (thy) chosen race,

Und zum Gebete deiner Knechte!
And to-the prayers of-thy servants!

Ach, laß vor dich
Ah, (Lord,) let before thee—

Durch ein inbrünstig Singen
Through - ardent singing—
{Ah Lord, through ardent singing, let before thee}

Der Lippen Opfer bringen!
(Our) lips' offering be-brought!

Wir weihen unsre Brust dir offenbar
We dedicate our breast to-thee manifestly
{We manifestly dedicate our heart to thee}

Zum Dankaltar.
As (an) altar-of-thanksgiving.

Du, den kein Haus, kein Tempel faßt,
(O) thou, whom no house, no temple can-contain,

Da du kein Ziel noch Grenzen hast,
For thou no end nor limits hast—
{For thou art without end or limits—}

Laß dir dies Haus gefällig sein,
Let to-thee this house pleasing be,
{Let this house be pleasing to thee,}

es sei dein Angesicht
(may) it (become) for-thy countenance

Ein wahrer Gnadenstuhl, ein Freudenlicht.
A true mercyseat, a light-of-joy.

3. Bass Aria

●God's radiance fills the sanctuary he has chosen (194-3)
Was des Höchsten Glanz erfüllt,
What the Highest-One's radiance does-fill,
{Whatever the Highest One fills with his radiance,}

Wird in keine Nacht verhüllt;
Shall in no night be-veiled;
{Shall never be veiled in night;}

---

1 Kings 8:22-23, 52-53. Then Solomon stood before the altar of the Lord in the presence of all the assembly of Israel and spread forth his hands toward heaven; and said, "O Lord, God of Israel, there is no God like thee...Let thy eyes be open to the supplication of thy servant, and to the supplication of thy people Israel...For thou didst separate them from among all the peoples of the earth, to be thy heritage..." (Also Ps. 33:12, 1 Pet. 2:9, 2 Thess. 2:13.)
2 Chron. 5:1, 11, 13-14. Thus all the work that Solomon did for the house of the Lord was finished...Now when the priests came out of the holy place...and when the song was raised, with trumpets and cymbals and other musical instruments, in praise to the Lord, "For he is good, for his steadfast love endures for ever," the house...of the Lord, was filled with a cloud...for the glory of the Lord filled the house of God. (Also 1 Kings 8:10-11.)
Ps. 116:12. What shall I render to the Lord for all his bounty...?
Heb. 13:15. ...Let us continually offer up a sacrifice of praise to God, that is, the fruit of lips that acknowledge his name.
Ps. 50:14, 23 [God]: Offer to God a sacrifice of thanksgiving, and pay your vows to the Most High...He who brings thanksgiving as his sacrifice honors me; to him who orders his way aright I will show the salvation of God! (Also Ps. 51:15-17.)
Rom. 12:1. ...Present your bodies as a living sacrifice, holy and acceptable to God, which is your spiritual worship.
2 Chron. 6:12-14, 18-20. Solomon stood before the altar of the Lord in the presence of all the assembly of Israel...and spread forth his hands toward heaven; and said, "O Lord, God of Israel, there is no God like thee, in heaven or on earth, keeping covenant and showing steadfast love to thy servants...Behold, heaven and the highest heaven cannot contain thee; how much less this house which I have built! Yet have regard to the prayer of thy servant and to his supplication, O Lord my God, hearkening to the cry and to the prayer which thy servant prays before thee; that thy eyes may be open day and night toward this house, the place where thou hast promised to set thy name, that thou mayest hearken to the prayer which thy servant offers toward this place." (Also 1 Kings 8:22-23, 27-29.)
Ex. 25:22 [God]: ...From above the mercy seat (Luther: Gnadenstuhl), from between the two cherubim that are upon the ark of the testimony [in my house], I will speak with you of all that I will give you in commandment for the people of Israel.
Ps. 89:15. Blessed are the people who know the festal shout, who walk, O Lord, in the light of thy countenance.

Ps. 50:2. Out of Zion, the perfection of beauty, God shines forth.
1 Jn. 1:5. God is light and in him is no darkness at all.
Jn. 1:4-5. In [Christ, the divine Word] was life, and the life was the light of men. The light shines in the darkness, and the darkness has not overcome it.
Heb. 1:3. [The Son] reflects the glory of God (Luther: der Glanz seiner Herrlichkeit) and bears the very stamp of his nature (Luther: das Ebenbilde seines Wesens)...
1 Tim. 6:15-16. ...[He is] the King of kings and Lord of lords, who alone has immortality and dwells in unapproachable light, whom no man has ever seen or can see...

Was des Höchsten heilges Wesen
Whatever the Highest-One's holy nature

Sich zur Wohnung auserlesen,
For-himself as dwelling has-chosen,
{For his dwelling has chosen,}

Wird in keine Nacht verhüllt,
Will in no night be-veiled,
{Shall never be veiled in night;}

Was des Höchsten Glanz erfüllt.
Whatever the Highest-One's radiance does-fill.
{Whatever the Highest One fills with his radiance.}

4. Soprano Recit.
●Church Dedication: May God accept our offerings (194–4)
Wie könnte dir, du höchstes Angesicht,
How could to-thee, thou most-sublime countenance—

Da dein unendlich helles Licht
Since thy infinitely brilliant light

Bis in verborgne Gründe siehet,
- Into (the) hidden depths doth-see—

Ein Haus gefällig sein?
A house pleasing be?
{How could a house be pleasing to thee, O thou most sublime countenance, since thy infinitely brilliant light sees into all the hidden depths?}

Es schleicht sich Eitelkeit allhie an allen Enden ein.
(For) creeps-in - vanity here on every (side)
{For vanity doth creep in here on every side.}

Wo deine Herrlichkeit einziehet,
Where'er thy glory takes-up-residence,

Da muß die Wohnung rein
There must the dwelling clean
{There must the dwelling be clean}

Und dieses Gastes würdig sein.
And of-this guest worthy be.
{And worthy of this guest.}

Hier wirkt nichts Menschenkraft,
Here avail nothing human-powers,
{Here human powers avail nothing,}

Drum laß dein Auge offenstehen
Therefore let thine eye stand-open

Ex. 34:29–30, 33–35. When Moses came down from Mount Sinai, with the two tables of the testimony in his hand as he came down from the mountain, Moses did not know that the skin of his face shone because he had been talking with God. And when Aaron and all the people of Israel saw Moses, behold, the skin of his face shone, and they were afraid to come near him...And...Moses...put a veil on his face; but whenever Moses went in before the Lord to speak with him, he took the veil off, until he came out; and when he came out, and told the people of Israel what he was commanded, the people of Israel saw the face of Moses, that the skin of Moses' face shone; and Moses would put the veil upon his face again, until he went in to speak with him.
2 Cor. 3:7–8. Now if the dispensation of death, carved in letters on stone, came with such splendor that the Israelites could not look at Moses' face because of its brightness, fading as this was, will not the dispensation of the spirit be attended with greater splendor?
2 Cor. 4:6. For it is the God who said, "Let light shine out of darkness," who has shone in our hearts to give the light of the knowledge of the glory of God in the face of Christ.

*Rev. 21:2–3. I saw the holy city, new Jerusalem, coming down out of heaven from God, prepared as a bride adorned for her husband; and I heard a loud voice from the throne saying, "Behold, the dwelling of God is with men. He will dwell with them, and they shall be his people, and God himself will be with them."
1 Kings 8:27. But will God indeed dwell on the earth? Behold, heaven and the highest heaven cannot contain thee; how much less this house... (Also 2 Chron. 6:18.)
1 Tim. 6:15–16. [He is] the blessed and only Sovereign, the King of kings and Lord of lords, who alone has immortality and dwells in unapproachable light... (Also Rev. 21:23–24, 22:5, +Rom. 11:33–36.)
Dan. 2:22. He reveals deep and mysterious things; he knows what is in the darkness, and the light dwells with him.
Ps. 139:11–12, 15. If I say, "Let only darkness cover me, and the light about me be night," even the darkness is not dark to thee, the night is bright as the day; for darkness is as light with thee...My frame was not hidden from thee, when I was being made in secret, intricately wrought in the depths of the earth. (Also Prov. 15:3, 11, Jer. 23:24.)
Acts 7:48–50. The Most High does not dwell in houses made with hands; as the prophet says, "Heaven is my throne, and earth my footstool. What house will you build for me, says the Lord, or what is the place of my rest? Did not my hand make all these things?" (See Is. 66:1; also 2 Chron. 2:4–6, 1 Kings 8:27, Acts 17:24–25.)
Ps. 8:3. [O Lord,] when I look at thy heavens, the work of thy fingers... what is man that thou art mindful of him...? (Also Ps. 144:3–4, Heb. 2:5–8.)
*Lk. 19:5–7. When Jesus came to the place [where Zacchaeus was in the sycamore tree], he looked up and said to him, "Zacchaeus, make haste and come down; for I must stay at your house today." So he made haste and came down and received him joyfully. And when they saw it they all murmured, "He has gone in to be the guest of a man who is a sinner." (Also Mt. 8:8, Lk. 7:6.)

Und gnädig auf uns gehen;
And graciously upon us (fall);

So legen wir in heilger Freude dir
Then lay we in holy joy for-thee
{Then we, in holy joy,}

Die Farren und die Opfer unsrer Lieder
(Our) bullocks and the offerings of-our songs
{Will lay down our bullocks and offerings of song}

Vor deinem Throne nieder
Before thy throne down
{Before thy throne}

Und tragen dir den Wunsch in Andacht für.
And bring-before thee (our) hope with devotion - .

5. Soprano Aria
●Prayer to be sanctified by Spirit as Isaiah was (194–5)
Hilf, Gott, daß es uns gelingt,
Help, (O) God, that this for-us (would) succeed,
{Help, O God, that this would prove successful in us,}

Und dein Feuer in uns dringt,
And thy fire into us penetrate,
{That thy fire might penetrate into us,}

Daß es auch in dieser Stunde
That it (might) also in this hour,

Wie in Essaiae Munde
As (it did) in Isaiah's mouth,

Seiner Wirkung Kraft erhält
Its (effective) power retain

Und uns heilig vor dich stellt.
And us holy before thee bring.
{And bring us sanctified before thee.}

6. Chorale (New to this version)
●Prayer: Holy Ghost, complete thy work of grace in me
(194–6)
   Heilger Geist ins Himmels Throne,
(O) Holy Ghost on heaven's throne,

Gleicher Gott von Ewigkeit
Equally God from (all) eternity

Mit dem Vater und dem Sohne,
With the Father and the Son,
{Coequal with the Father and the Son from all eternity,}

Is. 57:15. Thus says the high and lofty One who inhabits eternity, whose name is Holy: "I dwell in the high and holy place, and also with him who is of a contrite and humble spirit..."
1 Cor. 6:19–20. Do you not know that your body is a temple of the Holy Spirit within you, which you have from God?...So glorify God in your body. (Also 1 Cor. 3:16.)
2 Chron. 6:18–20. [O Lord,] behold, heaven and the highest heaven cannot contain thee; how much less this house which I have built! Yet have regard to the prayer of thy servant...that thy eyes may be open day and night toward this house... (Also 1 Kings 8:22–23, 27–29.)
Hos. 14:2. Take with you words and return to the Lord; say to him "Take away all iniquity; accept that which is good and we will render the fruit (Luther: Farren) of our lips."
Ps. 19:14. Let the words of my mouth and the meditation of my heart be acceptable in thy sight... (Also Ps. 104:34.)

Is. 6:1–7. In the year that King Uzziah died I saw the Lord sitting upon a throne, high and lifted up; and his train filled the temple. Above him stood the seraphim; each had six wings: with two he covered his face, and with two he covered his feet, and with two he flew. And one called to another and said: "Holy, holy, holy is the Lord of hosts; the whole earth is full of his glory." And the foundations of the thresholds shook at the voice of him who called, and the house was filled with smoke. And I said: "Woe is me! For I am lost; for I am a man of unclean lips, and I dwell in the midst of a people of unclean lips; for my eyes have seen the King, the Lord of hosts!" Then flew one of the seraphim to me, having in his hand a burning coal which he had taken with tongs from the altar. And he touched my mouth, and said: "Behold, this has touched your lips; your guilt is taken away, and your sin is forgiven."
Lk. 3:16. John [said to the people], "I baptize you with water; but he who is mightier than I is coming, the thong of whose sandals I am not worthy to untie; he will baptize you with the Holy Spirit and with fire." (Also Mt. 3:11, Mk. 1:7–8, Jn. 1:26–27, 33.)

Rom. 8:91. You are not in the flesh, you are in the Spirit, if in fact the Spirit of God dwells in you. Any one who does not have the Spirit of Christ does not belong to him.
Eph. 5:18. ...Be filled with the Spirit.
Eph. 2:18. Through [Christ] we...have access in one Spirit to the Father.
Mt. 28:19. ...in the name of the Father and of the Son and of the Holy Spirit.
+Jn. 3:3, 5–6. Jesus [said], "...Truly, truly, I say to you, unless one is born of water and the Spirit, he cannot enter the kingdom of God. That which is born of the flesh is flesh, and that which is born of the Spirit is spirit. Do not marvel that I said to you, 'You must be born anew.' The wind blows where it wills, and you hear the sound of it, but you do not know whence it comes or whither it goes; so it is with every one who is born of the Spirit."

Der Betrübten   Trost und Freud!
Of-the sorrowing (the) comfort and joy!
{Comfort and joy of all the sorrowing!}

Allen Glauben, den ich find,
All-the faith, which I find (within me),

Hast du in mir angezündt,
Hast thou in me kindled;

Über mir in Gnaden walte,
Over me in mercy hold-sway,
{Hold sway over me in mercy,}

Ferner   deine Gab erhalte.
Furthermore thy (favor) maintain.
{And maintain thy favor furthermore.}

///

Deine Hilfe zu mir sende,
Thy help to me send,
{Send thy help to me,}

O du edler Herzensgast!
O thou noble guest-of-(my)-heart!

Und das gute Werk vollende,
And that good work complete,
{And complete that good work,}

Das du angefangen hast.
Which thou begun hast.
{Which thou hast begun.}

Blas in mir das Fünklein auf,
Blow in me that spark (alive),
{Fan alive the flame,}

Bis daß nach vollbrachtem Lauf
Till, after - completed course
{Till, after my course is run}

Ich den Auserwählten gleiche
I the chosen-ones resemble
{I become like the chosen ones}

Jn. 14:16–17 [Christ]: I will pray the Father, and he will give you another Counselor (Luther: Tröster), to be with you for ever, even the Spirit of truth...you know him, for he dwells with you, and will be in you.

Jn. 16:8 [Christ]: When [the Counselor] comes, he will convince the world concerning sin and righteousness and judgment.

1 Cor. 12:3. ...No one can say "Jesus is Lord" except by the Holy Spirit.

Rom. 8:14, 16. For all who are led by the Spirit of God are sons of God...It is the Spirit himself bearing witness with our spirit that we are children of God.

1 Thess. 1:5–6. Our gospel came to you not only in word, but also in power and in the Holy Spirit and with full conviction...You received the word in much affliction, with joy inspired by the Holy Spirit. (Also Acts 9:31, 13:52, Rom. 14:17, Gal. 5:22.)

1 Cor. 2:12, 14. Now we have received not the spirit of the world, but the Spirit which is from God, that we might understand the gifts bestowed on us by God...The unspiritual man does not receive the gifts of the Spirit of God, for they are folly to him, and he is not able to understand them because they are spiritually discerned.

Heb. 6:4–5. ...[We] have tasted the heavenly gift, and have become partakers of the Holy Spirit, and have tasted the goodness of the word of God...

Ps. 103: 11. As the heavens are high above the earth, so great is [the Lord's] steadfast love (Luther: läßt er seine Gnade walten) toward those who fear him.

Phil. 1:6. I am sure that he who began a good work in you will bring it to completion at the day of Jesus Christ.

Phil. 2:13. For God is at work in you, both to will and to work for his good pleasure. (Also Ps. 138:8.)

Col. 1:27. ...Christ in you, the hope of glory.

*Rev. 21:3. ...Behold, the dwelling of God is with men. He will dwell with them, and they shall be his people...

*Lk. 19:5–6. When Jesus came to the place [where Zacchaeus was in the sycamore tree], he looked up and said to him, "Zacchaeus, make haste and come down; for I must stay at your house today." So he made haste and came down and received him joyfully.

Jn. 20:22. ...[Jesus] said to [his disciples], "Receive the Holy Spirit."

Jn. 14:16–17 [Christ]: ...The Father...will [send] you another Counselor, to be with you for ever, even the Spirit of truth...He dwells with you, and will be in you.

Acts 2:1, 3–4. When the day of Pentecost had come, [the disciples] were all together in one place...And there appeared to them tongues as of fire, distributed and resting on each one of them. And they were all filled with the Holy Spirit...

1 Cor. 3:16. Do you not know that you are God's temple and that God's Spirit dwells in you?

Heb. 12:1–2. ...Let us run with perseverance the race that is set before us, looking to Jesus the pioneer and perfecter of our faith...

2 Tim. 4:7–8. I have fought the good fight, I have finished the race (Luther: Lauf vollendet), I have kept the faith. Henceforth there is laid up for me the crown of righteousness, which the Lord, the righteous judge, will award to me on that Day, and not only to me but also to all who have loved his appearing.

Rev. 3:4 [Christ]: ...[The righteous] shall walk with me in white, for they are worthy.

Und des Glaubens Ziel erreiche.
And - faith's goal attain.
{And attain the goal of my faith.}

Part II

7. Tenor Recit.
●Rejoice, hasten to meet Trinity in his sanctuary! (194–7)
Ihr Heiligen, erfreuet euch,
Ye saints, rejoice,

Eilt, eilet, euren Gott zu loben:
Hasten, hasten, your God to praise:

Das Herze sei erhoben
(Your) heart be lifted-up
{Lift up each heart}

Zu Gottes Ehrenreich,
To God's realm-of-glory,

Von dannen er auf dich,
From there he over thee,
{From there he watches over thee—}

Du heilge Wohnung, siehet
Thou holy dwelling, watches
{His holy dwelling—}

Und ein gereinigt Herz zu sich
And a purified heart to himself
{And draws every purified heart}

Von dieser eitlen Erde ziehet.
From this vain world draweth.
{Away from the world to himself.}

Ein Stand, so billig selig heißt,
A station, which rightly blest is-called,
{This station can rightly be called blessed,}

Man schaut hier Vater, Sohn und Geist.
(We) behold here Father, Son, and Spirit.

Wohlan, ihr gotterfüllte Seelen!
Well-then, ye divinely-filled souls!

Rev. 17:14. ...[Those who are with Christ] are called and chosen and faithful (Luther: Auserwählten und Gläubigen).
Phil. 3:14. I press on toward the goal for the prize of the upward call of God in Christ Jesus.

Ps. 96:7–9/1 Chron. 16:28–30. Ascribe to the Lord, O families of the peoples, ascribe to the Lord glory and strength! Ascribe to the Lord the glory due his name; bring an offering, and come into his courts! Worship the Lord in holy array; tremble before him, all the earth!
Ps. 122:1. I was glad when they said to me, "Let us go to the house of the Lord!"
Lam. 3:41. Let us lift up our hearts and hands to God in heaven.
Acts 7:48–50. The Most High does not dwell in houses made with hands; as the prophet says, "Heaven is my throne, and earth my footstool. What house will you build for me, says the Lord, or what is the place of my rest? Did not my hand make all these things?"
Acts 7:55–56. [Stephen], full of the Holy Spirit, gazed into heaven and saw the glory of God, and Jesus standing at the right hand of God; and he said, "Behold, I see the heavens opened, and the Son of man standing at the right hand of God."
Col. 3:1–2. If then you have been raised with Christ, seek the things that are above, where Christ is, seated at the right hand of God. Set your minds on things that are above, not on things that are on earth. (Also 2 Cor. 4:16–18.)
Ps. 14:2. The Lord looks down from heaven upon the children of men, to see if there are any...that seek after God.
1 Kings 8:28–29. [O Lord,] have regard to the prayer of thy servant... that thy eyes may be open night and day toward this house [that I have built]...
1 Cor. 3:16–17. Do you not know that you are God's temple and that God's Spirit dwells in you?...God's temple is holy, and that temple you are.
1 Cor. 6:19–20. ...Your body is a temple of the Holy Spirit within you, which you have from God. You are not your own; you were bought with a price. So glorify God in your body.
Jms. 1:27. Religion that is pure and undefiled before God and the Father is this...to keep oneself unstained from the world.
1 Jn. 2:15. Do not love the world or the things in the world. If any one loves the world, love for the Father is not in him.
Jms. 4:4. ...Do you not know that friendship with the world is enmity with God? Therefore whoever wishes to be a friend of the world makes himself an enemy of God.
Jn. 6:44 [Christ]: No one can come to me unless the Father who sent me draws him (Luther: ihn ziehe)... (Also Jn. 6:65, 12:32, S. of S. 1:4.)
Ps. 24:3–4. Who shall ascend the hill of the Lord? And who shall stand in his holy place? He who has clean hands and a pure heart...
Ps. 27:4. One thing have I asked of the Lord, that will I seek after; that I may dwell in the house of the Lord all the days of my life, to behold the beauty of the Lord, and to inquire in his temple.
Ps. 73:25–26. [O Lord,] whom have I in heaven but thee? And there is nothing upon earth that I desire besides thee. My flesh and my heart may fail, but God is the strength of my heart and my portion (Luther: Trost und Teil) for ever.

Ihr werdet nun das beste Teil erwählen;
Ye will now the best part choose;
{Ye shall now choose the best part;}

Die Welt kann euch kein Labsal geben,
The world can ye no comfort give,
{The world can give ye no comfort,}

Ihr könnt in Gott allein vergnügt und selig leben.
Ye can in God alone content and blessed live.
{Only in God can ye live contentedly and blessedly.}

8. Tenor Aria
●God's presence alone is source of our joy (194-8)
Des Höchsten Gegenwart allein
The Highest's presence alone
{Only the presence of the Most High}

Kann unsrer Freuden Ursprung sein.
Can our joy's (fountainhead) be.
{Can be the source of our joy.}

Vergehe, Welt, mit deiner Pracht,
Vanish, (O) world, with thy pomp,

In Gott ist, was uns glücklich macht!
In God is, what us happy makes!
{In God we find that which makes us happy!}

9. Soprano & Bass Recit.
●Dialogue between Doubt & Confirmation (194-9)
Bass:
Kann wohl ein Mensch zu Gott im Himmel steigen?
Can indeed a mortal to God in heaven ascend?
{Can a mortal indeed ascend to God in heaven?}

Soprano:
Der Glaube kann den Schöpfer zu ihm neigen.
- Faith can the Creator (down) to itself (draw).
{Faith can draw the Creator down.}

Er ist oft ein zu schwaches Band.
It is oft a too weak bond.
{But faith is oft too weak a bond.}

Gott führet selbst und stärkt des Glaubens Hand,
God leads himself and strengthens - faith's hand,
{God himself leads and strengthens the hand of faith,}

Lk. 10:39–42. [Martha] had a sister called Mary, who sat at the Lord's feet and listened to his teaching. But Martha was distracted with much serving; and she went to him and said, "Lord, do you not care that my sister has left me to serve alone? Tell her then to help me." But the Lord answered her, "Martha, Martha, you are anxious and troubled about many things; one thing is needful. Mary has chosen the good portion (Luther: gute Teil erwählt), which shall not be taken away from her."
Ps. 16:11. [O Lord,] thou dost show me the path of life; in thy presence there is fulness of joy, in thy right hand are pleasures for evermore.

*Rev. 21:2–4. I saw the holy city, new Jerusalem, coming down out of heaven from God, prepared as a bride adorned for her husband; and I heard a loud voice from the throne saying, "Behold, the dwelling of God is with men. He will dwell with them, and they shall be his people, and God himself will be with them; he will wipe away every tear from their eyes, and death shall be no more, neither shall there be mourning nor crying nor pain any more, for the former things have passed away." (Also Is. 25:8. Rev. 7:15–17.)
1 Jn. 2:15–17. Do not love the world or the things in the world. If any one loves the world, love for the Father is not in him. For all that is in the world, the lust of the flesh and the lust of the eyes and the pride of life, is not of the Father but is of the world. And the world passes away, and the lust of it; but he who does the will of God abides for ever. (Also Jms. 4:4.)
Ps. 73:25. [O Lord,] whom have I in heaven but thee? And there is nothing upon earth that I desire besides thee.

Rom. 10:6–11. The righteousness based on faith says, Do not say in your heart, "Who will ascend into heaven?" (that is, to bring Christ down) or "Who will descend into the abyss?" (that is, to bring Christ up from the dead). But what does it say? The word is near you, on your lips and in your heart (that is, the word of faith which we preach); because if you confess with your lips that Jesus is Lord and believe in your heart that God raised him from the dead, you will be saved. For man believes with his heart and so is justified, and he confesses with his lips and so is saved. (Also Prov. 30:4.)
+Jn. 3:12–13 [Christ]: If I have told you earthly things and you do not believe, how can you believe if I tell you heavenly things? No one has ascended into heaven but he who descended from heaven, the Son of man. (Also Eph. 4:8–9, Ps. 113:4–8.)
Mk. 9:23–24. Jesus said to [the father of the sick child], "If you can! All things are possible to him who believes." Immediately the father of the child cried out and said, "I believe; help my unbelief!"
Phil. 2:13. God is at work in you, both to will and to work for his good pleasure.
1 Pet. 5:10. ...The God of all grace, who has called you to his eternal glory in Christ, will himself restore, establish, and strengthen you.
2 Thess. 1:11. To this end we always pray for you, that our God may make you worthy of his call, and may fulfil every good resolve and work of faith by his power.

Den Fürsatz zu erreichen.
(Its) purpose to achieve.

Wie aber, wenn des Fleisches Schwachheit wollte weichen?
But-what, if the flesh's weakness would give-way?

Des Höchsten Kraft wird mächtig in den Schwachen.
The Highest's power (proves) mighty in the weak.

Die Welt wird sie verlachen.
The world will them laugh-to-scorn.
{But the world will laugh them to scorn.}

Wer Gottes Huld besitzt, verachtet solchen Spott.
Whoever God's favor possesses, disdains such scorn.
{Whoever possesses God's favor disdains such scorn.}

Was wird ihr außer diesen fehlen?
What will it besides this lack?
{Besides this, what else would faith's hand lack?}

Ihr einzger Wunsch, ihr Alles ist in Gott.
Its sole wish, its all is (found) in God.

Gott ist unsichtbar und entfernet:
God is invisible and distant:
{But God is invisible and distant:}

Wohl uns, daß unser Glaube lernet,
Good-for us, that our faith learns,
{We are blessed if our faith learns}

Im Geiste seinen Gott zu schauen.
In-the spirit its God to see.
{To see its God in the spirit.}

Ihr Leib hält sie gefangen.
Its flesh holds it captive.
{But the hand of faith is held captive by the flesh.}

Des Höchsten Huld befördert ihr Verlangen,
The Highest's grace assists its desire,
{The grace of the Highest One assists its desire,}

Denn er erbaut den Ort, da man ihn herrlich schaut.
For he builds the place, where one him in-glory beholds.
{For he builds that place where we may behold him in his glory.}

Mk. 14:38 [Christ]: Watch and pray that you may not enter into temptation; the spirit indeed is willing, but the flesh is weak. (Also Mt. 26:41.)

2 Cor. 12:9–10. [The Lord] said to me, "My grace is sufficient for you, for my power is made perfect in weakness." I will all the more gladly boast of my weaknesses, that the power of Christ may rest upon me. For the sake of Christ, then, I am content with weaknesses, insults, hardships, persecutions, and calamities; for when I am weak, then I am strong.

Josh. 24:15. ...Choose this day whom you will serve...

Jms. 4:4. ...Do you not know that friendship with the world is enmity with God? Therefore whoever wishes to be a friend of the world makes himself an enemy of God. (Also 1 Jn. 2:15–17.)

Jn. 15:18–19 [Christ]: If the world hates you, know that it has hated me before it hated you. If you were of the world, the world would love its own; but because you are not of the world, but I chose you out of the world, therefore the world hates you. (Also Jn. 17:14, Mt. 5:10–12, 10:24–25, 1 Jn. 3:13.)

Ps. 73:25. ...[O Lord,] there is nothing upon earth that I desire besides thee.

Ps. 27:4. One thing have I asked of the Lord (Luther: eins bitt ich vom Herrn), that will I seek after; that I may dwell in the house of the Lord all the days of my life, to behold the beauty of the Lord, and to inquire in his temple.

Ps. 95:3. The Lord is a great God, and a great King above all gods. (Also Ps. 97:9.)

1 Tim. 6:15–16. ...[He is] the blessed and only Sovereign, the King of kings and Lord of lords, who alone has immortality and dwells in unapproachable light, whom no man has ever seen or can see...

Jn. 20:29. Jesus said to [Thomas], "Have you believed because you have seen me? Blessed are those who have not seen and yet believe."

Mt. 26:41 [Christ]: ...The spirit indeed is willing, but the flesh is weak. (Also Mk. 14:38.)

Rom. 7:15, 18, 24–25. I do not understand my own actions. For I do not do what I want, but I do the very thing I hate...For I know that nothing good dwells within me, that is, in my flesh. I can will what is right, but I cannot do it...Wretched man that I am! Who will deliver me from this body of death? Thanks be to God through Jesus Christ our Lord!... (Also Gal. 5:17.)

Rom. 8:26. The Spirit helps us in our weakness...

Jn. 14:1–3 [Christ]: Let not your hearts be troubled; believe in God, believe also in me. In my Father's house are many rooms; if it were not so, would I have told you that I go to prepare a place for you? And when I go and prepare a place for you, I will come again and will take you to myself, that where I am you may be also. (Also Jn. 12:26.)

Ps. 84:4, 7. Blessed are those who dwell in thy house, ever singing thy praise!...The God of gods will be seen in Zion.

Ps. 26:8. O Lord, I love the habitation of thy house, and the place where thy glory dwells.

Heb. 11:6. ...[But] whoever would draw near to God must believe that he exists and that he rewards those who seek him.

Jn. 1:12. To all who...believed in [Christ's] name, he gave power to become children of God.

Eph. 3:17. ...Christ [will] dwell in your hearts through faith...

Soprano & Bass:
Da er den Glauben nun belohnt
Since he - faith now rewards

Und bei uns wohnt,
And with us dwells—

Bei uns als seinen Kindern,
With us as his (very) children—

So kann die Welt und Sterblichkeit
Thus can the world and (our) mortality

die Freude nicht vermindern.
(this) joy not diminish.
{not diminish this joy.}

10. Soprano & Bass Duet
●God has chosen this as his house; how good for us! (194-10)
O wie wohl ist uns geschehn,
O how good (it) has for-us (turned-out),
{O how we have been blessed,}

Daß sich Gott ein Haus ersehn!
That - God a house has-chosen!

Schmeckt und sehet doch zugleich,
(O) taste and see indeed together,
{O, both taste and see,}

Gott sei freundlich gegen euch.
God is gracious to you.
{How gracious God is toward you.}

Schüttet eure Herzen aus
Pour your hearts out
{Pour out your hearts}

Hier vor Gottes Thron und Haus!
Here before God's throne and house!

11. Bass Recit.
●God dwells in this building as well as our hearts (194-11)
Wohlan demnach, du heilge Gemeine,
Come-on, (then), thou holy congregation,

Bereite dich zur heilgen Lust!
Prepare thyself for holy delight!

Gott wohnt nicht nur in einer jeden Brust,
God dwells not only in every individual breast,

1 Jn. 3:1-3. See what love the Father has given us, that we should be called children of God; and so we are. The reason why the world does not know us is that it did not know him. Beloved, we are God's children now; it does not yet appear what we shall be, but we know that when he appears we shall be like him, for we shall see him as he is. And every one who thus hopes in him purifies himself as he is pure.
+Jn. 3:6 [Christ]: That which is born of the flesh is flesh, and that which is born of the Spirit is spirit.
Rom. 8:9-11, 14-16. You are not in the flesh, you are in the Spirit, if in fact the Spirit of God dwells in you...If Christ is in you, although your bodies are dead because of sin, your spirits are alive because of righteousness. If the Spirit of him who raised Jesus from the dead dwells in you, he who raised Christ Jesus from the dead will give life to your mortal bodies also through his Spirit which dwells in you...All who are led by the Spirit of God are sons of God. For you did not receive the spirit of slavery to fall back into fear, but you have received the spirit of sonship. When we cry, "Abba! Father!" it is the Spirit himself bearing witness with our spirit that we are children of God.

Ezra 3:10-11. When the builders laid the foundation of the temple of the Lord, the priests in their vestments came forward with trumpets, and the Levites, the sons of Asaph, with cymbals, to praise the Lord... and they sang responsively, praising and giving thanks to the Lord, "For he is good, for his steadfast love endures for ever toward Israel." And all the people shouted with a great shout, when they praised the Lord, because the foundation of the house of the Lord was laid.
Zech. 2:10. Sing and rejoice, O daughter of Zion; for lo, I come and I will dwell in the midst of you, says the Lord.
Ps. 46:7/11. The Lord of hosts is with us...
Ps. 34:8. O taste and see that the Lord is good! Happy is the man who takes refuge in him! (Also 1 Pet. 2:3.)
Ps. 62:8. Trust in him at all times, O people; pour out your heart before him; God is a refuge for us.
Ezek. 43:4-7. As the glory of the Lord entered the temple by the gate facing east, the Spirit lifted me up, and brought me into the inner court; and behold, the glory of the Lord filled the temple. While the man was standing beside me, I heard one speaking to me out of the temple; and he said to me, "Son of man, this is the place of my throne ...where I will dwell in the midst of the people of Israel for ever..."

*Lk. 19:5-6. When Jesus came to the place [where Zacchaeus was in the sycamore tree], he looked up and said to him, "Zacchaeus, make haste and come down; for I must stay at your house today." So he made haste and came down and received him joyfully.
*Rev. 21:3. ...Behold, the dwelling of God is with men. He will dwell with them, and they shall be his people, and God himself will be with them.
Zech. 2:10. Sing and rejoice, O daughter of Zion; for lo, I come and I will dwell in the midst of you, says the Lord. (Also Zech 8:3, 8:8, Ezek. 43:9.)
Ps. 16:11. ...[O Lord], in thy presence there is fulness of joy, in thy right hand are pleasures for evermore.

Er   baut   sich   hier ein Haus.
He (also) builds for-himself here a   house.
{He also builds a house here for himself.}

Wohlan,   so rüstet   euch
Come-on, then (clothe) yourselves

        mit   Geist und   Gaben aus,
        with (the) Spirit and (his) gifts   - ,

Daß ihm sowohl dein Herz als auch dies Haus gefalle!
That him (both) thine heart as well-as this house please!
{That both thy heart and this house might be pleasing to him!}

12. Chorale (New to this version)
●Prayer that God accept our efforts & bless them (194–12)
Sprich Ja zu meinen Taten,
Say   "Yes" to   my   endeavors,

Hilf selbst das Beste raten;
Help, thyself, the best to-advise;
{Advise me thyself so I will choose the best part;}

Den Anfang, Mittl und Ende,
The beginning, middle, and end,

Ach, Herr, zum besten wende!
Ah Lord, to-the best   turn!
{Ah Lord, make them all turn out for the best!}

///

Mit   Segen mich beschütte,
With (thy poured-out) blessing me   cover,
{Pour over me thy blessing,}

    Mein Herz sei deine Hütte,
    (May) my heart be thy shelter,
    {May my heart be thy abode,}

    Dein Wort sei meine Speise,
    (May) thy Word be   my   food,

Bis ich gen Himmel reise!
Till I to   heaven journey!

Is. 57:15. Thus says the high and lofty One who inhabits eternity, whose name is Holy: "I dwell in the high and holy place, and also with him who is of a contrite and humble spirit..."
Eph. 3:17, 19. ...Christ [will] dwell in your hearts through faith...that you may be filled with all the fulness of God.
Eph. 5:18. ...Be filled with the Spirit.
1 Cor. 12:11. All these [gifts] are inspired by one and the same Spirit, who apportions to each one individually as he wills. (Also 1 Cor. 2:12, 14; 12:4.)
2 Chron. 7:11–12. Thus Solomon finished the house of the Lord...Then the Lord appeared to Solomon in the night and said to him: "I have heard your prayer, and have chosen this place for myself as a house of sacrifice." (Also 1 Kings 9:1–3.)

Ps. 90:17. Let the favor of the Lord our God be upon us, and establish thou the work of our hands upon us, yea, the work of our hands establish thou it.
2 Cor. 1:18–20. As surely as God is faithful, our word to you has not been Yes and No. For the Son of God, Jesus Christ...was not Yes and No; but in him it is always Yes. For all the promises of God find their Yes in him. That is why we utter the Amen through him, to the glory of God.
Rom. 8:28. ...In everything God works for good with those who love him, who are called according to his purpose.
Jms. 1:5. If any of you lacks wisdom, let him ask God...and it will be given him.
Ps. 16:7. I bless the Lord who gives me counsel (Luther: geraten hat); in the night also my heart instructs me. (Also Prov. 2:6, Ps. 32:8, 147:5, Is. 28:29.)

Gen. 32:26. ...I will not let you go, unless you bless me.
Deut. 26:15. [O Lord,] look down from thy holy habitation, from heaven, and bless thy people...
Ps. 28:9. O save thy people, and bless thy heritage; be thou their shepherd, and carry them for ever.
1 Kings 8:57–58. [May] the Lord our God be with us, as he was with our fathers; may he not leave us or forsake us; that he may incline our hearts to him, to walk in all his ways, and to keep his commandments, his statutes, and his ordinances...
Eph. 3:17, 19. ...[May] Christ...dwell in your hearts through faith...that you may be filled with all the fulness of God.
Col. 3:16. Let the word of Christ dwell in you richly...
Mt. 4:4 [Christ]: ...Man shall not live by bread alone, but by every word that proceeds from the mouth of God. (See Deut. 8:3, also Lk. 4:4.)
1 Thess. 5:23. May the God of peace himself sanctify you wholly; and may your spirit and soul and body be kept sound and blameless at the coming of our Lord Jesus Christ.

BWV 195
Dem Gerechten muß das Licht immer wieder aufgehen
(NBA I/33; BC B14a-c)

Marriage Ceremony[1] (BWV 196, 195, 197)
[1]The bridegroom was likely a lawyer; hence the numerous references to righteousness. See Dürr, *Die Kantaten*, p. 830. Librettist: Unknown. An earlier version of this cantata apparently included a Part II that has been replaced here with a chorale.

Part I

1. Chorus
●Light dawns for the righteous: Ps. 97:11–12 (195–1)
Dem Gerechten muß das Licht immer wieder aufgehen
For-the righteous must the light again-and-again dawn
{Light dawns again and again for the righteous}

und Freude den frommen Herzen.
and joy for-the godly in-heart.

Ihr Gerechten, freuet euch des Herrn und
Ye righteous, rejoice in-the Lord and

danket ihm und preiset seine Heiligkeit.
thank him, and praise his holiness.

2. Bass Recit. (Probably new to this version)
●Wedding day represents dawning of new blessing (195–2)
Dem Freudenlicht gerechter Frommen
To-the light-of-joy of-righteous saints
{The joyous light of righteous saints}

Muß stets ein neuer Zuwachs kommen,
Must ever - new growth come,
{Must ever increase,}

Der Wohl und Glück bei ihnen mehrt.
Which prosperity and happiness (for) them multiplies.
{Multiplying their prosperity and happiness.}

Auch diesem neuen Paar,
Also for-this new couple,

An dem man so Gerechtigkeit
In whom (we) - righteousness
{Whose righteousness}

Als Tugend ehrt,
As-well-as virtue do-honor,
{And virtue we honor,}

Ist heut ein Freudenlicht bereit,
Is today a light-of-joy prepared;
{Is today a joyous light ordained;}

Ps. 97:10–12. The Lord loves those who hate evil; he preserves the lives of his saints; he delivers them from the hand of the wicked. *Light dawns for the righteous, and joy for the upright in heart. Rejoice in the Lord, O you righteous, and give thanks to his holy name!* (Also Ps. 145:20.)

Prov. 4:18–19. The path of the righteous is like the light of dawn, which shines brighter and brighter until full day. The way of the wicked is like deep darkness; they do not know over what they stumble.

Prov. 13:9. The light of the righteous rejoices, but the lamp of the wicked will be put out.

Ps. 32:10–11. Many are the pangs of the wicked; but steadfast love surrounds him who trusts in the Lord. Be glad in the Lord, and rejoice, O righteous, and shout for joy, all you upright in heart!

Ps. 33:1. Rejoice in the Lord, O you righteous! Praise befits the upright.

Ps. 64:10. Let the righteous rejoice in the Lord, and take refuge in him! Let all the upright in heart glory!

Ps. 99:5, 9. Extol the Lord our God; worship at his footstool! Holy is he!...Extol the Lord our God, and worship at his holy mountain; for the Lord our God is holy!

Ps. 112:4–7. Light rises in the darkness for the upright; the Lord is gracious, merciful, and righteous. It is well with the man who deals generously and lends, who conducts his affairs with justice. For the righteous will never be moved; he will be remembered for ever. He is not afraid of evil tidings; his heart is firm, trusting in the Lord.

Ps. 5:12. Thou dost bless the righteous, O Lord; thou dost cover him with favor as with a shield.

Ps. 84:11. The Lord God is a sun and shield; he bestows favor and honor. No good thing does the Lord withhold from those who walk uprightly.

Is. 61:10. I will greatly rejoice in the Lord, my soul shall exult in my God; for he has clothed me with the garments of salvation, he has covered me with the robe of righteousness, as a bridegroom decks himself with a garland, and as a bride adorns herself with her jewels.

Prov. 18:22. He who finds a wife finds a good thing, and obtains favor from the Lord.

Prov. 5:18–19. ...Rejoice in the wife of your youth, a lovely hind, a graceful doe. Let her affection fill you at all times with delight, be infatuated always with her love.

Heb. 13:4. Let marriage be held in honor among all...

Mt. 19:4–6. [Jesus said], "Have you not read that he who made them from the beginning made them male and female, and said, 'For this reason a man shall leave his father and mother and be joined to his wife, and the two shall become one flesh'? So they are no longer two but one flesh. What therefore God has joined together, let not man put asunder." (Also Mk. 10:6–9.)

Das   stellet   neues Wohlsein dar.
Which (shall-bring) new   blessedness - .

O!   ein erwünscht Verbinden!
Oh! (What) a desirable   union!

So können zwei ihr Glück eins an dem andern finden.
Thus can two their happiness in-one-another   find.
{Thus can two find their happiness in one another.}

3. Bass Aria
●Wedding praise: Praise God for expected bliss (195–3)
Rühmet Gottes Güt   und   Treu,
Praise   God's goodness and faithfulness,

Rühmet ihn mit reger Freude,
Praise him with lively joy,

Preiset Gott,   Verlobten beide!
Praise God, (O) betrothed-ones, both!

Denn eu'r heutiges Verbinden
For   your today's   union
{For your union today}

Läßt euch lauter Segen finden,
Lets (you) nought-but blessing find,
{Brings you nought but blessing;}

Licht und Freude werden neu.
Light and joy   become new.
{Light and joy are ever renewed.}

4. Soprano Recit. (Probably new to this version)
●Marriage blessing pronounced as couple is united (195–4)
Wohlan, so knüpfet denn ein Band,
Come-on, then, join   then (this) bond,
{Come then, seal this bond,}

Das so viel Wohlsein prophezeihet.
Which so much well-being prophesies.
{Which promises so much happiness.}

Des Priesters Hand
The priest's   hand
{The priest}

Wird jetzt den Segen
Will now the blessing
{Will now lay his hand of blessing}

Auf euren Ehestand,
Upon your married-state,

Auf eure Schritte legen.
Upon your steps lay.
{And upon your way.}

1 Cor. 6:16. ...It is written, "The two shall become one flesh." (Also Eph. 5:31.)
1 Cor. 7:3–4, 33–34. The husband should give to his wife her conjugal rights, and likewise the wife to her husband. For the wife does not rule over her own body, but the husband does; likewise the husband does not rule over his own body, but the wife does...The married man is anxious...how to please his wife...and...the married woman is anxious ...how to please her husband.

Ps. 106:1. Praise the Lord! O give thanks to the Lord, for he is good; for his steadfast love endures for ever (Luther: seine Güte währet ewiglich)! Who can utter the mighty doings of the Lord, or show forth all his praise? (Also Ps. 107:1, 118:1, 136: 1, 2, 3, etc...)
Ps. 138:2. [O Lord,] I...give thanks to thy name for thy steadfast love and thy faithfulness (Luther: Güte und Treue)... (Also Ps. 86:15.)
Ps. 135:3. Praise the Lord, for the Lord is good; sing to his name, for he is gracious! (Also Ps. 147:1.)
Ps. 118:24. This is the day which the Lord has made; let us rejoice and be glad in it. (Also Ps. 126:2–3.)
S. of S. 3:11. ...Behold King Solomon, with the crown with which his mother crowned him on the day of his wedding, on the day of the gladness of his heart.
Prov. 5:18–19. ...Rejoice in the wife of your youth, a lovely hind, a graceful doe. Let her affection fill you at all times with delight, be infatuated always with her love.
Lam. 3:22–23. The steadfast love of the Lord never ceases, his mercies never come to an end; they are new every morning; great is thy faithfulness.
Prov. 4:18. The path of the righteous is like the light of dawn, which shines brighter and brighter until full day.

Prov. 18:22. He who finds a wife finds a good thing, and obtains favor from the Lord.
Prov. 31:10–12, 28–30. A good wife who can find? She is far more precious than jewels. The heart of her husband trusts in her, and he will have no lack of gain. She does him good, and not harm, all the days of her life...Her children rise up and call her blessed; her husband also, and he praises her: "Many women have done excellently, but you surpass them all." Charm is deceitful, and beauty is vain, but a woman who fears the Lord is to be praised.
Gen. 1:26–28. God created man in his own image, in the image of God he created him; male and female he created them. And God blessed them, and God said to them, "Be fruitful and multiply, and fill the earth and subdue it..."
Num. 6:24–27 [Aaronic (priestly) benediction]: The Lord bless you and keep you: The Lord make his face to shine upon you, and be gracious to you: The Lord lift up his countenance upon you, and give you peace.
Ps. 37:23–24. The steps of a man are from the Lord, and he establishes him in whose way he delights; though he fall, he shall not be cast headlong, for the Lord is the stay of his hand.
Gen. 28:15 [God]: Behold, I am with you and will keep you wherever you go... (Also Josh. 1:9.)

Und wenn des Segens Kraft   hinfort   an euch gedeihet,
And   when the blessing's power henceforth upon you   flourishes,
{And when the power of this blessing flourishes upon you henceforth,}

So   rühmt des Höchsten   Vaterhand.
Then praise the Most-High's paternal-hand.
{Then praise the paternal hand of the Almighty.}

Er knüpfte selbst eu'r Liebesband
He (tied)   himself your bond-of-love
{He himself sealed your bond of love}

Und   ließ   das, was er angefangen,
And allowed that which he had-begun,

Auch ein erwünschtes End erlangen.
Also (its)   desired   end   attain.
{To attain its desired end.}

5. Chorus
●Blessing's completion guaranteed by God's power (195-5)
Wir kommen, deine Heiligkeit,
We   come,   thy   holiness,

Unendlich großer Gott, zu preisen.
(O) infinitely   great   God, to praise.
{We come, O infinitely great God, to praise thy holiness,}

Der Anfang   rührt   von deinen Händen,
The beginning (proceeds) from thy   hands,

Durch   Allmacht kannst du es vollenden
By   (thine) omnipotence canst thou it complete
{And by thine almighty power thou canst complete it}

Und deinen Segen   kräftig   weisen.
And   thy   blessing powerfully manifest.
{And mightily direct thy blessing upon it.}

Part II

6. Chorale
●Praise to Him who is praised in heaven by angels (195-6)
Nun danket all   und bringet Ehr,
Now thank ye-all and   bring praise,

Ihr Menschen in der Welt,
(O) ye   people   (of) the world,

Dem, dessen Lob der Engel Heer
To-him, whose praise the angel host

In Himmel   stets   vermeldt.
In heaven continually proclaims.

Ps. 127:1. Unless the Lord builds the house, those who build it labor in vain...
Is. 41:20. ...Men [will] see and know, [and] consider and understand together, that the hand of the Lord has done this...
Ps. 109:27. Let them know that this is thy hand; thou, O Lord, hast done it! (Also Job 12:9.)
Jer. 29:11. I know the plans I have for you, says the Lord, plans for welfare and not for evil, to give you a future and a hope. (Also Prov. 23:18.)
Mk. 10:5-9. Jesus said to them, "...From the beginning of creation, 'God made them male and female.' 'For this reason a man shall leave his father and mother and be joined to his wife, and the two shall become one flesh.' So they are no longer two but one flesh. What therefore God has joined together, let not man put asunder." (Also Gen. 2:22-23, Mt. 19:4-6, Eph. 5:31.)
Phil. 1:6. And I am sure that he who began a good work in you will bring it to completion at the day of Jesus Christ. (Also Ps. 138:8.)

Ps. 97:12. Rejoice in the Lord, O you righteous, and give thanks to his holy name (Luther: preiset seine Heiligkeit)!
Rev. 15:3-4. ...Great and wonderful are thy deeds, O Lord God the Almighty! Just and true are thy ways, O King of the ages! Who shall not fear and glorify thy name, O Lord? For thou alone art holy...
Ps. 22:3. ...Thou art holy, enthroned on the praises of Israel.
Ps. 71:19. ...Thou who hast done great things, O God who is like thee?
Deut. 3:24. O Lord God, thou hast only begun to show thy servant thy greatness and thy mighty hand; for what god is there in heaven or on earth who can do such works and mighty acts as thine?
Rev. 1:8. "I am the Alpha and the Omega," (Luther: das A und das O, der Anfang und das Ende) says the Lord God, who is and who was and who is to come, the Almighty. (Also Rev. 21:6, 22:13.)
Phil. 1:6. ...He who began a good work in you will bring it to completion... (Also Ps. 138:8.)

Sirach (Apocrypha) 50:22. And now bless the God of all (Luther: Nun danket alle Gott), who in every way does great things...
Ps. 106:48. Blessed be the Lord, the God of Israel, from everlasting to everlasting! And let all the people say, "Amen!" Praise the Lord!
Ps. 117:1. Praise the Lord, all nations! Extol him, all peoples!
Ps. 136:26. O give thanks to the God of heaven, for his steadfast love endures for ever. (Also Ps. 96:1-4.)
Rev. 7:11-12. And all the angels stood round the throne and round the elders and the four living creatures, and they fell on their faces before the throne and worshiped God, saying, "Amen! Blessing and glory and wisdom and thanksgiving and honor and power and might be to our God for ever and ever! Amen." (Also Rev. 5:11-14.)
Rev. 4:8. And the four living creatures, each of them with six wings... day and night they never cease to sing, "Holy, holy, holy, is the Lord God Almighty, who was and is and is to come!"

BWV 196
Der Herr denket an uns
(NBA I/33; BC B11)

Marriage Ceremony (BWV 196, 195, 197)
Librettist: Scripture (Ps. 115:12–15)

1. Sinfonia

2. Chorus

●Lord remembers and blesses his people: Ps. 115:12 (196-2)
Der Herr denket an uns und segnet uns. Er segnet das Haus
The Lord thinks of us and blesses us. He blesses the house

Israel, er segnet das Haus Aaron.
of-Israel, he blesses the house of-Aaron.

3. Soprano Aria

●God blesses all who fear him: Ps. 115:13 (196-3)
Er segnet, die den Herrn fürchten, beide, Kleine
He blesses, those-who the Lord fear, both small
{He blesses those who fear the Lord, both small}

und Große.
and great.
{and great.}

4. Tenor & Bass Duet

●Blessing on you and your children: Ps. 115:14 (196-4)
Der Herr segne euch je mehr und mehr,
(May) the Lord bless you ever more and more,

euch und eure Kinder.
you and your children.

5. Chorus

●You are the Creator's blessed ones: Ps. 115:15 (196-5)
Ihr seid die Gesegneten des Herrn, der Himmel und Erde
You are the blessed of-the Lord, who heaven and earth

gemacht hat. Amen.
hath-made. Amen.

Ps. 115:12. *The Lord has been mindful of us; he will bless us; he will bless the house of Israel; he will bless the house of Aaron.*
Ps. 28:8–9. The Lord is the strength of his people, he is the saving refuge of his anointed. O save thy people, and bless thy heritage; be thou their shepherd, and carry them for ever. (Also Deut. 26:15.)
Ps. 67:1. May God be gracious to us and bless us and make his face to shine upon us.
Ps. 95:6–7. O come, let us worship and bow down, let us kneel before the Lord, our Maker! For he is our God and we are the people of his pasture, and the sheep of his hand.

Ps. 115:13. *He will bless those who fear the Lord, both small and great.*
Ps. 103:11, 13. As the heavens are high above the earth, so great is his steadfast love toward those who fear him...As a father pities his children, so the Lord pities those who fear him.
Ps. 25:12–13. Who is the man that fears the Lord? Him will he instruct in the way that he should choose. He himself shall abide in prosperity, and his children shall possess the land.

Ps. 115:14. *May the Lord give you increase, you and your children!*
Gen. 1:27–28. God created man in his own image, in the image of God he created him; male and female he created them. And God blessed them, and God said to them, "Be fruitful and multiply..."
Ps. 127:3. Lo, sons are a heritage from the Lord, the fruit of the womb a reward.
Ps. 128:1–4. Blessed is every one who fears the Lord, who walks in his ways! You shall eat the fruit of the labor of your hands; you shall be happy, and it shall be well with you. Your wife will be like a fruitful vine within your house; your children will be like olive shoots around your table. Lo, thus shall the man be blessed who fears the Lord.
Ps. 102:28. The children of thy servants shall dwell secure; their posterity shall be established before thee. (Also Ps. 103:17.)

Ps. 115:15. *May you be blessed by the Lord, who made heaven and earth!*
Ps. 100:3. Know that the Lord is God! It is he that made us, and we are his; we are his people, and the sheep of his pasture.
1 Pet. 2:9. You are a chosen race, a royal priesthood, a holy nation, God's own people...
Ps. 33:12. Blessed is the...people whom he has chosen as his heritage!

BWV 197
Gott ist unsre Zuversicht
(NBA I/33; BC B16)

Marriage Ceremony (BWV 196, 195, 197)
Librettist: Unknown. Certain movements were adapted from earlier works.

Part I (Exhortation to put trust in God)

1. Chorus
●God's sovereign rule brings blessing to us (197-1)
Gott ist unsre Zuversicht,
God is our   confidence,

Wir vertrauen   seinen Händen.
We   trust   (the way of) his   hands.

Wie   er unsre Wege führt,
The-way he   our   paths does-lead,

Wie   er unser Herz regiert,
The-way he   our   heart does-rule,

Da   ist Segen aller Enden.
That-way (there) is   blessing everywhere.
{That is the way of blessing in all things.}

2. Bass Recit.
●God is the best manager of our household (197-2)
Gott ist und bleibt der beste Sorger,
God is and remains the   best provider,

Er hält am besten   Haus.
He keeps - best (the) house.
{He is the best household manager.}

Er   führet   unser Tun   zuweilen wunderlich,
He works-out our   affairs at-times in-strange-ways,
{He sometimes works out our affairs in strange—}

Jedennoch   fröhlich aus,
Yet-nevertheless happily   -,
{Yet utimately happy—ways,}
          [ausführen = to work out]

Wohin   der Vorsatz nicht gedacht.
To-where (our) intention not had-thought.
{To ends different from what we had imagined.}

Was die Vernunft unmöglich macht,
What (our) reason impossible (thinks),
{What our reason thinks impossible,}

Das füget sich.
That comes-to-pass.

Ps. 46:1. God is our refuge (Luther: Zuversicht) and strength, a very present help in trouble. (Zuversicht: also Ps. 61:3, 62:7, 71:5, 7, 91:2, 142:5).
Is. 48:17. Thus says the Lord, your Redeemer...: "I am the Lord your God...who leads you in the way you should go."
Ps. 25:10. All the paths of the Lord are steadfast love and faithfulness... (Also Ps. 111:7.)
Ps. 31:14–15. I trust in thee, O Lord, I say, "Thou art my God." My times are in thy hand... (Also Job 23:10.)
Ps. 139:9–10. If I take the wings of the morning and dwell in the uttermost parts of the sea, even there thy hand shall lead me, and thy right hand shall hold me.
Ps. 10:14. [O Lord,] thou dost see; yea thou dost note trouble and vexation, that thou mayest take it into thy hands; the hapless commits himself to thee...
Ps. 16:7. I bless the Lord who gives me counsel; in the night also my heart instructs me.
Ps. 40:8. I delight to do thy will, O my God; thy law is within my heart.
Col. 3:15. Let the peace of Christ rule in your hearts (Luther: regiere in euren Herzen)...
Phil. 4:7. The peace of God, which passes all understanding, will keep your hearts and your minds in Christ Jesus.
Mk. 7:37. [The people] were astonished beyond measure [at Jesus], saying, "He has done all things well..."
Rom. 8:28. ...In everything God works for good with those who love him, who are called according to his purpose.

Prov. 24:3–5. By wisdom a house is built, and by understanding it is established; by knowledge (Luther: ordentliches Haushalten) the rooms are filled with all precious and pleasant riches.
Prov. 31:10–11, 15, 21, 27–30. A good wife who can find? She is far more precious than jewels. The heart of her husband trusts in her, and he will have no lack of gain...She rises while it is yet night and provides food for her household and tasks for her maidens...She is not afraid of snow for her household, for all her household are clothed in scarlet...She looks well to the ways of her household, and does not eat the bread of idleness. Her children rise up and call her blessed; her husband also, and he praises her: "Many women have done excellently, but you surpass them all." Charm is deceitful, and beauty is vain, but a woman who fears the Lord is to be praised.
Ps. 127:1. Unless the Lord builds the house, those who build it labor in vain...
Prov. 3:5–6. Trust in the Lord with all your heart, and do not rely on your own insight. In all your ways acknowledge him, and he will make straight your paths.
1 Pet. 5:7. Cast all your anxieties (Luther: alle eure Sorge) on him, for he cares about you (Luther: sorgt für euch). (Also Ps. 55:22, Mt. 6:25–32, Phil. 4:6.)
Is. 55:8–9. My thoughts are not your thoughts, neither are your ways my ways, says the Lord. For as the heavens are higher than the earth, so are my ways higher than your ways and my thoughts than your thoughts. (Also Job 11:7–9, 12:13.)
Jms. 4:7. Submit yourselves therefore to God...
Lk. 18:27 [Christ]: ...What is impossible with men is possible with God. (Also Mt. 19:26, Mk. 10:27.)

Er hat das Glück der   Kinder, die ihn lieben,
He has the fortune of (those) children, who him love,
{He has written the fortune of those children who love him}

Von Jugend an in seine Hand geschrieben.
From youth on upon his hand   written.
{Upon his hand from their youth on.}

3. Alto Aria (New to this version)
●Anxiousness quieted by trust in God's watchful care (197-3)
    Schläfert allen   Sorgenkummer
(Now) lull   all (your) anxious-care

In den Schlummer
Into the   slumber

Kindlichen Vertrauens ein.
Of-childlike   trust   -.
    [einschläfern = to lull to sleep]

Gottes Augen, welche wachen
God's   eyes,   which keep-watch (over us)

Und die unser Leitstern sein,
And which our guiding-star are,
{And which are our guiding star,}

Werden alles   selber machen.
Will   everything, themselves, do.
{Will, themselves, take care of everything for us.}

4. Bass Recit.
●God's ways lead through testing to Canaan (197-4)
Drum folget Gott und seinem Triebe.
So   follow God and   his   urging.

Das ist die rechte Bahn.
That is the proper course.

Die führet durch Gefahr
It   leads through peril (but)

Auch endlich in das Kanaan
Also finally into - Canaan

Und durch von ihm geprüfte Liebe
And through by him tested love
{And through divinely tested love}

Is. 49:15-16 [God]: Can a woman forget her sucking child, that she should have no compassion on the son of her womb? Even these may forget, yet I will not forget you. Behold, I have graven you on the palms of my hands; your walls are continually before me.
1 Cor. 2:9. As it is written, "What no eye has seen, nor ear heard, nor the heart of man conceived...God has prepared for those who love him."

Phil. 4:6-7. Have no anxiety about anything, but in everything by prayer and supplication with thanksgiving let your requests be made known to God. And the peace of God, which passes all understanding will keep your hearts and your minds in Christ Jesus.
Ps. 127:1-2. Unless the Lord builds the house, those who build it labor in vain. Unless the Lord watches over the city, the watchman stays awake in vain. It is in vain that you rise up early and go late to rest, eating the bread of anxious toil; for he gives to his beloved sleep.
Ps. 4:8. In peace I will both lie down and sleep; for thou alone, O Lord, makest me dwell in safety.
Ps. 131:2. I have calmed and quieted my soul, like a child quieted at its mother's breast... (Also Lam. 3:26.)
Ps. 121:2-4, 7-8. My help comes from the Lord, who made heaven and earth. He will not let your foot be moved, he who keeps you will not slumber. Behold, he who keeps Israel will neither slumber nor sleep...The Lord will keep you from all evil; he will keep your life. The Lord will keep your going out and your coming in from this time forth and for evermore.
Ps. 32:8 [God]: I will instruct you and teach you the way you should go; I will counsel you with my eye upon you (Luther: mit meinen Augen leiten). (Also Ps. 33:18, 34:15.)

Rom. 8:14. All who are led by the Spirit of God (Luther: welche der Geist...treibt) are sons of God.
Heb. 11:8-9. By faith Abraham obeyed when he was called to go out to a place which he was to receive as an inheritance; and he went out, not knowing where he was to go. By faith he sojourned in the land of promise, as in a foreign land, living in tents with Isaac and Jacob, heirs with him of the same promise.
Gen. 12:1, 4-7. The Lord said to Abram, "Go from your country and your kindred...to the land that I will show you..." So Abram went, as the Lord had told him...Abram took Sarai his wife...and all their possessions...and they set forth to go to the land of Canaan. When they had come to the land of Canaan, Abram passed through the land to the place at Shechem, to the oak of Moreh...Then the Lord appeared to Abram, and said, "To your descendants I will give this land." So he built there an altar (Luther: Altar) to the Lord, who had appeared to him.
Gen. 22:1-3, 9-17. After these things God tested Abraham, and said, "...Take your son...and go to the land of Moriah, and offer him there as a burnt offering..." So Abraham rose early...and took his son Isaac... When they came to the place of which God had told him, Abraham built an altar there, and laid the wood in order, and bound Isaac his son, and laid him on the altar...and took the knife to slay his son. But the angel of the Lord called to him from heaven, and said, "Abraham, Abraham!" And he said, "Here am I." He said, "Do not lay your hand on the lad...for now I know that you fear God, seeing you have not withheld your son...from me." And Abraham lifted up his eyes and

Auch an sein heiliges Altar
Also to his holy altar

Und bindet Herz und Herz zusammen,
And binds heart and heart together;

Herr! sei du selbst   mit diesen Flammen!
Lord, be thou, thyself, (present) in these   flames!

looked, and behold, behind him was a ram, caught in a thicket...and Abraham went and took the ram, and offered it up as a burnt offering instead of his son. So Abraham called the name of that place The Lord will provide...And the angel of the Lord called to Abraham a second time from heaven, and said, "By myself I have sworn, says the Lord, because you...have not withheld your son...I will indeed bless you, and I will multiply your descendants as the stars of heaven..."
Gen. 1:27–28. God created man in his own image...male and female he created them. And God blessed them, and God said to them, "Be fruitful and multiply..."
Heb. 13:4. Let marriage be held in honor among all...
Mt. 19:4–6. [Jesus] answered, "Have you not read that he who made them from the beginning made them male and female, and said, 'For this reason a man shall leave his father and mother and be joined to his wife, and the two shall become one flesh'? So they are no longer two but one flesh. What therefore God has joined together, let not man put asunder." (Also Gen. 2:22–23, Mk. 10:6–9, 1 Cor. 6:16, Eph. 5:31.)
S. of S. 8:6 [Bridegroom]: Set me as a seal upon your heart, as a seal upon your arm; for love is strong...Its flashes are flashes of fire, a most vehement flame.

5. Chorale (See also 169–7.)
●Loving one another: Prayer for divine help (197–5)
   Du süße Liebe, schenk uns deine Gunst,
(O) thou sweet Love, grant us thy favor,

Laß uns empfinden der Liebe Brunst,
Let us experience - love's ardor,

Daß wir uns von   Herzen einander lieben
That we - from (our) hearts one-other might-love
{That we might love one another from the bottom of our hearts}

Und in Fried auf einem Sinn bleiben.
And in peace, of one mind continue.
{And continue of one mind in peace.}

Kyrie eleis!
Kyrie eleis!

Rom. 5:5. ...God's love has been poured into our hearts through the Holy Spirit which has been given to us.
1 Jn. 4:16. So we know and believe the love God has for us. God is love, and he who abides in love abides in God, and God abides in him.
1 Pet. 1:22. ...Love one another earnestly from the heart.
Eph. 5:25–27. Husbands, love your wives, as Christ loved the church and gave himself up for her.
Phil. 2:1–2. So if there is any encouragement in Christ, any incentive of love, any participation in the Spirit, any affection and sympathy, complete my joy by being of the same mind (Luther: eines Sinnes), having the same love, being in full accord and of one mind. (Also Phil. 1:27, Jn. 17:21, 23, Rom. 12:16.)
Eph. 4:1–3. I...beg you to lead a life worthy of the calling to which you have been called, with all lowliness and meekness, with patience, forbearing one another in love, eager to maintain the unity of the Spirit in the bond of peace.
2 Jn. 1:3. Grace, mercy, and peace will be with us, from God the Father and from Jesus Christ the Father's Son, in truth and love.

Part II (God's constant blessing on those who trust him)

6. Bass Aria (Parody of BWV 197a–4)
●Wedding couple promised God's blessing (197–6)
O du angenehmes Paar,
O you   lovely   couple,

Dir wird   eitel   Heil   begegnen,
You will (by) nought-but well-being (be-met),
{You will encounter nought but well-being;}

Gott wird dich aus Zion segnen
God will you from Zion bless
{God will bless you from Zion}

Ps. 128:1–6. Blessed is every one who fears the Lord, who walks in his ways! You shall eat the fruit of the labor of your hands; you shall be happy, and it shall be well with you. Your wife will be like a fruitful vine within your house; your children will be like olive shoots around your table. Lo, thus shall the man be blessed who fears the Lord. The Lord bless you from Zion! May you see the prosperity of Jerusalem all the days of your life! May you see your children's children!...
Ps. 134:3. May the Lord bless you from Zion, he who made heaven and earth!
Ps. 115:14–15. May the Lord give you increase, you and your children!

Und dich leiten immerdar,
And you   lead evermore,
{And lead you evermore,}

O du angenehmesPaa r!
O you   lovely   couple!

7. Soprano Recit.
●God well-intentioned toward you since infancy (197-7)
So wie es Gott   mit   dir
Just-as - God towards you

Getreu und väterlich von Kindesbeinen an   gemeint,
Faithful and fatherlike from childhood on was-intentioned,
{Just as God has been faithful and fatherly towards you since
childhood,}

So will er für und für
So would he evermore

Dein allerbester Freund
Your very-best friend

Bis an das Ende bleiben.
Until   the end remain.
{Remain your very best friend until the end.}

Und also kannst du sicher glauben,
And therefore can you safely believe,
{And therefore you can be certain,}

Er wird dir nie
He will you never
{He will never let you—}

Bei   deiner Hände Schweiß und Müh
Amidst your hands' sweat and toil—

Kein   Gutes   lassen fehlen.
(Any) good-thing   let   lack.
{Lack any good thing.}

Wohl dir,   dein Glück ist nicht zu zählen.
How-blessed-you-are; your (joys) can not be numbered.

8. Soprano Aria (Parody of BWV 197a-6)
●Earthly bliss & satisfaction promised (197-8)
Vergnügen und Lust,
Pleasure   and delight,

Gedeihen und   Heil
Flourishing and well-being
{Prosperity and health}

May you be blessed by the Lord, who made heaven and earth!
Ps. 48:14. This is God, our God for ever and ever. He will be our guide for ever. (Also Ps. 32:8.)
Ps. 28:8-9. The Lord is the strength of his people, he is the saving refuge of his anointed. O save thy people, and bless thy heritage; be thou their shepherd, and carry them for ever.

Ps. 71:5-6. Thou, O Lord, art my hope, my trust, O Lord, from my youth. Upon thee I have leaned from my birth; thou art he who took me from my mother's womb...
Ps. 103:13. As a father pities his children, so the Lord pities those who fear him.
Ps. 37:25-26. I have been young, and now am old; yet I have not seen the righteous forsaken or his children begging bread. He is ever giving liberally and lending, and his children become a blessing.
Jms. 2:23. ...[By his actions Abraham showed that he] believed God, and it was reckoned to him as righteousness; and he was called the friend of God.
Jn. 15:14-16 [Christ]: You are my friends if you do what I command you. No longer do I call you servants, for the servant does not know what his master is doing; but I have called you friends...You did not choose me, but I chose you...
S. of S. 6:3 [Bride]: I am my beloved's and my beloved (Luther: Freund) is mine...
Mt. 28:20 [Christ]: ...Lo, I am with you always, to the close of the age. (Also Ps. 48:14.)
Ps. 34:10. The young lions suffer want and hunger; but those who seek the Lord lack no good thing.
Ps. 121:7-8. The Lord will keep you from all evil; he will keep your life. The Lord will keep your going out and your coming in from this time forth and for evermore.
Ecc. 5:18. Behold, what I have seen to be good and to be fitting is to eat and drink and find enjoyment in all the toil with which one toils under the sun the few days of his life which God has given him, for this is his lot.
Gen. 3:19 [God]: In the sweat of your face you shall eat bread till you return to the ground, for out of it you were taken; you are dust, and to dust you shall return.
Ps. 90:17. Let the favor of the Lord our God be upon us, and establish thou the work of our hands upon us, yea, the work of our hands establish thou it.
Ps. 84:11. For the Lord God is a sun and shield; he bestows favor and honor. No good thing does the Lord withhold from those who walk uprightly.
Ps. 40:5. Thou hast multiplied, O Lord my God, thy wondrous deeds and thy thoughts toward us; none can compare with thee! Were I to proclaim and tell of them, they would be more than can be numbered. (Also Ps. 71:15, 139:17-18.)

Ps. 37:4. Take delight (Luther: Lust) in the Lord, and he will give you the desires of your heart.
Jer. 17:7-8. Blessed is the man who trusts in the Lord, whose trust is the Lord. He is like a tree planted by water, that sends out its roots by the stream, and does not fear when heat comes, for its leaves remain green, and is not anxious in the year of drought, for it does not cease to bear fruit. (Also Ps. 1:3.)
Is. 58:11. The Lord will guide you continually, and satisfy your desire with good things, and make your bones strong; and you shall be like

Wird wachsen und stärken und laben.
Shall grow and strengthen and delight.
{Shall increase, become stronger, and delight you.}

Das Auge, die Brust
The eye, the breast

Wird ewig sein Teil
Shall ever its portion
{Shall ever have its portion}

An süßer Zufriedenheit haben.
Of sweet satisfaction have.
{Of sweet satisfaction.}

a watered garden, like a spring of water, whose waters fail not.
Deut. 28:2–6, 8, 12. All these blessings shall come upon you and overtake you, if you obey the voice of the Lord your God. Blessed shall you be in the city, and blessed shall you be in the field. Blessed shall be the fruit of your body, and the fruit of your ground, and the fruit of your beasts, the increase of your cattle, and the young of your flock. Blessed shall be your basket and your kneading-trough. Blessed shall you be when you come in, and blessed shall you be when you go out...The Lord will command the blessing upon your barns, and in all that you undertake; and he will bless you in the land which the Lord your God gives you...The Lord will open to you his good treasury the heavens, to give the rain of your land in its season and to bless all the work of your hands... (Also Deut. 7:13–15.)

9. Bass Recit.
•Blessed state will last, for God's love has no end (197-9)
Und dieser frohe Lebenslauf
And this happy course-of-life

Wird bis in späte Jahre währen.
Shall until latter years continue.
{Shall continue into old age.}

Denn Gottes Güte hat kein Ziel,
For God's loving-kindness has no end,

Die schenkt dir viel,
It gives you much,

Ja mehr, als selbst das Herze kann begehren.
Yes, more, than even the heart can desire.

Verlasse dich gewiß darauf.
(You may) rely - assuredly on-it.

Ps. 92:12, 14. The righteous flourish like the palm tree, and grow like a cedar in Lebanon...They still bring forth fruit in old age, they are ever full of sap and green.
Is. 46:3–4. Hearken to me, O house of Jacob...[you] who have been borne by me from your birth, carried from the womb; even to your old age I am He, and to gray hairs I will carry you... (Also Ps. 71:9.)
Lam. 3:22. The steadfast love of the Lord never ceases, his mercies never come to an end.
Ps. 106:1. ...His steadfast love endures for ever (Luther: seine Güte währet ewiglich)! (Also Ps. 107:1, 118:1, 136: 1, 2, 3, etc...)
Ps. 71:15. [O Lord,] my mouth will tell of thy righteous acts, of thy deeds of salvation all the day, for their number is past my knowledge.
Ps. 23:6. Surely goodness and mercy shall follow me all the days of my life...
1 Cor. 2:9. ...What no eye has seen, nor ear heard, nor the heart of man conceived, what God has prepared for those who love him...

10. Chorale[1]
•Walk in God's ways & he will continue to bless you (197-10)
So wandelt froh auf Gottes Wegen,
So journey joyfully on God's pathways,

Und was ihr tut, das tut getreu!
And whatever you do, that do faithfully!

Verdienet eures Gottes Segen,
Earn your God's blessing,

Denn der ist alle Morgen neu:
For it is every morning new:
{For it is new every morning:}

Denn welcher seine Zuversicht
For whoever his confidence
{For whoever has placed his confidence}

Deut. 30:15–18. See, I have set before you this day life and good, death and evil. If you obey the commandments of the Lord your God which I command you this day, by loving the Lord your God, by walking in his ways, and by keeping his commandments and his statutes and his ordinances, then you shall live and multiply, and the Lord your God will bless you in the land which you are entering to take possession of it. But if your heart turns away, and you will not hear, but are drawn away to worship other gods and serve them, I declare to you this day, that you shall perish... (Also Deut. 10:12–13.)
Ps. 119:1–3. Blessed are those whose way is blameless, who walk in the law of the Lord! Blessed are those who keep his testimonies, who seek him with their whole heart, who also do no wrong, but walk in his ways!
Lam. 3:22–23. The steadfast love of the Lord never ceases, his mercies never come to an end; they are new every morning; great is thy faithfulness.
Ps. 62:7–8. ...My refuge is God (Luther: meine Zuversicht ist auf Gott). Trust in him at all times, O people; pour out your heart before him; God is a refuge (Luther: Zuversicht) for us.

---

[1]Untexted in Bach's original; later sources have the text given here, which is a modified version of Vs. 7 of **Wer nur den lieben Gott läßt walten.**

Auf Gott setzt, den verläßt er nicht.
In God places, him forsakes he not.
{In God will not be forsaken by him.}

BWV 198
Laß, Fürstin, laß noch einen Strahl
(NBA I/38; BC G34)

Funeral Service (BWV 106, 157, 198)
This text is a funeral ode written for the memorial service of Christiane Eberhardine, protestant wife of August the Strong. The princess died on Sept. 5, 1727; the service was held on Oct. 17, 1727.
Librettist: Johann Christoph Gottsched

Part I

1. Chorus
●Mourning at the tomb of the Princess (198–1)
Ode Vs. 1:

Laß, Fürstin, laß noch einen   Strahl
Let, Princess, let but one (more) ray
{O Princess, let one more ray}

Aus Salems Sterngewölben schießen,
From Salem's starry-vault shoot-forth,
{Shoot forth from Salem's starry vault,}

Und sieh, mit wieviel Tränengüssen
And see, with how-many tearful-torrents

Umringen wir dein Ehrenmal.
Encircle we thy monument.
{We encircle thy monument.}

2. Soprano Recit.
●Mourning: Grief shared by everyone in the land (198–2)
Dein Sachsen, dein bestürztes Meißen
Thy Saxony, thy dismayed Meissen,

Erstarrt bei deiner Königsgruft;
Stands-numb beside thy royal-tomb;

Das Auge tränt, die Zunge ruft:
The eye weeps, the tongue cries-out:

Mein Schmerz kann unbeschreiblich heißen!
My pain can "indescribable" be-called!
{One could say my pain is indescribable!}

Ode Vs. 2:
Hier klagt August und Prinz und Land,
Here laments (King) August, and Prince, and land,
{Here King August laments, the Prince, and the entire land,}

Ps. 9:10. Those who know thy name put their trust in thee, for thou, O Lord, hast not forsaken those who seek thee.
Deut. 31:8. It is the Lord who goes before you; he will be with you, he will not fail you or forsake you; do not fear or be dismayed. (Also Deut. 31:6, Josh. 1:7, 9, Heb. 13:5.)

Jn. 11:32–33, 35–36. [After Lazarus had died] Mary, when she came where Jesus was and saw him, fell at his feet, saying to him, "Lord, if you had been here, my brother would not have died." When Jesus saw her weeping, and the Jews who came with her also weeping, he was deeply moved in spirit and troubled...[and he] wept. So the Jews said, "See how he loved him!"
Lam. 3:49–50. My eyes will flow without ceasing, without respite, until the Lord from heaven looks down and sees.
Ps. 76:2. [God's] abode has been established in Salem, his dwelling place in Zion. (Salem: Gen. 14:18–20, Heb. 7:1–3)
Heb. 12:22–23. But you have come to Mount Zion and to the city of the living God, the heavenly Jerusalem, and to innumerable angels in festal gathering, and to the assembly of the first-born who are enrolled in heaven, and to a judge who is God of all, and to the spirits of just men made perfect.
Rev. 21:1–4. Then [in my vision] I saw a new heaven and a new earth; for the first heaven and the first earth had passed away... And I saw the holy city, new Jerusalem, coming down out of heaven from God... and I heard a loud voice from the throne saying, "Behold, the dwelling of God is with men. He will dwell with them, and they shall be his people, and God himself will be with them; he will wipe away every tear from their eyes, and death shall be no more, neither shall there be mourning nor crying nor pain any more, for the former things have passed away." (Also Is. 25:8. Rev. 7:15–17.)
Rev. 3:12 [Christ]: He who conquers, I will make him a pillar in the temple of my God; never shall he go out of it, and I will write on him the name of my God, and the name of the city of my God, the new Jerusalem which comes down from my God out of heaven, and my own new name.

[No identifiable allusions to biblical passages or themes]

Lam. 1:12. Is it nothing to you, all you who pass by? Look and see if there is any sorrow like my sorrow...

Der Adel ächzt, der Bürger trauert,
The nobleman moans, the commoner grieves;

Wie hat dich nicht das Volk bedauert,
How did (with) thee not the nation commiserate,
{How the nation commiserated with thee,}

Sobald es deinen Fall empfand!
As-soon-as it thy condition perceived!
{When it learned of thy condition!}

3. Soprano Aria
●Mourning: Music silenced in time of royal mourning (198-3)
Verstummt, verstummt, ihr holden Saiten!
Be-silent, be-silent, ye charming lyres!

Kein Ton vermag der Länder Not
No sound can the land's distress

Bei ihrer teuren Mutter Tod,
At their beloved mother's death—

O Schmerzenswort! recht anzudeuten.
O painful-word!— properly express.
{No sound can properly express the land's distress at their beloved mother's death—O painful word!}

4. Alto Recit.
●Mourning: Tolling bells ring day after day (198-4)
Ode Vs. 3:
Der Glocken bebendes Getön
The (tolling) bells' vibrating clamour
{The vibrating clamour of the tolling bells}

Soll unsrer trüben Seelen Schrecken
Shall our downcast souls' terror
{Will yet frighten our downcast souls}

Durch ihr geschwungnes Erze wecken
By their swinging bronze awaken
{By their swinging bronze}

Und uns durch Mark und Adern gehn.
And us through marrow and veins go.
{And go through us to the core.}

O, könnte nur dies bange Klingen,
Oh, could but this anxious ringing,
{Oh, if only this sad ringing,}

Davon das Ohr uns täglich gellt,
From-which (our) ear - daily does-shrill,
{Which shrills in our ear day after day,}

Der ganzen Europäerwelt
To-the entire European-world

Job 2:11-13. When Job's three friends heard of all this evil that had come upon him...and when they saw him...they did not recognize him; and they raised their voices and wept... And they sat with him on the ground seven days and seven nights, and no one spoke a word to him, for they saw that his suffering was very great.

Is. 24:8. The mirth of the timbrels is stilled, the noise of the jubilant has ceased, the mirth of the lyre is stilled.
Ezek. 26:13 [God]: I will stop the music of your songs, and the sound of your lyres shall be heard no more.
Rev. 18:22. And the sound of harpers and minstrels, of flute players and trumpeters, shall be heard in thee no more...

1 Sam. 25:1. Now [the prophet] Samuel died; and all Israel assembled and mourned for him, and they buried him in his house at Ramah.
2 Chron. 35:24. ...[King Josiah] died, and was buried in the tombs of his fathers. All Judah and Jerusalem mourned for Josiah.
1 Macc. 9:19-21. Then Jonathan and Simon took Judas [Maccabeus] their brother and buried him in the tomb of their fathers at Modein, and wept for him. And all Israel made great lamentation for him; they mourned many days and said, "How is the mighty fallen, the savior of Israel!"
1 Macc. 13:26. All Israel bewailed [Jonathan, the brother of Judas Maccabeus] with great lamentation and mourned for him many days.

[No identifiable allusions to specific biblical passages or themes]

Ein Zeugnis unsres Jammers bringen!
A   testimony of-our lamentation bring!
{Might bring a testimony of our lamentation to the
entire European world!}

5. Alto Aria
●Death conquered Princess's body but not her spirit (198–5)
Ode Vs. 4:
Wie starb die Heldin so vergnügt!
How died (our) heroine so content!
{How contentedly our heroine died!}

Wie   mutig hat ihr Geist gerungen,
How valiantly did her spirit   struggle,
{How valiantly her spirit struggled}

Da   sie des Todes Arm bezwungen,
When her -   death's arm did-vanquish,
{When death's arm vanquished her,}

Noch   eh er ihre Brust   besiegt.
(But) before it her breast did-conquer.
{But her spirit did not fail before she died.}

6. Tenor Recit.
●Funeral tribute: She lived life ready for death (198–6)
Ihr Leben ließ die Kunst zu sterben
Her life   let the   art of   dying
{In her life}

In unverrückter Übung sehn;
In   steadfast practice be-seen;
{She steadily demonstrated the art of dying;}

Unmöglich konnt es denn   geschehn,
Impossible could it therefore happen, (for her)
{It were impossible, then, for her}

Sich   vor   dem Tode zu entfärben.
 - In-the-face-of -   death to blanch.
{To blanch in the face of death.}

Ode Vs. 5:
Ach selig!   wessen großer Geist
Ah, blessed (is) he-whose noble spirit

Sich über die Natur erhebet,
Itself above (our) nature raises,
{Rises above human nature,}

Vor Gruft und Särgen   nicht erbebet,
Before tomb and coffins (does) not tremble,

Wenn ihn sein Schöpfer scheiden heißt.
When him his   maker   to-part bids.
{When his maker bids him depart.}

Rev. 2:10–11 [Christ]: Do not fear what you are about to suffer. Behold, the devil is about to throw some of you into prison, that you may be tested, and for ten days you will have tribulation. Be faithful unto death, and I will give you the crown of life. He who has an ear, let him hear what the Spirit says to the churches. He who conquers shall not be hurt by the second death.
Mt. 10:28 [Christ]: Do not fear those who kill the body but cannot kill the soul; rather fear him who can destroy both soul and body in hell. (Also Lk. 12:4–5.)
Mt. 10:22 [Christ]: ...He who endures to the end will be saved. (Also Mt. 24:13, Mk. 13:13, Lk. 21:19.)
Rev. 14:13. And [in my vision] I heard a voice from heaven saying, "Write this: Blessed are the dead who die in the Lord henceforth." "Blessed indeed," says the Spirit, "that they may rest from their labors, for their deeds follow them!" (Also Ps. 116:15, Heb. 4:9–11.)

Jn. 12:24–25 [Christ]: ...Unless a grain of wheat falls into the earth and dies, it remains alone; but if it dies, it bears much fruit. He who loves his life loses it, and he who hates his life in this world will keep it for eternal life.
Ps. 90:10, 12. The years of our life are threescore and ten, or even by reason of strength fourscore; yet their span is but toil and trouble; they are soon gone, and we fly away...So teach us to number our days that we may get a heart of wisdom.
Jms. 4:13–15. Come now, you who say, "Today or tomorrow we will go into such and such a town and spend a year there and trade and get gain"; whereas you do not know about tomorrow. What is your life? For you are a mist that appears for a little time and then vanishes. Instead you ought to say, "If the Lord wills, we shall live and we shall do this or that."
Lk. 12:20. God said to [the rich man], "Fool! This night your soul is required of you; and the things you have prepared, whose will they be?"
Ps. 23:4. Even though I walk through the valley of the shadow of death, I fear no evil; for thou art with me; thy rod and thy staff, they comfort me.
Mt. 26:38–41. [In the garden of Gethsemane, Jesus] said to [his disciples], "My soul is very sorrowful, even to death; remain here, and watch with me." And going a little farther he fell on his face and prayed, "My Father, if it be possible, let this cup pass from me; nevertheless, not as I will, but as thou wilt." And he came to the disciples and found them sleeping; and he said to Peter, "So, could you not watch with me one hour? Watch and pray that you may not enter into temptation; the spirit indeed is willing, but the flesh is weak." (Also Mk. 14:38.)
Heb. 2:14–16. Since...the children share in flesh and blood, [Christ] himself likewise partook of the same nature, that through death he might destroy him who has the power of death, that is, the devil, and deliver all those who through fear of death were subject to lifelong bondage. (Also 1 Cor. 15:26, 2 Tim. 1:10, Is. 25:8.)

7. Chorus

●Funeral tribute: Nobility of Queen's faith exemplary (198–7)

An dir,   du Fürbild großer Frauen,
In thee, (O) thou model of-great women,
{In thee, O thou model of exalted women,}

An dir,   erhabne Königin,
In thee, (O) prominent queen,

An dir,   du Glaubenspflegerin,
In thee, (O) thou guardian-of-the-faith,

War dieser Großmut   Bild zu schauen.
Was of-this (noble-spirit) (the) image to be-seen.
{Could the image of such noble faith be seen.}

Heb. 13:7. Remember your leaders, those who spoke to you the word of God; consider the outcome of their life, and imitate their faith.
Heb. 11:13–16. These [heroes] all died in faith...having acknowledged that they were strangers and exiles on the earth. For people who speak thus make it clear that they are seeking a homeland. If they had been thinking of that land from which they had gone out, they would have had opportunity to return. But as it is, they desire a better country, that is, a heavenly one. Therefore God is not ashamed to be called their God, for he has prepared for them a city.
Heb. 13:14. ....We have no lasting city, but we seek the city which is to come.
Num. 23:10. ...Let me die the death of the righteous, and let my end be like his!

Part II

8. Tenor Aria

●Transfiguration of Queen as she is drawn to heaven (198–8)
Ode Vs. 6:

Der Ewigkeit saphirnes Haus
 - Eternity's sapphire house

Zieht,   Fürstin, deine heitern Blicke
Draws, (O) Princess, thy (serene) glances

Von   unsrer Niedrigkeit zurücke
Away-from our   low-estate   -

Und tilgt   der Erden Dreckbild aus.
And blots-out (this) earth's miry-image - .

Ein starker Glanz von hundert Sonnen,
A powerful radiance of a-hundred suns,

Der   unsern Tag zur Mitternacht
Which (turns) our   day to   midnight (and)

Uns unsre Sonne finster macht,
 - Our   sun   dark makes,
{Makes our sun seem dark,}

Hat dein verklärtes Haupt umsponnen.
Hath thy transfigured head   (encircled).

Ex. 24:10. [Moses and the elders of Israel] saw the God of Israel [on the mountain of Sinai]; and there was under his feet as it were a pavement of sapphire stone, like the very heaven for clearness.
Rev. 21:10–11, 19, 21. In the Spirit [the angel] carried me away to a great, high mountain, and showed me the holy city Jerusalem coming down out of heaven from God, having the glory of God, its radiance like a most rare jewel, like a jasper, clear as crystal...The foundations of the wall of the city were adorned with every jewel; the first was jasper, the second sapphire...And the twelve gates were twelve pearls, each of the gates made of a single pearl, and the street of the city was pure gold, transparent as glass.
Col. 3:1–3. If then you have been raised with Christ, seek the things that are above, where Christ is, seated at the right hand of God. Set your minds on things that are above, not on things that are on earth. For you have died and your life is hid with Christ in God. (Also 2 Cor. 4:16–18.)
Mt. 17:1–2. ...Jesus took with him Peter and James and John his brother, and led them up a high mountain apart. And he was transfigured (Luther: verklärt) before them, and his face shone like the sun, and his garments became white as light.
Acts 6:15, 7:54–56. Gazing at [Stephen, who was being stoned to death], all who sat in the council saw that his face was like the face of an angel...Now when they heard these things they ground their teeth against him. But he, full of the Holy Spirit, gazed into heaven and saw the glory of God, and Jesus standing at the right hand of God; and he said, "Behold, I see the heavens opened, and the Son of man standing at the right hand of God."

9. Bass Recit, Arioso, & Recit.

●Transfiguration of Queen well-earned; land mourns (198–9)
Ode Vs. 7:

Was Wunder ist's? Du bist es wert,
What wonder is-this? Thou art of-it worthy,
{Why should we wonder at this? Thou art worthy of it,}

Du Fürbild aller Königinnen!
Thou model of-all   queens!

Rev. 3:4–5 [Christ]: ...[The righteous] shall walk with me in white, for they are worthy. He who conquers shall be clad thus in white garments...
Rev. 19:6–8. [In my vision] I heard what seemed to be the voice of a great multitude...crying, "Hallelujah! For the Lord our God the Almighty reigns. Let us rejoice and exult and give him the glory, for the marriage of the Lamb has come, and his Bride has made herself ready; it was granted her to be clothed with fine linen, bright and pure"—for the fine linen is the righteous deeds of the saints. (Also Ezek. 16:9–13.)

Du mußtest allen   Schmuck gewinnen,
Thou hadst   all (this) adornment   to-win,
{Thou hadst to win all this adornment,}

Der deine Scheitel itzt verklärt.
Which thy   head now transfigures.
{Which now transfigures thy brow.}

Nun trägst du   vor des Lammes Throne
Now wearest thou before the Lamb's throne
{Now thou dost wear, before the Lamb's throne—

Anstatt des Purpurs Eitelkleit
Instead of purple's vanity—

Ein perlenreines Unschuldskleid
A   pearl-(white) robe-of-innocence

Und spottest der verlaßnen Krone.
And dost-scorn the forsaken crown.
{And dost scorn the crown thou didst leave behind.}

Arioso:
Ode Vs. 8:
Soweit der volle Weichselstrand,
As-far-as the brimming   Vistula,

Der Niester und die Warthe fließet,
The Dniester, and the Warthe do-flow,

Soweit   sich   Elb' und Muld' ergießet,
As-far-as themselves Elbe and Mulde discharge,
{As far as Elbe and Mulde discharge themselves,}

Erhebt dich beides Stadt und Land.
Extol   thee both   town and country.
{Do both town and country extol thee.}

Recit:
Dein Torgau geht im   Trauerkleide,
Thy Torgau walks in garments-of-mourning,

Dein Pretzsch wird   kraftlos, starr und matt;
Thy Pretzsch becomes powerless, rigid, and lifeless;

Denn da es dich verloren hat,
For since it thee   hath-lost,
{For with its loss of thee,}

Verliert es   seiner Augen Weide.
Loseth it (also) its   eyes' pasture.
{It also loses the delight of its eyes.}

Rev. 7:9–10. After this I looked, and behold, a great multitude which no man could number, from every nation, from all tribes and peoples and tongues, standing before the throne and before the Lamb, clothed in white robes, with palm branches in their hands, and crying out with a loud voice, "Salvation belongs to our God who sits upon the throne, and to the Lamb!"

Dan. 12:3. Those who are wise shall shine like the brightness of the firmament; and those who turn many to righteousness, like the stars for ever and ever.

2 Cor. 4:17. This slight momentary affliction is preparing for us an eternal weight of glory beyond all comparison. (Also Rom. 8:18.)

Phil. 3:7–8. Whatever gain I had, I counted as loss for the sake of Christ...For his sake I have suffered the loss of all things, and count them as refuse, in order that I may gain Christ...

Ps. 49:12–13, 16–19. Man cannot abide in his pomp, he is like the beasts that perish. This is the fate of those who have foolish confidence, the end of those who are pleased with their portion...Be not afraid when one becomes rich, when the glory of his house increases. For when he dies he will carry nothing away; his glory will not go down after him...Though a man gets praise when he does well for himself, he will go to the generation of his fathers... (Also Ps. 49:20, 62:9–11, 89:48, Rev. 18:16–17.)

1 Cor. 2:9. As it is written, "What no eye has seen, nor ear heard, nor the heart of man conceived...God has prepared for those who love him."

[No further identifiable allusions to specific biblical passages or themes]

10. Chorus

●Queen's fame and legacy lives on (198–10)

Ode Vs. 9:

Doch,   Königin! du stirbest nicht,
Yet (O) queen! Thou diest   not,
{Yet, O queen, thou dost not die,}

Man weiß, was man an dir   besessen;
(We) know, what (we) in thee have-possessed;
{We know what we have possessed in thee;}

Die Nachwelt wird dich nicht vergessen,
  - Posterity will thee not   forget,
{Posterity will not forget thee,}

Bis dieser Weltbau einst   zerbricht.
Till this universe one-day breaks-to-pieces.
{Till, one day, this universe dissolves.}

Ihr Dichter, schreibt! wir wollen's lesen:
Ye poets, write!   We would-it read:
{Ye poets, write! We will read it:}

Sie ist der Tugend Eigentum,
She was - virtue's possession,

Der Untertannen Lust und Ruhm,
(Her) subjects' delight and glory,
{The delight and glory of her subjects,}

Der Königinnen   Preis gewesen.
Of   queens (the) praise   - .
{The praise of queens.}

Ps. 112:1–3, 6. ...Blessed is the man who fears the Lord, who greatly delights in his commandments! His descendants will be mighty in the land; the generation of the upright will be blessed. Wealth and riches are in his house; and his righteousness endures for ever...The righteous will never be moved; he will be remembered for ever.
Prov. 10:7. The memory of the righteous is a blessing, but the name of the wicked will rot.
2 Pet. 3:10–12. But the day of the Lord will come like a thief, and then the heavens will pass away with a loud noise, and the elements will be dissolved with fire, and the earth and the works that are upon it will be burned up. Since all these things are thus to be dissolved, what sort of persons ought you to be in lives of holiness and godliness, waiting for and hastening the coming of the day of God, because of which the heavens will be kindled and dissolved, and the elements will melt with fire! (Also Is. 34:4, Heb. 1:10–11, Rev. 21:1.)
2 Chron. 35:24–25. ...[King Josiah] died, and was buried in the tombs of his fathers. All Judah and Jerusalem mourned for Josiah. Jeremiah also uttered a lament for Josiah; and all the singing men and singing women have spoken of Josiah in their laments to this day. They made these an ordinance in Israel; behold, they are written in the Laments.

BWV 199
Mein Herze schwimmt im Blut
(NBA I/20; BC A120a-c)

11. S. after Trinity (BWV 199, 179, 113)
*1 Cor. 15:1–10 (Paul writes of his apostleship and lists post-resurrection appearances of Jesus)
*Lk. 18:9–14 (Parable of the Pharisee and the tax collector in the temple to pray)
Librettist: Georg Christian Lehms

1. Soprano Recit.
●Depravity of my heart makes me utterly wretched (199–1)
Mein Herze schwimmt im Blut,
My heart swims in blood,
{My heart is bathed in blood}

Weil mich der Sünden Brut
Because me (my) sins' brood
{Because my sins' large brood}

In Gottes heilgen Augen
In God's   holy   eyes

Jer. 17:9–10. The heart is deceitful above all things, and desperately corrupt; who can understand it? "I the Lord search the mind and try the heart, to give to every man according to his ways, according to the fruit of his doings."
Gen. 6:5. The Lord saw that the wickedness of man was great in the earth, and that every imagination of the thoughts of his heart was only evil continually.
Job 15:15–16. Behold, God puts no trust in his holy ones, and the heavens are not clean in his sight; how much less one who is abominable and corrupt, a man who drinks iniquity like water!

Zum Ungeheuer macht;
Into-a monster make;
{Make a monster of me in God's holy eyes;}

Und mein Gewissen fühlet Pein,
And my conscience experiences pain,

Weil mir die Sünden nichts
Because to-me (my) sins nought
{Because my sins are nought}

Als Höllenhenker sein.
But hell's-hangmen are.
{But hell's hangmen to me.}

Verhaßte Lasternacht!
(O) hated night-of-depravity!
{O hated darkness of my depravity!}

Du, du allein
Thou, thou alone

Hast mich in solche Not gebracht!
Hast me into such distress brought!
{Hast brought me into such distress!}

Und du, du böser Adamssamen,
And thou, thou wicked seed-of-Adam,

Raubst meiner Seele alle Ruh
Dost-rob my soul of-all rest

Und schließest ihr den Himmel zu!
And dost-lock-up to-it - heaven - !
{And dost shut heaven to it!}

Ach! unerhörter Schmerz!
Ah! Unheard-of pain!

Mein ausgedorrtes Herz
My dried-up heart

Will ferner mehr kein Trost befeuchten;
Will furthermore no comfort moisten;
{Can no longer be softened with any comfort;}

Und ich muß mich vor dem verstecken,
And I must myself from him hide,
{And I must hide myself from him}

Vor dem die Engel selbst ihr Angesicht verdecken.
Before whom the angels themselves their face(s) cover.
{Before whom the angels themselves cover their faces.}

2. Soprano Aria
●Sighs & tears show my unspoken remorse (199-2)
Stumme Seufzer, stille Klagen,
Mute sighs, silent cries:

Ps. 14:2–3. The Lord looks down from heaven upon the children of men, to see if there are any that act wisely, that seek after God. They have all gone astray, they are all alike corrupt; there is none that does good, no, not one.
Ps. 143:2. [O Lord]...no man living is righteous before thee. (Also Ps. 130:3.)
Ps. 51:3. I know my transgressions, and my sin is ever before me.
Rom. 7:15–20, 22–24. I do not understand my own actions. For I do not do what I want, but I do the very thing I hate. Now if I do what I do not want, I agree that the law is good. So then it is no longer I that do it, but sin which dwells within me. For I know that nothing good dwells within me, that is, in my flesh. I can will what is right, but I cannot do it. For I do not do the good I want, but the evil I do not want is what I do. Now if I do what I do not want, it is no longer I that do it, but sin which dwells within me...For I delight in the law of God, in my inmost self, but I see in my members another law at war with the law of my mind and making me captive to the law of sin which dwells in my members. Wretched man that I am! Who will deliver me from this body of death? (Also Gal. 5:17.)
Rom. 5:12, 17, 19. ...Sin came into the world through one man and death through sin, and so death spread to all men because all men sinned...Because of one man's trespass, death reigned through that one man...By one man's disobedience many were made sinners...
Ps. 51:5. Behold, I was brought forth in iniquity (Luther: aus sündlichem Samen gezeugt), and in sin did my mother conceive me.
Is. 57:20–21. The wicked are like the tossing sea; for it cannot rest, and its waters toss up mire and dirt. There is no peace, says my God, for the wicked. (Also Is. 48:22.)
Deut. 11:16–17. Take heed lest your heart be deceived, and you turn aside and serve other gods and worship them, and the anger of the Lord be kindled against you, and he shut up the heavens (Luther: und schließe den Himmel zu)...
Gal. 5:19, 21. The works of the flesh are plain...I warn you, as I warned you before, that those who do such things shall not inherit the kingdom of God. (Also 1 Cor. 6:9–10.)
Heb. 3:12–13. Take care, brethren, lest there be in any of you an evil, unbelieving heart, leading you to fall away from the living God...that none of you may be hardened by the deceitfulness of sin.
1 Sam. 6:6. Why should you harden your hearts as the Egyptians and Pharaoh hardened their hearts?... (Also Heb. 3:8, 12–13, 15).
Gen. 3:8–10. [After they had sinned, Adam and Eve] heard the sound of the Lord God walking in the cool of the day, and [they] hid themselves from the presence of the Lord God among the trees of the garden. But the Lord God called to the man, and said to him, "Where are you?" And he said, "I heard the sound of thee in the garden, and I was afraid..." (Also 1 Jn. 2:28.)
Is. 6:1–2. ...I saw the Lord sitting upon a throne, high and lifted up; and his train filled the temple. Above him stood the seraphim; each had six wings: with two he covered his face...

*Lk. 18:9–13. [Jesus] also told this parable to some who trusted in themselves that they were righteous and despised others: "Two men went up into the temple to pray, one a Pharisee and the other a tax collector. The Pharisee stood and prayed thus with himself, 'God, I

Ihr mögt meine Schmerzen sagen,
Ye may my sorrows tell,

Weil der Mund geschlossen ist.
For (my) mouth locked is.
{For my mouth is locked.}

Und ihr nassen Tränenquellen
And ye wet fountains-of-tears

Könnt ein sichres Zeugnis stellen,
Can a certain testimony furnish,
{Can furnish certain testimony}

Wie mein sündlich Herz gebüßt.
Of-how my sinful heart does-penance.

Mein Herz ist itzt ein Tränenbrunn,
My heart is now a well-of-tears,

Die Augen heiße Quellen.
(My) eyes hot fountains.

Ach Gott! wer wird dich doch zufriedenstellen?
Ah God! Who will thee indeed satisfy?
{Ah God! Who will indeed satisfy thee?}

3. Soprano Recit.
●Mercy will be shown to me by God for I repent (199-3)
Doch Gott muß mir genädig sein,
Yet God must to-me merciful be,
{Yet God must be merciful to me,}

Weil ich das Haupt mit Asche,
For I (my) head with ashes,
{For I bathe my head with ashes,}

Das Angesicht mit Tränen wasche,
(My) face with tears do-bathe,
{My face with tears,}

Mein Herz in Reu und Leid zerschlage
My heart in remorse and sorrow do-batter
{And batter my heart in remorse and sorrow,}

Und voller Wehmut sage:
And full-of sadness (I) say:

Gott sei mir Sünder gnädig!
God be to-me, (a) sinner, merciful!
{God be merciful to me, a sinner!}

Ach ja! sein Herze bricht,
Ah, yes! His heart breaks,

Und meine Seele spricht:
And my soul says:

thank thee that I am not like other men, extortioners, unjust, adulterers, or even like this tax collector. I fast twice a week, I give tithes of all that I get.' But the tax collector, standing far off, would not even lift up his eyes to heaven, but beat his breast, saying, 'God be merciful to me a sinner!'"
Ps. 38:6–10, 13–14, 18. I am utterly bowed down and prostrate; all the day I go about mourning. For my loins are filled with burning, and there is no soundness in my flesh. I am utterly spent and crushed; I groan because of the tumult of my heart. Lord, all my longing is known to thee, my sighing is not hidden from thee. My heart throbs, my strength fails me; and the light of my eyes—it also has gone from me...I am like a deaf man, I do not hear, like a dumb man who does not open his mouth. Yea, I am like a man who does not hear...I confess my iniquity, I am sorry for my sin.
Lk. 7:37–38. Behold, a woman of the city, who was a sinner...brought an alabaster flask of ointment, and standing behind [Jesus] at his feet, weeping, she began to wet his feet with her tears, and wiped them with the hair...
Mic. 6:6–7. With what shall I come before the Lord, and bow myself before God on high?...Will the Lord be pleased with thousands of rams, with ten thousands of rivers of oil? Shall I give my first-born for my transgression, the fruit of my body for the sin of my soul?
Ps. 76:7. [O Lord]...who can stand before thee when once thy anger is roused? (Also Ps. 130:3, Ps. 143:2, Nah. 1:6, Mal. 3:2, Rev. 6:17.)

2 Chron. 7:14 [God]: If my people who are called by my name humble themselves, and pray and seek my face, and turn from their wicked ways, then I will hear from heaven, and will forgive their sin... (Also 1 Kings 8:33–34, 2 Chron. 6:24–25.)
Job 42:6. I despise myself, and repent in dust and ashes.
Dan. 9:3–6. I turned my face to the Lord God, seeking him by prayer and supplications with fasting and sackcloth and ashes. I prayed...and made confession, saying, "O Lord...we have sinned and done wrong and acted wickedly and rebelled, turning aside from thy commandments and ordinances; we have not listened to thy servants..."
Ezra 9:6. O my God, I am ashamed and blush to lift my face to thee, my God, for our iniquities have risen higher than our heads, and our guilt (Luther: Schuld) has mounted up to the heavens. (Also Rev. 18:5.)
Ps. 39:12. Hear my prayer, O Lord, and give ear to my cry; hold not thy peace at my tears!... (Also Ps. 56:8.)
Ps. 6:6–7. I am weary with my moaning; every night I flood my bed with tears; I drench my couch with my weeping. My eye wastes away because of grief... (Also Jer. 45:3.)
***Lk. 18:13.** The tax collector, standing far off, would not even lift up his eyes to heaven, but beat his breast, saying, 'God be merciful to me a sinner!'
Jer. 31:20 [God]: Is Ephraim my dear son? Is he my darling child? For as often as I speak against him, I do remember him still. Therefore my heart yearns for him (Luther: bricht mir mein Herz); I will surely have mercy on him, says the Lord.

4. Soprano Aria
●Confession: I confess my guilt; have patience! (199-4)
Tief gebückt und voller Reue
Deeply bowed and filled-with remorse

Lieg ich, liebster Gott, vor dir.
Lie I, dearest God, before thee.
{I lie, dearest God, before thee.}

Ich bekenne meine Schuld,
I confess my guilt,

Aber habe doch Geduld,
But have, please, patience,
{But please have patience,}

Habe doch Geduld mit mir!
Have, please, patience with me!
{Please have patience with me!}

5. Soprano Recit.
●Repentance brings God's word of comfort (199-5)
Auf diese Schmerzensreu
Upon this pain-of-remorse

Fällt mir alsdenn dies Trostwort bei:
Occurs to-me then this word-of-comfort - :
{Comes this word of comfort to me:}

6. Chorale: Soprano
●Christ's wounds provide salvation for sinners (199-6)
Ich, dein betrübtes Kind,
I, thy sorrowful child,

Werf alle meine Sünd',
Cast all my sins—

Soviel ihr' in mir stecken
As many (as) in me hide
{As many as hide within me}

Und mich so heftig schrecken,
And me so severely frighten,
{And so severely frighten me—}

In deine tiefen Wunden,
Into thy deep wounds,

Da ich stets Heil gefunden.
Where I ever Salvation have-found.
{Where I have ever found Salvation.}

7. Soprano Recit.
●Christ's wounds become my resting place by faith (199-7)
Ich lege mich in diese Wunden
I lay myself into these wounds

Lk. 18:13. The tax collector, standing far off, would not even lift up his eyes to heaven...
Ps. 51:1-3. Have mercy on me, O God, according to thy steadfast love; according to thy abundant mercy blot out my transgressions. Wash me thoroughly from my iniquity, and cleanse me from my sin! For I know my transgressions, and my sin is ever before me.
Ps. 32:5. [O Lord,] I acknowledged my sin to thee (Luther: Darum bekenne ich dir meine Sünde)...
Mt. 18:23-27 [Christ]: The kingdom of heaven may be compared to a king who wished to settle accounts with his servants. When he began the reckoning, one was brought to him who owed him ten thousand talents; and as he could not pay, his lord ordered him to be sold, with his wife and children and all that he had, and payment to be made. So the servant fell on his knees, imploring him, "Lord, have patience with me (Luther: habe Geduld mit mir), and I will pay you everything." And out of pity for him the lord of that servant released him and forgave him the debt (Luther: Schuld).

Ps. 38:17-18. ...My pain is ever with me. I confess my iniquity, I am sorry for my sin.
Ps. 32:5. [O Lord,] I acknowledged my sin to thee, and I did not hide my iniquity; I said, "I will confess my transgressions to the Lord"; then thou didst forgive the guilt of my sin. (Also Job 31:33, 37.)
Ps. 51:17. The sacrifice acceptable to God is a broken spirit; a broken and contrite heart, O God, thou wilt not despise.

1 Cor. 15:3. ...Christ died for our sins...
Is. 53:4-6, 10, 12. Surely he has borne our griefs and carried our sorrows...He was wounded for our transgressions, he was bruised for our iniquities; upon him was the chastisement that made us whole, and with his stripes we are healed. All we like sheep have gone astray; we have turned every one to his own way; and the Lord has laid on him the iniquity of us all...It was the will of the Lord to bruise him; he has put him to grief; when he makes himself an offering for sin...He bore the sin of many, and made intercession for the transgressors.
Rev. 5:9. ...Worthy art thou [O Lamb of God]...for thou wast slain and by thy blood didst ransom men for God from every tribe and tongue and people and nation.
Gal. 3:13. Christ redeemed us from the curse of the law, having become a curse for us—for it is written, "Cursed be every one who hangs on a tree."
1 Pet. 2:24. [Christ] himself bore our sins in his body on the tree, that we might die to sin and live to righteousness. By his wounds you have been healed.
Rom. 5:6, 8-9. While we were still weak, at the right time Christ died for the ungodly...God shows his love for us in that while we were yet sinners Christ died for us. Since, therefore, we are now justified by his blood, much more shall we be saved by him from the wrath of God.

1 Pet. 2:24. ...By [Christ's] wounds you have been healed.
Is. 53:5. ...With his stripes we are healed.
Col. 2:13-14. You, who were dead in trespasses...God made alive together with [Christ], having forgiven us all our trespasses, having

Als in den   rechten Felsenstein;
As into the (one) true   rock;

Die sollen meine Ruhstatt sein.
They shall   my   resting-place be.

In diese will ich mich im Glauben schwingen
Into these would I   -   in   faith   soar
{Into these wounds would I soar by faith}

Und drauf vergnügt und fröhlich singen.
And thus contentedly and joyously sing.

8. Soprano Aria
●Reconciliation with God brings this song of joy (199–8)
Wie freudig ist mein Herz,
How joyful is my heart,
{How joyful my heart is,}

Da Gott versöhnet ist
Since God reconciled is
{Since God has been reconciled}

Und mir auf   Reu und Leid
And to-me upon (my) remorse and sorrow
{And will—upon my remorse and sorrow—}

Nicht mehr   die Seligkeit
No   longer (from) that blessedness
{No longer exclude me from that blessedness}

Noch auch   sein Herz verschließt.
Nor yet (from) his heart will-exclude.
{Nor yet from his heart.}

canceled the bond which stood against us with its legal demands...
nailing it to the cross.
Ps. 62:5–7. For God alone my soul waits in silence, for my hope is
from him. He only is my rock and my salvation, my fortress...On God
rests my deliverance and my honor; my mighty rock (Luther: Fels) my
refuge is God.
1 Cor. 10:4. All [our fathers] drank...from the supernatural Rock which
followed them, and the Rock was Christ.
Mt. 16:18 [Christ]: ...On this rock I will build my church, and the
powers of death (Luther: Pforten der Hölle) shall not prevail against
it.
Rom. 5:1–2. Therefore, since we are justified by faith, we have peace
with God through our Lord Jesus Christ. Through him we have
obtained access to this grace in which we stand, and we rejoice in our
hope...

Ps. 32:1–2. Blessed is he whose transgression is forgiven, whose sin is
covered. Blessed is the man to whom the Lord imputes no iniquity...
(Also Rom. 4:7–8.)
Rom. 5:10–11. If while we were enemies we were reconciled to God
by the death of his Son, much more, now that we are reconciled, shall
we be saved by his life. Not only so, but we rejoice in God through
our Lord Jesus Christ, through whom we have now received our
reconciliation. (Also 2 Cor. 5:17–19.)
Col. 1:19–23. In [Christ] all the fulness of God was pleased to dwell,
and through him to reconcile to himself all things, whether on earth
or in heaven, making peace by the blood of his cross. And you, who
once were estranged and hostile in mind, doing evil deeds, he has now
reconciled in his body of flesh by his death... (Also 1 Pet. 3:18.)
Jn. 6:35, 37. Jesus said... "...Him who comes to me I will not cast out."
1 Jn. 1:9. If we confess our sins, he is faithful and just, and will forgive
our sins and cleanse us from all unrighteousness. (Also 2 Chron. 7:14,
1 Kings 8:33–34.)
*Lk. 18:14 [Christ]: I tell you, this [repentant tax collector] went
down to his house justified...

BWV 200
Bekennen will ich seinen Namen (Fragment)
(NBA I/28; BC A192)

Perhaps for Mary's Purification (Candlemas) (BWV 83, 125, 82, 157, 158, [161], [200])
*Mal. 3:1–4 (The Lord will suddenly come to his temple and purify his people)
*Lk. 2:22–32 (Mary presents Jesus at the temple; Nunc dimittis)

Or perhaps for Epiphany (BWV 65, 123, 248-VI, [200])
+Is. 60:1–6 (Prophecy: the Lord will shine upon you and nations will come to your light)
+Mt. 2:1–12 (The Magi come from the East)

Librettist: Unknown

1. Alto Aria
●Christ is light of salvation to all who confess him (200-1)
Bekennen will ich seinen Namen,
Confess   will I   his   name,
{I will confess his name,}

Er ist der Herr, er ist der Christ,
He is the Lord, he is the Christ,

In welchem aller Völker Samen
In whom   all nations' seed
{In whom the seed of all nations}

Gesegnet und erlöset ist.
Blessed   and redeemed is.
{Is blessed and redeemed.}

Kein Tod raubt mir die Zuversicht:
No death robs me of-this confidence:

Der Herr ist meines Lebens Licht.
The Lord is   my   life's light.
{The Lord is the light of my life.}

Heb. 13:15. Through [Christ]...let us continually offer up a sacrifice of praise to God, that is, the fruit of lips that acknowledge his name (Luther: seinen Namen bekennen).
Rom. 10:9–10. If you confess (Luther: so du bekennest) with your lips that Jesus is Lord and believe in your heart that God raised him from the dead, you will be saved. For man believes with his heart and so is justified, and he confesses (Luther: bekennt) with his lips and so is saved.
Mt. 16:15–16. [Jesus] said to them, "But who do you say that I am?" Simon Peter replied, "You are the Christ, the Son of the living God." (Also Mk. 8:29, Lk. 9:20.)
+Mt. 2:1–2. When Jesus was born in Bethlehem of Judea in the days of Herod the king, behold, wise men from the East came to Jerusalem, saying, "Where is he who has been born king of the Jews? For we have seen his star in the East, and have come to worship him."
*Lk. 2:25–32. Now there was a man in Jerusalem, whose name was Simeon, and this man was righteous and devout, looking for the consolation of Israel, and the Holy Spirit was upon him. And it had been revealed to him by the Holy Spirit that he should not see death before he had seen the Lord's Christ. And inspired by the Spirit he came into the temple; and when the parents brought in the child Jesus, to do for him according to the custom of the law, he took him up in his arms and blessed God and said, "Lord, now lettest thou thy servant depart in peace, according to thy word; for mine eyes have seen thy salvation which thou hast prepared in the presence of all peoples, a light for revelation to the Gentiles, and for glory to thy people Israel." (See Is. 42:6, 49:6.)
Gal. 3:8, 14, 16, 29. The scripture, foreseeing that God would justify the Gentiles by faith, preached the gospel beforehand to Abraham, saying, "In you shall all the nations be blessed."...That in Christ Jesus the blessing of Abraham might come upon the Gentiles, that we might receive the promise of the Spirit through faith...Now the promises were made to Abraham and to his offspring...which is Christ...And if you are Christ's, then you are Abraham's offspring, heirs according to promise. (Also Gen. 18:18, 22:18, 26:4, Acts 3:25.)
Lk. 1:78–79. ...The day shall dawn upon us from on high to give light to those who sit in darkness and in the shadow of death... (Also Mt. 4:16.)
+Is. 60:1–5. Arise, shine; for your light has come, and the glory of the Lord has risen upon you...The Lord will arise upon you, and his glory will be seen upon you. And nations shall come to your light, and kings to the brightness of your rising. Lift up your eyes round about, and see; they all gather together, they come to you; your sons shall come from far...Then you shall see and be radiant, your heart shall thrill and rejoice...
Heb. 2:14–16. Since...the children share in flesh and blood, [Christ] himself likewise partook of the same nature, that through death he might destroy him who has the power of death, that is, the devil, and deliver all those who through fear of death were subject to lifelong bondage.
Jn. 11:25–26. Jesus said to [Martha], "I am the resurrection and the life; he who believes in me, though he die, yet shall he live, and whoever lives and believes in me shall never die. Do you believe this?"
Ps. 27:1. The Lord is my light and my salvation; whom shall I fear? The Lord is the stronghold of my life; of whom shall I be afraid?

BWV 248 (Christmas Oratorio)

I. Jauchzet, frohlocket, auf, preiset die Tage
(NBA II/6; BC D7)

Christmas Day (BWV 63, 91, 110, 248-I, 191)
*Tit. 2:11–14 (The grace of God has appeared)
or: *Is. 9:2–7 (The people who walked in darkness have seen a great light; unto us a child is born)
*Lk. 2:1–14 (The birth of Christ, announcement to the shepherds, the praise of the angels)
Librettist: Unknown. The six cantatas that comprise the Christmas Oratorio borrow heavily from BWV 213, 214, 215 and other, only partially extant, works)

1. Chorus (Parody of BWV 214-1)
●Christmas: Come praise our Sovereign with music! (248-1)
Jauchzet, frohlocket, auf, preiset die Tage,
Shout-for-joy, rejoice, rise-up, exalt (these) days,

Rühmet, was heute der Höchste getan!
Extol, what today the Most-High has-done!

Lasset das Zagen, verbannet die Klage,
Leave-off - faintheartedness, banish - lamentation,

Stimmet voll Jauchzen und Fröhlichkeit an!
{Strike-up-a-song filled-with rejoicing and mirth - !}

Dienet dem Höchsten mit herrlichen Chören,
Serve the Most-High with magnificent choirs,

Laßt uns den Namen des Herrschers verehren!
Let us the name of (our) Sovereign honor!
{Let us honor the name of our Sovereign!}

2. Tenor Recit. (Evangelist) (New)
●Christmas Story: Trip to Bethlehem: Lk. 2:1, 3–6 (248-2)
Es begab sich aber zu der Zeit, daß ein Gebot
It came-to-pass - at that time, that a decree

von dem Kaiser Augusto ausging, daß alle Welt
from - Caesar Augustus went-out, that all-the world

geschätzet würde. Und jedermann ging, daß er sich
enrolled should-be. And everyone went, that he -

schätzen ließe; ein jeglicher in seiner Stadt. Da
be-enrolled; - each-one to his city. Then

machte sich auch auf Joseph aus Galiläe, aus der
set-out also - Joseph from Galilee, from the

Stadt Nazareth, in das jüdische Land zur Stadt
city (of) Nazareth, into the Judean land, to-the city

David, die da heißet Bethlehem; darum, daß
of-David, which - is-called Bethlehem; because -

Ps. 95:1. O come, let us sing to the Lord (Luther: dem Herrn frohlocken); let us make a joyful noise (Luther: jauchzen) to the rock of our salvation.

Ps. 118:24. This is the day which the Lord has made; let us rejoice and be glad in it. (Also Ps. 126:2–3.)

***Is. 9:2, 6–7.** The people who walked in darkness have seen a great light; those who dwelt in a land of deep darkness, on them has light shined...For to us a child is born, to us a son is given; and the government will be upon his shoulder, and his name will be called "Wonderful Counselor, Mighty God, Everlasting Father, Prince of Peace." Of the increase of his government and of peace there will be no end, upon the throne of David, and over his kingdom, to establish it, and to uphold it with justice and with righteousness from this time forth and for evermore... (Also Mt. 4:16.)

***Tit. 2:11.** The grace of God has appeared for the salvation of all men.

Ps. 100:1–2. Make a joyful noise to he Lord (Luther: jauchzet dem Herrn), all the lands! Serve (Luther: dienet) the Lord with gladness! Come into his presence with singing! (Also Ps. 66:1, 81:1, 95:1, 2, 98:4, 6.)

Ps. 8:1/9. O Lord, our Lord (Luther: Herr unser Herrscher), how majestic is thy name (Luther: wie herrlich ist dein Name) in all the earth!...

***Lk. 2:1–6.** *In those days a decree went out from Caesar Augustus that all the world should be enrolled.* This was the first enrollment, when Quirinius was governor of Syria. *And all went to be enrolled, each to his own city. And Joseph also went up from Galilee, from the city of Nazareth, to Judea, to the city of David, which is called Bethlehem, because he was of the house and lineage of David, to be enrolled with Mary, his betrothed, who was with child. And while they were there, the time came for her to be delivered.*

Mic. 5:2, 4. But you, O Bethlehem Ephrathah, who are little to be among the clans of Judah, from you shall come forth for me one who is to be ruler in Israel, whose origin is from of old, from ancient days... And he shall stand and feed his flock in the strength of the Lord, in the majesty of the name of the Lord his God. And they shall dwell secure, for now he shall be great to the ends of the earth.

Mt. 2:4–6. Assembling all the chief priests and scribes of the people, [King Herod] inquired of them where the Christ was to be born. They told him, "In Bethlehem of Judea; for so it is written by the prophet: 'And you, O Bethlehem, in the land of Judah, are by no means least among the rulers of Judah; for from you shall come a ruler who will govern my people Israel.'"

er von dem Hause und Geschlechte Davids war: auf daß
he from the house and lineage of-David was: so that

er sich schätzen ließe mit Maria, seinem vertrauten
he - enrolled might-be with Mary, his betrothed

Weibe, die war schwanger. Und als sie daselbst waren,
wife; she was with-child. And while they there were,

kam die Zeit, daß sie gebären sollte.
came the time, that she delivered should-be.
{the time came, that she should be delivered.}

3. Alto Recit. (Voice of betrothed) (Newly composed)
●Christmas: Promised Messiah, Zion's bridegroom born (248-3)
Nun wird mein liebster Bräutigam,
Now will my dearest bridegroom,

Nun wird der Held aus Davids Stamm
Now will the champion of David's lineage

Zum Trost, zum Heil der Erden
For-the comfort, for-the salvation of-the earth

einmal geboren werden.
finally be-born.

Nun wird der Stern aus Jakob scheinen,
Now will the star out-of Jacob shine,

Sein Strahl bricht schon hervor.
Its ray breaks already forth.
{Its ray already breaks forth.}

Auf, Zion, und verlasse nun das Weinen,
Rise-up, (O) Zion, and forsake now (thy) weeping,

Dein Wohl steigt hoch empor!
Thy welfare ascends high aloft!

4. Alto Aria (Parody of BWV 213-9)
●Christmas: Zion, prepare to receive thy bridegroom! (248-4)
Bereite dich, Zion, mit zärtlichen Trieben
Prepare thyself, (O) Zion, with tender desire

Den Schönsten, den Liebsten bald bei dir zu sehn!
The fairest-one, the dearest-one soon by thee to see!
{The fairest one, the dearest one soon to receive!}

Deine Wangen müssen heut viel schöner prangen,
Thy cheeks must today much lovelier shine,
{Today thy cheeks must shine much lovelier,}

Jn. 7:40–42. When [the people] heard [Jesus'] words, some of the people said, "This is really the prophet." Others said, "This is the Christ." But some said, "Is the Christ to come from Galilee? Has not the scripture said that the Christ is descended from David, and comes from Bethlehem...?"
Mt. 1:23. All this took place to fulfil what the Lord had spoken by the prophet: "Behold, a virgin shall conceive and bear a son, and his name shall be called Emmanuel" (which means, God with us). (See Is. 7:14.)

Hos. 2:19–20 [God]: I will betroth you to me for ever... (Also Is. 62:5, Jn. 3:29, 2 Cor. 11:2, Eph. 5:25–27, Rev. 19:7–9.)
Mt. 25:6. At midnight there was a cry, "Behold, the bridegroom! Come out to meet him."
*Lk. 2:11. ...To you is born this day in the city of David a Savior, who is Christ the Lord.
Lk. 1:32. [This child] will be great, and will be called the Son of the Most High; and the Lord God will give to him the throne of his father David.
Gen. 49:10. The scepter shall not depart from Judah...until he comes to whom it belongs (Luther: bis das der Held komme)...
Jer. 23:5. ...The days are coming, says the Lord, when I will raise up for David a righteous Branch, and he shall reign as king and deal wisely, and shall execute justice and righteousness in the land... (Also Ezek. 34:23–24.)
Is. 11:1–3, 10. There shall come forth a shoot from the stump of Jesse, and a branch shall grow out of his roots. And the Spirit of the Lord shall rest upon him, the spirit of wisdom and understanding, the spirit of counsel and might, the spirit of knowledge and the fear of the Lord. And his delight shall be in the fear of the Lord...In that day the root of Jesse shall stand as an ensign to the peoples; him shall the nations seek...
Num. 24:17. ...A star shall come forth out of Jacob, and a scepter shall rise out of Israel...
Gal. 4:4. When the time had fully come, God sent forth his Son, born of woman...
*Is. 9:2, 6. The people who walked in darkness have seen a great light; those who dwelt in a land of deep darkness, on them has light shined... For to us a child is born, to us a son is given; and the government will be upon his shoulder, and his name will be called "Wonderful Counselor, Mighty God, Everlasting Father, Prince of Peace."
Is. 25:8. He will swallow up death for ever, and the Lord God will wipe away tears from all faces...
Zech. 2:10. Sing and rejoice, O daughter of Zion; for lo, I come and I will dwell in the midst of you, says the Lord.

S. of S. 3:11. Go forth, O daughters of Zion, and behold King Solomon, with the crown with which his mother crowned him on the day of his wedding...
S. of S. 2:8 [Bride]: The voice of my beloved! Behold, he comes...
Mt. 25:1, 5–6 [Christ]: The kingdom of heaven shall be compared to ten maidens who took their lamps and went to meet the bridegroom... As the bridegroom was delayed, they all slumbered and slept. But at midnight there was a cry, "Behold, the bridegroom! Come out to meet him."
Is. 61:10. I will greatly rejoice in the Lord, my soul shall exult in my God; for he has clothed me with the garments of salvation, he has

Eile, den Bräutigam sehnlichst zu lieben!
Hasten, the bridegroom ardently to love!
{O hasten, to welcome the bridegroom with thy love!}

5. Chorale (New)
●Corporate prayer: How shall I meet the bridegroom? (248-5)
Wie soll ich dich empfangen,
How shall I thee receive,
{How shall I receive thee?}

Und wie begegn' ich dir?
And how meet I thee?
{And how shall I meet thee?}

O aller Welt Verlangen,
O (thou-who-art) all-the world's desire,
{O thou who art the desire of the whole world,}

O meiner Seelen Zier!
O my soul's adornment!

O Jesu, Jesu, setzte
O Jesus, Jesus, (bring)

Mir selbst die Fackel bei,
Me thyself the torch -,
{The torch to me thyself,}

Damit, was dich ergötze,
So-that, what thee delights,

Mir kund und wissend sei!
To-me made-known and understandable be!
{So that I might know and understand what pleases thee!}

6. Tenor Recit. (Evangelist)
●Christmas Story: Jesus is born: Lk. 2:7 (248-6)
Und sie gebar ihren ersten Sohn und wickelte
And she bore her first-born son and wrapped

ihn in Windeln, und legte ihn in eine Krippen,
him in swaddling-cloths, and laid him in a manger,

denn sie hatten sonst keinen Raum in der Herberge.
for they had otherwise no room in the inn.

7. Chorale (Soprano) & Recit. (Bass) (New)
●Christmas: God became poor so we could be rich (248-7)
Er ist auf Erden kommen arm,
He is to earth come poor,
{He came to earth poor,}

Wer kann die Liebe recht erhöhn,
Who can the love properly exalt,
{Who can properly exalt the love,}

covered me with the robe of righteousness, as a bridegroom decks himself with a garland, and as a bride adorns herself with her jewels. (Also Is. 62:5, Ezek. 16:9–13, Hos. 2:20, Jn. 3:29, 2 Cor. 11:2, Eph. 5:25–27, Rev. 19:7–8, 21:2.)

Mt. 25:1, 5–6 [Christ]: The kingdom of heaven shall be compared to ten maidens who took their lamps and went to meet the bridegroom... As the bridegroom was delayed, they all slumbered and slept. But at midnight there was a cry, "Behold, the bridegroom! Come out to meet him."
S. of S. 2:8 [Bride]: The voice of my beloved! Behold, he comes...
Mic. 6:6. With what shall I come before the Lord, and bow myself before God on high? Shall I come before him with burnt offerings...? (Also Ps. 40:6–8, 51:16–17.)
Eph. 5:10. Try to learn what is pleasing to the Lord.
Mic. 6:8. He has showed you, O man, what is good...
Jn. 1:9. [In Christ] the true light that enlightens every man was coming into the world.
***Is. 9:2.** The people who walked in darkness have seen a great light; those who dwelt in a land of deep darkness, on them has light shined.
Jn. 8:12. Jesus spoke to [the people], saying, "I am the light of the world; he who follows me will not walk in darkness, but will have the light of life." (Also Jn. 1:4, 9:5, 11:9, 12:46, Ps. 36:9.)
Eph. 1:16. [I pray that you may have] the eyes of your hearts enlightened, that you may know what is the hope to which he has called you, what are the riches of his glorious inheritance in the saints.
1 Cor. 2:12, 16. Now we have received not the spirit of the world, but the Spirit which is from God..."For who has known the mind of the Lord so as to instruct him?" But we have the mind of Christ.

***Lk. 2:7.** And she gave birth to her first-born son and wrapped him in swaddling cloths, and laid him in a manger, because there was no place for them in the inn.*
Mt. 8:19. A scribe came up and said to [Jesus], "Teacher, I will follow you wherever you go." And Jesus said to him, "Foxes have holes, and birds of the air have nests; but the Son of man has nowhere to lay his head." (Also Lk. 9:57–58.)

***Lk. 2:7.** And [Mary]...laid him in a manger, because there was no place for them in the inn.
2 Cor. 8:9. You know the grace of our Lord Jesus Christ, that though he was rich, yet for your sake he became poor, so that by his poverty you might become rich. (Also Col. 1:27, 2:2–3.)
Jn. 3:16–17. God so loved the world that he gave his only Son, that whoever believes in him should not perish but have eternal life. For

Die   unser Heiland für uns   hegt?
Which   our   Savior   for us   cherishes?
{Which our Savior holds for us?}

Daß er unser   sich erbarm',
That he on-us (might) have-mercy,
{That he might have mercy on us,}

Ja, wer vermag es einzusehen,
Yes, who is-able it to-comprehend,
{Yes, who is able to comprehend it,}

Wie ihn der Menschen Leid bewegt?
How him (our) human suffering moves?
{How our human suffering moves him?}

Uns in dem Himmel   mache reich
Us in - heaven (might) make rich
{That he might make us rich in heaven}

Des Höchsten Sohn kömmt in die Welt
The Most-High's Son comes into the world
{The Son of the Most High comes into the world}

Weil   ihm ihr   Heil so wohl gefällt,
Because him her salvation so greatly pleases,
{Because her salvation so greatly pleases him,}

Und seinen lieben Engeln   gleich.
And to-his   dear angels (make) similar.
{And make us like his dear angels.}

So   will er selbst als Mensch geboren werden.
Thus desires he himself as mortal   to-be-born.
{Thus he desires to be born as a mortal himself.}

Kyrieleis!
Kyrie-eleis!

8. Bass Aria (Parody of BWV 214-7)
●Christmas: Creator rejects earthly pomp for a manger
(248-8)
Großer Herr und starker König,
(O) great Lord and mighty King,

Liebster Heiland, o wie wenig
Dearest Savior, O how trifling

Achtest du der Erden Pracht!
Regardest thou the earth's pomp!
{Thou dost regard earthly pomp!}

Der die ganze Welt   erhält,
(Thou) who the whole world dost-uphold,

Ihre Pracht und Zier erschaffen,
Its splendor and finery hast-created,

Muß   in harten Krippen schlafen.
Must (here) in (a) hard manger   sleep.

God sent the Son into the world, not to condemn the world, but that the world might be saved through him.
1 Jn. 4:10. In this is love, not that we loved God but that he loved us and sent his Son to be the expiation for our sins.
Phil. 2:5–8. ...Though [Christ Jesus] was in the form of God, did not count equality with God a thing to be grasped, but emptied himself, taking the form of a servant, being born in the likeness of men. And being found in human form he humbled himself and became obedient unto death, even death on a cross.
1 Jn. 3:16. By this we know love, that he laid down his life for us...
Rom. 5:7–8. Why, one will hardly die for a righteous man—though perhaps for a good man one will dare even to die. But God shows his love for us in that while we were yet sinners Christ died for us.
Jn. 15:13 [Christ]: Greater love has no man than this, that a man lay down his life for his friends.
Heb. 2:14–15. Since...the children share in flesh and blood, [Christ] himself likewise partook of the same nature, that through death he might destroy him who has the power of death, that is, the devil, and deliver all those who through fear of death were subject to lifelong bondage. (Also 1 Jn. 3:8, Is. 25:8, 1 Cor. 15:26.)
2 Tim. 1:10. ...Our Savior Christ Jesus...abolished death and brought life and immortality to light...
Eph. 2:4–7. God, who is rich in mercy, out of the great love with which he loved us, even when we were dead through our trespasses, made us alive together with Christ (by grace you have been saved), and raised us up with him, and made us sit with him in the heavenly places in Christ Jesus, that in the coming ages he might show the immeasurable riches of his grace in kindness toward us in Christ Jesus. (Also Eph. 3:8, 3:16, Col. 1:27, 2:2, 2 Cor. 8:9.)
Phil. 3:20–21. Our commonwealth is in heaven, and from it we await a Savior, the Lord Jesus Christ, who will change our lowly body to be like his glorious body, by the power which enables him even to subject all things to himself.
Mt. 22:30. In the resurrection [we]...are like angels in heaven.

1 Kings 8:27 [King Solomon]: Will God indeed dwell on the earth? Behold, heaven and the highest heaven cannot contain thee; how much less this house which I have built!
Is. 57:15. Thus says the high and lofty One who inhabits eternity, whose name is Holy: "I dwell in the high and holy place, and also with him who is of a contrite and humble spirit, to revive the spirit of the humble, and to revive the heart of the contrite."
Ps. 138:6. Though the Lord is high, he regards the lowly; but the haughty he knows from afar.
Jn. 1:1–3, 14, 18. In the beginning was the Word, and the Word was with God, and the Word was God. He was in the beginning with God; all things were made through him, and without him was not anything made that was made...And the Word became flesh and dwelt among us, full of grace and truth; we have beheld his glory, glory as of the only Son of the Father...No one has ever seen God; the only Son, who is in the bosom of the Father, he has made him known.
＊Lk. 2:7. And she...laid him in a manger, because there was no place for them in the inn.

707

9. Chorale (New)
●Christmas Prayer: Let my heart be thy bed! (248–9)
Ach, mein herzliebes Jesulein!
Ah, my dearest little-Jesus!

Mach' dir ein rein sanft Bettelein,
Make for-thyself a pure, soft little-bed,
{Make a pure, soft little bed for thyself,}

Zu ruhn in meines Herzens Schrein,
To rest in my heart's shrine,

Daß ich nimmer vergesse dein!
That I (might) never forget thee!

II. Und es waren Hirten in derselben Gegend
(NBA II/6; BC D7)

2. Day of Christmas (BWV 40, 121, 57, 248-II)
*Tit. 3:4–7 (The mercy of God appeared in Christ)
*Lk. 2:15–20 (The shepherds go to the manger)

This day also celebrated as the festival of St. Stephen the Martyr.
*Acts 6:8–15; 7:54–60 (Martyrdom of Stephen)
*Mt. 23:34–39 (Jesus' lament: Jerusalem kills the prophets sent to her)
Librettist: Unknown

10. Sinfonia (New)

11. Tenor Recit. (Evangelist) (New)
●Christmas Story: Angels & shepherds: Lk. 2:8–9 (248-11)
Und es waren Hirten in derselben Gegend auf dem Felde
And there were shepherds in the-same region, in the field

bei den Hürden, die hüteten des Nachts ihre Herde.
with the flocks; they watched at night their flock.

Und siehe, des Herren Engel trat zu ihnen, und die
And lo, the Lord's angel appeared to them, and the

Klarheit des Herren leuchtet um sie, und sie
glory of-the Lord shone about them, and they

furchten sich sehr.
feared - greatly.

12. Chorale (New)
●Christmas: Christchild brings the dawn of new age (248-12)
Brich an, o schönes Morgenlicht,
Break forth, O lovely light-of-morning,

Und laß den Himmel tagen!
And let - heaven dawn!

Jn. 1:9–12. The true light that enlightens every man was coming into the world. He was in the world, and the world was made through him, yet the world knew him not. He came to his own home, and his own people received him not. But to all who received him, who believed in his name, he gave power to become children of God.
1 Pet. 3:15. In your hearts reverence Christ as Lord...
Eph. 3:16–19. That according to the riches of his glory he may grant you to be strengthened with might through his Spirit in the inner man, and that Christ may dwell in your hearts through faith; that you, being rooted and grounded in love, may have power to comprehend with all the saints what is the breadth and length and height and depth, and to know the love of Christ which surpasses knowledge, that you may be filled with all the fulness of God.

*←Lk. 2:8–9 [Gospel of preceding day]. And in that region there were shepherds out in the field, keeping watch over their flock by night. And an angel of the Lord appeared to them, and the glory of the Lord shone around them, and they were filled with fear.

*←Lk. 2:9–11 [Gospel of preceding day]. An angel of the Lord appeared to [the shepherds], and the glory of the Lord shone around them, and they were filled with fear. And the angel said to them, "Be not afraid; for behold, I bring you good news of a great joy which will come to all the people; for to you is born this day in the city of David a Savior, who is Christ the Lord."
*←Is. 9:2, 6–7 [Epistle from previous day]. The people who walked in darkness have seen a great light; those who dwelt in a land of deep

Du   Hirtenvolk,   erschrecke nicht,
Thou shepherd-people, be-alarmed   not,
{O, thou shepherd people, be not alarmed,)

Weil   dir   die Engel sagen,
For to-thee the angels   say,

Daß dieses schwache Knäbelein
That   this   weak   little-boy-child

Soll unser Trost und Freude sein,
Shall our comfort and   joy   be,
{Shall be our comfort and joy,}

Dazu   den Satan zwingen
To-that-end - Satan vanquish
{And that he shall vanquish Satan}

Und letzlich Frieden bringen.
And finally peace   bring.
{And ultimately bring peace.}

13. Tenor & Soprano Recit. (Evangelist & Angel) (New)
●Christmas Story: Angels & shepherds: Lk. 2:10-11 (248-13)
Und der Engel sprach zu ihnen: Fürchtet euch nicht,
And the angel   said to them: Fear   - not,

siehe, ich verkündige euch große Freude, die allem
behold, I   proclaim to-you great   joy,   which all

Volke widerfahren wird. Denn euch ist heute der
people   will-befall.   For to-you is today the

Heiland geboren, welcher ist Christus, der Herr,
Savior   born,   which is Christ, the Lord,

in der Stadt Davids.
in the city of-David.

14. Bass Recit. (New)
●Christmas fulfils promise to Abraham, a shepherd (248-14)
Was Gott dem Abraham verheißen,
What God   to Abraham did-promise,
{What God promised to Abraham,}

Das läßt er nun dem   Hirtenchor   erfüllt
That lets he now to-the shepherd-choir as-fulfilled

        erweisen.
        be-demonstrated.
{That he now shows the shepherd choir as having been fulfilled.}

darkness, on them has light shined...For to us a child is born, to us a son is given; and the government will be upon his shoulder, and his name will be called "Wonderful Counselor, Mighty God, Everlasting Father, Prince of Peace." Of the increase of his government and of peace there will be no end, upon the throne of David, and over his kingdom, to establish it, and to uphold it with justice and with righteousness from this time forth and for evermore. The zeal of the Lord of hosts will do this.
Lk. 1:78-79. ...Through the tender mercy of our God...the day shall dawn upon us from on high to give light to those who sit in darkness and in the shadow of death, to guide our feet into the way of peace.
*Tit. 3:4-5. When the goodness and loving kindness of God our Savior appeared, he saved us...
2 Cor. 4:6. It is the God who said, "Let light shine out of darkness," who has shone in our hearts to give the light of the knowledge of the glory of God in the face of Christ.
Heb. 2:14-15. Since...the children share in flesh and blood, [Christ] himself likewise partook of the same nature, that through death he might destroy him who has the power of death, that is, the devil, and deliver all those who through fear of death were subject to lifelong bondage. (Also 1 Jn. 3:8.)
Ps. 85:8. ...He will speak peace to his people...
Zech. 9:9-10. Rejoice greatly, O daughter of Zion! Shout aloud, O daughter of Jerusalem! Lo, your king comes to you...He shall command peace to the nations; his dominion shall be from sea to sea...

*←Lk. 2:10-11 [Gospel of preceding day]. *And the angel said to them, "Be not afraid; for behold, I bring you good news of a great joy which will come to all the people; for to you is born this day in the city of David a Savior, who is Christ the Lord."*
Lk. 1:26, 27-28, 30-32. ...The angel Gabriel [had been] sent from God ...to a virgin...and the virgin's name was Mary. And he came to her and said, "Hail, O favored one, the Lord is with you!...Do not be afraid, Mary, for you have found favor with God. And behold, you will conceive in your womb and bear a son, and you shall call his name Jesus. He will be great, and will be called the Son of the Most High; and the Lord God will give to him the throne of his father David."

Heb. 11:8-9. By faith Abraham obeyed when he was called to go out to a place which he was to receive as an inheritance; and he went out, not knowing where he was to go. By faith he sojourned in the land of promise, as in a foreign land, living in tents with Isaac and Jacob, heirs with him of the same promise.
Gen. 12:1-4, 8; 13:2, 5. The Lord said to Abram, "Go from your country and your kindred...to the land that I will show you. And I will make of you a great nation, and I will bless you, and make your name great, so that you will be a blessing...and by you all the families of the earth shall bless themselves." So Abram went, as the Lord had told him...He removed to the mountain on the east of Bethel, and pitched his tent...Now Abram was very rich in cattle...And Lot, who went with Abram also had flocks and herds and tents.

Ein Hirt hat Alles das zuvor
A shepherd did all of-it beforehand
{A shepherd learned of this}

Von Gott erfahren müssen.
From God learn - .
{Beforehand from God,}

Und nun muß auch ein Hirt die Tat,
And now must also a shepherd the deed,

Was er damals versprochen hat,
Which he at-that-time promised - ,

Zuerst erfüllet wissen.
First as-fulfilled know.
{And now a shepherd must also be the first to know the fulfillment of that promise.}

15. Tenor Aria (Parody of BWV 214-5)
●Christmas: Admonition to shepherds to go quickly (248-15)
Frohe Hirten, eilt, ach eilet,
(O) joyful shepherds, hasten, ah, hasten,

Eh' ihr euch zu lang verweilet,
Lest you - too long tarry,
{Lest you tarry too long,}

Eilt, das holde Kind zu sehn!
Hasten, the lovely child to see!
{Hasten to see the lovely child!}

Geht, die Freude heißt zu schön,
Go; (this) joy is too (wonderful),

Sucht die Anmut zu gewinnen,
Seek that charming-sweetness to obtain,
{Seek to obtain that charming-sweetness for yourselves,}

Geht und labet Herz und Sinnen.
Go and refresh (your) heart and senses.

16. Tenor Recit. (Evangelist) (New)
●Christmas Story: Babe will be in a manger: Lk. 2:12 (248-16)
Und das habt zum Zeichen: Ihr werdet finden
And this (you shall) have for-a sign: You shall find

das Kind in Windeln gewickelt, und in einer Krippe
the child in swaddling-cloths wrapped, and in a manger

liegen.
lying.

Lk. 1:54-55. [The Lord] has helped his servant Israel, in remembrance of his mercy, as he spoke to our fathers, to Abraham and to his posterity for ever.
Lk. 1:67-68, 73. ...Zechariah was filled with the Holy Spirit, and prophesied, saying, "Blessed be the Lord God of Israel, for he has visited and redeemed his people...to perform the mercy promised to our fathers, and to remember his holy covenant, the oath wich he swore to our father Abraham."
Gal. 3:8-9, 14, 16, 26, 29. The scripture, foreseeing that God would justify the Gentiles by faith, preached the gospel beforehand to Abraham, saying, "In you shall all the nations be blessed." So then, those who are men of faith are blessed with Abraham who had faith... that in Christ Jesus the blessing of Abraham might come upon the Gentiles, that we might receive the promise of the Spirit through faith ...Now the promises were made to Abraham and to his offspring... which is Christ...for in Christ Jesus you are all sons of God, through faith...And if you are Christ's, then you are Abraham's offspring, heirs according to promise.

Gen. 12:1, 4. Now the Lord said to Abram, "Go from your country and your kindred...to the land that I will show you..." So Abram went, as the Lord had told him...
Ps. 119:60. [O Lord,] I hasten and do not delay to keep thy commandments.
Heb. 3:7-8, 12. Therefore, as the Holy Spirit says, "Today, when you hear his voice, do not harden your hearts..." ...Take care, brethren, lest there be in any of you an evil, unbelieving heart, leading you to fall away from the living God. (Also vs. 3:15, 4:6-7, Ps. 95:8).
2 Thess. 2:13-14. ...God chose you from the beginning to be saved, through sanctification by the Spirit and belief in the truth. To this he called you (Luther: euch berufen hat) through our gospel, so that you may obtain the glory of our Lord Jesus Christ.
2 Pet. 1:3. His divine power has granted to us all things that pertain to life and godliness, through the knowledge of him who called us (Luther: uns berufen hat) to his own glory and excellence.
Gal. 3:14. That in Christ Jesus the blessing of Abraham might come upon the Gentiles, that we might receive the promise of the Spirit through faith.
2 Cor. 9:15. Thanks be to God for his inexpressible gift!

*←**Lk. 2:12.** [Gospel of preceding day]. *And this will be a sign for you: you will find a babe wrapped in swaddling cloths and lying in a manger.*
Is. 7:14. The Lord himself will give you a sign. Behold, a young woman shall conceive and bear a son, and shall call his name Immanuel.
Mt. 1:22-23. All this took place to fulfil what the Lord had spoken by the prophet: "Behold, a virgin shall conceive and bear a son, and his name shall be called Emmanuel" (which means, God with us).

17. Chorale (New)
●Christmas: Christ lies in yonder stall (248–17)
Schaut hin!   Dort liegt im finstern Stall,
Look there! Yonder lies in-a dark stable,
{Look there! Yonder, in a dark stable, lies}

Des   Herrschaft gehet   überall!
He-whose dominion extends everywhere!

Da   Speise vormals sucht ein Rind,
Where (its) food formerly sought an ox,
{Where formerly an ox sought its food,}

Da   ruhet jetzt der Jungfrau'n Kind.
There rests now   the   virgin's   child.
{There the virgin's child now rests.}

18. Bass Recit. (New)
●Christmas: Shepherds sent to cradle to sing lullaby (248–18)
So geht denn hin,
So go then forth,
{So go forth, then,}

Ihr   Hirten geht,
You shepherds, go,

Daß ihr das Wunder seht:
That you the wonder see:
{That you see this wonder:}

Und findet ihr des Höchsten Sohn
And find you the Highest's Son
{And when you find the Highest's Son}

In einer harten Krippe liegen,
In a   hard   manger lying,
{Lying in a hard manger,}

So singet ihm bei seiner Wiegen
Then sing to-him at his   cradle

Aus einem süßen Ton,
With a   sweet tone,

Und mit   gesamtem Chor
And with (the) united   choir
{And with united voices}

Dies Lied zur Ruhe vor!
This song for rest   - !
{This lullaby!}

19. Alto Aria (Parody of BWV 213–3)
●Christmas lullaby for child who is the Savior (248–19)
Schlafe, mein Liebster, genieße der Ruh
Sleep,   my   dearest,   take (thy) rest

Wache nach diesem vor aller   Gedeihen!
Awake after   this for everyone's prospering!

Mt. 8:19. A scribe came up and said to [Jesus], "Teacher, I will follow you wherever you go." And Jesus said to him, "Foxes have holes, and birds of the air have nests; but the Son of man has nowhere to lay his head." (Also Lk. 9:57–58.)
Phil. 2:5–9. ...Christ Jesus...though he was in the form of God, did not count equality with God a thing to be grasped, but emptied himself, taking the form of a servant, being born in the likeness of men. And being found in human form he humbled himself and became obedient unto death, even death on a cross. Therefore God has highly exalted him and bestowed on him the name which is above every name.
2 Cor. 8:9. You know the grace of our Lord Jesus Christ, that though he was rich, yet for your sake he became poor, so that by his poverty you might become rich.

*←Lk. 2:12. [Gospel of preceding day]. This will be a sign for you: you will find a babe wrapped in swaddling cloths and lying in a manger.

*Lk. 2:15–16. When the angels went away from them into heaven, the shepherds said to one another, "Let us go over to Bethlehem and see this thing that has happened, which the Lord has made known to us." And they went with haste...
[Note: Non-synchronization of lesson with libretto is especially evident here. While the trip of the shepherds to the manger has already occurred in the day's lesson, it has not yet happened in the oratorio's libretto. Here, the shepherds appear to be reluctant to go.]

Mt. 1:22–23. All this took place to fulfil what the Lord had spoken by the prophet: "Behold, a virgin shall conceive and bear a son, and his name shall be called Emmanuel" (which means, God with us).
Mt. 1:21. ...You shall call [this child] Jesus, for he will save his people from their sins.

Labe   die Brust,
Refresh (thy) breast,

Empfinde die Lust,
Experience the delight,

Wo   wir unser Herz   erfreuen!
There-where we our   heart(s) do-gladden!
{In that slumberland where we gladden our hearts!}

20. Tenor Recit. (Evangelist) (New)
●Christmas Story: Heavenly host appears: Lk. 2:13 (248-20)
Und alsobald war da bei dem Engel die Menge
And immediately was there with the angel the multitude

der himmlischen Heerscharen, die lobten Gott,
of-the heavenly   hosts;   they praised God,

und sprachen:
and   said:

21. Chorus ("Evangelist") (Unknown origin)
●Christmas Story: Glory to God in Highest: Lk. 2:14 (248-21)
Ehre   sei Gott in der Höhe und Friede auf Erden,
Glory be-to God in the highest and peace on   earth,

und den   Menschen ein Wohlgefallen.
and to (all) people   -   goodwill.

22. Bass Recit. (New)
●Christmas: Angels' song shall be joined by humans (248-22)
So recht, ihr Engel,   jauchzt   und singet,
So right: ye angels, shout-for-joy and sing
{Go on then, ye angels, shout for joy and sing}

Daß es uns heut' so schön   gelinget!
That it us today so beautifully hath-prospered!
{That this day hath been so prosperous for us!}

Auf denn! wir   stimmen   mit euch ein,
Rise-up then! We (shall) begin-to-sing with you - ,
{Rise up then! We shall join your singing,}

Uns kann es, so wie euch erfreu'n.
Us   can it, as (it does) you, gladden.
{This gladdens us as well as you.}

23. Chorale (New)
●Christmas: We join angelic praise for Christ's birth (248-23)
Wir singen dir   in deinem Heer
We sing to-thee within thy   host

Mt. 20:28 [Christ]: ...The Son of Man came not to be served but to serve, and to give his life as a ransom for many. (Also Mk. 10:45.)
Jn. 10:10 [Christ]: ...I came that they may have life, and have it abundantly.
Jn. 2:4 [Christ]: ...My hour has not yet come.
Ps. 127:2. It is in vain that you rise up early and go late to rest, eating the bread of anxious toil; for [God] gives to his beloved sleep.
Prov. 3:24. ...When you lie down, your sleep will be sweet.
Ps. 4:8. In peace I will both lie down and sleep; for thou alone, O Lord, makest me dwell in safety. (Also Ps. 3:5.)
Jer. 31:26. Thereupon I awoke and looked, and my sleep was pleasant to me.

*←Lk. 2:13–14 [Gospel of preceding day]. *And suddenly there was with the angel a multitude of the heavenly host praising God and saying,*

"Glory to God in the highest, and on earth peace among men with whom he is pleased!"

Ps. 148:1–2, 11–14. Praise the Lord! Praise the Lord from the heavens, praise him in the heights! Praise him, all his angels, praise him, all his host!...Kings of the earth and all peoples, princes and all rulers of the earth! Young men and maidens together, old men and children! Let them praise the name of the Lord, for his name alone is exalted; his glory is above earth and heaven. He has raised up a horn for his people, praise for all his saints, for the people of Israel who are near to him. Praise the Lord!
Ps. 118:24. This is the day which the Lord has made; let us rejoice and be glad in it.
Ps. 126:3. The Lord has done great things for us; we are glad.
Ps. 34:3. O magnify the Lord with me, and let us exalt his name together!

Rev. 5:11–13. I looked, and I heard around the throne and the living creatures and the elders the voice of many angels, numbering myriads of myriads and thousands of thousands, saying with a loud voice,

Aus aller   Kraft: Lob, Preis und Ehr,
With all (our) might: laud, praise, and honor,

Daß du, o lang gewünschter Gast,
That thou, O long   awaited   guest,

Dich nunmehr eingestellet hast.
-    Now   appeared   hast.
{Now hast appeared.}

"Worthy is the Lamb who was slain, to receive power and wealth and wisdom and might and honor and glory and blessing!" And I heard every creature in heaven and on earth and under the earth and in the sea, and all therein, saying, "To him who sits upon the throne and to the Lamb be blessing (Luther: Lob) and honor (Luther: Ehre) and glory (Luther: Preis) and might for ever and ever!"
Is. 25:9. ...Lo, this is our God; we have waited for him, that he might save us. This is the Lord; we have waited for him; let us be glad and rejoice in his salvation.

III. Herrscher des Himmels, erhöre das Lallen
(NBA II/6; BC D7)

3. Day of Christmas (BWV 64, 133, 151, 248-III)
*Heb. 1:1–14 (Christ is superior to the angels)
*Jn. 1:1–14 (Prologue: In the beginning was the Word...and the Word became flesh)
Librettist: Unknown

24. Chorus (Parody of BWV 214-9)
●Zion praises Ruler of Heaven for Salvation (248-24)
Herrscher des Himmels,   erhöre   das Lallen,
Ruler   of heaven, hear-favorably the stammering,
{Ruler of heaven, accept our stammering,}

Laß dir die matten Gesänge gefallen,
Let thee the feeble   songs   please,
{Let our feeble songs please thee,}

Wenn dich dein Zion mit Psalmen erhöht!
When thee thy Zion with psalms doth-exalt!
{When thy Zion exalts thee with psalms!}

Höre der Herzen frohlockendes Preisen,
Hear (our) hearts'   rejoicing   praise,
{Hear the joyous praise of our hearts,}

Wenn wir dir jetzo die Ehrfurcht erweisen,
When we to-thee now - reverence do-show,
{When we now pay homage to thee,}

Weil uns're Wohlfahrt befestiget steht!
Because our   welfare firmly-established doth-stand!
{Because our welfare has been so firmly established!}

25. Tenor Recit. (Evangelist) (New)
●Christmas Story: When the angels had gone: Lk. 2:15 (248-25)
Und da die Engel von ihnen gen Himmel fuhren,
And as the angels from them to heaven went,

sprachen die Hirten untereinander:
said   the shepherds to-one-another:

*←Lk. 2:20 [Gospel of preceding day].** And the shepherds returned, glorifying and praising God for all they had heard and seen, as it had been told them.
2 Cor. 9:15. Thanks be to God for his inexpressible gift!
Ps. 119:108. Accept my offerings of praise, O Lord...
Ps. 136:26. O give thanks to the God of heaven, for his steadfast love endures for ever.
Ps. 47:7. God is the king of all the earth; sing praises with a psalm!
Heb. 1:1–3, 5–6. In many and various ways God spoke of old to our fathers by the prophets; but in these last days he has spoken to us by a Son...He reflects the glory of God and bears the very stamp of his nature, upholding the universe by his word of power...To what angel did God ever say, "Thou art my Son, today I have begotten thee"? Or again, "I will be to him a father, and he shall be to me a son"? And again, when he brings the first-born into the world, he says, "Let all God's angels worship him." [Note: This scriptural lesson "praises God with a psalm" in that it quotes Ps. 2:7. Numerous other psalms are quoted in the rest of the day's Epistle.]
Ps. 95:1. O come, let us sing to the Lord (Luther: dem Herrn frohlocken); let us make a joyful noise to the rock of our salvation.
Ps. 135:21. Blessed be the Lord from Zion, he who dwells in Jerusalem! Praise the Lord! (Also Ps. 65:1.)
Ps. 102:21–22. [Let] men...declare in Zion the name of the Lord, and in Jerusalem his praise, when peoples gather together and kingdoms, to worship the Lord. (Also Ps. 147:12, Zeph. 3:14, Zech. 2:10.)
Lk. 1:68–69. Blessed be the Lord God of Israel, for he has visited and redeemed his people, and has raised up a horn of salvation for us...

*←Lk. 2:15 [Gospel of preceding day].** *When the angels went away from them into heaven, the shepherds said to one another...*

26. Chorus (Unknown origin)
●Christmas Story: Shepherds decide to go see: Lk. 2:15
(248–26)
Lasset uns nun gehen gen Bethlehem, und die Geschichte
Let us now go to Bethlehem, and the event

sehen, die da geschehen ist, die uns der Herr
see, which there has-happened, which to-us the Lord

kundgetan hat.
made-known has.

27. Bass Recit. (Voice of Old Testament prophet) (New)
●Christmas: God has comforted & redeemed his people
(248–27)
Er hat sein Volk getröst',
He has his people comforted,
{He has comforted his people,}

Er hat sein Israel erlöst,
He has his Israel redeemed,
{He has redeemed his Israel,}

Die Hülf' aus Zion hergesendet
The help out-of Zion sent
{Sent help out of Zion}

Und unser Leid geendet.
And our suffering ended.
{And ended our suffering.}

Seht, Hirten, dies hat er getan;
See, shepherds, this has he done;
{See, O shepherds, this he has done;}

Geht, dieses trefft ihr an!
Go, this (is what) you-will-find!

28. Chorale (New) (See also 64-2, 91-6.)
●Christmas: Praise to God for showing his love (248–28)
Dies hat er Alles uns getan,
This has he all for-us done,
{All this he has done for us,}

Sein groß Lieb zu zeigen an;
His great love to show - ;
{To show his great love;}

        Des freu sich alle Christenheit
(Let) over-this rejoice all Christendom
{Let all Christendom rejoice over this}

Und dank ihm des in Ewigkeit.
And thank him for-this (through) (all) eternity.

Kyrieleis!
Kyrie-eleis!

*←Lk. 2:15 [Gospel of preceding day]. ..."*Let us go over to Bethlehem and see this thing that has happened, which the Lord has made known to us.*"

Is. 49:13. Sing for joy, O heavens, and exult, O earth; break forth, O mountains, into singing! For the Lord has comforted his people...
Is. 52:9. Break forth together into singing, you waste places of Jerusalem; for the Lord has comforted his people, he has redeemed Jerusalem.
Lk. 1:68. Blessed be the Lord God of Israel, for he has visited and redeemed his people.
Is. 44:23. Sing, O heavens, for the Lord has done it; shout, O depths of the earth; break forth into singing, O mountains, O forest, and every tree in it! For the Lord has redeemed Jacob, and will be glorified in Israel.
Ps. 20:2. May [the Lord] send you help from the sanctuary, and give you support from Zion!
Ps. 14:7. O that deliverance for Israel would come out of Zion! When the Lord restores the fortunes of his people, Jacob shall rejoice, Israel shall be glad. (Also Ps. 14:7.)
Is. 40:1–2. Comfort, comfort my people, says your God. Speak tenderly to Jerusalem, and cry to her that her warfare is ended, that her iniquity is pardoned...
Is. 62:11–12. Behold, the Lord has proclaimed to the end of the earth: Say to the daughter of Zion, "Behold, your salvation comes; behold, his reward is with him, and his recompense before him." And they shall be called The holy people, The redeemed of the Lord...

Jn. 3:16. God so loved the world that he gave his only Son, that whoever believes in him should not perish but have eternal life.
Phil. 2:6–8. Though he was in the form of God, [Christ Jesus] did not count equality with God a thing to be grasped, but emptied himself, taking the form of a servant, being born in the likeness of men. And being found in human form he humbled himself and became obedient unto death, even death on a cross. 1 Jn. 4:10. In this is love, not that we loved God but that he loved us and sent his Son to be the expiation for our sins.
Rom. 5:8. God shows his love for us in that while we were yet sinners Christ died for us.
2 Cor. 9:15. Thanks be to God for his inexpressible gift!
Rev. 7:12. Amen! Blessing and glory and wisdom and thanksgiving and honor and power and might be to our God for ever and ever! Amen.
2 John 1:3. Grace, mercy, and peace will be with us, from God the Father and from Jesus Christ the Father's Son, in truth and love.
Lk. 18:13. ...God be merciful to me a sinner!

29. Soprano & Bass Duet (Parody of BWV 213-11)
●Christmas: Praise to God for his mercy to us (248-29)
Herr, dein   Mitleid, dein Erbarmen,
Lord, thy compassion, thy   mercy,

Tröstet uns und macht uns frei.
Comforts us and makes us free.

Deine holde Gunst und Liebe,
Thy   gracious favor and love,

Deine wundersamen   Triebe
Thy   wondrous, (loving) impulses

Machen deine   Vatertreu
Make   thy paternal-faithfulness

Wieder neu.
Again   new.
{These all renew thy paternal faithfulness to us.}

Jer. 15:5. Who will have pity on you (Luther: sich dein erbarmen), O Jerusalem, or who will bemoan you (Luther: Mitleiden mit dir haben)?...

*←Tit. 3:4–5 [Epistle of preceding day]. When the goodness and loving kindness of God our Savior appeared, he saved us, not because of deeds done by us in righteousness, but in virtue of his own mercy (Luther: Barmherzigkeit)...

Gal. 4:4–5. When the time had fully come, God sent forth his Son, born of woman...so that we might receive adoption as sons.

Lk. 4:16–19, 21. [Jesus] came to Nazareth, where he had been brought up; and he went to the synagogue...and he stood up to read...He opened the book...where it was written, "The Spirit of the Lord is upon me, because he has anointed me to preach good news to the poor, He has sent me to proclaim release to the captives and recovering of sight to the blind, to set at liberty those who are oppressed, to proclaim the acceptable year of the Lord."...And he began to say to them, "Today this scripture has been fulfilled in your hearing." (See Is. 61:1–2.)

Heb. 4:15. We have not a high priest who is unable to sympathize (Luther: Mitleiden haben) with our weaknesses, but one who in every respect has been tempted as we are, yet without sin.

1 Pet. 1:3. Blessed be the God and Father of our Lord Jesus Christ! By his great mercy (Luther: Barmherzigkeit) we have been born anew to a living hope...

Ps. 103:13. As a father pities his children, so the Lord pities those who fear him.

Lam. 3:22–23. The steadfast love of the Lord never ceases, his mercies (Luther: Barmherzigkeit) never come to an end; they are new every morning; great is thy faithfulness (Luther: Treue).

30. Tenor Recit. (Evangelist) (New)
●Christmas Story: Shepherds tell story: Lk. 2:16–19 (248-30)
Und sie kamen eilend, und funden beide, Mariam
And they came in-haste, and found both,   Mary

und Joseph dazu das Kind in der Krippe liegen.
and Joseph and the child in the manger lying.

Da   sie es aber gesehen hatten, breiteten sie das
When they it however seen   had,   spread   they the

Wort aus, welches zu ihnen   von   diesem Kind
Word abroad, which -   them concerning this   child

gesaget war. Und alle, vor die es kam, wunderten sich
had-been-told. And all, to whom it came, wondered   -

der   Rede, die ihnen die Hirten gesaget hatten.
at (the) (things), which them the sheperds told   - .

Maria   aber behielt alle diese Worte, und bewegte sie
Mary, however, kept   all these words, and pondered them

in ihrem Herzen.
in her   heart.

*←Lk. 2:16–19 [Gospel of preceding day]. *And they went with haste, and found Mary and Joseph, and the babe lying in a manger. And when they saw it they made known the saying which had been told them concerning this child; and all who heard it wondered at what the shepherds told them. But Mary kept all these things, pondering them in her heart.*

31. Alto Aria (Voice of Mary) (New[1])
●Christmas: Embrace this miracle in your heart! (248-31)
Schließe,   mein Herze, dies selige Wunder
Enclose, (O) my   heart,   this blessed miracle
{O my heart, embrace this wonder}

Fest   in   deinem Glauben ein!
Firmly within thy   faith - !
{Firmly with thy faith!}

Lasse dies Wunder der göttlichen Werke
Let   this miracle of   divine   deeds

Immer zur Stärke
Ever to-the strength
{Ever serve to strengthen}

Deines schwachen Glaubens sein!
Of-thy   weak   faith   be!
{Thy weak faith!}

32. Alto Recit. (Voice of Mary) (New)
●Christmas: I will preserve this miracle in my heart (248-32)
Ja, ja, mein Herz soll es bewahren,
Yes, yes, my heart will (that) preserve,
{Yes, my heart will preserve that}

Was es an dieser holden Zeit
Which it in   this propitious time

Zu   seiner Seligkeit
Regarding its   salvation

Für sicheren Beweis   erfahren.
As positive   proof has-experienced.
{Which it has experienced in this propitious time as positive proof
of its salvation.}

33. Chorale (New)
●Declaration: I will preserve Christ in my heart (248-33)
Ich will dich mit Fleiß bewahren,
I   will thee with diligence preserve,
{I will preserve thee in my heart with diligence,}

Ich will dir
I   will for-thee

Leben hier,
Live   here,
{I will live for thee here,}

*←Lk. 2:19 [Gospel of preceding day]. But Mary kept all these things,
pondering them in her heart.
Lk. 1:45. Blessed is she who believed...what was spoken to her from
the Lord.
*Heb. 1:5-6. To what angel did God ever say, "Thou art my Son,
today I have begotten thee"? Or again, "I will be to him a father, and
he shall be to me a son"? And again, when he brings the first-born
into the world, he says, "Let all God's angels worship him."
Jn. 20:31. These [signs] are written that you may believe that Jesus is
the Christ, the Son of God and that believing you may have life in his
name.
Jn. 10:24-25. The Jews gathered round [Jesus] and said to him, "How
long will you keep us in suspense? If you are the Christ, tell us
plainly." Jesus answered them, "I told you, and you do not believe.
The works (Luther: Werke) that I do in my Father's name, they bear
witness to me."
Jn. 2:23. ...Many believed in his name when they saw the signs which
[Jesus] did.
Jn. 7:31. Many of the people believed in him; they said, "When the
Christ appears, will he do more signs than this man has done?" (Also
Jn. 11:45.)
Lk. 12:28 [Christ]: ...O [ye] of little faith! (Also Mt. 6:30, 8:26, 14:31,
16:8, 17:20.)
Mk. 9:24. The father of the [sick] child cried out and said [to Jesus],
"I believe; help my unbelief!"

*←Lk. 2:19 [Gospel of preceding day]. But Mary kept all these things,
pondering them in her heart. (Luther: Maria aber behielt alle diese
Worte und bewegte sie in ihrem Herzen).
Ps. 105:5. Remember the wonderful works that [the Lord] has done,
his miracles...
*Jn. 1:14. The Word became flesh and dwelt among us, full of grace
and truth; we have beheld his glory, glory as of the only Son from the
Father.
1 Jn. 4:14. And we have seen and testify that the Father has sent his
Son as the Savior of the world.
1 Chron. 16:12. Remember the wonderful works that he has done, the
wonders he wrought...
Ps. 77:11-14. I will call to mind the deeds of the Lord; yea, I will
remember thy wonders of old. I will meditate on all thy work, and
muse on thy mighty deeds. Thy way, O God, is holy. What god is great
like our God? Thou art the God who workest wonders, who hast
manifested thy might among the peoples.

*←Lk. 2:19 [Gospel of preceding day]. But Mary kept all these things,
pondering them in her heart.
Prov. 4:23. Keep your heart with all vigilance (Luther: behüte dein
Herz mit allem Fleiß); for from it flow the springs of life.
Eph. 3:17-19. [I pray] that Christ may dwell in your hearts through
faith; that you, being rooted and grounded in love, may have power
to comprehend...what is the breadth and length and height and depth,
and to know the love of Christ which surpasses knowledge, that you
may be filled with all the fulness of God.

---

[1]This is the only newly-composed aria in the entire oratorio.

Dir will ich abfahren.
To-thee will I depart.
{And will depart to thee there.}

Mit dir will ich endlich schweben
With thee will I finally soar—

Voller Freud,
Filled-with joy,

Ohne Zeit
Without time—
{Beyond time—}

Dort im andern Leben.
Over-there in that-other life.

34. Tenor Recit. (Evangelist) (New)
●Christmas Story: Shepherds return: Lk. 2:20 (248-34)
Und die Hirten kehrten wieder um, preiseten und
And the shepherds turned back-again, glorified and

lobten Gott um alles, das sie gesehen und gehöret
praised God for all that they seen and heard

hatten, wie denn zu ihnen gesaget war.
had, as (it) to them had-been-told.

35. Chorale (New)
●Christmas: Rejoice! Salvation has come in Christ! (248-35)
Seid froh, dieweil, seid froh, dieweil,
Be glad, meanwhile, be glad, meanwhile,

Daß euer Heil
That your Salvation

Ist hie ein Gott und auch ein Mensch geboren,
Has here (as) God and also (as) man been-born,
{Has here been born as God and also as man:}

Der, welcher ist
He, who is

Der Herr und Christ
The Lord and Christ;

In Davids Stadt, von vielen auserkoren.
In David's city, from (amongst) many chosen.
{Born in David's city, chosen from amongst many.}

Rom. 14:8. If we live, we live to the Lord, and if we die, we die to the Lord; so then, whether we live or whether we die, we are the Lord's. **Phil. 1:20-21.** ...That...Christ will be honored in my body, whether by life or by death. For to me to live is Christ, and to die is gain. **2 Cor. 5:6-9.** So we are always of good courage; we know that while we are at home in the body we are away from the Lord, for we walk by faith, not by sight. We are of good courage, and we would rather be away from the body and at home with the Lord. So whether we are at home or away, we make it our aim to please him. **1 Thess. 4:16-17.** The Lord himself will descend from heaven with a cry of command, with the archangel's call, and with the sound of the trumpet of God. And the dead in Christ will rise first; then we who are alive, who are left, shall be caught up together with them in clouds to meet the Lord in the air; and so we shall always be with the Lord. **Rev. 10:5-6.** And the angel whom I saw standing on sea and land lifted up his right hand to heaven and swore...that there should be no more delay (Luther: das hinfort keine Zeit [= time] mehr sein soll).

***←Lk. 2:20 [Gospel of preceding day].** And the shepherds returned, glorifying and praising God for all they had heard and seen, as it had been told them.*

Lk. 2:10, 14. ...Behold, I bring you good news of a great joy which will come to all the people...Glory to God in the highest, and on earth peace among men with whom he is pleased! **Rom. 1:3-4.** [This is] the gospel concerning his Son, who was descended from David according to the flesh and designated Son of God in power according to the Spirit of holiness by his resurrection from the dead, Jesus Christ our Lord. ***Jn. 1:1, 14.** In the beginning was the Word, and the Word was with God, and the Word was God...And the Word became flesh and dwelt among us, full of grace and truth; we have beheld his glory, glory as of the only Son of the Father. **Jn. 1:18.** No one has ever seen God; the only Son, who is in the bosom of the Father, he has made him known. **Acts 2:36.** Let all the house of Israel therefore know assuredly that God has made him both Lord and Christ, this Jesus... **S. of S. 5:10 [Bride]:** My beloved is all radiant and ruddy, distinguished among ten thousand (Luther: auserkoren unter viel Tausenden). ***Heb. 1:5.** To what angel did God ever say, "Thou art my Son, today I have begotten thee"? Or again, "I will be to him a father, and he shall be to me a son"? **Lk. 2:11.** To you is born this day in the city of David a Savior, who is Christ the Lord.

IV. Fallt mit Danken, fallt mit Loben
(NBA II/6; BC D7)

New Year/Circumcision and Name of Jesus
(BWV 143, 190, 41, 16, 171, 248-IV)
*Gal. 3:23–29 (Through faith we are heirs of the promise)
*Lk. 2:21 (Circumcision and naming of Jesus)
Librettist: Unknown

36. Chorus (Parody of BWV 213-1)
●Praise God for his Son who is our victorious Savior (248–36)
Fallt   mit Danken,
Prostrate-yourselves in thanksgiving,

      fallt   mit Loben
      prostrate-yourselves in   praise

Vor   des Höchsten Gnadenthron!
Before the Most-High's throne-of-grace!

Gottes Sohn
God's   Son

Will   der Erden
Would the earth's

Heiland und Erlöser werden,
Savior   and Redeemer become,

Gottes Sohn
God's   Son

Dämpft der Feinde Wut und Toben.
Subdues the foe's rage and bluster.

37. Tenor Recit. (Evangelist) (New)
●Circumcision and naming of Jesus: Lk. 2:21 (248–37)
Und da acht Tage um waren, daß das Kind beschnitten
And when eight days were past, when the child circumcised

würde; da ward sein Name genennet Jesus, welcher
was; then was his name called Jesus, which (he)

genennet war von dem Engel, ehe denn er im
was-named   by the angel, before - he in-the

Mutterleibe empfangen ward.
womb   conceived was.

38. Bass Recit. & Soprano Chorale[1] (New)
      [1]Chorale continued in 248–40
●Emmanuel, Jesus' name, means everything to me (248–38)
Immanuel, o süßes Wort!
Emmanuel, O sweet word!

1 Jn. 4:14. We have seen and testify that the Father has sent his Son as the Savior of the world.

Rev. 5:8–13. ...The four living creatures and the twenty-four elders fell down before the Lamb...and they sang a new song, saying, "Worthy art thou...for thou wast slain and by thy blood didst ransom men for God from every tribe and tongue and people and nation, and hast made them a kingdom and priests to our God, and they shall reign on earth." Then I looked, and I heard around the throne and the living creatures and the elders the voice of many angels, numbering myriads of myriads and thousands of thousands, saying with a loud voice, "Worthy is the Lamb who was slain, to receive power and wealth and wisdom and might and honor and glory and blessing!" And I heard every creature in heaven and on earth and under the earth and in the sea, and all therein, saying, "To him who sits upon the throne and to the Lamb be blessing and honor and glory and might for ever and ever!" (Also Rev. 4:10–11, 19:4–5.)

Lk. 1:68–71. Blessed be the Lord God of Israel, for he has visited and redeemed his people, and has raised up a horn of salvation for us in the house of his servant David, as he spoke by the mouth of his holy prophets from of old, that we should be saved from our enemies, and from the hand of all who hate us.

1 Jn. 3:8. ...The reason the Son of God appeared was to destroy the works of the devil.

Heb. 2:14–15. Since therefore the children share in flesh and blood, [Christ] himself likewise partook of the same nature, that through death he might destroy him who has the power of death, that is, the devil, and deliver all those who through fear of death were subject to lifelong bondage.

***Lk. 2:21.** And at the end of eight days, when he was circumcised, he was called Jesus, the name given by the angel before he was conceived in the womb.*
Mt. 1:21. ...You shall call his name Jesus, for he will save his people from their sins.

Mt. 1:20–23. ...An angel of the Lord appeared to [Joseph] in a dream, saying, "Joseph, son of David, do not fear to take Mary your wife, for that which is conceived in her is of the Holy Spirit; she will

Mein Jesus heißt mein   Hirt,
My   Jesus is   my shepherd,
    [Heißen = to be called, to signify; hence the context
    here is "What does Jesus' name mean to me?"]

Mein Jesus heißt mein Leben.
My   Jesus is   my life.

Mein Jesus hat sich   mir ergeben,
My   Jesus has himself to-me devoted,
{My Jesus has devoted himself to me,}

Mein Jesus soll mir immerfort
My   Jesus shall - evermore

Vor   meinen Augen schweben;
Before my   eyes   hover;
{Hover before my eyes;}

Mein Jesus heißet meine Lust,
My   Jesus is   my delight,

Mein Jesus labet Herz und Brust.
My   Jesus refreshes heart and breast.

Bass & Soprano Arioso:
Komm! ich will dich mit Lust umfassen,
Come! I would thee with delight embrace,
{Come! I would embrace thee with delight,}

Mein Herze soll dich nimmer lassen,
My   heart shall thee never leave,
{My heart shall never leave thee;}

Ach! so nimm mich zu dir!
Ah! Then take me   to thee!

Jesu du mein liebstes Leben,
Jesus, thou, my   dearest   life,

Meiner Seelen Bräutigam,
My   soul's bridegroom,

Der du   dich vor mich gegeben
Thou-who thyself for me didst-give
{Thou who didst give thyself for me}

An des bittern Kreuzes Stamm!
On the bitter   cross's   beam!

Bass Recit:
Auch in dem Sterben
Even in -   dying

Sollst du mir das Allerliebste sein;
Shalt thou to-me the most-dearest be;

In Not, Gefahr und Ungemach
In distress, peril, and trouble

bear a son, and you shall call his name Jesus, for he will save his people from their sins." All this took place to fulfil what the Lord had spoken by the prophet: "Behold, a virgin shall conceive and bear a son, and his name shall be called Emmanuel" (which means, God with us). (See Is. 7:14.)

Zech. 2:10. Sing and rejoice...for lo, I come and I will dwell in the midst of you, says the Lord.

Ps. 23:1. The Lord is my shepherd, I shall not want...

Jn. 9:41, 10:11. Jesus said... "...I am the good shepherd... The good shepherd lays down his life for the sheep."

1 Thess. 5:9–10. God has not destined us for wrath, but to obtain salvation through our Lord Jesus Christ, who died for us so that...we might live with him.

Jn. 10:10 [Christ]: ...I came that they may have life, and have it abundantly.

Phil. 1:21. To me to live is Christ (Luther: Christus ist mein Leben)...

2 Tim. 1:10. ...Our Savior Christ Jesus...abolished death and brought life and immortality to light...

Jn. 17:3. This is eternal life, that they know thee the only true God, and Jesus Christ whom thou hast sent.

Gal. 2:20. ...Christ...lives in me; and the life I now live in the flesh I live by faith in the Son of God who loved me and gave himself for me.

Ps. 16:5, 8. The Lord is my chosen portion and my cup...I keep the Lord always before me...

Ps. 37:4. Take delight (Luther: Lust) in the Lord, and he will give you the desires of your heart.

Ps. 73:25. [O Lord,] whom have I in heaven but thee? And there is nothing upon earth that I desire besides thee.

S. of S. 3:4 [Bride]: ...I found him whom my soul loves. I held him, and would not let him go...

Gen. 32:26. ...Jacob said, "I will not let you go, unless you bless me."

Ps. 63:8. [O Lord,] my soul clings to thee (Luther: hanget dir an)... (Also Deut. 13:4, 2 Kings 18:6.)

Deut. 6:5. You shall love the Lord your God with all your heart, and with all your soul, and with all your might. (Also Mt. 22:37, Mk. 12:30, Lk. 10:27.)

Lk. 2:29–32. Lord, now lettest thou thy servant depart in peace, according to thy word; for mine eyes have seen thy salvation which thou hast prepared in the presence of all peoples, a light for revelation to the Gentiles, and for glory to thy people Israel.

S. of S. 2:16 [Bride]: My beloved is mine and I am his... (Also S. of S. 6:3.)

2 Cor. 11:2. ...I betrothed you to Christ to present you as a pure bride to her one husband. (Also Hos. 2:20, Eph. 5:25–27, Ezek. 16:9–13, Is. 61:10, 62:5, Jn. 3:29, Rev. 19:7–9.)

Eph. 5:2. ...Christ loved us and gave himself up for us... (Also Gal. 1:3–4, Eph. 5:25, 1 Tim. 2:6, Tit. 2:14.)

1 Pet. 2:24. He himself bore our sins in his body on the tree...

2 Cor. 5:6–8. So we are always of good courage; we know that while we are at home in the body we are away from the Lord, for we walk by faith, not by sight. We are of good courage, and we would rather be away from the body and at home with the Lord.

Phil. 1:21–23. To me to live is Christ, and to die is gain...Which I shall choose I cannot tell. I am hard pressed between the two. My desire is to depart and be with Christ, for that is far better.

Seh ich dir sehnlichst nach.
Look I thee longingly after.
{Do I look longingly after thee.}

Was jagte mir zuletzt
(How) should-instill in-me in-the-end
{How should death instill in me}

Der Tod für Grauen ein?
 - Death (any) dread - ?
{Any dread?}

Mein Jesus! Wenn ich sterbe,
My Jesus! When I die,

So weiß ich, daß ich nicht verderbe.
Then know I, that I (shall) not perish.
{Then I know that I shall not perish.}

Dein Name steht in mir geschrieben,
Thy name stands in me inscribed,
{Thy name is inscribed in me,}

Der hat des Todes Furcht vertrieben.
It hath - death's fear dispelled.
{It hath dispelled death's fear.}

39. Soprano Aria with Echo (Parody of BWV 213-5)
●Jesus' name inspires no fear of death, rather joy (248-39)
Flößt, mein Heiland, flößt dein Namen,
Inspires, (O) my Savior, inspires thy name,
{O my Savior, does thy name inspire}

Auch den allerkleinst en Samen
Even the very-smallest seed

Jenes strengen Schreckens ein?
Of-that severe terror - (that is to come)?

Nein, du sagst ja selber nein!
No, thou sayest indeed, thyself, no!
{No, thou thyself sayest, no!}

Sollt ich nun das Sterben scheuen?
Should I then - dying shun?
{Should I then shun dying?}

Nein, dein süßes Wort ist da!
No, thy sweet word is there!

Oder sollt ich mich erfreuen?
Or should I - rejoice?

Ja, du Heiland, sprichst selbst ja!
Yes, thou, (O) Savior, sayest thyself, yes!
{Yes, thou, O Savior, thyself sayest, yes!}

Acts 1:9–11. ...As [the disciples] were looking on, [Jesus] was lifted up, and a cloud took him out of their sight. And while they were gazing into heaven as he went, behold, two men stood by them in white robes, and said, "Men of Galilee, why do you stand looking into heaven?..."
Rom. 8:35, 38–39. Who shall separate us from the love of Christ? Shall tribulation, or distress, or persecution, or famine, or nakedness, or peril, or sword?...I am sure that neither death, nor life...nor anything else in all creation, will be able to separate us from the love of God in Christ Jesus our Lord.
Jn. 11:25–26. Jesus said to [Martha], "I am the resurrection and the life; he who believes in me, though he die, yet shall he live, and whoever lives and believes in me shall never die. Do you believe this?"
1 Cor. 15:55. O death, where is thy victory? O death, where is thy sting?
Jn. 3:16. God so loved the world that he gave his only Son, that whoever believes in him should not perish but have eternal life.
Lk. 10:20 [Christ]: ...Rejoice that your names are written in heaven.
Rev. 14:1. Then I looked, and lo, on Mount Zion stood the Lamb, and with him a hundred and forty-four thousand who had his name and his Father's name written on their foreheads.
Heb. 2:14–15. Since therefore the children share in flesh and blood, [Christ] himself likewise partook of the same nature, that through death he might destroy him who has the power of death, that is, the devil, and deliver all those who through fear of death were subject to lifelong bondage.

Phil. 2:9–10. ...God has highly exalted [Christ] and bestowed on him the name which is above every name, that at the name of Jesus every knee should bow...
Rom. 14:10–11. ...We shall all stand before the judgment seat of God; for it is written, "As I live, says the Lord, every knee shall bow to me..." (Also 2 Cor. 5:10, 2 Tim. 4:1.)
Heb. 9:27. ...It is appointed for men to die once, and after that comes judgment. (Also Heb. 10:26–27.)
1 Jn. 4:17–18. In this is love perfected with us, that we may have confidence for the day of judgment, because as he is so are we in this world. There is no fear in love, but perfect love casts out fear. For fear has to do with punishment, and he who fears is not perfected in love.
Heb. 2:15. [Christ delivered] all those who through fear of death were subject to lifelong bondage.
Jn. 5:22–24 [Christ]: The Father judges no one, but has given all judgment to the Son, that all may honor the Son, even as they honor the Father...Truly, truly, I say to you, he who hears my word and believes him who sent me, has eternal life; he does not come into judgment, but has passed from death to life.
Phil. 1:21. To me to live is Christ, and to die is gain.
2 Cor. 5:8. We are of good courage, and we would rather be away from the body and at home with the Lord.
2 Cor. 1:18–20. As surely as God is faithful, our word to you has not been Yes and No. For the Son of God, Jesus Christ...was not Yes and No; but in him it is always Yes. For all the promises of God find their Yes in him. That is why we utter the Amen through him, to the glory of God.

40. Bass Recit./Arioso & Soprano Chorale[1] (New)
[1]Continuation of chorale from 248-38
●Jesus' name alone shall be in my heart (248-40)
Wohlan, dein Name soll allein
Well-then, Thy name shall alone
{Well then, thy name alone shall}

In meinem Herzen sein.
In my heart be.
{Find place in my heart.}

Jesu meine Freud und Wonne
Jesus my joy and bliss

Meine Hoffnung, Schatz und Teil,
My hope, treasure, and portion,

So will ich dich entzücket nennen,
This shall I thee enraptured call,
{This is what, enraptured, I shall call thee,}

Wenn Brust und Herz zu dir vor Liebe brennen.
When (my) breast and heart for thee with love do-burn.

Mein Erlösung, Schutz und Heil,
My redemption, refuge, and Salvation,

Hirt und König, Licht und Sonne!
Shepherd and king, light and sun!

Doch, Liebster, sage mir:
Yet dearest, tell me:

Wie rühm ich dich, wie dank ich dir?
How extol I thee, how thank I thee?
{How do I extol thee; how do I thank thee?}

Ach! wie soll ich würdiglich,
Ah, how shall I worthily—

Mein Herr Jesu, preisen dich?
(O) my Lord Jesus— praise thee?

41. Tenor Aria (Parody of BWV 213-7)
●Prayer: Help me to live only for thy honor (248-41)
Ich will nur dir zu Ehren leben,
I would only for-thy honor live,

Mein Heiland, gib mir Kraft und Mut,
My Savior, grant me strength and courage,

Daß es mein Herz recht eifrig tut!
That it my heart right zealously might-do!
{So that my heart might do this right zealously!}

Stärke mich,
Strengthen me,

1 Pet. 3:15. In your hearts reverence Christ as Lord...
2 Thess. 1:12. [May] the name of our Lord Jesus...be glorified in you...
Ps. 43:4. I will go to the altar of God, to God my exceeding joy (Luther: Freude und Wonne); and I will praise thee with the lyre, O God, my God.
Ps. 146:5. Happy is he whose help is the God of Jacob, whose hope (Luther: Hoffnung) is in the Lord his God.
Ps. 71:5-6. Thou, O Lord, art my hope, my trust (Luther: Hoffunung), O Lord, from my youth. Upon thee I have leaned from my birth; thou art he who took me from my mother's womb. My praise is continually of thee.
Ps. 73:25-26. [O Lord,] whom have I in heaven but thee? And there is nothing upon earth that I desire besides thee. My flesh and my heart may fail, but God is the strength of my heart and my portion (Luther: Trost und Teil) for ever.
Mt. 13:44-46 [Christ]: The kingdom of heaven is like treasure (Luther: Schatz) hidden in a field, which a man found and covered up; then in his joy he goes and sells all that he has and buys that field.
Ps. 16:5, 8. The Lord is my chosen portion and my cup (Luther: Gut und Teil); thou holdest my lot...I keep the Lord always before me... (Also Ps. 142:5, Lam. 3:24.)
Is. 63:16. ...Thou, O Lord, art our Father, our Redeemer (Luther: Erlöser) from of old is thy name.
Ps. 59:9. O my Strength, I will sing praises to thee; for thou, O God, art my fortress (Luther: Schutz). (Schutz: also Ps. 18:2, 46:7/11, 48:3, 59:17, 94:22)
Ps. 23:1. The Lord is my shepherd, I shall not want; he makes me lie down in green pastures...
Ps. 44:4. [O Lord,] thou art my King and my God, who ordainest victories for Jacob.
Ps. 27:1, 3. The Lord is my light (Luther: Licht) and my salvation (Luther: Heil); whom shall I fear? The Lord is the stronghold of my life; of whom shall I be afraid?
Ps. 109:30. With my mouth I will give great thanks to the Lord (Luther: sehr danken); I will praise him (Luther: ihn rühmen) in the midst of the throng.
Ps. 116:12. What shall I render to the Lord for all his bounty to me?
Ps. 35:18. [O Lord,] I will thank thee (Luther: dir danken) in the great congregation; in the mighty throng I will praise thee (Luther: dich rühmen).

Ps. 115:1. Not to us, O Lord, not to us, but to thy name give glory (Luther: Ehre), for the sake of thy steadfast love and thy faithfulness!
2 Cor. 5:9. ...We make it our aim to please him.
1 Cor. 10:31. ...Whatever you do, do all to the glory of God (Luther: zu Gottes Ehre).
Tit. 2:11-12, 14. The grace of God has appeared for the salvation of all men, training us to renounce irreligion and worldly passions, and to live sober, upright, and godly lives in this world...a people of his own who are zealous for good deeds.
1 Cor. 16:13. ...Stand firm in your faith, be courageous, be strong.
Phil. 1:27. Let your manner of life be worthy of the gospel of Christ... (Also Eph. 4:1, 1 Thess. 2:12.)

Deine Gnade würdiglich
Thy   grace   worthily
{To exalt thy grace worthily}

Und mit   Danken   zu erheben!
And with thanksgiving to   exalt!
{With thanksgiving!}

42. Chorale (New)
●Prayer for Jesus to direct & keep us true always (248-42)
   Jesus richte mein Beginnen,
(O) Jesus direct   my   commencing,

   Jesus bleibe stets bei mir,
(O) Jesus remain ever with me,

   Jesus zäume mir die Sinnen,
(O) Jesus bridle my - senses,

   Jesus sei nur mein Begier.
(O) Jesus be alone my   desire.

   Jesus sei mir in Gedanken,
(O) Jesus be in-my   thoughts,

   Jesu, lasse mich nicht wanken!
(O) Jesus, let   me   not   waver!

V. Ehre sei dir Gott, gesungen
(NBA II/6; BC D7)

1. S. after New Year (BWV 153, 58, 248-V)
*1 Pet. 4:12-19 (Sharing the sufferings of Christ)
*Mt. 2:13-23 (Mary & Joseph's flight to Eygpt)
Librettist: Unknown

43. Chorus (Origin unknown)
●God exalted by whole world for his Salvation (248-43)
   Ehre sei dir   Gott, gesungen,
May "glory" be to-thee, (O) God,   sung,
{May praise be sung to thee, O God,}

Dir   sei Lob und   Dank   bereit',
To-thee be laud and thanksgiving rendered,
{May laud and thanksgiving be rendered to thee,}

Col. 1:9-10. ...We have not ceased to pray for you, asking that you... lead a life worthy of the Lord, fully pleasing to him, bearing fruit in every good work and increasing in the knowledge of God.
Col. 3:17. And whatever you do, in word or deed, do everything in the name of the Lord Jesus, giving thanks to God the Father through him.

*Lk. 2:21. ...He was called Jesus...
2 Thess. 1:11-12. ...We always pray for you, that our God may make you worthy of his call, and may fulfil every good resolve and work of faith by his power, so that the name of our Lord Jesus may be glorified in you...
Ps. 115:1. [O Lord]...to thy name give glory...
Phil. 2:9 God has...bestowed on [Christ] the name which is above every name.
Col. 3:11. ...Christ is all and in all.
Lk. 24: 29. [The disciples] constrained [Jesus], saying, "Stay with us..."
Mt. 28:20 [Christ]: ...Lo, I am with you always, to the close of the age. (Also Ps. 48:14.)
Heb. 13:8. Jesus Christ is the same yesterday and today and for ever.
Jude 1:24-25. Now to him who is able to keep you from falling and to present you without blemish before the presence of his glory with rejoicing...be glory...
Gal. 5:16-17. ...Walk by the Spirit, and do not gratify the desires of the flesh. For the desires of the flesh are against the Spirit, and the desires of the Spirit are against the flesh; for these are opposed to each other...
Ps. 91:14 [God]: Because he cleaves to me in love, (Luther: begehrt mein) I will deliver him; I will protect him, because he knows my name.
Ps. 73:25. [O Lord,] whom have I in heaven but thee? And there is nothing upon earth that I desire besides thee.
2 Tim. 2:8. Remember Jesus Christ (Luther: halt im Gedächtnis), risen from the dead, descended from David, as preached in my gospel.
Heb. 10:23. Let us hold fast the confession of our hope without wavering (Luther: wanken), for he who promised is faithful. (Also Heb. 10:39.)

[Note: This cantata already explores the theme of Epiphany (manifestation of the gospel to the gentiles as represented by the magi) despite the fact that Epiphany proper falls on the following day. (See Cantata VI.)]
Lk. 2:13-14. Suddenly there was with the angel a multitude of the heavenly host praising God and saying, "Glory to God in the highest, and on earth peace among men with whom he is pleased!" (Luther: Ehre sei Gott in der Höhe und Friede auf Erden und den Menschen ein Wohlgefallen!)
Ps. 117:1. Praise the Lord, all nations! Extol him, all peoples!
Ps. 67:3/5. ...O God; let all the peoples praise thee!
Ps. 66:4. [O Lord,] all the earth worships thee; they sing praises to thee... (Also 1 Chron. 16:23, Ps. 96:1.)
Rev. 5:6, 9. Between the throne and the four living creatures and among the elders, I saw a Lamb standing, as though it had been slain... and they sang a new song, saying, "Worthy art thou...for thou wast slain and by thy blood didst ransom men for God from every tribe and tongue and people and nation."

Dich erhebet alle Welt,
Thee exalts the-whole world,
{The whole world exalts thee,}

Weil dir unser Wohl gefällt,
Because thee our welfare pleases,
{Because it pleases thee to establish our welfare,}

Weil anheut unser aller Wunsch gelungen,
Because today our every wish hath-come-true,

Weil uns dein Segen so herrlich erfreut.
Because us thy blessing so splendidly doth-gladden.
{Because thy blessing gladdens us so splendidly.}

44. Tenor Recit. (Evangelist) (New)
●Epiphany: Magi come from the East: Mt. 2:1 (248–44)
Da Jesus geboren war zu Bethlehem im jüdischen Lande,
When Jesus born was in Bethlehem in-the Judean land,

zur Zeit des Königes Herodes, Siehe, da kamen die
in-the time of King Herod, behold, there came -

Weisen vom Morgenlande gen Jerusalem, und sprachen:
wisemen from the-East to Jerusalem, and said:

45. Chorus & Alto Recit. (Magi & Christ's betrothed)
(Probably adapted from BWV 247)
●Epiphany: Magi seek source of light: Mt. 2:2 (248–45)
Chorus:
Wo ist der neugeborne König der Jüden?
Where is the new-born king of-the Jews?

Alto Recit:
Sucht ihn in meiner Brust,
Seek him in my breast,

Hier wohnt er, mir und ihm zur Lust!
Here dwells he, me and him for delight!
{Here he dwells, to his and my delight!}

Chorus:
Wir haben seinen Stern gesehen im Morgenlande, und sind
We have his star seen in-the East, and have

kommen ihn anzubeten.
come him to-worship.

Wohl euch! die ihr dies Licht gesehen!
Blessed-are you, you-who this light have-seen!
{Blessed are you who have seen this light!}

Es ist zu eurem Heil geschehen.
It has for your salvation happened.
{It has happened for your salvation.}

Rev. 14:6–7. Then I saw another angel flying in midheaven, with an eternal gospel to proclaim to those who dwell on earth, to every nation and tribe and tongue and people; and he said with a loud voice, "Fear God and give him glory..."
Acts 28:28. Let it be known to you...that this salvation of God has been sent to the Gentiles...
Rom. 15:8–12. ...Christ became a servant to the uncircumcised...in order to confirm the promises given to the patriarchs, and in order that the Gentiles might glorify God for his mercy. As it is written, "Therefore I will praise thee among the Gentiles, and sing to thy name"; and again it is said, "Rejoice, O Gentiles, with his people"; and again, "Praise the Lord, all Gentiles, and let all the peoples praise him"; and further Isaiah says, "The root of Jesse shall come, he who rises to rule the Gentiles; in him shall the Gentiles hope." (See 2 Sam. 22:50, Ps. 18:49, Deut. 32:43, Is. 11:10, 52:15.)

*→Mt. 2:1 [Gospel of forthcoming day - Epiphany]. Now when Jesus was born in Bethlehem of Judea in the days of Herod the king, behold, wise men from the East came to Jerusalem, saying,

*→Mt. 2:2 [Gospel of forthcoming day - Epiphany]. Where is he who has been born king of the Jews?...
Col. 1:27. ...How great among the Gentiles are the riches of the glory of this mystery, which is Christ in you, the hope of glory.
Eph. 3:17–19. [I pray] that Christ may dwell in your hearts through faith; that you, being rooted and grounded in love, may have power to comprehend with all the saints what is the breadth and length and height and depth, and to know the love of Christ which surpasses knowledge, that you may be filled with all the fulness of God.
Jn. 14:23 [Christ]: If a man loves me, he will keep my word, and my Father will love him, and we will come to him and make our home with him.
S. of S. 2:16 [Bride]: My beloved is mine and I am his... (Also S. of S. 6:3.)

*→Mt. 2:2 [Gospel of forthcoming day - Epiphany]. ...For we have seen his star in the East, and have come to worship him.

*→Is. 60:1–6 [Epistle of forthcoming day - Epiphany]. Arise, shine; for your light has come, and the glory of the Lord has risen upon you. For behold, darkness shall cover the earth, and thick darkness the peoples; but the Lord will arise upon you, and his glory will be seen upon you. And nations shall come to your light, and kings to the brightness of your rising. Lift up your eyes round about, and see; they all gather together, they come to you...Then you shall see and be radiant, your heart shall thrill and rejoice...A multitude of camels shall cover you, the young camels of Midian and Ephah; all those from

Mein Heiland, du, du bist das Licht,
My Savior, thou, thou art the light,

Das auch den Heiden scheinen sollen,
Which also on-the Gentiles was-to-shine,
{Which was to shine on the Gentiles, also,}

Und sie, sie kennen dich noch nicht,
And they, they know thee yet not,
{And they, they do not yet know thee,}

Als sie dich schon verehren wollen.
When they thee already worship would.
{Even though they already come to worship thee.}

Wie hell, wie klar muß nicht dein Schein,
How bright, how clear must not thy radiance—
{How bright, how clear thy radiance must be,}

Geliebter Jesu, sein!
Beloved Jesus—be!
{O beloved Jesus!}

46. Chorale (New)
●Epiphany: God's radiance dispells all darkness (248-46)
Dein Glanz all Finsternis verzehrt,
Thy radiance (doth) all darkness consume;

Die trübe Nacht in Licht verkehrt.
The gloomy night into light doth-transform.
{Doth transform the gloomy night into light.}

Leit uns auf deinen Wegen,
Lead us in thy ways,

Daß dein Gesicht und herrlichs Licht
That thy face and glorious light

Wir ewig schauen mögen!
We eternally may-behold!
{That we may behold thy faith and glorious light eternally!}

47. Bass Aria (Parody of BWV 215-7)
●Epiphany prayer: Illumine me so I do no evil (248-47)
Erleucht auch meine finstre Sinnen,
Illumine also my dark thoughts,

Erleuchte mein Herze
Illumine my heart

Durch der Strahlen klaren Schein!
Through (thy) rays' clear gleam!

Sheba shall come. They shall bring gold and frankincense, and shall proclaim the praise of the Lord.
2 Cor. 4:6. It is the God who said, "Let light shine out of darkness," who has shone in our hearts to give the light of the knowledge of the glory of God in the face of Christ.
Jn. 8:12. Jesus spoke to [the people], saying, "I am the light of the world; he who follows me will not walk in darkness, but will have the light of life."
Jn. 12:44, 46. Jesus cried out and said, "...I have come as light into the world, that whoever believes in me may not remain in darkness."
Rom. 15:8-12. ...Christ became a servant to the uncircumcised...in order that the Gentiles might glorify God for his mercy. As it is written, "Therefore I will praise thee among the Gentiles, and sing to thy name"; and again it is said, "Rejoice, O Gentiles, with his people"; and again, "Praise the Lord, all Gentiles, and let all the peoples praise him"; and further Isaiah says, "The root of Jesse shall come, he who rises to rule the Gentiles; in him shall the Gentiles hope." (See 2 Sam. 22:50, Ps. 18:49, Deut. 32:43, Ps. 117:1, Is. 11:10, 52:15.)
Jn. 1:9. [In Christ] the true light that enlightens every man was coming into the world. (Also Jn. 1:4, 9:5, 11:9, Ps. 36:9.)

Is. 9:2. The people who walked in darkness have seen a great light; those who dwelt in a land of deep darkness, on them has light shined. (Also Mt. 4:16, 2 Cor. 4:6.)
Jn. 12:44, 46. Jesus cried out and said, "...I have come as light into the world, that whoever believes in me may not remain in darkness."
Is. 42:16 [God]: I will lead the blind in a way that they know not, in paths that they have not known I will guide them. I will turn the darkness before them into light...
Jn. 8:12. Jesus spoke to [the people], saying, "I am the light of the world; he who follows me will not walk in darkness, but will have the light of life."
Jn. 12:35-36. Jesus said to them, "The light is with you for a little longer. Walk while you have the light, lest the darkness overtake you; he who walks in the darkness does not know where he goes. While you have the light, believe in the light, that you may become sons of light." (Also Eph. 5:8, 1 Thess. 5:5-6.)
Rev. 21:23. The [heavenly] city has no need of sun or moon to shine upon it, for the glory of God is its light, and its lamp is the Lamb.

Jn. 3:19. This is the judgment, that the light has come into the world, and men loved darkness rather than light, because their deeds were evil.
*→Mt. 2:7-8 [Gospel of forthcoming day - Epiphany]. Then Herod summoned the wise men secretly and ascertained from them what time the star appeared; and he sent them to Bethlehem, saying [deceptively], "Go and search diligently for the child, and when you have found him bring me word, that I too may come and worship him."
Jer. 17:9. The heart is deceitful above all things, and desperately corrupt...
Jn. 12:35-36. Jesus said... "The light is with you for a little longer. Walk while you have the light, lest the darkness overtake you; he

Dein Wort soll   mir die hellste Kerze
Thy Word shall for-me the brightest candle
{Thy Word shall serve as the brightest candle for me}

In allen meinen Werken sein;
In all   my   enterprises be;
{In all my enterprises;}

Dies lässet die Seele nichts Böses beginnen.
This allows the soul   nothing evil to-undertake.
{This keeps the soul from undertaking anything evil.}

who walks in the darkness does not know where he goes. While you have the light, believe in the light, that you may become sons of light."
Eph. 5:8. Once you were darkness, but now you are light in the Lord; walk as children of light. (Also 1 Thess. 5:5.)
Ps. 119:105. [O Lord,] thy word is a lamp to my feet and a light to my path.
Ps. 18:28. Yea, thou dost light my lamp; the Lord my God lightens my darkness.
2 Cor. 4:6. It is the God who said, "Let light shine out of darkness," who has shone in our hearts to give the light of the knowledge of the glory of God in the face of Christ.
1 Jn. 1:7. If we walk in the light, as he is in the light, we have fellowship with one another, and the blood of Jesus his Son cleanses us from all sin.

48. Tenor Recit. (Evangelist) (New)
●Epiphany: King Herod is frightened: Mt. 2:3 (248-48)
Da das der König Herodes hörte, erschrak er, und mit
When this - King Herod heard, alarmed-was he, and with

ihm das ganze Jerusalem.
him   -   all   Jerusalem.

*→Mt. 2:3 [Gospel of forthcoming day - Epiphany]. When Herod the king heard this, he was troubled, and all Jerusalem with him.

49. Alto Recit. (Voice of Christ's betrothed) (New)
●Epiphany: Why be frightened of Jesus' presence? (248-49)
Warum wollt ihr erschrecken?
Why   are you frightened?

Kann meines Jesu Gegenwart euch solche Furcht
Can   my Jesus' presence in-you such   fear

     erwecken?
     awaken?
{Can my Jesus' presence awaken such fear in you?}

O! solltet ihr euch nicht vielmehr darüber freuen,
Oh! Should you - not   rather   over-that rejoice,
{Oh! Should you not rather rejoice,}

Weil   er dadurch verspricht
Because he thereby promises
{Because, by his presence, he promises}

Der Menschen Wohlfahrt zu erneuen.
  -   Mankind's welfare to   renew.
{To renew mankind's welfare?}

1 Jn. 4:16-18. So we know and believe the love God has for us. God is love, and he who abides in love abides in God, and God abides in him. In this is love perfected with us, that we may have confidence for the day of judgment, because as he is so are we in this world. There is no fear in love, but perfect love casts out fear. For fear has to do with punishment, and he who fears is not perfected in love.
Rev. 6:15-17. The kings of the earth and the great men and the generals and the rich and the strong, and every one, slave and free, hid in the caves and among the rocks of the mountains, calling to the mountains and rocks, "Fall on us and hide us from the face of him who is seated on the throne, and from the wrath of the Lamb; for the great day of their wrath has come, and who can stand before it?" (Also Is. 2:19, Lk. 23:30.)
Jn. 3:17. God sent the Son into the world, not to condemn the world, but that the world might be saved through him.
Lk. 2:8-10. ...There were shepherds out in the field, keeping watch over their flock by night. And an angel of the Lord appeared to them, and the glory of the Lord shone around them, and they were filled with fear. And the angel said to them, "Be not afraid; for behold, I bring you good news of a great joy which will come to all the people."

50. Tenor Recit. (Evangelist) (New)
●Epiphany: Herod assembles chief priests: Mt. 2:4-6 (248-50)
Und   ließ versammeln alle   Hohepriester und
And (he) let   assemble all (the) high-priests and

Schriftgelehrten unter dem Volk, und erforschete von
scribes   among the people, and   inquired   of

ihnen, wo Christus sollte geboren werden. Und sie sagten
them, where Christ should   be-born.   And they said

*→Mt. 2:4-6 [Gospel of forthcoming day - Epiphany]. And assembling all the chief priests and scribes of the people, he inquired of them where the Christ was to be born. They told him, "In Bethlehem of Judea; for so it is written by the prophet: 'And you, O Bethlehem, in the land of Judah, are by no means least among the rulers of Judah; for from you shall come a ruler who will govern my people Israel.'"
Mic. 5:2, 4. But you, O Bethlehem Ephrathah, who are little to be among the clans of Judah, from you shall come forth for me one

ihm: zu Bethlehem im jüdischen Lande; denn also
to-him: in Bethlehem in-the Judean land; for thus (it)

stehet geschrieben durch den Propheten: Und du
stands written by the prophets: And thou

Bethlehem im jüdischen Lande bist mit nichten die
Bethlehem in-the Judean land art by no-means the

Kleinste unter den Fürsten Juda; denn aus dir soll mir
smallest among the princes of-Judah; for out-of thee shall -

kommen der Herzog, der über mein Volk Israel
come the (prince), who over my people Israel

ein Herr sei.
a ruller shall-be.

51. Soprano, Alto, & Tenor Trio (Origin unknown)
●Christ's coming not recognized by some (248-51)
Ach, wenn wird die Zeit erscheinen?
Ah, when will the time appear?

Ach! Wann kommt der Trost der Seinen?
Ah! When comes the consolation of his-own (people)?
{Ah, when will the consolation of his people come?}

Schweigt, er ist schon würklich hier!
Hush! He is already really here!

Jesu, ach, so komm zu mir!
Jesus, ah, then come to me!

52. Alto Recit. (Voice of Christ's betrothed) (New)
●Hearts given to Christ become his throne (248-52)
Mein Liebster herrschet schon.
My beloved rules already.

Ein Herz, das seine Herrschaft liebet,
A heart, that his dominion loves,
{A heart that loves his rulership,}

Und sich ihm ganz zu eigen gibet,
And itself to-him completely for his-own gives,
{And gives itself completely to him to own,}

Ist meines Jesu Thron.
Is my Jesus' throne.
{Is the throne for my Jesus.}

who is to be ruler in Israel, whose origin is from of old, from ancient days...And he shall stand and feed his flock in the strength of the Lord, in the majesty of the name of the Lord his God. And they shall dwell secure, for now he shall be great to the ends of the earth.

Lk. 2:25–32. Now there was a man in Jerusalem, whose name was Simeon, and this man was righteous and devout, looking for the consolation of Israel (Luther: Trost Israels), and the Holy Spirit was upon him. And it had been revealed to him by the Holy Spirit that he should not see death before he had seen the Lord's Christ. And inspired by the Spirit he came into the temple; and when the parents brought in the child Jesus, to do for him according to the custom of the law, he took him up in his arms and blessed God and said, "Lord, now lettest thou thy servant depart in peace, according to thy word; for mine eyes have seen thy salvation which thou hast prepared in the presence of all peoples, a light for revelation to the Gentiles, and for glory to thy people Israel." (See Is. 40:1, 49:13; 42:6, 49:6, 52:10.)
Jn. 1:9–11. [In Christ] the true light that enlightens every man was coming into the world. He was in the world, and the world was made through him, yet the world knew him not. He came to his own home, and his own people (Luther: die Seinen) received him not.
Acts 28:28. Let it be known...then that this salvation of God has been sent to the Gentiles; they will listen.
Rom. 11:11. ...Salvation has come to the Gentiles, so as to make Israel jealous. (Also Rom. 10:19–11:14.)

Jn. 18:36. Jesus answered [Pilate], "My kingship is not of this world; if my kingship were of this world, my servants would fight...but my kingship is not from the world." Pilate said to him, "So you are a king?" Jesus answered, "You say that I am a king. For this I was born, and for this I have come into the world..."
Lk. 17:20–21. Being asked by the Pharisees when the kingdom of God was coming, [Jesus] answered them, "The kingdom of God is not coming with signs to be observed; nor will they say, 'Lo, here it is!' or 'There!' for behold, the kingdom of God is in the midst of you (Luther: inwendig in euch)."
Jn. 14:23. Jesus [said]... "If a man loves me, he will keep my word, and my Father will love him, and we will come to him and make our home with him."
Eph. 3:16–19. [I pray] that according to the riches of [God's] glory he may grant you to be strengthened with might through his Spirit in the inner man, and that Christ may dwell in your hearts through faith; that you, being rooted and grounded in love, may have power to comprehend with all the saints what is the breadth and length and height and depth, and to know the love of Christ which surpasses knowledge, that you may be filled with all the fulness of God.

53. Chorale (New)
●Heart is no fine residence but God illumines it (248-53)
Zwar   ist solche   Herzensstube
To-be-sure is   such (a) heart's-chamber
{To be sure, such a heart's chamber is}

Wohl kein schöner Fürstensaal,
Indeed no beautiful hall-of-princes,

Sondern eine finstre Grube;
But-rather a   dark   cavity;

Doch, sobald dein Gnadenstrahl
Yet,   As-soon-as thy ray-of-grace
{Yet, just as soon as thy ray of grace}

In denselbe nur wird blinken,
Into the-same just will flash,
{Flashes into it,}

Wird es voller Sonnen dünken.
Will it full-of sunshine seem.
{It will seem filled with sunshine.}

VI. Herr, wenn die stolzen Feinde schnauben
(NBA II/6; BC D7)

Epiphany (BWV 65, 123, 248-VI, [200])
*Is. 60:1-6 (Prophecy: the Lord will shine upon you and
nations will come to your light)
*Mt. 2:1-12 (The Magi come from the East)
Librettist: Unknown

54. Chorus (Adapted from nonextant BWV 248a-1)
●Escape from murderous foe assured by God's help (248-54)
Herr, wenn die stolzen Feinde   schnauben,
Lord, when (our) proud   foes (breathe-vengeance),

So   gib, daß wir im festen Glauben
Then grant, that we in firm   faith
{Then grant that, firm in faith, we}

Nach deiner Macht und Hülfe   sehn!
To   thy   might and help would-look!
{Would look to thy might and thy help!}

Wir wollen dir allein vertrauen,
We would thee alone   trust,
{We want to trust thee alone,}

So können wir den scharfen Klauen
Thus can   we the sharp   claws
{Thus we can escape the sharp claws}

*→Is. 60:1-2 [Epistle of forthcoming day - Epiphany]. Arise, shine;
for your light has come, and the glory of the Lord has risen upon you.
For behold, darkness shall cover the earth, and thick darkness the
peoples; but the Lord will arise upon you, and his glory will be seen
upon you.
Is. 9:2. The people who walked in darkness have seen a great light;
those who dwelt in a land of deep darkness, on them has light shined.
(Also Mt. 4:16.)
Eph. 4:17-18. ...[The unregenerate Gentiles] are darkened in their
understanding, alienated from the life of God because of the
ignorance that is in them, due to their hardness of heart.
Jer. 17:9-10. The heart is deceitful above all things, and desperately
corrupt; who can understand it?
2 Cor. 4:6. It is the God who said, "Let light shine out of darkness,"
who has shone in our hearts to give the light of the knowledge of the
glory of God in the face of Christ.
Ps. 18:28. ...The Lord my God lightens my darkness.
Jn. 1:9. [In Christ] the true light that enlightens every man was coming
into the world.
2 Pet. 1:19. And we have the prophetic word made more sure. You
will do well to pay attention to this as to a lamp shining in a dark
place, until the day dawns and the morning star rises in your hearts.
1 Pet. 2:9. You are a chosen race, a royal priesthood, a holy nation,
God's own people, that you may declare the wonderful deeds of him
who called you out of darkness into his marvelous light.

Acts 9:1. Saul [was] still breathing threats and murder (Luther:
schnaubte noch mit Drohen und Morden) against the disciples of the
Lord...
Ps. 56:1-2. Be gracious to me, O God, for...many fight against me
proudly. (Also Sirach 51:10.)
Ps. 25:19-20. Consider how many are my foes, and with what violent
hatred they hate me. Oh guard my life, and deliver me; let me not be
put to shame, for I take refuge in thee. (Also Ps. 3:1-8, 60:11/108:12.)
Mt. 2:13-17. Now...behold, an angel of the Lord appeared to Joseph
in a dream and said, "Rise, take the child and his mother, and flee to
Egypt, and remain there till I tell you; for Herod is about to search
for the child, to destroy him." And he rose and took the child and his
mother by night, and departed to Egypt, and remained there until the
death of Herod...Then Herod, when he saw that he had been tricked
by the wise men, was in a furious rage, and he sent and killed all the
male children in Bethlehem and in all that region who were two years
old or under, according to the time which he had ascertained from the
wise men.
Ps. 124:2-7. If it had not been the Lord who was on our side, when
men rose up against us, then they would have swallowed us up alive,
when their anger was kindled against us; then the flood would have
swept us away, the torrent would have gone over us; then over us
would have gone the raging waters. Blessed be the Lord, who has

Des Feindes unversehrt entgehn.
Of-the foe   uninjured   escape.
{Of the foe uninjured.}

not given us as prey to their teeth! We have escaped as a bird from the snare of the fowlers; the snare is broken, and we have escaped!

55. Tenor & Bass Recit. (Evangelist & Herod) (New)
●Herod plots to kill Christchild: Mt. 2:7–8 (248-55)
Da   berief Herodes die Weisen heimlich, und erlernet
Then summoned Herod the wise-men secretly,   and ascertained

mit Fleiß von ihnen, wenn der Stern erschienen wäre.
with diligence from them, when the star   had-appeared.

Und weiset sie gen Bethlehem, und sprach: Ziehet hin, und
And sent them to Bethlehem, and said: Go   and

forschet fleißig nach dem Kindlein, und wenn ihr's
search diligently for the child,   and when you-it

findet, sagt mir's wieder, daß ich auch   komme und
find,   bring-me-word, so-that I also (may) come and

es anbete.
it worship.

***Mt. 2:7–8.** Then Herod summoned the wise men secretly and ascertained from them what time the star appeared; and he sent them to Bethlehem, saying, "Go and search diligently for the child, and when you have found him bring me word, that I too may come and worship him."*

56. Soprano Recit. (Adapted from BWV 248a-2)
●Herod's deceitful heart is known to the Son (248-56)
Du   Falscher,   suche nur den Herrn zu fällen,
You treacherous-one, seek just the Lord to bring-down,
{You treacherous one, just try to bring down the Lord,}

Nimm alle   falsche List,
(Use) all (the) deceitful cunning (you can)

Dem Heiland nachzustellen;
The Savior   to-waylay;
{To waylay the Savior;}

Der, dessen Kraft kein Mensch ermißt,
He whose power no   man can-measure,

Bleibt   doch   in sich'rer Hand.
Remains nevertheless in secure hand(s).
{Remains in secure hands despite your plans.}

Dein falsches Herz ist schon,
Your deceitful heart is already,
{Your deceitful heart}

Nebst aller seiner List,
With all   its cunning,
{With all its cunning,}

Des   Höchsten Sohn,
To-the Most-High's Son,
{Is already very well known to the Most High's Son,}

Den du zu stürzen suchst, sehr wohl bekannt.
Whom you to overthrow do-seek, very well known.
{Whom you seek to overthrow.}

Ps. 2:1–9. Why do the nations conspire, and the peoples plot in vain? The kings of the earth set themselves, and the rulers take counsel together, against the Lord and his anointed, saying, "Let us burst their bonds asunder, and cast their cords from us." He who sits in the heavens laughs; the Lord has them in derision. Then he will speak to them in his wrath, and terrify them in his fury, saying, "I have set my king on Zion, my holy hill." I will tell of the decree of the Lord: He said to me, "You are my son, today I have begotten you. Ask of me, and I will make the nations your heritage, and the ends of the earth your possession. You shall break them with a rod of iron, and dash them in pieces like a potter's vessel."
Prov. 21:30. No wisdom, no understanding, no counsel, can avail against the Lord.
Prov. 26:23–26. Like the glaze covering an earthen vessel are smooth lips with an evil heart. He who hates, dissembles with his lips and harbors deceit in his heart; when he speaks graciously, believe him not, for there are seven abominations in his heart; though his hatred be covered with guile, his wickedness will be exposed... (Also Job 15:34–35, Ps. 28:3, 62:4.)
Jer. 17:9–10. The heart is deceitful above all things, and desperately corrupt; who can understand it? "I the Lord search the mind and try the heart, to give to every man according to his ways, according to the fruit of his doings."
Is. 47:10 [God]: You felt secure in your wickedness, you said, "No one sees me"...
Ps. 33:13–15. The Lord looks down from heaven, he sees all the sons of men; from where he sits enthroned he looks forth on all the inhabitants of the earth, he who fashions the hearts of all, and observes all their deeds.
1 Sam. 16:7. ...Man looks on the outward appearance, but the Lord looks on the heart. (Also Lk. 16:15.)
Jn. 2:25. [Jesus] knew all men and needed no one to bear witness of man; for he himself knew what was in man.

57. Soprano Aria (Adapted from BWV 248a–3)
● Mortal schemes easily overthrown by God (248-57)
Nur ein Wink von seinen Händen
Just one wave of   his   hands

Stürzt   ohnmächt'ger Menschen Macht.
Overthrows feeble   human   might.
{Can overthrow the feeble might of humans.}

Hier wird alle Kraft   verlacht!
Here is   all strength laughed-at!
{Here all such strength is laughed at!}

Spricht der Höchste nur ein Wort
Says   the Most-High but one word
{If the Most High says but one word}

Seiner Feinde Stolz zu enden,
His   foes' arrogance to end,
{To end his foes' arrogance,}

O, so müssen sich sofort
Oh, then are   - immediately (their)
{Oh, then their mortal designs}

Sterblicher Gedanken wenden.
Mortal   designs changed.
{Are immediately thwarted.}

2 Maccabees (Apocrypha) 8:18. They trust to arms and acts of daring... but we trust in the Almighty God, who is able with a single nod to strike down those who are coming against us and even the whole world.

Job 34:24–25. [God] shatters the mighty (Luther: Stolzen) without investigation, and sets others in their place. Thus, knowing their works, he overturns them in the night, and they are crushed.

Ps. 2:1–4. Why do the nations conspire (Luther: toben), and the peoples plot in vain? The kings of the earth set themselves, and the rulers take counsel together, against the Lord and his anointed, saying, "Let us burst their bonds asunder, and cast their cords from us." He who sits in the heavens laughs; the Lord has them in derision.

Ps. 59:8. Thou, O Lord, dost laugh at them; thou dost hold all the nations in derision.

Ezek. 12:25, 28 [God]: I the Lord will speak the word which I will speak, and it will be performed. It will no longer be delayed...None of my words will be delayed any longer, but the word which I speak will be performed, says the Lord God.

Lk. 1:51–52. [God] has shown strength with his arm, he has scattered the proud in the imagination of their hearts, he has put down the mighty from their thrones...

Is. 13:11 [God]: ...I will put an end to the pride of the arrogant, and lay low the haughtiness of the ruthless.

1 Sam. 2:10. The adversaries of the Lord shall be broken to pieces; against them he will thunder in heaven...

Ps. 33:10. The Lord brings the counsel of the nations to nought; he frustrates the plans of the peoples.

Prov. 21:30. No wisdom, no understanding, no counsel, can avail against the Lord.

58. Tenor Recit. (Evangelist) (New)
● Magi present their gifts to Christchild: Mt. 2:9-11 (248-58)
Als   sie nun den König gehöret hatten, zogen sie hin.
When they - the king   had-heard, departed they - .

Und siehe, der Stern, den sie im Morgenlande
And lo, the star, which they in   the-East

gesehen hatten, ging für ihnen hin, bis daß er kam,
had-seen,   went before them - , till - it came,

und stund oben über, da das Kindlein war. Da sie den
and stood - over, where the child was. When they the

Stern sahen, wurden sie hoch erfreuet; und gingen in
star saw, were they greatly cheered; and went into

das Haus, und funden das Kindlein mit Maria, seine Mutter,
the house, and found the child with Mary, his mother,

und fielen nieder, und beteten es an und taten ihre
and fell down, and worshiped him - and opened their

Schätze auf und schenkten ihm Gold, Weihrauch, und
treasures - and   gave   him gold, frankincense, and

Myrrhen.
myrrh.

*Mt. 2:9–11. *When they had heard the king they went their way; and lo, the star which they had seen in the East went before them, till it came to rest over the place where the child was. When they saw the star, they rejoiced exceedingly with great joy; and going into the house they saw the child with Mary his mother, and they fell down and worshiped him. Then, opening their treasures, they offered him gifts, gold and frankincense and myrrh.*

*Is. 60:1–6. *Arise, shine; for your light has come, and the glory of the Lord has risen upon you. For behold, darkness shall cover the earth, and thick darkness the peoples; but the Lord will arise upon you, and his glory will be seen upon you. And nations shall come to your light, and kings to the brightness of your rising. Lift up your eyes round about, and see; they all gather together, they come to you...Then you shall see and be radiant, your heart shall thrill and rejoice...A multitude of camels shall cover you, the young camels of Midian and Ephah; all those from Sheba shall come. They shall bring gold and frankincense, and shall proclaim the praise of the Lord.*

59. Chorale (New)
●Gift I bring to Christ in manger is my very self (248-59)
Ich steh an deiner Krippen hier,
I stand by thy manger here,

O Jesulein, mein Leben;
Oh little-Jesus, (thou who art) my life;

Ich komme, bring und schenke dir,
I come, bring, and give thee,

Was du mir hast gegeben.
What thou to-me hast given.
{What thou hast given to me.}

Nimm hin! es ist mein Geist und Sinn,
Accept (it)! It is my spirit and mind,

Herz, Seel und Mut, nimm alles hin,
Heart, soul, and mettle: accept (it) all - ,

Und laß dir's wohl gefallen.
And let it-thee well please.
{And let it please thee well.}

*Mt. 2:11. Going into the house [the wise men] saw the child with Mary his mother, and they fell down and worshiped him. Then, opening their treasures, they offered him gifts, gold and frankincense and myrrh.
Ps. 116:12. What shall I render to the Lord for all his bounty to me?
Rom. 14:8. If we live, we live to the Lord...
Phil. 1:21. To me to live is Christ...
1 Cor. 4:7. ...What have you that you did not receive? If then you received it, why do you boast as if it were not a gift?
1 Chron. 29:12, 14, 16. [O Lord,] both riches and honor come from thee...All things come from thee, and of thy own have we given thee... O Lord our God, all this abundance that we have provided...comes from thy hand and is all thy own. (Also Jms. 1:17.)
Rom. 12:1. I appeal to you therefore, brethren, by the mercies of God, to present your bodies as a living sacrifice, holy and acceptable to God, which is your spiritual worship.
2 Cor. 8:3, 5. [The believers of the churches in Macedonia] gave according to their means, as I can testify, and beyond their means, of their own free will...and this, not as we expected, but first they gave themselves to the Lord...

60. Tenor Recit. (Evangelist) (New)
●Magi warned to return by a different way: Mt. 2:12 (248-60)
Und Gott befahl ihnen im Traum, daß sie sich nicht
And God commanded them in-a dream, that they - not

sollten wieder zu Herodes lenken. Und zogen durch
should again to Herod (return). And (they) went by

einen andern Weg wieder in ihr Land.
a different way (back) to their country.

Mt. 2:12. And being warned in a dream not to return to Herod, they departed to their own country by another way.

61. Tenor Recit. (Adapted from BWV 248a-4)
●Jesus remains with me though the wise men depart (248-61)
So geht!
So go!

Genug, mein Schatz geht nicht von hier,
Enough (for me that) my treasure goes not from here,
{It is enough for me that my treasure does not leave,}

Er bleibet da bei mir,
He remains (here) by me;

Ich will ihn auch nicht von mir lassen.
I will him also not from me let-part.
{I will also not let him part from me.}

Sein Arm wird mich aus Lieb,
His arm will me in love,
{His arm will embrace me in love,}

*Mt. 2:11-12. ...Opening their treasures, [the wise men] offered him gifts, gold and frankincense and myrrh. And...they departed to their own country...
Ps. 73:25. [O Lord,] whom have I in heaven but thee? And there is nothing upon earth that I desire besides thee.
Mt. 28:20 [Christ]: ...Lo, I am with you always to the close of the age.
Heb. 13:5-6. ...[God] has said, "I will never fail you nor forsake you." Hence we can confidently say, "The Lord is my helper, I will not be afraid; what can man do to me?" (See Deut. 31:6, 8; Josh. 1:5.)
Gen. 32:26. ...Jacob said, "I will not let you go, unless you bless me."
S. of S. 3:4 [Bride]: ...I found him whom my soul loves. I held him, and would not let him go...
Ps. 63:8. [O Lord,] my soul clings to thee; thy right hand upholds me.

Mit sanftmutsvollem Trieb
With gentle desire

Und größter Zärtlichkeit umfassen;
And (the) greatest tenderness embrace;
{And with the greatest tenderness;}

Er soll mein Bräutigam verbleiben,
He shall my bridegroom remain,
{He shall remain my bridegroom,}

Ich will ihm Brust und Herz verschreiben.
I will to-him (my) breast and heart assign.
{I will assign my breast and heart to him.}

Ich weiß gewiß, er liebet mich,
I know assuredly, he loves me,

Mein Herz liebt ihn auch inniglich
My heart loves him, too, fervently,

Und wird ihn ewig ehren.
And will him eternally honor.
{And will honor him eternally.}

Was könnte mich nun für ein Feind
How could me now (any) - foe
{How could any foe hurt me now}

Bei solchem Glück versehren?
Amidst such prosperity hurt?
{Amidst such prosperity?}

Du, Jesu, bist und bleibst mein Freund;
Thou, Jesus, art and remainest my friend;

Und werd ich ängstlich zu dir flehn:
And (if) I anxiously to thee do-cry:

Herr, hilf!, so laß mich Hülfe sehn!
"Lord help!" then let me help see!
{"Lord help," then let me see thy help!}

62. Tenor Aria (Adapted from BWV 248a–5)
●Foe cannot hurt me if Jesus is with me (248–62)
Nun mögt ihr stolzen Feinde schrecken,
Now may you proud foes terrify,
{So now you proud foes can try to terrify me;}

Was könnt ihr mir für Furcht erwecken?
How can you in-me (any) fear awaken?
{How can you awaken any fear in me?}

Mein Schatz, mein Hort ist hier bei mir.
My treasure, my refuge is here with me.

Ihr mögt euch noch so grimmig stellen,
You may yourselves yet so fierce present,
{Though you appear ever so fierce,}

S. of S. 2:6 [Bride]: O that his left hand were under my head, and that his right hand embraced me!

Hos. 2:19–20 [God]: I will betroth you to me for ever; I will betroth you to me in righteousness and in justice, in steadfast love, and in mercy. I will betroth you to me in faithfulness; and you shall know the Lord.

2 Cor. 11:2. I feel a divine jealousy for you, for I betrothed you to Christ to present you as a pure bride to her one husband.

Rev. 19:6–9. Then I heard what seemed to be the voice of a great multitude, like the sound of many waters and like the sound of mighty thunderpeals, crying, "Hallelujah! For the Lord our God the Almighty reigns. Let us rejoice and exult and give him the glory, for the marriage of the Lamb has come, and his Bride has made herself ready; it was granted her to be clothed with fine linen, bright and pure"—for the fine linen is the righteous deeds of the saints. And the angel said to me, "Write this: Blessed are those who are invited to the marriage supper of the Lamb."... (Also Eph. 5:25–27, Ezek. 16:9–13, Is. 61:10, 62:5, Jn. 3:29.)

Mt. 22:37 [Christ]: ...You shall love the Lord your God with all your heart, and with all your soul, and with all your mind. This is the great and first commandment.

S. of S. 2:16 [Bride]: My beloved (Luther: Freund) is mine and I am his... (Also S. of S. 6:3.)

Ps. 118:6–7. With the Lord on my side I do not fear. What can man do to me? The Lord is on my side to help me; I shall look in triumph on those who hatA me. (Also Ps. 27:1–3, 56:3–4.)

Rom. 8:31. What then shall we say to this? If God is for us, who is against us?

Jn. 15:14–15 [Christ]: You are my friends if you do what I command you. No longer do I call you servants, for the servant does not know what his master is doing; but I have called you friends, for all that I have heard from my Father I have made known to you.

Ps. 27:7. Hear, O Lord, when I cry aloud, be gracious to me and answer me! (Also Ps. 4:1, 28:2.)

Ps. 102:2. Do not hide thy face from me in the day of my distress! Incline thy ear to me; answer me speedily in the day when I call! (Also Ps. 13:1, 44:24, 69:17, 88:14, 143:7.)

Ps. 17:6–7. I call upon thee, for thou wilt answer me, O God; incline thy ear to me, hear my words. Wondrously show thy steadfast love, O savior of those who seek refuge from their adversaries at thy right hand.

Ps. 27:1, 3. The Lord is my light and my salvation; whom shall I fear? The Lord is the stronghold of my life; of whom shall I be afraid?... Though a host encamp against me, my heart shall not fear; though war arise against me, yet I will be confident.

Rom. 8:31. 35–37. What then shall we say to this? If God is for us, who is against us?...Who shall separate us from the love of Christ? Shall tribulation, or distress, or persecution, or famine, or nakedness, or peril, or sword? As it is written, "For thy sake we are being killed all the day long; we are regarded as sheep to be slaughtered." No, in all these things we are more than conquerors through him who loved us.

Ps. 37:12–15. The wicked plots against (Luther: droht) the righteous, and gnashes his teeth at him; but the Lord laughs at the wicked, for he sees that his day is coming. The wicked draw the sword and bend

Droht   nur mich ganz und gar zu   fällen;
Threaten - me   completely   to bring-down;
{Threaten to bring me down completely;}

Doch seht! mein Heiland wohnet hier.
Yet   see! My   Savior   dwells   here.

63. S.A.T.B. Recit. (Adapted from BWV 248a–6)
●Hell can do nothing; we are in Jesus' hands (248-63)
Was will der Hölle Schrecken   nun,
What would - hell's   terror   (do) now,
{What can hell's terror do now,}

Was   will uns Welt und Sünde tun,
What would to-us world and   sin   do,
{What can the world and sin do to us,}

Da   wir in Jesu Händen ruhn?
Since we in Jesus' hands   rest?
{Since we rest in Jesus' hands?}

64. Chorus (Chorale) (Adapted from BWV 248a–7)
●Foes have all been conquered in Christ (248-64)
Nun seid ihr wohl gerochen
Now are you well avenged
{Now you are well avenged}

An eurer Feinde Schar,
On your foe's host,
{On your host of foes,}

Denn Christus hat zerbrochen
For   Christ has   broken

Was euch zuwider war.
What to-you contrary was.
{That which was opposing you.}

Tod, Teufel, Sünd und Hölle
Death, devil, sin, and hell

Sind ganz und gar geschwächt;
Are   completely   weakened;

Bei Gott hat   seine Stelle
With God has (as) its   place

Das menschliche Geschlecht.
The   human   race.
{The human race has now been given a place with God.}

their bows, to bring down (Luther: fällen) the poor and needy, to slay those who walk uprightly; their sword shall enter their own heart, and their bows shall be broken.
Ps. 118:6–7. With the Lord on my side I do not fear. What can man do to me? The Lord is on my side to help me; I shall look in triumph on those who hate me.

Mt. 16:17, 18 [Christ]: ...I will build my church, and the powers of death (Luther: Pforten der Hölle) shall not prevail against it.
Jn. 16:33 [Christ]: I have said this to you, that in me you may have peace. In the world you have tribulation; but be of good cheer, I have overcome the world. (Also 1 Jn. 2:13, 14.)
1 Jn. 4:4. Little children, you are of God, and have overcome [the spirits that are not of God]; for he who is in you is greater than he who is in the world.
Rom. 8:38–39. I am sure that neither death, nor life, nor angels, nor principalities, nor things present, nor things to come, nor powers, nor height, nor depth, nor anything else in all creation, will be able to separate us from the love of God in Christ Jesus our Lord.

Rom. 8:37. In all these things we are more than conquerors through him who loved us.
Is. 9:4. For the yoke of his burden, and the staff for his shoulder, the rod of his oppressor, thou [O Lord] hast broken... (Also Is. 10:27, 14:25.)
Col. 2:13–15. And you, who were dead in trespasses and the uncircumcision of your flesh, God made alive together with him, having forgiven us all our trespasses, having canceled the bond which stood against us with its legal demands; this he set aside, nailing it to the cross. He disarmed the principalities and powers and made a public example of them, triumphing over them in him.
1 Cor. 15:25–26. [Christ] must reign until he has put all his enemies under his feet. The last enemy to be destroyed is death. (Also 2 Tim. 1:10, Is. 25:8.)
1 Cor. 15:54–55, 57. When the perishable puts on the imperishable, and the mortal puts on immortality, then shall come to pass the saying that is written: "Death is swallowed up in victory." "O death, where is thy victory? O death, where is thy sting?"...Thanks be to God, who gives us the victory through our Lord Jesus Christ.
Heb. 2:14–15. ...[Christ] himself...partook of [flesh and blood], that through death he might destroy him who has the power of death, that is, the devil, and deliver all those who through fear of death were subject to lifelong bondage.
1 Jn. 3:8. He who commits sin is of the devil; for the devil has sinned from the beginning. The reason the Son of God appeared was to destroy the works of the devil.
Jn. 16:33 [Christ]: I have said this to you, that in me you may have peace. In the world you have tribulation; but be of good cheer, I have overcome the world. (Also 1 Jn. 2:13, 14; 4:4.)
Eph. 2:4–6. God...made us alive together with Christ...and raised us up with him, and made us sit with him in the heavenly places in Christ Jesus.

BWV 249 Easter Oratorio
Kommet, eilet und laufet
(NBA II/7; BC D8a/b)

Easter Sunday (BWV 4, 31, 249)
*1 Cor. 5:6–8 (Christ, our paschal lamb has been sacrificed)
*Mk. 16:1–8 (The resurrection of Christ)
Librettist: perhaps Picander (Christian Friedrich Henrici).
With the exception of the recitatives, which are newly
composed, this cantata is an adaptation of secular cantata
BWV 249a.

1. Sinfonia

2. Adagio

3. Tenor & Bass Duet (Peter & John)
●Easter: Run to the empty tomb where Christ was! (249-3)
Kommt, eilet und laufet, ihr flüchtigen Füße,
Come, hurry and run, ye fleet feet,

Erreichet die Höhle, die Jesum bedeckt!
Get-to the cave, which Jesus doth-cover!
{Get to the cave which hath concealed Jesus!}

Lachen und Scherzen
Laughter and jesting

Begleitet die Herzen,
Accompanies (our) hearts (as we go),

Denn unser Heil ist auferweckt.
For our Salvation (has-been) restored-to-life.

4. S.A.T.B. Recit.
●Easter: Embalming spices & tears prepared in vain (249-4)
Alto: (Mary Magdalene)
O kalter Männer Sinn!
O cold male disposition!

Wo ist die Liebe hin,
Where has that love gone,

Die ihr dem Heiland schuldig seid?
Which you to-the Savior do-owe?
{Which you owe the Savior?}

Soprano: (Mary, mother of James)
Ein schwaches Weib muß euch beschämen!
A weak woman must you shame!
{A weak woman must put you to shame in this!}

Tenor: (Peter)
Ach, ein betrübtes Grämen
Ah, a disconsolate grieving
{Ah, in our disconsolate grieving}

Jn. 20:1–9. Now on the first day of the week Mary Magdalene came
to the tomb early, while it was still dark, and saw that the stone had
been taken away from the tomb. So she ran, and went to Simon Peter
and the other disciple, the one whom Jesus loved, and said to them,
"They have taken the Lord out of the tomb, and we do not know
where they have laid him." Peter then came out with the other
disciple, and they went toward the tomb. They both ran, but the other
disciple outran Peter and reached the tomb first; and stooping to look
in, he saw the linen cloths lying there, but he did not go in. Then
Simon Peter came, following him, and went into the tomb; he saw the
linen cloths lying, and the napkin, which had been on his head, not
lying with the linen cloths but rolled up in a place by itself. Then the
other disciple, who reached the tomb first, also went in, and he saw
and believed; for as yet they did not know the scripture, that he must
rise from the dead.
Mt. 28:6. ...He has risen, as he said...
Lk. 24:34. ...The Lord has risen indeed...!

Mt. 28:1. ...Toward the dawn of the first day of the week, Mary
Magdalene and the other Mary went to see the sepulchre.
Lk. 24:1–26. On the first day of the week, at early dawn, [the women]
went to the tomb, taking the spices which they had prepared. And
they found the stone rolled away from the tomb, but when they went
in they did not find the body. While they were perplexed about this,
behold, two men stood by them in dazzling apparel; and as they were
frightened and bowed their faces to the ground, the men said to them,
"Why do you seek the living among the dead? Remember how he told
you, while he was still in Galilee, that the Son of man must be
delivered into the hands of sinful men, and be crucified, and on the
third day rise." And they remembered his words, and returning from
the tomb they told all this to the eleven and to all the rest. Now it was
Mary Magdalene and Joanna and Mary the mother of James and the
other women with them who told this to the apostles; but these words
seemed to them an idle tale, and they did not believe them. That very
day two of them were going to a village named Emmaus...and talking
with each other about all these things that had happened. While they
were talking and discussing together, Jesus himself drew near and
went with them. But their eyes were kept from recognizing him. And

Bass: (John)
Und banges Herzeleid
And anxious sorrow
{And in our anxious sorrow}

Tenor/Bass: (Peter & John)
Hat mit gesalznen Tränen
Did with salty tears

Und wehmutsvollem Sehnen
And melancholy yearning—

Ihm eine Salbung zugedacht,
For-him an annointing intend,
{And in our anxious sorrow we intended—with salty tears and melancholy yearning—to bring an annointing of a different sort,}

Soprano/Alto: (Mary & Mary Magdalene)
Die ihr, wie wir, umsonst gemacht.
Which you, as we, in-vain have-prepared.
{Which you, as we, have prepared in vain.}

5. Soprano Aria (Mary, mother of James)
●Easter promise: Myrrh will be exhanged for laurel (249-5)
Seele, deine Spezereien
(O) soul, thy spices

Sollen nicht mehr Myrrhen sein.
Shall no longer myrrh be.
{Shall no longer consist of myrrh.}

Denn allein
For only

Mit dem Lorbeerkranze prangen,
With (a) laurel-wreath resplendent,

Stillt dein ängstliches Verlangen.
Is-stilled thy anxious longing.
{Will thy anxious longing be stilled.}

6. Alto, Tenor, Bass Recit.
●Easter: Disciples arrive at tomb and find it empty (249-6)
Tenor: (Peter)
Hier ist die Gruft
Here is the tomb

he said to them, "What is this conversation which you are holding with each other as you walk?" And they stood still, looking sad. Then one of them, named Cleopas, answered him, "Are you the only visitor to Jerusalem who does not know the things that have happened there in these days?" And he said to them, "What things?" And they said to him, "Concerning Jesus of Nazareth, who was a prophet mighty in deed and word before God and all the people, and how our chief priests and rulers delivered him up to be condemned to death, and crucified him. But we had hoped that he was the one to redeem Israel. Yes, and besides all this, it is now the third day since this happened. Moreover, some women of our company amazed us. They were at the tomb early in the morning and did not find his body; and they came back saying that they had even seen a vision of angels, who said that he was alive. Some of those who were with us went to the tomb, and found it just as the women had said; but him they did not see." And he said to them, "O foolish men, and slow of heart to believe all that the prophets have spoken! Was it not necessary that the Christ should suffer these things and enter into his glory?"

Jn. 19:38-42. ...Joseph of Arimathea, who was a disciple of Jesus, but secretly, for fear of the Jews, asked Pilate that he might take away the body of Jesus, and Pilate gave him leave. So he came and took away his body. Nicodemus also, who had at first come to him by night, came bringing a mixture of myrrh and aloes, about a hundred pounds' weight. They took the body of Jesus, and bound it in linen cloths with the spices, as is the burial custom of the Jews. Now in the place where he was crucified there was a garden, and in the garden a new tomb where no one had ever been laid. So because of the Jewish day of Preparation, as the tomb was close at hand, they laid Jesus there.
Jn. 16:20, 22 [Christ]: ...You will be sorrowful, but your sorrow will turn into joy...I will see you again and your hearts will rejoice, and no one will take your joy from you.
Ps. 30:5. ...Weeping may tarry for the night, but joy comes with the morning.
Jer. 31:13 [God]: Then shall the maidens rejoice in the dance, and the young men and the old shall be merry. I will turn their mourning into joy, I will comfort them, and give them gladness for sorrow. (Also Ps. 30:11.)
1 Cor. 9:24-25. Do you not know that in a race all the runners compete, but only one receives the prize? So run that you may obtain it. Every athlete exercises self-control in all things. They do it to receive a perishable wreath, but we an imperishable.
2 Tim. 4:6-8. The time of my departure has come. I have fought the good fight, I have finished the race, I have kept the faith. Henceforth there is laid up for me the crown of righteousness, which the Lord, the righteous judge, will award to me on that Day, and not only to me but also to all who have loved his appearing. (crown: also Is. 28:5, 1 Pet. 5:4, Jms. 1:12, Rev. 2:10)

*Mk. 16:1-7. And when the sabbath was past, Mary Magdalene, and Mary the mother of James, and Salome, bought spices, so that they

Bass: (John)
Und hier der Stein,
And here the stone,

Der solche zugedeckt.
Which it did-cover.
{Which covered it.}

Wo aber wird mein Heiland sein?
Where, however, can my Savior be?

Alto: (Mary Magdalene)
Er ist vom Tode auferweckt!
He is from death raised-up!
{He has been raised from the dead!}

Wir trafen einen Engel an,
We met an angel - ,

Der hat uns solches kundgetan.
He has us of-this informed.
{Who informed us of this.}

Tenor: (Peter)
Hier seh ich mit Vergnügen
Here see I with pleasure
{Here I see with pleasure}

Das Schweißtuch abgewickelt liegen.
The napkin unwound lying.
{The unwound napkin lying.}

7. Tenor Aria (Peter)
●Resurrection assures us of comfort after death (249-7)
Sanfte soll mein Todeskummer,
Gentle shall my death's-trouble,
{My passage of death shall be gentle,}

Nur ein Schlummer,
Only a slumber,

Jesu, durch dein Schweißtuch sein.
Jesus, through thy napkin be.
{O Jesus, through thy napkin.}

Ja, das wird mich dort erfrischen
Yes, that will me there refresh
{Yes, that will refresh me there}

Und die Zähren meiner Pein
And the tears of-my pain
{And wipe the tears of my pain}

might go and anoint him. And very early on the first day of the week they went to the tomb when the sun had risen. And they were saying to one another, "Who will roll away the stone for us from the door of the tomb?" And looking up, they saw that the stone was rolled back—it was very large. And entering the tomb, they saw a young man sitting on the right side, dressed in a white robe; and they were amazed. And he said to them, "Do not be amazed; you seek Jesus of Nazareth, who was crucified. He has risen, he is not here; see the place where they laid him. But go, tell his disciples and Peter that he is going before you to Galilee; there you will see him as he told you."
Jn. 20:3–8. Peter then came out with the other disciple, and they went toward the tomb. They both ran, but the other disciple outran Peter and reached the tomb first; and stooping to look in, he saw the linen cloths lying there, but he did not go in. Then Simon Peter came, following him, and went into the tomb; he saw the linen cloths lying, and the napkin, which had been on his head, not lying with the linen cloths but rolled up in a place by itself. Then the other disciple, who reached the tomb first, also went in, and he saw and believed.
Jn. 11:38–41, 43–44. [When Lazarus, the brother of Mary and Martha, had died and been buried] Jesus...came to the tomb; it was a cave, and a stone lay upon it. Jesus said, "Take away the stone." Martha, the sister of the dead man, said to him, "Lord, by this time there will be an odor, for he has been dead four days." Jesus said to her, "Did I not tell you that if you would believe you would see the glory of God?" So they took away the stone...[Then] he cried out with a loud voice, "Lazarus, come out." The dead man came out, his hands and feet bound with bandages, and his faces wrapped with a cloth. Jesus said to them, "Unbind him, and let him go."

1 Cor. 15:17–23. If Christ has not been raised, your faith is futile and you are still in your sins. Then those also who have fallen asleep in Christ have perished. If for this life only we have hoped in Christ, we are of all men most to be pitied. But in fact Christ has been raised from the dead, the first fruits of those who have fallen asleep. For as by a man came death, by a man has come also the resurrection of the dead. For as in Adam all die, so also in Christ shall all be made alive. But each in his own order: Christ the first fruits, then at his coming those who belong to Christ. (Also Jn. 6:40/44/54, Rom. 8:11.)
Jn. 14:19 [Christ]: ...Because I live, you will live also. (Also 2 Tim. 2:11.)
Jn. 16:33 [Christ]: ...In the world you have tribulation; but be of good cheer, I have overcome the world.
Mt. 26:75. [When Peter had denied Christ three times, he] remembered the saying of Jesus, "Before the cock crows, you will deny me three times." And he went out and wept bitterly. (Also Mk. 14:72.)
Ps. 42:3. My tears have been my food day and night...
Rev. 21:3–4. I heard a loud voice from the throne saying, "Behold, the dwelling of God is with men. He will dwell with them, and they shall be his people, and God himself will be with them; he will wipe away every tear from their eyes, and death shall be no more, neither

Von den Wangen tröstlich wischen.
From (my) cheeks comfortingly wipe.
{Comfortingly from my cheeks.}

8. Soprano & Alto Recit. (Mary & Mary Magdalene)
●Yearning for death: We long to see the Savior soon! (249-8)
Indessen seufzen wir
Meanwhile sigh we
{Meanwhile we sigh}

Mit brennender Begier:
With burning desire:

Ach, könnt es doch nur bald geschehen,
Ah, might it indeed but soon happen,
{Ah, if only it would happen soon,}

Den Heiland selbst zu sehen!
The Savior himself to see!
{That we see the Savior himself!}

9. Alto Aria (Mary Magdalene)
●Easter: Where can I find him whom my soul loves? (249-9)
Saget, saget mir geschwinde,
Tell, tell me quickly,

Saget, wo ich Jesum finde,
Tell, where I Jesus might-find,

Welchen meine Seele liebt!
Whom my soul loves!

Komm doch, komm, umfasse mich;
Come, please, come, embrace me;

Denn mein Herz ist ohne dich
For my heart is without thee
{For without thee my heart is}

Ganz verwaiset und betrübt.
Completely orphaned and distressed.

10. Bass Recit. (John)
●Easter: Christ's resurrection turns our pain to joy (249-10)
Wir sind erfreut,
We are delighted,
{We rejoice,}

Daß unser Jesus wieder lebt,
That our Jesus again does-live,
{That our Jesus lives again,}

Und unser Herz,
And our heart,

shall there be mourning nor crying nor pain any more, for the former things have passed away." (Also Is. 25:8, Rev. 7:15-17.)

S. of S. 3:4 [Bride]: ...Have you seen him whom my soul loves?
Rom. 8:22-24, 26. We know that the whole creation has been groaning in travail together until now; and not only the creation, but we ourselves, who have the first fruits of the Spirit, groan inwardly as we wait for adoption as sons, the redemption of our bodies. For in this hope we were saved...Likewise the Spirit helps us in our weakness; for we do not know how to pray as we ought, but the Spirit himself intercedes for us with sighs too deep for words.
1 Jn. 3:2. Beloved, we are God's children now; it does not yet appear what we shall be, but we know that when he appears we shall be like him, for we shall see him as he is.
1 Cor. 13:12. Now we see in a mirror dimly, but then face to face...
2 Cor. 5:6-8. ...We know that while we are at home in the body we are away from the Lord, for we walk by faith, not by sight...We would rather be away from the body and at home with the Lord.

S. of S. 3:1-4 [Bride]: ...I sought him whom my soul loves; I sought him, but found him not; I called him, but he gave no answer. "I will rise now and go about the city, in the streets and in the squares; I will seek him whom my soul loves." I sought him, but found him not. The watchmen found me, as they went about in the city. "Have you seen him whom my soul loves?" (Also S. of S. 5:6.)
S. of S. 2:6 [Bride]: O that his left hand were under my head, and that his right hand embraced me!
Jn. 20:11-16. Mary stood weeping outside the tomb, and as she wept she stooped to look into the tomb; and she saw two angels in white, sitting where the body of Jesus had lain, one at the head and one at the feet. They said to her, "Woman, why are you weeping?" She said to them, "Because they have taken away my Lord, and I do not know where they have laid him." Saying this, she turned round and saw Jesus standing, but she did not know that it was Jesus. Jesus said to her, "Woman, why are you weeping? Whom do you seek?" Supposing him to be the gardener, she said to him, "Sir, if you have carried him away, tell me where you have laid him, and I will take him away." Jesus said to her "Mary." She turned and said to him in Hebrew, "Rabboni!" (which means Teacher).

*Mt. 28:1-2, 5-8. Now after the sabbath, toward the dawn of the first day of the week, Mary Magdalene and the other Mary went to see the sepulchre. And behold, there was a great earthquake; for an angel of the Lord descended from heaven and came and rolled back the stone, and sat upon it...But the angel said to the women, "Do not be afraid; for I know that you seek Jesus who was crucified. He is not here; for he has risen, as he said. Come, see the place where he lay. Then go quickly and tell his disciples that he has risen from the dead, and behold, he is going before you to Galilee; there you will see him. Lo, I have told you." So they departed quickly from the tomb with fear and great joy, and ran to tell his disciples.

So   erst in Traurigkeit zerflossen und geschwebt,
Which at-first in   sadness   was-dissolved and suspended,
{Which at first was dissolved and suspended in sadness,}

Vergißt den Schmerz
Forgets the   pain

Und sinnt auf Freudenlieder ;
And   devises   songs-of-joy;

Denn unser Heiland lebet wieder.
For   our   Savior   lives   again.

11. Chorus (Mary, Mary Magdalene, Peter, & John)
●Praise God for Christ's victory over hell & devil! (249-11)
        Preis und Dank
(May) glory and thanks

Bleibe,   Herr, dein Lobgesang.
Remain, (O) Lord, thy song-of-praise.

Höll und Teufel sind bezwungen,
Hell and devil   are   vanquished,

Ihre Pforten sind zerstört.
Their gates   are destroyed.

Jauchzet,   ihr erlösten Zungen,
Shout-for-joy, ye redeemed tongues,

Daß man es im Himmel hört.
(Till) they it in heaven can-hear.
{Till they can hear it in heaven.}

Eröffnet, ihr Himmel, die prächtigen Bogen,
Open,   ye heavens, your magnificent arches,

Der Löwe von Juda kommt siegend gezogen!
The lion of Judah comes victoriously marching!
{The lion of Judah comes marching victorious!}

Jn. 16:16, 20–22. [Jesus said], "A little while, and you will see me no more; again a little while, and you will see me...Truly, truly, I say to you, you will weep and lament, but the world will rejoice; you will be sorrowful, but your sorrow will turn into joy. When a woman is in travail she has sorrow, because her hour has come; but when she is delivered of the child, she no longer remembers the anguish, for joy that a child is born into the world. So you have sorrow now, but I will see you again and your hearts will rejoice, and no one will take your joy from you."

Rev. 5:9–13. And [in paradise] they sang a new song, saying, "Worthy art thou...for thou wast slain and by thy blood didst ransom men for God from every tribe and tongue and people and nation, and hast made them a kingdom and priests to our God, and they shall reign on earth." Then I looked, and I heard around the throne and the living creatures and the elders the voice of many angels, numbering myriads of myriads and thousands of thousands, saying with a loud voice, "Worthy is the Lamb who was slain, to receive power and wealth and wisdom and might and honor and glory and blessing!" And I heard every creature in heaven and on earth and under the earth and in the sea, and all therein, saying, "To him who sits upon the throne and to the Lamb be blessing (Luther: Lob) and honor (Luther: Ehre) and glory (Luther: Preis) and might for ever and ever!" (Also Rev. 7:11–12.)
Rom. 14:11. ...Every tongue shall give praise to God.
Ps. 66:1–2. Make a joyful noise (Luther: jauchzet) to God, all the earth; sing the glory of his name; give to him glorious praise! (Also Ps. 81:1, 95:1,2, 98:4, 6, 100:1–2.)
1 Jn. 3:8. ...The reason the Son of God appeared was to destroy the works of the devil. (Also Heb. 2:14–15.)
Col. 2:13. He disarmed the principalities and powers and made a public example of them, triumphing over them in him.
Rev. 5:5. Then one of the elders said to me, "...Lo, the Lion of the tribe of Judah, the Root of David, has conquered..." (Also Gen. 49:9.)
Ps. 24:7–8. Lift up your heads, O gates! and be lifted up, O ancient doors! that the King of glory may come in. Who is the King of glory? The Lord, strong and mighty, the Lord, mighty in battle! (Also Ps. 24:9–10.)

SELECTED BIBLIOGRAPHY

Ambrose, Z. Philip. "Another Lament in 'Weinen, Klagen, Sorgen, Zagen.'" *BACH: The Journal of the Riemenschneider Bach Institute* 13 (July 1982): 20–22.

Ambrose, Z. Philip, ed. and trans. *The Texts to Johann Sebastian Bach's Church Cantatas.* Neuhausen-Stuttgart: Hänssler, 1984.

Ambrose, Z. Philip. "'Weinen, Klagen, Sorgen, Zagen' und die antike Redekunst." *Bach-Jahrbuch* 1980: 35–45.

Arnold, Denis. *Bach.* London: Oxford University Press, 1984.

Axmacher, Elke. *"Aus Liebe will mein Heyland sterben." Untersuchungen zum Wandel des Passionsverständnisses im frühen 18. Jahrhundert.* Neuhausen-Stuttgart: Hänssler, 1984.

Axmacher, Elke. "Bachs Kantatentexte in auslegungsgeschichtlicher Sicht." *Bach als Ausleger der Bibel.* Theologische und musikwiss. Studien zum Werk Johann Sebastian Bachs, ed. M. Petzoldt. Göttingen: Vandenhoeck & Ruprecht, 1985, pp. 15–32.

Axmacher, Elke. "Die Texte zu Johann Sebastian Bachs Choralkantaten." *Bachiana et alia musicolgica.* Festschrift Alfred Dürr zum 65. Geburtstag. Kassel: Bärenreiter, 1983, pp. 3–16.

Axmacher, Elke. "'Ein feste Burg ist unser Gott' (BWV 80): Theologische Interpretation des Textes." *Beiträge zur theologischen Bachforschung I*, edited by Walter Blankenburg & Renate Steiger. Neuhausen-Stuttgart: Hänssler, 1987, pp. 117–125.

Axmacher, Elke. "Zur Theologie von J. S. Bachs Kirchenkantaten. Eine theologisch-germanistische Untersuchung der Kantatentexte im Blick auf ihre Beziehung zur Predigt des Barockzeitalters." Dissertation, Berlin, 1976.

Barker, Kenneth, general editor. *The NIV Study Bible.* Grand Rapids, MI: Zondervan, 1985.

Baron, Samuel. "Bach's Text Settings: Schweitzer and Pirro Revisited." In: *A Bach Tribute. Essays in Honor of William H. Scheide.* Published simultaneously in the United States and Germany. Kassel: Bärenreiter; Chapel Hill: Hinshaw Music; 1993, pp. 17–26.

Blankenburg, Walter. "Eine neue Textquelle zu sieben Kantaten Johann Sebastian Bachs und zu achtzehn Kantaten Johann Ludwig Bachs." *Bach-Jahrbuch* 1977: 7–25.

Blankenburg, Walter. "Mystik in der Musik J. S. Bachs." *Theologische Bach-Studien I*, edited by Walter Blankenburg & Renate Steiger. Neuhausen-Stuttgart: Hänssler, 1987, pp. 47–66.

Blume, Friedrich. "Die Kirchenkantaten J. S. Bachs." In: F. Blume, *Syntagma Musicologicum II.* Kassel: Bärenreiter, 1973, pp. 205–231.

Blume, Friedrich. "Outlines of a New Picture of Bach." *Music and Letters* 44 (1963) trans. from *Musica* 16 (1962): 169ff.

Brainard, Paul. "The regulative and generative roles of verse in Bach's 'thematic' invention." In: *Bach Studies.* Edited by Don O. Franklin. Cambridge: Cambridge University Press, 1989, pp. 54–74.

Buelow, George J. "Expressivity in the accompanied recitatives of Bach's cantatas." In: *Bach Studies.* Edited by Don O. Franklin. Cambridge: Cambridge University Press, 1989, pp. 18–35.

Chafe, Eric T. "Bach's First Two Leipzig Cantatas: A Message for the Community." In: *A Bach Tribute. Essays in Honor of William H. Scheide.* Published simultaneously in the United States and Germany. Kassel: Bärenreiter; Chapel Hill: Hinshaw Music; 1993, pp. 71–86.

Chafe, Eric T. *Tonal Allegory in the Music of J. S. Bach.* Berkeley: University of California Press, 1991.

Cowart, Georgia. "Symbolic Correspondence in the Duets of Bach's *Mass in B Minor.*" *BACH: The Journal of the Riemenschneider Bach Institute* 15 (January 1984): 17–24, (April 1984): 17–25.

Cox, Howard H. "Bach's Conception of his Office." *BACH: The Journal of the Riemenschneider Bach Institute* 20 (Spring 1989): 22–30.

Cox, Howard H. "Bach's Knowledge of the Bible." In: *A Bach Tribute. Essays in Honor of William H. Scheide.* Published simultaneously in the United States and Germany. Kassel: Bärenreiter; Chapel Hill: Hinshaw Music; 1993, pp. 87–99.

Cox, Howard H. *The Calov Bible of J. S. Bach.* Ann Arbor: UMI Research Press, 1985.

Crist, Stephen A. "Aria forms in the Cantatas from Bach's first Leipzig *Jahrgang.*" In: *Bach Studies.* Edited by Don O. Franklin. Cambridge: Cambridge University Press, 1989, pp. 36–53.

David, Hans T. "Bach's Problems and Artistic Creed." *BACH: The Journal of the Riemenschneider Bach Institute* 1 (April 1970): 6–13.

David, Hans T. and Arthur Mendel, eds. *The Bach Reader: A Life of Johann Sebastian Bach in Letters and Documents.* Revised edition. New York: W. W. Norton, 1966.

Day, James C. F. *The Literary Background to Bach's Cantatas.* London: D. Dobson, 1961.

Drinker, Henry S. *Texts of the Choral Works of J. S. Bach in English Translation.* 4 vols. New York: Association of American Colleges Arts Program, 1942-43.

Dürr, Alfred. "Bachs Kantatentexte. Probleme und Aufgaben der Forschung." *Bach-Studien* 5: 49-61.

Dürr, Alfred. "Bach's Chorale Cantatas." *Cantors at the Crossroads. Essays on Church Music in honor of Walter E. Buszin.* St. Louis, MO: Concordia, 1967, pp. 507-517.

Dürr, Alfred. *Die Kantaten von Johann Sebastian Bach mit ihren Texten.* 2 vols. Kassel: Bärenreiter, 1985.

Dürr, Alfred. "Noch einmal: Wo blieb Bachs fünfter Kantatenjahrgang?" *Bach-Jahrbuch* 1986: 121-122.

Dürr, Alfred. "Zur Entstehungsgeschichte des Bachschen Choralkantaten-Jahrgangs." *Bach-Interpretationen.* Göttingen: Vandenhoeck & Ruprecht, 1969, pp. 7-11, 207ff.

Dürr, Alfred. "Zur Textvorlage der Choralkantaten Johann Sebastian Bachs." *Kerygma und Melos. Christhard Mahrenholz 70 Jahre.* Kassel: Bärenreiter, 1970, pp. 222-236.

Gojowy, Detlef. "Wort und Bild in Bachs Kantatentexten." *Die Musikforschung* 25 (1972): 24-39.

Gudewill, Kurt. "Über Formen und Texte der Kirchenkantaten Johann Sebastian Bachs" *Festschrift Friedrich Blume zum 70. Geburtstag.* Kassel: Bärenreiter, 1963, pp. 162-175.

Emery, Walter and Arthur Mendel. "Views: Bach versus the Bible." *American Choral Review* 4 (April 1962):12-15.

Häfner, Klaus. "Der Picander-Jahrgang." *Bach-Jahrbuch* 1975: 70-113.

Häfner, Klaus. "Picander, der Textdichter von Bachs viertem Kantatenjahrgang. Ein neuer Hinweis." *Die Musikforschung* 35 (1982): 156-162.

Herz, Gerhard, ed. *Cantata 140.* With annotations. New York: W. W. Norton, 1972.

Herz, Gerhard. "More on Bach's Cantata No.4: Date and Style." *American Choral Review* 21 (April 1979): 3-19.

Herz, Gerhard. "Toward a New Image of Bach." *BACH: The Journal of the Riemenschneider Bach Institute* 1 (October 1970): 9-27; 2 (January 1971): 7-27. Reprinted 16 (January 1985): 12-52.

Herz, Gerhard. "Yoshitake Kobayashi's Article 'On the Chronology of the Last Phase of Bach's Work—Compositions and Performances: 1736 to 1750'—An Analysis with Translated Portions of the Original Text." *BACH: The Journal of the Riemenschneider Bach Institute* 21 (Spring 1990): 3-25.

Hirsch, Arthur. *Die Zahl im Kantatenwerk Johann Sebastian Bachs.* Neuhausen-Stuttgart: Hänssler, 1986.

Hirsch, Artur. "Johann Sebastian Bach's Cantatas in Chronological Order." *BACH: The Journal of the Riemenschneider Bach Institute* 11 (July 1980): 18-35.

Hobohm, Wolf. "Neue 'Texte zur Leipziger Kirchen-Musik'" *Bach-Jahrbuch* 1973: 5-32.

Irwin, Joyce. "German Pietists and Church Music in the Baroque Age." *Church History* 54 (1985): 29-40.

Jeffers, Ron. *Translations and Annotations of Choral Repertoire, Volume I: Sacred Latin Texts.* Corvallis, OR: Earthsongs, 1988.

Killy, Walther. "Über Bachs Kantatentexte." *Musik und Kirche* 52 (1982): 271-281.

Koch, Ernst. "Tröstendes Echo. Zur theologischen Deutung der Echo-Arie im IV. Teil des Weihnachts-Oratoriums von Johann Sebastian Bach." *Bach-Jahrbuch* 1989: 203-211.

Krapf, Gerhard. "Bach's Use of the Chorale as an agent of Exegesis." *Religious Studies and Theology* (University of Alberta, Canada) 6:1 & 2 (January, May 1986): 20-26.

Krausse, Helmuth K. "Eine neue Quell zu drei Kantatentexten Johann Sebastian Bachs." *Bach-Jahrbuch* 1981: 7-22.

Krausse, Helmuth K. "Erdmann Neumeister und die Kantatentexte Johann Sebastian Bachs." *Bach-Jahrbuch* 1986: 7-31.

Kobayashi, Yoshitake, trans. Jeffrey Baxter. "Universality in Bach's B Minor Mass: A Portrait of Bach in his Final Years (In Memoriam Dietrich Kilian)." *BACH: The Journal of the Riemenschneider Bach Institute* 24 (Fall/Winter 1993): 3-25.

Kobayashi, Yoshitake. "Zur Chronologie der Spätwerke Johann Sebastian Bachs." *Bach-Jahrbuch* 1988: 7-72.

Krummacher, Friedhelm. "Bachs Vokalmusik als Problem der Analyse." *Bachforschung und Bachinterpretation heute.*

Bericht über das Bachfest-Symposium 1978 der Philipps-Universität Marpurg, ed. Reinhold Brinkmann. Kassel: Bärenreiter, 1981, pp. 97–126.

Leaver, Robin A. "Der Text von Bachs Kantate Nr. 79: Eine Mutmaßung." *Theologische Bach-Studien I*, edited by Walter Blankenburg & Renate Steiger. Neuhausen-Stuttgart: Hänssler, 1987, pp. 109–116.

Leaver, Robin A. *J. S. Bach and Scripture, Glosses from the Calov Bible Commentary*. St. Louis, MO: Concordia, 1985.

Leaver, Robin A. "Parody and Theological Consistency." *BACH: The Journal of the Riemenschneider Bach Institute* 21 (Winter 1990): 30–43.

Luther, Martin. *The German Mass and Order of Service (1526)*. Trans. by Bard Thompson, in *Liturgies of the Western Church*. Philadelphia: Fortress Press, 1982, pp. 123–137.

Mann, Alfred. *Approaches to the B Minor Mass*. Published as a special issue of the *American Choral Review*: 27 (1985).

Marshall, Robert L. "Bach the Progressive: Observations on his Later Works." *Musical Quarterly* 62 (July 1976): 313–357. Reprinted with "Postcript" in: *The Music of Johann Sebastian Bach. The Sources, the Style, the Significance*. New York: Schirmer Books, 1990, pp. 23–58.

Marshall, Robert L. "On Bach's Universality." In: *The Music of Johann Sebastian Bach. The Sources, the Style, the Significance*. New York: Schirmer Books, 1990, pp. 65–79.

Meyer, Ulrich. "Überlegungen zu Bachs Kantate 'Gott der Herr ist Sonn und Schild' (BWV 79)." *Theologische Bach-Studien I*, edited by Walter Blankenburg & Renate Steiger. Neuhausen-Stuttgart: Hänssler, 1987, pp. 99–107.

Mies, Paul. *Die geistlichen Kantaten Johann Sebastian Bachs und der Hörer von heute*. Wiesbaden: Breitkopf & Härtel, Part I (1958), II (1959), III (1964).

Naumann, Martin J. "Bach the Preacher." In: *The Little Bach Book*, ed. Theodore Hoelty-Nickel. Valparaiso, IN: Valparaiso University Press, 1950.

Neumann, Werner and Hans-Joachim Schulze, eds. *Bach-dokumente*. 3 vols. Leipzig: Bach-Archiv, 1963, 1969, 1972.

Neumann, Werner. *Handbuch der Kantaten Johann Sebastian Bachs*. Leipzig: Breitkopf and Härtel, 1947, rev. 3/1967 4/1971; 5th ed. unrevised, Wiesbaden, 1984.

Pelikan, Jaroslav. *Bach Among the Theologians*. Philadelphia: Fortress Press, 1986.

Petzoldt, Martin. "'Ut probus & doctus reddar.' Zum Anteil der Theologie bei der Schulausbildung Johann Sebastian Bachs in Eisenach, Ohrdruf und Lüneburg." *Bach-Jahrbuch* 1985: 7–42.

Petzoldt, Martin & Joachim Petri. *Johann Sebastian Bach. Ehre sei dir Gott gesungen. Bilder und Texte zu Bachs Leben als Christ und seinem Wirken für die Kirche*. Berlin: Evangelische Verlaganstalt, Göttingen: Vandenhoeck & Ruprecht, 1988.

Poos, Heinrich. "Christus Coronabit Crucigeros: Hermeneutischer Versuch über einen Kanon Johann Sebastian Bachs." *Theologische Bach-Studien I*, edited by Walter Blankenburg & Renate Steiger. Neuhausen-Stuttgart: Hänssler, 1987, pp. 67–97.

Reed, Luther D. *The Lutheran Liturgy*. Rev. ed. Philadelphia: Muhlenberg Press, 1947.

Rilling, Helmuth. "Bach's Significance." Translated by Gordon Paine, *The Choral Journal* 25 (June 1985): 7–14.

Rosand, Ellen. "The Descending Tetrachord: an Emblem of Lament." *Musical Quarterly* 65 (July 1979): 346–359.

Scheide, William H. "Bach und der Picander-Jahrgang–Eine Erwiderung." *Bach-Jahrbuch* 1980: 47–51.

Scheide, William H. "Eindeutigkeit und Mehrdeutigkeit in Picanders Kantatenjahrgangs-Vorbemerkung und im Werkverzeichnis des Nekrologs auf Johann Sebastian Bach." *Bach-Jahrbuch* 1983: 109–113.

Scheide, William H. "Johann Sebastian Bachs Sammlung von Kantaten seines Vetters Johann Ludwig Bach." *Bach-Jahrbuch* 1959: 52–94, 1961: 5–24, 1962: 5–32.

Scheide, William H. "Zum Verhältnis von Textdrucken und musikalischen Quellen der Kirchenkantaten Johann Sebastian Bachs." *Bach-Jahrbuch* 1976: 79–94.

Schellhous, Rosalie Athol. "Form and Spirituality in Bach's *St. Matthew Passion*." *Musical Quarterly* 71 (1985): 295–326.

Schering, Arnold. *Johann Sebastian Bachs Leipziger Kirchenmusik*. 3rd ed. Wiesbaden: Breitkopf & Härtel, 1968.

Schmieder, Wolfgang. *Thematisches Verzeichnis der musikalischen Werke von Johann Sebastian Bach*, rev. & expanded ed. Wiesbaden: Breitkopf & Härtel, 1990.

Schmitz, Arnold. *Die Bildlichkeit der wortgebundenen Musik Johann Sebastian Bachs*. Mainz: Schott's Söhne, 1950. Neue Studien zur Musikwissenschaft 1. Reprinted Laaber: Laaber-Verlag, 1980.

Schrade, Leo. *Bach: The Conflict Between the Sacred and Secular.* New York: Merlin Press, 1955, reprinted 1973.

Schulze, Hans-Joachim. "The Parody Process in Bach's Music: An Old Problem Reconsidered." *BACH: The Journal of the Riemenschneider Bach Institute* 20 (Spring 1989): 7-21.

Schulze, Hans-Joachim and Christoph Wolff. *Bach Compendium.* 7 vols. Frankfurt: C. F. Peters, 1988.

Schweitzer, Albert. *J. S. Bach.* Trans. Ernest Newman. 2 vols. London: Breitkopf and Härtel, reissued Boston: Bruce Humphries Publishers, 1962.

Siegele, Ulrich. "Bachs Ort in Orthodoxie und Aufklarung." *Musik und Kirche* 51 (1981): 3-14.

Siegele, Ulrich. *Bachs theologischer Formbegriff und das Duett F-Dur: Ein Vortrag.* Neuhausen-Stuttgart: Hänssler, 1978.

Siegele, Siegele, trans. Gerhard Herz. "'I Had to be Industrious...' Thoughts about the Relationship between Bach's Social and Musical Character." *BACH: The Journal of the Riemenschneider Bach Institute* 24 (Fall/Winter 1991): 5-12.

Smend, Friedrich. *Joh. Seb. Bach: Kirchen-Kantaten.* Berlin: Christlicher Zeitschriftenverlag, 1947-9, 3/1966.

Smith, Timothy A. "Bach and the Cross." *Christian Scholar's Review* Vol. 22 (1993), No. 3: 267-290.

Spitta, Philipp. "Über die Beziehungen Sebastian Bachs zu Christian Friedrich Hunold und Mariane von Ziegler." *Historische und Philologische Aufsätze, Ernst Curtius zu seinem siebenzigsten Geburtstage am zweiten September 1884 gewidmet.* Berlin: A. Ascher & Co., 1884, pp. 403-434. Reprint: "Mariane von Zegler und Joh. Sebastian Bach," in: *Ph. Spitta, Zur Musik. Sechzehn Aufsätze,* Berlin: Gebrüder Paetel, 1892, pp. 93-118; "Bach und Christian Friedrich Hunold," in: *Musikgeschichtliche Aufsätze,* Berlin: Gebrüder Paetel, 1894, pp. 89-100.

Stiller, Günther. *Johann Sebastian Bach and Liturgical Life in Leipzig.* Translated by Herbert J. A. Bowman, Daniel F. Poellot, and Hilton C. Oswald. Edited by Robin A. Leaver. St. Louis, MO: Concordia, 1984.

Streck, Harald. *Die Verskunst in den poetischen Texten zu den Kantaten J. S. Bachs.* Hamburger Beiträge zur Musikwissenschaft, vol. 5, Hamburg: Verlag der Musikalienhandlung, 1971.

Tagliavini, Luigi Ferdinando. *Studi sui testi delle cantate sacre di J. S. Bach.* Padova: CEDAM, 1956.

Terry, C. S. *Bach: the Cantatas and the Oratorios.* London: Oxford University Press, 1925, reprinted 1972.

Terry, Charles Sanford. *Joh. Seb. Bach, Cantata Texts Sacred and Secular With a Reconstruction of the Leipzig Liturgy of his Period.* London: Constable, 1926; reprinted, London: Holland Press, 1964.

Terry, Charles Sanford. *The Four-Part Chorales of J. S. Bach.* London: Oxford University Press, 1929; reprinted (with a new foreword) 1964.

Unger, Melvin P. *The German Choral Church Compositions of Johann David Heinichen (1683-1729).* New York: Peter Lang, 1990.

Werthemann, Helene. *Die Bedeutung der alttestamentlichen Historien in Johann Sebastian Bachs Kantaten.* Beiträge zur Geschichte der biblischen Hermeneutik 3. Tübingen: J. C. B. Mohr, 1960.

Westrup, Jack. *Bach's Cantatas.* London: British Broadcasting Corporation, 1966, Seattle: University of Washington Press edition, 1969.

Wolff, Christoph. *Bach. Essays on his Life and Music.* Cambridge, MA: Harvard University Press, 1991.

Wolff, Christoph. "Wo blieb Bachs fünfter Kantatenjahrgang?" *Bach-Jahrbuch* 1982: 151-152.

Whittaker, William Gillies. *The Cantatas of Johann Sebastian Bach, Sacred and Secular.* 2d ed. 2 vols. London: Oxford University Press, 1959.

Wustmann, Rudolf. "Sebastian Bachs Kirchenkantatentexte." *Bach-Jahrbuch* 1910: 44-62.

Young, W. Murray. *The Cantatas of J. S. Bach, An Analytical Guide.* Jefferson, North Carolina and London: McFarland & Company, 1989.

Zander, Ferdinand. "Die Dichter der Kantatentexte Johann Sebastian Bachs." Ph.D. dissertation, Cologne, 1967. Partially reproduced in *Bach-Jahrbuch* 1968: pp. 9-64.

Ziebler, Karl. *Das Symbol in der Kirchenmusik Joh. Seb. Bachs.* Kassel: Bärenreiter, 1930.

ALPHABETICAL INDEX OF MOVEMENT SUMMARIES

Accompanying Christ through humiliation and death (159-2)
Accompanying Christ to his passion as his disciples did (22-2)
Accuser commanded to be silent (5-5)
Acknowledging Christ sincerely before men (45-5)
Advent: Christ's coming brings ever new blessings (61-2)
Advent: God's Son, the champion of Judah, comes (62-3)
Advent: Meet king Jesus, my bridegroom, with music! (36-4)
Advent: Praise to God for glorious gift in manger! (62-5)
Advent: Prepare the way for the coming Messiah! (132-1)
Advent: Preparing my heart to be his dwelling (61-5)
Advent: The Lord of Glory draws near to Zion! (36-1)
Advent: The Savior of the Gentiles is coming! (36-2)
Advent: Welcome, heavenly bridegroom, into my heart! (36-5)
Advent mystery: Ruler of heaven comes to earth (62-2)
Advent prayer: Come, my crown of joy, do not tarry! (61-6)
Advent prayer: Come, Savior of the Gentiles! (61-1, 62-1)
Advent prayer: Show thyself mighty in human flesh! (62-4)
Advent preparation requires clearing away sin (132-2)
Adversity: I've been given a bitter cup of tears (138-2)
Affliction: God is my confidence so I am content (58-3)
Affliction: Think not that God has forsaken you! (93-5)
Affliction caused by sin-seeking nature and pride (114-3)
Affliction fills the narrow path of pilgrimage (44-4)
Affliction is the Christian's lot in life (12-2)
Affliction purifies the Christian so be patient! (2-5)
Affliction sent as test; wormwood will turn to wine (155-3)
Affliction-filled ways accepted in faith (92-9)
Afflictions accepted with joy in view of heaven (75-5)
Agnus Dei: Lamb of God, have mercy on us! (23-4)
All we have is given by God; he has need of nothing (39-5)
Alleluia: Corporate praise to God for this day (110-7)
Alleluia (51-5)
Alleluia! Christ is our comfort (66-6)
Angel host encamps around God's people (19-3)
Angel host has defeated the dragon; praise God! (19-2)
Angel Michael battles with Satan, the dragon (19-1)
Angels: Praise to God for angels around God's throne (130-1)
Angels addressed: Protect me and teach me to sing! (19-5)
Angels are our chariot to heaven, let us love them (19-6)
Angels guard us like they did Daniel and his friends (130-4)
Angels of God keep watch over me wherever I go (149-4)
Angels' mission: to encircle Christ and his children (130-2)
Annunciation: Joyous, long-awaited news (1-2)
Antichrist persecutes, hates our teaching but in vain (44-5)
Anticipation of heaven where all is perfect (146-8)
Anticipation of heaven's bliss after earth's pain (146-7)
Anxiety concerning death (8-3)
Anxiousness quieted by trust in God's watchful care (197-3)
Apostasy: A prayer for aid in time of apostasy (2-1)
Apostasy: False teachers are like whited sepulchres (2-2)
Apostasy: Prayer to stop false teachers (2-3)
Appointed time of joy determined by God for us (93-4)
Ascension: Angels proclaim his return: Acts 1:10-11 (11-7a)
Ascension: Christ goes to prepare a place for me (43-10)

Ascension: Christ receives the appointed kingdom (43-8)
Ascension: Christ victorious; yearning to join him (43-11)
Ascension: Disciples return: Lk. 24:52, Acts 1:12 (11-7c)
Ascension: His love stays here as prospect of heaven (11-8)
Ascension of Christ: All things put under his feet (11-6)
Ascension of Christ: Jesus has finished his work (43-5)
Ascension of Christ: Lk. 24:50-51 (11-2)
Ascension of Christ: Mk. 16:19 (43-4)
Ascension of Christ: The basis for my own ascension (128-1)
Ascension of Christ: The grief of bereavement (11-3)
Ascension of Christ in a cloud: Acts 1:9, Mk. 16:19 (11-5)
Atonement: In judgment I plead Christ's saving work (55-4)
Awake lost sheep before trumpet of judgment sounds! (20-8)
Away anxieties! Jesus calls me to a glorious future! (8-4)
Baptism: Christ commanded disciples to baptize (7-5)
Baptism: Eye sees water, faith sees blood of Christ (7-7)
Baptism: See what God has said it means (7-2)
Baptism: We are lost unless we believe and are baptized (7-6)
Baptism by Spirit and water brings us into kingdom (165-1)
Baptism by water and Spirit heals us of sin's disease (165-2)
Baptism of blood and water provides clean raiment (132-5)
Baptism, Word, and Eucharist guard us from evil (165-6)
Baptismal vows often broken, sanctification needed (165-4)
Battle led by Christ; victory assured for God's child (80-2)
Believe his Word rather than appearances (9-7, 155-5, 186-6)
Blessed are the merciful; they shall receive mercy (39-7)
Blessed is the land and city in which God dwells (119-2)
Blessed state of ours will last, for God's love has no end (197-9)
Blessing for those who faithfully walk in God's ways (93-7)
Blessing on government brings justice and faithfulness (120-4)
Blessing on you and your children: Ps. 115:14 (196-4)
Blessing sought on anointed one and entire land (190-6)
Blessing's completion guaranteed by God's power (195-5)
Blessings await those who know Jesus' voice (184-4)
Blessings of body and spirit are gifts of grace (17-6)
Blindness to own faults; splinter in neighbor's eye (185-4)
Blood of Christ cleanses and frees entire world (136-6)
Body consumed in the earth but later transfigured (161-6)
Body is temporal but Word's manna feeds our souls (186-4)
Bride (Zion) rejoices over bridegroom's arrival (140-4)
Bride lovely in salvation's garment of righteousness (49-4)
Bridegroom seeks bride, his perfect dove (49-2)
Bridegroom's arrival from heaven announced to bride (140-2)
Brotherly love shown us in Christ is to be our example (76-12)
Canticle of Zechariah: God's promises now fulfilled (167-4)
Carrying the cross: it leads me to paradise (56-1)
Cast all your cares, your sorrows' yoke, on God (155-4)
Certainty of salvation based on coming of Spirit (108-3)
Certainty of salvation based on Jesus' parting words (108-2)
Charity makes us like God and earns heavenly blessing (39-3)
Chastisement of the Lord is well deserved by all (114-1)
Cheerfulness despite cross, storm, death, and hell (150-3)
Christ as physician and balm; our only hope (103-3)
Christ as victor: The heavenly host praises him (43-2)

Christ as victor over all: thousands praise him (43-3)

Christ as victor over Satan, death, and sin (43-6)

Christ as victor trod the winepress to save the lost (43-7)

Christ calms our accusing conscience and gives hope (78-6)

Christ came not to judge but save; no one excluded (68-3)

Christ came to destroy works of devil: 1 Jn. 3:8 (40-1)

Christ conquered death and hell for us (134-3)

Christ conquered sin and death for us (4-4)

Christ died as our paschal lamb (4-6, 158-4)

Christ died for our sins; rose for our life! (4-2)

Christ does wonders among the weak and dead (48-5)

Christ exalted because he suffered and died (31-4)

Christ fulfilled law, providing salvation by faith (9-4)

Christ helps his own in battle between doubt and faith (109-5)

Christ invites sinners to come and be cleansed (113-6)

Christ is light and salvation for Gentiles (125-6)

Christ is light for the Gentiles and glory of Israel (83-5)

Christ is light of salvation to all who confess him (200-1)

Christ is only begotten Son of God and morning star (96-1)

Christ is our helper; we cry to God in Jesus' name (116-1, 143-2)

Christ is with us, who can condemn us? (40-3)

Christ, our Alpha and Omega, shall return for us (1-6)

Christ present where two or three are gathered in his name (42-3)

Christ risen but I still experience inner strife (67-2)

Christ shelters me in storm; keeps me safe from foe (81-7)

Christ the morning star, root of Jesse, bridegroom (1-1)

Christ victorious can be seen at God's right hand (43-9)

Christ will place me at his right hand (128-5)

Christ's baptism: God's object lesson; hear him! (7-3)

Christ's baptism shows baptism confirmed by Trinity (7-4)

Christ's birth: A glad welcome to Jesus, my brother (133-1)

Christ's birth: How sweet the news is! (133-4)

Christ's birth: Praise Son of Mary to ends of earth! (121-1)

Christ's birth: Reconciling sinful mankind to God (122-2)

Christ's birth: The long-awaited day has come! (122-5)

Christ's birth begins true year of Jubilee, rejoice! (122-6)

Christ's birth brings a new year to Christendom (122-1)

Christ's birth makes heaven certain; yearning for it (64-6)

Christ's birth restores our relations with heaven (122-3)

Christ's birth signifies my election for heaven (151-1)

Christ's blood alone saves from hell and makes us heirs (74-7)

Christ's blood cancels guilt and makes us victorious (78-4)

Christ's blood is powerful enough for entire world (5-6)

Christ's children sent among wolves as he too was (139-3)

Christ's coming not recognized by some (248-51)

Christ's coming to earth takes away fear of death (133-5)

Christ's condescension opened heaven for us (151-4)

Christ's exaltation to God's right hand unfathomable (128-4)

Christ's forgiveness sufficient for great sin (33-3)

Christ's love: I could not bear to live without it (57-3)

Christ's passion is my joy for it offers me heaven (159-5, 182-7)

Christ's passion led to blessing; I offer my heart (78-5)

Christ's passion now over and salvation accomplished (159-4)

Christ's poverty has made us rich (151-3)

Christ's rebuke to raging sea: Be still! (81-5)

Christ's return: Longing for it to be soon (11-9)

Christ's return: Prayer that it might be soon (11-7b)

Christ's victory: May we appreciate and appropriate it (134-5)

Christ's wounds become my resting place by faith (199-7)

Christ's wounds provide salvation for sinners (199-6)

Christmas: Admonition to shepherds to go quickly (248-15)

Christmas: Angels' song shall be joined by humans (248-22)

Christmas: Blessed day when God came to deliver us (63-2)

Christmas: Celebrate and give thanks for salvation (63-5)

Christmas: Christ lies in yonder stall (248-17)

Christmas: Christchild brings the dawn of new age (248-12)

Christmas: Come praise our Sovereign with music! (248-1)

Christmas: Commemorate this day and render thanks (63-1)

Christmas: Creator rejects earthly pomp for a manger (248-8)

Christmas: Embrace this miracle in your heart! (248-31)

Christmas: God became poor so we could be rich (248-7)

Christmas: God has come; we will not hide like Adam (133-3)

Christmas: God has comforted and redeemed his people (248-27)

Christmas: God sent his Son to earth to deliver us (151-2)

Christmas: I will preserve this miracle in my heart (248-32)

Christmas: Let all praise God for this gift of love! (91-6)

Christmas: Let your ardor ascend to God like flames! (63-6)

Christmas: Praise to God for his mercy to us (248-29)

Christmas: Praise to God for showing his love (248-28)

Christmas: Prepare to receive Creator as thy guest! (91-4)

Christmas: Promised Messiah, Zion's bridegroom born (248-3)

Christmas: Rejoice! Salvation has come in Christ! (248-35)

Christmas: Shepherds sent to cradle to sing lullaby (248-18)

Christmas: The lion of Judah has appeared to free us (63-4)

Christmas: We join angelic praise for Christ's birth (248-23)

Christmas: Zion, prepare to receive thy bridegroom! (248-4)

Christmas fulfils promise to Abraham, a shepherd (248-14)

Christmas, God's gift of salvation: we build on it (63-3)

Christmas lullaby for child who is the Savior (248-19)

Christmas prayer: Look with favor on us worshipers (63-7)

Christmas Prayer: Let my heart be thy bed! (248-9)

Christmas Story: Angels and shepherds: Lk. 2:10-11 (248-13)

Christmas Story: Angels and shepherds: Lk. 2:8-9 (248-11)

Christmas Story: Babe will be in a manger: Lk. 2:12 (248-16)

Christmas Story: Glory to God in Highest: Lk. 2:14 (248-21)

Christmas Story: Heavenly host appears: Lk. 2:13 (248-20)

Christmas Story: Jesus is born: Lk. 2:7 (248-6)

Christmas Story: Shepherds decide to go see: Lk. 2:15 (248-26)

Christmas Story: Shepherds return: Lk. 2:20 (248-34)

Christmas Story: Shepherds tell story: Lk. 2:16-19 (248-30)

Christmas Story: Trip to Bethlehem: Lk. 2:1, 3-6 (248-2)

Christmas Story: When the angels had gone: Lk. 2:15 (248-25)

Church Dedication: A celebration of praise (194-1)

Church Dedication: May God accept our offerings (194-4)

Circumcision and naming of Jesus: Lk. 2:21 (248-37)

Cleansing from sin sought like David and Manasseh did (131-4)

Clinging to Jesus: Walking with him brings blessing (124-6)

Clinging to Jesus affords entrance to heaven (157-4)

Clinging to Jesus for comfort; fixing faith on him (157-2)

Clinging to Jesus, he leads me to streams of life (157-5)

Clinging to Jesus in life: Giving him all I am (124-2)

Clinging to Jesus in the pangs of death (124-3)

Clinging to Jesus in trouble, who else is there? (157-3)

Clinging to Jesus so not to lose him (124-1)

Clinging to Jesus till he blesses: Gen. 32:26 (157-1)

Clinging to Jesus; he leads me to streams of life (154-8)

Comfort extended to the soul: Ps. 116:7 (21-9)

Comfort sought; how can God be praised in death? (135-3)

Commit body and soul to God for your eternal welfare (114-6)

Condemnation removed for those in Christ: Rom. 8:1 (74-6)

Confessing Christ: He constrains weak flesh and mouth (147-9)

Confessing Christ: Jesus' help sought (147-7)

Confessing Christ with heart, mouth, deeds, and life (147-1)

Confession: I confess my guilt; have patience! (199-4)

Confession of faith: sufficiency of Christ's work of salvation (68-4)

Confession of sin; plea not to be cast away (105-2)

Confession of sinful nature: it makes me transgress (78-3)

Confession of unfaithfulness to God (132-4)

Confidence in face of trouble, that prayers are heard (86-2)

Conscience pangs turn to joy of reconciliation (113-4)

Conscience stilled by God; promise of eternal life (105-6)

Conscience tortures sinner; accuses and excuses him (105-3)

Consider God's blessing on city of Linden-trees (119-3)

Contentment experienced while journeying to heaven (75-6)

Contentment is a great treasure in this life (144-5)

Contentment now since eternal well-being is assured (84-5)

Contentment now; looking to eternal compensation (84-4)

Contentment of soul found only in concord and virtue (170-1)

Contentment with my lot though others have more (84-3)

Contentment with one's lot exhorted (144-2)

Contentment with what I have, though it be little (84-1)

Cornerstone laid by God: don't stumble but believe! (152-2)

Cornerstone laid in Israel for fall and rising of many (152-3)

Corporate prayer: How shall I meet the bridegroom? (248-5)

Courage! God promises eternal life by faith (176-5)

Creation looks to God for sustenance: Ps. 104:27-28 (187-1)

Creatures fill whole world: who could feed them all? (187-2)

Cross and crown related; Christ's wounds our comfort (12-4)

Cross bitter to flesh; endure it for future reward (99-5)

Crying from the depths to the Lord: Ps. 130:1-2 (131-1)

Cup given us may be bitter but is our medicine (99-3)

Damnation that never ends: attempts to imagine it (20-4)

Darkness has triumphed in many places (6-4)

Darkness of death and doubt turned to light by Christ (83-4)

Day of Judgment will destroy hypocrites (136-3)

Death: Committing spirit into God's hand: Ps. 31:5 (106-3a)

Death: Our imminent legacy from Adam (8-1)

Death: Prayer that faith may conquer in death's hour (111-5)

Death: The body even now bends toward the dust (8-2)

Death accepted with joy as entrance to paradise (106-3b)

Death always imminent; forsake lusts of the world! (20-9)

Death approaching: I look to Jesus, he looks on me (125-2)

Death brings down the greatest splendor (26-5)

Death comes at any time, only God knows how soon (27-1, 166-6)

Death conquered Princess' body but not her spirit (198-5)

Death decreed for all: Sirach (Apocrypha) 14:17, Rev. 22:20 (106-2d)

Death inevitable; prayer to be reminded: Ps. 90:12 (106-2b)

Death is coming; set your house in order: Is. 38:1 (106-2c)

Death is gateway to God; Christ wakes me from sleep (95-6)

Death is welcome for my soul is in his hands (127-3)

Death is welcome; I take afflictions to the grave (27-3)

Death is welcomed with peace and joy: Simeon (125-1)

Death, my way to freedom, no longer frightens me (114-5)

Death not feared: Christ our light and salvation has come (125-3)

Death welcomed by believers of new covenant (83-1)

Death's sleep welcomed for Jesus will awaken me (161-4)

Debt of sin paid by Christ on the cross (105-4)

Declaration: I will preserve Christ in my heart (248-33)

Deliverance from the furious waves of our foe (14-4)

Denial of Christ now means denial by him later (147-3)

Depravity of my heart makes me utterly wretched (199-1)

Despair: God's promise to help has not come true (13-3)

Despair: I cry to God but he does not answer (13-2)

Despair: My days are filled with sighs and tears (13-1)

Despair not when under foe's attack, little band! (42-4)

Devil not to be feared because he has been judged (80-5)

Dialogue: Anxious care and sorrow vs. trust in God (138-1)

Dialogue: Bride (Soul) and Bridegroom (Christ) (140-3)

Dialogue: Bridegroom and Bride (Christ and Believer) (49-5)

Dialogue: Doubting anxiety vs. trust in God (138-3)

Dialogue: Fear of eternity; Hope's response (60-1)

Dialogue: Fear vs. Christ's word as I consider death (60-4)

Dialogue: Fear vs. Hope as I consider death (60-2, 60-3)

Dialogue: Fear vs. Hope regarding resurrection (66-4)

Dialogue: Fear Vs. Hope that Christ is taken away (66-5)

Dialogue: Jesus and Soul list benefits of resurrection (145-1)

Dialogue: Love duet between Soul and Christ (140-6)

Dialogue: Love duet between Soul and Holy Spirit (172-5)

Dialogue: Wedding banquet is ready for the bride (49-3)

Dialogue (Christ and Believer): Christ extends hand (57-4)

Dialogue (Christ and Believer): Despair vs. comfort (21-8)

Dialogue (Christ and Believer): Fear vs. comfort (21-7)

Dialogue (Christ and Believer): United in paradise (49-6)

Dialogue (Christ and Believer): Way to heaven is worth it (58-5)

Dialogue (Christ and Believer): Way to heaven is hard (58-1)

Dialogue (Christ and Believer): Yearning for death (57-6)

Dialogue (Christ and believing Soul): Mystical union (32-5)

Dialogue (Christ and Soul); they meet in God's house (32-4)

Dialogue (Soul and Jesus): How must Jesus be received? (152-6)

Dialogue between Doubt and Confirmation (194-9)

Dialogue regarding Jesus' plan to go to Jerusalem (159-1)

Discipleship: Willing acceptance of the cross (12-5)

Discontent: Where it rules there is much grief (144-4)

Divine aid against enemies assured; sun will shine (57-5)

Divine fire: Yearning for its filling (1-3)

Doubt: Is this the one who is to help me? (186-3)

Doubt not, but trust him who is called Immanuel (107-1)

Doxology: Praise to Father, Son, and Holy Ghost (10-7, 33-6, 36-8, 62-6, 135-6, 192-3)

Doxology (Greater): Excerpt: Lk. 2:14 (191-1)

Doxology (Lesser): Part A (191-2)

Doxology (Lesser): Part B (191-3)

Doxology; prayer for victory through Jesus (106-4)

Dragon tirelessly seeks to devour God's children (130-3)

Earthly bliss and satisfaction promised (197-8)

Easter: Christ's resurrection turns our pain to joy (249-10)

Easter: Disciples arrive at tomb and find it empty (249-6)

Easter: Embalming spices and tears prepared in vain (249-4)

Easter: Jesus appears; thank God for his goodness! (66-3)

Easter: Rejoice and put away sorrow; Christ is risen (66-1)

Easter: Resurrection made everything turn out well (66-2)

Easter: Run to the empty tomb where Christ was! (249-3)

Easter: Where can I find him whom my soul loves? (249-9)

Easter promise: Myrrh will be exhanged for laurel (249-5)

Elect protected by God and Word in time of judgment (90-4)

Emmanuel: Heavenly prince has captured my heart (123-1)

Emmanuel, Jesus' name, means everything to me (248-38)

Encouragement to pray fervently in care-filled times (83-3)

Epiphany: God's radiance dispells all darkness (248-46)

Epiphany: Gold compared with heart as a fitting gift (65-4)

Epiphany: Herod assembles chief priests: Mt. 2:4-6 (248-50)

Epiphany: King Herod is frightened: Mt. 2:3 (248-48)

Epiphany: Magi come from the East: Mt. 2:1 (248-44)

Epiphany: Magi seek source of light: Mt. 2:2 (248-45)

Epiphany: My votive gift is my heart and all I am (65-6)

Epiphany: My votive gifts of faith, prayer, patience (65-5)

Epiphany: Prayer of personal surrender (65-7)

Epiphany: Prophecy fulfilled; Kings brought gifts (65-2)

Epiphany: Visitors from Sheba prophesied: Is. 60:6 (65-1)

Epiphany: What gift can I bring to Christ? (65-3)

Epiphany: Why be frightened of Jesus' presence? (248-49)

Epiphany prayer: Illumine me so I do no evil (248-47)

Escape from murderous foe assured by God's help (248-54)

Eternal damnation is like nothing on earth (20-2)

Eternal destiny kept in mind at all times (166-2)

Eternal flames of hell are no frivolous matter (20-3)

Eternal praise for divine deliverance (25-6)

Eternal torments will end when God ceases to be (20-7)

Eternal wealth ours if we abide in Christ, deny self (75-11)

Eternity, is a frightening word, receive me Jesus! (20-11)

Eternity is a thunderous word that frightens me! (20-1)

Exhortation: Bless the Lord, O my soul: Ps. 103:1-6 (28-2)

Exhortation: Heed God's invitation of grace in Christ (76-3)

Exhortation to flee sin and its judgment (20-6)

Exhortation to repent: Life can quickly end! (102-7)

Exhortation to repent: Think of your judgment! (102-5)

Exhortation to repent: Waiting is very dangerous! (102-6)

Exhortation to soul: Why are you cast down? Ps. 42:12 (21-6)

Exhortation to trust sovereignty of God (44-7)

Eyes of all wait upon the Lord: grant me light (23-3)

Failure to pray despite deliberate transgressions (87-2)

Faith alone, not good works, brings justification (37-4)

Faith and baptism lead to salvation: Mk. 16:16 (37-1)

Faith brings salvation, baptism is its seal (37-5)

Faith confessed despite circumstance: Mk. 9:24 (109-1)

Faith in adversity: Hope in God and wait for him! (155-2)

Faith in affliction; it is based on eternal covenant (99-4)

Faith in the promise that Jesus will act (109-4)

Faith is the sign of Jesus' love for his own (37-2)

Faith, not works makes us righteous before God (9-5)

Faith that God will rescue my foot out of net: Ps. 25:15 (150-6)

Faith unwavering sought despite opposition (178-7)

Faithfulness of God preserves me when worlds attacks (52-4)

Faithfulness of God to those who trust him (107-2)

Faithfulness to God avowed; world scorned (52-5)

Farewell given to world, heaven's splendor preferred (158-2)

Farewell to the world; comparing world and heaven (27-6)

Farewell world! I am going to heaven! (27-5)

Fatherly mercy: God knows we are dust: Ps. 103:13-16 (17-7)

Favor of this world rejected in favor of Christ (76-10)

Fear keeps me from seeking God openly; yet I believe (176-4)

Fear keeps me from seeking omnipotent God by day (176-3)

Fear not but trust God; no one can stop his plans! (111-2)

Fear not, I am with thee: Is. 41:10 (153-3)

Fear of foe still with me but God will work in me (67-5)

Fear of judgment: I recognize my sin (55-1)

Fear of judgment: My sin is great, where can I flee? (55-2)

Firmament of godly souls shall declare love of God (76-13)

Flesh and blood exalted by God's acceptance of it (173-1)

Flesh and blood understands Mt. Tabor but not Golgotha (22-3)

Flesh recalcitrant; but God became man to help us (3-2)

Flock of Jesus receive kindness now and reward later (104-5)

Foe cannot hurt me if Jesus is with me (248-62)

Foe's plots will fail; God will protect us (178-2)

Foes batter Christ's kingdom like waves do a ship (178-3)

Foes have all been conquered in Christ (248-64)

Foes like a lion; champion of Judah destroys them (178-5)

Foes seek our blood but call themselves Christians (178-4)

Foes would have killed us if God had not intervened (14-3)

Following Jesus into Zion; he opens way of salvation (182-8)

Foolishness of God is greater than wisdom of world (152-5)

Forsaking the world: Future in heaven with Jesus (124-5)

Forsaking what God hates; loving what he loves (30-8)

Fountain of blood cleanses me (5-3)

Funeral tribute: Nobility of Queen's faith exemplary (198-7)

Funeral tribute: She lived life ready for death (198-6)

Future blessing: Jesus alone shall be our wealth (16-5)

Future blessing requested on church, school, and state (16-4)

Future comfort greater than present cup of suffering (100-5)

Future glory much greater than present sufferings (75-7)

Garment of righteousness now; robe of glory later (162-5)

Gift I bring to Christ in manger is my very self (248-59)

Giving up life for Christ (183-3)

Glory be to God for anticipated splendor of heaven (140-7)

Glory to God in the highest: Lk. 2:14 (110-5)

Goal of my life is to prepare for death (27-2)

God and his ways trusted; his purpose revealed someday (100-4)

God as friend: Relying on him in times of opposition (139-1)
God as friend allows me to to defy all foes (139-6)
God as friend in times of adversity (139-4)
God as friend means the foe presents no danger (139-2)
God as great provider; may we praise him rightly (187-7)
God as refuge; fleeing from him like Jonah did is foolish (111-3)
God as shepherd: I need not fear anything (85-6)
God as sun and shield: Gratefulness for his protection (79-2)
God blesses all who fear him: Ps. 115:13 (196-3)
God comforted me in my grief: Ps. 94:19 (21-2)
God compassionate; his promise to hear our prayers (98-4)
God dwells in this building as well as our hearts (194-11)
God exalted by whole world for his Salvation (248-43)
God has chosen this as his house; how good for us! (194-10)
God has done all things well: daily blessings (35-4)
God has gone up with a shout: Ps. 47:5-6 (43-1)
God heals deaf, dumb, blind: we marvel (35-3)
God hears the oppressed when they cry to him (2-4)
God indwells the elect: what greater blessing is there? (34-3)
God is fountain, light, treasure, to his followers (28-4)
God is just: eternal damnation for temporal sin (20-5)
God is my confidence when all around me fails (188-2)
God is sun and shield for righteous: Ps. 84:11 (79-1)
God is the best manager of our household (197-2)
God keeps watch, hates dark, desires enlightenment (115-3)
God of Zion is king forever: Ps. 146:10 (143-5)
God ordains course of whole universe: Ps. 74:16-17 (71-4)
God owes me nothing; I have but done my duty (84-2)
God seeks people by sending fishermen: Jer. 16:16 (88-1)
God seeks sinners even though we reject him (88-2)
God seeks us when we stray from proper path (88-3)
God sent his Son so all might have eternal life (68-1)
God sustains all creatures; he will also help me (187-5)
God well-intentioned toward you since infancy (197-7)
God's attributes can be seen in heavens: Ps. 36:5 (17-3)
God's blessing assured if we are faithful stewards (88-5)
God's children lost without his aid: Ps. 124:1-3 (14-1)
God's chosen dwelling receives his blessing (34-4)
God's commissioning assures success despite obstacles (88-6)
God's continuing blessing on governors sought (119-7)
God's counsel needed for successful endeavors (97-1)
God's favor sure for those who love God completely (77-2)
God's grace keeps from harm if commandments obeyed (97-4)
God's grace sought in forgiveness of sins (97-5)
God's greatness is beyond all else: Jer. 10:6 (110-3)
God's hand works in unseen places to move the flesh (147-8)
God's help is only sure defense against the foe (178-1)
God's intentions are kind despite his angry look (188-3)
God's invitation came to us Gentiles and enlightened us (76-6)
God's invitation of grace spurned by many (76-4)
God's invitation rejected by perverse; I will accept (76-5)
God's judgment breaks like a storm on Jerusalem (46-3)
God's kindness is in vain: no repentance produced (90-2)
God's love shown: we are God's children: 1 Jn. 3:1 (64-1)
God's love shown in Christ's birth: give thanks! (64-2)
God's name and praise reach ends of earth: Ps. 48:10 (171-1)

God's name is exalted by all creation (171-2)
God's people to reflect his glory despite persecution (76-9)
God's praise expressed by his people in good deeds (76-14)
God's presence alone is source of our joy (194-8)
God's promises of a Savior have now been fulfilled (167-3)
God's purposes prevail despite opposition of devils (153-5)
God's radiance fills the sanctuary he has chosen (194-3)
God's sovereign rule brings blessing to us (197-1)
God's sovereign ways accepted, even affliction (100-6)
God's sovereign ways trusted and accepted as just (100-1)
God's sovereign will: I shall trust it always (72-2b)
God's sovereign will: Submission brings blessings (72-2a)
God's sovereign will accepted, even affliction (75-14, 99-6)
God's sovereign will accepted; acceptance of death (73-4)
God's sovereign will desired at all times (72-5)
God's sovereign will is that he should bless you! (72-3)
God's sovereign will is to sweeten thy cross! (72-4)
God's sovereign will to be trusted even in suffering (73-1)
God's sovereign will trusted and accepted (98-1, 99-1, 144-3)
God's sovereign will trusted in good and bad times (72-1)
God's sovereignty: In affliction God comforts (12-7)
God's sovereignty complete: to accomplish or hinder (107-5)
God's sovereignty complete and may be relied upon (107-3)
God's sovereignty is Alpha and Omega in weal and woe (41-3)
God's time is best; for living or dying: Acts 17:28 (106-2a)
God's ways are best; what seems bad is my gain (92-1)
God's ways are unfathomable but ever for our best (188-4)
God's ways lead through testing to Canaan (197-4)
God's ways trusted though they be like medicine (100-3)
God's ways trusted; he will change my misfortune (100-2)
God's will accepted and followed, even to death (111-4)
God's will accepted regarding life or death (97-8)
God's will best for me; I gladly accept it (97-3)
God's will is made known, servants must obey (45-2)
God's will is to extend grace to us in Christ (73-5)
God's will trusted and accepted, building on him (111-1)
God's wisdom perfect; he knows when to allow grief (92-4)
God's wisdom trusted; his providence accepted (97-9)
God's wonders make us speechless with astonishment (35-2)
God's Word comforts in all circumstances of life (97-6)
God's Word is my true treasure, all else is trickery! (18-4)
God's Word manifested: God protects church in peace (126-5)
Golden Rule is central: Mt. 7:12 (24-3)
Government is gift and image of God (119-5)
Grain of wheat dies to produce fruit; so our body (114-4)
Gratitude: What can I do for God's blessings? (39-6)
Grief and suffering has sapped all my strength (135-4)
Guardian of Israel does not sleep (193-2)
Guilt: No one justified before God: Ps. 143:2 (105-1)
Hallelujah, strength and might to name of Almighty (29-7)
Happy is he whose help is God of Jacob: Ps. 146:5 (143-3)
Hastening to Jesus for healing with feeble steps (78-2)
Hatred manifested by a world alienated from God (170-2)
Healing sought from physician of souls (135-2)
Heart as coin of tribute, God's image on it restored (163-3)
Heart held captive by world, freed by God's grace (163-4)

Heart is fallen: it bears thorns and will be judged (136-2)
Heart is no fine residence but God illumines it (248-53)
Heart is obstinate and hopeless: Jer. 17:9 (modified) (176-1)
Heart's ardor offered in devotion to infinite Father (173-5)
Hearts given to Christ become his throne (248-52)
Heaven anticipated; freed like an eagle (56-3)
Heaven entered only by bearing one's cross (146-6)
Heaven glimpsed with its robe and crown (162-6)
Heaven's manna delights me now on earth already (123-2)
Heavenly feast of love's sweet manna already begun (76-11)
Heavenly sabbath sought; ensured by God's indwelling (148-5)
Heavens tell the glory of God: Ps. 19:1, 3 (76-1)
Hell can do nothing; we are in Jesus' hands (248-63)
Herod plots to kill Christchild: Mt. 2:7-8 (248-55)
Herod's deceitful heart is known to the Son (248-56)
Holding fast to Jesus in life and death (133-6)
Honesty is rare; we are not honest by nature (24-2)
Hope: Exhortation to trust God's sovereignty (13-6)
Hope: Sorrow real yet God can change it to joy (13-4)
Hope gained by looking to heaven; weeping of no use (13-5)
Hope in the Lord for he will pardon: Ps. 130:7-8 (131-5)
Hope is placed in Christ alone; only he can help (33-1)
Hope of heaven comforts me in present suffering (57-2)
Hope rewarded in God's own time; he may be trusted (86-6, 186-11)
Hope vs. Fear: Doubt lets faith's wick almost go out (109-3)
Hope vs. Fear: vacillation between the two (109-2)
Hope's response to Christ's word: Death not feared (60-5)
Human will perverse: it vacillates and rejects dying (73-3)
Humility: Man is but dust, should he exalt himself? (47-3)
Humility is mark of true Christian; God hates pride (47-2)
Hypocrisy and deceit is rampant in the world (52-2)
Hypocrisy and dishonesty, etc. is of the devil (24-4)
Hypocrisy plagues all Christendom (179-2)
Hypocrisy warned against: Sirach (Apocrypha) 1:28 (179-1)
Hypocrites outwardly beautiful but inwardly filthy (179-3)
Hypocritical world hates me but God is my friend! (52-3)
Impenitence: God's discipline in vain: Jer. 5:3 (102-1)
Impenitence: God's forbearance will end! Rom. 2:4-5 (102-4)
Impenitence: Woe to the soul that persists in it! (102-3)
Impenitence nullifies God's attempts to work in us (102-2)
In life or death, Christ saves us from Adam's curse (114-7)
Incarnation: Christ became poor so we might be rich (91-5)
Incarnation: Creator exalts us by becoming flesh (121-2)
Incarnation: Eternal good clothed in flesh and blood (91-2)
Incarnation: Eternal light becomes a tiny child (91-3)
Incarnation: God became servant; do not take offence! (186-1)
Incarnation: Incomprehensible mystery of grace (121-3)
Incarnation: Love shown when God became son of David (96-2)
Incarnation: Man lowly yet exalted in incarnation (110-4)
Incarnation: Praise God for coming down from heaven (110-2)
Incarnation: Praise to Christ for his human birth (91-1)
Incarnation: We see God face to face! (133-2)
Incarnation: Word became flesh; the Lord became a servant (40-2)
Individual's response to God who fulfilled promise (30-7)

Integrity makes us like God and angels (24-5)
Invitation of grace is offered by the Savior! (30-5)
Jerusalem brings flood of judgment on itself (46-2)
Jesus appears to disciples secretly gathered: Jn. 20:19 (42-2)
Jesus appears to gathered disciples: a lesson for us (42-5)
Jesus as good shepherd: he gave his life for sheep (85-2)
Jesus as Lord and Prince of Peace confessed by church (67-7)
Jesus as physician; the balm of Gilead for sin (25-3)
Jesus as shepherd shows his love by dying for sheep (85-5)
Jesus at God's right hand; I will join him there (128-3)
Jesus conquered death, yet I still experience fear (67-3)
Jesus foretells his death: Lk. 18:31, 34 (22-1)
Jesus forgives, frees, and comforts us (5-4)
Jesus found; I will rejoice and not let him go (154-7)
Jesus heals our body and soul by faith (48-6)
Jesus heard in his Word and found in Father's house (154-6)
Jesus is a shield for believers in persecution (42-6)
Jesus is gone; this brings despair to my soul! (154-1)
Jesus is gone; where might I find him whom I love? (154-2)
Jesus recognized as true shepherd (175-4)
Jesus remains my delight, comfort, and sustenance (147-10)
Jesus remains with me though the wise men depart (248-61)
Jesus shall be everything to me; my beginning and end (190-5)
Jesus sleeps in boat during storm; I am without hope (81-1)
Jesus who suffered leads me through death to life (127-2)
Jesus will gather us like chicks in hell's storm (40-7)
Jesus would shelter righteous like sheep or chicks (46-5)
Jesus' baptism commences his ministry: bath for sin (7-1)
Jesus' name alone shall be in my heart (248-40)
Jesus' name inspires no fear of death, rather joy (248-39)
Jesus' name is my first and last word (171-4)
Jesus' name means everything to me in the new year (171-3)
Jesus' passion tore my soul from darkness (78-1)
Jesus' word brings salvation despite weak faith (38-4)
Jesus' word comes to comfort me in my suffering (38-3)
Jesus' words not understood by reason: Jn. 10:6 (175-5)
Jesus' words promise abundant life to all who follow (175-6)
John the Baptist: A herald announcing the King (30-4)
John the Baptist: A voice crying in the wilderness (30-6)
John the Baptist: Praise God for sending his servant! (30-3)
Judgment: Light of Word taken from desecrated temple (90-3)
Judgment Day: Many rejected as evildoers: Mt. 7:22-23 (45-4)
Judgment Day is near so let us watch and pray (115-6)
Judgment escaped by faith in the Son: Jn. 3:18 (68-5)
Judgment is imminent yet sinners disregard judge (90-1)
Judgment like that of Sodom falls on unmerciful (89-3)
Judgment not feared if Christ is guarantor of debts (168-4)
Judgment not reserved for Jerusalem alone (46-4)
Judgment self-determined; God helps us do his will (45-6)
Judgment well-deserved; man himself shows no mercy (89-2)
King of Heaven welcomed into the Zion of our hearts (182-2)
Kingdom of heaven sought: there triune God praised (176-6)
Lamb is worthy to receive all honor: Rev. 5:12-13 (21-11)
Lament: My cup is filled with woe, joy's wine fails (155-1)
Lamentation: Sighings, tears, etc. fill my days (21-3)
Languishing yet relying on Jesus' steadfast love (3-4)

Last day: Frightening, yet Jesus comforts me (70-9)
Last Day: Frightening for sinners, joyful for chosen (70-2)
Last Day: God remembers his servants (70-6)
Last Day: Lift up your heads, O ye righteous! (70-8)
Last Day: Yearning for exodus out of this world (70-3)
Last Day anticipated: Joy as soul thinks of heaven (70-7)
Last Day anticipated despite cataclysmic events (70-10)
Last Day will come despite scoffers (70-5)
Laughter for great things God has done: Ps. 126:2-3 (110-1)
Law discloses sin; gospel gives future beyond death (9-6)
Law given to show us we were too weak to keep it (9-2)
Law shows me guilty; repentance brings forgiveness (33-2)
Lay down your very being before the entering king (182-5)
Leipzig blessed like Jerusalem with peace and justice (193-4)
Leprosy of sin has infected entire world (25-2)
Life and death confront me on way to heavenly wedding (162-1)
Life devoured death by dying (4-5)
Life is like a journey by ship through stormy seas (56-2)
Light dawns for the righteous: Ps. 97:11-12 (195-1)
Light fills world; promise of salvation by faith (125-4)
Light from God promises blessing greater than earthly (1-4)
Loathing to live here; yearning for tranquil heaven (170-5)
Longing for God; He is my indwelling rest (148-3)
Longing for heavenly pastures, tents of Kedar (30-10)
Lord crowns the year with his blessing (187-3)
Lord hears our cry in Christ's name; wants to help (115-5)
Lord remembers and blesses his people: Ps. 115:12 (196-2)
Lord shows mercy to needy, giving them Word of life (186-8)
Lord's table: A mystery beyond human understanding (180-4)
Lord's table: Yearning for its blessings (180-3)
Losing Jesus: Reunion with him after death (124-4)
Love draws the heart gently to Jesus like a bride (36-3)
Love for God declared; prayer that it be constant (77-3)
Love for Jesus and faith in him confessed (75-12)
Love God with all your heart, soul, mind: Lk. 10:27 (77-1)
Love imperfect: I want to love yet lack the power (77-5)
Love made Christ leave glory and sacrifice himself (182-4)
Love of God constant despite billows and storms (92-2)
Love of God fully satisfies and opens heaven to us (169-4)
Love of God practised; love of world put to death (169-5)
Love of God that gave Son as ransom is like no other (174-3)
Loving God alone despite the world's wooing (169-2)
Loving God alone; he is the highest worth (169-3)
Loving God with all one's heart because he loved us (174-2)
Loving one another: Prayer for divine help (197-5)
Loving one's neighbor: Prayer for divine help (169-7)
Loving one's neighbor required of those who love God (169-6)
Magi present their gifts to Christchild: Mt. 2:9-11 (248-58)
Magi warned to return by a different way: Mt. 2:12 (248-60)
Magnificat: God casts down proud, exalts lowly (10-4)
Magnificat: God helps lowly but scatters proud (10-3)
Magnificat: God remembers his mercy: Lk. 1:54 (10-5)
Magnificat: Mary as favored among women: Lk. 1:46-48 (10-1)
Magnificat: Mary's confession and our stubborn silence (147-2)
Magnificat: Promise to Abraham fulfilled (10-6)
Magnificat: The holy, mighty God has blessed richly (10-2)

Mammon and world rejected in favor of Christ (105-5)
Man is only a worm yet God protects him with angels (19-4)
Mark of Christian is non-judging generosity (185-5)
Marriage blessing pronounced as couple is united (195-4)
Menacing judgment and peril; we cry out in his name (116-2)
Mercy and favor shown by God to those who show mercy (164-5)
Mercy seat established, grace extended in Christ (125-5)
Mercy taught by Christ yet we ignore the needy (164-2)
Mercy will be shown to me by God for I repent (199-3)
Mighty fortress is our God against ancient foe (80-1)
Misfortune accepted if God has chosen it for me (97-7)
Morning of comfort comes; Jesus rescues us (38-5)
Mortal schemes easily overthrown by God (248-57)
Mourning: Grief shared by everyone in the land (198-2)
Mourning: Music silenced in time of royal mourning (198-3)
Mourning: Tolling bells ring day after day (198-4)
Mourning at the tomb of the Princess (198-1)
Mourning for Jesus; deferring pleasure till heaven (159-3)
Murderous foe too strong for our small strength (14-2)
Mystic union with Christ (172-6) See also "Dialogue," "Clinging", "Bride"
National blessing requested of God (29-5)
National misfortune strikes other lands but not ours (143-4)
National response to continued blessing (29-6)
Nature and grace tell of God's gracious invitation (76-2)
Nature testifies of God's majesty (17-2)
New Year: Committing year to God in praise and faith (41-6)
New Year: Prayer to end year as well as it is begun (41-2)
New Year: Thanks for old year; prayer for new (41-1)
New Year's prayer: Come and bless thy church! (61-3)
New Year's prayer for blessing as in the past year (28-5)
New Year's prayer for protection and blessing (143-6)
New Year's prayer; thanks for blessings in Christ (28-6)
New Year's wish: Only to have Jesus as shepherd (190-4)
Offering of thanks to God at end of election day (119-6)
Old age: Blessing to old age: Deut. 33:25; Gen. 21:22 (71-3)
Old age reminisces about God's help: Ps. 74:12 (71-1)
Old age too feeble for new tasks: 2 Sam. 19:35, 37 (71-2)
Old year comes to close: praise God for blessings (28-1)
Out of the depths I cry to thee: Ps. 130:1-3 (38-1)
Parable of vineyard laborers (excerpt): Mt. 20:14 (144-1)
Paradise reopened to us today (151-5)
Pardon for sin sought since God sees contrite heart (87-4)
Paschal feast: we celebrate it in the light of joy (4-7)
Pasture is Word of God, sheepfold is heaven (104-4)
Patience in affliction is rewarded by Father's help (93-3)
Patience! Soon life's imperfections gone in heaven (30-11)
Pay to every man what is due him (163-1)
Pay vows to God for civic blessings, seek further blessing (120-3)
Paying God, giver of all, his due: our poor hearts (163-2)
Peace be upon Israel; God blesses with peace (34-5)
Peace in face of foes, God's angel hosts protect me (149-3)
Peace offered by Christ to troubled conscience (158-1)
Pentecost: God dwells in us; we shall live with him (59-4)
Pentecost: God honors mortals by indwelling them (59-2)

Pentecost: Prayer and praise for Holy Ghost (59-3)
Perform allotted tasks, trusting God's sovereignty (88-7)
Persecution: God rescues us like Joseph from Herod (58-2)
Persecution: God shows me a new land (58-4)
Persecution and death accepted without fear (183-2)
Persecution awaits true disciples of Christ (44-3)
Persecution of disciples foretold: Jn. 16:2 (44-1) cf. 183-1
Persecution's storms: God watches over church (44-6)
Persecutors think they please God: Jn. 16:2 (44-2)
Persevering in prayer until God hears and blesses (98-5)
Physical dearth but spiritual nourishment (186-7)
Pity the hearts who scoff at law against hatred! (170-3)
Ponder Christ's love which enlists us to the fight (80-3)
Posessing Jesus is the greatest blessing and comfort (147-6)
Poverty strikes Christ as well as his members (186-2)
Poverty vs. wealth: Believer also spiritually poor (75-9)
Poverty vs. wealth: Earthly wealth can lead to hell (75-2)
Poverty vs. wealth: Jesus shall be everything to me (75-3)
Poverty vs. wealth: positions reversed in eternity (75-4)
Poverty vs. wealth: The hungry shall eat: Ps. 22:26 (75-1)
Praise and honor to God for his protection and blessing (107-7)
Praise and honor to God who does wonders and comforts (117-1)
Praise for knowledge of salvation; prayer for others (79-4)
Praise God all ye lands, for his help in trouble! (51-1)
Praise God for blessing Jerusalem: Ps. 147:12-14 (119-1)
Praise God for blessings that are new each morning (16-3)
Praise God for Christ's victory over hell and devil! (249-11)
Praise God for his Son who is our victorious Savior (248-36)
Praise God for the blessing of good government (69-4)
Praise God in his glory! (11-1)
Praise God that he sent his Son, preceded by John (167-2)
Praise God who leads us to pasture like a shepherd (190-3)
Praise God with ardent songs for blessings to Zion (16-2)
Praise offered and vows paid to God in Zion: Ps. 65:1 (120-1)
Praise the Lord: all that is in me; that hath breath (137-5)
Praise the Lord, O my soul, for blessings: Ps. 103:2 (69-1)
Praise the Lord, O my soul!: Ps. 146:1 (143-1)
Praise the Lord, the mighty king, with psaltry and lyre (137-1)
Praise the Lord who bears you on eagles' wings (137-2)
Praise the Lord who fashions you, covers with wings (137-3)
Praise the Lord who has poured blessings on us (137-4)
Praise the Lord with music: Ps. 149:1, 150:4, 6 (190-1)
Praise to Christ who rose victorious and comforts us (134-6)
Praise to God: Creator himself supplies our needs (117-6)
Praise to God: Humans exhorted to musical praise (110-6)
Praise to God: Music as thanksgiving and sacrifice (1-5)
Praise to God: Praise him all who confess his name! (117-8)
Praise to God: Rejoice before Lord and pay your vows! (117-9)
Praise to God by people for national blessings (69-6)
Praise to God for blessing our city and borders (29-4)
Praise to God for gifts of grace through his Spirit (173-4)
Praise to God for help when I cried to him in need (117-4)
Praise to God for his goodness to sanctified spirits (173-2)
Praise to God for his sustenance of all creatures (69-2)
Praise to God for mighty power which keeps our land (71-5)

Praise to God for never deserting his people (117-5)
Praise to God for reappearance of victorious Christ (134-4)
Praise to God for renewed national blessings (190-2)
Praise to God for sending His Son, our Salvation (167-1)
Praise to God for sustaining his creation (117-3)
Praise to God from heaven's host and all creatures (117-2)
Praise to God that Zion is still his city (29-3)
Praise to God the Creator: my light and life (129-1)
Praise to God the Holy Ghost: my comfort and strength (129-3)
Praise to God the Son: my Salvation, my life (129-2)
Praise to Him who is praised in heaven by angels (195-6)
Praise to the Lamb who conquered Satan by his blood (149-2)
Praise to the Trinity, who is praised by all (129-4)
Praise to the Trinity; singing "Holy" with angels (129-5)
Praises that are weak but sincere heard in heaven (36-7)
Praising Christ's name at all times (148-6)
Praising God all life long; reaching all the earth (117-7)
Praising God in his temple for his daily blessings (51-2)
Praising God with angels; prayer that they protect us (130-6)
Pray as you watch: beg for mercy on your debt (115-4)
Prayer: Accept my imperfect, earthly songs (25-5)
Prayer: Add spiritual blessings to our temporal ones (41-4)
Prayer: Be my advocate when trumpet sounds judgment (127-4)
Prayer: Behold my foes; without thy help I am ruined! (153-1)
Prayer: Bless Christendom, grant a peaceful year (40-8)
Prayer: Bless us anew each morning and we will live godly (51-3)
Prayer: Bless us this new year for thy name's sake (171-6, 190-7)
Prayer: Bread of Life, revive my soul, I hunger for thee (162-3)
Prayer: Bring my soul to thee and raise my body on last day (149-7)
Prayer: Cast down the pride of the enemy (126-4)
Prayer: Christ who suffered for me, have mercy! (127-1)
Prayer: Come, bring me to thee in heavenly Salem (128-2)
Prayer: Conquer the flesh so it may hold thy divine power (36-6)
Prayer: Cornerstone, help me to find salvation in thee (152-4)
Prayer: Crucify fleshly desires in me (22-4)
Prayer: Crucify old nature so the new nature may live (22-5, 132-6, 164-6)
Prayer: Defeat Satan who seeks to harm thine elect (41-5)
Prayer: Destroy my sinful flesh but spare my soul (48-4)
Prayer: Dispel the derision of church's enemies (126-2)
Prayer: Do not hide thyself in the cloud of my sins! (154-4)
Prayer: Do not take Word away, it is our confidence (18-5)
Prayer: Dwell in me by a faith expressed through love (77-6)
Prayer: Enlighten mind and heart as only Christ can (116-6)
Prayer: Fight our foes: false brethren and lastly death (126-3)
Prayer: Forgive, keep us steadfast till death (127-5)
Prayer: Forgive me and break sin's yoke (113-7)
Prayer: Forgive me and break sin's yoke (113-7)
Prayer: Forgive me and break sin's yoke (113-7)
Prayer: God, why have you turned from me? (21-4)
Prayer: Good Shepherd, lead us to life (184-6)
Prayer: Grant humility that I not forfeit salvation (47-4)
Prayer: Grant me faith, forgive my sins as promised (37-6)
Prayer: Grant peace and good government (42-7, 126-6)
Prayer: Grant that I do thy will diligently (45-7)
Prayer: Have mercy on me, a sinner, for Jesus' sake (55-3)
Prayer: Have mercy on me, burdened with sin! (113-2)

Prayer: Help me surrender myself to thee (163-5)
Prayer: Help me to live faithfully until I reach heaven (153-9)
Prayer: Help me to live only for thy honor (248-41)
Prayer: Holy Ghost, complete thy work of grace in me (194-6)
Prayer: I love thee above all else, even in sorrow! (174-5)
Prayer: I trust in thee; let me not be confounded! (52-6)
Prayer: I turn to Jesus for relief in my heartache (48-7)
Prayer: Jesus, keep us with the light of thy Word (6-5)
Prayer: Jesus, Son of David (Messiah), have mercy on me! (23-1)
Prayer: Keep my soul in death until the resurrection (19-7)
Prayer: Lead me in thy truth; I wait on thee: Ps. 25:5 (150-4)
Prayer: Let my heart be like fertile soil (18-3)
Prayer: Let not evil infiltrate us (2-6)
Prayer: Lord of all grace, see how burdened I am with sin (113-1)
Prayer: Lord of life and death, let me die well (8-6)
Prayer: Make soil of our heart receptive to thy Word (181-5)
Prayer: May angels protect us; take us up like Elijah (130-5)
Prayer: May I be a child of peace until I enter heaven (158-3)
Prayer: May my baptism's healing purpose ever be realized (165-3)
Prayer: May thy invitation to thy table not be in vain (180-7)
Prayer: Melt my heart so I will show love to others (164-4)
Prayer: My end is near, take my soul into thy hands (156-2)
Prayer: My heart is prepared as thy dwelling (74-3)
Prayer: O Christ, remain our light (6-2)
Prayer: O God of love, kindle a heart of love in me! (185-1)
Prayer: Open to me the portals of thy sweet blessing (32-6)
Prayer: Pass not by without healing and blessing me (23-2)
Prayer: Peace comes from thee; keep us faithful (101-3)
Prayer: Plea for Christ not to leave (11-4)
Prayer: Pour Spirit of joy into my despairing heart (73-2)
Prayer: Preserve and keep me; then will I praise God (69-5)
Prayer: Preserve us from thy enemies by thy Word (126-1)
Prayer: Remain with us for night approaches: Lk. 24:29 (6-1)
Prayer: Remember Jesus' death and have mercy on me! (101-6)
Prayer: Rescue us from the chastisement of war (116-5)
Prayer: Sanctify me till death; You conquered death and sin (165-5)
Prayer: Search me O God and try my heart: Ps. 139:23 (136-1)
Prayer: Send love's fire into our hearts, thy temple (34-1)
Prayer: Since we are thy people, hear one final request (119-8)
Prayer: Source of all, grant health to body and soul (24-6)
Prayer: Spare us from judgment of national disasters (101-1)
Prayer: Spare us from thy zealous wrath! (101-4)
Prayer: Spare us from war, our deserved judgment (101-2)
Prayer: Spare us in judgment for Jesus' sake (46-6)
Prayer: Stir our spirits with thy Spirit (173-6)
Prayer: Strengthen, heal, wash me; take me home (113-8, 168-6)
Prayer: Take up residence in our heart as promised (34-2)
Prayer: That I avoid sin and maintain union with Christ (5-7)
Prayer: That I live or die in Christ (3-6)
Prayer: Thy will be done in living and dying (156-6)
Prayer: Thy Word is our light, help us keep it to end (6-3)
Prayer: Wedding garment of salvation sought (162-4)
Prayer: Why dost thou stand far off in my peril? (81-2)

Prayer claiming God's promise to indwell our hearts (74-2)
Prayer dedicating new sanctuary and our hearts to God (194-2)
Prayer for a compassionate heart toward neighbor (77-4)
Prayer for blessing all our days: Sirach (Apocrypha) 50:23-24 (192-2)
Prayer for blessing and spiritual protection on nation (90-5)
Prayer for blessing on just administrators (193-5)
Prayer for blessing on nation and spiritual protection (101-7)
Prayer for blessing; to be led in God's ways forever (108-5)
Prayer for constancy; ensured by grace, not works (177-4)
Prayer for continued blessing on new government (71-7)
Prayer for divine indwelling (172-3)
Prayer for forgiving spirit and Word's nourishment (177-3)
Prayer for grace to keep true faith of God's Word (177-1, 185-6)
Prayer for healing and cleansing; promise to praise God (25-4)
Prayer for help and protection in spiritual battle (177-5)
Prayer for help in face of growing threat from foes (153-4)
Prayer for help in face of lions and dragons (153-2)
Prayer for help; declaration of confidence in God (98-2)
Prayer for hope in death; not relying on good works (177-2)
Prayer for Jesus to direct and keep us true always (248-42)
Prayer for King of Kings to protect Christendom (6-6)
Prayer for mercy: I sink in the deep mire of sin! (179-5)
Prayer for mercy and lenient judgment (179-6)
Prayer for mercy on this poor sinner (135-1)
Prayer for new government: righteousness and blessing (120-5)
Prayer for protection and preservation in the truth (79-6)
Prayer for protection and the light of God's Word (79-5)
Prayer for protection from enemies: Ps. 74:19 (71-6)
Prayer for Spirit's intercession (183-4)
Prayer for stronger faith in face of sin and death (78-7)
Prayer for victory when temptation assails (111-6)
Prayer in Jesus' name: Bless us all this year! (171-5)
Prayer longing for Jesus, my all, to come (154-3)
Prayer of application: Touch my ears and tongue (35-6)
Prayer of confession; faith will produce good deeds (33-4)
Prayer of confession; request for advocacy (87-3)
Prayer of hope and trust in God: Ps. 25:1-2 (150-2)
Prayer of lament: the narrow way full of affliction (3-1)
Prayer of praise and dedication to Trinity (29-8, 51-4, 167-5)
Prayer of repentance, returning to God (55-5)
Prayer of Soul offering itself to Christ (147-5)
Prayer of submission to God's will in all things (156-4)
Prayer offering weak faith to him who can illumine me (180-5)
Prayer that Christ act as Prince of Peace for us (143-7)
Prayer that Christ illuminate and kindle the soul (96-3)
Prayer that God accept our efforts and bless them (194-12)
Prayer that God bless us and bring salvation to others (76-7)
Prayer that God enlighten soul and lead to right path (96-4)
Prayer that God guide my wayward steps (96-5)
Prayer that God will keep his own until eternity (184-5)
Prayer that God's love to me not be in vain (180-6)
Prayer that old nature would die and new nature live (96-6)
Prayer to avoid sin by Spirit's power (163-6)
Prayer to be sanctified by Spirit as Isaiah was (194-5)
Prayer to keep resolve firm until I reach heaven (166-3)

Prayer to love God with complete devotion (33-5)

Prayers answered eventually, though help be deferred (86-5)

Prepare for judgment day: watch and pray! (115-1)

Promise of God's indwelling: Jn. 14:23 (59-1, 172-2)

Promises of God fulfilled, unlike those of world (86-4)

Promises of God's Word are sure and bring us to heaven (86-3)

Queen's fame and legacy lives on (198-10)

Reason silenced; hope and comfort extended in Christ (178-6)

Receiving God with heart and mouth; resting in him (148-4)

Reconciled with God: now Satan can not harm us (122-4)

Reconciliation with God brings this song of joy (199-8)

Refuge only in Christ; where else could I turn? (114-2)

Rejecting the world; looking to blessings hereafter (8-5)

Rejecting world and yielding life to Christ (123-6)

Rejection of world in favor of Jesus (70-11)

Rejoice, for Christ loves and defends his flock! (184-3)

Rejoice, for Christ will return, though Satan attacks! (74-5)

Rejoice, hasten to meet Trinity in his sanctuary! (194-7)

Rejoice in Zion's pastures (heavenly Jerusalem)! (30-12)

Rejoice in Zion's tents, O redeemed multitude! (30-1)

Rejoice, O my heart, because thy Jesus has come! (68-2)

Rejoice Zion, you are God's people! (193-1, 193-6)

Relief that Christ speaks a word and calms the storm (81-6)

Religion acceptable to God helps the poor: Is. 58:7-8 (39-1)

Remain faithful in suffering; a crown awaits you (186-10)

Remember Christ, risen from the dead: 2 Tim. 2:8 (67-1)

Reminding Jesus that he is a God of love and peace (116-3)

Repentance brings God's word of comfort (199-5)

Repentance sought so an angel will take me to heaven (149-5)

Resolve to serve and praise despite fickle tendencies (30-9)

Resound ye songs! God prepares souls as his temples (172-1)

Response at manger: Recognizing Messiah as John did (121-4)

Response at manger: Wonder that Christ is so lowly (121-5)

Response at manger: Worshipful doxology (121-6)

Resurection is foundation for our faith (145-3)

Resurrected Jesus encountered and praised (134-1)

Resurrected with Christ: we flee sin and bear fruit (31-5)

Resurrection: Alpha and Omega has keys to death and hell (31-3)

Resurrection: Praise to Christ for his resurrection (145-5)

Resurrection assures us of comfort after death (249-7)

Resurrection guarantees freedom from indictment (145-2)

Resurrection light has come: Offer praise to God! (134-2)

Resurrection of Christ: Heaven and earth rejoice (31-2)

Resurrection of Christ assures my ascension (95-7)

Resurrection of Jesus gives me hope in death (145-4)

Reward comes after suffering; this is our comfort (12-6)

Righteous living is what God requires: Mic. 6:8 (45-1)

Righteousness and purity found only in Christ's blood (136-4)

Rise, O my soul, and sing a song of thanks to God! (69-3)

Sabbath: Hastening with joy to God's house (148-2)

Salvation brought by Jesus' grace alone (38-2)

Salvation, for which the fathers longed, has come (30-2)

Salvation has come: faith, not works, count with God (9-1)

Salvation is a gift of which no one is worthy (74-8)

Salvation offered in love, gained by faith: believe! (174-4)

Samaritan leper returns to give thanks: Lk. 17:15-16 (17-4)

Satan cannot prevail against thee; God is with thee! (107-4)

Savior knocks at thy heart's door; open to him! (180-2)

Savior powerfully manifested, nurturing body and soul (186-5)

Seed lies dormant unless soil is prepared (181-4)

Self-examination: The law shows us to be sinners (132-3)

Serpent brought death; woman's seed brings salvation (40-5)

Serpent, he who will bruise your head is born! (40-4)

Serpent vanquished by Christ's passion (40-6)

Sevants of God will have to give strict account (45-3)

Sharing pleases God; do not neglect it: Heb. 13:16 (39-4)

Sharing the pain of others makes us like God (164-3)

Sheep come to Jesus and scorn the enticing world (184-2)

Shepherd calls sheep by name and leads them: Jn. 10:3 (175-1)

Shepherd hidden; Fearful, I cry "abba" in faith (104-3)

Shepherd of Israel sought in prayer: Ps. 80:1 (104-1)

Shepherd on high cares for me, why should I worry? (104-2)

Shepherd that was long-awaited has now come (184-1)

Shepherd watches sheep when hirelings sleep (85-4)

Shepherd's Psalm: paraphrase of Ps. 23:1-2 (112-1)

Shepherd's Psalm: paraphrase of Ps. 23:2-3 (112-2)

Shepherd's Psalm: paraphrase of Ps. 23:4 (112-3)

Shepherd's Psalm: paraphrase of Ps. 23:5 (112-4)

Shepherd's Psalm: paraphrase of Ps. 23:6 (112-5)

Shepherd's Psalm: Ps. 23:1-2 (85-3, 104-6)

Shortcomings acknowledged; adequacy in Christ's blood (89-6)

Sickness: Nothing sound is in my body: Ps. 38:3 (25-1)

Sighs and tears show my unspoken remorse (199-2)

Silence impossible after great things God has done (173-3)

Simon Peter sent by Christ to fish for men: Lk. 5:10 (88-4)

Sin: Resist it or its poison will eventually kill you (54-1)

Sin came through Adam; cleansing through Christ (136-5)

Sin caused us all to be enslaved by death (4-3)

Sin is a poison that infects body; even more the soul (48-2)

Sin outwardly appealing but like a whitewashed tomb (54-2)

Sin's account paid by Jesus' drops of blood (89-5)

Sin's burden is greatest foe; removed by the Savior (139-5)

Sin's burden removed in Christ: Ps. 130:3-4 (131-2)

Sin's wage is suffering: I would rather suffer now (48-3)

Sincerity is a mark of the Christian (24-1)

Siners are of the devil; resist him and he flees (54-3)

Sinful nature, devil and world makes us prone to sin (101-5)

Sinking into the abyss with no one to help (9-3)

Sins abhorrent to God; in Christ we find cleansing (5-2)

Sins' debt forgiven in Jesus who is end of the law (89-4)

Sleeping still? Judgment will awaken you! (115-2)

Sodom rejected for prospect of heaven (146-3)

Song of praise for Christ's victory in resurrection (67-4)

Songs of praise only gift of thanks I can bring (17-5)

Sorrow: Is there any like mine? Lam. 1:12 (46-1)

Sorrow brief and will turn to joy; Jesus comforts us (103-6)

Sorrow turned to joy; water of weeping into wine (21-10)

Sorrow will turn to joy when Christ returns (103-4)

Sorrow will turn to joy; I will see Jesus again (103-5)

Sorrows are best born with composure (93-2)

Soul, prepare thyself for the Spirit's entrance (172-4)

Sow plentifully in this age to gather a rich harvest (185-3)
Sowing in tears, reaping with joy (146-5)
Spirit leads all who love God in paths of blessing (108-6)
Spirit teaches us how to pray effectively (183-5)
Spirit will come and lead into all truth: Jn. 16:13 (108-4)
Spirit's help sought to accept word of new life (175-7)
Spiritual death and resurrection: old and new life (31-6)
Spiritual health desired more than physical health (156-5)
Spiritual wealth given by Christ through Spirit (75-10)
Stand firm with Christ in battle; victory assured (80-6)
Staying with Jesus through persecution and woe (182-6)
Stewardship: All my debts are engraved in God's book (168-3)
Stewardship: Frightening command to give account (168-1)
Stewardship: Unfaithfulness brings fear of judgment (168-2)
Stewardship: Wealth used to ensure heavenly treasure (168-5)
Storm waves of Belial assail the Christian (81-3)
Storms defied; God has promised to be with me (153-6)
Storms of life break whatever God does not hold (92-3)
Storms of life do not frighten me, Jesus sends aid (123-3)
Storms produce fruit; trusting God's discipline (92-6)
Stubborness warned against: receive Christ today! (147-4)
Success not guaranteed by human effort but God's will (97-2)
Suffering accepted; Christ will help and comfort (87-6)
Suffering ends in heaven where it changes to rapture (153-8)
Suffering endured with God's help; future joy seen (150-7)
Suffering outwardly; rejoicing inwardly (3-3)
Suffering passes; Jesus comforts; foe is dispersed (135-5)
Suffering turned into joy if Jesus loves me (87-7)
Suffering, yet I can sing by faith (3-5)
Sufferings faced with faith and patience as Christ did (92-5)
Sufferings of Christchild gives us courage (153-7)
Surrendering to God; accepting hardship as beneficial (92-7)
Te Deum: Bless this people, thine inheritance (119-9, 120-6)
Te Deum: Lord, we praise thee! (16-1)
Temporal honor given up for eternal reward (47-5)
Temporal treasures a seduction: they vanish quickly (26-4)
Thank God for his blessings through good government (119-4)
Thanks for blessings in Christ; prayer for new year (16-6)
Thanks for blessings since infancy: Sirach (Apocrypha) 50:22 (79-3, 192-1)
Thanks for love given in Christ; betrothal to Christ (37-3)
Thanks to God and proclamation of his wonders: Ps. 75:1 (29-2)
Thanks to God for his fatherly devotion (193-3)
Thanks to God that we escaped like a bird (14-5)
Thanksgiving as a sacrifice of praise: Ps. 50:23 (17-1)
Time brings joy, beauty, learning, etc. to an end (26-3)
Time passes like a rushing stream of water (26-2)
Timid Nicodemus, unlike Joshua, prefers night (176-2)
Transfiguration of Queen as she is drawn to heaven (198-8)
Transfiguration of Queen well-earned; land mourns (198-9)
Transience of life is like a mist that disappears (26-1)
Transience of the earthly; whoever fears God abides (26-6)
Trembling seizes me when I think of my sin (113-3)
Trials: Whoever endures receives the crown: Jms. 1:12 (57-1)
Tribulation precedes entrance to kingdom: Acts 14:22 (12-3, 146-2)

True Christian admits his sin like the publican (179-4)
Trust in God exercised: all cares rejected (138-6)
Trust in God exercised: calmness in suffering (138-5)
Trust in God exercised: earth affords no comfort (138-7)
Trust in God exercised: patience in adversity (138-4)
Trusting and accepting God's will, building on him (144-6)
Trusting God in fear and distress; he can deliver (188-6)
Trusting God like a child; he will give me my share (187-6)
Trusting God who exalts the poor and humbles the rich (93-6)
Trusting God's sovereignty and yielding to his will (107-6)
Trusting God's ways is like building on solid ground (93-1)
Trusting the shepherd of my soul despite affliction (92-8)
Union with Christ in suffering and exaltation (31-7)
Unleavened bread: We eat only it, which is Christ (4-8)
Unlimited redemption available from God our shepherd (38-6)
Victory of Christ's kingdom over Satan: Rev. 12:10 (50-1)
Victory over hell and death is assured in Jesus (123-4)
Victory song of Lord's triumph: Ps. 118:15-16 (149-1)
Victory sure for those holding God in hearts by faith (80-7)
Victory ultimately assured despite temporal losses (80-8)
Voice of believing soul: Where find I thee, Jesus? (32-1)
Voice of God: Israel deserves no mercy: Hos. 11:8 (89-1)
Voice of Simeon (Nunc dimittis): Lk. 2:29-32 (82-1, 83-2)
Voices raised in praise to God for his goodness (120-2)
Vox Christi: Bride (Soul) welcomed by Christ (140-5)
Vox Christi: Do not worry: Mt. 6:31-32 (187-4)
Vox Christi: Eternal bliss assured (57-8)
Vox Christi: God's promise of blessing: Jer. 32:41 (28-3)
Vox Christi: Holy Spirit promised: Jn. 14:23 (74-1)
Vox Christi: I am the good shepherd: Jn. 10:12 (85-1)
Vox Christi: I come to do God's will: Ps. 40:7-8 (182-3)
Vox Christi: I stand at the door and knock: Rev. 3:20 (61-4)
Vox Christi: I will come again: Jn. 14:28 (74-4)
Vox Christi: I will grant your requests: Jn. 16:23 (86-1)
Vox Christi: I will send the Comforter: Jn. 16:7 (108-1)
Vox Christi: Jesus as a boy in the temple: Lk. 2:49 (154-5)
Vox Christi: My Word will produce fruit: Is. 55:10-11 (18-2)
Vox Christi: O ye of little faith, why fear? Mt. 8:26 (81-4)
Vox Christi: Peace be with you: Jn. 20:19, 21 (67-6)
Vox Christi: Persecution is coming: Jn. 16:2 (183-1) cf. 44-1
Vox Christi: Promise of divine indwelling: Jn. 14:23 (172-2)
Vox Christi: Where goest thou? Jn. 16:5 (166-1)
Vox Christi: Why did you seek me? Lk. 2:49 (32-2)
Vox Christi: World of fear overcome: Jn. 16:33 (87-5)
Vox Christi: You have not asked in my name: Jn. 16:24 (87-1)
Vox Christi: You will find me in the house of God (32-3)
Waiting for the Lord; hoping in his Word: Ps. 130:5 (131-3)
Walk in God's ways and he will continue to bless you (197-10)
Warning: Show mercy so that you receive mercy (185-2)
Watch and pray; be prepared for Day of Judgment! (70-1)
Watchmen of Jerusalem announce bridegroom's arrival (140-1)
Waves of affliction overwhelm my boat (21-5)
We confess our sin and beg for mercy shown in Christ (116-4)
Wealth is a blessing of God meant to be shared (39-2)
Wealth vs. poverty: Rejecting world for Christ (75-13)
Wedding couple promised God's blessing (197-6)

Wedding day represents dawning of new blessing (195-2)
Wedding feast: Prepare to receive Lord's invitation! (180-1)
Wedding of heaven is great honor for earthly bride (162-2)
Wedding praise: Praise God for expected bliss (195-3)
Weeping because Jesus, our refuge, taken from us (103-2)
Weeping ceases despite heavy yoke; God abandons none (98-3)
Weeping foretold; it will turn to joy: Jn. 16:20 (103-1)
Where can I turn with my many sins? (5-1)
Where is your love, the mark of a Christian? (164-1)
Whoever exalts himself shall be humbled: Lk. 14:11 (47-1)
Whoever trusts in God shall never be put to shame (109-6)
Willingness to suffer and die; yielding to God's will (156-3)
Winds may twist cedars but not him who trusts in God (150-5)
Word leads and sustains us on hard course to paradise (186-9)
Word of comfort and life: Jesus accepts sinners (113-5)
Word of God assures me of his help in misfortune (99-2)
Word rendered ineffective by fickle spirit and Belial (181-1)
Word sown among worldly thorns, which will burn (181-3)
Word that falls on hard hearts is ineffective (181-2)
World and its treasures rejected in favor of Christ (94-1)
World and Satan rejected; Christ invited into heart (80-4)
World and sin rejected to avoid fate of rich man (20-10)
World and this life given farewell (64-8)
World deluded by Mammon; Jesus is true wealth (94-4)
World passes away but Christ remains my confidence (94-2)
World rejected and given farewell; heaven anticipated (95-3)
World rejected as loathsome; true riches in Jesus (94-7)
World rejected for pleasure of having Jesus (64-4, 94-8)
World rejected in view of possessing heaven's riches (64-3)
World rejects me, I reject it in favor of Christ (123-5)
World surrendered for heaven and eternal life (64-7)
World's riches pass away; Jesus' gifts are eternal (64-5)
World's ridicule accepted for sake of heaven's honor (94-5)
Worldly good fortune can change before nightfall (166-5)
Worldly pleasures and life itself can vanish quickly (166-4)
Worldly pleasures are empty illusions (94-6)
Worldly pleasures deceitful; rejected for heaven (95-2)
Worldly pleasures detested; death yearned for (161-2)
Worldly power temporal but God is an eternal refuge (188-5)
Worldly success is temporal; I choose Jesus (94-3)
Worship: Give the Lord glory due his name: Ps. 29:2/96:8-9
  (148-1)
Wretched man that I am, who will deliver me? Rom. 7:24 (48-1)
Yearning for death: Body to earth, soul to heaven (161-5)
Yearning for death: Christ is my life, death is gain (95-1)
Yearning for death: Here is only misery, there peace (82-3)
Yearning for death: it brings me to port of rest (56-5)
Yearning for death: it will mark the end of all woe (95-4)
Yearning for death: may the hour soon strike! (95-5)
Yearning for death: Prayer offering soul to God (57-7)
Yearning for death: Sweetness comes out of death (161-1)
Yearning for death: We long to see the Savior soon! (249-8)
Yearning for death and heaven, our true inheritance (35-7)
Yearning for death and light of heaven (31-8)
Yearning for death as escape from woe (82-5)
Yearning for death's sleep: Christ will awaken me (31-9)

Yearning for God: Where do I find thee? (175-3)
Yearning for heaven because of oppression by world (146-4)
Yearning for heaven where the Lamb and bridegroom is (27-4)
Yearning for heaven; my inheritance: rest and comfort (56-4)
Yearning for heaven; spirit is willing, flesh weak (70-4)
Yearning for heaven; the night watch is almost over (149-6)
Yearning for shepherd and green pasture (175-2)
Yearning to depart and be with Christ in heaven (161-3)
Yearning to depart with Simeon and be with Christ (82-2)
Yearning to die and begin rest; farewell to world (82-4)
Yearning to leave hate-filled world for heaven (170-4)
You are the Creator's blessed ones: Ps. 115:15 (196-5)
Zion praises Ruler of Heaven for Salvation (248-24)

ALPHABETICAL INDEX OF CHORALE STANZAS[1]

[1]Information provided here based primarily on Hans-Joachim Schulze and Christoph Wolff, *Bach Compendium*; Alfred Dürr, *Die Kantaten von Johann Sebastian Bach mit ihren Texten*. Where these sources disagreed the former was usually favored.

Ach bleib bei uns, Herr Jesu Christ = Vs. 1 of **Ach bleib bei uns, Herr Jesu Christ** [Philipp Melanchthon, 1579] (6-3)

Ach Gott, vom Himmel sieh darein = Vs. 1 [Martin Luther, 1524] (2-1)

Ach Gott, wie manches Herzeleid = Vs. 1 [Martin Moller, 1587] (3-1, 44-4, 58-1)

Ach Herr, laß dein lieb Engelein = Vs. 3 of **Herzlich lieb hab ich dich, o Herr** [Martin Schalling, 1571] (149-7)

Ach Herr, mich armen Sünder = Vs. 1 [Cyriakus Schneegaß, 1597] (135-1)

Ach, Herr, vergib all unsre Schuld = Vs. 8 of **Herr Jesu Christ, wahr' Mensch und Gott** [Paul Eber, 1562] (127-5)

Ach, ich habe schon erblicket = Vs. 7 of **Alle Menschen müssen sterben** [Johann Rosenmüller or Johann Georg Albinus, 1652] (162-6)

Ach, lieben Christen, seid getrost = Vs. 1 [Johannes Gigas, 1561] (114-1)

Ach, mein herzliebes Jesulein! = Vs. 13 of **Vom Himmel hoch, da komm ich her** [Martin Luther, 1535] (248-9)

Ach wie flüchtig, ach wie nichtig ist der Menschen Leben = Vs. 1 [Michael Franck, 1652] (26-1)

Ach wie flüchtig, ach wie nichtig sind der Menschen Sachen! = Vs. 13 of **Ach wie flüchtig, ach wie nichtig** [Michael Franck, 1652] (26-6)

Ach, wie hungert mein Gemüte = Vs. 4 of **Schmücke dich, o liebe Seele** [Johann Franck, 1653] (180-3)

Ach! Herr Gott, durch die Treue dein = Vs. 3 of **Nimm von uns, Herr, du treuer Gott** [Martin Moller, 1584] (101-3)

All solch dein Güt wir preisen = Vs. 6 (final vs.) of **Helft mir Gotts Güte preisen** [Paul Eber, c.1580] (16-6, 28-6)

Allein zu dir, Herr Jesu Christ = Vs. 1 [Konrad Hubert, 1540] (33-1)

Alleluja! Alleluja! Gelobt sei Gott = Vs. 5 of **Wir Christenleut** [Kaspar Füger, 1592] (110-7)

Alleluja! Des solln wir alle froh sein = Vs. 3 of **Christ ist erstanden** [c.1090] (66-6)

Alsdenn so wirst du mich = Vs. 4 of **O Jesu, meine Lust** [Matthäus Avenarius, 1673] (128-5)

Also hat Gott die Welt geliebt = Vs. 1 [Salomo Liscow, 1675] (68-1)

Amen, Amen. Komm, du schöne Freudenkrone = End of final vs. of **Wie schön leuchtet der Morgenstern** [Philipp Nicolai, 1599] (61-6)

Amen zu aller Stund = Vs. 6 of **Auf meinen lieben Gott** [Lübeck, before 1603] (148-6)

Auf Christi Himmelfahrt allein = Vs. 1 [Ernst Sonnemann, 1661; based on Josua Wegelin, 1636] (128-1)

Auf daß wir also allzugleich = Vs. 8 of **Was alle Weisheit in der Welt** [Paul Gerhardt, 1653] (176-6)

Auf ihn magst du es wagen = Vs. 3 of **Was willst du dich betrüben** [Johann Heermann, 1630] (107-3)

Auf meinen lieben Gott = Vs. 1. [Lübeck, before 1603] (188-6)

Auf sperren sie den Rachen weit = Vs. 5 of **Wo Gott der Herr nicht bei uns hält** [Justus Jonas, 1524] (178-5)

Aus tiefer Not schrei ich zu dir = Vs. 1 [Martin Luther, 1524] (38-1)

Beweis dein Macht, Herr Jesu Christ = Vs. 2 of **Erhalt uns, Herr, bei deinem Wort** [Martin Luther, 1542] (6-6)

Bin ich gleich von dir gewichen = Vs. 6 of **Werde munter, mein Gemüte** [Johann Rist, 1642] (55-5)

Brich an, o schönes Morgenlicht = Vs. 9 of **Ermuntre dich, mein schwacher Geist** [Johann Rist, 1641] (248-12)

Christ lag in Todesbanden = Vs. 1 [Martin Luther, 1524] (4-2)

Christ unser Herr zum Jordan kam = Vs. 1 [Martin Luther, 1541] (7-1)

Christe, du Lamm Gottes = German Agnus Dei [Martin Luther, 1528] (23-4)

Christum wir sollen loben schon = Vs. 1 [Martin Luther, 1524] (121-1)

Christus, der ist mein Leben = Vs. 1 [S. Graff, before 1609] (95-1)

Dahero Trotz der Höllen Heer! = Vs. 5 of **Wohl dem, der sich auf seinen Gott** [Johann Christoph Rube, 1692] (139-6)

Darum wir billig loben dich = Vs. 11 of **Herr Gott, dich loben alle wir** [Paul Eber, c.1561] (130-6)

Das Aug allein das Wasser sieht = Vs. 7 of **Christ unser Herr zum Jordan kam** [Martin Luther, 1541] (7-7)

Das hat er alles uns getan = Vs. 7 of **Gelobet seist du, Jesu Christ** [Martin Luther, 1524] (64-2, 91-6, 248-28)

Das ist des Vaters Wille = Vs. 9 (final vs.) of **Von Gott will ich nicht lassen** [Ludwig Helmbold, 1563] (73-5)

Das macht Christus, wahr' Gottes Sohn = Vs. 2 of **Mit Fried und Freud ich fahr dahin** (paraphrased Nunc dimittis) [Martin Luther 1524] (125-3)

Das neugeborne Kindelein = Vs. 1 [Cyriakus Schneegaß, 1597] (122-1)

Das wollst du, Gott, bewahren rein = Vs. 6 of **Ach Gott vom Himmel sieh darein** [Martin Luther, 1524] (2-6)

Das Wort sie sollen lassen stahn = Vs. 4 of **Eine feste Burg ist unser Gott** [Martin Luther, 1526/1528] (80-8)

Dein Blut, der edle Saft = Vs. 9 of **Wo soll ich fliehen hin** [Johann Heermann, 1630] (136-6)

Dein Geist, den Gott vom Himmel gibt = Vs. 10 of **Gott Vater, sende deinen Geist** [Paul Gerhardt, 1653] (108-6)

Dein Glanz all Finsternis verzehrt = Vs. 5 of **Nun, liebe Seel, nun ist es Zeit** [Georg Weissel, 1642] (248-46)

Dein ist allein die Ehre = Vs. 3 of **Jesu, nun sei gepreiset** [Johannes Herman, 1593] (41-6)

Deine Hilfe zu mir sende = Vs. 7 of **Treuer Gott, ich muß dir klagen** [Johann Heermann, 1630] (194-6)

Dem wir das Heilig itzt Mit Freuden lassen klingen = Vs. 5 of **Gelobet sei der Herr** [Johann Olearius, 1665] (129-5)

Den Glauben mir verleihe = Vs. 4 of **Ich dank dir, lieber Herre** [Johann Kolrose, c.1535] (37-6)

Den Himmel und auch die Erden = Vs. 8 of **Wo Gott der Herr nicht bei uns hält** [Justus Jonas, 1524] (178-7)

Den Tod niemand zwingen kunnt = Vs. 2 of **Christ lag in Todesbanden** [Martin Luther, 1524] (4-3)

Denk nicht in deiner Drangsalshitze = Vs. 5 of **Wer nur den lieben Gott läßt walten** [Georg Neumark, 1657] (21-9, 93-5)

Denn er hat seine elende Magd angesehen = Vs. 2 of **Meine Seele erhebt den Herren** [German Magnificat] (10-1)

Denn Gott verlässet keinen = Vs. 2 of **Was willst du dich betrüben** [Johann Heermann, 1630] (107-2)

Denn wer selig dahin fähret = Vs. 9 of **Lasset ab von euren Tränen** [Gregorius Richter, 1658] (146-8)

Der du bist dem Vater gleich = Vs. 6 of **Nun komm, der Heiden Heiland** [Martin Luther, 1524] (36-6)

Der ewig reiche Gott = Vs. 2 of **Nun danket alle Gott** [Martin Rinckart, 1636] (192-2)

Der Gott, der mir hat versprochen = Vs. 2 of **Zion klagt mit Angst und Schmerzen** [Johann Heermann, 1636] (13-3)

Der Herr ist mein getreuer Hirt, dem ich mich ganz vertraue = Vs. 1 [Cornelius Becker, 1598] (85-3, 104-6)

Der Herr ist mein getreuer Hirt, hält mich = Vs. 1 [Wolfgang Meuslin, 1530] (112-1)

Der Herr ist noch und nimmer nicht = Vs. 5 of **Sei Lob und Ehr dem höchsten Gut** [Johann Jakob Schütz, 1673] (117-5)

Der Leib zwar in der Erden = Vs. 4 of **Herzlich tut mich verlangen** [Christoph Knoll, 1611] (161-6)

Der zeitlichen Ehrn will ich gern entbehrn = Vs. 11 of **Warum betrübst du dich, mein Herz?** [Nürnberg, c.1560] (47-5)

Des ewgen Vaters einigs Kind = Vs. 2 of **Gelobet seist du, Jesu Christ** [Martin Luther, 1524] (91-2)

Die Feind sind all in deiner Hand = Vs. 7 of **Wo Gott der Herr nicht bei uns hält** [Justus Jonas, 1524] (178-7)

Die Hoffnung wart' der rechten Zeit = Vs. 11 of **Es ist das Heil uns kommen her** [Paul Speratus, 1524] (86-6, 186-11)

Die Kön'ge aus Saba kamen dar = Vs. 4 of **Ein Kind geborn zu Bethlehem** [German version of **Puer natus in Bethlehem**: J. Spangenberg, 1545] (65-2)

Die Sünd hat uns verderbet sehr = Vs. 5 of **Nimm von uns, Herr, du treuer Gott** [Martin Moller, 1584] (101-5)

Die Sünd macht Leid = Vs. 3 of **Wir Christenleut** [Kaspar Füger, 1592] (40-3)

Die Welt bekümmert sich = Vs. 5 of **Was frag ich nach der Welt** [Balthasar Kindermann, 1664] (94-5)

Die Welt sucht Ehr und Ruhm = Vs. 3 of **Was frag ich nach der Welt** [Balthasar Kindermann, 1664] (94-3)

Dies hat er Alles uns getan: See "Das hat er Alles uns getan"

Drum fahrt nur immer hin, ihr Eitelkeiten = Vs. 6 of **Liebster Immanuel, Herzog der Frommen** [Ahasverus Fritsch, 1679] (123-6)

Drum ich mich ihm ergebe = Vs. 6 of **Was willst du dich betrüben** [Johann Heermann, 1630] (107-6)

Drum so laßt uns immerdar = Vs. 10 of **Mache dich, mein Geist, bereit** [Johann Burchard Freystein, 1697] (115-6)

Drum will ich, weil ich lebe noch = Vs. 16 of **Ach Gott, wie manches Herzeleid** [Martin Moller, 1587] (153-9)

Drum wir auch billig fröhlich sein = Vs. 14 of **Erschienen ist der herrlich Tag** [Nikolaus Herman, 1560] (145-5)

Du bereitest für mir einen Tisch = Vs. 4 of **Der Herr ist mein getreuer Hirt, hält mich** [Wolfgang Meuslin, 1530] (112-4)

Du bist ein Geist, der lehret = Vs. 5 of **Zeuch ein zu deinen Toren** [Paul Gerhardt, 1653] (183-5)

Du Friedefürst, Herr Jesu Christ = Vs. 1 [Jakob Ebert, 1601] (67-7, 116-1, 143-2)

Du Lebensfürst, Herr Jesu Christ = Vs. 1 [Johann Rist, 1641] (43-11)

Du süße Liebe, schenk uns deine Gunst = Vs. 3 of **Nun bitten wir den Heiligen Geist** [Martin Luther, 1524] (169-7, 197-5)

Du wollest deinen Geist und Kraft = Litany [Martin Luther, 1528/1529] (18-3)

Ehr sei Gott in dem höchsten Thron = Vs. 4 of **Allein zu dir, Herr Jesu Christ** [This stanza from Nürnberg, 1540; other stanzas by Konrad Hubert, 1540] (33-6)

Ehr sei ins Himmels Throne = Vs. 6 of **Ach Herr, mich armen Sünder** [Cyriakus Schneegaß, 1597] (135-6)

Ei nun, mein Gott, so fall ich dir = Vs. 10 of **Ich hab in Gottes Herz und Sinn** [Paul Gerhardt, 1647] (65-7, 92-7)

Ein feste Burg ist unser Gott = Vs. 1 [Martin Luther, 1526/1528] (80-1)

Eine Stimme läßt sich hören = Vs. 3 of **Tröstet, tröstet meine Lieben** [Johann Olearius, 1671] (30-6)

Er denket der Barmherzigkeit = Vs. 8 of **Meine Seele erhebt den Herren** [German Magnificat] (10-5)

Er ist auf Erden kommen arm = Vs. 6 of **Gelobet seist du, Jesu Christ** [Martin Luther, 1524] (248-7)

Er ist das Heil und selig Licht = Vs. 4 of **Mit Fried und Freud ich fahr dahin** (paraphrased Nunc dimittis) [Martin Luther, 1524] (83-5, 125-5)

Er kann und will dich lassen nicht = Vs. 2 of **Warum betrübst du dich, mein Herz** [Nürnberg, 1561] (138-3)

Er kennt die rechten Freudenstunden = Vs. 4 of **Wer nur den lieben Gott läßt walten** [Georg Neumark, 1657] (93-4)

Er richt's zu seinen Ehren = Vs. 5 of **Was willst du dich betrüben** [Johann Heermann, 1630] (107-5)

Er wolle meiner Sünden = Vs. 5 of **In allen meinen Taten** [Paul Fleming, 1642] (97-5)

Erbarm dich mein in solcher Last = Vs. 2 of **Herr Jesu Christ, du höchstes Gut** [Bartholomäus Ringwaldt, 1588] (113-2, 131-2)

Erhalt mein Herz im Glauben rein = Vs. 18 of **Ach Gott, wie manches Herzeleid** [Martin Moller, 1587] (3-6, 153-9)

Erhalt uns, Herr, bei deinem Wort = Vs. 1 [Martin Luther, 1542] (126-1)

Erhalt uns in der Wahrheit = Vs. 8 (final vs.) of **Nun laßt uns Gott, dem Herren** [Ludwig Helmbold, 1575] (79-6)

Erleucht auch unser Sinn und Herz = Vs. 7 of **Du Friedefürst, Herr Jesu Christ** [Jakob Ebert, 1601] (116-6)

Erschienen ist der herrlich Tag = Vs. 1 [Nikolaus Herman, 1560] (67-4)

Ertöt uns durch dein Güte = Vs. 5 of **Herr Christ, der einig Gotts Sohn** [Elisabeth Creutziger, 1524] (22-5, 96-6, 132-6, 164-6)

Es bringt das rechte Jubeljahr = Vs. 4 of **Das neugeborne Kindelein** [Cyriakus Schneegaß, 1597] (122-6)

Es danke, Gott, und lobe dich = Vs. 3 of **Es woll uns Gott genädig sein** [Martin Luther, 1524] (69-6, 76-14)

Es danken dir die Himmelsheer = Vs. 2 of **Sei Lob und Ehr dem höchsten Gut** [Johann Jakob Schütz, 1673] (117-2)

Es ist das Heil uns kommen her = Vs. 1 [Paul Speratus, 1524] (9-1)

Es ist genug; Herr, wenn es dir gefällt = Vs. 5 of **Es ist genug, so nimm, Herr, meinen Geist** [Franz Joachim Burmeister, 1662] (60-5)

Es kann mir fehlen nimmermehr! = Vs. 2 of **Ich hab in Gottes Herz und Sinn** [Paul Gerhardt, 1647] (92-2)

Es kann mir nichts geschehen = Vs. 3 of **In allen meinen Taten** [Paul Fleming, 1642] (97-3)

Es war ein wunderlicher Krieg = Vs. 4 of **Christ lag in Todesbanden** [Martin Luther, 1524] (4-5)

Es woll uns Gott genädig sein = Vs. 1 [Martin Luther, 1523] (76-7)

Freu dich sehr, o meine Seele...Aus Trübsal = Vs. 1 [Freiberg, 1620] [146-8]

Freu dich sehr, o meine Seele...Seine Freud = Vs. 10 (final vs.) of **Freu dich sehr, o meine Seele** [Freiberg, 1620] (70-7)

Führ auch mein Herz und Sinn = Vs. 11 of **Wo soll ich fliehen hin** [Johann Heermann, 1630] (5-7, 163-6)

Gedenk, Herr Jesu, an dein Amt = Vs. 3 of **Du Friedefürst, Herr Jesu Christ** [Jakob Ebert, 1601] (143-7)

Gelobet sei der Herr, Mein Gott, der ewig lebet = Vs. 4 of **Gelobet sei der Herr** [Johann Olearius, 1665] (129-4)

Gelobet sei der Herr, Mein Gott, mein Heil = Vs. 2 of **Gelobet sei der Herr** [Johann Olearius, 1665] (129-2)

Gelobet sei der Herr, Mein Gott, mein Licht = Vs. 1 [Johann Olearius, 1665] (129-1)

Gelobet sei der Herr, Mein Gott, mein Trost = Vs. 3 of **Gelobet sei der Herr** [Johann Olearius, 1665] (129-3)

Gelobet seist du, Jesu Christ = Vs. 1 [Martin Luther, 1524] (91-1)

Gib, daß ich tu mit Fleiß = Vs. 2 of **O Gott, du frommer Gott** [Johann Heermann, 1630] (45-7)

Gib unsern Fürsten und der Obrigkeit = Appended stanza [added in 1566 by Johann Walter as Vs. 2] of **Verleih uns Frieden gnädiglich** [Martin Luther, 1529]; sometimes appears as Vs. 7 of **Erhalt uns, Herr, bei deinem Wort** [First 3 stanzas by Martin Luther, 1542] (42-7, 126-6)

Gloria sei dir gesungen = Vs. 3 of **Wachet auf, ruft uns die Stimme** [Philipp Nicolai, 1599] (140-7)

Glorie, Lob, Ehr und Herrlichkeit = Vs. 7 of **In dich hab ich gehoffet, Herr** [Adam Reusner, 1533] (106-4)

Gott hat die Erde zugericht' = Vs. 4 of **Singen wir aus Herzensgrund** [Hans Vogel, 1563] (187-7)

Gott Heilger Geist, du Tröster wert = Vs. 3 of **Erhalt uns, Herr, bei deinem Wort** [Martin Luther, 1542] (126-3)

Gott Lob und Dank, der nicht zugab = Vs. 3 of **Wär Gott nicht mit uns** [Martin Luther, 1524] (14-5)

Gute Nacht, o Wesen = Vs. 5 of **Jesu, meine Freude** [Johann Franck, 1650] (64-8)

Gutes und die Barmherzigkeit = Vs. 5 of **Der Herr ist mein getreuer Hirt, hält mich** [Wolfgang Meuslin, 1530] (112-5)

Hat er es denn beschlossen = Vs. 7 of **In allen meinen Taten** [Paul Fleming, 1642] (97-7)

Heilger Geist ins Himmels Throne = Vs. 6 of **Treuer Gott, ich muß dir klagen** [Johann Heermann, 1630] (194-6)

Herr Christ, der einge Gottessohn = Vs. 1 [Elisabeth Creutziger, 1524] (96-1)

Herr, durch den Glauben wohn in mir = Vs. 8 of **O Gottes Sohn, Herr Jesu Christ** [David Denicke, 1657] (77-6)

Herr, gib, daß ich dein Ehre = Vs. 7 (final vs.) of **Was willst du dich betrüben** [Johann Heermann, 1630] (107-7)

Herr Gott, dich loben alle wir = Vs. 1 [Paul Eber, c.1561] (130-1)

Herr Gott, dich loben wir = Beginning of Vs. 1 of German Te Deum [Martin Luther, 1529] (16-1, 190-1, 190-2)

Herr Gott Vater, mein starker Held! = Vs. 5 of **Wie schön leuchtet der Morgenstern** [Philipp Nicolai, 1599] (37-3)

Herr, ich glaube, hilf mir Schwachen, = Vs. 12 of **Jesu, der du meine Seele** [Johann Rist, 1641] (78-7)

Herr, ich hoff je, du werdes die = Vs. 8 of **O Herre Gott, dein göttlich Wort** [Anarg von Wildenfels, 1526] (184-5)

Herr Jesu Christ, du höchstes Gut = Vs. 1 [Bartholomäus Ringwaldt, 1588] (113-1)

Herr Jesu Christ, einiger Trost = Vs. 12 of **Herr Jesu Christ, ich schrei zu dir** [Freiberg, 1620] (48-7)

Herr Jesu Christ, wahr' Mensch und Gott = Vs. 1 [Paul Eber, 1562] (127-1)

Herr, nun lässest du deinen Diener in Friede fahren = Canticum Simeonis (German Nunc dimittis) (83-2)

Herr, wie du willt, so schick's mit mir = Vs. 1 [Kaspar Bienemann, 1582] (73-1, 156-6)

Herrscher über Tod und Leben = Vs. 6 of **Liebster Gott, wenn werd ich sterben** [Caspar Neumann, c.1690] (8-6)

Herzlich lieb hab ich dich, o Herr = Vs. 1 [Martin Schalling, 1571] (174-5)

Heut lebst du, heut bekehre dich = Vs. 6 of **So wahr ich lebe, spricht dein Gott** [Johann Heermann, 1630] (102-7)

Heut schleußt er wieder auf die Tür = Vs. 8 of **Lobt Gott, ihr Christen, allzugleich** [Nikolaus Herman, 1560] (151-5)

Hier ist das rechte Osterlamm = Vs. 5 of **Christ lag in Todesbanden** [Martin Luther, 1524] (4-6, 158-4)

Hilf deinem Volk, Herr Jesu Christ = from end of Vs. 4 of German Te Deum [Martin Luther, 1529] (119-9)

Hilf mir mein Sach recht greifen an = Vs. 17 of **Ach Gott, wie manches Herzeleid** [Martin Moller, 1587] (153-9)

Hilf, o Herr Jesu, hilf du mir = Vs. 7 of **So wahr ich lebe, spricht dein Gott** [Johann Heermann, 1630] (102-7)

Ich armer Mensch, ich armer Sünder = Vs. 1 [Christoph Tietze, 1663] (179-6)

Ich bitt noch mehr, o Herre Gott = Vs. 2 of **Ich ruf zu dir, Herr Jesu Christ** [Johann Agricola, c.1530] (177-2)

Ich bitt, o Herr, aus Herzens Grund = Vs. 8 of **Durch Adams Fall ist ganz verderbt** [Lazarus Spengler, 1524] (18-5)

Ich bitte dich, Herr Jesu Christ = Vs. 3 of **Herr Jesu Christ, ich weiß gar wohl** [Bartholomäus Ringwaldt, 1582] (166-3)

Ich freue mich in dir = Vs. 1 [Caspar Ziegler, 1697] (133-1)

Ich hab dich einen Augenblick = Vs. 9 of **Barmherzger Vater, höchster Gott** [Paul Gerhardt, 1653] (103-6)

Ich hab in Gottes Herz und Sinn = Vs. 1 [Paul Gerhardt, 1647] (92-1)

Ich hab vor mir ein schwere Reis' = Vs. 2 of **O Jesu Christ, meins Lebens Licht** [Martin Behm, 1610] (58-5)

Ich leb indes in dir vergnüget = Vs. 12 of **Wer weiß, wie nahe mir mein Ende** [Ämilie Juliane von Schwarzburg-Rudolstadt, 1686] (84-5)

Ich lieg im Streit und widerstreb = Vs. 5 of **Ich ruf zu dir, Herr Jesu Christ** [Johann Agricola, c.1530] (177-5)

Ich rief dem Herrn in meiner Not = Vs. 4 of **Sei Lob und Ehr dem höchsten Gut** [Johann Jakob Schütz, 1673] (117-4)

Ich ruf zu dir, Herr Jesu Christ = Vs. 1 [Johann Agricola, c.1530] (177-1, 185-6)

Ich steh an deiner Krippen hier = Vs. 1 [Paul Gerhardt, 1656] (248-59)

Ich traue seiner Gnaden = Vs. 4 of **In allen meinen Taten** [Paul Fleming, 1642] (97-4)

Ich will alle meine Tage = Vs. 12 of **Treuer Gott, ich muß dir klagen** [Johann Heermann, 1630] (25-6)

Ich will dich all mein Leben lang = Vs. 7 of **Sei Lob und Ehr dem höchsten Gut** [Johann Jakob Schütz, 1673] (117-7)

Ich will dich mit Fleiß bewahren = Vs. 15 of **Fröhlich soll mein Herze springen** [Paul Gerhardt, 1653] (248-33)

Ich will hier bei dir stehen = Vs. 6 of **O Haupt voll Blut und Wunden** [Paul Gerhardt, 1656] (159-2)

Ich, dein betrübtes Kind = Vs. 3 of **Wo soll ich fliehen hin** [Johann Heermann, 1630] (199-6)

Ihm hab ich mich ergeben = Vs. 8 of **In allen meinen Taten** [Paul Fleming, 1642] (97-8)

Ihr, die ihr Christi Namen nennt = Vs. 8 of **Sei Lob und Ehr dem höchsten Gut** [Johann Jakob Schütz, 1673] (117-8)

In allen meinen Taten = Vs. 1 [Paul Fleming, 1642] (97-1)

In dich hab ich gehoffet, Herr = Vs. 1 [Adam Reusner, 1533] (52-6)

In dieser letzt'n betrübten Zeit = Vs. 2 of **Ach bleib bei uns, Herr Jesu Christ** [This stanza of 1572 by Nikolaus Selnecker was later added to the chorale of 1579 by Philipp Melanchthon] (6-3)

Ist Gott mein Schutz und treuer Hirt = Vs. 4 of **Ist Gott mein Schild und Helfersmann** [Ernst Christoph Homburg, 1658] (85-6)

Ist Gott versöhnt und unser Freund = Vs. 3 of **Das neugeborne Kindelein** [Cyriakus Schneegaß, 1597] (122-4)

Jedoch dein heilsam Wort, das macht = Vs. 4 of **Herr Jesu Christ, du höchstes Gut** [Bartholomäus Ringwaldt, 1588] (113-4)

Jesu, deine Passion = Vs. 33 of **Jesu Leiden, Pein und Tod** [Paul Stockmann, 1633] (159-5, 182-7)

Jesu, der du meine Seele = Vs. 1 [Johann Rist, 1641] (78-1)

Jesu, du mein liebstes Leben = Vs. 1 [Johann Rist, 1642] (248-38 & 40)

Jesu, mein Hort und Erretter = Vs. 2 of **Jesu, meiner Seelen Wonne** [Martin Jahn, 1661] (154-3)

Jesu, nimm dich deiner Glieder = Vs. 4 of **Freuet euch, ihr Christen alle** [Christian Keymann, 1646] (40-8)

Jesu nun sei gepreiset = Vs. 1 [Johannes Herman, 1593] (41-1)

Jesu, wahres Brot des Lebens = Vs. 9 of **Schmücke dich, o liebe Seele** [Johann Franck, 1653] (180-7)

Jesum laß ich nicht von mir: See "Meinen Jesum laß ich nicht, Geh ihm ewig..."

Jesus bleibet meine Freude = Vs. 16 of **Jesu, meiner Seelen Wonne** [Martin Jahn, 1661] (147-10)

Jesus Christus, Gottes Sohn = Vs. 3 of **Christ lag in Todesbanden** [Martin Luther, 1524] (4-4)

Jesus richte mein Beginnen = Vs. 15 of **Hilf, Herr Jesu, laß gelingen** [Johann Rist, 1642] (248-42)

Kein Frucht das Weizenkörnlein bringt = Vs. 3 of **Ach, lieben Christen, seid getrost** [Johannes Gigas, 1561] (114-4)

Kein Menschenkind hier auf der Erd = Vs. 2 of **Gott Vater, sende deinen Geist** [Paul Gerhardt, 1653] (74-8)

Komm, Heiliger Geist, Herre Gott = Vs. 1 [Martin Luther, 1524] (59-3)

Komm, o Tod, du Schlafes Bruder = Vs. 6 of **Du, o schönes Weltgebäude** [Johann Franck, 1653] (56-5)

Laß dein' Engel mit mir fahren = Vs. 9 of **Freu dich sehr, o meine Seele** [Freiberg, 1620] (19-7)

Laß mich kein Lust noch Furcht von dir = Vs. 4 of **Ich ruf zu dir, Herr Jesu Christ** [Johann Agricola, c.1530] (177-4)

Laß uns das Jahr vollbringen = Vs. 2 of **Jesu, nun sei gepreiset** [Johannes Herman, 1593] (171-6, 190-7)

Leg ich mich späte nieder = Vs. 6 of **In allen meinen Taten** [Paul Fleming, 1642] (97-6)

Leit uns mit deiner rechten Hand = Vs. 7 of **Nimm von uns, Herr, du treuer Gott** [Martin Moller, 1584] (90-5, 101-7)

Liebster Gott, wann werd ich sterben? = Vs. 1 [Caspar Neumann, c.1690] (8-1)

Liebster Immanuel, Herzog der Frommen = Vs. 1 [Ahasverus Fritsch, 1679] (123-1)

Lob, Ehr und Dank sei dir gesagt = Vs. 8 of **Christum wir sollen loben schon** [Martin Luther, 1524] (121-6)

Lob, Ehr und Preis sei Gott = Vs. 3 of **Nun danket alle Gott** [Martin Rinckart, 1636] (192-3)

Lob sei Gott, dem Vater, g'tan = Vs. 8 of **Nun komm, der Heiden Heiland** [Martin Luther, 1524] (36-8, 62-6)

Lob und Preis sei Gott dem Vater und dem Sohn = Vs. 10 of **Meine Seel erhebt den Herren** [German Magnificat] (10-7)

Lobe den Herren, den mächtigen König der Ehren = Vs. 1 [Joachim Neander, 1680] (137-1)

Lobe den Herren, der alles so herrlich regieret = Vs. 2 of **Lobe den Herren, den mächtigen König der Ehren** [Joachim Neander, 1680] (137-2)

Lobe den Herren, der deinen Stand sichtbar gesegnet = Vs. 4 of **Lobe den Herren, den mächtigen König der Ehren** [Joachim Neander, 1680] (137-4)

Lobe den Herren, der künstlich und fein dich bereitet = Vs. 3 of **Lobe den Herren, den mächtigen König der Ehren** [Joachim Neander, 1680] (137-3)

Lobe den Herren, was in mir ist, lobe den Namen! = Vs. 5 of **Lobe den Herren, den mächtigen König der Ehren** [Joachim Neander, 1680] (137-5)

Mach's mit mir, Gott, nach deiner Güt = Vs. 1 [Johann Hermann Schein, 1628] (156-2)

Mache dich, mein Geist, bereit = Vs. 1 [Johann Burchard Freystein, 1697] (115-1)

Mein Gott, öffne mir die Pforten = Vs. 12 of **Weg, mein Herz, mit den Gedanken** [Paul Gerhardt, 1647] (32-6)

Meine Seel erhebt den Herren = Vs. 1 [German Magnificat] (10-1)

Meinen Jesum laß ich nicht, Geh ihm ewig = Vs. 6 of **Meinen Jesum laß ich nicht** [Christian Keymann, 1658] (124-6, 154-8, 157-5)

Meinen Jesum laß ich nicht, Weil er sich = Vs. 1 [Christian Keymann, 1658] (124-1)

Mir mangelt zwar sehr viel = Vs. 7 of **Wo soll ich fliehen hin** [Johann Heermann, 1630] (89-6)

Mit Fried und Freud ich fahr dahin = Vs. 1 (paraphrased Nunc dimittis) [Martin Luther, 1524] (95-1, 106-3b, 125-1)

Mit Segen mich beschütte = Vs. 10 of **Wach auf, mein Herz, und singe** [Paul Gerhardt, 1647] (194-12)

Mit unserer Macht ist nichts getan = Vs. 2 of **Ein feste Burg ist unser Gott** [Martin Luther, 1526/1528] (80-2)

Muß ich sein betrübet? = Vs. 9 of **Selig ist die Seele** [Heinrich Müller, 1659] (87-7)

Nicht nach Welt, nach Himmel nicht = Vs. 5 of **Meinen Jesum laß ich nicht** [Christian Keymann, 1658] (70-11)

Nichts ist es spat und frühe = Vs. 2 of **In allen meinen Taten** [Paul Fleming, 1642] (97-2)

Nimm von uns, Herr, du treuer Gott = Vs. 1 [Martin Moller, 1584] (101-1)

Noch eins, Herr, will ich bitten dich = Vs. 4 of **Was mein Gott will, das g'scheh allzeit** [This stanza added in 1554 to Albrecht von Brandenburg's chorale of 1547] (111-6)

Nun danket all und bringet Ehr = Vs. 1 [Paul Gerhardt, 1647] (195-6)

Nun danket alle Gott = Vs. 1 [Martin Rinckart, 1636] (79-3, 192-1)

Nun hilf uns, Herr, den Dienern dein = Vs. 4 of German Te Deum [Martin Luther, 1529] (120-6)

Nun, ich weiß, du wirst mir stillen = Vs. 11 of **Jesu, der du meine Seele** [Johann Rist, 1641] (105-6)

Nun komm, der Heiden Heiland = Vs. 1 [Martin Luther, 1524] (36-2, 61-1, 62-1)

Nun lieget alles unter dir = Vs. 4 of **Du Lebensfürst, Herr Jesu Christ** [Johann Rist, 1641] (11-6)

Nun lob, mein Seel, den Herren = Vs. 1 [Johann Gramann, 1530] (28-2)

Nun seid ihr wohl gerochen = Vs. 4 of **Ihr Christen auserkoren** [Georg Werner, 1648] (248-64)

Nun, werter Geist, ich folge dir = Vs. 9 of **O Gottes Geist, mein Trost und Rat** [Johann Rist, 1651] (175-7)

O Ewigkeit, du Donnerwort...Mein ganz = Vs. 1 [Johann Rist, 1642] (20-1, 60-1)

O Ewigkeit, du Donnerwort...Nimm du = Final vs. (Vs. 16 of longer version or Vs. 12 of shortened version) of **O Ewigkeit du Donnerwort** [Johann Rist, 1642] (20-11)

O Gott, du frommer Gott = Vs. 1 [Johann Heermann, 1630] (24-6)

O großer Gott von Treu = Vs. 9 of **O großer Gott von Macht** [Matthäus Meyfart, 1633] (46-6)

Ob bei uns ist der Sünden viel = Vs. 5 of **Aus tiefer Not schrei ich zu dir** [Martin Luther, 1524] (38-6)

Ob sich's anließ, als wollt er nicht = Vs. 12 of **Es ist das Heil uns kommen her** [Paul Speratus, 1524] (9-7, 155-5, 186-6)

Richte dich, Leibste, nach meinem Gefallen und gläube = Vs. 6 of **Hast du denn, Jesu, dein Angesicht gänzlich verborgen** [Ahasverus Fritsch, 1668] (57-8)

Schau, lieber Gott, wie meine Feind = Vs. 1 [David Denicke, 1646] (153-1)

Schaut hin, Dort liegt im finstern Stall = Vs. 8 of **Schaut, schaut, was ist für Wunder dar** [Paul Gerhardt, 1667] (248-17)

Schmücke dich, o liebe Seele = Vs. 1 [Johann Franck, 1653] (180-1)

Schüttle deinen Kopf und sprich = Vs. 2 of **Schwing dich auf zu deinem Gott** [Paul Gerhardt, 1653] (40-6)

Sei Lob und Ehr dem höchsten Gut = Vs. 1 [Johann Jakob Schütz, 1673] (117-1)

Sei Lob und Preis mit Ehren = Vs. 5 [appended stanza: Königsberg, 1548] of **Nun lob, mein Seel, den Herren** [Johann Gramann, 1530] (29-8, 51-4, 167-5)

Seid froh, dieweil, seid froh, dieweil = Vs. 4 of **Laßt Furcht und Pein** [Christoph Runge, 1653] (248-35)

Sein Wort, sein Tauf, sein Nachtmahl = Vs. 5 of **Nun laßt uns Gott dem Herren** [Ludwig Helmbold, 1575] (165-6)

Selig sind, die aus Erbarmen = Vs. 6 of **Kommt, laßt euch den Herren lehren** [David Denicke, 1648] (39-7)

Sie stellen uns wie Ketzern nach = Vs. 4 of **Wo Gott der Herr nicht bei uns hält** [Justus Jonas, 1524] (178-4)

Sing, bet und geh auf Gottes Wegen = Vs. 7 of **Wer nur den lieben Gott läßt walten** [Georg Neumark, 1657] (88-7, 93-7)

So fahr ich hin zu Jesu Christ = stanza added in 1575 to **Wenn mein Stündlein vorhanden ist** [Nikolaus Herman, 1560] (31-9)

So feiern wir das hohe Fest = Vs. 6 of **Christ lag in Todesbanden** [Martin Luther, 1524] (4-7)

So kommet vor sein Angesicht = Vs. 9 of **Sei Lob und Ehr dem höchsten Gut** [Johann Jakob Schütz, 1673] (117-9)

So sei nun, Seele, deine = Vs. 9 (last) of **In allen meinen Taten** [Paul Fleming, 1642] (13-6, 44-7, 97-9)

So wandelt froh auf Gottes Wegen = Vs. 7 (modified) of **Wer nur den lieben Gott läßt walten** [Georg Neumarck, 1657] (197-10)

Solang ein Gott im Himmel lebt = Vs. 11 (16-stanza version) or Vs. 8 (12-stanza version) of **O Ewigkeit du Donnerwort** [Johann Rist, 1642] (20-7)

Soll ich auf dieser Welt = Vs. 6 of **O Gott, du frommer Gott** [Johann Heermann, 1630] (71-2)

Soll ich denn auch des Todes Weg = Vs. 12 of **Ich hab in Gottes Herz und Sinn** [Paul Gerhardt, 1647] (92-9)

Soll's ja so sein = Vs. 4 of **Ach Gott und Herr** [Martin Rutilius, 1604] (48-3)

Sprich Ja zu meinen Taten = Vs. 9 of **Wach auf, mein Herz, und singe** [Paul Gerhardt, 1647] (194-12)

Stärk mich mit deinem Freudengeist = Vs. 8 of **Herr Jesu Christ, du höchstes Gut** [Bartholomäus Ringwaldt, 1588] (113-8, 168-6)

Und bitten dich, wollst allezeit = Vs. 12 of **Herr Gott, dich loben alle wir** [Paul Eber, c.1561] (130-6)

Und ob gleich alle Teufel = Vs. 5 of **Befiehl du deine Wege** [Paul Gerhardt, 1653] (153-5)

Und ob ich wandert im finstern Tal = Vs. 3 of **Der Herr ist mein getreuer Hirt, hält mich** [Wolfgang Meuslin, 1530] (112-3)

Und was der ewig gütig Gott = Vs. 16 of **Kommt her zu mir, spricht Gottes Sohn** [Georg Grünwald, 1530] (86-3)

Und weil ich denn in meinem Sinn = Vs. 5 of **Herr Jesu Christ, du höchstes Gut** [Bartholomäus, Ringwaldt, 1588] (131-4)

Und wenn die Welt voll Teufel wär = Vs. 3 of **Ein feste Burg ist unser Gott** [Martin Luther, 1526/1528] (80-5)

Unter deinen Schirmen = Vs. 2 of **Jesu, meine Freude** [Johann Franck, 1650] (81-7)

Valet will ich dir geben = Vs. 1 [Valerius Herberger, 1613] (95-3)

Verleih, daß ich aus Herzensgrund = Vs. 3 of **Ich ruf zu dir, Herr Jesu Christ** [Johann Agricola, c.1530] (177-3)

Verleih uns Frieden gnädichlich = Vs. 1 of **Verleih uns Frieden gnädiglich** [Martin Luther, 1529]; sometimes appears as Vs. 6 of **Erhalt uns, Herr, bei deinem Wort** [First 3 stanzas by Martin Luther, 1542] (42-7, 126-6)

Verzage nicht, o Häuflein klein = Vs. 1 [Jacob Fabricius, c.1635] (42-4)

Von Gott kommt mir ein Freudenschein = Vs. 4 of **Wie schön leuchtet der Morgenstern** [Philipp Nicolai, 1599] (172-6)

Wachet auf, ruft uns die Stimme = Vs. 1 [Philipp Nicolai, 1599] (140-1)

Wär Gott nicht mit uns diese Zeit = Vs. 1 [Martin Luther, 1524] (14-1)

Warum betrübst du dich, mein Herz? = Vs. 1 [Nürnberg, 1561] (138-1)

Was frag ich nach der Welt, und allen ihren Schätzen = Vs. 1 [Balthasar Kindermann, 1664] (64-4, 94-1)

Was frag ich nach der Welt! Im Hui muß sie verschwinden = Vs. 7 of **Was frag ich nach der Welt** [Balthasar Kindermann, 1664] (94-8)

Was frag ich nach der Welt! Mein Jesus ist mein Leben = Vs. 8 of **Was frag ich nach der Welt** [Balthasar Kindermann, 1664] (94-8)

Was Gott tut, das ist wohlgetan, Dabei will ich = Vs. 6 of **Was Gott tut, das ist wohlgetan** [Samuel Rodigast, 1674] (12-7, 75-14, 99-6, 100-6)

Was Gott tut, das ist wohlgetan, Er ist mein Licht = Vs. 4 of **Was Gott tut, das ist wohlgetan** [Samuel Rodigast, 1674] (100-4)

Was Gott tut, das ist wohlgetan, Er wird mich nicht betrügen = Vs. 2 of **Was Gott tut, das ist wohlgetan** [Samuel Rodigast, 1674] (100-2)

Was Gott tut, das ist wohlgetan, Er wird mich wohl bedenken = Vs. 3 of **Was Gott tut, das ist wohlgetan** [Samuel Rodigast, 1674] (100-3)

Was Gott tut, das ist wohlgetan, Es bleibt gerecht = Vs. 1 [Samuel Rodigast, 1674] (98-1, 99-1, 100-1, 144-3)

Was Gott tut, das ist wohlgetan, Muß ich den Kelch = Vs. 5 of **Was Gott tut, das ist wohlgetan** [Samuel Rodigast, 1674] (75-7, 100-5)

Was helfen uns die schweren Sorgen = Vs. 2 of **Wer nur den lieben Gott läßt walten** [Georg Neumark, 1657] (21-9, 93-2)

Was mein Gott will, das g'scheh allzeit = Vs. 1 [Albrecht von Brandenburg 1547] (72-5, 111-1, 144-6)

Was Menschenkraft und -witz anfäht = Vs. 2 of **Wo Gott der Herr nicht bei uns hält** [Justus Jonas, 1524] (178-2)

Was unser Gott geschaffen hat = Vs. 3 of **Sei Lob und Ehr dem höchsten Gut** [Johann Jakob Schütz, 1673] (117-3)

Was willst du dich betrüben = Vs. 1 [Johann Heermann, 1630] (107-1)

Weil du mein Gott und Vater bist = Vs. 3 of **Warum betrübst du dich, mein Herz** [Nürnberg, 1561] (138-7)

Weil du vom Tod erstanden bist = Vs. 4 of **Wenn mein Stündlein vorhanden ist** [Nikolaus Herman, 1560] (95-7)

Was willst du dich betrüben = Vs. 1 [Johann Heermann, 1630] (107-4)

Welt, ade! ich bin dein müde = Vs. 1 [Johann Georg Albinus, 1649] (27-6, 158-2)

Wenn soll es doch geschehen = Vs. 7 of **Gott fähret auf gen Himmel** [Gottfried Wilhelm Sacer, 1697] (11-9)

Wenn Trost und Hülf ermangeln muß = Vs. 6 of **Sei Lob und Ehr dem höchsten Gut** [Johann Jakob Schütz, 1673] (117-6)

Wer hofft in Gott und dem vertraut = Vs. 7 of **Durch Adams Fall ist ganz verderbt** [Lazarus Spengler, 1524] (109-6)

Wer nur den lieben Gott läßt walten = Vs. 1 [Georg Neumark, 1657] (93-1)

Wer weiß, wie nahe mir mein Ende? = Vs. 1 [Ämilie Juliane von Schwarzburg-Rudolstadt, 1686] (27-1, 166-6)

Wie bin ich doch so herzlich froh = Vs. 7 of **Wie schön leuchtet der Morgenstern** [Philipp Nicolai, 1599] (1-6, 49-6)

Wie es war im Anfang = Vs. 11 of **Meine Seel erhebt den Herren** [German Magnificat] (10-7)

Wie schön leuchtet der Morgenstern = Vs. 1 [Philipp Nicolai, 1599] (1-1)

Wie schwerlich läßt sich Fleisch und Blut = Vs. 2 of **Ach Gott, wie manches Herzeleid** [Martin Moller, 1587] (3-2)

Wie sich ein Vatr erbarmet = Vs. 3 of **Nun lob, mein Seel, den Herren** [Johann Gramann, 1530] (17-7)

Wie soll ich dich empfangen = Vs. 1 [Paul Gerhardt, 1653] (248-5)

Wir danken sehr und bitten ihn = Vs. 6 of **Singen wir aus Herzensgrund** [Hans Vogel, 1563] (187-7)

Wir essen und wir leben wohl = Vs. 7 of **Christ lag in Todesbanden** [Martin Luther, 1524] (4-8)

Wir singen dir in deinem Heer = Vs. 2 of **Wir singen dir, Immanuel** [Paul Gerhardt, 1656] (248-23)

Wir wachen oder schlafen ein = Vs. 6 of **Ach, lieben Christen, seid getrost** [Johannes Gigas, 1561] (114-7)

Wo Gott der Herr nicht bei uns hält = Vs. 1 [Justus Jonas, 1524] (178-1)

Wo soll ich fliehen hin = Vs. 1 [Johann Heermann, 1630] (5-1)

Wohl dem, der sich auf seinen Gott = Vs. 1 [Johann Christoph Rube, 1692] (139-1)

Wohl mir, daß ich Jesum habe = Vs. 6 of **Jesu, meiner Seelen Wonne** [Martin Jahn, 1661] (147-6)

Wohlan, so will ich mich = Vs. 4 of **Ich freue mich in dir** [Caspar Ziegler, 1697] (133-6)

Zieh uns dir nach, so laufen wir = Vs. 13 of **Du Lebensfürst, Herr Jesu Christ** [Johann Rist, 1641] (43-11)

Zion hört die Wächter singen = Vs. 2 of **Wachet auf, ruft uns die Stimme** [Philipp Nicolai, 1599] (140-4)

Zudem ist Weisheit und Verstand = Vs. 5 of **Ich hab in Gottes Herz und Sinn** [Paul Gerhardt, 1647] (92-4)

Zum reinen Wasser er mich weist = Vs. 2 of **Der Herr ist mein getreuer Hirt, hält mich** [Wolfgang Meuslin, 1530] (112-2)

Zwar ist solche Herzensstube = Vs. 9 of **Ihr Gestirn, ihr hohlen Lüfte** [Johann Franck, 1655] (248-53)

Zwingt die Saiten in Cythara = Vs. 6 of **Wie schön leuchtet der Morgenstern** [Philipp Nicolai, 1599] (36-4)

INDEX OF CHORALE STANZAS APPEARING MORE THAN ONCE

1-6, 49-6
3-1, 44-4, 58-1
3-6, 153-9
4-6, 158-4
5-7, 163-6
9-7, 155-5, 186-6
12-7, 75-14, 99-6, 100-6
13-6, 44-7, 97-9
16-1, 190-1, 190-2
16-6, 28-6
20-1, 60-1
21-9, 93-2
21-9, 93-5
22-5, 96-6, 132-6, 164-6
27-1, 166-6
28-6, 16-6
29-8, 51-4, 167-5
36-2, 61-1, 62-1
36-8, 62-6
42-7, 126-6
42-7, 126-6
44-4, 58-1, 3-1
44-7, 13-6, 97-9
49-6, 1-6
51-4, 29-8, 167-5
58-1, 3-1, 44-4

60-1, 20-1
61-1, 36-2, 62-1
62-1, 36-2, 61-1
62-6, 36-8
64-2, 91-6, 248-28
64-4, 94-1
65-7, 92-7
67-7, 116-1, 143-2
69-6, 76-14
72-5, 111-1, 144-6
73-1, 156-6
75-7, 100-5
75-14, 12-7, 99-6, 100-6
76-14, 69-6
79-3, 192-1
83-5, 125-6
85-3, 104-6
86-6, 186-11
88-7, 93-7
90-5, 101-7
91-6, 64-2, 248-28
92-7, 65-7
93-2, 21-9
93-5, 21-9
93-7, 88-7
94-1, 64-4

95-1, 106-3b, 125-1
96-6, 22-5, 132-6, 164-6
97-9, 13-6, 44-7
98-1, 99-1, 100-1, 144-3
99-1, 98-1, 100-1, 144-3
99-6, 12-7, 75-14, 100-6
100-1, 98-1, 99-1, 144-3
100-5, 75-7
100-6, 12-7, 75-14, 99-6
101-7, 90-5
104-6, 85-3
106-3b, 95-1, 125-1
111-1, 72-5, 144-6
113-2, 131-2
113-8, 168-6
116-1, 67-7, 143-2
124-6, 154-8, 157-5
125-1, 95-1, 106-3b
125-6, 83-5
126-6, 42-7
126-6, 42-7
131-2, 113-2
132-6, 22-5, 96-6, 164-6
143-2, 67-7, 116-1
144-3, 98-1, 99-1, 100-1
144-6, 72-5, 111-1

153-9, 3-6
154-8, 124-6, 157-5
155-5, 9-7, 186-6
156-6, 73-1
157-5, 124-6, 154-8
158-4, 4-6
159-5, 182-7
163-6, 5-7
164-6, 22-5, 96-6, 132-6
166-6, 27-1
167-5, 29-8, 51-4
168-6, 113-8
169-7, 197-5
171-6, 190-7
177-1, 185-6
182-7, 159-5
185-6, 177-1
186-6, 9-7, 155-5
186-11, 86-6
190-1, 16-1, 190-2
190-2, 16-1, 190-1
190-7, 171-6
192-1, 79-3
197-5, 169-7
248-28, 64-2, 91-6

761

INDEX OF SCRIPTURAL QUOTATIONS AND STRICT PARAPHRASES

1 Cor. 10:13 (52–4, 104–2)
1 Jn. 3:1 (64–1)
1 Jn. 3:8 (40–1, 54–3)
1 Kings 18:39 (117–8)
2 Sam. 19:35, 37 (71–2)
2 Tim. 2:8 (67–1)
Acts 1:9 / Mk. 16:19 (11–5)
Acts 1:10–11 (11–7a)
Acts 1:12 / Lk. 24:52 (11–7c)
Acts 14:22 (12–3, 146–2)
Acts 17:28 (106–2a)
Deut. 4:7–8 (29–4)
Deut. 33:25; Gen. 21:22 (71–3)
Gen. 21:22 / Deut. 33:25 (71–3)
Gen. 32:26 (157–1)
Gen. 49:18 / Ps. 119:166 (60–1)
Heb. 13:16 (39–4)
Hos. 11:8 (89–1)
Is. 38:1 (106–2c)
Is. 41:10 (153–3)
Is. 55:10–11 (18–2)
Is. 58:7–8 (39–1)
Is. 60:6 (65–1)
Jer. 5:3 (102–1)
Jer. 10:6 (110–3)
Jer. 16:16 (88–1)
Jer. 17:9 (176–1)
Jer. 31:3 (49–6)
Jer. 32:41 (28–3)
Jms. 1:12 (57–1)
Jn. 3:16 (68–1)
Jn. 3:18 (68–5)
Jn. 10:3 (175–1)
Jn. 10:6 (175–5)
Jn. 10:12 (85–1)
Jn. 14:23 (59–1, 74–1, 172–2)
Jn. 14:28 (74–4)
Jn. 16:2 (44–1, 44–2, 183–1)
Jn. 16:5 (166–1)
Jn. 16:7 (108–1)
Jn. 16:13 (108–4)
Jn. 16:20 (103–1)
Jn. 16:23 (86–1)
Jn. 16:24 (87–1)
Jn. 16:33 (87–5)
Jn. 19:30 (159–4)
Jn. 20:19 (42–2, 67–6)
Jn. 20: 21 (67–6)
Lam. 1:12 (46–1)
Lk. 1:54 (10–5)
Lk. 1:68 (167–2)
Lk. 1:69 (167–1)
Lk. 1:46–48 (10–1)
Lk. 2:7 (248–6)

Lk. 2:8–9 (248–11)
Lk. 2:10–11 (248–13)
Lk. 2:12 (248–16)
Lk. 2:13 (248–20)
Lk. 2:14 (110–5, 191–1, 248–21)
Lk. 2:15 (248–25, 248–26)
Lk. 2:16–19 (248–30)
Lk. 2:20 (248–34)
Lk. 2:21 (248–37)
Lk. 2:29–32 (82–1, 83–2)
Lk. 2:49 (32–2, 154–5)
Lk. 5:10 (88–4)
Lk. 10:27 (77–1)
Lk. 14:11 (47–1)
Lk. 17:15–16 (17–4)
Lk. 18:31 (22–1, 159–1)
Lk. 18:34 (22–1)
Lk. 23:43 (106–3b)
Lk. 24:29 (6–1)
Lk. 24:50–51 (11–2)
Lk. 24:52 / Acts 1:12 (11–7c)
Mic. 6:8 (45–1)
Mk. 7:37 (35–4)
Mk. 9:24 (109–1)
Mk. 14:41 (60–5)
Mk. 16:15–16 / Mt. 28:19 (7–5)
Mk. 16:16 (37–1)
Mk. 16:19 (43–4)
Mk. 16:19 / Acts 1:9 (11–5)
Mt. 2:1 (248–44)
Mt. 2:2 (248–45)
Mt. 2:3 (248–48)
Mt. 2:4–6 (248–50)
Mt. 2:7–8 (248–55)
Mt. 2:9–11 (248–58)
Mt. 2:12 (248–60)
Mt. 3:17 (7–3)
Mt. 6:31–32 (187–4)
Mt. 7:12 (24–3)
Mt. 7:22–23 (45–4)
Mt. 8:26 (81–4)
Mt. 20:14 (144–1)
Mt. 28:19 / Mk. 16:15–16 (7–5)
Phil. 1:21 (95–1)
Ps. 19:1, 3 (76–1)
Ps. 22:26 (75–1)
Ps. 23:1–2 (85–3, 104–6, 112–1)
Ps. 23:2–3 (112–2)
Ps. 23:4 (112–3)
Ps. 23:5 (112–4)
Ps. 23:6 (112–5)
Ps. 25:1–2 (150–2)
Ps. 25:5 (150–4)
Ps. 25:15 (150–6)

Ps. 27:4 (190–4)
Ps. 29:2 / 96:8–9 (148–1)
Ps. 31:5 (106–3a)
Ps. 36:5 (17–3)
Ps. 38:3 (25–1)
Ps. 40:7–8 (182–3)
Ps. 42:5 (21–6)
Ps. 47:5–6 (43–1)
Ps. 48:10 (171–1)
Ps. 50:23 (17–1)
Ps. 65:1 (120–1)
Ps. 74:12 (71–1)
Ps. 74:16–17 (71–4)
Ps. 74:19 (71–6)
Ps. 75:1 (29–2)
Ps. 80:1 (104–1)
Ps. 84:11 (79–1)
Ps. 90:12 (106–2b)
Ps. 94:19 (21–2)
Ps. 97:11–12 (195–1)
Ps. 103:1–6 (28–2)
Ps. 103:2 (69–1)
Ps. 103:13–16 (17–7)
Ps. 104:27–28 (187–1)
Ps. 115:12 (196–2)
Ps. 115:13 (196–3)
Ps. 115:14 (196–4)
Ps. 115:15 (196–5)
Ps. 116:7 (21–9)
Ps. 118:15–16 (149–1)
Ps. 118:25 (18–3)
Ps. 119:166 / Gen. 49:18 (60–1)
Ps. 121:4–5 (193–2)
Ps. 124:1–3 (14–1)
Ps. 124:3–5 (14–3)
Ps. 124:6–8 (14–5)
Ps. 126:2–3 (110–1)
Ps. 128:6 (34–5)
Ps. 130:1–2 (131–1)
Ps. 130:1–3 (38–1)
Ps. 130:3–4 (131–2)
Ps. 130:5 (131–3)
Ps. 130:6 (131–4)
Ps. 130:7–8 (131–5)
Ps. 139:23 (136–1)
Ps. 143:2 (105–1)
Ps. 145:15 (23–3)
Ps. 146:1 (143–1)
Ps. 146:5 (143–3)
Ps. 146:10 (143–5)
Ps. 147:12 (190–3)
Ps. 147:12–14 (119–1)
Ps. 149:1 (190–1)
Ps. 150:4, 6 (190–1)

Rev. 2:10 (49–5)
Rev. 3:20 (61–4)
Rev. 5:11–12 (21–11)
Rev. 12:10 (50–1)
Rev. 14:13 (60–4)
Rev. 22:20 (106–2d)
Rom. 2:4–5 (102–4)
Rom. 7:24 (48–1)
Rom. 8:1 (74–6)
Sirach (Apocrypha) 1:28
   (179–1)
Sirach (Apocrypha) 14:17
   (106–2d)
Sirach (Apocrypha) 50:22 (79–3,
   192–1)
Sirach (Apocrypha) 50:23–24
   (191–2)

ALPHABETICAL INDEX OF LIBRETTISTS[1]

[1]Where an attribution is not certain, the cantata number appears in parentheses.

Chorale (Agricola, Johann 1494-1566): 177
Chorale (Fleming, Paul 1609-1640): 97
Chorale (Heermann, Johann 1585-1647): 107
Chorale (Luther, Martin 1483-1546): 4
Chorale (Meuslin, Wolfgang 1497-1563): 112
Chorale (Neander, Joachim 1650-1680): 137
Chorale (Olearius, Johann 1611-1684): 129
Chorale (Rinckart, Martin 1586-1649): 192
Chorale (Rodigast, Samuel 1649-1708): 100
Chorale (Schütz, Johann Jakob 1640-1690): 117
Doxologies (Traditional): 191
Eilmar, Georg Christian (1665-1715): (71), (131)
Franck, Salomon (1659-1725): (12), (21), 31, (67), (70a), 72, (80a), 132, (147), 152, 155, 161, 162, 163, 164, 165, 168, (172), (182), 185
Gottsched, Johann Christoph (1700-1766): 198
Heineccius, Johann Michael (1674-1722): (63)
Helbig, Johann Friedrich (c. 1720): 47
Helm, Christoph (?-1748): (17), (39), (43), (45), (88), (102), (187)
Knauer, Johann (c. 1720): 64, 77

Lehms, Georg Christian (1684-1717): 13, 16, 32, 35, 54, 57, 110, 151, 170, 199
Neumeister, Erdmann (1671-1756): 18, 24, 28, 59, 61, (79)
Picander (Christian Friedrich Henrici) (1700-1764): (30), (36), 84, 145, (148), 149, 156, 157, 159, 171, 174, 188, (249)
Psalm: 196
Rambach, Johann Jacob (? - ?): 25
Unknown: 1, 2, 3, 5, 7, 8, 9, 10, 11, 14, 19, 20, 22, 23, 26, 27, 29, 33, 34, 38, 40, 41, 46, 49, 50, 51, 52, 55, 56, 58, 60, 62, 65, 66, 69, 70, 73, 75, 76, 77, 78, 80, 81, 82, 83, 89, 90, 91, 92, 93, 94, 95, 96, 98, 99, 101, 105, 106, 109, 111, 113, 114, 115, 116, 119, 120, 121, 122, 123, 124, 125, 126, 127, 130, 133, 134, 135, 136, 138, 139, 140, 143, 146, 147, 148, 150, 153, 154, 158, 167, 169, 173, 178, 179, 180, 181, 184, 186, 190, 193, 194, 195, 197, 200, 248
Ziegler, Christiane Mariane von (1695-1760): 68, 74, 87, 103, 108, 128, 175, 176, 183
Weiß, Christian the elder (1671-1737): (6), (37), (42), (44), (79), (85), (86), (104), (144), (166)

Although many of the librettists are still unknown, Harald Streck has shown that several authors can be identified by their writing style, if not by name. He has identified four groups of cantatas, each of which may have been written by the same librettist. For a summary of Streck's findings, see Artur Hirsch, "Johann Sebastian Bach's Cantatas in Chronological Order," *BACH: The Journal of the Riemenschneider Bach Institute* 11 (July 1980): 18-35.

Group 1: 1, 5, 8, 26, 62, 78, 96, 115, 124, 181
Group 2: 9, 65, 101, 113, 180, 190 (also adaptations of 66, 134, 184)
Group 3: 3, 33, 38, 41, 91, 99, 111, 114, 116, 121, 122, 123, 125, 130, 133, 139
Group 4 (possibly by various authors; of inferior poetic quality): 2, 7, 10, 20, 92, 93, 94, 127, 135, 178

INDEX OF FIRST PERFORMANCE DATES[1]

[1]Dates of first performances (FP) or time of composition (TC) follow the *Bach Compendium* (taking corrigenda into account) and are given as year-month-date. Differing conclusions from recent studies by Yoshitake Kobayashi (KB) are indicated for BWV 171 and 195. Chronological positions are given in the far right column. (See Index of Cantatas in Chronological Order.)

BWV 1	Wie schön leuchtet der Morgenstern [FP 1725-3-25]	113
BWV 2	Ach Gott, vom Himmel sieh darein [FP 1724-6-18]	75
BWV 3	Ach Gott, wie manches Herzeleid I [FP 1725-1-14]	107
BWV 4	Christ Lag in Todesbanden [TC probably 1708 or earlier]	3
BWV 5	Wo soll ich fliehen hin [FP 1724-10-15]	92
BWV 6	Bleib bei uns, denn es will Abend werden [FP 1725-4-2]	115
BWV 7	Christ unser Herr zum Jordan kam [FP 1724-6-24]	76
BWV 8	Liebster Gott, wann werd ich sterben [FP 1724-9-24]	88
BWV 9	Es ist das Heil uns kommen her [TC 1732/1735, FP perhaps 1732-7-20]	183
BWV 10	Meine Seel erhebt den Herren [FP 1724-7-2]	78
BWV 11	Lobet Gott in seinen Reichen [FP 1735-5-19]	193
BWV 12	Weinen, Klagen, Sorgen, Zagen [FP 1714-4-22]	12
BWV 13	Meine Seufzer, meine Tränen [FP 1726-1-20]	137
BWV 14	Wär Gott nicht mit uns diese Zeit [FP 1735-1-30]	192
BWV 16	Herr Gott, dich loben wir [FP 1726-1-1]	135
BWV 17	Wer Dank opfert, der preiset mich [FP 1726-9-22]	148
BWV 18	Gleichwie der Regen und Schnee vom Himmel fällt [FP 1713/1714]	8
BWV 19	Es erhub sich ein Streit [FP 1726-9-29]	149
BWV 20	O Ewigkeit, du Donnerwort II [FP 1724-6-11]	74
BWV 21	Ich hatte viel Bekümmernis [FP perhaps 1713-12-? (some parts go back to earlier version)]	9
BWV 22	Jesus nahm zu sich die Zwölfe [FP 1723-2-7]	28
BWV 23	Du wahrer Gott und Davids Sohn [FP 1723-2-7]	27
BWV 24	Ein ungefärbt Gemüte [FP 1723-6-20]	32
BWV 25	Es ist nichts Gesundes an meinem Leibe [FP 1723-8-29]	41
BWV 26	Ach wie flüchtig, ach wie nichtig [FP 1724-11-19]	97
BWV 27	Wer weiß, wie nahe mir mein Ende [FP 1726-10-6]	150
BWV 28	Gottlob! nun geht das Jahr zu Ende [FP 1725-12-30]	134
BWV 29	Wir danken dir, Gott, wir danken dir [FP 1731-8-27]	180
BWV 30	Freue dich, erloste Schar [TC 1738-1742; FP probably 1738-6-24]	195
BWV 31	Der Himmel lacht! die Erde jubilieret [FP 1715-4-21]	19
BWV 32	Liebster Jesu, mein Verlangen [FP 1726-1-13]	136
BWV 33	Allein zu dir, Herr Jesu Christ [FP 1724-9-3]	85
BWV 34	O ewiges Feuer, o Ursprung der Liebe [TC ca. 1746/1747]	198
BWV 35	Geist und Seele wird verwirret [FP 1726-9-8]	147
BWV 36	Schwingt freudig euch empor [TC 1725-1730]	175
BWV 37	Wer da gläubet und getauft wird [FP 1724-5-18]	70
BWV 38	Aus tiefer Not schrei ich zu dir [FP 1724-10-29]	94
BWV 39	Brich dem Hungrigen dein Brot [FP 1726-6-23]	141
BWV 40	Dazu ist erschienen der Sohn Gottes [FP 1723-12-26]	53
BWV 41	Jesu, nun sei gepreiset [FP 1725-1-1]	104
BWV 42	Am Abend aber desselbigen Sabbats [FP 1725-4-8]	116
BWV 43	Gott fähret auf mit Jauchzen [FP 1726-5-30]	140
BWV 44	Sie werden euch in den Bann tun I [FP 1724-5-21]	71
BWV 45	Es ist dir gesagt, Mensch, was gut ist [FP 1726-8-11]	145
BWV 46	Schauet doch und sehet, ob irgendein Schmerz sei [FP 1723-8-1]	38
BWV 47	Wer sich selbst erhöhet, der soll erniedriget [FP 1726-10-13]	151
BWV 48	Ich elender Mensch, wer wird mich erlösen [FP 1723-10-3]	46
BWV 49	Ich geh und suche mit Verlangen [FP 1726-11-3]	155
BWV 50	Nun ist das Heil und die Kraft (fragment) [TC unknown]	200

BWV 51	Jauchzet Gott in allen Landen [FP 1730-9-17]	177
BWV 52	Falsche Welt, dir trau ich nicht [FP 1726-11-24]	158
BWV 54	Widerstehe doch der Sünde [TC Weimar period, perhaps FP 1714-3-4]	10
BWV 55	Ich armer Mensch, ich Sündenknecht [FP 1726-11-17]	157
BWV 56	Ich will den Kreuzstab gerne tragen [FP 1726-10-27]	153
BWV 57	Selig ist der Mann [FP 1725-12-26]	132
BWV 58	Ach Gott, wie manches Herzeleid II [FP 1727-1-5]	159
BWV 59	Wer mich liebet, der wird mein Wort halten I [TC 1723, 5, 16, FP 1724-5-28]	29
BWV 60	O Ewigkeit, du Donnerwort I [FP 1723-11-7]	50
BWV 61	Nun komm, der Heiden Heiland I [FP 1714-12-2]	15
BWV 62	Nun komm, der Heiden Heiland II [FP 1724-12-3]	99
BWV 63	Christen, ätzet diesen Tag [TC ca. 1714/1715]	17
BWV 64	Sehet, welch eine Liebe hat uns der Vater erzeiget [FP 1723-12-27]	54
BWV 65	Sie werden aus Saba alle kommen [FP 1724-1-6]	57
BWV 66	Erfreut euch, ihr Herzen [FP 1724-4-10]	64
BWV 67	Halt im Gedächtnis Jesum Christ [FP 1724-4-16]	66
BWV 68	Also hat Gott die Welt geliebt [FP 1725-5-21]	124
BWV 69	Lobe den Herrn, meine Seele II [FP probably 1748-8-26]	199
BWV 70	Wachet! betet! betet! wachet! [FP 1723-11-21]	52
BWV 71	Gott ist mein König [FP 1708-2-4]	4
BWV 72	Alles nur nach Gottes Willen [FP 1726-1-27]	138
BWV 73	Herr, wie du willt, so schick's mit mir [FP 1724-1-23]	59
BWV 74	Wer mich liebet der wird mein Wort halten II [FP 1725-5-20]	123
BWV 75	Die Elenden sollen essen [FP 1723-5-30]	30
BWV 76	Die Himmel erzählen die Ehre Gottes [FP 1723-6-6]	31
BWV 77	Du sollt Gott, deinen Herren, lieben [FP 1723-8-22]	40
BWV 78	Jesu, der du meine Seele [FP 1724-9-10]	86
BWV 79	Gott der Herr ist Sonn und Schild [FP 1725-10-31]	130
BWV 80	Ein feste Burg ist unser Gott [Largely based on BWVa: FP perhaps 1715-3-24. Revision 1727/1731. Last version: TC 1744/1747 or earlier.]	18
BWV 81	Jesus schläft, was soll ich hoffen [FP 1724-1-30]	60
BWV 82	Ich habe genug [FP 1727-2-2]	160
BWV 83	Erfreute Zeit im neuen Bund [FP 1724-2-2]	61
BWV 84	Ich bin vergnügt mit meinem Glücke [FP 1727-2-9]	162
BWV 85	Ich bin ein guter Hirt [FP 1725-4-15]	117
BWV 86	Wahrlich, wahrlich, ich sage euch [FP 1724-5-14]	69
BWV 87	Bisher habt ihr nichts gebeten in meinem Namen [FP 1725-5-6]	120
BWV 88	Siehe, ich will viel Fischer aussenden [FP 1726-7-21]	142
BWV 89	Was soll ich aus dir machen, Ephraim [FP 1723-10-24]	48
BWV 90	Es reißet euch ein schrecklich Ende [FP 1723-11-14]	51
BWV 91	Gelobet seist du, Jesu Christ [FP 1724-12-25]	100
BWV 92	Ich hab in Gottes Herz und Sinn [FP 1725-1-28]	109
BWV 93	Wer nur den lieben Gott läßt walten [FP 1724-7-9]	79
BWV 94	Was frag ich nach der Welt [FP 1724-8-6]	82
BWV 95	Christus, der ist mein Leben [FP 1723-9-12]	44
BWV 96	Herr Christ, der einge Gottessohn [FP 1724-10-8]	91
BWV 97	In allen meinen Taten [TC 1734, perhaps FP 1734-7-25]	185
BWV 98	Was Gott tut, das ist wohlgetan II [FP 1726-11-10]	156
BWV 99	Was Gott tut, das ist wohlgetan I [FP 1724-9-17]	87
BWV 100	Was Gott tut, das ist wohlgetan III [TC 1732/1735, probably 1734 or earlier]	184
BWV 101	Nimm von uns, Herr, du treuer Gott [FP 1724-8-13]	83
BWV 102	Herr, deine Augen sehen nach dem Glauben [FP 1726-8-25]	146
BWV 103	Ihr werdet weinen und heulen [FP 1725-4-22]	118
BWV 104	Du hirte Israel, höre [FP 1724-4-23]	67
BWV 105	Herr, gehe nicht ins Gericht mit deinem Knecht [FP 1723-7-25]	37
BWV 106	Gottes Zeit ist die allerbeste Zeit [TC probably 1707/1708]	2

BWV 107	Was willst du dich betrüben [FP 1724-7-23]	80
BWV 108	Es ist euch gut, daß ich hingehe [FP 1725-4-29]	119
BWV 109	Ich glaube, lieber Herr [FP 1723-10-17]	47
BWV 110	Unser Mund sei voll Lachens [FP 1725-12-25]	131
BWV 111	Was mein Gott will, das g'scheh allzeit [FP 1725-1-21]	108
BWV 112	Der Herr ist mein getreuer Hirt [FP 1731-4-8]	179
BWV 113	Herr Jesu Christ, du höchstes Gut [FP 1724-8-20]	84
BWV 114	Ach, lieben Christen, seid getrost [FP 1724-10-1]	90
BWV 115	Mache dich, mein Geist, bereit [FP 1724-11-5]	95
BWV 116	Du Friedefürst, Herr Jesu Christ [FP 1724-11-26]	98
BWV 117	Sei Lob und Ehr dem höchsten Gut [TC 1728/1731]	167
BWV 119	Preise, Jerusalem, den Herrn [FP 1723-8-30]	42
BWV 120	Gott, man lobet dich in der Stille [TC of earlier version from before 1729]	168
BWV 121	Christum wir sollen loben schon [FP 1724-12-26]	101
BWV 122	Das neugeborne Kindelein [FP 1724-12-31]	103
BWV 123	Liebster Immanuel, Herzog der Frommen [FP 1725-1-6]	105
BWV 124	Meinen Jesum laß ich nicht [FP 1725-1-7]	106
BWV 125	Mit Fried und Freud ich fahr dahin [FP 1725-2-2]	110
BWV 126	Erhalt uns, Herr, bei deinem Wort [FP 1725-2-4]	111
BWV 127	Herr Jesu Christ, wahr' Mensch und Gott [FP 1725-2-11]	112
BWV 128	Auf Christi Himmelfahrt allein [FP 1725-5-10]	121
BWV 129	Gelobet sei der Herr, mein Gott [TC 1726/1727, FP probably before 1727, perhaps 1726-10-31]	154
BWV 130	Herr Gott, dich loben alle wir [FP 1724-9-29]	89
BWV 131	Aus der Tiefen rufe ich, Herr, zu dir [TC 1707/1708]	1
BWV 132	Bereitet die Wege, bereitet die Bahn [FP 1715-12-22]	23
BWV 133	Ich freue mich in dir [FP 1724-12-27]	102
BWV 134	Ein Herz, das seinen Jesum lebend weiß [FP 1724-4-11]	65
BWV 135	Ach Herr, mich armen Sünder [FP 1724-6-25]	77
BWV 136	Erforsche mich, Gott, und erfahre mein Herz [FP 1723-7-18]	36
BWV 137	Lobe den Herren, den mächtigen König der Ehren [FP 1725-8-19]	128
BWV 138	Warum betrübst du dich, mein Herz [FP 1723-9-5]	43
BWV 139	Wohl dem, der sich auf seinen Gott [FP 1724-11-12]	96
BWV 140	Wachet auf, ruft uns die Stimme [FP 1731-11-25]	181
BWV 143	Lobe den Herrn, meine Seele I [spurious? ca. 1708-1714]	7
BWV 144	Nimm, was dein ist, und gehe hin [FP 1724-2-6]	62
BWV 145	Ich lebe, mein Herze, zu deinem Ergötzen [FP presumably 1729-4-19]	172
BWV 146	Wir müssen durch viel Trübsal [TC uncertain. FP perhaps 1726-5-12 or 1728-4-18]	139
BWV 147	Herz und Mund und Tat und Leben [FP 1723-7-2]	34
BWV 148	Bringet dem Herrn Ehre seines Namens [FP perhaps 1723-9-19]	45
BWV 149	Man singet mit Freuden vom Sieg [FP probably 1729-9-29]	174
BWV 150	Nach dir, Herr, verlanget mich [TC unknown; during or before Bach's Weimar period]	6
BWV 151	Süßer Trost, mein Jesus kömmt [FP 1725-12-27]	133
BWV 152	Tritt auf die Glaubensbahn [FP 1714-12-30]	16
BWV 153	Schau, lieber Gott, wie meine Feind [FP 1724-1-2]	56
BWV 154	Mein liebster Jesus ist verloren [FP 1724-1-9]	58
BWV 155	Mein Gott, wie lang, ach lange [FP 1716-1-19]	24
BWV 156	Ich steh mit einem Fuß im Grabe [FP probably 1729-1-23]	170
BWV 157	Ich lasse dich nicht, du segnest mich denn [FP probably 1727-2-6]	161
BWV 158	Der Friede sei mit dir [TC probably in Leipzig period, before 1735]	176
BWV 159	Sehet, wir gehn hinauf gen Jerusalem [FP probably 1729-2-27]	171
BWV 161	Komm, du süße Todesstunde [FP 1716-9-27, later version ca. 1735]	25
BWV 162	Ach! ich sehe, itzt, da ich zur Hochzeit gehe [FP 1716-10-25]	26
BWV 163	Nur jedem das Seine [FP 1715-11-24]	22
BWV 164	Ihr, die ihr euch von Christo nennet [FP 1725-8-26]	129
BWV 165	O heiliges Geist- und Wasserbad [FP presumably 1715-6-16]	20

BWV 166	Wo gehest du hin [FP 1724-5-7]	68
BWV 167	Ihr Menschen, rühmet Gottes Liebe [FP 1723-6-24]	33
BWV 168	Tue Rechnung! Donnerwort [FP 1725-7-29]	127
BWV 169	Gott soll allein mein Herze haben [FP 1726-10-20]	152
BWV 170	Vergnügte Ruh, beliebte Seelenlust [FP 1726-7-28]	143
BWV 171	Gott, wie dein Name, so ist auch dein Ruhm [FP probably 1729-1-1; or 1736/1737? (KB)]	169
BWV 172	Erschallet ihr Lieder, erklinget, ihr Saiten [FP probably 1714-5-20]	13
BWV 173	Erhöhtes Fleisch und Blut [FP perhaps 1724-5-29]	72
BWV 174	Ich liebe den Höchsten von ganzem Gemüte [FP 1729-6-6]	173
BWV 175	Er rufet seinen Schafen mit Namen [FP 1725-5-22]	125
BWV 176	Es ist ein trotzig und verzagt Ding [FP 1725-5-27]	126
BWV 177	Ich ruf zu dir, Herr Jesu Christ [FP 1732-7-6]	182
BWV 178	Wo Gott, der Herr, nicht bei uns hält [FP 1724-7-30]	81
BWV 179	Siehe zu, daß deine Gottesfurcht nicht Heuchelei sei [FP 1723-8-8]	39
BWV 180	Schmücke dich, o liebe Seele [FP 1724-10-22]	93
BWV 181	Leichtgesinnte Flattergeister [FP 1724-2-13]	63
BWV 182	Himmelskönig, sei willkommen [FP 1714-3-25]	11
BWV 183	Sie werden euch in den Bann tun II [FP 1725-5-13]	122
BWV 184	Erwünschtes Freudenlicht [FP 1724-5-30]	73
BWV 185	Barmherziges Herze der ewigen Liebe [FP 1715-7-14]	21
BWV 186	Ärgre dich, o Seele, nicht [FP 1723-7-11]	35
BWV 187	Es wartet alles auf dich [FP 1726-8-4]	144
BWV 188	Ich habe meine Zuversicht [FP probably 1728-10-17; perhaps 1729-11-6]	166
BWV 190	Singet dem Herrn ein neues Lied [FP 1724-1-1]	55
BWV 191	Gloria in excelsis Deo [TC between ca. 1743 and ca. 1746 (based on Bm mass)]	197
BWV 192	Nun danket alle Gott [FP probably 1730, fall]	178
BWV 193	Ihr Tore zu Zion [FP 1727-8-25]	163
BWV 194	Höcherwünschtes Freudenfest [FP ca. 1723-11-2, RP 1724-6-4]	49
BWV 195	Dem Gerechten muß das Licht [TC 1727/1731 or between 1748/9 and 1749/10 (KB)]	165
BWV 196	Der Herr denket an uns [TC presumably 1707/1708]	5
BWV 197	Gott ist unsre Zuversicht [TC 1736/1737]	194
BWV 198	Laß, Fürstin, laß noch einen Strahl [TC 1727-10-?, FP 1727-10-17]	164
BWV 199	Mein Herze schwimmt im Blut [FP 1714-8-12]	14
BWV 200	Bekennen will ich seinen Namen [TC ca. 1742]	196
BWV 248-I	Jauchzet, frohlocket, auf, preiset die Tage (Christmas Oratorio I) [FP 1734-12-25]	186
BWV 248-II	Und es waren Hirten in derselben Gegend (Christmas Oratorio II) [FP 1734-12-26]	187
BWV 248-III	Herrscher des Himmels, erhöre das Lallen (Christmas Oratorio III) [FP 1734-12-27]	188
BWV 248-IV	Fallt mit Danken, fallt mit Loben (Christmas Oratorio IV) [FP 1735-1-1]	189
BWV 248-V	Ehre sei dir, Gott, gesungen (Christmas Oratorio V) [FP 1735-1-2]	190
BWV 248-VI	Herr, wenn die stolzen Feinde schnauben (Christmas Oratorio VI) [FP 1735-1-6]	191
BWV 249	Kommet, eilet und laufet [FP 1725-4-1]	114

INDEX OF CANTATAS IN CHRONOLOGICAL ORDER[1]

[1]Based on dates of first performances (FP) or time of composition (TC) as listed in the *Bach Compendium* (taking corrigenda into account), given here as year-month-date. Differing conclusions from recent studies by Yoshitake Kobayashi (KB) are indicated for BWV 171 and 195.

BWV 131	Aus der Tiefen rufe ich, Herr, zu dir [TC 1707/1708]	1
BWV 106	Gottes Zeit ist die allerbeste Zeit [TC probably 1707/1708]	2
BWV 4	Christ Lag in Todesbanden [TC probably 1708 or earlier]	3
BWV 71	Gott ist mein König [FP 1708-2-4]	4
BWV 196	Der Herr denket an uns [TC presumably 1707/1708]	5
BWV 150	Nach dir, Herr, verlanget mich [TC unknown; during or before Bach's Weimar period]	6
BWV 143	Lobe den Herrn, meine Seele I [spurious? ca. 1708-1714]	7
BWV 18	Gleichwie der Regen und Schnee vom Himmel fällt [FP 1713/1714]	8
BWV 21	Ich hatte viel Bekümmernis [FP perhaps 1713-12-? (some parts go back to earlier version)]	9
BWV 54	Widerstehe doch der Sünde [TC Weimar period, perhaps FP 1714-3-4]	10
BWV 182	Himmelskönig, sei willkommen [FP 1714-3-25]	11
BWV 12	Weinen, Klagen, Sorgen, Zagen [FP 1714-4-22]	12
BWV 172	Erschallet ihr Lieder, erklinget, ihr Saiten [FP probably 1714-5-20]	13
BWV 199	Mein Herze schwimmt im Blut [FP 1714-8-12]	14
BWV 61	Nun komm, der Heiden Heiland I [FP 1714-12-2]	15
BWV 152	Tritt auf die Glaubensbahn [FP 1714-12-30]	16
BWV 63	Christen, ätzet diesen Tag [TC ca. 1714/1715]	17
BWV 80	Ein feste Burg ist unser Gott [Largely based on BWVa: FP perhaps 1715-3-24. Revision 1727/1731. Last version: TC 1744/1747 or earlier.]	18
BWV 31	Der Himmel lacht! die Erde jubilieret [FP 1715-4-21]	19
BWV 165	O heiliges Geist- und Wasserbad [FP presumably 1715-6-16]	20
BWV 185	Barmherziges Herze der ewigen Liebe [FP 1715-7-14]	21
BWV 163	Nur jedem das Seine [FP 1715-11-24]	22
BWV 132	Bereitet die Wege, bereitet die Bahn [FP 1715-12-22]	23
BWV 155	Mein Gott, wie lang, ach lange [FP 1716-1-19]	24
BWV 161	Komm, du süße Todesstunde [FP 1716-9-27, later version ca. 1735]	25
BWV 162	Ach! ich sehe, itzt, da ich zur Hochzeit gehe [FP 1716-10-25]	26
BWV 23	Du wahrer Gott und Davids Sohn [FP 1723-2-7]	27
BWV 22	Jesus nahm zu sich die Zwölfe [FP 1723-2-7]	28
BWV 59	Wer mich liebet, der wird mein Wort halten I [TC 1723, 5, 16, FP 1724-5-28]	29
BWV 75	Die Elenden sollen essen [FP 1723-5-30]	30
BWV 76	Die Himmel erzählen die Ehre Gottes [FP 1723-6-6]	31
BWV 24	Ein ungefärbt Gemüte [FP 1723-6-20]	32
BWV 167	Ihr Menschen, rühmet Gottes Liebe [FP 1723-6-24]	33
BWV 147	Herz und Mund und Tat und Leben [FP 1723-7-2]	34
BWV 186	Ärgre dich, o Seele, nicht [FP 1723-7-11]	35
BWV 136	Erforsche mich, Gott, und erfahre mein Herz [FP 1723-7-18]	36
BWV 105	Herr, gehe nicht ins Gericht mit deinem Knecht [FP 1723-7-25]	37
BWV 46	Schauet doch und sehet, ob irgendein Schmerz sei [FP 1723-8-1]	38
BWV 179	Siehe zu, daß deine Gottesfurcht nicht Heuchelei sei [FP 1723-8-8]	39
BWV 77	Du sollt Gott, deinen Herren, lieben [FP 1723-8-22]	40
BWV 25	Es ist nichts Gesundes an meinem Leibe [FP 1723-8-29]	41
BWV 119	Preise, Jerusalem, den Herrn [FP 1723-8-30]	42
BWV 138	Warum betrübst du dich, mein Herz [FP 1723-9-5]	43
BWV 95	Christus, der ist mein Leben [FP 1723-9-12]	44
BWV 148	Bringet dem Herrn Ehre seines Namens [FP perhaps 1723-9-19]	45
BWV 48	Ich elender Mensch, wer wird mich erlösen [FP 1723-10-3]	46
BWV 109	Ich glaube, lieber Herr [FP 1723-10-17]	47
BWV 89	Was soll ich aus dir machen, Ephraim [FP 1723-10-24]	48
BWV 194	Höcherwünschtes Freudenfest [FP ca. 1723-11-2, RP 1724-6-4]	49

BWV 60	O Ewigkeit, du Donnerwort I [FP 1723-11-7]	50
BWV 90	Es reißet euch ein schrecklich Ende [FP 1723-11-14]	51
BWV 70	Wachet! betet! betet! wachet! [FP 1723-11-21]	52
BWV 40	Dazu ist erschienen der Sohn Gottes [FP 1723-12-26]	53
BWV 64	Sehet, welch eine Liebe hat uns der Vater erzeiget [FP 1723-12-27]	54
BWV 190	Singet dem Herrn ein neues Lied [FP 1724-1-1]	55
BWV 153	Schau, lieber Gott, wie meine Feind [FP 1724-1-2]	56
BWV 65	Sie werden aus Saba alle kommen [FP 1724-1-6]	57
BWV 154	Mein liebster Jesus ist verloren [FP 1724-1-9]	58
BWV 73	Herr, wie du willt, so schick's mit mir [FP 1724-1-23]	59
BWV 81	Jesus schläft, was soll ich hoffen [FP 1724-1-30]	60
BWV 83	Erfreute Zeit im neuen Bund [FP 1724-2-2]	61
BWV 144	Nimm, was dein ist, und gehe hin [FP 1724-2-6]	62
BWV 181	Leichtgesinnte Flattergeister [FP 1724-2-13]	63
BWV 66	Erfreut euch, ihr Herzen [FP 1724-4-10]	64
BWV 134	Ein Herz, das seinen Jesum lebend weiß [FP 1724-4-11]	65
BWV 67	Halt im Gedächtnis Jesum Christ [FP 1724-4-16]	66
BWV 104	Du hirte Israel, höre [FP 1724-4-23]	67
BWV 166	Wo gehest du hin [FP 1724-5-7]	68
BWV 86	Wahrlich, wahrlich, ich sage euch [FP 1724-5-14]	69
BWV 37	Wer da gläubet und getauft wird [FP 1724-5-18]	70
BWV 44	Sie werden euch in den Bann tun I [FP 1724-5-21]	71
BWV 173	Erhöhtes Fleisch und Blut [FP perhaps 1724-5-29]	72
BWV 184	Erwünschtes Freudenlicht [FP 1724-5-30]	73
BWV 20	O Ewigkeit, du Donnerwort II [FP 1724-6-11]	74
BWV 2	Ach Gott, vom Himmel sieh darein [FP 1724-6-18]	75
BWV 7	Christ unser Herr zum Jordan kam [FP 1724-6-24]	76
BWV 135	Ach Herr, mich armen Sünder [FP 1724-6-25]	77
BWV 10	Meine Seel erhebt den Herren [FP 1724-7-2]	78
BWV 93	Wer nur den lieben Gott läßt walten [FP 1724-7-9]	79
BWV 107	Was willst du dich betrüben [FP 1724-7-23]	80
BWV 178	Wo Gott, der Herr, nicht bei uns hält [FP 1724-7-30]	81
BWV 94	Was frag ich nach der Welt [FP 1724-8-6]	82
BWV 101	Nimm von uns, Herr, du treuer Gott [FP 1724-8-13]	83
BWV 113	Herr Jesu Christ, du höchstes Gut [FP 1724-8-20]	84
BWV 33	Allein zu dir, Herr Jesu Christ [FP 1724-9-3]	85
BWV 78	Jesu, der du meine Seele [FP 1724-9-10]	86
BWV 99	Was Gott tut, das ist wohlgetan I [FP 1724-9-17]	87
BWV 8	Liebster Gott, wann werd ich sterben [FP 1724-9-24]	88
BWV 130	Herr Gott, dich loben alle wir [FP 1724-9-29]	89
BWV 114	Ach, lieben Christen, seid getrost [FP 1724-10-1]	90
BWV 96	Herr Christ, der einge Gottessohn [FP 1724-10-8]	91
BWV 5	Wo soll ich fliehen hin [FP 1724-10-15]	92
BWV 180	Schmücke dich, o liebe Seele [FP 1724-10-22]	93
BWV 38	Aus tiefer Not schrei ich zu dir [FP 1724-10-29]	94
BWV 115	Mache dich, mein Geist, bereit [FP 1724-11-5]	95
BWV 139	Wohl dem, der sich auf seinen Gott [FP 1724-11-12]	96
BWV 26	Ach wie flüchtig, ach wie nichtig [FP 1724-11-19]	97
BWV 116	Du Friedefürst, Herr Jesu Christ [FP 1724-11-26]	98
BWV 62	Nun komm, der Heiden Heiland II [FP 1724-12-3]	99
BWV 91	Gelobet seist du, Jesu Christ [FP 1724-12-25]	100
BWV 121	Christum wir sollen loben schon [FP 1724-12-26]	101
BWV 133	Ich freue mich in dir [FP 1724-12-27]	102
BWV 122	Das neugeborne Kindelein [FP 1724-12-31]	103
BWV 41	Jesu, nun sei gepreiset [FP 1725-1-1]	104
BWV 123	Liebster Immanuel, Herzog der Frommen [FP 1725-1-6]	105

BWV 124	Meinen Jesum laß ich nicht [FP 1725-1-7]	106
BWV 3	Ach Gott, wie manches Herzeleid I [FP 1725-1-14]	107
BWV 111	Was mein Gott will, das g'scheh allzeit [FP 1725-1-21]	108
BWV 92	Ich hab in Gottes Herz und Sinn [FP 1725-1-28]	109
BWV 125	Mit Fried und Freud ich fahr dahin [FP 1725-2-2]	110
BWV 126	Erhalt uns, Herr, bei deinem Wort [FP 1725-2-4]	111
BWV 127	Herr Jesu Christ, wahr' Mensch und Gott [FP 1725-2-11]	112
BWV 1	Wie schön leuchtet der Morgenstern [FP 1725-3-25]	113
BWV 249	Kommet, eilet und laufet [FP 1725-4-1]	114
BWV 6	Bleib bei uns, denn es will Abend werden [FP 1725-4-2]	115
BWV 42	Am Abend aber desselbigen Sabbats [FP 1725-4-8]	116
BWV 85	Ich bin ein guter Hirt [FP 1725-4-15]	117
BWV 103	Ihr werdet weinen und heulen [FP 1725-4-22]	118
BWV 108	Es ist euch gut, daß ich hingehe [FP 1725-4-29]	119
BWV 87	Bisher habt ihr nichts gebeten in meinem Namen [FP 1725-5-6]	120
BWV 128	Auf Christi Himmelfahrt allein [FP 1725-5-10]	121
BWV 183	Sie werden euch in den Bann tun II [FP 1725-5-13]	122
BWV 74	Wer mich liebet der wird mein Wort halten II [FP 1725-5-20]	123
BWV 68	Also hat Gott die Welt geliebt [FP 1725-5-21]	124
BWV 175	Er rufet seinen Schafen mit Namen [FP 1725-5-22]	125
BWV 176	Es ist ein trotzig und verzagt Ding [FP 1725-5-27]	126
BWV 168	Tue Rechnung! Donnerwort [FP 1725-7-29]	127
BWV 137	Lobe den Herren, den mächtigen König der Ehren [FP 1725-8-19]	128
BWV 164	Ihr, die ihr euch von Christo nennet [FP 1725-8-26]	129
BWV 79	Gott der Herr ist Sonn und Schild [FP 1725-10-31]	130
BWV 110	Unser Mund sei voll Lachens [FP 1725-12-25]	131
BWV 57	Selig ist der Mann [FP 1725-12-26]	132
BWV 151	Süßer Trost, mein Jesus kömmt [FP 1725-12-27]	133
BWV 28	Gottlob! nun geht das Jahr zu Ende [FP 1725-12-30]	134
BWV 16	Herr Gott, dich loben wir [FP 1726-1-1]	135
BWV 32	Liebster Jesu, mein Verlangen [FP 1726-1-13]	136
BWV 13	Meine Seufzer, meine Tränen [FP 1726-1-20]	137
BWV 72	Alles nur nach Gottes Willen [FP 1726-1-27]	138
BWV 146	Wir müssen durch viel Trübsal [TC uncertain. FP perhaps 1726-5-12 or 1728-4-18]	139
BWV 43	Gott fähret auf mit Jauchzen [FP 1726-5-30]	140
BWV 39	Brich dem Hungrigen dein Brot [FP 1726-6-23]	141
BWV 88	Siehe, ich will viel Fischer aussenden [FP 1726-7-21]	142
BWV 170	Vergnügte Ruh, beliebte Seelenlust [FP 1726-7-28]	143
BWV 187	Es wartet alles auf dich [FP 1726-8-4]	144
BWV 45	Es ist dir gesagt, Mensch, was gut ist [FP 1726-8-11]	145
BWV 102	Herr, deine Augen sehen nach dem Glauben [FP 1726-8-25]	146
BWV 35	Geist und Seele wird verwirret [FP 1726-9-8]	147
BWV 17	Wer Dank opfert, der preiset mich [FP 1726-9-22]	148
BWV 19	Es erhub sich ein Streit [FP 1726-9-29]	149
BWV 27	Wer weiß, wie nahe mir mein Ende [FP 1726-10-6]	150
BWV 47	Wer sich selbst erhöhet, der soll erniedriget [FP 1726-10-13]	151
BWV 169	Gott soll allein mein Herze haben [FP 1726-10-20]	152
BWV 56	Ich will den Kreuzstab gerne tragen [FP 1726-10-27]	153
BWV 129	Gelobet sei der Herr, mein Gott [TC 1726/1727, FP probably before 1727, perhaps 1726-10-31]	154
BWV 49	Ich geh und suche mit Verlangen [FP 1726-11-3]	155
BWV 98	Was Gott tut, das ist wohlgetan II [FP 1726-11-10]	156
BWV 55	Ich armer Mensch, ich Sündenknecht [FP 1726-11-17]	157
BWV 52	Falsche Welt, dir trau ich nicht [FP 1726-11-24]	158
BWV 58	Ach Gott, wie manches Herzeleid II [FP 1727-1-5]	159
BWV 82	Ich habe genug [FP 1727-2-2]	160

BWV 157	Ich lasse dich nicht, du segnest mich denn [FP probably 1727-2-6]	161
BWV 84	Ich bin vergnügt mit meinem Glücke [FP 1727-2-9]	162
BWV 193	Ihr Tore zu Zion [FP 1727-8-25]	163
BWV 198	Laß, Fürstin, laß noch einen Strahl [TC 1727-10-?, FP 1727-10-17]	164
BWV 195	Dem Gerechten muß das Licht [TC 1727/1731 or between 1748/9 and 1749/10 (KB)]	165
BWV 188	Ich habe meine Zuversicht [FP probably 1728-10-17; perhaps 1729-11-6]	166
BWV 117	Sei Lob und Ehr dem höchsten Gut [TC 1728/1731]	167
BWV 120	Gott, man lobet dich in der Stille [TC of earlier version from before 1729]	168
BWV 171	Gott, wie dein Name, so ist auch dein Ruhm [FP probably 1729-1-1; or 1736/1737? (KB)]	169
BWV 156	Ich steh mit einem Fuß im Grabe [FP probably 1729-1-23]	170
BWV 159	Sehet, wir gehn hinauf gen Jerusalem [FP probably 1729-2-27]	171
BWV 145	Ich lebe, mein Herze, zu deinem Ergötzen [FP presumably 1729-4-19]	172
BWV 174	Ich liebe den Höchsten von ganzem Gemüte [FP 1729-6-6]	173
BWV 149	Man singet mit Freuden vom Sieg [FP probably 1729-9-29]	174
BWV 36	Schwingt freudig euch empor [TC 1725-1730]	175
BWV 158	Der Friede sei mit dir [TC probably in Leipzig period, before 1735]	176
BWV 51	Jauchzet Gott in allen Landen [FP 1730-9-17]	177
BWV 192	Nun danket alle Gott [FP probably 1730, fall]	178
BWV 112	Der Herr ist mein getreuer Hirt [FP 1731-4-8]	179
BWV 29	Wir danken dir, Gott, wir danken dir [FP 1731-8-27]	180
BWV 140	Wachet auf, ruft uns die Stimme [FP 1731-11-25]	181
BWV 177	Ich ruf zu dir, Herr Jesu Christ [FP 1732-7-6]	182
BWV 9	Es ist das Heil uns kommen her [TC 1732/1735, FP perhaps 1732-7-20]	183
BWV 100	Was Gott tut, das ist wohlgetan III [TC 1732/1735, probably 1734 or earlier]	184
BWV 97	In allen meinen Taten [TC 1734, perhaps FP 1734-7-25]	185
BWV 248-I	Jauchzet, frohlocket, auf, preiset die Tage (Christmas Oratorio I) [FP 1734-12-25]	186
BWV 248-II	Und es waren Hirten in derselben Gegend (Christmas Oratorio II) [FP 1734-12-26]	187
BWV 248-III	Herrscher des Himmels, erhöre das Lallen (Christmas Oratorio III) [FP 1734-12-27]	188
BWV 248-IV	Fallt mit Danken, fallt mit Loben (Christmas Oratorio IV) [FP 1735-1-1]	189
BWV 248-V	Ehre sei dir, Gott, gesungen (Christmas Oratorio V) [FP 1735-1-2]	190
BWV 248-VI	Herr, wenn die stolzen Feinde schnauben (Christmas Oratorio VI) [FP 1735-1-6]	191
BWV 14	Wär Gott nicht mit uns diese Zeit [FP 1735-1-30]	192
BWV 11	Lobet Gott in seinen Reichen [FP 1735-5-19]	193
BWV 197	Gott ist unsre Zuversicht [TC 1736/1737]	194
BWV 30	Freue dich, erloste Schar [TC 1738-1742; FP probably 1738-6-24]	195
BWV 200	Bekennen will ich seinen Namen [TC ca. 1742]	196
BWV 191	Gloria in excelsis Deo [TC between ca. 1743 and ca. 1746 (based on Bm mass)]	197
BWV 34	O ewiges Feuer, o Ursprung der Liebe [TC ca. 1746/1747]	198
BWV 69	Lobe den Herrn, meine Seele II [FP probably 1748-8-26]	199
BWV 50	Nun ist das Heil und die Kraft (fragment) [TC unknown]	200

INDEX OF CANTATAS IN LITURGICAL ORDER[1]

[1]Cantatas with secondary or unconfirmed designations are given in square brackets: [ ].

ADVENT
1. S. in Advent (BWV 61, 62, 36)
2. S. in Advent
3. S. in Advent
4. S. in Advent (BWV 132)

CHRISTMASTIDE
Christmas Day (BWV 63, 91, 110, 248-I, 191)
2. Day of Christmas (BWV 40, 121, 57, 248-II)
3. Day of Christmas (BWV 64, 133, 151, 248-III)
1. S. after Christmas (BWV 152, 122, 28)
New Year/Circumcision and Name of Jesus (BWV 143, 190, 41, 16, 171, 248-IV)
1. S. after New Year (BWV 153, 58, 248-V)
Epiphany (BWV 65, 123, 248-VI, [200])
1. S. after Epiphany (BWV 154, 124, 32)
2. S. after Epiphany (BWV 155, 3, 13)
3. S. after Epiphany (BWV 73, 111, 72, 156)
Mary's Purification (Candlemas) (BWV 83, 125, 82, 157, 158, [161], [200])
4. S. after Epiphany (BWV 81, 14)
5. S. after Epiphany
6. S. after Epiphany

SEPTUAGESIMA
Septuagesima (BWV 144, 92, 84)
Sexagesima (BWV 18, 181, 126)
Estomihi (Quinquagesima) (BWV 23, 22, 127, 159)
The Annunciation: Mar. 25 (BWV [182], 1)

LENT
Ash Wednesday
Invocavit: 1. S. in Lent
Reminiscere: 2. S. in Lent
Oculi: 3. S. in Lent (BWV 54)
Laetare: 4. S. in Lent
Judica: 5. S. in Lent
Palmarum: Palm Sunday (BWV 182)

PASCHALTIDE
Easter Sunday (BWV 4, 31, 249)
Easter Monday (BWV 66, 6)
3. Easter Day (BWV 134, 145, 158)
Quasimodogeniti (Low Sunday): 1. S. after Easter (BWV 67, 42)
Misericordias Domini: 2. S. after Easter (BWV 104, 85, 112)
Jubilate: 3. S. after Easter (BWV 12, 103, 146)
Cantate: 4. S. after Easter (BWV 166, 108)
Rogate: 5. S. after Easter (BWV 86, 87)
Ascension (BWV 37, 128, 43, 11)
Exaudi: 1. S. after Ascension (BWV 44, 183)

TIME AFTER PENTECOST
Pentecost (Whitsunday) (BWV 172, 59, 74, 34)
2. Day of Pentecost (BWV 173, 68, 174)
3. Day of Pentecost (BWV 184, 175)
Trinity Sunday (BWV 165, [194], 176, 129)
1. S. after Trinity (BWV 75, 20, 39)
2. S. after Trinity (BWV 76, 2)
3. S. after Trinity (BWV 21, 135)
Feast of St. John the Baptist: June 24 (BWV 167, 7, 30)
4. S. after Trinity (BWV 185, 24, 177)
The Visitation: July 2 (BWV 147, 10)
5. S. after Trinity (BWV 93, 88)
6. S. after Trinity (BWV 170, 9)
7. S. after Trinity (BWV 186, 107, 187)
8. S. after Trinity (BWV 136, 178, 45)
9. S. after Trinity (BWV 105, 94, 168)
10. S. after Trinity (BWV 46, 101, 102)
11. S. after Trinity (BWV 199, 179, 113)
12. S. after Trinity (BWV 137, 35)
13. S. after Trinity (BWV 77, 33, 164)
14. S. after Trinity (BWV 25, 78, 17)
15. S. after Trinity (BWV 138, 99, 51)
16. S. after Trinity (BWV 161, 95, 8, 27)
17. S. after Trinity (BWV 148, 114, 47)
St. Michael's Day: Sept. 29 (BWV 130, 19, 149, [50])
18. S. after Trinity (BWV 96, 169)
19. S. after Trinity (BWV 48, 5, 56)
20. S. after Trinity (BWV 162, 180, 49)
21. S. after Trinity (BWV 109, 39, 98, 188)
Reformation Day (BWV 80, 79)
22. S. after Trinity (BWV 89, 115, 55)
23. S. after Trinity (BWV 163, 139, 52)
24. S. after Trinity (BWV 60, 26)
25. S. after Trinity (BWV 90, 116)
26. S. after Trinity (BWV 70)
27. S. after Trinity (BWV 140)

Change of Town Council (BWV 71, 119, 193, 120, 29, 69)
Church & Organ Dedication (BWV 194)
Marriage Ceremony (BWV 196, 195, 197)
Funeral Service (BWV 106, 157, 198)
Occasion Unknown (BWV 131, 150, 117, 192, 100, 97)

ALPHABETICAL INDEX OF CANTATAS WITH CHRONOLOGICAL ORDER NUMBERS[1]

[1]See Index of Cantatas in Chronological Order.

BWV 2	Ach Gott, vom Himmel sieh darein [FP 1724-6-18]	75
BWV 3	Ach Gott, wie manches Herzeleid I [FP 1725-1-14]	107
BWV 58	Ach Gott, wie manches Herzeleid II [FP 1727-1-5]	159
BWV 135	Ach Herr, mich armen Sünder [FP 1724-6-25]	77
BWV 162	Ach! ich sehe, itzt, da ich zur Hochzeit gehe [FP 1716-10-25]	26
BWV 114	Ach, lieben Christen, seid getrost [FP 1724-10-1]	90
BWV 26	Ach wie flüchtig, ach wie nichtig [FP 1724-11-19]	97
BWV 33	Allein zu dir, Herr Jesu Christ [FP 1724-9-3]	85
BWV 72	Alles nur nach Gottes Willen [FP 1726-1-27]	138
BWV 68	Also hat Gott die Welt geliebt [FP 1725-5-21]	124
BWV 42	Am Abend aber desselbigen Sabbats [FP 1725-4-8]	116
BWV 186	Ärgre dich, o Seele, nicht [FP 1723-7-11]	35
BWV 128	Auf Christi Himmelfahrt allein [FP 1725-5-10]	121
BWV 131	Aus der Tiefen rufe ich, Herr, zu dir [TC 1707/1708]	1
BWV 38	Aus tiefer Not schrei ich zu dir [FP 1724-10-29]	94
BWV 185	Barmherziges Herze der ewigen Liebe [FP 1715-7-14]	21
BWV 200	Bekennen will ich seinen Namen [TC ca. 1742]	196
BWV 132	Bereitet die Wege, bereitet die Bahn [FP 1715-12-22]	23
BWV 87	Bisher habt ihr nichts gebeten in meinem Namen [FP 1725-5-6]	120
BWV 6	Bleib bei uns, denn es will Abend werden [FP 1725-4-2]	115
BWV 39	Brich dem Hungrigen dein Brot [FP 1726-6-23]	141
BWV 148	Bringet dem Herrn Ehre seines Namens [FP perhaps 1723-9-19]	45
BWV 4	Christ Lag in Todesbanden [TC probably 1708 or earlier]	3
BWV 7	Christ unser Herr zum Jordan kam [FP 1724-6-24]	76
BWV 63	Christen, ätzet diesen Tag [TC ca. 1714/1715]	17
BWV 121	Christum wir sollen loben schon [FP 1724-12-26]	101
BWV 95	Christus, der ist mein Leben [FP 1723-9-12]	44
BWV 122	Das neugeborne Kindelein [FP 1724-12-31]	103
BWV 40	Dazu ist erschienen der Sohn Gottes [FP 1723-12-26]	53
BWV 195	Dem Gerechten muß das Licht [TC 1727/1731 or between 1748/9 and 1749/10 (KB)]	165
BWV 158	Der Friede sei mit dir [TC probably in Leipzig period, before 1735]	176
BWV 196	Der Herr denket an uns [TC presumably 1707/1708]	5
BWV 112	Der Herr ist mein getreuer Hirt [FP 1731-4-8]	179
BWV 31	Der Himmel lacht! die Erde jubilieret [FP 1715-4-21]	19
BWV 75	Die Elenden sollen essen [FP 1723-5-30]	30
BWV 76	Die Himmel erzählen die Ehre Gottes [FP 1723-6-6]	31
BWV 116	Du Friedefürst, Herr Jesu Christ [FP 1724-11-26]	98
BWV 104	Du hirte Israel, höre [FP 1724-4-23]	67
BWV 77	Du sollt Gott, deinen Herren, lieben [FP 1723-8-22]	40
BWV 23	Du wahrer Gott und Davids Sohn [FP 1723-2-7]	27
BWV 248-V	Ehre sei dir, Gott, gesungen (Christmas Oratorio V) [FP 1735-1-2]	190
BWV 80	Ein feste Burg ist unser Gott [Largely based on BWVa: FP perhaps 1715-3-24. Revision 1727/1731. Last version: TC 1744/1747 or earlier.]	18
BWV 134	Ein Herz, das seinen Jesum lebend weiß [FP 1724-4-11]	65
BWV 24	Ein ungefärbt Gemüte [FP 1723-6-20]	32
BWV 175	Er rufet seinen Schafen mit Namen [FP 1725-5-22]	125
BWV 136	Erforsche mich, Gott, und erfahre mein Herz [FP 1723-7-18]	36
BWV 66	Erfreut euch, ihr Herzen [FP 1724-4-10]	64
BWV 83	Erfreute Zeit im neuen Bund [FP 1724-2-2]	61
BWV 126	Erhalt uns, Herr, bei deinem Wort [FP 1725-2-4]	111
BWV 173	Erhöhtes Fleisch und Blut [FP perhaps 1724-5-29]	72
BWV 172	Erschallet ihr Lieder, erklinget, ihr Saiten [FP probably 1714-5-20]	13

BWV 184	Erwünschtes Freudenlicht [FP 1724-5-30]	73
BWV 19	Es erhub sich ein Streit [FP 1726-9-29]	149
BWV 9	Es ist das Heil uns kommen her [TC 1732/1735, FP perhaps 1732-7-20]	183
BWV 45	Es ist dir gesagt, Mensch, was gut ist [FP 1726-8-11]	145
BWV 176	Es ist ein trotzig und verzagt Ding [FP 1725-5-27]	126
BWV 108	Es ist euch gut, daß ich hingehe [FP 1725-4-29]	119
BWV 25	Es ist nichts Gesundes an meinem Leibe [FP 1723-8-29]	41
BWV 90	Es reißet euch ein schrecklich Ende [FP 1723-11-14]	51
BWV 187	Es wartet alles auf dich [FP 1726-8-4]	144
BWV 248-IV	Fallt mit Danken, fallt mit Loben (Christmas Oratorio IV) [FP 1735-1-1]	189
BWV 52	Falsche Welt, dir trau ich nicht [FP 1726-11-24]	158
BWV 30	Freue dich, erloste Schar [TC 1738-1742; FP probably 1738-6-24]	195
BWV 35	Geist und Seele wird verwirret [FP 1726-9-8]	147
BWV 129	Gelobet sei der Herr, mein Gott [TC 1726/1727, FP probably before 1727, perhaps 1726-10-31]	154
BWV 91	Gelobet seist du, Jesu Christ [FP 1724-12-25]	100
BWV 18	Gleichwie der Regen und Schnee vom Himmel fällt [FP 1713/1714]	8
BWV 191	Gloria in excelsis Deo [TC between ca. 1743 and ca. 1746 (based on Bm mass)]	197
BWV 79	Gott der Herr ist Sonn und Schild [FP 1725-10-31]	130
BWV 43	Gott fähret auf mit Jauchzen [FP 1726-5-30]	140
BWV 71	Gott ist mein König [FP 1708-2-4]	4
BWV 197	Gott ist unsre Zuversicht [TC 1736/1737]	194
BWV 120	Gott, man lobet dich in der Stille [TC of earlier version from before 1729]	168
BWV 169	Gott soll allein mein Herze haben [FP 1726-10-20]	152
BWV 171	Gott, wie dein Name, so ist auch dein Ruhm [FP probably 1729-1-1; or 1736/1737? (KB)]	169
BWV 106	Gottes Zeit ist die allerbeste Zeit [TC probably 1707/1708]	2
BWV 28	Gottlob! nun geht das Jahr zu Ende [FP 1725-12-30]	134
BWV 67	Halt im Gedächtnis Jesum Christ [FP 1724-4-16]	66
BWV 96	Herr Christ, der eine Gottessohn [FP 1724-10-8]	91
BWV 102	Herr, deine Augen sehen nach dem Glauben [FP 1726-8-25]	146
BWV 105	Herr, gehe nicht ins Gericht mit deinem Knecht [FP 1723-7-25]	37
BWV 130	Herr Gott, dich loben alle wir [FP 1724-9-29]	89
BWV 16	Herr Gott, dich loben wir [FP 1726-1-1]	135
BWV 113	Herr Jesu Christ, du höchstes Gut [FP 1724-8-20]	84
BWV 127	Herr Jesu Christ, wahr' Mensch und Gott [FP 1725-2-11]	112
BWV 248-VI	Herr, wenn die stolzen Feinde schnauben (Christmas Oratorio VI) [FP 1735-1-6]	191
BWV 73	Herr, wie du willt, so schick's mit mir [FP 1724-1-23]	59
BWV 248-III	Herrscher des Himmels, erhöre das Lallen (Christmas Oratorio III) [FP 1734-12-27]	188
BWV 147	Herz und Mund und Tat und Leben [FP 1723-7-2]	34
BWV 182	Himmelskönig, sei willkommen [FP 1714-3-25]	11
BWV 194	Höcherwünschtes Freudenfest [FP ca. 1723-11-2, RP 1724-6-4]	49
BWV 55	Ich armer Mensch, ich Sündenknecht [FP 1726-11-17]	157
BWV 85	Ich bin ein guter Hirt [FP 1725-4-15]	117
BWV 84	Ich bin vergnügt mit meinem Glücke [FP 1727-2-9]	162
BWV 48	Ich elender Mensch, wer wird mich erlösen [FP 1723-10-3]	46
BWV 133	Ich freue mich in dir [FP 1724-12-27]	102
BWV 49	Ich geh und suche mit Verlangen [FP 1726-11-3]	155
BWV 109	Ich glaube, lieber Herr [FP 1723-10-17]	47
BWV 92	Ich hab in Gottes Herz und Sinn [FP 1725-1-28]	109
BWV 82	Ich habe genug [FP 1727-2-2]	160
BWV 188	Ich habe meine Zuversicht [FP probably 1728-10-17; perhaps 1729-11-6]	166
BWV 21	Ich hatte viel Bekümmernis [FP perhaps 1713-12-? (some parts go back to earlier version)]	9
BWV 157	Ich lasse dich nicht, du segnest mich denn [FP probably 1727-2-6]	161
BWV 145	Ich lebe, mein Herze, zu deinem Ergötzen [FP presumably 1729-4-19]	172
BWV 174	Ich liebe den Höchsten von ganzem Gemüte [FP 1729-6-6]	173
BWV 177	Ich ruf zu dir, Herr Jesu Christ [FP 1732-7-6]	182

BWV 156	Ich steh mit einem Fuß im Grabe [FP probably 1729-1-23]	170
BWV 56	Ich will den Kreuzstab gerne tragen [FP 1726-10-27]	153
BWV 164	Ihr, die ihr euch von Christo nennet [FP 1725-8-26]	129
BWV 167	Ihr Menschen, rühmet Gottes Liebe [FP 1723-6-24]	33
BWV 193	Ihr Tore zu Zion [FP 1727-8-25]	163
BWV 103	Ihr werdet weinen und heulen [FP 1725-4-22]	118
BWV 97	In allen meinen Taten [TC 1734, perhaps FP 1734-7-25]	185
BWV 248-I	Jauchzet, frohlocket, auf, preiset die Tage (Christmas Oratorio I) [FP 1734-12-25]	186
BWV 51	Jauchzet Gott in allen Landen [FP 1730-9-17]	177
BWV 78	Jesu, der du meine Seele [FP 1724-9-10]	86
BWV 41	Jesu, nun sei gepreiset [FP 1725-1-1]	104
BWV 22	Jesus nahm zu sich die Zwölfe [FP 1723-2-7]	28
BWV 81	Jesus schläft, was soll ich hoffen [FP 1724-1-30]	60
BWV 161	Komm, du süße Todesstunde [FP 1716-9-27, later version ca. 1735]	25
BWV 249	Kommet, eilet und laufet [FP 1725-4-1]	114
BWV 198	Laß, Fürstin, laß noch einen Strahl [TC 1727-10-?, FP 1727-10-17]	164
BWV 181	Leichtgesinnte Flattergeister [FP 1724-2-13]	63
BWV 8	Liebster Gott, wann werd ich sterben [FP 1724-9-24]	88
BWV 123	Liebster Immanuel, Herzog der Frommen [FP 1725-1-6]	105
BWV 32	Liebster Jesu, mein Verlangen [FP 1726-1-13]	136
BWV 137	Lobe den Herren, den mächtigen König der Ehren [FP 1725-8-19]	128
BWV 143	Lobe den Herrn, meine Seele I [spurious? ca. 1708-1714]	7
BWV 69	Lobe den Herrn, meine Seele II [FP probably 1748-8-26]	199
BWV 11	Lobet Gott in seinen Reichen [FP 1735-5-19]	193
BWV 115	Mache dich, mein Geist, bereit [FP 1724-11-5]	95
BWV 149	Man singet mit Freuden vom Sieg [FP probably 1729-9-29]	174
BWV 155	Mein Gott, wie lang, ach lange [FP 1716-1-19]	24
BWV 199	Mein Herze schwimmt im Blut [FP 1714-8-12]	14
BWV 154	Mein liebster Jesus ist verloren [FP 1724-1-9]	58
BWV 10	Meine Seel erhebt den Herren [FP 1724-7-2]	78
BWV 13	Meine Seufzer, meine Tränen [FP 1726-1-20]	137
BWV 124	Meinen Jesum laß ich nicht [FP 1725-1-7]	106
BWV 125	Mit Fried und Freud ich fahr dahin [FP 1725-2-2]	110
BWV 150	Nach dir, Herr, verlanget mich [TC unknown; during or before Bach's Weimar period]	6
BWV 101	Nimm von uns, Herr, du treuer Gott [FP 1724-8-13]	83
BWV 144	Nimm, was dein ist, und gehe hin [FP 1724-2-6]	62
BWV 192	Nun danket alle Gott [FP probably 1730, fall]	178
BWV 50	Nun ist das Heil und die Kraft (fragment) [TC unknown]	200
BWV 61	Nun komm, der Heiden Heiland I [FP 1714-12-2]	15
BWV 62	Nun komm, der Heiden Heiland II [FP 1724-12-3]	99
BWV 163	Nur jedem das Seine [FP 1715-11-24]	22
BWV 34	O ewiges Feuer, o Ursprung der Liebe [TC ca. 1746/1747]	198
BWV 60	O Ewigkeit, du Donnerwort I [FP 1723-11-7]	50
BWV 20	O Ewigkeit, du Donnerwort II [FP 1724-6-11]	74
BWV 165	O heiliges Geist- und Wasserbad [FP presumably 1715-6-16]	20
BWV 119	Preise, Jerusalem, den Herrn [FP 1723-8-30]	42
BWV 153	Schau, lieber Gott, wie meine Feind [FP 1724-1-2]	56
BWV 46	Schauet doch und sehet, ob irgendein Schmerz sei [FP 1723-8-1]	38
BWV 180	Schmücke dich, o liebe Seele [FP 1724-10-22]	93
BWV 36	Schwingt freudig euch empor [TC 1725-1730]	175
BWV 64	Sehet, welch eine Liebe hat uns der Vater erzeiget [FP 1723-12-27]	54
BWV 159	Sehet, wir gehn hinauf gen Jerusalem [FP probably 1729-2-27]	171
BWV 117	Sei Lob und Ehr dem höchsten Gut [TC 1728/1731]	167
BWV 57	Selig ist der Mann [FP 1725-12-26]	132
BWV 65	Sie werden aus Saba alle kommen [FP 1724-1-6]	57
BWV 44	Sie werden euch in den Bann tun I [FP 1724-5-21]	71

BWV 183	Sie werden euch in den Bann tun II [FP 1725-5-13]	122
BWV 88	Siehe, ich will viel Fischer aussenden [FP 1726-7-21]	142
BWV 179	Siehe zu, daß deine Gottesfurcht nicht Heuchelei sei [FP 1723-8-8]	39
BWV 190	Singet dem Herrn ein neues Lied [FP 1724-1-1]	55
BWV 151	Süßer Trost, mein Jesus kömmt [FP 1725-12-27]	133
BWV 152	Tritt auf die Glaubensbahn [FP 1714-12-30]	16
BWV 168	Tue Rechnung! Donnerwort [FP 1725-7-29]	127
BWV 248-II	Und es waren Hirten in derselben Gegend (Christmas Oratorio II) [FP 1734-12-26]	187
BWV 110	Unser Mund sei voll Lachens [FP 1725-12-25]	131
BWV 170	Vergnügte Ruh, beliebte Seelenlust [FP 1726-7-28]	143
BWV 140	Wachet auf, ruft uns die Stimme [FP 1731-11-25]	181
BWV 70	Wachet! betet! betet! wachet! [FP 1723-11-21]	52
BWV 86	Wahrlich, wahrlich, ich sage euch [FP 1724-5-14]	69
BWV 14	Wär Gott nicht mit uns diese Zeit [FP 1735-1-30]	192
BWV 138	Warum betrübst du dich, mein Herz [FP 1723-9-5]	43
BWV 94	Was frag ich nach der Welt [FP 1724-8-6]	82
BWV 99	Was Gott tut, das ist wohlgetan I [FP 1724-9-17]	87
BWV 98	Was Gott tut, das ist wohlgetan II [FP 1726-11-10]	156
BWV 100	Was Gott tut, das ist wohlgetan III [TC 1732/1735, probably 1734 or earlier]	184
BWV 111	Was mein Gott will, das g'scheh allzeit [FP 1725-1-21]	108
BWV 89	Was soll ich aus dir machen, Ephraim [FP 1723-10-24]	48
BWV 107	Was willst du dich betrüben [FP 1724-7-23]	80
BWV 12	Weinen, Klagen, Sorgen, Zagen [FP 1714-4-22]	12
BWV 37	Wer da gläubet und getauft wird [FP 1724-5-18]	70
BWV 17	Wer Dank opfert, der preiset mich [FP 1726-9-22]	148
BWV 59	Wer mich liebet, der wird mein Wort halten I [TC 1723, 5, 16, FP 1724-5-28]	29
BWV 74	Wer mich liebet der wird mein Wort halten II [FP 1725-5-20]	123
BWV 93	Wer nur den lieben Gott läßt walten [FP 1724-7-9]	79
BWV 47	Wer sich selbst erhöhet, der soll erniedriget [FP 1726-10-13]	151
BWV 27	Wer weiß, wie nahe mir mein Ende [FP 1726-10-6]	150
BWV 54	Widerstehe doch der Sünde [TC Weimar period, perhaps FP 1714-3-4]	10
BWV 1	Wie schön leuchtet der Morgenstern [FP 1725-3-25]	113
BWV 29	Wir danken dir, Gott, wir danken dir [FP 1731-8-27]	180
BWV 146	Wir müssen durch viel Trübsal [TC uncertain. FP perhaps 1726-5-12 or 1728-4-18]	139
BWV 166	Wo gehest du hin [FP 1724-5-7]	68
BWV 178	Wo Gott, der Herr, nicht bei uns hält [FP 1724-7-30]	81
BWV 5	Wo soll ich fliehen hin [FP 1724-10-15]	92
BWV 139	Wohl dem, der sich auf seinen Gott [FP 1724-11-12]	96

About the Author

A native Albertan, Melvin P. Unger is currently Professor of Music at North American Baptist College in Edmonton, Alberta, Canada, and artistic director of the Edmonton Da Camera Singers. He earned his D.M.A. degree while a doctoral fellow at the University of Illinois, and received M. Mus and B. Mus. degrees from the Universities of Oregon and Saskatchewan, respectively. As a recipient of a scholarship from the *Deutscher Akademischer Austauschdienst,* he also studied at the *Hochschule für Musik und Darstellende Kunst* in Frankfurt under Bach specialist Helmuth Rilling. His choirs have appeared at numerous festivals and choral conventions, including provincial music conferences, national conventions of the Association of Canadian Choral Conductors, Expo '86, the Toronto International Choral Festival, and the Classical Music Seminar-Festival in Eisenstadt, Austria. His publications include *The German Choral Church Compositions of Johann David Heinichen (1683-1729)* (Peter Lang, 1990), some first editions of compositions by Heinichen (Carus-Verlag, 1989, 1991), and articles in the *Choral Journal.* For research related to the final preparation of this present volume, he received the 1991 research award of the American Choral Directors Association.